**Hermeneia
—A Critical
and Historical
Commentary
on the Bible**

Mark

A Commentary

by Adela Yarbro Collins

Edited by
Harold W. Attridge

Mark
A Commentary

Cover and interior design by Kenneth Hiebert
Typesetting and page composition by
The HK Scriptorium

Library of Congress Cataloging-in-Publication Data

Collins, Adela Yarbro.
  Mark : a commentary / Adela Yarbro Collins ; Harold W. Attridge, editor.
    p. cm. — (Hermeneia—a critical and historical commentary on the Bible)
  Includes bibliographical references and indexes.
  ISBN 978-0-8006-6078-9 (alk. paper)
  1. Bible. N.T. Mark—Commentaries. I. Attridge, Harold W. II. Title.
    BS2585.53.C65   2007
    226.3'077—dc22

                              2007009718

The paper used in this publication meets the minimum requirements of American National Standard for Information Sciences—Permanence of paper for Printed Library Materials, ANSI Z329.48–1984.

Manufactured in the U.S.A.

11   10   09   08   07   1   2   3   4   5   6   7   8   9   10

■ *Dedicated to the Faculty of Theology*
of the University of Oslo, Norway, in gratitude
for the award in 1994 of the degree
Doctor theologiae honoris causa

The Author

Adela Yarbro Collins is the Buckingham Professor of New Testament Criticism and Interpretation at the Yale University Divinity School. She studied science and humanities at the University of Portland in Oregon and Salzburg, Austria; religion and history at Pomona College in Claremont, California; and New Testament, philosophy, and theology at the Eberhard-Karls-Universität in Tübingen, Germany. She received the Ph.D. in the Study of Religion (New Testament and Christian Origins) at Harvard University. From 1973 until 1985, she taught at McCormick Theological Seminary in Chicago, Illinois; from 1985 to 1991 in the Theology Department of the University of Notre Dame, Notre Dame, Indiana; and at the University of Chicago Divinity School from 1991 to 2000. Since 2000, she has been at the Yale Divinity School. She is the author of *The Combat Myth in the Book of Revelation* (1976); *Crisis and Catharsis: The Power of the Apocalypse* (1984); *The Beginning of the Gospel: Probings of Mark in Context* (1992); and *Cosmology and Eschatology in Jewish and Christian Apocalypticism* (1996). She has also edited four books and served on the editorial boards of the *Journal of Biblical Literature*, the *Catholic Biblical Quarterly*, the *Journal of Religion*, *Biblical Interpretation*, and the *Journal for the Study of the New Testament*.

Contents
Mark

■ **End Matter** 821

The name *Hermeneia*, Greek ἑρμηνεία, has been chosen as the title of the commentary series to which this volume belongs. The word *Hermeneia* has a rich background in the history of biblical interpretation as a term used in the ancient Greek-speaking world for the detailed, systematic exposition of a scriptural work. It is hoped that the series, like its name, will carry forward this old and venerable tradition. A second, entirely practical reason for selecting the name lies in the desire to avoid a long descriptive title and its inevitable acronym, or worse, an unpronounceable abbreviation.

The series is designed to be a critical and historical commentary to the Bible without arbitrary limits in size or scope. It will utilize the full range of philological and historical tools, including textual criticism (often slighted in modern commentaries), the methods of the history of tradition (including genre and prosodic analysis), and the history of religion.

Hermeneia is designed for the serious student of the Bible. It will make full use of ancient Semitic and classical languages; at the same time, English translations of all comparative materials—Greek, Latin, Canaanite, or Akkadian—will be supplied alongside the citation of the source in its original language. Insofar as possible, the aim is to provide the student or scholar with full critical discussion of each problem of interpretation and with the primary data upon which the discussion is based.

Hermeneia is designed to be international and interconfessional in the selection of authors; its editorial boards were formed with this end in view. Occasionally the series will offer translations of distinguished commentaries which originally appeared in languages other than English. Published volumes of the series will be revised continually, and eventually, new commentaries will replace older works in order to preserve the currency of the series. Commentaries are also being assigned for important literary works in the categories of apocryphal and pseudepigraphical works relating to the Old and New Testaments, including some of Essene or Gnostic authorship.

The editors of *Hermeneia* impose no systematic-theological perspective upon the series (directly, or indirectly by selection of authors). It is expected that authors will struggle to lay bare the ancient meaning of a biblical work or pericope. In this way the text's human relevance should become transparent, as is always the case in competent historical discourse. However, the series eschews for itself homiletical translation of the Bible.

The editors are heavily indebted to Fortress Press for its energy and courage in taking up an expensive, long-term project, the rewards of which will accrue chiefly to the field of biblical scholarship.

The editor responsible for this volume is Harold W. Attridge, Lillian Claus Professor of New Testament and Dean at the Yale Divinity School.

Peter Machinist
For the Old Testament
Editorial Board

Helmut Koester
For the New Testament
Editorial Board

■ Epigram

My Markman

I do not live by the sea but I have
    A friend who lives by the sea. On him
        The wind sheds images of the far shore

When he walks in the wind. On me the wind
    Does not shed images, but I know of
        The far shore because he tells me of it.

Where he walks the Monarchs in their season
    Come across tacking and swooping over
        The wave crests from the far shore, and then over

The salt marsh and the sea grass, one by one
    Battering toward sleep in the Sierra Madre.
        Also whole days come to him on the wind

To which he gives a name, such as Storm Day
    or Wash Day or Death Day. He marks each one
        With a clear mark, a term. In Winter he

Takes account of the six wings of the snow.
    On the far shore where gulls nest in the clearness
        Of his thinking are treasuries of snow

And the wild horns from which spill butterflies.
    I love my markman who lives by the sea
        On whom the winds shed images he knows

I love him for the waking and for the time,
    The whole days, and for the Monarch on the
        Wind road to the mother mountain of sleep.

Allen Grossman
used by permission

The commentary by Adela Yarbro Collins contains a fresh translation of the text of the Gospel of Mark. Translations from the rest of the New Testament are hers as well, unless otherwise noted. Passages from the Hebrew Bible are usually quoted from the New Revised Standard Version. Quotations of Latin and Greek authors, except where noted, follow the texts and translations of the Loeb Classical Library.

The endpapers display folio 6 verso (Mark 7:25—8:1) and folio 7 recto (Mark 8:34—9:8) of $\mathfrak{p}^{45}$, a third-century witness to the Gospel of Mark. We are grateful to the Chester Beatty Library for permission to reprint these images. Photo © The Trustees of the Chester Beatty Library, Dublin. Used by permission.

The New Testament editorial board of the Hermeneia commentary series gave me the honor and the challenge of writing this commentary in 1987, at which time I began to focus my research and writing on the Gospel of Mark. In 1991 a Theological Scholarship and Research Grant, awarded by the Association of Theological Schools, and in 1995–1996 a Fellowship for University Teachers, awarded by the National Endowment for the Humanities, allowed me to make significant progress on the commentary. I am grateful to the University of Chicago Divinity School for granting me academic leaves so that I could make use of these grants. I am also grateful to the Yale University Divinity School for granting me academic leaves in the fall of 2001 and the fall of 2004, in which much of the writing was done.

I have learned much from former teachers and from past and present colleagues and students. A small portion of this debt is acknowledged in the footnotes. I am grateful to my colleague and Dean, Harold W. Attridge, for taking time out from his busy schedule to edit this volume in his erudite and skillful way. I am also grateful to Neil Elliott and Joshua Messner for coordinating the publication project so well; to Maurya Horgan, Paul Kobelski, and Jeska Horgan-Kobelski for their wonderful work in copyedting, typesetting, and page composition; to Chuck John and Christopher Stroup for their careful proofreading; and to Christopher Stroup and Joshua Hill for their good work on the indexes. My husband, John J. Collins, has been consistently encouraging and supportive. Finally, I dedicate this commentary to the Faculty of Theology at the University of Oslo in Norway as an expression of gratitude for the award of an honorary doctorate in 1994.

Guilford, Connecticut

Adela Yarbro Collins
August, 2007

1. Sources and Abbreviations

Abbreviations for ancient sources follow, with minor modifications, the *Theological Dictionary of the New Testament*, ed. Gerhard Kittel, trans. Geoffrey W. Bromiley, vol. 1 (Grand Rapids/London: Eerdmans, 1964) xvi–xl. Abbreviations in text-critical notes follow the Nestle-Aland, 27th edition (Eberhard Nestle, Erwin Nestle, Barbara Aland, Kurt Aland, et al., *Novum Testamentum Graece* [Stuttgart: Deutsche Bibelgesellschaft, 1993]; abbreviated Nestle-Aland [27th ed.]). All citations from the Greek New Testament are from this edition and all translations of such citations are mine, unless otherwise noted.

The following abbreviations have also been used:

AAAbo	Acta Academiae Aboensis
AAABO.H	—Ser. A, Humaniora
AARSR	American Academy of Religion Studies in Religion
AAWG.PH	Abhandlungen der Akademie der Wissenschaften in Göttingen, Philologisch-historische Klasse
AB	Anchor Bible
ABD	*The Anchor Bible Dictionary*, ed. David Noel Freedman (6 vols.; New York: Doubleday, 1992).
ʿAbod. Zar.	tractate ʿAboda Zara, Idolatry
ʾAbot R. Nat.	ʾAbot de Rabbi Nathan
ABRL	Anchor Bible Reference Library
Acta-Rom	Acta Instituti Romani Regni Sueciae
ad loc.	*ad locum*, at the place
Aeschylus	
Ag.	*Agamemnon*
Eum.	*Eumenides*
Prom.	*Prometheus vinctus*
AGJU	Arbeiten zur Geschichte des antiken Judentums und des Urchristentums
AGSU	Arbeiten zur Geschichte des Spätjudentums und Urchristentums
AGWG.PH	Abhandlungen der (Königlichen) Gesellschaft/Akademie der Wissenschaften zu Göttingen, Philologisch-historische Klasse
AnBib	Analecta biblica
ANF	*Ante-Nicene Fathers*, ed. Alexander Roberts and James Donaldson
ANRW	*Aufstieg und Niedergang der römischen Welt*, ed. Hildegard Temporini and Wolfgang Haase
ANTC	Abingdon New Testament Commentaries

ANWAW	Abhandlungen der Nordrhein-Westfälischen Akademie der Wissenschaften
aor.	aorist
AOT	*The Apocryphal Old Testament*, ed. H. F. D. Sparks (Oxford: Clarendon, 1984).
AOTC	Abingdon Old Testament Commentaries
APA.PM	American Philological Association, Philological Monographs
Ap. Jas.	*Apocryphon of James*
Ap. John	*Apocryphon of John*
Apoc. Abr.	*Apocalypse of Abraham*
Apoc. Pet.	*Apocalypse of Peter*
Apoc. Zeph.	*Apocalypse of Zephaniah*
Apuleius	Apuleius of Madaura in Numidia
Apol.	*Apology*
Met.	*Metamorphoses*
Aristotle	
Eth. Nic.	*Ethica Nicomachea*
HA	*Historia Animalium*
Poet.	*Poetica*
Rhet.	*Rhetorica*
Artemidorus	
Oneirocr.	*Oneirocriticum*
Asc. Isa.	*Ascension of Isaiah*
ASGB	Academia Scientiarum Germanica Berolinensis
ASGW	Abhandlungen der (Königlichen) Sächsischen Gesellschaft der Wissenschaften
ASGW.PH	—Philologisch-historische Klasse
As. Mos.	*Assumption of Moses*
ASOR	American Schools of Oriental Research
AThANT	Abhandlungen zur Theologie des Alten und Neuen Testaments
ATLAMS	American Theological Library Association Monograph Series
ATR	*Anglican Theological Review*
AUSDDS	Andrews University Seminary Doctoral Dissertation Series
AUSS	*Andrews University Seminary Studies*
Auth. Teach.	*Authoritative Teaching*, third tractate in Codex VI from Nag Hammadi
b.	Babylonian Talmud
BAGD	Walter Bauer, *A Greek-English Lexicon of the New Testament and Other Early Christian Literature*, ed. William F. Arndt, F. Wilbur Gingrich; 3rd ed. rev. by Frederick W.

	Danker (Chicago: University of Chicago Press, 2000).
Bar.	*Baraita*, a tannaitic text not included in the Mishnah
2 Bar.	*Syriac Apocalypse of Baruch*
BAR, B.A.R.	British Archaeological Reports
BARev	*Biblical Archaeology Review*
Barn.	*Epistle of Barnabas*
BASOR	*Bulletin of the American Schools of Oriental Research*
B. Batra	tractate *Baba Batra, The Last Gate*
BBB	Bonner biblische Beiträge
BCE	Before the Common Era
BDB	William Gesenius, *Hebrew and English Lexicon of the Old Testament*; trans. Edward Robinson; ed. F. Brown, S. R. Driver, and C. A. Briggs (Oxford: Clarendon, 1972).
BDF	F. Blass and A. Debrunner, *A Greek Grammar of the New Testament and Other Early Christian Literature*, ed. Robert W. Funk (Chicago: University of Chicago Press, 1961).
Bek.	tractate *Bekorot, Firstlings*
Ber.	tractate *Berakot, Blessings*
BEThL	Bibliotheca Ephemeridum Theologicarum Lovaniensium
BGBE	Beiträge zur Geschichte der biblischen Exegese
BHS	*Biblia Hebraica Stuttgartensia*, rev. ed., ed. K. Elliger and W. Rudolph (Stuttgart: Deutsche Bibelstiftung, 1967/1977).
BI	*Biblical Interpretation*
Bib	*Biblica*
Bib. Ant.	Pseudo-Philo, *Biblical Antiquities*
BibOr	Biblica et orientalia
BIS	Biblical Interpretation Series
BJRL	*Bulletin of the John Rylands Library*
BJS	Brown Judaic Studies
BMAP	*Brooklyn Museum Aramaic Papyri*, ed. E. G. Kraeling (New Haven: Yale University Press, 1953).
BNTC	Black's New Testament Commentary
bot.	bottom
B. Qam.	tractate *Baba Qamma, The First Gate*
BR	*Biblical Research*
BRS	Biblical Resource Series
BSGRT	Bibliotheca Scriptorum Graecorum et Romanorum Teubneriana
BSt	Biblische Studien, Neukirchen
BWANT	Beiträge zur Wissenschaft vom Alten und Neuen Testament
ByZ	*Byzantinische Zeitschrift*
BZ	*Biblische Zeitschrift*
BZNW	Beihefte zur *ZNW*, Supplements to *ZNW*
c.	circa; about, approximately
CahRB	Cahiers de la *Revue biblique*
Callimachus	Callimachus
Aet.	*Aetia*
Cant	Canticles, the Song of Songs
CB	Coniectanea Biblica
CBNTS	—New Testament Series
CBA	Catholic Biblical Association of America
CBQ	*Catholic Biblical Quarterly*
CBQMS	Catholic Biblical Quarterly Monograph Series
CBR	*Currents in Biblical Research*
CChr	Corpus Christianorum
CChrSL	—Series latina
CD	Cairo (Genizah) text of the *Damascus Document*
CE	Common Era
cent.	century or centuries
cf.	*confer*, compare
CGL	Coptic Gnostic Library
CGTC	Cambridge Greek Testament Commentary
chap(s).	chapter(s)
Cicero	
Att.	*Ad Atticum, Letters to Atticus*
Tusc.	*Tusculanae Disputationes, Tusculan Disputations*
Verr.	*In Verrem*, oration against Verres
CIJ	*Corpus inscriptionum iudaicarum*. ed. Jean-Baptiste Frey (2 vols.; SSAC 1 and 3; Vatican City/Rome: Pontificio istituto di archeologia cristiana, 1936–52).
CJA	Christianity and Judaism in Antiquity (monograph series)
Clement of Alexandria	
Quis div. salv.	*Quis dives salvetur, Who Is the Rich Man That Will be Saved?*
Strom.	*Stromata, Stromateis, Miscellanies*
col(s).	column(s)
ConBOT	Coniectanea biblica, Old Testament
cp.	compare
CPJ	*Corpus papyrorum Judaicarum*, ed. Victor A. Tcherikover, A. Fuks, and M. Stern (3 vols.; Cambridge, MA: Harvard University Press, 1957–64).
CRINT	Compendia Rerum Iudaicarum ad Novum Testamentum
CSCO	Corpus scriptorum christianorum orientalium

CSHJ	Chicago Studies in the History of Judaism	esp.	especially
CThM	Calwer theologische Monographien	ET	English translation
		et al.	*et alii* or *et alia*, and others
CTSRR	College Theology Society Resources in Religion	EtB	Études bibliques
DDD	*Dictionary of Deities and Demons in the Bible*, ed. Karel van der Toorn et al. (2nd rev. ed.; Leiden: Brill; Grand Rapids: Eerdmans, 1999).	*EThL*	*Ephemerides theologicae Lovanienses*
		Euripides	
		Hec.	*Hecuba*
		Eusebius	
		Hist. eccl.	*Historia ecclesiastica*
Demosthenes		*Praep. Ev.*	*Praeparatio Evangelica*
Or.	*Orationes*	*EvTh*	*Evangelische Theologie*
Did.	*Didache*	*ExpT*	*Expository Times*
Dio Cassius		F.	Folge, series
Hist. Rom.	*Roman History*	f(f).	the following (year[s] or item[s])
Dio Chrysostom	Dion of Prusa in Bithynia, later called Chrysostomos	FB	Forschung zur Bibel
		FBBS	Facet Books, Biblical Series
Or.	*Orationes, Orations*	fem.	feminine grammatical gender
Diogenes	Diogenes	fl.	floruit; flourished
Ep.	*Epistles*	FOTL	Forms of the Old Testament Literature
Diogenes Laertius			
Vit. Phil.	*Vitae Philosophorum*	frg(s).	fragment(s)
Diogn.	*Epistle to Diognetus*	FRLANT	Forschungen zur Religion und Literatur des Alten und Neuen Testaments
DJD	Discoveries in the Judaean Desert		
DK	Hermann Diels and Walther Kranz, *Die Fragmente der Vorsokratiker*, vol. 1 (6th ed.; Berlin: Weidmann, 1951).		
		FS	Festschrift
		FTS	Frankfurter Theologische Studien
		GBS	Guides to Biblical Scholarship
DSD	*Dead Sea Discoveries*	Germ.	German
DSS	Dead Sea Scrolls	*Giṭ.*	tractate *Giṭṭin, Bills of Divorce*
eadem	the same, the same as previously mentioned (feminine)	*Gos. Eb.*	*Gospel of the Ebionites*
		Gos. Pet.	*Gospel of Peter*
		Gos. Thom.	*Gospel of Thomas*
ed.	editor, edition, or edited by	*Ḥag.*	tractate *Ḥagiga, The Festal Offering*
eds.	editors	Hatch-Redpath	Edwin Hatch and Henry A. Redpath, eds., *A Concordance to the Septuagint and Other Greek Versions of the Old Testament* (Oxford: Clarendon, 1897).
ʿEd.	tractate *ʿEduyyot, Testimonies*		
EdF	Erträge der Forschung		
EDNT	*Exegetical Dictionary of the New Testament*, ed. Horst Balz and Gerhard Schneider (3 vols.; Grand Rapids: Eerdmans, 1990–93).		
EDSS	*Encyclopedia of the Dead Sea Scrolls*, ed. Lawrence H. Schiffman and James C. VanderKam (2 vols.; New York: Oxford University Press, 2000).	*HBD*	*Harper's Bible Dictionary*, ed. Paul J. Achtemeier (San Francisco: HarperSanFrancisco, 1996).
		HDR	Harvard Dissertations in Religion
		Hdt.	Herodotus
		Hermas	*The Shepherd of Hermas*
EHS.T	Europäische Hochschulschriften, Reihe 23, Theologie	*Man.*	*Mandate*
		Sim.	*Similitude*
Eidos	Eidos: Studies in Classical Kinds	*Vis.*	*Vision*
EKK	Evangelisch-Katholischer Kommentar zum Neuen Testament	Hesiod	
		Op.	*Opera et Dies, Works and Days*
Ep. Arist.	*Epistle of Aristeas*	*Sc.*	*Scutum Herculis, The Shield of Heracles*
Epictetus			
Diss.	*Dissertationes, Discourses*	Hippocrates	
Ench.	*Enchiridion, Handbook*	*Aph.*	ἀφορισμοί, *Aphorisms*
EPRO	Études préliminaires aux religions orientales dans l'empire Romain	*Morb. Sacr.*	*Morbus Sacer, The Sacred Disease*
		Hippolytus	
ʿErub.	tractate *ʿErubin, The Fusion of Sabbath Limits*	*Ref.*	*Refutatio Omnium Haeresium, Refutation of all Heresies*

HNT	Handbuch zum Neuen Testament
HNTC	Harper's New Testament Commentaries
HO	Handbuch der Orientalistik
Homer	
Il.	*Iliad*
Od.	*Odyssey*
Hom. Hymn.	*Homeric Hymn*
Ad Aphr.	*to Aphrodite*
Ad Dem.	*to Demeter*
Ad Hel.	*to Helios*
Hor.	tractate *Horayot, Instructions*
HSM	Harvard Semitic Monographs
HTK	Herder's theologischer Kommentar zum Neuen Testament
HTR	*Harvard Theological Review*
HTS	Harvard Theological Studies
HUCA	*Hebrew Union College Annual*
Ḥul.	tractate *Ḥullin, Animals Killed for Food*
HUTh	Hermeneutische Untersuchungen zur Theologie
Iamblichus	
Vit. Pyth.	*Vita Pythagorae* or *De Vita Pythagorica*
ibid.	*ibidem*, in the same place
IBS	*Irish Biblical Studies*
ICC	International Critical Commentary
IDB	*The Interpreter's Dictionary of the Bible*, ed. George Arthur Buttrick et al. (4 vols.; Nashville: Abingdon, 1962).
idem	the same, the same as previously mentioned (masculine)
IG	*Inscriptiones Graecae*
Ignatius	Ignatius of Antioch
Magn.	*Letter to the Magnesians*
Phld.	*Letter to the Philadelphians*
Smyrn.	*Letter to the Smyrnaeans*
Trall.	*Letter to the Trallians*
IGR	*Inscriptiones Graecae ad res Romanas pertinentes*
i.e.	*id est*, that is
IEJ	*Israel Exploration Journal*
Irenaeus	
haer.	*adversus haereses, Against Heresies*
ISFCJ	International Studies in Formative Christianity and Judaism
Isocrates	
Panath.	*Panathenaicus*
Jastrow	Marcus Jastrow, *Sepher Millim: A Dictionary of the Targumim, the Talmud Babli and Yerushalmi and the Midrashic Literature* (New York: Judaica, 1971).
JBL	*Journal of Biblical Literature*
JBLMS	—Monograph Series
JCPS	Jewish and Christian Perspectives Series
JECS	*Journal of Early Christian Studies*
Jerome	
Com. on Mt.	*Commentary on Matthew*
JHS	*Journal of Hellenic Studies*
JJS	*Journal of Jewish Studies*
Jos. Asen.	*Joseph and Aseneth*
Josephus	
Ant.	*Antiquities of the Jews*
Ap.	*Contra Apionem, Against Apion*
Bell.	*Bellum Judaicum, The Jewish War*
Vit.	*Vita, The Life of Josephus*
JPS	Jewish Publication Society
JR	*Journal of Religion*
JSJ	*Journal for the Study of Judaism*
JSJSup	Supplements to the Journal for the Study of Judaism, formerly Studia Post-Biblica
JSNT	*Journal for the Study of the New Testament*
JSNTSup	Journal for the Study of the New Testament Supplement Series
JSOT	*Journal for the Study of the Old Testament*
JSOTSup	Journal for the Study of the Old Testament Supplement Series
JSP	*Journal for the Study of the Pseudepigrapha*
JSPSup	Journal for the Study of the Pseudepigrapha Supplement Series
JTS	*Journal of Theological Studies*
JTS	Jewish Theological Seminary of America
Jub.	*Jubilees*
Justin Martyr	
1 Apol.	*First Apology*
Dial.	*Dialogue with Trypho*
KBANT	Kommentare und Beiträge zum Alten und Neuen Testament
Ketub.	tractate *Ketubot, Marriage Deeds*
KlT	Kleine Texte für Vorlesungen und Übungen
KNT	Kommentar zum Neuen Testament, edited by Theodor Zahn
κτλ.	*καὶ τὰ λοιπά*, and the rest
L.A.B.	*Liber antiquitatum biblicarum, Biblical Antiquities* (Pseudo-Philo)
LBS	Library of Biblical Studies
LCL	Loeb Classical Library
LD	Lectio divina
lit.	literally
LJPPSTT	The Literature of the Jewish People in the Period of the Second Temple and the Talmud

LQ	*Lutheran Quarterly*	NHS	Nag Hammadi Studies
LS	Charlton T. Lewis and Charles Short, *A Latin Dictionary* (Oxford: Clarendon, 1879; reprinted 1984).	NIBC	New International Biblical Commentary
		Nid.	tractate *Niddah, The Menstruant*
LSJ	Henry George Liddell, Robert Scott, and Henry Stuart Jones, *Greek-English Lexicon* (9th ed.; Oxford: Clarendon, 1940; reprinted 1966).	n(n).	note(s)
		NN	a name or names to be inserted by the reader
		no(s).	number(s)
Lucian		*NovT*	*Novum Testamentum*
Nec.	*Necyomantia* or *Menippus*	NovTSup	Novum Testamentum, Supplements
Peregr. mort.	*De Peregrini morte*		
Philops.	*Philopseudes, Lover of Lies*	Nr.	Nummer, number
Pisc.	*Piscator, The Dead Come to Life* or *The Fisherman*	NRSV	New Revised Standard Version
		n.s.	Neue Serie, new series, or nouvelle série
Pseudolog.	*Pseudologista, Mistaken Critic*	NT	New Testament
LXX	The Septuagint; all citations are from Rahlfs and translations by author, unless otherwise noted.	NTAbh	Neutestamentliche Abhandlungen
		NTApoc	*New Testament Apocrypha*, ed. Wilhelm Schneemelcher (2 vols.; rev. ed.; Cambridge: James Clarke; Louisville: Westminster John Knox, 1991, 1992).
m.	*Mishnah*		
Mak.	tractate *Makkot, Stripes*		
Mart. Pol.	*Martyrdom of Polycarp*		
Martyrol. Roman.	*Martyrologium Romanum, Roman Martyrology*	NTL	New Testament Library
Meʿil.	tractate *Meʿila, Sacrilege*	NTOA	Novum Testamentum et Orbis Antiquus
Mek.	*Mekilta*	*NTS*	*New Testament Studies*
Menaḥ.	tractate *Menaḥot, Meal-Offerings*	NTTS	New Testament Tools and Studies
metaph.	metaphorical	NumenSup	Studies in the History of Religions (Supplements to *Numen*)
MeyerK	H. A. W. Meyer, Kritisch-Exegetischer Kommentar über das Neue Testament	OCA	Orientalia Christiana analecta
		OCD	*Oxford Classical Dictionary*, ed. Simon Hornblower and Anthony Spawforth (3rd ed.; Oxford: Oxford University Press, 1996).
MGWJ	*Monatschrift für Geschichte und Wissenschaft des Judentums*		
Mid.	tractate *Middot, Measurements*		
Midr.	*Midrash*, a commentary	ODCC	*Oxford Dictionary of the Christian Church*, ed. F. L Cross and E. A. Livingstone (2nd ed.; Oxford: Oxford University Press, 1983).
Miqw.	tractate *Miqwaʾot, Immersion-Pools*		
Mn.S	Mnemosyne Supplement		
MS(S)	manuscript(s)		
MT	Masoretic Text of the Hebrew Bible	*OEANE*	*The Oxford Encyclopedia of Archaeology in the Near East*, ed. Eric M. Meyers (5 vols.; New York: Oxford University Press, 1997).
MThS	Münchener theologische Studien		
MThS.H	–Historische Abteilung		
NCBC	New Century Bible Commentary		
NEAEHL	*The New Encyclopedia of Archaeological Excavations in the Holy Land*, ed. Ephraim Stern et al. (4 vols.; New York: Simon & Schuster, 1993).	OECT	Oxford Early Christian Texts
		OG	Old Greek; to be distinguished from later Greek translations of Hebrew scriptures. Citations are from Rahlfs and translations by author.
Ned.	tractate *Nedarim, Vows*		
n.F.	Neue Folge, new series		
NGWG	Nachrichten (von) der Gesellschaft der Wissenschaften (zu) in Göttingen	*OGIS*	*Orientis Graeci Inscriptiones Selectae*, ed. W. Dittenberger (Leipzig, 1903–5; reprinted Hildesheim: G. Olms, 1960).
NGWG.PH	–Philologisch-historische Klasse		
		Origen	
NHLE	*The Nag Hammadi Library in English*, ed. James M. Robinson (3rd rev. ed.; San Francisco: Harper & Row, 1988).	*Comm. in Joh.*	*Commentary on John*
		Con. Cels.	*Contra Celsum*
		Princ.	*De Principiis*
		OT	Old Testament

ÖTBK	Ökumenischer Taschenbuchkommentar zum Neuen Testament
OTL	Old Testament Library
OTP	*The Old Testament Pseudepigrapha*, ed. James H. Charlesworth (2 vols.; Garden City, NY: Doubleday, 1983–85).
Ovid	P. Ovidius Naso
Met.	*Metamorphoses*
Pap.	Papyrus, shortened to P. when specific editions are quoted
P. Beatty	*Chester Beatty Biblical Papyri*, 8 vols.; ed. Frederic G. Kenyon, 1933–41.
P. Flor.	*Papiri Fiorentini*, 3 vols.; 1905–15.
P. Med.	*Papyri Mediolanii, Papiri Milanesi*
P. Oxy.	*The Oxyrhynchus Papyri*, ed. B. Grenfell and A. Hunt, 1898ff.
Pap. Eg.	Papyrus Egerton
par(s).	parallel(s)
Paralip. Jer.	*Paralipomena Jeremiou, The Things Omitted from Jeremiah*
Patrologia graeca	Jacques-Paul Migne, ed., *Patrologiae cursus completus: Series graeca*, 162 vols. (Paris, 1857–86).
Patrologia latina	Jacques-Paul Migne, ed., *Patrologiae cursus completus: Series latina*, 221 vols. (Paris, 1844–64).
pc	*pauci*, a few
Pesaḥ.	tractate *Pesaḥim, Feast of Passover*
Pesiq. R. Kah.	*Pesiqta de Rab Kahana*
PGC	Pelican Gospel Commentaries
PGM	*Papyri Graecae Magicae*, the Greek Magical Papyri; all references to this collection refer to the edition by Karl Preisendanz and Albert Henrichs (rev. ed.; Stuttgart: Teubner, 1973–74).
Philo	
Abr.	*De Abrahamo*
Conf. ling.	*De confusione linguarum*
Decal.	*De decalogo*
Det. pot. ins.	*Quod deterius potiori insidiari solat*
Ebr.	*De ebrietate*
Flacc.	*In Flaccum*
Jos.	*De Josepho*
Leg. Gaj.	*Legatio ad Gajum*
Mut. nom.	*De mutatione nominum*
Omn. prob. lib.	*Quod omnis probus liber sit*
Op. mun.	*De opificio mundi*
Praem. Poen.	*De Praemiis et Poenis*
Rer. div. her.	*Quis rerum divinarum heres sit*
Sacr. AC.	*De sacrificiis Abelis et Caini*
Som.	*De Somniis*
Spec. leg.	*De specialibus legibus*
Virt.	*De virtutibus*
Vit. cont.	*De vita contemplativa*
Vit. Mos.	*De vita Mosis*
Quaest. in Ex.	*Quaestiones in Exodum*
PhilologusSup	Philologus, Supplements
Philostratus	
Vita Ap.	*Vita Apollonii, Life of Apollonius*
pl(s).	plate(s)
Plato	
Ap.	*Apologia*
Leg.	*Leges*
Phaed.	*Phaedo*
Phaedr.	*Phaedrus*
Resp.	*Respublica*
Symp.	*Symposion*
Pliny	
Hist. nat.	*Naturalis Historia*
Plutarch	
Moralia	*Moralia*
Apoph.	*Apophthegmata Regum et Imperatorum*
Apoph. Lac.	*Apophthegmata Laconica*
Cons. ad Apoll.	*Consolatio ad Apollonium*
Def. orac.	*De defectu oraculorum*
Sera	*De sera numinis vindicta*
Superst.	*De superstitione*
Vit.	*Vitae, Lives*
Cato Minor.	*De Cato Minore*
Rom.	*Romulus*
pm	*per multi*, a large number
Polycarp	
Phil.	*Letter to the Philippians*
Porphyry	
Vit. Pyth.	*Vita Pythagorae*
Ps(s). Sol.	*Psalms of Solomon*
PVTG	Pseudepigrapha Veteris Testamenti graece
PW	Pauly-Wissowa, *Real-encyclopädie der classischen Altertumswissenschaft* 49 vols. (Munich, 1980).
Q	*Quelle*, source; the Synoptic Sayings Source
Qoh	Qoheleth, Ecclesiastes
Quintilian	= M. Fabius Quintilianus
Inst. Orat.	*Institutio Oratoria*
Qumran	
1Q, 4Q, etc.	Qumran Cave 1, Cave 4, etc.
1QapGen	The *Genesis Apocryphon* from Qumran Cave 1
1QH	*Hôdāyôt* (*Thanksgiving Hymns*) from Qumran Cave 1
1QM	*Serek hammilḥāmāh* (*War Scroll*) from Qumran Cave 1
1QpHab	*Pešer on Habakkuk* from Qumran Cave 1
1QS	*Serek hayyaḥad* (*Community Rule* [*Manual of Discipline*])

1QSa	*Serek lĕkôl ʿădath yiśrāʾēl* (*Rule of the Congregation*)	SBLSymS	—Symposium Series
4QDᵃ	*Damascus Document*, MS a, from Qumran Cave 4	SBLTT	—Texts and Translations
		GRRS	Graeco-Roman Religion Series
4QDᵇ	MS b	PS	Pseudepigrapha Series
4QDᵈ	MS d	SBS	Stuttgarter Bibelstudien
4QDᵉ	MS e	SBT	Studies in Biblical Theology
4QDᶠ	MS f	SbWGF	Sitzungsberichte der Wissenschaftlichen Gesellschaft an der Johann Wolfgang Goethe-Universität Frankfurt am Main
4QMMT	*Miqṣat maʿaśe ha-torah* (*Some of the Works of the Law* [*Halakhic Letter*]), from Qumran Cave 4		
4QPrNab	The *Prayer of Nabonidus* from Qumran Cave 4	SC	Sources chrétiennes
		scil.	*scilicet*, namely
4QTestim	*Testimonia* from Qumran Cave 4	SD	Studies and Documents
		Šeb.	tractate *Šebiʿit, The Seventh Year*
11QapPsᵃ	*Apocryphal Psalms*, MS a, from Qumran Cave 11	*Šebu.*	tractate *Šebuʿot, Oaths*
		sect.	section
11QMelch	*Melchizedek Scroll* from Qumran Cave 11	SemSup	Semeia Supplements
		Seneca	
11QT	*Temple Scroll* from Qumran Cave 11	*Ep. Mor.*	*Epistulae Morales, Moral Letters*
		Šeqal.	tractate *Šeqalim, The Shekel Dues*
11QTᵃ	MS a	SFISFCJ	South Florida International Studies in Formative Christianity and Judaism
Rab.	*Rabbah*, following abbreviation of the biblical book, *Midrash Rabbah*		
RAC	*Reallexikon für Antike und Christentum*, ed. Franz Josef Dölger et al. (Stuttgart: Hiersemann, 1950–).	SFSHJ	South Florida Studies in the History of Judaism
		SHAW.PH	Sitzungsberichte der Heidelberger Akademie der Wissenschaften, Philosophisch-historische Klasse
RB	*Revue biblique*		
RechBib	Recherches bibliques		
RevQ	*Revue de Qumran*		
RGRW	Religions in the Graeco-Roman World, formerly Études préliminaires aux religions orientales dans l'empire romain	SHR	Studies in the History of Religions, Supplements to *Numen*
		Sib. Or.	*Sibylline Oracles*
		sic	Thus, so
Rhet. Her.	*Rhetorica ad Herennium*	SJLA	Studies in Judaism in Late Antiquity
RNT	Regensburger Neues Testament and The Regensburg New Testament		
		SJT	*Scottish Journal of Theology*
RSV	Revised Standard Version	SNTSMS	Society for New Testament Studies Monograph Series
Šabb.	tractate *Šabbat, The Sabbath*		
SacP	Sacra pagina	SNTW	Studies of the New Testament and Its World
Sanh.	tractate *Sanhedrin, The Sanhedrin*		
SANT	Studien zum Alten und Neuen Testament	*Soph. Jes. Chr.*	*Sophia of Jesus Christ*
		Sophocles	
SAOC	Studies in Ancient Oriental Civilization	*Oed. Tyr.*	*Oedipus Tyrannus*
		Phil.	*Philoctetes*
SBB	Stuttgarter biblische Beiträge	SO.S	Symbolae Osloenses Supplements
SBL	Society of Biblical Literature	SP	Scholars Press
SBLAB	—Academia Biblica	SPHS	—Homage Series
SBLDS	—Dissertation Series	SPRTS	—Reprints and Translations Series
SBLEJL	—Early Judaism and Its Literature		
		SSAC	Sussidi allo studio delle antichità cristiane
SBLMS	—Monograph Series		
SBLSBS	—Sources for Biblical Study	SSEJC	Studies in Scripture in Early Judaism and Christianity
SBLSCS	—Septuagint and Cognate Studies		
		STDJ	Studies on the Texts of the Desert of Judah
SBLSPS	—Seminar Papers Series		
SBLSS	—Semeia Studies		

Str-B	[Hermann L. Strack and] Paul Billerbeck, *Kommentar zum Neuen Testament aus Talmud und Midrasch*; 6 vols. (Munich: Beck, 1926–61).
StTh	*Studia Theologica*
StUNT	Studien zur Umwelt des Neuen Testaments
Suetonius	Suetonius, *The Twelve Caesars*
Aug.	*Augustus*
C. Caligula	*Gaius Caligula*
Claud.	*Claudius*
Dom.	*Domitian*
Jul.	*Julius*
Tib.	*Tiberius*
Vesp.	*Vespasian*
SUKHVL	Skrifter utgivna av Kungl. Humanistiska Vetenskapssamfundet i Lund
suppl.	supplementary
SUSIR	Skrifter utgivna av Svenska Institutet i Rom
s.v(v).	*sub verbo* or *sub voce*, under the word(s) (entry[ies])
SVTP	Studia in Veteris Testamenti Pseudepigrapha
t.	Tosephta
T. Abraham	*Testament of Abraham*
T. 12 Patr.	*Testaments of the Twelve Patriarchs*
T. Benj.	*Testament of Benjamin*
T. Dan	*Testament of Dan*
T. Iss.	*Testament of Issachar*
T. Jos.	*Testament of Joseph*
T. Jud.	*Testament of Judah*
T. Levi	*Testament of Levi*
T. Sim.	*Testament of Simeon*
T. Zeb.	*Testament of Zebulon*
T. Job	*Testament of Job*
T. Sol.	*Testament of Solomon*
Ta'an.	tractate *Ta'anit, Days of Fasting*
Tacitus	
Hist.	*Histories*
Ann.	*Annals*
TANZ	Texte und Arbeiten zum neutestamentlichen Zeitalter
TBAW	Tübinger Beiträge zur Altertumswissenschaft
TDNT	*Theological Dictionary of the New Testament*, ed. G. Kittel and G. Friedrich; trans. and ed. Geoffrey W. Bromiley (10 vols.; Grand Rapids: Eerdmans, 1964–76).
Tg. Onq.	*Targum Onqelos*
ThBü	Theologische Bücherei
Θ	Theodotion; a translation of the Hebrew scriptures attributed to a man of that name. Citations are from Rahlfs and translations by author.
ThHKNT	Theologischer Handkommentar zum Neuen Testament
ThLZ	*Theologische Literaturzeitung*
Thom. Cont.	*Book of Thomas the Contender*
Tohar.	tractate *Ṭoharot, Cleannesses*
trans.	translation(s); translated by
TS	*Theological Studies*
TSAJ	Texte und Studien zum antiken Judentum/Texts and Studies in Ancient Judaism
TU	Texte und Untersuchungen zur Geschichte der altchristlichen Literatur
TZ	*Theologische Zeitschrift*
TzF	Texte zur Forschung
UBSGNT³	*United Bible Societies' Greek New Testament*, 3rd ed.
UNDCSJCA	University of Notre Dame Center for the Study of Judaism and Christianity in Antiquity
UNT	Untersuchungen zum Neuen Testament
USQR	*Union Seminary Quarterly Review*
UTR	Utrechtse Theologische Reeks
VC	*Vigiliae christianae*
VCSup	Supplements to Vigiliae Christianae
Vg.	Vulgate
v(v).l(l).	*varia(e) lectio(nes),* variant reading(s)
v(v).	verse(s)
Virgil	P. Vergilius Maro
Aen.	*Aeneid*
Vit. proph.	*Vitae prophetarum*
VTSup	*Vetus Testamentum,* Supplements
WBC	Word Biblical Commentary
WMANT	Wissenschaftliche Monographien zum Alten und Neuen Testament
WSC	Wisconsin Studies in Classics
WUNT	Wissenschaftliche Untersuchungen zum Neuen Testament
Xenophon	
Hell.	*Hellenica*
Mem.	*Memorabilia Socratis*
y.	Jerusalem Talmud
Yad.	tractate *Yadayim, Hands*
Yeb.	tractate *Yebamot, Sisters-in-law*
ZKWL	*Zeitschrift für kirchliche Wissenschaft und kirchliches Leben*
ZNW	*Zeitschrift für die neutestamentliche Wissenschaft*
ZPE	*Zeitschrift für Papyrologie und Epigraphik*
ZThK	*Zeitschrift für Theologie und Kirche*

2. Short Titles of Commentaries, Studies, and Articles Often Cited

Commentaries on Mark and certain works of reference are cited by the author's name only. Other frequently mentioned monographs or articles are cited by author and short title. In all cases full bibliographical information accompanies the first citation.

Abrahams, *Studies in Pharisaism*
Israel Abrahams, *Studies in Pharisaism and the Gospels* (2 vols.; Cambridge: Cambridge University Press, 1917–24; reprinted 2 vols. in 1; LBS; New York: Ktav, 1967). The original two volumes are cited in this commentary.

Achtemeier, "'And He Followed Him'"
Paul J. Achtemeier, "'And He Followed Him': Miracles and Discipleship in Mark 10:46-52," *Semeia* 11 (1978) 115–45.

Achtemeier, *1 Peter*
Paul J. Achtemeier, *1 Peter: A Commentary on First Peter* (Hermeneia; Minneapolis: Fortress, 1996).

Achtemeier, "*Omne Verbum Sonat*"
Paul J. Achtemeier, "*Omne Verbum Sonat*: The New Testament and the Oral Environment of Late Western Antiquity," *JBL* 109 (1990) 3–27.

Achtemeier, "Miracle Catenae"
Paul J. Achtemeier, "Toward the Isolation of Pre-Markan Miracle Catenae," *JBL* 89 (1970) 265–91.

Ahearne-Kroll, "Suffering of David"
Stephen P. Ahearne-Kroll, "The Suffering of David and the Suffering of Jesus: The Use of Four Psalms of Individual Lament in the Passion Narrative of the Gospel of Mark" (2 vols.; Ph.D. diss., University of Chicago, 2005).

Aland, "Bemerkungen"
Kurt Aland, "Bemerkungen zum Schluss des Markusevangeliums," in E. Earle Ellis and Max Wilcox, eds., *Neotestamentica et Semitica: Studies in Honour of Matthew Black* (Edinburgh: T & T Clark, 1969) 157–80.

Aland, "Der Schluss des Markusevangeliums"
Kurt Aland, "Der Schluss des Markusevangeliums," in Maurits Sabbe, ed., *L'Évangile selon Marc: tradition et redaction* (BEThL 34; 2nd rev. ed.; Leuven: Leuven University Press/Peeters, 1988; 1st ed. 1974) 435–70.

Aland, *Synopsis*
Kurt Aland, ed., *Synopsis Quattuor Evangeliorum* (15th rev. ed.; Stuttgart: Deutsche Bibelgesellschaft, 1996).

Aland and Aland
Kurt Aland and Barbara Aland, *The Text of the New Testament* (2nd rev. ed.; Grand Rapids: Eerdmans; Leiden: Brill, 1989; German 2nd rev. ed., 1981).

Albl, "*And Scripture Cannot Be Broken*"
Martin C. Albl, "*And Scripture Cannot Be Broken*": *The Form and Function of the Early Christian* Testimonia *Collections* (NovTSup 96; Leiden: Brill, 1999).

Alexander, "Demonology of the Dead Sea Scrolls"
Philip S. Alexander, "The Demonology of the Dead Sea Scrolls," in Peter W. Flint and James C. VanderKam, eds., *The Dead Sea Scrolls after Fifty Years: A Comprehensive Assessment* (2 vols.; Leiden/Boston/Cologne: Brill, 1998–99) 2:331–53.

Alexander, "Jesus and the Golden Rule"
Philip S. Alexander, "Jesus and the Golden Rule," in James H. Charlesworth and Loren L. Johns, eds., *Hillel and Jesus: Comparative Studies of Two Major Religious Leaders* (Minneapolis: Fortress, 1997) 363–88.

Allen
W. C. Allen, *The Gospel according to Saint Mark: With Introduction, Notes and Map* (Oxford Church Biblical Commentary; London: Rivingtons, 1915).

Anderson and Moore
Janice Capel Anderson and Stephen D. Moore, eds., *Mark and Method: New Approaches in Biblical Studies* (Minneapolis: Fortress, 1992).

Asher, *Polarity and Change*
Jeffrey R. Asher, *Polarity and Change in 1 Corinthians 15* (HUTh 42; Tübingen: Mohr Siebeck, 2000).

Attridge, *Hebrews*
Harold W. Attridge, *The Epistle to the Hebrews: A Commentary on the Epistle to the Hebrews* (Hermeneia; Philadelphia: Fortress, 1989).

Aune, "Magic"
David E. Aune, "Magic in Early Christianity," *ANRW* 2.23.2 (1980) 1507–57.

Aune, *Literary Environment*
David E. Aune, *The New Testament in Its Literary Environment* (Philadelphia: Westminster, 1987).

Aune, *Prophecy*
David E. Aune, *Prophecy in Early Christianity and the Ancient Mediterranean World* (Grand Rapids: Eerdmans, 1983).

Babbitt, *Plutarch's Moralia*
Frank Cole Babbitt, *Plutarch's Moralia* (15 vols.; LCL; Cambridge, MA: Harvard University Press, 1931).

Bammel and Moule, *Jesus*
Ernst Bammel and Charles F. D. Moule, eds., *Jesus and the Politics of His Day* (Cambridge/New York: Cambridge University Press, 1984).

Bauckham, *Jude, 2 Peter*
Richard J. Bauckham, *Jude, 2 Peter* (WBC 50; Waco, TX: Word Books, 1983).

Baumgarten, *Qumran Cave 4*
Joseph M. Baumgarten et al., eds., *Qumran Cave 4: XIII The Damascus Document (4Q266–273)* (DJD 18; Oxford: Clarendon, 1996).

Becker, *Markus-Evangelium*
Eve-Marie Becker, *Das Markus-Evangelium im Rahmen antiker Historiographie* (WUNT 194; Tübingen: Mohr Siebeck, 2006).

Bedenbender, "Orte mitten im Meer"
Andreas Bedenbender, "Orte mitten im Meer," *Texte & Kontexte* 86 (2000) 31–60.

Benovitz, *KOL NIDRE*
Moshe Benovitz, *KOL NIDRE: Studies in the Development of Rabbinic Votive Institutions* (BJS 315; Atlanta: Scholars Press, 1998).

Berger, *Gesetzesauslegung*
Klaus Berger, *Die Gesetzesauslegung Jesu: Ihr historischer Hintergrund im Judentum und im Alten Testament*, Teil I, *Markus und Parallelen* (WANT 40; Neukirchen-Vluyn: Neukirchener Verlag, 1972).

Berger, "Hellenistische Gattungen"
Klaus Berger, "Hellenistiche Gattungen im Neuen Testament," *ANRW* 2.25.2 (1984) 1031–1885.

Best, *Following Jesus*
Ernest Best, *Following Jesus: Discipleship in the Gospel of Mark* (JSNTSup 4; Sheffield: JSOT Press, 1981).

Best, *Temptation*
Ernest Best, *The Temptation and the Passion: The Markan Soteriology* (2nd ed.; SNTSMS 2; Cambridge: Cambridge University Press, 1990; 1st ed. 1965).

Betz, *Galatians*
Hans Dieter Betz, *Galatians: A Commentary on Paul's Letter to the Churches in Galatia* (Hermeneia; Philadelphia: Fortress, 1979).

Betz, *Magical Papyri*
Hans Dieter Betz, ed., *The Greek Magical Papyri in Translation Including the Demotic Spells* (Chicago: University of Chicago Press, 1986; 2nd ed. 1992).

Betz, *Sermon*
Hans Dieter Betz, *The Sermon on the Mount: A Commentary on the Sermon on the Mount, Including the Sermon on the Plain* (Hermeneia; Minneapolis: Fortress, 1995).

Beyer, *Semitische Syntax*
Klaus Beyer, *Semitische Syntax im Neuen Testament*, vol. 1: *Satzlehre, Teil 1* (2nd rev. ed.; StUNT 1; Göttingen: Vandenhoeck & Ruprecht, 1968).

Binder, *Into the Temple Courts*
Donald D. Binder, *Into the Temple Courts: The Place of the Synagogue in the Second Temple Period* (SBLDS 169; Atlanta: Society of Biblical Literature, 1999).

Black, *Apocalypsis Henochi Graece*
Matthew Black, ed., *Apocalypsis Henochi Graece* (PVTG 3; Leiden: Brill, 1970).

Black, *Mark*
C. Clifton Black, *Mark: Images of an Apostolic Interpreter* (Studies on Personalities of the New Testament; Columbia: University of South Carolina Press, 1994).

Black, "Oration at Olivet"
C. Clifton Black, "An Oration at Olivet: Some Rhetorical Dimensions of Mark 13," in Duane F. Watson, ed., *Persuasive Artistry: Studies in New Testament Rhetoric in Honor of George A. Kennedy* (JSNTSup 50; Sheffield: Sheffield Academic Press, 1991) 66–92.

Blackburn, *Theios Anēr*
Barry Blackburn, *Theios Anēr and the Markan Miracle Traditions* (WUNT 2.40; Tübingen: Mohr Siebeck, 1991).

Blackman, *Mishnayoth*
Philip Blackman, *Mishnayoth* (2nd rev. ed.; Gateshead [Durham]: Judaica Press, 1983).

Blenkinsopp, *Isaiah 1–39*
Joseph Blenkinsopp, *Isaiah 1–39: A New Translation with Introduction and Commentary* (AB 19; New York/London: Doubleday, 2000).

Blenkinsopp, *Isaiah 56–66*
Joseph Blenkinsopp, *Isaiah 56–66: A New Translation with Introduction and Commentary* (AB 19B; New York: Doubleday, 2003).

Boling and Wright, *Joshua*
Robert G. Boling and G. Ernest Wright, *Joshua: A New Translation with Notes and Commentary* (AB 6; Garden City, NY: Doubleday, 1982).

Bonner, "Thaumaturgic Technique"
Campbell Bonner, "Traces of Thaumaturgic Technique in the Miracles," *HTR* 20 (1927) 171–81.

Boobyer, "Galilee and Galileans"
George H. Boobyer, "Galilee and Galileans in St. Mark's Gospel," *BJRL* 35 (1952–53) 334–48; reprinted in *Galilee and Galileans in St. Mark's Gospel* (Manchester: John Rylands Library/Manchester University Press, 1953).

Booth, *Jesus and the Laws of Purity*
Roger P. Booth, *Jesus and the Laws of Purity: Tradition History and Legal History in Mark 7* (JSNTSup 13; Sheffield: JSOT Press, 1986).

Bornkamm, "Doppelgebot"
Günther Bornkamm, "Das Doppelgebot der Liebe," in Walther Eltester, ed., *Neutestamentliche Studien für Rudolf Bultmann zu seinem 70. Geburtstag* (2nd rev. ed.; BZNW 21; Berlin: Töpelmann, 1957) 85–93.

Borrell, *Peter's Denial*
Agustí Borrell, *The Good News of Peter's Denial: A Narrative and Rhetorical Reading of Mark 14:54.66-72* (SFISFCJ 7; Atlanta: Scholars Press/University of South Florida, 1998).

Bover
José Maria Bover, *Novi Testamenti Biblia Graeca et Latina* (Madrid, 1943; 5th ed. 1968).

Bradshaw, *Search*
Paul F. Bradshaw, *The Search for the Origins of Christian Worship: Sources and Methods for the Study of Early Liturgy* (New York/Oxford: Oxford University Press, 1992).

Brandenburger, *Markus 13 und die Apokalyptik*
Egon Brandenburger, *Markus 13 und die Apokalyptik* (Göttingen: Vandenhoeck & Ruprecht, 1984).

Brandt, *Die jüdischen Baptismen*
Wilhelm Brandt, *Die jüdischen Baptismen oder das religiöse Waschen und Baden im Judentum mit Einschluss des Judenchristentums* (BZNW 18; Giessen: Töpelmann, 1910).

Brown, *Bede*
George Hardin Brown, *Bede the Venerable* (Boston: Twayne/G. K. Hall, 1987).

Brown, *Death*
Raymond E. Brown, *The Death of the Messiah: From Gethsemane to the Grave: A Commentary on the Passion Narratives in the Four Gospels* (2 vols.; ABRL; New York/London: Doubleday, 1994).

Bruce, "Render to Caesar"
Frederick F. Bruce, "Render to Caesar," in Ernst Bammel and Charles F. D. Moule, eds., *Jesus and the Politics of His Day* (Cambridge/New York: Cambridge University Press, 1984.

Bultmann, *History*
Rudolf Bultmann, *The History of the Synoptic Tradition* (trans. John Marsh from the 2nd Germ. ed. 1931; New York: Harper & Row, 1963; rev. ed. with additions from the 1962 supplement, 1968).

Burchard, "Das doppelte Liebesgebot"
Christoph Burchard, "Das doppelte Liebesgebot in der frühen christlichen Überlieferung," in Eduard Lohse, ed., *Der Ruf Jesu und die Antwort der Gemeinde: Exegetische Untersuchungen Joachim Jeremias zum 70. Geburtstag* (Göttingen: Vandenhoeck & Ruprecht, 1970).

Burnett et al., *Roman Provincial Coinage*
Andrew Burnett, Michel Amandry, and Père Pau Ripollès, *Roman Provincial Coinage*, vol. 1: *From the Death of Caesar to the Death of Vitellius (44 BC–AD 69)*, part I: *Introduction and Catalogue* (London: British Museum Press; Paris: Bibliothèque Nationale, 1992).

Burridge, *What Are the Gospels?*
Richard A. Burridge, *What Are the Gospels? A Comparison with Graeco-Roman Biography* (SNTSMS 70; Cambridge: Cambridge University Press, 1992; 2nd rev. ed. Grand Rapids/Cambridge: Eerdmans; Dearborn, MI: Dove Booksellers, 2004).

Cahill, *Expositio Evangelii*
Michael Cahill, ed., *Expositio Evangelii secundum Marcum* (CChrSL 82; Scriptores Celtigenae pars 2; Turnhout: Brepols, 1997).

Cahill, *First Commentary*
Michael Cahill, *The First Commentary on Mark: An Annotated Translation* (New York/Oxford: Oxford University Press, 1998).

Camery-Hoggatt, *Irony*
Jerry Camery-Hoggatt, *Irony in Mark's Gospel: Text and Subtext* (SNTSMS 72; Cambridge/New York: Cambridge University Press, 1992).

Campbell, "Engagement"
William Sanger Campbell, "Engagement, Disengagement and Obstruction: Jesus' Defense Strategies in Mark's Trial and Execution Scenes (14.53-64; 15.1-39)," *JSNT* 26 (2004) 283–300.

Cancik, "Lucian on Conversion"
Hubert Cancik, "Lucian on Conversion: Remarks on Lucian's Dialogue *Nigrinos*," in Adela Yarbro Collins, ed., *Ancient and Modern Perspectives on the Bible and Culture: Essays in Honor of Hans Dieter Betz* (SPHS; Atlanta: Scholars Press, 1998) 26–48.

Cancik, *Markus-Philologie*
Hubert Cancik, ed., *Markus-Philologie: Historische, literargeschichtliche und stilistische Untersuchungen zum zweiten Evangelium* (WUNT 33; Tübingen: Mohr Siebeck, 1984).

Cancik et al., *Geschichte*
Hubert Cancik, Hermann Lichtenberger, and Peter Schäfer, eds., *Geschichte–Tradition–Reflexion: Festschrift für Martin Hengel zum 70. Geburtstag* (3 vols.; Tübingen: Mohr Siebeck, 1996).

Carlston, "Transfiguration and Resurrection"
Charles E. Carlston, "Transfiguration and Resurrection," *JBL* 80 (1961) 233–40.

Catchpole, "'Triumphal' Entry"
David R. Catchpole, "The 'Triumphal' Entry," in Ernst Bammel and Charles F. D. Moule, eds., *Jesus and the Politics of His Day* (Cambridge/New York: Cambridge University Press, 1984) 319–34.

Chancey, *Gentile Galilee*
Mark A. Chancey, *The Myth of a Gentile Galilee* (SNTSMS 118; Cambridge/New York: Cambridge University Press, 2002).

Charlesworth, *Dead Sea Scrolls*
James H. Charlesworth et al., eds., *The Dead Sea Scrolls: Hebrew, Aramaic, and Greek Texts with English Translations* (Princeton Theological Seminary Dead Sea Scrolls Project; Tübingen: Mohr Siebeck; Louisville: Westminster John Knox Press, 1993ff.)

Chazon, *Liturgical Perspectives*
Esther G. Chazon, ed., *Liturgical Perspectives: Prayer and Poetry in Light of the Dead Sea Scrolls* (STDJ 48; Leiden: Brill, 2003).

Cheesman, *Auxilia of the Roman Imperial Army*
George L. Cheesman, *The Auxilia of the Roman Imperial Army* (Oxford: Clarendon, 1914; reprinted Chicago: Ares, 1975).

Childs, *Exodus*
Brevard S. Childs, *The Book of Exodus* (OTL; Philadelphia: Westminster, 1974).

Chronis, "Torn Veil"
Harry L. Chronis, "The Torn Veil: Cultus and Christology in Mark 15:37-39," *JBL* 101 (1982) 97–114.

Cohn, *Trial*
Haim Cohn, *The Trial and Death of Jesus* (New York/London: Harper & Row, 1971).

Collins, "Afterlife in Apocalyptic Literature"
John J. Collins, "The Afterlife in Apocalyptic Literature," in Alan J. Avery-Peck and Jacob Neusner, eds., *Judaism in Late Antiquity*, part 4: *Death, Life-after-Death, Resurrection and the World-to-Come in the Judaisms of Antiquity* (HO 1, Der Nahe und Mittlere Osten/The Near and Middle East 49; Leiden: Brill, 2000) 119–39.

Collins, *Apocalyptic Imagination*
John J. Collins, *The Apocalyptic Imagination: An Introduction to Jewish Apocalyptic Literature* (2nd ed.; Grand Rapids: Eerdmans, 1998).

Collins, *Apocalypticism*
    John J. Collins, *Apocalypticism in the Dead Sea Scrolls* (Literature of the Dead Sea Scrolls; London/New York: Routledge, 1997).

Collins, *Daniel*
    John J. Collins, *Daniel: A Commentary on the Book of Daniel* (Hermeneia; Minneapolis: Fortress, 1993).

Collins, *Scepter and the Star*
    John J. Collins, *The Scepter and the Star: The Messiahs of the Dead Sea Scrolls and Other Ancient Literature* (New York: Doubleday, 1995).

Colson and Whitaker, *Philo*
    Francis H. Colson and George H. Whitaker, *Philo* (10 vols.; LCL; London: Heinemann; Cambridge, MA: Harvard University Press, 1934).

Conzelmann, *Acts*
    Hans Conzelmann, *Acts of the Apostles: A Commentary on the Acts of the Apostles* (Hermeneia; Philadelphia: Fortress, 1987).

Cook, *Structure*
    John G. Cook, *The Structure and Persuasive Power of Mark: A Linguistic Approach* (SBLSS; Atlanta: Scholars Press, 1995).

Cotter, *Miracles*
    Wendy Cotter, *Miracles in Greco-Roman Antiquity: A Sourcebook* (London/New York: Routledge, 1999).

Cox, *History and Critique*
    Steven Lynn Cox, *A History and Critique of Scholarship concerning the Markan Endings* (Lewiston, NY: Edwin Mellen, 1993) 13–51.

Coxe, *Apostolic Fathers*
    A. Cleveland Coxe, *The Apostolic Fathers with Justin Martyr and Irenaeus* (ANF 1; American Reprint of the Edinburgh Edition; Grand Rapids: Eerdmans, 1985).

Cranfield
    C. E. B. Cranfield, *The Gospel according to Saint Mark* (rev. ed.; CGTC; Cambridge/New York: Cambridge University Press, 1977; 1st ed. 1959).

Croy, *Mutilation*
    N. Clayton Croy, *The Mutilation of Mark's Gospel* (Nashville: Abingdon, 2003).

Daly, *Aesop without Morals*
    Lloyd W. Daly, *Aesop without Morals* (New York/London: Thomas Yoseloff, 1961).

Daly-Denton, *David*
    Margaret Daly-Denton, *David in the Fourth Gospel: The Johannine Reception of the Psalms* (AGJU 47; Leiden: Brill, 2000).

Danby, *Mishnah*
    Herbert Danby, *The Mishnah* (London: Oxford University Press, 1933).

D'Angelo, "Gender and Power"
    Mary Rose D'Angelo, "Gender and Power in the Gospel of Mark: The Daughter of Jairus and the Woman with the Flow of Blood," in John C. Cavadini, ed., *Miracles in Jewish and Christian Antiquity: Imagining Truth* (Notre Dame Studies in Theology 3; Notre Dame, IN: University of Notre Dame Press, 1999).

Danove, *End of Mark's Story*
    Paul L. Danove, *The End of Mark's Story: A Methodological Study* (BIS 3; Leiden: Brill, 1993).

Daube, *New Testament*
    David Daube, *The New Testament and Rabbinic Judaism* (New York: Arno Press, 1973; 1st ed. 1956).

Davidsen, *Narrative Jesus*
    Ole Davidsen, *The Narrative Jesus: A Semiotic Reading of Mark's Gospel* (Aarhus: Aarhus University Press, 1993).

Davies and Allison, *Matthew*
    W. D. Davies and Dale C. Allison, Jr., *A Critical and Exegetical Commentary on the Gospel according to Saint Matthew* (3 vols.; Edinburgh: T. & T. Clark, 1988, 1991, 1997).

Deines, *Die Pharisäer*
    Roland Deines, *Die Pharisäer: Ihr Verständnis im Spiegel der christlichen und jüdischen Forschung seit Wellhausen und Graetz* (WUNT 101; Tübingen: Mohr Siebeck, 1997).

de Jonge, "Cleansing"
    Henk J. de Jonge, "The Cleansing of the Temple in Mark 11:15 and Zechariah 14:21," in Christopher Tuckett, ed., *The Book of Zechariah and Its Influence* (Aldershot, Hampshire/Burlington, VT: Ashgate, 2003) 87–99.

de Jonge, *Testaments of the Twelve Patriarchs*
    Marinus de Jonge, *The Testaments of the Twelve Patriarchs: A Critical Edition of the Greek Text* (PVTG 1.2; Leiden: Brill, 1978).

Deming, "First Century Discussion"
    Will Deming, "Mark 9.42–10.12; Matthew 5.27-32, and *B. Nid.* 13b: A First Century Discussion of Male Sexuality," *NTS* 36 (1990) 130–41.

Denis and Janssens, *Concordance grecque*
    Albert-Marie Denis and Yvonne Janssens, *Concordance grecque des pseudépigraphes d'Ancien Testament* (Louvain-la-Neuve: Université Catholique de Louvain; Leiden: Brill/Peeters, 1987).

Derrett, "Law in the New Testament"
    J. Duncan M. Derrett, "Law in the New Testament: *Si scandalizaverit te manus tua abscinde illam* (Mk.IX.42) and Comparative Legal History," in idem, *Studies in the New Testament,* vol. 1: *Glimpses of the Legal and Social Presuppositions of the Authors* (Leiden: Brill, 1977) 4–31.

Dewey, *Markan Public Debate*
    Joanna Dewey, *Markan Public Debate: Literary Technique, Concentric Structure, and Theology in Mark 2:1–3:6* (SBLDS 48; Chico, CA: Scholars Press, 1980).

Dibelius, *From Tradition to Gospel*
    Martin Dibelius, *Die Formgeschichte des Evangeliums* (Tübingen: Mohr Siebeck, 1919; 2nd ed., 1933); ET *From Tradition to Gospel* (New York: Scribner's Sons, 1935).

Dibelius-Conzelmann, *Pastoral Epistles*
Martin Dibelius and Hans Conzelmann, *The Pastoral Epistles: A Commentary on the Pastoral Epistles* (Hermeneia; Philadelphia: Fortress, 1972).

Dibelius-Greeven, *James*
Martin Dibelius, *James: A Commentary on the Epistle of James* (rev. by Heinrich Greeven; Hermeneia; Philadelphia: Fortress, 1976).

Dihle, *Entstehung*
Albrecht Dihle, *Die Entstehung der historischen Biographie* (SHAW.PH 1986.3; Heidelberg: Carl Winter/Universitätsverlag, 1987).

Dihle, *Studien*
Albrecht Dihle, *Studien zur griechischen Biographie* (AAWG.PH, 3. F., Nr. 37; Göttingen: Vandenhoeck & Ruprecht, 1956).

Dillon and Hershbell
John Dillon and Jackson Hershbell, eds., *Iamblichus: On the Pythagorean Way of Life* (SBLTT 29; GRRS 11; Atlanta: Scholars Press, 1991).

Dimant and Rappaport
Devorah Dimant and Uriel Rappaport, eds., *The Dead Sea Scrolls: Forty Years of Research* (STDJ 10; Leiden: Brill; Jerusalem: Magnes Press/Yad Izhak Ben-Zvi, 1992).

Dixon, *Roman Family*
Suzanne Dixon, *The Roman Family* (Baltimore/London: Johns Hopkins University Press, 1992).

von Dobbeler, *Gericht und Erbarmen*
Stephanie von Dobbeler, *Das Gericht und das Erbarmen Gottes: Die Botschaft Johannes des Täufers und ihre Rezeption bei den Johannesjüngern im Rahmen der Theologiegeschichte des Frühjudentums* (BBB 70; Frankfurt am Main: Athenäum, 1988).

von Dobschütz, "Erzählerkunst"
Ernst von Dobschütz, "Zur Erzählerkunst des Markus," *ZNW* 27 (1928) 193–98.

Dodd, *According to the Scriptures*
C. H. Dodd, *According to the Scriptures: The Substructure of New Testament Theology* (London: Collins/Fontana Books, 1965; 1st ed. 1952).

Doering, *Schabbat*
Lutz Doering, *Schabbat: Sabbathalacha und -praxis im antiken Judentum und Urchristentum* (TSAJ 78; Tübingen: Mohr Siebeck, 1999).

Döller, "Der Wein in Bibel und Talmud"
Johannes Döller, "Der Wein in Bibel und Talmud," *Bib* 4 (1923) 143–67, 267–99.

Donahue, *Are You the Christ?*
John R. Donahue, *Are You the Christ? The Trial Narrative in the Gospel of Mark* (SBLDS 10; Missoula, MT: SBL/Scholars Press, 1973).

Donahue, *Discipleship*
John R. Donahue, *The Theology and Setting of Discipleship in the Gospel of Mark* (The 1983 Père Marquette Theology Lecture; Milwaukee: Marquette University Press, 1983).

Donahue, "Neglected Factor"
John R. Donahue, "A Neglected Factor in the Theology of Mark," *JBL* 101 (1982) 563–94.

Donahue, "Quest"
John R. Donahue, "The Quest for the Community of Mark's Gospel," in van Segbroeck et al., *The Four Gospels 1992,* 823–28, 832–35.

Donahue and Harrington
John R. Donahue and Daniel J. Harrington, *The Gospel of Mark* (SacP 2; A Michael Glazier Book; Collegeville, MN: Liturgical Press, 2002).

Dormeyer, *Evangelium*
Detlev Dormeyer, *Evangelium als literarische und theologische Gattung* (EdF 263; Darmstadt: Wissenschaftliche Buchgesellschaft, 1989).

Dormeyer, *Die Passion Jesu*
Detlev Dormeyer, *Die Passion Jesu as Verhaltensmodell: Literarische und theologische Analyse der Traditions- und Redaktionsgeschichte der Markuspassion* (NTAbh n.F. 11; Münster: Aschendorff, 1974).

Dowd, *Prayer*
Sharyn Echols Dowd, *Prayer, Power, and the Problem of Suffering: Mark 11:22-25 in the Context of Markan Theology* (SBLDS 105; Atlanta: Scholars Press, 1988).

Duling, "Solomon, Exorcism"
Dennis C. Duling, "Solomon, Exorcism, and the Son of David," *HTR* 68 (1975) 235–52.

Dwyer, *Wonder*
Timothy Dwyer, *The Motif of Wonder in the Gospel of Mark* (JSNTSup 128; Sheffield: Sheffield Academic Press, 1996).

Edelstein and Edelstein
Emma J. Edelstein and Ludwig Edelstein, *Asclepius: Collection and Interpretation of the Testimonies* (2 vols.; Baltimore: Johns Hopkins University Press, 1945; reprinted with a new introduction by Gary B. Ferngren, 1998).

Edwards, "Markan Sandwiches"
James R. Edwards, "Markan Sandwiches: The Significance of Interpolations in Markan Narratives," *NovT* 31 (1989) 193–216.

Ehrman, *Apostolic Fathers*
Bart Ehrman, ed. and trans., *The Apostolic Fathers* (2 vols.; LCL; Cambridge, MA/London: Harvard University Press, 2003).

Ehrman, *Orthodox Corruption*
Bart D. Ehrman, *The Orthodox Corruption of Scripture: The Effect of Early Christological Controversies on the Text of the New Testament* (New York/Oxford: Oxford University Press, 1993).

Eitrem, *Some Notes*
Samson Eitrem, *Some Notes on the Demonology in the New Testament* (SO.S 12; Oslo: A. W. Brøgger, 1950).

Elliott, "Eclectic Textual Commentary"
James K. Elliott, "An Eclectic Textual Commentary on the Greek Text of Mark's Gospel," in Elliott, *Language and Style,* 189–201.

Elliott, *Language and Style*
James K. Elliott, ed., *The Language and Style of the Gospel of Mark: An Edition of C. H. Turner's "Notes on Marcan Usage" Together with Other Comparable Studies* (NovTSup 71; Leiden: Brill, 1993).

Elliott, "Mark 1.1-3"
James K. Elliott, "Mark 1.1-3—A Later Addition to the Gospel?" *NTS* 46 (2000) 584–88.

Elliott, "Text and Language of the Endings to Mark's Gospel"
James K. Elliott, "The Text and Language of the Endings to Mark's Gospel," in Elliott, *Language and Style*, 203–11.

Elliott, "Jesus Movement"
John H. Elliott, "The Jesus Movement Was Not Egalitarian but Family-Oriented," *BI* 11 (2003) 173–210.

Ellis and Wilcox, *Neotestamentica et Semitica*
E. Earle Ellis and Max Wilcox, eds., *Neotestamentica et Semitica: Studies in Honour of Matthew Black* (Edinburgh: T & T Clark, 1969).

Ennulat, *Minor Agreements*
Andreas Ennulat, *Die "Minor Agreements": Untersuchungen zu einer offenen Frage des synoptischen Problems* (WUNT 2.62; Tübingen: Mohr Siebeck, 1994).

Epp, "Dynamic View"
Eldon Jay Epp, "The Significance of the Papyri for Determining the Nature of the New Testament Text in the Second Century: A Dynamic View of Textual Transmission," in William L. Petersen, ed., *Gospel Traditions in the Second Century: Origins, Recensions, Text, and Transmission* (CJA 3; Notre Dame, IN: University of Notre Dame Press, 1989) 1–32; reprinted in Eldon Jay Epp and Gordon D. Fee, *Studies in the Theory and Method of New Testament Textual Criticism* (SD 45; Grand Rapids: Eerdmans, 1993) 274–97. Cited according to the original publication.

Eshel, "Demonology in Palestine"
Esther Eshel, "Demonology in Palestine during the Second Temple Period" (Ph.D. diss., Hebrew University in Jerusalem, 1999) [Hebrew with an English abstract (pp. I–XIV)].

Eshel, "Genres of Magical Texts"
Esther Eshel, "Genres of Magical Texts," in Lange et al., *Demons*, 395–415.

Evans
Craig A. Evans, *Mark 8:27–16:20* (WBC 34B; Nashville: Thomas Nelson, 2001).

Fallon, "Law in Philo and Ptolemy"
Francis T. Fallon, "The Law in Philo and Ptolemy: A Note on the Letter to Flora," *VC* 30 (1976) 45–51.

Feigel, *Der Einfluss des Weissagungsbeweises*
Friedrich Karl Feigel, *Der Einfluss des Weissagungsbeweises und anderer Motive auf die Leidensgeschichte: Ein Beitrag zur Evangelienkritik* (Tübingen: Mohr Siebeck, 1910).

Finegan, *Archaeology*
Jack Finegan, *The Archaeology of the New Testament*
(rev. ed.; Princeton, NJ: Princeton University Press, 1992).

Fitzmyer, *Essays*
Joseph A. Fitzmyer, *Essays on the Semitic Background of the New Testament* (London: G. Chapman, 1971; Missoula, MT: Scholars Press, 1971). Reprinted in Fitzmyer, *The Semitic Background*.

Fitzmyer, *Luke*
Joseph A. Fitzmyer, *The Gospel according to Luke: Introduction, Translation, and Notes*, vol. 1: *I–IX;* vol. 2: *X–XXIV* (AB 28, 28A; Garden City, NY: Doubleday, 1981, 1985).

Fitzmyer, "Matthean Divorce Texts"
Joseph A. Fitzmyer, "The Matthean Divorce Texts and Some New Palestinian Evidence," *TS* 37 (1976) 213–23; reprinted idem, *To Advance the Gospel: New Testament Studies* (BRS; Grand Rapids: Eerdmans; Livonia, MI: Dove Booksellers, 1981; 2nd ed., 1998) 79–111.

Fitzmyer, *Semitic Background*
Joseph A. Fitzmyer, *The Semitic Background of the New Testament: Combined Edition of Essays on the Semitic Background of the New Testament and A Wandering Amamean: Collected Aramaic Essays* (BRS; Grand Rapids: Eerdmans; Livonia, MI: Dove Booksellers, 1997).

Fitzmyer and Harrington, *Palestinian Aramaic Texts*
Joseph A. Fitzmyer and Daniel J. Harrington, *A Manual of Palestinian Aramaic Texts: Second Century B.C.–Second Century A.D.* (BibOr 34; Rome: Biblical Institute Press, 1978).

Fleddermann, "Discipleship Discourse"
Harry T. Fleddermann, "The Discipleship Discourse (Mark 9:33-50)," *CBQ* 43 (1981) 57–75.

Fleddermann, *Mark and Q*
Harry T. Fleddermann, *Mark and Q: A Study of the Overlap Texts* (BEThL 122; Leuven: Leuven University Press/Peeters, 1995).

Flesseman-van Leer, "Die Interpretation der Passionsgeschichte"
Ellen Flesseman-van Leer, "Die Interpretation der Passionsgeschichte vom Alten Testament aus," in Hans Conzelmann et al., *Zur Bedeutung des Todes Jesu: Exegetische Beiträge* (Gütersloh: Mohn, 1967) 81–96.

Fornara, *Nature of History*
Charles William Fornara, *The Nature of History in Ancient Greece and Rome* (Eidos; Berkeley: University of California Press, 1983).

Foster, "Why Did Matthew Get the *Shema* Wrong"
Paul Foster, "Why Did Matthew Get the *Shema* Wrong? A Study of Matthew 22:37," *JBL* 122 (2003) 309–33.

Fowler, *Let the Reader Understand*
Robert M. Fowler, *Let the Reader Understand: Reader-Response Criticism and the Gospel of Mark* (Minneapolis: Fortress, 1991).

Fraade, "Moses and the Commandments"
Steven D. Fraade, "Moses and the Commandments: Can Hermeneutics, History, and Rhetoric Be Disentangled?" in Hindy Najman and Judith H. Newman, eds., *The Idea of Biblical Interpretation: Essays in Honor of James Kugel* (JSJSup 83; Leiden: Brill, 2004) 399–422.

Frankemölle, *Evangelium–Begriff und Gattung*
Hubert Frankemölle, *Evangelium: Begriff und Gattung: Ein Forschungsbericht* (2nd ed.; Stuttgart: Katholisches Bibelwerk, 1994).

Frenschkowski, *Offenbarung und Epiphanie*
Marco Frenschkowski, *Offenbarung und Epiphanie* (2 vols.; WUNT 2.79–80; Tübingen: Mohr Siebeck, 1995, 1997).

Freyne, *Galilee*
Seán Freyne, *Galilee, from Alexander the Great to Hadrian: 323 B.C.E. to 135 C.E.* (UNDCSJCA 5; Wilmington, DE: Michael Glazier; Notre Dame, IN: University of Notre Dame Press, 1980).

Freyne, "Galilee in the Hellenistic through Byzantine Periods"
Seán Freyne, "Galilee in the Hellenistic through Byzantine Periods," *OEANE* 2:370–76.

Froehlich, *Biblical Interpretation*
Karlfried Froehlich, trans. and ed., *Biblical Interpretation in the Early Church* (Philadelphia: Fortress, 1984).

Furnish, *II Corinthians*
Victor Paul Furnish, *II Corinthians: Translated with Introduction, Notes, and Commentary* (AB 32A; Garden City, NY: Doubleday, 1984).

Furnish, *Love Command*
Victor Paul Furnish, *The Love Command in the New Testament* (Nashville: Abingdon, 1972; London: SCM, 1973).

Gamble, *Books and Readers*
Harry Y. Gamble, *Books and Readers in the Early Church: A History of Early Christian Texts* (New Haven/London: Yale University Press, 1995).

García Martínez and Tigchelaar, *Dead Sea Scrolls*
Florentino García Martínez and Eibert J. C. Tigchelaar, eds., *The Dead Sea Scrolls Study Edition* (2 vols.; Leiden: Brill, 1997–98).

García Martínez et al., *Qumran Cave 11*
Florentino García Martínez, Eibert J. C. Tigchelaar and Adam S. van der Woude, eds., *Qumran Cave 11*, vol. 2: *11Q2–18, 11Q20–31* (DJD 23; Oxford: Clarendon, 1998).

Glancy, "Unveiling Masculinity"
Jennifer A. Glancy, "Unveiling Masculinity: The Construction of Gender in Mark 6:14-29," *BI* 2 (1994) 34–50.

Gnilka
Joachim Gnilka, *Das Evangelium nach Markus* (3rd ed.; 2 vols.; EKK II/1, 2; Zurich: Benziger; Neukirchen-Vluyn: Neukirchener Verlag, 1989).

Goldstein, *I Maccabees*
Jonathan A. Goldstein, *I Maccabees: A New Transla-*

tion, with Introduction and Commentary (AB 41; Garden City, NY: Doubleday, 1976).

Goldstein, *II Maccabees*
Jonathan A. Goldstein, *II Maccabees: A New Translation, with Introduction and Commentary* (AB 41A; Garden City, NY: Doubleday, 1983).

Gould
Ezra P. Gould, *A Critical and Exegetical Commentary on the Gospel according to Mark* (ICC; Edinburgh: T & T Clark, 1896).

Grundmann
Walter Grundmann, *Das Evangelium nach Markus* (ThHKNT 2; Berlin: Evangelische Verlagsanstalt, 1959).

Guelich
Robert A. Guelich, *Mark 1–8:26* (WBC 34A; Dallas, TX: Word Books, 1989).

Gundry
Robert H. Gundry, *Mark: A Commentary on His Apology for the Cross* (Grand Rapids: Eerdmans, 1993).

Haenchen, *Acts*
Ernst Haenchen, *The Acts of the Apostles: A Commentary* (Philadelphia: Westminster, 1971; 14th Germ. ed., 1965).

Hagedorn and Neyrey, "'It Was Out of Envy'"
Anselm C. Hagedorn and Jerome H. Neyrey, "'It Was Out of Envy That They Handed Jesus Over' (Mark 15:10): The Anatomy of Envy and the Gospel of Mark," *JSNT* 69 (1998) 15–56.

Harmon, *Lucian*
Austin M. Harmon, *Lucian* (8 vols.; LCL; Cambridge, MA: Harvard University Press; London: Heinemann, 1921; reprint, 1972).

Harrington, "Holiness and Law"
Hannah K. Harrington, "Holiness and Law in the Dead Sea Scrolls," *DSD* 8 (2001) 124–35.

Hartman, *Prophecy Interpreted*
Lars Hartman, *Prophecy Interpreted: The Formation of Some Jewish Apocalyptic Texts and of the Eschatological Discourse Mark 13 Par.* (CBNTS 1; Lund: Gleerup, 1966).

Hayes, *Gentile Impurities*
Christine E. Hayes, *Gentile Impurities and Jewish Identities: Intermarriage and Conversion from the Bible to the Talmud* (Oxford/New York: Oxford University Press, 2002).

Heaton, *School Tradition*
Eric W. Heaton, *The School Tradition of the Old Testament* (Oxford: Oxford University Press, 1994).

Hedrick and Olympiou, "Secret Mark: New Photographs"
Charles W. Hedrick and Nikolaos Olympiou, "Secret Mark: New Photographs, New Witnesses," *The Fourth R: An Advocate for Religious Literacy* 13 (2000) 3–16.

Heil, "Mark 14,1-52"
John Paul Heil, "Mark 14,1-52: Narrative Structure and Reader-Response," *Bib* 71 (1990) 305–32.

Heil, *Transfiguration*
John Paul Heil, *The Transfiguration of Jesus: Narrative Meaning and Function of Mark 9:2-8, Matt 17:1-8 and Luke 9:28-36* (AnBib 144; Rome: Editrice Pontificio Istituto Biblico, 2000).

Henderson, "'Salted with Fire'"
Ian H. Henderson, "'Salted with Fire' (Mark 9:42-50): Style, Oracles and (Socio)Rhetorical Gospel Criticism," *JSNT* 80 (2000) 44–65.

Hengel, *Charismatic Leader*
Martin Hengel, *The Charismatic Leader and His Followers* (SNTW; Edinburgh: T & T Clark, 1981; Germ. ed. 1968).

Hengel, *Crucifixion*
Martin Hengel, *Crucifixion in the Ancient World and the Folly of the Message of the Cross* (Philadelphia: Fortress, 1977).

Hengel, *Evangelienüberschriften*
Martin Hengel, *Die Evangelienüberschriften* (Vorgetragen am 18. Oktober, 1981; SHAW.PH 1984, 3; Heidelberg: Carl Winter/Universitätsverlag, 1984); ET: *Studies in Mark* (Philadelphia: Fortress, 1985).

Hengel, *"Hellenization" of Judaea*
Martin Hengel, *The "Hellenization" of Judaea in the First Century after Christ* (London: SCM; Philadelphia: Trinity Press International, 1989).

Hengel, *Judaism and Hellenism*
Martin Hengel, *Judaism and Hellenism: Studies in Their Encounter in Palestine during the Early Hellenistic Period* (2 vols.; Philadelphia: Fortress; London: SCM, 1974).

Hengel, *Studies in Mark*
Martin Hengel, *Studies in the Gospel of Mark* (Philadelphia: Fortress, 1985).

Hengel, *Zealots*
Martin Hengel, *The Zealots: Investigations into the Jewish Freedom Movement in the Period from Herod I until 70 A.D.* (Edinburgh: T & T Clark, 1989; Germ. ed., 1961; 2nd Germ. ed., 1976).

van Henten, *Maccabean Martyrs*
Jan Willem van Henten, *The Maccabean Martyrs as Saviours of the Jewish People: A Study of 2 and 4 Maccabees* (JSJSup 57; Leiden/New York: Brill, 1997).

Hicks, *Diogenes Laertius*
R. D. Hicks, *Diogenes Laertius: Lives of Eminent Philosophers* (2 vols.; LCL; Cambridge, MA: Harvard University Press, 1925; rev. ed. vol. 1, 1972; rev. ed. vol. 2, 1931).

Hilgert, "Son of Timaeus"
Earle Hilgert, "The Son of Timaeus: Blindness, Sight, Ascent, Vision in Mark," in Elizabeth A. Castelli and Hal Taussig, eds., *Reimagining Christian Origins: A Colloquium Honoring Burton I. Mack* (Valley Forge, PA: Trinity Press International, 1996) 185–98.

Holladay, *Jeremiah*
William L. Holladay, *Jeremiah: A Commentary on the Book of the Prophet Jeremiah* (2 vols.; Hermeneia; Minneapolis: Fortress, 1986, 1989).

Hollander and de Jonge
H. W. Hollander and M. de Jonge, *The Testaments of the Twelve Patriarchs: A Commentary* (SVTP 8; Leiden: Brill, 1985).

Hooker
Morna D. Hooker, *The Gospel according to St. Mark* (BNTC 2; London: A & C Black; Peabody, MA: Hendrickson, 1991).

Hooker, *Signs*
Morna D. Hooker, *The Signs of a Prophet: The Prophetic Actions of Jesus* (Harrisburg, PA: Trinity Press International, 1997).

Horsley and Hanson, *Bandits*
Richard A. Horsley and John S. Hanson, *Bandits, Prophets and Messiahs: Popular Movements in the Time of Jesus* (Minneapolis: Winston, 1985).

Huck-Greeven
Albert Huck, *Synopse der drei ersten Evangelien mit Beigabe der johanneischen Parallelstellen/Synopsis of the First Three Gospels with the Addition of the Johannine Parallels* (13th ed., fundamentally revised by Heinrich Greeven; Tübingen: Mohr Siebeck, 1981).

Hull, *Hellenistic Magic*
John M. Hull, *Hellenistic Magic and the Synoptic Tradition* (SBT 2nd series 28; Naperville, IL: Alec R. Allenson, 1974).

Hurtado
Larry W. Hurtado, *Mark* (NIBC 2; Peabody, MA: Hendrickson, 1983).

van Iersel, *Reading Mark*
Bas van Iersel, *Reading Mark* (Edinburgh: T & T Clark; Collegeville, MN: Liturgical Press, 1988).

Ilan, "Notes and Observations"
Tal Ilan, "Notes and Observations on a Newly Published Divorce Bill from the Judaean Desert," *HTR* 89 (1996) 195–202.

Incigneri, *Gospel to the Romans*
Brian J. Incigneri, *The Gospel to the Romans: The Setting and Rhetoric of Mark's Gospel* (BIS 65; Leiden/Boston: Brill, 2003).

Instone-Brewer, *Divorce and Remarriage*
David Instone-Brewer, *Divorce and Remarriage in the Bible: The Social and Literary Context* (Grand Rapids/Cambridge: Eerdmans, 2002).

Jeremias, *Parables of Jesus*
Joachim Jeremias, *The Parables of Jesus* (trans. S. H. Hooke; London: SCM, 1955; rev. ed., New York: Scribner, 1962).

Johnson, "Mark VIII.22-26"
E. S. Johnson, "Mark VIII.22-26: The Blind Man from Bethsaida," *NTS* 25 (1978–79) 370–83.

Johnson
Sherman E. Johnson, *A Commentary on the Gospel according to St. Mark* (HNTC; New York: Harper; London: A & C Black, 1960).

Joynes, "Reception History"
Christine E. Joynes, "The Reception History of Mark's Gospel," *Scripture Bulletin* 36 (2006) 24–32.

Juel, *Messianic Exegesis*
Donald Juel, *Messianic Exegesis: Christological Inter-pretation of the Old Testament in Early Christianity* (Philadelphia: Fortress, 1988).

Kadman, "Temple Dues" (*Israel Numismatic Bulletin*)
Leo Kadman, "Temple Dues and Currency in Ancient Palestine in the Light of Recent [*sic*] Discovered Coin-Hoards," *Israel Numismatic Bulletin* 1 (1962) 9–11.

Kadman, "Temple Dues" (*Congresso internazionale*)
Leo Kadman, "Temple Dues and Currency in Ancient Palestine in the Light of Recent [*sic*] Discovered Coin-Hoards," in *Congresso internazionale di numismatica, Roma, 11–16 settembre 1961* (2 vols.; Commission internationale de numismatique/Istituto italiano di numismatica; Rome: Istituto italiano di numismatica, 1961–65).

Kazen, *Jesus and Purity* Halakhah
Thomas Kazen, *Jesus and Purity* Halakhah*: Was Jesus Indifferent to Impurity?* (CBNTS 38; Stockholm: Almqvist & Wiksell International, 2002).

Kealy, *Mark's Gospel*
Sean P. Kealy, *Mark's Gospel: A History of Its Interpretation from the Beginning until 1979* (New York: Paulist, 1982).

Kee, *Medicine*
Howard Clark Kee, *Medicine, Miracle and Magic in New Testament Times* (Cambridge: Cambridge University Press, 1986).

Kee, "Transfiguration in Mark"
Howard Clark Kee, "The Transfiguration in Mark: Epiphany or Apocalyptic Vision?" in John Reumann, ed., *Understanding the Sacred Text: Essays in Honor of Morton S. Enslin on the Hebrew Bible and Christian Beginnings* (Valley Forge, PA: Judson, 1972) 135–52.

Kelber, *Gospel*
Werner H. Kelber, *The Oral and the Written Gospel* (Philadelphia: Fortress, 1983).

Kelber, "Hour of the Son of Man"
Werner H. Kelber, "The Hour of the Son of Man and the Temptation of the Disciples (Mark 14:32-42)," in idem, *Passion*, 41–60.

Kelber, *Kingdom*
Werner H. Kelber, *The Kingdom in Mark* (Philadelphia: Fortress, 1974).

Kelber, *Mark's Story*
Werner H. Kelber, *Mark's Story of Jesus* (Philadelphia: Fortress, 1979).

Kelber, *Passion*
Werner H. Kelber, ed., *The Passion in Mark: Studies on Mark 14–16* (Philadelphia: Fortress, 1976).

Kelhoffer, *Miracle and Mission*
James A. Kelhoffer, *Miracle and Mission: The Authentication of Missionaries and Their Message in the Longer Ending of Mark* (WUNT 2.112; Tübingen: Mohr Siebeck, 2000).

Kennard, *Render to God*
J. Spencer Kennard, Jr., *Render to God: A Study of the Tribute Passage* (New York: Oxford University Press, 1950).

Keppie, *Making of the Roman Army*
Lawrence J. F. Keppie, *The Making of the Roman Army: From Republic to Empire* (Norman: University of Oklahoma Press, 1998).

Kermode, *Genesis of Secrecy*
Frank Kermode, *The Genesis of Secrecy: On the Interpretation of Narrative* (Cambridge, MA/London, UK: Harvard University Press, 1979).

Kilpatrick, "Recitative λέγων"
G. D. Kilpatrick, "Recitative λέγων," in Elliott, *Language and Style,* 175–77.

Kister, "Divorce, Reproof"
Menahem Kister, "Divorce, Reproof and Other Sayings in the Synoptic Gospels: Jesus Traditions in the Context of 'Qumranic' and Other Texts," in Daniel R. Schwartz and Ruth A. Clements, eds., *Text, Thought, and Practice in Qumran and Early Christianity: Proceedings of a Joint Symposium Sponsored by the Orion Center for the Study of the Dead Sea Scrolls and Associated Literature and the Hebrew University Center for the Study of Christianity, 11–13 January, 2004* (STDJ; Leiden: Brill, forthcoming).

Klauck, *Allegorie und Allegorese*
Hans-Josef Klauck, *Allegorie und Allegorese in synoptischen Gleichnistexten* (NTAbh n.F. 13; Münster: Aschendorff, 1978; 2nd rev. ed., 1986).

Klauck, *Judas*
Hans-Josef Klauck, *Judas–Ein Jünger des Herrn* (Quaestiones Disputatae 111; Freiburg/Basel/Vienna: Herder, 1987).

Klauck, *Vorspiel im Himmel?*
Hans-Josef Klauck, *Vorspiel im Himmel? Erzähltechnik und Theologie im Markusprolog* (Biblisch-Theologische Studien 32; Neukirchen-Vluyn: Neukirchener Verlag, 1997).

Klawans, *Impurity and Sin*
Jonathan Klawans, *Impurity and Sin in Ancient Judaism* (New York: Oxford University Press, 2000).

Klostermann
Erich Klostermann, *Das Markusevangelium erklärt* (HNT 3; 4th ed.; Tübingen: Mohr Siebeck, 1950).

Knibb, *Enoch*
Michael A. Knibb, *The Ethiopic Book of Enoch: A New Edition in Light of the Aramaic Dead Sea Fragments* (2 vols.; Oxford: Clarendon, 1978).

Kobelski, *Melchizedek*
Paul J. Kobelski, *Melchizedek and Melchireša^c* (CBQMS 10; Washington, DC: CBA, 1981).

Koester, "Apocryphal and Canonical Gospels"
Helmut Koester, "Apocryphal and Canonical Gospels," *HTR* 73 (1980) 105–30.

Koester, *Gospels*
  Helmut Koester, *Ancient Christian Gospels: Their History and Development* (Philadelphia: Trinity; London: SCM, 1990).
Koester, "History and Development"
  Helmut Koester, "History and Development of Mark's Gospel," in Bruce Corley, ed., *Colloquy on New Testament Studies: A Time for Reappraisal and Fresh Approaches* (Macon, GA: Mercer University Press, 1983) 35–57.
Kokkinos, *Herodian Dynasty*
  Nikos Kokkinos, *The Herodian Dynasty: Origins, Role in Society and Eclipse* (JSPSup 30; Sheffield: Sheffield Academic Press, 1998).
Kollmann, *Wundertäter*
  Bernd Kollmann, *Jesus und die Christen als Wundertäter: Studien zu Magie, Medizin und Schamanismus in Antike und Christentum* (FRLANT 170; Göttingen: Vandenhoeck & Ruprecht, 1996).
Kraus, *Psalms 60–150*
  Hans-Joachim Kraus, *Psalms 60–150: A Commentary* (Minneapolis: Augsburg, 1989; 5th Germ. ed., 1978).
Kuhn, *Ältere Sammlungen*
  Heinz-Wolfgang Kuhn, *Ältere Sammlungen im Markusevangelium* (StUNT 8; Göttingen: Vandenhoeck & Ruprecht, 1971).
Kümmel, *New Testament*
  Werner Georg Kümmel, *The New Testament: The History of the Investigation of Its Problems* (Nashville: Abingdon, 1972).
Lagrange
  Marie-Joseph Lagrange, *Évangile selon saint Marc* (5th ed.; EtB; Paris: Gabalda, 1929; reprinted, 1966).
Lake, *Apostolic Fathers*
  Kirsopp Lake, *The Apostolic Fathers* (2 vols.; LCL; Cambridge, MA: Harvard University Press; London: Heinemann, 1912).
Lambrecht, *Redaktion*
  Jan Lambrecht, *Die Redaktion der Markus-Apocalypse: Literarische Analyse und Strukturuntersuchung* (AnBib 28; Rome: Pontifical Biblical Institute, 1967).
Lane
  William L. Lane, *The Gospel according to Mark: The English Text with Introduction, Exposition and Notes* (NICNT; Grand Rapids: Eerdmans, 1974).
Lange et al., *Demons*
  Armin Lange, Hermann Lichtenberger and K. F. Diethard Römheld, eds., *Die Dämonen: Die Dämonologie der israelitisch-jüdischen und frühchristlichen Literatur im Kontext ihrer Umwelt = Demons: The Demonology of Israelite-Jewish and Early Christian Literature in [the] Context of Their Environment* (Tübingen: Mohr Siebeck, 2003).
Layton, *Gnostic Scriptures*
  Bentley Layton, *The Gnostic Scriptures* (Garden City, NY: Doubleday, 1987).

Lefkowitz, *Lives of the Greek Poets*
  Mary R. Lefkowitz, *The Lives of the Greek Poets* (Baltimore: Johns Hopkins University Press, 1981).
Lehtipuu, *Afterlife Imagery*
  Outi Lehtipuu, *The Afterlife Imagery in Luke's Story of the Rich Man and Lazarus* (NovTSup 123; Leiden: Brill, 2006).
Lentzen-Deis, *Die Taufe Jesu*
  Fritzleo Lentzen-Deis, *Die Taufe Jesu nach den Synoptikern: Literarkritische und gattungsgeschichtliche Untersuchungen* (FTS 4; Frankfurt am Main: Josef Knecht, 1970).
Leo, *Biographie*
  Friedrich Leo, *Die griechisch-römische Biographie nach ihrer literarischen Form* (Leipzig: Teubner, 1901).
Leppä, *Making of Colossians*
  Outi Leppä, *The Making of Colossians: A Study on the Formation and Purpose of a Deutero-Pauline Letter* (Publications of the Finnish Exegetical Society 86; Helsinki: Finnish Exegetical Society; Göttingen: Vandenhoeck & Ruprecht, 2003).
Levine, *Feminist Companion*
  Amy-Jill Levine, ed., *A Feminist Companion to Mark* (Sheffield: Sheffield Academic Press, 2001).
Levine, *Numbers 1–20*
  Baruch A. Levine, *Numbers 1–20: A New Translation with Introduction and Commentary* (AB 4; New York: Doubleday, 1993).
Levine, "Nature and Origin"
  Lee I. Levine, "The Nature and Origin of the Palestinian Synagogue Reconsidered," *JBL* 115 (1996) 425–48.
Lichtenberger, *Baupolitik*
  Achim Lichtenberger, *Die Baupolitik Herodes des Großen* (Abhandlungen des Deutschen Palästina-Vereins 26; Wiesbaden: Harrassowitz, 1999).
Liebers, "Wie geschrieben steht"
  Reinhold Liebers, *"Wie geschrieben steht": Studien zu einer besonderen Art frühchristlichen Schriftbezuges* (Berlin/New York: de Gruyter, 1993).
Lightfoot, *Gospel Message*
  R. H. Lightfoot, *The Gospel Message of St. Mark* (Oxford: Clarendon, 1950).
Lindars, *New Testament Apologetic*
  Barnabas Lindars, *New Testament Apologetic: The Doctrinal Significance of the Old Testament Quotations* (London: SCM, 1961).
Lindton, "Der vermißte Markusschluß"
  Olof Lindton, "Der vermißte Markusschluß," *Theologische Blätter* 8 (1929) 229–34.
Linnemann, *Studien zur Passionsgeschichte*
  Eta Linnemann, *Studien zur Passionsgeschichte* (FRLANT 102; Göttingen: Vandenhoeck & Ruprecht, 1970).
Lohmeyer
  Ernst Lohmeyer, *Das Evangelium des Markus übersetzt und erklärt* (MeyerK 1.2; Göttingen: Vandenhoeck & Ruprecht, 1937; 17th ed. 1967).

Lohmeyer, *Galiläa und Jerusalem*
Ernst Lohmeyer, *Galiläa und Jerusalem* (Göttingen: Vandenhoeck & Ruprecht, 1936).

Lohmeyer, "Die Verklärung"
Ernst Lohmeyer, "Die Verklärung Jesu nach dem Markus-Evangelium," *ZNW* 21 (1922) 185–215.

Lohse, *Colossians and Philemon*
Eduard Lohse, *Colossians and Philemon: A Commentary on the Epistles to the Colossians and to Philemon* (trans. William R. Poehlmann and Robert J. Karris; Hermeneia; Philadelphia: Fortress, 1971).

Loisy
Alfred Loisy, *L'Évangile selon Marc* (Paris: Émile Nourry, 1912).

van der Loos, *Miracles*
H. van der Loos, *The Miracles of Jesus* (NovTSup 9; Leiden: Brill, 1965).

Lührmann
Dieter Lührmann, *Das Markusevangelium* (HNT 3; Tübingen: Mohr Siebeck, 1987).

Lührmann, *Fragmente*
Dieter Lührmann, *Fragmente apokryph gewordener Evangelien in griechischer und lateinischer Sprache* (Marburger Theologische Studien 59; Marburg: Elwert, 2000).

Lundbom, *Jeremiah 1–20*
Jack R. Lundbom, *Jeremiah 1–20: A New Translation with Introduction and Commentary* (AB 21A; New York: Doubleday, 1999).

Luz, *Matthew 1–7*
Ulrich Luz, *Matthew 1–7* (Minneapolis: Fortress, 1989).

Maccoby, *Ritual and Morality*
Hyam Maccoby, *Ritual and Morality: The Ritual Purity System and Its Place in Judaism* (Cambridge/New York: Cambridge University Press, 1999).

Mack and Robbins, *Patterns of Persuasion*
Burton L. Mack and Vernon K. Robbins, *Patterns of Persuasion in the Gospels* (Foundations and Facets: Literary Facets; Sonoma, CA: Polebridge, 1989).

Madigan, *Passions of Christ*
Kevin Madigan, *The Passions of Christ in High Medieval Thought: An Essay on Christological Development* (New York: Oxford University Press, 2008)

Malbon, *In the Company of Jesus*
Elizabeth Struthers Malbon, *In the Company of Jesus: Characters in Mark's Gospel* (Louisville: Westminster John Knox Press, 2000).

Malbon, *Narrative Space*
Elizabeth Struthers Malbon, *Narrative Space and Mythic Meaning in Mark* (San Francisco: Harper & Row, 1986).

Malherbe, *Cynic Epistles*
Abraham J. Malherbe, ed., *The Cynic Epistles: A Study Edition* (SBLSBS 12; Atlanta: Scholars Press, 1977).

Marcus
Joel Marcus, *Mark 1–8: A New Translation with Introduction and Commentary* (AB 27; New York: Doubleday, 2000).

Marcus, "Jewish War"
Joel Marcus, "The Jewish War and the *Sitz im Leben* of Mark," *JBL* 111 (1992) 441–62.

Marcus, *Way of the Lord*
Joel Marcus, *The Way of the Lord: Christological Exegesis of the Old Testament in the Gospel of Mark* (Louisville: Westminster John Knox, 1992).

Marrou, *History of Education*
Henri I. Marrou, *A History of Education in Antiquity* (WSC; Madison: University of Wisconsin Press, 1956; 3rd French ed., 1948).

Marshall, *Faith*
Christopher D. Marshall, *Faith as a Theme in Mark's Narrative* (SNTSMS 64; Cambridge/New York: Cambridge University Press, 1989).

Martin, *Corinthian Body*
Dale B. Martin, *The Corinthian Body* (New Haven/London: Yale University Press, 1995).

Marxsen, *Der Evangelist Markus*
Willi Marxsen, *Der Evangelist Markus: Studien zur Redaktionsgeschichte des Evangeliums* (2nd ed.; Göttingen: Vandenhoeck & Ruprecht, 1959; 1st ed., 1956); ET *Mark the Evangelist: Studies on the Redaction History of the Gospel* (Nashville: Abingdon, 1969).

Massaux, *Influence*
Édouard Massaux, *The Influence of the Gospel of Saint Matthew on Christian Literature before Saint Irenaeus* (New Gospel Studies 5.1-3; Leuven: Peeters; Macon, GA: Mercer University Press, 1990, 1992–93; 1st French ed., 1950).

Mayser
Edwin Mayser, *Grammatik der griechischen Papyri aus der Ptolemäerzeit mit Einschluss der gleichzeitigen Ostraka und der in Ägypten verfassten Inschriften: Laut- und Wortlehre* (Leipzig: Teubner, 1906).

McCown, *Testament of Solomon*
Chester Charlton McCown, *The Testament of Solomon* (Leipzig: Hinrichs, 1922).

Meier, "Circle of the Twelve"
John P. Meier, "The Circle of the Twelve: Did It Exist during Jesus' Public Ministry?" *JBL* 116 (1997) 635–72.

Meier, "Debate on the Resurrection"
John P. Meier, "The Debate on the Resurrection of the Dead: An Incident from the Ministry of the Historical Jesus?" *JSNT* 77 (2000) 3–24.

Meier, "Historical Jesus and the Historical Law"
John P. Meier, "The Historical Jesus and the Historical Law: Some Problems with the Problem," *CBQ* 65 (2003) 52–79.

Meier, *Marginal Jew*
John P. Meier, *A Marginal Jew: Rethinking the Historical Jesus*, vol. 1: *The Roots of the Problem and the*

Person (ABRL; New York/London: Doubleday, 1991); vol. 2: *Mentor, Message and Miracle* (1994); vol. 3: *Companions and Competitors* (2001).

Merk
Augustin Merk, *Novum Testamentum Graece et Latine* (Rome, 1933; 9th ed. 1964).

Merritt, "Jesus Barabbas"
Robert L. Merritt, "Jesus Barabbas and the Paschal Pardon," *JBL* 104 (1985) 57–68.

Metzger, *Early Versions*
Bruce Metzger, *The Early Versions of the New Testament: Their Origin, Transmission, and Limitations* (Oxford: Clarendon, 1977).

Metzger, *Textual Commentary*
Bruce M. Metzger, *A Textual Commentary on the Greek New Testament: A Companion Volume to the United Bible Societies' Greek New Testament (fourth revised edition)* (2nd ed.; Stuttgart: Deutsche Bibelgesellschaft, 1994).

Metzger and Ehrman, *Text*
Bruce M. Metzger and Bart D. Ehrman, *The Text of the New Testament: Its Transmission, Corruption, and Restoration* (4th ed.; New York/Oxford: Oxford University Press, 2005).

Meyers and Meyers, *Zechariah 9–14*
Carol L. Meyers and Eric M. Meyers, *Zechariah 9–14: New Translation with Introduction and Commentary* (AB 25C; New York: Doubleday, 1993).

Milgrom, *Leviticus*
Jacob Milgrom, *Leviticus: A New Translation with Introduction and Commentary* (3 vols.; AB 3, 3A, 3B; New York: Doubleday, 1991, 2000, 2001).

Mitchell, "Patristic Counter-Evidence"
Margaret M. Mitchell, "Patristic Counter-Evidence to the Claim that 'The Gospels Were Written for All Christians,'" *NTS* 51 (2005) 36–79.

Mitchell, *Rhetoric of Reconciliation*
Margaret M. Mitchell, *Paul and the Rhetoric of Reconciliation: An Exegetical Investigation of the Language and Composition of 1 Corinthians* (Louisville: Westminster John Knox, 1991).

Moeser, *Anecdote*
Marion C. Moeser, *The Anecdote in Mark, the Classical World and the Rabbis* (JSNTSup 227; Sheffield: Sheffield Academic Press, 2002).

Mohr, *Markus- und Johannespassion*
Till Arend Mohr, *Markus- und Johannespassion: Redaktions- und traditionsgeschichtliche Untersuchung der Markinischen und Johanneischen Passionstradition* (AThANT 70; Zurich: Theologischer Verlag, 1982).

Momigliano, *Greek Biography*
Arnaldo Momigliano, *The Development of Greek Biography* (Cambridge, MA: Harvard University Press, 1971).

Montefiore, *Synoptic Gospels*
C. G. Montefiore, *The Synoptic Gospels* (3 vols.; London: Macmillan, 1909).

Moo, *Old Testament*
Douglas J. Moo, *The Old Testament in the Gospel Passion Narratives* (Sheffield: Almond, 1983).

Morgan Gillman, *Herodias*
Florence Morgan Gillman, *Herodias: At Home in That Fox's Den* (Collegeville, MN: Liturgical Press, 2003).

Moss, "Transfiguration"
Candida R. Moss, "The Transfiguration: An Exercise in Markan Accommodation," *BI* 12 (2004) 69–89.

Motyer, "Rending of the Veil"
Stephen Motyer, "The Rending of the Veil: A Markan Pentecost?" *NTS* 33 (1987) 155–57.

Moulton
James Hope Moulton, *A Grammar of New Testament Greek*, vol. 1: *Prolegomena* (3rd ed.; Edinburgh: T & T Clark, 1906).

Moulton-Geden
Moulton and Geden: Concordance to the Greek New Testament (6th rev. ed.; ed. I. Howard Marshall; London/New York: T & T Clark/Continuum, 2002).

Moulton-Howard
James Hope Moulton and Wilbert Francis Howard, *A Grammar of New Testament Greek*, vol. 2: *Accidence and Word-Formation with an Appendix on Semitisms in the New Testament* (Edinburgh: T & T Clark, 1928; reprinted 1986).

Moulton-Milligan
James Hope Moulton and George Milligan, *The Vocabulary of the Greek Testament Illustrated from the Papyri and Other Non-Literary Sources* (Grand Rapids: Eerdmans, 1930).

Moulton-Turner
Nigel Turner, *Syntax* (Edinburgh: T & T Clark, 1963), which is vol. 3, and idem, *Style* (Edinburgh: T & T Clark, 1976), which is vol. 4 of James Hope Moulton, *A Grammar of New Testament Greek* (4 vols.; Edinburgh: T & T Clark, 1906–76).

Müller, *In der Mitte der Gemeinde*
Peter Müller, *In der Mitte der Gemeinde: Kinder im Neuen Testament* (Neukirchen-Vluyn: Neukirchener Verlag, 1992).

Musurillo, *Christian Martyrs*
Herbert Musurillo, *The Acts of the Christian Martyrs* (OECT; Oxford: Clarendon, 1972).

Musurillo, *Pagan Martyrs*
Herbert A. Musurillo, *The Acts of the Pagan Martyrs* (Oxford: Clarendon, 1954).

Myllykoski, *Die letzten Tagen*
Matti Myllykoski, *Die letzten Tagen Jesu: Markus und Johannes, ihre Traditionen und die historische Frage* (2 vols.; Suomalaisen Tiedeakatemian Toimituksia [Annales Academiae Scientiarum Fennicae] B. 256, 272; Helsinki: Suomalainen Tiedeakatemia, 1991, 1994).

Neirynck, "Apocryphal Gospels"
Frans Neirynck, "The Apocryphal Gospels and the

Gospel of Mark," in Jean-Marie Sevrin, ed., *The New Testament in Early Christianity: La réception des écrits néotestamentaires dans le christianisme primitif* (BEThL 86; Leuven: Leuven University Press/Peeters, 1989) 123–75.

Neirynck, "Assessment"
Frans Neirynck, "Assessment," in Fleddermann, *Mark and Q,* 261–303.

Neirynck, *Duality in Mark*
Frans Neirynck, *Duality in Mark: Contributions to the Study of the Markan Redaction* (BEThL 31; rev. ed.; Leuven: Leuven University Press/Peeters, 1988).

Neirynck, "La Fuite du jeune homme"
Frans Neirynck, "La Fuite de jeune homme en Mc 14,51-52," *EThL* 55 (1979) 43–66.

Neirynck, *Minor Agreements*
Frans Neirynck, ed., *The Minor Agreements of Matthew and Luke against Mark with a Cumulative List* (BEThL 37; Leuven: Leuven University Press, 1974).

Nestle-Aland
Eberhard Nestle, Erwin Nestle, Kurt Aland, Barbara Aland et al., *Novum Testamentum Graece* (27th ed.; Stuttgart: Deutsche Bibelgesellschaft, 1993; 26th ed. 1979; 25th ed. 1963).

Nickelsburg, *1 Enoch 1*
George W. E. Nickelsburg, *1 Enoch 1: A Commentary on the Book of 1 Enoch, Chapters 1–36; 81–108* (Hermeneia; Minneapolis: Fortress, 2001).

Nickelsburg, *Jewish Literature*
George W. E. Nickelsburg, *Jewish Literature between the Bible and the Mishnah: A Historical and Literary Introduction* (Philadelphia: Fortress, 1981).

Nickelsburg, "Judgment, Life-after-Death, and Resurrection"
George W. E. Nickelsburg, "Judgment, Life-after-Death, and Resurrection in the Apocrypha and the Non-Apocalyptic Pseudepigrapha," in *Judaism in Late Antiquity,* part 4: *Death, Life-after-Death, Resurrection and the World-to-Come in the Judaisms of Antiquity* (HO 1, Der Nahe und Mittlere Osten/The Near and Middle East 49; Leiden: Brill, 2000) 141–62.

Nickelsburg and VanderKam
George W. E. Nickelsburg and James C. VanderKam, *1 Enoch: A New Translation* (Minneapolis: Fortress, 2004).

Niederwimmer, "Johannes Markus"
Kurt Niederwimmer, "Johannes Markus und die Frage nach dem Verfasser des zweiten Evangeliums," *ZNW* 58 (1967) 172–88.

Nineham
D. E. Nineham, *The Gospel of St. Mark* (PGC; Baltimore: Penguin Books, 1963).

Öhler, *Elia*
Markus Öhler, *Elia im Neuen Testament: Untersuchungen zur Bedeutung des alttestamentlichen Propheten im frühen Christentum* (BZNW 88; Berlin/New York: de Gruyter, 1997).

Osiek, *Shepherd of Hermas*
Carolyn Osiek, *Shepherd of Hermas: A Commentary* (Hermeneia; Minneapolis: Fortress, 1999).

Osiek and Balch, *Families*
Carolyn Osiek and David L. Balch, *Families in the New Testament World: Households and Household Churches* (The Family, Religion, and Culture; Louisville: Westminster John Knox, 1997).

Park, *Mission Discourse*
Eung Chun Park, *The Mission Discourse in Matthew's Interpretation* (WUNT 2.81; Tübingen: Mohr Siebeck, 1995).

Perrin, *Pilgrimage*
Norman Perrin, *A Modern Pilgrimage in New Testament Christology* (Philadelphia: Fortress, 1974).

Perrin, *Plutarch's Lives*
Bernadotte Perrin, *Plutarch's Lives* (11 vols.; LCL; Cambridge, MA: Harvard University Press; London: Heinemann, 1914).

Perrin, *Redaction Criticism*
Norman Perrin, *What Is Redaction Criticism?* (GBS; Philadelphia: Fortress, 1969).

Perrin, *Rediscovering*
Norman Perrin, *Rediscovering the Teaching of Jesus* (New York: Harper & Row, 1967).

Perrin, "Towards an Interpretation"
Norman Perrin, "Towards an Interpretation of the Gospel of Mark," in Hans Dieter Betz, ed., *Christology and a Modern Pilgrimage: A Discussion with Norman Perrin* (Claremont, CA: New Testament Colloquium, 1971) 1–78.

Perry, *Aesopica*
Ben Edwin Perry, *Aesopica*, vol. 1: *Greek and Latin Texts* (Urbana: University of Illinois Press, 1952; reprinted New York: Arno Press, 1980).

Pesch
Rudolf Pesch, *Das Markusevangelium* I. Teil: *Einleitung und Kommentar zu Kap. 1,1–8,26* (HTK 2.1; Freiburg: Herder, 1976; 5th ed. 1989) and *Das Markusevangelium* II. Teil: *Kommentar zu Kap. 8,27–16,20* (HTK 2.2; Freiburg: Herder, 1977; 4th ed. 1991).

Petersen, *Literary Criticism*
Norman R. Petersen, *Literary Criticism for New Testament Critics* (GBS; Philadelphia: Fortress, 1978).

Petersen, *Tatian's Diatessaron*
William L. Petersen, *Tatian's Diatessaron: Its Creation, Dissemination, Significance, and History in Scholarship* (VCSup 25; Leiden: Brill, 1994).

Petersen, *Zechariah 9–14*
David L. Petersen, *Zechariah 9–14 and Malachi: A Commentary* (OTL; Louisville, KY: Westminster John Knox Press, 1995).

Phillips, "Ritual Kiss"
L. Edward Phillips, "The Ritual Kiss in Early Christian Worship" (Ph.D. diss., University of Notre Dame, 1992).

Preisendanz-Henrichs
  Karl Preisendanz, *Papyri Graecae Magicae: Die griechischen Zauberpapyri* (rev. Albert Henrichs; 2nd ed.; 2 vols.; Stuttgart: Teubner, 1973–74).
Preisigke, *Gotteskraft*
  Friedrich Preisigke, *Die Gotteskraft der frühchristlichen Zeit* (Papyrusinstitut Heidelberg Schrift 6; Berlin/Leipzig: de Gruyter, 1922).
Pritchard, *Atlas*
  James B. Pritchard, ed., *The Harper Atlas of the Bible* (New York: Harper & Row, 1987).
Pryke, *Redactional Style*
  E. J. Pryke, *Redactional Style in the Markan Gospel* (SNTSMS 33; Cambridge: Cambridge University Press, 1978).
Rahlfs
  Alfred Rahlfs, *Septuaginta* (vol. 1; 7th ed.; Stuttgart: Württembergische Bibelanstalt, 1935); vol. 2: *Libri poetici et prophetici* (7th ed.; Stuttgart: Württembergische Bibelanstalt, 1935).
Räisänen, *Messianic Secret*
  Heikki Räisänen, *The 'Messianic Secret' in Mark* (SNTW; Edinburgh: T & T Clark, 1990).
Rawson, *Marriage, Divorce, and Children*
  Beryl Rawson, ed., *Marriage, Divorce, and Children in Ancient Rome* (Canberra: Humanities Research Centre; Oxford: Clarendon, 1991).
Reardon, *Ancient Greek Novels*
  Bryan P. Reardon, "Chariton: Chaereas and Callirhoe; Introduction," in idem, ed., *Collected Ancient Greek Novels* (Berkeley: University of California Press, 1989).
Reinbold, *Der älteste Bericht*
  Wolfgang Reinbold, *Der älteste Bericht über den Tod Jesu: Literarische Analyse und historische Kritik der Passionsdarstellungen der Evangelien* (BZNW 69; Berlin/New York: de Gruyter, 1994).
Rhoads, *Reading Mark*
  David Rhoads, *Reading Mark, Engaging the Gospel* (Minneapolis: Fortress, 2004).
Riesner, *Jesus als Lehrer*
  Rainer Riesner, *Jesus als Lehrer: Eine Untersuchung zum Ursprung der Evangelien-Überlieferung* (WUNT 2.7; Tübingen: Mohr Siebeck, 1981).
Robbins, "Healing of Blind Bartimaeus"
  Vernon K. Robbins, "The Healing of Blind Bartimaeus (19:46-52) in the Marcan Theology," *JBL* 92 (1973) 224–43.
Robbins, *Jesus the Teacher*
  Vernon K. Robbins, *Jesus the Teacher: A Socio-Rhetorical Interpretation of Mark* (Philadelphia: Fortress, 1984).
Robinson, *Problem of History*
  James M. Robinson, *The Problem of History in Mark* (SBT; Naperville, IL: Allenson, 1957), reprinted in idem, *The Problem of History in Mark and Other Markan Studies* (Philadelphia: Fortress, 1982). The reprint is cited in this commentary.

Robinson et al., *Critical Edition of Q*
  James M. Robinson, Paul Hoffmann, and John Kloppenborg, eds., *The Critical Edition of Q* (Hermeneia; Minneapolis: Fortress; Leuven: Peeters, 2000).
Rofé, *Prophetical Stories*
  Alexander Rofé, *The Prophetical Stories: The Narratives about the Prophets in the Hebrew Bible, Their Literary Types and History* (Publications of the Perry Foundation for Biblical Research in the Hebrew University of Jerusalem; Jerusalem: Magnes, 1988; 1st Heb. ed. 1982; rev. Heb. ed. 1986).
Rolfe, *Suetonius*
  John C. Rolfe, *Suetonius* (2 vols.; LCL; Cambridge, MA: Harvard University Press, 1924; rev. ed. 1997–1998).
Roskam, *Purpose of Mark*
  Hendrika N. Roskam, *The Purpose of the Gospel of Mark in Its Historical and Social Context* (NovTSup 114; Leiden/Boston: Brill, 2004).
Rothschild, *Baptist Traditions and Q*
  Clare K. Rothschild, *Baptist Traditions and Q* (WUNT 190; Tübingen: Mohr Siebeck, 2005).
Sabbe, *L'Évangile selon Marc*
  M. Sabbe, ed., *L'Évangile selon Marc: tradition et redaction* (BEThL 34; 2nd rev. ed.; Leuven: Leuven University Press/Peeters, 1988; 1st ed. 1974).
Saldarini, *Pharisees*
  Anthony J. Saldarini, *Pharisees, Scribes and Sadducees in Palestinian Society: A Sociological Approach* (Wilmington, DE: Michael Glazier, 1988; reprinted BRS; Grand Rapids: Eerdmans, 2001).
Sanders, *Jesus and Judaism*
  E. P. Sanders, *Jesus and Judaism* (Philadelphia: Fortress, 1985).
Sanders, *Jewish Law*
  E. P. Sanders, *Jewish Law from Jesus to the Mishnah: Five Studies* (London: SCM; Philadelphia: Trinity Press International, 1990).
Schenke
  Ludger Schenke, *Das Markusevangelium: Literarische Eigenart–Text und Kommentierung* (Stuttgart: Kohlhammer, 2005).
Schenke, *Der gekreuzigte Christus*
  Ludger Schenke, *Der gekreuzigte Christus: Versuch einer literarkritischen und traditionsgeschichtlichen Bestimmung der vormarkinischen Passionsgeschichte* (SBS 69; Stuttgart: Katholisches Bibelwerk, 1974).
Schenke, *Passionsgeschichte*
  Ludger Schenke, *Studien zur Passionsgeschichte des Markus: Tradition und Redaktion in Markus 14, 1-42* (FB 4; Würzburg: Echter Verlag; Stuttgart: Katholisches Bibelwerk, 1971).
Schiffman, *Halakhah*
  Lawrence H. Schiffman, *The Halakhah at Qumran* (SJLA 16; Leiden: Brill, 1975).
Schildgen, *Power and Prejudice*
  Brenda Deen Schildgen, *Power and Prejudice: The*

Reception of the Gospel of Mark (Detroit: Wayne State University Press, 1999).

Schmid
Josef Schmid, *The Gospel according to Mark* (RNT; Staten Island, NY: Alba House, 1968).

Schmidt, *Place of the Gospels*
Karl Ludwig Schmidt, *The Place of the Gospels in the General History of Literature* (Columbia: University of South Carolina Press, 2002), ET of "Die Stellung der Evangelien in der allgemeinen Literaturgeschichte," in Hans Schmidt, ed., *ΕΥΧΑΡΙΣΤΗΡΙΟΝ: Studien zur Religion und Literatur des Alten und Neuen Testaments Hermann Gunkel zum 60. Geburtstag . . . dargebracht* (2 vols.; FRLANT 36; Göttingen: Vandenhoeck & Ruprecht, 1923) 2:50–134.

Schmidt, *Der Rahmen*
Karl Ludwig Schmidt, *Der Rahmen der Geschichte Jesu: Literarkritische Untersuchungen zur ältesten Jesusüberlieferung* (Berlin: Trowitzsch & Sohn, 1919; reprinted Darmstadt: Wissenschaftliche Buchgesellschaft, 1964).

Schmidt, "Mark 15.16-32"
T. E. Schmidt, "Mark 15.16-32: The Crucifixion Narrative and the Roman Triumphal Procession," *NTS* 41 (1995) 1–18.

Schmithals
Walter Schmithals, *Das Evangelium nach Markus* (2 vols.; ÖTBK 2.1-2; Gütersloh: Mohn, 1979).

Schmithals, *Wunder*
Walter Schmithals, *Wunder und Glaube: Eine Auslegung von Markus 4,35—6,6a* (BSt 59; Neukirchen-Vluyn: Neukirchener Verlag, 1970).

Schneider, "Die Verhaftung Jesu"
Gerhard Schneider, "Die Verhaftung Jesu: Traditionsgeschichte von Mk 14.43-52," *ZNW* 63 (1972) 188–209.

Scholtissek, *Die Vollmacht Jesu*
Klaus Scholtissek, *Die Vollmacht Jesu: Traditions- und redaktionsgeschichtliche Analysen zu einem Leitmotiv markinischer Christologie* (NTAbh 25; Münster: Aschendorff, 1992).

Schürer, *History*
Emil Schürer, *The History of the Jewish People in the Age of Jesus Christ (175 B.C.–A.D. 135)* (rev. ed. by Geza Vermes, Fergus Millar et al.; 3 vols. in 4; Edinburgh: T & T Clark, 1973–87).

Schüssler Fiorenza, *In Memory of Her*
Elisabeth Schüssler Fiorenza, *In Memory of Her: A Feminist Theological Reconstruction of Christian Origins* (New York: Crossroad, 1983).

Schweizer
Eduard Schweizer, *The Good News according to Mark* (Atlanta: John Knox, 1970); trans. of *Das Evangelium nach Markus übersetzt und erklärt* (Das Neue Testament Deutsch 1; Göttingen: Vandenhoeck & Ruprecht, 1967).

van Segbroeck et al., *Four Gospels 1992*
F. van Segbroeck, C. M. Tuckett, G. Van Belle, and J. Verheyden, eds., *The Four Gospels 1992: Festschrift Frans Neirynck* (3 vols.; BEThL 100; Leuven: Leuven University Press, 1992).

Seim, *Double Message*
Turid Karlsen Seim, *The Dougle Message: Patterns of Gender in Luke-Acts* (SNTW; Edinburgh: T & T Clark, 1994).

Sellew, "Composition"
Philip Sellew, "Composition of Didactic Scenes in Mark's Gospel," *JBL* 108 (1989) 613–34.

Sellew, "Secret Mark"
Philip Sellew, "*Secret Mark* and the History of Canonical Mark," in Birger A. Pearson, ed., *The Future of Early Christianity: Essays in Honor of Helmut Koester* (Minneapolis: Fortress, 1991) 242–57.

Van Seters, *In Search of History*
John Van Seters, *In Search of History: Historiography in the Ancient World and the Origins of Biblical History* (New Haven: Yale University Press, 1983).

Shepherd, *Markan Sandwich Stories*
Tom Shepherd, *Markan Sandwich Stories: Narration, Definition, and Function* (AUSDDS 18; Berrien Springs, MI: Andrews University Press, 1993).

Shiner, "Ambiguous Pronouncement"
Whitney T. Shiner, "The Ambiguous Pronouncement of the Centurion and the Shrouding of Meaning in Mark," *JSNT* 78 (2000) 3–22.

Shiner, *Proclaiming the Gospel*
Whitney T. Shiner, *Proclaiming the Gospel: First Century Performance of Mark* (Harrisburg, PA: Trinity Press International/Continuum, 2003).

Shuler, *Genre*
Philip L. Shuler, *A Genre for the Gospels: The Biographical Character of Matthew* (Philadelphia: Fortress, 1982).

Simonetti, *Biblical Interpretation*
Manlio Simonetti, *Biblical Interpretation in the Early Church: An Historical Introduction to Patristic Exegesis* (Edinburgh: T & T Clark, 1994; Italian ed. 1981).

Smalley, *Gospels in the Schools*
Beryl Smalley, *The Gospels in the Schools c. 1100–c. 1280* (London/Ronceverte, WV: Hambledon, 1985).

Smith, *Clement of Alexandria*
Morton Smith, *Clement of Alexandria and a Secret Gospel of Mark* (Cambridge, MA: Harvard University Press, 1973).

Smyth
Herbert Weir Smyth, *Greek Grammar* (rev. by Gordon M. Messing; Cambridge, MA: Harvard University Press, 1956); cited by section number.

von Soden
Hermann Freiherr von Soden, *Die Schriften des Neuen Testaments in ihrer ältesten erreichbaren Textgestalt hergestellt auf Grund ihrer Textgeschichte*, vol. 1, part 1: *Untersuchungen* (Berlin: Verlag von Alexander Duncker, 1902); vol. 1, part 2: *Die Textformen, A. Die Evangelien* (Berlin: Verlag von

Arthur Glaue [Duncker], 1907); vol. 2: *Text mit Apparat nebst Ergänzungen zu Teil I* (Göttingen: Vandenhoeck und Ruprecht, 1913).

Sommer, "Did Prophecy Cease?"
Benjamin D. Sommer, "Did Prophecy Cease? Evaluating a Reevaluation," *JBL* 115 (1996) 31–47.

Standaert, *Évangile selon Marc*
Benoit H. M. G. M. Standaert, *L'Évangile selon Marc: Composition et genre litteraire* (Nijmegen: Stichting Studentenpers Nijmegen, 1978).

Stegner, "Use of Scripture"
William Richard Stegner, "The Use of Scripture in Two Narratives of Early Jewish Christianity (Matthew 4.1-11; Mark 9.2-8)," in Craig A. Evans and James A. Sanders, eds., *Early Christian Interpretation of the Scriptures of Israel: Investigations and Proposals* (JSNTSup 148; SSEJC 5; Sheffield: Sheffield Academic Press, 1997) 98–120.

Stein, "Misplaced Resurrection-Account?"
Robert H. Stein, "Is the Transfiguration (Mark 9:2-8) a Misplaced Resurrection-Account?" *JBL* 95 (1976) 79–96.

Stemberger, "Galilee—Land of Salvation?"
Günter Stemberger, "Galilee—Land of Salvation?" Appendix IV in W. D. Davies, *The Gospel and the Land* (Berkeley: University of California Press, 1974).

Stern, *Parables in Midrash*
David Stern, *Parables in Midrash: Narrative and Exegesis in Rabbinic Literature* (Cambridge, MA/London: Harvard University Press, 1991).

Stone, *Fourth Ezra*
Michael Edward Stone, *Fourth Ezra: A Commentary on the Book of Fourth Ezra* (Hermeneia; Minneapolis: Fortress, 1990).

Stone, *Jewish Writings*
Michael E. Stone, ed., *Jewish Writings of the Second Temple Period* (CRINT 2, LJPPSTT 2; Assen: Van Gorcum; Philadelphia: Fortress, 1984).

Stuhlmacher, *Gospel and the Gospels*
Peter Stuhlmacher, ed., *The Gospel and the Gospels* (Grand Rapids: Eerdmans, 1991).

Suhl, *Funktion*
Alfred Suhl, *Die Funktion der alttestamentlichen Zitate und Anspielungen im Markusevangelium* (Gütersloh: Mohn, 1965).

Sukenik
E. L. Sukenik, ed., *The Dead Sea Scrolls of the Hebrew University* (Jerusalem: Magnes Press/Hebrew University, 1955).

Swete
Henry Barclay Swete, *The Gospel according to Mark* (London: Macmillan, 1913); reprinted as *Commentary on Mark: The Greek Text with Introduction, Notes and Indexes* (Grand Rapids: Kregel, 1977).

Talbert, "Biographies"
Charles H. Talbert, "Biographies of Philosophers

and Rulers as Instruments of Religious Propaganda in Mediterranean Antiquity," *ANRW* 2.16.2 (1978) 1619–51.

Talbert, *What Is a Gospel?*
Charles H. Talbert, *What Is a Gospel? The Genre of the Canonical Gospels* (Philadelphia: Fortress, 1977).

Tannehill, "Disciples in Mark"
Robert C. Tannehill, "The Disciples in Mark: The Function of a Narrative Role," *JR* 57 (1977) 386–405.

Tannehill, "Introduction"
Robert C. Tannehill, "Introduction: The Pronouncement Story and Its Types," *Semeia* 20 (1981) 1–13.

Tannehill, *Sword*
Robert C. Tannehill, *The Sword of His Mouth: Forceful and Imaginative Language in Synoptic Sayings* (SemSup 1; Philadelphia: Fortress; Missoula, MT: Scholars Press, 1975).

Tannehill, "Varieties"
Robert C. Tannehill, "Varieties of Synoptic Pronouncement Stories," *Semeia* 20 (1981) 101–19.

Taylor
Vincent Taylor, *The Gospel according to St. Mark: The Greek Text with Introduction, Notes, and Indexes* (2nd ed.; Grand Rapids: Baker Book House, 1966).

Taylor, *Formation*
Vincent Taylor, *The Formation of the Gospel Tradition* (London: Macmillan, 1933).

Taylor, "Golgotha"
Joan Taylor, "Golgotha: A Reconsideration of the Evidence for the Sites of Jesus' Crucifixion and Burial," *NTS* 44 (1998) 180–203.

Telford, *Barren Temple*
William R. Telford, *The Barren Temple and the Withered Tree: A Redaction-critical Analysis of the Cursing of the Fig-Tree Pericope in Mark's Gospel and Its Relation to the Cleansing of the Temple Tradition* (JSNTSup 1; Sheffield: JSOT Press, 1980).

Thackeray, *Josephus*
Henry St. J. Thackeray, Ralph Marcus, Allen Wikgren, Louis Feldman, *Josephus* (9 vols.; LCL; Cambridge, MA: Harvard University Press; London: Heinemann, 1926–66).

Theissen, *Gospels in Context*
Gerd Theissen, *The Gospels in Context: Social and Political History in the Synoptic Tradition* (Minneapolis: Fortress, 1991). ET of Gerd Theißen, *Lokalkolorit und Zeitgeschichte in den Evangelien: Ein Beitrag zur Geschichte der synoptischen Tradition* (NTOA 8; Freiburg, Schweiz: Universitätsverlag Freiburg; Göttingen: Vandenhoeck & Ruprecht, 1989).

Theissen, *Miracle Stories*
Gerd Theissen, *The Miracle Stories of the Early Christian Tradition* (SNTW; Edinburgh: T & T Clark; Philadelphia: Fortress, 1983). ET of Gerd Theißen, *Urchristliche Wundergeschichten: Ein Beitrag zur*

formgeschichtlichen Erforschung der synoptischen Evangelien (Gütersloh: Mohn, 1974).

Tiller, *Animal Apocalypse*
Patrick A. Tiller, *A Commentary on the Animal Apocalypse of 1 Enoch* (SBLEJL 4; Atlanta: Scholars Press, 1993).

Tischendorf
Constantinus Tischendorf, *Novum Testamentum Graece*, vol. 1 (8th ed.; Leipzig: Giesecke & Devrient, 1869).

Tolbert, *Sowing the Gospel*
Mary Ann Tolbert, *Sowing the Gospel: Mark's World in Literary-Historical Perspective* (Minneapolis: Fortress, 1989).

Torijano, *Solomon the Esoteric King*
Pablo A. Torijano, *Solomon the Esoteric King: From King to Magus, Development of a Tradition* (JSJSup 73; Leiden/Boston: Brill, 2002).

Tuckett, *Scriptures*
Christopher M. Tuckett, ed., *The Scriptures in the Gospels* (BEThL 131; Leuven: Leuven University Press/Peeters, 1997).

Tuckett, *Zechariah*
Christopher M. Tuckett, ed., *The Book of Zechariah and Its Influence* (London: Ashgate, 2003).

Turner
C. H. Turner, *The Gospel according to St. Mark: Introduction and Commentary* (London: SPCK; New York: Macmillan, 1931).

Turner, "Marcan Usage"
C. H. Turner, "Marcan Usage: Notes, Critical and Exegetical, on the Second Gospel," *JTS* 25 (1924) 377–86; 26 (1924) 12–20; 26 (1925) 145–56, 225–40, 337–46; 27 (1926) 58–62; 28 (1926) 9–30; 28 (1927) 349–62; 29 (1928) 275–89; 346–61; reprinted in Elliott, *Language and Style,* 3–136.

Turner, "A Textual Commentary"
C. H. Turner, "A Textual Commentary on Mark 1," *JTS* 28 (1927) 145–58.

Turner, "Western Readings"
C. H. Turner, "Western Readings in the Second Half of St. Mark's Gospel," *JTS* 29 (1927) 1–16.

Ulansey, "Heavenly Veil Torn"
David Ulansey, "The Heavenly Veil Torn: Mark's Cosmic *Inclusio*," *JBL* 110 (1991) 123–25.

VanderKam, *Book of Jubilees*
James C. VanderKam, *The Book of Jubilees* (CSCO 511, Scriptores Aethiopici 88; Leuven: Peeters, 1989).

VanderKam, "Righteous One"
James C. VanderKam, "Righteous One, Messiah, Chosen One, and Son of Man in 1 Enoch 37–71," in James H. Charlesworth, ed., *The Messiah: Developments in Earliest Judaism and Christianity* (Minneapolis: Fortress, 1992).

Vermes, *Dead Sea Scrolls*
Geza Vermes, *The Complete Dead Sea Scrolls in English* (rev. ed.; London: Penguin Books, 2004).

Versnel, "What Did Ancient Man See"
H. S. Versnel, "What Did Ancient Man See When He Saw a God? Some Reflections on Greco-Roman Epiphany," in Dirk van der Plas, ed., *Effigies Dei: Essays on the History of Religions* (Leiden/New York: Brill, 1987) 42–55.

Vielhauer, *Aufsätze*
Philipp Vielhauer, *Aufsätze zum Neuen Testament* (ThBü 31; Munich: Kaiser, 1965).

Vielhauer, *Geschichte*
Philipp Vielhauer, *Geschichte der urchristlichen Literatur* (Berlin/New York: de Gruyter, 1975).

Vielhauer, "Gottesreich und Menschensohn"
Philipp Vielhauer, "Gottesreich und Menschensohn in der Verkündigung Jesu," in Wilhelm Schneemelcher, ed., *Festschrift für Günther Dehn zum 75. Geburtstag* (Neukirchen: Kreis Moers, 1957) 51–79; reprinted in Vielhauer, *Aufsätze,* 55–91. Citations follow the pagination of the reprint.

Vogels
Heinrich Joseph Vogels, *Novum Testamentum Graece et Latine* (Düsseldorf: L. Schwann, 1920; 4th ed.; Freiburg-im-Breisgau: Herder, 1955).

Vorster, "Function"
W. S. Vorster, "The Function of the Use of the Old Testament in Mark," *Neotestamentica* 14 (1980) 62–72.

Votaw, *Gospels*
Clyde Weber Votaw, *The Gospels and Contemporary Biographies in the Greco-Roman World* (FBBS 27; Philadelphia: Fortress, 1970); reprint of idem, "The Gospels and Contemporary Biographies," *American Journal of Theology* [the forerunner of the *Journal of Religion*] 19 (1915) 45–73, 217–49.

Wasserman, "Death of the Soul"
Emma Wasserman, "The Death of the Soul in Romans 7: Sin, Death, and the Law in Light of Hellenistic Moral Psychology" (Ph.D. diss., Yale University, 2005).

Weeden, *Traditions in Conflict*
Theodore J. Weeden, Sr., *Mark–Traditions in Conflict* (Philadelphia: Fortress, 1971).

Wellhausen
Julius Wellhausen, *Das Evangelium Marci übersetzt und erklärt* (2nd ed.; Berlin: G. Reimer, 1909; 1st ed. 1903).

Westcott and Hort
Brooke Foss Westcott and Fenton John Anthony Hort, *The New Testament in the Original Greek*, vol. 1: *Text* (London, 1881; 2nd ed. 1896; work cited: London/New York: Macmillan, 1898); vol. 2: *Introduction and Appendix* (London, 1881; 2nd ed. 1896; work cited: New York: Harper & Brothers, 1882).

Wibbing, *Die Tugend- und Lasterkataloge*
Siegfried Wibbing, *Die Tugend- und Lasterkataloge im Neuen Testament und ihrer Traditionsgeschichte unter besonderer Berücksichtigung der Qumran-Texte* (BZNW 25; Berlin: Töpelmann, 1959).

Winter, *Trial*
Paul Winter, *On the Trial of Jesus* (2nd ed.; Studia Judaica 1; Berlin/New York: de Gruyter, 1974).

Wrede, *Messianic Secret*
William Wrede, *The Messianic Secret* (Cambridge/London: James Clarke, 1971). ET of William Wrede, *Das Messiasgeheimnis in den Evangelien: Zugleich ein Beitrag zum Verständnis des Markusevangeliums* (Göttingen: Vandenhoeck und Ruprecht, 1901; reprinted 1969).

Yarbro Collins, "Apocalyptic Rhetoric"
Adela Yarbro Collins, "The Apocalyptic Rhetoric of Mark 13 in Historical Context," *BR* 41 (1996) 5–36.

Yarbro Collins, *Beginning of the Gospel*
Adela Yarbro Collins, *The Beginning of the Gospel: Probings of Mark in Context* (Minneapolis: Fortress, 1992).

Yarbro Collins, "Charge of Blasphemy"
Adela Yarbro Collins, "The Charge of Blasphemy in Mark 14.64," *JSNT* 26 (2004) 379–401.

Yarbro Collins, *Cosmology and Eschatology*
Adela Yarbro Collins, *Cosmology and Eschatology in Jewish and Christian Apocalypticism* (JSJSup 50; Leiden: Brill, 1996).

Yarbro Collins, "Finding Meaning"
Adela Yarbro Collins, "Finding Meaning in the Death of Jesus," *JR* 78 (1998) 175–96.

Yarbro Collins, "Genre"
Adela Yarbro Collins, "The Genre of the Passion Narrative," *Studia Theologica* 47 (1993) 3–28.

Yarbro Collins, "Jesus' Action in Herod's Temple"
Adela Yarbro Collins, "Jesus' Action in Herod's Temple," in eadem and Margaret M. Mitchell, eds., *Antiquity and Humanity: Essays on Ancient Religion and Philosophy Presented to Hans Dieter Betz on His 70th Birthday* (Tübingen: Mohr Siebeck, 2001) 45–61.

Yarbro Collins, "From Noble Death"
Adela Yarbro Collins, "From Noble Death to Crucified Messiah," *NTS* 40 (1994) 481–503.

Yarbro Collins, "Origin of the Designation"
Adela Yarbro Collins, "The Origin of the Designation of Jesus as 'Son of Man,'" *HTR* 80 (1987) 391–407.

Yarbro Collins, *Perspectives*
Adela Yarbro Collins, ed., *Ancient and Modern Perspectives on the Bible and Culture: Essays in Honor of Hans Dieter Betz* (SPHS; Atlanta: Scholars Press, 1998).

Yarbro Collins, "Psalms of Individual Lament"
Adela Yarbro Collins, "The Appropriation of the Psalms of Individual Lament by Mark," in Tuckett, *Scriptures,* 223–41.

Yarbro Collins, "Rulers, Divine Men"
Adela Yarbro Collins, "Rulers, Divine Men, and Walking on the Water (Mark 6:45-52)," in Lukas Bormann, Kelly Del Tredici, and Angela Standhartinger, eds., *Religious Propaganda and Missionary Competition in the New Testament World: Essays Honoring Dieter Georgi* (NovTSup 74; Leiden/New York: Brill, 1994).

Yarbro Collins, "Son of God among Greeks and Romans"
Adela Yarbro Collins, "Mark and His Readers: The Son of God among Greeks and Romans," *HTR* 93 (2000) 85–100.

Yarbro Collins, "Son of God among Jews"
Adela Yarbro Collins, "Mark and His Readers: The Son of God among Jews," *HTR* 92 (1999) 393–408.

Zager, *Gottesherrschaft und Endgericht*
Werner Zager, *Gottesherrschaft und Endgericht in der Verkündigung Jesu: Eine Untersuchung zur markinischen Jesusüberlieferung einschliesslich der Q-Parallelen* (BZNW 82; Berlin: de Gruyter, 1996).

Ziesler, "Name of Jesus"
John A. Ziesler, "The Name of Jesus in the Acts of the Apostles," *JSNT* 4 (1979) 28–41.

Zimmerli, *Ezekiel 1*
Walther Zimmerli, *Ezekiel 1: A Commentary on the Book of the Prophet Ezekiel, Chapters 1–24* (Hermeneia; Philadelphia: Fortress, 1979).

Although the place of the Gospel of Mark in the Christian canon has always been secure, it was long neglected as an epitome of Matthew with little to offer in its own right.[1] It came into its own in the late eighteenth and especially in the nineteenth century in relation to the quest of the historical Jesus, when it began to be regarded as the oldest of the Gospels and as a reliable source for the life of Jesus.[2] Scholars soon raised questions about its historical reliability, and form critics in the early twentieth century described Mark as a collector of early Christian traditions shaped by the needs of the early church. But the majority continued to consider it to be the earliest of the canonical Gospels. Redaction criticism, aesthetic literary criticism, and other methods applied to the Gospels in the mid- and later twentieth century evoked appreciation for the originality and achievement of the author of Mark. The growing recognition of the independence and intentionality of the author, combined with the acceptance of Mark as the oldest Gospel, led to the insight that he was the first to attempt a narrative account of the events associated with the post-Easter proclamation of the followers of Jesus, the "gospel," in a sense that included the activity of Jesus before his arrest and execution.

This narrative account manifests both cultural tension and cultural adaptation. As the section below on the genre of Mark will argue and the commentary will show in detail, the author has created an eschatological counterpart of an older biblical genre, the foundational sacred history. The biblical story describes God's activity through Moses to establish a people and to instruct them in the proper way of life. Mark's story describes God's activity through Jesus to reform the people and to bring in the new age. Like the books of Moses, Mark is the product of a long process of tradition involving many authors and editors. In both cases, the story is told by one who believes it and in order to persuade others, and in neither case does the narrator speak in his own name. The author of Mark has taken the model of biblical sacred history and transformed it, first, by infusing it with an eschatological and apocalyptic perspective and, second, by adapting it to Hellenistic historiographical and biographical traditions. The latter was accomplished by the focus on the person of Jesus and by the presentation of his life and teaching in a way that assimilated him to the Hellenistic philosophers.

Another major achievement of Mark is the presentation of the significance of Jesus' life, death, and resurrection to a Hellenistic audience in a way that assimilated him to the heroes of Greek and Hellenistic tradition. The section on the interpretation of Jesus below will explore the affinities of the Markan Jesus with Hellenistic philosophers and heroes.

---

1   See Henry Barclay Swete, *The Gospel according to Mark* (London: Macmillan, 1913); reprinted as *Commentary on Mark: The Greek Text with Introduction, Notes and Indexes* (Grand Rapids: Kregel, 1977) xxxi–xxxv; and Helmut Koester, *Ancient Christian Gospels: Their History and Development* (Philadelphia: Trinity; London: SCM, 1990) 273–75.

2   See the discussion by James M. Robinson, *The Problem of History in Mark* (SBT; Naperville, IL: Allenson, 1957), reprinted in idem, *The Problem of History in Mark and Other Markan Studies* (Philadelphia: Fortress, 1982), 55–58. See also Werner Georg Kümmel, *The New Testament: The History of the Investigation of Its Problems* (Nashville: Abingdon, 1972) 75–76, 82, 147–55.

The second Gospel in the canonical order is said to be "according to Mark."[1] Apart from the title of this Gospel, the name "Mark" appears eight times in the New Testament.[2] It should be noted that none of the eight passages states that the man in question wrote a Gospel. To put this fact in perspective, however, one should remember that the book of Acts gives no hint that Paul wrote letters!

In New Testament scholarship from World War II until the 1980s at least, it was commonplace to say that the Gospels circulated anonymously at first and that their titles are late and secondary.[3] The consequence usually drawn is that the attributions of authorship are historically unreliable, since there was a tendency to claim apostolic authority for sacred texts. Martin Hengel challenged this consensus in 1981.[4]

It is true that in antiquity titles were not absolutely essential and that they were not universally and consistently used. If a work was intended for private use by an individual, family, or small group, it did not need a title. But if the author intended the work to be read by a wider public, if it was to be produced in multiple copies for wider circulation, usually in the context of the book trade, the author would be quite likely to give the work a title right from the start.[5] At the latest, the bookseller or whoever was managing the circulation of the work would give it a title. Titles were especially important in scrolls or codices that contained more than one work and in places where a number of scrolls or codices were collected, for example, in public and private libraries. In these contexts, the titles served to distinguish one work from another and to avoid confusion. In a scholarly con-

text, they also made citation of other works possible for authors. Given these circumstances, it is fair to say that in antiquity the giving and use of titles belonged somewhat more to the reception of works than to their production.[6]

It has often been pointed out that many biblical and Jewish works are anonymous, and it has been argued that the anonymity of the Gospels is part of this tradition. It is quite plausible that the author of the second Gospel modeled his work, at least in part, on the narrative books of the Old Testament.[7] The use of this model would explain the lack of any self-reference in the opening of the work itself. It does not compel the conclusion, however, that the Gospel circulated anonymously, that is, without a title that mentioned the author's name. The issue of authority was a live one from the beginning of the proclamation of the gospel, at least by the time Paul was active in that regard, as his letters show. A number of members of the movement wrote in their own names, for example, Paul; John, the prophet who authored the book of Revelation; and Hermas, who composed the *Shepherd of Hermas*. Thus, even if the author did not give his work a title, it is likely that whoever copied it and circulated it to other communities in other geographical locations gave it a title that mentioned Mark.

Support for this hypothesis is provided by Galen, the philosopher and physician active in the second century. He states that he did not write any of his works for publication, but only for pupils and friends who asked for written works to help them remember what they had heard. Galen, in his book on his own books (*De libris propriis liber*), says that he did not give any of his works

---

1　See the commentary on the title below.

2　Acts 12:12, 25; 15:37, 39; Col 4:10; 2 Tim 4:11; Phlm 24; 1 Pet 5:13. These references will be discussed below.

3　So still Harry Y. Gamble, *Books and Readers in the Early Church: A History of Early Christian Texts* (New Haven/London: Yale University Press, 1995) 153–54. According to John R. Donahue, the affirmation that John Mark of Acts was the author of Mark characterized much of British and American scholarship even after World War II ("The Quest for the Community of Mark's Gospel," in F. van Segbroeck et al., eds., *The Four Gospels 1992: Festschrift Frans Neirynck* [BEThL 100; Leuven: Leuven University Press, 1992] 2:817–18 and n. 4).

4　Martin Hengel, *Die Evangelienüberschriften* (Vorgetragen am 18. Oktober, 1981; SHAW.PH 1984, 3; Heidelberg: Carl Winter/Universitätsverlag, 1984); ET *Studies in the Gospel of Mark* (Philadelphia: Fortress, 1985) 64–84.

5　See the section of this introduction on *Audiences of Mark* below.

6　Hengel, *Evangelienüberschriften*, 28–33; ET *Studies in Mark*, 74–75; Carl Werner Müller, review of Egidius Schmalzriedt, Περὶ Φύσεως: *Zur Frühgeschichte der Buchtitel*, in *Gnomon* 50 (1978) 628–38.

7　See the section of this introduction on *Genre* below.

titles, but that, as they began to circulate, the same work was given different titles in varying circumstances.[8] This evidence suggests that, if the second Gospel had circulated without a title, it would have acquired two or more different titles in the course of its early transmission. Such a process, however, does not seem to have occurred.

Most of the oldest uncial manuscripts of the second Gospel, for example, have the title "(The) Gospel according to Mark" (εὐαγγέλιον κατὰ Μᾶρκον). Two very important manuscripts, Vaticanus and Sinaiticus, have simply "according to Mark" (κατὰ Μᾶρκον), which is most likely an abbreviated form of the standard title. The antiquity of this standard title is supported by the few fragments of papyrus manuscripts that preserve titles and by the Old Latin and the Coptic translations.

Of the twenty, in part quite fragmentary, papyri of canonical Gospels from the second and third centuries, only three preserve the titles either at the beginning or at the end of the work in question. Papyrus 66, which dates to about 200 CE, has the title "(The) Gospel according to John" (ΕΥΑΓΓΕΛΙΟΝ ΚΑΤΑ ΙΩΑΝΝΗΝ) at the beginning. Papyrus 75, which is slightly later, has the title "(The) Gospel according to Luke" (ΕΥΑΓΓΕΛΙΟΝ ΚΑΤΑ ΛΟΥΚΑΝ) at the end. On the same page, after a small blank space, the same papyrus has the title "(The) Gospel according to John" (ΕΥΑΓΓΕΛΙΟΝ ΚΑΤΑ ΙΩΑΝΝΗΝ) preceding the beginning of that Gospel. A leaf belonging to a document preserved by papyri 64 and 67 contains the title "(The) Gospel according to Matthew" (ΕΥΑΓΓΕΛΙΟΝ ΚΑΤΑ ΜΑΘΘΑΙΟΝ). This leaf may have been the title of a codex. It has been dated to the second century, so the manuscript from which it was copied must be dated to a point well within that century.[9] The oldest manuscript of Mark, papyrus 45, does not contain the opening of Mark.[10]

Justin Martyr, writing around the middle of the second century, preferred to describe the relevant texts as "reminiscences of the apostles," but he comments that they were usually called "Gospels" (1 Apol. 66).[11] Although Paul used the term "gospel" to designate the content of the oral proclamation, Mark is the only one of the canonical Gospels to use the term at the beginning as a summary of its own content. Since the noun "gospel" does not occur at all in Luke and John, and since it plays a much more important role in Mark than in Matthew, it is likely that the practice of referring to the four works as "Gospels" ultimately derives from Mark.

Papias, who was bishop of the Christian community in Hierapolis, a city of Asia Minor, in the early second century, does not call the work that Mark wrote a Gospel or use a term indicating his understanding of the kind of writing that it was, as Justin did:

> And the Presbyter used to say this, "Mark became Peter's interpreter and wrote accurately all that he remembered, not, indeed, in order, of the things said or done by the Lord. For he had not heard the Lord, nor had he followed him, but later on, as I said, followed Peter, who used to give teaching as necessity demanded but not making, as it were, an arrangement of the Lord's oracles, so that Mark did nothing wrong in thus writing down single points as he remembered them. For to one thing he gave attention, to leave out nothing of what he had heard and to make no false statements in them."[12]

Although Papias gives no label to Mark's work, the fact that he says that Mark wrote down the things said and done by the Lord suggests that it was a narrative work that included teaching, that is, something similar to the

---

8 Hengel, *Evangelienüberschriften*, 30; ET *Studies in Mark*, 74.
9 Hengel, *Evangelienüberschriften*, 11; ET *Studies in Mark*, 66.
10 See Nestle-Aland (27th ed.), 686.
11 On Justin's terminology, see the section of this introduction on *Genre* below.
12 Papias cited by Eusebius *Hist. eccl.* 3.39.15; trans. Kirsopp Lake, *Eusebius: The Ecclesiastical History* (2 vols.; LCL; Cambridge, MA/London: Harvard

University Press, 1926) 1:297. For discussion, see Josef Kürzinger, *Papias von Hierapolis und die Evangelien des Neuen Testaments: Gesammelte Aufsätze, Neuausgebung und Übersetzung der Fragmente, kommentierte Bibliographie* (Eichstätter Materialien 4; Regensburg: Pustet, 1983); Ulrich H.-J. Körtner, *Papias von Hierapolis: Ein Beitrag zur Geschichte des frühen Christentums* (FRLANT 133; Göttingen: Vandenhoeck & Ruprecht, 1985).

Gospel of Mark as we know it. Even though Papias does not quote the title of the Gospel, it is likely that he knew it, since he mentions a work attributed to Mark alongside one attributed to Matthew. A further important observation is that Papias has information about Mark as an author, not just from the title of the Gospel but also from oral tradition, which he claims to have at third hand.[13]

Kurt Niederwimmer has questioned the reliability of Papias's attribution of this tradition about Mark to John the Elder.[14] He argued that Papias invented the tradition in order to endow the second Gospel with apostolic authority. This argument, however, overlooks the fact that Papias is quite critical of the written work by Mark. The remark that it is "not in order" implies that it does not measure up to Papias's standard of what a Gospel should be; nevertheless, he defends it. This state of affairs makes it more likely that he inherited the tradition of the apostolic authority of Mark and had to come to terms with it, rather than that he invented it.

Jürgen Regul has also argued that Papias invented the pedigree of the Gospel of Mark by spinning this story out of one of the references to a man called Mark in the New Testament, namely, 1 Pet 5:13.[15] 1 Peter was probably written in Rome[16] between 80 and 100 CE.[17] Although most scholars today conclude that the letter was not written by Peter himself, the consensus is that it is an expression of the Christian tradition at Rome that was associated with Peter.[18]

According to Eusebius, Papias knew this letter.[19] The relevant verse (1 Pet 5:13) has the alleged author of the letter, Peter, refer to "my son Mark" (Μᾶρκος ὁ υἱός μου). The consensus is that the term "son" is meant metaphorically, as other familial terms, such as "sister" and "brother" were used in the early communities of the followers of Jesus. It is interesting that the previous verse refers to Silvanus as the one who physically wrote the letter or as the emissary who bore the letter to the addressees.[20] If Papias had looked to this letter for a way to connect the second Gospel with Peter, Silvanus would have been a more logical choice than Mark. If this hypothesis is correct, 1 Peter and Papias may be two independent witnesses to an association between Peter and Mark.

Given the common, and probably independent, association of the man with Peter, it is likely that Papias and 1 Peter refer to the same person named Mark. The possibility, however, that one or more other New Testament texts speak about someone else who also happened to be named Mark must be taken into account.

The New Testament book that says most about someone named Mark is Acts. According to Acts 12:12, set in Jerusalem, when Peter had been miraculously released from prison, he went to the house of Mary, where many had gathered to pray. In an apparent editorial aside, the author states that Mary was the mother of John who was also called Mark. Gerd Lüdemann argued that the reference to John Mark was added to a traditional story by Luke in order to prepare for the remark in v. 25 that Barnabas and Paul took him with them when they returned to Antioch. He seems to doubt the historical reliability of the relationship between Mary and Mark

13 William R. Schoedel, "Papias," *ABD* 5:140–42, esp. 141.

14 Kurt Niederwimmer, "Johannes Markus und die Frage nach dem Verfasser des zweiten Evangeliums," *ZNW* 58 (1967) 172–88, esp. 185–88.

15 Jürgen Regul, *Die Antimarcionitischen Evangelienprologe* (Vetus Latina 6; Freiburg: Herder, 1969) 96.

16 The apparent allusion to the community in Rome as "she who is in Babylon" supports this inference. Rome, as the second destroyer of the temple and Jerusalem, is given the name of the first destroyer (Paul J. Achtemeier, *1 Peter: A Commentary on First Peter* [Hermeneia; Minneapolis: Fortress, 1996] 353–54; cf. Raymond E. Brown, *An Introduction to the New Testament* [ABRL; New York: Doubleday, 1997] 719).

17 Achtemeier, *1 Peter*, 49–50.

18 C. Clifton Black, *Mark: Images of an Apostolic Inter-preter* (Studies on Personalities of the New Testament; Columbia: University of South Carolina Press, 1994) 61; cf. Achtemeier, *1 Peter*, 41–43.

19 Eusebius *Hist. eccl.* 3.39.17: "The same writer [Papias] used quotations from the first Epistle of John, and likewise also from that of Peter" (Κέχρηται δ'ὁ αὐτὸς μαρτυρίαις ἀπὸ τῆς Ἰωάννου προτέρας ἐπιστολῆς καὶ ἀπὸ τῆς Πέτρου ὁμοίως); text and trans. from Lake, *Eusebius*, 1:298–99.

20 Leonhard Goppelt argued that Silvanus was the author of the letter (*A Commentary on I Peter* [Grand Rapids: Eerdmans, 1993; Germ. ed., 1978] 369–70). Norbert Brox concluded that this reference to Silvanus is based on his role as emissary described in Acts 15:22–23 ("Zur pseudepigraphischen Rahmung des ersten Petrusbriefes," *BZ* n.F. 19 [1975] 78–96,

because of the redactional character of its attestation.[21] In any case, one may conclude that the author of Luke-Acts knew a tradition that there was a Mark who was a resident, perhaps a native, of Jerusalem and that this man was a Christian Jew, since he had both a Hebrew and a Greek or Roman name.[22]

According to Acts 13, John (Mark) assisted Barnabas and Paul in proclaiming the word of God in Cyprus and then sailed with them to Perga on the southern coast of Asia Minor (Acts 13:5, 13). But instead of continuing on with them in their work, at this point John (Mark) returned to Jerusalem. According to Acts 15:36–41, this incident was the cause of a later split between Barnabas and Paul. The outcome was that Barnabas continued his work with Mark as a companion, whereas Paul set out with Silas, whose other name was apparently Silvanus and who is probably the same person who is mentioned in 1 Peter.[23] Thus, the book of Acts presents a fairly negative portrait of Mark as a backslider or reluctant missionary to the Gentiles.[24] Since the author of Acts also wrote the Gospel according to Luke, it could be that this critical portrait was intended to undercut the authority of the second Gospel.

A man named Mark is mentioned also in Paul's letter to Philemon in connection with the closing greetings and benediction. Writing from prison, Paul conveys greetings from Epaphras, Mark, Aristarchus, Demas, and Luke (vv. 23–24). He calls Epaphras his fellow prisoner and the rest his fellow workers. The most plausible setting for the letter is an imprisonment in Ephesus in the mid-fifties.[25] Philemon was probably a resident of Colossae, so the letter is addressed to that locality.[26] It is striking that the list of co-workers contains two names that coincide with those of two evangelists. There are three possibilities: (1) The men named Mark and Luke mentioned here are different from the men named in the titles of the two Gospels. (2) The Gospel of Mark at first circulated anonymously; at some point, someone gave it the title "(The) Gospel according to Mark," taking the name from Philemon 24 in order to give the Gospel the apostolic authority of Paul. Later, someone else, who knew the Gospel attributed to Mark and had a copy of the third Gospel, which was anonymous at the time, gave it the title "(The) Gospel according to Luke," using the title of the older Gospel as a model, and taking the second name also from Philemon 24. (3) The second and third Gospels were written by the men named Mark and Luke who are mentioned in Philemon; the titles may have been added somewhat later than the time of composition, but they reflect accurate tradition concerning authorship.

The second possibility is unlikely, as argued earlier, because of the unanimity of the attribution of these Gospels to Mark and Luke by the middle of the second century. Many scholars would argue against the third possibility because of the significant differences between the Gospels of Mark and Luke and the letters of Paul in linguistic usage, tradition-history, and theology. But if they were young men when they had contact with Paul and wrote fifteen or more years later, after exercising their own leadership in the movement and experiencing individual and communal change and development, such differences would be not only explicable but expected. Although the possibility of coincidence must be taken into account, the third option cannot be ruled out either.

In the closing greetings, the letter to the Colossians contains the following statement:

Aristarchus my fellow prisoner greets you, as does Mark the cousin of Barnabas, concerning whom you have received instructions—if he comes to you welcome him. And Jesus who is called Justus (greets you).

esp. 84–90). Black is more inclined to agree with Brox than with Goppelt (*Mark*, 63, 72 n. 52).

21 Gerd Lüdemann, *Early Christianity according to the Traditions in Acts: A Commentary* (London: SCM, 1987) 141, 146.

22 "John" (Ἰωάννης) derives from the Hebrew name "Yohanan" (see the commentary on 3:17 below). The Roman praenomen "Marcus" was "in common use among Greek-speaking peoples from the Augustan age onwards" (Swete, xiii; see also Black, *Mark*, 17 n. 20).

23 John Gillman, "Silas," *ABD* 6:22–23.

24 Black, *Mark*, 25–44, esp. 43.

25 Eduard Lohse, *Colossians and Philemon: A Commentary on the Epistles to the Colossians and to Philemon* (trans. William R. Poehlmann and Robert J. Karris; Hermeneia; Philadelphia: Fortress, 1971) 188.

26 Ibid., 186.

These, being the only ones of the circumcision among my co-workers for the kingdom of God, have been a comfort to me. (Col 4:10–11)

This letter was probably written by a close associate of Paul not long after Paul's death.[27] The fact that the letter is pseudonymous, however, does not necessarily mean that all the information about persons in it is fictional. It is unlikely that the author of Colossians knew Acts, which was probably composed later.[28] There is no evidence for the dependence of Acts on Colossians. Thus, the information about Mark in Colossians is independent tradition that in part confirms and in part supplements the data in Acts. Both works link Mark with Barnabas, but only Colossians states that they were cousins. Both state or imply that Mark was a Christian Jew. This mutual confirmation supports the hypothesis that the Mark mentioned in Philemon is the same man who is mentioned in Acts.[29]

Many New Testament scholars assume that Mark was written by a Christian Gentile because of the Gospel's interest in and concern for the mission to the Gentiles and because of an allegedly negative attitude toward and assumed ignorance of the Jewish law. These, however, are not compelling reasons for concluding that the author was a Gentile.[30]

The judgment that Mark was written by a Gentile is based primarily on the remarks about Passover and the Feast of Unleavened Bread in 14:1 and 12 and on the opening verses of chap. 7. The problems in chap. 14 can be explained on the assumption that Mark departed from the Jewish calculation of days from sunset to sunset and substituted the reckoning of days from sunrise to sunrise. The reason for the change may well have been to make the account intelligible to a wider audience.

In chap. 7, vv. 1–2 constitute the introduction to a controversy-dialogue in which Jesus responds to the criticism of the Pharisees that his disciples do not live according to the tradition of the elders but eat with defiled hands. Already in v. 2, the evangelist explains that "defiled hands" means "unwashed hands." Then, in vv. 3–4, in an aside to the audience, he explains the relevant Jewish customs. This explanation has been criticized by some as inaccurate.[31] First of all, it should be noted that our knowledge of such customs in this period, both for Palestine and the Diaspora, is quite limited. On what grounds, therefore, can we say that Mark, one of our primary sources for Palestinian Jewish practices in the first century, is inaccurate? Secondly, it may well be that the evangelist is not attempting to be precise, but is giving a generalized, perhaps even exaggerated and polemical description of such customs.[32] Later in the chapter, Mark interprets a saying of Jesus as a declaration that all foods are clean. The argument that a Jew, even as a member of the messianic movement in the name of Jesus, could not have made such a statement or described Jewish customs as the author does in vv. 3–4, is refuted by analogous statements by Paul.

In this commentary, "Mark" will be used as a designation of the author of the second Gospel, as shorthand for "the author of the Gospel known as the Gospel according to Mark." The expression "Mark" will also be used for the text of this Gospel. It should be clear from the context which referent is intended.

---

27 Angela Standhartinger, *Studien zur Entstehungsgeschichte und Intention des Kolosserbriefs* (Leiden: Brill, 1999); Outi Leppä, *The Making of Colossians: A Study on the Formation and Purpose of a Deutero-Pauline Letter* (Publications of the Finnish Exegetical Society 86; Helsinki: Finnish Exegetical Society; Göttingen: Vandenhoeck & Ruprecht, 2003) 9–15.

28 Acts is not one of the works that Leppä thinks were known to the author of Colossians; Mark, however, is (*Making of Colossians*, 256–59).

29 For a more skeptical view of the evidence, see the latter part of the subsection of this introduction on *Audience and Purpose* below.

30 See Hengel, *Studies in Mark*, 148–49 n. 52.

31 E.g., Morna D. Hooker, *The Gospel according to St. Mark* (BNTC 2; London: A & C Black; Peabody, MA: Hendrickson, 1991) 174–75; Niederwimmer, "Johannes Markus," 183–85; John P. Meier, *A Marginal Jew: Rethinking the Historical Jesus*, vol. 3: *Companions and Competitors* (ABRL; New York/London: Doubleday, 2001) 316–17. For a different view, see the commentary on 7:2–4 below.

32 Martin Hengel, "Problems in the Gospel of Mark," in Peter Stuhlmacher, ed., *The Gospel and the Gospels* (Grand Rapids: Eerdmans, 1991) 230–31 and n. 52.

Irenaeus, who wrote around 180 CE, does not explicitly say that Mark was written in Rome, but he seems to assume it. Near the beginning of the third book of his work *Against Heresies*, he mentions the activity of Peter and Paul in Rome, preaching and laying the foundations of the church. Then he says, "After their departure [that is, their deaths], Mark, the disciple and interpreter of Peter, did also hand down to us in writing what had been proclaimed by Peter" (3.1.1).[1] The description of Mark as the disciple and interpreter of Peter is close to what Papias said about Mark.[2] Since Irenaeus quotes Papias elsewhere in this work, it is likely that he is dependent on Papias for this information about the Gospel of Mark. Since Papias apparently said nothing about the place of writing or whether Mark wrote during Peter's lifetime or afterward, it may be that Irenaeus drew these conclusions himself. If Irenaeus lived and studied for a time in Rome, as some scholars have conjectured, he may have taken these additional details from local tradition.[3] If so, it is difficult to say whether they are reliable or legendary. In any case, more recently scholars acknowledge only that Irenaeus was sent by the Christians of Vienne and Lyon in Gaul on an embassy to the bishop of Rome.[4]

Clement of Alexandria, according to a quotation by Eusebius, stated in the *Hypotyposeis* that the Gospel of Mark was written in Rome, but during Peter's lifetime.[5] John Chrysostom says that Mark was written in Egypt.[6]

An introductory note to the Gospel of Mark, found in some manuscripts of the Old Latin version, states the following:

> . . . Mark . . . was called "stumpy-fingered" [*colobodactylus*], because for the size of the rest of his body he had fingers that were too short. He was Peter's interpreter [*interpres*]. After the departure [or "death," *post excessionem*] of Peter himself, the same man wrote this Gospel in the regions of Italy.[7]

The text seems to be dependent on Irenaeus for the tradition that Mark was Peter's interpreter and that he wrote the Gospel after Peter's death in Italy. The additional detail about Mark's fingers appears also in Hippolytus's *Refutation of All Heresies*,[8] which was composed in Rome in the early part of the third century. The motif may well be legendary, but its origin and significance are obscure.[9]

---

1 Trans. (slightly modified) from A. Cleveland Coxe, *The Apostolic Fathers with Justin Martyr and Irenaeus* (ANF 1; American reprint of the Edinburgh Edition; Grand Rapids: Eerdmans, 1985) 414. See also the Latin text and ET in Margaret M. Mitchell, "Patristic Counter-Evidence to the Claim that 'The Gospels Were Written for All Christians,'" *NTS* 51 (2005) 36–79, esp. 64.

2 See the section of this introduction on *Authorship* above.

3 W. H. C. Frend, *The Early Church* (Knowing Christianity; Philadelphia: Lippincott, 1966) 77; Jean Daniélou and Henri Marrou, *The Christian Centuries*, vol. 1: *The First Six Hundred Years* (New York: McGraw-Hill, 1964) 110.

4 Eusebius *Hist. eccl.* 5.4.1–2; Denis Minns, "Truth and Tradition: Irenaeus," in Margaret M. Mitchell and Frances M. Young, eds., *The Cambridge History of Christianity*, vol. 1: *Origins to Constantine* (Cambridge/New York: Cambridge University Press, 2006) 261–73, esp. 262; Robert M. Grant, *Irenaeus of Lyons* (Early Church Fathers; London/New York: Routledge, 1997) 5.

5 Eusebius *Hist. eccl.* 6.14.5–7. Greek text and ET in Mitchell, "Patristic Counter-Evidence," 49. Another version of this tradition is given in Eusebius *Hist.*

eccl. 2.15.1–2; see the LCL edition of Eusebius or Bart Ehrman, ed. and trans., *Apostolic Fathers* (2 vols.; LCL; Cambridge, MA/London: Harvard University Press, 2003) 2:96–97; or Mitchell, "Patristic Counter-Evidence," 50–51 (note that "shown" in the first line of her ET should be "shone").

6 John Chrysostom *Homily [1.7] on Matthew*; Greek text and ET in Mitchell, "Patristic Counter-Evidence," 70–71, who notes, following Swete, that Chrysostom's placement of the writing of Mark in Egypt may be due to a misunderstanding of Eusebius *Hist. eccl.* 2.16 (Mitchell, 71 n. 99; Swete, xxxix).

7 Trans. from Black, *Mark*, 119.

8 Black (*Mark*, 116) cites *Ref.* 7.30.1 from Miroslav Marcovich, ed., *Hippolytus: Refutatio Omnium Haeresium* (Patristische Texte und Studien 25; Berlin/New York: de Gruyter, 1986) 311–12. In the ET by J. H. MacMahon in A. Cleveland Coxe, *Apostolic Fathers* (ANF 5; Grand Rapids: Eerdmans, 1985) 112, the passage occurs at 7.18.

9 See the discussion by Black, *Mark*, 115–20.

The external evidence thus points to Rome, or at least Italy. Much of the internal evidence, on the other hand, suggests the East.[10] For example, in passages that are likely to be editorial, Mark speaks of the "Sea of Galilee" (θάλασσα τῆς Γαλιλαίας), a usage that does not correspond to the usual Greek and Latin names for that body of water, but reflects exactly Hebrew and Aramaic word formation.[11] The use of such an expression points to a milieu in which Aramaic was spoken as well as Greek. The citation of words and sayings in Aramaic, as well as in Greek, is a sign that the author and at least some members of his audiences knew Aramaic as well as Greek.[12] These features are compatible with the hypothesis that Mark was written in Rome on the assumption that the author and part of his audience had come from Judea (including Galilee) or Syria and were living in Rome.[13]

Some New Testament scholars have argued for a location outside Palestine as the place of composition because of the author's alleged ignorance of Palestinian geography. The most problematic geographical reference occurs at the beginning of chap. 5, the story about the man possessed by a "legion" of demons: "And they came to the opposite shore of the sea, to the district of the Gerasenes." The point from which they traveled is not specified, but the overall context suggests a place near Capernaum, on the northwest coast of the lake. The problem with the description of the point of arrival is that Gerasa is quite distant from the lake. Even if we assume that the evangelist is speaking of the countryside belonging to the city, and not of the city itself, the reference is still problematic, since there were other major cities closer to the lake, which also had surrounding territory, so the likelihood of the territory of Gerasa reaching to the coast of the lake at any time in the relevant period is very low.

The problem with this line of argumentation, however, is the assumption that anyone living near a region would be precisely informed about its geography. Such an assumption is dubious. Modern New Testament exegetes with scholarly maps and atlases are better informed about the geography of the ancient world than many of its inhabitants were. Lack of knowledge of even relatively nearby regions would be likely if the author had not actually visited them in person. Even modern Americans are ignorant of parts of our country, including some that are quite nearby![14]

The ending of the story makes clear that the author has a setting in the Decapolis in mind: "And he went away and began to proclaim in the Decapolis how much Jesus had done for him, and everyone marveled" (5:20). The Decapolis was a region consisting of ten free cities, which included a small area between Galilee and Samaria west of the Jordan River. Most of the region lay to the east of the Jordan, extending from the east coast of the Sea of Galilee almost down to the Dead Sea. The mistake in 5:1 would be intelligible if Gerasa was the city of the Decapolis most familiar to Mark, as possibly the most renowned of the cities of the district, and yet he was not knowledgeable of its precise location.

Another geographical oddity occurs in 7:31. The previous incident, the healing of the daughter of the Syro-Phoenician woman, is set in the region of Tyre. The following incident, the healing of a deaf man with a speech impediment, takes place somewhere in the Decapolis. The verse in question describes Jesus' journey from the region of Tyre to the Decapolis. The geographical problem lies in the fact that Mark has Jesus going

10   For a discussion of the views of scholars who locate the writing of Mark near Palestine, most likely in southern Syria, see Donahue, "Quest, " 823–28, 832–35. To these add Ludger Schenke, *Das Markusevangelium: Literarische Eigenart–Text und Kommentierung* (Stuttgart: Kohlhammer, 2005) 41; and Joel Marcus, *Mark 1–8: A New Translation with Introduction and Commentary* (AB 27; New York: Doubleday, 2000) 33–37.

11   Gerd Theissen, *The Gospels in Context: Social and Political History in the Synoptic Tradition* (Minneapolis: Fortress, 1991) 237–38, ET of Gerd Theißen, *Lokalkolorit und Zeitgeschichte in den Evangelien: Ein Beitrag zur Geschichte der synoptischen Tradition* (NTOA 8; Freiburg, Schweiz: Universitätsverlag Freiburg; Göttingen: Vandenhoeck & Ruprecht, 1989) 248–49.

12   Mark 5:41; 7:11, 34; 14:32; 15:22, 34.

13   Brian J. Incigneri, *The Gospel to the Romans: The Setting and Rhetoric of Mark's Gospel* (BIS 65; Leiden/Boston: Brill, 2003) 96–97. For a discussion of scholars who have argued that Mark was written in Rome, see Donahue, "Quest," 828–32.

14   For a German example, see Hengel, *Studies in Mark*, 148 n. 51.

north toward Sidon first of all, that is, apparently away from the Decapolis, and then to the Sea of Galilee through the midst of the Decapolis, a region south of the direct route from Sidon to the lake. Such a journey would be like going from Chicago to Indiana by going north through Wisconsin and then east and south through Michigan to Indiana.

The problem, however, may lie more in the picture New Testament scholars have of the Decapolis than in Mark's text.[15] In his *Natural History*, Pliny the Elder says that the region of the Decapolis bordered Judea on the side of Syria. He also states that writers do not agree on which cities belonged to this region. He then gives a list of the ones most commonly included. The first one he mentions is Damascus (5.16.74). Now Damascus is roughly at the same latitude as Sidon. Pliny seems to have a view of the location of the Decapolis similar to Mark's. After a description of the (Palestinian) coast, he lists cities of Phoenicia, mentioning Achzib, Tyre, Zarephath, and Sidon. Then he says that behind Sidon begins the Lebanon mountain range. Facing that range (to the east) is the Counter-Lebanon range. Behind Counter-Lebanon inland, he continues, is the Decapolis (5.17.75). Since Damascus is located just south of the southern end of the Counter-Lebanon range, this statement makes sense if Damascus is one of the ten cities, although it places the northern border of the region quite a bit farther north than is usual in today's scholarly maps.

Since the Decapolis may have been understood by Mark to include cities from Damascus in the north to Gerasa and Philadelphia in the south, his description of Jesus' route may be understood as the deliberate construction of a wide-ranging journey in a great arc, approximately 270 degrees of a rough circle. Theissen

has argued that Mark constructed this brief account in order to include the territory of the community for which the Gospel was composed and conjectures that this community may have been located in Chalcis,[16] Damascus, or the southern valley of the Orontes River.[17] This conjecture is overly speculative. Mark may simply have wanted to show that Jesus traveled in these regions, thus prefiguring, or perhaps even inaugurating, the mission to the Gentiles.

Some scholars have argued that the use of the term "Syro-Phoenician" in the story about the woman with a demon-possessed daughter is evidence that Mark was written in Rome (Mark 7:26).[18] The argument is that the term "Syro-Phoenician" was coined to distinguish the Phoenicians of the eastern Mediterranean coast from the Libyan-Phoenicians of north Africa. The term makes sense only in a context, such as Rome, where it was necessary to distinguish the two groups. Theissen, however, has shown that the Latin word *Syrophoenix* is a loanword from the Greek and that the term makes sense in the East as a nonofficial designation of a resident of southern Syria.[19]

Another important argument for the Roman provenance of Mark has been based on the story of the widow's offering in 12:41–44. According to v. 42, the woman put in two *lepta*, which, the evangelist explains in an aside to the audience, were equivalent to a *quadrans*. The argument is that Mark must have been written in Rome because Greek coins are explained in terms of a Roman copper coin that did not circulate in the East.[20] It is true that the *quadrans* did not circulate in the East, but its name became proverbial as the minimum unit of money. The spread of the concept without the coin is to be explained by the fact that the local copper coin took on the role, and sometimes the name, of the *quadrans*.[21]

---

15 See the discussion by Friedrich Gustav Lang, "'Über Sidon mitten ins Gebiet der Dekapolis': Geographie und Theologie in Markus 7,31," *Zeitschrift des Deutschen Palästina-Vereins* 94 (1978) 145–60. See also Theissen, *Gospels in Context*, 243–44 (*Lokalkolorit*, 254–55).

16 Chalcis was a city in the Lebanon valley, northeast of Sidon and northwest of Damascus.

17 This valley, like the city of Chalcis, was between the Lebanon mountain range and the Counter-Lebanon, but farther north. Theissen makes this conjecture in *Gospels in Context*, 244–45 (*Lokalkolorit*, 255–56).

18 Hengel, *Studies in Mark*, 29; Niederwimmer, "Johannes Markus," 182; Incigneri, *Gospel to the Romans*, 98.

19 Theissen, *Gospels in Context*, 245–47 (*Lokalkolorit*, 256–58).

20 Hengel, *Studies in Mark*, 29; Incigneri, *Gospel to the Romans*, 98.

21 Theissen, *Gospels in Context*, 248 and the literature cited in n. 28 (*Lokalkolorit*, 259 and n. 28).

The copper *lepton* was the smallest Greek coin denomination. The name *lepton* was used for whatever was the smallest denomination of coins in the Syrian-Nabatean region. In Syria and Judea, Roman and local coin denominations coexisted, and local coins were understandable in terms of Roman denominations.[22] For this reason, the use of the term *quadrans* (more precisely, the Greek loanword κοδράντης with the same meaning) here may not be taken as evidence that Mark was written in Rome. In fact, mention of the two *lepta* makes it more likely that Mark was written in one of the eastern provinces.[23]

For further discussion, see the section of this introduction on *Audience and Purpose* below.

---

22 See the commentary on 12:42 below.
23 Theissen, *Gospels in Context*, 247–49 (*Lokalkolorit*, 259–61).

The best evidence for the date of Mark is provided by the eschatological discourse of Jesus in chap. 13.[1] Most scholars have concluded that this discourse reflects some knowledge or even experience of the first Jewish war with Rome, which lasted from 66 to 74 CE. The major difference of opinion concerns whether the Gospel was written before or after the destruction of the temple, which occurred in 70 CE.

Chapter 13 begins with a brief dialogue between Jesus and one of his disciples that occurs as Jesus is leaving the temple precinct, that is, the temple mount. The disciple says, "Teacher, look how grand the stones and buildings are!" Jesus answers, "Do you see these great buildings? There will surely not be left here a stone upon a stone that will not be thrown down." Some scholars argue that this prediction has been shaped by the actual events and, therefore, that it is a prophecy after the fact. That would mean that Mark was written after 70 CE.[2] Some point to a passage in Josephus's history of the Jewish war indicating that, after the Romans had taken possession of the temple and the whole city, they razed them both to the ground.[3] But the passage goes on to say "leaving only the loftiest of the towers, . . . and the portion of the wall enclosing the city on the west: the latter as an encampment for the garrison that was to remain, and the towers to indicate to posterity the nature of the city and of the strong defences which had yet yielded to Roman prowess."[4] Thus, the prophecy of 13:2 was not fulfilled precisely. This lack of correlation raises doubt about its being a prophecy after the fact.

Theissen noticed this problem and tried to solve it by arguing that the word "here" (ὧδε) in the prophecy limits its application, indicating that only the structures on the temple platform would be destroyed, whereas the foundation walls would remain intact.[5] It seems rather that the "here" is added for dramatic effect. It paints a vivid picture of Jesus standing in the temple area (or just outside it, looking back at the whole), gesturing to the magnificent buildings and prophesying their doom. It is unlikely that the word has a limiting function, since the text does not say exactly where Jesus was standing and thus does not distinguish between buildings and foundations.

Incigneri takes a different approach. He notes that "all other predictions of events after Jesus' death had already been fulfilled at the time of writing" and that "Mark never gives details of such events." He admits that the predictions "relating to his return (8:38; 13:26-27; 14:62)" constitute an exception.[6] Further, he argues that Mark could not have been sure that the Romans would destroy the temple before the destruction occurred and that he would not have taken the risk of including the prophecy of 13:2 if it had not yet been fulfilled.[7] These are not compelling arguments. The expectation of the destruction of the temple may have been an eschatological dogma for Mark, as was the expectation of the coming of the Son of Man. The author of the book of Daniel risked making predictions that could be falsified, for example, the time and manner of the death of Antiochus (Dan 11:45).[8]

In the next, closely related scene, Jesus is sitting on the Mount of Olives opposite the temple. Peter, James, John, and Andrew ask him privately, "Tell us when this will be and what the sign will be when all these things are about to be accomplished" (13:4). The question clearly implies that the destruction of the temple is perceived as part of the sequence of events that constitutes the end, or the eschatological turning point, when all things would be fulfilled (συντελεῖσθαι).[9] Jesus' response is the discourse that follows in 13:5-37.

---

1   This datum was not recognized by many scholars before 1956; see Donahue, "Quest," 817–18 and n. 3; Incigneri, *Gospel to the Romans*, 116.

2   E.g., Theissen, *Gospels in Context*, 259 (*Lokalkolorit*, 271); John S. Kloppenborg, "*Evocatio deorum* and the Date of Mark," *JBL* 124 (2005) 419–50. For other scholars who date Mark after 70, see Donahue, "Quest," 821–23.

3   Josephus *Bell.* 7.1.1 §1; cf. 6.9.1 §413.

4   Ibid. 7.1.1 §1–2; trans. H. St. J. Thackeray, *Josephus* (9 vols.; Cambridge, MA: Harvard University Press; London: Heinemann, 1928) 3:505.

5   Theissen, *Gospels in Context*, 259 (*Lokalkolorit*, 271).

6   Incigneri, *Gospel to the Romans*, 118.

7   Ibid., 119–20.

8   See John J. Collins, *Daniel: A Commentary on the Book of Daniel* (Hermeneia; Minneapolis: Fortress, 1993) 389–90.

9   This implication is made explicit in Matt 24:3, "Tell us when this will be and what the sign will be of your coming and of the consummation (συντέλεια) of the age."

The warning not to be led astray introduces an important theme of the discourse taken up again in vv. 21–23. This theme will be discussed below. Beginning with v. 7, the background for this theme is sketched: "Now when you hear of wars and reports of wars, do not be disturbed. It must happen, but the end is not yet." Verse 8 continues, "For nation will rise up against nation and kingdom against kingdom; there will be earthquakes in various regions; there will be famines. This is the beginning of the birth-pains."

These verses may simply set the scene and evoke typical eschatological lore, without any precise contemporary historical application. The visions associated with the first four seals in Revelation 6 are analogous. If the traditional motifs are also intended to have applications, the war between Herod Antipas and the Nabataean king, Aretas IV, in the mid-thirties could qualify,[10] or the Roman invasion of Armenia in 58–60 CE,[11] or the civil wars in Rome in 69.[12] In any case, the motifs of war, earthquakes, and famine in vv. 7-8 are very general apocalyptic commonplaces. It is usually easy for audiences to associate these motifs with historical events in their own immediate situation. Nevertheless, their purpose here seems to be primarily to define the appearance of the deceivers (v. 6) as one of the events of the last days.[13]

The next section, vv. 9–13, warns about persecutions involving councils (συνέδρια), synagogues, governors, and kings. Verse 12 again brings in typical eschatological motifs: "And brother will hand brother over to death,

and a father (his) child, and children will rise in rebellion against (their) parents and put them to death." The prophecy of persecution is often related to the police action instigated against Christians in Rome by Nero, and this interpretation is used to support the conclusion that Mark was written in Rome.[14] Given the considerable amount of traveling that Christians engaged in during the first century,[15] it is likely that members of the movement in the East had heard about this event and that it had a tremendous impact on them.[16] There were probably sporadic persecutions in the East as well. There were certainly persecutions of Jews by Gentiles in Antioch and Alexandria,[17] and it is likely that these also affected the communities that met in the name of Jesus. The two groups had a great deal in common, and the similarities were, no doubt, noticed by Gentiles, who belonged to neither group.

An outburst of violence against Jews in Alexandria occurred in 37 CE and another in Antioch around 40 CE.[18] In addition, Josephus says that, near the beginning of the Jewish–Roman war in 66, there were massacres and imprisonments of Jews in nearly all the cities of Syria.[19] He also comments that each city also had its Judaizers (ἰουδαΐζοντες), who aroused suspicion.[20] These "Judaizers" were probably partial proselytes like those the book of Acts calls "God-fearers," but it is likely that Christian Gentiles were affected also.[21]

Josephus narrates an incident that took place near the beginning of the war, in which a son denounced his own

---

10 Josephus *Ant.* 18.5.1 §109–15; Theissen, *Gospels in Context*, 137 (*Lokalkolorit*, 146).

11 See Margaret S. Drower, Eric W. Gray, and Susan M. Sherwin-White, "Armenia," *OCD* 170–71, and especially Drower and Barbara M. Levick, "Tiridates (4)," ibid., 1531; and Josef Wiesehöfer, "Tigranes (4) V," ibid., 1525.

12 Hengel, *Studies in Mark*, 22.

13 See the commentary on 13:7-8 below.

14 E.g., Hengel, *Studies in Mark*, 23. See the section of this Introduction, *Place of Writing*, above.

15 See Gamble, *Books and Readers*, 96, 142–43.

16 Adela Yarbro Collins, *Crisis and Catharsis: The Power of the Apocalypse* (Philadelphia: Westminster, 1984) 100–101.

17 On the persecution of Jews in Alexandria during the reign of Gaius Caligula, see John M. G. Barclay, *Jews in the Mediterranean Diaspora from Alexander to Trajan (323 BCE–117 CE)* (Edinburgh: T & T Clark, 1996)

51–55; on similar incidents in Antioch, see ibid., 251–57.

18 F. E. Peters, *The Harvest of Hellenism: A History of the Near East from Alexander the Great to the Triumph of Christianity* (New York: Simon & Schuster, 1970) 510–12.

19 Josephus *Bell.* 2.18.1–5 §457–80.

20 Ibid., 2.18.2 §463.

21 Cilliers Breytenbach, *Nachfolge und Zukunftserwartung nach Markus: Eine methodenkritische Studie* (AThAnt 71; Zurich: Theologischer Verlag Zürich, 1984) 311–30, esp. 327; Theissen, *Gospels in Context*, 268–69 (*Lokalkolorit*, 281–82). Incigneri's confidence that Christians and Jews could easily be distinguished in Antioch at this period (*Gospel to the Romans*, 84–86) is unwarranted. The name *Christianoi* in Acts 11:26 need not be understood as an exclusive alternative to *Ioudaioi* (Judeans or Jews).

father, who was the chief magistrate of the Jewish community in Antioch, and others, accusing them of a design to burn down the city.[22] Whether or not Mark had heard of this incident, it illustrates the kind of tragic event that could occur under the circumstances and shows that the typical motifs of eschatological lore reflect human experience and history.

Jesus' response to the question of the disciples comes in the next section, 13:14-20. Although the word "sign" ($\sigma\eta\mu\epsilon\hat{\iota}o\nu$) is not repeated, it is clear that v. 14 is so presented: "Now when you see 'the desolating sacrilege' standing where he should not—let the reader understand—then let those who are in Judea flee to the mountains. . . ." The desolating sacrilege is a sign in two senses: it is a signal for those in Judea to flee, as this verse itself shows, and it is an event that reveals, to those who have been instructed, that the final sequence of eschatological events is about to begin, as the continuation of the discourse shows.

The aside to the audience, "let the reader understand," has led some scholars to conclude that Mark has made use of a written source here, a kind of apocalyptic fly sheet or handbill,[23] that was produced around 40 CE during the crisis caused by the emperor Gaius Caligula's attempt to have his statue placed in the temple of Jerusalem.[24] But the aside can more simply be understood as a remark of the evangelist to his audience.[25] If these words are to be so understood, they indicate the author's emphasis on this event. The question then is whether the desolating sacrilege represents an event that is already past, of which Mark wishes to remind his audience, or whether it is still a prophecy from the author's point of view.

In the latter case, the reason for the special address to the reader is to encourage the one who read the Gospel aloud and the audience to recognize that the phrase "desolating sacrilege" ($\tau\grave{o}\ \beta\delta\acute{\epsilon}\lambda\nu\gamma\mu\alpha\ \tau\hat{\eta}\varsigma\ \acute{\epsilon}\rho\eta\mu\acute{\omega}\sigma\epsilon\omega\varsigma$) is an allusion to the book of Daniel. It is important for us twenty-first century readers to remember that Jews and Christians in Mark's time did not understand Daniel as an apocalyptic interpretation of the crisis created by the persecution of Antiochus Epiphanes. Rather, they understood Daniel as a prophecy of the eschatological kingdom of God, which was about to be inaugurated, perhaps during their own lifetimes. Thus, for Mark, the passages in Daniel about the "desolating sacrilege"[26] did not refer to the profanation of the altar in the second century BCE, but to an event of the future that would precede the establishment of the rule of God through the Son of Man who was about to come.

The wording of 13:14 provides a clue about how Mark conceived of this future event. The Greek noun translated "abomination" ($\beta\delta\acute{\epsilon}\lambda\nu\gamma\mu\alpha$) is neuter, but the participle modifying it and translated "standing" ($\acute{\epsilon}\sigma\tau\eta\kappa\acute{\omega}\varsigma$) is masculine. The masculine participle and the notion of something being set up or standing suggest that Mark's interpretation of the prophecy of Daniel has been influenced by the crisis under Caligula. He need not have had a written source from that time for such to be the case. Stories about the crisis had no doubt been handed down and thus entered into the living memory of people at the time.

There are three accounts of that crisis, two by Josephus and one by Philo. In all three accounts, the word for the object that the emperor wished to place in the temple is masculine: $\dot{\alpha}\nu\delta\rho\iota\acute{\alpha}\varsigma$, meaning "image of a man" or "statue."[27] According to Philo, Gaius said that he "ordered a statue of Zeus to be set up in the temple" ($\dot{\epsilon}\mu o\hat{\upsilon}\ \kappa\epsilon\lambda\epsilon\acute{\upsilon}\sigma\alpha\nu\tau o\varsigma\ \dot{\epsilon}\nu\ \tau\hat{\omega}\ \iota\epsilon\rho\hat{\omega}\ \Delta\iota\grave{o}\varsigma\ \dot{\alpha}\nu\delta\rho\iota\acute{\alpha}\nu\tau\alpha$

---

22 Josephus *Bell.* 7.3.3 §§46–53; Theissen, *Gospels in Context,* 269–70 (*Lokalkolorit,* 282–83).

23 E.g., Emanuel Hirsch, according to Egon Brandenburger, *Markus 13 und die Apokalyptik* (Göttingen: Vandenhoeck & Ruprecht, 1984) 25 n. 37. The notion of a flier or handbill fits a situation after the printing press has come into common use better than the ancient world.

24 E.g., Theissen, *Gospels in Context,* 125–65 (*Lokalkolorit,* 133–76).

25 See the commentary on 13:14–20 below. The "reader" is not an individual reading a private copy in solitude, but the one whom the evangelist

expected to read the Gospel aloud to a group assembled for that purpose.

26 Dan 9:27; 11:31; 12:11; cf. 8:13 and 1 Macc 4:36–59.

27 Josephus *Bell.* 2.10.1–5 §§184–203; the term $\dot{\alpha}\nu\delta\rho\iota\acute{\alpha}\varsigma$ is used in 2.10.1 §185; *Ant.* 18.8.1–9 §§257–309; the term $\dot{\alpha}\nu\delta\rho\iota\acute{\alpha}\varsigma$ is used most relevantly in 18.8.2 §261; Philo *Leg. Gaj.* 30–42 §§197–337; according to Philo, Gaius ordered that "a colossal statue ($\kappa o\lambda o\sigma\sigma\iota\alpha\hat{\iota}o\varsigma\ \dot{\alpha}\nu\delta\rho\iota\acute{\alpha}\varsigma$) coated with gold, should be set up in the mother city" (30 §203); text and trans. from F. H. Colson, *Philo* (10 vols.; LCL; Cambridge, MA: Harvard University Press; London: Heinemann, 1962) 10:104–5. See also 39 §306.

ἀνατεθῆναι).[28] In the context, however, it is stated that Gaius wished to be thought of as a god and wanted to punish the Jews for withholding divine honors by defiling their temple.[29] This juxtaposition suggests that the statue was of Zeus, but with the head of Gaius (or that Gaius was identified with Zeus in some other way).

Gaius's attempt failed. The success of such a project, however, would qualify as a fulfillment of Daniel's prediction of the "desolating sacrilege." In the context of the Jewish war, eschatologically interpreted, Mark may have expected the Romans to try again to set up a statue of the emperor as Zeus and to succeed this time.

If this interpretation is correct, it is highly unlikely that the Gospel was written after 70. When the outer buildings were already burning, Titus entered the temple and saw "the holy place of the sanctuary" (παρελθὼν . . . ἔνδον ἐθεάσατο τοῦ ναοῦ τὸ ἅγιον),[30] an act similar to what Pompey had done in 63 BCE.[31] But no sacrifices to other gods were offered on the altar of burnt offering, and no statue of a god or of the emperor was set up. Some have suggested that the "desolating sacrilege" was interpreted as the destruction itself, or that people expected the Romans to use the surviving platform of the temple to build a temple dedicated to Zeus (Jupiter) and that then the prophecy of Daniel would be fulfilled. These suggestions make a good deal of sense with regard to how this discourse would have been interpreted by audiences after 70. But they are not convincing as explanations of the author's purpose in composing it. The passage makes more sense as a genuine prophecy that was not fulfilled precisely and therefore had to be reinterpreted.

The continuation of the discourse supports this interpretation. The next section takes up the warning enunciated at the beginning of the speech, "And at that time if anyone says to you, 'Look, here is the Messiah,' 'Look there,' do not believe (him or her); for false messiahs and false prophets will rise up and will produce signs and wonders in order to deceive, if possible, the elect. As for you, watch out then; I have told you everything beforehand." This warning is best understood as directed against the messianic pretenders and the prophets who were active during the first Jewish war with Rome. Josephus gives detailed accounts of the messianic pretenders Menahem and Simon son of Gioras, and of the many prophets who were active at the time and the omens that were perceived during the war.[32]

The transition to the next section shows that Mark expected the coming of the risen Jesus as Son of Man to occur at the climax of the war, "But in those days after that tribulation, the sun will be darkened and the moon will not give its light and the stars will be falling from heaven, and the powers that are in the heavens will be shaken. And then the Son of Man will be seen coming in clouds with great power and glory" (13:24–26). The prophecy of Daniel about the desolating sacrilege was to be fulfilled first and then his prophecy of the "coming of one like a son of Man" (Dan 7:13). Some scholars argue that Mark saw himself and his community as living in the period between the Jewish war and the coming of the Son of Man, or living after the destruction of the temple but still awaiting the fulfillment of the two prophecies of Daniel.[33] Again, it was possible to interpret "in those days after that tribulation" (ἐν ἐκείναις ταῖς ἡμέραις μετὰ τὴν θλῖψιν ἐκείνην) in v. 24 in such a way, after it had become necessary to do so,[34] but it is less likely that the passage was originally composed for such a situation.

Thus, the Gospel according to Mark was probably composed after Menahem began to exercise a messianic role in 66 CE, or more likely after 68 or 69 when Simon, son of Gioras, emerged as the major messianic leader of the revolt.[35] These are the best candidates for the interpretation of the remark of the Markan Jesus, "many will come in my name," in 13:6. Since the "desolating sacrilege" and the destruction of the temple still seem to belong to the future from the point of view of the evangelist, the Gospel was probably written before 70 CE.

---

28 Philo *Leg. Gaj.* 35 §265; text and trans. from Colson, *Philo*, 10:134–35. From a Roman point of view, the deity in question would be Jupiter.

29 Ibid., 30 §198; similarly 31 §218.

30 Josephus *Bell.* 6.4.7 §260; text and trans. from Thackeray, *Josephus*, 3:450–51.

31 Ibid., 1.7.6 §§152–53.

32 See the commentary on 13:5-6 and 21-23 below.

33 E.g., Theissen, *Gospels in Context*, 134, 194

(*Lokalkolorit*, 143, 206); Marcus, 38–39.

34 The author of Matthew, surely writing after the destruction of the temple in 70 (22:7), adopted such an interpretation, as is evident from 24:29, the parallel to Mark 13:24, "Immediately then, after the tribulation of those days, the sun will be darkened etc." (εὐθέως δὲ μετὰ τὴν θλῖψιν τῶν ἡμερῶν ἐκείνων ὁ ἥλιος σκοτισθήσεται κτλ.).

35 See the commentary on 13:5-6 below.

The question what kind of literary work the Gospel of Mark is seems to be settled from the point of view of Christian tradition, since the work has long been called a "Gospel" and that label seems to answer the question of its literary character.[1] The issue begins to become complicated, however, when viewed historically. One complicating factor is that there were other early Christian works given the label "Gospel" that do not seem to belong to the same literary category at all. For example, the *Gospel of Thomas* is a collection of sayings of Jesus and short dialogues between him and his disciples. This work contains no miracle stories and no passion narrative. In fact, it has no narrative framework at all. It is best understood as an instruction or some other type of wisdom book.[2] Another example is the *Gospel of Truth*, which is a Christian mystical sermon on the theme of salvation.[3]

This variety in the use of the word "Gospel" in relation to early Christian works is less surprising when we consider the usage of the term in the oldest texts of Christian literature, namely, the letters of the apostle Paul. He used the word to mean the announcement of God's plan of salvation, proclaimed by the prophets and realized through the death and resurrection of Christ.[4] This announcement was originally oral, and its social setting was the missionary work carried out by Christians in the eastern Mediterranean world in the first century.

Given this original meaning and use of the term, it is not surprising that later writers communicated the Christian message in a variety of literary types.

In Paul's oldest letter, the First Letter to the Thessalonians, he uses the noun "gospel" ($\epsilon\dot{\upsilon}\alpha\gamma\gamma\dot{\epsilon}\lambda\iota\upsilon$) six times. In three of those cases (2:2, 8, 9), he speaks of "the gospel of God" ($\tau\dot{o}$ $\epsilon\dot{\upsilon}\alpha\gamma\gamma\dot{\epsilon}\lambda\iota\upsilon$ $\tau\upsilon\hat{\upsilon}$ $\vartheta\epsilon\upsilon\hat{\upsilon}$).[5] This qualification of the gospel means that God is the author of the gospel; not that God proclaims the good news directly, but that God established the plan for salvation, revealed it in Scripture, and made it known, for example, in revealing God's son to Paul.[6] In one case in 1 Thessalonians (3:2), Paul speaks of "the gospel of Christ" ($\tau\hat{\omega}$ $\epsilon\dot{\upsilon}\alpha\gamma\gamma\epsilon\lambda\dot{\iota}\omega$ $\tau\upsilon\hat{\upsilon}$ $X\rho\iota\sigma\tau\upsilon\hat{\upsilon}$). Here, and in the numerous other passages in which Paul uses this phrase, he means the good news *about* Jesus Christ, not the good news that Jesus himself proclaimed.[7]

The Gospel of Mark opens with the words "(The) beginning of the good news of Jesus Christ" ($\dot{\alpha}\rho\chi\dot{\eta}$ $\tau\upsilon\hat{\upsilon}$ $\epsilon\dot{\upsilon}\alpha\gamma\gamma\epsilon\lambda\dot{\iota}\upsilon\upsilon$ $I\eta\sigma\upsilon\hat{\upsilon}$ $X\rho\iota\sigma\tau\upsilon\hat{\upsilon}$). The following words, "Son of God" ($\upsilon\dot{\iota}\upsilon\hat{\upsilon}$ $\vartheta\epsilon\upsilon\hat{\upsilon}$), were probably added later, either by a pious scribe or by a leader in the early church who wanted to oppose the doctrine that Jesus only became the Son of God when the Spirit descended upon him at his baptism.[8] Scholars have debated whether the phrase "the gospel (or good news) of Jesus Christ" ($\tau\upsilon\hat{\upsilon}$ $\epsilon\dot{\upsilon}\alpha\gamma\gamma\epsilon\lambda\dot{\iota}\upsilon\upsilon$ $I\eta\sigma\upsilon\hat{\upsilon}$ $X\rho\iota\sigma\tau\upsilon\hat{\upsilon}$) in 1:1 means the gospel

1   See, e.g., Irenaeus *haer.* 3.11.7; Clement of Alexandria *Quis div. salv.* 5.1.

2   James M. Robinson, "LOGOI SOPHON: On the Gattung of Q," in idem and Helmut Koester, *Trajectories through Early Christianity* (Philadelphia: Fortress, 1971) 75–80; John S. Kloppenborg, *The Formation of Q: Trajectories in Ancient Wisdom Collections* (Studies in Antiquity and Christianity; Philadelphia: Fortress, 1987) 27–34, 327–28. The *Gospel of Thomas* survives in fragments in Greek and in its entirety only in a single Coptic MS. The title of the work appears at the end as "The Gospel according to Thomas"; see Bentley Layton, *The Gnostic Scriptures* (Garden City, NY: Doubleday, 1987) 377–80. For the critical edition, see Bentley Layton, ed., *Nag Hammadi Codex II, 2–7: Together with XIII, 2*, Brit. Lib. Or. 4926(1), and P.Oxy 1, 654, 655* (NHS 20; Leiden/New York: Brill, 1989).

3   So Layton, *Gnostic Scriptures*, 250–51; Harold W. Attridge refers to it as a homily or meditation ("The Gospel of Truth as an Exoteric Text," in Charles W. Hedrick and Robert Hodgson, Jr., eds., *Nag Ham-*

madi, Gnosticism, and Early Christianity [Peabody, MA: Hendrickson, 1986] 241). For a critical edition, see Harold W. Attridge, ed., *Nag Hammadi Codex I (The Jung Codex)* (NHS 22, 23; Leiden: Brill, 1985). The MSS do not specify the title of the work, but Irenaeus probably referred to this work as a "Gospel of Truth," apparently using the opening words as a title; see Layton, *Gnostic Scriptures*, 251. On the variety of the genres of works labeled "Gospels" in antiquity, see Wilhelm Schneemelcher, "A. Gospels: Non-Biblical Material about Jesus," *NTApoc*, 1:77–87.

4   So Adolf von Harnack, quoted by Peter Stuhlmacher, "The Pauline Gospel," in idem, ed., *Gospel and the Gospels*, 150.

5   This phrase occurs also in Rom 1:1; 15:16; 2 Cor 11:7.

6   Compare Gal 1:12 with 1:15-16.

7   The same phrase is used also in Rom 15:19; 1 Cor 9:12; 2 Cor 2:12; 9:13; 10:14; Gal 1:7; Phil 1:27. Analogous phrases are used in Rom 1:9; 2 Cor 4:4.

8   See the note on the trans. of 1:1 below.

about Jesus Christ, which, as we have seen, is what this phrase meant when Paul used it, or the gospel proclaimed *by* Jesus Christ. Some light is shed on the question by a passage a little further down: "after John was handed over, Jesus went into Galilee, proclaiming the good news of God and saying, 'The time is fulfilled and the kingdom of God has drawn near; repent and trust in the good news'" (1:14–15). Here we find another phrase that is common in the letters of Paul: "the gospel of God" ($\tau\grave{o}$ $\epsilon\dot{v}\alpha\gamma\gamma\acute{\epsilon}\lambda\iota o\nu$ $\tau o\hat{v}$ $\vartheta\epsilon o\hat{v}$). The statement attributed to Jesus summarizes the meaning of this phrase. The references to the time being fulfilled and the kingdom drawing near suggest a meaning similar to that expressed by Paul: the good news is that the divine plan, which had been foretold, is about to be put into effect.

So, like Paul, Mark attributes the gospel ultimately to God. But unlike Paul, he portrays Jesus as proclaiming the good news. If, as some scholars argue, the Greek technical term $\epsilon\dot{v}\alpha\gamma\gamma\acute{\epsilon}\lambda\iota o\nu$ ("good news" or "gospel") in the singular, and the concept for which it stood, was a new formulation by Greek-speaking Christian missionaries as a shorthand expression for the message that they traveled the world to announce to all who would hear,[9] then Mark is portraying Jesus as the founder of that missionary movement.

We see then that the opening words of the work as a whole are ambiguous. Anyone in the audience familiar with the usage of Paul, either from his letters or from contact with Christian missionaries, would understand the phrase to mean "the good news *about* Jesus Christ." But in light of the following portrait of Jesus as proclaimer, the phrase also takes on the meaning "the good news announced *by* Jesus Christ."

A further question is whether the word $\epsilon\dot{v}\alpha\gamma\gamma\acute{\epsilon}\lambda\iota o\nu$ ("good news" or "gospel") in Mark 1:1 was intended by the author to be understood as a literary self-definition of the work or as a reference to its content. Apparently the authors of Matthew and Luke did not take the word as a literary designation, or if they did, they chose not to adopt it. Matthew refers to itself (or to some part of the work) as a $\beta\acute{\iota}\beta\lambda o\varsigma$ ("account" or "book") in 1:1. Luke designates itself quite generally as a $\delta\iota\acute{\eta}\gamma\eta\sigma\iota\varsigma$ ("narration" or "narrative") in 1:1.

The earliest author who provides explicit evidence for early Christian reflection on the literary nature of the works that eventually became the canonical Gospels, Justin Martyr, favored the term $\dot{\alpha}\pi o\mu\nu\eta\mu o\nu\epsilon\acute{v}\mu\alpha\tau\alpha$ ("reminiscences" or "notes"). He did not, however, use the term as a precise literary definition, but rather to characterize the Gospels as historical sources in the ancient sense.[10] Origen referred to the Gospels, or to their content, as $\iota\sigma\tau o\rho\acute{\iota}\alpha\iota$ ("histories" or "investigations"), although he argued at the same time that some of the events that they record did not actually occur.[11]

---

9   See the discussion by Hubert Frankemölle in Detlev Dormeyer and Frankemölle, "Evangelium als literarische Gattung und als theologischer Begriff: Tendenzen und Aufgaben der Evangelienforschung im 20. Jahrhundert, mit einer Untersuchung des Markusevangeliums in seinem Verhältnis zur antiken Biographie," in *ANRW* 2.25.2 (1984) 1543–1704, esp. 1676, 1687–94. See also Hubert Frankemölle, *Evangelium–Begriff und Gattung: Ein Forschungsbericht* (2nd ed.; Stuttgart: Katholisches Bibelwerk, 1994) 251–62.

10 See the review of scholarship and critical discussion by Detlev Dormeyer, *Evangelium als literarische und theologische Gattung* (EdF 263; Darmstadt: Wissenschaftliche Buchgesellschaft, 1989), 11–16. Mark I. Wegener argued that a distinction should be made between "memorabilia" ($\dot{\alpha}\pi o\mu\nu\eta\mu o\nu\epsilon\acute{v}\mu\alpha\tau\alpha$), which recount anecdotes, "and a true 'life' (*bios*, $\beta\acute{\iota}o\varsigma$) or 'biography' which tells a person's story from birth to death" (*Cruciformed: The Literary Impact of Mark's Story of Jesus and His Disciples* [Lanham, MD: University Press of America, 1995] 29–30).

11 "The exacting reader can observe innumerable examples in the Gospels similar to these, in order to agree that other things, which did not occur, are woven together with the histories which happened literally" ($\pi\alpha\rho\alpha\pi\lambda\eta\sigma\acute{\iota}\omega\varsigma$ $\delta\grave{\epsilon}$ $\tau o\acute{v}\tau o\iota\varsigma$ $\kappa\alpha\grave{\iota}$ $\ddot{\alpha}\lambda\lambda\alpha$ $\mu\nu\rho\acute{\iota}\alpha$ $\dot{\alpha}\pi\grave{o}$ $\tau\hat{\omega}\nu$ $\epsilon\dot{v}\alpha\gamma\gamma\epsilon\lambda\acute{\iota}\omega\nu$ $\ddot{\epsilon}\nu\epsilon\sigma\tau\iota$ $\tau\grave{o}\nu$ $\dot{\alpha}\kappa\rho\iota$-$\beta o\hat{v}\nu\tau\alpha$ $\tau\eta\rho\hat{\eta}\sigma\alpha\iota$ $\dot{v}\pi\grave{\epsilon}\rho$ $\tau o\hat{v}$ $\sigma\nu\gamma\kappa\alpha\tau\alpha\vartheta\acute{\epsilon}\sigma\vartheta\alpha\iota$ $\sigma\nu\nu$-$\nu\phi\alpha\acute{\iota}\nu\epsilon\sigma\vartheta\alpha\iota$ $\tau\alpha\hat{\iota}\varsigma$ $\kappa\alpha\tau\grave{\alpha}$ $\tau\grave{o}$ $\dot{\rho}\eta\tau\grave{o}\nu$ $\gamma\epsilon\gamma\epsilon\nu\eta\mu\acute{\epsilon}\nu\alpha\iota\varsigma$ $\iota\sigma\tau o\rho\acute{\iota}\alpha\iota\varsigma$ $\ddot{\epsilon}\tau\epsilon\rho\alpha$ $\mu\grave{\eta}$ $\sigma\nu\mu\beta\epsilon\beta\eta\kappa\acute{o}\tau\alpha$ [Origen *Princ.* 4.3.1 = 4.1.16]). The Greek text is cited from Herwig Görgemanns and Heinrich Karpp, eds., *Origenes Vier Bücher von den Prinzipien* (TzF 24; Darmstadt: Wissenschaftliche Buchgesellschaft, 1985) 734; trans. by author. Cf. Dormeyer, *Evangelium*, 22. The examples to which Origen refers are reported events that could not have happened, including the statement that God walked about in Paradise, that one became a partaker of good and evil by eating fruit, and that the devil led Jesus up on a high mountain in order to show him all the kingdoms of the earth.

Like Justin, Origen does not seem to be interested in defining the literary nature of the Gospels precisely, but in claiming historical reliability for the more important events that they narrate. This conclusion is supported by the fact that he also refers to "the history" ($\tau\grave{\eta}\nu$ $\iota\sigma\tauo$-$\rho\acute{\iota}\alpha\nu$) recorded by the apostles as well as by the evangelists. With the term "apostles" he seems to refer to the letters of the New Testament, which also recount the main events of salvation.[12]

Justin was also the first author, as far as we know, to use the term $\epsilon\grave{\upsilon}\alpha\gamma\gamma\acute{\epsilon}\lambda\iotao\nu$ ("good news" or "gospel") in the plural to refer to what later became the four canonical Gospels. In the passage cited above, Origen also refers to them as "Gospels" as well as "histories." It is likely that this usage, like that of $\grave{\alpha}\pi o\mu\nu\eta\mu o\nu\epsilon\acute{\upsilon}\mu\alpha\tau\alpha$ ("memoirs" or "notes") and $\iota\sigma\tauo\rho\acute{\iota}\alpha$ ("history"), refers more to content than to literary form.

In the usage of Paul, an important aspect of the gospel was that it was foretold in Scripture. This element appears in Mark immediately after the opening words: "As it is written in the book of Isaiah the prophet" ($\kappa\alpha\vartheta\grave{\omega}\varsigma$ $\gamma\acute{\epsilon}\gamma\rho\alpha\pi\tau\alpha\iota$ $\grave{\epsilon}\nu$ $\tau\hat{\omega}$ $H\sigma\alpha\acute{\iota}\alpha$ $\tau\hat{\omega}$ $\pi\rho o\varphi\acute{\eta}\tau\eta$). The verses cited, a conflation of Isaiah, Exodus, and Malachi, are interpreted by juxtaposition with the following narrative as a prophecy of the appearance of John the Baptist, and his activity is defined as preparation for the mission of Jesus. Both John and Jesus are presented as agents of God, sent to fulfill the divine plan for human salvation.

Mark departs from Paul, however, in expanding the referent of the term "gospel" to include more than the death and resurrection of Jesus. To the extent that Mark is a passion narrative with an extended introduction, his use of the term "gospel" may be seen to be similar to Paul's. But once we recognize the profound difference between the primarily discursive language of Paul's letters and the narrative character of Mark, we begin to appreciate the magnitude of Mark's innovation. Mark has taken a term coined as a summary of oral preaching and used it to describe (the content of) an extended narrative. How to characterize that narrative is the question to which we now turn.

Before we assess the answers that have been given to that question, we should reflect briefly on what is at stake. When we read Mark, we rely, even if unconsciously, on some understanding of what kind of text it is and thus what its purpose is. The basic options with regard to the kind of text Mark is include "gospel," "history,"[13] and "life" or "biography."[14] The decision about the genre of Mark is not merely a matter of finding the right pigeonhole for the work or of academic debate in an ivory tower. Assumptions about the literary form of Mark affect the way this work is allowed to function in the lives of readers, in the life of the church, and in society.

The judgment that Mark is a "gospel" has taken several different forms. One is the classic form-critical position, most fully articulated by Karl Ludwig Schmidt, that the notion of genre in any precise sense is inappropriate, because the canonical Gospels do not really belong to the category of literature. At the same time, he did not claim that the Gospels are unique works, but compared

---

12 "The Spirit arranged things in this way not only with regard to the writings before the coming (of Christ); on the contrary, since he is the same (in both periods) and comes from the one God, he did the same thing in the case of the Gospels and the apostles. Not even these contain the history entirely free from elements interwoven with it but which never occurred in the bodily sense, and thus the legislation and the commands which they contain do not always immediately manifest a rational sense" ($o\grave{\upsilon}$ $\mu\acute{o}\nu o\nu$ $\delta\grave{\epsilon}$ $\pi\epsilon\rho\grave{\iota}$ $\tau\hat{\omega}\nu$ $\pi\rho\grave{o}$ $\tau\hat{\eta}\varsigma$ $\pi\alpha\rho o\upsilon\sigma\acute{\iota}\alpha\varsigma$ $\tau\alpha\hat{\upsilon}\tau\alpha$ $\tau\grave{o}$ $\pi\nu\epsilon\hat{\upsilon}\mu\alpha$ $\grave{\omega}\kappa o\nu\acute{o}\mu\eta\sigma\epsilon\nu$, $\grave{\alpha}\lambda\lambda\grave{\alpha}$ $\gamma\grave{\alpha}\rho$ $\breve{\alpha}\tau\epsilon$ $\tau\grave{o}$ $\alpha\grave{\upsilon}\tau\grave{o}$ $\tau\upsilon\gamma$-$\chi\acute{\alpha}\nu o\nu$ $\kappa\alpha\grave{\iota}$ $\grave{\alpha}\pi\grave{o}$ $\tau o\hat{\upsilon}$ $\grave{\epsilon}\nu\grave{o}\varsigma$ $\vartheta\epsilon o\hat{\upsilon}$, $\tau\grave{o}$ $\acute{o}\mu o\iota o\nu$ $\kappa\alpha\grave{\iota}$ $\grave{\epsilon}\pi\grave{\iota}$ $\tau\hat{\omega}\nu$ $\epsilon\grave{\upsilon}\alpha\gamma\gamma\epsilon\lambda\acute{\iota}\omega\nu$ $\pi\epsilon\pi o\acute{\iota}\eta\kappa\epsilon$ $\kappa\alpha\grave{\iota}$ $\grave{\epsilon}\pi\grave{\iota}$ $\tau\hat{\omega}\nu$ $\grave{\alpha}\pi o$-$\sigma\tau\acute{o}\lambda\omega\nu$, $o\grave{\upsilon}\delta\grave{\epsilon}$ $\tau o\acute{\upsilon}\tau o\iota\varsigma$ $\pi\acute{\alpha}\nu\tau\eta$ $\breve{\alpha}\kappa\rho\alpha\tau o\nu$ $\tau\grave{\eta}\nu$ $\iota\sigma\tauo\rho\acute{\iota}\alpha\nu$ $\tau\hat{\omega}\nu$ $\pi\rho o\sigma\upsilon\varphi\alpha\sigma\mu\acute{\epsilon}\nu\omega\nu$ $\kappa\alpha\tau\grave{\alpha}$ $\tau\grave{o}$ $\sigma\omega\mu\alpha\tau\iota\kappa\grave{o}\nu$ $\grave{\epsilon}\chi\acute{o}\nu\tau\omega\nu$ $\mu\grave{\eta}$ $\gamma\epsilon\gamma\epsilon\nu\eta\mu\acute{\epsilon}\nu\omega\nu$, $o\grave{\upsilon}\delta\grave{\epsilon}$ $\tau\grave{\eta}\nu$ $\nu o\mu o\vartheta\epsilon\sigma\acute{\iota}\alpha\nu$ $\kappa\alpha\grave{\iota}$ $\tau\grave{\alpha}\varsigma$ $\grave{\epsilon}\nu\tauo\lambda\grave{\alpha}\varsigma$ $\pi\acute{\alpha}\nu\tau\omega\varsigma$ $\tau\grave{o}$ $\epsilon\breve{\upsilon}\lambda o\gamma o\nu$ $\grave{\epsilon}\nu\tau\epsilon\hat{\upsilon}\vartheta\epsilon\nu$ $\grave{\epsilon}\mu\varphi\alpha\acute{\iota}\nu o\nu\tau\alpha$ [Origen *Princ.* 4.2.9 = 4.1.16; Görgemanns and Karpp, *Origenes*, 728, 730; trans. by author]).

13 Samuel Byrskog argues that eyewitness testimony played a role in the composition of Mark, along with the interpretative and narrativizing procedures of the author; thus, in his view, Mark is "story as history" and also "history as story" (*Story as History–History as Story: The Gospel Tradition in the Context of Ancient Oral History* [WUNT 123; Tübingen: Mohr Siebeck, 2000] 297–99; quotation from 299).

14 The term $\beta\iota o\gamma\rho\alpha\varphi\acute{\iota}\alpha$ ("biography") appears first in fragments of a text composed in the fifth century CE, Damascius's *Life of Isidorus*, and preserved by the

them to folk literature from various cultures and times.[15] This point of view implies that Mark is a practical work that grew out of the activities of a community, especially those related to proclamation, worship, and edification, and which has no interest in literary quality because of its pragmatic character.[16]

A related position is that a "gospel" is a unique Christian literary form. This judgment sets it aside as a "holy" text, as an instance of Scripture, a book unlike other books.[17] Its alleged uniqueness is associated with its character as theological proclamation.[18] Some who hold this view emphasize form and content, describing Mark as a unique, new type of narrative. Others focus on function, inferring a missionary, instructional, or polemical purpose.

Other scholars have attempted to identify Mark as an instance or adaptation of an existing genre, such as biography. The conclusion that Mark is a life of Jesus or a biography implies that it is a record of an individual who serves as a model for others. In ancient times and modern, people have read biography, in part at least, to find out what another person was like and to compare oneself with him or her, often to imitate or avoid the person's example. Virtue and vice are primary categories of biography. So this understanding of Mark implies that it presents Jesus as a model to be imitated. Such a model may function in the shaping of individuals, communities, or both. The focus on Jesus, seen as the subject of a biography, is appealing to those with an interest in Christology.[19]

The significance of the conclusion that Mark belongs to the category of history or historiography depends on the type of history it is judged to be. Historical works in antiquity often focused on one ethnic group, its origins, contributions, and destiny. The Gospel of Mark owes much to Israelite and Jewish historiography, which belongs to this type. Mark's interest lies in the significance of the culmination of this particular ethnic history for all of humankind, especially those shaped by Hellenistic culture. The universal perspective of Mark is expressed in the saying, "And the gospel must first be preached to all the nations" (13:10). Underlying this statement is the conviction that the world must be converted and reformed before its imminent end. From this point of view the cosmic perspective of Mark becomes visible. On the one hand, the author's reach exceeds his grasp. The Gospel of Mark is rooted in specific Jewish, Christian, and Hellenistic traditions. On the other, if the attempt to achieve a universal perspective is taken seriously, we allow the significance of the text to extend beyond personal and exclusivist communal piety to the situation of the entire human race in the world. Even for those who do not share Mark's expectation of an imminent end, its perspective challenges modern readers to reflect on the situation and destiny of humanity as a whole.

In what follows, I will discuss the genre of Mark from several points of view: Mark as a "gospel," that is, a new and unique genre; Mark as "biography;" and Mark as "history." Finally, I will argue that Mark is best understood as an eschatological historical monograph. In each case, I will give a brief review of scholarship and analyze the issues involved.

---

ninth-century Byzantine scholar Photius. See Arnaldo Momigliano, *The Development of Greek Biography* (Cambridge, MA: Harvard University Press, 1971) 12; Richard A. Burridge, *What Are the Gospels? A Comparison with Graeco-Roman Biography* (SNTSMS 70; Cambridge: Cambridge University Press, 1992; 2nd rev. ed., Grand Rapids/Cambridge: Eerdmans; Dearborn, MI: Dove Booksellers, 2004) 61–62 (2nd ed., 59).

15   Karl Ludwig Schmidt referred to Mark as a "Volksbuch" ("folk-book") and considered the historical books of the OT to have the same character; Karl Ludwig Schmidt, *The Place of the Gospels in the General History of Literature* (Columbia: University of South Carolina Press, 2002) 17–18, ET of "Die Stellung der Evangelien in der allgemeinen Literaturgeschichte," in Hans Schmidt, ed., *ΕΥΧΑΡΙΣΤΗΡΙΟΝ: Studien zur Religion und Literatur des Alten und Neuen Testaments Hermann Gunkel zum 60. Geburtstag . . . dargebracht* (FRLANT 36 = n.F., 19; 2 vols.; Göttingen: Vandenhoeck & Ruprecht, 1923) 2:50–134, esp. 66–68.

16   For discussion of the views of form critics on the literary nature of the Gospels, see Dormeyer, *Evangelium*, 2–3, 76–107; see also Schmidt, *Place of the Gospels*, 65–74 ("Stellung," 114–21).

17   By means of his doctrine of verbal inspiration, Origen was the first Christian thinker to distinguish Scripture, as a divine document, from profane literature; see Dormeyer, *Evangelium*, 23–24.

18   This view is typical of redaction critics; see Dormeyer, *Evangelium*, 2–3, 108–30.

19   E.g., Burridge, *What Are the Gospels?* 256–59 (2nd ed., 248–51).

Mark as a New Genre, a "Gospel"

The position that the term "gospel" adequately defines the literary form of Mark and reflects the fact that a new genre emerged in early Christian literature has its roots in the thought and writings of Johann Gottfried Herder. A forerunner of the Romantic movement who published his work near the end of the eighteenth century, he argued that the Gospels belong to the category of folk literature and thus were not composed in accordance with the ideals of Greek and Roman biography. He did acknowledge their debt to the Old Testament type of historiography. Yet he did not recognize the sophistication of the biblical histories, but assigned them to the childhood of the human race.[20] Franz Overbeck, writing in 1882, took a position similar to Herder's without explicit reference to him. He argued that the New Testament is what remains of a more extensive early Christian primitive literature that had nothing to do with the types or genres of ancient profane literature, that is, with literature in the true sense of the word. Rather, the various genres of the New Testament were modeled on traditional types of religious literature. He concluded that the Gospel genre is the only original Christian literary type. Overbeck's ideas concerning the originality of the Gospels and their anonymous production by the Christian community were taken up by the form critics and thus had a tremendous impact on New Testament scholarship in the twentieth century.[21]

The form critics and their heirs defined the new Christian genre "gospel" as an account of the "good news" that centers on the life, death, and resurrection of Jesus Christ. In their view, this account, like a sermon, had as its primary function the evocation of repentance and faith. The use of the term $\epsilon\dot{\upsilon}\alpha\gamma\gamma\dot{\epsilon}\lambda\iota\upsilon\nu$ ("good news" or "gospel") in the opening statement of Mark is not seen as a self-definition of literary form, but those who hold this position argue that it represents an important stage in the development of the new genre.[22]

The process envisaged by those who hold this position is analogous to the relationship of the book of Revelation to the genre "apocalypse." Prior to the writing of the book of Revelation, the term $\dot{\alpha}\pi\sigma\kappa\dot{\alpha}\lambda\upsilon\psi\iota\varsigma$ ("apocalypse" or "revelation") was used to mean the process or content of revelation or simply a "secret." It was not used to designate a kind of literary work. The word $\dot{\alpha}\pi\sigma\kappa\dot{\alpha}\lambda\upsilon\psi\iota\varsigma$ is used in the opening statement of the book of Revelation to characterize the content of the work as a whole and to indicate the means by which it had been made known. Later, in dependence on the book of Revelation, the term came to be used for a type of literature.[23]

The notion that the genre of Mark is best described as "gospel," a newly created early Christian genre, is closely tied to the form-critical view of the origin of Mark. One of the pioneers of the form-critical method in New Testament studies was Martin Dibelius. In 1919 he distinguished between *Kleinliteratur* and *Hochliteratur*. By *Kleinliteratur* he meant informal, popular works that emerged as the end-product of a process of handing on tradition and story-telling. *Hochliteratur*, on the other hand, included formal works which were "literary" in the proper sense, that is, produced by a self-conscious author applying a well defined method. He argued that the Gospels were the end-products of a process of oral tradition, produced by many anonymous individuals and not stamped by the intentions or personality of an individual author.[24] Rudolf Bultmann argued that the Gospels are expanded cult legends and that the literary type "gospel" developed out of the kerygma, that is, the preaching of the early Christian missionaries. He even concluded that the whole notion of "kind" of literary text is inappropriate for the Gospels: "the Gospel belongs to the history of dogma and worship."[25]

---

20 See the quotation cited by Dormeyer and his critical discussion, *Evangelium*, 32.

21 For discussion and bibliography, see Dormeyer, *Evangelium*, 26–27, 31–33, and 48–51.

22 See the discussion of Vielhauer below.

23 Morton Smith, "On the History of *ΑΠΟΚΑΛΥΠΤΩ* and *ΑΠΟΚΑΛΥΨΙΣ*," in David Hellholm, ed., *Apocalypticism in the Mediterranean World and the Near East* (Tübingen: Mohr Siebeck, 1983) 9–20.

24 Martin Dibelius, *Die Formgeschichte des Evangeliums* (Tübingen: Mohr Siebeck, 1919; 2nd ed., 1933); ET *From Tradition to Gospel* (New York: Scribner's Sons, 1935) 1–4. Dibelius's distinction has roots in Franz Overbeck's notion of *Urliteratur* (preliterary writings) and Paul Wendland's notion of folk literature; for discussion, see Dormeyer, *Evangelium*, 49–51, 68; Burridge, *What Are the Gospels?* 7–9 (2nd ed., 7–9).

25 Rudolf Bultmann, *The History of the Synoptic Tradi-*

The form-critical view was articulated more recently by Philipp Vielhauer.[26] The root metaphors of this view are organic growth and evolutionary development. The starting point is the fact that the term εὐαγγέλιον ("good news" or "gospel") is used in two different ways in early Christianity. The first is as a designation of the early Christian message. This usage is typical of the writings that were eventually collected and known as the New Testament. Although the term εὐαγγέλιον appears with this meaning in such writings, its origin was in the oral proclamation of early Christian missionaries. An example of this usage is Rom 1:1–7. "Gospel" in this sense is never used in the plural. The term is also used for a book that reports about Jesus' life, death, and resurrection. This usage does not appear in the New Testament, except for the titles that were secondarily attached to the works attributed to Matthew, Mark, Luke, and John.[27] The earliest datable instance of this use of "gospel" as a literary term is in the writings of Justin Martyr (*1 Apol.* 66.3). The starting point for this literary use was apparently the opening statement of Mark that equates the story of Jesus' life with the proclamation of salvation. This is an incipient literary usage, but it is not taken up by the authors of Matthew and Luke. Perhaps the reason is that it was not perceived as a literary term but as a description of the content of the work: as many had announced the good news in oral form, it was now to be recorded in written form. In the extracanonical "apostolic" literature, the term "gospel" seems to refer at times to the (oral) teaching of Jesus and at times to a written document. Even when "gospel" seems to refer to a document, for example in *Did.* 15:3–4 and *2 Clem.* 8:5, the reference seems to be to content rather than to a literary form.[28]

According to Vielhauer, following Bultmann, the collection of the tradition about Jesus and the process of writing it down in historical-biographical form constituted a natural development.[29] Nevertheless, he discussed four theories regarding the origin of Mark: (1) Mark is a composition following the model of the Hellenistic βίος ("life" or "way of life"); (2) Mark is the expansion of a previously existing "frame" or summary of the gospel, that is, the oral proclamation of early Christians; (3) Mark is the result of an immanent development of the tradition about Jesus; (4) Mark is an original literary creation.[30] Vielhauer rejected the theory of immanent development because such development seems to have led only to collections of units of the same form. Small collections of controversy stories, parables, and miracle stories have been discerned as sources used by the author of Mark. Documents such as the *Gospel of Thomas* and the infancy Gospels may also be seen as products of such an immanent development. Vielhauer also rejected the theory that Mark was composed on the model of the Greek and Roman "lives," at least as argued by Siegfried Schulz.[31] His reasons were that the examples cited by Schulz, the life of Apollonius of Tyana by Philostratus and the lives of Alexander of Abonuteichus and Peregrinus by Lucian, are later than Mark. A further argument is that those writings are on a higher literary level than Mark, in particular, that they are less episodic. The theory that Mark is an original literary creation was put forward in a weak form by Willi Marxsen, since he presupposed that the author made use of sources, such as a preexistent passion narrative and certain collections. Vielhauer had no great objection to the weak form of this theory. Erhardt Güttgemanns presented a strong form, arguing that Mark must be understood in, by, and for itself. The creation of the gospel form and the fixing

tion (trans. John Marsh from the 2nd Germ. ed., 1931; New York: Harper & Row, 1963; rev. ed. with additions from the 1962 supplement, 1968) 368–74.

26 Philipp Vielhauer, *Geschichte der urchristlichen Literatur* (Berlin/New York: de Gruyter, 1975) 252–58, 348–55.

27 For an argument that the titles of the Gospels are original, or were added by someone who knew the author as soon as the text circulated beyond the community in which it was written, see Hengel, *Studies in Mark*, 64–84.

28 Vielhauer, *Geschichte*, 253–54. See also Koester, *Gospels*, 17–18, 353–55.

29 Vielhauer, *Geschichte*, 349; cf. Bultmann, *History*, 370.

30 Vielhauer, *Geschichte*, 349; he took these four categories from the discussion by Gerd Theißen in the Ergänzungsheft to Rudolf Bultmann, *Die Geschichte der synoptischen Tradition mit einem Nachwort von Gerd Theißen* (10th ed.; Göttingen: Vandenhoeck & Ruprecht, 1995); Vielhauer, *Geschichte*, 124–25. In his "Nachwort," Theissen discussed only two theories, namely, the "analogy-model" and the "development-model" (pp. 446–51).

31 Siegfried Schulz, "Die Bedeutung des Mk für die Theologiegeschichte des Urchristentums," TU 87 (1964); cited by Vielhauer, *Geschichte*, 330, 350.

of the tradition about Jesus in writing were one and the same event. Vielhauer rejected this theory as nonexplanatory and because it is refuted by the evidence for pre-Markan Christian writings. It is not clear whether Vielhauer had in mind here primarily the letters of Paul and the hypothetical Sayings Source (Q), the date of which is in any case uncertain, or sources used by Mark, assuming that they were sources already fixed in writing.[32] The theory positing an already existing "frame" or "summary" used by the author of Mark was advocated by Dibelius, Bultmann, and C. H. Dodd. The main evidence is provided by the summaries of the early Christian message in the book of Acts. The problem is that it is by no means certain that these summaries are older than Mark.[33] To avoid this problem, Vielhauer adopted a simpler version of the theory by agreeing with Bultmann that the proclamation of the death and resurrection of Jesus constitutes the seed from which Mark was cultivated and that other material was added because of various needs of the community.[34] The early emphasis on the death and resurrection is attested in the letters of Paul.

Vielhauer's position, thus, is that Mark was formed neither by a free creative act nor by mechanically adding together previously composed material. The author of Mark received traditional material *and* limits to that material in the form of a chronological framework. This framework was bounded at the end by the death and resurrection of Jesus and at the beginning by the activity of John the Baptist. Vielhauer followed Theißen in emphasizing the significance of the death of Jesus as a fixed chronological point that signifies both the end of an actual life and a literary ending as well. Although Vielhauer was aware that some ancient biographies were not organized chronologically, he considered chronological organization to be the most natural. Further, he viewed the death of Jesus as the origin of the whole tradition about Jesus, since it was universally viewed by early Christians as a salvific event.[35] Since the evidence for a preexisting "frame" or "summary" of the life, death, and resurrection of Jesus is not strong, Vielhauer argued for a framing consciousness rather than a literary frame. The individual forms in the tradition about Jesus—parables, miracle stories, and so on—show that there were centrifugal forces (increasing diversity) at work in the tradition and that there were different Christologies. Vielhauer did not, however, conclude that the centripetal forces (increasing unity) were created by the author of Mark. Rather, they were already in the tradition. Behind the formation and transmission of every unit of tradition is the consciousness of the identity of the earthly and exalted Jesus. For Vielhauer, the awareness of this identity implied a consciousness of the meaning of Jesus' death and resurrection, a consciousness that the author of Mark made explicit. Therefore, the composition of Mark brings nothing in principle new but completes what began with the earliest oral tradition.

It is certainly correct to say that every unit of the tradition presupposes that the crucifixion of Jesus was not counterevidence to the claim that he was the agent of God. It is not clear, however, that every unit is based on the assumption that Jesus had been "exalted." Further, it seems impossible to defend the hypothesis that each unit originates in the conviction that Jesus' death was a saving event. The Sayings Source (Q), as reconstructed from Matthew and Luke, on the contrary, seems to have treated the death of Jesus as a typical instance of the suffering of a prophet.[36] The miracle stories do not necessarily imply that Jesus' death was salvific. For them it may simply be irrelevant. The later controversies over views labeled "docetic" show that such an attitude was conceivable.[37] If Jesus' death as a saving event was not the source of all the tradition, then the composition of Mark seems to be much less a natural outgrowth of it.

Another argument expressed by Vielhauer seems stronger. He concluded that Mark is not an example of a Greco-Roman "life" because, unlike the typical ancient biography, it shows no interest in the origins, education, and inner development of Jesus. According to Vielhauer,

---

32   Vielhauer, *Geschichte*, 350; cf. 353.

33   David E. Aune argues in addition that there are major differences between Mark and the reconstructed oral kerygma in form, content, and function (*The New Testament in Its Literary Environment* [Philadelphia: Westminster, 1987] 24–25, 43).

34   Vielhauer, *Geschichte*, 350.

35   Ibid., 352–53.

36   See Luke 11:47-51 || Matt 23:29-36 and Luke 13:34-35 || Matt 23:37-39.

37   E.g., Ignatius of Antioch criticized those who argued that the suffering of Jesus was only a semblance (*Trall.* 10).

this lack is due to the character of the Gospel as proclamation; it may also be due, however, to the influence of another genre, a point to which we shall return. The smaller forms within the Gospel are borrowed, according to Vielhauer, from the surrounding culture, but the gospel form itself is something new. The fact that Mark does not begin with Jesus' genealogy, family, and birth is striking in comparison with the majority of the ancient accounts of lives and is surely significant. The lack of interest in the inner development of Jesus is a somewhat different matter. A psychological interest is characteristic of modern biography.[38] Interest in the inner life of historical figures was relatively much lower in antiquity. Nevertheless, authors of ancient "lives" did often show an interest in the unfolding of the character of the subject. Thus, although the lack of interest in the inner development of Jesus is not a strong argument against the hypothesis that Mark is an example of a Hellenistic "life," it does raise some doubt about it.

Mark as Biography

In Germany Johannes Weiss, writing in 1903, departed to some degree from the strict position of Franz Overbeck and interpreted Mark in an ancient literary context.[39] Two years before, Friedrich Leo had published what proved to be a very influential book on Greek and Roman biography.[40] This work led Weiss to compare Mark with the ancient biographies.

Leo had argued that there were three types of ancient biography: the encomium, the peripatetic type, and the Alexandrian type. The term "encomium" was originally applied by Pindar to the songs with which a victor was escorted home from an athletic contest[41] and was sometimes applied to speeches praising a deceased person.[42] The term was also applied to written laudatory works.[43] The form of the encomium used by Xenophon has a double structure. The "deeds" ($\pi\rho\acute{\alpha}\xi\epsilon\iota\varsigma$) are recounted in chronological order and then the "virtue" ($\dot{\alpha}\rho\epsilon\tau\acute{\eta}$) is discussed according to categories. The conclusion is a "recapitulation" ($\dot{\alpha}\nu\alpha\kappa\epsilon\varphi\alpha\lambda\alpha\acute{\iota}\omega\sigma\iota\varsigma$) of the subject's virtue.[44]

The peripatetic type of biography, as the name implies, developed in the Aristotelian tradition. Aristotle combined "way of life" ($\beta\acute{\iota}o\varsigma$) and "word" or "speech" ($\lambda\acute{o}\gamma o\varsigma$) in contrast with one another.[45] Here the idea is clearly expressed that actions constitute the $\beta\acute{\iota}o\varsigma$ ("way

---

38 See Momigliano, *Greek Biography*, 1, 6; Aune, *Literary Environment*, 28.

39 See the summary and critical discussion in Dormeyer, *Evangelium*, 58–64; see also Schmidt, *Place of the Gospels*, 6–7, 11–13 ("Stellung," 54–55, 60–62).

40 Friedrich Leo, *Die griechisch-römische Biographie nach ihrer literarischen Form* (Leipzig: Teubner, 1901). Albrecht Dihle argued that Leo's thesis regarding two independent genres of ancient biography, the peripatetic and the Alexandrian, was refuted by the publication of two important papyri. One of these, P. Oxy. 1176, which was published in 1912, contains a fragment of the life of Euripides by Satyrus and shows that the Alexandrian scholar Satyrus wrote biographies in the form of a dialogue. The other, *Papyrus Graeca Hauniensis* 6, published by T. Larsen in 1942, seems to contain short biographies of Ptolemies of the third century BCE arranged in the framework of a family tree and shows that political figures did not always receive extended artistic treatment. In other words, these papyri show that historical personalities, as well as literary figures, were given short, nonliterary, summary treatment (the Alexandrian type) and that artfully arranged biogra-

phical works (the peripatetic type) were sometimes composed about literary personalities; see Albrecht Dihle, *Studien zur griechischen Biographie* (AAWG.PH, 3. F., Nr. 37; Göttingen: Vandenhoeck & Ruprecht, 1956) 7; cf. idem, "Die Evangelien und die griechische Biographie," in Peter Stuhlmacher, ed., *Das Evangelium und die Evangelien* (Tübingen: Mohr Siebeck, 1983) 383–413; ET Dihle, "The Gospels and Greek Biography," in Stuhlmacher, ed., *Gospel and the Gospels*, 361–86, esp. 371. But Leo did not argue that the two subtypes were entirely independent or that political figures were always handled with the peripatetic type and literary figures always with the Alexandrian type. Such rigid distinctions are due to the summarizers of Leo, not to Leo himself. Dihle is right, however, that the evidence for ancient biography is very limited and that many of Leo's hypotheses are very speculative; see also Momigliano, *Greek Biography*, 80, 85.

41 John F. Dobson, "Encomium," in N. G. L. Hammond and H. H. Scullard, eds., *OCD* 315; the 3rd ed. of the *OCD* does not have an entry on the encomium.

42 E.g., Isocrates *Evagoras* and Xenophon *Agesilaus*.

43 David E. Aune, *The Westminster Dictionary of New*

of life"), the mode of being, the nature of a person. It is in the actions that talent, disposition, and education are reflected; it is not appearance and words that play this role. So "way of life and deeds" (βίος καὶ πράξεις) became synonymous and were often combined in a single concept, especially in the biographies of Plutarch; so also ἦθος καὶ βίος ("custom" or "habit and way of life") and βίος καὶ τρόπος ("way of life and character"), sometimes in reverse order. The βίος ("way of life") is the human being, in practice as he lives, in theory as he ought to live. The same circle of scholars, Aristotle and his followers, carried on research into the history of the sciences and arts and of the deeds of leaders in the intellectual area, on the one hand, and, on the other hand, pursued the disciplined observation of what was characteristic in human life. Out of this coincidence grew scientific interest in the literary personality. Among the pupils of Aristotle who pursued the history of science, Aristoxenus appears as the founder of literary biography.[46] His works were apparently entitled "the way of life of X" (βίος τοῦ δεῖνα). The lives he wrote were all written with emotion—some out of hate, some out of love; that of Pythagoras out of religious veneration. They were written for a broad audience; this is indicated by Plutarch, who names them in connection with Herodotus, Xenophon, and Homer. We can tell from Plutarch and from individual fragments that their form

was free narration, which depicted the personality of the man, as well as the nature of his environment, by following the thread of his experiences.[47] Thus, the "peripatetic type" of biography, according to Leo, focused in its origins on leaders in literature, philosophy, and religion. Later, in the work of Plutarch,[48] this primarily chronological type was employed, often in connection with statesmen and generals.

In content, Alexandrian biography differs from peripatetic only in degree. According to Leo, the essential difference is in the form. The most important representatives of pre-Alexandrian biography depicted lives in a free-flowing narrative; in the type represented by Chamaeleon,[49] they followed the lead of the tragedies and comedies. Antigonus of Carystus,[50] in contrast, arranged his presentation according to key words that related to the individual qualities of the philosophers.[51] This schema derives from the encomion as it developed from Isocrates to Xenophon. Antigonus's arrangement of his material according to key words presupposes that, before the systematic treatment of the personality, the information on γένος ("origin" or "descent") and external experiences was already given. The account of experiences was perhaps divided into two parts, so that the report about the death and age at death concluded the whole. The form used by Antigonus, however, is not yet that of Alexandrian biography, although it may be seen

Testament and Early Christian Rhetoric (Louisville/London: Westminster John Knox, 2003) 145–47, s.v. "encomium."

44 Leo, *Biographie*, 91.

45 Aristotle *Eth. Nic.* 1127a 24.

46 Aristoxenus of Tarentum was born between 375 and 360 BCE; the date of his death is unknown. He was a Pythagorean before becoming a pupil of Aristotle. He wrote numerous works on music and works of a biographical, historical, and miscellaneous nature. His fragments were edited by Fritz Wehrli, *Die Schule des Aristoteles: Texte und Kommentar*, vol. 2: *Aristoxenos* (2nd rev. ed.; Basel/Stuttgart: Schwabe, 1967).

47 Leo, *Biographie*, 96–97, 101–3.

48 Plutarch of Chaeronea (c. 50–c. 120 CE) was a philosopher, biographer, and a priest at Delphi.

49 Athenaeus (fl. c. 200 CE) of Naucratis in Egypt, whose only surviving work is *The Learned Banquet* (*Deipnosophistae* or *Deipnosophists*), written in the form of a symposium, provides information about Chamaeleon (c. 350–c. 281 BCE) of Heraclea Pontica.

Chamaeleon wrote studies of poets, such as Sophocles and Euripides, deducing biographical data from their works and from references to them in comedy. Athenaeus's work is available in the LCL in seven volumes.

50 Antigonus of Carystus (fl. 240 BCE) wrote reminiscences or character sketches of philosophers of the Academy after Plato, whom he knew personally. This work was later incorporated into a longer biographical work on the same subject, which was used by Diogenes Laertius in composing his *Lives and Opinions of Eminent Philosophers*; see Leo, *Biographie*, 66–67.

51 E.g., ὀργίλος ("prone to anger," "passionate"), ἡδονῶν ἥττων ("yielding to pleasures"), and διακεχυμένος ("immoderate").

as a mediating form between the old and the new. The personal style, which creates from the whole, divides Antigonus from the Alexandrian form, but it is also distinct from the conversational style of the Peripatetics.[52]

The Alexandrian type was supposed to have originated among the scholars of that Egyptian city, the grammarians and philologists. Whereas Plutarch's main interests may be said to have been the ethical and historical and he wrote for a general, educated audience, the Alexandrian scholars wrote most often for other scholars and were motivated primarily by antiquarian interests.[53] The subject was generally a poet or playwright; the form was more topical than chronological; and the purpose was to preserve knowledge, to facilitate literary imitation, or to enhance understanding of the subject's works.

According to Weiss, Mark shares an important feature with the peripatetic type, which is best represented by the parallel lives written by Plutarch. This feature is the method employed to express the $\ἦθος$ ("custom," "habit," or "character") of the protagonist. Rather than preferring explicit description and commentary on the subject's virtues or vices, as in the Alexandrian type of biography, Plutarch and Mark emphasized the indirect approach. They described the protagonist's "deeds" ($\πράξεις$) and thus illustrated his character.[54] This similarity in characterization, however, is too small a basis on which to build a theory of literary dependence or even analogy. Weiss recognized that this technique was not confined to the biographical genre and concluded that Mark should not be assigned to the category of biographical literature.[55] In any case, it is doubtful that Mark, like Plutarch, presupposed an Aristotelian theory of ethics. But the notions that character is revealed in deeds and that teaching is better accomplished through deeds than words were probably commonplaces of popular philosophy in Mark's context and may well have been known to him as such.

In the American scholarly context, Clyde Votaw published two essays in 1915 in which he compared the Gospels to ancient biography.[56] He admitted that, in comparison with the elaborate literary productions of the Greeks and Romans, the Gospels are brief, special, and popular writings. In character a Gospel is a religious tract intended to promote the Christian movement. Nevertheless, the Gospels may be called biographies of Jesus, depending on the connotation given to the term "biography." He then distinguished biography in a historical sense from biography in a popular sense. Historical biography "is a writing which aims to present all the important dates and facts about a person, with perspective and exactness, including his relations to other persons and to his times. This involves research, criticism, and interpretation, according to the current principles of history-writing. It is obvious that the Gospels are not biographies in this sense of the term."[57] A popular biography is

any writing which aims to make one acquainted with a historical person by giving some account of his deeds and words, sketchily chosen and arranged, even when the motive of the writer is practical and hortatory rather than historical. The amount, character, order, and accuracy of the historical information contained in these pragmatic writings vary greatly, according to the purposes, interests, abilities, and resources of the several authors. The Gospels may be classified with productions of this kind. . . .[58]

He argued further that the closest parallels to the Gospels are the works about Socrates written by his

---

52 Leo, *Biographie*, 133.

53 On the distinction between political historiography and antiquarian erudition, see Arnaldo Momigliano, "Historiography on Written Tradition and Historiography on Oral Tradition," in idem, *Studies in Historiography* (London: Weidenfeld & Nicolson, 1966) 211–20, esp. 217–20.

54 Johannes Weiss, *Das älteste Evangelium: Ein Beitrag zum Verständnis des Markus-Evangeliums und der ältesten evangelischen Überlieferung* (Göttingen: Vandenhoeck & Ruprecht, 1903) 11, 15.

55 Ibid., 16, 22. See also Schmidt, *Place of the Gospels*, 11–13 ("Stellung" 50–62).

56 Clyde Weber Votaw, "The Gospels and Contemporary Biographies," *American Journal of Theology* [the forerunner of the *Journal of Religion*] 19 (1915) 45–73, 217–49, reprinted as Clyde Weber Votaw, *The Gospels and Contemporary Biographies in the Greco-Roman World* (FBBS 27; Philadelphia: Fortress, 1970).

57 Votaw, *Gospels*, 1–5; quotation from 5.

58 Ibid., 5.

pupils in order to rehabilitate his reputation after he had been executed by the state. He thus compared the Gospels with the dialogues of Plato and with Xenophon's recollections of Socrates.[59] Since the latter works are among the classics of high literature, most scholars have rejected Votaw's description of them as "biography in a popular sense." Furthermore, while the dialogues of Plato have a biographical aspect, they can hardly be defined as biographies in terms of literary genre.[60] Votaw was correct in his observation that some ancient texts maintain distance from their subjects and assess them critically, whereas others aim to persuade their readers, either by blaming or praising their subjects, but this difference does not correspond neatly to two distinct genres or subtypes.

The hypothesis that the Gospels should be defined as biographical works was eclipsed during much of the twentieth century by the form-critical thesis of their non- or pre-literary character and by the neo-orthodox and redaction-critical emphasis on their uniqueness.[61] But since the biographical hypothesis was revived by Charles H. Talbert in 1977, it has received growing attention.[62] In spite of Leo's extensive and detailed study of ancient biography, defining biography has been a problem in recent research. In light of the growing recognition of the differences between ancient and modern biography, scholars have attempted to reconstruct the ancient understanding of biography. But there is no ancient definition and no ancient literary-critical discussion of how a biography should be written, what its essential features are, and what its purpose is.[63] There was a great deal of

ancient literary-critical discussion of the poetic kinds of texts, but very little of prose works. The only prose genres that were discussed extensively in antiquity are history and the main types of speeches. Since ancient definitions are lacking, modern scholars have attempted to fill the gap. Arnaldo Momigliano defined biography as an account of the life of a man [sic] from birth to death.[64] Other scholars have been critical of his inclusion of parts of longer works in the category of biography. Joseph Geiger, for example, proposed the definition of the *Oxford English Dictionary* to solve this problem, namely, "The history of the lives of individual men [sic], as a branch of literature."[65] Similarly, David Aune argued that the category should be delimited as follows: "Biography may be defined as a discrete prose narrative devoted exclusively to the portrayal of the whole life of a particular individual perceived as historical."[66] Some would argue further against Momigliano that an account of the subject's birth, while frequently included, is not an essential part of a biography.[67] While it is true that no single topic defines the genre "biography" or is absolutely essential to it, the absence of any account of the protagonist's birth, ancestry, education, and childhood, as in Mark, may be a sign that the focus of the work is on something other than the life or personality of the subject and thus that its genre may be something else.[68] The reader is indeed given some information about Jesus' family in Mark (3:21, 31-35; 6:1-6a), but the author communicates it through anecdotes, whereas a more abstract, though sometimes brief, discussion of origin, descent, and status is usually given at the beginning of ancient

---

59   Ibid., esp. 33–34, 58–59.

60   But see Leo's concluding comment that Plato invented his own biographical form (*Biographie*, 323).

61   See the discussion of the form critics in the subsection *Mark as Gospel* above. For a summary and critical discussion of the theories of redaction critics about the literary nature of the Gospels, see Dormeyer, *Evangelium*, 108–30.

62   Charles H. Talbert, *What Is a Gospel? The Genre of the Canonical Gospels* (Philadelphia: Fortress, 1977); see also idem, "Biographies of Philosophers and Rulers as Instruments of Religious Propaganda in Mediterranean Antiquity," *ANRW* 2.16.2 (1978) 1619–51.

63   Plutarch and Cornelius Nepos make remarks in passing about the differences between history and biography, but the significance of these remarks is

disputed. See Charles William Fornara, *The Nature of History in Ancient Greece and Rome* (Eidos; Berkeley: University of California Press, 1983) 185; Burridge, *What Are the Gospels?* 63–65 (2nd ed., 60–62).

64   Momigliano, *Greek Biography*, 11.

65   Jospeh Geiger, *Cornelius Nepos and Ancient Political Biography* (Historia Einzelschriften 47; Stuttgart: Franz Steiner Verlag Wiesbaden, 1985) 14 n. 21.

66   Aune, *Literary Environment*, 29.

67   So, e.g., Dormeyer (*Evanglium*, 59–60) against Weiss.

68   The contrary is also true: the presence of stories about birth and childhood alone does not define a work as a biography. Schmidt rightly argued, against Weiss, that the presence of birth stories in Matthew and Luke is not a sufficient reason to define them as biographies (Schmidt, "Place of the Gospels,"11 ["Stellung" 60]).

biographies.[69] A problem with Aune's defintion is that the phrase "whole life" is ambiguous. Does it include a birth account or not? Does it include childhood stories and an account of the subject's education? A problem with all three definitions is that they do not address the question of the purpose or function of biography.[70]

Apparently because of the variety of purposes that may be inferred from individual biographical works, some scholars have attempted to define subtypes of biography and to show that each subtype has its own purpose or function. In his 1975 dissertation, part of which was eventually published in 1982, Philip Shuler defined a subtype of biography that he called "encomium" or laudatory biography.[71] The members of the subgroup are characterized as impressionistic portraits, rather than detailed, critical reports, exhibiting the presentation of the pattern of a life from birth to death; the use of the rhetorical techniques of amplification and comparison; and the aim of praising the central character.[72] Some of the Greek and Latin works that he wishes to classify as laudatory biography do not seem best defined as such.[73] A further problem is that he fails to account for the admitted difference between the function of the Gospels in eliciting faith in their central character and the aim of ancient encomiastic biographies in praising their subjects.[74]

In *What Is a Gospel?*, published in 1977, Talbert defined ancient biography as "prose narration about a person's life, presenting supposedly historical facts which are selected to reveal the character or essence of the individual, often with the purpose of affecting the behavior of the reader."[75] This definition is more helpful than those of Momigliano, Geiger, and Aune in that it attempts to define the purpose of the genre both in terms of the focus of its subject matter and the intended effect on the reader. Talbert also attempted to classify ancient biographies on the basis of how they functioned in their social, intellectual, and spiritual contexts. He first reviewed Friedrich Leo's three types of biography and accepted them. He proposed, however, that a fourth type be added, "the popular or romantic life."[76] He did not define this latter category in the same way as Clyde Votaw, but seems to mean by it works that are similar to the Greek novels or "romances" and that are less demanding or ambitious in form and style than the classical works. After establishing these four types, Talbert proposed a new approach which would divide all ancient biographies into two main categories, rather than four, by distinguishing between didactic or propagandistic lives, on the one hand, and nondidactic lives, on the other.[77] He argued that only the Alexandrian or grammatical type of lives were nondidactic. Unlike the majority of ancient lives, these were unconcerned with moral

---

69 E.g., Lucian *Demonax* 3; see also the examples given by Leo, *Biographie*, 11–15, 18, 27–31, 33–34, 115, 163, 173–74, 180–81. The presence of the γένος topic and its usual place at the beginning of the work are typical of both the Alexandrian and the peripatetic types of biography.

70 On the importance of purpose or function in the definition of a genre, see David Hellholm, "The Problem of Apocalyptic Genre and the Apocalypse of John," in Adela Yarbro Collins, ed., *Early Christian Apocalypticism: Genre and Social Setting*, Semeia 36 (1986) 1–64, esp. 1–27. Of course as a group, and even as individual works, they may have more than one function, depending on the level of abstraction in the definition of function. Aune discussed the obvious and latent functions of Greco-Roman biography (*Literary Environment*, 35–36).

71 Philip L. Shuler, *A Genre for the Gospels: The Biographical Character of Matthew* (Philadelphia: Fortress, 1982). See also the summary and critical discussion by Dormeyer, *Evangelium*, 165; and Burridge, *What Are the Gospels?*, 86–89 (2nd ed., 83–86).

72 Shuler, *Genre*, 45–57.

73 E.g., Philo's *Life of Moses* is better classified as a didactic biography (see below); Tacitus's *Life of Agricola* has strong affinities with history and ethnography; and Philostratus's *Life of Apollonius of Tyana* has important similarities to the ancient novel.

74 Cf. Burridge, *What Are the Gospels?*, 88–89 (2nd ed., 85).

75 Talbert, *What Is a Gospel?*, 17.

76 Ibid., 92–93; only two examples of this fourth type are given, the *Life of Aesop* and *Secundus the Silent Philosopher*. These two works are quite different in form, especially overall structure, and in content. Klaus Berger also argued that a fourth type be added, which he called "Populär-romanhafter Typ" (the "popular, novelistic type"), "Hellenistische Gattungen im Neuen Testament," *ANRW* 2.25.2 (1984) 1031–1885. He lists the same two examples of this fourth type. See also the summary and critical discussion of Berger's classification in Dormeyer, *Evangelium*, 166–68.

example. The other, larger group includes the encomium, the peripatetic type, and the popular type.[77]

Talbert's next step was to subdivide the didactic biographies into five types on the basis of their more specific functions. Type A includes lives whose function is simply to provide the readers with a model to imitate. Lucian's life of *Demonax* is an example. The purpose of the lives that belong to type B is to dispel a false image of the teacher or ruler and to provide a true model to follow, such as Xenophon's *Memorabilia*[79] and Philostratus's *Life of Apollonius of Tyana*. Xenophon was responding to an imaginary speech against Socrates composed by a sophist after Socrates had died. Philostratus was responding to the charge that Apollonius was a charlatan addicted to magical practices. According to Talbert, the Gospels of Mark and John belong to this type. Lives of type C discredit a given teacher or ruler by exposé. Examples are Lucian's satirical *Passing of Peregrinus* and *Alexander the False Prophet*.[80] By heaping ridicule on Peregrinus and Alexander, Lucian hopes to discourage readers from joining the groups preserving their memory and teachings. Talbert argued that other lives, type D, indicated where the "living voice" was to be found in the period after the death of the founder. His examples are a life of Aristotle, written in the third century BCE but known only from fragments, and various collections of "successions," of which the best preserved are those used as sources by Diogenes Laertius in his *Lives and Opinions of Eminent Philosophers*.[81] In these works, the life of the founder of a philosophical school is followed by a list of or a narrative about his successors and selected other disciples, which tells where the true tradition of the school is to be found. Talbert argued that the Gospel of Luke is

a life of the "founder" and that the book of Acts is a narrative concerning his successors. The final group, type E, consists of lives that aim at validating or providing the hermeneutical key for the teacher's doctrine, such as Porphyry's *Life of Plotinus*, the life of Aristotle used as an introduction to his works, and *Secundus the Silent Philosopher*.[82] Talbert concluded that the Gospel of Matthew is a life of this type.

A problem with Talbert's classification is that he defines "didactic" so broadly that a hortatory or propagandistic purpose may be attributed to almost any life. A further problem is that the functional types seem to be defined from the point of view of the Gospels and Acts, rather than to emerge from the functions of Greek and Roman biographies in their own contexts. If the proposed types do not reflect accurately the nature of Greek and Roman biography, then their application to the Gospels is called into question, as well as the conclusion that the Gospels belong to the category of ancient biography.

A dissertation by Richard Burridge, accepted by the University of Nottingham in England, had as its purpose either to refute the hypothesis that the Gospels are biographies or to put it on a firm scholarly footing.[83] Burridge's starting point was genre criticism and literary theory. He agreed with René Wellek and Austin Warren that genre should be conceived as a regulative concept, an underlying pattern or convention that is effective in molding the writing of concrete works.[84] He agreed further with Alastair Fowler that genre should be taken as an instrument not of classification or prescription but of meaning.[85] In considering how this convention functions, he followed E. D. Hirsch and Jonathan Culler in speaking

---

77 This distinction is very similar to the main difference that Votaw perceived between "biography in a historical sense" (exact, critical, and thus nondidactic, nonpropagandistic) and "biography in a popular sense" (hortatory and thus didactic, propagandistic) (*Gospels*, 5).

78 Talbert, *What Is a Gospel?*, 93; see also idem, "Biographies," 1619–20.

79 Xenophon's Greek title is ἀπομνημονεύματα ("reminiscences" or "notes"); see the discussion of Justin above in the introduction to this section on *Genre*. Talbert translated Xenophon's title as *Recollections* in *What Is a Gospel?* and as *Memorabilia* in "Biographies."

80 This is the same work referred to above as the life of Alexander of Abonoteichus; see the discussion of Vielhauer in the subsection *Mark as a Gospel* above.

81 Talbert, *What Is a Gospel?*, 94–97; see also idem, "Biographies," 1620–24, 1647–50.

82 Talbert, *What Is a Gospel?*, 96; idem, "Biographies," 1622–23, 1624, 1650.

83 Burridge, *What Are the Gospels?*, 24 (2nd ed., 24).

84 René Wellek and Austin Warren, *Theory of Literature* (3rd ed.; Harmondsworth: Penguin/Pelican, 1982; reprint of 1963 ed.).

85 Alastair Fowler, *Kinds of Literature: An Introduction to the Theory of Genres and Modes* (Oxford: Oxford University Press, 1982).

of a system or sets of expectations, and Heather Dubrow in positing a generic contract between author and reader.[86] He defined genre as "a group of literary works sharing certain 'family resemblances' operating at a level between Universals [Aristotle's genres of epic, lyric, and drama] and actual texts and between modes and specific subgroups, and functioning as a set of expectations to guide interpretation."[87] His own proposed solution to the problem begins with a list of generic features that are likely to reveal the particular pattern for each genre that constitutes the "contract" between author and reader. These include opening features (title, opening words, prologue, or preface), subject (subject matter or content), external features (mode of representation, meter, size or length, structure or sequence, scale, sources, methods of characterization), and internal features (setting, topics, style, tone, mood, attitude, values, quality of characterization, social setting, occasion of writing, author's intention or purpose).[88] He applied this model to two groups of ancient lives, one group of five that predate the Gospels and another of five that are later than the Gospels. The first group includes the *Evagoras* by Isocrates, the *Agesilaus* of Xenophon,[89] the fragmentary *Euripides* by Satyrus, the *Atticus* by Nepos, and Philo's *Life of Moses*.[90] The second group consists of Tacitus's *Agricola*, Plutarch's *Cato Minor*, Suetonius's *Lives of the Caesars*, Lucian's *Demonax*, and Philostratus's *Apollonius of Tyana*.[91] He concluded that these works exhibit a similar range of generic features within a flexible pattern. The primary similarity derives from their subject, the account of a person, which is usually signaled by the title, the subject's name, or by the word βίος itself, meaning "an account of the life."[92] The final step involves the

analysis of the four canonical Gospels according to the same model. Burridge concluded that there is a high degree of correlation between the Greco-Roman lives and the Gospels and that therefore the Gospels are lives of Jesus. They may constitute their own subgenre because of their shared content, but the ancient lives establish the "family" to which they belong. The differences are not sufficiently marked or significant to prevent the Gospels from belonging to the genre "life."[93]

The significance of Burridge's conclusion is undercut by his admission that "the narrower the genre proposed for the gospels, the harder it is to prove the case, but the more useful the hermeneutical implications; whereas the wider the genre, the easier it is to demonstrate that the gospels belong to it, but the less helpful the result."[94] His argument that the Gospels belong to the genre "life" is strong, but the genre is very wide.[95] In spite of Burridge's criticisms of Talbert, Talbert was right (or at least more helpful and interesting) to attempt to articulate a primary or typical function of the ancient biography and the more specific functions of its subgenres. The exemplary purpose of the ancient lives and their focus on character as a matter of virtue and vice is a significant theme in Burridge's treatment of Greco-Roman biography[96] and qualifies as the most distinctive purpose of the genre. In spite of Burridge's attempt to find something analogous in the Gospels, it is clear that their portrayal of Jesus' so-called character and virtues belongs to a different cultural context and has a purpose beyond the exemplary.

Burridge rightly criticized Bultmann for arguing that the Gospel of Mark simply evolved from early Christian preaching of the death and resurrection of Jesus and that

---

86 Eric Donald Hirsch, *Validity in Interpretation* (New Haven: Yale University Press, 1967); Jonathan Culler, *Structuralist Poetics: Structuralism, Linguistics and the Study of Literature* (London: Routledge & Kegan Paul, 1975); Heather Dubrow, *Genre* (Critical Idiom Series 42; London: Methuen, 1982).

87 Burridge, *What Are the Gospels?*, 42 (2nd ed., 40–41).

88 Ibid., 111 (2nd ed., 107).

89 Isocrates' *Evagoras* and Xenophon's *Agesilaus* are encomia, but it is generally agreed that they overlap with the genre βίος ("life").

90 Burridge, *What Are the Gospels?*, 128 (2nd ed., 124).

91 Ibid., 155–60 (2nd ed., 151–56).

92 Ibid., 152, 189 (2nd ed., 148, 184).

93 Ibid., 218–19, 238–39, 243 (2nd ed., 211–12, 231–32, 236).

94 Ibid., 255 (2nd ed., 247–48).

95 For more detailed criticism, see Adela Yarbro Collins, "Genre and the Gospels: A Review Article on Richard A. Burridge, *What Are the Gospels? A Comparison with Graeco-Roman Biography*," *JR* 75 (1995) 239–46.

96 Burridge, *What Are the Gospels?*, 63, 67, 76, 136, 145, 150, 176, 252 (2nd ed., 61, 64–65, 72, 132, 141, 145–46, 171, 244).

the Gospels belong to no literary genus. It is more credible that the Gospel as a whole was based on a particular literary model or that its author attempted to fuse two or more literary types. The Hellenistic and Roman "lives" may have been one such model. But Burridge should have taken the biographical material in 1–2 Samuel and 1–2 Kings more seriously as another likely model. The story of Elijah, for example, contains miracle stories and climaxes in an extraordinary death-account. The story of Moses is similar, especially as interpreted in the early Roman period. The Gospels' interest in eschatology or the meaning of history also requires explanation.

Burridge's case for defining the Gospels as βίοι ("lives") appears strong in large part because he did not seriously consider any alternative. The very brief review of scholarship under the heading "The Jewish Background" does not constitute a serious consideration of the relevant genres of Jewish literature.[97] It is certainly essential to interpret the Gospels in light of Greek and Roman literature, but it is equally essential to interpret them in light of Jewish literature. The fact that the Dead Sea Scrolls and rabbinic literature pay far less attention to individuals than Greek and Roman literature does not free us from that responsibility. Philo's *Life of Moses* is included by Burridge as an example of a Jewish βίος ("life"), but biblical and postbiblical Jewish historiography is not taken seriously as a possible generic model for the Gospels. The relevance of the latter genre depends to some degree on whether there was a pre-Hellenistic biblical or Jewish genre that could be defined as βίος ("life") or biography and that existed independently of historiography.

The book of Nehemiah has an autobiographical character and may have been inspired by Persian models, as Momigliano has suggested.[98] There was a much older biographical and autobiographical tradition in the ancient Near East. For example, the oldest type of Egyptian autobiographical text is a kind of funerary inscription, consisting primarily of a catalogue of virtues practiced and wrongs not committed, which Egyptologists call the "ideal biography." It is ideal in the sense that the shortcomings of the subject and the ephemera of his life are not recorded; in fact, the same catalogue may be used for many individuals. This genre took shape in the Fifth Dynasty of the Old Kingdom (c. 2500–2350 BCE). In the Sixth Dynasty (c. 2350–2190 BCE), truly autobiographical inscriptions were created, in the sense that they recorded specific information about a person's life that applied only to that person. Egyptian autobiographical fiction emerged already in the Middle Kingdom (c. 2106–1786 BCE) with the Story of Sinuhe. Both genres continued to flourish in the New Kingdom (c. 1550–1069 BCE). As Eberhard Otto has shown, the tradition of autobiographical inscriptions flourished throughout the Late Period (c. 664–332 BCE) and on into the Greek and Roman periods of Egyptian history.[99]

With reference to this Egyptian material, Klaus Baltzer argued that there are now passages in the Hebrew Bible that can be called "biographies," that these once had an independent existence apart from their present contexts, and that they have been secondarily incorporated into larger contexts, often as source material for historiography.[100] Baltzer takes "The Last Words of David" in 2 Samuel 23 as an example of an "ideal biography." Unlike the Egyptologists, he does not use this term to designate a text that could apply to various subjects. Rather, it signifies a summary of a life, as opposed to the recounting of particular events, and the instructional or exemplary character of the summary. David is presented as an example for those who come

---

97   Ibid., 19–21 (2nd ed., 19–21).

98   Momigliano, *Greek Biography*, 35–37. But the memoirs of Nehemiah have striking similarities to Egyptian biographies of the Late Period; see John Van Seters, *In Search of History: Historiography in the Ancient World and the Origins of Biblical History* (New Haven: Yale University Press, 1983) 186–87.

99   For the texts in English translation with introductions and notes, see Miriam Lichtheim, *Ancient Egyptian Literature: A Book of Readings*, 2 vols. (Berkeley: University of California Press, 1973, 1976). For the Late Period, see Eberhard Otto, *Die biographischen Inschriften der ägyptischen Spätzeit: Ihre geistesgeschichtliche und literarische Bedeutung* (Leiden: Brill, 1954).

100 Klaus Baltzer, *Die Biographie der Propheten* (Neukirchen-Vluyn: Neukirchener Verlag, 1975) 23–24, 29, 35–36, 39, 88, 105, 126–28.

after, that is, the kings who succeed him. In Judges 6–8, the story of Gideon, Baltzer finds an example of narrative biography. Following Wolfgang Richter, he argues that this passage is a unified composition, created by editing older, originally independent traditions. Baltzer assumed that this unified composition was also originally independent of its present context, but it is not at all clear that this assumption is justified. It may just as well have been composed precisely for the present context.[101] Similarly, it is not obvious that the books of Isaiah, Jeremiah, and Ezekiel incorporate originally independent, extended narrative biographies of these prophets. Thus, with the possible exceptions of Nehemiah and the Joseph story, it is not clear that we are justified in speaking of biography as a pre-Hellenistic biblical genre. It seems more appropriate to speak of the use of biographical elements in other biblical genres. For example, the book of Judges and 1 and 2 Samuel may be interpreted as historical fiction or historiography that centers on the activities of certain charismatic leaders. The books of Kings and Chronicles may be seen as annalistic historiography that focuses on the deeds of kings. The genre of the prophetic books is more difficult to articulate, but they should probably not be defined as biographies.

Detlev Dormeyer argued that the redactors of the Gospels conceived the idea of composing an "ideal biography" of Jesus from the biographical traditions of the Old Testament and Judaism.[102] Since these earlier texts did not provide a sufficiently clear literary model for such a work, they adopted further literary patterns from the literature of the Hellenistic culture in which they lived. The result was a new subgenre of historiographical biography.[103]

Dormeyer's proposal brings us back to the question of the types of the genre biography in antiquity. I would like to propose a new classification according to function, which seeks to avoid the problems of Talbert's. I do not claim that any particular ancient biography fits one of these types exactly and this one only. It is more a matter of emphasis; each ancient biography will probably fit one of these types better than it fits the others. The first type is encomiastic. The subjects of this type are typically kings, generals, and statesmen, although in principle any prominent person could be so honored. The encomiastic biography is based on a common rhetorical genre, the encomium, which was one of the three main types of epideictic rhetoric.[104] The prototype is the prose work honoring Evagoras, who ruled Cyprus in the late fifth and early fourth centuries BCE. It was written by Isocrates in the fourth century BCE. Xenophon's *Agesilaus* also belongs in this category. A later example is the lost life of Philopoimen by Polybius, which he describes in his *Histories*.[105] His life of Philopoimen was written in the first half of the second century BCE. It was widely recognized that the encomium and the encomiastic biography did not attempt to give an accurate, balanced portrait of the person honored. The aims of encomium were not the same as those of historiography. The author of an encomiastic work was expected to select and even exaggerate the positive aspects of the subject's character and deeds. He was permitted to omit entirely any vices or evil deeds and to overlook embarrassing facts, such as the fact that Evagoras had been murdered. In spite of Shuler's attempt to prove otherwise, it seems that the Gospels have little in common with this type.[106] The Synoptic Gospels lack the rhetorical techniques associated with it; further, they do not hesitate to include incidents that Hellenists would have considered embarrassing, such as the agony in the garden and the crucifixion itself.

101 Van Seters argued that the author of the Deuteronomistic history was responsible for the collection of old folk legends in Judges and cited Hans-Detlef Hoffmann's argument that Judg 6:1—8:35 is a carefully constructed work of the Deuteronomistic historian (van Seters, *In Search of History*, 343–44 and n. 74).

102 Dormeyer, *Evangelium*, 168–73; he used the term "ideal biography" in contrast with the modern notion of biography to emphasize the concern with the typical in ancient lives, as opposed to the individual and the psychological.

103 Ibid., 173. See also Detlev Dormeyer, *Das Markusevangelium als Idealbiographie von Jesus Christus, dem Nazarener* (SBB 43; Stuttgart: Katholisches Bibelwerk, 1999).

104 Aune, *Westminster Dictionary*, s.v. "encomium," 145.

105 Polybius *Histories* 10.21. See the discussion in Albrecht Dihle, *Die Entstehung der historischen Biographie* (SHAW.PH 1986.3; Heidelberg: Carl Winter/Universitätsverlag, 1987) 9–10, 12.

106 See the discussion of Shuler above.

The second type is the scholarly biography. The subjects of this type are typically authors of literary works and philosophers, although Suetonius used it also for Roman emperors.[107] The earliest example to survive, although in fragmentary form, is the life of Euripides, written by Satyrus, who probably lived in Alexandria in the third century BCE. The work is of high literary quality and was composed in dialogue form. It is related to a group of lost works entitled "Concerning X," X standing for the name of a writer. Such works are often attributed to scholars in the peripatetic or Aristotelian tradition. These were probably not biographies, but historical interpretations of selected passages from one classical author.[108] Using a method pioneered by those earlier works, Satyrus deduced many of the biographical details about Euripides from the text of Euripides' tragedies. Satyrus's work manifests an interest in literary history in his attempt to link the new comedy of Menander with Euripides.[109] Although Satyrus's biography is distinctive in form, its function is similar to that of the "Alexandrian type" of biography as defined by Leo.[110] The works assigned by Leo to the latter type may thus be included in the category "scholarly biography," for example, the *Lives and Opinions of Eminent Philosophers*, written by Diogenes Laertius in the early part of the third century CE.[111] Diogenes made use of many earlier books in composing his own, some of which go back to the early Hellenistic period. The aim of the work is to write a history of philosophy that divides philosophers into two main successions, an Ionian or Eastern and an Italian or Western. The last section deals with "sporadics," important philosophers who did not found successions. The author shows impartiality toward all the schools. A satirical, irreverent attitude toward individual philosophers frequently appears. It should be clear, in spite of Talbert's arguments, that this type of biography has little in common with the Gospels.

A third type may be named "didactic," because a primary aim is to instruct the reader, not only about the life of a particular individual but also about the way of life that he founded. The goal is to win respect for and perhaps also allegiance to that way of life. The subjects of this type are thus typically religious leaders and philosophers, especially those who founded communities or schools. A good example is the life of Moses written by the Jewish philosopher Philo of Alexandria in the first century CE.[112] In writing this life, Philo apparently intended not only to inform his audience about the achievements and virtues of Moses but also to present a summary of the Jewish way of life, emphasizing its admirable aspects. Another example is the work entitled *On the Pythagorean Way of Life*, written by the Neoplatonist philosopher Iamblichus in the late third or early fourth century CE.[113] The Gospels clearly have an affinity with this type. All four contain extensive teaching of Jesus, and discipleship is a major theme in each. The life of Jesus is told, at least in part, to inform the audience about Christian teaching and the Christian way of life.

The fourth type may be designated "ethical biography." An ancient biography may fit this type in a general sense by conceiving of and depicting the course of a particular life as determined by a self-conscious, individual

---

107 See below on the historical type of biography.

108 See the discussion by Momigliano, *Greek Biography*, 69–71; see also Dihle, *Entstehung*, 7–8.

109 Momigliano, *Greek Biography*, 80–81.

110 See the discussion of Leo above at the beginning of this subsection, i.e., *Mark as Biography*.

111 Dihle (*Studien*, 115) assigned this work to the scientific type of biography, following Leo.

112 On the relation of Philo's lives of Abraham, Joseph, and Moses to Greek and Roman lives, see Anton Prießnig, "Die literarische Form der Patriarchenbiographien des Philon von Alexandrien," *MGWJ* 37 (1929) 143–55. On Philo's *Life of Moses* as an elementary introduction to the ideals of Judaism, see Erwin R. Goodenough, "Philo's Exposition of the Law and his De vita Mosis," *HTR* 26 (1933) 109–25, in which he shows also that the *Exposition* and the *Life of Moses* were companion pieces; idem, *By Light, Light: The Mystic Gospel of Hellenistic Judaism* (New Haven: Yale University Press, 1935) 181–98; idem, *An Introduction to Philo Judaeus* (New Haven: Yale University Press, 1940) 37–40; see also the summary of his hypothesis by Talbert, "Biographies," 1624.

113 On the literary character of this work, see Anton Prießnig, "Die literarische Form der spätantiken Philosophenromane," *ByZ* 30 (1929–30) 23–30, esp. 26–28. For an introduction, text, trans. and notes, see John Dillon and Jackson Hershbell, eds., *Iamblichus: On the Pythagorean Way of Life* (SBLTT 29; GRRS 11; Atlanta: Scholars Press, 1991).

morality. Or it may adopt a particular ethical-psychological system, such as the doctrine of the peripatetic tradition, as the theoretical framework for the account of a person's life.[114] Three parts of Aristotle's systematic doctrine are important for later biography: (1) the relation of the deeds ($\pi\rho\acute{\alpha}\xi\epsilon\iota\varsigma$) of a human being to his character ($\mathring{\eta}\vartheta o\varsigma$); this relation is discussed in the *Nicomachean Ethics*; (2) the teaching on suffering or emotion ($\pi\acute{\alpha}\vartheta o\varsigma$) in the *Rhetoric*; and (3) the teaching on ethical types, formulated in the *Nicomachean Ethics* and clarified in a practical way in Theophrastus's work entitled *Characters*, and the teaching on human forms of life, which is related to the ethical types.[115] The emphasis on character is related to the aim of this type of biography: to encourage imitation of the virtues of the subjects and avoidance of their vices. Some of the biographies of Plutarch fit this type, for example, the lives of Cato the Younger and Pompey. Both emphasize the character of the subjects, and the controlling interest is ethical, not political.[116] The Gospels certainly manifest interest in ethical issues, but the conceptual context in which they are presented is very different from that of Hellenistic ethics.

The fifth type may be called the entertaining type of biography. If Momigliano is right, this may be the oldest and originating type of biography in the Greek tradition. The aim of this kind of work was to satisfy an audience's curiosity about heroes, poets, and prominent men, such as kings and tyrants. Reading a biography of this sort was analogous to traveling in foreign lands.[117]

Momigliano argued that there is sufficient evidence to support the hypothesis that biographies of poets and wise men were written already in the fifth century BCE. The later extant lives of Homer, Aesop, and Secundus the Silent Philosopher fit this type.[118] Skylax, the Ionian sailor of the early fifth century BCE, apparently wrote a life of Heraclides, the tyrant of Mylasa, as well as an autobiographical account of his own travels and geographical explorations.[119] In the later period, some of Plutarch's lives can be placed in this category, for example, his life of Antony. This work shows little interest in the historical context of Antony's life, but focuses on the personalities of Antony and the other characters in the narrative, especially Cleopatra. There is an important ethical element, but it does not dominate the narrative throughout. Rather, the focus is on a powerful story, artistically told; it is the tragic depiction of a noble nature, cruelly undone by the man's flaws.[120] This is entertainment in the highest sense.

The sixth type is the historical biography. Lives of this type have the same aims as historiography: to give an account of an important series of events and to explain the events in terms of their causes. Plutarch's life of Caesar is an example of this type. He pays little attention to Caesar's private life and character, in order to focus on posing and answering the questions how and why Caesar came to be a tyrant.[121] Another example is Tacitus's account of the life of his father-in-law, Agricola, written around 98 CE. In this work Tacitus was critical of the

---

114 Cf. the discussion in Dihle, *Studien*, 11.

115 See ibid., 59–60.

116 See the discussion by Christopher B. R. Pelling, "Plutarch's Adaptation of His Source-Material," *JHS* 100 (1980) 127–40, esp. 135–36.

117 Momigliano, *Greek Biography*, 21–22. For a more recent assessment of the role of travel in ancient historiography and the writing of biographies, see Judith Mossman, "Travel Writing, History, and Biography," in Brian McGing and eadem, eds., *The Limits of Ancient Biography* (Swansea, Wales: Classical Press of Wales, 2006) 281–303.

118 For Greek texts of various versions of the life of Homer, see Ulrich von Wilamowitz-Moellendorff, ed., *Vitae Homeri et Hesiodi* (KlT 137; Berlin: de Gruyter, 1929); for discussion, an ET, and bibliography, see Mary R. Lefkowitz, *The Lives of the Greek Poets* (Baltimore: Johns Hopkins University Press, 1981) 12–24, 139–55. For the life of Aesop, see Ben

Edwin Perry, *Aesopica*, vol. 1: *Greek and Latin Texts* (Urbana: University of Illinois Press, 1952; reprinted New York: Arno Press, 1980). See also Lloyd W. Daly, *Aesop without Morals* (New York/London: Thomas Yoseloff, 1961). On Secundus the Silent Philosopher, see Ben Edwin Perry, *Secundus the Silent Philosopher: The Greek Life of Secundus Critically Edited and Restored So Far as Possible Together with Translations of the Greek and Oriental Versions, the Latin and Oriental Texts, and a Study of the Tradition* (APA.PM 22; Ithaca, NY: American Philological Association/ Cornell University Press, 1964).

119 Momigliano, *Greek Biography*, 28–30, 36–38.

120 See the discussion by Pelling, "Plutarch's Adaptation of His Source-Material," 138.

121 Ibid., 136–37. See also Christopher Pelling "Breaking the Bounds: Writing about Julius Caesar," in McGing and Mossman, eds., *Ancient Biography*, 255–80, esp. 266–69.

ostentatious deaths of the Stoic opponents of the principate and endeavored to show that a good man was able to contribute to the welfare of the state, even during the rule of a despot.[122] Suetonius's *Lives of the Caesars* also belongs in this category. His method of collecting, ordering, and presenting material is that of the learned grammarian and antiquarian. In his *Lives of the Caesars*, however, he moved beyond the scholarly type into the historical type, because his aim was to communicate in an orderly way all the information about a person that is worth knowing and of significance for the field in which that person had distinguished himself. Since the emperors' field of activity was Roman history, he founded a new type of historiography: the narration of the history of a period by focusing on the lives of a series of supreme political rulers in that period.[123] The historical type of biography is the one that is most similar to the Gospels. Mark, for example, apparently intended to narrate the history of the fulfillment of the divine promises; in other words, to describe in mimetic fashion the sequence of events in which the gospel of God was proclaimed and had an effect on human beings as actors in a historical process. He chose to narrate this sequence of events by telling the story of Jesus' life, because he was the primary agent of God in the unfolding of this history. Further, the focus on a single life, from the beginning of the public life of the protagonist to his death and vindication, provides a pleasing artistic and dramatic unity.[124]

The Gospel of Mark, then, has an important affinity with what I am calling the didactic type of ancient biography. It is also analogous to the historical type of ancient biography, in that the life of Jesus is told, not for its own sake, not to illustrate his character or cultural achievement, but because his life was at the center of a crucial period of history from the point of view of Christian proclamation. The historical type of biography is very close to the historical monograph, which focuses on a single person. Whether one defines Mark as a historical biography or a historical monograph depends on one's perception of where the emphasis in Mark lies: on the activity and fate of Jesus or on God's plan for the fulfillment of history in which he played a decisive role.[125]

Mark as History

As noted above, Justin and Origen referred to the Gospels in ways that associated them with historiography and claimed for them reliability on major points, if not in every detail.[126] In the context of the German Enlightenment, Hermann Samuel Reimarus and Gotthold Ephraim Lessing applied the tools of critical historiography to the Gospels, taking them as imperfect historical documents on which a reliable reconstruction of events could be based.[127] Similarly, David Friedrich Strauss understood the Gospels to be historical works that had been embellished with mythic elements; that is, the basically historical account of Jesus had been expanded with stories in which traditional Jewish and folk ideas about Jesus as the Messiah were given historylike form.[128] Theodor Zahn compared Mark with the historiography of the Old Testament, which he characterized as didactic,

---

122 See the discussion by Dihle, *Entstehung*, 27–32, 80. For a recent treatment of the political ambiguities and genre of this text, see Tim Whitmarsh, "This In-Between Book: Language, Politics and Genre in the Agricola," in McGing and Mossman, eds., *Ancient Biography*, 305–33.

123 Ibid., 64–80. See also idem, *Studien*, 116. See below the discussion of histories that focus on an individual leader.

124 Leo pointed out how often the motif of the vengeance of the gods occurs at the end of Plutarch's lives and the dramatic effect of this motif and its placement (*Biographie*, 159, 165, 183).

125 Wegener concluded that Mark is best viewed as belonging to the genre "Hellenistic biography" from a historical point of view, but as dramatic history in the tragic mode as a more helpful category for modern readers (*Cruciformed*, 30–31).

126 See the introduction to this section above.

127 See Charles H. Talbert, ed., *Reimarus: Fragments* (Philadelphia: Fortress, 1970; reprinted SPRTS; Chico, CA: Scholars Press, 1985). See also Kümmel, *New Testament*, 76–77, 89–90; Dormeyer, *Evangelium*, 26–31; Eve-Marie Becker, *Das Markus-Evangelium im Rahmen antiker Historiographie* (WUNT 194; Tübingen: Mohr Siebeck, 2006) 37–38.

128 David Friedrich Strauss, *The Life of Jesus Critically Examined* (trans. from 4th Germ. ed.; 3 vols.; London: Chapman Brothers, 1846) esp. 1:85–87. On the issue of the relation of myth and history in the history of scholarship on Mark, see Becker, *Markus-Evangelium*, 56–61.

hortatory narrative, associated by later Jews with the prophets. He contrasted anonymous biblical historiography with the Greek, in which the person of the author and the verification of sources played major roles.[129]

The view that Mark is a historical work was undercut by the argument of Karl Ludwig Schmidt that the chronological and topographical framework of the Gospels is fictional.[130] It was further undermined by William Wrede's conclusion that the messianic secret in Mark does not reflect an actual, historical development in the self-understanding or self-revelation of Jesus, but is rather a theological construct of the postresurrection period.[131] The form critics then took Strauss's approach further and argued that not only the miracle stories but the entire Synoptic tradition was shaped by the beliefs and intentions of the tradents.[132] The redaction-critical method was introduced under the assumption that the Gospels are to be understood as kerygmatic expressions of faith in Jesus Christ and not as belonging to any genre of ancient literature.[133]

Up to this point in the history of scholarship, most scholars assumed that a work should not be classified as "history" unless it represented events accurately and reliably. James M. Robinson argued that such a point of view was based on a nineteenth-century understanding of the nature of history. He suggested that newer, twentieth-century insights had led to a new understanding of history and that a reassessment of the character of the Gospel of Mark was in order. It should not be understood as immanent, objective history (the nineteenth-century view), as nonhistorical theology (as Wrede and the redaction critics had argued), or as mythology (as Strauss and the form critics had defined it in part). Rather, it could be seen from a twentieth-century point of view as existential, communal history.[134]

In spite of Robinson's manifesto, in the second half of the twentieth century two main obstacles continued to stand in the way of a serious consideration of the hypothesis that the Gospel of Mark should be understood as a type of history. Both of these are modern ideas that have colored the perception of Mark. One is the positivistic understanding of history, according to which a historical work must be reliable in the details reported and have as its primary intention the aim of communicating information.[135] The other is the idea that Mark, as an early Christian theological work, belongs to a special category of writing that expresses faith and was written for the purpose of proclamation, and thus cannot be assigned to any type of literature current at the time. A further deterrent has been the tendency to assume that ancient canons of historical writing have more in common with modern historiography than they do with Mark.

In 2006, however, Eve-Marie Becker argued, on the one hand, that the genre of Mark and the other canonical Gospels is *sui generis*.[136] On the other hand, she argued that, in terms of historiographical theory, historicity, and the history of literature, Mark can be placed in the context of ancient historiography.[137] Furthermore, Mark can be identified as the historical beginning of Christian historiography.[138] Like ancient historians, the author of Mark used and edited historical sources and

---

129 Theodor Zahn, "Der Geschichtsschreiber und sein Stoff im Neuen Testament," *ZKWL* 9 (1888) 581–96; for critical discussion, see Dormeyer, *Evangelium*, 51–52; Becker, *Markus-Evangelium*, 39–40.

130 Karl Ludwig Schmidt, *Der Rahmen der Geschichte Jesu: Literarkritische Untersuchungen zur ältesten Jesusüberlieferung* (Berlin: Trowitzsch & Sohn, 1919; reprinted Darmstadt: Wissenschaftliche Buchgesellschaft, 1964) 152.

131 William Wrede, *The Messianic Secret* (Cambridge/London: James Clarke, 1971). ET of William Wrede, *Das Messiasgeheimnis in den Evangelien: Zugleich ein Beitrag zum Verständnis des Markusevangeliums* (Göttingen: Vandenhoeck & Ruprecht, 1901; reprinted 1969).

132 Dibelius, *From Tradition to Gospel*, 12–14; Bultmann, *History*, 1–7; cf. Dormeyer, *Evangelium*, 37.

133 This position was taken by Günther Bornkamm in his article on the stilling of the storm in Matthew; see the quotation and critical discussion in Dormeyer, *Evangelium*, 114–15.

134 Robinson, *Problem of History*.

135 For a discussion of this problem from the point of view of semiotics and Paul Ricoeur's notion of "historical narration of the first and second order," see Detlev Dormeyer, *Das Neue Testament im Rahmen der antiken Literaturgeschichte: Eine Einführung* (Darmstadt: Wissenschaftliche Buchgesellschaft, 1993) 59–62; ET *The New Testament among the Writings of Antiquity* (Sheffield: Sheffield Academic Press, 1998) 68–75.

136 Becker, *Markus-Evangelium*, 50, 52.

137 Ibid., 51–52.

138 Ibid., 52, 400–1.

traditions.[139] Becker concluded that the author was neither merely a transmitter, collector, or composer of tradition nor only a theologian, in the sense of one who
reformulates and interprets tradition. Rather, the author
and his work were "pre-historiographic," in the sense
that he took up traditions and sources and conceived
and shaped them in at least an incipient historiographical way.[140]

It seems worthwhile, at this point in the discussion of
the genre of Mark, to review briefly some ancient
notions about history and some examples of ancient historical writing in order to see whether or to what extent
Mark belongs in this context. The ancient definition of
history may be inferred from a passing remark of
Aristotle:

It is clear, therefore, that for legislation books of travel
are useful, since they help us to understand the laws
of other nations, and for political deliberations, the
investigations of those who write about deeds (ὥστε
δῆλον ὅτι πρὸς μὲν τὴν νομοθεσίαν αἱ τῆς γῆς
περίοδοι χρήσιμοι (ἐντεῦθεν γὰρ λαβεῖν ἔστι
τοὺς τῶν ἐθνῶν νόμους), πρὸς δὲ τὰς πολιτικὰς
συμβουλὰς αἱ τῶν περὶ τὰς πράξεις γραφόντων
ἱστορίαι).[141]

Quintilian's observation is similar:

Now there are three forms of narrative, without counting the type used in legal cases. First, there is the ficti-
tious narrative as we get it in tragedies and poems,

which is not merely not true but has little resemblance
to truth. Secondly, there is the realistic narrative as
presented by comedies, which, though not true, has
yet a certain verisimilitude. Thirdly there is the historical narrative, which is an exposition of something
done (Et quia narrationum, excepta qua in causis
utimur, tres accepimus species, fabulam, que versatur
in tragoediis atque carminibus, non a veritate modo
sed etiam a forma veritatis remota; argumentum,
quod falsum sed vero simile comoediae fingunt; histo-
riam, in qua est gestae rei expositio).[142]

In both cases, it is probably assumed that the deeds in
question are not just any deeds, but memorable deeds
worth telling, especially glorious achievements in war
and politics. Polybius refers to a work by Aulus Postumius
Albinus as "pragmatic history" (πραγματικὴ ἱστορία),
that is, narrative and explanatory political and military
history.[143] As Charles Fornara has argued, the defining
quality of all types of ancient history (monographs, universal histories, and Greek histories or *Hellenica*) was
their direct concern with the description of *res gestae*, the
actions performed in politics, diplomacy, and war in the
far and near past.[144]

It is generally agreed that, for the Greek cultural
realm at least, Herodotus was the inventor of historical
writing. He used the methods and incorporated the
results of older genres, such as mythography, ethnography, local history, and chronography.[145] All of these
result from the collecting and reporting of data. History
emerged as a genre when Herodotus decided to describe

---

139 Ibid., 52, 401–7.

140 Ibid., 407.

141 Aristotle *Rhet.* 1.4.13 = 1360A. Text and trans. (modified) from John Henry Freese, ed., *Aristotle* (23 vols.;
LCL; Cambridge, MA: Harvard Univeristy Press;
London: Heinemann, 1982) 22:46–47. For discussion, see Fornara, *Nature of History*, 1–46, esp. 1–2.

142 Quintilian *Inst. Orat.* 2.4.2; text and trans. (modified) from H. E. Butler, ed., *The Institutio Oratoria of
Quintilian* (4 vols.; LCL; Cambridge, MA: Harvard
University Press; London: Heinemann, 1980) 1:224–
25.

143 Polybius 39.1.4; he understood his own work to
belong to the same category; cf. 1.2.8. Cf. also his
criticism of the methods and style of the historian
Phylarchus and the related remarks on the purpose

of historical writing and the methods proper to it;
Polybius 2.56. For a Greek text and ET of these passages, see William R. Paton, ed., *Polybius: The Histories* (LCL; London: Heinemann; New York: Putnam's
Sons, 1922) 1:374–81 (for 1.2.8 and 2.56); idem, *Polybius: The Histories* (1960) 6:440–41 (for 39.1.4); Paton
translates ὁ τῆς πραγματικῆς ἱστορίας τρόπος as
"the systematic treatment of history" in 1.2.8 and
πραγματικὴ ἱστορία as "a serious history" in
39.1.4. See also the discussion in Fornara, *Nature of
History*, 26 n. 47; Becker, *Markus-Evangelium*, 149–
52.

144 Fornara, *Nature of History*, 3.

145 The classic work of mythography is Hesiod's
Theogony. Hecataeus's comparative treatment of foreign customs exemplifies ethnography; see Felix

and explain a sequential development and not merely to report it. In comparison with the previously mentioned genres, history is the only one that has a mimetic quality. In other words, it is the only one that recreates events in a representational way, rather than simply reporting them or listing them. As Fornara has persuasively argued, this quality is probably due to the influence of the *Iliad*.[146] It should be noted that this characteristic reveals the similarity of ancient historical writing to epic and tragedy and makes it less like the modern positivistic ideal of historiography. The more the historian must use imagination to paint a picture of events he did not actually witness, the less similar the result is to the positivistic ideal.[147]

The fact that the Greek word for "inquiry," "research," "investigation" ($i\sigma\tau o\rho i\alpha$) became the name of a particular class of literature indicates that a certain method was the defining characteristic of the genre, namely, the interrogation of witnesses and other informed parties and the synthesis of the answers in a continuous narrative.[148] Thucydides emphasized the evaluation of the sources as to their accuracy and reliability, but this methodological aspect was more important to some historians than to others. Although the laws of evidence and obedience to truth were at least in theory mandatory in history, the adaptation of ethnography permitted the publication of the unconfirmed report of even the improbable. The nature of ethnography was $i\sigma\tau o\rho i\alpha$ in the original sense: "inquiry" into what was "worthy of relation," "marvelous," "deserving to be heard." Whether something was true or likely to be true was secondary to the fact that it was "a report" ($\lambda\delta\gamma o\varsigma$) told by an informant.[149] Even though the historian would often distance himself from such tall tales, their acceptability in historical works paved the way for the use of miraculous tales in an encomiastic, missionary, or propagandistic sense.

Tension is evident also between the emphasis on personal observation, the recording of oral reports from the participants in events, and investigative travel, on the one hand, and the likelihood of the use of written sources and the free shaping or even invention of material, on the other.[150] Once again, the ancient canons of history meticulously articulated and applied by Thucydides were not always so strictly put into practice but may have been, more often than not, literary conventions to which only lip service was paid.

The genre of history was transformed in a momentous way by the emergence of powerful personalities at the dawn of the Hellenistic age. Socrates in the realm of ideas and Alexander in the public domain especially had tremendous impact on the shape of subsequent literature.[151] The influence of historical personalities and philosophical and literary interest in personality as such led to the emergence of a new kind of history. Xenophon's use of the phrase "the deeds of Jason" ($\tau\grave{\alpha}\varsigma$ $\pi\varepsilon\rho\grave{\iota}$ $\Iota\acute{\alpha}\sigma o\nu o\varsigma$ $\pi\rho\acute{\alpha}\xi\varepsilon\iota\varsigma$) reflects a conceptualization that would eventually be expressed in a type of history, "memorable deeds," which centers on a single person.[152] Theopompus, a historian of the fourth century BCE, continued the older type of historical writing in his *Hellenica*, which is a continuation of Thucydides. But he introduced a new type with a strong biographical interest

---

Jacoby, "Hekataios," *PWRE* 14 (1912) col. 2682. Local history, or "horography" (from $\mathring{\omega}\rho o\varsigma$, "year") gave the record of a city's life year by year; on the origin and purpose of this genre, see Fornara, *Nature of History*, 16–28.

146 Fornara, *Nature of History*, 16, 29, 31–32.

147 Polybius's ideal, following Thucydides, was to report, as far as possible, what was actually said and done; he criticized Phylarchus for being too mimetic, i.e., for writing history that had too much in common with tragedy (2.56).

148 Fornara, *Nature of History*, 47–48.

149 See, e.g., Herodotus 1.23–24; 2.123, 125; 3.9; 7.152. See Fornara, *Nature of History*, 15. On the positive role of miracles in the work of Herodotus, see Thomas Harrison, *Divinity and History: The Religion*

of Herodotus (Oxford: Clarendon, 2000) 64–101. On the role of prodigies in Josephus's history of the Jewish war and in Mark, see Becker, *Markus-Evangelium*, 304–40, and on the role of healing miracles in Tacitus and in Mark, see ibid., 350–61, 382–98.

150 See the discussion of the sources of Herodotus in Van Seters, *In Search of History*, 40–47.

151 This development is traced by Leo, *Biographie*, 85, 107–9, 234, 242, 251, 317, 323. See also Fornara, *Nature of History*, 34–36.

152 Xenophon *Hell.* 6.1.19; for a Greek text and ET, see Carleton L. Brownson, ed., *Xenophon: Hellenica, Books VI & VII; Anabasis, Books I–III* (LCL; London: Heinemann; Cambridge, MA: Harvard University Press, 1950) 16–17. See also Fornara, *Nature of History*, 34.

in his universal history entitled *Philippica*, because of its focus on Philip of Macedon, who provided its unifying theme.[153] The climax of the development was the series of historical works that focused on the deeds of Philip's son, Alexander the Great. The first of these was the lost work of Callisthenes, Aristotle's nephew. It is not known whether this work was entitled *History of Greece* (*Hellenica*) or *Deeds of Alexander* (πράξεις Ἀλεξάνδρου).[154] In any case, although this work widened the subject matter of history to include Greek affairs in general and not just war and politics, it narrowed the focus to one individual. This tendency became explicit and marked in the other historical works related to the deeds of Alexander and in their successors. Fornara spoke of "a sort of biographical history."[155] Leo commented that all the historians of this time offered material for biographies on their heroes, even though they did not write biographies, and later biographers were dependent on them for much of their material.[156] Once personality had emerged as a dominant theme in the Hellenistic period, the focus remained on the individual instead of on the history of the people. Roman annalistic writing went in the same direction.[157]

We see, then, that although Greek history was typically perceived as an account of memorable deeds in politics and war, it contained a variety of other materials at its origin (Herodotus) and was later expanded to include other topics, such as cultural and religious affairs. Furthermore, it came to focus more and more on individuals, sometimes on a single person.

Unlike the Greeks, the Israelites did not reflect directly on the nature of historical writing and its methods; at least no such reflections have been preserved. For this reason, John Van Seters had to turn elsewhere for a definition in his study of the origins of biblical history.

He adopted the definition proposed by the Dutch historian J. Huizinga: "History is the intellectual form in which a civilization renders account to itself of its past."[158] This definition is too narrow to cover at least some types of Greek and Roman history, especially the universal histories, but it does seem to express the intention of Israelite historical writing rather well. Van Seters also articulated a number of criteria for identifying historical writing in ancient Israel, some of which bear repeating here: any explanation of the genre as the mere result of an accidental accumulation of tradition is inadequate; historical writing is not primarily the accurate reporting of past events, but also considers the significance of those events; historical writing is national or corporate in character; thus, a report of the deeds of the king is only biographical unless they are viewed as part of the national history.[159]

Van Seters rejected the older views that historiography in Israel flowered during the early monarchy, the prime examples being the Story of David's Rise and the Succession Story (also known as the Court History of David), and that the oldest Israelite historical writing was essentially secular or profane; and that it was only later, under the influence of prophecy, that historiography was given a clear theological stamp.[160] Van Seters has argued instead, quite persuasively, that the history of the early monarchy is the work of the Deuteronomistic historian, making his case on the basis of editorial technique and thematic unity.[161] He has also argued brilliantly that the Court History of David is not an early profane history produced by an age of enlightenment at the height of the monarchy, but is rather an antilegitimation story, added to the Deuteronomistic history to balance or even negate its stories that legitimate the royal house of David.[162]

---

153 Fornara, *Nature of History*, 34; cf. Leo, *Biographie*, 108–9; Godfrey Louis Barber, "Theopompus (3)," *OCD* 1059.

154 Fornara concluded that the title was probably *Hellenica* (*Nature of History*, 34), whereas Leo opted for πράξεις Ἀλεξάνδρου (*Biographie*, 108).

155 Fornara, *Nature of History*, 35.

156 Leo, *Biographie*, 109.

157 Ibid., 234. Leo also points out that the way in which the personality of the leading persons comes naturally into the foreground in the narration of history is perfectly exemplified already by Herodotus, especially in books 7–9, in which Xerxes dominates on the one side and Themistocles on the other (ibid., 242).

158 Quoted by Van Seters, *In Search of History*, 1.

159 Ibid., 4–5.

160 See the discussion of previous scholarship in ibid., 209–48, esp. 209–20.

161 Ibid., 249–70.

162 Ibid., 277–91.

Van Seters's conclusions suggest that historical writing did not evolve from fairy tales or folktales through legends and novellas to objective history. Rather, historical writing emerged in Israel, probably in the mid-sixth century BCE, as an attempt to record and interpret in theological terms the experience of the people from Moses through the monarchy to the exile. The reconstructed editorial process is analogous to that employed by the author of Mark: a mixture of free composition and the creation of redactional links between independent blocks of material of different types and genres, some of which already existed in written form.[163] A major task of the Deuteronomistic history appears to have been the combination and reconciliation of the northern Mosaic traditions, reflected in Deuteronomy, with the royal ideology of the house of David in the south.[164] The Gospel of Mark seems to have had an analogous aim: to combine the traditions about Jesus preserved in apophthegmata, miracle stories, sayings, and parables with the passion kerygma, the proclamation of the death and resurrection of Jesus as saving events.[165] The assumption that the Jesus-traditions circulated primarily in Palestine and the passion kerygma primarily in the Diaspora is an oversimplification, so the geographical aspect of the analogy does not hold. Nevertheless, both the Deuteronomistic historian and Mark attempted to synthesize diverse traditions and theological perspectives.

One type of material included in the Deuteronomistic history is the prophetic legend.[166] Van Seters has shown that the Elijah stories are well integrated into the chronological framework of the Deuteronomistic history and that they bear the stamp of the historian's concerns. The Elisha stories, on the other hand, with the exception of 2 Kings 3 and 9–10, have not been well integrated into the larger work and show no signs of the historian's editing. Van Seters inclined to the conclusion that the collection of stories about Elisha was added to the Deuteronomistic history at a later stage, although he admits that it could have existed as a separate literary work known to the historian. The clear literary dependence of some of the stories about Elijah on certain of those about Elisha, which both Van Seters and Alexander Rofé have noted, supports the latter conclusion.[167] It may even be the case that the Elisha collection was simply incorporated into the Deuteronomistic history and that the editorial work was focused on the Elijah stories and on 2 Kings 3, 9–10. In any case, Van Seters notes that the inclusion of such uncritical tales in a history is not surprising for antiquity, since Herodotus's work contains many similar stories.[168]

Although some of these legends express a biographical interest in the prophet, they have been edited so that the prophet appears not only, or not even primarily, as a wonder-worker, but as the medium of the divine oracle, as the divine messenger. In this way, the stories and the prophets they speak of have been integrated into the national history. Similar legends are recorded concerning Moses.

The history of the composition of the Pentateuch and the Former Prophets was, of course, unknown to the author of Mark, but the hypotheses that we as modern readers hold about these matters have an impact on how

163 Ibid., 258.
164 Ibid., 360.
165 Cf. the argument of Talbert, following Paul J. Achtemeier, that the narrative framework was employed by Mark in order to give a controlling context for the interpretation of individual Jesus-traditions; Talbert, "Once Again: Gospel Genre," in Mary Gerhart and James G. Williams, eds., *Genre, Narrativity, and Theology*, Semeia 43 (1988) 63–64.
166 Alexander Rofé called them "prophetical stories" or "prophetical narratives" and divided them into twelve distinct genres (*The Prophetical Stories: The Narratives about the Prophets in the Hebrew Bible, Their Literary Types and History* [Publications of the Perry Foundation for Biblical Research in the Hebrew University of Jerusalem; Jerusalem: Magnes, 1988; 1st Heb. ed. 1982; rev. Heb. ed. 1986]). This book is an expansion of two earlier essays: Rofé, "The Classification of the Prophetical Stories," *JBL* 89 (1970) 427–40; idem, "Classes in the Prophetical Stories: Didactic Legenda and Parable," in G. W. Anderson et al., eds., *Studies on Prophecy: A Collection of Twelve Papers* (VTSup 26; Leiden: Brill, 1974) 143–64; see also the summary of these essays in Van Seters, *In Search of History*, 303–4.
167 On the probable dependence of the story about Elijah's sustenance at Zarephath by a widow (1 Kgs 17:8-24) on the parallel tale of Elisha's multiplication of a widow's oil (2 Kgs 4:1-7, 18-37), see Rofé, *Prophetical Stories*, 132–35; see also idem, "Classes in the Prophetical Stories," 148–50.
168 Van Seters, *In Search of History*, 305–6.

we view the end-products and how we imagine that Mark viewed them. If the biographical traditions about Moses, Samuel, Elijah, and Elisha have been thoroughly integrated into the national history, so that they appear not so much as personalities in their own right but as successive mediators between the deity and the people, it may well be that this way of portraying the prophets served as a model for Mark's presentation of Jesus. From this point of view, Mark presented Jesus as the last and the greatest of these mediators.

The presence of prophetic legends in biblical history and of improbable λόγοι ("reports" or "accounts") in Herodotus settles the question whether the miraculous and the divine may play a role in ancient historical writing. As noted earlier, Herodotus included such materials under the rubric of ethnography, at times pointing out contradictions and distancing himself from improbable reports, but at other times reporting remarkable events without questioning them.[169] The biblical historian included the prophetic legends to present the prophets as divine messengers and to make theological and didactic points.[170] The question remains, however, whether such elements are peripheral to the real business of historical writing, presented for secondary purposes of entertainment or propaganda. From this point of view, the primary task of the historian is to describe and explain events in a human context. Hermann Gunkel's ideal was the alleged "profane" or "secular" history of the early monarchy. Such history told what really happened and therefore excluded miracles, direct appearances, and physical intervention by the deity. But Gunkel did not draw the conclusion that profane or secular history excluded God altogether. Rather, divine power may be discerned indirectly in historical works worthy of the name.[171]

It seems useful to distinguish two main ways in which historical events and developments were related to divine power in antiquity. The older of the two involves appearances of deities and their direct intervention in human affairs. This type is well represented by the *Iliad* and the *Odyssey*. Later Greeks of course did not consider the Homeric epics to be examples of historical writing, but they were convinced that these works preserved the memory of real individuals and actual events.[172] Related to this type is the notion that the external, visible aspect of historical events is merely a veil, an outward form, in which the act of a deity realized itself. This idea is expressed in many texts from the ancient Near East that have a wide range of dates and belong to various literary genres: historical texts, hymns, prayers, and rituals.[173] Military conquest is interpreted in terms of the god(s) delivering a city into the hand of the king, a motif that occurs in both extrabiblical and biblical texts, for example, Josh 2:24.[174] Political and military decisions made by human beings are sometimes attributed to what seems to be the direct influence of the deity, as in 2 Sam 17:14. In contrast to the Court History, in the Story of David's Rise the author (the Deuteronomistic historian) frequently asserts that Yahweh is with David and that David constantly receives guidance for all his military and political actions.[175]

Certain aspects of Mark reflect this way of showing the influence of divine power on events. The splitting of the heavens in 1:10 and the cloud in 9:7 signify the self-revelation or presence of God. The Spirit of God "appears" as a dove that descends upon Jesus in 1:10. The voice from heaven that addresses or speaks of Jesus as "my beloved son" in 1:11 and 9:7 is a further manifestation of God. The events surrounding the baptism of Jesus in 1:9-11 constitute Jesus' call or installation as an agent of God, in which the endowment with the Spirit has both prophetic and messianic connotations. But

---

169 He tells the story of Arion's rescue by a dolphin, e.g., without overt skepticism (Herodotus 1.23–24).

170 On the theological and didactic emphases of the Deuteronomistic editorial incorporation of the Elijah stories, see Van Seters, *In Search of History*, 305–6.

171 See the discussion in ibid., 211–12, pointing out that Gunkel found such indirect discernment of divine causation both in parts of the OT and in Herodotus.

172 Fornara, *Nature of History*, 5.

173 See Bertil Albrektson, *History and the Gods: An Essay on the Idea of Historical Events as Divine Manifestations in the Ancient Near East and in Israel* (ConBOT 1; Lund: CWK Gleerup, 1967) esp. 28, 34. The extrabiblical examples are from Mesopotamia and the Hittite empire.

174 Ibid., 38–39.

175 Van Seters, *In Search of History*, 284; the Lord is said to be with David in 1 Sam 16:18; 18:12, 14, 28; 20:13; 2 Sam 5:10. The Lord's guidance of David is mentioned in 1 Sam 22:5, 9-15; 23:1-5, 9-13; 30:7-8; 2 Sam 2:1-2; 5:10, 12, 19, 23-25.

from this point onward, Jesus, unlike David in the Story of David's Rise, acts independently. His exorcisms, healings, and authoritative teaching are made possible, to be sure, by his endowment with the Spirit, but this endowment has become a permanent characteristic, as in the stories about Elijah and Elisha. Jesus does not need to inquire of the Lord, as David did, but is able to predict the future on his own. The divine voice of Mark 9:7 legitimates Jesus and interprets him for the three disciples present in the narrative setting and for the audience of Mark; it does not provide power, information, or guidance for Jesus himself.

The difference between the first and second type may be illustrated by contrasting the *Iliad* and Herodotus. Homer stated his theme, Achilles' anger, and asked which of the gods was responsible for the quarrel. Herodotus dispensed with the regular intervention of the Olympian gods in human affairs and usually explained events in terms of human motivations and reactions. Nevertheless, divine agency is always implicitly at work and shows itself to be the most important causal agency in his history, when Xerxes and Artabanus are persuaded by repeated dream-visions that the Persian invasion of Greece is divinely ordained.[176] A pale reflection of this "theological" view of history is present in the universal history of Polybius (1.4). It takes the form of the conclusion that Fortune ($T\acute{v}\chi\eta$) had determined the course of events through which Rome rose to a dominant role in the world. There is a certain tension between the preface, in which Polybius reflected generally on the rise of Rome, and the detailed narrative of the related events. In the preface, he attributed the rise of Rome to a real power directing events. This perspective leads to the attribution of greater single-mindedness to the Romans in their imperial expansion and to the perception of a greater inevitability in the course of events than the detailed description warrants.[177] His didactic aim is also

apparent: Fortune favored the Romans because of their merit.[178] The discernment of the hand of Fortune in the events is after the fact and does not determine how the historian shapes events.[179]

In Mark the divine plan is manifest in Scripture and in the predictions of the events of the passion which "must" ($\delta\epsilon\hat{\iota}$) take place.[180] Mark is more like Herodotus than Polybius in this regard. The perception of the influence of the divine plan does determine to a considerable degree the shaping of events. The audience of Jesus in the narrative, friend and foe alike, are prevented from understanding his teaching and his deeds. Whereas they should have evoked repentance and trust, instead they led to violent opposition and abandonment. The divine intervention in history is predicted in parabolic form in the parable of the wicked tenants (12:1-9) and in prophetic form in the apocalyptic discourse of Jesus (13:5-37).

With regard to the relation between historical events and divine power, Mark differs from Homer and the editorial comments of the Deuteronomistic historian about David in minimizing the role of God as a character in the narrative, describing very few direct divine interventions (primarily the descent of the Spirit of God and the resurrection, which is reported but not narrated), and in portraying Jesus as acting independently, rather than directly guided by God. In the depiction of Jesus as an independent miracle-worker, Mark is similar to the folktales about Elijah and Elisha incorporated into the Deuteronomistic history. Like Herodotus, Mark focuses on human interaction and interprets events as the results of this interaction. But like Herodotus and the Deuteronomistic historian, Mark places this human interaction in the context of a divine plan that underlies and indirectly controls events.

In previous scholarship, three main objections have been raised to the hypothesis that the Gospel of Mark

---

176 See the excellent discussion by Fornara, *Nature of History*, 77–79. See also Hermann Strasburger, *Die Wesensbestimmung der Geschichte durch die antike Geschichtsschreibung* (SbWGF 5.3 [1966]; 3rd ed.; Wiesbaden: Steiner, 1975) 70–71; Thomas Harrison, *Divinity and History: The Religion of Herodotus* (Oxford: Clarendon, 2000) esp. chaps. 2–5.

177 On the Romans' alleged single-minded scheme of universal aggression, see Polybius 1.3.6–10.

178 The merit of the Romans is hinted at in the preface;

Polybius 1.1.5–6; 1.2.7–8. It is explicitly discussed in book 6. See the discussion by Frank William Walbank, "Polybius (1)," *OCD* 853–54; idem, *A Historical Commentary on Polybius*, vol. 1: *Commentary on Books I–VI* (Oxford: Clarendon, 1957) 16–26.

179 Fornara, *Nature of History*, 81–82. On Fortune ($T\acute{v}\chi\eta$) as a "meta-historische Deutungskategorie" in Polybius, see Becker, *Markus-Evangelium*, 151–52.

180 See the commentary below on 8:31.

belongs to the category of history. The first concerns literary style: Mark is an example of folk or practical literature, whereas history is a type of high literature or literature properly speaking. It is striking that the author of Mark wrote anonymously; that is, he did not introduce himself, his aims, and his methods in a formal preface as Herodotus, Thucydides, and other historians did. This fact, however, is not an argument that Mark is nonliterary or preliterary, since he was probably following the precedent of the biblical historians. The Deuteronomistic historian, for example, apparently did not present himself, his aims, and his methods in a formal preface. The style of Mark is paratactic or episodic; that is, the work is composed of many blocks of independent material of different genres that are unified by being placed in a rough overall chronological framework. They are linked by the development of a few major themes; ring composition; the coupling of thought and action or word and deed through the pattern of advice and its execution or of oracle, dream, or prediction and its fulfillment; repetition of similar events, speeches, phrases, or formulaic expressions; analogies and contrasts between major figures; and the use of editorial comment to introduce or sum up the theme of a unit. This style is also characteristic of Herodotus's work and of the historical books of the Old Testament.[181] The closely related "dramatic episodic style" was used by a number of later historians, such as Cleitarchus, Duris, Curtius Rufus, and Livy.[182] Thus, the style of Mark is appropriate for an ancient historical work.

The second argument against understanding Mark as a work of history is that history is concerned with the accurate transmission of historical information, whereas Mark's concern is proclamatory and the work is full of miraculous events. As pointed out above, we must be careful not to attribute aspects of the modern, positivistic ideal of historiography to ancient writers and readers. Certain scientific or scholastic genres apparently did originate and flourish on the assumption that unvarnished facts were of intrinsic importance. History, however, was a mimetic (representational) and explanatory genre. The challenge of depicting events that the author did not see personally required the exercise of the imagination and a certain degree of invention. The resources used in the task of explanation were not always limited to the empirically verifiable kind. As we have seen, the presence of the miraculous in historical works was legitimated by ethnography. The question of the attitude of the author of Mark to such elements is difficult to discern. It may be that he believed that the mighty deeds of Jesus were actual historical events. Alternatively, he may have seen them as figurative expressions of the role and power of Jesus. In any case, their presence does not disqualify the Gospel of Mark as a work of history.

The third argument concerns scope and subject. Works of history treat military and political affairs at length, in several volumes or more. We have already discussed the broadening of the scope of history in the Hellenistic period to include human affairs besides the military and the political. Cultural and religious subjects began to be included, as well as information about outstanding individuals. Some histories focused on a single individual. Besides Alexander the Great, Agathocles of Syracuse, Attalus of Pergamum, Ptolemy IV Philopator, Antiochus the Great, Hannibal, Tigranes of Armenia, and Pompey were honored in this way.[183] In terms of length, histories with broad themes, especially universal histories, did tend to be much longer than Mark. More limited subjects, however, were treated in shorter works, which are often designated historical monographs.[184]

---

181 Van Seters, *In Search of History*, 31–40, 258, 312, 320–21, 358.

182 Eckhard Plümacher, *Lukas als hellenistischer Schriftsteller: Studien zur Apostelgeschichte* (StUNT 9; Göttingen: Vandenhoeck & Ruprecht, 1972) 111–36; Plümacher also argues that the same style is employed in Acts (ibid., 80–111). See also the discussion by Cilliers Breytenbach of Mark's episodic style in relation to Aristotle's *Poetics* and modern narratological theory ("Das Markusevangelium als episodische Erzählung: Mit Überlegungen zum 'Aufbau' des zweiten Evangeliums," in Ferdinand Hahn, ed., *Der Erzähler des Evangeliums: Methodische Neuansätze in der Markusforschung* [SBS 118/119; Stuttgart: Katholisches Bibelwerk, 1985] 137–69, esp. 157–62).

183 Fornara, *Nature of History*, 35–36; see also Leo, *Biographie*, 108.

184 On the historical monograph in relation to the work of Sallustius Crispus, see Becker, *Markus-Evangelium*, 213, 219–21.

Mark may thus be seen as a historical monograph that focuses on the deeds of Jesus.

All this is not to say that Mark can be entirely explained by analogy with historical works. The way in which the various literary influences were transformed into something new and distinctive will be treated below in the concluding section.

Mark as an Eschatological Historical Monograph

With the Gospel of Mark, a new type of writing emerged, but if it had been entirely new, it could not have been understood. Thus, it is important to determine which types of works it is most like, how it differs from those, and how it attempts to create its effect.[185] Although Mark lacks a formal preface in which the author introduces himself, his methods, and his subject matter, a good deal may be learned from the opening of the work. The first word, "beginning" (ἀρχή) reflects the historian's decision about the proper starting point for the descriptive and explanatory narrative.[186] The next phrase indicates that it is with the beginning "of the good news" or "of the gospel" (τοῦ εὐαγγελίου) that the narration commences. As we saw above, the good news is that the divine plan, foretold in Scripture, is about to be fulfilled. The citation of the book of Isaiah (and implicitly of Malachi and Exodus) that follows in 1:2-3 supports this interpretation. The fulfillment of Scripture alluded to here should not be taken as an isolated case in which a specific scriptural motif or even a few related passages are fulfilled in a single event, namely, the appearance and activity of John the Baptist. Rather, this is only the first in a sequence of events that constitute the fulfillment of the divine plan. The meaning of this fulfillment, as noted above, is summarized in 1:14-15 and focuses on the kingdom of God. The narrative of Mark as a whole suggests that the kingship of God on earth is to be realized in his Son Jesus (1:11) in an anticipatory way and later in a definitive way in his role as the heavenly Son of Man (8:38; 13:24-27; 14:62).

The activity of Jesus in Mark is modeled on that of the leaders of Israel in the biblical narrative: Moses as teacher and interpreter of the law, Elijah and Elisha as wonder-working prophets, and David as anointed king, although Mark's Jesus is like David only in a mysterious and ironic way.[187] Jesus resumes and fulfills the work of the earlier agents of God. But Van Seters is quite right in pointing out that there is no eschatology in the Israelite histories.[188] Mark, on the other hand, does imply that there is a divine plan in history that unfolds in stages. First, John the Baptist appears, proclaims his message of repentance and performs his preparatory baptism (1:4-8). Then Jesus proclaims the good news of the kingdom of God and makes it present in his teaching, meal fellowship, and mighty deeds (1:14-15, 22; 2:19; 3:23-27; 4:11; 7:37). But the good news, according to Mark, also includes the death of Jesus, as his comment in 14:9 on his anointing by the anonymous woman in the house of Simon makes clear: "Truly I say to you, wherever the good news is proclaimed in the whole world, what this woman has done will be made known also in memory of

---

185 Michael E. Vines, following Mikhail Bakhtin, argued that the most appropriate context for the interpretation of Mark is "the authorially determined ideological perspective that dictated its creation" (Vines, *The Problem of Markan Genre: The Gospel of Mark and the Jewish Novel* [SBLAB 3; Leiden/Boston: Brill, 2002] 66). He concludes that the Jewish novels are works that are ideologically similar to Mark because they all share the "use of a realistic-apocalyptic chronotope" (ibid., 159). The apocalyptic perspective, however, is much more characteristic of Mark than it is of Daniel 1–6, Tobit, Esther, Judith, and *Joseph and Aseneth*.

186 Compare Polybius 1.3.5: "And this is my reason for beginning where I do" (διὸ καὶ τὴν ἀρχὴν τῆς αὐτῶν πραγματείας ἀπὸ τούτων πεποιήμεθα τῶν καιρῶν); text and trans. from Paton, *Polybius*,

1.8–9. On the polyvalence of the term "beginning" (ἀρχή) in Mark 1:1 and Luke 1:2, see Becker, *Markus-Evangelium*, 111–12, 120.

187 See esp. 10:47-48; 11:9-10; 12:35-37; 15:16-20, 26. The Markan Jesus is like David also in his suffering, since David was understood to be the author of the Psalms, including the Psalms of individual lament; see Stephen P. Ahearne-Kroll, "The Suffering of David and the Suffering of Jesus: The Use of Four Psalms of Individual Lament in the Passion Narrative of the Gospel of Mark" (2 vols.; Ph.D. diss., University of Chicago, 2005).

188 Van Seters, *In Search of History*, 8–9.

her" (ἀμὴν δὲ λέγω ὑμῖν, ὅπου ἐὰν κηρυχϑῇ τὸ εὐαγγέλιον εἰς ὅλον τὸν κόσμον, καὶ ὃ ἐποίησεν αὔτη λαληϑήσεται εἰς μνημόσυνον αὐτῆς). This saying links the "good news" with the preparation of Jesus' body for burial, and thus indirectly with his death and resurrection.

The discourse of Jesus in chap. 13 also makes clear that a divine plan is in the process of unfolding: the "beginning of the birth-pains" (ἀρχὴ ὠδίνων) of 13:8 will be followed by the "tribulation" (ϑλῖψις) of 13:19, which in turn will be succeeded by the appearance of the Son of Man (13:24-27). But before "the end" (τὸ τέλος), mentioned in 13:7, the good news must "first" (πρῶτον) be proclaimed to all nations (13:10). Mark's notion of an eschatological fulfillment, of course, has its origin in the prophetic books of the Old Testament or Jewish Bible. His overall conception of history, however, with its notion of a fixed divine plan (8:31; 13:7, 20; 14:36, 49) and its incipient periodization (see the discussion above of the sequence of eschatological events) is due to the influence of apocalyptic tradition and literature. This debt will be traced in detail in the commentary below. From the point of view of its Jewish heritage, Mark may be seen as an eschatological and apocalyptic counterpoint to the biblical foundational histories. It continues Israelite and Jewish ethnic sacred history and illustrates the fulfillment of the universalist tendency in Israelite and Jewish literature through the extension of the revitalization movement begun by John and Jesus to the Gentiles.

From the point of view of its Hellenistic context, the Gospel of Mark may be seen as a historical monograph that focuses on the activity of a leading individual. He is the Jewish messiah, a royal figure whose kingship has been reinterpreted, so that the military aspect is removed and the usual political context is transcended. The "memorable deeds" (πράξεις) of Jesus include his authoritative teaching, the benefactions accomplished by his wonder-working, and his effective death.[189]

Since the history narrated by Mark coincides in large part with the life of Jesus, it is similar to the historical type of biography. The Gospel of Mark is similar to Plutarch's life of Caesar, for example, in the focus on a sequence of historical events that coincide to a great degree with the life of an individual. In *Caesar*, the narrative explains how Caesar became a tyrant, why he was loved by some and hated by others and why he was killed. Mark's narrative explains and defines the identity of Jesus, in what sense he is the Messiah, how he attracted a great following, and why he was killed. In both narratives there is an emphasis on prodigies connected with the death and the vindication of the subject after death. The style of *Caesar*, however, is much less episodic than that of Mark. Further, Plutarch includes more explicit commentary on Caesar's character and personality, a discursive summary of his achievements in warfare and generalizaing comments on his health, personal habits, austerity, and ambition.[190] Mark includes nothing of this sort about Jesus.

Finally, the presentation of Jesus as a teacher and interpreter of the law and the frequent use of illustrative anecdotes results in a similarity between the Gospel of Mark and certain lives of philosophers, such as Lucian's *Demonax*.[191] As with Plutarch's *Caesar*, however, the biographical interest is stronger than that in Mark and is manifest in the generalizing summary of Demonax's life with explicit commentary on his way of life and relationships (*Demonax* 1–11). The biographical focus is also clear in the brief epilogue to the work (67), in which the author states that the few things he has recorded are enough to enable the readers to infer "what sort of man he was" (ὁποῖος ἐκεῖνος ἀνὴρ ἐγένετο). Mark's interest was not so much in what sort of man Jesus was, in general, as it was in what sort of messiah, prophet, or divine mediator he was. But, like Lucian, he was interested also in the correspondence between Jesus' way of life and teaching and how it ought to be put into practice by his followers.

---

189 See the section of this introduction on the *Interpretation of Jesus* below.
190 Plutarch *Caesar* 5.5; 15.1–5; 17.2–11; 58.4–10.
191 On the similarities and differences between Lucian's *Demonax* and the Gospel of Mark, see Hubert Cancik, "Bios und Logos: Formengeschichtliche Untersuchungen zu Lukians 'Demonax,'" in idem, *Markus-Philologie*, 115–30; see also idem, "Die Gattung Evangelium: Das Evangelium des Markus im Rahmen der antiken Historiographie," in ibid., 85–113.

It is preferable to speak of the "interpretation of Jesus" in Mark, rather than the "Christology" of Mark, because systematic, philosophical reflection on the nature of Christ had not yet begun in the movement carried on by the followers of Jesus. In composing his narrative, the author of Mark made use of traditions that already expressed an implicit interpretation of the person and activity of Jesus. He affirmed all of these by incorporating them into his narrative, even though, to a modern reader, there seem to be tensions among them. He highlighted some traditions by including a large number of examples—for example, miracle stories and didactic anecdotes—and others by placing them at prominent points in the narrative, for example, the epithets χριστός ("messiah" or "Christ") in 1:1 and "son of God" (υἱὸς θεοῦ) in 15:39. The result is a complex portrayal of Jesus, multifaceted and somewhat ambiguous. Certain epithets and narrative accounts would evoke one set of associations and responses from the point of view of Jewish scripture and tradition, but another set from the point of view of Greek literature and tradition. In the sections that follow, this complex portrayal will be approached from several perspectives.

a. Jesus as Prophet

Israelite prophecy declined and then ceased sometime after the Babylonian exile.[1] But during the Second Temple period and later the belief that prophecy was a thing of the past was combined with the expectation that the end of days and the coming of redemption would be accompanied by the return of prophecy. The account of the rededication of the temple under Judas Maccabeus states that the stones of the defiled altar were stored until a prophet came to say what should be done with them. This statement reflects the attitude that prophecy belongs to the past and the future, but not to the present.[2] Certain rabbinic traditions associated the hoped-for rebuilding of the (third) temple with the return of the holy spirit, that is, of prophecy.[3] These passages suggest that the evidence for prophetic phenomena supplied by the Dead Sea Scrolls, Josephus, and the New Testament should not be taken as supporting the hypothesis that prophecy had not died out, but rather as evidence for the revival of prophecy toward the end of the Second Temple period among those who believed that the end of days was near.

The community associated with the Dead Sea Scrolls expected an eschatological prophet, as well as a Messiah of Aaron and a Messiah of Israel; that is, they looked forward to the appearance of a prophetic, a priestly, and a royal messiah.[4] The expectation of an eschatological prophet was apparently based on Deut 18:18-19.[5] Further light on the latter expectation is thrown by a fragmentary, poetic text discovered in Cave 4 that incorporates elements of Psalm 146 and Isa 61:1.[6] Fragment 2, col. 2, reads as follows:

> [the hea]vens and the earth will listen to His Messiah, and none therein will stray from the commandments of the holy ones.
> Seekers of the Lord, strengthen yourselves in His service!
> All you hopeful in (your) heart, will you not find the Lord in this?
> For the Lord will consider the pious (ḥasidim) and call the righteous by name.
> Over the poor His spirit will hover and will renew the faithful with His power.

1   This scholarly consensus was defended recently in a persuasive manner against recent challengers by Benjamin D. Sommer, "Did Prophecy Cease? Evaluating a Reevaluation," *JBL* 115 (1996) 31–47.

2   1 Macc 4:46; see also 14:41 and Sommer, "Did Prophecy Cease?" 37 and n. 25.

3   *Tanḥuma Běhaʿălōteka* 6 (cited by Sommer, "Did Prophecy Cease?" 36) and *Num. Rab.* 15:10 on the return of the holy spirit. Because of the association of the holy spirit with prophecy, *b. Sanh.* 93a-b implies that the Messiah will have the gift of prophecy (so Sommer).

4   1QS 9:10-11; John J. Collins, *The Scepter and the Star: The Messiahs of the Dead Sea Scrolls and Other Ancient Literature* (New York: Doubleday, 1995) 74–95, 116–22.

5   4QTestim 1–8. Mal 3:1, 23-24 MT (3:1; 4:5 RSV) may also have played a role.

6   Preliminary publications have been issued by Émile Puech, "Une apocalypse messianique (4Q521)," *RevQ* 15 (1992) 475–522, and Geza Vermes, "Qumran Forum Miscellanea," *JJS* 43 (1992) 303–4. For discussion see Collins, *Scepter and the Star*, 117–22. See now the official publication by Émile Puech,

And He will glorify the pious on the throne of the
eternal Kingdom,
He who liberates the captives, restores sight to the
blind, straightens the b[ent] (Ps. 146:7-8).
And f[or]ever I will clea[ve to the h]opeful and in His
mercy . . .
And the fr[uit . . .] will not be delayed for anyone
And the Lord will accomplish glorious things which
have never been as [He . . .]
For He will heal the wounded, and revive the dead
and bring good news to the poor (Isa 61:1).
. . . He will lead the uprooted and make the hungry
rich . . .[7]

In Isa 61:1, the speaker is a prophet who is sent by God
to bring good news. The allusion to a messiah or
anointed one at the beginning of this fragment, combined with the allusion to the prophet in Isa 61:1, who
also describes himself as anointed, suggests that the
eschatological deeds narrated in the poem will be accomplished by God through the eschatological prophet or
the prophetic messiah.[8] This hypothesis is supported by
the fact that the opening statement, "[the hea]vens and
the earth will listen to His Messiah," is reminiscent of Elijah's control over the heavens, manifested in his power to
prevent and to cause rain (1 Kgs 17–18; cf. Sir 48:3).
Thus, in his control over the heavens and the earth, the
eschatological prophet recapitulates the work and powers
of Moses and Elijah (cf. Rev 11:6).

Josephus summarized the prophetic movements of his
time as follows:

Deceivers and imposters, under the pretence of divine
inspiration fostering revolutionary changes, they persuaded the multitude to act like madmen, and led
them out into the desert under the belief that God
would there give them tokens of deliverance (πλάνοι
γὰρ ἄνθρωποι καὶ ἀπατεῶνες, (ὑπὸ) προσχήματι
θειασμοῦ νεωτερισμοὺς καὶ μεταβολὰς πραγμα-
τευόμενοι, δαιμονᾶν τὸ πλῆθος ἔπειθον καὶ προ-
ῆγον εἰς τὴν ἐρημίαν, ὡς ἐκεῖ τοῦ θεοῦ δείξοντος
αὐτοῖς σημεῖα ἐλευθερίας). (Josephus Bell. 2.13.4
§259)[9]

When one reads between the lines and compensates for
the polemic of Josephus, this passage provides evidence
for the widespread belief in the first century CE that a
divine intervention was about to occur, analogous to the
exodus and gift of the land described in the foundational
sacred history. One of the figures discussed by Josephus
was Theudas, who claimed to be and was recognized as a
prophet by many of the Jews around 45 CE. Josephus says
that he led his followers to the Jordan River and said that
at his command, the river would part and allow them an
easy crossing (Ant. 20.5.1 §97–99).[10] This claim evokes
the memory and mighty deeds of Moses, through whom
the parting of the Red Sea occurred (Exodus 14), and
especially Joshua, under whose leadership the Jordan
River was parted so that the people of Israel could cross
over (Joshua 3). Elijah and Elisha were also said to have
parted the waters of the Jordan.[11] By the first century CE,
all of these leaders could be numbered among the
prophets.[12] The leader whom Josephus calls "the

Qumrân Grotte 4, vol. 18, *Textes Hébreux (4Q521–
4Q528, 4Q576–4Q579)* (DJD 25; Oxford: Clarendon,
1998) 1–38.

7 Trans. (slightly modified) from Geza Vermes, *The
Complete Dead Sea Scrolls in English* (London: Allen
Lane/Penguin Press, 1997) 412–13.

8 The prophets are called "anointed ones" in CD 2:12;
6:1; and 1QM 11:7; see Collins, *Scepter and the Star*,
118. Frans Neirynck has argued that the text implies
that the eschatological deeds are works of the Lord,
with no mediator ("Q 6,20b-21; 7,22 and Isaiah 61,"
in Christopher M. Tuckett, ed., *The Scriptures in the
Gospels* [BEThL 131; Leuven: Leuven University
Press/Peeters, 1997] 27–64, esp. 56–58).

9 Text and trans. from Henry St. J. Thackeray, Ralph
Marcus, Allen Wikgren, and Louis Feldman, *Josephus*

(9 vols.; LCL; Cambridge, MA: Harvard University
Press; London: Heinemann, 1926–66) 2:424–25. For
a recent discussion of these figures, see Rebecca
Gray, *Prophetic Figures in Late Second Temple Judaism:
The Evidence from Josephus* (New York/Oxford:
Oxford University Press, 1993) 112–44.

10 See the discussion in Richard A. Horsley and John
S. Hanson, *Bandits, Prophets and Messiahs: Popular
Movements in the Time of Jesus* (Minneapolis: Winston,
1985) 164–67.

11 Elijah in 2 Kgs 2:6-8 and Elisha in 2:13-14.

12 Joshua is described as "the successor of Moses in the
prophetic office" (διάδοχος Μωυσῆ ἐν προφη-
τείαις) in Sir 46:1 LXX.

Egyptian false prophet" evidently presented himself as a new Joshua by claiming that at his command the walls of Jerusalem would fall down (*Ant.* 20.8.6 §170).[13]

Josephus's account of John the Baptist is positive; he neither calls him a false prophet nor recognizes him as a genuine prophet (*Ant.* 18.5.2 §116–19). His dress, activity, and message, however, clearly express a prophetic role.[14] The Gospels indicate that John was widely recognized as a prophet (Mark 11:32; Matt 14:5). Like the classical prophets of Israel, he indicted the people for their sins and called for repentance under the threat of divine punishment. The eschatological character of the impending judgment, however, is heightened in comparison with the canonical prophetic books.[15]

Another figure mentioned by Josephus fits the social role of prophet, even though Josephus does not use the term. As with John the Baptist, Josephus does not group this figure with the false prophets, but implies that he was divinely inspired, since his oracular pronouncements were indeed fulfilled. The man in question is one Jesus, son of Ananias (*Bell.* 6.5.3 §300–9). Four years before the first Jewish war with Rome broke out, he went to Jerusalem for the Feast of Booths and, standing in the temple, began to cry out, "A voice from the east, a voice from the west, a voice from the four winds; a voice against Jerusalem and the sanctuary, a voice against the bridegroom and the bride, a voice against all the people" (ibid., §301).[16] That Josephus regarded this man as directed by God is indicated not only by the account of the fulfillment of this prophecy but also by his comment that follows:

Reflecting on these things one will find that God has a care for human beings, and by all kinds of premonitory signs shows His people the way of salvation, while they owe their destruction to folly and calamities of their own choosing (Ταῦτά τις ἐννοῶν εὑρήσει τὸν μὲν θεὸν ἀνθρώπων κηδόμενον καὶ παντοίως προσημαίνοντα τῷ σφετέρῳ γένει τὰ σωτήρια, τοὺς δ᾽ ὑπ᾽ ἀνοίας καὶ κακῶν αὐθαιρέτων ἀπολλυμένους). (ibid., §309)[17]

Although the Gospel of Mark certainly presents Jesus as more than a prophet, his portrayal includes a number of distinctly prophetic characteristics. The endowment with the Spirit in Mark 1:10 has both prophetic and messianic connotations.[18] In the story about how Elisha succeeded Elijah, endowment with the spirit signifies installation into the prophetic office (2 Kgs 2:9, 15; cf. 1 Kgs 19:16). A similar idea is expressed in Isa 42:1, a passage to which the divine voice in Mark 1:11 alludes. In the former passage, God speaks about the servant as God's chosen, in whom God takes delight; God then says, "I have put my spirit upon him" (ἔδωκα τὸ πνεῦμά μου ἐπ᾽ αὐτόν).[19] It is likely that the servant was conceived originally as an anonymous prophetic figure.[20] The author of Mark was probably aware of the prophetic connotations of the passage, but may have interpreted it messianically.[21] In any case, this aspect of the divine statement implies that the descent of the Spirit qualifies Jesus as a commissioned prophet.

The next event in the narrative of Mark is the driving of Jesus into the wilderness by the Spirit (1:12). This

---

13 Cf. Joshua 6. This claim is not mentioned in the parallel passage, *Bell.* 2.13.5 §261–63. The Egyptian prophet was active around 56 CE; see Horsley and Hanson, *Bandits*, 167–70.

14 See the discussion in Horsley and Hanson, *Bandits*, 175–81; they classify John the Baptist as an oracular prophet.

15 That this characteristic is missing from the account of Josephus is due to his biases; it is preserved especially clearly and without obvious Christian adaptation in Matt 3:7-10.

16 Trans. from Thackeray, *Josephus*, 3:463, 465.

17 Text and trans. (slightly modified) from Thackeray, *Josephus*, 3:466–67.

18 On the messianic connotations, see the next subsection below, *Jesus as Messiah*.

19 In the LXX, the servant is identified with Jacob and Israel in 42:1; it is not certain that the author of Mark was familiar with this reading, or, if he was, how he interpreted it.

20 See the discussion and the literature cited in Christopher R. Seitz, "How Is the Prophet Isaiah Present in the Latter Half of the Book? The Logic of Chapters 40–66 within the Book of Isaiah," *JBL* 115 (1996) 219–40, esp. 238–39.

21 I.e., in terms of a royal messiah. The messianic (in the general sense of anointed) and the prophetic interpretations are not exclusive alternatives; see the discussion above about the expectation in the Dead Sea Scrolls of a prophetic messiah. Michael Stone has argued that the Messiah is called the servant of God in *4 Ezra* 7:29 and 13:32 (*Fourth Ezra: A Commentary on the Book of Fourth Ezra* [Hermeneia; Minneapolis: Fortress, 1990] 202, 207–13, 392, 402).

occurrence is reminiscent of biblical accounts according to which the divine Spirit carried the prophets from place to place.[22] Jesus' sojourn in the wilderness for forty days, during which time he is served by angels, recalls Elijah's flight into the wilderness, where an angel appears to him and gives him food and drink, which enables him to make a journey of forty days and forty nights to Mount Horeb.[23]

In Mark 1:14, the activity of Jesus is summarized as "proclaiming the good news of God" ($\kappa\eta\rho\acute{\upsilon}\sigma\sigma\omega\nu$ $\tau\grave{o}$ $\epsilon\mathring{\upsilon}\alpha\gamma\gamma\acute{\epsilon}\lambda\iota o\nu$ $\tau o\hat{\upsilon}$ $\vartheta\epsilon o\hat{\upsilon}$). As was discussed above, the Messiah of God, probably the eschatological prophet, was expected by the community associated with the Dead Sea Scrolls to "bring good news to the poor," in analogy with, or more likely, in fulfillment of Isa 61:1 understood as an eschatological prophecy. The Greek version of this passage reads "to bring good news to the poor" ($\epsilon\mathring{\upsilon}\alpha\gamma\gamma\epsilon\lambda\acute{\iota}\sigma\alpha\sigma\vartheta\alpha\iota$ $\pi\tau\omega\chi o\hat{\iota}\varsigma$). It is noteworthy that the verb used in the LXX is the cognate of the noun used in Mark 1:14.[24] A related passage, Isa 52:7, reads, according to the LXX, "as a season upon the mountains, as the feet of one bringing good news of peace, as one bringing good news, for I will make known your salvation, saying, 'Zion, your God reigns'" ($\acute{\omega}\varsigma$ $\acute{\omega}\rho\alpha$ $\mathring{\epsilon}\pi\grave{\iota}$ $\tau\hat{\omega}\nu$ $\mathring{o}\rho\acute{\epsilon}\omega\nu$, $\acute{\omega}\varsigma$ $\pi\acute{o}\delta\epsilon\varsigma$ $\epsilon\mathring{\upsilon}\alpha\gamma\gamma\epsilon\lambda\iota\zeta o\mu\acute{\epsilon}\nu o\upsilon$ $\mathring{\alpha}\kappa o\grave{\eta}\nu$ $\epsilon\mathring{\iota}\rho\acute{\eta}\nu\eta\varsigma$, $\acute{\omega}\varsigma$ $\epsilon\mathring{\upsilon}\alpha\gamma\gamma\epsilon\lambda\iota\zeta\acute{o}\mu\epsilon\nu o\varsigma$ $\mathring{\alpha}\gamma\alpha\vartheta\acute{\alpha}$, $\acute{o}\tau\iota$ $\mathring{\alpha}\kappa o\upsilon\sigma\tau\grave{\eta}\nu$ $\pi o\iota\acute{\eta}\sigma\omega$ $\tau\grave{\eta}\nu$ $\sigma\omega\tau\eta\rho\acute{\iota}\alpha\nu$ $\sigma o\upsilon$ $\lambda\acute{\epsilon}\gamma\omega\nu$ $\Sigma\iota\grave{\omega}\nu$ $B\alpha\sigma\iota\lambda\epsilon\acute{\upsilon}\sigma\epsilon\iota$ $\sigma o\upsilon$ $\acute{o}$ $\vartheta\epsilon\acute{o}\varsigma$). This passage is quoted in Hebrew in a document from Qumran that reads

This is the day of [Peace/Salvation] concerning which [God] spoke [through Isa]iah the prophet, who said, *[How] beautiful upon the mountains are the feet of the messenger who proclaims peace, who brings good news, who proclaims salvation, who says to Zion: Your ELOHIM [reigns]* (Isa 52:7). Its interpretation: the mountains are the prophets . . . and the messenger is the Anointed one of the spirit concerning whom Dan[iel] said. . . .[25]

The citation from Daniel is missing. Most scholars have concluded that it was a reference to Dan 9:25, which speaks of a משיח נגיד ("an anointed prince," or "an anointed ruler").[26] It may be, however, that the reference is to Dan 9:26, which mentions an anointed one who will be cut off.[27] Since the messenger of Isa 52:7 is a prophetic figure, like the servant of 42:1 and the anonymous speaker in 61:1, the messenger of the Qumran text is probably a prophetic figure also.[28] Since the context concerns the eschatological future,[29] this figure is probably the eschatological prophet. The good news that Jesus proclaims according to Mark 1:14 is elaborated in v. 15 with the words "The time is fulfilled and the kingdom of God has drawn near" ($\pi\epsilon\pi\lambda\acute{\eta}\rho\omega\tau\alpha\iota$ $\acute{o}$ $\kappa\alpha\iota\rho\grave{o}\varsigma$ $\kappa\alpha\grave{\iota}$ $\acute{\eta}\gamma\gamma\iota\kappa\epsilon\nu$ $\acute{\eta}$ $\beta\alpha\sigma\iota\lambda\epsilon\acute{\iota}\alpha$ $\tau o\hat{\upsilon}$ $\vartheta\epsilon o\hat{\upsilon}$). Thus, Mark 1:14-15 has two elements in common with Isa 52:7, a messenger or herald who proclaims good news and the content of the good news focusing on the reign or kingdom of God.

---

22   1 Kgs 18:12; 2 Kgs 2:16; Ezek 3:12-15; 8:3; 11:1, 24; 37:1; 43:5.

23   Cf. Mark 1:13 with 1 Kgs 19:4-8.

24   Hubert Frankemölle has argued that the use of the noun $\epsilon\mathring{\upsilon}\alpha\gamma\gamma\acute{\epsilon}\lambda\iota o\nu$ ("good news") in the singular was a Christian innovation, but that it was inspired in part by the use of the related verb in Isa 61:1 and other passages in Deutero-Isaiah ("Zweiter Teil: Evangelium als theologischer Begriff und sein Bezug zur literarischen Gattung 'Evangelium,'" in Detlev Dormeyer and Frankemölle, "Evangelium als literarische Gattung und als theologischer Begriff," *ANRW* 2.25.2 [1984] 1676; see also Frankemölle, *Evangelium–Begriff und Gattung*, 253).

25   11QMelch (11Q13) 2:15-16; trans. (slightly modified) from Vermes, *The Complete Dead Sea Scrolls in English* (rev. ed.; London: Penguin Books, 2004), 533. For the Hebrew text and an English translation, see Paul J. Kobelski, *Melchizedek and Melchireša^c* (CBQMS 10; Washington, DC: CBA, 1981) 6, 8; Florentino García Martínez, Eibert J. C. Tigchelaar and Adam S. van der Woude, eds., *Qumran Cave 11*,

vol. 2: *11Q2–18, 11Q20–31* (DJD 23; Oxford: Clarendon, 1998) 225, 229.

26   In the original context of the book of Daniel, 9:25 probably referred to Joshua the high priest, who, according to Zech 4:14, was one of the two anointed (lit., "sons of oil") who stand by the Lord. In the history of interpretation, however, this משיח נגיד ("anointed prince," or "anointed ruler") was taken as the Messiah; see Collins, *Daniel*, 355.

27   The reference was probably originally to the high priest Onias III, who was murdered; see 2 Macc 4:33-38. Christian commentators understood it as a prophecy of the death of Christ. The medieval Jewish commentator Rashi interpreted it in terms of the death of Agrippa, the last Jewish king, and a commentary attributed to an earlier Jewish commentator, Saadia Gaon, referred it to the end of the priestly line. See Collins, *Daniel*, 356; cf. 86.

28   See the discussion in Collins, *Scepter and the Star*, 119.

29   See Kobelski, *Melchizedek*, esp. 64.

Thus, for a Jewish audience or anyone familiar with the eschatological tradition and scriptural exegesis of the Qumran community, Jesus is presented here as an eschatological prophet.

The scenes in which Jesus calls disciples (1:16-20; 2:14) may be read as indicating a social role of either teacher or prophet.[30] In relation to prophetic tradition, the narratives of Mark are similar to the account of Elijah's call of Elisha (1 Kgs 19:19-21). In all three accounts, those called are engaged in work for a livelihood, which they abandon to answer the call. Both Jesus and Elijah take the initiative, Jesus with speech and Elijah at first with a symbolic gesture. James and John abandon their father, Zebedee, just as Elisha leaves his father and mother behind. All three narratives use language of "following." Elisha's remark to Elijah in 1 Kgs 19:20, "I will follow you" (ἀκολουθήσω ὀπίσω σου), for example, corresponds to the narrator's comment in Mark 1:20, "they followed him" (ἀπῆλθον ὀπίσω αὐτοῦ).[31]

According to the Gospel of Mark, the first thing that Jesus does after calling the first four disciples is to go into the synagogue in Capernaum and to teach.[32] It is noteworthy in this connection that the community of the Dead Sea Scrolls expected an eschatological teacher, as well as an eschatological prophet, priest, and king. The *Damascus Document* contains the following prophetic interpretation:

And the *star* is the Interpreter of the Law who will come to Damascus, as it is written, *A star shall come forth out of Jacob and a sceptre shall rise out of Israel* (Num 24:17). The *sceptre* is the prince of the whole congregation, and when he comes *he shall smite all the children of Seth* (Num 24:17). (CD 7:18-21 [MS A])[33]

This Interpreter of the Law who is to come in the future is probably the same figure referred to earlier in the same document with the words "until he arises who will teach righteousness at the end of days" (CD 6:10-11 [MS A]).[34] A collection of eschatological interpretations of biblical passages contains a similar interpretative prophecy:

The Lord declares to you that he will build you a House (2 Sam 7:11c). *I will raise up your seed after you* (2 Sam 7:12). *I will establish the throne of his kingdom [for ever]* (2 Sam 7:13). *[I will be] his father and he shall be my son* (2 Sam 7:14). He is the Branch of David who shall arise with the Interpreter of the Law [to rule] in Zion [at the end] of time. (4QFlor [4Q174] 1:10-12)[35]

The Interpreter of the Law is thus a teacher who was expected to appear at the end of days to teach righteousness to the members of the new covenant. There is some evidence that this eschatological teacher should be identified with the eschatological prophet expected by the community.[36] The latter expectation was based on Deut 18:18-19, which is quoted in the *Messianic Anthology* or *Testimonia* from Qumran:

I will raise up for them a Prophet like you from among their brethren. I will put my words into his mouth and he shall tell them all that I command him. And I will require a reckoning of whoever will not listen to the words which the Prophet shall speak in my Name (Deut 18:18-19). (4QTestim [4Q175] 5–8)[37]

This description of the role of the eschatological prophet is equivalent to "teaching righteousness." Further support for this identification is that the text applied to the

---

30 For a discussion of these scenes in terms of a teacher calling disciples, see the subsection below, *Jesus as Teacher*.

31 See also Josephus's version of the call of Elisha in *Ant.* 8.13.7 §353–54 and the discussion in Martin Hengel, *The Charismatic Leader and His Followers* (SNTW; Edinburgh: T & T Clark, 1981; Germ. ed., 1968) 16–18.

32 See also the subsection below, *Jesus as Teacher*.

33 Trans. (modified) from Florentino García Martínez and Eibert J. C. Tigchelaar, eds., *The Dead Sea Scrolls Study Edition* (2 vols.; Leiden: Brill, 1997–98) 1:561.

34 Trans. (modified) from García Martínez and

Tigchelaar, *Dead Sea Scrolls*, 1:559. The language is drawn from Hos 10:12.

35 Trans. (slightly modified) from Vermes, *Dead Sea Scrolls*, 526.

36 Collins, *Scepter and the Star*, 113–14. Another possibility is that the eschatological prophet was identified with the Messiah of Aaron (ibid., 114–15).

37 Trans. (slightly modified) from Vermes, *Dead Sea Scrolls*, 527.

eschatological prophet in CD 6:11 (Hos 10:12)[38] is applied to Elijah in later Jewish tradition.[39] Thus, the prominence of Jesus' role as teacher in Mark is compatible with his portrayal in prophetic terms.[40]

Exorcisms are the most prominent among the mighty deeds done by Jesus, according to Mark. Jesus' first miracle is an exorcism (1:23-28). Evidence for the practice of exorcism among Jews comes primarily from the latter part of the Second Temple period, although David and Solomon were later understood to be exorcists.[41] Exorcisms are not recorded among the mighty deeds accomplished by Elijah and Elisha in the books of Kings. The *Genesis Apocryphon*, a work discovered at Qumran, however, includes an account of an exorcism performed by Abraham. This account is part of a retelling of the story in Genesis 12 according to which Abram, while sojourning in Egypt, says that Sarai is his sister.[42] When Pharaoh hears of her beauty, he takes her into the palace. But the Lord afflicts Pharaoh and his household with great plagues because of Sarai. So Pharaoh, realizing that she is Abram's wife, restores her to him and sends them away. The account in the *Genesis Apocryphon* conflates this story with the parallel in Gen 20:1-18. In the latter version, Abraham and Sarah are sojourning in Gerar, and the king of Gerar, Abimelech, takes Sarah into his house. But God warns him in a dream not to touch her because she is married. God also tells Abimelech that Abraham is a prophet (20:7) and instructs him to ask Abraham to pray for him, that he may live and not die. Although no illness had been mentioned (but cf. 12:17), the narrative closes with the statement that, when Abra-

ham prayed for Abimelech, he was healed, as were his wife and female slaves, whose wombs God had closed (20:17-18).

According to the *Genesis Apocryphon*, God sent an evil spirit to afflict Pharaoh and all the men of his household, before Pharaoh could have contact with Sarai and in answer to Abram's prayer.[43] When all the wise men, magicians, and physicians of Egypt could not cure the Pharaoh, Abram is asked to come and pray "that this evil spirit may be commanded (to depart) from us" (1QapGen 20:28).[44] When Sarai was returned to Abram, he went to Pharaoh, prayed for him and laid his hands upon his head. "The plague was removed from him, and the evil [spirit] was commanded (to depart) [from him], and he was cured" (20:28-29).[45] This account qualifies as an exorcism. Although Abram is not called a prophet in the *Genesis Apocryphon*, he is so designated in Gen 20:7. Philo also considered Abraham to be a prophet.[46]

Other mighty deeds of Jesus recall even more clearly the miracles worked by the prophets of old or those expected to be performed by the eschatological prophet. The healing of the leper by Jesus in Mark 1:40-45 has as precedent the healing of Naaman the Syrian by Elisha (2 Kings 5). As Jesus raised the daughter of Jairus from the dead (Mark 5:22-43), so Elijah raised the son of the widow of Zarephath (1 Kgs 17:17-24) and Elisha the son of the Shunammite (2 Kgs 4:8-37). Elisha's multiplication of loaves (2 Kgs 4:42-44) may have been a prototype of the accounts of the corresponding miracles of Jesus (Mark 6:35-44; 8:1-10). Similar in type are the accounts of the creation of an unending supply of meal and oil by

---

38 See above.

39 See the discussion in Collins, *Scepter and the Star*, 113.

40 See also the discussion of the royal Messiah as teacher in the subsections *Jesus as Messiah* and *Jesus as Teacher* below.

41 See below, *Jesus as Messiah*.

42 Gen 12:10-20; cf. Gen 20:1-18 and 26:6-11. On exorcisms in the DSS, see Bernd Kollmann, *Jesus und die Christen als Wundertäter: Studien zu Magie, Medizin und Schamanismus in Antike und Christentum* (FRLANT 170; Göttingen: Vandenhoeck & Ruprecht, 1996) 131–37.

43 The spirit is called רוח מכדש ("an afflicting spirit") in 1QapGen 20:16, רוח באשא ("an evil spirit") in lines 16–17; and רוח שחלניא ("a spirit of purulence")

in line 26; for a text and trans., see Joseph A. Fitzmyer and Daniel J. Harrington, *A Manual of Palestinian Aramaic Texts: Second Century B.C.–Second Century A.D.* (BibOr 34; Rome: Biblical Institute Press, 1978) 100–27, esp. 114–15. For commentary, see Joseph A. Fitzmyer, *The Genesis Apocryphon of Qumran Cave 1: A Commentary* (BibOr 18a; 2nd ed.; Rome: Biblical Institute Press, 1971) esp. 131, 136.

44 Trans. from Fitzmyer and Harrington, *Palestinian Aramaic Texts*, 117.

45 Trans. from ibid.

46 Philo *Rer. div. her.* 52–53 §258, 263–66 (with reference to Gen 20:7); *Virt.* 39 §218.

Elijah (1 Kgs 17:8-16) and the multiplication of oil (for sale to pay debts) by Elisha (2 Kgs 4:1-7). Jesus' cursing of the fig tree is an example of a miraculously effective curse and is similar to Elisha's curse of the boys in Bethel and its effect (2 Kgs 2:23-25).

A joyful poem envisioning the restoration of Zion is preserved in Isa 35:1-10. The anonymous speaker exhorts, "Be strong, weak hands and disabled knees" (ἰσχύσατε, χεῖρες ἀνειμέναι καὶ γόνατα παραλελυμένα) (v. 3), and predicts, "Then the eyes of the blind shall be opened, and the ears of the deaf will hear; then shall the lame man leap like a hart, and the tongue of the impeded in speech will speak clearly" (τότε ἀνοιχθήσονται ὀφθαλμοὶ τυφλῶν, καὶ ὦτα κωφῶν ἀκούσονται. τότε ἁλεῖται ὡς ἔλαφος ὁ χωλός, καὶ τρανὴ ἔσται γλῶσσα μογιλάλων) (vv. 5-6). The acclamation of the witnesses to a healing by Jesus alludes to this passage: "he makes both the deaf hear and the speechless speak" (καὶ τοὺς κωφοὺς ποιεῖ ἀκούειν καὶ τοὺς ἀλάλους λαλεῖν) (Mark 7:37). The use of the word μογιλάλον ("impeded in speech") in Mark 7:32 supports the conclusion that the allusion is intentional. The context in Mark suggests that the poetic hyperbole of the passage in Isaiah was understood literally and prophetically in the first century CE, at least in some circles. In this passage (Mark 7:31-37), Jesus is portrayed as fulfilling part of the prophecy of Isaiah: he made a deaf man hear and an impeded tongue speak clearly. He fulfills other parts of the prophecy on other occasions: he opens the eyes of the blind (8:22-26 and 10:46-52), makes the lame walk (2:1-12),[47] and strengthens a weak hand (3:1-6). Further, the prophetic servant of the Lord is commissioned to open the eyes that are blind (Isa 42:7).[48]

As noted above, 4Q521 cites Ps 146:8, "the Lord opens the eyes of the blind," and implies that this prophecy will be fulfilled through the activity of the eschatological prophet. The same text expands Isa 61:1, so that this prophet will not only proclaim good news to the poor but also raise the dead. Jesus' healing of the two blind men and his raising of Jairus's daughter from the dead would thus imply for members of the audience of Mark familiar with these traditions that he is the eschatological prophet.

When the Markan Jesus meets with skepticism in Nazareth, he says, "A prophet is not without honor, except in his hometown and among his relatives and in his house" (οὐκ ἔστιν προφήτης ἄτιμος εἰ μὴ ἐν τῇ πατρίδι αὐτοῦ καὶ ἐν τοῖς συγγενεῦσιν αὐτοῦ καὶ ἐν τῇ οἰκίᾳ αὐτοῦ) (Mark 6:4). Although this saying does not necessarily imply that Jesus himself is a prophet, it does at least make an analogy between his role and that of a prophet. According to Mark 6:15, some of the people who encountered or heard about Jesus believed that he was Elijah or "a prophet like one of the prophets (of old)" (προφήτης ὡς εἷς τῶν προφητῶν).[49]

Although Jesus, according to the Gospels, did not use the messenger formula typical of the classical prophets of Israel,[50] a considerable portion of the sayings attributed to him may be classified as prophetic or apocalyptic sayings. Rudolf Bultmann defined four types of sayings in this category: the preaching of salvation, minatory sayings, admonitions, and apocalyptic predictions.[51] Furthermore, the narrative of the Gospel of Mark is structured in part by means of prediction-fulfillment techniques. Older Scripture predicts or prophesies the appearance of John the Baptist (1:2-3), a prediction whose fulfillment is then narrated (1:4-6). John predicts the coming of one stronger than he (1:7-8), a prophecy that is then fulfilled by the arrival of Jesus on the scene (1:9-13). Jesus prophesies his arrest, execution, and resur-

---

47 Note the similarity between the παραλελυμένα ("disabled," "paralyzed," or "lame") of Isa 35:3 LXX and the παραλυτικός ("lame man" or "paralytic") of Mark 2:3-5, 9-10.

48 The immediate context of Isa 42:7 suggests that the blindness spoken of may be symbolic; cf. Isa 42:16-17, 18-20; 43:8; 59:9-10. But the healing of blindness in Mark is symbolic as well as literal; see the commentary below on 8:22-26 and 10:46-52.

49 The disciples report similar opinions in Mark 8:28, including the belief that Jesus is John the Baptist; this identification is to be explained in light of Mark 6:14-16, in which Herod is said to believe that Jesus is John the Baptist risen from the dead.

50 See Claus Westermann, *Basic Forms of Prophetic Speech* (Philadelphia: Westminster, 1967) 98–128.

51 Bultmann, *History*, 108–25. Under the subtype "preaching of salvation," Bultmann discussed the sayings attributed to Jesus in Mark 10:29-30; 8:35; and the messianic preaching of John the Baptist in Mark 1:7-8. Minatory sayings in Mark include 8:38 and 12:38-40, as well as the logia in 10:23, 25; 8:12. Among the admonitions, he classified Mark 1:15 and 13:33-37. Apocalyptic predictions in Mark

rection (8:31; 9:31; 10:32-34), events that are later narrated in detail (14:43–16:8). In 14:27, Jesus predicts that his disciples will abandon him, when he is "struck," an event that is reported in 14:50-52. In 14:30, he predicts the denial of Peter, which is narrated in 14:66-72.[52] Although this is a literary device, it has the effect of presenting John the Baptist and Jesus as prophets, or at least as having the predictive powers of prophets.[53]

Finally, it should be noted that Jesus is presented as a clairvoyant, and that clairvoyance is another prophetic gift. In 11:1-7, Jesus sends two of the disciples to fetch a young donkey. He tells them where they will find it, predicts the response of the bystanders, and instructs the disciples about what to say. Events unfold exactly as he has foreseen and foretold. Similarly, in 14:12-16, he sends two disciples into the city to prepare for him to eat the Passover with his disciples. He foresees that they will meet a man with a water jug, instructs them to follow him, and tells them what to say to the master of the house that he enters. These anecdotes recall the exploits of Samuel, the judge and prophet, who was able to tell Saul that his father's donkeys had been found (1 Sam 9:20).[54] He also told Saul that, when he left Samuel, he would meet two men by Rachel's tomb; he predicts what they will say to Saul and predicts a further series of events. The fulfillment of these predictions will be signs for Saul, and he is instructed what to do afterward (10:2-8).

As noted above, Mark reports that many of the people who encountered Jesus concluded that he was a prophet (6:15; 8:28). Even though Peter's affirmation, σὺ εἶ ὁ χριστός ("You are the Messiah" or "You are the Christ"),

is in need of interpretation,[55] it is affirmed indirectly by the comment "And he rebuked them so that they would speak to no one about him" (καὶ ἐπετίμησεν αὐτοῖς ἵνα μηδενὶ λέγωσιν περὶ αὐτοῦ) (8:30). Thus, according to Mark, "Messiah" is a more appropriate designation of Jesus than "prophet." Nevertheless, he reports the popular reception of Jesus as a prophet, and his portrayal of Jesus has many prophetic characteristics, as has been pointed out above. This paradox implies two things. First, there had long been some overlap between the roles of king and royal messiah, on the one hand, and prophet, on the other. Just as kingship was depicted as a charismatic office during the period of its origin, so the eschatological king could be seen as a charismatic leader. According to 1 Samuel, for example, the spirit of the Lord came mightily upon Saul and he prophesied (10:6, 10-13; 19:18-24). The Messiah or eschatological king described in the *Psalms of Solomon* 17–18 is primarily a military leader who will drive out foreign overlords and reestablish an autonomous kingdom of Israel.[56] But he will also accomplish deeds more typical of a teacher, priest, or prophet:

He will not tolerate unrighteousness (even) to pause among them, and any person who knows wickedness shall not live with them. For he shall know them that they are all children of their God (καὶ οὐκ ἀφήσει ἀδικίαν ἐν μέσῳ αὐτῶν αὐλισθῆναι ἔτι, καὶ οὐ κατοικήσει πᾶς ἄνθρωπος μετ᾽ αὐτῶν εἰδὼς κακίαν· γνώσεται γὰρ αὐτοὺς ὅτι πάντες υἱοὶ θεοῦ εἰσιν αὐτῶν) (Ps. Sol. 17:27)[57]

---

include 13:2; 14:58; cf. 15:29; 9:1; 13:5-27, 28-29, 30, 31, 22; 9:12-13. See also David E. Aune, *Prophecy in Early Christianity and the Ancient Mediterranean World* (Grand Rapids: Eerdmans, 1983) 164–69; Detlev Dormeyer, *Das Neue Testament im Rahmen der antiken Literaturgeschichte: Eine Einführung* (Darmstadt: Wissenschaftliche Buchgesellschaft, 1993) 103–8; ET *The New Testament among the Writings of Antiquity* (Sheffield: Sheffield Academic Press, 1998) 119–23.

52 Cf. Norman R. Petersen, *Literary Criticism for New Testament Critics* (GBS; Philadelphia: Fortress, 1978) 49–80; W. S. Vorster, "The Function of the Use of the Old Testament in Mark," *Neotestamentica* 14 (1980) 69.

53 On the prophecies attributed to Jesus, see also Aune, *Prophecy*, 171–88.

54 According to Sir 46:13-14, Samuel was a "prophet of

the Lord" (προφήτης κυρίου) who "judged the congregation" (ἔκρινεν συναγωγήν), i.e., the people of Israel. Philo called Samuel "the greatest of kings and prophets" (βασιλέων καὶ προφητῶν μέγιστος) (*Ebr.* 36 §143).

55 The affirmation of Peter occurs in 8:29 and is interpreted in 8:31; see the commentary below.

56 So esp. *Ps. Sol.* 17:21-25. The *Psalms of Solomon* are usually dated to the first century BCE, not long after Pompey's conquest of Palestine for Rome in 63 BCE. Kenneth Atkinson has argued that *Ps. Sol.* 17 should be dated between 37 and 30 BCE ("Herod the Great, Sosius, and the Siege of Jerusalem [37 B.C.E.] in Psalm of Solomon 17," *NovT* 38 [1996] 313–22).

57 Text from Rahlfs; trans. from R. B. Wright, "Psalms of Solomon," in *OTP* 2:667.

And he will purge Jerusalem (and make it) holy as it was even from the beginning (καὶ καθαριεῖ Ιερουσαλημ ἐν ἁγιασμῷ ὡς καὶ τὸ ἀπ ἀρχῆς). (17:30)

And he himself (will be) free from sin, (in order) to rule a great people. He will expose officials and drive out sinners by the strength of his word. And he will not weaken in his days, (relying) upon his God, for God made him powerful in the holy spirit and wise in the counsel of understanding, with strength and righteousness (καὶ αὐτὸς καθαρὸς ἀπὸ ἁμαρτίας τοῦ ἄρχειν λαοῦ μεγάλου, ἐλέγξαι ἄρχοντας καὶ ἐξᾶραι ἁμαρτωλοὺς ἐν ἰσχύι λόγου. καὶ οὐκ ἀσθενήσει ἐν ταῖς ἡμέραις αὐτοῦ ἐπὶ θεῷ αὐτοῦ· ὅτι ὁ θεὸς κατειργάσατο αὐτὸν δυνατὸν ἐν πνεύματι ἁγίῳ καὶ σοφὸν ἐν βουλῇ συνέσεως μετὰ ἰσχύος καὶ δικαιοσύνης). (17:36-37)

His words will be purer than the finest gold, the best. He will judge the peoples in the assemblies, the tribes of the sanctified. His words will be as the words of the holy ones (i.e., angels), among sanctified peoples (τὰ ῥήματα αὐτοῦ πεπυρωμένα ὑπὲρ χρυσίον τὸ πρῶτον τίμιον, ἐν συναγωγαῖς διακρινεῖ λαοῦ φυλὰς ἡγιασμένου, οἱ λόγοι αὐτοῦ ὡς λόγοι ἁγίων ἐν μέσῳ λαῶν ἡγιασμένων). (17:43)

The refusal to tolerate unrighteousness, the verbal conviction of officials, and the endowment with the Holy Spirit are typically prophetic qualities. According to *4 Ezra*, a Jewish apocalypse written around 95 CE, the Davidic messiah would reprove the leaders of the fourth kingdom in prophetic style before destroying them (11:36-46; 12:31-33).[58] Furthermore, according to this work, the Messiah will work wonders (*4 Ezra* 13:50; cf. 7:27). Since these Jewish portrayals of the expected Messiah from the first century BCE and the first century CE reflect to some degree a conflation of the roles of charismatic leadership, it is not surprising that the followers of Jesus depicted him in a way that similarly conflated such roles.

---

58   On the date of this work, see Stone, *Fourth Ezra*, 9–10. For further discussion of the Messiah in this work, see below *Jesus as Messiah*.

b. Jesus as Messiah

Like the institution of prophecy, Israelite kingship came to an end with the destruction of Jerusalem in 586 BCE and the exile. A descendant of David, Zerubbabel, was appointed governor by the Persians in c. 538 BCE, but soon both political and religious leadership in Judah was concentrated in the hands of the high priest. The prophets Haggai and Zechariah probably regarded Zerubbabel as a royal messiah, in the sense that he was the focus of their hopes for an imminent restoration of the Davidic monarchy.[1] But in spite of these hopes and the promise in 2 Samuel 7, the Davidic line died out during the Persian period.

The theocratic system under the leadership of the high priest worked well, first under the Persians and then under the successors of Alexander, until the crisis of the early second century BCE, which led to the Maccabean revolt. This family then established the Hasmonean dynasty, the first autonomous, native monarchy since the exile. This line of rulers, by means of both their accomplishments and their shortcomings, provided a context for the revival of the hope for the restoration of the Davidic monarchy. The oldest evidence for this revived hope is provided by the Dead Sea Scrolls and the *Psalms of Solomon*.

As noted above in the subsection *Jesus as Prophet*, a passage in the *Rule of the Community* expresses the expectation of an eschatological prophet and Messiahs of Aaron and Israel (1QS 9:10-11). The latter figure is probably the eschatological Davidic king whose arrival is predicted in other texts from Qumran. For example, a commentary on the book of Isaiah (4QpIsaᵃ) contains a description of the shoot of Jesse, the Messiah of the Davidic line, based on Isa 11:1-5. Although the text is fragmentary, it is clear that the author interpreted the latter passage eschatologically and with reference to the Qumran community. There is reference to "the end of days" and to a battle with the Kittim, the eschatological enemy of the community.[2] The name "Kittim" probably refers here to the Romans.[3] The association of the royal messiah with a battle against the Romans suggests that the conquest of Judah by the Roman general Pompey in 63 BCE provided an impetus to the revival of hope for the restoration of the Davidic monarchy.

The Davidic messiah also plays a role in the *War Scroll*. A section of this work entitled "The rule for the standards of the congregation" includes the following instructions:

> "And on the sh[ield of] the Prince of the congregation they shall write his name, together with the names of Israel, Levi and Aaron, and the names of the twelve tribes of Israel according to the order of their precedence, with the names of their twelve chiefs." (1QM 5:1-2)[4]

The epithet "Prince of the congregation" probably derives from the use of the term נשׂיא ("prince") in the book of Ezekiel.[5] It was an old Israelite title that Ezekiel used both for the king of Judah who was sent into exile by the Babylonians and for the future king who would restore the Davidic monarchy.[6] Whereas the future king could be called either מלך ("king") or נשׂיא ("prince"), the

---

1 Hag 2:21-23; Zech 3:8; 4:11-14. For discussion, see Collins, *Scepter and the Star*, 31–32.

2 For text, translation, and notes, see Maurya P. Horgan, "Isaiah Pesher 4," in Charlesworth, *Dead Sea Scrolls*, 6B:83–97; see also Maurya P. Horgan, *Pesharim: Qumran Interpretations of Biblical Books* (CBQMS 8; Washington, DC: Catholic Biblical Association of America, 1979) 70–86.

3 Collins, *Scepter and the Star*, 57–58.

4 Trans. from Vermes, *Dead Sea Scrolls*, 170.

5 In Ezekiel, the title נשׂיא ("prince") is used for lesser kings, whereas the title מלך ("king") is usually reserved for the emperors in Mesopotamia and Egypt; see the trans. and textual note on Ezek 7:27 in Walther Zimmerli, *Ezekiel 1: A Commentary on the Book of the Prophet Ezekiel, Chapters 1–24* (Hermeneia; Philadelphia: Fortress, 1979) 200; see also the commentary on 7:27a (ibid., 209). The use of נשׂיא ("prince") for the Davidic kings in Ezekiel has a theological, reflective character (ibid., 273, 364). It is the preferred title for the king of Jerusalem in Ezekiel, but the title מלך ("king") is not avoided; see Walther Zimmerli, *Ezekiel 2: A Commentary on the Book of the Prophet Ezekiel, Chapters 25–48* (Hermeneia; Philadelphia: Fortress, 1983) 277–78.

6 That נשׂיא ("prince") is an old title is attested by Exod 22:27 MT (22:28 RSV); see Zimmerli, *Ezekiel 1*, 209. The term is used of the king in Jerusalem in Ezek 7:27; 12:10; and of the future Davidic king in 34:24 and 37:25; on the former two passages, see the

latter title is preferred in the later sections of Ezekiel.[7] That "the Prince of the congregation" refers to the Messiah of Israel in the *War Scroll* is indicated by the fact that the oracle of Balaam from Num 24:15-19 is cited in column 11. Although the "scepter" that shall arise out of Israel is not interpreted in the latter passage, it is interpreted as "the Prince of the whole congregation" in the *Damascus Document* (7:20), a work also found at Qumran.[8]

A text that has been identified as a fragment of the *War Scroll* or *War Rule* implies that the Prince of the congregation will take an active part in the war against the Kittim:

> [. . .] wickedness shall be beaten [. . .] [. . . the Prin]ce of the Congregation and all Is[rael . . .] [which i]s written [. . .] [. . .] upon the mountains [. . .] [. . .] the Kittim. *Blank* [. . .] [. . . the Pri]nce of the Congregation as far as the [great] sea [. . .] [. . . and they will flee] from Israel at that time [. . .] (he) will station himself opposite them and they shall be stirred against them [. . .] [. . .] they shall return to dry land at th[at] time [. . .] [. . .] they shall bring him before the Prince [of the Congregation . . .]. (4Q285 frg. 6 + 4)[9]

The same text announces, "*And there shall come forth a shoot from the stump of Jesse*" (frg. 7),[10] a prediction of the arrival of the Davidic messiah based on Isa 11:1. It goes on to identify this figure with "the Branch of David," another messianic epithet, derived from Jer 23:5-6. Since these two epithets are applied by this text to the Prince of the congregation, it seems clear that the latter is understood as the Davidic messiah or Messiah of Israel. According to this text, the Davidic messiah "will kill him. . . ."[11] Some scholars have argued that the text should be translated to mean that the Messiah is killed, but it is more likely that the fragment predicts the defeat of the king of the Kittim by the Messiah of Israel. This interpretation is supported by a passage in the *War Scroll*:

> All those [who are ready] for battle shall march out and shall pitch their camp before the king of the Kittim and before all the host of Belial gathered about him for the Day [of Revenge] by the Sword of God. (1QM 15:2-3)[12]

The identification of the Prince of the congregation with the Davidic messiah is supported also by the *Rule of the Blessings*, a collection of blessings appended to the *Rule of the Community*. The relevant passage reads:

> The Master (= Maskil) shall bless the Prince of the Congregation . . . and shall renew for him the Covenant of the Community that he may establish the kingdom of His people for ever, [that he may judge the poor with righteousness and] dispense justice with {equity to the oppressed} of the land, and that he may walk perfectly before Him in all the ways [of truth], and that he may establish His holy Covenant at the time of the affliction of those who seek God.
>
> May the Lord raise you up to everlasting heights, and as a fortified tower upon a high wall!
> [May you smite the peoples] with the might of your hand[13] and ravage the earth with your sceptre; may you bring death to the ungodly with the breath of your lips!
> [May He shed upon you the spirit of counsel] and everlasting might, the spirit of knowledge and of the fear of God; may righteousness be the girdle

references to Zimmerli, *Ezekiel 1*, cited in the previous note. On 34:24, see Zimmerli, *Ezekiel 2*, 218.

7 Zimmerli, *Ezekiel 2*, 277–78.

8 Trans. from Vermes, *Dead Sea Scrolls*, 135.

9 Trans. from García Martínez and Tigchelaar, *Dead Sea Scrolls*, 2:641, 643.

10 Trans. from Vermes, *Dead Sea Scrolls*, 189.

11 Trans. from Vermes, *Dead Sea Scrolls*, 189; so also García Martínez and Tigchelaar, *Dead Sea Scrolls*, 2:643 (in their trans. of frg. 5 = 11Q14 1 i).

12 Trans. from Vermes, *Dead Sea Scrolls*, 181; for discussion, see Collins, *Scepter and the Star*, 58–59.

13 In line 24, García Martínez and Tigchelaar restore "mouth" instead of "hand" (*Dead Sea Scrolls*, 1:109); see the discussion of *4 Ezra 13* below. Eduard Lohse also restored *Mund* ("mouth"), rather than "Hand" (idem, ed., *Die Texte aus Qumran* [Darmstadt: Wissenschaftliche Buchgesellschaft, 1971] 59).

[of your loins] and may your reins be girdled [with faithfulness]!

May He make your horns of iron and your hooves of bronze; may you toss like a young bull [and trample the peoples] like the mire of the streets!

For God has established you as the sceptre. The rulers . . . [and all the kings of the] nations shall serve you. He shall strengthen you with His holy Name and you shall be as a [lion; and you shall not lie down until you have devoured the] prey which naught shall deliver. . . . (1QSb = 1Q28b 5:20-29)[14]

The evidence from Qumran makes clear that the community associated with the scrolls expected an eschatological leader who would lead the faithful in battle against their enemies, especially the Romans, reestablish an autonomous kingdom of Israel, and rule as king with wisdom and justice. Although, as we have seen, the picture of the Messiah in the *Psalms of Solomon* has prophetic elements, it also emphasizes the role of the Davidic messiah in defeating the nations and driving them out of the land of Israel:

See, Lord, and raise up for them their king, the son of David, to rule over your servant Israel in the time known to you, O God.

Undergird him with the strength to destroy the unrighteous rulers, to purge Jerusalem from gentiles who trample her to destruction; in wisdom and in righteousness to drive out the sinners from the inheritance;

to smash the arrogance of sinners like a potter's jar;

To shatter all their substance with an iron rod;

to destroy the unlawful nations with the word of his mouth;

At his warning the nations will flee from his presence;

and he will condemn sinners by the thoughts of their hearts. (*Ps. Sol.* 17:21-25)[15]

Thereafter, he will rule the people as an ideal king: "And he will be a righteous king over them, taught by God" ($\kappa\alpha\grave{\iota}\ \alpha\grave{\upsilon}\tau\grave{o}\varsigma\ \beta\alpha\sigma\iota\lambda\epsilon\grave{\upsilon}\varsigma\ \delta\acute{\iota}\kappa\alpha\iota o\varsigma\ \delta\iota\delta\alpha\kappa\tau\grave{o}\varsigma\ \acute{\upsilon}\pi\grave{o}\ \vartheta\epsilon o\hat{\upsilon}\ \acute{\epsilon}\pi'\ \alpha\grave{\upsilon}\tau o\acute{\upsilon}\varsigma$) (*Ps. Sol.* 17:32).[16]

Besides this evidence for the expectation of a Davidic messiah in the Dead Sea Scrolls and the *Psalms of Solomon*, Josephus provides documentation for the appearance of messianic pretenders toward the end of the Second Temple period. One group of these appeared after the death of Herod I (the Great) near the end of the first century BCE. Like the conquest by the Romans, the death of Herod was a significant turning point in the political history of the Jewish people and thus stimulated hopes for the restoration of the Davidic monarchy. Further, the death of Herod created a power vacuum.[17] The other occasion for the appearance of such pretenders was the Jewish revolt that led to the first Jewish war with Rome, beginning in 66 CE.

Josephus comments that the disorder that followed the death of Herod induced many to aspire to sovereignty ($\beta\alpha\sigma\iota\lambda\epsilon\acute{\iota}\alpha$) (*Bell.* 2.4.1 §55). Since Josephus avoided traditional Jewish messianic language, his references to those who sought kingship or tyranny may be taken as unsympathetic reports of messianic movements. One of these (4 BCE) was led by Judas, son of Hezekiah, with headquarters in Sepphoris (*Bell.* 2.4.1 §56). Hezekiah had been a powerful bandit leader when Herod was a young man, newly appointed governor of Galilee by his father, Antipater. Herod caught and killed him (c. 47 BCE) and a number of his followers, thus establishing his reputation with the Syrians and the Roman governor of Syria.[18] The royal aspirations of Hezekiah's son, Judas, are explicitly stated in the account in the *Antiquities*.[19] In both passages, he is said to have taken up

---

14   Trans. (slightly modified) from Vermes, *Dead Sea Scrolls*, 389–90.
15   Trans. from R. B. Wright, "Psalms of Solomon," in *OTP* 2:667.
16   Trans. from ibid. See also 4QpGen^a (4Q252) 5:1-7; this text, commenting on Gen 49:10, refers to the messiah of justice (or righteousness), the branch of David (lines 3–4).
17   The harsh response in 4 BCE of Herod's son Archelaus to the people's request for reform and

leniency exacerbated the situation; see *Bell.* 2.1.1–3 §§1–13; see also the discussion in Horsley and Hanson, *Bandits*, 110–11.
18   Josephus *Ant.* 14.9.2 §§158–60; cf. *Bell.* 1.10.5 §§204–5.
19   Josephus speaks of his "ambition for royal rank" ($\zeta\acute{\eta}\lambda\omega\sigma\iota\varsigma\ \beta\alpha\sigma\iota\lambda\epsilon\acute{\iota}o\upsilon\ \tau\iota\mu\hat{\eta}\varsigma$); *Ant.* 17.10.5 §272; text and trans. from Ralph Marcus and Allen Wikgren, in Thackeray, *Josephus*, 8:498–99.

arms. This Judas may be the same person referred to by Josephus as "a Gaulanite from a city named Gamala," who, with a Pharisee by the name of Zadok, led a rebellion against the census initiated by Quirinius (6 CE).[20] In the parallel passage in the *Jewish War*, Judas the Gaulanite is identified with "a Galilean, named Judas" (*Bell.* 2.8.1 §118),[21] whom Josephus names as the founder of "the fourth philosophy."[22]

Two other messianic leaders who came forward after the death of Herod were Simon and Athronges. Josephus describes the movement associated with Simon as follows:

There was also Simon, a slave of King Herod but a handsome man, who took pre-eminence by size and bodily strength, and was expected to go farther. Elated by the unsettled conditions of affairs, he was bold enough to place the diadem on his head, and having got together a body of men, he was himself also proclaimed king by them in their madness, and he rated himself worthy of this beyond anyone else. After burning the royal palace in Jericho, he plundered and carried off the things that had been seized there. He also set fire to many other royal residences in many parts of the country and utterly destroyed them after permitting his fellow-rebels to take as booty whatever had been left in them. And he would have done something still more serious if attention had not quickly been turned to him. For Gratus, the officer of the royal troops, joined the Romans and with what forces he had went to meet Simon. A long and heavy battle was fought between them, and most of the Peraeans, who were disorganized and fighting with more recklessness than science, were destroyed. As for Simon, he tried to save himself by fleeing through a ravine, but Gratus intercepted him and cut off his head. (*Ant.* 17.10.6 §273–77)[23]

We infer from this account an acclamation of Simon as Messiah by his followers and note the military engagement, specifically a battle with the allies of Rome. Josephus gives the following account of Athronges:

Then there was a certain Athronges, a man distinguished neither for the position of his ancestors nor by the excellence of his character, nor for any abundance of means, but merely a shepherd completely unknown to everybody although he was remarkable for his great stature and feats of strength. This man had the temerity to aspire to the kingship, thinking that if he obtained it he would enjoy freedom to act more outrageously; as for meeting death, he did not attach much importance to the loss of his life under such circumstances. He also had four brothers, and they too were tall men and confident of being very successful through their feats of strength, and he believed them to be a strong point in his bid for the kingdom. Each of them commanded an armed band, for a large number of people had gathered round them. Though they were commanders, they acted under his orders whenever they went on raids and fought by themselves. Athronges himself put on the diadem and held a council to discuss what things were to be done, but everything depended upon his own decision. This man kept his power for a long while, for he had the title of king and nothing to prevent him from doing as he wished. He and his brothers also applied themselves vigorously to slaughtering the Romans and the king's men, toward both of whom they acted with a similar hatred, toward the latter

---

20 Josephus *Ant.* 18.1.1 §§4–10; quotation from §4; trans. from Louis Feldman, in Thackeray, *Josephus,* 9:5.

21 Trans. from Thackeray, *Josephus,* 2:367.

22 In *Bell.* 2.8.1 §118, he says that Judas was "a sophist who founded a sect (αἵρεσις) of his own (Thackeray, *Josephus,* 2:368–69). In *Ant.* 18.1.6 §23, he refers to this sect as "the fourth philosophy" (τετάρτη φιλοσοφία) (Feldman in Thackeray, *Josephus,* 9:20–21). Martin Hengel explained the lack of explicit identification of Judas, the son of Hezekiah,

with Judas the Gaulanite or Galilean as due to the use of different sources in the various accounts; see Martin Hengel, *The Zealots: Investigations into the Jewish Freedom Movement in the Period from Herod I until 70 A.D.* (Edinburgh: T & T Clark, 1989; Germ. ed., 1961; 2nd Germ. ed., 1976) 331.

23 Trans. from Marcus and Wikgren in Thackeray, *Josephus,* 8:499, 501; cf. *Bell.* 2.4.2 §§57–59.

because of the arrogance that they had shown during the reign of Herod, and toward the Romans because of the injuries that they were held to have inflicted at the present time. But as time went on they became more and more savage (toward all) alike. And there was no escape for any in any way, for sometimes the rebels killed in hope of gain and at other times from the habit of killing. On one occasion near Emmaus they even attacked a company of Romans, who were bringing grain and weapons to their army. Surrounding the centurion Arius, who commanded the detachment, and forty of the bravest of his foot-soldiers, they shot them down. The rest were terrified at their fate, but with the protection given them by Gratus and the royal troops that were with him they made their escape, leaving their dead behind. This kind of warfare they kept up for a long time and caused the Romans no little trouble while also afflicting much damage on their own nation. (*Ant.* 17.10.7 §§278–83)[24]

The great bodily strength of these two leaders may have supported their messianic claims through allusion to scriptural traditions of the *gibbôr* as the strong leader in holy war. Athronges especially could have called David to mind as the shepherd who became king.[25]

The second wave of messianic movements occurred in connection with the first Jewish war. The first of these was led by a certain Menahem, whom Josephus describes as the son of Judas the Galilean (*Bell.* 2.17.8 §433).[26] Because of the intervening time of sixty years, many scholars assume that he was actually the grandson of Judas.[27] Josephus says:

(Menahem) took his intimate friends off with him to Masada, where he broke into king Herod's armoury and provided arms both for his fellow-townsmen and for other brigands; then, with these men for his bodyguard, he returned like a veritable king to Jerusalem, became the leader of the revolution, and directed the siege of the palace. (*Bell.* 2.17.8 §§433–34)[28]

But the reduction of the strongholds and the murder of the high-priest Ananias inflated and brutalized Menahem to such an extent that he believed himself without a rival in the conduct of affairs and became an insufferable tyrant. (*Bell.* 2.17.9 §442)[29]

Josephus goes on to describe how the partisans of Eleazar, son of Ananias the high priest and himself captain of the temple,[30] rose against him. When Menahem disgracefully hid himself, they dragged him out into the open, tortured him, and put him to death (*Bell.* 2.17.9 §§443–48). Martin Hengel has argued that the insurgents originally thought of a dual rule by Eleazar as the Messiah of Aaron and Menahem as the Messiah of Israel, in accordance with the eschatological ideal of the Essenes, that is, the community associated with the Dead Sea Scrolls.[31]

The most prominent messianic pretender during the first Jewish war, who was also recognized as the leader of the revolt by the Romans, was Simon bar Giora. Josephus describes him as follows:

But another war was now impending over Jerusalem. There was a certain Simon, son of Gioras and a native of Gerasa, a youth less cunning than John,[32] who was already in possession of the city, but his superior in physical strength and audacity; the latter quality had led to his expulsion by the high priest Ananus from the province of Acrabetene, once under his com-

---

24 Trans. from Marcus and Wikgren in Thackeray, *Josephus*, 8:501, 503, 505; cf. *Bell.* 2.4.3 §§60–65.

25 See the discussion in Hengel, *Zealots*, 292; see also Horsley and Hanson, *Bandits*, 111–17.

26 Menachem emerged as a leader after the summer of 66 CE and was murdered in the same year.

27 So, e.g., Hengel, *Zealots*, 332 n. 105.

28 Trans. from Thackeray, *Josephus*, 2:493.

29 Trans. from Thackeray, *Josephus*, 2:497.

30 Eleazar the son of Ananias played a major role in the outbreak of the war by persuading the other priests to accept no gift or sacrifice from a for-

eigner. This meant the end of the offering of sacrifices for Rome and the emperor, a step tantamount to declaring a war of independence; see Josephus *Bell.* 2.17.2 §§409–10; see also Horsley and Hanson, *Bandits*, 80.

31 Hengel, *Zealots*, 294.

32 John, son of Levi, a native of Gischala (Heb. Gush Halav) in Upper Galilee; he became an important leader in the war from about 68 CE and was sentenced to life imprisonment by the Romans. See Josephus *Bell.* 4.2.4 §§106–16; 4.3.1 §§121–27; 4.7.1 §§389–97; 6.9.4 §434. Hengel suggests that John of

mand, whereupon he had joined the brigands who had seized Masada. (*Bell.* 4.9.3 §§503–4)[33]

He, on the contrary, was aspiring to despotic power and cherishing high ambitions; accordingly on hearing of the death of Ananus, he withdrew to the hills, where, by proclaiming liberty for slaves and rewards for the free, he gathered around him the villains from every quarter. (*Bell.* 4.9.3 §508)[34]

According to Josephus, Simon had been involved in the repulsion of the attack by the Syrian legate, Cestius Gallus, on Jerusalem in 66 (*Bell.* 2.19.2 §521). He was then active as a brigand in Acrabatene and Idumaea in the winter of 66–67 (*Bell.* 2.22.2 §§652–54). After the death of Ananus, the former high priest and leader of the pro-Roman faction during the war, Simon emerged as a messianic leader. His messianic pretensions can be discerned in the words of Josephus: "He, on the contrary, was aspiring to despotic power and cherishing high ambitions" (ὁ δὲ τυραννιῶν καὶ μεγάλων ἐφιέμενος) (*Bell.* 4.9.3 §508).[35] His acceptance as a messianic leader by many from various social statuses can be inferred from Josephus's statement "and his was no longer an army of mere serfs or brigands, but one including numerous citizen recruits, subservient to his command as to a king" (καὶ οὐκέτι ἦν δούλων μόνων οὐδὲ λῃστῶν στρατός, ἀλλὰ καὶ δημοτικῶν οὐκ ὀλίγων ὡς πρὸς βασιλέα πειθαρχία) (*Bell.* 4.9.4 §510).[36] In the spring of 69, Simon was invited by an alliance of Idumaeans and chief priests to enter Jerusalem and overcome the Zealots. He was acclaimed by the people as "savior and protector" (σωτὴρ . . . καὶ κηδεμὼν) (*Bell.* 4.9.11 §575).[37] During the desperate fighting in the spring of 70, Simon was regarded with such "reverence and awe" (αἰδὼς ἦν καὶ δέος) that those under his command were quite pre-

pared to take their own lives if he commanded it (*Bell.* 5.7.1 §§26–29).[38] When the Romans had entered the city and escape had proved impossible, Simon dressed in white tunics with a purple mantle and arose out of the ground at the very spot on which the temple stood. His clothing suggested royal status, and he may have expected a miracle or divine intervention to give him the victory at this point (*Bell.* 7.2.2 §§26–29).[39] He was captured, however, and executed during the celebration of the triumph of Vespasian and Titus in Rome (Josephus *Bell.* 7.5.6 §§153–55).

Most of these messianic pretenders differ from Jesus in their violent or military activities. They are similar to him, however, in the circumstance that many of them were killed or executed by the Romans. In any case, it is clear that, in some circles in the first century CE, the anticipated Davidic messiah was expected to be a military and political leader who would defeat foreign rulers, that is, the Romans, and their Jewish collaborators and reestablish an autonomous kingdom of Israel.

According to the Dead Sea Scrolls, the *Psalms of Solomon,* and the evidence from Josephus, the Davidic messiah would be endowed with divine gifts and powers and would appear at the end of days, or at least at a great turning point in history. Two other Jewish texts from the first century CE present portrayals of the Messiah in which his extraordinary nature is heightened. One of these is the Similitudes or Parables of Enoch, an originally independent Jewish apocalypse that was incorporated into the work known as *Ethiopic Enoch* or *1 Enoch*. The Similitudes of Enoch is difficult to date, but was probably composed around the turn of the era, that is, in the late first century BCE or the early first century CE.[40] In this work, a redeemer figure has a prominent role and is given several epithets: the Righteous One,[41] the Chosen

---

Gischala also strove for messianic dignity (*Zealots,* 117–18).

33 Trans. from Thackeray, *Josephus,* 3:151. His name indicates that he was the son of a proselyte; see Hengel, *Zealots,* 374.

34 Trans. from Thackeray, *Josephus,* 3:151, 153.

35 Thackeray, *Josephus,* 3:150–51.

36 Thackeray, *Josephus,* 3:152–53.

37 Thackeray, *Josephus,* 3:170–71.

38 Thackeray, *Josephus,* 3:296–97.

39 Josephus implies that Simon foolishly thought that

he could cheat the Romans by creating a scare. For discussion, see Hengel, *Zealots,* 297–98.

40 The Similitudes of Enoch constitute *1 Enoch* 37–71. See George W. E. Nickelsburg, *Jewish Literature between the Bible and the Mishnah: A Historical and Literary Introduction* (Philadelphia: Fortress, 1981) 214–23; the date is discussed on pp. 221–23.

41 *1 Enoch* 38:2; 53:6. In 38:2, some MSS attest the reading "righteousness," rather than "the Righteous One," and the former is probably the earlier reading; see the trans. and n. in George W. E. Nickels-

One or Elect One,[42] that Son of Man,[43] and his [God's] Messiah.[44]

"The Righteous One" and "the Chosen One" or "the Elect One" are epithets that correspond to designations of the community to be redeemed. This community is called "the community of the righteous" in *1 Enoch* 38:1, and its members "the chosen righteous" in 38:2.[45] The designation "the Righteous One" may derive from Isa 53:11, which reads "by his knowledge shall the righteous one, my servant, make many to be accounted righteous" (RSV).[46] "The Chosen One" or "the Elect One" as a name for the redeemer may have been inspired by the use of this epithet for the (prophetic) servant of the Lord in Isa 42:1.[47] The Similitudes of Enoch appears to be the oldest witness for the messianic interpretation of the Servant of the Lord in Deutero-Isaiah.[48] The use of this epithet in Isaiah also for Israel could explain the double usage in the Similitudes of Enoch.[49]

In *1 Enoch* 53:6, "the Righteous One" and "the Chosen One" are explicitly identified. "The Chosen One" and "his Messiah" are clearly synonymous in 52:1-9. Further, since the same role and activities are ascribed to both "the Chosen One" and "that Son of Man," it is clear that the two epithets refer to the same figure. They are both said to sit upon a throne of glory.[50] They are both to judge angels.[51] More generally, they both take the role of judge.[52] It is said of each of them that he will dwell with the redeemed community in the eschatological future.[53] Both are portrayed as revealers of secret wisdom.[54] A military role or at least violent action against the mighty and the wicked is ascribed to each.[55] Furthermore, in chap. 62, the epithets "the Chosen One" and "that Son of Man" seem to be used synonymously, and in 46:3 it is stated that the Lord of Spirits has chosen that Son of Man. Finally, "his Messiah" in 48:10 seems to be the same figure as the one designated "that Son of Man" in 48:2.

burg and James C. VanderKam, *1 Enoch: A New Translation* (Minneapolis: Fortress, 2004) 51, and esp. the discussion by James C. VanderKam, "Righteous One, Messiah, Chosen One, and Son of Man in 1 Enoch 37–71," in James H. Charlesworth, ed., *The Messiah: Developments in Earliest Judaism and Christianity* (Minneapolis: Fortress, 1992) 170.

42   *1 Enoch* 45:3, 4; 49:2; 51:3, 5; 52:6, 9; 55:4; 61:5, 8, 10; 62:1. See the discussion by VanderKam, "Righteous One," 172–74.

43   *1 Enoch* 46:2, 3, 4; 48:2; 62:7, 9, 14; 63:11; 69:26, 27, 29 (twice); 70:1; 71:17. For discussion of "that Son of Man" and related epithets, see VanderKam, "Righteous One," 174–75.

44   *1 Enoch* 48:10; 52:4. That the four epithets refer to the same individual has been argued by several scholars; see VanderKam, "Righteous One," 185–86.

45   The members of the community to be redeemed are also called "the righteous and the chosen who dwell on the dry ground" in *1 Enoch* 38:2; cf. 39:6, 7; 58:1, 2; 60:8; 61:13; 62:13, 15; 70:3; "the righteous" or "my righteous ones" in 38:3; 39:4; 45:6; 47:1, 2, 4; 48:7, 9; 50:2; 51:5; 53:7; 56:7; 58:3, 4; 61:3; 62:12; 71:17 (twice); "the chosen" or "my chosen ones" in 38:3; 41:2; 45:5; 48:9; 56:6 (twice); 58:3; 60:6; 61:4, 12; 62:7, 8, 12; "the holy, the righteous and the chosen" in 38:4; cf. 48:1; "the righteous and the holy" in 38:5; 48:4; cf. 48:7; 51:2; and "the holy and the chosen" in 50:1; 62:8.

46   See VanderKam, "Righteous One," 189.

47   The term in the MT is בחיר; in the LXX ἐκλεκτός. See VanderKam, "Righteous One," 189.

48   So VanderKam, "Righteous One," 190. He also notes rightly that the theme of the suffering of the Servant is not taken up in the Similitudes of Enoch. Thus, the latter work is a precedent for the messianic interpretation of Isaiah 53 in the *Targum of Jonathan*, in which the suffering is attributed to others and not to the Servant; see VanderKam, "Righteous One"; for an ET of the latter passage, see Samuel Rolles Driver and Adolf Neubauer, eds., *The Fifty-Third Chapter of Isaiah according to the Jewish Interpreters*, vol. 2: *Translations* (New York: Ktav, 1969) 5–6.

49   The term ἐκλεκτός ("Elect One" or "Chosen One") is applied to Israel as the servant of the Lord in Isa 42:1 and 45:4; the plural ἐκλεκτοί ("elect ones" or "chosen ones") is used in 65:9, 15, 23. See also Pss 88:4; 104:6, 43; 105:5 LXX. In Ps 105:23 LXX, the singular ἐκλεκτός ("Elect One" or "Chosen One") is applied to Moses. The phrase τὸ γένος μου τὸ ἐκλεκτόν ("my chosen people") is used in Isa 43:20 LXX.

50   The Chosen One in *1 Enoch* 45:3; 55:4; 61:8; cf. 51:3; the Son of Man in 69:27, 29.

51   The Chosen One in 61:8; the Son of Man in 69:28.

52   The Chosen One in 49:4; the Son of Man in 69:27-28.

53   The Chosen One in 45:3-4; the Son of Man in 62:13-16; 71:16-17.

54   The Chosen One in 51:3; the Son of Man in 46:3.

55   To the Chosen One in 52:6-9; to the Son of Man in 46:5; cf. 62:9-12; 63:11. A similar role is ascribed to "the Righteous One" in 38:5.

The epithet "that Son of Man" is a clear allusion to Daniel 7:13. The identification of the "one like a son of man" in the latter passage with "his Messiah" in the Similitudes suggests that the figure of Dan 7:13 was identified with the Davidic messiah by the author of this work and his circle.[56] The redeemer figure of the Similitudes of Enoch is similar to the Davidic messiah as reflected in the Dead Sea Scrolls, the *Psalms of Solomon*, and Josephus, insofar as he was expected to defeat the enemies of the community. Although these are not specified in the Similitudes, they were probably Roman officials and their local collaborators, especially the rich and powerful.[57] The expectation associated with him is different, however, in that the new age that he will inaugurate is not primarily a reestablished, autonomous kingdom of Israel, but a qualitatively new age that will begin with the resurrection from the dead and the radical transformation of the natural world.[58] For example, one account of the reign of "that Son of Man" includes the following:

And from then on there will be nothing that is corruptible;
  for that Son of Man has appeared.
And he has sat down on the throne of his glory,
  and all evil will vanish from his presence.
And the word of that Son of Man will go forth
  and will prevail in the presence of the Lord of Spirits. (*1 Enoch* 69:29)[59]

The defeat of the kings and the mighty does not simply imply loss of hegemony, but eternal punishment as well.[60]

One of the most striking characteristics of "that Son of Man" in the Similitudes, which is new in relation to the other works and evidence discussed above, is the motif of his hiddenness. This motif is introduced as follows:

Even before the sun and the constellations were created,
  before the stars of heaven were made,
  his name was named before the Lord of Spirits.
He will be a staff for the righteous,
  that they may lean on him and not fall;
And he will be the light of the nations,
  and he will be a hope for those who grieve in their hearts.
All who dwell upon the earth will fall down and worship before him,
  and they will glorify and bless and sing hymns to the name of the Lord of Spirits.
For this (reason) he was chosen and hidden in his presence
  before the world was created and for ever.
And the wisdom of the Lord of Spirits has revealed him to the holy and the righteous;
  for he has preserved the portion of the righteous.
For they have hated and despised this world of unrighteousness;
  Indeed, all its deeds and its ways they have hated in the name of the Lord of Spirits.
For in his name they are saved,
  and he is the vindicator of their lives. (48:3-7)[61]

The motif of hiddenness may have been inspired by Isa 49:2:

He made my mouth like a sharp sword,
in the shadow of his hand he hid me;
he made me a polished arrow,
in his quiver he hid me away. (RSV)[62]

---

56   A similar identification is implied by *4 Ezra* 13; see below.

57   Mention is made of the Parthians and the Medes in *1 Enoch* 56:5; the text may allude to the invasion of Judea by the Parthians and the Medes in 40 BCE, or it may be a prophecy of a future invasion. In any case, the frequent references to the kings and the mighty should probably be understood as allusions to the Romans and their collaborators; see Nickelsburg, *Jewish Literature*, 223.

58   Resurrection is described in *1 Enoch* 61:5 and 62:15-16. On the transformation of nature, see 45:4-5.

59   Trans. (slightly modified) from Nickelsburg and VanderKam, 92.

60   *1 Enoch* 46:6; 48:9-10; and esp. 53:2-5; 56:8; 62:11-13; 63:6, 10.

61   Trans. from Nickelsburg and VanderKam, 62.

62   The speaker is the Servant of the Lord; cf. Isa 49:3. The motif according to which the Son of Man is "a light to the nations" also comes from the poems about the Servant in Deutero-Isaiah, i.e., from Isa 42:6.

Scholars have debated whether the motif of hiddenness implies preexistence, that is, that the Son of Man existed before the creation of the world.[63] The following passage seems to support such an inference:

> For from the beginning the Son of Man was hidden,
>   and the Most High preserved him in the presence
>   of his might,
>   and he revealed him to the chosen. (*1 Enoch* 62:7)[64]

In any case, what is emphasized in the Similitudes is the revelation of the Son of Man before the day of judgment to the community that will be redeemed and the surprise that the kings and the mighty will experience when they see him on his throne of glory.[65] Thus, according to the Similitudes of Enoch, the Son of Man is revealed secretly to the community of the righteous beforehand and publicly in the last days, in particular on the day of judgment.

The redeemer figure in *4 Ezra*, like that of the Similitudes of Enoch, shows both continuity with older traditions about the Messiah, on the one hand, and transformation and innovation, on the other. The book is very clearly divided into seven sections, which are usually called "Visions." The first mention of the Messiah occurs in the exceptionally long and complex third vision (6:35—9:25).[66] In this section, 7:26-44 is a direct angelic prediction of the entire eschatological scenario.[67] The prediction opens as follows:

> For behold, the time will come, when the signs which I have foretold to you will come, that the city which

now is not seen shall appear, and the land which now is hidden shall be disclosed. And everyone who has been delivered from the evils that I have foretold shall see my wonders.[68] For my Messiah shall be revealed and those who are with him, and he shall make rejoice those who remain for four hundred years. And after these years my son (or: servant)[69] the Messiah shall die, and all who draw human breath. (*4 Ezra* 7:26-29)[70]

It is striking that in this passage, the Messiah has no role in the eschatological battle or in the final judgment.[71] His designated role is simply to be revealed, along with those who accompany him, and to dwell with rejoicing among those who survive the messianic woes. The language concerning the revelation of the Messiah here implies that he is preexistent.[72]

The Messiah also plays a role in the fifth vision (*4 Ezra* 11—12). The vision proper (11:1—12:3) concerns an eagle with twelve wings and three heads, which represents the Roman empire.[73] After the middle head had disappeared and the head on the right side had devoured the head on the left (11:33-35), that is, after the death of Vespasian and the (alleged) murder of Titus by Domitian,[74] a voice spoke to Ezra that introduced a new phase of the vision:

> Then I heard a voice saying to me, "Look before you and consider what you see." And I looked, and behold, a creature like a lion was aroused out of the forest, roaring; and I heard how he uttered a man's voice to the eagle, and spoke, saying, "Are you not the one that remains of the four beasts which I had made

---

63   See the discussion by VanderKam, "Righteous One," 179–82.

64   Trans. (slightly modified) from Nickelsburg and VanderKam, 80.

65   The motif of his revelation to the community occurs also in 48:6-7; cf. 69:26. The surprise and dismay of the kings and the mighty are described in 62:1-6. The judgment scene in *1 Enoch* 62–63 is similar to that in the Wisdom of Solomon 2; 4–5; see Nickelsburg, *Jewish Literature*, 222.

66   See Stone, *Fourth Ezra*, 50.

67   Ibid., 204.

68   Those who have been delivered from the evils that have been foretold are the ones who survive the messianic woes; see, e.g., *4 Ezra* 6:18-27.

69   The Latin version reads *filius meus Iesus* ("my son Jesus"). Stone argued that comparison with the

other versions makes clear that the lost Greek version probably read παῖς ("servant" or "son") and that the Hebrew original was probably עבד ("servant") (*Fourth Ezra*, 207). But the dependence of the portrayal of the Messiah in *4 Ezra* 13 on Psalm 2 makes it likely that the Hebrew original read בן ("son"); see Collins, *Scepter and the Star*, 165.

70   Trans. from Stone, *Fourth Ezra*, 202.

71   After the death of the Messiah, the resurrection will occur and then the judgment, in which the Most High will act as judge (*4 Ezra* 7:30-44).

72   See the discussion of the fifth vision below.

73   The eagle is described in 11:1-35 and interpreted in 12:11-30.

74   See Stone, *Fourth Ezra*, 10.

to reign in my world, so that the end of the times might come through them?" (*4 Ezra* 11:36-39)[75]

The lion then indicts and sentences the eagle in the style of the prophets of the Jewish scriptures.[76] On the one hand, the lion is a symbol of the Davidic messiah.[77] But this Messiah of Israel also acts and speaks like a prophet.

The Messiah of *4 Ezra*, like that of the Similitudes of Enoch, is preexistent. In the interpretation of the eagle vision, the angel says to Ezra:

> And as for the lion whom you saw rousing up out of the forest and roaring and speaking to the eagle and reproving him for his unrighteousness, and as for all his words that you have heard, this is the Messiah whom the Most High has kept until the end of days, who will arise from the posterity of David, and will come and speak to them; he will denounce them for their ungodliness and for their wickedness, and will cast up before them their contemptuous dealings. For first he will set them living in judgment, and when he has reproved them, then he will destroy them. But he will deliver in mercy the remnant of my people, those who have been saved throughout my borders, and he will make them joyful until the end comes, the day of judgment, of which I spoke to you at the beginning. (*4 Ezra* 12:31-34)[78]

As noted above, the figure of the Messiah here fuses traditional prophetic and Davidic messianic elements. The reproving mentioned in vv. 31 and 33 indicates a prophetic role. The Davidic descent affirmed in v. 32 is similar to the expectations of the Dead Sea Scrolls and the *Psalms of Solomon*. The role of the Davidic messiah as a warrior who defeats the enemies of the people in battle, also found in the Dead Sea Scrolls, the *Psalms of Solomon,* and in the accounts of the messianic pretenders in Josephus, surfaces here as well: after the Messiah reproves those symbolized by the eagle, he will destroy them (*4 Ezra* 12:33; cf. 12:1-3). The notion that the Mes-

siah would arise from the posterity of David is in some tension with the affirmation that the Most High has kept the Messiah until the end of days (12:32; cf. 7:28). The intimation of preexistence suggests a heightening of the charismatic and extraordinary character of the Messiah; it also offers comfort to the audience in its reassurance that the Messiah is already in existence, just waiting for the right time to be revealed.

The next description of the redeemer figure in *4 Ezra* occurs in the sixth vision, chap. 13, which focuses on "something like the figure of a man" that comes up from the heart of the sea. Like "that Son of Man" in the Similitudes of Enoch, "the man from the sea" in *4 Ezra* 13 is an image that alludes to and develops further the "one like a son of man" in Dan 7:13. This portion of *4 Ezra* thus also provides evidence for the messianic interpretation of the human figure in Dan 7:13 in the first century CE. In the vision proper, the "man from the sea" is presented primarily as a warrior.[79] Although he is not explicitly identified as the Davidic messiah, his role in defeating the nations in battle implies such an identification. It is further supported by the scriptural echoes of the description of his victory in battle:

> After this I looked, and behold, all who had gathered together against him, to wage war with him, were much afraid, yet dared to fight. And when he saw the onrush of the approaching multitude, he neither lifted his hand nor held a sword or any weapon of war; but I saw only how he sent forth from his mouth as it were a stream of fire, and from his lips a flaming breath, and from his tongue he shot forth a storm of fiery coals. All these were mingled together, the stream of fire and the flaming breath and the great storm, and fell on the onrushing multitude which was prepared to fight, and burned them all up, so that suddenly nothing was seen of the innumerable multitude but only the dust of ashes and the smell of smoke. When I saw it, I was amazed. (*4 Ezra* 13:8-11)[80]

---

75 Trans. from Stone, *Fourth Ezra*, 344.
76 See the discussion of the *Psalms of Solomon* and *4 Ezra* above in the section *Jesus as Prophet.*
77 This idea is a reinterpretation of Gen 49:9-10. See also 1QSb = 1Q28b 5:29, in which the Prince of the congregation, who is equivalent to the Davidic messiah, is addressed, "you shall be as a lion"; see the

discussion of the Messiah of Israel in the Dead Sea Scrolls above.
78 Trans. from Stone, *Fourth Ezra*, 360.
79 On the connections with Daniel 7 and on the presentation of the man from the sea as a divine warrior, see Stone, *Fourth Ezra*, 212.
80 Trans. from Stone, *Fourth Ezra*, 381–82.

It is clear from the outcome of the battle that the stream of fire from the mouth of the Messiah, from the point of view of the vision proper, should be taken as a miraculous means of destruction and not as a peaceful method of persuasion. A similar expectation is expressed with similar language in the blessing of the Prince of the congregation in the *Rule of Blessings* from Qumran:

> May [you strike the peoples] with the power of your mouth. With your sceptre may you lay waste *Blank* the earth. With the breath of your lips may you kill the wicked. (1QSb = 1Q28b 5:24-25)[81]

Both *4 Ezra* 13:8-11 and this passage from Qumran reflect a messianic interpretation of Isa 11:4, which reads:

> and he shall smite the earth with the rod of his
> mouth,
> and with the breath of his lips he shall slay the
> wicked.[82]

A similar idea is expressed in Ps 2:8-9:

> Ask of me, and I will make the nations your heritage,
> and the ends of the earth your possession.
> You shall break them with a rod of iron,
> and dash them in pieces like a potter's vessel. (NRSV)

The overlap of the rod or staff and the messianic interpretation of both passages in the later Second Temple period led to the combination of Isa 11:4 and Ps 2:9 in *Ps. Sol.* 17:21-24:

> See, Lord, and raise up for them their king, the son of David, to rule over your servant Israel . . . to smash the arrogance of sinners like a potter's jar; to shatter

all their substance with an iron rod; to destroy the unlawful nations with the word of his mouth.[83]

After the battle, the Messiah will gather the exiles of Israel (the joyful),[84] and the surviving Gentiles (the sorrowful) will be subjected to him as well.

The interpretation of the sixth vision (13:20-55) emphasizes the motif of the preexistence and hiddenness of the Messiah:

> This is the interpretation of the vision: As for your seeing a man come up from the heart of the sea, this is he whom the Most High has been keeping for many ages, through whom he will deliver his creation; and he will direct those who are left. (13:25-26)[85]

> I said, "O sovereign Lord, explain this to me: Why did I see the man coming up from the heart of the sea?" He said to me, "Just as no one can explore or know what is in the depths of the sea, so no one on earth can see my servant or those who are with him, except in the time of his day." (13:51-52)[86]

As noted above, the theme of the revelation of the Son of Man to the community of the chosen is explicit in the Similitudes of Enoch. That theme is not explicit in *4 Ezra*, but it is implicit in that the existence and future activity of the man from the sea are revealed to Ezra, who in turn reveals the information, apparently only in secret, to the wise (cf. *4 Ezra* 14:23-26).

The destruction of the innumerable multitude in the vision is explained in the interpretation of the vision in prophetic and legal terms: the fiery breath and the storm are interpreted as reproof (13:27-28, 37); the flames as verbal reproach and subsequent punishment (13:38);[87] and the fire as the Law (13:38).[88] An important

---

81   Trans. from Florentino García Martínez, *The Dead Sea Scrolls Translated: The Qumran Texts in English* (2nd ed.; Leiden: Brill; Grand Rapids: Eerdmans, 1996) 433. In *Dead Sea Scrolls,* García Martínez and Tigchelaar translate line 24 as follows, "May you be [. . .] with the power of your [mouth]" (1:109).

82   Trans. from Stone, *Fourth Ezra,* 386; see the discussion there.

83   See the fuller citation of this passage above in the discussion of the Messiah in the *Psalms of Solomon* 17–18; for discussion, see Stone, *Fourth Ezra,* 386.

84   *4 Ezra* 13:12-13; cf. Isa 66:20; for discussion, see Stone, *Fourth Ezra,* 387. The exiles of Israel are interpreted as the nine and one-half tribes in 13:40-47; see Stone, *Fourth Ezra,* 393, 404–5.

85   Trans. from Stone, *Fourth Ezra,* 392.

86   Trans. from Stone, *Fourth Ezra,* 394.

87   For discussion, see Stone, *Fourth Ezra,* 387.

88   See ibid., 212.

aspect of the role of the Messiah is his protection and leadership of those who survive the messianic woes. It is noteworthy that this role is not described in language of kingship (13:26, 48-49).[89] A further prophetic element that has been integrated into this portrayal of the Messiah is the affirmation that he will perform wonders for the survivors (13:50; cf. 4:26-27; 7:27).

It is in this context of first-century Jewish texts that the theme "Jesus as Messiah" in the Gospel of Mark must be approached. This theme is initiated already in the opening verse of Mark, "The beginning of the good news of Jesus Christ" ('Αρχὴ τοῦ εὐαγγελίου Ἰησοῦ Χριστοῦ).[90] As is clear from the discussion of the Dead Sea Scrolls above, the term χριστός ("anointed one" or "Messiah") could refer to a royal, prophetic, or priestly figure of the past or the eschatological future. The connotations of the epithet in Mark depend on the narrative development of the relevant themes. As shown in the subsection *Jesus as Prophet* above, from the point of view of the Jewish scriptures and eschatological traditions, the Gospel of Mark leads its audience to view Jesus, at least in part, as the eschatological prophet. In what follows, the narrative development of the theme "Jesus as (Davidic) Messiah" will be explored.

The theme of Jesus' role as royal messiah is subtly introduced in the saying of John the Baptist:

And he was proclaiming, saying, "The one who is stronger than I is coming after me; I am not fit to crouch and untie the strap of his sandals. I have baptized you with water, but he will baptize you in (the) Holy Spirit." (Mark 1:7-8)

It is not at first apparent why Jesus should be designated as "the one stronger than I" (ὁ ἰσχυρότερός μου) in v. 7.

Perhaps his strength has something to do with his imminent endowment with the Holy Spirit, as v. 8 suggests. In any case, the root word of the epithet, "the strong one" (ὁ ἰσχυρός), has connotations of the divine warrior and his (royal) messiah or other agent in battle. According to 1 Sam 16:18, David was a גבור חיל ("a mighty man" or "a man of valor").[91] Gideon, a leader of the Israelites in holy war, is addressed by the angel of the Lord as גבור החיל ("you mighty man of valor") (Judg 6:12 MT).[92] In Psalm 24, the Lord is acclaimed as גבור מלחמה ("mighty in battle") (v. 8 MT).[93] The king is addressed as גבור ("O mighty one") in Ps 45:4.[94] The statement in Ps 89:20, "I have set the crown on one who is mighty (גבור)," refers to David.[95] The prediction concerning the "child born to us" in Isa 9:5, that he would be אל גבור ("mighty God"), could have been interpreted messianically in the first century CE.[96] Judas Maccabeus is described as "a mighty warrior" (ἰσχυρὸς δυνάμει) (1 Macc 2:66). As noted above, Josephus commented on the bodily strength of a messianic pretender, Simon the slave of Herod, and the feats of strength accomplished by Athronges, another would-be Messiah. In a liturgical section of the *War Scroll* from Qumran, God is addressed twice as "Mighty One" or "Hero" (גבור) (1QM 12:9, 10).[97]

If the historical John the Baptist announced that a "stronger one" was coming after him, he may have been referring to an as-yet-unknown Messiah of Israel or to God as the divine warrior. In any case, in the present context of the Gospel of Mark, the "stronger one" is Jesus, and the term could well have had connotations of the Davidic messiah as God's agent in the eschatological battle. According to Mark, Jesus does not carry out such a role during his lifetime, but the expectation may have been elicited in some circles of the audience that he would carry out such a role upon his return as Son of Man.

---

89 See ibid., 405–6.

90 The reading υἱοῦ θεοῦ ("son of God") is most likely secondary; see the commentary below.

91 So the MT; the LXX reads ὁ ἀνὴρ συνετός ("a man of understanding").

92 In the LXX, B (Codex Vaticanus) reads ἰσχυρὸς τῶν δυνάμεων ("you mighty of deeds"); A (Codex Alexandrinus) reads δυνατὸς τῇ ἰσχύι ("you mighty in strength").

93 The Greek reads δυνατὸς ἐν πολέμῳ ("mighty in battle") (Ps 23:8 LXX).

94 Ps 45:4 MT; 45:3 RSV. Ps 44:4 LXX reads δυνατέ ("O mighty one").

95 Ps 89:20 MT; 89:19 RSV. Ps 88:19 LXX reads δυνατός ("a mighty one").

96 Isa 9:5 MT; 9:6 RSV. Isa 9:5 LXX reads Μεγάλης βουλῆς ἄγγελος ("Messenger of great counsel").

97 In a context of eschatological warfare, God is described as "Mighty One" or "Hero" (גבור) in 1QH 14:30 (= 6:30 in the old numbering).

As noted in the subsection *Jesus as Prophet* above, the descent of the Holy Spirit upon Jesus on the occasion of his baptism by John has both prophetic and messianic connotations. It is by the Spirit of the Lord that the prophet is able to speak the truth about the present and the future (1 Kgs 22:24). But the event also has messianic connotations in a historical and cultural context in which Isa 11:1-4 was read messianically:[98]

> There shall come forth a rod from the root of Jesse,
> and a flower shall grow out of his root.
> And the spirit of the Lord shall rest upon him,
> the spirit of wisdom and understanding,
> the spirit of counsel and might,
> the spirit of knowledge and the fear of the Lord
> (Καὶ ἐξελεύσεται ῥάβδος ἐκ τῆς ῥίζης Ιεσσαι,
> καὶ ἄνθος ἐκ τῆς ῥίζης ἀναβήσεται.
> καὶ ἀναπαύσεται ἐπ᾿ αὐτὸν πνεῦμα τοῦ θεοῦ,
> πνεῦμα σοφίας καὶ συνέσεως,
> πνεῦμα βουλῆς καὶ ἰσχύος,
> πνεῦμα γνώσεως καὶ εὐσεβείας). (Isa 11:1-2 LXX)

It is noteworthy that the phrase "spirit of might" or "spirit of strength" (πνεῦμα ἰσχύος) occurs in this passage, a phrase that the description of Jesus by John the Baptist as "the one stronger than I" (ὁ ἰσχυρότερός μου) in v. 7 echoes. The event of Jesus' endowment with the Spirit of God in the scene of his baptism in Mark thus appears to the knowledgeable members of the audience as a fulfillment of the prophecy of Isaiah understood in terms of an ideal, messianic king.

The descent of the Spirit upon Jesus is followed by a voice from heaven, the divine voice, that says: "You are my beloved son; I take delight in you" (σὺ εἶ ὁ υἱός μου ὁ ἀγαπητός, ἐν σοὶ εὐδόκησα). The first part of the divine statement alludes to Ps 2:7 LXX, which reads: "The Lord said to me, 'You are my son; today I have begotten you'" (Κύριος εἶπεν πρός με Υἱός μου εἶ σύ, ἐγὼ σήμερον γεγέννηκά σε).[99]

Psalm 2 speaks of the Lord and his anointed (king). As noted above, *Ps. Sol.* 17:21-24 reflects a messianic reading of this psalm. In the Gospel of Mark, therefore, the divine voice suggests to an audience familiar with the messianic reading of Psalm 2, that Jesus is the royal messiah or the Messiah of Israel.

"Son of God" is also an epithet of the Davidic messiah in the Dead Sea Scrolls. This conclusion is supported by a passage in a collection of eschatological interpretations of biblical passages from Qumran (4QFlor [4Q174] 1:10-12):

> The Lord declares to you that he will build you a House (2 Sam 7:11c). I will raise up your seed after you (2 Sam 7:12). I will establish the throne of his kingdom [for ever] (2 Sam 7:13). [I will be] his father and he shall be my son (2 Sam 7:14). He is the Branch of David who shall arise with the Interpreter of the Law [to rule] in Zion [at the end] of time.[100]

That the "Branch of David," designated here indirectly as "son of God," is the Messiah of Israel is made clear by a passage in the *Commentary on Genesis* (4QpGen[a] [4Q252] 5:1-4):

> The sceptre [shall not] depart from the tribe of Judah . . . [Gen 49:10]. Whenever Israel rules, there shall [not] fail to be a descendant of David upon the throne [Jer 33:17]. For the ruler's staff [Gen 49:10] is the Covenant of kingship, [and the clans] of Israel are the divisions, until the Messiah of Righteousness comes, the Branch of David. For to him and his seed is granted the Covenant of kingship over his people for everlasting generations . . . .[101]

It is likely that the figure declared to be "son of God" and "son of the Most High" in a controversial Aramaic fragment from Qumran is also the Davidic messiah.[102] Thus, from the point of view of these Jewish traditions,

---

98 See the discussion above for the messianic reading of Isa 11:1-4 in the DSS and the *Psalms of Solomon*.

99 The statement Υἱός μου εἶ σύ, ἐγὼ σήμερον γεγέννηκά σε ("You are my son, today I have begotten you") is quoted in Heb 1:5a.

100 Trans. (slightly modified) from Vermes, *Dead Sea Scrolls*, 526. The statement "I will be his father and he shall be my son" is quoted in Heb 1:5b.

101 Trans. from Vermes, *Dead Sea Scrolls*, 494; see also García Martínez and Tigchelaar, *Dead Sea Scrolls*, 1:505.

102 4QAramaic Apocalypse (4Q246) 2:1; Vermes, *Dead Sea Scrolls*, 618; García Martínez and Tigchelaar, *Dead Sea Scrolls*, 1:495; for discussion, see Collins, *Scepter and the Star*, 154–64.

the voice from heaven in Mark 1:11 is a clear attestation of Jesus as the Davidic messiah.

Jesus is addressed as "teacher" ten times in the Gospel of Mark and is referred to as "the teacher" twice; in one case it is a self-designation.[103] This activity or social role seems at first glance to be incompatible with the office of royal messiah. One way of solving this apparent anomaly is to note that, according to Mark, Jesus is appointed Messiah at his baptism, but only enters into his messianic office after his resurrection (see 9:9; 14:61-62). It is better, however, to observe that kingship and the teaching office are not mutually exclusive in Jewish tradition. Solomon held royal office but was also renowned as a wise man and a teacher of wisdom. The Davidic messiah of *Psalms of Solomon* 17–18 is described with attributes and activities that characterize the teacher as much as the king. He will be "taught by God" ($\delta\iota\delta\alpha\kappa\tau\grave{o}\varsigma\ \acute{v}\pi\grave{o}\ \vartheta\epsilon o\widehat{v}$) (*Ps. Sol.* 17:32).[104] His speech is extraordinary:

His words will be purer than the finest gold, the best.
He will judge the peoples in the assemblies, the tribes
    of the sanctified.
His words will be as the words of the holy ones
    (angels), among sanctified peoples
($\tau\grave{\alpha}\ \acute{\rho}\acute{\eta}\mu\alpha\tau\alpha\ \alpha\grave{v}\tau o\widehat{v}\ \pi\epsilon\pi\upsilon\rho\omega\mu\acute{\epsilon}\nu\alpha\ \acute{v}\pi\grave{\epsilon}\rho\ \chi\rho\upsilon\sigma\acute{\iota}o\nu\ \tau\grave{o}$
    $\pi\rho\widehat{\omega}\tau o\nu\ \tau\acute{\iota}\mu\iota o\nu,$
$\grave{\epsilon}\nu\ \sigma\upsilon\nu\alpha\gamma\omega\gamma\alpha\widehat{\iota}\varsigma\ \delta\iota\alpha\kappa\rho\iota\nu\epsilon\widehat{\iota}\ \lambda\alpha o\widehat{v}\ \phi\upsilon\lambda\grave{\alpha}\varsigma\ \acute{\eta}\gamma\iota\alpha\sigma\mu\acute{\epsilon}\nu o\upsilon,$
$o\acute{\iota}\ \lambda\acute{o}\gamma o\iota\ \alpha\grave{v}\tau o\widehat{v}\ \acute{\omega}\varsigma\ \lambda\acute{o}\gamma o\iota\ \acute{\alpha}\gamma\acute{\iota}\omega\nu\ \grave{\epsilon}\nu\ \mu\acute{\epsilon}\sigma\omega\ \lambda\alpha\widehat{\omega}\nu$
    $\acute{\eta}\gamma\iota\alpha\sigma\mu\acute{\epsilon}\nu\omega\nu$). (*Ps. Sol.* 17:43)[105]

The Messiah will be sent by God to accomplish the following:

to direct a man in righteous acts, in the fear of God,
to set them all in the presence of the Lord,
a good generation (living) in the fear of God in the
    days of mercy
($\kappa\alpha\tau\epsilon\upsilon\vartheta\widehat{\upsilon}\nu\alpha\iota\ \acute{\alpha}\nu\delta\rho\alpha\ \grave{\epsilon}\nu\ \acute{\epsilon}\rho\gamma o\iota\varsigma\ \delta\iota\kappa\alpha\iota o\sigma\acute{\upsilon}\nu\eta\varsigma\ \phi\acute{o}\beta\omega$
    $\vartheta\epsilon o\widehat{v}$

$\kappa\alpha\tau\alpha\sigma\tau\widehat{\eta}\sigma\alpha\iota\ \pi\acute{\alpha}\nu\tau\alpha\varsigma\ \alpha\grave{v}\tau o\grave{v}\varsigma\ \grave{\epsilon}\nu\acute{\omega}\pi\iota o\nu\ \kappa\upsilon\rho\acute{\iota}o\upsilon$
$\gamma\epsilon\nu\epsilon\grave{\alpha}\ \acute{\alpha}\gamma\alpha\vartheta\grave{\eta}\ \grave{\epsilon}\nu\ \phi\acute{o}\beta\omega\ \vartheta\epsilon o\widehat{v}\ \grave{\epsilon}\nu\ \acute{\eta}\mu\acute{\epsilon}\rho\alpha\iota\varsigma\ \grave{\epsilon}\lambda\acute{\epsilon}o\upsilon\varsigma$).
    (*Ps. Sol.* 18:8-9)[106]

The Chosen One, who is also the Messiah in the Similitudes of Enoch, is described as a teacher of revealed wisdom: "and all the secrets of wisdom will go forth from the counsel of his mouth" (*1 Enoch* 51:3).[107] Similarly, it is said of "that Son of Man," who is also the Messiah according to this work: "all the treasuries of what is hidden he will reveal" (*1 Enoch* 46:3).[108] As noted in the subsection *Jesus as Prophet* above, the role of eschatological teacher was combined with that of eschatological prophet in the Dead Sea Scrolls.[109] In the *Psalms of Solomon* and the Similitudes of Enoch, the role of (Davidic or royal) Messiah is combined with that of teacher or revealer. It is not surprising, therefore, that the Gospel of Mark presents Jesus both as the Davidic messiah and as a teacher.

As noted in the subsection *Jesus as Prophet*, the exorcisms of Jesus are the most prominent of the mighty deeds that he performs in the Gospel of Mark. Once again, this type of activity seems incompatible at first glance with the role of Davidic or royal messiah. The combination seems much less odd, however, when one recalls that David is presented in 1 Samuel as a kind of proto-exorcist:

Now the Spirit of the Lord departed from Saul, and an evil spirit from the Lord tormented him. And Saul's servants said to him, "Behold now, an evil spirit from God is tormenting you. Let our lord now command your servants, who are before you, to seek out a man who is skilful in playing the lyre; and when the evil spirit from God is upon you, he will play it, and you will be well." . . . Therefore Saul sent messengers to Jesse, and said, "Send me David your son, who is with the sheep." . . . And David came to Saul, and entered his service. . . . And whenever the evil spirit

---

103 See the discussion in the subsection *Jesus as Teacher* below.

104 This is an allusion to Isa 54:13; the same allusion is made in 1 Thess 4:9 and John 6:45.

105 Text from Rahlfs; trans. from Wright in *OTP* 2:668.

106 Text from Rahlfs; trans. modified from Wright in *OTP* 2:669.

107 Trans. from Nickelsburg and VanderKam, 65.

108 Trans. from Nickelsburg and VanderKam, 60.

109 Or with that of eschatological priest, or perhaps with both.

from God was upon Saul, David took the lyre and played it with his hand; so Saul was refreshed, and was well, and the evil spirit departed from him. (1 Sam 16:14-16, 19, 21, 23 RSV)

By the later part of the Second Temple period, a tradition had developed according to which Solomon was an exorcist and the source of exorcistic lore in use at the time.[110] This tradition developed in connection with the statement in 1 Kgs 5:9-14 (RSV 4:29-34) that Solomon's wisdom surpassed the wisdom of all the people of the East and all the wisdom of Egypt; he spoke three thousand parables and one thousand and five songs and spoke about plants and animals. According to the book of Wisdom attributed to Solomon, his knowledge included "the powers of spirits and the reasonings of human beings, the varieties of plants and the virtues of roots" (πνευμάτων βίας καὶ διαλογισμοὺς ἀνθρώπων, διαφορὰς φυτῶν καὶ δυνάμεις ῥιζῶν) (Wis 7:20).[111]

In his account of Solomon, Josephus refers to the passage in 1 Kings mentioned above and goes on to say:

And God granted him knowledge of the art used against demons for the benefit and healing of men. He also composed incantations by which illnesses are relieved, and left behind forms of exorcisms with which those possessed by demons drive them out, never to return. And this kind of cure is of very great power among us to this day, for I have seen a certain Eleazar, a countryman of mine, in the presence of Vespasian, his sons, tribunes and a number of other soldiers, free men possessed by demons (παρέσχε δ᾽ αὐτῷ μαθεῖν ὁ θεὸς καὶ τὴν κατὰ τῶν δαιμόνων τέχνην εἰς ὠφέλειαν καὶ θεραπείαν τοῖς ἀνθρώποις· ἐπῳδάς τε συνταξάμενος αἷς παρηγορεῖται τὰ νοσήματα καὶ τρόπους ἐξορκώσεων κατέλιπεν, οἷς οἱ ἐνδούμενοι τὰ δαιμόνια ὡς μηκέτ᾽ ἐπανελθεῖν ἐκδιώκουσι. καὶ αὕτη μέχρι νῦν παρ᾽ ἡμῖν ἡ θεραπεία πλεῖστον ἰσχύει· ἱστόρησα γάρ τινα

Ἐλεάζαρον τῶν ὁμοφύλων Οὐεσπασιανοῦ παρόντος καὶ τῶν υἱῶν αὐτοῦ καὶ χιλιάρχων καὶ ἄλλου στρατιωτικοῦ πλήθους τοὺς ὑπὸ τῶν δαιμονίων λαμβανομένους ἀπολύοντα τούτων). (Ant. 8.2.5 §45–46)

He then goes on to give an account of an exorcism performed by Eleazar. Without making an explicit connection between the Essenes and Solomon, Josephus makes the following remark in his description of the former:

They display an extraordinary interest in the writings of the ancients, singling out in particular those which make for the welfare of soul and body; with the help of these, and with a view to the treatment of diseases, they make investigations into medicinal roots and the properties of stones (σπουδάζουσι δ᾽ ἐκτόπως περὶ τὰ τῶν παλαιῶν συντάγματα, μάλιστα τὰ πρὸς ὠφέλειαν ψυχῆς καὶ σώματος ἐκλέγοντες· ἔνθεν αὐτοῖς πρὸς θεραπείαν παθῶν ῥίζαι τε ἀλεξητήριοι καὶ λίθων ἰδιότητες ἀνερευνῶνται). (Bell. 2.8.6 §136)[112]

There is evidence from the Dead Sea Scrolls that David was considered to be an exorcist of sorts:

And David, son of Jesse, was wise, and a light like the light of the sun, /and/ learned, *Blank* and discerning, and perfect in all his paths before God and men. And *Blank* YHWH gave him a discerning and enlightened spirit. And he wrote psalms: three thousand six hundred; . . . *And songs to perform over the possessed: four.* The total was four thousand and fifty. All these he spoke through (the spirit of) prophecy which had been given to him from before the Most High.[113]

It also seems likely that exorcism was practiced by members of the Qumran community. A scroll discovered in Cave 11, 11QApocryphal Psalms[a], contains fragments of

---

110 Much of the evidence has been collected by Dennis C. Duling, "Solomon, Exorcism, and the Son of David," *HTR* 68 (1975) 235–52.

111 Text from Rahlfs; trans. RSV modified.

112 Text and trans. from Thackeray, *Josephus*, 2:374–75.

113 From the "Compositions of David," a portion of the *Psalms Scroll* from Cave 11; the text quoted is 11QPs[a]

(11Q5) 27:2-5, 9-11; trans. from García Martínez and Tigchelaar, *Dead Sea Scrolls*, 2:1179 (emphasis added).

apocryphal psalms followed by a version of Psalm 91. The apocryphal texts seem to be closely related to the practice of exorcism. The surviving portions of col. 1 mention an "oath," a "dragon," the term "exorcising" and "the demon." The remaining portions of col. 2 mention "Solomon," who "will invoke," as well as "demons," "the Prince of Animosity" or enmity, the "abyss" and the term "cure."[114] Col. 4 reads:

> [and] great [. . .] adjuring [. . .] and the great [. . .] powerful and [. . .] the whole earth [. . .] heavens and [. . .] YHWH will strike you with a [mighty] bl[ow] to destroy you [. . .] and in the fury of his anger [he will send] a powerful angel against you, [to carry out] [all] his [com]mand, (one) who [will not show] you mercy, wh[o . . .] [. . .] above all these, who will [bring] you [down] to the great abyss, [and to] the deepest [Sheol.] . . . (11QPsAp [= 11Q11] 3)[115]

Col. 5 speaks of Raphael healing "them," possibly the possessed ones, who are mentioned in the previous line. A text attributed to David follows. The reader is instructed to say an incantation when a demon comes upon him at night, namely:

> Who are you, [O offspring of] man and of the seed of the ho[ly] ones? Your face is a face of [delus]ion, and your horns are horns of illu[si]on. You are darkness and not light, [injus]tice and not justice. (11QPsAp [= 11Q11] 5:6-8)[116]

Then the demon is to be threatened with being shut up by YHWH in the deepest Sheol, in utter darkness. Most of the remaining portion of col. 6 consists of a version of Psalm 91. The hypothesis that Psalm 91 was also used to exorcise finds support in the fact that this psalm is known in rabbinic literature as the "song for the stricken," the "song referring to evil spirits" and the "song for demons."[117]

The connection of Solomon with control over demons and exorcism is especially clear and strong in the apocryphal work entitled the *Testament of Solomon*.[118] Since David and Solomon were associated with exorcism in the time of Jesus, it is not strange that the Gospel of Mark could present him both as the Davidic messiah and as a powerful exorcist.

The other miracles of Jesus are reminiscent of the mighty deeds of Elijah and Elisha and are presented as fulfillments of the prophecies of restoration in Deutero-Isaiah, read as eschatological prophecies. These connections were noted in the subsection *Jesus as Prophet* above. But, as pointed out in the survey of Jewish messianism in the late Second Temple period above, there was an expectation that the Messiah would be associated with or even perform "wonders." In *4 Ezra* 7:26-29 (quoted above), it is said that everyone who has been delivered from the messianic woes will see divine wonders; the revelation of the Messiah itself is apparently one of these wonders. A parallel passage gives a more detailed picture of the "wonders" in question:

> And it shall come to pass that whoever remains after all that I have foretold to you shall himself be saved and shall see my salvation and the end of my world. And they shall see the men who were taken up, who from their birth have not tasted death; and the heart of the earth's inhabitants shall be changed and converted to a different spirit. (*4 Ezra* 6:25-26)[119]

A closer analogy to the portrayal of Jesus in Mark occurs in the description of the activities of the "man from the sea," a messianic figure in *4 Ezra* 13 (see the discussion above). After he destroys the nations that have assembled against him, he will defend those who remain[120] and show them very many wonders (*4 Ezra* 13:49-50). We see, then, that the performance of miracles is a typically prophetic element in Jewish tradition; given the conflation of roles in the Second Temple period, however,

---

114 See García Martínez and Tigchelaar, *Dead Sea Scrolls*, 2:1201.

115 Trans. from García Martínez and Tigchelaar, *Dead Sea Scrolls*, 2:1203.

116 Trans. from García Martínez and Tigchelaar, *Dead Sea Scrolls*, 2:1203.

117 *Y. Šabb.* 6:8b; *b. Šebu.* 15b; *y. ʿErub.* 10:26c; see Dul-ing, "Solomon, Exorcism," 239, and the literature cited in n. 17.

118 For an introduction and ET, see D. C. Duling in *OTP* 1:935–87; see also Duling, "Solomon, Exorcism," 242–44.

119 Trans. from Stone, *Fourth Ezra*, 163.

120 Those who remain are the righteous; cf. 4:27.

miracle-working can also be associated with the Davidic messiah. *4 Ezra*, which dates to the early part of the post-Second Temple period, is evidence that such a connection was indeed made.

In Mark 3:13-19, Jesus chooses twelve disciples to be with him, to be sent out to proclaim, and to cast out demons. The number twelve probably reflects the twelve tribes of Israel. The purposes for which these are selected reflect the intention of preparing the people of Israel for the dawning kingdom of God (cf. Mark 6:7-13). The act of choosing a special group of twelve for such a purpose fits well with the presentation of Jesus as the Davidic messiah or the Messiah of Israel.[121] As noted above, the Prince of the congregation was to have the names of the twelve tribes of Israel written upon his shield, according to the *War Scroll* from Qumran (1QM 5:1-2).

A very important passage for the development of the theme of "Jesus as Messiah" in Mark is the scene in which Peter declares, "You are the Messiah" (σὺ εἶ ὁ χριστός) (Mark 8:27-30). It is clear from the context that χριστός (lit. "anointed") means Davidic messiah or royal messiah here, because the acclamation is offered as an alternative to the opinion of some of the people that Jesus is "one of the prophets" (εἷς τῶν προφητῶν). The response of Jesus (v. 30) makes clear that the acclamation is accepted; the immediate response is not to reject or reinterpret but to command the disciples to keep the identity of Jesus secret.

The reinterpretation comes in the next, closely related scene. Evidently, Jesus and the disciples, as characters in the narrative, on the one hand, and the author of Mark and his audience, on the other, have a shared understanding of the notion of the Davidic messiah and a shared assumption that "the Messiah" and "the Son of Man" are equivalent. That such information is commonly understood is clear from the fact that it needs no com-

ment, explanation, or defense.[122] The speech of Jesus in v. 31, however, does introduce new, or least controversial, information: that the Messiah, the Son of Man, must suffer, etc. *4 Ezra* does allow for the death of the Messiah, but it is to be a natural death after a four hundred-year reign, belonging to the passing away of all temporal things and part of the transition to the new, incorporeal age (7:28-31). Many of the messianic pretenders described by Josephus died violent deaths, but such deaths were taken to indicate the falsehood of their claims and the failure of their movements.[123] As shown above, the expectation reflected in the Dead Sea Scrolls and the *Psalms of Solomon* was that the Messiah of Israel would be a successful military leader, who would throw off the foreign yoke and then rule as an autonomous king. Suffering, rejection, and death were not part of the picture. But suffering and rejection, even death, were typically associated with the prophetic role.[124] The combination of the rebuking, indicting, sentencing, and teaching activities of the prophet with the royal messianic role was not unusual in Jewish circles at the time of Mark, as the *Psalms of Solomon*, the Similitudes of Enoch, and *4 Ezra* make clear. The combination of the prophetic motifs of suffering, rejection, and even death with the royal messianic role, however, was very unusual. That this was so is indicated by the reaction of Peter and Jesus' strong correction of his attitude (Mark 8:32-33).

Jesus' command that his identity be kept secret (8:30) is an important element of the so-called messianic secret in the Gospel of Mark.[125] According to Martin Dibelius, the theory of the messianic secret reveals the purpose and standpoint of the author of Mark in undertaking a synthesis of various traditions about Jesus:

To the evangelist the life of Jesus as a whole is only comprehensible on the assumption that Jesus intentionally kept His real status secret. He was the Son of

---

121 For further discussion, see the commentary below.

122 On the equivalence of "Messiah" and "Son of Man" in the first century CE, see the discussion of the Similitudes of Enoch and *4 Ezra* above; see also Adela Yarbro Collins, "The Influence of Daniel on the New Testament," in Collins, *Daniel*, 90–112, esp. 90–105.

123 See the discussion above.

124 See, e.g., Reinhold Liebers, *"Wie geschrieben steht"*:

Studien zu einer besonderen Art frühchristlichen Schriftbezuges (Berlin/New York: de Gruyter, 1993) 369–76.

125 The term originated with William Wrede; for a history and critical assessment of scholarship and a new interpretation of the theme, see Heikki Räisänen, *The 'Messianic Secret' in Mark* (Edinburgh: T & T Clark, 1990).

God, but He did not reveal to the people who He was. This is the reason why He could be so much misunderstood and even sent to the Cross. . . . In this way, the gospel of Mark was written as *a book of secret epiphanies*.[126]

Dibelius's characterization of Mark as "a book of secret epiphanies" is very apt. He did not, however, take sufficient notice of the fact that the theme of Jesus' secret identity is closely related to his presentation as the Son of Man.[127] A certain analogy between Mark and the Similitudes of Enoch suggests that the theme of the secret identity of Jesus should be seen as the literary adaptation of an apocalyptic motif.

According to the Similitudes of Enoch, the Son of Man was named in the presence of the Lord of Spirits before the sun and the constellations were created (*1 Enoch* 48:2-3).[128] But from the beginning the Son of Man was hidden and the Most High revealed him only to the chosen (62:7-8).[129] He will be revealed publicly only on the day of judgment.[130] Before the day of judgment, including the time during which his identity is known to the chosen community, the Son of Man is kept in the presence of the Most High (62:7). The climax of the Similitudes of Enoch is the revelation of the fact that Enoch, the patriarch who did not taste death, but was taken up to heaven according to Gen 5:22-24, is the Son of Man (*1 Enoch* 70–71).[131]

It is not possible to determine whether the author of Mark knew a written text of the Similitudes of Enoch or was simply familiar with the oral tradition reflected in it.

In any case the analogy is striking. The author of Mark seems to have adapted the tradition of the hidden Son of Man in composing an account of the earthly life of Jesus. Rather than being hidden in the presence of the Lord in heaven, Jesus, the secret Son of Man, walked the earth and revealed his identity to a chosen few.[132] This secret revelation usually takes the form of teaching, but is also communicated through the transfiguration, an epiphany of Jesus as "Son of God," whose equivalence to "Son of Man" is made clear in the context (Mark 9:2-8).[133] On that occasion, Jesus appears with Moses and Elijah, who were believed, at the time of Mark, to have been taken up to heaven as Enoch was.[134] As in the Similitudes of Enoch, the Son of Man, according to Mark, will be revealed to opponents of the community and to the general public only at the end or at a major eschatological turning point. This conviction is clear from the Markan Jesus' statement to the high priest (14:62) and from the prophecy that the Son of Man will be revealed after the great tribulation (13:24-27). The affinity of the Gospel of Mark with the Similitudes of Enoch in this regard is accented by the use of the term ἐκλεκτοί ("elect" or "chosen") for those who will survive the messianic woes in Mark 13.[135]

According to Mark 13:1-2, Jesus predicted the destruction of the Second Temple. During his interrogation by the high priest, he is accused, falsely according to Mark, of having said, "I will destroy this sanctuary, which is made with hands, and in the course of three days I will build another, which is not made with hands" (Mark 14:58). These traditions are related to the statement in

---

126   Dibelius, *From Tradition to Gospel*, 229, 230.
127   Mark 8:30-31; 9:9; 9:30-32; cf. 10:32-34.
128   See the discussion above of the hiddenness of the Son of Man in the Similitudes of Enoch.
129   Cf. 48:6-7; 69:26.
130   *1 Enoch* 48:8-10; 62:3-6, 9-16; 69:27-29.
131   The interpretation of these chaps. is disputed as well as the question whether they were originally part of the work or added later; see VanderKam, "Righteous One," 177–85; Collins, *Scepter and the Star*, 178–81.
132   Because of the Hebrew and Aramaic idiom, the use of the epithet "Son of Man" in 2:10 and 2:28 is sufficiently ambiguous that the secret is not broken. The epithet functions in these cases like the parables in chap. 4; it is intelligible to the insiders, but not to the outsiders. See the commentary on these passages below.
133   Cf. Mark 9:7 with 9:9 for the equivalence of "Son of God" and "Son of Man." For further discussion, see the commentary below.
134   According to *4 Ezra* 14:9, Ezra was granted a similar honor. See also Adela Yarbro Collins, *The Beginning of the Gospel: Probings of Mark in Context* (Minneapolis: Fortress, 1992) 138–43, and the commentary below.
135   Mark 13:20, 22, 27. For the use of the term "chosen" for those who will survive the messianic woes in the Similitudes of Enoch, see n. 45 above.

the Similitudes of Enoch that "after this, the Righteous and Chosen One will cause the house of his congregation to appear;[136] from then on, they will not be hindered in the name of the Lord of Spirits. . . . and the righteous will rest from the oppression of the sinners" (*1 Enoch* 53:6-7).[137] The "house of his congregation" is probably the new, heavenly temple.[138] According to this passage, the Messiah will cause the temple to appear after the judgment; then he will rejoice with the righteous.[139] Similarly, according to Mark 13, the judgment will occur first (vv. 14-23),[140] and then the elect will be gathered to the Son of Man (v. 27).

This pattern of judgment followed by the gathering of the survivors by the Messiah or Son of Man occurs also in *4 Ezra*. After the Messiah has reproved and destroyed those represented by the eagle,

> he will deliver in mercy the remnant of my people, those who have been saved throughout my borders, and he will make them joyful until the end comes, the day of judgment, of which I spoke to you at the beginning. (*4 Ezra* 12:34)[141]

This passage presupposes two judgments: the first is executed by the Messiah against the Romans; the second is the general judgment presided over by the Most High.[142] Mark 13 implies that the judgment will be executed by divine power and that it will be directed against Jerusalem; it will fall upon both the Jewish rebels and the Romans laying siege to the city.[143] A second, general judgment is not mentioned in this chapter, but may be implied by Mark 9:42-48. According to the interpretation of the vision of the man from the sea, the latter will direct those who are left (*4 Ezra* 13:26). The peaceable multitude who come to him are the lost nine and one-half tribes (13:39-47). He will defend the children of Israel who remained within the borders of the holy land and who survived (13:48-49). Mark 13 has a similar distinction between "those who are in Judea" who belong to the elect (vv. 14-23) and the elect who must be gathered from the ends of the earth (v. 27).

The request of the sons of Zebedee, "Grant us that we sit, one on your right and one on your left, in your glory," implies that Jesus, in the future as Son of Man, will be exalted and seated on a throne of glory. The same is said of that Son of Man in the Similitudes of Enoch.[144]

In Mark 11:1-10, Jesus enters the city of Jerusalem in a way that suggests the fulfillment of Zech 9:9-10, understood as a messianic prophecy. The people acclaim Jesus as "the coming one" and associate him with the kingdom of their father David (vv. 9-10).

The passion narrative of Mark is full of ironic affirmations of the kingship of Jesus. The anonymous woman of Mark 14:3-9 is an unlikely choice, probably made deliberately, for the role of choosing and anointing Jesus as king, but her actions suggest that this is what she is doing.[145] Yet the gesture is reinterpreted by Jesus as anointing for burial; this reinterpretation is part of the author's redefinition of messiahship.

There is one scene in the passion narrative in which the kingship of Jesus is directly affirmed, in a nonironic way. When the high priest asks him, "Are you the Messiah, the son of the Blessed?" Jesus responds, "I am, and you will see the Son of Man sitting on the right of the Power and coming with the clouds of heaven" (14:61-62). The relation between the question and the answer, especially the opening statement "I am," shows clearly the equivalence of "Messiah" and "Son of Man" for the

---

136 When this term appears in the plural, "the houses of his congregation" (*1 Enoch* 46:8), it probably refers to houses of prayer or synagogues; when it appears, as here, in the singular, it is more likely to refer to the eschatological temple.

137 Trans. from Nickelsburg and VanderKam, 67.

138 Cf. *4 Ezra* 7:26, according to which the "city which now is not seen" and "the land which now is hidden shall be disclosed" after the messianic woes; cf. 9:40-54.

139 Cf. *1 Enoch* 45:2-6; 62:13-16; 71:16-17. See also the Animal Apocalypse (*1 Enoch* 85–90), which dates to the second century BCE, according to which the old (second) city of Jerusalem will be removed and a new one set up by God after the judgment (*1 Enoch* 90:20-29). On this work, see Nickelsburg, *Jewish Literature*, 90–94; and especially Patrick A. Tiller, *A Commentary on the Animal Apocalypse of* 1 Enoch (SBLEJL 4; Atlanta: Scholars Press, 1993).

140 See the commentary below.

141 Trans. from Stone, *Fourth Ezra*, 360.

142 Cf. *4 Ezra* 7:33-44.

143 See the commentary below.

144 See n. 50 above.

145 Cf. 1 Sam 10:1; 1 Kgs 19:15-16; 2 Kgs 8:7-15. See the commentary on 14:3-9 below.

author of Mark and the assumption that the audience would understand and accept it. This passage shows clearly that the rejection and suffering of Jesus belong to the period in which he is the hidden Son of Man (cf. Mark 8:30-31) and that his exercise of the messianic office will commence after his resurrection and exaltation.

The interrogation of Jesus by Pilate forms a transition from Jesus' direct affirmation of his messiahship to the irony that characterizes the period of the hiddenness of the Son of Man. Pilate asks him, "Are you the king of the Jews?" Jesus' response, "You say (so)," is affirmative but evasive and noninformative. The irony reappears in full strength in the scene in which the crowd rejects the nonviolent Jesus for the rebel Barabbas (15:6-15). It is present in powerful and poignant form in the mocking of Jesus as king by the Roman soldiers (15:16-20), in the inscription of the charge against him, "the king of the Jews" (15:26), and in the mockery of the passersby (15:32). The irony is shattered by the acclamation of the centurion, "This man really was God's son" (15:39).[146] Just as it is not entirely clear how Peter came to the insight that Jesus is the Messiah, so the reason for the centurion's affirmation in the narrative logic of the scene is somewhat obscure. Nevertheless, the link between the affirmation and the death of Jesus is unmistakable. This scene, thus, is the climax of the reinterpretation by the author of Mark of the traditional understanding of the royal messiah.

The denouement comes in Mark 16:1-8. Mark, following early Christian tradition, innovates in his portrayal of Jesus as Messiah by including the resurrection of the Messiah from the dead. In an analogous way, the authors of the Similitudes of Enoch and *4 Ezra*, in large part through their appropriation of Daniel 7, transformed the expectation of a royal messiah, who would be primarily a warrior and a king, into belief in an exalted, heavenly messiah whose role would be to execute judgment and to inaugurate a new age of peace and rejoicing.

---

146 On the ambiguity of the centurion's statement, see the commentary on 15:39 below.

c. Jesus as Teacher

As pointed out above in the subsection *Jesus as Prophet*, the prominence in Mark of Jesus' role as teacher is compatible with his portrayal in prophetic terms. Toward the end of the Second Temple period, the prophet was understood as a charismatic leader who was, among other things, a teacher. Furthermore, in the *Psalms of Solomon* and the Similitudes of Enoch, the role of (Davidic or royal) Messiah is combined with that of teacher or revealer. It is not surprising, therefore, that the Gospel of Mark presents Jesus both as the Davidic messiah and as a teacher.[1] In this subsection, Mark's portrayal of Jesus as teacher will be examined in relation to the social role of teacher (in the narrow sense) in the cultural context of the first century CE.

Possibly during preexilic times and probably in the period of the Second Temple, priests and Levites were educated in scribal schools in Jerusalem and possibly elsewhere in Palestine to prepare them to make legal decisions and to instruct the people in the Law.[2] A decree of Antiochus III dating to about 200 BCE and preserved by Josephus attests a fixed group of experts in the Law associated with the temple, γραμματεῖς τοῦ ἱεροῦ (lit., "scribes of the temple").[3] These schools in effect trained civil servants in a long tradition of scribal culture in the ancient Near East.[4] There may also have been wis-

dom schools apart from the temple and priestly tradition.[5] The popularization of the Torah by Ezra created a situation that favored the democratization and intensification of education. Such a development may have encouraged the establishment of schools for education beyond the instruction given within the family.[6] In any case, schools began to flourish under Hellenistic influence.[7] The school of Ben Sira was not a specialized school for professional experts in the Law, but provided instruction in wisdom for a wider circle. The techniques used, however, suggest that it was similar to the postexilic temple-school.[8]

The aristocratic priestly tradition did not break off with the rise of the new "democratic" form of school; Josephus still knows about the special teaching reserved for the priests.[9] His aristocratic attitude is evident in the following comment:

> For our people do not favour those persons who have mastered the speech of many nations, or who adorn their style with smoothness of diction, because they consider that not only is such skill common to ordinary freemen but that even slaves who so choose may acquire it. But they give credit for wisdom to those alone who have an exact knowledge of the law and who are capable of interpreting the meaning of the Holy Scriptures (παρ᾽ ἡμῖν γὰρ οὐκ ἐκείνους ἀποδέ-

---

1   See the subsection above, *Jesus as Messiah*.

2   Deut 33:8-11; Jer 2:8; 1 Chr 2:55; 2 Chr 34:13; Sir 45:17. For discussion see Martin Hengel, *Judaism and Hellenism: Studies in Their Encounter in Palestine during the Early Hellenistic Period* (2 vols; Philadelphia: Fortress; London: SCM, 1974) 1:78; Rainer Riesner, *Jesus als Lehrer: Eine Untersuchung zum Ursprung der Evangelien-Überlieferung* (WUNT 2.7; Tübingen: Mohr Siebeck, 1981) 160–61; Eric William Heaton, *The School Tradition of the Old Testament* (Oxford: Oxford University Press, 1994) 185.

3   Josephus *Ant.* 12.3.3 §§138–44; see Hengel, *Judaism and Hellenism*, 1:78; Riesner, *Jesus als Lehrer*, 162. Temple scribes are also mentioned in a letter from Xerxes to Ezra that Josephus quotes (*Ant.* 11.5.1 §128).

4   See Henri I. Marrou, *A History of Education in Antiquity* (WSC; Madison: University of Wisconsin Press, 1956; 3rd French ed., 1948) xiv–xvii. Roger Norman Whybray has challenged this consensus, but without success (*The Intellectual Tradition in the Old Testament* [BZAW 135; Berlin/New York: de Gruyter, 1974]

31–43). See the criticism by Heaton, *School Tradition*, 1–6. The consensus has also been challenged by Friedemann W. Golka, *The Leopard's Spots: Biblical and African Wisdom in Proverbs* (Edinburgh: T & T Clark, 1993).

5   Bernhard Lang, "Schule und Unterricht in Israel," in Maurice Gilbert, ed., *La Sagesse de l'Ancien Testament* (Leuven: Leuven University Press, 1990) 192–201.

6   Riesner, *Jesus als Lehrer*, 163; Heaton, *School Tradition*, 186–90.

7   See the discussion by Riesner (*Jesus als Lehrer*, 200–206) of the tradition preserved in *b. B. Batra* 21a, that Joshua b. Gamala decreed (first cent. CE) that teachers of children be appointed in every district and town.

8   Riesner, *Jesus als Lehrer*, 167.

9   Hengel, *Judaism and Hellenism*, 1:80. Hengel gives no references to Josephus here; one might point to *Ap.* 1.10 §54, where he speaks of the special knowledge that he has as a priest, and *Ap.* 1.23 §218, where he speaks of others who lack such specialized knowledge.

χονται τοὺς πολλῶν ἐθνῶν διάλεκτον ἐκμαθόντας καὶ γλαφυρότητι λέξεων τὸν λόγον ἐπικομψεύοντας διὰ τὸ κοινὸν εἶναι νομίζειν τὸ ἐπιτήδευμα τοῦτο μόνον οὐκ ἐλευθέροις τοῖς τυχοῦσιν ἀλλὰ καὶ τῶν οἰκετῶν τοῖς θέλουσι, μόνοις δὲ σοφίαν μαρτυροῦσιν τοῖς τὰ νόμιμα σαφῶς ἐπισταμένοις καὶ τὴν τῶν ἱερῶν γραμμάτων δύναμιν ἑρμηνεῦσαι δυναμένοις). (*Ant.* 20.12.1 §264)[10]

But a new idea gained currency, that anyone who belonged to the people of God, even the proselyte, could study wisdom and become a great teacher of the Law. This attitude "was foreign to early Israel and the ancient Orient in general, but was part and parcel of the liberal Hellenistic ideal."[11] It was in this cultural context that Jesus came forward as a teacher, even though he was not a priest and apparently lacked a scribal education.

As argued in the subsection *Jesus as Prophet* above, the summary of Jesus' activity and message in Mark 1:14-15 presents him as an eschatological prophet. The passage may also be read as the inauguration of his teaching activity, since the proclamation in public places of a message calling for a reorientation of self-understanding and lifestyle was typical of popular philosophers of the time.[12] In the same subsection above, it was noted that the scenes in which Jesus calls disciples (1:16-20; 2:14) may be read as indicating a social role of either teacher or prophet. In relation to prophetic tradition, the narratives of Mark are similar to the account of Elijah's call of Elisha (1 Kgs 19:19-21).[13] The most striking parallel to

Mark 1:16-20 in the Hellenistic philosophical tradition is the call of Xenophon by Socrates:

Xenophon, the son of Gryllus, was a citizen of Athens and belonged to the deme Erchia; he was a man of rare modesty and extremely handsome. The story goes that Socrates met him in a narrow passage, and that he stretched out his stick to bar the way, while he inquired where every kind of food was sold. Upon receiving a reply, he put another question, "And where do men become good and honourable?" Xenophon was fairly puzzled; "Then follow me," said Socrates, "and learn." From that time onward he was a pupil of Socrates (Ξενοφῶν Γρύλλου μὲν ἦν υἱός, Ἀθηναῖος, τῶν δήμων Ἐρχιεύς· αἰδήμων δὲ καὶ εὐειδέστατος εἰς ὑπερβολήν. τούτῳ δὲ ἐν στενωπῷ φασιν ἀπαντήσαντα Σωκράτην διατεῖναι τὴν βακτηρίαν καὶ κωλύειν παριέναι, πυνθανόμενον ποῦ πιπράσκοιτο τῶν προσφερομένων ἕκαστον· ἀποκριναμένου δὲ πάλιν πυθέσθαι, ποῦ δὲ καλοὶ κἀγαθοὶ γίνονται ἄνθρωποι· ἀπορήσαντος δέ, "ἕπου τοίνυν," φάναι, "καὶ μάνθανε." καὶ τοὐντεῦθεν ἀκροατὴς Σωκράτους ἦν). (Diogenes Laertius *Vit. Phil.* 2.48)[14]

Socrates has to bar Xenophon's way to get his attention. Then he engages him in a dialogue that piques his interest in what Socrates has to offer. In contrast, Jesus merely passes by and invites the four young men to follow him. They instantly abandon everyone and everything and do so. The situation is similar in the story

---

10 Text and trans. from Louis H. Feldman, in Thackeray, *Josephus*, 9:526–29.

11 Hengel, *Judaism and Hellenism*, 1:80, citing William F. Albright; further references are given in ibid., 2:54 n. 171.

12 Cf., e.g., the typical message of the Cynic philosopher, as summarized by Epictetus (*Diss.* 3.22.26–49). But in the LXX, the prophetic proclamation of the coming salvation is never the object of the verb διδάσκειν ("to teach"); see Karl Heinrich Rengstorf, "διδάσκω," *TDNT* 2 (1964) 137.

13 Samuel Byrskog discusses Elijah, Elisha, the "Sons of the Prophets," "Isaiah and His Disciples," and Jeremiah and Ezekiel and their "Followers" under the heading "The Teacher-Pupil Relationship" in idem, *Jesus the Only Teacher: Didactic Authority and Transmis-*

sion in Ancient Israel, Ancient Judaism and the Matthean Community (CBNTS 24; Stockholm: Almqvist & Wiksell International, 1994) 7, 36–45. He does this *"from the perspective of the ancient transmitters as users of texts"* (ibid., 36).

14 Text and trans. from Robert Drew Hicks, *Diogenes Laertius: Lives of Eminent Philosophers* (2 vols.; LCL; Cambridge, MA: Harvard University Press; London: Heinemann, 1925; rev. ed. 1931, 1972) 1:176–79. For further parallel accounts and discussion, see Hengel, *Charismatic Leader*, 27–29, 76–77; and Vernon K. Robbins, *Jesus the Teacher: A Socio-Rhetorical Interpretation of Mark* (Philadelphia: Fortress, 1984) 89–94.

about Levi (Mark 2:13-14). The contrast makes clear that, according to the Gospel of Mark, the appeal and authority of Jesus are more than human and beyond the rational.

In Mark 1:17, Jesus tells Simon and Andrew that he will make them "fishers of human beings" ($\dot{\alpha}\lambda\iota\epsilon\hat{\iota}\varsigma$ $\dot{\alpha}\nu\theta\rho\dot{\omega}\pi\omega\nu$), implying that he himself has "caught" them. A similar metaphor is used in the story of the conversion of Polemo to philosophy. After bursting in a drunken state into the school of Xenocrates, while the teacher was lecturing on temperance, and listening awhile, Polemo was "caught" ($\dot{\epsilon}\vartheta\eta\rho\dot{\alpha}\vartheta\eta$), like a wild beast being hunted.[15] Timon of Phlius, the skeptical philosopher, wrote a lampoon against Pythagoras, in which he called him a "hunter of human beings" ($\vartheta\dot{\eta}\rho\eta$ $\dot{\epsilon}\pi$ $\dot{\alpha}\nu\theta\rho\dot{\omega}\vartheta\omega\nu$).[16] This metaphor, common to the Hellenistic philosophical tradition and to Mark, suggests that Jesus the Messiah, like some philosophers, took the initiative in winning followers, and that in both cases a conversion from a former lifestyle was necessary.[17]

In the narrative of Mark, the first reported activity of Jesus after he has called the first four disciples is teaching in a synagogue on the Sabbath (1:21).[18] The narrator's comment in v. 22, "And they were amazed at his teaching; for he was teaching them with authority, not as the scribes taught" ($\kappa\alpha\grave{\iota}$ $\dot{\epsilon}\xi\epsilon\pi\lambda\dot{\eta}\sigma\sigma\sigma\nu\tau o$ $\dot{\epsilon}\pi\grave{\iota}$ $\tau\hat{\eta}$ $\delta\iota\delta\alpha\chi\hat{\eta}$ $\alpha\dot{\upsilon}\tauo\hat{\upsilon}\cdot$ $\dot{\eta}\nu$ $\gamma\grave{\alpha}\rho$ $\delta\iota\delta\dot{\alpha}\sigma\kappa\omega\nu$ $\alpha\dot{\upsilon}\tauo\grave{\upsilon}\varsigma$ $\dot{\omega}\varsigma$ $\dot{\epsilon}\xi o\upsilon\sigma\dot{\iota}\alpha\nu$ $\dot{\epsilon}\chi\omega\nu$ $\kappa\alpha\grave{\iota}$ $o\dot{\upsilon}\chi$ $\dot{\omega}\varsigma$ $o\dot{\iota}$ $\gamma\rho\alpha\mu\mu\alpha\tau\epsilon\hat{\iota}\varsigma$), immediately informs the reader that Jesus is no ordinary teacher. He is not a $\gamma\rho\alpha\mu\mu\alpha\tau\epsilon\dot{\upsilon}\varsigma$ ("scribe" or "expert in the Law"). The ordinary Greek sense of $\gamma\rho\alpha\mu\mu\alpha\tau\epsilon\dot{\upsilon}\varsigma$ was "clerk" or "secretary."[19] It was used among Greek-speaking Jews, however, to translate the Hebrew סופר and the Aramaic ספרא, which meant "one learned in the Torah."[20] This is the sense in which it is used in the Gospel of Mark.[21] Philo and Josephus generally avoided using $\gamma\rho\alpha\mu\mu\alpha\tau\epsilon\dot{\upsilon}\varsigma$ in this sense, probably to avoid confusion with the "clerk" or "secretary." Josephus referred to those learned in the Law as claiming to possess, aspiring to, or possessing "wisdom" ($\sigma o\varphi\dot{\iota}\alpha$).[22] When his own opinion differs from that of a particular scholar or group of experts in the Law, he refers to them as $\sigma o\varphi\iota\sigma\tau\alpha\dot{\iota}$ ("teachers," "sophists").[23] In rabbinic literature, סופרים ("scribes") is used historically for scholars of an earlier period and in a contemporary sense for schoolteachers (those who taught reading on the basis of the Torah) and secretaries; those learned in the Law are called חכמים ("the wise" or "the sages").[24]

Jesus is addressed as "teacher" ($\delta\iota\delta\dot{\alpha}\sigma\kappa\alpha\lambda o\varsigma$) ten times in the Gospel of Mark and referred to as "the teacher" ($\dot{o}$ $\delta\iota\delta\dot{\alpha}\sigma\kappa\alpha\lambda o\varsigma$) twice; in one of these cases it appears to be a self-designation.[25] In non-Jewish, non-Christian Greek, the $\delta\iota\delta\dot{\alpha}\sigma\kappa\alpha\lambda o\varsigma$ is not a teacher in general but a teacher of specific skills.[26] The noun occurs

---

15 Diogenes Laertius *Vit. Phil.* 4.16; Hicks, *Diogenes Laertius*, 1:392–93. Polemo, in turn, "captured" Crantor ($\vartheta\eta\rho\alpha\vartheta\hat{\eta}\nu\alpha\iota$ $K\rho\dot{\alpha}\nu\tau o\rho\alpha$ $\dot{\upsilon}\pi$ $\alpha\dot{\upsilon}\tauo\hat{\upsilon}$), i.e., won him for philosophy (ibid., 4.17; Hicks, 1:394–95).

16 Diogenes Laertius *Vit. Phil.* 8.36; Hicks, *Diogenes Laertius*, 2:352–53.

17 In rabbinic literature, it is usually the disciple who takes the initiative; see Robbins, *Jesus the Teacher*, 101–3.

18 He is also portrayed as teaching in the open air (Mark 2:13; 4:1) and in the temple (12:35).

19 $\gamma\rho\alpha\mu\mu\alpha\tau\epsilon\dot{\upsilon}\varsigma$ is used in this sense in Acts 19:35.

20 Joachim Jeremias, "$\gamma\rho\alpha\mu\mu\alpha\tau\epsilon\dot{\upsilon}\varsigma$," *TDNT* 1 (1964) 740. The clearest early example is perhaps Ezra 7:6 (LXX 2 Esdr 7:6).

21 With the partial exception of the scribes associated with the chief priests, who had administrative duties as well as expertise in the Law. See the commentary on 11:18 and 14:1-2 below.

22 Josephus *Ant.* 18.3.5 §§81–82; 20.12.1 §264.

23 Josephus *Bell.* 1.33.2 §§648, 650; *Ant.* 17.6.2 §§152, 155; in these passages he applies the label $\sigma o\varphi\iota\sigma\tau\alpha\dot{\iota}$ ("teachers," "sophists") to Judas, son of Sepphoraeus, and Matthias, son of Margalus, who persuaded some Jewish youths to tear down the golden eagle from over the great gate of the temple. He uses the term also for Judas the Galilean, who incited a revolt under the Roman governor Coponius (6–9 CE) (*Bell.* 2.8.1 §118), and for Gentile writers with whom he disagrees (*Ap.* 2.33 §236). See Ulrich Wilckens, "$\sigma o\varphi\dot{\iota}\alpha$, $\sigma o\varphi\dot{o}\varsigma$," *TDNT* 7 (1971) 502–3.

24 Jeremias, "$\gamma\rho\alpha\mu\mu\alpha\tau\epsilon\dot{\upsilon}\varsigma$," 741. See also Riesner, *Jesus als Lehrer*, 184–85.

25 Jesus is addressed as "teacher" in Mark 4:38; 9:17, 38; 10:17, 20, 35; 12:14, 19, 32; he is referred to as "the teacher" by someone else in 5:35 and by himself in 14:14.

26 Karl Heinrich Rengstorf, "$\delta\iota\delta\dot{\alpha}\sigma\kappa\alpha\lambda o\varsigma$," *TDNT* 2 (1964) 149.

only twice in the LXX (Esth 6:1; 2 Macc 1:10).[27] More common in this corpus is the use of the verb "to teach" (διδάσκειν). It is not used in the ordinary Greek sense of acquiring knowledge or a skill; rather, it is used in the absolute sense, like the Hebrew למד ("to teach"). This usage of the later parts of the LXX and rabbinic literature denotes the exposition of the Law as the revealed will of God. This exposition aims at the ordering of the relationship between the individual and God, on the one hand, and between the individual and his or her neighbor, on the other.[28] Jesus is frequently presented in Mark as teaching in an absolute or unqualified sense.[29] This presentation is more like the traditional Jewish understanding of a teacher than the Greek. The activity of teaching associated with Jesus in Mark has something like the meaning associated with the relevant terms in the later LXX and rabbinic literature, but they are not as focused on the Law. As some of the Pharisees and Herodians say in Mark 12:14, Jesus teaches "the way of God" (ἡ ὁδὸς τοῦ θεοῦ). As the acquaintances of Jesus in Nazareth say in 6:2, Jesus' teaching may be described as "wisdom" (σοφία).[30] But the first time that the content of Jesus' teaching is reported (4:1-34), it takes the form of parables associated with "the mystery of the kingdom of God" (τὸ μυστήριον τῆς βασιλείας τοῦ θεοῦ) (4:11). When the teaching of Jesus to his disciples is reported in plain language, it concerns the suffering of the Son of Man (8:31; 9:31). Thus, the teaching of Jesus has to do with the eschatological plan of God. The interpretation of the Law and the exposition of Scripture, elements also present in the teaching of Jesus, are determined by the eschatological context in which they occur.[31]

These findings are supported by the use of the noun "teacher" (διδάσκαλος) in Mark. The first four times that this epithet is applied to Jesus, it occurs in the context of miracle-working (4:38; 5:35; 9:17, 38). In two other cases, it appears in the context of eschatological tradition and interpretation of Scripture (10:35; 13:1). It is associated with Jesus in the context of the Law or the will of God in five passages, all of which occur in chaps. 10 and 12 (10:17, 20; 12:14, 19, 32). In one case, the self-designation (14:14), it occurs in a situation in which the relationship between Jesus and his disciples is prominent.

Jesus is also addressed as "Rabbi" (ῥαββί) several times in Mark. He is so addressed by Peter in 9:5 and 11:21 and by Judas in 14:45. This usage probably reflects contemporary Jewish custom, attested by later rabbinic texts, in accordance with which the pupil (תלמיד) addressed his teacher as רבי (lit., "my master").[32] This usage corresponds to the absolute use of διδάσκειν ("to teach") in Mark, which is characteristic of a strand of Jewish tradition. When Bartimaeus, however, addresses Jesus as ῥαββουνί ("my master" or "master") in 10:51, the epithet may simply be an expression of respect.[33] The contexts are similar to those in which διδάσκαλος ("teacher") is used. Peter's first address of Jesus as "Rabbi" (ῥαββί) occurs in the context of the transfiguration. In this context, Jesus is associated with Moses and Elijah, but is shown to be greater than they, because he is the beloved son or the only Son of God (ὁ υἱός μου ὁ ἀγαπητός) (9:7). The second such address by Peter occurs in the miracle story (or account of an effective curse) involving the fig tree (11:21). The address of Jesus by Judas emphasizes the master–pupil relationship and thus heightens the drama of the scene of betrayal (14:45). The address of Jesus by Bartimaeus as ῥαββουνί ("my master" or "master") also appears in the context of a miracle story.

As pointed out earlier, Jesus is distinguished from the γραμματεῖς ("scribes" or "experts in the Law") in Mark 1:21-22. The narrator's comment that he teaches "with authority" (ἐξουσίαν ἔχων) is illustrated and corroborated by the following exorcism (1:23-28). Similarly, the people of Nazareth link his astonishing teaching with δυνάμεις ("mighty deeds" or "miracles") in 6:2. The teaching about the eschatological role of the Son of Man in 8:31 and 9:31 follows upon Peter's acclamation of

---

27   For discussion, see Rengstorf, "διδάσκαλος," 151.

28   See the citation of 2 Chr 17:7-9 below and Rengstorf, "διδάσκω," 137.

29   Mark 1:21; 2:13; 4:1; 6:2, 6b, 34; 10:1; 14:49.

30   Compare Josephus's characterization of those learned in the Law discussed above.

31   Mark 10:1-12; 11:17; 12:13-17; 12:35-37.

32   For discussion and references, see Eduard Lohse, "ῥαββί, ῥαββουνί," *TDNT* 6 (1968) 961–65. See also the commentary on 9:5 below.

33   Cf. ibid., 961.

Jesus as the Messiah (8:29), and the teachings about the temple (11:17) and about the Messiah as son of David (12:35-37) follow the triumphal entry into Jerusalem, during which Jesus is associated with the kingdom of David that is coming (11:10). The teaching of Jesus in Mark, therefore, is not part of the chain of tradition that goes back to Moses and Sinai, but is a new, authoritative teaching based on his eschatological role.[34]

One of the most striking characteristics of the presentation of Jesus as a teacher in the Gospel of Mark is the itinerant character of his teaching activity.[35] Jesus' traveling from place to place is explained in 1:38 in terms of his intention to proclaim the good news of God in various places (cf. 1:14-15). It is difficult to find analogies to this activity and its rationale. The prophet Elijah went from place to place, sometimes in the normal way, but at the direct command of God or the angel of the Lord for some specific reason,[36] and sometimes transported by the spirit of God (1 Kgs 18:12, 46). When he is reported as traveling on his own initiative, it is to escape death at the hands of Jezebel (1 Kgs 19:3-4, 9-10). Elisha moves from place to place independently,[37] but it is not to proclaim a message to all the people, as is the case with Jesus.

An interesting but isolated parallel to the activity of Jesus may be found in 2 Chr 17:7-9 LXX:

And in the third year of his [Jehoshaphat's] reign he sent his leading men and the sons of the prominent people . . . to teach in the cities of Judah; and with them the Levites . . . the Levites, and with them . . . the priests; and they taught in Judah, and with them (was) the book of the Law of the Lord, and they passed through the cities of Judah and taught the people (καὶ ἐν τῷ τρίτῳ ἔτει τῆς βασιλείας αὐτοῦ ἀπέστειλεν τοὺς ἡγουμένους αὐτοῦ καὶ τοὺς υἱούς τῶν δυνατῶν, . . . διδάσκειν ἐν πόλεσιν Ιουδα, καὶ μετ᾽ αὐτῶν οἱ Λευῖται . . . οἱ Λευῖται, καὶ μετ᾽ αὐτῶν . . . οἱ ἱερεῖς, καὶ ἐδίδασκον ἐν Ιουδα, καὶ μετ᾽ αὐτῶν βύβλος νόμου κυρίου, καὶ διῆλθον ἐν ταῖς πόλεσιν Ιουδα καὶ ἐδίδασκον τὸ λαόν).

Here, according to the Chronicler, the old ideal, according to which the people are to be instructed in the Law by the priests and Levites, is fulfilled at the initiative of the king. Jesus' activity reflects a new ideal: the instruction of all the people about the good news of God, the eschatological plan about to be fulfilled.

In Greek cultural history, the social role of teacher and an itinerant lifestyle were combined for the first time in the second half of the fifth century BCE by the group of innovators who have come to be known as the sophists.[38] Their goal was to train statesmen, to serve the new ideal of political ἀρετή ("valor," "competitive achievement"). They offered their services to anyone who wished to succeed in the political arena. They did not open schools in the institutional sense of the word, but employed a method of collective tutoring. They charged a fixed sum of money for training that lasted three or four years. Since they were the first to offer to teach for a fee in this way, they had to create their own market. Thus, the sophist went from city to city in search of pupils, taking with him those whose fathers had already engaged his services. In order to attract students, he would give a "demonstration" (ἐπίδειξις) of his knowledge and skill, which might be a previously prepared lecture, an improvisation on a theme or a free debate on a topic proposed by his audience. Their rival and contemporary, Socrates, confined his activity to Athens, but similarly taught in public places and attracted pupils (or, in his view, companions) by his skill in reasoning and speaking.

---

34 See also Hengel, *Charismatic Leader*, esp. 38–83.

35 This wandering with a fixed purpose but no clear destination characterizes Jesus' activity in Mark 1:35–8:26. Beginning with 8:27, Jesus' movement follows the pilgrimage route from Caesarea Philippi to Jerusalem. See Detlev Dormeyer, "Jesus as Wandering Prophetic Wisdom Teacher," *Hervormde Teologiese Studies* 49 (1993) 101–17, esp. 105–11.

36 1 Kgs 17:2-5, 8-10; 18:1-2, 15-17; 19:15-16, 19; 21:17-20; 2 Kgs 1:3-4, 15; 2:1-2.

37 2 Kgs 2:23, 25; 4:8, 11, 38; 6:19-20; 8:7; cf. 4:25; 5:3; 6:13, 32.

38 Protagoras of Abdera, Gorgias of Leontini, Antiphon of Athens, Prodicus of Ceos, and Hippias of Elis; see Plato *Ap.* 19E. See also the discussions by Marrou, *History of Education*, 47–57; and Robbins, *Jesus the Teacher*, 88.

The teachers of the following generation, exemplified by Plato and Isocrates, opened schools, primarily in Athens, and were not itinerant. It became typical for the students to come to the teacher, rather than vice versa.[39] But in the Hellenistic and early Roman period, there were wandering philosophers who proclaimed their messages in public places. Such popular teachers were especially identified with the Cynic tradition of philosophy, but some Stoics adopted this mode of communication as well.[40] According to the popular image summarized by Epictetus, the Cynic was one who "went around begging from those he met" (περιερχόμενος αἰτεῖν . . . ἀπαντῶντας) (*Diss.* 3.22.10). He cannot be exiled, because the universe is his home, and wherever he goes there are sun, moon, stars, dreams, omens, his converse with the gods (*Diss.* 3.22.22; cf. 3.22.45–47).

The motif of itinerancy is most prominent in the letters attributed to Diogenes, in the discourse of Dio of Prusa (Dio Chrysostom), and in Lucian's accounts of Peregrinus and other Cynics.[41] In an apocryphal letter of Diogenes to his father that has been dated to the first century BCE, he describes how Socrates spoke of two roads to happiness. When Diogenes chose the short, steep, difficult road, Socrates fitted him out with a double, coarse cloak; a wallet containing bread, drink, a cup, and a bowl; an oil flask with scraper; and a staff. When Diogenes inquired about the wallet, Socrates replied, "'So that you might carry your house with you everywhere,' he explained" ("ἵνα πάντῃ τὴν οἰκίαν" εἶπε "περιφέρῃς").[42]

At the beginning of Letter 31, Diogenes mentions meeting a man on the road to Olympia who had been victorious at the games. Letter 35 opens with his account

of his arrival at Miletus. Letter 36 describes his teaching activity in Cyzicus, and Letter 37 begins with his journey from Ephesus to Rhodes and tells of his teaching there.[43] Lucian accused Peregrinus of going into exile and roaming about, going from one country to another, to escape punishment for the murder of his father (*Peregr. mort.* 10). He says that Peregrinus then settled in Palestine, where he became a Christian and was imprisoned for his membership in this new cult. After being freed by the governor of Syria, he returned home to the city of Parium (in the Hellespont) and avoided punishment for the death of his father by donating his inherited property to the state (ibid., 11–15). He then roamed about a second time, returned home again, went to Egypt, to Italy, and finally to Greece (ibid., 16–19).

The motif of exile, which occurs occasionally in the Cynic and Stoic popular philosophical traditions, is not present explicitly in Mark's narrative of Jesus. His rejection at Nazareth and the request of the Gerasenes that he leave their territory, however, are analogous. Further, the call to leave everything and follow Jesus (1:16-20; 2:13-14; 10:17-31) has some of the same religious and social connotations as the theme of exile in the philosophical traditions. Like the traditions about Diogenes and Peregrinus, Mark's portrayal of Jesus involves traveling from place to place in order to convey a specific message that took various concrete forms. Although the travels attributed to Peregrinus, a figure of the second century CE, cover much more of the known world, the range of Jesus' activity (Galilee, southern Syria, Gaulanitis, the Decapolis, Perea, Judea) is comparable to that attributed to Diogenes (mainland Greece, the islands of the Aegean, the Hellespont).

---

39 Before the rise of the sophists, in the late sixth century or the early fifth century, Pythagoras had founded a religious society that was also a philosophical school. This school became the model for Plato's Academy, Aristotle's Lyceum, and the school of Epicurus; see Marrou, *History of Education*, 47.

40 Marrou, *History of Education*, 207; Gerd Theissen, *Studien zur Soziologie des Urchristentums* (3rd ed.; WUNT 19; Tübingen: Mohr Siebeck, 1989) 89–90 and the lit. cited on p. 89 n. 28. F. Gerald Downing rightly pointed out that some of the most famous Cynics were not actually itinerant (*Cynics and Christian Origins* [Edinburgh: T & T Clark, 1992] 33).

41 As in the Gospel of Mark, teaching and discipleship are placed in an itinerant context in the *Life of Apollonius of Tyana*, written by Flavius Philostratus around the beginning of the third cent. CE; see Robbins, *Jesus the Teacher*, 105–7.

42 Pseudo-Diogenes 30. *To Hicetas, do well* 4; text and trans. from Abraham J. Malherbe, ed., *The Cynic Epistles: A Study Edition* (SBLSBS 12; Atlanta: Scholars Press, 1977) 132–33. On the date of this letter, see ibid., 14–15.

43 These letters also date to the first century BCE (Malherbe, *Cynic Epistles*, 14–15).

In addition to the shared motif of itinerancy, an analogy to the divine mission of Jesus may be found in Epictetus's description of the true Cynic:

> In the next place, the true Cynic, when he is thus prepared, cannot rest contented with this, but he must know that he has been sent by Zeus to human beings, partly as a messenger, in order to show them that in questions of good and evil they have gone astray, and are seeking the true nature of the good and the evil where it is not, but where it is they never think; and partly, in the words of Diogenes, when he was taken off to Philip, after the battle of Chaeroneia, as a scout (Εἶθ' οὕτως παρασκευασάμενον οὐκ ἔστι τούτοις ἀρκεῖσθαι τὸν ταῖς ἀληθείαις Κυνικόν, ἀλλ' εἰδέναι δεῖ, ὅτι ἄγγελος ἀπὸ τοῦ Διὸς ἀπέσταλται καὶ πρὸς τοὺς ἀνθρώπους περὶ ἀγαθῶν καὶ κακῶν ὑποδείξων αὐτοῖς, ὅτι πεπλάνηνται καὶ ἀλλαχοῦ ζητοῦσι τὴν οὐσίαν τοῦ ἀγαθοῦ καὶ τοῦ κακοῦ, ὅπου οὐκ ἔστιν, ὅπου δ' ἔστιν, οὐκ ἐνθυμοῦνται, καὶ ὡς ὁ Διογένης ἀπαχθεὶς πρὸς Φίλιππον μετὰ τὴν ἐν Χαιρωνείᾳ μάχην κατάσκοπος εἶναι). (Diss. 3.22.23–24)[44]

Similarly, Epictetus describes the Cynic as "the messenger, the scout, the herald of the gods" (τὸν ἄγγελον καὶ κατάσκοπον καὶ κήρυκα τῶν θεῶν) (Diss. 3.22.69).[45]

The images of messenger and herald had different associations for the audiences of Mark, depending on the cultural context in which they were perceived. From the point of view of Jewish traditions, these images would have recalled the prophetic figure of Isaiah 61 and its later interpretation.[46] In a context in which the teaching of Epictetus was well known, they would have recalled the true Cynic. The text of Mark goes beyond both sets of contemporary connotations. The Jesus of Mark is more than a messenger, scout, or herald of God. He is the Messiah, whose death and resurrection prepare the way for the full manifestation of the kingdom of God with his return as the heavenly Son of Man. But it is noteworthy that Jesus, like Epictetus's true Cynic, does act as a herald of God. Although Mark does not use the noun "herald" (κῆρυξ), the verb κηρύσσω ("to act as a herald" or "proclaim") does occur frequently.[47] John the Baptist appears first as the herald of Jesus: "And he was proclaiming, saying (καὶ ἐκήρυσσεν λέγων), 'The one who is stronger than I is coming after me'" (1:7). Then Jesus acts as a herald of God: "After John was handed over, Jesus went into Galilee, proclaiming the good news of God (κηρύσσων τὸ εὐαγγέλιον τοῦ θεοῦ) and saying, 'The time is fulfilled and the kingdom of God has drawn near; repent and trust in the good news'" (1:14-15).[48] Mark's Jesus is thus, among other things, the herald of God.

The messages, however, of the Cynic herald and Jesus as herald are quite different. According to Epictetus's true Cynic, the good is "serenity, happiness, freedom from restraint" (τὸ εὔρουν, τὸ εὐδαιμονικόν, τὸ ἀπαραπόδιστον) (Diss. 3.22.39).[49] The achievement of this goal is entirely in the power of the individual human being: to desire, to avoid, to choose, to refuse, to prepare, to set something before oneself—the human being is free to do or not to do these things (Diss. 3.22.43–44).[50] The kingdom of God, according to the Markan Jesus, must be met by human beings with repentance and trust (1:14-15). But its full manifestation is accomplished by divine power alone (9:1; 13:20, 24-27, 32).[51]

---

44 Text and trans. (modified) from William Abbott Oldfather, *Epictetus: The Discourses as Reported by Arrian, the Manual, and Fragments* (2 vols.; LCL; Cambridge, MA: Harvard University Press; London: Heinemann, 1925, 1928; reprinted 1989, 1985) 2:136–39.

45 Oldfather, *Epictetus*, 2:154–55.

46 See the subsection *Jesus as Prophet* above.

47 The activities of the prophetic figure in Isa 61:1 are described in the LXX as "to bring good news to the poor" (εὐαγγελίσασθαι πτωχοῖς), "to heal the broken-hearted" (ἰάσασθαι τοὺς συντετριμμένους τῇ καρδίᾳ), and "to proclaim liberty to the captives and recovery of sight to the blind" (κηρύξαι αἰχμαλώτοις ἄφεσιν καὶ τυφλοῖς ἀνάβλεψιν).

48 Later in the Gospel, when Jesus is portrayed as proclaiming without further specification, the audience would recall the summary in 1:14-15 and supply the content of his proclamation accordingly. The later passages are 1:38 and 1:39.

49 Oldfather, *Epictetus*, 2:144–45.

50 Oldfather, *Epictetus*, 2:146–47.

51 For a critique of the hypothesis that the historical Jesus was a Cynic, see Paul Rhodes Eddy, "Jesus as Diogenes? Reflections on the Cynic Jesus Thesis," *JBL* 115 (1996) 449–69 and the literature cited there, esp. Hans Dieter Betz, "Jesus and the Cynics: Survey and Analysis of a Hypothesis," *JR* 74 (1994) 453–75.

d. The Death of Jesus

The death of Jesus is presented, narrated, and interpreted in a variety of ways in Mark. Like the other writings that eventually became part of the New Testament, Mark does not give a single, clear and precise explanation of why Jesus died. Even less does he give a single, logically clear and conceptually precise interpretation of Jesus' death. Meaning is found and attributed to that event in a variety of ways that will be explored in this subsection.

The Gospel opens with the titular sentence "The beginning of the good news of Jesus Christ." In the oral proclamation of Paul, an important element of "the good news" was "that Christ died for our sins in accordance with the scriptures" (ὅτι Χριστὸς ἀπέθανεν ὑπὲρ τῶν ἁμαρτιῶν ἡμῶν κατὰ τὰς γραφάς) (1 Cor 15:3).[1] In summarizing "the good news" that Jesus proclaimed, however, Mark shifts the emphasis from the death and resurrection of Jesus to the fulfillment of "the time" (ὁ καιρός) and the nearness of the kingdom of God (1:14-15). Yet the account of an anonymous woman's anointing of Jesus in 14:3-9 makes clear that the death of Jesus is part of "the good news" from the point of view of Mark as well. In commenting on her deed, Jesus says, "Truly I say to you, wherever the good news is proclaimed in the whole world, what this woman has done will also be spoken of in memory of her" (14:9). Since, in the previous verse, the Markan Jesus has interpreted her act as anointing his body for burial beforehand, it is clear that his death is an important part of the good news or gospel for the author of this work as well.

In the controversy-dialogue about the question of fasting, the death of Jesus is referred to for the first time, although indirectly. In reply to the question why his disciples do not fast, the Markan Jesus contrasts the present time of rejoicing with a future time of mourning. The disciples do not fast while Jesus is with them, just as the groomsmen do not fast when the bridegroom is in their company. "But days will come when the bridegroom is taken away (ἀπαρθῇ) from them, and then they will fast on that day" (Mark 2:20). It is not made clear who will take "the bridegroom" away or why.[2]

The second incident following the question about fasting describes Jesus' healing a man with a withered hand on the Sabbath. The result of this deed is that "the Pharisees immediately went out and held a consultation with the Herodians against him, in order that they might destroy him" (Mark 3:6). In this concluding statement, the evangelist acts as a historian insofar as he attempts to explain, with reference to a sequence of events, the reason (αἰτία) why Jesus was crucified.[3] From a literary point of view, 3:6 builds suspense and prepares for the narration of the arrest, suffering, and death of Jesus.

The next time the death of Jesus is mentioned is in the first passion prediction of 8:31. Here an important interpretative step is taken in saying that the death of Jesus "must" (δεῖ) take place. This step evokes the story of Daniel's interpretation of Nebuchadnezzar's dream, in which Daniel tells the king that "there is a God in heaven revealing mysteries, who has made known to the king, Nebuchadnezzar, what must take place (ἃ δεῖ γενέσθαι) in the time of the last days" (Dan 2:28 OG). This text inspired, at least in part, and was incorporated into the apocalyptic understanding of creation and history expressed in the Dead Sea Scrolls.[4] Mark does something similar. The statement that Jesus "must" suffer and die implies that Jesus' death is part of the divine plan for human history. That Jesus speaks about such things indicates that he knows beforehand and accepts his suffer-

---

1   That this event is a key part of "the good news" (τὸ εὐαγγέλιον) is shown by 15:1. In making their argument that the "ransom" saying in Mark 10:45 does not mean that Jesus' death ransomed people from sin, Sharyn Dowd and Elizabeth Struthers Malbon overlook the link between Mark's use of the term "gospel" and the pre-Pauline summary of the oral gospel in 1 Cor 15:1-4 (Dowd and Malbon, "The Significance of Jesus' Death in Mark: Narrative Context and Authorial Audience," *JBL* 125 [2006] 271–97, esp. 280–81 n. 27).

2   On the significance of the wedding-metaphor, see the commentary on 2:19 below.

3   Becker, *Markus-Evangelium*, 126, 168. Mark does not use the term αἰτία in this context, but 3:6 shows a concern analogous to those of the ancient historians who do use the term. The term appears in 15:26 in a different type of usage.

4   See the commentary on 8:30-31 below.

ing, rejection, and death. From a literary point of view, 8:31, like 3:6, builds suspense and prepares the audience for the passion narrative.

The idea that the Son of Man[5] suffers and is treated with contempt in accordance with Scripture is expressed in the dialogue between Jesus and the three disciples who witnessed the transfiguration (9:12b). The allusion is probably to Psalm 22 (21 LXX), a psalm to which the passion narrative also alludes: "But I am a worm and no man, an object of reproach for a man and an object of contempt for the people" (Ps 21:7 LXX).[6] The whole dialogue works as another prediction of the passion of Jesus, and it does so by creating an analogy between the death of the Son of Man and the death of Elijah. Both were prefigured or prophesied in Scripture, and the prophecy concerning Elijah has already been fulfilled in the death of John the Baptist.[7] Like 8:31, this passage implies that there is a divine plan for history, specifically for the last days. Both John and Jesus were sent by God with a message to proclaim. Although many among the people responded favorably, both John and Jesus were rejected by the leaders.

In what is usually called the second prediction of the passion (9:31), the Markan Jesus states, "The Son of Man will be handed over ($\pi\alpha\rho\alpha\delta\acute{\iota}\delta\sigma\tau\alpha\iota$) into the hands of human beings, and they will kill him, and when he has been killed, after three days he will rise." With regard to a sequence of historical (or historylike) events, the verb $\pi\alpha\rho\alpha\delta\acute{\iota}\delta\omega\mu\iota$ has the sense "to hand over a person into the custody of officials." With regard to the interpretation of the passion of Jesus, it alludes to the Greek version of Isa 53:12, "Therefore, he will be the heir of many and will apportion the spoils of the mighty, because he was handed over ($\pi\alpha\rho\epsilon\delta\acute{o}\vartheta\eta$) to death and was reckoned among the lawless. And he has borne the sins of many and was handed over ($\pi\alpha\rho\epsilon\delta\acute{o}\vartheta\eta$) on account of their sins." Since this verb is used repeatedly in Mark, the allusion appears to be deliberate. The passive voice suggests divine agency.[8]

The same verb appears twice in the third passion prediction, "See, we are going up to Jerusalem, and the Son of Man will be handed over ($\pi\alpha\rho\alpha\delta\sigma\vartheta\acute{\eta}\sigma\epsilon\tau\alpha\iota$) to the chief priests and the scribes, and they will condemn him to death and hand him over ($\pi\alpha\rho\alpha\delta\acute{\omega}\sigma\sigma\upsilon\sigma\iota\nu$) to the nations, and they will mock him and spit on him and whip him and kill him, and after three days he will rise" (10:33-34). This is the most detailed of the three passion predictions. Literarily speaking, it provides a detailed summary of the passion narrative and thus prepares the audience for it, encouraging them to wonder how all this will take place. From the point of view of historiography, its purpose is to summarize events. Yet the double use of the verb "to hand over," like its use in the second prediction, hints at an interpretation. The poem about the Suffering Servant in Isaiah, especially 53:12 (LXX), is evoked and applied to Jesus. This application probably means that the passage is interpreted messianically.

In 3:6 the question "why" Jesus died and is raised begins to be answered from a historiographic point of view. The first time that this question is raised from an interpretative point of view is in the instruction on leadership related to the question of James and John (10:35-45). As Paul does in the prose hymn in Philippians 2, the author of Mark makes a significant christological statement in presenting the death of Jesus as an example or model for the audience to imitate in their interaction with one another. In advocating a leadership of service, the Markan Jesus states, "whoever wants to be first among you will be slave of all; for the Son of Man did not come to be served, but to serve and to give his life as a ransom ($\lambda\acute{\upsilon}\tau\rho\sigma\nu$) in behalf of ($\grave{\alpha}\nu\tau\acute{\iota}$) many" (10:44-45). The idea of dying for the benefit of others is present in both the Hebrew and the Greek version of Isa 53:11-12. But the notion of "ransom" ($\lambda\acute{\upsilon}\tau\rho\sigma\nu$) does not appear anywhere in the context (Isa 52:13—53:12). The usage of $\lambda\acute{\upsilon}\tau\rho\sigma\nu$ elsewhere in the LXX makes it probable that Mark and his audiences understood the "ransom" effected by Jesus as an expiation accomplished "in behalf of" or "in place of" ($\grave{\alpha}\nu\tau\acute{\iota}$) many.[9] The notion of expiation is sometimes associated with the ritual of sacrifice,

---

5   On the use of the title "Son of Man" for Jesus in Mark synonymously with "Messiah," see the commentary on 8:30-31 below.

6   See the commentary on 9:12-13 below.

7   See the commentary on 9:12-13 below.

8   See the commentary on 9:31 below. Dowd and Mal-

bon deny any allusion to Isaiah 53 in Mark ("Jesus' Death in Mark," 283–85).

9   See the commentary on 10:45 below.

but expiation of an offense or propitiation (presumably of God) may be made in other ways as well. The text lays empasis on the voluntary character of Jesus' death. His life was not taken from him; rather, he "came" "to give" it.[10]

After Jesus' actions and accompanying teaching in the temple, the following comment is made: "And the chief priests and the scribes heard (what he said) and were looking for a way to destroy him; for they feared him, for the whole crowd was amazed at his teaching" (11:18). Like the comment in 3:6, this statement has a historiographic purpose, namely, to explain "why" and "how" Jesus came to be crucified.[11] In the earlier context, it was the Pharisees and the Herodians who were conspiring to destroy Jesus. Here, for the first time, hostility on the part of the chief priests is mentioned. The audience has been prepared for this hostility by the first and third passion predictions (8:31; 10:33). The scribes join the chief priests in 11:18 in their incipient efforts to destroy Jesus. The theme of conflict between Jesus and the scribes is introduced already in 1:22, when the people in the synagogue at Capernaum are said to be amazed at his teaching, which was authoritative and not like that of the scribes. This theme is elaborated in several subsequent incidents.[12] The emergence of more deadly opposition on the part of the scribes, like that of the chief priests, is prepared for by the first and third passion predictions.

Jesus' death is dealt with allegorically in the parable of the vineyard and the tenants (12:1-12). The vinedressers declare, "This is the heir; come on, let's kill him, and the inheritance will be ours" (12:7). From an allegorical point of view, this statement may be interpreted as signifying that the leaders of the people wish to destroy Jesus because he is God's heir, that is, the son of God or Messiah. They kill him in order to keep leadership and power for themselves. The "others" to whom the vineyard will be given are presumably the leaders among the followers

of Jesus (12:9). So far, the parable addresses historiographic concerns in an indirect way. The reference to Scripture in vv. 10-11 concerns the interpretation of Jesus' death, the "why" as a theological question. Jesus is compared to the stone that the builders rejected, which has become the cornerstone. The primary rhetorical point made by the citation is that God will (has) reverse(d) the rejection and execution of Jesus by raising him from the dead. The imagery of building may presuppose the idea that the communities that meet in the name of Jesus constitute a living temple.[13] The last part of the quotation of Ps 118:23 (117:23 LXX) reads "this was the Lord's doing and it is marvelous in our eyes" (12:11). In the psalm, what is marvelous is the striking reversal in the situation of the one who was surrounded by enemies and near death. By the power of God he could celebrate a victory. Similarly, in Mark what is marvelous is the radical change in the status of Jesus from one who was rejected and shamefully treated to the exalted Son of Man.

Since they fear the crowd, the Markan chief priests and scribes decide to arrest Jesus "by deceit" or "by stealth" ($\dot{\epsilon}\nu$ $\delta\acute{o}\lambda\dot{\omega}$) (14:1). Judas, one of the Twelve, provides the means by his unmotivated offer to "hand over" Jesus to them (14:10). The decision and act of Judas are unmotivated from the point of view of Judas as a character in the narrative. But a scene at the last supper makes clear that he is playing a role in the divine drama. Although he is God's instrument in bringing about the death of Jesus, he is nonetheless culpable for this deed (14:17-21). God's will is discovered by means of a strategy for reading Scripture.[14]

As in the ransom saying, the interpretation of Jesus' death is taken up in the sayings about the bread and the cup (14:22-25). In the context of a Passover meal (14:12-16), the statement related to the bread, "Take, this is my body," suggests that Jesus' body is analogous to the

---

10   Emphasizing the literary context of the saying, Dowd and Malbon interpret 10:45 to mean that Jesus ransoms the majority from the tyranny of the elite ("Jesus' Death in Mark," 287). A problem with this view is that the Markan Jesus does not speak about his audience being under the tyranny of the (Gentile) elite. Rather he speaks about the Gentiles' rulers lording it over *them* and being tyrants over *them* (v. 42).

11   Becker, *Markus-Evangelium*, 168.
12   Mark 2:6, 16; 3:22; 7:1, 5.
13   See the commentary on 12:10-11 below.
14   See the commentary on 14:18, 20 below.

Passover lamb, that is, that Jesus' death is a metaphorical Passover sacrifice (cf. 1 Cor 5:7). The saying related to the cup, "This is my blood of the covenant," suggests that the death of Jesus is a sacrifice of covenant renewal. The pouring out of Jesus' blood, which is mentioned next, reinforces the impression of a metaphorical sacrifice, since the "pouring of blood" is technical sacrificial language.[15] That the blood of Jesus "is poured out for many (ὑπὲρ πολλῶν)" suggests a sacrifice offered to atone for sin. Or the sacrificial language of pouring out blood may be combined here with the idea and language of the vicarious suffering of the Servant of Isaiah 53.[16]

That the death of Jesus is God's will is implied by Jesus' citation of Zech 13:7b, "You will all take offense, for it is written, 'I will strike the shepherd, and the sheep will be scattered'" (14:27). The action of striking the shepherd is described indirectly as God's will in the text of Zechariah, in both the Hebrew and the Greek version: God gives the command to others to strike the shepherd. So Mark makes more explicit the idea that Jesus' death is God's will; in fact, it is described here as God's act. The portrayal of Jesus' death as God's will is also effected in the quotation of Jesus' prayer in 14:36, "Abba! Father! All things are possible for you; remove this cup from me. But (let) not what I want (be), but what you want." Since Jesus receives no response to his prayer and his death is narrated later on, his death must be what God wants. The same idea is expressed in Jesus' comment in 14:49; his arrest takes place in fulfillment of the scriptures.

The tension being built up by this harsh emphasis on Jesus' death as God's will is relieved somewhat by the prophecy that Jesus makes before the high priest. When asked whether he is the Messiah, Jesus replies, "I am, and you will see the Son of Man sitting on the right of the Power and coming with the clouds of heaven" (14:62). According to the passages discussed above, the death of Jesus itself has meaning as an event that takes place to benefit others (as atonement for sin, as an example to be

followed, as a renewed Passover or covenant). But the prophecy before the high priest makes clear that Jesus will not remain as one rejected and treated with contempt. As the rejected stone became the cornerstone, so the rejected and crucified Jesus will be exalted to the right hand of God. His coming with power implies that, after he is raised from the dead, Jesus will exercise his messianic role.

In the account of the crucifixion and death of Jesus, no explicit or transparent interpretation is given of that death (15:21-39). The narrative is open to a variety of interpretations. One way of reading the text is to see analogies with the scapegoat, or in Greek terms, the *pharmakos*.[17] Another is to read it as an account of a noble death or a martyrdom.[18] Another is to focus on the role of Scripture in the narrative. The text most frequently alluded to is Psalm 22 (21 LXX). Since the significance of the link between the events narrated and this psalm is not explained in the text of Mark itself, a variety of views have been expressed. One is that the allusions signify simply that all these events were foretold in Scripture. This point is apologetic: the fact that Jesus was rejected and crucified does not mean that he was deluded or was a false prophet; it does not invalidate the claim that he is the Messiah. The link has also been explained as a way of defining the character or role of Jesus. A widespread view is that the use of Psalm 22 portrays Jesus as the suffering just one or the righteous sufferer. Donald Juel has argued credibly that Mark and his predecessors did not read this and other psalms of individual lament in terms of innocent suffering in general, but with reference to the Messiah.[19]

The use of these psalms may also be understood in terms of Mark's reinterpretation of the role of the Messiah in relation to the widespread view among late Second Temple Jews that the Messiah of Israel would be a military leader and a king in the normal political sense. Since David was both the model for this typical view of

---

15 Adela Yarbro Collins, "Finding Meaning in the Death of Jesus," *JR* 78 (1998) 176.

16 Ibid., 177. Dowd and Malbon rightly conclude that the phrase "blood of the covenant" alludes to Exod 24:8 ("Jesus' Death in Mark," 292). But they overlook the fact that language about pouring out blood *for many* is not typical of accounts of covenant sacrifices (ibid., 293–94).

17 Yarbro Collins, "Finding Meaning," 186–87.

18 See the excursus on the passion narrative, the section on "Genre," in the commentary on 14:1-11 below.

19 On all these views, see the excursus on the passion narrative below. See also the commentary on 15:24 below.

the Messiah and also universally regarded at the time as the author of all the psalms, the memory and character of David could be used as one of the means of redefining the messianic role.[20] The story of David in 1–2 Samuel, especially as read in light of the psalms of individual lament, is not only a story of a victorious warrior and successful ruler. It is also a story of hardship, betrayal, and suffering. David as a suffering figure validates Jesus as a suffering Messiah. At the same time, Jesus' messiahship is portrayed as heavenly and eternal, not just earthly and temporally limited. This is why the Markan Jesus raises the question how the Messiah can be David's son, if David called him Lord.[21] As the hidden Son of Man on earth, Jesus suffered and died like David. But after his resurrection, he was installed as a heavenly Messiah, more like "that Son of Man" in the Similitudes of Enoch than like David.[22]

With regard to discipleship, the Markan Jesus warns his followers that they must suffer as he did (8:34-35). Yet, if they are loyal and endure, they will share his glory as well (8:34—9:1; 13:9-13, 27).

---

20   See Ahearne-Kroll, "Suffering of David."
21   See the commentary on 12:35-37 below.

22   See the subsection of this introduction above on *Jesus as Messiah*.

In the section of this introduction on authorship above, Papias's remarks about Mark and Peter were quoted. Much of that quotation is important also for the topic of the composition and structure of Mark. The relevant parts read as follows:

> Mark became Peter's interpreter and wrote accurately all that he remembered, not, indeed, in order (οὐ μέντοι τάξει), of the things said or done by the Lord. For he had not heard the Lord, nor had he followed him, but later on, as I said, followed Peter, who used to give teaching as necessity demanded but not making, as it were, an arrangement (σύνταξις) of the Lord's oracles. . . . Matthew collected [or better, systematically arranged] (συνετάξατο) the oracles in the Hebrew language, and each interpreted them as best he could.[1]

The point of interest for our topic is the remark that Mark "wrote accurately all that he remembered, not, indeed, in order, of the things said or done by the Lord." This remark has been interpreted in various ways. The most basic question is what kind of "order" is meant. One main possibility is that Papias refers to historically reliable chronological order. The other is that "order" (τάξις) is a rhetorical term that refers to the organization of a work as a whole, which may include the arranging of sayings according to topic.[2] Some scholars understand the word "order" chronologically and conclude that Papias prefers the depiction of the public life of Jesus in the Gospel of John to that of Mark.[3] Other scholars interpret Papias as meaning that the literary structure of Mark is deficient. Some of these conclude that Papias prefers Luke's literary arrangement, pointing to his claim in the preface of that Gospel that he has provided Theophilus with "an orderly account" (καθεξῆς σοι γράψαι) (Luke 1:3).[4] Others argue that Mark is being unfavorably compared with Matthew.[5]

The sentence that immediately follows the remark about Mark's lack of order seems to support the chronological interpretation. The fact that Mark was not a follower of Jesus would imply that he did not know the historical order of events, whereas a disciple of Jesus, such as Matthew or John, would have known such things firsthand. The next remark, however, regarding the teaching of Peter, supports the literary interpretation. Peter selected from the sayings and deeds of Jesus according to the circumstances of his teaching.[6] This procedure is explicitly contrasted with the literary activity of making a systematic arrangement of "the oracles" (τὰ λόγια) of the Lord. Finally, the statement that Matthew "systematically arranged the oracles" (τὰ λόγια συνετάξατο) shows that Papias's concern is a literary one. The statement that Mark was not a direct disciple of Jesus seems to imply not that he lacked knowledge about the sequence of historical events but that he had not mastered the teaching of Jesus sufficiently to be able to make a topical arrangement of it, but simply reported Peter's ad hoc teaching.

There is of course some systematic arrangement of Jesus' teaching in Mark. For example, parables have been collected and formed into a speech in chap. 4, and escha-

---

1   Papias cited by Eusebius *Hist. eccl.* 3.39.15–16; text and trans. from Kirsopp Lake, *Eusebius: The Ecclesiastical History* (2 vols.; LCL; Cambridge, MA: Harvard University Press; London: Heinemann, 1926) 1:296–97.

2   The Latin equivalent of the Greek rhetorical concept of τάξις or σύνταξις is *dispositio*. On the latter, see Quintilian *Inst. Orat.* 7.preface. David Aune takes the term σύνταξις in the quotation from Papias as a technical literary term meaning "artistically arranged" or "finished composition" (*Literary Environment*, 65–67). See also idem, "Arrangement," in idem, *The Westminster Dictionary of New Testament and Early Christian Rhetoric* (Louisville/London: Westminster John Knox Press, 2003) 62–64.

3   Martin Hengel, "Literary, Theological and Historical Problems in the Gospel of Mark," in Stuhlmacher,

Gospel and the Gospels, 234, 237; Helmut Merkel, cited by Pesch, 1:5–6 n. 6; and others (see Black, *Mark*, 110 n. 68).

4   Robert M. Grant and Ralph Martin (see Black, *Mark*, 92, 110 n. 68).

5   Josef Kürzinger, *Papias von Hierapolis und die Evangelien des Neuen Testaments: Gesammelte Aufsätze, Neuausgebung und Übersetzung der Fragmente, kommentierte Bibliographie* (Eichstätter Materialien 4; Regensburg: Pustet, 1983). Pesch also thinks that Papias is contrasting Mark and Matthew, but seems to interpret "order" chronologically or at least historically (Rudolph Pesch, *Das Markusevangelium I. Teil: Einleitung und Kommentar zu Kap. 1, 1–8,26* [HTK 2.1; Freiburg: Herder, 1976; 5th ed. 1989] 1:5 and n. 5).

6   Aune translates ὃς πρὸς τὰς χρείας ἐποιεῖτο τὰς διδασκαλίας as "who formulated his teachings in

tological teaching has been arranged in the eschatological discourse of chap. 13. Yet some of the teaching that Matthew places in the introduction to the teaching of Jesus, the Sermon on the Mount (chap. 5–7),[7] in the mission discourse in chap. 10, and in the instructions for the church in chap. 18 may have appeared to Papias to be scattered about in Mark's Gospel and lacking orderly arrangement.

Some modern scholars agree with Papias that Mark is a simple narrative, close to oral tradition, without a complex structure or sophisticated arrangement. Others argue that the Gospel in fact does have a highly detailed and sophisticated structure. It is important to clarify this question, since decisions about composition and structure bear directly on issues of interpretation, particularly of the portrayal of Jesus in Mark.

One type of structure is segmentation. The oldest manuscript of Mark, Chester Beatty Papyrus I, designated p[45] by textual critics, was probably copied in the first half of the third century.[8] It was, like most manuscripts of the time, written in continuous script; that is, the scribe left no spaces between words and sentences. The purpose was probably to economize, since writing materials were expensive. Punctuation was used only sporadically before the eighth century.[9] In the papyri, works were not divided into chapters.[10] The lengths of works were calculated according to lines ($\sigma\tau\acute{\iota}\chi\omicron\iota$). Such calculations made possible a rough check of a copy to see if it agreed in the number of lines with the original. Some ancient manuscripts provide information on the number of lines of the Gospels. Mark is usually said to consist of 1,600 lines.[11]

Eventually, what may be called "helps for readers" were introduced into the manuscripts, presumably to aid in both the private and public reading of Scripture. One of these was the division of works into chapters ($\kappa\epsilon\phi\acute{\alpha}\lambda\alpha\iota\alpha$), a simple way in which order may be perceived in a text. The oldest system is that preserved in the margins of Codex Vaticanus, designated "B" by textual critics, a parchment manuscript that was copied about the middle of the fourth century.[12] In this manuscript, Mark is divided into sixty-two sections. A more common system is preserved in the fifth-century parchment manuscript known as Codex Alexandrinus, referred to as "A" by textual critics. In this system there are forty-eight sections in Mark. The beginning of the first chapter is never placed at the beginning of a work, because it was customary to speak of the opening of a book as the introduction or preface ($\pi\rho\omicron\omicron\acute{\iota}\mu\iota\omicron\nu$). Thus, in the system represented by Alexandrinus and most other Greek manuscripts, chap. 1 of Mark begins at what we know as 1:23.[13]

Each of the chapters of the system found in Alexandrinus and most other late Greek manuscripts was given a title ($\tau\acute{\iota}\tau\lambda\omicron\varsigma$). This was placed in the margin, usually began with the word "about" or "concerning" ($\pi\epsilon\rho\acute{\iota}$), and summarized the content of the chapter. In many manuscripts, all the chapter titles for one book are gathered and listed before that book as a summary of its content.[14]

The text of the New Testament was divided into verses for the first time in the fourth edition published by the Parisian printer and publisher Robert Estienne, whose name is often cited in its Latinized form, Stephanus. This edition, published in 1551, contained the Greek text and two Latin versions.[15]

Modern scholars have divided the Gospels into small units, each of which is called a "pericope," a noun related to the Greek verb $\pi\epsilon\rho\iota\kappa\acute{o}\pi\tau\omega$, which means "to cut around." The idea is that there are passages that

---

the form of anecdotes" rather than as "who used to give teaching as necessity demanded," as Lake translated the phrase in Eusebius *Hist. eccl.* 3.39.15 (Lake, *Eusebius*, 296–97; Aune, *Literary Environment*, 66).

7 The Sermon on the Mount appears to be an introduction to the teaching of Jesus, since it comes near the beginning of Jesus' public activity and especially because it occurs at a place in Matthew that corresponds to Mark's first mention of Jesus' teaching without reporting it. Cf. Matt 4:18-25 with Mark 1:16-39 and Matt 8:1-4 with Mark 1:40-45.

8 Bruce M. Metzger and Bart D. Ehrman, *The Text of the New Testament: Its Transmission, Corruption, and Restoration* (4th ed.; New York/Oxford: Oxford University Press, 2005) 54.

9 Ibid., 22.

10 But a manuscript from the late second century (known as p[4], p[64], p[67]) uses an organized text division (ibid., 53).

11 Ibid., 26.

12 Ibid., 68.

13 Ibid., 34.

14 Ibid., 36.

15 Ibid., 149–50.

form units of thought and thus may figuratively be "cut around" or "cut away" from their contexts. The notion of a pericope is closely related to form criticism and its assumption that short passages in the Gospel, such as a parable or a pronouncement story, once circulated independently in the oral tradition. In the critical editions of the Greek New Testament, the pericopes are indicated by the indentation of paragraphs. In the *Synopsis of the First Three Gospels* prepared by Heinrich Greeven, there are 275 pericopes that occur in one or more of the first three Gospels.[16] Of these 104 occur in Mark.

The criteria for delimiting pericopes are explicit changes in spatial location or temporal setting, the introduction of one or more characters, or a shift in topic. Proponents of the newer discipline of text-linguistics or discourse analysis have attempted to refine these criteria and, using them, to define sections and subsections of texts of the New Testament.[17]

Besides segmentation, scholars have searched for other kinds of signals in Mark that reveal its structure. A number of these efforts have focused on the opening words, "(The) beginning of the good news of Jesus Christ." Several important issues related to these words concern composition and structure. One is whether these are the opening words of the work itself, often referred to with the Latin term *incipit*, or whether they should be seen as a title; the equivalent Latin term is *inscriptio* or *superscriptio*. Rudolf Pesch, in his two-volume commentary on Mark, first published in 1976 and 1977, labeled these words as a title and argued that the editor composed it by imitating a Jewish literary practice. This practice involved introducing a literary work with a sen-

tence lacking a verb that outlines briefly the content and external circumstances of the book.[18] He mentions Hosea as a formal parallel. Actually, the book of Hosea has two such opening sentences. The first reads "The word of the Lord that came to Hosea son of Beeri, in the days of Kings Uzziah, Jotham, Ahaz, and Hezekiah of Judah, and in the days of King Jeroboam son of Joash of Israel" (Hos 1:1 NRSV). The second is more similar to Mark and reads "(The) beginning of the word of the Lord to Hosea."[19]

The argument that Mark's opening words were modeled on Jewish precedents is persuasive. It is confusing, however, to refer to these words as a title, since ancient manuscripts distinguish between the opening words proper and the title, which may be placed either at the beginning or at the end of the work. The opening words may function in the same way as a title, but there is an important difference. The opening words are more likely to have been written by the author than the formal title.[20]

The second issue related to the opening words is the question whether v. 2 continues v. 1 or introduces v. 3. The third is whether the word "beginning" in v. 1 refers to the Gospel as a whole (Mark 1:2–16:8) or just to the introduction to the Gospel. If the latter, then how much of Mark belongs to the introduction?

As noted above, the ancient system of dividing Mark attested by Codex Alexandrinus designates 1:1-22 as the introduction to the Gospel. Most modern scholars have argued for a shorter introduction. In the 1960s and 1970s, most scholars concluded that Mark 1:1-13 was the introduction to the Gospel.[21] Beginning already in the

---

16   See Albert Huck, *Synopse der drei ersten Evangelien mit Beigabe der johanneischen Parallelstellen/Synopsis of the First Three Gospels with the Addition of the Johannine Parallels* (13th ed., fundamentally revised by Heinrich Greeven; Tübingen: Mohr Siebeck, 1981).

17   See, e.g., John G. Cook, *The Structure and Persuasive Power of Mark: A Linguistic Approach* (SBLSS; Atlanta: Scholars Press, 1995); Paul L. Danove, *The End of Mark's Story: A Methodological Study* (BIS 3; Leiden: Brill, 1993) 132–66; Lars Hartman, *Text-Centered New Testament Studies: Text-Theoretical Essays on Early Jewish and Early Christian Literature* (ed. David Hellholm; WUNT 102; Tübingen: Mohr Siebeck, 1997); David Hellholm, "The Problem of Apocalyptic Genre and the Apocalypse of John," in Adela Yarbro

Collins, ed., *Early Christian Apocalypticism: Genre and Social Setting*, Semeia 36 (1986) 1–64.

18   Pesch follows Ernst Lohmeyer on this point (Lohmeyer, 10; Pesch, 1:74–75).

19   Ἀρχὴ λόγου κυρίου πρὸς Ωσηε (Hos 1:2a LXX).

20   See the section on *Authorship* above.

21   E.g., Werner Georg Kümmel, *Introduction to the New Testament* (rev. ed.; Nashville: Abingdon, 1975) 82; C. E. B. Cranfield, *The Gospel according to Saint Mark* (rev. ed.; CGTC; Cambridge/New York: Cambridge University Press, 1977; 1st ed. 1959) 14; Vincent Taylor, *The Gospel according to St. Mark: The Greek Text with Introduction, Notes, and Indexes* (2nd ed.; Grand Rapids: Baker, 1966) 107.

1960s, a number of scholars argued that vv. 14-15 should be attributed to the introduction as well, although some continued to argue for vv. 1-13 only.[22] The strongest arguments for making a division between v. 13 and v. 14 are (1) there is a major change in spatial location (from the desert to Galilee), a clear temporal shift (after John had been arrested) and a major change with regard to the activity of Jesus (from the testing in the desert to proclaiming the good news); (2) the shift from v. 15 to v. 16 is less marked: Jesus remains in Galilee; there is no explicit temporal change; and the activity of calling disciples is closely related to announcing the good news. On the other hand, vv. 14-15 have an expository character; they depict the beginning of Jesus' ministry in a way that is at the same time a summary of it, and there is nothing analogous in the rest of the Gospel. Thus, it seems best to reckon these verses to the introduction, but to acknowledge their transitional character.

Opinions vary even more widely on the division of the rest of the Gospel. Some argue for a division into two main parts, others into three and some for as many as seven. Spatial indicators or geographical settings have often been employed as a major criterion for discerning the structure of Mark. On this basis Mary Ann Tolbert has argued for a two-part division of the material that follows the introduction. Part 1 consists of the first ten chapters, since all of the action in them takes place in and around Galilee.[23] Part 2 comprises chaps. 11 through 16, which take place in and around Jerusalem.[24] Kümmel isolated five parts, using geographical criteria: (1) Jesus in Galilee (1:14—5:43); (2) travels inside and outside of Galilee (6:1—9:50); (3) journey to Jerusalem (chap. 10); (4) Jesus in Jerusalem (chaps. 11–13); (5) passion and resurrection narratives (chaps. 14–16).[25] The last section is defined in terms of content rather than setting.

Another criterion for determining the divisions in the Gospel was proposed by Norman Perrin. He suggested that the editorial summaries be taken as transitional signals. Given that the early manuscripts lacked divisions into chapters, verses, or even individual words, the audience needed such signals to follow the progression of the narrative. He accepted the list of Markan summaries defined by Karl Ludwig Schmidt, an early form critic, and combined these with geographical and thematic indicators to isolate seven major sections. He took 1:14-15 as the first transitional summary, the summary of the preaching of Jesus, which demarcates the introduction from the first major section. Perrin defined the latter as 1:16—3:6 and described it as "the authority of Jesus exhibited in word and deed." The second summary is 3:7-12, which demarcates the boundary between the first and second major sections. The second extends from 3:13 to 6:6a and is described as "Jesus as Son of God and as rejected by his own people." The third summary is 6:6b, which is followed by the third major section, that is, 6:7—8:21, entitled "Jesus as Son of God and as misunderstood by his own disciples." The element that divides the third from the fourth major section is a miracle story, rather than an editorial summary, namely, the healing of the blind man in Bethsaida in 8:22-26. The fourth major section consists of 8:27—10:45 and concerns "Christology and Christian discipleship in light of the passion." The boundary between this section and the next is another account of the healing of a blind man, namely, the cure of Bartimaeus in 10:46-52. The fifth major section extends from 11:1 to 12:44 and is entitled "The days in Jerusalem prior to the passion." The "introduction to the apocalyptic discourse" (13:1-5a) plays the role of a summary in forming a transition from the fifth to the sixth major section, which consists of the apocalyptic dis-

---

22 Those who argue for 1:1-15 include Leander E. Keck, "The Introduction to Mark's Gospel," *NTS* 12 (1965–66) 352–70; Pesch, 1:71–73. Those who argue for 1:1-13 include Cook, *Structure*, 157, 343; Ole Davidsen, *The Narrative Jesus: A Semiotic Reading of Mark's Gospel* (Aarhus, Denmark: Aarhus University Press, 1993) 38; Danove, *End of Mark's Story*, 134–35. Bas van Iersel defines vv. 14-15 as a "hinge" linking the introduction and the first major section (*Reading Mark* [Edinburgh: T & T Clark; Collegeville, MN: Liturgical Press, 1988] 20). See also the section

"Narrative Unity" in the commentary on 1:2-15 below.

23 This description is an oversimplification; see the excursus "Galilee and Jerusalem in Mark" in the commentary on 14:26-31 below.

24 Mary Ann Tolbert, *Sowing the Gospel: Marks' World in Literary-Historical Perspective* (Minneapolis: Fortress, 1989) 113–14.

25 Kümmel, *Introduction*, 82–84.

course proper (13:5b-37). Similarly, the introduction to the passion narrative (14:1-12), including the inserted story about the woman anointing Jesus, provides the transition from the sixth to the seventh major section, which is the passion narrative proper (14:13—16:8).[26]

The most persuasive approach is to make use of several criteria, as Perrin did, such as the geographical and the thematic, and to discern the divisions where these criteria reinforce one another. Perrin's outline is problematic, however, because the transitional passages are not all summaries and the definition of the themes is sometimes rather subjective. But the two stories about the healing of blindness do seem to have an important function. We will return to this point below.

The analyses of the structure of Mark mentioned so far are based on (1) the ancient practice of providing a work with an introduction; (2) form-critical insights, especially the isolation of editorial summaries; and (3) general literary-critical observations regarding geographical and thematic indicators. Others have attempted a more detailed architectural analysis based on certain rhetorical features of ancient literature. One of these is the device called "chiasmus," which means a marking with diagonal lines like an X, which is the shape of the Greek letter *chi*. The technique involves the crosswise arrangement of contrasted pairs to give alternate stress. An English example is Milton's line, "Sweet is the breath of morn, her rising sweet."[27] Chiasmus is a device often found in ancient texts; and although the term is often used by modern critics, it is not found in the handbooks of the classical period. It appears for the first time in a

work entitled *On Invention*, attributed to Hermogenes and perhaps written in the fourth century CE. There "it is applied to a reversed arrangement of clauses in a sentence."[28]

Another device that was used, but not discussed, in antiquity is often cited in modern literature.[29] It is called *inclusio* and means the repetition of the same word or phrase, not always in identical form, at or near the beginning and ending of some unit, for example, a sentence, a pericope, or a larger section of a work. One sometimes finds a noun and a verb from the same root used in this way. An *inclusio* is not always easy to distinguish from coincidental repetition or repetition for a nonstructural reason. As Joanna Dewey put it, "the rhetorical critic by designating certain repetitions as inclusios is making a judgment about the limits of some unit of narrative."[30]

A number of scholars have argued, or proceeded on the assumption, that these devices, originally designed for use on the level of the sentence or small section of a work, came to be used in larger contexts, even to structure an entire work. According to Dewey, a chiasm may involve words or larger elements such as pericopes. It may have the form: a b : b' a', in which words or units are repeated in inverse order; or the form: a b c b' a', in which the middle element is not repeated.[31]

The device called *inclusio* is sometimes designated "ring composition."[32] According to Dewey, ring composition, in its simplest form, is the device of *inclusio*, that is, the repetition of a word or phrase at the beginning and end of a passage, marking it as a rhetorical unit. She goes on to say, however, that "ring composition, like chiasm,

---

26   Dennis C. Duling and Norman Perrin, *The New Testament: Proclamation and Parenesis, Myth and History* (3rd ed.; New York: Harcourt Brace College Publishers, 1994) 305. For an earlier form of this outline, see Norman Perrin, "Towards an Interpretation of the Gospel of Mark," in Hans Dieter Betz, ed., *Christology and a Modern Pilgrimage: A Discussion with Norman Perrin* (Claremont, CA: New Testament Colloquium, 1971) 3–6.

27   Definition and example from Herbert Weir Smyth, *Greek Grammar* (rev. by Gordon M. Messing; Cambridge, MA: Harvard University Press, 1956) §3020.

28   George A. Kennedy, *New Testament Interpretation through Rhetorical Criticism* (Chapel Hill/London: University of North Carolina Press, 1984) 28, discussing Pseudo-Hermogenes *On Invention* 4.3 (p. 182 Rabe).

29   Joanna Dewey commented that "chiasm" and "ring composition" (*inclusio*) are standard terms in classical scholarship, although neither was employed by the ancient rhetoricians; this comment is supported with a reference to Lausberg (Joanna Dewey, *Markan Public Debate: Literary Technique, Concentric Structure, and Theology in Mark 2:1–3:6* [SBLDS 48; Chico, CA: Scholars Press, 1980] 206 n. 123).

30   Ibid., 31. She also notes that *inclusio* "is a recognized technique of oral literatures" (ibid.).

31   Ibid., 32–33.

32   Ibid., 33. See also Willem A. A. van Otterlo, *Untersuchungen über Begriff, Anwendung und Entstehung der griechischen Ringkomposition* (Amsterdam: Noord-Hollandsche uitgevers maatschappij, 1944).

may be defined by content rather than verbal repetition and may encompass larger sections of narrative, parts of a pericope or three or more pericopes."[33]

Dewey defines "extended concentric structure" as the symmetrical arrangement or introverted parallelism of four, five, or more pericopes or items of narrative. Extended symmetrical patterns are recognized by multiple congruent parallelisms of content, of form and structure, and of repetitions of words.[34] The main thesis of her book on Markan public debate is that the series of controversy stories in 2:1–3:6 has a concentric structure.

On the assumption that Mark has a symmetrical structure, Rudolf Pesch discerned six major sections in the Gospel, each of which has three subsections.[35] In each set of subsections, the first and third are roughly the same length, whereas the middle one is considerably shorter. Pesch estimated the length of each subsection by counting the lines of the Greek text edited by Nestle and Aland, attempting to approximate the number of lines the text would have had in the continuous writing of the early manuscripts. He also attempted to determine the literary midpoint of the Gospel, physically speaking. According to his calculations, 1:2–8:26 consists of 708 lines, and 8:31–16:8 occupies 706 lines. The center of the Gospel is thus 8:27-30, the passage in which Peter acknowledges Jesus as the Christ. There is, however, a major problem with this analysis. Since Pesch concluded that chap. 13 was a later addition to the Gospel, he did not include that material in his calculations.

In a study of the composition and genre of Mark published in 1978, Benoit Standaert argued that Mark was composed on the model of the typical rhetorical speech and thus that the Gospel has the following pattern: introduction (1:1-13); narration (1:14–6:13); argumentation (6:14–10:52); denouement (11:1–15:47); and conclusion (16:1-8).[36] The main problem with this approach is that 6:14 to 10:52 is still narration, even if it has a more strongly didactic character than the preceding material.

Argumentation is generally discursive speech, like most of the material in the letters of Paul. Fiction has a rhetoric and an evaluative character,[37] but it is still narrative, and not argumentative, in form. Although the Gospels, especially Matthew, were influenced to some degree by the rhetorical practice of antiquity, we cannot assume that narratives and speeches were composed according to the same pattern. Standaert also viewed the Gospel of Mark concentrically and argued that the central section, which he called the argumentation, is the focus. He further analyzed this central section, 6:14–10:52, into a concentric pattern and concluded that the very center of the book is the passage extending from Jesus' question to the disciples about his identity in 8:27 through 9:13, which records the end of the discussion that took place on the way down from the mountain on which the transfiguration had occurred. He took the concentric analysis one step further to highlight the teaching on discipleship given in 8:34–9:1 as the innermost heart of the Gospel.[38]

One of the most interesting proposals about the structure of Mark is that of van Iersel.[39] He argues that Mark has a concentric structure based on spatial indicators. He sets aside 1:1 as the "title," but dispenses with the category "introduction." Apart from the so-called title, he divides the Gospel into five sections structured in a pattern in which there is a middle section that is not repeated, in the form: a b c b' a'. In between these sections are four "hinges" or transitional passages. The *inclusio* or repetition relating the beginning and ending of the Gospel is seen in the fact that the action in 1:2-13 is set in the desert and that of 16:1-8 at the tomb. In terms of cultural views at the time, both are places uninhabited by human beings but beset by demons. (Compare the account of the Gerasene demoniac in chap. 5, who lived among the tombs, presumably because he was possessed by demons.) Nevertheless, in both passages "new life springs up in these places of death."[40]

33   Dewey, *Markan Public Debate*, 33.

34   Ibid. She states that, strictly speaking, an arrangement of four narrative units is an extended chiasm (ibid., 206 n. 122).

35   Rudolf Pesch, *Naherwartungen: Tradition und Redaktion in Mk 13* (KBANT; Düsseldorf: Patmos-Verlag, 1968) 50–73.

36   Benoit H. M. G. M. Standaert, *L'Évangile selon Marc: Composition et genre littéraire* (Nijmegen: Stichting Studentenpers Nijmegen, 1978) 25–64.

37   Wayne C. Booth, *The Rhetoric of Fiction* (Chicago: University of Chicago Press, 1961).

38   Standaert, *Évangile selon Marc*, 47, 51.

39   Van Iersel, *Reading Mark*, 18–26.

40   Ibid., 21.

Like Pesch, van Iersel sees the summarizing depiction of Jesus' proclamation of the Gospel in 1:14-15 as a transition from the first section to the second. The corresponding "hinge" that links the last two sections is the introduction of the women who watched the crucifixion from afar in 15:40-41. The second section, consisting of 1:16—8:21, is set in Galilee. This corresponds to the fourth section, 11:1—15:39, which is set in Jerusalem. In this case there is a contrast, rather than a parallel, in the location. The two transitional passages that connect the second and the fourth sections to the third (central) section are the two healings of blindness to which Perrin also assigned a transitional function. The central, unrepeated section is defined as 8:27 to 10:45, which van Iersel entitled "On the Way,"[41] suggesting that Jesus turns figuratively, if not literally, toward Jerusalem in 8:27. Van Iersel also argued that the two longest sections, the second and the fourth, were also structured in a concentric arrangement and that they are parallel to each other.[42] This part of the argument is not convincing.

One of the strengths of van Iersel's structure is its interpretation of the two healings of blindness as transitional passages. This argument works if the two stories are taken symbolically. The interpreter of Mark must take care not to overinterpret, not to find symbolism where none was intended—in other words, not to engage in inappropriate allegorization of the text. Heikki Räisänen has shown how easily the methods of redaction criticism and literary criticism slide into subjective interpretations of this type.[43] In the case of the two healings of blindness, however, there are good reasons for a symbolic intepretation. First of all, they are the only healings of blindness in Mark. Second, they frame a section in which Jesus instructs the disciples and they fail to understand. Third, Paul Achtemeier has shown that Mark made use of two chains of miracle stories and that he moved the healing of the blind man of Bethsaida from its original place in the source. The implication is that the framing of the middle section with healings of the blind was deliberate.

What, then, is the symbolism involved? On the one hand, the healing of the blind man of Bethsaida is a fitting conclusion to the second section, as defined by van Iersel, since that section contains many miracle stories. On the other hand, it introduces the following section, which is the third and also the middle of the Gospel. It does so by constituting a symbolic parallel to the confession of Peter. After Jesus' first attempt to heal the blind man, he acquires partial sight: the people he sees look like trees. Similarly, Peter has partial insight into the identity of Jesus. He recognizes that Jesus is the Messiah, but he does not accept the revelation that the Messiah must suffer. Thus, this healing introduces and prefigures the opening scene of the middle section.

The healing of blind Bartimaeus both concludes the third section and introduces the fourth. The healing is an ironic conclusion to the middle section. The disciples, who are sighted and who receive private and detailed instruction, nevertheless fail to grasp the significance of Jesus' teaching. In spite of his blindness, Bartimaeus "sees" who Jesus is. He acclaims Jesus as "the son of David," a title that announces beforehand an important theme of the next section. In the first pericope of the following section, the crowd associates Jesus with the kingdom of David that is coming. But later in that section, Jesus challenges the idea that the Messiah is the son of David (12:35-37). It would seem, then, that the understanding of Bartimaeus is only partial as well.

The approaches to the composition and structure of Mark discussed so far are concerned mainly with the segmentation of the text and the relation of such segmentation to meaning. Another approach is to observe the flow of the narrative, including the twists and turns that it takes. An example of this approach is the argument that Mark is a well-arranged dramatic narrative—in other words, that the flow and function of the work have important analogies in ancient tragedy. Gilbert Bilezikian went too far in defining the genre of Mark as "tragedy."[44] Richard Burridge was right in arguing that Mark may have been written in the tragic mode, but it is not a tragedy.[45] But Bilezikian and others have pointed out

---

41 Ibid., 20.
42 Ibid., 24–26.
43 Räisänen, *Messianic Secret*, 3–9, 12–15.
44 For more appropriate definitions of the genre of Mark, see the section of this introduction above on *Genre*.
45 Gilbert G. Bilezikian, *The Liberated Gospel: A Comparison of the Gospel of Mark and Greek Tragedy* (Grand Rapids: Baker, 1977); Burridge, *What Are the Gospels?*, 247 (2nd ed., 239–40).

important points of contact between Mark and some of the typical features of tragic plots.[46]

In his *Poetics*, Aristotle argued that the most important aspect of a tragedy is the arrangement of the incidents (ἡ τῶν πραγμάτων σύστασις), which he also calls the "plot" (ὁ μῦθος). This aspect is important because a tragedy is not a representation of character, "but of a piece of action, of life, of happiness and unhappiness."[47] He goes on to say that two of the most important elements in the emotional effect of tragedy are the parts of the plot called "reversals" (περιπέτειαι) and "discoveries" or "recognitions" (ἀναγνωρίσεις).[48] A "reversal" is a change of situation or fortune into the opposite, this change being probable or inevitable.[49]

In the first chapter of Mark, Jesus' situation may be described as one of good fortune or success. Yet already in 3:6 it is stated that "the Pharisees immediately went out and held a consultation with the Herodians against him, in order that they might destroy him." This verse constitutes a "reversal" of fortune analogous to those of Greek tragedy. It is made probable, if not inevitable, by the controversies narrated in chap. 2, in which "some of the scribes" (v. 6; cf. v. 16) and Pharisees (v. 24) take offense at the speech and activity of Jesus.

The other important element in the plot is the "discovery" or "recognition." Aristotle defines this element as "a change from ignorance to knowledge, producing either friendship or hatred in those who are destined to good fortune or ill. A discovery is most effective when it coincides with reversals, such as that involved by the discovery in the *Oedipus*."[50] He says a bit later that the coincidence of a discovery and reversal of fortune will involve either pity or fear.[51]

From the announcement of the plot against Jesus' life in 3:6 onward, he experiences both acclamation and opposition. Although resistance gradually increases, he seems nevertheless to be in control of the situation. Then, in 8:27, he asks the disciples who people say that he is. This question leads to Peter's discovery that he is the Messiah. This discovery coincides with a reversal in the action, because Jesus' response is the prediction of his own suffering and death. The description of the conspiracy of the Pharisees and the Herodians in 3:6 made Jesus' death probable, but his prophecy makes it inevitable. This self-revelation of Jesus leads to enmity between himself and Peter, since Peter cannot accept the linkage of messiahship with suffering and death. For the audience, the announcement of Jesus' fate evokes pity. The following teaching on discipleship (8:34—9:1) evokes fear because it makes clear that they as disciples must share this fate.

Aristotle also discusses a third element characteristic of a tragic plot, namely, a calamity (πάθος), which he defines as "a destructive or painful occurrence, such as a death on the stage, acute suffering and wounding and so on."[52] Following Peter's confession, the Gospel focuses more and more on the suffering and death of Jesus. The central calamity is, of course, the crucifixion, but the agony in the garden, the mistreatment, mocking, and scourging are preparatory calamities that evoke pity, and fear as well, and heighten the tension until the crucifixion is portrayed.

Another way to relate Mark to Aristotle's description of tragedy would be to understand 1:16—8:26 as the complication of the plot, literally, "the tying" (of a knot) (δέσις). The confession of Peter and its immediate aftermath would then be the resolution, literally, "the untying" (λύσις), which concludes with the crucifixion.[53]

According to Aristotle, the constituent parts of a tragedy are prologue, episode, exode, and choral song.[54]

---

46 See the discussion in Hengel, "Literary, Theological and Historical Problems in the Gospel of Mark," in Stuhlmacher, *Gospel and the Gospels*, 213–17.

47 Aristotle *Poetics* 6.12–13 (1450a); text and trans. from W. Hamilton Fyfe, ed. and trans. *Aristotle*, vol. 23: *The Poetics; "Longinus," On the Sublime* (LCL; rev. ed.; Cambridge: Harvard University Press; London: Heinemann, 1932) 24–25.

48 Ibid. 6.17 (1450a); Fyfe, *Aristotle*, 26–27.

49 Ibid. 11.1 (1452a); Fyfe, *Aristotle*, 40–41.

50 Ibid. 11.4–5 (1452a); Fyfe, *Aristotle*, 40–41.

51 Ibid. 11.7 (1452a-b); Fyfe, *Aristotle*, 40–43.

52 Ibid. 11.9–10 (1452b); Fyfe, *Aristotle*, 42–43.

53 For a discussion of complication and resolution, see ibid. 18.1–3 (1455b); Fyfe, *Aristotle*, 66–69.

54 Ibid. 12.1 (1452b); Fyfe, *Aristotle*, 42–43.

The play concluded with the exode, a final scene that was variable in structure.[55] The scene at the empty tomb, and perhaps all of 15:40–16:8, may be seen as equivalent to the exode. The presence of the young man in the tomb who brings joyful news has been compared to the *deus ex machina* of the tragedies of Euripides, who brings about the miraculous change that creates a happy ending.[56]

Although the genre of Mark is not "tragedy," it is illuminating to consider the similarities of its plot with the main features of the typical plot of a tragic drama as defined by Aristotle. Thus, it may be said that the "mode" of Mark, if not the "genre," is tragic.

The particular structure of Mark presupposed by this commentary is evident in the division of the Gospel into units on which comment is made. This division is explained and supported by the commentary itself, especially in the sections on "the narrative unity" of a particular segment or its relation to what precedes and follows.

55   A. W. Pickard-Cambridge and D. W. Lucas, "Tragedy, Greek," *OCD* (2nd ed., 1970) 1086.

56   Hengel, "Literary, Theological and Historical Problems in the Gospel of Mark," 216, with reference to Standaert in n. 20. Standaert discusses the composition of Mark in relation to ancient drama (*Évangile selon Marc*, 64–108).

A helpful way of understanding Mark is to view the Gospel as part of the history of early Christian tradition. This tradition begins with the actual Jesus, who can be known in two ways: by reconstructing the historical Jesus by means of historical-critical methods or by engaging with the Christ of faith through a believing community. This commentary is based, to some degree, on the conclusion that the historical Jesus was an eschatological prophet who proclaimed the kingdom of God, a teacher of wisdom, an interpreter of the Torah, and probably an exorcist. It is not clear whether Jesus considered himself to be the Messiah, but he probably taught, drawing upon Daniel 7, that a heavenly Messiah would establish the kingdom of God, as God's agent, in the near future.[1] After Jesus was crucified by the Romans, some of his followers experienced him as risen from the dead. Out of these experiences arose the proclamation (*kerygma* in Greek) of Jesus as the Messiah by members of the Jewish messianic movement that eventually grew into the early Christian church. Those who proclaimed Jesus as the Messiah also remembered him as a teacher, prophet, and miracle-worker. These people shaped the tradition about Jesus and originated new traditions as they addressed new situations in light of his memory. As these traditions were handed on, new traditions were created and older traditions updated and applied to ever changing circumstances.

With regard to the relationships among the four works that eventually became the canonical Gospels, there are two main problems: (1) the literary relations among Mark, Matthew, and Luke (called the Synoptic Gospels because they are similar enough to be read "synoptically," that is, in parallel columns) and (2) the relation of John to the other three. Solving these problems, or at least taking a position on them, is important for three reasons: (1) for reconstructing the historical Jesus, since earlier traditions are more likely to be historical than later ones; (2) for writing the history of the movement that founded the diverse communities that may be defined as or that became the earliest "Christianities"; and (3) for interpreting the Gospels, since they will be read differently depending on judgments about early and late, literary dependence or independence, and editorial activity.

In the history of the interpretation of the Gospels, a number of theories have been proposed about their relative dates and literary relationships. Augustine at the end of the fourth century offered the classical formulation of the traditional explanation of their similarities and differences: Matthew was written first; Mark is an abbreviation of Matthew; the author of Luke used Matthew and Mark; and the author of John wrote last and used all of the earlier three.[2] In 1789, Johann Jakob Griesbach opposed the traditional view and argued that the author of Mark had used both Matthew and Luke, sometimes following one, at times the other. Mark occasionally substituted for both of his sources something he knew from oral tradition.[3] A neo-Griesbachian hypothesis has been espoused by William R. Farmer, David L. Dungan, and others, namely, that Matthew is the earliest Gospel, Luke used Matthew, and Mark was written last of the three as

---

1   Adela Yarbro Collins, "The Origin of the Designation of Jesus as 'Son of Man,'" *HTR* 80 (1987) 391–407.

2   Augustine *De consensu evangelistarum* 1.2. For an ET, see Stewart D. F. Salmond and Matthew B. Riddle, "Harmony of the Gospels," in Philip Schaff, ed., *A Select Library of the Nicene and Post-Nicene Fathers: Saint Augustine* (First Series; Grand Rapids: Eerdmans, 1980) 6:78–79. See the discussion in Kümmel, *Introduction*, 44–45.

3   Johann Jakob Griesbach, *Commentatio qua Marci Evangelium totum e Matthaei et Lucae commentariis decerptum esse monstratur* (Jena, 1789); the Latin text, in Gabler's 1825 edition, is reprinted in Bernard Orchard and Thomas R. W. Longstaff, eds., *J. J. Griesbach: Synoptic and Text-critical Studies 1776–1976*

(Johann Jakob Griesbach Bicentenary Colloquium at Münster, Germany; Cambridge: Cambridge University Press, 1978) 74–102, with an introduction by Bo Reicke (ibid., 68–73) and an ET by Orchard (ibid., 103–35). See also the discussion in Kümmel, *Introduction*, 47; idem, *New Testament*, 75; William Baird, *History of New Testament Research*, vol. 1: *From Deism to Tübingen* (Minneapolis: Fortress, 1992) 143–48. Griesbach also invented the synopsis, a term apparently coined by him (Baird, *From Deism to Tübingen*, 143; see also Kümmel, *New Testament*, 74–75).

a digest of both.[4] This hypothesis is sometimes called the "two-gospel hypothesis."[5]

In the nineteenth century, the view became widely accepted that Mark was the first to be written of the canonical four.[6] During the same century, a consensus also developed that Matthew and Luke had used a second source, in addition to Mark, that consisted mainly of discourses.[7] This source is often referred to as "Q" (from the German *Quelle*, meaning "source"). Even some scholars who deny the existence of Q support Markan priority.[8]

Although the two-source theory (that the authors of Matthew and Luke used Mark and Q as their main sources) cannot explain all the similarities and differences among the Synoptic Gospels, it is widely accepted today because it provides a more adequate explanation of more of the data than any other hypothesis.[9]

A problem with the two-source theory is the so-called minor agreements of Matthew and Luke against Mark. Each of these must be treated separately,[10] and will be treated in the commentary below. A further issue concerns the hypothetical compositional procedures followed by the evangelists in relation to what is known about ancient practices.[11]

---

4 William R. Farmer, *The Synoptic Problem: A Critical Analysis* (New York: Macmillan; London: Collier-Macmillan, 1964); David Laird Dungan, "Mark—The Abridgement of Matthew and Luke," in David G. Buttrick, ed., *Jesus and Man's Hope* (2 vols.; Pittsburgh: Perspective: A Journal of Pittsburgh Theological Seminary, 1970–71) 1:51–97; Bernard Orchard, *The Griesbach Solution to the Synoptic Question*, vol. 1: *Matthew, Luke & Mark* (no further vols. have appeared; Manchester, UK: Koinonia, 1976); William R. Farmer, "Modern Developments of Griesbach's Hypothesis," *NTS* 23 (1977) 275–95.

5 David J. Neville, *Mark's Gospel–Prior or Posterior? A Reappraisal of the Phenomenon of Order* (JSNTSup 222; Sheffield: Sheffield Academic Press, 2002) 78. He concludes that "[a]ll formal arguments based on the phenomenon of order are inconclusive" (ibid., 335).

6 Kümmel, *New Testament*, 75–76, 82, 147–51.

7 Ibid., 78, 82, 147–55; cf. 327.

8 Mark S. Goodacre, *Goulder and the Gospels: An Examination of a New Paradigm* (JSNTSup 133; Sheffield: Sheffield Academic Press, 1996); idem, *The Case against Q: Studies in Markan Priority and the Synoptic Problem* (Harrisburg, PA: Trinity Press International, 2002).

9 Similarly, François Bovon, *Luke 1: A Commentary on the Gospel of Luke 1:1–9:50* (Hermeneia; Minneapolis: Fortress, 2002) 6; Ulrich Luz, *Matthew 1–7* (Minneapolis: Fortress, 1989) 46; Christopher M. Tuckett, "Synoptic Problem," *ABD* 6:263–70, esp. 270.

10 Luz, *Matthew 1–7*, 47–48.

11 Sharon Lea Mattila, "A Question Too Often Neglected," *NTS* 41 (1995) 199–217.

The traditional view of the origin and purpose of Mark's Gospel is that it was composed in Rome soon after the death of Peter in the 60s CE. From this point of view, Mark's purpose was to give an account of Jesus' words and deeds based on Peter's recollections and to preserve the traditions about Jesus.[1] William Wrede and the form critics, however, argued that much of the tradition in Mark was created after the death of Jesus and that Mark's interests were more theological than historical.[2] In the second half of the twentieth century, the origin and purpose of Mark were debated, but no consensus emerged.[3]

When this debate was well under way, Nils Dahl noted two general views: (1) that Mark was written "with the 'intention to preserve that tradition which was applied on various occasions to the upbuilding of the church,'"[4] and (2) "that this Gospel has no other 'tendency' than that which every Gospel must have."[5] He explained the latter view as "a reaction against the *Tendenzkritik* of the Tübingen school." At the time he wrote, however, Dahl found "such general characterizations of Mark's purpose" to be "insufficient."[6] In his own determination of the purpose of Mark, he focused on three features: (1) the selection of sayings of Jesus; (2) the "messianic secret" and related conceptions; and (3) the ending of the Gospel.[7] He concluded:

> The evangelist is not writing with a missionary aim but wants those who already believe to understand the proper significance of the Gospel. He reminds them that the Christ in whom they believe is the one who lived as the hidden Son of man and died as the rejected Messiah. The emphasis on those points in the narrative which evoke fear and astonishment is a cry to awaken, addressed to a church in danger of taking the Gospel for granted. This call to faith, to

endurance in affliction, and to watchfulness is combined with a warning against self-assurance and ambitious strivings.[8]

In 1956, Willi Marxsen argued that the ending of Mark implies that the evangelist expected the parousia to take place shortly in Galilee. In relation to this hypothesis, he argued further that chap. 13 reveals that the Gospel was written for a community that had fled from Jerusalem during the Jewish war of 66–74 and was awaiting the return of Jesus in Galilee.[9]

In his review of scholarship on the Markan community, John R. Donahue noted that "[a]lmost a generation after Marxsen's work no consensus has emerged on the community and setting of the Gospel of Mark."[10] Most of the studies he discussed addressed the purpose of the Gospel in the context of a hypothesis concerning the date and place of writing. In his conclusions, he noted that Mary Ann Tolbert had raised "interesting questions about the whole enterprise of the quest for the communities behind the gospels." She rejected the assumption "that some identifiable, individualized local group—that is a *specific* community—and its problems provide the setting for Mark." Rather than use the model of the Pauline letters and communities in this quest, scholars should consider the analogy of the ancient novels, which were written "for a wide readership."[11] Donahue himself took the position that "this total skepticism [scil. concerning a specific community as the addressees of Mark] may be unwarranted."[12] Finally, he noted that the works of Howard Clark Kee, Gerd Theissen, and Herman Waetjen are welcome exceptions to the focus of other scholars on "the external factors of the location and date of the Gospel rather than the kind of community to which such a work is directed," but as yet "there is no agreed upon

---

1   See the discussion in Hendrika N. Roskam, *The Purpose of Mark in Its Historical and Social Context* (NovTSup 114; Leiden/Boston: Brill, 2004) 2–3; Incigneri, *Gospel to the Romans*, 116.

2   Roskam, *Purpose of Mark*, 3–5.

3   Ibid., 5–11.

4   Nils Dahl, "The Purpose of Mark's Gospel," in idem, *Jesus in the Memory of the Early Church* (Minneapolis: Augsburg, 1976) 52–65, citing Holger Mosbech (ibid., 52 n. 1).

5   Dahl, citing Adolf Jülicher (ibid., 52 n. 2).

6   Ibid., 52.

7   Ibid., 53–63.

8   Ibid., 63–64.

9   Willi Marxsen, *Der Evangelist Markus: Studien zur Redaktionsgeschichte des Evangeliums* (2nd ed.; Göttingen: Vandenhoeck & Ruprecht, 1959; 1st ed., 1956) 59–61, 73–77, 112–28 (ET *Mark the Evangelist: Studies on the Redaction History of the Gospel* [Nashville: Abingdon, 1969] 92–95, 111–16, 166–89).

10   Donahue, "Quest," 817–38; quotation from 835.

11   Tolbert, *Sowing the Gospel*, 303–4; Donahue, "Quest," 835–36.

12   Donahue, "Quest," 836.

method available for describing, on the basis of a text, the social make-up of a given community."[13]

Like Tolbert, but with different kinds of arguments, Richard Bauckham contrasted the Gospels with the Pauline letters and rejected the view that "each Gospel addresses a localized community in its own, quite specific context and character."[14] One main characteristic of this premise is "the development of more or less allegorical readings of the Gospels in the service of reconstructing not only the character but the history of the community behind the Gospel. . . . The principle that the Gospels inform us not about Jesus but about the church is taken so literally that the narrative, ostensibly about Jesus, has to be understood as an allegory in which the community actually tells its own story."[15] He also contrasted the written Gospels with oral teaching and concluded that they were probably written for a wider audience right from the start. In other words, they were written "for Greek-speaking Christians everywhere."[16] He supported this claim with a discussion of the evidence from the New Testament and other early Christian literature that "mobility and communication in the first-century Roman world were exceptionally high."[17]

Bauckham's arguments have persuaded some scholars.[18] Others have been critical.[19] Two years after the publication of Bauckham's work, Joel Marcus reaffirmed against Bauckham that the author of Mark "seems to

have written his work first and foremost for the Christian community of which he was a member."[20] One of his better arguments is that Alexander and Rufus are mentioned in 15:21 because they were known to Mark's audience. Since both Matthew and Luke omit these names, it is likely that they did not expect the two men to be known to any of their audiences.[21] Another is his proposal that the composition and circulation of Mark was analogous to that of *Hermas*. Although his conclusion that Hermas "was intended first and foremost for the instruction of the leaders and members of the local churches in and around Rome" may be somewhat overstated, the passages he cites (*Vis.* 2.2.6; 3.8.10; 3.9.7) are open to such an interpretation. In any case, the passage cited by Bauckham, *Vis.* 2.4.3, makes clear that the work was intended both for local communities ("this city") and for communities outside the area ("the cities abroad").[22]

Margaret Mitchell agreed with Bauckham that "redaction-critical readings can dissolve into excessive 'allegorical' readings of the gospels as 'nothing but' projections onto the life of Jesus of concerns of a hypothetically reconstructed church community."[23] She also agreed that "his [Bauckham's] emphasis on travel and networks in the early missionary movements provides a very serious objection to the idea that gospel communities were completely isolated and that their authors had a

---

13 Ibid., 838.

14 Richard Bauckham, "For Whom Were Gospels Written?" in idem, ed., *The Gospels for All Christians: Rethinking the Gospel Audiences* (Grand Rapids/Cambridge: Eerdmans, 1998) 9–48; quotation from 11.

15 Ibid., 19–20. Bauckham mentions Theodore Weeden, *Mark: Traditions in Conflict* (Philadelphia: Fortress, 1968) for Mark (ibid., 17, 19–20), and James Louis Martyn, *History and Theology in the Fourth Gospel* (Nashville: Abingdon, 1968) for John.

16 Ibid., 28–30; quotation from 30.

17 Ibid., 32.

18 E.g., Dwight N. Peterson, *The Origins of Mark: The Markan Community in Current Debate* (BIS 48; Leiden/Boston: Brill, 2000) 200–1; Whitney Shiner, *Proclaiming the Gospel: First Century Performance of Mark* (Harrisburg, PA: Trinity Press International/Continuum, 2003) 26–27. Apparently independently of Bauckham, Martin Hengel also concluded that "none of the four Gospels was written only for one particular community" (*The Four Gospels and the One Gospel of Jesus Christ: An Investiga-*

tion of the Collection and Origin of the Canonical Gospels [Harrisburg, PA: Trinity Press International, 2000] 106). He also concluded that Mark was "sent from Rome to the communities of the empire" (ibid., 110).

19 Philip F. Esler, "Community and Gospel in Early Christianity: A Response to Richard Bauckham's *Gospels for All Christians*," *SJT* 51 (1998) 235–48; David C. Sim, "The Gospels for All Christians? A Response to Richard Bauckham," *JSNT* 84 (2001) 3–27. See also Richard Bauckham, "Response to Philip Esler," *SJT* 51 (1998) 249-53.

20 Marcus, 25.

21 Ibid., 25, 27–28.

22 αὕτη ἡ πόλις and αἱ ἔξω πόλεις; text and trans. from Kirsopp Lake, *The Apostolic Fathers* (2 vols.; LCL; Cambridge, MA: Harvard University Press; London: Heinemann, 1913) 2:24–25. Cf. the trans. of Bart Ehrman, "this city" and "the foreign cities" in idem, *Apostolic Fathers*, 193.

23 Mitchell, "Patristic Counter-Evidence," 36–79; quotation from 37.

knowledge of *only one* local house church."[24] But she objected to Bauckham's exclusive dichotomy between two options: either the Gospels were written for specific communities or they were written for all Christians.[25] She wished to resituate the debate Bauckham views as resulting from the excesses of modern critical methodologies as "another instance of a very old and enduring hermeneutical problem in the exegesis of Christian literature: the relationship between the particularity and universality of the gospels."[26] Perhaps most importantly, Mitchell showed that Bauckham's claim "that no one until the late nineteenth century read the gospels by reference to a reconstructed original, local audience" is contradicted by the patristic evidence.[27] According to Clement, Mark wrote in Rome at the request of people there.[28] Gregory of Nazianzus says that Mark wrote (the marvels of Christ) for Italy.[29] According to John Chrysostom, Mark "did this very thing" (left for people in writing the things he had said orally) in Egypt.[30]

Two years after the publication of Bauckham's work, Dwight Peterson disputed the view that "the Markan community is the necessary solid ground on which scholars who would produce valid or convincing readings of Mark *must* stand." He argued that "the Markan community cannot perform these functions because it is the product of highly speculative, viciously circular and ultimately unpersuasive and inconclusive reading. . . . there is not even 'a' Markan community; instead there are as many so-called Markan communities as there are scholars to produce them." Nevertheless, reconstructed Markan communities provide provisional vantage points that are "serviceable for different readers under different circumstances."[31]

Five years after the publication of Bauckham's work, Brian Incigneri published a book whose title expressed his disagreement with Tolbert and Bauckham: *The Gospel*

to the Romans. In it he made a case for the composition of Mark in Rome in the latter months of 71 CE.[32] Although he revived the idea that each Gospel has a specific audience and purpose,[33] he distanced himself from redaction-critical and aesthetic literary-critical methods, including forms of reader-response criticism that ignore the actual readers addressed by the actual author.[34] His "aim is to show that recognition of the social, political and religious context and its effects on the local Christians is the key to understanding the Gospel's design and provides explanations for many literary features that have long puzzled scholars," and he defines his approach as the treatment of Mark "as a rhetorical text, crafted to persuade."[35] He rejects the hypothesis that Mark was written with a missionary purpose and instead emphasizes the passages concerning persecution.[36]

Incigneri argues that "[t]he strong motif of persecution in the Gospel has to be explained, not in relation to random attacks by mobs, but to executions by legal authorities for being a Christian, because Mark's text demands this."[37] He argues further:

The specific mention of the cross in 8:34 shows that it is the prime fear in the community. Indeed the whole Gospel implies that it is a possibility for the reader, as it graphically depicts Jesus leading the way for all of his followers. . . . Any proposed scenario therefore has to demonstrate a plausible threat of crucifixion. As crucifixion could only be carried out by Roman authorities throughout the Empire, a setting that involves a legal Roman trial has to be found. Indeed, for a capital offence in the provinces, the governor himself would have to be involved. The fact remains that we have no evidence at all for Roman executions of Christians in the East at this time.[38]

---

24   Ibid., 37–38 (emphasis original).

25   Ibid., 44; cf. Esler, "Community and Gospel," 242–43.

26   Mitchell, "Patristic Counter-Evidence," 38.

27   Ibid., 47, 54–77.

28   Ibid., 49–51. Note that the word "shown" in the first line of the ET on p. 51 should be "shone."

29   Ibid., 67.

30   Ibid., 71. Mitchell cites Swete to the effect that Chrysostom may have misunderstood Eusebius's statement about Mark and Egypt in *Hist. eccl.* 2.16 (Mitchell, "Patristic Counter-Evidence," 71 n. 99; Swete, xxxix).

31   Peterson, *Origins of Mark*, 196 (emphasis in first quotation original).

32   Incigneri, *Gospel to the Romans*, 2.

33   See his criticisms of Tolbert and Bauckham (ibid., 32–34).

34   Ibid., 3–30.

35   Ibid., 2; cf. 14. See also the discussion of rhetoric (ibid., 36–43) and of *pathos* (ibid., 51–56).

36   Ibid., 30–31. So also Marcus, 28–29.

37   Incigneri, *Gospel to the Romans*, 90.

38   Ibid., 91–92.

Incigneri argues that "persecution" in the sense of "subjection to legal penalties for their religious beliefs" should be considered a continuous state of affairs once being a Christian became a capital offence."[39] He concludes that the latter was the case beginning with Nero's persecution in Rome.[40]

Tacitus describes Nero's treatment of the Christians as follows:

> And derision accompanied their end: they were covered with wild beasts' skins and torn to death by dogs; or they were fastened on crosses, and, when daylight failed, were burned to serve as lamps by night (Et pereuntibus addita ludibria, ut ferarum tergis contecti laniatu canum interirent, aut crucibus adfixi aut flammandi, atque ubi defecisset dies, in usum nocturni luminis urerentur). (Ann. 15.44.4)[41]

William H. C. Frend infers that the burning was performed by means of the *molesta tunica*, a dress of pitch, in which a malefactor was burned.[42]

Incigneri infers that the allusion to crucifixion in 8:34 implies that Mark was written in Rome.[43] Yet, as he himself admits, the punishment of crucifixion could have been carried out anywhere in the Roman empire, including the East, by a Roman official, most likely the governor of a province.

It should be remembered that, although the Romans employed crucifixion as a mode of execution, it was not invented by them.[44] The case of the crucifixion of Jesus by Pontius Pilate shows that Roman officials could and did order crucifixion in the eastern provinces. According to Josephus, crucifixion was practiced among Jews in the Hellenistic-Hasmonean period. Antiochus IV crucified some of those who refused "to give up the worship of their own God, and to do reverence to the gods in whom he believed."[45] Alexander Jannaeus had 800 men of his own people crucified at some point between 103 and 76 BCE.[46] Two documents from Qumran connect Deut 21:22-23 with crucifixion.[47]

Given that Jesus was crucified, that being a Christian was a capital offense, and that crucifixion was well known in the East, the allusion to crucifixion in 8:34 does not compel the conclusion that Mark was written in Rome. Furthermore, the allusion to carrying one's cross may not signify that the author and earliest audience(s) expected or feared being crucified literally. Such language may be used metaphorically for any kind of death in a context of persecution. A comment by Plutarch provides evidence for such a metaphorical usage:

> and whereas every criminal who goes to execution must carry his own cross on his back, vice frames out of itself each instrument of its own punishment (καὶ τῷ μὲν σώματι τῶν κολαζομένων ἕκαστος κακούργων ἐκφέρει τὸν αὑτοῦ σταυρόν, ἡ δὲ κακία τῶν κολαστηρίων ἐφ᾽ ἑαυτὴν ἕκαστον ἐξ αὑτῆς τεκτείνεται). (Moralia Sera 554A–B)[48]

It is unlikely that Plutarch meant to say that all criminals condemned to death were executed by crucifixion.

Another argument for placing Mark in Rome is "the

---

39 Ibid., 106–7.

40 Ibid.; implied on 106; stated on 213.

41 Text and trans. (punctuation slightly modifed) from John Jackson, *Tacitus: The Histories, The Annals* (4 vols.; LCL; Cambridge, MA: Harvard University Press; London: Heinemann, 1937) 4:284–85; see n. 1 to the text on 284. Cited also by Martin Hengel, *Crucifixion in the Ancient World and the Folly of the Message of the Cross* (Philadelphia: Fortress, 1977), 26. Incigneri seems to imply that burning and crucifying were two separate modes of execution employed by Nero's agents (*Gospel to the Romans*, 217).

42 William H. C. Frend, *Martyrdom and Persecution in the Early Church: A Study of a Conflict from the Maccabees to Donatus* (Oxford: Blackwell, 1965) 162; definition from LS, s.v. *molestus*. See also Harald Fuchs,

"Tacitus über die Christen," *VC* 4 (1950) 65–93, esp. 87–93.

43 Incigneri, *Gospel to the Romans*, 243.

44 Hengel, *Crucifixion*, 22–25; Gerald G. O'Collins, "Crucifixion," *ABD* 1:1207–10, esp. 1207.

45 Josephus *Ant.* 12.5.4 §§253, 256; quotation from 253; trans. from Ralph Marcus, in Thackeray, *Josephus*, 7:131. O'Collins says that this took place in 267 BCE, but he must mean 167 ("Crucifixion," 1207).

46 Josephus *Ant.* 13.14.2 §380; cf. *Bell.* 1.4.6 §97; O'Collins, "Crucifixion," 1207.

47 The commentary on Nahum (4Q169) and 11QTemple (11Q19) 64:6-13 (O'Collins, "Crucifixion," 1207).

48 Text and trans. from Philip H. De Lacy and Benedict Einarson, *Plutarch's Moralia* (16 vols.; LCL;

presence in the Gospel of a large number of Latinisms."[49] Incigneri criticizes the view that these "are all military or economic terms, and are more likely to have been employed in an area under Roman occupation."[50] He concludes instead that "Rome is *the* place where all of these Latin terms came together most commonly."[51]

There are several problems with this view. First of all, many of the expressions taken over directly from Latin occur in Matthew, Luke, or John, often independently of Mark. Were those Gospels also written in Rome? Second, "Many of these loanwords are shown to be in general usage by their frequent appearance elsewhere in every type of Hellenistic literature"; some, like μόδιος, ξέστης, and δηνάριον,[52] are shown by their Modern Greek "descendants to be words belonging to the common language."[53] "Phraseological Latinisms are scarce and used mostly in connection with Roman authorities and the like."[54] This is where Mark's τὸ ἱκανὸν ποιεῖν (15:15) belongs;[55] also συμβούλιον διδόναι/ποιεῖν (3:6; 15:1); probably τιϑέναι τὰ γόνατα (15:19). The same and similar phrases occur also in Luke, Acts, and Matthew,[56] so the argument that Mark's use of them implies a setting in Rome is weak. Although he advocated the Roman provenance of Mark, Benjamin Bacon admitted, with regard to the Latinisms, "All these expressions had passed over into the current speech of Jews throughout the empire, so that their mere occurrence in Mark cannot prove anything as to its origin in a Latin-speaking region."[57]

Incigneri reads Mark against his reconstruction of events in Rome in 71, such as the triumph celebrated by Vespasian and Titus. The result is interesting, but it sometimes appears allegorical in the sense criticized by Bauckham and Mitchell.[58]

In a book published in 2004, Hendrika Roskam rejected the arguments of Bauckham for an intended audience of all Christians[59] and concluded that Mark wrote "for a Christian audience in Galilee sometime after the destruction of the Jerusalem temple in 70 A.D."[60] The persecution reflected in the Gospel is "the threat of persecutions by leading Jews." The threat existed because the evangelist may have believed that "the Markan Christian community" was perceived by outsiders as "a subversive Jewish movement that does not accept Roman rule in Palestine." Such a suspicion of subversiveness, especially after the Jewish revolt, "might lead the Romans to intervene violently against the Christians," an intervention that would also harm Jews in the area.[61] She defined the literary character of Mark as "an apologetic tract in biographical form" and its purpose as "to eliminate the political connotations of the title 'Christ' and Jesus' crucifixion," "to strengthen and encourage his Christian readers to resist the pressure caused by the persecu-

Cambridge: Harvard University Press; London: Heinemann, 1959) 7:214–15. Cited by Hengel, *Crucifixion*, 77; O'Collins, "Crucifixion," 1207.

49 Incigneri, *Gospel to the Romans*, 100.
50 Ibid., 100–1.
51 Ibid., 101.
52 Mentioned ibid., 101.
53 BDF §5 (1) (p. 4).
54 Ibid., §5 (3) (b) (p. 5).
55 Mentioned by Incigneri, *Gospel to the Romans*, 102.
56 BDF §5 (3) (b) (p. 6).
57 Benjamin W. Bacon, *Is Mark a Roman Gospel?* (HTS 7; Cambridge, MA: Harvard University Press; London: Humphrey Milford/Oxford University Press, 1919) 53–54. See the evidence cited above in relation to nn. 52 and 53.
58 E.g., the argument that the ambitious sons of Zebedee in 10:35-40 and the two robbers crucified with Jesus in 15:27 would call to mind Titus and Domitian, the sons of Vespasian, for the audience of Mark (Incigneri, *Gospel to the Romans*, 184); see also the argument that "Mark may offer special tribute" to the martyrs under Nero through his depiction of the woman who anoints Jesus in 14:3-9 and the widow who contributed her whole life/livelihood in 12:41-44 (ibid., 221–22).

59 Roskam, *Purpose of Mark*, 17–21. Her reasons are similar to those of Marcus (25–28). She argues further that, in addition to Alexander and Rufus, the sons of Simon of Cyrene, Mark assumed that his audience knew James and Joses, the sons of the Mary mentioned in 15:40. She assumes that the epithet "Magdalene" (15:40, 47; 16:1) implies knowledge of the place-name Magdala; familiarity with that place-name and Dalmanutha (8:10) suggests that the author and audience "lived at the same time and in the same area" (Roskam, *Purpose of Mark*, 15–16).
60 Roskam, *Purpose of Mark*, 237.
61 Ibid.

tions," and "to warn them not to falter in their faith."[62] On the basis of her analysis of 13:9-13, she concluded that the evangelist thought that "the Markan Christians" were

> to be persecuted by Jewish as well as non-Jewish authorities. The pre-Markan tradition used in Mk 13:9 spoke only of the handing over of Christians to the Jewish synagogues, not of their being handed over to secular courts. Mark revised the tradition, however, so as to include references to the corporal punishment inflicted on Christians by Jewish sanhedrins as well as Christians being brought up for trial before secular authorities. The interests of the Jewish leaders and the Roman "occupiers" "ran parallel."[63]

A problem with locating the composition of Mark in Galilee is that there probably was no major Christian community there in the earliest period.[64] The production of a Gospel would presumably require considerable financial support,[65] a need that points to a major community. I agree, on the whole, with Roskam that an important purpose of Mark was to redefine the notion of messiahship, but I would hesitate to say that he eliminated the political connotations of the title "Christ" or "Messiah" entirely.[66] The fear that the movement was subversive would seem to be at least as lively in the lead-up to the revolt and during it, perhaps of even more concern, than after the revolt was virtually quashed in 70 CE.[67]

Early Christian tradition associated Mark with Peter.[68] If one were to take a skeptical point of view, one could argue that this link is not necessarily historical, but may simply have been inferred from the text of Mark. Papias associates Mark with Peter, but does not place that association in any locality. Nor does he mention the place where the Gospel was written.[69] 1 Pet 5:13 implies that Mark was with Peter in Rome. Even if this tradition is reliable, it does not necessarily imply that the Gospel was written in Rome. Irenaeus, perhaps in dependence on Papias, mentions the association of Mark with Peter.[70] He adds the detail (perhaps an inference on his part) that Mark wrote his Gospel after the death of Peter. It is this detail that suggests that Mark was written in Rome, on the assumption that Peter died there.

If we assume, for the sake of argument, that there was some kind of association between Mark and Peter, we ought to remember that Peter was active in other places besides Rome. He was a leader of the Jerusalem community and, after leaving the city to work elsewhere, returned to the city from time to time.[71] According to Acts 9:32–10:48, he was also active in Lydda, Joppa, and Caesarea. 1 Cor 1:12 implies that he had visited Corinth (cf. 1 Cor 3:22; 9:5). Gal 2:11-14 attests to his presence in Antioch. Antioch is especially interesting as a possible setting for the composition of Mark. It "contained a large Aramaic-speaking and also a Jewish community."[72] Such a setting would explain Mark's use of Aramaic words and sayings, as well as his translation of them into Greek. It would also explain the Latinisms, since Antioch had been the capital of the Roman province of Syria since the time of Pompey.[73]

The evidence is not strong enough to point definitively to either Rome or Antioch, but it is compatible with both locations (and others). With regard to the pur-

---

62 Ibid., 238.

63 Ibid., 73–74.

64 See the excursus on Galilee and Jerusalem in Mark in the commentary on 14:26-31 below.

65 Gamble, *Books and Readers*, 42–143.

66 See the commentary below on 1:11; 12:37; 13:1-37; 15:8, 27, 29-32.

67 In favor of a date after 70, Roskam cites 12:9; 13:2; 13:14; and 15:38. But note that in 12:9 the Markan Jesus does not talk about destroying the city (as Matthew does in 22:7), but about destroying the tenants of the vineyard (the leaders of the people) and giving it to others (new leaders). On 13:2, 14, see the subsection of this introduction on *Date* above. On 15:38, see the commentary on that verse below.

68 See the subsections of this introduction on *Authorship* and *Place of Writing* above.

69 See the quotation of Papias in *Authorship* above.

70 See the discussion of Irenaeus in *Place of Writing* above.

71 Gal 1:18; 2:7-9; Acts 1–6; 8:14, 25; 11:1-18; 12:1-19; 15:7.

72 A. H. M. Jones, Henri Seyrig, W. Liebeschuetz, Susan Sherwin-White, "Antioch," *OCD* 107.

73 Ibid.

pose of Mark, it is likely that the author had more than one aim. One was to reassert the messiahship of Jesus and to redefine it over against the messianic pretenders during the Jewish war that began in 66 CE.[74] Another was to interpret actual or expected persecution (or both) as discipleship in imitation of Christ.[75]

---

74   See the discussion of Roskam's work above and also the commentary on chap. 13 below.

75   See the commentary on 8:27–9:1; 13:9-13 and 14:32-42 below. On the relation of Mark to persecution, actual or expected, see B. M. F. van Iersel, "The Gospel according to St. Mark—Written for a Persecuted Community?" *Nederlands Theologisch Tijdschrift* 34 (1980) 15–36, esp. 35.

On the basis of the two-source theory,[1] it can be inferred that Mark circulated widely in the first and early second centuries and that the authors of Matthew and Luke were the first interpreters of Mark.[2] A manuscript from the late second century apparently contained all four of the Gospels that eventually became canonical, although no fragments of Mark survive from it.[3] The oldest surviving fragments of Mark belong to 𝔓[45], one of the Chester Beatty papyri, which dates to the first half of the third century.[4] The next oldest texts of Mark are Codex Sinaiticus (fourth century) and Codex Vaticanus (mid-fourth century).[5] More papyrus fragments of Matthew, John, and Luke survive than of Mark.[6] This state of affairs may reflect the accidents of preservation, but more likely indicates the wider circulation and greater popularity of the other three.[7]

Apart from the use of Mark by the other two Synoptic authors, Helmut Koester has argued that "there is no certain quotation from Mark before Irenaeus and Clement of Alexandria."[8] He argued, however, that the *Gospel of the Ebionites* "possibly also [in addition to Matthew and Luke] drew materials from Mark."[9] Since Irenaeus refers to it and "the extant quotations show similarities to the gospel harmomy of the 2d-century apologist Justin Martyr," the *Gospel of the Ebionites* was apparently written in the mid-second century or earlier.[10] Frans Neirynck argued that two fragments of the *Gospel* are probably dependent on Mark 1:4-6 and a third on 1:9.[11]

The so-called Unknown Gospel, Papyrus Egerton 2, may be dependent on Mark 12:14.[12] The manuscript of Pap. Eg. 2 may have been written as early as the first half of the second century.[13] Some, however, are inclined to date it later, perhaps as late as the third century.[14] The reference to the master coming suddenly in *Hermas Sim.* 9.7.6 may be dependent on Mark 13:36. Neither Matthew nor Luke has anything as similar. *Hermas* dates to a period extending from the end of the first century to the first half of the second.[15] The *Gospel of Peter* 50–57 is probably dependent on Mark 16:1-8.[16] The *Gospel of Peter* was written before the late second or early third century, since the oldest surviving fragment of it dates to that

---

1 See the section of this introduction on the *Synoptic Problem* above.

2 See, e.g., the commentary on 13:5-6 below concerning the interpretation of 13:6 in Matt 24:5. On the way in which Matthew, Luke (and John) interpreted the passages in Mark that seem to attribute fear, sorrow, and ignorance to Jesus, see Kevin Madigan, *The Passions of Christ in High Medieval Thought: An Essay on Christological Development* (New York: Oxford University Press, 2007) esp. the introduction.

3 The fragments of this manuscript are known as 𝔓[4], 𝔓[64] and 𝔓[67] (Metzger and Ehrman, *Text*, 53).

4 Ibid., 54. Papyrus fragments of Mark survive also in 𝔓[84] (sixth cent.) and 𝔓[88] (fourth cent.); see Nestle-Aland (27th ed.), 688–89.

5 Metzger and Ehrman, *Text*, 62, 68.

6 Helmut Koester, "Apocryphal and Canonical Gospels," *HTR* 73 (1980) 105–30, esp. 108.

7 Ibid., 107. See also idem, "History and Development of Mark's Gospel," in Bruce Corley, ed., *Colloquy on New Testament Studies: A Time for Reappraisal and Fresh Approaches* (Macon, GA: Mercer University Press, 1983) 37; Brenda Deen Schildgen, *Power and Prejudice: The Reception of the Gospel of Mark* (Detroit: Wayne State University Press, 1999) 39–42.

8 Koester, "History and Development," 37.

9 Helmut Koester, *Introduction to the New Testament*, vol. 2: *History and Literature of Early Christianity* (2nd ed.; New York/Berlin: de Gruyter, 2000) 208.

10 Ibid. See also Frans Neirynck, "The Apocryphal Gospels and the Gospel of Mark," in Jean-Marie Sevrin, ed., *The New Testament in Early Christianity: La réception des écrits néotestamentaires dans le christianisme primitif* (BEThL 86; Leuven: Leuven University Press/Peeters, 1989) 123–75, esp. 157 and the literature cited in n. 183.

11 Ibid., 159.

12 The same possibility exists for *Gos. Thom.* 100. See the commentary on 12:13-17 below on both possibilities. With regard to Pap. Eg. 2, see also Édouard Massaux, *The Influence of the Gospel of Saint Matthew on Christian Literature before Saint Irenaeus* (New Gospel Studies 5.1–3; Leuven: Peeters; Macon, GA: Mercer University Press, 1990, 1992–1993; 1st French ed. 1950) 5.2:174–75; Neirynck, "Apocryphal Gospels," 161; Sean P. Kealy, *Mark's Gospel: A History of Its Interpretation from the Beginning until 1979* (New York: Paulist, 1982) 13.

13 Koester, "Apocryphal and Canonical Gospels," 108; Neirynck, "Apocryphal Gospels," 161.

14 Neirynck, "Apocryphal Gospels," 162.

15 Carolyn Osiek, *Shepherd of Hermas: A Commentary* (Hermeneia; Minneapolis: Fortress, 1999) 20.

16 Massaux, *Influence*, 5.2:214–16; Neirynck, "Apocryphal Gospels," 140–57, 170.

time.[17] Finally, Justin Martyr is dependent on Mark 3:17 in *Dial.* 106.3, in his reference to "Boanerges, that is, Sons of Thunder."[18]

In discussing the four Gospels and their symbols (taken from Rev 4:7), Irenaeus associates Mark with the fourth living creature, which was like an eagle, "pointing out the gift of the Holy Spirit hovering with His wings over the Church." A bit further along, he continues:

> Mark, on the other hand, commences with [a reference to] the prophetical spirit coming down from on high to men, saying, "The beginning of the Gospel of Jesus Christ, as it is written in Esaias the prophet,"—pointing to the winged aspect of the Gospel; and on this account he made a compendious and cursory narrative, for such is the prophetical character. (*Haer.* 3.11.8)[19]

In the same context, Irenaeus says that the heretics who attempt to establish their own peculiar doctrines on the basis of the Gospels are nevertheless refuted by them. With regard to Mark, he says:

> Those, again, who separate Jesus from Christ, alleging that Christ remained impassible, but that it was Jesus who suffered, preferring the Gospel by Mark, if they read it with a love of truth, may have their errors rectified. (*Haer.* 3.11.7)[20]

Irenaeus's remarks on the sacred character of the four Gospels that later became canonical attests to the early circulation of Mark.[21] "From the end of the second century, the literary history of" Mark merges with that of the four-Gospel "canon."[22] The evidence for the liturgical reading of Mark dates to the second century and later.[23]

A fragment of a letter attributed to Clement of Alexandria was discovered and published in the twentieth century, which mentions several versions of Mark, including one called the Secret Gospel of Mark. But doubts have been raised about the authenticity of this fragment.[24]

At some point between 165 and 180, probably between 172 and 175 CE, Tatian composed the *Diatessaron*, that is, "a conflation of passages from the four Gospels to make a complete account of the life of Jesus without repetitions."[25] The availability of Mark to Tatian and his recognition of its significance by including it in his harmony provide evidence for the wide circulation of

---

17 Neirynck, "Apocryphal Gospels," 141–42.

18 Wolf-Dietrich Köhler, *Die Rezeption des Matthäusevangeliums in der Zeit vor Irenäus* (WUNT 2.24; Tübingen: Mohr Siebeck, 1987) 255–56; for further literature, see Neirynck, "Apocryphal Gospels," 123 n. 4. See also Swete, xxx–xxxi.

19 Trans. from Coxe, *Apostolic Fathers*, 428. For a similar association of Mark with an eagle, see *The Explanation by Blessed Theophylact, Archbishop of Ochrid and Bulgaria, of the Holy Gospel according to St. Mark; translated from the original Greek* (Bl. Theophylact's Explanation of the New Testament 2; House Springs, MO; Chrysostom Press, 1993) 9. This trans. is based on the Greek text of *Patrologia graeca* 123:491–682. On Theophylact (eleventh cent.), see below.

20 Trans. from Coxe, *Apostolic Fathers*, 428. Matti Myllykoski discusses this passage in the context of "possession Christology" in the early second century ("Cerinthus," in Antti Marjanen and P. Luomanen, eds., *The Other Side: Second Century "Heretics"* [Edinburgh: T & T Clark, 2005] 213–46, esp. 233–35). On the use of Mark by Gnostic and "heretical" groups, see Swete, xxxi.

21 Swete, xxxi–xxxii.

22 Ibid., xxxiii. On the use of Mark by Irenaeus, see Schildgen, *Power and Prejudice*, 52–53. On the exegetical methods of Irenaeus, see Manlio Simonetti, *Biblical Interpretation in the Early Church: An Historical Introduction to Patristic Exegesis* (Edinburgh: T & T Clark, 1994; Italian ed. 1981) 21–24; on his hermeneutical principles, see Karlfried Froehlich, trans. and ed., *Biblical Interpretation in the Early Church* (Philadelphia: Fortress, 1984) 13–14.

23 Schildgen, *Power and Prejudice*, 50–52. The following passages (in the order given here) are included in the Christian Palestinian Syriac [Aramaic] lectionary in three MSS dating to the eleventh and twelfth cent.: 16:9-20; 12:28-37; 5:24-34; 9:32-40; 12:38-44; 6:1-5; 1:1-8; 1:9-11; 6:14-30; see Agnes Smith Lewis and Margaret Dunlop Gibson, eds., *The Palestinian Syriac Lectionary of the Gospels* (London: Kegan Paul, Trench, Trübner, 1899) 218, 232–33, 248–51, 258, 262–63, 265, 293–95.

24 See the excursus on the Secret Gospel of Mark in the commentary on 10:32b-34 below.

25 On authorship and date, see William L. Petersen, *Tatian's Diatessaron: Its Creation, Dissemination, Significance, and History in Scholarship* (VCSup 25; Leiden: Brill, 1994) 426–27. On the definition, see Simonetti, *Biblical Interpretation*, 63. See also Schildgen, *Power and Prejudice*, 45–46.

Mark in the second half of the second century. The *Diatessaron* was written in the East or during Tatian's journey from Rome to the East.[26] It was written in Syriac, but was soon translated into Latin and Armenian and later into many other languages.[27]

Although a commentary on Mark by Origen does not survive, one may infer how he would have commented on Mark by reading his commentary on Matthew.[28] In addition, Origen at times cites Mark in his commentaries on Matthew and John and in some of his other works.[29] He cites Mark 4:12 (that seeing they may not see, etc.) in a discussion of free will.[30] In commenting on John 1:3, he cites Mark 10:18 (None is good but one, etc.) to show that "the good" is the same as "he who is."[31]

A text from the early fourth century,[32] *On the Origin of the World*, may allude to Mark 4:22.[33] The relevant passage reads:

> Now the Word (*Logos*) that is superior to all beings was sent for this purpose alone: that he might proclaim the unknown. He said (Mk 4:22 par.), "There is nothing hidden that is not apparent, and what has not been recognized will be recognized." (125, 14–19)[34]

The allusion, however, could be to Matt 10:26 or Luke 8:17.

In the fourth century, interpreters long identified by the misnomer "Arians" used Mark and the other Gospels to show that Jesus was a creature and not fully divine. Members of the "Nicene" party attempted to counter their exegesis of the texts.[35]

In the fourth century, Ephraem the Syrian commented on the healing of the deaf and mute man (7:33) in a homily "On Our Lord." Section 10 opens with a doxology: "Glory be to him who received from us that he might give to us; that through that which is ours we might more abundantly receive of that which is his!"[36] After commenting on the slaying of the Mediator, he alludes to the healing in question:

> That power which may not be handled came down and clothed itself in members that may be touched; that the needy may draw near to him, that in touching his manhood they may discern his Godhead. For that dumb man [whom the Lord healed] with the fingers of the body, discerned that he had approached his ears and touched his tongue; no, with his fingers that may be touched, he touched Godhead, that may not be touched; when it was loosing the string of his tongue, and opening the clogged doors of his ears. For the architect of the body and artificer of the flesh came to him, and with his gentle voice pierced without pain his thickened ears. And his mouth which was closed up, that it could not give birth to a word, gave

26 Petersen, *Tatian's Diatessaron*, 427, 428–32.

27 Ibid., 2, 84–356, 428.

28 Robert Girod, ed., trans., and annotator, *Origène: Commentaire sur l'Évangile selon Matthieu*, tome 1: *Livres X et XI* (SC 162; Paris: Les Éditions du Cerf, 1970); see also Hermann J. Vogt, ed., *Origenes: Der Kommentar zum Evangelium nach Mattäus* (3 vols.; Bibliothek der Griechischen Literatur 18, 30, 38; Stuttgart: Hiersemann, 1983, 1990, 1993).

29 Schildgen, *Power and Prejudice*, 53–54.

30 Origen *Princ.* 3.1.7, 16; A. Cleveland Coxe, *Fathers of the Third Century* (ANF 4; American Reprint of the Edinburgh Edition; Grand Rapids: Eerdmans, 1985) 307, 317.

31 Origen *Comm. in Joh.* 2.7; Allan Menzies, trans. "Origin's Commentary on John," in idem, ed., *Original Supplement to the American Edition* (5th ed.; ANF 10; Grand Rapids: Eerdmans, 1986) 330.

32 So Hans-Gebhard Bethge, introduction to "On the Origin of the World (II,5 and XIII,2)," in *NHLE*, 170–71.

33 So Craig A. Evans, "The Interpretation of Scripture in the New Testament Apocrypha and Gnostic Writings," in Alan J. Hauser and Duane F. Watson, eds., *A History of Biblical Interpretation*, vol. 1: *The Ancient Period* (Grand Rapids: Eerdmans, 2003) 430–56, esp. 451.

34 Trans. by Hans-Gebhard Bethge, Bentley Layton, and the Societas Coptica Hierosolymitana in *NHLE*, 171–89; quotation from 188.

35 Madigan, *Passions of Christ*, chap. 2.

36 Ephraem Syrus *On Our Lord* 10; trans. (capitalization modified) by John Gwynn in Philip Schaff and Henry Wace, eds., *A Select Library of the Nicene and Post-Nicene Fathers*, second series, vol. 13: *Gregory the Great, Ephraim Syrus, Aphrahat* (Grand Rapids: Eerdmans, 1979) 309.

birth to praise to him who made its barrenness fruitful in the birth of words. He, then, who gave to Adam that he should speak at once without teaching, himself gave to the dumb that they should speak easily, tongues that are learned with difficulty.[37]

Also in the fourth century, John Chrysostom urged his audience to rebuke any of their fellow Christians whom they heard blaspheming God.[38] In support of this exhortation, he cited the example of John the Baptist, who "laid down his head" "for the sacred laws that were despised."[39] Possibly as early as the late fourth century, but certainly later, interest in the person of Mark and his martyrdom increased.[40]

Jerome wrote *Tractates on Mark* in the first decade of the fifth century. He "treats the text of Mark in homilies arranged in ten 'treatises.'"[41] In the last of these, he treats 13:32. He asks, "if God is one, how can there be different degrees of knowledge (*diuersa scientia*) in one God?" Since all things were made through Christ, he must have known when the day of judgment would be. It was not revealed in this discourse because it is better for us humans not to know the date.[42]

Both Jerome and Peter Chrysologus[43] wrote homilies on Mark 5:21-43.[44] They use this passage polemically, interpreting the woman with the flow of blood and Jairus's daughter as types of the church and the synagogue, respectively.[45] Jerome advocated a mission to the Jews and followed Paul (Rom 11:25-26) in expecting all Israel to be saved. According to Peter Chrysologus, the synagogue has died in order to live to Christ.

Augustine uses the passage more consistently for moral exhortation.[46] He relates Jairus's daughter to two other persons raised from the dead by Jesus, the widow's son (Luke 7:12-15) and Lazarus (John 11:11-14). He compares them to three sorts of sinners: those who sin in their hearts but not in deed (Jairus's daughter, who is dead inside the house), those who sin both in thought and deed (the widow's son, who is dead outdoors but not yet in the grave), and those for whom sinning is a "malignant habit" or an "addiction" (Lazarus, who is both dead and buried).[47]

---

37 Ibid.; trans. (slightly modified) Gwynn, 309. See also the trans. in Thomas C. Oden and Christopher A. Hall, eds., *Mark* (Ancient Christian Commentary on Scripture, NT 2; Downers Grove, IL: InterVarsity, 1998) 103. On the latter work in general, see the review by Robert F. Hull, Jr., in *JECS* 8 (2000) 297–98.

38 On the exegetical methods of John Chrysostom and his place in the history of exegesis, see Simonetti, *Biblical Interpretation*, 53, 60, 74, 88, 127.

39 John Chrysostom, *Homilies concerning the Statues* 1.32; trans. by W. R. W. Stephens, in Philip Schaff, ed., *A Select Library of Nicene and Post-Nicene Fathers*, first series, vol. 9: *Saint Chrysostom* (Grand Rapids: Eerdmans, 1983) 343; Christine E. Joynes, "The Reception History of Mark's Gospel," *Scripture Bulletin* 36 (2006) 24–32, esp. 29–30; eadem, "John the Baptist's Death: Irrelevant Legend or Political Challenge?" in John Vincent, ed., *Mark: Gospel of Action; Personal and Community Responses* (London: SPCK, 2006) 143–53.

40 Allen Dwight Callahan, "The *Acts of Saint Mark*: An Introduction and Commentary" (Ph.D. diss., Harvard University, 1992); abstract in *HTR* 85 (1992) 494–95. See also idem, "The Acts of Saint Mark: An Introduction and Translation," *Coptic Church Review* 14 (1993) 3–10.

41 Madigan, *Passions of Christ*, 45.

42 Ibid. Augustine came to a similar conclusion, arguing that some scriptural texts refer to the Son "according to the form of God" and others "according to the form of a servant." Mark 13:32 belongs to the second group (ibid., [MS 99]).

43 Peter Chrysologus was bishop of Ravenna in the fifth century (*ODCC* 285; Charles Kannengiesser, *Handbook of Patristic Exegesis: The Bible in Ancient Christianity* [2 vols.; Leiden: Brill, 2004] 2:1261–71). On Jerome's exegetical methods and place in the history of exegesis, see Simonetti, *Biblical Interpretation*, 99–103.

44 On the homilies of Jerome on Mark, see Schildgen, *Power and Prejudice*, 54–56.

45 Jerome *Homily 77*; in Sister Marie Liguori Ewald, trans., *The Homilies of Saint Jerome* (2 vols.; Fathers of the Church; Washington, DC: Catholic University of America Press, 1964–66) 2:148–51; Peter Chrysologus *Sermon 36*; in George E. Ganss, trans., *Saint Peter Chrysologus: Selected Sermons; Saint Valerian: Homilies* (Fathers of the Church; New York: Fathers of the Church, 1953) 75–80; Joynes, "Reception History," 28–29.

46 On Augustine's homilies on Mark, see Schildgen, *Power and Prejudice*, 54. On Augustine as an exegete, see Simonetti, *Biblical Interpretation*, 103–8.

47 Augustine *Sermon 98*; trans. and notes by Edmund Hill, in John E. Rotelle, ed., *The Works of Saint Augus-*

There is evidence to indicate that, in the sixth century, a certain presbyter, Victor of Antioch, wrote a commentary on Mark that is actually a compilation of passages from earlier writers (primarily from homilies and commentaries on Matthew and Luke).[48] Sean P. Kealy gives, as a sample of Victor's work, some comments on the healing of a deaf man in Mark 7:31-37.[49] Matthew and Luke probably omitted this story because of its apparently magical elements.[50] Victor interprets Jesus' taking the man "apart from the multitude" as a lesson for the audience that they should "put away vain glory and pride." This is a moral interpretation of what was probably originally a motif expressing the mysterious character of the healing.[51] The motifs of healing by touch, Jesus putting his fingers into the man's ears and applying his saliva to the man's tongue, are typical of ancient popular thought and practice.[52] Victor interprets Jesus putting his fingers into the man's ears as a way of showing "that the body united to his divinity, and to its operation, was endowed with divine power." Here we have a christological interpretation of a popular motif. The same gesture and the application of saliva show "the perfection of human nature" possessed by Adam before his sin. Here we find an anthropological interpretation of popular motifs. Victor says that Jesus "also groaned" (ἐστέναξεν; translated as "sighing" in the commentary on 7:34 below) "as taking our cause upon himself, and as

having compassion on human nature, seeing the misery into which humanity had fallen." In this case, a motif akin to magical practices[53] is interpreted as part of a merciful and empathetic portrayal of Jesus. As writers before him had done, Victor gives an edifying interpretation of elements of the text that could have been offensive in a more historical or contextual interpretation.[54]

Victor also commented on another passage unique to Mark, the parable about the seed that grows by itself (4:26-29). Victor interpreted the sleep of the man in v. 27 christologically as an allusion to the ascension and "the bringing forth of fruit" ethically as "the practice of justice" and "patience in time of affliction."[55] The "sower's ignorance of the manner of the growth and the sprouting of the seed of itself" are interpreted anthropologically as allusions to "the free will of man who has to do good works." Green shoot, head (of grain), and fully ripened wheat "are images of the different stages of the Christian life, which is meant to sprout and blossom forth not merely through obedience but by courage in trials" and which "must strive upward for heaven and carry the sheaves of good works." The parable probably had an allegorical significance for the evangelist and his first audiences.[56] Victor and his sources allegorized the parable in new ways.[57]

A Latin commentary on Mark was attributed to Jerome until its first critical edition by Erasmus. Since

---

tine: A Translation for the 21st Century, Part III—*Sermons*, vol. 4: *Sermons 94A-147A* (Augustinian Heritage Institute; Brooklyn, NY: New City Press, 1992) 43–49; Joynes, "Reception History," 29.

48 Kealy, *Mark's Gospel*, 28. For a detailed study of this commentary or catena, see Joseph Reuss, *Matthäus-, Markus- und Johannes-Katenen nach den handschriftlichen Quellen untersucht* (NTAbh 18.4–5; Münster: Aschendorff, 1941) 118–47. He distinguished two recensions; the textual attestation of the first is described on 118–29, the second on 129–33. He discussed the sources of the commentary (138–40), authorship (140), and date (140–41). The greatest portion derives from Chrysostom, then Origen, Cyril of Alexandria, and Titus of Bostra. Other writers are cited sparingly. According to Reuss, the best edition (primarily of the first recension) available is that by Ch. F. Matthaei (1775) (ibid., 137–38). Reuss declared (137 n. 16) that Otto Bardenhewer's evaluation of Matthaei's edition is in error (Bardenhewer, *Geschichte der altkirchlichen Literatur* [5 vols.; Freiburg:

Herder, 1924; reprinted Darmstadt: Wissenschaftliche Buchgesellschaft, 1962] 4:257). According to Reuss, the edition by J. A. Cramer (1840; reprinted 1967) is the most extensive, but also the worst (137–38). On Victor's sources, see also Harold Smith, "The Sources of Victor of Antioch's Commentary on Mark," *JTS* 19 (1918) 350–70.

49 Kealy, *Mark's Gospel*, 28. Quotations of this passage are from Kealy.

50 See the commentary on 7:32-36 below.

51 See the commentary on 5:37 and 7:33 below.

52 See the commentary on 5:21-43 and 7:33 below.

53 See the commentary on 7:34 below.

54 Theophylact's interpretation of this miracle is similar (*Explanation by Blessed Theophylact*, 62–63). On Theophylact's commentary, see below.

55 This and subsequent quotations are from Kealy's paraphrase (*Mark's Gospel*, 29).

56 See the commentary on 4:26-29 below.

57 On the difference between allegorical composition and allegorical reading, see Hans-Josef Klauck, *Alle-*

then it has been available among the writings of "Pseudo-Jerome" under the title *Commentarius in Euangelium secundum Marcum*.[58] Michael Cahill produced a new critical edition in 1997 under the title of *Expositio Evangelii secundum Marcum*.[59] He argued that this work is "the first full-length continuous commentary by a single author on the Gospel according to Mark."[60] Earlier Bernhard Bischoff had argued that the author was the Irish monk Comianus who wrote in the first half of the seventh century.[61] Cahill himself concluded that "the evidence supports an early seventh-century date, but Irish authorship needs more positive demonstration."[62] According to Cahill, the author "appears to belong to a young church, the result of a Roman mission" and "is aware of the ongoing evangelization of the world in his day." He has a "strong self-awareness as a gentile" and sees his own western people as barbarian.[63] He was probably the abbot of a monastery, since he was apparently in a position of authority, and his spiritual teaching fits the monastic life.[64] The author used the works of Gregory the Great as a major source for his commentary.[65]

Following Origen[66] indirectly and Hilary of Poitiers (*De Mysteriis*)[67] more directly, the author used the alle-gorical method and emphasized the unity of the OT and NT, using the former to explain the latter, focusing on Mark.[68] In the prologue, he states that he will, with God's help, make known the story or literal sense (*historia*) and the spiritual or mystical sense of Mark.[69] Cahill's conclusion that the author emphasizes the mystical sense[70] is supported by the commentary on the healing of a deaf man in 7:32-36. As Gregory the Great often did with characters in biblical narratives, the Expositor allegorizes the man and his physical ailments as the human race with its physical and spiritual weaknesses.[71] Jesus touching the man is interpreted as the incarnation with the remark, "*Many righteous people* and patriarchs *and prophets* hoped and desired that the Lord would become incarnate."[72] Jesus taking the man aside from the crowd is interpreted in terms of the spiritual life: "Whoever deserves to be healed is always led aside from confused thoughts, disordered actions, and undisciplined talk."[73] The fingers of Jesus, which he puts into the man's ears, are interpreted theologically and spiritually as "the words of the Spirit, of whom it is said, *This is the finger of God*, and the heavens are *the works of your fingers*."[74] Following Gregory's homily on Ezekiel, the

gorie und Allegorese in synoptischen Gleichnistexten (NTAbh n.F. 13; Münster: Aschendorff, 1978; 2nd rev. ed., 1986) 354–55.

58 *Patrologia latina*, 30:589–644. See Michael Cahill, ed., *Expositio Evangelii secundum Marcum* (CChrSL 82; Scriptores Celtigenae, pars 2; Turnholt: Brepols, 1997) 9*. See also the summary of its contents and perspective by Kealy, who attributes it tentatively to "Cummeanus" and dates it to c. 650 (*Mark's Gospel*, 36–37); so also Schildgen, *Power and Prejudice*, 78.

59 Cahill, *Expositio Evangelii*.

60 Michael Cahill, *The First Commentary on Mark: An Annotated Translation* (New York/Oxford: Oxford University Press, 1998) 3.

61 Bernhard Bischoff, "Wendepunkte in der Geschichte der lateinischen Exegese im Frühmittelalter," *Sacris Erudiri* 6 (1954) 189–279; reprinted in idem, *Mittelalterliche Studien: Ausgewählte Aufsätze zur Schriftkunde und Literaturgeschichte* (3 vols.; Stuttgart: Hiersemann, 1966–81) 1:205–73; ET "Turning Points in the History of Latin Exegesis in the Early Middle Ages," in Martin McNamara, ed., *Biblical Studies: The Medieval Irish Contribution* (Proceedings of the Irish Biblical Association 1; Dublin: Dominican Publications, 1976) 73–16.

62 Cahill, *First Commentary*, 4; see also idem, *Expositio Evangelii*, 116–17*.

63 Cahill, *Expositio*, 117*.

64 Ibid., 118*.

65 Ibid., 72–73*.

66 On Origen as an exegete and his influence, see Simonetti, *Biblical Interpretation*, 38–48, 53–55, 64–65, 75–82, 87–90, 99–102, 118–19; on Alexandrian hermeneutics, see Froehlich, *Biblical Interpretation*, 16–18.

67 On Hilary's place in the history of Western exegesis, see Simonetti, *Biblical Interpretation*, 88–89, 99, 117, 130. On Hilary's interpretation of Mark 13:32, see Madigan, *Passions of Christ*, chap. 4.

68 Cahill, *Expositio Evangelii*, 90*.

69 Cahill, *First Commentary*, 19–20; for the Latin text, see Cahill, *Expositio Evangelii*, 1.

70 Cahill, *Expositio Evangelii*, 90*.

71 Cahill, *First Commentary*, 65 n. 14.

72 Cf. Matt 13:17; Cahill, *First Commentary*, 65 and n. 17.

73 Cahill, *First Commentary*, 65 and n. 18.

74 Exod 8:19; Ps 8:4a (8:3a RSV); Cahill, *First Commentary*, 65 and n. 19.

Expositor interprets "the spit from the flesh of the Lord" as "divine wisdom."[75] The author develops this idea in his own way by commenting that this wisdom "loosens the bond of the lips of the human race so that it can recite, 'I believe in God, the Father almighty, etc.'"[76] The groan is interpreted as Jesus teaching us to sigh with "heartfelt compunction" through which "the frivolous joy of the flesh is purged." The command to silence, which leads to the broadcasting of what Jesus has done, is interpreted as an indication that "humility always comes before glory."[77]

The Expositor notes that the parable of the seed that grows by itself is peculiar to Mark. His treatment of it is the longest of his expositions of uniquely Markan material.[78] Perhaps under the influence of Gregory the Great, he takes the kingdom of God here as "the church which is ruled by God and which in turn rules humanity."[79] "The man sowing the seed is the Son of Man, the seed is the word of life, and the soil is the hearts of the people. The sleep of the man represents the death of the Savior." The growth refers to the growing number of believers.[80] The stalk (or green shoot) is "fear. *The beginning of wisdom, the fear of the Lord.*'"[81] The ear (or head of grain) is "tearful repentance." The fully developed grain in the ear (or fully ripened wheat) is "charity, since charity is the *fullness* of the law."[82] The sickle represents death or the judgment "which cuts through everything," and the

harvest is "the end of the age, when the righteous who sowed in tears will rejoice."[83]

Cahill rightly comments that a feature of the commentary "is the ingenious, often esthetically pleasing, suggestion of parallels and symbolism in materials that we would not normally associate with one another."[84] It had considerable influence on the history of the exegesis of Mark because it was believed to have been written by Jerome.[85] The two great exegetical compendia, the *Glossa Ordinaria* and Aquinas's *Catena Aurea*, quote it extensively.[86]

Also dating to the seventh century, a product of the Canterbury school of Archbishop Theodore and Abbot Hadrian, is what Bischoff and Michael Lapidge dubbed a "supplementary commentary on Genesis, Exodus and the Gospels."[87] The Greek of Mark 9:49 states that everyone will be salted with fire. Codex Bezae and the Old Latin manuscripts read "every sacrifice" instead of "everyone."[88] In the Vulgate, this verse was 9:48, and in it the two readings were conflated: everyone and every sacrifice will be salted with fire.[89] The "supplementary commentary" cites only the second part of the verse and explains it in terms of Jewish customs: "it was a custom for the Jews to sprinkle the fire and the sacrificial victim with salt at the same time."[90]

Another work from the same school, dubbed "second commentary on the Gospels" by the editors, has a sec-

---

75 Cahill, *First Commentary*, 66 and n. 20.

76 Ibid., 66 and n. 21.

77 Ibid., 67.

78 Ibid., 50 and n. 7.

79 The next sentence alludes to Matt 8:9; Cahill, *First Commentary*, 50 and n. 8.

80 Cf. Acts 6:7; 11:21; Cahill, *First Commentary*, 50–51 and n. 9.

81 Ps 111:10; Cahill, *First Commentary*, 51 and n. 12.

82 Cf. Rom 13:10; Cahill, *First Commentary*, 51 and n. 13.

83 The prologue of the commentary concludes in a similar manner; Cahill, *First Commentary*, 23–24, 51 and n. 14.

84 Cahill, *Expositio Evangelii*, 91*.

85 Ibid., 98*.

86 Ibid., 99*. On the *Catena Aurea*, see Schildgen, *Power and Prejudice*, 65, 81, 153 n. 10. For a description of the typical catena, see Simonetti, *Biblical Interpretation*, 113–14; see also Kannengiesser, *Handbook of Patristic Exegesis*, 2:978–87. On the "gloss," see Robert M. Grant with David Tracy, *A Short History of*

the Interpretation of the Bible (2nd ed., rev. and enlarged; Philadelphia: Fortress, 1984) 83–84; on *glossa* and the *Glossa Ordinaria*, see Schildgen, *Power and Prejudice*, 76; Beryl Smalley, *The Gospels in the Schools c. 1100–c. 1280* (London/Ronceverte, WV: Hambledon, 1985) 3–30.

87 Bernhard Bischoff and Michael Lapidge, eds., *Biblical Commentaries from the Canterbury School of Theodore and Hadrian* (Cambridge Studies in Anglo-Saxon England 10; Cambridge: Cambridge University Press, 1994) v, vii (capitalization modified in quotation).

88 See the note to the trans. of 9:49 below.

89 Omnis enim igne salietur, et omnis victima sale salietur; text from Alberto Colunga and Laurentio Turrado, eds., *Biblia Sacra Vulgatae Editionis* (Milan: San Paolo, 1995) 1001. This comment occurs also in the "second commentary on the Gospels" in section 78 (Bischoff and Lapidge, *Biblical Commentaries*, 410–11); see below.

90 *Omnis uictima salietur* [Mark IX.48]. Mos fuit Iudaeis

109

tion devoted to Mark.[91] It states that John the Baptist was eating "locusts of the land," rather than "locusts of the sea," which are lobsters.[92] It also comments that the sons of Zebedee were called "sons of thunder" (Mark 3:17) because they were sons of the Holy Spirit.[93] A comment on 7:32 states that some commentators attribute deafness and dumbness to an evil spirit, but physicians say "that they arise from contracted and dormant veins." The lack of clarity with which the man saw after Jesus had healed him (8:24) is explained thus: "sometimes Jesus did these things through his humanity."[94] Jesus said "My soul is sorrowful" (14:34) "so that no-one would believe the Jews and Manichees who say that Christ was not crucified, but only a phantasmal part of Him." With respect to 15:40, it is noted that "John Chrysostom said that there were seven Marys."[95] These and other interpretations make clear that the commentaries follow Antiochene exegesis.[96]

Bede, who was a younger contemporary of Theodore and Hadrian,[97] wrote a commentary on Mark in four books, the whole of which survives.[98] This commentary was written between about 725 and 731 CE.[99] According to Arthur E. Holder, "the theological ecclesiology expressed in Bede's biblical commentaries is for the most part derived from Augustine of Hippo and Augustine's disciple and interpreter Gregory the Great."[100] The commentary on Mark contains "a long story about the finding of John the Baptist's head and the chapter of accidents by which this precious relic came to be buried at Edessa." Bede adapted this material from a chronicle by Marcellinus Comes.[101]

Although he was not innovative doctrinally, Bede's biblical commentaries "are artful compositions that exhibit broad scholarship, pastoral sensitivity, and spiritual depth."[102] According to George Hardin Brown, Bede's biblical commentaries are indebted to Ambrose[103] and Jerome, as well as to Augustine and Gregory. In his commentary on Mark, "contrary to the usual medieval practice, he often gives specific citations in the text" and

ignem et uictimam insimul sale aspergere (text and trans. from Bischoff and Lapidge, *Biblical Commentaries*, 394–95).

91   Bischoff and Lapidge, *Biblical Commentary*, 406–13.

92   *Locustas* [I.6]: sunt locustae maris quas lopustran uocant; et sunt agrestes quas comedebat Iohannes (Bischoff and Lapidge, *Biblical Commentary*, 408–9).

93   Ibid.: Ipsi filii fuerunt spiritus sancti; ibid.

94   Ibid., 409; capitalization modified.

95   Ibid., 413.

96   Ibid., 243–49. On the origin and development of Antiochene exegesis, see Simonetti, *Biblical Interpretation*, 59–60, 67–77, 100–1, 110–11, 122–23; on Antiochene hermeneutics, see Froehlich, *Biblical Interpretation*, 19–23. See also Grant and Tracy, *Short History*, 63–72.

97   "Bede, St.," *ODCC*, 149–50; "Hadrian the African," *ODCC*, 612; "Theodore of Tarsus, St.," *ODCC*, 1360. On the place of Bede in the history of Christian scholarship in general, see Joseph F. Kelly, "1996 NAPS Presidential Address: On the Brink: Bede," *JECS* 5 (1997) 85–103. "Scholars have long noted how Bede wrote commentaries on biblical books" (Mark among others) "for which there were no or few patristic exemplars. Any book left unstudied represented a spiritual loss" (ibid., 100). See also Kealy, *Mark's Gospel*, 38; Schildgen, *Power and Prejudice*, 79–80. In her view, Bede's is the first major commentary on Mark (ibid., 80).

98   David Hurst, ed., *Bedae Venerabilis Opera*, Pars 2.3: *Opera Exegetica: In Lucae Evangelium Expositio; In* *Marci Evangelium Expositio* (CChrSL 120; Turnhout: Brepols, 1960) 427–648. An older edition was done by John Allen Giles, *The Complete Works of Venerable Bede in the Original Latin*, [part] 10, *Commentaries on the Scriptures*, vol. 4: *Comment. in Novum Testamentum* (London: Whittaker, 1844) ix, 1–264. According to Charles W. Jones, Giles was incompetent as an editor; *Bedae Pseudepigrapha: Scientific Writings Falsely Attributed to Bede*, p. 18; reprinted with same page numbering in idem, *Bede, the Schools and the Computus* (ed. Wesley M. Stevens; Aldershot, Hampshire, UK: Variorum; Brookfield, VT: Ashgate, 1994).

99   George Hardin Brown, *Bede the Venerable* (Boston: Twayne/G. K. Hall, 1987) 51, 119 n. 19.

100 Arthur G. Holder, "The Venerable Bede on the Mysteries of Our Salvation," *American Benedictine Review* 42 (1991) 140–62; quotation from 143. On Bede's debt to Augustine and on the exegetical methods of each of them, see Roger D. Ray, "Bede, the Exegete, as Historian," in Gerald Bonner, ed., *Famulus Christi: Essays in Commemoration of the Thirteenth Centenary of the Birth of the Venerable Bede* (London: SPCK, 1976) 125–40. See also Max L. W. Laistner, "Bede as a Classical and as a Patristic Scholar," in idem, *The Intellectual Heritage of the Early Middle Ages* (ed. Chester G. Starr; New York: Octagon Books, 1983) 93–116, esp. 110; idem, "The Library of the Venerable Bede," in Laistner, *Intellectual Heritage*, 117–49, esp. 121, 130–33.

101 Laistner, "Bede as a Scholar," 100.

102 Holder, "Venerable Bede," 144.

in the margins.[104] He "strove to convey the deepest meaning of the text by way of an intelligent interpretation. That interpretation was often allegorical."[105] Two books of his homilies were well known in the Middle Ages, which contain "fifty reflections on the Gospels, many excerpted from his gospel commentaries."[106] The text of one of his Advent homilies was Mark 1:4-8.[107] A homily for Holy Saturday had 7:31-37 as its text.[108] In Bede's interpretation, the deaf-mute "represents those members of the human race who merit being freed by divine grace from the error brought on by the devil's deceit."[109] The Lord's saliva is "the word of his gospel" for the healing of the world.[110] Bede compares the healing gestures of the Lord to the ritual of baptism.[111] The command to silence is interpreted as "an example, so that, when we perform acts of virtue, we would avoid the vice of boasting." The proclaiming of Jesus' deed in spite of the command to silence signifies "that if our good deeds are worthy of imitation, they cannot be hidden, but will be revealed for the purpose of fraternal correction" like the city on a mountain-top.[112]

The commentary on Mark was published after the one on Luke, and much of it is taken from the Lukan commentary, when the two Gospels agree. Yet the commentary on Mark "manifests some of Bede's finest and most mature exegesis."[113] His comment on 11:11 is tropological (ethical or moral): as the Lord went immediately to the temple when he entered Jerusalem, so we should enter a house of prayer whenever we enter a village, town, or other place. Then we can turn to "temporal affairs." He has two comments on the driving of the money-changers out of the temple: "the church can also be polluted by gossip and chatter." He also comments that "the individual soul is the temple that the Lord cleanses and purifies."[114]

Among the people and in the monasteries in the Middle Ages, little attention was paid to Mark as a distinct Gospel.[115] Along with the other Gospels, Mark played a role in popular genres, such as harmonies, biographies, dramas, and poems.[116] In the twelfth century, the Psalter and the letters of Paul were most often commented upon. In the twelfth and thirteenth centuries, the Gospels "took a more central place in the syllabus" of the schools.[117] In the twelfth century, Peter Comestor wrote commentaries on all four Gospels, which have survived in reports of lectures he gave in Paris from 1159 to 1178.[118] Under the influence of the movement begun by Hugh of St. Victor, Peter attempted to deepen understanding of the literal historical sense.[119] Passages in Mark played a role in the high Middle Ages, for example, in the work of Peter Lombard, Bonaventure, and Thomas Aquinas, in the discussion of whether fear, sorrow, ignorance, and submission to God in prayer could be attributed to Jesus.[120]

103   On Ambrose's interpretation of Mark 13:32, see Madigan, *Passions of Christ*, chap. 4.

104   Brown, *Bede*, 20; see also Max L. W. Laistner, "Source-Marks in Bede Manuscripts," *JTS* 34 (1933) 350–54, esp. 350–52; idem, "Bede as a Scholar," 103–4.

105   Brown, *Bede*, 20.

106   Ibid., 21; see also 62–65. For an ET of the homilies, see Lawrence T. Martin and David Hurst, trans., *Bede the Venerable: Homilies on the Gospels* (2 vols.; Cistercian Studies Series 110, 111; Kalamazoo, MI: Cistercian Publications, 1991).

107   Homily I.1 (Martin and Hurst, 1:1–8).

108   Homily II.6 (Martin and Hurst, 2:51–57).

109   Martin and Hurst, 2.51.

110   Ibid., 53.

111   Ibid., 54.

112   Ibid., 56.

113   Brown, *Bede*, 56.

114   Ibid., 57. For the Latin text, see David Hurst, ed., *Bedae Venerabilis Opera*, Pars 2.3, *Opera Exegetica: In*

Lucae Evangelium Expositio; In Marci Evangelium Expositio (CChrSL 120; Turnhout: Brepols, 1960) 575, 578–79.

115   Kealy, *Mark's Gospel*, 31–43; Schildgen, *Power and Prejudice*, 63–84. On medieval exegesis, see Henri de Lubac, *Medieval Exegesis* (2 vols.; Grand Rapids: Eerdmans; Edinburgh: T & T Clark, 1998–2000; French ed., 1959).

116   Schildgen, *Power and Prejudice*, 65–75, 83–84.

117   Smalley, *Gospels in the Schools*, 1–2.

118   Fridericus Stegmüller, *Repertorium Biblicum Medii Aevi* (11 vols.; Matriti: Instituto Francisco Suárez, 1950–), vol. 4: *Commentaria, Auctores N–Q* (1955) nos. 6575–78; Smalley, *Gospels in the Schools*, 4, 58.

119   Smalley, *Gospels in the Schools*, 103.

120   Madigan, *Passions of Christ*.

Evidence also exists for lectures on the Gospels in the Paris schools from 1173 to 1245.[121] Peter the Chanter considered Peter Comestor's work to be flawed by too much attention to trivial detail. His main concern was how to "reconcile Gospel teaching, taken literally, with current practice."[122] Commentaries survive on all four Gospels by the Dominican Hugh of St. Cher, the Franciscan Alexander of Hales, and by Alexander's student John of LaRochelle.[123] Hugh of St. Cher "was a compiler, working in the tradition of the 'biblical moral' school."[124] Both Hugh and Alexander moralize the blood in the story of the woman with a flow of blood as "sin added to sin."[125] Alexander wrote an allegorical treatment "of the types of sin signified by the unclean spirits and their entry into the swine (Mark 5:1-13)."[126]

John of LaRochelle commented self-consciously as a friar, which not even Hugh of St. Cher did.[127] A second Franciscan trait evident in his work is Joachite eschatology.[128] In commenting on the mocking of Jesus by the soldiers, he argued that the suffering of Christ prefigured that of the church in the last days. The royal cloak represented earthly power, which many leaders of the church had sought, inappropriately usurping a kind of power that does not pertain to them. The removal of the cloak and return of Christ's own clothing signified that the church would return to poverty, "her true garment."[129] All three, Hugh, Alexander, and John, "share a lack of interest in research on the literal historical sense of the Gospels," an interest manifested by Peter Comestor.[130]

From the mid-thirteenth century onward, writing on the Gospels took on a polemical tone, as the secular masters' attacks on the mendicants led to counterattacks. From this time also, lectures focus more on understanding the text and less on how to preach it. The tension between earthly power (*regnum*) and priestly power (*sacerdotium*) found in the Gospels was resolved in favor of the papacy. The anti-Jewish polemic of the patristic writers is maintained, but not increased or developed in new ways.[131] In the twelfth and thirteenth centuries, on the whole, the masters paid more attention to and gave a more significant place to the literal sense of the Gospels.[132]

In the East, Theophylact, a Byzantine exegete of the eleventh century and a native of Euboea, had been made archbishop of Achrida (Ochrida) in the country of the Bulgarians. He wrote commentaries on several books of the Old Testament and on all the books of the New Testament except Revelation.[133] His commentary on Mark stands in the Antiochene tradition, focusing on the "literal" sense by engaging philological and historical issues.[134]

In commenting on Mark's parable about the seed that grows by itself, Theophylact interprets the kingdom of God as "God's economy for us [that is, His ordering of His creation towards our salvation]."[135]

The "man" is God himself, who became man for our sake. The seed which he cast onto the earth is the preaching of the gospel. After he had cast it, he slept, meaning, he ascended into heaven. . . . The seed grows, "He knows not how." For we have free will, and

121 Smalley, *Gospels in the Schools*, 99.
122 Ibid., 103. His lectures can be dated to 1187–1197 (ibid., 107).
123 Ibid., 118.
124 Ibid., 143.
125 Ibid., 161–62.
126 Ibid., 170; Alexander's allegorical and moral interpretations are more sustained than those of Hugh (ibid.). Hugh's work, however, manifests "something of the ethos of a Friar Preacher," whereas "nothing in Alexander's gives an inkling that he was a potential or actual recruit to the Order of Friars Minor" (ibid., 171).
127 Ibid., 181–82.
128 On Joachite eschatology, see Bernard McGinn, *The Calabrian Abbot: Joachim of Fiore in the History of Western Thought* (New York: Macmillan; London: Collier Macmillan, 1985; Marjorie Reeves, *The Influence of Prophecy in the Later Middle Ages: A Study in Joachimism* (Notre Dame/London: University of Notre Dame Press, 1993; first ed. Oxford University Press, 1969).
129 Smalley, *Gospels in the Schools*, 183.
130 Ibid., 190.
131 Ibid., 276–77.
132 Ibid., 277–78.
133 *ODCC* 1364; on his commentary on the four Gospels, see Schildgen, *Power and Prejudice*, 65, 153 n. 12.
134 Schildgen, *Power and Prejudice*, 65.
135 *Explanation by Blessed Theophylact*, 40.

whether the seed increases or not depends on our own inclination. For we do not bear fruit by necessity, but by own our will, first producing the leaf and showing forth the beginnings of good when we are infants and have not yet reached the measure of maturity in Christ. Then we produce the ear, when we are able to withstand the storms of temptations. . . . Then comes the full grain in the ear when one bears the good fruit. "When the crop is brought forth," then the sickle gathers the fruit. The sickle means the Word of God, and the harvest signifies the end of the world.[136]

Theophylact agrees with Victor of Antioch in interpreting the sleep of the man christologically as the ascension and the bringing forth of fruit ethically. They also agree in explaining the sower's ignorance in terms of human free will. These similarities may be due to their common dependence on the Antiochene exegetical tradition. Theophylact agrees with the Expositor (the author of the Latin commentary edited by Cahill) that the harvest is the end of the age or world.

In commenting on Mark 16:18, Theophylact interprets the serpents spiritually and connects this interpretation with Luke 10:19. He also remarks that the text may refer to literal serpents and alludes to Paul's being unhurt by the viper (Acts 28:3-6).[137] He comments as follows on Mark 16:20:

The apostles preached everywhere, "the Lord working with them, and confirming the word with signs following." See that we must do our part first, and then follows God's collaboration with us. When we have acted and made a beginning, then the Lord works with us. . . . Consider this as well: after the word come works, and the word is confirmed by works, just as it was with the apostles then, when the works and the signs which followed confirmed the word.[138]

Then he prays that "our words which we speak concerning virtue" may be "confirmed by our labors and deeds. As ones perfected, may we stand by your side so that you may work with us in all our deeds and words."[139] This verse is also discussed in Thomas Aquinas's *Catena Aurea*, in a passage from Gregory the Great's *Explanations and Reflections on the Ascension*.[140]

Albertus Magnus, the teacher of Thomas Aquinas, composed a major commentary on Mark in the thirteenth century.[141] His procedure was to cite an entire chapter of Mark, then to cite a whole verse and make a general statement about it and finally to gloss, word by word or phrase by phrase, every verse in the chapter. He used allegorical, moral, literal, and anagogical approaches to the text.[142] In his treatment of the feeding of the four thousand (8:1-3), he interpreted the seven loaves as the seven virtues.[143] He also related them to the seven sacraments and to "the seven effects of the Word of God, for those who partake." These allegorical interpretations reflect Albertus's "effort to rationalize the problems posed by the literal level of" miracle stories, which conflicts with science and philosophy.[144]

The methods of Erasmus were similar to those of the medieval exegetes, but he enriched that tradition with newly recovered Greek and Latin texts. He wrote Latin paraphrases of all the Gospels, publishing the one on Mark last, in 1523.[145] Abandoning the practice of commenting word by word or phrase by phrase, Erasmus rewrote each chapter expressing his own humanist and spiritual ideas. Albertus had interpreted John the Baptist

---

136 Ibid.; trans. slightly modified.
137 Kealy, *Mark's Gospel*, 39; *Explanation by Blessed Theophylact*, 143.
138 *Explanation by Blessed Theophylact*, 144.
139 Ibid.; cf. Kealy, *Mark's Gospel*, 39.
140 Kealy, *Mark's Gospel*, 41–42.
141 Albertus Magnus, *Secundum Marcum* in Steph. Caes. Aug. Borgnet, ed., *Enarrationes in Matthaeum (XXI–XXVIII)–in Marcum, Opera Omnia*, vol. 21 (Paris: Apud Ludovicum Vives, Bibliopolam Editorem, 1894) 339–761; Schildgen, *Power and Prejudice*, 65, 153 n. 9, 80; Kealy, *Mark's Gospel*, 42.

142 Schildgen, *Power and Prejudice*, 80.
143 The three theological virtues—faith, hope, and love—and the four cardinal virtues—prudence, justice, fortitude, and temperance (Schildgen, *Power and Prejudice*, 81, 156 n. 64).
144 Ibid., 81.
145 Erasmus *Paraphrasis in Marcum*; Erika Rummel, trans. and annotator, *Paraphrase on Mark* (NT Scholarship of Erasmus: Collected Works of Erasmus 49; Toronto/Buffalo/London: University of Toronto Press, 1988). See also Schildgen, *Power and Prejudice*, 65, 81–82, 153 n. 13; Kealy, *Mark's Gospel*, 43–44.

in Mark 1 "as a model for monastic asceticism."[146] Erasmus, in contrast, wrote that "John taught that the teacher must acquire authority, not by the splendour of his garment or the pomp of his life, but by the integrity of his character."[147] This comment reveals the reforming spirit of the times, characteristic of those who criticized the extravagant lifestyle of authoritative leaders of the church, and recommends a simple, spiritual life.[148] Erasmus dedicated the work to Francis I of France, manifesting a major shift in patronage from monasteries and bishoprics to monarchs. He also testifies to the current revolution in technology and economy by referring to his work as "a saleable object."[149]

Luther wrote commentaries on the Old Testament and much of the New Testament. He wrote three volumes on John, but commented only on the Magnificat (Luke) and the Sermon on the Mount (Matthew) from the Synoptics.[150] He did, however, comment on the Synoptics in his sermons and other works.[151]

In his Christology, Luther emphasized the truly human (*vere homo*) nature of Christ. To illustrate this true humanity, he used the Synoptic Gospels as illustrations.[152] In discussing Jesus' associations with human beings, he emphasized his gentleness and goodness. He remarks how kindly Jesus instructed the ambitious disciples (Mark 10:35-45). He chastised the disciples for their unbelief (16:14), but did not reject them. He bore with them for having little faith before the feeding of the four thousand (8:1). In seeing the misery of one man, he saw that of all of humanity (7:31-32).[153] As Nicholas of Lyra had done before him,[154] Luther harmonzied Mark 4:12

with Matt 13:13, so that the difference between Mark's "in order that" and Matthew's "because" loses its force. He attributed all the responsibility to the human heart in order to affirm the divine will for salvation.[155]

Luther was critical of allegorical readings (of nonallegorical texts)[156] after 1525 and more so after 1529. After 1529, he treated only four texts allegorically, including Mark 7:31-37.[157] His principle of interpretation was that all the miracle stories have a spiritual sense that is more important than the outward event. The deaf and mute man is an image for the human being when determined by reason. The Decapolis stands for the Ten Commandments that such persons attempt to fulfill by their own power. The men who bring him to Christ are the proclaimers, the apostles. In order to help him, Christ must separate him from people who are involved in works. With the healing gestures, Christ wanted to demonstrate that it takes a lot of effort to make a mute man speak. The sighing relates to the misery of all human beings, not to that of this man alone.[158] When Christ puts his fingers in the man's ears, he pours the Holy Spirit into him through the word. The saliva is the word of God. The homely image signifies that the gospel is despised. It is the word of the cross.[159]

Calvin did not write commentaries on any of the individual Synoptic Gospels. He wrote a commentary on John and another on a harmony of Matthew, Mark, and Luke.[160] With regard to Mark 4:26, he says:

[Here] Christ seems particularly to refer to ministers of the Word, lest they should execute their office with

146 Schildgen, *Power and Prejudice*, 82; see also 90–91.
147 Rummel, *Paraphrase on Mark*, 18.
148 Schildgen, *Power and Prejudice*, 82.
149 See the dedicatory letter prefixed to the paraphrase in Rummel, *Paraphrase on Mark*, 10–11; Schildgen, *Power and Prejudice*, 82–83, 157 n. 70.
150 Schildgen, *Power and Prejudice*, 83. On the biblical interpretation of other reformers, see ibid.
151 D. Walther von Loewenich, *Luther als Ausleger der Synoptiker* (Forschungen zur Geschichte und Lehre des Protestantismus, series 10, vol. 5; Munich: Kaiser, 1954).
152 Loewenich, *Luther als Ausleger*, 132. On Luther as an interpreter of Scripture, see Grant and Tracy, *Short History*, 93–95, 99.
153 Loewenich, *Luther als Ausleger*, 135–36.
154 A Franciscan scholar (c. 1270–1340); see *ODCC* 972–73; see also Schildgen, *Power and Prejudice*, 87–89.
155 Loewenich, *Luther als Ausleger*, 33.
156 On this distinction, see Klauck, *Allegorie und Allegorese*, 354–55.
157 Loewenich, *Luther als Ausleger*, 16.
158 Cf. the interpretations of this passage by Victor of Antioch and the author of the seventh-century commentary discussed above.
159 Loewenich, *Luther als Ausleger*, 23.
160 John Calvin, *Commentarius in harmoniam evangelicam* in Guilielmus Baum, Eduardus Cunitz, Eduardus Reuss, eds., *Ioannis Calvini Opera quae supersunt omnia*, vol. 45 (Corpus Reformatorum 73; Brunsvigae: C. A. Schwetschke, 1891). There is an index of passages of Mark commented upon on pp. VII–VIII.

less enthusiasm when no fruit of their labours appears immediately.

They should not be "worried and anxious," but "get on with their daily work" and be "refreshed by a good night's sleep," until at last the crop is ripe. Lack of trust should not "diminish their zeal."[161]

In remarks on the healing of a deaf man in 7:31-37, Calvin interprets the "anointing of the dumb man's tongue" with the saliva of Jesus as a symbol indicating that "the faculty of speech flows from Himself alone." By putting his finger into the man's ears, Jesus "taught that it was His proper office to perforate, as it were, deaf ears." He goes on:

> There is no need to flee to allegories, and we see that those who have played that game the most subtly have offered nothing substantial but rather made the explaining of Scripture a mockery.[162]

Calvin rejects the idea that the command to tell no one about what had happened was a deliberate attempt by Jesus to stir "them up to publish abroad the news of the miracle." Rather, "[h]e only wanted this to be deferred to a more opportune and ripe time." The people were carried away by "an immoderate zeal," but Jesus "turns their imprudence to His glory, for the miracle was made known and all that region was made inexcusable for despising the author of the heavenly gifts."[163]

In the fifteenth and sixteenth centuries, the philological approach to the Bible was revived and transformed into a critical method by the separation of doctrinal and philological interests. This change was initiated, or at least anticipated, by the work of the early humanist Lorenzo Valla, who paid attention only to philological matters.[164] His primary concern was to establish an accurate text. "In contrast to all the harmonies, commentaries, and translations from the fourth through the fourteenth centuries," Valla agreed with Jerome that Mark originally ended with 16:8.[165] Valla's work was continued by Erasmus and others.[166] This new approach led to greater attention to the Gospel of Mark in its own right.

In the eighteenth century, patronage shifted in a major way once again from the aristocracy to universities and independent scholars. Educated men and women "began to trust their own rational capacities in a way that had not previously been apparent in Western intellectual activity."[167] A self-educated commoner numbered among the English Deists, Thomas Chubb (1697–1747), regarded Mark as the oldest Gospel and concluded that the other Gospels used it as a source. He also concluded that Mark "rested on oral tradition and made use of information that was second- or third-hand."[168] His view on the priority of Mark, however, had little effect. At the time of Johann Jakob Griesbach (1745–1812), the major views of the relationships among the Synoptic Gospels did not include the use of Mark by any of the others as a source.[169] Griesbach's view was that "the entire Gospel of Mark was extracted from the records of Matthew and Luke."[170] In his later work, Johann Gottfried Herder (1744–1803) concluded that Mark was the earliest of the canonical Gospels and independent of the others.[171] The growing interest in philology and history led to a diminishment of concern for the Gospels as literary works. Commentators in the eighteenth century lost or rejected the notion of "literary depiction" in biblical narratives. In its place they established "their conception of the literal sense, a philological or 'grammatical-historical' understanding of the texts rather than a literary one."[172]

161 John Calvin, *A Harmony of the Gospels: Matthew, Mark and Luke* (3 vols.; Calvin's Commentaries 1–3; trans. A. W. Morrison and H. W. Parker; ed. David W. Torrance and Thomas F. Torrance; Edinburgh: Saint Andrew Press, 1972; reprinted Grand Rapids: Eerdmans; Carlisle: Paternoster, 1994–95) 2:80.

162 Ibid., 2:173.

163 Ibid., 2:174.

164 Lorenzo Valla, *Collatio Novi Testamenti* (ed. Alessandro Perosa; Florence: Sansoni Editore, 1970; 1st ed. Paris, 1501; composed 1449–50); Schildgen, *Power and Prejudice*, 87, 89–91, 158 n. 8.

165 Schildgen, *Power and Prejudice*, 91.

166 Ibid., 94–100.

167 Ibid., 112.

168 William Baird, *History of New Testament Research*, vol. 1: *From Deism to Tübingen* (Minneapolis: Fortress, 1992) 54–55; quotation from 55.

169 Ibid., 138, 144.

170 Ibid., 145. See also the section of this introduction above on the *Synoptic Problem*; Schildgen, *Power and Prejudice*, 114–15, 118–21.

171 Baird, *From Deism to Tübingen*, 177, 181.

172 Schildgen, *Power and Prejudice*, 121–22, with refer-

Biblical scholars of the nineteenth century focused on three topics: the historical Jesus, the relations among the Gospels, and establishing the text of the Greek New Testament.[173] Christian Gottlob Wilke (1786–1854) argued in detail for the priority of Mark.[174] Christian Hermann Weisse (1801–1866) formulated the two-source theory and argued that Mark was the narrative source used by Matthew and Luke.[175] But it was not until Heinrich Julius Holtzmann published a work on the Synoptic Gospels in 1863 that the majority of scholars were persuaded that Mark was the earliest Gospel and that it was used by Matthew and Luke as a source.[176] The establishment of the theory of Markan priority greatly increased scholarly interest in Mark because of the assumption that the earliest Gospel provided reliable information about the historical Jesus.[177]

In 1901, however, William Wrede argued that Mark does not provide a reliable account of the development of Jesus' messianic consciousness. Rather, the "messianic secret" is an interpretative construct.[178] Although an important part of Wrede's contribution focused on the history of tradition between Jesus and the writing of Mark, his literary focus in some ways anticipated the method of "redaction criticism"[179] pioneered with respect to Mark by Willi Marxsen in 1956.[180]

Marxsen argued, against the form critics, that the unity given to many pieces of tradition by Mark is the result of deliberately planned activity, not the "fulfillment" or "end-point" of the anonymous stages of the process of transmission. That process leads to fragmentation, whereas redaction (editorial work) sets itself against that tendency.[181] Apart from certain collections of material and a passion narrative, Mark had only individual units of tradition with which to work. His achievement is thus much more remarkable than those of Matthew and Luke. This achievement is discerned first of all in the "framework" of the Gospel. This term includes the overall itinerary, the settings given to individual units, and the connections created between them, as well as the changes made within the traditional units themselves.

Joachim Jeremias distinguished two social settings: the activity of Jesus and the situation of the earliest community; redaction criticism concerns itself with a third social setting.[182] What actually happened is of secondary interest to the redaction critic. Such a critic asks rather about the situation of the community in which the Gospel originated. Whether or not this community can be defined as located in a specific place, the focus should be on what is typical about it.[183] Although Marxsen specifically stated that this community need not necessarily be defined as limited in a local sense, redaction critics came to assume that it could and should be so defined.[184] He attempted to recover the perspective of Mark in two ways. The one was analytical, the effort to distinguish tradition from redaction. The other was constructive, the attempt to reveal and explain the process of composition.[185] He also tried to discover what was typi-

---

ence to Hans W. Frei, *The Eclipse of Biblical Narrative: A Study in Eighteenth and Nineteenth Century Hermeneutics* (New Haven: Yale University Press, 1974) 9.

173 Schildgen, *Power and Prejudice*, 113.

174 Baird, *From Deism to Tübingen*. See also Albert Schweitzer, *The Quest of the Historical Jesus: First Complete Edition* (Minneapolis: Fortress, 2001) 112.

175 Baird, *From Deism to Tübingen*, 305–6.

176 Kümmel, *New Testament*, 151; see also William Baird, *History of New Testament Research*, vol. 2: *From Jonathan Edwards to Rudolf Bultmann* (Minneapolis: Fortress, 2003) 115–16; Schildgen, *Power and Prejudice*, 127.

177 For the importance of this point for Weisse, see Schweitzer, *Quest*, 110–23. On the new focus on Mark in the nineteenth century, see Schildgen, *Power and Prejudice*, 125, 127.

178 See the excursus on the messianic secret following

the commentary on 1:24 below. See also Baird, *From Jonathan Edwards to Rudolf Bultmann*, 148–49; Kümmel, *New Testament*, 284–87; Schweitzer, *Quest*, 296–314; Schildgen, *Power and Prejudice*, 113, 127–29.

179 On the origin of the method in historical context, see Schildgen, *Power and Prejudice*, 131–32.

180 See Marxsen, *Der Evangelist Markus*, 1–12; ET *Mark the Evangelist*, 21–22.

181 Ibid., 9; ET 18.

182 Ibid., 12; ET 23.

183 Ibid., 12–13; ET 23–24.

184 On Richard Bauckham's challenge to the assumption that the Gospels were addressed to specific, local communities, see the section of this introduction on *Audience and Purpose* above.

185 Marxsen, *Der Evangelist Markus*, 16; ET 28. For an excellent application of these two methods to Matthew, see Kari Syreeni, *The Making of the Sermon on the Mount: A Procedural Analysis of Matthew's*

cally Markan by looking at the later developments in the Gospels of Matthew and Luke.[186]

Apart from the methodological introduction, Marxsen's book consisted of four studies on Mark focusing on John the Baptist, the geographical outline, the term "gospel," and the apocalyptic discourse of chap. 13. The first study led to the conclusion, among others, that the opening part of Mark has the greatest density. Here unity is created by giving the tradition a "prehistory" and Jesus a "forerunner."[187] In the second study, Marxsen concluded that "Mark writes a Galilean Gospel." He used "Galilee" as a unifying redactional device, a locality that had more theological importance for the evangelist than historical, because he expected the parousia to take place there in the near future.[188] An important conclusion of the third study is that, in Mark, two streams that flow through earliest Christianity come together: the conceptual-theological, represented in the early period by Paul, and the kerygmatic-representational, typified by the Synoptic tradition. The union of the two is evident in Mark's use of the term "gospel" or "good news" ($\varepsilon\dot{\nu}\alpha\gamma\gamma\acute{\varepsilon}\lambda\iota o\nu$).[189] The fourth study leads to the conclusion that Mark, unlike Matthew, is one sermon, in which

chap. 13 plays an integral and important role.[190] In his concluding remarks, Marxsen argued that the inner goal of the whole Gospel is evident in its concluding inconclusiveness: the orientation toward Galilee and the imminent expectation of the parousia there constitute the formative motif. Mark must be interpreted against this background.[191]

Other influential redaction critics of Mark include Ernest Best,[192] Eduard Schweizer,[193] and Norman Perrin.[194] Perrin's most important contribution concerns the composition and structure of Mark.[195] His argument that all the Son of Man sayings originated after Easter is not persuasive.[196] His argument that Mark rejected the title "Son of God" by replacing it with "Son of Man" has been refuted by Jack Dean Kingsbury.[197]

In the nineteenth century and at least the first half of the twentieth century, especially in German-language scholarship, "literary criticism" meant, in effect, "source criticism."[198] In the second half of the twentieth century,[199] it began to be used for aesthetic literary criticism, an approach to the New Testament similar to the approaches used in departments of literature in universities. Pioneers of this approach were Amos Wilder,[200]

Redactoral Activity (Annales Academiae Scientiarum Fennicae; Dissertationes humanarum litterarum 44; Helsinki: Suomalainen Tiedeakatemia, 1987).

186 Marxsen, *Der Evangelist Markus*, 16; ET 28–29.

187 Ibid., 32; ET 52.

188 Ibid., 59; ET 92. For criticism of this view, see the excursus on Galilee and Jerusalem in Mark in the commentary on 14:26-31 below.

189 Marxsen, *Der Evangelist Markus*, 99; ET 147.

190 Ibid., 139–40; ET 204–5.

191 Ibid., 142; ET 208–9.

192 Ernest Best, *The Temptation and the Passion: The Markan Soteriology* (2nd ed.; SNTSMS 2; Cambridge: Cambridge University Press, 1990; 1st ed., 1965); idem, *Following Jesus: Discipleship in the Gospel of Mark* (JSNTSup 4; Sheffield: JSOT Press, 1981); idem, *Mark: The Gospel as Story* (Studies of the New Testament and Its World; Edinburgh: T & T Clark, 1983); idem, *Disciples and Discipleship: Studies in the Gospel according to Mark* (Edinburgh: T & T Clark, 1986).

193 Eduard Schweizer, *The Good News according to Mark* (Atlanta: John Knox, 1970); trans. of *Das Evangelium nach Markus* (Göttingen: Vandenhoeck & Ruprecht, 1968).

194 Norman Perrin, "Towards an Interpretation," in

Christology and a Modern Pilgrimage: A Discussion with Norman Perrin, ed. Hans Dieter Betz (Claremont, CA: New Testament Colloquium, 1971) 1–78; idem, *What Is Redaction Criticism?* (GBS; Philadelphia: Fortress, 1969).

195 See the section of this introduction on *Composition and Structure* above.

196 See the excursus on the Son of Man tradition in the commentary on 2:10 below.

197 Jack Dean Kingsbury, *The Christology of Mark's Gospel* (Philadelphia: Fortress, 1983).

198 For general essays on individual methods in biblical studies, from historical criticism to socioeconomic criticism, see Steven L. McKenzie and Stephen R. Haynes, eds., *To Each Its Own Meaning: An Introduction to Biblical Criticisms and Their Applications* (rev. and expanded ed.; Louisville: Westminster John Knox, 1999).

199 On the "new interest in a conscious hermeneutics of inquiry" in the second half of the twentieth century, which "has led to an expansion of various kinds of self-conscious theoretical approaches to biblical interpretation," see Schildgen, *Power and Prejudice,* 132. Her discussion begins with Marxist and liberationist readings of Mark (ibid., 132, 168 nn. 22–23).

200 Amos Niven Wilder, *The Language of the Gospel: Early*

William A. Beardslee,[201] and Robert Tannehill.[202] Among the many practicioners of this approach with respect to Mark are Norman Petersen,[203] Frank Kermode,[204] David Rhoads,[205] Joanna Dewey,[206] Elizabeth Struthers Malbon,[207] Tom Shepherd,[208] George Aichlele,[209] and Sharyn Echols Dowd.[210]

Subdisciplines of literary criticism include narrative criticism,[211] reader-response criticism,[212] and deconstructive criticism.[213]

Feminist studies of Mark include works by Rita Nakashima Brock, Monika Fander, Janice Capel Anderson, Hisako Kinukawa, and the essays edited by A. J. Levine.[214] David Rhoads has written a social-scientific study of Mark, and Benny Liew a postcolonial study.[215] The field of gender studies includes studies of masculinity. Several studies have been written of masculinities in Mark.[216]

Reception history is a broader category than the history of interpretation, including the use of Mark by poets and artists and the Gospel's influence on them. An example is the *St. Mark Passion* composed by Osvaldo Golijov.[217]

Christian Rhetoric (New York: Harper & Row, 1964); idem, *The Bible and the Literary Critic* (Minneapolis: Fortress, 1991).

201 William A. Beardslee, *Literary Criticism of the New Testament* (Philadelphia: Fortress, 1969).

202 Robert C. Tannehill, *The Sword of His Mouth: Forceful and Imaginative Language in Synoptic Sayings* (SemSup 1; Philadelphia: Fortress; Missoula, MT: Scholars Press, 1975).

203 Petersen, *Literary Criticism*.

204 Frank Kermode, *The Genesis of Secrecy: On the Interpretation of Narrative* (Cambridge, MA/London: Harvard University Press, 1979).

205 David Rhoads and Donald Michie, *Mark as Story: An Introduction to the Narrative of a Gospel* (Philadelphia: Fortress, 1982); David Rhoads, *Reading Mark, Engaging the Gospel* (Minneapolis: Fortress, 2004).

206 David Rhoads, Joanna Dewey, and Donald Michie, *Mark as Story: An Introduction to the Narrative of a Gospel* (2nd ed.; Minneapolis, MN: Fortress, 1999); see also Dewey, *Markan Public Debate*.

207 Malbon, *Narrative Space and Mythic Meaning in Mark*; eadem, *In the Company of Jesus: Characters in Mark's Gospel* (Louisville: Westminster John Knox Press, 2000); eadem, *Hearing Mark: A Listener's Guide* (Harrisburg, PA: Trinity Press International, 2002).

208 Tom Shepherd, *Markan Sandwich Stories: Narration, Definition, and Function* (AUSDDS 18; Berrien Springs, MI: Andrews University Press, 1993).

209 George Aichele, *Jesus Framed* (Biblical Limits; London/New York: Routledge, 1996).

210 Sharyn Echols Dowd, *A Literary and Theological Commentary on the Second Gospel* (Macon, GA: Smyth & Helwys, 2000); see also eadem, *Prayer, Power, and the Problem of Suffering* (SBLDS 105; Atlanta: Scholars Press, 1988).

211 Elizabeth Struthers Malbon, "Narrative Criticism: How Does the Story Mean?" in Janice Capel Anderson and Stephen D. Moore, eds., *Mark & Method: New Approaches in Biblical Studies* (Minneapolis, MN: Fortress, 1992) 23–49; Davidsen, *Narrative Jesus*; Stephen H. Smith, *A Lion with Wings: A Narrative-Critical Approach to Mark's Gospel* (Biblical Seminar 38; Sheffield: Sheffield Academic Press, 1996). Cf. the linguistic approach of Cook, *Structure*. Danove (*End of Mark's Story*) attempts to combine linguistic and literary methods.

212 Robert M. Fowler, "Reader-Response Criticism: Figuring Mark's Reader," in Anderson and Moore, 50–83; see also Fowler, *Let the Reader Understand: Reader-Response Criticism and the Gospel of Mark* (Minneapolis: Fortress, 1991).

213 Stephen D. Moore, "Deconstructive Criticism: The Gospel of the Mark," in Anderson and Moore, 84–102; in the original publication, the word "Mark" in the title of this article is crossed out with a large "X."

214 Rita Nakashima Brock, *Journeys by Heart: A Christology of Erotic Power* (New York: Crossroad, 1988). See also Elisabeth Schüssler Fiorenza, *In Memory of Her: A Feminist Theological Reconstruction of Christian Origins* (New York: Crossroad, 1983); eadem, ed., with Shelly Matthews, *Searching the Scriptures* (2 vols.; New York: Crossroad, 1993–94). Monika Fander, *Die Stellung der Frau im Markusevangelium unter besonderer Berücksichtigung kultur- und religionsgeschichtlicher Hintergründe* (2nd ed.; Altenberge: Telos, 1990); Janice Capel Anderson, "Feminist Criticism: The Dancing Daughter," in Anderson and Moore, 103–34; Hisako Kinukawa, *Women and Jesus in Mark: A Japanese Feminist Perspective* (Maryknoll, NY: Orbis, 1994); Amy-Jill Levine, ed., *A Feminist Companion to Mark* (Sheffield: Sheffield Academic Press, 2001).

215 David Rhoads, "Social Criticism: Crossing Boundaries," in Anderson and Moore, 135–61; Tat-Siong Benny Liew, *Politics of Parousia: Reading Mark Inter(con)textually* (BIS 42; Leiden: Brill, 1999); see also idem, "Tyranny, Boundary and Might: Colonial Mimicry in Mark's Gospel," *JSNT* 73 (1999) 7–31.

216 Jennifer A. Glancy, "Unveiling Masculinity: The Construction of Gender in Mark 6:14-29," *BI* 2

All of these newer approaches enrich and complicate the task of interpreting Mark. This commentary emphasizes the interpretation of Mark in its original and earliest contexts. It will discuss the history of scholarship and newer approaches when they are especially important for that project.

(1994) 34–50; Tat-Siong Benny Liew, "Re-mark-able Masculinities: Jesus, the Son of Man, and the (Sad) Sum of Manhood?" in Stephen D. Moore and Janice Capel Anderson, eds., *New Testament Masculinities* (SBLSS 45; Atlanta: SBL, 2003) 93–135; Eric Thurman, "Looking for a Few Good Men: Mark and Masculinity," in Moore and Anderson, *New Testament Masculinities,* 137–61; Yii-Jan Singh, "Mark and Masculinity: A Narrative Critical Analysis of the Second Gospel" (M.A. thesis, Trinity International University, 2005).

217 Joynes, "Reception History," 24–32; Osvaldo Golijov, *La Pasión según Marcos* (2 CD-set; available through Hänssler Classic; recorded by Südwestrundfunk, Germany; live recording of the first performance on September 5, 2000). Joynes is writing the Blackwell Bible Commentary on Mark's Gospel, which will emphasize its reception history.

From the late second century, the manuscript tradition of Mark merges with that of the four (canonical) Gospels. Fragments of a manuscript from that time survive and provide evidence that it contained all four Gospels, but no fragments of Mark from this manuscript survive.[1] A manuscript dating between 175 and 225 CE, however, may have contained only Luke and John.[2]

The principal witnesses, with the portion of Mark included in each, are:

Papyri

p[45]	P. Beatty (3rd cent.): 4:36-40; 5:15-26; 5:38—6:3, 16-25, 36-50; 7:3-15; 7:25—8:1, 10-26; 8:34—9:9, 18-31; 11:27—12:1, 5-8, 13-19, 24-28
p[84]	Leuven, University Library, and Palestine Archaeological Museum, Khirbet Mird 4, 11, 26, 27 (6th cent.): 2:2-5, 8-9; 6:30-31, 33-34, 36-37, 39-41
p[88]	P. Med. Inv. 69, 24 (4th cent.), Milano, Università Cattolica: 2:1–26

Uncial Codices or Codex Fragments

ℵ (01)	Codex Sinaiticus (4th cent.): complete
A (02)	Codex Alexandrinus (5th cent.): complete
B (03)	Codex Vaticanus (4th cent.): complete
C (04)	Codex Ephraemi rescriptus (5th cent.): 1:18–6:31; 8:6–12:29; 13:20–16:20
D (05)	Codex Bezae (5th cent.): complete; in Greek and Latin; Gospels in the "Western" order: Matthew, John, Luke, and Mark
L (019)	Codex Regius (8th cent.): 1:1—10:15; 10:31—15:1; 15:21—16:8 + shorter additional ending + 16:9-20
W (032)	Codex Washingtonianus (or Freerianus) (5th cent.): 1:1–15:12; 15:39—16:8 + 16:9-14 + Freer Logion +16:15b-20; Gospels in the "Western" order
Θ (038)	Codex Koridethi (9th cent.): complete
Ψ (044)	Codex Athous Laurae (9th–10th cent.): 9:6–16:8 + shorter additional ending + 16:9-20
059 with 0215 (parts of same MS)	(4th–5th cent.): 15:20-21, 26-27, 29-38
067	(6th cent.): 9:14-22; 14:58-70
069	(5th cent.): 10:50-51; 11:11-12
072	(5th–6th cent.): 2:23–3:5
083 with 0112 and 0235 (parts of same MS)	(6th–7th cent.): 13:12-14, 16-19, 21-24, 26-28; 14:29-45; 15:27—16:8 + shorter additional ending + 16:9-10
087 with 092b (parts of same MS)	(6th cent.): 12:32-37
099	(7th cent.): 16:6-8 + shorter additional ending + 16:9-18
0107	(7th cent.): 4:24-35; 5:14-23
0126	(8th cent.): 5:34—6:2
0130	(9th cent.): 1:31–2:16
0131	(9th cent.): 7:3, 6-8; 7:30—8:16; 9:2, 7-9
0132	(9th cent.): 5:16-40
0143	(6th cent.): 8:17-18, 27-28
0146	(8th cent.): 10:37-45
0167	(7th cent.): 4:24-29, 37-41; 6:9-11, 13-14, 37-39, 41, 45
0184	(6th cent.): 15:36-37, 40-41 in Greek; 15:29-31, 33-34 in Coptic
0187	(6th cent.): 6:30-41
0188	(4th cent.): 11:11-17
0213	(5th–6th cent.): 3:2-3, 5
0214	(4th–5th cent.): 8:33-37
0269	(9th cent.): 6:14-20
0274	(5th cent.): 6:56—7:4, 6-9, 13-17, 19-23, 28-29, 34-35; 8:3-4, 8-11; 9:20-22, 26-41; 9:43—10:1, 17-22

Important Minuscule Witnesses

f[1]	1, 118, 131, 209, 1582 et al.[3]
f[13]	13, 69, 124, 174, 230, 346, 543, 788, 826, 828, 983, 1969, 1709 et al.[4]

---

1. Metzger and Ehrman, *Text*, 53. See also the beginning of the section of this introduction on the *History of Interpretation* above.

2. p[75] (Metzger and Ehrman, *Text*, 58–59).

3. Kirsopp Lake, *Codex 1 of the Gospels and Its Allies* (Texts and Studies 7.3; Cambridge: Cambridge University Press, 1902; reprinted 1967); Metzger and Ehrman, *Text*, 86–87.

4. Kirsopp and Silvia Lake, *Family 13 (the Ferrar Group): The Text according to Mark with a Collation of Codex 18 of the Gospels* (SD 11; London: Christophers; Philadelphia: University of Pennsylvania Press, 1941); Metzger and Ehrman, *Text*, 87.

33	(9th cent.): 1:1–9:30; 11:12–13:10; 14:61–16:20[5]	q (13)	Codex Monacensis (6th–7th cent.): 1:1-6; 1:22–15:4; 15:37–16:20
2427	Archaic Mark; University of Chicago MS 972 (14th cent.?[6]): 1:1–16:20	r¹ (14)	Codex Usserianus I (7th cent.): 1:1–14:57; 15:9-31
		t (19)	Fragmenta Bernensia (5th–6th cent.): 1:2-23; 2:22-27; 3:11-18

Versions
  Old Latin

a (3)	Codex Vercellensis (4th cent.): 1:1-21; 1:35–15:14	*Syriac*	
aur (15)	Codex Aureus Holmiensis (7th cent.): complete	syˢ	Syrus Sinaiticus (4th–5th cent.): 1:12b-44a; 2:21–4:17; 5:1-26a; 6:5b–16:8
b (4)	Codex Veronensis (5th cent.): 1:1–13:10, 17-26; 14:25-55	syᶜ	Syrus Curetonianus (5th cent.): 16:17b-20
c (6)	Codex Colbertinus (12–13th cent.): complete	syᵖ	Peshitta (5th–6th cent.): complete
		syᵖʰ	Philoxeniana (Monophysite) (6th cent.): complete
d (5)	Codex Cantabrigiensis = Codex Bezae (D) (5th cent.): 1:1–16:5	syʰ	Harklensis (7th cent.): complete
		syᵖᵃˡ ᵐˢ	Codex Climaci rescriptus (6th cent.): 1:1-10, 20b-30a; 2:2b-11, 18b-24; 15:16-19
e (2)	Codex Palatinus (5th cent.): 1:21–4:7; 4:20–6:9; 12:38-39; 13:25-26, 34-35		
f (10)	Codex Brixianus (6th cent.): 1:1–12:4; 13:33–14:52; 14:63-69	*Coptic*	
ff² (8)	Codex Corbeiensis II (5th cent.): complete	sa	Sahidic dialect
g¹ (7)	Codex Sangermanensis I (8th–9th cent.): complete	P. Palau Rib. Inv.-Nr. 182 with variants of M 569	(5th cent.): complete; ends with 16:8[7]
i (17)	Codex Vindobonensis (5th cent.): 2:17–3:29; 4:4–10:1; 10:33–14:36; 15:33-40	bo	Bohairic dialect
k (1)	Codex Bobiensis (4th–5th cent.): 8:8-11, 14-16; 8:19–16:8 + shorter additional ending		
l (11)	Codex Rhedigeranus (7th–8th cent.): complete		
n (16)	Codex Sangallensis, St. Gall, Stiftsbibliothek 1394 II (5th cent.): 7:13-31; 8:32–9:10; 13:2-20; 15:22–16:13		
o (16)	Codex Sangallensis, St. Gall, Stiftsbibliothek 1394 III (7th cent.): 16:14-20		

Older scholarship used to classify p⁴⁵, the earliest papyrus text of Mark, as belonging to what was considered a well-defined text-type, the "Caesarean." More recent scholarship has determined that this papypus manuscript is neither "Caesarean" nor "pre-Caesarean" in Mark. It "has no significant connections with its previously regarded 'Caesarean' fellow-members, chief among which were Codex Koridethi (Θ) and minuscule 565." p⁴⁵ does, however, have significant connections with Codex Washingtonianus (W) in Mark 5:31–16:20.[8] Thus, it is more appropriate to consider p⁴⁵ and W as constituting their own group, "with further developments evident in

---

5   Metzger and Ehrman, *Text*, 87–88.
6   See the discussion of this MS below.
7   Hans Quecke, ed., *Das Markusevangelium saïdisch: Text der Handschrift PPalau Rib. Inv.-Nr. 182 mit den Varianten der Handschrift M569* (Papyrologica Castroctaviana, Studia et textus 4; Barcelona: Papyrologica Castroctaviana, 1972); Metzger and Ehrman, *Text*, 112–13.
8   W "is a classic example of block mixture." See Eldon Jay Epp, "The Significance of the Papyri for Determining the Nature of the New Testament Text in the

Second Century: A Dynamic View of Textual Transmission," in William L. Petersen, ed., *Gospel Traditions in the Second Century: Origins, Recensions, Text, and Transmission* (CJA 3; Notre Dame, IN: University of Notre Dame Press, 1989) 71–103, esp. 97; reprinted in idem and Gordon D. Fee, *Studies in the Theory and Method of New Testament Textual Criticism* (SD 45; Grand Rapids: Eerdmans, 1993) 274–97.

f^{13}."[9] This group may be identified as the "C" text-group, for convenience and because their text is midway between the "B" group, represented by Codex Vaticanus (B), and the "D" group, the kind of text found in $\mathfrak{p}^{29}$, $\mathfrak{p}^{48}$, and $\mathfrak{p}^{38}$, which is found in a later form in Codex Bezae (D).[10]

$\mathfrak{p}^{84}$ belongs to the "A" text-group, "variously called the Majority text, or the Koine, or the later Byzantine."[11] The "A" may suggest the "average," "accepted" or "ascendent" text, or recall Codex Alexandrinus, which (only in the Gospels) is the oldest representative of the group.[12]

Aland and Aland assigned $\mathfrak{p}^{88}$ to their "Category III," which they define as follows:

> Manuscripts with a small but not a negligible proportion of early readings, with a considerable encroachment of polished readings (a relatively strong Byzantine influence), and significant readings from other sources as yet undefined.[13]

The uncial manuscript 059 (with 0215) is also assigned to category III.[14] MS 067 is assigned to category III, but with influence from category V, that is, from a purely or predominantly Byzantine text.[15]

Codex Sinaiticus and Codex Vaticanus belong to text-group "B," which, in older scholarship, was called the "neutral text" and is still often called the "Alexandrian text."[16] Both of these manuscripts end with 16:8. The Old Syriac manuscript Sinaiticus (sy^s) and the Sahidic Coptic manuscript P. Palau Rib. Inv.-Nr. 182 also end with 16:8.[17] The minuscules of Family 1 contain a note indicating that some manuscripts end with 16:8, but some contain also 16:9-20.[18]

Codex Ephraemi is a mixed, composite manuscript.[19] Codex Regius (L) is an eighth-century representative of the "B" text-group.[20] This MS is interesting with regard to the ending of Mark. It conflates the shorter additional ending and the longer additional ending.[21] Codex Koridethi (Θ) is a MS of the Gospels that is "Byzantine" in Matthew, Luke, and John, but in Mark is "akin to the type of text that Origen and Eusebius used in the third and fourth centuries at Caesarea."[22] Like Codex Regius, Codex Athous Laurae (Ψ) contains both the shorter and the longer additional endings.[23]

The minuscule manuscripts identified by Kirsopp Lake as belonging to what he called Family 1 date from the twelfth century to the fourteenth. In Mark they often

9   Ibid.

10   Ibid., 87–88.

11   Ibid., 87, 100.

12   Ibid., 87; on "Byzantine Text," see also Metzger and Ehrman, *Text*, 279–80.

13   Kurt Aland and Barbara Aland, *The Text of the New Testament* (2nd rev. ed.; Grand Rapids: Eerdmans; Leiden: Brill, 1989; German 2nd rev. ed., 1981) 235; cf. 102 on $\mathfrak{p}^{88}$.

14   Ibid., 119; so also MSS 069 (ibid.), 072 (ibid., 120), 0107 (ibid., 121), 0126, 0131, 0143 (ibid., 122), 0146, 0167 (ibid., 123), 0187 (ibid., 124), 0213 and 0214 (ibid., 125). MS 0188 is also assigned to category III, but with the comment that it has "many singular readings" (ibid., 124).

15   Ibid., 119, 336. MSS 0130, 0132, and 0269 are similarly described (ibid., 122, 127).

16   Epp uses the term "textual group 'B'" ("Dynamic View," 87, with reference to Vaticanus; p. 102, with reference to Sinaiticus). On the term "neutral," see ibid., 85. On the "Alexandrian text," see Metzger and Ehrman, *Text*, 277–78.

17   Bruce Metzger, *The Early Versions of the New Testament: Their Origin, Transmission, and Limitations* (Oxford: Clarendon, 1977) 42, 11; Quecke, *Das Markusevangelium*, 179. The Sahidic MS M 569, however,

ends with 16:9-20; Quecke, Appendix I (p. 181). For an edition of M 569, see Gonzalo Aranda Pérez, *El Evangelio de San Marcos en Copto Sahídico (Texto de M 569 y Aparato Crítico)* (Consejo Superior de Investigaciones Científicas: Textos y Estudios "Cardenal Cisneros" 45; Madrid: Instituto de Filología, 1988).

18   See the section "Attestation of the Longer (Additional) Ending" in the commentary on 16:9-20 below.

19   Epp, "Dynamic View," 102; Metzger and Ehrman, *Text*, 69–70.

20   Epp, "Dynamic View," 96. Aland and Aland classify L, Θ, 087 (with 092b), 0184, and 0274 as belonging to category II, i.e., MSS with "a considerable proportion" of early readings, but "marked by alien influences" (pp. 120, 124, 127, 335).

21   See the comment on the shorter (additional) ending in the commentary on 16:9-20 below. See also Metzger and Ehrman, *Text*, 77.

22   Metzger and Ehrman, *Text*, 83.

23   See the commentary on 16:9-20 below; its text of Mark is an early one (Metzger and Ehrman, *Text*, 84–85). MS 083 (with 0112 and 0235) and 099 also attest both additional endings (Aland and Aland, 120–21).

agree with Codex Koridethi (Θ). These readings may go back to the third and fourth centuries in Caesarea.[24] As noted above, f^{13} is related to the same text-group as p[45], namely, the "C" group.[25] The manuscripts of Family 13 "were copied between the eleventh and fifteenth centuries and are descendants of an archetype that came either from Calabria in southern Italy or from Sicily."[26]

The minuscule manuscript 33 (ninth cent.) contains the entire NT except the book of Revelation. It is related to the "B" text-group.[27]

The minuscule 2427 is an illuminated miniature manuscript "smaller in dimension than a Loeb Classical Library volume."[28] "The precise history" of the manuscript "cannot at present be traced back before 1917, when it was found among the possessions of Mr. John Askitopoulos, an Athenian collector and dealer of antiquities, after his death in that year."[29] It was acquired by the University of Chicago at some point between 1935 and 1941.[30] It contains "the full text of a single document, the Gospel of Mark." One "bifolium (12r-v and 13r-v)" is transposed with the result that 5:38—6:9 follow 5:19a and 5:19b-38 follow 6:9. There is no "critical apparatus (canon tables, page headings, marginal textual notes, etc.)," but it does contain "gilt marginal initials," "a vividly colored brocade at the incipit (fol. 2r)," and sixteen "color illuminations of narrative scenes" "set roughly into their places within the text" "and an author portrait of the evangelist on the verso facing the incipit (1v)." Only the portrait of the evangelist and the illustration of the crucifixion occupy a full page, respectively. Since "the four-fold gospel book is the customary format for gospel codices since late antiquity" and if the codex was "originally planned just to contain Mark, the choice of only one gospel—and Mark, at that—is most curious."[31]

Manuscript 2427 has "an extraordinary degree of correspondence with" Codex Vaticanus (B). It departs from B in having the longer (additional) ending (16:9-20), although it does have a small mark (defined by Margaret M. Mitchell and Patricia A. Duncan as a lozenge) at the end of 16:8.[32] Folio 44 is now scored, but blank. Traces of letters indicate that the manuscript may once have had a colophon. Without a colophon, dating depends on the physical characteristics of the codex, the orthography, and the textual character and iconography of the manuscript. Assessments of the date have ranged from the thirteenth century to the twentieth. Kirsopp Lake and Hermann von Soden dated the manuscript early on the basis of their paleographic judgments. Others have thought the correspondence with Codex Vaticanus to be "too good to be true" and thus to depend on some modern edition of the text. In this case it would be a forgery of the nineteenth or twentieth century.[33] The orthography is "not at all the usual Byzantine book hand" and combines ancient and modern features.[34] A multiauthored article that applies chemical analysis to art-historical questions concludes that "the miniatures [of MS 2427] are based on the cycle in a late 12th-century gospel book in the National Library in Athens, codex 93 [MS 777]."[35] Analysis of the pigmentation of the miniatures led to the conclusion that "[t]he ubiquitousness of an iron blue in [MS 2427] raises doubts about the authenticity of this manuscript." The blue pigment in question was

24   Metzger and Ehrman, *Text*, 86–87.
25   Epp, "Dynamic View," 97.
26   Metzger and Ehrman, *Text*, 87.
27   Epp, "Dynamic View," 96–97; Metzger and Ehrman, *Text*, 87–88.
28   Margaret M. Mitchell and Patricia A. Duncan, "Chicago's 'Archaic Mark' (MS 2427): A Reintroduction to Its Enigmas and a Fresh Collation of Its Readings," *NovT* 48 (2006) 1–35; quotation from 1. The manuscript may be viewed online at http://goodspeed.lib.uchicago.edu.
29   Ibid., 3.
30   Ibid., 3 and n. 9.
31   Ibid., 4–5.
32   Ibid.
33   Ibid., 6.
34   Ibid., 9-10.
35   Mary Virginia Orna, Patricia L. Lang, J. E. Katon, Thomas F. Mathews, and Robert S. Nelson, "Applications of Infrared Microspectroscopy to Art Historical Questions about Medieval Manuscripts," in Ralph O. Allen, ed., *Archaeological Chemistry IV* (Advances in Chemistry Series 220; Washington, DC: American Chemical Society, 1989) 265–88; quotation from 270; cf. Mitchell and Duncan, "Chicago's 'Archaic Mark,'" 13 n. 44.

identified as "an iron blue" or "Prussian blue" that "was made by the Berlin color maker Diesbach in or around 1704. Moreover, according to Gettens and Stout, the material is so complex in composition and method of manufacture that there is practically no possibility that it was invented independently in other times or places."[36] The results of the chemical analysis "in addition to the evidence indicating that both the Archaic Mark and the Leningrad gospel fragment [MS 2357] were copies of the Athens codex 93 [MS 777]" suggested that "their origin may very well be during the flurry of Athenian forgeries that came to the market in the 1920s."[37] Mitchell and Duncan argue that "much more work needs to be done"[38] on the provenance of MS 2427.

Stephen C. Carlson had already noticed that a line from Mark 8:11 appeared to have been omitted from 2427. Following Paul Maas, he realized that line omissions in a manuscript provide important evidence about the manuscript's exemplar, that is, the text that its scribe copied. He checked a facsimile of Codex Vaticanus and found that its line breaks could not explain the omission that he had found.[39] After Mitchell and Duncan had published their collation of 2427, he noticed two other possible line omissions at Mark 6:2 and 14:14.[40] He eventually discovered a printed text that had line breaks that corresponded to those of MS 2427. This text is Philipp Buttmann's 1860 edition of the New Testament for the Teubner classical library, based primarily on Codex Vaticanus.[41]

Carlson noted that MS 2427 is closer to Codex Vaticanus than any other minuscule. It preserves many of its singular readings, yet avoids some of its errors. This data, in addition to the matching line breaks, led him to conclude that the exemplar or model of 2427 was Buttmann's 1860 edition of the NT or one of its reprints. The latter edition was based on inaccurate collations of B and preceded by just a few years Tischendorf's most accurate transcription of B.[42] Buttmann's edition departs from B in seventy places. 2427 follows Buttmann in each of these cases except those in which 2427 has its own error. After a detailed analysis of the character of the text of 2427, Carlson concluded that the scribe was concerned with appearances and had little regard for the proper text-type. He thus concluded that the manuscript was produced as an art forgery. Carlson also discovered that the 1871, 1882, and 1910 publications of Buttmann's edition are in Athenian libraries, whereas none of these can be found in the library of the University of Chicago or in Claremont. These data help to explain why the forgery was not detected earlier.[43] Given the likelihood that 2427 is a forgery, it has been cited sparingly in this commentary.

The Old Latin versions have clear affinities with the "Western" text-type. "On the whole, the African form of the Old Latin presents the larger divergences from the generally received text [the "A" text-type], and the European the smaller." The text of the Old Latin was not fixed, and scribes exercised considerable freedom in incorporating traditions known to them.[44] Codex Bobiensis (k) is the only manuscript that attests the shorter additional ending without the longer additional ending. Although the longer additional ending was at some point added to Codex Vercellensis (a), there is evidence that, originally, it contained (like k) only the shorter additional ending.[45]

36 Orna et al., "Applications," 275; cf. Mitchell and Duncan, "Chicago's 'Archaic Mark,'" 7 n. 23.

37 Orna et al., 275–78 (table intervening); cf. Mitchell and Duncan, "Chicago's 'Archaic Mark,'" 10–11, 13 n. 44.

38 Mitchell and Duncan, "Chicago's 'Archaic Mark,'" 15.

39 Paul Maas, *Textual Criticism* (Oxford: Clarendon, 1958) 4; Stephen C. Carlson, "'Archaic Mark' (MS 2427) and the Finding of a Manuscript Fake," *SBL Forum* (an online publication available at http://www.sbl-site.org), fourth paragraph and n. 2. On November 1, 2006, Carlson's article was available at http://www.sbl-site.org/Article.aspx?ArticleId=577.

40 Carlson, "'Archaic Mark,'" par. 5.

41 Ibid., par. 6.

42 Ibid. and Stephen C. Carlson, "The Nineteenth Century Exemplar of Archaic Mark," a presentation made in the New Testament Textual Criticism section at the annual meeting of the Society of Biblical Literature on November 21, 2006, in Washington, DC.

43 Carlson, "Nineteenth Century Exemplar."

44 Metzger, *Early Versions*, 325.

45 Kurt Aland, "Bemerkungen zum Schluss des Markusevangeliums," in E. Earle Ellis and Max Wilcox, eds., *Neotestamentica et Semitica: Studies in Honour of Matthew Black* (Edinburgh: T & T Clark, 1969) 176–77.

The Old Syriac manuscripts (sy[s] and sy[c]) belong to the "D" group, referred to as the "Western" text-type by Metzger, who notes that they preserve "many typically Alexandrian readings."[46] The Peshitta (s[p]) text of Mark has no strong connection to "the Neutral, Caesarean, or Western" text-types. It is dependent on the Old Syriac and agrees with the "A" text-type ("Koine") about half the time. When it differs from the "A" text-type, it agrees 29.1 percent of the time with the Old Latin.[47]

The Sahidic Coptic version of the Gospels is connected to the "B" text-type, being closer to Codex Vaticanus than to Codex Sinaiticus. It also preserves some "Western" readings, but lacks the longer additions typical of Codex Bezae.[48] The Bohairic Coptic version is also connected to the "B" text-type, especially to the text preserved by Codex Regius (L). In the Synoptic Gospels, it is closer to Sinaiticus than to Vaticanus. The Bohairic Gospels in their later forms were revised in accordance with the "Byzantine type" of text.[49]

It is difficult to know what changes the text of Mark underwent from the time of composition until the third century, when its textual attestation begins.[50] From the third century onward, many details of the text of Mark were remarkably fluid, such as the tenses of the verbs.[51] The major elements of the text, however, seem to have been well transmitted and preserved, with the exception of the beginning and especially the ending of the Gospel. In the opening titular sentence, manuscripts are divided as to whether the words υἱοῦ θεοῦ ("Son of God") should be included after Ἰησοῦ Χριστοῦ ("Jesus Christ" or "Jesus Messiah"). The following lack the words υἱοῦ θεοῦ ("Son of God"): Codex Sinaiticus, as originally written; Codex Koridethi (Θ); MS 28 as corrected; MS 1555, as originally written; Codex Climaci rescriptus (sy[pal ms]); a number of Armenian manuscripts; a Sahidic manuscript (no. 182 in the Palau-Ribes collection) and references to the passage in Origen, Serapion, and Cyril of Jerusalem.[52] J. K. Elliott has argued that 1:1-3 is a later addition to the Gospel.[53] N. Clayton Croy has argued that 1:1 is secondary and that the original beginning of the Gospel (the length of which cannot be known) has been lost.[54]

As noted above, Codex Sinaiticus, Codex Vaticanus, the Old Syriac manuscript Sinaiticus (sy[s]), and the Sahidic Coptic manuscript P. Palau Rib. Inv.-Nr. 182 end with 16:8. Other manuscripts have one or more additional endings.[55] Although the majority of scholars today conclude that the Gospel originally ended with 16:8, Croy has recently revived the argument that the original ending of Mark has been lost.[56] The positions taken in this commentary are that the beginning of Mark has been reliably preserved, that the words υἱοῦ θεοῦ ("Son of God") are not original, and that the Gospel originally ended with 16:8.

---

46 Metzger, *Early Versions*, 43; Metzger and Ehrman, *Texts*, 97. See above on the ending of sy[s].

47 Metzger, *Early Versions*, 61–62.

48 Ibid., 134.

49 Ibid., 137–38.

50 For an imaginative reconstruction of the early history of Mark's text, see Koester, "History and Development."

51 See the notes to the trans. of Mark below.

52 See Adela Yarbro Collins, "Establishing the Text: Mark 1:1," in Tord Fornberg and David Hellholm, eds., *Texts and Contexts: The Function of Biblical Texts in Their Textual and Situative Contexts* (Oslo: Scandinavian University Press, 1995) 111–27, esp. 112, and the commentary on 1:1 below.

53 J. K. Elliott, "Mark 1.1-3—A Later Addition to the Gospel?" *NTS* 46 (2000) 584–85.

54 N. Clayton Croy, *The Mutilation of Mark's Gospel* (Nashville: Abingdon, 2003) 113–36.

55 See above and the commentary on 16:9-20 below.

56 Croy, *Mutilation*, 45–71, 137–63.

Commentary

Title of the Gospel

(The good news) according to Mark[a]	a	Most MSS have the title "(The) good news according to Mark" (εὐαγγέλιον κατὰ Μᾶρκον). A few, including ℵ and B, have a shorter reading, "according to Mark" (κατὰ Μᾶρκον). The antiquity of the longer reading is supported by the few fragments of papyrus manuscripts that preserve the titles of John, Luke, and Matthew and by the old Latin and the Coptic translations. For the priority of the shorter title, nevertheless, see Comment.

Comment

A few manuscripts, including Sinaiticus, Vaticanus, and Codex Boreelianus (F[e] 09), have a short form of the title or *inscriptio*, namely, "according to Mark" (κατὰ Μᾶρκον). Most of the rest of the MSS have a slightly longer form, "(the) good news according to Mark" (εὐαγγέλιον κατὰ Μᾶρκον). Martin Hengel has argued that the shorter reading is probably an abbreviation of the standard title.[1] He is probably right with regard to the particular manuscripts that have the shorter reading. But this conclusion does not necessarily imply that the longer title goes back to the autograph, that is, to the author of Mark in its present form. One reason for this conclusion is that, in ancient book pro-duction and publication, the title belonged more to the stage of reception than to that of production.[2] It is unlikely, however, that the Gospels were issued anonymously.[3] Those who made copies of Mark for other communities probably knew who the author was and communicated this information along with the work in some kind of title or label, or at least by word of mouth.[4]

James A. Kelhoffer has shown that the *Didache*, *2 Clement*, and Marcion himself already presuppose the use of the term εὐαγγέλιον ("good news" or "gospel") for "written 'Gospel' materials."[5] Although the term "good news" or "gospel" originally meant the Christian message and its oral proclamation, Marcion was probably not an innovator in using it to indicate a written document.[6]

1   Hengel, *Die Evangelienüberschriften,* 11–12; ET *Studies in Mark,* 66–67.
2   Carl Werner Müller, review of Egidius Schmalzriedt, Περὶ Φύσεως: *Zur Frühgeschichte der Buchtitel,* in *Gnomon* 50 (1978) 628–38, esp. 628–29.
3   Contra Gamble, *Books and Readers,* 153–54.
4   Helmut Koester allows that "Hengel's claim that the canonical Gospels must have circulated from the very beginning under the name of specific authors may be correct" (*Gospels,* 26–27).
5   James A. Kelhoffer, "'How Soon a Book' Revisited: ΕΥΑΓΓΕΛΙΟΝ as a Reference to 'Gospel' Materials in the First Half of the Second Century," *ZNW* 95 (2004) 1–34; quotation from 34.
6   Contra Koester, *Gospels,* 4–7, 35–37.

1/	**The beginning of the good news of Jesus Christ.**[a]

a The reading $\upsilon\grave{\iota}o\hat{\upsilon}\ \vartheta\epsilon o\hat{\upsilon}$, "Son of God" ($\aleph^1$ B D L *pc* latt sy co; Ir[lat], but $\tau o\hat{\upsilon}\ \vartheta\epsilon o\hat{\upsilon}$ A $f^{1.13}$ 𝔐), is most likely secondary, because an accidental omission in the opening words of a work is unlikely. The shorter reading has early, extensive, and independent attestation; it is easier to understand why some copyists would add this phrase than why some would omit it. See Adela Yarbro Collins, "Establishing the Text: Mark 1:1," in Tord Fornberg and David Hellholm, eds., *Texts and Contexts: The Function of Biblical Texts in Their Textual and Situational Contexts* (Oslo: Scandinavian University Press, 1995) 111–27; Bart Ehrman, "The Text of Mark in the Hands of the Orthodox," in Mark Burrows and Paul Rorem, eds., *Biblical Hermeneutics in Historical Perspective: Essays in Honor of Karlfried Froehlich* (Grand Rapids: Eerdmans, 1991) 19–31; reprinted, *LQ* 5 (1991) 143–56; Ehrman, *The Orthodox Corruption of Scripture: The Effect of Early Christological Controversies on the Text of the New Testament* (New York/Oxford: Oxford University Press, 1993), 72–75; Peter M. Head, "A Text-Critical Study of Mark 1.1: 'The Beginning of the Gospel of Jesus Christ,'" *NTS* 37 (1991) 621–29.

Comment

■ **1** Mark 1:1 is an independent sentence, without a predicate, which both summarizes and introduces the rest of the work, that is, Mark 1:2—16:8.[1] In these opening words, the author seems to presuppose that the audience is familiar with the phrase "good news of Jesus Christ" ($\epsilon\grave{\upsilon}\alpha\gamma\gamma\acute{\epsilon}\lambda\iota o\nu\ \text{'}I\eta\sigma o\hat{\upsilon}\ X\rho\iota\sigma\tau o\hat{\upsilon}$).[2] The earliest evidence we have for the Christian use of the noun $\epsilon\grave{\upsilon}\alpha\gamma\gamma\acute{\epsilon}\lambda\iota o\nu$ ("good news") is its appearance in the letters of Paul to designate the message of the early Christian missionaries and its oral proclamation.[3] It would seem, then, that the introductory sentence summarizes the content of the work as an account of how the early Christian proclamation about Jesus originated.[4] On the one hand, the author took up the familiar meaning of the term $\epsilon\grave{\upsilon}\alpha\gamma\gamma\acute{\epsilon}\lambda\iota o\nu$ ("good news") as the oral announcement and explanation of the salvific significance of the life and work of Jesus, especially his death and resurrection. On the other, he used the word in a new way, to refer to

1 Eve-Marie Becker has argued that the concept of the "beginning" ($\grave{\alpha}\rho\chi\acute{\eta}$) in Mark 1:1 is polyvalent: it is the beginning of a book, the title of the book, and the beginning of the description of a series of events (*Markus-Evangelium*, 112).

2 On the origin of the Christian usage of $\epsilon\grave{\upsilon}\alpha\gamma\gamma\acute{\epsilon}\lambda\iota o\nu$ ("good news" or "gospel") as a technical term, see Helmut Koester, "The Origin of the Term 'Gospel,'" in *Gospels*, 1–4, who argues that the early Christian usage was influenced by the use of the plural form of this noun in relation to Roman imperial propaganda, especially in connection with the benefactions of Augustus. Hubert Frankemölle concludes that the Christian use of the singular noun is semantically unique, but that it was inspired by the use of the related verb in Deutero-Isaiah (*Evangelium–Begriff und Gattung*, 253–54); similarly, Peter

Stuhlmacher, *Das paulinische Evangelium: I. Vorgeschichte* (FRLANT 95; Göttingen: Vandenhoeck & Ruprecht, 1968) 286–89. Graham N. Stanton argues that "the imperial cult was not *the source* of early Christian use of the word group, but it was *the background* against which distinctively Christian usage was forged and first heard" (*Jesus and Gospel* [Cambridge: Cambridge University Press, 2004] 2 [emphasis his]).

3 See Koester, "The Use of the Term 'Gospel' in the Pauline Tradition," in *Gospels*, 4–9, esp. 4–7. See also the commentary on 14:9 below.

4 According to Loveday Alexander, the earliest Greek historians, like early writers in other fields, used the opening words of the first sentence to indicate the subject of their work (*The Preface to Luke's Gospel: Literary Convention and Social Context in Luke 1:1-4 and*

the content of a written work, in particular a narrative closely related to historical events of an eschatological nature.[5]

In this opening, Mark differs from the older historical and narrative books of scripture, most of which begin directly with an account of action, usually with a finite verb. The quasi-autobiographical book of Nehemiah is an exception; it opens with the sentence "The words of Nehemiah, son of Hacaliah" ($\Lambda \acute{o} \gamma o \iota \ N \epsilon \epsilon \mu \iota \alpha \ \upsilon \acute{\iota} o \upsilon \ A \chi \alpha \lambda \iota \alpha$).[6] Another exception is the book of Tobit, which begins "(The) book of the words of Tobit, the son of Tobiel . . ." ($B \acute{\iota} \beta \lambda o \varsigma \ \lambda \acute{o} \gamma \omega \nu \ T \omega \beta \iota \tau \ \tau o \hat{\upsilon} \ T \omega \beta \iota \eta \lambda \ . . .$). The use of such an introductory sentence is typical of the older wisdom books and the prophetic books (Prov 1:1; Eccl 1:1; Cant 1:1; Hos 1:2a LXX).[7]

The book of Hosea has two introductory, titular sentences. The first characterizes the content of the work as "(The) word of the Lord" ($\Lambda \acute{o} \gamma o \varsigma \ \kappa \upsilon \rho \acute{\iota} o \upsilon$). It also mentions Hosea as the recipient of God's word, gives the name of his father, and specifies the time of the reception in terms of the kings of Judah and Israel (1:1). The second sentence is shorter and more like that of Mark in wording: "(The) beginning of the word of the Lord to Hosea" ($A \rho \chi \grave{\eta} \ \lambda \acute{o} \gamma o \upsilon \ \kappa \upsilon \rho \acute{\iota} o \upsilon \ \pi \rho \grave{o} \varsigma \ \Omega \sigma \eta \epsilon$) (1:2a). In this context, the word "beginning" ($\grave{\alpha} \rho \chi \acute{\eta}$) seems to mean that the oracle that follows was the first one spoken to the prophet by God. The word seems to have a more complex function in Mark, since what follows immediately is a quotation from scripture. On the one hand, the events recounted in the entire work constitute only "the beginning" of the good news. The narrative as a whole is open-ended, and important predictions and promises remain unfulfilled when the account ends. On the other hand, the account of the life and work of Jesus, which constitutes the beginning and cause of the proclamation of the good news, must also have a particular beginning. Thus, Mark 1:1 also introduces the first unit of the text, Mark 1:2-15, which introduces the rest.[8]

As argued in the note to the translation above, the only epithet given to Jesus in this titular, introductory sentence is "Christ," meaning "anointed one" or "messiah." The lack of an article may be taken as support for the argument that "Christ" has become a proper name and has lost its messianic connotations. But the response of Peter in 8:29, "You are the messiah" ($\Sigma \grave{\upsilon} \ \epsilon \hat{\iota} \ \acute{o} \ X \rho \iota \sigma \tau \acute{o} \varsigma$), makes clear that the messianic connotations of the epi-

---

Acts 1:1 [SNTSMS 78; Cambridge: Cambridge University Press, 1993] 29, with reference to E. Herkommer, "Die Topoi in der Proömien der römischen Geschichtswerke," [Diss., Tübingen, 1968], and numerous primary texts). James K. Elliott has argued that the phrase "good news/gospel of Jesus Christ" is exceptional in Mark, in terms of both usage and meaning; for this reason, among others, he concludes that 1:1-3 is a later addition to the Gospel ("Mark 1.1-3—A Later Addition to the Gospel?" *NTS* 46 [2000] 584–88, esp. 584–85). But, as argued above, the author probably used the phrase here in a traditional way in order to reinterpret the notion of "gospel" for the intended audience.

5   John P. Dickson has argued that both the noun and the verb consistently and cross-culturally have the connotation of expressing something that is "news" to the audience ("Gospel as News: $\epsilon \upsilon \alpha \gamma \gamma \epsilon \lambda$- from Aristophanes to the Apostle Paul," *NTS* 51 [2005] 212–30; see 220 on the Synoptic Gospels). For an argument that $\epsilon \upsilon \alpha \gamma \gamma \acute{\epsilon} \lambda \iota o \nu$ ("good news") in Mark 1:1 has a literary meaning, see Detlev Dormeyer, "Die Kompositionsmetapher 'Evangelium Jesu Christi, des Sohnes Gottes' Mark 1.1: Ihre theologische und literarische Aufgabe in der Jesus-Biographie des Markus," *NTS* 33 (1987) 452–68. On the relation of Mark to historiography, see the section on *Genre* in the introduction to the commentary above.

6   In spite of this independent, introductory titular sentence, however, Nehemiah is not a separate book in the MSS of the LXX, but constitutes chaps. 11–23 of 2 Esdras; that is, it is the continuation of the canonical book of Ezra.

7   Ernst Lohmeyer, *Das Evangelium des Markus* (MeyerK I.2: Göttingen: Vandenhoeck & Ruprecht, 1937; 17th ed. 1967) 10. For further examples, see W. D. Davies and Dale C. Allison, Jr., *A Critical and Exegetical Commentary on the Gospel according to Saint Matthew* (3 vols.; Edinburgh T & T Clark, 1988, 1991, 1997) 1:151–52. In addition to those cited by Lohmeyer and Davies and Allison, see Isa 1:1; Jer 1:1; Obad 1:1a; Hab 1:1; Zeph 1:1; and Mal 1:1 (1:1a LXX).

8   Elliott has argued that "(the) beginning" in 1:1 simply signals that "here now is the start of the account of Jesus Christ's ministry" ("Mark 1.1-3," 585).

thet are deliberately evoked by the narrative of Mark.[9] Elliott has pointed out that the phrase "Jesus Christ" appears only here in Mark and concludes from this feature, among others, that 1:1-3 is a later addition to the Gospel.[10] It is to be expected, however, that the author would depart from his normal narrative usage in fashioning a suitable opening for the work as a whole.[11]

---

9   For further discussion, see the section *Jesus as Messiah* in the Introduction above. Hengel has shown that Paul used the term χριστός ("Christ" or "Messiah") with the sense "Messiah" and not only as a proper name for Jesus ("Jesus, the Messiah of Israel," in idem, *Studies in Early Christology* [Edinburgh: T & T Clark, 1995] 1–72, esp. 1–7).

10   Elliott, "Mark 1.1-3," 584.

11   Contra ibid., 586.

1

1:2-15 Narrative Introduction: The Beginning of the End as Fulfillment of Prophecy

2/ As it is written in the book of Isaiah the prophet,[a] "See, I am sending my messenger before your[b] face, who will prepare your way; 3/ the voice of one calling out in the wilderness, 'Prepare the way of the Lord, make straight his paths,'" 4/ [so] John was baptizing in the wilderness and proclaiming a baptism of repentance for the forgiveness of sins.[c] 5/ And the whole district of Judea and all the inhabitants of Jerusalem were going out to him and were being baptized by him in the Jordan River, confessing their sins. 6/ And John was wearing (a garment of) camel's hair[d] and a leather belt around his waist,[e] and eating grasshoppers and wild honey. 7/ And he was proclaiming, saying, "The one who is stronger than I is coming after me; I am not fit to crouch[f] and untie the strap of his sandals. 8/ I have baptized you with water, but he will baptize you in (the) Holy Spirit."[g]

9/ And in those days, Jesus came from Nazareth in Galilee and was baptized in the Jordan by John. 10/ And immediately, while he was coming up out of the water, he saw the heavens split and the Spirit coming down (in)to him[h] like a dove. 11/ And a voice came[i] from the heavens, "You are my beloved son; I take delight in you."

12/ And immediately the Spirit drove him out into the wilderness. 13/ And he was in the wilderness forty days, being put to the test by Satan. And he was with the wild animals, and the angels were serving him.

14/ After[j] John was handed over, Jesus went into Galilee, proclaiming the good news of God[k] 15/ and saying, "The time is fulfilled and the kingdom of God has drawn near; repent and trust in the good news."

a   The reading "the prophets" ($\tau o\hat{\iota}\varsigma\ \pi\rho o\varphi\acute{\eta}\tau\alpha\iota\varsigma$) (A W $f^{1.13}$ 𝔐 sy[h] bo[mss]) is a correction of "Isaiah the prophet," since parts of the following quotation come from Exodus and Malachi rather than from Isaiah.

b   Singular ($\sigma o\upsilon$).

c   The reading $\dot{o}\ \beta\alpha\pi\tau\acute{\iota}\zeta\omega\nu$ ("the baptizer") in B 33 et al. is probably secondary, since the addition of the article may be due to the use of this epithet of John elsewhere in Mark (6:14, 24) or to the use of the similar sobriquet $\dot{o}\ \beta\alpha\pi\tau\iota\sigma\tau\acute{\eta}\varsigma$ ("the Baptist") in the Synoptic Gospels (Matt 3:1; 11:11, 12; 14:2, 8; 16:14; 17:13; Mark 6:25; 8:28; Luke 7:20, 33; 9:19). The omission of $\kappa\alpha\acute{\iota}$ ("and") in the same MSS is probably a correction that was needed once the article was added, since $\dot{o}\ \beta\alpha\pi\tau\acute{\iota}\zeta\omega\nu$ ("the baptizer") was taken as a title. The placement of $\dot{\epsilon}\nu\ \tau\hat{\eta}\ \dot{\epsilon}\rho\acute{\eta}\mu\omega$ ("in the wilderness") before $\beta\alpha\pi\tau\acute{\iota}\zeta\omega\nu$ ("baptizing") in D Θ et al. may be due to an effort to emphasize the wilderness in order to bring out more clearly the fulfillment of prophecy.

d   Codex Bezae (D) and a fourth-century Old Latin manuscript (a) support the reading $\delta\acute{\epsilon}\rho\rho\iota\nu$ ("skin" or "garment of leather") instead of $\tau\rho\acute{\iota}\chi\alpha\varsigma$ ("hair").

e   D and the majority of the Old Latin manuscripts (it) lack $\kappa\alpha\grave{\iota}\ \zeta\acute{\omega}\nu\eta\nu\ \delta\epsilon\rho\mu\alpha\tau\acute{\iota}\nu\eta\nu\ \pi\epsilon\rho\grave{\iota}\ \tau\grave{\eta}\nu\ \dot{o}\sigma\varphi\grave{\upsilon}\nu\ \alpha\dot{\upsilon}\tau o\hat{\upsilon}$ ("and a leather belt around his waist") or its equivalent. Since this family of texts tends to be expansive, it is possible that these words constitute a secondary addition to the text, a so-called Western non-interpolation. On the other hand, these words associate John with Elijah (cf. 2 Kgs 1:8), an association that is implied elsewhere in Mark (9:11-13).

f   A number of MSS (D Θ f^{13} et al.) lack $\kappa\acute{\upsilon}\psi\alpha\varsigma$ ("to crouch"; lit., "having crouched"). This lack is probably due to the omission of the word under the influence of the parallel passages (Luke 3:16; John 1:27; Acts 13:25).

g   The MSS are divided on whether the two nouns $\ddot{\upsilon}\delta\alpha\tau\iota$ ("water") and $\pi\nu\epsilon\acute{\upsilon}\mu\alpha\tau\iota$ ("Spirit") should both be simple datives of means (B 2427. most MSS of Vg), objects of the preposition $\dot{\epsilon}\nu$ ("in" or "with"), so A (D) W (Θ) $f^{1.13}$ it, or one of each. Of the latter group, most have $\ddot{\upsilon}\delta\alpha\tau\iota$ ("with water") and $\dot{\epsilon}\nu\ \pi\nu\epsilon\acute{\upsilon}\mu\alpha\tau\iota\ \dot{\alpha}\gamma\acute{\iota}\omega$ ("in Holy Spirit" or "with Holy Spirit"), namely, ℵ Δ et al., and one (L) has $\dot{\epsilon}\nu\ \ddot{\upsilon}\delta\alpha\tau\iota$ ("in water" or "with water") and $\pi\nu\epsilon\acute{\upsilon}\mu\alpha\tau\iota\ \dot{\alpha}\gamma\acute{\iota}\omega$ ("with Holy Spirit"). The stronger attestation and the fact that scribes were more likely to create parallel expressions than destroy them indicate that the combination of $\ddot{\upsilon}\delta\alpha\tau\iota$ ("with water") and $\dot{\epsilon}\nu\ \pi\nu\epsilon\acute{\upsilon}\mu\alpha\tau\iota\ \dot{\alpha}\gamma\acute{\iota}\omega$ ("in/with Holy Spirit") is the earliest attested reading. See Bruce M. Metzger, *A Textual Commentary on the Greek New Testament: A Companion Volume to the United Bible Societies' Greek New Testament (fourth revised edition)* (2nd ed.; Stuttgart: Deutsche Bibelgesellschaft, 1994) 63.

h   The translation is based on the reading $\epsilon\dot{\iota}\varsigma\ \alpha\dot{\upsilon}\tau\acute{o}\nu$

("to him" or "into him") in B D *f*[13] 2427 *pc*. The rest of the MSS read ἐπ᾽ αὐτόν ("upon him"), probably under the influence of one or more of the parallels in Matt 3:16; Luke 3:22; and John 1:32. Ehrman argues that Mark's preposition εἰς was changed to ἐπί because the earlier reading was used by some ("Gnostics") to support their claim that a divine being had entered into Jesus at the time of his baptism and thus separating "Jesus" from "the Christ" (*Orthodox Corruption of Scripture*, 141–43).

i The translation is based on the reading καὶ φωνὴ ἐγένετο ἐκ τῶν οὐρανῶν ("and a voice came from the heavens") in ℵ[2] A B L (W) *f*[1.13] et al. The shorter reading, καὶ φωνὴ ἐκ τῶν οὐρανῶν ("and a voice from the heavens"), in ℵ* D ff[2] t has a claim to be the earliest, since it could explain the origin of the other two, the third being καὶ φωνὴ ἐκ τῶν οὐρανῶν ἠκούσϑη ("and a voice was heard from the heavens") in Θ

28. 565 (*l*2211) *pc*. But since the witnesses supporting the first reading are so numerous and some are independent of each other, this reading is likely to be the earliest attested.

j A few MSS (B D 2427 et al.) read καὶ μετά ("And after") a formulation more typical of Markan style than μετὰ δέ ("After"), attested by ℵ A L W Θ *f*[1.13] 33 𝔐 et al. Nonetheless, the latter reading is likely to be earlier, since it has such strong external attestation.

k A D W 𝔐 lat sy[p] bo[pt] read τὸ εὐαγγέλιον τῆς βασιλείας τοῦ ϑεοῦ ("the good news of the kingdom of God"). This reading is no doubt an assimilation of the phrase τὸ εὐαγγέλιον τοῦ ϑεου ("the good news of God"), which is unusual in the Gospels (but see 1 Thess 2:2, 8, 9; Rom 1:1; 15:16; 2 Cor 11:7), to the more common notion of the βασιλεία τοῦ ϑεοῦ ("kingdom of God"). See also Metzger, *Textual Commentary*, 64.

Narrative Unity

Although 1:1 is set off from 1:2-15 and the rest of the work as an introductory titular sentence, it nevertheless has thematic links with what follows.[1] The juxtaposition of vv. 1 and 2 suggests that the "beginning of the good news" is related to scripture in general, since the formula "as it is written" (καϑὼς γέγραπται) is regularly used in Jewish cultural contexts for the citation of scripture; more particularly, it suggests that this "beginning" is related to the book of Isaiah.[2]

The announcement of the proclamation of Jesus' messiahship and the implication that scripture is being fulfilled capture the attention of the audience and signify the importance of the subject matter of the work.[3]

The correspondence between the voice of the messenger crying out in the wilderness (vv. 2-3) and the description of John proclaiming in the wilderness (v. 4) suggests that in the activity of John the cited scripture has been fulfilled. This inference is reinforced by the congruence of the messenger's task of preparing the way with the narrated relationship between the activity of John and that of Jesus. John proclaimed a baptism of repentance for the forgiveness of sins (v. 4); this proclamation is taken up by Jesus' call for repentance (v. 15) but extended with the announcement of the good news of God, namely, that the time is fulfilled and the kingdom of God near.[4]

The notion of fulfillment in v. 15 resonates with the implied fulfillment of scripture in the sequence from

1 Robert A. Guelich defined Mark 1:1-3 as the "heading" of the Gospel (5–12); Jean Delorme has described 1:1-4 as "*L'incipit du livre*" ("Évangile et récit: La narration evangélique en Marc," *NTS* 43 [1997] 367–84, esp. 378). Hans-Josef Klauck has made an excellent case for the literary unity of 1:1-15 (*Vorspiel im Himmel? Erzähltechnik und Theologie im Markusprolog* [Biblisch-Theologische Studien 32; Neukirchen-Vluyn: Neukirchener Verlag, 1997] 13–35).

2 The formula "as it is written" (καϑὼς γέγραπται) occurs in the LXX: 4 Kgdms 14:6; 23:21; 2 Chr 23:18; 25:4; Tob 1:6; Dan 9:13 θ. An equivalent formula occurs in the DSS (כאשר כתוב): 1QS 5:17; 8:14; CD 7:19; 4QFlor 1:12; 4QpIsa[c] 6–7 ii 18; 4QCatena[a] 1:11; 4Q178 frg. 3:2; see Joseph Fitzmyer, "The Use of Explicit Old Testament Quotations in

Qumran Literature and in the New Testament," in idem, *Essays on the Semitic Background of the New Testament* (London: G. Chapman, 1971; Missoula, MT: Scholars Press, 1971), 3–58; reprinted in idem, *The Semitic Background of the New Testament: Combined Edition of Essays on the Semitic Background of the New Testament and A Wandering Aramean: Collected Aramaic Essays* (BRS; Grand Rapids: Eerdmans; Livonia, MI: Dove Booksellers, 1997) 3–58.

3 Shiner, *Proclaiming the Gospel*, 184.

4 Whether vv. 14-15 conclude the introduction or belong with the following section has been debated. Cook (*Structure*, 157, 343) takes these verses with what follows because vv. 2-13 are set in the wilderness and vv. 14-15 and what follows are set in Galilee. Davidsen (*Narrative Jesus*, 38) also takes vv. 14-15 with what follows, but the sole criterion

quotation to narration in vv. 2-4. The notion of the kingdom of God takes up the designation of Jesus as "Christ," an epithet whose connotation "anointed one" was apparent to members of the audience familiar with Jewish messianic traditions. The designation of Jesus as "my beloved son" in v. 11, that is, as the Son of God, makes clear to the reader that "anointed one" should be understood as "anointed king," since the king of Israel was frequently called God's son.[5] This inference is reinforced by the reference to the kingdom of God in v. 15.

Jesus' proclamation of the "good news of God" in v. 14 and his call to trust in the good news in v. 15 take up the key theme of the introductory titular sentence of v. 1. Given the evidence of the letters of Paul, as noted above, it is likely that the audience initially understood "the good news of Jesus Christ" in v. 1 to mean the proclamation of the salvific work of God in Jesus, especially in his death and resurrection. Vv. 14-15 lead the audience to modify this understanding. That is not to say that they are led to reject it, but rather to enrich and complicate it. The good news is to be understood not only as a message *about* Jesus but also as a message proclaimed *by* Jesus. The work of Jesus is to be seen not only in his death and resurrection but in all of his reported activity and teaching, beginning with his baptism, as narrated in the good news according to Mark.

Comment

■ **2** The opening part of this verse, "As it is written in the book of Isaiah the prophet" (Καθὼς γέγραπται ἐν τῷ Ἠσαΐᾳ τῷ προφήτῃ) is the most complete and explicit citation of scripture in the Gospel of Mark.[6] Other passages cite written scripture but name neither the book cited nor its author.[7] Some passages refer to particular laws of Moses, without referring to the book in which they occur.[8] Some passages refer quite generally to "the scriptures," and it is not clear to what passage or passages allusion is made.[9] The passages that are closest to this one are Mark 7:6 and 12:26. In the former, Jesus says to the Pharisees and the scribes, "Well did Isaiah prophesy concerning you hypocrites, as it is written," and proceeds to cite Isa 29:13. In the latter, he says to some Sadducees, "Have you not read in the book of Moses in the passage about the thorn-bush how God said to him," and proceeds to cite Exod 3:6. Mark 1:2 is unique insofar as it is the only scriptural citation made by the narrator, whereas the others are made by characters in the narrative.[10]

The first part of the quotation in Mark 1:2-3, the portion that appears in v. 2, "See, I am sending my messenger before your face, who will prepare your way" (ἰδοὺ ἀποστέλλω τὸν ἄγγελόν μου πρὸ προσώπου σου, ὃς κατασκευάσει τὴν ὁδόν σου), however, is not from Isaiah. It is similar in wording to Exod 23:20 LXX: "And see, I am sending my messenger before your face, in order that he may protect you on the way" (Καὶ ἰδοὺ ἐγὼ ἀποστέλλω τὸν ἄγγελόν μου πρὸ προσώπου σου, ἵνα φυλάξῃ σε ἐν τῇ ὁδῷ). It is also similar to Mal 3:1 LXX: "See, I am sending out my messenger, and he will inspect the way before my face" (ἰδοὺ ἐγὼ ἐξαποστέλλω

---

that he uses is the presence of a change in the relationship between God and Jesus. Danove (*End of Mark's Story,* 134–35) defines vv. 2-15 as a unit because of its thematic unity and because this unit has a concentric relationship with 15:42–16:8. Van Iersel (*Reading Mark,* 20) defines vv. 14-15 as a "hinge" linking 1:2-13, in which action takes place in the desert, and 1:16–8:21, in which action takes place in Galilee. He argues that 1:14-15 is concentrically parallel to the only other such "hinge" in Mark, 15:40-41.

5   See, e.g., Ps 2:7; 2 Sam 7:14.

6   On the quotation formula καθὼς γέγραπται ("as it is written"), see the section on the narrative unity of vv. 2-15 above.

7   Mark 10:6-8 cites Gen 1:27 and 2:24; Mark 11:17 cites Isa 56:7; Mark 12:10 cites Ps 118:22-23; Mark 12:29 cites Deut 6:4; Mark 14:27 cites Zech 13:7.

8   Mark 10:4 (cf. Deut 24:1-4); Mark 12:19 (cf. Deut 25:5).

9   Mark 9:12-13; 14:21, 49; on this type of reference to scripture, see Liebers, *"Wie geschrieben steht"*. On the use of scripture in Mark in general, see Joel Marcus, *The Way of the Lord: Christological Exegesis of the Old Testament in the Gospel of Mark* (Louisville: Westminster John Knox, 1992).

10 For this reason, along with the fact that, elsewhere in Mark, καθώς ("as") follows a main clause, J. K. Elliott has argued for the secondary nature of 1:1-3 ("Mark 1.1-3," esp. 585). It is not surprising, however, that the author would deviate from his normal narrative usage in shaping a formal introduction to the work as a whole; see the commentary on v. 1 above.

τὸν ἄγγελόν μου, καὶ ἐπιβλέψεται ὁδὸν πρὸ προσώπου μου). Although the similarities in wording between Mark 1:2 and Exod 23:20 are greater, it is likely that allusion is also made to Mal 3:1 in Mark 1:2, since the context in Malachi is similar to the context in Mark. The task of the messenger in Mal 2:17–3:5 is to prepare the people of Israel for the coming judgment; this is also the task of John and the purpose of his ritual washing in Mark. In Mal 3:23-24 MT (4:5-6 LXX), the messenger of 3:1 is identified with Elijah, who will be sent by God for the purpose of reconciliation.[11] In Mark, John is portrayed as Elijah returned.[12]

The fact that the author attributes the whole quotation to Isaiah has been explained in various ways. Some have argued that he took the citation from a collection of testimonies and did not notice that only part of the composite quotation was from Isaiah.[13] It is unlikely that the author of Mark was unaware of the allusion to Malachi because of the similarities in the contexts mentioned above. Another possibility is that he created the composite citation himself and attributed the whole to Isaiah, since he was better known than Malachi.[14] Or the author may have conflated three scriptural texts and attributed the conflation to Isaiah for theological reasons.[15] As many scholars have noted, Mark and Q overlap in Mark 1:2 and Q 7:27.[16] Harry T. Fleddermann has attempted to show that Mark 1:2 is dependent on redactional Q, that is, not only on the traditions or sources that Mark and Q have in common, but on a form of the Q-document itself.[17] But this conclusion is dubious.[18]

■ **3** The second part of the quotation in Mark 1:2-3, the portion that appears in v. 3, "(the) voice of one calling out in the wilderness, 'Prepare the way of the Lord, make straight his paths'" (φωνὴ βοῶντος ἐν τῇ ἐρήμῳ· ἐτοιμάσατε τὴν ὁδὸν κυρίου, εὐθείας ποιεῖτε τὰς τρίβους αὐτοῦ) is, as announced in the introductory comment, from the book of Isaiah and is closely related to the OG translation of Isa 40:3, "(the) voice of one calling out in the wilderness, 'Prepare the way of the Lord, make straight the paths of our God'" (φωνὴ βοῶντος ἐν τῇ ἐρήμῳ Ἑτοιμάσατε τὴν ὁδὸν κυρίου, εὐθείας ποιεῖτε τὰς τρίβους τοῦ θεοῦ ἡμῶν).

As recognized above, the context of Mark implies that the "messenger" in the first part of the quotation is John the Baptist, who is associated later in the text with Elijah. Similarly, in the second part of the quotation, the "voice

11   On Mal 3:1 and 3:23-24 (4:5-6 RSV), see Markus Öhler, *Elia im Neuen Testament: Untersuchungen zur Bedeutung des alttestamentlichen Propheten im frühen Christentum* (BZNW 88; Berlin/New York: de Gruyter, 1997) 2-6.

12   See Mark 1:6; 9:11-13 and the commentary on these passages below. See also Öhler, *Elia*, 31-47. Christine E. Joynes has argued that v. 2 refers to an angelic figure that is identified with the human John the Baptist ("The Returned Elijah? John the Baptist's Angelic Identity in the Gospel of Mark," *SJT* 58 [2005] 1-13).

13   This hypothesis was suggested by Francis Crawford Burkitt, *The Gospel History and Its Transmission* (Edinburgh: T & T Clark, 1906); and James Rendel Harris, *Testimonies* (2 vols.; Cambridge: Cambridge University Press, 1916, 1920); for discussion of their theories, see Martin C. Albl, *"And Scripture Cannot Be Broken": The Form and Function of the Early Christian Testimonia Collections* (NovTSup 96; Leiden: Brill, 1999) 18-22. The discovery of a document at Qumran, 4QTestimonia (4Q175), that consists of a string of quotations from authoritative texts, most of them from Scripture, that relate to and reinforce the perspective of the community at Qumran, supports the hypothesis that followers of Jesus compiled analogous collections and shows that there was precedent for such a practice. See the discussion by Fitzmyer, "'4QTestimonia' and the New Testament," in *Essays on the Semitic Background of the New Testament*, 59-89; reprinted in *The Semitic Background of the New Testament*, 59-89.

14   Detlev Dormeyer suggested that in doing so, the evangelist followed ancient conventions related to the genre of the cento ("Mk 1,1-15 als Prolog des ersten idealbiographischen Evangeliums von Jesus Christus," *BI* 5 [1997] 181-211, esp. 197).

15   So Marcus, *Way of the Lord*, 17.

16   Q 7:27 is the hypothetically common source of Matt 11:10 and Luke 7:27. See James M. Robinson, Paul Hoffmann, and John Kloppenborg, eds., *The Critical Edition of Q* (Hermeneia; Minneapolis: Fortress; Leuven: Peeters, 2000) 134-35, and the review of scholarship in Harry T. Fleddermann, *Mark and Q: A Study of the Overlap Texts* (BEThL 122; Leuven: Leuven University Press/Peeters, 1995) 25-31.

17   Ibid.

18   Frans Neirynck, "Assessment," in Fleddermann, *Mark and Q*, 263-307, esp. 268-70.

of one calling out in the wilderness" is also to be identified with John, since it is explicitly said that he was baptizing "in the wilderness" and "proclaiming" a baptism of repentance there (v. 4). Most immediately, the "Lord" in the quotation is to be identified with Jesus. That John's task is to prepare the way for the activity of Jesus is implied in the context in several ways. As noted above, in the section on the narrative unity of 1:2-15, the sequence of events in the narrative of this passage implies that John prepares the way for Jesus. Further, the sayings attributed to John in vv. 7-8 imply the same conclusion. John proclaims that one mightier than he is coming after him who will baptize the people in the Holy Spirit. That this coming one is Jesus and not God is made clear by the reference to his sandals in v. 7. This conclusion is supported by the subsequent association of Jesus with the Spirit in v. 10. That John's activity was preparation for that of Jesus is further suggested by the statement in v. 14 that the public activity of Jesus began only after the end of John's.

In the context of Mark as a whole, to prepare the way of Jesus as Lord is also to prepare a way for the Lord God. The clearest use of the epithet "Lord" ($K\acute{\upsilon}\rho\iota o\varsigma$) for God occurs in Mark 12:29-30, in the quotation of Deut 6:4. In Jesus' words to the healed demoniac in 5:19, however, "Go home to your family and report to them how much the Lord has done for you and had mercy on you," it is not entirely clear who the referent of "Lord" is. If it is God, as seems likely, then it is apparent that the activity of God and of Jesus are intimately related.[19] Such a relationship is apparent also in 1:2-15. As John's baptism of repentance prepared the way for the public activity of Jesus, that activity of Jesus is defined as proclaiming "the good news of God" (v. 14). That good news is further characterized as the announcement that "[t]he time is fulfilled and the kingdom of God has drawn near; repent and trust in the good news" (v. 15). Thus the task of

Jesus is to prepare the people for the full manifestation of the rule of God, which is imminent.

It is noteworthy that Isa 40:3 is cited also in the *Community Rule* discovered at Qumran. After stating that those who have been confirmed by two years of probation may be set apart as holy within the council of the men of the community, the text goes on to state:

> And when these become members of the Community in Israel according to all these rules, they shall separate from the habitation of unjust men and shall go into the wilderness to prepare the way of Him; as it is written, *Prepare in the wilderness the way* (דרך) *of . . . , make straight in the desert a path for our God* (Isa 40:3). This is the study of the Law which He commanded by the hand of Moses, that they may do according to all that has been revealed from age to age, and as the Prophets have revealed by His Holy Spirit. (1QS 8:12-16)[20]

The same passage is alluded to again a little further on, in the conclusion to a list of precepts for the Instructor (משכיל):

> He shall impart true knowledge and righteous judgment to those who have chosen the way (דרך). . . . This is the time for the preparation of the way into the wilderness, and he shall teach them to do all that is required at that time and to separate from all those who have not turned aside from all injustice. (1QS 9:17-20)[21]

These two passages suggest that the community related to the Dead Sea Scrolls interpreted Isa 40:3 as a prophecy that was being fulfilled in their own time and in the life of their community. The foundation of the communal settlement at Qumran, probably in the first half of the first century BCE,[22] and their life in accor-

---

19   See also Mark 12:36, where, in dependence on Ps 110:1 (109:1 LXX), both God and the Messiah (from the perspective of the author of Mark) are given the epithet "Lord" ($\kappa\acute{\upsilon}\rho\iota o\varsigma$).

20   Trans. (modified) from Vermes, *Dead Sea Scrolls*, 109. It is noteworthy that the text of Mark connects the phrase "in the wilderness" ($\dot{\epsilon}\nu\ \tau\hat{\eta}\ \dot{\epsilon}\rho\acute{\eta}\mu\hat{\varphi}$) with "the voice of one calling out" ($\varphi\omega\nu\grave{\eta}\ \beta o\hat{\omega}\nu\tau o\varsigma$) in its reception of Isa 40:3, whereas the reading reflected in the *Community Rule* links "in the wilderness"

(במדבר) with "prepare the way of the Lord" (פנו דרך יהוה). On this point, see Marcus, *Way of the Lord*, 13, 15 n. 9.

21   Trans. (modified) from Vermes, *Dead Sea Scrolls*, 111.

22   Jodi Magness's study of the stratigraphy and especially the coins from Qumran support this dating ("Qumran Archaeology: Past Perspectives and Future Prospects," in Peter W. Flint and James C. VanderKam, eds., *The Dead Sea Scrolls after Fifty*

dance with the interpretation of the Law revealed to the Teacher of Righteousness were seen as the first stages in this process of fulfillment. The culmination of that process was probably identified with the definitive visitation of the Lord to renew the creation in the new age:

> For God has established the spirits in equal measure until the final age, and has set everlasting hatred between their divisions. . . . But in the mysteries of His understanding, and in His glorious wisdom, God has ordained an end for injustice, and at the time of the visitation He will destroy it for ever. . . . God will then purify every deed of man with His truth; He will refine for Himself the human frame by rooting out all spirit of injustice from the bounds of his flesh. . . . For God has chosen them for an everlasting Covenant and all the glory of Adam shall be theirs. (1QS 4:16-23)[23]

The Gospel of Mark implies an analogous final visitation in its use of Isa 40:3 and in the announcement by Jesus in the narrative that the "time is fulfilled and the kingdom of God has drawn near." In both texts, a human response is expected to the divine revelation of the coming visita-

tion. According to Mark, the expected response is twofold: the acceptance of the baptism of repentance proclaimed by John and the repentance and trust in the good news called for by Jesus.

Excursus: The Baptism of John[24]

The ritual administered by John, immersion in the Jordan River, has its model, as a ritual action, in the commandments in the book of Leviticus that those to be cleansed of various kinds of ritual impurity are to bathe their bodies in water.[25] Apparently because the word רחץ ("bathe") was felt to be imprecise, connoting both ordinary and ritual washing, the rabbis consistently used the word טבל ("to dip," "to immerse") for ritual immersion, except when quoting scripture.[26] This word occurs in Biblical Hebrew meaning "dip" in, for example, Lev 14:16. It occurs once in the Bible with the sense "immerse" in 2 Kgs 5:14. In an earlier verse, Elisha commands Naaman to go and bathe (רחץ) in the Jordan seven times to be cleansed of his leprosy (2 Kgs 5:10). Eventually, Naaman complies and immerses himself (טבל) seven times in the Jordan (v. 14). The substitution of טבל ("immerse") in ordinary language for רחץ ("bathe") to refer to ritual immersion probably occurred at some point during the Second Temple period, since its Greek equivalent,

---

Years: A Comprehensive Assessment [2 vols.; Leiden/Boston/Cologne: Brill, 1998–99] 1:47–77, esp. 65). See also eadem, *The Archaeology of Qumran and the Dead Sea Scrolls* (Grand Rapids/Cambridge: Eerdmans, 2002) 47–72.

23   Trans. from Vermes, *Dead Sea Scrolls*, 102–3.

24   For a discussion of the *status quaestionis* on the quest of the historical John the Baptist, see Clare K. Rothschild, *Baptist Traditions and Q* (WUNT 190; Tübingen: Mohr Siebeck, 2005) 29–82.

25   The leper who is to be cleansed (Lev 14:9) "shall bathe his body in water" (ורחץ את בשרו במים); the man being cleansed of a long-term genital discharge (Lev 15:13) "shall bathe his body in spring water" (ורחץ בשרו במים חיים); the man being cleansed of an emission of semen (Lev 15:16) "shall bathe his whole body in water" (ורחץ במים את כל בשרו); the man and the woman being cleansed after intercourse (Lev 15:18) "shall bathe in water" (ורחצו במים); on the Day of Atonement, the high priest, before putting on the holy linen garments and entering the Holy of Holies (Lev 16:4) and again after performing his service in the most holy place and removing the holy garments (Lev 16:24), "shall bathe his body in water" (ורחץ את בשרו במים); the man who lets the goat go to Azazel (Lev 16:26), before re-

entering the camp, "shall bathe his body in water" (ורחץ את בשרו במים); the man who burns the skin, flesh and dung of the sin offerings (Lev 16:27-28), before he re-enters the camp, "shall bathe his body in water" (ורחץ את בשרו במים); the priest who touches anyone or anything unclean (Lev 22:6) shall not eat of the holy offerings "unless he has bathed his body in water" (כי אם רחץ בשרו במים); the priest, after he has performed the ritual related to the sacrifice of the red cow outside the camp and before he re-enters the camp (Num 19:7), "shall bathe his body in water" (ורחץ בשרו במים); and the one who has burned the cow outside the camp before he re-enters the camp (Num 19:8) "shall bathe his body in water" (ורחץ בשרו במים). For discussion of the passages in Leviticus, see Jacob Milgrom, *Leviticus: A New Translation with Introduction and Commentary* (3 vols.; AB 3, 3A, 3B; New York: Doubleday, 1991–2001) ad loc.; for the passages in Numbers, see Baruch A. Levine, *Numbers 1–20: A New Translation with Introduction and Commentary* (AB 4; New York: Doubleday, 1993) ad loc.

26   Milgrom, *Leviticus*, 1:841–42.

βαπτίζω ("immerse"), occurs with this sense in Jdt 12:7 and Sir 34:25. In the Dead Sea Scrolls, however, the word טבל ("to dip," "to immerse") is never used to mean "immerse."

Although the concepts of ritual impurity and sin are distinct, there is some overlap between the two in the Levitical laws. Sexual intercourse between husband and wife and childbirth render people unclean (טמא). These activities, however, are not only not sinful; they are commanded by God according to Gen 1:28. The leper (more accurately, one with a scale disease), however, is not only unclean (טמא). He must offer a reparation offering (אשם) to expiate the sacrilege caused by his disease (Lev 14:12).[27] Thus, he is responsible for the effects of his disease, even though he could not help contracting it. The moral connotations are even stronger in the LXX. The reparation-offering (אשם) is rendered by πλημμέλεια ("trespass-offering" or "sin-offering") and is explicitly said to be equivalent to the sin-offering (τὸ περὶ ἁμαρτίας) (Lev 14:12-13 LXX).

In Mark 1:4 it is stated that the purpose of John's baptism was the remission of sins (εἰς ἄφεσιν ἁμαρτιῶν). It is possible that the sins in question were related to ritual impurity. Since, however, John is presented as a prophet, it is likely that his baptism had a broader meaning.[28] The introduction of John and his baptism in 1:2-3, as noted above, associates his activity with the fulfillment of scripture. His ritual for removing sins by immersing people in water and his prophecy of a coming baptism or immersion in the Holy Spirit evoke the prophecy of Ezekiel:

> I will sprinkle clean water upon you, and you shall be clean from all your uncleannesses, and from all your idols I will cleanse you. A new heart I will give you, and a new spirit I will put within you; and I will take out of your flesh the heart of stone and give you a heart of flesh. And I will put my spirit within you, and cause you to walk in my statutes and be careful to observe my ordinances. You shall dwell in the land which I gave to your fathers; and you shall be my people, and I will be your God. (Ezek 36:25-28 RSV)

In its original context, this prophecy anticipated a definitive restoration after the exile that would be, in effect, a new creation. As alluded to by Mark, these promises take on eschatological connotations, since their fulfillment is the first stage in the definitive manifestation of the kingdom of God.

Like Isa 40:3, Ezekiel 36 was also important for the community of the Dead Sea Scrolls, and an eschatological allusion and interpretation of it appear in the *Rule of the Community*:

> But in the mysteries of His understanding, and in His glorious wisdom, God has ordained an end for injustice, and at the time of His visitation He will destroy it for ever. . . . He will refine for Himself the human frame by rooting out all spirit of injustice from the bounds of his flesh. He will cleanse him of all wicked deeds with the spirit of holiness; like purifying waters He will shed upon him the spirit of truth (to cleanse him) of all abomination and injustice. And he shall be plunged into the spirit of purification, that he may instruct the upright in the knowledge of the Most High and teach the wisdom of the sons of heaven to the perfect of way. For God has chosen them for an everlasting Covenant and all the glory of Adam shall be theirs. There shall be no more lies and all the works of injustice shall be put to shame. (1QS 4:18-23)[29]

At an early stage in research on the relation of the Dead Sea Scrolls to the New Testament, William H. Brownlee argued, on the basis of 1QS 5:13-14, that full admission into the community involved a bath that marked the initiate off as belonging to the "holy men."[30] Similarly, Otto Betz argued that the passage declaring that any hypocritical member of the community could not be cleansed by any ablution (1QS 3:4-9), since it is in proximity to the description of the ceremony of entry into the covenant community (1QS 1:16—2:18), implies that the community had an initiation ritual involving immersion in water that could be called a baptism, and that the baptism of John derived from this ritual.[31]

---

27   For discussion see Milgrom, *Leviticus*, 1:320.

28   The association of John with Elijah (Mark 1:6; 9:11-13) and his presentation as an advisor to "King" Herod Antipas (6:14-29) imply that he was a prophet.

29   Trans from Vermes, *Dead Sea Scrolls*, 103. See the citation and discussion of this passage above.

30   William H. Brownlee, "John the Baptist in the New Light of Ancient Scrolls," in Krister Stendahl, ed., *The Scrolls and the New Testament* (New York: Harper & Row, 1957) 33–53, esp. 38–39. He also suggests

31   that the allusion to Ezek 36:25-26 in 1QS 4:21 implies that the fulfillment of the prophecy was expected to occur in the sect's lustral rites (p. 43). Otto Betz, "Die Proselytentaufe der Qumransekte und die Taufe im Neuen Testament," *RevQ* 1 (1958) 213–34, esp. 216–17. Joachim Gnilka, however, emphasized the distinctiveness of John's ritual and argued that it had both priestly and prophetic roots ("Die essenischen Tauchbäder und die Johannestaufe," *RevQ* 3 [1961] 185–207).

The similarities between the baptism of John as described by Mark and the ritual immersions at Qumran are indeed striking. Both involved withdrawal to the desert to await the Lord with reference to Isa 40:3; both were linked to an ascetic lifestyle;[32] both included immersion of the whole body in water; and both were performed in the context of the expectation of a definitive divine visitation. But the passages that describe the ceremony by which individuals joined the community (1QS 1:16–2:18 and 5:7-13) do not mention a water ritual as part of the ceremony. The passage that declares that the hypocritical member of the community is not cleansed by purifying waters is a sophisticated reflection on the relationship between regular ritual washing and moral conversion (1QS 2:25–3:12).[33] It does not imply that one immersion was singled out as a ritual of initiation or as a ritual that effected a personal transformation. Nor does the passage that states that outsiders "shall not enter the water to partake of the pure Meal of the men of holiness" imply such a ritual (1QS 5:13).[34] It implies rather that there was a strict separation between members of the community and outsiders and that only (full) members of the community were allowed to use certain installations for ritual immersion (*mikvaoth*) at the site and to participate in the communal meal, which was eaten in a state of ritual purity.[35] Thus, the differences between the immersions at Qumran and that associated with John are equally striking. The community at Qumran was an exclusive, priestly community, whereas John acted as a charismatic prophet in a public setting. The full members of the community at Qumran immersed themselves at

least once a day, but the immersion administered by John was apparently a singular event for each participant. Finally, the reinterpreted Levitical immersions at Qumran were self-administered, whereas John immersed others or at least supervised the process.[36] Thus, John's baptism should be understood as a transformation of the Levitical type of immersion in light of eschatological expectation based on prophetic texts.[37]

Both in the *Community Rule* and in Mark 1:4, the emphasis is on the divine initiative. There is little evidence for understanding "repentance" in Mark as a human decision in a context of penitence and striving toward virtue.[38]

■ **4** John proclaimed a "baptism of repentance" ($\beta\acute{\alpha}\pi$-$\tau\iota\sigma\mu\alpha\ \mu\epsilon\tau\alpha\nuo\acute{\iota}\alpha\varsigma$). This phrase is ambiguous. It could mean a baptism intended to move God to repent with regard to his decision to punish the people. There is a biblical tradition that God's decisions regarding punishments and blessings are conditional and may be altered:

If I pronounce a decree upon a nation or a kingdom to cut them off and to destroy them, and that nation turn from all their sins, then I will repent ($\mu\epsilon\tau\alpha\nuo\acute{\eta}\sigma\omega$) of the evils which I had decided to do to them. And if I pronounce a decree upon a nation and a kingdom to rebuild and to plant it, and they do evil before me, so that they do not listen to my voice, then

---

32   See also Josephus's description of Bannos, who lived in the desert and practiced frequent ablutions in cold water, by day and night, and who wore only what the trees provided and ate only things that grew of themselves (*Vita* 11).

33   Compare Josephus's statement that John required moral conversion as a necessary preliminary to baptism; the ritual washing did not remove sin but only consecrated the body of a person whose soul had already been thoroughly cleansed by right behavior (*Ant.* 18.5.2 §116–119). Mark's account of John's baptism shows no awareness of such distinctions.

34   Trans. from Vermes, *Dead Sea Scrolls*, 104. For discussion, see Robert L. Webb, *John the Baptizer and Prophet: A Socio-Historical Study* (JSNTSup 62; Sheffield: JSOT Press, 1991) 152–56.

35   Compare Josephus's statement that the Essenes bathe their bodies in cold water before assembling for a meal in a place to which outsiders are denied entrance and that they enter their refectory in a pure state, as if it were a shrine (*Bell.* 2.8.5 §129).

36   For a discussion of John's procedure and practice of immersion, see Joan E. Taylor, *The Immerser: John the Baptist within Second Temple Judaism* (Grand Rapids/Cambridge: Eerdmans, 1997) 49–58; see also eadem, "John the Baptist and the Essenes," *JJS* 47 (1996) 256–85, in which she concludes that John had no direct connection to the Essenes.

37   See Adela Yarbro Collins, "The Origin of Christian Baptism," *Studia Liturgica* 19 (1989) 28–46; reprinted in eadem, *Cosmology and Eschatology in Jewish and Christian Apocalypticism* (JSJSup 50; Leiden: Brill, 1996) 218–38; Fritzleo Lentzen-Deis, *Die Taufe Jesu nach den Synoptikern: Literarkritische und gattungsgeschichtliche Untersuchungen* (FTS 4; Frankfurt am Main: Josef Knecht, 1970) 92.

38   David Lambert has shown that, in a few Second Temple texts, the Hebrew word שוב cannot be translated as repentence ("Did Israel Believe that Redemption Awaited Their Repentance? The Case of *Jubilees* 1," *CBQ* 68 [2006] 631–50, esp. 648–49; idem, "Topics in the History of Repentance: From

I will repent of the good which I said that I would do for them. (Jer 18:7-10 LXX)[39]

If such is the meaning of Mark's portrayal of John's "baptism of repentance," it has an analogy in an oracle of the fourth book of the *Sibylline Oracles*, a passage added in the first century CE by a Jewish writer to an originally non-Jewish Hellenistic political oracle:

> But when faith in piety perishes from among men,
> and justice is hidden in the world,
> untrustworthy men, living for unholy deeds,
> will commit outrage, wicked and evil deeds.
> No one will take account of the pious, but they will even
> destroy them all, by foolishness, very infantile people,
> rejoicing in outrages and applying their hands to blood.
> Even then know that God is no longer benign
> but gnashing his teeth in wrath and destroying the entire
> race of men at once by a great conflagration.
> Ah, wretched mortals, change these things, and do not
> lead the great God to all sorts of anger, but abandon
> daggers and groanings, murders and outrages,
> and wash your whole bodies in perennial rivers.
> Stretch out your hands to heaven and ask forgiveness
> for your previous deeds and make propitiation
> for bitter impiety with words of praise; God will grant repentance
> and will not destroy. He will stop his wrath again if you all

practice honorable piety in your hearts. (*Sib. Or.* 4:152-70)[40]

The context suggests that the word "repentance" in line 168 of this oracle refers to a change in God's plan for the future.

It is of course also possible that the "baptism of repentance" proclaimed by John was a ritual to be performed as part of a process in which human beings repented of their sins.[41] As noted in the discussion of the allusion to Malachi above, Elijah was expected to return in the last days to reconcile fathers and children. In the passage praising famous men (44:1–50:24), Sirach says that the assignment of Elijah is "to calm the fury of the wrath of God, to turn the heart of the father to the son, and to restore the tribes of Jacob" (Sir 48:10).[42] Immediately following the account of his mighty deeds, which alludes also to those of his successor Elisha, the following statement is made:

> For all this the people did not repent (οὐ μετενόησεν) and did not turn aside from their sins, until they were raided (and removed) from their land and were scattered in all the earth. (Sir 48:15)

The portrayal of John as a second Elijah or as Elijah returned fits well then with the proclamation of a baptism of repentance, an occasion on which the people are given a second and presumably final opportunity for repentance.[43]

In the context of Second Temple Jewish texts, however, it may well be that "repentance" signifies primarily

---

the Hebrew Bible to Early Judaism and Christianity" [Ph.D. diss., Harvard University, 2004] 137–46). He has also argued for the primacy of divine initiative over human repentance in sectarian thought ("Did Israel Believe," 631–50; "Topics," 84–146).

39 See also Jer 38:19; Amos 7:3, 6; Joel 2:13; Jonah 3:9-10; 4:2. There are also passages that speak of God's refusal or inability to repent of his decisions: 1 Kgdms 15:29; Jer 4:27-28; Zech 8:14-15.

40 Trans. from John J. Collins, "Sibylline Oracles," in *OTP* 1:388; on the date and Jewish character of this oracle, see ibid., 381.

41 The theme of the confession of sins will be discussed in the comments on v. 5.

42 On the treatment of Elijah in Sir 48:1-11, see Öhler, *Elia*, 6–11.

43 Elijah is mentioned in a fragmentary text from Qumran (4Q558) that appears to cite an Aramaic form of Mal 3:23; all that can be determined from the context is that Elijah is expected to come at some point in the last days; see Öhler, *Elia*, 17. 4Q521 may also refer to Elijah as an anointed eschatological prophet or to a prophet like Elijah; see the discussion of this text in the introduction to the commentary, the section *Jesus as Prophet*.

On the biblical theme of human repentance in general, see Wis 5:3; Sir 17:24; Isa 46:8; Jer 8:6. For a discussion of John's call for repentance in relation to the Deuteronomistic understanding of history and to apocalypticism, see Stephanie von Dobbeler, *Das Gericht und das Erbarmen Gottes: Die Botschaft Johannes des Täufers und ihre Rezeption bei den Johan-*

a positive response to the initiative of God taken through the agency of John.[44]

■ **5** The statement that "the whole district of Judea and all the inhabitants of Jerusalem were going out to him" implies that John was accepted as a prophet, as an eschatological agent of God, by the Jewish people, at least by the vast majority of the inhabitants of Judea and Jerusalem. The remark that they were baptized or immersed by John indicates, as noted in the excursus above, that this ritual immersion was administered by John, a feature that differs from most Jewish ritual immersions before John's time and contemporary with him. Later on, Jewish proselyte baptism was also administered, but the evidence for this practice is not earlier than the second century CE.[45]

The fact that John baptized in the Jordan River is significant for several reasons. It was and is the primary river in the land of Israel, a perennial stream. Thus, when the foreigner Naaman (see the excursus above) is instructed by Elisha to bathe in the Jordan, the Syrian becomes angry because he thinks the rivers of Damascus are greater than all the waters of Israel (2 Kgs 5:10-11). When he finally complies and is healed, the implication is not only that the God of Israel is powerful, but that the land of Israel and the River Jordan are holy. The Jordan River also has symbolic significance as the site of the miraculous entrance of the tribes of Israel into the promised land, an event analogous to the miraculous crossing of the Red Sea.[46] This foundational significance apparently gave rise to eschatological expectations in the late Second Temple period.[47] The hope evidently was that

God would restore the land to the people of Israel, driving out their enemies, who at this time were primarily the Romans and those who collaborated with them.

This verse also states that the people who were being immersed or baptized were also "confessing their sins" (ἐξομολογούμενοι τὰς ἁμαρτίας αὐτῶν). This description can be understood in various ways. It could refer to a communal or an individual confession; the confession may be public, in the hearing of all present, or private, in the hearing of John alone. It could be a confession of general sinfulness, of specific sins for which the people as a whole considered themselves accountable, of specific but unnamed sins, or of specific sins described in more or less detail. The ancient Assyrians, Babylonians, and Hittites confessed their sins directly to a deity in his or her temple. This confession was accompanied by self-humiliation as an expression of repentance and the hope of forgiveness. They composed or commissioned hymns in which their confessions were written down. The Egyptians commissioned stone tablets on which their confessions of sin were written. In all these cases, the confession is public, in the sense that it is written down, and of a general sinfulness, not of specific sins. Inscriptions from Lydia and Phrygia (first through third centuries CE) and curse tablets from Cnidos (second and first centuries BCE) show that such practices endured and spread. Some of the inscriptions state explicitly that the confession is public in order to serve as an example or warning to others.[48] There are also reports by Greek and Roman writers of the practice of public oral confession of sins and self-humiliation among worshipers of Isis, the

nesjüngern im Rahmen der Theologiegeschichte des Frühjudentums (BBB 70; Frankfurt am Main: Athenäum, 1988) 83–150.

44 According to Lambert, the term שוב signifies a divinely ordained turn that is predicted in Deuteronomy 4 and 30; i.e., the action in question is not on the level of specific human action, but describes a broader national change. He sees, however, the acknowledgment or confession of sin and the process of emphasizing divine grace as specific human responses ("Did Israel Believe," 631–50, esp. 648–49; idem, "Topics in the History of Repentance," 84–146, esp. 137–46).

45 Proselyte baptism is administered in the sense that it is witnessed and the witnesses lead the person being immersed in a ceremony involving instruction and prayer. Thus, the immersion is part of an initiation

ritual; see *b. Yeb.* 46a. For discussion, see Yarbro Collins, "Origin of Christian Baptism," 32–35; eadem, *Cosmology and Eschatology*, 224–28.

46 Cf. Joshua 3 with Exodus 14.

47 See the discussion of Theudas and his followers in the introduction to the commentary, the section *Jesus as Prophet*.

48 Fridolf Kudlien, "Beichte und Heilung," *Medizin historisches Journal* 13 (1978) 1–14, esp. 2–3. The Egyptian practice is attested in inscriptions from Thebes dating to the Nineteenth Dynasty (c. 1300 BCE); see Raffaele Pettazzoni, "Confession of Sins and the Classics," *HTR* 30 (1937) 1–14, esp. 1; reprinted, with minor changes, in idem, *Essays on the History of Religions* (SHR 1; Leiden: Brill, 1954) 55–67. Pettazzoni argues that, although most of the inscriptions from Lydia and Phrygia date to the second and third

Anatolian Great Mother and the Syrian goddess. For example, a passage attributed to Menander states:

Take, for example, the Syrians. Whenever they eat fish, by a kind of incontinence their feet and belly swell up; they put on sackcloth and then go and seat themselves on a dung heap by the wayside and propitiate the goddess by excessive self-humiliation.

(παράδειγμα τοὺς Σύρους λαβέ·
ὅταν φάγωσ᾽ ἰχθὺν ἐκεῖνοι, διά τινα
αὐτῶν ἀκρασίαν τοὺς πόδας καὶ γαστέρα
οἰδοῦσιν, ἔλαβον σακίον, εἶτ᾽ εἰς τὴν ὁδὸν
ἐκάθισαν αὐτοὺς ἐπὶ κόπρου, καὶ τὴν θεὸν
ἐξιλάσαντο τῷ ταπεινοῦσθαι σφόδρα.)[49]

An inscription related to the cult of Asklepios in Epidauros attests to a detailed, public confession of sin. Two further, unfortunately fragmentary, inscriptions from Epidauros contain the verb ὁμολογέω ("to confess").[50] The verb used in Mark 1:5, "to confess" (ἐξομολογέω), occurs in some of the inscriptions from Lydia and Phrygia mentioned above; these were dedicated by individuals and some of them contain references to sins for which the perpetrators have been punished by a deity.[51] Many of these inscriptions imply that atonement was made for such sins by paying a sum of money or making some gift to the shrine of the deity, by offering sacrifice, by making amends to the person(s) one has wronged, or simply

centuries CE and a few to the first century CE, they most likely "represent the late survival and continuance *in situ* of a confessional practice of very ancient origin" ("Confession of Sins and the Classics," 3–4). Kudlien concludes, following Pettazzoni, that the confession of sins was foreign to and rejected by the Greeks because of their distaste for self-humiliation.

49   Text and trans. from Francis G. Allinson, *Menander: The Principal Fragments* (LCL; London: Heinemann; New York: Putnam's Sons, 1921; rev. 1930) 342–43; Plutarch *Superst.* 168–71, esp. 168D and 170D; Ovid *Ex Ponto* 1.1.51–58; for discussion, see Kudlien, "Beichte und Heilung," 3–4; and Pettazzoni, "Confession of Sins and the Classics," 1–14. See also Hildebrecht Hommel, "Antike Bußformulare: Eine religionsgeschichtliche Interpretation der ovidischen Midas-Erzählung," in idem, *Sebasmata: Studien zur antiken Religionsgeschichte und zum frühen Christentum* (2 vols.; WUNT 31–32; Tübingen: Mohr Siebeck, 1983, 1984) 1:351–70. Ritual ablutions were conducted in the cults of Isis and Sarapis in the Hellenistic and Roman periods; the literary evidence emphasizes purification; see Robert A. Wild, *Water in the Cultic Worship of Isis and Sarapis* (EPRO 87; Leiden: Brill, 1981) esp. 143–48.

50   All three inscriptions date to around 300 BCE or earlier and belong to the *Iamata* of Asklepios; see Kudlien, "Beichte und Heiling," 5. The Greek text of the complete inscription may be found in J. D. E. Hondius, ed., *Supplementum Epigraphicum Graecum* (Leiden: Sijthoff, 1924) 2:10–11, no. 58; the text and a German trans. may be found in Rudolf Herzog, *Die Wunderheilungen von Epidauros: Ein Beitrag zur Geschichte der Medizin und der Religion* (Philologus-Sup 22.3; Leipzig: Dieterich'sche Verlagsbuchhandlung, 1931) 26–29, no. 47. Partial Greek texts and

German translations of the two fragmentary inscriptions may be found in Herzog, *Die Wunderheilungen*, 28–31, nos. 54 and 58. No. 58 mentions someone injured by a spear in a battle; after he confessed (ὡμολόγησε), he was healed.

51   E.g., an inscription dedicated to the deity Men, dated to 164/65 CE, states that the god punished a thief, who then brought to the god a garment that he had stolen and ἐξωμολογήσατο, i.e., "confessed (his sin)"; for a Greek text and German translation, see Georg Petzl, ed., *Die Beichtinschriften Westkleinasiens* (Epigraphica Anatolica: Zeitschrift für Epigraphik und historische Geographie Anatoliens 22; Bonn: Rudolf Habelt, 1994) no. 3, p. 3. The verb "to confess" (ἐξομολογέω) also occurs in an inscription dedicated by a woman to Apollo Bozenos. She was punished by him with an illness because she entered a holy place wearing a dirty or impure tunic; after she confessed (ἐξωμολογησάμην; lit., "I confessed"), she was healed; for a Greek text, German translation, and discussion, see Petzl, *Die Beichtinschriften*, no. 43, pp. 52–53. The same verb occurs in similar contexts also in Petzl, *Die Beichtinschriften*, nos. 109 (pp. 126–28), 111 (pp. 130–31), 112 (pp. 132–33), and 116 (p. 136). The verb "to confess" (ὁμολογέω) occurs in Petzl, *Die Beichtinschriften*, no. 100 (p. 117); this inscription may also be found in Eugene N. Lane, *Corpus Monumentorum Religionis Dei Menis*, vol. 1: *The Monuments and Inscriptions* (EPRO 19; Leiden: Brill, 1971) no. 77. On these "confessional inscriptions," see Hans-Josef Klauck, "Die kleinasiatischen Beichtinschriften und das Neue Testament," in Hubert Cancik, Hermann Lichtenberger, and Peter Schäfer, eds., *Geschichte–Tradition–Reflexion: Festschrift für Martin Hengel zum 70. Geburtstag* (3 vols.; Tübingen: Mohr Siebeck,

by setting up a stele recording the sinner's confession and desire to propitiate the deity.[52]

If a public communal confession of sins was part of the ceremony that centered on the baptism administered by John, some texts from Qumran provide analogies. According to the *Community Rule*, the community held a ceremony each year in which new members joined the (new or renewed) covenant (the community), and those who were already members renewed their commitment.[53] This ceremony apparently began with the members who were priests and Levites blessing God and reciting an account of all the favors bestowed by God upon Israel (1QS 1:18-22). Then

> the Levites shall recite the iniquities of the children of Israel, all their guilty rebellions and sins during the dominion of Belial. And after them, all those entering the Covenant shall confess and say: "We have strayed! We have [disobeyed!] We and our fathers before us have sinned and done wickedly in walking [counter to the precepts] of truth and righteousness. [And God has] judged us and our fathers also; but He has bestowed his bountiful mercy on us from everlasting to everlasting." (1QS 1:22–2:1)[54]

This text could be interpreted as a communal confession of specific sins for which the members of the sect, representing the people as a whole, considered themselves accountable, for example, idolatry and failure to observe the Law as interpreted by the Teacher. Or it may be understood as implying that "[a]cknowledgment of sin exonerates God by blaming Israel and thereby further augments the magnitude of God's grace. . . ."[55]

Fragments of a liturgical text from Qumran should also be noted. These seem to be part of a communal confession of sins. Column 1 contains the following:

> Our God, hide Thy face from [our] si[ns and] blot out [al]l our iniquities and create in us a new spirit, O Lord . . . . [do not] withhold faithfulness and to rebels . . . and bring back sinners to Thee. And [do not] reject from Thee the broken [spir]it, O God. (4Q393)[56]

Given the associations of the account of John and his activity with scripture and its analogies with the Dead Sea Scrolls, it is likely that the confession of sins was communal and general and that it signified acceptance of John's prophetic mission and a plea for forgiveness

1996) 3:63–87; and Adela Yarbro Collins, "The Signification of Mark 10:45 among Gentile Christians," in François Bovon, ed., *Jesus' Sayings in the Life of the Early Church: Papers Presented in Honor of Helmut Koester's Seventieth Birthday*, HTR 90 (1997) 371–82.

52 Pettazzoni cites evidence for the linking of immersion or sprinkling with the confession of sin in Anatolian ritual and ritual related to the worship of Isis ("Confession of Sins and the Classics," 2–3, 4–5).

53 Klaus Baltzer has argued that 1QS 1:18–2:10 is a traditional liturgy for a covenant renewal into which a confession of sins (1:22-23) has been interpolated; the confession of sins is necessary because the human party has broken the covenant (*The Covenant Formulary in Old Testament, Jewish, and Early Christian Writings* [Oxford: Basil Blackwell, 1971] 49–50, 167–69, 189–91).

54 Trans. from Vermes, *Dead Sea Scrolls*, 99. Cf. Ezra 9:5-15; Dan 9:4-19; and the call to repentance in *Sib. Or.* 4:152-70, cited above in the comments on v. 4.

55 Lambert, "Did Israel Believe," 648.

56 Trans. from Vermes, *Dead Sea Scrolls*, 381; see also Daniel Falk, "4Q393: A Communal Confession," *JJS* 45 (1994) 184–207, who interprets this text as a type of postexilic prayer that responds to the admonition

of Lev 26:40-45 that the people should confess their sins and the sins of their fathers. He identifies Nehemiah 9, Ezra 9, Daniel 9, Psalm 106, Daniel 3 LXX, 1 Bar 1:15–3:8, 1QS 1-2, and 4QDibHam as other examples of the genre. Robert H. Eisenman and Michael Wise have argued that 4Q414 is a "baptismal hymn" (Eisenman and Wise, *The Dead Sea Scrolls Uncovered* [Shaftesbury, Dorset/Rockport, MA/Brisbane, Queensland: Element Books, 1992] 230–33; so also Martin G. Abegg, "A Baptismal Liturgy," in Michael O. Wise, Martin Abegg, Jr., and Edward Cook, eds., *The Dead Sea Scrolls: A New Translation* [San Francisco: HarperSanFrancisco, 1996] 390–91). This document is included in García Martínez and Tigchelaar, *Dead Sea Scrolls*, under the title "4QRitual of Purification (4Q414)" (2:842-45). It is not included in Vermes, *Dead Sea Scrolls*. The document contains the phrase "to atone for us" (ולכפר לנו) in frg. 1 col. 1.3 in the text of Eisenman and Wise and in frgs. 1 col. 2 and 2 col. 1.3 in the reconstruction by García Martínez and Tigchelaar. But otherwise the language is about purity, impurity, and purification, not sin and repentance. This document is better described as a purification ritual than as a baptismal hymn or liturgy. Cf. 4Q512,

and thus for being spared from or in the eschatological judgment and punishment of God.

■ **6** The description of John as wearing (a garment of) camel's hair and a leather belt around his waist portrays him as a prophet.[57] This portrayal, especially in light of the allusion to Mal 3:1 in Mark 1:2, also associates him with Elijah.[58] According to 2 Kgs 1:8, Elijah was "a hairy man" (אִישׁ בַּעַל שֵׂעָר). The LXX correctly translates the Hebrew phrase with ἀνὴρ δασύς ("a hairy man").[59] But apparently the Hebrew phrase (and perhaps the Greek also) was later understood to allude to a hairy garment. Zech 13:4, for example, states, "On that day every prophet will be ashamed of his vision when he prophesies; he will not put on a hairy mantle (אַדֶּרֶת שֵׂעָר) in order to deceive, but will say 'I am no prophet. . . .'"[60] The text of *1 Clement* states that "those who went about 'in the skins (δέρμασιν) of goats and sheep' (cf. Heb

11:37), heralding the coming of Christ" were Elijah, Elisha, Ezekiel, the prophets, and the famous men of old.[61] In any case, part of Mark 1:6 is a clear allusion to the LXX of 2 Kgs 1:8. Compare Mark's "and a leather belt around his waist" (καὶ ζώνην δερματίνην περὶ τὴν ὀσφὺν αὐτοῦ) with the LXX's "and girded with a leather belt around his waist" (καὶ ζώνην δερματίνην περιεζωσμένος τὴν ὀσφὺν αὐτοῦ). This allusion implies a close association or an identification of John with Elijah.[62]

The significance of John's diet, grasshoppers and wild honey, may be explained in various ways.[63] The simplicity of the food may indicate asceticism.[64] Another possibility is that the motivating factor was the maintenance of purity, since the grasshoppers and honey would not have been handled by anyone else, and wild honey would not be subject to tithing.[65] Wild honey, "honey from the

---

which both Vermes (*Dead Sea Scrolls*, 382) and García Martínez and Tigchelaar (*Dead Sea Scrolls*, 2:1036–41) identify as a purification ritual.

57   See von Dobbeler, *Gericht und Erbarmen*, 192–93.

58   Rothschild, *Baptist Traditions and Q*, 129–30.

59   On the MT of 2 Kgs 1:8, see Mordechai Cogan and Hayim Tadmor, *II Kings: A New Translation with Introduction and Commentary* (AB 11; New York: Doubleday, 1988) 26.

60   The LXX of Zech 13:4 reads δέρριν τριχίνην ("a hairy leather garment") for the MT's phrase אַדֶּרֶת שֵׂעָר ("a hairy mantle"). Another possibility is that, independently of 2 Kgs 1:8, a hairy garment came to be associated with prophets as a sign of asceticism. Cf. *Asc. Isa.* 2:10, according to which all the prophets of the First Temple period wore a coarse cloth of hair (σάκκος); for the Greek text of this passage, see Albert-Marie Denis and Yvonne Janssens, *Concordance grecque des pseudépigraphes d'Ancien Testament* (Louvain-la-Neuve: Université Catholique de Louvain; Leiden: Brill/Peeters, 1987) 904; for an English translation, see C. Detlef and G. Müller in *NTApoc*, 2:607.

61   *1 Clem.* 17:1; text and trans. from Lake, *Apostolic Fathers*, 1:38–39. Bart Ehrman translates similarly, but has "proclaiming" rather than "heralding" (κηρύσσοντες) (*Apostolic Fathers*, 1:66–67). Although he refers to 2 Kgs 1:8, Zech 13:4, *Asc. Isa.* 2:10-12, and *1 Clem.* 17:1 as evidence that the description of John's manner of dress, especially the leather belt, could bring Elijah to mind, Josef Ernst argued that the motif originally expressed simply a prophetic self-understanding. The citation of Mal 3:1 in Mark 1:2 links the motif more strongly with Elijah

(*Johannes der Täufer: Interpretation–Geschichte–Wirkungsgeschichte* [BZNW 53; Berlin: de Gruyter, 1989] 8–9).

62   So also Öhler, *Elia*, 36.

63   For a discussion of the history of scholarship, see James A. Kelhoffer, "'Locusts and Wild Honey' (Mk 1.6c and Mt 3.4c): The *Status Quaestionis* concerning the Diet of John the Baptist," *CBR* 2 (2003) 104–27; idem, *The Diet of John the Baptist: "Locusts and Wild Honey" in Synoptic and Patristic Interpretation* (WUNT 176; Tübingen: Mohr Siebeck, 2005) 12–35.

64   See the discussion of Bannos's diet in the excursus on baptism above. See also *Asc. Isa.* 2:11, according to which the prophets of the First Temple period had nothing to eat except wild herbs (βοτάναι), which they gathered on the mountains, cooked, and ate in the company of Isaiah; for the Greek text, see Denis and Janssens, *Concordance grecque*, 904; for an ET, see Müller in *NTApoc*, 2:607. According to von Dobbeler, grasshoppers, like fish, were not considered to be meat, since they lacked blood, and the avoidance of meat is typical of ancient asceticism (*Gericht und Erbarmen*, 192). On the ascetic and vegetarian interpretations, see Kelhoffer, *Diet of John the Baptist*, 134–93.

65   2 Chr 31:5 implies that honey from domesticated bees was subject to the tithe; see J. F. Ross, "Honey," *IDB* 2:639. If wild honey was not subject to tithing, then one did not have to worry about whether the honey that one was eating came from a batch that had been properly tithed. According to Lev 11:22, the grasshopper (ἀκρίς in the LXX) is a clean animal.

rock," was not only pure, but evoked traditions of God's care for Israel.[66] In later Christian literature, the diet of John is often interpreted figuratively or as a model to be imitated.[67]

■ **7-8** As noted in the introduction to the commentary in the section *Jesus as Prophet*, Jesus' designation as "the one stronger than I" (ὁ ἰσχυρότερός μου) in v. 7 evokes connotations of the divine warrior and his (royal) messiah or other agent in battle. The saying of v. 7 exalts Jesus as a royal figure and strongly subordinates John to him. As noted in the excursus on baptism above, the saying of v. 8 evokes Ezek 36:25-28. In the passage from Ezekiel itself and in its adapted form in 1QS 4:18-23, the cleansing with water and the gift of the Holy Spirit are two aspects of the same event or process. Mark 1:8, however, divides the eschatological renewal into two stages. The cleansing with water has become a preparatory rite of repentance in the public activity of John, whereas the gift of the Holy Spirit is reserved for a second stage, the activity of Jesus.

Mark 1:7-8 overlaps with Q 3:16-17.[68] Fleddermann's reconstruction of the history of the saying preserved in Mark 1:8 is persuasive in its main features.[69] The oldest form of the saying did not mention the Spirit; it contrasted baptism in water with baptism in fire. Although, as noted in the excursus on baptism above, water and spirit are associated in Ezekiel 36 and in the *Community Rule*, another Jewish text supports the hypothesis that the earliest form of this saying expressed a contrast between water and fire. The passage from book 4 of the *Sibylline Oracles* cited in the comment on v. 4 above continues as follows:

> But if you do not obey me, evil-minded ones, but love
> impiety, and receive all these things with evil ears,
> there will be fire throughout the whole world, and a
>   very great sign
> with sword and trumpet at the rising of the sun.
> The whole world will hear a bellowing noise and
>   mighty sound.
> He will burn the whole earth, and will destroy the
>   whole race of men
> and all cities and rivers at once, and the sea.
> He will destroy everything by fire, and it will be smok-
>   ing dust. (*Sib. Or.* 4:171-78)[70]

Thus, the "baptism in fire" would be punishment for sin.[71] According to Fleddermann, the reference to the Holy Spirit was added at a second stage. This is the form of the saying preserved in Matt 3:11 and Luke 3:16. In the third stage, the form of the saying reflected in Mark 1:8, the reference to fire was omitted and the emphasis was placed on the Spirit and the subordination of John to Jesus. That Mark 1:8 is a later form of the saying than the one that probably stood in Q, however, does not necessarily imply that Mark is dependent on some form of the Q-document.[72]

■ **9-11** Bultmann's arguments are persuasive—that this brief narrative is not an account of Jesus being called or commissioned on the model of Isaiah 6, Jeremiah 1, or

---

66   Deut 32:13; Ps 81:16 (81:17 MT; 80:17 LXX). The
    motif present in both these passages, that God gives
    Israel "honey from the rock," may be related to the
    stock phrase "a land flowing with milk and honey,"
    an expression signifying the abundance of the land;
    Exod 3:8; Num 13:27; Deut 6:3; Jer 11:5; Sir 46:8;
    1 Bar 1:20; see J. F. Ross, "Milk," *IDB* 3:379–80. This
    connotation of honey is in tension, however, with
    John's location in the wilderness.
67   Kelhoffer, *Diet of John the Baptist*, 153–71.
68   Q 3:16-17 is the hypothetically common source of
    Matt 3:11-12 and Luke 3:16-17. For discussion, see
    Fleddermann, *Mark and Q*, 31–39.
69   Ibid., 36–37.
70   Trans. from Collins, "Sibylline Oracles," in *OTP*
    1:388.
71   Cf. von Dobbeler, *Gericht und Erbarmen*, 77, who
    concludes that the baptism of John was intended to

preserve people from judgment, whereas the baptism in fire was the punitive expression of divine judgment.
72   Fleddermann concludes that "Mark may show knowledge of redactional Q" in this case (*Mark and Q*, 37), but Neirynck is not persuaded ("Assessment," 270–71).

Ezekiel 1–2. He concluded that it is a faith legend, because it tells of Jesus' consecration as messiah. This conclusion is no doubt related to his assumption that the account originated in the oral tradition of the early church. Literarily speaking, as Bultmann also noted, the account is a biographical legend.[73] A feature that led Bultmann to define the account as a legend is what he called the miraculous moment, the way in which divine characters and power break into the world of human experience and transform the subject of the narrative.

Ancient biographies of poets contain similar accounts near the beginning of the narrative about their main subjects. In the popular biography of Aesop, he is portrayed as a slave, extraordinarily ugly, and unable to speak because of a severe speech impediment.[74] This low status is somewhat mollified by divine power. Near the beginning of the narrative, Aesop assists a priestess of Isis. As a reward Isis grants him the power of speech, and the nine Muses bestow upon him the power to devise stories and the ability to conceive and elaborate tales, as well as other gifts of excellent speech. A story was told about the archaic lyric poet Archilochus involving an extraordinary experience which revealed that he would be a poet. When he was leading a cow to market at night while the moon was shining, he met a crowd of women who offered to buy his cow. When he had agreed and they had promised to give him a good price, both the women and the cow disappeared, and before his feet he saw a lyre. He was overcome and realized that they were the Muses.[75] Like Archilochus, the Jesus of Mark has an experience near the beginning of the narrative that trans-

forms him and prepares him for his life's work. Archilochus experienced an epiphany or vision of the Muses, who enabled him to be a poet; Jesus sees the heavens open and the Holy Spirit descending like a dove and hears the divine voice address him as beloved son. The allusions to scripture in the words of the divine voice suggest that Jesus is being appointed as messiah or prophet or to an eschatological role that combines both offices. As Aesop was given gifts of wise speech by Isis and the Muses, Jesus is endowed with the divine Spirit on this occasion, the power that enables him to teach with authority, to heal, and to cast out demons.[76]

In relation to the overall narrative of Mark, the account of the baptism of Jesus is a biographical legend. In relation to at least part of the audience of Mark, the passage seems to have functioned as a cult legend.[77] The reference to baptism in the Holy Spirit in v. 8 would have called to mind the ritual of initiation into the community of the followers of Jesus (1 Cor 6:11; Acts 2:38). In light of that ritual and communal context, the narrative of Jesus' baptism in vv. 9-11 would call to mind the baptism of his followers, their reception of the Holy Spirit, and their being made sons and daughters of God. It has been argued that Paul alludes to an early tradition that links the reception of the status of sonship with the reception of the Holy Spirit and that this tradition was associated with the ritual of baptismal initiation.[78]

■ **9** This verse indicates a change in time ("And in those days") and introduces a new character on the scene ("Jesus came from Nazareth in Galilee"). These shifts introduce, on a narrative level, the transition from the

73 Bultmann, *History*, 247–48. Robert Tannehill understands the baptismal scene as the communication of God's commission to Jesus, but he uses the term "commission" in a special literary sense ("The Gospel of Mark as Narrative Christology," *Semeia* 16 [1980] 57–95, esp. 60–62).

74 For the texts of the two Greek MSS and of a shorter Latin version, see Perry, *Aesopica*; for an English translation, see Daly, *Aesop without Morals*, or Lawrence M. Wills, *The Quest of the Historical Gospel: Mark, John, and the Origins of the Gospel Genre* (London/New York: Routledge, 1997) appendix.

75 Lefkowitz, *Lives of the Greek Poets*, 27–28. This story appears on an inscription discovered on the island of Paros and published by Nikolaos Kontoleon in 1954. The marble orthostates on which the text was

inscribed belonged to the heroon of Archilochus that was built near the city of Paros in the third century BCE. For the Greek text and discussion, see Carl Werner Müller, "Die Archilochoslegende," *Rheinisches Museum für Philologie* n.F. 128 (1985) 99–151, especially 100–10. For the Greek text and a German translation of the story, see Max Treu, *Archilochos* (Munich: Ernst Heimeran, 1959) 42–45.

76 For further discussion of the similarities of Mark to the ancient popular biographies, see the introduction to the commentary, the section on *Genre*, and Yarbro Collins, "Finding Meaning," 175–96.

77 Cf. Bultmann, *History*, 250–53.

78 Gal 4:4-7; Rom 8:3-4, 14-15, 17. For discussion of the pre-Pauline tradition, see Ulrich Wilckens, *Der Brief an die Römer* (3 vols.; EKK 6; Zurich: Benziger;

period of John's public activity to the time of Jesus' public life (cf. v. 14). The context makes clear that Jesus is the one addressed by the quotation in v. 2 and the one referred to as "Lord" in v. 3. Although very little biographical information about Jesus is given, the audience is at least informed that he came from Nazareth, a village of the region of Galilee. The statement that Jesus was baptized by John in the Jordan River provides narrative continuity.

■ **10** The phrase "the heavens split" ($\sigma\chi\iota\zeta o\mu\acute{\epsilon}\nu o\upsilon\varsigma\ \tau o\grave{\upsilon}\varsigma\ o\grave{\upsilon}\rho\alpha\nu o\acute{\upsilon}\varsigma$) is an unusual expression. It does not occur in the LXX. It occurs nowhere else in the New Testament or in the apostolic literature. A similar phrase does occur in *Joseph and Aseneth*, according to which text the heaven was split ($\grave{\epsilon}\sigma\chi\acute{\iota}\sigma\vartheta\eta\ \acute{o}\ o\grave{\upsilon}\rho\alpha\nu\acute{o}\varsigma$) near the morning star. A great light appeared that proved to be a "man," that is, an angel, who came down to Aseneth from heaven (*Jos. Asen.* 14:1-3).[79] The verb "to open" ($\grave{\alpha}\nu o\acute{\iota}\gamma\omega$) was more often used to express the idea of the heaven(s) opening for theophanic, epiphanic, or revelatory purposes.[80]

The Holy Spirit is not presented as or compared with a dove in the MT or the LXX, but the use of the piel participle of רחף ("brooding" or "hovering over") to describe the activity of the "Spirit of God" (רוח אלהים) in Gen 1:2 may have given rise to the idea.[81] According to *b. Ḥag.* 15a, Ben Zoma stated that he "was gazing between the upper and the lower waters, and there is only a bare three fingers' [breadth] between them, for it is said: *And the spirit of God hovered over the face of the waters*—like a dove which hovers over her young without touching [them]."[82] Similarly, the targum of Cant 2:12 interprets the voice of the turtledove as the voice of the Holy Spirit. The first part of Cant 2:12, "The flowers appear on the earth," is interpreted as the appearance of Moses and Aaron; the second, "the time of singing," is read as "the time for pruning" and interpreted as "the time for the slaying of the firstborn"; and the third part, "and the voice of the turtledove is heard in our land," is interpreted as "and the voice of the Holy Spirit of salvation, which I spoke unto Abraham . . . , 'The nation that they serve I will judge. . . .'"[83]

The association of the Spirit of God with a human being in the Bible has different connotations according to the context.[84] It may endow a man with extraordinary physical strength (Judg 14:6, 19); it may induce ecstasy (Num 11:25; 1 Sam 10:6, 10); it may transport a person

Neukirchen-Vluyn: Neukirchener Verlag, 1978–83) 2:138–39; Klaus Berger, *Exegese des Neuen Testaments: Neue Wege vom Text zur Auslegung* (Heidelberg: Quelle & Meyer, 1977) 55–57. For the baptismal context of this tradition, see Henning Paulsen, *Überlieferung und Auslegung in Römer 8* (WMANT 43; Neukirchen-Vluyn: Neukirchener Verlag, 1974) 86–96.

79   For the Greek text of this passage, see Christoph Burchard, "Ein vorläufiger Text von Joseph und Aseneth," *Dielheimer Blätter zum Alten Testament* 14 (1979) 2–53, esp. 23; or Denis and Janssens, *Concordance grecque*, 854. For discussion, see Gideon Bohak, *Joseph and Aseneth and the Jewish Temple in Heliopolis* (SBLEJL 10; Atlanta: Scholars Press, 1996) 2–3; Angela Standhartinger, *Das Frauenbild im Judentum der hellenistischen Zeit: Ein Beitrag anhand von 'Joseph und Aseneth'* (AGJU 26; Leiden: Brill, 1995) 108–25.

80   Isa 63:19 LXX; Ezek 1:1 LXX; *Hermas, Vis.* 1.1.4; *T. Levi* 2:6; 18:6. Cf. *2 Bar.* 22:1; *Apoc. Abr.* 19:4 (no Greek version of the latter two passages has survived).

81   As Ephraim A. Speiser has pointed out, the same stem is used in Deut 32:11 of eagles in relation to their young (*Genesis: Introduction, Translation, and*

Notes [AB 1; Garden City, NY: Doubleday, 1964] 5). In the *Sipre* on Deut 32:10-12, the eagle's activity is compared to that of God's self-revelation on the occasion of the giving of the Torah; it is also compared to God's activity in the age to come, with reference to Cant 2:8, "Hark my beloved, behold he comes." For the text of the *Sipre*, see *Sifre on Deuteronomy* (New York: Jewish Theological Seminary, 1969) 356–57; for an ET, see Jacob Neusner, *Sifre to Deuteronomy: An Analytical Translation*, vol. 2: *Pisqaot One Hundred Forty-Seven through Three Hundred Fifty-Seven* (BJS 101.2; Atlanta: Scholars Press, 1987) 337. This text is cited by Israel Abrahams, *Studies in Pharisaism and the Gospels* (2 vols.; Cambridge: Cambridge University Press, 1917–24; reprinted 2 vols. in 1; LBS; New York: Ktav, 1967) 1:49.

82   Trans. from Morris Ginsberg in Isidore Epstein, ed., *The Babylonian Talmud: Seder Moʿed, Ḥagigah* (London: Soncino Press, 1935–52) 15a (section a).

83   For the Aramaic text, see Alexander Sperber, ed., *The Bible in Aramaic*, vol. 4A: *The Hagiographa* (Leiden: Brill, 1968) 131; trans. (modified) from Bernard Grossfeld, ed., *The Targum to the Five Megilloth* (New York: Hermon Press, 1973) 197–98; Hooker acknowledges that *b. Ḥag.* 15a and the tar-

miraculously from one place to another (1 Kgs 18:12; 2 Kgs 2:16; Ezek 3:12, 14; 8:3; 11:1, 24; 43:5); or it may endow the charisma of leadership (Judg 3:10; 1 Sam 16:13).[85] The Spirit of God is associated also with the charisma of the prophet (Mic 3:8; Neh 9:30) and with the qualities of the ideal king (Isa 11:1-9, esp. v. 2).[86] The narrative context of Mark, however, points to Isa 61:1-2 as an important precedent for Mark 1:10 and suggests an intertextual relationship. The former passage reads:

> The Spirit of the Lord is upon me, because he has
> anointed me;
> He has sent me to proclaim good news to the poor,
> To heal those whose hearts are broken,
> To proclaim release to the captives,
> The recovery of sight to the blind,
> To announce the year of the Lord's favor,
> And the day of recompense of our God,
> To comfort all who mourn . . . . (Isa 61:1-2 LXX)

The introduction of the quotations in Mark 1:2-3 with the words "As it is written in the book of Isaiah the prophet" and the relation of those quotations to the narration that follows suggest that the activities of John and Jesus are at least prefigured by, if not prophesied by, the book of Isaiah. "The Spirit of the Lord is upon me" (Isa 61:1a) is congruent with or fulfilled in the description of the descent of the Spirit upon Jesus in Mark 1:10c. The clause "because he has anointed ($\ddot{\epsilon}\chi\rho\iota\sigma\epsilon\nu$) me" (Isa 61:1b) has a similar relation to the epithet $\chi\rho\iota\sigma\tau\acute{o}\varsigma$ ("anointed" or "Christ") applied to Jesus in Mark 1:1. The idea of sending in the statement "He has sent me to

proclaim good news ($\epsilon\dot{\upsilon}\alpha\gamma\gamma\epsilon\lambda\acute{\iota}\sigma\alpha\sigma\vartheta\alpha\iota$) to the poor" (Isa 61:1c) is expressed in Mark 1:2-15 by the implication that the activity of Jesus comes to pass in fulfillment of scripture. The task of "proclaiming good news to the poor" is reflected in the summary of Jesus' activity as "proclaiming the good news of God" ($\kappa\eta\rho\acute{\upsilon}\sigma\sigma\omega\nu$ $\tau\grave{o}$ $\epsilon\dot{\upsilon}\alpha\gamma\gamma\acute{\epsilon}\lambda\iota\sigma\nu$ $\tau\sigma\hat{\upsilon}$ $\vartheta\epsilon\sigma\hat{\upsilon}$) in Mark 1:14 and in his call "repent and trust in the good news" ($\mu\epsilon\tau\alpha\nu\sigma\epsilon\hat{\iota}\tau\epsilon$ $\kappa\alpha\grave{\iota}$ $\pi\iota\sigma\tau\epsilon\acute{\upsilon}\epsilon\tau\epsilon$ $\dot{\epsilon}\nu$ $\tau\hat{\omega}$ $\epsilon\dot{\upsilon}\alpha\gamma\gamma\epsilon\lambda\acute{\iota}\omega$) in v. 15. The tasks of healing those whose hearts are broken and proclaiming release to the captives and recovery of sight to the blind (Isa 61:1d-f) are congruent with the miracles of Jesus narrated later in Mark. Announcing the year of the Lord's favor and the day of God's recompense (Isa 61:1g-h) are activities similar to announcing, "The time is fulfilled and the kingdom of God has drawn near" (Mark 1:15).

In addition to such interpretations based on the Old Testament and postbiblical Judaism, one must pay attention also to the Hellenistic context of Mark. Edward P. Dixon has argued persuasively that the simile of the Spirit's descent like a dove was modeled on Homer's depiction of the descents of gods from the heavenly realm to earth. In the Homeric epics, such descents are described with similes involving the descent of birds. On the basis of stylistic analysis, he argues further that the phrase $\epsilon\dot{\iota}\varsigma$ $\alpha\dot{\upsilon}\tau\acute{o}\nu$ in v. 10 signifies that the Spirit entered "into Jesus." In relation to the transfiguration in 9:2-8, members of the audience familiar with Greek mythology would understand v. 10 to mean that the earthly Jesus, from the time of his baptism, was a divine being walking the earth.[87]

---

gum of Cant 2:12 are later than the Gospel of Mark, but argues that they support the implication of Mark 1:10 that the image of the dove was already associated with the Holy Spirit in the first century (46). See also Abrahams, who points out that the association of the heavenly voice and the dove in Mark is illuminated by the fact that the former (*Bath-Qol*) is represented in several rabbinic passages as piping or chirping like a bird. He cites, e.g., *b. Ber.* 3a, "I heard a *Bath-Qol moaning as a dove* and saying: Woe to the children through whose iniquities I laid waste My Temple" (*Studies in Pharisaism*, 1:47; trans. and emphasis his). Lentzen-Deis discusses the targum of Cant 2:12 (*Die Taufe Jesu*, 180).

84   For a survey of themes and passages in the OT and

Jewish literature related to the descent of the Spirit upon Jesus, see Lentzen-Deis, *Die Taufe Jesu*, 127–70.

85   Friedrich Baumgärtel categorized these examples and others under the heading of the Spirit of God as "the effective power of God" ("Spirit in the OT," *TDNT* 6 [1968] 362–63).

86   Ibid., 363.

87   Edward P. Dixon, "Descending Spirit and Descending Gods: An Interpretation of the Spirit's 'Descent as a Dove' in Mark 1:10," (forthcoming in *JBL*).

■ **11** The best indicator of the significance of the descent of the Spirit is the saying of the divine voice from heaven.[88] The first part of the saying is an actualization or fulfillment of Ps 2:7, a line from a royal psalm in which the Lord says to the king of Israel, his anointed, "You are my son." The wording of Mark 1:11, "You are my son" (σὺ εἶ ὁ υἱός μου), is almost identical to that of the LXX, "You are my son" (Υἱός μου εἶ σύ). This statement implies that God recognizes or establishes Jesus as his "son" with these words. The widespread view that the language of Ps 2:7 implies adoption in its original social and historical contexts is not tenable.[89] Yet it may be that this language evoked ideas of adoption in at least some of the early social contexts in which Mark was read and heard. In any case, the allusion to Psalm 2 suggests that, when the Spirit enters into Jesus and he is addressed as God's "son," God thus appoints him as the messiah. The implied use of Psalm 2 at the coronation or installation of a king supports this inference.[90]

To the saying from Ps 2:7 the text of Mark adds the words "the beloved one" (ὁ ἀγαπητός). The source or model of this term is difficult to determine.[91] One possibility is that Mark 1:11 alludes to the story of the near-sacrifice of Isaac, implying that the near-death of Isaac prefigures the actual death of Jesus and its symbolic meaning.[92] Another, more likely explanation is that the expression "the beloved one"(ὁ ἀγαπητός) was inspired

by the other passage that is actualized or fulfilled in the speech of the divine voice, Isa 42:1, the first part of which reads, "Behold my servant, whom I uphold, my chosen, in whom my soul delights." The authors of Mark and Matthew may have known a text of Isa 42:1 in which the word "beloved" occurred.[93] Or the term may have been inspired by the use of the related verb in "the parallel and related passages Isa 41:8-9 and 44:2" in the Greek version.[94] These passages suggest that "chosen" and "beloved" are synonyms.[95]

The second part of the saying of the divine voice in Mark 1:11, "I take delight in you" (ἐν σοὶ εὐδόκησα), is closer to the MT than to the LXX. In the former, Isa 42:1b reads "my soul takes delight (in him)" (רצתה נפשי), whereas the LXX reads "my soul receives him" (προσεδέξατο αὐτὸν ἡ ψυχή μου). This passage also has an intertextual relationship with the description of the descent of the Spirit in Mark 1:10, since Isa 42:1continues "I have put my Spirit upon him."[96]

By combining Ps 2:7 and Isa 42:1, the text of Mark interprets Jesus both as the messiah and as the Servant of the Lord. This close association of the two epithets has several implications. One is that the author of Mark, or the tradents upon whom he was dependent, read the poems about the Servant of the Lord in Second Isaiah messianically, at least in part. The striking similarities between the fate of the Servant as described in Isaiah 53,

---

88   For a review of the relevant primary texts and a critical assessment, see Lentzen-Deis, *Die Taufe Jesu*, 183–93. He concludes that Isa 42:1 is significant for the interpretation of both the descent of the Spirit (156–58) and the heavenly voice (192).

89   For the view that Ps 2:7 implies adoption, see, e.g., Mitchell Dahood, *Psalms: Introduction, Translation, and Notes*, vol. 1: *1–50* (AB 16; Garden City, NY: Doubleday, 1966) 11–12. This view has been criticized by John J. Collins in idem and Adela Yarbro Collins, *Messiah and Son of God: Early Christology in Light of Biblical and Jewish Traditions* (Grand Rapids: Eerdmans, forthcoming) [John's first lecture, manuscript pages 10–11, 15–16].

90   On Jesus as messiah in Mark, see the introduction to the commentary, the section *Jesus as Messiah*. In relation to Mark 1:11, see also 2 Sam 7:14, "I will be his Father, and he shall be my son," which also implies that God recognizes or establishes the king as his "son."

91   For a discussion of the various theories, see Marcus,

Way of the Lord, 51–53; Richard J. Bauckham, *Jude, 2 Peter* (WBC 50; Waco, TX: Word Books, 1983) 207–10.

92   Gen 22:2 LXX reads "your beloved son" or "your son, the beloved one") τὸν υἱόν σου τὸν ἀγαπητόν; cf. Gen 22:12, 16. For an example of this interpretation, see Jon D. Levenson, *The Death and Resurrection of the Beloved Son: The Transformation of Child Sacrifice in Judaism and Christianity* (New Haven: Yale University Press, 1993) 30–31, 200–2, 228–29. See also Jeffrey B. Gibson, "Jesus' Wilderness Temptation according to Mark," *JSNT* 53 (1994) 3–34, esp. 25–26, and the literature cited by Marcus, *Way of the Lord*, 52 n. 16; Bauckham, *Jude, 2 Peter*, 208.

93   Cf. Mark 1:11 with Matt 12:17-21, esp. v. 18.

94   Marcus, *Way of the Lord*, 51.

95   This is the explanation that Marcus finds most persuasive (*Way of the Lord*, 52); Bauckham finds the fewest difficulties with it (*Jude, 2 Peter*, 208–9). The verb "to love" (ἀγαπάω) is used of God's relation to Israel, his servant, in Isa 41:8; 44:2 LXX.

on the one hand, and the fate of Jesus as interpreted by his followers, on the other, may have been the impetus for the messianic interpretation of these poems. Another implication is that the messiahship of Jesus is not presented in royal and military terms; instead the idea of the messiah of Israel is reinterpreted in prophetic terms.

■ **12-13** The statement "And immediately the Spirit drove[97] him out into the wilderness" is reminiscent of the passages in 1 and 2 Kings and in Ezekiel according to which the Spirit of God miraculously transported the prophet from one place to another.[98] The forty days during which Jesus was in the wilderness recalls the forty days that Moses spent on Mount Sinai (Exod 24:18; 34:28).[99] But Moses was with the Lord receiving revelation and instruction, whereas Jesus was being tested by Satan. The narrative constellation of Satan, wild animals ($\vartheta\eta\rho i\alpha$), and ministering angels in v. 13 is analogous to the reception of Psalm 91 at Qumran.[100]

The portion of Psalm 91 most similar to Mark 1:13 reads as follows:

For he will give his angels charge of you to guard you
    in all your ways.
On their hands they will bear you up, lest you dash
    your foot against a stone.
You will tread on the lion and the adder, the young
    lion and the serpent you will trample under
    foot. (Ps 91:11-13 RSV)[101]

In the tractate on oaths in the Babylonian Talmud, Psalm 91 is called the "song against evil occurrences" or "the song against plagues," that is, the psalm that protects against evil spirits or demons. Those who call it a song against plagues do so because of the line "no plague shall come near your tent" (v. 10), and those who call it a song against evil occurrences do so because of the line "a thousand may fall at your side" (v. 7); that is, the evil spirits will depart. It is stated further that Rabbi Joshua ben Levi recited these verses (Ps 91:1-9) when retiring to sleep, in order to protect himself (from evil spirits) (b. Šebu. 15b).[102]

---

96   $\check\epsilon\delta\omega\kappa\alpha$ $\tau\dot{o}$ $\pi\nu\epsilon\hat{v}\mu\dot{\alpha}$ $\mu o\upsilon$ $\dot{\epsilon}\pi$' $\alpha\dot{v}\tau\dot{o}\nu$ (Isa 42:1c).

97   Lit., "the Spirit drives him out" ($\tau\dot{o}$ $\pi\nu\epsilon\hat{v}\mu\alpha$ $\alpha\dot{v}\tau\dot{o}\nu$ $\dot{\epsilon}\kappa\beta\acute{a}\lambda\lambda\epsilon\iota$). This is the first use of the historic present in Mark, which is characteristic of the author's style; see Taylor, 163.

98   See the comments on v. 10 above. Susan R. Garrett has argued that the sequence of events from the baptism of Jesus to the Spirit's driving Jesus into the wilderness to confront Satan corresponds to a traditional model attested in the book of Job: declaration of divine approval, followed by satanic testing (Job 1:8-12; 2:3-6) (*The Temptations of Jesus in Mark's Gospel* [Grand Rapids: Eerdmans, 1998] 55–56). The motif of "testing" is not explicit in Job, and the Hebrew root (נסה), which is equivalent to the Greek terms $\pi\epsilon\iota\rho\acute{a}\zeta\epsilon\iota\nu$, $\pi\epsilon\iota\rho\hat{a}\nu$, does not occur with this sense in Job, but Garrett also mentions the story of the testing of Abraham in *Jub.* 17:15-16 (ibid., 46–47). The term נסה ("to test") does occur in the story of Isaac (Gen 22:1), and the motif occurs in the retelling of the story in *Jub.* 17:15-18. See the trans. of the latter passage by James C. VanderKam, *The Book of Jubilees* (CSCO 511, Scriptores Aethiopici 88; Leuven: Peeters, 1989) 105.

99   Some interpreters relate the forty days during which Jesus was in the wilderness to the forty years during which God humbled and tested Israel in the wilderness (Deut 8:2-4); see, e.g., Klauck, *Vorspiel im Himmel?* 56–57.

100   Gibson has noted that Mark 1:13 alludes to Ps 91:11-

13, but he did not observe the use of Psalm 91 at Qumran nor its connection with exorcism ("Jesus' Wilderness Temptation according to Mark," 21–22). Garrett argued that the mention of wild beasts in v. 13 alludes to Psalm 91 and that the wild beasts symbolize the dangers that Jesus faced and from which he was protected (*Temptations of Jesus*, 57). She also mentions the use of Psalm 91 for protection against demonic powers (ibid., 58; and eadem, *The Demise of the Devil: Magic and the Demonic in Luke's Writings* [Minneapolis: Fortress, 1989] 139 n. 71).

101   Jacques Dupont noted that the text of Mark, like Ps 91:11-12, connects the two motifs of the service of angels and the threat of wild animals; but he concluded that the allusion to Psalm 91 was made in a more detailed way by Mark's source and that it no longer makes sense at the Markan redactional level ("L'arrière-fond biblique du récit des tentations de Jesus," *NTS* 3 [1956–57] 287–304, esp. 294).

102   Trans, by Alec E. Silverstone in Isidore Epstein, ed., *The Babylonian Talmud: Shebuʿoth* (London: Soncino Press, 1935–52) 15b (section c). In Biblical Hebrew the noun פגע means "occurrence," "chance," or "evil occurrence" (BDB, s.v.). In Rabbinic Hebrew, the plural also has the meanings "evil spirits," "demons" (Jastrow, s.v.). According to Jastrow, *y. ʿErub.* 10.26ᶜ bot. refers to a "song of demons" that they used to recite in Jerusalem (in the temple, when one was threatened with insanity) (ibid.). A little further on in the tractate, this song is identified with Ps 3:2-3 and

151

Six fragmentary columns of a scroll containing psalms were discovered in Cave 11 near Qumran.[103] Several apocryphal psalms clearly intended for use in exorcism are followed by a recension of the canonical Psalm 91. Column 2 mentions Solomon and may have contained a list of types of demons, such as "spirits of the angels of destruction," "spirits of the bastards" (i.e., the spirits of the Giants, the dead offspring of the Watchers), "demons," "Lilith," "howlers," and "yelpers."[104] The language of exorcism found here and in other parts of the scroll is reinforced by the mention of Solomon, who was renowned for his exorcistic expertise around the turn of the era.[105] The inclusion of Psalm 91 in this collection (col. 5:3-14) suggests that this psalm was already used for exorcistic purposes in the Herodian period or even earlier.[106]

A Greek magical amulet found on the Crimean peninsula and probably dating to the late Roman period attests to the equivalence of wild beasts and demons in popular religion. It contains a brief spell for the exorcism of a young girl:

Ps 91:1-9; see Jacob Neusner, *The Talmud of the Land of Israel: A Preliminary Translation and Explanation*, vol. 12: *Erubin* (CSHJ; Chicago: University of Chicago Press, 1991) 290. Neusner translates, "They would recite a psalm for the suffering in Jerusalem," and categorizes the passage as *y. ʿErub.* 10:11 N-R. Similarly, Jastrow (s.v. פגע) refers to *y. Šabb.* 6:8b, where Ps 91:1-9 is designated a "song for the stricken"; Neusner translates, "They would recite the psalm for the afflicted in Jerusalem," and categorizes the passage as *y. Šabb.* 6:2 [7.H-L] (*The Talmud of the Land of Israel: A Preliminary Translation and Explanation*, vol. 11: *Shabbat* [CSHJ; Chicago: University of Chicago Press, 1991] 198-99).

103 11QapPsᵃ (11Q11); Florentino García Martínez, Eibert J. C. Tigchelaar, and A. S. van der Woude, eds., *Qumran Cave 11*, vol. 2: *11Q2-18, 11Q20-31* (DJD 23; Oxford: Clarendon, 1998) 181-205. Preliminary editions were published by J. P. M. van der Ploeg, "Le Psaume XCI dans une recension de Qumrân," *RB* 72 (1965) 210-17, pls. 8-9; idem, "Un petit rouleau de psaumes apocryphes (11QPsApᵃ)," in Gert Jeremias et al., eds., *Tradition und Glaube: Das frühe Christentum in seiner Umwelt: Festgabe für Karl Georg Kuhn* (Göttingen: Vandenhoeck & Ruprecht, 1971) 128-39, pls. 2-7; and Émile Puech, "Les deux derniers psaumes davidiques du rituel d'exorcisme, 11QPsApᵃ IV 4-V 14," in Devorah Dimant and Uriel Rappaport, eds., *The Dead Sea Scrolls: Forty Years of Research* (STDJ 10; Leiden: Brill; Jerusalem: Magnes Press/Yad Izhak Ben-Zvi, 1992) 64-89; Émile Puech, "11QPsApᵃ: Un rituel d'exorcismes: Essai de reconstruction," *RQ* 14 (1990) 377-408. See also James A. Sanders, "A Liturgy for the Healing of the Stricken (11QPsApᵃ = 11Q11)," in Charlesworth, *Dead Sea Scrolls*, vol. 4A: *Pseudepigraphic and Non-Masoretic Psalms and Prayers* (Tübingen: Mohr Siebeck; Louisville: Westminster John Knox, 1997) 216-33; Pablo A. Torijano, *Solomon the Esoteric King: From King to Magus, Development of a Tradition* (JSJSup 73;

Leiden/Boston: Brill, 2002) 43-53; Esther Eshel, "Genres of Magical Texts in the Dead Sea Scrolls," in Armin Lange, Hermann Lichtenberger, and K. F. Diethard Römheld, eds., *Die Dämonen: Die Dämonologie der israelitisch-jüdischen und frühchristlichen Literatur im Kontext ihrer Umwelt = Demons: The Demonology of Israelite-Jewish and Early Christian Literature in [the] Context of Their Environment* (Tübingen: Mohr Siebeck, 2003) 395-415, esp. 398-401; Eshel, "Apotropaic Prayers in the Second Temple Period," in Esther G. Chazon, ed., *Liturgical Perspectives: Prayer and Poetry in Light of the Dead Sea Scrolls* (STDJ 48; Leiden: Brill, 2003) 69-88, esp. 85-86; eadem, "Demonology in Palestine during the Second Temple Period" (Ph.D. diss., Hebrew University in Jerusalem, 1999; Hebrew with an English abstract [pp. I-XIV]) chap. 5.

104 See Philip S. Alexander, "The Demonology of the Dead Sea Scrolls," in Peter W. Flint and James C. VanderKam, eds., *The Dead Sea Scrolls after Fifty Years: A Comprehensive Assessment* (2 vols.; Leiden/Boston/Cologne: Brill, 1998-99) 2:332-33. Cf. the *Songs of the Maskil* (4Q510) frg. 1. 5-6; on that text, and on the related text 4Q511, see Eshel, "Genres of Magical Texts," 406-9.

105 Josephus *Ant.* 8.2.5 §42-49; *Testament of Solomon*; for discussion, see Duling, "Solomon, Exorcism," 235-52. See also Philip S. Alexander, "Incantations and Books of Magic," in Emil Schürer, *The History of the Jewish People in the Age of Jesus Christ (175 B.C.-A.D. 135)* (rev. ed. by Geza Vermes, Fergus Millar et al.; 3 vols. in 4; Edinburgh: T & T Clark, 1973-87) 3:342-79, esp. 372-79.

106 The original editors dated the scroll paleographically to the late Herodian period. See García Martínez et al., *Qumran Cave 11*, 2:184. So also Puech ("Les deux derniers psaumes davidiques," 80). Eshel defines the version of Psalm 91 in 11Q11 as an "apotropaic hymn" ("Genres of Magical Texts," 398).

I adjure you [pl.] by the living God, that every spirit and apparition and every beast, be gone from the soul of this woman . . . (Ὁρκίζω ὑμᾶς, κατὰ τοῦ θεοῦ τοῦ {ζω}ζῶ(ν)τος, πᾶν πνεῦμα καὶ φάντασμα καὶ πᾶν θηρίον ἀποστῆνε ἀπὸ {ψυχῆς} ψυχῆς τῆς γυνα(ι)κὸς ταύτης).[107]

The association of wild animals and demons was already made in the prophetic oracle of judgment against Babylon in Isaiah 13:

It will never be inhabited for all time, and no one will enter it for many generations; the Arabs will not pass through it, and shepherds will not rest there. Wild animals (θηρία) will rest there, and the houses will be filled with howling, and Sirens will rest there, and demons will dance there, and ape-demons will dwell there, and hedgehogs will build their nests in their houses. It is coming quickly and it will not delay. (Isa 13:20-22 LXX)[108]

The brief account of Jesus' testing in the wilderness in Mark 1:12-13 pits Jesus, the Spirit of God, and the angels, on the one hand, against Satan, wild animals, and (it is implied) demons, on the other. The text does not reveal exactly how and why Jesus was tested. His ability to withstand Satan and the wild beasts attests to his trust in God and to the favor bestowed by God on him.[109] But the contest also implies that, although John has prepared the way for Jesus and made straight his paths (v. 3), and even though God has designated him as the messiah (v. 11), Jesus will encounter opposition in his mission.[110]

■ **14-15** The statement in v. 14 that "Jesus went into Galilee, proclaiming (κηρύσσων) the good news of God" is parallel to the statement in v. 4 that "John was baptizing in the wilderness and proclaiming (κηρύσσων) a baptism of repentance for the forgiveness of sins." Like the contrast between the baptism with water and the baptism in the Holy Spirit (v. 8), this parallel presentation suggests that John's activity both precedes and prepares for that of Jesus. Furthermore, Jesus' public activity is pre-

---

107 Text and trans. from Roy Kotansky, *Greek Magical Amulets: The Inscribed Gold, Silver, Copper, and Bronze Lamellae, Part 1: Published Texts of Known Provenance* (ANWAW Papyrologica Coloniensia 22.1; Düsseldorf: Westdeutscher Verlag, 1994) no. 67, p. 383. On p. 385, Kotansky gives a list of spells against noxious animals and concludes that the generic θηρία ("wild animals") can refer to predatory animals or demons in animal form.

108 See also Isa 34:8-17, esp. vv. 11, 13-14; 1 Bar 4:35.

109 Cf. Mark 1:11c; Ps 91:1-2, 11-13; Job 5:17-23. Garrett argued that the testing of Jesus was a real one in which he was free to choose whether to follow God's way or not; the model for the scene is the testing of Job in Job 1–2 and of Abraham in *Jub.* 17:15—18:16. But these passages portray quite clearly and directly a contest between God and the Adversary, whereas Mark 1:12-13 implies that the contest is between Jesus and Satan. Garrett also refers to a Greek fragment of *Jubilees* (equivalent to 10:9) that mentions testing: "And a tenth [of the unclean demons] was given to [Mastema] in accordance with the divine decree, so that he might test human beings to examine each one's devotion to God; the other nine-tenths were thrown into the abyss" (καὶ ἐδόθη αὐτῷ τὸ δέκατον αὐτῶν κατὰ πρόσταξιν θείαν ὥστε πειράζειν τοὺς ἀνθρώπους πρὸς δοκιμὴν τῆς ἑκάστου πρὸς θεὸν προαιρέσεως τὰ δὲ λοιπὰ ἐννέα μέρη ἐβλήθη εἰς τὴν ἄβυσσον); text from Denis and Janssens, *Concordance grecque*, 903; my

trans. Cf. the trans. by VanderKam: "A tenth of them were given to him, in accord with the divine command, in order to tempt people as a test of each one's preference for God; the nine remaining parts were thrown into the depth(s)" (*Book of Jubilees*, 335). The term translated "devotion" by the author and "preference" by VanderKam is προαίρεσις ("a choosing of one thing over another"). It appears in Greek and Hellenistic ethical discussions; see Aristotle *Rhet.* 1.9.32; Plutarch *Mor.* 551E: a preference of evil (προαίρεσις τοῦ αἰσχροῦ). The motifs of faithfulness to God and of ethical choice are not explicit in Mark 1:12-13.

110 Cf. James M. Robinson's interpretation of the testing of Jesus in the context of (1) the apocalyptic idea that, when the consummation is near, victory will come only after an intensified struggle and (2) of the eschatological hope that the devil will be overthrown ("The Markan Introduction: 1:1-13," in *Problem of History*, 69–80, esp. 76). Klauck argued that Jesus appears in vv. 12-13 as a new Adam who withstands the test of Satan and thus initiates a new time of salvation (*Vorspiel im Himmel?* 55–60). Dieter Lührmann rejects the typology of a first and a second Adam and argues rather that Jesus restores the glory of Adam by means of his righteousness (*Das Markusevangelium* [HNT 3; Tübingen: Mohr Siebeck, 1987] 39).

sented as beginning only "after John was handed over" (v. 14).[111] This temporal distinction, along with the temporal expression in 1:1, "(The) beginning of the good news," and the qualitative contrast between the work of John and that of Jesus in v. 8, suggests that the time of eschatological fulfillment, the time of the fulfillment of scripture (cf. vv. 2-3), is divided into periods. First comes the time of John's activity, then the time of Jesus' public work. Similarly, the theme and the setting of "the wilderness" ($\dot{\eta}$ $\ddot{\epsilon}\rho\eta\mu o\varsigma$) in vv. 2-13 contrast with the setting given to Jesus' proclamation in v. 14 (Galilee). The text prepares for this shift in setting by mentioning Jesus' origin in Nazareth of Galilee in v. 9. The geographical contrast suggests a thematic and qualitative distinction between the time of repentance and asceticism in the wilderness and the time of good news, fulfillment and trust in Galilee. The distinction is of course not absolute. The activity of John is also fulfillment of scripture, and Jesus also calls for repentance (v. 15). Further, it is noteworthy that the verb "to hand over" ($\pi\alpha\rho\alpha\delta\dot{\iota}\delta\omega\mu\iota$), used of John in v. 14, is used of Jesus elsewhere in the Gospel.[112] This usage suggests that John is portrayed as a prototype of Jesus, and it explains why John's activity is included in the eschatological period of the proclamation of the good news (1:1-3).[113] On the phrase "the good news of God," see the introduction to the commentary, the section on *Genre*.

As noted in the section "Narrative Unity" above, the relation of the citation of scripture in vv. 2-3 to the activity of John and the appearance of Jesus in vv. 4-9 suggests that the events being narrated occur in fulfillment of the scriptures. Similarly, the announcement of Jesus in v. 15, "The time is fulfilled and the kingdom of God has drawn near," implies that the prophecies of scripture and the hopes of the people are in the process of being fulfilled.[114] This narrative presentation of the announcement of fulfillment is analogous to the argument made in the *Melchizedek Scroll* by assembling and interpreting various passages from scripture. Mark's Jesus announces that "the time is fulfilled" ($\pi\epsilon\pi\lambda\dot{\eta}\rho\omega\tau\alpha\iota$ $\dot{o}$ $\kappa\alpha\iota\rho\dot{o}\varsigma$). The *Melchizedek Scroll* speaks about "the end of days" (אחרית הימים) and "the end of the tenth jubilee" (סוף היובל העשירי) (11QMelch 2:4, 7).[115] In the Dead Sea Scrolls, the phrase "the end of days" (אחרית הימים) refers to a period of separation and affliction for the pious, a time of temptation and suffering in which the community had to stand the test. This final period of history included events that were already past from the point of view of the community; the present time, from the point of view of sectarian works from the oldest to the latest; and events of the future, such as the coming of the messiahs.[116] According to another document from Qumran, 4QPseudo-Ezekiel (4Q385), the history of the world is divided into ten jubilee periods, each of which is subdivided into weeks of years, as in the *Melchizedek Scroll* (11QMelch).[117] The end of the tenth jubilee, therefore, would be the end or fulfillment of history. This end-time is called "the day of salvation" (יום הישועה) (11QMelch 2:15-16).[118] Like Mark, the *Melchizedek Scroll* associates the time of fulfillment with the prophecies of Isaiah:

This is *the day [of salvation* (Isa 49:8) about w]hich [God] spoke [through the mouth of Isa]iah the

---

111 On the connotations of this language, see the commentary on 3:19 below.

112 Mark 3:19; 9:31; 10:33; 14:10, 21, 44; 15:1, 15.

113 On John as the prototype of Jesus, see Ernst, *Johannes der Täufer*, 4–5, 20–23. See also Lentzen-Deis, *Die Taufe Jesu*, 89, and the literature cited in n. 140; and Webb, *John the Baptizer and Prophet*, 55.

114 The process becomes complete only with the coming of the Son of Man; see 9:1; 13:24-27, and the commentary below.

115 For an edition of the Hebrew text and an ET, see García Martínez et al., *Qumran Cave 11*, 2:224–25, 229; see also Kobelski, *Melchizedek*, 5–10.

116 A persuasive case is made for these conclusions by Annette Steudel, "אחרית הימים in the Texts from Qumran," *RevQ* 16 (1993) 225–46. The Qumran

authors also referred to this period of time as the עת המצרף הבאה. Steudel translates this with "the time of refining that has come" (ibid., 228–29); García Martínez and Tigchelaar, however, translate "the time of trial which co[mes" (*Dead Sea Scrolls*, 354–55). Although Steudel refers to 4QMidrEschat 4:1ff. and García Martínez and Tigchelaar to 4QFlorilegium (4Q174) frg. 1 2:1, they actually refer to the same text.

117 Kobelski, *Melchizedek*, 14, 49–51. There are five significant fragments of this work: A = 4Q385; B = 4Q386; C = 4Q385c; D = 4Q388; E = 4Q391.

118 For the arguments in favor of this restoration, see Kobelski, *Melchizedek*, 20.

prophet who said, ["How] beautiful on (the) mountains are the feet of the heral[d who pro]claims peace, the her[ald of good who proclaims salvati]on, saying to Zion, 'Your God [is king.'"] (Isa 52:7) (11QMelch 2:15-16)[119]

Like the proclamation of Jesus in Mark 1:15, this text associates the fulfillment of history with the kingship of God.[120]

The מבשר ("herald") mentioned in 11QMelch 2:16, 18-19 is probably identical with the eschatological prophet expected by the community.[121] An aspect of the role of the herald is to announce to the members of the covenant community that Melchizedek is king. This constellation of eschatological ideas is strikingly analogous to the narrative introduction of Mark, in which the baptism performed by the prophetic figure John provides the occasion for the appointment of Jesus as messiah.[122]

The use of the term "repent" ($\mu\epsilon\tau\alpha\nu\circ\epsilon\hat{\iota}\tau\epsilon$) in v. 15 does not yet connote a penitential discipline or primarily a human decision that begins a process of moral reform.[123] Rather, it signifies a turning away from one's previous way of life, determined by particular sets of convictions, practices, and social affiliations and a turning to and acceptance of the new divine initiative through the agency of Jesus. For the author and audiences of Mark, this turning and adherence to Jesus and his message have already led to involvement in a new set of convictions, practices, and social affiliations.

---

119 Trans. from Kobelski, *Melchizedek*, 8. García Martínez et al. read שלום instead of ישועה and thus translate "the day of the peace" instead of "the day of salvation" (García Martínez et al., *Qumran Cave 11*, 2:225, 229).

120 11QMelch 2:24-25 interprets "God" in Isa 52:7 as referring to Melchizedek, who is an angel and probably equivalent to Michael, but this figure is clearly the agent of God in God's eschatological rule. See Kobelski, *Melchizedek*, 62–64, 71–74; cf. García Martínez et al., *Qumran Cave 11*, 2:233.

121 1QS 9:11; 4QTestim 5–8 citing Deut 18:18-19; see Kobelski, *Melchizedek*, 61–62. So also García Martínez et al., *Qumran Cave 11*, 2:232.

122 Daniel 7:22 Θ also links the terms "time" ($\kappa\alpha\iota\rho\acute{o}\varsigma$) and "kingdom" ($\beta\alpha\sigma\iota\lambda\epsilon\acute{\iota}\alpha$), and this text may have influenced the formulation of Mark 1:15.

123 Cf. Lambert, "Did Israel Believe," 648–49; idem, "Topics in the History of Repentance," 137–46.

1:16-20 Jesus Calls Four Disciples

16/ **And while he was passing by along the Sea of Galilee, he saw Simon and Andrew, the brother of Simon, casting (their nets)ᵃ in the sea; for they were fishers. 17/ And Jesus said to them, "Come after me, and I will make you fishers of human beings." 18/ And immediately they left the netsᵇ and followed him. 19/ And when he had gone a little farther, he saw James the son of Zebedee and his brother John, and they were in the boat, putting the nets in order. 20/ And immediately he called them, and they left their father Zebedee in the boat with the hired men and went away after him.ᶜ**

a The earliest attested reading is that of ℵ B L et al., "casting" ($\dot{\alpha}\mu\varphi\iota\beta\acute{\alpha}\lambda\lambda o\nu\tau\alpha\varsigma$). In order to clarify the text, some scribes added "the nets" ($\tau\grave{\alpha}\ \delta\acute{\iota}\kappa\tau\nu\alpha$), perhaps on the basis of v. 18; this reading is attested by D (Θ) f^{13} et al. Others added $\dot{\alpha}\mu\varphi\acute{\iota}\beta\lambda\eta\sigma\tau\rho o\nu$ ("a net"), a word that occurs in the Matthean parallel (4:18). Finally, a few simply changed the text to agree with Matt 4:18 (Γ et al.).

b Codex Bezae (D) and the majority of the Old Latin manuscripts (it) read $\pi\acute{\alpha}\nu\tau\alpha$ ("all things") instead of $\tau\grave{\alpha}\ \delta\acute{\iota}\kappa\tau\nu\alpha$ ("the nets"). The former is probably secondary, since it can be explained as a heightening and generalizing of the response of Simon and Andrew. This tendency is present also in Luke 5:11.

c Most mss read "they went away after him" ($\dot{\alpha}\pi\tilde{\eta}\lambda\vartheta o\nu\ \dot{o}\pi\acute{\iota}\sigma\omega\ \alpha\dot{v}\tau o\tilde{v}$). D W 1424 latt read "they followed him" ($\dot{\eta}\kappa o\lambda o\acute{v}\vartheta\eta\sigma\alpha\nu\ \alpha\dot{v}\tau\tilde{\omega}$). The latter reading is probably secondary, since it may have been inspired by the parallels in Matt 4:22 and Luke 5:11.

Narrative Unity of 1:16-45

As argued above, 1:1 is an introductory titular sentence, and 1:2-15 is a narrative introduction to the Gospel as a whole. Vv. 14-15 summarize the proclamation of Jesus. With v. 16 begins the narrative proper, the representation of specific deeds and sayings of Jesus. In the section 1:16-45, mention is made of Jesus' teaching (1:21-22, 27) and proclaiming (1:38-39), but the emphasis is on the mighty deeds of Jesus, exorcising (1:23-28, 32, 34, 39) and healing (1:29-31, 32, 34, 40-45). The authoritative teaching and the mighty deeds are manifestations of the nearness of the kingdom of God (1:15), and in this section they evoke a positive response from those who experience them or hear reports of them (1:27-28, 33, 37, 45). In 1:2-15 it is implied that Jesus has a divine mission that includes proclamation. The beginning and ending of

1:16-45 show the importance of the followers of Jesus, who share in that task of proclaiming (1:16, 45).

Comment

■ **16-20** Verse 16 marks a new unit in two ways. In the previous section, Jesus moved from the wilderness (vv. 12-13) to Galilee (v. 14). In v. 16 his whereabouts within Galilee is specified as beside the Sea of Galilee.[1] In addition, new characters are introduced in this verse, Simon and his brother Andrew. Mark 1:16-20 actually consists of two units. The incident regarding Simon and Andrew ends with v. 18. V. 19 introduces a new unit with a geographical shift: "And when he had gone a little farther" ($K\alpha\grave{\iota}\ \pi\rho o\beta\grave{\alpha}\varsigma\ \dot{o}\lambda\acute{\iota}\gamma o\nu$). Furthermore, two more new characters are introduced in this verse, James and John. But the identical structuring of the two incidents

---

1 The body of fresh water separating Galilee from the regions of the Gaulan and the Decapolis on the East is called "the Sea of Chinnereth" (יָם־כִּנֶּרֶת) in the Hebrew Bible, e.g., Num 34:11. Hebrew, like other ancient Semitic languages, used the same word for bodies of salt water and bodies of fresh water. The Septuagint translates this name as $\vartheta\acute{\alpha}\lambda\alpha\sigma\sigma\alpha\ X\epsilon\nu\alpha\rho\alpha$ (Num 34:11) or $\vartheta\acute{\alpha}\lambda\alpha\sigma\sigma\alpha\ X\epsilon\nu\epsilon\rho\epsilon\vartheta$ (Josh 12:3). The Gospels according to Mark and Matthew, like some other texts in Koine Greek, reflect this Semitic usage by calling this body of water "the Sea of Galilee" ($\dot{\eta}\ \vartheta\acute{\alpha}\lambda\alpha\sigma\sigma\alpha\ \tau\tilde{\eta}\varsigma\ \Gamma\alpha\lambda\iota\lambda\alpha\acute{\iota}\alpha\varsigma$) (BAGD,

s.v. $\vartheta\acute{\alpha}\lambda\alpha\sigma\sigma\alpha$). Jerome argued, against Porphyry, that the Hebrew word יָם can mean either "sea" or "lake" (Seán Freyne, "Galilee, Sea of," ABD 2:899–901, esp. 900). Josephus usually calls this body of water "Lake Gennesar" ($\Gamma\epsilon\nu\nu\eta\sigma\grave{\alpha}\rho\ \dot{\eta}\ \lambda\acute{\iota}\mu\nu\eta$) in, e.g., Bell. 2.20.6 §573. The Gospel according to Luke calls it "Lake Gennesaret" ($\dot{\eta}\ \lambda\acute{\iota}\mu\nu\eta\ \Gamma\epsilon\nu\nu\eta\sigma\alpha\rho\acute{\epsilon}\tau$) in, e.g., 5:1. The Gospel of John speaks of "the Sea of Galilee of Tiberias" ($\dot{\eta}\ \vartheta\acute{\alpha}\lambda\alpha\sigma\sigma\alpha\ \tau\tilde{\eta}\varsigma\ \Gamma\alpha\lambda\iota\lambda\alpha\acute{\iota}\alpha\varsigma\ \tau\tilde{\eta}\varsigma\ T\iota\beta\epsilon\rho\iota\acute{\alpha}\delta o\varsigma$) in 6:1.

Given this linguistic data, it is unlikely that the word $\vartheta\acute{\alpha}\lambda\alpha\sigma\sigma\alpha$ ("sea") was chosen to designate the

suggests that they belong together. Verse 21 marks a new unit with its indications of geographical, topographical, and temporal changes.

Bultmann rightly argued that the story involves no psychological interest in those who are called and that it is not a simple historical report. He classified the double story as a "biographical apophthegm."[2] Dibelius, in contrast, argued that the story of the calling of the disciples is the "opening bar" of the description of a day's work and that the point of the narrative is found in the general healings mentioned in 1:32-34. It is thus not isolated and lacks an external rounding off, so that it may not be classified as a paradigm.[3] He even argues that 1:16-20 is not a narrative at all, because it lacks all the conditions for making a plot. He concluded that the evangelist invented the scene on the basis of the saying about fishers of people and the tradition of the disciples' names.[4]

Although the double narrative lacks verisimilitude, owing to its disinterest in the motivation of the characters, especially those who are called, it is rounded off, as Bultmann recognized. His definition "biographical apophthegm" may be further specified as "call story."[5] The motif of the sudden summons from business to "coming after" or "following" may have been inspired by 1 Kgs 19:19-21, the story of how Elisha left his plowing to follow Elijah.[6] The details and wording are, on the whole, different, but compare the statements in Mark 1:18,

"they followed him" ($\mathring{\eta}\kappa o\lambda o\acute{v}\vartheta\eta\sigma\alpha\nu$ $\alpha\mathring{v}\tau\tilde{\wp}$) and 20, "they went away after him" ($\mathring{\alpha}\pi\tilde{\eta}\lambda\vartheta o\nu$ $\mathring{o}\pi\acute{\iota}\sigma\omega$ $\alpha\mathring{v}\tau o\tilde{v}$) with 1 Kgs 19:20, "and I will follow you" ($\kappa\alpha\mathring{\iota}$ $\mathring{\alpha}\kappa o\lambda o\upsilon\vartheta\acute{\eta}\sigma\omega$ $\mathring{o}\pi\acute{\iota}\sigma\omega$ $\sigma o\upsilon$). If there is an allusion to the story about Elijah calling Elisha, then the Markan story is a deliberate intensification of it. When Elijah casts his mantle upon Elisha, Elisha asks permission to take leave of his parents before going off to follow Elijah. When Jesus calls the four disciples in Mark 1:16-20, however, they immediately drop everything and follow him; James and John do not even take leave of their father (v. 20).[7]

Call stories also occur in Greek literature. A letter attributed to Diogenes of Sinope (fourth cent. BCE, but actually dating to the first cent. BCE) records the following story, allegedly told by Diogenes himself:

And indeed, once when I went to the house of a lad, the son of extremely prosperous parents, I reclined in a banquet hall adorned all about with inscriptions and gold, so that there was no place where you could spit. Therefore, when something lodged in my throat, I coughed and glanced around me. Since I had no place to spit, I spit at the lad himself. When he rebuked me for this, I retorted, "Well then, So-and-So (speaking to him by name), do you blame me for what happened and not yourself? It was you who decorated the walls and pavement of the banquet hall, leaving only your-

---

lake by the evangelist consciously to evoke the ancient Semitic and biblical mythological connotations associated with the sea. But the use of the word certainly evoked those traditions; see the discussion by Malbon, *Narrative Space,* 76–79. Although the use of the name "Sea of Galilee" ($\mathring{\eta}$ $\vartheta\acute{\alpha}\lambda\alpha\sigma\sigma\alpha$ $\tau\tilde{\eta}\varsigma$ $\Gamma\alpha\lambda\iota\lambda\alpha\acute{\iota}\alpha\varsigma$) does not allow us to determine the place in which Mark was written, it does indicate that the author's Greek was influenced by Semitic usage and that he was not concerned to conform his diction to a higher standard; cf. the discussion in Theissen, *Gospels in Context,* 237–39. Theissen infers from this usage that the Gospel was written in a rural area in the East.

2 Bultmann, *History,* 27–28. Arthur J. Droge has argued that the call stories of the Synoptic tradition belong to the ancient rhetorical category of the *chreia* ("Call Stories in Greek Biography and the Gospels," in Kent Harold Richards, ed., *Society of Biblical Literature 1983 Seminar Papers* (SBLSPS 22; Chico, CA: Scholars Press, 1983) 245–57. For a criti-

cal assessment of Droge's article, see James R. Butts, "The Voyage of Discipleship: Narrative, Chreia, and Call Story," in Craig A. Evans and William F. Stinespring, eds., *Early Jewish and Christian Exegesis: Studies in Memory of William Hugh Brownlee* (SPHS; Atlanta: Scholars Press, 1987) 199–219. Butts argues that the call stories of the Gospels fit the rhetorical category of the "narrative" ($\delta\iota\acute{\eta}\gamma\eta\sigma\iota\varsigma$) better than that of the *chreia* (pronouncement story).

3 Dibelius, *From Tradition to Gospel,* 44.
4 Ibid., 111–12.
5 See Arthur J. Droge, "Call Stories," *ABD* 1:821–23.
6 Roger David Aus, *The Stilling of the Storm: Studies in Early Palestinian Judaic Traditions* (ISFCJ; Binghamton, NY: Global Publications, 2000) 89–96, 98–100.
7 Cf. Droge, "Call Stories," 821–22.

self unadorned, as a place fit to spit onto!" He answered, "You appear to be criticizing my lack of education, but you won't be able to say this anymore. I don't intend to fall one step behind you." From the next day, after he distributed his property to his relatives, he took up his wallet, doubled his coarse cloak, and followed me (εἵπετο). (Pseudo-Diogenes 38.4-5)[8]

Diogenes' style is very different from that of Mark's Jesus, but the way in which the young man gives up his property and follows Diogenes is similar to the response of the four who follow Jesus. Also significant is the story about Xenophon recorded by Diogenes Laertius:

Xenophon, the son of Gryllus, was a citizen of Athens and belonged to the deme Erchia; he was a man of rare modesty and extremely handsome. The story goes that Socrates met him in a narrow passage, and that he stretched out his stick to bar the way, while he inquired where every kind of food was sold. Upon receiving a reply, he put another question, "And where do men become good and honourable?" Xenophon was fairly puzzled; "Then follow me (ἕπου τοίνυν)," said Socrates, "and learn (καὶ μάνθανε)."

From that time onward he was a pupil (ἀκροατής) of Socrates. (*Vit. Phil.* 2.48)[9]

Unlike the Jesus of Mark, Socrates offers Xenophon some indication of what he has to offer as a teacher. The motivation of those who follow Jesus is a gap in the narrative that may be filled in various ways. It could be the appearance of Jesus, his "presence," or personality that draws the four to follow him. Or it could be inferred that they are drawn to Jesus by some divine force of election or because they have been endowed with supernatural revelation about the identity and role of Jesus. The least likely inference is that they have heard the saying of John in 1:7-8 and concluded that Jesus is the one "stronger" than John who will baptize "in the Holy Spirit." The text says nothing about anyone except Jesus going from Galilee to be baptized by John, and the descent of the Spirit upon Jesus and the voice from heaven in vv. 10-11 are not described as public events. In any case, as noted earlier, the text shows no interest in what motivates the four. Nevertheless, their immediate and total response to Jesus makes a powerful impact on the audience of the Gospel and enhances the authority of Jesus.[10]

---

8   Text and trans. from Malherbe, *Cynic Epistles*, 162–63.

9   Text and trans. from Hicks, *Diogenes Laertius*, 1:176–79. This passage is similar to Mark 1:16-20 in the motif according to which the leading figure calls or invites the other to follow him. Other passages manifest a turning from one form of life to another, a conversion to philosophy; for references and discussion, see Hengel, *Charismatic Leader*, 27–30. See also Arthur Darby Nock, *Conversion: The Old and the New in Religion from Alexander the Great to Augustine of Hippo* (Oxford: Clarendon, 1933; reprinted Oxford/New York: Oxford University Press, 1961) 164–86; Hubert Cancik, "Lucian on Conversion: Remarks on Lucian's Dialogue *Nigrinos*," in Adela Yarbro Collins, ed., *Ancient and Modern Perspectives on the Bible and Culture: Essays in Honor of Hans Dieter Betz* (SPHS; Atlanta: Scholars Press, 1998) 26–48.

10   The immediate and total response of the four to Jesus' call may be seen as the result of the kind of attraction that Plato's Alcibiades says that Socrates exercised upon him and others: ". . . but so soon as we hear you, or your discourses in the mouth of another, . . . we are all astounded and entranced (ἐκπεπληγμένοι ἐσμὲν καὶ κατεχόμεθα). . . .

For when I hear him I am worse than any wild fanatic (πολύ μοι μᾶλλον ἢ τῶν κορυβαντιώντων); I find my heart leaping and my tears gushing forth at the sound of his speech. . . . So I withhold my ears perforce as from the Sirens, and make off as fast as I can, for fear that I should go on sitting beside him till old age was upon me" (Plato *Symp.* 215D-216A; text and ET from Walter R. M. Lamb, *Plato*, vol. 3: *Lysis, Symposium, Gorgias* [LCL; Cambridge, MA: Harvard University Press; London: Heinemann, 1961] 218–21). The reaction of astonishment (ἐκπεπληγμένοι ἐσμέν) on the part of those who heard Socrates, according to this text, is analogous to that of the people in the synagogue of Capernaum who listened to Jesus according to Mark 1:22, "And they were amazed at his teaching" (καὶ ἐξεπλήσσοντο ἐπὶ τῇ διδαχῇ αὐτοῦ); see below. As in this passage, Alcibiades a little further on again compares his reaction to Socrates to the divine madness associated with the worship of deities like Dionysos, "every one of you has had his share of philosophic frenzy and transport (τῆς φιλοσόφου τε καὶ βακχείας)" (*Symp.* 218B; Lamb, *Plato*, 226–27). An important difference, however, is that Alcibiades has this attraction

Fishing was a vital industry in the tetrarchy of Herod Antipas (Galilee) and in the tetrarchy of Philip (Gaulanitis).[11] Fishing with nets (τὰ δίκτυα; vv. 18-19) was one of several methods in use in Greek and Roman times.[12] The presentation of Zebedee as a fisher who has hired men to work with him (v. 20) suggests that his sons did not come from Palestine's lowest social stratum.[13]

Jesus' saying in v. 17, "Come after me, and I will make you fishers of human beings," may be an allusion to the oracle of judgment against Judah in Jer 16:16-18, especially to the announcement of judgment in v. 16, "I am now sending for many fishers, says the Lord, and they shall catch them; and afterward I will send for many hunters, and they shall hunt them from every mountain and every hill, and out of the clefts of the rocks."[14] If the Markan passage alludes to the one in Jeremiah with attention to the context, then the saying of Jesus would mean that the disciples are to bring sinners to judgment. This interpretation seems unlikely in light of the announcement of good news that immediately precedes (vv. 14-15), but is not impossible in light of later developments in the narrative. The speaker of one of the *Thanksgiving Hymns* discovered at Qumran alludes to Jer 16:16 and apparently understands the "fishers" and "hunters" to be the righteous, perhaps members of the community, who "hunt" the children of iniquity.[15]

Similar to Jesus' saying about "fishers of human beings" is a saying attributed to Aristippus by Diogenes Laertius. When Aristippus was reproached for allowing Dionysius, the king of Syracuse, to spit upon him, he replied:

If the fishers let themselves be drenched with seawater in order to catch a minnow, ought I not to endure to be wetted with mixed wine in order to take a carp? (εἶτα οἱ μὲν ἁλιεῖς, εἶπεν, ὑπομένουσι ῥαίνεσθαι τῇ θαλάττῃ, ἵνα κωβιὸν θηράσωσιν· ἐγὼ δὲ μὴ ἀνάσχωμαι κράματι ῥανθῆναι, ἵνα βλέννον λάβω;). (*Vit. Phil.* 2.67; my trans.)[16]

If this saying is understood to mean that Aristippus tolerated Dionysius's behavior in order to win him over to the philosophical way of life, then it could be taken as analogous to the saying of Jesus in Mark 1:17. The latter would then mean that the disciples are to win people over to a way of life that would prepare them for the kingdom of God (cf. 1:4-5 and the call to repent and trust in v. 15).[17]

In light of the saying in v. 17, Jesus himself may be seen in this narrative as a fisher, catching disciples. Analogous to this portrayal is the notion in the biographies by Antigonus of Carystus, according to which a young man, a philosopher-to-be, is hunted and caught (ἐθηράθη) by an older philosopher. The result is that the young man is brought to a lasting dedication to phi-

---

because of Socrates' discourses, whereas the four disciples of Jesus respond to his brief call and perhaps to his person or "presence."

11 On these rulers and their territories, see the section "Historical Context" in the comment on 1:21-28 below. On fishing as an industry in the late Second Temple period, see Wilhelm H. Wuellner, *The Meaning of "Fishers of Men"* (NTL; Philadelphia: Westminster, 1967) 26–63.

12 Wuellner, *"Fishers of Men"*, 16–20.

13 Contrary to the polemic of Celsus and the apologetic response of Origen; see Wuellner, *"Fishers of Men"*, 27, 47–49.

14 Cited by Lohmeyer, 32 n. 5. He, however, seems to have understood the passage in Jeremiah to mean that the people of Israel will "catch" the nations. On God as a hunter of human beings in the biblical tradition and God's commission of human fishers of other humans, see Wuellner, *"Fishers of Men"*, 88–107.

15 1QH 13:8-9 (E. L. Sukenik, ed., *The Dead Sea Scrolls of the Hebrew University* [Jerusalem: Magnes Press/Hebrew University, 1955] 5:8-9); for discussion, see Wuellner, *"Fishers of Men"*, 129–30. Hengel argued that the saying of Jesus in Mark 1:17 is based on an Aramaic logion and that Jesus reversed the use of the metaphor attested in the DSS and meant by it that his disciples were to deprive the "strong man" of his booty and to free those who were bound (*Charismatic Leader*, 76–78).

16 The passage is cited by Lohmeyer, 32 n. 4.

17 The stranger from Elea in Plato's *Sophist* defines fishing as a kind of hunting (220) and the pedagogical activity of the Sophists as a metaphorical hunting (223).

losophy.[18] For example, Diogenes Laertius, quoting Antigonus, says that the fact that Polemo never lost control of his voice was the means by which he "captured" Crantor (διὸ καὶ θηραθῆναι Κράντορα ὑπ' αὐτοῦ) (*Vit. Phil.* 4.17).[19]

Fishing and hunting metaphors play a role in Jewish missionary language. In Aseneth's psalm in the ostensibly Hellenistic-Jewish work *Joseph and Aseneth*, she says:

> . . . until Joseph the Powerful one of God came. . . . by his beauty he caught me, and by his wisdom he grasped me like a fish on a hook, and by his spirit, as by bait of life, he ensnared me, . . . and brought me to the God of the ages . . . and I became his bride for ever and ever" (ἕως οὗ ἦλθεν Ἰωσηφ ὁ δυνατὸς τοῦ θεοῦ . . . καὶ τῷ κάλλει αὐτοῦ ἤγρευσέ με καὶ τῇ σοφίᾳ αὐτοῦ ἐκράτησέ με ὡς ἰχθὺν ἐπ' ἀγκίστρῳ καὶ τῷ πνεύματι αὐτοῦ ὡς δελεάσματι ζωῆς ἐδελέασέ με . . . καὶ ἤγαγέ με τῷ θεῷ τῶν αἰώνων . . . καὶ ἐγενόμην αὐτοῦ νύμφη εἰς τοὺς αἰῶνας τῶν αἰώνων). (21:21)[20]

In this text, the erotic and the missionary senses of the metaphors are combined. Josephus refers to the theological views of the Essenes on the soul as the irresistible bait (ἄφυκτον δέλεαρ) by which they snare those who have tasted their wisdom even only once (*Bell.* 2.8.11 §158).

The image is used negatively in the anticosmic, dualist *Authoritative Teaching*, dating to the second century CE, in a discussion of the condition of the soul in the world:

> For this reason, then, we do not sleep, nor do we forget [the] nets that are spread out in hiding, lying in wait for us to catch us. . . . For eaters of human beings will seize us and swallow us, rejoicing like a fisher casting a hook into the water. For [the fisher] casts many kinds of food into the water because each one of the fish has his own food. He smells it and pursues its odor. But when he eats it, the hook hidden within the food seizes him and brings him up by force out of the deep waters. No one is able, then, to catch that fish down in the deep waters, except for the trap that the fisher sets. By the ruse of food he brought the fish up on the hook. In this very way we exist in this world, like fish. The adversary spies on us, lying in wait for us like a fisher, wishing to seize us, rejoicing that he might swallow us. . . . so that he may seize us with his hidden poison and bring us out of freedom and take us into slavery. (29.3–30.20)[21]

The use of the metaphor in Mark 1:17 must be interpreted in light of the summary of Jesus' proclamation in vv. 14-15. It is striking that the first reported deed of Jesus' public activity is the calling of disciples. In light of vv. 14-15, it is clear that v. 17 implies that those whom Jesus has called are to assist him in the task of proclaiming the good news and moving others to repentance and trust.[22]

---

18 Berger, "Hellenistische Gattungen," 1240, citing Dihle, *Studien*, 114 n. 1.

19 See also 4.24: He is said to have been asked by what means Polemo had "caught" him, and to have replied, "The fact that I never heard him raise or lower his voice in speaking" (φασὶ δὲ αὐτὸν ἐρωτηθέντα τίνι θηραθείη ὑπὸ Πολέμωνος, εἰπεῖν τῷ μήτ' ὀξύτερον μήτε βαρύτερον ἀκοῦσαι φθεγγομένου).

20 Text (accents and breathing marks added) is cited from Christoph Burchard, "Ein vorläufiger griechischer Text von Joseph und Aseneth," *Dielheimer Blätter zum Alten Testament* 14 (1979) 37; translation by idem, "Joseph and Aseneth," in *OTP* 2:237–38.

21 The Coptic text (with some loanwords from Greek) and an ET are available in the contribution by George W. MacRae in Douglas M. Parrott, ed., *Nag Hammadi Codices V, 2–5 and VI with Papyrus Berolinensis 8502, 1 and 4* (CGL; NHS 11; Leiden: Brill, 1979) 274–77; an ET is also available in George W. MacRae, "Authoritative Teaching (VI,3)," *NHLE* 308. The trans. cited above is MacRae's modified. On the date, see the note by Parrot added to MacRae's introduction to the work (*NHLE* 305).

22 Wuellner (*"Fishers of Men"*, 166–231) interprets the saying "I will make you fishers of human beings" in Mark 1:17 in a general theological way as "partnership with Jesus."

1

1:21-28 A New Teaching with Authority

21/ **And they went into Capernaum.[a] So then on the Sabbath, he taught in the synagogue.[b] 22/ And they were amazed at his teaching; for he was teaching them with authority, not as the scribes taught.**

23/ **So then there was in their synagogue a man with an unclean spirit and he cried out, 24/ saying, "What have we to do with you, Jesus of Nazareth? Have you come to destroy us? I know[c] who you are, the Holy One of God." 25/ And Jesus rebuked him, saying, "Be muzzled and come out of him." 26/ And the unclean spirit convulsed him, cried out[d] with a loud voice, and came out of him. 27/ And all were amazed, so that they discussed with one another, saying, "What is this? A new teaching with authority;[e] he commands even the unclean spirits, and they obey him." 28/ And his fame immediately went forth in all directions[f] in the whole region around Galilee.**

a The English spelling "Capernaum" derives from the spelling of the Greek name of the locality in the Textus Receptus, $Καπερναούμ$. This spelling is attested also by A C L f^1. The spelling $Καφαρναούμ$ ("Capharnaum"), attested by ℵ B D W $Δ$ $Θ$ f^{13} et al., is also attested by Josephus (*Bell.* 3.10.8 §519) and is closer to the probable Hebrew name of the place, כְּפַר נָחוּם ("village of Nahum").

b The translation is based on the reading $ἐδίδασκεν$ $εἰς$ $τὴν$ $συναγωγήν$ ("he taught in the synagogue"), attested by (ℵ C) L f^{13} et al. Since the phrase $ἐν$ $τῇ$ $συναγωγῇ$ ("in the synagogue") would normally be expected with a verb like $ἐδίδασκεν$ ("he taught"), this reading was corrected through the addition of $εἰσελθών$ ("having entered"). The latter reading is attested by A B W f^1 et al. See C. H. Turner, "Markan Usage: Notes, Critical and Exegetical, on the Second Gospel," *JTS* 26 (1924) 15 (James K. Elliott, ed., *The Language and Style of the Gospel of Mark: An Edition of C. H. Turner's "Notes on Marcan Usage" Together with Other Comparable Studies* [NovTSup 71; Leiden: Brill, 1993] 16–17); C. H. Turner, "A Textual Commentary on Mark 1," *JTS* 28 (1927) 153, who is followed by Taylor. See also the note to v. 39 below. For a different judgment concerning 1:21, see Klaus Scholtissek, *Die Vollmacht Jesu: Traditions- und redaktionsgeschichtliche Analysen zu einem Leitmotiv markinischer Christologie* (NTAbh 25; Münster: Aschendorff, 1992) 83–84.

c ℵ L $Δ$ 892 et al. read $οἴδαμεν$ ("we know") instead of $οἶδα$ ("I know"). The former is probably a change introduced to harmonize this statement with the plurals in the previous two sentences.

d Most MSS (A C $Θ$ $f^{1.13}$ $\mathfrak{M}$) read $κράξαν$ ("cried out"; lit., "having cried out") instead of $φωνῆσαν$ ("cried out"; lit., "having cried out"), the reading of ℵ B L et al. Since $κράζω$ ("cry out") is more commonly used in Mark (3:11; 5:5, 7; 9:26) and elsewhere in the NT (Matt 8:29; Luke 4:41; 9:39; Acts 16:17) of demons and demoniacs than $φωνέω$ ("call" or "cry out"; only here in Mark with a demon as subject and nowhere else in the NT), the latter is more likely to be the earlier reading; similarly, Scholtissek, *Die Vollmacht Jesu*, 84.

e The variants seem to be attempts to clarify the reading found in ℵ B L 33. 2427; see Metzger, *Textual Commentary*, 64. Similarly, Scholtissek, *Die Vollmacht Jesu*, 84.

f $εὐθύς$ ("immediately") is lacking in ℵ* W $Θ$ f^1 et al. $πανταχοῦ$ ("in all directions") is lacking in ℵ* A D $Θ$ f^1 et al. Both words occur in (ℵ²) B C L $f^{1.13}$ et al. Both words were probably deliberately omitted in efforts to improve the redundant style of Mark. See Turner, "Textual Commentary," 155.

Narrative Unity of 1:21-28

As noted above in the comment on 1:16-20, v. 21 introduces a new unit of text by indicating a new setting. In a steady progression of locative terms, the settings have become more and more specific. Jesus went into Galilee (v. 14), then passed by the Sea of Galilee (v. 16), entered the village of Capernaum (v. 21a), and taught in the synagogue (v. 21b). A new temporal setting is also given in v. 21b, "on the Sabbath." While the presence of Jesus and the four whom he called provides continuity with the preceding unit (vv. 16-20), the introduction of new characters, the unnamed people in the synagogue (v. 22), is another sign that a new unit is beginning. Verses 21-22, on the one hand, and vv. 23-28, on the other, are distinguished in that the former describe Jesus' teaching and its effects, whereas the latter narrate an exorcism. The two passages are held together, however, by the fact that the temporal and locative settings are the same, apart from the shift indicated by εὐθύς ("then" or "immediately"). The characters are the same, except for the new character who is the subject of the exorcism, "a man with an unclean spirit" (ἄνθρωπος ἐν πνεύματι ἀκαθάρτῳ). Most importantly, the two subunits are held together by the linking of teaching and authority in vv. 22 and 27b.[23] Furthermore, the scene as a whole expresses the idea that both the teaching and power of Jesus to exorcise have their basis in the authority of Jesus.[24]

Historical Context of 1:21-28

During the reign of Herod Antipas over Galilee and Perea (4 BCE–39 CE)[25] and that of Philip over Batanaea, Trachonitis, Auranitis, Gaulonitis, and portions of the "domains of Zenodorus" in the vicinity of Panias (4 BCE–33/34 CE),[26] Capernaum was a small border village that had been populated continuously since the Persian period.[27] The monumental synagogue, remains of which are visible today, was built at the end of the fourth and in the fifth century CE; the initial construction goes back to the third century CE at the earliest. But underneath its central nave, a large floor of basalt stones was found which dates to the beginning of the first century CE. Since it was common practice in the East to build synagogues and churches on the identical sites of earlier ones, this floor may have belonged to an earlier synagogue building or to a large home that was used as a gathering place for the Jewish community.[28]

The domains of Philip were awarded to Agrippa I with the title of king by Gaius in 37 CE. Upon the exile of Antipas, Agrippa received Galilee and Perea as well.[29] When Agrippa died in 44 CE, his son was considered too young to succeed him, so the whole of Palestine once more became part of the Roman province of Judea.[30] But in 53 CE, Claudius awarded Agrippa II the former domains of Philip, and Nero gave him parts of Galilee and Perea, most importantly Tiberias and Tarichea (= Magdala) in Galilee and Julias in Perea, some possibly in 56 and others in 61 CE.[31] Thus, at the time that Mark was written, Capernaum was probably part of the Roman province of Judea. Gessius Florus, whom Josephus blamed for provoking the Jewish revolt, was procurator from 64 to 66 CE.[32]

Comment

■ **21-28** The text of Mark describes a situation in which people gather in a building called a synagogue to be taught. Some have argued that this picture is anachronistic and that there were no synagogue buildings in the

---

23 On the unity of Mark 1:21-28, see also Scholtissek, *Die Vollmacht Jesu*, 81–83.

24 For discussion of this point, see Scholtissek, *Die Vollmacht Jesu*, 122–24.

25 David C. Braund, "Herod Antipas," *ABD* 3:160.

26 David C. Braund, "Philip. 5," *ABD* 5:310–11. Philip refounded the city of Panias (modern Banias) and renamed it Caesarea; this is the Caesarea Philippi ("Philip's Caesarea") mentioned in Mark 8:27 (ibid.).

27 Stanislao Loffreda, "Capernaum," *NEAEHL* 1:291–95.

28 Ibid., 294; he argues that the floor must have belonged to a public building, since he thinks that

its area is too large for a domestic dwelling. See also E. P. Sanders, *The Historical Figure of Jesus* (London: Allen Lane; New York: Penguin, 1993) 103.

29 David C. Braund, "Agrippa 1," *ABD* 1:99.

30 David C. Braund, "Agrippa 2," *ABD* 1:99; cf. Seán Freyne, *Galilee, from Alexander the Great to Hadrian: 323 B.C.E. to 135 C.E.* (UNDCSJCA 5; Wilmington, DE: Michael Glazier; Notre Dame, IN: University of Notre Dame Press, 1980) 72.

31 Braund, "Agrippa 2," 99. On the identification of Tarichea or Tarichaeae with Magdala, see Seán Freyne, "Galilee, Sea of," *ABD* 2:900.

land of Israel until after the destruction of the temple in 70 CE.[33] The earliest concrete evidence for the existence of synagogues as buildings consists of papyri and inscriptions from Ptolemaic Egypt.[34] A Greek inscription found in Jerusalem and dating to the period before 70 CE refers to a synagogue that was at least three generations old. It had recently been expanded by a priest, Theodotus, who was head of the synagogue. In the inscription he mentions his father and grandfather, who also had been heads of the synagogue.[35] Although other terms were used for such buildings, προσευχή ("place of prayer") and συναγωγή ("synagogue") are the dominant ones.[36] Philo and Josephus provide evidence for the nature of these buildings and how they were used.[37] The syna-

32 Freyne, *Galilee*, 73; Horsley and Hanson, *Bandits*, 42–43; see Josephus *Bell.* 2.14.2-16.3 §§277–343; 2.16.5-17.4 §§402–20; 2.19.4 §531; 2.20.1 §558; *Ant.* 18.1.6 §25; 19.9.2 §366; 20.9.5 §215; 20.11.1 §§252–57.

33 Howard Clark Kee has argued that, prior to 70 CE, Jews living in Galilee met in homes or in small public halls for study of the scriptures, worship, and instruction ("The Transformation of the Synagogue after 70 C.E.: Its Import for Early Christianity," *NTS* 36 [1990] 1–24; idem, "Early Christianity in the Galilee: Reassessing the Evidence from the Gospels," in Lee I. Levine, ed., *The Galilee in Late Antiquity* [New York/Jerusalem: Jewish Theological Seminary; Cambridge, MA/London: Harvard University Press, 1992] 3–22, esp. 12). Heather A. McKay, *Sabbath and Synagogue: The Question of Sabbath Worship in Ancient Judaism* (RGRW 122; Leiden: Brill, 1994), argues not only that there were no "synagogue" buildings in first-century Palestine but also that there were no Sabbath worship "services" at that time. She accepts the testimony of Philo and Josephus that Torah was read and studied in communal gatherings, but concludes that these activities were philosophical and educational, not part of a ceremony of worship (see esp. 250–51). Kee's conclusions have been criticized by E. P. Sanders, *Jewish Law from Jesus to the Mishnah: Five Studies* (London: SCM; Philadelphia: Trinity Press International, 1990) 341–43 n. 29; Richard E. Oster, Jr., "Supposed Anachronism in Luke-Acts' Use of ΣΥΝΑΓΩΓΗ: A Rejoinder to H. C. Kee," *NTS* 39 (1993) 178–208; Kenneth Atkinson, "On Further Defining the First-Century CE Synagogue: Fact or Fiction? A Rejoinder to H. C. Kee," *NTS* 43 (1997) 491–502; and Anders Runesson, *The Origins of the Synagogue: A Socio-Historical Study* (CBNTS 37; Stockholm: Almqvist & Wiksell International, 2001) esp. 485–86. For comprehensive studies of synagogues in the Second Temple period, see Donald D. Binder, *Into the Temple Courts: The Place of the Synagogues in the Second Temple Period* (SBLDS 169; Atlanta: Society of Biblical Literature, 1999); Runesson, *Origins of the Synagogue*; Birger Olsson and Magnus Zetterholm, eds., *The Ancient Synagogue from Its Origins until 200 C.E.*

(CBNTS 39; Stockholm: Almqvist & Wiksell International, 2003). See also Peter Richardson, *Building Jewish in the Roman East* (JSJSup 92; Waco, TX: Baylor University Press; Leiden: Brill, 2004) 111–33.

34 An inscription from Egypt dated to 246–221 BCE states that the Jews (have dedicated) a "house of prayer" (προσευχή) in honor of Ptolemy, his wife Berenice, and their children; for the Greek text and a French trans., see *CIJ* 2:366–67, no. 1440; the Greek text and an ET may be found in *CPJ* 3:141, no. 1440; an inscription from the same period states that the Jews of Krokodilopolis in Egypt (dedicated) a "house of prayer" (προσευχή) in honor of the same persons (*CPJ* 3:164, no. 1532A). These two inscriptions are the oldest references to "houses of prayer" or synagogues anywhere. See also *CPJ* 3:139–40, no. 1433; 141–42, no. 1441; 142, nos. 1442 and 1443; 143, no. 1444; 144, no. 1449; *CPJ* 1:247–49, no. 134; 2:220–24, no. 432. For discussion see Hengel, *Charismatic Leader*, 44–45; Lee I. Levine, "The Nature and Origin of the Palestinian Synagogue Reconsidered," *JBL* 115 (1996) 425–48, esp. 427, 429. On the synagogues of the Diaspora, see also Binder, *Into the Temple Courts*, 227–341; Alf Thomas Kraabel, "The Diaspora Synagogue: Archaeological and Epigraphic Evidence since Sukenik," *ANRW* 2.19.1 (1979) 477–510.

35 Sanders, *Jewish Law*, 77; Levine, "Nature and Origin," 429. Binder concludes that synagogue buildings in Palestine date at least to the beginning of the Common Era and probably from the early part of the first century BCE (*Into the Temple Courts*, 226).

36 Levine, "Nature and Origin," 429–30. The term προσευχή ("place of prayer") was common in Egypt, and the term συναγωγή ("synagogue") is used consistently for such buildings in Palestine with one exception.

37 Philo says that the Essenes of Palestinian Syria live in villages (κωμηδὸν οἰκοῦσι) and that they gather in sacred places (ἱεροὶ τόποι) called synagogues (συναγωγαί) on the seventh days; one takes the scrolls and reads aloud, and another of special competence comes forward and expounds (ἀναδιδάσκει) what is not understood (*Omn. prob. lib.* 12 §§75–82); see Francis H. Colson and George H.

gogue at Gamla in Gaulanitis, the modern Golan Heights, has provided the best archaeological evidence for a building designed and constructed for religious purposes in the pre-70 CE period. It was built in the early first century CE.[38] Lee I. Levine has argued that the synagogue was essentially a communal institution that served the full range of needs of a particular community, as a place for political meetings, social gatherings, courts, schools, hostels, charitable activities, manumission of slaves, meals, and religious and liturgical activities.[39] The literary sources, understandably, emphasize the activity that was unique to its Jewish setting, namely, the regular communal reading and expounding of the scriptures.[40] It is in the context of such activity that the text of Mark presents the teaching of Jesus in Capernaum.

The irregular (metaplastic) dative σάββασιν ("Sabbath") is regularly used in the New Testament.[41]

■ **22** This verse contrasts the teaching of Jesus with that of the "scribes."[42] Historically speaking, in the first century CE, the scribes of Jerusalem were officials, and those of Galilean villages were copyists and low-level officials.[43] Mark may not be historically accurate in portraying the scribes as a unified group opposed to Jesus.[44] Here Mark presents them as teachers and may have in mind the role of some scribes as experts in the Law.[45] Such teachers did not lack authority and power among the people.[46] According to Mark, however, the teaching of Jesus, unlike theirs, is with authority.[47] This idea is repeated in the declaration of the people in the synagogue and further developed by their remark that Jesus' teaching is "new"

Whitaker *Philo* (10 vols.; and 2 supp. vols.; LCL; London: Heinemann; Cambridge, MA: Harvard University Press, 1941) 9:52–59); see also *Spec. leg.* 2.15 §62–63. Josephus mentions the "house of prayer" (προσευχή) in Tiberias and alludes to activities there, i.e., public meetings and prayer (*Vit.* 276–303); he mentions the "synagogue" (συναγωγή) in Caesarea, indicates that the Jews gathered in this building on the Sabbath, and implies that the local Jewish community had scrolls containing the Torah (τοὺς νόμους) that were kept in the building (*Bell.* 2.14.4-5 §284–92). For discussion see Sanders, *Jewish Law*, 73–74, 77–81; E. P. Sanders, *Judaism: Practice and Belief 63 BCE–66 CE* (London: SCM; Philadelphia: Trinity Press International, 1992) 198–202. See also Lee I. Levine, "The Second Temple Synagogue: The Formative Years," in idem, ed., *The Synagogue in Late Antiquity* (Philadelphia: ASOR/JTS, 1987) 7–31, esp. 15–16.

38 See Levine, "Nature and Origin," 428–29; Atkinson, "First-Century CE Synagogue," 492–93; Sanders, *Judaism: Practice and Belief*, 200.

39 Levine, "Nature and Origin," 430–31. Binder, however, rightly points out that the "religious" dimensions of the activities in the synagogue were intertwined with the "nonreligious" aspects (*Into the Temple Courts*, 226).

40 E.g., Philo *Omn. prob. lib.* 12 §§75–82; *Spec. leg.* 2.15 §§62–63; Levine, "Nature and Origin," 431–32.

41 Swete, 17. On metaplastic forms, see Smyth, §282b. On the Jewish practices related to the observance of the Sabbath during the Second Temple period, see Lutz Doering, *Schabbat: Sabbathalacha und -praxis im antiken Judentum und Urchristentum* (TSAJ 78; Tübingen: Mohr Siebeck, 1999) 23–397, 479–565.

42 In its ordinary Greek sense, the word translated here as "scribe" (γραμματεύς) means "clerk" or "secretary." In the LXX, γραμματεύς is a translation of the Hebrew סוֹפֵר or the Aramaic סָפְרָא and has a wide range of meaning; see Anthony J. Saldarini, *Pharisees, Scribes and Sadducees in Palestinian Society: A Sociological Approach* (Wilmington, DE: Michael Glazier, 1988; reprinted BRS; Grand Rapids: Eerdmans, 2001) 241–76; idem, "Scribes," *ABD* 5:1012–16.

43 Saldarini, "Scribes," 1015.

44 Ibid. Mark does, however, present the scribe of 12:28-34 as approving, even praising, Jesus.

45 Joachim Jeremias, "γραμματεύς," *TDNT* 1 (1964) 740–41. Michael J. Cook argued that Mark was mistaken in distinguishing "scribes" and "Pharisees"; he did so because he used three written sources, two of which mentioned "scribes" but never "Pharisees," while the third depicted "Pharisees" but never "scribes." Cook himself assumed that "[t]he two terms refer to the same element of society," but such is not necessarily always the case (*Mark's Treatment of the Jewish Leaders* [NovTSup 51; Leiden: Brill, 1978] 4–5).

46 So also Demetrios Trakatellis, *Authority and Passion: Christological Aspects of the Gospel according to Mark* (Brookline, MA: Holy Cross Orthodox Press, 1987) 10. Stephen Westerholm has argued that the authority of the Pharisaic scribes was based on their knowledge of the Sacred Scriptures and the "traditions of the fathers" and was confirmed in the eyes of the people by their disciplined lives (*Jesus and Scribal Authority* [CBNTS 10; Lund: CWK Gleerup, 1978] 28–30).

47 Abrahams (*Studies in Pharisaism*, 1:14), following August Wünsche, argued that the phrase ὡς ἐξουσίαν ἔχων ("with authority"; lit., "as having author-

(v. 27). The description of Jesus as one having authority recalls the scene related to his baptism (vv. 9-11) in which he is endowed with the Holy Spirit and appointed Son of God, that is, messiah.[48] The "newness" of his teaching derives from this extraordinary authority and also from the newness of the situation. The fulfillment of the appointed period of time and the drawing near of the kingdom of God (v. 15) have created a new period of history and have put into motion new kinds of events.[49] Comparison with Mark 7:1-23 suggests that the contrast in 1:22 implies that Jesus, as the messiah, proclaims and expounds the commandments of God and the word of God, but the scribes who are experts in the Law teach merely the tradition of human beings.[50] The text of Mark thus suppresses the relative authority of the experts in the Law in order to attribute absolute authority to Jesus, the messiah.[51] This suppression is probably due in part to conflict among followers of Jesus and Jews who did not accept him as the messiah and the resulting polemical rhetoric of the Gospel of Mark.

In terms of genre, vv. 23-28 constitute an account of an exorcism.[52] Although he labeled vv. 21-28 as a healing, Bultmann concluded that the evangelist's source for this passage was an exorcism. He described the typical features (all found in 5:1-20) of an exorcism as follows: (1) meeting with the demon(s); (2) description of the dangerous character of such a sickness; (3) the demon recognizing the exorcist; (4) the exorcism; (5) demonstrative departure of the demon; (6) the impression on the spectator(s). The story in 1:23-28 has four of these typical features: (3) the demon recognizes the exorcist and puts up a struggle (v. 24); (4) there is a threat and a command by the exorcist, that is, the exorcism proper (v. 25); (5) the demon comes out making a demonstration (v. 26); and (6) an impression is made on the spectators (v. 27).[53]

The genre "account of an exorcism" is not unique to early Christian literature. Such an account is related by Josephus:

> [Solomon] also composed incantations by which illnesses are relieved, and left behind forms of exorcisms ($\tau\rho\acute{o}\pi o\upsilon\varsigma\ \acute{\epsilon}\xi o\rho\kappa\acute{\omega}\sigma\epsilon\omega\nu$) with which those possessed by demons ($\tau\grave{a}\ \delta\alpha\iota\mu\acute{o}\nu\iota\alpha$) drive them out, never to return. And this kind of cure is of very great power among us to this day, for I have seen ($\acute{\iota}\sigma\tau\acute{o}\rho\eta\sigma\alpha$) a certain Eleazar, a countryman of mine, in the

---

ity") is similar to the rabbinic idiom of speaking "from the mouth of power" (מפי הגבורה) with the connotation of direct divine inspiration. This connotation would fit well with the close association of teaching and exorcising in Mark 1:21-28, implying that both are activities in which the Spirit works through Jesus or Jesus works by the power of the Spirit.

48 Compare Dan 7:14a OG, "and authority was given to him," ($\kappa\alpha\grave{\iota}\ \acute{\epsilon}\delta\acute{o}\vartheta\eta\ \alpha\grave{\upsilon}\tau\tilde{\omega}\ \acute{\epsilon}\xi o\upsilon\sigma\acute{\iota}\alpha$), and 7:14c OG and Θ, "and his authority (is) an everlasting authority" ($\acute{\eta}\ \acute{\epsilon}\xi o\upsilon\sigma\acute{\iota}\alpha\ \alpha\grave{\upsilon}\tau o\tilde{\upsilon}\ \acute{\epsilon}\xi o\upsilon\sigma\acute{\iota}\alpha\ \alpha\grave{\iota}\acute{\omega}\nu\iota o\varsigma$). On the messianic interpretation of the one like a son of man in Jewish circles in the first century CE, see the introduction to this commentary, the section *Jesus as Messiah*. Scholtissek (*Die Vollmacht Jesu*, 126–27) argues that the author of Mark brought the early Christian theme of the authority of Jesus to the level of a concept by drawing upon biblical and Jewish notions of the authority of the ideal king or messiah, the prophet, and the heavenly Son of Man.

49 Cf. Scholtissek, *Die Vollmacht Jesu*, 123–24, 127–28. Jean Delorme has argued that, according to this passage, the authority of Jesus is legitimated not by its source or institutional framework but by its reception ("Prises de parole et parler vrai dans un récit de

Marc (1,21-28)," in Pietro Bovati and Roland Meynet, eds., *"Ouvrir les écritures": Mélanges offerts à Paul Beauchamp* [LD 162; Paris: Cerf, 1995] 179–99, esp. 184–85).

50 Mark's Jesus associates himself with the commandments of God and the word of God (7:8, 9, 13), the scribes who are experts in the Law with the tradition of the elders (v. 3), the commandments of human beings (v. 7), and the tradition of human beings (v. 8; cf. v. 13).

51 Cf. Trakatellis, *Authority and Passion*, 10.

52 Rhoads (*Reading Mark*, 69), following Robert Alter, refers to exorcisms, healings, nature miracles, and other types of anecdotes as "type-scenes." On the literary form "exorcism," see Eshel, "Demonology in Palestine," part 2 (chaps. 3–4).

53 Bultmann, *History*, 209–10. Dibelius classifies 1:23-27 as a paradigm, not a miracle story, because the interest is focused on the identity of Jesus as the envoy of God (*From Tradition to Gospel*, 43, 54–55). Gerd Theissen classifies 1:21-28 as an exorcism (*The Miracle Stories of the Early Christian Tradition* [SNTW; Edinburgh: T & T Clark; Philadelphia: Fortress, 1983]. ET of Gerd Theißen, *Urchristliche Wundergeschichten: Ein Beitrag zur formgeschichtlichen Erforschung der synoptischen Evangelien* [Gütersloh:

presence of Vespasian, his sons, tribunes and a number of other soldiers, free men possessed by demons, and this was the manner of the cure: he put to the nose of the possessed man ($\tau o\hat{\upsilon}$ $\delta\alpha\iota\mu o\nu\iota\zeta o\mu\acute{\epsilon}\nu o\upsilon$) a ring which had under its seal one of the roots prescribed by Solomon, and then, as the man smelled it, drew out the demon through his nostrils, and when the man at once fell down, adjured the demon never to come back into him, speaking Solomon's name and reciting the incantations which he had composed. Then, wishing to convince the bystanders and prove to them that he had this power, Eleazar placed a cup or footbasin full of water a little way off and commanded the demon, as it went out of the man, to overturn it and make known to the spectators that he had left the man. And when this was done, the understanding and wisdom of Solomon were clearly revealed. . . . (*Ant.* 8.2.5 §§45–49)[54]

This account has some of the features defined by Bultmann: the exorcism (4) is performed by means of a ring with a powerful root, by pronouncing the name of Solomon and reciting the incantations composed by him; the demonstrative departure of the demon (5) involves (a) the falling down of the man who had just been freed from the demon and (b) the demon's fulfillment of Eleazar's command to overturn a cup or footbasin of water; the impression on the spectators (6) is not narrated directly, but is implied by the statement that the understanding and wisdom of Solomon were revealed to them. Although the genre is the same, the presentation of the two exorcists differs significantly. Eleazar uses material and verbal techniques that derive from his famous ancestor, Solomon, and also exorcises in Solomon's name. Jesus uses no material means; he exor-

cises by a simple command and does not call upon the name of any other authority, not even God.

A non–Jewish-Hellenistic example of an account of an exorcism is given by Lucian. In Lucian's dialogue *The Lover of Lies*, Tychiades tells his friend Philocles about a conversation that took place in the house of Eucrates concerning extraordinary things. Tychiades reports the following remarks by a certain Ion:

"You act ridiculously," said Ion, "to doubt everything. For my part, I should like to ask you what you say to those who free possessed men ($\delta\alpha\iota\mu o\nu\hat{\omega}\nu\tau\alpha\varsigma$) from their terrors by exorcising the spirits ($\grave{\epsilon}\xi\acute{\alpha}\delta o\nu\tau\epsilon\varsigma$ $\tau\grave{\alpha}$ $\phi\acute{\alpha}\sigma\mu\alpha\tau\alpha$) so manifestly. I need not discuss this: everyone knows about the Syrian from Palestine, the adept in it ($\tau\grave{o}\nu$ $\grave{\epsilon}\pi\grave{\iota}$ $\tau o\acute{\upsilon}\tau\omega$ $\sigma o\phi\iota\sigma\tau\acute{\eta}\nu$), how many he takes in hand who fall down in the light of the moon and roll their eyes and fill their mouths with foam; nevertheless, he restores them to health and sends them away normal in mind, delivering them from their straits for a large fee. When he stands beside them as they lie there and asks: 'Whence came you into his body?' the patient himself is silent, but the spirit ($\grave{o}$ $\delta\alpha\acute{\iota}\mu\omega\nu$) answers in Greek or in the language of whatever foreign country he comes from, telling how and whence he entered into the man; whereupon, by adjuring ($\grave{o}$ $\delta\grave{\epsilon}$ $\acute{o}\rho\kappa o\upsilon\varsigma$ $\grave{\epsilon}\pi\acute{\alpha}\gamma\omega\nu$) the spirit and if he does not obey, threatening him, he drives him out. Indeed, I actually saw one coming out, black and smoky in colour." (Lucian *Philops.* 15–16)[55]

This account also has some of the features described by Bultmann: the dangerous character of the sickness (Bultmann's item 2) is highlighted by the description of the symptoms (the afflicted person falls down in the light of

Mohn, 1974] 321; cf. 85–90. See also Campbell Bonner, "The Technique of Exorcism," *HTR* 36 [1943] 39–49).

54 Text and trans. from Thackeray, *Josephus*, 5:594–97. For discussion, see David R. Jordan and Roy D. Kotansky, "IV. Magisches. 338. A Solomonic Exorcism," in Michael Gronewald et al., eds., *Kölner Papyri (P. Köln)* (ANWAW: Papyrologica Coloniensia 7.8; Düsseldorf: Westdeutscher Verlag, 1997) 53–69, esp. 59–61. Note also the story of the exorcism performed by R. Simeon b. Yoḥai, a rabbi who lived in

the second cent. CE, in *b. Meʿil.* 17b; for discussion, see Abrahams, *Studies in Pharisaism*, 1:92, 111.

55 Text and trans. from Austin M. Harmon, *Lucian* (8 vols.; LCL; London: Heinemann; Cambridge, MA: Harvard University Press, 1921) 3:344–45. See also Philostratus *Vita Ap.* 4.20, according to which a demon threw down a statue, obeying the command of Apollonius to show by a visible sign that he had departed from a young man.

the moon, eyes rolling and mouth filling with foam); the exorcism itself (4) is accomplished by adjuring and threatening the spirit; the spirit can actually be seen coming out (5); and Ion is clearly impressed by the exorcist's power (6). Like Jesus, this exorcist drives the demon out by verbal means only. Unlike Jesus, he charges a large fee for his services. Neither the passage from Josephus nor the one from Lucian involves the recognition of the exorcist by the spirit.[56] This motif is, however, of special importance in Mark (see below on v. 24).

As noted above, members of the community of the Dead Sea Scrolls apparently practiced exorcism.[57] In addition to the apocryphal psalms and the *Songs of the Maskil*, a fragment of a work has been discovered at Qumran (4Q560) that refers to demons and contains incantations.[58] This text is evidence for the practice of exorcism in the cultural context of the historical Jesus.

The means is verbal, as in Mark, but the exorcist in 4Q560 adjures the demon "by the Name of Him who forgives sins and transgression" (4Q560 1:4) whereas Mark's Jesus does not call upon the name of God as he casts out demons.[59]

■ **23** The text describes the entity that was besetting or possessing the man as "an unclean spirit" ($\pi\nu\epsilon\hat{\nu}\mu\alpha$ $\dot{\alpha}\kappa\dot{\alpha}\vartheta\alpha\rho\tau\text{o}\nu$). This is a Jewish formulation that may be related to the story of the fallen angels (Gen 6:1-4; *1 Enoch* 6–11).[60] In *1 Enoch* God instructs Enoch to rebuke the fallen angels, the Watchers, and to ask them, "Why have you forsaken the high heaven, the eternal sanctuary; and lain with women, and defiled yourselves with the daughters of men . . . ? You were holy ones and spirits, living forever. With the blood of women you have defiled yourselves . . ." (15:3-4).[61] Similarly, the book of *Jubilees* states that one of the three causes of the flood

---

56 Philostratus *Vita Ap.* 4.20 has something like this motif: "Now when Apollonius gazed on him, the ghost in him began to utter cries of fear and rage, such as one hears from people who are being branded or racked" (trans. from Frederick C. Conybeare, *Philostratus: The Life of Apollonius of Tyana* [2 vols.; Cambridge, MA: Harvard University Press, 1912] 1:388–91).

57 See the comments on 1:12-13 above. Further, the *Songs of the Maskil* (4Q510) 1:4-5 indicates that one of the leaders of the community, the *Maskil*, or the Sage, composed or performed songs intended to ward off demons; see Vermes, *Dead Sea Scrolls*, 420; García Martínez and Tigchelaar, *Dead Sea Scrolls*, 2:1026–29; see also 4Q511, another copy of the same work (ibid., 2:1029–37). On the *Songs of the Maskil*, see Bilha Nitzan, "Hymns from Qumran— 4Q510–4Q511," in Dimant and Rappaport, 53–63; Bilhah Nitzan, *Qumran Prayer and Religious Poetry* (STDJ 12; Leiden: Brill, 1994) 235–72; W. J. Lyons and A. M. Reimer, "The Demonic Virus and Qumran Studies: Some Preventative Measures," *DSD* 5 (1998) 16–32. On the officials of the community, see James C. VanderKam, *The Dead Sea Scrolls Today* (Grand Rapids: Eerdmans; London: SPCK, 1994) 112.

58 See Robert H. Eisenman and Michael Wise, *The Dead Sea Scrolls Uncovered* (Shaftesbury, Dorset/ Rockport, MA/Brisbane, Queensland: Element Books, 1992) 265–67; Douglas L. Penney and Michael O. Wise, "By the Power of Beelzebub: An Aramaic Incantation Formula from Qumran (4Q560)," *JBL* 113 (1994) 627–50; cf. García

Martínez and Tigchelaar, *Dead Sea Scrolls*, 2:1116–17; this text is not included in Vermes, *Dead Sea Scrolls*. According to Alexander, this fragment comes from a nonsectarian "recipe book containing the texts of amulets, which a professional magician would have copied out and personalized for a client's use." He concludes that the texts are apotropaic, rather than intended "to heal someone who has been attacked" ("Demonology of the Dead Sea Scrolls," 345).

59 Trans. (modified) from Eisenman and Wise, *Dead Sea Scrolls Uncovered*, 267.

60 References to unclean spirits also occur in the DSS: 11QPs[a] (11Q5) 19:15 (רוח טמאה); 4Q444 1 i 8 (רוח הטמאה); see Alexander, "Demonology of the Dead Sea Scrolls," 349; Eshel, "Demonology in Palestine," chap. 1. The specification "wicked spirits" (רוחי רשע or רוחי רשעה) occurs in 4Q511 1 6; 4Q444 1 i 4 (Alexander, "Demonology of the Dead Sea Scrolls," 332). Alexander points out that the language of impurity is applied to spirits already in Zech 13:2 (ibid., 349). The LXX of Zech 13:2 has a phrase similar to Mark's, τὸ πνεῦμα τὸ ἀκάθαρτον ("the unclean spirit" or "the spirit of impurity"). According to Carol L. Meyers and Eric M. Meyers, the corresponding Hebrew phrase is elliptical and denotes the unclean state that prophets bring upon themselves when they do not speak Yahweh's message (*Zechariah 9–14: A New Translation with Introduction and Commentary* [AB 25C; New York: Doubleday, 1993] 372). See also Clinton Wahlen, *Jesus and the Impurity of Spirits in the Synoptic Gospels* (WUNT 2.185; Tübingen: Mohr Siebeck, 2004) 24–59.

61 Trans. from Nickelsburg and VanderKam, 36.

was fornication, "that the Watchers had illicit inter-course—apart from the mandate of their authority—with women. When they married of them whomever they chose they committed the first (acts) of uncleanness" (7:21).[62] Thus, *Jubilees* can refer generally to "impure demons" (10:1).[63] The expression "evil spirits" occurs also in Jewish literature of the Second Temple period.[64]

■ **24** The spirit addresses Jesus first. Note that the Syrian exorcist in Lucian's dialogue (cited above) addresses the spirit first and finds out how it came into the victim's body; the implication may be that this information was then used to force the spirit to depart. Similarly, in an encounter between Solomon and a demon in the *Testament of Solomon*, Solomon speaks first, asking, "Who are you? What is your name?" (τίς εἶ σύ, καὶ τίς ἡ κλῆσίς σου;).[65] The demon then replies, "I am called Ornias" (Ὀρνίας καλοῦμαι) (*T. Sol.* 2:1).[66] Again, when the ruler of the demons, Beelzeboul, approaches Solomon, Solomon speaks first, glorifying God and then asking the demon, "Tell me, who are you?" (λέγε μοι, τίς εἶ σύ;). The demon replies, "I am Beelzeboul, the ruler of the demons" (ἐγώ εἰμι Βεελζεβοὺλ τῶν δαιμονίων ὁ ἔξαρχος) (3:5-6).[67] This pattern is varied when the evil demon Asmodeus is brought bound to Solomon:

I asked him, "Who are you?" He scowled at me and said, "And who are *you*?" I said to him, "You (dare to) answer (so arrogantly) when you have been punished like this?" He continued to give forth the same look and said to me, "How *should* I answer you? You are the son of a man, but although I was born of a human mother, I (am the son) of an angel (καὶ ἐπηρώτησα αὐτόν· σὺ τίς εἶ; ὁ δὲ ἀπειλητικὸν βλέμμα ῥίψας λέγει· σὺ δὲ τίς εἶ; καὶ εἶπον αὐτῷ· οὕτως τετιμωρημένος ἀποκρίνῃ; ὁ δὲ τῷ αὐτῷ βλέμματι προσχὼν εἶπέ μοι· πῶς ἔχω σοι ἀποκριθῆναι; σὺ μὲν υἱὸς ἀνθρώπου εἶ, κἀγὼ ἀγγέλου). (5:2-3)[68]

---

62 Trans. from Vanderkam, *Book of Jubilees*, 47.

63 Trans. from Vanderkam, *Book of Jubilees*, 58. See also the *Gospel of Philip* from Nag Hammadi, which speaks of "male spirits that have sexual intercourse with souls who conduct their lives within a female shape, and female ones that mingle promiscuously with those within a male shape" (65.1–8; trans. from Layton, *Gnostic Scriptures*, 340). These are the same as, or at least included among, the "unclean spirits" mentioned a little further on in the text: "For if they possessed the holy spirit, no unclean spirit could attach itself to them" (66.2–4; Layton, 340). There is also a spell for driving out demons that shows Jewish influence and includes the words "until you drive away this unclean daimon Satan (ἀκάθαρτος δαίμων Σατανᾶς), who is in him" (trans. by M. W. Meyer in Hans Dieter Betz, ed., *The Greek Magical Papyri in Translation Including the Demotic Spells* [Chicago: University of Chicago Press, 1986; 2nd ed. 1992] 62).

64 E.g., "But now the giants who were begotten by the spirits and flesh—they will call them evil spirits on the earth" (*1 Enoch* 15:8; trans. from Nickelsburg and VanderKam, 37). See also the passage from *Genesis Apocryphon* cited below. The expression "every wicked and evil spirit" (πᾶν πνεῦμα πονηρὸν καὶ κακόν) occurs in lines 1–2 of a Solomonic exorcistic text dating to the third or fourth cent. CE; see Jordan and Kotansky, "Solomonic Exorcism," 53–69. In later Christian exorcistic texts, "unclean" (ἀκάθαρτος) is more common than "evil" (πονηρός), but both terms occur with no clear distinction in usage (ibid., 57).

65 The antiquity of this formula is proved by its use in 11QPsApᵃ (= 11QApocryphal Psalms [11Q11]) 4:5-6, "When Belial comes to you, say to him, 'Who are you?'" For discussion, see Émile Puech, "Les deux derniers psaumes davidiques du rituel d'exorcisme, 11QPsApᵃ IV 4–V 14," in Dimant and Rappaport, 64–89, esp. 68–69; cf. Torijano, *Solomon the Esoteric King*, 43–53. See also Esther Eshel, "Genres of Magical Texts in the Dead Sea Scrolls," in Lange et al., *Demons*, 395–415, esp. 398–401; eadem, "Apotropaic Prayers in the Second Temple Period," in Chazon, *Liturgical Perspectives*, 69–88, esp. 85–86; eadem, "Demonology in Palestine," chap. 5.

66 Text from Chester C. McCown, *The Testament of Solomon* (Leipzig: Hinrichs, 1922) 13*; trans. from Dennis C. Duling, "Testament of Solomon," in *OTP* 1:935–87; citation is from 963. This work was written at some point in the period from the first to the third cent. CE; see Duling, *OTP* 1:940–43. On the use of the formula "Who are you?" in this text, see Torijano, *Solomon the Esoteric King*, 53–68.

67 Text from McCown, *Testament of Solomon*, 17*; trans. from Duling, *OTP* 1:964. Solomon also speaks first when he is approached by the female demon Onoskelis; he says, "Tell me who you are," and she answers, "My name is Onoskelis," and provides further information about herself (*T. Sol.* 4:3-7). See also *T. Sol.* 8:1-12; 9:1-2; 12:1-5; 14:1-8; 15:1-6; 17:1-5; 18:1-42; 22:16-19; 25:1-4.

Solomon binds Asmodeus with greater care, has him flogged, and commands him to defend himself by stating his name and activity. The demon then complies.

In one case, the encounter begins in a way similar to that between Jesus and the unclean spirit in the synagogue of Capernaum. When the doglike demon Scepter comes before Solomon, he speaks first, in a loud voice, saying, "Hail, O King Solomon" (χαῖρε, ὦ βασιλεῦ Σολομῶν). Solomon is astounded and says, "Who are you, dog?" (τίς εἶ σύ, κύον;) (10:1-2). But unlike the situation in the Gospel of Mark, this reversal seems to have no narrative significance in the *Testament of Solomon*.[69] In another case the reversal serves to demonstrate the great power of this demon and the difficulty Solomon has in subduing him.[70]

The unclean spirit in Mark says, "What have we to do with you, Jesus of Nazareth?" (τί ἡμῖν καὶ σοί, Ἰησοῦ Ναζαρηνέ;). The formula τί ἡμῖν (ἐμοὶ) καὶ σοί ("What have we/I to do with you?" or "Of what concern is that to us/me or you?") is common, but its meaning varies according to the context.[71] Otto Bauernfeind argued that the question is an attempt to ward off the impending destruction mentioned in the spirit's next question, "Have you come to destroy us?" (ἦλθες ἀπολέσαι ἡμᾶς;).[72] Dietrich-Alex Koch, however, has argued against Bauernfeind that the question is an expression of submission on the part of the unclean

spirit.[73] But the spirit's following declaration, "I know who you are, the Holy One of God" (οἶδά σε τίς εἶ, ὁ ἅγιος τοῦ θεοῦ), does not express submission. Although he does not flaunt the authority of Jesus as blatantly as Asmodeus challenged that of Solomon, the unclean spirit is presented as attempting to gain control over Jesus. The spirit expects that the knowledge he has about Jesus will allow him to control Jesus and to resist being driven out of the man. Compare the statements of a magician who expects to gain power over the moon:

You'll, willy-nilly, do the NN task
Because I know your lights in full detail, . . .
I truly know that you are full of guile . . .
As I instruct you, hurl him to this ill
Because, Kore, I know your good and great
Majestic names . . . .

(τὸ δεῖνα ποιήσεις, κἂν θέλῃς κἂν μὴ θέλῃς, ὅτι οἶδά σου τὰ φῶτα πρὸ(ς) στιγμῆς μέτρον. . . . δόλου γέμουσαν. . . σ᾽ οἶδα. . . . οἷον λέγω σοι, εἴσβαλε εἰς τοῦτον κακόν, ὅτι οἶδα σὲ τὰ καλὰ καὶ μεγάλα, Κόρη, ὀνόματα σεμνά).[74]

In the narrower context of the passage as a traditional exorcism, the words of the spirit constitute an attempt to exert power over Jesus. In the broader context of Mark as

---

68 Text from McCown, *Testament of Solomon*, 21*; trans. from Duling, *OTP* 1:965. Another variation occurs in the encounter between Solomon and Lix Tetrax, the demon of the wind. Before Solomon says anything to this demon, he attacks the king by hurling a great cloud of dust at him many times; Solomon gets him under control and then asks his name. After some resistance, the demon finally complies (*T. Sol.* 7:1-7; see also 13:1-7).

69 Text from McCown, *Testament of Solomon*, 37*; trans. from Duling, *OTP* 1:971–72. See also 16:1-7.

70 *T. Sol.* 11:1-7; in this passage a lion-shaped demon appears, roaring, and questions Solomon before the king can speak. Solomon is able to control him, however, by adjuring him by the name of the great God Most High.

71 See BDF §299.3; cf. John 2:4; Rudolf Bultmann, *The Gospel of John: A Commentary* (Philadelphia: Westminster, 1971) 116; Ernst Haenchen, *John 1* (Hermeneia; Philadelphia: Fortress, 1984) 173.

72 Cf. the question and reproach of the widow of

Zarephath in 1 Kgs 17:18; Otto Bauernfeind, *Die Worte der Dämonen im Markusevangelium* (BWANT 3.8; Stuttgart: Kohlhammer, 1927) 3–12. See also Burke O. Long, *1 Kings with an Introduction to Historical Literature* (FOTL 9; Grand Rapids: Eerdmans, 1984) 185, on 1 Kgs 17:18.

73 Dietrich-Alex Koch, *Die Bedeutung der Wundererzählungen für die Christologie des Markusevangeliums* (BZNW 42; Berlin/New York: de Gruyter, 1975) 57–61. This interpretation is supported by the similar question in 2 Chr 35:21; for discussion see Simon J. De Vries, *1 and 2 Chronicles* (FOTL 11; Grand Rapids: Eerdmans, 1989) 417–18, who defines it as a formula of appeasement. See also Otto Bächli, "Was habe ich mit Dir zu schaffen? Eine formelhafte Frage im A.T. und N.T.," *TZ* 33 (1977) 69–80, who argues that the question generally reflects the inferiority of the questioner to the one questioned.

74 *PGM* IV. 2251-53; 2289; 2343-45; Karl Preisendanz, *Papyri Graecae Magicae: Die griechischen Zauberpapyri* (rev. Albert Henrichs; 2nd ed.; 2 vols.; Stuttgart:

a whole, they are also revelatory of the identity of Jesus. The holiness of Jesus is the polar opposite of the uncleanness of the spirit. The unclean spirit is unclean like the Watchers who descended from heaven; Jesus is holy like Enoch, who ascended to heaven. But the definite article in the phrase "the holy one of God" (ὁ ἅγιος τοῦ θεοῦ) exalts Jesus over Enoch and all other mere human beings as the holiest of God's elect.

The words of the spirit also suggest that he has special knowledge, concealed from the human beings who surround Jesus. This special knowledge is analogous to the knowledge of the future that the demons are said to have in the *Testament of Solomon*.[75] Ornias explains this knowledge as follows:

We demons go up to the firmament of heaven, fly around among the stars, and hear the decisions which issue from God concerning the lives of men (ἡμεῖς οἱ δαίμονες ἀνερχόμεθα ἐπὶ τοῦ στερεώματος τοῦ οὐρανοῦ καὶ μέσον τῶν ἄστρων ἱπτάμεθα καὶ ἀκούομεν τὰς ἀποφάσεις τὰς ἐξερχομένας ἀπὸ τοῦ θεοῦ ἐπὶ τὰς ψυχὰς τῶν ἀνθρώπων). (20:12)[76]

The allusion to the special knowledge of the demon and the identification of Jesus as "the Holy One of God" introduce an important theme in the Gospel of Mark, the question of the identity of Jesus.

Excursus: The Messianic Secret

The "messianic secret" is a concept in the history of interpretation of the Gospel of Mark, not a phrase that occurs in the text itself.[77] William Wrede coined the term "the messianic secret" (*das Messiasgeheimnis*) and used it in the title of his very influential study of Mark that appeared in 1901.[78] He developed a hypothesis to explain a number of features of Mark that he believed had the same purpose, namely, the commands to demons and disciples not to reveal the identity of Jesus,[79] the instructions to those who are healed by Jesus not to speak about their healing,[80] the lack of understanding by the disciples,[81] certain individual features that betray a tendency against publicity, and the so-called parable theory. The latter is expressed in the enigmatic and shocking saying of Jesus addressed to a restricted group of those around him together with the Twelve, "To you has been given the mystery of the kingdom of God, but to those who are outside, everything happens in parables, in order that, seeing, they may see and not perceive, and hearing, they may hear and not comprehend, lest they turn and it be forgiven them" (4:11-12).[82] Wrede did not believe that the messianic secret in Mark reflected historical reality. Rather, he treated it as a development in the pre-Markan Christian tradition, intended to explain the difference between the situation before the resurrection of Jesus and the situation afterward. He believed that the key to the meaning and function of the messianic secret is the statement that, after his transfiguration, Jesus ordered Peter, James, and John to tell no one what they had seen, "except when the Son of Man had risen from the dead" (9:9). Wrede believed that the various types of the secrecy theme were all intended to explain the fact that Jesus' life and work were nonmessianic, whereas his followers came to believe that he was the messiah after they experienced him as risen from the dead.

Other scholars have argued that the messianic secret has some basis in the life of Jesus.[83] Beginning

Teubner, 1973–74) 1:142, 144; trans. by Edward N. O'Neil in Betz, *Magical Papyri*, 78–81. The parallel with Mark 1:24 was pointed out by Bauernfeind (*Die Worte der Dämonen*, 14) and noted by Robinson (*Problem of History*, 84). See also *PGM* VIII. 6–14; 20–21. The phrases "you are" and "your name is" without "I know" appear in *PGM* IV. 1636–49 and elsewhere; Bauernfeind, *Die Worte der Dämonen*, 21–23; Robinson, *Problem of History*, 84.

75   *T. Sol.* 5:5; 20:1-21. See also *b. Ḥag* 16a (a female demon states that she heard a statement in heaven regarding Hanina ben Dosa) and *b. Giṭ.* 68a (Asmodeus predicts the fate of a bride and groom).

76   Text from McCown, *Testament of Solomon*, 62*; trans. from Duling, *OTP* 1:983.

77   See also Adela Yarbro Collins, "Messianic Secret and the Gospel of Mark: Secrecy in Jewish Apocalyp-

cism, the Hellenistic Mystery Religions, and Magic," in Elliott R. Wolfson, ed., *Rending the Veil: Concealment and Secrecy in the History of Religions* (New York/London: Seven Bridges Press, 1999) 11–30.

78   Wrede, *Messianic Secret*.

79   E.g., Mark 1:34 (demons), 3:12 (unclean spirits), and 8:30 (disciples).

80   E.g., the leper in Mark 1:44.

81   E.g., Mark 8:14-21.

82   Mark 4:11-12; see the commentary below.

83   Albert Schweitzer, *The Quest of the Historical Jesus: First Complete Edition* (Minneapolis: Fortress, 2001) 319; Oscar Cullmann, *Peter: Disciple–Apostle–Martyr* (rev. ed.; Philadelphia: Westminster, 1962) 176–80; Taylor, 123; Julius Schniewind, "Messiasgeheimnis und Eschatologie," in *Nachgelassene Reden und Aufsätze* (Berlin: Töpelmann, 1952) 1–13; and Erik

with Bultmann, however, many scholars have interpreted the theory of secrecy as a creation of the evangelist. Bultmann argued that the device served to link the Hellenistic Christian community's proclamation of the Son of God coming down to earth, that is, the Christ-myth, with the narrative traditions about Jesus.[84] Dibelius argued that the secrecy theory had an apologetic function. It was intended to explain why, in spite of so many proofs of his supernatural power, Jesus was not recognized as the messiah during his lifetime.[85] Some scholars have argued against Wrede's thesis that the several secrecy themes have the same origin and purpose.[86] Ulrich Luz argued that the "miracle secret" and the "messianic secret proper" should be distinguished. According to him, the miracle secret is an independent motif that serves to highlight the glory of Jesus, which manifests itself irresistibly. He interpreted the messianic secret proper as a qualification of the nature of Jesus' messiahship, which can be understood only from the perspective of the cross and resurrection.[87] Jürgen Roloff agreed with Luz's separation of these two motifs but argued that the messianic secret proper should also be divided into two parts: commands to silence addressed to demons and commands addressed to disciples.[88] Schuyler Brown, Heikki Räisänen, and others have argued that the parable theory should be interpreted without reference to the messianic secret.[89]

In the scholarship reviewed up to this point, the primary methods employed are the reconstruction of the history of tradition in historical context and literary-theological interpretations of the text of Mark. More recently Gerd Theissen has taken a different approach. Applying the perspective of the sociology of knowledge, he has suggested that the secrecy motifs had a pragmatic function. That which is kept secret is removed from social sanctions. It is kept secret to avoid the imposition of such sanctions by those with the power to enforce them. As a rule, he suggests, every secret is an attempt by a group to protect itself. When the secret is broken, the group is endangered. Assuming a correspondence between the world of the text and the social world of the audience, Theissen suggests that the tension between keeping their Christian identity secret and revealing it was a problem for the audience, just as an analogous tension was a problem for Jesus as a character in the narrative with whom the audience would identify. By telling the story of Jesus, the Gospel of Mark offers advice to the audience. They may keep their identity secret with a good conscience. But they are warned that it will be impossible to do so in the long run. When they are discovered, they must confess their identity bravely, as Jesus did, and risk conflict that may lead to death. By means of this approach, Theissen is able to make a case for the unity of the secrecy themes, since they all have the same basic purpose.[90] The social functions of secrecy, however, are more varied and complex than Theissen allowed in that study. This commentary takes a comparative, history-of-religions approach to the question of the "messianic secret."[91]

Sjöberg, *Der verborgene Menschensohn in den Evangelien* (SUKHVL 53; Lund: Gleerup, 1955) 246; for criticism of these positions, see Räisänen, *Messianic Secret*, 48–54.

84 Bultmann, *History*, 347–48; see also Räisänen, *Messianic Secret*, 55.

85 Dibelius, *From Tradition to Gospel*, 223. Dibelius had many followers, e.g., T. Alec Burkill, *Mysterious Revelation: An Examination of the Philosophy of St. Mark's Gospel* (Ithaca, NY: Cornell University Press, 1963) 68–69; and Walter Schmithals, *Das Evangelium nach Markus* (2 vols.; ÖTBK 2.1-2; Gütersloh: Mohn, 1979) 1:52–53, 58–59; for a critical assessment, see Räisänen, *Messianic Secret*, 56–60.

86 Andreas Bedenbender argues that the messianic secret is a bundle of distinct themes; each type must be interpreted on its own terms, and the coherence of the whole can only be a differentiated one ("Das Messiasgeheimnis im Markusevangelium," *Texte und Kontexte* 27.3-4 [2004] 1–96, esp. 35).

87 Ulrich Luz, "Das Geheimnismotiv und die markinische Christologie," *ZNW* 56 (1965) 9–30; ET "The Secrecy Motif and the Marcan Christology," in

Christopher Tuckett, ed., *The Messianic Secret* (Issues in Religion and Theology; Philadelphia: Fortress; London: SPCK, 1983) 75–96.

88 Jürgen Roloff, "Das Markusevangelium als Geschichtsdarstellung," *EvTh* 29 (1969) 73–93; he concluded that the commands to the disciples reflect the author's intention to distinguish between the life of Jesus as a historical past that can be reported, on the one hand, and the time of Easter onward, the time of the eschatological activity of God to which one can only bear witness, on the other.

89 Schuyler Brown, "'The Secret of the Kingdom of God' (Mark 4:11)," *JBL* 92 (1973) 60–74; Räisänen, *Messianic Secret*, 73.

90 Gerd Theißen, "Die pragmatische Bedeutung der Geheimnismotive im Markusevangelium: Ein wissenssoziologischer Versuch," in Hans G. Kippenberg and Guy G. Stroumsa, eds., *Secrecy and Concealment: Studies in the History of Mediterranean and Near Eastern Religions* (SHR 65; Leiden: Brill, 1995) 225–45.

91 See the commentary on 4:1-34 and 8:27-33 below.

Wrede was right that all the secrecy motifs in the Gospel of Mark have the same purpose, or at least very similar purposes. His explanation of that purpose, however, is inadequate. As noted above, Wrede took the saying of Jesus after the transfiguration as the key to the messianic secret. According to Wrede, when Jesus told the disciples not to tell anyone what they had seen until the Son of Man had risen from the dead, that meant that the identity of Jesus would only be revealed or could only be comprehended after his resurrection. Other scholars have noted that Jesus' declaration to the high priest and the acclamation of the centurion beneath the cross call this hypothesis into question (Mark 14:62; 15:39). The saying of Jesus after the transfiguration should rather be interpreted as a signal that the transfiguration serves as a preview of the resurrected state of Jesus. Mark offers this account instead of a description of an appearance of the risen Jesus later on. In sum, Wrede did not take a sufficiently literary and comparative approach to the theme of secrecy in Mark.

Hans Jürgen Ebeling was closer to the mark in his thesis that the secrecy theme is a *literary device* intended to make it clear to the *reader* of the Gospel the importance of the things dealt with in it.[92] Ebeling argued that the unifying conception of the Gospel of Mark is the revelation of the Christ-event.[93] There is of course great tension between the theory that Mark is an account of the process of revelation, on the one hand, and the observation that secrecy is an important theme, on the other. He resolves this tension by pointing to the dialectic between revelation and secrecy in various texts from antiquity and to the tension between the activity of God and that of human beings in religious experience. Another way of expressing this tension is the felicitous description of the Gospel of Mark by Dibelius as a series of secret epiphanies.[94]

The theme of secrecy appears for the first time in Mark in the account of this first miracle, the exorcism that Jesus performs in the synagogue in Capernaum. His command to the spirit, "Be muzzled and come out of him," in v. 25 is a typical exorcistic technique. But Mark has employed a variant of the typical genre of the exorcism in order to allow the demon to identify Jesus. This identification has importance primarily for the reader and those to whom the Gospel is read

aloud. Those present in the narrative scene comment on how the demons obey Jesus, but not on the demon's revelation of Jesus' identity (Mark 1:27). The intention of the evangelist comes out even more clearly in the editorial summary given in 1:34: "And he healed many who were sick, and he drove out many demons, and he would not allow the demons to speak, because they knew him" (see also 3:11-12). The demons recognize Jesus because of their knowledge of heavenly matters, but his identity is not grasped by the human beings in the narrative.

The various themes of secrecy in Mark—the commands to demons and disciples not to reveal the identity of Jesus, the instructions to those who are healed by Jesus not to speak about their healing, the lack of understanding by the disciples, and the "parable theory"—are all literary devices created or adapted by the author of the Gospel to reveal and yet conceal Jesus and to imply that, during his lifetime, his identity was similarly revealed yet concealed.

■ **25** As noted above, the parallels to the speech of the unclean spirit in the Greek Magical Papyri are spoken by the magician in attempts to control suprahuman beings. In v. 24 it is the unclean spirit who attempts to control Jesus. While such reversals occur in other texts (see the discussion of the *Testament of Solomon* above), the turning of the tables in Mark provides an occasion for the mysterious revelation of the identity of Jesus and initiates the development of the related theme in the Gospel as a whole.

After the speech of the demon, Jesus rebukes the unclean spirit (v. 25). According to the *Genesis Apocryphon* (1Q20), a work read by the community at Qumran but probably not composed by them, the king of Egypt and all the men of his household were afflicted by an evil spirit because of the presence of Sarai, the wife of Abram, in the king's house. Pharaoh discovers the reason and asks Abram to pray that the evil spirit may be "rebuked" (ותתגער).[95]

Jesus also commands the unclean spirit, "Be muzzled," that is, "Be silent" (φιμώθητι). This response of

---

92   Hans Jürgen Ebeling, *Das Messiasgeheimnis und die Botschaft des Marcus-Evangelisten* (BZNW 19; Berlin: Töpelmann, 1939) 167-69, 170-72, 177-78. But some aspects of Ebeling's argument are untenable; see Räisänen's summary and criticism of Ebeling's interpretation (*Messianic Secret*, 60-62).

93   Ebeling, *Das Messiasgeheimnis*, 221-24.

94   Dibelius, *From Tradition to Gospel*, 230.

95   1QapGen 20:28; text and trans. may be found in Joseph A. Fitzmyer and Daniel J. Harrington, *A Manual of Palestinian Aramaic Texts: Second Century B.C.– Second Century A.D.* (BibOr 34; Rome: Biblical Institute Press, 1978) 116-17. They translate ותתגער with "may be commanded (to depart)," but Fitzmyer

Jesus makes clear that the speech of the unclean spirit is not a simple expression of submission. Rather, the speech, because of its special knowledge about Jesus, is dangerous. The spirit's speech is an attack, and it must be met with a counterattack.[96] Within the dramatic context of the exorcism itself, Jesus' command to silence is first and foremost a "muzzling" of the spirit, which is analogous to the "binding" involved in many effective rituals. Usually a human being makes use of a spell to "bind" and silence another human being:

> say "I bind NN with regard to NN [thing]. Let him not speak, not be contrary, not oppose; let him not be able to look me in the face nor speak against me; let him be subjected to me, so long as this ring is buried. I bind his mind and his brains, his desire, his actions, so that he may be slow [in his dealings] with all men" (λέγε· 'καταδεσμεύω τὸν δεῖνα πρὸς τὸ δεῖνα· μὴ λαλησάτω, μὴ ἀντισπ(ασ)άτω, μὴ ἀντειπάτω, μή μοι δύναιτο ἀντιβλέψαι ἢ ἀντιλαλῆσαι, ὑποτεταγμένος δέ μοι ἤτω, ἐφ' ὅσον οὗτος ὁ κρίκος κέχωσται. καταδεσμεύω δὲ αὐτοῦ τὸν νοῦν καὶ τὰς φρένας, τὴν ἐνθύμησιν, τὰς πράξεις, ὅπως νωχελὴς ᾖ πρὸς πάντας ἀνθρώπους'). (PGM V. 320-29)[97]

The text in Mark transposes this motif so that it works upon a suprahuman being rather than a human. Another difference is that Jesus' technique is a simple command; no ring or spell is involved. Jesus' command overpowers the spirit by nullifying and ending its speech.

But in the context of the Gospel as a whole, the command to silence takes on the connotations of the secret of Jesus' identity.[98]

■ **25-28** Jesus then commands the spirit to come out of the man (v. 25) and the spirit does so, convulsing the man and crying out with a loud, presumably inarticulate voice (v. 26). This is the exorcism proper, although the verbal adjuration from which the mighty deed gets its name, the formula involving the term ἐξορκίζω ("to adjure" or "to charge under oath") does not occur.[99] This victory of Jesus in a struggle with an unclean spirit takes up the theme of conflict with Satan and the demons introduced in the scene of Jesus' testing in the wilderness.[100] In the earlier passage the conflict was only implicit, but in vv. 23-28 it is explicit. Jesus, as the messiah and Servant of the Lord, must engage in a struggle with the powers that oppose God. As the herald and chief agent of the kingdom of God, he must do battle with the kingdom of Satan.[101]

As noted above, v. 27 expresses the typical motif of the reaction of the spectators to the exorcism. The acclamation "he commands even the unclean spirits, and they obey him" is appropriate to the genre exorcism and to this specific context. The exclamation "What is this? A new teaching with authority," however, seems out of place. It takes up, however, the teaching of Jesus in the synagogue just prior to the exorcism and the reaction of those who heard it (vv. 21-22). In that context the narrator notes that "he was teaching them with authority, not as the scribes taught." As noted above, this remark implies that Jesus' teaching was different from that of the

---

points out (*The Genesis Apocryphon of Qumran Cave 1: A Commentary* [2nd rev. ed.; BibOr 18A; Rome: Biblical Institute Press, 1971] 138) that in Zech 3:2 and in Ps 68:31 (MT) the LXX (Ps 67:31) renders this root with ἐπιτιμάω ("rebuke"). He cites Kee's conclusion (Howard Clark Kee, "The Terminology of Mark's Exorcism Stories," *NTS* 14 [1967–68] 232–46) with approval that in the DSS נער means the pronouncement of a commanding word by God or his agent by which evil powers are brought under control. See also the other literature cited by Fitzmyer, *Genesis Apocryphon*, 138.

96 Bauernfeind, *Die Worte der Dämonen*, 31–34.

97 Preisendanz-Henrichs, 1:192; trans. by Morton Smith in Betz, *Magical Papyri*, 106. This text is cited also by Theissen, *Miracle Stories*, 141, as an example of the category "Commands to fall silent."

98 See the excursus on the messianic secret above and the commentary on 1:32-34 below. See also Theissen, *Miracle Stories*, 144, who argues that the typical word of power becomes in Mark a command to secrecy. Bernd Kollmann makes too sharp a distinction between the use of φιμόω to mean "tie shut" or "muzzle," on the one hand, and "to silence," on the other ("Jesu Schweigegebote an die Dämonen," *ZNW* 82 [1991] 267–73).

99 The term ὁρκίζω ("to adjure" or "to implore") occurs in Mark 5:7; see the commentary below and Bauernfeind, *Die Worte der Dämonen*, 32.

100 See the commentary on 1:12-13 above.

101 See the commentary on 3:22-27 below.

experts in the Law in its warrants and style and perhaps also in content. The acclamation of the crowd in v. 27 implies that the power exercised by Jesus over the demon legitimates his teaching. Both the authority to teach and the power to exorcise have a divine source.[102] Although the spectators have apparently not drawn this conclusion, the audience knows that this authority is rooted in Jesus' appointment as the messiah and his endowment with the Holy Spirit. Verse 28 elaborates and extends the reaction of the spectators. They tell others about Jesus' accomplishments until his fame has spread throughout Galilee and beyond.[103]

1

1:29-31 Jesus Heals Simon's Mother-in-Law

29/ **So then, when they had gone out of the synagogue, they went into the house of Simon and Andrew, with James and John.[a] 30/ Now the mother-in-law of Simon was lying down, sick with a fever, and so they told him about her. 31/ And he went to her, took hold of her hand, and raised her up. And the fever left her and she began to serve them.**

a   B D W Θ $f^{1.13}$ et al. have singular verbal forms in this sentence. Although Turner's claim that the usage reflects the point of view of an eyewitness is untenable, he was correct in observing that the shift from an impersonal plural to the singular is characteristic of Mark's style (but note that the opposite shift is more likely to be original in 3:20; see below). The change to singular forms here was made to increase the focus on Jesus and to give a clearer antecedent for $\alpha\dot{\nu}\tau\hat{\varphi}$ ("him") in v. 30; the parallels in Matt 8:14 and Luke 4:38 may also have had an influence. See Turner, "Marcan Usage," 26 (1925) 225–31 (Elliott, *Language and Style*, 36–42); Turner, "Textual Commentary," 155. See also Metzger, *Textual Commentary*, 64.

Comment

■ **29-31** The story is brief and narrated entirely in the third person. A dialogue is summarized in v. 30b. These features may indicate that the evangelist has rewritten in concise form a longer account of the healing of Simon's mother-in-law.[104] The description of the event of healing itself is "And the fever left her" ($\kappa\alpha\grave{\iota}$ $\dot{\alpha}\phi\hat{\eta}\kappa\epsilon\nu$ $\alpha\dot{\nu}\tau\grave{\eta}\nu$ $\dot{o}$ $\pi\nu\rho\epsilon\tau\acute{o}\varsigma$). This formulation suggests that the fever is an entity that can enter and leave a human body, like an unclean spirit a or demon.[105] It thus creates an affinity between this example of an account of a healing and the typical account of an exorcism.[106] The typical features of this account of healing in Mark include (1) the coming of the miracle-worker: "when they had gone out of the synagogue, they went into the house of Simon and Andrew"; (2) description of the illness: she "was lying down, sick with a fever"; (3) request for healing: "they told him about her"; (4) the technique or means of healing: "he went to her, took hold of her hand, and raised her up"; (5) the event of healing: "And the fever left her"; and

---

102 Paul J. Achtemeier argues that the Markan Jesus' "power as a teacher is made visible in the acts of power he regularly performed" ("'He Taught Them Many Things': Reflections on Marcan Christology," *CBQ* 42 [1980] 465–81; citation from 480).

103 Cf. Mark 1:45; 5:14, 20; Matt 9:26, 31; Luke 7:17; Acts 9:42; see Theissen, *Miracle Stories*, 72.

104 The author of Matthew has rewritten the account of Mark in an even more concise style, eliminating mention of a dialogue (Matt 8:14-15; cf. Theissen, *Miracle Stories*, 177–78, 180).

105 On the widespread opinion in the ancient world that certain diseases were caused by a god, goddess, or daimon, see Dale B. Martin, *Inventing Superstition: From the Hippocratics to the Christians* (Cambridge, MA/London: Harvard University Press, 2004) 37–38, 53–54, 190, 271–72 n. 14.

106 The author of Luke has rewritten the account in a way that brings out this affinity more explicitly (Luke 4:38-39; see Theissen, *Miracle Stories*, 86–87, 185).

(6) demonstration of the healing: "she began to serve them."[107] It is noteworthy that Jesus heals in this case only by touch; no healing word is spoken.[108]

■ **29** The movement of Jesus, Simon, Andrew, James, and John creates a strong element of continuity in the narrative.[109] The names of the four disciples link this passage to the calling of the four in 1:16-20. The movement from the synagogue to the house reinforces the impres-

sion that the four were with Jesus as he taught and exorcised in the synagogue of Capernaum. It also implies that Simon and Andrew lived in Capernaum. The fact that Jesus accompanies Simon and Andrew to their home is in tension with the impression created by their call (vv. 16-18) that they abandoned everyone and everything to follow Jesus. But this tension is resolved in vv. 35-39.[110]

1

1:32-34 Summary of Activity in Capernaum

32/ When evening had come, when the sun had set, they brought to him all those who were sick and those who were possessed by demons. 33/ And the whole city was gathered together at the door. 34/ And he healed many who were sick, and he drove out many demons, and he would not allow the demons to speak, because they knew him.[a]

a B L W Θ f^1 et al. read $\alpha\dot{\upsilon}\tau\grave{o}\nu$ $\chi\rho\iota\sigma\tau\grave{o}\nu$ $\epsilon\dot{\imath}\nu\alpha\iota$, "that he was anointed" or "that he was (the) messiah," instead of $\alpha\dot{\upsilon}\tau\grave{o}\nu$ ("him"). A number of other MSS have a similar but more explicit reading, $\tau\grave{o}\nu$ $\chi\rho\iota\sigma\tau\grave{o}\nu$ $\alpha\dot{\upsilon}\tau\grave{o}\nu$ $\epsilon\dot{\imath}\nu\alpha\iota$, "that he was the Messiah." These MSS, some with a slightly different word order, are $\aleph^2$ C f^{13} et al. These are clarifying changes, probably made under the influence of the parallel in Luke 4:41. See Metzger, *Textual Commentary*, 64. For an argument that the changes were polemical, see Ehrman, *Orthodox Corruption*, 159.

Comment

■ **32-34** Dibelius and Bultmann have persuaded most scholars that these verses result from the editorial work of the evangelist.[111] The description of Jesus' healings and exorcisms is general; it lacks the vividness of the individual accounts that were handed down to the evangelist, but is based on them. Theissen has argued that the independent summary of vv. 32-34 is an expansion of the motif of the appearance of the crowd in relation to the miracle-worker.[112]

■ **32** The temporal setting, "When evening had come, when the sun had set" ($\dot{o}\psi\dot{\iota}\alpha\varsigma$ $\delta\grave{\epsilon}$ $\gamma\epsilon\nu\omega\mu\acute{\epsilon}\nu\eta\varsigma$, $\check{o}\tau\epsilon$ $\check{\epsilon}\delta\upsilon$ $\acute{o}$ $\check{\eta}\lambda\iota\omega\varsigma$), links the editorial summary to the two preceding scenes. The teaching and exorcism in the synagogue and the healing of Simon's mother-in-law all take place on the same day, a Sabbath (v. 21). The fact that the people of Capernaum waited until the sun had gone down to bring the sick and possessed to Jesus implies that either the activity of bringing them or healing them, or perhaps both, is unlawful on the Sabbath.[113] If such is indeed implied, then it is noteworthy that Mark's Jesus

---

107 See Bultmann, *History*, 221–26; see also motifs 1 (The Coming of the Miracle Worker), 8 (Description of the Distress), 22 (Touch), and 27 (Demonstration) in Theissen, *Miracle Stories*, 48–67. For a nuanced feminist reading of this passage, see Deborah Krause, "Simon Peter's Mother-in-law—Disciple or Domestic Servant? Feminist Biblical Hermeneutics and the Interpretation of Mark 1.29-31," in Levine, *Feminist Companion*, 37–53.

108 On the motif of "the miracle-working word," see Theissen, *Miracle Stories*, 63–65.

109 Cf. Bultmann, *History*, 212.

110 See the commentary on vv. 35-39 below.

111 Dibelius, *From Tradition to Gospel*, 44, 224; Bultmann, *History*, 341.

112 Theissen, *Miracle Stories*, 48.

113 CD 11:11 states that no one minding an infant shall carry it from one place to another on the Sabbath; see Lawrence Schiffman, *The Halakhah at Qumran* (SJLA 16; Leiden: Brill, 1975) 119–20. It would seem, then, that carrying an ill person would also be unlawful; *m. Šabb.* 14.3 and 4 imply that healing activities are unlawful on the Sabbath; cf. 22.6. See the commentary on 3:1-6 below.

nevertheless exorcises (vv. 21-28) and heals (vv. 29-31) on the Sabbath.

■ **33-34** The description of the whole city gathered at the door of Simon's house is a dramatic illustration of the authority and fame of Jesus and the positive response to him on the part of the people of Capernaum. The audience might expect a crowd assembled from other places in and around Galilee, given the statement about the spread of Jesus' fame to that distance in v. 28. But the spatial specificity of v. 33 continues the concreteness of the temporal setting given in v. 32. Verse 34 takes up Jesus' command that the unclean spirit be silent in v. 25. As noted above, that command, as part of a traditional exorcism, belongs to a description of a contest or strug-gle between Jesus and the unclean spirit and is meant to nullify the potential power that the special knowledge of the spirit might give it over Jesus. The statement in v. 34, however, "he would not allow the demons to speak, because they knew him," implies something more. It suggests that Jesus does not wish his identity to become known. The evangelist here takes the first step in devel-oping a traditional exorcistic motif into the theme of the secret identity of Jesus.[114] The shift from the expression "unclean spirit" ($\pi\nu\epsilon\hat{\upsilon}\mu\alpha\ \dot{\alpha}\kappa\dot{\alpha}\vartheta\alpha\rho\tau\sigma\nu$), which occurs in vv. 23, 26, and 27, to the term "demons" ($\delta\alpha\iota\mu\acute{\sigma}\nu\iota\alpha$) in v. 34 (cf. v. 39), may be due simply to stylistic variation.[115] Or, more likely, the evangelist uses both terms in order "to speak 'bilingually'" to both Jews and Gentiles.[116]

---

1 | **1:35-39 Withdrawal and Statement of Purpose**

35/ And he rose early in the morning, while it was still very dark, went out, and went away[a] to an unpop-ulated place, and began to pray there. 36/ Simon and those with him searched for him eagerly, 37/ and they found him and said to him,[b] "All are looking for you." 38/ And he said to them, "Let us go elsewhere, to the neighboring market-towns, in order that I may proclaim there also; for I came out for this purpose."[c] 39/ And he was proclaiming[d] in their syna-gogues in all Galilee and driving out the demons.

a   Some MSS (W *pc*) omit $\dot{\epsilon}\xi\hat{\eta}\lambda\vartheta\epsilon\nu\ \kappa\alpha\dot{\iota}$ ("went out and"); others (B 28. 565 *pc*) omit $\kappa\alpha\dot{\iota}\ \dot{\alpha}\pi\hat{\eta}\lambda\vartheta\epsilon\nu$ ("and went away"). These changes appear to be attempts to improve the redundant style of Mark.

b   The earliest recoverable text has three finite verbs connected with $\kappa\alpha\dot{\iota}$. The variants may be explained as attempts to improve this simple, paratactic style. See Turner, "Textual Commentary," 156.

c   The aorist tense of the verb $\dot{\epsilon}\xi\hat{\eta}\lambda\vartheta\sigma\nu$ ("I came out") indicates that the reference is to Jesus' departure from Capernaum, narrated in v. 35. This specific event is generalized in some MSS by a change in the tense of the verb or by the substitution of another verb which refers to Jesus' mission as a whole. W $\Delta\ f^{13}$ *pm* read $\dot{\epsilon}\lambda\dot{\eta}\lambda\upsilon\vartheta\alpha$ ("I have come"); A D K $\Gamma\ f^1$ *pm* read $\dot{\epsilon}\xi\epsilon\lambda-\dot{\eta}\lambda\upsilon\vartheta\alpha$ ("I have come out"); 2542 reads $\dot{\alpha}\pi\epsilon\sigma\tau\dot{\alpha}\lambda\eta\nu$ ("I was sent").

d   The translation is based on the reading attested by A C D W $f^{1.13}$ et al., "he was proclaiming" ($\hat{\eta}\nu\ \kappa\eta\rho\dot{\upsilon}\sigma-\sigma\omega\nu$). Since one would expect the phrase "in their syn-agogues" ($\dot{\epsilon}\nu\ \tau\alpha\hat{\iota}\varsigma\ \sigma\upsilon\nu\alpha\gamma\omega\gamma\alpha\hat{\iota}\varsigma\ \alpha\dot{\upsilon}\tau\hat{\omega}\nu$) with a verb of this sort, instead of "in their synagogues" or "into their synagogues" ($\epsilon\dot{\iota}\varsigma\ \tau\dot{\alpha}\varsigma\ \sigma\upsilon\nu\alpha\gamma\omega\gamma\dot{\alpha}\varsigma\ \alpha\dot{\upsilon}\tau\hat{\omega}\nu$), this reading was corrected by the addition of $\hat{\eta}\lambda\vartheta\epsilon\nu$ ("he came"). The latter reading is attested by $\aleph$ B L Θ et al. See Turner, "Marcan Usage," 26 (1924) 15–16 (Elliott, *Language and Style*, 17); Turner, "Textual Commen-tary," 156; so also Taylor, ad loc. For a different opin-ion, see Metzger, *Textual Commentary*, 64–65.

---

114   See the excursus above on the messianic secret.
115   The expression "unclean spirit" ($\pi\nu\epsilon\hat{\upsilon}\mu\alpha\ \dot{\alpha}\kappa\dot{\alpha}\vartheta\alpha\rho-\tau\sigma\nu$), as noted in the commentary above on vv. 23-28, has Jewish roots. The term "demons" ($\delta\alpha\iota\mu\acute{\sigma}\nu\iota\alpha$) is related to the Greek term $\delta\alpha\acute{\iota}\mu\omega\nu$ ("a deity"), but in this usage it also has Jewish analogies; see Josephus *Ant.* 6.8.2 §166, where the term $\delta\alpha\iota\mu\acute{\sigma}-\nu\iota\alpha$ ("demons" or "evil spirits") is used of the enti-ties troubling Saul.

116   Wahlen, *Jesus and the Impurity of Spirits*, 106.

Comment

■ **35-39** Bultmann rightly identified this passage as editorial.[117] The saying of Jesus in v. 38, therefore, is not a traditional "I-saying" that reflects on the person of Jesus and his coming.[118] It is rather bound to the context and moves the narrative along.

■ **35** Jesus rises early and goes out of Simon's house to pray alone. This brief description of Jesus praying near the beginning of his public activity corresponds to his prayer in Gethsemane near the end of his life.[119] The context of 1:35 and the correspondence with 14:32-42 imply that Jesus prays near the beginning of his activity for divine guidance and support.

■ **36-39** As noted in the comment on v. 29 above, the fact that Jesus goes with Simon and Andrew to their home in Capernaum is in some tension with the narrative of their call in vv. 16-20. Jesus' visit to their home and his healing of Simon's mother-in-law seem to imply that they need not leave everyone and everything to follow Jesus. This implication may explain why Peter and the others come out looking for Jesus and try to take him back to their home to meet the people who are looking for him (vv. 36-37), but Jesus' response makes clear that his activity of proclaiming (cf. vv. 14-15) is not to be confined to Capernaum. He will not make his headquarters in Simon's home and wait for the people to come to him. He will go out to them, but he leads his followers to perceive the scope of his mission gradually. He asks them simply to go out with him to the neighboring market-towns, for that is why he has left Simon's house (v. 38). Verse 39 is another summary of Jesus' activity. It extends the spatial scope of his activity from the neighboring market-towns to all Galilee. It also reflects the two foci of Jesus' activity depicted in vv. 21-28. On the one hand, he "proclaims" (the message summarized in vv. 14-15), as he "taught" in the synagogue of Capernaum. On the other hand, he casts out demons, as he drove out the unclean spirit from the afflicted man in Capernaum.[120]

1

1:40-45 The Healing of a Leper

40/ And a leper came to him, entreating him, falling on his knees before him,[a] and saying to him, "If you want, you are able to make me clean." **41/** And he had pity on him,[b] extended his hand, touched him, and said to him, "I do so want; be made clean." **42/** And immediately the leprosy left him, and he was made clean. **43/** And after he had upbraided him, he immediately drove him out **44/** and said to him, "See that you say nothing[c] to anyone, but go, show yourself to the priest and offer for your cleansing what Moses commanded, as a proof for them." **45/** But when he had gone away, he began to proclaim energetically and to spread the word widely, so that he was no longer able to enter a city openly, but remained outside in unpopulated places; and they were coming to him from everywhere.

a A strong combination of manuscripts (B D W Γ et al.) lacks the reference to the leper's kneeling. If the original reading was γονυπετῶν αὐτόν ("falling on his knees before him"), attested by A C et al., this phrase could have been omitted accidentally, because the scribe's eye may have skipped from the αὐτόν ("him") following παρακαλῶν ("entreating") to the one following γονυπετῶν ("falling on his knees"). Cf. Metzger, *Textual Commentary*, 65; Turner, "Textual Commentary," 156–57.

b A few manuscripts (D a ff² r1*) read ὀργισθείς ("having become angry") rather than σπλαγχνισθείς ("having taken pity"); the former reading may have been inspired by ἐμβριμησάμενος ("having warned sternly") in v. 43. See Metzger, *Textual Commentary*, 65. For a different view, see Turner, "Textual Commentary," 157. Bart Ehrman argues that ὀργισθείς ("having become angry") is the earlier reading ("Text and Tradition: The Role of New Testament Manuscripts in Early Christian Studies; The Kenneth W. Clark Lectures, Duke Divinity School, 1997," *TC: A Journal of Biblical Textual Criticism* [http://purl.org/TC] 5 [2000] Lecture 1).

c Some MSS (א A D L W et al.) lack μηδέν ("nothing").

---

117 Bultmann, *History*, 155.
118 The tendency to read it in such a way led to the variants discussed above in the note related to the translation of v. 38.
119 Mark 14:32-42, esp. vv. 32, 35, 39.
120 See the commentary on vv. 21-28 on the close relationship between Jesus' teaching and exorcising.

The inclusion of the word is probably the earlier reading, since it is characteristic of Mark's pleonastic style. The omission may have been inspired by the parallels in Matt 8:4 and Luke 5:14. See Turner, "Textual Commentary," 158.

Comment

■ **40-45** This miracle story, an account of healing, has a number of typical features: (1) the encounter: "a leper came to him"; (2) request for healing: "entreating him, falling on his knees before him, and saying to him, 'If you want, you are able to make me clean'"; (3) the technique of healing, in this case involving both touch and a simple oral formula: "extended his hand, touched him, and said to him, 'I do so want; be made clean'";[121] (4) the event of healing: "And immediately the leprosy left him, and he was made clean"; (5) the demonstration of the healing anticipated: "go, show yourself to the priest and offer for your cleansing what Moses commanded, as a proof for them"; (6) instead of the usual reaction of the spectators, the result of the healing as the proclaiming and spreading of the news on the part of the healed leper and the widespread response to his testimony (v. 45).[122]

In addition to the parallel versions of this story in Matt 8:1-4 and Luke 5:12-16, a version of it occurs in the unknown Gospel preserved in Papyrus Egerton 2.[123] Koester argued that the version preserved by the latter text is earlier than the Synoptic Gospels, whereas Neirynck concluded that its author knew all three of those Gospels.[124] The most likely explanation is that the version of the unknown Gospel is an example of secondary orality. The text is not independent of the Synoptic Gospels, but is not dependent on them in a literary sense.[125]

121 Kirsopp Lake argued that the reading ὀργισθείς ("having become angry") in v. 41 is the earlier reading (see the notes on the trans. of v. 41 above) and that it was the leper who became angry, not Jesus. He proposed the following translation: "And there came to him a leper beseeching him and kneeling and saying to him, If thou wilt, thou canst make me clean; and he [the leper] put out his hand in a passion of rage and touched him. And he [Jesus] said, I will, be thou clean. And immediately the leprosy departed from him and he was clean. And he rebuked him and immediately drove him out" ("ΕΜΒΡΙΜΗΣΑΜΕΝΟΣ and ὈΡΓΙΣΘΕΙΣ, Mark 1, 40-43," *HTR* 16 [1923] 197-98). This punctuation and translation are unpersuasive because they imply a sudden change in mood and attitude on the part of the leper. There is nothing in v. 40 to prepare for a sudden burst of anger on the part of the leper in v. 41.

122 On the technique of the therapy and proofs of the reality of the recovery, see Dibelius, *From Tradition to Gospel*, 54, 70-71, 80-81, 83, 87. Bultmann concluded that the healing gesture and the command that the man show himself to the priest as a demonstration of the healing are typical features (*History*, 212). See also motifs 3 (The Appearance of the Distressed Person), 10 (Falling to the Knees), 12 (Pleas and Expressions of Trust), 22 (Touch), 26 (Recognition of the Miracle), and 33 (The Spread of the News) in Theissen, *Miracle Stories*, 49-72.

123 Pap. Eg. 2 (1 recto 34-48); in 1987, Pap. Köln 255 was published, which comprises the lower lines of both sides of frg. 1 of Pap. Eg. 2. For a Greek text, ET, discussion, and bibliography, see Stephen R. Llewelyn, ed., *New Documents Illustrating Early Christianity*, vol. 9: *A Review of the Greek Inscriptions and Papyri Published in 1986-87* (North Ryde, N.S.W., Australia: Ancient History Documentary Research Centre, Macquarie University; Grand Rapids: Eerdmans, 2002) 99-101. For a Greek text, German translation, introduction, and bibliography, see Dieter Lührmann, *Fragmente apokryph gewordener Evangelien in griechischer und lateinischer Sprache* (Marburger Theologische Studien 59; Marburg: Elwert, 2000) 142-53; see also Koester, *Gospels*, 205-16; John P. Meier, *A Marginal Jew: Rethinking the Historical Jesus*, vol. 1: *The Roots of the Problem and the Person* (ABRL; New York/London: Doubleday, 1991); vol. 2: *Mentor, Message and Miracle* (1994); vol. 3: *Companions and Competitors* (2001) 1:118-20, 149 nn. 39-40; Thomas Kazen, "Sectarian Gospels for Some Christians? Intention and Mirror Reading in the Light of Extra-Canonical Texts," *NTS* 51 (2005) 561-78, esp. 569-73 and the literature cited there. See also the anecdote about the healing of ten lepers in Luke 17:11-19.

124 Koester, *Gospels*, 211-13; Frans Neirynck, "Papyrus Egerton and the Healing of the Leper," *EThL* 61 (1985) 153-60; reprinted in idem, *Evangelica II* (BEThL 99; Leuven: Leuven University Press/Peeters, 1991) 773-83. Neirynck reproduces the Greek text from Harold I. Bell and Theodore C.

■ **40-43** The humble gesture of kneeling and the pure and simple declaration of trust on the part of the leper (v. 40) awaken the pity of Jesus (v. 41).[126] He then heals the man by touch and speech (vv. 41-42).[127] So far the plot is typical and clear. But then the characterization of Jesus shifts from compassion to anger in v. 43: "And after he had upbraided him, he immediately drove him out" (ἐμβριμησάμενος αὐτῷ εὐθὺς ἐξέβαλεν αὐτόν). It has been suggested that the verbal form ἐμβριμησάμενος ("after he had upbraided him," lit., "having upbraided him") is a trace of a thaumaturgic technique or an indication of the pneumatic excitement of the healer.[128] But this interpretation is unlikely, since the pneumatic excitement of the healer should play a role before or during the healing, not afterward. It is more likely that the term in this context means that Jesus scolded or warned the man sternly in the context of instructing him to depart from himself and to go to the priest.[129]

The request of the leper is that Jesus "make me clean" (με καθαρίσαι). This verb is used in Lev 14:2, 4, not for the healing of a skin disorder but for the process by which the person is declared ritually "clean" or "pure" and thus reintegrated into society. Here, however, it is clear that the verb is used for the process of physical healing; v. 42 equates the man's "being made clean" with "the leprosy leaving him." After Jesus has healed the man, he instructs him to go to the priest to initiate the process described in Lev 14:1-32.[130]

■ **44** In the immediate context of this traditional account of a healing, Jesus' command, "See that you say nothing to anyone," is simply an expression of urgency. The man should go directly to the priest and show himself to him, "as a proof for them." The healing is to demonstrate to the authorities that Jesus has the power to heal and therefore is God's agent.[131] But in the larger context of the Gospel as a whole, this command to silence contributes to the theme of the mysterious and secret identity of Jesus.[132]

■ **45** No indication is given that the healed man obeyed Jesus' command to go to the priest. Rather, "he began to proclaim energetically and to spread the word widely." In the immediate context, the "word" is the fact that Jesus has healed him. In the larger context, however, his activity takes on the connotation that he is proclaiming the good news of God (cf. vv. 14-15) that Jesus also proclaims. This good news is the nearness of the kingdom of

Skeat, *Fragments of an Unknown Gospel and Other Early Christian Papyri* (London: Trustees of the British Museum, 1935) 10–11, Koester gives an ET.

125 Similarly, Meier, *Marginal Jew*, 1:119; Kazen, "Sectarian Gospels for Some Christians?" 570–71. It is possible, however, that the text of Pap. Eg. is a rewriting of one or more of the Synoptic Gospels, as Neirynck argued. See the commentary on 12:13-17 below.

126 Theissen (*Miracle Stories*, 57) argues that σπλαγχνισθείς ("he had pity on him") indicates "pneumatic excitement"; it is more likely, however, that the word expresses simple compassion.

127 It should be noted that the portrayal of Jesus touching a leper is "not in line with the prevailing legal interpretation" (Thomas Kazen, *Jesus and Purity Halakhah: Was Jesus Indifferent to Impurity?* [CBNTS 38; Stockholm: Almqvist & Wiksell International, 2002] 127). See the commentary on 5:33-34 below.

128 Campbell Bonner, "Traces of Thaumaturgic Technique in the Miracles," *HTR* 20 (1927) 171–81; Theissen, *Miracle Stories*, 57–58.

129 So also Lake, "Mark 1, 40–43," 197–98; Dibelius, *From Tradition to Gospel*, 73–74.

130 According to 11QT (11Q19), no leper may enter the sanctuary until he has purified himself and made an offering (45:17-18); in every city an area is to be set aside for lepers and others who may not enter the city because they would defile it (48:14-15). 4QMMT has similar regulations and, in addition, the stipulation that a leper is not to eat any holy food until the sun sets on the eighth day (after his ritual purification) (4QMMT 71–72); see Elisha Qimron and John Strugnell, *Qumran Cave 4*, vol. 5: *Miqṣat Maʿaśe Ha-Torah* (DJD 10; Oxford: Clarendon, 1994) 54–55; see also García Martínez and Tigchelaar, *Dead Sea Scrolls*, 2:796–97 (4Q396 3:11–4:1).

131 I cannot agree with Gerd Theißen's conclusion that Jesus commands the man to conceal from the authorities how he was cured ("Die pragmatische Bedeutung," 243). The phrase "as a proof for them" (εἰς μαρτύριον αὐτοῖς) tells against this hypothesis.

132 Anselm C. Hagedorn and Jerome H. Neyrey have argued that Jesus' command to the leper not to spread the news is part of a persistent strategy of avoiding excessive attention that would result in Jesus being envied by the scribes and Pharisees ("'It Was Out of Envy That They Handed Jesus Over' [Mark 15:10]: The Anatomy of Envy and the Gospel of Mark," *JSNT* 69 [1998] 15–56, esp. 52–53).

God, and that nearness is manifested in the authoritative teaching and healing of Jesus. This interpretation is supported by the similarity between the reaction of the people to the healed man's word and the spread of the news about Jesus after his activity in the synagogue of Capernaum (vv. 28, 32-33). Although Jesus tries to keep his identity a secret, his activity constitutes a series of secret epiphanies in which the divine glory cannot be hidden. Further, the healed man, like the four disciples called in vv. 16-20, joins Jesus in his mission. While the four are still in training to be fishers of men, the cleansed leper is already contributing to the missionary catch.

2

2:1-12 The Healing of the Paralytic

1/ And after several days he entered again into Capernaum, and it was heard that he was at home.[a] 2/ And many were gathered together, so that there was no longer any room, not even near the door; and he was speaking the word to them. 3/ And (some) came, bringing to him a paralytic, who was being carried by four (persons).[b] 4/ And when they were unable to bring[c] (him) to him on account of the crowd, they removed the roof where he was. And when they had dug through (the roof), they let down the pallet where the paralytic was lying. 5/ And when Jesus saw their faith, he said to the paralytic, "Child, your sins are forgiven."[d] 6/ Now some of the scribes were sitting there and considering in their hearts, 7/ "Why does this man speak in such a way? He blasphemes. Who is able to forgive sins except the one God?" 8/ And since Jesus knew immediately in his spirit that they were considering in this way within themselves, he said to them, "Why are you considering these things in your hearts? 9/ Which is easier, to say to the paralytic, 'Your sins are forgiven',[e] or to say, 'Get up and lift up your pallet and walk'?[f] 10/ Now in order that you may know that the Son of Man has authority to forgive sins on earth[g]—" he said to the paralytic, 11/ "I say to you, get up, lift up your pallet, and go home." 12/ And he got up and immediately lifted up his pallet and went out in the presence of all, so that all were amazed and glorified God, saying, "We have never seen anything like this."

a   A strong combination of MSS (p[88] ℵ B D et al.) read ἐν οἴκῳ ("at home" or "in a house"). The rest read εἰς οἶκον ("in a house" or "at home"). Although the latter phrase occurs three times elsewhere in Mark (3:20; 7:17; 9:28), it never occurs with ἐστίν ("he is"). The strong external attestation supports the conclusion that ἐν οἴκῳ ("at home" or "in a house") is the earlier reading. See also Metzger, *Textual Commentary*, 66.

b   The translation is based on the reading of p[88] ℵ B et al., καὶ ἔρχονται φέροντες πρὸς αὐτὸν παραλυτικὸν αἰρόμενον ὑπὸ τεσσάρων. The variants all seem to be attempts to improve the style of this reading.

c   Some MSS (A C D f[1.13] 𝔐 it?) read προσεγγίσαι ("to approach, come near") and others (W sa[ms] it?) read προσελθεῖν ("to go to, approach") instead of the reading adopted here, προσενέγκαι ("to bring to [someone]"). These readings seem to reflect attempts to improve on Mark's style or to clarify the original reading. See also Metzger, *Textual Commentary*, 66.

d   Some MSS, p[88] ℵ A C D et al., read ἀφέωνται ("have been forgiven") and others, (Δ) Θ, read ἀφίωνται ("may [your sins] be forgiven"). The former reading seems to be an attempt to improve the Greek, possibly under the influence of the parallel in Luke 5:20 (so Metzger, *Textual Commentary*, 66). The latter reading may be due to an attempt to soften Jesus' claim to be able to forgive sins.

e   See n. d above. p[88] is apparently illegible in this place. ℵ reads ἀφίενται ("[your sins] are forgiven") here, instead of ἀφέωνται ("have been forgiven"), which it has in v. 5.

f   p[88] ℵ L Δ 892 bo? read ὕπαγε ("go") and D (33) a ff[2] r[1] read ὕπαγε εἰς τὸν οἶκόν σου ("go home"). Both readings are probably secondary attempts to make this statement of Jesus conform to what he then says to the paralytic in v. 11.

g   p[88] ℵ C D L and many other MSS place ἐπὶ τῆς γῆς ("on earth") before ἀφιέναι ("to forgive"). A K Γ f[1.13] 28. 565 *pm* sy[h] place the same phrase before ἁμαρτίας ("sins"). Both readings, probably secondary, have the effect of emphasizing the spatial limitation of Jesus' power to forgive sins.

Narrative Unity and Literary History of 2:1—3:6

In the section designated "Jesus' First Mighty Deeds" in this commentary (1:16-45), as noted in the section above on its narrative unity, Jesus' teaching and mighty deeds evoke positive responses. The disciples he calls follow him (vv. 16-20); the people in the synagogue of Capernaum are amazed at the newness and authority of his teaching and at the fact that he controls the unclean spirits (v. 27). The whole city gathers at the door of Simon's house with their sick and possessed, confident that Jesus will heal them (vv. 32-33). His fame spreads to such a degree that he can no longer enter a city; he stays in unpopulated areas and people come to him from everywhere (vv. 28, 45). There are hints in that section, however, of conflict to come. The narrator contrasts Jesus' authoritative teaching with that of the scribes who were experts in the Law, implying that the latter lack authority. Jesus commands the healed leper to show himself to the priest to demonstrate the power of Jesus, but the leper apparently does not obey this command (vv. 43-45). In this section, 2:1–3:6, the latent conflict hinted at in the previous section becomes manifest. Some scribes think that Jesus blasphemes when he forgives the paralytic's sins (2:6); the scribes belonging to the party or voluntary association of the Pharisees object to his eating with sinners and tax collectors (2:16); the question is raised why the disciples of Jesus do not fast (2:18); the Pharisees object to the disciples of Jesus making their way by plucking heads of grain (2:23-24) and to Jesus' healing on the Sabbath (3:2, 6).

Furthermore, this section (2:1–3:6) is unified as a collection of stories with the same literary form or genre, controversy-apophthegm or conflict story.[1] The section is framed by the conclusion of the story about the healing of a leper (1:40-45), on the one hand, and the Markan summary in 3:7-12, on the other. According to 1:45, people were coming to Jesus from everywhere ($\pi\acute{\alpha}\nu\tau o\vartheta\epsilon\nu$). In 3:7-12, the localities from which people gathered to Jesus are listed: Galilee, Judea, Jerusalem, Idumea, Perea, and the regions around Tyre and Sidon. The earlier passage states that so many people came to Jesus that he could not go openly into a city. In 3:9-10, so many people

were pressing upon Jesus that he asked his disciples to have a boat ready for him lest the crowd crush him.[2]

As Joanna Dewey has shown, the section has a concentric structure.[3] The first (2:1-12) and last (3:1-6) units are the only two that involve healing. The first two units (2:1-12 and 2:13-17) share the theme of sin and sinners. The last two (2:23-28 and 3:1-6) share the theme of what is permitted on the Sabbath. The second, third, and fourth (2:13-17; 2:18-22; and 2:23-28) share the theme of eating (or not eating, that is, fasting). The first two and the last two all have a three-part structure, whereas the middle unit (2:18-22) has a two-part structure.[4]

The literary and topical unity of this section, which contrasts with the loosely organized character of much of the rest of the Gospel, has led many scholars to conclude that the evangelist drew upon a pre-Markan, probably written, collection of apophthegms or conflict stories. Martin Albertz was the first to make a detailed case for the use of an earlier written collection in this section.[5] He argued that the stories were originally independent accounts of conflicts between Jesus and the Jews over matters relating to the Law.[6] Although there is no progression in the seriousness of the issues or in the identification of the opponents, Albertz did find a crescendo in the expression of hostility to Jesus in the movement from silent to spoken questioning, which reaches a climax in the open hostility evident in the plot

---

1   "Controversy-apophthegm" or "controversy-dialogue" is Bultmann's term (*History*, 11–12). The term "conflict story" was proposed by Arland J. Hultgren, *Jesus and His Adversaries: The Form and Function of the Conflict Stories in the Synoptic Tradition* (Minneapolis: Augsburg, 1979). The "controversy-apophthegm" or "conflict story" may be understood as a subtype of the more inclusive genre "apophthegm," "pronouncement story," or "anecdote." Dibelius noted the similarities between the "paradigms" (Bultmann's apophthegms) and the *chreiae* of Greek literature, but emphasized the differences (*From Tradition to Gospel*, 152–64). More recent research has tended to emphasize the similarities; see Vernon K. Robbins, "Chreia and Pronouncement Story in Synoptic Studies," in Burton L. Mack and Vernon K. Robbins, *Patterns of Persuasion in the Gospels* (Foundations and Facets: Literary Facets; Sonoma, CA: Polebridge, 1989) 1–29.

2   Compare the discussion in Dewey, *Markan Public Debate*, 42, 105; for a discussion of the literary technique of "framing," see ibid., 23.

3   Ernest Best (*Mark: The Gospel as Story* [SNTW; Edinburgh: T & T Clark, 1983] 104–6) concluded that Dewey had made a good case for this thesis, but he questioned some details.

4   Dewey, *Markan Public Debate*, 109–16.

5   Martin Albertz, *Die synoptischen Streitgespräche: Ein Beitrag zur Formengeschichte des Urchristentums* (Berlin: Trowitzsch & Sohn, 1921) 5–16; see the summary and criticism of Albertz's arguments by Heinz-Wolfgang Kuhn, *Ältere Sammlungen im Markusevangelium* (StUNT 8; Göttingen: Vandenhoeck & Ruprecht, 1971) 18–24; Dewey, *Markan Public Debate*, 43–45; and Wolfgang Weiß, "*Eine Neue Lehre in Vollmacht*": Die Streit- und Schulgespräche des Markus-Evangeliums (BZNW 52; Berlin: de Gruyter, 1989) 20–23.

6   Albertz posited actual oral interchanges in Aramaic between Jesus and his opponents at the beginning of the history of these traditions; a second stage involved the shaping and repetition of accounts of these incidents in the oral tradition of the followers of Jesus after his death; finally these accounts were

182

to destroy him (3:6). Further arguments are based on how this section relates to the Gospel as a whole: the title "Son of Man" (2:10, 28) is not used in an eschatological sense, as it is elsewhere in Mark; the allusion to Jesus' death is premature, since he does not reveal its necessity until 8:31; and the mention of the plot against Jesus in 3:6 comes too early in the narrative. The purpose of the collection was to explain Jesus' death in terms of the historical conflict between him and his opponents.[7]

Criticisms of these arguments include the observation that, since the Gospel includes suffering Son of Man sayings as well as eschatological ones, sayings about the present authority of the Son of Man could have been included as well. There are other foreshadowings of the death of Jesus early in the Gospel, for example, the remark that Judas Iscariot was the one who handed Jesus over (3:19). Finally, the argument that the plot against Jesus comes too early in the Gospel is not compelling. The evangelist may have introduced this theme early but left its development until later. In fact, Albertz's argument that 3:6 was the conclusion and climax of a pre-Markan collection has been challenged by scholars who have argued that this verse is redactional and by the observation that it points ahead to the further progress and outcome of the plot against Jesus.[8]

Heinz-Wolfgang Kuhn avoids the latter problem by arguing that the pre-Markan collection is represented by Mark 2:1-28.[9] He argued that the four pericopes in the collection, individually and collectively, reflect conflict within the Christian movement over the continuing validity of certain Jewish practices. The collection also functions to stress the full, earthly authority of Jesus as the Son of Man. This emphasis does not occur elsewhere in Mark.

Although it is possible to explain the literary features of Mark 2:1—3:6 as the result of Markan compilation of various traditions, the fact that the rhetorical richness and elegance of this section exceeds that of most of the literary structures elsewhere in the Gospel makes it somewhat more likely that the evangelist made use of a source consisting roughly of 2:3-28.[10] The argument, however, that the primary purpose of the collection was to address an inner Christian debate on the continuing validity of certain Jewish practices is not compelling, since the legal premises and practices are not at all elaborated. It seems more likely that it was a collection of historical reminiscences about conflict between Jesus and other Jewish teachers. These reminiscences were shaped in a way that reflects a primary interest in the identity and authority of Jesus. They manifest a secondary interest in the implications of his authoritative activities and teachings for the way of life to be adopted by his followers.

Kuhn argued that the controversy over eating with tax collectors and sinners reflects debate within the early Christian movement regarding whether Jewish Christians could share in table-fellowship with Gentile Christians. Such a conflict is attested for Antioch (Gal 2:11-14).[11] He suggested that the reflection of this conflict, concern with Jewish practices, and the use of the epithet "Son of Man," because of its Semitic roots, would fit a Syrian provenance. These features, however, would fit a situation in Palestine equally well, especially cities like Caesarea Maritima, where both Jewish and Gentile converts may have joined the local community of the followers of Jesus.[12]

---

written down and collected (*Die synoptischen Streitgespräche*, 57–117). Although acknowledging that many members of the communities were bilingual, Albertz concluded that the collections were written, at least at first, in Aramaic (ibid., 110).

7 Ibid., 106–7.

8 Dewey, *Markan Public Debate*, 46–47.

9 Kuhn argues that 2:28 was the original conclusion to the collection and that the author of Mark added 3:1-6 (*Ältere Sammlungen*, 75, 86–88); see the discussions by Dewey (*Markan Public Debate*, 49–52) and Weiß ("*Eine Lehre*," 23–25). Other scholars have argued that the pre-Markan collection extended from 2:15 to 3:6, e.g., Ingrid Maisch and Rudolf Pesch (see Weiß, 24–25; Dewey, 48–49).

10 Note the observations of Dewey, *Markan Public Debate*, 192–93. Kuhn made the important literary observation that the conflict stories in Mark 2 all consist of dialogues of two verbal interchanges, whereas those of chap. 10 each contain more than two. He also noted that Jesus' response is consistently introduced with καί ("and") in chap. 2 and consistently with δέ ("then") in chap. 10 (*Ältere Sammlungen*, 82).

11 Kuhn, *Ältere Sammlungen*, 58–61, 91–95, 98, 232–34.

12 Kuhn's rejection of a Palestinian provenance is not well founded (ibid., 98, 232–34).

Comment

■ **1-12** Dibelius defined this unit as a story that represents in noteworthy purity the type that he called the paradigm.[13] He does not classify it as a tale (miracle story), because "its middle point is not the healing, but the forgiveness. The healing, when at last completed, shows to everyone the right of Jesus to forgive sins."[14] The paradigm, with its social connection to proclamation, focuses on this right, because the question of the worth of the miracle-worker is more important for preaching than the miracle itself. But the passage is a unity and one may not reconstruct two originally separate accounts, one of a miracle and the other a dispute.[15] Bultmann, however, argued that this unit was originally a miracle story and that vv. 5b-10 constitute a secondary interpolation. These verses, however, never formed an independent unit, but were composed for the context.[16]

Dewey argued that there are three subgroups of controversy-apophthegms or conflict stories: those occasioned by Jesus' healing, those occasioned by some other type of behavior of Jesus or his disciples, and those initiated by questions of opponents. Some stories belonging to the first subgroup, controversies in which Jesus' healing plays a role, follow the same pattern as the second subgroup, namely, "behavior–objection–vindication." Others, including this passage, do not. The healing occurs at the end, after Jesus' sayings, rather than at the beginning. This dislocation modifies the typical dialogue form, so that Jesus may take the initiative and the opponents may remain silent.[17] Her analysis shows that the passage is a literary unity with a circular rhythm or ring composition. The passage may have a literary history like that proposed by Bultmann, but such a conclusion may no longer be based on the argument of stylistic awkwardness or clumsiness.[18]

■ **1** It is not entirely clear whether the circumstantial phrase "after several days" ($\delta\iota'\,\dot{\eta}\mu\epsilon\rho\hat{\omega}\nu$) modifies "entered" ($\epsilon\dot{\iota}\sigma\epsilon\lambda\vartheta\dot{\omega}\nu$) or "it was heard" ($\dot{\eta}\kappa o\acute{\upsilon}\sigma\vartheta\eta$). The translation above is based on the former possibility.[19] This translation implies that the proclamation in the surrounding market-towns spoken of in 1:38 was completed in a few days. Such a picture fits with the account of Jesus' day in Capernaum in 1:21-34, according to which he accomplished a great deal in a short time. Furthermore, given Jesus' fame, it is unlikely that his return to Capernaum could remain undetected for several days.

As indicated in the note on the translation of v. 1 above, the phrase $\dot{\epsilon}\nu$ $o\check{\iota}\kappa\varphi$ could be translated either "at home" or "in a house." Although the latter translation is possible, the Greek phrase is idiomatic for "at home."[20] The precise meaning of the idiom here, however, is far from clear. The most that can be said reliably is that it refers to whatever place Jesus happened to be staying while in Capernaum.

■ **2-3** The assembling of a great crowd recalls the scene at the end of Jesus' first day in Capernaum (1:32-34). The depiction of Jesus speaking "the word" ($\tau\grave{o}\nu$ $\lambda\acute{o}\gamma o\nu$) to the people echoes the portrait of the healed leper spreading "the word" ($\tau\grave{o}\nu$ $\lambda\acute{o}\gamma o\nu$) (1:45). It is likely that Jesus' speaking the word in the house in 2:2 is equivalent to his teaching in the synagogue in 1:21. Both are related to the summary of Jesus' proclamation in 1:14-15. Similarly, the group of people bringing the paralytic to Jesus is a further instance of the summary in 1:32, according to which the people of Capernaum were bringing all their sick to Jesus for healing.

■ **4-5** As Jesus' teaching in the synagogue was interrupted by the appearance of a man with an unclean spirit (1:23), so here his speaking the word in the house is interrupted by the group with the paralytic digging through the roof and lowering the paralyzed man down on his pallet. But here the similarity ends. The unclean spirit, as we have seen, challenged and resisted Jesus, but was defeated. Here the efforts of the representatives of the paralyzed man express such trust or faith in the power of Jesus to heal that they take extraordinary means to overcome the obstacle posed by the crowd

13 Dibelius, *From Tradition to Gospel*, 43.
14 Ibid., 54.
15 Ibid., 66–67.
16 Bultmann, *History*, 14–15, 212–13.
17 Dewey, *Markan Public Debate*, 28–29.
18 Ibid., 66–76.
19 Cf. Taylor, 192.

20 James Hope Moulton, *A Grammar of New Testament Greek*, vol. 1, *Prolegomena* (3rd ed.; Edinburgh: T & T Clark, 1906) 81–82; Taylor, 193.

blocking their access to Jesus. The narrator remarks that Jesus saw their faith.[21]

■ **5-7** Jesus' response to the manifestation of their trust is to say to the paralyzed man, "Child, your sins are forgiven" (τέκνον, ἀφίενταί σου αἱ ἁμαρτίαι). The address "child" is one of the typical ways in which the wise man, sage, or teacher addresses his pupil.[22] Although the passive voice implies that it is God who forgives, the simple declaration "your sins are forgiven" (ἀφίενταί σου αἱ ἁμαρτίαι) is unusual in the context of Jewish tradition. There was a precedent for the communal declaration that God had forgiven all the sin of Israel in the past (Ps 85:1-3). Prophets and holy men of the past were credited with the ability to win forgiveness from God for the sins of others through their prayers.[23] But there is no precedent for a human being making a simple declaration that God is at this moment forgiving another human being's sin.[24] It is not surprising, therefore, that some scribes[25] who were present could be portrayed as thinking to themselves, "He blasphemes. Who is able to forgive sins except the one God?" (βλασφημεῖ· τίς δύναται ἀφιέναι ἁμαρτίας εἰ μὴ εἷς ὁ θεός;). A passage that could be cited in support of this scribal position is Ps 130:4, "But there is forgiveness with thee," that is, with God and no one else.[26]

An important underlying question is *how* God forgives sins. The means by which God forgives sins is specified in the Torah. For example, the priest is to make atonement for the sin of the whole congregation of Israel, and they shall be forgiven (Lev 4:20).[27] In the lifetime of Jesus, the setting in which this scene in Mark is placed, it was still possible for sins to be forgiven by means of sacrifice in the temple. When Mark was being written, the temple was probably still standing, although it was under threat. A further underlying issue is revealed in the wording of the scribes' objection: εἷς ὁ θεός ("the one God"). What Jesus has said calls the unity of God into question. The implication is that the simple declaration of Jesus that the man's sins are forgiven is blasphemy because he does not entreat God for forgiveness in behalf of the paralyzed man, but presumes to speak for God. He bypasses the procedures established by God for forgiving sins and challenges, in a way that appears to the scribes to be unwarranted, the authority of the officials who have the right to carry out those procedures. But the perspective of the narrator of the Gospel, and presumably of the actual author and most of the audience, is that Jesus has the authority to speak for God, since he is God's chief agent, the messiah.[28]

■ **8-9** The statement that "Jesus knew immediately in his spirit" (εὐθὺς ἐπιγνοὺς ὁ Ἰησοῦς τῷ πνεύματι αὐτοῦ) that they were considering in this way within themselves implies that Jesus has special insight not available to ordinary human beings. His question whether it is easier *to*

---

21 See Theissen's discussion of the typical motif "Difficulties in the Approach" (*Miracle Stories*, 52–53).

22 Prov 31:2; Sir 2:1; 3:1, 17; 4:1; 6:18, 23, 32; 10:28; 11:10; 14:11; 16:24; 18:15; 21:1; 23:7; 31:22; 37:27; 38:9, 16; 40:28; 41:14.

23 Moses in Exod 32:32 and Num 14:19; Job in Job 42:10 LXX.

24 The nearest thing to a precedent is Nathan's declaration to David that God has put away his sin (2 Sam 12:13; cited by Kuhn, *Ältere Sammlungen*, 56 n. 20, with other, less striking examples).

25 On the scribes, see the commentary on 1:22 above.

26 The Greek version highlights the process of forgiveness, namely, expiation: "For with you is expiation" (ὅτι παρὰ σοὶ ὁ ἱλασμός ἐστιν) (Ps 129:4 LXX). The idea that God alone could forgive sins does not seem to have been a contested issue in Second Temple Judaism; see Kuhn, *Ältere Sammlungen*, 55–56 n. 19. It could be that the response of the scribes is deliberately and polemically portrayed as an immediate rejection of Jesus as the agent of God. This

intention may be reflected in the emphasis on the unity of God in the thought attributed to the scribes.

27 The LXX uses the same verb, ἀφιέναι ("to forgive"), that appears in Mark 2:5 and 7. Similar statements are made in Lev 4:26, 31, 35; 5:6, 10, 13, 16, 18, 26; 19:22. See also Num 15:25 and 26.

28 The authority of the messiah to forgive sins as God's agent is an eschatological phenomenon, i.e., an event that belongs to the time of the fulfillment of the promises to Israel. A certain precedent to this idea may be found in Isa 33:17-24, a passage in which the ideal king will reign and the people who dwell in Zion will be forgiven their iniquity. See also the expectation expressed in the Melchizedek scroll from Qumran that Melchizedek, who will act as God's agent in the eschatological judgment, will relieve those belonging to his inheritance of the burden of all their iniquities; i.e., he will forgive or expiate their sins in the last days (11QMelch 2:4-8, 13).

say "Your sins are forgiven" or *to say* "Get up and lift up your pallet and walk" indicates that in both cases it is a matter of powerful, effective, authoritative speech. This question and the healing that follows it make explicit what is implied in the scene in the synagogue at Capernaum (1:21-28). Jesus' power to exorcise and to heal signifies that he speaks with the authority of God. Because of the Holy Spirit at work within him, he can proclaim "the good news of God" (1:14), teach with divine authorization (1:21-22, 27), and forgive sins as God's representative.[29]

■ **10** Following the rhetorical question of v. 9, Jesus does not simply say "Get up and lift up your pallet and walk," but introduces the act of healing by stating that he heals in order to demonstrate to the scribes "that the Son of Man has authority to forgive sins on earth." Heikki Räisä-nen has argued that this saying—indeed this passage as a whole—is in tension with the theme of the messianic secret. Jesus performs the healing openly, not in secret; does not command the spectators or the man healed to keep the healing secret; and even announces that the miracle is performed in order to legitimate the authority of the Son of Man to forgive sins. But Wrede had already argued, as Räisänen himself pointed out, that such tension is inevitable. If Jesus' identity were totally secret, there would be no point in telling the story of his life.[30] Things are actually more complicated, and there is great tension even within this account between the revelation and the concealment of Jesus' identity. The plot of the story pushes toward the revelation of Jesus and his identity, as Wrede pointed out. But the use of the epithet

"the Son of Man" (ὁ υἱὸς τοῦ ἀνθρώπου) conceals as much as it reveals about who Jesus is.[31] The critical reader of Mark today cannot assume that everyone in the audience of Mark understood this epithet as a title. Since ὁ υἱὸς τοῦ ἀνθρώπου is not an idiom in Greek, an ordinary Greek speaker of the time would have understood ὁ υἱὸς τοῦ ἀνθρώπου to mean "the son of the man" or "the man's son" and would have wondered about whom Jesus was speaking. A Jewish member of the audience who knew Hebrew or Aramaic, as well as Greek, would recognize a Semitic literary expression in Greek dress, but would be puzzled at the use of the definite form.[32] A Jew instructed in the scriptures might think that Jesus was alluding to the messiah, who, like the king, is the definitive "man."[33] Such a hearer might even recognize an allusion to Daniel 7:13.[34] Only those instructed by Christian leaders, however, would fully understand that Jesus is being presented here as the exalted Son of Man of Daniel 7 in a radically new reception of that text.[35]

The saying would also be opaque for the characters within the narrative. In fact, 2:1-12 initiates a division between two groups of characters within the narrative. As the call of the first four disciples creates a circle of insiders, the healing of the paralytic creates the category of outsiders within the narrative. First of all, Jesus offends some scribes by declaring that the sins of the paralyzed man are forgiven. This division is then heightened by the saying in v. 10, which also draws a veil over the person of Jesus. What would the scribes, as characters in the narrative, make of this phrase? Their reaction is not described. As noted above, the phrase alludes to

29   On the connection of sin and illness, see the commentary on 2:15 below.

30   Wrede, *Messianic Secret*, 124–29; see also the discussion in Räisänen, *Messianic Secret*, 43–44, 156–57.

31   Harry L. Chronis comes to a similar conclusion by a different route ("To Reveal and To Conceal: A Literary-Critical Perspective on 'the Son of Man' in Mark," *NTS* 51 [2005] 459–81, esp. 464–65, 472, 475). He puts too much weight, however, on the "title" "Son of God" in Mark and seems to interpret that epithet from the perspective of later Christian doctrine (ibid., 466–67 and n. 27; 468–69, 476).

32   On the Hebrew and Aramaic literary expression, see Paul Owen and David Shepherd, "Speaking up for Qumran, Dalman and the Son of Man: Was *Bar Enasha* a Common Term for 'Man' in the Time of

Jesus?" *JSNT* 81 (2001) 81–122; see also the excursus on the Son of Man tradition below.

33   Cf. Psalm 8, esp. v. 4, with Gen 1:26-27. On the royal connotations of the phrase "image of God," see Phyllis A. Bird, "'Male and Female He Created Them': Gen 1:27b in the Context of the Priestly Account of Creation," *HTR* 74 (1981) 129–59; see also the comment on v. 28 below.

34   Although the "one like a son of man" in Dan 7:13 in the original context of the book of Daniel as a whole should be interpreted as an angel, this figure was interpreted as the messiah in the first century CE; see Collins, *Daniel*, 72–86.

35   See Adela Yarbro Collins, "The Influence of Daniel on the New Testament," in Collins, *Daniel*, 90–105.

Daniel 7:13, but in a very indirect and cryptic way. Its use by Jesus in his dialogue with the scribes is, in effect, a riddle. Jesus issues them a challenge to discern his identity, a challenge that they apparently failed to meet.[36] The informed members of the audience, however, can discern the hidden meaning. Jesus can declare the man's sins forgiven at the moment that he makes the declaration (v. 5) because he is the chief and fully authorized agent of God on earth (v. 10).[37]

Excursus: The Son of Man Tradition

The question of the origin of the designation of Jesus as "Son of Man" has significant bearing on the reconstruction of the historical Jesus and the emergence of early Christology, that is, the interpretation by his followers after his death of the person and work of Jesus.[38] Bultmann concluded that a few Son of Man sayings were spoken by the historical Jesus, that is, those that distinguished Jesus from a Son of Man figure who was to play a role in the eschatological judgment.[39] This conclusion was disputed by Philipp

Vielhauer and Norman Perrin.[40] Both argued that none of the Son of Man sayings goes back to Jesus and that the tradition originated as one of several attempts to make sense of the death of Jesus and to express the conviction that he had been vindicated. According to Vielhauer, the designation of Jesus as Son of Man was the earliest Christology that arose in the experience of Easter.[41] Because of their affinites with Daniel 7 and the Similitudes of Enoch (*1 Enoch* 37-71), the Son of Man sayings that speak of a future Son of Man are generally recognized as apocalyptic sayings. The conclusion that Jesus did not speak such sayings is based on a theological tendency to value "eschatology" and to devalue "apocalypticism."[42]

As noted above in the comment on v. 10, the expression ὁ υἱὸς τοῦ ἀνθρώπου ("the Son of Man," lit., "the son of the man" or "the man's son") is not an idiom in Greek. For this reason, most scholars have concluded that it is a translation or a mistranslation of a Semitic idiom. Since both nouns in the Greek phrase have the article, the Semitic original probably consisted of two nouns in a construct chain, both nouns being made definite by the definite character

---

36 Julius Wellhausen argued that, in the context of the narrative, the saying in v. 10 does not remove the veil of secrecy over the identity of Jesus, since "son of man" simply means "man" in Aramaic. The scribes would have understood Jesus to mean that, although only God can forgive sins in heaven, a human being may forgive them on earth (Wellhausen, *Das Evangelium Marci übersetzt und erklärt* [2nd ed.; Berlin: George Reimer, 1909; 1st ed. 1903] 16).

37 Kuhn argued that the function of this controversy-story in its pre-Markan social setting was to justify the practice in the community of forgiving sins through Jesus or in his name (*Ältere Sammlungen*, 57, 90-91). Such a function is possible, but the emphasis of the passage is on the question of the identity of Jesus and his authority.

38 See Yarbro Collins, "Origin of the Designation," 391-407; reprinted with minor changes in Yarbro Collins, *Cosmology and Eschatology*, 139-58; see also eadem, "Influence of Daniel," 90-112, esp. 90-105.

39 Bultmann, *History*, 112, 122, 128, 151-52.

40 Philipp Vielhauer, "Gottesreich und Menschensohn in der Verkündigung Jesu," in Wilhelm Schneemelcher, ed., *Festschrift für Günther Dehn zum 75. Geburtstag* (Neukirchen: Kreis Moers, 1957) 51-79; reprinted in Vielhauer, *Aufsätze zum Neuen Testament* (ThBü 31; Munich: Kaiser, 1965) 55-91; idem, "Jesus und der Menschensohn: Zur Diskussion mit Heinz Eduard Tödt und Eduard Schweizer," *ZThK* 60 (1963) 133-77; reprinted in idem, *Aufsätze*, 92-

140 (subsequent references to this and all other reprinted essays in this footnote are to the reprint). Norman Perrin, "Mark XIV.62: The End Product of a Christian Pesher Tradition?" *NTS* 12 (1965-66) 150-55; reprinted in Perrin, *Pilgrimage*, 10-22; idem, "The Son of Man in Ancient Judaism and Primitive Christianity: A Suggestion," *BR* 11 (1966) 17-28 (*Pilgrimage*, 23-40); idem, "The Creative Use of the Son of Man Traditions by Mark," *USQR* 23 (1967-68) 357-65 (*Pilgrimage*, 84-93); idem, "The Son of Man in the Synoptic Tradition," *BR* 13 (1968) 3-25 (*Pilgrimage*, 57-83). See also idem, *Rediscovering the Teaching of Jesus* (New York: Harper & Row, 1967) 154-206; the review of scholarship by John R. Donahue, "Recent Studies on the Origin of 'Son of Man' in the Gospels," in Raymond E. Brown and Alexander A. Di Lella, eds., *A Wise and Discerning Heart: Studies Presented to Joseph A. Fitzmyer, S.J. in Celebration of His Sixty-Fifth Birthday* = *CBQ* 48 (1986) 484-98.

41 Vielhauer, "Gottesreich und Menschensohn," 90-91.

42 See Yarbro Collins, "Origin of the Designation," in *Cosmology and Eschatology*, 141-43.

of the second. The relevant expressions are בן האדם in Hebrew and בר נשא or בר אנשא in Aramaic. It is notable that the definite forms of these expressions in Hebrew and Aramaic are relatively rare, especially in earlier material.[43] For this reason the indefinite forms בן אדם in Hebrew and בר נש in Aramaic have also been studied. Aramaic philologists have agreed that the relevant Semitic terms may have a generic sense, "a human being," or an indefinite sense, "someone."[44] Geza Vermes's claim that these terms were also used as a circumlocution for "I" has been disputed.[45] In each of the examples that he produces as evidence, the speaker is included in a general statement about human beings.[46]

A number of scholars have argued that the phrase "the Son of Man" (ὁ υἱὸς τοῦ ἀνθρώπου) in Mark 2:10 derives from a translation of one of the Semitic phrases discussed above.[47] Vermes concluded that

"Son of Man" is not a title here, but a circumlocution for "I." Such circumlocutions, he argued, were idiomatic, when the context was one of awe, reserve, or humility.[48] Jesus did not simply say "I have authority to forgive sins" because it would have seemed immodest. But if Mark 2:10 derives from a translation of an older saying in Hebrew or Aramaic, in which the phrase "son of man" was used idiomatically, the meaning of the older saying would have been "human beings have authority on earth to forgive sins."[49] It is unlikely that the historical Jesus made such a proclamation. The Lord's Prayer, which probably goes back to Jesus, teaches his disciples to forgive others for the sins that they have committed against *them*, that is, against the one making the act of forgiveness.[50] It is not implied that any human being, including the one who follows Jesus, has the authority to forgive sins committed by others against God or against other

---

43 See the survey of the evidence by Joseph A. Fitzmyer, "The New Testament Title 'Son of Man' Philologically Considered," in idem, *A Wandering Aramean: Collected Aramaic Essays* (SBLMS 25; Chico, CA: Scholars Press, 1979) 143–60; reprinted in idem, *Semitic Background*, 143–60.

44 Geza Vermes, "The Use of בר נשא/בר נש in Jewish Aramaic," Appendix E in Matthew Black, *An Aramaic Approach to the Gospels and Acts* (3rd ed.; Oxford: Clarendon, 1967) 310–30, esp. 311–19; Fitzmyer, "New Testament Title," 147–48; Vermes, "The 'Son of Man' Debate," *JSNT* 1 (1978) 19–32, esp. 20.

45 Joachim Jeremias, "Die älteste Schicht der Menschensohn-Logien," *ZNW* 58 (1967) 165 and n. 9; Joseph A. Fitzmyer, Review of Matthew Black, *An Aramaic Approach*, 3rd ed., in *CBQ* 30 (1968) 426–27; Fitzmyer, "New Testament Title," 152–53; idem, "Another View of the Son of Man Debate," *JSNT* 4 (1979) 58–65, esp. 58–60. See also the criticisms of Frederick H. Borsch, *The Son of Man in Myth and History* (Philadelphia: Westminster, 1967) 23 n. 4; Carsten Colpe, "υἱὸς τοῦ ἀνθρώπου," *TDNT* 8 (1972) 403–4; John Bowker, "The Son of Man," *JTS* n.s. 28 (1977) 19–48; and Maurice Casey, "The Son of Man Problem," *ZNW* 67 (1976) 147–54; adapted in idem, *Son of Man: The Interpretation and Influence of Daniel 7* (London: SPCK, 1979) 224–40; idem, "Idiom and Translation: Some Aspects of the Son of Man Problem," *NTS* 41 (1995) 164–82.

46 The fullest collection of examples is given in Vermes, "Use of בר נשא/בר נש," 320–27; many of these are also given in idem, *Jesus the Jew: A Historian's Reading of the Gospels* (Philadelphia: Fortress, 1973) 163–68. Even in the two parallel examples that

Fitzmyer accepts as circumlocutions for "I," the speaker, Cain, is including himself in a general statement that applies to any human being; see Fitzmyer, "New Testament Title," 152–53; idem, "Another View," 58.

47 Barnabas Lindars, *Jesus Son of Man: A Fresh Examination of the Son of Man Sayings in the Gospels and in the Light of Recent Research* (Grand Rapids: Eerdmans, 1983) 44–47; A. J. B. Higgins, *The Son of Man in the Teaching of Jesus* (SNTSMS; Cambridge: Cambridge University Press, 1980) 2, 24–25.

48 Vermes, *Jesus the Jew*, 163–68, 180.

49 Wellhausen argued that this is in fact what the saying means, or at least what it originally meant (*Einleitung in die ersten drei Evangelien* [2nd ed.; Berlin: G. Reimer, 1911] 129; reprinted in idem, *Evangelienkommentare* [Berlin/New York: de Gruyter, 1987] 129). Colpe, Casey, and Lindars take the saying in Mark 2:10 as originally an example of the indefinite Semitic idiom ("a human being" or "a man") but deny that it refers to *any* human being, including the speaker. Colpe claims that the saying refers to Jesus' authority only ("υἱὸς τοῦ ἀνθρώπου," 430–31); Casey implies that it refers to healers (*Son of Man*, 228–29); Lindars explicitly argues that it applies only to "*some* people who have God's mandate to heal" (*Jesus Son of Man*, 46). Such interpretations are not supported by the Aramaic evidence collected by Vermes, "Use of בר נשא/בר נש," 320–27.

50 Matt 6:12; Luke 11:4; *Did.* 8:2; cf. Mark 11:25-26; Luke 17:3-4; see Hans Dieter Betz, *The Sermon on the Mount: A Commentary on the Sermon on the Mount, Including the Sermon on the Plain* (Hermeneia; Minneapolis: Fortress, 1995) 400–404.

human beings. Certain other passages imply that the followers of Jesus have authority to forgive sins in general, presumably the sins of the members of the community of Jesus' followers.[51] This idea, however, does not go back to the historical Jesus, but is part of the development of rules for disciplining the community.[52] If the historical Jesus had spoken a saying like that in Mark 2:10 and if he had meant that he *as a human being* had the authority to forgive sins, it is likely that the Aramaic phrase would have been translated with "human being" or "man" ($\check{\alpha}\nu\theta\rho\omega\pi o\varsigma$ or $\acute{o}$ $\check{\alpha}\nu\theta\rho\omega\pi o\varsigma$) rather than with "the Son of Man" ($\acute{o}$ $\upsilon\acute{i}o\varsigma$ $\tau o\hat{\upsilon}$ $\mathring{\alpha}\nu\theta\rho\acute{\omega}\pi o\upsilon$). In the oral stage of transmission, an idiomatic expression would probably have been translated idiomatically.[53] It seems likely then that this saying originated after the death of Jesus and that it presupposed the identification of Jesus with the one like a son of man in Daniel 7. In the pre-Markan collection of controversy-apophthegms preserved in Mark 2, the force of this saying, in the context of the healing of the paralytic and in the context of the col-

lection as a whole, was that Jesus has power to forgive sins because he is the chief agent of God, the messiah prefigured in Daniel 7. Although in the *narrative* context of the Gospel of Mark as a whole, the epithet "Son of Man" in 2:10 is ambiguous, especially for uninformed members of the audience, it acclaims Jesus as the figure of Daniel 7, as interpreted by the followers of Jesus, for informed members of the audience.

■ **11-12** The passage ends with the typical elements of an account of a healing. Verse 11, the command of Jesus that the paralyzed man get up, lift up his pallet, and go home, is the technique or means of healing. The description of the man's actions in v. 12a is the demonstration of the healing. The depiction of the spectators as amazed and as glorifying God and the quotation of their exclamation, "We have never seen anything like this," in v. 12b constitute the typical conclusion of such an account.[54]

2

2:13-17 Levi and Eating with Tax Collectors and Sinners	a
13/ And he went out again along the sea. And the whole crowd was coming to him, and he was teaching them. **14/** And as he was passing by, he saw Levi[a] the son of Alphaeus sitting at the revenue office, and he said to him, "Follow me." And he rose and followed him. **15/** And it happened that he was dining in his house, and many tax collectors and sinners were eating with Jesus and his disciples, for they were many and they were following him.[b] **16/** And when the scribes belonging to the Pharisees[c] saw that he was eating with the sinners and tax	b c

a Some MSS (D Θ f^{13} 565 *pc* it) read Ἰάκωβον ("James") apparently to harmonize this text with Mark 3:18.

b Some MSS imply that "and they were following him" ($\kappa\alpha\grave{\iota}$ $\mathring{\eta}\kappa o\lambda o\acute{\upsilon}\theta o\upsilon\nu$ $\alpha\mathring{\upsilon}\tau\hat{\varphi}$) goes with what precedes: B W 28 et al., and some with what follows: ($\mathfrak{p}^{88}$) ℵ L et al. The former group supports the translation given here. The latter group supports a translation such as the following: "for they were many. And the scribes belonging to the Pharisees were also following him." This reading may be due to a perceived redundancy in the remark that disciples were following Jesus or to the difficulty copyists may have found in the sudden and unmotivated appearance of the scribes of the Pharisees in v. 16.

c Some manuscripts read "the scribes and the Pharisees" ($o\grave{\iota}$ $\gamma\rho\alpha\mu\mu\alpha\tau\epsilon\hat{\iota}\varsigma$ $\kappa\alpha\grave{\iota}$ $o\grave{\iota}$ $\Phi\alpha\rho\iota\sigma\alpha\hat{\iota}o\iota$): A C (D) Θ et al. The more unusual "scribes belonging to the Pharisees" ($\gamma\rho\alpha\mu\mu\alpha\tau\epsilon\hat{\iota}\varsigma$ $\tau\hat{\omega}\nu$ $\Phi\alpha\rho\iota\sigma\alpha\acute{\iota}\omega\nu$) is to be

51 Matt 9:8; 18:15-18; John 20:23.

52 Bultmann, *History*, 141.

53 Casey's arguments in support of the likelihood of a literal translation apply to the written or literary stage of the transmission of the sayings of Jesus, not to the oral stage ("Idiom and Translation," 170–78).

54 On the impression that the miracle creates on the crowd as a typical motif, see Bultmann, *History*, 225–26; Theissen classifies the amazement of the spectators in v. 12b under the motif "Wonder" (*Miracle Stories*, 69–70) and their glorifying God under the

motif "Acclamation" (ibid., 71; cf. 91). He categorizes the account of the healing of the paralytic in Mark as a "rule miracle" that confirms the authority to forgive sins (ibid., 106, 111), but he does not clarify whose authority is at issue. He discusses the literary-critical problem whether vv. 5b-10 constitute a secondary addition to the story without attempting to solve the issue (ibid., 164–65).

189

collectors, they began to say to his disciples, "Why does he eat with the tax collectors and sinners?" 17/ And when he heard, Jesus said to them, "Those who are in good health have no need for a physician, but those who are sick; I did not come to call righteous people, but sinners."

preferred, since copyists were more likely to change the unusual expression into the usual than vice versa.

Comment

■ **13-14** These verses constitute a call story like those in 1:16-20. In v. 13 the notice that "he went out" provides a transition from the spatial setting within the house (2:1) to the outdoors. The new setting is further specified as "along the sea." The adverb "again" ($\pi\acute{\alpha}\lambda\iota\nu$) alludes to the scene in 1:16, in which Jesus "was passing by along the Sea of Galilee." The account in 2:13-14 thus recalls those in 1:16-20 in its similarity in both genre and setting.

The reference to the "crowd" recalls the crowd gathered around Jesus in the house (2:4). It is probably not implied, however, that the crowd in v. 13 is identical with that of v. 4 because the further statement that the crowd "was coming to him" recalls the summary of 1:45, according to which people "were coming to him from everywhere." The remark that Jesus "was teaching them" recalls the scene in 1:21-28, in which Jesus "was teaching" in the synagogue. It is also analogous to the report in 1:39 that Jesus "was proclaiming in their synagogues in all Galilee." In 2:13 Jesus is portrayed explicitly as teaching outdoors for the first time, but such may be implied by 1:45.

■ **14** As can be seen from the comments on vv. 13-14, v. 13 is an editorial composition linking the call story proper of v. 14 to the preceding narrative. The circumstantial participle and main verb of v. 14a, $\pi\alpha\rho\acute{\alpha}\gamma\omega\nu$ $\epsilon\hat{\iota}\delta\epsilon\nu$ ("as he was passing by, he saw") may also be editorial, since the same verbal forms appear in 1:16. The finite verb in the present tense of v. 14b, however, $\lambda\acute{\epsilon}\gamma\epsilon\iota$

("he said," lit., "he says"), differs from the aorist tense of $\epsilon\hat{\iota}\pi\epsilon\nu$ ("he said") in 1:17 and the $\acute{\epsilon}\kappa\acute{\alpha}\lambda\epsilon\sigma\epsilon\nu$ ("he called") of 1:20. The editorial elements show that, if the evangelist used a written collection of controversy-apophthegms, he edited them extensively.

The Gospels of Mark and Luke record the call by Jesus of a tax collector named Levi, who becomes a disciple of Jesus (Mark 2:14; Luke 5:27, 29).[55] Both Mark and the *Gospel of Peter* refer to the disciple Levi as a son of Alphaeus (Mark 2:14; *Gos. Pet.* 14:60). In the list of the Twelve in Mark 3:13-19, the name Levi does not appear, but there is a "James, the son of Alphaeus" ($\acute{I}\acute{\alpha}\kappa\omega\beta o\varsigma$ $\acute{o}$ $\tauo\hat{v}$ $\acute{A}\lambda\varphi\alpha\acute{\iota}ov$) (Mark 3:18).[56] In Matt 9:9, which is parallel to Mark 2:14, the man who is called by Jesus from the revenue office is named "Matthew" ($M\alpha\vartheta\vartheta\alpha\hat{\iota}o\varsigma$), not "Levi" ($\Lambda\epsilon\upsilon\acute{\iota}$), and he is not designated the son of Alphaeus.[57] In the list of the Twelve in Matt 10:1-4, there is a "James, the son of Alphaeus" ($\acute{I}\acute{\alpha}\kappa\omega\beta o\varsigma$ $\acute{o}$ $\tauo\hat{v}$ $\acute{A}\lambda$-$\varphi\alpha\acute{\iota}ov$), as in Mark. Both lists also have the name "Matthew" ($M\alpha\vartheta\vartheta\alpha\hat{\iota}o\varsigma$), but in the Gospel according to Matthew this name has the epithet "the tax collector" ($\acute{o}$ $\tau\epsilon\lambda\acute{\omega}\nu\eta\varsigma$), which is lacking in Mark (cf. Matt 10:3 and Mark 3:18). The author of Matthew may have changed the name "Levi" ($\Lambda\epsilon\upsilon\acute{\iota}$) in rewriting Mark 2:14 to "Matthew" ($M\alpha\vartheta\vartheta\alpha\hat{\iota}o\varsigma$) because he assumed that the tax collector must have been one of the Twelve. He then would have added the epithet "the tax collector" ($\acute{o}$ $\tau\epsilon\lambda\acute{\omega}$-$\nu\eta\varsigma$) to the name of Matthew in the list of the Twelve in order to make clear that the two Matthews were identical. There is insufficient evidence to decide whether this Gospel was associated with the disciple Matthew because

---

55   The call of Levi may be mentioned in *Gos. Pet.* 14:60.

56   See the note on the trans. of 2:14 above.

57   The *Gospel of the Ebionites*, as cited by Epiphanius, also gives the name Matthew to the disciple called from the revenue house; see *Gos. Eb.* frag. 4 in *NTApoc*, 1:170. Like the Gospel according to

Matthew, this text also lacks any mention of the name of this disciple's father.

of these changes, on the assumption that the author was Matthew himself, or whether these changes were made because the author and his audience considered themselves to stand in the tradition of Matthew.[58]

At the time of Jesus' public activity, Herod Antipas was tetrarch of Galilee and Perea.[59] During his reign, taxes were collected by officials employed and supervised by him.[60] The principal tax was probably the land tax.[61] There were also various indirect taxes, including taxes on the transport of goods, that is, tolls or custom duties.[62] The term $\tau\epsilon\lambda\acute{\omega}\nu\eta\varsigma$ ("tax collector") could be applied to various officials of varying rank and status. The brief portrait of Levi in v. 14 suggests that he is one of those of the lowest rank, an employee who collected custom duties at a public building called a $\tau\epsilon\lambda\acute{\omega}\nu\iota\nu$ ("tax office" or "revenue office").[63]

As in the call stories in 1:16-20, Jesus makes no attempt to persuade Levi to follow him, and the motivation of Levi in doing so is left unexplored. On one level, 2:14 reinforces the impression made by the earlier stories that the "presence" or person of Jesus alone had great power to attract disciples. On another level, this brief call story introduces the following scene.

■ **15-17** Bultmann defined this passage as a controversy-dialogue occasioned by the conduct of Jesus. He concluded that the point of the story lies in the saying of Jesus in v. 17. Since it has no very close connection with the situation described, he concluded further that v. 15 constitutes a story designed for the saying.[64]

Verse 15 portrays Jesus dining in the home of Levi with many tax collectors and sinners who were following Jesus.[65] The call of Levi has prepared for the presence of tax collectors with Jesus. The presence of sinners recalls the summary of his proclamation in 1:14-15 that called for repentance and trust in the good news. The appearance of sinners in 2:15 suggests that many sinners responded to this call for repentance. The kinds and seriousness of their sins, whether they actually repented, and, if so, what that repentance involved are questions that the narrative does not address.[66] Jesus is also por-

---

58   J. C. Fenton mentions the latter possibility but admits that it is pure conjecture (*The Gospel of Saint Matthew* [PGC; Baltimore: Penguin Books, 1963] 136).

59   David C. Braund, "Herod Antipas," *ABD* 3:160.

60   John R. Donahue, "Tax Collector," *ABD* 6:337-38.

61   See the section "*Local Color in 12:13-17*" in the commentary on that passage below.

62   On customs or duties imposed on goods in transit, see Schürer, *History*, 1:373-74.

63   Donahue, "Tax Collector," 337; Daniel C. Snell, "Tax Office," *ABD* 6:338. For a summary of the evidence from the Mishnah and Babylonian Talmud, see Ze'ev W. Falk, *Introduction to Jewish Law of the Second Commonwealth* (2 vols.; AGJU 11.1-2; Leiden: Brill, 1972, 1978) 1:77.

64   Bultmann, *History*, 18; Dibelius argued that the saying in v. 17 originally justified the call of the tax collector in v. 14, not the table-fellowship with sinners in v. 15 (*From Tradition to Gospel*, 64). Robert C. Tannehill classified the passage as an "objection story" ("Varieties of Synoptic Pronouncement Stories," *Semeia* 20 (1981) 107. Mack and Robbins defined it as a *chreia* (*Patterns of Persuasion*, 206-7).

65   See the note on the trans. of v. 15 above.

66   E. P. Sanders has argued that Jesus said or was understood to say that even heinous sinners who followed him were acceptable to God, and that he did not require of them the standard acts of atonement which are provided for in the Law ("Sin, Sinners [NT]," *ABD* 6.43; see also idem, *Jesus and Judaism*

[Philadelphia: Fortress, 1985] 210). Sanders claims that in no instance is Jesus said to recommend confession to a priest and sacrifice. This is accurate in the strict sense, but it should be noted that, according to Mark 1:44, Jesus commanded the leper to show himself to the priest and offer (a sacrifice) for his purification in accordance with the commands of Moses. The conclusion that Sanders drew from the lack of recommendations to go to a priest, confess, and sacrifice is that the offense Jesus caused to the leaders of the people was his self-assertion rather than his belief in grace ("Sin, Sinners," 44). Mark 1:44 shows that such self-assertion is compatible with compliance to the commands of Moses; the centrality of Jesus is expressed in the phrase "as a proof for them" (see the commentary on 1:44 above). Since Jesus, at least according to Mark, called for repentance, it is likely that he required, or at least expected, the reformation of the lives of sinners who accepted his proclamation. It may well be, however, as Mark 2:5 implies, that he, as God's agent, considered his announcement of forgiveness of sins to make atoning sacrifice unnecessary for those so forgiven. Abrahams concludes that the Pharisees and rabbis were inclined to leave the initiative for repentance to the sinner, whereas Jesus was inclined to take the initiative (*Studies in Pharisaism*, 1:58); he cites many examples, however, in which rabbis took the initiative in such matters (ibid., 59-61).

trayed as healing the sick (Mark 1:29-31, 32-34, 39-45; 2:1-12). Sickness was understood as a punishment for some sin or offense against a deity in many cultures of the ancient world.[67] The *Prayer of Nabonidus* from Qumran presupposes that illness is a punishment for sin:

The words of the p[ra]yer which Nabonidus, king of [Baby]lon, [the great] king, prayed [when he was smitten] with a bad disease by the decree of G[o]d in Teima. [I, Nabonidus, with a bad disease] was smitten for seven years and sin[ce] G[od] set [his face on me, he healed me] and as for my sin, he remitted it. A diviner (he was a Jew fr[om among the exiles) came to me and said:] "Pro[cla]im and write to give honour and exal[tatio]n to the name of G[od Most High", and I wrote as follows:] "I was smitten by a b[ad] disease in Teima [by the decree of the Most High God.] For seven years [I] was praying [to] the gods of silver and gold, [bronze, iron,] wood, stone, clay, since [I thoug]ht that th[ey were] gods. . . .[68]

The narrative of Mark implies that many in the crowd who followed Jesus were people whom he had healed.

His association with "sinners" in such a context may imply that many of those who were healed had been defined or had defined themselves as sinners in their social context on account of their illnesses.

Verse 16 does not paint a realistic picture. The audience of Mark is not told how the scribes belonging to the Pharisees[69] happened to see that Jesus was eating with tax collectors and sinners. But it is a reasonable assumption that word would get around in a small town or village about who was associating with whom. The narrative compresses the meal, the reaction of the scribes, and the response of Jesus into a concise story. The question of the scribes implies that Jesus broke a social convention by eating with tax collectors and sinners. It is relatively easy to explain the implied protest at Jesus' association with sinners. It was a commonplace of the wisdom tradition that the wise and the righteous should avoid association with the foolish and the wicked.[70] Eating a meal in common is a rather intimate instance of association. Restrictions on association in general and eating in particular may also relate to the issue of purity.[71] The members of the community of the Dead Sea Scrolls separated themselves from sinners, and

---

67 In a Jewish context, illness could be interpreted as the manifestation of the curse upon those who disobeyed the commandments of God; see Deut 28:21-22; Job 15:20-21; Psalm 32. For the link between illness and sin in other cultures, see the commentary on 1:5 above; see also Hans-Josef Klauck, "Heil ohne Heilung? Zu Metaphorik und Hermeneutik der Rede von Sünde und Vergebung im Neuen Testament," in Hubert Frankemölle, ed., *Sünde und Erlösung im Neuen Testament* (Freiburg/Basel/Vienna: Herder, 1996) 18–52; on the link between illness and sin in the NT, 22–23; in the Hebrew Bible and Second Temple Jewish texts, 23–24; and on non-Jewish, non-Christian ancient thought, 24; see also Abrahams, *Studies in Pharisaism*, 1:108–10.

68 4QPrNab (4Q242) frgs. 1–3; trans. by John Collins in *Qumran Cave 4*, vol. 17: *Parabiblical Texts, Part 3* (DJD 22; Oxford: Clarendon, 1996) 89; see also García Martínez and Tigchelaar, *Dead Sea Scrolls*, 1:486–87; Eshel, "Demonology in Palestine," chap. 3.

69 On the scribes, see the commentary on 1:22 above.

70 Prov 1:8-19; 4:7; cf. 1 Cor 15:33; *Barn.* 4:1-2. On 1 Cor 15:33, see Margaret M. Mitchell, *Paul and the Rhetoric of Reconciliation: An Exegetical Investigation of the Language and Composition of 1 Corinthians* (Louisville: Westminster John Knox, 1991) 176, who

cites Plutarch *Mor.* 491E as an analogy: so that they may not "enter into association with knaves or sluggards." Elsewhere Plutarch implies that even a good nature can be corrupted by bad company (*Mor.* 551D). See also Lucian *Pseudolog.* 30–31, cited below. For rabbinic passages in which men are warned of the personal dangers of associating with men or women of low morals, see Abrahams, *Studies in Pharisaism*, 1:57. Compare the argument of Christine Hayes that some of the literature of the Second Temple period opposes commensality and friendship with Gentiles, not because of the fear of ritual defilement by physical contact with Gentiles but because contact with idolators may have negative moral and religious effects (*Gentile Impurities and Jewish Identities: Intermarriage and Conversion from the Bible to the Talmud* [Oxford/New York: Oxford University Press, 2002] 47–50).

71 Sanders proposed that the significance of Jesus' eating with sinners did not have to do primarily with purity (*Jesus and Judaism*, 209). *M. Ṭohar.* 7.6, however, states, "If taxgatherers entered a house [all that is within it] becomes unclean" (trans. Herbert Danby, *The Mishnah* [London: Oxford University Press, 1933] 726); this text is cited by Mikeal C. Parsons, "'Short in Stature': Luke's Physical Description

only full members of the group, after a ritual ablution, could join in the pure meal:

And he shall undertake by the Covenant to separate from all the men of injustice who walk in the way of wickedness. For they are not reckoned in His Covenant. They have neither inquired nor sought after Him concerning His laws that they might know the hidden things in which they have sinfully erred; and matters revealed they have treated with insolence. Therefore Wrath shall rise up to condemn, and Vengeance shall be executed by the curses of the Covenant, and great chastisements of eternal destruction shall be visited on them, leaving no remnant. They shall not enter the water to partake of the pure Meal of the men of holiness, for they shall not be cleansed unless they turn from their wickedness: for all who transgress His word are unclean. (1QS 5:10-14)[72]

It is likely that the Pharisees similarly separated themselves from those who did not accept their distinctive regulations regarding ritual purity, tithes, and other food laws.[73] For the community of the Dead Sea Scrolls, those who did not accept what they considered to be the authoritative interpretations of the Torah were "sinners" in the deepest and broadest sense of the word.[74] The Pharisees may not have condemned as sinners those who followed interpretations of Torah different from theirs, but they may well have questioned Jesus, who presented himself as a teacher, about the regulations he followed and his criteria for table-fellowship. The question put to the disciples of Jesus in Mark 2:16 regarding "sinners" thus implies that he was not paying sufficient attention to the pursuit of holiness.[75] As the dominant religious group among Palestinian Jews at the time, (the scribes belonging to) the Pharisees were expected to take a position with regard to the teaching and activities of Jesus.[76]

In vv. 15-16, tax collectors are singled out from the general group of sinners for special mention. In some Greek texts, the Synoptic Gospels, and rabbinic literature, a deep disdain for tax collectors is evident.[77] In one of the epistles attributed to the Cynic philosopher Diogenes, a τελώνης ("tax collector") is called ἄνθρωπος ἀγοραῖος ("a huckster") (*Ep.* 36.2).[78] The following exchange is presented in one of the discourses of Dio Chrysostom:

Dio. Well then, do you think that it is permitted to *you* to do all things, which, while they are not expressly forbidden by the laws, yet are regarded as base and unseemly by humanity? I mean, for example, collecting taxes, or keeping a brothel, or doing other such things.

of Zacchaeus," *NTS* 47 (2001) 50–57; citation on 56. Hyam Maccoby, however, argued that this passage has limited applicability (*Ritual and Morality: The Ritual Purity System and Its Place in Judaism* [Cambridge/New York: Cambridge University Press, 1999] 150).

72   Trans. from Vermes, *Dead Sea Scrolls*, 104.

73   Anthony J. Saldarini, "Pharisees," *ABD* 5:291, 302–3.

74   See Sanders's discussion of sin as complete alienation from God ("Sin, Sinners," 43).

75   The fact that the disciples are questioned rather than Jesus himself has been taken by some scholars as an indication that the anecdote was composed in the context of controversies between followers of Jesus and (other) Jews or Jewish Christians (Bultmann, *History*, 49; Kuhn, *Ältere Sammlungen*, 61). Kuhn suggests that, from the point of view of the Christian community, the "tax collectors and sinners" stand for the Gentiles. This interpretation, however, is somewhat forced. It seems more likely that the controversy-story preserves a memory of the historical Jesus and that it was preserved because of

interest in his person and mission. His association with tax collectors and sinners could then secondarily have been understood as justifying the mission to the Gentiles.

76   Roland Deines, *Die Pharisäer: Ihr Verständnis im Spiegel der christlichen und jüdischen Forschung seit Wellhausen und Graetz* (WUNT 101; Tübingen: Mohr Siebeck, 1997) 554–55; see also his summary and critique of the conclusions of Heinrich Graetz regarding the "sinners" in this passage and their relation to the Pharisees (189–90). On the Pharisees as a historical group, see also Meier, *Marginal Jew*, 3:289–388.

77   Donahue, "Tax Collector," 337; Martin Goodman, *The Ruling Class of Judaea: The Origins of the Jewish Revolt against Rome A.D. 66–70* (Cambridge: Cambridge University Press, 1987) 131; Parsons, "'Short in Stature,'" 56.

78   Text from Malherbe, *The Cynic Epistles*, 148; trans. by author. This epistle has been dated to the first cent. BCE; Malherbe, *The Cynic Epistles*, 14–15.

O no, indeed. I should say that it is not permissible for the free to do such things either. And indeed for these acts the penalty fixed is to be hated or abominated by humanity

(Τί δέ; οἴει σοι ἐξεῖναι, ὅσα μὴ ἀπείρηται μὲν ὑπὸ τῶν νόμων ἐγγράφως, αἰσχρὰ δὲ ἄλλως δοκεῖ τοῖς ἀνθρώποις καὶ ἄτομα· λέγω δὲ οἷον τελωνεῖν ἢ πορνοβοσκεῖν ἢ ἄλλα ὅμοια πράττειν;

Οὐ μὰ Δία φαίην ἂν οὐδὲ τὰ τοιαῦτα ἐξεῖναι τοῖς ἐλευθέροις. καὶ γὰρ περὶ τούτων ἐπίκειται ζημία τὸ μισεῖσθαι ἢ δυσχεραίνεσθαι ὑπὸ τῶν ἀνθρώπων). (Or. 14.14)[79]

Lucian equates tax collecting (τελωνέω) with robbing (λωποδυτέω). He can excuse a person for plying this trade and doing other shameful things if he is hungry and thus bound by necessity. But Lucian has the following to say about those whose shameful behavior has no excuse:

It is not decent to ask people who so act to the same table, to share a cup with them, and to partake of the same food (οὐ γὰρ ὅσιον ἐπὶ τὴν αὐτὴν ἑστίαν τοὺς ταῦτα διατιθέντας καλεῖν καὶ φιλοτησίας προπίνειν καὶ ὄψων τῶν αὐτῶν ἄπτεσθαι). (Pseudolog. 30–31)[80]

This text shows that reluctance to share a meal with people considered to be morally deficient is not a uniquely Jewish characteristic and that it is not necessarily a matter of ritual purity in a specifically Jewish sense. Abrahams has argued that, in ancient Jewish circles, the motive for refusing to eat with sinners was primarily the desire to have fit comrades for learned and edifying discourse in connection with the meal.[81]

Tax collectors are linked with sinners in other passages of the New Testament besides this one.[82] Rabbinic texts link tax collectors with robbers, murderers, and sinners; tax collecting appears in rabbinic lists of despised trades that no observant Jew should practice.[83] The Mishnah states that men may vow to murderers, robbers, or tax collectors that what they have is heave-offering even though it is not heave-offering; or that they belong to the king's household even though they do not belong to the king's household (m. Ned. 3.4).[84] According to b. Ned. 28a, Samuel said, "The law of the country is law," implying that lawful taxes should be paid. R. Ḥinena said in the name of R. Kahana in the name of Samuel, "The Mishnah refers to a tax collector who is not limited to a legal due," implying that one need not pay more than the legal tax to those who would extort more.[85] Some scholars have found that the precise reasons for the massive disdain of tax collectors are difficult to determine.[86] Collecting tolls was not illegal, and there is no evidence that the lowest-ranking collectors were more dishonest than shopkeepers and others who might be tempted to overcharge people. Tax collectors may, however, have overcharged or extorted, or there may have been the common perception that they did. Another factor may have played a role in some circles. The tax collectors of Galilee in the time of Jesus were employees of Herod Antipas, not of Rome. But Herod Antipas was ruling at

79 Trans. slightly modified from James W. Cohoon, Dio Chrysostom (5 vols.; LCL; Cambridge, MA: Harvard University Press; London: Heinemann, 1939) 2:132–35. This speech may be dated c. 100 CE.

80 Text and trans. from Harmon, Lucian, 5:410–11. In a description of judgment in Hades, Lucian places together in one group adulterers, procurers, tax collectors (τελῶναι), flatterers, and informers (Nec. 11; text and trans. [modified] from Harmon, Lucian, 4:90–91).

81 Abrahams, Studies in Pharisaism, 1:55–56.

82 See the parallel passages Matt 9:10-11 and Luke 5:30; the link is also made in Matt 11:19||Luke 7:34 and Luke 15:1-2. In Matt 21:31-32 tax collectors are linked with prostitutes. In Matt 5:46-47 and 18:17 they are considered to be analogous to Gentiles.

83 Donahue, "Tax Collector," 337–38.

84 The Terumah or heave-offering was forbidden to Gentiles; the ruling presupposes that murderous or oppressive Gentiles would respect this religious rule.

85 The same point is made in b. B. Qam. 113a; according to b. Sanh. 25b, tax collectors and publicans may not serve as witnesses or judges because they overcharge. According to b. Bek. 31a, a tax collector could not be a ḥābēr. For discussion of these passages, see Abrahams, Studies in Pharisaism, 1:54–55.

86 Goodman, Ruling Class, 131–32; Sanders, "Sin, Sinners," 43.

the pleasure of Rome and tried to please the Roman authorities. Although he was at least somewhat respectful of Jewish tradition, he grew up in Rome and built cities reflecting Roman culture.[87] The hostility to tax collectors in the New Testament and rabbinic literature may have been due at least in part to dissatisfaction with (even indirect) Roman rule as foreign and thus as incompatible with the rule of God. This particular tension was an instance of the general tension between Roman and Hellenistic culture, on the one hand, and traditional Jewish values, on the other.

Jesus' metaphorical saying in v. 17 reflects the traditional link between sickness and sin discussed above, even though the saying speaks of metaphorical illness. "Those who are in good health" are likened to righteous people, and "those who are sick" to sinners. In the Greek philosophical tradition, the philosopher was often compared to the physician,[88] as in the following anecdotes:

I did not dine with everyone, but only with those in need of therapy. These are the ones who imitate the kings of the Persians (ἐδείπνουν δὲ οὐ παρὰ πᾶσι, παρὰ μόνοις δὲ τοῖς θεραπείας δεομένοις. ἦσαν δ᾽ οὗτοι οἱ τοὺς Περσῶν βασιλεῖς μιμούμενοι). (Diogenes *Ep.* 38.4)[89]

[Demonax] was never known to make an uproar or excite himself or get angry, even if he had to rebuke someone; though he assailed sins, he forgave sinners, thinking that one should pattern after doctors, who heal sicknesses but feel no anger at the sick (οὐδεπώποτε γοῦν ὤφθη κεκραγὼς ἢ ὑπερδιατεινόμενος ἢ

ἀγανακτῶν, οὐδ᾽ εἰ ἐπιτιμᾶν τῷ δέοι, ἀλλὰ τῶν μὲν ἁμαρτημάτων καθήπτετο, τοῖς δὲ ἁμαρτάνουσι συνεγίνωσκεν, καὶ τὸ παράδειγμα παρὰ τῶν ἰατρῶν ἠξίου λαμβάνειν τὰ μὲν νοσήματα ἰωμένων, ὀργῇ δὲ πρὸς τοὺς νοσοῦντας οὐ χρωμένων). (Lucian *Demonax* 7)[90]

In answer to one who remarked that he always saw philosophers at rich men's doors, [Aristippus] said "So, too, physicians are in attendance on those who are sick, but no one for that reason would prefer being sick to being a physician" (εἰπόντος τινὸς ὡς ἀεὶ τοὺς φιλοσόφους βλέποι παρὰ ταῖς τῶν πλουσίων θύραις, "καὶ γὰρ καὶ οἱ ἰατροί," φησί, "παρὰ ταῖς τῶν νοσούντων· ἀλλ᾽ οὐ παρὰ τοῦτό τις ἂν ἕλοιτο νοσεῖν ἢ ἰατρεύειν"). (Diogenes Laertius 2.70)[91]

One day when he was censured for keeping company with evil men, the reply [Antisthenes] made was, "Well, physicians are in attendance on their patients without getting the fever themselves (ὀνειδιζόμενός ποτ᾽ ἐπὶ τῷ πονηροῖς συγγενέσθαι, "καὶ οἱ ἰατροί," φησί, "μετὰ τῶν νοσούντων εἰσίν, ἀλλ᾽ οὐ πυρέττουσιν"). (Diogenes Laertius 6.6)[92]

In the anecdotes about Diogenes and Aristippus, it is the rich who need to be "cured" of their dependence on luxurious living. The stories about Demonax and Antisthenes are closer to Mark 2:17 in that it is sinners (οἱ ἁμαρτάνοντες) or evil people (πονηροί) who need to be "healed."[93] The motif of an immoral life as a metaphorical illness is common in Cynic-Stoic moral

87   Braund, "Herod Antipas," 160.

88   Martha C. Nussbaum, *The Therapy of Desire: Theory and Practice in Hellenistic Ethics* (Martin Classical Lectures n.s. 2; Princeton, NJ: Princeton University Press, 1994); Emma Wasserman, "The Death of the Soul in Romans 7: Sin, Death, and the Law in Light of Hellenistic Moral Psychology" (Ph.D. diss., Yale University, 2005) 22–30, 38–49.

89   Text and trans. from Malherbe, *Cynic Epistles*, 162–63. Like *Ep.* 36, cited above, this epistle dates to the first cent. BCE (ibid., 14–15). Epictetus compared the lecture room of the philosopher to a hospital (*Diss.* 3.23.23-38); see Abraham J. Malherbe, *Moral Exhortation: A Greco-Roman Sourcebook* (Library of Early Christianity; Philadelphia: Westminster, 1986) 122–24.

90   Text and trans. from Harmon, *Lucian*, 1:146–47.

91   Text and trans. from Hicks, *Diogenes Laertius*, 1:198–99.

92   Text and trans. from Hicks, *Diogenes Laertius*, 2:6–9. Hengel referred to this passage as related to Mark 2:17 (*Charismatic Leader*, 29 n. 43).

93   Less similar in content, but more similar in form, to Mark 2:17 is Plutarch *Apoph. Lac.* 230F: "When, in Tegea, after he had been exiled, [Pausanias, the son of Pleistoanax] commended the Spartans, someone said, 'Why did you not stay in Sparta instead of going into exile?' And he said, 'Because physicians, too, are wont to spend their time, not among the healthy, but where the sick are'" (Ἐπαινοῦντος δὲ αὐτοῦ ἐν Τεγέᾳ μετὰ τὴν φυγὴν τοὺς Λακεδαιμονίους, εἶπέ τις, "διὰ τί οὖν οὐκ ἔμενες ἐν Σπάρτῃ ἀλλ᾽ ἔφυγες;" "ὅτι οὐδ᾽ οἱ ἰατροί," ἔφη, "παρὰ τοῖς ὑγιαίνουσιν, ὅπου δὲ οἱ νοσοῦντες,

philosophy.[94] Dio Chrysostom argued that the best and most important teacher was the one who taught the virtues. As a physician knows how to heal the infirmities of the body (τὰ νοσήματα τοῦ σώματος), such a philosopher-teacher is competent to heal the maladies of the soul (τὰς τῆς ψυχῆς νόσους), namely, licentiousness, covetousness, and all such infirmities.[95]

A distinctive feature of the saying of Jesus is the motif that "I came to call sinners" (ἦλθον καλέσαι ἁμαρτωλούς). The remark "I came" recalls the statement in 1:14 that, after his endowment with the Spirit and his being tested in the wilderness, "Jesus came [or went] into Galilee proclaiming the good news etc." (ἦλθεν ὁ Ἰησοῦς εἰς τὴν Γαλιλαίαν κηρύσσων τὸ εὐαγγέλιον κτλ.). As noted earlier, part of his proclamation was a

call to repentance. Similarly, John proclaimed a baptism of repentance for the forgiveness of sins (1:4). The activity of both John and Jesus comes under the rubric of the citation of the divine promise in scripture, cited in 1:2, "See, I am sending my messenger before your face, who will prepare your way." Although the scripture has been rewritten to imply that John prepares the way for Jesus, since Jesus proclaims "the good news of God" (1:14), the implication is that Jesus has come as an agent of God to "call" sinners to repentance. The verb καλέω can also mean "invite," a connotation that is appropriate to this scene of table-fellowship. It also recalls Jesus' invitation or call of Levi to follow him in 2:14.[96]

2

2:18-22 The Question of Fasting

18/ And the disciples of John and the Pharisees were fasting. And people came and said to him, "Why do the disciples of John and the disciples of the Pharisees fast, but your disciples do not fast?" 19/ And Jesus said to them, "Can the groomsmen fast while the bridegroom is with them? As long as they have the bridegroom with them, they cannot fast.[a] 20/ But days will come when the bridegroom is taken away from them, and then they will fast on that day. 21/ No one sews a patch (made) of unshrunken cloth onto

a   This sentence is lacking in D W *f*[1] et al. It is probably original, however, since it fits with the pleonastic style of Mark. It may have been omitted under the influence of the parallels in Matt 9:15 and Luke 5:34.

b   Some mss, ℵ A C D et al. read "[the wine] is poured out and the wineskins are destroyed" (ἐκχεῖται καὶ οἱ ἀσκοὶ ἀπολοῦνται). This reading is probably due to the influence of the parallels in Matt 9:17 and Luke 5:37. See also Metzger, *Textual Commentary*, 67.

c   Some mss, D 2427 it bo[ms], lack this phrase, either because of a mistake or because it was felt to be redundant. Others, W (e f) sy[s-p], have the additional word βάλλουσιν ("they put"), perhaps following Matt 9:17, and yet others, p[88] ℵ[1] A C et al., βλητέον ("ought to be put"), perhaps following Luke 5:38. Those responsible for these additions either did not recog-

διατρίβειν εἰώθασιν"); text and trans. from Frank Cole Babbitt, *Plutarch's Moralia* (15 vols.; LCL; Cambridge, MA: Harvard University Press, 1931) 3:382–83. Cf. also an anecdote about Diogenes: "Accordingly, just as the good physician should go and offer his services where the sick are most numerous, so, said he, the man of wisdom should take up his abode where fools are thickest in order to convict them of their folly and reprove them" (δεῖν οὖν τὸν φρόνιμον ἄνδρα, ὥσπερ τὸν ἀγαθὸν ἰατρόν, ὅπου πλεῖστοι κάμνουσιν, ἐκεῖσε ἰέναι βοηθήσοντα, οὕτως ὅπου πλεῖστοί εἰσιν ἄφρονες, ἐκεῖ μάλιστα ἐπιδημεῖν ἐξελέγχοντα καὶ κολάζοντα τὴν ἄνοιαν αὐτῶν) (Dio Chrysostom *Or.* 8.5); text and trans. from Cohoon, *Dio Chrysostom,* 1:378–79. See also *Or.* 8:6-8. An ET of Dio Chrys. *Or.* 8.4-5, 9-16 is given in Malherbe, *Moral Exhortation*, 26–28.

94   Klauck, "Heil ohne Heilung?" 25.
95   Dio Chrysostom *Or.* 13.31-32; text and trans. from Cohoon, *Dio Chrysostom*, 2:116–17; see also *Or.* 17.1-6; 27.7-8; 32.17-18; 33.6-7, 44. In *Or.* 34, Dio Chrysostom compares discord to disease and the gradual establishment of concord to the healing process (34.17-18). Only the "physician" who has observed all the "symptoms" is in a position to "cure" the vices that create discord (34.19-26).

96   Cf. Klauck, "Heil ohne Heilung?," 22. As Morna Hooker has pointed out, the use of the verb καλέω ("invite") here may suggest that table-fellowship with Jesus is a foretaste of the messianic banquet (*The Signs of a Prophet: The Prophetic Actions of Jesus* [Harrisburg, PA: Trinity Press International, 1997] 40).

an old cloak; otherwise, the patch takes (something) away from it, the new from the old, and a worse tear occurs. 22/ And no one puts new wine into old wineskins; otherwise, the wine will burst the wineskins, and the wine is lost and the skins (as well).[b] But (one puts) new wine into new wineskins."[c]

nize that the earlier verb βάλλει ("puts") governs this phrase, or they wished to clarify or improve the style. Cf. Metzger, *Textual Commentary*, 67–68.

Comment

■ **18-22** Like 2:15-17, this passage was classified by Bultmann as a controversy-dialogue, but in this case the controversy is occasioned by the conduct of the disciples rather than that of Jesus.[97] It is noteworthy that the situation is quite indefinite; no particular setting or occasion is given, and the controversy is about the custom of fasting in general. It is also striking that those who question Jesus are unidentified. They seem not to be among the disciples of John or the Pharisees, but simply people who knew that those two groups observed the custom of fasting and wondered why the group associated with Jesus did not.[98] Bultmann concluded from these features, especially the fact that it is the conduct of the disciples that is in question, that the saying of v. 19a originated in the community of the followers of Jesus after his death and that its purpose is to defend the decision of the community not to fast by appeal to the authority of Jesus.[99] A problem for this hypothesis is the statement that they cannot fast "while the bridegroom is with them." Such a rationale fits the time of the historical Jesus better than the period of the postresurrection community.[100] The saying can be interpreted metaphorically, however, to refer to the presence of the risen Lord among his followers.[101] A metaphorical reading would support Bultmann's

conclusion. But another saying, which probably reflects a negative reaction to the historical Jesus, supports the hypothesis that v. 19a is a saying of Jesus:

> The Son of Man came eating and drinking, and they say, "See, a glutton and a drunkard, a friend of tax collectors and sinners" (ἦλθεν ὁ υἱὸς τοῦ ἀνθρώπου ἐσθίων καὶ πίνων, καὶ λέγουσιν· ἰδοὺ ἄνθρωπος φάγος καὶ οἰνοπότης, τελωνῶν φίλος καὶ ἁμαρτωλῶν). (Matt 11:19||Luke 7:34)[102]

Verses 18b-19a constitute a classic controversy-dialogue or pronouncement story in which the main character is challenged and responds with a striking saying that is both the climax and the end of the brief narrative. Vv. 19b-20 represent a reinterpretation or update of the original saying. Vv. 21 and 22 are metaphorical sayings that may have originated in another context and were then added to the dialogue because of their conceptual affinity with v. 19a. Alternatively, they may have been composed for the context in order to elaborate and reinforce the point of the saying of v. 19a.

■ **18** The introductory statement in v. 18a indicates that the disciples of John and the Pharisees had the custom of fasting, but no details are given. Fasting was one of the traditional ways of mourning the dead.[103] In other con-

---

97 Bultmann, *History*, 18–19.
98 The subject of ἔρχονται ("people came," lit., "they came") in v. 18 is not the disciples of John or the Pharisees, but is indefinite. This conclusion is supported by the formulation of the question, which refers to those groups without identifying the speakers with either of them.
99 Bultmann, *History*, 19, 48–49.
100 See the commentary on v. 19 below.
101 Such a notion is expressed, e.g., in Matt 18:20; 28:20. It seems to be implied in Luke 24:35 and possibly also in 1 Cor 10:21 and Acts 2:46-47.
102 Perrin argued that 2:19a is a saying of the historical Jesus and that Matt 11:16-19 provides information about him (*Rediscovering*, 79–80, 105–6).
103 1 Sam 31:13; 2 Sam 1:12; 3:35; Jdt 8:6; Roland de Vaux, *Ancient Israel*, vol. 1: *Social Institutions* (New York/Toronto: McGraw-Hill, 1961) 59.

texts, it was a way of attempting to gain divine aid or favor (2 Sam 12:15-23; Jdt 4:9).[104] It was also practiced in holy war (1 Sam 14:24-30; 1 Macc 3:47).[105] A custom evidently developed of fasting on the anniversary of the destruction of the First Temple (Zech 7:1-7).[106] The people were commanded "to afflict themselves" on the tenth day of the seventh month, the Day of Atonement, that is, to fast (Lev 16:29, 31).[107] During the Second Temple period, voluntary fasting was a mark of religious devotion (Tob 12:8; Philo *Vit. Cont.* 34).[108] The *Psalms of Solomon*, a work that may be representative of the Pharisaic point of view, portrays the righteous person as one who atones for unwitting sins by fasting and humbling one's soul (3:8).[109] Roman writers were familiar with the Jewish practice of fasting (Suetonius *Aug.* 76).[110] That John fasted is attested independently of Mark in the saying of Matt 11:18.[111]

The question of the anonymous interlocutors of Jesus in v. 18b is analogous to the question of the scribes in

v. 16. Eating with tax collectors and sinners was not universally accepted as a grievous sin. Similarly, the people were obliged to fast only on the Day of Atonement. The questioners wonder why it is that Jesus, who behaves like a prophet and a teacher, is not teaching his disciples to adopt a widely accepted devotional practice.

■ **19** The phrase οἱ υἱοὶ τοῦ νυμφῶνος (lit., "the sons of the wedding hall" or "sons of the bridal chamber") has been translated by some scholars as "the wedding guests" and by others as "the groomsmen."[112] The word νυμφῶν is used in Tobit to mean "bridal chamber," in the sense of the room where the bride and groom would spend their first night together (Tob 6:14, 17 LXX; 6:13, 16 RSV). It is used in Matt 22:10 to mean the room in which the wedding banquet was eaten. The Matthean usage supports the translation "the wedding guests," but the analogy with the phrase ὁ φίλος τοῦ νυμφίου ("the friend of the bridegroom" or "the best man") in John 3:29 supports the translation "the groomsmen."[113] In any

---

104 See also Ps 35:13; for further references see John Muddiman, "Fast, Fasting," *ABD* 2:774. See also Abrahams, *Studies in Pharisaism*, 1:122–23.

105 De Vaux, *Social Institutions*, 262, 265.

106 Roland de Vaux, *Ancient Israel*, vol. 2: *Religious Institutions* (New York/Toronto: McGraw-Hill, 1961) 387. Later on, the destruction of both temples was mourned on the same day, the ninth of Ab; see Sanders, *Jewish Law*, 83.

107 De Vaux, *Social Institutions*, 75; idem, *Religious Institutions*, 507. The penitential character of the fast is underlined by the terminology; see Muddiman, "Fast, Fasting," 773; Abrahams, *Studies in Pharisaism*, 1:123–24.

108 On fasting as preparation for the reception of revelation, see Abrahams, *Studies in Pharisaism*, 1:124.

109 *Ps. Sol.* 3:8. In rabbinic literature, the practice of fasting for rain is frequently mentioned; see Sanders, *Jewish Law*, 82.

110 Suetonius and other Latin classical writers state that Jews fasted on the Sabbath. According to *Jub.* 50:12-13, anyone who fasts on the Sabbath shall die. Judith avoided fasting on the day before the Sabbath and the Sabbath itself (Jdt 8:6). Lawrence H. Schiffman suggested that some Jews may have fasted on the Sabbath and that the halakic texts forbidding doing so may be protests against the practice. If יתערב ("enter partnership" or "intermingle") in line 4 should be emended to יתרעב ("starve himself" or "fast"), CD 11:4-5 is an example of such a protest (Schiffman, *Halakhah*, 110–11). In his edition, Elisha

Qimron does not emend the text in this place; idem, "The Text of CDC," in Magen Broshi, ed., *The Damascus Document Reconsidered* (Jerusalem: Israel Exploration Society/Shrine of the Book, Israel Museum, 1992) 9–49, esp. 31. The parallel passage in 4QD[f] (4Q271) 5 i 1 also reads יתערב ("enter partnership" or "intermingle") (Joseph M. Baumgarten et al., eds., *Qumran Cave 4: XIII The Damascus Document (4Q266-273)* [DJD 18; Oxford: Clarendon, 1996] 180).

111 The parallel in Luke 7:33 does not imply fasting in the strict sense; the formulation "neither eating bread nor drinking wine" may be Luke's attempt to clarify or to soften the formulation in Q preserved by Matthew, which does imply fasting: "neither eating nor drinking."

112 For literature and discussion, see Taylor, ad loc. For a discussion of the duties of the bridegroom's attendants according to rabbinic literature and in relation to John 3:29, see J. Jeremias, "νύμφη, νυμφίος," *TDNT* 4 (1967) 1101. The phrase οἱ υἱοὶ τοῦ νυμφῶνος (lit., "the sons of the wedding hall" or "sons of the bridal chamber") reflects Semitic interference in Markan Greek; see Elliott C. Maloney, *Semitic Interference in Marcan Syntax* (SBLDS 51; Chico, CA: Scholars Press, 1981) 169–71.

113 2 Cor 11:2 also supports the translation "the groomsmen"; see below.

case, the point of the comparison is that, just as one does not fast during a wedding, so Jesus and his disciples do not fast.

Jeremias suggested that the saying originally had nothing to do with the allegory in which the bridegroom stands for the messiah. Rather, the choice of metaphor was simply due to the common comparison of the age of salvation with a wedding.[114] But if the simple metaphor was intended, one would expect the saying to be formulated more generally. The focus on the bridegroom, rather than on the wedding feast, turns the attention of the audience to Jesus. Further, it implies that the presence of Jesus is equivalent to the presence of God. The metaphor of God's marriage to Israel was known in Jewish tradition from the time of Hosea. Mark 2:19 resonates even more clearly with Isa 62:5b: "And it will be so: in the way that a bridegroom will rejoice over his bride, so will the Lord rejoice over you" (καὶ ἔσται ὃν τρόπον εὐφρανθήσεται νυμφίος ἐπὶ νύμφῃ, οὕτως εὐφρανθήσεται κύριος ἐπὶ σοί). The historical Jesus may have made an indirect claim with this saying to be the chief agent of God and thus to mediate the presence of God in the last days. In any case, it is clear that the allegorical complex of images in Mark 2:19 was already known to Paul. He portrays himself as the best man, who plays a role in the wooing and betrothal of the bride: Christ as the bridegroom and the members of the Corinthian community as the bride (2 Cor 11:2). Here Paul, as an apostle, is analogous to the disciples of Jesus, who assist in proclaiming the good news.

■ **20** The sentence in v. 19b, "As long as they have the bridegroom with them, they cannot fast," belongs with the saying of v. 20, since it forms a transition from the saying of v. 19a to that of v. 20. Since vv. 21-22 continue the thought of v. 19a, and not that of vv. 19b-20, and

since vv. 21-22 fit so well in the overall conception of Jesus in the Gospel of Mark, the latter verses may constitute an addition by the author of Mark to the form of the controversy-dialogue as it appeared in his source. The saying of v. 20 is the first hint in the Gospel of Mark that a violent fate will befall Jesus. It implies that Jesus will die and that fasting will be an appropriate response at that time.[115] It also creates a contrast between the time of the earthly Jesus as a time of divine presence and joy and the time after the resurrection of Jesus in which he will be absent. God will still be with the followers of Jesus through the activity of the Spirit (13:10), but the presence of the risen Jesus with them is never promised in Mark.

■ **21-22** As noted above, when Jesus forgives the sins of the paralytic in 2:5-10, he speaks cryptically about "the Son of Man" having authority on earth to forgive sins. In this controversy about fasting, Jesus again speaks cryptically. He speaks metaphorically about groomsmen and a bridegroom, but leaves his audience guessing about the second level of meaning. Mention of specific roles suggests an allegorical interpretation, but the identities of the groomsmen, the groom, and the bride are unspecified, as is the reason for choosing the metaphor of a wedding. In vv. 21-22, Jesus continues to speak in figurative language. In v. 21 he speaks of an old cloak that needs mending. He draws upon common sense and experience to argue that it should not be patched with a piece of unshrunken cloth. If it were, at the next washing, the cloak would be further damaged. The clue to the metaphorical level of meaning is given in the words "the new from the old" (τὸ καινὸν τοῦ παλαιοῦ). In the present context of this saying, this expression recalls the exclamation of the people in the synagogue at Capernaum, "What is this? A new teaching with authority" in

---

114 Jeremias, "νύμφη, νυμφίος," 1101–3.

115 Kuhn concluded, along with other scholars to whom he refers, that "on that day" in v. 20 attests the practice of fasting on Fridays in commemoration of the death of Jesus and that the story reflects conflict between followers of Jesus and (other) Jews or Jewish Christians about which day(s) of the week should be fast-day(s) (*Ältere Sammlungen*, 69–71). It is also possible, however, that ἐν ἐκείνῃ τῇ ἡμέρᾳ should be translated "in that day" and that it is simply synonymous with ἡμέραι ("days"), the expression that occurs at the beginning of v. 20. Kuhn also suggests

that vv. 21-22 relate to vv. 18-20 as a whole, not just to v. 19a. If that were so, the implication would be that the newness of the events associated with Jesus, expressed in these vivid metaphors, could be expressed simply by fasting on Fridays instead of on Mondays and Thursdays. This interpretation seems unlikely. The metaphorical sayings of vv. 21-22 seem rather to treat vv. 19b-20 as an aside and to return to the theme of the newness and distinctiveness of the time of Jesus. The emphasis of the story as a whole thus lies on the joyful character of the activity of the earthly Jesus and the newness of his teaching.

1:27. The contrast between new and old also recalls the contrast drawn in 1:22 between the teaching of Jesus with authority and the teaching of the scribes.[116] In the context of Mark as a whole, this contrast must be seen in light of the summary of the proclamation of Jesus in 1:14-15. His teaching is "new" because he announces that the "time" is fulfilled and the kingdom of God has drawn near. If this saying (2:21) was spoken by the historical Jesus, he was challenging the current modes of interpreting scripture, the current applications of the Torah, and the current structure of leadership. In the qualitatively new situation that he announced, all these traditions had to be reevaluated and reformed. From the point of view of the followers of Jesus after Easter, the saying legitimated the new social formations and religious innovations of the communities founded in his name. In v. 21 the incompatibility of used, shrunken, old cloth and unused, unshrunken, new cloth is the focal point of the figurative language. In v. 22, the "new" is expressed with the image of "new wine." This wine is fresh and young, like the "good news" and the manifestation of the kingdom of God on earth alluded to in 1:14-15. Like the new wine, this new phenomenon will go through a process of change, a kind of "fermentation." This process is desirable but unsettling, even dangerous. If one tries to contain it within old structures, it will burst them, causing damage. Such a metaphorical warning could well have been issued by the historical Jesus. Later on, it expressed the perception that social and religious change was desirable, but also disruptive.

2

2:23-28 Plucking Grain on the Sabbath

23/ And it happened that on the Sabbath he was passing by through the grain-fields, and his disciples began to make a way by plucking the heads of grain.[a] 24/ And the Pharisees began to say to him, "Look, why are they doing on the Sabbath that which is not permitted?" 25/ And he said to them, "Have you never read what David did when he was in need and when he himself and those with him were hungry, 26/ how he went into the house of God, in the time of Abiathar the high priest,[b] and ate the bread of the Presence, which it is not permitted (for anyone) to eat, except the priests,[c] and gave (some) also to those who were with him?" 27/ And he said to them, "The Sabbath came into being on account of man, not man on account of the Sabbath; 28/ so the Son of Man is master also of the Sabbath."[d]

a   B f^1 et al. read ὁδοποιεῖν τίλλοντες ("to make a way by plucking"), substituting the complex infinitive ὁδοποιεῖν ("to make a way") for the less elegant simple infinitive with a noun object ὁδὸν ποιεῖν ("to make a way"). D W it read simply τίλλειν ("[began] to pluck"); this reading was probably introduced to eliminate the apparent contradiction between the motive of making a way in this verse and the motive of hunger implied by vv. 25-26; cf. Matt 12:1 and Luke 6:1.

b   Some MSS (D W *pc* it sy^s) omit the words "in the time of Abiathar the high priest" (ἐπὶ Ἀβιαθὰρ ἀρχιερέως) presumably because, according to 1 Sam 21:2-10 (21:1-9 RSV), Ahimelech was the priest in question. Matthew (12:4) and Luke (6:4) also lack reference to Abiathar. See also Metzger, *Textual Commentary*, 68.

c   The earliest recoverable reading (ℵ B et al.) is τοὺς ἱερεῖς ("the priests"), in the accusative case as the subject of the infinitive φαγεῖν ("to eat"), an unusual, but correct, construction. Most MSS have a reading with the dative, construing the noun in relation to the main verb ἔξεστιν ("it is permitted"). Cf. Taylor, ad loc.

d   Two MSS, W (sy^s), omit the second part of the saying in v. 27, and others, D (it), omit it entirely either by accident or to make Mark conform to Matthew (12:8) or Luke (6:5).

---

116   See the commentary on 1:22 and 27 above.

Comment

■ **23-28** Dibelius listed this passage as one of those that represent the "paradigm" in noteworthy purity.[117] He argued that it was an illustration used in early Christian preaching and that the final saying in v. 28 is a saying from a sermon.[118] Bultmann defined the passage as a controversy-dialogue occasioned by the behavior of the disciples. He concluded that it, like the dialogue about fasting in vv. 18-22, was the work of the church and that here the church justifies its conclusion that the Sabbath may be broken to satisfy hunger by ascribing this judgment to Jesus.[119] It is quite plausible, however, that the original dialogue consisted of vv. 23-26. Verses 27-28 have their own introduction, "And he said to them" (καὶ ἔλεγεν αὐτοῖς). The incident described in vv. 23-26 and the style and content of the argumentation are quite credible in the context of disputes among interpreters of the Law in the first century CE.[120] Verses 27-28, however, manifest reflection on the person of Jesus and his role that fits better in a post-Easter context.

■ **23-24** One of the reasons that Dibelius selected this passage as an example of the pure type of paradigm is that it is isolated from its context. There is no editorial connection or transition from the anecdote about fasting to the one about plucking grain. Two specific details of the setting are given in v. 23: it is the Sabbath and Jesus and his disciples are walking through the grain-fields. But the setting is quite general in other ways. The audience is not told which Sabbath it is, that is, whether it is the next Sabbath after the one mentioned in 1:21 or a later one. Nor are they told where Jesus and his disciples are going, for what purpose, or why they walk through the grain-fields rather than on a road.

The description of the scene does not imply that they are hungry or that they are plucking grain to eat. Rather, they pluck the heads of grain as they make their way through the field. The Pharisees are introduced abruptly, just as the scribes of the Pharisees are in v. 16. The verb "pass by" (παραπορεύεσθαι) in v. 23, however, may be taken as preparing for the appearance of the Pharisees.[121] The implication may be that Jesus and his disciples were passing a place where the Pharisees happened to be. The question of the Pharisees implies that the activity of the disciples described in v. 23b is not permitted on the Sabbath. The implication is that the Pharisees define the "plucking" of the disciples as "reaping."[122] The discrepancy between what the disciples are described as doing and the objection of the Pharisees puts the latter in a bad light. The disciples are not actu-

---

117 Dibelius, *From Tradition to Gospel*, 43.
118 Ibid., 64–65.
119 Bultmann, *History*, 16.
120 This conclusion does not imply that vv. 23-26 report accurately an actual incident in the life of the historical Jesus; rather they represent the sort of debate he may well have engaged in and the manner of his argumentation. Cf. Dibelius, *From Tradition to Gospel*, 64.
121 "Go past, pass by" is the second main usage of this verb according to LSJ; the first is "go beside" or "go alongside" (ibid.).
122 According to Exod 20:8-11 and Deut 5:12-16, working was forbidden on the Sabbath; according to *m. Šabb.* 7.2, reaping (קצר; text: הקוצר) is one of the thirty-nine main classes of work; Exod 34:21 implies that reaping is not permitted on the Sabbath. Note also the regulations for observing the Sabbath in the *Damascus Document* (CD 10:14—11:18). According to CD 10:20-21, "No man shall walk in the (or his) field to do business on the Sabbath" (trans. slightly modified from Vermes, *Dead Sea Scrolls*, 139). García Martínez and Tigchelaar give a more literal translation, "No-one is to walk in the field to do the work

which he wishes <on> the sabbath <day>" (*Dead Sea Scrolls*, 1:569). Schiffman pointed out that this law was derived from Isa 58:13 and concluded that it forbids either walking to the farthest extent of the Sabbath limit in order to leave on a journey immediately after nightfall or walking about in the field to determine what work needs to be done after the Sabbath (*Halakhah*, 90–91). Mark 2:23-28, however, says nothing about Jesus and his disciples doing business or work apart from "plucking." According to CD 10:21, "He shall not walk more than one thousand cubits beyond his town" (trans. from Vermes, *Dead Sea Scrolls*, 139). Schiffman concluded that this law is the result of a *midrash halakah*, based on a combination of Exod 16:29 and Num 35:2-5 (*Halakhah*, 91–98). Again, Mark 2:23-28 says nothing about how far outside the town Jesus and the disciples were or even what town they had been in last. Finally, CD 10:22-23 states, "No man shall eat on the Sabbath day except that which is already prepared. He shall eat nothing lying in the fields. He shall not drink except in the camp" (trans. from Vermes, *Dead Sea Scrolls*, 139). The second regulation seems similar to the issue at stake in Mark 2:23-28, but the grain or other ally reaping but simply making their way through a field of grain.[123] The Pharisees thus are portrayed as excessively strict in their observance and as attempting to impose their views on others.[124] Given that the Pharisees are criticized in the Dead Sea Scrolls as lax, the portrayal of them in Mark as overly strict is clearly relative to the perspective of the author of Mark.[125] This polemical view of the Pharisees, however, does not exclude the possibility that they and Jesus criticized one another. The historical Jesus may have taken positions more lenient than those of the Pharisees.

■ **25-26** Instead of arguing that the disciples were not actually reaping, Jesus in vv. 25-26 seems to accept the conclusion that they were reaping and argues that those who are hungry are allowed to reap on the Sabbath.[126] He does not make that point explicitly but argues by analogy. The argument is in part based on the precedent of an authoritative example from the past, the action of David.[127] The Markan Jesus may have chosen this example because he and others at the time inferred that the incident involving David occurred on the Sabbath.[128] As soon as this authoritative person is mentioned, stress is laid on the fact that "he was in need" and that "he himself and those with him were hungry." The Markan Jesus takes David's claim that his men were with him at face value.[129] But he also emphasizes the transgression of

---

produce in question in CD seems already to have been plucked or reaped; or perhaps the reference is to fruit that has fallen from a tree of itself. Schiffman translated, "No one shall eat (anything) on the Sabbath day except that which has been prepared (*mukhan*) (in advance) or from that which is decaying in the field" and concluded that the sect permitted the eating of fruit that had fallen from a tree if it had started to decay. The decay indicated that it had not fallen off the tree on the Sabbath, in which case it would be prohibited (*Halakhah*, 100–101).

123 Deut 23:25 seems to distinguish between reaping and plucking; it is permitted to pluck (קָטַף) with one's hand the standing grain in a neighbor's field, but not to put a sickle to it. One could infer that the use of a sickle defines "reaping," but later "reaping" covered a variety of harvesting activities; see *y. Šabb.* 7:2, 9a-g; *b. Šabb.* 73b sections B-C. Philo states that the Sabbath holiday "extends also to trees and plants; for it is not permitted to cut any shoot or branch, or even a leaf, or to pluck any fruit whatsoever" (*Vit. Mos.* 2.4 §22). But the verbs that Philo uses, τεμεῖν ("to cut") and δρέψασθαι ("to break off, pluck"), suggest intentional agricultural or horticultural work. Similarly, when plucking (אָרָה; text: הָאוֹרֶה) is prohibited on the Sabbath, the context implies that it is the pulling off and collecting of produce for consumption that is forbidden (*y. Šabb.* 7:2, 9a, c). This is not what the disciples of Jesus were doing (contra William L. Lane, *The Gospel according to Mark* [NICNT; Grand Rapids: Eerdmans, 1974] 115 n. 80).

124 Sanders has argued that the Pharisees and other pietist groups did not try to force others to follow their rules when they were stricter than those of the Bible (*Jewish Law*, 12). He does admit, however, that such a group often criticized others for observing rules that they believed to be wrong (ibid., 8–13).

125 The DSS refer to "seekers after smooth things" (דורשי החלקות), that is, those who interpret the Law in a way that makes it easier to observe it (cf. Isa 30:10); 4QpNah frgs. 3–4, col. 1, lines 2, 7; col. 2, lines 2, 4; col. 3, lines 3, 6–7; García Martínez and Tigchelaar, *Dead Sea Scrolls*, 1:336–41; Maurya P. Horgan, "Habakkuk Pesher," in Charlesworth, *Dead Sea Scrolls*, 6B:148–53. For further references and discussion, see Saldarini, "Pharisees," *ABD* 5:301. Most scholars conclude that the epithet "seekers after smooth things" in the DSS refers to the Pharisees or at least to a coalition that includes Pharisees.

126 Similarly, Sven-Olav Back, *Jesus of Nazareth and the Sabbath Commandment* (Åbo: Åbo Akademi University Press, 1995) 90.

127 Øivind Andersen and Vernon K. Robbins define a "paradigm" as "a summary of a significant situation in the past that is placed in a speech at a particular point to establish the *ethos* of the speaker or support the thesis or some part of the argument" ("Paradigms in Homer, Pindar, the Tragedians, and the New Testament," *Semeia* 64 [1993] 3–31; quotation from p. 20). They argue further that Jesus' appeal to David in Mark 2:23-28 is a paradigm in this sense. If it functions to confirm the *ethos* of the speaker, it implies that Jesus has authority to interpret commands regarding the Sabbath because he is the son of David. If it functions to confirm the speaker's understanding of the situation, it provides a rationale for the behavior of the disciples when they are with Jesus (ibid., 27–28).

128 A discussion of *m. Menaḥ.* 11.2 in *b. Menaḥ.* 95b involves the argument that the incident in 1 Sam 21:2-10 occurred on the Sabbath.

129 1 Sam 21:2-3 MT; 21:1-2 RSV; David is fleeing from Saul and comes to Ahimelech alone, yet makes up a story to reassure the priest. David Daube has argued

David. According to 1 Samuel 21, David asks the priest for some of the bread of the Presence, bread placed before the Lord in the sanctuary at Nob.[130] The priest agrees on the condition that David and his men are ritually pure. But according to the Markan Jesus, David enters the house of God and eats the bread. In the time of Jesus, such a deed would have been highly offensive. Only priests were allowed to enter the temple building proper, and the bread of the Presence, because of its placement on a golden table near the Holy of Holies, was holier than ordinary sacrifices.[131] The Markan Jesus even states explicitly that no one was allowed to eat this bread except the priests (v. 26).[132] But in spite of his offense, the Markan Jesus not only exonerates David because he was in need and hungry but generalizes from that example and implies that anyone who is hungry may perform work on the Sabbath to satisfy that hunger.[133] This position does not go so far as to reject the commandment not to work on the Sabbath as it is found in Exodus and Deuteronomy. But it does provide a criterion for interpreting that prohibition. The criterion is that any work that meets a basic and immediate human need is permitted on the Sabbath, because that need overrides the prohibition of work on the Sabbath.

■ **27** The dialogue, logically and literarily speaking, is complete with v. 26. The Pharisees have questioned Jesus and he has responded to their question with another that expresses his position. The introductory phrase in v. 27, "And he said to them," may be evidence that sayings material was added to an originally shorter and simpler dialogue. As suggested above, the counterquestion of Jesus implies a criterion for interpreting the prohibition of work on the Sabbath. The antithetical saying of v. 27 may have been added to make that criterion explicit. The criterion, however, is stated not in legal language but in an evocative and poetic way.[134] The first part of the antithesis, "The Sabbath came into being on account of man" ($\tau\grave{o}$ $\sigma\acute{\alpha}\beta\beta\alpha\tau o\nu$ $\delta\iota\grave{\alpha}$ $\tau\grave{o}\nu$ $\mathring{\alpha}\nu\vartheta\rho\omega\pi o\nu$ $\mathring{\epsilon}\gamma\acute{\epsilon}\nu\epsilon\tau o$), evokes the creation account of Gen 1:1—2:4a.[135] According to this account, God created human beings on the sixth day (1:26-31) and rested on the seventh day (2:1-3). The positive part of the antithetical saying in Mark 2:27 infers from this sequence that God created the Sabbath for human beings. The implication seems to be that, if the Sabbath was created for human beings, then it is meant to benefit them. The negative part of the saying then deduces the contrary: if the Sabbath is meant to benefit human beings, then they are not meant to observe the Sabbath in ways that harm them. It is highly likely that most Jews at the time of Jesus and afterward would agree with that principle.[136] In fact a similar saying

---

that the companions of David are included in Jesus' allusion to 1 Samuel 21 because they are necessary for the passage to be a model that exonerates the disciples ("Responsibilities of Master and Disciples in the Gospels," *NTS* 19 [1972] 1-15, esp. 5).

130 As noted above in the note on the trans. of v. 26, Ahimelech was the priest to whom David appealed, according to 1 Samuel 21, and he was not the high priest. Abiathar was a son of Ahimelech and is mentioned for the first time in 1 Sam 22:20. He did serve as high priest and was better known as an associate of David. The reference to Abiathar in Mark 2:26 is probably due to the tendency in the transmission of an anecdote to transfer a story about an unknown or less famous person to a more famous person. Compare the transferral of a story about Nabonidus to Nebuchadnezzar (Collins, *Daniel*, 33). For a discussion of attempts to reconcile the text of Mark with 1 Samuel 21, see Lane, ad loc. Daube argued that the reference to Abiathar was a mistake due to the reliance on memory ("Responsibilities," 6).

131 Paul V. M. Flesher, "Bread of the Presence," *ABD* 1:780-81.

132 This statement is based on Lev 25:5-9, a tradition that may not have been known to the author of 1 Samuel 21:2-10 MT; 21:1-9 RSV.

133 Rabbi Simeon maintained that the bread that David ate had already been removed from the presence of the Lord; but it would even have been permissible for the priest to give David the bread that was supposed to be placed before the Lord that very day because his life was in danger (*b. Menaḥ.* 95b-96a).

134 Robbins argued, developing a suggestion of Lane, that the saying of v. 27 reforms the "letter" of the Law in terms of the "intent" of the Law ("Plucking Grain on the Sabbath," in Mack and Robbins, *Patterns of Persuasion*, 128-29).

135 This is the first usage of the singular $\sigma\acute{\alpha}\beta\beta\alpha\tau o\nu$ ("Sabbath") in Mark. The translators of the LXX used both the singular and the plural to indicate a single Sabbath (Swete, 17). The singular is also used in 2:28; 6:2; 16:1.

136 Abrahams argued that, in a higher sense, man *was* made for the Sabbath; but in its practical application to ordinary human life, the Gospel rule is salutary (*Studies in Pharisaism*, 1:129).

occurs in rabbinic literature.[137] But Jesus and some of his fellow Jews may have disagreed about how to apply the principle.[138] The same applies even more to his followers at a later date.

■ **28** The saying of v. 28 relates to that of v. 27 in terms of a play on words. The ἄνθρωπος ("human being" or "man") of v. 27 is generic and also calls to mind the first human being, Adam. If ὁ υἱὸς τοῦ ἀνθρώπου ("the Son of Man" or "the son of man") in v. 28 is understood as a literal translation of the Semitic idiom discussed above in the excursus on the Son of Man, then v. 28 draws a conclusion from the saying of v. 27, namely, that if the Sabbath was made for (to benefit) human beings (and not to harm them), then the human being (in the generic sense) is master of the Sabbath.[139] The contrary is also implied. If human beings were not made for the Sabbath, then the Sabbath is not master of the human being (in the generic sense). In light of the example of David, the point would seem to be that human beings are free to interpret the prohibition of work on the Sabbath in ways

that meet basic human needs, that is, in ways that benefit and do not harm them.[140]

The saying of v. 28 is analogous to that of v. 10. If the saying is understood in terms of the Semitic idiom, the saying expresses something comprehensible to the dialogue partners of Jesus, but something that is puzzling and challenging to them. In the account of the healing of the paralytic, the question that the saying of v. 10 evoked was which human being(s) have the authority to mediate the forgiveness of God. Here the question that v. 28 evokes is which human being(s) have the authority to interpret the prohibition of work on the Sabbath. Both sayings, in the literary context of Mark as a whole, are like riddles that challenge the dialogue partners to draw the correct conclusion. A clue to the solution lies in the link between the first or ideal human being and the king. The first man was created in the image of God. The "image of God" is associated with having dominion in Genesis 1, and it was a typical epithet of the king in the ancient Near East.[141] The solution to the riddle is that "the son of man"

137 According to *b. Yoma* 85b, R. Jonathan b. Joseph said that the text "For it is holy unto you" (Exod 31:14) means היא מסורה בידכם ולא אתם מסורים בידה ("it [the Sabbath] is committed to your hands, not you to its hands"); text and trans. from Leo Jung and I. Epstein, eds., *Hebrew-English Edition of the Babylonian Talmud: Yoma* (London/Jerusalem/New York: Soncino Press, 1974) 85b. According to *Mek. de-Rabbi Ishmael*, *Šabb.*, R. Simon b. Menasiah said, interpreting the same passage from Exodus, "The Sabbath is given to you but you are not given to the Sabbath" (לכם שבת מסורה ואין אתם מסורין לשבת); text and trans. (modified) from Jacob Z. Lauterbach, *Mekilta de-Rabbi Ishmael* (Philadelphia: Jewish Publication Society of America, 1935; reprinted 1961) 198. Abrahams points out that both of these authorities were tannaim, R. Jonathan b. Joseph being from the early second cent. and R. Simon b. Menasiah from the end of that cent. CE. He argues that the saying is older than both of them and goes back to Mattathias. Whereas *Jub.* 50:12-13 forbids making war on the Sabbath, the father of Judas Maccabeus, under the pressure of necessity, established the principle that self-defense was lawful on the Sabbath (1 Macc 2:39-41) (*Studies in Pharasaism*, 1:129). Josephus attributes to Mattathias the saying that, if they did not fight on the Sabbath, "for the sake of the observance of the Law, they would be their own enemies" (φυλαττό-μενοι τὸ νόμιμον, αὐτοῖς ἔσονται πολέμιοι) (*Ant.* 12.6.2 §276); text and trans. (modified) from Ralph

Marcus, in Thackeray, *Josephus*, 7:142–43. See also Lutz Doering, *Schabbat: Sabbathalacha und -praxis im antiken Judentum und Urchristentum* (TSAJ 78; Tübingen: Mohr Siebeck, 1999) 416–19.

138 Abrahams argued that Jesus took the position that no act of mercy, whether the need pressed or not, was to be avoided because of the Sabbath (*Studies in Pharasaism*, 1:135). In an earlier passage, he argued even more strongly that Jesus asserted a general right to abrogate the Sabbath law for a person's ordinary convenience (ibid., 134). It is difficult to determine whether this judgment holds for the historical Jesus, but it is a plausible interpretation for the Jesus of Mark 2:23-28. See the discussion of Abrahams's views on the Pharisees by Deines, *Die Pharisäer*, 369–73, esp. 373 n. 208.

139 So, e.g., Wellhausen, 20.

140 Doering argued that the passage was intended to meet the objection that Christians broke the Sabbath arbitrarily (*Schabbat*, 432).

141 Bird, "'Male and Female He Created Them,'" 137–44. In Psalm 8, "man" and "the son of man" are part of the language of coronation and dominion and are used to describe the distinctive status and role of humanity in creation (ibid., 144). When "the son of man," however, is understood as the king or the messiah, then he becomes the human being par excellence who is God's particular agent on earth. Cf. the interpretation in Heb 2:5-9 of the "man" or "son of man" in Psalm 8 as references to Jesus; see

is "the Son of Man," that is, the messiah. Neither v. 10 nor v. 28 alludes explicitly to Dan 7:13. But the informed member of the audience knows that Jesus is the one like a son of man alluded to in Daniel 7, that he is the messianic Son of Man in an understanding of Dan 7:13 characteristic of the followers of Jesus.[142]

For the informed member of the audience, the allusion to Jesus' status as the messiah in vv. 27-28 puts the appeal to the example of David in a new light. The incident is no longer seen primarily as an argument about human hunger and need in general, but about David as

king and his authority. Just as David had authority to override conventional interpretations of the will of God because he was God's chosen one, so also Jesus has authority to interpret and proclaim the will of God in the last days.[143] If the ruling of *m. Sanh.* 2.4 was known already in the first century CE, it would explain the relationship between Jesus' reference to David and the activity of the disciples: "[The king] may break through [the private domain of any man] to make himself a road and none may protest against him: the kings's road has no prescribed measure."[144]

3

3:1-6 Healing of a Man with a Withered Hand

1/ **And he entered a synagogue again.**[a] **And a man who had a withered hand was there. 2/ And they were watching him carefully (to see) whether he would heal him on the Sabbath, in order that they might bring charges against him. 3/ And he said to the man who had the withered hand, "Rise, (go) to the center." 4/ And he said to them, "Is it permitted to do good**[b] **on the Sabbath or to do harm, to save a life or to kill?" They remained silent. 5/ And he looked around at them with anger, deeply grieved at the hardening of their hearts, and said to the man, "Hold out your hand." And he held it out and his hand was restored. 6/ And the Pharisees immediately went out and held a consultation with the Herodians against him, in order that they might destroy him.**

a Most MSS read $\epsilon i \varsigma \ \tau \grave{\eta} \nu \ \sigma \upsilon \nu \alpha \gamma \omega \gamma \acute{\eta} \nu$ ("into the synagogue"), but two important MSS (ℵ B) lack the article. The article is probably secondary, added either in an attempt to improve the style or to conform the text of Mark to Matt 12:9 or Luke 6:6. The article may have been added in most MSS of Mark and by Matthew and Luke because it was assumed that the synagogue in Capernaum was meant (cf. 1:21; 2:1). Cf. Taylor, ad loc.

b Although relatively few MSS (ℵ D W b e) use the simple infinitive with object, $\grave{\alpha} \gamma \alpha \vartheta \grave{\delta} \nu \ \pi o \iota \hat{\eta} \sigma \alpha \iota$ ("to do good") rather than a complex infinitive ($\grave{\alpha} \gamma \alpha \vartheta o \pi o \iota \hat{\eta} - \sigma \alpha \iota$ in most MSS), the former construction fits with Mark's style. Cf. the discussion of $\grave{\delta} \delta \grave{\delta} \nu \ \pi o \iota \epsilon \hat{\iota} \nu$ ("to make a way") in the note on the trans. of 2:23 above.

Comment

■ **1-6** Bultmann defined this passage as a controversy-dialogue occasioned by Jesus' healings.[145] Dibelius

defined it as a clear example of the paradigm, except for the remark of the evangelist in v. 6.[146] Theissen designated the passage as a "justificatory rule miracle," that is, a healing that justifies the conclusion that the obligation

also the discussion by Harold W. Attridge, *The Epistle to the Hebrews: A Commentary on the Epistle to the Hebrews* (Hermeneia; Philadelphia: Fortress, 1989) 69–77, esp. 73–75.

142 See the commentary on 2:10 and the excursus on the Son of Man above.

143 Andersen and Robbins see two ways in which the example of David works in this passage, one of

which is to confirm the *ethos* of Jesus as a descendant of David ("Paradigms in Homer," 27).

144 Trans. from Danby, *Mishnah*, 384. See also J. Duncan M. Derrett, *Studies in the New Testament*, vol. 1: *Glimpses of the Legal and Social Presuppositions of the Authors* (Leiden: Brill, 1977) 94.

145 Bultmann, *History*, 12.

146 Dibelius, *From Tradition to Gospel*, 43, 45. Bultmann

to help others prevails over the prohibition of work on the Sabbath.[147] Although v. 6 plays a role in the plot of Mark as a whole by preparing for the passion narrative, it also has a part to play in this controversy-miracle, namely, to express the rejection of the miracle-worker, a rejection that takes the place of the more usual motifs in which amazement is expressed or the miracle-worker is acclaimed.[148] Even if this account was not part of the pre-Markan collection of controversy-dialogues, the evangelist may have made use of a traditional story in constructing this conclusion to the controversies in Galilee.[149] Verse 1 consists of introductory motifs: the coming of the miracle-worker and the appearance of the distressed person. Verses 2-5a contain expositional motifs: criticism from opponents (v. 2); argument (v. 4); anger and grief of the miracle-worker because of the resistance of the opponents (v. 5a) and one central motif: setting the scene for the healing (v. 3). The rest of v. 5 is comprised of central motifs: the command of the miracle-worker to the distressed person; the fulfillment of the command; and the recognition of the miracle. Verse 6 contains the concluding motif: the rejection of the miracle-worker.[150]

■ **1** The first four words of this verse, "And he entered again," are similar to those of 2:1, "And having entered again." The setting of 3:1 in a synagogue is similar to the setting of 1:21-28. The introduction of the person to be

healed in 3:1, "And a man was there" (καὶ ἦν ἐκεῖ ἄνθρωπος), is similar to that of the possessed person in 1:23, "And then there was . . . a man" (καὶ εὐθὺς ἦν . . . ἄνθρωπος). These literary features are probably editorial.

The use of the word ἐξηραμμένη ("withered," lit., "dried up" or "desiccated") in this verse and of ξηρός ("dry" or "dried up") in v. 3 may show awareness of the doctrine of the humors, which was fundamental for ancient medicine. Here, however, the problem of dryness is corrected through miraculous healing and not through a medical regimen.[151]

■ **2** The verb παρατηρεῖν ("to watch carefully") may have a negative connotation, for example, "to lie in wait for" someone, as it has here.[152] The unidentified opponents of Jesus were watching to see whether he would heal the man with the withered hand on the Sabbath. The tractate Šabbat of the Mishnah contains the following remarks about healing:

> Greek hyssop [a remedy for worms in the stomach] may not be eaten on the Sabbath since it is not the food of them that are in health, but a man may eat pennyroyal [a remedy for worms in the liver] or drink knotgrass-water [an antidote to harmful liquids; both pennyroyal and knotgrass-water were also consumed by those in health]. He may eat any foodstuffs that

also noted that v. 6 is an editorial addition revealing a biographical interest (*History*, 12). Both concluded that the main point is the controversy over healing on the Sabbath (Dibelius, *From Tradition to Gospel*, 55).

147 Theissen, *Miracle Stories*, 106, 113. Doering defined it as a mixed form combining features of the miracle story and the controversy-dialogue, since Jesus' healing on the Sabbath evoked controversy (*Schabbat*, 443–46).

148 Cf. Theissen, *Miracle Stories*, 72.

149 See the section on the narrative unity and literary history of 2:1–3:6 above.

150 Cf. Theissen, *Miracle Stories*, 73–74. According to Theissen, the expositional motifs are typically stressed in rule miracles (ibid., 113).

151 Dieter Lührmann, "Neutestamentliche Wundergeschichten und antike Medizin," in Lukas Bormann, Kelly del Tredici, and Angela Standhartinger, eds., *Religious Propaganda and Missionary Competition in the New Testament World: Essays Honoring Dieter*

Georgi (NovTSup 74; Leiden: Brill) 195–204, esp. 201. On the humors, see Celsus *De medicina* proem. 15; Howard Clark Kee, *Medicine, Miracle and Magic in New Testament Times* (Cambridge: Cambridge University Press, 1986) 48, 57–59. Another form of the verb ξηραίνω ("to dry up") occurs in 3 Kgdms 13:4 in the context of a miracle of punishment; for discussion of the similarities and differences between Mark 3:1-5 and 3 Kgdms 13:1-10, see Kollmann, *Wundertäter*, 240–41 and the older literature cited on 241 n. 9.

152 Cf. Aristotle *Rhet.* 2.6.20 (1384b 7): "Now those who are inclined to gossip are those who have suffered wrong, because they always have their eyes upon us" (ἐξαγγελτικοὶ δὲ οἵ τε ἠδικημένοι διὰ τὸ παρατηρεῖν); text and trans. from John Henry Freese, *Aristotle*, vol. 22 (LCL; Cambridge, MA: Harvard University Press; London: Heinemann, 1982) 216–17.

serve for healing or drink any liquids except purgative water or a cup of root-water, since these serve to cure jaundice; but he may drink purgative water to quench his thirst, and he may anoint himself with root-oil if it is not used for healing.

If his teeth pain him he may not suck vinegar through them but he may take vinegar after his usual fashion, and if he is healed, he is healed. If his loins pain him, he may not rub thereon wine or vinegar, yet he may anoint them with oil but not with rose-oil. Kings' children may anoint their wounds with rose-oil since it is their custom so to do on ordinary days. R. Simeon says: All Israelites are kings' children! (*m. Šabb.* 14.3-4)[153]

These remarks make clear that it is the intention of healing and the performance of any activity for the purpose of healing that are forbidden on the Sabbath. The issue does not seem to be whether what one does is otherwise defined as work or not, since the same activity is permitted if it is not done with the intention of healing. In other words, anything done with the intention of healing is defined as work, even if the same activity done without the intention of healing would not be classified as work.[154]

According to the narrator of this account, if Jesus did heal the man on the Sabbath, his opponents intended to bring charges against him. Exod 31:14 states that every one who profanes the Sabbath shall be put to death and that whoever does any work on it shall be cut off from among his people. The anecdote about the man gather-ing sticks on the Sabbath day in Num 15:32-36 implies that the death penalty should be carried out by ston-ing.[155] According to *Jubilees*, the angel of the presence said to Moses:

> He created the heavens, the earth, and everything that was created in six days. The Lord gave a holy festal day to all his creation. For this reason he gave orders regarding it that anyone who would do any work on it was to die; also, the one who would defile it was to die. Now you command the Israelites to observe this day so that they may sanctify it, not do any work on it, and not defile it for it is holier than all (other) days. Anyone who profanes it is to die and anyone who does any work on it is to die eternally so that the Israelites may observe this day throughout their his-tory and not be uprooted from the earth. For it is a holy day; it is a blessed day. (*Jub.* 2:25-27)[156]

The importance of the Sabbath for *Jubilees* is made clear by the appearance of a similar passage at the climactic endpoint of the book. In this passage the death penalty is emphasized once again for anyone who desecrates the Sabbath or does work on it (*Jub.* 50:6-13).[157]

It is apparent, however, from the *Damascus Document* that at least some Jews of the late Second Temple period, perhaps the majority, did not believe that the biblical command regarding the death penalty for profaning or working on the Sabbath ought to be carried out. Accord-ing to this text:

---

153 Trans. from Danby, *Mishnah*, 113. Some of Danby's comments in the notes have been incorporated into the translation in brackets. According to *t. Šabb.* 12:8, it is not permissible to chew balsam resin or to rub dry salve onto one's teeth on the Sabbath if the activity is intended for a remedy, but it is permitted if it is done on account of bad breath. According to 12:13, a person may not bathe in a pond for steep-ing flax nor in the Sea of Sodom if the bath is intended as a remedy, but it is permitted for purifi-cation. See Jacob Neusner, *The Tosefta: Second Divi-sion, Moed (The Order of Appointed Times)* (New York: Ktav, 1981) 44–45, 46.

154 If this line of argumentation is correct, then Sanders is mistaken in arguing that Jesus heals the man with the withered hand without doing any work (*Jewish Law*, 21). On the role of intention in halakic debates about ritual impurity, see Eric Ottenheijm, "Impu-rity between Intention and Deed: Purity Disputes in First Century Judaism and in the New Testament," in Marcel J. H. M. Poorthuis and J. Schwartz, eds., *Purity and Holiness: The Heritage of Leviticus* (JCPS 2; Leiden/Boston/Cologne: Brill, 2000) 135–43.

155 If the profanation of the Sabbath or the perform-ance of work on that day was done unwittingly, pre-sumably Lev 4:27-35 would apply, and the guilty party would make a sin-offering instead of being put to death (Sanders, *Jewish Law*, 16).

156 Trans. from VanderKam, *Book of Jubilees*, 14.

157 The death penalty is mentioned in 50:8, 12-13.

Every man who preaches apostasy under the dominion of the spirits of Belial shall be judged according to the law relating to those possessed by a ghost or familiar spirit (Lev 20:27). But no man who strays so as to profane the Sabbath and the feasts shall be put to death; it shall fall to men to keep him in custody. And if he is healed of his error, they shall keep him in custody for seven years and he shall afterwards approach the Assembly. (CD 12:2-6)[158]

Since this passage is attested also in a copy of this work found at Qumran, it is likely that this regulation is sectarian.[159] Instead of the death penalty, an imprisonment of seven years is specified.[160]

According to the Mishnah:

"He that profanes the sabbath"[161] [is liable, after warning, to death by stoning] if he committed an act which renders him liable to Extirpation[162] if he acted wantonly, or to a Sin-offering[163] if he acted in error. (*m. Sanh.* 7.8)[164]

According to another tractate of the Mishnah (*m. Mak.* 3.15), all those liable to "cutting off" are no longer liable if they have been scourged, that is, if they have been given the forty lashes save one, presumably at the order of the proper officials. Since Paul states that he received this penalty by order of Jews (2 Cor 11:24), we may infer that it was given occasionally in the time of Jesus. In light of these various traditions, the portrayal of the opponents of Jesus in this account implies that they intended to accuse Jesus of deliberately profaning the Sabbath or working on the Sabbath. In principle the penalty for this offense was death. In practice, a scourging was the more likely outcome.[165]

The account in Mark does not specify to whom the charges against Jesus would have been brought. As noted above, at the time of Jesus' public activity, Herod Antipas was tetrarch of Galilee and Perea. Local government was probably in the hands of local priests, Levites, and elders, organized into courts or councils.[166] The account in Mark, therefore, seems to presuppose that the opponents of Jesus intended to accuse him of profaning the Sabbath before such a local court or council.

■ **3-4** The account in v. 2 establishes the presence of opponents and their intention to watch Jesus and accuse him. In v. 3, the narrative continues with the beginning of the fulfillment of the expectations of the opponents. Jesus takes the initiative and calls the disabled man into the center of the room.[167] In v. 4, he is the first to speak, as in the account of the healing of the paralytic in 2:1-12. Although it is not explicitly stated here, it seems to be implied, especially in light of 2:8, that Jesus was aware that his opponents were watching him and intending to accuse him. Jesus' saying in v. 4 is a powerful indictment of the motives of his opponents and also a highly polemical reflection on the tradition that the need to save a life overrides the prohibition of work on the Sabbath. In its first part, the saying implies that because Jesus wishes "to do good" on the Sabbath, that is, to heal a man, his opponents wish "to do harm," that is to spy on him and accuse him. In the second part, "doing good" is height-

---

158 Trans. from Vermes, *Dead Sea Scrolls*, 141.

159 4QDᶠ (4Q271) 5 i 19-21; see Baumgarten, *Qumran Cave 4*, 181–82.

160 Schiffman interpreted the passage to mean that the man who went astray and violated the Sabbath was to be deprived of his position in the congregation (קהל) for seven years, during which time he was to be observed. If he mended his ways, he was readmitted (*Halakhah*, 78). The verbal forms translated "keep in custody" by Vermes and "guarded" by Baumgarten all derive from the root שמר ("to watch," "to keep," or "to guard").

161 Cf. Num 15:32-36.

162 That is, to "cutting off"; according to Exod 31:14, "whoever does any work on [the Sabbath], that soul shall be cut off from among his people."

163 Cf. Lev 4:27-35.

164 Trans. from Danby, *Mishnah*, 393. Cf. *m. Šabb.* 7.1 and the discussion in Sanders, *Jewish Law*, 18–19.

165 Schiffman disagreed with Chaim Rabin's argument that the sect related to the DSS "abolished" the death penalty. Since it is a biblical penalty, the term "abolish" is inappropriate. Schiffman concluded that even if the death penalty for transgressing the Sabbath remained "on the books," it need not ever have been carried out (*Halakhah*, 78).

166 When Josephus organized Galilee at the beginning of the first war with Rome, he established seventy magistrates over the whole region and seven judges in each city (*Bell.* 2.20.5 §570–71). See Sanders, *Jewish Law*, 17–18.

167 Contrast an apocryphal version of the story in which the man takes the initiative and begs Jesus to heal him because he cannot carry on his trade, masonry,

ened and redefined as "saving a life." This redefinition implies that the man is as good as dead without the use of his hand or with whatever social stigmas accrued to his disability. Jesus' intended act of "saving a life" is then contrasted with "killing," which was the penalty for profaning the Sabbath, at least in principle. The contrast between the honorable motivation of Jesus and the shameful motivation of his opponents forces them to maintain silence.

As noted above, the redefinition of healing as "saving a life" evokes the tradition that the need to save a life overrides the prohibition of work on the Sabbath. In the Mishnah, the following ruling is recorded:

> Moreover R. Mattithiah b. Heresh said: If a man has a pain in his throat they may drop medicine into his mouth on the Sabbath, since there is doubt whether life is in danger, and whenever there is doubt whether life is in danger, this overrides the Sabbath. (*m. Yoma* 8.6)[168]

This ruling apparently expresses a liberal view that permits healing on the Sabbath, as long as there is any possibility that life may be in danger. There does not seem to be any possibility that the life of the man with the withered hand was in danger. In any case, Jesus' implied ruling seems to take "life" metaphorically, rather than to raise the question whether there is doubt concerning a life being in danger. As in the account involving the plucking of heads of grain on the Sabbath, Jesus here implies that human need and well-being override the prohibition of work on the Sabbath.[169]

■ **5** Jesus takes the silence of his opponents as a refusal to reconsider their opposition to "doing good" on the Sabbath, that is, to healing on the Sabbath, and as persistence in their plan to accuse him. His response is anger and grief at their hardness of heart. Although the Greek vocabulary differs, the theme of hardness of heart in early Christian tradition probably originated in reflection on the narrative theme of the hardening of Pharaoh's heart in the book of Exodus and the prophetic theme of the "fat" or unfeeling heart of the people of Israel. In Exod 4:21, God informs Moses, "I will harden [Pharaoh's] heart" (ἐγὼ δὲ σκληρυνῶ τὴν καρδίαν αὐτοῦ).[170] In Isa 6:10, God commands the prophet: "Make the heart of this people fat, and their ears heavy, and shut their eyes; lest they see with their eyes and hear with their ears, and understand with their hearts and turn and be healed.)[171] The Greek verb πωρόω ("to harden") is used in John 12:40 in a citation of this passage. Paul uses the same verb to speak about the "hardening" of some of the people of Israel with reference to a similar passage from Isaiah (Rom 11:7-8; Isa 29:10). He uses the same noun that appears in Mark 3:5, πώρωσις ("hardening"), later in the same passage, in which he describes the "hardening" of part of Israel as a "mystery" (μυστήριον). The "mysteries" to which Paul refers here and elsewhere are early Christian prophetic insights, sometimes apparently based on inspired exegesis of scripture. It would seem, then, that both Paul and the author of Mark were aware of an earlier exegetical tradition according to which some of the Jews were "hardened" and therefore refused to accept Jesus as the messiah.

---

with his disablity (Jerome *Com. on Mt.* on 12:13; for Latin text and English trans., see Albert F. J. Klijn and Gerrit J. Reinink, *Patristic Evidence for Jewish-Christian Sects* [NovTSup 36; Leiden: Brill, 1973] 216–17; see also *NTApoc*, 1:160).

168 For discussion, see Abrahams, *Studies in Pharasaism*, 1:132. See also the discussion of the principle that the Sabbath may be violated to save a life in relation to CD 11:16-17 (the case of a human being falling into a place of water on the Sabbath) in Schiffman, *Halakhah*, 125–28. See also the parallel in 4QD^f (4Q271) 5 i 10-11 (Baumgarten, *Qumran Cave 4*, 180–81).

169 Doering, *Schabbat*, 453.

170 The Hebrew root translated by σκληρύνω ("to

harden") in Exod 4:21 is חזק (in the piel "to harden"). In Exod 8:11 and 28 (8:15 and 32 in RSV), the Greek word βαρύνω (in this case "to make stubborn" or "to harden," lit., "to weigh down") is used to translate the Hebrew root כבד (in the piel "to make heavy, hard, or dull"). In 1QM 14:7, the phrase לבב קושי ("hard of heart") is used for the wicked.

171 The Hebrew root שמן (in the hiphil "to make fat, unfeeling") in Isa 6:10 is translated by παχύνω ("to thicken, to fatten"; to make dull of understanding") in the LXX.

Now the passages cited above, Exod 4:21 and Isa 6:10, imply that the "hardening" is intended and effected by God. If the hardness of heart of Jesus' opponents was in accordance with the divine will, it is strange that the evangelist would portray Jesus as angry and grieved about it, unless he wished to portray Jesus as a fully human being struggling with the difficult and mysterious character of God's will. Besides portraying the hardness of Pharaoh's heart as the result of divine activity, however, the book of Exodus also speaks about Pharaoh hardening his own heart.[172] So another way of interpreting the anger and grief of Jesus in Mark 3:5 is that it is directed against a choice made by the opponents, for which they can be held responsible.[173]

In spite of the resistance of the opponents, Jesus then commands the man to hold out his hand. When the man does so, expressing in this way his desire to be healed and his confidence in Jesus' ability to heal, he is healed.[174]

■ 6 As noted above, the action taken by the Pharisees in this verse serves as a conclusion to the account: their reaction to the miracle is the rejection of the miracle-worker. In this concluding motif, the unnamed opponents of Jesus, introduced in v. 2, are identified as Pharisees. As soon as Jesus had healed the man, they went out and held a consultation with the Herodians. As noted in the comment on v. 2, anyone seeking to bring charges against another for profaning the Sabbath would probably have gone to a local court or council. The term "Herodians" ($Ἡρῳδιανοί$) means an adherent of Herod the Great or of his dynasty.[175] In this context, the term probably refers to members of a local court or council, approved or appointed by Herod Antipas, or perhaps to officials close to Herod himself in his capital city of Tiberias.[176] The reference, however, is vague and may simply reflect knowledge that Galilee was under Herodian rule during the time of Jesus.

The text states that the goal of the Pharisees was "to destroy" ($ἀπόλλυμι$) Jesus, to have him put to death. In light of the discussion above, it is historically unlikely that the Pharisees sought the death penalty against Jesus for healing on the Sabbath. But this notice serves well the theological and literary purposes of the evangelist. In the immediate context it brings the thematic and polemical contrasts of "doing good" and "doing harm," of "saving a life" and "killing" to a climax. In the context of the Gospel as a whole, it builds suspense and prepares for the narration of the arrest, suffering, and death of Jesus.[177]

---

172 Exod 8:11 and 28 (8:15 and 32 in RSV); see the note on the citation of Exod 4:21 above.

173 A list of sins or vices in the *Community Rule* includes "heaviness of heart" or "hardness of heart" (כיבוד לב) (1QS 4:11); Siegfried Wibbing, *Die Tugend- und Lasterkataloge im Neuen Testament und ihrer Traditionsgeschichte unter besonderer Berücksichtigung der Qumran-Texte* (BZNW 25; Berlin: Töpelmann, 1959) 57–58. These sins are the result of the domination of human beings by the Spirit of Wickedness, but the human beings who commit them are nonetheless culpable.

174 According to 1QM 14:7, the triumph of the God of Israel will involve the triumph of the poor in spirit over the hard of heart; see the trans. by Vermes, *Dead Sea Scrolls*, 178.

175 See Samuel Sandmel, "Herodians," *IDB* 2:594–95; Meier, *Marginal Jew*, 3:560–65, esp. 564. The term is a Greek noun with an ending modeled on a Latin ending; other examples are "the adherents of Pompey" ($οἱ Πομπηιανοί$) and "the adherents of Caesar" ($Καισαριανοί$) (BAGD, *s.v.* $Ἡρῳδιανοί$). A truly Greek form of the word is $οἱ Ἡρωδεῖοι$ ("the adherents of Herod"), which appears in Josephus only once, *Bell.* 1.16.6 §319 (Meier, *Marginal Jew*, 3:561). Josephus also used the expression $οἱ τὰ Ἡρώδου φρονοῦντες$ ("the adherents/partisans of Herod") (*Ant.* 14.15.10 §450). According to Freyne, the Herodians are the new nobility centered on the court of Antipas, who replaced the Hasmonean nobles (*Galilee*, 199–200). For a discussion of older scholarship on the Herodians, see Deines, *Die Pharisäer*, 182 n. 138.

176 Herod Antipas founded the city of Tiberias between 18 and 20 CE, built a royal palace there and made it his capital. Josephus says that some of those who were forced to settle there were magistrates ($οἱ ἐν τέλει$) (*Ant.* 18.2.3 §37). He also says that Herod attracted some residents by giving them houses and land (ibid., §38). See also Yizhar Hirschfeld, "Tiberias," *NEAEHL* 4:1464–70. Meier interprets the Herodians here as "the servants, courtiers, or officials of Herod Antipas" (*Marginal Jew*, 3:562).

177 V. 6 is probably Markan composition (Doering, *Schabbat*, 441–43).

3:7   And Jesus withdrew with his disciples to the sea, and a great multitude from Galilee[a] and Judea 8/ and from Jerusalem and from Idumea[b] and Perea and (from) around Tyre and Sidon,[c] a great multitude[d] came to him, when they heard about the things that he was doing. 9/ And he told his disciples that a boat should stand ready for him on account of the crowd, to prevent them from pressing upon him; 10/ for he had healed many, with the result that they approached him eagerly, in order that those of them who had (bodily) torments might touch him. 11/ And the unclean spirits, whenever they saw him, would fall down before him and cry out, saying, "You are the Son of God!" 12/ And he rebuked them sternly so that they would not make him known.

a   Some MSS., B L et al., add "followed" in the singular (ἠκολούθησεν) after "Galilee"; others, A et al., add the same verb plus αὐτῷ ("him"). Other MSS., ℵ C et al., add "followed" in the plural (ἠκολούθησαν); yet others, K* 1241 et al., add the same verb plus αὐτῷ ("him"). A few (W b c) place the words ἠκολούθουν αὐτῷ ("were following [plural] him") later in the verse, after Σιδῶνα ("Sidon"). All these additions can be explained as independent attempts to clarify the long sentence in vv. 7-8. The earliest recoverable reading is thus preserved by D it et al. For similar views, see Taylor, ad loc.; and C. H. Turner, *The Gospel according to St. Mark: Introduction and Commentary* (London: SPCK; New York: Macmillan, 1931), ad loc. For a different view, see Metzger, *Textual Commentary*, 68.

b   Some MSS (ℵ* W Θ et al.) omit the words "and from Idumea" (καὶ ἀπὸ τῆς Ἰδουμαίας), either by mistake or under the influence of the parallels in Matt 4:25 and Luke 6:17.

c   Many MSS, A D Θ et al., add οἱ ("people [who lived]") before περὶ Τύρον καὶ Σιδῶνα ("around Tyre and Sidon"). This addition was apparently an attempt to clarify the phrase, when a copyist failed to notice that it, like the previous phrase, is the object of the preposition ἀπό ("from"), which is to be supplied.

d   The omission of the words πλῆθος πολύ ("a great multitude") in W a b c sy[s] is due to an attempt to improve the pleonastic style of the earlier reading (so also Metzger, *Textual Commentary*, 68). See n. a above.

Comment

■ **7-12** This passage is an editorial formulation that emphasizes the huge following acquired by Jesus, gives a general description of his healing activity, and develops the theme of his mysterious identity.[1] It is a transitional passage, having both concluding and introductory elements.[2]

■ **7-8** The statement in v. 7 that "Jesus withdrew with his disciples to the sea" forms a transition from the collection of controversies to a new situation. The verb "to withdraw," "to retire" (ἀναχωρέω) in this context has the connotation of withdrawing from a situation of conflict. It is now taken for granted that Jesus' disciples accompany him (cf. Mark 1:38; 2:15, 23). That Jesus returns to

---

1   Butlmann designates this passage as an editorial formulation that describes the healing activity of Jesus (*History*, 341).

2   See the discussion of the view that 3:7-12 introduces a new section in Leander E. Keck, "Mark 3:7-12 and Mark's Christology," *JBL* 84 (1965) 341–58, esp. 342–43. Keck himself argued that this passage concludes the section 1:16–3:12 (ibid., 343–45). He also argued that the evangelist did not compose 3:7-12 freely, but expanded a traditional summary (ibid.,

346–48). The attribution of προσέπιπτον ("they would fall down before him") in v. 11 to Mark and ἐπιπίπτειν ("they approached him eagerly") in v. 10 to the traditional summary and the like, however, is not persuasive. Such differences may simply be deliberate variations in style to avoid monotony.

the sea recalls his activity by the sea in earlier scenes (Mark 1:16; 2:13).

When Jesus returns to the sea, he is followed by a great multitude (πολὺ πλῆθος). This statement recalls 2:13, according to which "the whole crowd was coming to him" (πᾶς ὁ ὄχλος ἤρχετο πρὸς αὐτόν), but at the same time it goes beyond it by implying that an even greater number of people were coming to Jesus at this later point in the narrative. In 1:28 the narrator states that Jesus' fame spread to "the whole region around Galilee." In 3:7-8 it is made clear that Jesus' fame has spread to Idumea on the south, to the area beyond the Jordan on the east and to the territories of Tyre and Sidon on the north. It is of course also noteworthy that some of the people are said to come to Jesus from Judea and Jerusalem. These place-names call to mind 1:5, which states that "the whole district of Judea and all the inhabitants of Jerusalem were going out to [John]." A comparison of the two passages leads the audience to conclude that the activity of Jesus has already had a greater and more extensive effect than that of John. It is emphasized that the people came because of "the things that he was doing," presumably his mighty deeds of healing.

■ **9-10** The size of the crowd and the intensity of their interest in Jesus are portrayed vividly by means of Jesus' request that the disciples arrange to have a boat ready in case the pressure of the crowd becomes too great. In v. 10, "the things that he was doing" that attracted the multitude are specified as many healings. This picture is analogous to the one painted by the seer-philosopher Empedocles of his own public reception:

Friends, who live in the great city of the yellow Acragas, up on the heights of the citadel, caring for good deeds, I give you greetings. An immortal god, mortal no more, I go about honoured by all, as is fitting, crowned with ribbons and fresh garlands; and by all whom I come upon as I enter their prospering towns, by men and women, I am revered. They follow me in

their thousands, asking where lies the road to profit, some desiring prophecies, while others ask to hear the word of healing for every kind of illness, long transfixed by harsh pains (ὦ φίλοι, οἳ μέγα ἄστυ κάτα ξανθοῦ Ἀκράγαντος ναίετ' ἀν' ἄκρα πόλεος, ἀγαθῶν μελεδήμονες ἔργων, χαίρετ'· ἐγὼ δ' ὑμῖν θεὸς ἄμβροτος, οὐκέτι θνητὸς πωλεῦμαι μετὰ πᾶσι τετιμένος, ὥσπερ ἔοικα, ταινίαις τε περίστεπτος στέφεσίν τε θαλείοις· <πᾶσι δὲ> τοῖς ἂν ἵκωμαι ἐς ἄστεα τηλεθάοντα, ἀνδράσιν ἠδὲ γυναιξί, σεβίζομαι· οἱ δ' ἅμ' ἕπονται μυρίοι ἐξερέοντες, ὅπη πρὸς κέρδος ἀταρπός, οἱ μὲν μαντοσυνέων κεχρημένοι, οἱ δ' ἐπὶ νούσων παντοίων ἐπύθοντο κλύειν εὐηκέα βάξιν, δηρὸν χαλεπῆσι πεπαρμένοι <ἀμφ' ὀδύνῃσιν>).[3]

Although Mark does not portray Jesus explicitly as a god or as God, the text does present him as God's agent, endowed with the Spirit, in whose mighty deeds the power of God is present. Like Empedocles, the Markan Jesus combines the activities of the teacher, the prophet, and the healer. Porphyry drew a similar picture of Pythagoras:

His speech was so persuasive that, according to Nicomachus, in one address made on first landing in Italy, he made more than two thousands adherents. Out of desire to live with him, these built a large auditorium, to which both women and boys were admitted. [Foreign visitors were so many that] they built whole cities, settling that whole region of Italy now known as Magna Graecia (οὕτως δὲ πάντα εἰς ἑαυτὸν ἐπέστρεψεν ὥστε μιᾷ μόνον ἀκροάσει, ὡς φησὶ Νικόμαχος, ἣν ἐπιβὰς τῆς Ἰταλίας πεποίηται, πλέον ἢ δισχιλίους ἑλεῖν τοῖς λόγοις, ὡς μηκέτι οἴκαδ' ἀποστῆναι, ἀλλ' ὁμοῦ σὺν παισὶ καὶ γυναιξὶν ὁμακόιόν τι παμμέγεθες ἱδρυσαμένους πολίσαι τὴν πρὸς πάντων ἐπικληθεῖσαν μεγάλην Ἑλλάδα ἐν Ἰταλίᾳ). (*Vit. Pyth.* 20)[4]

---

3   Empedocles Καθαρμοί ("Purifications") frg. 112 (DK); frg. 102 in M. R. Wright, *Empedocles: The Extant Fragments* (New Haven: Yale University Press, 1981); and 399 in Geoffrey S. Kirk, John E. Raven, and Malcolm Schofield, *The Presocratic Philosophers: A Critical History with a Selection of Texts* (2nd ed.; Cambridge: Cambridge University Press, 1983); text

and trans. from the latter (p. 313); the fragment is cited by Hengel, *Charismatic Leader*, 25.

4   Text from Augustus Nauck, ed., *Porphyrii Philosophi Platonici: Opuscula Tria* (Leipzig: Teubner, 1860) 21; trans. from Kenneth Sylvan Guthrie et al., *The Pythagorean Sourcebook and Library* (Grand Rapids: Phanes, 1987) 126–27. A related passage in

In v. 10 also the pressure of the crowd is specified as people approaching Jesus eagerly, pushing against or falling upon him (ἐπιπίπτειν), in order to touch him and thus be healed. These people are those "who had (bodily) torments" (ὅσοι εἶχον μάστιγας). The word translated "torments" (μάστιγες) has also the concrete meaning "whip" and the other metaphorical meanings "scourge" or "plague." Since unclean spirits are mentioned in v. 11, the implication seems to be that the diseases or disabilities suffered by the people in question were caused by such spirits. This inference is supported by a spell in a Greek magical papyrus that may date to the fourth century CE:

> Write the formula on a new sheet of papyrus, and after extending it from one of your temples to the other read the 6 names, while you face north, saying "Subject to me all daimons, so that every daimon, whether heavenly or aerial or earthly or subterranean or terrestrial or aquatic, might be obedient to me and every enchantment and scourge which is from God." And all daimons will be obedient to you (γράψας τὸ ὄνομα εἰς καινὸν χαρτάριον καὶ διατείνας ἀπὸ κροτάφου εἰς κρόταφον σεαυτοῦ ἐντύγχανε πρὸς βορέαν τοῖς ϛ´ ὀνόμασι λέγων· ὑπόταξόν μοι πάντα τὰ δαιμόνια, ἵνα μοι ἦν ὑπήκοος πᾶς δαίμων οὐράνιος καὶ αἰθέριος καὶ ἐπίγειος καὶ ὑπόγειος καὶ χερσαῖο(ς) καὶ ἔνυδρος καὶ πᾶσα ἐπιπομπὴ καὶ μάστιξ ἡ θεοῦ.' καὶ ἔσται σοι τὰ δαιμόνια πάντα ὑπηκοα). (PGM V. 160–170)[5]

In this text a "scourge" (μάστιξ) is an instrument of a divine being. In Mark 3:10, the "torments" or "scourges" (μάστιγας) seem to result from the activity of the unclean spirits that possess or influence people.

■ **11-12** The mention of unclean spirits (τὰ πνεύματα τὰ ἀκάθαρτα) recalls the unclean spirit that Jesus encountered in the synagogue at Capernaum and the acclamation of the people who witnessed the exorcism, "he commands even the unclean spirits, and they obey him" (Mark 1:23, 26, 27). The whole scene in 3:7-12 is analogous to that in 1:32-34, but intensified. In chap. 1, the scene is calmer, and the audience infers that only the sick of Capernaum are brought to Jesus. That scene concludes with the remark by the narrator, "He would not allow the demons to speak, because they knew him." That remark calls to mind the cry of the unclean spirit in 1:24 and his address of Jesus by name (Jesus of Nazareth) and as "the Holy One of God." All these motifs are recapitulated and lifted to a new level in 3:11, when the unclean spirits prostrate themselves before Jesus and acclaim him "Son of God." Since the words "Son of God" (υἱοῦ θεοῦ) in 1:1 were not originally part of the text of the Gospel, this is the first time in Mark that this epithet is explicitly applied to Jesus.[6] It is, of course, implied in the words of the voice from heaven in 1:11, "You are my beloved son." As argued in the comment on 1:11 above, this address implies that Jesus is the messiah of Israel, the eschatological king. Similarly, the obeisance of the unclean spirits in 3:11 is a fitting complement to the acclamation of a king.

In v. 12, however, Jesus forbids the unclean spirits to make him known. As noted above in connection with 1:24 and 34, the spirits know who Jesus is because, as suprahuman beings, they have knowledge of things inaccessible to human beings. The Markan Jesus opposes the

---

Iamblichus *Vit. Pyth.* 6.30 reads: "in only one lecture, so they say, which he made on his first arrival in Italy, to the general public, more than two thousand were captivated by his words, so powerfully that they no longer returned home, but together with children and women, they established a very great school, and built a community in that which is called by all Magna Graecia" (ἐν μιᾷ μόνον ἀκροάσει, ὥς φασιν, ἣν πρωτίστην καὶ πάνδημον μόνος ἐπιβὰς τῆς Ἰταλίας ὁ ἄνθρωπος ἐποιήσατο, πλέονες ἢ δισχίλιοι τοῖς λόγοις ἐνεσχέθησαν, αἱρεθέντες αὐτοὶ κατὰ κράτος οὕτως, ὥστε οὐκέτι οἴκαδε ἀπέστησαν, ἀλλὰ ὁμοῦ παισὶ καὶ γυναιξὶν ὁμακοεῖόν τι παμμέγεθες ἱδρυσάμενοι

καὶ πολίσαντες αὐτοὶ τὴν πρὸς πάντων ἐπικληθεῖσαν Μεγάλην Ἑλλάδα); text and trans. from Dillon and Hershbell, 52, 54–55.

5 Preisendanz-Henrichs, 1:186; trans. by David E. Aune in Betz, *Magical Papyri*, 103. In a love spell, the god Anubis is asked to drive the desired woman by means of his scourge (τῇ σῇ μάστιγι ἐλαυνομένην) to the man who desires her (PGM XVIIa.25; Preisendanz-Henrichs, 2:139; trans. by Edward N. O'Neil in Betz, *Magical Papyri*, 254). Cf. line 16 of the same text.

6 See the note on the translation of 1:1 above.

revelation of his messianic identity to the people at this point in the narrative primarily because his exercise of the office of messiah, at least during his earthly life, would not conform to the expectations of the people (as these can be discerned from the literature of the late Second Temple period).[7] The secrecy also has the effect of building suspense in the narrative unfolding of the identity of Jesus, and it implies that the nature of his identity is something sacred that cannot be revealed in an indiscriminate manner.[8]

3

3:13-19 Jesus Appoints the Twelve

13/ And he went up on the mountain and summoned those whom he wanted, and they went to him. 14/ And he appointed twelve[a] in order that they might be with him and he might send them to proclaim[b] 15/ and to have authority[c] to drive out the demons. 16/ So he appointed the Twelve,[d] and he gave to Simon the surname Rock (Peter), 17/ and (he appointed) James the son of Zebedee and John the brother of James, and he gave them the surname Boanerges, that is, Sons of Thunder; 18/ and Andrew and Philip and Bartholomew and Matthew and Thomas and James the son of Alphaeus and Thaddaeus[e] and Simon the zealot[f] 19/ and Judas Iscariot,[g] who also handed him over.

a Some MSS, ℵ B (C*) et al., add "whom he also named apostles" (οὓς καὶ ἀποστόλους ὠνόμασεν); one MS (W; similarly Δ) adds these words after the next clause: "in order that they might be with him" (ἵνα ὦσιν μετ᾽ αὐτοῦ). This addition was probably made under the influence of Luke 6:13. Cf. Metzger, *Textual Commentary*, 69.

b Some MSS, D W et al., add the phrase "the good news" (τὸ εὐαγγέλιον) to clarify what it is they were to proclaim; cf. 1:14-15. But Mark uses forms of the verb κηρύσσειν ("to proclaim") without objects in 1:37 and 39. In any case, 6:12 suggests that the proclamation of the Twelve was similar to that of Jesus as summarized in 1:14-15.

c Most MSS, A C² D W et al., add at this point "to heal diseases and" (θεραπεύειν τὰς νόσους καί). This addition may have been made under the influence of the parallel in Matt 10:1 or in Luke 9:1, but both of those passages mention the unclean spirits or demons before the disease(s).

d The words "So he appointed the Twelve" (καὶ ἐποίησεν τοὺς δώδεκα), which resume the statement at the beginning of v. 14, are attested by ℵ B C* et al. Although such repetition, to resume the train of thought after a digression, is typical of ancient documents (see Willem A. A. van Otterlo, *Untersuchungen über Begriff, Anwendung und Entstehung der griechischen Ringkomposition* [Amsterdam: Noord-Hollandsche uitgevers maatschappij, 1944]), it is somewhat awkward here since the digression is so short. For this reason, the words were omitted in most MSS (A C² D L Θ et al.). Similarly, Swete, ad loc. For a different view, see Taylor, ad loc. See also Metzger, *Textual Commentary*, 69.

e Some MSS (D it) read "Lebbaeus" (Λεββαῖον) instead of "Thaddaeus" (Θαδδαῖον). The same variant occurs in some MSS of Matt 10:3. The variant apparently represents a different tradition from the one represented by most MSS. In many MSS of Matt 10:3, the two traditions are conflated by an indication that they are names of the same person (C L W Θ et al.). Cf. Metzger, *Textual Commentary*, 69; and Taylor, ad loc.

---

7 See the section of the introduction to the commentary *Jesus as Messiah* above.

8 See the excursus on the messianic secret, following the commentary on 1:24 above.

f   Some MSS (A *Θ* et al.) read *Κανανίτην* ("Cananite," or "a man from Cana") instead of *Καναναῖον* ("Cananean," from קַנְאָן, the Aramaic for "zealous"), a reading attested by ℵ B C D et al. The latter may have been changed to the former because the latter was no longer understood. The Aramaic meaning is correctly translated into Greek in Luke 6:15. Cf. Taylor, ad loc.

g   Some MSS (D lat) read *Σκαριώθ* ("Scarioth") instead of

Ἰσκαριώθ ("Iscariot," probably from the Aramaic אִישׁ קְרִיּוֹת, "a man from Kerioth," a locality in southern Judea). Other MSS, A (W) et al., read *Ἰσκαριώτην*, a declinable form of *Ἰσκαριώθ*. The variant in D has given rise to many theories, but none of them are compelling; see BAGD, s.v. *Ἰσκαριώθ*; Metzger, *Textual Commentary*, 69; cf. 21–22; Taylor, ad loc.

Comment

■ **13** The fact that the mountain which Jesus climbs is not named allows it to take on connotations of the mountain of God or the cosmic mountain, the place where heaven and earth meet and where a holy man encounters God and the people receive revelation.[9] Jewish tradition presents Mount Sinai as such a place, where Moses, his close associates and seventy elders, "the chief men of the people of Israel," met God (Exod. 24:9-11 *RSV*). Analogously, in this passage Jesus summons his close associates to join him on the mountain.[10]

■ **14-15** The statement "And he appointed twelve" (*καὶ ἐποίησεν [τοὺς] δώδεκα*) may have been the pre-Markan introduction to the traditional list of names that appears in vv. 16-19.[11] The repetition of the statement in v. 16 could be a sign that the author returned to his source after inserting his own introduction concerning the purpose of the appointment in vv. 14-15.

The Markan Jesus appoints twelve men "to be with him" (*ἵνα ὦσιν μετ' αὐτοῦ*). Although the terminology of teacher (*διδάσκαλος*) and disciple (*μαθητής*) does occur in Mark but is avoided by both Xenophon and

Plato in describing the relationship between Socrates and his followers, there is an analogy between this statement in Mark and the term that Xenophon used most frequently to describe that relationship, namely, *συνόντες* ("those who were with him").[12]

Both the motif of "being with him" and the motif of twelve close associates are found in a passage from the *Temple Scroll* that describes the law for the king:

[They shall count,] on the day that they appoint hi[m] king, the sons of Israel from the age of twenty to sixty years according to their standard (units). He shall install at their head captains of thousands, captains of hundreds, captains of fifties and captains of ten in all their cities. He shall select from among them one thousand by tribe to be with him: twelve thousand warriors who shall not leave him alone to be captured by the nations. All the selected men whom he has selected shall be men of truth, God-fearers, haters of unjust gain and mighty warriors. They shall be with him always, day and night. They shall guard him from anything sinful, and from any foreign nation in order not to be captured by them. The twelve princes of his

---

9   The mountain of God may be Mount Horeb (Exod 3:1), Mount Sinai (Exod 19:1-2, 11), or Mount Zion (Ps 2:6; 48:2). Traditions about the cosmic mountain are applied to any great mountain with springs at its base or side where a sanctuary exists; see Frank Moore Cross, *Canaanite Myth and Hebrew Epic: Essays in the History of the Religion of Israel* (Cambridge, MA: Harvard University Press, 1973) 38, and Richard J. Clifford, *The Cosmic Mountain in Canaan and the Old Testament* (HSM 4; Cambridge, MA: Harvard University Press, 1972).

10   Cf. Klemens Stock, *Boten aus dem Mit-Ihm Sein: Das Verhältnis zwischen Jesus und den Zwölf nach Markus* (AnBib 70; Rome: Biblical Institute Press, 1975) 9–10.

11   Wolfgang Trilling, "Zur Entstehung des Zwölfer-

kreises: Eine geschichtskritische Überlegung," in Rudolf Schnackenburg, Josef Ernst and Joachim Wanke, eds., *Die Kirche des Anfangs: Festschrift für Heinz Schürmann zum 65. Geburtstag* (Leipzig: St. Benno, 1977) 201–22, esp. 204–6.

12   Xenophon *Mem.* 1.1.4, 5; 1.2.8, 18, 39, 51, 64; 2.1.1; 2.5.1; 3.1.1; 3.12.1; 4.5.1; 4.6.1; 4.7.1, 8; 4.8.7; for further references, see Catharina Maria Gloth and Maria Francisca Kellogg, *Index in Xenophontis Memorabilia* (Cornell Studies in Classical Philology 11; New York: Macmillan, 1900) 82. See also Whitney Taylor Shiner, *Follow Me! Disciples in Markan Rhetoric* (SBLDS 145; Atlanta: Scholars Press, 1995) 47–48.

people shall be with him, and twelve from among the priests, and from among the Levites twelve. They shall sit together with him to (proclaim) judgement and the law so that his heart shall not be lifted above them, and he shall not do anything without them concerning any affair. (11QT 57:2-15)[13]

Since the *Temple Scroll* is a rewriting of portions of the Torah, this passage refers to the future historical king of Israel, in terms of its literary point of view. As read by the community at Qumran, however, it portrayed the ideal king of the eschatological future as well as of the historical past. The twelve princes, twelve priests, and twelve Levites are to form a council to advise the king and to assist him in making decisions.[14]

Both this passage from the *Temple Scroll* and Mark 3:13-19 must be seen in the context of the expectation of the restoration of the twelve tribes of Israel in the last days. This hope was already expressed in the late exilic period as the restoration under Cyrus was anticipated:

And now the Lord says, who formed me from the womb to be his servant, to bring Jacob back to him, and that Israel might be gathered to him, for I am honored in the eyes of the Lord, and my God has become my strength—he says: "It is too light a thing that you should be my servant to raise up the tribes of Jacob and to restore the preserved of Israel; I will give

you as a light to the nations, that my salvation may reach to the end of the earth." (Isa 49:5-6 LXX)[15]

According to Ben Sira, one of the tasks that Elijah will accomplish in the last days is the restoration of the tribes of Israel:

הכתוב נכון לעת להשבית אף לפני בא יום ייי:[
להשיב לב אבות על בנים ולהכין ש]בטי ישרא[ל:

Of whom it is written that you are prepared for the proper time, to turn aside the wrath befor[e the day of the Lord comes,] to turn the hearts of the fathers to the sons and to establish the tr[ibes of Israel]. (Sir 48:10)[16]

Josephus may know this tradition, although he avoids stating it explicitly. He reports a decree of Xerxes allowing the Jews to return from Babylon to Jerusalem and states that many did so. He goes on to say, however:

But the Israelite nation as a whole remained in the country. In this way has it come about that there are two tribes in Asia and Europe subject to the Romans, while until now there have been ten tribes beyond the Euphrates—countless myriads whose number cannot be ascertained (ὁ δὲ πᾶς λαὸς τῶν Ἰσραηλιτῶν κατὰ χώραν ἔμεινεν· διὸ καὶ δύο φυλὰς εἶναι συμ-

---

13 Trans. from Vermes, *Dead Sea Scrolls*, 213. Joseph M. Baumgarten argues that 4Q159 (Ordinances) is an excerpt from the *Temple Scroll* and cites 1QM 2:1-3 as a parallel text. He suggests that this advisory body derives from the model of Jehoshaphat's central tribunal in 2 Chr 19:5-11 ("The Duodecimal Courts of Qumran, the *Apocalypse*, and the Sanhedrin," in idem, *Studies in Qumran Law* [SJLA 24; Leiden: Brill, 1977] 145–71). The number of judges appointed, however, and the number of the members of the tribunal are not specified in 2 Chronicles.

14 See also 4QpIsa^d (4Q164) frg. 1 1–8, according to which the rubies of Isa 54:12 represent the twelve chief priests, and the gates of carbuncles correspond to the chiefs of the tribes of Israel in the last days; see García Martínez and Tigchelaar, *Dead Sea Scrolls*, 1:326–27; David Flusser, "Qumran und die Zwölf," in C. J. Bleeker, ed., *Initiation* (NumenSup 10; Leiden: Brill, 1965) 134–46.

15 See also Isa 11:11-12, 15-16; 27:12-13; Jer 31:7-9.

16 Text from Francesco Vattioni, ed., *Ecclesiastico: Testo ebraico con apparato critico e versioni greca, latina e siriaca* (Pubblicazioni del Seminario di Semitistica; Testi 1; Naples: Istituto Orientale di Napoli, 1968) 263; my trans. For the Hebrew text, see also Pancratius C. Beentjes, *The Book of Ben Sira in Hebrew* (VTSup 68; Leiden: Brill, 1997) 86. The Greek text (LXX) reads ὁ καταγραφεὶς ἐν ἐλεγμοῖς εἰς καιροὺς κοπάσαι ὀργὴν πρὸ θυμοῦ, ἐπιστρέψαι καρδίαν πατρὸς πρὸς υἱὸν καὶ καταστῆσαι φυλὰς Ιακωβ ("Of whom it is written that you would cause the anger to abate before the (day of) wrath by means of punishments until the proper times, that you would turn the hearts of the fathers to the sons and establish the tribes of Jacob"). See also Sir 36:10 LXX (36:13 RSV).

βέβηκεν ἐπί τε τῆς Ἀσίας καὶ τῆς Εὐρώπης Ῥωμαίοις ὑπακουσάσας, αἱ δὲ δέκα φυλαὶ πέραν εἰσὶν Εὐφράτου ἕως δεῦρο, μυριάδες ἄπειροι καὶ ἀριθμῷ γνωσθῆναι μὴ δυνάμεναι). (*Ant.* 11.5.2 §133)[17]

Ἰησοῦς εἶπεν αὐτοῖς· ἀμὴν λέγω ὑμῖν ὅτι ὑμεῖς οἱ ἀκολουθήσαντές μοι ἐν τῇ παλιγγενεσίᾳ, ὅταν καθίσῃ ὁ υἱὸς τοῦ ἀνθρώπου ἐπὶ θρόνου δόξης αὐτοῦ, καθήσεσθε καὶ ὑμεῖς ἐπὶ δώδεκα θρόνους κρίνοντες τὰς δώδεκα φυλὰς τοῦ Ἰσραηλ).[22]

It is likely that the historical Jesus chose twelve special associates in order to symbolize the restoration of the twelve tribes of Israel that was about to take place.[18] Vielhauer argued that the idea of an inner circle of twelve within the group of Jesus' disciples, based on eschatological expectation, arose only after the death of Jesus.[19] The earliest tradition about the resurrection of Jesus is Paul's statement that "he was seen by Cephas, then by the Twelve" (καὶ ὤφθη Κηφᾷ εἶτα τοῖς δώδεκα) (1 Cor 15:5).[20] This early tradition implies that the Twelve constituted a definite group before the experience of Jesus as risen. If the vision of the Lord was the occasion for the formation of the Twelve, one would expect to find some trace of this idea in the various traditions about the resurrection. It is of course possible that the tradition that Jesus appeared to them was invented in order to legitimate a group of Twelve, but then one would expect them to play a larger role either in the leadership or the ideology of the early Christian movement.[21] The eschatological role of the Twelve is expressed in Matt 19:28:

Jesus said to them, "Truly I say to you that, in the new age, when the Son of Man sits on his glorious throne, you who have followed me will also sit on twelve thrones judging the twelve tribes of Israel" (ὁ δὲ

Since a similar saying occurs in Luke, the versions in Matthew and Luke may be based on a form of the saying in Q:

You are those who have remained with me during my trials; and, just as my Father has conferred a kingdom upon me, I also confer (it) upon you, in order that you may eat and drink at my table in my kingdom and sit upon thrones judging the twelve tribes of Israel (Ὑμεῖς δέ ἐστε οἱ διαμεμενηκότες μετ᾽ ἐμοῦ ἐν τοῖς πειρασμοῖς μου· κἀγὼ διατίθεμαι ὑμῖν καθὼς διέθετό μοι ὁ πατήρ μου βασιλείαν, ἵνα ἔσθητε καὶ πίνητε ἐπὶ τῆς τραπέζης μου ἐν τῇ βασιλείᾳ μου, καὶ καθήσεσθε ἐπὶ θρόνων τὰς δώδεκα φυλὰς κρίνοντες τοῦ Ἰσραήλ). (Luke 22:28-30)[23]

If the saying was not in Q, it nevertheless represents an early tradition compatible with the activity of the historical Jesus as an eschatological prophet.[24]

The author of Mark, however, emphasizes a more immediate role for the Twelve; the Markan Jesus wishes to send them out to proclaim and with authority to cast out demons.[25] Although the content of their proclamation is not specified here, it is likely that it is substantially

---

17 Text and trans. from Thackeray, *Josephus*, 6:376–79.

18 Meier, *Marginal Jew*, 3.128–47.

19 Vielhauer, "Gottesreich und Menschensohn," 68–71. For a list of other scholars who deny that the group of the Twelve existed during the lifetime of Jesus and further bibliography, see John P. Meier, "The Circle of the Twelve: Did It Exist during Jesus' Public Ministry?" *JBL* 116 (1997) 635–72, esp. 643 n. 22. Meier himself concludes that the circle of the Twelve did exist during Jesus' public ministry.

20 The variant "eleven" (ἕνδεκα) is clearly secondary, a correction in light of the betrayal of Judas; cf. Matt 28:16.

21 See also the arguments of Sanders, *Jesus and Judaism*, 98–106. For further bibliography and a list of other scholars who argue that Jesus appointed the Twelve, see Meier, "Circle of the Twelve," 643 n. 22.

22 Text from Nestle-Aland (27th ed.); my trans.

23 Text from Nestle-Aland (27th ed.); my trans.

24 See the reconstruction of the Q-saying in Robinson et al., *Critical Edition of Q*, 558–61. For a summary of the debate concerning whether this saying was in Q, see John S. Kloppenborg, *Q Parallels: Synopsis, Critical Notes & Concordance* (Foundations and Facets Reference Series; Sonoma, CA: Polebridge, 1988) 202. Meier accepts it as a Q-saying ("Circle of the Twelve," 653–59). For a discussion of Jesus as an eschatological prophet, see the section of the Introduction to the commentary above on *Jesus as Prophet*; Sanders, *Jesus and Judaism*; Meier, *Marginal Jew*, 2:237–507.

25 The twofold task anticipated here for the Twelve is similar to the summary of Jesus' activity in 1:39; see Suzanne Watts Henderson, "'Concerning the

the same as that of Jesus, as summarized in 1:14-15. This is the purpose for which the disciples were called; this is what it means to be "fishers of human beings" (cf. 1:16-20, esp. 17). Whereas the Q-saying discussed above deals with the role of the Twelve in the time of fulfillment, this passage in Mark portrays their role in the initial phase of the last days.

■ **16-19** Although the lists of the names of the Twelve in Mark, Matthew, Luke, and Acts vary in order and in the formulation of some of the epithets, the actual names are remarkably consistent. There is only one real difference among the lists. Mark and Matthew mention a Thaddaeus, whereas Luke-Acts mentions a Jude, the son of James.[26] This variation is evidence that the author of Luke-Acts had a tradition about the Twelve that was independent of Mark.[27] Although this independent attestation does not prove the historicity of the tradition, it at least provides evidence that the tradition is pre-Markan.

■ **16** The disciple of Jesus named Simon ($\Sigma i\mu\omega\nu$) was called in 1:16-17 and mentioned several times in incidents that follow his call (1:29, 30, 36). Joseph A. Fitzmyer has shown that the name שמעון ("Simeon" or "Symeon") or its Greek equivalent $\Sigma i\mu\omega\nu$ ("Simon") was the most common given name for Jewish males in the period from about 100 BCE to 200 CE.[28] Here Jesus renames him $\Pi\acute{\epsilon}\tau\rho\sigma\varsigma$ ("Rock" or "Peter"). From this point onward in the text of Mark, the disciple in question

is always called simply "Peter" with one exception—14:37.[29] It is probable that this disciple's change of name occurred for the first time in Aramaic, that is, from שמעון ("Simeon" or "Symeon") to כפא ("Rock"). This hypothesis is supported by the fact that Paul refers to this disciple regularly as $K\eta\varphi\hat{\alpha}\varsigma$ ("Cephas").[30] He uses the name $\Pi\acute{\epsilon}\tau\rho\sigma\varsigma$ ("Rock" or "Peter") for him only twice (Gal 2:7, 8).[31] $K\eta\varphi\hat{\alpha}\varsigma$ ("Cephas") is a Greek form of the Aramaic word כפא, which assimilates it to masculine nouns of the first declension.[32] In Aramaic כפא is a common noun meaning "rock" or "crag."[33] It is attested as a proper name in an Aramaic text from Elephantine that is dated to 416 BCE.[34] It is best understood as a shortened form of a name that once had a theophoric element; it is thus similar to the Biblical Hebrew name צור ("Rock").[35] This name is a short form of צוריאל ("God is my rock") or צורישדי ("The Almighty is my rock").[36]

The only clue that the context of Mark gives about the significance of the change of name from Simon to Peter is that it takes place in connection with the appointing of the Twelve and that Simon is at the head of the list of names. Although the name implies that ultimately God is the firm rock on which any building must be based, in its shortened form it suggests that Simon Peter is to be the foundation of the community anticipated by Jesus, namely, the restored Israel.[37] The addition of a surname for Simon is similar to the formal change of the name of

Loaves:' Comprehending Incomprehension in Mark 6:45-52," *JSNT* 83 (2001) 3–26, esp. 10–11.

26 Cf. Mark 3:16-19; Matt 10:2-4; Luke 6:14-16; Acts 1:13. See the discussion in Meier, "Circle of the Twelve," 645–52.

27 Cf. Meier, "Circle of the Twelve," 650–51.

28 Joseph A. Fitzmyer, "The Name Simon," in idem, *Essays;* reprinted in idem, *Semitic Background*, 105–12. See also BAGD, s.v. On the Hebrew name and its Greek equivalent, see Sharon Pace Jeansonne and Stanley E. Porter, "Simeon," *ABD* 6:26–28. On the Greek name, see Scott T. Carroll, Uriel Rappaport, and Robert F. Stoops, Jr., "Simon," *ABD* 6:28–31.

29 The verse reads καὶ λέγει τῷ Πέτρῳ· Σίμων, καθεύδεις; ("and he said to Peter, 'Simon, are you sleeping?'"); on this passage, see the commentary below.

30 1 Cor 1:12; 3:22; 9:5; 15:5; Gal 1:18; 2:9, 11, 14.

31 On the theory that Paul refers to two different people with the names "Cephas" and "Peter" respectively, see Joseph A. Fitzmyer, "Aramaic Kephaʾ and

Peter's Name in the New Testament," in E. Best and R. M. Wilson, eds., *Text and Interpretation: Studies in the New Testament Presented to Matthew Black* (Cambridge: Cambridge University Press, 1979) 121–32; reprinted in Joseph A. Fitzmyer, *To Advance the Gospel: New Testament Studies* (BRS; Grand Rapids: Eerdmans; Livonia, MI: Dove Booksellers, 1981; 2nd ed., 1998) 112–24, esp. 114–15; Hans Dieter Betz, *Galatians: A Commentary on Paul's Letter to the Churches in Galatia* (Hermeneia; Philadelphia: Fortress, 1979) 96–97.

32 Fitzmyer, "Aramaic Kephaʾ," 115.

33 Ibid.

34 BMAP 8:10; Fitzmyer, "Aramaic Kephaʾ," 116.

35 1 Chr 8:30; 9:36; Num 25:15; 31:8; Josh 13:21.

36 Num 3:35; 1:6; 2:12; Fitzmyer, "Aramaic Kephaʾ," 118.

37 The Gospel of Matthew updates this idea so that Peter becomes the foundation of the ἐκκλησία ("assembly" or "community") of the followers of Jesus in the postresurrection period; often trans.

Abram to Abraham and of Sarai to Sarah in Genesis 17. In the ancient Near East such a change was viewed as the external sign of an important change in the life or role of the bearer. The underlying concept is related to the king's assumption of a special throne name.[38] It is also similar to the change of Jacob's name to Israel (Gen 32:28). In both of these cases, it is a matter of the establishment of the people of Israel; in Mark 3:16, it is a matter of the eschatological renewal of Israel.

■ **17** Andrew, who was called along with Simon in 1:16-18, is listed not second but fourth. The two sons of Zebedee, James and John, called in 1:19-20, are mentioned in second and third place.[39] The first three listed here, Simon Peter, James, and John, are given a privileged role several times in the following narrative.[40] The first four listed here are named in the same order in 13:3 as putting the question to Jesus that evokes his eschatological discourse.[41]

The name Ἰάκωβος ("James") is a Greek form of Ἰακώβ ("Jacob"), the Greek equivalent of the Hebrew name יעקב ("Jacob").[42] Ζεβεδαῖος ("Zebedee") comes from the Aramaic זבדי ("gift of Yahweh").[43] The name Ἰωάννης ("John") is the Greek equivalent of the Hebrew name יוחנן ("Yohanan").[44]

The Markan Jesus gives James and John the surname Βοανηργές ("Boanerges"). It is highly likely that this surname is a transliteration of a Hebrew or Aramaic expression, but the original is difficult to reconstruct.[45] The first part Βοανη- ("Boane-") probably represents the Hebrew בני ("sons of"). The second part ργες- ("rges") could derive from the Hebrew רֹגֶז ("agitation" or "tumult"). This word occurs in the following passage of Job:

At this also my heart trembles, and leaps out of its place. Hearken to the thunder (רֹגֶז) of his voice and the rumbling that comes from his mouth. Under the whole heaven he lets it go, and his lightning to the

---

with "church"). There is continuity between the two insofar as ἐκκλησία ("assembly") evokes the קהל ("the assembly" of the Israelites). In the DSS, the term קהל ("assembly") is used for the community understood as the eschatological Israel in the wilderness; CD 14:18; 11QT 16:18; 1QM 4:10. See also CD 7:17; 4QDᵃ (4Q266) 3 iii 18 (for text and trans. of the latter, see Baumgarten, *Qumran Cave 4*, 44); 4QDᵃ (4Q266) 10 i 11 (Baumgarten, *Qumran Cave 4*, 72–73); 4QDᵈ (4Q269) 11 i 1 (Baumgarten, *Qumran Cave 4*, 134–35); the latter two passages are parallel to CD 14:18, cited above. Finally, see 4QDᶠ (4Q271) 5 i 21 (Baumgarten, *Qumran Cave 4*, 181–82).

Richard M. Meyer interpreted the renaming of Simon in a more individual and moral sense, arguing that the simultaneous bestowal of leadership and the name "Peter" implies that the disciple should always be aware of the meaning of his name in order to be challenged to fulfill it ("Der Namenwitz: Ein Beitrag zur Theorie des Witzes," in *Neue Jahrbücher für das klassische Altertum und deutsche Literatur* (Neue Jahrbücher für das klassische Altertum, Geschichte und deutsche Literatur und für Pädagogik 11; Leipzig: Teubner, 1903) 122–45, esp. 132.

38 Ephraim A. Speiser, *Genesis: Introduction, Translation, and Notes* (AB 1; Garden City, NY: Doubleday, 1964) 127. Cf. Neh 9:7-8 = 2 Esdr 19:7-8, a passage remarking on the change of Abram's name to Abraham. See also 2 Kgs 24:17, according to which the king of Babylon appoints a new king of Judah and gives him a new name.

39 The listing of Peter, James, and John together at the head of the list may reflect their prominence in the early Christian movement; cf. Gal 2:9, where Paul says that they were reputed to be pillars. See Roger D. Aus, "Three Pillars and Three Patriarchs: A Proposal concerning Gal 2:9," *ZNW* 70 (1979) 252–61.

40 They alone are allowed to accompany Jesus to the house of Jairus and to witness his raising Jairus's daughter from the dead (5:37); they alone witness the transfiguration of Jesus (9:2); and they alone are taken aside with Jesus as he prays in Gethsemane (14:33).

41 In Mark 1:29 the four names are given in a different order, which is the same as that in which they were called.

42 BAGD, s.v. The Hebrew name is interpreted as "heel-grabber" (Gen 25:26) or "supplanter" (Gen 27:36); see John G. Gammie, "Jacob," *HBD* 443.

43 BAGD, s.v.; E. P. Blair, "Zebedee," *IDB* 4:940.

44 The Hebrew means "Yahu has been gracious" (B. T. Dahlberg, "Johanan," *IDB* 2:929). The Greek form of the name is attested for Jews in 1 and 2 Maccabees and in Josephus; see S. Sandmel, "John," *IDB* 2:930.

45 Neither Matthew nor Luke includes the surname of the sons of Zebedee in the parallel passages, perhaps because it was not intelligible to their respective authors.

corners of the earth. After it his voice roars; he thunders with his majestic voice and he does not restrain his lightnings when his voice is heard. (Job 37:1-4 RSV)[46]

This usage explains the translation offered in Mark for the enigmatic expression Βοανηργές ("Boanerges"), namely, υἱοὶ βροντῆς ("Sons of Thunder"). The latter Greek phrase is a Semitism, in which υἱός ("son") is used with a following genitive of origin or definition.[47] Since thunder is one of the primary elements of the motif of "theophany," the significance of the epithet seems to be that God is manifest in the activity of these two disciples.[48] Such an interpretation fits with the context of Mark, in which they are to be sent out to proclaim and with authority to drive out the demons. The fact that only these two are given this epithet, although all Twelve are sent out, is explained by the facts that Simon has acquired his own epithet commensurate with his role and that James and John, along with Simon, have greater authority and prominence than the others.[49]

The fact that the two brothers receive a common surname is perhaps related to the custom among the Greeks of referring to pairs of brothers or sisters with a special name, for example, the sons of Xenophon, the follower of Socrates:

According to Demetrius of Magnesia [Xenophon] was accompanied by his wife Philesia, and, in a speech written for the freedman whom Xenophon prosecuted for neglect of duty, Dinarchus mentions that his two sons Gryllus and Diodorus, the Dioscuri as they were called, also went with him (εἵπετο δὲ αὐτῷ καὶ γύναιον ὄνομα Φιλησία, καθά φησι Δημήτριος ὁ Μάγνης, καὶ δύο υἱεῖς, Γρύλλος καὶ Διόδωρος, ὡς φησι Δείναρχος ἐν τῷ πρὸς Ξενοφῶντα ἀποστασίου, οἳ καὶ Διόσκουροι ἐπεκαλοῦντο). (Diogenes Laertius Vit. Phil. 2.52)[50]

"Dioscuri" means "sons of Zeus," and typically refers to Castor and Polydeuces (latinized, Pollux). Castor was killed in battle, but Polydeuces shared his immortality with him.[51] Harris, following a suggestion of James G. Frazer, argued that the name given to James and John by Jesus was originally a title of the Dioscuri and that it was given to James and John because of twinlike features in their appearance or conduct.[52] Since Zeus was associated with thunder, such an epithet for the Dioscuri is plausible, but Harris did not provide evidence that it is actually attested for them.[53] Although the connection with the Dioscuri is dubious, the Greek cultural context suggests another connotation of the epithet "Sons of Thunder." According to Homer, Zeus might signal his will by

---

46 On the derivation of Βοανηργές ("Boanerges") from בְּנֵי ("sons of") and רְגֶז ("agitation" or "tumult") and the occurrence of the latter in Job 37:2, see Taylor, ad loc. James Rendel Harris at first argued against this explanation but later came to accept it; contrast idem, "Sons of Thunder," Expositor 3 (1907) 146–52, esp. 146–48, with idem, The Twelve Apostles (Cambridge: Heffer & Sons, 1927) 102 n. 1.

47 James Hope Moulton and Wilbert Francis Howard, A Grammar of New Testament Greek, vol. 2: Accidence and Word-Formation with an Appendix on Semitisms in the New Testament (Edinburgh: T & T Clark, 1928; reprinted 1986) 440–41.

48 Swete's comment (ad loc.) is persuasive, that James and John were called "Sons of Thunder" not because of the impetuousness of their characters but because of their place in the new order. On the role of the thunderstorm in theophanies, see Theodore Hiebert, "Theophany in the OT," ABD 6:505–11. According to the so-called Mithras Liturgy, the initiate hears thunder (βροντή) as he or she ascends to heaven and sees the gods and angels (PGM IV. 571,

621). The Pole Lords of heaven are addressed as those who send out thunder and lightning (ibid., 681); see Betz, Magical Papyri, 49–51.

49 W and three Old Latin MSS state that the epithet "Sons of Thunder" was given to all of the Twelve (see Taylor, ad loc.). Although this reading is not original, it is based on the insight that the epithet has more to do with a role in the history of salvation than with individual characteristics of personality, temperament, or natural gifts. The latter motivation is prominent in the story that Aristotle gave his follower Tyrtamus the name Theophrastus (Θεόφραστος) on account of his graceful style (Diogenes Laertius Vit. Phil. 5.38).

50 Text and trans. from Hicks, Diogenes Laertius, 1:180–83. This passage is cited, along with other examples, by BAGD, xxv.

51 See R. C. T. Parker, "Dioscuri," OCD 484.

52 Harris, "Sons of Thunder," 149–52.

53 On the association of Zeus with thunder, see Fritz Graf, "Zeus," in DDD 934–40, esp. 934; on the Dioscuri, see Ken Dowden, "Dioskouroi," ibid., 258–

sending thunder and lightning as signs when asked in prayer to do so.[54] Among those familiar with this motif, the epithet "Sons of Thunder" might have suggested that James and John were prophets.

■ **18** As mentioned above, Andrew, the brother of Simon, called in 1:16-18, is listed here in fourth place and receives no special epithet. It is noteworthy that Ἀνδρέας ("Andrew") and Φίλιππος ("Philip") are purely Greek names, whereas the names of the first three members of the Twelve have Hebrew equivalents.[55]

The name Βαρθολομαῖος ("Bartholomew") is a Greek form of the Aramaic epithet בר תלמי ("son of Talmai"). The name Talmai appears in the Bible as the name of the king of Geshur, whose daughter married David. The Greek equivalent of this name in the Roman period was Θολομαῖος ("Tholomaios").[56]

The name Μαθθαῖος ("Matthew") is also spelled Ματθαῖος ("Matthew").[57] This name is probably the Greek form of the Hebrew name מתי ("Mattai") or the Aramaic מתאי ("Mattai"), which are shortened forms of מתתיה ("Mattithiah," which means "gift of Yahweh") or מתני ("Mattenai," also "gift of Yahweh").[58] The name מתתיה ("Mattithiah") occurs in 1 and 2 Chronicles and in Ezra-Nehemiah.[59] The name מתני ("Mattenai") occurs in Ezra-Nehemiah.[60]

The name Θωμᾶς ("Thomas") is a Greek proper name that was sometimes associated with the Aramaic word for "twin," תאומא, which was phonetically similar to the former. The Aramaic term, however, was not a proper name.[61] In Mark, Matthew, and Luke-Acts, this disciple is simply called "Thomas." In three of the seven times that he is mentioned in the Gospel of John, however, he is called Θωμᾶς ὁ λεγόμενος Δίδυμος ("Thomas, who is called Didymos [which means "twin"]).[62] Unlike the Aramaic תאומא ("twin"), the Greek term Δίδυμος ("Didymos" or "twin") was used as a proper name.[63] In John nothing is said about Thomas's twin. By the time that the *Acts of Thomas* was written in the early third century CE, however, the legend had developed that this disciple's full name was Judas Thomas and that he was the twin brother of Jesus.[64] The Coptic *Gospel of Thomas* presents itself as written by Didymus Judas Thomas.[65]

Nothing reliable is known about James the son of Alphaeus (Ἰάκωβος ὁ τοῦ Ἀλφαίου) beyond his consistent inclusion in the four lists of the Twelve.[66] J. M.

59, who does not mention any association of them with thunder, although they "specialized in the rescue of sailors in distress" (ibid., 258).

54 Homer *Od.* 20.102-5 (thunder); *Il.* 2.353 (lightning); cited by Graf, "Zeus," 936.

55 BAGD, s.v.

56 2 Sam 3:3; 13:37. The Semitic name תלמי ("Talmai") is transliterated in the LXX as Θολμι ("Tholmi") in 2 Kgdms 3:3 and as Θολμαι ("Tholmai") in 13:37. Josephus renders the name of the king of Geshur as Θολομαῖος ("Tholomaios") (*Ant.* 7.1.4 §21). Josephus also mentions a brigand leader by the name of Θολομαῖος ("Tholomaios") or Θολεμαῖος ("Tholemaios") who was executed by Fadus around 44–46 CE (*Ant.* 20.1.1 §5–6).

57 BAGD, s.v.

58 E. P. Blair, "Matthew," *IDB* 3:301–2. See also Dennis Duling, "Matthew," *ABD* 4:618–22.

59 1 Chr 9:31; 16:5; Ezra 10:43; Neh 8:4; the equivalent name מתתיהו ("Mattithiah") occurs in 1 Chr 15:18, 21; 25:3, 21. In 1 Esdr 9:43 (= Neh 8:4) the name מתתיה ("Mattithiah") is rendered in Greek as Ματταθίας ("Mattathias"). This Greek name occurs in Luke 3:25 and 26 for ancestors of Jesus.

60 Ezra 10:33, 37; Neh 12:19.

61 BAGD, s.v.

62 The occurrences with the surname "Didymos" are John 11:16; 20:24; 21:2; those without it are 14:5; 20:26, 27, and 28.

63 BAGD, s.v.

64 He is called Ἰούδας Θωμᾶς ("Judas Thomas"), Ἰούδας ὁ καὶ Θωμᾶς ("Judas who (is) also (called) Thomas"), and Ἰούδας Θωμᾶς ὁ καὶ Δίδυμος ("Judas Thomas who (is) also (called) Didymos [which means 'twin']") in the *Acts of Thomas;* see Han J. W. Drijvers, "The Acts of Thomas," in *NTApoc,* 2:322–411, esp. 324. On the date of this work, see ibid., 323.

65 *Gos. Thom.* prologue; see Beate Blatz, "The Coptic Gospel of Thomas," in *NTApoc,* 1:110–33. In *Gos. Thom.* 13, Thomas is presented as having greater understanding of the identity of Jesus than Simon Peter and Matthew.

66 Mark 3:18; Matt 10:3; Luke 6:15; Acts 1:13. On the attempts to identify him with other men by the name of James and on the legends that were later attached to his name, see Donald A. Hagner, "James," *ABD* 3:616–18.

Norris has argued that the name of the father of this disciple should have a smooth breathing and that it is a purely Greek name.[67] Other scholars, however, see it as the Greek form of an Aramaic name, חלפי ("Halphai"), and thus give it a rough breathing.[68] Such a name does not occur in the Bible, but it does occur in a work by Procopius of Gaza.[69]

The name Θαδδαῖος ("Thaddaeus") occurs in both Mark's and Matthew's lists of the Twelve (Mark 3:18; Matt 10:3). Luke and Acts, however, list Ἰούδας Ἰακώβου ("Judas the son of James") instead of Thaddaeus (Luke 6:16; Acts 1:13). This discrepancy has been resolved by identifying Thaddaeus with Judas the son of James. The *Passio Simonis et Judae (latina),* a work dating to the fourth century CE or later, describes the deeds and martyrdom of Simon the Canaanite (also one of the Twelve according to Mark and Matthew) and Judas Thaddaeus.[70] Thaddaeus is also associated with the Abgar legend. Eusebius is the earliest writer to refer to it (*Hist. eccl.* 1.13; 2.1.6-8). The story goes that Abgar, the king of Edessa, wrote a letter to Jesus because he had heard of his miraculous healings. He invited Jesus to come to Edessa to heal him. Jesus wrote a letter in return to decline the invitation, but promised to send one of his disciples. After Jesus had ascended, Judas Thomas sent Thaddaeus to Edessa, who healed the king and converted the city to the Christian faith. H. J. W. Drijvers has suggested that the legend originated in Syria at the end of the third century and that the disciple in question was Addai, not Thaddaeus. The name Addai was so strange to Eusebius that he transformed it to the Greek name Thaddaeus and identified Thaddaeus with one of the seventy missionaries mentioned in Luke 10:1.[71]

Mark and Matthew mention Σίμων ὁ Καναναῖος (lit., "Simon the Cananean"), whereas Luke calls this disciple Σίμων ὁ καλούμενος ζηλωτής ("Simon who is called the zealot").[72] As indicated in note f on the translation of v. 18 above, some manuscripts of Mark give the name as Σίμων ὁ Κανανίτης ("Simon the Cananite" or "Simon, the man from Cana"). It is likely that Luke has given the correct sense of the epithet and that it is based on the Aramaic term קנאן ("zealous"). It is not likely that this disciple belonged or had belonged to the political party called "the Zealots."[73] This party did not come into being until the winter of 67-68.[74] The notion of "zeal" is closely related to that of "jealousy"; the Hebrew root קנא is used in both senses. The idea that Yahweh is a jealous God is closely related to the command to worship him alone.[75] Thus, a zealous Israelite was one who strongly opposed the worship of any other deity. The classic example of the "zealot" in this sense is Phinehas, who killed the man of Israel who had married a Midianite woman. The context suggests that the reason was that the Midianite women had led the men of Israel into idol-

---

67 J. M. Norris, "Alphaeus," *IDB* 1:96.

68 BAGD, s.v.

69 Procopius Gazaeus *Epistolae* 99; the name appears with a smooth breathing in the edition by Richard Hercher, *Epistolographoi hellenikoi: Epistolographi graeci* (Bibliotheca scriptorum Graecorum; Paris: Didot, 1873) 571. Procopius wrote in the fifth or sixth century CE.

70 See Aurelio de Santos Otero, "Later Acts of Apostles," in *NTApoc,* 2:481-82. Note also that the two persons are identified in some modern reference works; the entry "Thaddaeus" in *IDB* 4:614 directs the reader to the entry "Judas 8," by E. P. Blair, *IDB* 2:1008. The latter article identifies Thaddaeus with Judas the son of James mentioned in Luke and Acts. The article "Thaddeus" in the *ABD* takes a similar position, namely, that the descriptions "Lebbaeus" and "Thaddeus" were used instead in order to avoid confusion with Judas Iscariot the traitor (JoAnn Ford Watson, "Thaddeus," *ABD* 6:435). It is more likely that "Lebbaeus," "Thaddeus," and "Judas the

son of James" reflect minor variations in the traditional list of the Twelve. See note e on the translation of v. 18 above and Wolfgang A. Bienert, "The Concept of the Apostle in Primitive Christianity," in *NTApoc,* 1:5-25, esp. 17.

71 H. J. W. Drijvers, "The Abgar Legend," in *NTApoc,* 1:492-500.

72 Mark 3:18; Matt 10:4; Luke 6:15. In Acts 1:13 he is called Σίμων ὁ ζηλωτής ("Simon the Zealot").

73 Contra BAGD, s.v. Καναναῖος; see the literature cited there.

74 According to the reconstruction of Horsley and Hanson (*Bandits,* 216-43), based on Josephus, the Zealots were a coalition of peasant-bandits who rendered ineffective the attempt of the chief priests (including Josephus) and leading Pharisees to reach an accommodation with the Romans in the middle of the first war with Rome.

75 Exod 34:14; Deut 29:19 (29:20 RSV); 32:21; 1 Kgs 14:21-24; Ezek 8:1-6; 16:35-43.

atry (Num 25:1-18).[76] During the Second Temple period, however, the focus of zeal was extended to include all offenses against the Law. Those who were zealous in this sense would endure any hardship, even death, rather than transgress the Law. Some would also take it upon themselves to punish transgressors of the Law, and Simon, the disciple of Jesus, may have earned his epithet by doing so.[77]

■ **19** The list of the Twelve ends dramatically with the name of the one who handed Jesus over, Ἰούδας Ἰσκαριώθ ("Judas Iscariot"). The name Ἰούδας ("Judas" or "Jude") is the Greek form of the name of the patriarch יהודה ("Judah") (Gen 29:35; 49:8-12). It has been proposed that the patriarch Judah is a type of Judas because he sold his brother Joseph into slavery.[78] The motifs of treachery committed against a close associate and a transaction involving money are common to both. Judah, however, proposed to his brothers that they sell Joseph into slavery rather than killing him, since he was their brother, their own flesh (Gen 37:26-27). Nevertheless, the profit motive is clear in his words.

The surname Ἰσκαριώθ ("Iscariot") applies both to Judas and his father; thus it is unlikely to refer to some personal characteristic unique to Judas.[79] It is probably a Greek transcription of the Hebrew אִישׁ קְרִיּוֹת ("a man from Kerioth").[80] This Kerioth is probably the village of Kerioth-Hezron, which was about twelve miles south of Hebron in Judea (Josh 15:25).[81]

The reference to Judas as the one who handed Jesus over (ὃς καὶ παρέδωκεν αὐτόν)[82] calls to mind the remark that Jesus began his public activity in Galilee after John was handed over (μετὰ δὲ τὸ παραδοθῆναι τὸν Ἰωάννην) (Mark 1:14). This verb is used to express the idea of giving a city or a person into another's hands, especially as a hostage or to an enemy. It may have the connotation of treachery and in such contexts may be translated "betray."[83] Now the two primary sources of information about the death of John agree that Herod Antipas sent his agents to seize John and later put him to death.[84] It seems, then, that the idea of John's "being handed over" results from his being symbolically likened to Jesus.[85] This parallel also suggests that the primary significance of Judas's handing over of Jesus is not betrayal, but the result of the handing over of Jesus, namely, his death and its significance. The repetition of this word in association with the deaths of John and Jesus emphasizes it and evokes reflection on its significance. It is probably not a coincidence that this verb occurs twice in the poem about the Suffering Servant in Isaiah:

> We all have gone astray like sheep; each has gone astray on his own path. And the Lord has handed him

76 Other biblical figures expressed similar zeal; see David Rhoads, "Zealots," *ABD* 6:1043–54, esp. 1044.

77 Ibid., 1044.

78 See Kim Paffenroth, *Judas: Images of the Lost Disciple* (Louisville/London: Westminster John Knox, 2001) 5 and the literature cited in 146 n. 14.

79 Judas is named Ἰούδας Σίμωνος Ἰσκαριώτου ("Judas the son of Simon Iscariot") in John 6:71; 13:26; the text is less certain in 13:2.

80 Hans-Josef Klauck, *Judas–Ein Jünger des Herrn* (Quaestiones Disputatae 111; Freiburg/Basel/Vienna: Herder, 1987) 40–44.

81 See Joseph A. Fitzmyer, *The Gospel according to Luke: Introduction, Translation, and Notes* (2 vols.; AB 28, 28A; Garden City, NY: Doubleday, 1981, 1985) 1:620; see also Jeffrey R. Zorn, "Kerioth-Hezron," *ABD* 4:24; and BAGD, s.v. Ἰσκαριώθ. Charles C. Torrey's argument that אִישׁ ("man"), as Hebrew, could not have been part of the surname, because it was given to Judas by the common people, who spoke Aramaic, is invalid because the origin of the surname is unknown (Torrey, "The Name 'Iscariot,'" *HTR* 36 [1943] 51–62, esp. 54). His own thesis, that Ἰσκαριώτης ("Iscariōtēs") is the original form of the surname and that it derived from אִשְׁקַרְיָא, a Palestinian Aramaic by-form of שְׁקַרְיָא ("the liar" or "the false one"), the definite form of שְׁקַר ("liar"), is intriguing but overly speculative. Cf. the sobriquet אִישׁ הכוב ("man of the lie" or "Liar") in 1QpHab 2:1-2. For discussion of other theories, see Paffenroth, *Judas*, 5–6 and the literature cited on 146–47 nn. 17-29.

82 William Klassen has argued that the epithet of Judas should be translated "the one who handed Jesus over" and not "the traitor" or "the one who betrayed him" (*Judas: Betrayer or Friend of Jesus?* [Minneapolis: Fortress, 1996] 41–58; so also Wolfgang Reinbold, *Der älteste Bericht über den Tod Jesu: Literarische Analyse und historische Kritik der Passionsdarstellungen der Evangelien* [BZNW 69; Berlin/New York: de Gruyter, 1994] 316).

83 LSJ, s.v.

84 Josephus *Ant.* 18.5.2 §116–19; Mark 6:17.

85 See the commentary on 1:14-15 above on John as a prototype of Jesus.

over for our sins (πάντες ὡς πρόβατα ἐπλανήθη-
μεν, ἄνθρωπος τῇ ὁδῷ αὐτοῦ ἐπλανήθη· καὶ
κύριος παρέδωκεν αὐτὸν ταῖς ἁμαρτίαις ἡμῶν).

For this reason he will be the heir of many, and he
will distribute the spoils of the mighty, because he was
handed over to death, and he was considered to be
among the lawless. And he bore the sins of many and
was handed over on account of their sins (διὰ τοῦτο
αὐτὸς κληρονομήσει πολλοὺς καὶ τῶν ἰσχυρῶν
μεριεῖ σκῦλα, ἀνθ᾽ ὧν παρεδόθη εἰς θάνατον ἡ
ψυχὴ αὐτοῦ, καὶ ἐν τοῖς ἀνόμοις ἐλογίσθη· καὶ
αὐτὸς ἁμαρτίας πολλῶν ἀνήνεγκεν καὶ διὰ τὰς
ἁμαρτίας αὐτῶν παρεδόθη). (Isa 53:6, 12 LXX)

Although Judas is not relieved of responsibility, this allusion to Isaiah 53 suggests that the death of Jesus was
divinely ordained. This verse then, is the second allusion
to the death of Jesus in the narrative of Mark, the first
being the elaboration in 2:19b-20 of the saying about the
bridegroom in 2:19a.[86]

Excursus: The Historicity of Judas

Some scholars argue that the betrayal of Jesus by
Judas and Judas' label as "one of the Twelve" constitute the strongest argument for the historical reliability of the inclusion of Judas among the Twelve and for
the existence of this group during the lifetime of
Jesus.[87] But the historicity of the Twelve does not
depend on the historicity of Judas and his membership in this circle. On the contrary, Paul's mention of
the Twelve as a group seeing the risen Lord suggests
that he knew nothing of Judas. His lack of knowledge

of Judas, however, does not necessarily imply that the
group was first constituted by an appearance of the
risen Jesus. The number was the significant element,
right from the beginning, not the names of the twelve
individuals. It could be that the original Twelve did
not include Judas and that the list was redefined at
some point after the death of Jesus to include him.

The symbolic role of Judas raises doubt about his
historicity. The notion of betrayal by an intimate
friend is a scriptural motif.[88] The motif of "handing
over" could also have been inspired by the tendency to
interpret the death of Jesus as the fulfillment of scripture.[89] The fact that Judas is the only one of the
Twelve from Judea is also suspect. His Judean origin
could be exploited in making him a symbolic representative of "the Jews." The tradition that Jesus had
been betrayed by one of his inner circle made followers of Jesus vulnerable to critics later on, but at the
earliest stages of the movement few would have been
concerned about such polemics. The betrayal of Judas
was part of the scandal of the cross and thus part of
the divine plan.

If the figure of Judas had been invented for the
reasons described above, however, it is hard to explain
why he is identified as "Iscariot," that is, as a native of
the village of Kerioth. If he were a fictional character,
it is more likely that he would have been either from
Galilee like the rest or from Jerusalem as the capital
of Judea. This minor detail supports the historicity
of Judas as a disciple of Jesus at least and perhaps as a
member of the Twelve as well.[90] If Judas is historical
and actually did hand Jesus over to the authorities,
then Paul's mention of "the Twelve" in 1 Cor 15:5 may
be taken as a reference to the group as such, regardless of whether it still actually had twelve members.[91]

3

3:20-35 Jesus, His Family, and Satan

a   Many MSS (א[2] A C L Θ et al.) read "they went" (ἔρχονται) instead of "he went" (ἔρχεται); D reads "they
went in" (εἰσέρχονται). The singular was probably
changed to the plural, since Jesus and the Twelve are
mentioned together in the previous passage. Another
reason for changing the singular to the plural may
have been to prepare for αὐτούς ("they [were not even

20/ And he[a] went home. And the[b]
crowd gathered again, so that
they were not even able to eat.
21/ And when his family heard
(about it),[c] they went out to

---

86   See the commentary on these verses above.
87   Trilling, "Zur Entstehung des Zwölferkreises," 208–
13; Klauck, *Judas*, 33–38.
88   Mark 14:18; Ps 41:10 (41:9 RSV).
89   Mark 3:19 pars.; Mark 14:10-11 pars.; Mark 14:18
par.; Luke 22:21; Mark 14:21 pars.; Mark 14:41-42
par.; Mark 14:44 par.; Luke 22:48; Isa 53:6, 12 LXX.
90   Paffenroth concluded that the historicity of Judas is

likely, but for reasons different from those presented
here (*Judas*, 9–10).
91   Joseph Ysebaert concluded that Paul referred to the
remaining eleven of the inner circle of the Twelve as
"the Twelve" because the term was already technical
at the time that he wrote (*Die Amtsterminologie im
Neuen Testament und in der alten Kirche: Eine lexiko-
graphische Untersuchung* [Breda: Eureia, 1994] 3, 27).

restrain him; for they said, "He has lost his senses." 22/ And the scribes who had come down from Jerusalem said, "He is possessed by Beelzebul,"[d] and "By the ruler of the demons he drives out demons." 23/ And he summoned them and began to speak to them in parables, "How can Satan drive out Satan? 24/ And if a kingdom is divided against itself, that kingdom is not able to stand. 25/ And if a house is divided against itself, that house will not be able to stand. 26/ And if Satan has rebelled against himself and is divided, he is not able to stand, but is at an end. 27/ But no one is able to enter a strong man's house and steal his property, unless he first binds the strong man; then he will thoroughly plunder his house. 28/ Truly I say to you, all sins will be forgiven the sons of men and whatever abusive remarks[e] they utter; 29/ but whoever insults the Holy Spirit does not obtain forgiveness for all eternity,[f] but will be[g] guilty of an eternal sin."[h] 30/ For they said, "He has an unclean spirit."

31/ And his mother and his brothers came, and standing outside, sent (someone) to him to call him. 32/ And a crowd was sitting around him, and they said to him, "See, your mother and your brothers[i] are looking for you outside." 33/ And he answered them, "Who is my mother and (who are) my brothers?" 34/ And he looked around at those who were sitting in a circle around him and said, "Look, (here are) my mother and my brothers. 35/ For whoever does the will of God, such a person is my brother and sister and mother."

able]") later in the verse, understood as Jesus and his disciples. Note that the opposite shift in 1:29 is likely to be original (see the note on the trans. of 1:29 above).

b Some MSS (ℵ* C L* W Θ et al.) omit the article. The article was probably omitted either by accident or because copyists thought it unlikely that the same crowd could be meant as in 3:9.

c Some MSS (D W it) read "when the scribes and the rest heard about him" (ἀκούσαντες [ὅτε ἤκουσαν D] περὶ αὐτοῦ οἱ γραμματεῖς καὶ οἱ λοιποί). Clearly the original reading οἱ παρ᾽ αὐτοῦ ("his family") was so offensive that some copyists changed it, so that the standard opponents of Jesus, rather than his family, said that he had lost his senses.

d The spelling of the name varies in the MSS; B has Βεεζεβούλ ("Beezebul"); vg sy[s.p] attest Βεελζεβούβ ("Beelzebub"); the rest have βεελζεβούλ ("Beelzebul"). The reading of B may be dependent on Symmachus; see W. Herrmann, "Baal Zebub," DDD 154–56. The reading of vg sy[s.p], Βεελζεβούβ ("Beelzebub"), is a secondary correction of the earliest reading, βεελζεβούλ ("Beelzebul"), to make it conform to the Hebrew בעל זבוב ("Baal Zebub") of 2 Kgs 1:2, 3, 6, 16; see Herrmann, "Baal Zebub," 293–94.

e In Greek there is a play on words linking abusive remarks against other human beings and blasphemy against the Holy Spirit, a play that cannot be reproduced in English; see Adela Yarbro Collins, "The Charge of Blasphemy in Mark 14.64," in JSNT 26 (2004) 379–401.

f Some MSS (D W Θ et al.) omit the words "for all eternity" (εἰς τὸν αἰῶνα), perhaps to avoid redundancy (see the next clause).

g Most MSS read "is" (ἐστιν), whereas some (ℵ D L Δ et al.) read "will be" (ἔσται). The future tense is probably original, because the reference is to the eschatological judgment. Copyists evidently changed the future to the present to agree with the preceding clause.

h Many MSS, A C[2] et al., read "judgment" (κρίσεως) and some (348. 1216 pc) read "punishment" (κολάσεως); others (C*[vid] D W f[13]) use a different Greek word meaning "sin" (ἁμαρτίας). The first two readings probably arose as attempts to clarify the implications of the text. The third simply substitutes the more familiar word ἁμαρτίας ("sin") for the less familiar ἁμαρτήματος ("sin"). Cf. Metzger, Textual Commentary, 70.

i Some MSS (A D Γ 700 et al.) add "and your sisters" (καὶ αἱ ἀδελφαί σου); these words were probably added to the text to prepare for Jesus' reference to his "sister" in v. 35. For a discussion of other explanations, see Metzger, Textual Commentary, 70.

Narrative Unity

As was noted by Klostermann, von Dobschütz, and many others since, the author of Mark sometimes begins a story, interrupts it to tell a second story, and then concludes the first.[92] Mark 3:20-35 is not a classic example of this technique, since vv. 20-21 may be taken as an introduction to the story of vv. 22-30 and the anecdote of vv. 31-35 may be understood independently of vv. 20-21. The two framing units, however, do illuminate each other. The account in vv. 31-35 suggests that those who are described as intending to seize Jesus in v. 21 are his mother and brothers, who are mentioned explicitly in v. 31. The incident in vv. 20-21, in turn, explains why the mother and brothers of Jesus are seeking him in v. 31.[93]

Comment

■ **20-21** Although the earliest recoverable reading is "he went home" (ἔρχεται εἰς οἶκον), it is assumed that the disciples went with Jesus.[94] The phrase εἰς οἶκον could be translated either "into a house" or "home," as in the translation above. The use of the preposition εἰς ("to" or "into") with οἶκον ("house" or "home") is idiomatic for "(going) home."[95] It is likely that reference is being made to the place where Jesus was staying in Capernaum.[96] The statement that the crowd gathered again recalls the scene described in vv. 7-12 in which a multitude had gathered and was pressing upon Jesus, seeking healing. Here the emphasis is on the time it took to deal with the crowd, so that Jesus and his disciples did not even have leisure to eat.[97] It is implied that they were alone in the interlude on the mountain (vv. 13-19), but when they descended the crowd quickly overwhelmed them again.

The phrase οἱ παρ᾽ αὐτοῦ is used in Koine Greek to denote those who are intimately connected with someone, for example, family or relatives.[98] What they heard is not specified, but the context suggests that they heard about Jesus healing people and casting out unclean spir-

92 Erich Klostermann, *Das Markusevangelium* (HNT 3; 4th ed.; Tübingen: Mohr Siebeck, 1950) 36; Ernst von Dobschütz, "Zur Erzählerkunst des Markus," *ZNW* 27 (1928) 193–98. On the history of scholarship on the Markan intercalations, see Geert van Oyen, "Intercalation and Irony in the Gospel of Mark," in van Segbroeck et al., *Four Gospels 1992*, 2:949–74. David Friedrich Strauss, followed by Dibelius, argued that the evangelist composed vv. 20-21 as an introduction to vv. 31-35 (Strauss, *The Life of Jesus Critically Examined* [trans. from 4th Germ. ed.; 3 vols.; London: Chapman Brothers, 1846] 2:201–3; Dibelius, *From Tradition to Gospel*, 47). On more recent scholarship on this literary technique, see James R. Edwards, "Markan Sandwiches: The Significance of Interpolations in Markan Narratives," *NovT* 31 [1989] 193–216, esp. 193–96. Edwards also cites a few comparable examples in Homer, 2 Maccabees, and the Hebrew Bible (ibid., 200–203).

93 Von Dobschütz distinguished two literary techniques employed by the author of Mark. One is the insertion of an unrelated story in the middle of another to allow for the passage of time and to build suspense (6:12-30; 14:1-11; 5:21-43). Another is the linking of two originally unrelated stories by composing an introduction that prepares for the second (3:20-35; 3:7-9 + 4:1 + 4:35-41; 11:11-25; 14:53-72) ("Erzählerkunst," 196–98). Von Dobschütz believed that the juxtaposition of the two accounts in 3:20-35

created a contrast between the benign concern of the relatives of Jesus and the hostility of the scribes from Jerusalem (ibid., 196). As argued below, the reaction of the relatives is in fact a rejection of Jesus and his work, although there is certainly a difference in degree between the two forms of rejection. Edwards goes too far in arguing that the juxtaposition implies that the activity of the relatives of Jesus is satanic ("Markan Sandwiches," 210).

94 See n. a above; contra Theodore C. Skeat, who argued that Jesus went alone (*ΑΡΤΟΝ ΦΑΓΕΙΝ: A Note on Mark iii. 20-21*," in Traianos Gagos and Roger S. Bagnall, eds., *Essays and Texts in Honor of J. David Thomas* [American Studies in Papyrology 42; Oakville, CT: American Society of Papyrologists, 2001] 29–30). I am grateful to Bruce Griffin for bringing this article to my attention.

95 Cf. Aeschylus *Eum.* 459; Sophocles *Phil.* 240.

96 See the commentary on 2:1 above. Skeat argued that "home" here refers to Nazareth ("*ΑΡΤΟΝ ΦΑΓΕΙΝ*," 29).

97 Skeat takes αὐτούς ("they") as referring to the crowd, not to Jesus and the disciples. He argues that the text originally read ὥστε μὴ δύνασθαι αὐτὸν μηδὲ φανῆναι ("so that [Jesus] could not even be seen") (ibid., 30).

98 BAGD, s.v. παρά.

its (cf. vv. 10-11). Their response is to attempt to restrain Jesus from these activities. A brief explanation of their reaction is given: "for they said, 'He has lost his senses'" (ἔλεγον γὰρ ὅτι ἐξέστη). The context suggests that Jesus' family, who lack understanding of his identity and role, think that he is out of his mind. He is actually filled with the divine Spirit that empowers him to heal and cast out demons.[99] An analogous contrast is expressed explicitly by Plato's Socrates:

> And therefore it is just that the mind of the philosopher only has wings, for he is always, so far as he is able, in communion through memory with those things the communion with which causes God to be divine. Now a man who employs such memories rightly is always being initiated into perfect mysteries and he alone becomes truly perfect; but since he separates himself from human interests and turns his attention toward the divine, he is rebuked by the vulgar, who consider him mad and do not know that he is inspired (διὸ δὴ δικαίως μόνη πτερροῦται ἡ τοῦ φιλοσόφου διάνοια· πρὸς γὰρ ἐκείνοις ἀεί ἐστιν μνήμη κατὰ δύναμιν, πρὸς οἷσπερ θεὸς ὢν θεῖός ἐστιν. τοῖς δὲ δὴ τοιούτοις ἀνὴρ ὑπομνήμασιν ὀρθῶς χρώμενος, τελέους ἀεὶ τελετὰς τελούμενος, τέλεος ὄντως μόνος γίγνεται· ἐξιστάμενος δὲ τῶν ἀνθρωπίνων σπουδασμάτων καὶ πρὸς τῷ θείῳ γιγνόμενος νουθετεῖται μὲν ὑπὸ τῶν πολλῶν ὡς παρακινῶν, ἐνθουσιάζων δὲ λέληθε τοὺς πολλούς). (*Phaedr.* 249C–D)[100]

Philo makes a similar point in his interpretation of the story of Hannah, the mother of Samuel:

> Now when grace fills the soul, that soul thereby rejoices and smiles and dances, for it is possessed and inspired, so that to many of the unenlightened it may seem to be drunken, crazy and beside itself (χάριτος δ᾽ ἥτις ἂν πληρωθῇ ψυχή, γέγηθεν εὐθὺς καὶ μει-

διᾷ καὶ ἀνορχεῖται· βεβάκχευται γάρ, ὡς πολλοῖς τῶν ἀνοργιάστων μεθύειν καὶ παρακινεῖν καὶ ἐξεστάναι ἂν δόξαι). (*Ebr.* 36 §145–46)[101]

The Gospel of Mark speaks about a miracle-working messiah, the *Phaedrus* about the philosopher, and Philo about Jewish philosophy as a divine gift. In all three cases, however, the point is made that ordinary people will not understand the person and activity of the divinely inspired person and will think that he or she is out of his or her senses.

A striking and distinctive element in this scene in Mark is the powerful expression of the theme of rejection by one's own family. This element echoes a motif that occurs in one of the psalms of individual lament:

> For it is for your sake that I have borne reproach, that shame has covered my face. I became alienated from my brothers and a stranger to the sons of my mother (ὅτι ἕνεκα σοῦ ὑπήνεγκα ὀνειδισμόν, ἐκάλυψεν ἐντροπὴ τὸ πρόσωπόν μου. ἀπηλλοτριωμένος ἐγενήθην τοῖς ἀδελφοῖς μου, καὶ ξένος τοῖς υἱοῖς τῆς μητρός μου). (Ps 68:8-9 LXX)[102]

Although the brothers of Jesus are not mentioned explicitly in Mark 3:21, his family (οἱ παρ᾽ αὐτοῦ) is further defined in v. 31 as his mother and his brothers. Like Psalm 22, Psalm 69 is a psalm of individual lament that is also cited in the Markan passion narrative.[103] Here, however, it echoes in a quite different way. The reproach and shame borne by the speaker are connected not primarily with the physical suffering and death of Jesus but with the misunderstanding of his charismatic activity. This misunderstanding is tantamount to a rejection of his divine mission, and thus, in the context of Mark as a whole, of his messianic role.[104]

■ **22-30** In Mark, this passage is a controversy-dialogue occasioned by the exorcisms of Jesus in general, not by a particular case. The observation that the author of

---

99 Cf. 1:10 and 3:28-30; see the commentary on the latter verses below.

100 Text and trans. from Harold North Fowler, *Plato*, vol. 1 (LCL; Cambridge, MA: Harvard University Press; London: Heinemann, 1914) 480–83.

101 Text and trans. from Colson and Whitaker, *Philo*, 3:394–95.

102 Cf. Ps 69:9 MT (69:8 RSV).

103 Ps 69(68):22 is probably alluded to in Mark 15:36.

104 See Adela Yarbro Collins, "The Appropriation of the Psalms of Individual Lament by Mark," in Christopher M. Tuckett, ed., *The Scriptures in the Gospels* (BEThL 131; Leuven: Leuven University Press/Uitgeverij Peeters, 1997) 223–41, esp. 235–36.

Matthew combined Mark's version of this passage with another that Luke follows exclusively indicates the existence of a parallel passage in Q.[105] Q's version begins with an account of a specific exorcism, although it is very brief. Bultmann argued that the Q version has the older form.[106] Theissen concluded that the miracle story in Matthew's version serves as the introduction to an apophthegm.[107] Robert C. Tannehill defined each of the Synoptic versions of this narrative as an "objection story."[108]

■ **22** Scribes have been mentioned several times so far in the narrative, but this is the first time that they are said to have come down from Jerusalem.[109] This portrayal is historically plausible, since, if any urban area had a dominant influence on the people of Galilee, it was Jerusalem, not the Herodian cities.[110] The objection or accusation of these scribes is twofold, first, that Jesus is possessed by Beelzebul and, second, that he drives out demons by the ruler of the demons.[111] They attempt to discredit Jesus and his exorcisms by arguing that he is able to exorcise only because he is possessed by the prince of demons. Although no formal legal charge is mentioned, that the officials come from Jerusalem and the nature of their charge against Jesus signify the seriousness of the situation. The description calls to mind, for those familiar with Jewish tradition, two passages in Leviticus and their interpretation in the first century CE:

Do not turn to mediums (האבת) or wizards (הידענים); do not seek them out, to be defiled by them: I am the Lord your God. (Lev 19:31 RSV)

A man or a woman who is a medium (אוב) or wizard (ידעני) shall be put to death; they shall be stoned with stones, their blood shall be upon them. (Lev 20:27 RSV)

In the LXX, the term אוב ("medium") is translated with ἐγγαστρίμυθος in both passages.[112] In these contexts

---

105 The occurrence of such a saying in Q and its wording are uncertain (Robinson et al., *Critical Edition of Q*, 234–35; cf. lxxxii–lxxxiii for an explanation of the sigla). For a detailed comparison of the three accounts and a reconstruction of the version of Q, see Fleddermann, *Mark and Q*, 41–73. His argument that Mark is dependent on Q (p. 61), however, is not compelling; the two documents may be dependent on a common source, written or oral. He also discusses the parallel in *Gos. Thom.* 35, which is more similar to Mark than the versions in Matt 12:29 and Luke 11:21–22; the version in *Thomas* may be dependent on Mark as Fleddermann argues; on the version in *Gos. Thom.*, see also Robinson et al., *Critical Edition of Q*, 234.

106 Bultmann, *History*, 13.

107 Theissen, *Miracle Stories*, 114.

108 Robert C. Tannehill, "Introduction: The Pronouncement Story and Its Types," *Semeia* 20 (1981) 8–9; idem, "Varieties," 107, 110.

109 Mark 1:22 refers simply to "scribes" (γραμματεῖς); 2:6 to "some of the scribes" (τινες τῶν γραμματέων); and 2:16 to "the scribes belonging to the Pharisees" (οἱ γραμματεῖς τῶν Φαρισαίων). On the historical scribes and the scribes as a group in Mark, see the commentary on 1:22 above.

110 Seán Freyne, "Urban-Rural Relations in the Light of the Literary Sources," in idem, *Galilee and Gospel: Collected Essays* (Tübingen: Mohr Siebeck, 2000) 51.

111 According to Mark 3:22, the scribes say, literally, that Jesus "has Beelzebul" (Βεελζεβοὺλ ἔχει). The primary significance of this statement is that Jesus is possessed by Beelzebul, as the man Jesus exorcised

in chap. 5 was possessed by a legion of demons: τὸν ἐσχηκότα τὸν λεγιῶνα (literally, "the one who had had the legion," which means "the one who had been possessed by the legion") (5:15). In the case of Jesus, however, since he is able to cast out demons, a further connotation may be that he has Beelzebul at his disposal. Compare a statement from a magical spell addressed to a deity: "For you are I, and I, you. Whatever I say must happen, for I have your name as a unique phylactery in my heart, and no flesh, although moved, will overpower me; no spirit will stand against me—neither daimon nor visitation nor any other of the evil beings of Hades, because of your name, which I have in my soul and invoke" (σὺ γὰρ εἶ ἐγὼ καὶ ἐγὼ σύ. ὃ ἐ(ὰν) εἴπω, δεῖ γενέσθαι. τὸ γὰρ ὄνομά σου ἔχω ἐν φυλακτήριον ἐν καρδίᾳ τῇ ἐμῇ, καὶ οὐ κατισχύσει με ἄπασα σὰρξ κινουμένη, οὐκ ἀντιτάξεταί μοι πᾶν πνεῦμα—οὐ δαιμόνιον, οὐ συνά(ν)τημα οὐδὲ ἄλλο τι τῶν καθ᾿ Ἅιδου πονηρῶν, δι(ὰ) τὸ σὸν ὄνομα ὃ ἐν τῇ ψυχῇ ἔχω καὶ ἐπικαλοῦμαι) (*PGM* XIII. 795–800; Preisendanz-Henrichs, 2:123; trans. by Morton Smith in Betz, *Magical Papyri*, 191). In another spell (*PGM* IV. 2241–2358) addressed to the moon, the speaker says, "To Hermes, leader of the gods, you promised to contribute to this rite. Aye, in my power I hold (ἔχω) you" (IV. 2330–2332; trans. E. N. O'Neil in Betz, *Magical Papyri*, 80).

112 In one usage, the term ἐγγαστρίμυθος implies that some entity speaks from the belly of the person so described. If the person him- or herself is thought to be the speaker, the appropriate translation is "ven-

the Greek term implies that the medium or prophet has a familiar spirit who enables him or her to prophesy or bring up the dead. Compare the Greek version of 1 Sam 28:8:

> Saul disguised himself and dressed in other clothes and went, he and two men with him, and they went to the woman by night, and he said to her, "Prophesy for me by your familiar spirit and bring up for me whomever I say to you" (Καὶ συνεκαλύψατο Σαουλ καὶ περιεβάλετο ἱμάτια ἕτερα καὶ πορεύεται αὐτὸς καὶ δύο ἄνδρες μετ᾽ αὐτοῦ καὶ ἔρχονται πρὸς τὴν γυναῖκα νυκτὸς καὶ εἶπεν αὐτῇ Μάντευσαι δή μοι ἐν τῷ ἐγγαστριμύθῳ καὶ ἀνάγαγέ μοι ὃν ἐὰν εἴπω σοι). (1 Kgdms 28:8 LXX)[113]

The second passage from Leviticus cited above is referred to in a passage from the *Damascus Document*:

> Every man who preaches apostasy under the dominion of the spirits of Belial shall be judged according to the law relating to those possessed by a ghost or familiar spirit [Lev. xx, 27]

(כל איש אשר ימשלו בו רוחות בליעל ודבר סרה

כמשפט האוב והידעוני ישפט)

(CD 12:2-3)[114]

A similar law occurs in the Mishnah:

> "He that has a familiar spirit" (such is the Python which speaks from his armpits), "and the soothsayer" (such is he that speaks with his mouth), these are [to be put to death] by stoning, and he that inquires of them transgresses against a warning. (m. Sanh. 7.7)[115]

In the cultural contexts in which these traditions were known, the accusation of the officials from Jerusalem implies that Beelzebul is Jesus' familiar spirit and that Jesus deserves a death by stoning.[116]

As noted above in the note on the translation of v. 22, the name Βεελζεβούλ ("Beelzebul") is related to the name בעל זבוב in 2 Kings ("Baal Zebub," which means "Lord of the Flies").[117] The OG translation of this name is Βααλ μυῖα ("Baal the fly").[118] It is likely that בעל זבוב ("Baal Zebub") is a pejorative or mocking play on the name of a well-known Semitic deity, בעל זבל ("Baal Zabul," which means "Baal the prince").[119] The fact that

---

triloquist." Often, however, the context suggests that it is a spirit that speaks through the person; in such contexts the person may be described as ἐγγαστρίμυθος ("one that prophesies from the belly" = ἐγγαστρίμαντις) or the spirit may be so designated; see the discussion above. See also Plutarch's criticism of the popular idea that Apollo enters into the bodies of his prophets and prompts their utterances, using their mouths and voices as instruments (*Def. orac.* 414E). He calls such prophets ἐγγαστρίμυθοι, which, in this context, should probably be translated "ventriloquist." So Babbitt, *Plutarch's Moralia*, 5:376–77. Philo uses the same term in describing the seers of Egypt (*Som.* 1.38 §220). Here also the term should probably be translated "ventriloquist." So Colson and Whitaker, *Philo*, 5:414–15.

113 Compare the parody of this idea in Lucian *Lexiphanes* 20: ἐγγαστρίμυθόν τινα ἔοικα πεπωκέναι ("I would seem to have swallowed a familiar spirit"); text and trans. from Harmon, *Lucian*, 5:320–21.

114 Text from Elisha Qimron, "The Text of CDC," in Magen Broshi, ed., *The Damascus Document Reconsidered* (Jerusalem: Israel Exploration Society/Shrine of the Book, Israel Museum, 1992) 9–49, esp. 33; trans. from Vermes, *Dead Sea Scrolls*, 141. See also 4QD^b (4Q267) frg. 4, 11–12; Baumgarten restores a phrase

את א[ו]בות וא[ת] [ידעוני]ם and translates "ghosts and [familiar spirits]" (*Qumran Cave 4*, 100); 4QD^e (4Q270) 2 i 10; the phrase או ידרוש באוב ובידעונים occurs here and Baumgarten translates ". . . or inquires of ghosts and familiar spirits . . ." (*Qumran Cave 4*, 142–43).

115 Trans. from Danby, *Mishnah*, 392–93; the quotations are from Lev 20:27; the "warning" alludes either to Lev 19:31 or to Deut 18:11.

116 Compare the tradition (a baraita) preserved in some MSS of *b. Sanh.* 43a (part e) that Jesus was condemned to be stoned (and was hanged) because he practiced sorcery and enticed Israel to apostasy. Following this baraita is the statement of the Amora Ulla that Jesus was an enticer (מסית), citing Deut 13:9 (13:8 RSV). For a brief discussion of these passages, see Joseph Klausner, *Jesus of Nazareth: His Life, Times, and Teaching* (New York: Macmillan, 1925) 27–28.

117 See 2 Kgs 1:2, 3, 6, 16; see Herrmann, "Baal Zebub," 293–94.

118 Josephus says that the name of the god was Μυῖα ("Fly") (*Ant.* 9.2.1 §19); the Hebrew name of the deity is transliterated as Beelzebub in the Vulgate (Herrmann, "Baal Zebub," 293).

119 This is the explanation of W. F. Albright, based on

the Synoptic Gospels have something close to the name of this ancient deity, rather than the name that appears in 2 Kings and passages dependent on it, suggests that the deity was still known in Palestine in the first century CE, but as a demon rather than a deity.[120] Although the idea of a prince or ruler could have been derived by speakers of Aramaic from the *Baal*-part of the name, it may be that the author of Mark, followed by the authors of Matthew and Luke, was aware that the *zebul*-part of the name is equivalent to the epithet "prince" or "ruler" ($\overset{\text{?}}{\alpha}\rho\chi\omega\nu$, the term used in v. 22).[121]

The hypothesis that the demon $B\epsilon\epsilon\lambda\zeta\epsilon\beta o\acute{\nu}\lambda$ ("Beelzebul") was known in Palestine in the first century CE is supported by the appearance of a demon of that name in the *Testament of Solomon*, although its date is uncertain. According to this text, the demon Ornias interfered with the building of the First Temple. With the help of the archangels Michael and Ouriel, Solomon overcame this demon and forced him to bring the ruler of the demons ($\acute{o}$ $\overset{\text{?}}{\alpha}\rho\chi\omega\nu$ $\tau\hat{\omega}\nu$ $\delta\alpha\iota\mu o\nu\acute{\iota}\omega\nu$) into Solomon's presence, whose name is $B\epsilon\epsilon\lambda\zeta\epsilon\beta o\acute{\nu}\lambda$ ("Beelzebul").[122] Later, when Solomon asked Beelzebul why he alone was ruler of the demons, he informed Solomon about his origin:

Because I alone am left of the heavenly angels. For I was a holy angel among those of the first rank, the one called "Beelzebul" [Prince Baal] ($\delta\iota\grave{\alpha}$ $\tau\grave{o}$ $\mu\acute{o}\nu o\nu$ $\mu\epsilon$ $\acute{\nu}\pi o\lambda\epsilon\iota\varphi\vartheta\hat{\eta}\nu\alpha\iota$ $\tau\hat{\omega}\nu$ $o\grave{\nu}\rho\alpha\nu\acute{\iota}\omega\nu$ $\grave{\alpha}\gamma\gamma\acute{\epsilon}\lambda\omega\nu.$ $\grave{\epsilon}\gamma\grave{\omega}$ $\gamma\grave{\alpha}\rho$ $\overset{\text{?}}{\eta}\mu\eta\nu$ $\grave{\epsilon}\nu$ $\pi\rho\acute{\omega}\tau o\iota\varsigma$ $o\grave{\nu}\rho\acute{\alpha}\nu\iota o\varsigma$ $\overset{\text{?}}{\alpha}\gamma\gamma\epsilon\lambda o\varsigma$ $\acute{o}$ $\pi\rho o\sigma\alpha\gamma o-\rho\epsilon\nu\acute{o}\mu\epsilon\nu o\varsigma$ $B\epsilon\epsilon\lambda\zeta\epsilon\beta o\acute{\nu}\lambda$). (*T. Sol.* 6:2)[123]

When Solomon asked about his activities, he replied:

For my part, I destroy through tyrants, I cause demons to be worshiped among human beings, and I awaken holy men and chosen priests to desire. I instigate envy and murders in cities and bring on wars ($\kappa\grave{\alpha}\gamma\grave{\omega}$ $\kappa\alpha\vartheta\alpha\iota\rho\hat{\omega}$ $\delta\iota\grave{\alpha}$ $\tau\nu\rho\acute{\alpha}\nu\nu\omega\nu$ $\kappa\alpha\grave{\iota}$ $\tau\grave{\alpha}$ $\delta\alpha\iota\mu\acute{o}\nu\iota\alpha$ $\pi o\iota\hat{\omega}$ $\pi\alpha\rho\grave{\alpha}$ $\grave{\alpha}\nu\vartheta\rho\acute{\omega}\pi o\iota\varsigma$ $\sigma\acute{\epsilon}\beta\epsilon\sigma\vartheta\alpha\iota$ $\kappa\alpha\grave{\iota}$ $\tau o\grave{\nu}\varsigma$ $\grave{\alpha}\gamma\acute{\iota}o\nu\varsigma$ $\kappa\alpha\grave{\iota}$ $\tau o\grave{\nu}\varsigma$ $\grave{\epsilon}\kappa\lambda\epsilon\kappa\tau o\grave{\nu}\varsigma$ $\acute{\iota}\epsilon\rho\epsilon\hat{\iota}\varsigma$ $\epsilon\grave{\iota}\varsigma$ $\grave{\epsilon}\pi\iota\vartheta\nu\mu\acute{\iota}\alpha\nu$ $\grave{\epsilon}\gamma\epsilon\acute{\iota}\rho\omega.$ $\kappa\alpha\grave{\iota}$ $\varphi\vartheta\acute{o}\nu o\nu\varsigma$ $\grave{\epsilon}\nu$ $\pi\acute{o}\lambda\epsilon\sigma\iota$ $\kappa\alpha\grave{\iota}$ $\varphi\acute{o}\nu o\nu\varsigma$ $\grave{\alpha}\pi o\tau\epsilon\lambda\hat{\omega}$ $\kappa\alpha\grave{\iota}$ $\pi o\lambda\acute{\epsilon}-\mu o\nu\varsigma$ $\grave{\epsilon}\pi\acute{\alpha}\gamma\omega$). (*T. Sol.* 6:4)[124]

This self-description suggests that Beelzebul was one of "the sons of God" who took to wife some of "the daughters of men" according to Gen 6:1-4. His indirect claim to leadership may imply that he is equivalent to Semyaza, said to be the leader of "the watchers, the sons of

---

the Ugaritic texts from Ras Shamra and summarized by Herrmann, "Baal Zebub," 295. According to 2 Kings 1, the oracle of this god was in Ekron, a Philistine town. Evidently the cult of this Semitic deity was taken over by the Philistines of Ekron and incorporated into their local cult (ibid., 293).

120 Note that the phrase דבב בעל (*bēl dēbāb*, "enemy") occurs, partially restored, in 4Q560 1:1; see Douglas L. Penney and Michael O. Wise, "By the Power of Beelzebub: An Aramaic Incantation Formula from Qumran (4Q560)," *JBL* 113 (1994) 627–50, esp. 631–33, who interpret the term as "The Accuser" and conclude that it is equivalent to Beelzebul. See also Alexander, "Demonology of the Dead Sea Scrolls," 341 n. 31, who accepts the equivalence with Beelzebub and understands it as a designation for the leader of the demons. See also Esther Eshel, "Genres of Magical Texts," in Lange et al., *Demons*, 396–98; Eshel, "Apotropaic Prayers in the Second Temple Period," in Chazon, *Liturgical Perspectives*, 69–88, esp. 84.

121 See also Matt 12:24 and Luke 11:15, where the name $B\epsilon\epsilon\lambda\zeta\epsilon\beta o\acute{\nu}\lambda$ ("Beelzebul") is combined with the epithet $\overset{\text{?}}{\alpha}\rho\chi\omega\nu$ $\tau\hat{\omega}\nu$ $\delta\alpha\iota\mu o\nu\acute{\iota}\omega\nu$ ("ruler of the demons"). See Herrmann, "Baal Zebub," 294. L. K. Handy argued that זבל ("Zabul") should be translated

"ruler," since it designates a person who is governing or ruling; see the summary and literature cited by Herrmann, 295–96. On the Jewish and Christian tendency to identify pagan gods with demons, see Adela Yarbro Collins, "Pergamon in Early Christian Literature," in Helmut Koester, ed., *Pergamon: Citadel of the Gods* (Harrisburg, PA: Trinity Press International, 1998) 163–84.

122 The "ruler of the demons" ($\acute{o}$ $\overset{\text{?}}{\alpha}\rho\chi\omega\nu$ $\tau\hat{\omega}\nu$ $\delta\alpha\iota-\mu o\nu\acute{\iota}\omega\nu$) is mentioned in *T. Sol.* 2:8; that his name is "Beelzebul" ($B\epsilon\epsilon\lambda\zeta\epsilon\beta o\acute{\nu}\lambda$) becomes clear in 3:1; cf. 3:5. In 3:6 he calls himself "Beelzebul, the chief of the demons" ($B\epsilon\epsilon\lambda\zeta\epsilon\beta o\grave{\nu}\lambda$ $\tau\hat{\omega}\nu$ $\delta\alpha\iota\mu o\nu\acute{\iota}\omega\nu$ $\acute{o}$ $\overset{\text{?}}{\epsilon}\xi\alpha\rho\chi o\varsigma$). Text from McCown, *Testament of Solomon*, 16*; my trans. D. C. Duling translates $\acute{o}$ $\overset{\text{?}}{\alpha}\rho\chi\omega\nu$ $\tau\hat{\omega}\nu$ $\delta\alpha\iota\mu o\nu\acute{\iota}\omega\nu$ as "the Prince of Demons" and $\tau\hat{\omega}\nu$ $\delta\alpha\iota-\mu o\nu\acute{\iota}\omega\nu$ $\acute{o}$ $\overset{\text{?}}{\epsilon}\xi\alpha\rho\chi o\varsigma$ as "the ruler of the demons" ("The Testament of Solomon," in *OTP* 1:964).

123 Text from McCown, *Testament of Solomon*, 25*; my trans.

124 Text from McCown, *Testament of Solomon*, 26*; my trans.

heaven" who chose human wives, according to the elaboration of the Genesis passage in the Book of the Watchers (*1 Enoch* 6:1-3).[125] Other passages imply that Azazel was their leader, and his association with the weapons of war fits with Beelzebul's activity of bringing on wars.[126]

In the *Testament of Solomon*, another demon clarifies Beelzebul's role as ruler of the demons:

> Seeing that he is the master of the spirits in the air, on the earth and under the earth, Beelzebul gives advice regarding the activities of each one of us, and for this reason I too came up from the sea to receive some decree from him (ἐπεὶ δὲ ὁ Βεελζεβοὺλ ὁ τῶν ἀερίων καὶ ἐπιγείων καὶ καταχθονίων πνευμάτων δεσπότης συμβουλεύει εἰς τὰς καθ' ἑνὸς ἑκάστου ἡμῶν πράξεις, διὰ τοῦτο κἀγὼ ἀνέβην ἐκ τῆς θαλάσσης σκέψιν τινὰ λαβεῖν παρ' αὐτῷ). (*T. Sol.* 16:3)[127]

This demon, Kunopegos, then tells how, when he went to Beelzebul for a consultation, the ruler of the demons bound him and forced him to stand before Solomon. These traditions make clear why the enemies of the Markan Jesus, seeing that he was a successful exorcist, linked him to Beelzebul, the one who controlled all the demons.

■ **23-26** In his initial response to the scribes, the Markan Jesus constructs an argument using "parables," or better "comparisons" (παραβολαῖς), in the classic rhetorical sense.[128] The metaphorical language is clear and straightforward in order to point out to Jesus' opponents the illogical character of their accusation.

The phrase "And he summoned them" in v. 23 indicates a slight shift of scene or setting from the general statement about the accusation made by Jesus' opponents in v. 22 to his response in vv. 23-30. This is the first time in Mark that Jesus is said to speak "in parables" or "in comparisons" (ἐν παραβολαῖς). According to Aristotle, the "comparison" (παραβολή) is one of the proofs common to all branches of rhetoric. It belongs to the category of the example, which has two kinds, historical and fictional. The comparison is a fictional argument but, unlike the fable, one that is based on a plausible situation in daily life.[129] In a rhetorical situation, the speaker makes a point by a simple, clear illustration. If the metaphorical meaning is not clear, the argument is not effective. In the first part of his response, Jesus argues in just such a straightforward manner. When the scribes accuse him of being possessed and of casting out demons because of a pact with the ruler of the demons, Jesus points out the illogical character of this accusation.

In v. 23 the Markan Jesus assumes that his audience will accept "Satan" (σατανᾶς) as the equivalent of Beelzebul. The context makes it clear that σατανᾶς ("Satan") is a personal name. The noun שָׂטָן in the Hebrew Bible is not a personal name (with perhaps one exception), and its meaning varies with the context. Its usage includes "adversary," "opponent," "accuser," "enemy," and "slanderer." In Job 1–2 and Zech 3:1-2, it is used with the definite article for a celestial being who takes the role of the accuser in the heavenly court.[130] In 1 Chr 21:1, the noun is used without the article, either in an indefinite sense ("an adversary") or as a proper name,

---

125 Trans. from Nickelsburg and VanderKam, 23. Cf. *1 Enoch* 9:7; 10:11.

126 *1 Enoch* 8:1 (where weapons are mentioned); 9:6; 10:4, 8. The fact that two leaders are mentioned may be due to the combination of two different traditions about the fallen angels or Watchers. The *Apocalypse of Abraham* alludes to the role of Azazel as leader of the fallen angels (14:1-14).

127 Text from McCown, *Testament of Solomon*, 48*; my trans.

128 For a rhetorical analysis of Mark 3:22-30 pars., see Vernon K. Robbins, "Rhetorical Composition & the Beelzebul Controversy," in Mack and Robbins, *Patterns of Persuasion*, 161–93.

129 Aristotle *Rhet.* 2.20.1-4 (1393 a-b). Aristotle defines the comparison (παραβολή) functionally, not for-

mally. Later rhetoricians, e.g., Longinus and Demetrius, used the term for a specific stylistic device; see Elian Cuvillier, *Le concept de ΠΑΡΑΒΟΛΗ dans le second évangile: Son arrière-plan littéraire, sa signification dans le cadre de la rédaction marcienne, son utilisation dans la tradition de Jésus* (EtB n.s. 19; Paris: Gabalda, 1993) 22–24, 35–40.

130 In both cases, the LXX renders הַשָּׂטָן ("the accuser") with ὁ διάβολος ("the slanderer" or "the Slanderer," i.e., "the Devil"). Peggy L. Day has argued that the use of the term הַשָּׂטָן ("the accuser") should not be understood in terms of a specific role or office, since no such office has been convincingly identified in ancient Israel; the idea is rather that the individual has the current and temporary status of accuser ("Satan (I-III)," *DDD* 726–30).

"Satan."[131] Whereas 2 Sam 24:1 states that God incited David to take a census of the people, 1 Chr 21:1 portrays an (angelic) adversary or Satan as the instigator of the census. Thus, the ambiguity of the character of God is reduced, and incitement to sin becomes the work of a lesser being. "Satan" as a personal name appears seldom in the Jewish apocryphal and pseudepigraphical literature. As noted above, the leaders of the evil spirits in *1 Enoch* are Semyaza and Azazel.[132] In *Jubilees*, it is Mastema who plays this role (*Jub.* 10:8; 19:28).[133] Although "Belial" is the most common name for the evil angel in the Dead Sea Scrolls, the name "Satan" is occasionally used.[134] In rabbinic literature, שׂטן ("Satan") is used regularly as a proper name.[135]

The varied usage in the extracanonical Jewish literature, as well as the substitution of σατανᾶς ("Satan") for Βεελζεβούλ ("Beelzebul") in this passage, indicates that, although the concept of a leader of the evil spirits had emerged, that being was called by various names. Since it is a transliteration from Hebrew or Aramaic, and the LXX and most Greek works from the Second Temple period prefer ὁ διάβολος ("the slanderer" or "the Slanderer," i.e., "the Devil"), the use of σατανᾶς ("Satan") here is a clear Semitism.[136]

The comparisons in vv. 24 and 25 are hypothetical; they express principles based on common sense. The saying about a divided kingdom (v. 24) is a present general condition, and the one about a divided house or household (v. 25) is a future more vivid condition.[137] These are the "parables" or "comparisons" proper. They are framed by references to the actual accusation against Jesus made by the scribes: "How can Satan drive out Satan?" (v. 23) and "And if Satan has rebelled against himself and is divided, he is not able to stand, but is at an end" (v. 26). The latter saying is a past condition.[138] In this saying, the Markan Jesus does not necessarily grant that Satan has rebelled against himself, but he points out what the consequences would be if Satan had done so. Even if the officials were right about what Jesus was doing, the result would be that the power of Satan was coming to an end.

The figurative language about a divided kingdom in relation to Satan suggests that Satan has a kingdom, opposed to the kingdom of God although permitted as part of the divine plan. Jesus confronts Satan in the wilderness (1:12-13) and then begins to proclaim the nearness of the kingdom of God (1:14-15). The implied notion

---

131 Victor P. Hamilton concluded that each of these translations is valid ("Satan," *ABD* 5:985–89, esp. 987). Day argued that the noun is not a proper name here ("Satan (I-III)," 729–30).

132 "Semyaza" is a transliteration from the Ethiopic; "Shemihazah," from the Aramaic of the same name; see *1 Enoch* 6:3, 7. The name "Azazel" derives from the name עזאזל ("Azazel"), which appears in the account of the scapegoat ritual in Leviticus 16. This name is probably a metathesis of עזזאל ("fierce god" or "Mot is fierce"). If so, then Azazel may be identified with the Canaanite god Mot, whom the biblical tradition has demoted to a demon. See Jacob Milgrom, *Leviticus: A New Translation with Introduction and Commentary* (3 vols.; AB 3, 3A, 3B; New York: Doubleday, 1991, 2000, 2001) 1:1021. If this interpretation is correct, the figure of Azazel is analogous to Beelzebul, who is also a demoted Canaanite deity. The most common designation of the leader of the evil spirits in the DSS is "Belial." The name derives from the Hebrew word בליעל ("worthlessness" or "wickedness"). See Theodore J. Lewis, "Belial," *ABD* 1:654–55.

133 In *Jub.* 11:5, this spirit is called "Prince Mastema." The name "Mastema" derives from the verb שׂטם

("to treat as an enemy," "to hate"), which is a byform of the verb שׂטן ("to treat as an enemy"), from which the noun שׂטן ("adversary" or "accuser" and eventually "Satan") derives. The noun משׂטמה (*maśṭēmâ*, meaning "hostility") appears in Hos 9:7-8 and in the DSS. See Jan Willem van Henten, "Mastemah," *DDD* 553–54.

In *Jub.* 10:11, the noun שׂטן ("accuser") is used with the article, thus not as a proper name. Hamilton concluded that this noun without the article in *Jub.* 23:29 is used as a proper name ("Satan," 987), but VanderKam translates "a satan" (*Book of Jubilees*, 149). The trans. by R. H. Charles (revised by C. Rabin) apparently takes the noun as a proper name in both passages, since it is capitalized (*AOT*, 42, 76), although "adversary" is given as an alternative translation in 23:29.

134 11QPsᵃ (11Q5) 19:15; see Alexander, "Demonology of the Dead Sea Scrolls," 341. On Belial and Mastema, see Eshel, "Demonology in Palestine," chap. 2.

135 Hamilton, "Satan," 988.

136 Cilliers Breytenbach, "Satan (I, IV)," *DDD* 726–27, 730–32.

137 See Smyth §2297.

138 Smyth §2291.2; cf. 2289 (apodosis without ἄν).

of a "kingdom of Satan" is analogous to the "dominion of Belial" (ממשלת בליעל) in the Dead Sea Scrolls.[139]

■ **27** In this saying, Jesus' argument returns to figurative language and reaches its climax. Here, however, he does not use a comparison in the classic rhetorical sense. This brief saying is more like a fable in that it veils a claim that the Markan Jesus does not want to make explicit.

Karl Meuli has shown that the ancient $\alpha\hat{\imath}\nu o\varsigma$, the original, living fable, was a cryptic, meaningful story that veiled the essential thing that needed to be said. It may, for example, disguise a request or a warning. Often it is a weaker, lesser person directing a request or a warning to a superior, powerful person. When it is a more powerful person addressing weaker ones, it may have an element of threatening irony. Originally, the fable was not the vehicle of a universal truth, a moral that could apply to any time and place. It was rather the diplomatic mediator of a very particular, urgent truth, meant to affect a particular hearer in a concrete situation. It is an artistic way of speaking the truth that emerges, on the one hand, out of the need to remove the sting from the dangerous, wounding sharpness of critical truth and, on the other, from the pleasure and competence in fable-making and in persuading with this art. The better and more impressive the comparison, the more reconciling and persuasive it will be.[140] If Jesus is viewed as the partner with lower status in this dialogue and the authoritative officials from Jerusalem as having high status, this saying can be seen as an indirect claim of Jesus that he is a messianic figure. He diplomatically invites the scribes to

infer from his exorcisms that he is an authoritative agent of God. If, however, Jesus is viewed as the more powerful partner, in view of his messianic status, then the saying may be read as an ironic threat. If Jesus has the power to bind Satan, he has power over the officials as well!

In any case, the comparison with the strong man and his house makes clear that Jesus rejects the scribes' premise that Satan has rebelled against himself. Rather, someone stronger than Satan has bound him. Satan is strong ($\iota\sigma\chi\nu\rho\acute{o}\varsigma$), but Jesus is stronger. This argument recalls the saying of John the Baptist in 1:7, "The one who is stronger than I ($\acute{o}\ \iota\sigma\chi\nu\rho\acute{o}\tau\epsilon\rho\acute{o}\varsigma\ \mu o\nu$) is coming after me." This designation of Jesus evokes connotations of the divine warrior and his (royal) messiah or other agent in battle.[141]

On the literal level, Satan is compared to any strong man with household goods, and Jesus to a stronger man who is able to bind the first man and take his goods. Jesus' metaphorical "binding" ($\delta\acute{\epsilon}\omega$), however, has a range of intertextual associations. Jesus' binding of Satan is analogous to God's binding ($\delta\acute{\epsilon}\omega$) of Leviathan in the book of Job and Raphael's binding ($\delta\acute{\epsilon}\omega$) of Azazel, the leader of the fallen angels, in *1 Enoch*.[142] The result of the binding of Leviathan is the (re-)establishment of God's rule over the earth, and of the binding of Azazel, the restoration of the earth that had been ruined by the works of the teaching of Azazel.[143] For certain members of the audience, the notion of Jesus binding Satan might have evoked the Greek binding spells.[144] In certain Jewish texts, although angels accomplish the binding, the context suggests a

---

139 1QS 2:19; cf. 3:23–24; 1QM 1:14–15; Alexander, "Demonology of the Dead Sea Scrolls," 351–52 n. 55.

140 Karl Meuli, "Herkunft und Wesen der Fabel," in *Schweiz. Archiv für Volkskunde* 50 (1954) 65–88; also issued separately and also appeared as "Herkunft und Wesen der Fabel: Ein Vortrag," in idem, *Gesammelte Schriften* (Basel/Stuttgart: Schwabe, 1975) 2:731–56, especially 742–44.

141 See the commentary on 1:7-8 above and the Introduction, *Jesus as Prophet*. According to *T. Levi* 18:12, the eschatological priest, perhaps a priestly messiah, will bind Beliar: "and Beliar will be bound by him" ($\kappa\alpha\grave{\imath}\ \acute{o}\ B\epsilon\lambda\iota\grave{\alpha}\rho\ \delta\epsilon\vartheta\acute{\eta}\sigma\epsilon\tau\alpha\iota\ \acute{\nu}\pi'\ \alpha\acute{\nu}\tau o\hat{\nu}$); text from Marinus de Jonge, *The Testaments of the Twelve Patriarchs: A Critical Edition of the Greek Text* (PVTG 1.2; Leiden: Brill, 1978) 49; ET idem, "The Testaments of the Twelve Patriarchs," *AOT* 537. Cf. *T. Dan* 5:10–11.

142 Job 40:26, 29 LXX; *1 Enoch* 10:4; cf. 18:16; for the Greek text, see Matthew Black, ed., *Apocalypsis Henochi Graece* (PVTG 3; Leiden: Brill, 1970) 24–25, 31; cf. *Jub.* 10:5-11. See also the binding of the ancient serpent, identified with Satan, by an angel in Rev 20:1-3.

143 Job 41:1-2 LXX; *1 Enoch* 10:8; Black, *Apocalypsis Henochi Graece*, 25. The binding of Beliar in *T. Levi* 18:12 is associated with the opening of the gates of Paradise and eschatological joy; in *T. Dan* 5 with eternal peace, with rest in Eden, and with joy in the new Jerusalem.

144 The technical term for a binding spell, $\kappa\alpha\tau\acute{\alpha}\delta\epsilon\sigma\mu o\varsigma$, derives from the verb $\kappa\alpha\tau\alpha\delta\acute{\epsilon}\omega$ ("bind down" or "bind fast"); see Christopher A. Faraone, "The Agonistic Context of Early Greek Binding Spells," in idem and Dirk Obbink, eds., *Magika Hiera: Ancient Greek Magic and Religion* (New York/Oxford: Oxford

magical procedure or exorcism (Tob 8:3; *Jub.* 48:15-19).[145] In any case, the comparison in this verse suggests that the exorcisms of Jesus constitute a struggle with Satan in which Jesus will be victorious and that the result will be the reestablishment of God's rule over the earth.

The specific wording of the saying, with its emphasis on "first" binding the strong man and "then" plundering his house, suggests that Jesus had "bound" Satan before he began performing his exorcisms. The reference may be to the scene described in 1:12-13, in which Jesus is tested by Satan. In that context the outcome is not explicitly stated. The saying in v. 27, however, suggests that the outcome was Jesus' victory over Satan and the subsequent waning of Satan's power.[146]

■ **28-30** The controversy-dialogue concludes with a nonparabolic saying (vv. 28-29) and its application (v. 30).[147] Bultmann classified the saying about the sin against the Spirit (vv. 28-29) as a legal saying or church rule.[148] M. Eugene Boring defined it as a prophetic saying.[149]

The earliest recoverable form of the saying probably stated that all abusive remarks will be forgiven the "son of man," that is, any human being, except insults of the Holy Spirit. The "son of man" became "the sons of men" in Mark and "Son of Man" in Q.[150]

The idea of an unforgivable sin is attested in an inscription from Attica dated to the late second century CE that contains rules for the cult of Men related to a temple in Sounion. It states that anyone who meddles with the property of the god commits a sin against Men Tyrannos that cannot be expiated ($\mathrm{^{\circ}O\varsigma\ \mathring{a}\nu\ \delta\grave{e}\ \pi o\lambda\upsilon\pi\rho\alpha\gamma}$-$\mu o\nu\acute{\eta}\sigma\eta\ \tau\grave{\alpha}\ \tau o\hat{\upsilon}\ \vartheta\epsilon o\hat{\upsilon}\ \mathring{\eta}\ \pi\epsilon\rho\iota\epsilon\rho\gamma\acute{\alpha}\sigma\eta\tau\alpha\iota,\ \mathring{\alpha}\mu\alpha\rho\tau\acute{\iota}\alpha\nu$ $\mathring{o}\varphi\epsilon\iota\lambda\acute{\epsilon}\tau\omega\ M\eta\nu\grave{\iota}\ T\upsilon\rho\acute{\alpha}\nu\nu\omega\iota,\ \mathring{\eta}\nu\ o\mathring{\upsilon}\ \mu\grave{\eta}\ \delta\acute{\upsilon}\nu\alpha\tau\alpha\iota\ \mathring{e}\xi$-$\epsilon\iota\lambda\acute{\alpha}\sigma\alpha\sigma\vartheta\alpha\iota$).[151] This instance supports Bultmann's definition of Mark 3:28-29 as a legal saying.

Verse 30 makes clear that the legal saying of vv. 28-29 is applied in the context to the accusers of the Markan Jesus, the scribes from Jerusalem. Their claim that Jesus exorcised by the power of a demon was an offense

---

University Press, 1991) 3–32, esp. 21 n. 3; see also John G. Gager, ed., *Curse Tablets and Binding Spells from the Ancient World* (New York/Oxford: Oxford University Press, 1992); Fritz Graf, *Magic in the Ancient World* (Cambridge, MA/London: Harvard University Press) 118–74.

145   See Klauck, *Allegorie und Allegorese*, 181. It is striking that, according to *Jub.* 48:18, the leader of the evil spirits is bound so that the Israelites may plunder the utensils of the Egyptians; cf. the plunder of the strong man's σκεῦα (lit., "utensils") in Mark 3:27. For the translation "utensils" in *Jub.* 48:18, see VanderKam, *Book of Jubilees*, 314–15.

146   See Robinson, *Problem of History*, 76–80.

147   The use of an "introductory Amen" is found in the OT, but it regularly confirms what precedes, not what follows, as here and elsewhere in the Gospels. The formula "Amen (truly) I say to you" is a distinctive element of the Gospel tradition (Swete, 67). It occurs only on the lips of Jesus in the Gospels (John R. Donahue and Daniel J. Harrington, *The Gospel of Mark* [SacP 2; Collegeville, MN: Liturgical Press, 2002] 131). The word "Amen" may, as Wellhausen suggested, have been retained in Hebrew transliteration because it was characteristic of the speech of Jesus (ad loc.). But the use of the formula does not guarantee that the saying in question goes back to the historical Jesus.

148   Bultmann, *History*, 130–31.

149   M. Eugene Boring, "The Unforgivable Sin Logion Mark III 28-29/Matt XII 31-32/Luke XII 10: Formal

Analysis and History of the Tradition," *NovT* 18 (1976) 258–79, esp. 258 and n. 2.

150   So Bultmann (*History*, 131), following Wellhausen, who argued that the version with "Son of Man" arose out of a misunderstanding. It may, however, have been a deliberate change in order to adapt the saying to a context of mission. Those who had rejected Jesus (the Son of Man on earth) have a second chance to respond to the preaching of his followers who possess the Holy Spirit. Those who reject their message will not have another chance, but will be condemned. The parallel in *Gos. Thom.* 44 seems to be a further development of the Q-form of the saying. Boring reconstructed a pre-Markan form of the saying and concluded that the underlying Aramaic saying referred to "the son of man" (בר נשא) ("Unforgivable Sin Logion," 274–76). He discusses the possibility that the first part of the Q-form of the saying refers not to the rejection of the earthly Jesus as Son of Man but to the denial of the exalted Son of Man by Christians under duress (ibid., 278).

151   Text from Eugene N. Lane, *Corpus Monumentorum Religionis Dei Menis*, vol. 1: *The Monuments and Inscriptions* (EPRO 19; Leiden: Brill, 1971) no. 13, lines 14–16; p. 9. For discussion see ibid., vol. 3, *Interpretations and Testimonia* (1976) 7–16, esp. 12. Cf. Hans-Josef Klauck, "Die kleinasiatischen Beichtinschriften und das Neue Testament," in Cancik et al., *Geschichte*, 3:63–87, esp. 74–75.

against the Holy Spirit, the power by which he cast out demons (cf. 1:10), and was an unforgivable sin. Although we cannot be certain about it, the occasion for the inclusion of this saying here may have been controversies at the time of the evangelist, regarding either Jesus' exorcisms or those performed at the time by his followers.

■ **31-35** Bultmann classified Mark 3:20-21, 31-35 as a biographical apophthegm. He concluded that the oldest part of the passage is the saying about those who do the will of God in v. 35; the narrative was composed to give concrete form to the saying in an impressively symbolic fashion. Those who do God's will are depicted as an audience gathered around Jesus eager to learn from him. He also concluded that v. 21 rests on good and ancient tradition.[152]

It is likely, however, that the story was preserved, if not composed, because of the ongoing importance of the tension between doing God's will and family ties. Such tension was often expressed in ancient texts. It had two dimensions; on the one hand, ties of kinship were to be ignored if close relatives attempted to lead one away from God or the good; on the other hand, those who shared devotion to God or to the good were one's true kin. Both themes are expressed in Philo's discussion of Deut 13:1-11. He first argues that any prophet who advocates worship of the gods recognized in the different cities should be rejected as a false prophet. He goes on to say that, even if one's brother or son or daughter or wife, the mistress of one's household, or true friend urges one to do so, one should not only refuse, but punish that person as a public enemy, taking little thought for the close relationship (οἰκειότης) involved:

Let there be then for us one close relationship and one mark of friendship, namely, the desire to please God and the saying and doing of everything that fulfills our duty to God (ἔστω γὰρ ἡμῖν μία οἰκειότης καὶ φιλίας ἓν σύμβολον ἡ πρὸς θεὸν ἀρέσκεια καὶ τὸ πάντα λέγειν τε καὶ πράττειν ὑπὲρ εὐσεβείας). (Philo *Spec. leg.* 1.58 §316)[153]

The Markan passage expresses the same pattern, but inverted. According to Deuteronomy and Philo, religious people should reject a prophet who attempts to lead them astray. According to Mark, Jesus, who is among other things a true prophet, rejects his family because they try to prevent him from continuing his work as God's agent (vv. 20-21).

Similar themes are sounded in Xenophon's defense of Socrates against the charge that he corrupted the youth:

"But," said his accuser, "Socrates taught sons to treat their fathers with contempt: he persuaded them that he made his companions wiser than their fathers." . . . "But," said his accuser, "Socrates caused his companions to dishonour not only their fathers, but their other relations as well, by saying that invalids and litigants get benefit not from their relations, but from their doctor or their counsel. Of friends too he said that their goodwill was worthless, unless they could combine with it some power to help one: only those deserved honour who knew what was the right thing to do, and could explain it. Thus by leading the young to think that he excelled in wisdom and in ability to make others wise, he had such an effect on his companions that no one counted for anything in their estimation in comparison with him" (Ἀλλὰ Σωκράτης γ᾽, ἔφη ὁ κατήγορος, τοὺς πατέρας προπηλακίζειν ἐδίδασκε, πείθων μὲν τοὺς συνόντας ἑαυτῷ σοφωτέρους ποιεῖν τῶν πατέρων . . . Ἀλλὰ Σωκράτης γε, ἔφη ὁ κατήγορος, οὐ μόνον τοὺς πατέρας, ἀλλὰ καὶ τοὺς ἄλλους συγγενεῖς ἐποίει ἐν ἀτιμίᾳ εἶναι παρὰ τοῖς ἑαυτῷ συνοῦσι, λέγων, ὡς οὔτε τοὺς κάμνοντας οὔτε τοὺς δικαζομένους οἱ συγγενεῖς ὠφελοῦσιν, ἀλλὰ τοὺς μὲν οἱ ἰατροί, τοὺς δὲ οἱ συνδικεῖν ἐπιστάμενοι. ἔφη δὲ καὶ περὶ τῶν φίλων αὐτὸν λέγειν, ὡς οὐδὲν ὄφελος εὔνους εἶναι, εἰ μὴ καὶ ὠφελεῖν δυνήσονται· μόνους δὲ φάσκειν αὐτὸν ἀξίους εἶναι τιμῆς τοὺς εἰδότας τὰ δέοντα καὶ ἑρμηνεῦσαι δυναμένους· ἀναπείθοντα οὖν τοὺς νέους αὐτόν, ὡς αὐτὸς εἴη

---

152 Bultmann, *History*, 29–30. For a summary of recent redaction-critical studies of this passage, see Stephen C. Barton, *Discipleship and Family Ties in Mark and Matthew* (SNTSMS 80; Cambridge/New York: Cambridge University Press, 1994) 69–76.

153 Text from Colson and Whitaker, *Philo*, 7:282; my

trans. See also Barton, *Discipleship and Family Ties*, 24–25. Compare also Philo *Abr.* 6 §31.

σοφώτατός τε καὶ ἄλλους ἱκανώτατος ποιῆσαι σοφούς, οὕτω διατιθέναι τοὺς ἑαυτῷ συνόντας, ὥστε μηδαμοῦ παρ᾽ αὐτοῖς τοὺς ἄλλους εἶναι πρὸς αὐτόν). (*Mem.* 1.2.49-52)[154]

Xenophon admits that Socrates spoke in this way and stresses that his aim was to teach that reason and usefulness are more important than the bond of familiarity.[155]

It is noteworthy that Xenophon includes fathers, whereas Philo and the author of Mark omit them. The reason is probably that neither of the latter two authors wished to make explicit the possibility that a father would oppose what was best for his son or daughter or seem to encourage rebellion against one's father.[156]

A letter attributed to Diogenes of Sinope (fourth cent. BCE), which was probably written at the end of the second or the beginning of the third century CE, criticizes Homer for referring to Zeus as the father of both men and the gods:

Now when the son of Meles called Zeus the father of both men and gods, he did not do him any honor, but degraded him, since I find it difficult to believe those to be children of Zeus whose own parents repudiate them because of their wickedness (οὐδὲ γὰρ ὁ τοῦ Μέλετος εἰπὼν τὸν Δία πατέρα ἀνδρῶν τε θεῶν τε ἐκύδηνεν ἀλλ᾽ ἐμείωσεν, ἐπεὶ χαλεπόν, εἰ οὓς οἱ γεννήσαντες διὰ πονηρίαν ἀπολέγονται, Διὸς εἶναι παῖδας πιστεύομεν). (Pseudo-Diogenes 41)[157]

Here we see an example of a related theme, that good parents should dissociate themselves from their, presumably grown, children when they do evil.

The Markan scene, then, functions not primarily to record an incident in the life of Jesus but to make the point that doing the will of God is more important than one's relationships with mother, brothers, and sisters. It also suggests that listening to Jesus (or to the tradition about him) is the way that one discerns the will of God.[158] It may also imply that the followers of Jesus formed communities that they considered to be metaphorical families. There is evidence that adherents of the Qumran community who practiced marriage referred to certain leaders of the community as "fathers" and "mothers." The offenses of "murmuring (לון) against the fathers" and "murmuring against the mothers" are mentioned in a fragmentary penal code from Cave 4 (4Q270 frg. 7 i 13-14) that is related to the *Damascus Document* (CD).[159] Those who "murmur" or rebel against the "fathers" are to be expelled from the community, whereas those who do so against the "mothers" are to be penalized for ten days. Another fragmentary text from Qumran attests to a group of metaphorical "brothers" (אחים) who seem to be equivalent to the group called "mature men (but younger than the elders)" (אשישים) (4Q502 frg. 9 lines 4, 9, 11).[160] It also refers to a group of elderly women called "sisters" (אחיות) (frg. 96).[161]

Certain of Philo's remarks may indicate a similar notion of a metaphorical family among the Essenes and the Therapeutae. Concerning the Essenes he says:

The old men too even if they are childless are treated as parents of a not merely numerous but very filial family and regularly close their life with an exceed-

154 Text and trans. from Edgar C. Marchant and Otis J. Todd, *Xenophon: Memorabilia, Oeconomicus, Symposium, Apology* (LCL; Cambridge/London: Harvard University Press, 1923) 4:36-37.

155 Ibid., 53-55.

156 For other explanations, see Schüssler Fiorenza, *In Memory of Her*, 146-48; Detlev Dormeyer, "Die Familie Jesu und der Sohn der Maria im Markusevangelium (3,20f.31-35; 6,3)," in Hubert Frankemölle und Karl Kertelge, eds., *Vom Urchristentum zu Jesus: Für Joachim Gnilka* (Freiburg/Basel/Vienna: Herder, 1989) 109-35; and Halvor Moxnes, "What Is Family? Problems in Constructing Early Christian Families," in idem, ed., *Constructing Early Christian Families: Family as*

Social Reality and Metaphor (London/New York: Routledge, 1997) 13-41, esp. 34-35.

157 *To Melesippus*; text and trans. from Malherbe, *Cynic Epistles*, 172-73; on the date, see ibid., 14-15.

158 On the theme "To do the will of God" in early Christian morality, see Wayne A. Meeks, *The Origins of Christian Morality: The First Two Centuries* (New Haven/London: Yale University Press, 1993) 84-86, 150-57.

159 See text, trans., and comments in Baumgarten, *Qumran Cave 4*, 163-64.

160 See Joseph M. Baumgarten, "4Q502, Marriage or Golden Age Ritual?" *JJS* 35 (1983) 125-35, esp. 129, 133.

161 Ibid., 133, 135.

ingly prosperous and comfortable old age; so many are those who give them precedence and honour as their due and minister to them as a duty voluntarily and deliberately accepted rather than enforced by nature (οἱ δὲ δὴ πρεσβῦται, κἂν εἰ τύχοιεν ἄτεκνοι, καθάπερ οὐ πολύπαιδες μόνον ἀλλὰ καὶ σφόδρα εὔπαιδες, ἐν εὐτυχεστάτῳ καὶ λιπαρω-τάτῳ γήρᾳ τὸν βίον εἰώθασι καταλύειν, ὑπὸ τοσούτων προνομίας ἀξιούμενοι καὶ τιμῆς ἑκ-ουσίῳ γνώμῃ μᾶλλον ἢ φύσεως ἀνάγκῃ θερα-πεύειν ἀξιούντων). (*Hypothetica* 11.13)[162]

Concerning the Therapeutae he remarks:

They do not have slaves to wait upon them as they consider that the ownership of servants is entirely against nature. . . . but the services are rendered by free men who perform their tasks as attendants not under compulsion nor yet waiting for orders, but with deliberate goodwill anticipating eagerly and zealously the demands that may be made. For it is not just any free men who are appointed for these offices but young members of the association. . . . They give their services gladly and proudly like sons to their real fathers and mothers, judging them to be the parents of them all in common, in a closer affinity than that of blood, since to the right minded there is no closer tie than noble living (διακονοῦνται δὲ οὐχ ὑπ᾽ ἀν-δραπόδων, ἡγούμενοι συνόλως τὴν θεραπόντων κτῆσιν εἶναι παρὰ φύσιν· . . . ἐλεύθεροι δὲ ὑπηρε-

τοῦσι, τὰς διακονικὰς χρείας ἐπιτελοῦντες οὐ πρὸς βίαν οὐδὲ προστάξεις ἀναμένοντες, ἀλλ᾽ ἐθελουσίῳ γνώμῃ φθάνοντες μετὰ σπουδῆς καὶ προθυμίας τὰς ἐπικελεύσεις. οὐδὲ γὰρ οἱ τυχόν-τες ἐλεύθεροι τάττονται πρὸς ταῖς ὑπουργίαις ταύταις, ἀλλ᾽ οἱ νέοι τῶν ἐν τῷ συστήματι . . . οἳ καθάπερ υἱοὶ γνήσιοι φιλοτίμως ἄσμενοι πατράσι καὶ μητράσιν ὑπουργοῦσι, κοινοὺς αὐτῶν γονεῖς νομίζοντες οἰκειοτέρους τῶν ἀφ᾽ αἵματος, εἴ γε καλοκἀγαθίας οὐδὲν οἰκειότερόν ἐστι τοῖς εὖ φρονοῦσιν). (*Vit. cont.* 70-72)[163]

The narrative of Mark to this point hints at a new social world in the making that began with Jesus calling disci-ples. The call of the disciples (1:16-20; 2:13-14) and the naming of an inner circle of Twelve (3:13-19) suggest a new social formation. This scene indicates that there is a boundary between those who follow Jesus and those who remain "outside" like his mother and brothers (vv. 31, 32). This sense of "insiders" and "outsiders" is reinforced by the conflict with the scribes in vv. 22-30. The passage as a whole (vv. 20-35) may be read as reflecting or legiti-mating the social displacement and relativization of social norms that members of the audience have experi-enced as they moved from communities based on ties of kinship and traditional ethnic identities to voluntary associations of followers of Jesus.[164] At the same time, these new voluntary associations were based on the social model of the ancient Mediterranean family.[165]

---

162 Text and trans. from Colson and Whitaker, *Philo*, 9:440–43.
163 Colson and Whitaker, *Philo*, 9:156–57.
164 Similarly Barton, *Discipleship and Family Ties*, 82.
165 Joseph H. Hellerman argues that the early Christian congregations understood themselves as "surrogate patrilineal kinship groups" (*The Ancient Church as Family* [Minneapolis: Fortress, 2001] 25). See also John H. Elliott, "The Jesus Movement Was Not Egal-itarian but Family-Oriented," *Biblical Interpretation* 11 (2003) 173–210.

4

1/ And again he began to teach beside the sea. And a very large crowd gathered in his presence, so that he got into a boat[a] and sat on the sea, and the whole crowd was[b] on the land facing the sea.[c] 2/ And he was teaching them many things in parables and he said to them in his teaching, 3/ "Listen. See, the sower went out to sow. 4/ And while he was sowing,[d] the one (seed)[e] fell along the road, and the birds came and devoured it. 5/ And another seed fell on stony ground, where[f] it did not have much earth; and it sprang up immediately because the earth was not deep. 6/ And when the sun rose, it was scorched, and it withered because it had no root. 7/ And another seed fell among thorn-plants, and the thorn-plants came up and choked it, and it did not bear fruit. 8/ And other seeds[g] fell upon good ground and began to give fruit by coming up and growing,[h] and some of them bore up to thirty (grains per seed), and (others bore fruit) amounting to sixty (grains per seed) and (others) amounting to a hundred (grains per seed)."[i] 9/ And he said, "Let anyone who has ears to hear, hear!"

a   Some MSS, B[2] D W et al., add the article, presumably because some copyists assumed, probably rightly, that the boat ($\pi\lambda o\hat{\iota}o\nu$) mentioned here is the $\pi\lambda o\iota\acute{\alpha}\rho\iota o\nu$ ("boat") introduced in 3:9. The addition of the article is then an improvement in the style.

b   A D W et al. read the singular form $\mathring{\eta}\nu$ ("was"), whereas ℵ B C et al. read the plural form $\mathring{\eta}\sigma\alpha\nu$ ("was"). The plural is probably the earlier reading and some copyists changed it to the more usual singular. Mark uses singular verbs and participles elsewhere with the noun $\mathring{o}\chi\lambda o\varsigma$ ("crowd"), when it is in the singular, except in 9:15, where the phrase $\pi\hat{\alpha}\varsigma\ \mathring{o}\ \mathring{o}\chi\lambda o\varsigma$ ("all the crowd") occurs, as here. But cf. 11:18, where the singular form of the verb is better attested, although the phrase $\pi\hat{\alpha}\varsigma\ \mathring{o}\ \mathring{o}\chi\lambda o\varsigma$ ("all the crowd") occurs there as well.

c   Instead of $\pi\rho\grave{o}\varsigma\ \tau\grave{\eta}\nu\ \vartheta\acute{\alpha}\lambda\alpha\sigma\sigma\alpha\nu\ \mathring{\epsilon}\pi\grave{\iota}\ \tau\hat{\eta}\varsigma\ \gamma\hat{\eta}\varsigma$ ("facing the sea on the land"), D reads $\pi\acute{\epsilon}\rho\alpha\nu\ \tau\hat{\eta}\varsigma\ \vartheta\alpha\lambda\acute{\alpha}\sigma\sigma\eta\varsigma$ ("on the other side of the sea") and W it attest the reading $\mathring{\epsilon}\nu\ \tau\hat{\omega}\ \alpha\mathring{\iota}\gamma\iota\alpha\lambda\hat{\omega}$ ("on the shore"). Both of these readings probably originated in attempts to simplify the original wording.

d   Most MSS read $\mathring{\epsilon}\gamma\acute{\epsilon}\nu\epsilon\tau o\ \mathring{\epsilon}\nu\ \tau\hat{\omega}\ \sigma\pi\epsilon\acute{\iota}\rho\epsilon\iota\nu$ ("while he was sowing," lit., "it happened during the sowing"); W lacks this clause and D lat sy[s.p] sa attest a reading lacking $\mathring{\epsilon}\gamma\acute{\epsilon}\nu\epsilon\tau o$ ("it happened"). The last two readings arose as attempts to improve the Greek style of the sentence.

e   The construction here, $\mathring{o}\ \mu\grave{\epsilon}\nu\ \ldots\ \kappa\alpha\grave{\iota}\ \mathring{\alpha}\lambda\lambda o$, is analogous to $\mathring{o}\varsigma\ \mu\grave{\epsilon}\nu\ \ldots\ \mathring{o}\varsigma\ \delta\acute{\epsilon}$ (BAGD, s.v. $\mathring{o}\varsigma$, $\mathring{\eta}$, $\mathring{o}$, 2. b). See also Arland J. Hultgren, *The Parables of Jesus: A Commentary* (Grand Rapids/Cambridge: Eerdmans, 2000) 181–82.

f   B 2427 read $\kappa\alpha\grave{\iota}\ \mathring{o}\pi o\upsilon$ ("and where"); D W it attest the reading $\kappa\alpha\grave{\iota}\ \mathring{o}\tau\iota$ ("and since"). The copyist of B evidently understood $\tau\grave{o}\ \pi\epsilon\tau\rho\hat{\omega}\delta\epsilon\varsigma$ ("stony ground") to mean stones and introduced the $\kappa\alpha\acute{\iota}$ to distinguish between stones and places with shallow soil. The other reading also seems to be an attempt at clarification.

g   Some MSS (ℵ[1] A D et al.) have the singular, $\kappa\alpha\grave{\iota}\ \mathring{\alpha}\lambda\lambda o$, "and another seed," instead of the plural, $\kappa\alpha\grave{\iota}\ \mathring{\alpha}\lambda\lambda\alpha$, "and other seeds," which is attested by ℵ[*.2] B C L W Θ et al. Some copyists apparently changed the plural to the singular to make this sentence conform to the two previous ones.

h   The reading adopted is attested by ℵ B et al. and involves the neuter plural nominative passive participle $\alpha\mathring{\upsilon}\xi\alpha\nu\acute{o}\mu\epsilon\nu\alpha$ ("growing"). This participle agrees with the subject of the first clause of this sentence, $\mathring{\alpha}\lambda\lambda\alpha$, "other seeds," and with the preceding participle $\mathring{\alpha}\nu\alpha\beta\alpha\acute{\iota}\nu o\nu\tau\alpha$ ("coming up"). Instead of $\alpha\mathring{\upsilon}\xi\alpha\nu\acute{o}\mu\epsilon\nu\alpha$ ("growing"), some MSS (A D L W et al.) read $\alpha\mathring{\upsilon}\xi\alpha\nu\acute{o}\mu\epsilon\nu o\nu$ ("growing"); this form is either the neuter singular nominative passive participle or the masculine singular accusative. In the former case, the neuter plural may have been changed to the neuter singular to agree with the singular subject of the previous clause attested in some MSS (see above). In the latter case, the preceding participle, ἀναβαίνοντα ("coming up"), was mistakenly read as a masculine singular accusative and both participles were taken as agreeing with καρπόν ("fruit"). Other MSS (C Θ et al.) read αὐξάνοντα ("growing," the present active participle having an intransitive sense). In this case the neuter plural passive participle was changed either to the neuter plural active or, more likely, to the masculine accusative singular, as above. Cf. Metzger, *Textual Commentary*, 71.

i My trans. of the last part of this verse is based on the original reading of Codex Vaticanus (B), καὶ ἔφερεν εἰς τριάκοντα καὶ ἐν ἑξήκοντα καὶ ἐν ἑκατόν. This reading is the earliest recoverable one, since all the others can be explained as deriving from it. A corrector of B (B²) understood this reading as καὶ ἔφερεν εἰς τριάκοντα καὶ ἐν ἑξήκοντα καὶ ἐν ἑκατόν and added accents and breathing marks accordingly (my trans. assumes the same understanding). But at least one copyist (L) understood the reading as εἰς . . . ἕν . . . ἕν, "and (one part) bore (fruit) up to thirty, and one (bore) sixty, and another (bore) a hundred." Some copyists "corrected" the perceived incon-

sistency of the original reading to εις . . . εις . . . εις, which, assuming smooth breathings, is translated "up to thirty . . . up to sixty . . . up to a hundred" (ℵ C*vid Δ), and others to ἐν . . . ἐν . . . ἐν, which, assuming smooth breathings, is translated "amounting to thirty . . . amounting to sixty . . . amounting to a hundred" (A C² D Θ). (The Curetonian Syriac seems to presuppose the Greek ἐν τριάκοντα καὶ ἐξήκοντα καὶ ἑκατόν, "and it gave (fruit) amounting to thirty and sixty and a hundred." See F. Crawford Burkitt, *Evangelion Da-Mepharreshe: The Curetonian Version of the Four Gospels, with the readings of the Sinai Palimpsest and the Early Syriac Patristic Evidence* [2 vols.; Cambridge: Cambridge University Press, 1904] 1:182). Smooth breathing marks were added to the former reading in 28. 700 *pc*. Some copyists and translators interpreted the latter reading as ἐν . . . ἐν . . . ἐν, "amounting to" three times (0133 *f*¹ 𝔐 sy^h), whereas others read it as ἕν . . . ἕν . . . ἕν, "one (part) (bore) . . . another . . . another" (*f*¹³ *pc* lat syr^p). Finally, at least one copyist understood the latter reading as ἕν . . . ἕν . . . ἕν, but "improved" it to τὸ ἕν . . . τὸ ἕν . . . τὸ ἕν, "the one (part) (bore) . . . the other . . . the other" (W). The hypothesis of Aramaic influence is unnecessary; contra Metzger, *Textual Commentary*, 71, and Elliott C. Maloney, *Semitic Interference in Marcan Syntax* (SBLDS 51; Chico, CA: Scholars Press, 1981) 150–52.

The Parable Speech in Literary Context

The scene in which Jesus speaks in parables is introduced (4:1) in a way suggesting that it is a typical scene in the life of Jesus: "And again (πάλιν) he began to teach beside the sea." A scene in which Jesus teaches a crowd by the sea is introduced also in 2:13. In 4:1, the size of the crowd forces Jesus to get into a boat and to address the crowd opposite him on the land. Just such a situation is anticipated in 3:9. Jesus' teaching in parables is also portrayed in 3:23. These features all integrate Mark 4:1-34 into its context in the Gospel as a whole. There is tension, however, between certain elements of the speech in parables and other passages in Mark. Such tension will be addressed in the section on the literary history of the passage below.

Literary History of 4:1-34

A number of tensions within this passage and between aspects of it and other passages in Mark have provided grounds for source-critical theories. In the passage itself,

the first problem is that in v. 10, those who were around him with the Twelve asked him about the parables (plural). The response in vv. 11-12 fits well with this question, but then in v. 13, Jesus gives another response, as if the question had been about the parable (singular) that he has just spoken, the parable of the sower. A second problem is that, at the beginning of the passage, Jesus is sitting in a boat on the Sea of Galilee addressing a crowd that stands opposite him on the shore. The scene shifts in v. 10, so that Jesus is alone with a group of disciples. But vv. 33-34 imply that some or all of the material in vv. 21-32 was spoken to the crowd, although no transition from solitude to being with the crowd again was narrated. Verses 35-36 imply that Jesus remained in the boat the whole time or was in the boat again by the end of the speech in parables. A third problem is that v. 33 seems to indicate that Jesus spoke to the crowd in parables in order to teach them, on the assumption that they could understand the parables, whereas vv. 11-12 state that Jesus spoke in parables in order that "those outside," presumably those who are not technically disciples of Jesus, including the crowd, would not understand what he was saying. A fourth problem is that v. 34 seems to contradict v. 33. Verse 34 fits well with vv. 11-12; Jesus spoke in parables to the crowd and explained them only to his disciples. Finally, the many introductory formulas (vv. 9, 13, 21, 24, 26, 30) provide evidence of the secondary combination of originally independent units.[1]

Two main tensions have been observed between Mark 4:11-12, on the one hand, and the rest of Mark, on the other. The so-called parable theory of vv. 11-12 makes a sharp distinction between insiders and outsiders, who are taken to be equivalent to the disciples and all other people, respectively. Yet elsewhere in Mark, Jesus shows concern for the crowd, and they manifest sympathy and some understanding of Jesus.[2] In contrast, the disciples, who have been given the secret of the kingdom of God, show the same lack of understanding as the outsiders.[3] The second type of tension lies in the fact that, apparently contrary to the parable theory, the opponents of Jesus seem to understand Jesus' speech in parables elsewhere in the Gospel.[4]

The second tension, however, may be only apparent. Verse 12 speaks of seeing but not perceiving, and of hearing but not comprehending. The point is not that those who are preeminently outsiders, the opponents of Jesus, fail to understand the rhetorical force of Jesus' parables (they do "see" and "hear"), but rather that their hearts are hardened so that they do not accept Jesus' point of view and therefore reject his proclamation (they do not "perceive" and "comprehend").

In any case, the tensions within the passage are sufficient to warrant the conclusion that the evangelist made use of two sources in composing Jesus' speech in parables. The similarity in theme, outlook, and structure among the parable of the sower (vv. 3-8), the similitude of the seed growing by itself (vv. 26-29), and the similitude of the mustard seed (vv. 30-32) supports the hypothesis that these constituted a source used by the evangelist. They all use the image of the growth of seed; the two similitudes explicitly compare the kingdom of God with this growth. Various features indicate that this source was orally composed and transmitted, such as the use of a group of three units, but it may have been committed to writing by the time the author of Mark received it. Verse 33 represents the conclusion of this source.[5]

The second source was a brief didactic dialogue, including a version of the parable of the sower (vv. 3-8) and the interpretation of this parable (vv. 13-20). It probably also included the saying about having ears to hear in v. 9, and the "parable theory" in vv. 11-12. This source portrays Jesus' parables as riddles or symbolic sayings requiring interpretation through the use of established techniques. Verse 34 represents the conclusion of this source. It was almost certainly written, since it makes use of an interpretive schema characteristic of prophetic and apocalyptic literature, namely, a formal pattern used in the interpretation of dreams and visions. The pattern, as adapted, contained a saying, a request for interpretation, and a structured explanation.[6]

The ways in which the author of Mark combined these sources and the meaning of the resulting composition will be discussed in the comments on the component parts of the discourse below.

Literary Unity of 4:1-34

Although the respective texts differ greatly in date, it seems relevant to the interpretation of Mark 4:1-34 that the Jewish exegetical texts called *midrashim* sometimes contain chains or series of parables or *meshalim*. In the Hebrew Bible, the term *mashal* is used for a variety of types of figurative sayings, and it is often translated by the Greek word παραβολή, "parable." In rabbinic literature the *mashal* is usually a brief narrative in the past tense and thus is similar to the Greek fables and the New Testament parables. Nearly all rabbinic *meshalim* have two parts. The fictional narrative proper is called the *mashal*, and its application is the *nimshal*. Each begins with a formulaic phrase. The *mashal* usually begins with

---

1   Räisänen, *Messianic Secret*, 85; see also Philip Sellew, "Oral and Written Sources in Mark 4.1-34," *NTS* 36 (1990) 234-67. Both of these studies contain bibliographical information and discussion of older theories.

2   Mark 1:21-28; 3:32-34; 6:34; 7:37; 12:37b; 11:18b; Räisänen, *Messianic Secret*, 92–96.

3   Mark 4:40; 6:51-52; 7:18; 8:17-21; cf. Räisänen, *Messianic Secret*, 97–101.

4   Mark 3:22-27; and esp. 12:12; cf. Räisänen, *Messianic Secret*, 87–92.

5   Sellew, "Oral and Written Sources," 251–60.

6   Sellew, "Oral and Written Sources," 255, 260–63; Klauck, *Allegorie und Allegorese*, 67–91; Joel Marcus,

the phrase "It is like" or the equivalent. The *nimshal* usually opens with the word "similarly." The *nimshal* usually concludes by citing a verse from scripture, the *mashal's* proof text. The citation from scripture is both the exegetical occasion for the *mashal* and its climax.[7]

According to David Stern, the parables in a rabbinic chain or series usually have parallel narratives and parallel applications.[8] Sometimes a group of parables is used to transport the audience from an opening verse to a proof text. He cites an example in which the opening verse is Jer 9:17, "Thus said the Lord of Hosts: Listen! Summon the dirge-singers, let them come." The proof text is Lam 1:1, "How lonely sits the city that was full of people etc." Three parables lead from the first text to the second. They each have the same themes and purposes, but each one arranges them differently so that the three are similar, yet distinct. The changes result in a movement that leads to a suprising conclusion. The speaker in the opening verse of Lamentations is no longer personified Zion, but God.[9]

An analogous movement may be seen in Mark 4:1-34. The parable of the sower itself, the fictional narrative, may be seen as an introduction to the parabolic discourse. It does not have an explicit theme, and it also lacks an application. The lack of these makes the parable somewhat opaque, although, as will be shown below, the imagery was familiar enough to lead members of the audience to recall themes that they knew from oral discourse or other texts in their respective cultures.

Jesus' dialogue with his disciples forms a transition from the fictional narrative about the sower to its application. In the dialogue, a theme or topic is expressed: the mystery of the kingdom of God. In the interpretation or application of the parable of the sower, the mystery of the kingdom of God is not mentioned, but another theme or topic is introduced, "the word." "The word," as will be shown below, is equivalent in Mark to the "good news" or "gospel." The summary of Jesus' proclamation in 1:14-15 shows that the "good news" is that the time has been fulfilled and the kingdom of God has drawn

near. Thus, the fictional narrative, the transitional dialogue, and the interpretation or application all treat the theme of the kingdom of God in different ways.

The two-part saying that follows the interpretation of the parable of the sower (vv. 21-22) continues the theme of the "mystery of the kingdom of God" by substituting for that phrase first "what is hidden" and then "what is secret." This saying suggests that the mystery is not to be kept secret but to be proclaimed. The following three-part saying (vv. 24-25) develops first the theme of proclaiming and then the theme contrasting the insiders and outsiders, which was introduced in vv. 11-12.[10]

The shifts introduced by the sayings in vv. 21-25 lead the audience to infer that the sower in the parable of the seed growing by itself represents the followers of Jesus carrying on his proclamation, rather than Jesus himself. This parable and the following one about the mustard seed, both explicitly related to the kingdom of God, have the effect of encouraging the audience to be patient in their efforts to spread the gospel and in their expectations of the fulfillment of the kingdom. The parable of the mustard seed, with its parody of messianic expectation, alludes to the suffering and death of Jesus. Thus, the collection of figurative sayings or parables in 4:1-34 transports the audience from a focus on God's act through Jesus in announcing the good news of the kingdom of God (vv. 3-9) to a foreshadowing of the surprising turn of events in which the messiah must die before the full manifestation of that kingdom (vv. 30-32).

Support for this analysis may be found in the argument that there is an analogous movement in the sequence of three parables in Matt 21:28–22:22. The three parables may be seen as linked by a chronological succession of topics. The parable about the two sons concerns response to the mission of John the Baptist (21:32). The parable about the wicked tenants depicts response to the mission of Jesus as "the son" of the owner of the vineyard (21:37-39) and the consequences of that response (21:40-44). Finally, the parable about the wedding banquet concerns the mission of the apostles after Jesus'

The Mystery of the Kingdom of God (SBLDS 90; Atlanta: Scholars Press, 1986) 62–64.

7 David Stern, *Parables in Midrash: Narrative and Exegesis in Rabbinic Literature* (Cambridge, MA/London: Harvard University Press, 1991) 8.

8 Ibid., 176.

9 Ibid., 160–62.

10 For a fuller treatment, see the commentary below.

death (22:9-10). Both the good and the bad are invited, but the bad will be judged at the final judgment (22:13).

Comment

■ **1-9** In the context of ancient figurative speech, it is odd that this parable expresses only one element of the comparison. Both elements are expressed in Aristotle's instances of the figure of speech he calls "parable" (παραβολή), for example, Socrates' saying that choosing government officials by lot is like choosing athletes by lot instead of by ability (*Rhet.* 1393b = 2.20.4). One could explain the lack of the second element in the parable of the sower by arguing that it belongs to a different genre. Aristotle's "parable" (παραβολή) is actually a simile or similitude in the present tense, whereas the parable of the sower is a metaphorical narrative in the past tense. Aristotle refers to fictional, metaphorical narratives in the past tense as "fables" (λόγοι). His illustrations of this literary type, however, also express both elements of the comparison. He tells the fable, for example, devised by Stesichorus about Phalaris. When the people of Himera had made Phalaris a dictator over them and were about to appoint a bodyguard for him, Stesichorus told the following story:

A horse was in sole occupation of a meadow. A stag having come and done much damage to the pasture, the horse, wishing to avenge himself on the stag, asked a man whether he could help him to punish the stag. The man consented, on condition that the horse submitted to the bit and allowed him to mount him javelins in hand. The horse agreed to the terms and the man mounted him, but instead of obtaining vengeance on the stag, the horse from that time

became the man's slave (ὡς ἵππος κατεῖχε λειμῶνα μόνος, ἐλθόντος δ᾽ ἐλάφου καὶ διαφθείροντος τὴν νομὴν βουλόμενος τιμωρήσασθαι τὸν ἔλαφον ἠρώτα τινὰ ἄνθρωπον εἰ δύναιτ᾽ ἂν μετ᾽ αὐτοῦ κολάσαι τὸν ἔλαφον, ὁ δ᾽ ἔφησεν, ἐὰν λάβῃ χαλινὸν καὶ αὐτὸς ἀναβῇ ἐπ᾽ αὐτὸν ἔχων ἀκόντια· συνομολογήσαντος δὲ καὶ ἀναβάντος, ἀντὶ τοῦ τιμωρήσασθαι αὐτὸς ἐδούλευσεν ἤδη τῷ ἀνθρώπῳ). (*Rhet.* 1393b = 2.20.5)[11]

Stesichorus told the people that they should be careful, in their desire to avenge themselves on their enemy, not to end up like the horse. They already wore the bit, since they had made him dictator; if they gave him a bodyguard and allowed him to mount them, they would immediately become his slaves.[12]

Like the Greek fables, rabbinic parables regularly express both elements of the comparison. According to Stern, nearly all rabbinic parables have two parts: a fictional narrative, the parable or *mashal* proper; and the narrative's application, the *nimshal*.[13]

The parable of the sower was probably orally composed, perhaps by the historical Jesus.[14] Whether it was composed by Jesus or by one of his followers after his death, the parable originally had a rhetorical purpose. Its significance would have been clear in the situation in which it was told.[15] In an oral collection of parables, such as the source mentioned above (Literary History of 4:1-34), the rhetorical situation would still provide the application. Once the collection was written down, however, the rhetorical situation was lost and is virtually unrecoverable. In the second source utilized by the evangelist, the second element of the comparison was deliberately omitted in order to evoke the question of the disciples regarding the meaning of the parable.

11   Text and trans. from John Henry Freese, *Aristotle* (LCL; Cambridge, MA: Harvard University Press; London: Heinemann, 1926) 22:274–77.

12   On the rhetorical use of fables in antiquity, see Gert-Jan van Dyck, *ΑΙΝΟΙ, ΛΟΓΟΙ, ΜΥΘΟΙ: Fables in Archaic, Classical, and Hellenistic Greek Literature with a Study of the Theory and Terminology of the Genre* (Mn.S 166; Leiden: Brill, 1997).

13   Stern, *Parables in Midrash*, 8.

14   For attempts to reconstruct the original form of the parable, see John Dominic Crossan, *In Parables: The Challenge of the Historical Jesus* (New York: Harper &

Row, 1973) 39–44; Klauck, *Allegorie und Allegorese*, 188–89; Marcus, *Mystery*, 31–33.

15   For a critique of New Critical approaches to the parables of Jesus and for an argument that they had a primarily rhetorical significance, see William F. Brosend II, "The Recovery of Allegory" (Ph.D. diss., University of Chicago, 1993). For a case study on the rhetorical use of a parable by a folklorist, see Barbara Kirshenblatt-Gimblett, "A Parable in Context: A Social Interactional Analysis of Storytelling Performance," in Dan Ben-Amos and Kenneth S. Goldstein, eds., *Folklore: Performance and Communication*

As noted in the section on Literary History above, the interpretation of the parable of the sower, now found in vv. 14-20, was part of the source consisting of a brief, written, didactic dialogue. It is generally agreed that the parable of the sower is older than this interpretation.[16] Since the pre-Markan rhetorical situation of the parable is unknown, the interpretation of vv. 14-20 is later, and the parable itself does not indicate the second element in the comparison, the best way to understand the significance of the parable is to investigate whether the imagery of the parable was used in specific ways in its cultural settings.[17]

The most striking and most fully elaborated analogous use of the image of sowing in roughly contemporary Jewish literature is *4 Ezra* 8:37-41:

[The angel] answered [Ezra] and said, "Some things you have spoken rightly, and it will come to pass according to your words. For indeed I will not concern myself about the fashioning of those who have sinned, or about their death, their judgment, or their destruction; but I will rejoice over the creation of the righteous, over their pilgrimage also, and their life, and their receiving their reward. As I have spoken, therefore, so it shall be. For just as the farmer sows many seeds and plants a multitude of seedlings, and yet not all that have been sown will live in due season, and

not all the plants will take root; so also those who have been sown in the world will not all live."[18]

In this text, God is the sower, and the results of sowing and planting are human beings. "Living in due season" alludes to a happy, eternal afterlife. Those who do not "live" are the wicked, who are eternally damned.[19] As Klauck has pointed out, the imagery of this passage has precedents in the Bible.[20] In Hos 2:23-25 (2:21-23 RSV), God is the sower and what is sown is the people of Israel.[21]

Another Jewish apocalyptic work roughly contemporary with Mark, the Similitudes of Enoch (*1 Enoch* 37–71), uses the imagery of sowing and applies it specifically to the new age, rather than to the present:

For from the beginning the son of man was hidden, and the Most High preserved him in the presence of his might, and he revealed him to the chosen. And the congregation of the chosen and the holy will be sown; and all the chosen will stand in his presence on that day. (*1 Enoch* 62:7-8)[22]

The context implies that the community of the holy and the chosen will be established at the beginning of the new age, when the Son of Man is revealed.

(Approaches to Semiotics 40; The Hague/Paris: Mouton, 1975) 105–30. See also Mary Ann Beavis, "The Power of Jesus' Parables: Were They Polemical or Irenic?" *JSNT* 82 (2001) 3–30.

16 The case for this conclusion was made persuasively by Joachim Jeremias, *The Parables of Jesus* (rev. ed.; New York: Scribner's Sons, 1963; trans. from 6th Germ. ed., 1962) 77–79. The fact that the version of the parable in *Gos. Thom.* 9 is briefer than Mark's and lacks the interpretation does not constitute evidence that the version of *Gos. Thom.* is older than that of Mark. The version in *Gos. Thom.* could well have resulted from the commonly practiced technique of reformulating a text in a more concise manner; see Mack and Robbins, *Patterns of Persuasion*, 17–18. The omission of the interpretation is also in keeping with the cryptic style of *Gos. Thom.*

17 See Klauck's investigation of the parable's "field of images" (*Bildfeld*) (*Allegorie und Allegorese*, 192–96); for an explanation of the concept "field of images," see 142–43).

18 Trans. from Stone, *Fourth Ezra*, 276. Note that the Latin version reads *salvatio* ("salvation") rather than "life" and *salvabuntur* ("will be saved") instead of "live."

19 Stone, *Fourth Ezra*, 283–84.

20 Klauck, *Allegorie und Allegorese*, 193 and n. 43.

21 Cf. Jer 31:27-28 (38:27-28 LXX), which alludes to and elaborates the passage in Hosea cited above; see William L. Holladay, *Jeremiah: A Commentary on the Book of the Prophet Jeremiah* (2 vols.; Hermeneia; Minneapolis: Fortress, 1986, 1989) 2:196–97. See also Ezek 36:8-11; Zech 10:9 LXX. See also *4 Ezra* 9:18-22, where God's saving of a remnant is portrayed as exercising agricultural labor.

22 Trans. from Nickelsburg and VanderKam, 80.

One of the *Thanksgiving Hymns* from Qumran speaks about the members of the community as follows:

> Their root] will sprout like a flo[wer of the field
> f]orever,
> and shall cause a shoot to grow into the boughs of an
> everlasting Plant.
> It shall cover the whole ea[rth] with its shade [and] its
> [crown] (shall reach) up to the sk[y].
> Its roots (shall go down) to the Abyss, and all the
> rivers of Eden [shall water] its [branches]. (1QH
> 14:14-16)[23]

In this text, the community has already been planted, and its members express hope that it will grow and flourish.[24]

In Greek literature, the image of sowing was also used for the generation of human beings by divine power.[25] In his discussion of the creation of the universe, Plato has the Demiurge instruct the younger gods to create the bodies of mortal living creatures and state that he himself will deliver to them the immortal part when he has "sown it and given it origin."[26] After he had produced these immortal souls, "He proceeded to sow them, some in the Earth, some in the Moon," and the others in various stars.[27]

Analogously, Seneca wrote:

> The gods are not disdainful or envious; they open the door to you; they lend a hand as you climb. Do you marvel that a human being goes to the gods? God comes to humans; no, he comes nearer,—he comes into humans. No mind that has not God is good. Divine seeds are scattered throughout our mortal bodies; if a good cultivator receives them, they spring up in the likeness of their source and of a parity with

those from which they came. If, however, the cultivator is bad, like a barren or marshy soil, he kills the seeds, and causes tares to group up instead of wheat (Non sunt di fastidiosi, non invidi; admittunt et ascendentibus manum porrigunt. Miraris hominem ad deos ire? Deus ad homines venit, immo quod est proprius, in homines venit; nulla sine deo mens bona est. Semina in corporibus humanis divina dispersa sunt, quae si bonus cultor excipit, similia origini prodeunt et paria iis, ex quibus orta sunt, surgunt; si malus, non aliter quam humus sterilis ac palustris necat ac deinde creat purgamenta pro frugibus). (*Ep. Mor.* 73.16)[28]

These texts, the Greek, the Latin, and the Jewish, suggest that the sower in the parable of the sower is God, or perhaps Jesus as the agent of God. Since Mark summarizes Jesus' teaching with the words "The time is fulfilled, and the kingdom of God has drawn near" (1:15), the parable probably addresses the crisis of the last days. Like *4 Ezra*, the Markan parable does not expect all seeds to bear fruit. In *4 Ezra*, the characteristic that is analogous to bearing fruit is righteousness, ethical living in response to God's instruction. Similarly, in the Similitudes of Enoch, the community that is "sown" are the holy, who will be rewarded, whereas the wicked will be punished. The latter text adds the theme of the oppression of the poor righteous by the wealthy wicked. The *Thanksgiving Hymns* from Qumran also imply that the community is holy and righteous, but a new element there is loyalty to the community and its divinely revealed teaching. It is likely, at least for members of the audience familiar with these traditions, that analogous connotations were present in the Markan parable as well. Those who bear fruit are the members of the eschatolog-

---

23   Sukenik, col. 6 + frg. 26:

שׁוֹרשׁם] פרח כצין] שׂדה ע]ד עולם
לגדל נצר לעופי מטעת עולם
ויצל צל על כול תבל ועני]מו עד שחק]ם
ו]שׁרשׁיו עד תהום וכול נהרות עדן [תשקו
את ד]לן]ותיו.

Text and trans. (modified) from García Martínez and Tigchelaar, *Dead Sea Scrolls*, 1:174–75.

24   The apocalyptic use of the image of planting has a precedent in Isa 60:19-21.

25   Jeffrey R. Asher, *Polarity and Change in 1 Corinthians 15* (HUTh 42; Tübingen: Mohr Siebeck, 2000) 137–38.

26   σπείρας καὶ ὑπαρξάμενος ἐγὼ παραδώσω (Plato *Timaeus* 41C); text and trans. from Robert G. Bury, *Plato*, vol. 9 (LCL; Cambridge, MA/London: Harvard University Press, 1929) 9:88–89.

27   ἔσπειρε τοὺς μὲν εἰς γῆν, τοὺς δ᾽εἰς σελήνην, τοὺς δ᾽εἰς τἆλλα ὅσα ὄργανα χρόνου (*Timaeus* 42D); Bury, *Plato*, 9:92–93.

28   Text and trans. (modified) from Richard Gummere, *Seneca: Ad Lucilium Epistulae Morales* (3 vols.; London: Heinemann, 1917–25) 2:112–13. This passage is cited by Joseph B. Lightfoot as analogous to Jesus' parables (*St. Paul's Epistle to the Philippians* [London:

ical community constituted by those who respond positively to the proclamation of Jesus.

Those educated in Greek and Hellenistic literature and tradition would also recognize the description of sowing and its results as an analogy to or allegory of education. The *Law* is a brief statement of the characteristics desirable in a student of medicine. This work is attributed to Hippocrates, the great Greek physician. It includes the following statement:

> The learning of medicine may be likened to the growth of plants. Our natural ability is the soil. The views of our teachers are as it were the seeds. Learning from childhood is analogous to the seeds' falling at the right time upon the prepared ground. The place of instruction is as it were the nutriment that comes from the surrounding air to the things sown. Diligence is the working of the soil. Time strengthens all these things, so that their nurture is perfected (Ὁκοίη γὰρ τῶν ἐν γῇ φυομένων θεωρίη, τοιήδε καὶ τῆς ἰητρικῆς ἡ μάθησις. ἡ μὲν γὰρ φύσις ἡμέων ὁκοῖον ἡ χώρη· τὰ δὲ δόγματα τῶν διδασκόντων ὁκοῖον τὰ σπέρματα· ἡ δὲ παιδομαθίη, τὸ καθ' ὥρην αὐτὰ πεσεῖν ἐς τὴν ἄρουραν· ὁ δὲ τόπος ἐν ᾧ ἡ μάθησις, ὁκοῖον ἡ ἐκ τοῦ περιέχοντος ἠέρος τροφὴ γιγνομένη τοῖσι φυομένοισιν· ἡ δὲ φιλοπονίη, ἐργασίη· ὁ δὲ χρόνος ταῦτα ἐνισχύει πάντα, ὡς τραφῆναι τελέως). (*Law* 3)[29]

This passage is a simile rather than a fable, but the points of comparison are very similar to those implied by the parable of the sower. It is noteworthy, however, that the element of "industrious toil" is missing from the parable of the sower. In a similar vein, Diogenes Laertius wrote concerning the Stoics:

> Or, again, they liken Philosophy to a fertile field: Logic being the encircling fence, Ethics the crop,

Physics the soil or the trees (ἢ ἀγρῷ παμφόρῳ· οὗ τὸν μὲν περιβεβλημένον φραγμὸν τὸ λογικόν, τὸν δὲ καρπὸν τὸ ἠθικόν, τὴν δὲ γῆν ἢ τὰ δένδρα τὸ φυσικόν). (*Vit. Phil.* 7.40)[30]

This passage is an extended metaphor, rather than a metaphorical narrative or parable, but like the *Law*, it suggests that agricultural metaphors were common in ancient discourse about education.

Seneca compared educating people in philosophy to sowing seed:

> Words should be scattered like seed; no matter how small the seed may be, if it has once found favorable ground, it unfolds its strength and from an insignificant thing spreads to its greatest growth. Reason grows in the same way; it is not large to the outward view, but increases as it does its work. Few words are spoken; but if the mind has truly caught them, they come into their strength and spring up. Yes, precepts and seeds have the same quality; they produce much, and yet they are slight things. Only, as I said, let a favorable mind receive and assimilate them. Then of itself the mind also will produce bounteously in its turn, giving back more than it has received (Seminis modo spargenda sunt, quod quamvis sit exiguum, cum occupavit ideoneum locum, vires suas explicat et ex minimo in maximos auctus diffunditur. Idem facit ratio; non late patet, si aspicias; in opere crescit. Pauca sunt, quae dicuntur, sed si illa animus bene excepit, convalescunt et exurgunt. Eadem est, inquam, praeceptorum condicio quae seminum; multum efficiunt, et angusta sunt. Tantum, ut dixi, idonea mens capiat illa et in se trahat. Multa invicem et ipsa generabit et plus reddet quam acceperit). (*Ep. Mor.* 38.2)[31]

An analogous notion appears in *4 Ezra* in the prayer of Ezra that precedes his vision of the heavenly Jerusalem. He attributes the following speech to God on the occasion of the giving of the Law in the wilderness:

Macmillan, 1913; reprinted Grand Rapids: Zondervan, 1953] 285–86).

29   Text and trans. (modified) from William H. S. Jones, *Hippocrates* (LCL; Cambridge, MA: Harvard University Press; London: Heinemann, 1923) 2:264–65.

30   Text and trans. from Hicks, *Diogenes Laertius*, 2:150–51.

31   Text and trans. from Gummere, *Seneca*, 1:256–59. This passage is cited in relation to the parable of the mustard seed and the parable of the sower by Bertram T. D. Smith, *The Parables of the Synoptic Gospels: A Critical Study* (London: Cambridge University Press; New York: Macmillan, 1937) 120, 125–26.

Hear me, O Israel, and give heed to my words, O seed of Jacob. For behold, I sow my law in you, and it shall bring forth fruit in you, and you shall be glorified through it forever. (9:30-31)[32]

Once again, God is depicted as the sower, but this time it is the Law, the instruction of God, that is sown in the people. By analogy with this text, the Markan parable of the sower could be understood as God sowing "the good news of God" (τὸ εὐαγγέλιον τοῦ θεοῦ) into the people through the agency of the proclamation and teaching of Jesus.[33]

■ **3** The analogous Jewish texts suggest that the sower represented God in the original context of the parable. In the context of Mark, he probably represents Jesus as the agent of God.

■ **4-7** Since the original rhetorical context of the parable is lost, it is uncertain whether the three ways in which some seeds fail to thrive were intended to be interpreted allegorically. It is noteworthy, however, that Ezra, as a character in *4 Ezra*, attributes the failure of the Law to bear fruit in the people of Israel to the "evil heart" with which human beings apparently were created (3:20).

■ **8** Although, again, no precise allegorical interpretation of the threefold fruitfulness may be recovered, the imagery does imply that there are degrees of insight, righteousness, or other appropriate response to the sowing. The author of *1 Clement* offers the following interpretation:

"The sower went out" and cast each of the seeds onto the soil. Because they are dry and barren they decay when they fall onto the soil. But the magnificent providence of the Master raises them up out of their decay, and from the one seed more grow and bring forth fruit (ἐξῆλθεν ὁ σπείρων καὶ ἔβαλεν εἰς τὴν γῆν ἕκαστον τῶν σπερμάτων, ἅτινα πεσόντα εἰς τὴν γῆν ξηρὰ καὶ γυμνὰ διαλύεται· εἶτ᾽ ἐκ τῆς διαλύσεως ἡ μεγαλειότης τῆς προνοίας τοῦ

δεσπότου ἀνίστησιν αὐτά, καὶ ἐκ τοῦ ἑνὸς πλείονα αὔξει καὶ ἐκφέρει καρπόν). (24.5)[34]

The context is an argument that there will be a future resurrection. The interpretation seems to be an allegorical one, in which the sowing of seed represents death, and the plants and fruit the resurrected body. Irenaeus takes the different degrees of fruitfulness as representing degrees of reward in the afterlife. He says that, according to the elders, those who are deemed worthy of an abode in heaven will go there, others will be in Paradise, and yet others will inhabit the new Jerusalem. The first are those who, according to the parable of the sower, bear one-hundredfold, the second those who bear sixtyfold, and the third those who bear thirtyfold (Irenaeus *Haer.* 5.36.1-2). The readings of *1 Clement* and Irenaeus are analogous to the eschatological employment of the imagery in *4 Ezra* and the Similitudes of Enoch (see above). Col 1:5b-6, probably dependent on this verse, speaks about the true word of the gospel "bearing fruit and growing in the whole world" (ἐν παντὶ τῷ κόσμῳ ἐστὶν καρποφορούμενον καὶ αὐξανόμενον).[35]

The reference to seed yielding a hundredfold is not unrealistic.[36]

■ **9** This exhortation to hear repeats the invitation to listen in v. 3, using the same Greek verb (ἀκούειν). The invitation of v. 3 is addressed to the whole crowd. The exhortation of v. 9, on the literal level, implies that all who have the physical ability to hear are able to understand the parable. On the metaphorical level, however, it prepares for the parable theory that follows by hinting that not all who have the physical ability to hear have also the capacity to understand.[37] According to the *Thanksgiving Hymns* from Qumran, it is God who opens a human being's ears "to wondrous mysteries" (לרזי פלא) (1QH 9:21; Sukenik, 1:21).

---

32 Trans. from Stone, *Fourth Ezra*, 306.
33 According to Stern, the rabbinic parables are "about events and characters, and particularly one character—the king, or God" (*Parables in Midrash*, 93). This centrality of God as a character in rabbinic parables supports the inference that God or God's agent is the sower in the Markan parable.
34 Text and trans. (modified) from Ehrman, *Apostolic Fathers*, 1:80–81; see also Lake, *Apostolic Fathers*, 1:52–53.
35 Leppä, *Making of Colossians*, 219, 257–58.
36 John T. Fitzgerald, "Gadara: Philodemus' Native City," in idem, Dirk Obbink, and Glenn S. Holland, eds., *Philodemus and the New Testament World* (NovTSup 111; Leiden: Brill, 2004) 343–97, esp. 387.
37 Cf. Marcus, 297.

4

4:10-12 The Mystery of the Kingdom of God

10/ And when they were alone, those who were around him with the Twelve[a] asked him about the parables.[b] 11/ And he said to them, "To you has been given the mystery of the kingdom of God, but to those who are outside, everything happens[c] in parables, 12/ in order that, seeing, they may see and not perceive, and hearing, they may hear and not comprehend, lest they turn and it[d] be forgiven them."[e]

a   A number of MSS read μαθηταὶ αὐτοῦ, "his disciples," instead of περὶ αὐτὸν σὺν τοῖς δώδεκα, "who were around him with the Twelve," namely, D W Θ f[13] et al. The latter was changed to the former either to simplify the expression or under the influence of the parallel in Luke 8:9; cf. Matt 13:10.

b   Since the earliest recoverable reading has those around Jesus ask him about "the parables" (τὰς παραβολάς), whereas he has told only one parable according to the context in the narrative, some copyists changed the reading to τὴν παραβολήν, "the parable" (A f[1] 𝔐 et al.) and others to τίς ἡ παραβολή αὕτη, "What is this parable?" (D W Θ f[13] et al.).

c   One or more copyists (see D Θ et al.) attempted to clarify the meaning by changing γίνεται, "happens," to λέγεται, "is spoken."

d   Instead of ἀφεθῇ, "it be forgiven them," D* reads ἀφεθήσομαι, "I shall forgive them" (D[2] it attest ἀφήσω, which has the same meaning). These changes move the allusion closer to Isa 6:10 LXX.

e   A D Θ f[13] et al. read τὰ ἁμαρτήματα, "(their) sins," after αὐτοῖς, "them." This reading is an addition intended to clarify the meaning.

Comment

■ **10** This is the first of several occasions in Mark when Jesus makes a public statement or performs a public deed and then is asked about it in private by a smaller group, usually the disciples.[38] The presence of this typical pattern here suggests that v. 10 is Markan redaction. The use of the plural, παραβολαί ("parables"), takes up the editorial comment in v. 2, that "he was teaching them many things in parables."

■ **11-12** Jesus' response is twofold. The first statement is "To you has been given the mystery of the kingdom of God." Matthew and Luke agree against Mark in adding the word γνῶναι ("to know") and in reading τὰ μυστήρια ("the mysteries") instead of τὸ μυστήριον ("the mystery"). This is one of the famous "minor agreements" of Matthew and Luke against Mark. These agreements became a problem when the consensus about

Markan priority emerged.[39] Helmut Koester concluded that Matthew and Luke preserve the original wording of Mark 4:11.[40] Andreas Ennulat has argued that the three agreements between Matthew and Luke against Mark in Mark 4:11 pars. must be understood in terms of a post-Markan, pre-Matthean and pre-Lukan revision of Mark with regard to its secret-theory and theme of the misunderstanding of the disciples.[41] Mark expresses the idea of the perception of a phenomenon (without that phenomenon necessarily being understood), whereas Matthew and Luke refer to a knowledgeable understanding of this phenomenon. Ennulat explains the shift from the singular τὸ μυστήριον ("the mystery") in Mark to the plural τὰ μυστήρια ("the mysteries") in Matthew and Luke by noting that in the Greek versions of Daniel, the singular is used for the dream-vision of Nebuchadnezzar (before it is understood), whereas the plural is used for the

38   The others are 7:14-17; 9:27-28 (note v. 18b); 10:2-12; 13:1-4.

39   Frans Neirynck, ed., *The Minor Agreements of Matthew and Luke against Mark with a Cumulative List* (BEThL 37; Leuven: Leuven University Press, 1974) 11. This work contains a history of scholarship on the minor agreements, a cumulative list, a classification of stylistic agreements, and an appendix on the

argument from order. Mark 4:11 pars. are presented on p. 89.

40   Koester, *Gospels*, 279–80.

41   Andreas Ennulat, *Die "Minor Agreements": Untersuchungen zu einer offenen Frage des synoptischen Problems* (WUNT 2.62; Tübingen: Mohr Siebeck, 1994) 124–26.

dream-vision as interpreted (or about to be interpreted).[42] Another possibility is that Matthew and Luke independently added γνῶναι ("to know") as a clarification, overlooking (or correcting) the fact that, in Mark, the "giving" of the mystery does not yet imply its "being known." They may also have changed τὸ μυστήριον ("mystery") to τὰ μυστήρια ("the mysteries") independently. They may have understood each parable as a "mystery" to be explained.[43] Or they may have made the change in accordance with the usage in Daniel or the Wisdom of Solomon; furthermore, the plural was typically used in speaking about the mystery religions of antiquity.[44] The exact correspondence between Matthew and Luke in the order of words, however, is difficult to explain in terms of independent redaction.[45]

Language about "mystery" and "mysteries" in the New Testament, however, derives from the use of the Persian loanword *rāz* in Hebrew and Aramaic texts of the Second Temple period.[46] In the Dead Sea Scrolls, both the plural and the singular are used. An example of the plural usage is a passage in the commentary on Habakkuk which states that God made known to the Teacher of Righteousness "all the mysteries of the words of his ser-

vants, the prophets."[47] In certain sapiential works from Qumran, the plural רזים ("mysteries") refers to natural phenomena and to processes of history, all of which embody divine wisdom.[48] The singular occurs in the formula רז נהיה ("the mystery that is to be" or "the mystery that is to come"). The contexts in which it appears suggest that it has "both cosmic and eschatological dimensions, as well as moral or practical consequences."[49] For example, *Sapiential Text A* contains the following passage:

> [Gaze upon the mystery] that is to come, and comprehend the birth-times of salvation, And know who is to inherit glory (= glorious immortality?) and toil

> ([הבט ברז] נהיה וקח מולדי ישע)
> (ודע מי נוחל כבוד ועמל)
> (4QInstruction[c] [4Q417] frg. 2 1:10-11)[50]

The inference that "inheriting glory" refers to immortality is supported by the rhetorical question that follows immediately regarding the eternal joy that awaits those who mourn.[51] The "mystery that is to come" includes "the entire divine plan from creation to eschatological judgment."[52] The eschatological dimension expresses

---

42 The singular is used in Dan 2:27, 30, 47; 4:9 *Θ*; the plural in Dan 2:28, 29, 47; Ennulat, *Minor Agreements*, 125–26.

43 Koester uses this argument to support the conclusion that τὰ μυστήρια ("the mysteries") is the original wording (*Gospels*, 279–80).

44 Dan 2:28, 29, 47 LXX; Wis 2:22. On the mystery religions, see Walter Burkert, *Ancient Mystery Cults* (Cambridge, MA: Harvard University Press, 1987).

45 On the whole issue of the relation between source criticism of the Gospels and textual criticism, as well as for a criticism of Koester's hypothesis, see David C. Parker, *The Living Text of the Gospels* (Cambridge: Cambridge University Press) 104–18, 183.

46 Raymond E. Brown, *The Semitic Background of the Term "Mystery" in the New Testament* (FBBS 21; Philadelphia: Fortress, 1968); Joel Marcus, "Mark 4:10-12 and Markan Epistemology," *JBL* 103 (1984) 557–74; Daniel J. Harrington, "Mystery," *EDSS* 1:588–91.

47 כול רזי דברי עבדיו הנבאים (1QpHab 7:4-5); text and trans. from García Martínez and Tigchelaar, *Dead Sea Scrolls*, 1:16–17.

48 Lawrence H. Schiffman, "Mysteries," in Torleif Elgvin et al., *Qumran Cave 4*, vol. 15: *Sapiential Texts, Part 1* (DJD 20; Oxford: Clarendon, 1997) 31–32.

49 The second word in the formula, נהיה, is a niphal participle of the verb to be (היה). In many contexts in which the formula occurs, this participle appears to have a future sense; see Daniel J. Harrington, *Wisdom Texts from Qumran* (London/New York: Routledge, 1996) 48–49. Armin Lange concluded that the formula designates a phenomenon that unites ethical, historical, legal, eschatological, and primordial elements. It concerns a world order or order of creation that will be fulfilled in the eschaton (*Weisheit und Prädestination: Weisheitliche Urordnung und Prädestination in den Textfunden von Qumran* [STDJ 18; Leiden/New York: Brill, 1995] 60).

50 Formerly numbered frg. 1; text and trans. from John Strugnell and Daniel Harrington, *Qumran Cave 4*, vol. 24: *Sapiential Texts, Part 2* (DJD 34; Oxford: Clarendon, 1999) 173, 176.

51 Harrington, *Wisdom Texts from Qumran*, 51–52.

52 John J. Collins, *Jewish Wisdom in the Hellenistic Age* (OTL; Louisville: Westminster John Knox, 1997) 122.

both the fulfillment of the divine plan and the fact that only at the end will the plan become evident to all.

The notion of "the mystery to come" in the Dead Sea Scrolls is analogous to the idea of "the mystery of the kingdom of God" in Mark 4:11. The mystery of the kingdom is the divinely willed way in which the rule of God will manifest itself and come to fulfillment through the agency of Jesus. The statement that "it has been given" to the inner circle refers to the teaching of Jesus that they have already heard.[53] This teaching is summarized by Mark in 1:15, "The time is fulfilled and the kingdom of God has drawn near; repent and trust in the good news." Up to this point in the narrative, many have heard this teaching, not just the inner circle. Jesus' saying implies that the inner circle alone will receive a more complete revelation of the significance of this teaching. This process begins to occur with the interpretation of the parable of the sower and becomes the focus of the narrative from 8:27—10:45.

It is only in this middle section of the Gospel of Mark that Jesus reveals the most difficult aspect of the "mystery of the kingdom of God," the "gospel," and the "word," namely, that he, God's anointed, must suffer and die. The disciples' question about the parables may foreshadow their difficulties in understanding and accepting this revelation. This hypothesis is supported by the fact that in 4:2 Jesus speaks "in parables" ($\dot{\epsilon}\nu$ $\pi\alpha\rho\alpha\beta o\lambda\alpha\hat{\iota}\varsigma$), whereas in 8:32 he is explicitly said to speak "openly" ($\pi\alpha\rho\rho\eta\sigma\dot{\iota}\alpha$). The contrast seems to be deliberate.

The second part of Jesus' response is "to those who are outside, everything happens in parables, in order that, seeing, they may see and not perceive, and hearing, they may hear and not comprehend, lest they turn and it

be forgiven them" (vv. 11b-12). Many interpreters understandably object to the implication of the text that God predestines some people for damnation. The passage seems to have a more limited goal when seen in its historical context. The latter part of the statement alludes to Isa 6:9-10, in which Isaiah's prophetic mission to the people of Judah and Jerusalem is portrayed as doomed from the start. The passage in Isaiah may have been written after the fact, and thus may be an attempt to understand and explain why the people did not respond to God's revelation and teaching through Isaiah.[54] It is also a way of affirming the sovereignty of God: whatever happens is God's will and human beings must accept it as such. The situation may have been analogous with Mark and his audience. The passage may have been composed after many people to whom the word had been proclaimed had rejected it. This discouraging situation is made bearable by interpreting it in terms of an authoritative text and by accepting it as part of the divine plan.[55]

Mark links the concealment of the mystery of the kingdom of God with the "blindness" and "deafness" of the outsiders. The insiders are given special instruction by Jesus. *Sapiential Text A* (4QInstruction) from Qumran encourages the addressee, presumably a sectarian "insider," to honor his parents because they "opened your ears" (גלה אוזנכה) to the mystery to come.[56] He is also exhorted to "look at" (הבט) or consider the mystery to come.[57] Both texts use language of seeing and hearing with regard to the divine mystery.

A literary approach to vv. 11-12 leads to the inference that only a member of the community of followers of Jesus is able to understand his parables. The capacity for understanding is created by identification with the com-

---

53 In the context of Mark, the relevant occasions are 1:21-22, 39; 2:2, 13; 4:1-9.

54 Joseph Blenkinsopp concludes that it was written in response to the rejection of the prophet's message by Ahaz and those who supported his pro-Assyrian policy (*A History of Prophecy in Israel* [rev. ed.; Louisville: Westminster John Knox, 1996] 102).

55 Mark's use of Isa 6:9-10 implies that the failure of the outsiders to understand, and thus "turn" or repent and be forgiven, is the will of God brought about by Jesus as God's agent. This interpretation is all the more striking in comparison with the "softening" of the passage in the DSS and in the versions; see Craig A. Evans, *To See and Not Perceive: Isaiah 6.9-*

10 in Early Jewish and Christian Interpretation (JSNTSup 64; Sheffield: JSOT Press, 1989) esp. 53–80. Mark's usage is analogous to Paul's, though apparently not dependent on it. On Paul's use of Isa 6:9-10, see ibid., 81–89; on Mark's, 91–106.

56 4Q416 (4QInstruction[b]) 2 iii 18 (*Qumran Cave 4, XXIV: 4QInstruction (Sapiential Texts), Part 2* [ed. John Strugnell, Daniel J. Harrington, and Thorlief Elgvin; DJD 34; New York: Oxford University Press, 2000) 110, 113.

57 4Q416 (4QInstruction[b]) 2 i 5; Strugnell et al., *Qumran Cave 4, XXIV*, 88.

munity. The community has its own language, and only a member of it can speak and understand that language.[58] This insight is appropriate for the Markan and later stages of the literary history of the passage, since it fits the hermeneutic of the passion narrative of Mark (see the commentary on chap. 15 below). Another kind of literary approach leads to the conclusion that "Mark is a strong witness to the enigmatic and exclusive character of narrative, to its property of banishing interpreters from its secret places."[59]

The notion of "seeing" but not "perceiving" here has a certain analogy in the Dead Sea Scrolls. In the *Community Rule*, blindness was a culpable failure to discern the will of God. "Light," however, which enables "sight," that is, an understanding of the will and plan of God, is a divine gift.[60] A similar analogy to "hearing" but not "comprehending" occurs in the same context.[61]

4

4:13-20 The Interpretation of the Parable of the Sower

13/ And he said to them, "Do you not understand this parable? How then will you understand all the parables? 14/ The sower sows the word. 15/ And these are the ones who (are) along the road[a] where the word is sown; and when they hear, immediately Satan comes and takes away the word which has been sown in them.[b] 16/ And these are[c] the ones who are sown on stony ground, who, when they hear the word, receive it[d] immediately with joy, 17/ and they do not have a root in themselves, but are ephemeral; then, when tribulation or persecution on account of the word occurs, they immediately take offense. 18/ And others are the ones who are sown among thorn-plants: these are they who have heard the word,[e] 19/ and the anxieties of the age[f] and the seduction by wealth[g] and the desires for other things[h] enter (into them) and choke the word and it becomes unfruitful. 20/ And those are the ones who have been sown upon good ground, the ones who hear the word and accept it and bear fruit amounting to thirty and sixty and a hundred."[i]

a Nestle-Aland (27th ed.) places a colon after ὁδόν ("road"). But the clause ὅπου σπείρεται ὁ λόγος ("where the word is sown") fits better with what precedes than with what follows; thus the author follows the punctuation of Tischendorf (Constantinus Tischendorf, *Novum Testamentum Graece*, vol. 1 [8th ed.; Leipzig: Giesecke & Devrient, 1869]) and of Westcott and Hort (Brooke Foss Westcott and Fenton John Anthony Hort, *The New Testament in the Original Greek* [2 vols.; 2nd ed.; London/New York: Macmillan, 1898 (vol. 1); New York: Harper & Brothers, 1882 (vol. 2)] ad loc.).

b One uncial (A), one Old Latin MS (l), and, according to Tischendorf (ad loc.), the Ethiopic version attest the reading ἀπὸ τῆς καρδίας αὐτῶν ("from their hearts") instead of εἰς αὐτούς ("in them"), the reading attested by B W *f*[1.13] et al. The former reading is due to the influence of the parallel in Luke 8:12. The reading of D Θ 33 𝔐 et al., ἐν ταῖς καρδίαις αὐτῶν ("in their hearts"), may also have been influenced by the Lukan parallel. The reading of ℵ C L et al., ἐν αὐτοῖς ("in them"), represents a stylistic improvement or variant.

c Some MSS (A B 2427 𝔐 et al.) read ὁμοίως ("similarly") after εἰσιν ("are") and some (ℵ C L et al.) before it. Both of these readings are probably stylistic improvements, although Tischendorf (ad loc.) accepted the latter as original and Nestle (25th ed.) and Westcott and Hort (ad loc.) accepted the former.

d A number of MSS (Θ *f*[1.13] et al.) lack αὐτόν ("it") or its equivalent; this lack is due either to a stylistic improvement or to accidental omission.

e Some MSS (A 33 𝔐 et al.) read καὶ οὗτοί εἰσιν οἱ εἰς τὰς ἀκάνθας σπειρόμενοι οἱ τὸν λόγον ἀκού-

---

58 Stern, *Parables in Midrash*, 204–5.

59 Kermode, *Genesis of Secrecy*, 33–34.

60 "Blindness of the eyes" (עורון עינים) is a sin or vice in a list of such in 1QS 4:11; cf. 11:3-7 (Wibbing, *Die Tugend- und Lasterkataloge*, 56–57).

61 "Deafness of the ear" (כבוד אוזן) is listed following "blindness of the eyes" in 1QS 4:11 (Wibbing, *Die Tugend- und Lasterkataloge*, 57).

σαντες ("And these are the ones who are sown among thorn-plants, who have heard the word"). This reading apparently resulted from an effort to conform the structure of this sentence to v. 16. Other MSS (W Θ f¹·¹³ et al.) read καὶ οἱ εἰς τὰς ἀκάνθας σπειρό-μενοι· οὗτοί εἰσιν οἱ τόν λόγον ἀκούσαντες ("And the ones who are sown among thorn-plants: these are they who have heard the word"). This reading probably arose as an attempt to clarify the earliest recoverable reading or to improve its style.

f   Some MSS (D W Θ et al.) read βίου ("of life"); this reading resulted from a change intended to make the text more generally applicable by eliminating the apocalyptic term αἰῶνος ("age").

g   Some MSS, W (1424) f, read ἀπάται ("seductions" or "deceits") instead of the singular ἀπάτη ("seduction" or "deceit"). The former reading probably results from a change intended to make this noun conform to the plurals that precede and follow, respectively. Other MSS, D (Θ 565) it, also reading the plural ἀπάται ("seductions" or "deceits"), read κόσμου ("world") instead of πλούτου ("wealth"). The former reading resulted either from a desire to generalize or from a more positive attitude to wealth. One MS (Δ) reads ἡ ἀγάπη, "the love" (of wealth), instead of ἀπάτη ("seduction" or "deceit"); this reading resulted either from an attempt at clarification or a mistake.

h   D (Θ) W f¹ et al. lack καὶ αἱ περὶ τὰ λοιπὰ ἐπιθυμί-αι ("and the desires for other things"). The omission may have been deliberate, since the clause does not contribute much.

The textual issues here are analogous to those in v. 8. See p. 239 n. i above. In v. 20, the original reading of Codex Vaticanus (B*) was εν τριάκοντα καὶ ἑξ-ήκοντα καὶ ἑκατόν (which, assuming a smooth breathing, is translated "amounting to thirty and sixty and a hundred"). This is probably the earliest recoverable reading, since the other variants may be explained as deriving from it. At least two later copyists (1424 and 2427) read the εν as ἐν (as in the author's translation). Some copyists attempted to clarify the reading with the single εν, either by adding one more εν before ἑκατόν (C*vid pc), or by adding two more, one before ἑξήκοντα and the other before ἑκατόν (ℵ A C² D). Some copyists and translators understood the latter reading (εν . . . εν . . . εν) as ἐν . . . ἐν . . . ἐν, "amounting to thirty and amounting to sixty and amounting to a hundred" (f¹·¹³ 33 𝔐 sy), whereas others read it as ἓν . . . ἓν . . . ἓν, "one (bore) thirty and another sixty and another a hundred" (Θ pc lat; L reads ἐν, then twice ἓν, but not ἓν, "amounting to thirty; (one bore) sixty, another a hundred"; see Tischendorf, ad loc.). Finally, the reading ἓν . . . ἓν . . . ἓν, "one (bore) thirty and another sixty and another a hundred" was "improved" to το εν . . . το εν . . . το εν, "the one (bore) thirty and another sixty and another a hundred" (W).

Comment

■ **13** As noted above (Literary History of 4:1-34), v. 13 stands in some tension with vv. 10-12. In v. 10, the inner circle asks about "the parables," and Jesus gives a general response about parables in vv. 11-12. In v. 13, however, he responds as if they had inquired only about the parable of the sower. This tension results from the Markan or pre-Markan combination of the parable of the sower and its interpretation, on the one hand, with the "parable-theory" of vv. 11-12, on the other. Jesus' chiding of the inner circle for not understanding the parable of the sower seems to be a rhetorical device. It highlights the importance of what follows and engages the audience's attention. It may also foreshadow the disciples' difficulty in understanding the revelation of the necessity of Jesus' suffering in the middle section of Mark.

■ **14-20** The interpretation that follows remains to a significant degree on the figurative level. V. 14 reveals that what is sown is ὁ λόγος ("the word"). Jeremias demonstrated that this absolute use of the word is a technical term for the gospel in the early church.[62] In the context of Mark, its use here recalls 2:2, "And many were gathered together, . . . and he was speaking the word to them." In order to understand the nature of this "word," the audience must have recourse to the summary of Jesus' teaching in 1:15. So, although the interpretation does not explicitly identify the sower, the context of Mark suggests that this figure represents Jesus. Furthermore, the relationship between 1:14-15 and 2:2 suggests

---

62   Jeremias, *Parables of Jesus*, 77.

that for Mark, "the good news" or "gospel" and "the word" are equivalent.

In 4:15, the interpretation of the sowing along the road is introduced by the demonstrative pronoun οὗτοι ("these"). The use of such demonstratives is typical of the interpretation of dreams and of scripture in the Joseph story, prophetic vision reports, Daniel, apocalyptic literature, the Dead Sea Scrolls, and rabbinic literature.[63] The audience is not told how Satan's taking away the word that had been sown would be experienced. Presumably Satan was thought to work through other human beings to persuade those who had accepted the word to change their minds and to commit or recommit themselves to other points of view and ways of life. Another possibility is that Satan was believed to work directly by inspiring certain thoughts, words, and actions. Jesus' rebuke of Peter in 8:33 may indicate that the author of Mark considers Peter's response to Jesus' prediction of his sufferings to be an example of Satan's taking away the word from Peter.[64]

In vv. 16-17, the explanation of the rocky ground is illuminating in its reference to "tribulation or persecution on account of the word." This detail reveals that some of those who accepted the message of Jesus experienced social pressure to reject it later. This pressure may have taken a variety of forms, anything from being ostracized to being executed. The implied invitation to "take up your cross and follow me" in 8:34 suggests that some had died or at least that death was a threatening possibility.

The explanation of the thorns (vv. 18-19) in terms of the cares of the world, the delight in riches and other things, suggests that at least some in the movement or community of Jesus' followers were committed to an ascetic lifestyle. This commitment was probably related to the perceived need to travel about and proclaim the word.[65]

The interpretation, like the parable, ends on a positive note (v. 20). Even though many seeds fail to bear fruit, those that do will bear in extraordinary abundance. As Jeremias has shown, the metaphorical use of the verb καρποφορεῖν ("bearing fruit") and the notion of the word bearing fruit do not occur in the Synoptic Gospels apart from this passage and those dependent on it, but they do occur in other early Christian literature.[66] In Romans, Colossians, and *4 Ezra*, the image represents living in accordance with the will of God; it has a primarily ethical force.[67] As in Colossians, the image in Mark is closely related to the "growth" of the word, that is, the spread of the gospel throughout the world.[68]

4

	4:21-23 What Is Hidden Will Be Revealed	a	Some MSS, D (W *f*[13]) et al., read ἅπτεται ("is lighted") instead of ἔρχεται ("come"); the change was clearly made as an intended improvement.
21/	And he said to them, "Does a lamp come[a] in order to be put under the container or under the bed? Doesn't it (come) in order to be put on[b] the lampstand? 22/ For there is nothing hidden that will not be revealed, and nothing concealed that will not come out into the open. 23/ If anyone has ears to hear, let him hear!"	b	ℵ B* *f*[13] 33 *pc* read ὑπό ("under") instead of ἐπί ("on"). The former reading is due to an early error; see Westcott and Hort, 2:24.

---

63 Klauck, *Allegorie und Allegorese*, 67–91. See also Martha Himmelfarb, *Tours of Hell: An Apocalyptic Form in Jewish and Christian Literature* (Philadelphia: University of Pennsylvania Press, 1983) 41–67.

64 Mary Ann Tolbert argued in this way (*Sowing the Gospel*, 148–59, 195–203).

65 Cf. Mark 10:17-31 and the commentary below.

66 Jeremias, *Parables of Jesus*, 77–78.

67 Rom 7:4; Col 1:6, 10; *4 Ezra* 3:20; 9:31; see the discussion in Lohse, *Colossians and Philemon*, 19–20, 29.

68 Cf. Mark 4:8b, 20 with Col 1:6.

Comment

■ **21-22** Following the interpretation of the parable of the sower is a pair of sayings that comes close to the classic rhetorical comparison.[69] Just as a lamp is put on a stand, what is hidden or secret must come out into the open. The kingdom of God is not an explicit theme here, but this pair of sayings contrasts with the transitional dialogue between Jesus and his disciples. There it is said that the mystery of the kingdom is given to the disciples and withheld from outsiders. The term "mystery" is given two substitutes in this pair of sayings: $\kappa\rho\upsilon\pi\tau\acute{o}\nu$ ("what is hidden") and $\dot{\alpha}\pi\acute{o}\kappa\rho\upsilon\varphi\rho\nu$ ("what is secret"). The comparison with the lamp suggests that the mystery of the kingdom is not to be kept secret but is to be proclaimed.[70] There will always be outsiders who will reject the proclamation, but the circle of insiders is an open, not a closed, one.

■ **23** This exhortation to hear or listen continues the theme introduced in v. 3. There a simple call to listen ($\dot{\alpha}\kappa o\acute{u}\epsilon\tau\epsilon$) focused the audience's attention on the parable of the sower. Verse 9, a variant of the saying in v. 23, hints that this parable may not be easy to understand, or that its meaning, when grasped, may be difficult to accept. If the interpretation of vv. 21-22 above is correct, the exhortation to hear in v. 23 may call attention to a shift from the secrecy expressed in vv. 11-12 to the revelation advocated in vv. 21-22.

4

4:24-25 By the Measure with Which You Measure

24/ And he said to them, "Pay attention to what you hear. By the measure with which you measure, it will be measured to you and it will be added to you.[a] 25/ For with regard to the one who has, it will be given to him; and the one who does not have, even what he has will be taken away from him."

a   Some MSS (D W 565 et al.) lack $\kappa\alpha\grave{\iota}$ $\pi\rho o\sigma\tau\epsilon\vartheta\acute{\eta}\sigma\epsilon\tau\alpha\iota$ $\acute{\upsilon}\mu\hat{\iota}\nu$ ("and it will be added to you"). This clause was omitted either as a stylistic improvement or under the influence of the parallel in Matt 7:2 or Luke 6:38. For another explanation, see Metzger, *Textual Commentary*, 71–72. Other MSS (A Θ et al.) read the clause just discussed and, following it, the words $\tauo\hat{\iota}\varsigma$ $\dot{\alpha}\kappa o\acute{u}ou\sigma\iota\nu$ ("who hear"). These words were probably added to qualify the statement with some indication of worthiness on the part of those who receive. Cf. Metzger, *Textual Commentary*, 71–72.

Comment

■ **24-25** This three-part saying is a "parable" in the sense attested in the LXX, namely, an enigmatic or riddling saying.[71] If the previous pair of sayings (vv. 21-22) alludes to the proclamation of the mystery of the kingdom, this unit may develop that theme further. The introductory statement, "Pay attention to what you hear" (v. 24a), stands in some tension with the metaphorical saying, "By the measure with which you measure, it will be measured to you and it will be added to you" (v. 24b). The opening statement seems to define the addressees as those who hear the proclamation, whereas the first metaphorical saying seems to identify them as those who proclaim. The tension is resolved by the assumption that, as soon as one has grasped what one has heard, one is called to proclaim it to others. The third part of the saying, "For with regard to the one who has, it will be given to him; and the one who does not have, even that which he has will be taken away from him," seems to refer to the insiders and the outsiders of the dialogue (vv. 11-12) once again. Those who have the mystery of the kingdom will proclaim it and thus receive a greater reward, whereas those who do not have it, will not understand the parables and thus lose their opportunity to participate in the kingdom of God.

---

69   See the commentary above on vv. 1-9.
70   On the lamp as a symbol for God's word, see Marcus, 318.
71   Ps 77:2 LXX; Prov 1:6; Sir 39:3; Ezek 17:2; Dan 12:8 OG.

4:26-29 The Seed Grows by Itself

26/ And he said, "So is the kingdom of God, as a man throws seed upon the earth[a] 27/ and sleeps and wakes up night and day, and the seed sprouts and grows high, how he does not know. 28/ The earth bears fruit by itself,[b] first (the) green shoot, then[c] (the) head (of grain), then (the) fully ripened wheat[d] in the head. 29/ And when the (condition of the) crop permits, he immediately puts in the sickle, because the harvest-time has come."

a   ℵ B D L et al. read ὡς ἄνθρωπος ("as a man"); this is the reading adopted in the translation here. In a simple comparison, one would expect ὡς ("as") to be followed by a verb in the indicative mood. The fact that it is followed by a verb in the subjunctive has given rise to several readings that attempt to improve on the syntax. W f¹ et al. attest the reading ὡς ἄνθρωπος ὅταν, "as a man, whenever (he throws)"; A C et al. read ὡς (ἐ)ὰν ἄνθρωπος, "as, if a man (throws)." The reading of Θ f¹³ et al., ὥσπερ ἄνθρωπος, "just as," intensifies the comparison somewhat.

b   Some MSS attest the reading αὐτομάτη γάρ, "for of itself" (W Θ et al.) and others ὅτι αὐτομάτη, "because of itself" (D 565. et al.). These readings resulted from a perceived need for a connection between this clause and the preceding.

c   (ℵ*) B* L Δ have the Ionic-Hellenistic form εἶτεν ("then") instead of the more usual εἶτα ("then") here and in the following phrase. See Taylor, ad loc.

d   The earliest recoverable reading is that of C*vid 28. 2542ᶜ, πλήρης σῖτον ("fully ripened wheat"), in which the adjective is indeclinable (nominative in form) and the noun is in the accusative. This reading apparently gave rise to various "corrections": in some MSS, the noun has been put into the nominative to agree with the adjective (B 2427 *pc*; similarly, D W); in others, the adjective has been changed to the accusative to agree with the noun (ℵ A C² L Θ et al.). See Westcott and Hort, 2:24; and Taylor, ad loc. Cf. Nigel Turner, *Syntax* (Edinburgh: T & T Clark, 1963) 315–16.

Comment

■ **26-29** Unlike the parable of the sower, which is a narrative, a story told by verbs in the past tense, this parable is a simile, a comparison made in the present tense. Unlike the classic rhetorical comparisons, however, its point is not crystal clear. The kingdom of God is compared with a man who sows seed on the ground. Without his further participation, the seed sprouts and grows. The earth produces of itself. But when the grain is ready, the man puts in the sickle, because the harvest-time has come. No application or interpretation is explicit.

The parable discourse began with the parable of the sower, in which the sower was likely to be identified by the audience with God or with Jesus as God's agent. The sayings of vv. 21-25, however, have suggested that those to whom the mystery of the kingdom of God has been given are expected to proclaim it. Since this mystery is equivalent to the "word," which in turn is equivalent to the "good news" or the "gospel," these individuals may also be seen as sowers of the seed or word.

If the man sowing seed in the simile of vv. 26-29 represents the disciples of Jesus, then the emphasis on his not knowing how the seed sprouts and grows and on the earth producing of itself implies that the disciples should not become impatient or discouraged. They cannot control the manifestation of the kingdom nor force it. They are expected only to proclaim and to trust that the kingdom will be manifested at the proper time.

This interpretation implies a correspondence between the divine mysteries related to the growth of plants and those related to historical and eschatological events. The first speech of the angel Uriel in *4 Ezra* implies a similar correspondence: Ezra cannot weigh the weight of fire or measure the wind or call back a day that is past; likewise, he cannot understand the way of the Most High with regard to history (*4 Ezra* 4:1-12).[72] Uriel presents a positive analogy for eschatology from the processes of pregnancy and birth. When Ezra asks when the final judgment will occur, Uriel compares Hades to a pregnant woman's womb. Just as delivery takes place after nine months, so Hades will give up the souls in it at the proper time (*4 Ezra* 4:40-43).

Although it lacks the agricultural simile, the commentary on Habakkuk from Qumran includes a saying that expresses a conviction analogous to the rhetorical force of the parable of the seed growing by itself. After quot-

ing Hab 2:3b to the effect that the final age will definitely come, though it tarry, and one should wait for it, the commentator reassures the audience that:

כול קיצי אל יבואו לתכונם
כאשר חקק להם ברזי ערמתו

("all the ages of God will come at the right time, as he established for them in the mysteries of his prudence"). (1QHab 7:13-14)[73]

4

4:30-32 The Parable of the Mustard Seed

30/ And he said, "How should we figure the kingdom of God or with what illustration should we compare it?[a] **31/** (We shall figure it) as a mustard seed,[b] which, when it is sown upon the earth, is the smallest of all the seeds which are upon the earth, **32/** and when it is sown, it rises up and becomes larger[c] than all the shrubs, and it produces large branches, so that the birds of the air are able to live in its shade."

a The trans. is based on the reading of A C² D Θ et al., παραβολῇ παραβάλωμεν αὐτήν ("illustration should we compare it"), because it can best explain the origin of the other readings. The other readings can be explained as attempts to eliminate a perceived tautology in the use of the same root in the noun and the verb; see Moulton-Howard, 419; cf. 319.

b A L W Θ et al. read the noun in the accusative case, κόκκον ("seed"), rather than in the dative, κόκκῳ ("seed"), the reading of ℵ B C^vid D et al. The reading with the dative case, which is strongly attested by a combination of ℵ B and D, takes the noun as governed by the verb ὁμοιώσωμεν ("should we figure") in the previous verse. The reading with the accusative case takes it as the direct object of one of the verbs in the previous verse. The reading with the dative case is the basis of the trans. given here.

c D Δ f¹ et al. read μείζων ("larger") in the masculine gender, rather than μεῖζον ("larger") in the neuter, the reading of ℵ B C L W et al. The former reading is a "correction" of the latter, to make the adjective agree with its antecedent κόκκος ("seed"), which is masculine.

Comment

■ **30-32** Like the preceding parable, that of the mustard seed is actually a simile. Here again, the kingdom of God is the point of comparison, but there is no explicit interpretation or application. A link with the previous simile may be found in the likelihood that the implied impatience or discouragement of the previous comparison is directly addressed in this final one. It addresses discour-

agement and frustration by alluding to a passage from scripture and transforming it. The older passage is Ezekiel 17. As noted above, it is presented as a "parable" in the LXX; it is actually a political allegory. In it, an eagle represents the king of Babylon, the top of the cedar stands for the house of David, and a vine by many waters is Jehoiakin, the exiled king of Judah who rebelled against the king of Babylon. This rebellion is condemned, and God promises to plant a twig from the

---

72 For discussion, see Karina Martin Hogan, "Theologies in Conflict in 4 Ezra: Wisdom Debate and Apocalyptic Solution" (Ph.D. diss., University of Chicago, 2002) chap. 4.

73 Text and trans. from García Martínez and Tigchelaar, *Dead Sea Scrolls*, 1:16–17.

cedar that will become a noble cedar under which all kinds of beasts will dwell and in whose branches birds of every sort will nest (vv. 22-24). This last part of the parable or allegory expresses hope for the restoration of the house of David. From the point of view of eschatologically oriented groups in the late Second Temple period, one could call it a messianic parable.[74]

In the concluding parable of the collection in 4:1-34, the starting point is a mustard seed rather than a twig from a cedar. The end point is a shrub, rather than a noble cedar. The author of Mark has chosen to place this simile in a climactic position in order to parody overblown messianic expectations. As argued above, the most difficult aspect of the mystery of the kingdom of God in Mark is the revelation that the messiah, Jesus, must suffer and die. Mark has arranged the parable discourse so that it transports the audience from an initial emphasis on the proclamation of Jesus to a foreshadowing of his passion and its results. Jesus, who was handed over, scourged, and executed, was not the military leader and king that some groups were expecting. Instead of a cedar they got a shrub. Nevertheless, the kingdom of God will become manifest through him. The shrub will be capacious enough for the birds of the air to make nests in its branches.

---

4   4:33-34 Conclusion

33/   **And by means of many such parables he spoke the word to them, to the degree that they were able to hear. 34/ Now he did not speak to them without a parable, but he explained everything privately to his own disciples.**

Comment

■ **33** As noted above (Literary History of 4:1-34), v. 33 seems to imply that some or all of the material from v. 21 to v. 32 was spoken to the crowd and not just to the inner circle, although there is no indication of a transition from the private conversation that began in v. 10 back to public speech. Furthermore, the statement in v. 33 that Jesus spoke "the word" to them "in parables" "as they were able to hear" or understand is in tension with vv. 11-12, which state that Jesus spoke in parables to the outsiders so that they could not understand the mystery of the kingdom of God. These tensions suggest that v. 33 probably represents the conclusion to one of the two sources used in the composition of vv. 1-34, namely, a collection of parables consisting of a version of the parable of the sower (vv. 3-8), the similitude of the seed growing by itself (vv. 26-29), and the similitude of the mustard seed (vv. 30-32).

■ **34** As noted above (Literary History of 4:1-34), v. 34 fits well with the "parable theory" of vv. 11-12. Jesus speaks to the crowd or the outsiders only in parables, but reveals their meaning only to the disciples, the insiders. This private instruction fits also with the interpretation of the parable of the sower (vv. 13-20), which only the insiders hear. Thus, v. 34 probably represents the conclusion of the second source used by the evangelist, a brief didactic dialogue that included a version of the parable of the sower (vv. 3-8), its interpretation (vv. 13-20), the saying about having ears to hear in v. 9, and the "parable theory" in vv. 11-12. This source portrays Jesus' parables as enigmatic sayings requiring interpretation through the use of traditional techniques.

In this second source, οἱ ἴδιοι μαθηταί ("his own disciples") probably refers to "those who were around [Jesus] with the Twelve."[75] It is thus not clear that "the disciples" here refers to the Twelve, even from the point of view of the evangelist.[76]

---

74   Zimmerli (*Ezekiel 1*, 366) defines Ezek 17:22-24 as an oracle of salvation.

75   Cf. v. 10 above.

76   Rhoads (*Reading Mark*, 125) argued that, after 3:13-19, all the instances of "the disciples" refer to the Twelve.

4:35—6:6a **Epiphanies of Divine Power**

4

4:35-41 The Stilling of the Storm

35/ And he said to them on that day, when evening had come, "Let us go to the shore on the other side." 36/ And, having dismissed the crowd,[a] they took him along, as he was, in the boat; and other boats were with him.[b] 37/ And a mighty blast of wind arose and the waves beat against the boat, so that it was quickly filled with water. 38/ He himself was in the stern, asleep on the cushion. They woke[c] him and said to him, "Teacher, don't you care that we are perishing?" 39/ And when he had awakened, he rebuked the wind and said to the sea, "Be silent; be muzzled." And the wind abated and there was a great calm. 40/ And he said to them, "Why are you cowardly?[d] Do you not yet have trust?" 41/ And they were very fearful and were saying among themselves, "Who then is this that both the wind and the sea obey him?"[e]

a The surviving portion of the oldest witness to the text of Mark, p[45], begins with this verse; it appears to read, along with D W Θ *f*[13] et al., ἀφίουσιν τὸν ὄχλον καί ("they dismissed the crowd and"), rather than ἀφέντες τὸν ὄχλον ("having dismissed the crowd"). If this part of the verse is redactional, the latter reading is more likely, since the use of an aorist participle with a main verb is typical of Markan style; see Moulton-Turner, 4:26. It is possible, however, that the former reading is original and represents the style of Mark's source. Instead of τὸν ὄχλον ("the crowd"), A reads αὐτόν ("him"), most likely by mistake, since it contradicts the following clause.

b Some MSS (D L 33 *pm*) read the diminutive form πλοιάρια (lit., "little boats," but at this period probably just "boats") instead of πλοῖα ("boats"). The diminutive form occurs in 3:9.

c Many MSS (A B[1] C[2] L et al.) read διεγείρουσιν, "they woke (him) up," instead of ἐγείρουσιν, "they woke (him)," the reading of ℵ B* C* Δ 2427 et al. The latter is somewhat more likely to be earlier, since the former may be seen as a secondary intensification or a change made to prepare for the use of διεγερθείς ("when he had awakened" or "having awakened") in v. 39. Most of the MSS that read the finite verb instead of the participle at the beginning of v. 36 have the participle, διεγείραντες ("having waked [him] up"; except *f*[13] which reads ἐγείραντες, "having waked"), here instead of the finite verb. The reading of ℵ B* C* Δ 2427 et al. is again more likely to be earlier, since it can explain the origin of these two readings as well.

d The trans. given here is based on ℵ B D L et al., which attest the reading τί δειλοί ἐστε; οὔπω, "Why are you cowardly? (Do you) not yet." Many MSS (A C 33 𝔐 et al.) attest the addition of οὔτως ("so") after ἐστε ("are you"), which resulted from an attempt at intensification or improvement of the style. These same MSS also change οὔπω ("not yet") to πῶς οὐκ ("how not"). The addition of πῶς ("how") may have been made to soften Jesus' reproach; so Metzger, *Textual Commentary*, 72. Other MSS (p[45vid] *f*[1.13] et al.) add the word οὔτως ("so") before δειλοί ("cowardly").

e Many MSS (D A W Θ 33 𝔐 lat) read ὑπακούουσιν, "(they) obey," rather than ὑπακούει, "(it) obeys." This change was made either as a correction or under the influence of the parallel in Matt 8:27 or Luke 8:25.

The Stilling of the Storm in Literary Context

The miracle story about the stilling of the storm is closely linked to the preceding parable discourse. The opening clause, "and he said to them," is connected to what goes before in that "disciples" in v. 34 is the antecedent of "them" in v. 35. Further, the temporal reference in v. 35, "on that day," indicates that the mighty deed occurred on the evening of the same day as the parable discourse. The taking leave of the crowd and the mention of the boat in v. 36 link the miracle story to the setting of the parable discourse in 4:1, where the crowd is introduced and Jesus is described as teaching from a boat on the Sea of Galilee.

The shift from discourse to mighty deed, however, indicates a transition to a new section of the Gospel, 4:35—6:6a, devoted to epiphanies of the divine power at work in Jesus and the various responses to it. This section is unified by the keywords πίστις ("faith" or "trust") and ἀπιστία ("unbelief" or "lack of trust"). As Gerd Theissen has pointed out, these are typical miracle motifs. Furthermore, both the first and the last passages in this section express the theme of Jesus' identity. In 4:41 the disciples ask, "Who is this . . . ?," and in 6:3 the residents of Jesus' hometown ask, "Is this not. . . ?"[1]

The History of the Tradition

Paul J. Achtemeier has argued persuasively that the material not dealing with miracles in Mark 4:35—8:26 is heavily redacted.[2] His argument that there is relatively little redaction in the miracle stories in Mark 4–6 is generally persuasive.[3] He was also able to show that the original order of the miracle-stories in 6:45—8:26 is remarkably similar to the order of those in 4:35—6:44, namely, a sea miracle, three healing miracles, and the feeding of a multitude. Thus, his thesis that the author of Mark made use of two collections of miracle stories is credible. The stilling of the storm was apparently the first unit in one of these sources.

Genre

Dibelius defined 4:35-41 as a "Tale" (German *Novelle*).[4] He argued that the Tales of the Synoptic tradition are "*Epiphanies* in which the divine power of the divine wonder-worker becomes manifest."[5] The purpose of the Tales is not edification, nor to indicate what the will of God is; rather, the miracle is told for the sake of the divine epiphany itself.[6] Bultmann classified this passage as a "nature miracle."[7] Theissen placed it in the category of "rescue miracles." He rejected the category of "nature miracles," arguing that there is little justification for distinguishing between miracles in the human domain and those in the natural world. He included stories about rescue from prison in this category, as well as those about rescue at sea. Both, he suggested, depict victory over hostile forces, the power of nature and that of the state.[8]

Comment

■ **35** For the temporal references, see "The Stilling of the Storm in Literary Context" above. Jesus' remark, "Let us go to the shore on the other side," indicates the first occasion on which Jesus leaves Galilee since the notice in 1:14 that he went into Galilee after John the Baptist "was handed over." Judging from 5:1, the intended destination is the territory of the Decapolis.[9] No motivation for the journey is given, but the audience may recall that Jesus said earlier in the narrative, "Let us go elsewhere, to the neighboring market-towns, in order that I may proclaim there also; for I came out for this purpose" (1:38).

■ **36** On the crowd and the boat, see "The Stilling of the Storm in Literary Context" above. The statement that "other boats were with him" has been explained in various ways. Bultmann concluded that this mention "is old, and has been rendered unintelligible by the editing."[10] Theissen suggested that Mark has compressed a longer story in which the sinking of the other boats depicted the dangerous character of the storm.[11] Recently Dennis R. MacDonald has argued that the narrative of the stilling of the storm was modeled on Homer's *Odyssey*. The mention of other boats being with Jesus echoes *Od.* 10.1-69, according to which Odysseus left the island of Aeolus with twelve ships.[12] If the miracle story of Mark is based, in part, on Ps 107:23-32 (106:23-32 LXX), however, the presence of "other boats" may be inspired by v. 23a, "Those who go down to the sea in boats" (οἱ καταβαίνοντες εἰς τὴν θάλασσαν ἐν πλοίοις).

1   Theissen, *Miracle Stories*, 208; cf. 129–40. On the unity of 4:35—6:6a, see also Schmithals, *Wunder,* 7.

2   Paul J. Achtemeier, "Toward the Isolation of Pre-Markan Miracle Catenae," *JBL* 89 (1970) 266–74.

3   Ibid., 274–81.

4   Dibelius, *From Tradition to Gospel,* 71.

5   Ibid., 94 (emphasis original).

6   Ibid.

7   Bultmann, *History*, 215–16.

8   Theissen, *Miracle Stories*, 99–100.

9   See the commentary on 5:1 below.

10   Bultmann, *History*, 215–16.

11   Theissen, *Miracle Stories*, 102, 180.

12   Dennis R. MacDonald, *The Homeric Epics and the*

■ **37** Although its setting is on a relatively small lake, the storm described here is assimilated to the awesome storms at sea that figure in historical writings and also provided many an ancient writer with a realistic motif in fictional writing or a powerful image for the experience of divine benevolence or vengeance. For example, in one of the *Thanksgiving Hymns* from Qumran, the speaker, opposed by the wicked, describes himself as a sailor on a ship amid furious seas, against which their waves and billows roar (1QH 14:22-24; Sukenik, 6:22-24). In another hymn, the image is used eschatologically. When the marvelous mighty counselor appears, those who practice injustice will be like sailors on the deeps, and the abyss will swallow them up forever (1QH 11:9-18; Sukenik, 3:9-18).

The term λαῖλαψ ("mighty blast" or "furious storm") occurs six times in the *Odyssey*, but is typical of literary accounts of storms in general.[13] In the LXX, λαῖλαψ ("mighty blast" or "whirlwind") is used to translate הסערה ("whirlwind," "storm," or "tempest") in Job 38:1. The reference is to the whirlwind out of which God spoke to Job. It is the Greek word used in Sirach to describe the whirlwind that took Elijah to heaven (Sir 48:9, 12). It is also used in Jer 32:32 LXX in the context of a theophany.[14] Although in these texts the whirlwind represents the power of God, rather than that of an opponent, these biblical passages support the epiphanic interpretation of the stilling of the storm. The image of the waves beating against the boat and the boat filling is a concrete variant of a widespread motif of the danger of a storm or other adverse conditions at sea.[15]

■ **38** The depiction of Jesus asleep at the stern is reminiscent of Odysseus and Aeneas.[16] It is also reminiscent of an ancient Near Eastern symbol of the sleeping deity. The divine king could sleep undisturbed because his authority was unquestioned.[17] The portrayal of the disciples waking Jesus and saying, "don't you care that we are perishing?" is a variant on the motif of the terror of sailors tossed by a violent storm at sea.[18] The disciples' statement is not a confident prayer for help, as Jesus' rebuke in v. 40 indicates. Other stories about rescue at sea do contain such confident requests.[19] The disciples address Jesus as "teacher" (διδάσκαλε), an address that, at first sight, seems inappropriate in the context of a miracle story. Matthew changes the address to κύριε ("Lord") and also changes their question to a confident prayer for help (Matt 8:25). Luke replaces "teacher" with "Master, Master" (ἐπιστάτα ἐπιστάτα) (Luke 8:24). The linking of the title "teacher" with miracle-working is characteristic of Mark. As in 1:21-28, so here, the implication is that the teaching of Jesus is validated and illustrated by his miracle-working power.

Although close verbal similarity is lacking, the general situation in Mark 4:37-38 is similar to that in Jonah 1:4-6.[20] According to Mark 4:37, a mighty blast of wind arose (γίνεται λαῖλαψ μεγάλη ἀνέμου); in the book of Jonah, the Lord raised up a wind upon the sea (κύριος ἐξήγειρεν πνεῦμα εἰς τὴν θάλασσαν; 1:4 LXX). In Mark's account, the waves beat against the boat, so that it was immediately filled with water (τὰ κύματα ἐπέβαλλεν εἰς τὸ πλοῖον, ὥστε ἤδη γεμίζεσθαι τὸ πλοῖον). In the story about Jonah, there was a great

---

Gospel of Mark (New Haven/London: Yale University Press, 2000) 58–61.

13 Ibid., 59.

14 Cf. Jer 25:32 MT and the comments of Holladay, *Jeremiah*, 1:677–81.

15 Ps 107:25b (106:25b LXX); 1QH 11:15 (Sukenik, 3:15); 14:23 (Sukenik, 6:23); *Hom. Hymn.* 33.11-12; Plutarch *Vit. Caesar* 38. On Caesar's unsuccessful attempt to cross the Adriatic Sea during a severe storm and its relation to this passage in Mark, see Roger David Aus, *The Stilling of the Storm: Studies in Early Palestinian Judaic Traditions* (ISFCJ; Binghamton, NY: Global Publications, 2000) 56–71.

16 Homer *Od.* 10.47-49; 13.73-80; for discussion, see MacDonald, *Homeric Epics*, 59, 221 n. 18; Virgil *Aen.* 4.553; see Rick Strelan: "A Greater than Caesar:

Storm Stories in Lucan and Mark," *ZNW* 91 (2000) 166–79, esp. 178 n. 47.

17 Bernard F. Batto, "The Sleeping God: An Ancient Near Eastern Motif of Divine Sovereignty," *Bib* 68 (1987) 153–77; Batto discusses the influence of this motif on the Hebrew Bible and on Mark 4:35-41 pars. Batto concludes that the sleep of Jesus in Mark 4:38 signifies his possession of absolute authority (175).

18 Ps 107:26-28a (106:26-28a LXX); 1QH 11:14 (Sukenik, 3:14); 14:24 (Sukenik, 6:24).

19 Ps 107:28b (106:28b LXX); *Hom. Hymn.* 33.8-10.

20 On the similarities and differences between the Jonah story and Mark 4:35-41, see Klauck, *Allegorie und Allegorese*, 345–46. See also Aus, *Stilling of the Storm*, 3–55.

storm on the sea and the ship was in danger of being broken up (ἐγένετο κλύδων μέγας ἐν τῇ θαλάσσῃ καὶ τὸ πλοῖον ἐκινδύνευεν συντριβῆναι). According to Mark 4:38, Jesus was in the stern, asleep on the cushion (αὐτὸς ἦν ἐν τῇ πρύμνῃ ἐπὶ τὸ προσκεφάλαιον καθεύδων). According to Jonah 1:5, Jonah had gone down into the hold of the ship and was sleeping and snoring (Ιωνας δὲ κατέβη εἰς τὴν κοίλην τοῦ πλοίου καὶ ἐκάθευδεν καὶ ἔρρεγχεν). In Mark's account, the disciples (cf. 4:34) wake Jesus and ask, "Teacher, don't you care that we are perishing?" (καὶ ἐγείρουσιν αὐτὸν καὶ λέγουσιν αὐτῷ· διδάσκαλε, οὐ μέλει σοι ὅτι ἀπολλύμεθα; 4:38). In the narrative about Jonah, the shipmaster goes to him and says, "Why are you snoring? Arise and call upon your god, in order that god may save us and we may not perish" (καὶ προσῆλθεν πρὸς αὐτὸν ὁ πρωρεὺς καὶ εἶπεν αὐτῷ Τί σὺ ῥέγχεις; ἀνάστα καὶ ἐπικαλοῦ τὸν θεόν σου, ὅπως διασώσῃ ὁ θεὸς ἡμᾶς καὶ μὴ ἀπολώμεθα; 1:6). The outcome is also narrated in a similar way. According to Mark 4:39b, the wind abated and there was a great calm (ἐκόπασεν ὁ ἄνεμος καὶ ἐγένετο γαλήνη μεγάλη). In Jonah 1:15 it is said that, when Jonah had been cast into the sea, the sea ceased from its raging (ἔστη ἡ θάλασσα ἐκ τοῦ σάλου αὐτῆς).

In both stories there is a contrast between the relaxed attitude of the one sleeping and the anxiety of the others in the vessel. Jonah's ability to sleep is ironic, because he is the one on whose account the storm was caused by divine power.[21] Although the question of the disciples may owe something to the humor and realism of the Jonah story, the sleep of Jesus in the context of Mark, especially in light of Jesus' question about trust later in this story, shows that his serenity is due to his trust in God. It is likely that the evangelist is deliberately alluding to the Jonah story here, since the book of Jonah is also alluded to in the scene in Gethsemane[22] and since Jonah was an antitype of Jesus in early Christian tradition.[23]

■ **39** Jonah is asked by the shipmaster to pray to his god. He does not do so, but proposes that the sailors throw him overboard. Jesus' response to the disciples' question is not to pray but to rebuke the wind and the sea (καὶ διεγερθεὶς ἐπετίμησεν τῷ ἀνέμῳ καὶ εἶπεν τῇ θαλάσσῃ· σιώπα, πεφίμωσο). The narrative thus portrays Jesus behaving not like a devout human person but like God, who caused the sea to cease from its raging in the Jonah story. Thus, Jesus is portrayed not so much as a human being who has trust in God's power to save, but as a divine being.[24] The amazement of the disciples is intelligible in light of the cultural context and parallel texts: they have God manifest in the boat with them!

The depiction of Jesus sleeping, being awakened by the disciples, and then stilling the storm is reminiscent of a motif in the Hebrew Bible that involves the metaphor of God being roused from sleep by the people in order to deliver them by performing a mighty deed. For example:

Awake! Why are you sleeping, Lord?
Rise up and do not reject (us) forever.
Why do you turn your face away,
(And) forget our poverty and tribulation?
For our soul has been abased to the dust,
Our belly is bound to the ground.
Arise, Lord, help us
And redeem us for the sake of your name
(ἐξεγέρθητι· ἵνα τί ὑπνοῖς, κύριε; ἀνάστηθι καὶ μὴ ἀπώσῃ εἰς τέλος. ἵνα τί τὸ πρόσωπόν σου ἀποστρέφεις, ἐπιλανθάνῃ τῆς πτωχείας ἡμῶν καὶ τῆς θλίψεως ἡμῶν;

---

21   The idea that a deity would send a storm to punish a wrongdoer occurs in Acts 28:4 and is widespread in Greek literature. See Jack M. Sasson, *Jonah: A New Translation with Introduction, Commentary, and Interpretation* (AB 24B; New York: Doubleday, 1990) 91–92.

22   See the commentary on 14:32-42 below.

23   Matt 12:39-41; 16:4; Luke 11:29-30, 32; on Jonah in early Christian art, see Graydon F. Snyder, *Ante Pacem: Archaeological Evidence of Church Life before Constantine* (Macon, GA: Mercer University Press, 1985) 45–49.

24   On God's power over the sea, see Ps 64:8 LXX (65:8 MT; 65:7 NRSV). The Greeks and Romans turned with prayers and sacrifices to the gods for help with the storms of the sea, i.e., to Zeus, Apollo, Hera, Poseidon, or to the special gods of the winds like Boreas and Zephyrus, and they created the cult of the winds in many places; see Paul Stengel, *Opferbräuche der Griechen* (Leipzig/Berlin: Teubner, 1910) 146–53; Stefan Weinstock, *Divus Julius* (Oxford: Clarendon, 1971) 121. For a sea rescue by Aphrodite, see Wendy Cotter, *Miracles in Greco-Roman Antiquity: A Sourcebook* (London/New York:

ὅτι ἐταπεινώθη εἰς χοῦν ἡ ψυχὴ ἡμῶν,
ἐκολλήθη εἰς γῆν ἡ γαστὴρ ἡμῶν.
ἀνάστα, κύριε, βοήθησον ἡμῖν
καὶ λύτρωσαι ἡμᾶς ἕνεκεν τοῦ ὀνόματός σου). (Ps 43:24-27 LXX)[25]

After he awoke, the Markan Jesus rebuked (ἐπετίμησεν) the wind and commanded the sea to be muzzled (πεφίμωσο).[26] These terms recall the exorcism that was Jesus' first mighty deed. At that time he rebuked (ἐπετίμησεν) the unclean spirit and commanded it to be muzzled (φιμώθητι) (Mark 1:25).[27] The reason why the wind and sea are treated like demons is that demons or evil spirits were thought to be responsible for inclement weather.[28] There is evidence in both Greek and Jewish literature, early and late, for the personification or demonization of wind and sea.[29]

Herodotus tells how Xerxes had bridges built across the Hellespont from Asia to Europe. The distance was seven-eighths of a mile. In the first attempt, he had the Phoenicians make a bridge of flaxen cables, the Egyptians one of papyrus. No sooner was the strait bridged than a great storm occurred and destroyed their work. Xerxes was very angry and commanded that the Hellespont be scourged with three hundred lashes (ἐκέλευσε τριηκοσίας ἐπικέσθαι μάστιγι πληγάς) and a pair of fetters be thrown into the sea (καὶ κατεῖναι ἐς τὸ πέλαγος πεδέων ζεῦγος). He sent branders with the rest to brand the Hellespont (στιγέας ἅμα τούτοισι ἀπέπεμψε στίξοντας τὸν Ἑλλήσποντον). He charged them while they scourged to utter words, which were in

Herodotus's view, outlandish and presumptuous (ἐνετέλλετο δὲ ὧν ῥαπίζοντας λέγειν Βάρβαρά τε καὶ ἀτάσθαλα): "You bitter water," they should say, "our master thus punishes you, because you did him wrong although he had done no wrong to you. Yes, Xerxes the king will pass over (διαβήσεται) you, whether you wish it or not; it is but just that no man offers you sacrifice, for you are a turbid and a briny river." Thus he commanded that the sea should be punished (τήν τε δὴ θάλασσαν ἐνετέλλετο τούτοισι ζημιοῦν) and they who had been overseers . . . should be beheaded (7.34-35).[30] Whether or not this story is historically reliable and in spite of Herodotus's obvious disapproval, the account indicates that some people at the time of Herodotus personified the sea or treated it as they would a demon.

A spell that was written down in the 4th cent. CE, but may be older, implies that there are names that may be recited to control winds:

Taking a three-cornered sherd from the fork of a road—pick it up with your left hand—inscribe it with myrrhed ink and hide it. [Write:] ASSTRAELOS CHRAELOS, dissolve every enchantment against me, NN, for I conjure you / by the great and terrible names which the winds fear and the rocks split when they hear it (Λαβὼν ὄστρακον ἀπὸ τριόδου τρίγωνον, τῇ ἀριστερᾷ χειρὶ ἄρας, γράφε ζμυρνομελανίῳ καὶ κρύψον· Ἀσστράηλος Χράηλος λύσατε πᾶν φάρμακον γενόμενον κατ᾽ ἐμοῦ τοῦ δεῖνα, ὅτι ὀρκίζω ὑμᾶς κατὰ τῶν μεγάλων καὶ φικτρῶν ὀνο-

---

Routledge, 1999) §3.1 (pp. 132–33); for Poseidon as a saver of ships, §3.2 (p. 133); for the Dioscuri as deliverers of sailors and calmers of storms, §§3.4 and 3.5 (p. 134).

25 See also Pss 7:7; 58:5b-6; 77:65-66; Isa 51:9-11 MT.

26 The use of the term θάλασσα (lit., "sea") for this relatively small lake is a sign of a Koine Greek influenced by Semitic languages and possibly of the locally limited world in which the story was told; see Theissen, *Gospels in Context*, 105–8, and the commentary above on 1:16-20. On the use of φιμώθητι ("be muzzled") in the *PGM*, see Samson Eitrem, *Some Notes on the Demonology in the New Testament* (SO.S 12; Oslo: A. W. Brøgger, 1950) 30–31.

27 See also 3:12; 9:25. On the link between the stilling of the storm and the exorcisms, see Theissen, *Miracle Stories*, 99, 140–41.

28 H. van der Loos, *The Miracles of Jesus* (NovTSup 9; Leiden: Brill, 1965) 642. *Jub.* 2:2 refers to "the angels of the spirit of the winds" (trans. VanderKam, *Book of Jubilees*, 7); *1 Enoch* 69:22 refers to the spirits of the winds; according to *1 Enoch* 60:16, "the wind of the sea is male and strong" (trans. Nickelsburg and VanderKam, 73); see Kollmann, *Wundertäter*, 272–73.

29 On various kinds of weather demons, see Wilhelm Fiedler, *Antiker Wetterzauber* (Würzburger Studien zur Altertumswissenschaft 1; Stuttgart: Kohlhammer, 1931) 25–72.

30 Text and trans. (modified) from Alfred D. Godley, *Herodotus* (4 vols.; LCL; Cambridge, MA: Harvard University Press; London: Heinemann, 1922) 3:334–71.

μάτων, ὧν οἱ ἄνεμοι φρίζουσιν καὶ αἱ πέτραι ἀκούσαντες διαρήσσονται). (PGM XXXVI. 256–64)[31]

Psalm 106 is a national confession of sin that contains a historical poem (vv. 7–46) and ends with a prayer for help.[32] One of the events recounted is the exodus:

and [God] rebuked the Red Sea, and it dried up,
and he guided them through the deep as through the
wilderness
(καὶ ἐπετίμησεν τῇ ἐρυθρᾷ θαλάσσῃ, καὶ
ἐξηράνθη,
καὶ ὡδήγησεν αὐτοὺς ἐν ἀβύσσῳ ὡς ἐν ἐρήμῳ).
(Ps 105:9 LXX)

In this passage, the Red Sea is personified and probably assimilated to the mythic pattern of God doing battle with Sea, Leviathan, Tannin, or Rahab.[33]

The *Testament of Solomon* presents a dialogue between Solomon and a demon who has the form of a horse in front and a fish in back. He identifies himself as "a cruel spirit of the sea" (θαλάσσιον πνεῦμα χαλεπόν). He raises himself up like a wave and, being transformed, comes in against the ships. He gives his name as Kunopegos, which may be another name for Poseidon (*T. Sol.* 16).[34]

■ **40** As noted above, the contrast between Jesus' serene attitude and the fear of the disciples implies Jesus' trust in God. But the question he asks the disciples, combined with their address of him as "teacher," implies much more than that.[35] The storm is an occasion for teaching about trust. As in 11:22–23, Jesus instructs the disciples that, if they have trust (or faith) in God, they too will have the extraordinary power over the elements that Jesus exercises. Just as divine power manifests itself in Jesus, so also will it become manifest in his followers, if they have this trust or faith.[36]

■ **41** The ending of the story about the stilling of the storm in Mark displays elements related to epiphanies, namely, the great fear of the disciples and·their exclamation, "Who then is this that both the wind and the sea obey him?"[37] In the context of Mark as a whole, it is clear that the disciples are not ready to think of themselves as individuals able to control the natural elements through trust or faith in God. The stilling of the storm is the most astounding mighty deed that they have seen Jesus perform so far, and it leads them to ponder his identity and the source of his power. As Jesus' address of the wind and sea in v. 39 echoed his commands addressed to the unclean spirit in 1:25, so the question of the disciples echoes the question and acclamation of the people in the synagogue in Capernaum. Compare "Who then is this"

---

31 Preisendanz-Henrichs, 2:171; trans. by Morton Smith in Betz, *Magical Papyri*, 275; on the date of the manuscript, see p. xxiv. See also John G. Gager, ed., *Curse Tablets and Binding Spells from the Ancient World* (New York/Oxford: Oxford University Press, 1992) 237. Compare the depiction in the book of Revelation of angels controlling winds (7:1).

32 Mitchell Dahood, *Psalms III: 101–150: Introduction, Translation, and Notes* (AB 17A; Garden City, NY: Doubleday, 1970) 67.

33 Cf. Isa 27:1; Job 9:13; 26:12; Isa 51:9; Ps 89:10; 74:13.

34 Text from McCown, *Testament of Solomon*, 48*; trans. from D. C. Duling in *OTP* 1:976. Contrast *Hom. Hymn.* 22, which describes Poseidon as a savior of ships.

35 On the two-step progression or duality of Jesus' question, see Christopher D. Marshall, *Faith as a Theme in Mark's Narrative* (SNTSMS 64; Cambridge/New York: Cambridge University Press, 1989) 215–16.

36 So also Ian G. Wallis, *The Faith of Jesus Christ in Early*

Christian Traditions (SNTSMS 84; Cambridge/New York: Cambridge University Press, 1995) 36–39. Marshall (*Faith*, 217) concluded, "This view has much to commend it."

37 The concept "theophany" is closely related to that of "epiphany." On theophanies in the OT and NT, see G. Henton Davies, "Theophany," *IDB* 4:619–20; and on theophanies in the OT, see Theodore Hiebert, "Theophany in the OT," *ABD* 6:505–11; the latter has a bibliography of works up to 1992. On the phenomenon of "epiphany" in Greek and Roman religion, see H. S. Versnel, "What Did Ancient Man See When He Saw a God? Some Reflections on Greco-Roman Epiphany," in Dirk van der Plas, ed., *Effigies Dei: Essays on the History of Religions* (Leiden/New York: Brill, 1987) 42–55 (with a large bibliography). Timothy Dwyer concludes that the terror of the disciples is "an unavoidable reaction to uncanny power" (*The Motif of Wonder in the Gospel of Mark* [JSNTSup 128; Sheffield: Sheffield Academic Press, 1996] 111).

(4:41) with "What is this? (1:27) and "both the wind and the sea obey him" (4:41) with "he commands even the unclean spirits, and they obey him" (1:27). Thus, the rhetorical question of the disciples here is a kind of

acclamation. From the point of view of the audience, these mighty deeds are part of the unfolding of the significance of Jesus' portrayal as "messiah" or "Christ" (1:1) and as God's son (1:11 and 3:11).[38]

5

5:1-20 The Gerasene Demoniac

1/ And they came[a] to the opposite shore of the sea, to the district of the Gerasenes.[b] 2/ When he came out of the boat, a man with an unclean spirit immediately came out[c] from among the tombs to meet him. 3/ This man was living among the tombs, and no one was able to bind him anymore, not even with a chain, 4/ for he had often been bound with fetters and handcuffs, but the handcuffs were torn apart by him and the fetters broken, and no one was able to subdue him. 5/ And night and day he was crying out among the tombs and on the mountains and beating himself with stones. 6/ And having seen Jesus from a distance, he ran and showed him[d] reverence 7/ and he cried out with a loud voice and said, "What have I to do with you, Jesus, son of the most high God? I adjure you by God, do not torment me." 8/ For he (had) said to him, "Come out of the man, you unclean spirit." 9/ And he asked him, "What is your name?" And he said to him, "Legion[e] is my name, because we are many." 10/ And he entreated him strongly not to send them[f] out of the region. 11/ Now there was a large herd of pigs there, grazing beside the mountain; 12/ and they entreated him, saying,[g] "Send us into the pigs, so that we may enter into them." 13/ And he allowed them[h] (to do so). And

a ℵ* A B D Π et al. read ἦλθον ("they came"), giving this reading very strong external support. ℵ^cvid C G M L et al. attest the reading ἦλθεν ("he came"). Heinrich Greeven adopted the singular reading, arguing that the plural was introduced under the influence of the Lukan parallel (Luke 8:26; see Huck-Greeven, ad loc.). Tischendorf and Westcott and Hort adopted the plural reading. The plural is probably original, because a scribe may have changed such a reading to agree with the reference to Jesus alone in the following verse. Turner argued that the use of the plural in describing the coming and going of Jesus and the disciples, followed at once by the singular in reference to Jesus alone, is typical Markan style ("Marcan Usage," 26 [1925] 225–26, 228; Elliott, Language and Style, 36–37, 39).

b The reading Γερασηνῶν ("Gerasenes") is supported by ℵ* B D 2427^vid latt sa. This reading has strong external support but is problematic because Gerasa, modern Jerash, is located more than thirty miles southeast of the Sea of Galilee. It is unlikely that its surrounding district ever extended to the shores of the lake. Other MSS support the reading Γαδαρηνῶν ("Gadarenes"), namely, A C et al. Although Gadara, modern Um Qeis, was about five miles southeast of the Sea of Galilee, its territory probably did border on the lake during the time of Jesus; see Metzger, Textual Commentary, 18–19; James B. Pritchard, The Harper Atlas of the Bible (New York: Harper & Row, 1987) 164, 181; John McRay, "Gerasenes," ABD 2:991–92, esp. 991; John T. Fitzgerald, "Gadara: Philodemus' Native City," in idem, Dirk Obbink and Glenn S. Holland, eds., Philodemus and the New Testament World (NovT-Sup 111; Leiden: Brill, 2004) 343–97, esp. 344–45, 347–48, 386–87. This reading, however, probably resulted from scribal attempts to conform Mark to MSS of Matt 8:28 that had this reading. It is likely that this reading is the original one for Matthew and that it

---

38 Günter Kettenbach notes that the question of the disciples (v. 41) is answered by the centurion under the cross (15:39) (Einführung in die Schiffahrtsmetaphorik der Bibel [EHS.T 512; Frankfurt am Main/New York: Peter Lang, 1994] 260). The confession of Peter in 8:29b is at least as important (cf.

Schmithals, Wunder, 57–58). Kettenbach also argues that, in this passage, the author of Mark founded the symbol of the ship as the church (270). Klauck entertains this possibility but is more cautious (Allegorie und Allegorese, 347).

the unclean spirits went out (of the man) and entered into the pigs, and the herd rushed down the steep bank into the sea, about two thousand in number, and they were drowned in the sea. 14/ And those who were tending them fled and brought a report[i] into the city and to the farms; and they came to see what it was that had happened, 15/ and they came to Jesus and saw the demoniac sitting, clothed and in his right mind, who had had the legion,[j] and they were afraid. 16/ And those who had seen told them how it had happened to the demoniac and concerning the pigs. 17/ And they began to entreat him[k] to leave their region. 18/ And as he was getting into the boat, the former demoniac began to entreat him that he might be with him. 19/ He did not allow him (to do so), but said to him, "Go home to your family and report[l] to them how much the Lord has done for you[m] and had mercy on you." 20/ And he went away and began to proclaim in the Decapolis how much Jesus had done for him, and everyone marveled.

was a correction of Mark's Γερασηνῶν ("Gerasenes"). The reading Γεργεσηνῶν ("Gergesenes") is supported by ℵ² L Δ et al. This reading may derive from Origen, who proposed it without mentioning manuscript support (*Comm. in Joh.* 6.24); see Tjitze Baarda, "Gadarenes, Gerasenes, Gergesenes and the 'Diatessaron' Traditions," in Ellis and Wilcox, *Neotestamentica et Semitica*, 181–97. Origen says that he had visited Gergesa (modern El Kursi), that it was an old town near the lake called Tiberias in his time (i.e., the Sea of Galilee), that on the edge of it there was a steep place abutting on the lake, and that the local people said that the swine had been cast down by the demons from that place. He also supports the identification with a dubious etymology. One MS (W) reads Γεργυστηνῶν ("Gergustenes"). The reading Γερασηνῶν ("Gerasenes") in Mark 5:1 is probably original because of its strong external support and its status as the most difficult reading.

c   Nestle-Aland (26th and 27th eds.) place ὑπήντησεν ("he came out to meet") in the text, following ℵ B C D et al. Tischendorf and Westcott and Hort also adopted this reading. Greeven accepts the reading ἀπήντησεν ("he came out to meet"), following A W 33 𝔐. The latter reading is somewhat more likely to be original, since the same verb appears in Mark 14:13, whereas ὑπαντάω is not used anywhere else in Mark. If this hypothesis is correct, then Matthew and Luke independently changed Mark's ἀπήντησεν to ὑπήντησεν. The latter inference is supported by the fact that the latter verb occurs also in Matt 28:9 and twice in Luke (14:31; 17:12), whereas the former verb does not occur at all in Matthew and only once as a *v.l.* in Luke 17:12.

d   Nestle-Aland (26th and 27th eds.) place αὐτῷ ("him" in the dative case) in the text, following ℵ D W et al. Tischendorf also adopted this reading. Greeven and Westcott and Hort, on the other hand, accept the reading αὐτόν ("him" in the accusative case), following A B C L et al. The former reading is more likely, since the dative was used by preference with the verb προσκυνέω ("show reverence") in Koine Greek, whereas the accusative was preferred in Attic Greek and its later imitators (see BAGD, s.v.).

e   ℵ* B* C (D) L et al. attest the spelling λεγιών ("legion"); ℵ² A B² W et al. attest the spelling λεγεών ("legion"). The two spellings are about equally represented in antiquity; see BAGD, s.v.

f   The earliest recoverable reading is probably that attested by B C Δ (Θ), the neuter plural pronoun αὐτά ("them"). The noun is in the neuter to agree with πνεῦμα, "(unclean) spirit" in vv. 2, 8, and plural because the plurality of the demons has just been revealed in the name and its explanation in v. 9 (cf. also v. 13). The reading attested by D f¹³ 𝔐, the mas-

culine plural pronoun αὐτούς, "them," may be understood as a "correction" to conform the pronoun to the
masculine plural πολλοί, "many" in v. 9. The reading
attested by ℵ L 2427 et al., the masculine singular pronoun αὐτόν, "him," resulted from a change based on
the opinion that only one spirit was involved. Joachim
Gnilka points out that this reading conforms to Billerbeck's interpretation of the name as a member of a
legion (*Das Evangelium nach Markus* [3rd ed.; 2 vols.;
EKK II/1, 2; Zurich: Benziger; Neukirchen-Vluyn:
Neukirchener Verlag, 1989] ad loc.)

g   The earliest recoverable reading is that attested by ℵ B
C L et al., παρεκάλεσαν αὐτὸν λέγοντες ("they
entreated him, saying"). This construction is typical of
Mark's style; see G. D. Kilpatrick, "Recitative λέγων,"
in Elliott, *Language and Style,* 175–77. The reading
attested by W *f*[13] et al., παρακαλέσαντες εἶπον
("entreating him, they said"), is a stylistic variant. The
other variants may be explained as resulting from
attempts to clarify that the subject is the demons (and
not the pigs mentioned in the previous verse).

h   The reading attested by A *f*[13] et al. has the additional
words εὐθέως ὁ Ἰησοῦς, "immediately Jesus," following the words ἐπέτρεψεν αὐτοῖς, "he permitted them
(to do so)." This addition has the effect of emphasizing the role of Jesus in the miraculous event. The
other major variant shows a more marked tendency of
this type. Some MSS (D Θ 565 et al.) reflect a change
from the verb ἐπέτρεψεν, "he permitted," to
ἔπεμψεν, "he sent," in order to show that Jesus was in
firm control of the demons.

i   Some MSS (W Δ *f*[13] et al.) read ἀνήγγειλαν instead of
ἀπήγγειλαν (both meaning "brought a report" or
"reported"). The two readings are stylistic variants; cf.
v. 19 below.

j   Some MSS (ℵ[1] A B C W et al.) have the spelling λεγε-
ῶνα ("legion") rather than λεγιῶνα ("legion"); see
the note on v. 9 above. Other MSS (D lat sy[s] bo) attest a
reading that lacks this whole participial clause; this
reading is probably due to an "improvement" of
Mark's pleonastic style. On the use of ἔχω in Mark,
see Turner, "Marcan Usage," 28 (1927) 357–60
(Elliott, *Language and Style,* 99–102).

k   Some MSS (D Θ 565. et al.) attest the reading
παρεκάλουν ("were entreating") rather than ἤρξαντο
παρακαλεῖν ("began to entreat"). The former reading reflects an intended stylistic improvement,
whereas the latter is typical Markan style. On the use
of the verb ἄρχομαι with present infinitive as auxiliary for the imperfect in Mark, see Turner, "Markan
Usage," 28 (1927) 352–53 (Elliott, *Language and Style,*
93–95).

l   Some MSS (p[45] D W *f*[1.13] et al.) read διάγγειλον
("report"); others (A L 0132. 33 𝔐) read ἀνάγγειλον
("report"); and yet others (ℵ B C et al.) read
ἀπάγγειλον ("report"). The three readings are stylistic variants.

m   The earliest recoverable reading is that attested by (ℵ)
B C et al., ὁ κύριός σοι, "the Lord (has done) for
you." Some MSS (A L W et al.) read the word σοι ("for
you") before ὁ κύριος ("the Lord"). Others, D (1241),
read σοι ὁ θεός, "God (has done) for you." Both of
the latter two readings probably result from changes
to the Markan text to bring it into conformity with
Luke 8:39. For an argument that the change was made
to emphasize the divinity of Jesus, see Ehrman, *Orthodox Corruption,* 114–15 n. 189.

Literary Context

The opening words of this passage, "And they came to
the opposite shore of the sea, to the district of the
Gerasenes," link it closely to the preceding passage,
which includes the following statement by Jesus near the
beginning, "Let us go to the shore on the other side"
(4:35b). Furthermore, in 4:36, Jesus is portrayed as in a
boat, and in 5:2 as getting out of the boat. Achtemeier
has made a reasonable case that the link between the two
miracle stories is pre-Markan.[39] The exorcism of the
Gerasene demoniac was probably the second of five miracle stories in one of the two collections used by the
author of Mark. The temporal connection between 4:35-
41 and 5:1-20 is problematic. Jesus and the disciples leave
the spot where Jesus was teaching from the boat, presumably a point near Capernaum, in the evening (4:35).
There is no indication, however, that it took the whole
night to cross the "sea," nor that the encounter with the
Gerasene demoniac takes place at night. This discontinuity may be an indication that the temporal reference in
4:35 is redactional.

---

39   Achtemeier, "Miracle Catenae," 275–76.

Genre

Dibelius classified this passage as a "Tale," like the stilling of the storm. He pointed out that the Tales tend to be longer than the paradigms, and that they manifest delight in the storyteller's art. He cited "The Demons and the Swine" as an example of a Tale that is vivid and reflects attention to detail.[40] Bultmann categorized it as a miracle story of the subtype exorcism.[41] Theissen defined it as an exorcism.[42]

History of the Tradition

John F. Craghan argued that Mark 5:1-20 "may be divided into a threefold 'Sitz im Leben'": Jesus' actual exorcism; the primitive community's presentation of the event in terms of universal salvation (drawing upon Isaiah 65); and the evangelist's redaction, which makes the healed demoniac into an apostle to the nations.[43]

Rudolf Pesch argued that there were three stages in the history of this miracle story prior to Mark. The first stage was the oral telling of an exorcism, perhaps in Hellenistic-Jewish Christian circles in Galilee, similar to and perhaps modeled on the one now found in 1:21-28. The narrative setting of this story was the land of the Gerasenes. Its social setting was the Galilean Hellenistic-Jewish Christian mission to the Gentiles. The second stage involved an expansion of the story that demonstrated Jesus' triumph over the disturbing way of life of Gentiles. At this stage, the demoniac is portrayed as representative of this offensive way of life (vv. 3-5); he came from a distance, like the Gentiles, and subjected himself to Jesus (v. 6). Jesus succeeded in subduing him, whereas others had failed (vv. 3-4). Pesch also attributed vv. 9-12 to this stage. He attributed the third stage to the editor of the collection of miracles, who added vv. 18-20, transforming the epiphanic exorcism into a story about mission.[44]

Dibelius argued that the point of the story was the recognition of God's true envoy by a demon on foreign soil. He thought that the story was originally Jewish and was only later applied to Jesus. He concluded that vv. 18-20 constitute a secondary conclusion, added by Mark.[45] Bultmann follows Wellhausen in concluding that the story was secondarily applied to Jesus.[46]

There is no reason to think that the story was not originally about Jesus. It is clear, however, that it originated in a setting characterized by a Jewish perspective. It is also unnecessary to reconstruct additional stages in the history of the tradition of the story beyond the pre-Markan and the Markan.[47] The tensions within it may be explained by its oral origin.[48]

Comment

■ 1 As indicated above,[49] a major textual and interpretive problem is how the action can be set in Gerasa, modern Jerash, since this city is located more than thirty miles southeast of the Sea of Galilee, and the pigs are depicted as rushing off of a presumably nearby cliff into the sea (v. 13). It could be that the oral version of the story simply indicated that it took place in (one of the cities of) the Decapolis (cf. v. 20). Either when it was included in the written collection of miracles that Mark used as a source or at the time that Mark incorporated it into his Gospel, the place may have been specified as "the district of the Gerasenes."[50] The specification must have been made by someone who did not realize how far Gerasa was from the Sea of Galilee.[51]

40 Dibelius, *From Tradition to Gospel*, 71, 76–77. On the way in which Matthew has compressed the detailed story of Mark, see Theissen, *Miracle Stories*, 176, 178.

41 Bultmann, *History*, 210–11; see the discussion of specific features on 220–21, 223–24.

42 Theissen, *Miracle Stories*, 321.

43 John F. Craghan, "The Gerasene Demoniac," *CBQ* 30 (1968) 522–36. Craghan gives a summary of scholarship on the historical reliability of the account (522–24).

44 Pesch, 1:292–93. He apparently also attributed v. 13b to the second stage (1:284). Meier (*Marginal Jew*, 2:650–53) agrees with Pesch.

45 Dibelius, *From Tradition to Gospel*, 54–55, 74, 89. Theissen also emphasizes the contrast between Jews and Gentiles in this passage (*Miracle Stories*, 254).

46 Wellhausen, 39; Bultmann, *History*, 210.

47 See "Literary Context" above.

48 Theissen, *Miracle Stories*, 129, 193.

49 See the second note on the trans. of 5:1 above.

50 Cf. Theissen, *Miracle Stories*, 129.

51 Andreas Bedenbender has suggested that the name

The Gentile character of Gerasa in particular and the Decapolis in general should not be overemphasized. The cities of the Decapolis were "eastern cities with a Hellenistic overlay that often facilitated the expression of aspects of Semitic religion and practice, including Judaism. Jewish remains from the Roman period are well known from Gerasa, Gadara, Abila, and possibly Capitolias, all in the Decapolis."[52]

■ **2-5** Verse 2 tells how a man with an unclean spirit immediately came out from among the tombs to meet Jesus when he disembarked. Verses 3-5 then digress to describe the condition and activities of the possessed man. The fact that two synonyms are used in vv. 2-3, $\mu\nu\eta\mu\epsilon\hat{\iota}o\nu$ ("monument, memorial," "grave, tomb") in v. 2 and $\mu\nu\hat{\eta}\mu\alpha$ ("sign of remembrance," "grave, tomb") in vv. 3 and 5, should not be taken as a sign of editorial expansion. A single author may have used two different words for the sake of variety.[53] Both nouns occur in 15:46.

The phrase "unclean spirit" ($\pi\nu\epsilon\hat{\upsilon}\mu\alpha$ $\dot{\alpha}\kappa\dot{\alpha}\theta\alpha\rho\tau o\nu$) in v. 2 does not necessarily allude to Gentile impurity, since the same phrase is used of the demon possessing the man whom Jesus heals in the synagogue in Capernaum (Mark 1:23, 26, 27). The uncleanness of the spirit is probably not due to its association with tombs and thus with the impurity of corpses. Rather, it is unclean because of its origin.[54] The association with tombs may indicate that the man is possessed by the spirits of those who died untimely or violent deaths.[55]

The man is described as living among the tombs; as being so violent that the local people had tried, unsuccessfully, to subdue him by binding his hands and feet with chains; as crying out, day and night, among the tombs or on the hills; and as beating himself with stones. This vivid description shows that the man is out of his senses and isolated. The terrible and dangerous character of the possession is also a feature of the exorcism in 9:14-29.[56]

■ **6** The first part of this verse, "And having seen Jesus from a distance, he ran" ($\kappa\alpha\grave{\iota}$ $\iota\delta\grave{\omega}\nu$ $\tau\grave{o}\nu$ $\mathrm{\iota}\eta\sigma o\hat{\upsilon}\nu$ $\dot{\alpha}\pi\grave{o}$ $\mu\alpha\kappa\rho\acute{o}\theta\epsilon\nu$ $\acute{\epsilon}\delta\rho\alpha\mu\epsilon\nu$), has often been seen as a sign of editorial expansion, since it repeats the substance of v. 2. Such repetition or recapitulation, however, is typically used by writers who digress, in order to return to the original train of thought.

Since vv. 3-5 depict the man as lacking control over himself, the reverential gesture is probably an act initiated by the unclean spirit. This inference is supported by the fact that the man's speech in v. 7 clearly comes from the demon. The act of bowing down before Jesus expresses the demon's recognition of Jesus' power and status.[57]

"Gerasa" is related to the root גרשׁ ("to drive away, to expel"), which is regularly translated with ἐκβαλλεῖν ("to throw or cast out") in the LXX, and that the localization of this story in Gerasa is due, in part, to the connection between this name and the same Greek verb, which is often used in exorcisms ("Orte mitten im Meer," *Texte & Kontexte* 86 [2000] 43–44).

52   Eric M. Meyers, "Jesus and His Galilean Context," in Douglas R. Edwards and C. Thomas McCollough, eds., *Archaeology and the Galilee: Texts and Contexts in the Graeco-Roman and Byzantine Periods* (SFSHJ 143; Atlanta: Scholars Press, 1997) 57–66, esp. 62. See also Fitzgerald, "Gadara," 358–59, 374–75, 380 n. 171.

53   Craghan, "Gerasene Demoniac," 525. Pesch implies that the shift in vocabulary supports the conclusion that vv. 3-5 are redactional; he also suggests that the term $\mu\nu\hat{\eta}\mu\alpha$ ("sign of remembrance," "grave, tomb") in v. 3 comes from Isa 65:4 LXX; he sees Isaiah 65 as the foundational text for the description of the demoniac (1:286). He interprets Isaiah 65 as a description of Gentiles as such, although the passage is addressed to the people of God. According to Brevard S. Childs, Isa 65:1-7 is addressed to "apostate Jews" (*Isaiah* [OTL; Louisville: Westminster John Knox, 2001] 534–35). Paul applies Isa 65:1 to the Gentiles and 65:2 to Israel in Rom 10:20-21.

54   See the commentary on 1:23 above.

55   On "the unsettled dead" in relation to this passage, see Douglas W. Geyer, *Fear, Anomaly, and Uncertainty in the Gospel of Mark* (ATLAMS 47; Lanham, MD/London: Scarecrow, 2002) 132–35; see also Sarah Iles Johnston, *Restless Dead: Encounters between the Living and the Dead in Ancient Greece* (Berkeley: University of California Press, 1999).

56   For this motif, see Bultmann, *History*, 221; cf. Theissen, *Miracle Stories*, 51–52.

57   Theissen calls it "capitulation" (*Miracle Stories*, 57). Heinrich Greeven argued that, in the LXX, the use of the word with human beings as the object always implies "a recognition that the one thus honored is God's instrument" ("$\pi\rho o\sigma\kappa\upsilon\nu\acute{\epsilon}\omega$, $\pi\rho o\sigma\kappa\upsilon\nu\eta\tau\acute{\eta}\varsigma$," *TDNT* 6 [1968] 758–66; quotation from 761).

■ 7 The submission quickly turns to resistance. The man (demon) cries out with a loud voice (κράξας φωνῇ μεγάλῃ).[58] He asks Jesus, "What have I to do with you, Jesus, son of the most high God?" (τί ἐμοὶ καὶ σοί, Ἰησοῦ υἱὲ τοῦ θεοῦ τοῦ ὑψίστου;). This question is analogous to that of the unclean spirit in 1:24. In both cases, the demon attempts to control Jesus, or at least to ward him off or resist him, by pronouncing his name and demonstrating that he knows Jesus' identity.[59] In the context of Mark as a whole, this declaration by the demon serves to develop the theme of Jesus' identity: the demon as a supernatural entity knows who Jesus is.

The title "God the Most High" (ὁ θεὸς ὁ ὑψίστος) was not unknown among Jews as an epithet of the God of Israel.[60] In the Greek translations of the Hebrew Bible, עליון ("Elyon") is always translated by (ὁ) ὑψίστος, but in non-Jewish, non-Christian Greek texts, the expression occurs as a divine name for Zeus. Zeus Hypsistos was revered from Athens, through Asia Minor, Syria, and on into Egypt.[61] An inscription dating to 22 or 23 CE attests a temple and cult of Zeus Olympius in Gerasa.[62] Thus, for members of Mark's audience familiar with this cult, the demon's address of Jesus is equivalent to "son of Zeus."[63]

The demon goes on to say, "I adjure you by God, do not torment me" (ὁρκίζω σε τὸν θεόν, μή με βασανίσῃς). The verb ὁρκίζω ("to make one swear, bind by an oath," "adjure") and its synonym ὁρκόω ("to make one swear, bind by an oath," "adjure") are usually used by the exorcist to force the demon to depart from the possessed person.[64] The demon's use of the term signifies his resistance to Jesus and that a struggle is taking place between them.[65] The demon's request that Jesus not torment him signifies that exorcism is painful or at least distressing for the spirit.[66]

■ 8 This statement is clearly an afterthought. Its purpose is to explain why the demon addressed Jesus through the possessed man so aggressively (v. 7). Some interpreters conclude on this basis that v. 8 belongs to a later stage than the original account.[67] Pesch argued that v. 8 was added when vv. 9-12 were inserted, in order to introduce the question about the demon's name and the demons' request to be allowed to enter the swine.[68] Such theories become unnecessary when the oral character of the account is recognized. In the telling of a story, the storyteller sometimes has to fill in information parenthetically that is required for understanding the course of events.[69]

■ 9 Asking a demon to reveal his name is a typical exorcistic technique.[70] The demon responds, "Legion is

---

58 Cf. 3:11, according to which the unclean spirits, whenever they saw Jesus, "would fall down before him and cry out (προσέπιπτον αὐτῷ καὶ ἔκραζον)." There, however, they simply declare that Jesus is the Son of God and offer no resistance. Cf. also 1:26, according to which the unclean spirit "cried out with a loud voice" (φωνῆσαν φωνῇ μεγάλῃ) as it went out of the man.

59 It is more typical for the exorcist to force the demon to reveal his name and identity, so that the exorcist can control him; see the commentary on 1:24 above.

60 Deut 32:8; 1QapGen 21:2 (this text says that Abraham offered sacrifices to the God Most High); 4QAramaic Apocalypse (4Q246, also referred to as the "son of God" text) 2:1 (this text refers to someone who will be called "son of the Most High").

61 Ciliers Breytenbach, "Hypsistos," *DDD* 439–43.

62 Carl H. Kraeling, ed., *Gerasa: City of the Decapolis* (New Haven: American Schools of Oriental Research, 1938) 373–74.

63 Adela Yarbro Collins, "Mark and His Readers: The Son of God among Greeks and Romans," *HTR* 93 (2000) 85–100.

64 Josephus *Ant.* 8.2.5 §47; the verb ὁρκόω ("to make one swear, bind by an oath," "adjure") is used, but

here, as usual, the subject is the exorcist. On the use of the Hebrew equivalent of ὁρκίζω, [אני] משבע ("[I] adjure"), in 8Q5; 11Q11 1:7; 4:1 and the Aramaic incantation אומיתך רוחא ("I adjured you, O spirit) in 4Q560, see Eshel, "Genres of Magical Texts," 396–402; eadem, "Demonology in Palestine," part 3.

65 Theissen, *Miracle Stories*, 57, 88–89. Robert H. Gundry describes the spirit as trying "to exorcise Jesus out of exorcising it" (*Mark: A Commentary on His Apology for the Cross* [Grand Rapids: Eerdmans, 1993] 250).

66 Theissen goes further and speaks of the exorcist treating the demon violently (*Miracle Stories*, 57).

67 Craghan, "Gerasene Demoniac," 525; cf. Dibelius, *From Tradition to Gospel*, 83.

68 Pesch, 1:288.

69 Theissen, *Miracle Stories*, 192–93.

70 See the commentary on 1:24 above. See also Campbell Bonner, "The Technique of Exorcism," *HTR* 36 (1943) 39–49, esp. 44–45. Note also the demand of the exorcist that the demon reveal what type of demon he is in *PGM* IV: 3038–39, 3041, and 3045; Bonner argued that the purpose was simply to make the demon speak, in order to drive him out more effectively (41–42). Pablo Torijano concludes that

---

my name, because we are many."[71] It is likely that the demon is not portrayed as giving his actual name, but that the response is a clever evasion.[72] The rest of the story, however, shows that the response is accurate insofar as it reveals that the man is possessed by at least two thousand demons.[73] During the first century CE, a Roman legion consisted of fifty-four hundred men, including 120 legionary cavalry.[74] The Latin word *legio* ("legion") could also be used in a transferred sense to refer to (1) the troops of other nations; (2) an army, a large body of troops; or (3) a large body of men.[75]

It may be that, in the original form of the account, the "name" Legion was chosen to express an anti-Roman sentiment.[76] Caesar's tenth legion (Legio X *Fretensis*) had, among other things, the image of a boar on its standards

and seals.[77] This legion was stationed in Cyrrhus, a city of northwestern Syria, from 17 CE to 66 CE, when it was moved to Alexandria for the projected campaign against Ethiopia. Instead, it took part in the first Jewish war and was subsequently stationed in Jerusalem.[78] The author of Mark was probably familiar with this legion and its symbol, but it is doubtful that the pre-Markan composer of the story was.

There is, however, no theme of opposition to Rome in Mark. Assuming that the remark of the centurion at the foot of the cross is not ironic, this Roman soldier expresses faith in Jesus as the Son of God, or at least as the son of a god.[79] It is more likely that the earliest audiences would have read the story of the Gerasene demoniac in connection with the theme of the battle between

---

the formula "Who are you?" in an exorcistic context is apotropaic (*Solomon the Esoteric King*, 68). On the question "Who are you" in 11Q11 5:6, see Eshel, "Demonology in Palestine," part 3.

71 The word λεγιών ("legion") is a Latin loanword. Its use here does not provide evidence for the composition of Mark in Rome, since the term and the concept were widely known in the Mediterranean world. Theissen suggests that the Latin word here fits with the use of foreign words of power in miracle stories (*Miracle Stories*, 255), but the word may no longer have been perceived as foreign in the Greek of the first century CE.

72 Bonner, "Technique of Exorcism," 44. "Legion" seems to be taken as the actual name of the demon by Hans Dieter Betz, "Legion (Λεγιών)," *DDD* 508. But Betz (ibid.) also cites *T. Sol.* 11, in which Solomon interrogates a demon who identifies himself as πνεῦμα δυνάμενον μηδόλως δεθῆναι ("a spirit that can never be bound"; cf. Mark 5:4). This demon's name is Λεοντοφόρον ("the Lion-Shaped Demon"), but the name for all the demons under him is λεγεῶνες ("legions"); text from McCown, *Testament of Solomon*, 39*–40*; trans. (modified) from Duling, *OTP* 1:972–73. This passage is evidence for an early reading according to which "Legion" is not the actual name of the demon(s) in Mark 5:1-20.

73 Note the neuter plural pronoun αὐτά ("them") in v. 10 (see the note on the trans. above); the plural forms in vv. 12-13; and especially the demonic possession of the two thousand pigs that were drowned (vv. 12-13). The story may imply that one demon entered each pig, but since all the demons had been inhabiting one man, this is not necessarily the case. The *Epistula Apostolorum* interprets the story to

mean that there was one demon (chap. 5; see *NTApoc*, 1:253). According to *T. Sol.* 11, the demon Legion explains his name as follows: "I assault (people) with the legions of demons subject to me. . . . The name for all demons which are under me is legion."

74 J. B. Campbell, "Legion," *OCD* 839. Gundry's suggestion (263), following Jeremias, that λεγιών ("legion") here is equivalent to τέλος ("a force of 2,048 infantry"; LSJ s.v. 10b), since Josephus uses the latter term to designate Roman soldiers (*Ant.* 14.16.2 §472), is far-fetched.

75 LS s.v. *legio*, II.

76 Eitrem, *Some Notes*, 56; Theissen, *Miracle Stories*, 255; Ched Myers, *Binding the Strong Man: A Political Reading of Mark's Story of Jesus* (Maryknoll, NY: Orbis, 1988) 191–92. Myers's claim that Josephus's account of Vespasian's assault on Gerasa is relevant for this passage is called into question by archaeological evidence; Shimon Applebaum and Arthur Segal state that most scholars conclude that Josephus is not talking about the Transjordanian town ("Gerasa," *NEAEHL* 2:471). See also Rasiah S. Sugirtharajah, *Postcolonial Criticism and Biblical Interpretation* (Oxford/New York: Oxford University Press, 2002) 91–94.

77 Van der Loos, *Miracles*, 383; Theissen, *Gospels in Context*, 110.

78 Campbell, "Legion," 841.

79 See Yarbro Collins, "Son of God among Greeks and Romans," 94–97, and the commentary on 15:39 below.

Jesus and Satan. Daniel and the book of Revelation speak of heavenly armies. The Matthean Jesus, rebuking the disciple who cut off the ear of the slave of the high priest, said to him, "Do you think that I am not able to appeal to my Father, and he will send to me immediately more than twelve legions ($\lambda\epsilon\gamma\iota\hat{\omega}\nu\epsilon\varsigma$) of angels?" (Matt 26:53). As the Markan Jesus alluded to a kingdom of Satan in the Beelzebul controversy, so here he implies that one of Satan's legions has taken possession of the unfortunate man. The aim of the story is not—at least not primarily—to make a statement about the Romans, but to show how Jesus rescued the man from his plight and restored him to a normal life.

Just as, however, the heavenly armies of Daniel and Revelation are correlated with earthly events, so there may be a secondary political implication to the story of the Gerasene demoniac in Mark. It would be a culturally logical step for the audience to link the kingdom of Satan with Rome and the healing activity of Jesus with the restored kingdom of Israel.

■ **10** The spirits (speaking through the man) entreat Jesus strongly not to send them out of the region. This motif is in some tension with the idea of the unclean spirits being the spirits of the Giants, offspring of the Watchers, or fallen angels under the leadership of Satan. It suggests that the unclean spirits are the souls of the local dead. This implication fits with the description of the man as dwelling among the tombs. Another possibility is that the request is simply part of the ongoing power struggle between Jesus and the unclean spirits.[80] It also prepares narratively for the sending of the spirits into the pigs.

■ **11** It has been argued that the story originally depicted the spirits as entering into a herd of cattle or oxen.[81] Two arguments may be made against this view. First, whether pigs occur in large herds or not, some ancient people apparently thought that they did.[82] Second, various kinds of illness were believed to be transferable to various kinds of animals in antiquity and the Middle Ages.[83]

■ **12** The demons' request that Jesus send them into the pigs may be interpreted as a plea for a concession that

---

80   Theissen, *Miracle Stories*, 57.

81   Roy Kotansky argued that, since pigs do not occur in large herds, the story originally spoke about cattle or oxen ("Jesus and Heracles in Cádiz ($\tau\grave{\alpha}$ $\Gamma\acute{\alpha}\delta\epsilon\iota\rho\alpha$): Death, Myth, and Monsters at the 'Straits of Gibraltar' [Mark 4:35–5:43]," in Adela Yarbro Collins, ed., *The Bible and Culture: Ancient and Modern Perspectives* [SBLSymS; Atlanta: Scholars Press, 1998] 199–200). According to Walter Burkert, the ancients believed that insanity could not be eliminated, only shifted. The panic of the herd was understood to be visible proof that the insanity had been transferred to the animals. Pigs appear in this story rather than wild goats because pigs are unclean in a Jewish context. Unclean spirits belong in unclean animals ("Psychotherapy from Ancient Greece to Gerasa" [lecture given at the University of Chicago on April 1, 1993]). According to Marten Stol, the pig was an unclean animal in Babylonia as well. Babylonian texts imply that pigs and goats were used as substitutes for various diseases; similarly in Hittite magic, pigs and dogs were considered able to absorb impurity (*Epilepsy in Babylonia* [Cuneiform Monographs 2; Groningen: Styx, 1993] 101).

82   In describing the shield of Heracles, Hesiod *Sc.* 168 mentions $\sigma\nu\hat{\omega}\nu$ $\mathring{\alpha}\gamma\acute{\epsilon}\lambda\alpha\iota$ ("herds of wild boars" or "herds of pigs"). The Markan word $\chi o\hat{\iota}\rho o\varsigma$ ("young pig" or simply "pig") is a synonym of $\sigma\hat{\upsilon}\varsigma$ ("wild boar" or "pig"); see LSJ s.v. $\chi o\hat{\iota}\rho o\varsigma$.

83   An Akkadian incantation contains the following prayer, "May Ninkilim, lord of the animals, transfer his grave illness to the vermin of the earth" (*Šurpu* 7.69-70); trans. from Erica Reiner, *Šurpu: A Collection of Sumerian and Akkadian Incantations* (Archiv für Orientforschung 11; Graz: Ernst Weidner, 1958) 38. See also $\mathring{\eta}\lambda\theta\epsilon$ $\delta\grave{\epsilon}$ $\nu o\hat{\upsilon}\sigma o\varsigma$, $\alpha\hat{\iota}\gamma\alpha\varsigma$ $\mathring{\epsilon}\varsigma$ $\mathring{\alpha}\gamma\rho\iota\acute{\alpha}\delta\alpha\varsigma$ $\tau\grave{\eta}\nu$ $\mathring{\alpha}\pi o\pi\epsilon\mu\pi\acute{o}\mu\epsilon\theta\alpha$, $\psi\epsilon\upsilon\delta\acute{o}\mu\epsilon\nu o\iota$ $\delta'\iota\epsilon\rho\grave{\eta}\nu$ $\varphi\eta\mu\acute{\iota}\zeta o\mu\epsilon\nu$ ("the disease seized her, which we send into the wild goats and which we falsely call sacred") (Callimachus frg. 75.12–14 = *Aet.* 3.1.13; text and trans. [modified] from C. A. Trypanis, Thomas Gelzer, and Cedric Whitman, *Callimachus; Musaeus* [LCL; Cambridge, MA: Harvard University Press; London: Heinemann, 1958] 54–55; cited by Burkert; see the first note on v. 11 above). Owsei Temkin argues that the disease in question here is quartan fever (*The Falling Sickness: A History of Epilepsy from the Greeks to the Beginnings of Modern Neurology* [2nd rev. ed.; Baltimore/London: Johns Hopkins University Press, 1971] 18–19). A medieval *historiola*, based on older models, has Christ sending a personified headache into the wild mountains to settle in a bull's head (Kotansky, *Greek Magical Amulets*, Part I: *Published Texts of Known Provenance* [ANWAW, Sonderreihe, Papyrologica Coloniensia 22.1; Opladen: Westdeutscher Verlag, 1994] 60–61). *PGM* VII. 429–58 is a spell: "The spell [in it], when said, conjures daimons [out] and makes them enter [objects or

mediates the tension between resistance and capitulation in the struggle between demons and exorcist.[84] They desire not only to remain in the district (v. 10) but also to have a physical body in which to dwell.[85]

Jesus' aim is to drive the demons out of the man (cf. v. 8). Such an act may be called an ἀποπομπή ("a sending away"). The demons ask to be sent to a particular place; they request an ἐπιπομπή ("a sending to [a place]"). Such actions are common cross-culturally, including in Greco-Roman antiquity, in spells and incantations.[86]

■ **13** Jesus grants the demons' request. In the second clause of this verse, the narrator relates that the unclean spirits came out of the man and went into the pigs. On one level, the rest of the verse may be seen as confirmation of that statement. The panic of the herd is visible proof that the demons have entered the pigs.[87] Some visible proof that the demon has left the possessed person is a typical motif of accounts of exorcism.[88] As Campbell Bonner rightly pointed out with regard to the pigs rushing down the steep bank into the sea and drowning, "This is the act of physical violence that bears witness to the reality of the expulsion; and in the source from which Mark drew it is probable that there was no more thought of the ethical or social problems that might arise from the incident than there was in the stories of exorcism as practiced by Eleazar and Apollonius."[89]

The demons, according to the narrative, did not foresee that the pigs would rush into the sea and drown.[90] They wanted to remain in the district of the Gerasenes. So, on another level of meaning, the implication of the latter part of this verse is that Jesus has outwitted the demons.[91] By allowing them to enter the swine, apparently foreseeing that the swine would go mad, Jesus has sent them into the sea, where they can no longer harm human beings.[92] Another possibility is that Jesus has sent them to their proper dwelling-place. The "sea" is symbolically equivalent to the "abyss," and the "abyss," or Sheol, is the home of the demons.

Evidence for this conclusion may be found in an apocryphal psalm from Qumran. According to this text, when a demon comes by night, one should attack him verbally, for example, by threatening him that "the chief of the army, YHWH, [will bring] you [down] [to the] deepest [Sheo]l."[93] Similarly, one is to say "YHWH will strike you with a [grea]t b[low] to destroy you[And in his fury[he will send] against you a powerful angel[to carry out] his [entire comm]and, who[will not show] you mercy, . . . who[will bring] you [down] to the great abyss [and to] the deepest [Sheol.] . . . and it will be very dark [in the gr]eat [abyss."[94]

This text is similar in some ways to the *Songs of the Maskil* from Qumran.[95] These texts are remarkable in that songs of praise are explicitly intended to frighten

---

people]" (ὁ δὲ λόγος λεγόμενος ὁρκίζει δαίμονας καὶ εἰσκρίνει) (Preisendanz-Henrichs, 2:20; trans. by Morton Smith in Betz, *Magical Papyri*, 129).

84　Theissen, *Miracle Stories*, 57.

85　Wellhausen, 39.

86　Otto Weinreich, "Gebet und Wunder: Zwei Abhandlungen zur Religions- und Literaturgeschichte: Erste Abhandlung: Primitiver Gebetsegoismus (Ein Beitrag zu Terenz, Andria 232f.)," in Friedrich Focke et al., *Genethliakon Wilhelm Schmid* (TBAW 5; Stuttgart: Kohlhammer, 1929) 169–99, esp. 175–76; cited by Pesch, 1:290.

87　Burkert suggested that the tendency of herds to panic gave rise to the ancient idea that insanity could be transferred to them (see the comment on v. 11 above).

88　Josephus *Ant.* 8.2.5 §48 (Eleazar); Philostratus *Vita Ap.* 4.20 (Apollonius); Bonner, "Technique of Exorcism," 47–49.

89　Ibid., 49.

90　Cf. Wellhausen, 39. The fact that pigs are good

swimmers is irrelevant to the story, since the entry of the demons into the pigs drove them mad; contra Kotansky, "Jesus and Heracles in Cádiz (τὰ Γάδειρα)," 200.

91　Bultmann, *History*, 210, following Wellhausen, 39.

92　Weinreich, "Gebet und Wunder," 175; Rudolf Pesch, *Der Besessene von Gerasa* (SBS 56; Stuttgart: Katholisches Bibelwerk, 1972) 37.

93　שׂר הצבה יהוה [יוריד]ך [לשאו]ל תחתית (11QapPsª [11Q11] 5:8-9; text and trans. from García Martínez et al., *Qumran Cave 11*, 2:198–200).

94　יככה יהוה מ]כה גדול[ה אשר לאבדך]
ובחרון אפו] ישלח]עליך מלאך תקיף[לעשות]
[כול דב]רו אשר] בלוא] רחמ]ים[עליך . . .
. . . אשר] יורידו]ך לתהום רבה
[ולשאול] התחתית ומי] [כב וחשך
[בתהום ר]בה
(11QapPsª [11Q11] 4:4-9; text and trans. from García Martínez et al., *Qumran Cave 11*, 2:195–97; see also Eshel, "Genres of Magical Texts," 403–4).

95　On the *Songs of the Maskil* (4Q510 and 511), see

and terrify evil spirits.[96] The songs of the Maskil are more apotropaic in character than exorcistic.[97] The demons mentioned in the Dead Sea Scrolls are "the supernatural forces of the realm of evil which dominate the earth until the final Judgment Day." It follows that the Maskil wages a kind of war against evil by singing God's praises in his Songs.[98] The songs constitute instruments of war in a battle that is analogous to and anticipates the eschatological conflict described in the *War Scroll*. The Maskil says, "And as for me, I spread the fear of God *in the ages of my generations* to exalt the name and to terrify with his power all spirits of the *mamzerim*."[99] According to Nitzan, the power of the Songs "may be defined as a temporary power used by mortals, until the expected ultimate power of the Almighty will make its mighty appearance in the final judgment at the end of days."[100]

Like the *Songs of the Maskil*, Mark links the practice of exorcism with an apocalyptic understanding of the times. The evangelist presents Jesus in conflict with Satan immediately following his baptism (1:9-11) and in the controversy over his exorcisms (3:22-30). His first mighty deed in Mark is an exorcism, and this deed is closely linked with his teaching, namely, that "the time is fulfilled and the kingdom of God has drawn near" (1:15). Jesus' exorcisms are not the definitive manifestation of the kingdom of God. Rather, they constitute a struggle with Satan that prefigures and anticipates the final, full manifestation of the kingdom of God that will take place with the coming of the Son of Man.

■ **14-17** The fate of the pigs and the demons is only half of the proof of the miracle.[101] Those tending the pigs reported to many people in the district what had happened (v. 14a). These came to see for themselves (v. 14b). At this point the narrative focus shifts from the pigs and the demons to the man who is now healed (v. 15). The statement that he was sitting (with Jesus) clothed ($\kappa\alpha\vartheta\acute{\eta}$-$\mu\epsilon\nu o\nu$ $\acute{\iota}\mu\alpha\tau\iota\sigma\mu\acute{\epsilon}\nu o\nu$) has led to the inference that he had been naked while he was possessed. But the description of the man's wild state (vv. 2-5) contains no mention of nakedness.[102] The participle $\acute{\iota}\mu\alpha\tau\iota\sigma\mu\acute{\epsilon}\nu o\nu$ ("to be dressed" or "to be furnished with clothing") may simply imply that his healing resulted in his interest and ability to be properly dressed.[103] His being properly dressed corresponds to his being in his right mind ($\sigma\omega\varphi\rho o\nu\hat{\omega}\nu$) (v. 15).

A text that sheds some light on how demoniacs were expected to behave is a story about Nicias that Plutarch included in his *Life of Marcellus*. Nicias pretended to be "possessed and crazed" ($\delta\alpha\iota\mu o\nu\hat{\omega}\nu$ $\kappa\alpha\grave{\iota}$ $\pi\alpha\rho\alpha\varphi\rho o\nu\hat{\omega}\nu$) in order to avoid arrest and probable death. Among other things, he "tore off his mantle, rent his tunic, and leaping up half naked, ran toward the exit of the theatre" ($\acute{\alpha}\pi o\rho$-$\rho\acute{\iota}\psi\alpha\varsigma$ $\tau\grave{o}$ $\acute{\iota}\mu\acute{\alpha}\tau\iota o\nu$ $\kappa\alpha\grave{\iota}$ $\pi\epsilon\rho\iota\rho\rho\eta\xi\acute{\alpha}\mu\epsilon\nu o\varsigma$ $\tau\grave{o}\nu$ $\chi\iota\tau\omega$-$\nu\acute{\iota}\sigma\kappa o\nu$, $\acute{\eta}\mu\acute{\iota}\gamma\upsilon\mu\nu o\varsigma$ $\acute{\alpha}\nu\alpha\pi\eta\delta\acute{\eta}\sigma\alpha\varsigma$ $\acute{\epsilon}\vartheta\epsilon\epsilon$ $\pi\rho\grave{o}\varsigma$ $\tau\grave{\eta}\nu$ $\acute{\epsilon}\xi o\delta o\nu$ $\tau o\hat{\upsilon}$ $\vartheta\epsilon\acute{\alpha}\tau\rho o\upsilon$). (*Vit. Marcellus* 20.5)[104]

When the people see the transformation of the demoniac, they become fearful ($\acute{\epsilon}\varphi o\beta\acute{\eta}\vartheta\eta\sigma\alpha\nu$) (v. 15). This reaction suggests that this miracle story is an epiphany of

Bilha Nitzan, "Hymns from Qumran—4Q510–4Q511," in Dimant and Rappaport, 53–63; Bilhah Nitzan, *Qumran Prayer and Religious Poetry* (STDJ 12; Leiden/New York: Brill, 1994) 235–72.

96 4Q510 1 4-5; Nitzan, *Qumran Prayer*, 237.

97 Alexander, "Demonology of the Dead Sea Scrolls," 344. Similarly, Eshel defines 4Q510 and 511 as "apotropaic prayers" ("Genres of Magical Texts," 406–11).

98 Nitzan, *Qumran Prayer*, 237.

99 ואני מירא אל בקצי דורותי לרומם שם דב. [...] ולפחד [בגבורתו כו]ל]רוחי ממזרים (4Q511 frg. 35 6-7; text and trans. [modified and emphasis added] from García Martínez and Tigchelaar, *Dead Sea Scrolls*, 2:1032–33). The spirits of the *mamzerim* are the demons, who are the spirits of the Giants, the unclean offspring of the Watchers and human

women. See Alexander, "Demonology of the Dead Sea Scrolls," 337–41.

100 Nitzan, "Hymns from Qumran," 63.

101 On the demonstration of a miracle by a new act, see Theissen, *Miracle Stories*, 66–67.

102 Theissen concludes that the belated implication of the man's nakedness is an oral feature (*Miracle Stories*, 193).

103 Dibelius, *From Tradition to Gospel*, 87.

104 Text and trans. from Bernadotte Perrin, *Plutarch's Lives* (11 vols.; LCL; Cambridge, MA: Harvard University Press; London: Heinemann, 1914) 5:490–91; cf. Wendy Cotter, *Miracles in Greco-Roman Antiquity: A Sourcebook* (London/New York: Routledge, 1999) 79.

divine power, since fear is the appropriate human response to such a manifestation.[105]

Verse 16 reprises v. 14a; the tenders of the pigs had presumably told the whole story as they hurried through the district. The miracle is summarized in v. 16 to introduce the second response of the assembled people: "they began to entreat him to leave their region" (v. 17).[106] Dibelius concluded insightfully that here Jesus is presented "not as the benign Saviour who helps, but as the strange miracle man who terrifies."[107] As the local people tried to control the suprahuman power of the demoniac by binding him, here they try to control or ward off the suprahuman power of Jesus by asking him to leave their district.

■ **18-20** Jesus complies immediately with the people's request (v. 18). As he is getting into the boat, however, the (former) demoniac entreats him "that he might be with him" (ἵνα μετ' αὐτοῦ ᾖ). This request is reminiscent of the appointment of the Twelve in 3:13-19. In that text, one of the reasons that Jesus appoints the Twelve is "that they might be with him" (ἵνα ὦσιν μετ' αὐτοῦ). It is likely that the historical Jesus chose twelve special associates in order to symbolize the restoration of the twelve tribes of Israel that was about to take place.[108] The evangelist and his first audiences were no doubt aware of this symbolic role. The Markan Jesus may therefore reject the man's request (v. 19a), because only members of the people of Israel could play this role.

Another reason that the Markan Jesus appoints the Twelve is that "he might send them to proclaim and to have authority to drive out the demons" (3:14-15). Jesus commands the former demoniac simply to report (ἀπαγγελλεῖν) to the members of his household "how much the Lord has done for you and had mercy on you" (5:19). But the evangelist portrays him as proclaiming (κηρύσσειν) in the Decapolis[109] "how much Jesus had done for him" (v. 20). There is a certain analogy here with the healing of the leper in 1:40-45. The leper is told "go, show yourself to the priest and offer for your cleansing what Moses commanded, as a proof for them" (1:44). Instead of doing what Jesus told him, the former leper began to proclaim energetically and to spread the word widely, so that huge crowds began to come to Jesus from everywhere (1:45). Although the former leper and the former demoniac do not have "the mystery of the kingdom of God" (4:11), they nevertheless perform an important preliminary role in describing the mighty deeds of Jesus to many people. In the evangelist's view, they may be seen as preparing the ground into which the seed will later be sown.[110]

The account closes with the remark, "and everyone marveled" (καὶ πάντες ἐθαύμαζον). This is the only miracle story in the early Christian tradition in which the motif of wonder constitutes the actual conclusion. This type of conclusion became typical in Christian miracle stories of the second to the tenth centuries.[111] The wonder expressed here, however, is a direct response not to the exorcism but to the proclamation of the former demoniac.[112]

---

105 Timothy Dwyer interprets this fear as "the awe which attends the supernatural" (*Wonder*, 113; cf. Schmithals, *Wunder*, 33).

106 Theissen classified this reaction as "rejection" and noted that it is unique to the NT; he interpreted the motif of "rejection" as a paradigmatic variant of the motif of "acclamation" (*Miracle Stories*, 72).

107 Dibelius, *From Tradition to Gospel*, 87. According to Schmithals (*Wunder*, 33), the people ask Jesus to leave because they cannot bear the presence of his divine majesty.

108 See the commentary on 3:14-15 above.

109 Although the word "Decapolis" means "Ten Cities," the number was not strictly defined. All of them but Scythopolis were east of the Jordan River and the Sea of Galilee. They did not form a politically coherent unit. What unified them was their Hellenistic character, which distinguished them from neighboring populations. The references to the Decapolis in Mark are the oldest attestations of the term. See Jean-Paul Rey-Coquais, "Decapolis," *ABD* 2:116–21.

110 Bultmann rightly concludes that there is no command to silence in 5:19-20 (*History*, 220 n.1); Theissen finds Mark's theory of the secret here, but admits that it is weakly drawn (*Miracle Stories*, 146–48).

111 Theissen, *Miracle Stories*, 70–71. Note the similar expression in 1:27, "And all were astounded" (καὶ ἐθαμβήθησαν ἅπαντες).

112 Dwyer, *Wonder*, 115.

5:21-43 Two Healings

21/ **And when Jesus had crossed over in the boat[a] back to the other shore,[b] a large crowd was gathered to him, and he was beside the sea. 22/ And[c] a certain synagogue leader came to him, whose name was Jairus;[d] and when he saw him, he fell at his feet 23/ and entreated[e] him earnestly,[f] saying, "My daughter is at the point of death; come and lay your hands on her, in order that she may be saved and live." 24/ And he went away with him. And a large crowd was following him and pressing upon him. 25/ Now there was a woman who had had a flow of blood for twelve years 26/ and had suffered much under many physicians and had spent all that she had[g] and not been benefited at all, but rather had become worse. 27/ Having heard about Jesus,[h] she came from behind in the crowd and touched his cloak; 28/ for she was saying, "If I touch even his clothes, I shall be saved." 29/ And immediately the source of her blood was dried up and she knew in her body that she had been healed of the torment. 30/ And immediately Jesus knew in himself that power had gone out from him; he turned around in the crowd and said, "Who touched my clothes?" 31/ And his disciples said to him, "You see the crowd pressing upon you and you say, 'Who touched me?'" 32/ And he kept looking around to see who had done this. 33/ Then the woman, afraid and trembling,[i] knowing what had happened to her,[j] came and fell down before him and told him the whole truth. 34/ Then he said to her, "Daughter,[k] your trust has saved you; go in peace and be healthy (and freed) from your torment." 35/ While he was still speaking, (some people) from the (household) of the synagogue leader came, saying, "Your daughter has died. Why do you still trouble the teacher?" 36/ But Jesus overheard[l] the message as it was spoken and said to the synagogue leader, "Do not fear;**

a   The earliest recoverable reading is probably that of ℵ A (B) C L et al., τοῦ Ἰησοῦ ἐν τῷ πλοίῳ ("Jesus in the boat"). Some MSS (p⁴⁵ᵛⁱᵈ D Θ et al.) omit ἐν τῷ πλοίῳ ("in the boat") on the grounds that these words are superfluous; others (W saᵐˢˢ) move these words before τοῦ Ἰησοῦ ("Jesus") in order to achieve a better sequence. Cf. Metzger, *Textual Commentary*, 72–73.

b   The earliest recoverable reading is that of ℵ¹ A B C L W et al., πάλιν εἰς τὸ πέραν ("back to the other shore"); for the trans. of πάλιν as "back" here, see Turner, "Marcan Usage," 29 (1928) 284 (Elliott, *Language and Style*, 113). The variants seem to have resulted from a misunderstanding of this idiomatic use of πάλιν (here "back"; elsewhere in the Gospels, usually "again"). ℵ* D et al. attest the reading εἰς τὸ πέραν πάλιν ("to the other shore again"); this word order implies that the adverb "again" modifies the verb that follows, so that the meaning is "a great crowd gathered again." Similarly, p⁴⁵ f attest the reading πάλιν ("again"), in which the words εἰς τὸ πέραν ("to the other shore") have been omitted. The result is that πάλιν ("again") modifies the following verb. Θ pc et al. attest a reading in which πάλιν ("again") has simply been omitted.

c   p⁴⁵ A C W et al. attest a reading in which ἰδού ("see" or "behold") follows the opening καί ("and"). Since ℵ B D et al. lack this word, it is likely that the longer reading is due to the influence of the parallel in Matt 9:18 or Luke 8:41.

d   W Θ 565. 700 read ᾧ ὄνομα Ἰάϊρος ("whose name was Jairus") instead of ὀνόματι Ἰάϊρος ("whose name was Jairus"). The former reading is probably due to the influence of the parallel in Luke 8:41. D a e et al. attest a reading that has neither of these word-groups. The shorter reading is due either to deliberate abbreviation or, more likely, to an accidental omission. See Metzger, *Textual Commentary*, 73–74, for arguments against the hypothesis put forward by Taylor (ad loc.) that the shorter reading is original.

e   The earliest recoverable reading is probably the historical present indicative παρακαλεῖ, "(he) entreated," lit., "(he) entreats," attested by ℵ A C L et al., since this usage is characteristic of Mark's style. See John Charles Doudna, *The Greek of the Gospel of Mark* (SBLMS 12; Philadelphia: SBL, 1961) 40–42. B W Θ et al. attest the reading παρεκάλει, "(he) was entreating" or "(he) began to entreat." Taylor argues for this as the earliest reading (ad loc.). D (it syˢ) substitute the present participle παρακαλῶν ("entreating").

f   D et al. attest a reading without πολλά ("earnestly" or "at length," lit., "very much"). The omission may be due to a deliberate stylistic preference or to the influence of the parallel in Luke 8:41.

g   The earliest recoverable reading is attested by A B L

just trust." 37/ And he did not allow anyone to accompany him,[m] except Peter and James and John, the brother of James. 38/ And they went into the house of the synagogue leader, and he saw a disturbance and people who were weeping and wailing loudly, 39/ and when he had entered he said to them, "Why are you distressed and weeping? The child has not died, but is sleeping. 40/ And they began to laugh at him, but he[n] drove them all out and took the father of the child and the mother and those with him and went into (the room) where the child was. 41/ And he grasped the hand of the child and said to her, "Talitha koum,"[o] which means, "Girl, I say to you, wake up!" 42/ And immediately the girl arose and began to walk; for she was twelve years old. And they were immediately[p] amazed in great amazement. 43/ And he ordered them strongly that no one should know this, and he said that (something) should be given to her to eat.

et al., $\tau\grave{\alpha}\ \pi\alpha\rho'\ \alpha\dot{\upsilon}\tau\hat{\eta}\varsigma\ \pi\acute{\alpha}\nu\tau\alpha$ ("all that she had"). The readings of D W Θ et al., $\tau\grave{\alpha}\ \dot{\varepsilon}\alpha\upsilon\tau\hat{\eta}\varsigma\ \pi\acute{\alpha}\nu\tau\alpha$ ("all that she had"), and $\aleph$ C K et al., $\tau\grave{\alpha}\ \pi\alpha\rho'\ \dot{\varepsilon}\alpha\upsilon\tau\hat{\eta}\varsigma\ \pi\acute{\alpha}\nu\tau\alpha$ ("all that she had"), represent two independent corrections of the style.

h $\aleph$* B C* et al. read $\tau\grave{\alpha}\ \pi\varepsilon\rho\grave{\iota}\ \tau o\hat{\upsilon}\ \mathit{Ἰ}\eta\sigma o\hat{\upsilon}$ ("the things concerning Jesus"). This reading represents a secondary stylistic improvement; cf. Luke 24:19, 27; Acts 1:3; 18:25. Taylor argues for its originality (ad loc.).

i   D (Θ) et al. attest the secondary, explanatory comment $\delta\iota\grave{o}\ \pi\varepsilon\pi o\iota\acute{\eta}\kappa\varepsilon\iota\ \lambda\acute{\alpha}\vartheta\rho\alpha$ ("because of what she had done secretly").

j $\aleph$ B C D L et al. read $\alpha\dot{\upsilon}\tau\hat{\eta}$ ("to her"); A W Θ et al. read $\dot{\varepsilon}\pi'\ \alpha\dot{\upsilon}\tau\hat{\eta}$ ("to her"); $\Phi\ f^{13}$ et al. read $\dot{\varepsilon}\pi'\ \alpha\dot{\upsilon}\tau\acute{\eta}\nu$ ("to her"). These are stylistic variants. For the first two constructions, see BAGD, s.v. $\gamma\acute{\iota}\nu o\mu\alpha\iota$.

k   The earliest recoverable reading is probably the nominative $\vartheta\upsilon\gamma\acute{\alpha}\tau\eta\rho$ ("Daughter"), attested by B D W et al. Most of the documents that were eventually collected in the NT use nominative forms for the vocative; see Moulton-Turner, 3:3, 33–35. The reading of the vocative form $\vartheta\acute{\upsilon}\gamma\alpha\tau\varepsilon\rho$ ("Daughter"), attested by $\aleph$ A C[2vid] L Θ et al., thus represents a secondary correction.

l   The translation is based on the reading attested by $\aleph$*.c B L W et al., $\pi\alpha\rho\alpha\kappa o\acute{\upsilon}\sigma\alpha\varsigma$ ("overheard," lit., "having overheard"). Since this verb is ambiguous and could mean "ignore" or "disobey," it was corrected to $\dot{\alpha}\kappa o\acute{\upsilon}\sigma\alpha\varsigma$ ("heard," lit., "having heard"), a reading attested by $\aleph^2$ A C D et al. So Metzger, *Textual Commentary*, 74. Taylor accepts the former reading, but understands it to mean "ignored" (ad loc.).

m   The MSS show two kinds of stylistic variants: between $\alpha\dot{\upsilon}\tau\hat{\wp}$ ("with him") and $\mu\varepsilon\tau'\ \alpha\dot{\upsilon}\tau o\hat{\upsilon}$ ("with him") (for both constructions, see BAGD, s.v. $\sigma\upsilon\nu\alpha\kappa o\lambda o\upsilon\vartheta\acute{\varepsilon}\omega$); and among $\sigma\upsilon\nu\alpha\kappa o\lambda o\upsilon\vartheta\acute{\varepsilon}\omega$, $\dot{\alpha}\kappa o\lambda o\upsilon\vartheta\acute{\varepsilon}\omega$, and $\pi\alpha\rho\alpha\kappa o\lambda o\upsilon\vartheta\acute{\varepsilon}\omega$ (all meaning "follow" or "accompany someone").

n   Perhaps because the construction $\alpha\dot{\upsilon}\tau\grave{o}\varsigma\ \delta\acute{\varepsilon}$ ("but he," lit., "but he himself") was originally emphatic, the construction $\dot{o}\ \delta\acute{\varepsilon}$ ("but he") was substituted for it in a reading attested by A W et al. See Moulton-Turner, 3:40–41.

o   The earliest recoverable reading is $\tau\alpha\lambda\iota\vartheta\alpha\ \kappa o\upsilon\mu$ ("Talitha koum"), attested by $\aleph$ B C L et al. Since $\kappa o\upsilon\mu$ ("koum") represents an Aramaic masculine imperative, it is corrected to $\kappa o\upsilon\mu\iota$ ("koumi"), the feminine imperative, in a reading attested by A Θ et al. The reading of D, $\rho\alpha\beta\beta\iota\ \vartheta\alpha\beta\iota\tau\alpha\ \kappa o\upsilon\mu\iota$ ("rabbi Tabitha koumi"), may be a corruption of $\rho\alpha\beta\iota\vartheta\alpha\ \kappa o\upsilon\mu\iota$ ("rabitha koumi"), $\rho\alpha\beta\iota\vartheta\alpha$ meaning "girl" in an Aramaic dialect ($\tau\alpha\lambda\iota\vartheta\alpha$ represents a more common Aramaic word with a similar meaning). The less-familiar Aramaic word was associated with the proper name $T\alpha\beta\iota\vartheta\acute{\alpha}$ ("Tabitha"; cf. Acts 9:40). This name also

Literary Context

The description of Jesus crossing over in the boat back to the other side (of the Sea of Galilee) in v. 21 links the two healings in 5:21-43 closely to the preceding exorcism of the Gerasene demoniac. It also recalls the scene in 4:35, when Jesus, sitting in a boat, proposes to his disciples that they go to the other side of the shore. The mention of the large crowd in 5:21 is reminiscent of the crowd that was dismissed in 4:36, just before the boat carrying Jesus left from an area near Capernaum for the shore of the Decapolis. The statement that Jesus "was beside the sea" (ἦν παρὰ τὴν θάλασσαν) in v. 21 creates a typical Markan scene.[113] The presence of the crowd, however, is necessary for the story about the woman with a flow of blood. It is likely, therefore, that the first clause of v. 21 represents material that was in the source, a collection of five miracle stories, whereas the second clause may be a Markan addition.

Literary Relationship between the Two Stories

Until the 1920s, most scholars concluded that the two stories were intertwined because the events happened in that way.[114] This is unlikely, among other reasons, because the two stories are written in quite different styles. The story about Jairus's daughter uses verbs

mostly in the historical present and is written in short sentences with few participles. The story about the woman with the flow of blood is told with verbs in the aorist and imperfect tenses. The sentences are longer and there is a higher frequency of participles.[115] Since each story could stand alone and the insertion of one story into another is a feature of Markan style, it is likely that the two stories were separate in the source. The healing of the woman with the flow of blood probably preceded the raising of Jairus's daughter.[116]

The present form of the section containing the intertwined miracle stories is made up of a series of scenes in which the action moves progressively from a very public to a very private scene. This narrowing of the audience has the effect of highlighting the mysterious and miraculous character of the raising of the daughter of Jairus.[117] With regard to the inner story, the healing of the woman with the flow of blood, the opposite movement occurs, from a very private action to a public acknowledgment of the action and its effect.[118]

Genres

The healing of the woman with a flow of blood has a number of typical features. The descriptions of the length of the illness and of the failure of previous

---

113   Cf. "while he was passing by along the sea" (παρ-άγων παρὰ τὴν θάλασσαν) in 1:16; "he went out again along the sea" (ἐξῆλθεν πάλιν παρὰ τὴν θάλασσαν) in 2:13; "Jesus withdrew with his disciples to the sea" (ὁ Ἰησοῦς μετὰ τῶν μαθητῶν αὐτοῦ ἀνεχώρησεν πρὸς τὴν θάλασσαν) in 3:7; and "again he began to teach beside the sea" (πάλιν ἤρξατο διδάσκειν παρὰ τὴν θάλασσαν) in 4:1. As in 5:21, a crowd is also present in 2:13; 3:7; and 4:1.

114   For examples, see von Dobschütz, "Erzählerkunst," 195; Achtemeier, "Miracle Catenae," 276–77. For a

list of more recent scholars who take the same position, see Meier, *A Marginal Jew*, 2:708, 755, n. 140. To these may be added van der Loos, *Miracles*, 509.

115   Achtemeier, "Miracle Catenae," 277.

116   Ibid., 277–79.

117   Marshall, *Faith*, 91.

118   Shepherd, *Markan Sandwich Stories*, 139–40.

attempts at healing (vv. 25-26) illustrate the difficulty of the cure and thus the magnitude of the miracle.[119] Healing by means of touch and the instantaneousness of the cure (vv. 27-29) are also typical.[120] The motif of criticism of doctors is found in ancient literature, but not typically in miracle stories.[121]

With regard to the raising of the daughter of Jairus, the device of Jesus being summoned to cure a fatal illness but arriving only after the patient has died is an example of the typical motif of the heightening of the effect by demonstrating the difficulty of the task. The laughter of the mourners has the same effect (vv. 38-40a). Other typical motifs are the dismissal of the crowd (v. 40), the healing gesture, the words of power in a foreign language (v. 41), the instantaneousness of the miracle, the mention of the girl's age (v. 42), and the motif of demonstration of the miracle (the command in v. 43 that she be given something to eat shows that she is alive and not a ghost).[122]

According to the Hebrew Bible, Elijah raised the son of a widow from the dead, and Elisha raised the son of the Shunammite woman (1 Kgs 17:17-24; 2 Kgs 4:18-37). In the version of the Elijah story in the MT, he stretches himself out upon the child three times. In the LXX, he breathes on him three times. Josephus's version of the story lacks both of these details (*Ant.* 8.13.3 §325–27). Many Greek and Hellenistic miracle-workers were reputed to have raised the dead.[123]

The following story was written down between 160 and 170 CE, although there is evidence that a version of it was known as early as the time of the emperor Tiberius (14–37 CE):

The famous Asclepiades, who ranks among the greatest of doctors, indeed, if you except Hippocrates, as the very greatest. . . . It chanced that once, when he was returning to town from his country house, he observed an enormous funeral procession in the suburbs of the city. A huge multitude of men who had come out to perform the last honours stood round the bier, all of them plunged in deep sorrow and wearing worn and ragged apparel. He asked whom they were burying, but no one replied; so he went nearer to satisfy his curiosity and to see who it might be that was dead, or, it may be, in the hope to make some discovery in the interests of his profession. Be this as it may, he certainly snatched the man from the jaws of death as he lay there on the verge of burial. The poor fellow's limbs were already covered with spices, his mouth filled with sweet-smelling unguent. He had been anointed and was all ready for the pyre. But Asclepiades looked upon him, took careful note of certain signs, handled his body again and again, and perceived that the life was still in him, though scarcely to be detected. Straightway he cried out, "He lives! Throw down your torches, take away your fire, demolish the pyre, take back the funeral feast and spread it on his board at home." While he spoke, a murmur arose; some said that they must take the doctor's word, others mocked at the physician's skill. At last, in spite of the opposition offered even by his relations, perhaps because they had already entered into possession of the dead man's property, perhaps because they did not believe his words, Asclepiades persuaded them to put off the burial for a brief space. Having

---

119 For ancient texts mentioning the failure of the medical art, see Otto Weinreich, *Antike Heilungswunder: Untersuchungen zum Wunderglauben der Griechen und Römer* (Giessen: Töpelmann, 1909) 195–96.

120 Bultmann, *History*, 214, 221–22.

121 Cotter, *Miracles*, 204–5; note also the tradition that Empedocles (1.44) healed a woman on whom the physicians had given up (ibid., 39). The fifth epistle attributed to Heraclitus claims that "the original, untutored way of curing" is harmony with nature. "Only later do various men, when they imitate a variety of objects, call types of ignorance branches of knowledge." Trans. from Harold W. Attridge, *First Century Cynicism in the Epistles of Heraclitus: Introduction, Greek Text and Translation* (HTS 29; Missoula,

MT: Scholars Press, 1976) 63. The sixth epistle is more explicitly critical of physicians, arguing that "they understand neither medical science nor nature." They kill in the name of science and "sell for monetary gain artificial contrivances of science" (ibid., 65; see also the discussion on 7).

122 Bultmann, *History*, 214–15, 221–25.

123 Barry Blackburn, *Theios Anēr and the Markan Miracle Traditions* (WUNT 2.40; Tübingen: Mohr Siebeck, 1991) 192; Cotter, *Miracles*, 13–15, 24–30, 39, 45–47.

thus rescued him from the hands of the undertaker, he carried the man home, as it were from the very mouth of hell, and straightway revived the spirit within him, and by means of certain drugs called forth the life that still lay hidden in the secret places of the body (Asclepiades ille, inter praecipuos medicorum, si unum Hippocratem excipias ceteris princeps, ... is igitur cum forte in ciuitatem sese reciperet et rure suo suburbano rediret, aspexit in pomoeriis ciuitatis funus ingens locatum plurimos homines ingenti multitudine, qui exequias uenerant, circumstare, omnis tristissimos et obsoletissimo uestitu. propius accessit, utine cognosceret in ore mortui, quisnam esset, quoniam percontanti nemo responderat an uero ut ipse aliquid in illo ex arte reprehenderet? certe quidem iacenti homini ac prope deposito salutem adtulit. iam miseri illius membra omnia aromatis perspersa, iam os ipsius unguine odore delibutum, iam eum pollinctum, iam pyrae paratum contemplatus enim, diligentissime quibusdam signis animaduersis, etiam atque etiam pertrectauit corpus hominis et inuenit in illo uitam latentem. confestim exclamauit uiuere hominem: procul igitur faces abicerent, procul ignes amolirentur. rogum demolirentur, cenam feralem a tumulo ad mensam referrent. murmur interea exortum: partim medico credendum dicere, partim etiam inridere medicinam. postremo propinquis etiam hominibus inuitis, quodne iam ipsi hereditatem habebant, an quod adhuc illi fidem non habebant, aegre tamen ac difficulter Asclepiades impetrauit breuem mortuo dilationem atque ita uispillonum manibus extortum uelut ab inferis postliminio domum rettulit confestimque spiritum recreauit [confestim] animamque in corporis latibulis delitiscentem quibusdam medicamentis prouocauit). (Apuleius *Florida* 19)[124]

This story is not technically an account of the raising of the dead, but it is close to one. Another account blurs the distinction between healing someone near death and raising someone from the dead:

Here too is a miracle which Apollonius worked: A girl seemed to have died just in the hour of her marriage, and the bridegroom was following her bier lamenting as was natural his marriage left unfulfilled, and the whole of Rome was mourning with him, for the maiden belonged to a consular family. Apollonius then witnessing their grief, said: "Put down the bier, for I will stay the tears that you are shedding for this maiden." And at once he asked what was her name. The crowd accordingly thought that he was about to deliver such an oration as is commonly delivered as much to grace the funeral as to stir up lamentation; but he did nothing of the kind, but merely touching her and whispering in secret some spell over her, at once woke up the maiden from her seeming death; and the girl spoke out loud, and returned to her father's house, just as Alcestis did when she was brought back to life by Hercules. And the relations of the maiden wanted to present him with the sum of 150,000 sesterces, but he said that he would freely present the money to the young lady by way of a dowry. Now whether he detected some spark of life in her, which those who were nursing her had not noticed,—for it is said that although it was raining at the time, a vapor went up from her face—or whether life was really extinct, and he restored it by the warmth of his touch, is a mysterious problem which neither I myself nor those who were present could decide (Κἀκεῖνο Ἀπολλωνίου θαῦμα· κόρη ἐν ὥρᾳ γάμου τεθνάναι ἐδόκει, καὶ ὁ νυμφίος ἠκολούθει τῇ κλίνῃ βοῶν ὁπόσα ἐπ᾽ ἀτελεῖ γάμῳ, ξυνωλοφύρετο δὲ καὶ ἡ Ῥώμη, καὶ γὰρ ἐτύγχανεν οἰκίας ἡ κόρη τελούσης ἐς ὑπάτους. παρατυχὼν οὖν ὁ Ἀπολλώνιος τῷ πάθει, "κατάθεσθε," ἔφη, "τὴν κλίνην, ἐγὼ γὰρ ὑμᾶς τῶν ἐπὶ τῇ κόρῃ δακρύων παύσω." καὶ ἅμα ἤρετο, ὅ τι ὄνομα αὐτῇ εἴη. οἱ

---

124 Text from J. van der Vliet, ed., *Lvcii Apvlei Madavrensis Apologia, sive De magia liber et Florida* (Leipzig: Teubner, 1900) 185–86; trans. from H. E. Butler, *The Apologia and Florida of Apuleius of Madaura* (Oxford: Clarendon, 1909; reprinted Westport, CT: Greenwood, 1970) 207–8. The same trans. of this passage is cited by Cotter, *Miracles,* §1.57 (pp. 46–47). The *Florida* was written between 160 and 170 CE (S. J. Harrison, "Apuleius," *OCD* 131). That the story was known in the time of Tiberius is attested by Celsus *On Medicine* 2.6.15 (J. T. Vallance, "Cornelius Celsus, Aulus," *OCD* 392–93). An ET of the latter passage may be found in Cotter, *Miracles,* §1.56 (p. 46).

μὲν δὴ πολλοὶ ᾤοντο λόγον ἀγορεύσειν αὐτόν, οἷοι τῶν λόγων οἱ ἐπικήδειοί τε καὶ τὰς ὀλοφύρσεις ἐγείροντες, ὁ δὲ οὐδὲν ἄλλ᾽ ἢ προσαψάμενος αὐτῆς καί τι ἀφανῶς ἐπειπών, ἀφύπνισε τὴν κόρην τοῦ δοκοῦντος θανάτου, καὶ φωνήν τε ἡ παῖς ἀφῆκέ, ἐπανῆλθέ τε ἐς τὴν οἰκίαν τοῦ πατρός, ὥσπερ ἡ Ἄλκηστις ὑπὸ τοῦ Ἡρακλέους ἀναβιωθεῖσα. δωρουμένων δὲ αὐτῷ τῶν ξυγγενῶν τῆς κόρης μυριάδας δεκαπέντε φερνὴν ἔφη ἐπιδιδόναι αὐτὰς τῇ παιδί. καὶ εἴτε σπινθῆρα τῆς ψυχῆς εὗρεν ἐν αὐτῇ, ὃς ἐλελήθει τοὺς θεραπεύοντας—λέγεται γάρ, ὡς ψεκάζοι μὲν ὁ Ζεύς, ἡ δὲ ἀτμίζοι ἀπὸ τοῦ προσώπου—εἴτ᾽ ἀπεσβηκυῖαν τὴν ψυχὴν ἀνέθαλψέ τε καὶ ἀνέλαβεν, ἄρρητος ἡ κατάληψις τούτου γέγονεν οὐκ ἐμοὶ μόνον, ἀλλὰ καὶ τοῖς παρατυχοῦσιν). (Philostratus *Vita Ap.* 4.45)[125]

Philostratus leaves open whether the girl was only near death or had actually died. In either case, he does not present Apollonius as a physician, but as someone able to revive the girl or restore her to life by means of mere touch and some secret words.

Comment

■ **21-24** On v. 21, see "Literary Context" above. Jairus is portrayed as a "synagogue leader" or "ruler of a synagogue" (ἀρχισυνάγωγος) in v. 22. In a non-Jewish context, the word was used for the head of an association.[126] In a Jewish context, it refers to an official whose primary responsibility was to supervise the business of the local Jewish community.[127] Jairus appears as the representative of his daughter, who is the distressed person. Theissen has pointed out that the motif of a representative and the motif of faith or trust are associated motifs.[128] The distressed person or the representative falling at the feet of

the miracle-worker or kneeling before him is also a typical motif.[129]

Jairus's obeisance to Jesus and his words indicate complete confidence, or faith, that Jesus has the power to heal his daughter (vv. 22-23).[130] He is thus one of the few persons with religious authority or political power who is portrayed positively in Mark. Significantly, Jairus disregards his social status and humbles himself before Jesus.[131]

Jairus says, "My daughter is at the point of death" (τὸ θυγάτριόν μου ἐσχάτως ἔχει). Similar language is used in an inscription dating to about 200 BCE dedicated on the island of Cos in the Sporades, where Hippocrates was born and where there was a sanctuary of Asclepius. The inscription honors a physician by the name of Anaxippos, who "saved many of the citizens, when they had fallen into great sicknesses and life-threatening dangers" (πολλούς τε τῶν πολιτᾶν εἰς μεγ(ά)λας ἀρωστίας ἐμπεσόντας καὶ κινδύνους τοὺς ἐσχάτους διέσωισε).[132] Jairus asks Jesus to come and lay his hands upon the girl "in order that she may be saved and live" (ἵνα σωθῇ καὶ ζήσῃ) (v. 23). Here and elsewhere in Mark, the verb σῴζειν ("to save") is used in the sense of saving a person from a physical ailment or from death.[133] Elsewhere, however, the same verb is used with regard to eternal life (8:35; 10:26; 13:13). Jairus seeks his daughter's rescue from death; the members of the audience of Mark, however, who know the Gospel as a whole, may infer a second level of meaning relating to eternal life in the kingdom of God.

Without recording a verbal response on Jesus' part, the evangelist depicts Jesus' compliance with Jairus's request simply by reporting that "he went away with him" (v. 24). The large crowd that was introduced in v. 21 is mentioned again in v. 24, and the additional comment is added that the crowd was pressing upon him. This detail has a double function. On the one hand, it begins to

125 Text and trans. (modified) from Frederick C. Conybeare, *Philostratus: The Life of Apollonius of Tyana* (2 vols.; Cambridge, MA/London: Harvard University Press, 1912) 1:456–59. ET also in Cotter, *Miracles*, §1.55 (p. 45).

126 Franz Poland, *Geschichte des griechischen Vereinswesens* (Leipzig: Teubner, 1909) 355; cf. BAGD, s.v.

127 Schürer, *History*, 2:434.

128 Theissen, *Miracle Stories*, 49.

129 Ibid., 53. In Mark, cf. 1:40; 5:6; 7:25.

130 Cf. Schmithals, *Wunder*, 69–70.

131 Marshall, *Faith*, 90–91, 96.

132 Text from Jost Benedum, "Griechische Arztinschriften aus Kos," *ZPE* 25 (1977) 270; my trans.; cf. BAGD, s.v. ἐσχάτως.

133 Cf. 3:4; 5:28, 34; 6:56; 10:52; 13:20; 15:30, 31.

heighten the suspense about whether Jesus will arrive in time to heal the dying girl. On the other, it prepares for the secret approach of the woman with the flow of blood.

■ **25** The "flow of blood" (ῥύσις αἵματος) mentioned in v. 25 is no doubt a gynecological ailment. According to Aristotle:

> Further, of all female animals the human female has the most abundant blood, and menstrual flows are more plentiful in women than in any other animal. This blood if it has become diseased is known as flux (μάλιστα δὲ καὶ τῶν θηλέων ζῴων γυνὴ πολύαιμον, καὶ τὰ καλούμενα καταμήνια γίγνεται πλεῖστα τῶν ζῴων ταῖς γυναιξίν. νενοσηκὸς δὲ τοῦτο τὸ αἷμα καλεῖται ῥοῦς). (HA 3.19 [521a.25–27)[134]

The word that Hippocratic physicians of the classical period used for a pathological discharge from the womb was ῥόος or ῥοῦς ("flux" or "discharge"), and they considered it to be a ("disease").[135] Aretaeus the Cappadocian, a member of the Rationalist medical school active before Galen, defined the female flux as "an irregular, but sustained, flow of material of varied colour, consistency, and volume from the uterus."[136] Soranus of Ephesus, the physician who practiced in Rome under Trajan and Hadrian, distinguished carefully between hemorrhage, which was sudden and dangerous, and various female "fluxes" or discharges (3.10-11 §40–44).[137] Thus, Mark's ῥύσις αἵματος should not be translated as "hemorrhage," but as "flow of blood."[138]

The treatments recommended by Soranus for fluxes include douches, vaginal suppositories, measures to relieve pain, if needed, and appropriate diet and exercise (3.11 §44).[139] Remedies for such irregular bleeding or discharge are provided in the Demotic magical papyri and the tractate Šabbat in the Babylonian Talmud.[140]

The woman is said to have had this ailment "for twelve years." It is unlikely that this number is symbolic. It signifies that the woman has suffered for a long time and that, therefore, the illness would be difficult to heal.

■ **26** The remark that the woman "had suffered much under many physicians and had spent all that she had" indicates that at one time she could afford to consult not just one but many physicians. Her search for healing,

---

134 Text and trans. (modified) from Arthur L. Peck, *Aristotle: Historia Animalium* (3 vols.; LCL; Cambridge, MA: Harvard University Press; London: Heinemann, 1965) 1:220–23; cited by Lesley Dean-Jones, *Women's Bodies in Classical Greek Science* (Oxford: Clarendon, 1994) 129.

135 Dean-Jones, *Women's Bodies*, 129–30; Mary Rose D'Angelo, "Gender and Power in the Gospel of Mark: The Daughter of Jairus and the Woman with the Flow of Blood," in John C. Cavadini, ed., *Miracles in Jewish and Christian Antiquity: Imagining Truth* (Notre Dame Studies in Theology 3; Notre Dame, IN: University of Notre Dame Press, 1999) 83–109; Kevin Wilkinson, "'The fount of her blood was dried up': Desiccation, Gender, and Eschatology in Mark 5:25-34" (unpublished paper, 2001).

136 Rebecca Flemming, *Medicine and the Making of Roman Women: Gender, Nature, and Authority from Celsus to Galen* (New York/Oxford: Oxford University Press, 2000) 211–12. The author of *Medical Definitions*, attributed to Galen, and Archigenes of Apamea (who flourished under Trajan), both also Rationalists, defined female flux in the same way (ibid.). Galen discusses the female flux in *On the Difference between Symptoms*, in *On Tromos, Palmos, Spasmos, and Rigos* (Περὶ τρόμου καὶ παλμοῦ καὶ σπασμοῦ καὶ ῥίγος), and in *On the Affected Places* (ibid., 332, 336).

137 ET based on the Greek text of Johannes Ilberg by Owsei Temkin, *Soranus' Gynecology* (Baltimore/London: Johns Hopkins University Press, 1956) 161–68; D'Angelo, "Gender and Power," 92–93; on Soranus, a member of the Methodical school of medicine, see Helen King, "Soranus," *OCD* 1426; Flemming, *Medicine*, 248–49.

138 According to Origen (*Con. Cels.* 6.35), the Valentinians interpreted the woman with the flow of blood as a symbol of Sophia Prunikos (Vulgar Wisdom); van der Loos, *Miracles*, 510; on Sophia Prunikos, see Layton, *Gnostic Scriptures*, 164, 171.

139 Temkin, *Soranus' Gynecology*, 166–68; cf. D'Angelo, "Gender and Power," 93 and n. 58. The Hippocratic corpus includes a cure for ῥόος ἐρυθρός ("pathological menses") that involves applying cupping glasses to the breasts; Dean-Jones, *Women's Bodies*, 142.

140 D'Angelo, "Gender and Power," 93–94.

however, had resulted in the depletion of her assets, so that the audience may infer that she was desperate at this point.

The statement that "she had not been benefited at all, but rather had become worse" is an indictment of the medical profession of the time. First of all, this remark casts a critical light on the previous statement that she had spent all she had. Second, it raises a sharp question about the competence of doctors. That physicians were sometimes criticized or mocked as incompetent in antiquity is suggested by three epigrams of Martial, who wrote during the first century CE:

> Lately was Diaulus a doctor, now he is an undertaker. What the undertaker now does the doctor too did before (Nuper erat medicus, nunc est vispillo Diaulus: quod vispillo facit, fecerat et medicus).

> I was sickening; but you at once attended me, Symmachus, with a train of a hundred apprentices. A hundred hands frosted by the North wind have pawed me: I had no fever before, Symmachus; now I have (Languebam: sed tu comitatus protinus ad me venisti centum, Symmache, discipulis. centum me tetigere manus Aquilone gelatae: non habui febrem, Symmache, nunc habeo).

> You are now a gladiator: you were an eye-specialist before. You did as a doctor what you do now as a gladiator (Oplomachus nunc es, fueras opthalmicus ante. fecisti medicus quod facis oplomachus). (*Epigrams* 1.47; 5.9; 8.74)[141]

Physicians were also sometimes perceived as avaricious:

> Doctor Herodes had stolen a drinking-ladle from a sick patient. When detected he said: "You fool, why then do you drink?" (Clinicus Herodes trullam sub-

duxerat aegro: deprensus dixit "Stulte, quid ergo bibis?"). (Martial *Epigrams* 9.96)[142]

when his collarbone [lit., the keybone of his shoulder] had been broken in battle, and the attending physician insistently demanded a fee every day, [Philip the father of Alexander the Great] said, "Take as much as you wish; for you have the key in your charge!" (τῆς δὲ κλειδὸς αὐτῷ καταγείσης ἐν πολέμῳ καὶ τοῦ θεραπεύοντος ἰατροῦ πάντως τι καθ' ἡμέραν αἰτοῦντος, "λάμβανε," ἔφη, "ὅσα βούλει· τὴν γὰρ κλεῖν ἔχεις"). (Plutarch *Apoph.* = *Moralia* 177F [9])[143]

The Hippocratic work *Precepts* (4 and 6) advises physicians not to worry about their fees, but to enhance their reputations. It also recommends free treatment for the poor.[144]

■ **27-28** The woman, still suffering from her disease and having no more money for physicians (nor confidence in their ability to heal), heard about Jesus and went to him for healing (v. 27). Her decision to come up behind him and touch his cloak is not unusual or surprising, given the portrayal of Jesus healing the crowds elsewhere in Mark. According to 3:10, "he had healed many, with the result that they approached him eagerly, in order that those of them who had (bodily) torments might touch him." The evangelist may have composed 3:10, as part of the Markan summary of 3:7-12, in light of the story of the woman with a flow of blood that he found in a source. Or, as Leander Keck has argued, 3:10 may be part of a pre-Markan summary associated with (some of) the miracle stories of chaps. 4–6.[145] In either case, 3:10 shows that the evangelist found nothing problematic in the woman's behavior (cf. also 6:56).

The woman's remark in v. 28, "If I touch even his clothes, I shall be saved," is a soliloquy that makes the

---

141   Text and trans. from Walter C. A. Ker, *Martial: Epigrams* (2 vols.; LCL; Cambridge, MA: Harvard University Press; London: Heinemann, 1919–20) 1:58–59, 300–1; 2:58–59; ET given in Cotter, *Miracles*, §A.3–5 (p. 204). On the dates of Martial, see Mario Citroni, "Martial," *OCD* 930.

142   Text and trans. from Ker, *Martial: Epigrams*, 2:142–43; ET given in Cotter, *Miracles*, §A.6 (p. 204).

143   Text and trans. from Babbitt, *Plutarch's Moralia*, 3:44–45; cf. Cotter, *Miracles*, §A.7 (p. 204).

144   Cited by Eung Chun Park, *The Mission Discourse in Matthew's Interpretation* (WUNT 2.81; Tübingen: Mohr Siebeck, 1995) 101–2.

145   Leander E. Keck, "Mark 3:7-12 and Mark's Christology," *JBL* 84 (1965) 341–58.

audience aware of her great confidence or faith in Jesus' power to heal. The woman does not seem to think that Jesus' conscious desire to heal is a prerequisite for her healing. The remark in 3:10 is similar, although 6:56 seems to presuppose Jesus' permission to touch the edge (or tassel) of his outer garment.

Her soliloquy and the related passages in Mark express a belief in the transfer by touch of some quality of a charismatic person.[146] The idea is clearly expressed in an anecdote about the Roman general Sulla:

As she passed along behind Sulla, she rested her hand upon him, plucked off a bit of nap from his mantle, and then proceeded to her own place. When Sulla looked at her in astonishment, she said, "It's nothing of importance, Dictator, but I too wish to partake a little in your good luck" (αὕτη παρὰ τὸν Σύλλαν ἐξόπισθεν παραπορευομένη τήν τε χεῖρα πρὸς αὐτὸν ἀπηρείσατο καὶ κροκύδα τοῦ ἱματίου σπάσασα παρῆλθεν ἐπὶ τὴν ἑαυτῆς χώραν. ἐμβλέψαντος δὲ τοῦ Σύλλα καὶ θαυμάσαντος, "Οὐδέν," ἔφη, "δεινόν, αὐτόκρατορ, ἀλλὰ βούλομαι τῆς σῆς κἀγὼ μικρὸν εὐτυχίας μεταλαβεῖν"). (Plutarch Vit. Sulla 35.4)[147]

■ **29** The word εὐθύς ("immediately") indicates the instantaneous, and thus miraculous, quality of the cure. The statement that "the source of her blood was dried up" (ἐξηράνθη ἡ πηγὴ τοῦ αἵματος αὐτῆς) could simply mean that the cause of the abnormal bleeding was dried up.[148] Alternatively, it could mean that the woman's womb was dried up so that she became menopausal. If

the latter interpretation is correct, it may have eschatological connotations: the human being of the new age or the kingdom of God is beyond sexuality.[149]

The narrator's statement, "and she knew in her body that she had been healed of the torment (μάστιξ)," takes the place of the usual public demonstration of the reality of the miracle. The use of the term μάστιξ (lit., "whip"; metaph. "torment") here is another element that this passage has in common with 3:10. In the latter passage, the term is used for diseases and disabilities caused by unclean spirits.[150] In the story about the woman with the flow of blood, the wielder of the whip, so to speak, is left unspecified.[151]

■ **30-32** Just as the woman "knew in her body" (ἔγνω τῷ σώματι) that she had been healed, so Jesus "knew in himself that power had gone out from him" (ἐπιγνοὺς ἐν ἑαυτῷ τὴν ἐξ αὐτοῦ δύναμιν ἐξελθοῦσαν) (v. 30a). As Sulla's communicable charism was good luck, so Jesus' is healing power. Jesus' "power" (δύναμις) in this passage is analogous to that of ancient legendary figures, heroes, and deities. In his work *On the Pythagorean Way of Life*, Iamblichus refers to Abaris, the legendary priest of Apollo from the land of the Hyperboreans. Iamblichus states that Abaris crossed impassible places by riding an arrow, performed purifications, and drove off plagues and winds from cities that asked for his assistance. He concludes the list with the comment: "And other such signs of Abaris' power are on record" (καὶ ἄλλα τοιαῦτα τεκμήρια ἱστορεῖται τῆς τοῦ Ἀβάριδος δύναμεως) (Vit. Pyth. 92).[152] The closest parallel to this healing by touching Jesus' cloak is Acts 19:11-12:

---

146 Eitrem argued that Jesus' ability to heal by means of touch was understood in terms of power flowing out and simultaneously being replenished (*Some Notes*, 35). Friedrich Preisigke concluded that the woman's idea that the healing power of Jesus could be transmitted by contact with his clothing alone and without his conscious involvement was part of the religious thought of the masses at the time (*Die Gotteskraft der frühchristlichen Zeit* [Papyrusinstitut Heidelberg Schrift 6; Berlin/Leipzig: de Gruyter, 1922] 201; cf. David E. Aune, "Magic in Early Christianity," ANRW 2.23.2 [1980] 1536-37). Preisigke, like Eitrem, concluded that the power of Jesus was conceived of as being constantly replenished from the source, the Father of all (*Gotteskraft*, 207-8).

147 Text and trans. (modified) from Perrin, *Plutarch's Lives*, 4:436-39. Even though the woman's act was an eventually successful flirtation, her gesture implies that it was widely believed that power could be communicated by touch. Cf. Theissen, *Miracle Stories*, 134; D'Angelo, "Gender and Power," 98-99.

148 D'Angelo seems to presuppose this interpretation; she translates "the spring of her blood was dried up" ("Gender and Power," 98).

149 Wilkinson, "'The fount of her blood was dried up.'"

150 See the commentary on 3:9-10 above.

151 In Greek texts, the "whip" or "scourge" is often wielded by a deity; see LSJ, s.v. See also Eitrem, *Some Notes*, 28-29.

152 Text and trans. from Dillon and Hershbell, 114-17;

God was working mighty deeds, not the ordinary kind, through the hands of Paul, so that cloths or aprons were carried from his skin to the sick and the diseases departed from them and the evil spirits came forth from them (Δυνάμεις τε οὐ τὰς τυχούσας ὁ θεὸς ἐποίει διὰ τῶν χειρῶν Παύλου, ὥστε καὶ ἐπὶ τοὺς ἀσθενοῦντας ἀποφέρεσθαι ἀπὸ τοῦ χρωτὸς αὐτοῦ σουδάρια ἢ σιμικίνθια καὶ ἀπαλλάσσεσθαι ἀπ᾽ αὐτῶν τὰς νόσους, τά τε πνεύματα τὰ πονηρὰ ἐκπορεύεσθαι).[153]

An analogous phenomenon is the idea that a statue or other image of a hero or other extraordinarily accomplished person had the same power as the actual person.[154] Thus, these images were believed to have the power to heal diseases. Lucian of Samosata satirizes this belief in his *Lover of Lies* (18–21). Just as the fabric of Jesus' cloak can be a container, as it were, of divine power, so can such power reside in the wood of a divine image, according to folk belief.[155]

Underlying these phenomena is the ancient notion that certain objects and persons have a particular "power" (δύναμις), respectively, for example, to heal a certain disease.[156] The objects include certain stones, plants, animals, and parts of animals.

No reason is given for Jesus' desire to know "Who touched my clothes?" (v. 30b). This first question provides an occasion for presenting the disciples' reaction, "You see the crowd pressing upon you and you say, 'Who touched me?'" (v. 31). This response shows that the disciples have less understanding about the workings of Jesus' healing power than the woman does; it may imply that they have less trust as well. The question also, however, expresses the folk belief that Jesus could actually feel the power being transferred from his body to that of another person.[157] The text implies that ordinary, accidental touch does not effect the transfer of Jesus' power in this automatic way. Rather, only touch with the intention of being healed and with trust that Jesus is the bearer of power to heal creates this phenomenon.

The next verse, "And he kept looking around to see who had done this" (v. 32), describes the renewal of Jesus' search for the person who touched him and leads into the woman's coming forward.[158]

■ **33-34** The reaction of the woman, being frightened and in a state of trembling (v. 33), is sometimes explained in terms of the woman's impurity due to her genital discharge (Lev 15:25-30). She has touched Jesus by stealth, it is said, because, by doing so, she was communicating her ritual uncleanness to a holy man.[159] But ritual impurity is not an explicit theme in the story.[160] Furthermore, Shaye J. D. Cohen has argued that neither the menstruant nor the *zābâ* (a woman with a vaginal discharge) was socially isolated among Jews of the Second Temple period. With

---

they note that the legend of Abaris goes back to Herodotus (4.36).

153 Even if this passage is dependent on Mark 5:50 (cf. Luke 8:46), it nevertheless reflects popular ideas of the time. See also Acts 5:15. Both passages are cited by Aune in relation to Mark 5:30 ("Magic," 1537).

154 Weinreich, *Antike Heilungswunder*, 144; Aune, "Magic," 1537.

155 Preisigke, *Gotteskraft*, 204.

156 Julius Röhr, *Der okkulte Kraftbegriff im Altertum* (Philologus Supplements 17.1; Leipzig: Dieterich, 1923) 9–15; cited by Aune "Magic," 1537. Röhr compares the communication of power by touch in Mark 5:30 to the North African idea that one can acquire some of the *mana* of a charismatic person through touch and to the late antique and medieval cults of relics (p. 15). Preisigke compares it to electricity or magnetism, which operate according to certain fixed laws of nature (*Gotteskraft*, 201–2).

157 So Preisigke, *Gotteskraft*, 202–3.

158 The use of the feminine participle ποιήσασαν ("who had done") is from the point of view of the omniscient narrator and does not imply that Jesus already knew who had touched him in a way that drew power from him; so also Ezra P. Gould, *A Critical and Exegetical Commentary on the Gospel according to Mark* (ICC; Edinburgh: T & T Clark, 1896).

159 So Meier, *Marginal Jew*, 2:709; Walter Grundmann stated that the woman had transgressed a statute, since she, as unclean, mixed with the people and touched Jesus, thereby transmitting uncleanness to him (*Das Evangelium nach Markus* [ThHKNT 2; Berlin: Evangelische Verlagsanstalt, 1959] 115).

160 See the discussion in D'Angelo, "Gender and Power," 83–85. See also Charlotte Fonrobert, "The Woman with a Blood-Flow (Mark 5:24-34) Revisited: Menstrual Laws and Jewish Culture in Christian Feminist Hermeneutics," in Craig A. Evans and James A. Sanders, eds., *Early Christian Interpretation of the Scriptures of Israel: Investigations and Proposals* (JSNTSup 148; SSEJC 5; Sheffield: Sheffield Aca-

regard to this passage, he concludes that the account gives no hint that the woman was impure or suffered any kind of social isolation as a result of her condition.[161] Other explanations are that she was ashamed or embarrassed to reveal the nature of her ailment in public; she feared because she had stolen power without permission; she knew that some believed the touch of a bleeding woman to be harmful; she feared that Jesus would be angry and would undo the healing; or she was awed by the power and majesty of Jesus.[162] The only explanation given in the text is that she knew "what had happened to her." Although purity is not an explicit theme of the story, it is likely that some Jews at the time would have considered her ritually impure, for example, the members of the community of the Dead Sea Scrolls. In light of this likely religious-social context, the story portrays Jesus as relatively indifferent to the issue of the transmission of ritual impurity due to genital discharges.[163]

In any case, Mark portrays the woman as coming forward, making a gesture of respect to Jesus, and courageously telling the whole truth (v. 33). Jesus' response (v. 34) is that her trust has saved her. Unlike the disciples, who were unable to calm the storm because of their lack of trust or faith (4:40), this woman was able to heal herself by the power of her faith. By availing herself of the power of Jesus, she has saved herself from her torment and is able, as Jesus confirms, to go in peace.

■ **35-36** In the Markan source, before the story about the woman with the flow of blood was inserted into the account of the raising of Jairus's daughter, the person still speaking when the people from the household of the synagogue leader arrived was probably Jairus (v. 35). Thus, the earlier form of the story had the envoys arrive while Jairus was still saying to Jesus, "My daughter is at the point of death; come and lay your hands on her, in order that she may be saved and live" (v. 23).[164] The close relation of the plea and the announcement of death would have created a dramatic and tragic irony. In the present, combined form of the two stories, the envoys arrive while Jesus is speaking to the healed woman (v. 34). The question of the messengers, "Why do you still trouble the teacher?" indicates that even those who recognize Jesus as a gifted healer do not imagine that he could raise the dead.[165] Their attitude serves to indicate the difficulty of the task that Jesus will take up.

When the Markan Jesus overhears the report, he says to Jairus, "Do not fear; just trust" (v. 36). This instruction indicates that the evangelist did not combine the two stories merely to delay Jesus' arrival at Jairus's house, so that a sufficiently plausible amount of time could pass between Jairus's request and the announcement of his daughter's death.[166] Rather, the confidence, faith, or trust of the woman with the flow of blood was brought forward in order to illustrate for Jairus and the audience what kind of faith or trust Jesus is advocating.[167] The exhortation "Do not fear" is both an expression of conso-

demic Press, 1997) 121–40. Both D'Angelo and Fonrobert offer criticisms of certain Christian feminist-liberationist readings of this passage in light of their anti-Jewish implications. Maccoby also argued that ritual impurity is not an issue here (*Ritual and Morality*, 162–63). Susan Haber argued that the woman's health is the primary concern of the passage, not her ritual impurity ("A Woman's Touch: Feminist Encounters with the Hemorrhaging Woman in Mark 5:24-34," *JSNT* 26 [2003] 171–92).

161 Shaye J. D. Cohen, "Menstruants and the Sacred in Judaism and Christianity," in Sarah B. Pomeroy, ed., *Women's History and Ancient History* (Chapel Hill/London: University of North Carolina Press, 1991) 273–99, esp. 278–79. Amy-Jill Levine makes the same point with regard to the parallel in Matthew (9:18-26) ("Discharging Responsibility: Matthean Jesus, Biblical Law, and Hemorrhaging Woman," in David R. Bauer and Mark Allan Powell, eds., *Treasures New and Old: Recent Contributions to*

Matthean Studies [SBLSymS 1; Atlanta: Scholars Press, 1996] 379–97).

162 Theissen, *Miracle Stories*, 134; van der Loos, *Miracles*, 517. Klostermann rejects the impurity theory in favor of the hypothesis that the woman was ashamed on account of her medical condition (51).

163 Cf. Kazen, *Jesus and Purity* Halakhah, 127–64, esp. 164. Kazen argued that Jesus "placed relative importance on ethics, that he had a pragmatic, rural or locally based attitude, which did not allow purity rules to [interfere] with social network, table fellowship and community, and that his eschatological outlook made impurity subordinate to the kingdom" (ibid., 347).

164 Achtemeier, "Miracle Catenae," 277.

165 On the link between Jesus as teacher and miracle stories, see the commentary on 4:40 above; cf. Dwyer, *Wonder*, 117.

166 Cf. John 11:1-44, esp. v. 6.

167 Edwards, "Markan Sandwiches," 204–5.

lation and a call for courage. The encouragement "just trust" (μόνον πίστευε), as a present imperative, calls for continuing confidence in Jesus' ability to heal, in spite of the fact that death has intervened.[168]

■ **37** As Jesus sets off once again for the house of Jairus, he allows only Peter, James, and John to accompany him. No such stipulation was made when he set out the first time (v. 24). The reason that it is introduced here is the awesome character of a raising from the dead. A miracle is performed away from public view because it is not appropriate that divine power be seen at work.[169] Elsewhere in Mark's Gospel, Peter, James, and John are the only three allowed to see the transfiguration (9:2), and they are the only three that Jesus has near him in the Garden of Gethsemane (14:33).[170]

■ **38-40a** The description of the scene in the house of Jairus as "a disturbance" (θόρυβος) (v. 38) suggests that the girl has died recently and that the mourning is spontaneous rather than ritualized.[171] Jesus' statement, "The child has not died, but is sleeping," in v. 39, introduces an element of ambiguity into the narrative.[172] It raises the question, for those in the audience of Mark who are familiar with stories about people who only appear to be dead, whether the girl was really dead.[173] The narrative rhetoric of the story, however, makes clear that the girl is really dead. Jesus' remark is an indication of the ease with which he will be able to awaken her. The laughter of the people in the house (v. 40a), like the question of the envoys in v. 35, indicates that they have no idea that Jesus has the power to raise her from the dead. This element heightens the tension once again and illustrates the difficulty of the mighty deed that Jesus is about to perform.

■ **40b-43** Jesus drove everyone out of the house except the parents of the girl and the three disciples who had come with him (v. 40b). This is the second instance in this account of the motif of the removal of the public (cf. v. 37). This doubling may result from the editorial combination of the two stories.[174] In any case, the effect is to heighten the dramatic tension.[175]

When Jesus had gone to the place where the girl was, he grasped her hand (v. 41). As the woman with the flow of blood was healed by touching Jesus' cloak (vv. 27-29), here the girl is raised from the dead, in part, by the physical contact with Jesus.[176] He also said to her ταλιθα κουμ ("Talitha koum"), an Aramaic phrase that the evangelist translates as "Girl, I say to you, wake up!" (τὸ κοράσιον, σοὶ λέγω, ἔγειρε). Wellhausen argued that the original reading was ραβιθα ("girl"), which he reconstructed from the corrupt reading of Codex D, rather than ταλιθα ("girl"), because the latter word is more refined and less dialectical and thus a correction. He also argued that κουμι ("koumi," i.e., "arise" or "stand up"), read by Codex D, is original, as the Old Palestinian form of the second person singular feminine imperative; he considered κουμ ("koum," i.e., "arise" or "stand up") to be a later Mesopotamian form.[177]

One could argue that, since Jesus was an Aramaic speaker, there is nothing unusual in the evangelist quoting his speech in Aramaic here. It is also the case that what he says is not an incantation or magical formula. It is noteworthy, however, that the only words of Jesus that the evangelist gives in Aramaic in this context are the powerful words by which, in part, Jesus raised the girl from the dead. The implication is that, for Greek speak-

---

168 Marshall, *Faith*, 97–98.

169 Cf. 2 Kgs 4:4, 33; Bultmann, *History*, 224; Kollmann, *Wundertäter*, 263, 265. Theissen calls the motif of the removal of the public "a motif of mystery" (*Miracle Stories*, 149).

170 Four disciples are allowed to hear the eschatological discourse, Peter, James, John, and Andrew (13:3). Theissen argued that 5:37 is redactional (*Miracle Stories*, 184). Bultmann took the opposite view (*History*, 214, 345).

171 Cf. Gail Holst-Warhaft, *Dangerous Voices: Women's Laments and Greek Literature* (London: Routledge, 1992) 103.

172 Compare John 11:11-15.

173 See, e.g., the story about Asclepiades and the com-

ment at the end of the story about Apollonius, both cited in the section on "Genres" above. For further examples, see Kollmann, *Wundertäter*, 265. Van der Loos concluded that the girl was only apparently dead (*Miracles*, 569).

174 See above on v. 37.

175 Theissen, *Miracle Stories*, 183.

176 The phrase κρατήσας τῆς χειρός ("having grasped the hand [of someone]") occurs also in the healing of Peter's mother-in-law in 1:31 and in the exorcism of the boy in 9:27 (Kollmann, *Wundertäter*, 263). On the motif of touch, see Theissen, *Miracle Stories*, 62.

177 See the note on the trans. of v. 41 above; Wellhausen, 41–42.

ers in the audience, the Aramaic words were in themselves perceived to be mysterious and powerful.[178] Lucian of Samosata satirizes the use of holy names and foreign phrases in healing by having one of his characters ask whether the fever or inflammation is afraid of them and so takes flight.[179]

As noted in the section on "Genres" above, the instantaneous character of the miracle (v. 42) is a typical feature. Not only does the girl get up immediately, but she is also able to walk around right away. The age of the girl is given as twelve years. Since the clause giving this information is connected with the preceding one by the conjunction γάρ ("for"), it is evident that the datum is given in order to explain that she was old enough to walk.[180] That the girl is twelve years of age and the woman with the flow of blood had suffered for twelve years is sometimes taken as a sign that the two narratives should be interpreted in light of each other.[181] The two narratives should indeed be interpreted in light of each other, but there is no indication that either number is symbolic.[182]

The response of the disciples and the parents is described in very strong terms: "they were immediately amazed in great amazement" (ἐξέστησαν εὐθὺς ἐκστάσει μεγάλῃ). This response is the typical motif of the impression that the miracle creates on the crowd or the witnesses to it.[183] Their very strong reaction is appropriate in view of the unexpected and difficult character of the act of raising someone from the dead.[184] The statement may be interpreted in terms of a reaction of amazement or awe at the manifestation of divine power.[185]

The story ends with a command "that no one should know this" (v. 43a) and a second demonstration of the reality of the miracle: "he said that [something] should be given to her to eat" (v. 43b). The command to silence follows naturally enough on the amazement of the witnesses: the overwhelmingly impressive event should not be spoken about. The great mystery of the divine power at work in the raising of someone from the dead is probably a sufficient explanation of the command to silence, which was probably part of the source.[186] The placement at the end of the narrative of the remark that she should be given something to eat formed a literary bridge to the next passage in the source, the account of the multiplication of the loaves (now in 6:34-44).[187] It is noteworthy that the object of secrecy in v. 43a is not the identity of Jesus (in which Mark is interested) but a state of affairs (τοῦτο). This suggests that the command of secrecy is traditional and not an addition of Mark.[188]

178 Bultmann, *History*, 222–23. Koester ("History and Development," 38, 55) argues that the Aramaic spells or formulas—ταλιθα κουμ ("Girl, get up!) here and εφφαθα ("be opened") in 7:34—were added to the version of Mark used by Matthew by the editor who transformed that version into Secret Mark.

179 ὄνομα θεσπέσιον ἢ ῥῆσιν βαρβαρικήν ("a holy name or a foreign phrase") (Lucian *Philops.* 9); text and trans. from Harmon, *Lucian*, 3.334-35. On the motif of ῥῆσις βαρβαρική ("a foreign phrase" or "a foreign saying"), see Theissen, *Miracle Stories*, 149–51. Kollmann (*Wundertäter*, 263–64) suggested that ταλιθα κουμ ("Talitha koum") may be a traditional Jewish healing formula.

180 All but one of the nouns used to refer to the girl up to this point in the narrative are diminutives, so clarification may have seemed necessary; so also Gundry, 275.

181 Kermode, *Genesis of Secrecy*, 132; Dwyer, *Wonder*, 116–17.

182 For an interpretation of these two miracle-stories in terms of Jesus' kindness to these women and his benevolence, see Wendy Cotter, "Mark's Hero of the Twelfth-Year Miracles: The Healing of the Woman with the Hemorrhage and the Raising of Jairus's Daughter (Mark 5.21-43)," in Levine, *A Feminist Companion*, 54–78.

183 Bultmann, *History*, 225–26; the verb ἐξίστασθαι ("to be amazed") is used in a similar way also in 2:12 and 6:51.

184 Dwyer (*Wonder*, 120) suggests that it is the presence of divine power that gives rise to the exceedingly great amazement.

185 See the commentary on 16:8 below.

186 Theissen argued that motifs of the removal of the public and the magic words of v. 41 are associated with the command to silence (*Miracle Stories*, 148–49).

187 Achtemeier, "Miracle Catenae," 279.

188 Theissen concluded that all the commands to silence and secrecy in the miracle stories are traditional, where they were a standard device; Mark transferred them to other genres and applied them to the identity of Jesus (*Miracle Stories*, 151).

6

6:1-6a Offense and Unbelief in Nazareth

1/ And he went out from there and went into his hometown, and his disciples followed him. 2/ And when the Sabbath came, he began to teach in the synagogue, and many[a] of those who were listening[b] were amazed, saying, "From what source does he take these things and what sort of wisdom is it that has been given to him, such are the powerful works occurring through his hands?[c] 3/ Is not this the carpenter, the son[d] of Mary and brother of James and Joses[e] and Judas and Simon? And are not his sisters here with us? And they took offense at him. 4/ And Jesus said to them, "A prophet is not without honor, except in his hometown[f] and among his relatives and in his house." 5/ And he was not able to do any powerful work there, except that he laid his hands on a few who were ill and healed them. 6a/ And he marveled[g] at their unbelief.

a Some MSS, B L f^{13} et al., have the reading οἱ πολλοί ("most") instead of πολλοί ("many"). The former reading was adopted by Tischendorf, Westcott and Hort, Hermann Freiherr von Soden, *Die Schriften des Neuen Testaments in ihrer ältesten erreichbaren Textgestalt hergestellt auf Grund ihrer Textgeschichte* (2 vols.; Berlin: Alexander Duncker, 1902 [vol. 1, part 1]; Berlin: Arthur Glane, 1907 [vol. 1, part 2]; Göttingen: Vandenhoeck & Ruprecht, 1913 [vol. 2]), Augustin Merk, *Novum Testamentum Graece et Latine* (Rome, 1933; 9th ed., 1964), José Maria Bover, *Novi Testamenti Biblia Graeca et Latina* (Madrid, 1943; 5th ed., 1968), and Nestle-Aland (25th ed.), primarily because it is the reading of B, a MS regarded as highly reliable. Tischendorf also pointed to the use of the article in Mark 9:26 and 12:37 as support for this reading. But the reading in 12:37 is not certain, and the weight of the external evidence for the anarthrous πολλοί is very strong.

b The author's trans. is based on the present participle, ἀκούοντες ("listening"), read by ℵ A B C W et al., rather than the aorist participle ἀκούσαντες ("having heard"), read by D L Δ Θ et al. The latter is a stylistic improvement.

c The third question is elliptical and has thus given rise to variants. A corrector and at least one copyist recognized that an interrogative word, probably πόθεν ("from what source [are]" or "what is the source of") as in the first question, should be supplied, but they improved the syntax by adding two articles, one to transform the predicate position of the demonstrative adjective τοιαῦται ("such") to the attributive, which is more common in Attic Greek (see Smyth §1180), and the other to govern the participle. This reading is represented by ℵ[1] Δ and may be translated: "and (what is the source of) such powerful works which occur through his hands?" Rather than supplying an interrogative word, some copyists dropped the article before δυνάμεις ("powerful works") and changed the participle, γινόμεναι ("occurring"), to a finite verb, γίνονται ("occur"). This change had the effect of transforming the third question into a statement: "And such powerful works occur through his hands!" This variant is represented by A C[2] W et al. Other copyists apparently transformed the third question into a result clause, by dropping the article (as in the previous reading), prefixing the conjunction ἵνα ("so that") and changing the participle into a finite verb in the subjunctive mood, γίνωνται ("occur"): ". . . so that such powerful works occur through his hands?" This reading is represented by C* D K et al. My translation is based on the reading attested by ℵ* B et al. So also Metzger, *Textual Commentary*, 75.

d The earliest surviving MS (fragmentary) of Mark, p[45vid], a number of minuscules (f^{13} et al.), and some early versions (it vg[mss] bo[mss]) read τοῦ τέκτονος υἱὸς καί ("Is not this the) son of the carpenter and (of Mary)." This reading may have resulted from an assimilation of Mark's text to the parallel in Matthew 13:55, or it may be a correction based on the same reasoning that led Matthew to correct Mark. This reasoning may be a desire to deny that Jesus was a mere carpenter; according to Origen, Celsus made derogatory remarks about Jesus as a craftsman (*Con. Cels.* 6.34, 36; cf. Metzger, *Textual Commentary*, 75–76). Another reason may be that it was felt to be inappropriate to refer to Jesus as the son of his mother alone. In spite of belief in the virginal conception of Jesus (which may not be presupposed by Mark) or the supposed previous death of Joseph, it would have been expected in most social circumstances that Jesus would be named as the son of his (legal) or (deceased) father; see Detlev Dormeyer, "Die Familie Jesu und der Sohn der Maria im Markusevangelium (3,20f.31-35; 6,3)," in Hubert Frankemölle und Karl Kertelge, eds., *Vom Urchristentum zu Jesus: Für Joachim Gnilka* (Freiburg/Basel/Vienna: Herder, 1989) 109–35, esp. 127–31.

e   Three Old Latin MSS omit this name entirely (c ff² i). Many MSS give the name in the indeclinable form Ἰωσῆ (A C W et al.), and many others give the genitive form Ἰωσῆτος, B D L et al. Some MSS (ℵ *pc* lat) read Ἰωσήφ ("Joseph") instead of Ἰωσῆ or Ἰωσῆτος ("Joses"). The three names are related, since the Hebrew name יוֹסֵף was sometimes shortened to יוֹסֵה and then transliterated as Ἰωσῆ or Ἰωσῆς; see BDF §53 (2). According to Edwin Mayser (*Grammatik der griechischen Papyri aus der Ptolemäerzeit mit Einschluss der gleichzeitigen Ostraka und der in Ägypten verfassten Inschriften: Laut- und Wortlehre* [Leipzig: Teubner, 1906] 274), some foreign names were hellenized with the endings -ῆς, -ῆτος following the model of certain Ionic names. The name Ἰωσῆς is the only example in the NT of a name with the dental inflection; see BDF §55 (2); cf. Mayser, 273–75. The reading Ἰωσήφ ("Joseph") here is probably secondary and was introduced either under the influence of Matt 13:55 or because the Greek name "Joses" was known to be the equivalent of "Joseph"; see also BAGD, s.v. Ἰωσῆς and Ἰωσήφ.

f   The substitution of the reflexive pronoun ἑαυτοῦ ("his") for the simple personal pronoun αὐτοῦ ("his") in the readings attested by ℵ* Θ *f*¹³ 565 is probably a correction to conform the style to Attic.

g   The reading with the imperfect ἐθαύμαζεν ("he marveled"), attested by A C D L W et al., is probably the earlier reading, representing a Markan descriptive imperfect (see Moulton-Turner, 3:65–66). The reading with the aorist ἐθαύμασεν ("he marveled"), attested by ℵ B 565. 2427 *pc*, represents a change to the more usual narrative tense.

Literary Context

If Paul Achtemeier's thesis is correct, that the multiplication of the loaves (now in 6:34-44) followed upon the raising of Jairus's daughter in the evangelist's source, it follows that Mark inserted the material now in 6:1-35. As noted in the discussion of the stilling of the storm in literary context above, the section 4:35–6:1a is unified by the focus on epiphanies of divine power, the key words πίστις ("faith" or "trust") and ἀπιστία ("unbelief," "lack of trust"), and by the fact that the first and last units (4:35-41 and this passage) treat the theme of Jesus' identity. The anecdote in 6:1-6a thus forms the conclusion to the section designated here "Epiphanies of Divine Power."

Besides concluding the section in which it appears, 6:1-6a is also reminiscent of 1:21-28. In both cases Jesus goes into a village or small town with his disciples, enters the synagogue and begins to teach. In both accounts, those who hear his teaching are amazed (ἐξεπλήσσοντο). In 1:22, they are amazed at his authority (ἐξουσία); in 6:2 at his wisdom (σοφία). After the exorcism, the people of Capernaum marvel at his teaching, as illustrated and legitimated by his power over unclean spirits (1:27). In his hometown (presumably Nazareth), the people associate his teaching with his deeds of power (αἱ δυνάμεις) (6:2). But the latter story has a turning point in which the people of Nazareth take offense at Jesus (6:3) and the two stories end quite differently. Just as "those who are outside" (οἱ ἔξω) hear the parables but do not understand them (4:11), so there are those who observe (or at least hear about) Jesus' deeds of power and do not accept his proclamation or trust him. Faith generates miracles, but miracles do not necessarily generate faith.[189]

History of the Tradition

As one of three examples illustrating his thesis that a synchronic, text-semantic analysis ought to precede

---

189   Cf. Schmithals, *Wunder*, 95; also John 2:23-25.

redaction-critical or composition-critical analysis, Ciliers Breytenbach has assessed form-critical and redaction-critical approaches to this passage, as well as attempts to reconstruct the history of the traditions that appear in it.[190] For his conclusions, see below.

Bultmann argued that this passage is a classic example of the way in which an imaginary situation is created as a setting for an independently circulating saying. He concluded that the saying of Jesus preserved in P. Oxy. 1.5 [1.30-35] is more original than that of Mark 6:4-5.

A prophet is not acceptable in his hometown,
and a physician effects no cures for those who know him (οὐκ ἔστιν δεκτὸς προφήτης ἐν τῇ π(ατ)ρίδι αὐτ(ο)ῦ, οὐδὲ ἰατρὸς ποιεῖ θεραπείας εἰς τοὺς γεινώσκοντας αὐτό(ν)).[191]

The second half of the twin proverb is transposed in the Markan passage so that the phrase "those who know him" (τοὺς γινώσκοντας αὐτόν) becomes the "relatives" (συγγενεῖς) of v. 4. The contradiction between v. 5a ("he was not able to do any powerful work there") and v. 5b ("except that he laid his hands on a few who were ill and healed them") derives from the desire to avoid depicting a complete failure on Jesus' part. The tension between v. 2—and possibly the beginning of v. 3 (genuine admiration)—and the statement that "they took offense at him" at the end of v. 3 may be due, in Bultmann's opinion, to Markan editing of a pre-Markan account of some successful appearance of Jesus. In that case, the unit would have two originals: the saying and the scene of suc-

cess. The saying (and its imaginary setting) probably originated in the missionary experience of the early church.[192]

After the publication of the texts from Nag Hammadi, it became evident that the saying in P. Oxy. 1.5 [1.30-35] is part of the *Gospel of Thomas* (31).[193] Rather than arguing that one version of this saying is more original than another, it is better to see them as variants of a common saying or notion.[194]

It may well be that the evangelist composed this passage, using a common saying and certain traditions about Jesus, namely, that Jesus came from Nazareth; that Jesus was a carpenter or a woodworker; and the names of his mother, brothers, and sisters.[195]

Comment

■ **1** The introductory clause "And he went out from there" links this passage to the preceding account of the raising of Jairus's daughter, but only in a vague and loose way. This weak link makes it unlikely that the passage was part of the collection of miracle stories from which Mark drew the preceding four accounts.[196]

The use of the word πατρίς ("hometown"), rather than Ναζαρέτ ("Nazareth"), is an indication that the story was composed with the saying of v. 4 in mind.[197]

The formulation "and his disciples followed him" is unusual in Mark. The disciples are frequently portrayed as accompanying Jesus, but this explicit description of Jesus' entourage may prepare for the reaction of the people of his hometown: here is an ordinary handworker

---

190 Cilliers Breytenbach, "Das Markusevangelium als traditionsgebundene Erzählung? Anfragen an die Markusforschung der achtziger Jahre," in *The Synoptic Gospels: Source Criticism and the New Literary Criticism* (ed. Camille Focant; BEThL 110; Leuven: Leuven University Press/Peeters, 1993) 77–110, esp. 105–9.

191 Text from Harold W. Attridge, "Appendix: The Greek Fragments," in Bentley Layton, ed., *Nag Hammadi Codex II,2–7* (NHS 20; Leiden/New York: Brill, 1989) 1:120; my trans.

192 Bultmann, *History*, 31; see also Breytenbach, "Das Markusevangelium als traditionsgebundene Erzählung?" 105–6.

193 Attridge in Layton, *Nag Hammadi Codex II,2–7*. See also the discussion by Joseph A. Fitzmyer, "The

Oxyrhynchus Logoi of Jesus and the Coptic Gospel according to Thomas," in idem, *Essays*, 355–433, esp. 401–2; reprinted in idem, *Semitic Background*, 355–433.

194 Breytenbach refers to them as "logical variants" or "performancial variations" ("Das Markusevangelium als traditionsgebundene Erzählung?" 107).

195 Ibid., 109–10; Achtemeier concluded that vv. 1-6a "owe much of their present shape to Markan editorial activity" ("Miracle Catenae," 267–68). For sayings that express an idea similar to Mark 6:4, see M. Eugene Boring, Klaus Berger, and Carsten Colpe, eds., *Hellenistic Commentary to the New Testament* (Nashville: Abingdon, 1995) §106 (p. 96).

196 See "Literary Context" above.

197 See "History of the Tradition" above.

who is presenting himself as a teacher and gathering disciples.[198]

■ **2** The singular (τὸ) σάββατον ("Sabbath") is used here, rather than the plural τὰ σάββατα ("Sabbath"), which was used in 1:21.[199] Jesus' entry into a village or town, the setting being the Sabbath, and his teaching in the synagogue are features that 6:1-2 and 1:21 have in common.[200] The amazement of those who were listening in Jesus' hometown is similar to that of the people in Capernaum. The response of the people of Capernaum, however, both according to the narrator (1:22) and in their own words (1:27) is entirely positive. The opening statement of the people of Jesus' hometown, in contrast, is ambiguous. Their question, "From what source does he take these things?" is open to two interpretations. The presupposition or expected answer could be that he gets them from God; he has divine wisdom and power. Or the implication may be that he gets them from Beelzebul or Satan.[201] The rhetorical questions in v. 2 may originally have been positive.[202] In any case, in the present context, juxtaposed with v. 3, they take on an ironic, even sarcastic tone.[203]

■ **3** The first rhetorical question, "Is this not the carpenter?" may be read as an insult.[204] Criticism of social background was a standard mode of invective in antiquity. The compiler of the Life of Sophocles denied the statements of earlier writers that Sophocles' father was a carpenter, a bronzesmith, or a sword-maker, and defended his aristocratic background.[205] The writers of Old Comedy made fun of Euripides by calling him the son of a woman who sold vegetables.[206] The claim that Jesus himself was a carpenter could be an insult if taken literally.[207] Compare Lucian's mockery of Hesiod as a (mere) shepherd, an imposter (*Saturnalia* 6). If taken figuratively, however, "carpenter" is equivalent to "poet."[208] Note also the perspective of Sirach:

> The wisdom of the scribe [comes to be] in the opportunity for leisure, and the man who has less business will become wise. How will the man who lays hold of the plow become wise, who boasts in the shaft of an ox-goad, drives cattle and who is busy in their work, and whose conversation is about bullocks? He concentrates on producing furrows, and gives his attention to fodder for calves. In this way every carpenter and master-builder (does), whoever continues (working) by night and by day (Σοφία γραμματέως ἐν εὐκαιρίᾳ σχολῆς, καὶ ὁ ἐλασσούμενος πράξει αὐτοῦ σοφισθήσεται. Τί σοφισθήσεται ὁ κρατῶν ἀρότρου, καὶ καυχώμενος ἐν δόρατι κέντρου, βόας ἐλαύνων καὶ ἀναστρεφόμενος ἐν ἔργοις αὐτῶν, καὶ ἡ διήγησις αὐτοῦ ἐν υἱοῖς ταυρῶν; Καρδίαν αὐτοῦ δώσει ἐκδοῦναι αὔλακας, καὶ ἡ ἀγρυπνία αὐτοῦ εἰς χορτάσματα δαμάλεων. Οὕτως πᾶς τέκτων καὶ ἀρχιτέκτων, ὅστις νύκτωρ ὡς ἡμέρᾳ διάγει). (Sir 38:24-27a LXX)[209]

The reference to Jesus as "the son of Mary" could also be taken as an insult.[210] It was usual in Semitic cultures to refer to a man as the son of his father, even when the father was dead.[211] The reference to Jesus as "the son of Mary" could lead an uninformed or hostile reader to

---

198 Cf. Schmithals, *Wunder*, 94.

199 See the commentary on 1:21 and 27 above.

200 See "Literary Context" above.

201 Cf. 3:21, 22 and the commentary above.

202 See "History of the Tradition" above.

203 Cf. Jerry Camery-Hoggatt, *Irony in Mark's Gospel: Text and Subtext* (SNTSMS 72; Cambridge/New York: Cambridge University Press, 1992) 141.

204 The rest of this paragraph is based on Yarbro Collins, "Finding Meaning," 175–96.

205 Lefkowitz, *Lives of the Greek Poets*, 75.

206 Ibid., 88.

207 Some MSS at v. 3 read τοῦ τέκτονος υἱὸς καὶ "(Is not this the) son of the carpenter and (of Mary)." See the first note on the trans. of v. 3 above. Celsus mocked Jesus for being a carpenter; Origen replied

that in none of the Gospels was Jesus himself designated as a carpenter (*Con. Cels.* 6.36); see Lane, 202.

208 Gregory Nagy, *The Best of the Achaeans: Concepts of the Hero in Archaic Greek Poetry* (Baltimore: Johns Hopkins University Press, 1979) 297–300.

209 Referred to by Camery-Hoggat, *Irony*, 141.

210 That it is not necessarily an insult is demonstrated by Meier, *Marginal Jew*, 1:226–27.

211 Bultmann, *History*, 387 (addition to p. 31, n. 1); Theissen concluded, in another context, that "[i]dentification through the father was the norm in the whole ancient world" (*Gospels in Context*, 176 n. 24). Dormeyer ("Die Familie Jesu," 129; see the first note on the trans. of v. 3 above) argues that, from the perspective of Mark, the father should no longer be known, because of the breaking in of the kingdom

infer that the mother is named and not the father because the father was unknown and the son illegitimate. The author of Mark could leave open the possibility of such an inference, because it makes the origin of Jesus mysterious, like that of Homer, and suggests a semidivine or heroic status. According to Aristotle, Homer's mother was made pregnant by "some divinity" among the dancers in a festival of the muses.[212] This ambiguity is dissolved in Ephorus's account, according to which Homer was illegitimate.[213] The *Life of Homer* attributed to Herodotus, however, which dates to the late Hellenistic period, leaves the identity of Homer's father a mystery.[214]

Other analogies to the description of Jesus as "the son of Mary" include *1 Enoch* 62:5, in which the messianic figure of the Similitudes of Enoch is called "that Son of a Woman." One who is deemed insignificant (son of a woman) turns out to be the eschatological judge.[215] In Greek magical texts, it was customary to refer to the magician, or to the person to be helped or harmed, as the son of NN (his mother).[216]

The brothers and sisters of Jesus mentioned here, Ἰάκωβος ("Jacob" or "James"), Ἰωσῆς ("Joses"), Ἰούδας ("Judah," "Judas," or "Jude"), Σίμων ("Simon"), and two or more unnamed sisters, are apparently presented as true siblings of Jesus.[217]

After the rhetorical questions of the people of Jesus' hometown, the narrator remarks, "and they took offense at him" (καὶ ἐσκανδαλίζοντο ἐν αὐτῷ). As Gustav Stählin points out, the New Testament usage of σκάνδαλον ("trap" or "enticement to sin/apostasy") and σκανδαλίζω ("cause to sin" or "give offense") "is exclusively controlled by the thought and speech of the OT and Judaism."[218] The σκάνδαλον "is an obstacle in coming to faith and a cause of going astray in it."[219] The noun does not occur in Mark. All the other instances of the verb in Mark refer to the apostasy of those who have previously had faith or trust in Jesus (4:17; 9:42, 43, 45, 47; 14:27, 29). Here it indicates an obstacle to coming to faith. Either their inculpable familiarity with Jesus or their culpable resentment of his new roles prevents them from accepting his message and trusting his person. In either case, the attitude of "taking offense at him" (σκανδαλίζεσθαι ἐν αὐτῷ) is the opposite of "believing or trusting in him" (πιστεῦσαι εἰς αὐτόν).[220]

■ **4** As noted above in the section "History of the Tradition," Mark attributes to Jesus here a well-known saying. Matthew reproduces Mark's version of the saying, except that he omits καὶ ἐν τοῖς συγγενεῦσιν αὐτοῦ ("and among his relatives") (Matt 13:57). Luke and *Gos. Thom.* 31 offer similar versions, but in reverse order. The Greek text of the *Gospel of Thomas*'s version is preserved in P. Oxy. 1.5 [1.30-35].[221] Both Luke and the *Gospel of Thomas* reflect a two-part saying, one part being about a prophet and the other about a physician. The Lukan Jesus says to the people of Nazareth, "Surely you will say this parable to me, 'Physician, heal yourself'"; . . . He then said, "Truly I say to you that no prophet is acceptable in his hometown" (πάντως ἐρεῖτέ μοι τὴν παραβολὴν ταύτην· ἰατρέ, θεράπευσον σεαυτόν . . . εἶπεν δέ· ἀμὴν λέγω ὑμῖν ὅτι οὐδεὶς προφήτης δεκτός ἐστιν ἐν τῇ πατρίδι αὐτοῦ) (Luke 4:23-24).

---

of God; cf. Theissen, *Gospels in Context*, 180. Some have argued that the reference implies that Mary was a widow; see the list in Gustav Stählin, "χήρα," *TDNT* 9 (1974) 448 n. 74.

212 Lefkowitz, *Lives of the Greek Poets*, 13. According to other traditions, he was the son of a muse and Apollo or a direct descendant of Apollo through Orpheus or Musaeus (ibid., 12).

213 Ibid., 14.

214 Ibid., 20; *Life of Homer* 2; Ulrich von Wilamowitz-Moellendorff, ed., *Vitae Homeri et Hesiodi* (KIT; Berlin: de Gruyter, 1929); ET in Lefkowitz, *Lives of the Greek Poets*, 139–55; see esp. 139.

215 Cf. also Job 15:14; 25:4, where the context is also the confrontation with mighty potentates who are put to shame; see Leslie W. Walck, "The Son of Man in Matthew and the Similitudes of Enoch" (Ph.D. diss., University of Notre Dame, 1999) 172–73.

216 See, e.g., Greek magical amulets ##38 (line 8), 39 (lines 9–11), and 66 (lines 7–8) in Kotansky, *Greek Magical Amulets*, Part I: *Published Texts of Known Provenance*, 206–15, 379–82.

217 For a history of the research on this issue and an evaluation of the evidence, see Meier, *Marginal Jew*, 1:318–32.

218 Gustav Stählin, "σκάνδαλον, σκανδαλίζω," *TDNT* 7 (1971) 344.

219 Ibid., 345.

220 Ibid., 349; cf. Mark 9:42 (some MSS). See also Theissen, *Miracle Stories*, 72.

221 Cited above in the section "History of the Tradition."

Mark's version of the saying reflects his typical style in two ways. The first part of the saying has a double negative, and the saying as a whole is a double statement involving first a negative statement and then a positive one (in this case a negative followed by an exception):

οὐκ ἔστιν προφήτης ἄτιμος
εἰ μὴ ἐν τῇ πατρίδι αὐτοῦ . . .
("There is *not* a prophet *without* honor
except in his hometown. . .").[222]

The saying is plausible in the context of the historical Jesus. In that context, πάτρις would be translated "hometown" as here and applied to Nazareth or possibly to Capernaum.[223] According to Acts, Mary, the mother of Jesus, was among his followers after the experience of his resurrection (Acts 1:14). James (or Jacob), "the brother of the Lord," was a leader in the early church, and at least one other brother of Jesus belonged to the movement (Gal 1:19; 1 Cor 9:5).[224] It could be, however, that they opposed Jesus during his lifetime and came to believe in his message and person only after the experience of the resurrection.[225] In this case, the saying would have its ordinary, proverbial significance.

The saying would also have fit the missionary situation of the followers of Jesus after his death. In that context, πάτρις would be translated "homeland" and applied to Galilee or Judea or both. In this case, the saying would have a consoling effect upon those who were discouraged at the meager results of missionary efforts in the land of Israel. In the Gospel of John, the saying apparently is used with reference to Jerusalem or Judea as Jesus' home, the place that rejected him (John 4:43-45; cf. 1:11).

Finally, in the context of Mark and the other Gospels, the saying may have an apologetic function. It helps to explain why it is that the Christian movement, which claimed to be the fulfillment of the promises to Israel, was not accepted by the majority of the Jewish people.

■ **5-6a** The evangelist's emphasis, however, in the immediate context is on the relation between faith and miracles, or, more precisely, between lack of faith and the scarcity of miracles. As the disciples did not even attempt to still the storm by means of their own faith, so the people of Jesus' hometown do not experience the full power of Jesus' gift for performing mighty deeds. Mark actually says "And *he was not able* to do any powerful work there" (καὶ οὐκ ἐδύνατο ἐκεῖ ποιῆσαι οὐδεμίαν δύναμιν). Matthew revised this statement to "And *he did not do* many powerful works there" (καὶ οὐκ ἐποίησεν ἐκεῖ δυνάμεις πολλάς) (Matt 13:58). Luke omits the statement entirely. The disciples, however, in asking "Who then is this that both the wind and the sea obey him?" show their awakening faith in Jesus as one who has divine power. The people of Jesus' hometown, however, in asking "Is not this the carpenter?" indicate that their way to faith is blocked.

The power possessed by Jesus cannot be totally eclipsed even by lack of faith, so Mark qualifies the statement quoted above. In fact, the saying of v. 5 has the same stylistic elements as the one in v. 4: a double negative and double statement (negative-positive), again a negative followed by an exception:

οὐκ ἐδύνατο ἐκεῖ ποιῆσαι οὐδεμίαν δύναμιν,
εἰ μὴ ὀλίγοις ἀρρώστοις . . . ἐθεράπευσεν
("he was *not* able to do *any* mighty deed there,
except that he . . . healed a few who were ill").[226]

The account ends with Jesus marveling (θαυμάζειν) at their lack of faith (ἀπιστία). There is a certain ironic contrast here with the statement in 5:20 that all marveled at the proclamation of the former demoniac.[227]

---

222 See Frans Neirynck, *Duality in Mark: Contributions to the Study of the Markan Redaction* (BEThL 31; rev. ed.; Leuven: Leuven University Press/Peeters, 1988) 88, 89; see also Breytenbach, "Das Markusevangelium als traditionsgebundene Erzählung?" 110.

223 Mark 2:1 seems to imply that Jesus made his home in Capernaum during his activity in Galilee. Cf. 3:20 and the commentary above.

224 Meier, *Marginal Jew*, 1:57–58.

225 James, the brother of Jesus, may be the one referred to in 1 Cor 15:7. Cf. Mark 3:21, 31-35 and the commentary above.

226 See Neirynck, *Duality in Mark*, 88, 89.

227 Cf. Camery-Hoggatt, *Irony*, 141.

6

**6:6b-30 The Sending Out of the Twelve
and the Death of John the Baptist**

6b/ And he went around among the villages in a circle teaching. 7/ And
he summoned the Twelve and
began to send them out two by
two[a] and he gave them authority
over the unclean spirits, 8/ and he
gave them orders that they
should take[b] nothing but a staff
for the journey, no bread, no bag,
no money in their belts, 9/ but
(they should put) sandals on their
feet; and (he said,) "Do not put
on[c] two shirts." 10/ And he said to
them, "Whenever you enter a
house, stay there until you leave
that place. 11/ And when a place
does not welcome you[d] or listen
to you, as you go out from there,
shake off the dust which is under
your feet as testimony against
them."[e] 12/ And they went out
and proclaimed[f] that (people)
should repent,[g] 13/ and they
drove out many demons, and
they anointed many ill people
with oil and healed them. 14/ And
King Herod heard (about Jesus),
for his name had become known,
and they were saying[h] that John
the baptizer[i] had been raised
from the dead and for this reason
extraordinary powers were at
work in him. 15/ Others were saying that he was Elijah, and others
that he was a prophet like one of
the prophets (of old). 16/ But
when Herod heard (about him),
he said, "The one I beheaded,
John, has been raised."[j] 17/ For
Herod himself had ordered that
John be arrested and bound in
prison on account of Herodias,
the wife of Philip his brother,
because he had married her.
18/ For John said to Herod, "It is
not permitted for you to have the
wife of your brother." 19/ So
Herodias had a grudge against
him and wished to kill him, but
was not able (to do so). 20/ For
Herod respected John, knowing
him to be a just and holy man,
and he protected him. Having
heard him, he was greatly perplexed,[k] yet he heard him gladly.[k]
21/ And an opportune day came
when Herod on his birthday gave
a banquet for his courtiers and
military officers and the prominent people of Galilee. 22/ And
his daughter Herodias[l] came in

a   D et al. read "having summoned the twelve disciples,
he sent them out two by two" (προσκαλεσάμενος
τοὺς δώδεκα μαθητὰς ἀπέστειλεν αὐτοὺς ἀνὰ
δύο). The use of the participle προσκαλεσάμενος
("having summoned") rather than the finite verb
προσκαλεῖται ("he summoned," lit., "he summons,"
a historical present) and the insertion of the word
μαθητάς ("disciples") may have been inspired by the
parallel passage in Matt 10:1; the use of ἀπέστειλεν
("he sent out") rather than ἤρξατο ("[he] began")
with the present infinitive ἀποστέλλειν ("to send
out") and the substitution of ἀνὰ δύο ("two by two")
for δύο δύο ("two by two") may have been inspired by
the parallel passage in Luke 10:1. Or those who made
these changes in the MSS of Mark may have been motivated by the same stylistic concerns that motivated
Matthew and Luke. On the typical use of ἄρχομαι
with present infinitive as auxiliary for the imperfect in
Mark, see Turner, "Marcan Usage," 28 (1927) 352–53
(Elliott, *Language and Style*, 93–95).

b   ℵ C L W et al. read ἄρωσιν ("should take" in the
aorist subjunctive) rather than αἴρωσιν ("should take"
in the present subjunctive). The substitution was probably intended to be an improvement of Mark's syntax,
perhaps because no reason was perceived for the use
of the present. The present subjunctive is used with
ἵνα ("in order that") also in Mark 3:9, 14 (twice); 4:12;
6:41; 8:6.

c   The sudden shift from indirect to direct discourse is
disturbing (though not unusual; see Moulton-Turner,
3:325–26) and has given rise to variants. A few MSS (B*
33 pc) use the aorist imperative, ἐνδύσασθε, "do (not)
put on," which is rare in prohibitions (Smyth §1840);
its unusual character tends to support the originality
of this reading, but the external evidence for it is weak.
The aorist subjunctive, ἐνδύσησθε ("do not put on"),
is thus the earliest recoverable reading. A number of
MSS reflect the substitution of an infinitive for the prohibition, so that the indirect discourse may be preserved to the end of the sentence. Some of these (B²
892. 2427 pc) have the first aorist middle infinitive, ἐν-
δύσασθαι, "(not) to put on," and others (L N 1424 et
al.) the perfect middle, ἐνδεδύσθαι, "(not) to wear."

d   Instead of "when a place does not welcome you" (ὃς
ἂν τόπος μὴ δέξηται), many MSS (A C² D Θ et al.)
read "when some (people) do not welcome you" (ὅσοι
ἂν μὴ δέξωνται). The latter reading is an intended
improvement, probably evoked by the following clause
and either based on or analogous to Luke 9:5.

e   Many MSS (A f^1.13 et al.) add the saying "Truly I say to
you, it will be more bearable for the people of Sodom
or Gomorrah on the day of judgment than for that
city" (ἀμὴν λέγω ὑμῖν· ἀνεκτότερον ἔσται Σοδό-
μοις ἢ Γομόρροις ἐν ἡμέρᾳ κρίσεως ἢ τῇ πόλει
ἐκείνῃ). This addition was inspired by Matt 10:15.

and danced and pleased[m] Herod and his guests. So the king said[n] to the girl, "Ask of me whatever you wish and I will give it to you." 23/ And he swore to her,[o] "Whatever[p] you ask of me I will give you, up to half of my kingdom." 24/ And she went out and said to her mother, "What shall I ask for?" And she said, "The head of John the baptizer."[q] 25/ She went in immediately with haste to the king and asked, saying, "I wish that you give me at once, on a platter, the head of John the Baptist." 26/ And although the king was deeply grieved, he did not wish to refuse her on account of the oaths and those at table.[r] 27/ And immediately the king sent the executioner and commanded him to bring[s] his head. And he went out and beheaded him in the prison 28/ and brought his head upon a platter and gave it to the girl, and the girl gave it to her mother. 29/ And when his disciples heard (what had happened), they went and took away his corpse and put it in a tomb. 30/ And the apostles gathered together in the presence of Jesus and reported to him all that they had done and taught.

f   The scribes of some MSS (A W Θ et al.) changed the aorist ἐκήρυξαν ("they proclaimed") to the imperfect ἐκήρυσσον ("they proclaimed") to conform it to the three imperfect verbs that follow in v. 13.

g   Many MSS (ℵ A C f[1.13] 33 𝔐) have the aorist subjunctive, μετανοήσωσιν ("should repent"), rather than the present subjunctive, μετανοῶσιν ("should repent"). Since the former reading is an "improvement," and since the present is compatible with Mark's style (cf. 1:15 and n. b above), the latter reading is earlier.

h   Some MSS, B (D) W et al., support a reading with the third person plural, "they were saying" (ἔλεγον) and others (ℵ A C L Θ et al.) the third person singular, "he was saying" (ἔλεγεν). The former was changed to the latter to make this verb agree with the first verb of v. 14, "he heard" (ἤκουσεν). See Metzger, *Textual Commentary*, 76. The three opinions that follow this verb constitute a digression; the evangelist returns to Herod in v. 16.

i   A number of MSS (D W Θ et al.) read "the Baptist" (ὁ βαπτιστής) instead of "the baptizer" (ὁ βαπτίζων). The latter was changed to the former either under the influence of the parallel passage, Matt 14:2, or because the former is used in Mark 6:25 and 8:28.

j   The trans. is based on the earliest recoverable reading: ὃν ἐγὼ ἀπεκεφάλισα Ἰωάννην, οὗτος ἠγέρθη, attested by ℵ[2] B L W et al. This reading has two features that gave rise to variants. One is the inverse attraction of the case of the antecedent, Ἰωάννην ("John"), to that of the relative, ὅν ("the one [whom]"); see Moulton-Turner, 3:324. Some MSS read the nominative Ἰωάννης ("John") (ℵ Θ et al.) and one (D) omits the name. The other feature is the construction that allows an expression in casus pendens to be followed by a resumptive personal pronoun (see Moulton-Turner, 4:21; Taylor, ad loc.). Luke (9:9) has rewritten Mark to avoid this feature; the reading attested by Θ (f[1]) et al., "This (man) is John; he has been raised from the dead" (οὗτός ἐστιν Ἰωάννης· αὐτός ἐκ νεκρῶν ἠγέρθη) seems to reflect a similar process. The reading of A (C) 0269 𝔐 seems to conflate the latter reading with that attested by ℵ[2] B L W et al.

k   The two fourth-cent. MSS that include Mark, ℵ B, and other witnesses, L (W) Θ 2427 co, support the reading "and having heard him, he was greatly perplexed, yet he heard him gladly" (καὶ ἀκούσας αὐτοῦ πολλὰ ἠπόρει, καὶ ἡδέως αὐτοῦ ἤκουεν). The majority of the MSS support the reading "and he heard him often and heard him gladly" (καὶ ἀκούσας αὐτοῦ πολλὰ ἐποίει, καὶ ἡδέως αὐτοῦ ἤκουεν). It has been suggested that the reading ἠπόρει ("he was at a loss") was inspired by Luke 9:7; there Herod is the subject of διηπόρει ("was very perplexed"). The expression ἀκούσας αὐτοῦ πολλὰ ἐποίει ("he heard him often") may be a Semitism (BDF §414 [5]), or it may simply mean "after having heard him once (aorist), he did so often" (see Lohmeyer, ad loc.). The reading ἠπόρει ("he was at a loss") has significant external support, as noted above. This intrinsically appropriate and interesting reading may have been changed to the less interesting reading attested by the majority of MSS in order to heighten the tendency, already present in Mark, to exonerate Herod of responsibility for the death of John. Cf. Metzger, *Textual Commentary*, 76–77; Taylor, ad loc.; and G. D. Kilpatrick, "Some Notes on Marcan Usage," in Elliott, *Language and Style*, 159–74, esp. 173.

l   The reading "his daughter Herodias" (τῆς θυγατρὸς αὐτοῦ Ἡρῳδιάδος) has strong external support (ℵ B D L Δ 565 *pc*) and is the earliest recoverable reading, although it is in considerable tension with the description of the Herodian family given by Josephus (see Metzger, *Textual Commentary*, 77, and the commentary below). The reading "the daughter of Herodias" (τῆς θυγατρὸς τῆς Ἡρῳδιάδος), attested by *f*¹ *pc* (aur b c f) sy^{s.p}, may have been introduced to make the text of Mark conform to Josephus. The reading "Herodias's daughter herself" (τῆς θυγατρὸς αὐτῆς Ἡρῳδιάδος), attested by W a d et al. (see Tischendorf, ad loc.), may have a similar origin. The majority reading, τῆς θυγατρὸς αὐτῆς τῆς Ἡρῳδιάδος ("Herodias's daughter herself") would then be a conflation of the latter two. Elliott argued that this last reading is the earliest ("An Eclectic Textual Commentary," in idem, *Language and Style*, 197).

m   Instead of the aorist finite verb, some MSS (𝔭⁴⁵ A C³ D W et al.) have the aorist participle: καὶ ἀρεσάσης ("and having pleased"). It seems more likely that the finite verb is the earlier reading, since the statement that Herod and his guests were pleased is not a mere circumstance but an important development in the plot. The change of this verb to a participle was an attempt to improve the style, which overlooked the importance of this event in the unfolding of the plot.

n   Most of the MSS that read the participle instead of the finite verb in the previous sentence have no connective at the beginning of this clause. When the finite verb was changed to the participle, δέ ("so") was

dropped as unnecessary and the verb was placed before the subject. The earliest recoverable reading is thus ὁ δὲ βασιλεὺς εἶπεν ("So the king said"), attested by ℵ (A) B C* L et al.; so also Taylor, ad loc., and Nestle (25th edition).

o   The shortest variant, "and he swore" (καὶ ὤμοσεν), has a claim to be the earliest, since it could explain the origin of the others. But it is too weakly attested (L *pc* sa^{ms} bo^{ms}) to allow its adoption as the earliest recoverable reading. 𝔭⁴⁵ᵛⁱᵈ 28 read καὶ ὤμοσεν πολλά ("and he swore earnestly" or "many times"). Although this usage is typical of Markan style (see Metzger, *Textual Commentary*, 77), the word πολλά ("earnestly" or "many times") may have been added to prepare for the plural τοὺς ὅρκους ("the oaths") in v. 26. Thus, the earliest recoverable reading is probably καὶ ὤμοσεν αὐτῇ ("and he swore to her"), attested by ℵ A B C²ᵛⁱᵈ et al.

p   The earliest recoverable reading is probably "whatever" (ὅ τι ἐάν), attested by 𝔭⁴⁵ B Δ et al. Some copyists (ℵ A L Θ *f*¹³ 𝔐 latt) apparently took the generalizing relative pronoun ὅ τι ("whatever") as the conjunction ὅτι recitativum (introducing direct discourse and not to be translated) and so added the neuter relative pronoun ὅ ("what") after ὅτι (not to be translated); see Metzger, *Textual Commentary*, 77. The reading of D, "if (you ask) anything (of me)" (εἴ τι ἐάν), may have resulted from an attempt to avoid the ambiguity of the reading ὅ τι ("whatever").

q   The same MSS that read "the Baptist" (βαπτιστής) in v. 14 (except Θ) have the equivalent reading here; they are joined in this reading by A C *f*¹ and many others. The change from βαπτίζοντος ("baptizer") to βαπτιστοῦ ("Baptist") here may have occurred under the influence of v. 25 and its parallel in Matt 14:8.

r   Some MSS (ℵ A C² D et al.) read "those reclining with [him] at table" (συνανακειμένους) instead of "those reclining at table" (ἀνακειμένους). The former reading probably arose under the influence of the parallel in Matt 14:9.

s   The Hellenistic aorist active infinitive ἐνέγκαι ("bring") was replaced by the more typically Attic form ἐνεχθῆναι ("bring"); see LSJ, s.v. φέρω, III and V.

The Literary Unity of 6:6b-30

Ernst von Dobschütz named this passage as the best example of the storyteller's technique of occupying the audience's attention while some other action is going on and of giving them the impression that considerable

time has elapsed. The various opinions among the people about Jesus provide a context for the idea of Herod, born of a bad conscience, that Jesus is John the Baptist raised from the dead. This idea then provides the occasion for an excursus on the death of John the Baptist that ends with the mention of John's burial by his disciples. None of these elements has the least to do with the sending out of the disciples nor with the withdrawal of Jesus to a deserted place that follows.[1]

Frank Kermode criticized the theory that the episode was inserted in order to fill the gap between the departure of the Twelve and their return. He argued instead that it is a genuine example of what Gérard Genette called a "heterodiegetic analepsis," that is, a flashback belonging to a different story, namely, the story of John the Baptist, as opposed to the story of Jesus. But Kermode noted that the flashback is also "completive" of the main narrative of Mark because we already know about John's ministry (1:4-8) and his arrest (1:14). Thus 6:14-29 completes an account of the Baptist's career.[2]

James R. Edwards argued that Mark inserted one passage into the middle of another for a theological purpose. In his view the account of the death of John on one level prefigures that of Jesus. The reason for inserting it into the account of the sending out of the Twelve is to indicate "a relationship between missionaries and martyrdom, between discipleship and death."[3] Tom Shepherd has pointed out contrasts between the outer story and the inner story. The verb "to send" ($\dot{\alpha}\pi o\sigma\tau\dot{\epsilon}\lambda\lambda\epsilon\iota\nu$) is used of both the action of Jesus and that of Herod (v. 7 of Jesus; vv. 17, 27 of Herod). There is also a contrast between the Twelve, who go out with modest clothing and no provisions, and the lavish feast of Herod.[4]

Von Dobschütz was correct that the intercalation has the narrative function of filling the imagined time between the sending out of the Twelve and their return. The literary and theological observations made by Edwards and Shepherd may or may not have been intentional on the part of the evangelist, but the connections may well have been made by some ancient readers, just as they are by some modern readers.

The Sending Out of the Twelve in Literary Context

The transitional statement, "And he went around among the villages in a circle teaching" ($\kappa\alpha\grave{\iota}\ \pi\epsilon\rho\iota\hat{\eta}\gamma\epsilon\nu\ \tau\grave{\alpha}\varsigma\ \kappa\acute{\omega}\mu\alpha\varsigma\ \kappa\acute{\upsilon}\kappa\lambda\wp\ \delta\iota\delta\acute{\alpha}\sigma\kappa\omega\nu$), is reminiscent of Jesus' response when Peter tells him that everyone was searching for him, after his day of healing in Capernaum at the beginning of his public activity: "Let us go elsewhere, to the neighboring market-towns, in order that I may proclaim there also" (1:38). The similarity between the two passages suggests that the present section (6:6b—8:26) involves a renewal of the proclamation and the mighty deeds initiated in the earlier section (1:19-45). The use of the verb $\delta\iota\delta\acute{\alpha}\sigma\kappa\epsilon\iota\nu$ ("to teach") in 6:6b, rather than $\kappa\eta\rho\acute{\upsilon}\sigma\sigma\epsilon\iota\nu$ ("to proclaim"), as in 1:38, is an indication of the equivalence of the two activities of Jesus in Mark.

The sending out of the Twelve in 6:7-13 alludes back to the appointing of the Twelve in 3:13-19 and puts into action the intention of Jesus expressed in 3:14-15: "And he appointed twelve . . . in order that he might send them to proclaim and to have authority to drive out the demons."

Both accounts are associated with the Markan technique of intercalation, the intertwining of two accounts. The appointing of the Twelve is followed by the controversy over Jesus' exorcisms, which is inserted into an account of the attempt of Jesus' relatives to constrain him (3:20-35).[5] The sending out of the Twelve is the frame-story into which the narration of the death of John the Baptist has been inserted (6:7-29).

Much of the rest of the section consists of miracle stories. The first feeding story (6:31-44) probably came from the same collection that contained the stilling of the storm, the exorcism of the Gerasene demoniac, the healing of the woman with the flow of blood, and the raising of Jairus's daughter.[6] The account of Jesus' walking on

1   Von Dobschütz, "Erzählerkunst," 193–94. He also contrasts the literary procedures of Matthew and Luke in the parallel passages (ibid., 194). See also the commentary above on 3:20-35.

2   Kermode, *Genesis of Secrecy*, 128–31. On analepsis, see Shepherd, *Markan Sandwich Stories*, 84.

3   Edwards, "Markan Sandwiches," 205–6. Francis J. Moloney has argued that the intertwining of the two narratives implies that the disciples must carry out their mission without regard for the consequences to themselves, just as John the Baptist carried out his ("Mark 6:6b-30: Mission, the Baptist, and Failure," *CBQ* 63 [2001] 647–63, esp. 659, 661).

4   Shepherd, *Markan Sandwich Stories*, 174–75.

5   See the commentary above.

6   See the section "The History of the Tradition" following the translation of 4:35-41 above.

the water, the exorcism of the Syro-Phoenician woman's daughter, the healing of the deaf man, the second feeding story (8:1-10), and the healing of the blind man in Bethsaida probably belonged to the second collection of miracle stories used by the evangelist as a source. In their present context in Mark, the group of miracle stories in 6:30–8:26 continues the revelation of the divine power of Jesus. They also serve as occasions for Jesus to teach the disciples and for the evangelist to develop the theme of the misunderstanding of the disciples, especially Jesus' walking on the water and the two feeding miracles.[7]

History of the Tradition of the Sending of the Twelve

The instructions for mission given by Jesus to his disciples are preserved in a double tradition. Luke follows Mark in 9:1-6 and Q in 10:1-12. Matthew combines the Markan and the Q traditions in 9:35–10:16. The Q version included: (1) sayings about the harvest and about sheep among wolves, (2) instruction concerning equipment, (3) directives about behavior among those who welcome the missionary, (4) empowerment for miracle-working and proclaiming, and (5) rules for dealing with rejection.[8]

Harry T. Fleddermann has argued that the author of Mark created his mission discourse (6:7-13) by abbreviating and reformulating the mission discourse in Q.[9] The similarities between the Markan passage and Q, however, can be explained just as well by the hypothesis that both are dependent on a common source or tradition.

Genre

Bultmann placed 6:8-11 in the category of legal sayings and church rules. He concluded that the version of Q preserves the tradition more completely, whereas Mark offers an excerpt. He also argued that the material originated in the early church as instruction received from the risen Lord. He assumed that Mark was writing in a

different cultural context and did not recognize the ongoing authority of these instructions. That is why he made them into a charge for the mission of the Twelve during the life of Jesus. Matthew and Luke followed him in doing so.[10] Bernd Kollmann, however, argued for a historical core of this tradition. Jesus, like other miracle-workers of antiquity, passed on his wisdom concerning exorcism and healing to his followers and thereby founded a kind of school.[11] It is impossible to be certain about the origin of the material. It is also not as clear as Bultmann thought that the material has no relevance to the missionary activity of Mark and his audience.

Comment

■ **6b** This is a transitional verse. On its role in the literary context, see "The Sending Out of the Twelve in Literary Context" above. The description of Jesus going around "in a circle" ($\kappa\dot{\nu}\kappa\lambda\omega$) means that his journey ended at a point near where he started, that is, near the Sea of Galilee.[12]

■ **7** The purpose of the Twelve, for the historical Jesus and probably also for the author of Mark, was to symbolize and anticipate the eschatological restoration of the twelve tribes of Israel.[13] In Mark, Jesus' exorcisms signify his struggle with Satan, which prefigures and anticipates the reestablishment of the rule of God on earth.[14] The restoration of the twelve tribes was often associated with the period of eschatological fulfillment in Second Temple Jewish texts.[15] The mission of the Twelve is focused here on their having authority over the unclean spirits. The implication is that they share in the struggle of Jesus against Satan and thus also in the anticipation of the manifestation of the kingdom of God.

The verb used for the sending ($\dot{\alpha}\pi o\sigma\tau\acute{\epsilon}\lambda\lambda\epsilon\iota\nu$) is a technical term for delegation. It carries the notion of a special commission and the delegation of authority to accomplish that commission.[16] In this case, Jesus gives the Twelve the same "authority" ($\dot{\epsilon}\xi o\upsilon\sigma\acute{\iota}\alpha$) that he

---

7   Cf. Theissen, *Miracle Stories*, 208–9.
8   For a reconstruction of the text of the instructions for mission in Q, see Robinson et al., *Critical Edition of Q*, 160–81. On Matthew's version, see Park, *Mission Discourse*.
9   Fleddermann, *Mark and Q*, 116–24.
10 Bultmann, *History*, 145.
11 Kollmann, *Wundertäter*, 197–99.
12 Cf. 6:32; so Swete, ad loc.
13 See the commentary on 3:14-15 above.
14 See the commentary on 3:26-27 and 5:13 above.
15 See the commentary on 3:14-15 above.
16 Park, *Mission Discourse*, 91–92.

demonstrated in the synagogue in Capernaum when he taught and exorcised an unclean spirit (1:22, 27).

Jesus sends them out "two by two" or "in pairs" (δύο δύο). This distributive use of a number is acceptable Greek.[17] This detail calls to mind the fact that the first disciples called by Jesus were found by him and came to him in pairs (1:16-20). It also corresponds to Jesus' sending two disciples to fetch a young donkey in 11:1-2 and another two to prepare the Passover meal in 14:13. It may also correspond to early Christian mission practice.[18] The custom was probably a practical one: the two could support and defend each other.[19]

■ **8-9** The instruction in v. 8, "that they should take nothing for the journey" (ἵνα μηδὲν αἴρωσιν εἰς ὁδόν) is analogous to a custom of the Essenes, according to Josephus:

They occupy no one city, but settle in large numbers in every town. On the arrival of any of the sect from elsewhere, all the resources of the community are put at their disposal, just as if they were their own; and they enter the houses of men whom they have never seen before as though they were their most intimate friends. Consequently, they carry nothing whatever with them on their journeys, except arms as a protection against brigands. In every city there is one of the order expressly appointed to attend to strangers, who

provides them with raiment and other necessities. In their dress and deportment they resemble children under rigorous discipline. They do not change their garments or shoes until they are torn to shreds or worn threadbare with age (Μία δ᾽ οὐκ ἔστιν αὐτῶν πόλις, ἀλλ᾽ ἐν ἑκάστῃ μετοικοῦσιν πολλοί. καὶ τοῖς ἑτέρωθεν ἥκουσιν αἱρετισταῖς πάντ᾽ ἀναπέπταται τὰ παρ᾽ αὐτοῖς ὁμοίως ὥσπερ ἴδια, καὶ πρὸς οὓς οὐ πρότερον εἶδον εἰσίασιν ὡς συνηθεστάτους· διὸ καὶ ποιοῦνται τὰς ἀποδημίας οὐδὲν μὲν ὅλως ἐπικομιζόμενοι, διὰ δὲ τοὺς λῃστὰς ἔνοπλοι. κηδεμὼν δ᾽ ἐν ἑκάστῃ πόλει τοῦ τάγματος ἐξαιρέτως τῶν ξένων ἀποδείκνυται, ταμιεύων ἐσθῆτα καὶ τὰ ἐπιτήδεια. καταστολὴ δὲ καὶ σχῆμα σώματος ὅμοιον τοῖς μετὰ φόβου παιδαγωγουμένοις παισίν. οὔτε δὲ ἐσθῆτας οὔτε ὑποδήματα ἀμείβουσι πρὶν διαρραγῆναι τὸ πρότερον παντάπασιν ἢ δαπανηθῆναι τῷ χρόνῳ). (*Bell.* 2.8.4 §§124–26)[20]

In the context of the life of the Markan Jesus, it is unlikely that the mission instruction envisions the reception of those sent into homes of other followers of Jesus. In the context of missionaries of Mark's time, if the text was read as applying to the situations of Mark's audiences, the instruction may have been understood as envisioning such receptions. Christians developed the

---

17   See BAGD, s.v. δύο. Cf. the note to the translation of v. 7 above.

18   Acts 8:14; 13:2; 15:2, 39, 40; 1 Cor 1:1; 2 Cor 1:1; Phil 1:1; Col 1:1.

19   In expounding this passage, Theophylact, archbishop of Achridia (Ochrida) in Bulgaria (fl. 1077 CE), cited Eccl 4:9, "two are better than one" (ἀγαθοὶ δύο ὑπὲρ τὸν ἕνα) (quoted by Swete, ad loc.; cf. cxvi). Joachim Jeremias recognized the practical reasons for sending representatives or messengers out in pairs, but put more weight on rabbinic traditions in which a pair of pupils is sent out by the rabbis with an official message. He argued that this practice was rooted in the biblical requirement that two witnesses are necessary for conviction, especially in capital cases ("Paarweise Sendung im Neuen Testament," in Angus J. B. Higgins, ed., *New Testament Essays: Studies in Memory of Thomas Walter Manson* [Manchester: University of Manchester Press, 1959] 136–43). This thesis is interesting in light of the significance of the gesture of shaking off

the dust from the missionaries' feet; see the commentary on v. 11 below.

20   Text and trans. from Thackeray, *Josephus*, 2:370–71. Partial citation in Park, *Mission Discourse*, 104. Philo states briefly, "First of all then no one's house is his own in the sense that it is not shared by all, for besides the fact that they dwell together in communities, the door is open to visitors from elsewhere who share their convictions" (πρῶτον μὲν τοίνυν οὐδενὸς οἰκία τίς ἐστιν ἰδία, ἣν οὐχὶ πάντων εἶναι κοινὴν συμβέβηκε· πρὸς γὰρ τῷ κατὰ θιάσους συνοικεῖν ἀναπέπταται καὶ τοῖς ἑτέρωθεν ἀφικνουμένοις τῶν ὁμοζήλων) (*Omn. prob. lib.* 85; text and trans. from Colson and Whitaker, *Philo*, 9:58–59).

custom early on of receiving missionaries, providing them with hospitality, and giving them provisions for the journey to the next destination (1 Cor 16:6, 11; Rom 15:24).[21] In either context, v. 11 is best understood as referring to the possibility that outsiders will not accept the travelers.[22] Thus, the Markan text differs from the text from Josephus cited above in that the lack of provisions is not due to the assumption that members of the group will provide for other, traveling members. Nonetheless, the text from Josephus suggests that the reason for the lack of provisions in the Markan text is the assumption that hospitality will be extended by those to whom the mission is addressed.

The Markan text permits those sent to take along a ῥάβδος, which here has the sense of a "traveler's staff."[23] Travelers used staves to protect themselves from attacking animals and human beings.[24] The Markan missionary with staff is thus analogous to Josephus's Essenes traveling ἔνοπλοι ("armed" or "with weapons"). Josephus's description gives the impression of thriftiness at least, and perhaps of asceticism with regard to clothing. The permission to wear sandals, ὑποδεδεμένους σανδάλια— leather soles bound to the feet with leather thongs (v. 9)— may be a way of excluding more elaborate shoes that would cover the upper foot as well.[25] Similarly, the command not to wear two shirts is a rejection of the custom of wearing an inner and an outer shirt or tunic, a style of dress adopted by persons of distinction.[26] These analogies between Mark and Josephus's description of the

Essenes do not support the conclusion that the historical Jesus or his followers were connected to the Essenes but only suggest that they had certain similar values.

The Markan missionary instructions have some important similarities to and differences from traditions about the Cynics. The characteristic attributes of the Cynics were a threadbare double cloak (τρίβων διπλοῦν), a bag (πήρα), and a staff (βακτηρία, βάκτρον or ῥάβδος). For example, a letter attributed to Diogenes and addressed to his father Hicetas contains the following statement:

Do not be upset, Father, that I am called a dog [Cynic] and put on a double, coarse cloak, carry a bag over my shoulders, and have a staff in my hand. It is not worth while getting distressed over such matters, but you should rather be glad that your son is satisfied with little, while being free from popular opinion, to which all, Greeks and barbarians alike, are subservient (Μὴ ἀνιῶ, ὦ πάτερ, ὅτι κύων λέγομαι καὶ ἀμπέχομαι τρίβωνα διπλοῦν καὶ πήραν φέρω κατ᾽ ὤμων καὶ ῥάβδον ἔχω διὰ χειρός· οὐ γὰρ ἄξιον ἐπὶ τοῖς τοιούτοις ἀνιᾶσθαι, μᾶλλον δὲ ἥδεσθαι, ὅτι ὀλίγοις ἀρκεῖται ὁ παῖς σου, ἐλεύθερος δέ ἐστι δόξης, ᾗ πάντες δουλεύουσιν Ἕλληνές τε καὶ βάρβαροι).[27]

Park has shown that Cynics were despised by the public and that their cloak, begging bag, and staff were objects of contempt.[28]

---

21 For discussion, see Raymond E. Brown, *The Epistles of John: Translated with Introduction, Notes, and Commentary* (AB 30; Garden City, NY: Doubleday, 1982) 742. See also *Did.* 11–13.

22 3 John 5–8 presupposes and advocates the reception of Christian missionaries into Christian homes; vv. 9–10 envision a situation in which a Christian leader refuses to offer hospitality to Christian missionaries. For discussion, see Georg Strecker, *The Johannine Letters: A Commentary on 1, 2, and 3 John* (Hermeneia; Minneapolis: Fortress, 1996) 258–64.

23 Carl Schneider, "ῥάβδος, ῥαβδίζω, ῥαβδοῦχος," *TDNT* 6 (1968) 969.

24 Pesch, 1:328.

25 So Gould, 106. The participle ὑποδεδεμένους is imperative ("put on"); BDF §468 (2).

26 Gould, 107. According to Stobaeus, Musonius Rufus said: "It is more honorable to wear only one tunic than two, and to wear no tunic instead of one, but

only a cloak. And it is better, if possible, to go barefoot than to wear sandals" (καὶ τὸ μὲν ἑνὶ χρῆσθαι χιτῶνι τοῦ δεῖσθαι δυοῖν προτιμητέον, τοῦ δ᾽ ἑνὶ χρῆσθαι χιτῶνι τὸ μηδενί, ἀλλὰ ἱματίῳ μόνον. καὶ τοῦ γε ὑποδεδέσθαι τὸ ἀνυποδετεῖν τῷ δυναμένῳ κρεῖττον); text and trans. (modified) from Park, *The Mission Discourse*, 106 n. 133. He provides evidence that the practices of wearing no tunic and going barefoot are imitations of Socrates. Cf. Luke 3:11, according to which John the Baptist taught that he who had two shirts should share with him who had none.

27 Diogenes 7. *To Hicetas*; text and trans. (modified) from Malherbe, *Cynic Epistles*, 98–99; cited by Park, *Mission Discourse*, 107.

28 Park, *Mission Discourse*, 107–8.

There is little in the mission instruction of vv. 8-9 to link those sent with the Cynics. No mention is made of a threadbare, double cloak. A traveler possessing a staff but lacking a bag would not be identified as a Cynic by ancient observers. The command not to take a bag is explicable in terms of the general instruction that they should take nothing for the journey.

It is likely that the mission instruction of the Synoptic Sayings Source (Q) contained commands not to carry a bag, sandals, or a staff.[29] It could be that the rejection of the bag and the staff expresses the intention that Christian missionaries not be confused with Cynics. Such an intention could simply be a matter of self-definition, although it could be due to perceived public contempt for Cynics.[30] But the rejection of sandals is analogous to the extreme asceticism of some Cynics, or, more precisely to their attempt to be as close to nature as possible. It also reflects the practice of Socrates. It may be, therefore, that the mission instruction of Q was not anti-Cynic, but rather defined the Christian missionary as one who fulfilled Cynic values more completely than the Cynics themselves did.[31]

The larger framework of meaning in which the mission instruction in both Mark and Q has its place is very different from that of Cynic philosophy. The Cynics valued "frank speech" ($\pi\alpha\rho\rho\eta\sigma\acute{\iota}\alpha$) and "shamelessness" ($\mathring{\alpha}\nu\alpha\acute{\iota}\delta\epsilon\iota\alpha$) as expressions of the freedom and self-sufficiency of the philosopher. The perspective of Q involves the traditional Jewish call to repentance and the expectation of the imminent manifestation of the king-

dom of God.[32] Mark links the mission with exorcism, which is related to Jesus' proclamation of the nearness of the kingdom of God,[33] the call to repentance (v. 12), and healing (v. 13b).

■ **10** The command to stay in only one house in a particular locality is not accompanied by an explanation. The parallel passages do not clarify the prohibition either (Matt 10:11; Luke 9:3; 10:7). One possibility is that the command seeks to avoid the use of one's welcome for material gain.[34] Another possibility is that it seeks to avoid the appearance of begging, in an effort to distinguish Christian missionaries from Cynics.[35] The theory that the command seeks to avoid rivalries among the members of the community being founded[36] does not fit the context of the life of Jesus, but would fit a later Christian missionary context, especially in cities where there were several prominent families vying for honor.

■ **11** If the people of a place refuse to receive a pair of missionaries and to listen to them, the missionaries are to shake off the dust that is under their feet as testimony against that people, as they leave the place.[37] The meaning of this gesture is unexplained in Mark. The parallel in Matt 10:14 is followed by another saying that interprets it:

Truly I say to you, it will be more bearable for the land of Sodom and Gomorrah on the day of judgment than for that city ($\mathring{\alpha}\mu\grave{\eta}\nu$ $\lambda\acute{\epsilon}\gamma\omega$ $\mathring{\upsilon}\mu\hat{\iota}\nu$, $\mathring{\alpha}\nu\epsilon\kappa\tau\acute{o}\tau\epsilon\rho o\nu$ $\acute{\epsilon}\sigma\tau\alpha\iota$ $\gamma\hat{\eta}$ $\Sigma o\delta\acute{o}\mu\omega\nu$ $\kappa\alpha\grave{\iota}$ $\Gamma o\mu\acute{o}\rho\rho\omega\nu$ $\mathring{\epsilon}\nu$ $\mathring{\eta}\mu\acute{\epsilon}\rho\alpha$ $\kappa\rho\acute{\iota}\sigma\epsilon\omega\varsigma$ $\mathring{\eta}$ $\tau\hat{\eta}$ $\pi\acute{o}\lambda\epsilon\iota$ $\mathring{\epsilon}\kappa\epsilon\acute{\iota}\nu\eta$). (Matt 10:15)[38]

29 Robinson et al., *Critical Edition of Q*, 164; see "History of the Tradition of the Sending of the Twelve" above.

30 Theissen argued that the prohibition of bag and staff was probably intended to avoid giving the impression that Christian missionaries were beggars, like the Cynics ([Theißen], "Wanderradikalismus," *ZThK* 70 [1973] 245-71; ET [Theissen] "Itinerant Radicalism: The Tradition of Jesus Sayings from the Perspective of the Sociology of Literature," *Radical Religion* 2 [1975] 84-93).

31 John S. Kloppenborg concluded that "[r]eferences to the homeless and wandering existence of the Q missionaries, and especially the prohibition of carrying a wallet or sandals, strengthen the affinities of Q with Cynic chriae" (*The Formation of Q: Trajectories in Ancient Wisdom Collections* [Philadelphia: Fortress, 1987] 324).

32 Ibid.; cf. Gerd Theissen, *Sociology of Early Palestinian Christianity* (Philadelphia: Fortress, 1978) 15-16; Park, *Mission Discourse*, 112-13.

33 Cf. Mark 6:7, 13a with 3:22-27 and see the commentary on the latter verses above.

34 Theissen, "Itinerant Radicalism," 88.

35 Park, *Mission Discourse*, 117, 118-19.

36 François Bovon, *Das Evangelium nach Lukas*, vol. 2: *Lk 9,51–14,35* (EKK 3.2; Düsseldorf: Benziger; Neukirchen-Vluyn: Neukirchener Verlag, 1996) 53.

37 The dative $\alpha\mathring{\upsilon}\tauo\hat{\iota}\varsigma$ ("against them") is a dative of disadvantage; see Smyth §1481. Cf. Jas 5:3; for discussion, see H. Strathmann, "$\mu\acute{\alpha}\rho\tau\upsilon\varsigma$, $\mu\alpha\rho\tau\upsilon\rho\acute{\epsilon}\omega$, $\mu\alpha\rho\tau\upsilon\rho\acute{\iota}\alpha$, $\mu\alpha\rho\tau\acute{\upsilon}\rho\iota o\nu$," *TDNT* 4 (1967) 503; the $\mathring{\upsilon}\mu\hat{\iota}\nu$ in that passage is a dative of disadvantage (*dativus incommodi*) (Dibelius, *James*, 236-37 and n. 36).

38 The parallel command in the sending out of the Twelve in Luke (9:5) does not have this explanatory

Matthew has omitted the final phrase of v. 11, "as testimony against them" (εἰς μαρτύριον αὐτοῖς). It seems likely that Matthew omitted the phrase because he makes the testimony explicit with the saying about the judgment day.[39]

In the sending out of the Twelve in Luke (9:5), the evangelist reproduces the Markan phrase. He changes Mark's εἰς μαρτύριον αὐτοῖς ("as testimony against them") to εἰς μαρτύριον ἐπ' αὐτούς ("as testimony against them").[40] In the sending out of the seventy-(two), Luke omits the Markan phrase. He has the missionaries declare to the people publicly that they are wiping the dust of the place from their feet. He also has them say: "Only know that the kingdom of God has drawn near" (πλὴν τοῦτο γινώσκετε ὅτι ἤγγικεν ἡ βασιλεία τοῦ θεοῦ) (Luke 10:11). A version of the eschatological saying that Matthew gives in 10:15 then follows in Luke 10:12, but it is spoken by the Lord to the seventy-(two), not by the missionaries to the people who reject them. The juxtaposition of the two sayings, however, supports the inference that the statement about the kingdom of God is meant to be a witness against the people.

The meaning of the phrase "as testimony against them" in Mark is best illuminated by attempting to clarify the significance of the gesture of shaking off the dust from the feet. A number of suggestions have been offered. One is that shaking the dust of a city from one's feet in Matt 10:14 pars. indicates that one considers the place to be equivalent to Gentile territory, which was regarded as unclean, and that therefore one wanted to have no association with the inhabitants.[41] In the Hebrew Bible, Gentile land, like any land, could contract moral impurity through the presence of idols, their worship, and immoral and defiling acts. Gentile land was not intrinsically impure, and moral impurity did not entail ritual impurity.[42] The notion of the ritual impurity of foreign lands was an innovation in the Second Temple period. In the Mishnah, Gentile lands are compared to lands that are ritually impure because bones, corpses, and graves may be present.[43] The notion of the impurity of Gentile lands is thus old enough to be relevant to the interpretation of Mark 6:11. A problem with the explanation of (Strack and) Billerbeck, however, is that none of the texts cited in support of their thesis is really comparable to Matt 10:14 pars.[44]

Park argued that the dust from the sandals of the missionary represents his self and remains in the place as witness against those who have rejected him. He finds support for this view in a spell for a dream revelation:

> *This is the offering*: Take equal portions of dirt from your sandal, of resin, and of the droppings of a white dove, and while speaking [the invocation] burn them as an offering to the Bear (ἐπίθυμα τοῦτο· λαβὼν ῥύπον ἀπὸ σανδαλίου σου καὶ ῥητίνης καὶ κόπρου περιστερᾶς λευκῆς ἴσα ἴσων ἐπίθνε πρὸς τὴν ἄρκτον λέγων). (*PGM* VII. 484–86)[45]

But again, this text does not include a gesture of the type that we find in Mark 6:11.

The idea that the gesture is a curse is more illuminating.[46] An important analogy is found in Neh 5:13 (2 Esdras LXX 15:13). An internal crisis occurred among those who had returned from exile, because the poor had been forced to pledge their possessions in order to meet their basic needs. They protested, and Nehemiah called an assembly of the people, demanding the immediate return of property taken in pledge. The assembly agreed and the wealthy leaders were forced to comply with the assembly's decision. In order to be sure that

---

comment; in the sending out of the seventy-two, a saying similar to the explanatory comment in Matthew appears (10:15), but it is separated from the saying about the dust. Q probably had the command followed by the explanatory comment (Robinson et al., *Critical Edition of Q*, 176–81).

39 Park conjectured that Matthew wanted to reserve the word μαρτύριον ("witness") for positive witness, as in 10:18 (*Mission Discourse*, 122).

40 On the preposition ἐπί (here "against") with the accusative in a hostile sense, see Smyth §1689.3.d.

41 Str-B, 1:571.

42 Hayes, "Appendix A: The Impurity of Gentile Lands and Houses: A Refutation of Alon," in *Gentile Impurities*, 199–204.

43 Ibid.

44 As argued by Park, *Mission Discourse*, 123–24.

45 Preisendanz-Henrichs, 2:22; trans. by Hubert Martin, Jr., in Betz, *Magical Papyri*, 131. Park follows Betz in interpreting the phrase "dirt from your sandal" (ῥύπον ἀπὸ σανδαλίου σου) as "an instance of magical substance (οὐσία) representing the person's self" (Park, *Mission Discourse*, 124).

46 So also Park, *Mission Discourse*, 124.

they would act on that compliance, Nehemiah asked the leaders to take an oath before the priests. In relation to the oath, he performed a symbolic action that was, in effect, a curse:

> and I shook out my mantle and said, "So may God shake out every man who does not put this decree into force from his house and from his work, and he will be shaken out and empty in this way." And the whole assembly said "Amen," and they praised the Lord. And the people put what was said into action (καὶ τὴν ἀναβολήν μου ἐξετίναξα καὶ εἶπα Οὕτως ἐκτινάξαι ὁ θεὸς πάντα ἄνδρα, ὃς οὐ στήσει τὸν λόγον τοῦτον, ἐκ τοῦ οἴκου αὐτοῦ καὶ ἐκ κόπου αὐτοῦ, καὶ ἔσται οὕτως ἐκτετιναγμένος καὶ κενός. καὶ εἶπεν πᾶσα ἡ ἐκκλησία Αμην, καὶ ἤνεσαν τὸν κύριον· καὶ ἐποίησεν ὁ λαὸς τὸ ῥῆμα τοῦτο).
> (2 Esdr 15:13 LXX)[47]

The gesture commanded in Mark 6:11 probably had an analogous meaning, transformed by the eschatological context. The idea is that God or a divine agent will punish the people who reject the proclamation and the persons of the missionaries, presumably during the eschatological crisis of the last days or at the last judgment. In Acts 13:51, a similar use of the gesture of shaking dust off the feet occurs. In the context, some of the Gentiles of Antioch of Pisidia believed the proclamation of Paul and Barnabas. Some of the Jews of the locality stirred up persecution against them and drove them out of the district. In response, "[t]hey then shook off the dust of their feet against them and went to Iconium" (οἱ δὲ ἐκτιναξάμενοι τὸν κονιορτὸν τῶν ποδῶν ἐπ᾽ αὐτοὺς ἦλθον εἰς Ἰκόνιον). That this gesture implies eternal damnation is suggested by the contrast with the statement that as many Gentiles as were assigned to the destiny of eternal life believed the proclamation (Acts 13:48).[48]

The specific gesture chosen to embody the curse, however, is probably connected to customs related to hospitality. The refusal to accept the missionaries is linked to the refusal of hospitality and thus to the failure to wash the feet of the strangers.[49]

■ **12-13** After the instructions of vv. 8-11, the narrative resumes with the report that the Twelve went out, proclaimed that people should repent, drove out many demons, and anointed many sick people with oil and healed them. Like the introductory statement in v. 7, this report assimilates the activity of the Twelve to that of Jesus. Jesus' activity is summarized as proclaiming in 1:14; his proclamation included a call to repentance (1:15).[50] It is likely that the proclamation of the Twelve is meant to include an announcement of the nearness of the kingdom of God, as Jesus' did (1:15). Jesus is said on many occasions in the previous narrative to drive out unclean spirits or demons.[51] Similarly, he has been an active healer.[52]

The element of anointing sick people with oil is new in the narrative. It may indicate the practice of anointing the sick with oil in the time of the author and his first audiences.[53] In Jas 5:14, the anointing of the sick with oil is performed "in the name of the Lord" (ἐν τῷ ὀνόματι τοῦ κυρίου). The use of the name is an indication that a miraculous healing is in view; the anointing is thus not primarily a medical treatment. But a practice of folk medicine may have been taken over and transformed into a charismatic type of healing.[54] Dibelius-Greeven argued that Mark 6:13 presupposes a practice similar to that of Jas 5:14.

---

47 Cited by Conzelmann in relation to Acts 18:6 (Hans Conzelmann, *Acts of the Apostles: A Commentary on the Acts of the Apostles* [Hermeneia; Philadelphia: Fortress, 1987], 152); on Neh 5:13 and its context, see Jacob M. Myers, *Ezra, Nehemiah: Introduction, Translation and Notes* (AB 14; Garden City, NY: Doubleday, 1965) 129–31.

48 Conzelmann concluded that the gesture in Luke 9:5 and 10:11 is "a final sentence," but that it has been weakened in Acts to a symbolic act (*Acts*, 107).

49 T. J. Rogers, "Shaking the Dust off the Markan Mission Discourse," *JSNT* 27 (2004) 169–92.

50 Thus, "repent" (μετανοεῖν) here has the same con-

notations as Jesus' call to "repent" (see the commentary on 1:14-15 above).

51 Mark 1:23-28, 34, 39 (combined with proclaiming); 3:10-12 (implied), 22-30 (controversy over Jesus' exorcisms); 5:1-20.

52 Mark 1:29-31, 32-34, 40-45; 2:1-12; 3:1-6, 10; 5:21-24a, 24b-43; 6:5.

53 Kollmann, *Wundertäter*, 319.

54 Martin Dibelius, *James: A Commentary on the Epistle of James* (rev. by Heinrich Greeven; Hermeneia; Philadelphia: Fortress, 1976) , 252–54.

The Death of John the Baptist in Literary Context

Since the Twelve are presented as agents of Jesus and as carrying on his work, the shift from a report about their activity (vv. 12-13) to the reflections of Herod and others on the "the extraordinary powers at work in him" (αἱ δυνάμεις ἐν αὐτῷ) is logical enough (vv. 14-16). The various opinions of the people prepare for the question Jesus poses to the disciples and their response in 8:27-28. The opinion of Herod, that Jesus is John the Baptist, whom he had beheaded, risen from the dead, prepares for the account of John's death in vv. 17-29.[55] As noted above, the narrative about the death of John the Baptist may be read as a preview of the death of Jesus. Its insertion into the account of the mission of the Twelve may imply that violent death may result from missionary activity.[56]

Comment

■ **14-16** This is the first mention of "King Herod" (ὁ βασιλεὺς Ἡρῴδης) in Mark, although "the Herodians" (οἱ Ἡρῳδιανοί) were mentioned in 3:6.[57] The Herod in question here is Herod Antipas, the son of Herod the Great, who, when his father died in 4 BCE, became tetrarch of Galilee and Perea.[58] He governed those regions until 39 CE. Antipas's title, "tetrarch" (τετραάρχης), is attested by two inscriptions, one on Cos and one on Delos.[59] He sailed to Italy to seek the title "king" (βασιλεύς) from the emperor Gaius, but was unsuccessful. In fact, he was deposed and exiled to Lyons

or perhaps to northern Spain.[60] The use of the title "king" in v. 14 may reflect popular usage.[61]

The statement "for his name had become known" (φανερὸν γὰρ ἐγένετο τὸ ὄνομα αὐτοῦ) continues the theme of the spread of Jesus' fame.[62] This theme is initiated in 1:28, "And his fame immediately went forth in all directions in the whole region around Galilee" (καὶ ἐξῆλθεν ἡ ἀκοὴ αὐτοῦ εὐθὺς πανταχοῦ εἰς ὅλην τὴν περίχωρον τῆς Γαλιλαίας), following Jesus' first exorcism. It is continued in 1:45 with the remark, "so that he was no longer able to enter a city openly, but remained outside in unpopulated regions; and they were coming to him from everywhere" (ὥστε μηκέτι αὐτὸν δύνασθαι φανερῶς εἰς πόλιν εἰσελθεῖν, ἀλλ' ἔξω ἐπ' ἐρήμοις τόποις ἦν· καὶ ἤρχοντο πρὸς αὐτὸν πάντοθεν) (see also 3:7). In tension with this theme is another, the secret of Jesus' identity.[63] According to 3:12, Jesus rebuked the unclean spirits sternly, "so that they would not make him known" (ἵνα μὴ αὐτὸν φανερὸν ποιήσωσιν). The word φανερός ("known"), along with its cognate verb, φανεροῦν ("to make known"), is also used in the saying of 4:22, "For there is nothing hidden that will not be revealed [or made known], and nothing concealed that will not come out into the open [or become known]" (οὐ γάρ ἐστιν κρυπτὸν ἐὰν μὴ ἵνα φανερωθῇ, οὐδὲ ἐγένετο ἀπόκρυφον ἀλλ' ἵνα ἔλθῃ εἰς φανερόν). This lexical connection suggests that the identity of Jesus is part of the mystery of the kingdom that must be made known.

One of the opinions about Jesus circulating among the people, according to v. 14, was that he was John the

---

55 Von Dobschütz, "Erzählerkunst," 193.

56 See "The Literary Unity of 6:6b-30" above.

57 On the Herodians in 3:6, see the commentary above.

58 Antipas's territory was divided into two parts by the Decapolis, a region between Galilee and Perea (Schürer, *History*, 1:341). On the life of Antipas, his realm and reign, and the evidence for his interaction with John, Pilate, and Jesus, see Harold W. Hoehner, *Herod Antipas* (SNTSMS 17; Cambridge/New York: Cambridge University Press, 1972).

59 Braund, "Herod Antipas," 160.

60 Ibid.

61 Lane suggested that the title may have been used here ironically (ad loc.). Theissen suggested that it may reflect the environment of later narrators of

the story, in whose time the descendants of Herod did have the title (*Gospels in Context*, 87). Hoehner also argued for a Palestinian origin and that the title "king" is used in Mark and Matthew either in accordance with popular usage or as a courtesy (*Herod Antipas*, 117-20, 149-50).

62 Jesus' name becoming known is equivalent to his fame becoming widespread (BAGD, s.v. ὄνομα, 4).

63 See the excursus "The Messianic Secret" in the commentary on 1:16-45 above.

baptizer risen from the dead. This is not the type of resurrection to which Jesus' raising of Jairus's daughter belongs.[64] Furthermore, it does not necessarily imply the release of the powers of "the Age to Come."[65] Rather, this popular religious idea is that an especially good or especially evil person could come back from the dead by some mysterious process. The closest analogy is the notion of Nero *redivivus*.[66] The revived or resurrected (*redivivus*) figure was perceived to be more powerful than an ordinary human being. Thus, although John the baptizer did not work miracles (cf. John 10:41), it belongs to the logic of this popular idea that Jesus, as John *redivivus*, had extraordinary powers ($\alpha i\ \delta\upsilon\nu\dot\alpha\mu\epsilon\iota\varsigma$) working in him. This opinion about who Jesus was also reflects the observation of certain similarities between Jesus and John, for example, the proclaiming of the need to repent in light of the nearness of the kingdom. So Jesus could be viewed as carrying on the work of John.

The notion that Jesus was Elijah (v. 15a) is presented with no connection to the idea that he is John the baptizer risen from the dead.[67] This interpretation of Jesus, whether it is pre-Markan or formulated by Mark, supports the inference that the expectation of the return of Elijah as God's messenger in the last days was current among the people.[68] The evangelist takes up this notion by portraying Jesus in some ways as similar to Elijah.[69] But the text of Mark makes clear that this is not an adequate interpretation of Jesus by implying strongly that Elijah has already come in and through John.[70]

The opinion that Jesus was "a prophet like one of the prophets (of old)" ($\pi\rho o\varphi\dot\eta\tau\eta\varsigma\ \dot\omega\varsigma\ \epsilon\dot\iota\varsigma\ \tau\dot\omega\nu\ \pi\rho o\varphi\eta\tau\dot\omega\nu$) reflects the fact that there was a revival of prophecy in the late Second Temple period among those who believed that they were living in the last days or that the manifestation of the kingdom of God was near.[71]

The clause "But when Herod heard (about him), he said" ($\dot\alpha\kappa o\dot\upsilon\sigma\alpha\varsigma\ \delta\dot\epsilon\ \dot o\ \dot H\rho\dot\omega\delta\eta\varsigma\ \ddot\epsilon\lambda\epsilon\gamma\epsilon\nu$) in v. 16 resumes the opening clause of v. 14. In formulating Herod's comment about Jesus in v. 16, the evangelist portrays him as superstitious, fearing vengeance for his execution of John.[72] Or the comment could be read ironically; Herod had eliminated one troublemaker, and here was another one![73]

The Genre of the Account of John the Baptizer's Death

Bultmann classified the story as a legend.[74] Dibelius would have been willing to call it a legend if John were the main character; since he is not, Dibelius classified the story as an anecdote about Herod.[75] Klaus Berger defined it both as a report of a martyrdom and as a court tale.[76] Lohmeyer argued that it has the style of an ancient *novella*, reporting good and evil without praising or blaming.[77] Theissen rightly concluded that it is not a typical story of a martyrdom nor a typical legend of a holy man.[78] He himself argued, reasonably, that it is a court legend, in the sense of a court anecdote about intrigue and the misuse of power, in which the victim is a holy man.[79]

---

64 The rabbinic stories cited by Str-B (1:679) in relation to the Matthean parallel (Matt 14:2) are of the same type as the raising of Jairus's daughter and thus not illuminating for this passage.

65 Contra Lane, 212.

66 See Adela Yarbro Collins, *The Combat Myth in the Book of Revelation* (HDR 9; Missoula, MT: Scholars Press/Harvard Theological Review, 1976; reprinted Eugene, OR: Wipf & Stock, 2001) 176–83.

67 So, rightly, Lohmeyer, ad loc.

68 See the commentary on 1:2, 4, and 6 above and on 9:11-13 below.

69 See the section *Jesus as Prophet* in the introduction.

70 See 9:11-13 and the commentary below.

71 See the section *Jesus as Prophet* in the introduction.

72 Cf. Dale B. Martin, *Inventing Superstition: From the Hippocratics to the Christians* (Cambridge, MA: Harvard University Press, 2004) 29–30.

73 Cf. Lohmeyer, 117.

74 Bultmann, *History*, 301–2; see the brief review of scholarship on this point in Theissen, *Gospels in Context*, 81 n. 53. Dibelius simply calls it a fragment of tradition (*From Tradition to Gospel*, 218).

75 Martin Dibelius, *Die urchristliche Überlieferung von Johannes dem Täufer* (Göttingen: Vandenhoeck & Ruprecht, 1911) 80.

76 Klaus Berger, *Formgeschichte des Neuen Testaments* (Heidelberg: Quelle & Meyer, 1984) 334; he mentions Daniel 3–4; Esther; 1 Esdras, and *Ahiqar* as examples of court tales (also possibly Daniel 6).

77 Lohmeyer, 121.

78 Theissen, *Gospels in Context*, 81 n. 53. Not only is there no emphasis on the suffering of John or on his verbal self-defense, as Theissen pointed out; there is also no stress laid upon John's suffering for a principle, on his courage, indifference to death, etc.

An example of a court legend from Josephus is the story of the death of Glaphyra, a woman who had unlawfully married the brother of her dead husband, even though she and her first husband had had children:[79]

A similar thing happened also to his wife Glaphyra, the daughter of King Archelaus, to whom, as I said before, Alexander, the son of Herod and the brother of Archelaus, had been married while she was still a virgin. For when Alexander was put to death by his father, she married Juba, the king of Libya, and when, after the death of the Libyan king, she was living as a widow with her father in Cappadocia, Archelaus divorced his wife Mariamme to marry her, so overwhelming was his love for Glaphyra. And while she was the wife of Archelaus, she had the following dream. She seemed to see Alexander standing before her, and in her joy she embraced him warmly. But he reproached her and said, "Glaphyra, you certainly confirm the saying that women are not to be trusted. For though you were betrothed and married to me as a virgin, and children were born to us, you let yourself forget my love in your desire to marry again. But not content even with this outrage, you had the temerity to take still a third bridegroom to your bed, and in an indecent and shameless manner you again became a member of my family by entering into marriage with Archelaus, your own brother-in-law and my own brother. However, I will not forget my affection for you but will free you of all reproach by making you my own, as you were (before)." A few days after she had related these things to her women friends she died. (*Ant.* 17.13.4 §§349–53)[81]

Joachim Gnilka makes the following insightful remark about Mark 6:14-29 in its current form:

The story, which circulated independently, should not be described as Christian nor as a tradition of the disciples of John the Baptist. The death of the Baptist has virtually no meaning. The aim of the story could have been to denounce the godless carrying-on of the powerful in general, and of Herod Antipas and his court in particular, through this reminiscence.[82]

The Historical Context

As noted in the commentary on vv. 14-16 above, the "Herod" of this text is Herod Antipas, the first of three children whom Herod the Great fathered with his fourth wife, Malthace, who was a Samaritan.[83] Antipas's first wife was the daughter of King Aretas of Nabataea. He probably married her for a political reason, that is, to lessen the likelihood that Aretas would encroach upon his territory.[84] At some point between 29 and 39 CE,[85] he visited his half-brother, Herod, a son of Herod the Great and his third wife, Mariamme, the daughter of Simon the high priest.[86] This half-brother was married to Herodias, who was a daughter of Aristobulus.[87] Aristobulus was a son of Herod the Great and his second wife, Mariamme

---

79 Ibid. Florence Morgan Gillman argues for the historicity of the story (*Herodias: At Home in That Fox's Den* [Collegeville, MN: Liturgical Press, 2003] 91–95).

80 On the relevant laws, see the section "The Historical Context" below.

81 Cited by Theissen, *Gospels in Context*, 82.

82 "Die isoliert überlieferte Geschichte ist weder als christliche noch als Überlieferung der Täuferjünger, sondern also im Volk umlaufende Geschichte anzusprechen. Der Tod des Täufers wirkt nahezu sinnlos. Ziel der Geschichte könnte es gewesen sein, das gottlose Treiben der Mächtigen und konkret des Herodes Antipas und seines Hofes durch die Erinnerung zu brandmarken" (Gnilka, 1:246; my trans.; cited by Theissen, *Gospels in Context*, 85 n. 64, in support of his argument that the story is a popular tradition).

83 On Herod Antipas, see Schürer, *History*, 1:340–53. On Malthace and her children, see Nikos Kokkinos, *The Herodian Dynasty: Origins, Role in Society and Eclipse* (JSPSup 30; Sheffield: Sheffield Academic Press, 1998) 223–35.

84 The marriage may have been encouraged by the emperor Augustus (Schürer, *History*, 1:342). For further discussion, see Theissen, *Gospels in Context*, 82; Kokkinos, *Herodian Dynasty*, 229–30 and n. 90.

85 Or between 29 and 36, if the battle between Aretas and Agrippa can be reliably dated to 36 CE; see Morgan Gillman, *Herodias*, 30, 108–9.

86 On Mariamme and her children, see Kokkinos, *Herodian Dynasty*, 217–23.

87 Morgan Gillman, *Herodias*, 15–18; Kokkinos, *Herodian Dynasty*, 264–65.

the Hasmonean.[88] He and his brother Alexander were strangled, by Herod the Great's orders, in about 7 BCE (Josephus *Bell.* 1.27.6 §§550–51). Aristobulus was thus another half-brother of Antipas, so Herodias was the (half-)niece of both her husband and Antipas.[89] Herod, the half-brother of Antipas, and Herodias had a daughter, Salome.[90] At some point Salome married Philip, another son of Herod the Great, who was tetrarch of Trachonitis. When he died childless, she married Aristobulus, the son of her mother's brother, Herod, king of Chalcis. They had three sons (Josephus *Ant.* 18.5.4 §§136–37).[91]

According to Josephus, Antipas visited Herod and Herodias on his way to Rome. Antipas fell in love with Herodias and proposed marriage to her. She accepted, on the condition that he divorce his wife, the daughter of Aretas. He agreed and set sail for Rome.[92] When he returned, Antipas's wife returned to her father, who initiated a war with Antipas. Antipas's whole army was destroyed. He wrote the emperor Tiberius about the defeat, whose response was to ask Vitellius, the governor of Syria, to bring Aretas to him alive in chains, or, if he were killed, to send him his head.[93]

But many of the Jews thought that Antipas's defeat was divine vengeance for his treatment of John the Baptist. Antipas had put John to death, according to Josephus, even though John was a good man and had exhorted the people to practice piety toward God and justice toward each other, because he feared that John's eloquence and influence on the people could lead to some form of sedition (Josephus *Ant.* 18.5.1-2 §§109–19).[94]

Josephus disapproved of Antipas's proposal to Herodias (*Ant.* 18.5.1 §110) and also criticized Herodias for accepting it. He says:

> They [Herod and Herodias] had a daughter Salome, after whose birth Herodias, taking it into her head to flout the way of our fathers, married Herod [Antipas], her husband's brother by the same father, who was tetrarch of Galilee; to do this she parted from a living husband (καὶ αὐτοῖς Σαλώμη γίνεται, μεθ' ἧς τὰς γονὰς Ἡρωδιὰς ἐπὶ συγχύσει φρονήσασα τῶν πατρίων Ἡρώδῃ γαμεῖται τοῦ ἀνδρὸς τῷ ὁμοπατρίῳ ἀδελφῷ διαστᾶσα ζῶντος). (*Ant.* 18.5.4 §136)[95]

Josephus's disapproval of Herodias's marriage to her husband's brother is no doubt based upon Lev 18:16 (see also 20:21):

> You shall not uncover the nakedness of your brother's wife; she is your brother's nakedness. (RSV)

ערות אשת־אחיך לא תגלה ערות אחיך הוא (MT)

His remark that she parted from a living husband to marry his brother indicates that her marriage to Antipas was not justified by the statute regarding levirate marriage (Deut 25:5-10).[96]

Soon after Gaius (Caligula) became emperor in 37 CE, he assigned to Agrippa, Herodias's brother, the tetrarchy of Philip, who had died in 33 or 34 CE, and he also gave Agrippa the title "king" (βασιλεύς).[97] According to Jose-

---

88 Not the same person as Herod the Great's third wife, who was also named Mariamme.

89 Marriages between uncles and nieces were not expressly forbidden in the Bible, although those between aunts and nephews were (Lev 18:12-13). The rabbis considered marriages between uncles and nieces meritorious (*b. Yeb.* 62b). They were strictly forbidden, however, by the community at Qumran (CD 5:7-11; 11QT[a] [11Q19] 66:16-17); for discussion, see Milgrom, *Leviticus*, 2:1543. See also Theissen, *Gospels in Context*, 84 n. 61.

90 Kokkinos, *Herodian Dynasty*, 266.

91 Kokkinos concluded that this woman married neither Philip nor Aristobulus (*Herodian Dynasty*, 270).

92 Morgan Gillman, *Herodias*, 19–22. For Kokkinos's reconstruction and interpretation of these events, see *Herodian Dynasty*, 267–69.

93 Vitellius prepared for war with Aretas, but before he attacked, Tiberius died, so he returned to Antioch with his army, and Antipas's defeat remained unavenged (Schürer, *History*, 1:350; Kokkinos, *Herodian Dynasty*, 269).

94 Josephus's account is tendentious in that he omits the eschatological dimension of John's proclamation and denies that the baptismal ritual was effective in itself; cf. Theissen, *Gospels in Context*, 81 n. 54.

95 Text and trans. from Louis Feldman in Thackeray, *Josephus*, 9:92–93.

96 See Victor P. Hamilton, "Marriage: Old Testament and Ancient Near East," *ABD* 4:567–68.

97 Schürer, *History*, 1:351; on the date of the death of Philip, see David C. Braund, "Philip (5)," *ABD* 5:310–11.

phus, Herodias begrudged her brother his rise to a status higher than that of her husband. Because of her envy, she urged her husband to go to Rome to ask Gaius to give him the status of king as well. Antipas resisted at first, but eventually gave in, and the two of them sailed for Rome. Agrippa sent a freedman to Gaius, who arrived at the same time as Antipas and Herodias, to accuse Antipas of disloyalty to Gaius. Gaius believed the charge, deposed Antipas, exiled him to Lyons, and gave his property to Agrippa. Herodias went into exile with her husband. Josephus regarded this outcome as divine punishment upon Herodias for envy and upon Antipas for listening to her (*Ant.* 18.7.1-2 §§240–55).[98]

Comment

■ **17-18** According to the court legend incorporated into Mark, Antipas arrested and imprisoned John because he had declared Antipas's marriage to Herodias unlawful.[99] The declaration attributed to John, "It is not permitted for you to have the wife of your brother" (οὐκ ἔξεστίν σοι ἔχειν τὴν γυναῖκα τοῦ ἀδελφοῦ σου), alludes to Lev 18:16, cited above. The legend is less interested in the fine points of Jewish law than Josephus, since it does not mention the fact that the union was not legitimated by the statute of levirate marriage (Deut 25:5-10).[100] The court legend about Glaphyra, quoted in the section "The Genre of the Account of John the Baptizer's Death" above, also implies that it was wrong of Glaphyra to marry her dead husband's brother, since she and her first husband had had children.

Verse 17 states that Herodias had been the wife of Antipas's brother Philip. As noted in the section "The Historical Context" above, Herodias was the wife of Antipas's (half-)brother Herod when Antipas met and fell in love with her. It is virtually certain that "the wife of Philip his brother" (τὴν γυναῖκα Φιλίππου τοῦ ἀδελφοῦ αὐτοῦ) is the earliest recoverable reading of Mark. The explanation is probably that, in the course of oral transmission of the story, there was a shift from the less famous "Herod" to the more famous "Philip."[101]

■ **19-20** This passage seeks to exonerate Antipas for the execution of John and to place the blame on Herodias. It stands in tension with the account of the arrest of John and Antipas's reason for having him arrested in vv. 17-18 and with Antipas's reference to John as "the one I beheaded" (ὃν ἐγὼ ἀπεκεφάλισα) in v. 16.[102] Furthermore, Josephus does not report Herodias's involvement in Antipas's decision to execute John, even though he is otherwise quite critical of her and reports her role in Antipas's quest for kingship.[103] The shift of responsibility evident in Mark is due in part to the legendary assimilation of Herodias to Jezebel and John to Elijah.[104]

Verse 17 leaves open whether Antipas himself decided to arrest John or whether he did so at Herodias's request. Verse 19 indicates that Herodias bore ill will toward John because of his condemnation of her marriage to Antipas. Verse 20 explains why she was not able to kill him. Since Antipas had a deep reverence for John and heard him gladly, the narrative implies that he might divorce Hero-

---

98 See also Kokkinos, *Herodian Dynasty*, 269.

99 This motive is not necessarily unhistorical, even though Josephus does not mention it; see Hoehner, *Herod Antipas*, 136–46.

100 See "The Historical Context" above. See also Theissen, *Gospels in Context*, 83–84; Morgan Gillman, *Herodias*, 44–48. Morgan Gillman concludes that the evangelist understood John's condemnation of the marriage as based on the fact that both were divorced and remarried (ibid., 48). The text of Mark, however, makes explicit that the problem was Antipas's marriage to his *brother's wife* (v. 18).

101 So Theissen, *Gospels in Context*, 87–88; Morgan Gillman, *Herodias*, 40. Many scholars have solved the discrepancy by assuming that Herodias's husband, Herod, had "Philip" as a second name; see, e.g.,

Hoehner, *Herod Antipas*, 133–36. There is, however, no source attesting the name "Herod Philip"; see Gary Herion, "Herod Philip," *ABD* 3:160–61. Kokkinos concluded that the second husband of Herodias was indeed Philip the Tetrarch (*Herodian Dynasty*, 266–67).

102 The latter tension is pointed out by Jennifer A. Glancy, "Unveiling Masculinity: The Construction of Gender in Mark 6:14-29," *BI* 2 (1994) 38.

103 See "The Historical Context" above. Note also that Matthew 14:5 attributes the intention of killing John to Herod Antipas, not to Herodias.

104 Cf. 1 Kgs 16:29-34; 18:4, 13; 19:1-3; 21:1-29, esp. 25; 22:37-38; 2 Kgs 9:7-10, 30-37; cf. Lohmeyer, 121; Hoehner, *Herod Antipas*, 162; Janice Capel Anderson, "Feminist Criticism: The Dancing Daughter," in

dias. This possibility explains the strength of her desire to kill John.[105]

■ **21** The temporal reference to the arrival of an opportune day creates a link with v. 19. It recalls both Herodias's desire to kill John and her inability to persuade her husband to do so. This day should be interpreted as Antipas's birthday, not the anniversary of his accession to the throne.[106] The guests include "his courtiers" (οἱ μεγιστᾶνες αὐτοῦ), in this case probably the heads of the ten toparchies of his realm,[107] "the military officers" (οἱ χιλίαρχοι), and "the prominent people of Galilee" (οἱ πρῶτοι τῆς Γαλιλαίας), that is, the aristocrats.[108]

■ **22-23** As concluded in the first note on the translation of v. 22 above, the earliest recoverable reading is "his daughter Herodias" (τῆς θυγατρὸς αὐτοῦ Ἡρῳδιάδος).[109] This reading implies that the girl herself was named Herodias and that she was the daughter of Antipas and Herodias. At this time a daughter of Antipas and Herodias could have been, at most, ten years old,

since the couple met in 29 CE at the earliest, and Antipas was exiled from Galilee in 39 CE.[110] Such an age would fit with her designation as κοράσιον ("girl") later in this verse, the same term that is used for the twelve-year-old daughter of Jairus in 5:42.[111] It is likely, however, that Mark or his source mistakenly made the girl a daughter of Antipas, and that she was actually the daughter of Herodias and her first husband, Herod. According to Josephus, they had a daughter named Salome (*Ant.* 18.5.4 §136).[112] Salome must have been born in 20 CE at the latest, since she married Philip the tetrarch and he died in 34 CE. She must have been at least thirteen years old at the time of the marriage.[113] So she would have been at least of an age between nine and nineteen at the time of the festive banquet, assuming that the story had verisimilitude.[114]

The statement that the girl "danced and pleased Herod and his guests" (ὀρχησαμένης ἤρεσεν τῷ Ἡρῴδῃ καὶ τοῖς συνανακειμένοις) is a relatively

---

Anderson and Moore, 129–30; Morgan Gillman, *Herodias*, 84–85. Note that Matthew states explicitly that Antipas held John to be a prophet (14:5). Theissen cites evidence for the influence of Herodian women on legal decisions, but points out that they normally exercised their influence in beneficent ways (*Gospels in Context*, 88). He also discusses the malicious gossip about a number of Herodian women in the first cent. CE (ibid., 94–96).

105 Glancy refers to Herodias's vulnerable political position and also recalls her grandfather's use of assassination as a political tactic ("Unveiling Masculinity," 39).

106 Schürer, *History*, 1:346–47 n. 26. The same note (pp. 347–48) also includes evidence for the celebration of birthdays of ancient princes and private persons. See also Morgan Gillman, *Herodias*, 53 and n. 4.

107 Hoehner, *Herod Antipas*, 102 n. 3, 119 n. 3. Toparchies were administrative units that also served as tax districts (Schürer, *History*, 1:372, 2:186 n. 4, 195 n. 43. See also Pesch, 1:341 n. 16).

108 Freyne implies that all three designations refer to various groups of the "new nobility," centered on the court of Antipas, who replaced the old Hasmonean nobility (*Galilee*, 199–200). He also implies that οἱ μεγιστᾶνες αὐτοῦ ("his courtiers") were village leaders (ibid., 70).

109 Hoehner argued that the correct reading is θυγατρὸς αὐτῆς τῆς Ἡρῳδιάδος and that it should be translated "the daughter of the one who is called Herodias" or "the daughter of the aforementioned

Herodias," thus harmonizing Mark and Josephus (*Herod Antipas*, 151–54). Morgan Gillman correctly adopts the reading accepted here and concludes that Mark was mistaken about the relationship of Antipas and the girl (*Herodias*, 55 n. 6).

110 Cf. Schürer, *History*, 1:348–49 n. 28, where the opinion is expressed that such a daughter would have been only a year or two old. Morgan Gillman dates the marriage of Antipas and Herodias to about 23 CE. (*Herodias*, 25–27, 29; see also the literature cited in ibid., 26 n. 15).

111 The word κοράσιον, as the diminutive of κόρη ("girl"), would be translated literally "little girl," but diminutives had lost their force in the Koine Greek of the time; so rightly Morgan Gillman, *Herodias*, 56. Thus, the term could be used for a small child but most often refers to a young girl at marriageable age, i.e., a girl who had reached puberty. See n. 112 below.

112 See "The Historical Context" above; so also Theissen, *Gospels in Context*, 89.

113 Theissen, *Gospels in Context*, 90; Morgan Gillman, *Herodias*, 104, 119; cf. Hoehner, *Herod Antipas*, 155.

114 Since the dinner must have taken place (or been imagined as taking place) between 29 and 39 CE; see "The Historical Context" above. Theissen noted that the probably great discrepancy in age between Salome and her husband, Philip, could have led to the popular notion that she was Philip's daughter (which is implied by v. 17) (*Gospels in Context*, 90–91). Hoehner concluded that the word κοράσιον

restrained instance of the motif of sexual entertainment at such banquets. As Theissen has pointed out:

> The motif of dancing has no parallels. It takes the place of directly sexual motifs in the parallels that have been cited. The evident background for this motif is the fact that at symposia, hetaerae could be present, playing the flute and dancing—but not honorable women.[115]

Jennifer Glancy points out that the narrative implies that Herod Antipas responded to the dance with incestuous pleasure.[116] Given the ancient cultural context, this reading is persuasive.

The narrative does not specify who asked the girl to dance. The reference in v. 21 to the day as opportune may be read as implying that the girl's mother sent her to dance, anticipating that her husband would offer to grant the girl's wish. On the other hand, the implication may simply be that the opportunity arose when the girl consulted her mother about what she should say in response to Antipas's offer. If Herod Antipas had arranged for the dance, he is put in an even worse light, ogling and exploiting his own daughter.[117]

Herod Antipas was moved by the pleasure he took in the girl's dancing to say to her, "Ask of me whatever you wish and I will give it to you" ($αἴτησόν με ὃ ἐὰν θέλῃς, καὶ δώσω σοι$). This is an example of the motif involving a powerful man offering to grant a woman or a subject any wish he or she may have. A famous example in Greek literature is Herodotus's account of what Xerxes said to his daughter-in-law Artaÿnte, whom he had seduced: "he bade her ask for what she would have in return for her favours, for he would deny nothing at her asking. Thereat—for she and all her house were doomed to evil—she said to Xerxes, 'Will you give me whatever I ask of you?' and he promised and swore it" ($ἐκέλευσε αὐτὴν αἰτῆσαι ὅ τι βούλεταί οἱ γενέσθαι ἀντὶ τῶν αὐτῷ ὑπουργημένων· πάντα γὰρ τεύξεσθαι αἰτήσασαν. τῇ δὲ κακῶς γὰρ ἔδεε πανοικίῃ γενέσθαι, πρὸς ταῦτα εἶπε Ξέρξῃ "Δώσεις μοι τὸ ἄν σε αἰτήσω;" ὁ δὲ πᾶν μᾶλλον δοκέων κείνην αἰτῆσαι ὑπισχνέετο καὶ ὤμοσε$) (9.109).[118] She asked him for the brightly colored mantle that his wife, the queen, had made for him with her own hands. He offered her instead cities, great quantities of gold, and even an army for her to command, but she insisted on the mantle. He eventually gave it to her, and the gift led to dire consequences.

In the Bible, the motif occurs in the book of Esther. When Mordecai hears that Haman had persuaded King Ahasuerus (Artaxerxes in Greek) to allow him to destroy the Jews living in the Persian empire, he asks his adopted daughter, Esther, to intercede with the king. The king had made her his new queen and did not know that she was Jewish. Although it was against the laws of the Persians to approach the king in this way, Esther, who was very beautiful (2:7), put on her royal robes and stood in the inner court of the king's palace. She found favor in his sight, and he allowed her to approach and said, "What do you wish, Esther, and what is your request? (Ask for) up to half of my kingdom, and it will be yours" ($Τί θέλεις, Εσθηρ, καὶ τί σού ἐστιν τὸ ἀξίωμα; ἕως$

("girl") signifies a young girl at or near marriageable age and that Salome was twelve to fourteen years of age at the time John was beheaded (*Herod Antipas*, 156).

115 Theissen, *Gospels in Context*, 93. The motif is intended to attribute "shady morals" to the Herodian women (ibid., 91). The evidence discussed by Fritz Weege suggests that it was primarily $ἑταῖραι$ ("courtesans") who danced at banquets (*Der Tanz in der Antike* [Halle/Saale: Niemeyer, 1926] 118–24). For a different view, see Hoehner, *Herod Antipas*, 156–57.

116 Glancy, "Unveiling Masculinity," 39 n. 17. She also argues that the construction of feminine gender in this verse involves being looked at, and the construction of masculine gender involves voyeurism (39).

Capel Anderson argued that the text is indeterminate on this point ("Dancing Daughter," 121–26).

117 Cf. Glancy, "Unveiling Masculinity," 40–41.

118 Text and trans. from A. D. Godley, *Herodotus* (4 vols.; LCL; Cambridge, MA: Harvard University Press; London: Heinemann, 1925) 4:286–87; partial citation by Theissen, *Gospels in Context*, 86 n. 66; see also Carey A. Moore, *Esther: Introduction, Translation, and Notes* (AB 7B; Garden City, NY: Doubleday, 1971) 55.

τοῦ ἡμίσους τῆς βασιλείας μου καὶ ἔσται σοι) (5:3 LXX).[119] Esther at first invites the king and Haman to dinner and does so a second time but eventually asks for the deliverance of her people from destruction. The king grants her request and Haman is hanged on the gallows that he prepared for Mordecai (7:3-10).[120]

An example from Hellenistic Jewish literature occurs in Josephus's account of a banquet that King Agrippa, the brother of Herodias, gave for the emperor Gaius Caligula in Rome (*Ant.* 18.8.7-8 §§289–301).[121] Impressed with the lavishness of the banquet and Agrippa's desire to please him, Gaius said, "Indeed, all the gifts that I have allotted to you are but slight in amount; any service that can add its weight in the scale of prosperity shall be performed for you with all my heart and power" (ὀλίγον γὰρ πᾶν ὁπόσον σοι δωρεῶν ἐχόμενον ἀπεμοιρασάμην. τὸ πᾶν, ὅπερ σοι ῥοπὴν ἂν προσθείη τοῦ εὐδαίμονος, δεδιακονήσεται γὰρ σοι προθυμίᾳ τε καὶ ἰσχύι τῇ ἐμῇ) (*Ant.* 18.8.7 §293).[122] Josephus comments that Gaius expected Agrippa to ask for territory to be added to his kingdom or for the revenues of certain cities. Agrippa diplomatically replied at first that his present activities were in no way inspired by a desire for personal gain and that the previous gifts that Gaius had given him exceeded his thoughts and claims. Gaius was amazed at his character and listened all the more to what Agrippa might request. Finally, Agrippa asked Gaius to abandon the idea of erecting the statue that he had ordered the governor of Syria to install in the temple in Jerusalem. Josephus comments on how hazardous this request was, since, if Gaius did not receive it with favor, it could have cost Agrippa his life.[123] Josephus notes that Gaius was bound by Agrippa's attentions to him, that he thought it would be unseemly to break his word before so many witnesses,[124] and that he admired Agrippa for giving precedence to the laws and the divine over his personal power. So Gaius wrote Petronius saying that, if he had already set up the statue, it should stand. But if not, he should not install it, because Gaius wished to show favor to Agrippa. Although it is historically likely that Agrippa contributed to the resolution of the conflict between Gaius Caligula and the Jews over the statue, the form of this story is legendary.[125]

The legendary motif of the willingness to grant any request is combined in v. 23 with the motif of the foolish oath or vow. Here Herod Antipas restates his willingness to grant any wish of his daughter and adds the qualifier, "up to half of my kingdom" (ἕως ἡμίσους τῆς βασιλείας μου). This extravagant elaboration of the promise assimilates Herod to Ahasuerus (Artaxerxes in Greek).[126] This assimilation is ironic, since Herod rules over a small territory at the pleasure of Rome, whereas Ahasuerus ruled 127 provinces from India to Ethiopia (Esth 1:1). The detail that he swore to the girl and later regretted his oath but was powerless to undo it (v. 26) recalls the foolish vow of Jephthah (Judg 11:30-31, 35).

In the Bible, the "oath" (שבועה in the MT and ὅρκος in the LXX) is a curse that the person making the oath calls upon him- or herself if his or her words prove false.[127] In a future-oriented oath like this one, the curse will take effect if the oath is violated. So the implication is that Herod has invoked God to send some evil upon

---

119 Herod Antipas also offers his daughter anything she wishes, up to half of his kingdom (v. 23).

120 For a feminist analysis of the relation of the Markan story to that of Esther, see Capel Anderson ("Dancing Daughter," 127–28). See also Morgan Gillman, *Herodias*, 85–87.

121 On Agrippa I, the brother of Herodias, see Donald K. Berry, "Agrippa," *ABD* 1:98–99; Daniel R. Schwartz, *Agrippa I: The Last King of Judaea* (TSAJ 23; Tübingen: Mohr Siebeck, 1990). For discussion of the similarities between the account of Josephus and Mark 6, see Hoehner, *Herod Antipas*, 165–67.

122 Text and trans. from Louis Feldman, in Thackeray, *Josephus*, 9:170–71.

123 Cf. Esther's remark that anyone who approaches the king inside the inner court without having been summoned was liable to be put to death (Esth 4:10-11).

124 A similar motivation is attributed to Herod Antipas in v. 26 below.

125 Theissen, *Gospels in Context*, 86. Schürer seems to prefer Philo's account in *Legatio ad Gajum* but comments that the outcome in both sources is the same (1:395–97, esp. 396 n. 179).

126 See the citation of Esth 5:3 above.

127 The noun ὅρκος ("oath") is used in v. 26; here the verb ὀμνύω ("to swear an oath") is used. On oaths in the Hebrew Bible, see Moshe Benovitz, *KOL NIDRE: Studies in the Development of Rabbinic Votive Institutions* (BJS 315; Atlanta: Scholars Press, 1998) 127–32.

him if he does not grant the girl's request. In the Bible, the "vow" (נדר in the MT and εὐχή in the LXX) is a dedication of persons or property to God, either as a sacrifice or as a gift to the temple.[128] Jephthah vowed, "If you will really subject the Ammonites to my power, then anything coming out the doors of my house to meet me, when I return with victory from the Ammonites, shall belong to Yahweh; I will offer it up as a burnt offering" (Judg 11:30-31).[129] When his daughter is the first to come out of the doors of his house, he regrets his vow, but says, "I have opened my mouth to Yahweh, and I cannot retract" (Judg 11:35).[130]

■ **24-25** The fact that the girl had to go out of the banquet hall to speak to her mother is an indication that honorable women are not portrayed as joining in the banquet. The separation of the sexes at banquets was traditional. Even though respectable women began to participate in banquets in the Roman period, the rhetoric of the time stigmatized women who attended them as prostitutes.[131]

The daughter's consultation with her mother over what to request reveals the meaning of the temporal expression in v. 21, "And an opportune day came" (καὶ γενομένης ἡμέρας εὐκαίρου). Herodias makes use of the opportunity and instructs her daughter to ask for the head of John the baptizer. From the perspective of Greeks and Romans, cutting off and manipulating the heads of human beings was something that outsiders did. Thus, Herodotus claimed that the Tauri, neighbors of the Scythians, sacrificed all shipwrecked men and any Greeks that they captured in their sea-raiding to a goddess:

after the first rites of sacrifice, they smite the victim on the head with a club; according to some, they then throw down the body from the cliff whereon their temple stands, and place the head on a pole; others agree with this as to the head, but say that the body is buried, not thrown down from the cliff. This deity to whom they sacrifice is said by the Tauri themselves to be Agamemnon's daughter Iphigenia (καταρξάμενοι ῥοπάλῳ παίουσι τὴν κεφαλήν. οἱ μὲν δὴ λέγουσι ὡς τὸ σῶμα ἀπὸ τοῦ κρημνοῦ ὠθέουσι κάτω (ἐπὶ γὰρ κρημνοῦ ἵδρυται τὸ ἱρόν), τὴν δὲ κεφαλὴν ἀνασταυροῦσι· οἱ δὲ κατὰ μὲν τὴν κεφαλὴν ὁμολογέουσι, τὸ μέντοι σῶμα οὐκ ὠθέεσθαι ἀπὸ τοῦ κρημνοῦ λέγουσι ἀλλὰ γῇ κρύπτεσθαι. τὴν δὲ δαίμονα ταύτην τῇ θύουσι λέγουσι αὐτοὶ Ταῦροι Ἰφιγένειαν τὴν Ἀγαμέμνονος εἶναι). (4.103)[132]

Herodotus goes on to say that when the Tauri defeat their enemies in battle, each man cuts off an enemy's head and carries it away to his house, where he places it on a pole high above. It serves to guard the whole house.

Diodorus of Sicily, after praising the courage of the Gauls in battle, says:

When their enemies fall they cut off their heads and fasten them about the necks of their horses; . . . and these first-fruits of battle they fasten by nails upon their houses, just as men do, in certain kinds of hunting, with the heads of wild beasts they have mastered. The heads of their most distinguished enemies they embalm in cedar-oil and carefully preserve in a chest, and these they exhibit to strangers, gravely maintaining that in exchange for this head some one of their ancestors, or their father, or the man himself, refused the offer of a great sum of money (τῶν δὲ πεσόντων πολεμίων τὰς κεφαλὰς ἀφαιροῦντες περιάπτουσι τοῖς αὐχέσι τῶν ἵππων· . . . καὶ τὰ ἀκροθίνια ταῦτα ταῖς οἰκίαις προσηλοῦσιν ὥσπερ οἱ ἐν κυνηγίοις τισὶ κεχειρωμένοι τὰ θηρία. τῶν δ' ἐπιφανεστάτων πολεμίων κεδρώσαντες τὰς κεφαλὰς ἐπιμελῶς τηροῦσιν ἐν λάρνακι, καὶ τοῖς ξένοις ἐπιδεικνύουσι σεμνυνόμενοι διότι τῆσδε τῆς κεφαλῆς τῶν προγόνων τις ἢ πατὴρ ἢ καὶ αὐτὸς πολλὰ χρήματα διδόμενα οὐκ ἔλαβε). (5.29.4-5)[133]

---

128 On vows in the Hebrew Bible, see Benovitz, *KOL NIDRE*, 9–13.

129 Trans. from Robert G. Boling, *Judges: Introduction, Translation, and Commentary* (AB 6A; Garden City, NY: Doubleday, 1975) 206.

130 Trans. from ibid.

131 Glancy, "Unveiling Masculinity," 39 n. 17.

132 Text and trans. from Godley, *Herodotus*, 2:304–5.

133 Text and trans. from Charles H. Oldfather, *Diodorus of Sicily* (12 vols.; LCL; Cambridge, MA: Harvard University Press; London: Heinemann, 1939) 3:172–75.

Diodorus comments that it is noble to refuse to sell that which is a proof of one's valor; but to continue to fight against a human being after he is dead is to descend to the level of a beast. Plutarch notes that the head and right hand of Cyrus II were cut off by a eunuch of his brother, King Artaxerxes II of Persia, when the latter's forces defeated the former's rebellion.[134]

Decapitation occurs, at least as a literary motif, in the Bible. 2 Kgs 10:1-7 states that Jehu asked the rulers of Samaria to take the heads of Ahab's sons, put them in baskets, and send them to Jehu in Jezreel, to show their loyalty to him.[135]

According to Josephus, the outrage actually occurred in the Second Temple period. Antigonus, the Hasmonean king and high priest from 40 to 37 BCE, achieved rule through the favor of the Parthians. Herod the Great went to Rome to seek the kingship of Judea and was awarded it at a formal session of the Senate. Herod landed at Ptolemais in 39 BCE, assembled an army, and began to take possession of the land. While Herod went to Samosata in Commagene to pay his respects to Antony, he put his brother Joseph in charge of his army. Antigonus attacked, and Joseph fell in battle.[136] According to Josephus:

Not content with his victory, Antigonus was so far carried away by rage as actually to do outrage to Joseph's corpse. Being in possession of the bodies of the slain, he had his head cut off, notwithstanding the ransom of fifty talents with which Pheroras, the brother of the deceased, offered to redeem it (Ἀντιγόνῳ δὲ οὐκ ἀπέχρησεν ἡ νίκη, προῆλθεν δὲ εἰς τοσοῦτον ὀργῆς, ὥστε καὶ νεκρὸν αἰκίσασθαι τὸν Ἰώσηπον· κρατήσας γοῦν τῶν σωμάτων ἀποτέμνει τὴν κεφαλὴν αὐτοῦ, καίτοι πεντήκοντα τάλαντα λύτρον αὐτῆς Φερώρα τἀδελφοῦ διδόντος). (Bell. 1.17.2 §325)[137]

It is clear that Josephus disapproved of this deed as an irrational act.

Anaxarchus of Abdera was a philosopher with Skeptical tendencies who accompanied Alexander the Great on his Asiatic campaigns.[138] According to Diogenes Laertius, who wrote in the first half of the third century CE,[139]

Once at a banquet, when asked by Alexander how he liked the feast, he is said to have answered, "Everything, O king, is magnificent; there is only one thing lacking, that the head of some satrap should be served up at table." This was a hit at Nicocreon (καὶ ποτ᾽ ἐν συμποσίῳ τοῦ Ἀλεξάνδρου ἐρωτήσαντος αὐτὸν τί ἄρα δοκεῖ τὸ δεῖπνον, εἰπεῖν φασιν, "ὦ βασιλεῦ, πάντα πολυτελῶς· ἔδει δὲ λοιπὸν κεφαλὴν σατράπου τινὸς παρατεθεῖσθαι·" ἀπορρίπτων πρὸς τὸν Νικοκρέοντα). (9.58)[140]

This was no doubt an example of the "frank speech" (παρρησία) of the philosopher in criticizing a tyrant. Nicocreon was offended, however, and, after Alexander died, he had Anaxarchus brutally killed.

When Pompey, the Roman general, was defeated by Caesar in 48 BCE, he fled to Egypt. He was stabbed to death as he landed.[141] According to Plutarch:

But they cut off Pompey's head, and threw the rest of his body unclothed out of the boat, and left it for those who craved so pitiful a sight. Philip [Pompey's freedman], however, stayed by the body, until such had taken their fill of gazing; then he washed it in sea-water, wrapped it in a tunic of his own, since he had no other supply, sought along the coast until he found the remnants of a small fishing-boat, old stuff, indeed, but sufficient to furnish a funeral pyre that would answer for an unclothed corpse, and that not too entire (τοῦ δὲ Πομπηΐου τὴν μὲν κεφαλὴν ἀπο-

---

134 Plutarch Vit., Artaxerxes 17 (1019); this passage was referred to by Bultmann, History, 301 n. 5. On Cyrus II, see Pierre Briant, "Cyrus (2)," OCD 423; on Arta-xerxes II, see idem, "Artaxerxes (2)," ibid., 182.

135 See also Morgan Gillman, Herodias, 88–89.

136 Schürer, History, 1:281–83.

137 Text and trans. from Thackeray, Josephus, 2:152–53.

138 David N. Sedley, "Anaxarchus," OCD 86.

139 H. S. Long and R. W. Sharples, "Diogenes (6) Laertius," OCD 474–75.

140 Text and trans. from Hicks, Diogenes Laertius, 2:470–73.

141 G. E. F. Chilver and Robin J. Seager, "Pompeius Magnus (1), Gnaeus (Pompey)," OCD 1216.

τέμνουσι, τὸ δὲ ἄλλο σῶμα γυμνὸν ἐκβαλόντες
ἀπὸ τῆς ἁλιάδος τοῖς δεομένοις τοιούτου θεά-
ματος ἀπέλιπον. παρέμεινε δὲ αὐτῷ Φίλιππος,
ἕως ἐγένοντο μεστοὶ τῆς ὄψεως· εἶτα περιλούσας
τῇ θαλάσσῃ τὸ σῶμα καὶ χιτωνίῳ τινὶ τῶν ἑαυτοῦ
περιστείλας, ἄλλο δὲ οὐδὲν ἔχων, ἀλλὰ περισκο-
πῶν τὸν αἰγιαλὸν εὗρε μικρᾶς ἁλιάδος λείψανα,
παλαιὰ μέν, ἀρκοῦντα δὲ νεκρῷ γυμνῷ καὶ οὐδὲ
ὅλῳ πυρκαϊὰν ἀναγκαίαν παρασχεῖν). (Vit., Pompey
80 [661])[142]

The girl is portrayed as an extension of her mother
and as desiring intensely what her mother wishes; the girl
goes in again to the banqueting hall *immediately* and *with
haste*. When she makes her request to the "king," she
even goes beyond what her mother has told her, "I wish
that you give me *at once, on a platter*, the head of John the
Baptist (θέλω ἵνα ἐξαυτῆς δῷς μοι ἐπὶ πίνακι τὴν
κεφαλὴν Ἰωάννου τοῦ βαπτιστοῦ) (emphasis added).
The result is grotesque.[143] A young girl is portrayed as
requesting that a severed head be given her on a platter
as if it were food.[144] This image is even more shocking
than that of Anaxarchus.

The following text from Livy, when compared with
the account of the death of John in Mark, casts light on
the probable intent (or effect) of the pre-Markan story to
disparage the Herodian women:

[Valerius Antias] writes that at Placentia a notorious
woman, with whom [Flamininus] was desperately in
love, had been invited to a dinner. There he was
boasting to the courtesan, among other things, about
his severity in the prosecution of cases and how many
persons he had in chains, under sentence of death,
whom he intended to behead. Then the woman,
reclining below him, said that she had never seen a
person beheaded and was very anxious to behold the
sight. Hereupon, he says, the generous lover, ordering
one of the wretches to be brought to him, cut off his
head with his sword. This deed, whether it was performed in the manner for which the censor rebuked
him, or as Valerius reports it, was savage and cruel; in
the midst of drinking and feasting, where it is the custom to pour libations to the gods and to pray for blessings, as a spectacle for a shameless harlot, reclining in
the bosom of a consul, a human victim sacrificed and
bespattering the table with his blood! (Placentiae
famosam mulierem, cuius amore [Flamininus]
deperiret, in convivium arcessitam [Valerius Antias]
scribit. Ibi iactantem sese scorto inter cetera rettulisse
quam acriter quaestiones exercuisset et quam multos
capitis damnatos in vinculis haberet, quos securi per-
cussurus esset. Tum illam infra eum accubantem
negasse umquam vidisse quemquam securi ferientem,
et pervelle id videre. Hic indulgentem amatorem
unum ex illis miseris attrahi iussum securi percussisse.
Facinus sive eo modo quo censor obiecit, sive, ut
Valerius tradit, commissum est, saevum atque atrox:
inter pocula atque epulas, ubi libare diis dapes, ubi
bene precari mos esset, ad spectaculum scorti procacis,
in sinu consulis recubantis, mactatam humanam victi-
mam esse et cruore mensam respersam!). (39.43)[145]

■ **26-28** The "king" was deeply grieved because he had a
great reverence for John, knowing him to be a just and
holy man, and because he had been protecting him, presumably from Herodias's desire to kill him.[146] The conflict in which the "king" finds himself is due to his own
foolishness.[147] He does not want to have John executed,
but he is no doubt afraid to put the curse upon himself

---

142 Text and trans. from Perrin, *Plutarch's Lives*, 5:322–
23. The author of *Psalms of Solomon* 2 concluded that
the ignominious death of Pompey occurred as
divine vengeance for his entering into the Holy of
Holies in the temple in Jerusalem (esp. vv. 26-29).

143 Glancy, "Unveiling Masculinity," 41. Capel Anderson points out that in "the Middle Ages, veneration
of *Johannisschüsseln*, devotional images of John's
head on the platter, was popular in Europe. Herod's
banquet foreshadowed the Last Supper, and John's
head was a type of the eucharistic body and blood of
Christ" ("Dancing Daughter," 127).

144 Shepherd, *Markan Sandwich Stories*, 206.

145 Text and trans. from Evan T. Sage, *Livy* (14 vols.;
LCL; Cambridge, MA: Harvard University Press;
London: Heinemann, 1936) 11:356–59; this passage
was referred to by Bultmann, *History*, 301 n. 5.

146 Cf. vv. 19-20 and the commentary above.

147 The statement that he swore to the girl (v. 23) is
restated here in terms of a plurality of oaths; see the
first note on the translation of v. 23 above.

into effect, and he is ashamed to refuse the girl in front of his guests.[148] In a similar way, when Jephthah returned home after defeating the Ammonites and his daughter was the first to come out of his house to greet him, he tore his clothes and exclaimed, "Ahh! My child! You have brought me low! You have become a stumbling block before me. You have become my great misfortune! I have opened my mouth to Yahweh, and I cannot retract" (Judg 11:35).[149]

The noun "executioner" ($\sigma\pi\epsilon\kappa o\upsilon\lambda\acute{a}\tau\omega\rho$) is a Latin loanword. The proper meaning of the Latin noun *speculator* was "scout (in the Roman imperial army)." It was also used to designate one of the *principales* ("attendants") of a provincial governor. It is used analogously here of a member of Herod Antipas's staff, whose responsibility included executions.[150]

The "king" resolves the dilemma depicted in v. 26 by sending the executioner and commanding him to bring the head of John (v. 27).[151] The command is portrayed as being carried out immediately.

Josephus says that John was executed at Herod Antipas's fortified palace in Perea, Machaerus (*Ant.* 18.5.2 §119).[152] It is highly likely, however, that Mark's narrative presupposes that the banquet took place in the royal palace in Tiberias and that John was executed in a prison nearby.[153]

The grotesque character of the girl's request is mirrored by the gruesome report of its fulfillment in v. 28. The portrayal of the girl as an extension of her mother in vv. 24-25 is replicated in v. 28, as the girl receives the platter with John's head on it and gives it to her mother.

■ **29** Disciples of John were mentioned in 2:18 as practicing the ritual of fasting, as the disciples of the Phar-

isees did. This verse then links the account of the death of John to the overall narrative. The reference to his arrest (lit., "being handed over") in 1:14 is completed by the narrative of 6:17-29.[154]

The word "corpse" ($\pi\tau\hat{\omega}\mu\alpha$), used here of John, is used of Jesus in 15:45. The disciples of John perform an act of piety by burying the remains of their teacher. This report awakens the expectation that the disciples of Jesus will do the same. They abandon him, however, and he is buried by Joseph, a stranger.

The Conclusion to the Sending of the Twelve: Comment

■ **30** In literary terms, one task of this verse is to enclose the account of the death of John the Baptist within the report of the sending out of the Twelve. A summary of their activities had already been given in vv. 12-13. Verse 30 does bring a new element, namely, that they were teaching as they traveled about. This notice is probably equivalent to the statement in v. 12, "they proclaimed that (people) should repent" ($\dot{\epsilon}\kappa\acute{\eta}\rho\upsilon\xi\alpha\nu$ $\ddot{\iota}\nu\alpha$ $\mu\epsilon\tau\alpha\nu o\hat{\omega}\sigma\iota\nu$). As in the case of Jesus, proclaiming the gospel of God, that the kingdom of God has drawn near (1:14-15), is equivalent to teaching the people (1:21) or speaking the word to them (2:1). Another task of this verse is to reunite the Twelve with Jesus for the continuation of the narrative.

Another new element in this verse is the designation of the Twelve as "apostles" ($\dot{\alpha}\pi\acute{o}\sigma\tau o\lambda o\iota$). In 3:14, some manuscripts include the statement "whom he also named apostles" ($o\mathring{\upsilon}\varsigma$ $\kappa\alpha\grave{\iota}$ $\dot{\alpha}\pi o\sigma\tau\acute{o}\lambda o\upsilon\varsigma$ $\mathring{\omega}\nu\acute{o}\mu\alpha\sigma\epsilon\nu$), but this is not the earliest recoverable reading of the text.[155] This, then, is the only use of the term $\dot{\alpha}\pi\acute{o}\sigma\tau o\lambda o\varsigma$ ("apostle")

148 Cf. the reaction of Gaius to Agrippa's request in Josephus *Ant.* 18.8.8 §§299–300, paraphrased in the commentary on vv. 22-23 above.

149 Trans. from Boling, *Judges*, 206. Note that Jephthah's foolishness continues in his blaming his daughter for the misfortune. From the point of view of the narrator, the daughter exhibits wisdom that contrasts with her father's foolishness; cf. ibid., 209 (note on v. 36).

150 LSJ, s.v. See also Hoehner, *Herod Antipas*, 119–20 n. 3.

151 Shepherd points out the ironic parallel between Jesus sending the Twelve ($\dot{\alpha}\pi o\sigma\tau\acute{\epsilon}\lambda\lambda\epsilon\iota\nu$) and Herod sending ($\dot{\alpha}\pi o\sigma\tau\acute{\epsilon}\lambda\lambda\epsilon\iota\nu$) the executioner (*Markan*

Sandwich Stories, 181); see "The Literary Unity of 6:6b-30" above.

152 Morgan Gillman, *Herodias*, 31.

153 Cf. Theissen, *Gospels in Context*, 86–87; contra Hoehner, *Herod Antipas*, 146–48. On the royal palace in Tiberias, see Josephus *Vit.* 12 §65; Schürer, *History*, 1:342–43.

154 Cf. Kermode's argument that 6:14-19 is a "completive" narrative as well as a "heterodiegetic" one; see the section "The Literary Unity of 6:6b-30" above.

155 See the first note on the trans. of 3:14 above.

in Mark. It is likely that the word is used here in the usual sense of a delegate.[156] It does not seem to be a technical term here, as it is in other writings of the Christ-movement. Paul used the word ἀπόστολος ("apostle") in the earliest attested Christian technical sense, that is, a wit-

ness to the resurrection of Jesus who has been commissioned by the risen Lord to proclaim the Christ-event.[157] The author of Luke-Acts endowed the word with a different technical sense: he identified "the apostles" with the Twelve (Luke 9:13).[158]

---

156 See the comments on the use of the verb ἀποστέλλειν ("to send") in v. 7 above.

157 1 Cor 9:1; 15:7-8; Gal 1:15-16; Fitzmyer, *Luke,* 1:615.
158 Fitzmyer, *Luke,* 1:254, 615–16.

31/ And he said to them, "Come, you yourselves privately, to an unpopulated place and rest a little while." For those who were coming and going were many, and they did not even have an opportunity to eat. 32/ And they went away in the boat to an unpopulated place by themselves. 33/ And many saw them going and recognized[a] (them), and they ran by land from all the cities, gathering at that place, and arrived before them.[b] 34/ And when he disembarked, he saw a large crowd and he had pity on them[c] because they were like sheep without a shepherd, and he began to teach them many things. 35/ And when it became late, his disciples went to him and said,[d] "The place is unpopulated and the hour is already late; 36/ dismiss them so that they may go to the surrounding farms and villages to buy something for themselves to eat." 37/ He then answered them, "You give them (something) to eat." And they said to him, "Shall we go and buy loaves for two hundred denarii and give[e] (them) to them to eat?" 38/ He then said to them, "How many loaves do you have?[f] Go see." And when they had found out, they said, "Five;[g] and two fish." 39/ And he commanded them to have them all recline[h] in parties on the green grass. 40/ And they reclined in groups of one hundred and groups of fifty. 41/ And he took the five loaves and the two fish, looked up to heaven, gave praise (to God) and broke the loaves (into pieces) and gave (them) to his disciples[i] to set before them, and he distributed the two fish to all. 42/ And they all ate and were satisfied, 43/ and they picked up (enough) broken pieces to fill twelve baskets[j] and (pieces) from the fish. 44/ And those who had eaten the loaves[k] were five thousand men. 45/ And immediately he compelled his disciples to get into the boat and to go ahead (of him) to the other shore, to Bethsaida, while he himself dismissed[l] the crowd. 46/ And having said farewell to them, he went away to the moun-

a   In the earliest recoverable form of this sentence, attested by B D W Θ f^1 et al., the verb ἐπέγνωσαν ("recognized") had no expressed object. This ambiguity gave rise to variants. Some MSS (ℵ A K et al.) read αὐτούς ("them"), as the object of the verb, and others (Γ f^{13} 565 *pm*) αὐτόν ("him").

b   It is likely that the reading attested by p84vid (A, f^{13}) 𝔐 et al., namely, "and they arrived before them and gathered in his presence" (καὶ προῆλθον αὐτοὺς καὶ συνῆλθον πρὸς αὐτόν) is a conflation of two other attested readings. One of these is "and they arrived before them" (καὶ προῆλθον αὐτούς), reflected in ℵ B et al.; the other is "and they came together here" (καὶ συνῆλθον αὐτοῦ), reflected in D (28. 700, 33 *pc*) b. See the discussion in Westcott and Hort, 2:Introduction, §§134–38. It is difficult to determine which of these is prior (or whether one of the other variants has a claim to be earlier). The reading "and they arrived before them" (καὶ προῆλθον αὐτούς) may have a slightly better claim than the others; see Metzger, *Textual Commentary*, 78.

c   The reading ἐπ᾽ αὐτούς ("on them"), attested by ℵ B D et al., is earlier than ἐπ᾽ αὐτοῖς ("on them"), attested by p84vid A L W Θ $f^{1.13}$ 33 𝔐, since the latter improves the syntax of the former.

d   The majority of MSS read the historical present λέγουσιν ("they said," lit., "they say") rather than the imperfect ἔλεγον, attested by ℵ¹ (ℵ* Θ 579; 2–5) B L Δ et al. The former reading may have arisen under the influence of Matt 15:33 or of the λέγουσιν ("they said," lit., "they say") in Mark 6:37.

e   The earliest recoverable reading is the syntactically problematic future indicative verbal form δώσομεν ("give"), attested by p45 A B L Δ et al. Taylor (ad loc.) judged this reading to be a mistake for δώσωμεν ("give") since it is preceded by a subjunctive, but Moulton-Turner (3:98) considered it a viable reading. The variants with the first aorist subjunctive δώσωμεν ("give"), attested by ℵ D N f^{13} et al., and the second aorist subjunctive δῶμεν ("give"), attested by W Θ f^1 𝔐, are syntactical improvements.

f   The word order varies in the MSS; B L Δ Θ et al. read πόσους ἔχετε ἄρτους ("how many loaves do you have?"), a reading accepted by Taylor (ad loc.), following Westcott and Hort. p45 ℵ A D W $f^{1.13}$ 33 𝔐 read πόσους ἄρτους ἔχετε. The former reading appears without variants in Mark 8:5. Matthew has no exact parallel to the clause in Mark 6:38, but the parallel to 8:5 reads πόσους ἄρτους ἔχετε. There is no close parallel in Luke. The reading πόσους ἔχετε ἄρτους may have been deliberately introduced in some MSS of Mark 6:38 to conform this verse to 8:5, or it may have arisen as an unconscious stylistic variant.

g   A number of MSS (D 565. et al.) include the word ἄρτους ("loaves") after the word πέντε ("five"); this tain to pray. 47/ And when evening had come, the boat was[m] in the middle of the sea, and he himself was alone on the land. 48/ And when he saw them impeded in their progress, for the wind was against them, at about the fourth watch of the night, he came to them, walking on the sea; and he wanted to pass by them. 49/ Now those who saw him walking on the sea thought that he was a ghost, and they cried out. 50/ For they all saw him[n] and were terrified. But he spoke with them immediately, and said to them, "Have courage! It is I; do not be afraid." 51/ And he stepped into the boat with them, and the wind abated, and they were very, exceedingly amazed[o] within themselves.[p] 52/ For they did not comprehend with regard to the loaves, but their hearts had become hardened. 53/ And having crossed over to the land, they came to Gennesaret[q] and went into the harbor.[r] 54/ And when they disembarked, (people) immediately recognized him 55/ and they ran about that whole region and began to carry about those who were ill on pallets (to the place) where they heard that he was. 56/ And wherever he went, into villages or cities or farms, they put the sick in the marketplaces and entreated him that they might touch even the edge of his cloak; and as many as touched him were saved.[s]

variant probably arose under the influence of the parallel in Matt 14:17.

h The reading καὶ ἐπέταξεν αὐτοῖς ἀνακλῖναι πάντας ("and he ordered them [the disciples] to have them all [the crowd] recline") is attested by A B¹ D L W 𝔐 et al. This is the earliest recoverable reading, which was modified in the direction of the parallel in Matt 14:19, as attested by ℵ B* et al. This secondary reading is καὶ ἐπέταξεν αὐτοῖς ἀνακλιθῆναι πάντας ("and he ordered them [the disciples] that all [the crowd] should recline"). The awkwardness of the shift in antecedent from the indirect object to the subject of the infinitive is relieved by the reading καὶ ἐπέταξεν αὐτοῖς πᾶσιν ἀνακλιθῆναι ("and he ordered them all [the crowd] to recline"), attested by Or^pt and the reading καὶ ἐπέταξεν αὐτοῖς ἀνακλιθῆναι ("and he ordered them [the crowd] to recline") attested by 700.

i The reading τοῖς μαθηταῖς αὐτοῦ ("to his disciples") is attested by 𝔓⁴⁵ A D W Θ f¹·¹³ 𝔐 et al. Taylor (ad loc.) adopts this reading against Westcott and Hort, since it is typically Markan. A number of MSS lack αὐτοῦ ("his"), namely, ℵ B L Δ et al. The latter reading may be due to the influence of the parallel passages in Matt 14:19 and Luke 9:16. Cf. Metzger, *Textual Commentary*, 78. See also the note on 8:1.

j Two variants, κλασμάτων δώδεκα κοφίνους πλήρεις ("twelve baskets full of broken pieces"), attested by A D Θ 𝔐 et al., and περισσεύματα κλασμάτων δώδεκα κοφίνους πλήρεις ("the remainder of the broken pieces, twelve baskets full"), attested by (33, 700). 1241. 1424 *pc* lat, show the influence of the parallel in Matt 14:20.

k Some MSS (𝔓⁴⁵ ℵ D W Θ et al.) lack τοὺς ἄρτους ("the loaves"), probably because of the influence of the parallel in Matt 14:21. Cf. Metzger, *Textual Commentary*, 78–79.

l The earliest recoverable reading is the present indicative ἀπολύει ("he dismissed," lit., "he dismisses"), attested by ℵ B D L Δ et al. The indicative is acceptable in the Koine, but the subjunctive would be expected in Attic; see Moulton-Turner, 3:110 and Smyth §§2422–23. This state of affairs gave rise to variants: 𝔓⁴⁵ A N W et al. read the aorist subjunctive ἀπολύσῃ ("he dismissed"), and K Γ f¹³ et al. read the future indicative ἀπολύσει ("he dismissed," lit., "he will dismiss"). The former variant may have been inspired by the parallel in Matt 14:22.

m 𝔓⁴⁵ D f¹ et al. read ἦν πάλαι ("was already"); Taylor (ad loc.) adopted this reading against Westcott and Hort, who placed it in the margin. On the one hand, Matthew's ἤδη ("already") in 14:24 may be taken as evidence that he read πάλαι ("already") in his copy of Mark; on the other hand, πάλαι ("already") may have entered the text under the influence of Matthew. The latter seems more likely, given the weak external support for the reading. See Metzger, *Textual Commentary*, 79.

n   D Θ 565. 700 it lack the words γὰρ αὐτὸν εἶδον ("for they saw him"), so that πάντες ("all") becomes the subject of ἀνέκραξαν ("they cried out"). This reading probably represents a secondary omission, either by error or because these words were thought to be redundant after οἱ δὲ ἰδόντες αὐτόν ("those who saw him") in v. 49. Alternatively, γὰρ αὐτὸν εἶδον could be a later addition to make the point that "those who saw him" were all of the Twelve.

o   A D W Θ f¹³ 33. (565) 𝔐 et al. read καὶ ἐθαύμαζον, "and they marveled" after ἐξίσταντο, "(they) were amazed." This reading is a secondary heightening of the effect of the miracle; cf. Metzger, *Textual Commentary*, 79–80.

p   Θ reads περιέσωσεν αὐτοὺς καί ("he saved them from death and") instead of λίαν ἐκ περισσοῦ ἐν ἑαυτοῖς ("very, exceedingly in themselves"). This reading is a secondary attempt at improvement that eliminates a group of words perceived as pleonastic and sharpens the point of the story. Since the earliest recoverable reading, λίαν ἐκ περισσοῦ ἐν ἑαυτοῖς ("very, exceedingly in themselves"), attested by A f¹³ et al., was perceived to be pleonastic, it was simplified in two apparently independent ways: ℵ B (L) Δ et al.

attest the reading λίαν ἐν ἑαυτοῖς ("very in themselves"), and D (W, f¹, 28, 2542) et al. the reading περισσῶς ἐν ἑαυτοῖς ("exceedingly in themselves"). Φ attests a reading that is a conflation of those of Θ and A f¹³ et al.

q   B* K N Θ f¹.¹³ et al. attest the reading Γεν(ν)ησαρεθ ("Gennesaret"). This name occurs also in the parallel in Matt 14:34 and in an unrelated passage in Luke 5:1. D it vg^mss et al. attest the reading Γεννησαρ ("Gennesar"). The latter reading is probably a secondary correction inspired by 1 Macc 11:67 or the usage of Josephus.

r   D W Θ f¹.¹³ et al. lack the words καὶ προσωρμίσθησαν ("and went into the harbor"). This reading probably reflects an omission inspired by the parallel in Matt 14:34.

s   The earliest recoverable reading is probably ὅσοι ἂν ἥψαντο ("as many as touched him"). The use of the indicative with ἄν here is correct and has affinities with the iterative use of ἄν with the indicative; see Moulton, 167–68; Smyth §§1790–92. But the reading that lacks ἄν, attested by ℵ D Δ et al., probably reflects an intended correction on the assumption that ἄν should be used with the subjunctive. The reading attested by A 𝔐 sy^h, the imperfect indicative ἥπτοντο ("touched"), is also a correction, since the imperfect is more appropriate for repeated action in the past.

Comment

■ 31-34

■ 31 Jesus' proposal that they go "to an unpopulated place" (εἰς ἔρημον τόπον) and rest a little while recalls the scene in 1:35 when Jesus "rose early in the morning, while it was still very dark, went out, and went away to an unpopulated place, and began to pray there" (πρωΐ ἔννυχα λίαν ἀναστὰς ἐξῆλθεν καὶ ἀπῆλθεν εἰς ἔρημον τόπον κἀκεῖ προσηύχετο). The similarity suggests that here Jesus proposes a time of rest and perhaps prayer so that the disciples can renew themselves after the intense activity of their itinerant preaching, exorcising, and healing (vv. 12-13).

The remark that "those who were coming and going were many" (οἱ ἐρχόμενοι καὶ οἱ ὑπάγοντες πολλοί) recalls the situation in 1:45 caused by the healed leper's spreading the word: "they were coming to him from everywhere" (ἤρχοντο πρὸς αὐτὸν πάντοθεν). Perhaps

the implication in 6:31 is that people were streaming to the Twelve in the same way that they have been flocking to Jesus since the healing of the leper.[1]

Lexically, the statement, "they did not even have an opportunity to eat" (οὐδὲ φαγεῖν εὐκαίρουν), recalls Herodias's "opportune day" (ἡμέρα εὔκαιρος) in 6:21. Also lexically, but even more so substantively, it is reminiscent of the scene in 3:20 that led the family of Jesus to think that he was out of his senses, "the crowd gathered again, so that they were not even able to eat" (συνέρχεται πάλιν ὁ ὄχλος, ὥστε μὴ δύνασθαι αὐτοὺς μηδὲ ἄρτον φαγεῖν).

■ 32 The last time that "the boat" (τὸ πλοῖον) was mentioned was in 5:21. On that occasion, Jesus and his disciples had just returned to the area near Capernaum after visiting the Decapolis.[2] On this occasion, the implication is that they are going by boat to an unpopulated area, away from Capernaum. The rest of the verse recapitulates the proposal of Jesus in v. 31.

---

1   This phenomenon is foreshadowed by the response to Jesus in Capernaum (1:32-34).

2   On the geographical problem, see the commentary on 5:20.

■ **33** The repetition of Jesus' proposal of v. 32, that they go to an unpopulated place to be by themselves, contrasts sharply with the result of their attempt to be alone, described in this verse. Many people saw the boat, recognized Jesus and the disciples, anticipated the place to which they were heading, traveled there by land, and arrived before the boat landed. So the unpopulated place became "populated" before Jesus and the disciples could rest there.

■ **34** The Markan Jesus does not resent the presence of the large crowd, but rather has pity on them, just as he had pity on the leper (1:41). Jesus pities the crowd because they are like sheep without a shepherd. In the Bible, because of the pastoral component of the economy of Israel, God is frequently depicted as a "shepherd." So also are human rulers or leaders of Israel and of foreign nations.[3] The expression "sheep without a shepherd" is most frequently used in the Bible of a people without a king.[4] The motif of the people lacking a shepherd here could be a hint that Jesus is the messiah of Israel, the king whom they need. The phrase is also used by Moses in his request that a successor to him be appointed, so that the people of Israel will not be like sheep without a shepherd (Num 27:17). Joshua is appointed to succeed Moses, but the phrase in relation to Moses may also recall the promise that God would send a prophet like Moses (Deut 18:15-18).[5] From this point of view, v. 34 hints that Jesus is the eschatological prophet. The portrayal of Jesus as teaching the people here is compatible with either role, royal messiah or eschatological prophet.[6]

The Genre of 6:35-44

Bultmann classified this account as a nature miracle, implicitly placing the emphasis on the ability of Jesus to feed five thousand people with five loaves of bread and two fish. He points out that the dialogue between Jesus and his disciples increases the tension. The miracle itself is illustrated only by the successful distribution and the satisfaction of those fed. The narrative makes its impact in large part by showing that there was more food at the end than at the beginning, and the number of those fed is revealed impressively only at the end.[7]

Theissen categorizes this story as a "gift miracle," that is, a story in which "material goods are made available in surprising ways; they provide larger-than-life and extraordinary gifts, food transformed, increased, richly available." Such stories could also be called miracles of material culture, since they illustrate problems of human labor: how to get food to live and wine to feast. A typical feature is that gift miracles are never initiated by requests, but always by an act of the miracle-worker.[8] Bultmann's and Theissen's perspectives are complementary, rather than exclusive, alternatives.

Cultural Contexts

A number of passages, in the Bible and elsewhere, describe the miraculous provision of food or drink. According to 1 Kings 17, Elijah took an oath "As the Lord the God of Israel lives" that there would be neither dew nor rain except by his word.[9] God's second way of providing for Elijah during the drought was to send him to a widow in Zarephath, a town in the territory of Sidon. She had only a handful of meal in a jar and a little oil in a flask. She tells the prophet that she was about to prepare it for herself and her children, so that they could eat it and die. Elijah says to her:

> Have courage! Go in and do as you have said; but first make from it a little loaf for me and bring it out to me. Then make (loaves) for yourself and your children. For thus says the Lord, "The jar of meal will not fail, and the flask of oil will not be depleted until the day that the Lord sends rain upon the land" ($\vartheta\acute{\alpha}\rho\sigma\epsilon\iota$, $\epsilon\check{\iota}\sigma\epsilon\lambda\vartheta\epsilon$ $\kappa\alpha\grave{\iota}$ $\pi o\acute{\iota}\eta\sigma o\nu$ $\kappa\alpha\tau\grave{\alpha}$ $\tau\grave{o}$ $\acute{\rho}\hat{\eta}\mu\acute{\alpha}$ $\sigma o\nu\cdot$ $\grave{\alpha}\lambda\lambda\grave{\alpha}$ $\pi o\acute{\iota}\eta\sigma o\nu$ $\grave{\epsilon}\mu o\grave{\iota}$ $\grave{\epsilon}\kappa\epsilon\hat{\iota}\vartheta\epsilon\nu$ $\grave{\epsilon}\gamma\kappa\rho\upsilon\varphi\acute{\iota}\alpha\nu$ $\mu\iota\kappa\rho\grave{o}\nu$ $\grave{\epsilon}\nu$

---

3   See Meyers and Meyers, *Zechariah 9–14*, 195.

4   3 Kgdms 22:17; 2 Chr 18:16; Nah 3:18; Jdt 11:19; cf. 2 Kgdms 24:17.

5   See Lührmann, ad loc.

6   See the sections of the introduction *Jesus as Messiah* and *Jesus as Prophet*.

7   Bultmann, *History*, 217.

8   Theissen, *Miracle Stories*, 103.

9   On this form of oath, see M. H. Pope, "Oaths," *IDB* 3:577.

πρώτοις καὶ ἐξοίσεις μοι, σαυτῇ δὲ καὶ τοῖς τέκνοις σου ποιήσεις ἐπ᾽ ἐσχάτου· ὅτι τάδε λέγει κύριος Ἡ ὑδρία τοῦ ἀλεύρου οὐκ ἐκλείψει καὶ ὁ καψάκης τοῦ ἐλαίου οὐκ ἐλαττονήσει ἕως ἡμέρας τοῦ δοῦναι κύριον τὸν ὑετὸν ἐπὶ τῆς γῆς). (3 Kgdms 17:13-14)[10]

The woman did as Elijah had said, and he, she, and her household ate for many days.

The dialogue between Elijah and the widow is analogous to the dialogue between Jesus and the disciples in Mark 6:35-38. Elijah gives a command regarding food, and the woman demurs, emphasizing the scantiness of what she has. In both stories food is miraculously multiplied. In the story about Elijah, it occurs not to feed a large number of people once, but to feed a few over an extended period of time. The situation of need is greater in the Elijah story; there is a drought and the consequent famine. The woman is a widow and thus by definition needy. The mention of green grass in Mark 6:39 makes it clear that there is no drought. God plays a more direct role in the Elijah story: God sends Elijah to the widow and when Elijah announces the miracle, he does it in the form, "Thus says the Lord." Jesus looks to heaven, probably in prayer, and praises (God, although his words are not quoted), but there is little indication that the miracle is God's rather than Jesus.'

According to 2 Kgs 4:42, a man came from Baal-shalishah, bringing "the man of God," that is, Elisha, twenty loaves of barley. Elisha said:

"Give [second person plural] to the people and let them eat." And his servant said, "How may I give this to a hundred men?" And he said, "Give [second person singular] to the people and let them eat, for thus says the Lord, 'They will eat and will leave (some) remaining.'" And they ate and left (some) remaining,

according to the word of the Lord (Δότε τῷ λαῷ καὶ ἐσθιέτωσαν. καὶ εἶπεν ὁ λειτουργὸς αὐτοῦ Τί δῶ τοῦτο ἐνώπιον ἑκατὸν ἀνδρῶν; καὶ εἶπεν Δὸς τῷ λαῷ καὶ ἐσθιέτωσαν, ὅτι τάδε λέγει κύριος Φάγονται καὶ καταλείψουσιν. καὶ ἔφαγον καὶ κατέλιπον κατὰ τὸ ῥῆμα κυρίου). (4 Kgdms 4:42-44)[11]

The miraculous deed in this story is almost identical to that of Mark 6:35-44, except that in the Elisha story there are no fish. The LXX of 4 Kgdms 4:42 adds παλάθας (cakes made of preserved fruit, mostly of figs). The dialogue is present in the middle portion of the story, as in the Elijah story and the Jesus story. Elisha's first command to his servant (ὁ λειτουργὸς αὐτοῦ, more or less equivalent to a disciple) contains the same verb as the command given by Jesus to his disciples in v. 37a: δότε ("give" in the second person plural). Elisha's servant's response is similar to the response of the disciples of Jesus in v. 37b. The last part of Elisha's response to the servant uses the same verbal stem, φάγονται ("they will eat"), as the narrator's statement at the end of the Jesus story (Mark 6:42, 44).

Some differences are that Elisha begins with a larger number of loaves and provides for a smaller number of people. These differences may be due to the desire of the tradents of the Jesus-tradition to show that Jesus is greater than Elisha. Elisha does not take the food, praise God, break the bread, and give it back to his servant to distribute. These elements in the Jesus story probably reflect the communal meals of early members of the Christ-movement and perhaps the memory of meals with the historical Jesus. Elisha predicts the miracle and attributes it to divine power, whereas Jesus proceeds without reference to the intended results.[12]

According to *The Lives of the Prophets*, Ezekiel worked the following miracles:

---

10   This miracle is summarized in *The Lives of the Prophets* 21:6. 1 Kgs 17:8-16 (= 3 Kgdms 17:8-16) is cited by Theissen as a gift miracle (*Miracle Stories*, 104), but Bultmann concluded that it was irrelevant (*History*, 230). The similar story in 2 Kgs 4:1-7, a miracle of Elisha, is a counterexample to Theissen's claim that gift miracles are never initiated by requests. The woman does not request that the oil be multiplied, but she does ask for help to prevent

her two children from being sold as slaves. This miracle story is summarized in *The Lives of the Prophets* 22:8.

11   This miracle story is not summarized in *The Lives of the Prophets*.

12   Bultmann concluded that 2 Kgs 4:42-44 may be *one* source of the feeding stories in the Gospels (*History*, 230).

He, through prayer of his own accord, supplied abundant nourishment to them from fish, and for many who were dying, he summoned life from God (Οὗτος διὰ προσευχῆς αὐτομάτως αὐτοῖς δαψιλῆ τροφὴν ἰχθύων παρέσχετο καὶ πολλοῖς ἐκλείπουσι ζωὴν ἐλθεῖν ἐκ θεοῦ παρεκάλεσεν).[13]

The explicit reference to prayer is analogous to the actions of Jesus described in the Jesus story (looking to heaven, praising). The motif of abundance is present explicitly here and by implication in the concrete description of the leftovers in the Jesus story. Both miracles are performed unbidden. This gift motif is explicit here, and implicit in the Jesus story. Fish are involved in both stories. Dissimilarities include the fact that the Ezekiel story is a summary, whereas the Jesus story is a narrative. No bread is involved in the Ezekiel story. No servants or disciples are mentioned in the Ezekiel story.

In Euripides' *Bacchae*, a messenger reported that he had seen three revel-bands of women in the woods. Among other things, he reported that:

And one took her thyrsus and struck it into the earth, and forth there gushed a limpid spring; and another plunged her wand into the lap of earth and there the god sent up a fount of wine; and all who wished for draughts of milk had but to scratch the soil with their finger-tips and there they had it in abundance, while from every ivy-wreathed staff sweet rills of honey trickled.

(θύρσον δὲ τις λαβοῦσ᾽ ἔπαισεν ἐς πέτραν,
ὅθεν δροσώδης ὕδατος ἐκπηδᾷ νοτίς·
ἄλλη δὲ νάρθηκ᾽ ἐς πέδον καθῆκε γῆς,
καὶ τῇδε κρήνην ἐξανῆκ᾽ οἴνου θεός·
ὅσαις δὲ λευκοῦ πώματος πόθος παρῆν,
ἄκροισι δακτύλοισι διαμῶσαι χθόνα
γάλακτος ἑσμοὺς εἶχον· ἐκ δὲ κισσίνων

θύρσων γλυκεῖαι μέλιτος ἔσταζον ῥοαί.
ὥστ᾽, εἰ παρῆσθα, τὸν θεὸν τὸν νῦν ψέγεις
εὐχαῖσιν ἂν μετῆλθες εἰσιδὼν τάδε).
(704-13)[14]

Here a god provides his followers with water, wine, milk, and honey. These gifts are spontaneously given.

According to Philostratus, while Apollonius was visiting India and conversing with the sages there, a king arrived in the village below. Apollonius asked the sages whether a rich table would be laid for the king when he came. They replied affirmatively; although they lived simply, the king required and took pleasure in a great deal more. But he would not be given any living creature to eat. After the king arrived and had exchanged greetings with those present:

Thereupon four tripods stepped forth like those of the Pythian temple, but of their own accord, like those which advanced in Homer's poem, and upon them were cupbearers of black brass resembling the figures of Ganymede and of Pelops among the Greeks. And the earth strewed beneath them grass softer than any mattress. And dried fruits and bread and vegetables and the dessert of the season all came in, served in order, and set before them more agreeably than if cooks and waiters had provided it; now two of the tripods flowed with wine, but the other two supplied, the one of them a jet of warm water and the other of cold (τρίποδες μὲν ἐξεπορεύθησαν Πυθικοὶ τέτταρες αὐτόματοι, καθάπερ οἱ Ὁμήρειοι προϊόντες, οἰνοχόοι δ᾽ ἐπ᾽ αὐτοῖς χαλκοῦ μέλανος, οἷοι παρ᾽ Ἕλλησιν οἱ Γανυμήδεις τε καὶ οἱ Πέλοπες. ἡ γῆ δὲ ὑπεστόρνυ πόας μαλακωτέρας ἢ αἱ εὐναί. τραγήματα δὲ καὶ ἄρτοι καὶ λάχανα καὶ τρωκτὰ ὡραῖα, πάντα ἐν κόσμῳ ἐφοίτα διακείμενα ἥδιον ἢ εἰ ὀψοποιοὶ αὐτὰ παρεσκεύαζον, τῶν δὲ τριπόδων οἱ μὲν δύο οἴνου ἐπέρρεον, τοῖν δυοῖν

---

13 *De prophetarum vita et obitu*, recensio anonyma, γ΄. Ἰεζεκιήλ (3. Ezekiel); text from Theodorus Schermann, *Prophetarum vitae fabulosae* (Leipzig: Teubner, 1907) 75; my trans.; cf. trans by D. R. A. Hare, "The Lives of the Prophets," in *OTP* 2:389.

14 Text from E. R. Dodds, *Euripides: Bacchae* (2nd ed.; Oxford: Clarendon, 1960) 30; trans. from Edward B. Coleridge, "The Plays of Euripides," in Robert Maynard Hutchins, ed., *Great Books of the Western World* (Chicago/London: Encyclopaedia Britannica, 1952) 345. Cf. *Bacchae* 142–43. Blackburn refers to this text, but argues that the feeding stories of the Gospels are comprehensible in terms of the OT and Jewish sources (*Theios Anēr*, 195).

δὲ ὁ μὲν ὕδατος θερμοῦ κρήνην παρεῖχεν, ὁ δὲ αὖ ψυχροῦ). (*Vita Ap.* 3.27)[15]

This text is somewhat similar to the fairy-tale motif of the table that sets itself.[16] The soft grass provided for reclining upon is noteworthy in light of Mark 6:39.

The miraculous provision of bread in Mark 6:35-44 is also analogous to the biblical texts describing the miraculous provision of manna in the wilderness. According to Exodus 16, while the people of Israel were in the wilderness of Sin, they complained to Moses and Aaron that they were dying of hunger. In response, the Lord said to Moses:

See, I will rain bread for you [plural] from heaven, and the people will go out and will gather the portion of a day on the day, so that I may test them, whether they will walk in my Law or not (Ἰδοὺ ἐγὼ ὕω ὑμῖν ἄρτους ἐκ τοῦ οὐρανοῦ, καὶ ἐξελεύσεται ὁ λαὸς καὶ συλλέξουσιν τὸ τῆς ἡμέρας εἰς ἡμέραν, ὅπως πειράσω αὐτοὺς εἰ πορεύσονται τῷ νόμῳ μου ἢ οὔ). (Exod 16:4 LXX)

Moses says to the people:

When the Lord gives you meat to eat in the evening and bread in the morning in abundance because the Lord has heard your murmuring, which you murmured against us—what are we? For your murmuring is not against us, but against the Lord (Ἐν τῷ διδόναι κυρίον ὑμῖν ἑσπέρας κρέα φαγεῖν καὶ ἄρτους τὸ

πρωὶ εἰς πλησμονὴν διὰ τὸ εἰσακοῦσαι κύριον τὸν γογγυσμὸν ὑμῶν, ὃν ὑμεῖς διαγογγύζετε καθ᾽ ἡμῶν· ἡμεῖς δὲ τί ἐσμεν; οὐ γὰρ καθ᾽ ἡμῶν ὁ γογγυσμὸς ὑμῶν ἐστιν, ἀλλ᾽ ἢ κατὰ τοῦ θεοῦ). (Exod 16:8 LXX)

Here we see the motif of abundant miraculous provision. But the gift is requested (indirectly), and the people are condemned for that reason.[17] But the Lord reiterates the promise:

I have heard the murmuring of the sons of Israel; say to them, "Toward evening you will eat meat and in the morning you will be filled with bread; and you will know that I am the Lord your God" (Εἰσακήκοα τὸν γογγυσμὸν τῶν υἱῶν Ισραηλ· λάλησον πρὸς αὐτοὺς λέγων Τὸ πρὸς ἑσπέραν ἔδεσθε κρέα καὶ τὸ πρωὶ πλησθήσεσθε ἄρτων· καὶ γνώσεσθε ὅτι ἐγὼ κύριος ὁ θεὸς ὑμῶν). (Exod 16:12 LXX)

The last statement indicates that the purpose of the miracle is not only to provide the people with needed nourishment, but also to manifest the power and glory of God and to establish or reestablish a relationship between God and the people.[18]

The notion of an eschatological or messianic banquet is also of relevance to Mark 6:35-44.[19] Psalm 132 is a royal psalm that celebrates God's choice of Zion and the Davidic dynasty. God's promise is cited:

---

15 Philostratus *Vita Ap.* 3.27; text and trans. from Fredrick C. Conybeare, *Philostratus: The Life of Apollonius of Tyana* (2 vols.; Cambridge, MA/London: Harvard University Press, 1912) 1:288–91. Blackburn refers to this text (*Theios Anēr*, 195 n. 79). The Homeric text alluded to by Philostratus is *Il.* 18.375; it tells of the god Vulcan making twenty tripods that were to stand by the wall of his house. He set wheels of gold under each of them so that they could go of their own accord to the assemblies of the gods and come back again.

16 Note also the sacred rite for acquiring an assistant demon (*PGM* I. 96–107); the demon will bring, on request, water, wine, bread, and any kind of food, except fish and pork (Betz, *Magical Papyri*, 6). Blackburn refers to this text (*Theios Anēr*, 195 n. 79).

Theissen points out that the gift miracles have no analogies in visual experience; they owe more to imagination than any other type and have the light quality of a wish or unaffected fairy-tale (*Miracle Stories*, 105–6).

17 In Ps 105:40 (LXX 104:40), it is noted that the gift of quails and bread was in response to a request of Israel, but there is no condemnation of the request.

18 Cf. Exod 16:7 (the reference to the glory of God being manifested).

19 Blackburn refers to many of these texts under the rubric of the eschaton "as a time when God will provide abundant food and drink for His people" (*Theios Anēr*, 195).

Blessing, I will bless her hunting,
Her poor I will satisfy with bread
(τὴν θήραν αὐτῆς εὐλογῶν εὐλογήσω,
τοὺς πτωχοὺς αὐτῆς χορτάσω ἄρτων). (Ps 131:15
LXX)[20]

Originally, this text spoke about divine favor upon Jerusalem during the time of the monarchy. Later, when there was no autonomous monarchy, or when there was discontent with the Hasmoneans or the Herodians, it may have been read eschatologically. The word χορτάζειν ("to satisfy") occurs also in Mark 6:42.

The description of a banquet in Isa 25:6-8 alludes to Exod 24:11 and may have liturgical roots. In any case, it is the oldest reference to the eschatological banquet:[21]

And the Lord of Hosts will make [a banquet] upon this mountain for all the nations; they will drink good cheer, they will drink wine, they will anoint themselves with perfumed oil. On this mountain give all these things to the nations. For this is the will [of God] for all the nations. Death, having prevailed, has swallowed [people] up, and again God has removed every tear from every face. He has removed the reproach of the people from the whole earth, for the mouth of the Lord has spoken (καὶ ποιήσει κύριος σαβαωθ πᾶσι τοῖς ἔθνεσιν ἐπὶ τὸ ὄρος τοῦτο πίονται εὐφροσύνην, πίονται οἶνον, χρίσονται μύρον. ἐν τῷ ὄρει τούτῳ παράδος ταῦτα πάντα τοῖς ἔθνεσιν· ἡ γὰρ βουλὴ αὕτη ἐπὶ πάντα τὰ ἔθνη. κατέπιεν ὁ θάνατος ἰσχύσας, καὶ πάλιν ἀφεῖλεν ὁ θεὸς πᾶν δάκρυον ἀπὸ παντὸς προσώπου· τὸ ὄνειδος τοῦ λαοῦ ἀφεῖλεν ἀπὸ πάσης τῆς γῆς, τὸ γὰρ στόμα κυρίου ἐλάλησεν). (Isa 25:6-8 LXX; cf. 65:13-14)

According to *1 Enoch* 10, after the final judgment,

Then all the earth will be tilled in righteousness, and all of it will be planted with trees and filled with bless-

ing; and all the trees of joy will be planted on it. They will plant vines on it, and every vine that will be planted on it will yield a thousand jugs of wine, and of every seed that is sown on it, each measure will yield a thousand measures, and each measure of olives will yield ten baths of oil. (*1 Enoch* 10:18-19)[22]

In this text, a banquet is not described, but the theme of eschatological abundance of food and drink is clearly present.

According to the *Syriac Apocalypse of Baruch*, when all is accomplished that was to come to pass in the twelve periods before the end, the messiah will be revealed. Then the following events will take place:

And Behemoth shall appear from his place and Leviathan shall ascend from the sea—those two great monsters I created on the fifth day of creation and have kept until then; and then they shall serve as food for all that survive. The earth also shall yield its fruit ten thousand-fold; and on each vine there shall be a thousand branches, and each branch shall produce a thousand clusters, and each cluster produce a thousand grapes, and each grape produce a cor of wine. And those who have been hungry will rejoice; and, also, they shall see marvels every day. For winds shall go forth from me bearing the scent of aromatic fruits every morning, and, at the close of day, clouds distilling a health-giving dew. And at that time the storehouse of manna shall descend from on high again; and they shall eat of it in those years, because it is they who have come to the final consummation. (*2 Bar.* 29:4-8)[23]

Again, the banquet motif is not explicit, but the motif of an abundance of food and drink in the messianic reign is highly elaborated.

---

20   On the genre of Psalm 132 (131 LXX), see Mitchell Dahood, *Psalms III: 101–150: Introduction, Translation, and Notes* (AB 17A; Garden City, NY: Doubleday, 1970) 241.

21   Joseph Blenkinsopp, *Isaiah 1–39: A New Translation with Introduction and Commentary* (AB 19; New York/London: Doubleday, 2000) 357–60.

22   Trans. by Nickelsburg and VanderKam, 30.

23   Trans. by L. H. Brockington in *AOT*, 856–57.

Comment

■ **35-36** The disciples take the initiative here, but the concrete request they make of Jesus is not related to the miracle. On the contrary, since there is no food available, they ask Jesus to send the crowd away.[24] In spite of their success in proclaiming repentance, exorcising, and healing (vv. 12-13), they do not imagine that they or Jesus can feed the crowd.

■ **37-38** As Jesus upbraided the disciples for their lack of faith because it did not occur to them that they themselves could have stilled the storm,[25] so here he says, "You give them (something) to eat" ($\delta \acute{o} \tau \epsilon$ $\alpha \mathring{v} \tau o \hat{i} \varsigma$ $\mathring{v} \mu \epsilon \hat{i} \varsigma$ $\varphi \alpha \gamma \epsilon \hat{i} \nu$). Their response, "Shall we go and buy loaves for two hundred denarii and give (them) to them to eat?" ($\mathring{a} \pi \epsilon \lambda \vartheta \acute{o} \nu \tau \epsilon \varsigma$ $\mathring{a} \gamma o \rho \acute{a} \sigma \omega \mu \epsilon \nu$ $\delta \eta \nu \alpha \rho \acute{\iota} \omega \nu$ $\delta \iota \alpha \kappa o \sigma \acute{\iota} \omega \nu$ $\mathring{a} \rho \tau o \upsilon \varsigma$ $\kappa \alpha \grave{\iota}$ $\delta \acute{\omega} \sigma o \mu \epsilon \nu$ $\alpha \mathring{v} \tau o \hat{i} \varsigma$ $\varphi \alpha \gamma \epsilon \hat{i} \nu$;), remains on the mundane level and shows even more clearly than their initial proposal that they do not expect a miracle. Jesus then asks them to go and see how many loaves they have. They go to investigate, return, and tell Jesus that they have five loaves of bread and two fish. All of this conversation and investigation builds the suspense.[26] The reaction of the disciples to Jesus' request that they investigate how many loaves they had is not reported, but the audience may well imagine that they were puzzled.[27]

■ **39-40** Without replying to their report that they have five loaves and two fish, Jesus commands the disciples to have the crowd recline. The word $\mathring{a} \nu \alpha \kappa \lambda \hat{\iota} \nu \alpha \iota$ ("to cause to recline") has the sense "place as a guest" in v. 39.[28] The repetition of the word $\sigma \upsilon \mu \pi \acute{o} \sigma \iota \alpha$ ("parties" or "groups of people eating together") in a distributive sense is acceptable, though not elegant, Greek.[29]

The singular of the repeated noun, $\sigma \upsilon \mu \pi \acute{o} \sigma \iota o \nu$ (lit., "drinking party"), is well understood as a "banquet."[30]

The use of this word suggests that the meal hosted by Jesus is a kind of banquet. This connotation suggests a contrasting parallel with the festive dinner ($\delta \epsilon \hat{\iota} \pi \nu o \nu$) or banquet given by Herod Antipas (v. 21). Whereas Herod presumably provided a lavish menu, Jesus provides a simple meal of bread and fish. Whereas Herod invited the nobles of Galilee, Jesus welcomes a crowd of ordinary people and meets their basic needs. The imagery of banqueting is reminiscent of the eschatological banquet of Isa 25:6-8.

The Markan Jesus commands the disciples to have the crowd recline "on the green grass" ($\mathring{\epsilon} \pi \grave{\iota}$ $\tau \hat{\omega}$ $\chi \lambda \omega \rho \hat{\omega}$ $\chi \acute{o} \rho \tau \omega$). This simple but adequate support for the guests is analogous to the remark of Philostratus concerning the meal at which the Indian sages hosted a king, "And the earth strewed beneath them grass softer than any mattress" ($\mathring{\eta}$ $\gamma \hat{\eta}$ $\delta \grave{\epsilon}$ $\mathring{v} \pi \epsilon \sigma \tau \acute{o} \rho \nu \upsilon$ $\pi \acute{o} \alpha \varsigma$ $\mu \alpha \lambda \alpha \kappa \omega \tau \acute{\epsilon} \rho \alpha \varsigma$ $\mathring{\eta}$ $\alpha \mathring{\iota}$ $\epsilon \mathring{v} \nu \alpha \acute{\iota}$).[31]

The distributive repetition of the word $\pi \rho \alpha \sigma \iota \alpha \acute{\iota}$ ("groups") in v. 40 is the same construction as $\sigma \upsilon \mu \pi \acute{o} \sigma \iota \alpha$ $\sigma \upsilon \mu \pi \acute{o} \sigma \iota \alpha$ ("in parties") in v. 39. The word $\pi \rho \alpha \sigma \iota \acute{\alpha}$ ("group") was often used in Greek literature and documents with the sense "bed in a garden" or "garden plot."[32] This connotation of the word thus continues the imagery of a simple, outdoor banquet.

The immediate context, however, shows a shift in imagery. The people recline "in groups of one hundred and groups of fifty" ($\pi \rho \alpha \sigma \iota \alpha \grave{\iota}$ $\pi \rho \alpha \sigma \iota \alpha \grave{\iota}$ $\kappa \alpha \tau \grave{\alpha}$ $\mathring{\epsilon} \kappa \alpha \tau \grave{o} \nu$ $\kappa \alpha \grave{\iota}$ $\kappa \alpha \tau \grave{\alpha}$ $\pi \epsilon \nu \tau \acute{\eta} \kappa o \nu \tau \alpha$). The *Damascus Document* gives a "rule of the assembly of the cam[ps]" (סרך מושב המחן[נו]ת) (12:22-23).[33] During the time of wickedness, until there arises the messiah of Aaron and Israel, those who walk in the camps "shall be ten in number as a minimum to (form) thousands, hundreds, fifties and tens" (עד עשׂרה אנשים למועט לאלפים ומיאיות וחמשׁים ועשׂרות) (CD 13:1-

---

24 Cf. Theissen, *Miracle Stories*, 104.

25 See the commentary above on 4:40. For an argument that the disciples play an important role in this first feeding story, see Suzanne Watts Henderson, "'Concerning the Loaves': Comprehending Incomprehension in Mark 6:45-52," *JSNT* 83 (2001) 12–15.

26 Bultmann, *History*, 217.

27 Compare the literary functions of the dialogues in 1 Kgs 17:10-14 and 2 Kgs 4:42-44; see "Cultural Contexts" above.

28 BAGD, s.v.

29 As is the analogous construction $\delta \acute{v} o$ $\delta \acute{v} o$ ("two by

two" or "in pairs") in v. 7; see the commentary above.

30 BAGD, s.v. Abrahams argued that $\sigma \upsilon \mu \pi \acute{o} \sigma \iota o \nu$ ("banquet") is equivalent to "the Talmudic shura (שׁורה) row" (*Studies in Pharisaism*, 2:210–11).

31 See "Cultural Contexts" above.

32 BAGD, s.v.

33 Text and trans. from García Martínez and Tigchelaar, *Dead Sea Scrolls*, 1:570–71. The pattern of organization probably comes from Exod 18:21, 25; Deut 1:15.

2).[34] This passage suggests that the eschatological community, living already in the last days, was to be organized in groups of thousands, hundreds, fifties, and tens while they were awaiting the messiah(s). The mention of groups of hundreds and fifties in v. 40 may be a hint that the crowd around Jesus represents and anticipates the eschatological community.

Immediately following the rule of the assembly of the camps is the rule of the Inspector of the camp (המבקר למחנה):

He shall instruct the Many in the deeds of God, and shall teach them his mighty marvels, and recount to them the eternal events with <their explanations>. He shall have pity on them like a father on his sons, and will provide drink to all the <afflicted among them> like a shepherd his flock

> (ישכיל את הרבים במעשי אל ויבינם בגבורות פלאו
> ויספר לפניהם נהיות עולם בפרתיה [בפתריהם]
> וירחם עליהם כאב לבניו
> וישקה לכל מדהובם [מרהוב בם] כרועה עדרו).
> (CD 13:7-8)[35]

The similarities between this passage and the context of the feeding of the crowd in Mark 6 are striking. Like the Inspector, Jesus teaches the crowd (v. 34c) and has pity on them (v. 34b). The Inspector is to care for the Many as a shepherd his flock, which Jesus implicitly does in the Markan passage (v. 34b). These similarities reinforce the inference that the groups of hundreds and fifties in v. 40 draw upon scripture (Exod 18:21, 25; Deut 1:15) to speak about the eschatological community.

The *Rule of the Community* also depicts the community as organized in "thousands, hundreds, fifties, and tens" (לאלפים ומאות וחמשים ועשרות) so that each member may know his standing in God's community in conformity

with an eternal plan (1QS 2:21-23).[36] The *War Scroll* presupposes the restoration of the twelve tribes of Israel and links them to the organization of the army of Israel into thousands, hundreds, fifties, and tens (1QM [1Q33] 3:13—4:4). The *Rule of the Congregation* describes a gathering of the community with the messiah of Israel in which the seating arrangement seems to follow the same organization (1QSa 2:11-22).

■ **41** The action of Jesus taking the five loaves and two fish, looking up to heaven, praising God, breaking the loaves, and distributing the bread and the fish is the point at which the miracle takes place in a hidden and mysterious way. Theissen has argued that these gestures call to mind the early Christian ritual meal and thus indicate an allegorization of the miracle story.[37] But these gestures may have been typical of ordinary meals among Jews at the time.

The term used in Mark, Matthew, and Luke for Jesus' prayerful gesture is εὐλογεῖν ("to praise"), whereas John uses εὐχαριστεῖν ("to give thanks") (Matt 14:19; Luke 9:16; John 6:11).[38] The former is the Greek equivalent of the Hebrew ברך ("to bless" or "to praise"), which was probably the most commonly used term for prayer among Jews in the first century.[39] The latter is roughly equivalent to the Hebrew הודה ("to give thanks"). The latter is also the verb more commonly used in relation to early Christian ritual meals. At the same time, however, a prayer of praise or thanksgiving may have been said at the beginning of ordinary meals, both by Jews and Christians. The verb εὐχαριστεῖν ("to give thanks") is used in the Last Supper in Luke in relation to both the bread and the wine (22:17, 19), whereas it is used only in relation to the wine in Mark (14:23) and Matthew (26:27). In relation to the bread, both Mark (14:22) and Matthew (26:26) use εὐλογεῖν ("to praise").

The distribution of the bread and the fish among the people is the initial motif in the demonstration of the

---

34   Text and trans. from García Martínez and Tigchelaar, *Dead Sea Scrolls*, 1:570-71.

35   Text and trans. (modified) from García Martínez and Tigchelaar, *Dead Sea Scrolls*, 1:572-73.

36   Text and trans. from García Martínez and Tigchelaar, *Dead Sea Scrolls*, 1:72-73. The same organization appears in 1QSa (1Q28a) 1:14-15; 1:29—2:1.

37   Theissen suggested that the gift miracles were soon allegorized because they did not arise out of ordinary activity as other types of miracle stories did (*Miracle Stories*, 106).

38   Mark also uses εὐχαριστεῖν ("to give thanks") in the second feeding story (8:6).

39   Paul F. Bradshaw, *The Search for the Origins of Christian Worship: Sources and Methods for the Study of Early Liturgy* (New York/Oxford: Oxford University Press, 1992) 15-16.

miracle. That Jesus asks the disciples to distribute the bread is reminiscent of the story about Elisha and the twenty barley loaves, in which Elisha asks his servant to serve the bread to the people.[40]

■ **42-44** The statement that they all ate and were satisfied is the climactic moment in the demonstration of the miracle. The miracle itself is not described. It can only be inferred from its consequences.[41]

As noted above, one set of important intertexts for this miracle story involves the theme of the feeding of the people of Israel in the wilderness with manna and quails.[42] The presentation of this theme in Psalm 78 has an important similarity with v. 42, which reads, "And they all ate and were satisfied" (καὶ ἔφαγον πάντες καὶ ἐχορτάσθησαν). Psalm 78 is a didactic psalm that instructs the people on the basis of Israel's history.[43] The account of the gift of manna includes the following statement: "and they ate and were filled exceedingly, and he brought them their desire" (καὶ ἐφάγοσαν καὶ ἐνεπλή-σθησαν σφόδρα, καὶ τὴν ἐπιθυμίαν αὐτῶν ἤνεγκεν αὐτοῖς) (Ps 78:29 [77:29 LXX]). The word πάντες ("all") in v. 42 emphasizes the greatness of the miracle. It prepares for the revelation of the number of those who ate in v. 44. The use of the word χορτάζειν ("to satisfy"), rather than ἐμπιμπλάναι ("to fill quite full"), indicates the modest nature of the banquet hosted by Jesus. The expression "they ate and were filled exceedingly" (καὶ ἐφάγοσαν καὶ ἐνεπλήσθησαν σφόδρα) prepares for the criticism of the people's attitude in the following verses of the psalm.

In v. 43, the phrase δώδεκα κοφίνων πληρώματα (lit., "fullnesses of twelve baskets") is in apposition to ἦραν κλάσματα ("they picked up pieces").[44] The twelve baskets full of leftovers stand in stark contrast to the five loaves and two fish mentioned in vv. 38 and 41. The depiction of the huge amount of leftover pieces elaborates the demonstration of the miracle. The large remainder verifies that all the people were completely satisfied and indicates the greatness of Jesus' power. It is also reminiscent of the motif of abundance in the tradition of the eschatological banquet.[45] For those members of the audience who recognized in the groups of v. 40 an allusion to the organization of the eschatological community, the fact that the leftover pieces filled twelve baskets would probably recall the hope for the restoration of the twelve tribes in the time of fulfillment.[46]

The denouement of the story is the statement that those who had eaten the loaves were five thousand men (v. 44). The audience has known so far that those fed constituted a large crowd (v. 34), but no number had been given. This great number once again enhances the effect of the miracle and indicates the extraordinary power of Jesus.[47] The effect is heightened also by the fact that only the men are counted; if the women and children were counted, the number would be even greater. That only the men are counted here may owe something to the tradition that a census included only those males about to go to war (Num 1:2, 20). Given the patriarchal organization of society, the groups of "thousands, hundreds, fifties, and tens" in the *Damascus Document* and the *Rule of the Congregation* were probably enumerated only in terms of the men.[48]

The History of the Tradition of 6:45-52

As Paul Achtemeier has argued, the story about Jesus walking on the water was the first miracle story in the second of two collections used by the author of Mark. The hypothesis that it was followed by the healing of the blind man at Bethsaida is supported by the fact that in v. 45 Jesus proposes that they go to Bethsaida, but they arrive in Gennesaret in v. 53. They arrive in Bethsaida only in 8:22.[49] The motivation for Jesus' compelling the disciples to embark without him is double: he stayed

---

40 See "Cultural Contexts" above.
41 Theissen points out that gift miracles lack central motifs because the miraculous event itself is unobtrusive. This type of miracle therefore has the stress on the demonstration (*Miracle Stories*, 105).
42 See "Cultural Contexts" above.
43 Mitchell Dahood, *Psalms II: 51–100: Introduction, Translation, and Notes* (AB 17; Garden City, NY: Doubleday, 1968) 238.
44 Swete, ad loc.

45 See "Cultural Contexts" above.
46 See the commentary on 3:14-15 above.
47 The possibly deliberate outdoing of Elisha was mentioned above; see "Cultural Contexts."
48 See the commentary on v. 40 above. The *Rule of the Community*, however, probably applied only to the group living near the site of Qumran, which likely included only men.
49 Achtemeier, "Miracle Catenae," 281–84.

behind to dismiss the crowd (v. 45) and he wanted to be alone to pray (v. 46). The first motivation, "while he himself dismissed the crowd" (ἕως αὐτὸς ἀπολύει τὸν ὄχλον), is probably editorial. It is the means by which the evangelist connected this story to the account of the feeding of the five thousand.[50] The latter story was the last in the first collection.[51] The second motivation, "he went away to the mountain to pray" (ἀπῆλθεν εἰς τὸ ὄρος προσεύξασθαι), is pre-Markan.[52] Thus the participial phrase in v. 46, "having said farewell to them" (ἀποταξάμενος αὐτοῖς), referred originally to Jesus' saying farewell to the disciples, not to his dismissal of the crowd.[53] Verse 52 is also redactional since it develops the Markan theme of the misunderstanding of the disciples.[54] There is no compelling evidence of editorial activity in vv. 46-51.[55]

The form critics argued that the miracle stories were oral compositions designed to evoke interest in Jesus and to attract new members of the movement. Bultmann was inclined to exclude the possibility of the influence of older texts on this oral process. Literary factors no doubt, however, came into play when the stories were written down in collections and even more so when they were incorporated into the Gospels.[56]

The Genre of 6:45-52

Bultmann classifed this story as a nature miracle. He concluded that it is not a variant on the stilling of the storm. Rather, Jesus' walking on the water is the original motif, and the element of the storm was added secondarily, on the basis of 4:37-41.[57] He also noted the possibility that the story was originally a resurrection appearance, but concluded that certainty on this point was unobtainable.[58] Dibelius classified this story as a *Novelle* ("Tale").[59] He argued that the intention of the story is to present an epiphany of Jesus. He found support for this view in the detail that Jesus did not want to enter the boat, but wanted simply to reveal his nature to the disciples by walking on the water. This is the reason for the statement "he wanted to pass by them" (ἤθελεν παρελθεῖν αὐτούς).[60] Theissen defined it as a "soteriological epiphany" in his synchronic catalogue of themes.[61] The typical motifs that make up this theme are the extraordinary visual phenomenon, the "ghost" (φάντασμα) of v. 49; the withdrawal of the god, "(he wanted) to pass by (them)" (παρελθεῖν) in v. 48; the word of revelation, "It is I" (ἐγώ εἰμι) in v. 50; and the numinous amazement of the disciples. The disciples' perception that they saw a "ghost" (φάντασμα), however, is mistaken. The extraordinary visual phenomenon is that they see Jesus "walking on the sea" (περιπατῶν ἐπὶ τῆς θαλάσσης). The account is an epiphany, but the emphasis is on the manifestation of divine power in a miracle, rather than on the revelation of the person of the deity.[62] Theissen also concluded that an original epiphany on the water may have attracted motifs from a rescue story.[63]

Once the Markan editorial contributions are identified, the pre-Markan form of the story emerges as a complex one with more than one important theme. The relations among these themes can no longer be illuminated by diachronic analysis. The significant themes of

---

50 Bultmann, *History*, 216. The crowd of v. 45 is the same as that of v. 34.
51 Achtemeier, "Miracle Catenae," 276, 282, 291.
52 Bultmann, *History*, 216.
53 Achtemeier, "Miracle Catenae," 283.
54 Ibid., 282–83.
55 Adela Yarbro Collins, "Rulers, Divine Men, and Walking on the Water (Mark 6:45-52)," in Lukas Bormann, Kelly Del Tredici, and Angela Standhartinger, eds., *Religious Propaganda and Missionary Competition in the New Testament World: Essays Honoring Dieter Georgi* (NovTSup 74; Leiden/New York: Brill, 1994) 208.
56 Bultmann, *History*, 230; on the role of literary factors, see Yarbro Collins, "Rulers, Divine Men," 212.
57 Bultmann, *History*, 216.
58 Ibid., 230.
59 Dibelius, *From Tradition to Gospel*, 71.
60 Ibid., 95. Dibelius concluded that the epiphany motif is due to non-Christian influence (ibid., 100).
61 Theissen, *Miracle Stories*, 97.
62 According to H. S. Versnel, Greeks and Romans believed that "the presence of the god could find expression in other forms than personal manifestations" and one of these was the miracle that proves the arrival or presence (*parousia*) of the god ("What Did Ancient Man See," 52). So also Martin Dibelius and Hans Conzelmann, excursus "'Epiphany' in the Pastoral Epistles," in *The Pastoral Epistles: A Commentary on the Pastoral Epistles* (Hermeneia; Philadelphia: Fortress, 1972) 104. Cf. Yarbro Collins, "Rulers, Divine Men," 210.
63 Theissen, *Miracle Stories*, 186.

this story are Jesus' performance of a superhuman or divine deed—walking on the surface of the water; the assistance Jesus gives the disciples by overcoming the contrary wind (this theme has affinities with the theme of the storm); and the divine epiphany (this theme has affinities with the resurrection-appearance story).[64]

Cultural Contexts

The most distinctive and characteristic theme of this story is the extraordinary deed of walking on the sea.[65] As was the case with the feeding of the five thousand, this narrative has affinities with biblical, Jewish, Greek, and Roman traditions. The ability to control the sea is an important element in the portrayal of the God of Israel in both prose and poetry in the Hebrew Bible.[66]

In Greek tradition, Poseidon is the god of the sea rather than its opponent, as the God of Israel was portrayed. But like the God of Israel, Poseidon was depicted as having control over the sea. He is portrayed in epic poetry as traveling in his chariot along the surface of the sea:

Thither came [Poseidon], and let harness beneath his car his two bronze-hooved horses, swift of flight, with flowing manes of gold; and with gold he clad himself about his body, and grasped the well-wrought whip of gold, and stepped upon his car, and set out to drive over the waves. Then gamboled the sea-beasts beneath him on every side from out the deeps, for well they knew their lord, and in gladness the sea parted before him; right swiftly sped they on, and the axle of bronze was not wetted beneath; and unto the ships of the Achaeans did the prancing steeds bear their lord

(ἔνθ᾽ ἐλθὼν ὑπ᾽ ὄχεσφι τιτύσκετο χαλκόποδ᾽ ἵππω, ὠκυπέτα, χρυσέῃσιν ἐθείρῃσιν κομόωντε,

χρυσὸν δ᾽ αὐτὸς ἔδυνε περὶ χροΐ, γέντο δ᾽ ἱμάσθλην χρυσείην εὔτυκτον, ἑοῦ δ᾽ ἐπιβήσετο δίφρου, βῆ δ᾽ ἐλάαν ἐπὶ κύματ᾽· ἄταλλε δὲ κήτε᾽ ὑπ᾽ αὐτοῦ πάντοθεν ἐκ κευθμῶν, οὐδ᾽ ἠγνοίησεν ἄνακτα· γηθοσύνῃ δὲ θάλασσα διίστατο· τοὶ δὲ πέτοντο ῥίμφα μάλ᾽, οὐδ᾽ ὑπένερθε διαίνετο χάλκεος ἄξων, τὸν δ᾽ ἐς Ἀχαιῶν νῆας ἐΰσκαρθμοι φέρον ἵπποι).
(Homer Il. 13.23-31)[67]

In Roman tradition, Neptune is portrayed in a similar way. In the *Aeneid*, Neptune says to Venus:

Then Saturn's son, lord of the deep sea, spake thus: "You have every right, O Cytherean, to put trust in this, my realm, whence you draw birth. This, too, I have earned; often have I checked the fury and mighty rage of sea and sky"

(tum Saturnius haec domitor maris edidit alti: "fas omne est, Cytherea, meis te fidere regnis, unde genus ducis. merui quoque; saepe furores compressi et rabiem tantam caelique marisque").
(Virgil Aen. 5.799-802)[68]

After he has reassured the goddess, Neptune departs in this fashion:

When with these words he had soothed to gladness the goddess' heart, the Sire yokes his wild steeds with gold, fastens their foaming bits, and lets all the reins stream freely in his hand; then over the water's surface lightly he flies in azure car. The waves sink to rest, beneath the thundering axle the sea of swollen waters is smoothed, and the storm-clouds vanish from the wide sky

---

64   Yarbro Collins, "Rulers, Divine Men," 211.
65   For a comprehensive study of this motif in ancient literature, see Wendy Cotter, "The Markan Sea Miracles: Their History, Formation and Function" (Ph.D. diss., University of St. Michael's College, 1991). I am indebted to her fine research.
66   Yarbro Collins, "Rulers, Divine Men," 212–13.
67   Text and trans. from Augustus T. Murray, *Homer: The Iliad* (2 vols.; LCL; Cambridge, MA: Harvard

University Press; London: Heinemann, 1924–25) 2:4–5.
68   Text and trans. (modified) from H. Rushton Fairclough, *Virgil* (2 vols.; LCL; Cambridge, MA: Harvard University Press; London: Heinemann, 1974) 1:498–99.

(his ubi laeta deae permulsit pectora dictis,
iungit equos auro Genitor spumantiaque addit
frena feris manibusque omnis effundit habenas.
caeruleo per summa levis volat aequra curru;
subsidunt undae tumidumque sub axe tonanti
sternitur aequor acquis; fugiunt vasto aethere nimbi).
(Virgil *Aen.* 5.816-21)[69]

Jewish, Greek, and Roman traditions thus all included a portrayal of a deity controlling wind and sea and making a path through the sea.

In both Jewish and Greek traditions, a deity gives power over the sea or rivers to certain human beings. According to the book of Exodus (14:21-29), the Lord gave Moses power to divide the sea, so that the people of Israel might go on dry ground through the sea, and then to bring the water back upon the Egyptians.[70] The book of Joshua (3:7—4:18) narrates how God enabled Joshua to divide the waters of the Jordan River in a similar way so that the people would know that he was the authoritative successor to Moses. The power of Elijah is depicted in more autonomous terms, like that of Jesus. Elijah divided the waters of the Jordan, so that he and Elisha could cross over on dry ground, simply by rolling up his cloak and striking the river with it (2 Kgs 2:8). After Elijah is taken up, Elisha takes the cloak of Elijah, strikes the Jordan with it, and calls upon the God of Elijah. The subsequently narrated event, that the waters parted and Elisha crossed over on dry ground, portrays Elisha as the authoritative successor to Elijah (2 Kgs 2:14).[71]

Greek tradition also includes the endowment of human beings with power over the sea.[72] Typically, it is the sons of Poseidon by human mothers who have such power. According to an ancient commentary on Pindar's *Pythian Odes*, the hero Euphemus was given the ability to pass across the sea unharmed, as across land (τὴν θάλασσαν ἀπημάντως διαπορεύεσθαι ὡς διὰ γῆς).[73] This tradition is attributed to Asclepiades.[74] If the Asclepiades in question is Asclepiades of Tragilus, the tradition could be as old as the fourth century BCE.[75] If he is Asclepiades of Myrleia in Bithynia, it could be dated to the first century BCE.[76] In any case, a similar tradition is attested in the third century BCE by Apollonius of Rhodes, who lists Euphemus of Taenarum, whom Europa bore to Poseidon, among the heroes who went in quest of the Golden Fleece:

He was wont to skim the swell of the grey sea, and wetted not his swift feet, but just dipping the tips of his toes was borne on the watery path

(κεῖνος ἀνὴρ καὶ πόντου ἐπὶ γλαυκοῖο θέεσκεν οἴδματος, οὐδὲ θοοὺς βάπτεν πόδας, ἀλλ᾽ ὅσον ἄκροις ἴχνεσι τεγγόμενος διερῇ πεφόρητο κελεύθῳ). (Apollonius Rhodius *Argonautica* 1.182-84)[77]

Apollodorus preserved the following traditions about Orion:

And Artemis slew Orion in Delos. They say that he was of gigantic stature and born of the earth; but Pherecydes says that he was a son of Poseidon and Euryale. Poseidon bestowed on him the power of striding across the sea (Ὠρίωνα δὲ Ἄρτεμις ἀπέκτεινεν ἐν Δήλῳ. τοῦτον γηγενῆ λέγουσιν

---

69 Text and trans. from Fairclough, *Virgil*, 1:500–501.
70 Blackburn, *Theios Anēr*, 146.
71 Cf. A. M. Denis, "Jesus Walking on the Water," *Louvain Studies* 1 (1967) 292.
72 See the discussion in Blackburn, *Theios Anēr*, 145–47.
73 Greek text from A. B. Drachmann, ed., *Scholia Vetera in Pindari Carmina*, vol. 2: *Scholia in Pythionicas* (Leipzig: Teubner, 1910; reprinted, Amsterdam: Hakkert, 1967) 106.
74 The tradition cited above with almost identical wording is cited by Tzetzes in the twelfth century and attributed to Asclepiades in a *scholium* on Lycophron's *Alexandra* 886; see Eduard Scheer, ed.,

Lycophronis Alexandra, vol. 2: *Scholia continens* (Berlin: Weidmann, 1908) 287.
75 Ken Dowden, "Asclepiades (1)," *OCD* 187.
76 P. B. R. Forbes and K. S. Sachs, "Asclepiades (4)," *OCD* 187.
77 Text and trans. from R. C. Seaton, *Apollonius Rhodius: The Argonautica* (LCL; Cambridge, MA: Harvard University Press; London: Heinemann, 1912) 14–15. A similar tradition occurs in Hyginus *Fabulae* 14.15; see Yarbro Collins, "Rulers, Divine Men," 216 n. 32.

ὑπερμεγέθη τὸ σῶμα· Φερεκύδης δὲ αὐτὸν Ποσειδῶνος καὶ Εὐρυάλης λέγει. ἐδωρήσατο δὲ αὐτῷ
Ποσειδῶν διαβαίνειν τὴν θάλασσαν). (*Library*
1.4.3)[78]

A work called *Astronomy* or *Astrology* was attributed to
Hesiod. The surviving fragments indicate that it
described the principal constellations, their dates of
rising and setting, and the legends connected with
them.[79] One of these fragments concerns Orion:

Hesiod says that he was the son of Euryale, the daughter of Minos, and of Poseidon, and that there was
given to him as a gift the power of walking upon the
waves as though upon land

(τοῦτον Ἡσίοδός φησιν Εὐρυάλης τῆς Μίνωος καὶ
Ποσειδῶνος εἶναι, δοθῆναι δὲ αὐτῷ δωρεὰν ὥστε
ἐπὶ τῶν κυμάτων πορεύεσθαι καθάπερ ἐπὶ τῆς
γῆς).[80]

These sons of Poseidon are granted power in a way analogous to the working of the Lord through Moses and
Joshua.

The more autonomous power of Elijah has its analogue in traditions about Heracles. In Seneca's tragedy,
Hercules furens, Heracles' wife, Megara, and his reputed
father, Amphitryon, hope for his return from the underworld, where he has been sent to bring Cerberus to the
upper world; this task is the last of his twelve labors.
Megara asks what way he has to the upper air. Amphitryon replies:

The same he had when across the parched desert and
the sands, billowing like the stormy sea, he made his

way, and across the strait with twice-receding, twice-
returning waves; and when, his barque abandoned, he
was stranded, a prisoner on Syrtes' shoals, and,
though his vessel was held fast, he crossed o'er seas on
foot

(Quam tunc habebat cum per arentem plagam
et fluctuantes more turbati maris
adit harenas bisque discedens fretum
et bis recurrens, cumque deserta rate
deprensus haesit Syrtium brevibus vadis
et puppe fixa maria superavit pedes). (Seneca *Hercules
furens* 319-24)[81]

At least by the fifth cent. BCE, power over the sea
began to be associated with rulers and kings.[82] After
Xerxes had successfully bridged the Hellespont and his
army had crossed over it during seven days and seven
nights, a story circulated that Herodotus reports:

Having passed over to Europe, Xerxes viewed his
army crossing under the lash; seven days and seven
nights it was in crossing, with never a rest. There is a
tale that, when Xerxes had now crossed the Hellespont, a man of the Hellespont cried, "O Zeus, why
have you taken the likeness of a Persian man and
changed your name to Xerxes, leading the whole
world with you to remove Hellas from its place? For
that you could have done without these means"
(Ξέρξης δὲ ἐπεὶ διέβη ἐς τὴν Εὐρώπην, ἐθηεῖτο
τὸν στρατὸν ὑπὸ μαστίγων διαβαίνοντα· διέβη δὲ
ὁ στρατὸς αὐτοῦ ἐν ἑπτὰ ἡμέρῃσι καὶ ἐν ἑπτὰ
εὐφρόνῃσι, ἐλινύσας οὐδένα χρόνον. ἐνθαῦτα
λέγεται, Ξέρξεω ἤδη διαβεβηκότος τὸν Ἑλλήσποντον, ἄνδρα εἰπεῖν Ἑλλησπόντιον "Ὦ Ζεῦ, τί

---

78 Text and trans. from James George Frazer, *Apol-
    lodorus: The Library* (2 vols.; LCL; Cambridge, MA:
    Harvard University Press; London: Heinemann,
    1921) 1:30–31.
79 See Hugh Evelyn-White, *Hesiod, the Homeric Hymns
    and Homerica* (rev. ed.; Cambridge, MA: Harvard
    University Press; London: Heinemann, 1936) xix–xx.
80 Pseudo-Eratosthenes *Catasterismi* frg. 32 = (pseudo-)
    Hesiod *Astronomy* 4; text and trans. from Evelyn-
    White, *Hesiod*, 70–71.
81 Text and trans. from Frank Justus Miller, *Seneca* (10

vols.; LCL; Cambridge, MA: Harvard University
Press; London: Heinemann, 1917) 8:28–29. The
emperor Julian, in the fourth cent., wrote that it was
his belief that Heracles walked on the sea as though
it were dry land; see Yarbro Collins, "Rulers, Divine
Men," 218.
82 Cotter, "Markan Sea Miracles," 298–322.

δὴ ἀνδρὶ εἰδόμενος Πέρσῃ καὶ οὔνομα ἀντὶ Διὸς Ξέρξην θέμενος ἀνάστατον τὴν Ἑλλάδα θέλεις ποιῆσαι, ἄγων πάντας ἀνθρώπους· καὶ γὰρ ἄνευ τούτων ἐξῆν τοι ποιέειν ταῦτα"). (7.56)[83]

Xerxes' feat, in mythical form, was well known in the Roman imperial period in the East. In his third discourse on kingship, probably delivered in the presence of Trajan in 104 CE, Dio Chrysostom presented the views of Socrates in dialogue form and had his interrogator say:

"Socrates," said he, "you know perfectly well that of all men under the sun that man is most powerful and in might no whit inferior to the gods themselves who is able to accomplish the seemingly impossible—if it should be his will, to have men walk dryshod over the sea, to sail over the mountains, to drain rivers dry by drinking—or have you not heard that Xerxes, the king of the Persians, made of the dry land a sea by cutting through the loftiest of the mountains and separating Athos from the mainland, and that he led his infantry through the sea, riding upon a chariot just like Poseidon in Homer's description? And perhaps in the same way the dolphins and the monsters of the deep swam under his raft as the king drove along" (Ὦ Σώκρατες, ἔφη, τοῦτο μὲν ἐπίστασαι παντὸς μᾶλλον, ὅτι τῶν ὑπὸ τὸν ἥλιον ἀνθρώπων ἐκεῖνός ἐστιν ἰσχυρότατος καὶ μηδὲ τῶν θεῶν αὐτῶν ἥττονα ἔχων δύναμιν, ᾧ γε ἔνεστι καὶ τὰ ἀδύνατα δοκοῦντα ποιῆσαι δυνατά, εἰ βούλοιτο, πεζεύεσθαι μὲν τὴν θάλατταν, πλεῖσθαι δὲ τὰ ὄρη, τοὺς δὲ ποταμοὺς ἐκλείπειν ὑπὸ ἀνθρώπων πινομένους. ἢ οὐκ ἀκήκοας ὅτι Ξέρξης ὁ τῶν Περσῶν βασιλεὺς τὴν μὲν γῆν ἐποίησε θάλατταν, διελὼν τὸ μέγιστον τῶν ὁρῶν καὶ διαστήσας ἀπὸ τῆς ἠπείρου τὸν Ἄθω, διὰ δὲ τῆς θαλάττης τὸν πεζὸν στρατὸν ἄγων ἤλαυνεν ἐφ᾽ ἅρματος, ὥσπερ τὸν Ποσειδωνά φησιν Ὅμερος; καὶ τυχὸν ὁμοίως οἵ τε δελφῖνες καὶ τὰ κήτη κάτωθεν ὑπέπλει τὴν σχεδίαν, ὁπότε ἐκεῖνος ἤλαυνε). (Dio Chrysostom 3.30-31)[84]

Dio has Socrates reject this point of view, but the passage may be evidence that it was held by a sufficient number of people to require refutation.

Alexander was reputed to have similar power.[85] Menander, the Attic poet of the New Comedy, satirized this view of Alexander:

How very Alexander-like is this forthwith: "If I require someone's presence, of his own accord he will appear! And if, forsooth, I needs must tread some pathway through the sea, then it will give me footing!" (ὡς Ἀλεξανδρῶδες ἤδη τοῦτο· κἂν ζητῶ τινα, αὐτόματος οὗτος παρέσται· κἂν διελθεῖν δηλαδὴ διὰ θαλάττης δὴ πόρον τιν᾽, οὗτος ἔσται μοι βατός). (Menander frg. 924K)[86]

The target of the satire may well be those who are willing to attribute such powers to rulers, as well as the attitudes of the rulers themselves.

These passages from Dio and Menander show that the motif of walking on water had become proverbial for the (humanly) impossible and for the arrogance of the ruler aspiring to empire.[87] It appears in 2 Maccabees, a Hellenistic-Jewish text dating to the early first century BCE, characterizing the arrogance of Antiochus IV Epiphanes:

Then Antiochus departed for Antioch rather quickly, carrying off eight hundred talents from the temple in addition to the thousand, supposing arrogantly that he could make the land navigable and the sea passable (as if it were land), on account of the vain imagining of his heart (Ὁ γοῦν Ἀντίοχος ὀκτακόσια πρὸς τοῖς χιλίοις ἀπενεγκάμενος ἐκ τοῦ ἱεροῦ τάλαντα θᾶττον εἰς τὴν Ἀντιόχειαν ἐχωρίσθη οἰόμενος ἀπὸ τῆς ὑπερηφανίας τὴν μὲν γῆν πλωτὴν καὶ τὸ πέλαγος πορευτὸν θέσθαι διὰ τὸν μετεωρισμὸν τῆς καρδίας). (5:21 LXX)

This passage shows that, in a Hellenistic-Jewish cultural context, the idea of walking on water was associated with the arrogance of rulers who claimed to be divine.

---

83 Text and trans. (modified) from A. D. Godley, *Herodotus* (4 vols.; LCL; Cambridge, MA: Harvard University Press; London: Heinemann, 1922) 3:370–71.

84 Text and trans. from James W. Cohoon, *Dio Chrysostom* (5 vols.; LCL; London: Heinemann; Cambridge, MA: Harvard University Press, 1932) 1:116–19.

85 Cotter, "Markan Sea Miracles," 303–9.

86 Text and trans. from Francis G. Allinson, *Menander: The Principal Fragments* (LCL; Cambridge, MA: Harvard University Press; London: Heinemann, 1921) 532–33.

87 See further Cotter's discussion of Roman rulers of the first cent. CE ("Markan Sea Miracles," 312–22).

Probably in deliberate defiance of the proverbial impossibility of walking on water, the motif appears in magical and related texts as something that the properly trained or instructed person can accomplish. A text included in the Greek Magical Papyri, dating to the second or third century CE, that may be part of an ancient novel, contains the following statement:

> . . . [the sun] will stand still; and should I order the moon, it will come down; and should I wish to delay the day, the night will remain for me; and should we in turn ask for day, the light will not depart; and should I wish to sail the sea, I do not need a ship; and should I wish to go through the air, I will be lifted up. It is only an erotic drug that I do not find, not one that can cause, not one that can stop love. For the earth, in fear of the god, does not produce one (. . . στήσεται, κἂν σελήνη κελεύσω, καταβήσεται, κἂν κωλῦσαι θελ[ή]σω τὴν ἡμέραν, ἡ νύξ μοι μενεῖ, κἂν δεηθῶμεν πάλιν ἡμέρας, τὸ φῶς οὐκ ἀπελεύσεται, κἂν πλεῦσαι θελήσω τὴν θάλατταν, οὐ δέομαι νεώς, κἂν δι᾽ ἀέρος ἐλθεῖν, κουφισθή-σομ[α]ι. ἐρωτικὸν μόνον οὐχ εὑρίσκω φάρμακον, οὐ ποιῆσαι δυνάμενον, οὐ παῦσαι δυνάμενον· ἡ γῆ γάρ, φοβουμένη τὸν θεόν, οὐ φέρει). (PGM XXXIV 1–15)[88]

Certain Jewish magical texts provide instructions for walking on water.[89]

The motif of walking on water is also associated with dreams. According to Dio Chrysostom, the book "On Dreams" (Ὀνείρασιν) by a certain Horus listed experiences that people have in dreams, for example:

> and at times, possibly, flying offhand or walking on the sea. For this reason one might well call Homer's poetry a kind of dream, obscure and vague at that (καὶ οὕτως, εἰ τύχοι ποτέ, πέτεσθαι καὶ βαδίζειν ἐπὶ τῆς θαλάττης ὥστε καὶ τὴν Ὁμήρου ποίησιν

ὀρθῶς ἄν τινα εἰπεῖν ἐνύπιον, καὶ τοῦτο ἄκριτον καὶ ἀσαφές). (Dio Chrysostom 11.129)[90]

Here the motif represents not only what is humanly impossible but also the wild and unrealistic type of thing that one sometimes dreams. According to Artemidorus of Daldis in Lydia, a professional interpreter of dreams, the meaning of an unexpected and allegorical dream of walking on the sea depends on the gender, legal status, social location, and particular circumstances of the dreamer. For comparison with Jesus, the following is the most important example:

> On the other hand, for all those who earn their living from crowds, for statesmen, and popular leaders, (the dream of walking on the sea) prophesies extraordinary gain together with great fame. For the sea also resembles a crowd because of its instability (πᾶσι δὲ τοῖς ἐξ ὄχλου ποριζομένοις καὶ πολιτευταῖς καὶ δημαγωγοῖς μετὰ πολλῆς εὐκλείας πορισμὸν οὐ τὸν τυχόντα προαγορεύει· ἔοικε γὰρ καὶ ὄχλῳ ἡ θάλασσα διὰ τὴν ἀταξίαν). (Artemidorus Oneiro-critica 3.16)[91]

This passage reinforces the traditional link between rulers and the motif of walking on the sea and suggests that the deed symbolizes the power of the ruler.[92]

The creation of the account in Mark 6:45-52 was an act of early Christian *mythopoiesis*, the construction of an incident in the life of Jesus that was intended to honor him and to win adherents to his cause. Whether the story was originally intended to represent an actual event or was consciously composed as a symbolic or allegorical narrative is impossible to determine. It is likely that some in the audience of Mark took it literally and others symbolically or allegorically.[93]

As indicated above, the motif of walking on the sea or on water was known in Greek, Roman, biblical, and Jewish tradition. The members of the Christian communities in which Mark was read probably came from diverse

---

88 Preisendanz-Henrichs, 2:159; trans. by E. N. O'Neil in Betz, *Magical Papyri*, 267.

89 Yarbro Collins, "Rulers, Divine Men," 221.

90 Text and trans. from Cohoon, *Dio Chrysostom*, 1:544–45.

91 Text from Roger A. Pack, *Artemidori Daldiani: Oniro-criticon Libri V* (ASGB; BSGRT; Leipzig: Teubner,

1963) 211; trans. from Robert J. White, *The Interpretation of Dreams: Oneirocritica by Artemidorus* (Noyes Classical Studies; Park Ridge, NJ: Noyes Press, 1975) 162.

92 For a different interpretation of Artemidorus 3.16, see Cotter, "Markan Sea Miracles," 336–40.

93 Note that Clearchus of Soli, a student of Aristotle,

backgrounds. Those Jewish by birth and well instructed in biblical and Jewish tradition were likely to understand the account of Jesus walking on the Sea of Galilee in terms of Jewish cultural heroes and prophets. The fact that it is God alone in the Hebrew Bible who is said to walk on water, in addition to the theophanic elements in vv. 45-52, makes it likely that such members of the audience of Mark would have understood that the passage implies the divinity of Jesus.[94] The motif of a human or semi-divine being walking on water, however, is considerably more widespread in Greek and Roman tradition than in Jewish circles. This currency makes it likely that Gentile Christians, or anyone familiar with such traditions, would associate this story with Greek and Roman backgrounds, even if they had been instructed in the biblical and Jewish analogies.

The most probable focal point for a fusion of traditions is the messianic character attributed to Jesus. In certain Jewish circles, especially apocalyptic ones, the messiah was expected to assume some of the functions normally reserved to God.[95] Such assimilation of the messiah to God would provide a context for the attribution to Jesus of God's power to walk upon the sea. The association of the motif with rulers in Greek and Roman tradition would make the presentation of Jesus as messiah (king of Israel) intelligible to Greek and Roman Gentile members of the audience of Mark. The philosophical discussions of true kingship, for instance, in the discourses of Dio Chrysostom, would facilitate the acceptance of Jesus as a king, in spite of his lack of literal political power.

Comment

■ **45-46** As noted above, the pre-Markan form of this account portrayed Jesus as compelling his disciples to go on without him in the boat because he wanted to go up alone to the mountain to pray.[96] The goal to which Jesus directed them, Bethsaida, was also in the source, a pre-Markan collection of miracle stories, in which the healing of the blind man in Bethsaida followed this one. Mark's rearrangement of the stories explains why Jesus and the disciples arrive in Gennesaret in v. 53, rather than in Bethsaida.[97] The secondary motivation for Jesus' staying behind, "while he himself dismissed the crowd" (ἕως αὐτὸς ἀπολύει τὸν ὄχλον), is probably an editorial link between this miracle-story and the previous one, the multiplication of the loaves, which the author found in a different source.

■ **47-48** According to v. 47, when evening came, the period between late afternoon and darkness, the boat carrying the disciples was in the middle of the Sea of Galilee, while Jesus remained alone on the land.[98] The reference to "the fourth watch of the night" (τετάρτη φυλακή) in v. 48 reflects the Roman custom of dividing the night, roughly the period between 6:00 P.M. and 6:00 A.M., into four equal periods of time or watches, in which different people would be responsible for security.[99] The fourth watch would then be a period of time extending more or less from 3:00 A.M. to 6:00 A.M. Because of the darkness and the distance, Jesus' ability to see the disciples, even if he were on a mountain, is extraordinary.

The depiction of the disciples as "impeded in their progress, for the wind was against them" (βασανιζομένους ἐν τῷ ἐλαύνειν, ἦν γὰρ ὁ ἄνεμος ἐναντίος αὐτοῖς) has led many commentators to infer that the situation involved a storm.[100] Describing the situation as a storm seems to be an overstatement. The issue is rather whether they will be able to arrive at their intended destination.[101] It is difficult, however, to infer in what direction they were attempting to sail, since it is not clear where the multiplication of the loaves took place.[102]

---

    compared miracle stories to dreams; cited by Hengel, *Judaism and Hellenism*, 1:257.

94   Cf. the discussion in Adela Yarbro Collins, "The 'Son of Man' Tradition and the Book of Revelation," in James H. Charlesworth, ed., *The Messiah: Developments in Earliest Judaism and Christianity* (Minneapolis: Fortress, 1992) 536–68; reprinted in Yarbro Collins, *Cosmology and Eschatology*, 159–97; Blackburn, *Theios Anēr*, 145–82.

95   Collins, *Daniel*, 72–89; Blackburn, *Theios Anēr*, 171–73.

96   See "The History of the Tradition of 6:45-52" above.

97   Cf. 8:22-26; see "The History of the Tradition of 6:45-52" above.

98   Swete argued that ὀψία ("evening") here refers to the early hours of the night, as it does in 14:17 (ad loc.).

99   BAGD, s.v. φυλακή.

100 See "The Genre of 6:45-52" above.

101 Cf. Gundry, 335.

102 See the commentary on v. 32 above.

Rather than implying that they were blown off course, however, the narrative seems to imply that they made no progress in several hours.[103]

On the premise that the disciples were in distress because of a storm and by analogy with 4:35-41, many commentators find it odd that Jesus "wanted to pass by them" (ἤθελεν παρελθεῖν αὐτούς). The narrative, however, may be read as implying that the disciples' progress was restrained by divine power in order that Jesus might be manifested to them in a way that revealed his role as a divine messiah.[104] Compare the theophany to Moses: "And the Lord came down in a cloud, and he approached him there, and he proclaimed the name of the Lord. And the Lord passed by before his face" (καὶ κατέβη κύριος ἐν νεφέλῃ, καὶ παρέστη αὐτῷ ἐκεῖ, καὶ ἐκάλεσεν τῷ ὀνόματι κυρίου. καὶ παρῆλθεν κύριος πρὸ προσώπου αὐτοῦ) (Exod 34:5-6 LXX).[105] The theophany to Elijah also uses language of the deity "passing by" (παρελθεῖν): "And he said, 'You will go out tomorrow and stand before the Lord on the mountain; see, the Lord will pass by'" (καὶ εἶπεν Ἐξελεύσῃ αὔριον καὶ στήσῃ ἐνώπιον κυρίου ἐν τῷ ὄρει· ἰδοὺ παρελεύσεται κύριος) (3 Kgdms 19:11 LXX). The language of "passing by" suggests that Jesus appears to his disciples in a way analogous to the appearance of God to Moses and Elijah.

Jesus' depiction as "walking on the sea" (περιπατῶν ἐπὶ τῆς θαλάσσης) reveals that he is the agent of God who can perform deeds like those of the God of the Hebrew Bible. It also suggests that he is a king who, by divine power, can walk on water, unlike arrogant rulers who only vainly imagine that they can.[106]

■ **49-50** The disciples' reaction, thinking that they were seeing a ghost (φάντασμα), emphasizes, in a narrative way, that ordinary human beings are not able to walk on the surface of water.[107] The disciples literally cannot believe their eyes. This response heightens both the miraculous and the epiphanic dimensions of the portrayal of Jesus. They also cry out, an expression of fear appropriate to the context in reaction to the manifestation of divine power. This reaction is elaborated in v. 50. It is emphasized that they all saw him, a detail perhaps intended to underline the reality of the event.[108] The reaction of the disciples is described again as terror, a typical response to an epiphany or divine revelation.[109]

Jesus speaks to them immediately to calm them and says, "Have courage! It is I; do not be afraid" (θαρσεῖτε, ἐγώ εἰμι· μὴ φοβεῖσθε). The first of these verbs occurs also in the account of the theophany on Mount Sinai:

And the whole people saw the sound (of the thunder) and the flashes of lightning and the sound of the trumpet and the mountain which was smoking. Since, then, the whole people were afraid, they stood far off. And they said to Moses, "You speak to us, and let God not speak to us, in order that we may not die." And Moses said to them, "Have courage!" (καὶ πᾶς ὁ λαὸς ἑώρα τὴν φωνὴν καὶ τὰς λαμπάδας καὶ τὴν φωνὴν τῆς σάλπιγγος καὶ τὸ ὄρος τὸ καπνίζον· φοβηθέντες δὲ πᾶς ὁ λαὸς ἔστησαν μακρόθεν.

---

103 Gennesaret, where they are depicted as eventually landing, is on the northwestern coast of the Sea of Galilee. See Pritchard, *Atlas,* 163. Ancient Bethsaida was located near and to the east of the point where the Jordan River flows into the Sea of Galilee (Josephus *Ant.* 18.2.1 §28; *NEAEHL* 2:526).

104 As Dibelius pointed out, Jesus wishes to pass by the disciples because his intention is to reveal himself to them; see "The Genre of 6:45-52" above.

105 The subjects of the second two finite verbs in v. 5 are ambiguous; see Brevard S. Childs, *The Book of Exodus* (OTL; Philadelphia: Westminster, 1974) 603, 611.

106 See "Cultural Contexts" above.

107 The motif of antipathy of ghosts toward water, if known to the audiences of Mark, would make the disciples' surmise seem absurd (Jason Robert Combs, "A Ghost on the Water?: Understanding an Absurdity in Mark 6:49-50" [forthcoming in JBL]).

108 Or it may be an allusion to Exod 20:18 LXX; see the next paragraph.

109 The same verb, ταραχθῆναι ("to be terrified"), is used in Gen 19:16 LXX to describe the response of Lot and his family when the angels appear to take them out of Sodom; cf. Gen 40:6; 41:8 LXX (in relation to dreams); Ps 2:5 LXX (the Gentiles shall be terrified at the wrath of the Lord); Dan 2:1 LXX (Nebuchadnezzar is terrified at a dream); 7:15 LXX and Θ (Daniel is terrified by his visions); Dan 4:2 Θ (Nabuchadnezzar is terrified by a dream); Dan 5:9 Θ (Baltasar is terrified by the writing on the wall). See also Dwyer, *Wonder,* 131.

καὶ εἶπαν πρὸς Μωυσῆν Λάλησον σὺ ἡμῖν, καὶ μὴ λαλείτω πρὸς ἡμᾶς ὁ θεός, μήποτε ἀποθάνωμεν. καὶ λέγει αὐτοῖς Μωυσῆς Θαρσεῖτε). (Exod 20:18-20 LXX)

The command "do not be afraid" (μὴ φοβεῖσθε) is a typical element in an account of an epiphany. When Daniel is overwhelmed by the appearance of a mighty angel, the angel says to him, "Do not be afraid, Daniel" (Μὴ φοβοῦ, Δανιηλ) (Dan 10:12 LXX [and Θ]).[110]

Jesus' words, "It is I" (ἐγώ εἰμι), serve primarily to let the disciples know that it is Jesus whom they have seen. Occasionally in the LXX, God is portrayed as saying "It is I" or "I am" (ἐγώ εἰμι), but this expression is used of human beings as well.[111] According to Exodus, God said to Moses from the burning bush: "I am the one who is" (Ἐγώ εἰμι ὁ ὤν) (3:14 LXX). According to Deuteronomy, God said, "See, see that I am, and there is no God except me" (ἴδετε ἴδετε ὅτι ἐγώ εἰμι, καὶ οὐκ ἔστιν θεὸς πλὴν ἐμοῦ) (32:39 LXX). The book of Isaiah portrays God as saying "I, God, [am the] first, and in future time, I am" (ἐγὼ θεὸς πρῶτος, καὶ εἰς τὰ ἐπερχόμενα ἐγώ εἰμι) (41:4 LXX).[112] Those in the audience who had grasped the assimilation of Jesus to God in this passage and who were familiar with the passages cited here from Deuteronomy and Isaiah in which "It is I" or "I am" (ἐγώ εἰμι) functions as a divine name or quality may have understood the expression of Jesus in similar terms.[113] In any case, awareness of these intertextual connections is not necessary for the audience to realize that Jesus is being portrayed here as divine in a functional, not necessarily in a metaphysical, sense.

■ **51-52** Although Jesus had intended to pass by the disciples (v. 48), he nevertheless stepped into the boat with them. This gesture indicates not only Jesus' desire to reassure the disciples but also his concern to reveal himself to them and to teach them about his significance. After Jesus had stepped into the boat, the wind abated. This event is quite different from Jesus' stilling of the storm in 4:39, when he rebuked the wind and the sea. Here the wind abates automatically. As noted in the comment on v. 48 above, the wind here simply delays the progress of the disciples so that the epiphany of Jesus can occur by night in the middle of the Sea of Galilee.[114]

The close link between the abating of the wind and Jesus' stepping into the boat makes clear to the disciples that the wind was directly controlled by a divine force. This perception causes them to be "very, exceedingly amazed within themselves" (λίαν ἐκ περισσοῦ ἐν ἑαυτοῖς ἐξίσταντο). This amazement is a typical motif of miracle stories and is connected with a variety of other types of extraordinary phenomena (cf. Mark 2:12; 5:42).[115] As in 5:42, the reaction of amazement here signifies the extraordinary character of the phenomenon that has just been witnessed, including the walking on the sea.[116]

The pre-Markan version of the story may have ended with this reaction of exceeding amazement, or it may have concluded with either a titular or nontitular acclamation of Jesus.[117] In any case, the motif of amazement surely had a positive function in the pre-Markan source, as it has in 5:42. Some interpreters have concluded, however, that the evangelist, by adding v. 52, interprets the amazement here negatively.[118] It is more likely, however,

---

110 See also Dan 10:19 LXX and Θ. In Dan 5:9-10 Θ, Baltasar's terror is followed by the queen's admonition that he, in effect, have courage.

111 Of the angel or messenger of God, e.g., Judg 6:18; of God, e.g., 2 Kgdms 12:7b; in both of these cases, the phrase ἐγώ εἰμι ("It is I") is the subject of a verb, so that the εἰμι ("is" or "am") here results from an oddity of translation: the phrase ἐγώ εἰμι is apparently designed to correspond to אנכי ("I") in the MT. It is used of human beings in, e.g., Judg 5:3 (twice); 11:35, 37; Ruth 4:4. In some of these cases also, the phrase ἐγώ εἰμι ("It is I") is the subject of a verb, so that the εἰμι ("is" or "am") is redundant.

112 See also Isa 43:10; 46:4; 48:12.

113 Cf. Gundry, 337.

114 Gundry concluded that the wind died down in order to provide Jesus with an easy passage; Gundry cites Philostratus *Vita Ap.* 4.13, 15; 7.10; 8.15; Iamblichus *Vit. Pyth.* 28 §135.

115 Theissen, *Miracle Stories*, 69–71; Dwyer, *Wonder*, 100, 130–34. See also the commentary on 16:8 below.

116 See the commentary on 5:40b-43 above.

117 Cf. Yarbro Collins, "Rulers, Divine Men," 225–26. The evangelist may have intensified a motif of amazement in the source; see Dwyer, *Wonder*, 133–34.

118 See "The History of the Tradition of 6:45-52" above on the redactional character of v. 52. For a review of works that argue for the negative reinterpretation of the amazement, see Dwyer, *Wonder*, 132.

that v. 52 comments on the disciples' behavior in the account as a whole.[119]

It may well be that the narrative implies that Jesus' sending the disciples on without him was a test of their faith. After Moses exhorts the people, "Have courage!" (Θαρσεῖτε), in the text cited above, he goes on to say, "For God has come to you for the sake of testing you, so that the fear of him may be in you, in order that you may not sin" (ἔνεκεν γὰρ τοῦ πειράσαι ὑμᾶς παρεγενήθη ὁ θεὸς πρὸς ὑμᾶς, ὅπως ἂν γένηται ὁ φόβος αὐτοῦ ἐν ὑμῖν, ἵνα μὴ ἁμαρτάνητε) (Exod 20:20 LXX). Especially in the context of Mark as a whole, the implication in 4:40 that the disciples themselves could have stilled the storm and in 6:37 that they could have multiplied the loaves makes it likely that the hidden motivation of Jesus in 6:45-46 is to give the disciples yet another opportunity to exercise and demonstrate the power of their faith. When the experiment failed, Jesus took another tack and provided them with another educational epiphany of divine power. Their mistaking him for a ghost, however, indicates that they still have far to go in grasping the significance of Jesus.[120]

The reference to the loaves in v. 52, like the dismissal of the crowd in v. 45, links this story to the previous one, the feeding of the five thousand. The disciples fail to realize that they could have controlled the wind and to grasp the significance of Jesus' walking on the sea, because they could not conceive of the possibility of feeding the crowd themselves, nor did they understand the significance for his identity of Jesus' feeding the crowds.

The comment that "their hearts had become hardened" (ἦν αὐτῶν ἡ καρδία πεπωρωμένη) is a radical intensification of the theme of the misunderstanding of the disciples. The theme is introduced in 4:13, as Jesus chides them for not understanding the parable of the sower. Mark 4:34, however, implies that they received private instruction and gives no indication that they were not making progress. The theme intensifies with Jesus' admonishing the disciples for their lack of faith in the context of the stilling of the storm.[121] The disciples do not understand, when Jesus asks who touched him, that Jesus is not speaking about an ordinary touch.[122] The Twelve are successful when Jesus sends them out to proclaim, exorcise, and heal (Mark 6:7-13, 30). Yet their proposal that Jesus send the crowd away shows that they have not understood his divine power and their potential share in it (6:35-36).[123] The comment that their hearts had become hardened, however, implies that they are impeded in their progress in faith because of a habitual attitude. The language is shocking because it associates the disciples with the opponents of Jesus. According to 3:2, certain people were watching Jesus carefully to see whether he would heal the man with a withered hand on the Sabbath. If he did, they intended to bring charges against him. When Jesus questioned them about whether it was permitted to heal on the Sabbath or even to save a life on the Sabbath, they were silent. According to 3:5, Jesus was both angry and grieved "at the hardening of their hearts" (ἐπὶ τῇ πωρώσει τῆς καρδίας αὐτῶν). In Jesus' comments about the parables in 4:11-12 and in the narrator's comments in 4:34, a dichotomy is drawn between insiders, to whom the mystery of the kingdom of God is given and for whom the parables are interpreted, and outsiders, to whom everything happens in parables and who are prevented from perceiving and comprehending them. The innovation of 6:52 is the idea that the disciples are outsiders too; or at least, if they are insiders, they are not significantly different from the outsiders.

It is unlikely, as Theodore Weeden argued, that the evangelist is engaging in polemics against the Twelve or the Jerusalem community.[124] The relation of this story to older scripture suggests instead that the evangelist is expressing a profound sense of the difficulty human beings have in grasping divine revelation. The portrayal of Jesus walking on the sea in v. 48 (περιπατῶν ἐπὶ τῆς θαλάσσης) is reminiscent of the portrayal of God in Job 9:8 as the one who "trampled the back of the sea

119 So also Dwyer, *Wonder*, 132–33.
120 Cf. the interpretation of Watts Henderson, "'Concerning the Loaves,'" 16–24.
121 See the commentary on 4:40 above.
122 See the commentary on 5:30-32 above.
123 See the commentary on vv. 35-36 and 37-38 above. Theissen argued that the third group of miracles in Mark (6:30–8:26) makes the two feeding miracles the basis for the question about correct understanding; as "a new teaching" (διδαχὴ καινή) (cf. 1:27), they call for understanding (*Miracle Stories*, 208–9).
124 Theodore J. Weeden, *Mark—Traditions in Conflict* (Philadelphia: Fortress, 1971) 49–50, 148–49.

dragon" (παριπατεῖν . . . ἐπὶ θαλάσσης in the LXX).[125] Jesus' intention to "pass by" the disciples (παρελθεῖν αὐτούς) in the same verse of Mark resonates with another verse of Job in the same context:

Look, he passes by me, and I do not see him;
he moves on, but I do not perceive him

הן יעבר עלי ולא אראה)
ויחלף ולא־אבין לו).
(Job 9:11 MT; trans. RSV [modified])

The LXX reads:

If he steps over me, I do not see (him);
and if he passes by me, even so I do not know (it)

(ἐὰν ὑπερβῇ με, οὐ μὴ ἴδω·
καὶ ἐὰν παρέλθῃ με, οὐδ᾽ ὡς ἔγνων). (Job 9:11 LXX)

Ernst Lohmeyer argued that the term "pass by" (παρελθεῖν) in the LXX belongs to the motif of the divine epiphany.[126] But in Job 9:11 the term does not describe God's appearance in an epiphany.[127] In fact, one could argue that this verse in Job is an anti-epiphany; it calls into question the very possibility of such an event. Even if God were to pass directly by the speaker (a mere human being), that person would not be capable of perceiving or comprehending the divine presence.

The negative perspective of Job 9:11 is congenial to Mark's theme of the lack of understanding of the

disciples: "For *they did not comprehend* with regard to the loaves, but their hearts had become hardened" (οὐ γὰρ συνῆκαν ἐπὶ τοῖς ἄρτοις, ἀλλ᾽ ἦν αὐτῶν ἡ καρδία πεπωρωμένη). Mark is saying something about the difficulty of perceiving the divinity of Jesus on the part of mere human beings.

■ **53** Unlike the account in John 6:21, there is nothing miraculous about the way in which the boat reaches the shore. The coming up and abating of the wind seem to be miraculous, that is, controlled by divine power. But once the wind has abated, the boat sails in the ordinary way to the harbor of Gennesaret.[128]

It has been suggested that Mark 6:52-53 is represented on a Greek fragment from Qumran Cave 7 (7Q5).[129] This conclusion, however, is not likely to be correct.[130]

■ **54-55** When Jesus disembarks, people immediately recognize him. This scene is reminiscent of v. 33, which says that many people recognized Jesus and the disciples as they were sailing to an unpopulated place and attempting to be alone and to rest for a while. In the earlier passage, the people gathered to Jesus to be taught. In this case, they ran out and brought to Jesus those who were ill. That they bring the ill on pallets recalls the healing of the paralytic in 2:1-12, who was also brought to Jesus on a pallet.

The statement that the people "began to carry about those who were ill on pallets (to the place) where they heard that he was" (ἤρξαντο ἐπὶ τοῖς κραβάττοις τοὺς κακῶς ἔχοντας περιφέρειν ὅπου ἤκουον ὅτι ἐστίν) in v. 55, indicates that the specific account of Jesus arriving

---

125 It is unlikely that this passage played a role in shaping the oral form of this story (rightly, Bultmann, *History*, 230), but once the story was written down, especially when the tradents were educated in the Jewish Scriptures, as the evangelist probably was, the influence of such passages was likely to come into play.

126 Ernst Lohmeyer, "'Und Jesus ging vorüber': Eine exegetische Betrachtung," *Nieuw Theologisch Tijdschrift* 23 (1934) 206–24, esp. 216–19; reprinted in idem, *Urchristliche Mystik: Neutestamentliche Studien* (Darmstadt: Hermann Gentner, 1956) 57–79; see also John Paul Heil, *Jesus Walking on the Sea: Meaning and Gospel Functions of Matt 14:22-33, Mark 6:45-52 and John 6:15b-21* (AnBib 87; Rome: Biblical Institute Press, 1981) 69–72. See also Watts Henderson, "'Concerning the Loaves,'" 20–21.

127 Heil notes this fact (*Jesus Walking*, 71 n. 98), but does not draw out its implications for Job or for Mark.

128 Cf. the passages cited in n. 114 above.

129 José O'Callaghan, *Los primeros testimonios del Nuevo Testamento: Papirología neotestamentaria* (En los orígenes del Cristianismo 7; Cordoba: Ediciones el Almendro, 1995) 107–11; Albert Dou, "Epílogo," in ibid., 116–39; Carsten Peter Thiede, *The Earliest Gospel Manuscript? The Qumran Papyrus 7Q5 and Its Significance for New Testament Studies* (Exeter: Paternoster, 1992).

130 Robert H. Gundry, "No *Nu* in Line 2 of 7Q5: A Final Disidentification of 7Q5 with Mark 6:52-53," *JBL* 118 (1999) 698–707; Stefan Enste, *Kein Markustext in Qumran: Eine Untersuchung der These: Qumran-Fragment 7Q5 = Mk 6, 52-53* (NTOA 45; Freiburg,

at Gennesaret has been used to introduce a Markan summary of Jesus' activities over a period of time.[131]

■ **56** The summary continues, mentioning Jesus' visits to villages, cities, and farms. Wherever he went, the people placed the sick in the marketplaces. The statement that the people "entreated him that (the sick) might touch even the edge of his cloak" (παρεκάλουν αὐτὸν ἵνα κἂν τοῦ κρασπέδου τοῦ ἱματίου αὐτοῦ ἅψωνται) is reminiscent of the woman with a flow of blood, who knew that if she touched even the cloak of Jesus, she would be healed.[132] Here the confidence in the healing power of Jesus is heightened, so that it is necessary to touch only the edge (or tassel) of Jesus' cloak.[133] This statement, in a Markan summary, shows that the evangelist shared, or at least accepted, the popular belief that the healing power of Jesus could be transferred by touch.[134]

The woman with the flow of blood is portrayed as thinking, as she approached Jesus, "If I touch even his clothes, I shall be saved" (ἐὰν ἅψωμαι κἂν τῶν ἱματίων αὐτοῦ σωθήσομαι) (5:28). When she is healed, Jesus says to her, "your faith has saved you" (ἡ πίστις σου σέσωκέν σε) (5:34). Similarly, the narrator comments here, "and as many as touched him were saved" (καὶ ὅσοι ἂν ἥψαντο αὐτοῦ ἐσῴζοντο). Being "saved" in these contexts means being healed. This inference is confirmed by the comment of Jesus to the woman that follows the one cited, "go in peace and be healthy (and freed) from your torment" (ὕπαγε εἰς εἰρήνην καὶ ἴσθι ὑγιὴς ἀπὸ τῆς μάστιγός σου) (5:34).

Schweiz: Universitätsverlag; Göttingen: Vandenhoeck & Ruprecht, 2000).

131 Achtemeier argues credibly that this summary was composed by the evangelist to fill the gap created by his transposition of the healing of the blind man in Bethsaida to a later point in the narrative ("Miracle Catenae," 284–86).

132 See the commentary on 5:27-28 above.

133 The term κράσπεδον ("edge," "border," or "hem") was also used for the tassel (ציצת) that an Israelite was obliged to wear on the four corners of his outer garment; see Num 15:37-41; Deut 22:12; BAGD, s.v.

134 See the commentary on 5:30-32 above.

7

7:1-23 Dispute with the Pharisees

1/ And the Pharisees and some
scribes who had come from
Jerusalem gathered with him.
2/ And they saw some of his disciples, that[a] they were eating
their food with profane hands,
that is, with unwashed hands[b]—
3/ For the Pharisees and all the
Jews do not eat unless they wash
their hands up to the elbow,[c]
holding fast the tradition of the
elders, 4/ and when they return
from the market, they do not eat,[d]
unless they immerse.[e] And there
are many other things which they
receive (from the elders) to hold
fast, the immersing of cups and
pitchers and copper kettles and
dining couches[f]—5/ And the Pharisees and the scribes asked him,
"Why do your disciples not walk
in accordance with the tradition
of the elders, but eat bread with
profane[g] hands?" 6/ He then said
to them,[h] "Well did Isaiah prophesy concerning you hypocrites, as
it is written, 'This people[i] honors[j]
me with their lips, but their
hearts are far from me; 7/ they
worship me to no purpose, teaching as[k] (authoritative) teachings
commandments of human
beings.'[l] 8/ Abandoning the commandment of God, you keep the
tradition of human beings."
9/ And he said to them,[m] "How
well you nullify the commandment of God, in order that you
may preserve[n] your tradition!
10/ For Moses said, 'Honor your
father and your mother,' and
'Whoever reviles father or mother
shall die.' 11/ But you say, 'If a
man says to his father or mother:
whatever of mine may benefit
you is *korban*,' which means
gift—12/ You no longer allow him
to do anything for his father or
mother, 13/ making void the
word of God by means of your
tradition which you have handed
on. And you do many similar such
things."

14/ And he summoned the crowd
again[o] and said to them, "Listen
to me all of you and comprehend.
15/ There is nothing outside of a
human being which, by going
into him, is able to profane him;
rather, it is what goes out of a
human being that profanes him."[p]

a A D W Θ et al. omit ὅτι ("that") and change the finite
verb ἐσθίουσιν ("they ate," lit., "they eat") to the participle ἐσθίοντας ("eating"). The changes are due to
the rejection of the stylistic element of prolepsis; cf.
Moulton-Turner, 3:325. ℵ B L Δ et al. attest the earlier
reading.

b D adds κατέγνωσαν ("they condemned [them]"), in
order to complete this sentence before introducing
the parenthesis that follows; v. 2 in this MS may thus be
translated, "And having seen some of his disciples eating with defiled hands, that is, with unwashed hands,
they condemned them." K N W Θ et al. add the verb
ἐμέμψαντο ("they found fault with them") instead.

c The meaning of πυγμῇ ("up to the elbow," lit., "with
a fist" or "with the fist") is obscure; thus ℵ W (b) et al.
attest the reading πυκνά ("frequently"), a variant that
arose in an attempt to clarify the meaning. For the
same reason, some MSS (Δ sy^s sa) simply omit πυγμῇ
("up to the elbow"). See Metzger, *Textual Commentary*,
80. On the translation see Turner, "Marcan Usage," 29
(1928) 278–79 (Elliott, *Language and Style*, 107).

d The phrase ἀπ' ἀγορᾶς (lit., "from the marketplace")
is a pregnant constuction, meaning "after returning
from the marketplace"; see BAGD, s.v. ἀγορά. In
order to make this meaning explicit, D W et al. add
ὅταν ἐλθῶσιν ("when they come") after ἀπ' ἀγορᾶς
("from the market").

e Since the word βαπτίζειν (lit., "to immerse" or "to
dip") was closely associated with the Christian practice of baptism, some scribes changed the verb βαπτίσωνται ("they immerse") to ῥαντίσωνται ("they
purify by sprinkling"), which was used with reference
to objects as well as to people. The latter reading is
attested by ℵ B et al. Cf. Metzger, *Textual Commentary*,
80. See also Claus-Hunno Hunzinger, "ῥαντίζω,"
TDNT 6 (1968) 981 n. 23, who points out that it is
hard to link the form ῥαντίσωνται ("they sprinkle
themselves") with any known Jewish rite.

f The difficulty of the idea of immersing beds or dining
couches has apparently led to the omission of the
words καὶ κλινῶν ("and dining couches") in p^45vid ℵ B
L Δ et al. Cf. Metzger, *Textual Commentary*, 80–81.

g The reading attested by ℵ* B (D W) Θ et al., κοιναῖς
χερσίν ("with profane hands"), is probably the earliest recoverable reading. The reading ἀνίπτοις χερσίν ("with unwashed hands"), attested by ℵ² A L 𝔐 et
al., probably arose as a clarification based on v. 2. The
reading κοιναῖς χερσὶν καὶ ἀνίπτοις ("with profane
and unwashed hands") attested by p^45 (f^13) is a conflation of the other two readings or a clarification also
based on v. 2.

h p^45 A D W et al. read ὅτι (not to be translated in this
instance; introduces direct speech) following αὐτοῖς
("to them"), whereas ℵ B L Δ Θ et al. omit it. Following γέγραπται ("as it is written"), many of the MSS

17/ And when he had gone indoors, away from the crowd, his disciples asked him about the parable. **18/** And he said to them, "Are you thus also foolish? Do you not understand that nothing that is outside can profane a human being by going into him, **19/** because it does not go into his heart, but into the belly, and it goes out into the latrine?" making all (types of) food clean.[q] **20/** And he said, "That which comes out of a human being, that is what profanes him. **21/** For from within, from the hearts of human beings, come evil intentions, acts of unlawful intercourse, stealing, murder, **22/** adultery, greediness, and wickedness; deceit,[r] licentiousness, an evil eye, abusive speech, arrogance, foolishness; **23/** all this evil goes out from inside and profanes the human being."

line up in the opposite way: A D W et al. lack the conjunction and ℵ B L et al. include it. The usage of Mark suggests that ὅτι (not to be translated in either instance; introduces direct speech or quotation) should be read in both cases. See Turner, "Marcan Usage," 28 (1926) 9–15 (Elliott, *Language and Style*, 68–74).

i The word order varies in the MSS: most attest the reading οὗτος ὁ λαός ("this people"), but B D 2427 *pc* read ὁ λαὸς οὗτος ("this people"). The latter reading arose as an assimilation to the word order of the parallel in Matt 15:8 or of the text to which allusion is made, Isa 29:13 LXX.

j A few MSS (D W a b c) read ἀγαπᾷ ("loves") rather than τιμᾷ ("honors"). This reading may represent an otherwise lost variant of Isa 29:13 LXX or it may have been inspired by Mark 12:30, 33.

k Some witnesses (p[45] it vg[cl]) attest a reading with καί ("and") between διδασκαλίας ("teachings") and ἐντάλματα ("commandments"). This reading is translated "teaching teachings and commandments of human beings" and may have been inspired by the wording of Isa 29:13 LXX: διδάσκοντες ἐντάλματα ἀνθρώπων καὶ διδασκαλίας ("teaching commandments of human beings and teachings").

l Some MSS (D Θ et al.) add immediately after the quotation from Isaiah the words "(such as) the immersing of pitchers and cups; and you do many other such similar things" (βαπτισμοὺς ξεστῶν καὶ ποτηρίων καὶ ἄλλα παρόμοια τοιαῦτα πολλὰ ποιεῖτε) or their equivalent. The likelihood that this is a secondary addition based on vv. 4 and 13 is supported by the fact that an equivalent passage appears after ἀνθρώπων ("human beings") at the end of v. 8 in other MSS, namely, (A) *f*[13] 33 𝔐 et al. See Metzger, *Textual Commentary*, 81.

m One MS (sy[s]) omits the equivalent of the words from ἀφέντες ("abandoning") in v. 8 to αὐτοῖς ("to them") in v. 9, either by accident or because they seemed redundant.

n Most MSS attest either the aorist or the present subjunctive of the verb τηρέω ("to keep, preserve"): ℵ A (B 2427: τηρῆτε) L *f*[13] 33 𝔐 et al. Some (D W Θ *f*[1] et al.) attest the reading στήσητε ("establish, confirm"). Either reading could have given rise to the other, but the former is better attested. For a different view, see Metzger, *Textual Commentary*, 81.

o The earliest recoverable reading is probably πάλιν ("again"), attested by ℵ B D L et al. (contra Taylor, ad loc.). Since the adverb is difficult to construe (the crowd was last mentioned in 6:45), some MSS (A W Θ *f*[1.13] 33 𝔐 et al.) attest a reading in which it has been changed to πάντα ("all" or "the whole") and others (565. 579 et al.) a reading in which it has simply been omitted. Markan style supports the judgment that

$\pi \acute{\alpha} \lambda \iota \nu$ ("again") is the earliest recoverable reading; see Turner, "Marcan Usage," 29 (1928) 283–87 (Elliott, *Language and Style*, 111–15).

p Many MSS (A D W Θ $f^{1.13}$ 33 $\mathfrak{M}$ et al.) contain the following words, which constitute v. 16: $\epsilon \ddot{\iota}$ $\tau \iota \varsigma$ $\ddot{\epsilon} \chi \epsilon \iota$ $\ddot{\omega} \tau \alpha$ $\dot{\alpha} \kappa o \acute{\upsilon} \epsilon \iota \nu$ $\dot{\alpha} \kappa o \upsilon \acute{\epsilon} \tau \omega$ ("Let anyone who has ears to hear, hear!"). This statement may have been added to warn the audience not to take the clause immediately preceding it literally! Alternatively or in addition, it may have been added to complement the call to understanding in v. 14. Cf. 4:23 and Metzger, *Textual Commentary*, 81.

q The translation given here follows Origen and Chrysostom in taking the unexpressed subject of the verb $\lambda \acute{\epsilon} \gamma \epsilon \iota$ ("he said") in v. 18 as the antecedent of the participle $\kappa \alpha \vartheta \alpha \rho \acute{\iota} \zeta \omega \nu$ ("making clean") which is near the end of v. 19. The participial phrase would then be the evangelist's comment on the consequence of Jesus' explanation, rather than part of the explanation itself. The reading with a neuter participle, $\kappa \alpha \vartheta \acute{\alpha} \rho \iota \zeta o \nu$ ("making clean"), in K Γ 33. 700. 2542 *pm*,

may have arisen as a correction by a scribe who took $\tau \grave{o}$ $\ddot{\epsilon} \xi \omega \vartheta \epsilon \nu$ ("that which is outside") as the antecedent of the participle. The readings with the present indicative active, attested by D (i r¹), and middle, attested by 1047 syˢ, arose in attempts by those who took Jesus as the subject of the participle to clarify the syntax. See Moulton-Turner, 3:316; Taylor, ad loc.; Turner, "Marcan Usage," 26 (1925) 149 (Elliott, *Language and Style*, 27–28); Metzger, *Textual Commentary*, 81.

r The translation offered here follows $\aleph$ B L (Θ) et al. in the order of the vices listed. Many MSS place $\mu o \iota \chi \epsilon \hat{\iota} \alpha \iota$ ("adultery," lit., "acts of adultery") first instead of fourth: A (W) $f^{1.13}$ et al. Some of these also place $\phi \acute{o} \nu o \iota$ ("murder," lit., "acts of murder") before rather than after $\kappa \lambda o \pi \alpha \acute{\iota}$ ("stealing," lit., "acts of stealing"): A f^{1} $\mathfrak{M}$ et al. D differs from other MSS in expressing all but one of the vices, $\kappa \lambda \acute{\epsilon} \mu \mu \alpha \tau \alpha$ ("acts of stealing") in place of $\kappa \lambda o \pi \alpha \acute{\iota}$ ("stealing," lit., "acts of stealing"), in the singular. Most MSS have the first six in the plural and the last six in the singular.

The Dispute with the Pharisees in Literary Context

Just as this section (6:6b–8:26) contains renewed proclamation[1] and renewed epiphanies of the divine power at work in Jesus,[2] it also renews Jesus' conflict with his rivals for the leadership of the people of Israel (cf. 2:1–3:6). This passage (7:1-23) also provides some variety in subject matter in the immediate context: two miracle stories and a summary of miraculous healing precede it and three miracle stories follow it.

Rudolf Pesch pointed out that this is the second extensive speech of Jesus, the parable discourse of 4:1-34 being the first. Pesch concluded that this discourse concerning the Law was well placed, namely, before Jesus' activity in Gentile territory.[3]

The Genre of the Dispute with the Pharisees

Bultmann classified this passage as a controversy-dialogue occasioned by the behavior of the disciples. He argued that the section of vv. 9-13 is pure polemic, not a response to an attack.[4] He defined the form of the saying of v. 15 as "a double-stranded mashal," and regarded it as an enigma that required commentary.[5] It was originally a parable-like form of polemic but was turned into a church rule.[6] The original section, vv. 1-8, was expanded several times, with the result that the interlocutors, the Pharisees and the scribes, are forgotten. The scene has no real conclusion.[7]

Dibelius contrasted this passage and others like it, which he called extended "conversations," with para-

---

1 See the section "The Sending Out of the Twelve in Literary Context" above.

2 Mark 6:34-44; 6:53-56; and especially 6:45-52; see the section "The Genre of 6:45-52" above.

3 Pesch, 1:367. Jesus goes away into the region of Tyre in 7:24. But he soon returns to "Jewish" territory, in 8:10, if not already in 8:1. Note also that he was already active among Gentiles in 5:1-20. On the location of Dalmanutha (8:10), see Pritchard, *Atlas*, 165.

4 Bultmann, *History*, 17.

5 Ibid., 81, 92; see the next section, "The History of the Tradition."

6 Bultmann, *History*, 130, 147, 149.

7 Ibid., 17–18.

digms. The paradigms contain dialogues, but these are pointedly directed toward silencing or convicting the interlocutor of Jesus or in justifying the behavior or attitude of Jesus. In the "conversations" this pointedness is entirely lacking. The point lies in an individual saying or in groups of sayings, but these are united by elements of dialogue into highly artificial wholes. The "conversations" focus less on the kingdom of God than the paradigms do. The purpose of the conversations, and their organizing principle, is to gather sayings of Jesus on related topics in order to create a "teaching" of Jesus on an important topic for church life.[8]

Pesch follows Bultmann in defining the passage as a controversy-dialogue. Pesch discerned a three-part construction: (1) the description of the offensive situation (vv. 1-4); (2) the objection of the opponents (vv. 1, 2, 5); and (3) the response of Jesus (vv. 6-8, 9-13).[9]

Robert C. Tannehill defined 7:1-5 as an "objection story."[10] An "objection story" is a type of "pronouncement story." It presents a situation of conflict created by an objection to the behavior or views of the responder or his followers. The typical objection story has three parts: (1) the cause of the objection; (2) the objection itself; and (3) the response to the objection.[11] He concluded that objection stories frequently contain general statements of principle in the responses to the objection. These are often formulated antithetically, emphasizing the contrast between the speaker's perspective and another point of view. He included 7:15 in this category. The story thus moves from a specific occasion to a general disclosure of God's will, which provides a guideline for the audience's way of life.[12] He argued further that the unit in vv. 1-15 involves a sharp counterattack against the objecting group, which suggests hard lines of division between communities.[13] He defined 7:17-23 as a "dependent inquiry scene" in which Jesus gives additional explanation of the issues raised in the preceding objection story.[14]

In its present form, 7:1-23 has two main parts. Verses 1-13 constitute a scholastic or controversy dialogue in which the interlocutors are the Pharisees and the scribes. Verses 14-23 are structured as a typically Markan scene in which Jesus first instructs the crowd and then gives private instruction to his disciples.[15]

The History of the Tradition

Bultmann concluded that 7:1-8 is an artistically stylized composition that originated in the early Christian community. He found evidence for this conclusion in the presentation of Jesus as defending the behavior of the disciples (who represent the later community) and in the artificiality of the depiction of the scribes as coming from Jerusalem particularly to see the disciples eating. Furthermore, he argued that the reference to Isaiah in vv. 6-7 was derived from the traditional polemic of the church. He also concluded that this section came from the Palestinian church, because it was in that context that the relation of the "tradition of the elders" to the Law was a live issue (v. 8).

According to Bultmann, the structure of the whole was probably determined by Mark himself. He elaborated vv. 1-8, the basic section, by adding vv. 9-13. The latter section contains another traditional saying of the Lord, introduced by Mark with the formula "and he said to them" ($\kappa\alpha\grave{\iota}$ $\check{\epsilon}\lambda\epsilon\gamma\epsilon\nu$ $\alpha\grave{\upsilon}\tauo\hat{\iota}\varsigma$). Since the saying cites scripture, Bultmann inferred that its origin was in the polemic of the Christian community (that is, that it does not go back to the historical Jesus). He concluded that this section, too, originated in the Palestinian church because of the subject matter.

The evangelist added another item from the tradition, v. 15. Since he considered it to be a metaphor, he introduced the uncomprehending public, as was his practice, in v. 14. Bultmann concluded that the saying of v. 15 could belong to the oldest tradition.[16] He defended the

---

8 Dibelius, *From Tradition to Gospel*, 222.
9 Pesch, 1:369.
10 Tannehill, "Varieties," 107.
11 Tannehill, "Introduction," 8.
12 Tannehill, "Varieties," 110.
13 Ibid., 111.
14 Ibid., 114.
15 Cf. the public teaching of 4:1-9, followed by the private instruction of vv. 10-20. The order is reversed in chap. 8, with the private instruction coming first (vv. 31-33) and the public teaching following (8:34—9:1). The more typical pattern occurs again in the public teaching of 10:1-9 followed by the private instruction of vv. 10-12. Cf. 13:1-2 and vv. 3-37.
16 Bultmann, *History*, 17–18; see the section "The Genre of the Dispute with the Pharisees" above.

hypothesis that it goes back to the historical Jesus because it demands "a new disposition of mind" with regard to purity. It contains "something characteristic, new, reaching out beyond popular wisdom and piety," and yet it "in no sense [is] scribal or rabbinic nor yet Jewish apocalyptic. So here if anywhere we can find what is characteristic of the preaching of Jesus."[17]

According to Bultmann, v. 16 is a gloss (that is, not part of the original text of Mark).[18] The explanation of the saying of v. 15 preserved in vv. 18b, 19 came to the evangelist along with the saying. Mark introduces this commentary with a change of scene (vv. 17-18a), following his custom of having Jesus give metaphorical teaching to the crowd and explaining it to his disciples. He thought that 7:20-23 is later material than vv. 9-13. He distinguished it in part because of the new introductory formula, "And he said" ($\check{\epsilon}\lambda\epsilon\gamma\epsilon\nu \ \delta\acute{\epsilon}$). According to Bultmann, vv. 20-23 may have been composed by Mark, but in any case by "a Hellenistic author," as the catalogue of vices shows.

Dibelius argued that, in 7:5-23, originally isolated sayings have been brought together for a particular reason. Like Bultmann, Dibelius concluded that the introductory formula in v. 9a, "and he said to them" ($\kappa\alpha\grave{\iota} \ \check{\epsilon}\lambda\epsilon\gamma\epsilon\nu \ \alpha\mathring{\upsilon}\tauο\hat{\iota}\varsigma$), indicates that vv. 9-13 were originally independent. For Dibelius, this inference is reinforced by the fact that this section is about the practice of *korban*, whereas the subject of vv. 1-8 is hand-washing. He also concluded that v. 15 was originally independent, because it deals with eating and not with hand-washing. According to Dibelius, both of the explanations of "the saying about true cleanliness" in v. 15, namely, vv. 18-19 and vv. 20-23, are constructions of the early church. He concluded that the opponents' question about hand-washing (vv. 1-5) was placed at the beginning of the whole composition by the evangelist. He thought that the section of vv. 6-15, which begins with a citation of Isaiah, is older than vv. 1-5.[19]

Dibelius also concluded that this "conversation" was not created by Mark.[20] The evangelist's interest lies in the biographical motifs at the beginning. In other words, he is adapting this "teaching" of Jesus concerning ritual cleanness to a narrative about Jesus' work.[21]

Pesch argued that the evangelist combined two complexes of tradition (vv. 1-13 and 14-23), each with its own theme and tradition history. The first concerns ritual purity; the second, clean and unclean types of food. They were brought together because of their thematic similarity, shown especially in the use of the terms $\kappa ο\iota\nu\acute{ο}\omega, \ \kappa ο\iota\nu\acute{ο}\varsigma$ ("to consider profane" or "to defile"; "profane" or "defiled") in both.[22]

Roger P. Booth accepted the form-critical argument that the pre-Markan tradition was composite. He concluded that the earliest form of the dispute consisted of a simple question directed to Jesus—namely, why his disciples ate with profane hands—and the reply of Jesus, preserved in vv. 14b-15, minus the redactional elements.[23] He concluded further that the "medical" explanation of vv. 18-19 and the ethical explanation of vv. 20-22 are dependent on the original unit and did not circulate independently.[24] The "Isaiah reply" (vv. 6-7) and the "Korban reply" (vv. 9-12), however, "were each used as separate units in the polemic of the early church."[25]

These various theories will be evaluated in the commentary below.

Comment

■ **1** The opening statement is quite artificial and serves to set the scene for the observation described in v. 2 and the question put forward in v. 5. E. P. Sanders paraphrased Mark as presenting the Pharisees and scribes as "making a special trip from Jerusalem to Galilee to check on whether or not [Jesus'] disciples washed their hands," and John Meier spoke of "some sort of investigatory commission sent from Jerusalem to question or attack Jesus' activity in Galilee."[26] Mark's setting of the scene, however, simply says that "the Pharisees and some scribes who had come from Jerusalem gathered with

17 Bultmann, *History*, 105.
18 See the note on the trans. of v. 15 above.
19 Dibelius, *From Tradition to Gospel*, 220–21.
20 See the section "The Genre of the Dispute with the Pharisees" above.
21 Dibelius, *From Tradition to Gospel*, 222–23, 260.
22 Pesch, 1:367.

23 Roger P. Booth, *Jesus and the Laws of Purity: Tradition History and Legal History in Mark 7* (JSNTSup 13; Sheffield: JSOT Press, 1986) 74; cf. 53.
24 Ibid., 74; cf. 62.
25 Ibid., 74; cf. 61.
26 Sanders, *Jewish Law*, 1; Meier, *Marginal Jew*, 3:554.

him" (Καὶ συνάγονται πρὸς αὐτὸν οἱ Φαρισαῖοι καί τινες τῶν γραμματέων ἐλθόντες ἀπὸ Ἱεροσολύμων). Nothing is said about their purpose in coming to Jesus or their attitude.[27] The Beelzebul controversy gives the impression that scribes went to Galilee specifically to confront Jesus. Here, however, the audience must infer why the Pharisees and scribes gather in the presence of Jesus. If one assumes that the Pharisees here are the same as, or cooperating with, those who held a consultation with the Herodians against Jesus (3:6), one will conclude that their motivation is hostile. Yet the text does not indicate such. As noted in the commentary on 3:22, there were close religious and cultural ties between Galilee and Jerusalem in the first century CE, so the portrayal of scribes visiting Galilee from Jerusalem has verisimilitude.[28]

■ **2** The Pharisees and the scribes observe that some of the disciples of Jesus are eating their food[29] "with profane hands, that is, with unwashed hands" (κοιναῖς χερσίν, τοῦτ᾽ ἔστιν ἀνίπτοις). The term "profane" (κοινός) here signifies that which is not in a state of ritual purity and thus not fit for contact with what is sacred.[30] It may be, however, that during the Second Temple period, rit-

ual purity was valued for its own sake or at least as a prerequisite for holiness.[31] In any case, it is likely that at least "one current" among Second Temple Jews had an "expansionist" view of impurity which necessitated handwashing.[32] The phrase "with unwashed hands" (ἀνίπτοις χερσί) occurs in Homer, and Philo treats it as proverbial.[33] Mark added the latter phrase for those in his audience who may not have been familiar with the Jewish notion of ritual impurity.[34]

■ **3-4** Without completing the sentence begun in v. 2, the evangelist digresses in order to provide a context for the question of v. 5.[35] Matthew streamlines Mark's version by omitting this digression and making the point by having the Pharisees and scribes ask, "Why do your disciples transgress the tradition of the elders?" (διὰ τί οἱ μαθηταί σου παραβαίνουσιν τὴν παράδοσιν τῶν πρεσβυτέρων;) (Matt 15:2).[36]

According to the Mishnah, the hands need to be rinsed before eating unconsecrated food or food in the category of "second tithe" or "heave-offering" (m. Ḥag 2.5).[37] The hands must be immersed, however, before eating holy things, that is, things that need to be offered in the temple, are partly or entirely devoted to the altar,

---

27 Mark 2:15-17 is similar. Contrast 2:6-7; 3:2; 8:11; 10:2; 12:13. Mark 2:24 and 3:22 belong to a different category; in 2:24 the issue is more serious, because it concerns a biblical commandment; in 3:22 the statement of the scribes is openly hostile. Mark 11:27-28 also presents a direct confrontation. Matthew's rewriting of Mark's setting of the scene is explicitly confrontational (15:1-2).

28 See the commentary on 3:22 above; see also Seán Freyne, "Galilee-Jerusalem Relations according to Josephus' *Life*," *NTS* 33 (1987) 600–609; reprinted in idem, *Galilee and Gospel: Collected Essays* (Tübingen: Mohr Siebeck, 2000) 73–85. On the historical scribes and the scribes as a group in Mark, see the commentary on 1:22 above.

29 The word ἄρτος ("bread") often means simply "food," since bread was the main food of ordinary people at the time; see BAGD, s.v.

30 Hyam Maccoby has argued, rather unconvincingly, that the type of hand-washing mentioned here was simply a matter of "good manners and hygiene" (*Ritual and Morality*, 157).

31 John C. Poirier, "Purity beyond the Temple in the Second Temple Era," *JBL* 122 (2003) 247–65.

32 Kazen, *Jesus and Purity* Halakhah, 60–88; quotations from 74.

33 Homer *Il.* 6.266; Hector, returning from battle, says, "with hands unwashen, I have awe to pour libation of flaming wine to Zeus" (χερσὶ δ᾽ ἀνίπτοισιν Διὶ λείβειν αἴθοντα οἶνον ἅζομαι); text and trans. from Augustus T. Murray, *Homer: The Iliad* (2 vols.; LCL; Cambridge, MA: Harvard University Press; London: Heinemann, 1924–25) 1:280–81. Philo alludes to this passage, "'with unwashed hands,' as the phrase goes" (τὸ λεγόμενον δὴ τοῦτο, "ἀνίπτοις χερσὶ") in speaking about people who heedlessly invoke the name of God in their oaths (*Spec. leg.* 2.2 §6; text and trans. from Colson and Whitaker, *Philo* 7:308–11). Citations from BAGD, s.v. ἄνιπτος. On the importance of hand-washing for Hesiod, see Israel Abrahams, "ʿAM HĀ᾽ ĀREC," in Claude G. Montefiore, *The Synoptic Gospels* (2nd ed.; 2 vols.; London: Macmillan, 1927) 2:662 n. 1.

34 Cf. Lane, 245.

35 The evangelist begins a new sentence in v. 5, thus leaving the sentence begun in v. 2 incomplete; this figure of speech is called anacoluthon; see Smyth §§3004-8; cf. Pesch, 1:368.

36 Either Matthew assumes that his audience is familiar with the traditions elaborated in Mark 7:3-4 or considers it sufficient to make the point about "transgression."

and must be eaten in the court of the temple (ibid.).[38] Before one eats holy things, one's hands must be immersed in a valid immersion pool (מקוה) containing forty *seahs* of undrawn water (ibid.).[39] Since the same mishnah says that "if a man's hands are unclean his whole body is deemed unclean," the immersion of the whole body is probably required in the latter case, not just of the hands (ibid.).[40]

The requirement or custom of rinsing the hands before eating ordinary food has often been understood as an innovation of the sages (Pharisees) that was part of their tendency to extend the biblical regulations regarding the holiness of the priests to all the Jews.[41] Eyal Regev has argued, however, that this and related customs arose before the Hasmonean period and were observed by Jews in the land of Israel as well as in the Diaspora, that is, not only by the Pharisees.[42]

Mark's statement that the Pharisees and all the Jews do not eat unless they wash their hands has often been taken as an exaggeration, even as seriously in error. Archaeological evidence, however, indicates that many Jews of the first century CE attempted to live in a state of ritual purity.[43] The *Epistle of Aristeas*, probably written by an Alexandrian Jew,[44] states that the seventy-two translators of the LXX washed their hands in the sea in connection with their daily prayers:

Following the custom of all the Jews, they washed their hands in the sea in the course of their prayers to God, and then proceeded to the reading and explication of each point. I asked this question: "What is their purpose in washing their hands while saying their prayers?" They explained that it is evidence that they have done no evil, for all activity takes place by means of the hands. Thus they nobly and piously refer everything to righteousness and truth (ὡς δὲ ἔθος ἐστί πᾶσι τοῖς Ἰουδαίοις ἀπονιψάμενοι τῇ θαλάσσῃ τὰς χεῖρας ὡς ἂν εὔξωνται πρὸς τὸν θεὸν ἐτρέποντο πρὸς τὴν ἀνάγνωσιν καὶ τὴν ἑκάστου διασάφησιν. ἐπηρώτησα δὲ καὶ τοῦτο τίνος χάριν ἀπονιζόμενοι τὰς χεῖρας τὸ τηνικαῦτα εὔχονται; διεσάφουν δὲ ὅτι μαρτύριόν ἐστι τοῦ μηδὲν εἰργᾶσθαι κακὸν πᾶσα γὰρ ἐνέργεια διὰ τῶν χειρῶν γίνεται καλῶς καὶ ὁσίως μεταφέροντες ἐπὶ τὴν δικαιοσύνην καὶ τὴν ἀλήθειαν πάντα). (305-6)[45]

---

37 For an explanation of "second tithe," see Danby, *Mishnah*, 73 n. 6. "Terumah" or "heave-offering" was that portion of their harvests that Israelites must give to the priests (Num 18:8-20; Deut 18:4; see Danby, *Mishnah*, appendix I, no. 48).

38 Danby, *Mishnah*, 213 and n. 16.

39 Ibid., 213 and n. 17; Appendix II, D and E (on the *seah*).

40 Ibid., 213; Roland Deines interprets the mishnah in this way (*Jüdische Steingefäße und pharisäische Frömmigkeit: Ein archäologisch-historischer Beitrag zum Verständnis von Joh 2,6 und der jüdischen Reinheitshalacha zur Zeit Jesu* [WUNT 2.52; Tübingen: Mohr Siebeck, 1993] 229).

41 Cf. Exod 30:17-21; Wilhelm Brandt, *Die jüdischen Baptismen oder das religiöse Waschen und Baden im Judentum mit Einschluß des Judenchristentums* (BZNW 18; Gießen: Töpelmann, 1910) 38-39. See also Abrahams, "ʿAM HAʾAREC," 664. Jacob Neusner argued that one of the major characteristics of the Pharisees was the practice of eating ordinary food in a state of ritual purity (*The Rabbinic Traditions about the Pharisees before 70* [3 vols.; Leiden: Brill, 1971] 3:288-98). Deines rightly rejects the thesis, proposed as early as Maimonides and defended by Adolph Büchler, that the regulations regarding purity applied only to the priests in the temple and to ordinary Israelites when they visited the temple (*Die Pharisäer*, 364).

42 Eyal Regev, "Pure Individualism: The Idea of Non-Priestly Purity in Ancient Judaism," *JSJ* 31 (2000) 176-202, esp. 180-81, 188-89; idem, "Moral Impurity and the Temple in Early Christianity in Light of Ancient Greek Practice and Qumranic Ideology," *HTR* 97 (2004) 383-411, esp. 388-89. Poirier also criticizes the hypothesis of Pharisaic innovation ("Purity beyond the Temple," 247-65). The position of Deines is analogous (*Die Pharisäer*, 512-13 n. 313).

43 Regev, "Pure Individualism," 181-86. See also the arguments of Poirier ("Purity beyond the Temple," 247-65).

44 R. J. H. Shutt, "Letter of Aristeas," *OTP* 2:9; Katell Berthelot, "L'interprétation symbolique des lois alimentaires dans la Lettre d'Aristée: une influence pythagoricienne," *JJS* 52 (2001) 253-68, esp. 254-55.

45 Text from Denis and Janssens, *Concordance grecque*, 892; trans. from Shutt, "Letter of Aristeas," 33. Lane argued, on the basis of this text, that Mark was following a Jewish convention in generalizing the practice of hand-washing to "all the Jews" (245).

Since Aristeas, the supposed author of the *Epistle*, is portrayed as a Gentile, he asks the seventy-two the significance of a custom "of all the Jews."[46] The text suggests that the washing of hands in connection with prayer was a widespread custom of Jews around 170 BCE.[47] The actual author may have used the question as a rhetorical device, in order to provide an opportunity to present his allegorical interpretation of the rite. In Josephus's version of the story, "washing their hands in the sea" (τῇ θαλάσσῃ τὰς χεῖρας ἀπονιπτόμενοι) is equivalent to "purifying themselves" (καθαίροντες αὐτούς) (*Ant.* 12.2.13 §106).[48]

Largely because of Matthew's allusion to the phrase "Galilee of the Gentiles" in Isaiah (8:23), many interpreters have concluded that the Jews of Galilee were less observant than those of Judea.[49] But archaeological evidence suggests that many Jewish residents in the towns of Galilee were just as observant as those of Jerusalem.[50] Thus, the reference in the *Epistle of Aristeas* to "all the Jews" or "all the Judeans," could reflect the practice of Galileans as well.

Somewhat later than the *Epistle of Aristeas*, a Jewish Sibylline oracle was written that contained a eulogy of the Jews. It praises the Jews because they do not create images of humans or animals:

For on the contrary, at dawn they lift up holy arms
toward heaven, from their beds, always sanctifying
 their flesh
with water, and they honor only the Immortal who
 always rules,
and then their parents

(ἀλλὰ γὰρ ἀείρουσι πρὸς οὐρανὸν ὠλένας ἁγνὰς
ὄρθριοι ἐξ εὐνῆς αἰεὶ χρόα ἁγνίζοντες
ὕδατι καὶ τιμῶσι μόνον τὸν ἀεὶ μεδέοντα
ἀθάνατον καὶ ἔπειτα γονεῖς). (*Sib. Or.* 3.591–94)[51]

The text and translation follow Clement of Alexandria in reading χρόα ("flesh") in line 592; the MSS, however read χεῖρας ("hands").[52]

According to the book of Judith, while she was in the camp of Holofernes, she went out from her tent each night to the valley of Bethulia and immersed (ἐβαπτί-ζετο) in the spring in the camp (Jdt 12:5-7 LXX).[53] This immersion immediately preceded her activity of praying.

46 Shutt mistakenly identifies the actual author, an Alexandrian Jew, with Aristeas, the supposed author ("Letter of Aristeas," 7). That Aristeas is presented as a Gentile is clear from §16; Shutt's translation "Their name for him is Zeus and Jove" should be "Our name, etc."

47 On the date of *Ep. Arist.*, see Shutt, "Letter of Aristeas," 8–9. The washing of hands in the sea is compatible with the practice of immersion of the hands (see above). According to *b. Šabb.* 14b, however, it was (first) Hillel and Shammai who decreed uncleanness of the hands; see Brandt, *Die jüdischen Baptismen*, 38. Hillel and Shammai flourished at the end of the first cent. BCE; see Robert Goldenberg, "Hillel the Elder," *ABD* 3:201–2; idem, "Shammai, School of," *ABD* 5:1158. On the halakot attributed to Hillel and Shammai regarding nonpriestly purity, see Regev, "Pure Individualism," 180. See also Anders Runesson, "Water and Worship: Ostia and the Ritual Bath in the Diaspora Synagogue," in Birger Olsson, Dieter Mitternacht, and Olof Brandt, eds., *The Synagogue of Ancient Ostia and the Jews of Rome* (SUSIR 4.57; Acta-Rom 4.57; Stockholm: Paul Åströms Förlag, 2001) 116–18.

48 Text and trans. from Ralph Marcus in Thackeray, *Josephus*, 7:52–53.

49 Γαλιλαία τῶν ἐθνῶν ("Galilee of the Gentiles") (Matt 4:15). Isa 8:23 LXX has the same phrase; the Hebrew is גליל הגוים. See the excursus on Galilee and Jerusalem in Mark in the commentary on 14:26-31 below.

50 Jewish ritual baths and stoneware designed to meet the requirements of laws of purity have been found in Galilean towns; see James F. Strange, "First Century Galilee from Archaeology," in Douglas R. Edwards and C. Thomas McCollough, *Archaeology and the Galilee: Texts and Contexts in the Graeco-Roman and Byzantine Periods* (SFSHJ 143; Atlanta: Scholars Press, 1997) 44; Mark A. Chancey, *The Myth of a Gentile Galilee* (SNTSMS 118; Cambridge/New York: Cambridge University Press, 2002) 63–119.

51 Text from Denis and Janssens, *Concordance grecque*, 895; trans. from John J. Collins, "The Sibylline Oracles," *OTP* 1:375. This oracle is dated by Collins to the period 163–45 BCE (ibid., 355). The provenance of 3.75–92 is Egypt, and nothing in the rest of book 3 "is incompatible with Egyptian provenance" (ibid., 360).

52 See Collins, "Sibylline Oracles," 1:375 n. t3.

53 The book of Judith was probably written in Palestine about 104–103 BCE; see Carey A. Moore, *Judith: A New Translation with Introduction and Commentary* (AB 40; Garden City, NY: Doubleday, 1985) 67.

The text also implies that she remained in a state of purity until she ate her food toward evening (12:8-9). Regev's argument that she was purifying herself from Gentile impurity, following G. Alon, must be modified in light of the work of Christine E. Hayes.[54]

With regard to the ritual of hand-washing, John C. Poirier has argued that diasporic practices illuminate Palestinian practices. The point is not to live like priests but rather to avoid ingesting impurity. Defilement of the interior of one's body would make one unfit for prayer and Torah study.[55]

The custom of hand-washing is said in v. 3 to be πυγμῇ ("up to the elbow").[56] This description would fit the requirement that the hands must be immersed before eating holy things.[57]

The phrase "the tradition of the elders" (ἡ παράδοσις τῶν πρεσβυτέρων) is clarified by a passage in Josephus:

> For the present I wish merely to explain that the Pharisees had passed on to the people certain regulations handed down by former generations and not recorded in the Laws of Moses, for which reason they are rejected by the Sadducaean group, who hold that only those regulations should be considered valid which were written down (in Scripture), and that those which had been handed down by former generations need not be observed. And concerning these matters the two parties came to have controversies and serious differences, the Sadducees having the confidence of the wealthy alone, while the Pharisees have the support of the masses (νῦν δὲ δηλῶσαι βούλομαι ὅτι νόμιμά τινα παρέδοσαν τῷ δήμῳ οἱ Φαρισαῖοι ἐκ πατέρων διαδοχῆς, ἅπερ οὐκ ἀναγέγραπται ἐν τοῖς Μωυσέος νόμοις, καὶ διὰ τοῦτο ταῦτα τὸ τῶν Σαδ-

δουκαίων γένος ἐκβάλλει, λέγον ἐκεῖνα δεῖν ἡγεῖσθαι νόμιμα τὰ γεγραμμένα, τὰ δ᾽ ἐκ παραδόσεως τῶν πατέρων μὴ τηρεῖν. καὶ περὶ τούτων ζητήσεις αὐτοῖς καὶ διαφορὰς γίνεσθαι συνέβαινε μεγάλας, τῶν μὲν Σαδδουκαίων τοὺς εὐπόρους μόνον πειθόντων τὸ δὲ δημοτικὸν οὐχ ἑπόμενον αὐτοῖς ἐχόντων, τῶν δὲ Φαρισαίων τὸ πλῆθος σύμμαχον ἐχόντων). (Ant. 13.10.6 §§297–98)[58]

He uses another, similar expression, "tradition of their fathers" (ἡ πατρῴα παράδοσις) in a passage describing the period from 78–69 BCE:

> Alexandra then appointed Hyrcanus as high priest because of his greater age but more especially because of his lack of energy; and she permitted the Pharisees to do as they liked in all matters, and also commanded the people to obey them; and whatever regulations, introduced by the Pharisees in accordance with the tradition of their fathers, had been abolished by her father-in-law Hyrcanus, these she again restored. And so, while she had the title of sovereign, the Pharisees had the power (Ἡ δὲ ἀρχιερέα μὲν ἀποδείκνυσιν Ὑρκανὸν διὰ τὴν ἡλικίαν, πολὺ μέντοι πλέον διὰ τὸ ἄπραγμον αὐτοῦ, καὶ πάντα τοῖς Φαρισαίοις ἐπιτρέπει ποιεῖν, οἷς καὶ τὸ πλῆθος ἐκέλευσε πειθαρχεῖν, καὶ εἴ τι δὲ καὶ τῶν νομίμων Ὑρκανὸς ὁ πενθερὸς αὐτῆς κατέλυσεν ὧν εἰσήνεγκαν οἱ Φαρισαῖοι κατὰ τὴν πατρῴαν παράδοσιν, τοῦτο πάλιν ἀποκατέστησεν. τὸ μὲν οὖν ὄνομα τῆς βασιλείας εἶχεν αὐτή, τὴν δὲ δύναμιν οἱ Φαρισαῖοι). (Ant. 13.16.2 §§408–9)[59]

Paul, the Pharisee, uses a similar phrase, "the traditions of my fathers" (οἱ πατρικοί μου παραδόσεις) (Gal 1:14).[60]

---

54   Regev, "Pure Individualism," 178; Hayes, *Gentile Impurities*, 49. Moore concludes that the immersion was preparatory for prayer (*Judith*, 219).

55   John C. Poirier, "Why Did the Pharisees Wash Their Hands?" *JJS* 47 (1996) 217–33.

56   See the note on the trans. of v. 3 above.

57   See above. Lane argued that the ritual in question involved pouring water over the hands (*m. Yad.* 2.1). He also concluded that πυγμῇ ("up to the elbow") should be translated a "*handful of water*" (246).

58   Text and trans. from Marcus, in Thackeray, *Josephus*, 7:376–77. On the Pharisees as tradents, preservers,

and elaborators of legal tradition, see Deines, *Die Pharisäer*, 541 and n. 43.

59   Text and trans. from Marcus, in Thackeray *Josephus*, 7:432–33. In the first cent. CE the Pharisees lacked this kind of political support. On the reign of Alexandra, see Mitchell C. Pacwa, "Alexandra Salome," *ABD* 1:152. On "the tradition received from, or handed down by, the fathers," see David Daube, "Rabbinic Methods of Interpretation and Hellenistic Rhetoric," *HUCA* 22 (1949) 239–64, esp. 242–45, 248.

60   As pointed out by Sanders, *Jewish Law*, 108–9.

Mark's use of the term "tradition of the elders" (ἡ παράδοσις τῶν πρεσβυτέρων), instead of "tradition of the fathers" (ἡ παράδοσις τῶν πατέρων), may be due to familiarity with the tradition preserved in the mishnaic tractate "The Fathers":

> Moses received the Law from Sinai and committed it to Joshua, and Joshua to the elders, and the elders to the Prophets; and the Prophets committed it to the men of the Great Synagogue. They said three things: Be deliberate in judgment, raise up many disciples, and make a fence around the Law

מֹשֶׁה קִבֵּל תּוֹרָה מִסִּינַי וּמְסָרָהּ לִיהוֹשֻׁעַ וִיהוֹשֻׁעַ לִזְקֵנִים
וּזְקֵנִים לִנְבִיאִים וּנְבִיאִים מְסָרוּהָ לְאַנְשֵׁי כְנֶסֶת הַגְּדוֹלָה:
הֵם אָמְרוּ שְׁלשָׁה דְבָרִים הֱווּ מְתוּנִים בַּדִּין
וְהַעֲמִידוּ תַלְמִידִים הַרְבֵּה וַעֲשׂוּ סְיָג לַתּוֹרָה:

(*m. ʾAbot* 1.1)[61]

The elders referred to here may be the seventy men appointed by Moses according to Num 11:16-25. Or the allusion may be to Josh 24:31, to the elders who outlived Joshua and who had experienced the work that the Lord did for Israel.[62]

The expression "to hold fast to a tradition" (κρατεῖν παράδοσιν) in v. 3 has the sense of keeping or following a tradition. It is analogous to the phrase "keep the deposit (of faith)" or "guard the deposit" (τὴν παραθήκην φυλάσσειν) in 1 Tim 6:20. The use of ἀφεῖναι ("to abandon," lit., "to let go") in v. 8 as an antonym supports this interpretation.[63]

The phrase ἀπ' ἀγορᾶς in v. 4a is a pregnant construction meaning "after returning from the market."[64] It is most likely that βαπτίσωνται should be translated "they immerse (themselves)."[65] Alternatively, it could signify that they immerse their hands.[66] A full immersion would be performed in order to remove the impurity that may have been contracted by contact with a *zāb*, that is, a man with an abnormal discharge, or with someone who has a similar uncleanness (Lev 15:7-8, 11).[67] Such an immersion is not required by the Bible, unless the person who had been to the market was planning to go into the temple or eat consecrated food. It would be performed as an act of piety.[68] A fragmentary text from Qumran, however, indicates that the community associated with the Dead Sea Scrolls held the position that a *zāb* was obliged to fast until he performed an initial immersion and thus reduced his degree of impurity.[69] Philo and some, but not all, of the rabbis considered the regulations regarding nonpriestly purity to be biblical commands.[70]

The narrative in Luke that is roughly parallel to this passage in Mark portrays Jesus' host, who is a Pharisee, as astonished that Jesus did not immerse before the meal (ἐθαύμασεν ὅτι οὐ πρῶτον ἐβαπτίσθη πρὸ τοῦ ἀρίστου) (Luke 11:38). This incident is probably intended to represent a case of the principle that Mark articulates in v. 4a. In Luke, Jesus had just been portrayed as mixing with a crowd (Luke 11:29, 38).[71] The Levitical precepts, however, say nothing about abstaining from food while in a state of uncleanness. This detail in Mark 7:4 recalls the Essene practice of immersing before eating.[72]

---

61 Text from Philip Blackman, *Mishnayoth*, vol. 4: *Order Nezikin* (2nd rev. ed.; Gateshead [Durham]: Judaica Press, 1983) 489; trans. from Danby, *Mishnah*, 446. Cf. Pesch, 1:371.

62 So Danby, *Mishnah*, 446 n. 3.

63 Wilhelm Michaelis, "κρατέω," *TDNT* 3 (1965) 911–12.

64 See the first note on the trans. of v. 4 above; BAGD, s.v. ἀγορά; Taylor, ad loc.; Heinrich J. Holtzmann, *Hand-Commentar zum Neuen Testament*, vol. 1: *Die Synoptiker. Die Apostelgeschichte* (2nd rev. ed.; Freiburg i. B.: Mohr Siebeck, 1892) 178.

65 With Brandt, *Die jüdischen Baptismen*, 40–42, and against Pesch (1:371), who concluded that it is the things brought from the market that need to be sprinkled.

66 Hunzinger, "ῥαντίζω," 981 n. 23.

67 Brandt, *Die jüdischen Baptismen*, 40.

68 Regev has argued that the pursuit of purity became so important in the Second Temple period because purity was understood as a prerequisite of holiness ("Pure Individualism," 187).

69 4QOrd^c (4Q514); for text, trans., and discussion, see Milgrom, *Leviticus*, 1:972–76. See also Joseph M. Baumgarten, "The Purification Rituals in *DJD* 7," in Dimant and Rappaport, 199–209, esp. 208; Regev, "Pure Individualism," 179–80. See also 4Q274; Hannah K. Harrington, "Holiness and Law in the Dead Sea Scrolls," *DSD* 8 (2001) 126.

70 Regev, "Pure Individualism," 180, 190.

71 Alternatively, the term βαπτίζομαι ("to bathe") could be understood partitively, as referring only to washing the hands (and feet) (Brandt, *Die jüdischen Baptismen*, 40). Luke's use of βαπτίζομαι ("to

Some of the customs mentioned in v. 4b, the immersing of cups and pitchers and copper kettles, continue the theme introduced in v. 2 of concern about ingesting something impure.[73] According to Leviticus, articles of wood, fabric, leather, and goat hair must be immersed if any swarming creature has fallen onto them. After immersion, the article is unclean until evening; then it is clean (Lev 11:32). The underlying purpose is to avoid becoming unclean by ingesting something impure.[74]

Verse 4b also mentions the custom of immersing dining couches.[75] In the biblical period, most beds consisted of a mat, a quilt to lie upon, and a covering. The wealthy had ornamental bed frames that were raised above the floor. The beds of the poor probably included only a wicker mat and the owner's day clothes.[76] The situation was probably similar in the first century CE. Leviticus mentions that beds may become unclean and implies that they are to be dismantled and immersed, then being unclean until evening (Lev 15:4, 21, 23, 26).[77] *M. Kelim* 19.1 presupposes the practice of immersing beds.[78]

■ **5** The author uses the device of anacoluthon here, by beginning a new sentence without completing the one begun in v. 2.[79] As noted above, Bultmann argued that the disciples represent the later Christian community and, therefore, that vv. 1-8 is a composition of the early

church.[80] Another way of interpreting the role of the disciples is to infer that the evangelist is presenting the Pharisees and scribes as attempting to discern what kind of teacher Jesus is. If he does not teach his disciples to follow the tradition of the elders, why not, and what principles does he teach them instead?[81] The question is not overtly hostile. Contrast Mark's "Why do your disciples not *walk* in accordance with the tradition of the elders?" with Matthew's "Why do your disciples *transgress* the tradition of the elders?"[82]

■ **6-8** Whereas the question is not overtly hostile, Jesus' reply is highly polemical, quoting and applying scripture in an attack on his questioners.[83] Regev has argued that the Pharisees are condemned in this context "for a practice that is by no means exclusively Pharisaic" because they were viewed by Jesus or his followers later on as using such practices as means "to demonstrate their religious piety and to establish their reputation as religious leaders," in other words, "as a source of prestige."[84]

The formula "as it is written" ($\dot{\omega}\varsigma$ $\gamma\acute{\epsilon}\gamma\rho\alpha\pi\tau\alpha\iota$) shows that the evangelist regards the book of Isaiah as scripture.[85] The opening words, "Well did Isaiah prophesy" ($\kappa\alpha\lambda\tilde{\omega}\varsigma$ $\dot{\epsilon}\pi\rho\sigma\phi\acute{\eta}\tau\epsilon\upsilon\sigma\epsilon\nu$ $H\sigma\alpha\dot{\iota}\alpha\varsigma$), however, show that behind the book, the person of the inspired prophet is in view.[86] That the passage cited is taken as a prophecy

---

bathe") supports the inference that $\beta\alpha\pi\tau\acute{\iota}\sigma\omega\nu\tau\alpha\iota$ ("they immerse themselves") is an earlier reading in Mark 7:4a than $\dot{\rho}\alpha\nu\tau\acute{\iota}\sigma\omega\nu\tau\alpha\iota$ ("purify by sprinkling"); see the second note on the trans. of v. 4 above.

72　Josephus *Bell.* 2.8.5 §129. Cf. the discussion of 4QOrd^c above.

73　Cf. the exhortation "and do not touch (anything) unclean" ($\kappa\alpha\grave{\iota}$ $\dot{\alpha}\kappa\alpha\theta\acute{\alpha}\rho\tau\sigma\upsilon$ $\mu\grave{\eta}$ $\ddot{\alpha}\pi\tau\epsilon\sigma\theta\epsilon$) in 2 Cor 6:17.

74　Milgrom, *Leviticus,* 1:684–85; Brandt, *Die jüdischen Baptismen,* 42.

75　On the translation of $\kappa\lambda\acute{\iota}\nu\eta$ here as "dining couch" rather than "bed," see BAGD, s.v. $\kappa\lambda\acute{\iota}\nu\eta$; James G. Crossley, "Halakah and Mark 7.4: '. . . and Beds,'" *JSNT* 25 (2003) 433–47.

76　Milgrom, *Leviticus,* 1:909.

77　Milgrom, *Leviticus,* 1:910.

78　See also *m. Miqw.* 7.7. These mishnaic passages use the term מטה ("bed" or "dining couch") rather than משכב ("bed"), the term used in Leviticus 15. The LXX translates משכב ("bed") with $\kappa\sigma\acute{\iota}\tau\eta$ ("bed"). Crossley has argued that מטה ("bed" or "dining

couch") is roughly equivalent to $\kappa\lambda\acute{\iota}\nu\eta$ ("bed" or "dining couch") and that v. 4 shows that Mark had precise knowledge of the Law ("Halakah and Mark 7.4").

79　See the first paragraph of the commentary on vv. 3-4 above.

80　See the section "The History of the Tradition" above.

81　Similarly, Holtzmann, *Die Synoptiker,* 178.

82　On the "tradition of the elders," see the commentary on vv. 3-4 above. On "eating food with profane hands," see the commentary on v. 2 above.

83　The lack of hostility in the question of v. 5 could lead to the conclusion that this is a scholastic dialogue, rather than a controversy-dialogue. Bultmann concluded that, in either case, the material goes back to the debates of the church, sayings that have polemical and apologetic purposes, primarily in relation to Jewish opponents (*History,* 146).

84　Regev, "Moral Impurity," 389–90.

85　Gottlob Schrenk, "$\gamma\rho\acute{\alpha}\phi\omega$," *TDNT* 1 (1964) 747.

86　The emphasis is more on the book of Isaiah in Mark 1:2; see the commentary above. Pap. Eg. 2 cites the "concerning you" (περὶ ὑμῶν) indicates that the prophecy applies to the contemporaries of Jesus, and not only to those of Isaiah.[87]

The polemic emerges in the designation of the questioners as ὑποκριταί ("hypocrites," lit., "actors" here in the sense of "pretenders" or "dissemblers"). This epithet introduces and summarizes the first part of the quotation from Isa 29:13: "This people honors me with their lips, but their hearts are far from me" (οὗτος ὁ λαὸς τοῖς χείλεσίν με τιμᾷ, ἡ δὲ καρδία αὐτῶν πόρρω ἀπέχει ἀπ᾽ ἐμοῦ).[88] In its original context, the prophecy of Isaiah was directed against the official state cult by representing it "as driven by convention and routine." It also implicitly attacks an attitude of rejection or indifference to prophetic revelation.[89] Similarly here, Mark contrasts Jesus, who comes with God's good news about the kingdom, with the Pharisees and scribes whom he portrays as worshiping God with the lips but not with the heart. This image introduces the theme of the external versus the internal, which will be taken up again in v. 15.

The second part of the quotation implies that the questioners' worship of God is in vain, because they teach "commandments of human beings" (ἐντάλματα ἀνθρώπων) as if they were divine, authoritative "teachings" (διδασκαλίαι).[90] The commandments of human beings correspond to the worship of the lips, whereas the divine teachings correspond to the worship of the heart.

The statement of the Markan Jesus in v. 8 interprets the second part of the quotation, but in light also of the first part. Abandoning the commandment of God (ἀφέντες τὴν ἐντολὴν τοῦ θεοῦ) involves substituting commandments of human beings for divine, authoritative teachings; it is also equivalent to having a heart far from God and worshiping with the lips alone. In the main clause of v. 8, the phrase "the tradition of the elders" (ἡ παράδοσις τῶν πρεσβυτέρων), which was employed in vv. 3 and 5, is transformed polemically and in light of the quotation from Isaiah to the phrase "the tradition of human beings" (ἡ παράδοσις τῶν ἀνθρώπων).[91] Whereas the mishnaic tractate "The Fathers" assumes identity, or at least strong continuity, between the Law given on Sinai and the tradition of the elders, the Markan Jesus drives a wedge between the two by equating Isaiah's "commandments of human beings" with "the tradition of the elders."[92] Other rabbinic texts argue that the teaching of the elders is equivalent to the teaching of God.[93]

Although Jesus' response in vv. 6-8 does not address the question of hand-washing explicitly, it does respond to the question of v. 5. The questioners mention eating with profane hands, but ask Jesus more generally why he does not teach his disciples to "walk in accordance with the tradition of the elders." If the speech ended with v. 8, the audience of Mark might infer that "the command-

---

same passage from Isaiah in a similar way, following a passage similar to Mark 12:13-17; see Lührmann, *Fragmente*, 150–51, and the commentary on 12:13-17 below.

87 The authors of the biblical commentaries among the DSS also "found correspondences between contemporary events and figures of biblical prophecies" (Timothy Lim, *Holy Scripture in the Qumran Commentaries and Pauline Letters* [Oxford: Clarendon, 1997] 120).

88 The MSS used by Rahlfs in his edition of the LXX have οὗτος ("this") after ὁ λαός ("people"), rather than before, as in Mark; see the second note on the trans. of v. 6 above. These MSS also read τιμῶσιν ("[they] honor"), rather than τιμᾷ ("[it] honors") as in Mark. Otherwise, the wording of this part of the quotation in Mark is close to Rahlfs's critical text.

89 Blenkinsopp, *Isaiah 1–39*, 405–6.

90 The wording of the LXX differs; see the first note on the trans. of v. 7 above. The LXX also differs from the Hebrew; see the trans. and notes in Blenk-

insopp, *Isaiah 1–39*, 403. On the use of the phrase "commandments of human beings" by Hermann L. Strack to criticize the Judaism of his day, see Deines, *Die Pharisäer*, 239 n. 3.

91 Col 2:22 echoes Mark 7:7-8; it may be that Colossians also deals with the issue of the observance of the Jewish regulations regarding ritual purity; cf. Leppä, *Making of Colossians*, 262–63. Cf. Strabo, who says of the ordinances observed by both the Greeks and the barbarians that they are "twofold; for they come either from gods or from men" (τὸ δὲ πρόσταγμα διττόν· ἢ γὰρ παρὰ θεῶν ἢ παρὰ ἀνθρώπων); text and trans. from Horace Leonard Jones, *The Geography of Strabo* (8 vols.; Cambridge, MA: Harvard University Press; London: Heinemann, 1930) 7:286–87.

92 See the citation of *m. ʾAbot* 1.1 in the commentary on vv. 3-4 above.

93 E.g., *Mekilta of R. Shimʿon bar Yohai* 19:19; for a discussion of this text and the whole issue of the relation of the teaching of Moses, the elders, and the

ment of God" referred to the instruction to repent and believe or trust in the good news mediated by Jesus (cf. 1:14-15). This inference is not inappropriate, but the next section of the speech interprets the phrase otherwise.

As Claude G. Montefiore has pointed out, the logic of the argument in vv. 6-8 is not compelling.[94] It may well be that the underlying issue is actually competition for leadership of the people of Israel, as the original force of the quotation from Isaiah suggests. Whereas the Pharisees displayed a high degree of nonpriestly purity as a way of gaining social authority and status, and hoped thereby to bring the majority of the people to imitate this way of life, the Markan Jesus, and perhaps the historical Jesus, claimed a different sort of authority and had a different way of reforming the people. Rather than modeling a high degree of purity, he reached out more directly to the ordinary people, including sinners, and called them to repentance, that is, to return to obedience to God in light of the nearness of the kingdom and to accept Jesus as God's agent.[95]

■ **9-13** It may be, as Bultmann argued, that vv. 9-13 constitute an elaboration of an older unit, vv. 1-8. Such a conclusion is not necessary, however, since the reference to "the commandment of God" (ἡ ἐντολὴ τοῦ θεοῦ) in v. 8 already prepares for the citations in v. 10.[96] The introductory or transitional formula "And he said to them" (καὶ ἔλεγεν αὐτοῖς) in v. 9, however, does distinguish vv. 1-8 and vv. 9-13 as two sections of the overall speech or "conversation."

The statement of v. 9 summarizes the conclusion of v. 8 and intensifies it. In v. 9 the Markan Jesus accuses the questioners not only of *abandoning* the commandment of God but of *nullifying* it. Verses 10-12 elaborate and support this accusation. The introductory formula "For Moses said" (Μωϋσῆς γὰρ εἶπεν) in v. 10 implies that the words of Moses are equivalent to the commandments of God. Here there is even more emphasis on the person who mediates the divine revelation and less emphasis on the written scriptures than in v. 6. The citation of the commandment to honor one's parents agrees with Deut 5:16 LXX in having a second σου ("your") after μητέρα ("mother").[97] The wording of the commandment that one who speaks evil of either of his parents shall die is closer to Exod 21:16 LXX than to Lev 20:9 LXX.[98]

The opening words of v. 11, "But you say" (ὑμεῖς δὲ λέγετε), create an antithesis with the opening words of v. 10, "For Moses said" (Μωϋσῆς γὰρ εἶπεν). The implication is that Moses speaks the commandments of God, whereas the questioners speak only the commandments of human beings.

Verse 11 is a prohibitive vow. The prohibitive vow is not mentioned in the Bible. All biblical vows are dedicatory.

prophets to the teaching of God, see Steven D. Fraade, "Moses and the Commandments: Can Hermeneutics, History, and Rhetoric Be Distinguished?" in Hindy Najman and Judith H. Newman, eds., *The Idea of Biblical Interpretation: Essays in Honor of James Kugel* (JSJSup 83; Leiden: Brill, 2004) 399–422. Fraade discusses Mark 7:1-13 on 417.

94 Claude G. Montefiore, *The Synoptic Gospels* (3 vols.; London: Macmillan, 1909) 1:145–47.

95 Cf. Mark 1:14-15 and 2:15-17. On the Pharisees' display of purity and the competition between them and the historical Jesus, see Regev, "Pure Individualism," 192–201. Sanders's argument that the historical Jesus did not require repentance of sinners seems to be an overstatement (*Jesus and Judaism*, 210); see the commentary on 2:15-17 above. Members of the community at Qumran also strove for a higher degree of purity than the average Israelite (Harrington, "Holiness and Law," 127). On the interpretation of language about repentance, see David Lambert, "Did Israel Believe That Redemption Awaited Its Repentance? The Case of *Jubilees* 1,"

CBQ 68 (2006) 631–50; idem, "Topics in the History of Repentance: From the Hebrew Bible to Early Judaism and Christianity" (Ph.D. diss., Harvard University, 2004).

96 Booth, however, following E. J. Pryke, concludes that v. 8 is redactional (*Jesus and the Laws of Purity*, 40–43, 51–52).

97 Cf. Exod 20:12 LXX. On the use of scripture in this passage, in comparison with the use of the same passages in rabbinic literature and Philo, see Harry Jungbauer, *"Ehre Vater und Mutter": Der Weg des Elterngebots in der biblischen Tradition* (WUNT 2.146; Tübingen: Mohr Siebeck, 2002) 271–74.

98 Mark 7:10b and Exod 21:16 LXX both read ὁ κακολογῶν ("the one who speaks evil"), whereas Lev 20:9 LXX reads ἄνθρωπος ἄνθρωπος, ὃς ἂν κακῶς εἴπῃ ("any person who speaks evil"). Both Mark and Exod 21:16 use the verb τελευτᾶν ("to die"), whereas Lev 20:9 uses θανατοῦσθαι ("to be killed"). Codex Alexandrinus, in Exod 21:16, has the same verb as Mark: τελευτάτω ("he shall die").

A dedicatory vow is a promise to give persons or property to God. Sacrificial animals were offered on the altar, whereas other property was placed in the treasury of the temple. Such property was considered sacred until sold to a third party or redeemed by the votary at cost plus one-fifth.[99] Moshe Benovitz's analysis of prohibitive vows in Second Temple literature and rabbinic texts suggests that "originally, prohibitive vows were actually *dedicatory* vows of a specific type, which could not take effect for technical reasons. The only practical effect was a personal prohibition."[100] The prohibitive vows of Second Temple and New Testament texts constitute a transitional type between the biblical dedicatory vow and the rabbinic prohibitive vow. In the latter type, property is often *likened* to an offering, prohibiting its use *as if* it were actually an offering. This type of vow was regarded as an oath substitute. Oaths were discouraged because of the commandment not to take the name of the Lord in vain.[101]

The prohibitive vow originally had the form "*qorbān* the food that I shall eat."[102] The term *qorbān* is used in Second Temple literature for both sacrificial and non-sacrificial offerings, although the former is more common.[103] According to the Bible, vows are inviolable. Nonfulfillment makes the person liable for trespass against temple property (Deut 23:22; Lev 5:14-16).[104] Another common vow formula is "*qonam* is that which you benefit from me."[105] This formula, although it seems absurd, should be taken literally: any property of mine that you use is dedicated to the temple. The property is not dedicated to the temple unless and until the person mentioned in the vow derives benefit from it. Since this prohibitive vow is actually a dedicatory vow, it is "vested with Torah sanction."[106]

Verse 11 should be understood in the same way.[107] This vow is thus a clever way in which a son can prevent his parents from using any of his property. The only practical effect of the vow is that the parents would be liable to trespass against temple property if they made use of any of their son's belongings. In other words, the son is making cynical use of the biblical vow, a cultic form, in order to evade his obligations related to the commandment to honor one's father and mother. This interpretation reveals the logical connection between vv. 9-13 and vv. 5-8. The son's use of the biblical vow is a case of honoring God with the lips but not the heart, and of abandoning or nullifying the commandment of God. He is a pious dissembler. The Markan Jesus objects to the prohibitive vow because it is a dedicatory vow that is formulated in such a way that the votary intends that it never take effect. In the extreme case cited here, it is hypocritical.[108]

The accusation of substituting "the tradition/commandments of human beings" for the commandment of God may be clarified further. This charge is illuminated by a passage from Philo preserved by Eusebius:

> If a man has devoted his wife's sustenance to a sacred purpose he must refrain from giving her that sustenance; so with a father's gifts to his son or a ruler's to his subjects. The chief and most perfect way of releasing dedicated property is by the priest refusing it, for he is empowered by God to accept it or not. Next to this, that given by those who at the time have the higher authority may lawfully declare that God is propitiated so that there is no necessity to accept the dedication (ἐὰν ἐπιφημίσῃ τροφὴν γυναικὸς ἀνὴρ ἱερὰν εἶναι, τροφῆς ἀνέχειν· ἐὰν πατὴρ υἱοῦ, ἐὰν ἄρχων τοῦ ὑπηκόου, ταὐτόν. καὶ ἔκλυσις δὲ ἐπιφημισθέντων ἡ μὲν τελειοτάτη καὶ μεγίστη τοῦ ἱερέως ἀποφήσαντος· ὑπὸ γὰρ τοῦ θεοῦ κύριος

99 Benovitz, KOL NIDRE, 3, 9–13.
100 Ibid., 4.
101 Ibid., 3–4, 11–12.
102 Ibid., 6. The Hebrew is קרבן (*qorbān*, "offering"), which is transliterated by Mark in Greek as κορβᾶν (*korban*).
103 Benovitz, KOL NIDRE, 10.
104 Ibid., 7, 10.
105 *Qonam* is equivalent to *qorban* (ibid., 14).
106 Ibid., 16.
107 For a review and critical assessment of previous scholarship on this and related passages, see Benovitz, KOL NIDRE, 17–22.
108 Cf. ibid., 23. See also P. W. van Boxel, "Isaiah 29:13 in the New Testament and Early Rabbinic Judaism," in Pieter W. van der Horst, ed., *Aspects of Religious Contact and Conflict in the Ancient World* (UTR 31; Utrecht: Faculteit der Godgeleerdheid, Universiteit Utrecht, 1995) 81–90, esp. 89–90.

οὗτος δέξασθαι· καὶ μετὰ ταύτην δὲ ἡ παρὰ τῶν
μᾶλλον ἀεὶ κυρίων ὁσία ἵλεω τὸν θεὸν ἀπο-
φαίνειν, ὡς μηδὲ ἐπάναγκες τὴν ἀνάθεσιν
δέχεσθαι). (Eusebius *Praep. Ev.* 8.7.5 = Philo *Hypothetica* 7.5)[109]

Philo's remarks provide evidence that, in the Second Temple period, the treasurer of the temple, his agent, or influential laypeople had the authority to reject an offering at the request of the votary, that is, to annul a vow. Rabbinic literature indicates that the dissolution of vows was common in the rabbis' spheres of influence. Sages and rabbinic courts had the authority to declare that vows were not binding.[110] The Pharisees, however, apparently did not consider themselves authorized to nullify vows. They would certainly not have encouraged this type of cynical vow, but since they had endowed the prohibitive vow with the sanction of Torah, they were powerless to distinguish between moral and immoral uses of it.[111] From this perspective, the prohibitive vow itself is a "commandment of human beings" that has come into conflict with a "commandment of God."

The accusation of the Markan Jesus in vv. 12-13a, directed against the Pharisees and the scribes, criticizes the Pharisees' unwillingness to annul vows even when they put human beings in need of the most basic resources. According to Josephus, Theophrastus states, in his work on *Laws*, that the Tyrians prohibit the use of foreign oaths and mentions *korban* as one of these (Josephus *Ap.* 1.22 §§166–67).[112] The statement in v. 13b, "And you do many similar such things" (καὶ παρόμοια

τοιαῦτα πολλὰ ποιεῖτε), may allude to the Sabbath laws challenged by Jesus in chaps. 2–3.[113]

■ **14-15** As pointed out above, v. 14 begins the second major part of the unit 7:1-23.[114] Here Jesus turns his attention from the Pharisees and scribes to address the crowd. In the first part of the "conversation" or speech (vv. 1-13), Jesus responds to the interlocutors' question about what kind of teacher he is by challenging their authority as teachers. In the second part (vv. 14-23), he sets forth his own teaching on the relevant subject matter.

The second major part is divided into an address to the crowd (vv. 14-15) and instruction of the disciples in private (vv. 17-23).[115] The situation is analogous to that of 4:1-34. Jesus speaks in parables to the crowd; the saying of v. 15 is defined as a παραβολή ("parable" or "figurative saying") in v. 17.[116] The commands to listen and to comprehend in v. 14 do not necessarily mean, from the point of view of the evangelist, that the crowd is able to grasp the significance of the saying. As Jesus needed to interpret the parables and sayings of 4:1-34 for his disciples, so also does he need to interpret the saying of v. 15 for them.[117]

Bultmann, as noted above, argued that the saying of v. 15 goes back to the historical Jesus.[118] More recent scholarship has, on the whole, agreed with that assessment.[119] Heikki Räisänen, however, has argued that the saying is inauthentic because it is too radical for a Jew of the first century to have uttered.[120] But the saying is only radical in that sense if one interprets its meaning in light of v. 19c, "(Jesus said this) making all (types of) food

---

109　Text and trans. from Colson and Whitaker, *Philo*, 9:424–27.
110　Benovitz, *KOL NIDRE*, 7.
111　Ibid., 23, 25–26.
112　Jungbauer, *"Ehre Vater und Mutter,"* 274.
113　See the commentary on 2:23-28 and 3:1-6 above.
114　See the section "The Genre of the Dispute with the Pharisees" above.
115　V. 16 is a post-Markan gloss; see the note on the trans. of v. 15 above.
116　It may also be defined as an antithetical aphorism because of the contrast between "going in" and "coming out" (Tannehill, *Sword*, 89).
117　A similar structure of public teaching followed by private instruction of disciples is found in *Pesikta deRab Kahana* 14:14, which probably dates to the

sixth cent. CE; for discussion and comparison with Mark 7:1-23, see Eric Ottenheijm, "Impurity between Intention and Deed: Purity Disputes in First Century Judaism and in the New Testament," in M. J. H. M. Poorthuis and J. Schwartz, eds., *Purity and Holiness: The Heritage of Leviticus* (JCPS 2; Leiden/Boston/Cologne: Brill, 2000) 129–47, esp. 143–46.
118　See the section "The History of the Tradition" above.
119　Booth, *Jesus and the Laws of Purity*, 46–47 (with a review of redaction-critical scholarship on the verse), 53; Jonathan Klawans, *Impurity and Sin in Ancient Judaism* (Oxford/New York: Oxford University Press, 2000) 146–50.
120　Heikki Räisänen, "Jesus and the Food Laws: Reflec-

clean" ($\kappa\alpha\vartheta\alpha\rho\acute{\iota}\zeta\omega\nu$ $\pi\acute{\alpha}\nu\tau\alpha$ $\tau\grave{\alpha}$ $\beta\rho\acute{\omega}\mu\alpha\tau\alpha$). Yet this parenthetical remark is the evangelist's addition, not part of the teaching of the historical Jesus.[121]

Montefiore, who identified himself as a liberal Jew,[122] rightly concluded that, in the context, the saying of v. 15 must be connected with the question of hand-washing raised in v. 5. In other words, the issue is that a profane hand, in touching the bread, would cause "some particles of forbidden matter" to be eaten and thus the eater to be unclean.[123] Thus, the concern not to become unclean by ingesting something impure is an underlying idea that unites vv. 1-8 with v. 15 and what follows.[124] Montefiore, however, drew the conclusion that the saying has significance beyond the present literary context and that "the *principle* of the Logion goes beyond its actual wording." In other words, the saying "destroys the whole conception of *material* or ritual uncleanness" which occurs in a variety of religions. The historical Jesus taught that "no *thing* can make you unclean. You can only make yourself

unclean by sin."[125] Montefiore saw this teaching of Jesus as analogous to the teaching of the prophets who argued that God was moved not by "religious uncleanness" but by moral considerations only (counting idolatry as a part of morality in this context).[126]

Montefiore, however, doubted that Jesus was conscious of the underlying principle and its ramifications. Montefiore followed Alfred E. J. Rawlinson in arguing that the saying is an antithetical epigram that should not be taken literally. Just as Hos 6:6, "I desire mercy and not sacrifice," means that mercy is more important than sacrifice, so also the saying of Jesus means that avoiding the defilement of sin is more important that avoiding ritual impurity.[127] Mark's arrangement of the material perhaps implies that this traditional, nonliteral significance represents the crowd's understanding of the saying, whereas Jesus reveals to his disciples in v. 19c that a more radical, literal meaning is meant.

As Jonathan Klawans has pointed out, the idea that

tions on Mark 7.15," *JSNT* 16 (1982) 79–100. Another important argument of Räisänen is the lack of influence of the saying on subsequent Christian developments; but again, if the saying originally did not address the food laws, this lack of influence is not surprising. Sanders argued that v. 19c represents the "obvious" meaning of the saying in v. 15 and concluded that the historical Jesus could not have spoken this saying in a context like the one portrayed in 7:1-23, which would make it revolutionary (*Jewish Law*, 28).

121 Swete at first refers to this phrase as an addition of a teacher or editor, apparently prior to Mark, but then cites with approval Field's argument that 3:30 is "another instance of a brief explanation parenthetically added by Mc" (152). Those who clearly attribute the parenthesis to Mark include Taylor (345), Booth, *Jesus and the Laws of Purity*, 49–50; Bart D. Ehrman, *Jesus: Apocalyptic Prophet of the New Millennium* (Oxford/New York: Oxford University Press, 1999) 204–5; Jesper Svartvik, *Mark and Mission: Mk 7:1–23 in Its Narrative and Historical Contexts* (CBNTS 32; Stockholm: Almqvist & Wiksell, 2000) 406–7. Both Ehrman and Svartvik argue that the saying of v. 15 did not originally signify the abrogation of the food laws, as v. 19c suggests. The latter conclusion is supported by Menahem Kister, who argues that the first part of the saying, "There is nothing outside of a human being which, by going into him, is able to profane him," conforms to rabbinic system of purity, which assumes that "*according*

to the law of the Torah no food can defile a man* [that is, by eating], except the *nevela* (corpse) of a clean bird" ("Law, Morality and Rhetoric in Some Sayings of Jesus," in James L. Kugel, ed., *Studies in Ancient Midrash* [Harvard Center for Jewish Studies; Cambridge, MA: Harvard University Press, 2001] 145–54; citation from p. 151).

122 Montefiore, *Synoptic Gospels*, 1:ix. For a summary and critique of Montefiore's scholarship on the Pharisees, see Deines, *Die Pharisäer*, 365–69; on the interpretation of v. 15 by Montefiore, see ibid., 366–67; on his and other interpretations of 7:1-23, see ibid., 367 n. 192; cf. 466–67.

123 Montefiore, *Synoptic Gospels*, 1:152. Svartvik similarly concludes that the issue is the restricted topic of eating contaminated food, i.e., food that has been made impure (*Mark and Mission*, 406). It is interesting that *Gos. Thom.* 14 places a version of the saying of Mark 7:15 in a ritual context; it follows the command of Jesus, "when they receive you eat whatever they serve to you" (trans. from Layton, *Gnostic Scriptures*, 383). Cf. Luke 10:8.

124 See the commentary on vv. 3-4 above.

125 Montefiore, *Synoptic Gospels*, 1:153–54.

126 Ibid., 154. Ottenheijm similarly argued that the first clause of v. 15 denies "physical impurity as an existing negative power" ("Impurity between Intention and Deed," 146).

127 Montefiore, *Synoptic Gospels*, 1:155. Sanders (*Jewish Law*, 28, and p. 335, C. Food, n. 8) allows this meaning for Mark 7:15 interpreted apart from its present

sins are morally defiling was nothing new in the Jewish context in which Jesus taught. The "not . . . but" formula in v. 15 indicates that moral purity is given a higher priority than ritual purity. In this prioritization, the saying is similar to the arguments of Philo. Yet it is a significant difference that Jesus apparently did not present ritual purity as a symbol of moral purity, as Philo did. It is this lack of a symbolic link that may have opened the way for some of the followers of Jesus to cease to observe the ritual laws.[128]

A further interpretive issue is whether "moral impurity" in this context is metaphorical or literal, in the sense that sins such as those listed in vv. 21-22 produce a condition of impurity analogous to ritual impurity. The latter seems to be the view of Regev.[129] The former seems more likely.

■ **17-19** As noted above, this change of scene and the disciples' question belong to the Markan shaping of the material.[130] The fact that the disciples have to ask about the significance of the saying of v. 15 implies that it is a "parable" in the sense attested in the LXX, namely, an enigmatic or riddling saying.[131] The first part of Jesus' reply in v. 18, "Are you thus also foolish?" (οὕτως καὶ ὑμεῖς ἀσύνετοί ἐστε;), confirms this inference. As disciples of Jesus, they should already be wise enough to understand the saying. The "also" (καί) alludes to the crowd, the outsiders who are not expected to understand the saying properly.[132] Jesus' criticism of the disciples, however, is also a rhetorical device to call attention to what Jesus is about to say. Compare the following scene in the *Shepherd of Hermas*:

And I began to ask (the personified church) about the times, if the end were yet. But she cried out with a loud voice saying, "Foolish man, do you not see the tower still being built? Whenever therefore the building of the tower has been finished, the end comes" (ἐπηρώτων δὲ αὐτὴν περὶ τῶν καιρῶν, εἰ ἤδη συντέλειά ἐστιν. ἡ δὲ ἀνέκραγε φωνῇ μεγάλῃ λέγουσα· Ἀσύνετε ἄνθρωπε, οὐχ ὁρᾷς τὸν πύργον ἔτι οἰκοδομούμενον; ὡς ἐὰν οὖν συντελεσθῇ ὁ πύργος οἰκοδομούμενος, ἔχει τέλος). (*Hermas, Vis.* 3.8.9)[133]

Verse 18b restates the first part of the saying, previously expressed in v. 15a. The saying is reformulated, however, so that "There is nothing outside of a human being" (οὐδέν ἐστιν ἔξωθεν τοῦ ἀνθρώπου) in v. 15a becomes "everything which is outside" (πᾶν τὸ ἔξωθεν) in v. 18b, and "which is able to profane him" (ὃ δύναται κοινῶσαι αὐτόν) in v. 15a becomes "is not able to profane him" (οὐ δύναται αὐτὸν κοινῶσαι) in v. 18b. This shift from negative to positive and from positive to negative is probably a technique of stylistic variation.

Verse 19a gives an explanation for the first part of the saying: that which goes into a human being does not defile because it does not go into his "heart" (καρδία). In Akkadian, the word "heart" (*libbu*) is used to describe emotions such as joy, fear, and desire. In archaic Greece, the term "heart" (κῆρ or καρδίη) is often connected with courage, especially in battle.[134] In the Hebrew Bible, "heart" (לֵב and לֵבָב) is used both literally and figuratively. In general, its figurative usage signifies the innermost part of the human being. In particular, it is associated with courage; it is the seat of the rational functions; it is the center of planning and volition; and religious and moral conduct is portrayed as rooted in the heart.[135] In the LXX, καρδία ("heart") is "the true equivalent of the Heb. לֵב or לֵבָב," reflecting the "wealth of nuances" expressed by the corresponding Hebrew

context, following Andreas B. Du Toit; so also Svartvik (*Mark and Mission*, 406), following Sanders and Klawans (*Impurity and Sin*, 147), following James D. G. Dunn. Kazen also concluded that the saying expresses a way of setting priorities (*Jesus and Purity Halakhah*, 88). See the commentary on 5:33-34 above.

128　Klawans, *Impurity and Sin*, 149.
129　Regev, "Moral Impurity," 386–87.
130　See the section "The History of the Tradition" and the commentary on vv. 14-15 above.
131　See the commentary on 4:24-25 above.

132　Cf. v. 14 and the commentary above; cf. also 4:11-12, 33-34, and the commentary above.
133　Text and trans. from Lake, *Apostolic Fathers*, 2:48–49. Cf. *Vis.* 3.6.5; Osiek, *Shepherd of Hermas*, 78.
134　Walter Burkert, "Towards Plato and Paul: The 'Inner' Human Being," in Yarbro Collins, *Perspectives*, 64–65.
135　Friedrich Baumgärtel, "καρδία. A. לֵב, לֵבָב in the OT," *TDNT* 3 (1965) 606–7.

words.[136] The NT use of καρδία ("heart") agrees with the OT usage. Even more strongly than the LXX, it speaks of the "heart as the main organ of psychic and spiritual life." The "heart" stands for the whole of the inner being of a person in contrast to the external side, the πρόσωπον ("the entire bodily presence" or "person," lit., "face").[137]

The Markan Jesus provides evidence for the claim that things going from outside into the body do not enter the heart by pointing out that they go instead to the belly ("κοιλία") (v. 19b). The basic meaning of the term κοιλία is "hollow," especially with reference to the human or animal body. It often refers to the stomach or intestines. Philo used the term to denote the digestive system. It is surely in the latter sense that it is used here.[138] The comment that the things that come into the body from outside go out of it again and end up in the latrine (v. 19b) satirizes the great concern about ingesting something impure alluded to in vv. 3-4 and makes the point that such concern would be better directed elsewhere.

The participial phrase "making all (types of) food clean" (καθαρίζων πάντα τὰ βρώματα) in v. 19c is an explanatory comment, added by the evangelist.[139] The saying of v. 15 has a great deal in common with the prophetic devaluation of cult and emphasis on fidelity to God, justice, and other moral qualities. The comment of v. 19c takes a giant step further and implies, at the very least, that the observance of the food laws for followers of Jesus is not obligatory. The Markan declaration that Jesus made all types of food clean is analogous to principles enunciated by Paul:

Food will not bring us before (the judgment seat of) God; we are neither worse off if we do not eat, nor

better off if we do eat (βρῶμα δὲ ἡμᾶς οὐ παραστήσει τῷ θεῷ· οὔτε ἐὰν μὴ φάγωμεν ὑστερούμεθα, οὔτε ἐὰν φάγωμεν περισσεύομεν). (1 Cor 8:8; my trans.)

Paul first states that food is not a matter of great concern to God; it is irrelevant for the final judgment. The elaboration of this principle seems to be directed at those who pride themselves on not being bound by ritual laws related to food. It makes the point that those who avoid eating unclean food are not worse off in their relation to God because they do so. Likewise, those who make no distinctions in what they eat are not thereby more pleasing to God.[140] It seems intrinsically likely that the audience of Mark would include both those who observed the ritual laws related to food and those who did not. The comment of the evangelist should probably not be read as an indication that the evangelist and his entire audience had abandoned such observance. It does make the point, however, that such observance is not necessary for followers of Jesus.

■ 20-23 As noted above, v. 18b repeats the first part of the saying in v. 15, and v. 19 explains that part. Verse 20 then restates the second part of the saying in v. 15. The restatement in v. 20 varies the original formulation by using the singular "that which comes out of a human being" (τὸ ἐκ τοῦ ἀνθρώπου ἐκπορευόμενον), rather than the plural used in v. 15, literally, "the things that come out of a human being" (τὰ ἐκ τοῦ ἀνθρώπου ἐκπορευόμενα). The formulation of v. 20 also has the emphatic ἐκεῖνο ("that"), which is lacking in v. 15.[141]

Verses 21-22 then give the explanation for the second half of the saying, as reformulated in v. 20. The statement that evil intentions come from within the hearts of human beings in v. 21 seems to presuppose the idea of

---

136 Johannes Behm, "καρδία. C. The LXX, and Hellenistic and Rabbinic Judaism," *TDNT* 3 (1965) 609.

137 Johannes Behm, "καρδία. D. καρδία in the New Testament," *TDNT* 3 (1965) 611–13. Cf. Seneca, who wrote from a moral perspective about what is "in a man" (*in illo*) and what is "his" (*suus*), as opposed to what "does not belong to him" (*aliena*) or what is merely "around him" (*circa ipsum*) (*Ep. mor.* 41.6–8; text from Richard Gummere, *Seneca: Ad Lucilium Epistulae Morales* (3 vols.; London: Heinemann; Cambridge, MA: Harvard University Press, 1917) 1:274–76; my trans.

138 Johannes Behm, "κοιλία," *TDNT* 3 (1965) 786–88.

139 See the commentary on vv. 14-15 and the note on the trans. of v. 19 above. Cf. 13:14 and the commentary below.

140 The same point is made in Rom 14:1-4.

141 In keeping with the other changes, the plural attributive participle τὰ κοινοῦντα τὸν ἄνθρωπον (lit., "the things which profane him") of v. 15 becomes the finite verb κοινοῖ ("profanes") in v. 20.

the evil heart.[142] This idea seems to have originated in Gen 6:5:

> The Lord saw that the wickedness of humanity was great in the earth, and that every inclination of the intentions of their hearts was only evil continually

> (וירא יהוה כי רבה רעת האדם בארץ
> וכל־יצר מחשבת לבו רק רע כל־היום)[143]

The Septuagint version of Gen 6:5 reads:

> The Lord God saw that the evils of human beings had multiplied upon the earth and that every single one (of them) diligently considers in his heart evil things continually (Ἰδὼν δὲ κύριος ὁ θεὸς ὅτι ἐπληθύνθησαν αἱ κακίαι τῶν ἀνθρώπων ἐπὶ τῆς γῆς καὶ πᾶς τις διανοεῖται ἐν τῇ καρδίᾳ αὐτοῦ ἐπιμελῶς ἐπὶ τὰ πονηρὰ πάσας τὰς ἡμέρας).

According to *4 Ezra* 3:21, Adam "bore" or "was burdened" with an evil heart, as were all who were descended from him. Thus, the "disease" became permanent (3:22, 25-26).[144] The word διαλογισμός ("intention" or "thought"), which occurs in v. 21, is used in the LXX to translate מחשבה ("intention" or "thought"), which occurs in Gen 6:5, cited above.[145] In contrast to the idea of an evil heart, Seneca argued that the human being has a god within by nature, that is, the soul brought to perfection by reason. To be good is to live in accordance with nature; it is other human beings that push a person into vice (*Ep. mor.* 41.1, 9).[146]

Verses 21-23 imply that the evil thoughts or intentions in the heart lead to specific evil deeds or sins.[147] Verses 21b-22 constitute, form-critically speaking, a list of vices. The catalogue form originated in the Stoic school of philosophy.[148] The sins or vices are listed asyndetically; that is, they are coordinated without any connectives.[149] The asyndetic form probably arose in oral, popular philosophical teaching and is attested in non-Jewish, non-Christian Hellenistic, and Jewish Hellenistic texts. The lists of virtues and vices in the *Community Rule* are sometimes asyndetic, sometimes not.[150] The literary form has no fixed number of items or organizing principle.[151]

---

142 The idea of the evil intentions of the heart leading to the commission of specific sins in Mark 7:21-23 is analogous to Paul's notion of "the intentions of the flesh" (ἐπιθυμίαι τῆς σαρκός) which result in the "works of the flesh" (τὰ ἔργα τῆς σαρκός); see Betz, *Galatians*, 283. This similarity, however, does not necessarily imply the dependence of Mark on Paul. Although some of the same terms that occur in vv. 21-22 are found also in lists of vices in the Pauline letters, there is little reason to posit Pauline influence; so Cranfield (242–43) contra Taylor (346–47). Contrast the *Community Rule*, according to which evil deeds result from the domination of the "spirit of wickedness" or "spirit of perverseness" (רוח עולה) over a human being (1QS 4:9) (Wibbing, *Die Tugend- und Lasterkataloge*, 52).

143 Text from BHS; trans. (modified) from RSV. See also Gen 8:21; Jer 3:17; 7:24; 11:8; 16:12; 18:12. Cf. the heart of stone in Ezek 36:26 and the guilty heart of 1QS 1:6. On the related idea of the evil inclination, see Stone, *Fourth Ezra*, 63 nn. 17, 18.

144 See Stone, *Fourth Ezra*, 63–67.

145 Gottlob Schrenk, "διαλογισμός," *TDNT* 2 (1964) 96.

146 Seneca *Ep. Mor.* 41.1, 9; Gummere, *Seneca*, 1:272–73, 276–79.

147 Wibbing has argued persuasively that in the lists of virtues and vices in the OT, the *T. 12 Patr.*, the DSS, and the NT, the inner connection between disposition (*Gesinnung*) and concrete deeds is so strong that one may not separate the two (*Die Tugend- und Lasterkataloge*, 33, 108). The same strong connection is evident in Mark 7:21-22. Ottenheijm does not pay sufficient attention to this connection when he concludes that "Jesus reinterprets impurity by pointing to immoral intentions as defiling, evaluating intentions as equal to deeds" ("Impurity between Intention and Deed," 146).

148 Wibbing, *Die Tugend- und Lasterkataloge*, 15. Although tendencies in this direction can be found, there are no lists of virtues or vices in the OT (ibid., 26). The form emerges in Philo, Wisdom of Solomon, and 4 Maccabees; it has two roots: the Decalogue and the Stoic catalogues of virtues and vices (ibid., 26–27). In *1 Enoch* 91, 94; *2 Enoch*; and *Jubilees*, the catalogues of virtues and vices are set in opposition to one another in a way that recalls the tradition of the Two Ways (ibid., 42).

149 On asyndeton, see Smyth §2165; Wibbing points out that approximately half of the lists of virtues and vices in the NT are asyndetic, Mark 7:21-22 among them (*Die Tugend- und Lasterkataloge*, 79).

150 Wibbing, *Die Tugend- und Lasterkataloge*, 79.

151 Ibid., 81.

The flexible form and lack of a logical principle suggest that the NT lists are rooted in Jewish Hellenistic traditions.[152]

The first evil deeds that are mentioned are sexual sins, namely, πορνεῖαι ("acts of unlawful intercourse" or "sexual immorality"). Leviticus 18 forbids sexual relations between persons who are near of kin, sexual relations with a menstruating woman, sexual relations between a man and another man's wife, sexual relations between men, and between human beings and animals (Lev 18:6-20, 22-23). Such deeds are defined as defiling, but in a moral sense, not a ritual sense. They defile the land and lead to the expulsion of the nation to which the offenders belong (Lev 18:24-30; Ezek 33:26b).[153]

The next type of evil deed, however, κλοπαί ("acts of stealing"), is not a source of moral defilement according to the Bible, the Dead Sea Scrolls, or rabbinic literature.[154] On the other hand, in the LXX, stealing (κλέπτειν) is one of the chief sins, along with murder, adultery, false witness, and idolatry (Jer 7:9).[155] The commandment not to steal (οὐ κλέψεις) is unconditional (Exod 20:14; Deut 5:19).[156]

The third item in the list of evil deeds, φόνοι ("acts of murder"), like the first, is a heinous act that generates moral impurity. It pollutes the land and the people in the midst of whom God dwells. The threatened result is expulsion from the land.[157] Whereas the nouns πορνεία ("unlawful intercourse") and κλοπή ("stealing") do not occur elsewhere in Mark, the term φόνος ("murder") occurs also in 15:7 in association with the rebels who had been imprisoned, including Barabbas.[158]

The fourth item in the list, μοιχεῖαι ("acts of adultery"), includes specifically one of the more serious sexual sins mentioned under the general rubric of πορνεῖαι ("acts of unlawful intercourse") in the previous verse (21). Although the noun does not occur elsewhere in Mark, verbal forms are used in 10:11-12 and 10:19. In 10:11-12, the Markan Jesus takes the position that remarriage after divorce is equivalent to adultery. In 10:19 he cites the commandment against adultery in the dialogue with a young man.[159]

The fifth item, πλεονεξίαι ("acts of greediness"), may be understood in terms of power or material possessions. The basic usages of the word-group are "having more," "receiving more," and "wanting more." Another of its usages is "arrogance."[160] In Herodotus, πλεονεξία signifies "hunger for power." Thucydides used the related verb to signify "seeking political gain." Plato used the noun to mean both "insatiability" with regard to food and pleasure, on the one hand, and "the desire for power" or "the urge to assert oneself," on the other. Aristotle used it to mean "covetousness," for example, with respect to money, fame, and physical desires. In Hellenistic philosophy, the opposite of πλεονεξία is σωφροσύνη ("moderation") in the context of the ideals of the relative equality among men and a just society.[161]

Unlike non-Jewish, non-Christian Greek literature, πλεονεξία in the LXX usually has a negative connotation. It signifies a striving for wealth through dishonest, sometimes violent means. Philo's usage is always negative. In the *Life of Moses*, it usually means "covetousness."

---

152 Ibid., 86.
153 On the distinction between ritual impurity and moral impurity, see Klawans, *Impurity and Sin*, 22–31. Cf. the phrase מעשי תועבה ברוח זנות ("abominable deeds in a spirit of sexual immorality") in 1QS 4:10, which has both the connotation of unlawful intercourse and of idolatry (Wibbing, *Die Tugend- und Lasterkataloge*, 55). Wibbing, however, connects this phrase with "licentiousness" (ἀσέλγεια) and "acts of adultery" (μοιχεῖαι) in Mark 7:22 (ibid., 93).
154 Klawans, *Impurity and Sin*, 148.
155 Herbert Preisker, "κλέπτω, κλέπτης," *TDNT* 3 (1965) 754.
156 Ibid.
157 Num 35:29-34; Ezek 33:23-29; cf. Ps 106:37-42; Ezek 9:9-10; 22:1-5; Klawans, *Impurity and Sin*, 26, 28–29.

158 "Murder" (φόνος), "stealing" (κλοπή), "deceit" (δόλος), "adultery" (μοιχεία), and "licentiousness" (ἀσέλγεια) all occur in Wis 14:25-26 as well as in Mark 7:21-22 (Wibbing, *Die Tugend- und Lasterkataloge*, 29).
159 See the commentary on these passages below.
160 LSJ, s.v. The phrase רחוב נפש in 1QS 4:9 (in a list of sins or vices) may have the connotations of both greed and arrogance; cf. Prov 21:4; 28:25 (Wibbing, *Die Tugend- und Lasterkataloge*, 52).
161 Gerhard Delling, "πλεονέκτης, πλεονεκτέω, πλεονεξία," *TDNT* 6 (1968) 266–68.

In the series of ethical antitheses in *Omn. prob. lib.* 159, πλεονεξία is placed in opposition to δικαιοσύνη ("justice"). According to *Decal.* 155, πλεονεξία is one of the causes of oligarchy and mob rule.[162]

The six plural forms designating vices in vv. 21-22 may be viewed as organized into two groups of three, since each group begins with a type of sexual sin, followed by a sin that may be related to property.[163] In the context of Mark as a whole, however, πλεονεξία may have the sense of a desire for power and influence.[164]

Klawans has suggested that the commentary on Habakkuk from Qumran implies that "greed" or "avarice" (πλεονεξία) is a grave sin that leads to the moral defilement of the sanctuary (1QpHab 8:8-13; 12:6-10).[165] He concluded that the author of the commentary depicted acts of violent greediness as an abomination because this sort of behavior derives from arrogance. Klawans, following William H. Brownlee, discussed some of the biblical texts that may have inspired the idea that arrogance was abominable and thus a source of moral impurity.[166] As we have seen, one of the usages of πλεονεξία is to signify arrogance.

The general character of the last, πονηρίαι ("acts of wickedness"), supports the hypothesis that the six plural forms are treated as a group. In Aristotle's ethics, πονηρία is the "intentionally practised evil will." Plato and Aristotle used it as the antithesis of ἀρετή ("virtue" or "excellence").[167] Philo and Josephus use the term usually in the moral sense, although Philo uses the synonym κακία ("evil") more frequently. In the Dead Sea Scrolls, the term "wickedness" (רשע) often has the connotation of rebellion against God.[168] Lohmeyer argued that the pairing of πλεονεξίαι ("acts of greediness") and πονηρίαι ("acts of wickedness") here and of the corresponding singular forms in Rom 1:29 is evidence for a fixed catechetical formula.[169] This hypothesis goes beyond the evidence.

The six vices of the second set are given in singular form (v. 22). The first of these is δόλος ("deceit"). This noun occurs also in 14:1 as a characterization of the way in which the chief priests and scribes intended to arrest Jesus. Klawans argued that "deceit was considered a source of moral impurity in both the *Temple Scroll* and tannaitic sources, and it was understood as a defilement at Qumran as well."[170] The relevant passage of the *Temple Scroll*, however, condemns showing partiality in justice and taking bribes. Klawans has argued plausibly that Deut 25:15-16, combined with Lev 19:15 and 35, was the basis for the idea in the *Temple Scroll* that bribery defiles the sanctuary with moral impurity (11QT 51:11-15).[171] The issue in Deut 25:15-16 is accurate weights and measures. False weights and measures evoke the idea of deceit, although no term with this significance is used. Klawans also cites a tannaitic commentary on Leviticus, to the effect that deceit is a source of moral defilement.[172] The text, however, states that the judge who perverts justice is עול ("unjust"), not "deceitful."[173] This Hebrew word is apparently never translated with δόλος ("deceit") in the Greek versions of the Old Testament.[174] Philo, however, may provide some support for associating the notion of deceit with the context of Lev 19:15. Lev 19:16a reads: "You shall not go up and down as a slanderer among your people" (לא־תלך רכיל בעמיך) (trans. RSV). Philo cites this passage as follows:

The Law lays upon anyone who has undertaken to superintend and preside over public affairs a very just prohibition when it forbids him "to walk with deceit among the people," for such conduct shows an illiberal and thoroughly slavish soul which disguises its

---

162 Ibid., 269–70.

163 Ibid., 272.

164 Cf. 9:33-37, 50c; 10:35-45; see the commentary below.

165 Klawans, *Impurity and Sin*, 69–70, 148.

166 Ibid., 70.

167 Günther Harder, "πονηρία," *TDNT* 6 (1968) 563.

168 Wibbing, *Die Tugend- und Lasterkataloge*, 53, 94. This term occurs in 1QS 4:9 in a list of sins or vices.

169 Lohmeyer, 143. Lohmeyer is followed by Harder, who mistakenly states that the term κακία ("evil") occurs in Mark 7:22 ("πονηρία," 565).

170 Klawans, *Impurity and Sin*, 148.

171 Ibid., 49–50.

172 Ibid., 50.

173 Klawans translated this term with "deceitful" in one citation of this passage (*Sifra Kedoshim, Perek* 4:1 [ed. Weiss, 88d-89a]), but with "unjust" in another (*Impurity and Sin*, 50, 122).

174 According to Hatch-Redpath, s.v. The noun רמיה, which is translated three times in the LXX with δόλος, occurs in 1QS 4:9 in a list of sins or vices; cf. Wibbing, *Die Tugend- und Lasterkataloge*, 54. A word much more frequently translated with δόλος in the

malignant ways with hypocrisy (Ἀπαγορεύει δ᾽ ὁ νόμος τῷ τὴν προστασίαν καὶ ἐπιμέλειαν τῶν κοινῶν ἀνειληφότι δικαιοτάτην ἀπαγόρευσιν, μὴ πορεύεσθαι δόλῳ ἐν τῷ ἔθνει· ψυχῆς γὰρ ἀνελευθέρου καὶ σφόδρα δουλοπρεποῦς ἐπίβουλα ἤθη συσκιαζούσης ὑποκρίσει τὸ ἔργον). (Spec. leg. 4.35 §183)[175]

The editor comments that, although the statement is a general principle in both the Hebrew Bible and the LXX (that is, it applies to every member of the people), Philo may have applied it to a person in authority because the preceding verse of Leviticus gives instruction about just judgment.[176]

The word ἀσέλγεια ("licentiousness") signifies a lack of self-restraint that leads to conduct that is socially unacceptable.[177] In the New Testament it appears only with "the older and sensual sense of 'voluptuousness' or 'debauchery.'"[178] The connotation of sexual excess is probable in Gal 5:19 and certain in other passages of the New Testament and extracanonical early Christian literature.[179] If that connotation is present here, this vice may be seen as parallel to "acts of unlawful intercourse"

(πορνεῖαι) in v. 21 and to "acts of adultery" (μοιχεῖαι) in v. 22.

The phrase ὀφθαλμὸς πονηρός could be translated either "unhealthy eye" or "evil eye."[180] In the context of a list of vices, the latter must be intended here. The expression "evil eye" refers to an attitude of envy, jealousy, or stinginess. According to Sirach:

The man who envies (or who is grudging) is evil with respect to the eye, turning his face away and disdaining people. The eye of a greedy man is not satisfied with a portion, and evil iniquity dries up (his) soul. An evil eye is envious (or grudging) of bread, and it is wanting at his table

(πονηρὸς ὁ βασκαίνων ὀφθαλμῷ,
ἀποστρέφων πρόσωπον καὶ ὑπερορῶν ψυχάς.
πλεονέκτου ὀφθαλμὸς οὐκ ἐμπίπλαται μερίδι,
καὶ ἀδικία πονηρὰ ἀναξηραίνει ψυχήν.
ὀφθαλμὸς πονηρὸς φθονερὸς ἐπ᾽ ἄρτῳ
καὶ ἐλλιπὴς ἐπὶ τῆς τραπέζης αὐτοῦ). (Sir 14:8-10 LXX)

LXX is מרמה, which occurs in 1QS 10:22 in a brief list of vices (ibid., 93).

175 Text and trans. (modified) from Colson and Whitaker, Philo, 8:120–21.

176 Ibid., n. b.

177 BAGD, s.v.

178 Otto Bauernfeind, "ἀσέλγεια," TDNT 1 (1964) 490.

179 Rom 13:13; 2 Cor 12:21; 2 Pet 2:2, 18; Hermas, Vis. 2.2.2; 3.7.2; Man. 12.4.6; Sim. 9.15.3; Bauernfeind, "ἀσέλγεια," 490. J. Louis Martyn's comments on Gal 5:19 suggest a sexual meaning for ἀσέλγεια, which he translates as "uncontrolled debauchery"; Galatians: A New Translation with Introduction and Commentary (AB 33A; New York/London: Doubleday, 1997) 496. Joseph A. Fitzmyer translated ἀσέλγεια in Rom 13:13 as "sexual excess" (Romans: A New Translation with Introduction and Commentary [AB 33; New York/London: Doubleday, 1993] 681, 683). Victor Paul Furnish translated ἀσέλγεια in 2 Cor 12:21 with "licentiousness" and noted that "it is often associated specifically with illicit sexual behavior" (II Corinthians: Translated with Introduction, Notes, and Commentary [AB 32A; Garden City, NY: Doubleday, 1984] 562–63). Richard J. Bauckham translated the plural form of the noun in 2 Pet 2:2 and 18 with "dissolute practices" and com-

mented that the term usually means sensual indulgence, esp. sexual immorality (Jude, 2 Peter, 236, 241, 271, 274). In Hermas, Sim. 9.9.5, Hermas sees in a vision twelve beautiful women, clothed in black, girded, with their shoulders bare and their hair loose. They look cruel to him. In Sim. 9.15.3, the first four, the more powerful of these women, are interpreted as Ἀπιστία ("Unbelief" or "Faithlessness"), Ἀκρασία ("Self-Indulgence"), Ἀπείθεια ("Disobedience"), and Ἀπάτη ("Deceit"); the others, who follow them, are explained as Λύπη ("Grief"), Πονηρία ("Wickedness"), Ἀσέλγεια ("Licentiousness"), Ὀξυχολία ("Bitterness"), Ψεῦδος ("Lying"), Ἀφροσύνη ("Foolishness"), Καταλαλία ("Evilspeaking"), and Μῖσος ("Hate"). It may be implied here that ἀκρασία ("self-indulgence") leads to acts of licentiousness (ἀσέλγεια). Cf. Philo's personification of Virtue and Pleasure as two women, and Pleasure as a prostitute, who is followed by eleven other women who represent vices (Sacr. AC. 5 §§19–22; Wibbing, Die Tugend- und Lasterkataloge, 27).

180 For the usage of πονηρός meaning "unhealthy," see BAGD, s.v., 3.

The phrase "evil eye" sometimes has the connotation of types of black magic connected with envy.[181] The interpretation of the phrase here as "envy" is supported by the statement in 15:10 that Pilate knew that the chief priests had handed Jesus over to him out of envy (φθόνος).[182]

The fourth term of the second set of six is "abusive speech" (βλασφημία). In Greek literature it can signify a very strong form of personal mockery, defamation, or slander. It can also refer to speech that is offensive to the gods, for example, by mistaking their true nature or doubting their power.[183] Philo uses the verb on occasion for the reviling of one human being by another:

Another excellent injunction (of the Mosaic Law) is that no one is to revile or abuse any other, particularly a deafmute who can neither perceive the wrong he suffers nor retaliate in the same way, nor on an equal footing (Εὖ μέντοι κἀκεῖνο διείρηται, ὅπως μηδεὶς μηδένα βλασφημῇ καὶ κακηγορῇ, καὶ μάλιστα κωφὸν οὔτε αἴσθησιν ὧν ἀδικεῖται δυνάμενον λαβεῖν οὔτε ἐν τοῖς ἴσοις αὐτὸ τοῦτο ἀμύνασθαι). (*Spec. leg.* 4.38 §197)[184]

Hermann W. Beyer argued that the religious sense, "blasphemy," is present here in v. 22. It is true that a particular theological perspective is presupposed, so that any sin is a sin against God, but all of the other specific sins mentioned in vv. 21-22 concern relations among human beings. It seems unlikely that the term here means primarily speech that offends God directly. The verb is used in

a religious sense in 2:7, where Jesus is accused of blasphemy because he dares to forgive the paralytic's sins.[185] Both the noun and the verb are used in Mark 3:28, in which Jesus declares that all the abusive remarks that human beings utter will be forgiven. In the next verse, blaspheming the Holy Spirit is defined as an unforgivable sin. Here the religious sense is clearly intended.[186] In 14:64, the noun is used in the religious sense.[187] In 15:29, however, the verb is used in the general sense of abusive speech, although the religious sense may be a secondary connotation.[188]

The tannaitic rabbis used the expression קללת ה׳ to indicate "blasphemy," that is, abusive speech in the religious sense.[189] According to the *Sifre* to Deut 23:10, blasphemy is a source of moral defilement. Klawans has argued that this idea is probably based on a reading of Deut 21:22-23, which states that the impaled body of an executed criminal should be buried on the same day because it is an "affront" (קללת אלהים) to God. Since v. 23 implies that leaving the body on display any longer would defile the land, the inference was drawn that any "affront to God" or "blasphemy" created moral impurity. Some, but not all, tannaitic rabbis drew this conclusion.[190]

The phrase לשון גדופים in a list of sins or vices in the *Community Rule* probably has the general sense "a reviling tongue" or "a defiant tongue."[191] It may also have the more explicitly religious connotation of "a blasphemous tongue."[192]

In Greek literature, the adjective ὑπερήφανος and the noun derived from it, ὑπερηφανία, are used mainly

---

181 For literature on this topic, see Betz, *Sermon*, 451 n. 236.

182 On envy in the Bible, the literature of early Christianity and esp. in Greek and Hellenistic culture, see Matthew W. Dickie, "Envy," *ABD* 2:528–32. See also Rivka Ulmer, *The Evil Eye in the Bible and in Rabbinic Literature* (Hoboken, NJ: Ktav, 1994).

183 Hermann Wolfgang Beyer, "βλασφημέω, βλασφημία, βλάσφημος," *TDNT* 1 (1964) 621. Cf. LSJ and BAGD, s.v. βλασφημία. See also Yarbro Collins, "Charge of Blasphemy."

184 Text and trans. from Colson and Whitaker, *Philo*, 8:130–31; cf. Lev 19:14.

185 See the commentary on 2:7 above.

186 See the commentary on 3:28-29 above.

187 See Yarbro Collins, "Charge of Blasphemy," and the commentary on 14:63-64 below.

188 See the commentary on 15:29-32 below.

189 Klawans, *Impurity and Sin*, 124–25. קללה ("reviling" or "curse") is not one of the words in the Hebrew Bible translated with βλασφημία ("abusive speech" or "blasphemy") in the LXX; see Hatch-Redpath, 1:221.

190 Klawans, *Impurity and Sin*, 124–25.

191 So Wibbing, *Die Tugend- und Lasterkataloge*, 56.

192 So García Martínez and Tigchelaar, *Dead Sea Scrolls*, 1:76–77; Vermes, *Dead Sea Scrolls*, 102. See also Wibbing, *Die Tugend- und Lasterkataloge*, 93.

in the pejorative sense of pride, arrogance, and boasting. These terms are not usually associated with violence but rather with foolish, self-deceptive and deceiving empty boasting and despising.[193] In the biblical wisdom literature, especially in Sirach, these two words take on a negative ethical character, indicating the attitude that the righteous are to avoid.[194] Also in the LXX, the righteous person prays that God will destroy the proud. The reference may be to the arrogance of some among the people of Israel or to that of the enemies of the people, as in the oracles against foreign nations.[195] Under Stoic influence, the terms were included in the lists of vices found in Hellenistic Jewish and early Christian literature.[196] The noun in v. 22 has some overlap with the term $\pi\lambda\epsilon o\nu\epsilon\xi\iota\alpha\iota$ ("acts of greediness") in the same verse.[197] The evangelist may have included "arrogance" in this list in preparation for teaching about leadership in 9:33-50 and 10:35-45.[198]

The final type of sin or vice listed is $\mathring{\alpha}\varphi\rho o\sigma\acute{\upsilon}\nu\eta$ ("foolishness"). A Hebrew equivalent occurs in a list of sins or vices in the *Community Rule*, but not in last place.[199] According to Plato, $\varphi\rho\acute{o}\nu\eta\sigma\iota\varsigma$ ("practical wisdom") is "the right state of the intellect from which all moral qualities derive."[200] In the school tradition of the Stoa, $\mathring{\alpha}\varphi\rho o\sigma\acute{\upsilon}\nu\eta$ ("foolishness") was the first of the four cardinal vices, the opposite of $\varphi\rho\acute{o}\nu\eta\sigma\iota\varsigma$ ("practical wisdom").[201]

This term designates the wrong state of intellect from which all immoral qualities derive. Its presence at the end of the list may be taken as a restatement of the idea expressed in v. 21 that "evil intentions" in the "heart" lead to all sorts of evil deeds and qualities.[202]

Verse 23 is a summary and recapitulation of vv. 20-22. It also serves as a conclusion to the unit consisting of vv. 17-23, to the second main part of the section (vv. 14-23), and to the section as a whole (vv. 1-23).

Klawans has argued plausibly that the community of the Dead Sea Scrolls conflated ritual and moral impurity so that all sin was understood as ritually defiling as well as morally defiling.[203] In contrast, the Pharisees, like the tannaim, kept the two kinds of impurity separate. He concluded that Jesus was taking sides in a contemporary debate by arguing that immoral deeds are ritually defiling.[204] Klawans also concluded, however, that the rhetorical force of vv. 20-23 is that moral purity is more important than ritual purity.[205] This raises the question whether the language of moral defilement is hyperbolic or symbolic, rather than more literally symbolic, as at Qumran. In any case, Klawans's study is illuminating for many of the types of sins mentioned in vv. 21-22, if not all.

---

193 Georg Bertram, "$\mathring{\upsilon}\pi\epsilon\rho\acute{\eta}\varphi\alpha\nu o\varsigma$, $\mathring{\upsilon}\pi\epsilon\rho\eta\varphi\alpha\nu\acute{\iota}\alpha$," *TDNT* 8 (1972) 525.

194 Two of the Hebrew terms that are translated with $\mathring{\upsilon}\pi\epsilon\rho\acute{\eta}\varphi\alpha\nu o\varsigma$ and $\mathring{\upsilon}\pi\epsilon\rho\eta\varphi\alpha\nu\acute{\iota}\alpha$ in the LXX, namely, גוה and רום, occur in 1QS 4:9 in a list of sins or vices (Wibbing, *Die Tugend- und Lasterkataloge*, 53, 92).

195 E.g., Sir 10:7; Bertram, "$\mathring{\upsilon}\pi\epsilon\rho\acute{\eta}\varphi\alpha\nu o\varsigma$, $\mathring{\upsilon}\pi\epsilon\rho$-$\eta\varphi\alpha\nu\acute{\iota}\alpha$," 526.

196 Bertram, "$\mathring{\upsilon}\pi\epsilon\rho\acute{\eta}\varphi\alpha\nu o\varsigma$, $\mathring{\upsilon}\pi\epsilon\rho\eta\varphi\alpha\nu\acute{\iota}\alpha$," 525, 527–28.

197 See above. Klawans cites the *Mekhilta de Rabbi Ishmael*, a halakic midrash, which states, commenting on Exod 20:18, that all those who are arrogant (גבה לב) cause the land to be defiled (*Impurity and Sin*, 123); for an introduction to this work, see Hermann L. Strack and Günter Stemberger, *Introduction to the Talmud and Midrash* (Edinburgh: T & T Clark, 1991) 274–80. Cf. also the phrase קנאת זדון ("passionate pride" or "arrogant pride") in 1QS 4:10 (Wibbing, *Die Tugend- und Lasterkataloge*, 54–55).

198 See the commentary on these passages below.

199 The term occurs in the phrase רוב אולת ("much foolishness") in 1QS 4:10; cf. Wibbing, who argues

that the context gives the phrase the connotation of human action in opposition to God (*Die Tugend- und Lasterkataloge*, 54, 93); cf. also Hatch-Redpath, s.v. $\mathring{\alpha}\varphi\rho o\sigma\acute{\upsilon}\nu\eta$.

200 Georg Bertram, "$\varphi\rho\acute{\eta}\nu$, $\mathring{\alpha}\varphi\rho\omega\nu$, $\mathring{\alpha}\varphi\rho o\sigma\acute{\upsilon}\nu\eta$, $\varphi\rho o\nu\acute{\epsilon}\omega$, $\varphi\rho\acute{o}\nu\eta\mu\alpha$, $\varphi\rho\acute{o}\nu\eta\sigma\iota\varsigma$, $\varphi\rho\acute{o}\nu\iota\mu o\varsigma$," *TDNT* 9 (1974) 222. Zeno, according to Plutarch, similarly derived the other three cardinal virtues from $\varphi\rho\acute{o}\nu\eta\sigma\iota\varsigma$ ("practical knowledge of value" or "practical wisdom") (Wibbing, *Die Tugend- und Lasterkataloge*, 15–16).

201 Wibbing, *Die Tugend- und Lasterkataloge*, 17.

202 Cf. Bertram, "$\mathring{\upsilon}\pi\epsilon\rho\acute{\eta}\varphi\alpha\nu o\varsigma$, $\mathring{\upsilon}\pi\epsilon\rho\eta\varphi\alpha\nu\acute{\iota}\alpha$," 231.

203 Klawans, *Impurity and Sin*, 124. See, e.g., 1QS 4:10, where the phrase "impure ways in the service of uncleanness" (דרכי נדה בעבודת טמאה), which is the opposite of "ways of truth" or "ways of light," implies that all sin leads to impurity and uncleanness. Cf. Wibbing, *Die Tugend- und Lasterkataloge*, 56.

204 Ibid., 150.

205 Ibid., 149.

Svartvik has argued that, according to tannaitic hag-gadic texts, sinful speech renders a person metaphori-cally impure.[206] He suggested that Mark 7:15 be connected with the figure of Miriam, "the biblical arch-slanderer."[207] He concluded that the first part of v. 15 (things going in) refers to contaminated food, and that the second part (things coming out) refers to contami-nated speech.[208] The argument that the first part of v. 15 refers to contaminated food is persuasive.[209] But there are two problems with the hypothesis that the second part of the saying refers to evil speech. First, this inter-pretation relies more on the wording of Matt 15:11 and *Gos. Thom.* 14 (things that come out of the mouth) than on that of Mark 7:15. Second, the notion of evil speech fits at most only two of the sins or vices listed in vv. 21-22, "deceit" (δόλος) and "abusive speech" (βλασφημία). But Svartvik is certainly correct that the saying of v. 15 does not necessarily imply the cleansing of all foods.[210]

---

206 Svartvik, *Mark and Mission*, 402.
207 Ibid., 407–8.
208 Ibid., 409.

209 See the commentary on vv. 14-15 and vv. 17-19 above.
210 Svartvik, *Mark and Mission*, 411.

7:24-30 The Syro-Phoenician Woman

24/   Then he set out from there and went away into the region of Tyre.[a] And he entered into a house and wanted no one to know, yet he was not able to escape notice. 25/ But immediately a woman, whose daughter[b] had an unclean spirit, heard about him and came and fell at his feet. 26/ Now the woman was a Gentile, Syro-Phoenician in origin; and she asked him to drive the demon out of her daughter. 27/ And he said to her, "Let the children be satisfied first, for it is not good to take the bread of the children and throw it to the dogs."[c] 28/ Then she answered and said to him, "Sir,[d] even the dogs under the table eat of the children's crumbs." 29/ And he said to her, "Go (home); on account of this saying the demon has gone out of your daughter." 30/ And when she went into her house, she found the child lying on the bed and the demon gone out (of her).

a   ℵ A B et al. attest the reading in which the words καὶ Σιδῶνος ("and of Sidon") follow Τύρου ("of Tyre"). This reading is probably a secondary expansion inspired by the parallel in Matt 15:21 or by Mark 7:31. See Taylor, ad loc.; Metzger, *Textual Commentary*, 82.

b   The pleonastic αὐτῆς (lit., "of her"), attested by A B L 𝔐, is acceptable Greek (see Moulton-Turner, 3:325; cf. 4:21), but was omitted in readings attested by p⁴⁵ ℵ D W et al.

c   Although the form κυνάρια ("dogs") is diminutive, it probably did not have a diminutive sense in Mark's time. See Turner, "Marcan Usage," 29 (1928) 349–52 (Elliott, *Language and Style*, 123–26).

d   Many MSS, including ℵ A B L et al., attest readings in which the word ναί ("yes") occurs before κύριε ("sir"). Although this reading has strong external support, it is probably a secondary assimilation of the text of Mark to the parallel in Matt 15:27. See Metzger, *Textual Commentary*, 82.

The History of the Tradition

Verse 24a, the setting of the narrative in Tyre, is redactional.[1] In 3:8, people from the region around Tyre come to Jesus. Here he goes to that region himself. The evangelist seems to have placed the story about the Syro-Phoenician woman in Tyre in order to relate this story to the dispute with the Pharisees in 7:1-23. Verse 19c indicates that Mark reinterpreted the saying of v. 15 so that it signifies the abrogation of the food laws. In line with that interpretation, he presents Jesus here as initiating the mission to the Gentiles, although in a hidden and reluctant way.[2]

Verse 24b-c, however, probably belongs to the account of the miracle story as Mark found it in his source. In the second collection of miracle stories used by the evangelist, this account originally followed the healing of the blind man in Bethsaida.[3] Since Bethsaida is near Capernaum, it makes more narrative sense for Jesus to enter a house there and attempt to remain hidden. It makes less sense for him to do so in the region of Tyre. The description of the woman as a Syro-Phoenician may have prompted the relocation of the incident. As Achtemeier has pointed out, the story also has greater internal sense if it was originally located in Bethsaida. The journey of Jesus to Tyre suggests that he himself is not giving the "bread" to the "children" alone.[4] There is no mention of his seeking out a synagogue in order to proclaim the good news to the Jews of the area. Furthermore, the careful identification of the woman as "Gentile" (Ἑλληνίς; lit., "Greek"), as opposed to "Jewish" (Ἰουδαία), and as "Syro-Phoenician" makes more sense in Galilee than in the region around Tyre, where such a religious and ethnic identity would have been the rule, rather than the

---

1   Bultmann, *History*, 38, 64–65; Achtemeier, "Miracle Catenae," 287; Theissen, *Miracle Stories*, 125–26.

2   Cf. 5:18-20 and the commentary above.

3   Achtemeier, "Miracle Catenae," 283–84, 287–88.

4   Ibid., 287.

5   Cf. Theissen, *Miracle Stories*, 126, the literature cited there, and Chancey, *Gentile Galilee*, 120–66, esp. 150. For an anthropological approach to ethnic identity

exception.[5] Finally, the statement of Jesus that the "children" must be fed "first" ($\pi\rho\hat{\omega}\tau o\nu$) makes more sense in a Galilean context. The implication in the source was probably that Jesus' mission to the people of Israel precedes that of the disciples of Jesus to the Gentiles after the resurrection.[6] The adverb may also have the connotation of the qualitative priority of the Jews in the scheme of salvation.[7]

The Genre of the Story about the Syro-Phoenician Woman

Bultmann argued that this account belongs to the category of the apophthegms, even though its main point is not the saying of Jesus. He argued that the miracle is not told for its own sake but rather that the emphasis is on the change in Jesus' behavior.[8] The miraculous dimension, however, seems to be more important than Bultmann allowed.[9] Bultmann also saw the account as a controversy-dialogue of a sort, but one in which Jesus is not the victor. He rightly observed that this departure from the usual form is not in any way a denigration of Jesus.[10]

Theissen defines this passage as an exorcism.[11] It also belongs to the subcategory of a healing (or exorcism) from a distance.[12] He sees the dialogue between Jesus and the woman as part of the inner dynamic of the miracle story. The order of motifs is "petition, difficulty, overcoming of the difficulty, assurance."[13] Socioculturally speaking, the story emphasizes the contrast between Jews and Gentiles, which is related to the stress on the motif of resistance. The account reflects awareness of sociocul-tural boundaries and tension between cultures, but the implication is that these boundaries may be crossed.

Robert C. Tannehill argued that the narrative about the Syro-Phoenician woman is a quest story in which the climax of the story includes Jesus' response to an objection. It is thus a hybrid story.[14] It is a hybrid objection quest in which the objection must be overcome for the quest to be successful.[15] Quest stories are unique in that the quester is given a prominent role. This emphasis on the quester evokes empathy with that character and interest to see whether the quest succeeds or fails. The quester is often the object of prejudice, and the stories function to create openness for such people in the community.[16]

Comment

■ **24** As noted above, v. 24a is redactional.[17] The evangelist portrays Jesus here as moving from Galilee to the region around Tyre and as engaging in a reluctant mission to the Gentiles.[18] Verse 24b-c portrays Jesus as attempting to conceal himself, but as being unable to remain hidden. Even though this motif is a frequent one in Mark, the author may have found it in his source.[19]

■ **25** In keeping with the motif in v. 24b-c, that Jesus cannot remain hidden, it is narrated here that a woman whose daughter was possessed by an unclean spirit "immediately" ($\epsilon\dot{\upsilon}\vartheta\dot{\upsilon}\varsigma$) heard about him.[20] The woman's gesture, falling at the feet of Jesus, is typical of the suppliant in accounts of healing and exorcism.[21]

---

in ancient Greece, see Jonathan Hall, *Ethnic Identity in Greek Antiquity* (Cambridge/New York: Cambridge University Press, 1997).

6   This is also the schema of Matthew; cf. Matt 10:5-6 with 28:19-20. Cf. also Acts 13:46.

7   Cf. Rom 1:16; Marcus, 1:463.

8   Bultmann, *History*, 38, 66.

9   See the commentary below.

10   Bultmann, *History*, 38.

11   Theissen, *Miracle Stories*, 54–55, 114, 321.

12   Ibid., 113.

13   Ibid., 181.

14   Tannehill, "Varieties," 107.

15   Ibid., 113.

16   Ibid., 114.

17   See the section "The History of the Tradition" above.

18   Cf. 6:53; 7:1; on Jesus' mission to the Gentiles, see the section "The History of the Tradition" above. The reluctance may signify awareness of the problem of how the activity of the historical Jesus related to the later Gentile mission (Theissen, *Gospels in Context*, 64).

19   Cf. 1:35, 45; 2:1; 6:31-34. On the probability of v. 24b-c belonging to a source, see the section "The History of the Tradition" above.

20   The phrase "unclean spirit" ($\pi\nu\epsilon\hat{\upsilon}\mu\alpha$ $\dot{\alpha}\kappa\dot{\alpha}\vartheta\alpha\rho\tau o\nu$) is used frequently in Mark to designate evil spirits or demons: 1:23, 26, 27; 3:11, 30; 5:2, 8, 13; 6:7; 9:25 (for a total of eleven times). See the commentary on 1:23 above.

21   Cf. 1:40; 5:6, 22; Theissen, *Miracle Stories*, 53.

■ **26** Verse 26a, which gives information about the woman's religious and ethnic identity, gives the impression of being a digression or an afterthought. This feature is indicative of an oral style.[22] The term Ἑλληνίς here means "a Greek-oriented woman alien to Israel's life, *Greek* (polytheist)."[23]

The description of the woman as "Syro-Phoenician" (Συροφοινίκισσα) has been taken as evidence that the Gospel according to Mark was written in Rome.[24] Martin Hengel argued, citing Diodorus of Sicily, that the term distinguishes the Phoenicians of Syria from those of Libya.[25] Since there would have been no need to make such a distinction for an audience in Syria, Hengel concluded that the audience of Mark must have been in the West. He also argued that the oldest examples of the expression "Syro-Phoenician" occur in Roman writers (in Latin) of the second and first centuries BCE.

In response, Theissen argued that the Latin *syrophoenix* ("Syro-Phoenician") is borrowed from the Greek, although no instances survive that are older than the Latin ones cited by Hengel. He also argued persuasively that the expression "Syro-Phoenicia" originated in the East in order to distinguish southern from northern

Syria. The northern part was called Syria Coele and the southern Syria Phoenice.[26]

The woman asks Jesus to drive the demon (δαιμόνιον) out of her daughter.[27] In this miracle story, the woman comes to Jesus as the representative of her daughter, who is the distressed person.[28] Her statement represents the motif of "petition" or "plea."[29]

■ **27** Jesus, the miracle-worker, refuses to grant the woman's petition. This refusal constitutes the "difficulty" that the petitioner must overcome. It is an example of the "boundary-stressing motif" in miracle stories.[30] The reply of Jesus is in the form of a metaphor (cf. 2:17, 19; 3:24-25).[31] The contrast between the "children" and the "dogs" represents a contrast between Jews and Gentiles, for which the designation of the woman as "a Greek (polytheist)" (Ἑλληνίς) has prepared.[32]

The Hebrew (and Aramaic) word כלב ("dog") usually refers to the wild or semi-wild dogs of the streets, although occasionally the reference is to domestic pets.[33] To compare someone else with a dog was insulting and dishonoring, and to compare oneself with a dead dog was an extreme instance of self-abasement.[34] In Psalm 22, the speaker compares his ungodly opponents to wild

22 Theissen, *Miracle Stories*, 193.
23 BAGD, s.v. Cf. Gal 3:28.
24 Martin Hengel, "Entstehungszeit und Situation des Markusevangeliums," in Hubert Cancik, ed., *Markus-Philologie: Historische, literargeschichtliche und stilistische Untersuchungen zum zweiten Evangelium* (WUNT 33; Tübingen: Mohr Siebeck, 1984) 45; ET in Hengel, *Studies in Mark*, 29.
25 Diodorus Siculus 19.93.7; 20.55.4; he completed his history around 30 BCE (Kenneth S. Sacks, "Diodorus [3]," *OCD* 472).
26 Theissen, *Gospels in Context*, 245–47.
27 The term "demon" (δαιμόνιον) occurs nine times in Mark: 1:34, 39; 3:15, 22; 6:13; 7:26, 29, 30; 9:38. See the commentary on 1:33-34 above.
28 As Jairus represents his daughter in 5:22-23 and a man represents his son in 9:17-18 (Theissen, *Miracle Stories*, 49, 114).
29 See the section "The Genre of the Story about the Syro-Phoenician Woman" above.
30 Theissen, *Miracle Stories*, 77.
31 Bultmann, *History*, 41.
32 Theissen has also interpreted the story in the context of ethnic relationships, cultural circumstances, social status, economic conditions, and political and social-psychological relationships in the border

regions between Tyre and Galilee (*Gospels in Context*, 66–80). He concluded that the harshness of Jesus' refusal reflects various types of conflict in those regions, that the story originated in Palestine, and that it may have a historical core (ibid., 79).
33 Otto Michel, "κύων," *TDNT* 3 (1965) 1101. Most ancient dogs were mongrels; modern scholars refer to any stray dog as a "pariah," in keeping with ancient (and current) attitudes in the eastern Mediterranean world; see Douglas J. Brewer, "Ancient Egyptian Dogs," in idem, Terence Clark and Adrian Phillips, *Dogs in Antiquity, Anubis to Cerberus: The Origins of the Domestic Dog* (Warminster: Aris & Phillips, 2001) 39, 44–46; Terence Clark, "The Dogs of the Ancient Near East," in Brewer et al., *Dogs in Antiquity*, 66, 75; Adrian Phillips, "The Dogs of the Classical World," in Brewer et al., *Dogs in Antiquity*, 87. These authors also discuss dogs domesticated for hunting, herding, shepherding, and guarding.
34 1 Sam 17:43; 24:14; 2 Sam 9:8; 2 Kgs 8:13; Michel, "κύων," 1101. Tat-Siong Benny Liew concludes that the Markan Jesus insults the Syro-Phoenician woman and that the reason is the intersection of ethnocentrism and sexism (*Politics of Parousia: Reading Mark Inter(con)textually* [Leiden/Boston: Brill, 1999] 135–37).

bulls threatening to devour him and to the ravenous dogs of the streets (22:12-13, 16, 20).[35] Deut 23:18 uses the term "dog" for a male prostitute. According to the *Halakhic Letter* from Qumran, dogs are forbidden to enter Jerusalem "because they might eat [some of the bones from the temple with the flesh on] them. Because Jeru[sa]l[em] is the holy camp . . . ." (4QMMT B 58-62 [4Q396 2:9-11])[36]

In rabbinic literature, "dog" is used metaphorically for a person who is unlearned in the scripture, Mishnah, and Talmud; for ungodly people; and for Gentiles. In the Midrash on the Psalms, a parable is attributed to Rabbi Joshua ben Levi in which the guests arriving for a banquet in the king's palace see dogs coming out with the heads of pheasants, capons, and calves in their mouths. They exclaim, "If the dogs are so well fed, imagine what the banquet will be like!" The parable is applied to the great gifts given to the Gentiles in this world and to the even greater gifts that will be given to Israel in the next world. The Gentiles receive great gifts for observing the seven (Noachite) commandments; so the Israelites will receive even greater gifts for observing the 613 commandments (of the Torah).[37] Rabbi Akiba called his dogs Rufus and Rufina (Roman names), because the Gentiles are like dogs in their way of life. The reason that the Gentiles are regarded as inferior is that they do not have the Torah.[38]

Since the diminutive form of the word "dog" in v. 27 (κυνάριον) probably does not have a diminutive connotation in the colloquial language of Mark, the term proba-

bly refers to the scavenging dogs of the street.[39] This passage is evidence that the metaphorical use among Jews of "dogs" for Gentiles was already current in the first century CE.[40]

As noted above, the word "first" (πρῶτον) may signify the chronological and qualitative priority of the Jews in the history of salvation.[41] The image of "bread" here was probably originally strictly metaphorical. The collection of miracle stories in which the evangelist found this account ended with a feeding story.[42] In that context the image of bread may have prepared for the multiplication of the loaves. The present literary context in Mark is even more likely to lead readers to note connections among this passage, the dispute with the Pharisees, and the two feeding stories. The word "bread" (ἄρτος) occurs in all four passages, and the word "to be satisfied" (χορτασθῆναι) occurs in three of them.[43]

■ **28** The woman overcomes the difficulty posed by Jesus' refusal by means of wit and self-abasement. The wit consists in her transformation of the scavenging dogs of the street, used metaphorically by Jesus in his refusal, into domestic dogs, which have access to the part of the home in which the family has its table and eats its meals. Her self-abasement is expressed in her acceptance of this softened metaphor of "dogs" for "Gentiles."[44] Her faith (or confidence or trust) that Jesus is able to drive the demon out of her daughter is so great that she is willing to abase herself in order to secure his cooperation.[45] This self-abasement also implies acceptance of the chronological and qualitative superiority of the Jews in the history

---

35   Michel, "κύων," 1101.

36   Trans. (slightly modified) from García Martínez and Tigchelaar, *Dead Sea Scrolls*, 2:797; Harrington, "Holiness and Law," 128.

37   *Midr. Ps.* 4 §11 (24ᵃ); cited in Str-B, 1:724-25.

38   Michel, "κύων," 1102.

39   See the note on the trans. of v. 27 above; contra Michel, "κυνάριον," *TDNT* 3 (1965) 1104. Cf. *Jos. Asen.* 10:14; 13:8; Theissen, *Gospels in Context*, 62 n. 2.

40   This hypothesis also illuminates the way in which Paul turns the metaphor around. In defense of his gospel, he labels Jews or Judaizers "dogs" (κύνες) in Phil 3:2; see Carolyn Osiek, *Philippians, Philemon* (ANTC; Nashville: Abingdon, 2000) 82.

41   See the section "The History of the Tradition" above. Cf. Theissen's summary of the "salvation-historical interpretation" of this passage (*Gospels in Context*, 63). But the understanding of "first" (πρῶτον) offered

above does not necessarily lead to the type of overall interpretation summarized by Theissen.

42   See the section "The History of the Tradition" above.

43   "Bread" (ἄρτος) in 6:37, 38, 41, 44, 52; 7:2, 5, 27; 8:4, 5, 6; "to be satisfied" (χορτασθῆναι) in 6:42; 7:27; 8:4, 8; cf. Theissen, *Gospels in Context*, 64-65. He concluded that, although the saying of Jesus in v. 27 was not formulated in relation to the problem of common meals involving Jews and Gentiles in the early Christian communities, it was eventually secondarily applied to such a context.

44   According to Theissen, the woman's reply is a "declaration of humility and trust" provoked by Jesus' rejection (*Miracle Stories*, 54-55).

45   Theissen speaks of "tested faith" (*Gospels in Context*, 63) and of "(petitionary) faith" being tested (*Miracle Stories*, 137-38).

of salvation expressed by the claim of Jesus that the "children" must be fed "first."[46]

■ **29** Jesus recognizes and affirms the woman's wit and self-abasement by responding "Go (home); on account of this saying the demon has gone out of your daughter" (διὰ τοῦτον τὸν λόγον ὕπαγε, ἐξελήλυθεν ἐκ τῆς θυγατρός σου τὸ δαιμόνιον).[47] This statement also indicates that Jesus has exorcised the demon from a distance. The woman has contributed significantly to the healing of her daughter, just as the woman with the flow of blood virtually healed herself.[48]

In this narrative, the woman, as a Gentile, is an ambivalent figure. On the one hand, she, like all Gentiles, is depicted as worthless by means of the image of the "dogs." On the other, her great faith and humility are presented as a model to be imitated.[49]

■ **30** The woman arrives home and finds that the child has been healed, the demon having been driven out. This notice serves as the confirmation of the miracle.[50]

7

7:31-37 The Healing of a Deaf Man

31/ And again he left the region of Tyre and went through Sidon[a] to the Sea of Galilee through the middle of the region of (the) Decapolis. 32/ And they brought to him a (man who was) deaf and impeded in his speech, and they entreated him to lay his hand[b] upon him. 33/ And he took him away from the crowd in private and put his fingers into his ears and, having spat, touched his tongue.[c] 34/ And he looked up to heaven, sighed, and said to him, "Ephphatha," which means "Be opened." 35/ And[d] his ears were opened and[e] the bond of his tongue was untied (or loosened), and he began to speak correctly. 36/ And he ordered them to speak to no one; but the more he ordered them, so much more did they proclaim (what he had done). 37/ And they were amazed beyond all measure, saying, "He has done all things well; he makes both the deaf hear and the speechless speak."

a   p[45] A W et al. attest the reading καὶ Σιδῶνος ἦλθεν ("[of Tyre] and Sidon and went"). This reading results from a change introduced because Jesus' journey north to Sidon before traveling to the Sea of Galilee seemed unmotivated. The reading εἰς τὰ ὅρια Τύρου καὶ Σιδῶνος ("into the region of Tyre and Sidon") in v. 24 may also have had an influence. See Metzger, *Textual Commentary*, 82.

b   ℵ* N Δ Σ et al. (see Huck-Greeven, ad loc.) read τὰς χεῖρας ("hands") instead of the singular. This reading was introduced, either deliberately or accidentally, to make this passage conform to the much more common usage of the plural with the verb ἐπιτίθημι ("to lay upon"); Matt 9:18 is the only other passage in the NT with the singular.

c   0131 reads "he spit on his fingers and put (them) into the ears of the deaf man and touched the tongue of the man with impeded speech" (ἔπτυσεν εἰς τοὺς δακτύλους αὐτοῦ καὶ ἔβαλεν εἰς τὰ ὦτα τοῦ κωφοῦ καὶ ἥψατο τῆς γλώσσης τοῦ μογιλάλου). This change reflects the assumption that two men are mentioned in v. 32; it also seeks to clarify the technique employed by Jesus. Similarly, D Θ it move πτύσας ("having spat") close to ἔβαλεν ("put") in order to connect the spitting with the act of placing fingers in the ears, rather than with the touching of the tongue. W Φ sy[s] speak of two separate acts relating to the ears: "having also spat into his ears, he put his fingers (into them) and touched his tongue" (ἔβαλεν τοὺς δακτύλους αὐτοῦ καὶ πτύσας εἰς τὰ ὦτα αὐτοῦ ἥψατο τῆς γλώσσης αὐτοῦ). See Kurt Aland,

46   Cf. Theissen, *Gospels in Context*, 63–64 n. 12.

47   Theissen labels Jesus' response as "assurance"; see the section "The Genre of the Story about the Syro-Phoenician Woman" above.

48   See the commentary on 5:33-34 above.

49   Theissen, *Miracle Stories*, 254. For readings of this text from the point of view of issues related to gender and ethnicity, see Sharon Ringe, "A Gentile Woman's Story, Revisited: Rereading Mark 7.24-31," and Rajini Wickramaratne Rebera, "The Syrophoenician Woman: A South Asian Feminist Perspective," in Levine, *Feminist Companion*, 79–100 and 101–10.

50   Cf. 1:31b; 2:12a-b; 5:15, 42a; 6:43-44. Cf. Bultmann, *History*, 63, 66.

ed., *Synopsis Quattuor Evangeliorum* (15th rev. ed.; Stuttgart: Deutsche Bibelgesellschaft, 1996) 221.

d $\mathfrak{p}^{45}$ A W Θ et al. attest the reading εὐθέως ("immediately") after καί ("And"). ℵ B D W et al., however, lack this word. The evidence is difficult to evaluate. On the one hand, the older MSS that read εὐθέως ("immediately") often lack the word εὐθύς ("immediately") where other MSS have it but never seem to add it where others lack it. On the other hand, some impor-

tant MSS that lack εὐθέως here (ℵ B L) seldom or never omit εὐθύς where others read it. Since εὐθύς is typical of Markan style and εὐθέως is not, the balance of probability lies with the shorter reading. Cf. Metzger, *Textual Commentary*, 82–83.

e ℵ Δ (L 0274. 892) read εὐθύς ("immediately") after καί ("and"). Although this word is typical of Markan style, the reading is too weakly attested to have a claim to be early.

Comment

■ **31** This entire verse is a Markan editorial transition.[51] Localities are mentioned here that have been mentioned before: "the region of Tyre" (τὰ ὅρια Τύρου) in v. 24; "Sidon" (Σιδών) in 3:8; "the Sea of Galilee" (ἡ θάλασσα τῆς Γαλιλαίας) in 1:16;[52] and the Decapolis (Δεκάπολις) in 5:20.[53] The evangelist presents Jesus as beginning a journey from the region of Tyre to the Sea of Galilee. Since the Sea of Galilee is southeast of ancient Tyre, the journey portrayed is quite roundabout: first north to Sidon, then east and south to the Decapolis, and finally west from there to the Sea of Galilee.[54] One might conclude from this account of Jesus' itinerary that the evangelist was not familiar with the geography of Syria-Palestine and that, therefore, he must have written the Gospel somewhere else, for example, in Rome. Such an argument would not be compelling. It is possible, even likely, that someone living in Syria-Palestine would not know the geography exactly, since people at that time did not have maps or atlases. A better argument, however, is that the itinerary was made roundabout deliberately. Theissen has argued that the Gospel originated in Syria near Palestine and that the evangelist wished to place Jesus in those regions of Syria close to

"the neighborhood of Markan Christianity."[55] Alternatively, the evangelist may simply have known about the spread of the Jesus-movement into the Decapolis and southern Syria and wished to anticipate that development in his portrayal of Jesus' activity.

Heikki Räisänen argued that the expression ἀνὰ μέσον τῶν ὁρίων Δεκαπόλεως means "in the middle of the region of (the) Decapolis."[56] The preposition ἀνά with the accusative, however, usually expresses horizontal motion when used locally.[57] Since the Sea of Galilee is mentioned in the context as the end of Jesus' journey, it is likely that the evangelist intended to set the healing of the deaf man in the vicinity of the Sea of Galilee.[58] Further, Mark probably intended to portray the region of Tyre in the preceding passage as a primarily Gentile cultural area, even though there were Jews living in the area.[59] With the healing of the deaf man, however, the evangelist portrays Jesus as returning to a primarily Jewish region.

■ **32-36** The actual account of the healing has no parallel in Matthew or in Luke. Perhaps this account did not occur in the copies of Mark used by the authors of Matthew and Luke. It is more likely, however, that Matthew and Luke deliberately omitted this story because of its magical elements.[60]

---

51 Bultmann, *History*, 38; Achtemeier, "Miracle Catenae," 288.

52 The Sea of Galilee is of course mentioned many more times in abbreviated form.

53 Theissen, *Miracle Stories*, 126. On the Decapolis, see the commentary on 5:18-20 above.

54 The itinerary is like going from St. Louis to Dallas by way of Chicago and New York; cf. Theissen, *Gospels in Context*, 243.

55 Theissen, *Gospels in Context*, 242–45, 249.

56 Following D.-A. Koch; Räisänen, *Messianic Secret*, 153. The Sea of Galilee does not lie "in the middle of the Decapolis." Although the city and the region

of Scythopolis (Beth-Shean) did lie south of the Sea of Galilee and west of the Jordan, the other cities lay to the east and southeast of the lake.

57 Smyth, §1682.2.

58 Thus, the story about the Syro-Phoenician woman is the first story to be set in a Gentile area since the exorcism of the Gerasene demoniac; cf. Räisänen, *Messianic Secret*, 153.

59 Theissen, *Gospels in Context*, 68; on the primarily Gentile character of the region of Tyre, see Chancey, *Gentile Galilee*, 120–66, esp. 150.

60 So also Aune, "Magic," 1507–57, esp. 1537.

■ **32** The adjective κωφός can signify the lack of the capacity for speech ("mute"), the lack of the capacity for hearing ("deaf"), or both.[61] The adjective μογιλάλος can signify either the ability to speak only with difficulty ("impeded in speech") or the inability to articulate ("mute").[62] The meaning "impeded in speech" is supported by the description of the cure in v. 35, "he began to speak correctly" (ἐλάλει ὀρθῶς). The implication is that he could speak beforehand, but not correctly. Thus κωφός in this context means either "deaf" or "hard of hearing."[63]

Those who bring the man to Jesus entreat Jesus to lay his hand upon the man.[64] Jesus heals Peter's mother-in-law by grasping her hand and raising her up, and the leper with a touch of his hand (1:31, 41). Jairus's original request was that Jesus come and lay his hands upon Jairus's daughter, and Jesus raises her from the dead by grasping her hand and speaking to her (5:23, 41). The people of Jesus' hometown speak, perhaps metaphorically, about the "powerful works occurring through his hands," and he heals a few sick people there by laying his hands upon them (6:2, 5).[65] All these instances imply the belief that Jesus had a special healing power that was communicated through touch.[66] In the *Genesis Apocryphon,* Abram exorcises and heals Pharaoh by laying his hands upon him (1QapGen 20:28-29). According to Ovid, Asclepius healed Hippolytus by (among other things) touching him on the breast three times (*Fasti* 6.753).[67]

■ **33** The emphasis in this miracle story is on the therapeutic process.[68] Jesus does much more than simply lay a hand upon the man.[69] First of all, he takes the man away from the crowd to heal him in private. The logic of this motif is that it is not fitting for those not directly involved to see divine power at work.[70] Jesus then puts his fingers into the man's ears. This gesture is a specific application of the motif of healing by touch.

Jesus then applies his own saliva to the man's tongue. According to Pliny the Elder, saliva as such had healing power. He wrote that it was beneficial in the treatment of venom poisoning, as a deterrent to snakes, and for superficial ailments. He mentions its remedial uses some ten times throughout the *Natural History*.[71] He also said that saliva can calm mental anxiety if placed behind the ear with one's finger (*Hist. nat.* 28.5.25). He notes that saliva may be used to ward off witchcraft and that it increases the effectiveness of medical remedies; he recommends spitting on epileptics when they are having a seizure (28.4.35-39). The sweat and the saliva of people involved in witchcraft have curative powers (28.6.30-31). According to Pliny, saliva is used in healing according to custom (*mos*), not for any rational purpose (28.7.36).

Similarly, Galen says that chewed wheat heals boils when applied to them because "this phlegm [saliva] in the mouth is also a cure for lichens [perhaps psoriasis]" (*On the Natural Faculties* 3.7 §163).[72] It destroys scorpions and animals that emit venom; in any case it does them damage.

---

61 BAGD, s.v.

62 BAGD, s.v.

63 Pliny says that all those born deaf are also mute (*Nat. Hist.* 10.192).

64 Laying on a single hand is an unusual motif; see the note on the trans. of v. 32 above.

65 See also 8:23, 25; 9:27.

66 See the section "Genres" in the commentary on 5:21-43 and the commentary on 5:27-28 and 30-32 above. See also Bultmann, *History*, 222.

67 Emma J. Edelstein and Ludwig Edelstein, *Asclepius: Collection and Interpretation of the Testimonies* (2 vols.; Baltimore: Johns Hopkins University Press, 1945; reprinted with a new introduction by Gary B. Ferngren, 1998) no. 75 (1. 42).

68 Theissen, *Miracle Stories*, 113.

69 Bultmann concluded that the report of "special manipulation" signifies the difficulty of the healing (*History*, 221-22).

70 Cf. 5:37 and the commentary above.

71 E.g., *Hist. nat.* 28.7.37. In this passage he says that the saliva of a fasting person (*saliva ieiuni*; the saliva of one who was fasting was considered to have greater potency for certain ailments) can keep lichens [psoriasis ?] and leprous sores in check, also inflammation of the eye, etc. For a discussion of the magical and healing use of saliva in antiquity, see John M. Hull, *Hellenistic Magic and the Synoptic Tradition* (SBT 2nd series 28; Naperville, IL: Alec R. Allenson, 1974) 76-78.

72 τὸ γάρ τοι φλέγμα τουτὶ τὸ κατὰ τὸ στόμα καὶ λειχήνων ἐστὶν ἄκος; text and trans. from Arthur John Brock, *Galen: On the Natural Faculties* (LCL; London: Heinemann; Cambridge, MA: Harvard University Press, 1916) 252-53.

According to one of the testimonies from the shrine of Asclepius at Epidaurus:

A dog cured a boy from Aegina. He had a growth on the neck. When he had come to the god, one of the sacred dogs healed him—while he was awake—with its tongue and made him well (*Κύων ἰάσατο παῖδα Αἰ(γιν)άταν. οὗτος φῦμα ἐν τῶ(ι τρα)χάλωι εἶχε· ἀφικόμενο(ν) δ᾽ αὐτὸν ποὶ τ(ὸν) θε(ὸ)ν κύων τῶν ἱαρῶν ὕ(παρτ)αι γλώσσαι ἐθεράπευσε καὶ ὑγιῆ ἐπόη(σ)ε*).[73]

The comment that the boy was healed while he was awake differentiates this cure from most of those attributed to Asclepius, which occur while the suppliant is sleeping in the deity's shrine. Here the saliva is believed to be healing probably because the dogs are sacred.

In treating a boy who had been bitten by a dog and thereafter behaved like a dog, Apollonius of Tyana recommended that the dog who bit him lick the wound so that the agent of the wound might in turn be its healer (Philostratus *Vita Ap.* 6.43).

In his *Life of Vespasian*, Suetonius narrates an incident that occurred while Vespasian was in Alexandria.

Vespasian as yet lacked prestige and a certain divinity, so to speak, since he was an unexpected and still new-made emperor; but these also were given him. A man of the people who was blind, and another who was lame, came to him together as he sat on the tribunal, begging for the help for their disorders which Serapis had promised in a dream; for the god declared that Vespasian would restore the eyes, if he would spit on them, and give strength to the leg, if he would deign to touch it with his heel. Though he had hardly any faith that this could possibly succeed, and therefore shrank even from making the attempt, he was at last prevailed upon by his friends and tried both things in public before a large crowd; and with success (Auctoritas et quasi maiestas quaedam ut scilicet inopinato et adhuc novo principi deerat; haec quoque accessit. E plebe quidam luminibus orbatus, item alius debili crure sedentem pro tribunali pariter adierunt orantes opem valitudini demonstratam a Serapide per quietem: restituturum oculos, si inspuisset; confirmaturum crus, si dignaretur calce contingere. Cum vix fides esset ullo modo rem successuram ideoque ne experiri quidem auderet, extremo hortantibus amicis palam pro contione utrumque temptavit; nec eventus defuit). (*The Twelve Caesars, Vesp.* 7.2-3)[74]

Here, the saliva of Vespasian is effective presumably because he was the emperor of Rome. Similarly, Jesus' saliva is healing because he is endowed with divine power. Unlike the healing performed here in private by Jesus, however, those by Vespasian were done in public before a large crowd.

■ **34** Next Jesus looks up to heaven (or to the sky). This gesture may signify Jesus' calling on God to assist in the healing or an attempt to draw further upon the divine power.[75] After looking upward, Jesus sighs (*ἐστέναξεν*). In antiquity, the sigh sometimes signified the drawing in of spiritual power. In a collection of miscellaneous spells, the following instruction is given:

(Breathe out, in. Fill up); . . . (pushing more, bellowhowling.) "Come to me, god of gods, . . ." (Pull in, fill up, shutting your eyes. Bellow as much as you can, then, sighing, give out [what air remains] in a hiss.) (*πνεῦσον ἔξω, ἔσω. διαπλήρωσον· . . . ἔσω προσβαλόμενος μύκησαι. (ὀλολυγμός.) "δεῦρό μοι, θεῶν θεέ, . . ." ἕλκυσαι ἔσω, πληροῦ καμμύων, μύκησαι, ὅσον δύνασαι, ἔπειτα στενάξας συριγμῷ ἀνταπόδος*). (*PGM* XIII. 942–46)[76]

---

73 Text and trans. from Edelstein and Edelstein, no. 423.26 (1:226, 234). See also no. 423.20, according to which one of the dogs in the temple cured a blind boy, and 423.17, which states that a serpent that came out of the temple healed a man's toe with its tongue.

74 Text and trans. from John C. Rolfe, *Suetonius* (2 vols.; LCL; Cambridge, MA: Harvard University Press, 1914; rev. ed. 1997) 2:280–83. Other accounts of the incident are given by Tacitus (*Histories* 4.81) and Dio Cassius (*Roman History* 65.8.1). The latter uses the verb προσπτύειν ("to spit upon" or "spit forth"), which has the same root as Mark's πτύειν ("to spit") in this passage.

75 Meier defines both the looking up to heaven and the sighing as gestures of prayer (*Marginal Jew*, 2:713).

76 Text from Preisendanz-Henrichs, 2:127–28; trans. by Morton Smith in Betz, *Magical Papyri*, 193.

On the basis of this and other texts, Dibelius and Campbell Bonner concluded that the sigh of Jesus here belongs to the technique of, as Dibelius put it, "mystical magic."[77] This interpretation fits the immediate context better than the hypotheses that the sigh is a gesture of prayer or an expression of an emotion like compassion.[78]

Then Jesus says ἐφφαθα, which is אתפתח in Aramaic, meaning "Be opened."[79] As was the case with the words that Jesus spoke to Jairus's daughter, this verbal form is not a magical formula or an incantation.[80] Nevertheless, it is significant that what Jesus says is quoted in Aramaic, as well as in Greek. It is an indication that, for Greek speakers at least, the Aramaic words in themselves were believed to be powerful.[81]

■ **35** The use of the same verb here as in the Greek translation of Jesus' address to the man, "to open" (διανοίγειν), makes clear that Jesus' command was addressed to his ears (αὐτοῦ αἱ ἀκοαί), which represent the faculty of hearing in this context.[82] Not only were the man's ears opened, but "the bond of his tongue was untied" (ἐλύθη ὁ δεσμὸς τῆς γλώσσης αὐτοῦ).

A word related to the one used in Mark for "bond" (δεσμός), namely, κατάδεσμος, represents "a uniquely Greek form of cursing" and is usually translated "binding spell."[83] Judicial binding spells make up the largest category of binding spells in general. They were written prior to the outcome of a trial and represent attempts to bind "the opponent's ability to think clearly and speak effectively in court in the hope that a dismal performance will cause him to lose the case." A representative spell of this type involves the binding of the tongue among other things.[84] The statement that "the bond of his tongue was untied" in this verse may imply that someone had cast a spell on the unfortunate man to hinder his speech.[85]

The application of Jesus' saliva to the man's tongue, however, may imply a medical problem, rather than a spell. In that case, the verb ἐλύθη should be translated "was loosened." In the popular life of Aesop, he is portrayed as suffering from a similar problem, from which the goddess Isis frees him:

"I [the goddess, the lady Isis] restore his voice . . . ." Having said this and having cut off the rough (part) of (Aesop's) tongue, which was preventing him from speaking, Isis herself granted him his voice (ἐγὼ (ἡ θεός, ἡ κυρία Ἶσις) μὲν οὖν τὴν φωνὴν ἀποκαθίστημι . . . . εἰποῦσα δὲ ταῦτα καὶ τὸ τραχὺ τῆς γλώττης ἀποτεμοῦσα, τὸ κωλῦον αὐτὸν λαλεῖν, αὐτὴ δὴ ἡ Ἶσις ἐχαρίσατο <τὴν φωνήν>). (*Life of Aesop* 7 [Vita G])[86]

This text portrays a medical problem being solved by a divine being, as is the case in many of the testimonies to

---

77 Dibelius, *From Tradition to Gospel*, 85–86; Bonner, "Thaumaturgic Technique," 171–81. Hull concluded that the sigh here is an instance of sympathetic magic, the sighing being in imitation of the restoration of speech and of forcing out the in-dwelling demon (*Hellenistic Magic*, 84).

78 See the reference to Meier above; cf. also Blackburn, *Theios Anēr*, 216–18.

79 BAGD, s.v.; Wellhausen, 58; Lohmeyer, 150 n. 7.

80 Eitrem, however, referred to a magical spell for opening a door that uses the equivalent word in Coptic (*Some Notes*, 33).

81 Contra Blackburn, *Theios Anēr*, 219–21. See the commentary on 5:40b-43 above. Theissen argues that the Aramaic word here is "intended to demonstrate the superior power of eastern words of healing" (*Miracle Stories*, 254). Hull also concluded that the Aramaic word here is presented as a word of power (*Hellenistic Magic*, 85).

82 The noun ἀκοή is sometimes used in the plural for the organs of hearing, i.e., the ears; BAGD, s.v.

83 Christopher A. Faraone, "The Agonistic Context of Early Greek Binding Spells," in idem and Dirk Obbink, eds., *Magika Hiera: Ancient Greek Magic and Religion* (New York/Oxford: Oxford University Press, 1991) 3. According to LSJ, the word δεσμός is used at least once to mean *spell, charm* (s.v.).

84 Faraone, "Agonistic Context," 15. Adolf Deissmann pointed out that thirty Attic spells had been published that aimed at "binding" or "cursing" someone's tongue (*Licht vom Osten* [4th rev. ed.; Tübingen: Mohr Siebeck, 1923] 259; ET *Light from the Ancient East: The New Testament Illustrated by Recently Discovered Texts of the Graeco-Roman World* [London: Hodder & Stoughton, 1927] 305).

85 Deissmann concluded that the tongue of a mute person was "bound" by some demon in popular belief (*Licht vom Osten*, 258–61; *Light from the Ancient East*, 304–7); Lohmeyer, 151 n. 2. Hull agreed with Deissmann that the "bond of the tongue" is a phrase taken from the technical vocabulary of magic (*Hellenistic Magic*, 17, 81–82).

the healing power of Asclepius.[87] The Markan passage may be read in the same way.

The "rough (part) of (Aesop's) tongue" probably refers to some excess or deformity that prevented speech. Compare the following passage from Galen:

> Expiration is produced by the contraction of all muscles of the chest. Exsufflation, being a forceful expiration, results mainly from the action of the intercostal muscles. If it is noisy, the pharyngeal muscles are participating. But the sound is produced by the laryngeal muscles. The tongue, however, which articulates the sound, is needed to produce speech. This is accomplished by the aid of teeth and lips, the nasal communications, the palate, the uvula and, in addition, by the median ligament of the tongue itself. Those who speak in a lisping, inarticulate manner and those who have a related disturbance of the speech, suffer from a damage of the instruments of speech, either during their natural formation or at a later stage (ἐκπνοὴν μὲν γὰρ ἅπαντες οἱ συστέλλοντες τὸν θώρακα μύες· ἐκφύσησιν δὲ, οὖσαν ἐκπνοὴν σφοδρὰν, οἱ μεσοπλεύριοι μάλιστα· τὴν ψοφώδη δὲ οἱ τῆς φάρυγγος· αὐτὴν δὲ τὴν φωνὴν οἱ τοῦ λάρυγγος ἐργάζονται μύες· ἡ δὲ γλῶττα, διαρθροῦσα τὴν φωνὴν, εἰς τὸ διαλέγεσθαι χρήσιμος ὑπάρχει, συντελούντων δ᾽ εἰς τοῦτο καὶ τῶν ὀδόντων καὶ τῶν χειλῶν, ἔτι τε τῶν κατὰ τὴν ῥῖνα συντρήσεων, οὐρανίσκου τε καὶ γαργαρεῶνος, ἐπὶ τούτοις τε τοῦ συμμέτρου δεσμοῦ τῆς γλώττης αὐτῆς. οἱ μὲν οὖν τραυλοὶ, καὶ ψελλοὶ, καὶ τι τοιοῦτον κατὰ τὸ διαλέγεσθαι σφαλλόμενοι, τῶν διαλεκτικῶν ὀργάνων ἔχουσί τι βεβλαμμένον, ἢ κατὰ τὴν φυσικὴν διάπλασιν, ἢ μετὰ ταῦθ᾽ ὕστερον). (De locis affectis 4.9)[88]

The Greek phrase translated "the . . . ligament of the tongue" (ὁ . . . δεσμὸς τῆς γλώττης) is virtually identi-cal to the phrase used by Mark here (ὁ δεσμὸς τῆς γλώσσης). The only difference is that Galen used the Attic spelling of the word for "tongue." If, as is likely, the terminology of Galen was taken from ordinary usage, the author of Mark may have used the phrase to mean "the ligament of the tongue." In that case, the man's problem would have been that a ligament of the tongue was too tight or malformed in a way that impeded his speech.

Another approach to the statement is to see it as a metaphorical allusion to two prophecies in Isaiah, which, it would imply, are now being fulfilled.[89] According to these:

> I, the Lord God, have called you in righteousness and I will grasp your hand and I will strengthen you and I have given you for (the purpose of) a covenant of a people, for (the purpose of) a light of nations, to open the eyes of the blind, to lead out those who are bound from their bonds and those who are sitting in darkness from prison (ἐγὼ κύριος ὁ θεὸς ἐκάλεσά σε ἐν δικαιοσύνῃ καὶ κρατήσω τῆς χειρός σου καὶ ἐνισχύσω σε καὶ ἔδωκά σε εἰς διαθήκην γένους, εἰς φῶς ἐθνῶν ἀνοῖξαι ὀφθαλμοὺς τυφλῶν, ἐξαγαγεῖν ἐκ δεσμῶν δεδεμένους καὶ ἐξ οἴκου φυλακῆς καθημένους ἐν σκότει). (Isa 42:6-7 LXX)

> Thus says the Lord, ". . . I have given you for (the purpose of) a covenant of nations to establish the land and to inherit a desolate inheritance, saying to those in bonds, 'Come out,' and to those in the darkness, 'Be revealed'" (οὕτως λέγει κύριος . . . ἔδωκά σε εἰς διαθήκην ἐθνῶν τοῦ καταστῆσαι τὴν γῆν καὶ κληρονομῆσαι κληρονομίαν ἐρήμου, λέγοντα τοῖς ἐν δεσμοῖς Ἐξέλθατε, καὶ τοῖς ἐν τῷ σκότει ἀνακαλυφθῆναι). (Isa 49:8-9 LXX)

According to this interpretation, Jesus is the one being addressed by the Lord in the prophecies, and his break-

---

86 Text from Perry, *Aesopica*, 37; my trans.

87 One of the testimonies tells how Asclepius gave the power of speech to a speechless boy (παῖς ἄφωνος); for text and trans. see Edelstein and Edelstein, no. 423.5 (1:222–23, 230–31). In this case, however, no manipulation by the deity or anyone else is reported.

88 Text from D. Carolus Gottlob Kühn, *Claudii Galeni: Opera omnia* (Medicorum Graecorum Opera Quae Exstant; Leipzig: Knobloch, 1824) 8:271–72; trans. (slightly modified) from Rudolph E. Siegel, M.D., *Galen: On the Affected Parts* (Basel/New York: S. Karger, 1976) 126. I am grateful to Kevin Wilkinson for assistance in finding this reference.

89 See the commentary on v. 37 below. Cf. Lohmeyer, 151 n. 2.

ing the bond of the man's tongue is analogous to breaking the bonds of captives.

The statement that the man "began to speak correctly" (ἐλάλει ὀρθῶς) is proof that the bond of his tongue was untied or loosened and thus of the reality of the miracle.

■ **36** Bultmann argued that the command to silence breaks into the context and should, therefore, be recognized as a formulation by Mark.[90] Räisänen agreed and presented stylistic arguments supporting the hypothesis that v. 36 is a Markan composition.[91] He pointed out that the verb διαστέλλεσθαι ("to order" or "to command") occurs also in 5:43 and 9:9. The command to silence in 5:43, however, is probably from a source and not Markan composition.[92] The evangelist's use of the word in 9:9 may have been inspired by its usage in the sources.[93] Similar responses could be made to the other stylistic arguments.

Theissen argued that all the commands to silence in the miracle stories are from the tradition.[94] The commands to secrecy outside the miracle stories concern the identity of Jesus, a Markan theme, whereas that is never the case in the miracle stories themselves.[95] Since the command to silence in v. 36 fits well with the traditional motif of taking the person to be healed aside in v. 33, it was probably part of the story already in the collection of miracle stories used by the evangelist.

The identity of those who are commanded to be silent is somewhat unclear.[96] One manuscript modified the text to indicate that Jesus healed two men, one deaf and one with a speech impediment.[97] This change may have been made to prepare for v. 36, on the assumption that the word "them" (αὐτοῖς) refers to the person(s) healed. The ambiguity is most likely due to the terseness of the story.

It is implied, but not stated, that after Jesus healed the man, the two of them rejoined the people who had brought the man to Jesus in the first place.

The purpose of this command to silence is not to keep the identity of Jesus secret. It is rather a literary device. The command is given only to be broken. The goal is to impress on the audience that the mighty deeds of Jesus are so extraordinary that they cannot be hidden. His glory shines forth in spite of his attempt to conceal it. The same device is used in the account of the healing of the leper. The motif is most likely traditional in that story also, and not a Markan editorial addition.[98]

■ **37** Form-critically speaking, this verse has two parts: an expression of amazement on the part of those who have become aware of the miracle and an acclamation of the miracle-worker. The word ὑπερπερισσῶς ("beyond all measure") is rare.[99] This is its only occurrence in early Christian literature.[100]

Bultmann concluded that this verse was pre-Markan and that it represented the typical motif of the impression made by the miracle.[101] Dibelius pointed out that the acclamation was probably not part of the story in its original form, since the wording of the statement "He has done all things well; he makes both the deaf hear and the speechless speak" (καλῶς πάντα πεποίηκεν, καὶ τοὺς κωφοὺς ποιεῖ ἀκούειν καὶ (τοὺς) ἀλάλους λαλεῖν) implies that it was composed as the conclusion to a number of stories.[102] Achtemeier argued that this feature fits with his hypothesis that this story was the last of a group of three healings that followed the account of the walking on the water and preceded the feeding story represented by 8:1-10 in the second collection of miracle stories used by the evangelist.[103] The story about the raising of Jairus's daughter was the last of the three healing stories in the

90 Bultmann, *History*, 213. Similarly, Dibelius, *From Tradition to Gospel*, 74; Achtemeier, "Miracle Catenae," 288–89.

91 Räisänen, *Messianic Secret*, 150.

92 See the commentary on 5:40b-43 above.

93 Räisänen himself suggests that the secret features of the healing stories may have provided the starting point for the redactional secrecy theology (*Messianic Secret*, 222).

94 He concluded, however, that v. 36b is redactional (*Miracle Stories*, 162).

95 Ibid., 150–51; cf. Räisänen, *Messianic Secret*, 242–43.

96 One of Räisänen's arguments for the redactional

character of v. 36 is based on this ambiguity (*Messianic Secret*, 150).

97 See the note on the trans. of v. 33.

98 See the commentary on 1:44 and 45 above.

99 See LSJ, s.v.

100 BAGD, s.v. The related verb, however, occurs in Rom 5:20 and 2 Cor 7:4; Lohmeyer, 151 n. 3.

101 Bultmann, *History*, 213.

102 Dibelius, *From Tradition to Gospel*, 76. For others who have taken this position, see Achtemeier, "Miracle Catenae," 289 n. 93.

103 Achtemeier, "Miracle Catenae," 289.

first collection.[104] It is quite striking, therefore, that these two stories are the only ones that contain commands to silence and the motif of amazement on the part of the bystanders.[105] A deliberate pattern of composition or editing in the two sources could explain these phenomena.

Ancient acclamations take various forms. A very old one from Egypt takes the form "What Thoth does is great."[106] The Old Testament and the LXX contain responses to miracles that are similar to later acclamations. For example, after Elijah's fire miracle, the people proclaim:

Truly the Lord is God; he is God (Ἀληθῶς κύριός ἐστιν ὁ θεός, αὐτὸς ὁ θεός). (3 Kgdms 18:39)[107]

One of the additions to Daniel, the story of Bel and the Serpent, contains two acclamations:

Great is Bel, and there is no deceit with him (Μέγας ἐστὶν ὁ Βηλ, καὶ οὐκ ἔστι παρ' αὐτῷ δόλος). (Bel 18 OG)[108]

Great is the Lord God, and there is no other but him (Μέγας ἐστὶ κύριος ὁ θεός, καὶ οὐκ ἔστι πλὴν αὐτοῦ ἄλλος). (Bel 41 OG)[109]

The mother of the seven sons killed by Antiochus Epiphanes threatens that he will be brought by afflictions and plagues to confess:

He alone is God (μόνος αὐτὸς θεός ἐστιν). (2 Macc 7:37 LXX)[110]

Acclamations also occur in various books of the New Testament. For example, Matthew's version of the stilling of the storm concludes with an acclamation:

Truly you are God's son (Ἀληθῶς θεοῦ υἱὸς εἶ). (Matt 14:33)[111]

As Theissen has pointed out, it is striking that the acclamations in the Markan miracle stories are not titular. The only titular acclamation in Mark is that of the centurion at the crucifixion (15:39).[112] It may be that the evangelist deliberately avoided titular acclamations in the miracle stories in order to create a dramatic climax with the acclamation of the centurion.[113]

A distinctive characteristic of the acclamation in this verse is the way in which it echoes several passages in Isaiah:

Then will the eyes of the blind be opened, and the ears of the deaf hear. . . . and the tongue of the speech-impaired will be clear (τότε ἀνοιχθήσονται ὀφθαλμοὶ τυφλῶν, καὶ ὦτα κωφῶν ἀκούσονται. . . . καὶ τρανὴ ἔσται γλῶσσα μογιλάλων). (Isa 35:5-6 LXX)

And on that day the deaf will hear the words of a book (Καὶ ἀκούσονται ἐν τῇ ἡμέρᾳ ἐκείνῃ κωφοὶ λόγους βιβλίου). (Isa 29:18 LXX)

And the hearts of the feeble will pay attention so that they may hear, and the tongues of the inarticulate will quickly learn to speak peace (Καὶ ἡ καρδία τῶν ἀσθενούντων προσέξει τοῦ ἀκούειν, καὶ αἱ γλῶσσαι αἱ ψελλίζουσαι ταχὺ μαθήσονται λαλεῖν εἰρήνην). (Isa 32:4 LXX)

It seems likely that the original audience of the pre-Markan collection of miracle stories was expected to perceive the allusions, at least to Isa 35:5-6. The implication

---

104 Ibid., 279.

105 Ibid., 289.

106 Pap. Anastasi V. 9-10; dated to the thirteenth cent. BCE; cited by Theissen, *Miracle Stories*, 158–59.

107 Cf. Theissen, *Miracle Stories*, 159.

108 My trans.; Theissen, *Miracle Stories*, 159.

109 My trans. This work may be assigned tentatively to Jerusalem in the first quarter of the second cent. BCE; see Collins, *Daniel*, 418.

110 Cf. Theissen, *Miracle Stories*, 160, where the reference to 2 Macc 6:37 is incorrect.

111 Cf. John 1:49; 6:14; Acts 8:10; 14:11-12; 28:6; cf. Theissen, *Miracle Stories*, 161–62.

112 Theissen, *Miracle Stories*, 162–63. The nontitular acclamations in the miracle stories are 1:27; 4:41; and this verse.

113 Theissen, *Miracle Stories*, 171. He even claims that the composition of the Gospel of Mark as a whole is based on the compositional structure of the miracle stories (214–15).

is that the great day of the ransom of Zion is dawning (Isa 35:10). In other words, the acclamation of the people indicates the eschatological fulfillment of the prophecies of the Jewish Scriptures.[114] It is striking that this miracle story combines an image of Jesus as a charismatic healer, or even magician, with his acclamation as the agent of the divine eschatological fulfillment. This combination was evidently no problem for the pre-Markan tradents nor for the evangelist.[115]

The allusions to the Old Testament in this acclamation support the conclusion that this account is set in a Jewish region.[116] The acclamation may also echo Wis 10:20-21:

Therefore the righteous . . . sang hymns, O Lord, to your holy name, and praised with one accord your defending hand, because wisdom opened the mouth of the mute and made the tongues of babes speak

clearly (διὰ τοῦτο δίκαιοι . . . ὕμνησαν, κύριε, τὸ ὄνομα τὸ ἅγιόν σου τήν τε ὑπέρμαχόν σου χεῖρα ᾔνεσαν ὁμοθυμαδόν· ὅτι ἡ σοφία ἤνοιξεν στόμα κωφῶν καὶ γλώσσας νηπίων ἔθηκεν τρανάς). (Wis 10:20-21 LXX)[117]

Here we find hymns, similar to acclamations, combined with miracles of speech.

The statement "he has done all things well (καλῶς)" is reminiscent of Gen 1:31 (LXX): "And God saw all the things that he had made, and see, (they were) very good" (καὶ εἶδεν ὁ θεὸς τὰ πάντα, ὅσα ἐποίησεν, καὶ ἰδοὺ καλὰ λίαν).[118] Compare Sir 39:16 (LXX): "All things are the works of the Lord, for they are very good" (τὰ ἔργα κυρίου πάντα ὅτι καλὰ σφόδρα).[119] These echoes of scripture suggest that Jesus is the agent of God in the eschatological renewal of creation.

---

114 Lohmeyer, 151.
115 Lohmeyer concluded that the story originated in Palestine (151–52). The combination, or at least the thaumaturgical part of it, did apparently disturb the authors of Matthew and Luke, since Luke omitted the narrative entirely and Matthew has something very different in its place.
116 Räisänen, *Messianic Secret*, 153. Lohmeyer, however, argues that the evangelist puts these words in the mouths of Gentiles in order to show that they outdo the Jews (151 n. 4).

117 Trans. from RSV (modified); Lohmeyer argued that this passage is evoked by the remark in v. 35 that the man "spoke correctly" (151). Cf. also Exod 4:10; Philo *Mut. nom.* 7 §56; David Winston, *The Wisdom of Solomon: A New Translation with Introduction and Commentary* (AB 43; Garden City, NY: Doubleday, 1979) 222.
118 Cf. Lohmeyer, 151.
119 Trans. from RSV; cf. Lohmeyer, 151.

8

8:1-9 The Feeding of the Four Thousand

1/ In those days there was again a large crowd, and since they did not have anything to eat, he summoned his[a] disciples and said to them, 2/ "I have pity on the crowd, for they have remained with me for three days[b] now and they do not have anything to eat; 3/ and if I dismiss them hungry to their homes, they will become weary on the way; and some of them have come[c] from a distance." 4/ And his disciples answered him, "From what place will anyone be able to satisfy these (people) here with bread in an uninhabited region?" 5/ And he asked them, "How many loaves do you have?" They said, "Seven." 6/ And he ordered the crowd to recline on the ground; and he took the seven loaves, gave thanks, broke (them) and gave (them) to his disciples to set before (the crowd), and they set (them) before the crowd. 7/ And they had a few fish; and having blessed them,[d] he said that they should place these also before (the crowd).[e] 8/ And they ate[f] and were satisfied, and they picked up the remainder of the broken pieces, seven hampers. 9/ And they were about four thousand. And he dismissed them.

a   A B W et al. attest the reading τοὺς μαθητὰς αὐτοῦ ("his disciples"), whereas ℵ D et al. attest the reading τοὺς μαθητάς ("the disciples"). Since Hellenistic Greek made greater use of pronouns than classical Greek, stylistically conscious scribes were inclined to remove unnecessary pronouns. Thus, the former reading is more likely to be original; see Turner, "Marcan Usage," 26 (1925) 235–37 (Elliott, *Language and Style*, 47–48); Taylor, ad loc.; James K. Elliott, "An Eclectic Textual Commentary on the Greek Text of Mark's Gospel," in Elliott, *Language and Style*, 189–201, esp. 197–98.

b   The earliest recoverable reading is probably the parenthetic nominative ἡμέραι τρεῖς ("three days"). This construction appears elsewhere in the NT and frequently in the papyri (Taylor, ad loc.). The readings attested by B (2427), ἡμέραις τρισίν ("three days"), a temporal dative of the duration of time (see Moulton-Turner, 3:243–44), and D it, ἡμέραι τρεῖς εἰσίν ἀπὸ πότε ὦδε εἰσίν ("it is three days that they have been here"), reflect attempts at syntactical improvement.

c   The earliest recoverable reading is probably the present verb with a perfect ending ἥκασιν ("they have come"), attested by ℵ A D et al. This reading gave rise to variants. One reading attests a correction from the perfect ending to the present (0131 *f*[13] 𝔐). The reading attested by B L et al., εἰσίν ("are"), may be an Atticistic correction (Moulton-Turner, 3:82).

d   The earliest recoverable reading is probably εὐλογήσας αὐτά ("having blessed them"), attested by ℵ B C et al. Two of the variants may be explained as attempted improvements. N Γ 33 et al. omit the pronoun αὐτά ("them"), either as redundant in light of the following ταῦτα ("these") or to prevent the audience from losing sight of the fact that God was being blessed, not the fish. The variant attested by D 1009 et al., εὐχαριστήσας ("having given thanks"), addresses the same problem(s) as the previous reading and also conforms this verse to the description of the analogous action with the bread in v. 6. See Metzger, *Textual Commentary*, 83.

e   Moulton-Turner (3:137–38) takes the infinitive παραθεῖναι, attested by (N) W Θ et al., or παραθῆναι, attested by A et al. ("to place before"), as the direct object of εἶπεν ("he said"). ℵ[1] B L et al. attest the present active form of the infinitive, παρατιθέναι ("to place before"). Taylor accepts the latter reading and understands the construction as "the use of the infinitive after εἶπεν ["he said"] in the sense of 'to command'" (ad loc. and 62).

f   A few MSS (ℵ 33 *pc* vg[ms]) attest a reading with πάντες ("all") following ἔφαγον ("they ate"). The word πάντες ("all") represents a secondary addition inspired either by the parallel in Matt 15:37 or by the corresponding verse in the earlier account in Mark (6:42).

Comment

On the genre and cultural context of 8:1-9, see the sections "The Genre of 6:35-44" and "Cultural Contexts" in the commentary on 6:35-44 above.

It is often argued that the first feeding took place in a Jewish region as an expression of Jesus' beneficence to Jews and that the second feeding took place in a Gentile region and was directed to Gentiles.[1] The implied setting of the second feeding story in Mark, however, is also Galilee.[2]

■ **1-2** The first feeding account (6:35-44) is much more integrated into its literary context than this account. Here the temporal setting ("in those days") is general and connects the second feeding only loosely to the preceding account of a healing. Similarly, the presence of the crowd is merely noted here, whereas their gathering is described elaborately in 6:31-34. These observations suggest that the opening of this account reflects the wording of the source, with the possible exception of πάλιν ("again").[3] Paul J. Achtemeier has argued persuasively that the two feeding miracles were originally the last in each of the two chains of miracle stories used by the evangelist.[4]

Bultmann argued that the motif of Jesus' taking the initiative here is secondary in comparison with the disciples' initiative in 6:35-36.[5] Although the initiative of Jesus may be a secondary motif in some cases, it is not necessarily so here. Mark may have given the disciples the initiative in the first feeding story in order to highlight their lack of understanding of Jesus' power and the potential power of their own faith.[6] Theissen defines this account as a "gift miracle" and notes that such miracles are never initiated by requests. The motif "initiative of the miracle-worker" is typical of gift miracles.[7]

Jesus' statement in v. 2 that the crowd has remained with him for three days indicates a greater need for food on their part than that of the crowd in the first feeding story, who had been with Jesus for only one day. The presence of the crowd for a shorter time in the first story is dependent on the redactional description of the gathering of the crowd.

■ **3-4** This account contrasts with the first feeding story in that there is no question here of sending the people to the surrounding farms and villages to buy something for themselves to eat (cf. 6:36).[8] Rather, Jesus is concerned that they would become weary on the way to their homes. In the source collections, these elements may simply be variant ways of telling the traditional story. In the first feeding story, however, there is tension between the setting in an unpopulated place (ἔρημος τόπος) and the presence of relatively near surrounding farms and villages.[9] Here, in the disciples' response to Jesus in v. 4,

---

1   E.g., Werner H. Kelber, *Mark's Story of Jesus* (Philadelphia: Fortress, 1979) 39; Seán Freyne, "The Geography of Restoration: Galilee–Jerusalem Relations in Early Jewish and Christian Experience," *NTS* 47 (2001) 289–311, esp. 306.

2   See the commentary on 7:31 above and on 8:10 below.

3   Contra Achtemeier ("Miracle Catenae," 289) and with Bultmann (*History*, 217). Karl Ludwig Schmidt argued that πάλιν ("again") is the only editorial addition; he came to this conclusion because the word occurs so often in Mark (*Der Rahmen*, 192). Theissen assigns 8:1 to the oldest stratum (*Miracle Stories*, 125). Achtemeier is inclined to take ἐν ἐκείναις ταῖς ἡμέραις πάλιν ("in those days again") as redactional, because then the account would begin with a genitive absolute. He notes that three other miracle stories begin with genitive absolutes, but these are all from the first source, whereas 8:1-9 is from the second ("Miracle Catenae," 289 n. 95; cf. 291).

4   Achtemeier, "Miracle Catenae," 290.

5   Bultmann, *History*, 217; cf. 66. He argued also that Jesus' statement in 8:2 that he has pity on the crowd is secondary in comparison with the narrator's comment about his pity in 6:34 (ibid., 217). It could be so, but it is noteworthy that the narrator's description of Jesus' pity in 6:34 is combined with an allusion to the biblical motif of the king as a shepherd; see the commentary above ad loc.

6   See the commentary on 6:35-36 and 37-38 above.

7   Theissen, *Miracle Stories*, 103–4.

8   Bultmann, *History*, 217.

9   Achtemeier concluded that the reference to an unpopulated place was introduced into the first feeding story by Mark ("Miracle Catenae," 280).

a related but stronger word (ἐρημία) is used to set the feeding in the "wilderness" or "desert."[10] The assumption that the people would have to travel a considerable distance to their homes is compatible with this setting. Furthermore, the use of the noun "wilderness" (ἐρημία) here evokes more strongly than the setting of the first feeding the wandering of the people of Israel in the wilderness and their being fed with manna there.[11]

Achtemeier argued plausibly that the reaction of the disciples in v. 4 is possible only if this account was formulated completely independently of the first feeding story.[12] This conclusion is supported by the fact that there is no indication of a rebuke or didactic purpose on the part of Jesus, as one would expect if the disciples' question were meant to illustrate their lack of understanding.[13]

■ 5-6 This account differs from the first feeding story in that the disciples have five loaves in the first and seven loaves here. The different numbers are most likely variants in relation to the basic structure of the traditional story. They seem to have no symbolic meaning, at least not in the sources used by the evangelist. This account also differs from the first in that Jesus himself commands the crowd to recline here, whereas, according to the earliest recoverable reading of 6:39, in the first feeding story Jesus commands the disciples to have the people recline.[14] The greater involvement of the disciples in the first account is probably connected to the didactic motif that emerges in 6:37a.[15] The verb used here (v. 6) for "recline" (ἀναπίπτειν) appears also in 6:40, whereas a different verb with the same meaning is used in 6:39 (ἀνακλίνειν).

This account has Jesus command the people to recline simply "on the ground" (ἐπὶ τῆς γῆς). This motif contrasts with the more elaborate "on the green grass" (ἐπὶ τῷ χλωρῷ χόρτῳ) of 6:39, which is part of the depiction of the scene as an outdoor banquet in contrast to the banquet of Herod.[16]

The motif according to which Jesus looks up to heaven in 6:41 is lacking here. Furthermore, the first account has Jesus praise God (εὐλογεῖν), but here (v. 6) he gives thanks (εὐχαριστεῖν). The former verb is used in connection with Jesus' taking a loaf of bread at the Last Supper, and the latter is used in connection with the taking of the cup (14:22-23).[17] This variation is compatible with the diversity in the practice of prayers before and after meals among Jews in the late Second Temple period.[18] Philo consistently uses the expression "to give thanks" (εὐχαριστεῖν) to refer to prayer at meals, rather than the expression "to praise" or "to bless" (εὐλογεῖν).[19]

The primary significance of this miracle story is to depict the extraordinary power of Jesus and his use of that power to provide for people in need. On a secondary level, the use of the term "to give thanks" (εὐχαριστεῖν) is reminiscent of the early Christian eucharist (lit., "thanksgiving," εὐχαριστία) (Did. 9:1).[20]

As Achtemeier has pointed out, the fact that both collections of miracle stories seem to have ended with an account of Jesus feeding a multitude is significant for the reconstruction of their purpose and use.[21] He concluded:

> The most likely explanation lies in the suggestion that, at some point prior to Mark, the stories of the feeding had their locus in a liturgy accompanying a eucharistic celebration, either as an auxiliary to it, or as part of

---

10 In 1:3, 4, 12 and 13, the related adjective ἔρημος ("unpopulated") is used substantively to indicate the wilderness or desert.

11 See the section "Cultural Contexts" in the commentary on 6:35-44 above.

12 Achtemeier, "Miracle Catenae," 290 n. 98.

13 Contrast 6:37a; see the commentary on 6:35-36 and 37-38 above.

14 See the note on the trans. of 6:39 above.

15 See the commentary on 6:35-36 and 37-38 above.

16 See the commentary on 6:39-40 above.

17 Paul reports a tradition that Jesus, on the night on which he was handed over, took bread, gave thanks (εὐχαριστεῖν), and broke it (1 Cor 11:23-24).

18 According to Paul F. Bradshaw, among first century Jews either a "blessing" (berakah) or a "thanksgiving" (hodayah) could be said in connection with a meal (Search, 15–17). Cf. Paul's practice according to Acts 27:35.

19 Bradshaw, Search, 26.

20 Ibid., 47–55.

21 Paul J. Achtemeier, "The Origin and Function of the Pre-Markan Miracle Catenae," JBL 91 (1972) 198–221.

the catechism accompanying it, the point of which was to clarify the meaning and import of that celebration.[22]

He argued further that the group or groups that used the pre-Markan collections composed a liturgy that "used epiphanic events in the life of Jesus to give substance to [the primitive church's] epiphanic interpretation of the eucharistic meal."[23] Evidence for this type of epiphanic eucharist may be found especially in the account of the appearance of the risen Jesus to the disciples on the road to Emmaus and in the summary description of early Christian ritual meals in Acts 2:46.[24] In that they are manifestations of the power of Jesus, the miracles of the two collections may be described as epiphanic, especially the stilling of the storm, the exorcism of the Gerasene demoniac, and the account of Jesus walking on the water.[25] It is credible that the collections of miracle stories were read at early Christian ritual meals, at which the risen Jesus was believed to be present (cf. 1 Cor 10:21). The term "liturgy" may imply more formal, fixed practices than can reasonably be inferred from the evidence for this period. The stories may simply have been read or told as part of the edifying "table-talk" when Christians gathered to eat together.

■ 7 Bultmann was inclined to conclude that this verse is an addition to the text inspired by the account in 6:34-44.[26] Achtemeier argued that the fish motif here is intrusive and thus a redactional addition. He concluded that the evangelist called attention to the fish in order to deemphasize the eucharistic connotations in the account.[27] It seems more likely that the apparent intrusiveness of the mention of the fish is due to the oral character of the narrative. That the disciples had fish and that Jesus blessed and distributed them, as well as the bread, are elements of the story that are included as afterthoughts.[28]

The word for "fish" ($i\chi\vartheta\acute{v}\delta\iota o\nu$) here is diminutive in form. It probably did not have a diminutive meaning in

Mark's colloquial usage.[29] The size of the fish is not important for the miracle story. The miracle consists in the feeding of four thousand people with only seven loaves of bread and a few fish.

Jesus is depicted as "blessing" the fish (or blessing God over the fish) here, but he "gave thanks" over the bread (v. 6). This discrepancy may have played a role in the inclination of Bultmann to take this verse as an addition to the text based on 6:34-44. But given the diversity and fluidity in late Second Temple Jewish prayers, and thus very probably in early Christian prayers, this variation in terminology does not constitute evidence for the redactional character of v. 7.[30]

■ 8 The statement that the people ate and were satisfied constitutes the demonstration of the miracle and the climax of this short narrative. It is also reminiscent of the theme of the feeding of Israel with manna and quails in the Hebrew Bible.[31]

The description of the food left over also demonstrates that a miracle has occurred and indicates the great abundance associated with the power and beneficence of Jesus. The construction here, "the remainder of the broken pieces" ($\pi\epsilon\rho\iota\sigma\sigma\epsilon\acute{v}\mu\alpha\tau\alpha$ $\kappa\lambda\alpha\sigma\mu\acute{\alpha}\tau\omega\nu$), differs from that in 6:43.

Whereas five loaves resulted in twelve baskets ($\kappa\acute{o}\varphi\iota$-$\nu o\iota$) of leftovers in 6:35-44, here seven loaves result in seven hampers ($\sigma\pi\upsilon\rho\acute{\iota}\delta\epsilon\varsigma$) of superfluous bread. The difference between the number of loaves and baskets, as well as elements of the context, suggests that the numeral twelve in 6:43 is symbolic.[32] Here, however, the correspondence between seven loaves and seven hampers may simply be a way of expressing the greatness of the power of Jesus and the abundance resulting from the miracle: each loaf fed a large number of people and still filled a hamper with excess bread. Analogous to this correspondence is that between five loaves and five thousand people in 6:38 and 44.

■ 9 The comment that those who ate and were satisfied numbered four thousand people (v. 9a) is the denoue-

22   Ibid., 208.
23   Ibid., 209.
24   Ibid., 214–17.
25   See the commentary on 4:37 and 41; 5:14-17; 6:49-50 and 51-52; and the section "The Genre of 6:45-52" above.
26   Bultmann, *History*, 217.

27   Achtemeier, "Miracle Catenae," 220–21.
28   Cf. the commentary on 5:8 above.
29   Turner, "Marcan Usage," 29 (1928) 349–52 (Elliott, *Language and Style*, 123–26).
30   See the commentary on vv. 5-6 above.
31   See the commentary on 6:42-44 above.
32   See the commentary 6:42-44 above.

ment of the narrative. It also serves to elaborate the demonstration of the miracle expressed in v. 8 and to enhance its effect. In the context of this brief narrative itself, the number of people fed from so few loaves is astounding. In comparison with the first feeding, however, fewer people are fed with more loaves. The fact that there is no escalation from the first story to the second is in keeping with the concise, unelaborated character of the second in contrast with the richly detailed nature of the first.

If Achtemeier is correct that this narrative was the last in the second collection of miracle stories used by the evangelist, it is unlikely that v. 9b was part of that source. The statement that Jesus dismissed the people would make little sense in the last of a series of miracle stories told in the context of a ritual meal. Its primary function is to end this story and to prepare for what the Markan Jesus will do next.[33]

8 8:10-21 The Question of a Sign and Bread

10/ And immediately he got into the boat with his disciples and went to the district of Dalmanoutha.[a] 11/ And the Pharisees came out and began to discuss with him, demanding of him a sign from heaven, putting him to the test. 12/ And he sighed deeply in his spirit and said, "Why does this generation demand a sign? Truly I say to you,[b] a sign will not be given to this generation. 13/ And he left them, embarked again,[c] and went away to the other shore. 14/ And they had forgotten to bring bread, and they had (no bread) with them in the boat, except for one loaf.[d] 15/ And he ordered them, saying, "See, watch out[e] for the leaven of the Pharisees and the leaven of Herod."[f] 16/ And they were discussing among themselves that they did not have bread.[g] 17/ And he knew (what they were discussing) and said to them, "Why are you discussing that you do not have bread? Do you not yet understand or comprehend? Do you have hardened hearts?[h] 18/ Having eyes, do you not see, and having ears, do you not hear? And do you not remember, 19/ when I broke the five loaves for the five thousand, how many baskets full of fragments you picked up?" They said to him, "Twelve."

a   The earliest recoverable reading is $\tau\grave{\alpha}\ \mu\acute{\epsilon}\rho\eta\ \Delta\alpha\lambda\mu\alpha\nu\upsilon\vartheta\acute{\alpha}$ ("the district of Dalmanoutha"), attested by ℵ A (B) C et al. The phrase $\tau\grave{\alpha}\ \mu\acute{\epsilon}\rho\eta$ ("the district"), which occurs nowhere else in Mark, was replaced at some point by $\tau\grave{\alpha}\ \acute{o}\rho\iota\alpha$ ("the region" or "the district"), which occurs in Mark 5:17; 7:24, 31 (twice) and in the parallel in Matt 15:39. The latter reading is attested for Mark 8:10 by Δ. (N) 1241. 1424 pc f. Readings that seem to derive from this one appear in W (28 sy^s) D aur c (k). Perhaps because the location of Dalmanoutha was unknown or because the place was better known by another name, the author of Matthew changed the name to $M\alpha\gamma\alpha\delta\acute{\alpha}\nu$ ("Magadan" [15:39]). There are variants of Mark 8:10 that show the influence of the latter reading or of an analogous change: 28 565 it sy^s read $M\alpha\gamma\epsilon\delta\acute{\alpha}$ ("Mageda"); Θ $f^{1.13}$ 2542 pc read $M\acute{\alpha}\gamma\delta\alpha\lambda\alpha$ ("Magdala"); and D aur c (k) read $M\alpha\gamma\alpha\delta\acute{\alpha}$ ("Magada"). See also Metzger, *Textual Commentary*, 83.

b   B L 892 pc lack $\acute{v}\mu\tilde{\iota}\nu$ ("to you") and the word is omitted by Taylor (ad loc.), following Westcott and Hort. The shorter reading, however, is too weakly attested to have a good claim to be earlier.

c   The shorter reading, $\pi\acute{\alpha}\lambda\iota\nu\ \acute{\epsilon}\mu\beta\acute{\alpha}\varsigma$ ("embarked again"), is attested by ℵ B C et al. and was adopted by Tischendorf; Westcott and Hort; Taylor; Nestle (25th edition); Nestle-Aland (26th and 27th editions); Aland, *Synopsis*; and Huck-Greeven. The longer reading, $\pi\acute{\alpha}\lambda\iota\nu\ \acute{\epsilon}\mu\beta\grave{\alpha}\varsigma\ \epsilon\acute{\iota}\varsigma\ \tau\grave{o}\ \pi\lambda o\tilde{\iota}o\nu$ ("got into the boat again"), is attested by A 0131 f^1 𝔐 et al. Elliott has argued recently for this as the earlier reading on the grounds that it is a redundant expression characteristic of Mark ("Eclectic Textual Commentary," 194). But since the order of words varies among the witnesses to the longer reading, it is more likely that it arose as a clarifying expansion.

---

33   Contra Achtemeier, "Miracle Catenae," 289–90. See the discussion of v. 10 below.

20/ "When (I broke) the seven (loaves) for the four thousand, how many hampers were filled with the excess of the pieces that you picked up?" And they said to him, "Seven." **21/** And he said to them, "Do you not yet[i] comprehend?"

d   The earliest recoverable reading, καὶ εἰ μὴ ἕνα ἄρτον οὐκ εἶχον, "and they had (no bread) except for one loaf," is typical of Mark's style; it is a double statement involving a negative followed by a positive. See Neirynck, *Duality in Mark,* 89. The variants represent attempts at improving the style. D (it) attest the reading εἰ μὴ ἕνα ἄρτον εἶχον, "except (the) one loaf (which) they had." p[45vid] (W) Θ f[1] et al. attest the reading ἕνα μόνον ἄρτον ἔχοντες, "having only one loaf."

e   The reading ὁρᾶτε, βλέπετε ("See, watch out"), attested by ℵ A B L W et al., is probably the earliest recoverable reading, since it reflects Markan style in the double imperative (Neirynck, *Duality in Mark,* 84) and in the asyndeton (Turner, "Marcan Usage," 28 (1926) 15–19 [Elliott, *Language and Style,* 74–78]). In the reading attested by D Θ f[1] 565. 2542, βλέπετε ("Watch out"), the duality has been eliminated by the omission of the first imperative, ὁρᾶτε ("See"); in that attested by Δ 700, ὁρᾶτε ("See"), the same effect has been achieved by the omission of the second imperative. Another variant, ὁρᾶτε καὶ βλέπετε ("See and watch out"), attested by p[45] C 0131 et al., relieves the asyndeton by the addition of καί ("and").

f   The reading attested by p[45] W Θ et al., τῶν Ἡρῳδιανῶν ("the Herodians"), clearly resulted from an attempt to conform this verse to 3:6 and 12:13; see Metzger, *Textual Commentary,* 83.

g   A C L et al. attest a reading in which λέγοντες ("saying") follows ("one another"). Most of these MSS also read ἔχομεν ("we have"), rather than ἔχουσιν ("they did not have," lit., "they do not have"). These MSS have thus transformed the conjunction ὅτι ("that") to ὅτι-recitativum (introduces direct discourse and is not to be translated). Turner ("Markan Usage," 27 (1926) 58–60 [Elliott, *Language and Style,* 63–65]) and G. D. Kilpatrick ("Recitative λέγων," in Elliott, *Language and Style,* 175–77, esp. 175) take the ὅτι of the earliest reading as interrogative: "why (they had no loaves)." The readings that include λέγοντες ("saying") and ἔχομεν ("we have") are suspect because they may have arisen either through assimilation of the text of Mark to the parallel in Matt 16:7 or through intended improvement analogous to that carried out by Matthew. See also Taylor, ad loc.

h   D* reads πεπηρωμένη, "(Are your minds) incapacitated?," instead of πεπωρωμένην, "(Do you have) hardened hearts (or minds)?" The former verb appears as a variant in other passages of the NT, as well as in Job 17:7; see BAGD, s.v. πηρόω. (D) Θ (0143[vid]). 565 (it) co attest the reading πεπωρωμένη ὑμῶν ἐστὶν ἡ καρδία; ("Are your hearts hardened?"), rather than πεπωρωμένην ἔχετε τὴν καρδίαν ὑμῶν ("Do you have hardened hearts?"), the reading attested by p[45vid] ℵ B C et al. The latter reading is the earlier, since ἔχειν ("to have") is a verb used often by Mark, which Matthew and Luke frequently eliminate; so Turner, "Marcan Usage," 28 (1927) 357–60 (Elliott, *Language and Style*, 99–102). It is also better attested.

i B Γ 28 et al. attest the reading πῶς οὐ, "How (do you) not (comprehend)?" ℵ C K L et al. attest the reading οὔπω, "(Do you) not yet (comprehend)?" The latter is

more likely to be the earliest recoverable reading, since οὔπω ("not yet") is a favorite word of Mark; see John C. Hawkins, *Horae Synopticae: Contributions to the Study of the Synoptic Problem* (2nd ed.; Oxford: Clarendon, 1909) 13. The reading attested by A D N W Θ et al., πῶς οὔπω, "How (do you) not yet (comprehend)?," seems to be a conflation of the other two.

Comment

■ **10** Achtemeier concluded that vv. 9b-10 formed the original conclusion to the preceding narrative (the second feeding story) in the source collection, arguing that the description of the destination "the district of Dalmanoutha" (τὰ μέρη Δαλμανουθά) in v. 10 is specific, whereas the Markan summaries tend to mention either more general locations, for example, "beside the sea," or better-known places like Capernaum. He noted further that this place-name presented a problem from an early time, as the textual history of the verse indicates.[34] But if even the statement that Jesus dismissed the people (v. 9b) seems out of place in the concluding narrative of the source collection,[35] so much more would v. 10 be unlikely to conclude a collection being read in a meal setting.

The statement that Jesus and the disciples got into "the boat" and traveled, presumably on the Sea of Galilee, supports the conclusion that both the healing of the deaf man and the second feeding take place in the vicinity of the Sea of Galilee. The boat mentioned here is presumably the same one that is referred to in 6:54, which is part of a Markan summary.[36]

■ **11-13** According to Bultmann, this scene is a controversy-dialogue.[37] He placed the saying of Jesus that forms its climax (v. 12) in the general category of prophetic and apocalyptic sayings and defined it as a minatory saying or prophetic threat.[38] He was inclined to attribute the substance of this saying to the historical Jesus.[39] Robert C. Tannehill defined the scene as a whole as a correction story.[40] Bernd Kollmann has analyzed the history of the tradition in this passage and its relation to the parallels in Q.[41] Harry T. Fleddermann has argued that Mark is secondary to Q in this passage and shows knowledge of redactional Q, but this conclusion is dubious.[42] Many scholars have concluded that Mark's version is the oldest.[43]

The statement in v. 11 that the Pharisees "came out" suggests that they came to the harbor to meet Jesus when his boat landed. No reason is given for their demand of a sign from Jesus. The Pharisees last appeared in the controversy or scholastic dialogue in 7:1-13. Their reappearance here suggests that their demand for a sign is a response to the miracles that Jesus has done in the meantime.[44] In the Synoptic tradition, the demand for a sign

34 Achtemeier, "Miracle Catenae," 289–90. See the note on the trans. of v. 10 above. Andreas Bedenbender argued that "Dalmanoutha" is a symbolic name, meaning roughly "Doubts-City," created by Mark to characterize the Pharisees in the subsequent account of the request for a sign ("Orte mitten im Meer," 44–47).

35 See the commentary on v. 9 above.

36 See the commentary on 6:54-55 above.

37 Bultmann, *History*, 52. Dibelius concluded that vv. 11-12 are formally similar to ancient Greek *chreiai*, although they differ greatly in content from the *chreiai* (*From Tradition to Gospel*, 159–60).

38 Bultmann, *History*, 117.

39 Ibid., 128.

40 Tannehill, "Varieties," 1.1 (p. 102) and 1.3 (p. 103).

41 Kollmann, *Wundertäter*, 282–83; see also Olof Linton, "The Demand for a Sign from Heaven (Mk 8, 11-12 and Parallels)," *StTh* 19 (1965) 112–29, esp. 112–23. Linton argued that, in the context of the life of the historical Jesus, the "sign" requested was a testimony of trustworthiness, not of power (ibid., esp. 128).

42 Fleddermann, *Mark and Q*, 126–34; cf. Neirynck, "Assessment," 280–81.

43 See Kollmann, *Wundertäter*, 283, and the literature cited there.

44 The exorcism of the daughter of the Syro-Phoenician woman (7:24-30); the healing of a deaf man (7:31-37); and the feeding of the four thousand (8:1-9). Cf. Marshall, *Faith*, 66–67.

from Jesus typically relates to "the miracles of Jesus in which his authority is expressed."[45] The qualification of the sign as "from heaven" indicates that the Pharisees want verification that Jesus' miracle-working power comes from God. Their demand for a sign is thus analogous to the charge made by the scribes in 3:22 that Jesus casts out demons by the power of Beelzebul.[46] The narrator comments that the demand for a sign is a way of testing Jesus. The last time that Jesus was tested in Mark was during his sojourn in the wilderness after his baptism. On that occasion the tester was Satan. The depiction of both the Pharisees and Satan as testers of Jesus implies that both are opponents of Jesus in his role as God's agent.

In light of Jesus' response in v. 12, the Pharisees here play a role in the last days analogous to the role of the generation of the wilderness. That generation witnessed many divine signs, but continued to demand further interventions, behind which stood the question "Is the Lord among us or not?" (Exod 17:7).[47]

Campbell Bonner has argued that Jesus' deep sighing or groaning (ἀναστενάζειν) in v. 12 would signify to the ancient audience the typical deep inhalation of the wonder-worker or prophet before performing a mighty deed or making an authoritative utterance. The sound produced would have been taken as an indication of possession by a spirit.[48] Jeffrey B. Gibson has argued that elsewhere the use of this verb followed by a verb of speaking, as here, signifies distress as a result of being in

a hopeless situation.[49] He suggests that here Jesus sighs deeply because the Pharisees' request for a sign "tried not his patience but his faithfulness."[50] It may be that the text portrays Jesus as dismayed because he is being forced to choose between testing God by attempting a sign from heaven, on the one hand, and eventually being put to death, on the other.[51]

In his verbal response in v. 12, Jesus associates the Pharisees who demand a sign with "this generation" (ἡ γενεὰ αὕτη). It is likely that this label does not simply denote the contemporaries of Jesus, but expresses the judgment that those who reject the person and message of Jesus are like the rebellious generation of the wandering in the wilderness.[52] According to the song of Moses, the Lord said: "For it is a perverse generation, sons in whom there is no faithfulness" (ὅτι γενεὰ ἐξεστραμμένη ἐστίν, υἱοὶ οἷς οὐκ ἔστιν πίστις ἐν αὐτοῖς) (Deut 32:20 LXX). The generation of the wilderness was also known for testing God. For example, when the people complained of having no water to drink, Moses said to them: "Why do you revile me, and why do you test the Lord?" (Τί λοιδορεῖσθέ μοι, καὶ τί πειράζετε κύριον;) (Exod 17:2 LXX).[53]

In portraying Jesus as refusing absolutely to give a sign from heaven, the author of Mark may be drawing a contrast between him and the eschatological prophets discussed by Josephus.[54] The fulfillment of Theudas's prediction, in about 45 CE, that the waters of the Jordan would part at his command was no doubt expected to be

---

45   Karl Heinrich Rengstorf, "σημεῖον," TDNT 7 (1971) 200–261, esp. 234–35.

46   See the commentary on 3:20-35 above. Marshall interprets the demand of the Pharisees at face value and thus defines it as a separate false response to the miracles of Jesus, distinct from the hostility expressed in 3:22 (Faith, 66–67, 69).

47   Evald Lövestam, Spiritus Blasphemia: Eine Studie zu Mk 3,28f par Mt 12,31f, Lk 12,10 (Lund: Gleerup, 1968) 65.

48   Bonner, "Thaumaturgic Technique," 171–74. He suggests that such is the case even though here the refusal to work a miracle occurs rather than the performance of one (172). The use of the same verb (without the prepositional prefix) in 7:34 supports this hypothesis; see the commentary on that verse above.

49   Jeffrey B. Gibson, "Mark 8.12a: Why Does Jesus 'Sigh Deeply'?" Bible Translator 38 (1987) 122–25; his

interpretation of 2 Macc 6:30, however, is unpersuasive.

50   Ibid., 125.

51   Cf. the distress of Jesus in Gethsemane (14:32-36).

52   Cf. Evald Lövestam, "The ἡ γενεὰ αὕτη: Eschatology in Mk 13,30 parr.," in Jan Lambrecht, ed., L'Apocalypse johannique et l'Apocalyptique dans le Nouveau Testament (BEThL 53; Gembloux: Duculot; Leuven: Leuven University Press, 1980) 403–13, esp. 411; see also Evald Lövestam, Jesus and 'This Generation': A New Testament Study (CB 25; Stockholm: Almqvist & Wiksell International, 1995) esp. 21–37; Susan R. Garrett, The Temptations of Jesus in Mark's Gospel (Grand Rapids: Eerdmans, 1998) 22–23.

53   See also Num 14:22; Ps 77(78):18, 41, 56; 94(95):9; 105(106):14.

54   Cf. Jeffrey Gibson, "Jesus' Refusal to Produce a 'Sign' (Mk 8.11-13)," JSNT 38 (1990) 37–66.

a sign from heaven that Theudas was God's eschatological agent who would inaugurate the rule of God on earth. Similarly, "the Egyptian false prophet" claimed, around 56 CE, that at his word the walls of Jerusalem would fall down.[55] In this passage, Mark criticizes both those who rejected Jesus during his lifetime and those who believed the (false) popular prophets who arose after his death.

The rhetorical question of Jesus in v. 12b is followed by an oath in v. 12c. In the Bible, as in the ancient Near East generally, oaths usually involved a curse that would fall upon the one who swore the oath if it turned out to be false. Usually, only the self-imposed condition is stated, and the curse is left unexpressed.[56] This explains why the sentence in v. 12c is incomplete (lit., "Truly I say to you, if a sign will be given to this generation"). The Greek particle εἰ ("if") corresponds to the Hebrew particle אִם ("if"), which introduces such conditions in Hebrew oaths. This use of εἰ ("if") here is probably due to the influence of the LXX.[57] The oath formula here is equivalent to a strong negative.[58]

Jesus' strong reply to the Pharisees is reinforced by the narration of his immediate departure in v. 13. Their rejection of him, implied by their demand for a sign, is met by his refusal to associate with them.[59]

■ **14-21** This passage does not fit any of the classic form-critical literary types. Bultmann mentioned "instruction to the disciples" which is sometimes given "quite independent formulation."[60] He listed 8:14 as "an introduction to the saying about leaven" under the rubric of scenes in Mark "which are in the *highest degree formulations analogous to the apophthegms*."[61] He described 8:15 as "(Warning against the leaven of the Pharisees), a saying whose original form, like its original meaning, is almost beyond recovery."[62] Dibelius discussed Mark 8:14-21 only from the point of view of the evangelist's synthesis.[63]

Philip Sellew defined the passage as a "didactic scene." The typical such scene begins with public instruction by Jesus, continues with a change of place, questioning by Jesus' disciples, and a critical reply from Jesus, and ends with an explanation.[64] Sellew argued that this passage was composed by Mark on the model of the two earlier didactic scenes that he found in his source material (Mark 4:3-20; 7:14-23).

Verse 14 indicates that the setting is in the boat and the characters include the disciples and Jesus.[65] The narrator's remark that they had forgotten to bring bread and had only one loaf with them is ironic in the context of the feeding of the four thousand with seven loaves.[66] This circumstance, however, is not taken up immediately; rather, the narrative shifts abruptly to the command of Jesus in v. 15.

The double imperative involving synonymous expressions ("See, watch out") in v. 15 is typical of Mark's

---

55   See the introduction above on the Interpretation of Jesus, the section on "Jesus as Prophet."

56   Lawrence H. Schiffman, "Oaths and Vows," *EDSS* 2:621–23. See also Benovitz, *KOL NIDRE*, 10–11.

57   Moulton-Howard, 468–69.

58   Moulton-Turner, 333; Swete, ad loc. N. D. Coleman suggested that v. 12c is a strong affirmation, affirming in order to "exonerate our Lord from using the implied oath involved in the accepted Hebraistic interpretation of Mark viii 12" ("Some Noteworthy Uses of εἰ or εἶ in Hellenistic Greek, with a Note on St Mark viii 12," *JTS* 28 [1927] 159–67; citation from 164). F. C. Burkitt rejected the suggestion ("Mark VIII 12 and εἰ in Hellenistic Greek," *JTS* 28 [1927] 274–76).

59   Camery-Hoggatt describes Jesus' abrupt departure as "a sign of refusal" (*Irony*, 154).

60   Bultmann, *History*, 330.

61   Ibid., 331; emphasis original.

62   Ibid., 131; he placed the saying under the heading "Legal Sayings and Church Rules."

63   Dibelius, *From Tradition to Gospel*, 228–29.

64   Philip Sellew, "Composition of Didactic Scenes in Mark's Gospel," *JBL* 108 (1989) 613, 617.

65   Although the disciples are not mentioned in vv. 11-13, they are said to be with Jesus in the boat on the way to Dalmanoutha in 8:10. On the style of v. 14, see the note on the trans. above; see also Neirynck, *Duality in Mark*, 79.

66   Jeffrey Gibson has argued that the Markan disciples deliberately bring only one loaf to prevent Jesus from performing another miraculous feeding. He inferred from the narrator's comment in v. 13 that Jesus went away to the other shore that the disciples took this action because they perceived that they were going to Gentile territory and thus opposed Jesus' intention to offer salvation to the Gentiles ("The Rebuke of the Disciples in Mark 8.14-21," *JSNT* 27 [1986] 31–47). Jesus and the disciples, however, landed in Bethsaida, which had a significant Jewish population, at least until the first Jewish war with Rome; see Zvi Uri Maʿoz, "Golan," *NEAEHL*

style.[67] The more typical metaphorical uses of "leaven" or "yeast" in both Jewish and Roman culture derive from a comparison of leavening with defilement.[68] Philo interprets yeast allegorically in various ways, depending on the context.[69] In 1 Cor 5:6-8, Paul uses yeast as a symbol of wickedness and evil (κακία καὶ πονηρία). Just as yeast leavens a whole batch of dough, so the man living with his father's wife will corrupt the community, unless he is expelled. In Gal 5:7-12, the leaven signifies the corrupting influence of the teachers who have attempted to persuade the Galatian Christians to be circumcised.[70]

A variant of the saying in Mark 8:15 occurs in Luke 12:1. In the latter, the "leaven of the Pharisees" is interpreted as hypocrisy (ὑπόκρισις). Matthew's form of the saying is dependent on Mark's, but the author of Matthew has changed "Herod" to "the Sadducees" and interpreted the "leaven" as "teaching" (διδαχή) (Matt 16:6, 11-12). It may be that the image of "leaven" itself here is neutral, indicating that every person or group exerts an influence, whether good or bad. In this case, the emphasis would be on the genitives, the Pharisees and Herod, rather than on the image of yeast as such.[71]

Harold W. Hoehner has argued that the warning against the "leaven" of the Pharisees concerned their expectation of a messiah who would establish a national political kingdom based on "purely external-political power."[72] He interpreted the "leaven" of Herod in relation to "his desire to maintain his position as sovereign by external-political means."[73] The text of Mark, however, does not associate the theme of external political power

with the Pharisees or Herod. More plausibly, Roland Deines has suggested that the saying is a polemical adaptation of the self-understanding of the Pharisees as the leaven that makes the whole batch of dough rise (the holy remnant that makes the whole people holy). Their ability to compromise and to cooperate with the Herodians (and Sadducees; see the parallel in Matt 16:6) is criticized by the Markan Jesus as a turning aside from the new reality of the dawning kingdom of God.[74]

In the context of Mark, the warning of Jesus concerning the Pharisees refers to the implied hostility to Jesus in their demand for a sign in v. 11 and to the hostility explicitly attributed to them and the Herodians in 3:6. Besides 8:15, the only other time that Herod is mentioned in Mark is in the account of the death of John the Baptist in 6:17-29 and its introduction in 6:14-16. Although the narrative does not portray Herod as hostile to John, Herod does have John executed. Further, Herod associates Jesus with John. The intercalation of the passages dealing with Herod into the account of the sending out of the disciples suggests that they are in danger of meeting a fate analogous to John's, just as Jesus does later in the narrative. Finally, the attitudes and actions of the Pharisees and Herod may also be interpreted as resistance to Jesus and his mission based on a lack of understanding.[75]

In response to Jesus' warning, the disciples begin discussing among themselves the fact that they do not have bread (v. 16). The audience now becomes aware that the introductory statement in v. 14 has prepared for this

---

2:526. But see Chancey, *Gentile Galilee*, 106–8. In any case, there is no evidence that the disciples are portrayed as deliberately bringing only one loaf. On the contrary, it is stated explicitly that they had forgotten to bring (more) bread (v. 14).

67   See the note on the trans. above; see also Neirynck, *Duality in Mark*, 103. The reference to two entities (the Pharisees and Herod) is also typical of Mark's style (ibid., 109). The use of the preposition ἀπό ("from") with βλέπετε ("watch out") as an expression of what one should avoid is possible in classical Greek but was encouraged by Semitic influence (BDF §149).

68   Hans Windisch, "ζύμη, ζυμόω, ἄζυμος," *TDNT* 2 (1964) 902–6, esp. 905.

69   In *Quaest. in Ex.* 1.15, Philo speaks of leaven as a symbol of arrogance; in 2.14, it symbolizes sensual pleasures, as well as arrogance and foolish belief. In

contrast, he interprets leaven positively, in accordance with Stoic philosophy, in *Spec. leg.* 2.185 as joy, which is "the rational elevation or rising of the soul" (χαρά δὲ ψυχῆς ἐστιν εὔλογος ἔπαρσις); text and trans. from Colson and Whitaker, *Philo*, 7:422–23; see also the note on §185 on p. 628. See also Windisch, "ζύμη, ζυμόω, ἄζυμος," 904–5.

70   Cf. Windisch, "ζύμη, ζυμόω, ἄζυμος," 903–4, 905.

71   See ibid., 906, and the literature cited there; Harold W. Hoehner, *Herod Antipas* (SNTSMS 17; Cambridge/New York: Cambridge University Press, 1972) 203.

72   Hoehner, *Herod Antipas*, 204–7.

73   Ibid., 208.

74   Deines, *Die Pharisäer*, 514 and n. 316.

75   Cf. Marshall, *Faith*, 212; Camery-Hoggatt, *Irony*, 154.

reaction. The disciples' response is a case of misunderstanding based on the literal interpretation of a metaphor (leaven). This type of misunderstanding is typical of the Gospel of John.[76]

In v. 17 Jesus rebukes the disciples for this response and asks, "Do you not yet understand or comprehend?" (οὔπω νοεῖτε οὐδὲ συνίετε;).[77] The use of the verb "understand" (νοέω) here links this passage to 7:18, in which Jesus rebukes the disciples for not understanding the "parable" that Jesus spoke to the crowd in 7:15. The use of the verb "comprehend" (συνίημι) here recalls 6:52, according to which the disciples "did not comprehend with regard to the loaves, but their hearts had become hardened."[78] This link is reinforced by the next part of Jesus' reply in v. 17, "Do you have hardened hearts?" Thus, this passage continues the radical intensification of the theme of the misunderstanding of the disciples begun in 6:52.[79] The motif of "hardness of heart" (πώρωσις τῆς καρδίας) was introduced in 3:5.[80] In terms of biblical anthropology, a hard heart is equivalent to an obdurate mind.[81] The attribution of hard hearts to the disciples in 6:52 and 8:17 associates them with the opponents of Jesus, who object to his healing on the Sabbath and plot to kill him (3:1-6).

The use of the verb "comprehend" (συνίημι) in v. 17 also recalls Isa 6:9, which is cited in 4:12 in the saying about the negative purpose of the parables for outsiders.

This link assimilates the disciples to such outsiders. Here, in v. 18, an analogous passage is cited, Jer 5:21, in which the Lord rebukes the people, the household of Jacob, for being "senseless," literally, "without heart."[82] They are accused of having eyes but not seeing; of having ears but not hearing. Jeremiah may imply here that the prophecy of Isa 6:10 has come true.[83] After the citation, Jesus asks the disciples "And do you not remember?" and goes on to ask them about the feeding of the five thousand and the feeding of the four thousand. The implication is that they are blind and deaf with regard to the significance of those two events. As in the narrator's comment in 6:52, Jesus here implies that the disciples do not "comprehend about the loaves."

The detailed questioning in vv. 19-20 about how many baskets full of fragments they picked up after the feeding of the five thousand and how many hampers were filled with the excess of the pieces after the feeding of the four thousand, along with their specific answers, "twelve" and "seven," seems to be an exercise in shaming.[84] The exasperated teacher forces the pupils to repeat the elementary facts. When they repeat the data but give no indication that they grasp their meaning, Jesus scolds them with the final remark, "Do you not yet comprehend?" (v. 21).

The details are brought into the dialogue primarily to portray the disciples as dull pupils. Dibelius's hypothesis

---

76 As Dibelius pointed out (*From Tradition to Gospel*, 229). See, e.g., John 3:3-4; 4:10-11.

77 The use of two synonymous verbs is typical of Mark's style; see the commentary on v. 15 above.

78 Cf. Sellew, "Composition," 619.

79 See the commentary on 6:51-52 above.

80 On the relation of this theme to older scripture and for a discussion of its use in other early Christian writings, see the commentary on 3:5 above.

81 Friedrich Baumgärtel, "καρδία, A." *TDNT* 3 (1965) 606–7; Johannes Behm, "καρδία, C.-D.," ibid., 609–13.

82 ἀκάρδιος in the LXX; on the Hebrew text and its interpretation, see Holladay, *Jeremiah*, 1:195–96.

83 See ibid. Although he denies any historical or literary connection, Robert Renehan cited coincidental parallels to Mark 8:18 in Homer *Il.* 15.128–29; Aeschylus *Prom.* 447–48; idem, *Ag.* 1623; Sophocles *Oed. Tyr.* 413; idem, frg. 837 (Nauck) = frg. 923 (Pearson); Demosthenes *Or.* 25.89; Heraclitus frg. 34 (Diels-Kranz); see Renehan, "Classical Greek Quota-

tions in the New Testament," in David Neiman and Margaret Schatkin, eds., *The Heritage of the Early Church: Essays in Honor of the Very Reverend Georges Vasilievich Florovsky* (OCA 195; Rome: Pontifical Institute for Oriental Studies, 1973) 17–46, esp. 20. Renehan attributes the similarity among these passages, following Eduard Fraenkel, to a widespread popular pattern of thought.

84 So Sellew, "Composition," 618. John Drury drew a connection between v. 19a, where the feeding of five thousand with five loaves and the twelve baskets of leftovers are mentioned, and 2:23-27 and, via the latter, between this passage and 1 Samuel 21, where David takes five of the twelve loaves of the Presence ("Understanding the Bread: Disruption and Aggregation, Secrecy and Revelation in Mark's Gospel," in Jason P. Rosenblatt and Joseph C. Sitterson, Jr., eds., *"Not in Heaven": Coherence and Complexity in Biblical Narrative* [Bloomington/Indianapolis: Indiana University Press, 1991] 98–119, esp. 103–9). Inferring that David left seven loaves of the Presence behind,

that Jesus' questions are meant to lead the audience to the conclusion that "Jesus continually gives them true bread" is perhaps too Johannine a reading of the passage.[85] Kelber's argument that the "one loaf" of v. 14 embodies the oneness of Jews and Gentiles is rendered unlikely by the narrative evidence that the second feeding, like the first, is set in Galilee.[86] It was noted above that the twelve baskets of 6:43 may have recalled, for some in the audience of Mark, the hope for the restoration of the twelve tribes in the time of fulfillment.[87] It is unlikely, however, that the seven hampers are symbolic. François Bovon has argued that the twelve baskets "direct the attention to the pastoral responsibility of a Church placed under the leadership of the Twelve," and the seven hampers "evoke the Church of the Hellenists and its organization of seven leaders."[88] It is doubtful that the author of Mark knew the tradition about the seven leaders of the Hellenists recorded in Acts 6:1-6. Joel Marcus has argued that the number seven here symbolizes eschatological fullness.[89] Seven, however, was a

special number in antiquity, with many connotations.[90] There are insufficient indications in the text of Mark to associate the seven baskets with eschatological fulfillment.

As noted in the commentary on v. 17 above, there are significant links between this passage and 6:52. The comment by the narrator in the latter verse, that the disciples did not understand about the loaves, is given as an explanation for their failure to grasp the significance of Jesus' walking on the sea. This linking of the feedings with Jesus' self-revelation on the sea suggests that the issue in the dialogue of 8:17-21 is the identity of Jesus. Despite their "being with him" (3:14), their "having the mystery of the kingdom" (4:11), their being given private instruction by Jesus (4:10-20; 7:17-23), their authority over unclean spirits (6:7, 13), their proclamation of the need for repentance (6:12), and their ability to heal the sick (6:13), the disciples do not yet understand who Jesus is or the significance of his mighty deeds.

8

8:22-26 The Blind Man of Bethsaida

22/ **And they went to Bethsaida.[a] And they brought him a blind man and entreated him to touch him. 23/ And he took hold of the hand of the blind man and took him out of the village and, having spat on his eyes and laid his hands on him, he asked him, "Do you see anything?"[b] 24/ And having regained his sight, he said, "I see the people, for I see (something) like trees, (only they are)**

a   D 1424[mg] *pc* it attest the reading Βηθανίαν ("Bethany"). This reading may have arisen because of perceived tension between the designation of the place as Βηθσαϊδάν ("Bethsaida"), which was a city, and its description as a village in vv. 23 and 26; so Taylor, *ad loc.* Another possibility is that the name of the locality was changed to obscure the problem that Jesus and the disciples had set out for Bethsaida in 6:45, but had arrived in Gennesareth in 6:53.

b   The trans. is based on the reading attested by B C D* et al., in which the particle εἰ is taken as the introduction of a direct question (not to be translated in this instance; usually translated "if" or "whether"). This construction is common in the LXX and in the NT,

---

Drury also established a connection with the seven loaves and seven hampers of leftovers in v. 20 (ibid., 103). In other words, the total number of loaves broken and distributed by Jesus was twelve (ibid., 110–11).

85   Dibelius, *From Tradition to Gospel*, 229.
86   Kelber, *Mark's Story*, 40. See the commentary on 8:10 above. Drury's interpretation of the second feeding as imaging "the universality of the gospel for all humanity, for the lesser gentiles as well as the

privileged Jews," similarly depends on the location of the feeding in the Decapolis ("Understanding the Bread," 111). Drury interprets the one loaf of v. 14 as Jesus himself as their nourishment, referring to 14:22-25 (ibid., 113–14).

87   See the commentary on 6:42-43 above.
88   François Bovon, "Names and Numbers in Early Christianity," *NTS* 47 (2001) 267–88, esp. 284–85.
89   Marcus, 514.
90   Yarbro Collins, *Cosmology and Eschatology*, 55–138.

walking about."[c] 25/ Then he laid his hands upon his eyes again, and he saw clearly and was cured and looked at everything with a clear view. 26/ And he sent him home, saying, "Do not go into the village."[d]

especially in Luke and Acts; see Moulton-Turner, 3:333. This is the only example in Mark, since the question in 10:2 is indirect (so also Taylor, on 8:23). ℵ A D² et al. attest a reading in which εἰ is taken as the introduction of an indirect question, as in 10:2. The verb βλέπεις, "Do you see," was then "corrected" to βλέπει, "(whether) he saw (lit., "he sees") (anything)."

c   The trans. is based on the longer reading, which is the earlier, ὅτι ὡς δένδρα ὁρῶ περιπατοῦντας, "for I see (something) like trees, (only they are) walking about." On the trans. of this clause, see Taylor, ad loc. The shorter reading, ὡς δένδρα περιπατοῦντας, "like trees walking about," attested by C² D W Θ et al. (see Aland, *Synopsis*, 228), resulted from an attempt to smooth out the syntax; so also Taylor ad loc. The presence of ὁρῶ ("I see"), even after βλέπω ("I see") in the previous clause, is typical of Markan style (see Neirynck, *Duality in Mark*, 79).

d   ℵ* W read μὴ εἰς τὴν κώμην εἰσέλθῃς ("Do not go into the village"); Tischendorf adopted this reading. ℵ² B L et al. attest the reading μηδὲ εἰς τὴν κώμην εἰσέλθῃς ("Do not go into the village"); this reading was adopted by Westcott and Hort; von Soden; Aland, *Synopsis*; Nestle (25th edition); Nestle-Aland (26th edition), and Huck-Greeven. The Old Latin MS c attests the reading μηδενὶ εἰς τὴν κώμην εἴπῃς ("Do not speak to anyone in the village"); see von Soden, 2:168; Turner, "Marcan Usage," 26 (1926) 18 (Elliott, *Language and Style*, 19), and C. H. Turner, "Western Readings in the Second Half of St. Mark's Gospel," *JTS* 29 (1927) 2. This reading also appears as the second half of a longer reading in D: ὕπαγε εἰς τὸν οἶκόν σου καὶ μηδενὶ εἴπῃς εἰς τὴν κώμην ("Go home and speak to no one in the village"). On the basis of these two witnesses and the argument that Mark used the prepositions εἰς ("in" or "into") and ἐν ("in") interchangeably, a practice that was corrected by Matthew especially, but also by Luke and some scribes, Turner concluded that the earliest reading was μηδε(νὶ) εἰς τὴν κώμην εἴπῃς ("Do not speak in the village" or "Speak to no one in the village") (ibid). In this judgment he was followed by Taylor (ad loc.), who adopted the reading μηδενὶ εἰς τὴν κώμην εἴπῃς ("Speak to no one in the village"). Since the use of εἰς ("in" or "into") where ἐν ("in") would normally be expected was corrected elsewhere not by substitution, but by addition (see the notes on the trans. of 1:21 and 39 above), Turner's argument is not persuasive in this case. It is more likely that the reading attested by ℵ* W, μὴ εἰς τὴν κώμην εἰσέλθῃς ("Do not go into the village"), or by ℵ² B L et al., μηδὲ εἰς τὴν κώμην εἰσέλθῃς ("Do not go into the village"), is the earliest recoverable reading and that the other readings arose through attempts to clarify its meaning. For a reconstruction of the various developments, see Westcott and Hort, 2. §140, or Metzger, *Textual Commentary*, 84. Elliott argued that the reading attested by A C et al., μηδὲ εἰς τὴν κώμην εἰσέλθῃς μηδὲ εἴπῃς τινὶ ἐν τῇ κώμῃ ("Do not go into the village and do not speak to anyone in the village"), is original ("Eclectic Textual Commentary," 199). It is more likely, however, that this is a conflate reading, as Westcott and Hort argued (ibid.).

The History of the Tradition

As noted above, the account of the healing of the blind man in Bethsaida was probably the second of the five miracle stories in the second collection that the author of Mark used. In this source it followed the walking on the sea and preceded the exorcism of the Syro-Phoenician woman's daughter.[91] The evangelist apparently moved the story to this point in the narrative to encourage the audience to interpret the blind man as a symbol of the disciples.[92] The citation of Jer 5:21 in v. 18, "Having eyes, do you not see?" is the main clue that the audience should make a connection between the disciples and the blind man.

Bultmann argued that the introduction (v. 22) contradicts the account that follows in that v. 22 locates the story in Bethsaida, which is a city, whereas the narrative is set outside a village. He took this as evidence that v. 22 is editorial.[93] He apparently based his judgment that Bethsaida was a city on the statement by Josephus that Herod Philip "raised the village of Bethsaida on Lake Gennesaritis [Sea of Galilee] to the status of a city by adding residents and strengthening the fortifications. He named it after Julia, the emperor's daughter" (κώμην δὲ Βηθσαϊδὰ πρὸς λίμνῃ τῇ Γεννησαρίτιδι πόλεως παρασχὼν ἀξίωμα πλήθει τε οἰκητόρων καὶ τῇ ἄλλῃ δυνάμει Ἰουλίᾳ θυγατρὶ τῇ Καίσαρος ὁμώνυμον ἐκάλεσεν) (*Ant.* 18.2.1 §28).[94] Although Bethsaida may have been considered by Josephus to be a city, the evidence suggests that it remained a village.[95]

91 See the section "History of the Tradition of 6:45-52" and the commentary on 6:45-46 above. See also the section "The History of the Tradition" in the commentary on 7:24-30 above.

92 See Achtemeier, "Miracle Catenae," 286–87, and the older literature cited there; E. S. Johnson, "Mark VIII.22-26: The Blind Man from Bethsaida," *NTS* 25 (1978–79) 370–83, esp. 374–75. Tannehill argued that it was no accident that the scene "with Jesus' reproachful question about the disciples' inability to see and hear (8:18), is framed by stories of healing a deaf man and a blind man (7:31-37; 8:22-26)"; (Robert C. Tannehill, "The Disciples in Mark: The Function of a Narrative Role," *JR* 57 [1977] 399–400). For further discussion, see the commentary below.

93 Bultmann, *History*, 64–65, 213, 338; Johnson follows Bultmann on this point ("Mark VIII.22-26," 370–72).

94 Text and trans. from Louis Feldman in Thackeray, *Josephus*, 9:24–25. Schürer, *History*, 1:339; Zvi Uri Maʿoz, "Golan," *NEAEHL* 2:526. Fred Strickert and others have argued that the Julia in question was not the daughter of Augustus, but his wife, Livia, who was renamed Julia Augusta after the death of Augustus (Strickert, "The Coins of Philip," in Rami Arav and Richard A. Freund, eds., *Bethsaida: A City by the North Shore of the Sea of Galilee* [3 vols.; Bethsaida

Excavations Project; Kirksville, MO: Thomas Jefferson University Press/Truman State University Press, 1995, 1999, 2004] 1:165–89, esp. 183; Mark D. Smith, "A Tale of Two Julias: Julia, Julias, and Josephus," in Arav and Freund, *Bethsaida*, 2:333–46). Mark Appold states that Bethsaida was still a village in Jesus' time, since it was not elevated to city status until 29–31 CE ("The Mighty Works of Bethsaida," in Arav and Freund, *Bethsaida*, 1:229–42, esp. 236); this point is relevant only if the story and its location in Bethsaida go back to a time prior to 29 CE. See also John J. Rousseau and Rami Arav, *Jesus and His World: An Archaeological and Cultural Dictionary* (Minneapolis: Fortress, 1995) 66–67.

95 See Schürer, *History*, 2:172; Theissen, *Miracle Stories*, 127. The ambiguity of the locality's status is illustrated nicely by the fact that it had a temple dedicated to Livia/Julia, but otherwise was rural in character (Rami Arav, "Show Me Your Bethsaida," *BAR* 26.5 [Sept./Oct. 2000] 12, 14, 72, 74); on the temple, see John T. Greene, "Honorific Naming of Bethsaida-Julias," in Arav and Freund, *Bethsaida*, 2:307–31, esp. 309–10; Smith, "Tale of Two Julias," 341–42. Chancey, however, is skeptical about whether the relevant building is a temple of the imperial cult (*Gentile Galilee*, 107-8).

This ambiguity of status makes it less likely that v. 22 is editorial.[96]

Bultmann concluded that v. 26a constitutes the original conclusion. He argued that v. 26b is an editorial addition, apparently because he understood this instruction as a command to silence and thus as part of the "messianic secret."[97] Räisänen, however, has shown that v. 26b could just as well come from the tradition.[98]

The Literary Role of 8:22-26

The section of Mark designated here "Renewed Proclamation" began in 6:6b. The first subsection, 6:6b-30, is held together by the continuity between the sending out of the Twelve in 6:7-13 and their return in 6:30. Both 6:6b and 6:30 are transitional.[99] The close link between 6:30 and 6:31 unites 6:6b-30 with 6:31-56. The Dispute with the Pharisees (7:1-23), a subsection concerned with Jesus' teaching, is inserted between two series of miracle stories, just as 6:6b-31 was.[100] The miracles continue from 7:24 through 8:9. The controversy-dialogue with the Pharisees (8:10-13) is an illustration of the way in which Jesus' opponents misunderstand or reject his mighty deeds. It takes the first step in bringing this section to a close. The next step is taken by the didactic scene in 8:14-21, in which the disciples, like the Pharisees, fail to understand Jesus' mighty deeds, represented by the two feedings, and thus continue to be ignorant of who he is and what his mission is.[101]

The miracle story in 8:22-26 has both a concluding and an introductory role to play in the overall narrative.[102] The elements of continuity with the preceding material are (1) it continues the narration of Jesus' mighty deeds;[103] (2) it develops the theme of the disciples' "blindness" introduced in 8:18. The story is also integrally related to the next section, 8:27—10:45, because that section ends with the healing of a blind man (10:46-52), so that the two miracle stories form a literary bracket around the intervening material.[104]

The Genre of 8:22-26

Bultmann defined this story as a miracle of healing. He pointed out that it belongs to the same type as the healing of the deaf man in 7:32-37. Since these stories manifest most of the same characteristics, they are to be taken as variants.[105] He pointed out, however, that 8:22-26 is distinctive in its lack of a magic word and in the characteristic that the healing is by degrees.[106] Usually the healing is instantaneous, but there is some comparative material for a healing in stages. The motif enables a more detailed description of the miracle than an instant cure allows.[107]

The inscription from the temple of Asclepius in Epidaurus contains more than fifty testimonies to healings effected by him and dates to the second half of the fourth century BCE.[108] Several of these concern the heal-

---

96 Meier doubted that the reference to Bethsaida is editorial (*Marginal Jew*, 2:741 n. 71); Theissen takes it as pre-Markan (*Miracle Stories*, 127).

97 Bultmann, *History*, 213. He points out the similarity between Jesus' sending the man home in 8:26a to the language of 2:11 and 5:19, which he presumably takes as parts of pre-Markan stories.

98 Räisänen, *Messianic Secret*, 164; so also Johnson, "Mark VIII.22-26," 373.

99 See the sections "The Literary Unity of 6:6b-30" and "The Sending Out of the Twelve in Literary Context" above.

100 See Achtemeier, "Miracle Catenae," 286.

101 Theissen takes at least 6:30—8:26, and possibly 6:7—8:26, as a unity because the two feeding miracles are "the basis for the question about correct understanding" (*Miracle Stories*, 208).

102 So also, e.g., Best, *Following Jesus*, 134; Guelich, xxxvi–xxxvii.

103 In his text-linguistic study, Cook includes 8:22-26 in the section 1:14—8:26 (*Structure*, 343–46).

104 Perrin, "Towards an Interpretation," 4–5; Werner H. Kelber, *The Oral and the Written Gospel* (Philadelphia: Fortress, 1983) 110.

105 Bultmann, *History*, 213. Subsequent scholars have spoken of the two stories as a "pair of twins" (Räisänen, *Messianic Secret*, 151, 165; Meier, *Marginal Jew*, 2:691, and the older literature cited there; see also ibid., 739 n. 60).

106 Bultmann, *History*, 213.

107 Ibid., 224–25.

108 IG, IV², 1. nos. 121–22; text and trans. in Edelstein and Edelstein, no. 423 (1:221–37).

ing of blindness.[109] The most interesting of these for comparison with our text is number 18:

Alcetas of Halieis. This blind man saw a dream. It seemed to him that the god came up to him and with his fingers opened his eyes, and that he first saw the trees of the sanctuary. At daybreak he walked out sound (Ἀλκέτας Ἁλικός. οὗτος τυφλὸς ἐὼν ἐνύπνιον εἶδε· ἐδόκει οἱ ὁ θεὸς ποτελθὼν τοῖς δακτύλοις διάγειν τὰ ὄμματα καὶ ἰδεῖν τὰ δένδρη πρᾶτον τὰ ἐν τῶι ἰαρῶι. ἀμέρας δὲ γενομένας ὑγιὴς ἐξῆλθε).[110]

Although a healing by stages is not an explicit characteristic of this testimony, the implication that he saw trees during the night in his dream and then was fully cured the next morning is somewhat analogous to the Markan story. The motif that both blind men see trees or something like trees at first is also a similarity.

A healing of a blind man is attributed also to Vespasian:

Vespasian as yet lacked prestige and a certain divinity, so to speak, since he was an unexpected and still new-made emperor; but these also were given him. A man of the people who was blind, and another who was lame, came to him together as he sat on the tribunal, begging for the help for their disorders which Serapis had promised in a dream; for the god declared that Vespasian would restore the eyes, if he would spit upon them, and give strength to the leg, if he would deign to touch it with his heel. Though he had hardly any faith that this could possibly succeed, and therefore shrank even from making the attempt, he was at last prevailed upon by his friends and tried both

things in public before a large crowd; and with success. (Suetonius *Twelve Caesars, Vesp.* 7.2-3)[111]

In Mark's account, Jesus also spits on the man's eyes in order to heal his blindness (v. 24).[112] Another similarity is that both Jesus and Vespasian are rulers, if the epithet "Christ" or "messiah" attributed to Jesus is taken seriously.[113]

According to Philostratus, the sages of India healed a blind man whose eyes had been put out (*Vita Ap.* 3.39).[114] The existence of these texts makes it likely that the evangelist presents this narrative as a miracle story as well as a symbolic narrative representing the disciples.[115]

Theissen notes that Mark 8:22-26 emphasizes the motifs that occur in the middle of the story, that is, the therapeutic process. In this way it is similar to the testimonies from Epidaurus.[116]

It should also be noted that the giving of sight to the blind is part of the restorationist eschatology of the book of Isaiah (Isa 29:18; 35:5). This motif in Isaiah refers to both literal and metaphorical blindness.[117]

Comment

■ **22-26** This miracle story, like 7:32-36, has no parallel in Matthew or Luke. Again, the reason is probably not that the copies of Mark used by the authors of those Gospels lacked this healing of a blind man. It is more likely that they deliberately omitted this account because of its magical elements.[118] The omission of the healing of the blind man from Bethsaida may also owe something to the fact that it plays a role in Mark's theme of the blindness of the disciples, a theme that was not of interest to the authors of Matthew and Luke.[119]

■ **22** At this point, Jesus and the disciples arrive at Beth-

109 Nos. 4, 9, 11, 18, 20, 22, 32, and perhaps 40.

110 Edelstein and Edelstein, no. 423 (1:224–25, 233). See also Cotter, *Miracles,* 17–18.

111 For the Latin text, the source of the ET, and references to other versions of this story, see the commentary on 7:33 above.

112 On saliva as a healing substance, see Theissen, *Miracle Stories,* 63, 93; Howard Clark Kee, *Medicine, Miracle and Magic in New Testament Times* (Cambridge: Cambridge University Press, 1986) 104; and the commentary on 7:33 above.

113 See the section of the introduction above on the Interpretation of Jesus, the subsection on *Jesus as Messiah.* See also Cotter, *Miracles,* 40–41.

114 Cf. Cotter, *Miracles,* 43.

115 So also Räisänen (contra Luz), *Messianic Secret,* 163 n. 73.

116 Theissen, *Miracle Stories,* 113.

117 Blenkinsopp, *Isaiah 1–39,* 409.

118 So also Aune, "Magic," 1537.

119 Johnson, "Mark VIII.22-26," 370; Best, *Following Jesus,* 137.

saida, the destination to which he had directed them in 6:45.[120] At the end of that voyage, however, they arrived in Gennesaret. This oddity in the narrative is an indication that the healing of the blind man in Bethsaida followed the account of Jesus' walking on the water in a source used by the author of Mark.[121] Some people in Bethsaida bring a blind man to Jesus and ask him to touch him. The motif of touching (ἅπτομαι) here may be pre-Markan or Markan; it is impossible to be sure.[122] In any case, in its present context in Mark as a whole, it may remind the audience of the description of the healing of the leper by Jesus' touch (1:41). It also recalls the woman with a flow of blood who was healed by touching Jesus' cloak (5:27) and the description of Jesus touching the tongue of the man who was deaf and impeded in his speech (7:33). Most strikingly, the request is reminiscent of two Markan summaries. In 3:10 the narrator states that people approached Jesus eagerly, "in order that those of them who had (bodily) torments might touch him" (ἵνα αὐτοῦ ἅψωνται ὅσοι εἶχον μάστιγας). According to the summary in 6:56, wherever Jesus went, people "put the sick in the marketplaces and entreated him that they might touch even the edge of his cloak; and as many as touched him were saved" (ἐν ταῖς ἀγοραῖς ἐτίθεσαν τοὺς ἀσθενοῦντας καὶ παρεκάλουν αὐτὸν ἵνα κἂν τοῦ κρασπέδου τοῦ ἱματίου αὐτοῦ ἅψωνται· καὶ ὅσοι ἂν ἥψαντο αὐτοῦ ἐσῴζοντο). These other passages make clear that, for Mark, the request for Jesus' touch implies belief that his touch transmits healing power.[123]

The blind man himself, besides being an individual in need of physical healing, also represents the "blind" disciples.[124]

■ **23** Jesus' taking the man by the hand here is not yet the healing touch. He does so in order to lead the man outside the village. His taking him by the hand signifies either that the man needs guidance since he is blind, that Jesus is taking charge of the situation, or both.

On the alleged tension between the setting in (the city of) Bethsaida and the description of the locality as a village (κώμη) here, see "History of the Tradition" above.

Jesus takes the man outside the village so that the healing can be performed in private. Given the other magical elements in the story, it is likely that this motif has its origins in magical practice and that it would have been recognized as such by the audience.[125]

As noted above, Jesus' spitting on the man's eyes is a technique of healing, since saliva was believed to be a healing substance in antiquity.[126]

In addition to spitting on the man's eyes, Jesus lays his hands on the man. Both, especially the latter, signify the use of the healing touch.[127] The cultural assumption, on the part of both author and audience, was that "the touch transfers miraculous vital power to the sick person."[128] Sometimes, as here, this touch takes the form of the laying on of hands.[129]

Samson Eitrem argued that Jesus' hand (and arm) represented his power (δύναμις) in a higher degree than any other part of his body. In many cultures of antiquity, the hand was a symbol of intention and activity, power and authority. Jesus' extraordinary power was communicated through touch, especially by the hand.[130]

After performing these healing gestures, the Jesus of this text asks the man, in direct speech, whether he could

---

120 The site has been identified as et-Tell, an oval-shaped mound located north of the Sea of Galilee 250 meters east of the Jordan River (Arav and Freund, *Bethsaida*, 1:xi, xiv–xv, 3; see also Heinz-Wolfgang Kuhn, "An Introduction to the Excavations of Bethsaida (et-Tell) from a New Testament Perspective," in Arav and Freund, 2:283–94, esp. 283–84).

121 See the section "History of the Tradition" above.

122 Cf. Theissen, *Miracle Stories*, 127–28.

123 See the commentary on 5:27-28 and 30-32 above.

124 Cf. v. 18 and the sections on the "History of the Tradition" and the "The Literary Role of 8:22-26" above.

125 This conclusion seems to be implied by Aune's discussion of the passage ("Magic," 1537–38) although he does not explicitly say so.

126 See "The Genre of 8:22-26" above; see also John 9:6-7, 11; Aune, "Magic," 1537; Eitrem, *Some Notes*, 45–47.

127 See the commentary on v. 22 above.

128 Theissen, *Miracle Stories*, 62.

129 Otto Weinreich, *Antike Heilungswunder: Untersuchungen zum Wunderglauben der Griechen und Römer* (Giessen: Töpelmann, 1909) 14–37; Aune, "Magic," 1533.

130 Eitrem, *Some Notes*, 33–38. See also the commentary on 5:27-28 above. According to 4 Kgdms 5:11 LXX, Naaman expected Elisha to heal his leprosy by laying his hand on the (diseased) spot.

see anything.[131] One could argue that this question is necessary, since no one but the blind man himself could determine whether he could see. John 9:7-12 shows that there are other ways to narrate the healing of blindness. One should rather conclude, therefore, that this portrayal of Jesus as a healer is very different from most of the other exorcisms and healings in Mark. Jesus causes the demon to depart from the afflicted man in the synagogue in Capernaum with a simple, sovereign command (Mark 1:21-28).[132] Similarly, he heals the mother-in-law of Simon simply by taking her hand and lifting her up (1:29-31). He heals the leper by means of touch and a commanding word, and the leprosy leaves him instantly (1:41-42). Even more striking is the healing of the paralytic simply with the words, "I say to you, get up, lift up your pallet, and go home" (2:11).[133] In the healing of the deaf man with a speech impediment, which is very similar to this one in other respects, the recovery is again instantaneous (7:35). The healing of the other blind man, a narrative that, along with this one, brackets the section 8:27–10:45, also describes the healing as taking place instantly (10:52).

This distinctive feature of the healing of the blind man in Bethsaida, in comparison with other stories in Mark, could be due to Markan composition for his particular purposes in this context. It is more likely, as Achtemeier and others have argued, that the account is pre-Markan.[134] In that case, it is noteworthy that the evangelist, unlike Matthew and Luke, preserved this story in spite of this relative weakness of Jesus as a miracle-worker. Its placement in this position corresponds to the difficulty that Jesus had in teaching the disciples how his mighty deeds signify his identity and purpose.

■ **24** E. S. Johnson has argued persuasively that ἀνα-βλέψας here means "having regained his sight," rather than "having looked up."[135] In response to Jesus' question, the man says that he sees things that look like trees walking about, so he knows that they are actually people. The implication, of course, is that he has regained his sight to some degree but cannot yet see accurately. Because the preceding passage—the didactic scene in the boat—implies that the disciples understand nothing, the partial sight of the man probably alludes, on the symbolic level, to the statement of Peter in 8:29. Somehow Peter comes to know that Jesus is the messiah. But his knowledge is only partial because he does not have the proper understanding of the role of the messiah, which Jesus proceeds to teach him and the others in v. 31.[136]

■ **25** Jesus then expends further effort to heal the man more completely. In v. 23, it is said simply that Jesus laid his hands upon the man. Here, in the second attempt to heal the man, it is said that Jesus "then laid his hands upon his eyes again" (εἶτα πάλιν ἐπέθηκεν τὰς χεῖρας ἐπὶ τοὺς ὀφθαλμοὺς αὐτοῦ). The adverb "again" implies that Jesus had laid his hands upon the man's eyes also in v. 23. Thus, Jesus employs no new technique in this second attempt, but simply transfers more miraculous vital power to the man's eyes.

The result was that the man "saw clearly and was cured and looked at everything with a clear view."[137] Räisänen disputes the symbolic interpretation of this miracle story because the disciples either are granted full illumination by v. 29 or they continue to see dimly throughout the narrative of the Gospel.[138] The evidence of the text, however, supports a symbolic reading. The allusion to Jeremiah in v. 18 implies that the disciples are

131 See the note on the trans. above.
132 See the commentary on 1:24-25 above.
133 See also the instant healing of the man with the withered hand (3:5) and the instant stilling of the storm (4:39).
134 Achtemeier, "Miracle Catenae," 285–87; Theissen, *Miracle Stories*, 127–28.
135 Johnson, "Mark VIII.22-26," 376–77.
136 Räisänen, though he is skeptical about the symbolic interpretation, refers to earlier literature by scholars who advocate it (*Messianic Secret*, 203 n. 218; 204 n. 220). He also provides references to those who criticize it (204 n. 219).
137 Joel Marcus has argued that the text presupposed

the extramission theory of vision and suggested the following paraphrase, "And his vision broke through, and it was restored, and the far-shining beams of his eyesight fell on all things in the outside world from that moment on" ("A Note on Markan Optics," *NTS* 45 [1999] 250–56; citation from 256). Johnson's analysis of the vocabulary is more apposite ("Mark VIII.22-26," 377–79).
138 Räisänen, *Messianic Secret*, 204.

"blind." The section in which Jesus gives the disciples extensive private instruction (8:27–10:45) is framed by two stories about healing the blind.

A symbolic reading is supported also by the use of blindness as a metaphor in Greek and biblical traditions. In Greek tragedy, among the pre-Socratics, and in Plato's works, blindness is a metaphor for ignorance.[139] In the Bible, Isa 6:9-10 and Jer 5:21 use the metaphor of blindness for the impenitence and obstinacy of the people. Mark cites both of these passages.[140]

There are two ways to reconcile the conclusion that the story is symbolic with Räisänen's clear-sighted analysis. One is to conclude that a symbolic narrative need not be fully allegorical, in the sense that every element must have a secondary level of meaning.[141] A better way is to conclude that the text of Mark implies that the disciples do not "see clearly" until after the resurrection.[142] Such a transformation from partial sight (8:29) to clear sight is implied by chap. 13, especially vv. 9-13.

■ 26 As noted above, Bultmann argued that the first part of this verse, "And he sent him home," is the original conclusion of the miracle story, whereas the second part, "saying 'Do not go into the village,'" is an editorial addition.[143] Theissen argued that, "Since the blind man has been led out of the village, the natural conclusion would be his being sent away back into the village: 'and

he sent him home' is in this direction, but the subsequent instruction not to enter the village is in direct contradiction with it."[144] This argument, however, assumes that the man lived in the village. The narrative may imply, on the contrary, that he lived on a nearby farm. Räisänen argued that, if the author is responsible for the command to silence in v. 30 (after Peter's confession), he may be responsible for the analogous command in v. 26b, which he also calls a "command to silence."[145]

Eitrem has explained how all of v. 26 may be understood as part of the traditional story. He argued that interdictions of this sort are conventional in the practice of folk medicine: "The complete recovery of the patient depends upon his seclusion from any detrimental influence of the surroundings, eventually—and, at that time most of all—from the intrusion of spirits. Of course the attendance of distrusting unbelievers might be a serious hindrance to a miracle-doctor too."[146] The best conclusion seems to be that the command not to enter the village is pre-Markan and reflects the practice of folk medicine or magic. Once the miracle story became part of Mark, however, it took on connotations of the "messianic secret," or, more accurately, it became part of the theme of the mysterious identity of Jesus.[147]

139 Klauck, *Allegorie und Allegorese*, 348–49.

140 See the commentary on 4:12 and 8:18 above. For additional passages, see Klauck, *Allegorie und Allegorese*, 350. Carolyn J. Sharp has suggested that the halakic letter from Qumran includes a symbolic dimension in its references to the blind and the deaf (4QMMT B 50–54) ("Phinehan Zeal and Rhetorical Strategy in *4QMMT*," *RevQ* 70 [1997] 207–22, esp. 219).

141 Räisänen mentions this possibility himself (*Messianic Secret*, 165).

142 So also Johnson, "Mark VIII.22-26," 381–83; Best, *Following Jesus*, 137.

143 See the section "History of the Tradition" above.

144 Theissen, *Miracle Stories*, 148. He concludes that

Mark, by adding the negative to the second half of the verse, imposes the motif of secrecy on the "home" and opposes "home" to the village as the place of "public life."

145 Räisänen, *Messianic Secret*, 165. He concluded that the command in v. 26b "should probably be interpreted as being really concerned with Jesus' *identity* (corresponding to 8.30) and not with his *healing* activity (unlike 7.36)" (ibid.; emphasis original). Johnson rightly points out that v. 26b does not correspond to Mark's commands to silence elsewhere in the Gospel ("Mark VIII.22-26," 373).

146 Eitrem, *Some Notes*, 47.

147 See the excursus "The Messianic Secret" in the commentary on 1:24 above.

8:27—9:1 The Mystery Revealed

27/ And Jesus and his disciples went out to the villages of Caesarea Philippi. And on the way he asked his disciples, saying to them, "Who do people say that I am?" 28/ They then said to him,[a] "John the Baptist, and others Elijah, and others (say) that (you are) one of the prophets." 29/ And he asked them, "Who then do you say that I am?" Peter answered him, "You are the messiah."[b] 30/ And he rebuked them so that they would speak to no one about him. 31/ And he began to teach them that it was necessary that the Son of Man suffer much, and be rejected by the elders and the chief priests and the scribes, and be killed, and after three days[c] rise. 32/ And he was speaking the word openly. And Peter took him aside and began to rebuke him. 33/ But he turned around, saw his disciples, and rebuked Peter and said, "Get out of my sight, satan, because you do not set your mind on the affairs of God, but on human affairs."

34/ And he summoned the crowd with his disciples and said to them, "If anyone wants to come[d] after me, let him deny himself and take up his cross and follow me. 35/ For whoever wants to save his life will lose it; but whoever loses his life because of me and[e] the good news will save it. 36/ For how does it benefit a man to gain the whole world and yet suffer the loss of his life?[f] 37/ For what can a man give[g] in exchange for his life? 38/ For whoever is ashamed of me and of my words[h] in this adulterous and sinful generation, the Son of Man will also be ashamed of him, when he comes in the glory of his Father with[i] the holy angels."

9:1/ And he said to them, "Truly I say to you, some of those who are standing here will surely not experience death until they see that the kingdom of God has come with power."

a   The earliest recoverable reading is εἶπαν αὐτῷ λέγοντες ("said to him," lit., "said to him, saying") attested by ℵ B C[(2)] L et al. Since this formulation is awkwardly redundant, it has been replaced in some MSS (A f^1 𝔐 et al.) by ἀπεκρίθησαν ("they answered") and in others (D [W] Θ et al.) by ἀπεκρίθησαν αὐτῷ λέγοντες ("they answered him, saying"). The authors of Matthew and Luke made analogous changes. The words αὐτῷ λέγοντες ("to him, saying") are omitted from the parallel in Matt 16:14 and ἀποκριθέντες ("answering") is substituted for the same words in Luke 9:19. See Turner, "Marcan Usage," 28 (1926) 12 (Elliott, *Language and Style*, 71). On the Markan construction, see Max Zerwick, *Untersuchungen zum Markus-Stil: Ein Beitrag zur stilistischen Durcharbeitung des Neuen Testaments* (Scripta Pontificii Instituti Biblici; Rome: Pontifical Biblical Institute, 1937) 33–34.

b   The shortest reading, ὁ χριστός ("the messiah"), is surely the earliest. This reading was expanded by the addition of the words ὁ υἱὸς τοῦ θεοῦ ("the Son of God") in a reading attested by ℵ L *pc* r[1]. This expansion is analogous to that in 1:1; see the note on the trans. of that verse above. Another expansion, ὁ υἱὸς τοῦ θεοῦ τοῦ ζῶντος ("the son of the living God"), attested by W f^{13} et al., was evidently inspired by the parallel in Matt 16:16.

c   The trans. is based on the reading of the majority of the MSS, μετὰ τρεῖς ἡμέρας ("after three days"). W $f^{1.13}$ et al. attest the reading τῇ τρίτῃ ἡμέρᾳ ("on the third day"), which also appears as a variant in the MSS of 9:31 (see below). In both cases it represents an assimilation of the text of Mark to the more common formulation that appears, e.g., in variant forms in the two Synoptic parallels, Matt 16:21 and Luke 9:22. The formulation μετὰ τρεῖς ἡμέρας ("after three days") occurs in connection with the resurrection of Jesus in the NT only in Mark 8:31; 9:31; 10:34; and Matt 27:63. The two phrases do not necessarily refer to different periods of time; see Taylor, ad 8:31.

d   The reading ἐλθεῖν ("to come"), attested by ℵ A B C[2] et al., is probably earlier than the reading ἀκολουθεῖν ("to follow"), attested by p[45] C* D W et al. The direct parallels in Matt 16:24 (ἐλθεῖν, "to come") and Luke 9:23 (ἔρχεσθαι, "to come") suggest that the authors read ἐλθεῖν in Mark. The latter reading is also somewhat better attested. Note that a similar saying in Q is given in Matt 10:38 with ἀκολουθεῖ ("follow") and in Luke 14:27 with ἔρχεται ("come").

e   The words ἐμοῦ καί, "(because of) me and," do not occur in p[45] D 28 700 it (sy[s]). They are nevertheless probably part of the earlier text, since they appear in the parallels in Matt 16:25 and Luke 9:24 and since the double expression is typical of Markan style. See Taylor, ad loc.; Neirynck, *Duality in Mark*, 103.

f   p[45] A (C) D et al. read ἐὰν κερδήσῃ τὸν κόσμον ὅλον καὶ ζημιωθῇ ("if he gains the whole world and suffers the loss"). Apparently Matthew and Luke rewrote Mark differently and these MSS reflect the assimilation of Mark's text to Matthew's.

g   The earliest recoverable reading is δοῖ ("can give") attested by ℵ* B 2427[vid]. This is a Koine form of the 2nd aor. subjunctive; see BDF §95 (2). In the context it is a deliberative or dubitative subjunctive, which in classical Greek is seldom used in the third person; see BDF §366 (1). Thus Matthew changed the form to the future indicative, δώσει ("will give"; 16:26; Luke omits the saying). Similarly, a number of MSS of Mark reflect this correction: p[45] A C D W et al. Other MSS (ℵ[2] L) reflect a reading that is a correction to the more usual

spelling of the second aor. subjunctive, δῷ ("can give").

h   p[45vid] W k sa read καὶ τοὺς ἐμούς ("and of mine" or "and of my [disciples]") instead of καὶ τοὺς ἐμοὺς λόγους ("and of my words"), the reading of the rest of the MSS. Turner argued for the shorter reading as the earlier ("Western Readings," 2–3), but it is more likely that it is the result of accidental omission; see Metzger, *Textual Commentary*, 84.

i   p[45] W 2542 sy[s] read καί ("and") instead of μετά ("with"). This reading derives either from an independent attempt to reduce the mythic-realistic apocalyptic character of this saying or from the influence of the parallel in Luke 9:26.

Narrative Unity of 8:27—10:45

As noted above, the healing of the blind man in Bethsaida is a transitional narrative. It both concludes the section 6:6b—8:26 and introduces the section 8:27—10:45.[1] It belongs primarily to the section 6:6b—8:26, however, as the last in a series of miracle stories and as a comment on the theme of the "blindness" of the disciples introduced in 8:18. The section 8:27—10:45 is held together by the repetition of a three-part pattern: (1) prediction of the suffering, death, and resurrection of the Son of Man (8:31; 9:31; 10:32-34); (2) misunderstanding on the part of the disciples (8:32-33; 9:32; 10:35-41); and (3) teaching about discipleship (8:34-37; 9:33-37; 10:42-45).[2] This section is followed by another account of the healing of a blind man, 10:46-52. The two healing stories frame the section 8:27—10:45 and probably both relate to the theme of the disciples' "blindness." The healing of Bartimaeus in 10:46-52, however, belongs primarily to the next section, "Proclamation in Jerusalem" (10:46—13:37),

for two reasons: (1) the topographical change in 10:46, at which point Jesus and the disciples arrive in Judea (Jericho);[3] (2) the introduction of the epithet "son of David," which links the story to 11:10 and 12:35. Like the healing of the blind man in Bethsaida, the healing of Bartimaeus is also a transitional story.[4] When Bartimaeus is healed, he follows Jesus along the way (10:52). This statement, on the one hand, concludes the theme of following Jesus along the way, which is characteristic of 8:27—10:45. On the other hand, on the literal level, it signifies that Bartimaeus follows Jesus into Jerusalem. On the symbolic level, Bartimaeus is portrayed as a disciple who is willing to follow Jesus even into suffering and death.

It is in this middle section of Mark, 8:27—10:45, that Jesus teaches the disciples that the Son of Man must suffer and that discipleship involves faithful suffering. The section is structured as a journey, first northward to the villages of Caesarea Philippi (8:27) and Mount Hermon (9:2), and then southward toward Jerusalem.[5] The term

---

1   See the section "The Literary Role of 8:22-26" in the commentary on 8:22-26 above.

2   On these "passion prediction units," see Perrin, "Towards an Interpretation," 7–8; idem, *Redaction Criticism*, 45. Bultmann concluded that "Christian dogma has attained its point of greatest influence on the presentation" in 8:27—10:52 (*History*, 351).

3   See the note on the trans. of 10:1 below. Pesch argued that the pre-Markan passion narrative began with the scene preserved in 8:27-30 (2:1–28).

4   See the summary of older scholarship in Vernon K. Robbins, "The Healing of Blind Bartimaeus (10:46-52) in the Marcan Theology," *JBL* 92 (1973) 224–43, esp. 237–38. The division of opinion as to whether the story belongs to the preceding or the following section is an indication of its transitional character. Robbins himself places it in the section 10:46—12:44 (ibid., 241).

5   From the vicinity of the "high mountain" (9:2), they journey through Galilee (9:30), stopping in Caper-

"way" or "journey" (ὁδός) occurs frequently in this section.[6] Most of the occurrences refer to a literal road or journey. The usage in 10:32, however, is distinctive:

> Now they were on the way going up to Jerusalem, and Jesus was going ahead of them, and they were astounded, and those who followed were afraid. And he took the twelve again and began to tell them about the things that were about to happen to him.

The depiction of Jesus as going ahead of the disciples and of them as following him suggests that the literal journey to Judea symbolizes discipleship.[7] The portrayal of the disciples as astounded and afraid is unmotivated except for the remark that "they were on the way going up to Jerusalem." Their emotional state foreshadows what the Markan Jesus makes explicit in vv. 33-34, that the suffering and death of Jesus as Son of Man will take place in Jerusalem. As his disciples, they are in danger too. The journey from Mount Hermon to Judea is thus a path to suffering and death—actually for Jesus and potentially for his disciples.[8]

Genre of 8:27-30

Bultmann labeled this passage "Peter's Confession" and defined it as a legend, specifically a legend of faith in the messiahship of Jesus. He concluded that the narrative is fragmentary, "since it must originally have contained an account of the attitude Jesus himself took to the confession he had stimulated."[9] He argued that Mark omitted the original conclusion and substituted his own formulations and that the original conclusion has been preserved in Matt 16:17-19. He inferred that it was the risen Lord who blessed Peter in this original conclusion and that thus the whole narrative is an Easter story carried back into the life of Jesus for the first time by Mark.[10] Dibelius, in contrast, excluded this passage from consideration of the traditional forms because it is not "rounded-off." He assumed that the story is pre-Markan, but the evangelist has edited it so much as to obscure its original meaning and purpose.[11]

Bultmann also took the portrayal of Jesus taking the initiative by asking a question as evidence that the narrative is secondary; that is, it does not fit the usual pattern in which a disciple, rival, or opponent puts a question to Jesus. The content of the question is also extraordinary: "Why does Jesus ask about something on which he is bound to be every bit as well informed as were the disciples?" The question occurs simply to elicit an answer; in other words, it is a literary device.[12]

Robert C. Tannehill defined this passage as "an inverted testing inquiry, i.e., a testing inquiry in which the person featured in the writing (Jesus) does not respond to the test but poses the testing question."[13] He observed that Matthew has transformed the narrative into a commendation story.[14] Tannehill also noted that Jesus asks a preliminary question ("Who do people say that I am?") before asking the primary question ("Who then do you say that I am?"), thus eliciting a preliminary answer that contrasts with the final one.[15]

The difficulty involved in categorizing this passage in the usual form-critical terms, its distinctive features, its dramatic character, and its role as a virtual turning point in the narrative as a whole[16] all suggest that it is a Markan composition. It is not necessary, as Bultmann did, to posit a pre-Markan Easter story as a source used by the evangelist. The portrayal of Peter, throughout the narrative, as the most important of the disciples is sufficient explanation of the ascription of insight into Jesus'

---

naum (9:33), then going on to Perea (Transjordan) (see the note on the trans. of 10:1). From there they set out for Jerusalem (10:32), and arrive in Jericho (10:46), a city of Judea.

6   Seven of the sixteen occurences of the term are in this section plus 10:46-52, namely, 8:27; 9:33, 34; 10:17, 32, 46, 52.

7   Cf. Acts 9:2; 18:25; 19:9, 23; 22:4; 24:14, 22. Cf. also the use of the "way" (ὁδός) as an image for conversion in Lucian *Nigrinos*; Cancik, "Lucian on Conversion," 39.

8   Marcus connects the "way" of 10:32-34 with 1:3 and "the Deutero-Isaian picture of Yahweh's triumphant processional march" (*Way of the Lord*, 35).

9   Bultmann, *History*, 257–58.

10   Ibid., 258–59, 288–89.

11   Dibelius, *From Tradition to Gospel*, 44, 230.

12   Bultmann, *History*, 257–58.

13   Tannehill, "Varieties," 5.21 (p. 115).

14   Ibid., 118 n. 18.

15   Ibid., 5.22 (p. 116); p. 118 n. 20.

16   See, e.g., Hooker, 200.

messiahship to him, although the tradition that the risen Jesus appeared to Peter may have been the reason for this portrayal (1 Cor 15:4).

History of the Tradition of 8:27-30

Bultmann argued that v. 27a, the statement that Jesus and the disciples went out to the villages of Caesarea Philippi, is the conclusion of the miracle story about the healing of the blind man in Bethsaida.[17] He judged both of these topographical references to be Markan editorial additions.[18] He concluded that both the healing of the blind man and the confession of Peter were pre-Markan traditional units, but that "we must take Jesus' journey north as a phantasy, and eliminate it from history."[19]

Karl Ludwig Schmidt, however, took v. 27a as the introduction to the confession of Peter (vv. 27-30). Furthermore, he argued that, in spite of the plausible topographical connection between Bethsaida in the previous passage and the villages of Caesarea Philippi in this one, there is a "seam" between the two narratives. He agreed with Bultmann, however, that the narrative about the confession of Peter is pre-Markan tradition. But he concluded that the reference to Caesarea Philippi was part of this tradition from the beginning. Finally, he argued that the reference is part of the oldest tradition and that here we have a "genuinely remembered fact."[20] His warrants for the latter conclusion are the following: (1) the region of Caesarea Philippi is not mentioned elsewhere in the Gospel tradition; (2) it does not occur here

because of an itinerary assumed by Mark; (3) it was not invented by (tradents of) the pre-Markan tradition, since it has no didactic or symbolic meaning; (4) that Jesus did not enter Caesarea Philippi itself, the residence of Philip, is historically credible, since he is never depicted as entering Tiberias, the residence of Herod Antipas.[21] The second and third of these warrants will be questioned below.

Comment

■ **27a** The preceding healing of the blind man took place in Bethsaida, a city of the district of Gaulanitis, modern Golan, east of the Sea of Galilee. This district was part of the tetrarchy of Philip.[22] According to this verse, Jesus and his disciples left there and traveled to the villages of Caesarea Philippi. This means that they would have traveled north to the district of Panias, also part of the tetrarchy of Philip, which contained the sources of the Jordan River.[23]

From the third century BCE onward, there was a locality known as "the cave (or grotto) of Panias" ($\tau\grave{o}$ $\Pi\acute{a}\nu\epsilon\iota o\nu$ [$\check{a}\nu\tau\rho o\nu$]) beside "the mountain of Panias" ($\tau\grave{o}$ $\Pi\acute{a}\nu\epsilon\iota o\nu$ [$\check{o}\rho o\varsigma$]). The grotto was dedicated to the god Pan.[24] This deity played an important role in the Ptolemaic ruler cult and may have done so in the Seleucid ruler cult as well.[25] The region of Panias was granted to Herod (the Great) by Augustus in 20 BCE.[26] In association with the grotto, Herod built a temple of white marble dedicated to Augustus.[27] It is clear that Josephus

---

17 Bultmann, *History*, 64–65.

18 Ibid.; see also the section "The History of the Tradition" in the commentary on 8:22-26 above.

19 Bultmann, *History*, 65; cf. 213 and 257–59 on the traditional character of the two narratives.

20 Schmidt, *Der Rahmen*, 215–17 (my trans.).

21 Ibid., 216–17.

22 Schürer, *History*, 1:223 n. 17; ibid., 1:336–37.

23 Ibid., 1:336–37. This region was largely non-Jewish (2:169), as was the city founded by Philip (2:170).

24 Ibid., 2:169 and n. 454. On the history of the site, see Zvi Uri Maʿoz, "Banias," *NEAEHL* 1:136–43, esp. 137–39. Vassilios Tzaferis concludes that the cave became a sanctuary of Pan at least from the start of the second century BCE ("Cults and Deities Worshipped at Caesarea Philippi-Banias," in Eugene Ulrich, John W. Wright, Robert P. Carroll, and Philip R. Davies, eds., *Priests, Prophets and Scribes:*

Essays on the Formation and Heritage of Second Temple Judaism in Honour of Joseph Blenkinsopp [JSNTSup 149; Sheffield: Sheffield Academic Press, 1992] 190–201, esp. 191).

25 Achim Lichtenberger, *Die Baupolitik Herodes des Großen* (Abhandlungen des Deutschen Palästina-Vereins 26; Wiesbaden: Harrassowitz, 1999) 150.

26 Schürer, *History*, 2:169.

27 Tzaferis, "Cults and Deities," 196–97; Lichtenberger, *Baupolitik*, 150–53. Josephus certainly gives the impression that one of the three temples that Herod dedicated to Augustus was at the place called Panias (*Ant.* 15.10.3 §§363–64, esp. the end of that passage; *Bell.* 1.21.3 §§404–6). But J. Andrew Overman et al. claim to have found the relevant temple at Omrit, less than two miles from Panias (idem, Jack Olive, and Michael Nelson, "Discovering Herod's Shrine to Augustus: Mystery Temple Found at Omrit," *BAR*

connected the grotto and the temple with Mount Hermon.[28] Philip, a son of Herod the Great, inherited the region of Panias (along with Gaulanitis and neighboring districts). He built a city near the grotto and named it Caesarea ($Καισάρεια$) in honor of Augustus.[29] The city, identical with the Caesarea Philippi of the New Testament and modern Banias, was founded in 2 or 1 BCE.[30] Agrippa II enlarged the city and renamed it Neronias ($Νερωνίας$) in 53 CE in honor of the emperor Nero. The new name, however, did not catch on.[31] The "villages of Caesarea Philippi" mentioned here belonged to the territory of the city.[32]

Bultmann's conclusion that v. 27a belongs to the story of the healing of the blind man must be rejected.[33] The phrase "on the way" ($ἐν τῇ ὁδῷ$) in v. 27b links the two clauses firmly together. The verb "went out" ($ἐξῆλθεν$) in v. 27a refers back to Bethsaida in v. 22, but that connection is insufficient to warrant the inference that v. 27a is the conclusion of the healing story.[34] Schmidt is right that the setting of vv. 27-30 in Caesarea Philippi does not result from an itinerary taken over or assumed by Mark,[35] but it could well be that it is part of an itinerary deliberately created by the evangelist. Mark may have had his reasons for locating the confession of Peter, the teaching on discipleship, and the transfiguration in the region of Caesarea Philippi, and these reasons may have been symbolic.

One reason may be that it was an appropriate setting for revelation. According to 9:2, the transfiguration is set on a high mountain ($ὄρος ὑψηλόν$), and members of the audience familiar with the topography of Caesarea Philippi and Panias probably inferred that this mountain was Mount Hermon. George W. E. Nickelsburg has argued that "the region around Mount Hermon was sacred to Canaanites, Israelites, non-Israelites of the Greco-Roman period, and Christians."[36] Following Bultmann, Nickelsburg suggests that both the confession of Peter and the transfiguration are based on traditions about the appearance of the risen Jesus to Peter. Thus, these narratives are evidence for "a broader, post-resurrection revelatory tradition bound to the area of Hermon."[37]

In particular, in the Greco-Roman period the god of Mount Hermon (Baal identified with Zeus) was considered to be an oracular deity.[38] Peter's unexplained insight that Jesus is the messiah and Jesus' revelation of the necessity that the Son of Man must suffer take on the connotations of oracular utterances for those familiar with the oracular character of the region.

Another reason may be to contrast Jesus as messiah with other rulers.[39] As noted above, Herod built a temple dedicated to Augustus in or near Panias. This temple was at least maintained by Philip and Agrippa II, if not

29.2 [2003] 40–49, 67–68). Their claim, however, has been disputed by Andrea M. Berlin ("Debate: Where Was Herod's Temple to Augustus? Banias Is Still the Best Candidate," *BAR* 29.5 [2003] 22–24) and Ehud Netzer ("A Third Candidate: Another Building at Banias," *BAR* 29.5 [2003] 25).

28 Josephus *Bell.* 1.21.3 §§404–5; *Ant.* 15.10.3 §§360–64. The grotto and temple are "located at the foot of the southwest extremity of Mount Hermon (Jebel esh-Sheikh)" (Maʿoz, "Banias," 136). On the excavation of the sanctuary of Pan and the temple of Augustus, see ibid., 140.

29 Josephus *Ant.* 18.2.1 §28; *Bell.* 2.9.1 §168.

30 Maʿoz, "Banias," 138; or in 3 or 2 BCE (Schürer, *History*, 2:170). On the excavation of the city, see Maʿoz, "Banias," 141–42. Tzaferis dates the foundation to 3 BCE ("Cults and Deities," 190).

31 Schürer, *History*, 2:170; Josephus *Bell.* 3.10.7 §514; *Ant.* 20.9.4 §211; Tzaferis, "Cults and Deities," 197–98.

32 Schürer, *History*, 2:171.

33 See the section "History of the Tradition" above.

34 Schmidt notes rightly that in an oral story the question from where Jesus went out need not have arisen (*Der Rahmen*, 216).

35 Ibid.

36 George W. E. Nickelsburg, *1 Enoch 1: A Commentary on the Book of 1 Enoch, Chapters 1–36; 81–108* (Hermeneia; Minneapolis: Fortress, 2001), 238–47. Note the map on p. 240; the photographs of Mount Hermon on p. 241; and the photographs of the sanctuary of Pan on p. 243.

37 Ibid., 246; George W. E. Nickelsburg, "Enoch, Levi and Peter: Recipients of Revelation in Upper Galilee," *JBL* 100 (1981) 575–600, esp. 599 n. 106; cf. Bultmann, *History*, 257–59.

38 Youssef Hajjar, "Divinités oraculaires et rites divinatoires en Syrie et en Phénicie à l'époque gréco-romaine," in *ANRW* 2.18.4 (1990) 2236–2320, 2783–97, esp. 2252–53.

39 Bas van Iersel entertains the possibility that the narrator locates Peter's statement here in order to "con-

expanded.[40] Placing the confession of Peter at Caesarea Philippi makes the point for those aware of the imperial cult practiced there that *Jesus* is the agent of the supreme deity, not the emperor. The confession of the centurion in 15:39 makes the same point.[41]

Events related to the Jewish war with Rome in the time of the evangelist may have been the catalyst for drawing such a contrast. Modius, the viceroy of Agrippa II, imprisoned the Jews of Caesarea Philippi, apparently in reaction to the defeat of Cestius Gallus, the governor of Syria, in Jerusalem in 66 CE.[42] More importantly for Mark, Vespasian visited Caesarea Philippi for twenty days at some point between June and September of 67 CE. Agrippa II invited him in order to entertain the general and his troops and to seek their help in putting an end to the disorder in his realm. According to Josephus, Vespasian offered thank-offerings to (some pagan) god(s), while he was there, for his successes up to that point. These were presumably offered in the temple of Augustus.[43] Vespasian was in Palestine as an agent of the emperor Nero, who was probably worshiped in the temple of Augustus in the locality along with his predecessors. Agrippa II, as noted above, had renamed the city Neronias (Νερωνίας) in 53 CE in honor of Nero.

In the confession of Peter and the transfiguration, Mark portrays the revelation of the suffering mission of Jesus as Son of Man and his glorious status as Son of God to the disciples in a numinous setting characterized primarily by non-Jewish, non-Christian, Syrian, and Hellenistic religious practice.[44] The effect is to place the Christian reverence for Jesus in competition with pagan religious belief and practice and to co-opt the sacredness of the locality.

■ **27b-28** Jesus' preliminary question[45] takes up explicitly the theme of Jesus' identity in the Gospel.[46] This theme is introduced by the unclean spirit's declaration in 1:24, "I know who you are, the Holy One of God," and especially by the narrator's remark in 1:34, "he would not allow the demons to speak, because they knew him."[47] Although the demons know who Jesus is, human beings do not, at least not before this point in the narrative. After Jesus stills the storm, the disciples ask, "Who then is this that both the wind and the sea obey him?" They affirm his extraordinary power, but do not understand its source or purpose (4:41).[48] Jesus' identity is defined disparagingly by the residents of Nazareth as "the carpenter, the son of Mary and brother of James and Joses and Judas and Simon" (6:3).[49] They take offense at him because of the disparity between their alleged knowledge of who he is and his (authoritative) teaching in their synagogue. Jesus responds with the saying "A prophet is not without honor, except in his hometown and among his relatives and in his house," hinting, but not asserting, that he is a prophet of some sort.

jure up the thought of another king for Israel" in this "city of emperors and kings" (*Reading Mark*, 125–26).

40 Maʿoz, "Banias," 140.

41 See the commentary on 15:39 below.

42 Josephus *Vit.* 13 §74; cf. 6 §§24–25. The evangelist probably did not, however, choose Caesarea Philippi as a setting in order to relate the suffering of Jesus to the suffering of the Jews in the war (and thus depict Jesus as a representative of Israel) because Jews suffered more, and more famously, in other northern cities. For the view that the story of Jesus in Mark reflects events of the Jewish war, see Andreas Bedenbender (following Ton Veerkamp), "Römer, Christen und Dämonen: Beobachtungen zur Komposition des Markusevangeliums," *Texte und Kontexte* 67 (1995) 3–52, esp. 3–4.

43 Josephus *Bell.* 3.9.7 §§443–44. Cf. Maʿoz, "Banias," 138; Bedenbender, "Römer, Christen," 4. After the destruction of the temple and the city of Jerusalem and after Titus had deposited most of his spoils in Caesarea on the sea, he and his troops went to Cae-

sarea Philippi and celebrated the birthday of his brother Domitian. During this festival, many of the Jewish prisoners perished in contests with wild beasts and with one another (Josephus *Bell.* 7.2.1 §§23–24; 7.3.1 §§37–38). This event, however, probably took place after Mark was written; see the commentary on chap. 13 below.

44 Heinz-Wolfgang Kuhn entertained this possibility ("Jesu Hinwendung zu den Heiden im Markusevangelium im Verhältnis zu Jesu historischem Wirken in Betsaida mit einem Zwischenbericht zur Ausgrabung eines vermuteten heidnischen Tempels auf et-Tell (Betsaida)," in Klaus Krämer and Ansgar Paus, eds., *Die Weite des Mysteriums: Christliche Identität im Dialog für Horst Bürkle* [Freiburg: Herder, 2000] 204–40, esp. 211).

45 See the section "Genre" above.

46 See "Excursus: The Messianic Secret" in the commentary on 1:24 above.

47 See also 3:11-12 and the commentary above.

48 See the commentary above.

49 See the commentary above.

The theme of Jesus' identity is given significant development in 6:14-16. Verse 14 indicates that some people were interpreting Jesus as John the baptizer, raised from the dead, and thus possessing extraordinary power. Verse 15 implies that other people were saying that Jesus was Elijah, returned to earth from heaven, and others that Jesus was a prophet like one of the prophets (of old). According to v. 16, Herod agreed with the first opinion, that Jesus was John raised from the dead.[50] No assessment of these opinions is given in chap. 6, neither explicit nor clearly implied.

As suggested above, the Pharisees' demand for a sign is, in effect, a question about Jesus' identity or an indirect rejection of his implied claim to be a prophet or the messiah.[51] The didactic scene in which Jesus questions the disciples closely about the two feedings is also a dialogue about Jesus' identity, indirectly. The disciples do not understand about the loaves because they do not understand Jesus' identity and mission.[52] Finally, it was suggested above that the healing of the blind man near Bethsaida symbolized the removal of the disciples' "blindness" alluded to in 8:18.[53]

The preliminary answer of the disciples, in response to Jesus' preliminary question, summarizes the opinions of various people, including Herod (Antipas), given in 6:14-16. These opinions were not evaluated by the evangelist then, because they are to be evaluated in this context.

■ **29** Jesus then asks the more important question, "Who then do you say that I am?" Unlike Herod (Antipas), who simply chose one of the current theories about the identity of Jesus,[54] Peter gives a different answer, "You are the messiah." This response is clearly superior to those mentioned in v. 28 from the point of view of the implied author, since Jesus is declared to be the messiah in the introductory titular sentence of the Gospel.[55] The subsequent unfolding of the narrative (and the symbolic import of 8:22-26), however, indicates that Peter's response, although true, is ambiguous and thus in need of clarification.

■ **30-31** The initial response of the Markan Jesus to Peter's answer, rebuking the disciples so that they would speak to no one about him, is the same as his response to revelations of his identity by the demons, which are also called unclean spirits (1:34; 3:11-12). This rebuke does not signify that the answer is wrong. It signifies first and foremost that the identity of Jesus as messiah must be kept secret for the time being.[56]

Why that identity must be kept secret is illuminated by the use of the epithet "Son of Man" in the second response of Jesus, the teaching described in v. 31. The use of this epithet as a synonym for "messiah" indicates that the author and audience have a shared understanding of the Davidic or royal messiah and a shared assumption that "messiah" in this sense and "Son of Man" are equivalent.[57] The command to keep silent about Jesus' identity as the Son of Man is at least analogous to, if not dependent on, the portrayal of "that Son of Man" in the Similitudes of Enoch (*1 Enoch* 37–71), which is based on the "one like a son of man" in Daniel 7:13.

One of the most distinctive characteristics of the Son of Man in the Similitudes is his hiddenness. He is revealed to the community that will be redeemed, but his revelation on the day of judgment will surprise the kings and the mighty. The Son of Man is revealed secretly to the righteous and later publicly to the rest of humanity, in particular, on the day of judgment.[58] A difference between the Similitudes and Mark is that, according to the former, the Son of Man is a heavenly being, whereas in Mark, Jesus walks the earth as Son of Man. Nevertheless, one factor in the secrecy of Jesus' messiahship may be the idea that the Son of Man is revealed to the elect in a secret and anticipatory way.[59]

---

50   See the commentary on 6:14-16 above.
51   See the commentary on 8:11-13 above.
52   See the commentary on 8:14-21 and 6:51-52.
53   See the commentary on 8:22-26 above.
54   Cf. 6:16 with 6:14; see the first note on the trans. of 6:14 and the commentary on 6:14-16 above.
55   See the commentary on 1:1 above.
56   See "Excursus: The Messianic Secret" in the commentary on 1:24 above.

57   See the introduction above on the interpretation of Jesus, the subsection "Jesus as Messiah." That Peter's answer refers to the Davidic or royal messiah is implied by the rejection of the theory that Jesus is a(n anointed/messianic) prophet in the first answer.
58   See "Jesus as Messiah" in the introduction above.
59   The epithet "Son of Man" in 2:10, 28 may already have been in the evangelist's source; see "Narrative Unity and Literary History of 2:1–3:6" in the com-

This interpretation of the secret of Jesus' identity explains the apparent giving away of the secret in 14:62. William Wrede argued that the key to the secret was the saying in 9:9, that the three disciples who witnessed the transfiguration were not to speak of it until "the Son of Man had risen from the dead." Critics of Wrede argued that Jesus' remark to the high priest, "you will see the Son of Man sitting on the right of the Power and coming with the clouds of heaven," revealed the secret *before* Jesus had risen from the dead. The saying in 9:9, however, should be interpreted as a signal that the transfiguration serves as a preview of the resurrected state of Jesus. Mark offers this account instead of a description of an appearance of the risen Jesus later on. Analogously, the saying in 14:62 is a preview of the parousia, the day of the return of Jesus, on which his identity as the Son of Man will be revealed to all of humanity. That Jesus is the Son of Man will come as a surprise to the high priest and his allies, who rejected Jesus' claim to be the messiah (expressed in the first part of 14:62). The saying hints at a scenario like that described in *1 Enoch* 62:3-12.

The Dead Sea Scrolls, the *Psalms of Solomon,* and the events of the first Jewish war with Rome, as narrated by Josephus, provide evidence that a significant number of Jews in the first century CE anticipated a Davidic messiah who would defeat the Romans and their Jewish collaborators and reestablish an autonomous kingdom of Israel.[60] The Similitudes of Enoch (*1 Enoch* 37–71) and 2 Esdras 13 provide evidence that, in some circles in the same period of time, the "one like a son of man" in Dan 7:13 was interpreted as a heavenly messiah who would be God's agent in the eschatological judgment.[61] In this cultural context, the teaching of v. 31 is a shocking inversion of the standard expectation of the messiah and his deeds.

If the historical Jesus predicted his own death, it is likely that he expected to die along with others in the context of the messianic woes.[62] The details of this saying have certainly been influenced by knowledge of later events.[63] Opinions differ about whether the saying in v. 31 is traditional and slightly revised by Mark or is a Markan composition.[64]

The use of the term $\delta\epsilon\hat{\iota}$ ("it was necessary," lit., "it is necessary") implies a theological interpretation of the events mentioned in v. 31. Its usage here recalls Daniel's speech to Nebuchadnezzar:

but there is a God in heaven revealing mysteries, who has made known to the king, Nebuchadnezzar, what must take place in the time of the last days ($\dot{\alpha}\lambda\lambda'\,\ddot{\epsilon}\sigma\tau\iota$ $\theta\epsilon\grave{o}\varsigma\,\dot{\epsilon}\nu\,o\dot{\nu}\rho\alpha\nu\hat{\omega}\,\dot{\alpha}\nu\alpha\kappa\alpha\lambda\acute{\nu}\pi\tau\omega\nu\,\mu\nu\sigma\tau\acute{\eta}\rho\iota\alpha,\,\ddot{o}\varsigma\,\dot{\epsilon}\delta\acute{\eta}$-$\lambda\omega\sigma\epsilon\,\tau\hat{\omega}\,\beta\alpha\sigma\iota\lambda\epsilon\hat{\iota}\,N\alpha\beta o\nu\chi o\delta o\nu o\sigma o\rho\,\ddot{\alpha}\,\delta\epsilon\hat{\iota}\,\gamma\epsilon\nu\acute{\epsilon}\sigma\vartheta\alpha\iota$ $\dot{\epsilon}\pi'\,\dot{\epsilon}\sigma\chi\acute{\alpha}\tau\omega\nu\,\tau\hat{\omega}\nu\,\dot{\eta}\mu\epsilon\rho\hat{\omega}\nu$) (Dan 2:28 OG).

In the Dead Sea Scrolls, the Hebrew phrase (אחרית הימים), equivalent to Daniel's Aramaic phrase (באחרית יומיא) translated by the LXX as $\dot{\epsilon}\pi'\,\dot{\epsilon}\sigma\chi\acute{\alpha}\tau\omega\nu\,\tau\hat{\omega}\nu\,\dot{\eta}\mu\epsilon\rho\hat{\omega}\nu$ ("in the time of the last days"), is used to refer to the messianic age.[65] In Dan 2:28, the Aramaic term (רזין), translated by the LXX as $\mu\nu\sigma\tau\acute{\eta}\rho\iota\alpha$ ("mysteries"), refers to the dream of the king and related phenomena. In the Dead Sea Scrolls, the equivalent Hebrew term is used for the words of the prophets, which are regarded as mysteries in need of interpretation.[66]

Both types of mysteries are connected to the apocalyptic and sectarian view of the predetermined periods of history (קצים). Since the sequence of these periods according to the divine plan is hidden, they are called "the mysteries of God" (רזי אל) in the sectarian writings.[67] The *Community Rule* relates these "mysteries" to

---

mentary on 2:1-12 above. Furthermore, these occurrences of the epithet do not give away the "messianic secret" because they are so ambiguous. They conceal as much as they reveal about the identity of Jesus; see the commentary on 2:10 and 2:28 above.

60 See "Jesus as Messiah" in the introduction above.
61 See ibid.
62 Dale C. Allison, Jr., *The End of the Ages Has Come: An Early Interpretation of the Passion and Resurrection of Jesus* (Philadelphia: Fortress, 1985) 117–18.
63 Cf. Hooker, 205.
64 Räisänen, *Messianic Secret*, 177. It is likely, however,

that v. 31 and the other passion predictions are Markan composition; see below. E. J. Pryke concluded that the first two passion predictions are Markan composition and that the third may be either pre-Markan or Markan (*Redactional Style*, 163, 164, 166).

65 Collins, *Daniel*, 161.
66 Ibid.
67 Devorah Dimant, "Qumran Sectarian Literature," in Michael E. Stone, ed., *Jewish Writings of the Second Temple Period* (CRINT 2, LJPPSTT 2; Assen: Van Gorcum; Philadelphia: Fortress, 1984) 483–550,

the divine plan for the eschatological fulfillment.[68] 4QInstruction (now more commonly referred to as *Sapiental Work A*) may come from a pre-Qumranic phase of the sect's history or may have been written for Essenes who married and lived elsewhere than at Qumran. It uses the expression *rāz nihyeh* at key points.[69] It is best translated "mystery to come" and is a comprehensive term for God's plan for creation and history, especially for the eschatological period in which the elect will be redeemed.[70] The Markan Jesus' statement that the Son of Man *must* suffer is best understood in this context or one analogous to it. In other words, the necessity for the suffering, rejection, death, and resurrection of Jesus as Son of Man is part of the divine plan for the period of eschatological fulfillment. This plan is revealed in scripture, for those with the proper principles of interpretation, and is now being revealed by the Markan Jesus to his disciples.

The prophecy that the Son of Man must "suffer much" ($\pi o\lambda\lambda\dot{\alpha}\ \pi\alpha\theta\epsilon\hat{\iota}\nu$) is reminiscent of the account of the death of Eleazar:

Then, when he was about to die because of the wounds, he groaned and said, "It is evident to the Lord, who has holy knowledge, that, although I could have been acquitted of the death penalty, I am submitting to harsh pains as I am being whipped with respect to my body. But with respect to my soul, I suffer this gladly on account of my fear of him." And then this man died in this way, leaving behind his own death as an example of nobility of character and a memorial of virtue, not only for the young, but also for the greatest number of the nation ($\mu\dot{\epsilon}\lambda\lambda\omega\nu\ \delta\dot{\epsilon}$ $\tau\alpha\hat{\iota}\varsigma\ \pi\lambda\eta\gamma\alpha\hat{\iota}\varsigma\ \tau\epsilon\lambda\epsilon\nu\tau\hat{\alpha}\nu\ \dot{\alpha}\nu\alpha\sigma\tau\epsilon\nu\dot{\alpha}\xi\alpha\varsigma\ \epsilon\hat{\iota}\pi\epsilon\nu\ T\hat{\omega}$ $\kappa\nu\rho\dot{\iota}\omega\ \tau\hat{\omega}\ \tau\dot{\eta}\nu\ \dot{\alpha}\gamma\dot{\iota}\alpha\nu\ \gamma\nu\hat{\omega}\sigma\iota\nu\ \dot{\epsilon}\chi o\nu\tau\iota\ \phi\alpha\nu\epsilon\rho\dot{o}\nu\ \dot{\epsilon}\sigma\tau\iota\nu$ $\ddot{o}\tau\iota\ \delta\nu\nu\dot{\alpha}\mu\epsilon\nu o\varsigma\ \dot{\alpha}\pi o\lambda\nu\theta\hat{\eta}\nu\alpha\iota\ \tau o\hat{\nu}\ \theta\alpha\nu\dot{\alpha}\tau o\nu\ \sigma\kappa\lambda\eta\rho\dot{\alpha}\varsigma$

$\dot{\nu}\pi o\phi\dot{\epsilon}\rho\omega\ \kappa\alpha\tau\dot{\alpha}\ \tau\dot{o}\ \sigma\hat{\omega}\mu\alpha\ \dot{\alpha}\lambda\gamma\eta\delta\dot{o}\nu\alpha\varsigma\ \mu\alpha\sigma\tau\iota\gamma o\dot{\nu}$-$\mu\epsilon\nu o\varsigma,\ \kappa\alpha\tau\dot{\alpha}\ \psi\nu\chi\dot{\eta}\nu\ \delta\dot{\epsilon}\ \dot{\eta}\delta\dot{\epsilon}\omega\varsigma\ \delta\iota\dot{\alpha}\ \tau\dot{o}\nu\ \alpha\dot{\nu}\tau o\hat{\nu}\ \phi\dot{o}\beta o\nu$ $\tau\alpha\hat{\nu}\tau\alpha\ \pi\dot{\alpha}\sigma\chi\omega.\ \kappa\alpha\dot{\iota}\ o\hat{\nu}\tau o\varsigma\ o\dot{\nu}\nu\ \tau o\hat{\nu}\tau o\nu\ \tau\dot{o}\nu\ \tau\rho\dot{o}\pi o\nu$ $\mu\epsilon\tau\dot{\eta}\lambda\lambda\alpha\xi\epsilon\nu\ o\dot{\nu}\ \mu\dot{o}\nu o\nu\ \tau o\hat{\iota}\varsigma\ \nu\dot{\epsilon}o\iota\varsigma,\ \dot{\alpha}\lambda\lambda\dot{\alpha}\ \kappa\alpha\dot{\iota}\ \tau o\hat{\iota}\varsigma$ $\pi\lambda\epsilon\dot{\iota}\sigma\tau o\iota\varsigma\ \tau o\hat{\nu}\ \ddot{\epsilon}\theta\nu o\nu\varsigma\ \tau\dot{o}\nu\ \dot{\epsilon}\alpha\nu\tau o\hat{\nu}\ \theta\dot{\alpha}\nu\alpha\tau o\nu$ $\dot{\nu}\pi\dot{o}\delta\epsilon\iota\gamma\mu\alpha\ \gamma\epsilon\nu\nu\alpha\iota\dot{o}\tau\eta\tau o\varsigma\ \kappa\alpha\dot{\iota}\ \mu\nu\eta\mu\dot{o}\sigma\nu\nu o\nu\ \dot{\alpha}\rho\epsilon\tau\hat{\eta}\varsigma$ $\kappa\alpha\tau\alpha\lambda\iota\pi\dot{\omega}\nu).$ (2 Macc 6:30-31 LXX)

This passage and Mark 8:31 share the idea of the unjust suffering of an individual. But 2 Maccabees interprets the suffering of Eleazar in terms of fear of the Lord, nobility of character, and virtue, whereas v. 31 interprets the death of Jesus in terms of the divine plan for the last days.[71]

The idea that the Son of Man must "be rejected" ($\dot{\alpha}\pi o\delta o\kappa\iota\mu\alpha\sigma\theta\hat{\eta}\nu\alpha\iota$) is probably drawn from Psalm 118:

a stone, which the builders rejected,
this has become the cornerstone
($\lambda\dot{\iota}\theta o\nu,\ \ddot{o}\nu\ \dot{\alpha}\pi\epsilon\delta o\kappa\dot{\iota}\mu\alpha\sigma\alpha\nu\ o\dot{\iota}\ o\dot{\iota}\kappa o\delta o\mu o\hat{\nu}\nu\tau\epsilon\varsigma,$
$o\hat{\nu}\tau o\varsigma\ \dot{\epsilon}\gamma\epsilon\nu\dot{\eta}\theta\eta\ \epsilon\dot{\iota}\varsigma\ \kappa\epsilon\phi\alpha\lambda\dot{\eta}\nu\ \gamma\omega\nu\dot{\iota}\alpha\varsigma).$ (Ps 117:22 LXX)

In the Hebrew version of the psalm (118), this proverb is employed to celebrate how one who was despised has been honored.[72] This psalm is cited in Mark 12:10-11 as a comment on the parable of the wicked tenants. It is not explicitly interpreted with reference to Jesus, but if the beloved son of 12:6, in the context of Mark at least, represents Jesus, then the psalm text should be interpreted in terms of Jesus' death and exaltation. So the prophecy of Jesus' rejection in 8:31, for those who perceive the allusion to Psalm 118, already contains a hint of his vindication.

The "elders and the chief priests and the scribes" mentioned in v. 31 are equivalent in Mark to the (Judean) council or Sanhedrin.[73] The "tradition of the elders"

esp. 536. According to Torleif Elgvin, 4QInstruction shares this view of the predestined periods of history ("An Analysis of 4QInstruction" [Ph.D. diss., Hebrew University of Jerusalem, 1997] 79).

68 1QS 4:16-19; see also 1QM 3:7-9; 1QpHab 7:4-8, 10-14; *2 Bar.* 81:4; 2 Esdr 14:5; Elgvin, "4QInstruction," 79.

69 Daniel J. Harrington, "Sapiential Work," *EDSS* 2:825-26.

70 Elgvin, "4QInstruction," 80–81. See also the commentary on 4:11-12 above.

71 Pesch (2:49), following Lothar Ruppert, interprets the suffering of Jesus in terms of the tradition of the suffering righteous person.

72 Hans-Joachim Kraus, *Psalms 60–150: A Commentary* (Minneapolis: Augsburg, 1989; 5th Germ. ed. 1961/1978) 399–400.

73 Cf. 14:53 with 55; see also 15:1; Anthony J. Saldarini, "Sanhedrin," *ABD* 5:975-80. The term "scribes" here could simply refer to bureaucrats, judges, or officials in Jerusalem, rather than to experts in the Law related to the party or voluntary

mentioned in 7:3, 5 most likely had nothing to do with the (Judean) council or Sanhedrin.[74] It may be, however, that such tradition was associated with a Pharisaic organization.[75] In any case, some members of the audience may have associated the "elders" of chap. 7 with those of 8:31. Such auditors would, at least retrospectively, perceive the dispute with the Pharisees as less of a scholastic dialogue and more of a controversy-dialogue expressing (or evoking) conflict.

Socially speaking, the elders were the traditional leaders of the people, as senior members of prominent families.[76] The chief priests were probably the male members of the four or five families from whom the high priests were selected.[77] The "scribes" were educated leaders, but probably not a unified group. They were connected to the government in Jerusalem, as associates of the priests, and involved in the implementation of regulations for Jewish life. Outside of Jerusalem, they functioned as local officials.[78]

Matthew and Luke agree against Mark in reading "on the third day be raised" ($\tau\hat{\eta}$ $\tau\rho i\tau\eta$ $\dot{\eta}\mu\acute{e}\rho\alpha$ $\dot{e}\gamma\epsilon\rho\vartheta\hat{\eta}\nu\alpha\iota$) rather than "after three days rise" ($\mu\epsilon\tau\grave{\alpha}$ $\tau\rho\epsilon\hat{\iota}\varsigma$ $\dot{\eta}\mu\acute{e}\rho\alpha\varsigma$ $\dot{\alpha}\nu\alpha\sigma\tau\hat{\eta}\nu\alpha\iota$).[79] In the second prediction of the passion, Matt 17:23 differs from Mark 9:31 in the same ways, but there is no Lukan parallel. In the third prediction, Matt 20:19 differs from Mark 10:34 in the same ways; Luke 18:33 agrees with Matthew in reading "on the third day," but agrees with Mark in reading "he will rise." Andreas Ennulat argued that the agreements of Matthew and Luke against Mark in the passion predictions are evidence for a post-Markan, pre-Matthean, and pre-Lukan revision of Mark.[80] The Markan formulation can be explained as a paraphrasing adaptation of Hos 6:2 LXX:

he will heal us after two days, on the third day we shall rise and we shall live before him ($\dot{\upsilon}\gamma\iota\acute{\alpha}\sigma\epsilon\iota$ $\dot{\eta}\mu\hat{\alpha}\varsigma$ $\mu\epsilon\tau\grave{\alpha}$ $\delta\acute{\upsilon}o$ $\dot{\eta}\mu\acute{e}\rho\alpha\varsigma$, $\dot{e}\nu$ $\tau\hat{\eta}$ $\dot{\eta}\mu\acute{e}\rho\alpha$ $\tau\hat{\eta}$ $\tau\rho i\tau\eta$ $\dot{\alpha}\nu\alpha\sigma\tau\eta$-$\sigma\acute{o}\mu\epsilon\vartheta\alpha$ $\kappa\alpha\grave{\iota}$ $\zeta\eta\sigma\acute{o}\mu\epsilon\vartheta\alpha$ $\dot{e}\nu\acute{\omega}\pi\iota o\nu$ $\alpha\dot{\upsilon}\tauο\hat{\upsilon}$).

The Lukan and Matthean forms can be explained by their preference for the formulation also known to Paul, $\dot{e}\gamma\acute{\eta}\gamma\epsilon\rho\tau\alpha\iota$ $\tau\hat{\eta}$ $\dot{\eta}\mu\acute{e}\rho\alpha$ $\tau\hat{\eta}$ $\tau\rho i\tau\eta$ $\kappa\alpha\tau\grave{\alpha}$ $\tau\grave{\alpha}\varsigma$ $\gamma\rho\alpha\phi\acute{\alpha}\varsigma$ ("he was raised on the third day in accordance with the scriptures") (1 Cor 15:4).[81] Norman Perrin suggested credibly that Mark used the verb $\dot{\alpha}\nu i\sigma\tau\eta\mu\iota$ ("to rise") intransitively (it can be used either transitively or intransitively) in order to express the power of the Son of Man, as well as his suffering, in the predictions of the passion.[82]

It is striking that there is relatively little explicit interpretation of the suffering, rejection, death, and resurrection of the Son of Man in the saying.[83] This characteristic makes it unlikely that a form of this saying ever circulated independently. It is thus likely that the saying is a Markan composition. It plays a narrative role by bringing out into the open and stating with shocking directness what had only been hinted at earlier in the narrative (cf. 2:20; 3:6, 19).[84] It also predicts in summarizing detail what will be narrated in chaps. 14–16 and thus unifies the narrative as a whole. Finally, by foreshadowing the events of the passion narrative, it builds suspense and prepares the audience for that narrative. The prediction also demonstrates Jesus' foreknowledge and acceptance of his suffering, rejection, and death.

---

association of the Pharisees; see Saldarini, "Scribes," ibid., 1015, and the commentary on 1:22 above.

74 See the commentary on 7:3-4 above and Claudia J. Setzer, "Tradition of the Elders," ABD 6:638–39.

75 On the likely existence of executive, legislative, and disciplinary assemblies and bodies of Pharisees, Sadducees, and other groups, see Saldarini, "Sanhedrin," 979.

76 Saldarini, Pharisees, 154–55.

77 E. P. Sanders, Judaism: Practice and Belief 63 BCE–66 CE (London: SCM; Philadelphia: Trinity Press International, 1992) 328. Michael J. Cook, however, argued that the term "chief priests" simply refers to the "more important" priests and has "no technical import" (Mark's Treatment of the Jewish Leaders [NovTSup 51; Leiden: Brill, 1978] 17).

78 Saldarini, Pharisees, 148, 153; idem, "Scribes," 1012–16, esp. 1015.

79 Neirynck, Minor Agreements, 121. On the "minor agreements," see the commentary on 4:11-12 above.

80 Ennulat, Minor Agreements, 188–95.

81 But note that Paul used the verb "to rise" ($\dot{\alpha}\nu i\sigma\tau\eta\mu\iota$) in 1 Thess 4:14, 16.

82 Perrin, "Towards an Interpretation," 27.

83 E.g., there is no allusion to Isaiah 53 and no hint of vicarious suffering (Hooker, 205).

84 The death of John the Baptist also suggests that Jesus may meet the same fate (6:14-29).

■ **32a** This statement of the narrator, "And he was speaking the word openly" (καὶ παρρησίᾳ τὸν λόγον ἐλάλει), plays an important role in Mark's narrative, a role that was not important to the authors of Matthew and Luke, who omitted the remark. The depiction of Jesus speaking openly here contrasts with the conclusion of the parable discourse in which the narrator comments that "by means of many such parables he spoke the word to them" (τοιαύταις παραβολαῖς πολλαῖς ἐλάλει αὐτοῖς τὸν λόγον) and "he did not speak to them without a parable" (χωρὶς δὲ παραβολῆς οὐκ ἐλάλει αὐτοῖς) (4:33-34).

This antithetical parallel is closely related to the saying of Jesus in 4:11, that the mystery of the kingdom of God is given to "you," but hidden from "those outside." Those outside hear only parables without grasping their full significance, whereas Jesus "explained everything privately to his own disciples" (κατ᾽ ἰδίαν δὲ τοῖς ἰδίοις μαθηταῖς ἐπέλυεν πάντα) (4:34). As noted above, v. 31 implies that what *must* happen to the Son of Man is part of the mysterious divine plan. These two features support the hypothesis that the prophecy of the passion in v. 31 is an important aspect of the "mystery of the kingdom of God" mentioned in 4:11.[85]

The contrast between veiled speech and plain speech in the context of revelation occurs also in an ancient work on the interpretation of dreams by Artemidorus:

I have added this section to demonstrate that gods and all persons worthy of credence speak the truth in every instance, but sometimes they speak plainly, while at other times they speak in riddles (παρακείσθω σοι καὶ οὗτος ὁ λόγος, ὡς ἄρα οἱ θεοὶ καὶ πάντες οἱ ἀξιόπιστοι πάντως μὲν ἀληθῆ λέγουσιν, ἀλλὰ ποτὲ μὲν ἁπλῶς λέγουσι, ποτὲ δὲ αἰνίσσονται). (*Oneirocr.* 4.71)[86]

The Gospel of John contains a contrast analogous to that in Mark, either independently or as part of an extensive rewriting of Mark, in the farewell discourse:

I have spoken these things to you in figures of speech. The hour is coming when I will no longer speak to you in figures of speech, but will tell you openly of the Father (ταῦτα ἐν παροιμίαις λελάληκα ὑμῖν· ἔρχεται ὥρα ὅτε οὐκέτι ἐν παροιμίαις λαλήσω ὑμῖν, ἀλλὰ παρρησίᾳ περὶ τοῦ πατρὸς ἀπαγγελῶ ὑμῖν). (John 16:25)[87]

The "hour" apparently followed immediately, since after some further remarks of Jesus, the disciples say, "See, now you are speaking openly (ἐν παρρησίᾳ), and you do not say any figure of speech (παροιμία οὐδεμία)" (John 16:29).

An association is made between such plain speech and "the mysteries of the Father" in the *Epistle to Diognetus*, possibly in dependence on Mark or Matthew. The anonymous author asks rhetorically:

For who has been taught in the proper way and become friendly with *[Or pleasing to]* the word and yet does not seek to learn clearly the things which have been plainly shown the disciples through the word? The Word appeared to them and revealed these things, speaking openly. Even though he was not understood by unbelievers, he told these things to his disciples, who after being considered faithful by him came to know the mysteries of the Father (τίς γὰρ ὀρθῶς διδαχθεὶς καὶ λόγῳ προσφιλὴς γενηθεὶς οὐκ ἐπιζητεῖ σαφῶς μαθεῖν τὰ διὰ λόγου δειχθέντα φανερῶς μαθηταῖς, οἷς ἐφανέρωσεν ὁ λόγος φανείς, παρρησίᾳ λαλῶν, ὑπὸ ἀπίστων μὴ νοούμενος, μαθηταῖς δὲ διηγούμενος, οἳ πιστοὶ λογισθέντες ὑπ᾽ αὐτοῦ ἔγνωσαν πατρὸς μυστήρια;). (*Diogn.* 11.2)[88]

■ **32b-33** The comment of the narrator that Peter took Jesus aside implies that this scene is private and that the other disciples did not hear the dialogue between them.[89] Just as Jesus had rebuked the disciples so that

85 See the commentary on v. 31 and on 4:11-12 above.
86 Text from Roger A. Pack, *Artemidori Daldiani Oniro-criticon Libri V* (ASGB; BSGRT; Leipzig: Teubner, 1963) 292; trans. from Robert J. White, ed. and trans., *The Interpretation of Dreams: Oneirocritica by Artemidorus* (Noyes Classical Studies; Park Ridge, NJ: Noyes, 1975) 214.

87 On the relation of Mark and John, see the excursus on the passion narrative in the commentary on 14:1-11 below.
88 Text and trans. (modified) from Ehrman, *Apostolic Fathers*, 2:154-55.
89 This interpretation supports Timothy Wiarda's argument that, in this passage, Peter is presented as "an

they would not reveal to outsiders that he was the messiah (v. 30), so Peter here rebukes Jesus. Jesus' response in v. 33, that Peter does not set his mind on the affairs of God, implies that Peter has opposed the divine plan by rejecting the idea that the messianic Son of Man must suffer. Jesus' statement that Peter sets his mind on human affairs suggests that Peter's reason for rejecting the prophecy of the passion is that he is committed to the expectation of a Davidic messiah who would defeat the Romans and their Jewish collaborators and reestablish an autonomous kingdom of Israel.[90]

Jesus' reaction implies first of all that Peter is not behaving like a disciple. Jesus turns and sees the rest of the disciples behind him, whereas Peter has treated Jesus like his own disciple. Thus Jesus rebukes him, making the point that *he* has the authority to rebuke Peter and not the other way around. The first part of Jesus' verbal response to Peter, "Get out of my sight" ($\H{\upsilon}\pi\alpha\gamma\epsilon$ $\dot{o}\pi\dot{\iota}\sigma\omega$ $\mu o\upsilon$), could also be translated "Get behind me." The double meaning is effective. On the one hand, Jesus indicates clearly that he rejects Peter's attempt to persuade him to prevent the prophecy of suffering from being fulfilled. On the other, he lets Peter know that he should return to "following" Jesus, as a disciple should.[91]

It is highly unlikely that Jesus' address of Peter as "satan" indicates that Peter is identical with the leader of the evil spirits or that Satan has possessed him. The implication is rather that Peter is taking a role similar to the one that Satan usually plays. The text of Mark gives evidence for reconstructing that role. First of all, Satan put Jesus to the test in the wilderness immediately after his baptism. Exactly how he tested Jesus is not revealed, but the scene expresses the idea that Jesus will meet opposition in his mission.[92] The link between that passage and this one, created by the use of the term/name "satan/Satan," suggests that in both cases the expression

signifies the role of adversary or opponent, the basic meaning of the Hebrew equivalent (שָׂטָן).[93] The theme of opposition is continued in the Beelzebul controversy in the image of a kingdom of Satan opposed to the kingdom of God.[94] Satan is portrayed as an adversary also in the interpretation of the parable of the sower: he comes and takes away the word that was sown in those who are "along the road." This activity could be interpreted as taking place through the influence of other persons (for example, Peter trying to influence Jesus to nullify God's plan).[95]

■ 34 The section consisting of 8:27—9:1 is held together by the sequence (1) prediction of the suffering, death, and resurrection of the Son of Man in v. 31; (2) misunderstanding on the part of the disciples in vv. 32-33; and (3) teaching about discipleship in vv. 34-37.[96]

No temporal or spatial change is mentioned in v. 34, but there is a change in the characters of the narrative. Jesus here rather artificially summons "the crowd" and addresses teaching to them along with his disciples. In 7:14, "the crowd" appears in a similarly unmotivated way, introduced by an almost identical phrase, "And he summoned the crowd again." Bultmann explained the evangelist's way of proceeding in both passages as the creation of a situation for the insertion of speech material.[97] The comparison with 7:14 suggests that 8:27—9:1 is a kind of didactic scene created by Mark.[98] Unlike the other scenes, however, in which public teaching precedes the private instruction of the disciples, here the private instruction comes first. The introduction of the crowd may be a device to make the point that the teaching on discipleship applies to a wider group than the small circle of disciples around Jesus.

Bultmann also argued that in 8:34-37 at least three originally independent sayings are joined together.[99] The two sayings in vv. 34-35 occur in Matthew and Luke

---

opinion leader rather than a spokesman or typical disciple" ("Peter as Peter in the Gospel of Mark," *NTS* 45 [1999] 19–37, esp. 28–29).

90 See the commentary on vv. 30-31 above.

91 Cf. Grundmann, 170–71; Gundry, 432–33. Hooker suggests, as a secondary trans., "Get back into line, Peter" (206–7). See also Evans, 19.

92 See the commentary on 1:12-13 above.

93 See the commentary on 3:23 above.

94 See the commentary on 3:23-26 above.

95 See the commentary on 4:15 above.

96 See the section "Narrative Unity of 8:27—10:45" above.

97 Bultmann, *History*, 329–30.

98 See Sellew, "Composition," 613–34; Sellew does not discuss 8:27–9:1. On 8:27-30 as a Markan composition, see "Genre of 8:27-30" and the commentary on v. 31 above.

99 Bultmann, *History*, 82–83.

twice. They appear together in contexts parallel to that of Mark (Matt 16:24-25; Luke 9:23-24); they occur together a second time in Matthew (10:38-39) and separately in Luke (14:27; 17:33). This double attestation has led many to conclude that the sayings occurred in Q as well as in Mark, probably together as in Matthew.[100] Harry Fleddermann has argued that the sayings formed a unit in Q, that the Q form is older than the Markan, and that Mark is dependent on Q. The first two conclusions are plausible, but the third is dubious.[101]

In the saying of v. 34, the expression "If anyone wants to come after me" (εἴ τις θέλει ὀπίσω μου) recalls Jesus' command to Simon and Andrew, "Come after me" (δεῦτε ὀπίσω μου) in 1:17 and the narrator's comment that the sons of Zebedee "went away after him" (ἀπῆλθον ὀπίσω αὐτοῦ) in 1:20. The concluding formulation, "and let him follow me" (καὶ ἀκολουθείτω μοι) recalls the narrator's comment in 1:18 that Simon and Andrew "immediately left the nets and followed him" (εὐθὺς ἀφέντες τὰ δίκτυα ἠκολούθησαν αὐτῷ) and Jesus' command to Levi and his response in 2:14. The commitment that is dramatized in those passages is articulated explicitly here. In the context, there is surely an implied criticism of Peter, who needed to be told "Get out of my sight" (ὕπαγε ὀπίσω μου, lit., "Get behind me").[102]

The one who wants to come after Jesus must "deny himself" (ἀπαρνησάσθω ἑαυτόν). This command means that such a person must refuse to recognize or must

ignore oneself.[103] Such behavior is the opposite of denying Jesus, as Peter does in 14:68, 70. Thus, in 8:32-33 and in 14:66-72, Peter is a negative example for the audience.

The follower of Jesus must also "take up his cross" (ἀράτω τὸν σταυρὸν αὐτοῦ). Literally, to take up one's cross meant to carry the crossbeam that would be used in one's crucifixion.[104] The author of Luke transformed this command by adding the phrase "daily" (καθ' ἡμέραν), thus making clear to his audience that it was to be taken metaphorically (Luke 9:23). In Mark, the phrase may have a metaphorical dimension, but its force is primarily literal.[105] In v. 31 the Markan Jesus had simply predicted that the Son of Man would "be killed" (ἀποκτανθῆναι). Verse 34 shocks by simultaneously revealing (to the disciples and the audience, if not to the crowd) how the Son of Man will be killed, mentioning the word "cross" (σταυρός) for the first time in the Gospel, and demanding that the follower of Jesus be prepared to meet the same fate (cf. 15:21, 30, 32). The literal impact of the language here would have been strong because execution by crucifixion was well known in the history of Judea and a method used by the Romans in the cultural context of Mark, broadly speaking.[106] The language reflects at least the expectation of persecution, if not its actuality (cf. 13:9-11).[107]

■ **35** The saying in this verse was probably an independent one originally.[108] At that stage it was a proverbial wisdom saying, expressing a principle in personal terms,

100 John S. Kloppenborg, *Q Parallels: Synopsis, Critical Notes & Concordance* (Foundations and Facets; Sonoma, CA: Polebridge, 1988) 170; Robinson et al., *Critical Edition of Q*, 454–57. But see Neirynck, "Assessment," 283–84.

101 Fleddermann, *Mark and Q*, 135–45; cf. Neirynck, "Assessment," 282–84.

102 See the commentary on v. 33 above.

103 Swete, 182; cf. Heinrich Schlier, "ἀρνέομαι," TDNT 1 (1964) 469–71, esp. 471.

104 Cf. 15:21 and the commentary below.

105 Cf. Swete, 182. For reflections on how this passage might be read today, see Joanna Dewey, "'Let Them Renounce Themselves and Take Up Their Cross': A Feminist Reading of Mark 8.34 in Mark's Social and Narrative World," in Levine, *A Feminist Companion*, 23–36.

106 According to Josephus, Alexander Jannaeus crucified eight hundred Pharisees who had opposed his rule (*Bell.* 1.4.6 §§96–98; *Ant.* 13.14.2 §§380–81);

Schürer, *History*, 1:224. On the practice of crucifixion in antiquity, see Hengel, *Crucifixion*; also published as part two of idem, *The Cross of the Son of God* (London: SCM, 1986). The Greeks and Romans spoke of it as a "barbarian" practice, although they made use of it themselves (*Crucifixion*, 23).

107 Luise Schottroff has argued that the author understood the present time as "the beginning of the birth-pains" (13:8) ("Die Gegenwart in der Apokalyptik der synoptischen Evangelien," in David Hellholm, ed., *Apocalypticism in the Mediterranean World and the Near East: Proceedings of the International Colloquium on Apocalypticism* [Tübingen: Mohr Siebeck, 1983] 707–28, esp. 720).

108 Bultmann, *History*, 83. Bultmann concluded that the saying, without the christological expansion (see below), goes back to the historical Jesus (ibid., 105).

which belonged to the general category of sayings of the Lord.[109] Tannehill defined it as an antithetical aphorism.[110] If the saying ever had a purely proverbial form, it would have lacked the phrase "because of me and because of the good news" (ἕνεκεν ἐμοῦ καὶ τοῦ εὐαγγελίου).[111] This form of the saying is ambiguous in isolation. It is not clear whether the Greek word ψυχή should be understood to mean "life" or "soul." If it means "life," the saying is paradoxical if "life" is understood to mean one's physical life. This paradox could be resolved by understanding the proverb as a play on words, taking "life" sometimes as physical life and sometimes as eternal life or soul.[112] In the oral stage, the significance of the proverb would have been clear from its application or rhetorical force in a specific context.

This hypothetical proverb at some point would have received a christological expansion by the addition of the words "because of me" (ἕνεκεν ἐμοῦ).[113] This addition evokes a context of persecution and leads the audience to understand the saying as follows: For whoever wants to save his (physical) life will lose (eternal life); but whoever loses his (physical) life because of me will save it (that is, will save his soul or gain eternal life). This tendency was continued in the addition of "and the good news" (καὶ τοῦ εὐαγγελίου), either by Mark or at a pre-Markan stage.[114]

In the present context in Mark, the audience is led to interpret this saying in light of v. 34. Verse 35 advocates not wishing to save one's (physical) life. This is an illustration of what it means "to deny oneself." Similarly, "losing one's life because of (Jesus) and the good news"

is equivalent to "taking up one's cross" and following Jesus.

■ **36-37** Like vv. 34-35, vv. 36-37 were probably originally independent sayings.[115] Both are proverbial wisdom sayings attributed to Jesus that take the form of a question.[116] In combination, they take the form of a double-stranded *mashal*.[117]

As an isolated proverb, there is nothing particularly Christian about v. 36. It questions human striving for wealth and power by showing the insignificance of these pursuits in the face of death. The saying would be quite at home in Jewish wisdom literature.[118] The force of v. 37 is somewhat different; it evokes the thought that nothing is as valuable as life itself.[119]

These proverbs take on particular connotations, however, in their present context in Mark. Verse 36 continues the play on words begun in v. 35: "For how does it benefit a man to gain the whole world and yet suffer the loss of his life (or soul)?" The saying now expresses the idea that following Jesus, even if it means losing "the whole world," is the way to "life" or the way to save one's soul. Similarly, the word "life" (ψυχή) in v. 37 takes on the connotation of "soul." Physical life is less important than following Jesus.

■ **38** This is a prophetic saying that threatens those who are ashamed of Jesus and his words or sayings. When the Son of Man comes, he will likewise be ashamed of such people. Matthew has rewritten the saying thoroughly, so that the emphasis is on the coming of the Son of Man and his repaying each person according to his or her way of acting (Matt 16:27).[120] Luke follows Mark more closely,

---

109 Ibid., 69–72, 75. Bultmann describes it as a double-stranded *mashal* (ibid., 81). He also defines it as a prophetic saying and finds this judgment supported by its paradoxical character (ibid., 111). See also the discussion below.
110 Tannehill, *Sword*, 98.
111 Bultmann, *History*, 75.
112 Tannehill stresses that the saying "*intends* to be a paradox" (*Sword*, 99; emphasis original). Cf. Park on Matt 10:39 (*Mission Discourse*, 156).
113 Bultmann, *History*, 93, 151. This is probably the form that the saying had in Q; see Matt 10:39 and Robinson et al., *Critical Edition of Q*, 456. It is also the form found in Matt 16:25 and Luke 9:24, the parallels to Mark 8:35. The authors of Matthew and Luke omitted Mark's "and the good news" (καὶ τοῦ

εὐαγγελίου) either because they found it redundant or under the influence of the Q form of the saying.
114 Bultmann, *History*, 93, 111.
115 Ibid., 82–83. He doubts that either of these goes back to the historical Jesus (ibid., 102).
116 Ibid., 69–70, 72–73, 78–79.
117 Ibid., 81.
118 Ibid., 97.
119 The author of Luke omitted this saying, perhaps because he concluded that it was not sufficiently different from the previous saying to warrant inclusion; see Luke 9:25-26.
120 The Son of Man is clearly in the role of judge in this saying.

except that he omits the phrase "in this adulterous and sinful generation" (Luke 9:26).[121]

Matthew and Luke have a similar saying in non-Markan contexts, a prophetic saying that contains both a promise and a threat.[122] Those who acknowledge Jesus before human beings will be acknowledged by him (by the Son of Man, according to Luke) before Jesus' Father (before the angels of God, according to Luke). Those who deny him will be denied in the same way (Matt 10:32-33; Luke 12:8-9). As was the case with vv. 34-35, this double attestation makes it likely that a form of this saying was in Q.[123]

Perrin argued that v. 38 and the saying in Luke 12:8-9 are based on a saying of the historical Jesus. He reconstructed this saying as follows: "Everyone who acknowledges me before men, he will be acknowledged before the angels of God." He accepted this saying as authentic because of its Aramaic features and because this form could explain the rise of all the variants. In the earliest form of the saying, the passive voice of the verb in the apodosis is used as a circumlocution for divine activity. In the course of transmission, an increasing christological interest led to the ascription of God's activity to Jesus. This occurred in two ways. In one group of variants, "I" was used for the subject of the action, the speaker being Jesus. In another group, "the Son of Man" was used.[124]

Philipp Vielhauer argued that the saying in Luke 12:8-9 probably does not go back to the historical Jesus, because it presupposes a forensic situation, namely, a court setting in which the followers of Jesus were questioned about their relationship to him. Such an occasion was more likely to arise after Jesus' death than before.[125]

The same observation applies to Perrin's reconstruction of the earliest form of the saying, since ὁμολογέω is a term commonly used of forensic testimony.[126] Even if the use of the term includes acknowledging Jesus in non-forensic situations, such usage is more understandable if forensic interrogation were a real possibility. The saying thus probably arose in a post-Easter situation in which the earthly courts faced by the followers of Jesus are contrasted with the heavenly court in which God passes judgment. When God is portrayed as the judge, the role of Jesus is typically that of the advocate (παράκλητος) of his faithful followers.[127] Jesus himself, however, was sometimes envisioned as judge (as God's agent), as well as advocate.[128] Jesus' role as judge is clear in Matt 16:27.[129]

Bultmann argued that the Q form and the Markan saying distinguish between Jesus and the Son of Man. He argued further that the historical Jesus spoke about an apocalyptic, heavenly Son of Man, but did not identify himself with that figure.[130] If Bultmann is right on this point, as he may well be, Perrin's reconstruction of a form of the saying that does not include an allusion to the "Son of Man" is unnecessary. The earliest form spoke about the Son of Man of Dan 7:13, who was not identical with Jesus. Later, when Jesus was identified with the Son of Man, Mark and Luke (and probably Q) expressed the identification by means of the context, whereas Matthew used the personal pronoun to make the point. Luke 12:9 does not mention the Son of Man in order to avoid repetition.[131]

The Markan form of the saying does not evoke a forensic setting as clearly as the Q form.[132] In the first part of the saying, the verb "to be ashamed of" (ἐπαισχύνομαι) has the social sense of being ashamed about

---

121 On this phrase, see below.

122 Mark may present the saying in the form of a threat alone because the saying in 9:1 expresses the corresponding promise; so Perrin, *Redaction Criticism*, 47.

123 Robinson et al., *Critical Edition of Q*, 304–7; the Q-saying is probably better represented by Luke than by Matthew.

124 Perrin, *Rediscovering*, 185–91; see also idem, *Pilgrimage*, 35–36.

125 Vielhauer, "Gottesreich und Menschensohn," 76–79.

126 Otto Michel, "ὁμολογέω κτλ.," *TDNT* 5 (1967) 200–202.

127 Jarl Fossum, "Jewish-Christian Christology and Jewish Mysticism," *VC* 37 (1983) 260–87, esp. 275.

128 With regard to those who deny Jesus, he takes the role of accuser; cf. Lührmann, 153.

129 Jesus' role in Matt 10:32-33 and Luke 12:8-9 is ambiguous; it could be understood either as advocate or as judge.

130 Bultmann, *History*, 112, 128.

131 On the latter point, cf. Bultmann, *History*, 112. On the whole question, see "Excursus: The Son of Man Tradition" in the commentary on 2:10 above.

132 The Q form is attested by Luke 12:8-9 as noted above.

being associated with a dubious person or cause.[133] Such shame implies failing to proclaim the good news and probably also denying Jesus when interrogated.[134] Ernst Käsemann famously argued that the correspondence between humans being ashamed of Jesus and the Son of Man being ashamed of them indicates that the saying belongs to the form-critical category "sentences of holy law."[135] The idea of the punishment fitting the crime and the literary device of parallelism are not confined, however, to legal sayings.[136] In the second part of the saying, the Son of Man's being ashamed of such people suggests that he will refuse to associate with them. Such rejection means that they will not be included when the Son of Man sends his angels to gather the elect (13:27).

The phrase "in this adulterous and sinful generation" (ἐν τῇ γενεᾷ ταύτῃ τῇ μοιχαλίδι καὶ ἁμαρτωλῷ) does not occur in any of the other variants of this saying. Since the criticism of "this generation" was so widespread in early Christian tradition, this distinctiveness does not necessarily imply Markan editorial work.[137] The phrase "evil and adulterous generation" (γενεὰ πονηρὰ καὶ μοιχαλίς) occurs in Matt 12:39 and 16:4 in condemnation of those who seek a sign. The epithet "adulterous" no doubt comes from the prophetic image of the relationship between God and the people of Israel as a marriage; when the people worship other gods, they are accused of "adultery."[138] The epithet "sinful"

(ἁμαρτωλός) may simply be a synonym for "evil" (πονηρός).[139] "This adulterous and sinful generation" in v. 38, however, does not mean Israel in general or all Jews living at the time of Jesus. It refers to those living at the time of Jesus who reject his person and his message.[140] In its present Markan context, the phrase recalls Jesus' refusal to give a sign to "this generation" in 8:12.[141]

In its present context in Mark, the saying takes on new connotations. "Being ashamed" of Jesus is the opposite of "denying oneself" and "taking up one's cross and following" him (v. 34). Those who want "to save their lives" (v. 35) will find that the Son of Man is ashamed of them when he comes. Those who "are ashamed of the words" of Jesus are those who avoid losing their lives for the sake of "the gospel."[142] The context suggests that "this generation" is depicted as evil, not only for its rejection of Jesus and his words, but also because it persecutes his followers in the time of the author. The believers are placed in contrast with "this generation." Because they reject its values and advocate values that it rejects, the text implies an antipathy between them. The believers must, therefore, be prepared to be subjected to various trials. This tension and persecution are expected to continue until the return of the Son of Man.[143]

There is also a striking contrast between the suffering Son of Man portrayed in v. 31 and the Son of Man who will return "in the glory of his Father with the holy

---

133 Rudolf Bultmann, "αἰσχύνω κτλ.," *TDNT* 1 (1964) 189–91, esp. 190.

134 Paul's declaration that he is not ashamed of the gospel implies that he is willing to proclaim and explicate it (Rom 1:16). Mark advocates the proclamation of the good news on the part of Jesus' followers; see the commentary on 4:21-22, 24-25 above.

135 Ernst Käsemann, "Sätze heiligen Rechtes im Neuen Testament," *NTS* 1 (1954–55) 248–60; ET "Sentences of Holy Law in the New Testament," in idem, *New Testament Questions of Today* (London: SCM; Philadelphia: Fortress, 1969) 66–81, esp. 77.

136 Perrin redefined Käsemann's category as "eschatological judgment pronouncements" (*Pilgrimage*, 62–63).Tannehill defines it as "parenetic warning or prophetic threat" (*Sword*, 113).

137 For a study of this tradition as a whole, see Evald Lövestam, *Jesus and 'this Generation': A New Testament Study* (CB 25; Stockholm: Almqvist & Wiksell International, 1995); on the pre-Markan character of the phrase, see ibid., 58 n. 189.

138 Ibid., 36.

139 But see Isa 1:4 LXX; Swete, 185.

140 Lövestam, *Jesus and 'this Generation'*, 19. Note that in 1QpHab 2:3-10, the phrase הדור האחרון ("the last generation") probably refers to all the people of Israel living at a certain time, but the emphasis is on "the trait[ors to] the new [covenant]," "[. . . the trai]tors at the latter days," and "the ruthless [ones of the cove]nant." Text and trans. from Maurya P. Horgan, "Habakkuk Pesher," in Charlesworth, *Dead Sea Scrolls*, 6B:162–63; cf. also 1QpHab 7:2, where the phrase is interpreted in terms of both those who will be rewarded (7:3-14) and those who will be punished (7:14-16).

141 See the commentary on 8:11-13 above.

142 This suggests that "gospel" here refers to the gospel that Jesus proclaimed, not the gospel that is proclaimed about him (see the commentary on 1:14-15 above). On the link between "words" or "sayings" in v. 38 and "gospel" in v. 35, cf. Lührmann, 152–53.

143 Cf. Lövestam, *Jesus and 'this Generation'*, 57–59, 86

angels" in v. 38. The description of God as the Father of the Son of Man in v. 38 implies that he is also Son of God.[144] The equivalence of "Son of Man" and "Son of God" in v. 38 is analogous to the implied equivalence of "messiah" and "Son of Man" in vv. 29-31.[145]

■ **9:1** This saying is set off from the preceding sayings by the introductory phrase "And he said to them" (καὶ ἔλεγεν αὐτοῖς). Nevertheless, it belongs with the preceding sayings rather than with the following account of the transfiguration. The saying of 9:1 is connected thematically with the preceding material. The temporal change marked in 9:2, "And after six days" (καὶ μετὰ ἡμέρας ἕξ), clearly shows that a new unit begins at that point.[146] The current division of chapters, which associates 9:1 with the transfiguration, is probably due to the exegetical tradition that the saying is at least partially fulfilled in the latter event.[147] This interpretation, however, overlooks the imminent expectation of Mark.[148]

Some commentators have concluded that 9:1 preserves a saying of the historical Jesus.[149] In contrast, Bultmann argued that this was originally an isolated saying, an apocalyptic prediction, that served to console the

community because of the delay of the *parousia*. The consolation consisted in the thought that at least some would live to see it.[150] Perrin argued that Mark composed 9:1 using the saying of 13:30 as a model. He concluded that 13:30 was part of the Jewish Christian apocalyptic source that the evangelist used in composing chap. 13.[151] But it is unlikely that the author of Mark used such a source in composing chap. 13.[152] The saying of 13:30 is context-bound, and it is difficult to construe it as an independent saying.[153] It thus seems likely that 13:30 is a Markan composition.[154] In that case, 13:30 may have been composed on the model of 9:1 rather than vice versa.

Perrin's arguments in support of his conclusion that 9:1 is a Markan composition are (1) Mark uses verbs of "seeing" in connection with "the *parousia*" (the manifestation of the kingdom of God and the visible return of the Son of Man), whereas Matthew and Luke have this usage only in dependence on Mark; (2) Mark is distinctive in using the terms "glory" (δόξα) and "power" (δύναμις) in connection with the *parousia*, especially in combination.[155] These arguments are not compelling.

and n. 323, 96. He argues that "this generation" is expected to last until the return of the Son of Man (ibid., 56).

144 Ibid., 153.

145 See the commentary on vv. 30-31 above.

146 Cook takes 8:34—9:1 as a unit (*Structure*, 226).

147 Cf. Taylor, 385. For a history of the interpretation of 9:1 from the early church to 1976, see Martin Künzi, *Das Naherwartungslogion Markus 9,1 par: Geschichte seiner Auslegung* (BGBE 21; Tübingen: Mohr Siebeck, 1977).

148 Klostermann argued correctly that the transfiguration should not be interpreted as the fulfillment of the prophecy of 9:1 (86). Bruce D. Chilton's argument to the contrary is not persuasive ("The Transfiguration: Dominical Assurance and Apostolic Vision," *NTS* 27 [1980] 115–24, esp. 120). C. H. Dodd argued that the coming of the kingdom of God "with power" referred to the resurrection of Jesus, Pentecost, and the era of the church on earth; see the summary and criticism of this position by Norman Perrin, *The Kingdom of God in the Teaching of Jesus* (NTL; Philadelphia: Westminster, 1963) 67–68. Perrin himself argued credibly that the coming of the kingdom of God with power is the same event as the coming of the Son of Man, depicted with different imagery (ibid., 84–85).

149 E.g., Taylor, 385–86; Pesch, 2:66–67; Perrin, *Kingdom of God*, 188 (he changed his position later; see below); Chilton, "Transfiguration," 124.

150 Bultmann, *History*, 121.

151 Perrin, *Rediscovering*, 19–20, 199–201; idem, *Redaction Criticism*, 49–50. Pesch (2:311) also attributed 13:30 to a pre-Markan "apocalypse," but left open (unlike Perrin in his work after *Kingdom of God*) the possibility that it might be a saying of the historical Jesus.

152 Yarbro Collins, *Beginning of the Gospel*, 73–91; see also the commentary on chap. 13 below.

153 Perrin, *Redaction Criticism*, 49–50; Pesch, 2:308.

154 Perrin supports his argument that 13:30 is pre-Markan by noting that this is the only place where μέχρις οὗ ("until") is used in Mark; elsewhere ἕως ("until") is used (*Rediscovering*, 199, 201). But ἕως ("until") is also used in 13:19, which is normally attributed to the source (by those who accept the theory that Mark used a source in chap. 13); see Brandenburger, *Markus 13 und die Apokalyptik*, 166–67. Furthermore, Luke also uses μέχρι ("until") only once and ἕως ("until") often. Nevertheless, it is likely that ἕως ("until") in a Q-saying was changed by the author of Luke to μέχρι ("until") in Luke 16:16; see Robinson et al., *Critical Edition of Q*, 464.

155 Perrin, *Redaction Criticism*, 48–49.

They do not exclude the possibility that 9:1 is, in part at least, a traditional saying that has influenced Mark's usage elsewhere in the Gospel.

Perrin is right, however, in stressing the way in which the saying combines Jewish apocalyptic ideas with traditions about the kingdom of God that are typical of the Jesus-tradition.[156] A passage in 2 Esdras is quite similar to 9:1 in content:

> And it shall come to pass that whoever remains after all that I have foretold to you shall himself be saved and shall see my salvation and the end of my world. And they shall see the men who were taken up, who from their birth have not tasted death. (2 Esdr 6:25-26)[157]

The idea of the kingdom of God "coming," as Perrin has shown, is both typical of and distinctive to the Jesus-tradition.[158]

This is the second occurrence in Mark of the phrase "Amen (truly) I say to you" ('Αμὴν λέγω ὑμῖν).[159] Its use here is solemn, and it affirms the veracity of the following saying.

Although the verb "taste" is used metaphorically in classical and Hellenistic Greek, the phrase "experience death" (γεύομαι θανάτου, lit., "taste death") is not typical. The verb is also used metaphorically in the LXX, but the phrase "taste death" does not occur. It does occur in 2 Esdr 6:26 (see the citation above), and in rabbinic literature.[160]

The perfect participle "has come" (ἐληλυθυῖαν, lit., "having come") implies that the kingdom of God will arrive fully, that is, be fully manifested, before all those listening to the Markan Jesus have died.[161] This arrival is the next stage after the "drawing near" of the kingdom in the activity of the earthly Jesus.[162] The idea that the kingdom will come "with power" or "powerfully" (ἐν δυνάμει) is similar to the depiction of the coming of the Son of Man "with great power and glory" (μετὰ δυνάμεως πολλῆς καὶ δόξης) in 13:26.[163] Thus 9:1 should be interpreted as referring to the coming of the Son of Man. It is at that time that the kingdom of God will be manifested. The claim that some who heard Jesus (either those who heard the historical Jesus or those who heard him as members of the audience of Mark) would live until the coming of the Son of Man is evidence of the imminent expectation of that event on the part of the author of Mark.[164]

Together, 8:38 and 9:1 make a fitting conclusion to this speech of Jesus. The former expresses a threat to those who are ashamed of Jesus and his words and thus conform to "this adulterous and sinful generation." The latter expresses a promise to those who deny themselves, take up their crosses, and follow Jesus loyally. The coming of the kingdom with power will vindicate them before those who persecuted them and will console them after their trials. This prophetic-apocalyptic conclusion provides a powerful incentive to faithful discipleship.

---

156 Ibid., 50–51.

157 Trans. from Stone, *Fourth Ezra*, 163; passage cited by Perrin, *Redaction Criticism*, 50.

158 Perrin, *Rediscovering*, 58–60.

159 See the commentary on 3:28 above.

160 Str-B 1:751–52. The motif is used without the imminent eschatology in *Gos. Thom.* 1 (P. Oxy. 654.1). Luke's omission of "with power" may also be evidence of a tendency to remove the imminent eschatological expectation of the saying.

161 On the Semitic syntax of the conditional clauses in 9:1 and 13:30, see Klaus Beyer, *Semitische Syntax im Neuen Testament*, vol. 1: *Satzlehre, Teil 1* (2nd rev. ed.; StUNT 1; Göttingen: Vandenhoeck & Ruprecht, 1968) 132–33 n. 1.

162 See the commentary on 1:15 above.

163 According to 8:38, the Son of Man will come "in (or with) the glory of his Father" (ἐν τῇ δόξῃ τοῦ πατρὸς αὐτοῦ). Thus 8:38 and 9:1 together combine the motifs of "power" and "glory."

164 Cf. the implication of 8:38 that the generation living in the time of Jesus would experience the coming of the Son of Man. See the commentary on v. 38 above.

9:2-8 The Transfiguration

2/	**And after six days, Jesus took Peter** a **and James and John and led them up on a high mountain alone by themselves. And[a] he was transfigured in their presence, 3/ and his clothes became very white and they shone, as no cloth-handler on earth could whiten them. 4/ And Elijah with Moses appeared to them and they were conversing with Jesus. 5/ And Peter answered Jesus, "Rabbi, it is good that we are here; and let us make three tents, one for you and one for Moses and one for Elijah. 6/ For he did not know how he should respond, for they were terrified. 7/ And a cloud arose, overshadowing them, and a voice arose from the cloud, "This is my beloved son; listen to him." 8/ And suddenly, when they looked around, they no longer saw anyone, but[b] only Jesus with them.**

a $\mathfrak{p}^{45}$ W f^{13} (565) pc have the additional words $\dot{\epsilon}\nu\ \tau\hat{\wp}$ $\pi\rho\sigma\epsilon\dot{\nu}\chi\epsilon\sigma\vartheta\alpha\iota\ \alpha\dot{\nu}\tau\sigma\dot{\nu}\varsigma$ ("while they were praying"); Θ 28 pc read $\dot{\epsilon}\nu\ \tau\hat{\wp}\ \pi\rho\sigma\epsilon\dot{\nu}\chi\epsilon\sigma\vartheta\alpha\iota\ \alpha\dot{\nu}\tau\dot{\sigma}\nu$ ("while he was praying"). These closely related readings are probably due to the influence of the parallel in Luke 9:29, which is identical to the latter.

b $\aleph$ B D N et al. read $\epsilon\iota\ \mu\dot{\eta}$ ("except") instead of $\dot{\alpha}\lambda\lambda\dot{\alpha}$ ("but"), the reading of A C L W et al. The conjunction $\dot{\alpha}\lambda\lambda\dot{\alpha}$ ("but") sometimes has the sense "except" in vernacular idiom, but this usage was not common (Moulton, 241–42). Its oddity may have given rise to the variant with $\epsilon\iota\ \mu\dot{\eta}$ ("except") (Moulton-Turner, 4:13; Taylor, ad loc.).

Literary Unity of 9:2-29

The transfiguration; the conversation about resurrection, Elijah, and the Son of Man; and the exorcism of the epileptic young man are linked together topographically: on the mountain, on the way down from the mountain, and at the foot of the mountain. In all three units, disciples play an important role: Peter, James, and John in the first two, and the larger group in the exorcism. The second two accounts concern the instruction of the disciples, and the first climaxes with an imperative addressed to them (v. 7). The middle unit, like 8:27–9:1, focuses on the suffering of the Son of Man. Ernst Lohmeyer eloquently pointed out that in this section is depicted all that needs to be said about Jesus: divine glory, deadly suffering, and merciful help in the darkness of human life.[1]

History of the Tradition

Although a number of scholars had noted the similarities between the transfiguration and resurrection-appearance stories, Julius Wellhausen was the first to suggest that this account was originally a description of an appearance of the resurrected Jesus.[2] Wellhausen argued that the identity of the mountain was unknown to the composer of the account, but that it was surely the same one mentioned in Matt 28:16, where the risen Jesus appeared to the Eleven. He thus suggested that the account was originally about an appearance of the Crucified One to the three disciples.[3] Alfred Loisy found the suggestion somewhat credible but emphasized the connection with the baptismal story in the present Markan context.[4] Wilhelm Bousset noted the distinctive use of the expression "he was transfigured" or "he was transformed" ($\mu\epsilon\tau\epsilon\mu\rho\rho\phi\dot{\omega}\vartheta\eta$) in v. 2 and concluded that the description of Jesus' clothing signifies a superearthly being. He raised the question, without answering it, whether the source of the account is a theophany of three divine beings on a high mountain and whether the building of the "tents" or "huts" reflects the idea of creating a shrine for the appearing deity. Toward the end of

1   Lohmeyer, 172–73.
2   Joseph Blinzler, *Die neutestamentlichen Berichte über die Verklärung Jesu* (NTAbh 17.4; Münster: Aschendorff, 1937) 116 n. 90; Heinrich Baltensweiler, *Die*

Verklärung Jesu: Historisches Ereignis und synoptische Berichte (AThANT 33; Zurich: Zwingli, 1959) 91.
3   Wellhausen, 69, 71. He also interpreted 2 Pet 1:16-18 as an allusion to such an appearance (ibid., 71).

a long footnote, however, he mentioned the possibility that the account was based on an appearance of the risen Jesus.[5] Bultmann defined the passage in its present form as a legend but took it as established that it was originally a resurrection story.[6]

Theodore J. Weeden argued that Mark took up a narrative of the first resurrection appearance of Jesus, which was to Peter, reshaped it into a transfiguration narrative, and predated it by placing it in the life of the earthly Jesus. He agreed with some critics of the resurrection story hypothesis that the transfiguration-story, in its Markan context, is a proleptic experience of the *parousia*. He concluded that the pre-Markan narrative was a resurrection story that belonged to the *theios-anēr* (divine man) tradition of Mark's opponents. By placing it in the period of the public activity of Jesus, Mark undermined their proclamation of a glorious, pneumatic type of Christology and discipleship. In Mark's view, the glorification of Jesus was an event still in the future (the *parousia*).[7]

The hypothesis that the account of the transfiguration was originally a resurrection story is unwarranted.[8] But the depiction of Jesus in this account is similar to the appearance of human beings who have been glorified after death.[9] In a Greek fragment of the *Apocalypse of Peter*, the twelve disciples ask to see one of the departed righteous brethren in order to see in what form they are. An epiphany follows:

And as we prayed, suddenly there appeared *two men*, standing before the Lord, on whom we were not able to look. For there went forth from their *countenance a ray, as of the sun*, and their *raiment was shining, such as the eye of man never* <saw. For> no mouth can describe nor <heart conceive> the glory with which they were clad nor the beauty of their countenance. And when we saw them we were astonished, for their bodies were whiter than any snow and redder than any rose (Καὶ εὐχομένων ἡμῶν ἄφ<νω> φ<αίν>ονται δύο ἄνδρες ἑστῶτες ἔμπροσθε τοῦ κυρίου πρὸς ο<ὓς> οὐκ ἐδυνήθημεν ἀντιβλέψαι· ἐξήρχετο γὰρ ἀπὸ τῆς ὄψεως αὐτῶν ἀκτὶν ὡς ἡλίου καὶ φωτεινὸν ἦν αὐ<τῶν τὸ> ἔνδυμα ὁποῖον οὐδέποτε ὀφθαλμὸς ἀνθρώπ<ου εἶδεν· οὐδὲ γὰ>ρ στόμα δύναται ἐξηγήσασθαι, ἢ καρ<δία ἐπινοῆσα>ι τὴν δόξαν ἣν ἐνεδέδυντο καὶ τὸ κάλ<λος τῆς ὄ>ψεως αὐτῶν. οὓς ἰδόντες ἐθαμβώθημεν· τὰ μὲν γὰρ σώματα αὐτῶν ἦν λευκότερα πάσης χιόνος καὶ ἐρυθρότερα παντὸς ῥόδου).[10]

Bauckham has argued against this hypothesis (*Jude, 2 Peter*, 210–11).

4   Loisy, 259–60.

5   Wilhelm Bousset, *Kyrios Christos: Geschichte des Christusglaubens von den Anfängen des Christentums bis Irenaeus* (4th ed.; Göttingen: Vandenhoeck & Ruprecht, 1935; reprint of 2nd rev. ed., 1921) 61 and n. 2; cf. 268 n. 2; ET *Kyrios Christos: A History of the Belief in Christ from the Beginnings of Christianity to Irenaeus* (from 5th Germ. ed.; Nashville: Abingdon, 1970) 102 and n. 86; cf. 342 n. 377.

6   Bultmann, *History*, 259; Klostermann, 86, and many other scholars. For a list up to 1976, see Robert H. Stein, "Is the Transfiguration (Mark 9:2-8) a Misplaced Resurrection-Account?" *JBL* 95 (1976) 79–96.

7   Theodore J. Weeden, *Mark–Traditions in Conflict* (Philadelphia: Fortress, 1971) 118–37. The main proponent of the *parousia* interpretation is G. H. Boobyer, *St. Mark and the Transfiguration Story* (Edinburgh: T & T Clark, 1942) 48–87; see the commentary on v. 7 below.

8   See the systematic refutation by Stein, "Misplaced Resurrection-Account?" 79–96, and the brief but telling criticisms of John E. Alsup, *The Post-Resurrection Appearance Stories of the Gospel Tradition* (CThM A.5; Stuttgart: Calwer, 1975) 141–44. Brent Nongbri has argued plausibly, however, that the account of the transfiguration has been influenced by resurrection stories ("Mark 9:2-8: Transfiguring the Resurrection," unpublished paper, 2001).

9   On the transformation of the individual human being into a glorious or godlike state in Jewish apocalyptic texts and in texts relating to the Hellenistic mystery cults, respectively, see Johannes Behm, "μεταμορφόω," *TDNT* 4 (1967) 755–59, esp. 757. Good examples of the former are *2 Bar.* 51:10 and *2 Esdr* 7:97, referred to by Lohmeyer (174 n. 7); see the trans. of the former passage in *AOT*, 871. The idea is already present in Dan 12:3; it reappears in 2 Cor 3:18; 1 John 3:2. On the relation between v. 3 and 2 Cor 3:18, see Ernst Lohmeyer, "Die Verklärung Jesu nach dem Markus-Evangelium," *ZNW* 21 (1922) 185–215, esp. 206.

10   *Apoc. Pet.* (Greek fragment from Akhmim 6–8); text from Erwin Preuschen, ed., *Antilegomena: Die Reste der außerkanonischen Evangelien und urchristlichen Überlieferungen* (2nd rev. ed.; Gieszen [= Giessen]: Töpelmann, 1905) 84; trans. by C. Detlef G. Müller,

Even if this account is dependent on one or more of the Synoptic Gospels, it shows that a description like that of the transfigured Jesus could be associated with the glorified body of a deceased righteous person.

Although the resurrected Jesus is not depicted as luminous or in white clothing in the canonical and some extracanonical Gospels, the angels associated with his resurrection are so described.[11] For example, in the *Gospel of Peter*, the angels who accompany him as he rises from the dead have come down from heaven "in great brightness" (πολὺ φέγγος ἔχοντες), and the angel who announces the resurrection is clothed "with a brightly shining robe" (περιβεβλημένος στολὴν λαμπροτάτην) (*Gos. Pet.* 9 [36]; 13 [55]).[12] The Coptic-Gnostic *Pistis Sophia* describes the final (postresurrection) ascension of Jesus by means of "a great power (δύναμις) of light,

gleaming very bright, and the light that was in it was beyond measure" (2–3).[13] James M. Robinson has pointed out that in Gnostic texts, cast normally in the framework of resurrection appearances, a luminous apparition comparable to the transfiguration is the rule.[14] Often these appearances of the resurrected one in light take place on a mountain.[15] It is not clear, however, whether these later texts preserve an old Christian tradition or represent a later development on this point. In any case, radiance and shining garments are typical features of Greek and Roman epiphanies.[16]

Genre

The account of the transfiguration evokes the Old Testament genre of the theophany[17] and especially the

---

"Apocalypse of Peter," in *NTApoc*, 2:634; emphasis original. Cited by Bultmann, *History*, 260.

11 The motif of white or shining clothing is characteristic of heavenly beings in Second Temple Jewish and early Christian texts; e.g., Dan 7:9; Mark 16:5; Matt 28:3; Luke 24:4; John 20:12; Acts 1:10; Rev 4:4; 15:6; 19:14.

12 Text from M. G. Mara, *Évangile de Pierre* (SC 201; Paris: Cerf, 1973) 56, 64; trans. by Christian Maurer, "The Gospel of Peter," in *NTApoc*, 2:224–25. See also Matt 28:2-3; Luke 24:4.

13 Trans. by Henri-Charles Puech and Beate Blatz, "The Pistis Sophia," in *NTApoc*, 1:363–64. Bousset argued that the opening scene of the *Pistis Sophia* was dependent on the account of the transfiguration of Jesus (*Kyrios Christos*, 61–62 n. 2, 268 n. 2).

14 Robinson, *Problem of History*, 29–30. In addition to *Pistis Sophia* 2-3, he mentions the *Letter of Peter to Philip* (NH VIII, 2) 134:10; the *Ap. Jas.* (NH I, 2) 14:25-26, 35-36; *Ap. John* (NH II, 1) 1:33; 2:1-7; *Soph. Jes. Chr.* (NH III, 4) 91:13; 93:8-12; *Thom. Cont.* (NH II, 7) 139:20-24; 141:25-30.

15 Robinson, *Problem of History*, 30.

16 Frederick E. Brenk, "Greek Epiphanies and Paul on the Road to Damascus," in Ugo Bianchi, ed., *The Notion of "Religion" in Comparative Research: Selected Proceedings of the XVIth Congress of the International Association for the History of Religions* (Rome: "L'Erma" di Bretschneider, 1994) 415–24, esp. 420.

17 Theodore Hiebert, "Theophany in the OT," *ABD* 6:505–11; Jörg Jeremias, *Theophanie: Die Geschichte einer alttestamentlichen Gattung* (WMANT 10; Neukirchen-Vluyn: Neukirchener Verlag, 1965). Hans-Peter Müller argued that the transfiguration is

an adapted theophany report ("Die Verklärung Jesu: Eine motivgeschichtliche Studie," *ZNW* 51 [1960] 56–64, esp. 62). On Mark 9:2-8 as an epiphany, see Dibelius, *From Tradition to Gospel*, 43, 230, 275–76; Schmid, 170; Foster R. McCurley, Jr., "'And after Six Days' (Mk. 9:2): A Semitic Literary Device," *JBL* 93 (1974) 67–81, esp. 81; John Paul Heil, *The Transfiguration of Jesus: Narrative Meaning and Function of Mark 9:2-8, Matt 17:1-8 and Luke 9:28-36* (AnBib 144; Rome: Editrice Pontificio Istituto Biblico, 2000) 35–73; Heil defines the transfiguration as a "pivotal mandatory epiphany," a genre he defines and discusses only within biblical, Jewish, and early Christian tradition. Other scholars have argued that it is an apocalyptic vision: Maurice Sabbe, "La rédaction du récit de la transfiguration," in Edouard Massaux, ed., *La venue du messie: Messianisme et Eschatologie* (RechBib 6; Bruges: Desclée de Brouwer; Leuven: Leuven University Press, 1962) 65–100, esp. 67, 91; Howard Clark Kee, "The Transfiguration in Mark: Epiphany or Apocalyptic Vision?" in John Reumann, ed., *Understanding the Sacred Text: Essays in Honor of Morton S. Enslin on the Hebrew Bible and Christian Beginnings* (Valley Forge, PA: Judson, 1972) 135–52; William Richard Stegner, "The Use of Scripture in Two Narratives of Early Jewish Christianity (Matthew 4.1-11; Mark 9.2-8)," in Craig A. Evans and James A. Sanders, eds., *Early Christian Interpretation of the Scriptures of Israel: Investigations and Proposals* (JSNTSup 148; SSEJC 5; Sheffield: Sheffield Academic Press, 1997) 98–120. For surveys of generic proposals, see Dwyer, *Wonder*, 139–40; Heil, *Transfiguration*, 22–23.

Hellenistic and Roman genres of epiphany and metamorphosis.[18] The affinity with biblical theophany is especially apparent in comparison with the account of the theophany on Mount Sinai:

> And Moses and Joshua went up on the mountain, and the cloud covered the mountain. And the glory of God came down upon Mount Sinai, and the cloud covered it for six days; and the Lord called Moses on the seventh day from the midst of the cloud (καὶ ἀνέβη Μωυσῆς καὶ Ἰησοῦς εἰς τὸ ὄρος, καὶ ἐκάλυψεν ἡ νεφέλη τὸ ὄρος. καὶ κατέβη ἡ δόξα τοῦ θεοῦ ἐπὶ τὸ ὄρος τὸ Σινα, καὶ ἐκάλυψεν αὐτὸ ἡ νεφέλη ἓξ ἡμέρας· καὶ ἐκάλεσεν κύριος τὸν Μωυσῆν τῇ ἡμέρᾳ τῇ ἑβδόμῃ ἐκ μέσου τῆς νεφέλης). (Exod 24:15-16 LXX)

Although it is used differently, both texts have the period of "six days"; both have a cloud on a mountain signifying the presence of God; both have the presence of Moses on the mountain; and both report speech of God on the mountain.[19]

In Exodus, the speech of God is reported in 25:1–31:18. This speech concerns the construction of the "tent" or "tabernacle" in the wilderness, including its furniture and rituals:

> And you shall make a sanctuary for me, and I will appear to you (in it); and you shall make (it) for me in accordance with all the things that I show you on the mountain, the model of the tent and the model of all of its furnishings; so shall you make (it) (καὶ ποιήσεις μοι ἁγίασμα, καὶ ὀφθήσομαι ἐν ὑμῖν· καὶ ποιήσεις μοι κατὰ πάντα, ὅσα ἐγώ σοι δεικνύω ἐν τῷ ὄρει, τὸ παράδειγμα τῆς σκηνῆς καὶ τὸ παράδειγμα πάντων τῶν σκευῶν αὐτῆς· οὕτω ποιήσεις). (Exod 25:8-9 LXX)

The connection with the text from Exodus, however, does not explain the statement in v. 2 that Jesus was transfigured. A later passage in Exodus says that, when Moses came down from Mount Sinai, his face "shone" or "had been glorified" because he had been talking with God.[20] One could argue that, analogously, Jesus was transfigured because he was talking with two heavenly beings, the glorified Elijah and Moses. The text, however, seems to imply that Jesus' transfigured state is part of the revelation, rather than a result of it.

---

18 Elpidius Pax, *ΕΠΙΦΑΝΕΙΑ: Ein religionsgeschichtlicher Beitrag zur biblischen Theologie* (MThS.H 10; Munich: Karl Zink, 1955); Johannes Behm, "μορφή κτλ.," *TDNT* 4 (1967) 742–59, esp. 746, 756; Martin Dibelius and Hans Conzelmann, *The Pastoral Epistles: A Commentary on the Pastoral Epistles* (Hermeneia; Philadelphia: Fortress, 1972), excursus "'Epiphany' in the Pastoral Epistles" (p. 104); Versnel, "What Did Ancient Man See When He Saw a God?" 42–55; Marco Frenschkowski, *Offenbarung und Epiphanie* (2 vols.; WUNT 2.79–80; Tübingen: Mohr Siebeck, 1995, 1997); Samuel Vollenweider, "Die Metamorphose des Gottessohns: Zum epiphanialen Motivfeld in Phil 2,6-8," in Ulrich Mell and Ulrich B. Müller, eds., *Das Urchristentum in seiner literarischen Geschichte: Festschrift für Jürgen Becker* (BZNW 100; Berlin/New York: de Gruyter, 1999) 107–31; Dieter Zeller, "Die Menschwerdung des Sohnes Gottes im Neuen Testament und die antike Religionsgeschichte," in idem, ed., *Menschwerdung Gottes–Vergöttlichung von Menschen* (NTOA 7; Fribourg: Universitätsverlag; Göttingen: Vandenhoeck & Ruprecht, 1988) 141–76; idem, "La Metamorphose de Jésus comme épiphanie (Mc 9,2-8)," in Alain Marchadour, ed., *L'Évangile Exploré: Mélanges offerts à*

Simon Légasse à l'occasion de ses soixante-dix ans (LD 166; Paris: Cerf, 1996) 167–86; idem, "Bedeutung und religionsgeschichtlicher Hintergrund der Verwandlung Jesu (Markus 9:2-8)," in Bruce D. Chilton and Craig A. Evans, eds., *Authenticating the Activities of Jesus* (NTTS 28.2; Leiden/Boston: Brill, 1999) 303–21; idem, "New Testament Christology in Its Hellenistic Reception," *NTS* 47 (2001) 312–33; Candida R. Moss, "The Transfiguration: An Exercise in Markan Accommodation," *BI* 12 (2004) 69–89.

19 The MT states that Moses set out with Joshua, his assistant, but only Moses is said to go up on the mountain of God; Aaron, Hur, and the elders remain even further behind (vv. 13-14). In contrast, the LXX states that Joshua went up on the mountain with Moses (v. 15). The name "Joshua" is the same name as "Jesus" in Greek (Ἰησοῦς). This seems to be another point of contact between the two texts.

20 δεδόξασται ἡ ὄψις τοῦ χρώματος τοῦ προσώπου αὐτοῦ ἐν τῷ λαλεῖν αὐτὸν αὐτῷ (Exod 34:29 LXX).

The statement that Jesus was "transfigured" or "transformed" (μετεμορφώθη) evokes the Greek idea that gods sometimes walked the earth in human form.[21] In the *Iliad*, Apollo takes on the appearance of Lycaon, son of Priam, and the sound of his voice, in order to stir Aeneas up to do battle with Achilles (20.81–82). Hera then proposes that other gods stand by Achilles lest he become discouraged when he sees the strength of Apollo coming against him. She ends her speech by saying "for hard are the gods to look upon when they appear in their own forms" (20.131).[22] In the *Odyssey*, when Odysseus is entering Nausicaa's city, Athena meets him "in the guise of a young maiden carrying a pitcher" (7.20).[23] When Odysseus landed on Ithaca, not recognizing the place and thus discouraged, Athena "drew near him in the form of a young man, a herdsman of sheep, one most gentle, as are the sons of princes" (13.222–23).[24] Later, as she revealed her identity to him, she "changed herself to the form of a woman, beautiful and tall, and skilled in glorious handiwork" (13.288–89).[25] When one of the suitors abuses Odysseus, who himself has been disguised by Athena as an old man, another rebukes him, ironically warning him that the old man might be a god, since "the gods do, in the guise of strangers from afar, put on all manner of shapes, and visit the cities, beholding the violence and righteousness of men" (17.485–87).[26]

A passage that is analogous to the transfiguration of Jesus in Mark, since it describes a transfiguration from an ordinary human state to a glorified or divine state, is the account of the transformation of the humble wet-nurse Doso into the goddess Demeter in the presence of her human employer, Metaneira:

Thus speaking, the goddess changed her size and appearance, thrusting off old age. Beauty breathed about her and from her sweet robes a delicious fragrance spread; a light beamed far out from the goddess's immortal skin, and her golden hair flowed over her shoulders

(Ὣς εἰποῦσα θεὰ μέγεθος καὶ εἶδος ἄμειψε γῆρας ἀπωσαμένη, περί τ' ἀμφί τε κάλλος ἄητο· ὀδμὴ δ' ἱμερόεσσα θυηέντων ἀπὸ πέπλων σκίδνατο τῆλε δὲ φέγγος ἀπὸ χροὸς ἀθανάτοιο λάμπε θεᾶς, ξανθαὶ δὲ κόμαι κατενήνοθεν ὤμους). (*Hom. Hymn 2 ad Dem.* 275–80)[27]

Immediately preceding this self-revelation, Demeter commands that the people of Eleusis build her a temple and an altar and promises to teach them her rites, so that they may perform them and propitiate her spirit (*Hymn 2 ad Dem.* 268–74). In antiquity, the epiphany of a deity was regularly associated with the foundation of a cult or with the celebration of a festival.[28] Peter's proposal to

---

21 Yarbro Collins, "Son of God among Greeks and Romans," 90–92; Moss, "Transfiguration," 69–89.

22 χαλεποὶ δὲ θεοὶ φαίνεσθαι ἐναργεῖς; text and trans. [modified] from Augustus T. Murray, *Homer: The Iliad* (2 vols.; LCL; Cambridge, MA: Harvard University Press; London: Heinemann, 1924–25) 2:380–81; cited by Moss, "Transfiguration," 78 n. 38.

23 παρθενικῇ ἐϊκυῖα νεήνιδι, κάλπιν ἐχούσῃ; text and trans. from Augustus T. Murray and George E. Dimock, *Homer: The Odyssey* (2 vols; LCL; Cambridge, MA/London: Harvard University Press, 1995) 1:246–47.

24 ἀνδρὶ δέμας εἰκυῖα νέῳ, ἐπιβώτορι μήλων, παναπάλῳ, οἷοί τε ἀνάκτων παῖδες ἔασι; text and trans. from Murray and Dimock, *Homer: The Odyssey*, 2:18–19; Moss, "Transfiguration," 77.

25 δέμας δ' ἤϊκτο γυναικὶ καλῇ τε μεγάλῃ τε καὶ ἀγλαὰ ἔργα ἰδυίῃ; text and trans. from Murray and Dimock, *Homer: The Odyssey*, 2:22–23; Moss, "Transfiguration," 77.

26 καί τε θεοὶ ξείνοισιν ἐοικότες ἀλλοδαποῖσι, παντοῖοι τελέθοντες, ἐπιστρωφῶσι πόληας, ἀνθρώπων ὕβριν τε καὶ εὐνομίην ἐφορῶντες; text and trans. from Murray and Dimock, *Homer: The Odyssey*, 2:190–91; Yarbro Collins, "Son of God among Greeks and Romans," 91. Acts 14:8-18 presupposes that the people of Lystra hold a similar idea; cf. Vollenweider, "Metamorphose," 111, 113.

27 Text and trans. from Helene P. Foley, ed., *The Homeric Hymn to Demeter: Translation, Commentary, and Interpretive Essays* (Princeton, NJ: Princeton University Press, 1994) 16–17. Frenschkowski defines this text, among other things, as a "hidden epiphany" (*Offenbarung und Epiphanie*, 2:6–9).

28 According to Herodotus, the epiphany of Apis is closely linked to a festival (3.27.3); an epiphany of Pan is linked to the foundation of a cult (6.105). When Aphrodite grants Anchises a hidden epiphany, he offers to build an altar and offer sacrifices to her (*Hom. Hymn 5 ad Aphr.* 81–102). On the link between epiphany and cultic practice, see Moss,

build "three tents" or "three huts" is explicable in this context. He is proposing to establish cults in honor of the three beings who have appeared.[29]

Herodotus (fifth cent. BCE) and Polyaenus (second cent. CE) both claimed that epiphanies were staged for political or military purposes. According to Herodotus, when Pisistratus was seizing power for his second period of tyranny in Athens, Megacles assisted him in staging an epiphany of Athena in order to authorize his tyranny.[30] According to Polyaenus, a Spartan king staged an appearance of the Dioskouri to encourage his troops:

In Arcadia, when Archidamus was going to draw up his army for battle on the next day, he encouraged the Spartiates by erecting an altar during the night and decorating it with the most brilliant arms and leading two horses around it. At dawn, the squadron and division commanders, seeing the new arms, the footprints of two horses, and an altar built by itself, announced that the Dioscuri had come to fight as their allies. Taking courage and becoming, they thought, divinely inspired, the soldiers fought nobly and conquered the Arcadians (Ἀρχίδαμος ἐν Ἀρκαδίᾳ μέλλων παρατάσσεσθαι τῇ ὑστεραίᾳ ἐπέρρωσε τοὺς Σπαρτιάτας διὰ νυκτὸς βωμὸν ἱδρυσάμενος καὶ κοσμήσας ὅπλοις λαμπροτάτοις καὶ ἵππους δύο περιαγαγών. ἐπεὶ δὲ ἦν ἕως, οἱ λοχαγοὶ καὶ οἱ ταξίαρχοι καινὰ ὅπλα καὶ δυοῖν ἵπποιν ἴχνη καὶ βωμὸν αὐτόματον ἰδόντες διήγγειλαν, ὡς οἱ Διόσκουροι συμμαχήσοντες ἥκοιεν. οἱ στρατιῶται θαρρήσαντες καὶ τὰς γνώμας ἔνθεοι γενόμενοι γενναίως ἠγωνίσαντο καὶ τοὺς Ἀρκάδας ἐνίκησαν). (1.41.1)[31]

Although the epiphany of the Markan Jesus is depicted as real, rather than faked, it is staged in the sense that Jesus chooses the time and place.[32] It thus may be seen as a device for authorizing Jesus and instructing the disciples.[33]

The author of Mark, or his predecessor(s), appears to have drawn upon the Hellenistic and Roman genres of epiphany and metamorphosis, but in a way that adapts them to the biblical tradition, especially to that of the theophany on Sinai.[34] Mark's narrative, with its implied criticism of Peter's proposal, deliberately excludes the use of the epiphany of Jesus as a foundation legend for a cult.

Structure

Verse 2a-b indicates the time, place, and characters. Verse 8 reestablishes the opening situation. In between is an account of a miraculous process (vv. 2c-7). This account has three parts. The first miraculous event has

---

"Transfiguration," 81, 83–84. Ovid associates an epiphany of Jupiter and Mercury with the founding of a cult (*Met.* 8.618–724); Frenschkowski, *Offenbarung und Epiphanie*, 2:10–14; Vollenweider, "Die Metamorphose," 111.

29 Cf. Bousset's rhetorical question cited in "History of the Tradition" above. The "three tents" (τρεῖς σκηναί) also recall the tabernacle (σκηνή); see the discussion of the genre "theophany" above.

30 Herodotus 1.60; Rosalind Thomas, "Megacles," *OCD* 950; eadem, "Pisistratus," ibid., 1186–87.

31 Text and trans. from Peter Krentz and Everett L. Wheeler, eds., *Polyaenus: Stratagems of War*, vol. 1 (*Books I–V*) (Chicago: Ares, 1994) 90–93; the Greek text is the same as that of Eduard Woelfflin and Johannes Melber, eds., *Polyaeni: Strategematon libri octo* (BSGRT 1714; Stuttgart: Teubner, 1970) 46–47; see also John B. Campbell, "Polyaenus (2)," *OCD* 1209.

32 Cf. Lohmeyer, 174.

33 Clare Komoroske Rothschild argued in an unpub-

lished paper (1997) that the purposes of the transfiguration were divine sponsorship and validation of leadership.

34 Cf. Joseph A. Fitzmyer's argument: Paul's affirmation that the person who has faith in Christ Jesus is gradually "transformed" (μεταμορφόομαι) "is a mythological figure taken over from Greco-Roman metamorphosis literature"; at the same time, Paul has adapted this motif in terms of the story of Moses in Exodus 34 and an allusion to Genesis 1 ("Glory Reflected on the Face of Christ [2 Cor 3:7–4:6] and a Palestinian Jewish Motif," *TS* 42 [1981] 630–44, esp. 632–33, 639, 644). Pax argued that the account of the transfiguration was a pre-Markan "epiphany-pericope," but that the evangelist himself lacked the developed epiphany concept found in the Gospel of John (ΕΠΙΦΑΝΕΙΑ, 251).

two parts: the transfiguration of Jesus and the appearance of Elijah and Moses (vv. 2c-4). The second miraculous event also has two parts: the appearance of the cloud and the voice from the cloud (v. 7). In between is the human response: Peter's proposal and the fear of the three disciples (vv. 5-6).[35]

Comment

■ **2** In keeping with his theory that the transfiguration was originally a resurrection story, Wellhausen suggested that the six days refer to the period between Jesus' death and his appearance in Galilee.[36] Others have argued that they allude to the six days between the appearance of the cloud on Mount Sinai and God's calling Moses.[37] Yet others that "after six days" is equivalent to "on the seventh day" and that therefore the allusion is to the Sabbath.[38] Foster McCurley argued that "after six days" is a Semitic idiom in which decisive action is then described on the seventh day. Although the transfiguration lacks mention of "the seventh day," he argued on the basis of Hos 6:2 that it is implied that the transfiguration takes place on the seventh day in a series. He argued further that the

Markan text is primarily related to Exod 24:15-18.[39] McCurley's conclusions about the Semitic idiom and the relation to Exod 24:15-18 are credible, but his further theories about the passage are dubious.[40]

Since the account was probably not originally a resurrection-appearance story and since the other traditions about appearances do not mention a six-day interval, Wellhausen's theory is unwarranted. An allusion to Exod 24:16 is likely, a passage that is itself an instance of the Semitic idiom noted by McCurley.[41] Since we are not told on what day the six began, an allusion to the Sabbath is unlikely. In the present context of Mark, the six days separate the sudden insight of Peter and the disturbing teaching of Jesus, on the one hand, from the extraordinary experience of the transfiguration, on the other. The interval may be interpreted as a time for assimilation and reflection on the first stage of revelation before the second stage or as a time of preparation for the second stage.[42]

According to 8:27-33, only the disciples of Jesus hear Peter's answer to the question of Jesus' identity and Jesus' teaching about the necessity of the suffering of the

35 Lohmeyer, 173.
36 Wellhausen, 71.
37 See the citation of Exod 24:15-16 LXX above; Charles E. Carlston mentions this as a hypothesis frequently defended ("Transfiguration and Resurrection," *JBL* 80 [1961] 233-40, esp. 236); see also Stein, "Misplaced Resurrection-Account?" 82 n. 20. Stegner states that in both accounts "the six days precede the encounter with God" ("Use of Scripture," 114). Bruce D. Chilton concluded that the transfiguration is "a visionary representation of the Sinai motif of Exod. 24" ("The Transfiguration: Dominical Assurance and Apostolic Vision," *NTS* 27 [1980] 115-24, esp. 122). He defines its genre as "a Tabernacles Haggadah" (ibid., 124).
38 Carlston mentions this hypothesis, but considers it "improbable in the extreme" ("Transfiguration and Resurrection," 236 and n. 13); Stein, "Misplaced Resurrection-Account?" 82 n. 20. Margaret E. Thrall argued that "after six days" implies "on the seventh day" and that Mark implies that the resurrection of Jesus took place on the Sabbath; in this and other ways, the evangelist connects the transfiguration to the story of the empty tomb ("Elijah and Moses in Mark's Account of the Transfiguration," *NTS* 16 [1969-70] 305-17, esp. 310-11). Benjamin W. Bacon

suggested that the six days here and in John 1 reflect the practice of devoting six days of preparation for the feast of the Epiphany ("After Six Days: A New Clue for Gospel Critics," *HTR* 8 [1915] 94-121, esp. 111-12).
39 On Exod 24:15-18, see "Genre" above; McCurley, "'And after Six Days,'" 67-78.
40 He argues unpersuasively that "after six days" stood in the middle of the passage in the pre-Markan tradition and that the climax of the account was the ascension of Jesus (ibid., 79, 81). See the criticisms of Stein, "Misplaced Resurrection-Account?" 82-83.
41 Contra Bultmann, *History*, 260; but he is right that such an allusion by no means explains everything about the passage.
42 Lohmeyer argued that the six days probably signify a time of preparation for the reception of divine revelation (173-74). Childs interpreted the six days in Exod 24:16 as a period in which "Moses must wait in preparation" (*Exodus*, 508); see also Bacon, "After Six Days," 94-95. Jarl E. Fossum referred to the period of preparation (six or seven days) before receiving revelation in Jewish apocalyptic texts, e.g., *2 Bar.* 20:3-22:1; 2 Esdr 6:31-7:2 ("Ascensio, Metamorphosis," in idem, *The Image of the Invisible God: Essays on the Influence of Jewish Mysticism on Early*

Son of Man. According to 9:2, only three disciples, Peter and James and John, are allowed to experience the transfiguration of Jesus.[43] This narrowing of the group may be simply a literary device to heighten the awesome and secret character of the transformation. This hypothesis is supported by the phrase "alone by themselves" ($\kappa\alpha\tau$ $\grave{\iota}\delta\acute{\iota}\alpha\nu$ $\mu\acute{o}\nu o\iota$) (cf. 5:37, 40).[44] It is possible, however, that these three are chosen also to affirm their leadership role in the postresurrection community.[45]

If the account is pre-Markan,[46] the mountain was apparently unspecified at that stage of the tradition. Even though it is unlikely to have been Mount Sinai itself, the generic character of the mountain would allow that association to be made. Furthermore, "a high mountain" would, in Mark's cultural context, call to mind the mythic notion of the cosmic mountain or the mountain as the dwelling place of a god or of the gods.[47] In the present context in Mark, however, the implication is that the "high mountain" is Mount Hermon, a traditionally sacred place.[48]

The narrator's statement that "he was transfigured in their presence" evokes the ancient genre of the epiphany or metamorphosis.[49] This statement may be understood in either of two ways. One is that Jesus walked the earth as a divine being, whose true nature is momentarily revealed in the transfiguration (cf. Phil 2:6-11).[50] The other is that the transfiguration is a temporary change that Jesus undergoes here as an anticipation of his glorification after death (cf. 1 Cor 15:43, 49, 51-53).[51] The motif of a temporary transformation, anticipating the final one, is typical of a group of apocalypses, but there it is associated with a heavenly journey.[52]

■ **3** Jesus' clothing here is said to have "shone" ($\sigma\tau\acute{\iota}\lambda\beta\omega$). In the LXX, this verb is used "almost always of the radiance of stars or the luster of metals."[53] The verb is used in a depiction of the god Helios (the Sun), riding in his chariot:

Bright rays shine dazzlingly from him, and his bright locks streaming from the temples of his head grace-

---

Christology [NTOA 30; Freiburg, Schweiz: Universitätsverlag Freiburg; Göttingen: Vandenhoeck & Ruprecht, 1995] 71–94, esp. 79–80).

43   In the context of Mark, James and John are clearly the sons of Zebedee (cf. 1:19; 3:17; 10:35). Of the three "pillars" mentioned in Gal 2:9, Cephas is certainly the same as Peter here, John may be the son of Zebedee, but James is probably the brother of the Lord, not the son of Zebedee; cf. Gal 1:18-19; Betz, *Galatians*, 78–79, 99, 101.

44   Lohmeyer, 174; Frenschkowski, *Offenbarung und Epiphanie*, 2:187.

45   See "Genre" above. See also Müller, "Die Verklärung Jesu," 60; Stegner, "Use of Scripture," 112–13.

46   So, e.g., Bultmann, *History*, 243, 259–61; Stein, "Misplaced Resurrection-Account?" 83. See also "History of the Tradition" above.

47   See the commentary on 3:13 above; Richard J. Clifford, *The Cosmic Mountain in Canaan and the Old Testament* (HSM 4; Cambridge, MA: Harvard University Press, 1972); Adela Yarbro Collins, "Pergamon in Early Christian Literature," in Helmut Koester, ed., *Pergamon: Citadel of the Gods* (Harrisburg, PA: Trinity Press International, 1998) 163–184, esp. 168–70.

48   See the commentary on 8:27a above. The mountain was already identified by early Christian writers with Mount Tabor, as it often is today; for references see Lohmeyer, 174 n. 5; he himself identifies the mountain with Mount Hermon.

49   See "Genre" above. Lohmeyer argued in this way in

his article ("Die Verklärung," 203–5), but interpreted the metamorphosis of Jesus in apocalyptic terms in his commentary (174–75 n. 7), because he believed that literary unity implied a unified background in the history of religion.

50   Adela Yarbro Collins, "Psalms, Phil. 2:6-11, and the Origins of Christology," *BI* 11 (2003) 361–72; see also the commentary on v. 7 below. See also Lohmeyer, "Die Verklärung," 206.

51   A synonym of the verb "to be transfigured" ($\mu\epsilon\tau\alpha$-$\mu o\rho\varphi\acute{o}\omega$), used by Mark, occurs in 1 Cor 15:51-52, namely, "to be changed" ($\grave{\alpha}\lambda\lambda\acute{\alpha}\sigma\sigma\omega$) (Asher, *Polarity and Change*, 176–77). Paul uses the same verb as Mark in 2 Cor 3:18 in an analogous context; cf. D. E. Nineham, *The Gospel of St. Mark* (PGC; Baltimore: Penguin Books, 1963) 234.

52   Martha Himmelfarb, "Transformation and the Righteous Dead," in eadem, *Ascent to Heaven in Jewish and Christian Apocalypses* (New York: Oxford University Press, 1993) 47–71. Fossum argued that the "religio-historical derivation" of the transfiguration is from traditions of heavenly ascent and transformation ("Ascensio, Metamorphosis," 71–94).

53   BAGD, s.v.

fully enclose his far-seen face (λαμπραὶ δ' ἀκτῖνες ἀπ' αὐτοῦ αἰγλῆεν στίλβουσι παρὰ κροτάφων δέ τ' ἔθειραι λαμπραὶ ἀπὸ κρατὸς χαρίεν κατέχουσι πρόσωπον τηλαυγές). (*Hom. Hymn 31 ad Hel.* 10–13)[54]

Jesus is not depicted as luminous or as wearing white garments in the resurrection-appearance stories. He is so depicted, however, in epiphany stories. Compare the account of an epiphany of the risen Jesus in the book of Revelation: "and his face shone like the sun in its strength" (καὶ ἡ ὄψις αὐτοῦ ὡς ὁ ἥλιος φαίνει ἐν τῇ δυνάμει αὐτοῦ) (Rev 1:16c).[55]

Wellhausen pointed out that Mark's term "cloth-handler" or "fuller" (γναφεύς) was omitted by Matthew, Luke, and some MSS of Mark because it was considered too plebeian.[56] The Greek term probably occurred in the *Shepherd of Hermas*, but the relevant portion survives only in Latin.[57]

■ **4** Note the contrast between the verb used for the epiphany of Jesus, "he was transfigured" (μετεμορφώθη), and that used for the epiphany of Elijah and Moses, "appeared" (ὤφθη).[58] The latter verb is sometimes used of a resurrection appearance of Jesus (Luke 24:34),[59] but this verbal form (and the related participle)

is also used for a theophany (Acts 7:2; cf. Gen 12:7 LXX), for the appearance of an angel to a human being,[60] for an epiphany of the risen Jesus (Acts 9:17; 26:16), for the appearance of a vision to Paul (Acts 16:9), for a revelation of the ark of the covenant in the heavenly temple (Rev 11:9), and for the revelation of signs in heaven (Rev 12:1, 3). Jesus does not "appear" because he has been with them all the time.

Elijah "appears" because, in the cultural context of Mark, he was believed to have been taken up to heaven and made immortal (Josephus *Ant.* 9.2.2 §28).[61] The facts that Elijah is mentioned first here and that he was famous for his translation to heaven (cf. e.g., Sir 48:9) indicate that an important purpose of the transfiguration account is to foreshadow the transformation of Jesus' body and its translation to heaven.[62] In the early church the usual interpretation was that Moses and Elijah here represent the Law and the Prophets.[63] This interpretation fits the parallels in Matthew and Luke, which name Moses first, but it is not as appropriate for Mark. In Mark, Elijah appears "with" (σύν) Moses.[64] Moses also "appears" because, like Elijah, he was believed not to have died but to have been taken up to heaven and made immortal.[65]

54 Text and trans. (modified) from Hugh G. Evelyn-White, *Hesiod: The Homeric Hymns and Homerica* (rev. ed.; LCL; Cambridge, MA: Harvard University Press; London: Heinemann, 1936) 458–59. For further examples of radiance and shining garments in the *Odyssey* and other *Homeric Hymns*, see Brenk, "Greek Epiphanies," 420.

55 Cf. also Acts 9:3; 22:6, 9, 11; 26:13; C. H. Dodd, "The Appearances of the Risen Christ: An Essay in Form-Criticism of the Gospels," in Dennis E. Nineham, ed., *Studies in the Gospels: Essays in Memory of R. H. Lightfoot* (Oxford: Blackwell, 1955) 9–35, esp. 25.

56 Wellhausen, 69. Matthew and Luke omit the whole clause; some MSS of Mark simply change γναφεύς ("cloth-handler") to τις ("one" or "someone"); for the variants, see Aland, *Synopsis*, ad loc. Others omit the whole clause; see Lohmeyer, 175 n. 3.

57 *Hermas Sim.* 9.32.3-5; the Latin term is *fullo*. See the discussion of the trade in Osiek, *Shepherd of Hermas*, 257 and nn. 7 and 8.

58 Rothschild argues that ὤφθη ("appeared") is a technical term for "resurrection" and thus that Elijah here represents the resurrected John the Baptist (*Baptist Traditions and Q*, 136–37, 148, 153–54, 170).

In my view, the term is not technical. See the commentary immediately below.

59 "Truly the Lord has risen and has appeared to Simon" (ὄντως ἠγέρθη ὁ κύριος καὶ ὤφθη Σίμωνι); see also Acts 13:31; 1 Cor 15:5, 6, 7, 8.

60 Judg 6:12 LXX; Luke 1:11; 22:43; Acts 7:30 (an interpretation of the burning bush).

61 Yarbro Collins, *Beginning of the Gospel*, 142–43.

62 On Mark's understanding of the resurrection of Jesus as the transformation of his earthly body and his translation to heaven, see Yarbro Collins, *Beginning of the Gospel*, 146; and the commentary on 16:1-8 below.

63 Tertullian *Against Marcion* 4.22; Augustine *Homilies* 232; cited by Swete, 189. Taylor affirms this interpretation (ad loc.). Nineham combines it with the eschatological interpretation (234–35); on the latter, see below.

64 The order may be due to the fact that, at the end of Malachi in the LXX, Elijah and Moses are mentioned in close proximity and in that order (Nineham, 235); see also Lohmeyer, who mentions that the saying of Johanan ben Zakkai expects them to return together ("Die Verklärung," 190).

The significance of the appearance of Elijah and Moses is first and foremost to show that Jesus belongs in their company. They speak together like friends. Compare the following scene in the Jewish *Apocalypse of Zephaniah:*

> Then [the great angel, whose glory was great] ran to all the righteous ones, namely, Abraham and Isaac and Jacob and Enoch and Elijah and David. He spoke with them as friend to friend speaking with one another. (9:4-5)[66]

For Mark, Jesus belongs in their company in two senses. First, like them, he will be taken up bodily into heaven.[67] Second, like them he has an important role in the last days. According to scripture, Elijah was to return to earth:

> And see, I shall send to you Elijah the Tishbite before the great and manifest day of the Lord comes, who will restore the heart of a father (in friendly relations) with a son, and the heart of a man with his neighbor, lest I come and strike the earth (or the land) utterly (καὶ ἰδοὺ ἐγὼ ἀποστέλλω ὑμῖν Ἠλίαν τὸν Θεσβίτην πρὶν ἐλθεῖν ἡμέραν κυρίου τὴν μεγάλην καὶ ἐπιφανῆ, ὃς ἀποκαταστήσει καρδίαν πατρὸς πρὸς υἱὸν καὶ καρδίαν ἀνθρώπου πρὸς τὸν πλησίον αὐτοῦ, μὴ ἔλθω καὶ πατάξω τὴν γῆν ἄρδην). (Mal 3:22-23 LXX; 3:23-24 MT; 4:5-6 RSV)

The narrative of Mark as a whole creates the impression that, in Mark's cultural context, the expectation of Elijah's eschatological return was widespread.[68] The expectation of the return of Elijah was apparently alive in the community of the Dead Sea Scrolls. A fragmentary text associates the coming of Elijah with elements that may signify the dawning of the "Day of the Lord":

> to you I will send Eliyah, befo[re ...]
> power, lightning and met[eors . . .]
>
> (לכן אשלח לאליה קד[ם...]
> תו]ן קו[ף {ס} ברקא וזי]קיא [...]
> (4QVision[b]ar [4Q558] 4-5)[69]

In addition to the tradition of his translation to heaven, the inclusion of Moses may be explained in two major ways, both of which are probably relevant. One is that there was a lively expectation of the "prophet like Moses," mentioned in Deut 18:15, 18-19.[70] The expecta-

---

65 Josephus *Ant.* 4.8.48 §§325–26. In spite of the statement in Deut 34:5 that Moses died, Josephus did not believe that he did; see Christopher Begg, "Josephus' portrayal of the Disappearances of Enoch, Elijah and Moses: Some Observations," *JBL* 109 (1990) 691–93, esp. 692; Yarbro Collins, *Beginning of the Gospel,* 142–43.

66 Trans. by Orval S. Wintermute, *OTP* 1:514; it survives in Coptic and was probably written in Greek between 100 BCE and 175 CE (ibid., 500). Lohmeyer interprets the presence of Elijah and Moses similarly (175–76); cf. Heil, *Transfiguration,* 96.

67 Bultmann interpreted the transfiguration in its Markan context as "a prophecy of the Resurrection in pictorial form (cp. 8:31)" (*History,* 260). Heil argued that the significance of the appearance of Elijah and Moses is that Jesus will attain heavenly glory, as they did, but only after being raised by God after suffering the unjust death of a rejected prophet (*Transfiguration,* 98–100).

68 Mark 6:15; 8:28; 9:11. Cf. Sir 48:10. On eschatological traditions associated with Elijah, see Lohmeyer, "Die Verklärung," 188–89; Kee, "Transfiguration in Mark," 144–46.

69 Text and trans. from García Martínez and Tigchelaar, *Dead Sea Scrolls,* 2:1114–15; for discussion see Öhler, *Elia im Neuen Testament,* 16–22. See also *Sib. Or.* 2.187–89, which associates the return of Elijah with the final judgment; it is difficult to determine whether this text is Jewish or Christian; see John J. Collins, "Sibylline Oracles," *OTP* 1:330, 349–50; idem, "The Sibylline Oracles," in Stone, *Jewish Writings,* 357–81, esp. 377; Öhler, *Elia im Neuen Testament,* 14–15.

70 Howard M. Teeple, *The Mosaic Eschatological Prophet* (JBLMS 10; Philadelphia: SBL, 1957) 49–73; Marcus, *Way of the Lord,* 81 and n. 4. Richard A. Horsley argued that the expectation of an eschatological prophet was not widespread ("'Like One of the Prophets of Old': Two Types of Popular Prophets at the Time of Jesus," *CBQ* 47 [1985] 435–63, esp. 443). The expectation of a prophet like Moses may be reflected in John 6:14; this expectation is placed in cultural context by Wayne A. Meeks, *The Prophet-King: Moses Traditions and the Johannine Christology* (Leiden: Brill, 1967).

tion of such a prophet in the cultural context of Mark would explain why some people are portrayed as identifying Jesus as "a prophet like one of the prophets (of old)" (Mark 6:15; cf. 8:28).[71] It is likely that the community of the Dead Sea Scrolls expected an eschatological prophet inspired by Deut 18:18-19.[72] The other is that there may have been, already in the time of Mark, an expectation that Moses would return to play an eschatological role. In support of this hypothesis, one could point to a saying attributed to Johanan ben Zakkai and to Rev 11:3-13.[73] Moses is not named in Revelation 11, but the "two witnesses" have power to prevent rain, to turn the waters into blood, and to strike the earth with every kind of plague whenever they wish. The witnesses are thus modeled on the biblical accounts of Elijah and Moses. The respective allusions occur in the same order as the names are given in Mark. The idea of an eschatological role for Moses, or one like Moses, may be related to the notion of eschatological plagues.[74]

■ **5-6** Bultmann doubted that the account is a unity, even though he concluded that a literary analysis could not be made with certainty. He suggested that v. 7 originally followed v. 4.[75] This hypothesis is unlikely. There must have been spectators for whose benefit the epiphany took place. In that case, some kind of response on their part fits the context well. Furthermore, the interlude created by vv. 5-6 effectively slows down the action and builds suspense.[76]

The introduction to Peter's statement in v. 5 is virtually identical to the introduction of his answer to the question about Jesus' identity: "And Peter answered Jesus" (καὶ ἀποκριθεὶς ὁ Πέτρος λέγει τῷ Ἰησοῦ).[77] But here the verb has the sense of initiating a dialogue, rather than continuing one.[78]

This is the first time that the address "Rabbi" occurs in Mark.[79] It is a transliteration of the Hebrew term רבי, from the root רב, meaning "big" or "great." Judging from the immediate context, its primary connotation here is Jesus' greatness.[80] There is no hint that this form of address is inappropriate.

Although the expression "three tents" or "three huts" (τρεῖς σκηναί) is reminiscent of the "tent" or "tabernacle" (σκηνή) that God instructs Moses to make (Exodus 25–31), the plurality of the tents and their relation to the three epiphanic figures indicates that the Greek and Roman genres of epiphany and metamorphosis have had an influence on this passage.[81] In those traditions, an account of an epiphany is often associated with the foundation of a cult or a festival.[82] Peter is proposing that the triple epiphany be commemorated at least by the building of a shrine and perhaps by some regular ritual observance.

The narrator's comment, "For he did not know how he should respond" (οὐ γὰρ ᾔδει τί ἀποκριθῇ), uses the verb ἀποκρίνομαι (usually translated "answer") in yet another sense. Not preceded by a question, it rather

---

71 See also the section of the introduction "Jesus as Prophet" above.

72 1QS 9:11; *4QTestimonia* (4Q175) 5–8; Fitzmyer, "'4QTestimonia' and the New Testament," in *Essays*, 59–89, esp. 82–84; reprinted in idem, *Semitic Background*, 59–89; Collins, *Scepter and the Star*, 74–75; Kee, "Transfiguration in Mark," 146.

73 So Lohmeyer, 175; idem, "Die Verklärung," 189–90. Israel Abrahams found no reason to doubt that the saying went back to Johanan and gave the following translation, "In the world to come when I bring unto them Elijah the prophet, the two of you (Moses and Elijah) shall come together" (*Studies in Pharisaism*, 2:53 n. 5); Teeple, *Eschatological Prophet*, 45–46.

74 There are seven in Revelation 15–16, but ten in *Apoc. Abr.* 29:15-16.

75 Bultmann, *History*, 260–61. McCurley argued that vv. 5-6 are Markan ("And after Six Days," 77). Stein gives a list of scholars who hold that v. 6 is Markan ("Misplaced Resurrection-Account?" 86 n. 36).

76 Cf. Lohmeyer, 176 n. 1.

77 Mark 8:29: "Peter answered him" (ἀποκριθεὶς ὁ Πέτρος λέγει αὐτῷ).

78 BAGD, 114.

79 It occurs also in 11:21; 14:45; in addition, it occurs on the lips of disciples in John 1:38, 49; 9:2. A variant form of the term, ῥαββουνί, occurs in 10:51 on the lips of Bartimaeus and in John 20:16 on those of Mary Magdalene.

80 Hayim Lapin, "Rabbi," *ABD* 5:600–602.

81 Chilton (see commentary on v. 2 above) and Stegner associate the tents with the feast of Succoth (Lev 23:43; Stegner, "Use of Scripture," 114). Lohmeyer does also, but primarily in an eschatological sense ("Die Verklärung," 191–96).

82 See "Genre" above.

expresses a contrast with the situation described in vv. 2c-4 and should be translated "respond" or "reply."[83] The narrator goes on to give the reason why he did not know how to respond: they (all three disciples) were terrified.[84]

The narrator's comments indicate clearly that the idea of building a shrine is inappropriate, but Peter is not criticized as severely here as he is in 8:33. Peter's reaction here serves two purposes, besides the literary ones pointed out above. First, it makes the point that the scene is an epiphany for those in the audience familiar with the link between epiphanies and cult. Second, although the specific proposal is rejected, it serves to express the typical and appropriate human response of awe, reverence, and terror to the manifestation of divinity.[85]

■ **7** The cloud is a theophanic element, signifying the presence of God.[86] In Exod 24:15-16 LXX, the cloud's covering Mount Sinai is equivalent to the descent of God's "glory" upon the mountain.[87]

The statement in v. 7 that the cloud "overshadowed them" (ἐπισκιάζουσα αὐτοῖς) is also theophanic language:

And the cloud covered the tent of testimony, and the tent was filled with the glory of the Lord; and Moses was not able to enter the tent of testimony, because the cloud overshadowed it, and the tent was filled with the glory of the Lord (Καὶ ἐκάλυψεν ἡ νεφέλη τὴν σκηνὴν τοῦ μαρτυρίου, καὶ δόξης κυρίου ἐπλήσθη ἡ σκηνή· καὶ οὐκ ἠδυνάσθη Μωυσῆς εἰσελθεῖν εἰς τὴν σκηνὴν τοῦ μαρτυρίου, ὅτι ἐπεσκίαζεν ἐπ᾽ αὐτὴν ἡ νεφέλη καὶ δόξης κυρίου ἐπλήσθη ἡ σκηνή). (Exod 40:34-35 LXX)

Wellhausen commented that, in Luke 1:35, the notion of "overshadowing" has been preserved, but the Holy Spirit has taken the place of the cloud.[88]

It is not clear exactly who is overshadowed. It could be the three glorious figures alone, the three disciples alone, or all six. Evidently this detail was not important enough to be clarified. The important thing is that the disciples saw the cloud and recognized the divine presence.

Given the theophanic context, the voice from the cloud is clearly a divine voice.[89] Moreover, the "voice" that came "from the cloud" (ἐγένετο φωνὴ ἐκ τῆς νεφέλης) here is the same as the "voice" that came "from heaven" (φωνὴ ἐγένετο ἐκ τῶν οὐρανῶν) in 1:11. Jesus is referred to as God's beloved son in both passages. An important difference between the two is that, in the baptismal scene, the divine voice addresses Jesus in the second person singular, and, presumably, Jesus is the only one who hears the voice. Jesus is consecrated as messiah, but only he, the demons, and the audience of Mark know that such is the case. In the transfiguration, the divine voice speaks about Jesus in the third person

---

83 BAGD, 113.

84 Dwyer argues, unconvincingly, that the second clause in v. 6 does not give the reason for what is stated in the first clause (*Wonder*, 141). He cites, however, some illuminating passages in which the word ἔκφοβος ("terrified") and the related word φόβος ("fear") are used, including 4 Macc 4:10, where the term is also used in connection with an epiphany (Dwyer uses the term "vision" [ibid., 141–42]). Stegner compares this verse with the response of the people of Israel to a theophany on Mount Sinai (Exod 20:18 LXX) ("The Use of Scripture," 115).

85 Even though he agrees with those who take v. 6 as Markan, Dwyer does not interpret it as a polemic against Peter or all three disciples (*Wonder*, 142). Thrall argued that Peter's mistake was in attributing equality to the three figures; the divine voice corrects this view by indicating that Jesus alone is the messianic Son of God ("Elijah and Moses," 308–9).

86 Lohmeyer, "Die Verklärung," 196–98. Heil argued that it is an oracular cloud (the divine voice) and a vehicular cloud (it transports Elijah and Moses back to heaven) (*Transfiguration*, 129–49).

87 Exod 24:15-16 is cited in "Genre" above.

88 Wellhausen, 69. Fitzmyer argued that the verb "overshadow" (ἐπισκιάζω) in Luke 1:35 is used figuratively, signifying the presence of God to Mary (*Luke*, 1:351).

89 The motif of a voice from heaven is a commonplace in apocalypses: *1 Enoch* 13:8 (Greek); 65:4; *2 Bar.* 13:1; 22:1; Rev 10:4; 11:12; 14:13; cf. 4:1. Several scholars have argued that the account of the transfiguration has an apocalyptic character; see "Genre" and the commentary on v. 2 above; see also Bauckham, *Jude, 2 Peter*, 206.

and addresses the disciples in the second person plural. Thus, in keeping with the theme of the section 8:27–10:45, the identity of Jesus is revealed in a special way to three selected disciples. That only three disciples see the transfiguration indicates that Jesus' identity is still to some degree a secret.[90]

That the identity of Jesus is concealed here as much as it is revealed is supported by the ambiguity in the statement of the divine voice. When the text "This is my beloved son" was read, some members of the audience probably recalled the remark of the divine voice at the baptism and interpreted this statement as a further revelation and confirmation of Jesus' role as messiah.[91] This insight would also lead to the recognition that this divine announcement confirms the answer of Peter to the question of Jesus' identity (cf. 8:29).[92] For others, the phrase "my beloved son" (ὁ υἱός μου ὁ ἀγαπητός) evoked the story of the near-sacrifice of Isaac (Gen 22:2, 12, 16 LXX).[93] This intertextual relation also created a link with the first passion prediction in 8:31.[94] Those deeply influ-

enced by Greek literature and rituals understood this passage to mean that Jesus was a divine being walking the earth.[95]

The command "listen to him" (ἀκούετε αὐτοῦ) was probably taken by some members of the audience as a general expression of the authority of Jesus and the attitude that his followers should take toward him.[96] For those knowledgeable about scripture, it probably recalled the statement in Deut 18:15 LXX, "to him you shall listen" (αὐτοῦ ἀκούσεσθε).[97] Those familiar with the expectation of an eschatological prophet like Moses were especially likely to make this connection.[98] Those attentive to context probably linked the command to the teaching of Jesus concerning the suffering, rejection, death, and resurrection of the Son of Man (8:31) and concerning persecuted disciples, the *parousia*, and full manifestation of the kingdom of God (8:34–9:1). The divine voice confirms these prophecies and admonitions of Jesus.[99] This part of the divine speech also fits well

---

90   Cf. Wellhausen, 69–70. For Dibelius, the transfiguration is one of the typically secret epiphanies of Mark which indicate that the divine glory of the earthly Jesus was evident only to the smallest circle of the chosen; it discloses Jesus as the messiah, but also shows why he was not recognized as such (*From Tradition to Gospel*, 230); see also Zeller, "New Testament Christology," 326.

91   See the commentary on 1:11 above. Cf. Lohmeyer, "Die Verklärung," 199; Kee, "Transfiguration in Mark," 148–49.

92   Bultmann, *History*, 260; Boobyer, *St. Mark and the Transfiguration Story*, 18; Klostermann, 86; Carlston, "Transfiguration and Resurrection," 240 (he also sees the transfiguration as ratification of Jesus' prediction of his suffering and resurrection); Frenschkowski, *Offenbarung und Epiphanie*, 2:184. Boobyer argued that the primary significance of the account was the confirmation of Jesus' messiahship, but that it had further meaning as a reference to the *parousia* (*St. Mark and the Transfiguration Story*, 48–87).

93   See Marcus, *Way of the Lord*, 52; Bauckham, *Jude, 2 Peter*, 208; Jon D. Levenson, *The Death and Resurrection of the Beloved Son: The Transformation of Child Sacrifice in Judaism and Christianity* (New Haven: Yale University Press, 1993) 30–31, 200–202, 228–29; Stegner, "Use of Scripture," 116.

94   Joseph B. Bernardin interprets the transfiguration as a confirmation both of Peter's confession and of Jesus' prediction of his suffering, death, and resur-

rection ("The Transfiguration," *JBL* 52 [1933] 181–89, esp. 181).

95   Yarbro Collins, "Son of God among Greeks and Romans," 91–92; Moss, "Transfiguration," 76–84. See also "Genre" above. Dibelius argued that, besides disclosing Jesus as the messiah (see above), the transfiguration reveals him as the Son of God in such a way that excludes the idea that he was adopted as such (*From Tradition to Gospel*, 276). Bernardin argued that Mark was influenced by the Jewish notion of a heavenly, preexistent messiah, as well as by traditions such as Phil 2:6-11, in his portrait here of Christ as a preexistent being ("Transfiguration," 183–89).

96   Stegner concludes that the transfiguration and the heavenly voice establish Jesus as "God's spokesman for the end-time" ("The Use of Scripture," 118).

97   Cf. Lohmeyer, "Die Verklärung," 198–99; Marcus, *Way of the Lord*, 80–81; Stegner, "Use of Scripture," 115.

98   See the commentary on v. 4 above.

99   Carlston, "Transfiguration and Resurrection," 240 (he also understands the transfiguration as a confirmation of Peter's confession; see above).

with another theme of 8:27—10:45, the instruction of the disciples.[100]

■ **8** This verse implies that, immediately after the sound of the divine voice, the cloud, Elijah, and Moses disap-

peared, and Jesus returned to his normal state. This sudden change suggests that the divine voice is the climax of the account and expresses its primary purpose. It is also typical of the literary form of the epiphany.[101]

---

100 See above and Lohmeyer, 172.

101 Frenschkowski, *Offenbarung und Epiphanie*, 2:187.

9:9   **And as they were coming down from the mountain, he ordered them to tell no one what they had seen, until the Son of Man had risen from the dead. 10/ And they kept the saying to themselves, discussing what the resurrection from the dead was. 11/ And they asked him, saying, "Why do the scribes say that Elijah must come first?" 12/ He said to them, "Elijah does come first and restores all things; and yet how is it written with reference to the Son of Man that he is to suffer much and be treated with contempt? 13/ But I say to you that Elijah has indeed come, and they did to him what they wanted, as it is written with reference to him."**

History of the Tradition

Bultmann argued that v. 11 followed directly upon v. 1 in Mark's source.[1] The main reason for this conclusion is that he understood the question of the disciples in v. 11 as pointing out the tension between the saying about the imminent coming of the kingdom of God in 9:1 and the "Jewish theory of a forerunner to the Kingdom of God."[2] Jesus' response resolves the tension by explaining that the forerunner has already come. This source-critical theory is unnecessary, however, if the disciples' question points out the tension between the imminent resurrection of the Son of Man, alluded to in v. 9, and the theory that "Elijah must come first." Such tension is created by the assumption that the resurrection of the Son of Man would be part of the general resurrection or at least of the resurrection of the righteous.[3] A number of commentators take vv. 9-10 as Markan redaction and conclude that vv. 11-13 preserve pre-Markan material.[4] Maurice Casey has attempted to reconstruct the Aramaic source allegedly used by the evangelist in composing vv. 11-13.[5]

Genre

Bultmann defined v. 9 as part of the transfiguration account, v. 10 as Markan composition, the disciples' ques-

1   Bultmann, *History*, 124–25, 260; so also Karl Gerold Goetz, *Petrus als Gründer und Oberhaupt der Kirche und Schauer von Gesichten nach den altchristlichen Berichten und Legenden: Eine exegetisch-geschichtliche Untersuchung* (UNT 13; Leipzig: Hinrichs, 1927) 78; Klostermann, 88–89; similarly Justin Taylor, "The Coming of Elijah, Mt 17,10-13 and Mk 9,11-13: The Development of the Texts," *RB* 98 (1991) 107–19, esp. 118.

2   Bultmann, *History*, 124.

3   See the commentary on vv. 10-11 below.

4   See the assessment by Ciliers Breytenbach, "Das Markusevangelium als Traditionsgebundene Erzählung? Anfragen an die Markusforschung der achtziger Jahre," in Camille Focant, ed., *The Synoptic Gospels: Source Criticism and the New Literary Criticism* (BEThL 110; Leuven: Leuven University Press/Peeters, 1993) 77–110, esp. 102–5. Hermut Löhr argued that vv. 11-13 were not originally connected with the preceding material ("Bermerkungen zur Elia-Erwartung in den Evangelien: Ausgehend von Mk 9,11-13," in Klaus Grünwaldt and Harald Schroeter, eds., *Was suchst du hier, Elia? Ein hermeneutisches Arbeitsbuch* [Hermeneutica 4; Rheinbach-Merzbach: CMZ-Verlag, 1995] 85–95, esp. 88–89).

5   Maurice Casey, *Aramaic Sources of Mark's Gospel* (SNTSMS 102; Cambridge/New York: Cambridge University Press, 1998) 121.

tion in v. 11 as Markan composition, and the saying about the coming of Elijah in vv. 12a, 13 as a pre-Markan apocalyptic saying.[6] Tannehill defined vv. 9-13 as an objection story; he did not, however, explain to what he thought the disciples' question in v. 11 was objecting.[7]

It is more illuminating to interpret vv. 9-13 as a didactic scene, created by Mark, and attached to the transfiguration-story.[8]

Comment

■ **9** The syntax of this sentence reflects Semitic influence.[9] The change of scene sets this verse and what follows off from the transfiguration as a separate, though related, unit.

William Wrede argued that this command is the key to the meaning and function of the messianic secret in Mark. He believed that the various types of the theme of secrecy were all intended to explain the fact that Jesus' life and work were unmessianic, whereas his followers came to believe that he was the messiah after they experienced him as risen from the dead. The command of Jesus signified that his identity would be revealed or could be comprehended only after his resurrection.[10] A comparative approach, however, also sensitive to the immediate literary context, leads to the conclusion that the command to silence here is a signal that the transfiguration should be interpreted as an anticipation and pre-

view of the resurrected state of Jesus.[11] The reference to the "Son of Man" "rising from the dead" recalls the first prediction of the resurrection of the Son of Man in 8:31.

■ **10-11** The verb $\kappa\rho\alpha\tau\epsilon\omega$ here has the sense of "keep."[12] It is not clear whether the Greek phrase $\pi\rho\grave{o}\varsigma\ \dot{\epsilon}\alpha\upsilon\tau\upsilon\acute{\varsigma}$ modifies the verb "keep" or the participle "discussing" ($\sigma\upsilon\zeta\eta\tauo\hat{\upsilon}\nu\tau\epsilon\varsigma$). The translation given above is based on the first alternative. The second requires a translation like "discussing among themselves."

The import of v. 10 is that the command of Jesus has impressed the three disciples, but also thrown them into confusion. Verse 11 follows logically, as the disciples ask Jesus a question aimed at dispelling their confusion. The disciples' question alludes to Mal 3:22-23.[13] In the text of Malachi, Elijah must come before "the great and splendid day of the Lord" (Mal 3:22 LXX). The context of Mark, however, suggests that the disciples assume that Elijah must come before "the resurrection of the dead" (Mark 9:10).[14] The classic meaning of "the Day of the Lord" is "day of judgment." By the late Second Temple period, the notion of the Day of the Lord was associated with a complex of eschatological ideas.[15] Among early Christians, "the Day of the Lord" was interpreted as the return of the risen Jesus and surely included the notion of resurrection.[16] The Markan disciples thus associate the "Day of the Lord" with the resurrection of the righteous or the general resurrection of the dead and assume that the Son of Man will arise on that occasion.[17]

---

6   Bultmann, *History*, 67, 124–25, 330. He considered v. 12b to be a (post-Markan) interpolation (ibid., 125).

7   Tannehill, "Varieties," 3.1 (p. 107).

8   Cf. Bultmann, *History*, 330–32; Sellew, "Composition," 631–32; and the commentary on 8:14-21 and 8:34 above. Öhler concluded that vv. 9-13 were composed by Mark (*Elia*, 40).

9   Beyer, *Semitische Syntax*, 133–34.

10   Wrede, *Messianic Secret*, 67–70; see "Excursus: The Messianic Secret" in the commentary on 1:24 above.

11   See the commentary on 8:30-31 above.

12   BAGD, 565. According to BDF §5(b) (p. 6), this expression is a Latinism; $\kappa\rho\alpha\tau\epsilon\omega$ ("keep") = *(memoria) tenere*.

13   Cited in the commentary on v. 4 above. See Marcus, *Way of the Lord*, 94; Liebers, *"Wie geschrieben steht"*, 75; Öhler, *Elia*, 2–6.

14   So also Joseph A. Fitzmyer, "More about Elijah Coming First," *JBL* 104 (1985) 295–96, esp. 295; Markus

Öhler states that "the day of judgment is the day of the resurrection of the dead" ("The Expectation of Elijah and the Presence of the Kingdom of God," *JBL* 118 [1999] 461–76; citation from 464).

15   Sir 48:10 is evidence for the association of the return of Elijah with the (eschatological) restoration of the twelve tribes (Öhler, *Elia*, 6–11; see also K. J. Cathcart, "Day of Yahweh," *ABD* 2:84–85.

16   Cf. 1 Thess 4:16 with 5:2; see also Richard H. Hiers, "Day of the Lord," *ABD* 2:82–83.

17   *1 Enoch* 22:13 implies that some of the dead will rise on the great day of judgment (George W. E. Nickelsburg, "Resurrection [Early Judaism and Christianity]," *ABD* 5:684–91, esp. 685).

Their confusion is caused by the evidently imminent resurrection of the Son of Man, in spite of the fact that Elijah apparently has not yet come. The evangelist presents the disciples as unaware that the Son of Man would rise *before* the general resurrection.[18] There is thus insufficient tension between the "dialogue" of vv. 9-10 and the question of the disciples in v. 11 to warrant the conclusion that vv. 11-13 constitute a pre-Markan unit.[19]

The teaching of the scribes[20] alluded to in v. 11, therefore, is not that Elijah is the forerunner of the messiah.[21] There is virtually no evidence that the notion of Elijah as a forerunner of the messiah was widely known in the first century CE.[22] This idea, on the contrary, seems to be a Christian innovation.[23] In Mark, it is expressed most clearly in 1:7-8.

■ **12-13** The first part of Jesus' response confirms the contemporary Jewish tradition, based on Malachi, that Elijah would return in the last days. The Markan Jesus not only alludes to scripture here but also expands it, so that Elijah "restores" not only "hearts" but all things.[24] This expansion gives Elijah a significant eschatological role.[25]

In the second part of his response, Jesus introduces a new prophecy, that the Son of Man is to suffer much and be treated with contempt. The term "it is written" ($\gamma\acute{\epsilon}\gamma\rho\alpha\pi\tau\alpha\iota$) indicates that this prophecy is taken from scripture, but scholars disagree about whether this statement alludes to a specific passage of scripture. Those who think that it does disagree about which passage and whether one or several texts are in view.[26] C. E. B. Cran-

---

18 The (probably Gentile) interlocutors of Paul in 1 Corinthians 15 apparently had no problem in accepting the resurrection of Christ while denying the general resurrection. Paul's conviction that they belong together, although the general resurrection is delayed, is typical of Jewish eschatology in the Second Temple period.

19 With Hugh Anderson, "The Old Testament in Mark's Gospel," in James M. Efird, ed., *The Use of the Old Testament in the New and Other Essays: Studies in Honor of William Franklin Stinespring* (Durham, NC: Duke University Press, 1972) 280–306, esp. 294; contra Liebers, *"Wie geschrieben steht"*, 76–77. See also "History of the Tradition" above.

20 On the historical scribes and the scribes as a group in Mark, see the commentary on 1:22 above.

21 Contra Sigmund Mowinckel, *He That Cometh* (New York/Nashville: Abingdon, 1954; Norwegian ed. 1951) 299; Joachim Jeremias, "Ἠλ(ε)ίας," *TDNT* 2 (1964) 928–41, esp. 931, 936; Cranfield, 297–98; Dale C. Allison, Jr., "Elijah Must Come First," *JBL* 103 (1984) 256–58. Louis Ginzberg argued that Elijah appears as the precursor of the messiah in the Talmud and *midrashim* (*An Unknown Jewish Sect* [New York: Jewish Theological Seminary, 1976; copyright 1970] 212, 241; cf. 216). He also argued that the *Damascus Document* from the Genizah in Cairo portrayed Elijah as "the messianic herald" (ibid., 226). These views are no longer widely accepted today. There is evidence, however, for the expectation of an eschatological teacher in Second Temple and rabbinic Judaism, who was usually identified with Elijah (see Gert Jeremias, *Der Lehrer der Gerechtigkeit* [StUNT 2; Göttingen: Vandenhoeck & Ruprecht, 1963] 285–87).

22 John A. T. Robinson, "Elijah, John and Jesus," in idem, *Twelve New Testament Studies* (SBT; Naperville,

IL: Allenson, 1962) 28–52, esp. 34–36; J. Louis Martyn, "We Have Found Elijah," in Robert Hamerton-Kelly and Robin Scroggs, eds., *Jews, Greeks and Christians: Religious Cultures in Late Antiquity: Essays in Honor of William David Davies* (Leiden: Brill, 1976) 181–219, esp. 189–90 n. 17; Morris M. Faierstein, "Why Do the Scribes Say That Elijah Must Come First," *JBL* 100 (1981) 75–86; Fitzmyer, "More about Elijah Coming First," 295–96; Öhler, *Elia*, 29–30; idem, "Expectation of Elijah," 461–64.

23 Note the clearly Christian passage in the recension attributed to Dorotheus of *Vit. proph.* 21: "[Elijah] is the one who is reckoned worthy to be the forerunner of the second and manifest coming of the Lord Christ" (οὗτος ὁ τῆς δευτέρας καὶ ἐπιφανοῦς παρουσίας τοῦ δεσπότου Χριστοῦ ἀξιούμενος εἶναι πρόδρομος); text and trans. from Michael E. Stone and John Strugnell, eds., *The Books of Elijah: Parts 1–2* (SBLTT 18; PS 8; Missoula, MT: Scholars Press, 1979) 96–97. On the anonymous recension, considered to be the earliest, see Öhler, *Elia*, 12–13.

24 See the quotation of Mal 3:22-23 LXX in the commentary on v. 4 above.

25 Löhr, "Bermerkungen zur Elia-Erwartung," 89.

26 Alfred Suhl concluded that the suffering of the Son of Man is merely asserted to be in accordance with the scriptures here and that no specific passage is in view (*Die Funktion der alttestamentlichen Zitate und Anspielungen im Markusevangelium* [Gütersloh: Mohn, 1965] 44, 134). See the criticisms by Marcus, *Way of the Lord*, 95 n. 4; Anderson, "Old Testament in Mark's Gospel," 286, 306. Barnabas Lindars concluded that Isaiah 53 was alluded to here and that the motive was apologetic (*New Testament Apologetic: The Doctrinal Significance of the Old Testament Quotations* [London: SCM, 1961] 88).

field concluded that the reference here is primarily to Isa 52:13–53:12 and interpreted the suffering of the Son of Man as modeled on the suffering of the Servant of the Lord. He also mentioned several psalms to which the passage may allude.[27] Rudolf Pesch argued that the suffering of the Son of Man here is modeled primarily on that of the suffering righteous person in the psalms.[28] The epithet "Son of Man" most likely derives ultimately from Dan 7:13, but the link between that epithet and suffering does not derive from Daniel 7.[29] The idea that the Son of Man, that is, the messiah, must suffer much could equally well be based on Isaiah 53 as on the psalms of individual lament, on the assumption of a messianic rereading in each case. The use of the verb ἐξουδενέω ("treat with contempt") in v. 12 makes it somewhat more likely that the allusion is to Psalm 22 (21 LXX):

> But I am a worm and no man,
> an object of reproach for a man and an object of
> contempt for the people
> (ἐγὼ δέ εἰμι σκώληξ καὶ οὐκ ἄνθρωπος,
> ὄνειδος ἀνθρώπου καὶ ἐξουδένημα λαοῦ).
> (Ps 21:7 LXX)

Although forms of the related verb, ἐξουδενόω or ἐξουθενόω ("to treat with contempt") occur in the translations of Isa 53:3 attributed to Aquila, Symmachus, and Theodotion, neither verb occurs in the Old Greek of the verse or anywhere else in Isa 52:13–53:12.[30] The noun ἐξουδένωσις ("contempt") occurs in certain psalms, but the analogy between the situations of the speakers in these psalms and that of Jesus is less striking than in Psalm 22.[31] More significantly, neither of these psalms is cited anywhere else in Mark, whereas several allusions to Psalm 22 occur in Mark's passion narrative. Another striking parallel occurs in Psalm 89 (88 LXX):

> You have rejected and treated with contempt,
> you cast off your anointed;
> you have overturned the covenant of your servant,
> you have profaned to the ground his sanctuary
> (σὺ δὲ ἀπώσω καὶ ἐξουδένωσας,
> ἀνεβάλου τὸν χριστόν σου·
> κατέστρεψας τὴν διαθήκην τοῦ δούλου σου,
> ἐβεβήλωσας εἰς τὴν γῆν τὸ ἁγίασμα αὐτοῦ).
> (Ps 88:39-40 LXX)[32]

The "anointed" here is the king, rather than the "messiah" or "Christ," and God is reproached for events of the past. Nevertheless, the psalm is open to interpretation in terms of the sufferings of Jesus. Yet again, there is no allusion to this psalm elsewhere in Mark.

The statement regarding the Son of Man in v. 12b is probably a Markan composition.[33] It could be read as a prophecy of the rejection of the person and message of Jesus as the messiah,[34] but in the context, it is better understood as an allusion to the statement that the Son of Man must suffer much, be rejected (ἀποδοκιμασθῆναι) by the elders and the chief priests and the scribes, be killed, and after three days rise (8:31).[35] "Being rejected" and "being treated with contempt" are synonyms, and the motif of "suffering much" occurs in both sayings.

---

27 Pss 22:6 (21:7 LXX); 119:22 (118:22 LXX); 123:3 (122:3 LXX); Cranfield, 277, 298.

28 Pss 118:22; 22:6, 24; 69:33; and esp. 89:38 (88:39 LXX); Pesch, 2:79. The concept of a "suffering righteous" person as a key to the interpretation of the psalms of individual lament has been criticized; see the commentary on 14:18 below.

29 See "Excursus: The Son of Man Tradition" in the commentary on 2:10 above. See also Adela Yarbro Collins, "The Influence of Daniel on the New Testament," in Collins, *Daniel*, 90–105.

30 Cranfield (298) pointed out its presence in Aquila, Symmachus, and Theodotion. The verb does occur in Pss 22:24 (21:25 LXX); 69:33 (68:34 LXX), as Pesch pointed out (2:79), but these occurrences are in the thanksgiving parts of the psalm and do not fit the situation of the Markan Jesus as well as 22:6 (21:7 LXX).

31 Ps 123:3 (122:3 LXX); 119:22 (118:22 LXX); Cranfield, 298.

32 See Pesch, 2:79.

33 Liebers, *"Wie geschrieben steht"*, 83.

34 Adela Yarbro Collins, "The Appropriation of the Psalms of Individual Lament by Mark," in Tuckett, *Scriptures*, 223–41, esp. 234.

35 This statement in turn is based on scripture; see the commentary on 8:30-31 above.

The shift from the saying in v. 12a to that of v. 12b seems very harsh at first.[36] The third part of Jesus' response in v. 13, however, is the key to the relationship between the two sayings. It is generally agreed that the Markan Jesus refers to John the Baptist in saying, "Elijah has indeed come," and Matthew makes this explicit (17:3).[37] The remark "they did to him what they wanted" alludes to the account of the death of John in 6:14-29. The qualification "as it is written with reference to him" is problematic, since the motif that the returned Elijah would be persecuted is not attested in Jewish tradition prior to or contemporary with Mark.[38] It is likely that the indirect depiction of Elijah's being killed upon his return in Revelation 11 is Christian in origin. It is unlikely that the prophecy referred to here is a typological reading of the persecution of the earthly Elijah in 1 Kgs 19:2-10.[39] It is probable that the reference is to scripture, but not to a single passage. On the assumption that John the Baptist was a prophet, the Markan Jesus refers to a pervasive scriptural motif, namely, the rejection of the person and message of the prophet, which sometimes involves the threat or even the actuality of his death.[40]

Verses 12-13 establish a parallel between Elijah (John the Baptist) and Jesus (the Son of Man = messiah). Elijah has come, and, in fulfillment of scripture, has suffered. The messiah has come, and, in fulfillment of scripture, he will suffer. The placement of the saying about the suffering Son of Man in the center makes the whole speech another prophecy of the passion.[41]

This passage implies that the expanded eschatological role acknowledged for Elijah in v. 12a was not fulfilled because of the rejection of John by the leaders of the people and his death at the hands of Herod Antipas. A further implication is that Jesus, during his ministry and when he returns as Son of Man, will fulfill the hopes associated with Elijah and more.[42] This inference is supported by the subordination of Elijah to the transfigured Jesus, "the beloved Son" of God (9:7). The parallel between Jesus and John and the implication that Jesus will fulfill the hopes connected with Elijah imply, like 1:7-8, that John, as Elijah, was the forerunner of Jesus, the messiah.

9

	9:14-29 Exorcism and Faith	a
14/	**And when they came[a] to the disciples, they saw a large crowd around them and scribes[b] discussing with them.[c] 15/ And immediately the whole crowd was amazed when they saw him, and they ran up to[d] him and greeted him. 16/ And he asked**	

a   A C D et al. read ἐλθών ("when he came") and εἶδεν ("he saw") instead of ἐλθόντες ("when they came") and εἶδον ("they saw"), the readings of ℵ B L W et al. The plurals were probably changed to the singulars because the following verse speaks of the crowd's reaction to the presence of Jesus alone. The impersonal plural followed by the singular is typical of Markan style; see Turner, "Marcan Usage," 26. 229, 235 (Elliott, *Language and Style*, 40, 46).

---

36   Bultmann considered v. 12b to be a (post-Markan) interpolation; see "Genre" above. Clare Rothschild resolved this problem by arguing that "the Son of Man" in this verse refers to John the Baptist rather than to Jesus (*Baptist Traditions and Q*, 189). This solution is ingenious, but it is unlikely that the designation "Son of Man" would be used of Jesus in v. 9 (as Rothschild agrees; ibid., 191) and then of John so soon afterward in v. 12.

37   Öhler, "Expectation of Elijah," 465; Löhr, "Bermerkungen zur Elia-Erwartung," 91.

38   Marcus, *Way of the Lord*, 97–98; Liebers, "*Wie geschrieben steht*", 86–91.

39   Marcus, *Way of the Lord*, 97–98.

40   Jer 11:19, 21; 20:1-2; 26:8-11, 20-23; 37:14-16; 38:4-6;

2 Chr 16:10; 24:20-22; 1 Kgs 19:2, 10, 14; 22:19-28; Liebers, "*Wie geschrieben steht*," 369–75.

41   Martin Dibelius, *Die urchristliche Überlieferung von Johannes dem Täufer* (Göttingen: Vandenhoeck & Ruprecht, 1911) 30–31; Suhl, *Funktion*, 134; Liebers, "*Wie geschrieben steht*," 84–85; cf. Öhler, *Elia*, 47.

42   Christine E. Joynes argues that Jesus continues the work of John (Elijah) by cleansing the temple ("A Question of Identity: 'Who Do People Say That I Am?' Elijah, John the Baptist and Jesus in Mark's Gospel," in Christopher Rowland and Crispin H. T. Fletcher-Louis, eds., *Understanding, Studying and Reading: New Testament Essays in Honour of John Ashton* [JSNTSup 153; Sheffield: Sheffield Academic Press, 1998] 15–29, esp. 25).

them,ᵉ "What are you discussing with one another?"ᶠ 17/ And one (man) from the crowd answered him, "Teacher, I brought my son to you, because he has a mute spirit; 18/ and wherever it seizes him, it throws him down (to the ground),ᵍ and he foams at the mouth and grinds his teeth and becomes rigid; and I asked your disciples to drive it out, but they were not able." 19/ He then answered them, "O faithless generation, how long will I be with you? How long will I put up with you? Bring him to me." 20/ And they brought him to him. And when he saw him, the spirit immediately convulsed him, and he fell upon the ground and began to roll (himself around), foaming at the mouth. 21/ And he asked his father, "How long is it that this has been happening to him?" He said, "Since childhood. 22/ And it has often thrown him both into fire and into water in order to destroy him; but if you are able in any way, help us and have pity on us." 23/ Jesus then said to him, "If you are able!ʰ All things are possible for the one who trusts." 24/ Immediately the father of the child cried out and said,ⁱ "I trust; help my lack of trust!" 25/ Then, when Jesus saw that a crowd had run together, he rebuked the unclean spirit, saying to it, "(You) mute and deaf spirit, I command you, come out of him and from now on, do not enter into him." 26/ And, after crying out and convulsing (him) greatly, it came out. And he became like a corpse, so that most (of the crowd) were saying that he had died. 27/ Then Jesus took his hand and raised him up, and he rose.

28/ And when he had gone home, his disciples asked him privately, "Why were we not able to drive it out?" 29/ And he said to them, "This kind can be forced out in no way except by prayer."ʲ

b D Θ 067 Φ pc have, in addition, the article τούς ("the" [scribes]); see Aland, Synopsis, ad loc. The addition of the article may reflect the notion that the scribes, as a whole and as a social group, were the opponents of Jesus and his disciples. This would reinforce the tendency of the portrayal of the scribes in Mark as a whole, with the exception of 12:28-34. See the commentary on 1:22 above.

c A D N and many others read αὐτοῖς ("with them") instead of πρὸς αὐτούς ("with them"); see Aland, Synopsis, ad loc. This reading is a secondary grammatical improvement.

d D it attest the reading προσχαίροντες ("they were glad") instead of προστρέχοντες ("they ran up to"). The former reading is probably an early corruption; see Taylor, ad loc.

e C A N and many others attest the reading τοὺς γραμματεῖς ("the scribes"); see Aland, Synopsis, ad loc. This reading reflects a change from αὐτούς ("them") made to clarify and specify those addressed by Jesus.

f The rough breathing should be supplied in the word αὐτούς in the phrase πρὸς αὐτούς, read by ℵ¹ B Cᵛⁱᵈ et al. (see Tischendorf, 1:308) because the word is to be taken as reflexive (and thus as a contraction of ἑαυτούς). Some MSS reflect changes that make the reflexive character of the phrase unmistakable: ℵ* A W et al. read πρὸς ἑαυτούς; Θ 472. 565 read πρὸς ἀλλήλους; and D lat read ἐν ὑμῖν (see Aland, Synopsis, ad loc.).

g Almost all the MSS read ῥήσσει, "throws him down (to the ground)." It is unlikely, however, that this form is from ῥήσσω, the later form of ῥήγνυμι ("burst, tear"; cf. 2:22). Turner argued in favor of the reading attested by D 565 et al., ῥάσσει, "strikes," "dashes," or "overthrows (him)," a form of ῥάσσω, which is related to ἀράσσω; see idem, "Western Readings," 3–4. But this hypothesis is unnecessary, since ῥήσσει, "throws him down (to the ground)," may be taken as an Ionic form of ῥάσσω ("strike, dash, overthrow"); see LSJ, s.v.; Taylor, ad loc.

h The earliest recoverable reading is probably τὸ εἰ δύνῃ ("If you are able!"), in which the article τὸ (lit., "the") functions as quotation marks or an exclamation point and the words εἰ δύνῃ ("If you are able!") repeat part of the father's statement. This reading, with some MSS substituting δύνασαι ("you are able") for δύνῃ ("you are able"), is attested by ℵ B C* et al. The somewhat unusual use of the article and the ambiguity of the whole phrase gave rise to variants. One variant apparently arose from failure to note the play on the earlier statement by the father; it involves the addition of the infinitive πιστεῦσαι ("to believe"), which anticipates the following statement of Jesus, and is attested by A C³ D et al. Another variant lacks the τὸ (lit., "the") and is attested by p⁴⁵ D K et al.; W reads τοῦτο

i   The reading μετὰ δακρύων ("with tears"), attested by
      A² C³ D et al., is an early expansion of the text; see
      Taylor, ad loc., and Metzger, *Textual Commentary*, 85.

j   The translation is based on the shorter reading,
      attested by א* B et al. Most MSS attest the longer read-
      ing, καὶ νηστείᾳ ("and fasting"), which reflects an
      early expansion of the text. See Taylor, ad loc., and
      Metzger, *Textual Commentary*, 85.

History of the Tradition

Bultmann argued that two miracle stories were combined at the pre-Markan stage. The first, roughly vv. 14-
20, contrasted Jesus as miracle-worker with his disciples,
whose inability to exorcise the demon provided an
opportunity for the master to demonstrate his ability.
The second, more like an apophthegm in form and consisting roughly of vv. 21-27, describes the paradox of
unbelieving faith. The conclusion of the first story was
either broken off or is preserved in v. 25. The conclusion
of the second story has been replaced by vv. 28-29. His
arguments were as follows: (1) the disciples play a role
only in vv. 14-19, whereas the father takes the chief role
beginning with v. 21; (2) the illness is described twice, in
vv. 18 and 21-22; (3) the crowd is already present in v. 14,
yet comes on the scene for the first time in v. 25.[43]
Johannes Sundwall argued that the original story is represented by vv. 20-27 and that the evangelist expanded it
by adding vv. 14-19 and vv. 28-29.[44] Ludger Schenke
argued that vv. 19, 23-24 were added by the evangelist
and that vv. 28-29 are secondary, but pre-Markan.[45]

Helmut Koester noted that the account in Mark is
more than twice as long as the parallel narratives in
Matthew and Luke. Granted that Matthew often abbreviated Mark's miracle stories, he noted further that Luke's
version is abbreviated in much the same way. Mark 9:14b-
16, 21, 22b-24, parts of 25-27 and 28 do not appear in
either Matthew or Luke. He concluded that the version

of Mark we now have is longer in this passage than the
version read by the authors of Matthew and Luke.[46] The
evidence can, however, be explained just as well, if not
better, by the hypothesis that Matthew and Luke independently shortened the account of Mark.[47]

Gerd Theissen argued against Bultmann and others
that the middle section, beginning with v. 20, should be
regarded not as an originally independent story but as a
secondary accretion.[48] He explained the repetition of the
description of the symptoms as an intensification; that of
v. 20 is more violent than that of v. 18. Furthermore, the
attack of v. 20 is narratively motivated by the spirit seeing
Jesus (v. 20).[49] Further, he noted that the doubting plea
of v. 22 presupposes the disappointment with the disciples and that the motif of faith in vv. 23-24 picks up
Jesus' complaint in v. 19. Thus, whoever composed vv.
22-24 was working with vv. 14-19.[50] Finally, he argued
that the rush of the crowd in v. 25 was probably not originally motivated by the father's saying in v. 24, but by
some kind of threat, perhaps the attack described in v.
20.[51] The interpolation would then be vv. 21-24, perhaps
added by the evangelist.

Genre and Cultural Context

This account is an exorcism, which is a subtype of the
healing type of miracle story.[52] The Markan version of
this story is the only one that has "the complete form-
critical field of characters" as defined by Theissen.[53]

43   Bultmann, *History*, 211.
44   Johannes Sundwall, *Die Zusammensetzung des Markus-
      evangeliums* (AAABO.H 9.2; Åbo: Åbo Akademi,
      1934) 59; so also Karl Kertelge, *Die Wunder Jesu im
      Markusevangelium: Eine redaktionsgeschichtliche Unter-
      suchung* (SANT 23; Munich: Kösel, 1970) 175–77;
      but see the criticism by Ludger Schenke, *Die Wunder-
      erzählungen des Markusevangeliums* (SBB; Stuttgart:
      Katholisches Bibelwerk, 1974) 315–16.
45   Schenke, *Wundererzählungen*, 314–49, esp. 332, 335.
46   Koester, "History and Development," 50. He admits,
      however, that vv. 20-24 may be original (ibid., 51).
47   See Theissen, *Miracle Stories*, 177, who argues that
      compression is a tendency of transmission in gen-
      eral and not just a peculiarity of Matthew; see also
      the commentary below.
48   Theissen, *Miracle Stories*, 136.
49   Cf. Bultmann's second argument above.
50   Cf. Bultmann's first argument above.
51   Cf. Bultmann's third argument above.
52   On the genre "exorcism," see the commentary on
      1:21-28 above.
53   Theissen, *Miracle Stories*, 43–44.

In v. 17, the possessing demon is called "a mute spirit" (πνεῦμα ἄλαλον). Judging from the rest of the narrative, the reason is that the spirit does not speak through the afflicted person; the possession is manifested in physical symptoms. Or the description of the demon may derive from an ancient perception of the symptoms of epilepsy.[54]

The physical symptoms described in v. 18 are similar to those known today as manifestions of epilepsy. The modern name of the disease is related to the Greek name for it, ἐπιληψία or ἐπίληψις ("seizure" in the sense of "epileptic fit").[55] Many Greeks viewed the disease as a divine visitation and therefore called it "the sacred disease" (ἱερὰ νόσος).[56] A treatise attributed to Hippocrates, however, argues that it is no more sacred than any other disease.[57] Like other diseases, it has specific features and a particular cause. The author admits that the theory of divine origin is supported by the difficulty of understanding the illness but is undercut by the alleged simplicity of the cure: "purifications and incantations" (καθαρμοὶ καὶ ἐπαοιδαί).[58] In the opinion of the author of the treatise, those who first designated the disease as "sacred" were like the people called in his day "magicians, purifiers, charlatans and quacks" (μάγοι τε καὶ καθάρται καὶ ἀγύρται καὶ ἀλαζόνες).[59] Such people speak about "the intervention of gods and spirits" (ἐς τὸ θεῖον ἀφῆκει καὶ τὸ δαιμόνιον) and attribute the withdrawal of afflicted people from public view at the time of a seizure to "fear of the divine" (φόβος τοῦ δαιμονίου).[60] Among the symptoms listed are the following: "the patient becomes speechless and chokes; froth flows from the mouth; he gnashes his teeth and twists his hands; the eyes roll and intelligence fails" (ἄφωνος γίνεται καὶ πνίγεται, καὶ ἀφρὸς ἐκ τοῦ στόματος ἐκρεῖ, καὶ οἱ ὀδόντες συνηρείκασι, καὶ αἱ χεῖρες συσπῶνται, καὶ τὰ ὄμματα διαστρέφονται, καὶ οὐδὲν φρονέουσιν).[61] Kicking out with the feet, and jumping out of bed and running outside are also mentioned.[62] The author concluded that the disease is hereditary and that "phlegmatic" people are prone to it.[63] This remark makes clear that the author understood the disease as a result of an imbalance of humors.[64] Mark's attribution of the symptoms of the boy[65] to a spirit is similar to the popular or religious view of the sacred disease described in and rejected by this treatise.

Many Romans also considered the disease to be divine. During the reign of Tiberius,[66] Aulus Cornelius Celsus wrote an encyclopedia on medicine, in which he calls the disease *comitialis (morbus)* ("the disease pertaining to the *comitia*," i.e., "epilepsy") because a meeting of the *comitia* ("the assembly of the Romans for electing magistrates") was adjourned if anyone had an attack of epilepsy since this was considered a manifestation of divine power.[67] He also calls it *maior* ("the greater [disease])." Besides falling down and foaming at the mouth,

---

54 Owsei Temkin, *The Falling Sickness: A History of Epilepsy from the Greeks to the Beginnings of Modern Neurology* (2nd rev. ed.; Baltimore/London: Johns Hopkins University Press, 1971) 40; see also below.

55 LSJ, s.vv.; Hippocrates Aph. 3.16 (ἐπίληπτοι/ "[those] suffering from epilepsy"), 20 (τὰ ἐπιλη-πτικά/"epileptic [seizures]"), 22 and 29 (ἐπιλη-ψίαι/"epileptic seizures"); 5.7 (τὰ ἐπιληπτικά/ "epileptic [seizures]"); text from W. H. S. Jones, *Hippocrates* (LCL; Cambridge, MA: Harvard University Press; London: Heinemann, 1923) 4:126–33, 158–59; my trans.

56 The earliest attestations are found in fragments of Heraclitus and in Herodotus (Temkin, *Falling Sickness*, 15).

57 This work dates to about 400 BCE (Temkin, *Falling Sickness*, 4).

58 Hippocrates *Morb. Sacr.* 1.10; text and trans. from Jones, *Hippocrates*, 2:138–39.

59 *Morb. Sacr.* 2.1-5; Jones, *Hippocrates*, 2:140–41.

60 *Morb. Sacr.* 3.6-7; 15.1-8; Jones, *Hippocrates*, 2:144–45, 170–71.

61 *Morb. Sacr.* 10.3-6; Jones, *Hippocrates*, 2:158–59.

62 *Morb. Sacr.* 4.29-32; Jones, *Hippocrates*, 2:146–49. For a summary of symptoms noted by the ancients, see Temkin, *Falling Sickness*, 40–42.

63 *Morb. Sacr.* 5.7-8; 8.1-2; Jones, *Hippocrates*, 2:150–53, 154–55. See also Temkin, *Falling Sickness*, 31.

64 On the medical theory of the humors, see J. T. Valance, "Humours," *OCD* 733.

65 Verse 21 seems to imply that the man's son is no longer a child; but he is referred to as a παιδίον ("child") in v. 24.

66 J. T. Valance, "Cornelius Celsus, Aulus," *OCD* 392–93.

67 Celsus *De Medicina* 3.23.1; see W. G. Spencer, *Celsus: De Medicina* (3 vols.; LCL; Cambridge, MA: Harvard University Press; London: Heinemann, 1935) 1:332–33 and n. b. See also Temkin, *Falling Sickness*, 8.

he mentions *distentio nervorum* ("spasm of the sinews") as a symptom.[68] This feature seems similar to the rigidity described in Mark 9:18.

According to the Hippocratic treatise, *The Sacred Disease*, some people tried to cure epilepsy by "purification and magic" (καθαρμὸς καὶ μαγεία).[69] The *Apology* of Apuleius is evidence that some ancient people thought that epilepsy could also be the result of a spell. Apuleius was accused of casting a spell on a boy and a woman, but he defended himself by explaining that they were epileptics, so that their conditions were the result of disease, not of spells cast by Apuleius.[70] He knows that some people associate this illness with possession by a deity or daimon and believe that those who suffer from it may predict the future through a divine indwelling power that will manifest itself in the divination that occurs.[71] Apuleius himself, however, offers an explanation of epilepsy based on Plato's *Timaeus*.[72]

Some ancient people associated epileptic seizures with the power of the moon.[73] The parallel description of the illness in Matthew reflects this association by saying that the child was "moonstruck" (σεληνιάζεται) (17:15).[74] Similar language is used in a satirical dialogue by Lucian, in which Ion, a character who believes in exorcism, makes the following statement:

everyone knows about the Syrian from Palestine, the adept in it, how many he takes in hand who fall down in the light of the moon and roll their eyes and fill their mouths with foam; nevertheless, he restores them to health and sends them away normal in mind, delivering them from their straits for a large fee (πάντες ἴσασι τὸν Σύρον τὸν ἐκ τῆς Παλαιστίνης, τὸν ἐπὶ τούτῳ σοφιστήν, ὅσους παραλαβὼν καταπίπτοντας πρὸς τὴν σελήνην καὶ τὼ ὀφθαλμὼ διαστρέφοντας καὶ ἀφροῦ πιμπλαμένους τὸ στόμα ὅμως ἀνίστησι καὶ ἀποπέμπει ἀρτίους τὴν γνώμην, ἐπὶ μισθῷ μεγάλῳ ἀπαλλάξας τῶν δεινῶν). (Lucian *Philops.* 16)[75]

The text goes on to describe an exorcism.[76] Like Mark, this text associates the symptoms of epilepsy with possession by a demon and its cure with exorcism.

Comment

■ **14** This sentence describes Jesus and the three disciples who had seen the transfiguration being reunited with the rest of the disciples (cf. 9:2). The scribes may have been introduced here in order to prepare for Jesus' exclamation against this "faithless generation" (γενεὰ ἄπιστος) in v. 19.[77] That the rest of the disciples are portrayed as disputing with the scribes here, perhaps as a typical phenomenon, also recalls the knowledge of the scribes' teaching on the part of the three disciples who had gone with Jesus.[78]

---

68   Celsus *De Medicina* 3.23.2; text and trans. from Spencer, *Celsus*, 1:334–35.

69   Hippocrates *Morb. Sacr.* 21.26; Jones, *Hippocrates*, 2:182–83.

70   Apuleius *Apol.* 43–48; see the Latin text in Vincent Hunink, ed., *Apuleius of Madauros: Pro se de magia (Apologia): Edited with a Commentary* (2 vols.; Amsterdam: Gieben, 1997) 1:66–70 and the ET by Hunink, "Apology," in Stephen Harrison, ed., *Apuleius: Rhetorical Works* (Oxford/New York: Oxford University Press, 2001) 68–72; see also Kee, *Medicine*, 98.

71   Apuleius *Apol.* 42–43; Hunink, *Pro se de magia*, 65–66; idem, "Apology," 66–67.

72   Apuleius *Apol.* 49–51; Hunink, *Pro se de magia*, 70–71; idem, "Apology," 73–74; cf. Temkin, *Falling Sickness*, 6, 54, 59; Kee, *Medicine*, 98.

73   The association was made already in ancient Mesopotamia (Temkin, *Falling Sickness*, 3–4); in the second cent. CE, the physicians Aretaeus (ibid., 7) and Galen (ibid., 26), as well as the interpreter of

dreams Artemidorus (ibid., 11), also provide evidence for the association.

74   Cf. Matt 4:24, where the verb σεληνιάζομαι ("to be moonstruck") occurs; BAGD, s.v.

75   Text and trans. from A. M. Harmon, *Lucian* (8 vols.; LCL; London: Heinemann; Cambridge, MA: Harvard University Press, 1921) 3:344–45.

76   A trans. of the full passage is given in the commentary on 1:21-28 above.

77   Cf. 8:12, where Jesus refuses to give a sign to "this generation" (ἡ γενεὰ αὕτη); this expression does not refer to all people living at the time of Jesus, but to those who reject his person and message. See the commentary on 8:11-13 above. Matthew omits the reference to the scribes and relates the saying in Mark 9:19 to the disciples; cf. Matt 17:20. On the historical scribes and the scribes as a group in Mark, see the commentary on 1:22 above.

78   Cf. v. 11 and the commentary on vv. 10-11 above.

■ **15** The reaction of the crowd seems unmotivated. Their amazement (ἐκθαμβέομαι) is best understood as a literary device to highlight the significance and authority of Jesus.[79] The simple form of this verb (θαμβέομαι) occurs in 1:27, with reference to the authoritative teaching of Jesus and his power over demons. The analogous portrayal of Jesus here contributes to the contrast between the disciples and their master in the passage as a whole.

■ **16-19** Jesus' question in v. 16 begins the first dialogue between him and the father of the epileptic. He addresses the disciples and the scribes (cf. v. 14), but an individual from the crowd replies to him (v. 17). The man addresses Jesus as "teacher" (διδάσκαλε) and states that he had brought his son to Jesus because he had "a mute spirit."[80] An analogous link between authoritative teaching and the power to exorcise was made in 1:21-28. The underlying idea is that, in Jesus' case, both the authority to teach and the power to exorcise have a divine source.[81]

The man proceeds to describe the symptoms caused by the "mute spirit" (v. 18a). These are similar to those associated with epilepsy, from antiquity to today. The association of a particular disease with possession by a spirit was typical in some circles in antiquity.[82]

The man also reports the inability of the disciples to drive the spirit out (v. 18b). The failure of the disciples to cast out the demon is reminiscent of Gehazi's failure to raise the son of the Shunammite woman (2 Kgs 4:31). The motif occurs also in the Asclepius tradition. The servants of Asclepius removed a woman's head in order to remove a tapeworm from her. They were able to remove it, but then could not reattach her head. The god was provoked at them but with "a certain effortless divine power" was able to attach her head and raise her up.[83]

Jesus' remark about the faithless generation echoes Deut 32:20 LXX, "For it is a perverse generation, sons in whom there is no faithfulness" (ὅτι γενεὰ ἐξεστραμμένη ἐστίν, υἱοὶ οἷς οὐκ ἔστιν πίστις ἐν αὐτοῖς), whereas the parallels in Matt 17:17 and Luke 9:41 echo Deut 32:5 LXX, "a crooked and perverted generation" (γενεὰ σκολιὰ καὶ διεστραμμένη). This difference makes clear that "faith" or "trust" is the key theme in the Markan story. This theme has deep roots in scripture but has analogies also in the Asclepius tradition.[84]

The referent of the "faithless generation" is ambiguous. It could be the scribes, whose presence here is otherwise virtually unmotivated and unexplained.[85] It could be the disciples, on the assumption that their inability to cast out the spirit was due to their lack of faith or to the insufficiency of their faith.[86] Or it could be the father, whose own faith was insufficient to allow the exorcism to take place.[87]

The complaint of Jesus implies that it is a burden to be with "this faithless generation" and that he longs to go (or to return) to the divine world. It expresses impatience with the lack of faith he has encountered. The fact that he does not know how long this "exile" will last indicates that he is a creature whose mission and destiny are determined by God. Yet at the same time he possesses a hidden, divine power. In order to fulfill that mission and exercise that power he asks that the epileptic be brought to him.[88]

■ **20** In v. 18, the father described the typical seizures that the spirit caused in his son. Here, when the epileptic is brought to Jesus, one of those seizures occurs. The remark that the spirit convulsed the man immediately when it saw Jesus suggests that the seizure is an expression of the spirit's power and a kind of resistance to Jesus. Since it is mute, it cannot defend itself with

---

79 Cf. Georg Bertram, "θάμβος κτλ.," *TDNT* 3 (1965) 4–7, esp. 6.

80 On the significance of this description of the possessing spirit, see "Genre and Cultural Context" above.

81 See the commentary on 1:25-28 above.

82 See "Genre and Cultural Context" above.

83 Aelian *De natura animalium* 9.33; text and trans. in Edelstein and Edelstein, no. 422 (1:220–21).

84 Edelstein and Edelstein, no. 423.3 and 4 (1:222, 230); no. 423.9 (1:223, 231–32).

85 See the commentary on v. 14 above. This explanation is supported by the use of the expression "this generation" in 8:12 in a critical response to a request by the Pharisees; see the commentary on 8:11-13 above. See also 8:38 and the commentary above.

86 This is the interpretation of Matthew (see 17:20). See also the commentary on 4:40 and 6:37-38 above.

87 Contrast the woman with the flow of blood in 5:25-34; see the commentary on 5:33-34 above. This interpretation is supported by Jesus' statement in v. 23 and the father's response in v. 24.

88 Cf. Lohmeyer, 186–87. The exclamation of Jesus

speech, as the spirits in previous encounters with Jesus did (cf. 1:23; 5:6-7, 12).[89]

■ **21-24** Jesus initiates the second dialogue with the father by asking how long such seizures had been occurring (v. 21a). This question appears to be somewhat anticlimactic and thus has provided a basis for the argument that the story is not a unity.[90] In any case, the question provides an opportunity for renewed dialogue that explores the relation between healing or exorcising and faith or trust.

The father answers that his son has been having such seizures from childhood (v. 21b). This reply may indicate that he had reached puberty.[91] According to Celsus, the disease was sometimes spontaneously cured by the onset of puberty in the case of boys and of menstruation in the case of girls. But usually it persisted until the day of death without danger to life.[92] According to *The Sacred Disease*, when the disease has become chronic, it is incurable.[93] Galen wrote that a typical case of epilepsy began in childhood, and if it was not cured or did not disappear with puberty, it would increase and become worse and worse.[94]

The further description of the illness in v. 22a goes beyond ancient descriptions of epilepsy in attributing the intent to kill to the spirit. *The Sacred Disease* states that small children simply fall down wherever they happen to be when a seizure occurs. Later, they run to their mothers or someone else they know when they feel an attack coming on. Adults, having the same kind of premonition of an attack, seek privacy before a seizure commences.[95]

The drama is heightened when the father utters a "despairing plea" that expresses ambivalence toward Jesus as miracle-worker (v. 22b).[96] His call for help and pity expresses his desperation. The fact that he has brought his son to Jesus signifies his belief, or at least his hope, that Jesus has the power to heal his son. But the qualification "if you are able in any way" reveals his doubt. Nevertheless, the father is asking Jesus to go beyond the boundaries of what is humanly possible.[97]

Jesus' response in v. 23 plays on the qualification in the father's plea and turns the tables on him.[98] It is a question not of Jesus' ability but of the father's ability. The father's trust is the crucial factor in the healing of his son.[99] This response is an "exhortation" and an expression of "assurance" that evokes faith.[100] Most striking is the statement that "All things are possible for the one who trusts." Such ability is attributed only to God or the gods in antiquity.[101] According to the Markan Jesus, "trust" or "faith" is a quality that can endow human beings with divine power.

The climax of the story is the father's cry in v. 24, "I trust; help my lack of trust!" Here again there is ambivalence between his desire to trust and to step beyond the boundaries of human limitation, on the one hand, and his realization that he cannot do so without divine assistance, on the other.[102]

■ **25-27** In the present form of the story, the running together of the crowd is unmotivated. Verse 25 may have followed originally on v. 20. The crowd would then have run together because of the seizure described in v. 20 as an attack by the mute spirit. The reference to Jesus' seeing that the crowd had run together would then be a

---

may also be interpreted in terms of the pneumatic excitement of the miracle-worker; see Theissen, *Miracle Stories*, 57–58, and the literature cited there.

89 See the commentary above. See also Theissen, *Miracle Stories*, 136.

90 See "History of the Tradition" above.

91 But the use of the word παιδίον ("child") in v. 24 suggests otherwise.

92 Celsus *De Medicina* 3.23.1; Spencer, *Celsus*, 1:334–35.

93 Hippocrates *Morb. Sacr.* 14.19-20; Jones, *Hippocrates*, 2:168–69.

94 Temkin, *Falling Sickness*, 43.

95 Hippocrates *Morb. Sacr.* 15.1-14; Jones, *Hippocrates*, 2:170–71. See also Temkin, *The Falling Sickness*, 37–40.

96 Theissen, *Miracle Stories*, 54.

97 Ibid., 137.

98 See the note on the trans. of v. 23 above.

99 Compare Jesus' inability to perform mighty deeds in his hometown; see 6:5-6a and the commentary above.

100 Theissen, *Miracle Stories*, 54, 58.

101 Robert M. Grant, *Miracle and Natural Law in Graeco-Roman and Early Christian Thought* (Amsterdam: North Holland, 1952) 127–34; Theissen, *Miracle Stories*, 137.

102 Cf. Theissen, *Miracle Stories*, 137.

means of returning to the basic story line after the addition of vv. 21-24.[103]

The spirit is called "unclean" (ἀκάθαρτον) for the first time in v. 25.[104] Jesus rebukes it, as in the first exorcism in Mark.[105] As in 1:25, the verbal rebuke of Jesus is reported, but it is much longer here.[106] The spirit is addressed as "(You) mute and deaf spirit," probably because deafness and muteness were closely associated.[107] The point may be that the boy was unable to speak or to hear others during a seizure.[108]

Jesus' statement, "I command you . . . and from now on, do not enter into him" (ἐγὼ ἐπιτάσσω σοι . . . καὶ μηκέτι εἰσέλθῃς εἰς αὐτόν), is similar to Josephus's account of an exorcism performed by a certain Eleazar, "he made him swear that he would never come back into him" (μηκέτ᾽ εἰς αὐτὸν ἐπανήξειν ὥρκου).[109] Such commands appear to be a technique designed to prevent a relapse.[110]

The departure of the spirit (v. 26) is described in terms similar to those of Jesus' first exorcism (1:26). In both cases, the spirit "convulses" (σπαράσσω) the possessed person, although here "greatly" (πολλά) is added. In both cases, the spirit "cries out," although different terms are used.[111] Even if the cry is inarticulate, this element is an indication that the spirit itself is not mute; rather, it causes its victim to become mute (cf. T. Sol. 12:2). Distinctive here is the result of the departure of the spirit: the young man "became like a corpse" and the

bystanders thought that he had died. Jesus then "raised him up and he rose" (ἤγειρεν αὐτὸν καὶ ἀνέστη). Although the story does not imply that the boy was actually dead, the dual expression in v. 27 attracts the attention of the audience and may call to mind the raising of the daughter of Jairus who had died. Jesus also grasped her hand; he asked her to "wake up" or "rise up" (ἔγειρε); and she also rose (ἀνέστη) (5:41-42).[112] In both stories the extraordinary power of Jesus is gloriously manifested.

■ **28-29** The scene changes abruptly so that Jesus and the disciples are alone. This is a typically Markan formulation, in which private instruction of the disciples is attached to pronouncement stories and other types of narratives.[113] As elsewhere, the instruction follows a question asked by the disciples.[114] Here the disciples ask why they could not drive out the spirit (v. 28). It is striking that the means recommended, prayer, does not occur in the story itself.[115] Prayer does appear elsewhere in Mark as a miracle-working technique (11:23-24; cf. Jas 5:15; Acts 9:40).[116] Calling upon the name of Jesus is also a powerful technique (9:38-39; Matt 7:22; Luke 10:17; Acts 3:6).[117] The fact that neither of these techniques occurs in Synoptic miracle stories indicates that miracle workers and tellers of miracle-stories were probably not the same people at the oral stage.[118] The disjunction between vv. 14-17 and vv. 28-29 is probably due to the distinction between the two streams of tradition.

---

103 See "History of the Tradition" above.

104 Cf. 1:23, 26, 27; 3:11, 30; 5:2, 8, 13; 6:7; 7:25, and the commentary on 1:23 above.

105 In 1:25 the rebuke is a technique of exorcism; see the commentary on 1:24-25 above. In 3:12, Jesus rebukes the spirits so that they would not make him known; in 4:39, he rebukes the wind, thus stilling it.

106 According to Koester, it is the longest exorcistic formula reported in the Synoptic Gospels ("History and Development," 51).

107 See v. 17 and the commentary on 7:32 above.

108 The phenomenon was noted in the Hippocratic literature (Temkin, *Falling Sickness*, 40).

109 Josephus *Ant.* 8.2.5 §47; text from Thackeray, *Josephus*, 5:596; my trans. Cf. the full citation of this passage in the commentary on 1:21-28 above.

110 The saying of Matt 12:43-45//Luke 11:24-26 implies that such relapses were known and were viewed as a problem.

111 See the note on the trans. of 1:26 above.

112 Cf. Koester, "History and Development," 51.

113 Sellew, "Composition," 631–32.

114 Cf. 4:10-13; 7:17-23; 10:10-12; 13:3-37; Bultmann, *History*, 330.

115 Unless the command in v. 25 can be considered a prayer; see Ville Auvinen, *Jesus' Teaching on Prayer* (Åbo: Åbo Akademi, 2003) 160–61. Another possibility is that the cry of the father in v. 24 is construed here as a prayer.

116 Theissen, *Miracle Stories*, 262.

117 Ibid.

118 So, plausibly, Theissen, *Miracle Stories*, 262.

9:30 **And they went out from that place**
and were going through Galilee,
and he did not want anyone to
know; 31/ for he was teaching his
disciples and was saying to them,
"The Son of Man will be handed
over into the hands of human
beings, and they will kill him, and
when he has been killed, after
three days[a] he will rise." 32/ But
they did not understand the
statement, and they were afraid
to ask him.

a   The translation is based on the reading attested by ℵ
B C* D et al. A C³ W et al. attest the reading τῇ τρίτῃ
ἡμέρᾳ ("on the third day"), which is a secondary
assimilation of the text of Mark to the more common
early Christian formulation, perhaps in particular to
the parallel in Matt 17:23; see above on 8:31. Cf. also
Matt 16:21; 20:19; 27:64; Luke 9:22; 18:33; 24:7, 21,
46; Acts 10:40; 1 Cor 15:4.

Comment

■ **30** This verse marks a topographical shift from the
region around Caesarea Philippi southwestward to and
through Galilee. On the surface, the statement that Jesus
"did not want anyone to know" (οὐκ ἤθελεν ἵνα τις
γνοῖ) resembles the remark in 7:24, that Jesus "wanted
no one to know" (οὐδένα ἤθελεν γνῶναι) that he was
in a house in the region of Tyre, but the motif plays very
different roles in the two passages. In chap. 7, the point
is that Jesus cannot remain hidden because of his
extraordinary power and the way in which the news
about him spreads. This element may already have been
in Mark's source.[1] Here, however, the secrecy is associated with Jesus' rebuke of the disciples in 8:30 and the
need to keep his identity hidden.[2] This association is
made clear by the second prediction of the destiny of the
Son of Man, which follows immediately in v. 31.

■ **31** As noted above, the section 8:27—10:45 is unified
by the repetition of a threefold pattern: (1) prediction of
the suffering, death, and resurrection of the Son of Man;
(2) misunderstanding on the part of the disciples; and
(3) teaching about discipleship.[3] The second occurrence

of this pattern begins in this verse with the second prediction. It is noteworthy that Mark introduces this prediction as Jesus' "teaching" (διδάσκω), just as he did the
first one (8:31). The saying does not qualify as "teaching"
for Matthew and Luke, so they omit this introductory
remark, just as they modify the introduction to the first
prediction.[4]

Mark uses the present tense in order to express a confident assertion about the future: "The Son of Man will
be handed over" (παραδίδοται). This is a vernacular
usage, comparable to the historical present, and common
in the NT in prophecies.[5] Matthew and Luke revise this
to the more correct or more literary "is about to be
handed over" (μέλλει παραδίδοσθαι) (Matt 17:22;
Luke 9:44).

One of the main usages of the verb παραδίδωμι is as
a technical term signifying "to hand over a person into
the custody of officials."[6] Mark uses the verb in this sense
many times, in a way that constitutes a theme in the overall narrative.[7] It is used for the first time in 1:14 to signify the arrest of John the Baptist.[8] Then it is used in
3:19 with reference to Judas Iscariot's handing Jesus over
to the chief priests, the scribes, and the elders.[9] This

---

1   See the commentary on 7:24-25 above.
2   See the commentary on 8:30 above and "Excursus:
    The Messianic Secret" in the commentary on 1:24
    above.
3   See "Narrative Unity of 8:27—10:45" in the commen-
    tary on 8:27—9:1 above.
4   Matt 17:22; Luke 9:43; cf. Matt 16:21; Luke 9:22. Cf.
    Paul J. Achtemeier, "'He Taught Them Many
    Things': Reflections on Marcan Christology," *CBQ*
    42 (1980) 465–81, esp. 480. Nancy Pardee has
    argued that for Matthew, "teaching" (διδαχή) signi-
    fies instruction based on the revealed will of God

for the ordering of the relationship between the
individual and God and between the individual and
his or her neighbor ("The Genre of the Didache: A
Text-Linguistic Analysis" [Ph.D. diss., University of
Chicago, 2001] 141–47).
5   BDF §323 (1).
6   BAGD, s.v., 1b.
7   See the commentary on 1:14-15 above.
8   That this is the sense of 1:14 is made clear by 6:17.
9   The full significance of 3:19 becomes clear gradu-
    ally; cf. 14:10-11, 43-46.

verse (9:31) is the next time that it occurs in this sense. Here the passive voice is ambiguous. On the one hand, it picks up the remark that Judas would hand Jesus over. On the other, it is open to a reading that takes it as a divine passive. The use of the verb $\delta\epsilon\hat{\iota}$ ("must") in the first prediction (8:31) encourages such an inference.[10] The same verb, in the passive voice, is used of the Servant of the Lord in Isaiah:

> Therefore, he will be the heir of many and will apportion the spoils of the mighty, because he was handed over to death and was reckoned among the lawless. And he has borne the sins of many and was handed over on account of their sins ($\delta\iota\dot{\alpha}$ $\tau o\hat{\upsilon}\tau o$ $\alpha\dot{\upsilon}\tau\dot{o}\varsigma$ $\kappa\lambda\eta\rho o\nu o\mu\dot{\eta}\sigma\epsilon\iota$ $\pi o\lambda\lambda o\dot{\upsilon}\varsigma$ $\kappa\alpha\dot{\iota}$ $\tau\hat{\omega}\nu$ $\dot{\iota}\sigma\chi\upsilon\rho\hat{\omega}\nu$ $\mu\epsilon\rho\iota\epsilon\hat{\iota}$ $\sigma\kappa\hat{\upsilon}\lambda\alpha,$ $\dot{\alpha}\nu\vartheta'$ $\hat{\omega}\nu$ $\pi\alpha\rho\epsilon\delta\dot{o}\vartheta\eta$ $\epsilon\dot{\iota}\varsigma$ $\vartheta\dot{\alpha}\nu\alpha\tau o\nu$ $\dot{\eta}$ $\psi\upsilon\chi\dot{\eta}$ $\alpha\dot{\upsilon}\tau o\hat{\upsilon},$ $\kappa\alpha\dot{\iota}$ $\dot{\epsilon}\nu$ $\tau o\hat{\iota}\varsigma$ $\dot{\alpha}\nu\dot{o}\mu o\iota\varsigma$ $\dot{\epsilon}\lambda o\gamma\dot{\iota}\sigma\vartheta\eta\cdot$ $\kappa\alpha\dot{\iota}$ $\alpha\dot{\upsilon}\tau\dot{o}\varsigma$ $\dot{\alpha}\mu\alpha\rho\tau\dot{\iota}\alpha\varsigma$ $\pi o\lambda\lambda\hat{\omega}\nu$ $\dot{\alpha}\nu\dot{\eta}\nu\epsilon\gamma\kappa\epsilon\nu$ $\kappa\alpha\dot{\iota}$ $\delta\iota\dot{\alpha}$ $\tau\dot{\alpha}\varsigma$ $\dot{\alpha}\mu\alpha\rho\tau\dot{\iota}\alpha\varsigma$ $\alpha\dot{\upsilon}\tau\hat{\omega}\nu$ $\pi\alpha\rho\epsilon\delta\dot{o}\vartheta\eta$). (Isa 53:12 LXX)

The verb is used ten times in chaps. 14–15. This frequent usage makes it into a kind of refrain and surely signifies its theological significance and its allusion to Isaiah 53.[11] The destiny of "being handed over" does not belong exclusively to Jesus. As we have seen, John the Baptist was handed over, and Mark applies the idea also to the disciples.[12]

The generality of the Son of Man's being handed over "into human hands" ($\epsilon\dot{\iota}\varsigma$ $\chi\epsilon\hat{\iota}\rho\alpha\varsigma$ $\dot{\alpha}\nu\vartheta\rho\dot{\omega}\pi\omega\nu$) is in striking contrast with the specificity of 8:31. The formulation here recalls the rebuke of Peter for setting his mind on "human affairs" ($\tau\dot{\alpha}$ $\tau\hat{\omega}\nu$ $\dot{\alpha}\nu\vartheta\rho\dot{\omega}\pi\omega\nu$) (8:33). The rest of the prediction is substantially the same as the first one.[13]

■ **32** The narrator's remark that the disciples did not understand what Jesus had said makes explicit the second element of the threefold pattern mentioned above. In the first realization of this pattern, the theme of misunderstanding was indirectly expressed in Peter's rebuke of Jesus (8:32b).

The narrator's remark here also develops the theme of the disciples' lack of understanding in the Gospel as a whole (6:52; 7:18; 8:17). In 6:52 and 8:17, this theme concerned the identity of Jesus as revealed in his mighty deeds.[14] Here it concerns the destiny of the Son of Man, his being handed over, killed, and rising from the dead.

In some cases in Mark, fear is the typical response of a human being to the revelation of divine power (4:41; 5:15; perhaps also 5:33; 6:50). In other cases, fear arises out of self-interest and self-protection (11:18, 32; 12:12). The reason for the disciples' fear here is not clearly indicated. Some members of the audience might infer that it is the numinous character of the prophecy that provokes awe in them. The specific comment that they were afraid *to ask him* about the saying, however, suggests that they did not want to hear about Jesus' being handed over and killed. If he is handed over and killed, the same could happen to them. In fact, Jesus has already stated, "If anyone wants to come after me, let him deny himself and take up his cross and follow me" (8:34). So their lack of understanding is closely related to the instinct of self-preservation (contrast 8:35-38). In other words, their lack of understanding is related to resistance to Jesus and his teaching, a classic example of "hardness of heart" (cf. 6:52; 8:17). In this reaction, the disciples are negative examples for the audience.

9

9:33-50 Instruction on Rank, Outsiders, and Sexuality

33/ And they went[a] to Capernaum. And when he was at home, he asked them, "What were you discussing on the way?" 34/ They remained silent; for they were speaking

a   The trans. is based on the reading $\hat{\eta}\lambda\vartheta o\nu$ ("they went"), attested by א B D et al. The majority of the MSS read $\hat{\eta}\lambda\vartheta\epsilon\nu$ ("he went"), but this is an early correction to prepare for the singular participle and main verb in the following sentence; see Turner, "Marcan Usage," 26 (1925) 229 (Elliott, *Language and Style*, 40).

---

10   See the commentary on 8:30-31 above.
11   Adela Yarbro Collins, "From Noble Death to Crucified Messiah," *NTS* 40 (1994) 492–93.
12   Mark 1:14 (John the Baptist); 13:9, 11, 12 (disciples).
13   See the commentary on 8:30-31 above.
14   See the commentary on 8:14-21 above.

among themselves on the way[b] about who was the greatest. 35/ And he sat down and called the Twelve and said to them, "If anyone wants to be first, he will be last of all and servant of all."[c] 36/ And he took a child and placed him in their midst. And having taken him in his arms, he said to them, 37/ "Whoever welcomes one child such as this one in my name, welcomes me; and whoever welcomes me, does not welcome me, but the one who sent me."

38/ John said to him, "Teacher, we saw someone driving out demons in your name and we prohibited him (from doing so), because he was not following us.[d] 39/ Jesus, however, said, "Do not prohibit him; for there is no one who will do a powerful work in my name and be able soon afterward to revile me. 40/ For whoever is not against us is for us. 41/ For whoever gives you a cup of water on the ground that you belong to Christ,[e] truly I say to you, he will surely not lose his reward.

42/ "And whoever gives offense to one of these little ones who trust in me,[f] it would be better for him if a big millstone were hung around his neck and he were thrown into the sea. 43/ And if your hand gives you offense, cut it off; it is better that you enter into life maimed, than with your two hands go into Gehenna, into the unquenchable fire.[g] 45/ And if your foot gives you offense, cut it off; it is better that you enter into life lame, than with your two feet be thrown into Gehenna.[h] 47/ And if your eye gives you offense, take it out; it is better that you enter into the kingdom of God with one eye, than with your two eyes be thrown into Gehenna, 48/ where their worm does not die and the fire is not quenched.

49/ "For everyone will be salted with fire.[i] 50/ Salt is good; but if salt becomes unsalty, with what will you season it? Have salt within yourselves and be at peace with one another."

b   A D et al. lack the words ἐν τῇ ὁδῷ ("on the way"). This lack is due to the perception that these words are superfluous, since they occur in v. 33 as well. Such superfluity, however, is characteristic of Markan style (Neirynck, *Duality in Mark*, 117).

c   D k omit the words καὶ λέγει αὐτοῖς· εἴ τις θέλει πρῶτος εἶναι, ἔσται πάντων ἔσχατος καὶ πάντων διάκονος, "and he said to them, 'If anyone wants to be first, he will be last of all and servant of all.'" This omission is probably due to an attempt to improve the coherence and pointedness of the passage; see Taylor, ad loc.

d   Apart from minor variations, there are three forms of the text of this sentence. ℵ B et al. attest the reading καὶ ἐκωλύομεν αὐτόν, ὅτι οὐκ ἠκολούθει ἡμῖν, "and we prohibited him (from doing so), because he was not following us." This reading is preferred by Nestle-Aland (26th and 27th editions) and *UBSGNT* (3rd edition) because of the intrinsic value of the witnesses. D W *f*[1.13] et al. attest the reading ὃς οὐκ ἀκολουθεῖ ἡμῖν καὶ ἐκωλύομεν αὐτόν, "(casting out demons in your name) who was not following us, and we prohibited him (from doing so)." This reading was advocated by Turner because he believed that the reading of ℵ B et al. represents an assimilation of the text of Mark to the more logical arrangement of the clauses in Luke (idem, "Western Readings," 4); it was also adopted by Huck-Greeven, ad loc., and preferred by Taylor, ad loc. A 𝔐 sy[h] Bas attest the reading ὃς οὐκ ἀκολουθεῖ ἡμῖν καὶ ἐκωλύομεν αὐτόν ὅτι οὐκ ἠκολούθει ἡμῖν, "(casting out demons in your name) who was not following us, and we prohibited him (from doing so), because he was not following us." This reading was rejected as conflate by Turner (ad loc.), Nestle-Aland (26th and 27th editions), and *UBSGNT* (3rd edition) (see Metzger, *Textual Commentary*, 86). It was adopted, however, by Nestle (25th edition) and Aland, *Synopsis* (4th rev. ed., 1967); it is advocated by Elliott as typical of Mark's repetitive style ("Eclectic Textual Commentary," 199); so apparently also Neirynck, *Duality in Mark*, 99. But it seems more likely that the last reading is indeed due to conflation; it is more blatantly redundant than the usual type of Markan repetition and this quality is easier to understand as an attempt to reconcile two differing readings than as Markan composition. It is more difficult to decide between the first two readings, but one cannot be sure that the reading of ℵ B et al. reflects an assimilation to the text of Luke. It could just as well be that the text of Luke is dependent on the earliest recoverable reading of Mark. In that case the reading of D W et al. could be explained as an "improvement" of the earlier Markan text.

e   The earliest recoverable reading is probably ἐν ὀνόματι ὅτι Χριστοῦ ἐστε ("on the ground that you belong to Christ"), attested by ℵ² A B et al. In this context, ἐν ὀνόματι ὅτι ("on the ground that") is a standard Greek idiom; see Charles F. D. Moule, *An Idiom Book of New Testament Greek* (2nd ed.; Cambridge: Cambridge University Press, 1960) 79; BDF §397 (3); Taylor, ad loc. The fact that the phrase resonates with ἐπὶ τῷ ὀνόματί μου ("in my name"), which occurs in vv. 37 and 39, has given rise to the variant ἐν ὀνόματί μου, "(a cup of water) in my name," which is attested by ℵ* C³ et al. The oddity of Jesus referring to himself in the third person has perhaps given rise to the variant ὅτι ἐμόν ἐστε, "that you (pl.) are mine (sing.)," attested by ℵ*. The ungrammaticality of this reading has led to the proposed emendation ὅτι ἐμοί ἐστε, "that you are mine"; see Tischendorf, ad loc., and Taylor, ad loc.

f   ℵ C*vid Δ it omit εἰς ἐμέ ("in me"); these words may have been added in an assimilation of the text of Mark to the parallel in Matt 18:6 (see Metzger, *Textual Commentary*, 86). They were omitted by Nestle-Aland (25th edition), Aland, *Synopsis* (4th rev. ed., 1967) and Huck-Greeven. Taylor (ad loc.) places them in the margin but concludes that they probably should be read. The strong attestation of the words, along with the possibility that they were omitted from a few MSS by accident, makes it likely that they belong to the earliest recoverable text of Mark.

g   The long reading, εἰς τὴν γέενναν, εἰς τὸ πῦρ τὸ ἄσβεστον ("into Gehenna, into the unquenchable fire"), is attested by ℵ*.² A B et al. There are two short readings: ℵ¹ L Δ et al. attest the reading εἰς τὴν γέενναν ("into Gehenna"); W f¹.¹³ 28 *pc* syˢ attest the reading εἰς τὸ πῦρ τὸ ἄσβεστον ("into the unquenchable fire"). The former of the short readings may have

arisen under the influence of the related sayings in Matt 5:29-30, and the latter under the influence of the parallel in Matt 18:8. Or both readings may be due to independent attempts to improve Mark's redundant style.

h   Verse 44 in the traditional text of Mark, attested by A D Θ f¹³ 𝔐, but lacking in ℵ B C et al., is an early expansion of the text, based immediately on v. 48 and ultimately on Isa 64:24 LXX, to which v. 43 also alludes.

The shorter reading, εἰς τὴν γέενναν ("into Gehenna"), is attested by ℵ B C et al. The longer reading, εἰς τὴν γέενναν, εἰς τὸ πῦρ τὸ ἄσβεστον ("into Gehenna, into the unquenchable fire"), is attested by A D Θ f¹³ 𝔐 et al. Since the shorter reading is so well attested, it is likely that the longer reading arose under the influence of v. 43.

i   Verse 46 in the traditional text of Mark entered the text in the same way as v. 44; see above. The earliest recoverable reading, πᾶς γὰρ πυρὶ ἁλισθήσεται ("For everyone will be salted with fire"), attested by (ℵ) B L et al., gave rise to variants because of its obscurity and ambiguity. D it attest the alternative reading πᾶσα γὰρ θυσία ἁλὶ ἁλισθήσεται ("For every sacrifice will be salted with salt"). This reading arose in an attempt to clarify the Markan text under the influence of Lev 2:13 LXX. The reading attested by A 𝔐 et al., πᾶς γὰρ πυρὶ ἁλισθήσεται καὶ πᾶσα θυσία ἁλὶ ἁλισθήσεται ("For everyone will be salted with fire and every sacrifice will be salted with salt"), is a conflation of the former two readings. See Taylor, ad loc.; and Metzger, *Textual Commentary*, 87. Elliott argues for the priority of the double reading ("Eclectic Textual Commentary," 199).

Literary Unity of 9:33-50

The unity of this passage as a whole is indicated primarily by the *inclusio* formed by the dispute about greatness at the beginning (vv. 33-34) and the exhortation to "be at peace with one another" in v. 50.[15]

The fact that this section is a collection of sayings linked by catchword or theme does not necessarily imply that the collection as such is pre-Markan.[16]

History of the Tradition

Bultmann argued that the setting in Capernaum is editorial. In fact, the whole setting is an editorial creation in order to introduce a collection of sayings now found in vv. 33-50. A controversy among the disciples is used as an occasion for the sayings.[17] Thus vv. 33-34 were composed by Mark.[18] The controversy about who is the greatest provides a setting for the saying in v. 35 on the greatness of

---

15   Frans Neirynck, "The Tradition of the Sayings of Jesus: Mark 9, 33-50," in *The Dynamism of Biblical Tradition* (New York: Paulist, 1967) = *Concilium* 20 (1967) 62–74, esp. 64.

16   Perry V. Kea, "Salting the Salt: Q 14:34-35 and Mark 9:49-50," *Forum* 6, 3–4 (1990) 239–44, esp. 242.

17   Bultmann, *History*, 65, 66, 149–50, 330.

18   Ernest Best concluded that most, if not all of vv. 33-

service. Bultmann argued that it is the oldest element in vv. 33-37, 41, and that it once circulated independently.[19] He concluded that it probably does not go back to the historical Jesus and tentatively suggested that it came from Jewish tradition.[20] The portrayal of Jesus taking a child in his arms in v. 36 is a Markan construction based on the traditional portrait in 10:16.[21] It serves as a setting for the saying in v. 37.[22]

Bultmann concluded that v. 37 was originally a Jewish proverb making the point that kindness to children is equivalent to kindness to God. In the Christian form of the saying, Jesus, who speaks here as the risen Lord, takes the place of God. By a transference of ideas, the child is interpreted as an ordinary or unimportant Christian. In the saying, therefore, the risen Lord instructs his people on how to behave toward one another.[23] Bultmann's argument about the original significance of the saying is persuasive, but not his conclusion about its meaning in its present context.[24]

Genre of vv. 33-37

Bultmann defined vv. 33-37 as an apophthegm, and vv. 35 and 37 as dominical sayings of the type "church-rules."[25] Robert C. Tannehill defined vv. 33-37 as a "correction story," in which "the corrected attitude is paradoxically tied to its opposite" in v. 35.[26] Bultmann's analysis provides useful general categories, and Tannehill's gives more precise expression to the purpose of the story.

Comment

■ **33-34** This is the third and last time in Mark that Capernaum is explicitly mentioned (cf. 1:21 and 2:1).

The first specifically identified place in Galilee where Jesus was active was Capernaum (1:21); similarly, it is the last here. The section 9:33-50 is set there; in 10:1 he moves on to Perea and Judea. As in 2:1, Capernaum is the location of Jesus' home.

After questioning the disciples, Jesus discovers that they were discussing on the way which of them was the greatest. As Bultmann noted, the scene is an artificial construction, designed as a setting for the saying in v. 35.[27] At the same time, it develops the theme of the misunderstanding of the disciples. The controversy among the disciples is another instance of the theme. Just as they do not wish to hear any more about the suffering of the Son of Man and do not wish to suffer themselves,[28] so here they not only wish to be "great," but each wishes to be greater than the others. This is the opposite of "denying oneself" (8:34).

■ **35** This saying has its own introduction, "And he sat down and called the twelve" (καὶ καθίσας ἐφώνησεν τοὺς δώδεκα). This feature supports Bultmann's argument that it once circulated independently and that vv. 33-34 constitute a secondary introduction for the new context in Mark.[29] In any case, in the present context, the saying is addressed to the Twelve. Whatever the origin of the saying, its link to the Twelve in its present form suggests that it concerns the style of leadership in the early church. The historical Jesus probably chose twelve disciples to symbolize the restoration of the twelve tribes of Israel.[30] There is little evidence that all of the Twelve took on leadership roles in the early church, either collectively or individually.[31] It is unlikely that the author of Mark is here criticizing the Twelve. Rather, he uses the

---

34 come from the evangelist ("Mark's Preservation of the Tradition," in M. Sabbe, ed., *L'Évangile selon Marc: tradition and redaction* (BEThL 34; 2nd rev. ed.; Leuven: Leuven University Press/Peeters, 1988) 21–34, esp. 27.

19 On the history of the tradition preserved in v. 41, see the commentary below.

20 Bultmann, *History*, 143, 147.

21 Ibid., 61.

22 Harry Fleddermann also concluded that this scene is a Markan construction and argued that the dispute about greatness is based on the anecdote about the sons of Zebedee (10:35-45) ("The Discipleship Discourse [Mark 9:33-50]," *CBQ* 43 [1981] 57-75, esp. 58-61).

23 Bultmann, *History*, 142–44, 147, 149, 155.

24 See the commentary on vv. 36-37 below. On the history of the tradition of vv. 42-50, see below.

25 Bultmann, *History*, 61, 65, 66, 142–44.

26 Tannehill, "Varieties," 1.1 (p. 102); 1.4 (p. 104).

27 See "History of the Tradition" above.

28 See the commentary on v. 32 above.

29 See "History of the Tradition" above. So also Best, "Mark's Preservation of the Tradition," 28, and the scholars he cites in n. 21.

30 See the commentary on 3:14-15 above.

31 Karl Heinrich Rengstorf, "δώδεκα κτλ.," *TDNT* 2 (1964) 321–28, esp. 326–27.

group to represent Christian leaders in general. He and those who handed on the saying before him present Jesus as advocating a kind of leadership characterized by service.[32] The idea of making oneself "last of all" is similar to the saying of Jesus that the disciple must "deny oneself."[33] This link with 8:34 suggests that the saying applies to all the followers of Jesus, not only to the leaders.

■ **36-37** Bultmann's argument that the evangelist constructed v. 36 on the model of 10:16 is persuasive, because the presence of children in 10:13-16 is intrinsic to the story, which is not the case here. Verse 36 serves primarily to provide a setting for the saying in v. 37.[34] Jesus' gesture of hugging the child suggests that the following saying is about actual children. Thus, Bultmann's conclusion that, in the Markan context, the child represents ordinary or unimportant members of the Christian community, as distinct from the leaders, is unlikely.[35] The placement of the child "in their midst" (ἐν μέσῳ αὐτῶν) and the use of the verb "to welcome (or accept or receive)" (δέχομαι) suggest that the issue is whether children ought to be welcomed as members of the community or welcomed at communal gatherings.[36]

Apart from the central role of the child, the saying seems related to the context of missionary proclamation and the hospitality that was necessary to the success of such efforts.[37] It seems unlikely, however, that the acceptance or welcoming of a child here relates to a missionary context. Bultmann's insight that the saying itself concerns kindness to children may be correct. If the saying did circulate independently, it may represent an adaptation of missionary language to a new context, perhaps the acceptance of newborn children. Greeks and Romans exposed or killed some newborn children as a way to control the size of their families. Such practices were not considered to be murder.[38] For some Jews at least, however, the exposure of infants and infanticide were defined as murder.[39] Christians apparently adopted the

---

32 John R. Donahue has suggested that "the imagery of household service (*diakonia*) is to characterize the way of discipleship" (*The Theology and Setting of Discipleship in the Gospel of Mark* [The 1983 Père Marquette Theology Lecture; Milwaukee: Marquette University Press, 1983] 39.

33 See the commentary on 8:34 above.

34 Bultmann argued that it provided an introduction for a complex of sayings, i.e., vv. 37-50 (*History*, 61).

35 Hooker (*Signs of a Prophet*, 42–43), following Matthew Black, argued that v. 36 is an acted parable, playing on the double meaning of the Aramaic word טַלְיָא ("child" and "servant"); the child is a "dramatic representation of the servant whom the disciple is required to become." This interpretation does not explain the present text of Mark, however, which does not play on the double meaning of the Greek word παῖς ("child" and "servant") but uses διάκονος ("servant") and παιδίον ("child" or "infant").

36 Peter Müller argued that the child in this passage is an opposing image to the rivalry for leadership; Jesus' action in v. 36 and saying in v. 37 imply that anyone who cares for such a child is acting in the manner of Jesus and God; *In der Mitte der Gemeinde: Kinder im Neuen Testament* (Neukirchen-Vluyn: Neukirchener Verlag, 1992) 220.

37 Cf. Q 10:16; Robinson et al., *Critical Edition of Q*, 188–89; Park, *Mission Discourse*, 157–59; Müller, *In der Mitte der Gemeinde*, 214–18.

38 Abandonment of children was not illegal nor, often, considered to be immoral; see John Boswell, *The Kindness of Strangers: The Abandonment of Children in Western Europe from Late Antiquity to the Renaissance* (New York: Pantheon Books, 1988) 58–62, 83–91. It was a fact of life. See Suzanne Dixon, *The Roman Mother* (Norman: University of Oklahoma Press, 1988) 19, 23, 34; eadem, *The Roman Family* (Baltimore/London: Johns Hopkins University Press, 1992) 40–41, 47–48, 109, 122, 131; Beryl Rawson, "Adult–Child Relationships in Roman Society," in eadem, ed., *Marriage, Divorce, and Children in Ancient Rome* (Canberra: Humanities Research Centre; Oxford: Clarendon, 1991) 7–30, esp. 10–11; Müller, *In der Mitte der Gemeinde*, 108, 117; see also Carolyn Osiek and David L. Balch, *Families in the New Testament World: Households and Household Churches* (The Family, Religion, and Culture; Louisville: Westminster John Knox, 1997), 65–66, 246 n. 92; Judith M. Gundry-Volf, "The Least and the Greatest: Children in the New Testament," in Marcia J. Bunge, ed., *The Child in Christian Thought* (Grand Rapids: Eerdmans, 2001) 29–60, esp. 33–34.

39 Philo *Spec. leg.* 3.20 §§110–19; Josephus *Ap.* 2.24 §202; Pseudo-Phocylides 184–85 (for Greek text and trans. see Pieter W. van der Horst, *The Sentences of Pseudo-Phocylides: With Introduction and Commentary* [SVTP 4; Leiden: Brill, 1978] 232); John J. Collins, "Marriage, Divorce, and Family in Second Temple Judaism," in Leo G. Perdue et al., *Families in Ancient Israel* (The Family, Religion, and Culture; Louisville: Westminster John Knox, 1997) 104–62, esp. 140;

Jewish view.[40] Exposed children were sometimes taken, before they died, by people who raised them as slaves.[41]

In this cultural context, the saying of Jesus may be understood as an exhortation to parents to accept, rather than kill or expose their infants.[42] Such an exhortation may have been called for in the case of recent Gentile converts or in the case of poor parents, whether Jewish or Gentile.[43] Alternatively, or in addition, the saying may advocate that Christian couples "accept" or "welcome" exposed infants and bring them up as their own. Such infants represent Jesus in his role as the suffering Son of Man.[44]

Literary Context of 9:38-40

An important reason for the placement of vv. 38-40 here is the association of the phrase "in your name" ($\dot{\epsilon}\nu$ $\tau\hat{\omega}$ $\dot{o}\nu\dot{o}\mu\alpha\tau\acute{\iota}$ $\sigma o\nu$) in v. 38 with the phrase "in my name" ($\dot{\epsilon}\pi\grave{\iota}$ $\tau\hat{\omega}$ $\dot{o}\nu\dot{o}\mu\alpha\tau\acute{\iota}$ $\mu o\nu$) in v. 37.[45] The theme of exorcism also recalls the exorcism of the epileptic in vv. 14-29. This link encourages an ironic reading of vv. 38-40: the disciples were unable to drive out the spirit afflicting the epileptic, but a man who is not even following Jesus is exorcising successfully in his name. This comparison leads to a recognition of tension between two techniques of exorcism: prayer in v. 29 and calling upon the name of Jesus in v. 38.

Cultural Context of vv. 38-40

In Jesus' encounter with the Gerasene demoniac, the demon attempts to gain power over Jesus by adjuring him by God ($\dot{o}\rho\kappa\acute{\iota}\zeta\omega$ $\sigma\epsilon$ $\tau\grave{o}\nu$ $\vartheta\epsilon\acute{o}\nu$) (Mark 5:7). This attempt reflects typical magical practice.[46] Compare the following use of the name of Jesus in an exorcistic charm: "I conjure you by Jesus, the god of the Hebrews" ($\dot{o}\rho\kappa\acute{\iota}\zeta\omega$ $\sigma\epsilon$ $\kappa\alpha\tau\grave{\alpha}$ $\tau o\hat{\nu}$ $\vartheta\epsilon o\hat{\nu}$ $\tau\hat{\omega}\nu$ $\dot{E}\beta\rho\alpha\acute{\iota}\omega\nu$ $\dot{I}\eta\sigma o\hat{\nu}$).[47] Like the situation portrayed in Mark 9:38-40, this is an example of non-Christian use of the name of Jesus, perceived to be powerful in casting out or driving away possessing spirits.[48]

The Greek translation of the miracles of Elisha also reflects the idea that the name of a deity is powerful. Naaman, the leper, expected that Elisha would come to him and stand and call upon the name of his god ($\dot{\epsilon}\pi\iota\kappa\alpha$-$\lambda\acute{\epsilon}\sigma\epsilon\tau\alpha\iota$ $\dot{\epsilon}\nu$ $\dot{o}\nu\dot{o}\mu\alpha\tau\iota$ $\vartheta\epsilon o\hat{\nu}$ $\alpha\dot{\nu}\tau o\hat{\nu}$) (4 Kgdms 5:11 LXX). Elisha cursed, in the name of the Lord ($\dot{\epsilon}\nu$ $\dot{o}\nu\dot{o}\mu\alpha\tau\iota$ $\kappa\nu\rho\acute{\iota}o\nu$), the boys who taunted him (4 Kgdms 2:24 LXX).

The author of Acts portrays Peter healing a lame man by the effective power of the name "Jesus Christ of Nazareth" (Acts 3:6). The effective power of divine persons is made active by the use of their names in the cultural context of the New Testament. The reason is that, in certain contexts, no distinction was made between the

---

Osiek and Balch, *Families*, 66. Adele Reinhartz argued that Philo condemned exposure and infanticide because some Jews in Alexandria were, like their Gentile neighbors, engaging in these activities; "Philo on Infanticide," in David T. Runia, ed., *The Studia Philonica Annual: Studies in Hellenistic Judaism* (vol. 4; BJS 264; Atlanta: Scholars Press, 1992) 42–58.

40 *Did.* 2:2; 5:2; *Barn.* 19:5; 20:2; *Diog.* 5:6; for further references, see Osiek and Balch, *Families*, 272–73 n. 50.

41 Boswell, *Kindness of Strangers*, 62; Osiek and Balch, *Families*, 65.

42 The decision whether to accept or expose an infant was the father's (Osiek and Balch, *Families*, 66, 83; Dixon, *Roman Mother*, 61). Note that 4QInstruction (*Sapiental Work A*) contains an exhortation that the male addressee should accept the offspring of his wife (or daughter): 4Q415 11 11 and 4Q416 2 iii 20; John Strugnell and Daniel Harrington, eds., *Qumran Cave 4*, vol. 24: *Sapiential Texts, Part 2: 4QInstruction*

(DJD 34; Oxford: Clarendon, 1999) 58–59, 62, 110, 113, 123.

43 The exposure of children by poor parents was especially common (Dixon, *Roman Family*, 109).

44 Müller interprets the child in vv. 36-37 as a symbol of the opposite of striving to become "great"; he also sees v. 37 as possibly exhorting Christians to care for orphans (*In der Mitte der Gemeinde*, 219–21). Gundry-Volf makes a connection between exposed children and the suffering Son of Man; she, however, takes the saying to mean welcoming children in general ("Least and the Greatest," 44–46, 60).

45 Bultmann, *History*, 149.

46 On the use of the phrase "in the name of" and of particular powerful names, see André Bernand, *Sorciers grecs* (Paris: Fayard, 1991) 24–25; on using the name of someone in healing and exorcism as a way of invoking the power of that person, see John A. Ziesler, "The Name of Jesus in the Acts of the Apostles," *JSNT* 4 (1979) 28–41, esp. 28.

47 *PGM* IV. 3019–20; text (slightly modified) from

person and the name.[49] In a related speech of Peter, the effective power is explained in terms of "faith in his name" (ἐπὶ τῇ πίστει τοῦ ὀνόματος αὐτοῦ), although it is not clear whose faith is meant. Further, in the same context it is stated that it is the name that has healed the man (Acts 3:16; so also 4:10).[50] According to the communal prayer of Acts 4:24-30, signs and wonders are done in the name of Jesus by God who "stretches out [God's] hand to heal" (ἐν τῷ τὴν χεῖρα (σου) ἐκτείνειν σε εἰς ἴασιν) on such occasions (Acts 4:30).[51]

Acts also portrays Paul exorcising in the name of Jesus: "I command you in the name of Jesus Christ to come out from her" (παραγγέλλω σοι ἐν ὀνόματι Ἰησοῦ Χριστοῦ ἐξελθεῖν ἀπ᾽ αὐτῆς) (Acts 16:18). Like Mark, Acts also depicts non-Christian exorcists using the name of Jesus to cast out demons; these are itinerant Jewish exorcists, identified as "seven sons of the high priest Sceva." Unlike the portrayal in Mark, these exorcists are unsuccessful, not because the name lacks power but because the evil spirit recognizes that they have no connection with Jesus (Acts 19:13-17). Haenchen comments, "Jesus' name works only if he is called upon by a Christian."[52]

In light of these passages in Acts, it is striking that Luke 9:49-50 follows Mark 9:38-40 in portraying Jesus as approving the use of his name by exorcists who have no relation to him and as supporting this approval with the same saying. Luke also preserves the saying that makes the opposite point, which the author apparently found in Q (Luke 11:23||Matt 12:30).[53] There is no contradiction,

because it is characteristic of proverbial speech that advice is not absolute or universal but must fit the occasion.

That healing in the name of Jesus was practiced by early Christians is attested by Jas 5:14.[54]

The pronunciation of the divine name in the context of healing was criticized in the Mishnah:

And these are they who have no share in the life to come . . . R. Akiba says, also one who reads heretical books, or he that utters charms over a wound and says [Exod 15:26]. Abba Saul says, Also he that utters the Divine Name according to its letters

(ואלו שאין להם חלק לעולם הבא . . . רבי עקיבא
אומר אף הקורא בספרים החיצונים והלוחש
על המכה אומר [Exod 15:26] אבא שאול אומר
אף ההוגה את־השם באותיותיו).
(m. Sanh 10.1)[55]

A text from the Tosephta implies, probably in a polemical way, that healing in the name of Jesus is practicing magic.[56]

Genre of 9:38-40 and of 9:38-50

Bultmann defines vv. 38-40 as a scholastic dialogue in which a simple communication (v. 38) provides the starting point.[57] Tannehill defines it as a correction story. It contains a negation (v. 39) followed "by the reason for

---

Preisendanz-Henrichs, 1:170; trans. from Betz, *Magical Papyri*, 96.

48 The story about R. Eleazar ben Damma (*t. Ḥul.* 2.22–23) may be evidence for Jewish or Jewish-Christian use of the name of Jesus in healing; cf. Joshua Schwartz, "Ben Stada and Peter in Lydda," *JSJ* 21 (1990) 1–18, esp. 12 n. 47.

49 Ernst Haenchen, *The Acts of the Apostles: A Commentary* (Philadelphia: Westminster, 1971; 14th Germ. ed., 1965) 200; Ziesler concluded that, in this passage and other similar ones in Acts, the name of Jesus is used to latch on to the power latent in the name ("Name of Jesus," 33).

50 Acts 3:16 implies, according to Haenchen, that the name is ineffective without faith on the part of the sick man (*Acts*, 207). Ziesler argues more persuasively that it is the apostles' faith that is powerful here and that the author of Acts thereby implies that

healing relates to the gospel and is not just a matter of the right people using the right formula ("Name of Jesus," 34–35).

51 Cf. Haenchen, *Acts*, 227.

52 Haenchen, *Acts*, 564; so also Ziesler, "Name of Jesus," 34.

53 Robinson et al., *Critical Edition of Q*, 236–37.

54 Dibelius argued that such healing was, in effect, an exorcism; Dibelius-Greeven, *James*, 252–53. He also points out that those who heal here are the elders, to whom such power is attributed because of their official status.

55 Text and trans. from Blackman, *Mishnayoth*, vol. 4: *Order Nezikin*, 285–86.

56 *T. Ḥul.* 2.22-23; see Schwartz, "Ben Stada and Peter in Lydda," 12 n. 47.

57 Bultmann, *History*, 54.

the negative response," given here in a *gar*-clause.[58] Again, both definitions are helpful; Bultmann's in a general way and Tannehill's in a more pointed way.

The story about Eldad and Medad may have provided a model for this one.[59] They remained in the camp, rather than going with the seventy elders and Moses to the tent, where those elders received some of the spirit that was on Moses and prophesied. Nevertheless, Eldad and Medad prophesied in the camp. When this event was reported to Moses, Joshua, his assistant, proposed to Moses that he stop them from prophesying. Eldad and Medad, however, were not outsiders but were among those registered by Moses as elders (Num 11:26-30).[60] Moses' response is inclusive rather than restrictive. Jesus' response goes further in refusing to restrict divine power to the followers of Jesus.

The larger passage, vv. 38-50, may be defined as an elaborated chreia.[61] The brief literary form, a saying attributed to a (usually famous) person, was elaborated in school exercises by adding, for example, a brief word of praise concerning the speaker of the saying, a paraphase of the chreia in a way that articulates a thesis, and then an argument that supports the thesis.[62]

Comment

■ **38-39** The "John" in question here is the son of Zebedee and brother of James (1:19, 29; 3:17; 5:37; 9:2). He was one of the three allowed to accompany Jesus to the home of Jairus (5:37) and to see the transfiguration (9:2). Although Bultmann looked upon the use of specific names as a secondary, novelistic development, he concluded that the role of John here is part of the original story.[63]

Here, as often in Mark, the address "teacher" is used

in connection with the mighty deeds of Jesus, although the use of the term does not always reflect unambiguous faith in or full understanding of his power. In any case, the association reflects the evangelist's perspective that the teaching interprets the mighty deeds and those deeds legitimate the teaching (4:38; 5:35; 9:17).[64]

On the practice of driving out demons "in the name of" Jesus, see "Cultural Context of vv. 38-40" above. Adolf Deissmann credibly argued that the use of the dative in this phrase is instrumental.[65]

The dialogue presupposes that there are people driving out demons in the name of Jesus. This setting probably does not go back to the lifetime of the historical Jesus, but more likely reflects a post-Easter situation. Further, John states that the exorcist in question is "not following us" (οὐκ ἠκολούθει ἡμῖν) rather than "not following you, that is, Jesus."[66] Similarly, Jesus' response in v. 39 fits the situation of the early church better than the life of the historical Jesus. It fits well in a time in which early Christians are engaged in mission and thus emphasizing the power available through faith in Jesus and his name. In addition, the setting is one in which there is concern about people "reviling" (κακολογέω) Jesus and especially his followers.

■ **40** Bultmann argued that the dialogue reached its climax with v. 39 and that this saying is a secondary addition, perhaps even a variant of the saying in Matt 12:30.[67] He classified v. 40 as a dominical saying, that is, a once-independent, proverbial saying attributed to Jesus.[68] In its present form, however, the saying is linked to v. 39 by the conjunction γάρ ("for"). In this context, the conjunction marks a clarification.[69] The idea is that those who perform or benefit from exorcisms or other mighty deeds done in the name of Jesus, no matter who performs them, will not be "against us" (καθ' ἡμῶν), but

58 Tannehill, "Varieties," 1.1 (p. 102); 1.4 (p. 104).
59 Bultmann, *History*, 25.
60 Levine, *Numbers 1–20*, 325–26, 339.
61 Ian H. Henderson, "'Salted with Fire' (Mark 9:42-50): Style, Oracles and (Socio)Rhetorical Gospel Criticism," *JSNT* 80 (2000) 44–65, esp. 50, 60.
62 Mack and Robbins, *Patterns of Persuasion*, 57–63.
63 Bultmann, *History*, 68, 345.
64 See the commentary on 1:25-28 above; see also Achtemeier, "'He Taught Them Many Things,'" 480.
65 Adolf Deissmann, *Bible Studies: Contributions, chiefly from papyri and inscriptions, to the history of the language, the literature, and the religion of Hellenistic Judaism and primitive Christianity* (Edinburgh: T & T Clark, 1901) 197–98, esp. n. 1 on 198.
66 Bultmann, *History*, 25, 54; cf. Günter Klein, *Die Zwölf Apostel: Ursprung und Gehalt einer Idee* (Göttingen: Vandenhoeck & Ruprecht, 1961) 28–29.
67 Bultmann, *History*, 24–25. See "Cultural Context of vv. 38-40" above.
68 Bultmann, *History*, 75, 81.
69 It thus fits category 2 in BAGD, s.v.

rather "for us" (ὑπὲρ ἡμῶν). Like v. 39, this verse fits a situation in which early Christian communities are spreading and becoming more widely known and controversial. The different attitude expressed in Acts may derive from a stronger sense of communal boundaries and from a desire to differentiate early Christian practices from magic.[70]

■ **41** According to Bultmann, v. 41 originally followed upon v. 37 and they "belong together." He also concluded that v. 41 originally spoke about "children" (παιδία) rather than "you" (ὑμεῖς), just as Matt 10:40 originally spoke about "little ones" (μικροί), like 10:42, rather than "you" (ὑμεῖς). The changes were made to make the saying applicable to the early church.[71] Therefore, in his view, v. 41, like v. 37, is a saying about kindness to children that comes from Jewish tradition.[72] That v. 41 was edited to apply it to the early church is clear from the addition of ὅτι Χριστοῦ ἐστε ("because you belong to Christ").[73] It is the risen Christ who speaks here.[74] The name of Jesus has religious meaning because he is the messiah and judge of the world.[75] Bultmann classified the saying among the "I-sayings" and concluded that it was formulated in the Palestinian church.[76]

It is not so clear, however, that the saying in v. 41 ever spoke about "children" (παιδία). The giving of a cup of water seems to fit best in a missionary context, and children are unlikely to have played a leading role in such a context.[77] In the present form of the saying, the conjunction γάρ ("for") links it to the saying of v. 40. Like the γάρ ("for") of v. 40, which links it to v. 39, the conjunction here marks a clarification.[78] This link leads the audience to connect the saying of v. 41 with the uncertain social context implied by vv. 39-40. In a situation in which many people are hostile to members of the Christ-movement, outsiders who give them even a cup of water

will surely be rewarded. This reward may be given in this life[79] or at the judgment when the Son of Man comes (cf. 8:38; 9:43, 45, 47).

This saying was probably placed in its present context because of the association of the phrase ἐν ὀνόματι ὅτι Χριστοῦ ἐστε ("on the ground that you belong to Christ") with the phrase "in your name" (ἐν τῷ ὀνόματί σου) in v. 38 and the phrase "in my name" (ἐπὶ τῷ ὀνόματί μου) in v. 37.[80] The relevant phrase in v. 41 is a standard Greek idiom.[81] This qualification implies that those who will receive a reward for giving even just a cup of water are those who do so *because* the recipient "belongs to Christ." Christians offering hospitality to other Christians are probably included as well.

The History of the Tradition of vv. 42-50

Will Deming argued that Mark 9:42–10:12; Matt 5:27-32; and *b. Nid.* 13b each display pronounced similarities to both of the other two texts, even though none is directly dependent on the others. He concluded that all three derive from a common set of traditions, dating to the middle of the first century CE, that reflects a discussion on sexuality in which the concept of adultery is extended to include a variety of sexual sins. The result was that all these sins were defined as such over against heterosexual marriage as a norm. This discussion also reflects the extension to men of the idea that sexuality is legitimate only within marriage, a norm often applied only to women.[82]

Even if Matt 5:27-32 was composed with reference to Mark 9:43-48, the clear sexual interpretation of the offense caused by the eye in the Matthean context indicates that Matthew understood the Markan passage at least to be open to a sexual interpretation. The Matthean

---

70 See "Cultural Context of vv. 38-40" above and Susan R. Garrett, *The Demise of the Devil: Magic and the Demonic in Luke's Writings* (Minneapolis: Fortress, 1989) 92–93.

71 Bultmann, *History*, 142–43, 148; similarly Klein, *Die Zwölf Apostel*, 30–31. Park concluded that Matthew changed the "you" (ὑμεῖς) in Mark 9:41 to "one of these little ones" (μικροί) (*Mission Discourse*, 161).

72 Bultmann, *History*, 147.

73 Ibid., 148.

74 Ibid., 149.

75 Ibid., 151.

76 Ibid., 151, 163.

77 Cf. the commentary on v. 37 above.

78 See category 2 in BAGD, s.v.

79 Cf. the reward given Aesop for showing the way and offering hospitality to a priestess of Isis (*Life of Aesop* 4–8 [Vita G]; Greek text in Perry, *Aesopica*, 36–38; ET in Daly, *Aesop without Morals*, 32–34).

80 See "Literary Context of 9:38-40" above.

81 See the note on the trans. of v. 41 above.

82 Will Deming, "Mark 9.42–10.12; Matthew 5.27-32, and *B. Nid.* 13b: A First Century Discussion of Male Sexuality," *NTS* 36 (1990) 130–41.

exegesis of Mark, combined with the similarities between Mark and *b. Nid.* 13b, would thus indicate that both evangelists were familiar with the set of traditions postulated by Deming.

■ **42** Since actual children are the subject of vv. 33-37, it is likely that "these little ones who trust in me" (οἱ μικροὶ τούτοι οἱ πιστεύοντες εἰς ἐμέ) are actual children as well.[83] Deming argues that Mark understands "the little ones" in this verse as Jesus' disciples.[84] Apart from the fact, however, that v. 42 follows v. 41, there is no reason to identify the "little ones" of v. 42 with the "you" of v. 41. "Little ones" is first and foremost a synonym of παιδία ("children" or "infants"). It seems better to conclude, then, that v. 42 picks up the reference to children in vv. 36-37 after a discussion of outsiders in vv. 38-41. If this inference is correct, then vv. 42-48 have sexuality as their primary referent.[85]

The qualification "who trust in me" indicates that children belonging to the Christian community are in view.[86] In the Markan context, "giving offense" (σκανδαλίζω) to one of them probably means relating to a child in a sexual manner (cf. Sir 9:5; *Ps. Sol.* 16:7). This hypothesis is supported by the likelihood that vv. 43, 45, and 47 also refer to sexual temptations.[87]

Deming argued that the masculine form of the word "one" (εἷς) here originally designated a young boy and thus that pederasty was in view.[88] The masculine could, however, simply represent the masculine form of the adjective "little" (μικρός) used here inclusively of both male and female children.

The construction of the sentence involves a conclusion (apodosis) followed by an unreal condition (protasis) and shows Semitic influence.[89] The force of the condition is that it would be better for a person who molests a child to die the horrible death described than to face the final judgment without having been punished for the sin already.[90] The logic seems to be that punishment in this life is better than eternal punishment.

■ **43** In the Old Testament and the Dead Sea Scrolls, the Hebrew word יד ("hand") is sometimes used euphemistically for the penis (Isa 57:8; 11QT 46:13).[91] It is unlikely that this is the referent in v. 43; rather, the idea of the hand giving offense alludes to "adultery with the hand," that is, masturbation, probably by males.[92] In the Mish-

---

83 So also William Loader, *Sexuality and the Jesus Tradition* (Grand Rapids: Eerdmans, 2005) 22. Werner Zager argued that they are disciples, namely, the "elect" (*Gottesherrschaft und Endgericht in der Verkündigung Jesu: Eine Untersuchung zur markinischen Jesusüberlieferung einschliesslich der Q-Parallelen* [BZNW 82; Berlin: de Gruyter, 1996] 201); Henderson argued that they are "believers dependent on official disciples like John and the Twelve" ("'Salted with Fire,'" 53). His conclusion that vv. 42-50 constitute an argument that the leaders should "avoid injuring lesser believers by maintaining peace within the leadership cadre" applies much better to Matthew 18 than to Mark (ibid., 54; cf. 55).

84 Deming, "First Century Discussion," 132, 138.

85 See "The History of the Tradition of vv. 42-50" above.

86 Bultmann argued that the saying was originally an old, possibly Jewish, proverb that was taken over by Q without Christianization (*History*, 144, 147); cf. Robinson et al., *Critical Edition of Q*, 472–77. The phrase "who trust in me" is, according to Bultmann, a secondary Christianization (*History*, 144–45, 148).

87 Deming, "First Century Discussion," 135. Zager argued that the "offense" is a temptation or inclination to sin and that the self-mutilation is intended to prevent sin, not as a punishment (*Gottesherrschaft und*

Endgericht, 213–14). The drowning envisaged in this verse, however, must be a punishment rather than a prevention (see the last paragraph of the commentary on v. 42 in the text above). The self-mutilation demanded in vv. 43, 45, and 47, however, could function both as punishment for sins already committed and as prevention of further sins. But see the story of Nahum in the commentary on v. 45 below.

88 Deming, "First Century Discussion," 135. See also Loader, *Sexuality*, 23–24, 59–60.

89 Beyer, *Semitische Syntax*, 76 n. 1; 80 n. 1; 176.

90 According to Josephus, the Galileans, in a rebellion against the nobles of the region, drowned the partisans of Herod the Great in the lake, i.e., the Sea of Galilee (*Ant.* 14.15.10 §450); Taylor, ad loc.; J. Duncan M. Derrett, "Law in the New Testament: *Si scandalizaverit te manus tua abscinde illam* (Mk.IX.42) and comparative legal history," in idem, *Studies in the New Testament*, vol. 1: *Glimpses of the Legal and Social Presuppositions of the Authors* (Leiden: Brill, 1977) 4–31, esp. 25.

91 See also Marvin H. Pope, *Song of Songs* (AB 7C; Garden City, NY: Doubleday, 1977) 517–18 and plate V, following p. 360; Betz, *Sermon*, 238 n. 335, and the literature cited there. Cf. also Matt 19:12.

92 George Foot Moore interpreted the parallel in Matt 5:30 in this way (*Judaism in the First Centuries of the*

nah it is stated that "every hand which frequently examines [the genitals for symptoms, for example, of menstruation] is, among women, praiseworthy; but among men, let it be cut off" (*m. Nid.* 2.1).[93] In the Babylonian Talmud, this is explained as a punishment for masturbation by men (*b. Nid.* 13a–b). A debate is recorded in the same context as to whether this punishment is a law or merely an execration, that is, a cursing (*b. Nid.* 13b [section b]).[94] On the one hand, a case is cited in which R. Huna actually cut off the hand (of someone who was accustomed to strike other people) in accordance with an analogous command in Job 38:15 (*b. Sanh.* 58b [section d]). On the other hand, the decision of R. Tarfon is reported, "If his hand touched the membrum, let his hand be cut off upon his belly," and the objection is also reported that his belly would then be split. R. Tarfon's response is, "It is preferable that his belly shall be split rather than that he should go down into the pit of destruction" (*b. Nid.* 13b [section b]).[95] The discussion ends with approval of taking the command as a law.[96]

Masturbation by males was condemned by the rabbis because of the loss of seed, which meant loss of potential life (*b. Nid.* 13a [section c]; 13b [section a]). Male homosexual relations were condemned in Lev 18:22 for the same reason.[97]

The punishment of cutting off the hand occurs also in Deuteronomy:

If men are fighting in the same place, a man with his brother, and the wife of one of them comes to rescue her husband from the hand of the one who is beating him and, extending her hand, takes hold of his testicles, you shall cut off her hand; your eye shall not spare [that is, have pity on] her (Ἐὰν δὲ μάχωνται ἄνθρωποι ἐπὶ τὸ αὐτό, ἄνθρωπος μετὰ τοῦ ἀδελφοῦ αὐτοῦ, καὶ προσέλθῃ γυνὴ ἑνὸς αὐτῶν ἐξελέσθαι τὸν ἄνδρα αὐτῆς ἐκ χειρὸς τοῦ τύπτοντος αὐτὸν καὶ ἐκτείνασα τὴν χεῖρα ἐπιλάβηται τῶν διδύμων αὐτοῦ, ἀποκόψεις τὴν χεῖρα αὐτῆς· οὐ φείσεται ὁ ὀφθαλμός σου ἐπ᾽ αὐτῇ). (Deut 25:11-12 LXX)[98]

It is likely that the punishment is so severe in this case because such an action could lead to injury of the testicles and thus to the inability to father children.[99]

Philo, however, understood the issue to be the woman's immodesty. He states approvingly:

And the penalty shall be this—that the hand shall be cut off which has touched what decency forbids it to touch (ἔστω δ᾽ ἡ δίκη χειρὸς ἀποκοπὴ τῆς ἁψαμένης ὧν οὐ θέμις). (*Spec. leg.* 3.31 §175)[100]

He reports an allegorical interpretation that he has heard from "highly gifted men" (θεσπέσιοι ἄνδρες) and

---

Christian Era: The Age of the Tannaim [2 vols.; New York: Schocken Books, 1958] 2:268); for a different opinion, see J. Duncan M. Derrett, *Law in the New Testament* (London: Darton, Longman & Todd, 1970) xlv–xlvi. On Mark 9:43, see Deming, "First Century Discussion," 134; cf. Betz, *Sermon*, 238–39. Helmut Koester argued that the sayings of vv. 43, 45, and 47 must be interpreted in light of the image of the body as a communal metaphor: "members of the Christian church who give offense should be excluded" ("Mark 9:43-47 and Quintilian 8.3.75," *HTR* 71 [1978] 151–53). He makes his case, however, not on the basis of the Markan text but on Matthew 18 and passages from Paul; see also the criticism by Deming, "First Century Discussion," 139.

93 Trans. (modified) from Derrett, "Law in the New Testament," 23.

94 Henderson argued that vv. 42-50 constitute "an oracular curse on leaders-in-waiting" ("'Salted with Fire,'" 60–63); this reading is based more on pas-

sages from Paul than on Mark's text. He rightly points out, however, that the use of the word "Gehenna" is "code-switching into non-Greek" and that such switching in Mark is sometimes motivated by "a semi-magical sense of the evocative and performative power of Jesus' speech" (ibid., 62–63).

95 Trans. by Israel W. Slotki, in Israel Epstein, ed., *The Babylonian Talmud, Seder Ṭohoroth, Niddah* (London: Soncino, 1935–52).

96 Betz cites *b. Šabb.* 108b (section c)-109a (section a) as evidence that the command was taken by the rabbis as an execration. The passage in question, however, does not explicitly say that the command to cut off the hand is not meant literally, and the category "execration" is not mentioned (*Sermon*, 239).

97 Milgrom, *Leviticus*, 2:1567–68.

98 Cf. Swete, ad loc.

99 Jeffrey H. Tigay, *Deuteronomy* (JPS Torah Commentary; Philadelphia/Jerusalem: JPS, 1996) 234, 485.

100 Text and trans. from Colson and Whitaker, *Philo*, 7:584–85.

elaborates it himself.[101] He clearly approves of this interpretation, which rejects the literal execution of the punishment. He does not, however, explicitly reject it himself, even though he had argued against such a punishment in non-Jewish law. He rejected amputation in that case, however, in favor of the death penalty, in accordance with the Law.[102]

Josephus attests that Galileans cut off the hand of the brother of Justus for forging letters.[103] He also claims that he caused a leader of an instance of sedition to cut off his own left hand as a punishment.[104]

It may be, nevertheless, that the saying in v. 43 is hyperbolic (cf. 10:25).[105] Compare the remarks of the prophetess Diotima in Plato's *Symposium*:

For men are prepared to have their own feet and hands cut off if they feel these belongings to be harmful. The fact is, I suppose, that each person does not cherish his belongings except where a man calls the good his own property and the bad another's; since what men love is simply and solely the good (ἐπεὶ αὐτῶν γε καὶ πόδας καὶ χεῖρας ἐθέλουσιν ἀποτέμνεσθαι οἱ ἄνθρωποι, ἐὰν αὐτοῖς δοκῇ τὰ ἑαυτῶν πονηρὰ εἶναι. οὐ γὰρ τὸ ἑαυτῶν, οἶμαι, ἕκαστοι ἀσπάζονται, εἰ μὴ εἴ τις τὸ μὲν ἀγαθὸν οἰκεῖον καλεῖ καὶ ἑαυτοῦ, τὸ δὲ κακὸν ἀλλότριον· ὡς οὐδέν γε ἄλλο ἐστὶν οὗ ἐρῶσιν ἄνθρωποι ἢ τοῦ ἀγαθοῦ). (*Symp.* 205e–206a)[106]

The idea of cutting off one's own hand is so extreme that it shocks the imagination and creates the motivation to avoid the evil that is being condemned.[107] Although the primary force of the saying is probably sexual, as argued above, the reference to the hand's giving offense could apply to a range of forbidden actions, for example, stealing. The Markan audience is called upon to interpret the saying and to apply it to themselves.

The command to cut off your hand if it gives you offense is followed by an argument why this should be done (v. 43b): if you sin (and remain unpunished in this life), you will go with an intact body to a place of punishment after death; if you cut off your hand, and do not sin (anymore), you will enter, though maimed, into "life," a place of reward.[108] The form of the sentence could be a direct translation from an Aramaic or postbiblical Hebrew saying, except for the accusative with infinitive construction. The sentence as a whole is good Greek.[109] The construction with καλόν ("better"; lit., "good")... ἤ ("than") is modeled on the biblical "'better' saying," which uses the construction טוב ("better"; lit. "good")... מן ("than") in the MT and κρείσσων ("better")/ἀγαθόν ("good")... ἤ/ὑπέρ ("than") in the LXX (e.g., Prov 15:16; Eccl 7:2).[110]

"Life" (ἡ ζωή) in vv. 43 and 45 is parallel to "the kingdom of God" (ἡ βασιλεία τοῦ θεοῦ) in v. 47. This correspondence suggests that "life" signifies "eternal life."

---

101 Philo *Spec. leg.* 3.32 §178; Colson and Whitaker, *Philo*, 7:586–87.

102 Philo *Spec. leg.* 2.44 §§242–48. Betz concluded that Philo rejects the literal penalty (*Sermon*, 239 n. 347); see, however, Colson and Whitaker, *Philo*, 7:584–85 n. a.

103 Josephus *Vit.* 35 §177; Derrett, "Law in the New Testament," 13.

104 Josephus *Vit.* 34 §§169–73; *Bell.* 2.21.10 §§642–45; Derrett, "Law in the New Testament," 13–14.

105 Betz concluded that Matt 5:29-30 is hyperbolic in ideas, images, and functions (*Sermon*, 236). Zager concludes that Mark 9:43, 45, and 47 are probably intended to be taken metaphorically, although the literal sense cannot be ruled out, given the Jewish comparative material (*Gottesherrschaft und Endgericht*, 214–18).

106 Text and trans. from W. R. M. Lamb, *Plato* (12 vols.; LCL; Cambridge, MA: Harvard University Press; London: Heinemann, 1925) 3:188–89.

107 Cf. Tannehill's notion of the "focal instance" (*Sword*, 53); Henderson argued that "the vivid indetermi-

nacy of the threat makes it persuasive" ("'Salted with Fire,'" 63–64). The hyperbolic character of the saying is one of the reasons why Luz (*Matthew 1–7*, 291–92) concluded that it goes back to the historical Jesus; similarly Jacques Schlosser, *Le règne de Dieu dans les dits de Jesus* (2 vols.; EtB; Paris: Gabalda, 1980) 2:632–33. Zager concluded that Mark 9:43, 45, 47 go back to the historical Jesus (*Gottesherrschaft und Endgericht*, 218, 220–23).

108 Davies and Allison presuppose the resurrection or transformation of the body as a prelude to "entering into life" in Matt 18:8//Mark 9:43 and thus conclude that the saying is "unmistakably hyperbolic" (*Matthew*, 2:766). This, however, is not necessarily the case, since the afterlife was regularly conceived in bodily terms in ancient texts; see Outi Lehtipuu, *The Afterlife Imagery in Luke's Story of the Rich Man and Lazarus* (NovTSup 123; Leiden: Brill, 2006).

109 Beyer, *Semitische Syntax*, 80 n. 1.

110 Roland E. Murphy, *Wisdom Literature: Job, Proverbs, Ruth, Canticles, Ecclesiastes, and Esther* (FOTL 13;

The designation of the place of punishment as "the unquenchable fire" ($\tau\grave{o}$ $\pi\hat{v}\rho$ $\tau\grave{o}$ $\mathring{\alpha}\sigma\beta\epsilon\sigma\tau o\nu$) supports this reading.[111] Matthew rightly interpreted the phrase by providing the synonym "the eternal fire" ($\tau\grave{o}$ $\pi\hat{v}\rho$ $\tau\grave{o}$ $\alpha\mathring{i}\acute{\omega}\nu\iota o\nu$) (18:8).[112]

$\Gamma\acute{\epsilon}\epsilon\nu\nu\alpha$ ("Gehenna") is a Greek form of the Aramaic expression גי הנם ("Valley of Hinnom"), which is equivalent to the Hebrew גי בן־הנם ("Valley of ben Hinnom") (Josh 15:8).[113] This valley has been identified with "the broad and deep Wadi er-Rababeh circling the Old City of Jerusalem on the south and west."[114] The valley became a negative symbol because the kings of Judah—for example, Ahaz and Manasseh—engaged in child sacrifice to Molech there. The shrine was destroyed by Josiah during his reform (2 Kgs 16:3; 21:6; 23:10).[115] Its role as a place of punishment begins with the prophecies of Jeremiah, who renamed it "Valley of Slaughter" and predicted that it would be filled with corpses, which would become food for the birds and wild animals, during the destruction of Jerusalem (Jer 7:30-34; 19:1-13).[116] In Jewish apocalyptic literature, this valley provided the imagery for a place of eternal punishment by fire.[117] The name "Gehenna" became the regular designation for the place of the eternal punishment of the wicked.[118] This is the usage in Mark 9:43, 45, and 47, which thus refer to eternal punishment.[119]

■ **45** Verse 44 in the traditional text of Mark is a later expansion of the text.[120]

In Biblical Hebrew, the word "foot" (רגל) is sometimes used as a euphemism for the male genitals.[121] If the sexual readings of vv. 42 and 43 are correct, this verse probably refers primarily to "adultery with the foot," that is, adultery in the conventional sense.[122]

Elsewhere in the NT, the Greek word usually translated "foot" ($\pi o\acute{v}\varsigma$) often means the whole leg and its individual parts. This may be another level of meaning here. The "foot" or "leg" here may also mean the instrument with which one goes somewhere to perform any kind of evil act.[123] The description of a person who has carried out the command of this verse as "lame" ($\chi\omega\lambda\acute{o}\varsigma$) relates to this more general level of meaning.[124]

A story in the Babylonian Talmud about Nahum of Gamzu provides a certain analogy to the command here, read in the latter sense. Nahum was so righteous that a dilapidated house did not collapse as long as he was in it. He was, however, blind in both eyes; his two hands and legs were amputated; and his body was covered with boils. When his disciples asked why all this had befallen him, he explained that he had once delayed giving food to a poor man, and before he gave the food the man had died. In his remorse he prayed that his eyes, which had had no pity on the poor man's eyes, become blind, his legs be amputated, and his body covered with boils. When his disciples lamented his fate, Nahum said, "Woe would it be to me did you not see me in such a sore plight" (*b. Taʿan.* 21a [section b]).[125]

Grand Rapids: Eerdmans, 1981) 70, 139–40, 173; Davies and Allison, *Matthew*, 1:525; 2:766. See also Henderson, "'Salted with Fire,'" 55, and the literature cited in n. 23.

111 This phrase may have been inspired by Isa 66:24, which is cited in v. 48. See the commentary below.

112 Note that the MT of Job 20:26 speaks about "an unfanned flame," i.e., lightning, as the means of punishment of the wicked, whereas the LXX speaks about "unquenchable fire" ($\mathring{\alpha}\kappa\alpha\upsilon\sigma\tau o\nu$ in some MSS and $\mathring{\alpha}\sigma\beta\epsilon\sigma\tau o\nu$ in others; see Rahlfs, *ad loc.*).

113 Joachim Jeremias, "$\gamma\acute{\epsilon}\epsilon\nu\nu\alpha$," *TDNT* 1 (1964) 657–58, esp. 657.

114 Robert G. Boling and G. Ernest Wright, *Joshua: A New Translation with Notes and Commentary* (AB 6; Garden City, NY: Doubleday, 1982) 368.

115 Jeremias, "$\gamma\acute{\epsilon}\epsilon\nu\nu\alpha$," 657; Mordechai Cogan and Hayim Tadmor, *II Kings: A New Translation with Introduction and Commentary* (AB 11; New York: Doubleday, 1988) 287–88.

116 Jeremias, "$\gamma\acute{\epsilon}\epsilon\nu\nu\alpha$," 657; Holladay, *Jeremiah*, 1:267–68.

117 *1 Enoch* 90:24–27; cf. 27:1; 54:1-6; 56:1-4; Jeremias, "$\gamma\acute{\epsilon}\epsilon\nu\nu\alpha$," 657; Nickelsburg, *1 Enoch 1*, 403–4.

118 2 Esdr 7:36; Stone, *Fourth Ezra*, 203, 221. Cf. *2 Bar.* 59:10; 85:13; *Sib. Or.* 1.103; 4.186.

119 Jeremias, "$\gamma\acute{\epsilon}\epsilon\nu\nu\alpha$," 658.

120 See the note on the trans. of v. 43 above.

121 Isa 7:20; cf. Judg 3:24; 1 Sam 24:3; Ezek 16:25; Deut 28:57; 2 Kgs 18:27 = Isa 36:12; Isa 6:2; 2 Sam 11:8-11; Konrad Weiss, "$\pi o\acute{v}\varsigma$," *TDNT* 6 (1968) 624–31, esp. 627 and n. 35; Deming, "First Century Discussion," 134 n. 12.

122 Deming, "First Century Discussion," 134.

123 Weiss, "$\pi o\acute{v}\varsigma$," 628.

124 Cf. Deming, "First Century Discussion," 138.

125 Trans. by Joseph Rabbinowitz in Israel Epstein, ed., *The Babylonian Talmud: Seder Moʿed, Taʿanith* (London: Soncino, 1935–52) 21a. Note also that blinding one's fellow's eye, cutting off his hand, and breaking

The command to cut off the foot or the leg is exactly parallel to the command to cut off the hand in v. 43. The next sentence, which gives the reason for cutting off the foot, is parallel except that βληθῆναι ("be thrown") is substituted for ἀπελθεῖν ("go"). The verb "be thrown" expresses more clearly the idea that going to Gehenna is a result of divine punishment. The order of words is also varied somewhat, because exact repetition would be displeasing to the audience.[126]

■ **47-48** Verse 46 in the traditional text of Mark is a later expansion of the text.[127]

The idea of the eye "giving you offense" should be understood in the context of the erotic gaze. Matthew makes this connection (5:28-29), and it was common in ancient literature and philosophy.[128] The command is parallel to those in vv. 43 and 45, except for the substitution of "take it out" (ἔκβαλε αὐτόν) for "cut if off" (ἀπόκοψον αὐτήν/αὐτόν), in keeping with human anatomy.

The sentence giving the reason is parallel to those of vv. 43 and 45, except that "the kingdom of God" (ἡ βασιλεία τοῦ θεοῦ) is substituted for "life" (ἡ ζωή).[129] The context makes clear that "the kingdom of God" is not fully present or manifest during the lifetime of the earthly Jesus. Its full manifestation and human participation in it are expected in the future, in the time of eschatological fulfillment. This usage supports the translation "the kingdom of God has drawn near" in 1:15, rather than "the kingdom of God has arrived."[130] The use of the phrase "the kingdom of God" in this third saying gives it a climactic character and links it to 1:14-15 and especially 9:1.

The verb βληθῆναι ("be thrown") is used in v. 47, as in v. 45. The order of words here differs from that of the two preceding sayings, creating an aesthetically pleasing variation.

This third saying is given an even stronger climactic effect by the elaboration of Gehenna as a place "where their worm does not die and the fire is not quenched" (ὅπου ὁ σκώληξ αὐτῶν οὐ τελευτᾷ καὶ τὸ πῦρ οὐ σβέννυται). These clauses allude to Isaiah:

And they shall go out and look at the corpses of the people who have transgressed against me; for their worm shall not die, and their fire shall not be quenched, and they will be a spectacle for all flesh (καὶ ἐξελεύσονται καὶ ὄψονται τὰ κῶλα τῶν ἀνθρώπων τῶν παραβεβηκότων ἐν ἐμοί· ὁ γὰρ σκώληξ αὐτῶν οὐ τελευτήσει, καὶ τὸ πῦρ αὐτῶν οὐ σβεσθήσεται, καὶ ἔσονται εἰς ὅρασιν πάσῃ σαρκί). (Isa 66:24 LXX)

These clauses are probably part of the earliest recoverable text of Mark. Their climactic purpose was not recognized by scribes who inserted them after vv. 43 and 45.[131]

Although it is not explicit, the location of the corpses in question may be the Valley of ben Hinnom on the south and west of the old city of Jerusalem.[132] In any case, Isa 66:24 speaks about an everlasting punishment of the wicked, and it is this motif that is emphasized by Mark.

■ **49** This saying was probably placed in its present context because of the association of the word "fire" (πῦρ) with the same word in v. 48. Like vv. 43-48, this saying has an eschatological focus. It implies that each follower of Jesus will be tested by fire. What is worthless will be destroyed, and what is good will survive. Fire is thus analogous to salt, which preserves (cf. 1 Cor 3:13, 15).[133] This "fire" should be understood in the context of the eschatological woes or "birth-pangs." In 13:5-8, the appearance of those who lead people astray, wars and rumors of wars

---

his foot are given as examples of liable injury in *m. B. Qam.* 8.1. See also Philo's argument that it is better for sinners to be punished by God than to be let alone (*Det. pot. ins.* 40); for discussion see Emma Wasserman, "The Death of the Soul in Romans 7: Sin, Death, and the Law in Light of Hellenistic Moral Psychology" (Ph.D. diss., Yale University, 2005) 206–8.

126 Fleddermann, "Discipleship Discourse," 70.

127 See the note on the trans. of v. 45 above.

128 Deming, "First Century Discussion," 134–35; Betz,

Sermon, 232; on the sexual context in Matthew, see also Derrett, "Law in the New Testament," 8.

129 The three instances of Mark are compressed into two in the parallel in Matthew; "life" (ἡ ζωή) appears in both (Matt 18:8-9).

130 See the commentary on 1:14-15 above.

131 See the notes on the trans. of vv. 43 and 45 above.

132 Jeremias, "γέεννα," 657. See the commentary on v. 43 above.

133 Wellhausen, 76; Friedrich Hauck, "ἅλας," *TDNT* 1 (1964) 228–29, esp. 229. For brief surveys of other

are but "the beginning of the birth-pains." The tribulation itself (13:19) is compared to the destruction of
Sodom and Gomorrah by fire.[134]

■ **50** This group of sayings was probably placed here
because of the association of the noun "salt" ($\ddot{\alpha}\lambda\alpha\varsigma$) with
the verb "to be salted" ($\dot{\alpha}\lambda\iota\sigma\theta\dot{\eta}\sigma\sigma\mu\alpha\iota$) in v. 49. The first
saying, "Salt is good" ($\kappa\alpha\lambda\dot{o}\nu \tau\dot{o} \ddot{\alpha}\lambda\alpha\varsigma$), serves to introduce the second.[135] A variant of the second saying was
included in Q (Matt 5:13b–c||Luke 14:34-35).[136] This
proverb can have many applications.[137] Given the eschatological character of vv. 43-48, and especially of v. 49, one
expects a similar application in the next saying, "Have
salt within yourselves" ($\ddot{\epsilon}\chi\epsilon\tau\epsilon \,\dot{\epsilon}\nu \,\dot{\epsilon}\alpha\nu\tau\sigma\hat{\iota}\varsigma \,\ddot{\alpha}\lambda\alpha$). This
cryptic saying and its eschatological significance are illu-
minated by a passage in Ignatius's *Letter to the Magnesians*
10.2:

> Put aside then the evil leaven, which has grown old
> and sour, and turn to the new leaven, which is Jesus
> Christ. Be salted in him, that none among you may be
> corrupted, since by your savour you shall be tested
> ($\dot{\nu}\pi\dot{\epsilon}\rho\theta\epsilon\sigma\theta\epsilon \,\sigma\dot{\nu}\nu \,\tau\dot{\eta}\nu \,\kappa\alpha\kappa\dot{\eta}\nu \,\zeta\dot{\nu}\mu\eta\nu, \,\tau\dot{\eta}\nu \,\pi\alpha\lambda\alpha\iota\omega$-
> $\theta\epsilon\hat{\iota}\sigma\alpha\nu \,\kappa\alpha\dot{\iota} \,\dot{\epsilon}\nu\sigma\xi\dot{\iota}\sigma\alpha\sigma\alpha\nu, \,\kappa\alpha\dot{\iota} \,\mu\epsilon\tau\alpha\beta\dot{\alpha}\lambda\epsilon\sigma\theta\epsilon \,\epsilon\dot{\iota}\varsigma$
> $\nu\dot{\epsilon}\alpha\nu \,\zeta\dot{\nu}\mu\eta\nu, \,\ddot{o} \,\dot{\epsilon}\sigma\tau\iota\nu \,\dot{I}\eta\sigma\sigma\hat{\nu}\varsigma \,X\rho\iota\sigma\tau\dot{o}\varsigma. \,\dot{\alpha}\lambda\dot{\iota}\sigma\theta\eta\tau\epsilon \,\dot{\epsilon}\nu$
> $\alpha\dot{\nu}\tau\hat{\omega}, \,\ddot{\iota}\nu\alpha \,\mu\dot{\eta} \,\delta\iota\alpha\phi\theta\alpha\rho\hat{\eta} \,\tau\iota\varsigma \,\dot{\epsilon}\nu \,\dot{\nu}\mu\hat{\iota}\nu, \,\dot{\epsilon}\pi\epsilon\dot{\iota} \,\dot{\alpha}\pi\dot{o} \,\tau\hat{\eta}\varsigma$
> $\dot{o}\sigma\mu\hat{\eta}\varsigma \,\dot{\epsilon}\lambda\epsilon\gamma\chi\theta\dot{\eta}\sigma\epsilon\sigma\theta\epsilon$).[138]

"Have salt within yourselves" in Mark may be read as a
metaphor for protecting oneself against corruption, for
avoiding the kinds of sins and occasions of sin treated in
vv. 42-48. Only in this way can one avoid being consumed
by the testing fire of v. 49 or eternally punished by the
fire of vv. 43-48.[139]

Another, less likely possibility is that the exhortation
"Have salt within yourselves" should be interpreted in the
context of communal relations. In Col 4:6, the
addressees are exhorted, "Let your speech always be gracious, seasoned with salt, so that you may know how you
ought to answer everyone" ($\dot{o} \,\lambda\dot{o}\gamma\sigma\varsigma \,\dot{\nu}\mu\hat{\omega}\nu \,\pi\dot{\alpha}\nu\tau\sigma\tau\epsilon \,\dot{\epsilon}\nu$
$\chi\dot{\alpha}\rho\iota\tau\iota, \,\ddot{\alpha}\lambda\alpha\tau\iota \,\dot{\eta}\rho\tau\nu\mu\dot{\epsilon}\nu\sigma\varsigma, \,\epsilon\dot{\iota}\delta\dot{\epsilon}\nu\alpha\iota \,\pi\hat{\omega}\varsigma \,\delta\epsilon\hat{\iota} \,\dot{\nu}\mu\hat{\alpha}\varsigma \,\dot{\epsilon}\nu\dot{\iota}$
$\dot{\epsilon}\kappa\dot{\alpha}\sigma\tau\omega \,\dot{\alpha}\pi\sigma\kappa\rho\dot{\iota}\nu\epsilon\sigma\theta\alpha\iota$).[140] The context makes clear that
this speech "seasoned with salt" is directed toward
answering the questions and challenges of outsiders.[141] If
the Markan saying should also be interpreted in terms of
judicious, interesting, and well-chosen speech, it differs
from the exhortation in Colossians by being directed to
insiders. Such speech would have as its goal dissuading
other followers of Jesus from rivalry and conflict and
inculcating the values expressed in the collection as a
whole.[142]

The last saying leads the audience in a different direction, if the former interpretation of the preceding saying
given above is correct. The exhortation "be at peace with

---

interpretations, see Fleddermann, "Discipleship Discourse," 70; Urban C. von Wahlde, "Mark 9:33-50:
Discipleship: The Authority That Serves," *BZ* n.F. 29
(1985) 49–67, esp. 60–63.

134 See the commentary on 13:14-20 below. Cf. 1 Cor
5:5; Adela Yarbro Collins, "The Function of 'Excom-
munication' in Paul," *HTR* 73 (1980) 251–63; cf.
also 13:8 and the commentary below. Von Wahlde
concludes that the fire signifies punishment in
Gehenna for those disciples who have lost their salti-
ness, i.e., failed in discipleship ("Mark 9:33-50," 62–
63). A problem with this hypothesis, as he
recognizes, is that it would be better supported if
v. 49 followed v. 50 rather than vice versa.

135 Bultmann, *History*, 91.

136 Robinson et al., *Critical Edition of Q*, 458–61; Bultmann, *History*, 87.

137 Bultmann concluded that it was originally a "secular" proverb (*History*, 102).

138 Text and trans. from Lake, *Apostolic Fathers*, 1:206–7.
Bart D. Ehrman translates "So lay aside the bad
yeast, which has grown old and sour, and turn to the

new yeast, which is Jesus Christ. Be salted in him,
that no one among you become rotten; for you will
be shown for what you are by your smell" (*Apostolic
Fathers*, 1:251).

139 For discussion of other interpretations, see Fleddermann, "Discipleship Discourse," 73; Michael Lattke,
"Salz der Freundschaft in Mk 9 50c," *ZNW* 75 (1984)
44–59, esp. 48–53; von Wahlde, "Mark 9:33-50," 64–
65.

140 Jeremy F. Hultin interprets "gracious" and "seasoned with salt" in this passage as referring to "witti-
ness" ("Watch Your Mouth: The Ethics of Obscene
Speech in Early Christianity and Its Environment"
[Ph.D. diss., Yale University, 2003] 216–22).

141 Lohse, *Colossians and Philemon*, 168–69; Hultin,
"Watch Your Mouth," 224–25.

142 Lattke interprets the saying as an admonition to
share the "salt of friendship" and as a call to table
fellowship and thus to fellowship as such ("Salz der
Freundschaft in Mk 9 50c," 58). Von Wahlde interprets the salt as representing the message of Jesus,
which acts as a purifying agent ("Mark 9:33-50," 65).

one another" (εἰρηνεύετε ἐν ἀλλήλοις) shifts the focus to the relations among the members of the community. It recalls the controversy disclosed in vv. 33-34. That link suggests that the command here is directed especially to the leaders to dissuade them from rivalry and self-assertion. The saying thus serves to round off the collection of sayings by returning to the opening theme.[143]

---

143 Neirynck, "The Tradition of the Sayings of Jesus," 65.

10

10:1-12 The Question of Divorce

1/   And he set out from there and went into the region of Judea and[a] Perea, and crowds gathered to him again, and, as he was accustomed, he was teaching them again.
2/   And they asked him[b] whether a man is permitted to divorce his wife, putting him to the test. 3/ He then answered them, "What did Moses command you?" 4/ They said, "Moses allowed him to write a certificate of divorce and to divorce her." 5/ Jesus then said to them, "He wrote this commandment for you because of your hardness of heart. 6/ But from the beginning of creation, 'male and female he made them.'[c] 7/ 'For this reason, a man shall leave his father and mother and cling to his wife,[d] 8/ and the two will become one flesh,' so that they are no longer two, but one flesh. 9/ What therefore God has joined man shall not separate."
10/   And when they were at home again, the disciples asked him about this matter. 11/ And he said to them, "Whoever divorces his wife and marries another commits adultery against her; 12/ and if she divorces her husband and marries another, she commits adultery."[e]

a   The trans. is based on the reading attested by ℵ B C* et al., καὶ πέραν τοῦ Ἰορδάνου, "(the region of Judea) and Perea." The meaning is probably that Jesus traveled through Perea to Judea, but the wording seems to imply that he went to Judea first and then to Perea. That the meaning is the former is supported by 11:1, where the place arrived at last is mentioned first. But the ambiguity gave rise to variants. The reading attested by C² D W et al., πέραν τοῦ Ἰορδάνου, "(the region of Judea) beyond the Jordan," results either from an independent attempt at clarification or an assimilation to the text of the parallel in Matt 19:1. The reading attested by A 𝔐 sy^h, διὰ τοῦ πέραν, "(the region of Judea) through Perea," is a more successful attempt at clarification that probably expresses the meaning of the earliest recoverable wording, i.e., the reading attested by ℵ B et al. See Taylor, ad loc., and Metzger, *Textual Commentary*, 87–88.

b   Most MSS have a variant of the longer reading, καὶ προσελθόντες Φαρισαῖοι ἐπηρώτων αὐτόν ("And Pharisees came and asked him"), attested by A B et al. It is likely, however, that the shorter reading, καὶ ἐπηρώτων αὐτόν ("And they asked him"), attested by D it et al., is the earliest recoverable reading, since the impersonal plural is typically used in Mark as equivalent to the passive. The mention of the Pharisees derives either from an independent attempt at clarification or from the parallel in Matt 19:3. See Turner, "Marcan Usage," 25 (1924) 378–86, esp. 382 (Elliott, *Language and Style*, 4–12, esp. 8); Turner, "Western Readings," 5; Taylor, ad loc., and Metzger, *Textual Commentary*, 88. Bultmann speaks about a tendency always to present the opponents of Jesus as scribes or Pharisees (*History*, 52).

c   The words ἄρσεν καὶ θῆλυ ἐποίησεν αὐτούς ("he made them male and female") allude to Gen 1:27 LXX. The variant attested by D W *pc* it, ἄρσεν καὶ θῆλυ ἐποίησεν ὁ θεός ("God created male and female"), is probably due to concern that the allusion will be overlooked and the subject of ἐποίησεν ("he made" or "he created") misconstrued as Moses. The reading attested by A Θ et al., ἄρσεν καὶ θῆλυ ἐποίησεν αὐτούς ὁ θεός ("God made them male and female"), is a conflation of the two older readings. Cf. Taylor, ad loc., and Metzger, *Textual Commentary*, 88.

d   The words καὶ προσκολληθήσεται πρὸς τὴν γυναῖκα αὐτοῦ ("and cling to his wife") do not occur in ℵ B Ψ 892*. 2427 sy^s. This shorter reading is probably due to accidental omission, since the last part of the quotation (v. 8a) makes sense only if the wife is mentioned beforehand; cf. Metzger, *Textual Commentary*, 88–89. The shorter reading was preferred by Lagrange, ad loc., Nestle (25th edition), and Aland, *Synopsis* (4th rev. ed., 1967).

e   The second saying occurs in the MSS in three main forms. ℵ B (C) et al. (see Tischendorf, ad loc., Taylor, ad loc., and Nestle-Aland [26th and 27th editions]) attest the reading καὶ ἐὰν αὐτὴ ἀπολύσασα τὸν ἄνδρα αὐτῆς γαμήσῃ ἄλλον μοιχᾶται, "and if she divorces her husband and marries another, she commits adultery." A 𝔐 et al. attest the reading καὶ ἐὰν γυνὴ ἀπολύσῃ τὸν ἄνδρα αὐτῆς καὶ γαμηθῇ ἄλλῳ μοιχᾶται, "and if a woman divorces her husband and is married to another, she commits adultery." D (Θ) f[13] et al. attest the reading καὶ ἐὰν γυνὴ ἐξέλθῃ ἀπὸ τοῦ ἀνδρὸς καὶ γαμήσῃ ἄλλον μοιχᾶται, "and if a woman departs from her husband and marries another, she commits adultery." The reading attested by ℵ B et al. is probably the earliest recoverable reading. That attested by A 𝔐 et al. is virtually identical in meaning. The variant attested by D (Θ) et al. probably arose as a correction of the earliest recoverable reading on the basis of an inference from Matt 19:9 and Luke 16:18 that it was not customary for Jewish women to divorce their husbands. Cf. the discussion by Lagrange, ad loc., who reads καὶ ἐὰν γυνὴ ἀπολύσῃ τὸν ἄνδρα αὐτῆς καὶ γαμήσῃ ἄλλον μοιχᾶται ("and if a woman divorces her husband and marries another, she commits adultery"); and by Taylor, ad loc., who favors the reading of D (Θ) et al.

Narrative Unity of 10:1-31

This section deals with issues that concern families and households: divorce and remarriage (vv. 2-12), children (vv. 13-16), property (vv. 17-22), and families, households and farms (vv. 23-31).[1] Such issues were of concern also to religious associations such as the community of the Dead Sea Scrolls.[2] These issues were especially relevant for the early Christian communities, since their self-understanding and organization were based, at least in part, on those of the family and the household.[3]

History of the Tradition of 10:1-31

Joachim Jeremias argued that Mark 10:1-31 represents a small, pre-Markan catechetical collection containing teaching regarding marriage, children, and property.[4] Heinz-Wolfgang Kuhn agreed that the evangelist made use of a collection of texts here, but defined its scope as including 10:1-45.[5] Rudolf Pesch agreed in part with Kuhn and found such a collection represented in 10:2-12, 17-27, 35-45. He concluded that this was a written source.[6] Such hypotheses are speculative and difficult to prove. The related subject matter of the units in 10:1-31, however, makes it likely that Mark used a written document of some sort, perhaps even his own notes.[7]

Comment

■ **1** As noted above, the middle section of Mark, 8:27—10:45, is structured as a journey, first northward to the villages of Caesarea Philippi (8:27) and Mount Hermon (9:2), and then southward toward Jerusalem.[8] After the exorcism at the foot of Mount Hermon (9:14-29), Jesus and his disciples travel toward the southwest into and through Galilee (9:30a). Their time in Galilee is characterized as a period in which Jesus was teaching the disciples privately (9:30b-31). This teaching involves first of all the second prediction of the passion (9:31). The disciples are portrayed as lacking understanding, first explicitly in 9:31 and then indirectly in the argument concerning

1   Donahue, *Discipleship*, 41–46; Elliott, "Jesus Movement," 199–200.
2   Donahue, *Discipleship*, 39; Pesch, 2:128; Kuhn, *Ältere Sammlungen*, 169–70.
3   Elliott, "Jesus Movement," 177–78, 187–95, 198–200.
4   Joachim Jeremias, *Die Kindertaufe in den ersten vier Jahrhunderten* (Göttingen: Vandenhoeck & Ruprecht, 1958) 62; ET *Infant Baptism in the First Four Centuries* (London: SCM, 1960) 50. Ernest Best concluded that Jeremias was basically right in this hypothesis (*Following Jesus*, 99).
5   Kuhn, *Ältere Sammlungen*, 146–91. He excluded the anecdote about the children in 10:13-16 (because their significance is metaphorical) and the third passion prediction (vv. 32-34). He concluded that the tradents of the pre-Markan collection were teachers concerned with the organization of communities.
6   Pesch, 2:128–30.
7   On the practice of note-taking and its relation to the composition of longer works, see Paul J. Achtemeier, "*Omne Verbum Sonat*: The New Testament and the Oral Environment of Late Western Antiquity," *JBL* 109 (1990) 14.
8   See the section "Narrative Unity of 8:27—10:45" above.

who was the greatest (9:33b-34). The teaching of Jesus that follows (9:35-50) to correct this misunderstanding takes place in Capernaum (9:33a). In 10:1, Jesus, having left Galilee behind, journeys through the region beyond the Jordan (Perea) into Judea.[9]

Whereas private teaching of the disciples has just occurred in Galilee, here in Judea the crowds come to Jesus once again, and he resumes his public teaching. This context sets the scene for the dialogue about divorce.

Genre of 10:2-9

Although he was inclined to think that the reference to the Pharisees in v. 2 is a later addition,[10] Bultmann classified this story as belonging to the type of controversy- (or scholastic) dialogue in which the questions are asked by opponents.[11] The reason is probably the narrator's comment that the questioners were testing ($\pi\epsilon\iota\rho\acute{a}\zeta\epsilon\iota\nu$) Jesus. This verb may have the neutral sense "to endeavor to discover the nature or character of [someone or] something by testing," or the hostile sense "to attempt to entrap through a process of inquiry."[12] Robert C. Tannehill defined the story, presupposing less dramatic tension than Bultmann, as a "testing inquiry."[13] Whether the questioners are hostile opponents or merely skeptical inquirers should be discernible from the context. As Bultmann has shown, however, the story does not have the typical structure of such dialogues, a feature that reveals its artificiality. He concludes that the story is artificial because the debate originated in the early church rather than in the ministry of Jesus.[14] If so, it must have been a very early development, since Paul already knows of a commandment of the Lord that the wife shall not be separated from her husband and the husband shall not divorce his wife (1 Cor 7:10-11).[15]

Divorce in the Jewish Cultural Contexts of Mark

In antiquity generally, marriage was "a social and legal contract between two families" to promote the interests of both families in terms of offspring and property.[16] Among Jews, Deut 24:1-4 became the classic legal text regarding divorce in the Second Temple period and among the rabbis, although originally its point was to forbid a man to remarry a woman whom he had divorced, if she had been married to and divorced from someone else in the meantime.[17] Other passages in Deuteronomy forbid divorce under certain circumstances (22:13-21, 28-29),[18] but in doing so imply that, apart from those situations, divorce was permissible. Deut 24:1-4 of course implies the same thing. The marriage contracts from Elephantine show that in this Jewish colony in Egypt divorce was practiced in the fifth century BCE; they show further that Jewish women, as well as men, could initiate divorce, at least in that context.[19] According to

---

9   See the note on the trans. of 10:1 above.
10 Bultmann, *History*, 52; see the note on the trans. of 10:2 above.
11 Bultmann, *History*, 26–27.
12 BAGD, s.v. $\pi\epsilon\iota\rho\acute{a}\zeta\omega$.
13 More precisely, Tannehill defines the story as a hybrid, since "vv. 5-9 both answer the initial question and correct the Mosaic permission" ("Varieties," 5.21 [p. 115]; cf. his discussion of correction stories, 1. [pp. 102–5]).
14 Bultmann, *History*, 27.
15 Although Paul presupposes that married women among his addressees have the right to divorce their husbands (v. 13), the formulation of the saying in v. 10 may reflect a Jewish context in which divorce initiated by a woman was less common; cf. Joseph A. Fitzmyer, "The Matthean Divorce Texts and Some New Palestinian Evidence," *TS* 37 (1976) 213–23; reprinted idem, *To Advance the Gospel: New Testament Studies* (BRS; Grand Rapids: Eerdmans; Livonia, MI:

Dove Booksellers, 1981; 2nd ed., 1998) 79–111, esp. 81 and 102–3 n. 7 (the reprint is cited here).
16 Osiek and Balch, *Families*, 42; on the importance of legitimate children in Roman marriages, see Dixon, *Roman Family*, 62, 67–68.
17 John P. Meier, "The Historical Jesus and the Historical Law: Some Problems within the Problem," *CBQ* 65 (2003) 52–79, esp. 64–67. David Instone-Brewer has concluded that the reference to a divorce certificate in Deut 24:1 is unique in ancient Near Eastern sources (*Divorce and Remarriage in the Bible: The Social and Literary Context* [Grand Rapids/Cambridge: Eerdmans, 2002] 28–31).
18 Fitzmyer, "Matthean Divorce Texts," 102 n. 3.
19 Fitzmyer, "Matthean Divorce Texts," 85–86; Tal Ilan, "Notes and Observations on a Newly Published Divorce Bill from the Judaean Desert," *HTR* 89 (1996) 195–202, esp. 195 and n. 2; John J. Collins, "Marriage, Divorce, and Family in Second Temple Judaism," in Leo G. Perdue et al., *Families in Ancient*

the Law, a woman had the right to divorce her husband if he did not fulfill his obligations to her.[20]

A different perspective is apparently expressed in Mal 2:10-16. The passage is difficult to interpret and probably corrupt. The reason for the corruption, however, is most likely that the text originally expressed an unqualified rejection of divorce. Later scribes and translators attempted to reconcile this text with Deut 24:1-4 and the widespread practice of divorce.[21] For example, the Greek translation reads:

> and guard yourselves in spirit, and do not forsake the wife of your youth; but if you hate her, divorce her, says the Lord, the God of Israel (καὶ φυλάξασθε ἐν τῷ πνεύματι ὑμῶν, καὶ γυναῖκα νεότητός σου μὴ ἐγκαταλίπῃς· ἀλλὰ ἐὰν μισήσας ἐξαποστείλῃς, λέγει κύριος ὁ θεὸς τοῦ Ἰσραηλ). (Mal 2:15b-16 LXX)

Similarly, in the *Scroll of the Minor Prophets* from Qumran, Mal 2:16 reads "but if you hate [her], divorce [her]" (4Q12[a] ii.4-7).[22] This variant, like the Greek translation, reflects the need to avoid inconsistency with Deut 24:1-4. The biblical manuscripts among the Dead Sea Scrolls represent the shape of scripture at the time among Jews in general.[23] This text, therefore, does not necessarily represent the view of the Community concerning divorce.[24]

The question of the community's attitude toward divorce is contested. The most important text for this issue is the *Damascus Document*. In 4:13-14, Isa 24:17 is quoted: "Terror and the pit and the snare are upon you, O inhabitant of the earth!" (NRSV). In the interpretation that follows, the three items—terror, pit, and snare—are equated with three nets of Belial, namely, unchastity (זנות), wealth, and defilement of the temple. The issue of unchastity is elaborated as follows:

> *The builders of the wall* [Ezek 13:10] . . . have been caught in unchastity in two ways: by taking two wives in their lifetime, whereas the principle of creation (is) *'Male and female he created them'* [Gen 1:27]; and those who entered (Noah's) ark, *'two (by) two went into the ark'* [Gen 7:9]. And concerning the prince (it is) written: *'He shall not multiply wives for himself'* [Deut 17:17]

> (בוני החיץ . . . הם ניתפשים בשתים בזנות לקחת שתי
> נשים בחייהם ויסוד הבריאה זכר ונקבה ברא אותם
> ובאי התבה שנים שנים באו אל התבה vacat
> ועל הנשיא כתוב לא ירבה לו נשים). (CD 4:19–5:2)[25]

The "builders of the wall" may refer to the Pharisees or to all Jews outside the community.[26] The Hebrew word translated "in their lifetime" (בחייהם) has a masculine suffix and thus seems to condemn any man who marries

Israel (The Family, Religion, and Culture; Louisville: Westminster John Knox, 1997) 119-20; Instone-Brewer, *Divorce and Remarriage*, 75-80.

20 Instone-Brewer, *Divorce and Remarriage*, 24-26.

21 Collins, "Marriage, Divorce, and Family," 122-27; Andrew E. Hill, *Malachi: A New Translation with Introduction and Commentary* (AB 25D; New York: Doubleday, 1998) 222-24, 250; Gershon Brin, "Divorce at Qumran," in Moshe Bernstein et al., eds., *Legal Texts and Legal Issues* (STDJ 23; Leiden: Brill, 1997) 231-44, esp. 232-36.

22 Trans. by Instone-Brewer, *Divorce and Remarriage*, 56 n. 56; see also Meier, "Historical Jesus and the Historical Law," 74-75 and n. 52. The MS dates to the middle of the second cent. BCE; Eugene Ulrich et al., eds., *Qumran Cave 4*, vol. 10: *The Prophets* (DJD 15; Oxford: Clarendon, 1997) 221; see the transcription, notes, and variants (ibid., 224-26).

23 Eugene Ulrich, *The Dead Sea Scrolls and the Origin of the Bible* (Studies in the Dead Sea Scrolls and Related Literature; Grand Rapids: Eerdmans; Leiden: Brill, 1999) 8-9.

24 Brin's argument that the community "consciously chose to adopt a reading in the *Scroll of the Minor Prophets* advocating divorce" is not persuasive ("Divorce at Qumran," 237).

25 Text from García Martínez and Tigchelaar, *Dead Sea Scrolls*, 1:556; trans. by Fitzmyer, "Matthean Divorce Texts," 95.

26 Instone-Brewer, *Divorce and Remarriage*, 62. Jerome Murphy-O'Connor concluded that the positions condemned here were generally approved outside of the community ("An Essene Missionary Document? CD II, 14–VI, 1," *RB* 77 [1970] 201-29, esp. 220). Solomon Schechter argued that the reference is to the Pharisees, since "the builder of the wall" alludes to their motto, "Make a fence to the Torah" (*Documents of Jewish Sectaries* [2 vols.; Cambridge: Cambridge University Press, 1910] 1:xvii).

twice in his entire life. Marrying twice would include polygamy, remarriage after divorce, and remarriage after being widowed.[27] Some commentators have drawn the conclusion that the text condemns any second marriage whatsoever.[28]

Chaim Rabin suggested that "in their (masc.) lifetime" is an allusion to Lev 18:18, which forbids a man to marry his wife's sister, as long as his wife is alive. He thus interpreted CD 4:21 to mean "in their (fem.) lifetime." This reading means that a man could marry a second time after his first wife had died.[29]

In 1972, Yigael Yadin published, in a preliminary way, part of the *Temple Scroll* that relates to the issue of the community's attitude to divorce. The relevant passage reads:

And he shall not take a wife from among all the daughters of the nations, but instead take for himself a wife from his father's house from his father's family.

And he shall take no other wife in addition to her for she alone will be with him all the days of her life. And if she dies, he shall take for himself another from his father's house, from his family

(ואשה לוא ישא מכול בנות הגויים כי אם מבית אביהו
יקח לו אשה ממשפחת אביהו ולוא יקח עליה אשה
אחרת כי היאה לבדה תהיה עמו כול ימי חייה ואם
מתה ונשא לו אחרת מבית אביהו ממשפחתו).
(11QT[a] 57:15-19)[30]

Yadin argued that the community opposed both polygamy and divorce. Since this text clearly permits remarriage after the death of the first spouse, a prohibition of all second marriages should not be inferred from CD 4:21.[31] In order to reconcile the two passages, a number of scholars have argued that the masculine plural suffix in the phrase "in their lifetime" (בחייהם) in CD 4:21 refers to the man and the woman who are joined in mar-

---

27   Instone-Brewer, *Divorce and Remarriage*, 63.

28   Murphy-O'Connor, "An Essene Missionary Document?" 220; Hartmut Stegemann, "The Qumran Essenes—Local Members of the Main Jewish Union in Late Second Temple Times," in Julio Trebolle Barrera and Luis Vegas Montaner, eds., *The Madrid Qumran Congress* (2 vols.; Leiden: Brill; Madrid: Editorial Complutense, 1992) 1:83–166, esp. 133. For other scholars who hold this view, see Adiel Schremer, "Qumran Polemic on Marital Law: CD 4:20–5:11 and Its Social Background," in Joseph M. Baumgarten et al., eds., *The Damascus Document: A Centennial of Discovery* (STDJ 34; Leiden: Brill, 2000) 147–60, esp. 149 n. 6.

29   Chaim Rabin, *The Zadokite Documents* (Oxford: Clarendon, 1954) 16–17; cf. Instone-Brewer, *Divorce and Remarriage*, 63. Rabin (p. 17) states that Schechter concluded that this passage forbids divorce. Schechter's position is not entirely clear, however; in one place he says that our passage condemns polygamy and remarriage while the first wife is alive, even if she has been divorced (*Documents of Jewish Sectaries*, 1:xvii). In another place he states that the sect condemned a second marriage during the lifetime of the first husband, even after divorce (1:xix). In a third place, he says that the passage is directed against polygamy and divorce (1:xxxvi n. 3). R. H. Charles noted that "not infrequently in the O.T. the masc. suffix is used in reference to feminine nouns," and he gave Ruth 4:11 as an example (*The Apocrypha and Pseudepigrapha of the Old Testa-*

ment [2 vols.; Oxford: Clarendon, 1913] 2:810, n. to 7:1). His own position is not clear. In the note just cited, he says that the reference to David "would imply that we have here to do with polygamy only." In his introduction to the Zadokite work, however, he says, "Divorce is absolutely forbidden in our text. See vii. 1" (ibid., 2:796). Geza Vermes similarly pointed out that in both Biblical and Mishnaic Hebrew the third person masculine plural suffix occasionally refers to feminine subjects ("Sectarian Matrimonial Halakhah in the Damascus Rule," *JJS* 25 [1974] 197–202, esp. 198, 202). Yigael Yadin argued that בחייהם is a scribal error for בחייהן ("L'Attitude essénienne envers la polygamie et le divorce," *RB* 79 [1972] 98–99). For his interpretation of the passage, see below.

30   Text and trans. from García Martínez and Tigchelaar, *Dead Sea Scrolls*, 2:1278–79.

31   Yadin, "L'Attitude essénienne," 98–99; cf. also 11QT 54:4-5; 66:8-11. Murphy-O'Connor replied that one cannot suppose that all the doctrines expressed in the various DSS are homogeneous, nor can one exclude the possibility that the community's teaching changed over time ("Remarques sur l'exposé du Professeur Y. Yadin," *RB* 79 [1972] 99–100).

riage. According to this interpretation, the text condemns men who take a second wife while the first wife is still alive.[32]

The relevance of the *Temple Scroll* to the question of the community's attitude toward divorce, however, is dubious. The *Temple Scroll* is a rewriting of the book of Deuteronomy intended to regulate the life of Israel in the utopian future.[33] The regulations cited above refer to the king. Thus, the text does not refer to the daily life of the community during the period of its existence. Nonetheless, one could argue that these regulations reflect the ideal values of the group.

A more serious problem is that the *Temple Scroll* may not be a composition of the community of the Dead Sea Scrolls but may predate the origin of the group. Although the composition of the work has been dated at various points from the fifth century BCE to the first century CE, the most likely date is the middle of the second century BCE.[34] Some scholars argue that the work originated in a context that was completely independent of the sect, whereas others see it as a typical sectarian composition. Most persuasive is the hypothesis that it originated in the same priestly circles from which the sect later emerged; that is, that it belongs to the formative period of the Qumran community, a time before the settlement of the site at Qumran.[35] The implication is that the values expressed in the *Temple Scroll* are not necessarily those of the community living at or near Qumran, nor of the related communities living in the various towns of Israel.

It is generally agreed that the *Damascus Document* is a rule book related to the community at Qumran. Complicating the interpretation of CD 4:21 is the fact that this work mentions divorce as a fact of community life in 13:15-18.[36] Some scholars resolve this tension by arguing that CD 4:21 forbids polygamy, not divorce.[37] One of the arguments for this position is that all of the three scriptural examples argue against polygamy, not against divorce.[38] The citation of Deut 17:17, which stipulates that the king shall not multiply wives for himself, is a clear reference to polygamy. The other two citations, however, Gen 1:27 ("Male and female he created them") and 7:9 ("[they] two by two went into the ark") are open to several interpretations.[39]

A fragmentary passage of the *Damascus Document* discovered at Qumran is decisive for the question whether any remarriage whatsoever was permitted. It reads as follows:

---

32 Vermes, "Sectarian Matrimonial Halakhah," 202 (polygamy only); Fitzmyer, "Matthean Divorce Texts," 96 (second marriage while the first wife is alive, even if divorced); Lawrence H. Schiffman, "Laws pertaining to Women in the Temple Scroll," in Dimant and Rappaport, 210–28, esp. 217 (similar to Fitzmyer). For more scholars who conclude that CD 4:21 opposes polygamy and second marriage after divorce (while the first wife is still alive), see Schremer, "Qumran Polemic," 149 n. 5.

33 Michael Owen Wise, *A Critical Study of the Temple Scroll from Qumran Cave 11* (SAOC 49; Chicago: Oriental Institute of the University of Chicago, 1990) 200.

34 Ibid.; Florentino García Martínez, "New Perspectives on the Study of the Dead Sea Scrolls," in idem and Ed Noort, eds., *Perspectives in the Study of the Old Testament and Early Judaism* (VTSup 73; Leiden: Brill, 1998) 230–48, esp. 242–43; Lawrence H. Schiffman dated the work to the second half of the reign of John Hyrcanus, who ruled from 134 to 104 BCE ("Temple Scroll," *ABD* 6:348–50).

35 Wise, *Critical Study*, 203; García Martínez, "New Perspectives," 243.

36 Brin, "Divorce at Qumran," 238–39; Tom Holmén, "Divorce in *CD* 4:20–5:2 and *11QT* 57:17-28: Some Remarks on the Pertinence of the Question," *RevQ* 18 (1998) 397–408, esp. 403–4.

37 Louis Ginzberg, *An Unknown Jewish Sect* (New York: Jewish Theological Seminary, 1976; copyright 1970) 19–20; Rabin, *Zadokite Documents*, 17; Vermes, "Sectarian Matrimonial Halakhah," 199–202; Schiffman, "Laws pertaining to Women," 217; David Instone Brewer, "Nomological Exegesis in Qumran 'Divorce' Texts," *RevQ* 18 (1998) 561–79; idem, *Divorce and Remarriage*, 61–72. For more scholars who take this position, see Schremer, "Qumran Polemic," 148 n. 3; he himself comes to this conclusion as well (ibid., 160).

38 Gen 1:27; 7:9; Deut 17:17; see the citation of CD 4:19–5:2 above; Vermes, "Sectarian Matrimonial Halakhah," 200–201; Michael Knibb concluded that the passage condemns polygamy primarily (*The Qumran Community* [Cambridge: Cambridge University Press, 1987] 43).

39 Similarly, Holmén, "Divorce in *CD* 4:20–5:2 and *11QT* 57:17-28," 402.

Let no man bring [a woman into the ho]ly [covenant?] who has had sexual experience, (whether) she had such [experience in the home] of her father or as a widow who had intercourse after she was widowed. And any [woman upon whom there is a] bad [na]me in her maidenhood in her father's home, let no man take her, except [upon examination] by trustworthy [women] of repute selected by command of the supervisor over [the many. After]ward he may take her, and when he takes her he shall act in accordance with the l[a]w [and he shall not t]ell about [her]

אל יבא איש)

[אשה בבריתה](?) הקו[ד]ש אשר ידעה לעשות מעשה

מ/בדבר ואשר ידעה

[מעשה בבית] אביה או אלמנה אשר נשכבה מאשר

התארמלה וכול

[אשר עליה ש]ם רע בבתוליה בבית אביה אל יקחה איש

כי אם

[בראות נשים] נאמנות וידעות ברורות ממאמר המבקר

אשר על

[הרבים ואח]ר יקחנה ובלוקחו אותה יעשה כמ[ש]פט

[ולוא] יגיד

עלי[ה](.)

(4Q271 frg. 3, lines 10-15)[40]

This passage makes clear that a male member of the Community is permitted to marry a widow, as long as she has not had intercourse with anyone since her husband died. The evidence then supports the conclusion

that the *Damascus Document* permits divorce but condemns all second marriages as long as the first wife is still living.[41] The author(s) of this text may have justified this condemnation by reading the word אחותה/אחתה in Lev 18:18 as "other" instead of "sister."[42] Divorce was probably not permitted in the two situations described in Deut 22:13-19, 28-29.[43] The reason for forbidding polygamy and remarriage during the lifetime of the first spouse is probably a concern about purity. It is noteworthy that, according to Leviticus, priests are forbidden to marry divorced women and widows, "for [the priests] are holy to their God" (Lev 21:7, 13-14; quotation from v. 7 NRSV).

As indicated above, Jewish women in the colony at Elephantine had the right to initiate divorce. Whether women in Palestine in the late Second Temple period had this right has been debated. Josephus says that Salome, the sister of Herod the Great, sent her husband a document dissolving their marriage. Josephus comments that her doing so was not in accordance with the Law, according to which only the man had this right (*Ant.* 15.7.10 §259). His remarks, however, may reflect only one point of view in the pluralistic situation of first century Judea and Galilee.[44] Furthermore, he may be rejecting not the fact that she divorced her husband but the way in which she did so.[45] Deut 24:1-4, as read at the time, implies that only the husband was allowed or commanded to give the wife a document of divorce.[46]

In 1951 or 1952, Bedouin found texts allegedly from Naḥal Ṣeʾelim.[47] These included a document assigned to Josef Milik for preparation for publication; he published

40   Text and trans. from Baumgarten, *Qumran Cave 4*, 175–76.

41   Aharon Shemesh came to a similar conclusion; he pointed out that 4Q271 frg. 3 does not mention the possibility of marriage to a divorcée (גרושה) ("4Q271.3: A Key to Sectarian Matrimonial Law," *JJS* 49 [1998] 246). Schremer argues that the term that does occur in this text, אלמנה, means, in Mishnaic Hebrew, "a woman previously married," i.e., a widow or a divorcée ("Qumran Polemic," 159 n. 25). Jastrow, however, lists only "widow" as the meaning of this word (s.v. אַלְמָנָה). Similarly, he lists only "to become a widow" as the meaning of the verb ארמל, a form of which also occurs in line 12 of this text (s.v. אֲרְמֵל). Furthermore, the mishnaic texts to which he refers distinguish between becoming a widow and being divorced (*Ketub.* 1.2; 5.1).

42   Ginzberg, *Unknown Jewish Sect*, 19–20; Instone Brewer, "Nomological Exegesis," 574–76; idem, *Divorce and Remarriage*, 68–72.

43   Cf. 4QOrdᵃ (4Q159) frgs. 2–4; Brin, "Divorce at Qumran," 239–40; Holmén, "Divorce in *CD* 4:20–5:2 and 11QT 57:17-28," 407.

44   Ilan concluded that Josephus's comment reflects only the Pharisaic point of view ("Notes and Observations," 202).

45   Ralph Marcus, "Notes on Torrey's Translation of the Gospels," *HTR* 27 (1934) 211–39, esp. 221.

46   Instone-Brewer, *Divorce and Remarriage*, 89 and n. 12.

47   Jonas C. Greenfield, "The Texts from Naḥal Ṣeʾelim (Wadi Seiyal)," in Trebolle Barrera and Vegas Montaner, eds., *Madrid Qumran Congress*, 2:661–83, esp. 661.

an article in 1957 stating that he had in his possession and would publish a document, dated to 135 CE, in which a woman asked her husband for a divorce.[48] Milik eventually gave this text to Jonas Greenfield to publish. In 1992, Greenfield mentioned it in "a tentative catalogue." The document had been assigned the number Ṣeʾelim 13 by the Rockefeller Museum, and Greenfield continued to use that designation for convenience, even though in the meantime it had been demonstrated that the documents actually came from Naḥal Ḥever.[49] He described the document in question as an Aramaic contract, a

> [d]ivorce quittance, acknowledgment by wife that former husband is not indebted to her, 14 lines. Dated to 20 Sivan, 3rd year of Bar Kokhba. This document had previously been mistakenly interpreted as a divorce given by a wife to her husband.[50]

The text of the document was published by Ada Yardeni in Hebrew in 1995. She identified it as a receipt given by a woman to her husband in exchange for the sum of money that the marriage contract had stipulated that she was to receive if he divorced her.[51] She based this definition on the judgment that, whereas lines 1–5a and 9–10 were in the first person feminine and were thus the words of the wife, lines 5b–8 come from the scribe representing the husband.[52]

Tal Ilan was the first to publish an English translation of the document. She agreed with Milik that it is a divorce bill sent by a woman to her husband. She concluded that ancient Jewish women could in fact divorce their husbands and that it is an accident of transmission that we do not have more evidence attesting to that practice.[53]

In 1997, the official edition appeared with an English translation.[54] The editors describe the document as "a waiver of claims from a wife to her husband (or a divorce document written by the wife?)."[55] Adiel Schremer took the position that the document is a waiver or receipt. He translated lines 7–8 "this is to you from me a bill of divorce and release without reservation" and took this statement to be a quotation from the bill of divorce that the husband had given the wife, even though in lines 4–6, in the rest of line 8 and in line 9, it is the wife who is speaking in the first person.[56] David Instone-Brewer proposed a reasonable compromise. He translates lines 4–7 as follows:

> I, Shelamzion, daughter of Joseph Qebshan
> of Ein Gedi, with you, Eleazar son of Hananiah
> who had been *her* husband before this time,
> this is from *her* to you a bill of divorce and release.[57]

He concluded that the text was written by an authoritative scribe on her behalf. Thus, "although the document is theoretically from her, it also speaks about her in the third person."[58] It seems likely that this document provides evidence that a woman in the first half of the second century could and did initiate a divorce from her husband.[59]

48   Josef T. Milik, "Le travail d'édition des manuscrits du Désert de Juda," in International Organization for the Study of the Old Testament, *Volume du Congrès: Strasbourg, 1956* (VTSup 4; Leiden: Brill, 1957) 17–26, esp. 21. He translated the key stipulation (line 7) as follows: "Que te soit (notifié) de sa part l'acte de divorce et de répudiation" ("The document of divorce and repudiation is [served] upon you by her" [my trans.]).

49   Greenfield, "Texts from Naḥal Ṣeʾelim," 661–62, 664.

50   Ibid., 664.

51   Ilan, "Notes and Observations," 197–98; cf. *m. Giṭ.* 8.8; Danby, *Mishnah*, 318; 794, s.v. Ketubah.

52   Ilan, "Notes and Observations," 198.

53   Ibid., 198, 201.

54   Hannah M. Cotton and Ada Yardeni, *Aramaic, Hebrew and Greek Documentary Texts from Naḥal Ḥever and Other Sites* (DJD 27; Oxford: Clarendon, 1997) 65–70.

55   Ibid., 65; see also the note on lines 6–7 on p. 69.

56   Adiel Schremer, "Divorce in Papyrus Ṣeʾelim 13 Once Again: A Reply to Tal Ilan," *HTR* 91 (1998) 193–202, esp. 201–2.

57   David Instone-Brewer, "Jewish Women Divorcing Their Husbands in Early Judaism: The Background to Papyrus Ṣeʾelim 13," *HTR* 92 (1999) 349–57; citation from 351; emphasis original.

58   Ibid., 352.

59   The initiative of women is also illustrated by an aspect of the life of Josephus. At the command of Vespasian, he married a virgin (Jewish) captive from

Divorce in the Greek and Roman Cultural Contexts of Mark

Customs regarding marriage and divorce were generally similar among ancient Greeks and Romans.[60] A woman's family of origin provided her with a dowry when she married. While she was married, her husband administered this property. In case of divorce, the woman and the dowry returned to her family of origin.[61] Although marriage was a legal and social contract between families, marital affection "was considered essential to a true marriage, so much so that its cessation was cause for divorce."[62] Divorce was common in all ancient Mediterranean societies and apparently bore no social stigma.[63] Men initiated divorce more commonly than women, but women also had the right to do so, often through the intervention of a male relative for the purpose of protecting her honor or that of the family of origin. The two main causes of divorce were adultery and infertility, but mutual consent with the approval of both families was sufficient.[64] Many men and women married two or more times, but the *univira*, a woman married to only one husband, and lifelong marital fidelity were praised, at least in funerary monuments.[65]

Augustan legislation was designed to encourage Romans, especially those of high status, to marry and have children. It also "attempted to formalize divorce by requiring a formal letter of divorce and witnesses and by compelling husbands to divorce adulterous wives." Men who had sexual relations with married women (adultery) or with single women (*stuprum*) were to be punished as criminals. This legislation does not appear to have been particularly successful.[66]

Comment

■ **2** The earliest recoverable form of this verse in Mark probably did not identify the questioners of Jesus as Pharisees.[67] As argued in the section "Divorce in the Jewish Cultural Contexts of Mark" above, there is no evidence that any Jewish group in the first century CE forbade divorce. As pointed out in the section "Divorce in the Greek and Roman Cultural Contexts of Mark," divorce was an accepted fact of life in those contexts. So the question whether a man is permitted to divorce his wife is, culturally speaking, very odd. The artificiality of this introduction to the dialogue may indicate either that the evangelist needed to create a setting for a saying attributed to Jesus or that the whole dialogue has its social setting in the early church.[68] Matthew rewrote the question, making it more intelligible. His Pharisees ask whether a man is permitted to divorce his wife *for any reason* (19:3).[69]

Caesarea. She, in effect, divorced him (ἀπαλλάσσω), and he then remarried (*Vit.* 414–16; cf. Instone-Brewer, *Divorce and Remarriage*, 89 n. 12).

60   Osiek and Balch, *Families*, 61.

61   Ibid., 57; Dixon, *Roman Family*, 50–51, 65.

62   Osiek and Balch, *Families*, 42, 61 (citation from 61). On the public and communal character of marriage in Rome, see Dixon, *Roman Family*, 62–64; on marital affection and loyalty, 68–69; on marital partnership and harmony, 69–70. See also Suzanne Dixon, "The Sentimental Ideal of the Roman Family," in Beryl Rawson, ed., *Marriage, Divorce, and Children in Ancient Rome* (Canberra: Humanities Research Centre; Oxford: Clarendon, 1991) 99–113.

63   Osiek and Balch, *Families*, 62; the notion of fault had little significance in late republican divorce (Susan Treggiari, "Divorce Roman Style: How Easy and How Frequent Was It?" in Rawson, *Marriage, Divorce, and Children*, 30–46, esp. 38, 46; Dixon, *Roman Family*, 66, 69). "From the time of the late Republic at least, widows were likely to remarry, and divorce

became quite common and casual" (Dixon, *Roman Family*, 77).

64   Osiek and Balch, *Families*, 62; Susan Treggiari, *Roman Marriage: Iusti Coniuges from the Time of Cicero to the Time of Ulpian* (Oxford: Clarendon, 1991) 461–65; "gradually the separate marital regime, in which women could also initiate divorce, became dominant" ("Divorce Roman Style," 31, 37–38). In the latter work, Treggiari notes that by the time of Cicero, divorce could be initiated by either husband or wife; see also Dixon, *Roman Family*, 69.

65   Osiek and Balch, *Families*, 62; Treggiari, "Divorce Roman Style," 40–41; Dixon, *Roman Family*, 32–33, 66, 76–77, 89.

66   Dixon, *Roman Family*, 79–80; citation from 79.

67   See the note on the trans. of v. 2 above.

68   On the artificiality of the dialogue and the motif of "testing," see the section "Genre of 10:2-9" above.

69   Philo and Josephus both interpret Deut 24:1-4 to mean that a man may divorce his wife for any reason; Philo *Spec. leg.* 3.5 §§30–31; Josephus *Ant.*

■ 3-5 Jesus responds "What did Moses command you?" presumably to elicit a quotation of scripture.[70] Although Jesus had asked about a *command*, his questioners respond that Moses *allowed* a man to write a certificate of divorce and thus to divorce his wife, paraphrasing Deut 24:1-4.[71] The difference in terminology may indicate a common assumption of the two parties in the dialogue: that divorce was *allowed*, but, in case of divorce, the writing of a certificate was *commanded*. Jesus replied to their answer with the remark that Moses "wrote this commandment for you because of your hardness of heart." Here Jesus is not speaking about the Pharisees in particular, but about the people as a whole, who received the Torah.

Jesus' initial question and his reply to his interlocutors' response imply that the commandments regarding divorce come from Moses and not directly from God. As Stephen Fraade has pointed out, the precise nature and extent of Moses' role as an intermediary between God and the people is an issue that has occupied biblical interpreters from the beginning. One way to put the question is to ask to what degree Moses simply transmitted the commands of God and to what degree he was the "author" of some of them.[72] The Pentateuch, Joshua, 2 Kings, and 1 and 2 Chronicles speak about Moses commanding the people specific things, and Deut 33:4 speaks about Moses commanding them the Torah in general. It is rarely said that God commanded the people

(directly), although it is often said that God commanded "through Moses."[73]

The book of Deuteronomy is a notable instance of this problem, since it portrays Moses as summarizing what was previously commanded by God, yet contains commandments that are not in the earlier books of Moses and some that occur there but in different form. This discrepancy may explain why the *Temple Scroll* has God speaking in the first person, instead of Moses speaking about God in the third person. The *Temple Scroll* thus verifies that Moses spoke the words of God.[74]

Philo, in his retelling of the story of Korah's rebellion, speaks about "spiteful rumours that [Moses] had falsely invented the oracles" and had chosen Aaron as high priest "through family feeling and affection for his brother" (*Vit. Mos.* 2.33 §176; cf. §278).[75] Philo does distinguish, nevertheless, between the laws of God and the laws of Moses. The Ten Commandments come directly from God, whereas the particular laws come

through the most perfect of the prophets whom He selected for his merits and having filled him with the divine spirit, chose him to be the interpreter of His sacred utterances (διὰ τοῦ τελειοτάτου τῶν προφητῶν, ὃν ἐπικρίνας ἀριστίνδην καὶ ἀναπλήσας ἐνθέου πνεύματος ἑρμηνέα τῶν χρησμῳδουμένων εἵλετο). (*Decal.* 33 §175)[76]

4.8.23 §253. In *Vit.* 426, Josephus says that he divorced his wife because he was displeased with her behavior (μὴ ἀρεσκόμενος αὐτῆς τοῖς ἤθεσιν). Matthew's formulation of the Pharisees' question, in any case, seems to be evidence that the issue was contested in his cultural context (Meier, "Historical Jesus and the Historical Law," 77–78).

70 Bultmann, *History*, 27.

71 As Meier has pointed out, in the late Second Temple period, the act of giving the wife a certificate of divorce is treated as a distinct law within the Torah of Moses ("Historical Jesus and the Historical Law," 64–67). Instone-Brewer interprets the original significance of the mention of the divorce certificate as a law that gave women the right to remarry (*Divorce and Remarriage*, 30–31). On the "nomistic exegesis" of narrative and other nonlegal texts, see Menahem Kister, "Divorce, Reproof and Other Sayings in the Synoptic Gospels: Jesus Traditions in the Context of 'Qumranic' and Other Texts," in Daniel R. Schwartz and Ruth A. Clements, eds., *Text, Thought, and Prac-*

tice in Qumran and Early Christianity: Proceedings of a Joint Symposium sponsored by the Orion Center for the Study of the Dead Sea Scrolls and Associated Literature and the Hebrew University Center for the Study of Christianity, 11–13 January, 2004 (STDJ; Leiden: Brill, forthcoming), section I.2.(2) (MS p. 14).

72 Steven D. Fraade, "Moses and the Commandments: Can Hermeneutics, History, and Rhetoric Be Disentangled?" in Hindy Najman and Judith H. Newman, eds., *The Idea of Biblical Interpretation: Essays in Honor of James Kugel* (JSJSup 83; Leiden: Brill, 2004) 399–422.

73 Ibid., 400 n. 6.

74 Ibid., 400 n. 4.

75 Trans. from Colson and Whitaker, *Philo*, 6:535. Fraade concludes that Philo interpreted the incident as "a challenge to the divine origin of the commandments" ("Moses and the Commandments," 414 n. 41).

76 Text and trans. (modified) from Colson and Whitaker, *Philo*, 7:92–93. Cf. *Spec. leg.* 2.21 §104; for

Although Philo distinguishes among commandments as to their origin, he does not do so to argue that some laws are valid whereas others are not.[77]

In a tannaitic midrash, it is said, "One who says, 'All of the Torah is from the mouth of the Holy One, but this thing/commandment Moses said on his own (מפי עצמו),' is what is meant by 'for he has spurned the word of the Lord.'"[78] The latter passage seems to be polemical; it and others like it may have been written against some who argued in the way that it condemns. According to rabbinic tradition, the Ten Commandments had formerly been read aloud to the people in the temple, but that practice was ended in order not to encourage the heretics (*minim*) who said "these alone were given to Moses at Sinai."[79]

A second-century Valentinian text, *Ptolemy to Flora*, states that "our savior's words teach us" that the Pentateuch has three parts: one derives from God, one from Moses, and the third from the elders of the people who "must have inserted certain of their own commandments."[80] An early midrashic text, probably in response to those who argued in the way that *Ptolemy to Flora* does, affirms that Exod 19:7 teaches that what one hears from Moses' mouth is equivalent to what one hears from the mouth of the Holy One; likewise, what comes from the mouths of the elders and the prophets is equivalent to the words of God.[81]

The statement that Moses "wrote this commandment for you because of your hardness of heart" (v. 5) implies that divorce is not the will of God but was allowed by Moses only because of the people's stubbornness.

According to Fraade, Mark 10:2-9 implies that "the law of divorce was Moses' own invention and not indicative of the divine will, and hence only a temporally-bound concession to human weakness."[82]

■ **6-9** After relativizing the commandment of Moses concerning divorce, the Markan Jesus contrasts with it the will of God as manifested in the account of creation in Genesis.[83] In v. 6 he cites Gen 1:27, in exact correspondence with the LXX, "male and female he made them."[84] This text is used here, as in CD 4:19–5:1; *Jub.* 2:14; 3:8; and *b. Yeb.* 63a, to indicate that the man and the woman form a unit, "the human being" (האדם).[85]

He then cites Gen 2:24 in vv. 7-8a. In the context of Genesis 2, the phrase "for this reason" (ἕνεκεν τούτου) refers to Adam's immediately preceding statements that the woman is "bone of my bones and flesh of my flesh" and that "she was taken from the man" (Gen 2:23). These are the reasons why "a man shall leave his father and mother and cling to his wife, and the two will be one flesh." In the speech of Jesus, "for this reason" refers to the act of God in creating humanity. It is because God made man and woman as a unit that a man shall cling to his wife. The juxtaposition of Gen 1:27 and 2:23 leads to this conclusion.

Like 4QInstruction, this saying of Jesus interprets the statement in Gen 2:24, "and the two will be one flesh," as referring to the unity of the couple in marriage. The Samaritan text of the Pentateuch and Rashi's commentary on Gen 2:24 differ in taking the statement to refer to the couple's offspring, in whom they literally become one flesh.[86] Both 4QInstruction and this saying interpret

further relevant passages and discussion see Francis T. Fallon, "The Law in Philo and Ptolemy: A Note on the Letter to Flora," *VC* 30 (1976) 45–51, esp. 47–50; cited by Fraade, "Moses and the Commandments," 418 n. 47.

77 Contrast the letter of *Ptolemy to Flora*; see Fallon, "Law in Philo and Ptolemy," 51, and the discussion of *Ptolemy to Flora* below.

78 *Sifre Num.* 112 (ed. Horowitz, 121); trans. by Fraade, "Moses and the Commandments," 410.

79 Fraade, "Moses and the Commandments," 417–18 and n. 46.

80 *Ptolemy to Flora* 33.4.1–3; trans. by Layton, *Gnostic Scriptures*, 309; cited and discussed by Fraade, "Moses and the Commandments," 418–20. See also Fallon, "Law in Philo and Ptolemy," 45–47.

81 *Mekilta of R. Shimʿon bar Yoḥai* 19:9; cited and dis-

cussed by Fraade, "Moses and the Commandments," 404–7.

82 Fraade, "Moses and the Commandments," 417. The letter from *Ptolemy to Flora* 33.4.4–6 cites the parallel to this passage in Matthew and points out that the Law of Moses contradicts the law of God (Fallon, "Law in Philo and Ptolemy," 47).

83 The priority of the will of God to the Law of Moses is also based on the chronological priority of the creation to the giving of the Law (Marion C. Moeser, *The Anecdote in Mark, the Classical World and the Rabbis* [JSNTSup 227; Sheffield: Sheffield Academic Press, 2002] 222).

84 See the note on the trans. of v. 6 above. The same clause occurs also in Gen 5:2.

85 Kister, "Divorce, Reproof," section I.1 (MS p. 8).

86 Ibid., I.2.(1) (MS p. 13).

the human acts described in Gen 2:24 as divine acts. This exegesis implies that the "verse is either a commandment of God or a divine declaration concerning the validity of marriage."[87]

Some MSS omit the words καὶ προσκολληθήσεται πρὸς τὴν γυναῖκα αὐτοῦ ("and cling to his wife"). It may well be that these words were omitted simply by accident.[88] It could be, however, that they were omitted deliberately because they did not seem to be compatible with the virtue of self-mastery. In either case, the words probably belong to the earliest recoverable form of the text.

The comment on Gen 2:24 of the Markan Jesus in v. 8b, "so that they are no longer two, but one flesh," emphasizes the unity of the married couple. The context of the scriptural citation is important here, especially Gen 2:23. Just as Eve was taken from the very body of Adam by an extraordinary procedure, so every married couple are "one flesh." This emphasis prepares for the conclusion that is drawn in v. 9 from the citations of scripture, "What therefore God has joined man shall not separate."[89]

As Fraade has pointed out, the contrast between "God" and "man" in this verse seems also to be a contrast between "God" and "Moses" and thus to override the law of divorce in Deut 24:1-4.[90] It also resonates with the contrast between "the commandment of God" and "the tradition of human beings" in Mark 7:8. In Mark 7 one of the Ten Commandments is affirmed, but the "tradition of the elders" is rejected.[91]

Although the Markan Jesus implies that Deut 24:1-4 contradicts Gen 2:24, an exegetical connection between the two may be seen in the terminology used. The "certificate of divorce" or "bill of divorce" in Deut 24:1 is literally a "certificate/bill of cutting" (ספר כריתת). The link between the two passages may be the idea that Deuteron-

omy speaks of the "cutting" of the "cleaving" mentioned in Gen 2:24.[92]

Mark 10:2-9 may be described as a brief legal debate that "embodies a legal principle of Jesus arrived at by his interpretation of scriptural verses."[93] Like the Markan Jesus, the author(s) of the *Damascus Document* also used Gen 1:27 to support a legal principle regarding marriage.[94] That work also combines Gen 1:27 with another passage from Genesis, but instead of 2:24, it is 7:9, "two (by) two they went into the ark." Unlike the Markan Jesus, the *Damascus Document* does not forbid divorce but uses the passages from Genesis to forbid polygamy and remarriage after divorce, if the first spouse is still living.[95]

As argued above, no Jewish group in the first century CE forbade divorce. The teaching of the Markan Jesus is thus distinctive. The criterion of dissimilarity could be applied to conclude that the historical Jesus did in fact forbid divorce. Another possibility is that the dialogue arose in some of the communities of followers of Jesus after his death in response to a tendency toward sexual continence. The wish to divorce may have been connected with the ideal of sexual self-mastery. Paul's reiteration in 1 Cor 7:10 of the command of Jesus against divorce occurs in a context in which he is attempting to limit the desire of at least some of the Corinthians to put into practice the maxim "It is good for a man not to touch a woman" (7:1).[96] The Gospel of Luke also expresses an ascetic tendency. Unlike Mark and Matthew, Luke speaks about disciples leaving their wives for the sake of the kingdom of God (Luke 18:29; contrast Mark 10:29 and Matt 19:29). Luke also rewrote Mark's dialogue of Jesus with the Sadducees so that the idea of not marrying and being like the angels applies to the elect in the present, and not only to the eschatological future

---

87 Ibid., I.2.(2) (MS p. 14).

88 As argued in the note on the trans. of v. 7 above.

89 The verb used here, χωρίζειν ("to separate"), was often used in Greek literature and marriage contracts to mean divorce in the strict sense; BAGD, s.v.; Fitzmyer, "Matthean Divorce Texts," 89, 107 n. 55. The saying of v. 9 also makes a contrast between "joining" and "separating"; these contrasts indicate its artful character and define it as an antithetical aphorism. See Tannehill, *Sword*, 95–97.

90 On how Deut 24:4 was read in the Second Temple

period, see the section "Divorce in the Jewish Cultural Contexts of Mark" above.

91 Fraade, "Moses and the Commandments," 417.

92 Kister, "Divorce, Reproof," section I.4 (MS p. 17–18).

93 Moeser, *Anecdote*, 223.

94 See the section "Divorce in the Jewish Cultural Contexts of Mark" above.

95 Whatever biblical laws command regarding men, the *Damascus Document*, wherever possible, applies also to women (Instone-Brewer, *Divorce and Remarriage*, 68).

96 Dale B. Martin has argued that the slogan repre-

(Luke 20:34-36; contrast Mark 12:25 and Matt 22:30). Even the Matthean Jesus speaks about men becoming eunuchs for the sake of the kingdom of heaven (Matt 19:10-12). This ideal may be directed to men who have never married, as the question of the disciples in 19:10 may imply. But since the context concerns remarriage after divorce, it may apply also to men who are divorced. The saying could, conceivably, have the effect of encouraging divorce.

Mark 10:2-9 could, then, have arisen in order to discourage divorce for the sake of some ideal in tension with marriage, whether it be sexual self-mastery or dedication to the itinerant proclamation of the gospel. The teaching of the Markan Jesus in this passage is thus analogous to that of Paul: "Are you bound to a wife? Do not seek to be free" (1 Cor 7:27 NRSV).

■ **10-12** This is the fourth of five occasions on which the Markan Jesus makes a public statement or performs a public deed and then is asked about it in private by a smaller group, usually the disciples.[97] Thus, the attachment of sayings in vv. 11-12 to the dialogue of vv. 2-9 is likely to be Mark's editorial work. This judgment is confirmed by the fact that the sayings appear in a different context in Luke 16:18.[98] The literary form of vv. 10-12 may be defined as an anecdote that focuses on a saying that is a response to an inquiry.[99]

Privately, when the disciples are at home with Jesus, they ask for clarification of his legal statement in v. 9. Although it is not stated explicitly in v. 10, the sayings of vv. 11-12 imply that the question concerns the feasibility

of avoiding divorce altogether. The sayings presuppose the fact that sometimes divorce will be inevitable. But, in such cases, the Markan Jesus forbids remarriage as long as the former spouse is still living.[100] The saying in v. 11 states that any man who divorces his wife and marries another commits adultery *against her*, that is, against his first wife. If his first wife had died, the second marriage would presumably not be defined as adultery (cf. Rom 7:1-3).

In the scripture of Israel, the literature of the Second Temple period, and rabbinic literature, adultery is defined as a man having intercourse with a woman married or betrothed to another man. Adultery is the violation by one man of the marriage of another man (Deut 22:22-24; Lev 20:10).[101] In Greek and Roman cultures, the situation was similar. Unconditional fidelity was required of the woman alone. In Greek law, adultery was defined as "secret sexual intercourse with a free woman without the consent of her κύριος [lit., 'lord'; here, 'husband']."[102]

Thus, the Markan Jesus innovates significantly in teaching that any man who divorces his wife and marries another commits adultery *against his first wife*. Men are no longer responsible only to respect the rights of other men over their spouses and those they have betrothed. According to v. 11, men are responsible also to their own wives; that is, they are forbidden to have sexual relations with anyone other than their own wives. The rationale for this innovation is probably a heightened sense of purity, just as the condemnation in the *Damascus*

---

sents the position of "the strong" in the community at Corinth and that they valued sexual asceticism because of a concern for the continued strength and health of the body (*The Corinthian Body* [New Haven/London: Yale University Press, 1995] 208). Margaret Mitchell has pointed out that divorce can cause alienation and division within a community; prohibition of divorce thus contributes to group unity (*Rhetoric of Reconciliation*, 122–23, 236–37).

97 The others are 4:1-10; 7:14-17; 9:27-28 (note v. 18b); 13:1-4.

98 Luke probably took these sayings from Q (Robinson et al., *Critical Edition of Q*, 470–71). Matthew abbreviates the sayings of Mark 10:11-12 and combines the new saying with his famous exception clause in 19:9. He preserves the dual structure of Mark 10:2-12 but offers different additional teaching in 19:10-12. See also Matt 5:31-32.

99 Moeser, *Anecdote*, 223.

100 Cf. the teaching of the *Damascus Document*; see the section "Divorce in the Jewish Cultural Contexts of Mark" above. Fraade understands these verses as part of a larger argument that most of Mosaic Law "was a temporary concession to flawed human nature after the 'fall,' and that with the messianic undoing of that 'fall,' those laws which were concessions cease to be operative. However, what to do in a transitional period? Divorce (ideally) is prohibited, but what is the status of those who have previously divorced, or can't avoid divorce? They shouldn't remarry, at least not while the former spouse is still alive" (personal communication).

101 F. Hauck, "μοιχεύω κτλ.," *TDNT* 4 (1967) 729–35, esp. 730–32.

102 Hauck, "μοιχεύω κτλ.," 732–33; citation from 732.

Document of a second marriage while the first spouse is still living is probably a matter of purity.[103] Although the version of the saying in Luke 16:18a lacks the phrase "against her," the meaning is probably the same, since there is no mention of the second wife being (formerly) married to someone else.

Verse 12 makes the same point with regard to women. The first thing to note is that the same verb is used for a woman divorcing her husband as is used in v. 11 for a man divorcing his wife (ἀπολύειν). This symmetry between the rights of women and men may reflect a situation in Jewish contexts in which the right of women to take the initiative in divorce was generally recognized.[104] Josephus, however, uses this term, among others, in describing Salome divorcing her husband and says that her action (perhaps only sending her husband a document of divorce) was contrary to the Law (*Ant.* 15.7.10 §259).[105] Other Jewish attestations of the term use it only with the man as the subject.[106] In Roman sources, the vocabulary for each of the genders is distinct, with a few exceptions from the second century. In the early imperial period, the verb *repudiare* and the noun *repudium* were used of the husband's action in divorce. The verb *divertere/divortere* was used "to describe the wife's action in separating from her husband and adopting a different path in life, literally 'diverging.'"[107]

The usage of the Markan Jesus therefore appears to be at least somewhat innovative, taking an intercultural trend toward symmetry between the sexes to its logical conclusion. As noted above, an exegetical principle of the *Damascus Document* and the *Temple Scroll* is that laws binding on men are, mutatis mutandis, binding on women as well.[108] Such a principle may have been at work in the formation or transmission of the sayings in Mark 10:11-12 as well.

In any case, wives are held to the same ethical standard as husbands: if a woman divorces her husband, she may not remarry as long as her first husband is alive. Although it is not explicit, the phrase ἐπ᾿ αὐτόν ("against him," that is, the first husband) is probably understood.[109] The parallel saying in Luke 16:18 does not have the same symmetry as Mark 10:11-12.[110] In Luke 16:18b, the man who marries a divorced woman is condemned, since such a marriage is equivalent to adultery committed against her first husband.[111]

---

103 See the section "Divorce in the Jewish Cultural Contexts of Mark" above. Instone-Brewer argues that the teaching in the Gospels that a second marriage is equivalent to adultery is based on the idea of the invalidity of divorce (*Divorce and Remarriage*, 147–52).

104 See the section "Divorce in the Jewish Cultural Contexts of Mark" above; see also Str-B, 2:23–24.

105 On the terms used in the NT for divorce and their currency in non-Christian Greek literature, see Fitzmyer, "Matthean Divorce Texts," 89–91. In 1 Esdr 9:36, the term ἀπολύειν is used of men divorcing their (foreign) wives; it is also used of a man divorcing his wife in a divorce text from Murabbaʿat Cave 2 from the Bar Kokhba period (ibid., 90–91; 107 n. 59).

106 In 1 Esdr 9:36; a divorce text from Murabbaʿat Cave 2 from the Bar Kokhba period (Fitzmyer, "Matthean Divorce Texts," 90–91, 107 nn. 59, 61).

107 Treggiari, *Roman Marriage*, 436–37; citation from 437; eadem, "Divorce Roman Style," 34. Treggiari also notes that the immoral motives of women in divorcing is a misogynist theme in literature, but divorce by men "is material neither for ethics nor for satire" ("Divorce Roman Style," 42).

108 See the section "Divorce in the Jewish Cultural Contexts of Mark" above.

109 Marcus, "Notes on Torrey's Translation of the Gospels," 221.

110 Eric K. C. Wong points out that the sayings in 1 Cor 7:10-11 also lack the reciprocity of Mark 10:11-12, since in the former passage different verbs are used for the activity of the man and the woman in initiating a divorce ("The Deradicalization of Jesus' Ethical Sayings in 1 Corinthians," *NTS* 48 [2002] 181–94, esp. 183).

111 Ibid.

10 10:13-16 Children and the Kingdom
of God

13/ **And they were bringing children to
him in order that he might touch
them. But the disciples rebuked
them.ᵃ 14/ So when Jesus saw
(it), he became angry and said to
them, "Allow the children to
come to me, do not prohibit
them, for the kingdom of God
belongs to such as these.
15/ Truly I say to you, whoever
does not receive the kingdom of
God as a child (would receive it)
shall surely not enter into it."
16/ And having taken them in his
arms, he blessed them, putting
his hands upon them.**

a Most MSS, including A D et al., read ἐπετίμων τοῖς
προσφέρουσιν ("began to rebuke those who were
bringing") instead of ἐπετίμησαν αὐτοῖς ("rebuked
them"), which is attested by ℵ B C et al. The longer
reading apparently arose in an attempt to make clear
that the disciples were rebuking those who were bringing the children and not the children themselves. See
Metzger, *Textual Commentary*, 89.

History of the Tradition of vv. 13-16

It is likely that vv. 13-14, 16 represent a pre-Markan narrative and that Mark has added v. 15.[1] Bultmann concluded that v. 15 was a traditional saying attributed to
Jesus, originally independent of this context, that Mark
inserted here.[2] It seems more likely that Mark composed
the saying in order to link the traditional story about
children with the story about the rich man in vv. 17-22.
The rich man does not accept Jesus' advice about his
property, nor Jesus' invitation to follow him. His negative responses indicate that the likelihood of his entering
the kingdom of God is very low (vv. 23-25). A child, in
contrast, has virtually no possessions or responsibilities
and is thus much more likely to respond positively to the
opportunity to enter the kingdom (v. 15). The saying in
v. 15 thus sets the scene for the story about the rich man.

Genre of vv. 13-16

Bultmann defined the pre-Markan story as a biographical apophthegm, presumably because it serves to characterize Jesus as someone who welcomed and blessed

children.[3] Robert C. Tannehill argued that this passage is
a hybrid pronouncement story that combines correction
with commendation. Jesus corrects the disciples and
commends the children.[4] Robbins concluded that the
pronouncement story as presented in Mark and Matthew
is a mixed chreia; that is, it combines sayings and actions,
whereas the version of Luke is a sayings chreia.[5] Each of
these definitions points to a significant feature of the
passage.

Comment

■ **13** People were bringing children to Jesus in order
that he might *touch* (ἅψασθαι) them. This is the only
instance in Mark in which this verb is used in a context
other than a healing.[6] As argued above, the belief was
current in the cultural contexts of Mark that some quality of a charismatic person could be transferred by
touch. The pre-Markan miracle stories and the Markan
summaries in which Jesus' touch figures prominently
presuppose that his healing power can be transferred to
those desirous of being healed.[7] Such ideas seem to be
presupposed in this pre-Markan text as well. Given their

1 Müller, *In der Mitte der Gemeinde,* 54, and the literature cited in n. 60.
2 Bultmann, *History,* 32.
3 Ibid., 32, 55–57.
4 Tannehill, "Varieties," 1.1 (p. 103); see also 1.4
   (p. 104) and 2.1 (p. 105).
5 Vernon K. Robbins, "Pronouncement Stories and

Jesus' Blessing of the Children: A Rhetorical
Approach," *Semeia* 29 (1983) 43–74; Moeser also
defines Mark 10:13-16 as a mixed chreia (*Anecdote,*
227).
6 Cf. Mark 1:41; 3:10; 5:27, 28, 30, 31; 6:56; 7:33; 8:22;
   Müller, *In der Mitte der Gemeinde,* 59–60.
7 See the commentary on 5:27-28, 30-32 above.

prominence in the Markan summaries, Mark seems to affirm them also.

The narrator goes on to say that the disciples rebuked those who were bringing the children. No motivation for the rebuke is given, but the logic of the story seems to be analogous to the tale about Elisha's raising the son of the Shunammite (2 Kgs 4:8-37).[8] When Elisha sees the Shunammite coming toward him at an unexpected time, he sends his servant Gehazi to ask whether she, her husband, and their child are all right. She replies affirmatively (in spite of the fact that her son has died) and continues to approach Elisha. When she reaches him, she catches hold of his feet. Gehazi moves toward her to push her away, but Elisha replies, "Let her alone, for she is in bitter distress; the Lord has hidden it from me and has not told me" (2 Kgs 4:27).[9] In both cases, the attendant(s) of the charismatic figure assume(s) the role of gatekeeper, allowing or denying access to him, and presume(s) to know his wishes. A later rabbinic story is also analogous. Rabbi Akiva returned home with a crowd of disciples after being gone for many years. His wife came to him, fell on her face and kissed his feet. His disciples wanted to push her away, but he said, "Let her alone; what is mine and what is yours is hers (what I am and what you are we owe to her!)."[10]

■ **14** Like Elisha and Rabbi Akiva, Jesus corrects his disciples and instructs them to let the children come to him, "for the kingdom of God belongs to such as these." From the time of Origen onward, "such as these" (οἱ τοιοῦτοι) has been interpreted metaphorically. Bultmann, however, was probably right in arguing that the primary meaning of the saying is that children have a share in the kingdom of God.[11] In both the context of the historical Jesus and that of the evangelist, such an argument would have both a present and a future dimension. It means, for the present, that children may share in the group that forms around Jesus and in the early Christian communities. For the future, it means that they are included in the life of the new age.

The rabbis debated whether children would be raised from the dead and included in the age to come. Rabban Gamliel argued that the children of the impious in Israel would have no share in the age to come. Rabbi Joshua argued that they would. The rabbis agreed that the children of non-Israelites would neither be raised nor judged.[12] They debated what age an Israelite child had to have reached before death in order to be included in the age to come. One taught that all who had been born would be included; another, only those who had begun to speak; another, from the time when they could answer "Amen" in the synagogue with understanding; another, from the time when they are circumcised. Near the end of the collection of rabbinic views, the opinion that all those who have been born are included is restated. The passage ends with the declaration by Rabbi Elʿazar, that even children who have been miscarried will be raised; he based his opinion on a midrashic reading of Isa 49:6.[13]

The fact that the rabbis needed to engage in such a debate and the portrayal of the disciples as not wanting Jesus to be bothered with children both indicate the relatively low status of children in the ancient world in comparison with adults.[14] Jesus' indignation and his statement that "the kingdom of God belongs to such as these" indicate not only that children are included in the kingdom of God but also that they represent the type of person who is especially associated with the kingdom of God (cf. Mark 9:33-37). The perspective here is analogous to that expressed in the beatitudes of Luke and Matthew. In Luke 6:20-21, the kingdom of God belongs especially to the poor, the hungry, and those who weep. In Matt 5:5, it belongs, among others, to the meek.[15]

■ **15** As noted earlier, this verse is probably a Markan addition to a pre-Markan pronouncement story.[16] The

---

8 Bultmann, *History*, 32.

9 The initial word in both Jesus' and Elisha's (in the LXX) statements is the aorist imperative of ἀφιέναι ("let [someone] be"; "allow").

10 *B. Ketub.* 63a; *b. Ned.* 50a; Str-B, 1:808; Bultmann, *History*, 32.

11 Bultmann, *History*, 32.

12 *T. Sanh.* 13:1–2 (434); *Bar. Sanh.* 110b; ʾAbot R. Nat. 36; *p. Šeb.* 4, 35c, 29; Str-B, 1:786; Bultmann, *History*, 32.

13 *P. Šeb.* 4, 35c, 31; Str-B, 1:786; Bultmann, *History*, 32.

14 On the status of children in Greek and Roman societies, see Judith M. Gundry-Volf, "The Least and the Greatest: Children in the New Testament," in Marcia J. Bunge, ed., *The Child in Christian Thought* (Grand Rapids: Eerdmans, 2001) 29–60, esp. 31–34; on children in Jewish societies, see ibid., 34–36.

15 Ibid., 38.

16 See the section "History of the Tradition of vv. 13-16" above.

saying is elliptical and scholars have come to different conclusions about what words are omitted.[17] As indicated in the translation above, the word παιδίον ("child") should be taken as in the nominative case. So the saying threatens those who do not receive the kingdom in the way that a child receives it. How a child receives the kingdom is to be inferred from the context of the saying in Mark. The mention of a child here reminds the audience of the controversy about greatness in which Jesus took a child and placed it in the midst of the disciples. The connection between these two passages suggests that receiving the kingdom as a child means receiving it without the ambition to be a figure of authority, but being content to be "last of all and servant of all" (Mark 9:33-37; quotation from v. 35). The threat "shall surely not enter into it" in 10:15 foreshadows the saying of v. 25, "It is easier for a camel to pass through the eye of a needle than for a rich man to enter into the kingdom of God." This link suggests that receiving the kingdom as a child means receiving it without being held back by wealth and possessions.

The hypothesis that Mark added this verse to a traditional story is supported by the likelihood that Matthew found the saying to be out of place in this narrative and moved it to his version of the controversy about great-

ness (18:1-5). Matthew's rewriting of Mark 10:15 suggests that he also understood the noun παιδίον ("child") to be in the nominative case. His placing of the saying clearly indicates that he understood the dispute about greatness to be the best context in which to interpret what it means to receive the kingdom as a child. His elaboration of the saying in 18:3-4 goes beyond the implications of the Markan form of the saying. The Matthean Jesus calls for a personal transformation involving "becoming like children" and defines that as "humbling oneself." The *Gospel of Thomas* (22) interprets the saying (probably the Matthean version) as calling for the abolition of dichotomies, for example, that of male and female.

■ **16** The anecdote ends with actions of Jesus that demonstrate the significance of what he has said, especially in v. 14. The main action is his blessing of the children. In light of the intention expressed at the beginning of the story, "that he might touch them," this blessing is to be understood in the strong sense, as conveying some concrete benefit to the children. The motif of touching is continued in the action of putting his hands upon them. The initial action, putting his arms around the children, contrasts dramatically with the disciples' rebuke and illustrates Jesus' saying about the kingdom belonging to them.

10

10:17-31 Property and the Kingdom of God

17/ And as he was setting out on a journey, someone[a] ran up to him, fell on his knees before him, and asked him, "Good teacher, what should I do to inherit eternal life?" 18/ Jesus said to him, "Why do you call me good? No one is good except one, (namely) God. 19/ You know the commandments, 'You shall not murder, you shall not commit adultery,[b] you shall not steal, you shall not bear false witness, you shall not defraud,[c] honor your father and mother.'" 20/ And he said to him, "Teacher, I have observed all these things from my youth." 21/ Jesus then

a   Instead of προσδραμὼν εἷς ("someone ran up to him"), A K W et al. attest the reading ἰδού τις πλούσιος προσδραμών ("see, a certain rich man ran up to him"). The latter reading is probably secondary and arose either because εἷς ("someone") was perceived to be too vague or because of increasing interest in the character of the questioner. That he was rich was inferred from v. 22. Note that Matt 19:16 includes the word ἰδού ("see") and Luke 18:18 the word τις ("a certain"); these parallel passages may have influenced the text of Mark or changes analogous to those made by the other two evangelists may have been made in the transmission of Mark's text.

b   Some MSS (A W Θ et al.) reverse the order of the first two commandments mentioned here, apparently under the influence of the parallel in Luke 18:20. Cf. also Exod 20:13-15 LXX. On the other hand, the text of Mark could have been modified in the direction of the parallel in Matt 19:18. Turner argued that the

---

17   Moeser, *Anecdote*, 225–27.

looked intently at him, loved him, and said to him, "You lack one thing; go, sell what you possess and give to the poor, and you will have treasure in heaven, and come, follow me." 22/ But he was shocked at the saying and went away distressed; for he had many possessions.

23/ And having looked around, Jesus said to his disciples, "With what difficulty will those who have possessions enter into the kingdom of God!"[d] 24/ His disciples were astounded at his words. So Jesus said to them again, "Children, how difficult entering into the kingdom of God is![e] 25/ It is easier for a camel[f] to pass through the eye of a needle than for a rich man to enter into the kingdom of God."[g] 26/ Then they were extremely amazed, saying to one another,[h] "Who then can be saved?" 27/ Jesus looked at them intently and said, "For human beings it is impossible, but not for God, for all things are possible to God."

28/ Peter began to say to him, "See, we have left everything and followed you." 29/ Jesus said, "Truly I say to you, there is no one who has left house or brothers or sisters or mother or father[i] or children or farms because of me and because of the good news 30/ who will not receive a hundredfold now,[j] in this time, houses and brothers and sisters and mothers and children and farms with persecutions, and in the age to come eternal life.[k] 31/ And many (who are) first will be last and the last first."

c   earliest recoverable text (for the first two commandments) is the reading attested by D (Γ pc) k, $\mu\grave{\eta}$ $\mu o\iota\chi\epsilon\acute{v}\sigma\eta\varsigma$, $\mu\grave{\eta}$ $\pi o\rho\nu\epsilon\acute{v}\sigma\eta\varsigma$ ("you shall not commit adultery, you shall not have unlawful intercourse"); ("Western Readings," 5). Taylor adopted this reading, ad loc. It seems more likely, however, that this reading is due to an idiosyncratic revision.

c   A number of MSS (B* K W et al.) lack the words $\mu\grave{\eta}$ $\grave{\alpha}\pi o\sigma\tau\epsilon\rho\acute{\eta}\sigma\eta\varsigma$ ("you shall not defraud"). The words were probably omitted under the influence of the parallel in Matt 19:18-19 or in Luke 18:20 or because such words are lacking in the lists of commandments in Exod 20:12-16 and Deut 5:16-20. Cf. Metzger, *Textual Commentary*, 89.

d   Some MSS (D a b ff²) have a version of v. 25 here at the end of v. 23: $\tau\acute{\alpha}\chi\iota o\nu$ $\kappa\acute{\alpha}\mu\eta\lambda o\varsigma$ $\delta\iota\grave{\alpha}$ $\tau\rho\nu\mu\acute{\alpha}\lambda\iota\delta o\varsigma$ $\acute{\rho}\alpha\varphi\acute{\iota}\delta o\varsigma$ $\delta\iota\epsilon\lambda\epsilon\acute{v}\sigma\epsilon\tau\alpha\iota$ $\grave{\eta}$ $\pi\lambda o\acute{v}\sigma\iota o\varsigma$ $\epsilon\grave{\iota}\varsigma$ $\tau\grave{\eta}\nu$ $\beta\alpha\sigma\iota\lambda\epsilon\acute{\iota}\alpha\nu$ $\tauο\tilde{v}$ $\vartheta\epsilon o\tilde{v}$ ("a camel will pass through the eye of a needle more quickly than a rich person into the kingdom of God"). These MSS then omit v. 25. This arrangement is a secondary development, apparently intended to improve the logic in the sequence of sayings; cf. Metzger, *Textual Commentary*, 89–90. Taylor, however, concluded that the original order was vv. 23, 25, 24, 26–27 (ad loc.).

e   The trans. is based on the reading attested by ℵ B et al. This apparently absolute statement is qualified in some MSS. One MS (W) has the additional word $\pi\lambda o\acute{v}$-$\sigma\iota o\nu$, "rich (man)," which transforms the saying to "how difficult it is for a rich man to enter into the kingdom of God!" Other MSS (A C D et al.) have the additional words $\tauο\grave{v}\varsigma$ $\pi\epsilon\pi o\iota\vartheta\acute{o}\tau\alpha\varsigma$ $\grave{\epsilon}\pi\grave{\iota}$ $\chi\rho\acute{\eta}\mu\alpha\sigma\iota\nu$ ("those who put their confidence in possessions"), which produce the saying "how difficult it is for those who put their confidence in possessions to enter into the kingdom of God!" Both of the latter readings seem to be "improvements" that modify the saying to fit its context better; see Metzger, *Textual Commentary*, 90.

f   Instead of $\kappa\acute{\alpha}\mu\eta\lambda o\nu$ ("camel"), f^{13} 28. et al. attest the reading $\kappa\acute{\alpha}\mu\iota\lambda o\nu$ ("rope"). This reading could have arisen by mistake, but is probably a secondary attempt to reduce the extravagance of the hyperbole or to choose an image that corresponds better to the function of a needle. Cf. Metzger, *Textual Commentary*, 40, 90.

g   D a b ff² lack this sentence at this point, but place a version of it after v. 23; see above.

h   ℵ B C et al. read $\pi\rho\grave{o}\varsigma$ $\alpha\grave{v}\tau\acute{o}\nu$ ("to him") rather than $\pi\rho\grave{o}\varsigma$ $\grave{\epsilon}\alpha\nu\tauο\acute{v}\varsigma$ ("to one another"). The former reading seems to be a correction in light of the context. Cf. Metzger, *Textual Commentary*, 90.

i   There are three variants for this portion of the text. B C W et al. attest the reading $\grave{\eta}$ $\mu\eta\tau\acute{\epsilon}\rho\alpha$ $\grave{\eta}$ $\pi\alpha\tau\acute{\epsilon}\rho\alpha$ ("or mother or father"); ℵ A read $\grave{\eta}$ $\pi\alpha\tau\acute{\epsilon}\rho\alpha$ $\grave{\eta}$ $\mu\eta\tau\acute{\epsilon}\rho\alpha$

("or father or mother"); D a ff k (i) attest the reading ἢ μητέρα ("or mother"). Turner argued that the last reading is the earliest, because there is no mention of fathers in v. 30 and it can explain the other variants ("Western Readings," 6); Taylor agreed (*ad loc.*). But the last reading may be explained as a correction intended to bring v. 29 into harmony with v. 30. The discrepancy between the two verses is understandable, since, on the one hand, discipleship may involve leaving one's biological father (cf. 1:20), but, on the other, the criticism of hierarchy (cf. 9:33-37; 10:41-45) led to a lack of emphasis on the notion of spiritual or metaphorical fatherhood. Thus, the reading of B C et al. is probably the earliest, and that of ℵ A a correction to the more usual order.

A further issue is whether ἢ γυναῖκα ("or wife") should be read with A C et al. This reading is probably secondary; it is either an independent expansion or an assimilation to the parallel in Luke 18:29.

j   D 2542 et al. attest a reading without νῦν ("now"). This reading is probably due to a deliberate omission

to avoid redundancy. The double expression is typical of Markan style (Neirynck, *Duality in Mark*, 95).

k   ℵ¹ A C W et al. attest a reading with μητέρα ("mother") instead of μητέρας ("mothers"). This reading seems to be a correction on the presumption that the individual in the example would have only one mother. ℵ² K *f*¹ et al. attest a reading with πατέρα καὶ μητέρα ("father and mother"). This reading seems to be a correction intended to conform v. 30 to the list in v. 29. D (it) attest the reading ὃς δὲ ἀφῆκεν οἰκίαν καὶ ἀδελφὰς καὶ ἀδελφοὺς καὶ μητέρα καὶ τέκνα καὶ ἀγροὺς μετὰ διωγμοῦ ἐν τῷ αἰῶνι τῷ ἐρχομένῳ ζωὴν αἰώνιον λήμψεται ("he who has left house and sisters and brothers and mother and children and farms with persecution will receive eternal life in the age to come"). This is a secondary reading that may have been designed to improve the syntax but that also has the effect of lessening the emphasis on earthly rewards. The formulation of the saying by Clement of Alexandria has the same effect; see Taylor, ad loc.

History of the Tradition

Bultmann defined vv. 17-22 as a classic apophthegm, in which the master is questioned by the rich man. Only the introduction in v. 17a is likely to be an editorial addition. He argued that vv. 23, 25 constitute another old apophthegm that was already attached to the anecdote about the rich man in vv. 17-22 when Mark received it.[18] Mark then elaborated the simple anecdote in vv. 23 and 25 by adding vv. 24, 26, and 27.[19] The remark in v. 27 that "all things are possible for God" recalls 9:23, where Jesus says to the father of the epileptic young man, "All things are possible for the one who trusts."[20] This similarity supports the hypothesis that v. 27 is Markan elaboration. Bultmann's hypothesis that vv. 23, 25 constitute an old apophthegm is less convincing than the hypothesis that v. 25 is a pre-Markan saying for which Mark provides a setting in vv. 23-24, 26-27. The saying may have come to Mark as a brief anecdote, but, if so, its pre-Markan introduction can no longer be detected.

Mark also added vv. 28-31, perhaps making use of a traditional saying in vv. 29-30. It is likely that he composed v. 28 as an introduction to this section, which elaborates the significance of the story of the rich man for the disciples as characters in the narrative and for the audience of Mark. Verse 31 is also a traditional saying that occurs in several other contexts.[21]

Comment

■ **17** The genitive absolute with which the story begins, Καὶ ἐκπορευομένου αὐτοῦ εἰς ὁδόν ("And as he was setting out on a journey"), could be a link composed by Mark to connect the traditional story to the current context.[22] Or it could be part of the traditional story on which Mark modeled the introduction to the third passion prediction in v. 32. The use of the numeral "one" (εἷς) instead of the indefinite pronoun (τις) is typical of

18   Bultmann, *History*, 21–22.
19   Bultmann argued that Mark added vv. 24, 26, but he did not comment on the origin of v. 27.
20   See the commentary on 9:21-24 above.
21   Bultmann left open the possibility that v. 28 is the

introduction to another pre-Markan apophthegm (*History*, 22). The saying of v. 31 occurs in unrelated contexts in Matt 20:16; Luke 13:30; cf. also P. Oxy. 654.5-9 = *Gos. Thom.* 4; *Barn.* 6:13.
22   See the section "History of the Tradition" above.

unliterary Koine Greek.[23] The only other place in Mark in which someone "runs up" (προστρέχειν) to Jesus is 9:15. There it is a crowd who are amazed when they see Jesus. In both passages, this verb may be used to show the effect that Jesus, spirit-filled and charismatic, had on people. The only other place in which someone falls on his knees (γονυπετεῖν) before Jesus is 1:40. There it is a leper who is seeking healing from him. In both passages, the gesture expresses reverence for Jesus and intense petition. In 1:40, the petition is for healing; here it is for authoritative instruction.

The man who runs up and kneels before Jesus addresses him as "good teacher" (διδάσκαλε ἀγαθέ). This address implies that Jesus is pleasing to God and can show others how to become so.[24] The instruction that he seeks concerns what he must do "to inherit eternal life" (ἵνα ζωὴν αἰώνιον κληρονομήσω). In the Hebrew Bible, language of inheritance refers "originally and almost exclusively to the possession of land."[25] The land in question may be the land belonging to a particular family or the land of Canaan, the land flowing with milk and honey promised to Israel. In some texts from the Second Temple period and the rabbinic literature, inheritance still refers to land. In some of these cases, the reference is to the promised land; in others, to the whole earth. In many of these texts, the possession of the land or the earth is an eschatological expectation.[26]

Other texts from the Second Temple period are closer to the request of the man in Mark 10:17. *Psalms of Solomon* 14:9-10, for example, contrasts the devout and the sinners and warns that the inheritance (κληρονομία) of sinners is Hades and destruction. The devout will "inherit life in happiness" (κληρονομήσουσιν ζωὴν ἐν εὐφροσύνῃ).[27] The contrast between "life" and "Hades" suggests that "life" here means eternal life. More explic-

itly, *1 Enoch* 40:9 speaks about the angel Phanuel, "who (is) in charge of the repentance to hope of those who inherit everlasting life."[28] According to fragment 3 of the *Sibylline Oracles* (lines 46–49),

> But those who honor the true eternal God
> inherit life, dwelling in the luxuriant garden
> of Paradise for the time of eternity,
> feasting on sweet bread from starry heaven
> (οἱ δὲ θεὸν τιμῶντες ἀληθινὸν ἀέναόν τε ζωὴν κληρονομοῦσι, τὸν αἰῶνος χρόνον αὐτοί οἰκοῦντες παραδείσου ὁμῶς ἐριθηλέα κῆπον δαινύμενοι γλυκὺν ἄρτον ἀπ᾽ οὐρανοῦ ἀστερόεντος).[29]

The question of the man who runs up to Jesus presupposes expectations of this kind.

■ **18-19** Jesus' reply has two parts. In v. 18, he responds to the way the man addressed him, "good teacher" (διδάσκαλε ἀγαθέ). This part of Jesus' response also has two parts. First, he distances himself from the address by asking, "Why do you call me good?" Second, he explains why he refuses the characterization of himself as "good" by stating, "No one is good except one, (namely) God."[30] This statement reflects the typical summons in the Psalms, 1 and 2 Chronicles, and Ezra to give thanks to God because God is good. The goodness of God is associated in these passages with God's steadfast love (חסד) for Israel.[31]

Philo explains that God did not include any penalties in the Ten Commandments because "He was God, and it follows at once that as Lord He was good, the cause of good only and of nothing ill" (θεὸς ἦν, εὐθὺς δὲ κύριος ἀγαθός, μόνων ἀγαθῶν αἴτιος, κακοῦ δ᾽ οὐδενός) (*Decal.* 33 §176).[32] According to the tractate *Berakot* (*Blessings*) in the Mishnah, in thanksgiving for rain and good

23 Philip Sellew, "*Secret Mark* and the History of Canonical Mark," in Birger A. Pearson, ed., *The Future of Early Christianity* (Minneapolis: Fortress, 1991) 252.

24 Walter Grundmann, "ἀγαθός, κτλ.," *TDNT* 1 (1964) 10–18, esp. 12.

25 Johannes Herrmann, "B. נַחֲלָה and נָחַל in the OT," *TDNT* 3 (1965) 769–76; citation from 774.

26 Werner Foerster, "κλῆρος κτλ.," *TDNT* 3 (1965) 758–69, 776–85, esp. 779–80.

27 Trans. from R. B. Wright, "Psalms of Solomon," *OTP* 2:664; cited by Foerster, "κλῆρος κτλ.," 780.

28 Trans. from Nickelsburg and VanderKam, 55; Foer-

ster, "κλῆρος κτλ.," 780. Cf. the discussion of the two ages in the same portion of *1 Enoch*, the Similitudes of Enoch, below in the commentary on v. 30.

29 Trans. from J. J. Collins, "Sibylline Oracles," *OTP* 1:471. Text from Johannes Geffcken, *Die Oracula Sibyllina* (Griechische Christliche Schriftsteller der ersten drei Jahrhunderte 8; Leipzig: Hinrichs, 1902) 232.

30 Israel Abrahams pointed out that the idiom of this phrase, οὐδεὶς ἀγαθὸς εἰ μὴ εἷς ὁ θεός, is thoroughly Hebraic (*Studies in Pharisaism*, 2:186).

31 Pss 100:5; 106:1; 107:1; 118:1; 136:1; 1 Chr 16:34;

news, one should say "Blessed is he, the good and the doer of good" (הטוב והמיטיב) (*m. Ber.* 9.2).[33] It is rare, but not unheard of, for a rabbi to be called good. Israel Abrahams, following Gustav Dalman, cited a case in which a rabbi heard the following in a dream:

Good greeting to the good teacher from the good Lord, who of his goodness doeth good to his people

(שלם טב לרב טב מרבון טב דמיטוביה לעמיה:).[34]

Moses is also called "good."[35]

In the first part of his response in v. 18, the Markan Jesus shows his modesty and piety by not claiming for himself qualities or prerogatives that belong to God alone. This portrayal of him contrasts with the accusations of the scribes and the high priest and council elsewhere in Mark.[36]

In v. 19, Jesus replies to the man's question itself. The introductory statement, "You know the commandments," is open to several interpretations. In all Jewish contexts in the first century CE, ἐντολαί ("commandments") would signify at least all the individual precepts of the books of Moses.[37] Among Pharisees, the term would include the written precepts of Moses and also the unwritten ones of the tradition of the fathers (ἡ πατρῴα παράδοσις).[38] Among Essenes, it would signify the commandments of God as interpreted by the Teacher of Righteousness and the leaders who succeeded him. The question of the man who knelt before Jesus, "what should I do to inherit eternal life?" is illuminated by a passage in the *Damascus Document*:

But those who remained steadfast in God's precepts, with those who were left from among them, God established his covenant with Israel for ever, revealing to them hidden matters in which all Israel had gone astray: *blank* his holy sabbaths and his glorious feasts, his just stipulations and his truthful paths, and the wishes of his will which man must do in order to live by them

(ובמחזיקים במצות אל)
אשר נותרו מהם הקים אל את בריתו לישראל עד עולם לגלות
להם נסתרות אשר תעו בם כל ישראל *vacat* שבתות קדשו ומועדי
כבודו עידות צדקו ודרכי אמתו וחפצי רצונו אשר יעשה האדם וחיה בהם).
(CD 3:12-16)[39]

Here the commandments (מצות; translated "precepts" above) of God are equivalent to God's "just stipulations" (עידות צדקו), which have been revealed to the Teacher and his community. The expression "which man must do in order to live by them" is an allusion to Lev 18:5, "You shall keep my statutes and my ordinances; by doing so one shall live: I am the Lord" (NRSV).[40] In its early contexts, the latter passage referred to physical life.[41] In this context, however, it probably signifies eternal life, since the same work, a few lines later, speaks about the steadfast acquiring eternal life (CD 3:20).

Any application of the written commandments in Jesus' time would take place in the context of one or more interpretive traditions.[42] It is difficult to discern what interpretive tradition provided the context for the teaching of the historical Jesus and the earliest communities of his followers. For that reason it is not clear whether the pre-Markan story about the rich man

2 Chr 5:13; Ezra 3:11; Grundmann, "ἀγαθός, κτλ.," 13–14; Kraus, *Psalms 60–150*, 318; Jacob M. Myers, *I Chronicles: Introduction, Translation, and Notes* (AB 12; Garden City, NY: Doubleday, 1965) 121; idem, *II Chronicles: Translation and Notes* (AB 13; New York: Doubleday, 1965) 29–30.

32 Trans. from Colson, *Philo*, 7:92–93.

33 Hebrew from Grundmann, "ἀγαθός, κτλ.," 14; trans. from Danby, *Mishnah*, 9.

34 Abrahams, *Studies in Pharisaism*, 2:186.

35 *B. Menaḥ.* 53b; Abrahams, *Studies in Pharisaism*, 2:186.

36 See the commentary on 2:6-7 above and on 14:61-64 below.

37 Gottlob Schrenk, "ἐντέλλομαι, ἐντολή," TDNT 2 (1964) 544–56, esp. 546.

38 See the commentary on 7:3-4 above.

39 Text and trans. from García Martínez and Tigchelaar, *Dead Sea Scrolls*, 1:554–55.

40 A similar expression occurs in Ezek 20:11, 13, 21; Craig A. Evans, "Jesus and the Dead Sea Scrolls," in Peter W. Flint and James C. VanderKam, eds., *The Dead Sea Scrolls after Fifty Years: A Comprehensive Assessment* (2 vols.; Leiden: Brill, 1998–99) 2:573–98, esp. 594–95.

41 Milgrom, *Leviticus*, 2:1522.

42 Meier, "Historical Jesus and the Historical Law," 67.

rejected the view that "the commandments" included all the precepts of the books of Moses. In any case, the Jesus of this story emphasizes the Ten Commandments and, within these, the latter ones that concern the relations among human beings.

The first of the commandments cited, "You shall not murder," is an allusion to Exod 20:13/Deut 5:17, in wording close to that of the LXX.[43] The second, "you shall not commit adultery," is an allusion to Exod 20:14/Deut 5:18, again in wording close to the LXX.[44] In the Hebrew texts, the commandment not to commit adultery follows immediately on the commandment not to murder. In the LXX, the commandment concerning adultery precedes that concerning murder.[45] The third of the commandments cited, "you shall not steal," is an allusion to Exod 20:15/Deut 5:19, in wording close to the LXX.[46] The fourth, "you shall not bear false witness," is an abbreviated allusion to Exod 20:16/Deut 5:20, omitting "against your neighbor."[47]

The fifth of the commandments cited, "you shall not defraud," is not one of the Ten Commandments as such. That may be the reason why it is omitted in some MSS.[48] It could be a very concise summary of Lev 6:1-7 (5:20-26 LXX), which concerns defrauding a neighbor.[49] Another possible source is Malachi:

"And I will come near to you in judgment and I will be a swift witness against the sorceresses and against the adulteresses and against those who swear falsely in my name and against those who defraud a hired worker of his wages and those who exploit a widow and those who maltreat orphans and those who turn away from justice for the alien and those who do not fear me," says the Lord the Almighty (καὶ προσάξω πρὸς ὑμᾶς ἐν κρίσει καὶ ἔσομαι μάρτυς ταχὺς ἐπὶ τὰς φαρμακοὺς καὶ ἐπὶ τὰς μοιχαλίδας καὶ ἐπὶ τοὺς ὀμνύοντας τῷ ὀνόματί μου ἐπὶ ψεύδει καὶ ἐπὶ τοὺς ἀποστεροῦντας μισθὸν μισθωτοῦ καὶ τοὺς καταδυναστεύοντας χήραν καὶ τοὺς κονδυλίζοντας ὀρφανοὺς καὶ τοὺς ἐκκλίνοντας κρίσιν προσηλύτου καὶ τοὺς μὴ φοβουμένους με, λέγει κύριος παντοκράτωρ). (Mal 3:5 LXX)

In this text there are allusions to two of the Ten Commandments (adultery, false witness) and also to deeds of economic injustice. Another possibility is that the commandment not to defraud in v. 19 is a particular commandment based on the general one not to steal. Philo discusses the embezzlement of money or property given as a deposit on trust in his discussion of the commandment not to steal in the *Special Laws* (4.7 §§30–38). Or it may derive from ethical teaching rooted in the oral tradition and literature of Jewish wisdom. Sirach instructed his audience, "do not defraud the livelihood of one who is destitute and do not put off the eyes of the destitute" (τὴν ζωὴν τοῦ πτωχοῦ μὴ ἀποστερήσῃς καὶ μὴ παρελκύσῃς ὀφθαλμοὺς ἐπιδεεῖς) (Sir 4:1 LXX).[50] In any case, this commandment may be included by the narrator of the story because the man is rich (as becomes apparent in v. 22), and this commandment addresses one of the temptations of those with wealth.

The sixth and last of the commandments cited in

---

43 Exod 20:15/Deut 5:18 LXX both read οὐ φονεύσεις ("you shall not murder"). In Mark 10:19, μή with the subjunctive is used to express a prohibition; in the LXX, οὐ with the indicative is used. The same verb, however, is used in both contexts.

44 Exod 20:13/Deut 5:17 LXX both read οὐ μοιχεύσεις ("you shall not commit adultery"). In this case also, Mark has μή with the subjunctive.

45 In Exodus 20 LXX, the commandment not to steal follows immediately on the one not to commit adultery; the command not to murder then follows the one not to steal. In Deuteronomy 5 LXX, the commandment not to murder follows immediately upon the one not to commit adultery. The variation in order among the Hebrew text and the two chapters of the LXX may have been a factor in the variation

in the order of the commandments in the MSS of Mark; see the first note on the trans. of v. 19 above.

46 On the placement of this commandment in Exodus 20 and Deuteronomy 5 LXX, see the previous note.

47 Mark 10:19 reads simply μὴ ψευδομαρτυρήσῃς ("you shall not bear false witness"). Exod 20:16 and Deut 5:20 LXX read οὐ ψευδομαρτυρήσεις κατὰ τοῦ πλησίον σου μαρτυρίαν ψευδῆ ("you shall not bear false witness against your neighbor").

48 See the second note on the trans. of v. 19 above.

49 The verb ἀποστερεῖν ("to defraud"), however, does not occur in Lev 5:20-26 LXX. On the possible connection between the two passages, see BAGD, s.v. ἀποστερέω. Metzger concludes that this commandment is remininscent of Exod 20:17 or Deut 24:14 (*Textual Commentary*, 89).

v. 19, "honor your father and mother," is an abbreviated allusion to Exod 20:12/Deut 5:16. The wording of the Markan text agrees exactly with the first part of Exod 20:12 LXX.[51] In both the Hebrew Bible and the LXX, this commandment comes before the others of the Ten Commandments alluded to here. The placement of the commandment to honor father and mother immediately after the command not to defraud evokes in the Markan audience the memory of the saying of Jesus regarding the circumvention of the former by the *korban*-vow.[52] Such defrauding of one's parents may also have been viewed as a temptation especially for the wealthy.

■ **20-22** The man shows his responsiveness to instruction by dropping the word "good" and simply addressing Jesus as "Teacher." He replies that he has observed all these commandments since his youth. Jesus' looking intently at him and loving him indicate that he recognizes that the man has great potential as a disciple. He then tells the man that he lacks one thing. The dialogue seems to imply that, as far as Jesus is concerned, keeping the commandments is sufficient for inheriting eternal life.[53] The man, however, seeks something more.[54] Jesus then instructs him, "sell what you possess and give to the poor, and you will have treasure in heaven, and come, follow me." It is noteworthy that the stated motivation for selling his property and giving to the poor is not the neediness of the poor but the accumulation of "treasure in heaven." This motivation suggests that the man is seeking a greater than ordinary level of spiritual achievement.

There is an analogy between the man's desire for spiritual achievement and Jesus' advice, on the one hand, and Hellenistic texts that speak about self-mastery with regard to money and property, on the other. Epictetus, for example, argued that the lover of wisdom ought to be able to say

"If you want my property in the country," says he, "take it; take my servants, take my office, take my paltry body. But you will not make my desire fail to get what I will, nor my aversion fall into what I would avoid" (εἰ τὰ κατὰ τὸν ἀγρὸν θέλεις, λάβε· λάβε τοὺς οἰκέτας, λάβε τὴν ἀρχήν, λάβε τὸ σωμάτιον. τὴν δ' ὄρεξιν οὐ ποιήσεις ἀποτευκτικὴν οὐδὲ τὴν ἔκκλισιν περιπτωτικήν). (*Diss.* 3.6.6)[55]

In another place, he asks his audience:

And how shall I free myself?—Have you not heard over and over again that you ought to eradicate desire utterly, direct your aversion towards the things that lie within the sphere of the moral purpose, and these things only, that you ought to give up everything, your body, your property, your reputation, your books, turmoil, office, freedom from office? (Καὶ πῶς ἀπαλλάξω;—Οὐ πολλάκις ἤκουσας, ὅτι ὄρεξιν ἆραί σε δεῖ παντελῶς, τὴν ἔκκλισιν ἐπὶ μόνα τρέψαι τὰ προαιρετικά, ἀφεῖναί σε δεῖ πάντα, τὸ σῶμα, τὴν κτῆσιν, τὴν φήμην, τὰ βιβλία, θόρυβον, ἀρχάς, ἀναρχίαν;). (*Diss.* 4.4.33)[56]

Crates, the pupil of Aristotle and the teacher of Zeno, was attracted to the Cynic philosophy:

So he turned his property into money,—for he belonged to a distinguished family,—and having thus collected about 200 talents, distributed that sum among his fellow citizens. And (it is added) so sturdy a philosopher did he become that he is mentioned by the comic poet Philemon (ἐξαργυρισάμενόν τε τὴν οὐσίαν—καὶ γὰρ ἦν τῶν ἐπιφανῶν—ἀθροίσαντα πρὸς τὰ (ἑκατὸν) διαδόσια τάλαντα, τοῖς πολί-

---

50 See also Sir 34:21 LXX (34:25 NRSV); 34:22 LXX (34:27 NRSV).

51 Some MSS add the word σου ("your") and thus agree exactly with Deut 5:16 LXX.

52 See the commentary on 7:9-13 above.

53 Matthew makes this explicit by having Jesus preface his advice with the clause εἰ θέλεις τέλειος εἶναι ("If you wish to be perfect") (Matt 19:21).

54 This element of the story is recognized by Tannehill, who defines it as a "quest story" ("Varieties," 4.3 [p. 112]).

55 Text and trans. from W. A. Oldfather, *Epictetus* (2 vols.; LCL; Cambridge, MA: Harvard University Press; London: Heinemann, 1928) 2:46–47. See also *Diss.* 3.24.67–68; 4.1.81–83; 4.1.87; 4.1.128–30; 4.1.153; 4.3.10.

56 Text and trans. from Oldfather, *Epictetus*, 2:324–25. See also *Diss.* 4.6.34; 4.7.5; *Ench.* 1.

ταις διανεῖμαι ταῦτα. αὐτὸν δὲ καρτερῶς οὕτω φιλοσοφεῖν ὡς καὶ Φιλήμονα τὸν κωμικὸν αὐτοῦ μεμνῆσθαι). (Diogenes Laertius 6.87)[57]

Although the primary emphasis in Mark 10:21 is on the spiritual quest and achievement of the man, his divestment of his property is intended to benefit the poor. The Hellenistic texts lack this concern for alleviating the suffering of the needy, but both Mark and the Hellenistic texts call for a radical reorientation of one's life.[58]

The man does not respond in the way that Simon (Peter), Andrew, James, John, and Levi did (cf. 1:16-20; 2:13-14). On the contrary, he is appalled at Jesus' suggestion and goes away distressed. The narrator's comment, "for he had many possessions" (ἦν γὰρ ἔχων κτήματα πολλά), suggests that he lacked the philosophical or religious insight and the self-mastery to let go of his wealth and to choose a higher good. He is thus a negative example for the audience.[59]

■ **23-27** This paragraph is repetitive and contains redundancies, but such are typical of Markan style.[60] These features may have led one or more scribes to rearrange the passage.[61] If vv. 23 and 25 constitute an old anecdote placed by Mark in this context, he has woven at least v. 23 expertly into the new setting.[62] As he looked intently (ἐμβλέψας) at the man who had run up to him (v. 21), now he looks around (περιβλεψάμενος) at his disciples.[63] This verbal link may imply a contrast between the man with many possession who did not follow Jesus and the disciples, who were less wealthy and did accept Jesus' call.

The saying in v. 23, "With what difficulty will those who have possessions enter into the kingdom of God!" recalls the last time the kingdom of God was mentioned, the saying in v. 15, "Truly I say to you, whoever does not receive the kingdom of God as a child (would receive it) shall surely not enter into it." This textual link suggests another contrast, one between children who have no possessions legally their own and those who have many possessions at their disposal. The implication is that attachment to property is a hindrance in responding properly to the demands of the kingdom.

In v. 24a, the narrator remarks that the disciples were astounded at Jesus' words. In the context of Mark's narrative, Jesus' words here are not surprising, but the disciples' reaction may be narrated to reflect and to call into question a common cultural assumption rooted in scripture, that wealth is a blessing given by God, even a reward for obedience to God's commandments.[64] Jesus' saying in v. 23b subverts that cultural belief, just as the beatitudes and woes in Luke do (Luke 6:20-26). Like Epictetus, Jesus warns that property can be a major distraction from what is truly good and important.

The saying of v. 24b, "Children, how difficult entering into the kingdom of God is!" seems to generalize the saying of v. 23b and thus does not fit well into the context. These features explain the variations in the MSS.[65] If the generalization is significant for the social setting of the evangelist and his audiences, it may reflect an aspect of their experience, namely, that many Jews and non-Jews have rejected the proclamation of the good news. Alternatively, this saying may simply have been composed by Mark in order to introduce the traditional saying of v. 25.

The saying of v. 25 is vivid, arresting, and difficult in several senses of the word. At least one scribe may have found the juxtaposition of a camel and a needle too farfetched and thus substituted "rope" for "camel."[66] But the saying is hyperbolic and refers to something that is obviously impossible.[67] Much of the power of the saying lies in its evocation of the mental image of a huge camel

57   See also 6.88; Hengel, *Charismatic Leader*, 28–29 and n. 43.

58   Cf. Arthur Darby Nock, *Conversion: The Old and the New in Religion from Alexander the Great to Augustine of Hippo* (Oxford: Clarendon, 1933; reprinted Oxford/New York: Oxford University Press, 1961); Cancik, "Lucian on Conversion," 26–48.

59   Tannehill notes that this is the only "unsuccessful quest story" in the Synoptic Gospels ("Varieties," 4.3 [p. 112]).

60   Neirynck, *Duality in Mark*, 99.

61   See the note on the trans. of v. 23 above.

62   See the section "History of the Tradition" above.

63   Gundry, 555. See also v. 27, where Jesus "looks intently" (ἐμβλέψας) at the disciples.

64   Deut 28:1-14, esp. vv. 11-12; Prov 10:22; Gundry, 555.

65   See the note on the trans. of v. 24 above.

66   See the first note on the trans. of v. 25 above.

67   Tannehill, *Sword*, 76.

and a tiny needle with its yet tinier eye. The hyperbolic character of the saying catches the attention of the audience effectively and leads them to confront seriously the problem of wealth as a hindrance to entering the kingdom.

In v. 26 the response of the disciples is dramatically heightened in comparison with v. 24. In v. 24 they are simply astounded. In v. 26, they are extremely amazed. Since the saying of v. 25 is more imaginative and shocking than the one of v. 24b, the reaction is appropriately stronger. The disciples go on to ask one another, "Who then can be saved?" The question of the disciples seems, on the surface, nonsensical, since not everyone is rich (πλούσιος). Their question may be understood as part of the theme of the misunderstanding of the disciples, since it shows that they have not grasped Jesus' challenge to the traditional wisdom that wealth is a sign of God's blessing and favor. The question implies that if the rich cannot be saved, then no one can.[68]

Now (v. 27) Jesus looks intently at the disciples, just as he did at the man who had knelt at his feet.[69] This textual link suggests that Jesus' answer concerns the specific problem of how the rich can be saved, not the general one raised by the disciples in the specific wording of their question. His reply, "For human beings it is impossible, but not for God, for all things are possible to God," reveals a significant difference between the perspective of the Markan Jesus and the Hellenistic writers cited above.[70] For Epictetus and Diogenes Laertius' Crates, proper practices regarding property and the pursuit of the morally good life are matters under human control. For Jesus, it is God, not human beings, who is in control, even in matters that seem to center on human choices and decisions.[71]

Jesus' saying also addresses the social situation of Mark and his audiences. The communities of followers of Jesus had some members who were literate and had considerable property.[72] This saying acknowledges that such people may be saved and opposes the inference that only the poor will enter the kingdom of God.

■ **28-31** As pointed out above, the refusal of the man to accept Jesus' call contrasts with the acceptance of his call by Simon (Peter) and the others.[73] The story of the rich man provides a negative example for the audience, whereas the call stories of the disciples provide positive examples. The implicit comparison of the rich man with Peter and the rest becomes explicit in Peter's comment in v. 28, "See, we have left everything and followed you." This remark provides an opportunity for Jesus to speak in vv. 29-30 about the consequences of accepting his call. This saying of Jesus is significant on two levels. On one level, it concerns Peter and the other disciples who are characters in the narrative. On another level, it addresses the situation of the audiences of the Gospel. James and John are explicitly described in 1:20 as leaving their father, Zebedee. The mention of Simon's (Peter's) mother-in-law in 1:30-31 suggests that Peter left a wife and perhaps other family members as well to follow Jesus as his disciple. Levi left his work of collecting custom-duties (2:13-14). The disciples, however, belong to a special category. Mark does not imply that all who would be followers of Jesus and members of early Christian communities must leave families, farms, or other types of work in order to do so.[74] Nevertheless, when individuals or parts of households joined a community of those who belonged to Christ and the rest of their household did not join, it must have happened at times that the newly converted would become estranged from nonconverted members of their household. Although such converts might not have "left" parents and siblings physically, they

68 Cf. Gundry, 557. On the theme of the misunderstanding of the disciples, see the commentary on 9:32 and 9:33-34 above.

69 On the multiplication of cognate verbs in vv. 21, 23, and 27, see Neirynck, *Duality in Mark*, 79.

70 See the commentary on vv. 20-22 above.

71 On the phrase πάντα δυνατὰ παρὰ τῷ θεῷ ("all things are possible to God"), see the commentary on 9:21-24 above.

72 Wayne A. Meeks, *The First Urban Christians: The Social World of the Apostle Paul* (New Haven/London:

Yale University Press, 1983) 51–73; Gamble, *Books and Readers*, 5, 8–9.

73 See the commentary on vv. 20-22 above.

74 Stephen P. Ahearne-Kroll, "'Who Are My Mother and My Brothers?' Family Relations and Family Language in the Gospel of Mark," *JR* 81 (2001) 1–25, esp. 9, 17–18.

may have been forced to "leave" them in terms of allegiance and mutual support.

Mark 3:20-35 provides an important analogy to the saying of Jesus in 10:29-30.[75] The former passage frames the controversy over Jesus' exorcisms with two narratives that illuminate each other. According to 3:20-21, Jesus' family tried to restrain him, thinking that he had lost his senses. In 3:31-35, Jesus distances himself from his family and declares that those who are sitting and listening to him are his mother and his brothers; indeed, he says, whoever does the will of God is his brother and sister and mother. This narrative account of tension between Jesus and his family of origin is probably included by Mark as a way of addressing similar tensions being experienced by members of his audiences. The similarity between 3:20-35 and 10:29-30 suggests that the reception of a hundredfold, in this time, of brothers and sisters and mothers and children refers to the new family constituted by the early Christian communities.[76] This reading is supported by other early Christian texts that show that these communities were organized on the model of the ancient household.[77]

It is noteworthy that v. 29 speaks about leaving fathers, among others, but v. 30 does not mention receiving (new) fathers, along with brothers, sisters, mothers, and children. Nor is a father mentioned in 3:20-35. It would be awkward to portray Jesus, of course, as recognizing one of his followers as "father." In 10:29-30, the one who leaves parents to follow Jesus may take the role of "father" himself. Another explanation for the omission is that the saying embodies an "anti-patriarchal" ideology and reflects the "radically egalitarian" organization of the earliest Christian communities. In its strong form, this thesis is untenable, both historically and exegetically. The ancient household was not egalitarian, and the leaders took the role of the father. Paul refers to himself, for example, as the "father" of the communities that he founded (1 Cor 4:15).[78] Although the early Christian communities were not socially and economically egalitarian, it may be that Mark omitted "fathers" in v. 30 in order to make the point that the leaders should not insist on their superior role but rather should engage in a leadership of service. Such an aim would fit with Jesus' teaching in the controversies over rank in 9:33-37 and 10:35-45.

The leaving of "house" or "household" ($oἰκία$) and "farms" or "fields" ($ἀγροί$) may refer to those who leave home to proclaim the good news, like the disciples in the narrative, or to those who lose their place in their households and lose their share in the produce of the family's land because they have joined a Christian community. Those who travel to proclaim the gospel, the saying of Jesus promises, will be welcomed in the households and farms of others who will offer them hospitality. Similarly, the members of communities who have become estranged from their families of origin will not only be incorporated into a new household and family but will also share the goods of their fellow Christians, as they have need.

In v. 29, the Markan Jesus refers to leaving house and family "because of me and because of the good news" ($ἕνεκεν ἐμοῦ καὶ ἕνεκεν τοῦ εὐαγγελίου$). Matthew and Luke differ from Mark on this point. Matt 19:29 reads "because of my name" ($ἕνεκεν τοῦ ὀνόματός μου$); Luke 18:29 reads "because of the kingdom of God" ($ἕνεκεν τῆς βασιλείας τοῦ θεοῦ$). Helmut Koester has argued that the relevant text of Mark is a secondary expansion of an older saying that read simply "because of me" ($ἕνεκεν ἐμοῦ$). He concluded that the version of Mark used by Matthew had this shorter text.[79] It seems more likely that the double formulation of the Markan text is the earliest recoverable text.[80] Matthew and Luke found it redundant, so each rewrote the text independently.

Verse 30 states that the new family and property will be received "with persecutions" ($μετὰ διωγμῶν$). This phrase has two implications. One is that the follower of Jesus will necessarily experience rejection, estrangement,

---

75 See the commentary on 3:20-35 above.

76 Donahue, *Discipleship*, 32–42. David Rhoads argues that the allusion is "to solidarity through hospitality as the disciples journey from place to place" (*Reading Mark*, 100).

77 Elliott, "Jesus Movement," 177–78, 187–93, 198–200.

78 Elliott, "Jesus Movement," 173–210, esp. 192.

79 Koester, "History and Development," 43–44.

80 Neirynck, *Duality in Mark*, 104.

and other forms of persecution, even death, as he did.[81] The other is that the estrangement caused by leaving one's family of origin for the new family in Christ often leads to persecution.[82]

Verse 30 contrasts what those who have left house and family will receive "now, in this time" (νῦν ἐν τῷ καιρῷ τούτῳ) and what they will receive "in the age to come" (ὁ αἰών ὁ ἐρχόμενος). The notion of two ages or aeons, "this age" and "the age to come" is common in Jewish apocalyptic texts and in rabbinic literature. The word "age" or "aeon" (αἰών) can have either a temporal sense or a spatial sense and can thus be translated either "age" or "world."[83] The Similitudes of Enoch, a section of *1 Enoch* that is roughly contemporary with Mark, contrasts "this age of unrighteousness" with "the age that is to be" (48:7; 71:15).[84] The notion of "this age of unrighteousness" seems to be presupposed in Mark 4:19, where "the age" (αἰών) is associated with "anxieties" and the "seduction by wealth."[85] In the Jewish apocalypse of *4 Ezra*, written about thirty years after Mark, "this aeon" (*hoc saeculum, hoc tempus, hic mundus,* or *praesens saeculum*) is temporal, whereas "the aeon to come" (*futurum saeculum, saeculum venturum, saeculum sequens* or *saeculum maius*) is eternal.[86]

What the faithful followers of Jesus will receive in "the age to come" is "eternal life" (ζωὴ αἰώνιος). This is the eschatological reward that the man who had run up to Jesus was seeking.[87] The use of the same phrase here contrasts once again the rich man with the disciples of Jesus. This contrast prepares for v. 31, "And many (who are) first will be last and the last first." This saying takes up the theme of the subversion of the traditional view that the rich are blessed by God.[88] Many of the rich, who appear to be those to whom the kingdom of God belongs, will *not* enter into it, whereas many of the poor, who seem to be abandoned by God, *will* enter into it.

---

81 Donahue, *Discipleship*, 43.

82 Ibid., 44–45. For an ironic interpretation of the phrase, see Tannehill, *Sword*, 149–52.

83 BAGD, s.v. αἰών.

84 Trans. from Nickelsburg and VanderKam, 62, 95; Hermann Sasse, "αἰών, αἰώνιος," *TDNT* 1 (1964) 197–209, esp. 206.

85 See the trans. (and the note on the trans.) of 4:19 above.

86 Stone, *Fourth Ezra*, 284, on 8:46; see also the "Excursus on the Two Ages," ibid., 92–93; terminology for the two ages in *4 Ezra* provided by Sasse, "αἰών, αἰώνιος," 206.

87 See the commentary on v. 17 above.

88 See the commentary on vv. 23-27 above.

32/ Now they were on the way going up to Jerusalem, and Jesus was going ahead of them, and they were astounded, and those who followed were afraid.[a] And he took the twelve again and began to tell them about the things that were about to happen to him, 33/ "See, we are going up to Jerusalem, and the Son of Man will be handed over to the chief priests and the scribes, and they will condemn him to death and hand him over to the nations, 34/ and they will mock him and spit on him and whip him and kill him, and after three days[b] he will rise."	a The earliest recoverable reading, οἱ δὲ ἀκολου-θοῦντες ἐφοβοῦντο ("and those who followed were afraid"), attested by ℵ B C* et al. (see Tischendorf; and Aland, *Synopsis*, ad loc.), is ambiguous. It is not clear whether those who followed are identical with those ahead of whom Jesus went, a portion of that group, or a distinct group. This ambiguity has given rise to variants. D K 157. 700. et al. omit the clause. A C² N et al. read καὶ ("and") instead of δὲ ("and" or "but"). b The trans. is based on the reading attested by ℵ B C D et al., μετὰ τρεῖς ἡμέρας ("after three days"). The reading τῇ τρίτῃ ἡμέρᾳ ("on the third day"), attested by A(*) W Θ f¹·¹³ 𝔐 et al., is a secondary assimilation of the text of Mark to the more common formulation, perhaps specifically to the parallel in Matt 20:19; cf. Luke 18:33. See above on 8:31 and 9:31.

Comment

■ **32a** As noted above, the middle section of Mark, 8:27–10:45, is structured as a journey, first northward to the villages of Caesarea Philippi (8:27) and Mount Hermon (9:2), and then southward toward Jerusalem.[1] Like each of the first two passion predictions, the third marks a topographical shift.[2] According to 10:1, Jesus had arrived in Judea.[3] Here, they are "on the way" or "on the road" (ἐν τῇ ὁδῷ) to Jerusalem itself. The style of this verse is typically Markan.[4]

It is not clear who is going up to Jerusalem with Jesus, whom he is leading (προάγειν), who are astounded, and who are following him (v. 32a).[5] In v. 32b, he takes the Twelve aside, presumably for private instruction.[6] This gesture suggests that a larger group than the Twelve is following Jesus here.

In any case, the picture of Jesus going ahead and others following him suggests that the journey to Jerusalem is symbolic of discipleship.[7] The astonishment and fear of those following Jesus are unmotivated except for the remark that they were going up to Jerusalem and that Jesus was leading the way. Their depiction as fearful may anticipate Jesus' prediction in vv. 33-34 that the Son of Man will suffer and die in Jerusalem. As his disciples, they are vulnerable too. The journey to Jerusalem is the "way" to suffering and death.[8] But it is also the "way" to resurrection (v. 34), so the fear here may include the numinous sort.[9]

Helmut Koester has argued that the amazement and fear of the disciples and followers of Jesus in v. 32 make no sense in the context of Mark in its canonical form. He tried to explain their significance in relation to "Secret Mark," a version of Mark mentioned in a fragment of a letter of Clement discovered and published by Morton Smith.[10] According to this fragment, Secret Mark had a passage regarding the raising of a young man from the dead immediately following 10:34. Koester also argued

---

1 See the section "Narrative Unity of 8:27–10:45" above and the commentary on 10:1.

2 See the commentary on 8:27a and 9:30 above.

3 See the commentary on 10:1 and the note on the trans.

4 Neirynck, *Duality in Mark*, 79, 83, 99, 104, 115, 123; Dwyer, *Wonder*, 160–61.

5 See the note on the trans. of v. 32 above; see also Dwyer, *Wonder*, 157 n. 43, 159.

6 BAGD, s.v. παραλαμβάνω.

7 Jesus is acting here as a guide; see Earle Hilgert,

"The Son of Timaeus: Blindness, Sight, Ascent, Vision in Mark," in Elizabeth A. Castelli and Hal Taussig, eds., *Reimagining Christian Origins: A Colloquium Honoring Burton L. Mack* (Valley Forge, PA: Trinity Press International, 1996) 185–98, esp. 186; 195–96 n. 6.

8 See the section "Narrative Unity of 8:27–10:45" above.

9 See the commentary on 16:8 below.

10 See the excursus on the "Secret Gospel of Mark" below.

that an editor had transformed the exorcism of the epileptic in chapter 9 into a resurrection story. Since the amazement of the crowd in 9:15 is also unmotivated, Koester argued that the editor of 9:14-29, the editor of the third passion prediction, and the person who inserted the story of the raising of the youth in Secret Mark are one and the same person. He concluded that Secret Mark is a version of Mark that is older than canonical Mark; in fact, the latter was derived from the former.[11]

The most telling argument against this hypothesis is that the account of the raising of the young man from the dead disrupts an apparently carefully constructed pattern in the middle section of Mark. Each passion prediction (8:31; 9:31; 10:33-34) is followed immediately by an inappropriate reaction on the part of the disciples, manifesting rejection or misunderstanding (8:32; 9:32, 33-34; 10:35-40). Jesus then summons his disciples (8:34; 9:35; 10:42) and teaches them regarding self-denial and service (8:34; 9:35; 10:42-45). It is more likely that the story about the raising of the young man was added later and disrupted this careful structure than that the structure came about accidentally by the removal of that story.[12] If Secret Mark is authentic, it is more likely to be derived from canonical Mark than vice versa.[13]

■ **32b-34** As noted in the comment on v. 32a, Jesus here takes the Twelve aside, a gesture that implies that a larger group was following him on the way to Jerusalem. This third passion prediction is the only one that has an introductory summary in indirect discourse: "he began to tell them about the things that were about to happen to him" (ἤρξατο αὐτοῖς λέγειν τὰ μέλλοντα αὐτῷ συμβαίνειν). The simple λέγειν ("to tell") is used here rather than διδάσκειν ("to teach"), as in the first two predictions (8:31; 9:31).[14]

The opening statement in direct discourse, "See, we are going up to Jerusalem" (ἰδοὺ ἀναβαίνομεν εἰς Ἱεροσόλυμα), repeats a part of the narrative introduction to the saying, in a way typical of Markan style.[15] This prediction is the longest and most detailed of the three. Like the second (9:31), it begins with the Son of Man being "handed over" (παραδιδόναι); but whereas the second speaks generally about his being handed over into human hands, the third specifies that he will be handed over to the chief priests and the scribes.[16] Only the third prediction uses legal language descriptive of a trial and its verdict: "and they will condemn him to death" (καὶ κατακρινοῦσιν αὐτὸν θανάτῳ). This language alludes to the trial before the high priest and the Judean council in 14:53-65. Another unique feature of this prediction is the statement "and they will hand him over to the nations" (καὶ παραδώσουσιν αὐτὸν τοῖς ἔθνεσιν). This remark foreshadows the act of the chief priests in handing Jesus over to Pilate in 15:1; it also refers indirectly to

---

11 Koester, "History and Development," 52, 54–56; idem, "The Text of the Synoptic Gospels in the Second Century," in William L. Petersen, ed., *Gospel Traditions in the Second Century: Origins, Recensions, Text, and Transmission* (CJA 3; Notre Dame, IN: University of Notre Dame Press, 1989) 19–37, esp. 34–36; idem, *Ancient Christian Gospels*, 293–303.

12 Scott G. Brown, "On the Composition History of the Longer ('Secret') Gospel of Mark," *JBL* 122 (2003) 89–110, esp. 102–4. In a later work, Brown argues that the longer version was written by the same author as canonical Mark and that the two passages inserted, one before 10:35 and the other after 10:45, constitute a typical Markan intercalation (*Mark's Other Gospel: Rethinking Morton Smith's Controversial Discovery* [Studies in Christianity and Judaism 15; Waterloo: Wilfrid Laurier University Press/Canadian Corporation for Studies in Relgion, 2005] 163–238). He differs from Koester in concluding that the longer version is later than the shorter, canonical Mark (ibid., 111–20).

13 Eckhard Rau has argued that the two fragments of Secret Mark illuminate the reception of the Gospel of Mark (its *Nachgeschichte*) rather than the history of its tradition (its *Vorgeschichte*) ("Zwischen Gemeindechristentum und christlicher Gnosis: Das geheime Markusevangelium und das Geheimnis des Reiches Gottes," *NTS* 51 [2005] 482–504; quotations from 484). See also idem, *Das geheime Markusevangelium: Ein Schriftfund voller Rätsel* (Neukirchen-Vluyn: Neukirchener Verlag, 2003).

14 The latter has both verbs.

15 Neirynck, *Duality in Mark*, 115.

16 The first prediction speaks about the Son of Man being "rejected" (ἀποδοκιμάζειν) by the chief priests and the scribes. In both the first and the third, the "scribes" could simply be bureaucrats, judges, or officials, rather than experts in the Law belonging to the Pharisees; see the commentary on 8:31 above. On the historical scribes and the scribes as a group in Mark, see also the commentary on 1:22 above.

the trial before Pilate in 15:2-15. The third is also the only prediction to speak explicitly about the mistreatment of Jesus before the official penalties of whipping and crucifixion: "and they will mock him and spit on him" (καὶ ἐμπαίξουσιν αὐτῷ καὶ ἐμπτύσουσιν αὐτῷ). These two clauses allude to the scene in 15:16-20 in which Roman soldiers spit upon Jesus and mock him. Similarly, this prediction is the only one to refer explicitly to Jesus' being whipped prior to the crucifixion: "and they will whip him" (καὶ μαστιγώσουσιν αὐτόν).

In the last two clauses, the third prediction is more similar to the first two in speaking about Jesus' death and resurrection. Whereas the first prediction uses the expression "it is necessary that the Son of Man . . . be killed" (δεῖ τὸν υἱὸν τοῦ ἀνθρώπου . . . ἀποκτανθῆναι), both the second and the third use the active voice with respect to Jesus' death: "they will kill (him)" (ἀποκτενοῦσιν [αὐτόν]) (cf. 10:34 with 8:31 and 9:31). With regard to the resurrection, all three predictions use the verb ἀνιστάναι ("to rise"), and all three use the phrase "after three days" (μετὰ τρεῖς ἡμέρας).[17]

The first passion prediction uses scriptural language, and the context creates a connection with the mystery of the kingdom of God mentioned in 4:11. It constitutes a brief revelation of that "mystery," but also connects with the Markan narrative in its elaboration of the enemies of Jesus as the "elders and the chief priests and the scribes." The second prediction emphasizes the death and resur-

rection of Jesus, but also speaks about his being "handed over into human hands." The general reference to human beings fits the context of ethical instruction that follows, which explores the various weaknesses and temptations to which human beings are subject.[18] The third passion prediction, with its elaborated details, has an important role in the narrative of Mark. It prepares the listening audience for the passion narrative that follows, building suspense but also focusing their attention and alerting them as to what to expect.

Excursus: The Secret Gospel of Mark

In 1940 Morton Smith went to Palestine and stayed until 1945, when he returned to the United States. During the time he was in Jerusalem, he registered as a graduate student at the Hebrew University and wrote a Ph.D. thesis in Hebrew entitled "Tannaitic Parallels to the Gospels."[19] In 1941, he stayed for two months at Hagios Sabbas (in Arabic, Mar Saba), a Greek Orthodox monastery in the desert southeast of Jerusalem. In 1958, he returned to the monastery as a guest of the patriarch of the Greek Orthodox Church in Jerusalem, who sponsored Smith's research project, to search for Greek manuscripts and to examine early printed books in the library of the monastery to see whether ancient manuscripts or supplements thereto had been copied by hand into any of them. The results of his search were published in the patriarchate's journal, *Nea Sion*.[20]

---

17 On the use of the verb ἀνιστάναι ("to rise"), the phrase μετὰ τρεῖς ἡμέρας ("after three days"), and the passion predictions as Markan composition, see the commentary above on 8:31. The literary role of the third passion prediction as a foreshadowing plot summary makes it unlikely to be a pre-Markan saying; cf. E. J. Pryke, *Redactional Style in the Markan Gospel* (SNTSMS 33; Cambridge: Cambridge University Press, 1978) 166.

18 See the commentary on 9:33-50 above.

19 Morton Smith, *Maqbilot ben haBesorot le Sifrut ha Tanna'im* (Jerusalem, 1948); ET, rev. *Tannaitic Parallels to the Gospels* (JBLMS 6; Philadelphia: SBL, 1951); Guy G. Stroumsa, "Comments on Charles Hedrick's Article: A Testimony," *JECS* 11 (2003) 147-53, esp. 149. Smith wrote that he went to Jerusalem on a traveling fellowship from the Harvard Divinity School and "got stuck there when the Mediterranean was closed by the war" (*The Secret Gospel: The Discovery and Interpretation of the Secret Gospel accord-*

ing to Mark [New York: Harper & Row, 1973] 1). On his dissertation, see ibid., 8.

20 The letter attributed to Clement is no. 65 in the catalogue; Morton Smith, "Ἑλληνικὰ χειρόγραφα ἐν τῇ Μονῇ τοῦ ἁγίου Σάββα," *ΝΕΑ ΣΙΩΝ* 52 (1960) 110-25 and 55 (1960) 245-56; no. 65 is discussed on pp. 251-52; Morton Smith, *Clement of Alexandria and a Secret Gospel of Mark* (Cambridge, MA: Harvard University Press, 1973) ix. See also Charles W. Hedrick and Nikolaos Olympiou, "Secret Mark: New Photographs, New Witnesses," *The Fourth R: An Advocate for Religious Literacy* 13 (2000) 3-10, 16, esp. 3; Charles W. Hedrick, "The Secret Gospel of Mark: Stalemate in the Academy," *JECS* 11 (2003) 133-45, esp. 140 n. 24; Stroumsa, "Comments on Charles Hedrick's Article," 147 and n. 1. For Smith's account of the initial visit, see *Secret Gospel*, 3-6; for the invitation of the patriarch, see p. 9; on the research project and the discovery, see pp. 11-13.

During this search, as Smith later reported, he discovered a fragment of a letter attributed to Clement of Alexandria copied onto both sides of the last (blank) page and over half of the recto (front) of a sheet of binder's paper at the back of a printed book containing an edition of the letters of Ignatius of Antioch by Isaac Voss.[21] According to experts consulted by Smith, the handwriting is typical of the period from 1700 to 1800 or slightly earlier or later.[22] The fragment had the heading "From the letters of the most holy Clement, the author of the Stromateis. To Theodore" (ἐκ τῶν ἐπιστολῶν τοῦ ἁγιωτάτου κλήμεντος τοῦ στρωματέως· Θεοδώρῳ).[23]

The sender of the letter commends Theodore for opposing the Carpocratians.[24] These are the followers of Carpocrates, who, according to Irenaeus, styled themselves as Gnostics and declared that Jesus spoke in a mystery to his disciples and apostles privately. This esoteric teaching they handed on to those who were worthy.[25] According to an undisputedly authentic work of Clement, Carpocrates was an Alexandrian who had a son named Epiphanes.[26] The followers of Carpocrates and Epiphanes, he says, think that wives should be held in common.[27] He also says that they indulge in promiscuous fornication at their dinners, to which he refuses to give the name of a Christian love-feast.[28]

The sender of the letter goes on to say:

Such men are to be opposed in all ways and altogether. For, even if they should say something true, one who loves the truth should not, even so, agree with them. For not all true things are the truth, nor should that truth which merely seems true according to human opinions be preferred to the true truth, that according to the faith (τούτοις οὖν ἀντιστατέον πάντῃ τε καὶ πάντως· εἰ γὰρ καί τι ἀληθὲς λέγοιεν οὐδ᾽ οὕτω συμφωνοίη ἂν αὐτοῖς ὁ τῆς ἀληθείας ἐραστής· οὐδὲ γὰρ πάντα τἀληθῆ ἀλήθεια· οὐδὲ τὴν κατὰ τὰς ἀνθρωπίνας δόξας φαινομένην ἀλήθειαν προκριτέον τῆς ἀληθοῦς ἀληθείας τῆς κατὰ τὴν πίστιν).[29]

These remarks lead into a discussion of the inappropriate use of the Gospel according to Mark by the Carpocratians. The sender fills in the background by explaining that Mark "wrote an account of the Lord's doings" (αἱ πράξεις τοῦ κυρίου) while he was in Rome with Peter, but that he did not include all of them, especially not the "secret ones" (αἱ μυστικαί).[30] Then, he says, when Peter had given his testimony (i.e., died; μαρτυρεῖν), Mark went to Alexandria, "bringing both his own notes (ὑπομνήματα) and those of Peter," some of which he added "to his former book," namely, "the things most suitable to whatever makes for progress toward knowledge (γνῶσις).[31] The sender of the letter calls this

---

21 I[saacu]s Vossius, *Epistolae genuinae S. Ignatii Martyris* (Amsterdam: J. Blaeu, 1646); Smith, *Clement of Alexandria*, ix, 1; Hedrick, "Secret Gospel of Mark," 133. According to Stroumsa, he and his companions saw the book with "the three manuscript pages of Clement's letter written on the blank pages at the end of the book, exactly as described by Smith" ("Comments on Charles Hedrick's Article," 147).

22 Smith, *Clement of Alexandria*, 1; idem, *Secret Gospel*, 22–23; see the questions raised about this procedure by Quentin Quesnell, "The Mar Saba Clementine: A Question of Evidence," *CBQ* 37 (1975) 48–67, esp. 50–51.

23 Folio 1, recto, line 1; trans. and transcription from Smith, *Clement of Alexandria*, 446, 448.

24 Folio 1, recto, lines 2–7.

25 Irenaeus *Haer.* 1.25.1, 5–6. For the Greek/Latin text of the remarks of Irenaeus and Hippolytus on the Carpocratians, see Walther Völker, *Quellen zur Geschichte der christlichen Gnosis* (Tübingen: Mohr Siebeck, 1932) 36–38.

26 For the Greek text of Clement's quotation from Epiphanes' book *On Righteousness*, see Völker, *Quellen*, 33–36.

27 Clement of Alexandria *Strom.* 3.5.1; see John Ferguson, trans., *Clement of Alexandria: Stromateis Books*

One to Three (Fathers of the Church; Washington, DC: Catholic University of America Press, 1991) 258.

28 Clement of Alexandria *Strom.* 3.10.1; Ferguson, *Clement of Alexandria*, 262.

29 Folio 1, recto, lines 7–11; trans. and transcription from Smith, *Clement of Alexandria*, 446, 448.

30 Folio 1, recto, lines 15–17; trans. and transcription from Smith (446, 448). Brown translated the "spiritual" ones instead of the "secret" ones because he concluded that the former was more likely to represent the sense of the Greek μυστικός in the writings of Clement and his contemporaries ("On the Composition History," 89 n. 1; 96; idem, "The More Spiritual Gospel: Markan Literary Techniques in the Longer Gospel of Mark" [Ph.D. diss., University of Toronto, 1999] 143–78).

31 Folio 1, recto, lines 18–21; trans. and transcription from Smith (446, 448).

expanded Gospel "a more spiritual Gospel for the use of those who were being perfected" (πνευματικώ- τερον εὐαγγέλιον εἰς τὴν τῶν τελειουμένων χρῆσιν).[32] When Mark died, he left this writing to the church in Alexandria, where even yet it "is most carefully guarded, being read only to those who are being initiated into the great mysteries" (ὅπου εἰσέτι νῦν ἀσφαλῶς εὖ μάλα τηρεῖται· ἀναγινωσκόμενον πρὸς αὐτοὺς μόνους τοὺς μυουμένους τὰ μεγάλα μυστήρια).[33]

The sender goes on to say that Carpocrates obtained a copy of "the secret Gospel" (τὸ μυστικὸν εὐαγγέλιον) from a presbyter of the church in Alexandria.[34] He charges that Carpocrates interpreted this Gospel in a blasphemous and carnal manner and "polluted" (μιαίνειν) it by adding "shameless lies" (ἀναιδέστατα ψεύσματα) to the text.[35] The teaching of the Carpocratians is derived from this mixture of false interpretation of a sacred text and interpolated falsifications.[36] The sender then exhorts Theodore:

To them, therefore, as I said above, one must never give way; nor, when they put forward their falsifications, should one concede that the secret Gospel is by Mark, but should even deny it on oath. For, "Not all true things are to be said to all men" (τού- τοις οὖν· καθὼς καὶ προείρηκα· οὐδέποτε εἰκτέον· οὐδὲ προτείνουσιν αὐτοῖς τὰ κατεψευσμένα συγχωρητέον τοῦ μάρκου εἶναι τὸ μυστικὸν εὐαγγέλιον· ἀλλὰ καὶ μεθ' ὅρκου ἀρνητέον· οὐ γὰρ ἅπασι πάντα ἀληθῆ λεκτέον).[37]

After elaborating on the last point, the sender proceeds to answer the questions that Theodore has asked, "refuting the falsifications by the very words of the Gospel" (δι' αὐτῶν τοῦ εὐαγγελίου λέξεων τὰ κατεψευσμένα ἐλέγχων).[38] Then follows the first, and much longer, of the two citations from the secret Gospel of Mark:

For example, after "Now they were on the way going up to Jerusalem" and what follows, until "After three days he will rise," the secret Gospel brings the following material word for word: "And they come into Bethany. And a certain woman whose brother had died was there. And, coming,

she prostrated herself before Jesus and says to him, 'Son of David, have mercy on me.' But the disciples rebuked her. And Jesus, being angered, went off with her into the garden where the tomb was, and straightway a great cry was heard from the tomb. And going near Jesus rolled away the stone from the door of the tomb. And straightway, going in where the youth was, he stretched forth his hand and raised him, seizing his hand. But the youth, looking upon him, loved him and began to beseech him that he might be with him. And going out of the tomb they came into the house of the youth, for he was rich. And after six days Jesus told him what to do and in the evening, the young man comes to him, wearing a linen cloth over his naked body. And he remained with him that night, for Jesus taught him the mystery of the kingdom of God. And thence, arising, he returned to the other side of the Jordan." After these words follows the text, "And James and John come to him" and all that section. But "naked man with naked man," and the other things about which you wrote, are not found (ἀμέλει μετὰ τὸ· ἦσαν δὲ ἐν τῇ ὁδῷ ἀναβαίνοντες εἰς ἱεροσόλυμα· καὶ τὰ ἐξῆς ἕως· μετὰ τρεῖς ἡμέρας ἀναστήσεται· ὧδε ἐπιφέρει κατὰ λέξιν· καὶ ἔρχονται εἰς βηθανί- αν καὶ ἦν ἐκεῖ μία γυνὴ ἧς ὁ ἀδελφὸς αὐτῆς ἀπέθανεν· καὶ ἐλθοῦσα προσεκύνησε τὸ ιη- σοῦν καὶ λέγει αὐτῷ· υἱὲ Δαβὶδ ἐλέησόν με· οἱ δὲ μαθηταὶ ἐπετίμησαν αὐτῇ· καὶ ὀργισθεὶς ὁ ιησοῦς ἀπῆλθεν μετ' αὐτῆς εἰς τὸν κῆπον ὅπου ἦν τὸ μνημεῖον· καὶ εὐθὺς ἠκούσθη ἐκ τοῦ μνημείου φωνὴ μεγάλη· καὶ προσελθὼν ὁ ιη- σοῦς ἀπεκύλισε τὸν λίθον ἀπὸ τῆς θύρας τοῦ μνημείου· καὶ εἰσελθὼν εὐθὺς ὅπου ἦν ὁ νεανίσκος ἐξέτεινεν τὴν χεῖρα καὶ ἤγειρεν αὐτόν· κρατήσας τῆς χειρός· ὁ δὲ νεανίσκος ἐμβλέψας αὐτῷ ἠγάπησεν αὐτὸν καὶ ἤρξατο παρακαλεῖν αὐτὸν ἵνα μετ' αὐτοῦ ᾖ· καὶ ἐξ- ελθόντες ἐκ τοῦ μνημείου ἦλθον εἰς τὴν οἰκί- αν τοῦ νεανίσκου· ἦν γὰρ πλούσιος· καὶ μεθ' ἡμέρας ἓξ ἐπέταξεν αὐτῷ ὁ ιησοῦς· καὶ ὀψίας γενομένης ἔρχεται ὁ νεανίσκος πρὸς αὐτόν· περιβεβλημένος σινδόνα ἐπὶ γυμνοῦ· καὶ ἔμεινε σὺν αὐτῷ τὴν νύκτα ἐκείνην· ἐδίδασκε

---

32 Folio 1, recto, lines 21–22; trans. and transcription from Smith (446, 448).

33 Folio 1, recto, line 27 through folio 1, verso, line 2; trans. and transcription from Smith (446, 448, 450).

34 Folio 1, verso, lines 2–6; citation from line 6; trans. and transcription from Smith (446, 450).

35 Folio 1, verso, lines 6–9; citation from lines 8–9; trans. (446–47) and transcription (450) from Smith.

36 Folio 1, verso, lines 9–10; Smith translates, "From this mixture is drawn off the teaching of the Carpocrations" (447).

37 Folio 1, verso, lines 10–13; trans. (447) and transcription (450) from Smith.

38 Folio 1, verso, line 20; trans. (447) and transcription (450) from Smith.

γὰρ αὐτὸν ὁ ἰησοῦς τὸ μυστήριον τῆς
βασιλείας τοῦ θεοῦ· ἐκεῖθεν δὲ ἀναστὰς
ἐπέστρεψεν εἰς τὸ πέραν τοῦ ἰορδάνου· ἐπὶ μὲν
τούτοις ἕπεται τὸ· καὶ προσπορεύονται αὐτῷ
ἰάκωβος καὶ ἰωάννης· καὶ πᾶσα ἡ περικοπή· τὸ
δὲ γυμνὸς γυμνῷ καὶ τἆλλα περὶ ὧν ἔγραψας
οὐκ εὑρίσκεται).[39]

At the annual meeting of the Society of Biblical
Literature in 1960, Smith made a presentation
announcing his discovery.[40] Pierson Parker, who
responded to his presentation, accepted that the fragmentary letter was written by Clement, but questioned
Clement's statements about the attribution of the
additions to Mark. He noted that the style of the additions is not distinctively Markan; rather, it "points to
close acquaintance with *all* the canonical Gospels and
with other parts of the New Testament too."[41]

Fifteen years after the discovery (1973), Smith published the fragmentary letter in two books, one a
scholarly analysis of the text and the other a treatment
of the discovery for a wider audience.[42] In 1975, two
publications appeared expressing quite different reactions to Smith's books. Helmut Koester published a
review in which he accepted the fragmentary letter as
a work of Clement and also Smith's arguments that
the style of the additions is Markan. He dated the
additions to "somewhat before 125 A.D." He agreed
with Smith that the additions represent "a text of
Mark that is more primitive than the canonical text of
this Gospel." Koester criticized Smith's theories about
"the assumed intention of the secret baptismal rite:
ascent to the heavens" and questioned the logical connection between "ascent to the heavens" and "freedom from the law." Smith had argued that both were
features of the historical Jesus.[43]

In the same year, Quentin Quesnell published an
article in which he pointed out that the first responsibility of a scholar who finds a new manuscript is to make
it available for scientific examination to rule out the
possibility of its being a modern forgery. In the case of
the text written on the back pages of Voss's book, the
ink needs to be analyzed in order to determine the
period of time of its origin. Microscopic examination
of the impressions on the page could determine the
type of pen used and whether its date is consistent with
the eighteenth-century handwriting. A microscopic
analysis of the handwriting itself needs to be made to
see whether it is the free-flowing production of someone using his native script or whether it betrays the
careful copying of a forger. Quesnell lists other scientific studies that could also shed light on the likelihood
of a modern forgery.[44] He also discussed a number of
famous modern scholarly forgeries to show that failure
to check the authenticity of the manuscript leaves the
door open to fraud. He assembled an impressive body
of evidence and arguments to show the credibility of
the hypothesis that this manuscript was produced at
some point between 1936 and 1958.[45]

---

39 Folio 1, verso, line 20 through folio 2, recto, line 14; transcription (450, 452) and trans. (447) from Smith (both slightly modified). The second citation from the secret Gospel of Mark will be discussed in rela- tion to Mark 10:46 below.

40 The Editor [W. Taylor Stevenson], "Documentation and Reflection: Morton Smith and Clement's Letter about a Secret Gospel of Mark," *ATR* 56 (1974) 52; Frederick Fyvie Bruce, *The 'Secret' Gospel of Mark* (Ethel M. Wood Lecture, University of London, 11 February 1974; London: Athlone Press, 1974) 6.

41 Pierson Parker, "On Professor Morton Smith's Find at Mar-Saba," *ATR* 56 (1974) 53–57; first delivered as an address at the annual meeting of the SBL in 1960. Citation from p. 53. Frans Neirynck argued similarly and placed the additions in the category of "the harmonization of the Canonical Gospels" ("The Minor Agreements and Proto-Mark: A Response to Helmut Koester," in Frans van Seg- broeck, ed., *Evangelica II 1982–1991: Collected Essays of Frans Neirynck* [BEThL 99; Leuven: Leuven Uni- versity Press/Peeters, 1991] 59–73). Smith accepted the conclusion that the addition to Mark's Gospel contains "several apparently Lucan phrases and

many expressions found in Mt and Jn" ("On the Authenticity of the Mar Saba Letter of Clement," *CBQ* 38 [1976] 196–99; citation from 197). See also Morton Smith, "Clement of Alexandria and Secret Mark: The Score at the End of the First Decade," *HTR* 75 (1982) 449–61, esp. 453–54. James Kelhof- fer has argued that the Longer Ending of Mark (16:9-20) manifests an attempt to imitate traditional formulations, the majority of which find their clos- est analogies in Matthew, Luke, and John (*Miracle and Mission: The Authentication of Missionaries and Their Message in the Longer Ending of Mark* [WUNT 2. 112; Tübingen: Mohr Siebeck, 2000] 473).

42 Smith, *Clement of Alexandria*; idem, *The Secret Gospel*.

43 Helmut Koester, review of Morton Smith, *The Secret Gospel* and *Clement of Alexandria and a Secret Gospel of Mark* in *American Historical Review* 80 (1975) 620– 22; first two citations from 620; the rest are from 621.

44 Quesnell, "Mar Saba Clementine," 48–53.

45 Ibid., 53–58. See also the response by Smith, "On the Authenticity of the Mar Saba Letter of Clement," and the reply by Quesnell, "A Reply to Morton Smith," *CBQ* 38 (1976) 200–203.

Toward the end of the same year (December 1975), at a colloquy in Berkeley, California, Charles E. Murgia, a professor of classics at the University of California at Berkeley, applied the methods developed in detecting fakes in the Virgilian tradition to the fragmentary letter of Clement.[46] He pointed out that there was an opportunity that may have been exploited by a forger, namely, the fact that there was a fire in the monastery of Mar Saba in the eighteenth century. Since the letter is written in an eighteenth-century hand in a seventeenth century book, the "suspicion arises that the scribe chose a seventeenth century book for his pages in order to be able to pretend that the text was copied before the fire from an ancient manuscript which was since destroyed by the fire. He could therefore never be challenged to produce the original."[47]

The first paragraph of the alleged excerpt from the letters of Clement is an attack on the Carpocratians, Clement's "favorite target, in language reminiscent of Clement."[48] This part of the letter has the rhetorical effect of assuring modern readers that "this is indeed a letter of Clement of Alexandria."[49] Murgia concluded that every sentence of the letter, except for the quotations from Secret Mark, is designed to provide a "seal of authenticity" for those quotations. Great care is taken to explain to modern readers why they have never heard of this Gospel before, but he also pointed out a contradiction. The heading, "From the letters of the most holy Clement, the author of the Stromateis. To Theodore," presupposes a published collection of Clement's letters. Given ancient conventions, it should be Clement himself who published them. It is, however, ludicrous to urge someone to

commit perjury to conceal something that you yourself are making public. Smith pointed out two contradictions between the letter and the other works of Clement and argued that no imitator would have introduced them. Murgia concluded that the rhetorical purpose of the recommendation of perjury was so important that it was worth the contradiction.[50] He also pointed out that fakers often introduce contradictions in order to argue for the authenticity of the faked material.[51]

The advocacy of perjury is linked to another phenomenon: the longer fragment of Secret Mark reduces the supposedly exalted to a mundane level to the point of parodic humor.[52] Finally, the high incidence of parallels in this short passage from Secret Mark to canonical Mark and the other Gospels is a frequent feature of fakes.[53] Another telling sign of the rhetoric of authenticity is the pretense of giving an earlier version of the story of the raising of Lazarus in the Gospel of John. Finally, there is no serious textual error in the letter, whereas ancient fakes tend to survive in a badly corrupted state. This letter gives no evidence of any form of transmission, so Murgia concludes that "it is exactly what it appears to be, an autograph."[54]

Along similar lines, Ernest Best concluded that the passage allegedly cited by Clement from Secret Mark concerning the resurrection of the young man is "too much like Mark." His linguistic analysis "implies it was not written by Mark but by someone who knew Mark well and picked up his phrases. . . . Inadvertently he produced an 'overkill.' It is impossible to determine when or by whom this was done."[55]

---

46 Charles E. Murgia, "Secret Mark: Real or Fake?" in Reginald H. Fuller, ed., *Longer Mark: Forgery, Interpolation, or Old Tradition?* (Protocol of the Eighteenth Colloquy, 7 December 1975; Berkeley, CA: Center for Hermeneutical Studies in Hellenistic and Modern Culture, 1976) 35–40.

47 Ibid., 37.

48 Ibid.

49 Ibid.

50 The recommendation of perjury is part of the indirect explanation to modern readers of why they have not heard of this Gospel before.

51 Murgia, "Secret Mark," 38–39; cf. 36–37. Smith pointed out minor contradictions and ignored the big one, namely, that Clement must be seen as publishing what he is recommending be kept secret.

52 The mundane narration of extraneous detail contrasts with the supposedly exalted character of the initiation into the mystery of the kingdom of God.

53 E.g., Jesus taking a youth by the hand and raising

him up (Mark 9:27), the youth looking at Jesus and loving him (a reversal of Jesus looking at the young man and loving him (Mark 10:21), and the disciples rebuking a woman (Mark 14:4-5). A number of details recall the raising of Lazarus in John 11:1-44, namely, the link of Bethany with a woman whose brother had died (Mary or Martha), Jesus raising someone from a tomb, a loud cry (here that of the man in the tomb; in John that of Jesus).

54 Murgia, "Secret Mark," 39–40; citation from 40. Murgia means, of course, the "autograph" of a twentieth-century forger. According to Bruce, "The raising of the young man of Bethany is too evidently based—and clumsily based at that—on the Johannine story of the raising of Lazarus for us to regard it as in any sense an independent Markan counterpart to the Johannine story (not to speak of our regarding it as a *source* of the Johannine story)" (*'Secret' Gospel of Mark*, 20).

55 Ernest Best, review of Pryke, *Redactional Style*, in

In the spring of 1976, David Flusser, professor of New Testament; Shlomo Pines, professor of medieval Arabic and Jewish philosophy, both of the Hebrew University of Jerusalem; Archimandrite Meliton, from the Greek Patriarchate in Jerusalem; and Guy Stroumsa, then a graduate student at Harvard University and now professor of comparative religion at the Hebrew University, went to Mar Saba to look for the alleged letter of Clement. In the library they found Voss's edition of Ignatius with the handwritten text in the back pages. "Smith 65" was inscribed on the front page (with reference to Smith's research project of 1958). They took the book and deposited it in the library of the Patriarchate in Jerusalem for safekeeping. They hoped to have the manuscript examined scientifically, for example, to have the ink analyzed. At the National and University Library, however, they were told that the necessary experts were at the police headquarters. Father Meliton objected to handing the book over to the Israeli police, so the matter was dropped.[56]

In January of 1980, Thomas Talley, professor at General Theological Seminary in New York, went to the library of the Patriarchate in Jerusalem and asked about the letter attributed to Clement.[57] He was told by Archimandrite Meliton that it was at that time in that library.[58] Talley also reported that Father Kallistos, the librarian of the Patriarchate's library, had told him that the two folios of the manuscript had been removed from the book and were being restored.[59]

In the early 1980s, Quesnell was allowed to look at the two folios of the manuscript. He also obtained permission from the Patriarchate to have color photographs made of the folios by a firm in Jerusalem.[60]

At some point after 1992 and before 2000, Nikolaos Olympiou, professor of Old Testament at the Uni-

versity of Athens, informed Charles Hedrick, professor at Southwest Missouri State University, that Olympiou's former student, Archimandrite Kallistos Dourvas, had been librarian of the library of the Patriarchate in Jerusalem from 1975 to 1990.[61] Kallistos told Olympiou that he had removed the manuscript from the book at the time that he photographed it, shortly after he received it into the library of the Patriarchate. He gave black-and-white photographs of the manuscript to Olympiou, who later gave copies to Hedrick. Then Olympiou acquired color photographs from Kallistos and loaned them to Hedrick for publication.[62]

Smith's two books on the letter attributed to Clement and the "secret Gospel of Mark" have been widely reviewed and discussed. In 1982, he reviewed the discussion up to that point.[63] He noted that twenty-five scholars had accepted the fragmentary letter as a work of Clement of Alexandria. Johannes Munck, Walther Völker, Arthur Darby Nock, Werner Georg Kümmel, Charles Murgia, and Herbert Musurillo concluded that it was not by Clement.[64] Smith also noted that Clement's attribution to Mark of the citations from the Gospel he mentions in the letter has been universally rejected. Some scholars have argued that they come from an apocryphal Gospel dating to the second century. The most common opinion is that they constitute a pastiche based on the canonical Gospels. Others hold that they are an expansion of Mark in imitation of Mark's style.[65] In 1984, Hans-Martin Schenke published an article in which he summarized a number of responses to Smith's books.[66]

In 1995, A. H. Criddle published an article arguing that "the letter proper (i.e., excluding the heading and the extracts from the secret gospel), contains too

JSNT 4 (1979) 69–76; citations from 75–76. Similarly, Bruce concluded that the expansion is "an obvious pastiche . . . quite out of keeping with Mark's quality as a story-teller. Morton Smith indeed argues that it is no mere pastiche or cento, but I find his arguments unconvincing" (*'Secret' Gospel of Mark*, 12).

56 Stroumsa, "Comments on Charles Hedrick's Article," 147–48.

57 Hedrick and Olympiou, "Secret Mark: New Photographs," 7.

58 See the discussion about the visit to Mar Saba by Flusser et al. above. According to Hedrick and Olympiou, in 2000 Melito was assistant bishop of the Archbishopric of Athens as bishop of Marathon (ibid., 16 n. 14).

59 Thomas-Julian Talley, "Le temps liturgique dans l'Église ancienne: État de la recherche," *La Maison-*

Dieu 147 (1981) 29–60, esp. 52; Hedrick and Olympiou, "Secret Mark: New Photographs," 7, 16 n. 16.

60 Personal communication.

61 Hedrick and Olympiou, "Secret Mark: New Photographs," 8; in 2000, Kallistos was a parish priest in the Church of Eisodia tes Theotokou (Presentation of the the Mother of God/Virgin Mary) in Ano Glyfada near Athens (ibid.).

62 Ibid., 8, and accompanying photographs of the manuscript at 120% of acutal size.

63 Smith, "Clement of Alexandria and Secret Mark: The Score at the End of the First Decade," 449–61.

64 Ibid., 450.

65 Ibid., 457.

66 Hans-Martin Schenke, "The Mystery of the Gospel of Mark," *Second Century* 4 (1984) 65–82, esp. 69–71.

high a ratio of Clementine to non-Clementine traits to be authentic and should be regarded as a deliberate imitation of Clement's style."[67] His analysis leads to the conclusion that the letter contains four non-Clementine words and nine Clementine words used only once by Clement. Statistical analysis indicates that in the letter there are too many of the latter category of words (that is, words used only once in the undisputed works of Clement) and not enough of the former (words not previously found in Clement's works).[68] He noted further that "[t]he letter brings together words scattered throughout Clement's works and uses them often with new meanings, to put across rather non-Clementine ideas." He concluded that the author of the letter, in imitating Clement's style, aimed at using words found in Clement, but not in other patristic writers; in doing so "the writer brought together more rare words and phrases scattered throughout the authentic works of Clement than are compatible with genuine Clementine authorship."[69]

In 2001, Philip Jenkins found the location of the find "fascinating," since Mar Saba "was the scene of the forgery described" in a novel published around the time of Smith's first visit in 1940.[70] Since the novel was so popular, the find of Secret Mark at Mar Saba, in Jenkins's view, was either authentic or "a tribute to the unabashed *chutzpah* of a forger."[71]

In 2003, the *Journal of Early Christian Studies* published three short studies on the Secret Gospel, two of which also include summaries of reactions to Smith's two books.[72] One of these, by Bart Ehrman, concludes that "the jury is still out" on whether the manuscript is a forgery. Like Quesnell, he calls for a careful exam-

ination of the physical manuscript, under a microscope if possible.[73]

The whereabouts of the folios removed from Voss's book are currently unknown to the public. Three books, nevertheless, have been published in the early twenty-first century that deal, to a greater or lesser extent, with the question of authenticity. Brown defended the authenticity of the text (chapter 2) in his study arguing that "the passages quoted" from secret Mark "develop and elucidate aspects of Markan theology."[74] Stephen C. Carlson, working with photographs of the text and drawing upon his knowledge of the law and culture in the United States of the 1950s, argued that the handwriting is "a drawn imitation of an eighteenth-century style" and the letter fragment betrays its modern origin by an anachronism regarding "salt-making technology."[75] Further, "*Secret Mark* is also an imitation, with its Markan parallels deviating only at its climax, in language that resonates with mid-twentieth-century expressions of sexuality."[76]

In a very different but complementary way, Peter Jeffery has made a convincing case that the cultural context of the real author of the letter fragment and Secret Mark was the mid-twentieth century. He shows that the liturgy depicted in the first quotation does not fit the description in the undisputed works of Clement of the liturgical services of Alexandria in the second century. After demonstrating that it does not fit what we know about Alexandrian liturgy at any period, he shows that it fits quite well with what Anglican scholars of the mid-twentieth century thought ancient Christian liturgy was like.[77] He also makes a persuasive argument that the "homosexuality" presup-

---

67 A. H. Criddle, "On the Mar Sabba Letter Attributed to Clement of Alexandria," *JECS* 3 (1995) 215–20.

68 Ibid., 217–18. The argument is that none of the undisputed works of Clement has as few as four words never used elsewhere in his writings in such a short passage. It is also unusual to have in such a brief passage as many as nine words used only once elsewhere.

69 Ibid., 218. Further significant arguments are made on 218–19.

70 Philip Jenkins, *Hidden Gospels: How the Search for Jesus Lost Its Way* (Oxford/New York: Oxford University Press, 2001) 102; the novel is James Hogg Hunter, *The Mystery of Mar Saba* (Toronto: Evangelical Publishers, 1940; reprinted Grand Rapids: Zondervan, various dates); see also Peter G. Jeffery, *The Secret Gospel of Mark Unveiled: Imagined Rituals of Sex, Death and Madness in a Biblical Forgery* (New Haven/London: Yale University Press, 2007) 262 n. 63.

71 Jenkins, *Hidden Gospels*, 102.

72 Hedrick, "Secret Gospel of Mark: Stalemate," 135 and n. 5, 136–38; Bart D. Ehrman, "Response to Charles Hedrick's Stalemate," *JECS* 11 (2003) 155–63, esp. 155–56.

73 Ehrman, "Response to Charles Hedrick's Stalemate," 159–60.

74 Brown, *Mark's Other Gospel*, 21.

75 Stephen C. Carlson, *The Gospel Hoax: Morton Smith's Invention of* Secret Mark (Waco, TX: Baylor University Press, 2005) 60–62. See also the review article by Scott G. Brown, "Factualizing the Folklore: Stephen Carlson's Case against Morton Smith," *HTR* 99 (2006) 291–327.

76 Ibid.

77 Jeffery, *Secret Gospel*, chaps. 3–4.

posed by Secret Mark is unlike the ideas and practices of any Hellenistic "homosexuality." Rather, it fits "a homoerotic subculture in English universities" in the nineteenth century, a subculture well known to students of English literature and culture in the early and mid-twentieth century.[78]

Both Carlson and Jeffery, with humorous wit rivaling that of the subject of their studies, show that Smith's authorship of the letter fragment and Secret Mark is highly credible. If the jury is still out, it is seeming more and more likely that their verdict will be that the work is a modern forgery or hoax.[79]

10

10:35-45 Instruction on Leadership

35/ And James and John, the sons of Zebedee, came to him and said to him, "Teacher, we want you to do for us whatever we ask of you." 36/ He then said to them, "What do you want me to do for you?"[a] 37/ They then said to him, "Grant us that we sit, one on your right and one on your left,[b] in your glory." 38/ Jesus then said to them, "You do not know what you are asking. Are you able to drink the cup that I am about to drink or to be baptized with the baptism with which I am about to be baptized?" 39/ They then said to him, "We are able." Jesus then said to them, "You will drink the cup that I am about to drink and you will be baptized with the baptism with which I am about to be baptized, 40/ but to sit on my right hand or on my left is not mine to grant, except to those for whom[c] it has been prepared."

41/ And when the ten heard, they began to become angry at James and John. 42/ And Jesus summoned them and said to them, "You know that those who are recognized as ruling the nations are masters over them and those in high position among them exercise authority over them. 43/ It is[d] not so among you, but whoever wants to be in a high position among you will be[e] your servant, 44/ and whoever wants to be first among you will be slave of all; 45/ for the Son of Man did not come to be served,

a The reading, $\tau\acute{\iota}\ \vartheta\acute{\epsilon}\lambda\epsilon\tau\acute{\epsilon}\ \mu\epsilon\ \pi o\iota\acute{\eta}\sigma\omega\ \acute{\upsilon}\mu\hat{\iota}\nu$ ("what do you want me to do for you?"), attested by $\aleph^1$ B Ψ, is attractive as the most difficult reading; it was adopted by Tischendorf, Nestle-Aland (25th, 26th, and 27th ed.), and Aland, *Synopsis*. But it may be a conflation of the other two readings. The reading attested by C Θ $f^{1.13}$ et al., $\tau\acute{\iota}\ \vartheta\acute{\epsilon}\lambda\epsilon\tau\epsilon\ \pi o\iota\acute{\eta}\sigma\omega\ \acute{\upsilon}\mu\hat{\iota}\nu$ ("what do you want me to do for you?"), is typical of Markan style and thus is probably the earliest recoverable reading; cf. 10:51; 14:12; 15:9; and a variant of 15:12. For discussion see Turner, "Marcan Usage," 28 (1927) 357 (Elliott, *Language and Style*, 98). ($\aleph^2$) A (L W 2427*) $\mathfrak{M}$ read $\tau\acute{\iota}\ \vartheta\acute{\epsilon}\lambda\epsilon\tau\epsilon\ \pi o\iota\hat{\eta}\sigma\alpha\iota\ \mu\epsilon\ \acute{\upsilon}\mu\hat{\iota}\nu$ ("what do you want me to do for you?"). This reading was adopted by Huck-Greeven. It is most likely, however, to have originated as a correction of the reading of C Θ et al. and to be the source of the $\mu\epsilon$ ("me") in the reading attested by $\aleph^1$ B et al. Taylor (*ad loc.*) follows Westcott and Hort in reading $\tau\acute{\iota}\ [\vartheta\acute{\epsilon}\lambda\epsilon\tau\epsilon]\ \pi o\iota\acute{\eta}\sigma\omega\ \acute{\upsilon}\mu\hat{\iota}\nu$ ("what do you want me to do for you?" [including the word in brackets] or "what should I do for you?" [excluding the word in brackets]).

b The reading $\acute{\epsilon}\xi\ \grave{\alpha}\rho\iota\sigma\tau\epsilon\rho\hat{\omega}\nu$, "on (your) left," lit., "on the better side," attested by B et al., is probably the earliest recoverable reading, since it can explain the origin of the other readings. The reading attested by L Ψ 892*, $\sigma o\upsilon\ \acute{\epsilon}\xi\ \grave{\alpha}\rho\iota\sigma\tau\epsilon\rho\hat{\omega}\nu$, "on your left," is a correction to make this phrase parallel to the corresponding one about the right side. The other two readings, $\acute{\epsilon}\xi\ \epsilon\grave{\upsilon}\omega\nu\acute{\upsilon}\mu\omega\nu$, "on (your) left," lit., "on the side of good name," or "on the fortunate side," attested by D W et al., and $\acute{\epsilon}\xi\ \epsilon\grave{\upsilon}\omega\nu\acute{\upsilon}\mu\omega\nu\ \sigma o\upsilon$, "on your left," attested by ($\aleph$) A C et al., are then assimilations of the text of Mark to the parallel in Matt 20:21.

c Early mss of Mark probably read $A\Lambda\Lambda OI\Sigma$, which could be understood either as $\grave{\alpha}\lambda\lambda'\ o\hat{\iota}\varsigma$, "except to those for whom," or $\check{\alpha}\lambda\lambda o\iota\varsigma$ ("mine to grant; it has been prepared) for others." The former understanding is attested by B^2 Θ et al. and the latter by 225 it sa[ms]. The latter understanding may have arisen

---

78 Ibid., chaps. 8–10.

79 Carlson prefers the term "hoax," because "*Secret Mark* functions as a hoax designed to test, not a forgery designed to cheat" (*Gospel Hoax*, 79).

but to serve and to give his life as a ransom in behalf of many."

spontaneously or, as Taylor suggests (ad loc.), it may be a deliberate rereading from a Marcionite point of view. Cf. Metzger, *Textual Commentary*, 91.

d   The trans. is based on the reading ἐστιν ("it is"), attested by ℵ B C* D L W et al. The reading ἐσται ("it will be"), attested by A C³ *f*¹·¹³ 𝔐 et al., is a correction made either to soften the claim in light of the situation depicted in the previous scene or to conform this clause to the one which follows; cf. Metzger, *Textual Commentary*, 91. It may also be the case that ἐστιν (lit., "it is") has a futuristic sense here (cf. Moulton-Turner, 3:63) and that the secondary reading simply clarifies this aspect.

e   ℵ C Δ et al. read ἐστω ("let him be"). The future ἐσται ("he will be") should be understood as expressing a command; cf. Moulton-Turner, 3:86. The secondary reading with the third person imperative clarifies this connotation.

History of the Tradition

Bultmann argued that the apophthegm of vv. 35-40 is traditional, whereas vv. 41-45 is a typical Markan elaboration, since the former concerns precedence in the future kingdom, and the latter treats precedence within the communities of the followers of Jesus. He argued further that the apophthegm is not a unity, since the question of James and John receives two answers. In vv. 38-39, the response is that the way to greatness in the kingdom is through martyrdom; in v. 40 the request is denied without any reference to martyrdom. He concluded that vv. 38-39 constitute the secondary element, since it is a prophecy of the deaths of the two disciples after the fact. The remainder, vv. 35-37, 40, appears to be a unitary composition. He also concluded, because of the self-evident acceptance of the messiahship of Jesus, that the anecdote arose in the early church.[80]

Although Rudolf Pesch recognized that vv. 35-45 constitute an example of the misunderstanding of the disciples in the threefold pattern of the middle section of Mark, he concluded that Mark took the scene from a catechetical collection from which he also took vv. 2-12 and

17-31.[81] Pesch concluded, like Bultmann, that vv. 35-40 concern the future heavenly glory, whereas vv. 41-44 deal with rank in the community. He argued, unlike Bultmann, that the two passages were already linked when Mark received them. He concluded that v. 45 was also part of the pre-Markan catechetical collection and that it served to authorize the community rule in vv. 43-44. He considered the possibility that vv. 39-40 is a secondary expansion, added after the death of James.[82] He concluded that Luke 22:24-27 is not based on a tradition parallel to Mark 10:41-45 but rather on a Lukan transposition and editing of the Markan passage.[83]

It seems equally plausible that Mark composed the entire scene, making use of oral or written tradition. The double answer thus may be original. The first (vv. 38-39) makes the point that suffering is the characteristic of Jesus that calls for emulation, not his glorious greatness; it also probably alludes to the death of James and perhaps also to that of John.[84] The second answer (v. 40) is an exemplary refusal of a self-seeking request that prepares for the teaching in vv. 41-45.

Pesch argued that the saying of v. 45 is a product of Greek-speaking Jewish Christians.[85] Peter Stuhlmacher

---

80   Bultmann, *History*, 24.
81   Pesch, 2:153; see the section "History of the Tradition of 10:1-31" above.
82   Pesch, 2:153; cf. 164–65.
83   Ibid., 164–65; so also Calvin K. Katter, "Luke 22:14-38: A Farewell Address" (Ph.D. diss., University of Chicago, 1993) 192–203.

84   See the commentary on vv. 38-40 below.
85   Pesch, 2:162. Cilliers Breytenbach leaves open the possibility of an earlier Aramaic form of the saying, but doubts that it goes back to the historical Jesus (*Versöhnung: Eine Studie zur paulinischen Soteriologie* [WMANT 60; Neukirchen-Vluyn: Neukirchener Verlag, 1989] 208–9). For references to earlier scholars

argued that it preserves (in substance) tradition that goes back to the historical Jesus.[86]

Genre(s) of 10:35-45

Bultmann argued that the anecdote of vv. 35-37, 40 is typical in the way that it focuses on the concluding saying of Jesus. There is no interest in reporting what the sons of Zebedee had to say in response to Jesus' statement.[87] He argued further that the saying in vv. 43-44 was an old proverb about the greatness of service that was secondarily applied to the Christian church and thus became a legal saying or church rule. In the process, v. 42 was added as a foil and v. 45 as a reference to the example of Jesus.[88]

Robert C. Tannehill argued that 10:35-45 is a correction story, and he emphasized the negation followed by a strong "but" (ἀλλά) in vv. 43-45. He also noted that the saying of vv. 43-44 is "an antithetical aphorism, a brief saying in which the corrected attitude is paradoxically tied to its opposite."[89] Tannehill's analysis is more helpful for understanding the passage in its present form; nevertheless, Bultmann's is illuminating for perceiving the building blocks of the whole.

Comment

■ **35-37** This is the sixth time that James and John, the sons of Zebedee, have been mentioned in Mark. The others are 1:19 (their call by Jesus); 1:29 (they accompany Jesus to the house of Simon [Peter] and Andrew); 3:17 (they are chosen to be among the Twelve and are given the surname "Sons of Thunder"); 5:37 (they, along with Peter, are the only ones allowed to witness the raising of Jairus's daughter); 9:2 (they, along with Peter, are the only ones allowed to witness the transfiguration of Jesus). In the context of Mark as a whole, their request to Jesus appears to be an attempt to achieve ranks higher than that of Peter. Such an effort recalls the discussion among the disciples concerning who was the greatest among them (9:34). Their request creates a jarring contrast with the prediction of Jesus' suffering and death in vv. 33-34 and constitutes the climactic example of the disciples' misunderstanding of (or refusal to accept) Jesus' revelation, in the middle section of the Gospel, that the messiah must suffer.

The initial, general formulation of their request, "we want you to do for us whatever we ask of you" (θέλομεν ἵνα ὃ ἐὰν αἰτήσωμέν σε ποιήσῃς ἡμῖν) recalls the extravagant promise that Herod made to "his daughter Herodias," who danced for him and his guests: "Ask of me whatever you wish and I will give it to you" (αἴτησόν με ὃ ἐὰν θέλῃς, καὶ δώσω σοι) (Mark 6:22).[90] The similarity of the two statements suggests that James and John are speaking in an equally thoughtless and extravagant manner.

The specific request is "Grant us that we sit, one on your right and one on your left, in your glory" (δὸς ἡμῖν ἵνα εἷς σου ἐκ δεξιῶν καὶ εἷς ἐξ ἀριστερῶν καθίσωμεν ἐν τῇ δόξῃ σου).[91] The saying probably presupposes that Jesus will be enthroned as the king and judge of the new age as God's agent. The Similitudes of Enoch portrays God's "Chosen One," the messiah, as sitting on "the throne of glory" on "that day" (1 Enoch 45:3).[92] The Matthean Jesus prophesies that the Son of Man will sit on the throne of his glory and that the Twelve will sit on thrones as well, judging the twelve tribes of Israel (Matt 19:28; cf. 25:31).

The seat to the right of the king belongs to the one of highest rank and honor after the king.[93] This is clear

---

who conclude that the saying is a post-Easter formulation, see Wilfrid Haubeck, *Loskauf durch Christus: Herkunft, Gestalt und Bedeutung des paulinischen Loskaufmotivs* (Giessen: Brunnen Verlag, 1985) 231 n. 27.

86   Peter Stuhlmacher, *Versöhnung, Gesetz und Gerechtigkeit: Aufsätze zur biblische Theologie* (Göttingen: Vandenhoeck & Ruprecht, 1981) 27–42; ET *Reconciliation, Law and Righteousness* (Philadelphia: Fortress, 1986) 16–29; so also Haubeck, *Loskauf durch Christus*, 235–39.

87   Bultmann, *History*, 63.

88   Ibid., 143–44.

89   Tannehill, "Varieties," 1.1 (p. 102); 1.4 (p. 104); citation from 104.

90   On the name of the girl and her relationship to Herod, see the commentary on 6:22-23 above.

91   See the note on the trans. above.

92   Trans. by Nickelsburg and VanderKam, 59. See also *1 Enoch* 51:3; 55:4; 61:8; 62:5; 69:27, 29.

93   3 Kgdms 2:19; Bathsheba, the king's mother, sits at the right hand of Solomon (ἐκ δεξιῶν αὐτοῦ). The criticism of the behavior of the king's concubine in 1 Esdr 4:28b-30 presupposes that the seat at the right hand of the king is one of high rank and honor (ἐν δεξιᾷ τοῦ βασιλέως). Sir 12:12 implies that the

especially from Ps 110:1, in which God says to the king, "Sit at my right hand."[94] This passage is cited, in wording close to the LXX, in Mark 12:36. The context makes clear that Mark interprets the king in the psalm as the messiah.

The seat to the left of the king is the seat next in rank to that on his right. It is clear that this is the view of Josephus from the way in which he rewrites 1 Sam 20:25. According to the MT, when King Saul sat at the feast of the new moon to eat, Jonathan stood nearby and Abner sat by Saul's side. According to the LXX, Saul "went before Jonathan" (προέφθασεν τὸν Ιωναθαν), Abner sat by his side (ἐκάθισεν Αβεννηρ ἐκ πλαγίων Σαουλ) and David's place was empty (lit., "covered over") (1 Kgdms 20:25 LXX). Josephus writes:

The next day, which was the new moon, the king, after purifying himself as the custom was, came to the feast; and when his son Jonathan had seated himself on his right side and Abener, the commander of the army, on his left, he marked that David's seat was empty (Τῇ δ᾿ ἐχομένη, νουμηνία δ᾿ ἦν, ἁγνεύσας, ὡς ἔθος εἶχεν, ὁ βασιλεὺς ἧκεν ἐπὶ τὸ δεῖπνον, καὶ παρακαθεσθέντων αὐτῷ τοῦ μὲν παιδὸς Ἰωνάθου ἐκ δεξιῶν Ἀβενήρου δὲ τοῦ ἀρχιστρατήγου ἐκ τῶν ἑτέρων, ἰδὼν τὴν τοῦ Δαυίδου καθέδραν κενήν). (Ant. 6.11.9 §235)[95]

■ 38-40 The first part of Jesus' reply, "You do not know what you are asking" (οὐκ οἴδατε τί αἰτεῖσθε), implies that their request is thoughtless and superficial. The saying that follows indicates that the one who wishes to have a high rank in the messianic kingdom must be ready to suffer. The image of the cup (τὸ ποτήριον) here may be related to the scene of the Last Supper, in which Jesus takes a cup (ποτήριον) and, after the disciples have drunk from it, declares that it is his blood of the covenant (14:23-24; cf. Exod 24:8). Jesus, however, is not portrayed as drinking from that cup. It is more likely that the image of the cup here is related to the prophetic metaphor of drinking the cup of the divine wrath. For example:

Wake up, wake up, get up, Jerusalem, you who have drunk the cup of wrath from the hand of the Lord; for you have drunk and emptied the cup that makes you fall down, the glass of wrath (Ἐξεγείρου ἐξεγείρου ἀνάστηθι, Ιερουσαλημ ἡ πιοῦσα τὸ ποτήριον τοῦ θυμοῦ ἐκ χειρὸς κυρίου· τὸ ποτήριον γὰρ τῆς πτώσεως, τὸ κόνδυ τοῦ θυμοῦ ἐξέπιες καὶ ἐξεκένωσας). (Isa 51:17 LXX)

Here the image of a drunken woman is used to express the devastation of the destruction of the city by the Babylonians in the sixth century BCE. In Jer 25:15-29, the same metaphor is used. There the prophet is instructed to give the cup of wrath first to Jerusalem and then to the nations. The cup of divine wrath that must be drunk to the dregs is a graphic image of intoxication that expresses in a vivid and analogous way the effects of calamities on human beings.[96]

Rather than the scene of the Last Supper, the image of the cup in v. 38 is related to the prayer of Jesus in Gethsemane, "Abba, Father, all things are possible for you; take this cup away from me. But (let) not what I want (be), but what you want" (14:36). Here it is clear that the cup represents the suffering that Jesus is about to endure and that this suffering is part of the divine plan. In 10:38, Jesus makes this suffering real and vivid for James and John by using the traditional image of the cup of wrath.

The significance of the term βάπτισμα ("baptism") in the saying of v. 38 is difficult to determine. The referent is clearly the death of Jesus, but it is not clear how his death is being interpreted by the use of the term. This specific word is typically Christian, but Josephus used related words to speak of John as ὁ βαπτιστής ("the baptist") and to discuss his ritual activity as βαπτισμός or βάπτισις (both words may translated "baptism").[97]

seat on the right hand of others besides the king was also a place of relatively high rank and honor (ἐκ δεξιῶν σου).

94   Κάθου ἐκ δεξιῶν μου (Ps 109:1 LXX).
95   Text and trans. from Thackeray, Josephus, 5:282–83. Cited by Swete, ad loc.

96   Joseph Blenkinsopp, Isaiah 40–55 (AB 19A; New York: Doubleday, 2002) 336–37.
97   Josephus Ant. 18.5.2 §§116–17; Fitzmyer, Luke, 2:996; Albrecht Oepke, "βάπτω κτλ.," TDNT 1 (1964) 529–46, esp. 545–46.

The closest analogy to this saying in the New Testament is Luke 12:49-50:

> I came to cast fire upon the earth, and how I wish it were already kindled! I have a baptism with which to be baptized, and how distressed I am until it is accomplished! (Πῦρ ἦλθον βαλεῖν ἐπὶ τὴν γῆν, καὶ τί θέλω εἰ ἤδη ἀνήφθη. βάπτισμα δὲ ἔχω βαπτισθῆναι, καὶ πῶς συνέχομαι ἕως ὅτου τελεσθῇ).

Here "baptism" is used metaphorically and refers neither to the baptism of John nor to Christian baptism. The term "baptism" is also used metaphorically in Mark 10:38. Since the words βαπτίζειν ("immerse" or "baptize") and βαπτισμός ("immersion" or "baptism") were used in Mark 7:4 for Levitical washings, these or the baptism of John may provide the literal level of the metaphor here. The Levitical washings aim at the restoration of purity, whereas the baptism of John was concerned with repentance and the forgiveness of sins. The notion of a baptism for the forgiveness of sins would fit the context here well. It is analogous to the idea of Jesus' drinking the cup of the wrath of God. In both cases, it is presupposed that Jesus' death is vicarious.[98] This understanding becomes explicit in v. 45.[99]

One way to read Jesus' question in v. 38 is to infer that no one else can drink the cup and be baptized in the way that Jesus will, namely, as an act that is ἀντὶ πολλῶν ("in place of many" or "in behalf of many"; cf. v. 45). If such is the case, then the statement of Jesus in v. 39, "You will drink the cup which I am about to drink and you will be baptized with the baptism with which I am about to be baptized" (τὸ ποτήριον ὃ ἐγὼ πίνω πίεσθε καὶ τὸ βάπτισμα ὃ ἐγὼ βαπτίζομαι βαπτισθήσεσθε), would mean that they will share in the *form* of Jesus' death, but not in its *meaning*. It seems more likely that they share in its meaning as well, though in a limited way. According

to 8:34-35, the true followers of Jesus are those who take up their crosses and follow him, who are willing to die for his sake and for the sake of the gospel. The letter to the Colossians, written about the same time as Mark, has Paul say:

> Now I rejoice in my sufferings for your sake, and, in my flesh, I do my part to fill up what is lacking in the afflictions of Christ [or of the messiah] for the sake of his body, that is, the church (Νῦν χαίρω ἐν τοῖς παθήμασιν ὑπὲρ ὑμῶν καὶ ἀνταναπληρῶ τὰ ὑστερήματα τῶν θλίψεων τοῦ Χριστοῦ ἐν τῇ σαρκί μου ὑπὲρ τοῦ σώματος αὐτοῦ, ὅ ἐστιν ἡ ἐκκλησία). (Col 1:24)

This saying in no way denigrates the accomplishment of Christ. Rather, it reflects the notion of the messianic woes that afflict all of the elect. Related to this idea is that of "the measure" predetermined by God. When the messianic afflictions are complete, the new age will be manifested.[100] Similarly, Mark may express the idea in vv. 38-39 that the deaths of James and John are analogous to that of Jesus.

Jesus' statement in v. 39 that James and John will suffer like himself probably presupposes the execution of James mentioned in Acts 12:1-2. According to this brief account it was "King Herod" who executed James. Luke apparently refers here to Julius Agrippa I, a grandson of Herod the Great. In 37 CE, Gaius Caligula awarded him the territories of Philip the tetrarch and Lysanias with the title of king. When Antipas was exiled in 39 CE, Gaius gave Agrippa his territory as well (Galilee and Perea). In 41 CE, Claudius bestowed on him the rest of the territories once ruled by his grandfather. He possessed all of Judea as king from 41 to 44 CE. Since Agrippa died in 44 CE, James was killed before that date.[101] According to Acts, James was killed "with the

---

98 Henk J. de Jonge has argued that the "dying formula," which occurs eight times in Paul's letters, whose basic form is Χριστὸς ὑπὲρ ἡμῶν ἀπέθανεν ("Christ died for us"), describes Jesus' death as both atoning and vicarious or substitutionary ("The Original Setting of the *ΧΡΙΣΤΟΣ ΑΠΕΘΑΝΕΝ ΥΠΕΡ* Formula," in Raymond F. Collins, ed., *The Thessalonian Correspondence* [BEThL 87; Leuven: Leuven University Press/Peeters, 1990] 229–35, esp. 230). He

argues that the formula originated in "the exhortatory homily of the earliest, Greek-speaking, Christian community, which may well have been that of Jerusalem in the early thirties of the first century A.D." (ibid., 234).

99 See the commentary on v. 45 below.

100 Lohse, *Colossians and Philemon*, 68–71.

101 Conzelmann, *Acts of the Apostles: A Commentary on the Acts of the Apostles* (Hermeneia; Philadelphia:

sword" (μαχαίρῃ), which probably means that he was decapitated. From a Roman point of view, this was the most honorable method of execution.[102] Crucifixion, the way Jesus was executed, on the contrary, was the most shameful.[103] Clement of Alexandria says that James was beheaded. Neither Luke nor Clement mentions the death of John.[104]

The final part of Jesus' reply is the statement, "but to sit on my right hand or on my left is not mine to grant, except to those for whom it has been prepared" (τὸ δὲ καθίσαι ἐκ δεξιῶν μου ἢ ἐξ εὐωνύμων οὐκ ἔστιν ἐμὸν δοῦναι, ἀλλ᾽ οἷς ἡτοίμασται). Here Jesus flatly refuses to grant their request. This refusal instructs James and John, and the audiences of Mark as well, that a direct seeking of high rank is unworthy of the followers of Jesus. This saying prepares for the further instruction that is to come in vv. 41-45.

The Markan Jesus uses the word εὐώνυμος ("left," lit., "auspicious" or "fortunate") in v. 40 rather than the word used by the brothers in v. 37, ἀριστερός ("left," lit., "better"). Both words are euphemisms, since the left was associated with bad luck. It is likely that a different, but synonymous, word was chosen here simply in the interests of a pleasingly varied style.

■ **41** This remark by the narrator serves two purposes. First, it illustrates the ill effects of the ambition of James and John. Their efforts to achieve higher ranks than the other members of the Twelve evoke anger and strife within the group. At least one reason for advocating other-centered service is precisely to avoid such effects of ambitious self-seeking. It is likely that the evangelist constructed this scene in order to address analogous tensions in early Christian communities.[105] The letters of Paul provide evidence of tensions among both itinerant and local leaders. Whether there were tensions between Paul and Apollos personally is unclear, but 1 Corinthians

1–4 provides evidence that divisions arose among their respective followers. Galatians provides evidence for conflict between Paul and Peter and others, and 2 Corinthians documents strife between Paul and those he calls "super-apostles." Phil 2:1-13 and 4:2 attest to conflict within the community in Philippi. Mark may not have been aware of these particular cases but was probably familiar with analogous ones. The other purpose served by this verse is a literary one; it provides a transition from the anecdote involving James and John to the related teaching conveyed by Jesus to the Twelve.

The Literary Context of 10:42-45

This third instance of teaching about discipleship is designed to reprise and synthesize the first two. The first (8:34-37) exhorts the disciples to take up their crosses, as the master will take up his. The second (9:35-37) instructs them that the true disciple of Jesus takes the role of a servant. In the climactic saying of this third unit, it is made clear that being a servant means imitating Jesus and that servanthood and the cross are linked in the life and death of Jesus.[106]

Comment

■ **42** After the narrator's comment about the anger of the ten, Jesus summons "them," probably all those mentioned in v. 41, namely, the Twelve. This summons is part of the threefold pattern unifying this middle section of Mark.[107] The summons is followed by teaching, as in the first two units (cf. 8:34—9:1; 9:35-37). The first statement addresses what is commonly known: "You know that those who are recognized as ruling the nations are masters over them and those in high position among them exercise authority over them" (οἴδατε ὅτι οἱ δοκοῦντες ἄρχειν τῶν ἐθνῶν κατακυριεύουσιν αὐτῶν καὶ οἱ

Fortress, 1987) 93 (Excursus: "Herods"); David C. Braund, "Agrippa," *ABD* 1:98–99.

102 The simple Roman death penalty was death by decapitation; members of the higher social orders were often spared the death penalty and imprisoned or exiled instead. Crucifixion, burning alive, and condemnation to the beasts were aggravated forms of the death penalty. Crucifixion was the normal form of execution for slaves; see Peter Garnsey, *Social Status and Legal Privilege in the Roman Empire* (Oxford: Clarendon, 1970) 103–31, esp. 105 n. 1, 124, 127.

103 Hengel, *Crucifixion*, 87; idem, *The Cross of the Son of God* (London: SCM, 1986) 114–55.

104 Johannes Munck, *The Acts of the Apostles: Introduction, Translation, and Notes* (rev. by William F. Albright and C. S. Mann; AB 31; New York: Doubleday, 1967) 113.

105 See the commentary on 9:35 above.

106 Perrin, *Redaction Criticism*, 45–46.

107 Cf. 8:34; 9:35, and the commentary on 10:32a above.

μεγάλοι αὐτῶν κατεξουσιάζουσιν αὐτῶν). The synonymous, double character of the saying prepares for the more striking double antithetical aphorism in vv. 43-44.[108]

The phrase οἱ δοκοῦντες ἄρχειν τῶν ἐθνῶν ("those who are recognized as ruling the nations") is a term of honor and contains no hint of depreciation. Compare the following:

> For the same speech has quite a different force if it is spoken by a man of repute or by a nobody (λόγος γὰρ ἔκ τ᾽ ἀδοξούντων ἰὼν κἀκ τῶν δοκούντων αὐτὸς οὐ ταὐτὸν σθένει). (Eur. Hec. 294–95)[109]

■ **43-44** The first clause of Jesus' second statement, "It is not so among you" (οὐχ οὕτως δέ ἐστιν ἐν ὑμῖν), rejects the actual relations of power in the surrounding societies as a model for followers of Jesus. The rest of the statement is a double antithetical aphorism. The first aphorism replaces the role of one in high position (μέγας) with the role of servant (διάκονος). The second intensifies the first by beginning with the role of the "first," that is, the greatest of all (πρῶτος), and replacing it with the lowest social status of all, that of the slave (δοῦλος).[110] This double saying takes up the same theme that was introduced in 9:35.[111] The force of the statement is that leadership in the communities of followers of Jesus is not to be self-aggrandizing and self-serving; rather, it is to be characterized by service to the other members of the community and to the good of the community as a whole. Indeed, the leader should consider his or her role to be analogous to that of a slave belonging to the community. This model suggests that the leader's service should be centered on the needs of the community, not on her or his own.

As stated above, these verses reject the actual relations of power in the early Roman imperial period as a model for the followers of Jesus. The teaching expressed here, however, is not new. As Moshe Weinfeld has pointed out, 1 Kgs 12:7 already articulates the idea that the king should be a servant of the people. He also showed that the concept of the monarchy as an institution that should serve the people has its roots in the ancient Near East and has argued that the literary genre of advice to the king (περὶ βασιλείας) is of eastern origin.[112] The teaching of vv. 41-45 is also similar to widely expressed Greek and Roman ideals of leadership. For example, the Macedonian philosopher-king Antigonos Gonatas (c. 320–239 BCE) taught his son, "Do you not understand, my son, that our kingdom is held to be a noble servitude (ἔνδοξος δουλεία)?"[113] Populist or democratic leaders spoke about the ruler as a slave of the many.[114] Paul seems to adopt such language in 1 Cor 9:19-23, when he declares that he has made himself a slave to all, including those he is supposed to lead.[115]

■ **45** This saying provides both a warrant and a model for the teaching expressed in vv. 43-44. It is striking that this saying, one of the richest christological statements in Mark, is not included primarily because of an interest in defining the nature and work of Jesus as the Christ, but as a rhetorical example related to teaching that concerns

108 Tannehill, *Sword*, 102–3.

109 Text and trans. from David Kovacs, *Euripides: Children of Heracles, Hippolytus, Andromache, Hecuba* (LCL 484; Cambridge, MA/London: Harvard University Press, 1995) 424–25. The passage is cited (re Gal 2:2) by Joseph B. Lightfoot, *The Epistle of St. Paul to the Galatians* (Grand Rapids: Zondervan, 1957) 103.

110 Tannehill, *Sword*, 102.

111 Tannehill notes that the saying of 9:35 manifests partial doubling (ibid.). On the relation of 9:35 and 10:43-44 to other Synoptic sayings, see *Sword*, 190 n. 43.

112 Moshe Weinfeld, "The King as the Servant of the People: The Source of the Idea," *JJS* 33 (1982) 189–94.

113 Cited by Weinfeld, "King as the Servant," 189. See also the treatment of this saying by Hans Volkmann,

"Die Basileia als ἔνδοξος δουλεία," in idem, *ENDOXOS DULEIA: Kleine Schriften zur Alten Geschichte* (Berlin/New York: de Gruyter, 1975) 74–81.

114 Dale B. Martin, *Slavery as Salvation: The Metaphor of Slavery in Pauline Christianity* (New Haven/London: Yale University Press, 1990) 86–116. On kingship as service in "the political philosophy of Hellenistic kingship," see David Seeley, "Rulership and Service in Mark 10:41-45," *NovT* 35 (1993) 234–50. On (the appropriation of) these ideals in Jewish Hellenistic writings, see Martin, *Slavery as Salvation*, 113–14 (Philo); Oda Wischmeyer, "Herrschen als Dienen—Mk 10,41-45," *ZNW* 90 (1999) 28–44, esp. 36 (*Jos. Asen.*), 37 (*T. Job*), 37–38 (*Ep. Arist.* and Philo *Leg. Gaj.*).

115 Martin, *Slavery as Salvation*, 87, 117–35.

the formation of communities. As a unit, vv. 42-45 is intended to shape Christian identity both in terms of internal relations and in contrast to the practices of other social groups.[116]

The use of the epithet "Son of Man" for Jesus here in relation to his death is analogous to, if not dependent on, the usage of that designation in the Markan passion predictions.[117] Like them, this saying is paradoxical because, for Mark and his audiences, "Son of Man" and "messiah" were equivalent and because "Son of Man" evoked Dan 7:13, in which the "one like a son of man" is a glorious figure who is given universal kingship. Verse 45, with its vivid portrayal of the self-humbling of Jesus, lures the audiences to accept the paradoxical definition of leadership in vv. 43-44. The prose hymn of Philippians 2 has a similar rhetorical effect.[118]

Both parts of the saying are connected to the context. The claim that "the Son of Man did not come to be served, but to serve" presents Jesus as a model for leadership as service advocated in vv. 43-44. The remark that he came "to give his life as a ransom in behalf of many" clarifies the cryptic allusions to the "cup" and the "baptism" in vv. 38-39. The aim of giving his life makes clear that the two images relate to the death of Jesus. The second part of the remark introduces a new image, that his death is to be a "a ransom in behalf of many" (λύτρον ἀντὶ πολλῶν).

The saying of v. 45 has some important similarities to Isaiah 53:10b-12 LXX:

And the Lord intends to take away the suffering of his soul (or life), to show him light and to shape [him] with understanding, to vindicate the just one who serves many well; and he will bear their sins. Therefore, he himself will be the heir of many, and he will

divide the spoils of the mighty, because his soul (or life) was handed over to death, and he was reckoned among the wicked. And he himself has borne the sins of many and was handed over on account of their sins (καὶ βούλεται κύριος ἀφελεῖν ἀπὸ τοῦ πόνου τῆς ψυχῆς αὐτοῦ, δεῖξαι αὐτῷ φῶς καὶ πλάσαι τῇ συνέσει, δικαιῶσαι δίκαιον εὖ δουλεύοντα πολλοῖς, καὶ τὰς ἁμαρτίας αὐτῶν αὐτὸς ἀνοίσει. διὰ τοῦτο αὐτὸς κληρονομήσει πολλοὺς καὶ τῶν ἰσχυρῶν μεριεῖ σκῦλα, ἀνθ᾽ ὧν παρεδόθη εἰς θάνατον ἡ ψυχὴ αὐτοῦ, καὶ ἐν τοῖς ἀνόμοις ἐλογίσθη· καὶ αὐτὸς ἁμαρτίας πολλῶν ἀνήνεγκεν καὶ διὰ τὰς ἁμαρτίας αὐτῶν παρεδόθη).

The figure spoken about here is defined as the servant of God (ὁ παῖς μου) in Isa 52:13, just as Jesus as the Son of Man comes to serve. In addition, in 53:11, he is described as a just man "who serves many well" (δίκαιον εὖ δουλεύοντα πολλοῖς). As the Son of Man gives his life (δοῦναι τὴν ψυχὴν αὐτοῦ), the servant's soul or life is "handed over to death" (παρεδόθη εἰς θάνατον ἡ ψυχὴ αὐτου).[119]

A similarity with a difference is that the servant is cast in the image of the scapegoat by his portrayal as one who has borne the sins of many (καὶ αὐτὸς ἁμαρτίας πολλῶν ἀνήνεγκεν), whereas the Son of Man gives his life as a ransom in behalf of many (λύτρον ἀντὶ πολλῶν). No Hebrew term equivalent to λύτρον occurs in the MT of Isa 52:13—53:12, and the latter term does not occur in the LXX version of that passage.[120] The term λύτρον, both in the singular and the plural, does, however, occur elsewhere in the LXX.

The singular (λύτρον) occurs in Lev 27:31 (for גְּאֻלָּה) in a context concerning the redemption of tithes. The owner must pay the monetary value plus one-fifth to

---

116 Cf. the use to which Paul puts the prose hymn in Phil 2:6-11; on this text, see Adela Yarbro Collins, "The Psalms and the Origins of Christology," in Harold W. Attridge and Margot E. Fassler, eds., *Psalms in Community: Jewish and Christian Textual, Liturgical, and Artistic Traditions* (SBLSymS 25; Atlanta: SBL, 2003) 113–23; eadem, "Psalms, Phil. 2:6-11, and the Origins of Christology," in *BI* 11 (2003) 361–72.

117 See the commentary on 8:30-31 and the "Excursus: The Son of Man Tradition" related to the commentary on 2:10 above.

118 See note 116.

119 David Hill concluded that, although the language of v. 45 does not recall the exact words of Isaiah 53, the ideas in the two passages are similar (*Greek Words and Hebrew Meanings: Studies in the Semantics of Soteriological Terms* [SNTSMS 5; Cambridge: Cambridge University Press, 1967] 79).

120 Charles K. Barrett, "The Background of Mark 10:45," in Angus J. B. Higgins, ed., *New Testament Essays: Studies in Memory of Thomas Walter Manson 1893–1958* (Manchester: Manchester University Press, 1959) 1–18. In spite of this important differ-

retain in his possession any property that is holy to the Lord.[121] It also occurs in Prov 6:35 (for כֹּפֶר) in a statement that a wronged husband will accept no ransom (compensation); he will instead take revenge on the adulterer. The only other occurrence of the singular is in Prov 13:8 (again for כֹּפֶר); the rich man is able to pay a ransom for his life.[122] The reason why he would need to pay such a ransom is not stated. The plural occurs more frequently in the LXX, often in ways analogous to the usage of the singular. In Lev 19:20, λύτρα is used in connection with the manumission of a slave.[123] In Lev 25:24 it is used with regard to the redemption of land during the period between jubilee years.[124] It is used for the redemption of an Israelite who has lost his land and been "sold" as a hired, resident laborer in Lev 25:51-52.[125] In Isa 45:13, it is used with regard to a ransom paid for the release of prisoners of war.[126]

Other usages of the plural (λύτρα) are more complex and more illuminating for Mark 10:45. According to Exod 21:29, if an ox is accustomed to goring people and the owner has been warned but fails to restrain it with the result that the ox kills a man or a woman, the ox shall be stoned and its owner shall also be put to death. According to v. 30, if the relatives of the deceased are willing to accept a ransom (MT כֹּפֶר; LXX λύτρα) for the life of the owner, he should pay the redemption money (MT פִּדְיֹן; LXX λύτρα) in whatever amount they ask.[127] Here we have the notion of a payment of money as a substitution for the execution of a guilty person. Num 35:31-34, however, stipulates that no ransom (MT כֹּפֶר; LXX λύτρα) shall be accepted for a murderer subject to the death penalty. The reason is that the blood shed by the murderer pollutes the land in which the Lord dwells and that pollution can only be expiated (MT יְכֻפַּר; LXX ἐξιλασθήσεται) by the blood of the murderer.[128]

The term is also used in Exod 30:11-16 in the context of the taking of a census of the Israelites to register them. Verse 12 stipulates that each of them shall pay a ransom (MT כֹּפֶר; LXX λύτρα) for his life, so that no plague may come upon them for being registered. The underlying idea is probably that the primary purpose of a census is to determine the number of men eligible for military service; military duty involved a complex set of laws of ritual purity. Therefore, an Israelite enrolled in a census was subject to these laws, and any infraction could lead to disastrous results. The plague is the result of the violation of ritual taboos.[129] The ransom that each Israelite gives is a sum of money, which is also called an offering to the Lord (εἰσφορὰ κυρίῳ) in vv. 13 and 14. According to v. 15, the purpose of bringing the offering is "to make atonement for your lives" (ἐξιλάσασθαι περὶ τῶν ψυχῶν ὑμῶν). Verse 16 states that the money is to be used for the service of the tent of meeting (εἰς κάτεργον τῆς σκηνῆς τοῦ μαρτυρίου), and it will be a memorial offering (μνημόσυνον) for the Israelites before the Lord to atone (ἐξιλάσασθαι) for their lives. The idea seems to be that the sum of money, the offering, takes the place of the deaths that the plague related to the census would cause. The phrase "to make atonement for your lives" (ἐξιλάσασθαι περὶ τῶν ψυχῶν ὑμῶν) apparently means to propitiate or conciliate God, to cause God to be favorably inclined in the matter of

ence, Rikki E. Watts has argued that Isaiah 53 is the primary source of Mark 10:45 ("Jesus' Death, Isaiah 53, and Mark 10:45: A Crux Revisited," in William H. Bellinger, Jr., and William R. Farmer, eds., *Jesus and the Suffering Servant: Isaiah 53 and Christian Origins* [Harrisburg, PA: Trinity Press International, 1998] 125–51, esp. 149).

121 Milgrom, *Leviticus*, 3:2398.

122 R. B. Y. Scott, *Proverbs, Ecclesiastes: Introduction, Translation, and Notes* (AB 18; Garden City, NY: Doubleday, 1965) 93, 95.

123 The LXX of Lev 19:20 uses the expression καὶ αὐτὴ λύτροις οὐ λελύτρωται for the Hebrew וְהָפְדֵּה לֹא נִפְדָּתָה. Both phrases may be translated "And she has not been ransomed (manumitted)."

124 Milgrom, *Leviticus*, 3:2188–89. The term λύτρα is

used in a similar context in Lev 25:26 (ibid., 2195–96).

125 Ibid., 2234–39.

126 On the MT, see Klaus Baltzer, *Deutero-Isaiah: A Commentary on Isaiah 40–55* (Hermeneia; Minneapolis: Fortress, 2001) 237; Blenkinsopp, *Isaiah 40–55*, 251, 255.

127 Childs, *Exodus*, 443, 473; Bernd Janowski, "Auslösung des verwirkten Lebens: Zur Geschichte und Struktur der biblischen Lösegeldvorstellung," *ZThK* 79 (1982) 25–59, esp. 32–34.

128 Janowski, "Auslösung des verwirkten Lebens," 40–43.

129 Cf. 2 Samuel 24; P. Kyle McCarter, Jr., *II Samuel: A New Translation with Introduction, Notes, and Commentary* (AB 9; Garden City, NY: Doubleday, 1984) 512–

their lives. In other words, the census, or its results, potentially offends God, and the offering is a means of winning God's favor. As in Num 35:31-34 (cited above), this link of the notion of "ransom" to the notion of "propitiation" or "expiation" suggests that they are synonymous or at least closely related.

The term is used also in connection with the Levites:

And the Lord spoke to Moses saying, "And see, I claim the Levites from the midst of the sons of Israel in the place of every firstborn who opens the womb from the sons of Israel; they will be a ransom for them, and the Levites will be mine. For every firstborn is mine; on the day on which I struck every firstborn in the land of Egypt, I consecrated for myself every firstborn in Israel, from human beings and from animals. They will be mine; I am [the] Lord" (καὶ ἐλάλησεν κύριος πρὸς Μωυσῆν λέγων Καὶ ἐγὼ ἰδοὺ εἴληφα τοὺς Λευίτας ἐκ μέσου τῶν υἱῶν Ἰσραηλ ἀντὶ παντὸς πρωτοτόκου διανοίγοντος μήτραν παρὰ τῶν υἱῶν Ἰσραηλ· λύτρα αὐτῶν ἔσονται καὶ ἔσονται ἐμοὶ οἱ Λευῖται. ἐμοὶ γὰρ πᾶν πρωτότοκον· ἐν ᾗ ἡμέρᾳ ἐπάταξα πᾶν πρωτότοκον ἐν γῇ Αἰγύπτου, ἡγίασα ἐμοὶ πᾶν πρωτότοκον ἐν Ἰσραηλ ἀπὸ ἀνθρώπου ἕως κτήνους· ἐμοὶ ἔσονται, ἐγὼ κύριος). (Num 3:11-13 LXX)[130]

The logic seems to be that the Israelites must give their firstborn to God in return for God's delivering them from the land of Egypt. In any case, the use of the preposition ἀντί in v. 12 is interesting in comparison with the use of the same preposition in Mark 10:45. The usage of the preposition in the context of a "ransom" in Num 3:12 suggests that the relevant phrase in Mark 10:45 could be translated "and to give his life as a ransom in place of many" (καὶ δοῦναι τὴν ψυχὴν αὐτοῦ ἀντὶ πολλῶν).[131] The implication would be that the death of Jesus is a substitute for the deaths of many others.

The usage of λύτρον in the LXX makes it probable that Mark and his audiences understood the "ransom" (λύτρον) constituted by Jesus' giving of his life as an expiation accomplished "in behalf of" or "in place of" (ἀντί) many. This hypothesis is supported by the usage of the word-group λύτρον in a number of inscriptions from Asia Minor, called "confessional inscriptions" by modern scholars.[132] One of these is an undated inscription on a stele from Lydia that reads:

A female slave of the village of the Keryzeis [is dedicated] to [Men] Gallikos Asklepias as a ransom for Diogenes (Γαλλικῷ Ἀσκληπιᾶς κώμης Κερυζέων πα(ι)δίσκη (Δ)ιογένου λύτρον).

This inscription implies that a certain Diogenes dedicated a slave to the sacred village or to the god as compensation for some offense he had committed.[133] Another inscription, dated to 148–149 CE, reads:

Alexander, son of Thalouse, with Julius and his sister paid to the god Men of Diodotos a ransom for things known and not known. Year 233 (= 148–149 CE) (Μῆνα ἐγ Διοδότου Ἀλέξανδρος Θαλούσης μετὰ Ἰουλίου καὶ τῆς ἀδελφῆς ἐλυτρώσαντο τὸν θεὸν ἐξ εἰδότων καὶ μὴ εἰδότων. Ἔτους σλγ΄).[134]

Although the two instances of the participle εἰδώς are grammatically active, the only appropriate explanation of the inscription involves taking them in a passive sense.

---

14. Ephraim A. Speiser argued that in Israel and elsewhere in the ancient Near East, the very writing down of names was, in some circumstances, an ominous process and required prophylactic propitiation ("Census and Ritual Expiation in Mari and Israel," *BASOR* 149 [1958] 17–25).

130 See also Num 18:15.

131 Cf. Num 3:40-51, which stipulates that the firstborn male Israelites have to be "redeemed, bought back" from God by giving money to the priests. According to Baruch Levine, the "primary context is that of bondage, wherein the owner or master of one in service is compensated for the claim held on the person bound over to him. The Israelites had been in bondage to the Egyptians, and God bought them their freedom" (*Numbers 1–20*, 162). In the LXX, λύτρα occurs in vv. 46, 48, 49, 51.

132 For a more detailed discussion see Adela Yarbro Collins, "The Signification of Mark 10:45 among Gentile Christians," in François Bovon, ed., *Jesus' Sayings in the Life of the Early Church: Papers Presented in Honor of Helmut Koester's Seventieth Birthday*, HTR 90 (1997) 371–82, and the literature cited there.

133 Ibid., 373–74.

134 Ibid., 375.

The inscription thus attests a ritual act whereby people secured their release from the effects of both deliberate and unwitting sins. The fact that the noun θεός (God) is the object of the verb λυτρόομαι ("pay a ransom," "redeem") implies that this verb is synonymous here with ἱλάσκομαι ("propitiate," "cause a deity to become favorably inclined"). The implication is that the group who set up the stele had lost divine favor because of some offense for which the ritual act serves as expiation.[135] Although this inscription is later than Mark, the ritual practices and ideas to which it attests are considerably older.

The evidence thus suggests that the term λύτρον ("ransom") in v. 45 is a synonym of ἱλαστήριον ("expiation" or "propitiation"). Jesus' death is interpreted here as a metaphorical ritual act of expiation for the offenses of many. Verse 45 is thus analogous to the saying over the cup in 14:24, according to which the blood of Jesus was poured out for many. In the confessional inscriptions both words may be associated with sacrifice, but expiation may be made in other ways as well.[136] In v. 45 the metaphorical ritual act is a voluntary death, which may be understood either as a sacrifice or as some other kind of altruistic death.[137]

Paul describes Jesus' death both as an ἀπολύτρωσις ("ransoming") and as an ἱλαστήριον ("expiation" or "propitiation") in Rom 3:24-25.[138] Ernst Käsemann argued that the former term is liturgical and eschatological and that the latter is rooted in cultic language. He concluded that Paul was dependent on earlier Christian tradition in his formulation of vv. 24-26.[139] Given the variation in the terms, it is unlikely that Mark is dependent on Paul in v. 45. It is more likely that they drew independently upon similar earlier traditions.[140]

The book of Revelation is informed by an understanding of Jesus' death analogous to that of v. 45:

To the one who loves us and ransomed [lit., "released"] us from our sins by his blood . . . be glory

---

135 Ibid., 375–76.

136 Ibid., 381 and n. 56.

137 Cf. the saying attributed to the emperor Otho by Dio Cassius, "I shall free myself [take my own life], that all may learn from the deed that you chose for your emperor one who would not give you up to save himself, but rather himself to save you" (ὅστις οὐχ ὑμᾶς ὑπὲρ ἑαυτοῦ ἀλλ' ἑαυτὸν ὑπὲρ ὑμῶν δέδωκε) (Dio Cassius 63.13; text and trans. from Earnest Carey, Dio Cassius [9 vols.; LCL; Cambridge, MA: Harvard University Press, 1925] 8:214–17). The context is Otho's decision not to fight a losing battle in which many of his supporters would be killed. Max Wilcox has interpreted v. 45 historically rather than metaphorically and has argued that "Jesus himself was to be the actual price of (certain) other people's freedom; that in acutal historical fact he was to be taken as a hostage (or worse) against their safe-conduct." He attempts to make a case for this hypothesis on the basis of Josephus's use of the term λύτρον ("ransom") and on various passages in the Gospel of John ("On the Ransom-Saying in Mark 10:45c, Matt 20:28c," in Cancik et al., Geschichte, 3:173–86; citation from 179). Hill concluded that the most adequate interpretation of λύτρον in v. 45 is "atoning substitute" (Greek Words and Hebrew Meanings, 81); so also Knut Backhaus, "'Lösepreis für viele' (Mk 10,45): Zur Heilsbedeutung des Todes Jesu bei Markus," in Thomas Söding, ed., Der Evangelist als Theologe: Studien zum Markusevangelium (SBS 163; Stuttgart: Katholisches Bibelwerk, 1995) 91–118, esp. 108.

138 Cf. Heb 9:5, where ἱλαστήριον is used for the "mercy seat" or "place of atonement" in the Holy of Holies. Wolfgang Kraus argued that the pre-Pauline tradition in Rom 3:25-26a interprets the death of Jesus in the context of the Day of Atonement and the consecration of the eschatological temple (Der Tod Jesu as Heiligtumsweihe [WMANT 66; Neukirchen-Vluyn: Neukirchener Verlag, 1991] 260–61). Martin Gaukesbrink translates ἀπολύτρωσις with "redemption" (Erlösung) and ἱλαστήριον with "place of atonement" (Sühneort) or "monument of atonement" (Sühnemal), connecting the latter term with the ritual of the Day of Atonement; he concludes that the key interpretation of the death of Jesus in Paul's letters is that of atonement or expiation (Die Sühnetradition bei Paulus: Rezeption und theologischer Stellenwert [FB 82; Würzburg: Echter Verlag, 1999] 231–32, 285).

139 Ernst Käsemann, Commentary on Romans (Grand Rapids: Eerdmans, 1980; from German 4th ed. 1980) 96–97. Breytenbach argued that the pre-Pauline tradition preserved here reinterprets the cult of the temple so that the atoning presence of God is understood as being present in the crucified Jesus rather than in the Holy of Holies (Versöhnung, 167–68). See also 1 Cor 6:20.

140 Cf. Breytenbach, Versöhnung, 208–9. Kraus sees no connection between the history of the tradition of Mark 10:45 and that of Rom 3:25-26 (Der Tod Jesu, 261).

and power for ever. Amen (Τῷ ἀγαπῶντι ἡμᾶς καὶ λύσαντι ἡμᾶς ἐκ τῶν ἁμαρτιῶν ἡμῶν ἐν τῷ αἵματι αὐτοῦ ... ἡ δόξα καὶ τὸ κράτος εἰς τοὺς αἰῶνας τῶν αἰώνων· ἀμήν). (Rev 1:5b-6)[141]

4 Maccabees, a Jewish work composed in Greek around 100 CE[142] and characterized by Hellenistic philosophical language and ideas, describes the deaths of Eleazar and the woman and her seven sons as an expiation (ἱλαστήριον) (4 Macc 17:22).[143] Since this expiation is accomplished through their blood, the notion of sacrifice is evoked. The notion of ransom is also present in the context:

And these, therefore, having been consecrated on account of God, are honored, not only with this honor, but also with the fact that, on account of them, the enemies did not conquer our people and the tyrant was punished and the fatherland was purified,

since they became, as it were, a ransom for the sin of the people (καὶ οὗτοι οὖν ἁγιασθέντες διὰ θεὸν τετίμηνται, οὐ μόνον ταύτῃ τῇ τιμῇ, ἀλλὰ καὶ τῷ δι᾽ αὐτοὺς τὸ ἔθνος ἡμῶν τοὺς πολεμίους μὴ ἐπικρατῆσαι καὶ τὸν τύραννον τιμωρηθῆναι καὶ τὴν πατρίδα καθαρισθῆναι, ὥσπερ ἀντίψυχον γεγονότας τῆς τοῦ ἔθνους ἁμαρτίας). (4 Macc 17:20-21 LXX)

For comparison with Mark 10:45, it is interesting that the word used here meaning "ransom" (ἀντίψυχον) has the connotation of the giving of one life for another.[144] The prefix of this word, ἀντι-, is related to the preposition ἀντί in v. 45. Although 4 Maccabees was probably written later than Paul's letter to the Romans and Mark's Gospel, its similar terminology suggests that the early Christian traditions adapted in Mark 10:45 and Rom 3:24-25 were influenced by the ideas and language of Greek-speaking Jews.[145]

10

10:46-52 The Healing of Bartimaeus

46/ And they went to Jericho.[a] And as he and his disciples and a considerable crowd were setting out from Jericho, the son of Timaeus, Bartimaeus, a blind beggar, was sitting by the side of the road.[b] 47/ And when he heard that it was Jesus of Nazareth,[c] he began to cry out and to say, "Son of David, Jesus, have mercy on me." 48/ And many were rebuking him, so that he would be silent; but he cried out all the more, "Son of David, have mercy on me." 49/ And Jesus stopped and said, "Call him." And they called the blind man and said to him, "Have courage! Get up! He is calling you." 50/ He then threw off his cloak, jumped up, and went to

a   B* sa^ms lack this sentence. It may have been omitted accidentally. If the omission was deliberate, the reason may have been that Jesus is said to go to Jericho and then to leave the place, without description of any activity there.

b   The noun προσαίτης ("beggar") is a late and rather rare word; see LSJ s.v. Its use thus gave rise to variants. A C² W et al. have the participle προσαιτῶν ("begging") and D Θ 565 the related participle ἐπαιτῶν ("begging") instead. C* 579 attest a reading in which the noun προσαίτης ("beggar") has been omitted. Cf. Taylor, ad loc.

c   The spelling of this epithet varies in the MSS. The earliest recoverable reading is most likely Ναζαρηνός ("of Nazareth" or "Nazarene"), attested by B L W et al. This term occurs with no variants in 1:24; 14:67; and 16:6 (except that in the last passage, every such term is omitted by ℵ* D). In 10:47, however, ℵ A C et al. (see Tischendorf and Huck-Greeven, ad loc.) read Ναζωραῖος ("Nazoraean" or "Nazarene"), probably under the influence of the reading of the majority of

141 The verb λύω belongs to the same word-group as λύτρον; see Yarbro Collins, "Signification of Mark 10:45," 376–81.

142 Jan Willem van Henten, *The Maccabean Martyrs as Saviours of the Jewish People: A Study of 2 and 4 Maccabees* (JSJSup 57; Leiden/New York: Brill 1997) 78.

143 Van Henten interprets ἱλαστήριον here as "an atoning sacrifice" (*Maccabean Martyrs,* 152).

144 Van Henten, *Maccabean Martyrs,* 151–52.

145 Janowski rejects the hypothesis of the influence of the Hellenistic Diaspora on this saying and argues for its origin in OT Jewish traditions ("Auslösung des verwirkten Lebens," 54–55).

Jesus. 51/ And Jesus said to him, "What do you want me to do for you?" The blind man then said to him, "Rabbouni, that I might regain my sight." 52/ And Jesus said to him, "Go, your faith has saved you." And immediately he regained his sight and followed him on the way.

the MSS for the parallel in Luke 18:37. D 28 et al. read Ναζωρηνός ("Nazorene"), which looks like a conflation of the first two readings. For other minor variations in the spelling, see Tischendorf; and Huck-Greeven, *ad loc.*

Comment

■ **46a** Most MSS have the following reading for the first clause: Καὶ ἔρχονται εἰς Ἰεριχώ ("And they went [lit., "they go"][146] to Jericho"). Mark frequently uses the present tense of ἔρχεσθαι ("to go" or "to come") to introduce a location.[147] The fragmentary letter attributed to Clement and discovered by Smith attests a different reading of this verse: καὶ ἔρχεται εἰς ἰεριχώ ("And he went [lit., "he goes"] to Jericho").[148] According to F. F. Bruce, the latter is the Western reading, which could point to Clement as the author.[149] According to the letter, "the secret Gospel" (τὸ μυστικὸν εὐαγγέλιον) contained the following addition after this introductory statement: "And the sister of the youth whom Jesus loved and his mother and Salome were there, and Jesus did not receive them" (καὶ ἦσαν ἐκεῖ ἡ ἀδελφὴ τοῦ νεανίσκου ὃν ἠγάπα αὐτὸν ὁ ἰησοῦς· καὶ ἡ μήτηρ αὐτοῦ καὶ σαλώμη· καὶ οὐκ ἀπεδέξατο αὐτὰς ὁ ἰησοῦς).[150]

Several explanations for the presence of this material have been put forward. One is that an earlier version of Mark had gone on to report a conversation between Jesus and the three women mentioned whose content was not acceptable to the orthodox. Smith argued that the omitted material was a conversation between Jesus and Salome and that Salome was an authority for unorthodox or Gnostic groups.[151] The present form of Mark would thus be an edited version of an older, fuller text. Richard Bauckham and Scott Brown have argued persuasively against this explanation.[152] The second explanation, which can be combined with the first, is that the passage "can have been invented and preserved only as polemic against those women or their followers or persons who appealed to their authority (as the Carpocratians did to that of Salome. . .)."[153] Bauckham has pointed out that there are no parallels to this text (interpreted as polemic) and this lessens the likelihood of this explanation.[154] A third explanation is more likely than the first two. This interpretation depends on the hypothesis that the story about Jesus raising the young man, which allegedly followed the third passion prediction (vv. 33-34), is an addition to canonical Mark. According to this explanation, the primary purpose of the passage about the women is to assist in integrating the passage about the young man into the Gospel as a whole. The reference to the sister of the young man whom Jesus loved

146 On the use of the historic present, see the commentary on 1:12 above. See also Vernon K. Robbins, "The Healing of Blind Bartimaeus (10:46-52) in the Marcan Theology," *JBL* 92 (1973) 224-43, esp. 224, and the literature cited there.

147 Mark 3:20; 6:1; 8:22; 10:1; 11:15, 27; 14:32; Paul J. Achtemeier, "'And He Followed Him': Miracles and Discipleship in Mark 10:46-51," *Semeia* 11 (1978) 115-45, esp. 137 n. 2.

148 Folio 2, recto, line 14; transcription from Smith, *Clement of Alexandria*, 452; my trans. See "Excursus: The Secret Gospel of Mark" above.

149 Bruce, *'Secret' Gospel of Mark*, 9. According to Rueben J. Swanson, the singular verb is attested by D 2 788 (*New Testament Greek Manuscripts: Variant Readings Arranged in Horizontal Lines against Codex Vaticanus, Mark* [Sheffield: Sheffield Academic

Press; Pasadena, CA: William Carey International University Press, 1995] 172).

150 Folio 2, recto, lines 14-16; trans. (447) and transcription (452) from Smith, *Clement of Alexandria*.

151 Ibid., 122, 189-92. See also the discussion by Richard Bauckham, "Salome the Sister of Jesus, Salome the Disciple of Jesus, and the Secret Gospel of Mark," *NovT* 33 (1991) 245-75, esp. 245-67.

152 Bauckham, "Salome the Sister of Jesus," 269-75; Brown, "The More Spiritual Gospel," esp. 265-387; idem, "On the Composition History of the Longer ('Secret') Gospel of Mark," 101-10; idem, *Mark's Other Gospel*, 32.

153 Smith, *Clement of Alexandria*, 121.

154 Bauckham, "Salome the Sister of Jesus," 272.

links the second passage to the first. The mention of Salome links both passages with 15:40 and 16:1 where she appears as one of a group of three women, as here.[155] If one keeps the possibility of a modern forgery in mind, the reference here to the young man "whom Jesus loved" (ὂν ἠγάπα αὐτὸν ὁ Ἰησοῦς), could be an allusion to the problem of the Beloved Disciple in the Gospel according to John, thereby piquing the interest of New Testament scholars.[156] Finally, the refusal of Jesus to receive the women could reflect a particular modern presupposition about "homosexuality."[157]

The fact that v. 46a depicts Jesus (and the disciples) entering Jericho and v. 46b portrays them as leaving Jericho immediately is an oddity that may have prompted an ancient interpolator (or a modern forger) to select this place for an addition to Mark.[158]

Literary Context of 10:46b-52

Like the healing of the blind man in 8:22-26, the healing of blind Bartimaeus is a transitional narrative. It concludes the middle section in which Jesus instructs his followers about his own destiny of suffering, the necessity of suffering for his followers, and the ideal of a leadership of service. It also introduces the next section, in that the address of Jesus as "son of David" prepares for the acclamation of the crowd in 11:10 that associates Jesus' entrance into Jerusalem with the restoration of the kingdom of David.[159] Furthermore, the two healings of blind men form literary brackets around the middle section.[160] As noted above, the healing of the blind man in 8:22-26 is a pre-Markan miracle story about the giving of physical sight. Mark's placement of it suggests a second level of meaning, in which the disciples, like the man being healed, at first see but not clearly. Peter recognizes that

Jesus is the messiah, but he does not understand what messiahship entails.[161] The healing of Bartimaeus may be pre-Markan, but if so, it has been thoroughly rewritten by Mark and placed strategically. The literal level of meaning implies an actual healing. The placement of the story suggests that, unlike Bartimaeus, the disciples have not yet been healed of their "blindness." They continue to fail to grasp the ways in which the suffering service of Jesus is to be a model for their own way of life.

Genre of 10:46b-52

Both Bultmann and Dibelius note how unusual the naming of the person seeking healing is. The only other Synoptic miracle story that names the supplicant is the one about the raising of Jairus's daughter (Mark 5:22 par.).[162] Bultmann concluded, "It is hardly possible to believe that there is an original, conventionally narrated miracle story at the basis of this passage."[163] Typical features displayed by the healing of Bartimaeus are "cries for help" (v. 47), "pleas and expressions of trust" (vv. 47, 48b, 51), "rejection/obstacle" (v. 48a), "exhortation" (v. 49), and "dismissal/conclusion" (v. 52).[164]

Dibelius categorized this passage as a paradigm of a less pure type.[165] He surmised that originally it was a genuine paradigm that emphasized the compassion of Jesus and the faith of a nameless beggar. In its next stage, it was a hybrid, combining the features of the original paradigm with those of a tale, "without portraiture and without description of the healing." Eventually, the narrative became a legend, when the nameless beggar was identified with a well-known blind man of Jericho, Bartimaeus. The mention of the name would be understandable if the man had become a follower of Jesus and then a member of a post-Easter local community. The conclusion,

155 Ibid., 272–75.
156 On the possibility of the letter attributed to Clement being a modern forgery, see "Excursus: The Secret Gospel of Mark" above.
157 Jeffery, *Secret Gospel*, chap. 8, the section "Ancient Male Homosexuals on Women," 198–206; chap. 9, the section "A Strange Idolatry," 215–19.
158 On the abrupt arrival and departure of Jesus and his retinue at Jericho here, see Sellew, "*Secret Mark*," 245.
159 Robbins, "Healing of Blind Bartimaeus," 237–38, 242; Achtemeier, "'And He Followed Him,'" 136.
160 See the section "The Literary Role of 8:22-26" above.
161 See the commentary on 8:25 above.
162 Bultmann, *History*, 213; Dibelius, *From Tradition to Gospel*, 51–53.
163 Bultmann, *History*, 213. On the typical genre of the healing story, see the commentary on 1:40-45 above.
164 Theissen, *Miracle Stories*, 53–55, 143–44.
165 Dibelius, *From Tradition to Gospel*, 43.

"and he followed him on the way" (καὶ ἠκολούθει αὐτῷ ἐν τῇ ὁδῷ), may imply this.[166] It belongs to the character of the paradigm that the story reaches its climax in the proof and the consequence of faith. Typical of the paradigm is that the narrator's aim is devotional and didactic, not to impress with the miraculous element, as is typical of the tale.[167]

Hans Dieter Betz has argued that the story is a different kind of hybrid. It begins as a miracle story and then "flips over" into a call story in vv. 49-50.[168] This double genre explains the shift from the address of Jesus as "son of David" (υἱὲ Δαυίδ) in vv. 47-48 to "rabbouni" or "my master" (ῥαββουνί) in v. 51.[169] Betz leaves open the question whether the request "that I might regain my sight" (ἵνα ἀναβλέψω) has metaphorical overtones. In any case, he argues that the concluding scene (v. 52) "briefly describes Bartimaeus's new life as a disciple of Jesus and thus reveals again the intent of the whole story."[170]

Paul Achtemeier compared the story about Bartimaeus with the call story of Peter in Luke 5:1-11 and concluded that the former is a call story and not a miracle story.[171] Like Dibelius, he also defined the story as a legend because of its focus on a named person other than Jesus and because "the exemplary character of the actions of that person are traits of a 'legend' rather than a miracle story."[172] He interpreted the address of Jesus as ῥαββουνί ("rabbouni" or "my master") in v. 51 and the

confirmation of his faith in v. 51 as belonging to the language of discipleship.[173]

Every verse of this story displays characteristics of Markan style.[174] E. J. Pryke concluded that Mark came closest to the invention of new narrative in this passage.[175] The hypothesis of Markan composition can explain the hybrid character of the narrative as well as the theory that Mark adapted a preexisting story.[176] The attitude of faith or trust (πίστις or πιστεύειν) is a prerequisite for healing here and elsewhere in Mark.[177] This motif indicates the affinity of this story with the other miracle stories in Mark. The story of Bartimaeus also links the healing of blindness with discipleship. The Gospel of Mark contains references both to metaphorical and literal blindness. The theme of metaphorical blindness was introduced already in the statement about the parables in 4:11-12. It is continued with a not entirely surprising twist in 8:18, where it is the disciples who are "blind." The theme of literal blindness was introduced with the healing of the blind man in Bethsaida (8:22-26). This account is presented both as an actual healing and as a symbolic narrative that continues the theme of the disicples' "blindness."[178] In the case of 8:22-26, Mark made his point by using a traditional story and placing it at a strategic and suggestive point in his narrative. In the case of 10:46-52, Mark may have composed the story himself, drawing on some of the conventions of miracle

---

166 Ibid., 52–53, 115, 118, 290.

167 Ibid., 87. Robbins argued that the story was originally a tale or miracle story that later became an apophthegm with legendary force ("Healing of Blind Bartimaeus," 232–33).

168 Hans Dieter Betz, "The Early Christian Miracle Story: Some Observations on the Form Critical Problem," *Semeia* 11 (1978) 69–81, esp. 74–75. It should be noted, however, that v. 49 uses the verb φωνέω ("call to oneself, summon, invite") and not καλέω ("call"), which appears in the story of the call of the sons of Zebedee (1:20). The two other call stories, however, do not use any verb of "calling"; rather they use words of "following" metaphorically for discipleship (1:17-18; 2:14). The verb ἀκολουθεῖν ("to follow") occurs in 1:18; 2:14; and 10:52.

169 Ibid., 74–75.

170 Ibid., 75. Cf. Betz's analysis of the return of the healed Samaritan leper in Luke 17:15-19, which he interprets as a conversion story ("The Cleansing of

the Ten Lepers [Luke 17:11-19]," *JBL* 90 [1971] 314–28, esp. 318–19).

171 Achtemeier, "'And He Followed Him,'" 122–25; see also Robbins, "Healing of Blind Bartimaeus," 225 and n. 14.

172 Achtemeier, "'And He Followed Him,'" 115, 122.

173 Ibid., 115.

174 Neirynck, *Duality in Mark*, 80, 83, 84, 95, 99, 106, 107, 120, 121, 122, 123, 132, 135.

175 Pryke, *Redactional Style*, 145, 167.

176 Achtemeier argued for the latter hypothesis ("'And He Followed Him,'" 115–20, 130–31).

177 Cf. 10:52 with 2:5 and esp. 4:40; 5:34, 36; 9:23-24. See also 11:22-24.

178 See the section "History of the Tradition" of 8:22-26, the section "The Literary Role of 8:22-26," and the commentary on 8:22 above. On 8:22-26 as a "parade example" of a miracle story, see Achtemeier, "'And He Followed Him,'" 121–22.

stories in order to create a parallel with 8:22-26, but also departing from that model and including elements of the call story in order to present Bartimaeus as an ideal disciple in contrast to the Twelve.

Comment

■ **46b** As noted above, the fact that Jesus and his entourage arrive in Jericho and then leave immediately has often been seen as a problem.[179] Matthew solves it by not mentioning the arrival in Jericho and simply beginning with Jesus and the others leaving Jericho (10:29). Luke has Jesus heal the (unnamed) blind man on the way into Jericho (instead of on the way out, as in Mark) and then, when he has entered Jericho, he encounters Zacchaeus.[180] Mark's formulation is probably related to his portrayal of Jesus and the disciples as being on a journey to Jerusalem.[181]

The genitive absolute in v. 46b has sometimes been seen as "overloaded." This observation has given rise to the hypothesis that the words "and his disciples" (καὶ τῶν μαθητῶν αὐτοῦ) were added by Mark in order to include the disciples in the scene, since they are portrayed as accompanying Jesus on his journey to Jerusalem in the larger literary context.[182] This feature, however, may be due to the mode of production of the text, which, though written, still has many oral features.[183] The mention of the disciples could be the kind of afterthought that is characteristic of oral speech. The sequence of a third person plural verb in v. 46a followed by a singular verbal form with Jesus as the subject in v. 46b is typical of Markan style.[184]

The name of the blind man is given as "the son of Timaeus, Bartimaeus" (ὁ υἱὸς Τιμαίου Βαρτιμαῖος).[185] Although one would expect the order to be reversed, it is typical of Markan style to give an Aramaic phrase along with a translation in Greek.[186] As noted above, it is quite unusual for the supplicant in a miracle story to be named.[187] There are three explanations as to why he is named here. One is that he was known to Mark and at least some in his audiences.[188] Another is that a name is given simply to provide the story with vividness and verisimilitude.[189] The third is that Mark uses the name to allude to Plato's *Timaeus*.[190]

The name itself is problematic. It is not clear whether it is an originally Semitic name or an originally Greek name. If it were a Greek name, then the inclusion of the Aramaicizing form Βαρτιμαῖος ("Bartimaeus" or "son of Timaeus") would be odd. The common Greek name "Timaeus" is accented on the first syllable (Τίμαιος).[191] The genitive Τιμαίου in Mark could be derived either from the nominative Τίμαιος or Τιμαῖος.

Many commentators have concluded that the Greek name Τίμαιος or Τιμαῖος in Mark "covers a Semitic name which also underlies the patronymic Βαρτιμαῖος."[192] Jerome argued that the true form of the underlying Semitic name is Barsemia (*filius caecus* = blind son). Most modern commentators have rejected that theory, since the Greek MSS of Mark provide no evidence for it.[193] Gustav Volkmar argued that the Aramaic name is

---

179 See the commentary on v. 46a above.

180 Luke 18:35-43 (the blind man) and 19:1-10 (Zacchaeus); Achtemeier, "'And He Followed Him,'" 116–17.

181 See the commentary on v. 32a above. Swete interprets the portrayal as historically reliable and explains it in terms of the location and layout of the city of Jericho and its gates (241).

182 Achtemeier, "'And He Followed Him,'" 117, 137 n. 4; Robbins, "Healing of Blind Bartimaeus," 228, and the literature cited there.

183 Achtemeier, *"Omne Verbum Sonat,"* 9, 12–13, 17 n. 108, 26.

184 Robbins, "Healing of Blind Bartimaeus," 228–29; he also argues that the construction of the genitive absolute is typical of Markan style (230).

185 On the names Τιμαῖος and Βαρτιμαῖος, see Tal Ilan, *Lexicon of Jewish Names in Late Antiquity: Part I,*

Palestine 330 BCE–200 CE (TSAJ 91; Tübingen: Mohr Siebeck, 2002) 18, 308.

186 Neirynck, *Duality in Mark*, 106–7. Cf. v. 47, where Mark wrote υἱὲ Δαυὶδ Ἰησοῦ ("son of David, Jesus") where one would expect "Jesus, son of David" (Ἰησοῦ υἱὲ Δαυίδ) (Swete, 243).

187 See the section "Genre of 10:46b-52" above.

188 So Dibelius, as noted in the section "Genre of 10:46b-52" above; so also Swete, 242.

189 Or to create a wordplay; see below.

190 So Hilgert, "Son of Timaeus;" see below.

191 LSJ, s.v. τιμαῖος; Moulton-Milligan, s.v. Τιμαῖος. The name Τίμαιος appears in Josephus with regard to the Greek historian of that name (*Ap.* 1.3 §16; 1.24 §221).

192 Swete, 242.

193 Ibid.; Taylor, 448.

בר תמאא [sic] ("son of the unclean").[194] H. J. Holtzmann noted that the cognates of the Hebrew word טמא ("unclean") in Syriac and Arabic mean "blind."[195] Julius Wellhausen rejected this line of interpretation emphatically.[196] He himself suggested that the name in question is Timai and that it may be an abbreviation of Timotheus ($Τιμόθεος$ = Timothy).[197] He seems to presuppose that the name is originally Greek and that "Timai" is its Semitic form. Paul Billerbeck argued that $Βαρτιμαῖος$ ("Bartimaeus") presupposes the Aramaic spelling בר טימי (bar Timai). In a midrashic text, he found a reference to R. Joshua, the son of Rab Timai. This man could thus have been called bar Timai or Bartimaeus. The name in question is thus attested in rabbinic literature.[198]

Earle Hilgert has argued that the name of the blind man was introduced by Mark in order to allude to "Plato's famous encomium of eyesight in the *Timaeus*. The story of the Son of Timaeus is a story of the gift of eyesight and with it the gift of insight, a theme that is prominent in Plato's then widely known encomium."[199] This hypothesis is ingenious and attractive, but if Mark intended to make such an allusion it seems more likely that he would simply have used the name $Τίμαιος$ (Timaeus) or the phrase ὁ

υἱὸς $Τιμαίου$ ("the son of Timaeus") alone. The fact that he gives an Aramaic form of the name, $Βαρτιμαῖος$ ("Bartimaeus"), complicates the issue. It may well be, as Burton Mack has suggested, that Mark is making a deliberate Greek–Aramaic wordplay here, inverting the Aramaic טמא ("unclean") into the Greek $τιμαῖος$ ("highly prized").[200] The hypothesis of a wordplay would explain both the unusual placement of the Greek translation before the Aramaic word as well as the circumflex accent on $τιμαῖος$.[201] It is impossible to determine whether Mark intended to allude to Plato's *Timaeus*, but it is likely that the name would have brought that text to mind for those in the audience familiar with it.

The portrayal of a blind beggar sitting by the side of the road as pilgrims passed on their way to Jerusalem for Passover has verisimilitude.[202]

■ **47** When the man hears that it is Jesus of Nazareth who is passing, he begins to cry out. The epithet $Ναζαρηνός$ ("of Nazareth") is used here as a simple means of identifying Jesus.[203] Bartimaeus's cry is "son of David, Jesus, have mercy on me."[204] The address of Jesus as "son of David" in connection with a plea for the healing of blindness has seemed odd to some, because, they

194 Gustav Volkmar, *Die Evangelien: oder, Marcus und die Synopsis der kanonischen und ausserkanonischen Evangelien nach dem ältesten Text mit historisch-exegetischem Commentar* (Leipzig: Fues [R. Reisland], 1870) 502–3; cited (and corrected to בר טמאא) by Hilgert, "Son of Timaeus," 191, 197 n. 24.

195 H. J. Holtzmann et al., *Hand-Commentar zum Neuen Testament*, vol. 1 (by Holtzmann), *Die Synoptiker. – Die Apostelgeschichte* (Freiburg i. B.; Mohr Siebeck, 1889) 228; cited by Hilgert, "Son of Timaeus," 191, 197 n. 25.

196 Wellhausen, 85.

197 Ibid.

198 *Midr. Qoh* 9.9 (42a); Str-B, 2:25. Cohen, however, points the name differently and transliterates "Ṭimi"; A. Cohen, trans., *Midrash Rabbah: Ecclesiastes* (London/New York: Soncino, 1983) 237.

199 Hilgert, "Son of Timaeus," 191.

200 Burton L. Mack, *Mark and Christian Origins: A Myth of Innocence* (Philadelphia: Fortress, 1988) 297 n. 2.

201 The part of the only papyrus MS of Mark, p⁴⁵, that contained 10:46 is not extant (Aland and Aland, 98). Codex Vaticanus (B) has a circumflex accent on the second syllable of $Βαρτειμαῖος$ (the accent is over the alpha, rather than the iota). The following uncials have no accent at all on $Βαρτιμαῖος$ or its

equivalent: Sinaiticus (א); Alexandrinus (A); Bezae (D), which reads $ΒΑΡΙΤΕΙΜΙΑΣ$; Freerianus (W) lacks the name $Βαρτιμαῖος$ or its equivalent; Coridethianus (Θ); the author has consulted facsimiles of all of these. A printed version of Ephraemi Syri Rescriptus (C) that represents a facsimile lacks an accent on this name. The minuscule 892 (ninth cent.) has a circumflex on the second iota of $Βαρτιμαῖος$, according to the facsimile that the author has seen. I am grateful to Terence J. Rogers for his help in consulting these MSS.

202 Taylor, 447; Pesch, 2:170–71. Pesch argues that these details are based on reliable historical memory.

203 It is used in the same way in 1:24; 14:67; 16:6. In 1:24 the epithet is used by the unclean spirit in its struggle with Jesus; see the commentary above.

204 On this cry as a "cry for help," "plea," or "expression of trust," see the section "Genre of 10:46b-52" above.

argue, the messiah of Israel was not expected to perform miracles.[205] Some of the miracles attributed to Jesus in Mark are reminiscent of those of Elijah and Elisha and thus fit the category of prophecy better than that of messianism.[206] At least by the time of *4 Ezra* (c. 100 CE), the expectation was current that the messiah would be associated with or even perform "wonders."[207] So Mark's portrayal of Bartimaeus's plea may reflect such Jewish expectations.[208]

It may be, however, that the address of Jesus as son of David is not linked primarily to Jesus' power to heal, but rather manifests Bartimaeus's prophetic gift. In Greek myths the association of blindness with compensatory supernatural gifts was common.[209] Thus, Bartimaeus's cry is a revelation of Jesus' identity, comparable to Peter's confession in 8:29.[210]

Robbins has argued that the basic story is pre-Markan, but that Mark added the reference to the son of David and thus created "the first instance of an explicit Son of David healing tradition."[211] His analysis of the text leads him to conclude that Mark formulated the story so as "to get a clear acclamation of Jesus as Son of David before he entered into Jerusalem."[212] If Mark composed the account himself, these arguments are all the more persuasive.

■ **48-49** The rebuke of "many" in the crowd has several effects in the narrative. On one level, it is reminiscent of Jesus' rebuke of his disciples in 8:30 that they not reveal his identity, that is, that he is the messiah as Peter has just stated in v. 29. The evocation of that rebuke recalls the theme of the secret of Jesus' identity.[213] On another level, the rebuke plays the role of an obstacle to healing that is typical of miracle stories.[214] Thus, the rebuke provides an opportunity for Mark to portray the man as crying out all the more, manifesting his confidence and trust that Jesus will heal him. At the same time, it allows Mark to have the man cry "son of David" again, thus emphasizing the epithet right before the entry into Jerusalem.[215] Analogous is the disciples' rebuke in 10:13 of those bringing children to Jesus. It provides the Markan Jesus with an occasion for displaying his affirmation of the importance and worth of children.

■ **49-50** In this context (v. 49), the verb φωνεῖν ("to call," "to summon") is synonymous with καλεῖν ("to call"). Another feature that indicates this account's affinity with call stories is the use of the verb ἀκολουθεῖν ("to follow") in v. 52 to describe Bartimaeus's response to Jesus.[216] When Jesus stops and calls Bartimaeus, the crowd's attitude changes from rebuke to encouragement. This is a typical feature of miracle stories.[217]

The detail of Bartimaeus throwing off his cloak could simply be a way of showing in narrative form the eagerness of his response to Jesus.[218] It may also be interpreted as a literary motif with symbolic value. It signifies that

205 Klaus Berger, "Die königlichen Messiastraditionen des Neuen Testaments," *NTS* 20 (1973) 1–44, esp. 3 and n. 12.

206 See the section of the introduction above "Jesus as Prophet."

207 *4 Ezra* 6:25-26; 7:26-29; 13:49-50; see the section of the introduction above "Jesus as Messiah."

208 Others have argued that "son of David" here is an allusion to Solomon; Duling, "Solomon, Exorcism," 235–52; Bruce Chilton, "Jesus *ben David*: Reflections on the *Davidssohnfrage*," *JSNT* 14 (1982) 88–112; James H. Charlesworth, "The Son of David: Solomon and Jesus (Mark 10.47)," in Peder Borgen and Søren Giversen, eds., *The New Testament and Hellenistic Judaism* (Peabody, MA: Hendrickson, 1995) 72–87; Stephen H. Smith, "The Function of the Son of David Tradition in Mark's Gospel," *NTS* 42 (1996) 523–39. For criticism of this interpretation, see Marcus, *Way of the Lord*, 151–52.

209 Todd Compton, "The Trial of the Satirist: Poetic *Vitae* (Aesop, Archilochus, Homer) as Background

for Plato's *Apology*," *American Journal of Philology* 111 (1990) 330–47, esp. 343 n. 41.

210 Robbins, "Healing of Blind Bartimaeus," 227.

211 Ibid., 234. Achtemeier concluded that Mark could not have added the address of Jesus as son of David because of the "negative trajectory on Jesus' davidic sonship in Mark 11 and 12" ("'And He Followed Him,'" 130–31). This argument is not persuasive. See the commentary on 11:1-10 and 12:35-37 below.

212 Robbins, "Healing of Blind Bartimaeus," 236.

213 See "Excursus: The Messianic Secret" in the commentary on 1:24 above.

214 See the section "Genre of 10:46b-52" above.

215 Robbins, "Healing of Blind Bartimaeus," 235–36.

216 See the section "Genre of 10:46b-52" above.

217 Ibid.

218 Nineham, ad loc.; Robbins, "Healing of Blind Bartimaeus," 232–33.

the one called may be required to leave something behind. From that perspective it is related to the description of Peter and Andrew leaving their nets (1:18), the sons of Zebedee leaving their father (1:20), and Peter and the rest leaving everything to follow Jesus (10:28). It contrasts with the man who would not leave behind his many possessions (10:21-22). A cloak ($i\mu\acute{\alpha}\tau\iota o\nu$) is one of the very few possessions that a beggar would have. His leaving it behind is thus analogous to the widow who contributed "her whole livelihood" to the service of God in the temple (12:44).[219]

■ **51-52** Jesus' question in v. 51, "What do you want me to do for you?" ($\tau\acute{\iota}$ $\sigma o\iota$ $\vartheta\acute{\epsilon}\lambda\epsilon\iota\varsigma$ $\pi o\iota\acute{\eta}\sigma\omega;$), is reminiscent of his question to the sons of Zebedee in v. 36, "What do you want me to do for you?" ($\tau\acute{\iota}$ $\vartheta\acute{\epsilon}\lambda\epsilon\tau\acute{\epsilon}$ ($\mu\epsilon$) $\pi o\iota\acute{\eta}\sigma\omega$ $\acute{\upsilon}\mu\hat{\iota}\nu;$).[220] The similarity between the two leads the audiences to compare the two requests. Bartimaeus simply asks that his sight be restored, whereas James and John ask for status of the highest honor after Jesus. Again, James and John are cast as negative models and the blind man as a positive model.

In his response to Jesus, the blind man addresses him as $\acute{\rho}\alpha\beta\beta o\upsilon\nu\acute{\iota}$ ("rabbouni" or "my master"). This term is a variant of $\acute{\rho}\alpha\beta\beta\acute{\iota}$ ("rabbi" or "my master"). Originally this term was used for anyone occupying a high or respected position. Its use signified that the addressee held a position higher than the speaker. At least by the time of the Tannaim, the earliest rabbinical leaders, it was used for "teacher." In the Gospels it is sometimes used as a title of respect and sometimes to mean "teacher."[221] Since the blind man is "called" by Jesus and then "follows" him, it is likely that "teacher" is the meaning here.

Jesus' reply in v. 52, "Go, your faith has saved you" ($\acute{\upsilon}\pi\alpha\gamma\epsilon$, $\acute{\eta}$ $\pi\acute{\iota}\sigma\tau\iota\varsigma$ $\sigma o\upsilon$ $\sigma\acute{\epsilon}\sigma\omega\kappa\acute{\epsilon}\nu$ $\sigma\epsilon$), is similar to aspects of other miracle stories in Mark. The same formula of dismissal, "go" ($\acute{\upsilon}\pi\alpha\gamma\epsilon$), appears in the healing of the leper (1:44), the healing of the paralytic (2:11), and the exorcism of the Gerasene demoniac (5:19). The whole reply here is similar to the two-part statement of Jesus to the woman who had the flow of blood. He first says, "Daughter, your faith has saved you" ($\vartheta\upsilon\gamma\acute{\alpha}\tau\eta\rho$, $\acute{\eta}$ $\pi\acute{\iota}\sigma\tau\iota\varsigma$ $\sigma o\upsilon$ $\sigma\acute{\epsilon}\sigma\omega\kappa\acute{\epsilon}\nu$ $\sigma\epsilon$), and then "Go in peace, etc." ($\acute{\upsilon}\pi\alpha\gamma\epsilon$ $\epsilon\acute{\iota}\varsigma$ $\epsilon\acute{\iota}\rho\acute{\eta}\nu\eta\nu$, $\kappa\tau\lambda$.) (see also 7:29). This formula of dismissal is one of the typical features of the genre.[222]

The statement that the man immediately regained his sight is the announcement of the event of healing, a typical feature of a miracle story.[223] The hybrid character of this story is shown by the clause that follows this announcement: "and he followed him on the way" ($\kappa\alpha\grave{\iota}$ $\acute{\eta}\kappa o\lambda o\acute{\upsilon}\vartheta\epsilon\iota$ $\alpha\dot{\upsilon}\tau\hat{\omega}$ $\acute{\epsilon}\nu$ $\tau\hat{\eta}$ $\acute{o}\delta\hat{\omega}$). This simple statement contrasts with the urgent request of the healed Gerasene demoniac "that he might be with [Jesus]" ($\acute{\iota}\nu\alpha$ $\mu\epsilon\tau'$ $\alpha\dot{\upsilon}\tau o\hat{\upsilon}$ $\hat{\eta}$), which is rejected by Jesus (5:18-19). "Being with" Jesus is the prerogative of the Twelve (3:14). The demoniac seeks a position that is not planned for him, thus, like the sons of Zebedee, he must be corrected. In addition, the demoniac's request comes at the time of Jesus' epiphany to the public and before his teaching about suffering discipleship. Although Bartimaeus had not heard that teaching as a character in the narrative, the audiences know that "to follow Jesus on the way" means to follow him to suffering and death.

---

219 R. Alan Culpepper, "Mark 10:50: Why Mention the Garment?" *JBL* 101 (1982) 131–32.

220 On the construction of the Greek, see the note on the trans. of 10:36 above.

221 Eduard Lohse, "$\acute{\rho}\alpha\beta\beta\acute{\iota}$, $\acute{\rho}\alpha\beta\beta o\upsilon\nu\acute{\iota}$," *TDNT* 6 (1968)

961–65. On the affinity of this story with call stories, see the section "Genre of 10:46b-52" above.

222 See the section "Genre of 10:46b-52" above.

223 See the commentary on 1:40-45 above.

11

11:1-11 The Entry into Jerusalem

1/ And when they drew near[a] to Jerusalem, to Bethphage and Bethany, to the Mount of Olives, he sent two of his disciples 2/ and said to them, "Go into the village which is before you, and immediately as you enter it, you will find a young donkey tied up, upon which no human being has ever sat; untie it and bring it. 3/ And if anyone says to you, 'Why are you doing this?' say, 'The Lord needs it and will send it back here immediately.'"[b] 4/ And they went away and found a young donkey tied at a door outside on the street and they untied it. 5/ And some of those who were standing there said to them, "What are you doing, untying the donkey?" 6/ They then said to them as Jesus had said, and they allowed them (to take the donkey). 7/ And they brought the donkey to Jesus and laid their cloaks on it, and he sat on it. 8/ And many spread their cloaks on the road, and others cut leaves from the fields.[c] 9/ And those going ahead and those following were crying out, "Hosanna![d] Blessed is he who comes in the name of the Lord! 10/ Blessed is the coming kingdom of our father David! Hosanna in the highest heights!"[e] 11/ And he went into Jerusalem to the temple precinct and, after he had looked around at everything, since the hour was already late, he went out to Bethany with the Twelve.

a D it sy^p read ἤγγιζεν, "(And when) he drew near," rather than ἐγγίζουσιν, "they drew near," lit., "they draw near." The former reading seems to reflect a deliberate change to prepare for the third person singular verbal forms that follow. This shift from plural to singular, however, is typical of Markan style; see Turner, "Marcan Usage," 26 (1925) 230 (Elliott, *Language and Style*, 41).

b ℵ B C*vid D Δ et al. disagree on the order of the words αὐτὸν ἀποστέλλει πάλιν ("will send it back"), and Δ omits αὐτὸν ("it"), but all of these MSS include πάλιν ("back") and imply that this clause is part of what the disciples should say to the questioner. A C² G W et al. omit πάλιν ("back") and imply that this clause is part of Jesus' instructions to the disciples, so that one should translate "say 'The Lord needs it,' and he will send it here immediately." One could argue that πάλιν ("back") is an addition, since it precedes the verb in some MSS and follows it in others. Such an addition may have been made to solve a perceived moral problem in Jesus' conscription of an animal. But no such addition was made to the parallel in Matt 21:3, which also lacks πάλιν ("back"), and such differences in the order of words often occur in Mark as stylistic variants. It is more likely, then, that the reading with πάλιν ("back") is the earliest recoverable one. This rather banal statement was then rewritten by Matthew to create a more dramatic point to Jesus' statement. The reading without πάλιν ("back") then arose, either under the influence of the text of Matthew or as an analogous "improvement." See Taylor, ad loc.; and Metzger, *Textual Commentary*, 92.

c The earliest recoverable reading, κόψαντες ἐκ τῶν ἀγρῶν, "cut (leaves) from the fields," lit., "having cut (leaves) from the fields," attested by ℵ B (C) L et al., is somewhat awkward and elliptical. The reading ἔκοπτον ἐκ τῶν δένδρων καὶ ἐστρώννυον εἰς τὴν ὁδόν, "were cutting (leaves) from the trees and spreading (them) on the road," attested by A (D Θ) f$^{1.13}$ 𝔐 et al., represents a secondary clarification, perhaps inspired by the parallel in Matt 21:8.

d This simple exclamation, a transliteration of the Aramaic words נָא הוֹשַׁע or the Hebrew נָא הוֹשִׁיעָה (both meaning, originally, "Save, please!"), is probably the earliest reading. See the commentary on v. 9 below. It is omitted in D W et al., probably under the influence of the parallel in Luke 19:37-38. In other MSS (Θ f^{13} et al.), it is expanded with the words τῷ ὑψίστῳ ("to the Most High").

e If one were to presuppose the transliterated Aramaic or Hebrew, the whole phrase (ὡσαννὰ ἐν τοῖς ὑψίστοις) would mean "Save, please, (you who are) in the highest (heights or heavens)!" Two other readings arose either because the transliterated Aramaic or Hebrew was no longer intelligible or under the influence of the parallel in Luke 19:37-38. Some MSS (W 28. 700 sy^s) read εἰρήνη ("peace") instead of ὡσαννά ("Hosanna!"). Others, Θ (f^1) et al., have the same sub- stitution but add, after εἰρήνη ("peace"), the words ἐν οὐρανῷ καὶ δόξα ("in heaven and glory").

Narrative Unity of 11:1—13:37

A new section begins with 11:1 because it follows the self-contained middle section of Mark with its two framing stories about the healing of the blind (8:22—10:52). Another reason is that 11:1 marks the first time that Jesus enters the environs of Jerusalem.[1] This new section contains two significant events: the entry into Jerusalem (11:1-11) and the actions in the temple precinct (11:15-19). Apart from those, the focus is on Jesus' proclamation and teaching in Jerusalem, some of it addressed only to the disciples (11:20-25; 13:3-37) and the rest to the public. The passion narrative then begins with 14:1. The literary unity of chaps. 11–13 is indicated by the framing references to the Mount of Olives.[2]

The Historical Reliability of 11:1-11

The historicity of this passage has been doubted for several reasons. Those who believe, like William Wrede, that there was nothing messianic about Jesus and his activities conclude that the story is part of the attempt to transfer the later belief that Jesus was the messiah into the narration of the events of his lifetime. Although Mark does not explicitly quote Zechariah 9, the narrative of Jesus' entry has several points of contact with that text. So some argue that the whole scene has been created as a fulfillment of the older passage read as prophecy.[3] Others infer from the accounts about messianic pretenders and prophetic leaders in Josephus's works that, if the incident described here had actually occurred, the Romans would have intervened immediately.[4]

In the second half of the twentieth century, many scholars disagreed with Wrede and argued that Jesus was executed as a messianic pretender or a "would-be 'king of the Jews.'"[5] The Markan portrayal of Jesus' entry fits this charge and can explain why Jesus was so executed.[6] If Zechariah 9 was known to the evangelists, it was probably known to Jesus as well. Jesus could well have arranged his entry so that it recalled Zechariah 9 for all those present.[7] If vv. 7-10 more or less accurately describe how Jesus entered Jerusalem, the Romans may not have acted immediately because Jesus and those hailing him did not take up arms or commit any acts of violence. Two of the messianic pretenders in the period following the death of Herod the Great, Simon and Athronges, engaged in violent activities against the Jewish ruling class and the Romans. Simon was beheaded by Gratus, a Roman officer. Athronges and his brothers were caught and taken prisoner by Gratus and Ptolemy, a friend of Herod the Great.[8]

---

1   Cook, *Structure*, 159, 346.
2   Dowd, *Prayer*, 37.
3   Friedrich Karl Feigel, *Der Einfluss des Weissagungsbeweises und anderer Motive auf die Leidensgeschichte: Ein Beitrag zur Evangelienkritik* (Tübingen: Mohr Siebeck, 1910) 22–24. Bultmann argued that the historical event of Jesus' entry became a messianic legend under the influence of Zechariah 9 (*History*, 261–62).
4   Cf. Sanders's formulation of the problem (*Jesus and Judaism*, 306); see also the list of examples of Roman intervention in David R. Catchpole, "The 'Triumphal' Entry," in Ernst Bammel and Charles F. D. Moule, eds., *Jesus and the Politics of His Day* (Cambridge/New York: Cambridge University Press, 1984) 319–34, esp. 332.
5   The former formulation is that of Sanders (*Jesus and Judaism*, 294); the latter is mine (Yarbro Collins,

"From Noble Death," 487–88). See also the literature cited in both works.
6   The accounts of Matthew and Luke fit even better; Matt 21:9 quotes Zech 9:9, which contains the word "king" (βασιλεύς) and Luke has "the whole multitude of the disciples" acclaim him as "king" (βασιλεύς). John combines both of these elements (12:13-15). On the "fit" between the entry and the execution, see Sanders, *Jesus and Judaism*, 306; Catchpole, "'Triumphal' Entry," 328; but Catchpole is not persuaded by this argument (330).
7   Sanders concluded that Jesus "deliberately managed" the entry (with its allusion to Zechariah 9) "to symbolize the coming kingdom and his own role in it," but only for the sake of the disciples; it did not "attract large public attention" (*Jesus and Judaism*, 308).
8   See the section of the introduction "Jesus as Messiah" above.

After the death of Jesus, while Fadus was procurator of Judea, a prophet named Theudas led a large number of people out to the Jordan River, promising that the river would be parted at his command. Although there is no evidence that this group was armed or committed violent acts, they took their possessions with them and thus were apparently well organized and had a purpose that could have been viewed by the Romans as rebellious. Fadus sent a squadron (500 or 1000 men) of cavalry after them, and Theudas was beheaded.[9] In 56 CE, a prophet whom Josephus calls "the Egyptian" led a large crowd to the Mount of Olives and asserted that at his command the walls of Jerusalem would fall down. Josephus says that he intended to set himself up as a tyrant; this may be a pejorative paraphrase of a messianic claim and its acceptance by a large number of the people. The procurator Felix attacked the Egyptian and his followers, killing four hundred and taking two hundred prisoners.[10]

In light of the accounts of these two prophetic figures, one could argue that Jesus' entry into Jerusalem did not lead to Roman intervention for one or more of the following reasons: (1) the crowd hailing Jesus was not as large as those following Theudas and the Egyptian; (2) the crowd at Jesus' entry assembled spontaneously and was not an organized movement; (3) Pontius Pilate, as procurator, had a different way of responding to such an event than his successors had.

It is clear that the story about the finding of the donkey, as it stands in Mark, has legendary and miraculous features.[11] Furthermore, even if the rest of the story is based on historical memory, one cannot be certain that any one of its specific details is historically reliable.

The Genre of Mark 11:1-11

The account of Jesus' entry into Jerusalem in Mark has affinities with accounts of certain kinds of processions in ancient literary and inscriptional texts. Catchpole compared Mark 11:1-10 with "a family of stories detailing the celebratory entry to a city by a hero figure who has previously achieved his triumph."[12] He referred to the ceremonial entry of the newly anointed King Solomon into Jerusalem, the arrival of a king in procession in Zech 9:9-10, Josephus's account of the entry of Alexander the Great into Jerusalem, the reception of Apollonius in Jerusalem, the triumphal returns of Judas Maccabeus to Jerusalem after military victories, the entry of Jonathan into Askalon and of Simon into Gaza (or Gazara), the celebration following Simon's conquest of the citadel in Jerusalem, Marcus Agrippa's reception by the people of Jerusalem, Archelaus's procession as (provisional) king into Jerusalem and other similar passages.[13] He concluded that these stories have the following standard features, which are shared by Mark's account:

(a) A victory already achieved and a status already recognised for the central person. (b) A formal and ceremonial entry. (c) Greetings and/or acclamations together with invocations of God. (d) Entry to the city climaxed by entry to the Temple, if the city in question has one. (e) Cultic activity, either positive (e.g. offering of sacrifice), or negative (e.g. expulsion of objectionable persons and the cleansing away of uncleanness).[14]

---

9   Josephus *Ant.* 20.5.1 §§97–99; Horsley and Hanson, *Bandits,* 164–67.

10   Josephus *Ant.* 20.8.6 §170; *Bell.* 2.13.5 §§261–63; Horsley and Hanson, *Bandits,* 167–70.

11   Bultmann, *History,* 261; Hendrikus Boers, *Who Was Jesus? The Historical Jesus and the Synoptic Gospels* (New York: Harper & Row, 1989) 86–87.

12   Catchpole, "'Triumphal' Entry," 319. In the Roman triumphal procession and related rituals, the man celebrating the triumph rode in a chariot drawn by four horses, not sitting on a horse or a similar type of animal, as Jesus does in the Gospels; see Ernst Badian, "Triumph," *OCD* 1554; H. S. Versnel, *Triumphus: An Inquiry into the Origin, Development and Meaning of the Roman Triumph* (Leiden: Brill, 1970) index s.v. *quadriga.*

13   Catchpole, "'Triumphal' Entry," 319–21; Solomon: 1 Kgs 1:32-40; Alexander: Josephus *Ant.* 11.8.4–5 §§325–39; Apollonius: 2 Macc 4:21-22; Judas: 1 Macc 4:19-25; *Ant.* 12.7.4 §312; 1 Macc 5:45-54; *Ant.* 12.8.5 §348–49; Jonathan: 1 Macc 10:86; Simon: 1 Macc 13:43-48, 49-51; Agrippa: *Ant.* 16.2.1 §§12–15; Archelaus: *Ant.* 17.8.2–17.9.5 §§194–239.

14   Catchpole, "'Triumphal' Entry," 321.

Contra Reimarus and S. G. F. Brandon, Catchpole argued that Jesus was not aiming at a secular kingdom, since his "already achieved victory" was gained by healings, not social or political conquest.[15] He concluded that the story of Jesus' "triumphal entry" and the account of his actions in the temple precinct "have been welded into a single whole under the combined influence of an already existing Jewish pattern and a post-Easter christological conviction."[16]

It is questionable that Mark presents Jesus as having already achieved a victory. His status as messiah has been recognized by Peter, as Catchpole notes, but he has not yet undergone the necessary suffering, nor is he already exercising the role of messiah (cf. 14:62). But Catchpole has rightly emphasized the affinities of Mark with the other passages regarding the formal and ceremonial entry, the greetings and/or acclamations, and the role of temples and cultic activity.

Paul Duff, following Werner Kelber and especially Jacob Myers, argued that the entry in Mark is not triumphal and that there is no actual entry, except for the anticlimactic v. 11. The episode is "street theater," giving intentionally conflicting messianic signals in order to provoke the readers to reconsider their presuppositions about messiahship, discipleship, and the kingdom of God.[17] He argued that Mark awakens expectations of a triumphal entry with allusions to Zechariah 14 and by playing on the structure and elements of "contemporary Greco-Roman entrance processions." Mark draws on the readers' knowledge and/or experience of typical Greek and Roman entrance processions in order to highlight allusions to the divine warrior of Zechariah 14.[18] The examples of entrance processions that he cites are Josephus's account of Alexander's entry into Jerusalem (also cited by Catchpole), Antony's entry into Ephesus, the entry of King Attalus of Pergamum into Athens, and the arrival of Demetrius Poliocertes in Athens.[19] He also compared Mark's account with the Roman triumph, a subtype of entrance procession. He constructed a list of typical features from a variety of accounts by Greek and Roman writers and included Josephus's account of the joint triumph of Vespasian and Titus after the defeat of Judea.[20] He concluded that, although Mark portrays Jesus at first as a conquering ruler who has come to take possession of his city and temple, "this procession abruptly and comically ends." Instead of taking possession of the city and instituting his rule, Jesus just looks around and then leaves the city since it was late in the day. Duff argued further that Jesus' actions in the temple precinct (vv. 15-19) constitute a "symbolic appropriation," but with a twist.[21]

Duff seems to overgeneralize some features of narratives about entrance and to overemphasize an alleged "ritual of appropriation." Yet he rightly discerns the anticlimactic character of v. 11. That character, however, is open to other interpretations than his own.[22]

Brent Kinman has argued that the celebratory welcome ($\pi\alpha\rho o\upsilon\sigma\iota\alpha$) is a better analogy to Jesus' entry into Jerusalem than the Roman triumph: "The arrival of a royal or other dignitary was an occasion for an ostentatious display designed to court the favor and/or placate the wrath of the visiting celebrity."[23] This display began with the procession of the magistrates and citizens of the city, especially the elite, going forth from the city, often in festal clothing, to meet the dignitary well outside of the city walls. It continued with speeches of welcome given by selected members of the delegation. Finally, the guest was escorted into the city by those who had gone out to meet him. The $\pi\alpha\rho o\upsilon\sigma\iota\alpha$ often ended with a visit to the local temple. Among his examples are the visit of

---

15 Ibid., 322–23.

16 Ibid., 334.

17 Paul Brooks Duff, "The March of the Divine Warrior and the Advent of the Greco-Roman King: Mark's Account of Jesus' Entry into Jerusalem," *JBL* 111 (1992) 55–71, esp. 55–56.

18 Ibid., 56.

19 Ibid., 58–61. Alexander: Josephus *Ant.* 11.8.4–5 §§325–39; Antony: Plutarch *Vit. Antony* 24.3–4; Attalus: Polybius 16.25.1–9; Demetrius: Plutarch *Vit. Demetr.*, 8.4–9.1.

20 Duff, "March of the Divine Warrior," 62–63; Josephus *Bell.* 7.5.4–6 §§123–57.

21 Duff, "March of the Divine Warrior," 67–68.

22 See the discussion of Brent Kinman's work immediately below and the commentary on v. 11 below.

23 Brent Kinman, "Parousia, Jesus' 'A-Triumphal' Entry, and the Fate of Jerusalem (Luke 19:28-44)," *JBL* 118 (1999) 279–94; citation from 281.

King Attalus to his capital city of Pergamum in the second century BCE (also cited by Duff), Mithridates' reception by the cities of Asia Minor after his victory over the Romans in the first century BCE, Cicero's reception in the province of Asia, the reception of Demetrius by Athens (also cited by Duff), and the reception of Alexander by Jerusalem (also cited by Catchpole and Duff).[24] To these examples could be added the celebratory welcome of Vespasian by the people of Rome (an event distinct from the celebration of his joint triumph with Titus).[25]

The failure to extend the customary greeting could have dire consequences. Kinman pointed out that a Roman magistrate besieged the city of Vesontio because it did not receive him properly. At Florus's behest, the chief priests in Jerusalem warned the people to go out and meet courteously the two cohorts of Roman troops coming up from Caesarea lest the procurator Florus have reason to wreak further violence upon the city.[26] Kinman then showed that, in the context of normal celebratory welcomes in the ancient world, the response to Jesus' approach to Jerusalem in Luke is nothing short of insulting. The elite of the city do not go forth to meet him. Although he is a king, he is not so received by the leaders of the city; his entry is "a-triumphal." Luke makes plain the link between the failure to receive Jesus properly and the destruction of the city.[27] Although Mark's text is not as clear as Luke's on this point, ancient audiences familiar with the typical features of the celebratory welcoming of dignitaries may well have interpreted the anticlimax of v. 11 as due to the failure of the leaders of the city to welcome Jesus.

Comment

■ **1** As noted above, the narration of Jesus' and his entourage's drawing near to Jerusalem marks a major geographical shift in Mark and the beginning of a new section.[28] They do not go immediately into the city, however, but stop at a location that Mark identifies as "Bethphage and Bethany" and "the Mount of Olives." The Mount of Olives is part of a ridge of hills opposite Jerusalem on the other side of the Kidron Valley. The ridge has three main summits, Mount Scopus in the north, the Mount of Olives directly across from the temple mount, and the Mount of Corruption or the Mount of Offence, above the village of Silwan.[29] Since Jesus and his retinue are coming from Jericho (10:46), the narrative presupposes that they approach Jerusalem from the east on an ancient road that crossed the ridge south of the summit of Mount Scopus and north of the summit of the Mount of Olives.[30] In v. 2, Jesus sends two disciples "into the village which is before [them]." This is apparently Bethphage, whose location has been identified as south of the ancient road.[31] Mark adds the name of the village of Bethany, probably because it was better known.[32] The site is that of the present-day village of el ʿAzariyeh, which lies on the downslope of the ridge, southeast of Bethphage.[33] Thus both villages lay to the left of those journeying toward Jerusalem on the ancient road.

It may be that the names of the two villages have symbolic meaning or play on words in the text of Mark. The name of Bethany may have signified "House of Ananiah."[34] Mark may have played on the similarity of this proper name to the word עני ("poor, afflicted, humble").[35] The Onomastica inteprets Bethany as בית עניה.[36] This phrase could be translated "house of the [fem.] afflicted one." The form עניה ("afflicted one" [fem.]) occurs twice in Isaiah with reference to personified Jerusalem (Isa 51:21; 54:11). One of these instances occurs in the context of the divine promise "to set your stones in antimony, and lay your foundations with sap-

24 Ibid., 281–83. Attalus: Polybius 16.25.1–9; Mithridates: Diodorus Siculus 37.26; Cicero *Att.* 5.16 (letter 109 to Atticus); Demetrius: Plutarch *Vit. Demetr.,* 8.4–9.1; Alexander: Josephus *Ant.* 11.8.4–5 §§325–39.
25 Josephus *Bell.* 7.4.1 §§63–74.
26 Josephus *Bell.* 2.15.3 §§318–24; Kinman, "Parousia," 283.
27 Kinman, "Parousia," 290–94.
28 See the section "Narrative Unity of 11:1–13:37" above.
29 The Mount of Corruption or Mount of Offence

takes its name from the statement in 2 Kgs 23:13 that Solomon worshiped Astarte, Chemosh, and Milcom there (Jack Finegan, *The Archaeology of the New Testament* [rev. ed.; Princeton, NJ: Princeton University Press, 1992] 155).
30 Ibid., 152, 154.
31 Ibid., 154, 162.
32 Luke follows Mark in giving the names of both villages (Luke 19:29); Matthew mentions only Bethphage (21:1).
33 Finegan, *Archaeology*, 154–57.

phires. I will make your pinnacle of rubies, your gates of jewels, and all your wall of precious stones" (Isa 54:11-12 NRSV). This potential play on words is interesting in light of the charge in the trial before the Judean council that Jesus said he would destroy the current temple and build another, not made with hands, in three days.[37] More importantly, there may be a play on the word עני ("humble"), which is used in the MT of Zech 9:9 to describe the king.

The name Bethphage means "house of early figs."[38] The allusion to early figs may be related to the fig tree that Jesus curses on the following day.[39]

The depiction of Jesus as entering the city from the Mount of Olives may constitute an allusion to scripture.[40] According to Zechariah 14, the theophany of the divine warrior will take place on the Mount of Olives and initiate a radically new situation.[41] In the interpretation of this divine theophany in the late Second Temple period, it was probably associated with the activity of an agent of God, a prophet or the messiah. This hypothesis can explain the actions of the Egyptian prophet.[42]

■ **2-3** As noted above, Jesus sends two of his disciples into a village, probably Bethphage.[43] In v. 2, Jesus pre-dicts that they will find a "foal" ($\pi\hat{\omega}\lambda o\varsigma$). This word can refer to a young animal of any kind, depending on the context. Bauer argued that, when the noun is unqualified, it refers to a horse of any age.[44] It is unlikely, however, that Mark would depict the presence of a horse in a small village on the Mount of Olives. The context makes it much more likely that the foal of a donkey ($\check{o}\nu o\varsigma$) is meant.

In the second millennium BCE, human kings and deities were depicted as riding on donkeys. At that time, the donkey was a vehicle fit for a king.[45] The poem of Gen 49:1-27 deals with the royal destiny of Judah and associates him with a vigorous young male ass or donkey (MT עיר; LXX $\pi\hat{\omega}\lambda o\varsigma$) and with the foal of a she-ass (MT בני אתנו; LXX $\dot{o}$ $\pi\hat{\omega}\lambda o\varsigma$ $\tau\hat{\eta}\varsigma$ $\check{o}\nu o\upsilon$), reflecting the tradition of the donkey as a royal mount (Gen 49:11). Zech 9:9 depicts the king as riding on a donkey (MT חמור; LXX $\dot{\upsilon}\pi o\zeta\dot{\upsilon}\gamma\iota o\nu$), on a young male ass, the foal of a she-ass (MT עיר בן אתנות; LXX $\pi\hat{\omega}\lambda o\varsigma$ $\nu\acute{e}o\varsigma$). The second term in the synonymously parallel expression alludes to Gen 49:11 and thus evokes the ancient royal tradition.[46] The first term, however, as the translation in the LXX rightly indicates, signifies an ordinary beast of draught

---

34 Ibid., 155.

35 Bedenbender, "Orte mitten im Meer," 40. He interprets Bethany as "*bet ʿani*" ("house of the poor [man]").

36 BAGD, s.v. Βηθανία.

37 See the commentary on 14:58 below.

38 BDB, s.v. פגג for the translation "early figs"; Bedenbender interprets Bethphage as "house of figs" ("Orte mitten im Meer," 40); BAGD as "house of unripe figs" (s.v. Βηθφαγή).

39 See the commentary on vv. 12-14 below.

40 Henk Jan de Jonge considers the hypothesis of an allusion to Zech 14:4 in Mark 11:1 doubtful, but worth considering ("The Cleansing of the Temple in Mark 11:15 and Zechariah 14:21," in Christopher M. Tuckett, ed., *The Book of Zechariah and Its Influence* [London: Ashgate, 2003] 87–99, esp. 87–88).

41 I agree with Duff that there is an allusion to Zechariah 14 here, but I disagree with some elements of his interpretation, e.g., that the purpose of the rending of the Mount of Olives is to prepare a highway for Yahweh and his holy ones to enter Jerusalem ("March of the Divine Warrior," 58, 66). On the contrary, the purpose of the rending is to provide a means for Yahweh's people to escape from Jerusalem before Yahweh destroys the enemy (Mey-ers and Meyers, *Zechariah 9–14*, 421, 424; David L. Petersen, *Zechariah 9–14 and Malachi: A Commentary* [OTL; Louisville: Westminster John Knox, 1995], 142–43). Zechariah 14 does not describe Yahweh's entrance into the holy city in procession as Duff claims ("March of the Divine Warrior," 58, 66). Yahweh comes (v. 5c) to do battle (Meyers and Meyers, *Zechariah 9–14*, 429; Petersen, *Zechariah 9–14*, 143).

42 See the section "The Historical Reliability of 11:1-11" above; Josephus *Bell.* 2.13.5 §262; *Ant.* 20.8.6 §169; Bultmann, *History*, 261.

43 See the commentary on v. 1 above.

44 BAGD, s.v. πῶλος. Bauer's thesis has been refuted by Heinz-Wolfgang Kuhn, "Das Reittier Jesu in der Einzugsgeschichte des Markusevangeliums," *ZNW* 50 (1959) 82–91; Kinman, "Parousia," 286 n. 25. J. Duncan M. Derrett argued that the animal was an ass, not a horse, since horses were too valuable to be kept in the open street ("Law in the New Testament: The Palm Sunday Colt," *NovT* 13 [1971] 241–58, esp. 243–44).

45 Meyers and Meyers, *Zechariah 9–14*, 130; Petersen, *Zechariah 9–14*, 58.

46 Meyers and Meyers, *Zechariah 9–14*, 129–30.

or burden. This mount fits with the description of the king as עני (LXX πραΰς, "humble").[47]

The special arrangements described for obtaining a donkey imply that Jesus deliberately chose to *ride* into the city, rather than to walk. After the address of Jesus by Bartimaeus as "son of David," the choice of riding into Jerusalem on a donkey, rather than walking, is a nonverbal way of making a messianic claim.[48] This interpretation is supported by the benediction of the crowd in v. 10.

It is quite striking that Jesus rides a donkey and not a horse or even a mule. In keeping with the instruction about a leadership of service in 10:41-45, Jesus does not ride a horse or in a chariot, as a Roman celebrating a triumph would.[49] Nor does he ride a mule to recall the narrative about the succession of Solomon to the throne of David (1 Kgs 1:33).[50] Rather, he rides a donkey that evokes both the royal tradition of Gen 49:11 and the humility (or the gentle and benign exercise of power) of Zech 9:9.[51]

The prediction in v. 2 that, as soon as they enter the village, they will see a young donkey tied up on which no one has ever sat manifests Jesus' prophetic powers (cf. 14:12-16).[52] The description of the animal as being tied is perhaps an allusion to Gen 49:11, a royal passage open to a messianic reading.[53] The stipulation that the donkey should be one upon which no human being has ever sat is analogous to the requirement that the red heifer, which is to be used in the ritual of cleansing from the impurity resulting from contact with a corpse, must be one on which no yoke has been laid. The logic is that an animal that is to be used for a sacred purpose should not have been put to any profane use (Num 19:2; cf. Deut 21:3; 1 Sam 6:7).[54] In some cases the animal was to be sacrificed (cf. 1 Sam 6:7 with 6:14).[55] The command to untie the animal and to bring it to Jesus implies that it will be used for some sacred purpose.

Alternatively, or additionally, the detail that the donkey has never been ridden may have been inspired by Zech 9:9 LXX, which says that the king would come mounted on a "new [or young] foal" (πῶλος νέος).[56] According to the Mishnah, no one else is allowed to ride upon the animal that the king rides (*m. Sanh.* 2.5).[57]

In v. 3, Jesus gives further instructions. If anyone challenges them about taking the donkey, they are to say "The Lord needs it and will send it back here immediately" (ὁ κύριος αὐτοῦ χρείαν ἔχει καὶ εὐθὺς αὐτὸν ἀποστέλλει πάλιν ὧδε).[58] The second clause, about sending the animal back, makes clear that the first clause should not be translated "Its owner needs it."[59] The phrase "the Lord" (ὁ κύριος), therefore, is an honorary title for Jesus. The implication is—and v. 6 bears this out—that Jesus is well enough known and well enough respected that the people of Bethphage would allow him to borrow a young donkey. The language may imply that, as the messiah, he has the right to requisition anything he needs.[60] Something similar is implied in 2:23-28. In 2:25, the expression "to have need" (χρείαν ἔχειν) is used with David as the subject. Because he had need of

---

47 On the usage of πραότης/πραΰτης to signify "a populist bearing, a gentle and benign exercise of government," see Donald Dale Walker, *Paul's Offer of Leniency (2 Cor 10:1): Populist Ideology and Rhetoric in a Pauline Letter Fragment* (WUNT 2.152; Tübingen: Mohr Siebeck, 2002) 338.

48 Hooker, *Signs*, 43–44.

49 Horses (and chariots) are associated with kings and military actions in the Hebrew Bible; Hag 2:22; Meyers and Meyers, *Zechariah 9–14*, 129. On the chariot in the Roman triumph, see the discussion of Catchpole's interpretation in "The Genre of Mark 11:1-11" above.

50 MT פרדה ("mule"); LXX ἡμίονος ("mule"). Mordechai Cogan concludes that the mule was favored by the "upper class" in Israel (*1 Kings: A New Translation with Introduction and Commentary* [AB 10; New York: Doubleday, 2001] 161).

51 De Jonge considers the allusion to Zech 9:9 in Mark 11:2, 7 to be probable ("Cleansing of the Temple," 87). See also the discussion by Kuhn, "Das Reittier Jesu," 90.

52 Bultmann referred to both of these stories as legendary and as similar to motifs in fairy tales (*History*, 161).

53 Cf. 4Q252 5:1-4; Kuhn, "Das Reittier Jesu," 86–87.

54 Levine, *Numbers 1–20*, 461.

55 Homer *Il.* 6.93–94; for references to Latin literature, in addition to these texts, see Klostermann, 113.

56 Catchpole, "'Triumphal' Entry," 324.

57 Catchpole, "'Triumphal' Entry," 324.

58 See the note on the trans. of v. 3 above.

59 Contra Taylor (455) and Derrett, "Palm Sunday Colt," 246. The word αὐτοῦ should be taken as the complement of χρεία, not as modifying κύριος; see BAGD, s.v. χρεία.

60 Ethelbert Stauffer argued that the use of the terms κύριος ("lord" or "master") and χρεία ("need") are

it, he was allowed to take the holy bread of the Presence, even though normally only priests were allowed to eat it. The saying about the Son of Man being Lord (κύριος) of the Sabbath in v. 28 implies, among other things, that the messiah, like the king, "may break through [the private domain of any man] to make himself a road and none may protest against him: the kings's road has no prescribed measure" (*m. Sanh.* 2.4).[61]

■ **4-6** The disciples go and do as Jesus instructed them. They find a donkey tied up. Details are given to make the scene present before the inner eyes of the audience: the animal is tied at a door outside on the street. They untie it, and some of those who are standing there ask what they are doing. They reply as Jesus had commanded them and are allowed to take the animal.

■ **7-8** When the two disciples bring the donkey to Jesus, they place their cloaks upon the animal before Jesus mounts it. In addition, "many" (πολλοί) spread their cloaks on the road. These gestures of respect and honor are reminiscent of the gesture of the other commanders of the army when Jehu reveals to them that the young prophet has anointed him king over Israel: "they all took their cloaks and spread them for him on the bare steps" (2 Kgs 9:13).[62] The gesture is known to Roman culture as well:

When the time of Cato's military service came to an end, he was sent on his way, not with blessings, as is common, nor yet with praises, but with tears and insatiable embraces, the soldiers casting their cloaks down for him to walk upon, and kissing his hands, things which the Romans of that day rarely did, and only to a few of their imperators (Ἐπεὶ δὲ τέλος εἶχεν ἡ στρατεία τῷ Κάτωνι, προεπέμφθη, οὐκ εὐχαῖς, ὃ κοινόν ἐστιν, οὐδ᾽ ἐπαίνοις, ἀλλὰ δάκρυσι καὶ περιβολαῖς ἀπλήστοις, ὑποτιθέντων τὰ ἱμάτια τοῖς ποσὶν ᾗ βαδίζοι καὶ καταφιλούντων τὰς χεῖρας, ἃ τῶν αὐτοκρατόρων ὀλίγοις μόλις ἐποίουν οἱ τότε Ῥωμαῖοι). (Plutarch *Vit. Cato Minor.* 12)[63]

■ **9** Josephus also describes processions in which some people go before and some follow. Like Mark, Josephus uses προάγειν ("to go ahead") and ἀκολουθεῖν ("to follow") in his description of Herod the Great's funeral procession. The troops went ahead of the bier, and the servants and freedmen followed it (*Bell.* 1.33.9 §673).[64]

The exclamation "Hosanna" (ὡσαννά) is related to the Hebrew הושיעה נא ("Save, please!") of Ps 118:25.[65] It is probably a transliteration of the equivalent Aramaic expression הושע נא.[66] Mark does not translate it. The reason may be that the Hebrew phrase had been adopted, untranslated, in the ritual practices of his audiences.[67] By Mark's time it may have become a cry of jubilation.[68] The following benediction agrees exactly in wording with Ps 117:26a LXX as it has been transmitted to us.

indications that this sentence is an official formula of requisition, used, for example, to prepare for the ceremonious arrival of a ruler in a particular place ("Messias oder Menschensohn?" *NovT* 1 [1956] 81–102, esp. 85; see also Derrett, "Palm Sunday Colt," 243–44; Kinman, "Parousia," 287).

61 Trans. from Danby, *Mishnah*, 384. See the commentary on 2:23-28 above.

62 Jack Dean Kingsbury, *The Christology of Mark's Gospel* (Philadelphia: Fortress, 1983) 107. Both the LXX of 2 Kgs 9:13 and Mark 11:7 use the word ἱμάτιον ("cloak").

63 Trans. (modified) from Perrin, *Plutarch's Lives*, 8:260–61.

64 Catchpole, "'Triumphal' Entry," 325. In his account of the funeral of Abener (Abner), Josephus says that David commanded all the people to go ahead of the bier (προάγειν) and he himself followed it (ἐφέπειν) (*Ant.* 7.1.6 §§40–41).

65 See the note on the trans. of v. 9 above. The LXX translates הושיעה נא with σῶσον δή ("do save").

66 Joseph A. Fitzmyer, "Aramaic Evidence Affecting the Interpretation of *Hosanna* in the New Testament," in Gerald F. Hawthorne and Otto Betz, eds., *Tradition and Interpretation in the New Testament: Essays in Honor of E. Earle Ellis* (Grand Rapids: Eerdmans; Tübingen: Mohr Siebeck, 1987) 110–18, esp. 112.

67 Cf. Margaret Daly-Denton, *David in the Fourth Gospel: The Johannine Reception of the Psalms* (AGJU 47; Leiden: Brill, 2000) 179.

68 Hooker, 260. Fitzmyer describes it as "a spontaneous cry of greeting or a cry of homage" ("Aramaic Evidence," 115); Menahem Kister as "an exclamation" ("Words and Formulae in the Gospels in Light of Hebrew and Aramaic Sources," in Hans-Jürgen Becker and Serge Ruzer, eds., *The Sermon on the Mount and Its Jewish Setting* [CahRB 60; Paris: Gabalda, 2005] 117–47, esp. 120–22).

Psalm 118 (117) is a liturgy for a festival of thanksgiving. Verses 19-20 make clear that the singer who is presenting the thanksgiving of vv. 5-21 is in a festival procession that is on its way to the "portals of Yahweh."[69] It has been a problem for commentators that the thanksgiving of vv. 5-21 is an individual one, yet the context is a public liturgy.[70] Joseph Blenkinsopp has argued that the psalm is "a hymn of national thanksgiving after a victory (cf. Zech 9:9!) and was probably written for a royal entry or parousia in the first place . . . ."[71] He pointed out that both Luke and John gloss Mark's "he who comes" (ὁ ἐρχόμενος) as "king" and concluded that "he who comes" is an allusion to Gen 49:10, part of the oracle about the royal destiny of Judah.[72] According to this interpretation, Jesus is "he who comes," the messiah. Catchpole mentions the possibility that this psalm was interpreted messianically prior to the time of Jesus.[73]

In the late Second Temple period, David was considered to be the author of the Psalter, so the thanksgiving may have been interpreted in Jesus' time as spoken by David.[74] This hypothesis is supported by evidence that Psalm 118 was associated with David in early rabbinic literature.[75] From this perspective, the psalm is here applied to Jesus as the son of David.

The exclamation of Ps 118:25 is a cultic petition. In the Mishnah, it occurs as a petitionary cry for rain and fertility. The benediction of v. 26 "belongs to the liturgy of entry and the gate. From the inside of the sanctuary (מבית יהוה) the word of blessing is called out by priests to those coming in (cf. Ps 24:5)."[76] In the context of Mark, Jesus takes the role of the individual who is accompanied by the festival community. Here the blessing is spoken by the crowd instead of the priests.

■ **10** In this verse the crowd improvises, rather than quoting a psalm. They bless "the coming kingdom of our father David" (ἡ ἐρχομένη βασιλεία τοῦ πατρὸς ἡμῶν Δαυίδ). Although here Jesus is not hailed explicitly as king or as son of David, the context suggests that he is both. Such an inference is supported by the address of Jesus by Bartimaeus as son of David.[77]

The last three words of the petition, ὡσαννὰ ἐν τοῖς ὑψίστοις ("Save, please, [you who are] in the highest [heights or heavens]!"),[78] come from Ps 148:1b. Psalm 148 is a hymn for public worship from the postexilic period. The heading of this psalm in the LXX provides the information that it is to be associated with Haggai and Zechariah.[79] Verse 1 in both the Hebrew and the Greek calls upon the residents of the heavenly world to praise the Lord. It may be that "Hosanna" in Mark 11:9 and 10 has the sense of "praise" rather than "save."[80] In that case, the object of praise may be Jesus, as "Lord" (cf. v. 3), or God, whose agent Jesus is.

■ **11** This verse is anticlimactic because the honor paid to Jesus in the preceding verses leads the audience to expect his installation as king. Mark frustrates this expectation for several interrelated reasons. It should be noted first of all that we do not know, historically speaking, what happened when Jesus entered Jerusalem. There may have been tension, even conflict, between those who believed that he was the messiah and those who rejected such an idea. In any case, it is clear that he was not universally acclaimed as king. Mark portrays his kingship ironically in chaps. 14–15. Second, Mark redefines the role of the messiah. When Peter identifies Jesus as the messiah in 8:29, Jesus explains that messiahship involves suffering, death, and resurrection (8:31). Jesus cannot be enthroned as a king in the usual sense during his earthly lifetime because of this destiny of suffering and death. Finally, Mark does imply that Jesus will be enthroned as a messianic ruler but only after the resurrection. As Son of Man he will exercise the universal sovereignty prophesied in Dan 7:13-14.[81]

69 Kraus, *Psalms 60–150*, 394–95.
70 Ibid., 395–96.
71 Joseph Blenkinsopp, "The Oracle of Judah and the Messianic Entry," *JBL* 80 (1961) 55–64; citation from 59.
72 Ibid., 56–57, 59.
73 Catchpole, "'Triumphal' Entry," 325 n. 11.
74 Josephus *Ant.* 7.12.3 §305; Philo *Conf. ling.* 28 §149; Daly-Denton, *David*, 110–11.
75 Daly-Denton, *David*, 181–82.

76 Kraus, *Psalms 60–150*, 400.
77 See the commentary on 10:47 and 48-49 above; Frank J. Matera, *The Kingship of Jesus: Composition and Theology in Mark 15* (SBLDS 66; Chico, CA: Scholars Press/SBL, 1982) 73.
78 See the note on the trans. of v. 10 above.
79 Kraus, *Psalms 60–150*, 561–62.
80 Ibid., 400; Daly-Denton, *David*, 179.
81 Mark 12:35-37 (implied); 13:26; 14:62.

Mark also had literary reasons for composing v. 11 in the way that he did. He depicts Jesus' entry into the city as occurring late in the day so that he can have Jesus retire for the night and then, on his way into the city in the morning, see the fig tree. Verse 11 thus prepares for vv. 12-14 and 20-25. The statement that he looked around at everything ($\pi\epsilon\rho\iota\beta\lambda\epsilon\psi\acute{\alpha}\mu\epsilon\nu\sigma\varsigma\ \pi\acute{\alpha}\nu\tau\alpha$) may be included to prepare for vv. 15-19. Jesus sees things going on in the temple precinct of which he does not approve. He then expresses his disapproval at his second visit to the temple precinct on the next day.[82] Finally, it is explicitly mentioned that Jesus and the Twelve are staying in Bethany during the Passover feast. As noted earlier, the name "Bethany" may have symbolic significance here, or Mark may be encouraging the audiences to recognize a play on words.[83]

The frustration of expectations caused by the anticlimactic v. 11 would have been especially strong for those familiar with the practice of celebratory welcomes.[84] The prefects and procurators of Judea were probably welcomed by the leaders of the city of Caesarea (on the sea) when they arrived to take up office. Josephus mentions one or two visits of Vitellius, the governor of Syria and father of the later emperor of the same name, to Jerusalem and says that "the populace gave him a very splendid reception" ($\delta\epsilon\xi\alpha\mu\acute{\epsilon}\nu\sigma\upsilon\ \tau\sigma\hat{\upsilon}\ \pi\lambda\acute{\eta}\vartheta\sigma\upsilon\varsigma\ \alpha\grave{\upsilon}\tau\grave{\sigma}\nu\ \lambda\alpha\mu\pi\rho\acute{\sigma}\tau\alpha\tau\alpha\ \pi\acute{\alpha}\nu\upsilon$) (Ant. 15.11.4 §405).[85] It is possible that the author of Mark observed one or more such welcomes firsthand. If not, it is likely that he had heard about them and knew what their conventional features were. His audiences, inside and outside Palestine, would also have been familiar with this custom, either firsthand or by reputation.

From this perspective, the statement "And he went into Jerusalem to the temple precinct" ($\kappa\alpha\grave{\iota}\ \epsilon\grave{\iota}\sigma\hat{\eta}\lambda\vartheta\epsilon\nu\ \epsilon\grave{\iota}\varsigma\ \acute{I}\epsilon\rho\sigma\sigma\acute{\sigma}\lambda\upsilon\mu\alpha\ \epsilon\grave{\iota}\varsigma\ \tau\grave{\sigma}\ \acute{\iota}\epsilon\rho\acute{\sigma}\nu$) is what one would expect, given the typical features of ancient celebratory welcomes and entrance processions. It is odd, however, that Jesus enters the city only in the company of the Twelve. In a celebratory welcome, one would expect the leaders of the city to accompany the dignitary to the temple. For those who considered Jesus to be such a dignitary, his nonreception by the leaders of the city would be viewed as an affront.

---

82   Von Dobschütz, "Erzählerkunst," 197.
83   See the commentary on v. 1 above.
84   See the section "The Genre of Mark 11:1-11" above.
85   Text and trans. by Ralph Marcus, in Thackeray, *Josephus,* 8:194–95. In describing the same or another visit, he says that Vitellius was "received in magnificent fashion" ($\delta\epsilon\chi\vartheta\epsilon\grave{\iota}\varsigma\ \mu\epsilon\gamma\alpha\lambda\sigma\pi\rho\epsilon\pi\hat{\omega}\varsigma$ [Ant. 18.4.3 §90]). Text and trans. by Louis Feldman, in Thackeray, *Josephus,* 9:64–65. If there were two visits, it is likely that one occurred in c. 36 CE, the other in 37 (Feldman, 65, n. c).

11

11:12-25 The Fig Tree and the Temple

12/ And on the next day, as they were going out from Bethany, he was hungry. 13/ And when he saw from a distance a fig tree with leaves, he went (to it) (to see) if perhaps he would find something on it;[a] yet when he came to it, he found nothing except leaves. For it was not the time for figs. 14/ And he said to it, "May no one ever eat fruit from you again!" And his disciples heard (what he said).

15/ And they went into Jerusalem. And he went into the temple precinct and began to drive out those who were selling and those who were buying in the temple precinct, and he overturned the tables of the money-changers and the chairs of those who were selling the doves, 16/ and he would not allow anyone to carry a vessel through the temple precinct. 17/ And he taught and said to them, "Is it not written, 'My house shall be called a house of prayer for all the nations'? But you have made it 'a den of robbers.'" 18/ And the chief priests and the scribes heard (what he said) and were looking for a way to destroy him; for they feared him, for the whole crowd was amazed at his teaching. 19/ And when evening came, he[b] went outside the city.

20/ And as they were passing by early in the morning, they saw the fig tree withered from the roots. 21/ And Peter remembered and said to him, "Rabbi, look, the fig tree which you cursed has withered." 22/ And Jesus said to them, "Have trust in God.[c] 23/ Truly I say to you, that whoever says to this mountain, 'Be lifted up and thrown into the sea,' and does not doubt in his mind, but trusts that what he says will come to pass, it will be (so) for him. 24/ For this reason I say to you, whatever you pray and ask for, trust that you will obtain it,[d] and it will be (so) for you. 25/ And when you stand[e] praying, if you have anything against anyone, forgive (it), in order that your Father who is in the heavens also may forgive you your transgressions.[f]

a   The indirect question εἰ ἄρα τι εὑρήσει ("if perhaps he would find something") is loosely connected to the rest of the sentence and this fact gave rise to variants. The reading ὡς εὑρήσων τι ("to find something"), attested by Θ 0188. 565 et al., is probably an Atticistic correction; see Smyth §§2065, 2086 and BDF §§351 (1), 425 (3). The reading ἰδεῖν ἐάν τί ἐστιν ("to see whether there was something"), attested by D it, clarifies the connection between the indirect question and the main clause and gives ἐάν ("whether") as a variant of εἰ ("if"); see BDF §368 and Moulton-Turner, 3:113–14.

b   Although the plural ἐξεπορεύοντο ("they went") is attested by representatives of three different textual groups (A B W), this reading is probably due to an early assimilation of the earlier singular ἐξεπορεύετο ("he went") to the plural verb in v. 20. See Turner, "Marcan Usage," 26 (1925) 230 (Elliott, *Language and Style*, 41); Taylor, ad loc. For a different opinion, see Metzger, *Textual Commentary*, 92. On textual groups or clusters, see Epp, "A Dynamic View," 1–32.

c   א D Θ f13 et al. attest the reading εἰ ἔχετε πίστιν θεοῦ ("If you have trust in God"). This reading is probably a secondary assimilation to the saying found in Luke 17:6; cf. Matt 17:20 and 21:21. This conclusion is supported by the fact that the expression that follows, "Truly I say to you" (ἀμὴν λέγω ὑμῖν), elsewhere normally begins a sentence. See Taylor, ad loc., and Metzger, *Textual Commentary*, 92.

d   The earliest recoverable reading is the aorist ἐλάβετε, "you will obtain (it)," lit., "you obtained (it)"; the sense is, "If you trust, you will obtain (it)." This reading is attested by א B C L W et al. An aorist after a future condition (in this case, implied) "is, to a certain extent, futuristic," see BDF §333 (2). Moulton-Turner argue that it is a gnomic aorist (3:73), but this proposal does not suit the context. The other two readings are secondary attempts at clarification. A f13 33 𝔐 read the present tense, λαμβάνετε ("you receive") and D Θ f1 et al. attest the future tense, λή(μ)ψεσθε ("you will receive"). Elliott argued that the present is the earliest recoverable reading, since Matthew and scribes often altered Mark's historic presents to aorists ("An Eclectic Textual Commentary," 201). But this type of change was made when the event in question was assumed to have occurred in the past; such an assumption is not self-evident in this case. The committee of the UBSGNT accepted the aorist as the earliest reading, but concluded that it represents the Semitic prophetic perfect (Metzger, *Textual Commentary*, 93).

e   The earliest recoverable reading is the present indicative στήκετε ("you stand"); ὅταν ("when" or "whenever") is used with the indicative primarily to denote indefinite repetition in past time; cf. BDF §382 (4) and Mark 3:11. But it is also used, as here, with the present indicative, in the sense of ἐάν ("if"; ibid.). Since ὅταν ("when" or "whenever") was used with the subjunctive in Attic Greek, this reading gave rise to variants. B K N W Γ *pm* read the present subjunctive στήκητε ("you stand") and ℵ reads the second aorist subjunctive of a related verb στῆτε ("you stand").

f   Verse 26 in the traditional text of Mark is omitted by ℵ B L W et al. It is probably an early expansion inspired by Matt 6:15; see Taylor, ad loc.; Metzger, *Textual Commentary*, 93; Dowd, *Prayer*, 40.

The Literary Relationship between the Two Stories

Ernst von Dobschütz argued that Mark brought two originally unrelated stories together here and emphasized the way in which v. 11 prepares for vv. 15-19.[1] The placement of the account of Jesus' actions in the temple between the two parts of the story of the cursing of the fig tree simply allows for time to pass and for the effect of the curse to be noticed on the next day. He contrasted the way in which Matthew separated the two stories and portrayed the curse as taking effect immediately. He implies that Mark's narrative is more effective.[2]

Ernst Lohmeyer concluded that the cursing of the fig tree originally had no symbolic meaning, but that Mark constructed one by its placement. He described this meaning in two ways; generally speaking, it signifies that the Lord punishes everything that does not serve its divine purpose. Concretely, it implies that he punishes the people who do not respond to his challenge with obedience. In the latter sense, it serves as an effective introduction to the account of the cleansing of the temple and to the theme of judgment, which plays such an important role in chaps. 12 and 13.[3]

Heinz Giesen argued that the fig tree symbolizes Israel, which produces no fruit and therefore loses its privilege as God's people. Now everything depends on faith in God. He also argued that the story about the fig tree should be interpreted in the context of the cleansing of the temple.[4]

William R. Telford concluded that the fate of the unfruitful tree is "a proleptic sign prefiguring the destruction of the Temple cultus."[5] Although it was not the season for figs, the fig tree should have provided fruit for its rightful owner in the messianic age. The placement of the story of the fig tree in the context of the cleansing of the temple indicates that "the expected fruitfulness associated with that institution is not to be."[6] "Its spiritual authority is a sham and its pretense to uniting man and God fruitless." With the occupation of the temple by the Zealots, it had, for Mark and his audiences, become a brigand's cave.[7]

James R. Edwards argued for a symbolic interrelation between the two stories. He overstated his case that "the fig tree is often in the Old Testament a symbol for Israel, and more than once Israel is judged under this symbol."[8] The first passage that he cites to corroborate this statement is Isa 34:4, but the context is an oracle against the nations, not against Israel. The second, Jer 5:17, is part of an oracle directed against Israel and Judah, but the fig trees here are not symbolic: the enemy will devour the produce of vines and fig trees. There are similar problems with some of the other passages cited. In Hos 9:10, the ancestors of Israel are compared to "the first fruit on the fig tree, in its first season" (NRSV), but such

---

1   See the commentary on v. 11 above.
2   Von Dobschütz, "Erzählerkunst," 197. For a history of research on the cursing of the fig tree from 1830 to 1980, see William R. Telford, *The Barren Temple and the Withered Tree: A Redaction-critical Analysis of the Cursing of the Fig Tree Pericope in Mark's Gospel and Its Relation to the Cleansing of the Temple Tradition* (JSNTSup 1; Sheffield: JSOT Press, 1980) 1–38.
3   Mark 12:1-12, 38-40; 13:4-37; Lohmeyer, 235.
4   Heinz Giesen, "Der verdorrte Feigenbaum—Eine

symbolische Aussage: Zu Mk 11,12-14. 20f," *BZ* n.F. 20 (1976) 95–111, esp. 99, 102–3.
5   Telford, *Barren Temple*, 238.
6   Ibid., 196.
7   Ibid., 261.
8   Edwards, "Markan Sandwiches," 207.

comparisons do not imply that the fig tree is a symbol for Israel in general.[9] He also argued that the statement "it was not the season for figs" in v. 13 "has less to do with horticulture than with theology. . . . There is no fruit on the tree because its time has passed. The leafy fig tree, with all its promise of fruit, is as deceptive as the temple, which, with all its bustling activity, is really an outlaw's hideout (v. 17)."[10] He apparently understood the withering of the fig tree from its roots in v. 20 as an allusion to Hos 9:16 and inferred that, in Mark's view, "the temple's function is now 'withered from the roots.'"[11] Further connotations, in Edwards's view, are that the cursing and withering of the fig tree foreshadow the destruction of the temple and that "Jesus himself has replaced the temple as the center of Israel's faith (15:38-39); salvation is found in him, not in the temple."[12]

Christopher D. Marshall also concluded that the two "dovetailed episodes" have a "mutually interpretive relationship."[13] He argued that the audiences of Mark would connect this passage with Jer 8:12 (meaning, apparently, 8:13) and other passages, inferring that "the blasting of the fig tree could only be a token of eschatological judgment against the nation, . . . specifically against the corrupt temple cultus."[14]

Tom Shepherd argued that the two stories create a dramatized irony between the fig tree in the outer story and the temple in the inner story. The irony is dramatized by means of parallels and contrasts. The fig tree has leaves but no fruit; the temple is supposed to be a house of prayer but has become a den of robbers. Jesus curses the tree but cleanses the temple.[15] The contrasts are overcome by the fact that the action of Jesus in the temple leads to a plot to kill him, which leads to the destruction of the temple. The intercalation of the one story into the other thus concerns the fate of the leaders of the people.[16]

Philip F. Esler has argued that the author of Mark found the two-stage miracle story in a Jerusalemite source that he used in composing parts of chaps. 11–14. The evangelist made sense of this story by relating it to Jesus' teaching on faith and prayer.[17]

The analyses of von Dobschütz, Lohmeyer, and Shepherd are more persuasive than those of Giesen, Telford, Edwards, Marshall, and Esler. Von Dobschütz and Lohmeyer base their inferences closely on the text and its immediate context. Shepherd extends his analysis to other parts of the passion narrative but with more careful arguments than the others.

Recent studies of orality have placed the whole question of intercalation in a new light. In light of such studies, Paul J. Achtemeier argued that "[t]he Markan technique of intercalating stories is a way of allowing one story to function as an *inclusio* for a second, thus aiding the listener in determining when both stories have concluded."[18] In this regard, he cited Werner Kelber to the effect that "such intercalation is more likely to belong to the oral nature of the material than to anything like manipulation of the written text in the form of 'interpolations.'"[19] Since Mark was written to be read aloud by a single reader to a gathered group, the purpose of aiding the listener is likely to be the intention of the author. Modern literary critics should then be cautious about

---

9   Deborah Krause argued that Mark employed Hos 9:10-17 "to give form to the narrative of the cursing of the fig tree and the clearing of the temple" ("Narrated Prophecy in Mark 11.12-21: The Divine Authorization of Judgment," in Craig A. Evans and W. Richard Stegner, eds., *The Gospels and the Scriptures of Israel* [JSNTSup 104; SSEJC 3; Sheffield: Sheffield Academic Press, 1994] 235–48; quotation from 235). Edwards also cites Mic 7:1-6 ("Markan Sandwiches," 207 n. 40); J. Neville Birdsall argued that Jesus had this passage in mind in the incident reported by Mark ("The Withering of the Fig-Tree [Mark xi. 12-14, 20-22]," *ExpT* 73 [1961–62] 191). Arthur de Q. Robin argued that the historical Jesus alluded to Micah 7:1-6 MT by quoting its opening words in order to comment "on the state of the nation and its leaders, before pronouncing the judgement of God upon

them" by cursing the fig tree and cleansing the temple ("The Cursing of the Fig Tree in Mark XI: A Hypothesis," *NTS* 8 [1961–62] 276–81).

10   Edwards, "Markan Sandwiches," 207.
11   Ibid., 208.
12   Ibid.
13   Marshall, *Faith*, 160.
14   Ibid. Some of the passages he cites seem irrelevant: Isa 28:3-4; Joel 1:7, 12.
15   Shepherd, *Markan Sandwich Stories*, 217, 219.
16   Ibid., 227, 229.
17   Philip F. Esler, "The Incident of the Withered Fig Tree in Mark 11: A New Source and Redactional Explanation," *JSNT* 28 (2005) 41–67.
18   Achtemeier, "*Omne Verbum Sonat*," 21.
19   Kelber, *Gospel*, 67; Achtemeier, "*Omne Verbum Sonat*," 21 n. 133.

exaggerating the degree to which the intercalated stories are intended to interpret one another. The discernment of complex literary designs may indeed be illuminating of the Markan text, but they probably should not be attributed to the author's intention.

The Genre of the Story about the Fig Tree

Some scholars have argued that the incident actually occurred and that certain features of the story have become distorted in the process of transmission. Others have suggested that the passage is an aetiological legend that arose to explain how a particular tree near Jerusalem came to be withered. Others have concluded that it resulted from the transformation of a parable like the one in Luke 13:6-9 into a realistic narrative.[20] Some have categorized it as a miracle story belonging to the subtype of effective curse or miraculous punishment.[21] Others have defined it as an enacted parable or a prophetic symbolic action.[22] It is likely that Mark composed the narrative or rewrote an earlier story and, in doing so, pushed the genre miracle story in the direction of metaphorical narrative.[23]

Comment

■ **12-14** The mention of "the next day" ($\dot{\eta}\ \dot{\epsilon}\pi\alpha\dot{\upsilon}\rho\iota\upsilon\upsilon$ [$\dot{\eta}\mu\dot{\epsilon}\rho\alpha$]) in v. 12, the "evening" ($\dot{o}\psi\dot{\epsilon}$) in v. 19, and "the morning" ($\pi\rho\omega\dot{\iota}$) in v. 20, along with the temporal remarks in 14:1 and later passages, provide the basis for the definition of Jesus' time in Jerusalem as a "holy

week."[24] The temporal markers in vv. 12, 19 and 20, however, occur because of the way Mark narrates the story about the cursing of the fig tree. The repetition of the place-name "Bethany" in vv. 11 and 12 simply serves to assist the listening audience in following the thread of the narrative.

It is odd that Jesus is depicted as hungry, since the narrative context implies that he had enjoyed hospitality in Bethany.[25] It is also odd that the disciples are not portrayed as hungry as well.[26] These features indicate either that the story about the fig tree was placed in this context secondarily or that it was composed, probably by Mark, as a metaphorical narrative.[27]

Jesus' hunger, his seeing the fig tree from afar, his approaching it to look for figs, and his disappointment are analogous to the prophet's lament in Mic 7:1:

> Woe is me! For I have become like one who, after the summer fruit has been gathered, after the vintage has been gleaned, finds no cluster to eat; there is no first-ripe fig for which I hunger. (NRSV)

(אללי לי כי הייתי כאספי קיץ כעללת בציר
אין אשכול לאכול בכורה אותה נפשי)[28]

The next verse in Micah makes clear that the simile has to do with the lack of faithful people in the land. If one looks to the immediate context in Mark as a guide for the metaphorical meaning of the analogous brief narrative in Mark, one recalls that Jesus has just been hailed as "the coming one" who is associated with the "coming

---

20 Robin, "Cursing of the Fig Tree," 276–79; Robin himself takes the position that the incident is historical.

21 Grundmann, 228; Pesch, 2:191, 195–96; Pesch argued that the incident is historical. Bultmann defined the passage as a nature miracle (*History*, 218). Dibelius classified it as a legend that may have derived from a parable (*From Tradition to Gospel*, 106).

22 As enacted parable: Craig Blomberg, "The Miracles as Parables," in David Wenham and Craig Blomberg, eds., *Gospel Perspectives*, vol. 6: *The Miracles of Jesus* (Sheffield: JSOT Press, 1986) 327–59, esp. 332; as prophetic symbolic action: Hooker, *Signs*, 44.

23 See the commentary on vv. 12-14 and 20-25 below.

24 Lohmeyer organizes the material from 11:1 to 12:12

in relation to three days (228–38); Pesch in relation to two (2:189–90).

25 Grundmann, 228.

26 Giesen, "Der verdorrte Feigenbaum," 95.

27 Pryke concluded that v. 12, the last clause of v. 13, and vv. 14, 20-22 and the opening clause of v. 23 were composed by Mark (*Redactional Style*, 167–68). See "The Genre of the Story about the Fig Tree" above.

28 The LXX does not mention fig(s) here. Allusion may also be made to Jer 8:13, which occurs in the context of an indictment of the leaders of the people (8:8-13). Blomberg concluded that the historical Jesus alluded to these passages to depict the eschatological judgment of Israel if the people did not repent ("Miracles as Parables," 332; similarly, Lane, 401–2).

kingdom of our father David" by his disciples and the crowd. Yet he was not welcomed as such by the leaders of the city.[29] The "leaves" on the fig tree correspond to the acclamations of the crowd, and the lack of fruit corresponds to the missing welcome by the leaders.

Although the words for "fig" differ, the name "Bethphage" also refers to early figs, as does the passage from Micah cited above.[30] It seems likely that Mark deliberately alluded to Mic 7:1.[31] In any case, some members of the audiences of Mark would probably have made the connection.

The interpretation offered above, that the lack of figs on the tree corresponds to the leaders' failure to welcome Jesus, can explain the statement that "it was not the time for figs" (ὁ γὰρ καιρὸς οὐκ ἦν σύκων).[32] The tension between Jesus' searching for figs and it not being the season for figs is analogous to the tension created by the account of his entry into Jerusalem. On the one hand, the disciples and the crowd acclaim Jesus as the messiah; therefore, according to convention and given the audience's assumption that he is the messiah, the leaders of Jerusalem should have welcomed him. On the other hand, it was not yet the time for his enthronement as messiah. He had not yet suffered, been raised, and been exalted as the Son of Man. In other words, it was not the time for his exercise of messiahship, yet the leaders are culpable for not recognizing his status as messiah.

The culpability of the leaders on the narrative level is expressed figuratively by Jesus' curse, "May no one ever eat fruit from you again!" (μηκέτι εἰς τὸν αἰῶνα ἐκ σοῦ μηδεὶς καρπὸν φάγοι). The implication is that their role as leaders is forfeit. This rhetorical point is similar to the force of the parable in 12:1-12 about the murderous tenants. The owner of the vineyard "will come and destroy the vine-dressers and give the vineyard to others"

(v. 9). The chief priests, the scribes, and the elders recognize that Jesus had told the parable against them.[33]

The statement that his disciples heard what he said prepares for Peter's recognition that the tree had withered as a result of Jesus' curse (v. 21).

The History of the Tradition of 11:15-19

As Bultmann pointed out, it is highly likely that the first sentence of v. 15, "And they went into Jerusalem" (Καὶ ἔρχονται εἰς Ἱεροσόλυμα), and vv. 18-19 come from the editor, most likely the evangelist. But the remainder does not seem to be a unitary apophthegm, since the introduction to the saying in v. 17, "and he taught and said to them" (καὶ ἐδίδασκεν καὶ ἔλεγεν αὐτοῖς), "gives the impression that word and action did not originally belong together."[34] In its present form, vv. 15-17 constitute a mixed chreia, a brief narrative that has a dual focus on an action and a saying of the protagonist. In this subtype, the emphasis lies on the action.[35] Bultmann's conjecture that v. 17 is a secondary interpretation of the actions in vv. 15-16 is attractive. One reason for agreeing with it is that the saying in v. 17 makes better sense as addressed to a wider group than the buyers, the sellers, and the money-changers mentioned in v. 15. Another reason is that the Gospel of John reports a similar set of actions, but appends a different saying.[36] Whereas Mark's version alludes to Isa 56:7 and Jer 7:11, John's alludes to Zech 14:21. Finally, the saying of v. 17 does not fit Jesus' actions very well. The narrative description of Jesus' actions does not emphasize the Gentiles or their relation to the temple. This lack is especially important since the outer court, where the actions probably took place, was not called the "Court of the Gentiles" in the time of Jesus and Mark.[37]

---

29   See the section "The Genre of Mark 11:1-11" and the commentary on 11:11 above.

30   See the commentary on 11:1 above.

31   Robin and Birdsall argued that Jesus had the passage in mind; see the section "The Literary Relationship between the Two Stories" above.

32   This statement creates a deliberate incongruity as a signal that the event or narrative has a metaphorical or symbolic significance (Cranfield, 356; Lane, 401–2; Blomberg, "Miracles as Parables," 332; Hooker, 262). The term καιρός ("time" or "season") has two levels of meaning here. On one level, it refers to the

season in which figs ripen. On another level, it refers to a decisive moment of the last days; cf. 1:15; 13:33. Giesen rightly recognizes the eschatological level of meaning but offers a different interpretation from the one offered here ("Der verdorrte Feigenbaum," 104–5).

33   Cf. 11:27 with 12:12. See the commentary on 12:1-12 below.

34   Bultmann, *History*, 36.

35   On the mixed chreia, see Moeser, *Anecdote*, 70–71, 77.

36   Bultmann, *History*, 36.

The Historical Reliability of 11:15-17

As argued immediately above, v. 17 probably does not go back to the historical Jesus. The arguments that have been put forward against the historicity of vv. 15-16, however, are not persuasive.[38] Verse 16 is based on very old tradition and may go back to the historical Jesus. The saying clearly concerns the holiness of the temple mount and possibly ritual purity, a theme of little importance to Mark.[39] The saying fits with the significance of the actions of Jesus, as will be argued below. The concern for holiness or ritual purity expressed in Mark's version of the account, the oldest of the four versions; the rather opaque character of the actions of Jesus and their significance; and the likelihood that there were two independent accounts of the incident (Mark's and John's) support the conclusion that the accounts are based on an event in the life of the historical Jesus. The original significance of the event, however, has been obscured by subsequent reinterpretations.

As was the case with the account of Jesus' entry into Jerusalem, the question has been raised how Jesus could have accomplished the actions described in vv. 15-16 without evoking the immediate intervention of the Romans or the temple police.[40] Wellhausen and Grundmann concluded that the account is based on a historical event and that the authorities did not intervene because of the large numbers of Jesus' followers and the intensity of their commitment to Jesus.[41] As with the entry, there is a good fit between Jesus' action in the temple and the charges against him at the trial before the high priest:

blasphemy and the claim to be the messiah.[42] E. P. Sanders accepted the historicity of the event but solved this problem by arguing that "the action was not substantial enough even to interfere with the daily routine; for if it had been he would surely have been arrested on the spot."[43] It must be admitted that we do not know the details of Jesus' last days in Jerusalem. It may be that Mark's portrayal of the authorities' wish to arrest Jesus "by deceit" (ἐν δόλῳ) in 14:1, rather than publicly, is accurate. It is also conceivable that Mark and the pre-Markan passion narrative are unreliable in portraying Jesus' arrest as taking place several days after his actions in the temple. In any case, vv. 15-16 probably give us a glimpse of the activity of the historical Jesus in those last days.

Those who agree that the account is based on a historical event do not agree about its original significance. Some have argued that it was the activity of trade itself that needed to be "cleansed." Others have concluded that Jesus had a political purpose in carrying out these actions. Sanders has argued that the overturning of tables was symbolic of the destruction of the temple. Others have proposed that Jesus' motivation was primarily economic, that Jesus was protesting the exploitation of the poor by the temple authorities.[44]

It is more likely that Jesus' actions were aimed at the results of Herod's remodeling of the temple, which involved moving the sessions of the council (Sanhedrin) from "the Chamber of Hewn Stones" in the temple court to the Royal Portico bordering the outer courtyard. More pertinently, the remodeling encouraged the vendors of

---

37 Josephus simply calls it "the open court" (τὸ ὕπαιθρον) (Bell. 5.5.2 §192); Adela Yarbro Collins, "Jesus' Action in Herod's Temple," in eadem and Margaret M. Mitchell, eds., *Antiquity and Humanity: Essays on Ancient Religion and Philosophy Presented to Hans Dieter Betz on His 70th Birthday* (Tübingen: Mohr Siebeck, 2001) 45–61, esp. 46.

38 Yarbro Collins, "Jesus' Action in Herod's Temple," 45–46.

39 Ibid., 46–47.

40 See the section "The Historical Reliability of 11:1-11" above.

41 Wellhausen, 90; Grundmann, 230.

42 Klostermann, 117. Klostermann raises the question whether the whole incident may have been inspired by scripture, but does not adopt this view (ibid.).

The same issue has been discussed with regard to Jesus' entry into Jerusalem; see the section "The Historical Reliability of 11:1-11" above.

43 Sanders, *Jesus and Judaism*, 70; similarly, Richard A. Horsley, *Jesus and the Spiral of Violence: Popular Jewish Resistance in Roman Palestine* (San Francisco: Harper & Row, 1987) 299–300.

44 For criticism of these views, see Yarbro Collins, "Jesus' Action in Herod's Temple," 48–53. See also the discussion of the studies by L. D. Sporty and D. Bahat by Sarah Japp, *Die Baupolitik Herodes' des Großen: Die Bedeutung der Architektur für die Herrschaftslegitimation eines römischen Klientelkönigs* (Internationale Archäologie 64; Rahden, Westf.: Verlag Marie Leidorf, 2000) 59. She herself emphasizes the ways in which Herod followed Israelite-Jewish

doves to move from shops outside the temple mount to another part of the same portico. Herod's plan followed the traditional use of the outer courtyard of the temple as public space, analogous to the Greek marketplace (ἀγορά) or the Roman forum. The minority view, however, was that the outer court was to be holy as part of the sanctuary and was not to be used as civic space. This view was articulated in Ezekiel and the *Temple Scroll*. It appears that Herod's remodeling program increased the degree to which the outer court served as a profane civic center. He greatly enlarged the area of the temple mount. Thus, the ambiguous character of the outer court was increased. It appeared to be part of the *temenos*, the sacred area dedicated to the deity, but was also a great civic esplanade. Furthermore, Herod made use of an architectural form that was associated with both the older ruler cult and the emerging imperial cult.[45]

Although any reconstruction of the intention of Jesus must remain tentative, it is likely that his action against those buying and selling doves indicates his advocacy of an ideal temple along the lines of those described by Ezekiel and the *Temple Scroll*. The outer court was to be sacred space devoted to prayer and teaching, not civic space open to the general public and devoted to profane activities. Those who needed or wished to sacrifice doves could purchase them outside the temple mount.

According to Mark, Matthew, and John, Jesus also overturned the tables of the money-changers (Mark 11:15; Matt 21:12; John 2:15). This action may be a protest against the type of coins that had to be used to pay the temple tax of half a shekel. The bronze coins that were minted in Jerusalem conformed scrupulously to the current interpretation of the commandment against images by avoiding the representation of any animate being (Exod 20:4; Deut 5:8).[46] The temple tax, however, had to be paid in Tyrian silver coins.[47] These bore the head of the town god Melqart (identified with Heracles) on the front and an eagle standing on the prow of a ship on the back. If Jesus was concerned about the holiness and purity of the temple, he may have found these images, especially that of a foreign deity, offensive.[48] The use of such coins in the temple of the God of Israel dishonored the God to whom the temple was dedicated. In Mark 12:13-17, Jesus is asked whether it is lawful to pay taxes to Caesar. He asks for a coin, a *denarius*, and inquires whose image it bore. When told that of Caesar, he replied with the famous saying "Give back to Caesar what is Caesar's and to God what is God's." This saying may be interpreted as approving the use of foreign coins to pay taxes to Caesar but does not necessarily approve the use of such coins to pay the temple tax. In fact, the opposite is a more appropriate reading.[49]

---

and ancient Near Eastern traditions in remodeling the temple but acknowledges that Herod aimed at expressing his person and his rule in visible form by means of the colonnades and the Royal Portico (ibid., 58–59).

45 Ezekiel 40–48; 11Q19 40:5-6. For more detailed discussion, see Yarbro Collins, "Jesus' Action in Herod's Temple," 53–57.

46 On these coins, see Andrew Burnett, Michel Amandry and Père Pau Ripollès, *Roman Provincial Coinage*, vol. 1: *From the Death of Caesar to the Death of Vitellius (44 BC–AD 69)*, part I: *Introduction and Catalogue* (London: British Museum Press; Paris: Bibliothèque Nationale, 1992) 582. See also Yaʿakov Meshorer, *Ancient Jewish Coinage*, vol. 2: *Herod the Great through Bar Cochba* (Jerusalem: Israel Museum; Dix Hills, NY: Amphora Books, 1982) 18–33, 57–59.

47 This conclusion is contested; Donald T. Ariel rejects it; see his discussion of the variety of opinion in "A Survey of Coin Finds in Jerusalem (until the End of the Byzantine Period)," *Liber Annuus* 32 (1982) 273–326, esp. 284 n. 32.

48 The mint at Tyre, however, may have avoided using the imperial portrait in order to lessen the offense given to Jews (Burnett et al., *Roman Provincial Coinage*, 1/I:584). During the first year of the revolt that began in 66 CE, silver and bronze coins were minted in Jerusalem in Jewish types (John W. Betlyon, "Coinage," *ABD* 1:1076–89, esp. 1087; James S. McLaren, "The Coinage of the First Year as a Point of Reference for the Jewish Revolt [66–70 CE]," *Scripta Classica Israelica* 22 [2003] 135–52). This act, especially the minting of silver, was an assertion of independence, but it may also be evidence that many Jews, including members of the priestly elite, were offended by the Tyrian coin type. Peter Richardson has argued that "the primary reason for" Jesus' overturning the tables in the temple was "hostility to the use of Tyrian shekels to pay temple dues" (*Building Jewish in the Roman East* [JSJSup 92; Waco, TX: Baylor University Press; Leiden: Brill, 2004] 251).

49 Yarbro Collins, "Jesus' Action in Herod's Temple," 58–60. See also the commentary on 12:13-17 below.

Although Jesus challenged, or at least is portrayed as challenging, some of the regulations regarding the observance of the Sabbath and some of the customs regarding purity outside of the temple, such traditions are not incompatible with the interpretation of his actions in the temple offered here. He challenged some Sabbath and other practices when they conflicted with human need, especially hunger and illness. The need of pilgrims to purchase doves did not have to be met on the temple mount. This activity could take place elsewhere. The protest against the coins may represent something more fundamental than simply moving the money-changers away from the temple mount. It may call for the use of aniconic coins instead. In any case, Jesus seems in this instance to place the honor and dignity of God above human convenience. Or perhaps it would be better to say that he placed the honor of God above the architectural pretensions of Herod and the convenience of the chief priests.[50]

Comment

■ **15** The opening sentence of this unit, "And they went into Jerusalem," takes up the thread of the larger narrative. Jesus' first entry into the city was narrated in v. 11. On that occasion, it was late, so he and the Twelve left soon thereafter and went to Bethany where they were staying. Verse 12 narrates the beginning of their walk from Bethany to Jerusalem. The encounter with the fig tree occurs on this walk. The first sentence of v. 15 signals the conclusion of their walk into the city. The next clause, "And he went into the temple precinct" (καὶ εἰσελθὼν εἰς τὸ ἱερόν), indicates that on this second occasion, Jesus goes immediately to the temple, just as he did in v. 11.

On the first visit to the temple, however, Jesus simply "looked around at everything" (v. 11). Here he drives out those who were selling and those who were buying in the temple precinct. It is noteworthy that this general statement precedes more specific descriptions of Jesus' actions in the rest of v. 15 and in v. 16. It may be that the specific statements belong to an earlier stage of the history of the tradition of this account. The general statement near the beginning of v. 15 seems to have the purpose of linking Jesus' actions with Zech 14:21.[51]

The last sentence of Zech 14:21 in the MT reads as follows:

> And there shall no longer be a trader in the house of Yahweh Sabaoth on that day. (my trans.)

(ולא יהיה כנעני עוד בבית יהוה צבאות ביום ההוא).[52]

In its original context, this verse expressed the idea that, on the Day of the Lord, the temple precinct would no longer be the site of economic transactions, in keeping with its radical holiness.[53] The same sentence in the LXX reads as follows:

> And there shall no longer be a trader in the house of the Lord Almighty on that day (καὶ οὐκ ἔσται Χαναναῖος οὐκέτι ἐν τῷ οἴκῳ κυρίου παντοκράτορος ἐν τῇ ἡμέρᾳ ἐκείνῃ).[54]

The Greek version of Zechariah attributed to Aquila reads μετάβολος ("huckster" or "retail dealer"), which Jerome translates with *mercator* ("trader" or "merchant").[55] So, although כנעני and Χαναναῖος could be interpreted as "Canaanite," Mark 11:15 and John 2:16

---

50 Ibid., 60–61. On Herod's rebuilding of the temple, see Lichtenberger, *Baupolitik*, 131–42.

51 Cf. Henk Jan de Jonge, "The Cleansing of the Temple in Mark 11:15 and Zechariah 14:21," in Tuckett, *Zechariah*, 87–99, esp. 100.

52 The Hebrew word כנעני has two usages: "a Canaanite" and "a trader" or "merchant" (BDB, s.v.). The context, which speaks of cooking pots and bowls, fits better with the second usage. So Petersen, *Zechariah 9–14*, 160; for a different view, see Meyers and Meyers, *Zechariah 9–14*, 489–92.

53 Petersen, *Zechariah 9–14*, 160.

54 Like the Hebrew כנעני, the Greek word Χαναναῖος had two usages: "Canaanite" and "trader" or "merchant." It has the meaning "trader" or "merchant" in Prov 31:24 (LSJ, s.v. Χαναναῖος).

55 De Jonge, "Cleansing of the Temple," 100. See also his discussion of the whole translation issue on p. 90.

provide evidence that at least some early Christians read Zech 14:21 as referring to traders.

If the specific descriptions of Jesus' actions in the second half of v. 15 are historically reliable, it is likely that they express the view that the outer court should be sacred and, therefore, that the selling of doves and the changing of money should take place outside of the temple precinct altogether.[56] If so, then the allusions to Zech 14:21 in v. 15a and John 2:16 may reflect a view similar to that of the historical Jesus.

■ **16** The narrator states that, in addition to overturning the tables of the money-changers and the chairs of those selling doves, Jesus "would not allow anyone to carry a σκεῦος through the temple precinct." The basic meaning of the term σκεῦος is "vessel or implement of any kind."[57] It may refer to a container or tool of some sort, and the precise meaning must be determined from the context. Since the context here is the temple mount, the term should be seen in relation to "the holy vessels of the service" (τὰ ἅγια σκεύη τῆς λειτουργίας), the vessels and utensils used by the priests in association with the sacrificial cult.[58] The point seems to be that Jesus taught that it was improper to carry an ordinary, that is, a profane container or implement from outside the temple mount, through the temple area and out again. This teaching has two implications: (1) the whole temple-mount, including the outer court, is sacred and only sacred vessels and implements are allowed there; (2) it is improper to take a shortcut through the temple precinct while carrying a profane vessel or tool.[59] The saying clearly concerns the holiness of the temple and possibly ritual purity as well. The latter topic is of little importance in Mark.[60] It is thus likely that this verse represents

pre-Markan tradition. It fits well with the gestures against the money-changers and the sellers of doves as intepreted above.[61] If those gestures were performed by the historical Jesus, it is likely that the teaching of this verse goes back to him as well.[62]

■ **17** The style of this verse is Markan in its use of direct discourse preceded by qualifying verbs, "he taught and said" (ἐδίδασκεν καὶ ἔλεγεν), and in the antithetical parallelism created by the combination of the citation from Isa 56:7 and the allusion to Jer 7:11.[63] It may be that Mark replaced an earlier interpretation of Jesus' actions with this saying in order to relate the account to his own time.

In its original context, the citation from Isa 56:7 is linked to a general exhortation to avoid evildoing and to the particular advocacy of Sabbath observance. The latter is presented as the primary sign of fidelity to the covenant.[64] This opening oracle of Third Isaiah, Isa 56:1-8, also reassures eunuchs and individuals of foreign descent that their place in the people of God is secure. This "reassurance is conditional upon observing the Sabbath and holding fast to the covenant" (Isa 56:4, 6).[65] The author of the oracle even declares that people of foreign descent are eligible for the priesthood. The promise that their burnt offerings and sacrifices will be accepted on the altar of the temple in Jerusalem thus refers to the sacrifices that they will offer as priests.[66] It is clear, therefore, that, in its original context, the declaration "for my house shall be called a house of prayer for all peoples" does not mean that Gentiles will be admitted to the temple as Gentiles (Isa 56:7c).[67] It is presupposed that they will turn aside from their former practices and join the people of Israel.[68] Although sacrifices are mentioned in

56 See the section "The Historical Reliability of 11:15-17" above.

57 LSJ, s.v. σκεῦος.

58 *Paralip. Jer.* 3:9; cf. Heb 9:21; Josephus *Bell.* 6.8.3 §389; for further references, see Yarbro Collins, "Jesus' Action in Herod's Temple," 47 n. 11.

59 Yarbro Collins, "Jesus' Action in Herod's Temple," 47.

60 Contrast 7:1-23, esp. v. 19b.

61 See the section "The Historical Reliability of 11:15-17" and the commentary on v. 15 above.

62 Contra Sanders, *Jesus and Judaism*, 364 n. 1.

63 Neirynck, *Duality in Mark*, 123, 134.

64 Joseph Blenkinsopp, *Isaiah 56–66: A New Translation*

with Introduction and Commentary (AB 19B; New York: Doubleday, 2003) 135.

65 Blenkinsopp, *Isaiah 56–66*, 135, 140.

66 Ibid., 140.

67 MT: כי ביתי בית תפלה יקרא לכל העמים; LXX: ὁ γὰρ οἶκός μου οἶκος προσευχῆς κληθήσεται πᾶσιν τοῖς ἔθνεσιν; trans. above from NRSV.

68 The affiliation of the Gentiles to Israel is implied also by the parallel passage in Isa 66:23, "All flesh shall come to worship before me." On the literary relationship between the two passages, see Paul D. Hanson, *Isaiah 40–66* (Interpretation; Louisville: John Knox, 1995) 196.

the context as legitimate and necessary, the declaration shifts the emphasis from sacrifice to intercessory prayer (תפלה).[69]

Mark's citation of Isa 56:7 agrees exactly with the LXX as it has been transmitted. The condemnation of the leaders of the people implied by the cursing of the fig tree does not imply that Mark rejected sacrifice or that he denied the validity of the priestly service in the temple.[70] Members of the audience familiar with the context of the citation would probably not conclude that its use here implies that Gentiles would participate in the service of the temple as Gentiles.[71] Rather, the saying implies, also in its Markan context, the ideal that the Gentiles will turn to the God of Israel and adopt Jewish practices. Like the saying in Isa 56:7 itself, however, the Markan context implies a shift of emphasis from sacrifice to prayer. The theme of prayer introduced here prepares for the teaching about prayer in vv. 24-25.

The combination of Isa 56:7 with Jer 7:11, however, implies that the leaders of the people, especially the chief priests, are frustrating the divine plan. Instead of a house of prayer, they have made the temple "a den of robbers" (Jer 7:11a).[72] The phrase in Jeremiah occurs in the context of an oracle about the temple (7:8-11).[73] Verse 8 is a declaration that the addressees have broken the prohibition of the previous oracle, namely, not to trust in deceptive words (7:4). The deceptive words, a repetition of the phrase "the temple of Yahweh," represent the view that Jerusalem and the temple will surely not be destroyed.[74] Verses 9-10 express a rhetorical question: "Do you think you can steal, murder, commit adultery, bear false witness, burn incense to Baal and go after other gods that you have not known and then come and stand in my presence, in this house upon which my name is called, and say 'We are safe!'—only to keep doing all these abominations?" (Jer 7:9-10).[75] This question creates an incongruity between "unholy behavior and assumed protection in the holy sanctuary."[76] The "robbers' cave" or "bandits' den"[77] is clearly metaphorical. The sins of the addressees are not defined primarily as robbery or brigandage. Rather, it is the incongruity of their behavior with their expectation of security in the holy place that gives rise to the metaphor.

The incongruity in Mark, however, lies in the contrast between the intended purpose of the temple and its current state. This reformulation gives the connotations of robbery and brigandage a more direct force. In the late 50s and early 60s of the first century CE, four highpriestly families engaged in factional maneuvering that led to corruption and violence. Josephus says that the slaves of the high priest Ananias would take tithes from the ordinary priests by force, with the result that some priests starved to death (Ant. 20.9.2 §§205-7).[78] Ananias and others like him could well be called "robbers." Furthermore, according to Josephus, the peasant-brigands called "Zealots" "converted the temple of God into their fortress and refuge from any outbreak of popular violence, and made the Holy Place the headquarters of their tyranny" (Bell. 4.3.7 §151).[79] This event could very well have inspired the allusion to Jeremiah's "den of robbers."[80]

The saying in v. 17 may be read in several related ways. In relation to the entry of Jesus into Jerusalem, the incongruity of the behavior of the chief priests and other leaders lies in their continuing to serve God in the temple after having refused to welcome Jesus into the city as God's messiah.[81] In the combination of the citation of Isa 56:7 with an allusion to Jer 7:11, Mark also protests against the factionalism and violence of the high priestly families, which was a contributing factor to the outbreak

---

69   Blenkinsopp, *Isaiah 56–66*, 141.

70   See the commentary on vv. 12-14 above.

71   But note the accusation that Paul had brought Greeks, i.e., Gentiles, into the temple, recorded and refuted in Acts 21:27-29.

72   MT: מערת פרצים ("den of robbers"); LXX: σπήλαιον λῃστῶν ("den of robbers"); the basic meaning of מערת and σπήλαιον is "cave."

73   Jack R. Lundbom, *Jeremiah 1–20: A New Translation with Introduction and Commentary* (AB 21A; New York: Doubleday, 1999) 453.

74   Holladay, *Jeremiah*, 1:239, 248.

75   Trans by Lundbom, *Jeremiah 1–20*, 453 (modified).

76   Ibid., 458.

77   Holladay, *Jeremiah*, 1:246; Lundbom, *Jeremiah 1–20*, 467–68.

78   Yarbro Collins, "Jesus' Action in Herod's Temple," 51–53.

79   Trans. from Thackeray, *Josephus*, 3:47.

80   It took place during the winter of 67–68; Thackeray, *Josephus*, 3:21, 27, 121. Joel Marcus also links this event to v. 17 ("The Jewish War and the *Sitz im Leben* of Mark," *JBL* 111 [1992] 441–62, esp. 455).

81   See the commentary on v. 11 above.

of the revolt against Rome. Finally, he alludes to the occupation of the temple by the Zealots, in which the temple quite literally became a "brigands' den."[82]

■ **18** The statement in this verse that the chief priests and the scribes heard what Jesus had said and that they were looking for a way to destroy him supports the inference that those addressed in v. 17 ("But you have made it, etc.") are the leaders of the people, especially these two groups.[83] Indirectly, it confirms the reading of the cursing of the fig tree as a symbolic condemnation of the leaders of the people, not a rejection of the temple or the people as a whole. It is implied that the two groups mentioned know that the saying of v. 17 was spoken against them, just as the chief priests, scribes, and elders know that the parable about the tenants was spoken against them.[84]

The remark that the chief priests and the scribes feared Jesus is explained with reference to the crowd's amazement at his teaching. This implies that they were concerned that his actions and teaching in vv. 15-17 would lead to widespread agitation for reform of the practices related to the outer courtyard and perhaps also for recognition of Jesus as messiah or prophet. Both possibilities would limit their own influence and power and perhaps lead to unrest that would provoke Roman military action. Their hesitation here and in 12:12 prepares for the narration in 14:1 of the plan to arrest Jesus "by deceit."

■ **19** This verse continues the narrative thread of vv. 11, 12, and 15. After entering Jerusalem the first time, Jesus went out to spend the night in Bethany. On the next morning, he encountered the fig tree, then entered the city and the temple. Here he returns to Bethany for the second night.

The History of the Tradition of 11:20-25

Bultmann argued that the sayings in vv. 22-23, 24 and 25 originally circulated independently. Later, the sayings were attached to a miracle story "already in circulation whose original significance is uncertain." This process probably took place gradually; its continuation in the history of the text is clear from the secondary addition of v. 26.[85] Telford argued that vv. 24 and 25 were not part of the earliest recoverable text of Mark but were originally scribal glosses, just like v. 26.[86]

Another version of the saying of v. 25 appears in Matt 6:14, so this saying may have been known to both evangelists from another written source or from oral tradition. It is credible that the saying of v. 23 circulated independently of the story of the fig tree, since it appears in different contexts in Matt 17:20 and in Luke 17:6. It is likely that a form of this saying was included in Q.[87] In addition, Paul seems to allude to an oral version of this saying in 1 Cor 13:2.[88] It is likely that this saying goes back to the historical Jesus.[89]

Some scholars have argued that the sayings in vv. 22-25 were already attached to the miracle story in the pre-Markan stage of transmission, and others that the evangelist added them to the narrative himself.[90] E. J. Pryke concluded that vv. 20-22 and the opening phrase

82   The Greek word λῃστής, used in v. 17 and in Josephus, has a semantic range including "robber," "bandit," and "brigand"; on ancient Jewish social banditry, see Horsley and Hanson, *Bandits*, 48–87.

83   Here "the scribes" (οἱ γραμματεῖς), who are associated with the chief priests, are probably bureaucrats, judges, or officials in Jerusalem (see Anthony J. Saldarini, "Scribes," *ADB* 5:1015). See also the commentary on 10:33, 8:31, and 1:22 above.

84   Cf. Mark 11:18 with 12:12. Mark 11:18 and 12:12 are linked also by the common features of wanting to destroy or arrest Jesus and the crowd's positive reaction to Jesus and his teaching.

85   Bultmann, *History*, 25; see note f on the trans. of v. 25 above. Here a miracle story is used as the setting of an apophthegm, resulting in a scholastic dia-

logue; the whole is a formulation of the post-Easter community (ibid., 54).

86   Telford, *Barren Temple*, 50–56; Bultmann had raised the question whether v. 25 is genuine in Mark (*History*, 25). Sharyn Echols Dowd, however, has argued persuasively that vv. 24-25 were part of the original text of the Gospel (*Prayer*, 40–43). Marshall has argued similarly for v. 25 (*Faith*, 172–74).

87   Robinson et al., *Critical Edition of Q*, 492–93.

88   See also the adaptations of this saying in *Gos. Thom.* 48; 106.

89   Perrin, *Rediscovering*, 137–39. Perrin connects this saying also with the theme of "faith" in the miracle stories.

90   E.g., Pesch concluded that the sayings on faith in vv. 22-23 were attached to the story about the fig

of v. 23, "Truly I say to you, that" (ἀμὴν λέγω ὑμῖν ὅτι), were composed by Mark.[91]

The narrative of the cursing of the fig tree may be pre-Markan. If so, Mark has rewritten it and adapted it to his own purposes.[92] The curse, "May no one ever eat fruit from you again!" is portrayed in v. 20 as resulting in the total withering of the tree.[93] The remark of Peter in v. 21 picks up the comment of the narrator in v. 14b, that "his disciples heard (what he said)," and makes the significance of that comment clear. Peter recognizes the power of Jesus' speech. The initial brief saying in v. 22b serves as a heading or introduction to the rest of the sayings[94] and was probably composed by Mark. The three sayings in vv. 23-25 may once have circulated independently, but appear to be a brief catechetical collection of sayings.[95] It is not clear whether Mark created this collection or whether it is pre-Markan.[96]

Comment

■ **20** Like v. 19, the first part of this verse continues the thread of the narrative. After spending a second night in Bethany and on their walk back into the city, Jesus and the disciples see the same fig tree that they encountered on their way into the city on the previous morning.[97] They see that, in the meantime, the fig tree has "withered from the roots."

The expression "from the roots" (ἐκ ῥιζῶν) is biblical.[98] In two passages, the phrase is used in metaphorical and symbolic ways that resonate with v. 20. The first of these is Job 18:16. It occurs in a portion of

Bildad the Shuhite's second speech describing the wicked man and his fate:

From underneath his roots will wither,
and from above his harvest will fall
(ὑποκάτωθεν αἱ ῥίζαι αὐτοῦ ξηρανθήσονται,
καὶ ἐπάνωθεν ἐπιπεσεῖται θερισμὸς αὐτοῦ).
(Job 18:16 LXX)[99]

The other passage, Ezek 17:9, appears in the context of a riddle or parable concerning the king of Babylon, Nebuchadnezzar II; two kings of Judah, Jehoiachin and Zedekiah; and a pharaoh, Psammetichus II.[100] Nebuchadnezzar had placed Zedekiah on the throne as his vassal. This event is figured as a great eagle planting a seed in fertile soil that grows into a vine. But Zedekiah had been disloyal by making an alliance with Egypt, an event depicted as the transplanting of the vine. Verse 9 prophesies the fate of Zedekiah under the figure of the vine:

Will not the roots of its tenderness and its fruit become rotten, and will not all its new sprouts wither? And in order to pull it up from its roots, a mighty arm and a numerous people will not be necessary (οὐχὶ αἱ ῥίζαι τῆς ἀπαλότητος αὐτῆς καὶ ὁ καρπὸς σαπήσεται, καὶ ξηρανθήσεται πάντα τὰ προανατέλλοντα αὐτῆς; καὶ οὐκ ἐν βραχίονι μεγάλῳ οὐδ' ἐν λαῷ πολλῷ τοῦ ἐκσπάσαι αὐτὴν ἐκ ῥιζῶν αὐτῆς). (Ezek 17:9 LXX)

---

tree in the pre-Markan passion narrative, but that Mark added the sayings on prayer in vv. 24-25 because of catchword association and formal similarity (2:202). D. E. Nineham took the position that all the sayings of vv. 22-25 circulated independently prior to Mark and that the evangelist appended them to the story about the fig tree by means of artificial verbal connections (298, 300).

91 Pryke, *Redactional Style*, 168.

92 See the section "The Genre of the Story about the Fig Tree" above.

93 On the significance of this event, see the commentary below.

94 Cf. Lohmeyer, 238–39.

95 Taylor, 467.

96 See the sections "Literary Unity of 9:33-50" and "History of the Tradition of 10:1-31" above.

97 See the commentary on v. 15 above.

98 Job 28:9; 31:12; Ezek 17:9 LXX; Lohmeyer, 238.

99 The second line in the Hebrew of Job 18:16 reads וממעל ימל קצירו ("and from above his bough will wither"; my trans.). This verse in the LXX is marked with an asterisk in the Hexapla, which means that it stood in the Hebrew but not in the OG. Origen added the passage from one of the other Greek versions; see Emanuel Tov, *Textual Criticism of the Hebrew Bible* (Minneapolis: Fortress; Assen/Maastricht: Van Gorcum, 1992) 147–48.

100 Zimmerli, *Ezekiel 1*, 361–63. In 17:2, the terms in the MT are חידה ("riddle") and משל ("parable"); in the LXX they are διήγημα ("tale") and παραβολή ("parable"). On the general political situation presupposed by Ezekiel 17, see Robert R. Wilson, "The Community of the Second Isaiah," in Christopher R.

These examples suggest that the audiences of Mark would have understood the withering of the fig tree as representing a loss of power on the part of the leaders of the people. This reading supports the argument stated above, that the fig tree does not represent the people of Israel as a whole or the temple. Rather, it is the leaders of the people who reject and oppose Jesus who are to be defeated and judged.[101]

■ **21** The statement that Peter remembered (what Jesus had said on the previous morning) and his declaration to Jesus that "the fig tree which you cursed has withered" is an instance of the typical motif of the recognition that a miracle has occurred.[102] The statement of Peter also defines Jesus' exclamation in v. 14 as a curse. The narrator's remark that Peter "remembered" picks up the earlier comment that the disciples heard what Jesus had said in v. 14b.[103] These links with v. 14 tie the two halves of the story about the fig tree together.

Peter addresses Jesus as "Rabbi" here, as he did in 9:5. The connection with the miracle of the withering of the fig tree suggests that the significance of the title here is simply to express the greatness of Jesus.[104] Since immediately following Peter's remark Jesus teaches the disciples about faith or trust and prayer, the address may also have the connotation of "teacher" here.[105]

■ **22-23** Verse 22 has a transitional character. Insofar as it is a reply to what Peter has said, it implies that the power of Jesus' word comes ultimately from God. It also introduces the sayings on miracle-working trust, prayer, and forgiveness that follow.[106]

The sayings of Jesus in vv. 22-23 that follow Peter's recognition of the miracle continue the theme of miracle by portraying Jesus as instructing his disciples on how to work miracles. This instruction continues a related theme introduced in 3:14-15, where it is said that Jesus

appointed Twelve "to have authority to drive out the demons." In 4:40, as here, there is a link between performing miracles and having faith. The fact that the disciples wake Jesus and ask him to deal with the storm indicates their lack of faith and thus their inability to still the storm.[107] There Jesus asks them, "Do you not yet have trust?" Here he instructs them, "Have trust in God."

Similarly, in the account of the healing of the woman with the flow of blood, her awareness of Jesus' power and her confidence in it are contrasted with the disciples' lack of such understanding.[108] The link between miracles and trust or faith is emphasized also in the account of the raising of Jairus's daughter.[109] Analogously, a lack of trust or faith is linked with the absence of miracle-working power in the description of Jesus' rejection in Nazareth.[110] As in the passage of the appointment of the Twelve, when Jesus sends them out two by two later on (6:7), he gives them "authority over the unclean spirits" ($\dot{\epsilon}\xi o\upsilon\sigma\acute{\iota}\alpha\nu$ $\tau\hat{\omega}\nu$ $\pi\nu\epsilon\upsilon\mu\acute{\alpha}\tau\omega\nu$ $\tau\hat{\omega}\nu$ $\dot{\alpha}\kappa\alpha\vartheta\acute{\alpha}\rho\tau\omega\nu$). No advice is given them at that point about how to exercise that authority.

As Jesus challenged the disciples in the account of the stilling of the storm, he challenges them to provide food (miraculously) for the crowd just before he multiplies the loaves the first time.[111] Jesus' sending on the disciples ahead of him after the first feeding may be read as another test of their faith or trust. When they are unable to deal with the contrary wind, Jesus comes to them in an epiphanic moment and assists them. Their lack of understanding "with regard to the loaves" in 6:52 makes clear that they have failed the test.[112]

The first occasion on which Jesus gives the disciples instruction on how to perform miracles occurs in their brief conversation following the exorcism of the epileptic. The boy's father had asked the disciples to cast out

Seitz, ed., *Reading and Preaching the Book of Isaiah* (Philadelphia: Fortress, 1988) 53–70, esp. 56–57.

101   Job 18:16 and Ezek 17:9 are cited by Lohmeyer (238 n. 2), but he does not use them to illuminate v. 20 in the way proposed here.

102   Theissen, *Miracle Stories*, 65–66.

103   See the section "The History of the Tradition of 11:20-25" above.

104   See the commentary on 9:5-6 above.

105   See the commentary on 10:51-52 above.

106   Dowd, *Prayer*, 58–59.

107   See the commentary on 4:40 above.

108   See the commentary on 5:30-32 above.

109   See the commentary on 5:35-36 above.

110   See the commentary on 6:5-6a above.

111   See the commentary on 6:35-36 and 6:37-38 above.

112   See the commentary on 6:51-52 above.

the spirit that was possessing his son, but the disciples were unable to do so. After Jesus heals the boy, the disciples ask why they could not do so. Jesus replies, "This kind can be forced out in no way except by prayer." In the same context, as he does here Jesus teaches the father of the epileptic that "All things are possible for the one who trusts." The Markan Jesus teaches that "trust" or "faith" can endow human beings with divine power.[113]

The link between miracle-working and faith in v. 23 was recognized by the author of Matthew, who introduced another version of the saying into the healing of the epileptic. Instead of teaching the disciples that such a demon can be driven out only by prayer, as the Markan Jesus teaches, the Matthean Jesus attributes their failure to their lack of faith or trust and then introduces the relevant saying (Matt 17:19-20).[114]

As noted above, Jesus enunciates a principle in 9:23 that "All things are possible for the one who trusts." This principle is an extension of the ancient idea that "all things are possible to God" ($\pi\acute{\alpha}\nu\tau\alpha \ldots \delta\upsilon\nu\alpha\tau\grave{\alpha} \ \pi\alpha\rho\grave{\alpha} \ \tau\hat{\wp} \ \vartheta\epsilon\hat{\wp}$) (Mark 10:27).[115] This idea is related to the rhetorical and literary device of the $\grave{\alpha}\delta\acute{\upsilon}\nu\alpha\tau\upsilon\nu$ (that which is "impossible"). The saying in v. 23 is an example of an impossible event.[116] So in v. 23, Mark gives an instance of the principle of 9:23, that nothing is impossible for the one who trusts.

Some have argued that the reference to "this mountain" means that, in the context of Mark, a specific mountain was in view. Of these some have concluded that the reference is to the Mount of Olives and others to Mount Zion.[117] The proverbial and traditional character of the saying, however, makes it unlikely that a particular mountain is meant.[118] The argument for Mount Zion is based on the overinterpretation of the fig tree as representing all Israel or the temple.[119]

The implied advice not to doubt in one's heart but to believe or trust that what one says will come to pass makes explicit the kind of trust that characterized the woman with the flow of blood. The father of the epileptic prayed that he might be granted the same confident trust. Some have criticized the saying of v. 23 for tending to make faith a human achievement or for fostering expectations that will be cruelly disappointed.[120] But it should be recognized that the saying is hyperbolic. It grasps the imagination and encourages the fainthearted to imagine what they could accomplish by trusting in God.[121] The powerful incitement of this saying is not incompatible with the more realistic wisdom of the Rolling Stones, who sang, "You can't always get what you want; but if you try sometimes, you just might find, you get what you need."[122]

Another, more difficult issue is the tension between this saying and other parts of Mark. The saying suggests

---

113 See the commentary on 9:21-24 above.

114 See also the related sayings in *Gos. Thom.* 48; 106. Neither of these sayings links the removal of a mountain with faith (Maureen W. Yeung, *Faith in Jesus and Paul: A Comparison with Special Reference to 'Faith that Can Remove Mountains' and 'Your Faith Has Healed/Saved You'* [WUNT 2.147; Tübingen: Mohr Siebeck, 2002] 27–28).

115 Philo *Op. mun.* 14 §46; Robert M. Grant, *Miracle and Natural Law in Graeco-Roman and Early Christian Thought* (Amsterdam: North Holland, 1952) 127–34.

116 Dowd, *Prayer*, 69–72.

117 Taylor (466) and Cranfield (361) assumed that the Mount of Olives was the one in question; Lane (410) argued for this conclusion; for other scholars who took this position, see Marshall, *Faith*, 168 n. 3. Those who have argued for Mount Zion include Werner H. Kelber, *The Kingdom in Mark* (Philadelphia: Fortress, 1974) 103–4; Telford, *Barren Temple*, 59; for further references, see Marshall, *Faith*, 168 n. 4. Marshall himself takes the latter position.

Yeung argues that the mountain in question is either the Mount of Olives or Mount Zion (*Faith in Jesus and Paul*, 26–27). Her main point, however, is that the saying has to do with the moving of actual mountains, i.e., it is not a poetic expression (ibid., 24–25).

118 Cf. the version of the saying in 1 Cor 13:2.

119 See the section "The Literary Relationship between the Two Stories" and the commentary on vv. 12-14 above.

120 Marshall, *Faith*, 167–68.

121 Marshall (*Faith*, 168), following Tannehill, argued that the saying "exerts an imaginative shock."

122 Rolling Stones, "You Can't Always Get What You Want," recorded in their album *Let It Bleed* (Abkco, ASIN B0000 6AW2G; original release date, November 28, 1969).

that one's own suffering or the suffering of others can be removed by faith or confident trust. Yet the teaching on discipleship on 8:34—9:1 implies that suffering is a typical, if not a necessary, feature of a life modeled on that of Jesus. Jesus healed others but died on a cross himself. A way of resolving this tension may be found in the prayer of Jesus in Gethsemane (14:36). In that context, Jesus expresses confidence that all things are possible for God; nevertheless, he subordinates his own wishes to the wishes or plan of God. When read in light of these other passages, the saying of v. 23 must be qualified. The desire to escape suffering and death may not always be consistent with the divine will or plan. Recognition of that condition prevents the bold confidence inspired by the saying from becoming unrealistic or arrogant.

■ **24** As noted above, vv. 22-23 follow quite logically on v. 21 and continue the theme of miracle. Verse 24, however, shifts the topic from miracle-working to prayer. Verses 22-23 are addressed to the disciples, continuing their education and training as co-workers of Jesus. Verse 24 applies to them too, but is more open to application to the various audiences of Mark.[123] Just as miracle-workers are to speak powerful words to bring about extraordinary events, so every member of the community is encouraged to pray with confidence. The link between trust or faith and prayer and the exhortation to pray with confidence is also found in other early Christian texts.[124]

The context suggests that the kind of prayer envisioned here concerns requests for extraordinary events or miracles.[125] A similar link between miracle-working and prayer is made in John 14:8-14. This brief dialogue begins with Philip's request that Jesus show the disciples the Father (v. 8). Jesus' response shifts the topic to the relationship between himself and the Father (v. 9). Those who see Jesus have already seen the Father. This point is elaborated in v. 10, which ends with the statement that the Father does his works in or through Jesus. In this and other passages in John, "works" ($\check{\epsilon}\rho\gamma\alpha$) refers to the same type of events as "signs" ($\sigma\eta\mu\epsilon\hat{\iota}\alpha$) elsewhere in the Gospel.[126] If the disciples cannot believe (explicitly and directly) that Jesus is in the Father and the Father is in Jesus, they should believe "on account of the works themselves" ($\delta\iota\grave{\alpha}\ \tau\grave{\alpha}\ \check{\epsilon}\rho\gamma\alpha\ \alpha\dot{\upsilon}\tau\grave{\alpha}\ \pi\iota\sigma\tau\epsilon\acute{\upsilon}\epsilon\tau\epsilon$) (v. 11).

The topic then shifts to a link between faith and the ability to perform miracles: "Truly, truly I say to you, the one who believes in me will do the works that I am doing and will do greater works than these because I am going to the Father" ($A\mu\grave{\eta}\nu\ \dot{\alpha}\mu\grave{\eta}\nu\ \lambda\acute{\epsilon}\gamma\omega\ \dot{\upsilon}\mu\iota\nu,\ \dot{o}\ \pi\iota\sigma\tau\epsilon\acute{\upsilon}\omega\nu\ \epsilon\dot{\iota}\varsigma\ \dot{\epsilon}\mu\grave{\epsilon}\ \tau\grave{\alpha}\ \check{\epsilon}\rho\gamma\alpha\ \grave{\alpha}\ \dot{\epsilon}\gamma\grave{\omega}\ \pi\omicron\iota\hat{\omega}\ \kappa\dot{\alpha}\kappa\epsilon\hat{\iota}\nu\omicron\varsigma\ \pi\omicron\iota\acute{\eta}\sigma\epsilon\iota\ \kappa\alpha\grave{\iota}\ \mu\epsilon\acute{\iota}\zeta\omicron\nu\alpha\ \tau\omicron\acute{\upsilon}\tau\omega\nu\ \pi\omicron\iota\acute{\eta}\sigma\epsilon\iota,\ \dot{o}\tau\iota\ \dot{\epsilon}\gamma\grave{\omega}\ \pi\rho\grave{o}\varsigma\ \tau\grave{o}\nu\ \pi\alpha\tau\acute{\epsilon}\rho\alpha\ \pi\omicron\rho\epsilon\acute{\upsilon}\omicron\mu\alpha\iota$) (John 14:12). The last two verses speak about prayer, presumably prayer for extraordinary events: "And whatever you ask in my name, this I will do in order that the Father may be glorified in the Son. Whatever you ask me in my name, I will do" ($\kappa\alpha\grave{\iota}\ \dot{o}\ \tau\iota\ \dot{\alpha}\nu\ \alpha\dot{\iota}\tau\acute{\eta}\sigma\eta\tau\epsilon\ \dot{\epsilon}\nu\ \tau\hat{\omega}\ \dot{o}\nu\acute{o}\mu\alpha\tau\acute{\iota}\ \mu\omicron\upsilon\ \tau\omicron\hat{\upsilon}\tau\omicron\ \pi\omicron\iota\acute{\eta}\sigma\omega,\ \dot{\iota}\nu\alpha\ \delta\omicron\xi\alpha\sigma\vartheta\hat{\eta}\ \dot{o}\ \pi\alpha\tau\grave{\eta}\rho\ \dot{\epsilon}\nu\ \tau\hat{\omega}\ \upsilon\dot{\iota}\hat{\omega}.\ \dot{\epsilon}\acute{\alpha}\nu\ \tau\iota\ \alpha\dot{\iota}\tau\acute{\eta}\sigma\eta\tau\acute{\epsilon}\ \mu\epsilon\ \dot{\epsilon}\nu\ \tau\hat{\omega}\ \dot{o}\nu\acute{o}\mu\alpha\tau\acute{\iota}\ \mu\omicron\upsilon\ \dot{\epsilon}\gamma\grave{\omega}\ \pi\omicron\iota\acute{\eta}\sigma\omega$) (vv. 13-14). Mark 11:24, in light of its context, makes a similar point.[127]

■ **25** In this saying, God is mentioned explicitly, as in v. 22b, where the disciples are urged "Have trust in God." As argued above, the saying of v. 23 is an invitation to imitate or appropriate divine power. The preceding exhortation to trust God suggests that God is willing to share divine power with those who trust. In both sayings (vv. 23 and 25), however, human beings are expected to take the initiative. Just as they are to trust that they have the power to perform mighty deeds, so they are to for-

---

123 The verb in v. 22b is in the second person plural, addressed to the Twelve (cf. v. 11). Verse 23 begins with a second person plural address to the same group, but shifts into the third person singular in the pre-Markan saying. Verse 24 is entirely in the second person, which makes it easier for the audiences to assume that they are addressed as well. On the link between v. 23 and v. 24 and their parallel structure, see Dowd, *Prayer*, 63.

124 Jas 1:5-7; *Did.* 4:4; *Barn.* 19:6; *Hermas Man.* 9:1–2; Bultmann, *History*, 94; Dibelius-Greeven, *James*, 80–

81; Osiek, *Shepherd of Hermas*, 131–32. On the related Q-saying, Matt 7:8//Luke 11:10, and the similar saying in *Gos. Thom.*, see Fleddermann, *Mark and Q*, 182–86.

125 See the commentary on vv. 22-23 above.

126 See the commentary on 16:17 below.

127 But see the qualification based on other portions of Mark discussed in the commentary on vv. 23-24 above.

give anyone who has wronged them. Then, in response, God will forgive them their own trespasses.

The expression "your Father who is in the heavens" (ὁ πατὴρ ὑμῶν ὁ ἐν τοῖς οὐρανοῖς) occurs only here in Mark but is frequent in Matthew.[128] The saying in Mark 11:25 is especially similar to the double saying in Matt 6:14, where the human act of forgiving also precedes the divine.[129] The double saying in Matt 6:14-15 is the principle that stands behind one of the petitions of the Lord's

prayer, "And forgive us our debts, as we also forgive [or: have forgiven] our debtors" (Matt 6:12).[130] The similarity, however, does not mean that Mark knew a text of the Sermon on the Mount or of Matthew.[131] Rather, both evangelists knew a tradition linking prayer and forgiveness and adapted it independently to their respective contexts. Later, because of the similarity between Mark 11:25 and Matt 6:14, v. 26 was added to the text of Mark on the model of Matt 6:15.[132]

---

128 Matt 5:16, 45; 6:1; 7:11; 18:14. Betz holds the opinion that the term is "almost technical" in the Sermon on the Mount and in Matthew in general (*Sermon*, 315 n. 907). Note also the similar phrases, "your heavenly Father" (ὁ πατὴρ ὑμῶν ὁ οὐράνιος) in Matt 5:48; 6:14, 26, 32; 23:9; "my heavenly Father" (ὁ πατήρ μου ὁ οὐράνιος) in Matt 15:13; 18:35; "our Father who is in the heavens" (ὁ πατὴρ ἡμῶν ὁ ἐν τοῖς οὐρανοῖς) in Matt 6:9; and "my Father who is in (the) heavens" (ὁ πατήρ μου ὁ ἐν (τοῖς) οὐρανοῖς) in Matt 7:21; 10:32, 33; 12:50; 16:17; 18:10, 19.

129 The larger logical context may be that God has taken the initiative by forgiving the sins of those for whom the Son of Man has given his life (cf. 10:45). It is incumbent upon those who trust in God to forgive their fellow human beings thereafter. If they do not, they will not be forgiven at the last judgment. Cf. Betz, *Sermon*, 416.

130 Trans. from Betz, *Sermon*, 329.

131 So also Betz, *Sermon*, 408, 417 n. 605.

132 See note f on the trans. of v. 25 above.

27/   **And they went into Jerusalem again. And while he was walking in the temple precinct, the chief priests and the scribes and the elders came to him** 28/ **and said to him, "With what authority do you do this? Or who gave you the authority to do this?"** 29/ **Jesus then said to them, "I will ask you a question; answer me and I will tell you with what authority I do this.** 30/ **Did the baptism of John originate in heaven or among human beings? Answer me."** 31/ **And they were discussing with one another, saying "What shall we say?ᵃ If we say, 'In heaven,' he will say, 'Why did you not give him credence?'ᵇ** 32/ **But (if) we say, 'among human beings'—." They feared the peo-ple;ᶜ for they all thoughtᵈ that John was really a prophet.** 33/ **And they answered Jesus, "We do not know." And Jesus said to them, "I also will not say to you with what authority I do this."**

a   D Θ f¹³ et al. include the words τί εἴπωμεν ("What shall we say?"). This question, which is then resumed by the conditional clauses that follow, is characteristic of Markan repetitive style and thus is probably the ear-liest recoverable reading. See Turner, "Western Read-ings," 6; Taylor, ad loc.; G. D. Kilpatrick, "Recitative λέγων," in Elliott, *Language and Style*, 175; Elliott, "Eclectic Textual Commentary," 194.

b   א B C² D et al. read οὖν ("therefore") after διὰ τί ("why"). A C* L W et al. omit this word. The parallel in Matt 21:25 has οὖν ("therefore"), whereas the paral-lel in Luke 20:5 lacks it. This conjunction occurs most often in Matthew, less often in Luke, and least in Mark. These considerations lead to the conclusion that the earliest recoverable reading is the one lacking the conjunction and that it was added either inde-pendently or under the influence of Matthew. See Turner, "Marcan Usage," 28 (1926) 20 (Elliott, *Lan-guage and Style*, 80). For another opinion, see George D. Kilpatrick, "Particles," in Elliott, *Language and Style*, 184.

c   The trans. is based on the reading λαόν ("people"), attested by A D L W et al. The reading ὄχλον ("crowd") is attested by א B C et al. The former read-ing is attested by members of all four textual groups; on the groups, see Epp, "Dynamic View," 1–32. Fur-thermore, the same word is used in 14:2 in a similar context (but contrast 12:12). The latter reading is attested mostly by members of the "B" group (Codex Vaticanus and related MSS) and could be a correction, since a crowd is a more immediate and concrete threat.

d   The trans. is based on the reading εἶχον ("they thought," lit., "they held"). This is an idiomatic use of ἔχειν ("to have") that is attested in the papyri; see Taylor, ad loc., and BAGD s.v. D W Θ et al. read ᾔδεισαν ("they knew") and 700 reads οἴδασι ("they know"). These secondary readings arose either as "corrections" or clarifications of the idiom or in an effort to make the narrator sound less neutral about the status of John. For a different opinion, see Turner, "Western Readings," 7.

Comment

■ **27-28** The opening sentence of v. 27 takes up the thread of the narrative. The short speech of Jesus in vv. 22-25 was given to the Twelve as they walked from Bethany to the city on the second morning of their stay (cf. 11:11, 12, 15, 19, 20). Verse 27a reports their arrival in Jerusalem. Verse 27b implies that Jesus returned to the temple a third time since his arrival.

According to vv. 27b-28, the chief priests, the scribes,

and the elders approached Jesus to speak with him. The mention of the chief priests and the scribes recalls the earlier statement that these two groups were trying to destroy Jesus after his actions in the temple precinct (v. 18). The addition of the "elders" (πρεσβύτεροι) here is reminiscent of the first prediction of the suffering of the Son of Man, which says that he will be rejected by "the elders and the chief priests and the scribes" (8:31).[1]

The question they pose to Jesus is who gave him the authority to do "this" or "these things" (ταῦτα). Some scholars have argued that this passage followed immediately on the account of Jesus' actions in the temple (vv. 15-17) at a pre-Markan stage.[2] Some have suggested that the entry was followed immediately by the actions in the temple, which in turn were followed immediately by the question of authority.[3]

Others have pointed out that there is a double intercalation in chap. 11.[4] The narrative about the actions in the temple is inserted into the story about the fig tree, and the second half of the story about the fig tree, along with the sayings of vv. 22-25, is inserted between the account of the actions in the temple and the question of authority that logically follows it. This observation makes it difficult to decide whether Mark inherited a connected narrative of the three events (entry, actions in temple, question about authority), which he then broke up and expanded by adding the material related to the cursing of the fig tree, or whether he had access to several independent traditions, in oral or written form, which he then arranged in a characteristic way.

In any case, in the text of Mark as we have it, the "this" or "these things" ($\tau\alpha\hat{\upsilon}\tau\alpha$) refers at least to the actions in the temple and possibly also to the way in which Jesus entered the city, deliberately evoking Zechariah 9.[5]

■ **29-30** Jesus responds cleverly and evasively, or better, in a challenging manner, with a counterquestion.[6] He asks whether the baptism of John originated "in heaven" ($\dot{\epsilon}\xi$ $o\dot{\upsilon}\rho\alpha\nu o\hat{\upsilon}$) or "among human beings" ($\dot{\epsilon}\xi$ $\dot{\alpha}\nu\vartheta\rho\dot{\omega}\pi\omega\nu$). This reply has several implications. First of all, it suggests that the question of the leaders of the people concerned whether or not Jesus' authority derived from God. Underlying their question is doubt that it did and a challenge to prove his claim, if Jesus answered that his authority did come from God. Although, of course, Jesus is simply turning the tables on his interrogators, his counterquestion seems to imply that John's baptism did indeed originate "in heaven."[7] Jesus' strategy is made clear by the report of the leaders' deliberations in vv. 31-32.

■ **31-32** The leaders recognize that, if they say that John's baptism originated "in heaven," Jesus will reply "Why did you not give him credence?"[8] But they were afraid to say "among human beings" because the people were convinced that John was a prophet. The statement that "they feared the people" recalls v. 18, which says that the chief priests and the scribes feared Jesus, because the crowd was amazed at his teaching. So Jesus' counterquestion has prevented them from making any progress beyond the situation in v. 18. The leaders' question about the source of Jesus' authority (v. 28) was presum-

---

1   The term "scribes" here could simply refer to bureaucrats, judges, or officials in Jerusalem; see the commentary on 8:31 and 1:22 above.

2   Bultmann accepted this as a possibility for an earlier edition of Mark but doubted that such a connection was original, since the actions of Jesus in the temple did not seem to be an appropriate occasion for the rabbinic-style debate of this controversy-dialogue (*History*, 20). Robert C. Tannehill defines this passage as a testing inquiry ("Varieties," 3.2 [p. 107]; 5.21 [pp. 115–16]).

3   Telford, *Barren Temple*, 39–49, esp. 47. Henk Jan de Jonge concluded that the entry and the cleansing formed a unit in the pre-Markan tradition ("The Cleansing of the Temple in Mark 11:15 and Zechariah 14:21," in Tuckett, *Zechariah*, 87–99, esp. 91).

4   Dowd, *Prayer*, 38–40.

5   Timothy Dwyer concluded that $\tau\alpha\hat{\upsilon}\tau\alpha$ ("this" or "these things") refers to all of the activities of Jesus that have been recounted in the narrative of Mark up to this point, in particular, to his proclamation of the kingdom of God (*Wonder*, 167; see also the literature cited in ibid., n. 81).

6   On the use of a counterquestion as a response to a question in rabbinic literature, see Str-B, 1:861–62. Tannehill notes that through such questions "Jesus seizes the initiative in the testing situation" ("Varieties," 5.22 and 5.23 [p. 116]). See also Michael Tilly, *Johannes der Täufer und die Biographie der Propheten: Die synoptische Täuferüberlieferung und das jüdische Prophetenbild zur Zeit des Täufers* (BWANT 137 = 7.F. 17; Stuttgart: Kohlhammer, 1994) 62 and n. 110.

7   Cf. the discussion by Bultmann, *History*, 20.

8   Because of the use of $\pi\iota\sigma\tau\epsilon\acute{\upsilon}\epsilon\iota\nu$ ("to believe" or "to trust") here, Bultmann concluded that vv. 31-32 were composed by a "Hellenist," perhaps Mark himself (*History*, 20). E. J. Pryke assigns vv. 31-32 to Mark, along with v. 27 (*Redactional Style*, 168). Although he admitted the possibility "that the verb does not signal the same faith conception here as it does in other Markan passages," Christopher D. Marshall concluded that, for Mark, the "refusal by the nation's rulers to believe John and repent was the first step on the road to the passion of Jesus" (*Faith*, 195, 200).

ably intended to lure Jesus into making a claim about the divine source of his authority, which they could then use to accuse him of blasphemy.[9]

■ 33 The failure of the leaders' attempt to trap Jesus is manifest in their inept reply, "We do not know." Since they could not or would not rise to Jesus' challenge by answering his question, he is justified in refusing to answer theirs. The audiences of Mark must surely have enjoyed hearing about this battle of wits and especially about Jesus' victory over his opponents.

12

12:1-12 The Vineyard and the Tenants

1/ And he began to speak to them in parables, "A man planted a vineyard and placed a fence around it and dug out a vat and built a tower and leased it to vinedressers and went on a journey. 2/ And he sent a slave to the vinedressers at the right time, in order that he might receive from the vinedressers some of the fruit of the vineyard. 3/ And they took him and beat him and sent him away empty-handed. 4/ And again he sent to them another slave. And they struck that one on the head[a] and treated him shamefully. 5/ And he sent another; and that one they killed. And (he sent) many others, some of whom they beat and some they killed. 6/ He still had one, a beloved son. He sent him to them last, saying, 'They will have regard for my son.' 7/ But those vinedressers said to one another, 'This is the heir; come on, let's kill him, and the inheritance will be ours.' 8/ And they took him and killed him and threw him outside of the vineyard. 9/ What[b] will the owner of the vineyard do? He will come and destroy the vinedressers and give the vineyard to others. 10/ Have you not read this scripture, 'The stone that the builders rejected has become the cornerstone; 11/ this was the Lord's doing and it is marvelous in our eyes'?" 12/ And they were trying to arrest him, and yet they feared the crowd, for they knew that he had told this parable against them. And so they left him and went away.

a   ℵ B L Ψ 579. 892 read ἐκεφαλίωσαν. This is the only occurrence of this word in Greek literature; Swete (ad loc.) refers on this point to Christian August Lobeck's 1820 edition of Phrynichus Arabius. Swete accepted this as the earliest recoverable reading and argued that it was formed quite regularly from the diminutive form of the word for head, κεφάλιον ("little head" or perhaps simply "head") and that it means "they wounded (that one) on the head"; cf. BDF §108 (1). He agreed with the medieval commentator Euthymius that the word was used in place of τὴν κεφαλὴν συνέτριψαν ("they broke the head"). Taylor hesitated to accept this reading because it is exclusively "Alexandrian" (textual group "B"; see Epp, "Dynamic View," 285, 289–92). A C D Δ Θ et al. attest the reading ἐκεφαλαίωσαν. The meaning is "they brought under heads" or "they summed up." Nowhere else is the verb attested with a meaning like "strike on the head." Thus, Taylor concluded that either Mark used the word in an otherwise unattested sense or the text is corrupt (ad loc.). Turner proposed the emendation ἐφακελίωσαν, "trussed (him) up in a bundle" ("Marcan Usage," 29 [1928] 276–77 [Elliott, *Language and Style*, 105]). It is likely that the reading of ℵ B L et al. is the earliest recoverable reading and that it represents an otherwise unattested usage. The reading of A C D et al. seems to be a correction from an unknown or lesser known word to a known or better known word. It is not necessary to emend the text.

b   B L 892* et al. lack the conjunction οὖν ("therefore"). The shorter reading is in accordance with Markan style; see Turner, "Marcan Usage," 28. 17, 20 (Elliott, *Language and Style*, 76, 80); G. D. Kilpatrick, "Particles," in Elliott, *Language and Style*, 184.

9   See the commentary on 14:64 below.

History of the Tradition

Since the early twentieth century, scholarship on the parables has been deeply influenced by the work of Adolf Jülicher, who claimed that parables are not allegories.[10] Rather than multiple points of comparison, he argued that each parable has a single metaphorical point. Jülicher's approach to the parables has been heavily criticized, and his argument that the parables of the Synoptic Gospels were not originally allegories should no longer be taken for granted.[11]

Bultmann noted that the narrative of vv. 1-9 has no introductory formula explaining what the narrative illustrates or with what it is being compared. He concluded that it is an allegory, since the sequence of events is intelligible only under that assumption.[12] On the basis of its content, he concluded further that it is a community product; that is, it does not go back to the historical Jesus.[13] He argued that the author of the narrative gave it an ending typical of parables, namely, the question in v. 9a, which demands a response from the hearer. In this case, the narrator of the parable also gave the answer to the question in v. 9b. According to Bultmann, the scriptural quotation in vv. 10-11 was added by Mark.[14] If the parable was originally composed as an allegory about Jesus, however, the scriptural quotation could be original, since it demonstrates the vindication of Jesus after death, just as the passion predictions include the resurrection after the execution.

C. H. Dodd argued that the original narrative (disregarding the secondary citation of Psalm 118 and other secondary elements, in his view) "in its main lines is natural and realistic in every way."[15] The picture of an absentee landlord renting a vineyard to tenants reflects a common practice attested by some of the Oxyrhynchus Papyri.[16] He argued further that the parable reflected "the kind of thing that went on in Galilee during the half century preceding the general revolt of A.D. 66."[17] He concluded that the parable in its original form was spoken by the historical Jesus as a prediction in a nonclairvoyant sense of his death "and the judgment to fall upon His slayers."[18]

Joachim Jeremias, following Jülicher, assumed that the parables of the historical Jesus were simple illustrations of his eschatological proclamation of the kingdom of God. He argued, however, that "the process of treating the parables as allegories" began very early.[19] He concluded that, when Jesus told the parable, he had his own sending by God in mind when he spoke about the sending of the son by the owner of the vineyard. He argued further that Jesus' hearers could not have understood the messianic significance of the son in the story because "no evidence is forthcoming for the application of the title 'Son of God' to the Messiah in pre-Christian Palestinian Judaism."[20] Since the full publication of the Dead Sea Scrolls, this view can no longer be maintained.[21]

Jeremias explicated the allegorical character of Mark's version of the parable by pointing out that it alludes to "the Song of the Vineyard in Isa 5.1-7" so that "the vineyard is clearly Israel, the tenants are Israel's rulers and leaders, the owner of the vineyard is God, the messengers are the prophets, the son is Christ." So far the

---

10 Adolf Jülicher, *Die Gleichnisreden Jesu*, vol. 1: *Die Gleichnisreden Jesu im allgemeinen* (Freiburg i. B.: Mohr, 1886; 2nd ed., 1899; 3rd ed., Tübingen: Mohr Siebeck, 1910); vol. 2: *Auslegung der Gleichnisreden der drei ersten Evangelien* (Freiburg i. B.: Mohr, 1899; 2nd ed., Tübingen: Mohr Siebeck, 1910); reprinted (2 vols. in 1) Darmstadt: Wissenschaftliche Buchgesellschaft, 1969). On the allegorical interpretation of the parable prior to Jülicher, see the literature cited by George J. Brooke, "4Q500 1 and the Use of Scripture in the Parable of the Vineyard," *DSD* 2 (1995) 268–94, esp. 281 n. 39.

11 Klauck, *Allegorie und Allegorese*, 4–63; Stern, *Parables in Midrash*, 10–11, 48–49, 191–92; William F. Brosend II, "The Recovery of Allegory" (Ph.D. diss., University of Chicago, 1993).

12 Bultmann, *History*, 177.

13 Ibid., 177, 205.

14 Ibid., 177.

15 Charles H. Dodd, *The Parables of the Kingdom* (rev. ed.; New York: Scribner's Sons, 1961) 96.

16 Ibid.

17 Ibid., 97.

18 Ibid., 102.

19 Joachim Jeremias, *The Parables of Jesus* (rev. ed.; New York: Scribner, 1963; 6th German ed. 1962) 11–13.

20 Ibid., 72–73.

21 Adela Yarbro Collins, "Mark and His Readers: The Son of God among Jews," *HTR* 92 (1999) 393–408.

allegorical reading of Jeremias is plausible. When he goes on to say that "the punishment of the husbandmen symbolizes the ruin of Israel, the 'other people' (Matt. 21.43) are the Gentile Church,"[22] however, his reading is influenced by Christian anti-Jewish polemic.

The allegorical features of the parable in Mark and Matthew are secondary in Jeremias's view because they are lacking in the Lukan version and especially in that of the *Gospel of Thomas*.[23] He argued that the omission of the allusion to Isaiah 5 in Luke 20:9 indicates that the Lukan version is not an allegory. He noted that Luke did not take over the killing of the third servant nor Mark's allegorical conclusion to the part about the sending of the servants (v. 5b), which alludes to the prophets and their fate.[24] Although he recognized that the "perfect symmetry" of Luke 20:10-12 is typical of Luke's style, he left open the possibility that Luke differs from Mark because of his knowledge of an oral version of the parable.[25] The latter argument is weakened, however, by the

admission that the Lukan version has allegorical features.[26] Jeremias considered that his argument concerning Luke had been confirmed by the *Gospel of Thomas*. He pointed out that the allusion to Isaiah 5 is also lacking at the beginning of this Gospel's version of the parable.[27] He argued further that the parable is not an allegory in *Gos. Thom.* because it ends abruptly with the death of the son. Since "the resurrection of Jesus had such a central importance for the primitive Church . . . it must have been mentioned in the story" if it were an allegory.[28] It is, however, likely that the version in *Gos. Thom.* is a rewriting of one or more of the Synoptic versions.[29] It is also possible that *Gos. Thom.* 65 is a textualization of an oral parable that presupposed the allegorical reading in terms of Jesus. If one agrees with Jeremias that the text in *Gos. Thom.* is not an allegory, one must recognize the likelihood that it is a rewriting of an allegorical parable into a nonallegorical form with the purpose of adapting it to the perspective of the work as a whole.[30] Even

---

22   Jeremias, *Parables of Jesus*, rev. ed., 70.

23   Matt 21:33-46; Luke 20:9-19; *Gos. Thom.* 65; Jeremias, *Parables of Jesus*, rev. ed., 70–76. Brooke, however, points out that the question of the owner of the vineyard in Luke 20:13, "What shall I do?" is based on LXX Isa 5:4 ("4Q500 1 and the Use of Scripture in the Parable of the Vineyard," 283).

24   Jeremias, *Parables of Jesus*, rev. ed., 70–72.

25   Ibid., 72 and n. 84.

26   Ibid., 73.

27   Ibid., 70.

28   It should be noted, however, that a saying alluding to the vindication of Jesus in terms of Ps 118:22 occurs immediately after the parable in the *Gospel of Thomas*. See below.

29   Wolfgang Schrage concluded that *Gos. Thom.* 65 is a pastiche of the three Synoptic versions, esp. the Matthean and the Lukan; he stressed the fact that some of the similarities involve dependence on Lukan redactional elements (*Das Verhältnis des Thomas-Evangeliums zur synoptischen Tradition und zu den koptischen Evangelienübersetzungen* [BZNW 29; Berlin: Töpelmann, 1964] 139–40). Schrage's methods, however, have been criticized; see Christopher Tuckett, "Thomas and the Synoptics," *NovT* 30 (1988) 132–57, esp. 134–36. On the whole problem of the relation of *Gos. Thom.* and the Synoptics, see Tuckett's article and Meier, *Marginal Jew*, 1:124–39. Although he did not discuss *Gos. Thom.* 65 and 66, Tuckett has demonstrated that *Gos. Thom.* "sometimes shows parallels with redactional material in

the synoptics" and thus "that there is a measure of dependence between our version(s) of Th and our synoptic gospels" ("Thomas and the Synoptics," 157). Klyne R. Snodgrass argued that *Gos. Thom.* 65 is dependent on "a pre-Tatian harmonizing tradition" attested in certain Syriac manuscripts of Mark and Luke; thus, the "twofold sending of the servants" in *Gos. Thom.* 65 "stems from a post-Synoptic stage" of the transmission of the parable ("The Parable of the Wicked Husbandmen: Is the Gospel of Thomas Version the Original?" *NTS* 21 [1974–75] 142–44).

30   E.g., Jean-Marie Sevrin concluded that certain Synoptic parables were brought together into a new order by the author of *Gos. Thom.* (63, 64, 65) to argue that ties to the material world lead to death, whereas seeking self-knowledge leads to life ("Un groupement de trois paraboles contre les richesses dans l'Evangile selon Thomas: *EvTh* 63, 64, 65," in Jean Delorme, ed., *Les paraboles évangéliques: Perspectives nouvelles* [Paris: Cerf, 1989] 425–39, esp. 438). Martin Hengel, following Schrage, had concluded earlier that *Gos. Thom.* shows a tendency to remove allegorical elements ("Das Gleichnis von den Weingärtnern Mc 12 1-12 im Lichte der Zenonpapyri und der rabbinischen Gleichnisse," *ZNW* 59 [1968] 1–39, esp. 5–6).

Jeremias admits that there is an allegorical "hint" or "trait" in the context, in that the saying about the cornerstone is "attached as an independent logion (66) to the completed parable (65)."[31] According to Jeremias, the "original meaning of the parable" is the vindication of Jesus' proclamation of the gospel to the poor. These are the "others" to whom the vineyard of God is to be given.[32]

Martin Hengel followed Jülicher in concluding that vv. 1-9 represent the earliest form of the parable.[33] Like Dodd, he argued that the events of the parable are realistic.[34] He has shown that the picture of tenant-farming and the basic terms used to describe it in the narrative are attested in the Zenon papyri.[35] These papyri provide evidence related to commercial and agricultural activity in Palestine in the third century BCE.[36] Hengel argued further that the basic narrative of the parable is compatible with activities presupposed by a number of biblical narratives and rabbinic parables.[37] He also agreed with Dodd that the historical Jesus spoke this parable in his last confrontation with the leaders before his arrest. He recognized that they would murder him and pronounced judgment upon them.[38] The realistic character of the narrative, however, is an insufficient warrant for the conclusion that the narrative goes back to Jesus.[39]

Hans-Josef Klauck concluded that the vineyard was not metaphorical in the oldest form of the parable. He also concluded that the historical Jesus expressed in this parable, in an indirect and metaphorical way, his own destiny in relation to the kingdom of God. The additions to the parable in the pre-Markan stage of transmission indicate a new interpretation in which the vineyard and the servants are interpreted metaphorically. The servants are understood as the prophets, and the tenants are interpreted as Israel who murders the prophets, in accordance with the Deuteronomistic tradition. Verse 9 belongs to this stage and expresses a threat of judgment and the supersession of Israel.[40] More importantly, v. 9 reflects an eschatological expectation of the coming of the risen Lord. The only Markan redactional element in the parable itself is, according to Klauck, the qualification of the son as "beloved" ($\dot{\alpha}\gamma\alpha\pi\eta\tau\acute{o}\varsigma$). This addition relates the parable to the Markan theme of Jesus as the Son of God. Mark also added the citation of Psalm 118 in vv. 10-11. This citation is the answer to the question of Jesus' authority posed in 11:28.[41]

Under the influence of Jülicher, Dodd, and Jeremias, Klyne Snodgrass concluded that the parable "was told originally by Jesus toward the end of his ministry in the context of his conflict with the Jewish authorities" and that it originally had a single metaphorical point, "responsibility in the context of covenant."[42] The covenant involves possession of "the Law, the promises, and the working of God in the past and present. . . . That which is taken and given to others is the special relationship to God which results from being his elect or, in short, election itself."[43] He also concluded that the connection between the parable and the citation of Psalm 118 is original, since it is based on a wordplay on בֵּן ("son") and אֶבֶן ("stone").[44] Play on the same two words occurs in Exod 28:9-10 and Josh 4:6-7.[45]

George Brooke argued that the parable both was an

---

31 Jeremias, *Parables of Jesus*, rev. ed., 74 n. 94; cf. 77.

32 Ibid., 76. Note that the statement that the vineyard will be given to others does not occur in the version of the parable in *Gos. Thom.* 65.

33 Hengel, "Das Gleichnis von den Weingärtnern," 1–2.

34 Ibid., 3–11.

35 Ibid., 11–16, 19–28.

36 Schürer, *History*, 2:61–62.

37 Hengel, "Das Gleichnis von den Weingärtnern," 16–19, 28–31; on rabbinic analogies, see also Stern, *Parables in Midrash*, 324–25 n. 19.

38 Hengel, "Das Gleichnis von den Weingärtnern," 34, 37.

39 Klauck, *Allegorie und Allegorese*, 297.

40 The interpretation of v. 9 as portraying the supersession of Israel is an overinterpretation of the text influenced by Christian anti-Jewish polemic.

41 Klauck, *Allegorie und Allegorese*, 308–11.

42 Klyne Snodgrass, *The Parable of the Wicked Tenants* (WUNT 27; Tübingen: Mohr Siebeck, 1983) 111–12.

43 Ibid., 76.

44 Ibid., 62–65, 95–106, 113–18.

45 Brooke, "4Q500 1 and the Use of Scripture," 287. He suggested that the same wordplay may be present also in Lam 4:1-2 and Zech 9:16 and argued that the wordplay could work in both Hebrew and Aramaic. Josephus says that, during the siege of Jerusalem, the Romans would catapult stones at the Jewish defenders. When wanting to warn their fellows that such a stone was flying toward them, they would say, in their native language, "The son is coming" (*Bell.* 5.6.3 §272; Brooke, "4Q500 1 and the Use of Scripture," 287–88).

allegory in its earliest form and goes back to the historical Jesus. Building on an analysis of 4Q500 1 by Joseph M. Baumgarten, Brooke argued that this text from the Dead Sea Scrolls illustrates how Isa 5:1-7 was interpreted in the late Second Temple period. Whereas Isa 5:7 implies that "the vineyard represents the house of Israel in which are planted the people of Judah,"[46] the text from Qumran interprets the vineyard as Jerusalem. It thus provides evidence for the interpretation attested in the targum attributed to Jonathan. Its version of Isa 5:2 is "And I built my sanctuary among them and also my altar I gave as atonement for their sins." It thus interprets the tower of the vineyard as the temple and the vat as the altar of burnt offering in front of the temple.[47] The vineyard of the parable is thus "Israel in miniature, that is Jerusalem, its temple and its cult."[48] The parable indicts the leaders of the people for abusing their privileged role in Jerusalem and its temple.[49] He also concluded that the link between the parable and the citation of Ps 118:22-23 is original, since the catchword οἰκοδομεῖν ("to build") links the two (vv. 2, 10).[50] Finally, he argued that the motif of election is important, "not in terms of Christian displacement of Israel, but in terms of who may participate in the cult, in the right worship of God. It is the authorities in the temple who are undermined, challenged and displaced, not Israel as a whole."[51]

David Stern agreed with many other interpreters in concluding that the tenants correspond to the Jewish leaders, the owner is God, and the messengers are the various biblical prophets. He differed from most other interpreters, however, in arguing that the son in the parable represents John the Baptist. He based this argument on the context of Mark as a whole, including the question about the authority of Jesus, in 11:27-33, where John the Baptist is mentioned. Stern also concluded that the "stone that the builders rejected" is John.[52] This interpretation of the son in the parable is implausible. Mark reports that Herod, not the chief priests, scribes, and elders to whom the parable is addressed, killed John (6:17-29), as Stern himself admitted. An even more significant problem is that it is Jesus who is called "the beloved son" elsewhere in Mark, not John. Further, the idea that John "has become the cornerstone" does not fit with the rest of Mark's narrative. Stern is surely right that the destinies of John and Jesus are parallel in Mark, but the analogy between the two characters is insufficient to support the interpretation of the son in the parable as John.

John Kloppenborg has argued that the story is "a piece of realistic fiction" and that v. 9 is "a secondary allegorizing accretion to the story."[53]

Comment

■ **1** The parable is introduced with the words "And he began to speak to them in parables." The antecedent of "them" (αὐτοῖς) is "the chief priests and the scribes and the elders," who, according to 11:27-28, come to Jesus and question the origin of his authority.

The opening statements of the parable itself both describe a typical agricultural situation and allude to Isa 5:1-2.[54] In the MT, the passage begins with the following introduction:

Let me sing for my friend my love song about his vineyard

(אשירה נא לידידי שירת דודי לכרמו).[55]

The song is written and performed on behalf of God, whose epithet here ("friend" or "beloved") recalls ancient Near Eastern deities of vegetation, an epithet appropriate for a song about a vineyard.[56] The first line of the song reads:

46 Brooke, "4Q500 1 and the Use of Scripture," 284.
47 Ibid., 269–72.
48 Ibid., 284.
49 Ibid., 286.
50 Ibid., 288.
51 Ibid., 294.
52 Stern, *Parables in Midrash*, 193–94.
53 John S. Kloppenborg, "Self-Help or *Deus ex Machina* in Mark 12.9?" *NTS* 50 (2004) 495–518; quotations from 517.
54 See the section "History of the Tradition" above. For an excavated example of a country estate perhaps similar to the one envisioned by the parable, see Yizhar Hirschfeld with Miriam Feinberg Vamosh, "A Country Gentleman's Estate," *BAR* 31.2 (March/April 2005) 18–31.
55 Trans. from Blenkinsopp, *Isaiah 1–39*, 205.
56 Ibid., 207. The LXX translates this word with ἠγαπημένος ("beloved").

My friend had a vineyard on a hillside rich in soil

(כרם היה לידידי בקרן בן שמן).[57]

Whereas in Isaiah the "friend" already has the vineyard, the narrative in Mark begins with a man planting a vineyard.[58]

Although the Markan text omits some of the details and modifies the order of the activities, the next three clauses have close parallels in the LXX version of the song. Mark's "and he placed a fence around it" (καὶ περιέθηκεν φραγμόν) is close to the LXX's "and a fence I placed around it" (καὶ φραγμὸν περιέθηκα) (Mark 12:1 and Isa 5:2 LXX).[59] Mark's "and he dug out a vat" (καὶ ὤρυξεν ὑπολήνιον) alludes to the LXX's "and a vat (in front of the winepress) I dug out in it" (καὶ προλήνιον ὤρυξα ἐν αὐτῷ).[60] Similarly, Mark's "and he built a tower" (καὶ ᾠκοδόμησεν πύργον) evokes the LXX's "and I built a tower in the middle of it" (καὶ ᾠκοδόμησα πύργον ἐν μέσῳ αὐτῷ).[61]

According to Isa 5:7, the vineyard is the house of Israel and the vine is the people of Judah. In v. 3, the inhabitants of Jerusalem and the people of Judah are asked to judge between "me and my vineyard." It may be the mention of Jerusalem here that led to the interpretation, attested already in the Dead Sea Scrolls, of the vineyard as Jerusalem, the tower as the temple, and the vat as the altar of burnt offering in front of the temple.[62]

A new element in the Markan narrative, in comparison with the song of Isaiah, is the leasing of the vineyard to vinedressers and the departure of the owner. The motif of the owner/king leasing a field (vineyard, orchard, etc.) to tenants occurs in rabbinic parables.[63] In light of the statement that Jesus spoke the parable to "them," that is, to the chief priests and the scribes and the elders (see above) and the remark in v. 12 that "they knew that he had told this parable against them," it is apparent that the tenants represent these leaders of the people, to whom God has entrusted God's "vineyard" (Jerusalem as "Israel in miniature," as Brooke put it).[64]

■ **2-3** Although this part of Mark's narrative is concise and extreme, it would have had a degree of verisimilitude for its ancient audiences. For example, Hengel pointed out the similarity between Mark's scenario and the situation described in several of the Zenon papyri. In the third century BCE, Apollonius, the royal financier during the reign of Ptolemy II Philadelphus, owned an estate in Beth-Anath in Lower Galilee. Zenon, an agent of Apollonius, visited this estate, which was devoted primarily to vineyards and the production of wine, during a tour of inspection of the region. Shortly thereafter, another agent of Apollonius, Glaukias, also made an inspection, consulting with the manager of the estate, Melas. Wine from the estate was shipped to Alexandria for the use of the absentee owner. One of the papyri describes rebellious agricultural workers who created difficulties for Melas in the delivery of various products, especially wine. Melas referred to the contracted amounts, whereas the workers had petitioned that these be reduced. The workers apparently did not resort to violence, even though Melas admonished them to pay what they owed fully and on time. Hengel speculated, however, that they were a factor to be reckoned with.[65]

■ **4** Many commentators have argued that the narrative lacks verisimilitude at this point, since the owner would not simply have sent another slave after the first one had been beaten and sent away empty-handed. Hengel has shown, however, that it was not always so easy for the absentee owners of estates and their agents to collect what they were legally entitled to. Once again, the Zenon

---

57 Trans. from ibid., 205.

58 The planting of the vineyard (ἀμπελών) in Mark may allude to the planting of a vine (ἄμπελος) in Isa 5:2 LXX.

59 The MT does not contain this feature.

60 The MT reads ונם יקב חצב בו ("he hewed out a wine vat in it"); trans. from Blenkinsopp, *Isaiah 1–39*, 205.

61 The MT reads ויבן מגדל בתוכו ("he built a watch-tower inside it"); trans. from Blenkinsopp, *Isaiah 1–39*, 205.

62 4Q500 1; see the section "History of the Tradition" above. Note that in the Animal Apocalypse,

Jerusalem is portrayed as a "house" and the temple as a "tower" (*1 Enoch* 87:3; 89:50, 72-73; 90:29; Tiller, *Animal Apocalypse*, 248–50, 313–14, 339–40, 376).

63 Stern, *Parables in Midrash*, 324 n. 19.

64 See "History of the Tradition" above.

65 Hengel, "Das Gleichnis von den Weingärtnern," 12–16. See also Freyne, *Galilee*, 156–57. On the ownership of land in Galilee in the Hellenistic period in general, see Hengel, "Das Gleichnis von den Weingärtnern," 20–21; for the Hellenistic and Roman periods, see Freyne, *Galilee*, 156–70.

papyri provide relevant evidence. Although they describe an earlier period, the conditions they attest probably persisted into the first century CE with appropriate permutations.[66] When Zenon was making his tour of inspection in Palestine, he attempted to collect a debt from a certain Jeddua, apparently a Jewish leader or elder of a village. Zenon sent an official under his authority, Straton, to collect the debt and asked the local Ptolemaic authorities to support him in that endeavor. A certain Oryas, probably the chief of that district, delegated the responsibility for assisting Straton to Alexander, an official under him who was in charge of the relevant locality. Alexander begged off, on the basis of illness, and merely sent one of his slaves with Straton. He gave the slave a letter for Jeddua, presumably instructing him to pay his debt to Straton. Hengel speculated that Alexander was trying to avoid conflict with Jeddua. In any case, Jeddua not only did not pay the debt but, perhaps along with his allies, mistreated Straton and Alexander's slave physically and drove them out of the village.[67] Once again, the ancient hearers may have understood this part of the narrative as a concise and extreme example of the kind of thing that had happened or could happen.

At the same time, the event described by this verse may also be understood allegorically. Already in vv. 2-3, the word δοῦλος ("slave") could evoke the notion of God's servants or slaves, the prophets.[68] Furthermore, the unusual word used to describe what the tenants did to the second slave, κεφαλιοῦν ("to strike on the head"), may result from the evangelist's attempt to allude to the death of John the Baptist without being too obvious by using the word "to behead" (ἀποκεφαλίζειν) (cf. 6:16).[69] This interpretation is credible only on the assumption that the various sendings in vv. 2-5 are not strictly allegorical in the sense of being references to particular prophets in chronological order.

The implication, on the allegorical level, is that the leaders addressed by the Markan Jesus are the heirs of those who earlier rejected and mistreated the prophets.[70] Verse 4 also suggests that the leaders are likely to behave in the violent way that Herod Antipas did with regard to John the Baptist.[71]

■ **5** The killing of the third slave provides a preliminary climax in the folkloric threesome. On the narrative level, the violence escalates from beating, to striking on the head, to killing. The comment in v. 5b that he sent "many others, some of whom they beat and some they killed," is probably an allusion to the pervasive scriptural motif of the rejection of the person and message of the prophet, which may involve violence and even death.[72]

■ **6-9** The major climax of the story comes with the sending and the murder of the owner's son. Although this climax does not have much historical verisimilitude, it has narrative power.[73] The son is more valuable to the father than any slave: ἀγαπητός ("beloved") may have the connotation of "only (son)" or "favorite (son)." The rebellion of the tenants reaches its height in this incident. It escalates from refusing to pay what they owe to the owner to attempting to seize the property itself and to gain ownership of it. Finally, instead of giving the son's body a decent burial, they cast it out of the vineyard and abandon it to dogs, birds, and wild animals.[74]

---

66   Freyne, *Galilee*, 162.

67   Hengel, "Das Gleichnis von den Weingärtnern," 26; see also Freyne, *Galilee*, 156–58.

68   E.g., Amos 3:7 LXX refers to "the slaves of the Lord, the prophets" (οἱ δοῦλοι (κυρίου) οἱ προφῆται).

69   See note a on the trans. of v. 4 above.

70   Compare the criticism of the scribes and Pharisees as the heirs of those who killed the prophets in Matt 23:29-31//Luke 11:47-48. On references to the persecution of the prophets by leaders of the people in the Hebrew Bible and Second Temple Jewish texts, see Liebers, "*Wie geschrieben steht*", 370–73.

71   It is more likely that John the Baptist is alluded to with the slave of v. 4 than with the beloved son; see the discussion of Stern's interpretation in "History of the Tradition" above.

72   Liebers, "*Wie geschrieben steht*", 369–75; see the commentary on 9:12-13 above. See also Colleen Demetra Stamos, "The Killing of the Prophets: Reconfiguring a Tradition" (Ph.D. diss., University of Chicago, 2001).

73   Dodd, *Parables of the Kingdom*, 100–101; Hengel, "Das Gleichnis von den Weingärtnern," 30–31. Kloppenborg argued that v. 9 is unrealistic because resort to the courts was the norm at the time, not the use of violence to recover a debt ("Self-Help or *Deus ex Machina* in Mark 12.9?" 507–15).

74   Hengel, "Das Gleichnis von den Weingärtnern," 31.

This shocking portrayal of the tenants' deeds prepares well for the rhetorical question in v. 9a, "What will the owner of the vineyard do?"

As with the preceding verses, v. 6 is also easily read allegorically. The narrator's remark, "He still had one, a beloved son," places this last agent of God in the line of the prophets yet indicates that he is more than a prophet. According to Mark, Jesus has a prophetic role in some important ways yet is more appropriately described as "messiah" than as "prophet."[75] In the Markan form of the parable, the "beloved son" clearly refers to Jesus. God addresses him as "my beloved son" in the scene of his baptism (1:11) and declares to the disciples who witness the transfiguration that Jesus is "my beloved son" (9:7). Those two passages, along with this one, are the only places in Mark where the word $\dot{\alpha}\gamma\alpha\pi\eta$-$\tau\dot{o}\varsigma$ ("beloved") is used. The remark that the owner sent his son "last" ($\ddot{\epsilon}\sigma\chi\alpha\tau o\nu$) evokes the summary of Jesus' message in 1:15, "The time is fulfilled and the kingdom of God has drawn near; repent and trust in the good news." If the time is fulfilled, the narrative time of Mark belongs to the "last days" and Jesus is God's last agent. On the allegorical level, the statement attributed to the owner, "They will have regard for my son" ($\dot{\epsilon}\nu\tau\rho\alpha\pi\dot{\eta}\sigma o\nu$-$\tau\alpha\iota$ $\tau\dot{o}\nu$ $\upsilon\dot{\iota}\dot{o}\nu$ $\mu o\upsilon$), need not be read in terms of the patience or forbearance of God, but as indicating the proper response to Jesus.[76]

The second level of meaning of v. 7, in which the vinedressers recognize the son as the heir and kill him, sets Jesus as the messiah over against the chief priests and the scribes and the elders. Here is the answer to their question about the authority of Jesus.[77] He is the "son" who has authority over the "vineyard" because of his relationship to the Father, whereas the leaders who question his authority are only "tenants."[78] Their rejection of Jesus is tantamount to rebellion against God. The murder of the son and the casting out of his body in v. 8 do

not have a close allegorical relationship to the crucifixion of Jesus, to be described later in the narrative of Mark. Rather, this part of the narrative depicts the tenants/leaders as unscrupulous and sacrilegious.

In relation to the parable as a narrative, the word $\kappa\dot{\upsilon}\rho\iota o\varsigma$ ("owner," "lord") in the rhetorical question of v. 9a simply refers to the owner of the vineyard. On the allegorical level, however, it refers to the Lord God, the owner of the prototypical vineyard in Isaiah 5. According to Isa 5:5, the divine speaker will remove the hedge of the vineyard and allow it to become pastureland, will breach its wall and allow it to be trampled down, and will make it a wasteland. The audience of Mark might expect the answer given to the rhetorical question to be that the Lord will come and destroy the vineyard, that is, Jerusalem.[79] Such a response would fit with the prediction of the destruction of the temple and city in chapter 13. The response in v. 9b, however, is "He will come and destroy the vinedressers and give the vineyard to others." Here the focus is not on the destruction of Jerusalem, let alone the rejection of Israel as a whole. Rather it is on the removal from power of the leaders who oppose Jesus. The story about the cursing of the fig tree makes the same point.[80] Giving the vineyard to others implies that a new leadership will emerge among those who accept Jesus as the messiah.

■ **10-11** After both asking and answering a rhetorical question in v. 9, the Markan Jesus, without waiting for a response from the leaders, goes on to ask, "Have you not read this scripture, 'The stone that the builders rejected has become the cornerstone; this was the Lord's doing and it is marvelous in our eyes'?" Many commentators have concluded that this scriptural citation was added by Mark to an older parable.[81] In the light of later rabbinic practice, however, the citation may be taken as an integral part of the rhetorical use of the parable, corresponding to the *nimshal* (the application of the narrative

---

75   See the section of the introduction "Interpretation of Jesus," especially the subsection "Jesus as Prophet."

76   Lohmeyer saw the notion of the patience or forbearance of God expressed in the sending of one messenger after another (245), and Hengel affirmed this meaning for the later, Markan version of the parable ("Das Gleichnis von den Weingärtnern," 28 n. 91).

77   Klauck, *Allegorie und Allegorese*, 311.

78   Cf. the contrast between Jesus, the shepherd, and those who came before him, who are characterized as thieves and bandits, in John 10:1-18.

79   See the commentary on v. 1 above.

80   See the commentary on 11:12-14, 18, 20 above.

81   Klauck, *Allegorie und Allegorese*, 310–11; see also the section "History of the Tradition" above.

parable) in rabbinic parables. The citation does not provide an "explanation" for the narrative but confirms the rhetorical message expressed by the parable, giving it scriptural authority. Thus, this passage may be "one of the earliest testimonies to the inherently rhetorical use of scriptural exegesis in a narrative parable."[82] The narrative and the citation are also connected by the use of the word οἰκοδομεῖν ("to build") in vv. 1 and 10 and by the possible play on "son" (בן) and "stone" (אבן) in vv. 6 and 10.[83] If the latter is not mere coincidence, the parable, along with the scriptural citation, must have been formulated in Aramaic or Hebrew originally or in Greek by someone, like the author of Mark, competent in Aramaic and probably Hebrew and Greek.[84]

The passage cited is Ps 118:22-23 (Psalm 117 LXX). Mark's wording agrees exactly with the LXX text as it has come down to us. In the context of Mark as a whole, it is clear that the stone that the builders rejected (ἀποδοκιμάζειν) is Jesus, the Son of Man, who must be rejected (ἀποδοκιμάζειν) by the elders, chief priests, and scribes, according to 8:31. This textual link makes clear also that the "builders" of the psalm are the leaders to whom the parable is addressed. The latter identification is supported by the possible play on words with regard to the Hebrew version of the text between הבונים ("builders") and בנים ("the thinkers" or "the wise").[85] The latter epithet would fit especially the scribes, if they are to be understood as experts in the Law.

In the LXX, the phrase κεφαλὴν γωνίας is a literal translation of the rare Hebrew phrase ראש פנה. Both mean, literally, "head of the corner." These phrases refer to the most distant corner of a building at the horizontal level—in other words, the foundation stone of the corner at which a building is begun, fixing its site and orientation. Such stones were not below ground, but were visible.[86] In the Hebrew psalm, the saying about the rejected stone becoming the cornerstone was probably a proverb

that expressed the reversal effected by God: the one who was in danger of death has emerged victorious.[87]

In Mark, the citation may function in a similarly metaphorical way simply to indicate the divine reversal of the rejection and execution of Jesus by raising him from the dead. The imagery of building, however, may be significant. The implication may be that, with the resurrection of Jesus, God will begin to build a living temple that will consist of the communities founded in Jesus' name. Such an idea is analogous to the self-understanding of the community at Qumran as a metaphorical temple (1QS 8:4-10; 9:3-6).[88] The idea of the community of followers of Jesus as a living temple is expressed by Paul in 1 Cor 3:10-17 and 2 Cor 6:16. Eph 2:19-22 also refers to the community as a holy temple under construction with Christ Jesus as the cornerstone (ἀκρογωνιαῖος).[89] 1 Peter also portrays the community as a temple, with Jesus Christ as the cornerstone, citing Isa 28:16; Ps 118:22; and Isa 8:14.

Here the Markan Jesus cites Psalm 118 as scripture with the introductory formula, "Have you not read this scripture?" In the narrative of Jesus' entry into Jerusalem, the same psalm is alluded to in the exclamation and benediction shouted by the crowd, "Hosanna! Blessed is he who comes in the name of the Lord!" (11:9). In that context, the idea that David was the author of the psalm may have played a role in the benediction of "the coming kingdom of our father David!" in 11:10.[90] If that idea was familiar to Mark and his audiences, then the application of the psalm to Jesus here may also carry the connotation of Jesus being the son of David, the messiah, who, though rejected and killed, is the beginning of God's new creation.

Jesus' speech in Mark ends with the citation of Ps 117:23 LXX: "this was the Lord's doing and it is marvelous in our eyes" (παρὰ κυρίου ἐγένετο αὔτη καὶ ἔστιν θαυμαστὴ ἐν ὀφθαλμοῖς ἡμῶν). Luke omits this

---

82 Stern, *Parables in Midrash*, 196–97.

83 See "History of the Tradition" above.

84 On the use of the Hebrew word בן in Aramaic, see the discussion of Brooke's analysis in "History of the Tradition" above.

85 Stern, *Parables in Midrash*, 196.

86 Helmut Krämer, "γωνία κτλ.," *EDNT* 1 (1990) 267–69, esp. 268.

87 Cf. Kraus, *Psalms 60–150*, 400.

88 The community also understood itself as a living Jerusalem: 11QMelch 2:23-24; 4Q164, lines 1–7.

89 Eph 2:20 alludes to Isa 28:16; ἀκρογωνιαῖος ("cornerstone") here probably has the same meaning as κεφαλὴν γωνίας ("cornerstone") in Ps 117:22 LXX and in Mark 12:10; Krämer, "γωνία κτλ.," 268.

90 See the commentary on 11:9-10 above.

material and adds another saying about a metaphorical stone (Luke 20:18).[91] Matthew follows Mark by including the citation of Ps 117:23 LXX, but diminishes its significance by adding an emphatic saying of Jesus that elaborates the statement that the vineyard will be given to others. In Mark, however, the citation of v. 23 of the psalm has an emphatic position in the rhetorical conclusion of the parable. In the psalm, what is marvelous is the striking reversal in the situation of the one who was surrounded by enemies and near death. By the power of God he could celebrate a victory. Similarly, in Mark what is marvelous is the radical change in the status of Jesus from one who was rejected and shamefully treated to the exalted Son of Man.[92]

■ **12** The reaction of the addressees of the parable, the chief priests, scribes, and elders, is then reported. It is similar to the reaction of the chief priests and the scribes to the Markan Jesus' actions in the temple and the narrator's commentary on them, reported in 11:18. In chapter 11, they begin looking for a way to destroy him; here they begin seeking a way to arrest him. There they fear him because of the crowd's amazement at this teaching. Here they are hesitant to arrest him because they fear the crowd. Here Jesus is explicitly and temporarily victorious, since they leave him and go away.

The remark that they knew that the parable had been told against them reinforces the audience's tendency to understand the parable as an allegory. The portrayal of the leaders as grasping the significance of the parable immediately shows that this parable is like the figurative language used by Jesus in the first part of the controversy over his exorcisms and not like the enigmatic parables of 4:1-34.[93]

---

91   This saying may allude to Dan 2:34-35, 44-45 and to Isa 8:14-15.

92   Cf. 8:31; 9:31; 10:33-34 and esp. 14:62.

93   See the commentary on 3:23-26 and on 4:1-9, 11-12, 24-25, 26-29 above.

12:13-17 Tribute to Caesar

13/	And they sent some of the Pharisees and the Herodians to him in order that they might catch him in a statement. 14/ And they came and said to him, "Teacher, we know that you are truthful and court no man's favor; for you do not accommodate your teaching to humans, but teach the way of God in accordance with the truth. Is it permitted to pay tax[a] to Caesar or not? Should we pay or not pay?" 15/ He then, knowing their hypocrisy, said to them, "Why do you put me to the test? Bring me a denarius, so that I may see it." 16/ They then brought (one). And he said to them, "Whose portrait is this and whose legend?" They then said to him, "Caesar's." 17/ Jesus then said to them, "Give back to Caesar what is Caesar's and to God what is God's." And they marveled greatly at him.

a ℵ A B C L W et al. attest the reading κῆνσον ("tax," a loanword based on the Latin *census*). D Θ et al. attest the reading ἐπικεφάλαιον ("poll-tax," a Greek translation of the Latin *capitularium*). a b ff i read *tributum* ("a stated payment," or "contribution," or "tribute"). Since the latter translate κῆνσον ("tax") as *censum* in Matt 22:17, Turner thought that they did not read κῆνσον ("tax") in Mark ("Western Readings," 7–8). Although he does not make this suggestion, *tributum* ("a stated payment," or "contribution," or "tribute") may represent φόρον ("tribute"); since Luke 20:22 reads φόρον ("tribute"), it could be that Luke and the scribes in question read φόρον ("tribute") in Mark as well. But since κῆνσον ("tax") is so broadly attested and since it fits with the frequent use of Latinisms in Mark, it is most likely the earliest recoverable reading.

Literary Context

The passage about paying tax to Caesar is loosely connected to the preceding scene by the remark that "they sent some of the Pharisees and Herodians to him" in v. 13. Those who did the sending are the chief priests, scribes, and elders mentioned in 11:27, against whom Jesus told the parable of the tenants (12:12). The intention of catching Jesus in a statement (v. 13) continues the theme expressed in v. 12, that the chief priests and the others were trying to arrest Jesus. The Pharisees and Herodians are, however, new characters in this context.[1] The introduction of the Sadducees in the next passage and of a scribe in the following one has the effect of portraying Jesus as able to hold his own with or overcome in debate the main authoritative groups among the Jewish people at the time.[2]

David Daube has argued that the anecdotes in Mark 12:13-37 are united by a pattern of four types of question. This schema was of Hellenistic origin (Alexandria) and is attested in the Babylonian Talmud and the Passover liturgy.[3] This hypothesis is ingenious and attractive but overly speculative.

History of the Tradition of 12:13-40

Martin Albertz argued that Mark used a second collection of five controversy-dialogues in this context, like the one he drew on to compose 2:1—3:6. These five concerned the authority of Jesus (11:27-33), paying taxes to Caesar (12:13-17), resurrection (12:18-27), the greatest commandment (12:28-34), and the messiah as David's son (12:35-37).[4] The collection was framed by the actions of Jesus in the temple (11:15-17) and the denunciation of the scribes (12:38-40). The actions in the temple provide the motivation for the question about Jesus' authority in 11:28. The sayings about the scribes in 12:38-40 undercut their role as leaders and provide a fitting conclusion to

---

1 The Pharisees and the Herodians are mentioned in 3:6 as conspiring against Jesus; on the "Herodians," see the commentary on 3:6 above. On the Pharisees, see the commentary on 2:16 and 7:3-4 above.

2 Loisy, 345.

3 David Daube, "Four Types of Question," in idem,

The New Testament and Rabbinic Judaism (New York: Arno Press, 1973; 1st ed. 1956) 158–69.

4 Martin Albertz, *Die synoptischen Streitgespräche: Ein Beitrag zur Formengeschichte des Urchristentums* (Berlin: Trowitzsch & Sohn, 1921) 16–36; see also "Narrative Unity and Literary History of 2:1–3:6" above.

the whole.[5] Albertz argued that both collections were made in the circle related to Stephen.[6]

Vincent Taylor was at first inclined to accept Albertz's thesis, noting "a certain artificiality of form in the succession of the various deputations."[7] He also pointed out a certain tension between the picture of Jesus in chapter 12 as a successful controversialist, popular with the crowd, and the third passion prediction (10:32-34), which states that he went to Jerusalem to suffer and die.[8] He thus agreed with Albertz that the plot to kill Jesus does not grow out of the controversies but was already established beforehand (see 11:18).[9] Later, however, Taylor argued that Mark himself was the compiler of these controversy-dialogues; before composing the Gospel, he had "combined episodes from the life of Jesus for catechetical purposes."[10]

H.-W. Kuhn praised Albertz for raising the question of the social setting of the alleged collection.[11] But he rejected Albertz's two main arguments in favor of the hypothesis that a pre-Markan collection of five controversy-dialogues was used in the composition of chapters 11–12: the self-contained character of the collection and the tension between the collection and its present context.[12] With regard to the alleged tension with the context, Kuhn argued that all the conflict scenes are appropriate in the setting leading up to the arrest of Jesus, with the exception of the question about the highest commandment (12:28-34). He explained the presence of this positive scene by analogy with the placement of the healing of the leper immediately before the conflict dialogues of 2:1–3:6.[13]

Kuhn also criticized the argument that the collection is self-contained and unified. He noted that Albertz himself, in a later work, had retracted the hypothesis that the denunciation of the scribes (12:38-40) constituted the conclusion to the collection, since the scribes were only one of several groups contending with Jesus in the collected stories.[14] Kuhn also argued that the repeated mention of the temple in 12:35 (cf. 11:27) calls into question the idea that the collection as a whole was set in the temple at the pre-Markan stage. As is typical of Mark, the location of the scenes in 12:13-34 is left open. Kuhn also doubted Albertz's assignment of certain clauses to the pre-Markan editor of the collection.[15] From a form-critical point of view, Kuhn argued that the majority of the anecdotes do indeed reflect conflict between the followers of Jesus and Jewish groups, as Albertz had argued. But the topics have different levels of importance and three of the units are not even controversy-dialogues.[16]

Joanna Dewey concluded that Mark did not build "upon any premarkan collection or source" in composing 12:1-40. Rather, he composed the passage by joining together previously independent traditions.[17] The result is a symmetrical pattern.[18] Other scholars have also been skeptical with regard to Albertz's thesis.[19]

Taylor's suggestion that Mark himself compiled the anecdotes before composing his Gospel is appealing because it fits the way ancient authors apparently worked.[20] It also allows for the possibility that Mark may have composed one or more of these anecdotes.[21]

5   Albertz, *Die synoptischen Streitgespräche*, 34–35.
6   Ibid., 101–7.
7   Vincent Taylor, *The Formation of the Gospel Tradition* (London: Macmillan, 1933) 179.
8   Ibid.
9   Albertz, *Die synoptischen Streitgespräche*, 16. For other scholars who have agreed with Albertz, wholly or in part, see Kuhn, *Ältere Sammlungen*, 40 n. 179; Dewey, *Markan Public Debate*, 60, 217 n. 93.
10   Taylor, 101.
11   Kuhn, *Ältere Sammlungen*, 40.
12   Ibid.
13   Ibid., 41.
14   Ibid. In fact, the scribes as a group do not contend with Jesus in chap. 12 (ibid., 43 n. 189). Kuhn's point is that the denunciation of the scribes in vv.

38-40 does not recapitulate the conflict with the Pharisees, the Herodians, and the Sadducees.
15   Ibid.
16   I.e., the question about the greatest commandment (12:28-34); the discussion whether the messiah is David's son (12:35-37); and the denunciation of the scribes (12:38-40); Kuhn doubted that the same social setting can be attributed to anecdotes of different forms (literary types) (*Ältere Sammlungen*, 42).
17   Dewey, *Markan Public Debate*, 167; see also 60–61.
18   Ibid., 162.
19   Ibid., 60–61.
20   Achtemeier, *"Omne Verbum Sonat,"* 14.
21   See the commentary on vv. 18-27 below.

Genre and Style of 12:13-17

Bultmann defined the passage as a controversy-dialogue occasioned by a question put to Jesus by opponents. The saying at the end hardly circulated independently, so the dialogue is a unity. By rejecting the idea that the passage is a product of the community, he implied that it has a basis in the life of Jesus.[22] He concluded that it was probably formed orally in a Palestinian context.[23] He also noted that Jesus' reply takes the form of a question in v. 16. The question contains the implied answer, which is then expressed in v. 17.[24]

Robert Tannehill categorized the passage as a testing inquiry.[25] Differently from Bultmann, he noted that v. 16 is "a preliminary counterquestion" designed to evoke a response that will prepare for Jesus' actual answer. By means of this counterquestion, Jesus "seizes the initiative" from those who are testing him.[26] The dramatic tension is high in testing stories because the responder has something to gain or lose in the situation. This tension is heightened by the inclusion of several exchanges in the dialogue.[27] The tension is released in the saying of v. 17. It is "a short, pointed saying [aphorism] consisting of two halves."[28] The two clauses are tightly linked by the syntax of the sentence and lead the audience to reflect on the relation between the two proper nouns: "Caesar" and "God." The saying is too general to provide a practical guide for conduct. It is characterized by wit rather than serious argument.[29]

Daube argued that the question put to Jesus in this anecdote falls under the category of ḥokmâ; that is, it is halakic—it concerns a point of law.[30]

Local Color in 12:13-17

When Archelaus, a son of Herod the Great, was deposed from his office as ethnarch of Judea, Samaria, and Idumea in 6 CE, these territories became the Roman imperial province of Judea. The new province had its own governor, called a *praefectus* ("prefect"), of equestrian rank. This prefect was only to some extent subordinate to the imperial legate who governed the province of Syria.[31] The first prefect of Judea was Coponius. At the time of his appointment, Quirinius became the new legate to Syria. Quirinius was charged with the task of taking a census of the population of the newly acquired territory for the purpose of levying taxes according to Roman usage. At this time, 6 or 7 CE, Judas, a Galilean or a native of Gamala in Gaulanitis (now the Golan), called upon his countrymen to refuse to pay tax to the Romans and to recognize only God as their ruler. Josephus described this man as a "teacher" ($\sigma o \varphi \iota \sigma \tau \acute{\eta} \varsigma$). In the *Jewish War*, Josephus says that Judas founded his own school of thought among Jews, one that had nothing in common with the others (*Bell.* 2.8.1 §§117–18). In the *Antiquities*, Josephus says that Judas allied himself with Saddok, a Pharisee, in calling for refusal to pay taxes and inciting a rebellion for the purpose of achieving independence. In this passage, Josephus says that the two men founded "a fourth philosophy" among the Jews and sowed the seeds of the later revolt that led to the destruction of the temple (*Ant.* 18.1.1 §§1–10). In another passage, he says that the fourth philosophy agrees with the opinions of the Pharisees in every way, except that the former advocates freedom from foreign rule and recognizes God alone as leader and master (*Ant.* 18.1.6 §23).[32] Judas and his allies caused trouble for Quirinius, but the high priest Joazar persuaded the people to submit to the census and taxation.[33]

Originally, in the time of the Republic, the Roman census involved only Roman citizens. It was a registration of citizens and their property in relation to compulsory military service and the collection of direct taxes. Such

---

22 Bultmann, *History*, 26.

23 Ibid., 48.

24 Ibid., 41.

25 Tannehill, "Varieties," 5.21 (p. 115).

26 Ibid., 5.22 (p. 116).

27 Ibid., 5.23 (p. 116).

28 Tannehill, *Sword*, 173.

29 Ibid., 173–77. For a summary of exegetical attempts to relate this saying to the issue of the Christian and the state, see John R. Donahue, "A Neglected Factor in the Theology of Mark," *JBL* 101 (1982) 563–94, esp. 572 and n. 30; see also 573 and n. 35. Donahue himself interprets the passage theologically (572–75).

30 Daube, *New Testament*, 159.

31 Schürer, *History*, 1:354–58; Frederick F. Bruce, "Render to Caesar," in Bammel and Moule, *Jesus*, 249–63, esp. 253–54.

32 On the "fourth philosophy," see Horsley and Hanson, *Bandits*, 190–243; Schürer, *History*, 1:598–606.

33 Schürer, *History*, 1:381.

registrations were not common practice in the territories subject to Rome during the Republican period. In the late Republic and under the empire, Roman citizens were not subject to compulsory military service or to direct taxes. Any census in Italy or the colonies governed by Italian law during these later periods related only to statistics or religious practices. The practice of taking a census in the provinces, however, had taxation as its main goal. There were two kinds of direct taxes in the provinces: a tax on agricultural produce and a tax on each individual (poll tax). The first was paid partly in goods, partly in money. The second tax had two parts: a person paid a tax determined by the amount of property owned, and each person paid a specific amount as an individual. The latter amount apparently varied for the different categories of the population. Women and slaves had to pay the poll tax; only children and old people were exempt. The declaration of property and the payment of the tax had to take place in the main town of the tax district.[34] In Judea, these tax districts were probably the eleven toparchies characteristic of the Roman period. Jerusalem was the main city of one of these.[35] Although the revenues from Judea went into the public treasury (*aerarium*), rather than into the imperial treasury (*fiscus*), Mark 12:14 and its parallels speak about paying taxes "to Caesar."[36]

Fabian Udoh has argued persuasively that, prior to 70 CE, direct taxes in Judea were confined to agricultural tribute paid in kind. The poll tax (*tributum capitis*) was not levied in the province before that date.[37] If Mark was written prior to 70, as argued in the introduction above, Jesus' request for a denarius does not signify a literal payment of a tax in coin, but rather concretizes and symbolizes the general issue of paying tribute to Rome.

Coins and the Issue of Historical Reliability

In v. 15, Jesus asks his interlocutors to bring him a denarius. This detail raises the question of the historical reliability of the account, since the silver coinage circulating in Judea in the time of Jesus appears to have consisted mainly of Tyrian shekels.[38] There is, however, evidence that Roman denarii circulated in Judea, at least in a limited way, already in the period from the death of Caesar to the death of Vitellius.[39]

The mint at Tyre produced silver shekels and half-shekels, which corresponded to Hellenistic tetradrachms and didrachms, respectively.[40] The Roman denarius corresponded to the Attic drachma.[41] The Roman taxes were calculated in denarii but paid in the local provincial coinage.[42] The denarius did not circu-

---

34 Ibid., 1:401–3.

35 Ibid., 1:372; 2:190–96.

36 Ibid., 1:372.

37 Fabian E. Udoh, *To Caesar What Is Caesar's: Tribute, Taxes and Imperial Administration in Early Roman Palestine (63 B.C.E.–70 C.E.)* (BJS 343; Providence: Brown Judaic Studies, 2005) 241.

38 Donald T. Ariel, "A Survey of Coin Finds in Jerusalem (until the End of the Byzantine Period)," *Liber Annuus* 32 (1982) 273–326, esp. 283, 287, 290; Stefan Alkier, "'Geld' im Neuen Testament—Der Beitrag der Numismatik zu einer Enzyklopädie des Frühen Christentums," in idem and Jürgen Zangenberg, eds., *Zeichen aus Text und Stein: Studien auf dem Weg zu einer Archäologie des Neuen Testaments* (TANZ 42; Tübingen/Basel: Francke, 2003) 308–35, esp. 327–28.

39 See below for this evidence. Andrew Burnett, Michel Amandry, and Père Pau Ripollès argue that Roman denarii do not seem to have circulated in Syria before Vespasian or been made there and that the principal silver currencies in Syria were the

tetradrachms of Antioch and the shekels of Tyre (Burnett et al., *Roman Provincial Coinage*, 12). They state unequivocally that the silver coins that circulated in Egypt during this period were exclusively locally produced, but with regard to Syria, they state that this was only perhaps the case (ibid., 9; cf. 587).

40 Burnett et al., *Roman Provincial Coinage*, 655; Alkier, "'Geld' im Neuen Testament," 321; David R. Walker, *The Metrology of the Roman Silver Coinage*, Part 1: *From Augustus to Domitian* (British Archaeological Reports Series 5; Oxford: British Archaeological Reports, 1976) 80 n. 35.

41 Walker, *Metrology*, 1:70.

42 J. Spencer Kennard, Jr., *Render to God: A Study of the Tribute Passage* (New York: Oxford University Press, 1950) viii, 51–55. Cf. Burnett et al., *Roman Provincial Coinage*, 26, 29, 31, 587, 590; John F. Matthews, "The Tax Law of Palmyra: Evidence for Economic History in a City of the Roman East," *Journal of Roman Studies* 74 (1984) 157–80. The date of the tax law is 137 CE, but it quotes a letter dating to 18–19 CE that implies that the taxes are reckoned in Roman

late in significant numbers in greater Syria until the late first century CE.[43]

There is evidence that denarii had some, though limited, circulation in Judea in the first century CE Four denarii have been discovered in Jerusalem. One is from the Republican period (46 BCE).[44] A second was minted in Rome by Antony in 32/31 BCE and found near the southern wall of the temple mount.[45] Both of these coins probably "arrived in Jerusalem after Herod's accession to the throne," since it is likely that Roman coins began to circulate in Jerusalem during the reign of Herod.[46] The other two were minted at Lugdunum (modern Lyon), one under Augustus and the other under Tiberius.[47] Like the coin of Antony, both of these were discovered near the southern wall of the temple mount.[48] The hoard of coins found at Isfiya (or Ussfiya) on Mount Carmel in 1960 was reported to contain 160 Roman denarii minted under Augustus.[49] Later it became clear that at least thirty of these were minted under Tiberius.[50]

The hoard found at Isfiya contained about 4,500 coins, of which 3,400 were Tyrian shekels and 1000 Tyrian half-shekels.[51] Kadman wrongly assumed that the shekels and half-shekels were not "in regular currency in Palestine" at the time the hoard was hidden (after 53 CE), but were used exclusively for the payment of the temple dues. He thus concluded that the hoard could not have been "the property of a private owner, a local bank or a military chest."[52] The hoard was, in his opinion, a shipment of temple dues that could not be delivered and thus was buried.[53] The implication of his argument is that the coins of this hoard, including the denarii, never circulated in Palestine. Since shekels were in fact common currency at the time, these coins may very well have been in circulation.

The evidence for the circulation of denarii in the time of Jesus is strong enough to support the conclusion that Mark 12:13-17 is based on an incident in the life of the historical Jesus.[54] It is also strong enough to support the

denarii but paid in the local coinage. The inscription in question is *IGR* 3.1056 = *OGIS* 629, but these editions are unreliable. See the article by Matthews and his bibliography for supplementary information and corrections. The residents of the Roman province of Arabia also paid their taxes with local coins (Wolfram Weiser and Hannah M. Cotton, "'Gebt dem Kaiser, was des Kaisers ist . . .': Die Geldwährungen der Griechen, Juden, Nabatäer und Römer im syrisch-nabatäischen Raum unter besonderer Berücksichtigung des Kurses von Selaᶜ/Melaina und Lepton nach der Annexion des Königreiches der Nabatäer durch Rom," *ZPE* 114 [1996] 237–87, esp. 240–41).

43 Burnett et al., *Roman Provincial Coinage*, 12, 29, 587.

44 Ariel, "Survey of Coin Finds," 284; #22 in table 3 on p. 312.

45 Ibid., #31 on p. 313.

46 Ibid., 284.

47 Ibid., #54 on p. 313 and #60 on p. 314. Ariel states that the coin of Tiberius was minted in Rome, but the current view is that all the denarii from the reign of Tiberius were minted in Lugdunum (William Metcalf; personal communication).

48 Ariel, "Survey of Coin Finds," #54 and #60 (pp. 313–14). A gold coin (an aureus) minted under Tiberius in Lugdunum was also found in the same location (#61, p. 314). Two gold coins from the reign of Nero were found, one in the Jewish Quarter (#72, p. 314) and the other near the southern wall (#74, p. 314). A denarius from the reign of Vespasian (#189,

p. 315) and ten denarii from the second century (##190–99, p. 315) were also found in Jerusalem.

49 Leo Kadman, "Temple Dues and Currency in Ancient Palestine in the Light of Recent [*sic*] Discovered Coin-Hoards," *Israel Numismatic Bulletin* 1 (1962) 9–11, esp. 11. In another publication, Kadman stated that one of the 160 Roman denarii was minted by Tiberius ("Temple Dues and Currency in Ancient Palestine in the Light of Recent [*sic*] Discovered Coin-Hoards," in *Congresso internazionale di numismatica, Roma, 11–16 settembre 1961* [2 vols.; Commission internationale de numismatique/Istituto italiano di numismatica; Rome: Istituto italiano di numismatica, 1961–65] 2:69–76, esp. 69).

50 Hart, "The Coin of 'Render unto Caesar . . . ,'" 241–48, esp. 248.

51 Kadman, "Temple Dues" (*Israel Numismatic Bulletin*) 9; idem, "Temple Dues" (*Congresso internazionale*) 69.

52 Kadman, "Temple Dues" (*Israel Numismatic Bulletin*) 10; idem, "Temple Dues" (*Congresso internazionale*) 70. In the latter publication, Kadman stated that the hoard was concealed after 54 CE (ibid.).

53 Kadman, "Temple Dues" (*Israel Numismatic Bulletin*) 11; idem, "Temple Dues" (*Congresso internazionale*) 70–73. For criticism of some of the details of Kadman's argument, see D. Sperber, "Numismatics and Halacha," *Israel Numismatic Journal* 2 (1964) 16–18.

54 With Bultmann, *History*, 26, although he does not raise the issue of the numismatic evidence (see the section "Genre and Style of 12:13-17" above); Taylor, *Formation*, 179; Kennard, *Render to God*, viii–ix; Hart,

conclusion that Mark and his audiences, even if he wrote in Judea, Galilee, or Syria in the late 60s, were sufficiently familiar with the denarius to know that Roman taxes were calculated in terms of denarii and that this type of coin had the emperor's portrait (εἰκών) and legend (ἐπιγραφή) on it (Mark 12:16).[55] In the context of the evangelist and his first audiences, the account probably had the effect of dissociating Jesus and his followers from the program of the Zealots.[56]

Comment

■ **13-17** In addition to the parallel versions of this controversy-dialogue or testing inquiry in Matt 22:15-22 and Luke 20:20-26,[57] versions of it occur in the unknown Gospel preserved by Pap. Eg. 2 and in the *Gospel of Thomas*.[58] The version in Pap. Eg. 2 appears to be a pastiche of four different passages from the canonical Gospels.[59] Helmut Koester doubted that the passage was composed by selecting or imitating sentences from Mark, Luke, and John, because he saw no analogies to such a method of composition. A case has been made, however, by James Kelhoffer that the longer ending of Mark was composed in just this way.[60] Koester, on the contrary, concluded that the version in Pap. Eg. 2 preserves language that is both pre-Synoptic and pre-Johannine.[61] John Meier argued that the general question in Pap. Eg. 2, "Is it licit to pay *to the kings* what *pertains to the government?*," is likely to be a later reworking of the concrete Synoptic form, "to pay the *poll tax to Caesar*."[62] It could be that the version of Pap. Eg. 2 reflects secondary orality, as the story of the healing of the leper does.[63]

The relevant passage in the *Gospel of Thomas* reads:

> They showed Jesus a gold coin and said to him, "Caesar's agents are exacting taxes from us." He said to them, "Give unto Caesar the things that are Caesar's, give unto God the things that are God's, and give unto me that which is mine." (100)[64]

"Coin of 'Render unto Caesar . . . ,'" 242–48; Bruce, "Render to Caesar," 257–62. Martin Rist argued that the earliest form of the anecdote was closer to the version of Pap. Eg. 2 than to Mark's and that the motif of the denarius with its portrait and legend was added at a later stage, when Gentile Christians were expected to participate in the imperial cult ("Caesar or God," 317–31).

55 See the discussion of the date and place of the writing of Mark in the introduction.

56 According to Hippolytus, the Zealots refused to carry, look at, or manufacture coins bearing any sort of image (*Ref.* 9.26); for an ET of this passage, see Hengel, *Zealots*, 70–71; for discussion see 190–96. On the origins, goals, and tactics of the Zealots, see Horsley and Hanson, *Bandits*, 216–43. Alfred Loisy argued that the aim of this anecdote was to show that Jesus did not rebel against Rome and to prevent the association of Christians with Zealots (*L'Évangile selon Luc* [Paris: Émile Nourry, 1924] 483). Loisy is cited by Kennard, *Render to God*, 3, 17 n. 1.

57 The (very) minor agreements between Matthew and Luke against Mark in this passage are readily explicable as independent editorial changes, contra Ennulat, *Minor Agreements*, 269–73. For a listing of these agreements, see Neirynck, *Minor Agreements*, 153–54.

58 Pap. Eg. 2 (2 recto 43–59); *Gos. Thom.* 100. For a transcription and critical Greek text of Pap. Eg. 2 (2 recto 43–59), see H. Idris Bell and T. C. Skeat, *Frag-

ments of an Unknown Gospel and Other Early Christian Papyri* (London: Trustees of the British Museum, 1935) 10–13; for a reproduction of Bell and Skeat's text and a German trans., see Lührmann, *Fragmente*, 150–51. For a critical Coptic text and English trans. of *Gos. Thom.* 100, see Bentley Layton, ed., *Nag Hammadi Codex II,2–7* (2 vols.; NHS 20–21; Leiden/New York: Brill, 1989) 1:88–89. The surviving Greek fragments of *Gos. Thom.* do not include the relevant passage.

59 Mark 12:13-15; John 3:2; Luke 6:46; Mark 7:6-7||Matt 15:7-9; see the Synoptic chart in Koester, *Gospels*, 213–14.

60 Kelhoffer, *Miracle and Mission*, 48–150. The conflation of passages from the undisputed Pauline letters in Colossians is also analogous; see Leppä, *Making of Colossians*, 15–21, and the literature cited there.

61 Koester, *Gospels*, 215; cf. Thomas Kazen, "Sectarian Gospels for Some Christians? Intention and Mirror Reading in the Light of Extra-Canonical Texts," *NTS* 51 (2005) 561–78, esp. 572.

62 Meier, *Marginal Jew*, 1:119; emphasis in original.

63 See the commentary on 1:40-45 above. Bruce concluded that the version of Pap. Eg. 2 is later than that of Mark ("Render to Caesar," 249).

64 Trans. (slightly modified) from Layton, *Gnostic Scriptures*, 397. See also the ET in Koester, *Gospels*, 112.

Koester concludes that the version in *Gos. Thom.* is earlier than that of Mark because it lacks "all of the narrative and discourse sections" that link the story to its context in Mark,[65] but these details may have been omitted in adapting the Markan story to its new context in an anthology of sayings of Jesus. Ancient writers were trained to rewrite anecdotes in a more concise manner as well as to expand and elaborate them.[66]

■ **13** The chief priests, scribes, and elders send some of the Pharisees and Herodians to catch Jesus in an unguarded statement.[67] The purpose for doing so is left unstated, although the audience may infer that it is connected with the intention expressed in v. 12 of arresting Jesus. Luke makes explicit what is probably implied by Mark: they want to find or create grounds for making an accusation to the governor against Jesus (Luke 20:20). The Pharisees are brought in because the question that will be raised in vv. 14-15 concerns what is "permitted" or "lawful" (ἔξεστιν) and thus the interpretation of the Law. The Herodians may be included because Herod the Great and his descendants were allies of Rome and gave the Julio-Claudian emperors and their families numerous honors. Philip, one of Herod's sons, was the tetrarch of Gaulanitis, Trachonitis, Batanea, and Paneas from 4 BCE to 34 CE. His capital city was Caesarea Philippi.[68] He minted three types of copper-alloy coins with the portrait of Augustus on the obverse with the legend *ΚΑΙΣΑΡΟΣ ΣΕΒΑΣΤΟΥ* ("of Caesar Augustus") or variants of it. He minted two types with the portrait of Tiberius on the obverse with the legend *ΤΙΒΕΡΙΟΣ ΣΕΒΑΣ(ΤΟΣ)* ("Tiberius Augustus") or *ΤΙΒΕΡΙΟΣ ΣΕΒΑΣΤΟΣ ΚΑΙΣΑΡ* ("Tiberius Augustus Caesar").[69] In the late 30s and early 40s, Agrippa I minted copper-alloy coins at Caesarea Philippi with portraits of Caligula and Claudius.[70]

■ **14** Those who come to Jesus praise him as a teacher who truly teaches the way of God. Given their mission, such praise seems intended to encourage Jesus to teach the will of God, even if it may be unpopular with influential people, such as the Roman governor and the emperor. This is a tactic to put him off guard.

Then comes the question, "Is it permitted to pay tax to Caesar or not? Should we pay or not pay?" In the context, this question implies that there are some among the people of Judea and Galilee who believe that the tax should not be paid. The issue was raised by the resistance advocated by Judas in 6 or 7 CE.[71] It is not clear whether it was still a live issue in the time of Jesus.[72] In the time of Mark, Roman rule was being called into question by the revolt that erupted into open warfare in 66 CE.[73] The mention of the Herodians in v. 13 could have reminded Mark's audiences of the Zealot attacks on Herodian aristocrats reported by Josephus.[74]

■ **15** The statement that Jesus recognized their hypocrisy makes clear to the audience of Mark that Jesus was not taken in by the questioners' attempt to catch him off guard. His question, "Why do you put me to the test?" makes the same point for those testing Jesus within the narrative and for the crowd that was present (cf. v. 12). After putting his interlocutors in their place, Jesus seizes the initiative by asking them to bring him a denarius.[75]

■ **16-17** By cooperating with Jesus' request, the questioners implicitly accept Jesus' authority as a teacher.[76] Jesus' question, "Whose portrait is this and whose legend?" implies that he has taken the coin from one of the interlocutors and looked at it. They reply "Caesar's." The use of the simple name "Caesar," which applied to all the emperors, without the addition of a specific name, such as Augustus or Tiberius, allows the story to apply to the

65   Koester, *Gospels*, 112.

66   The exercise of rewriting a chreia in a more concise form was called συστολή ("condensation"); see Ronald F. Hock and Edward N. O'Neil, *The Chreia in Ancient Rhetoric*, vol. 1: *The Progymnasmata* (SBLTT 27; GRRS 9; Atlanta: Scholars Press, 1986) 36; Moeser, *Anecdote*, 55 n. 14. Bruce concluded that the version in *Gos. Thom.* is later than the one in Mark ("Render to Caesar," 249–50).

67   See the section "Literary Context" above.

68   See the commentary on 8:27a above.

69   Burnett et al., *Roman Provincial Coinage*, 680–81.

70   Ibid., 683–84.

71   See the section "Local Color in 12:13-17" above. See also Horsley and Hanson, *Bandits*, 196–97.

72   Horsley and Hanson, *Bandits*, 199.

73   Ibid., 41–46, 217–19.

74   Ibid., 223–29.

75   On Jesus seizing the initiative, see the section "Genre and Style of 12:13-17" above. On the historical reliability of the narrative detail that Jesus asked for a denarius, see the section "Coins and the Issue of Historical Reliability" above.

76   Alkier, "'Geld' im Neuen Testament," 323.

audience of Mark, as well as to those questioning Jesus and the crowd within the narrative.[77]

Jesus' concluding aphorism, "Give back to Caesar what is Caesar's and to God what is God's," suggests that, as he spoke, Jesus gave the coin back to the one who had handed it to him. It is inappropriate to derive an ethical teaching or social policy from this saying.[78] The main point is that Jesus was clever and witty enough to respond to the question without saying anything that would provide grounds for a charge against him before the Roman governor. Jesus turned the tables on the questioners, forcing them to decide what belonged to Caesar and what to God.

In his *First Apology*, Justin Martyr cites this passage in order to make the point that Christians worship God alone but are willing to pay taxes and obey the government in other matters (17).[79] Tertullian interprets the passage to mean that you give money to Caesar, since his image is on the coins, but you give yourself to God, since you bear God's image. In the context, the implication is that Christians should not worship any being but God.[80] In another work, he implies that some have used this passage to argue that it is permissible for Christians to avoid martyrdom by bribery. He rejects this interpretation, since bribery is not giving to Caesar what belongs to him. In any case, in such a situation, giving to God what belongs to God involves laying down one's life as Christ laid down his for humanity.[81]

It is not clear whether the concluding comment, "And they marveled greatly at him," applies to the interlocutors, to the crowd, or to both. Since the crowd is not explicitly mentioned, it is likely that the questioners are meant primarily. This wonderment seems to continue the theme of the acceptance of Jesus as a teacher by his interlocutors.[82] By the end of the story, those who came to entrap Jesus have become his admirers.

12

12:18-27 The Question of Resurrection

18/ **And Sadducees came to him, who say that there is no resurrection, and they asked him, saying, 19/ "Teacher, Moses wrote for us, 'If a man's brother dies and leaves behind a wife, and does not leave a child, let his brother take the wife and raise up children for his brother.' 20/ There were seven brothers; and the first took a wife, died, and left no offspring. 21/ And the second took her and died without leaving behind any offspring. And the third likewise. 22/ And none of the seven left offspring. Last of all, the woman also died. 23/ In the resurrection, when they rise,[a] to which of them will she be wife? For the seven had her as wife." 24/ Jesus said to them, "Is it not for this reason that you are mistaken, that you**

a   An impressive range of MSS lack the words ὅταν ἀναστῶσιν ("when they rise"), namely, ℵ B C D et al. But the shorter reading is almost certainly not the earlier. A Θ ƒ[1.(13)] 𝔐 et al. include the words; they were retained in the recension known as Syrian, Koine, or Byzantine (A et al.), because the reviser found them in at least one MS and elected to retain them according to his regular preference. This procedure, which often preserves secondary expansions, in this case has retained the earlier reading; so Turner, "Western Readings," 8. The longer reading is also in accordance with Markan style; the shorter reading arose either under the influence of the parallels in Matt 22:28 and Luke 20:33 or in an analogous attempt to eliminate the redundancy. See also Taylor, ad loc., Metzger, *Textual Commentary*, 93; Elliott, "Eclectic Textual Commentary," 194; Neirynck, *Duality in Mark*, 105.

---

77   Ibid., 330–31.
78   See the section "Genre and Style of 12:13-17" above.
79   Cited by Kennard, *Render to God*, 6; and Rist, "Caesar or God," 328.
80   Tertullian *On Idolatry* 15; cited by Rist, "Caesar or God," 328.
81   Tertullian *On Flight in Persecution* 12; cited by Kennard, *Render to God*, 6.
82   See the first remark on vv. 16-17 above.

know neither the scriptures nor the power of God? 25/ For when they rise from the dead, they neither marry nor are given in marriage, but they are like angels in the heavens. 26/ Now concerning the dead, that they are raised, have you not read in the book of Moses in the passage about the thornbush how God said to him, 'I am the God of Abraham and the God of Isaac and the God of Jacob'? 27/ [God] is not a God of the dead, but of the living. You are very much mistaken."

Genre of 12:18-27

Bultmann classified this anecdote as a controversy-dialogue centering on a question raised by opponents of Jesus.[83] He defined vv. 23-25 as a debate on the resurrection of the dead, belonging to the category of legal sayings, because Deut 25:5-6 is cited by the opponents of Jesus.[84] Such debating sayings serve apologetic and polemical purposes.[85] The anecdote portrays Sadducees as opponents because "it was traditional for them to deny the resurrection."[86] Bultmann concluded also that vv. 26-27 constitute a later addition, but not of a saying that circulated independently. Rather, the text was expanded on the basis of the theological activity of the church.[87] Verses 26-27 also comprise a legal saying, in which an appeal to Exod 3:6 justifies a new outlook over against the old.[88]

Tannehill further characterized this "pronouncement story" as a "correction story."[89] In correction stories, the "responder takes a position that contrasts with and corrects the position assumed through word or action by some other party."[90] The "climactic saying" often contrasts sharply the position of the other party with that of

the responder, as in vv. 25 and 27, with the use of ἀλλά ("but").[91] Although some Synoptic pronouncement stories are hybrids of the testing inquiry and the correction story, this one is a simple correction story, since Jesus does not respond to the question but simply corrects the view that gave rise to it. Nevertheless, the implication that Jesus is being tested heightens the tension in the story.[92]

Daube argued that the question posed by the Sadducees to Jesus here falls under the category of *boruth* ("vulgarity"). The point of such a question is to ridicule a belief held by the person being questioned.[93]

Comment

■ **18-27** Rudolf Pesch argued that this anecdote lacks a setting in space and time and that it was the evangelist who placed it in its present context.[94] Meier concluded that Mark brought together "various individual dispute stories" in this context in order "to dramatize the heightening tensions between Jesus and his opponents just before the passion."[95] Meier also argued that the unit is

83 Bultmann, *History*, 26.
84 Ibid., 136.
85 Ibid., 146.
86 Ibid., 26.
87 Ibid.
88 Ibid., 136. This saying may also serve a polemical or apologetic purpose (ibid., 146).
89 Tannehill, "Varieties," 1.1 (p. 102).
90 Ibid., 1.4 (pp. 103–4).
91 Ibid., (p. 104).
92 Ibid., 1.3 (p. 103).
93 Daube, *New Testament*, 160.
94 See "History of the Tradition of 12:13-40" above; Pesch, 2:229; Donahue, "Neglected Factor," 575. For a history of scholarship on this passage, see Otto Schwankl, *Die Sadduzäerfrage (Mk 12, 18–27 parr): Eine exegetisch-theologische Studie zur Auferstehungserwartung* (BBB 66; Frankfurt: Athenäum, 1987) 11–67.
95 John P. Meier, "The Debate on the Resurrection of the Dead: An Incident from the Ministry of the Historical Jesus?" *JSNT* 77 (2000) 3–24; quotations from 4–5.

pre-Markan.[96] All his arguments in favor of that conclusion, however, can be answered by the hypothesis that Mark had a limited goal in composing this narrative: to show that Jesus, as a teacher, was superior to the Sadducees and their teaching.[97] The two phrases that may have been added by Mark could equally well be interpreted as indications of Markan style.[98] Donahue also argued that Mark edited a traditional story in composing this correction story.[99] His arguments concerning Markan redaction are also compatible with the hypothesis of Markan composition.[100] It is certainly possible that Mark used tradition in composing this anecdote, but it is very difficult to prove that he did so. Meier concluded that "the text of the story as we have it is a Christian composition,"[101] but he made a case for the conclusion that the anecdote is based on an incident in the life of Jesus.[102]

■ **18-19** In v. 18, as in other ancient texts, the Sadducees are characterized as saying that there is no resurrection (ἀνάστασις).[103] The text makes clear that the Sadducees are testing Jesus because their "question is based on a premise that the questioners reject. It does not arise from a search for truth but is a trick question designed to embarrass Jesus."[104]

Like the Pharisees and Herodians in v. 14, the Sadducees address Jesus as "teacher" (διδάσκαλε) in v. 19. They acknowledge that he is recognized as a teacher but attempt to reveal weaknesses in his teaching. Jesus himself refers to the commandments of Moses elsewhere in Mark (Mark 1:44; 7:10; 10:3). Unlike the interlocutors of 10:4, who cite Moses' teaching in response to a question from Jesus, the Sadducees here take the initiative by referring to what Moses wrote. They do not cite scripture exactly but offer a conflated paraphrase of Deut 25:5-6 and Gen 38:8.[105] The topic that they raise with this double allusion is levirate marriage.

The English expression "levirate marriage" is based on the Latin word *levir* ("husband's brother" or "brother-in-law"). Deut 25:5-10 stipulates that, when brothers reside together and one of them dies and has no son, the widow shall not be married outside her husband's family. Rather, the surviving brother shall marry her, and the first son that she bears will take the name of the brother who died, so that his name will not be blotted out from Israel. It also stipulates that, if the surviving brother does not wish to marry the widow, this fact shall be made known to the elders, and the widow shall perform a

---

96 Ibid., 5–6.

97 One of Meier's arguments concerns the fact that Mark does not link this story to the passion narrative, which Meier finds especially strange since he assumes that the Jewish authorities involved in Jesus' arrest and trial were probably the leaders of the Sadducean party (ibid., 5). But as Anthony Saldarini has pointed out, one should not assume "that all or most of the priests and aristocrats were Sadducees" (*Pharisees*, 121).

98 Meier, "Debate on the Resurrection," 6–7. Meier himself concluded that both of these phrases "could well have stood in the pre-Markan text. Rudolf Pesch may thus be correct in maintaining that Mark took over this pericope unchanged" (ibid., 7).

99 Donahue, "Neglected Factor," 575–76.

100 The argument that v. 25 comes from tradition because it speaks about the dead rising (ἀναστῶσιν) whereas v. 26 is redactional since it speaks about them being raised (ἐγείρονται) is not compelling because Mark uses both verbs elsewhere; cf. Donahue, "Neglected Factor," 576 and n. 46.

101 Meier, "Debate on the Resurrection," 7.

102 Ibid., 7–23. Similarly, Schwankl, *Die Sadduzäerfrage*, 587.

103 Besides the parallels to this passage in Matt 22:23

and Luke 20:27, see Acts 4:1-2; 23:6-8. Josephus says that the Sadducees reject the idea of "the persistence of the soul after death, penalties in the underworld, and rewards" (ψυχῆς τε τὴν διαμονὴν καὶ τὰς καθ' ᾅδου τιμωρίας καὶ τιμάς) (*Bell.* 2.8.14 §165; text and trans. from Thackeray, *Josephus*, 2:386–87). In another passage, he says that "the Sadducees hold that the soul perishes along with the body" (Σαδδουκαίοις δὲ τὰς ψυχὰς ὁ λόγος συναφανίζει τοῖς σώμασι) (*Ant.* 18.1.4 §16; text and trans. from Louis Feldman, *Josephus*, 9:12–13). According to ʾAbot R. Nat. A.5, Zadok's followers broke away from Antigonus of Soco over the issue of resurrection; see Gary G. Porton, "Sadducees," *ABD* 5:892–95, esp. 892. See also Saldarini, *Pharisees*, 121, 154.

104 Tannehill, "Varieties," 1.3 (p. 103). Similarly, Suhl, *Funktion*, 67–68.

105 Suhl, *Funktion*, 67; Pesch, 2:231.

ceremony in which she pulls the sandal off from one of his feet. This ceremony is known as חליצה (halîṣâ) from the verbal root חלץ ("to draw off").[106]

Lev 18:16 and 20:21 prohibit absolutely the marriage between a brother-in-law and his sister-in-law. The rabbis reconciled the contradiction between these passages and Deut 25:5-10 by arguing that Leviticus expresses the general rule, whereas the law in Deuteronomy applies only when a married man dies without offspring.[107] Whether levirate marriage was practiced in the time of Jesus is unclear.[108]

Both the LXX and the rabbis stipulated that levirate marriage was necessary only if the deceased brother had no offspring whatsoever, unlike the MT, which refers to "a son" (בן) (Deut 25:5 MT). The LXX refers to "offspring" (σπέρμα) and "the child" (τὸ παιδίον) (Deut 25:5, 6 LXX).[109] Similarly, the Sadducees in v. 19 refer to "a child" (τέκνον) and "offspring" (σπέρμα).

■ **20-22** After alluding to the law of Deut 25:5-10, the Sadducees construct a hypothetical case. There were seven brothers.[110] The first married and died without leaving "offspring" (σπέρμα) (v. 20). The second married the widow and died without leaving behind any offspring. The implication is that, not only was he unable to provide a child for his deceased brother, but he did not have any children of his own either.[111] The same thing happened with the third brother (v. 21) and with the rest of the seven. Finally the woman died (v. 22).

■ **23** The Sadducees' question, "In the resurrection, when they rise, to which of them will she be wife? For the seven had her as wife," has several effects in the context. For one thing, it makes fun of the belief in resurrection. For another, it attempts to reduce the logic of belief in resurrection to an absurdity (*reductio ad absurdum*). Finally, it may imply that Moses did not teach resurrection, since he did not foresee such a problem.[112] There is perhaps an analogy in a question put by "the Alexandrians" to Rabbi Joshua ben Hananiah. They asked him whether the resurrected dead would need to be sprinkled with water on the third and the seventh days (to remove the ritual impurity resulting from contact with a corpse). Rabbi Joshua replied, "When they will be resurrected we shall go into the matter" (lit., "we shall be wise about them").[113]

The question has been raised whether any Jews in the time of Jesus believed in a type of resurrection in which marital relations would occur.[114] In the time prior to Jesus, there is evidence for two types of expectation of resurrection. 2 Macc 7:11 provides evidence for a bodily type of resurrection. Dan 12:2-3 envisages a spiritual or heavenly type of resurrection.[115] 2 Maccabees, however, does not mention marital relations as an aspect of resurrected life.[116]

---

106 The passage in Deuteronomy presents חליצה (halîṣâ) as a shameful alternative (Michael L. Satlow, *Jewish Marriage in Antiquity* [Princeton: Princeton University Press, 2001] 186). The practice of levirate marriage is reflected in Genesis 38, but that passage does not seem to recognize the option of חליצה (ibid.). Ruth 4 is an example of "an agnate marriage, which may have been connected to levirate marriage at some stage of development" (ibid., 343 n. 28). On Ruth 4, see also Edward F. Campbell, *Ruth: A New Translation with Introduction and Commentary* (AB 7; Garden City, NY: Doubleday, 1975) 156; Richard Kalmin, "Levirate Law," *ABD* 4:296–97 and the literature cited there.

107 Kalmin, "Levirate Law," 296. Note the broadening of the requirement from "son" to "offspring."

108 Satlow, *Jewish Marriage in Antiquity*, 186.

109 Josephus refers to "a woman left childless (τὴν ἄτεκνον) on her husband's death" (*Ant.* 4.8.23 §254; text and trans. from Thackeray, *Josephus*, 4:596–97).

110 The Palestinian Talmud contains an anecdote according to which one of thirteen brothers married

the twelve widows of his brothers according to the levirate law (Str-B, 1:887).

111 According to rabbinic law, the distinction would not pertain, since "the offspring of the levirate union are considered the levir's and the levir inherits his brother's estate" (Kalmin, "Levirate Law," 297, citing *m. Yeb.* 4.7).

112 Wellhausen, 95; Klostermann, 125; Suhl, *Funktion*, 67–68.

113 *B. Nid.* 69b, 70b; trans. by Israel W. Slotki in Isidore Epstein, ed., *The Babylonian Talmud: Seder Ṭohoroth, Niddah* (London: Soncino Press, 1935–52); this passage is cited by Str-B, 1:888. For the relation of this and similar questions to the Sadducees and the Hellenistic schools of philosophy, see David Daube, "Rabbinic Methods of Interpretation and Hellenistic Rhetoric," *HUCA* 22 (1949) 239–64, esp. 243.

114 Str-B, 1:888; Suhl, *Funktion*, 68 n. 4.

115 Yarbro Collins, *Beginning of the Gospel*, 125–26.

116 *1 Enoch* 22–27 seems to envisage "a resurrection to some kind of bodily life" (George W. E. Nickelsburg, "Resurrection: Early Judaism and Christianity," *ABD*

Two apocalypses written thirty to forty years after Mark express the expectation that there will be an earthly messianic reign followed by the eternal new age. *4 Ezra* 7:28-44 describes the revelation of the messiah, an earthly messianic reign for four hundred years, the death of the messiah and all others living at that time, seven days of primeval silence, and then the appearance of the new, incorruptible world, the resurrection, and the judgment. Although the messianic age is earthly, the resurrection takes place after its end.[117] The resurrection life is portrayed as spiritual and heavenly (*4 Ezra* 7:95-98).[118] *2 Baruch* 29 speaks about an earthly messianic reign in which those who have survived to that point will feast upon Behemoth and Leviathan, will have an abundance of wine, and will eat manna. But all this takes place before the resurrection, which is described briefly in chapter 30. In a more detailed discussion of the resurrection, it is stated that those who rise will be recognizable to those who knew them, but then they will be transformed into a glorious, heavenly form (*2 Baruch* 50–51).[119]

Paul Billerbeck concluded that the majority of Jews in the time of Jesus believed in the resurrection and expected marital relations to be a normal part of resurrected life. In support of this conclusion, he cited two rabbinic passages that commented on Ezekiel 37 to the effect that those who had been raised by Ezekiel had children afterward. But this interpretation is a case of the resuscitation of a corpse to ordinary human life, not the eschatological resurrection of the dead.[120] He cited a number of other passages but admitted that they may

refer to the earthly messianic age and not to the eternal new age.[121] In light of the evidence, it is likely that the question of the Sadducees is based on a caricature of the belief in resurrection current among Jews in the first century CE.

■ **24-25** The response of the Markan Jesus here differs from that of Rabbi Joshua ben Hananiah in the passage cited above and from his own response in vv. 13-17 to the question about paying tax to Caesar. In both of those cases, wit or humor is used to evade the question. Here Jesus takes the question seriously, not by answering it but by questioning its premise. The questioners are rebuked indirectly for taking as a premise a caricature of belief in resurrection. The explicit accusation in v. 24 is that they are mistaken because they know neither the scriptures nor the power of God.

The statement in v. 25 corrects the Sadducees' false premise: "For when they rise from the dead, they neither marry nor are given in marriage, but they are like angels in the heavens."[122] The proper understanding of resurrection is the spiritual one, not the bodily one. The picture of resurrection given here is quite similar to that of *2 Baruch* 51.[123] Those who are obedient and wise during their earthly lives will "be transformed so that they look like angels" after they are raised from the dead (*2 Bar.* 51:5). "For in the heights of [the world which is now invisible to them] shall they dwell, And they shall be made like the angels, And be made equal to the stars; And they shall be changed into whatever form they will, From beauty into loveliness, And from light into the splendour of glory" (*2 Bar.* 51:10).[124] They will see

---

5:684–691; quotation from 685). *1 Enoch* 92–105, however, portrays a heavenly type of resurrected life (ibid., 685–86).

117 For discussion, see Stone, *Fourth Ezra*, 215–23.

118 Ibid., 244–46.

119 See the ET by Robert H. Charles, rev. by Leonard H. Brockington, in Sparks, *AOT*, 869–71. The presence of this understanding of resurrection in a work that was probably composed in Hebrew (see John J. Collins, *The Apocalyptic Imagination: An Introduction to Jewish Apocalyptic Literature* [2nd ed.; Grand Rapids, MI: Eerdmans, 1998] 212) is an indication that caution is needed regarding the association of this anecdote with "the spiritualizing tendency of Hellenistic thought" (Donahue, "Neglected Factor," 577). Jewish ideas about resurrection were influenced by Hellenism from the beginning. See the dis-

cussion of Dan 12:2-3 above. On the influence of Hellenistic philosophy on the rabbis, see Daube, "Rabbinic Methods of Interpretation," 261.

120 Some rabbis, however, interpreted the raising of the dead by God through Elijah, Elisha, and Ezekiel as evidence for the resurrection of the new age (Str-B, 1:895).

121 Str-B, 1:888–89. See also the criticisms of Suhl, *Funktion*, 68 n. 4.

122 According to Acts 23:8, the Sadducees did not accept the existence of angels; the saying of Jesus in v. 25 perhaps corrects his interlocutors on this point also.

123 Suhl, *Funktion*, 68 n. 4.

124 Trans. by Charles, rev. Brockington, in Sparks, *AOT*, 871.

Paradise, the living creatures beneath the throne of God and the armies of the angels. "Then shall the splendour of the righteous exceed even the splendour of the angels" (*2 Bar.* 51:11-12).[125] There is no thought of marriage in this heavenly scenario.[126]

■ **26-27** Bultmann argued that these verses constitute a later expansion of an original controversy-dialogue that consisted of vv. 18-25.[127] Literary arguments can be made, however, for taking vv. 26-27 as an integral part of the anecdote. The controversy-dialogue has a concentric structure. The response of Jesus in v. 25 is directed to the explicit question of the Sadducees in vv. 19-23. The response in vv. 26-27, however, is directed to the description of the Sadducees in v. 18 as not accepting the idea of resurrection. The latter response either presupposes that Jesus knows that they are Sadducees and reject resurrection, or it is directed at the audience of Mark, who have been told about that rejection. Or, if one accepts Wellhausen's argument that the question of the Sadducees implies that Moses did not believe in resurrection,[128] then Jesus' allusion to Exod 3:6 may be taken as an argument that Moses did, on the contrary, accept the idea of resurrection. Jesus' argument is based on Moses' description of God as the God of Abraham, Isaac, and Jacob. But, since God is a God not of the dead but of the living,[129] Abraham, Isaac, and Jacob must be living now (or will live again in the future).

In any case, both v. 25 and vv. 26-27 constitute responses characteristic of a typical correction story. They express Jesus' own positions, which contrast sharply with those of his questioners.[130] Additional argu-ments for the unity of the anecdote as it occurs in Mark include the observation that the last two verses round out the anecdote with an interpretation of scripture that corresponds in a contrasting manner to the scriptural citation of the questioners in v. 19.[131] Furthermore, Jesus' initial statement in v. 24 introduces his whole argument. Because the interlocutors do not know the scriptures, they deny the reality of the resurrection (vv. 26-27); because they do not know the power of God, they misunderstand the nature of resurrected life (v. 25).[132]

Many scholars have concluded that, in v. 26, Jesus argues in a way similar to the rabbis.[133] Dan M. Cohn-Sherbok, however, has argued that the Synoptic Jesus "does not strictly follow the hermeneutical rules laid down by Tannaitic exegetes."[134] There are problems with Cohn-Sherbok's argument. First, it is not certain that the rules attributed to Hillel or R. Ishmael were in use in the time of Jesus.[135] Second, if they were in use in the time of Jesus, they may not have been applied exactly in the way that they are applied in later rabbinic literature. Third, one could make a case that Jesus' argumentation fits one or more of the rules attributed to Hillel.

The fifth rule attributed to Hillel, "the general and the particular, the particular and the general" (כלל ופרט ופרט וכלל), "stipulates that where particular terms are followed by a general term it is assumed that the law refers to anything included in the general—the particulars being regarded merely as illustrative examples."[136] The citation from Exod 3:16 in v. 26 could be taken here as the particular: God is the God of Abraham, Isaac, and Jacob. The statement in v. 27 could be taken as the gen-

---

125 Sparks, *AOT*, 871.

126 See also *1 Enoch* 51:4; 104:6; cited by Str-B, 1:891.

127 See the section "Genre of 12:18-27" above.

128 See the commentary on v. 23 above.

129 Ps 6:5; Isa 38:16-19; Sir 17:27-28.

130 See the discussion of Tannehill's conclusions in "Genre of 12:18-27" above.

131 Cf. Lohmeyer, 255. Dewey concluded that "Jesus first resolves the riddle and then argues for resurrection, answering the issues in reverse or chiastic order" (*Markan Public Debate*, 158).

132 Lohmeyer, 256. Note the chiastic arrangement of the two parts of the opening statement and the corresponding elaborations of them.

133 E.g., Lohmeyer, 256; Klostermann, 126; Taylor, 480, 484. For a defense of the hermeneutical appropriate-

ness of the argument, see J. Gerald Janzen, "Resurrection and Hermeneutics: On Exodus 3.6 in Mark 12.26," *JSNT* 23 (1985) 43–58.

134 Dan M. Cohn-Sherbok, "Jesus' Defence of the Resurrection of the Dead," *JSNT* 11 (1981) 64–73; quotation from 64.

135 The seven rules attributed to Hillel and the thirteen attributed to R. Ishmael are discussed by Cohn-Sherbok ("Jesus' Defence," 65–69) and Herman L. Strack and Günter Stemberger (*Introduction to the Talmud and Midrash* [Edinburgh: T. & T. Clark, 1991] 19–25). Daube discusses the first five and the seventh "norms" of Hillel in "Rabbinic Methods of Interpretation," 251–58, and the sixth, 259–60. He discusses "the systems of interpretation advocated by Ishmael and Akiba" in relation to contemporary

eral: God is not God of the dead but of the living. This latter statement is not a citation of scripture but does seem to express ideas based on one or more scriptural passages. In Ps 6:4-5, the Psalmist calls on God to save his life and then states, "For in death there is no remembrance of you; in Sheol who can give you praise?"[137] In the prayer of Hezekiah in Isaiah 38, he gives thanks that God has restored his life. Then he says, "For those who are in Hades will not praise you, and those who have died will not bless you, and those who are in Hades will not hope for your mercy. The living will bless you in the way that I also do."[138] If the general statement implies that God is the God of the living, then Abraham, Isaac, and Jacob must be living now or will live again.[139]

The sixth rule attributed to Hillel, "something similar to this in another passage," lit., "as it goes forth with this from another place" (כיוצא בו ממקום אחר), is an argument by analogy. If the statement "[God] is not a God of the dead, but of the living" can be seen as based on one of the scriptural passages mentioned above, then this rule could stand behind the Markan Jesus' argument. The logic is less apparent than the potential application of the fifth rule, discussed above.[140]

In any case, the argumentation of Jesus has some similarity to certain rabbinic arguments concerning the resurrection.[141] In the Mishnah, it is stated that all Israelites have a share in the world to come. But the unrighteous will not have a share, for example, "he that says that there is no resurrection of the dead prescribed in the Law" (m. Sanh. 10.1).[142] In the Babylonian Talmud, in relation to this mishnah, the question is raised, "How is resurrection derived from the Torah?" and answered, "As it is written, *And ye shall give thereof the Lord's heave offering to Aaron the priest* [Num 18:28]. But would Aaron live for ever; he did not even enter Palestine, that *terumah* [the heave offering] should be given him [the priestly dues were rendered only in Palestine]? But it teaches that he would be resurrected, and Israel give him *terumah*. Thus resurrection is derived from the Torah" (*b. Sanh.* 99b).[143] Another rabbinic argument is even more similar to that of the Markan Jesus: "R. Simai said: Whence do we learn resurrection from the Torah?—From the verse, *and I also have established my covenant with them,* [sc. the patriarchs] *to give them the land of Canaan* [Exod 6:4]: '[*to give*] you' is not said, but '*to give* them' [personally]; thus resurrection is proved from the Torah" (*b. Sanh.* 99b).[144] Both of these texts, however, unlike the Markan anecdote, seem to presuppose an earthly existence after the resurrection.

To support the idea that the dead rise, Jesus refers to "the book of Moses," which is equivalent to the Law of Moses or the commands of Moses.[145] The Markan Jesus here cites Exod 3:6 in a form close to that of the LXX, omitting the verb εἰμί ("I am") and the phrase τοῦ

---

non-Jewish rhetoric (261). Strack and Stemberger (Daube also) assume that these rules were used in the time of the historical Hillel, i.e., in the late first cent. BCE (19). Daube thinks it likely that Hillel's "seven norms of interpretation" were connected to the Hellenistic scholarship of Alexandria through his teachers, Shemaiah and Abtalion ("Rabbinic Methods of Interpretation," 241).

136 Cohn-Sherbok, "Jesus' Defence," 67–68. Daube notes that, according to the fifth norm, what was important was the term that came second. If the specific term comes second, then it restricts the first term; he also gives examples of the use of both parts of a similar norm by Roman jurists ("Rabbinic Methods of Interpretation," 252–54).

137 ὅτι οὐκ ἔστιν ἐν τῷ θανάτῳ ὁ μνημονεύων σου· ἐν δὲ τῷ ᾅδῃ τίς ἐξομολογήσεταί σοι (Ps 6:6 LXX; trans. NRSV [6:5]).

138 Isa 38:18-19 LXX: οὐ γὰρ οἱ ἐν ᾅδου αἰνέσουσίν σε, οὐδὲ οἱ ἀποθανόντες εὐλογήσουσίν σε, οὐδὲ ἐλπιοῦσιν οἱ ἐν ᾅδου τὴν ἐλεημοσύνην σου· οἱ

ζῶντες εὐλογήσουσίν σε ὃν τρόπον κἀγώ. See also Sir 17:27-28.

139 Cohn-Sherbok concluded that the argumentation of vv. 26-27 fits this rule only if the unexpressed copula in v. 26 is assumed to be in the present tense ("Jesus' Defence," 67–68). This seems to be an unnecessary restriction of the application and relevance of the rule.

140 Cohn-Sherbok rejects the applicability of this rule because, in his opinion, Exod 3:16 "simply points to God's identity" ("Jesus' Defence," 68).

141 George Foot Moore, *Judaism in the First Centuries of the Christian Era: The Age of the Tannaim* (2 vols.; New York: Schocken Books, 1958) 2:381–83.

142 Trans. Danby, *Mishnah*, 397.

143 Trans. Harry Freedman in Isidore Epstein, ed., *The Babylonian Talmud: Seder Nezîḳin. Sanhedrin* (London: Soncino Press, 1935–52).

144 Trans. Freedman. "The promise could be literally fulfilled only by the Patriarchs' resurrection" (ibid., n. 10).

145 Cf. 2 Chr 35:12; Lohmeyer, 256 n. 9; Jacob M.

πατρός σου ("of your father").[146] The interpretive comment following the citation, "[God] is not a God of the dead, but of the living," is similar to the second rabbinic argument cited above in that both focus on the relationship between God and the patriarchs.[147]

The afterlife of the patriarchs is treated in several ancient texts. The Similitudes or Parables of Enoch speak about "the first fathers and the righteous, who were dwelling . . . from of old" in the place to which Enoch was taken when he was removed, without dying, from among human beings. This place is probably Paradise (1 Enoch 70:4).[148] In the story of Luke 16:19-31, when the poor man Lazarus dies, he is taken by angels to a place of comfort in close fellowship with Abraham.[149] In the Testament of Benjamin, Benjamin teaches his children that Enoch, Noah, Shem, Abraham, Isaac, and Jacob will rise at the time when "the Lord reveals his salvation to all the Gentiles" (T. Benj. 10:5-6).[150] According to the Testament of Isaac, Isaac was taken immediately after his death by an angel in a chariot to the heavens to be with his father Abraham and all the saints. Jacob would join Isaac at the time of his death (T. Isaac 2:1-6; 12:1–13:1).

4 Maccabees is a Jewish text, but probably written later than Mark.[151] According to this work, those who can control the passions of the flesh can do so in part because "they believe that they, like our patriarchs Abraham and Isaac and Jacob, do not die to God, but live to God" (4 Macc 7:19 NRSV).[152] In this case, the underlying idea is the immortality of the soul, not resurrection.[153]

It is not clear exactly what vv. 26-27 presuppose about the current state of the patriarchs, whether they are in a place of comfort awaiting the general resurrection or already in the presence of God. The main points are that the patriarchs experience resurrection (vv. 26-27) and that resurrection is spiritual; that is, it does not involve an earthly type of life.

Jesus' entire reply to the Sadducees (vv. 24-27) ends with an *inclusio*. The statement opens and closes with the accusation "you are mistaken" (πλανᾶσθε).

Myers, *II Chronicles: Translation and Notes* (AB 13; New York: Doubleday, 1965) 213.

146 Ἐγώ εἰμι ὁ θεὸς τοῦ πατρός σου, θεὸς Αβρααμ καὶ θεὸς Ισαακ καὶ θεὸς Ιακωβ ("I am the God of your father, [the] God of Abraham and [the] God of Isaac and [the] God of Jacob") (Exod 3:6 LXX). The use of Exod 3:6 as proof for the general resurrection is unique to this passage and later texts dependent upon it (Meier, "Debate on the Resurrection," 11–14). For a comparison of Mark's citation of Exod 3:6 with those of Matthew and Luke and the relation of these citations to the LXX and the MT, see David S. New, *Old Testament Quotations in the Synoptic Gospels, and the Two-Document Hypothesis* (SBLSCS 37; Atlanta: Scholars Press, 1993) 68–70; see also 119.

147 On the theological implications of v. 27, see Donahue, "Neglected Factor," 577; Klaus Scholtissek, "'Er ist nicht ein Gott der Toten, sondern der Lebenden' (Mk 12,27): Grundzüge der markinischen Theo-logie," in Thomas Söding, ed., *Der lebendige Gott: Studien zur Theologie des Neuen Testaments; Festschrift für Wilhelm Thüsing zum 75. Geburtstag* (Münster: Aschendorff, 1996) 71–100, esp. 84–86.

148 Trans. from Nickelsburg and VanderKam, 93. Note the heading given to the relevant passage, "He Was Taken to Paradise" (ibid., 92).

149 According to *1 Enoch* 22, the spirits of the righteous dead (Abel is mentioned here) will abide until the day of judgment in four beautiful places with water and light; the spirits of sinners will dwell until the day of judgment in separate places of torment (Nickelsburg and VanderKam, 42–43; Nickelsburg, "Resurrection," 685). On the treatment of the afterlife in Luke 16:19-31, see Outi Lehtipuu, *The Afterlife Imagery in Luke's Story of the Rich Man and Lazarus* (NovTSup 123; Leiden: Brill, 2006), 153–226.

150 Trans. by M. de Jonge in Sparks, *AOT*, 599. *T. Jud.* 25:1 makes a similar point.

151 Van Henten, *Maccabean Martyrs*, 73–78.

152 See also 16:25.

153 Nickelsburg, "Resurrection," 686. According to *L.A.B.* 19:12, Moses is to rest until God raises him and his fathers at the time of God's visitation upon the world; see the discussion by Lehtipuu, *Afterlife Imagery*, 248–49.

12

12:28-34 The Greatest Commandment

28/ And one of the scribes, having come, heard them discussing and having seen that he answered them well, asked him, "Which commandment is first of all?" 29/ Jesus answered, "First is 'Hear, Israel, the Lord our God is one Lord; 30/ and you shall love the Lord your God with your whole heart and with your whole life and with your whole mind and with your whole strength.' 31/ This is second, 'You shall love your neighbor as yourself.' No other commandment is greater than these." 32/ And the scribe said to him, "Fittingly, Teacher, (and) in accordance with the truth you have said that 'He is one and there is no other except him' 33/ and 'to love him with the whole heart and with the whole understanding and with the whole strength' and 'to love one's neighbor as oneself' is much more than all whole burnt offerings and sacrifices." 34/ And Jesus, having seen him,[a] that he answered thoughtfully, said to him, "You are not far from the kingdom of God." And no one dared anymore to question him.

a   ℵ D L W et al. omit αὐτόν ("him"). This is a secondary reading, due to the failure to recognize (or the rejection of) the figure of speech, prolepsis, used here. On prolepsis, see Smyth §2182. This figure is also used in 7:2; see note a on the trans. of that verse above. Cf. Taylor, ad loc.

Literary Context and Genre

This passage is linked to the preceding one by the narrator's comments in v. 28 that the scribe heard them (Jesus and the Sadducees) discussing and perceived that Jesus answered them well. It lacks the polemical tone of the preceding anecdotes from 11:27 through 12:27 and thus contrasts with them. Dewey has argued that the three anecdotes concerning taxes, resurrection, and the first commandment constitute a rhetorical unit characterized by ring composition (12:13-34).[1] She also contrasted chapter 12 with 2:1—3:6 by pointing out that the most serious charges against Jesus appear in the first and last anecdotes of the latter section, whereas in chapter 12, there is a decline in the overt opposition to Jesus.[2]

This anecdote is "a pure scholastic dialogue in Mark, and it ends with the questioner being praised."[3] Robert C. Tannehill defines it as a quest story, but compares it with "inverted commendation stories in which the sage

1   *Markan Public Debate*, 157–59. John R. Donahue also observed similarities between this passage and the anecdote about paying taxes to Caesar ("Neglected Factor," 578). He concluded further that 12:13-34 is based on "an early Christian apologetic which is in debt to the missionary preaching of Hellenistic Judaism (esp. in 12:28-34) (580).

2   Dewey, *Markan Public Debate*, 163.

3   Bultmann, *History*, 51; followed by Günther Bornkamm, "Das Doppelgebot der Liebe," in Walther Eltester, ed., *Neutestamentliche Studien für Rudolf Bultmann zu seinem 70. Geburtstag* (2nd rev. ed.; BZNW 21; Berlin: Töpelmann, 1957) 85–93, esp. 85. This scholastic dialogue is turned into a controversy-dialogue by Matthew (22:34-40) and Luke (10:25-28), as Bultmann points out (*History*, 51).

or hero is praised, rather than praising another."[4] He notes that "the parallel versions are testing inquiries."[5] Bultmann and Tannehill are correct in their respective observations that the scribe and Jesus are both praised. But as Tannehill rightly points out, the statement of the scribe is unusually long (12:32-33).[6] This literary feature seems to suggest that the emphasis in the account is on the praise of Jesus.

David Daube argued that the question put to Jesus by the scribe falls under the category of *derek 'ereṣ*, which includes questions "concerned with the fundamental principles on which to base one's conduct, as opposed to detailed ritual."[7]

Relation to Jesus, Originality, and Cultural Context

The consensus is that the two passages cited here, Deut 6:5 and Lev 19:18, are not cited in combination in any ancient Jewish text.[8] But this fact does not necessarily lead to the conclusion that the double love-command goes back to the historical Jesus, because it is anticipated in substance and function in Jewish literature, especially texts written in Greek.[9] In formulation the closest parallels are *T. Iss.* 5:2 and *T. Dan* 5:3.[10] They read as follows:

So keep the law of God, my children, and try to live simply and in innocence; and do not be over-inquisitive about the Lord's commands, nor about the affairs of your neighbour. But love the Lord and your neighbour, and show compassion for the poor and the weak (Φυλάξατε οὖν νόμον θεοῦ, τέκνα μου, καὶ τὴν ἁπλότητα κτήσασθε, καὶ ἐν ἀκακίᾳ πορεύεσθε, μὴ περιεργαζόμενοι ἐντολὰς κυρίου καὶ τοῦ πλησίον τὰς πράξεις· ἀλλ' ἀγαπᾶτε κύριον καὶ τὸν πλησίον, πένητα καὶ ἀσθενῆ ἐλεᾶτε). (*T. Iss.* 5:1-2)[11]

Love the Lord throughout [or "with all"] your life, and one another with a true heart (ἀγαπᾶτε τὸν κύριον ἐν πάσῃ τῇ ζωῇ ὑμῶν, καὶ ἀλλήλους ἐν ἀληθινῇ καρδίᾳ). (*T. Dan* 5:3)[12]

Since the *Testaments of the Twelve Patriarchs* has been preserved by Christians and has some obvious Christian interpolations, it is not clear whether these passages are independent witnesses to the traditions of Greek-speaking Jews or whether they are dependent on the Markan passage and its parallels.[13] Nevertheless, there are other pieces of evidence that support the claim that

4 Tannehill, "Varieties," 4.3 (p. 112). Dewey defines it as a "school debate containing no hint of conflict" (*Markan Public Debate*, 17).

5 Tannehill, "Varieties," 4.3 (p. 112).

6 Ibid.

7 Daube, *New Testament*, 160.

8 Christoph Burchard, "Das doppelte Liebesgebot in der frühen christlichen Überlieferung," in Eduard Lohse, ed., *Der Ruf Jesu und die Antwort der Gemeinde: Exegetische Untersuchungen Joachim Jeremias zum 70. Geburtstag* (Göttingen: Vandenhoeck & Ruprecht, 1970) 39–62, esp. 55; Andreas Nissen, *Gott und der Nächste im antiken Judentum: Untersuchungen zum Doppelgebot der Liebe* (WUNT 15; Tübingen: Mohr Siebeck, 1974) 241 n. 642; Donahue, "Neglected Factor," 579 and n. 55.

9 Burchard, "Das doppelte Liebesgebot," 55. See also *T. Iss.* 7:6; *T. Jos.* 11:1 *T. Benj.* 3:1-3, 10:3. For discussion see Klaus Berger, *Die Gesetzesauslegung Jesu: Ihr historischer Hintergrund im Judentum und im Alten Testament*, Teil I: *Markus und Parallelen* (WANT 40; Neukirchen-Vluyn: Neukirchener Verlag, 1972) 160–62.

10 Burchard, "Das doppelte Liebesgebot," 55–56.

11 Text from Marinus de Jonge, *The Testaments of the Twelve Patriarchs: A Critical Edition of the Greek Text* (PVTG 1/2; Leiden: Brill, 1978), 85; trans. by idem in *AOT* 554.

12 Text from de Jonge, *Testaments of the Twelve Patriarchs*, 107; trans. by idem in *AOT* 564. Cf. also *T. Zeb.* 5:1, *T. Benj.* 10:3, which seem to sum up the commandments of the Lord in terms of right dealings with other human beings.

13 Nineham, 324; Donahue, "Neglected Factor," 579 n. 55; Oscar S. Brooks, "The Function of the Double Love Command in Matthew 22:34-40," *AUSS* 36 (1998) 7–22, esp. 15 n. 27; M. de Jonge, "The Two Great Commandments in the Testaments of the Twelve Patriarchs," *NovT* 44 (2002) 371–92. See also Hollander and de Jonge, 82–85; Harm W. Hollander, *Joseph as an Ethical Model in the Testaments of the Twelve Patriarchs* (SVTP 6; Leiden: Brill, 1981); M. de Jonge, "The Testaments of the Twelve Patriarchs: Central Problems and Essential Viewpoints," *ANRW* 2.20.1 (1987) 359–420.

the double command was anticipated in earlier Jewish texts. The command to love God in Deut 6:5 was already a kind of summarizing formula in the Deuteronomic tradition.[14] The exclusive allegiance to YHWH demanded here "means scrupulous observance of his commandments."[15] The tendency to present summarizing "main commandments" was present in the wisdom literature.[16]

The book of *Jubilees* was composed in Hebrew between 170 and 150 BCE. Fragments of the Hebrew work, discovered in caves near Qumran, and quotations from a Greek translation survive, but *Jubilees* is extant mainly in Ethiopic manuscripts. It is "a heavily edited retelling of Genesis 1—Exodus 12."[17] In a speech of Noah to his (grand)sons, the most important commandments are listed:

> He testified to his sons that they should do what is right, cover the shame of their bodies, bless the one who had created them, honor father and mother, love one another, and keep themselves from fornication, uncleanness, and from all injustice. (*Jub.* 7:20)[18]

Abraham's speech to his offspring does likewise:

> He ordered them to keep the way of the Lord so that they would do what is right and that they should love one another; that they should be like this in every war so that they could go against each one (who was) against them; and do what is just and right on the earth. (*Jub.* 20:2)[19]

The section of the speech that follows immediately upon this passage commands the practice of circumcision and the avoidance and punishment of sexual impurity and uncleanness (20:3). Thus the context makes clear that the listing of general, important commandments does not mean that the particular commandments need not be observed.

In his farewell speech to Esau and Jacob, Isaac also summarizes the main commandments, or, to put it another way, emphasizes his sons' main duties:

> Now I will make you swear with the great oath—because there is no oath which is greater than it, by the praiseworthy, illustrious, and great, splendid, marvelous, powerful, and great name which made the heavens and the earth and everything together—that you will continue to fear and worship him, as each loves his brother kindly and properly. One is not to desire what is bad for his brother now and forever, throughout your entire lifetime, so that you may be prosperous in everything that you do and not be destroyed. (*Jub.* 36:7-8)[20]

Here we have two main duties expressed, the fear and worship of God and the love of one's brother (that is, the members of one's people). This dual emphasis is analogous to the double love-command in Mark 12:28-34.[21]

The original meaning of the Decalogue was reinterpreted in the book of Deuteronomy.[22] This process was taken further by Greek-speaking Jews, especially Philo. Crucial to Philo's summarizing characterizations of the Law was the influence of Greek tradition about the virtues. Greek literature typically summed up human duties under two categories, τὸ ὅσιον ("holiness," lit., "the holy") or τὸ εὐσεβές ("piety," lit., "the pious"), on the one hand, and τὸ δίκαιον ("justice," lit., "the just"), on the other. So εὐσέβεια καὶ δικαιοσύνη ("piety and justice") were the two main virtues.[23] Philo spoke about the synagogues as schools teaching the virtues every

14 Berger, *Gesetzesauslegung*, 55–63.

15 Moshe Weinfeld, *Deuteronomy 1–11: A New Translation with Introduction and Commentary* (AB 5; New York: Doubleday, 1991) 328.

16 Berger, *Gesetzesauslegung*, 136–37, who cites, e.g., Sir 25:1; 32:23 LXX; Wis 6:18. He also notes that the opening and closing remarks of the work of Pseudo-Phocylides, a Greek-speaking Jew, identify the law of God with the collection of wisdom sayings that constitute the book (ibid., 47).

17 VanderKam, *Book of Jubilees*, V–XIX; quotation from V.

18 Trans. from VanderKam, *Book of Jubilees*, 46–47.

19 Trans. from VanderKam, *Book of Jubilees*, 115–16.

20 Trans. from VanderKam, *Book of Jubilees*, 238.

21 Cf. Berger, *Gesetzesauslegung*, 163; Reginald H. Fuller, "The Double Commandment of Love: A Test Case for the Criteria of Authenticity," in Luise Schottroff et al., *Essays on the Love Commandment* (Philadelphia: Fortress, 1978) 41–56, esp. 55 n. 22.

22 Berger, *Gesetzesauslegung*, 138; Weinfeld, *Deuteronomy 1–11*, 241–42.

23 Berger, *Gesetzesauslegung*, 143–51.

seventh day.[24] He went on to say that all the particular sayings (λόγοι) and decrees (δόγματα) studied there could be brought under two main heads:

But among the vast number of particular truths and principles there studied, there stand out, so to speak, high above the others two main heads: one of duty to God as shown by piety and holiness, one of duty to human beings as shown by kindness and justice, each of them splitting up into multiform branches, all highly laudable (ἔστι δ᾽ ὡς ἔπος εἰπεῖν τῶν κατὰ μέρος ἀμυθήτων λόγων καὶ δογμάτων δύο τὰ ἀνωτάτω κεφάλαια, τό τε πρὸς θεὸν δι᾽ εὐσεβείας καὶ ὁσιότητος καὶ τὸ πρὸς ἀνθρώπους διὰ φιλανθρωπίας καὶ δικαιοσύνης· ὧν ἑκάτερον εἰς πολυσχιδεῖς ἰδέας καὶ πάσας ἐπαινετὰς τέμνεται). (Spec. leg. 2.15 §63)[25]

Since the composition of Deuteronomy 5, the Decalogue as such apparently played no special role in Jewish writings until it was "rediscovered" by Philo, who was the first to write a treatise on it.[26] Following Deuteronomy and differently from Exodus,[27] Philo presents the Decalogue as the only laws that God gave "in His own person and by His own mouth alone" (Decal. 5 §19).[28] He goes on to say that the Decalogue is constituted by laws that are also "heads summarizing the particular laws" (καὶ νόμων τῶν ἐν μέρει κεφάλαια) (ibid.).[29] Later he argues that the ten are divided into two sets of five, which were engraved on two tables; the first five obtaining the first place, the second five the second place

(Decal. 12 §50).[30] With regard to the two sets of five, he wrote:

Thus one set of enactments begins with God the Father and Maker of all, and ends with parents who copy His nature by begetting particular persons. The other set of five contains all the prohibitions, namely adultery, murder, theft, false witness, covetousness or lust (ὡς εἶναι τῆς μιᾶς γραφῆς τὴν μὲν ἀρχὴν θεὸν καὶ πατέρα καὶ ποιητὴν τοῦ παντός, τὸ δὲ τέλος γονεῖς, οἳ μιμούμενοι τὴν ἐκείνου φύσιν γεννῶσι τοὺς ἐπὶ μέρους. ἡ δ᾽ ἑτέρα πεντὰς τὰς πάσας ἀπαγορεύσεις περιέχει· μοιχείας, φόνου, κλοπῆς, ψευδομαρτυριῶν, ἐπιθυμιῶν). (Decal. 12 §51)[31]

After discussing the first five, Philo refers to people who follow carefully one set of five but neglect the other. Those who follow the first set exclusively are those characterized by "yearning for piety" (ὁ εὐσεβείας πόθος), whereas those devoting themselves only to the second set think that the only good is practicing justice toward human beings (τὰ πρὸς ἀνθρώπους δικαιώματα) (Decal. 22 §§108–9).[32] The former are called "lovers of God" (φιλόθεοι), the latter "lovers of human beings" (φιλάνθρωποι). Both of these come only half-way in virtue (ibid. §110).[33] Philo characterizes the first set of five as those that command "the most sacred things" (τὰ ἱερώτατα) and the second as containing "just matters toward human beings" (τὰ πρὸς ἀνθρώπους δίκαια) (ibid. §106).[34]

---

24 Philo Spec. leg. 2.15 §62.
25 Text and trans. (modified) from Colson and Whitaker, Philo, 7:346–47.
26 Berger, Gesetzesauslegung, 138. The Decalogue is cited in the Nash Papyrus, but it is difficult to determine to what effect (Paul Foster, "Why Did Matthew Get the Shema Wrong? A Study of Matthew 22:37," JBL 122 [2003] 309–33, esp. 327–28).
27 Weinfeld, Deuteronomy 1–11, 241.
28 Trans. from Colson and Whitaker, Philo, 7:15.
29 Text and trans. from Colson and Whitaker, Philo, 7:14–15.
30 Colson and Whitaker, Philo, 7:30–31.
31 Colson and Whitaker, Philo, 7:30–33.
32 Text and trans. (modified) from Colson and Whitaker, Philo, 7:60–63.

33 Text and trans. (modified) from Colson and Whitaker, Philo, 7:62–63. Dale C. Allison, Jr., cites this passage, but does not note the critical, or even negative, context in which these terms appear ("Mark 12.28-31 and the Decalogue," in Craig A. Evans and W. Richard Stegner, eds., The Gospels and the Scriptures of Israel [JSNTSup 104; SSEJC 3; Sheffield: Sheffield Academic Press, 1994] 270–78, esp. 272).
34 Text and trans. (modified) from Colson and Whitaker, Philo, 7.60–61. See also Decal. 24 §121, where Philo describes the first set as more concerned with the divine (θειοτέρα) (Allison, "Mark 12.28-31 and the Decalogue," 272).

In one place, Philo says that the leading virtues are εὐσέβεια ("piety") and ὁσιότης ("holiness") (*Decal.* 23 §119).[35] This emphasis on the first table of the Decalogue reflects the importance of reverence and obedience to God in Jewish tradition. In another place, following Greek popular philosophy, he says that the leading virtues are εὐσέβεια ("piety") and φιλανθρωπία ("kindness") (*Virt.* 18 §95).[36]

As noted above, in *Spec. leg.* 2.15 §63, Philo states that the Ten Commandments are "headings" of all the particular commandments. He elaborated this point in *Decal.* and used it as an organizing principle in *Spec. leg.* It is clear, however, that Philo does not use the idea of summarizing headings to argue that only some laws are to be observed and others not. This is made clear, for example, in the separate treatment of circumcision as a particular law apart from the Decalogue in a kind of preface to the work (*Spec. leg.* 1.1-2 §§1–11). Further, in *Spec. leg.* 4.25 §§132–35, he recognizes that there are some laws that do not fit under the heading of any one of the Ten Commandments. He uses a new scheme in what follows by organizing the commandments according to virtues like justice and courage and claims that these commands are implied by all ten commandments of the Decalogue.[37]

As we have seen, the *T. 12 Patr.* speaks about loving both God and neighbor in the same context, but the Christian transmission of this document precludes using it with assurance as evidence for the attestation of the double love-command independently of the Gospels. *Jubilees* speaks occasionally of "loving one another" or "loving one's brother," but does not combine such commands with the command to love God. Philo speaks about "lovers (or friends) of God" (φιλόθεοι) and "lovers (or friends) of human beings" (φιλάνθρωποι), but this usage is not typical of his summarizing interpretation of the commandments. So the formulation of two most important or summarizing commandments in terms of love in Mark or the tradition to which the evangelist was heir was at least distinctive, if not original.

The idea and the activity of summarizing the commandments or selecting the most important ones apparently arose in Jewish circles primarily in response to popular Greek philosophical teaching about the virtues and its attempt to summarize all human duties in terms of two main virtues. The tannaim and later rabbis engaged in such activities, but it is uncertain whether the relevant texts represent traditions that go back to the time of Jesus.[38] It thus seems likely that the double love-command, as we find it in Mark, was formulated by a Greek-speaking Jew with knowledge of Greek popular ethics or Jewish adaptation of such ethics. This formulation did not necessarily take place outside Palestine,[39] where Jews had been in contact with Hellenistic culture for centuries.[40] There were Greek-speaking Jews living in

---

35   Text and trans. (modified) from Colson and Whitaker, *Philo*, 7:66–67.

36   Text and trans. (modified) from Colson and Whitaker, *Philo*, 8:220–21. See also *Virt.* 9 §51; *Abr.* 37 §208; *Vit. Mos.* 2.31 §163 (θεοφιλής should probably be translated "loving God" here, rather than in terms of "God's love for him," as Colson translates it); *Spec. leg.* 4.25-26 §§135–36. The typical pair in Greek texts is εὐσέβεια καὶ δικαιοσύνη ("piety and justice") or occasionally εὐσέβεια καὶ φιλανθρωπία ("piety and kindness"); Philo may have chosen φιλανθρωπία ("kindness") rather than δικαιοσύνη ("righteousness") to counter the accusation that the Jews were characterized by hatred of (other) human beings (μισανθρωπία). See Berger, *Gesetzesauslegung*, 137, 140, 143–60, 168. *Ep. Arist.* 131 summarizes the Law of Moses in terms of εὐσέβεια ("piety") and δικαιοσύνη ("justice"); text from Henry Barclay Swete, *An Introduction to the Old Testament in Greek* (Cambridge: Cambridge University Press, 1914) 574; trans. (modified) from R. J. H.

Shutt in *OTP*, 2:21; see also *Ep. Arist.* 18, 168, 228–29; Berger, *Gesetzesauslegung*, 155–56.

37   Colson and Whitaker, *Philo*, 7:xi.

38   P. S. Alexander, "Jesus and the Golden Rule," in James H. Charlesworth and Loren L. Johns, eds., *Hillel and Jesus: Comparative Studies of Two Major Religious Leaders* (Minneapolis: Fortress, 1997) 363–88, esp. 375, 382–88; cf. George Foot Moore, *Judaism in the First Centuries of the Christian Era: The Age of the Tannaim* (2 vols.; New York: Schocken Books, 1958) 2:83–88. See also the commentary below.

39   Contra Bornkamm, "Doppelgebot," 87–88; Burchard, "Das doppelte Liebesgebot," 55.

40   Hengel, *Judaism and Hellenism*, 1:58–106.

Palestine, especially in Jerusalem.[41] Some of these had contact with Jewish pilgrims from the Diaspora; some had visited or lived in Jewish communities of the Diaspora; and some were Jewish natives of some of those communities.[42] A Greek inscription found in Jerusalem in 1913/1914 attests to the presence of a synagogue of Greek-speaking Jews in the first century CE.[43] There were probably a number of synagogues in Jerusalem for Greek-speaking Jews who had returned from the Diaspora.[44]

As noted at the beginning of this section above, the most distinctive aspect of the double love-command in Mark is the combined citation of Deut 6:4-5 and Lev 19:18. In terms of substance, the reason for bringing these two passages together was to express, in a typically Jewish(-Christian) way, the two main virtues of piety ($\epsilon\dot{\upsilon}$-$\sigma\acute{\epsilon}\beta\epsilon\iota\alpha$) and justice ($\delta\iota\kappa\alpha\iota\sigma\acute{\upsilon}\nu\eta$) or kindness ($\varphi\iota\lambda\alpha\nu$-$\vartheta\rho\omega\pi\acute{\iota}\alpha$). Formally speaking, the justification for bringing the two passages together may be the second interpretive norm or hermeneutical principle attributed to Hillel, namely, גזרה שוה ("the same decree" or "the rule of analogy"). The use of the same term in the two passages, the verb "to love" (אהב in Hebrew and $\dot{\alpha}\gamma\alpha\pi\epsilon\hat{\iota}\nu$ in Greek) would thus have provided the rationale for joining the two texts.[45]

The combination of interest in Greek ethics and proto-rabbinic exegesis of scripture would fit well in a context in which Greek-speaking Jewish followers of Jesus were in dialogue, and perhaps to some degree in conflict, with primarily Aramaic-speaking followers of Jesus or with Jews who spoke either or both languages but did not follow Jesus. The origin of the formulation as preserved by Mark would thus fit the context of the group of Christians, originally located in Jerusalem, called "the Hellenists" by the author of Acts (6:1-6).[46]

If the formulation of the double love-command as Mark has preserved it does not go back to the historical Jesus, it is clear that it has important roots in his teaching and activity.[47] For example, the teaching to love one's enemies has a good claim to come from the historical Jesus.[48]

Relations among the Synoptic Gospels and Their Sources

Bultmann thought it likely that Luke used a version of the anecdote other than Mark's.[49] Bornkamm argued that Matthew and Luke knew an older version of the anecdote that lacked the second dialogical interchange in vv. 32-34. They found two variants of this older version in their respective copies of Mark; it thus lacked the perspective of Hellenistic apologetic that Bornkamm believed characterized the anecdote in the form of Mark that has come down to us.[50] Burchard rejected Bornkamm's conclusion, believing it to be based on the dubious hypothesis of an *Urmarkus*.[51] He argued instead that Matthew and Luke must have known another version of the anecdote in addition to the one now preserved in Mark. They probably knew this version from oral tradition.[52]

---

41   Martin Hengel, *The 'Hellenization' of Judaea in the First Century after Christ* (London: SCM; Philadelphia: Trinity Press International, 1989) 9–11. Gerd Theissen argued that the early Christian community in Jerusalem included Palestinians from Galilee and Hellenistis from the Diaspora (*Gospels in Context*, 180). See also Mark A. Chancey, *Greco-Roman Culture and the Galilee of Jesus* (SNTSMS; Cambridge/New York: Cambridge University Press, 2005) esp. chaps. 1–3.

42   Hengel, *'Hellenization' of Judaea*, 13–14.

43   For the Greek text and a French trans., see *CIJ* vol. 2, #1404 (pp. 332–35); for an ET, see Eric M. Meyers, "Synagogue," *ABD* 6:251–60, esp. 252. For discussion, see Hengel, *'Hellenization' of Judaea*, 11, 13, 21, 70 n. 60.

44   Hengel, *'Hellenization' of Judaea*, 13.

45   Asher Finkel, *The Pharisees and the Teacher of Nazareth* (AGSU 4; Leiden, Brill, 1964) 174; Victor Paul Fur-

nish, *The Love Command in the New Testament* (Nashville: Abingdon, 1972; London: SCM, 1973; the latter is cited here) 28; Berger, *Gesetzesauslegung*, 170. On the rules attributed to Hillel, see also the commentary on vv. 26-27 above.

46   On conflict between "the Hellenists" and Greek-speaking Jews who did not accept Jesus, see Acts 6:8-10; cf. 9:29.

47   Bultmann, *History*, 54–55; Burchard, "Das doppelte Liebesgebot," 61–62.

48   Bultmann, *History*, 105; Furnish, *Love Command*, 65–66.

49   Bultmann, *History*, 23.

50   Bornkamm, "Doppelgebot," 92; followed by Koester, "History and Development," 40.

51   Burchard, "Das doppelte Liebesgebot," 41.

52   Ibid., 43. He considered and rejected the possibility that the version common to Matthew and Luke stood in Q (ibid.). Material from Luke 10:25-28 is

The conclusion that Matthew and Luke must have known another version of the story is based on certain features that their accounts have in common that are different from Mark's version. One such feature is that Matthew and Luke identify the questioner as a νομικός ("legal expert," "jurist," or "lawyer"), whereas Mark describes him as a γραμματεύς ("scribe").[53] This agreement against Mark can easily be explained as coincidental, independent editing on the part of Matthew and Luke. In their contexts, most likely outside Palestine, the term γραμματεύς usually meant "secretary" or "clerk." They followed Mark and other sources in using this term much of the time, but here the character in question had to be presented as one with expertise in the Law. Thus, they chose a term better suited to the expectations of their audiences.

Two other features common to Matthew and Luke are both omissions: the citation of the *Shema*ᶜ (Deut 6:4)[54] and the second dialogical interchange (vv. 32-34) are lacking in those Gospels. The *Shema*ᶜ, however attractive and valuable it may have been, especially to Matthew, could easily have been omitted by both because it did not serve their immediate purposes. Neither may have understood Mark's purpose in portraying the scribe positively, so they both transformed the anecdote into the more common controversy-dialogue and, in the process, shortened Mark's version.[55]

Comment

■ **28** This scribe is portrayed as an interpreter of the Law; thus, he is presented as a legal expert or teacher like the scribes who are mentioned in 1:22.[56] The scribe asks Jesus, "Which commandment is first (πρώτη) of all?" Here the term πρώτη signifies the "first" with regard to importance or prominence, not the first in a sequence.[57] Matthew has the questioner ask which commandment is (the) great(est) (μεγάλη) in the Law (22:36), which is equivalent to the corresponding question in Mark.[58] Luke has him ask what he must do to inherit eternal life (10:25), a formulation that does not focus as clearly on the interpretation of commandments or the Law as the versions of Mark and Matthew do.

Matthew's formulation of the question is the closest of the three to the terminology of the rabbis. Rabbinic literature counted the commandments, 613 in all. Of these, 248 are positive commandments and 365 are prohibitions.[59] The 613 commandments were also divided into "light commandments" and "heavy commandments." The significance of this distinction varied. Sometimes the "light commandments" were defined as those that make little claim on one's power or possessions. In contrast, the "heavy commandments" are those that require the expenditure of a large amount of money or that involve a threat to one's life.[60] At other times, a "heavy commandment" was defined as an "important" commandment. In this case, a "light commandment" means one that is "unimportant." An "important" commandment could also be referred to as a "great commandment," as in Matt 22:36.[61] The "heavy" or "important" commandments were defined in one text as those for which extirpation or the judicial penalty of the death sentence is prescribed, and the "light" or "unimportant" commandments as those entailing offenses that can be

---

unlikely to have been included in Q (Robinson et al., *Critical Edition of Q*, 200–205).

53   Burchard, "Das doppelte Liebesgebot, 41.

54   On the *Shema*ᶜ, see the commentary on vv. 29-30 below.

55   On the practice of rewriting texts to make them more concise, see the commentary on vv. 13-17 above. Furnish also concluded that the differences among the three accounts are due to the editorial activity of Matthew and Luke (*Love Command*, 30–45, esp. 37–38).

56   On the historical scribes and the scribes as a group in Mark, see the commentary above on 1:22. On the "scribe" as an interpreter and teacher of the Law and wisdom, see Finkel, *Pharisees and the Teacher of Nazareth*, 18–22.

57   See BAGD, s.v. πρῶτος.

58   The Markan Jesus uses the comparative form of the same term in v. 31b; see the commentary below.

59   Str-B, 1:900. "By an ingenious conceit," these numbers were shown to be fitting by connecting the positive commandments with the 248 members and organs of the human body and the prohibitions with the 365 days in the solar year (Moore, *Judaism*, 2:83).

60   Str-B, 1:901.

61   Ibid. A "light" commandment could also be referred to as a "little commandment" (ibid., 901–2); cf. Matt 5:19.

expiated.[62] Most commonly, the "important" or "heavy" commandments were defined as those concerning idolatry, unchastity, the shedding of blood, profaning the divine name, keeping the Sabbath holy, calumny or slander against one's neighbor, studying the Torah, and the redemption of captives.[63] A text from the Babylonian Talmud reads:

> Now, which is the commandment that is as weighty as all other commandments? Surely (lit. be saying) it is that concerning idolatry. . . . Now which is the commandment that was given in the words of the Holy One, blessed be He, and also by the hand of Moses? Surely (lit. be saying) it is that of idolatry; for R. Ishmael recited: [The words] *I* (the first word of the first commandment, '*I am the Lord* etc.' Exod 20:2) and *Thou shalt not have* (first words of the second commandment, Exod 20:3) were heard (lit. we heard them) from the mouth of Omnipotence. (*b. Hor.* 8a §f)[64]

The commandment that "is as weighty as all other commandments" is equivalent to the "great(est)" commandment in Matt 22:36 and to the commandment that is "first of all" in Mark 12:28.

The command to "love the Lord your God" in Deut 6:5, cited in Mark 12:30, Matt 22:37, and Luke 10:27, is equivalent to the first two commandments cited in *b. Hor.* 8a. In all cases, the issue is the most important commandment.[65] The combination of Deut 6:5 and Lev 19:18, which occurs in this context in all three Synoptic Gospels (Mark 12:30-31; Matt 22:37-39; Luke 10:27), however, is, substantively speaking, a summary of the whole Law.[66] Analogously, Philo implies that the Law is summed up in the two main virtues of piety ($\epsilon\dot{\upsilon}\sigma\acute{\epsilon}\beta\epsilon\iota\alpha$) and kindness ($\phi\iota\lambda\alpha\nu\vartheta\rho\omega\pi\acute{\iota}\alpha$). These virtues characterize Abraham, who is a living law ($\ddot{\epsilon}\mu\psi\upsilon\chi\sigma\varsigma\ \nu\acute{o}\mu\sigma\varsigma$) (Philo *Abr.* 37 §208).[67] They also constitute the two main heads of the teaching that takes place every seventh day in the synagogues.[68] Some rabbinic texts contain discussions of "the great principle" (כלל גדול), that is, "a general principle underlying a series of concrete rulings."[69]

As noted above, this scribe is portrayed by Mark as approaching Jesus out of a genuine desire to learn from him, not to test him, as in Matt 22:35 and Luke 10:25.[70]

■ **29-30** The Markan Jesus responds to the scribe by presenting as the "first" commandment a citation of Deut 6:4-5. As noted above, Mark is the only Gospel to include Deut 6:4 in this context.[71] The citation of 6:4-5 would remind those in Mark's audiences who were familiar with it of the *Shema*.[72] Josephus quotes Moses as establishing a law about a twice-daily prayer that is most likely the *Shema* or something like it:

---

62 Ibid., 902.

63 Ibid.

64 Trans. by Israel W. Slotki in Isidore Epstein, ed., *The Babylonian Talmud: Seder Neziḳin, Horayoth* (London: Soncino Press, 1935–52); this passage is cited by Str-B, 1:904.

65 Cf. *Ep. Arist.* 228: "for God's very great commandment concerns the honor due to parents" ($\kappa\alpha\grave{\iota}\ \gamma\grave{\alpha}\rho$ $\dot{o}\ \vartheta\epsilon\grave{o}\varsigma\ \pi\epsilon\pi\sigma\acute{\iota}\eta\tau\alpha\iota\ \dot{\epsilon}\nu\tau\sigma\lambda\grave{\eta}\nu\ \mu\epsilon\gamma\acute{\iota}\sigma\tau\eta\nu\ \pi\epsilon\rho\grave{\iota}\ \tau\hat{\eta}\varsigma$ $\tau\hat{\omega}\nu\ \gamma\sigma\nu\acute{\epsilon}\omega\nu\ \tau\iota\mu\hat{\eta}\varsigma$); text from Swete, *Introduction to the Old Testament in Greek*, 590; trans. from Shutt in *OTP* 2:28.

66 This is made explicit in Matt 22:40; cf. Plutarch *Cons. ad Apoll.* 28, cited by Davies and Allison, *Matthew*, 3:240 n. 35. The trans. they cite is by Babbitt, *Plutarch's Moralia*, 2:183. This trans. has been unduly influenced by Matt 22:40, but nonetheless, the similarity is striking. On rabbinic traditions about a summary of the Law, see Abrahams, *Studies in Pharisaism*, 1:23–29; Alexander, "Jesus and the Golden Rule," 382–88.

67 On the patriarchs as "living laws," see Philo, *Abr.* 1

§§3–5. For discussion see Peder Borgen, "Philo of Alexandria," in Stone, *Jewish Writings*, 237–38. See the discussion in "Relation to Jesus, Originality, and Cultural Context" above.

68 See the citation and discussion of Philo *Spec. leg.* 2.15 §63 in "Relation to Jesus, Originality, and Cultural Context" above.

69 Alexander, "Jesus and the Golden Rule," 383–88.

70 See "Literary Context and Genre" above.

71 See "Relation to Jesus, Originality, and Cultural Context" and "Relations among the Synoptic Gospels and Their Sources" above.

72 Brooks argued that the audience of Matthew would have associated the citation of Deut 6:5 in Matt 22:37 with the *Shema* ("Function of the Double Love Command," 10–12); Joel Marcus assumes the same for Deut 6:4-5 in this verse (*Way of the Lord*, 145). Berger concluded that the intention of the author of the text preserved by Mark was to cite the commandment to worship only one God, not to cite the *Shema* as such (*Gesetzesauslegung*, 190–91).

Twice each day, at the dawn thereof and when the hour comes for turning to repose, let all acknowledge before God the bounties which He has bestowed on them through their deliverance from the land of Egypt: thanksgiving is a natural duty, and is rendered alike in gratitude for past mercies and to incline the giver to others yet to come. They shall inscribe also on their doors the greatest of the benefits which they have received from God and each shall display them on his arms; and all that can show forth the power of God and His goodwill towards them, let them bear a record thereof written on the head and on the arm, so that all may see on every side the loving care with which God surrounds them (Δὶς δ᾽ ἑκάστης ἡμέρας ἀρχομένης τε αὐτῆς καὶ ὁπότε πρὸς ὕπνον ὥρα τρέπεσθαι μαρτυρεῖν τῷ θεῷ τὰς δωρεάς, ἃς ἀπαλλαγεῖσιν αὐτοῖς ἐκ τῆς Αἰγυπτίων γῆς παρέσχε, δικαίας οὔσης φύσει τῆς εὐχαριστίας καὶ γενομένης ἐπ᾽ ἀμοιβῇ μὲν τῶν ἤδη γεγονότων ἐπὶ δὲ προτροπῇ τῶν ἐσομένων· ἐπιγράφειν δὲ καὶ τοῖς θυρώμασιν αὐτῶν τὰ μέγιστα ὧν εὐηργέτησεν αὐτοὺς ὁ θεὸς ἔν τε βραχίοσιν ἕκαστον διαφαίνειν, ὅσα τε τὴν ἰσχὺν ἀποσημαίνειν δύναται τοῦ θεοῦ καὶ τὴν πρὸς αὐτοὺς εὔνοιαν φέρειν ἐγγεγραμμένα ἐπὶ τῆς κεφαλῆς καὶ τοῦ βραχίονος, ὡς περίβλεπτον πανταχόθεν τὸ περὶ αὐτοὺς πρόθυμον τοῦ θεοῦ). (*Ant.* 4.8.13 §§212–13)[73]

According to the Mishnah, the *Shemaꜥ* is a benediction to be recited twice a day, in the morning and evening, by every adult male Israelite, in any language. It consisted at

that time (beginning of the third century CE) of Deut 6:4-9, Deut 11:13-21, and Num 15:37-41.[74] Deut 11:13 and Num 15:39-40 emphasize the keeping of all of God's commandments. Deut 11:16-17 warns against turning away to serve other gods.

In addition to evoking the *Shemaꜥ*, Jesus' citation of Deut 6:4 emphasizes the Jewish affirmation that there is only one God. The MT is ambiguous and could be translated as follows:[75]

Hear, O Israel: The Lord is our God, the Lord alone

(שְׁמַע יִשְׂרָאֵל יְהוָה אֱלֹהֵינוּ יְהוָה אֶחָד)

The manuscripts of the LXX, however, followed by Mark, make clear that the word meaning "alone" or "one" in the Hebrew text (אֶחָד) is to be taken as a predicate:

Hear, O Israel: The Lord our God is one Lord (or "The Lord our God, the Lord is one" or "The Lord is our God, the Lord is one") (Ἄκουε, Ἰσραηλ· κύριος ὁ θεὸς ἡμῶν κύριος εἷς ἐστιν). (Deut 6:4 LXX)[76]

The response of the scribe in v. 32 strengthens this affirmation of monotheism.[77]

The Markan Jesus goes on to quote Deut 6:5 in the first part of his reply to the scribe ("You shall love, etc."). Here, however, the Markan text differs from the LXX in having four instead of three phrases describing the manner in which one is commanded to love God.[78] The LXX reads:

---

73 Text and trans. (slightly modified) from Thackeray, *Josephus*, 4:576–79. Foster is right to question the notion that the *Shemaꜥ* had a fixed liturgical form in the first cent. CE, but he does not discuss this passage from Josephus ("Why Did Matthew Get the *Shemaꜥ* Wrong?" 321–31). Josephus mentions the deliverance from Egypt, which is referred to in Num 15:41; he also mentions inscribing the benefits of God on the Israelites' doors, arms, and heads; something similar is said in Deut 6:4-9 and in Deut 11:18, 20. The command to pray twice a day, morning and evening, at the beginning of the quotation from Josephus is echoed in Deut 6:7 and 11:19. See the discussion of the *Shemaꜥ* in the Mishnah immediately below.

74 *M. Ber.* 2.2; *m. Tamid* 5.1; Schürer, *History*, 2:454–55.

75 Text from *BHS*; trans. NRSV.

76 Text from Rahlfs; trans. from the note on this verse in the NRSV. Bornkamm argued that the LXX version of Deut 6:4 promotes monotheism by rendering the divine name with κύριος and by taking the phrase יְהוָה אֶחָד in a predicative manner ("Doppelgebot," 87 and n. 8).

77 Marcus, *Way of the Lord*, 145; see the commentary on vv. 32-33 below. This affirmation would be particularly important in the Gentile mission; cf. 1 Thess 1:9 (Pheme Perkins, *Love Commands in the New Testament* [New York: Paulist, 1982] 23).

78 The probable allusion to Deut 6:5 in 1QS 5:8-9 has only two of the three phrases from the MT: בכול לב ובכול נפש ("[He shall swear with a binding oath to revert to the Law of Moses . . .] with his whole

And you shall love the Lord your God
  with your whole heart and
  with your whole life and
  with your whole power
(καὶ ἀγαπήσεις κύριον τὸν θεόν σου
  ἐξ ὅλης τῆς καρδίας σου καὶ
  ἐξ ὅλῆς τῆς ψυχῆς σου καὶ
  ἐξ ὅλης τῆς δυνάμεώς σου). (Deut 6:5 LXX)[79]

Some manuscripts, including Codex Vaticanus, read "mind" (διανοίας) instead of "heart" (καρδίας).[80] This reading is preferred in the Göttingen edition of the LXX of Deuteronomy.[81] The reading καρδίας ("heart") is a more literal translation of לבב in the MT; διανοίας ("mind") is a more metaphorical one.[82]

The Markan text agrees with the LXX through the third line as quoted above. Then the phrase "with your whole mind and" (ἐξ ὅλῆς τῆς διανοίας σου καὶ) is added. Bornkamm argued that the *addition* of this clause in Mark, along with other related features of the text, indicates that this version of the anecdote continues and takes further the tendency of the LXX to transform the Hebrew text into a lexically and culturally Greek formulation.[83]

In the line corresponding to the last line of the LXX text as cited above, Mark reads "strength" (ἰσχύος) instead of "power" (δυναμέως).[84] All the surviving manuscripts of the LXX agree in translating the MT's מאד ("power" or "strength") with δύναμις ("power"). An unfamiliarity with the word ἰσχύς ("strength") in this context may be a reason why Matthew omitted this phrase.[85]

■ **31** Although the scribe only asked which commandment was the "first" (πρώτη) of all, the Markan Jesus goes on to explain what commandment is "second" (δευτέρα) in rank, namely, the command "You shall love your neighbor as yourself," expressed in Lev 19:18b. The implication is that these two together are the most important, or that they, as a unit, summarize the Law.[86]

The context of this command in Leviticus makes clear that "neighbor" (רע) refers to one's fellow Israelite (Lev 19:17, 18a).[87] In the book of *Jubilees*, the patriarchs similarly urge love for one's brothers, that is, fellow Israelites (7:20; 20:2; 36:7-8).[88] The *Epistle of Aristeas* 168, however, states that "Our Law commands that we harm no one, neither by word nor by deed" and that the justice commanded by the Law is to be extended to all (πάντες

---

heart and his whole life"); text and trans. (modified) from García Martínez and Tigchelaar, *Dead Sea Scrolls*, 1:80–81.

79   According to rabbinic tradition, Rabbi Akiva concluded that he fulfilled the command to love God with all your life in his death as a martyr (Abrahams, *Studies in Pharisaism*, 1.19; Daniel Boyarin, *Dying for God: Martyrdom and the Making of Christianity and Judaism* [Stanford: Stanford University Press, 1999] 106).

80   Bornkamm, "Doppelgebot," 88. Since διάνοια ("mind") is a frequently used equivalent for לב or לבב ("heart"), Bornkamm does not lay much weight on this variant (ibid.).

81   The reading of Vaticanus is due to a *rescriptor*; i.e., it is not the original reading of this MS but a correction that has obliterated the original. *Septuaginta: Vetus Testamentum Graecum/auctoritate Academiae Scientiarum Gottingensis editum*, vol. 3.2: John William Wevers, ed., *Deuteronomium* (Göttingen: Vandenhoeck & Ruprecht, 1977) ad loc. Other MSS that have this reading include 963 = P. Chester Beatty VI, which dates to the second cent., and W¹ = Washington MS (ibid.; cf. 8, 15).

82   Foster, "Why Did Matthew Get the *Shema* Wrong?" 320.

83   Bornkamm, "Doppelgebot," 88–89. On the other, related features of the text, see the commentary below.

84   The term "strength" (ἰσχύς) is used in 2 Kgs 23:25 LXX in a similar context (Abrahams, *Studies in Pharisaism*, 1:20).

85   Foster, "Why Did Matthew Get the *Shema* Wrong?" 320–21. The threefold structure of the passage in the LXX (in distinction from the fourfold structure in Mark) may be another reason (ibid., 321).

86   Furnish, *Love Command*, 26–27. In *Did.* 1:2, the "way of life" or "the path of life" is summarized by linking loving God, loving neighbor, and the so-called "negative" form of the golden rule; for a Greek text and ET, see Ehrman, *Apostolic Fathers*, 1:416–17. On the "negative" form of the golden rule, see Abrahams, *Studies in Pharisaism*, 1:21–23; Alexander, "Jesus and the Golden Rule," 377–79. Abrahams, following the midrash *Genesis Rabbah* 24, argued that the "first" commandment here logically implies the "second" (*Studies in Pharisaism*, 1:18); see also his discussion of rabbinic literature related to Lev 19:18 (ibid., 20–23).

87   Milgrom, *Leviticus*, 2:1646–56, esp. 1654.

88   See the citations and discussion in "Relation to Jesus, Originality, and Cultural Context" above.

ἄνθρωποι).[89] Philo also interprets the commandments concerning duties to human beings in universal terms.[90]

Paul applies the commandment to love your neighbor as yourself primarily to the members of the respective local Christian communities (Gal 5:14; Rom 13:8-10; cf. Rom 12:9-10).[91] There is no indication in either Mark's or Matthew's version of this anecdote that the command to love one's neighbor is understood to apply to all human beings. The author of Luke, by linking his version with the example story about the Good Samaritan, implies that one's enemies are also one's neighbors.[92] Attentive readers or hearers of Matthew and Luke would understand the love of neighbor in light of the teaching of Jesus to love one's enemies preserved elsewhere in those Gospels (Matt 5:43-48; Luke 6:27-36).[93]

Unlike *Jubilees* and Philo, Paul does imply that the summary of the Law in terms of love of neighbor should serve as a criterion for deciding which particular commandments are binding and which are not.[94] The statement in Mark 12:31b, "No other commandment is greater than these," in itself does not imply that some commandments are not binding.[95] The allusion to all foods being clean in 7:19, however, would provide a basis for such a reading of this anecdote.[96]

■ **32-33** The scribe affirms Jesus' statement and restates it. The adverb καλῶς ("fittingly" or "well") occurs also in the dispute with the Pharisees in 7:1-23. It is used straightforwardly in the statement that Isaiah had prophesied well concerning the Pharisees, but ironically in the description of the Pharisees' nullifying of the commandment of God.[97] The use of the word in praise of Jesus' miracle-working power in 7:37 is more similar to its use here.[98] The scribe's use of this word in v. 32 in praise of Jesus takes up the narrator's comment in v. 28.[99] The scribe also acknowledges Jesus' authority as a teacher by addressing him as "Teacher" (διδάσκαλε). Further affirmation is expressed by the phrase "in accordance with the truth" (ἐπ᾽ ἀληθείας). The same phrase occurs in 12:14 in the hypocritical praise of Jesus by the Pharisees and the Herodians.[100]

The scribe's restatement of Jesus' response to his question is formulated in two parts, but the two parts do not correspond to the two commands, that is, to love God and to love one's neighbor. Instead, the first part (v. 32) emphasizes the portion of Deut 6:4 LXX that expresses the idea of monotheism.[101] The scribe affirms that God is one on the basis of that verse (εἷς ἐστιν) and adds an allusion to Isa 45:21 LXX or Deut 4:35 or a combination of the two: "and there is no other except him" (καὶ οὐκ ἔστιν ἄλλος πλὴν αὐτοῦ).[102] This

---

89 Text from Swete, *Introduction to the Old Testament in Greek*, 580; my trans. See also *T. Zeb.* 5:1; 7:6.

90 See the discussion of Philo, especially in *Decal.* 22 §§106, 108-10, in "Relation to Jesus, Originality, and Cultural Context" above.

91 Cf. Furnish, *Love Command*, 99-106.

92 Although Paul does not speak explicitly in Romans 12-13 about loving one's enemies, he does urge kind treatment of them; cf. Furnish, *Love Command*, 106-10.

93 Furnish, *Love Command*, 45-59.

94 See the discussion of *Jubilees* and Philo in "Relation to Jesus, Originality, and Cultural Context" above; on Paul, see Furnish, *Love Command*, 95-98; Berger, *Gesetzesauslegung*, 50-51. Berger's further argument, however, is doubtful, namely, that this position was already adopted by Greek-speaking Jews before Paul. It is unlikely that they would have taken such a position at least with regard to full proselytes. Although they were interested in the question of how the Law could be summarized, the rabbis held that all commandments were equally binding (Abrahams, *Studies in Pharisaism*, 1:25; Bornkamm, "Doppelgebot," 86). According to Alexander, the particular laws consti-

tuted the criterion for assessing the general principle, not the other way around ("Jesus and the Golden Rule," 387-88).

95 Contra Bornkamm, "Doppelgebot," 86. One of Bornkamm's arguments in favor of the idea that the "principle" of the Law expressed in vv. 30-31 implies the abolition of some commandments is the Markan scribe's allusion to Hos 6:6 (ibid., 85); on that point, see the commentary on v. 33 below.

96 See the commentary on 7:17-19 above.

97 See the commentary on 7:6-8 and 9-13 above.

98 See the commentary on 7:37 above.

99 See "Literary Context and Genre" above.

100 See the commentary on 12:14 above.

101 See the commentary on vv. 29-30 above. See also Bornkamm, "Doppelgebot," 86-87.

102 Isa 45:21 LXX reads: Ἐγὼ ὁ θεός, καὶ οὐκ ἔστιν ἄλλος πλὴν ἐμοῦ ("I am God, and there is no other except me"); Deut 4:35 LXX reads: οὗτος θεός ἐστιν, καὶ οὐκ ἔστιν ἔτι πλὴν αὐτοῦ ("he is God, and, moreover, there is no other except him").

emphasis on monotheism suggests that the anecdote is formulated with the mission to the Gentiles in view.[103]

The double love-command is restated in the second part of the scribe's reformulation of Jesus' reply (v. 33). The first portion of this second part restates the command to love God in Deut 6:5. Unlike the allusion to Deut 6:5 in the reply of Jesus, which expresses four ways in which God is to be loved, the scribe's restatement has only three parts, like the corresponding statement in the LXX:

and "to love him
   with the whole heart and
   with the whole understanding and
   with the whole strength"
(καὶ τὸ ἀγαπᾶν αὐτὸν
   ἐξ ὅλης τῆς καρδίας καὶ
   ἐξ ὅλης τῆς συνέσεως καὶ
   ἐξ ὅλης τῆς ἰσχύος).[104]

The second line, about loving with one's whole heart, agrees with v. 30 and Deut 6:5 LXX, except for the omission of σου ("your"), which is lacking in all three adverbial clauses in the scribe's restatement. This omission is due to the abbreviating paraphrase of the text(s) in question. The second adverbial phrase in v. 30 and in the LXX, "with your whole life" (ἐξ ὅλης τῆς ψυχῆς σου) is omitted by the scribe. The effect is that the extra phrase in v. 30, "with your whole understanding" (ἐξ ὅλης τῆς διανοίας σου), is retained and paraphrased, with σύνεσις ("intelligence" or "insight") substituting for διάνοια ("understanding"). This emphasis on the activity of the mind reveals the influence of the high value placed upon reason in Greek popular philosophy, which would also fit the context of the Gentile mission.[105]

The scribe paraphrases the second love command by changing the legal usage of the second person singular verb in v. 31 to the infinitive and the second person reflexive pronoun to the third person.

A new element in v. 33 is the affirmation that the double love-command "is much more than all whole burnt offerings and sacrifices" (περισσότερόν ἐστιν πάντων τῶν ὁλοκαυτωμάτων καὶ θυσιῶν). This statement is an allusion to Hos 6:6 or 1 Sam 15:22 LXX. Hos 6:6 LXX reads:

For I want mercy and not sacrifice and full knowledge of God rather than burnt offerings (διότι ἔλεος θέλω καὶ οὐ θυσίαν καὶ ἐπίγνωσιν θεοῦ ἢ ὁλοκαυτώματα).

The text of 1 Sam 15:22 (1 Kgdms 15:22 LXX) reads as follows:

And Samuel said, "Are burnt offerings and sacrifices wished for by the Lord as [much as] the hearing of the voice of the Lord?" (καὶ εἶπεν Σαμουηλ Εἰ θελητὸν τῷ κυρίῳ ὁλοκαυτώματα καὶ θυσίαι ὡς τὸ ἀκοῦσαι φωνῆς κυρίου;).

Bornkamm interpreted this allusion as criticism of cultic sacrifices.[106] Although the verse is open to such a reading, it is by no means a necessary one. The two corresponding passages in older scripture just cited imply that mercy or kindness, knowledge of God, and hearing and obeying the voice of the Lord are more important than burnt offerings and sacrifices. That does not mean that cultic sacrifices do not need to be made, or still less that they ought to be abolished. The same can be said about the saying attributed to Jesus in 7:15 about what defiles a person. In itself, it does not mean that the food laws do not need to be observed. That idea comes in only with the last clause of 7:19.[107]

■ 34 The narrator's statement that Jesus saw that he answered thoughtfully (νουνεχῶς) corresponds to the statement in v. 28 that the scribe saw that Jesus responded well to the Sadducees. The word νουνεχῶς ("thoughtfully") occurs only here in the NT. It does not

---

103 Bornkamm, "Doppelgebot," 87; see also the commentary on vv. 29-30 above. This mission was important in Palestine, as well as in the Diaspora; see "Relation to Jesus, Originality, and Cultural Context" above.

104 On the text of Deut 6:5 in the LXX and the allusion to it in v. 30, see the commentary on vv. 29-30 above.

105 Cf. Bornkamm, "Doppelgebot," 86–87.

106 Ibid., 85, 89–90.

107 See the commentary on 7:14-15 and 17-19 above. On the last clause of 12:33, see Abrahams, *Studies in Pharisaism*, 2:197–99.

occur in any Greek version of the OT, including the apocrypha.[108] This term, along with διάνοια ("understanding") and σύνεσις ("intelligence"), is an indication of the affinity of this text with Greek popular philosophy, probably mediated by Greek-speaking Jews.[109]

Jesus praises the scribe by saying, "You are not far from the kingdom of God."[110] This remark is an example of the figure of speech called litotes (λιτότης).[111] The basic meaning of the term is "plainness, simplicity." As a figure of speech it means "understatement so as to intensify, affirmation by the negative of the contrary."[112] This means that Jesus' statement should be taken positively, not negatively. The understated emphasis is on the scribe's nearness to the kingdom of God, not the fact

that he does not yet belong to the kingdom. The point is that Jesus' double love-command expresses a genuinely Jewish understanding of the Law and that any Jew who agrees with that understanding is near the kingdom of God. The force of Jesus' statement again makes sense in the context of apologetic and mission, in this case in relation to Jews.[113]

The concluding remark by the narrator, "And no one dared any more to question him," is rather surprising after the positive exchange between Jesus and the scribe. It is probably an editorial comment by Mark, intended to apply to and to conclude the series of three anecdotes in vv. 13-34.[114]

12

| 12:35-37 | The Messiah and the Son of David |

35/ And Jesus said, teaching in the temple precinct, "How can the scribes say that the messiah is son of David? 36/ David himself said in the Holy Spirit, 'The Lord said to my Lord, sit on my right until I put your enemies under[a] your feet.' 37/ David himself calls him Lord; how then can he be his son?" And the mass of the people[b] heard him gladly.

a   The earliest recoverable reading, attested by B D W et al., is ὑποκάτω ("under"); the appearance of the same word in the preferred reading in the parallel in Matt 22:44 supports the conclusion that Matthew read this word in Mark. The reading ὑποπόδιον, "(until I make your enemies) a footstool," attested by ℵ A L Θ et al., is due either to an independent assimilation of the text of Mark to that of a Greek version of Ps 110:1 (109 LXX) or to the text of the parallel in Luke 20:43. See Taylor, ad loc., and Metzger, *Textual Commentary*, 94.

b   The trans. is based on the reading ὁ πολὺς ὄχλος ("the mass of the people," lit., "the big crowd"), attested by A B L et al.; see Turner, "Marcan Usage," 26 (1925) 238 (Elliott, *Language and Style*, 49) and Taylor, ad loc. A reading lacking the article ὁ ("the") is attested by ℵ D W et al. This reading is due to an attempt to clarify the unusual reading with the article; the phrase ὄχλος πολύς ("a big crowd") or its equivalent, πολὺς ὄχλος ("a big crowd"), occurs in 5:21, 24; 6:34; 8:1; 9:14.

---

108   Moulton-Geden, s.v. and xvii. According to Moulton-Milligan, it is common from Aristotle onward, "as equivalent to νουνεχόντως ('sensibly')" (s.v.).
109   Cf. Bornkamm, "Doppelgebot," 88–89.
110   See "Literary Context and Genre" above.
111   Bornkamm, "Doppelgebot," 90. Furnish goes too far in concluding that the figure of speech implies that

"the scribe is said to belong to the Kingdom" already (*Love Command*, 28–29 n. 12).
112   Smyth §3032. According to LSJ, it means "*assertion by means of understatement or negation*" (s.v.).
113   Cf. Bornkamm, "Doppelgebot," 91.
114   Burchard, "Das doppelte Liebesgebot," 43; see also "Literary Context and Genre" above.

Literary Context

In v. 35 it is noted that Jesus was teaching in the temple precinct. This is the first indication of spatial setting since 11:27, which states that, while Jesus was walking in the temple precinct, he was approached by the chief priests, the scribes, and the elders. They proceeded to question him about his authority (11:27-33). The passage in which Jesus tells the parable of the vineyard and the tenants (12:1-12) is closely linked to that scene, since there is no change in the temporal or spatial setting and the characters involved remain the same.[115] The next three scenes (12:13-17; 12:18-27; and 12:28-34) are distinguished only by changes in characters.[116] Although the spatial location mentioned in 12:35 is the same as the one given in 11:27, the mention of the spatial setting in v. 35 sets this passage off from the preceding ones.

This passage may be viewed as linked to the preceding one (vv. 28-34) and the following one (vv. 38-40) by the catchword γραμματεύς ("scribe").[117] Or it may be associated with the following one as examples of public teaching.[118] Dewey argued that the use of the otherwise redundant participle ἀποκριθείς ("having answered") in v. 35 indicates that this passage is linked to the preceding debates.[119] It seems more appropriate, however, to consider the use of a redundant participle as typical of Markan style.[120]

Genre, History of the Tradition, and Composition

Dibelius treated this passage in the chapter on sayings he defined as exhortations. He commented that it is a conversation only in Matthew and that in Mark it is simply a saying introduced into the evangelist's biographical framework.[121] Bultmann concluded that it is characteristic of the typical early apophthegm that the occasion of a saying of Jesus is something that happens to him. Jesus' taking the initiative is a sign of a secondary formation; in other words, in such cases the anecdote is a community product and is unlikely to have a root in the life of the historical Jesus. He defined this passage as such a formation by the community.[122]

Bultmann defined the genre of this passage as one of "the legal sayings . . . which, by means of a proverb or an appeal to scripture, justify or base the new outlook over against the old."[123] Robert C. Tannehill argued that this passage is a correction story if Jesus is rejecting the view that the messiah is David's son.[124] On the other hand, it may be an inverted testing inquiry. If Jesus is not denying that the Christ is David's son, he is posing a testing question.[125] The story as a whole concerns Jesus' authority and status.[126] A wide variety of views have been expressed regarding the origin and purpose of the passage.[127]

The difficulty of finding a typical form-critical category to which this passage may belong and the speculative character of the theories about its origin and purpose may indicate that this is a passage composed by the author of Mark.[128] Bultmann pointed out that another passage in which Jesus takes the initiative is 8:27b-30.[129] That passage was probably composed by Mark.[130]

---

115 The close link between 12:1-12 and the preceding passage, the question of authority, is a problem for Dewey's argument that 12:1-40 has a symmetrical pattern (*Markan Public Debate*, 162).

116 See "Literary Context and Genre" in the commentary on 12:28-34 above.

117 Dewey, *Markan Public Debate*, 62; implied perhaps, but not actually stated by John R. Donahue, *Are You the Christ? The Trial Narrative in the Gospel of Mark* (SBLDS 10; Missoula, MT: SBL/Scholars Press 1973) 116.

118 Dewey, *Markan Public Debate*, 59.

119 Ibid., 159, 242 n. 85.

120 Taylor, 63.

121 Matt 22:41-46; Luke 20:41-44 is similar to Mark's version; Dibelius, *From Tradition to Gospel*, 261. Cf. Bultmann, *History*, 51.

122 Bultmann, *History*, 66, 136.

123 Ibid., 136.

124 Tannehill, "Varieties," 1.1 (p. 102); p. 117 n. 5.

125 Ibid., 5.21 (pp. 115–16).

126 Ibid., 5.23 (p. 116).

127 Bultmann, *History*, 136–37, 407.

128 The difficulty of determining the form-critical category was also noted by Marcus, *Way of the Lord*, 132 n. 11. He, however, thinks that most of the passage comes from pre-Markan tradition (ibid., 131–32); so also Achtemeier, "'And He Followed Him,'" 127.

129 Bultmann, *History*, 331.

130 See the section "Genre of 8:27-30" above.

In any case, the anecdote as we now have it may be influenced by the diatribal use of "the 'Socratic' method of censure and protreptic."[131] In this method, the concern is to expose errors and lead the audience to the correct view.[132]

Comment

■ **35** The participle ἀποκριθείς ("having answered," not translated above) here is redundant.[133] The notice that Jesus was teaching in the temple precinct sets this passage off from the preceding three dialogues as public teaching.[134] The force of the interrogative adverb πῶς ("how") here implies that the scribes are wrong in concluding that the messiah is the son of David,[135] or at least that there is a problem with this conclusion. The question of the Markan Jesus is more like a rhetorical question calling an assumption into question[136] than one that could be paraphrased "With what right" or "On the basis of what evidence do the scribes say that the messiah is son of David?"[137] The term γραμματεῖς ("scribes") here, as in v. 28, signifies those who are interpreters and teachers of the Law.

■ **36** The Markan Jesus, and probably the author and audiences of Mark, assumes that David is the author of the psalms.[138] He also identifies David as a prophet, speaking "in the Holy Spirit" (ἐν τῷ πνεύματι τῷ ἁγίῳ).[139] The words of David apparently have the status of scripture for him. The quotation appears to be a conflation of elements from two psalms, 110:1 and 8:6. Ps 110:1 reads:

The Lord said to my Lord, "Sit on my right until I make your enemies a footstool for your feet" (Εἶπεν ὁ κύριος τῷ κυρίῳ μου Κάθου ἐκ δεξιῶν μου,
ἕως ἂν θῶ τοὺς ἐχθρούς σου ὑποπόδιον τῶν ποδῶν σου). (Ps 109:1 LXX)[140]

Ps 8:6 reads:

And you have placed him in a position of authority over the works of your hands (and) subjected all things under his feet (καὶ κατέστησας αὐτὸν ἐπὶ τὰ ἔργα τῶν χειρῶν σου,
πάντα ὑπέταξας ὑποκάτω τῶν ποδῶν αὐτοῦ). (Ps 8:7 LXX)[141]

The earliest recoverable reading of Matt 22:44 agrees with the earliest recoverable reading of Mark 12:36 in having ὑποκάτω ("under"), whereas the best available reading of Luke 20:43 is ὑποπόδιον ("footstool").[142]

The rhetorical context of the quotation implies that the author can assume that the audiences are familiar with the interpretation of these psalms as prophecies or prefigurations of the messiah. Simply quoting Psalm 110 proves something about the messiah.[143] Besides the relevant verses in Mark and Matthew, the two psalm passages are also linked in three other places in writings that eventually became part of the NT (1 Cor 15:25-27; Eph 1:20-22; Heb 1:13—2:8).[144] Since Psalm 110 apparently was not interpreted messianically in Second Temple Jewish texts,

---

131 Stanley Kent Stowers, *The Diatribe and Paul's Letter to the Romans* (SBLDS 57; Chico, CA: SBL/Scholars Press, 1981) 76; cf. 116. Stowers does not discuss the relation of the diatribe to Mark; his concern is to define the term and show that Paul imitated the style of school discourse.

132 Cf. ibid., 77.

133 See "Literary Context" above.

134 See ibid.

135 So Achtemeier, "'And He Followed Him,'" 127–30; Bultmann, *History*, 149.

136 BAGD, s.v., sect. 1.a.δ.

137 Ibid., sect. 1.a.α.

138 Daly-Denton, *David*, 5–6, 59–113; Ahearne-Kroll, "Suffering of David," 1:69–71.

139 On the conflation of royal messianic and prophetic messianic elements in Second Temple Judaism, see "Jesus as Messiah" and "Jesus as Prophet" in the introduction to this commentary above.

140 The phrase τῶν ποδῶν σου ("for your feet") is redundant in light of the presence of σου ("your") before ὑποπόδιον ("footstool"). The redundancy is preserved in the citation of this verse in Heb 1:13.

141 In Heb 2:5-8, Ps 8:5-7 LXX is cited, but the line καὶ κατέστησας αὐτὸν ἐπὶ τὰ ἔργα τῶν χειρῶν σου is omitted; see the discussion in Attridge, *Hebrews*, 71.

142 See note a on the trans. of v. 36 above.

143 Albl, *"And Scripture Cannot Be Broken,"* 227–28.

144 David M. Hay, *Glory at the Right Hand: Psalm 110 in Early Christianity* (Nashville: Abingdon, 1973) 35; Marcus, *Way of the Lord*, 130; Albl, *"And Scripture Cannot Be Broken,"* 227.

at least not to any significant degree, the Synoptic usage probably presupposes Christian exegetical activity.[145] Early Christian exegetes found in Ps 110:1 imagery for affirming the vindication, exaltation, and glorification of Jesus, and in Ps 8:4-6, an Adam/Christ typology.[146] It may well be that Mark had a written collection of passages from scripture that served as *testimonia*, which included a conflation of Ps 110:1 and Ps 8:6.[147]

The anonymous epistle attributed to Barnabas also quotes Ps 110:1 as follows:

> See again Jesus, not as Son of Man, but as Son of God, but manifested in a type in the flesh. Since therefore they are going to say that Christ is David's son, David himself prophesies, fearing and under-standing the error of the sinners, "The Lord said to my Lord sit on my right until I make your enemies a footstool for your feet." And again Isaiah speaks thus, "The Lord said to the Christ [Messiah] my Lord, whose right hand I held, that the nations should obey before him, and I will shatter the strength of kings." See how "David calls him Lord" and does not say "son" (ἴδε πάλιν Ἰησους, οὐχὶ υἱὸς ἀνθρώπου, ἀλλὰ υἱὸς τοῦ θεοῦ, τύπῳ δὲ ἐν σαρκὶ φανερωθείς. ἐπεὶ οὖν μέλλουσιν λέγειν, ὅτι Χριστὸς[148] υἱὸς Δαυείδ ἐστιν, αὐτὸς προφητεύει Δαυείδ, φοβούμενος καὶ συνίων τὴν πλάνην τῶν ἁμαρτωλῶν· Εἶπεν κύριος τῷ κυρίῳ μου· Κάθου ἐκ δεξιῶν μου, ἕως ἂν θῶ τοὺς ἐχθρούς σου ὑποπόδιον τῶν ποδῶν σου. καὶ πάλιν λέγει οὕτως Ἡσαΐας· Εἶπεν κύριος τῷ Χριστῷ μου κυρίῳ, οὗ ἐκράτησα τῆς

δεξιᾶς αὐτοῦ, ἐπακοῦσαι ἔμπροσθεν αὐτοῦ ἔθνη, καὶ ἰσχὺν βασιλέων διαρρήξω. ἴδε, πῶς Δαυεὶδ λέγει αὐτὸν κύριον, καὶ υἱὸν οὐ λέγει). (*Barn.* 12:10-11)[149]

The citation of Ps 110:1 agrees with the LXX and Luke in reading ὑποπόδιον ("footstool") rather than ὑποκάτω ("under") with Mark and Matthew. The citation of Isa 45:1 differs from the manuscripts of the LXX that have survived, which read:

> Thus says the Lord God to my anointed Cyrus, whose right hand I have held that the nations should obey before him, and I will shatter the strength of kings (Οὕτως λέγει κύριος ὁ θεὸς τῷ χριστῷ μου Κύρῳ, οὗ ἐκράτησα τῆς δεξιᾶς ἐπακοῦσαι ἔμπροσθεν αὐτοῦ ἔθνη, καὶ ἰσχὺν βασιλέων διαρρήξω). (Isa 45:1 LXX)[150]

The reading of *Barnabas*, τῷ Χριστῷ μου κυρίῳ ("to the Christ [messiah] my Lord"), rather than τῷ χριστῷ μου Κύρῳ ("to my anointed Cyrus"), was common among later Christian writers. The origin of the former reading is unclear.[151]

The author of *Barnabas* wished to demonstrate in this passage that Jesus is Son of God. Given the texts that he cites, it is clear that for him, "Son of God" and "Lord" are equivalent.[152] A number of scholars have argued for the independence of the text in *Barnabas* from the Synoptic Gospels.[153] Martin C. Albl has argued that the author of *Barnabas* was dependent in this passage on a

---

145 Albl, *"And Scripture Cannot Be Broken,"* 221–22, 227–28.

146 Ibid., 228.

147 Ibid., 236 n. 11. See also the commentary on 1:2-3 above.

148 Codex Sinaiticus attests this reading, i.e., "Christ" (Χριστός without the article); Codex Constantinopolitanus and the archetype of eight defective Greek MSS read ὁ Χριστός υἱός ἐστιν Δαυείδ ("the messiah is son of David"). In Codex Sinaiticus, *Barn.* follows immediately upon the book of Revelation, with no indication that it belongs to a different category (Lake, *Apostolic Fathers*, 1:386 n. 1; 338–39).

149 Text and trans. (modified) from Lake, *Apostolic Fathers*, 1:386–87.

150 The trans. follows Lake when the two texts agree.

151 Albl, *"And Scripture Cannot Be Broken,"* 232–33.

152 Ibid., 232.

153 Helmut Köster, *Synoptische Überlieferung bei den apostolischen Vätern* (TU 65; Berlin: Akademie-Verlag, 1957) 145–46; Christoph Burger, *Jesus als Davidssohn: Eine traditionsgeschichtliche Untersuchung* (FRLANT 98; Göttingen: Vandenhoeck & Ruprecht, 1970) 57–58; Wolf-Dietrich Köhler concluded that dependence on Matthew is possible but not likely; he does not discuss other possibilities (*Die Rezeption des Matthäusevangeliums in der Zeit vor Irenäus* [WUNT 2.24; Tübingen: Mohr Siebeck, 1987] 119); Marcus, *Way of the Lord*, 132; James Carelton Paget, *The Epistle of Barnabas: Outlook and Background* (WUNT 2.64; Tübingen: Mohr Siebeck, 1994) 161; Albl, *"And Scripture Cannot Be Broken,"* 232.

written collection of testimonies relating to the idea of two powers in heaven.[154] *Barn.* 12:10-11 and Mark 12:35-37 and its Synoptic parallels, however, are the only texts in which Ps 110:1 is used in connection with the question whether the messiah should be called son of David.[155] This agreement in theme suggests that the author of *Barnabas* was dependent on one or more of the Synoptic Gospels indirectly, perhaps through the phenomenon of secondary orality.[156]

■ **37** The Markan Jesus comments on the quotation, combining a statement with a question: "David himself calls him Lord; how then can he be his son?" As the anecdote is narrated in Mark, Jesus does not answer his own question. Rather, he poses a problem for his audience in the narrative, the mass of the people, and provokes them to reflect on the tension between the well-known idea that the messiah would be a descendant of David and the text of Ps 110:1. As the latter text was read in the first century CE by followers of Jesus, David calls the messiah "Lord."

The closing comment of the narrator, "And the mass of the people heard him gladly" (Καὶ ὁ πολὺς ὄχλος ἤκουεν αὐτοῦ ἡδέως), recalls an earlier remark (Mark 6:20) concerning Herod and John the Baptist: "Having heard him, he was greatly perplexed, yet he heard him gladly" (καὶ ἀκούσας αὐτοῦ πολλὰ ἠπόρει, καὶ ἡδέως αὐτοῦ ἤκουεν).[157] The parallel suggests that the people heard Jesus gladly, even though he did not dissolve the tension between the teaching of the scribes and Ps 110:1 explicitly.

It was suggested above that vv. 35-37 were composed by Mark.[158] In addition to 8:27b-30, discussed above, it is also likely that Mark composed 8:14-21 on the model of the didactic scenes that he found in his source material.[159] So it may be that Mark composed this scene by

using the chreia form to create a setting for a saying that he based on a collection of testimonies in his possession.[160] He may also have been influenced by the typical style of the discourse of the schools.[161]

In any case, whether the anecdote is traditional or not, Mark had a purpose in placing it here. The first mention of David occurs in 2:25. In that context, it is implied that Jesus is the messianic Son of Man.[162] Although the term "son of David" is not used, the appeal to David as an authoritative example implies that just as David had authority to override conventional interpretations of the will of God because he was God's chosen one, so also Jesus has authority to interpret and proclaim the will of God in the last days.

In the account of the healing of blind Bartimaeus, he calls upon Jesus as "son of David" to have mercy on him. This appellation of Jesus is strategically placed by Mark just before Jesus' entry into Jerusalem.[163] Jesus' reply to the man, "Go, your faith has saved you," in 10:52 implicitly affirms his designation of Jesus as "son of David."[164] Then, in the entry itself, the crowd blesses "the coming kingdom of our father David."[165] Although Jesus is not hailed explicitly as king in that passage nor as son of David, the context suggests that he is both. Such an inference is supported by the address of Jesus as "son of David" by Bartimaeus in the immediately preceding passage. There is no indication in 11:1-11 that the designation of Jesus as "son of David" is inadequate. The fact that the leaders of the city do not come out to meet Jesus suggests, however, that they do not recognize him as such.[166] The lack of a welcome of Jesus by the leaders of the people and the anticlimactic ending of the account of his entry into Jerusalem are hints that the role Jesus will play in the rest of the narrative is not the one most often

154 Albl, *"And Scripture Cannot Be Broken,"* 232, 236 n. 11. Paget also argued for a testimony source of some kind (*Epistle of Barnabas*, 161).

155 See the chart in Albl, *"And Scripture Cannot Be Broken,"* 217–19.

156 Cf. the commentary on 1:40-45 and 12:13-17 above.

157 Also noted by Marcus, *Way of the Lord*, 131. See the note on the trans. of 6:20 above.

158 See "Genre, History of the Tradition and Composition" above.

159 See the commentary on 8:14-21 above.

160 Study of and practice in writing chreiai were basic

parts of elementary education in Mark's time. See Mack and Robbins, *Patterns of Persuasion*; Ronald F. Hock and Edward N. O'Neil, *The Chreia in Ancient Rhetoric*, vol. 1: *The Progymnasmata* (SBLTT 27; GRRS 9; Atlanta: Scholars Press, 1986).

161 See "Genre, History of the Tradition and Composition" above.

162 See the commentary on 2:28 above.

163 See the commentary on 10:47 and 48-49 above.

164 So also Marcus, *Way of the Lord*, 138 n. 31.

165 See the commentary on 11:10 above.

166 See "The Genre of Mark 11:1-11" above.

associated with the messianic son of David among Jews of the time.[167]

In this passage, the voice of Jesus raises an explicit question about the adequacy of the epithet "son of David" for the messiah. It does so by quoting an early Christian testimony to the glorified state of Jesus after his crucifixion and exaltation. The reference to the enemies of Jesus being placed under his feet expresses in a concrete way the kingship that he is to exercise after his resurrection.[168] This glorified state is related to the portrayal of Jesus as the heavenly Son of Man elsewhere in Mark (8:38; 13:26-27; and esp. 14:62). The question about the messiah as son of David in this passage is thus part of a complex and nuanced narrative portrayal of Jesus as messiah. He is son of David, but not in the way that many in his time would expect. His identity is best expressed in terms of the juxtaposition of and tension between the suffering Son of Man and the glorious Son of Man related to the vision of a heavenly one like a son of man in Dan 7:13.[169]

	12:38-40 Denunciation of the Scribes	

12

38/ And in his teaching he said, "Watch out for the scribes, who want to walk around in long robes and (to receive) greetings in the marketplaces **39/** and seats of honor in the synagogues and the places of honor at dinners, **40/** they who devour[a] the houses of widows and pray at length for appearance' sake. These will receive a more severe condemnation."

a   The trans. is based on the earliest recoverable reading, οἱ κατεσθίοντες ("who devour"), attested by most MSS. The nominative participle creates an anacoluthon, since it should be genitive to agree with τῶν θελόντων ("who want") in v. 38. The lack of agreement gave rise to the variant attested by D (*f*[1.13] *pc*) co, κατεσθίουσιν ("they devour"); these MSS also omit the καὶ ("and") after χηρῶν ("widows"). See Taylor, ad loc.

Comment

■ **38-40** This passage is linked to the preceding one in two ways. First, the introductory phrase "in his teaching" (ἐν τῇ διδαχῇ αὐτοῦ) indicates that the spatial and temporal setting of the passage is the same as the preceding one. In addition, no characters depart and no new ones appear. Second, the two passages have the catchword "scribes" (γραμματεῖς) in common (vv. 35, 38). This feature links both of them to the passage about the greatest commandment, which opens with the same catchword (v. 28).

■ **38-39** The verbal form βλέπετε in the sense of "watch out for" was used in 8:15 when Jesus warned the disciples about "the leaven of the Pharisees and the leaven of Herod." That warning concerned the resistance of the Pharisees and Herod to Jesus and his mission.[170] Here the warning concerns the scribes, whose (negative) portrayal suggests that they are experts in and teachers of the Law, like those of the preceding two passages.

The movement from one to the next of these three passages is from approval of the scribe who questions Jesus about the greatest commandment to questioning the exegesis of the scribes in vv. 35-37, to outright denunciation of scribes in general in this passage. It may be that Matthew makes explicit what the text of Mark

---

167 See "Jesus as Messiah" in the introduction to this commentary above. See also Ahearne-Kroll, "Suffering of David," 1:187–230; 2:231–99.

168 Cf. the similar idea expressed by Paul in 1 Cor 15:24-28.

169 See "Excursus: The Son of Man Tradition" related to the commentary on 2:10 above. Achtemeier concluded that "Son of Man" is "the major christological title in Mark" ("'And He Followed Him,'" 128).

Cf. Marcus, *Way of the Lord*, 139–44. Marcus suggested that another reason for Mark's reserve with regard to the "title" "son of David" is the role of "messianic figures of Davidic stripe" in the Jewish war of 66–74 CE (ibid., 146).

170 See the commentary on 8:14-21 above.

implies, namely, that the point of attack in the denunciation is the failure to practice what they teach (cf. Matt 23:3).[171] This principle could explain how the Markan Jesus could approve of the scribe in vv. 28-34 but condemn scribes in general in this passage. Yet vv. 35-37 do not fit this pattern. The tension may simply be due to the combination of disparate traditions by catchword in this section.

According to Sirach, the social position of experts in the Law and teachers was relatively high already in his time (second cent. BCE) (Sir 39:4-11).[172] The most common outer garment for men in Palestine in the first century CE was the ἱμάτιον ("cloak"), consisting of a rectangular piece of fabric, the size of which varied. It was draped around the body. The στολή ("robe") was a long flowing robe that signified wealth.[173] In the LXX, the word is often used to refer to "particularly splendid clothing."[174] So wanting to walk around in such a robe indicates a desire to be able to display a symbol of high status. Similarly, wanting greetings in the marketplace shows a desire to be honored and recognized by people as someone important.[175]

Being able to sit in the "seats of honor" or "front seats" in the synagogues (πρωτοκαθεδρίαι ἐν ταῖς συναγωγαῖς) was also a sign of social status and a symbol of honor.[176] Some evidence suggests that it was the elders who were given seats of honor in synagogues, but this evidence is from a later period.[177] An inscription from Cyme in Asia Minor declares that the synagogue of the Jews in that city honored a woman, Tation, with a golden crown and a seat of honor (προεδρία) because she built the house and the colonnade around the courtyard and donated them to the Jews.[178]

The reference to the "places of honor at dinners" (πρωτοκλισίαι ἐν τοῖς δείπνοις)[179] evokes the meal customs of the ancient world according to which positions were assigned by social rank. Once again the issue here is one of honor and status. Normally, the host would "take the first position with his honored guest located to his right. Other rankings would also continue to the right."[180] These customs were sometimes criticized or suspended for practical reasons (Luke 14:7-11; Jas 2:2-4).[181] The Community (היחד) attested by the Dead Sea

---

171 In the case of Mark, the failure to practice would presumably be linked to the issue of the acceptance or rejection of Jesus and his mission.

172 Cited by Ulrich Luz, *Das Evangelium nach Matthäus (Mt 18–25)* (EKK 1.3; Zurich: Benziger; Neukirchen-Vluyn: Neukirchener Verlag, 1997) 306 n. 73. See also the commentary on 1:22 above.

173 Douglas R. Edwards, "Dress and Ornamentation," *ABD* 2:232–38, esp. 235–36. On the association of the στολή ("robe") with wealth, Edwards cites Luke 15:22 (where it is related to a celebration or feast); 20:46 (the Lukan parallel to this verse).

174 Fleddermann, *Mark and Q*, 188. He cites Gen 41:42; Exod 28:2; 29:21; 31:10; 2 Chr 18:9; 23:13; Esth 6:8; 8:15; 1 Macc 6:15; Jonah 3:6. Some of these involve priestly garments; others involve royal attire.

175 The phrase καὶ τοὺς ἀσπασμοὺς ἐν ταῖς ἀγοραῖς ("and greetings in the marketplaces") probably occurred also in Q (Robinson et al., *Critical Edition of Q*, 274). For discussion, see Fleddermann, *Mark and Q*, 186–89.

176 Analogously, the Roman senate passed a law stipulating that the first row of seats at any public show should be reserved for senators (Suetonius *Aug.* 44; cited by Davies and Allison, *Matthew*, 3:274). Cf. Bruce J. Malina, *The New Testament World: Insights from Cultural Anthropology* (3rd rev. ed.; Louisville: Westminster John Knox, 2001) 38–39. A phrase like

this probably occurred in Q (Robinson et al., *Critical Edition of Q*, 274). For discussion, see Fleddermann, *Mark and Q*, 186–89.

177 Rachel Hachlili, "Diaspora Synagogues," *ABD* 6:260–63, esp. 262.

178 Walter Ameling, ed., *Inscriptiones Judaicae Orientis*, vol. 2: *Kleinasien* (TSAJ 99; Tübingen: Mohr Siebeck, 2004) #36 (pp. 162–67); the editor found the inscription impossible to date (ibid., 164); previously published in *CIJ* vol. 2, #738 (p. 8); the latter cited by Davies and Allison, *Matthew*, 3:274.

179 A phrase similar to this one probably occurred in Q (Robinson et al., *Critical Edition of Q*, 274). For discussion, see Fleddermann, *Mark and Q*, 186–89. Fleddermann argued that Mark used Q in written form, but it may be that Mark and Q simply shared some common traditions; cf. the assessment by Neirynck (ibid., 291–92).

180 Dennis E. Smith, *From Symposium to Eucharist: The Banquet in the Early Christian World* (Minneapolis: Fortress, 2003) 136. Sometimes the honored guest would be given the position with the highest honor (ibid., 34). For an illustration and discussion of changing customs with regard to the location of the seat with the highest honor, see ibid., 17.

181 On "equality" at sacrificial meals, see Smith, *From Symposium to Eucharist*, 82–83.

Scrolls had strict rules about seating when they assembled to eat, drink, or take counsel:

This is the rule for the session of the Many. Each one by his rank: the priests will sit down first, the elders next and the remainder of all the people will sit down in order of rank

((ה{)}וזה הסרך למושב הרבים איש בתכונו הכוהנים
ישבו לרשונה והזקנים בשנית ושאר כול העם ישבו
איש בתכונו).

(1QS 6:8-9)[182]

■ **40** The first part of this verse (about the widows) has a parallel in Luke (20:47a). Some manuscripts of Matthew include a parallel to this verse, but its omission is the earliest recoverable reading.[183]

The verb κατεσθίειν ("devour") is used metaphorically here to denote an unethical appropriation of the property of widows. The term οἰκία has two main usages: (1) a house as a building, and (2) a household, consisting of the people who live together in the same building or house, as a social unit. Here it may mean the houses of widows as buildings, including their household goods.[184] Or it may be used here by metonymy[185] to mean the property of widows more generally.

It is not clear from the text whether the widows in question are poor and vulnerable or rich yet vulnerable to exploitation. From early times in the Near East, Greece, and Rome, the widow in these patriarchal societies was "disadvantaged and even oppressed from the social, economic, legal, and religious standpoint."[186] Widows and orphans are often linked as those who have lost their "sustainer and protector."[187] Some Jewish widows in the first century CE were no doubt poor and powerless, as were some of the widows in early Christian communities.[188] After legal changes favoring women in the early Hellenistic period, however, there were widowed women from families of high status who "controlled property and power."[189] Some widows in early Christian communities were apparently wealthy.[190]

In the ancient Near East, rulers were expected to help and protect widows.[191] In the Old Testament, every member of the people of God is admonished to deal justly with widows and to be benevolent toward them.[192] Ill treatment of widows is characteristic of the wicked (Wis 2:10) and of boasters (Philo *Vit. Mos.* 2.43 §240).[193] A portion of the *Assumption* (or *Testament*) *of Moses* is even more similar to the Markan passage, although the manuscript is damaged:

---

182 Text and trans. from García Martínez and Tigchelaar, *Dead Sea Scrolls*, 1:82–83; cf. 1QSa (1Q28a) 2:11-22; cited by Luz, *Das Evangelium nach Matthäus (Mt 18–25)*, 306 n. 72. According to Philo, the Therapeutae reclined according to the order of their admission to the group (*Vit. cont.* 67). "The custom of assigning positions by rank" was standard practice for Greco-Roman clubs (Smith, *From Symposium to Eucharist*, 124).

183 Nestle-Aland (27th ed.) omits Matt 23:14 from the critically reconstructed text; see also Turid Karlsen Seim, *The Double Message: Patterns of Gender in Luke-Acts* (SNTW; Edinburgh: T & T Clark, 1994) 230. Seim notes that widows play a much larger role in Luke-Acts than in Matthew (ibid., and n. 133, 258).

184 So BAGD, s.v.

185 On metonymy as a figure of speech, see Smyth §3033.

186 Gustav Stählin, "χήρα," TDNT 9 (1974) 440–65; quotation from 442; see also Seim, *Double Message*, 232–33.

187 Stählin, "χήρα," 442–43.

188 Seim points out that "early Christian communities

adopted the Jewish attitude and developed their own care for widows, as an important part of their provision for the poor" (*Double Message*, 234–35, 241); see also Osiek and Balch, *Families*, 166–67.

189 Stählin, "χήρα," 443.

190 Osiek and Balch, *Families*, 100; Seim, *Double Message*, 229–48, esp. 232 and n. 142. Abrahams chides "more recent writers" (than Jerome) for taking the polemic in this passage at face value without criticizing early Christians for exercising an analogous influence over such women (*Studies in Pharisaism*, 1:79). Polycarp, bishop of Smyrna in the second cent., exhorts widows to avoid love of money (φιλαργυρία) (Polycarp *Phil.* 4.3; text and trans. from Ehrman, *Apostolic Fathers*, 1:338–39). Cf. Osiek and Balch, *Families*, 122–23.

191 Stählin, "χήρα," 443–44; Seim, *Double Message*, 233.

192 Stählin, "χήρα," 446–47; Seim, *Double Message*, 233–34.

193 Cited by Stählin, "χήρα," 447.

And pestilent and impious men will rule over them, who proclaim themselves to be righteous. And they will excite their wrathful souls; they will be deceitful men, self-complacent, hypocrites in all their dealings, and who love to debauch each hour of the day, devourers, gluttons, . . . who eat the possessions of . . . , saying they do this out of compassion . . . murderers, complainers, liars, hiding themselves lest they be recognized as impious (Et regnabunt de his homines pestilentiosi et impii docentes se esse justos, et hi suscitabunt iram animorum suorum, qui erunt homines dolosi, sibi placentes, ficti in omnibus suis, et omni hora diei amantes convivia, devoratores, gulae . . . bonorum comestores, dicentes se haec facere propter misericordiam . . . exterminatores, quaeru<losi>, fallaces, celantes se, ne possent cognosci impii). (*As. Mos.* 7:3-7)[194]

Ps. Sol. 4:9-13 speaks about leaders of the people who destroy houses; the context suggests that the term translated "house" ($o\hat{\iota}\kappa o\varsigma$) in this passage refers to households as social units.

According to the rabbis, following, as they said, the people of Jerusalem and Galilee in earlier times, the widow had a right to live in her deceased husband's house and to receive maintenance from his goods as long as she remained a widow in his house.[195] Both the Old Testament and the rabbis mention wealthy widows.[196]

It is impossible to be more precise about the manner in which the scribes are portrayed here as "devouring the houses of widows."[197] Turid Seim concluded that the parallel phrase in Luke implies that poor widows are victims of the scribes' mismanagement of their finances.[198] She also argued that the following phrase $\mu\alpha\kappa\rho\grave{\alpha}\ \pi\rho o\sigma\epsilon\acute{\upsilon}$-$\chi o\nu\tau\alpha\iota$ ($\pi\rho o\sigma\epsilon\upsilon\chi\acute{o}\mu\epsilon\nu o\iota$ in Mark) is connected to the phrase about widows and that "the scribes are condemned because they extort from widows under the pretext of performing long (and well paid) prayers for them."[199] She sees irony in the contrast between these hypocritical prayers and the portrayal of widows elsewhere in Luke-Acts as models of persevering in prayer.[200] It seems better, however, to take the two parts of v. 40 as separate criticisms.[201]

The Markan Jesus also criticizes the scribes as those who "pray at length for appearance' sake" ($\kappa\alpha\grave{\iota}\ \pi\rho o\varphi\acute{\alpha}$-$\sigma\epsilon\iota\ \mu\alpha\kappa\rho\grave{\alpha}\ \pi\rho o\sigma\epsilon\upsilon\chi\acute{o}\mu\epsilon\nu o\iota$). In Matt 6:5, the "pretenders," "dissemblers," or "hypocrites" ($o\acute{\iota}\ \acute{\upsilon}\pi o\kappa\rho\iota\tau\alpha\acute{\iota}$) are criticized for praying publicly, in synagogues and on street corners, in order to impress people. The "hypocrite" here is "the 'typical' religious practitioner whose external performance sharply conflicts with fundamental religious and moral principles."[202] Those who pray in order to be recognized as pious and powerful by others have already received their reward, and thus there is no reason for God to reward them further.[203]

The Markan text links "for appearance' sake" with "praying at length" rather than with praying publicly. Praying at length is criticized also in Matt 6:7. There it is Gentiles who are criticized for praying verbosely. Hans Dieter Betz pointed out that this criticism was made also in Greek Jewish wisdom literature and in Greek popular philosophy.[204]

---

194 Text and trans. from Johannes Tromp, *The Assumption of Moses: A Critical Edition with Commentary* (Leiden: Brill, 1992) 16–17. Tromp concluded that this "description is heavily biased" and is not "drawn from life"; it is impossible to determine the identity of the wicked rulers; they are described as typical sinners (207, 209). The similarity with Mark 12:40 has led to the restoration of *viduarum* ("widows") as the owners of the possessions eaten or devoured by these wicked rulers, but Tromp inclines toward the more usual restoration: *pauperum* ("the poor") (ibid., 212).

195 *M. Ketub.* 4.12; the text comments that the people of Judea in earlier times would allow her to do so only until such time as the heirs are minded to give her the sum of money specified in her marriage document and let her go; cited by Stählin, "$\chi\acute{\eta}\rho\alpha$," 448.

196 Stählin, "$\chi\acute{\eta}\rho\alpha$," 445 n. 45; 448 n. 67.

197 For conjectures, see Stählin, "$\chi\acute{\eta}\rho\alpha$," 449; he wrongly attributes to Abrahams (*Studies in Pharisaism*, 1:80) a conjecture that the latter quotes and rejects. Fitzmyer lists six theories concerning the parallel in Luke, but emphasizes that the text does not give an explanation (*Luke*, 2:1318).

198 Seim, *Double Message*, 95.

199 Ibid., 245, following Stählin, $\chi\acute{\eta}\rho\alpha$, 449. Nineham entertains this interpretation as a possibility for the Markan parallel (333).

200 Seim, *Double Message*, 245–46.

201 Nineham also mentioned this possibility (333–34).

202 Betz, *Sermon*, 356–57.

203 Ibid., 362; cf. 358.

204 Ibid., 365–66.

Although Mark does not use the term "hypocrite" (ὑποκριτής), the criticism of the whole passage (vv. 38-40) could be summed up with that word. Those who are criticized are accused of focusing on externals rather than protecting and benefiting widows and praying sincerely. Luke T. Johnson has shown that certain types of polemic were conventional.[205] Nevertheless, what Luz says about Matt 23:6-7 applies also to this passage: the global attack on the scribes is unfair. Christian exegetes and preachers should take care to correct the impression of some in their audiences that this passage represents Jews as such. Rabbinic literature is full of self-criticism, and self-criticism is the best kind of criticism.[206]

The passage ends with the remark "These will receive a more severe condemnation" (οὖτοι λήμψονται περισσότερον κρίμα). The adjective περισσότερον ("more severe") is a true comparative here and should not be translated as a superlative.[207] Although κρίμα signifies a judicial verdict of any sort, it is used mostly in a negative sense.[208] The force of the comparative here seems to be that the scribes who are guilty as charged will receive a greater condemnation for the wrongs that they do, such as defrauding widows, than those who commit the same evil deeds but make no claim to being respected experts in the Law and moral and religious leaders.[209]

12

12:41-44 The Poor Widow's Contribution

41/ And he sat down opposite the treasury and was observing how the crowd was putting money into the treasury. And many rich people were putting in a lot of money. 42/ And a poor widow came and put in two lepta, which make a quadrans. 43/ And he summoned his disciples and said to them, "Truly I say to you, this poor widow put in more than all those who put (money) into the treasury. 44/ For they all put in out of their abundance, but she out of her need put in everything she had, her whole livelihood."

Comment

■ **41-44** This passage is distinguished from the preceding one by a change in the spatial setting. As noted above, vv. 38-40 are closely linked to vv. 35-37 by having the same temporal and spatial location and involving the same characters. Verse 35 locates both passages in "the temple precinct" (ἐν τῷ ἱερῷ). This passage is also within the temple precinct, but the location is given more precisely and movement on the part of Jesus to this specific location is implied: "And he sat down opposite the treasury" (Καὶ καθίσας κατέναντι τοῦ γαζοφυλακίου). There is also a change in characters. In

205 Luke T. Johnson, "The New Testament's Anti-Jewish Slander and the Conventions of Ancient Polemic," *JBL* 108 (1989) 419–41.
206 Luz, *Das Evangelium nach Matthäus (Mt 18–25)*, 306–7; ET Ulrich Luz, *Matthew 21–28: A Commentary* (Hermeneia; Minneapolis: Fortress, 2005) 105.
207 Contra Fitzmyer, *Luke*, 2:1319, with regard to the parallel in Luke.
208 With BAGD, s.v., and Fitzmyer, *Luke*, 2:1319, with regard to the parallel in Luke.
209 Cf. Jas 3:1, "Let not many of you become teachers, my brothers and sisters, knowing that we shall receive a greater condemnation" (Μὴ πολλοὶ διδάσκαλοι γίνεσθε, ἀδελφοί μου, εἰδότες ὅτι μεῖζον κρίμα λημψόμεθα).

v. 37, Jesus' audience is characterized as "the mass of the people" (ὁ πολὺς ὄχλος). Here "the crowd" (ὁ ὄχλος) is characterized as those putting money into the treasury, and the focus is on "the many rich people" (πολλοὶ πλούσιοι). "A poor widow" (μία χήρα πτωχή) is a new character, who is introduced as coming on the scene in v. 42. The disciples, whose implicit presence the Markan audience no doubt would assume, are reintroduced in v. 43.[210]

This anecdote is linked to the preceding one (vv. 38-40) by the catchword χήρα ("widow").[211] It has a parallel in Luke 21:1-4, but Matthew has omitted it.

Bultmann defined the genre of this passage as "biographical apophthegm."[212] It is not biographical in the strict sense, since it is an ideal scene that discusses "the proper standard for judging a sacrifice" for the benefit of the church.[213] In addition to the form of the anecdote and its content, the context (the setting of the scene in the temple) suggests that the story arose in "the Palestinian Church."[214] Tannehill defined the story as a hybrid pronouncement story that combines correction and commendation.[215] The correction is not as emphatic as in other hybrids of this type. The narrator expresses the ordinary view of economic values, in commenting that the rich put in much. Jesus corrects this view by saying that the widow, though she put in only two lepta, put in "more than all" (πλεῖον πάντων).[216]

It has often been pointed out that other cultural traditions contain sayings similar to that of Jesus or stories similar to this one. For example, Xenophon had the following to say about Socrates:

Though his sacrifices were humble, according to his means, he thought himself not a whit inferior to those who made frequent and magnificent sacrifices out of great possessions. The gods (he said) could not well delight more in great offerings than in small—for in that case must the gifts of the wicked often have found more favour in their sight than the gifts of the upright—and man would not find life worth having, if the gifts of the wicked were received with more favour by the gods than the gifts of the upright. No, the greater the piety of the giver, the greater (he thought) was the delight of the gods in the gift. He would quote with approval the line: "According to thy power render sacrifice to the immortal gods" (θυσίας δὲ θύων μικρὰς ἀπὸ μικρῶν οὐδὲν ἡγεῖτο μειοῦσθαι τῶν ἀπὸ πολλῶν καὶ μεγάλων πολλὰ καὶ μεγάλα θυόντων. οὔτε γὰρ τοῖς θεοῖς ἔφη καλῶς ἔχειν, εἰ ταῖς μεγάλαις θυσίαις μᾶλλον ἢ ταῖς μικραῖς ἔχαιρον· πολλάκις γὰρ ἂν αὐτοῖς τὰ παρὰ τῶν πονηρῶν μᾶλλον ἢ τὰ παρὰ τῶν χρηστῶν εἶναι κεχαρισμένα· οὔτ' ἂν τοῖς ἀνθρώποις ἄξιον εἶναι ζῆν, εἰ τὰ παρὰ τῶν πονηρῶν μᾶλλον ἦν κεχαρισμένα τοῖς θεοῖς ἢ τὰ παρὰ τῶν χρηστῶν· ἀλλ' ἐνόμιζε τοὺς θεοὺς ταῖς παρὰ τῶν εὐσεβεστάτων τιμαῖς μάλιστα χαίρειν. ἐπαινέτης δ' ἦν καὶ τοῦ ἔπους τούτου, Καδδύναμιν δ' ἔρδειν ἱέρ' ἀθανάτοισι θεοῖσι). (Mem. 1.3.3)[217]

■ **41** In his description of the temple as renovated by Herod, Josephus says that the inner walls of "the holy place" (τὸ ἅγιον), that is, the inner court, were lined with treasury chambers (γαζοφυλάκια) (Bell. 5.5.2 §200).[218] Elsewhere he says that, at the time the Romans burned the temple, these treasury chambers were filled with large sums of money, great stacks of clothing and other valuables:

210 The last time they were explicitly mentioned was in 11:14; their presence is implied by the plural verbal forms in 11:15, 20, 22-25, 27.

211 Stählin, "χήρα," 449; Donahue, Are You the Christ? 116.

212 Bultmann, History, 32–33.

213 Ibid., 56–57.

214 Ibid., 60.

215 Tannehill, "Varieties," 1.1 (p. 103).

216 Ibid., 2.1 (p. 106).

217 Text and trans. from Edgar C. Marchant Xenophon: Memorabilia, Oeconomicus (LCL; Cambridge/London: Harvard University Press, 1923) 44–47; the line quoted in the text is from Hesiod Op. 336. See also Josephus Ant. 5.7.4 §149; Midrash on Psalms (Midrash Tĕhillîm) on Psalm 22, section 31; Leviticus Rabbah 3:5.

218 Text and trans. from Thackeray, Josephus, 3:260–61. For discussion, see Th. A. Busink, Der Tempel von Jerusalem von Salamo bis Herodes, vol. 2: Von Ezechiel bis Middot (Leiden: Brill, 1980) 1097–1101. Cf. Theissen, Gospels in Context, 120 = Lokalkolorit, 128.

They further burnt the treasury-chambers, in which lay vast sums of money, vast piles of raiment, and other valuables; for this, in short, was the general repository of Jewish wealth, to which the rich had consigned the contents of their dismantled houses (ἔκαιον δὲ καὶ τὰ γαζοφυλάκια, ἐν οἷς ἄπειρον μὲν χρημάτων πλῆθος ἄπειροι δ᾽ ἐσθῆτες καὶ ἄλλα κειμήλια, συνελόντι δ᾽ εἰπεῖν, πᾶς ὁ Ἰουδαίων σεσώρευτο πλοῦτος, ἀνεσκευασμένων ἐκεῖ τοὺς οἴκους τῶν εὐπόρων). (*Bell.* 6.5.2 §282)[219]

The treasury chambers then were used in part in relation to the temple's role as a bank, a role played by many temples in antiquity (2 Macc 3:9-12).[220] The chambers were also used for gifts dedicated to God, for example, the gold chain dedicated by King Agrippa I that had been given to him by the emperor Gaius.[221] Some of these gifts may have been money paid for sacrificial offerings. The following passage from Josephus may be related to such gifts:

On a later occasion [Pilate] provoked a fresh uproar by expending upon the construction of an aqueduct the sacred treasure known as *Corbonas* (Μετὰ δὲ ταῦτα ταραχὴν ἑτέραν ἐκίνει τὸν ἱερὸν θησαυρόν, καλεῖται δὲ κορβωνᾶς, εἰς καταγωγὴν ὑδάτων ἐξαναλίσκων). (*Bell.* 2.9.4 §175)[222]

In the Second Temple period, the term *qorban* was used for both sacrificial and nonsacrificial offerings, although the former is more common.[223] In the parallel passage in his *Antiquities*, Josephus speaks about "the sacred funds" (τὰ ἱερὰ χρήματα) (*Ant.* 18.3.2 §60).[224] According to a passage in the Mishnah:

There were thirteen Shofar-chests in the Temple, whereon was inscribed: "New Shekel dues," "Old Shekel dues," "Bird-offerings," "Young birds for the Whole-Offering," "Wood," "Frankincense," "Gold for the Mercy-seat" (or "Vessels of Ministry"), and, on six of them, "Freewill-offerings". (*m. Šeqal.* 6.5)[225]

Chapters 3 and 4 of the same tractate mention "the Shekel-chamber." Perhaps this was one of the chambers that Josephus described as lining the inner walls of the inner court.

Mark, however, describes Jesus as sitting opposite the γαζοφυλάκιον ("treasury") and watching people coming and going and placing money in it. It seems to be out of the question that such a scene could have taken place in the inner court. Thus, it seems likely that γαζοφυλάκιον in this verse and in the parallel in Luke 21:1 has the sense of "collection box" or "receptacle."[226] If the story represents conditions in the temple in the time of Jesus or Mark, the box must have been in the outer court.

219 Thackeray, *Josephus*, 3:458–59.
220 Jonathan A. Goldstein, *II Maccabees: A New Translation with Introduction and Commentary* (AB 41A; Garden City, NY: Doubleday, 1983) 207–9; see also idem, *I Maccabees: A New Translation with Introduction and Commentary* (AB 41; Garden City, NY: Doubleday, 1976) 210; William A. Ward, "Temples and Sanctuaries," *ABD* 6:369–72, esp. 371.
221 Josephus *Ant.* 19.6.1 §§294–96; cf. Theissen, *Gospels in Context*, 120 = *Lokalkolorit*, 128. On Agrippa I, see David C. Braund, "Agrippa," *ABD* 1:98–100, esp. 98–99. In *Ant.* 17.10.3 §265, Josephus refers to the grief that the Jews felt when the Romans carried off "the dedicatory offerings" (τὰ ἀναθήματα) when Varus was putting down the Jewish revolt after the death of Herod the Great; text and trans. from Ralph Marcus, in Thackeray, *Josephus*, 8:494–95.
222 Text and trans. from Thackeray, *Josephus*, 2:390–91.
223 See the commentary on 7:11 above. In Matt 27:6, however, the term κορβανᾶς seems to be used quite generally to mean "the temple treasury" (BAGD, s.v.).
224 Text from Louis H. Feldman, in Thackeray, *Josephus*, 9:46; my trans. Feldman translates τὰ ἱερὰ χρήματα with "the sacred treasury." He concluded that the funds in question came from the annual contribution of a half-shekel from every Israelite twenty years old and upward (ibid., 46–47 n. b). Cf. *m. Šeqal.* 1.1; see Danby, *Mishnah*, 152 n. 2. Feldman referred to *m. Šeqal.* 3.2.
225 Trans. from Danby, *Mishnah*, 159. Danby explains that the purpose of these chests was to receive the Shekel dues and that "shofar" ("trumpet" or "horn") "possibly refers to the tapering shape of these money-chests" (ibid., 153 n. 10).
226 BAGD, s.v.; Busink, *Der Tempel von Jerusalem*, 1098. Cf. the description of a collection box in the First Temple in 2 Kgs 12:9-16. Oddly, John 8:20 depicts Jesus as teaching "in the treasury" (ἐν τῷ γαζοφυλακίῳ). Raymond E. Brown translated this phrase with "at the temple treasury" and concluded that Jesus was simply near the treasury, which he interpreted as a storage chamber abutting the Court of

The narrator states that Jesus was watching people putting χαλκός into the treasury or collection box. This term refers to "a metal of various types, such as copper, brass, or bronze." It can also refer to "Copper coin, small change."[227] Since, however, the narrator says that many rich people were putting in πολλά ("a lot"), it seems best to conclude that χαλκός refers here simply to "money."[228]

■ **42** After many rich people put a lot of money into the treasury or collection box, a poor widow comes along and puts in two lepta. The phrase λεπτὰ δύο is short for λεπτὰ δύο νομίσματα ("two small coins").[229] The copper lepton was the smallest Greek coin denomination.[230] The denomination "lepton" occurs in the papyri from Naḥal Ḥever. The documents also mention a Nabatean coin denomination called the *melaina*, which was a silver coin. One such coin was worth more than fifty-eight lepta. A *melaina* was worth less than a denarius.[231] The name λεπτὸν (νόμισμα) ("small coin") was used for whatever was the smallest denomination of coins in the Syrian-Nabatean region.[232] Under Herod the Great and after 6 CE, the smallest coin minted in Judea was the *perutah* or *prutah*. Since it was the smallest coin in circulation, it could be called a "lepton."[233]

Mark defines two lepta as equivalent to a *quadrans*. The quadrans was the smallest denomination of Roman coins.[234] In the first century CE, the most valuable bronze coin was the *as*; the half-piece of the *as* was the *semis*, and the *quadrans* was the quarter-piece of the *as*.[235] The Herodian equivalent of the quadrans was the *shamin*, which was worth two *prutot*.[236] In Syria and Judea, Roman and local coin denominations coexisted, and local coins were understood in terms of Roman denominations.[237] For this reason, the use of the term *quadrans* (more precisely, the Greek loanword κοδράντης with the same meaning) here may not be taken as evidence that Mark was written in Rome. In fact, mention of the two lepta makes it more likely that Mark was written in one of the eastern provinces.[238]

■ **43-44** After seeing the widow put her two little coins in the treasury or collection box, Jesus summoned his disciples in order to speak to them. This summons is similar to those in 8:34 and 10:42. In 8:34, Jesus summoned the crowd with his disciples in order to teach them about suffering discipleship.[239] In 10:42, Jesus summoned the Twelve in order to teach them about a discipleship of service.[240] This similarity suggests that the action of the widow is relevant to the question of discipleship.

Jesus begins his statement or teaching about the widow with the phrase ἀμὴν λέγω ὑμῖν ("Truly I say to you" or "Amen I say to you"). The Markan Jesus used this phrase earlier to introduce his prophetic saying about insulting the Holy Spirit.[241] It also precedes his declara-

---

the Women, presumably in the inner court; *The Gospel according to John (i–xii): Introduction, Translation, and Notes* (AB 29; Garden City, NY: Doubleday, 1966) 342.

227 BAGD, s.v.

228 A usage also documented by BAGD, s.v.

229 Cf. BAGD, s.v. λεπτός, ή, όν.

230 Alkier, "'Geld' im Neuen Testament," esp. 321.

231 Wolfram Weiser and Hannah M. Cotton, "'Gebt dem Kaiser, was des Kaisers ist . . .': Die Geldwährungen der Griechen, Juden, Nabatäer und Römer im syrisch-nabatäischen Raum unter besonderer Berücksichtigung des Kurses von Selaᶜ/Melaina und Lepton nach der Annexion des Königreiches der Nabatäer durch Rom," *ZPE* 114 (1996) 237–87, esp. 237–40.

232 Ibid., 247.

233 Ibid., 258, 260; the authors refer to Mark 12:42-43 to make this point. See also Alkier, "'Geld' im Neuen Testament," 321 n. 51; 322; Burnett et al., *Roman Provincial Coinage*, 678.

234 Alkier, "'Geld' im Neuen Testament," 321. The quadrans began to be produced in or shortly after

the second cent. BCE, replacing the *sextans* and valued at a quarter of an *as*. The *as* was the most valuable bronze coin in the Roman system (Michael Crawford, "Money and Exchange in the Roman World," *Journal of Roman Studies* 60 [1970] 40–48, esp. 40).

235 Crawford, "Money and Exchange in the Roman World," 41.

236 Alkier, "'Geld' im Neuen Testament," 322; cf. Burnett et al., *Roman Provincial Coinage*, 678.

237 Burnett et al., *Roman Provincial Coinage*, 590.

238 Theissen, *Gospels in Context*, 247–249 = *Lokalkolorit*, 259–61.

239 See the commentary on 8:34 above.

240 See "The Literary Context of 10:42-45" and the commentary on 10:42 above. Cf. Elizabeth Struthers Malbon, "The Poor Widow in Mark and Her Poor Rich Readers," *CBQ* 53 (1991) 589–604; reprinted in eadem, *In the Company of Jesus*, 166–88, esp. 183; reprinted also in Levine, *Feminist Companion*, 111–27 (*In the Company of Jesus* is cited here).

241 See the note on the trans. of 3:28 and the commentary on that verse above.

tion that a sign will not be given to this generation (8:12) and his prediction that "some of those who are standing here will surely not experience death until they see that the kingdom of God has come with power" (9:1). It also introduces the emphatic part of his promise that whoever gives a follower of Jesus a cup of water to drink will surely not lose his reward.[242] This phrase also introduces the saying that whoever does not receive the kingdom of God as a child (would receive it) shall surely not enter into it (10:15) and the promise "there is no one who has left house or brothers or sisters or mother or father or children or farms because of me and because of the good news, etc." (10:29). Finally, the same phrase introduces the promise that "whoever says to this mountain, 'Be lifted up and thrown into the sea,' etc." in 11:23. All these previous occurrences of the phrase in Mark produce an expectation of an important, emphatic statement here, either a prophetic saying or a saying about discipleship.[243]

Jesus' saying has two parts. The first part, "this poor widow put in more than all those who put (money) into the treasury," is surprising and counterintuitive. The narrator has just said that many rich people put a lot of money into the treasury or collection box and that the widow put in only two coins, the two coins of the least value in Judea at the time. The second part of the saying explains and defends the first part by contrasting the rich, who gave out of their abundance, with the widow, who gave out of her need. The statement in the first part of the saying, that the widow put in more than all the rest, corrects the view that the economic value is the primary thing and praises the widow for her generosity.[244]

The last portion of the second part of the saying goes even further, remarking that the widow "put in everything she had, her whole livelihood." The word trans-lated "livelihood" here is $\beta\iota\sigma\varsigma$, which also has the meaning "life," in the sense of "life and activity associated with it."[245] In Jesus' reply to the scribe's question about the greatest commandment, he quotes Deut 6:5, which uses another word for life: "and you shall love the Lord your God with your whole heart and with your whole life ($\dot{\epsilon}\xi$ $\ddot{o}\lambda\eta\varsigma$ $\tau\hat{\eta}\varsigma$ $\psi\upsilon\chi\hat{\eta}\varsigma$ $\sigma o\upsilon$) and with your whole mind and with your whole strength." The word $\ddot{o}\lambda\eta$ ("whole") also links the two passages.

The implication is that the scribe *knows* what the greatest commandment is, but the widow actually *fulfills* it.[246] By offering her last two coins to God (whose temple and treasury they ultimately are), she has demonstrated that she loves God "with her whole life."

A further consideration supports this interpretation. In both Jesus' and the scribe's formulations, the greatest commandment includes the command to love God "with your whole strength" ($\dot{\epsilon}\xi$ $\ddot{o}\lambda\eta\varsigma$ $\tau\hat{\eta}\varsigma$ $\dot{\iota}\sigma\chi\acute{\upsilon}o\varsigma$). As noted above, the word $\dot{\iota}\sigma\chi\acute{\upsilon}\varsigma$ ("strength") translates the MT's מאד ("power" or "strength").[247] In the exegesis of Deut 6:5 in the Dead Sea Scrolls, מאד ("power" or "strength") is interpreted as "wealth" or "property."[248] For members of the audience familiar with this interpretation of Deut 6:5, the implication is that the widow has also shown that she loves God "with her whole strength," that is, with all her property.

The behavior of the widow is also contrasted with that of the scribes who are denounced in vv. 38-40. She gives all, whereas they take all, they "devour the houses of widows."[249] Seim has a good discussion of the way the parallel in Luke develops the theme of the ideal or demand "of giving up possessions and realising [i.e., making use of] property for the benefit of the community" in Luke and the first part of Acts.[250]

---

242 See the trans. and the commentary on 9:41 above.

243 Cf. Malbon, "Poor Widow," 183–84.

244 See the discussion of Tannehill's definition of the genre of this anecdote in the commentary on 12:41-44 above.

245 BAGD, s.v.

246 Note that the scribe, in restating the greatest commandment, omits the phrase "with your whole life." This detail may not be accidental.

247 See the commentary on vv. 29-30 above.

248 CD 9:10b-12; 1QS 1:11-15; 3:2-3; Catherine M. Murphy, *Wealth in the Dead Sea Scrolls and in the Qumran Community* (STDJ 40; Leiden: Brill, 2002) 48–49,

118–25. See also the literature cited by Foster, "Why Did Matthew Get the *Shema* Wrong?" 329. He is right that the evidence does not necessarily reflect the liturgical use of the *Shema*ᶜ, but it does support the conclusion that these passages involve an interpretation of Deut 6:5.

249 With Malbon, "Poor Widow," 175–76; and Seim, *Double Message*, 95–96 (regarding the Lukan parallel), and contra Addison G. Wright, "The Widow's Mites: Praise or Lament?—A Matter of Context," *CBQ* 44 (1982) 256–65, esp. 261–62.

250 Seim, *Double Message*, 77–78. Cf. 2 Cor 8:1-4.

13

13:1-37 The Fall of the Temple

1/ And as he was going out of the temple precinct, one of his disciples said to him, "Teacher, look how grand the stones and buildings are!" 2/ And Jesus said to him, "Do you see these great buildings? There will surely not be left here[a] a stone upon a stone that will not be thrown down."[b]

3/ And when he was sitting on the Mount of Olives opposite the temple mount, Peter and James and John and Andrew asked him privately, 4/ "Tell us when this will be and what the sign will be when all these things are about to be accomplished." 5/ Then Jesus began to say to them, "Watch out, so that no one deceives you. 6/ Many will come in my name, saying 'I am he,' and they will deceive many. 7/ Now when you hear of wars and reports of wars, do not be disturbed. It must happen, but the end is not yet. 8/ For nation will rise up against nation and kingdom against kingdom; there will be earthquakes in various regions; there will be famines.[c] This is the beginning of the birth-pains.[d]

9/ "Now you watch out for yourselves.[e] They will hand you over to (local) councils and you will be beaten in synagogues and you will stand in the presence of governors and kings because of me in order to give testimony to them. 10/ And first it is necessary that the good news be proclaimed to all the nations.[f] 11/ And when they lead you to hand you over, do not be anxious beforehand about what you will say, but say whatever is given to you in that hour; for you are not the ones who are speaking, but the Holy Spirit. 12/ And brother will hand brother over to death, and a father (his) child, and children will rise in rebellion against (their) parents and put them to death. 13/ And you will be hated by all on account of my name. But the one who endures to the end will be saved.

14/ "Now when you see 'the desolating sacrilege' standing where he should not—let the reader understand—then let those who are in

a A K Γ 1241. 2542 *pm* lat omit ὧδε ("here"). Tischendorf, Huck-Greeven, Nestle-Aland (25th ed.), and Aland, *Synopsis*, follow these MSS. Greeven took the position that Luke represents the original text of Mark on this point and that the ὧδε ("here") was placed secondarily in the text of Mark under the influence of Matthew. Nestle-Aland (26th and 27th ed.) and Metzger (*Textual Commentary*, 94), however, are more likely to be correct in following the strong combined witness of ℵ B D L W et al. and including ὧδε ("here") in the text.

b D W, most of the Old Latin MSS and Cyprian add at this point the words καὶ διὰ τριῶν ἡμερῶν ἄλλος ἀναστήσεται ἄνευ χειρῶν ("and in three days another will rise up without hands"). One Old Latin MS (c) reads καὶ διὰ τριῶν ἡμερῶν ἀναστήσω αὐτόν ("and in three days I will raise it up"). These additions were probably inspired by Mark 14:58.

c Some MSS, A (W, Θ) *f*[1.13] et al., continue with καὶ ταραχαί ("and disturbances"); others, 2542 *pc*, with καὶ λοιμοί ("and diseases"); and yet others, Σ *pc*, with what appears to be a combination of the first two readings, καὶ λοιμοὶ καὶ ταραχαί ("and diseases and disturbances"). The shortest reading, on which the trans. is based, is the earliest recoverable reading, which was expanded in various ways (cf. Metzger, *Textual Commentary*, 95).

d The trans. is based on the reading of ℵ B D et al., ἀρχή ("beginning"). Many MSS read ἀρχαί ("beginnings") instead of the singular. The plural is probably an "improvement" on the original, an attempt to make the noun agree with the plurality of the events predicted. The subject ταῦτα ("this" or "these things") may be taken either as a singular collective or as a plural.

e D W Θ *f*[1] et al. omit this sentence, possibly under the influence of the parallel in Luke 21:12.

f That this apparent aside or digression was found to be difficult is shown by the variants; see the discussion of parentheses in Mark in Moulton-Turner, 4:26, reprinted in Elliott, *Language and Style*, 232. The earliest recoverable reading is probably that attested by ℵ[c] B D et al. The word order implies that "first" modifies "all the nations." This implication was apparently problematic and gave rise to two variants. Some MSS (A L *f*[1.13] et al.) reversed the order of πρῶτον ("first") and δεῖ ("it is necessary"); in light of the usual word order, "first" would now modify "it is necessary." This is probably the intended meaning, but the reading is secondary as an attempt to make that meaning clear. The original hand of Sinaiticus (ℵ*) added the word λαόν ("people") between πρῶτον ("first") and δεῖ ("it is necessary") to change the meaning to "And it is necessary that the first people proclaim the good news to all the nations." The reading attested by W Θ 565 et al., ἕνεκεν ἐμοῦ εἰς μαρτύριον αὐτοῖς καὶ εἰς

Judea flee to the mountains, 15/ let[g] him who is on the roof not come down[h] or go in to take something out of his house, 16/ and let him who is in the field not turn back to take his cloak. 17/ Woe to women who are pregnant and who are nursing infants in those days! 18/ Pray then that it not happen in winter.[i] 19/ For those days will be a tribulation the like of which has not occurred since the beginning of the creation which God created until now and surely will not occur (again). 20/ And if the Lord did not shorten the days, nobody would survive; but on account of the elect whom he had chosen, he shortened the days. 21/ And at that time if anyone says to you, "Look, here is the Messiah," "Look there,"[j] do not believe (him or her); 22/ for false messiahs[k] and false prophets will rise up and will produce[l] signs and wonders in order to deceive, if possible, the elect. 23/ As for you, watch out then; I have told you everything beforehand.

24/ "But in those days after that tribulation, the sun will be darkened and the moon will not give its light 25/ and the stars will be falling[m] from heaven, and the powers that are in the heavens will be shaken. 26/ And then the Son of Man will be seen coming in clouds with great power and glory. 27/ And then he will send the angels and he will gather the elect[n] from the four winds, from (one) end of the earth to the other.[o]

28/ "Now learn from the comparison with the fig tree. By the time its branch has sprouted and put forth leaves, you know[p] that summer is near. 29/ So also you, when you see these things happening, know that he is near, at the door. 30/ Truly I say to you, this generation will surely not pass away until all these things happen. 31/ The sky and the earth will pass away, but my words will surely[q] not pass away.

32/ "But concerning that day or the hour, no one knows, not even the angels in heaven, and not even the Son;[r] (no one knows) except

πάντα τὰ ἔθνη πρῶτον δὲ δεῖ κηρυχϑῆναι τὸ εὐαγγέλιον ("because of me in order to give testimony to them and to all the nations, but first it is necessary that the good news be proclaimed"), results from an attempt to link the parenthesis better to its context.

g   In the earliest recoverable form of the text, there was probably no conjunction linking this clause or sentence with the previous one; on asyndeton in Mark, see Moulton-Turner, 4:12, reprinted in Elliott, *Language and Style*, 216. This reading is preserved by B 1424. 2427. 2542 et al. Two "corrections" were later made; some MSS (ℵ A L W et al.) read ὁ δέ, "and (let) him" and others (D Θ 565. et al.) read καὶ ὁ, "and (let) him."

h   Some MSS (A D W et al.) include the words εἰς τὴν οἰκίαν ("into the house" or "into his house"), which apparently were added at some point to clarify the presumed meaning.

i   Some MSS reflect attempts to clarify the subject of the verb γένηται ("happen") by making it explicit. In some cases (Θ f¹³ et al.) it is ταῦτα ("these things" or "this"); in others (ℵ² A Ψ et al.), φυγὴ ὑμῶν ("your flight"). The latter reading probably arose under the influence of Matt 24:20.

j   In the earliest recoverable form of the text, attested by ℵ L W et al., the second saying followed the first without a conjunction. This instance of asyndeton (see n. g above on v. 15) was "corrected" or clarified in two ways, either by the addition of καί ("and"), so B 2427 et al., or ἤ ("or"), so A (C) D et al.

k   A few MSS (D *pc* i k) lack the words ψευδόχριστοι καί ("false messiahs and") or the equivalent, which were probably omitted by mistake.

l   A number of MSS (D Θ f¹³ 28. 565 *pc* a) read ποιήσουσιν ("do," "make," or "perform") instead of δώσουσιν ("produce," literally "give"). The former reading was accepted by Tischendorf, Bover, Nestle-Aland (25th ed.), and Huck-Greeven because they held that ποιήσουσιν ("do") had been changed to δώσουσιν ("produce") under the influence of the parallel in Matt 24:24. But it is more likely that the word δώσουσιν ("produce"), which reflects a Semitic idiom, was changed to the more normal Greek ποιήσουσιν ("do").

m   Some MSS (W 565. 700 e) change the periphrastic future ἔσονται . . . πίπτοντες ("will be falling") to the more common future middle form πεσοῦνται ("will fall"), either under the influence of Matt 24:29 or in an effort to improve the Greek. See Moulton-Turner (4.20–21, reprinted in Elliott, *Language and Style*, 225–26) on periphrastic tenses in Mark. ℵ B C D et al. read πίπτοντες ("falling"); a large number of MSS (f¹ 𝔐 et al.) read ἐκπίπτοντες ("falling from") instead. Von Soden, Vogels, and Huck-Greeven adopted this reading. Since, however, all the MSS

the Father. 33/ Watch out, stay awake;[s] for you do not know when the time is. 34/ (It is) like a man away on a journey, who has left his household and given to each of his slaves the authority (to do) his task; and he has given the doorkeeper orders to keep awake. 35/ So keep awake; for you do not know when the master of the household is coming, whether in the evening or at midnight or at cockcrow or early in the morning; 36/ (keep awake) so that he will not come unexpectedly and find you sleeping. 37/ Now what I say to you, I say to all: keep awake."

(except A) that have the latter reading also differ from ℵ B C Θ Ψ et al. in other and various ways, it seems more likely that πίπτοντες ("falling") is the earlier reading.

n The majority of MSS (ℵ A B C Θ et al.) have αὐτοῦ ("his") after τοὺς ἐκλεκτοὺς ("the elect"). A number of MSS lack αὐτοῦ ("his"), namely, D L W et al. It is difficult to decide between the two readings. Tischendorf, von Soden, Bover, and Huck-Greeven leave αὐτοῦ ("his") out of their critical texts, whereas Westcott and Hort and Nestle-Aland (25th and 26th ed.) print it in brackets. Since it is easier to understand how the word would have been added than omitted and since the shorter reading is represented by some MSS from both group "B" and group "D," the shorter reading is more likely to be earlier. On the textual groups, see Epp, "Dynamic View."

o Lit., "from (one) end of the earth to (one) end of the sky."

p Some MSS, namely, B² D L W et al., read γινώσκεται ("it is known" or "one knows") instead of γινώσκετε ("you know"). The former reading probably arose in an attempt to justify the emphatic ὑμεῖς ("you") near the beginning of the following verse A contrast between an impersonal expression and the emphatic second person plural is more elegant than one between an unemphatic second person plural and an emphatic one.

q B D* lack μή, "surely (not)." Westcott and Hort printed this word only in the margin and Nestle-Aland (25th ed.) omitted it. Given its overwhelming support in the MSS, however, it probably belonged to the earlier form of the text.

r A few MSS (X 983. 1689 et al.) omit οὐδὲ ὁ υἱός ("and not even the Son"); see Huck-Greeven, ad loc. These words were probably omitted deliberately because they seemed to contradict the doctrine of the divinity of Christ; see Taylor, ad loc.

s Most MSS, including ℵ A C L W, have the words καὶ προσεύχεσθε ("and pray") after ἀγρυπνεῖτε ("stay awake"). B D 122. 2427 et al. lack these words; cf. Huck-Greeven, ad loc. The shorter reading is probably earlier, since it is attested by representatives of both group "B" and group "D" and since the longer text could very well be the result of independent pious additions, perhaps based on Mark 14:38.

Literary Context and Genre

At the beginning of v. 1, Jesus is portrayed as leaving the temple mount. This change in location indicates the beginning of a new section within the larger unit depicting Jesus' proclamation in Jerusalem (11:1–13:37). In the previous section, 11:27–12:44, the scene of Jesus' activity is the temple mount. This new section ends with 13:37, the end of Jesus' speech. 14:1 begins another section with an indication of temporal setting and a change of characters.

13:1-2 is a short pronouncement story or chreia, in which a saying of Jesus is placed in a brief narrative setting. The disciple who speaks to Jesus and evokes the saying is unidentified. In v. 3, there is a change of location, as Jesus arrives on the Mount of Olives and takes his seat there in the posture of a teacher. A change of characters also occurs. The audience is likely to infer that all of the (twelve) disciples have followed Jesus as he left the temple mount, but according to v. 3, four named disciples ask Jesus a question privately, which is narrated in v. 4. Jesus' extended response constitutes vv. 5-37. Although the setting and characters change in v. 3, vv. 1-2 and vv. 3-37 are closely linked by the fact that both passages share the subject matter of the temple mount and its fate. This link is introduced already in the description of Jesus' sitting "opposite the temple mount" ($\kappa\alpha\tau\acute{\epsilon}\nu\alpha\nu\tau\iota$ $\tau o\hat{\upsilon}\ \acute{\iota}\epsilon\rho o\hat{\upsilon}$) in v. 3, which repeats the reference to the temple mount in v. 1.

The speech in vv. 5-37 is the longest and most coherent of all those attributed to Jesus in Mark. Only 4:3-32 is comparable. The length and coherence of 13:5-37 indicate the importance of the teaching there expressed from the point of view of the evangelist.

The anecdote in vv. 1-2 begins as a scholastic dialogue might: a disciple addresses Jesus as teacher ($\delta\iota\delta\acute{\alpha}\sigma\kappa\alpha\lambda\epsilon$), and a neutral remark by the disciple is the occasion for teaching on the part of Jesus.[1] The pronouncement of Jesus, however, is a prophetic saying. So a prophetic saying has been placed in a scholastic context.[2]

Jesus' monologue in vv. 5-37, set in the framework of a dialogue with the four named disciples, is often referred to as "the little apocalypse" or as a version of "the Synoptic apocalypse." An apocalypse, however, is best defined as a narrative account of the reception of revelation by a human seer from a heavenly being.[3] The Gospel of Mark identifies Jesus with the heavenly Son of Man, but he has not yet been exalted to that state in the narrative. In chapter 13, Jesus is presented as a teacher and prophet, not as a heavenly being. The speech, however, does contain apocalyptic eschatology, which may be defined as the types of ideas, symbols and teaching associated with the heavenly world and the future that one finds in the apocalypses.[4] Jesus' monologue is best described as a prophetic oracle or apocalyptic discourse.[5] Although the speech of Jesus in vv. 5-37 has some similarities with texts that belong to the genre "testament," it lacks some important typical features of that literary type.[6]

Like vv. 1-2, vv. 3-37 constitute a scholastic dialogue. A group of disciples ask their teacher a question seeking more information or greater understanding. As a prophetic saying is placed in a scholastic context in vv. 1-2, so an apocalyptic discourse is put in such a framework in vv. 3-37. Although there is no indication that the Gospel of Mark was an esoteric document, there are several scenes that are presented as private teaching or esoteric instruction.[7] The scene depicted in vv. 3-37 may thus be characterized as rhetorically shaped esoteric instruction of a prophetic and apocalyptic nature.[8]

Sources, Composition, and Performance

With regard to the use of sources, there are three main options: (1) Mark used a substantial, coherent written source; (2) Mark joined together a variety of materials, in oral or written form; (3) Mark took a more active role in composing the discourse, making use of scripture and other sources in written and oral form. Rudolf Pesch

1   Because of the relationship between the disciple's remark and Jesus' saying, Tannehill defines the anecdote as a correction story ("Varieties," 102).

2   Adela Yarbro Collins, "The Apocalyptic Rhetoric of Mark 13 in Historical Context," *BR* 41 (1996) 5–36, esp. 8.

3   John J. Collins, "Introduction: Towards the Morphology of a Genre," in idem, ed., *Apocalypse: The Morphology of a Genre, Semeia* 14 (1979) 9.

4   Collins, *Apocalyptic Imagination*, 11–12.

5   Adela Yarbro Collins, "The Early Christian Apocalypses," *Semeia* 14 (1979) 61–121, esp. 96–97; eadem, "Apocalyptic Rhetoric," 9–10.

6   Yarbro Collins, "Apocalyptic Rhetoric," 8–9.

7   Mark 4:10-20; 7:17-23; 9:9-13, 30-32; 10:32-43.

8   C. Clifton Black goes too far in classifying vv. 5b-37 as an epideictic oration ("An Oration at Olivet: Some Rhetorical Dimensions of Mark 13," in Duane F. Watson, ed., *Persuasive Artistry: Studies in New Testament Rhetoric in Honor of George A. Kennedy* [JSNTSup 50; Sheffield: Sheffield Academic Press, 1991] 66–92). See the critical discussion in Yarbro Collins, "Apocalyptic Rhetoric," 10–13.

advocated the first option, arguing that vv. 1-2 belonged to the pre-Markan passion narrative and most of vv. 3-31 represents a pre-Markan, Christian apocalypse written during the Jewish War. Mark added v. 6 to warn against parousia enthusiasts; v. 10 to indicate that the Gentile mission will take place before the end; vv. 23 and 32 to dampen imminent expectation; and vv. 33-37 to urge watchfulness in light of the parousia.[9]

Another advocate of the first option is Egon Brandenburger, according to whom the basis of Mark 13 is a Christian apocalyptic text written after the beginning of the Jewish War. He assigned less material to this source than Pesch, however, including mainly the narrative portions of the speech in the source: vv. 7-8, 14-20, and 24-27. He argued that vv. 1b-2, most of vv. 9-13, vv. 21-22, 30-32, and 34-36 come from oral tradition. The rest is Markan redaction, although some of the relevant verses may also be from oral tradition.[10] Lars Hartman argued that "the nucleus of the eschatological discourse consisted of a 'midrash' on Dn (2,31-35), 7,7-27, 8,9-26, 9,24-27 and 11,21—12,4(13)."[11] He does not argue that this "midrash" was written, but speaks about its "solidity and plasticity."[12] This source is represented by Mark 13:5b-8, 12-16, 19-22, and 24-27; he expressed some doubt about vv. 8b and 15a. He concluded that "the original 'midrash' originated in the teaching of Jesus."[13]

An article published by George R. Beasley-Murray is a good example of the second option.[14] He argued that the discourse was composed by "welding" together four groups of sayings and individual logia into a whole as a response to the Jewish War, either before or after 70 CE. The social context in which the respective groups of sayings were formed was early Christian catechesis, the instruction of new converts. One group of sayings concerned "the tribulation of Israel" and is now represented by Mark 13:14-20. Another related to "the tribulation of the disciples of Jesus," now found in vv. 9-13. The core of this group is two sayings (vv. 9, 11) related to the Q-saying that appears in Luke 12:11-12. A third group treated the theme "false messiahs and the true Messiah" and comprises vv. 21-27. The fourth expressed the theme "*parousia* and watchfulness" and consists of vv. 33-37.[15]

In *The Kingdom in Mark*, Werner Kelber followed earlier scholars in assuming that Mark used a source in composing chapter 13. His own approach to the passage, however, was the method of "composition criticism," and his aim was to interpret the discourse in the context of Mark as a whole. Because of its methodological focus, this book may serve as an example of the third option.[16] Kelber argued that the introduction to the speech, 13:1-4, is "a redactional product throughout."[17] Following others, he interpreted vv. 5b-6 and 21-22 as doublets that deal with the issue of deception and together serve as a framing device. These framing units "exercise a controlling influence upon the material they embrace." In other words, this large section of the speech must be interpreted in terms of false prophecy. He concluded further that this first main part of the speech was organized with the purpose of refuting a false viewpoint. In fact, the main purpose of the discourse as a whole, in his view, was to correct "an erroneously conceived realized eschatology."[18] He argued that "in Judea" in 13:14 is redactional; the phrase was added to signal, in symbolic fashion, that the audience should flee to Galilee: "The flight of the Judean Christians is an eschatological exodus out of the land of Satan into the promised land of the Kingdom."[19] In his analysis, the second and central part of the discourse consists of vv. 24-27. This section reaffirms the parousia as a future event. The third section, vv. 28-37, answers the question of the timing of the

---

9   Pesch, 2:266–67.

10   Brandenburger, *Markus 13 und die Apokalyptik*, 41–42, 166–67.

11   Lars Hartman, *Prophecy Interpreted: The Formation of Some Jewish Apocalyptic Texts and of the Eschatological Discourse Mark 13 Par.* (CBNTS 1; Lund: Gleerup, 1966) 235.

12   Ibid., 251.

13   Ibid., 247.

14   George R. Beasley-Murray, "Second Thoughts on the Composition of Mark 13," *NTS* 29 (1983) 414–20.

15   Ibid., 416–17.

16   Kelber, *Kingdom*, 109–10.

17   Ibid., 111.

18   Ibid., 114–15.

19   Ibid., 121. The identification of Judea with "the land of Satan" is an overinterpretation that reinforces, if it does not derive from, Christian anti-Judaism.

parousia and how it relates to the "experienced destruction of the temple."[20] Jan Lambrecht's work on Mark 13 acknowledges the use of sources, but emphasizes the freedom with which "the final editor" shaped the material.[21]

Although it is likely that Mark used one or more written sources in composing this chapter, it is unlikely that he used an extensive, coherent written source. One of the most influential arguments for the use of such a source is that the aside to the reader in v. 14 comes from the source and is not an aside directed by the evangelist to his audience. This parenthetical remark, "Let the reader understand," is open to a variety of interpretations.[22] One of the oldest of these argues that the object of understanding is the text of Daniel. As Morna D. Hooker has pointed out, this theory probably arose as an attempt to explain why Jesus, in speaking to the four disciples, would refer to a "reader."[23] From the point of view of this theory, the eschatological discourse is basically authentic.

The authenticity of the discourse was challenged by Timothée Colani in 1864. He argued that the aside was part of the text of a Jewish-Christian apocalypse mentioned by Eusebius (*Hist. eccl.* 3.5)[24] that was equivalent to the divine revelation instructing the members of the Christian community in Jerusalem to leave that city. The interpolated discourse (vv. 5-31) was written before the siege of Jerusalem had begun.[25] In 1933, Gustav Hölscher argued that "the little apocalypse" was a Jewish text written in 39/40 CE in the context of the crisis evoked by Gaius Caligula's attempt to install his statue in the temple in Jerusalem.[26] Some advocates of the "little apocalypse" theory suggested that this text circulated in Judea in the form of an apocalyptic flier.[27] Gerd Theissen has recently argued in favor of an apocalyptic flier circulating around 40 CE.[28] Those who use the expression "Let the reader understand" as evidence for a written source must conclude that the evangelist reproduced these words without realizing the absurdity of attributing this expression to Jesus in the context of a speech to four disciples.[29]

It is much more likely that the aside is a literary device to indicate that the preceding allusion to the "desolating sacrilege" or "abomination of desolation" is a cryptic saying that requires interpretation. This literary device belongs to ancient practical apocalyptic hermeneutics. Compare the exhortation to one with understanding to calculate the number of the beast in Rev 13:18.[30]

---

20 Ibid., 122, 124.

21 Jan Lambrecht, "Die Logia-Quellen von Markus 13," *Bib* 47 (1966) 321–60; idem, *Die Redaktion der Markus-Apocalypse: Literarische Analyse und Struktur-untersuchung* (AnBib 28; Rome: Pontifical Biblical Institute, 1967).

22 The fullest list of possible interpretations of which I am aware is that of Fowler, *Let the Reader Understand,* 83–87.

23 Hooker, 314. Representatives of the position that the object of understanding is Daniel include Cranfield, ad loc.; Rudolf Bultmann (with a question mark and in combination with the little apocalypse theory), "ἀναγινώσκω, ἀνάγνωσις," *TDNT* 1 (1964) 343–44; Evans, ad loc. Scholars who accept this argument, but only as a partial explanation or as one of two or more reasonable explanations, include Taylor, 511–12; Gundry, 742.

24 According to Eusebius, the revelation was given before the war; the whole body of the church left Jerusalem and settled beyond the Jordan in Pella.

25 T(imothée) Colani, *Jésus-Christ et les croyances messianiques de son temps* (2nd rev. ed.; Strasbourg: Treuttel et Wurtz, 1864) 202–9. For a discussion of the context and motivation of Colani's interpretation, see

George R. Beasley-Murray, *Jesus and the Last Days: The Interpretation of the Olivet Discourse* (Peabody, MA: Hendrickson, 1993) 13–20. Pesch's interpretation has been influenced, directly or indirectly, by Colani's (Pesch, 2:292).

26 Gustav Hölscher, "Der Ursprung der Apokalypse Mrk 13," *Theologische Blätter* 12 (1933) 193–202. For a recent discussion of this crisis, see James S. McLaren, "Jews and the Imperial Cult: From Augustus to Domitian," *JSNT* 27 (2005) 257–78.

27 Taylor, 498.

28 Theissen, *Gospels in Context,* 136–65 (= *Lokalkolorit,* 145–76).

29 Hooker, 314.

30 Brandenburger, *Markus 13 und die Apokalyptik,* 50; cf. also Rev 17:9. The juxtaposition of the statement that those who are wise will understand with the two calculations of the end in Dan 12:10-12 is also analogous. Those who follow this line of interpretation include Hooker, 315; Larry W. Hurtado, *Mark* (NIBC; Peabody, MA: Hendrickson, 1983) 220; Sherman E. Johnson, *A Commentary on the Gospel according to St. Mark* (HNTC; Peabody, MA: Hendrickson, 1960) 216; Lane, 467; Taylor, 511–12.

An important question in determining the significance of the aside is who the "reader" is who is exhorted to understand. Most of the commentators who do not accept the "little apocalypse" theory argue or assume that the individual "reader" of Mark's Gospel is meant.[31] A problem for this interpretation is the likelihood that the Gospel was composed to be read aloud to an assembled audience.[32] It would thus be odd for the evangelist to address both an "individual" (note the use of the singular here) and a member of the audience as a "reader."

Whitney Shiner cited Apuleius *Met.* 1.1 as evidence that the word "reader" could apply to an individual listening to the text being read, for example, by his slave.[33] The social contexts in which Apuleius was read and heard, however, were quite different from those in which Mark was. Shiner admitted that the "performer" of the Gospel would probably have had a certain degree of authority within the local church.[34] He also argued that Mark addressed the individual member of the audience here in order to draw each person into the story. He appealed to the ancient work *On the Sublime* for support. But the author of that work recommends a change of person, for example, from third person to second person singular, in order to set the *hearer* (ὁ ἀκροατής) in the center of the action.[35]

Ernest Best has argued that the phrase "let the reader understand" was a private note to the public reader, the person who read the Gospel aloud for an assembled group. The phrase was not meant to be read aloud. It was intended to draw attention to a "grammatical solecism," the fact that the neuter βδέλυγμα ("abomination" or "sacrilege") is followed by a masculine participle ἑστηκώς ("standing"). This shift in grammatical gender is important for interpretation. The private reader would have time to note it and reflect upon it, but the public reader would not have that leisure and needed to be warned not to perceive the incongruity as a mistake and correct it orally. To clarify his point, Best put the verse into a modern idiom as follows: "But when you see that thing, the abomination of desolation, standing where he [*sic*] should not then let those who are in Judea flee to the mountains."[36]

This theory is ingenious and attractive, but there are several problems with it. One is that public readers most likely did not read texts like Mark's Gospel to an assembled audience "cold," so to speak. Such readers had no doubt read the Gospel privately in advance, even studied it, and thus would not be taken by surprise by the shift in grammatical gender. Best himself admits that the "gloss" was very early, since Matthew evidently read it in the text of Mark that he used. He also points out that "[s]o long then as a living tradition of the way a text was read still existed, punctuation was unnecessary."[37] If no punctuation was necessary, then this alleged gloss would not have been necessary either. Another problem is that the shift in gender is not, strictly speaking, a solecism, since *constructio ad sensum* was widespread in Greek from early times. Elsewhere in Mark a masculine participle is used with a neuter noun, when the noun represents a personal being (Mark 9:20, 26).[38] So, ingenious as this hypothesis is, it should not be adopted.

Like Best, Wellhausen, following Carl Weizsäcker, argued that the aside is addressed to the person entrusted with the reading of the Gospel to the community. He defined the purpose, however, as alerting the reader and the listening audience to the fact that this

---

31 Cranfield, 403; Donahue and Harrington describe this as the most common view; they themselves allow that "the reader" could also be the one who read the Gospel to the assembly (372); Craig A. Evans, *Mark 8:27–16:20* (WBC 34B; Nashville: Thomas Nelson, 2001) 320; Fowler, *Let the Reader Understand*, 87 (he uses the term "narratee" rather than "reader"); Gould, 246–47; Gundry, 742 (he lists this as the first of two possibilities); Hooker, 314–15; Hurtado, 220; Lane, 467 n. 77.

32 So, among others, Fowler, *Let the Reader Understand*, 84.

33 Shiner, *Proclaiming the Gospel*, 15–16.

34 Ibid., 26.

35 "Longinus" *On the Sublime* 26; text and trans. from W. Hamilton Fyfe in idem and W. Rhys Roberts, *Aristotle: The Poetics; "Longinus"; Demetrius* (LCL; rev. ed.; Cambridge, MA: Harvard University Press; London: Heinemann, 1932) 200–201; Shiner, *Proclaiming the Gospel*, 177.

36 Ernest Best, "The Gospel of Mark: Who Was the Reader?" *IBS* 11 (1989) 124–32, esp. 128–30; my attention was brought to this article by Donahue and Harrington, 372.

37 Best, "Gospel of Mark," 130.

38 BDF §134 (3); §282 (4); §296.

public reader would be able to explain the allusion to the "abomination of desolation."[39] It has been argued against this interpretation that "understand" does not mean "interpret."[40] In the literary and social context, however, the two are closely related. Literate members of the community were likely to be leaders and teachers as well.[41]

Wellhausen also pointed out that, in the prologue to Sirach, "the reader" (ὁ ἀναγινώσκων) is one who is learned in the scriptures.[42] The relevant part of the prologue reads, "Now those who read the scriptures must not only themselves understand them, but must also as lovers of learning be able through the spoken and written word to help the outsiders" (Sir prol. 4–6 NRSV).[43] The outsiders (οἱ ἐκτός) are those outside the scribal or wisdom schools, who are unable to read the scriptures.[44] The situation was analogous in the early church. Most of the members of the local communities were probably illiterate, and copies of the Gospels were expensive and rare, so public reading by an individual before a local assembly was the rule (1 Thess 5:27; Col 4:16; Rev 1:3).[45] Although it was probably written considerably later than Mark, 1 Timothy provides a notable analogy to the probable social setting of the parenthetical comment in Mark. The alleged author of the letter, Paul, instructs his representative, Timothy, to devote himself to "public reading, exhortation, and teaching" (1 Tim 4:13). Here, as in Mark 13:14, it is implied that the ability to read a text aloud before an assembly of fellow believers is connected with the authority to exhort and to teach the members of such an assembly.[46]

The evidence supports the conclusion that the "reader" in the phrase "Let the reader understand" is the one who actually reads the text to the audience, rather than the individual member of the audience.[47] If the author wished to address such individuals directly, he probably would have used a formula like "Let anyone who has ears to hear, hear!" (Mark 4:9).[48] In any case, the social setting of the expression "Let the reader understand" was both oral and scribal. It is oral in the sense that the Gospel was publicly read aloud and probably interpreted and applied as well. It is scribal in the sense that the Gospel was a written text that the public reader had probably read privately and studied, but this private reading and study was most likely rooted in an oral context of teaching and handing on the tradition.

The other arguments for the use of an extensive written source are equally weak.[49] While the use of such a source cannot be ruled out with certainty, the evidence is insufficient to demonstrate its use.

History of the Tradition

It is clear that chapter 13 is composed of a variety of materials.[50] Scholars differ, however, on whether the

---

39 Wellhausen, 103; Carl Weizsäcker, *Das apostolische Zeitalter der christlichen Kirche* (2nd rev. ed.; Freiburg i. B.: Mohr Siebeck, 1892) 362.

40 Theissen, *Gospels in Context*, 128–29 (= *Lokalkolorit*, 137). Theissen contrasts the νοείτω ("understand") of Mark 13:14 with the διερμηνευέτω ("interpret" or "translate") in 1 Cor 14:27, but the latter passage comes from an entirely different context.

41 Gamble, *Books and Readers*, 5, 8–9.

42 Wellhausen, 103.

43 Rahlfs's numbering used here.

44 Cf. Ezra 7:11; Neh 8:1-4; cited by Patrick W. Skehan and Alexander A. Di Lella, *The Wisdom of Ben Sira: A New Translation with Notes* (AB 39; New York: Doubleday, 1987) 133; see also Bultmann, "ἀναγινώσκω, ἀνάγνωσις," 344. The social setting of Jewish scribes seems more relevant than the role of the *anagnōstēs* discussed by Fowler, who also acknowledges the relevance of the Jewish practice of the public reading of scripture (*Let the Reader Understand*, 84).

45 Bultmann, "ἀναγινώσκω, ἀνάγνωσις," 343; Fowler, *Let the Reader Understand*, 84.

46 Gordon D. Fee argues that the three activities are basically the same, "and as such are to be Timothy's positive way of countering the erroneous teachings (cf. 2 Tim 3:14-17)" (*1 and 2 Timothy, Titus* [NIBC 13; Peabody, MA: Hendrickson, 1984] 107–8).

47 Note that Josephus refers occasionally to his readers in the plural but never in the singular (*Bell.* 7.11.5 §455; *Ant.* 1.proem.4 §§18, 24; *Ant.* 11.3.10 §68; *Ant.* 14.10.9 §218; *Ant.* 14.10.26 §265; *Vita* 6 §27).

48 Cf. Rev 2:7, 11, 17; Theissen, *Gospels in Context*, 128–29 (= *Lokalkolorit*, 137).

49 Yarbro Collins, *Beginning of the Gospel*, 73–91.

50 See, e.g., the list in Brandenburger, *Markus 13 und die Apokalyptik*, 13.

emphasis should be placed on Mark as a compiler of traditions or on Mark as an author who had mastery of his materials. An underlying issue is the degree to which any of the material can be said to originate with the historical Jesus. A further issue is the significance of the presence of typical traditional motifs and structures. Hartman studied "certain structures in Jewish apocalyptic texts whose contents resemble that of" Mark 13 and the part that scripture played "in the building of those structures." He defined these structures as "patterns of thought or conceptual frameworks which seem to have played a part in the formation of individual portions of text."[51] Barry Henaut cited David Stern to the effect that "the parablist 'was able to draw upon a kind of ideal thesaurus of stereotyped traditional elements' in order to improvise a parable under spontaneous conditions." Yet, as Henaut pointed out, "[t]his thesaurus [of commonplace plots and characterizations] would have been equally available to the evangelists and the authors of any literary sources they inherited."[52] The same holds true for Hartman's "structures."

A question for which some evidence can be found is whether pre-Markan tradition can be discerned in the description of the coming of the Son of Man in vv. 24-27. Alfred Resch argued that Paul's description of the parousia in 1 Thess 4:13-18 is dependent on sayings of Jesus that are also found in the Synoptic Gospels. He interpreted the reference to a $\lambda \acute{o} \gamma o \varsigma \ \kappa \upsilon \rho \acute{\iota} o \upsilon$ ("word" or "saying" or "discourse of the Lord") in v. 15 to mean that Paul knew some sayings attributed to the historical Jesus. He proposed that "we will be taken up" ($\acute{\alpha} \rho \pi \alpha \gamma \eta \sigma \acute{o}$-

$\mu \epsilon \vartheta \alpha$) in v. 17 is related to "he will gather the elect" ($\acute{\epsilon} \pi \iota \sigma \upsilon \nu \acute{\alpha} \xi \epsilon \iota \ \tau o \grave{\upsilon} \varsigma \ \acute{\epsilon} \kappa \lambda \epsilon \kappa \tau o \acute{\upsilon} \varsigma$) in Mark 13:27 and that $\acute{\epsilon} \nu \ \nu \epsilon \varphi \acute{\epsilon} \lambda \alpha \iota \varsigma$ ("in clouds" or "on clouds") in 1 Thess 4:17 is related to the same Greek phrase in Mark 13:26.[53] Béda Rigaux concluded that the $\lambda \acute{o} \gamma o \varsigma \ \kappa \upsilon \rho \acute{\iota} o \upsilon$ ("word" or "saying" or "discourse of the Lord") in 1 Thess 4:15 refers to the same apocalyptic revelation attributed to Jesus that is recorded in Mark 13 and its parallels. In his view, there is a relationship between 1 Thess 4:16-17 and the Synoptic eschatological discourse.[54]

David Wenham interpreted the $\lambda \acute{o} \gamma o \varsigma \ \kappa \upsilon \rho \acute{\iota} o \upsilon$ ("word" or "saying" or "discourse of the Lord") as signifying "the traditional description of the Parousia."[55] He argued further that Paul did not quote the tradition verbatim but expounded it freely. If Paul's treatment of the tradition is related to a Synoptic saying, then Mark 13:27 would be a good candidate, since "will bring with him" ($\acute{\alpha} \xi \epsilon \iota \ \sigma \grave{\upsilon} \nu \ \alpha \grave{\upsilon} \tau \hat{\omega}$) in 1 Thess 4:14 is similar and perhaps related to "he will gather the elect" ($\acute{\epsilon} \pi \iota \sigma \upsilon \nu \acute{\alpha} \xi \epsilon \iota \ \tau o \grave{\upsilon} \varsigma \ \acute{\epsilon} \kappa \lambda \epsilon \kappa \tau o \acute{\upsilon} \varsigma$) in that Markan verse.[56] He concluded that the link is indirect through "the eschatological parenesis of the Greek-speaking church."[57]

Hartman argued that the phrase $\lambda \acute{o} \gamma o \varsigma \ \kappa \upsilon \rho \acute{\iota} o \upsilon$ in 1 Thess 4:15 does not necessarily mean an individual saying. It can also refer to a "discourse" or part of one. The phrase could thus be translated "a teaching of the Lord" or "an instruction of the Lord."[58] He argued further that in this verse Paul is not repeating a tradition as he does in 1 Corinthians 11 and 15. Here Paul refers to a teaching of the Lord and "interprets and supplements [it] for his own purpose."[59] Hartman concluded that

---

51   Hartman, *Prophecy Interpreted*, 13–14.

52   Barry W. Henaut, *Oral Tradition and the Gospels: The Problem of Mark 4* (JSNTSup 82; Sheffield: JSOT Press, 1993) 78.

53   1 Thess 1:10 also refers to the parousia (Alfred Resch, *Der Paulinismus und die Logia Jesu* [TU n.F. 12; Leipzig: Hinrichs, 1904] 38, 339). Traugott Holtz also concluded that the $\lambda \acute{o} \gamma o \varsigma \ \kappa \upsilon \rho \acute{\iota} o \upsilon$ ("word" or "saying" or "discourse of the Lord") in 1 Thess 4:15 is "a designation of a received saying of Jesus" ("Paul and the Oral Gospel Tradition," in Henry Wansbrough, ed., *Jesus and the Oral Gospel Tradition* [JSNTSup 64; Sheffield: Sheffield Academic Press, 1991] 380–93; citation from 385).

54   Béda Rigaux, *Saint Paul: Les Epitres aux Thessaloniciens* (EtB; Paris: Gabalda, 1956) 96–104, 539.

55   David Wenham, "Paul and the Synoptic Apocalypse," in Richard T. France and Wenham, eds., *Gospel Perspectives: Studies of History and Tradition in the Four Gospels* (Gospel Perspectives 2; Sheffield: JSOT Press, 1981) 345–75; citation from 367 n. 17. I. Howard Marshall takes a similar position (*1 and 2 Thessalonians* [NCBC; Grand Rapids: Eerdmans; London: Marshall Morgan & Scott, 1983] 126).

56   Wenham, "Paul and the Synoptic Apocalypse," 348 (g); 368 n. 17. He notes that the motifs of clouds and archangel/angels link the Pauline passage to Mark 13:26-27 (348 [c] and [d], 353).

57   Ibid., 349, 353.

58   Hartman, *Prophecy Interpreted*, 182.

59   Ibid., 188.

Paul knew the "midrash" on Daniel on which Mark 13 is based.[60]

Other scholars, however, have argued that the phrase λόγος κυρίου here refers to a saying of the risen Lord received by Paul as a prophet, which he then communicated to the Thessalonians.[61] The similarities between 1 Thessalonians 4 and the eschatological discourse of the Synoptic Gospels, however, make this hypothesis unnecessary.[62] The connection between 1 Thessalonians 4 and Mark 13 has also been called into question by the argument that the so-called "rapture," the idea that "we will be taken up" (ἁρπαγησόμεθα) in 1 Thess 4:17, is peculiar to Paul.[63] It is likely, on the contrary, that the description in Mark 13:27 of the Son of Man sending out the angels to gather the elect from the four winds presupposes an event similar to the one that Paul describes. Granted, the Markan passage does not specify where the elect will be taken once they are gathered, but the involvement of angels suggests that they are taken to heaven.

In light of the variability of oral tradition and its constant adaptation to new situations, the connection between Mark 13:26-27 and 1 Thess 4:15-17 could be explained by positing that each text has resulted from the textualization of a different version of the oral tradition about the parousia. Such a conclusion, however, must remain tentative, since it is equally possible that each text results from its respective author's adaptation and actualization of an earlier written text that involved rewriting the text in the author's own words.[64] Mark describes the event primarily in visual terms, whereas Paul emphasizes what will be heard.[65]

An aim of many who present Mark as a compiler of traditions is to show that at least some of those traditions go back to the historical Jesus. Now it may be that some of the traditions in Mark 13 do indeed go back to the historical Jesus. The description of the coming of the Son of Man on or in clouds in v. 27 may well go back to him. The hypothesis that best explains the Synoptic evidence concerning the Son of Man sayings is that the historical Jesus, alluding to Dan 7:13, spoke about a heavenly Son of Man figure to come in the future.[66] Yet, for a variety of reasons, not least among them the use of oral techniques in the composition of Mark 13, it is not possible to reconstruct earlier oral or even written traditions used by the evangelist in this chapter with a reasonable degree of certainty.

Comment

■ **1-2** As noted above, vv. 1-2 constitute a scholastic dialogue that focuses on a prophetic saying of the Markan Jesus.[67] Theissen has suggested that the remark of the disciple indicates "a dissociation from urban culture,"

---

60 Ibid., 188–90; he is followed by Charles A. Wanamaker, *1 and 2 Thessalonians* (NCBC; Grand Rapids: Eerdmans; London: Marshall Morgan & Scott, 1983) 171.

61 E.g., Abraham J. Malherbe, *The Letters to the Thessalonians: A New Translation with Introduction and Commentary* (AB 32B; New York: Doubleday, 2000) 267–69; he puts weight on the phrase λέγομεν ἐν λόγῳ κυρίου, which he translates "we tell you as a message from the Lord" and defines as a "prophetic claim." See also Bartholomäus Henneken, *Verkündigung und Prophetie im Ersten Thessalonicherbrief* (SBS 29; Stuttgart: Katholisches Bibelwerk, 1969) 88–91. For other scholars who take this position, see Malherbe, *Letters to the Thessalonians*, 268–69; Henneken, *Verkündigung*, 82 n. 28, and Wanamaker, *1 and 2 Thessalonians*, 170.

62 These similarities are recognized by Malherbe, *Letters to the Thessalonians*, 274, 276–77.

63 Marshall, *1 and 2 Thessalonians*, 130.

64 Vernon K. Robbins categorizes the latter procedure as "recitation of a saying using words different from the authoritative source." As an example, he mentions Paul's version (in 1 Cor 9:14) of the Synoptic saying "for laborers deserve their food" (Matt 10:10||Luke 10:7) (*Exploring the Texture of Texts: A Guide to Socio-Rhetorical Interpretation* [Valley Forge, PA: Trinity Press International, 1996] 42).

65 Kelber, *Gospel*, 143–44.

66 Adela Yarbro Collins, "The Influence of Daniel on the New Testament," in Collins, *Daniel*, 92–96; eadem, "The Apocalyptic Son of Man Sayings," in Birger A. Pearson et al., eds., *The Future of Early Christianity: Essays in Honor of Helmut Koester* (Minneapolis: Fortress, 1991) 220–28; eadem, "Daniel 7 and the Historical Jesus," in Harold W. Attridge et al., eds., *Of Scribes and Scrolls: Studies on the Hebrew Bible, Intertestamental Judaism, and Christian Origins, Presented to John Strugnell on the Occasion of His Sixtieth Birthday* (CTSRR 5; Lanham, MD: University Press of America, 1990) 187–93; eadem, "Origin of the Designation."

67 See "Literary Context and Genre" above.

since it is reminiscent of the reactions of people from the provinces who seldom go to the capital.[68]

The prophecy in v. 2 is probably a variant of a traditional saying attributed to Jesus, which may have some basis in the teaching of the historical Jesus (cf. Mark 14:58; 15:29; John 2:19; Acts 6:14). It is not possible to reconstruct an "original form" of the saying or to determine its "original" significance and historical context.[69] If the saying does go back to Jesus, however, it is likely that it was a prophetic or apocalyptic saying, rather than a prediction of a specific historical event.[70] The Dead Sea Scrolls provide evidence for the expectation of an eschatological temple. The members of the יחד ("community") believed that, in the new age, God would create a new temple that would last forever (11QT^a [11Q19] 29:6-10).[71] A similar expectation is expressed in *Jubilees*, a work closely related to the Dead Sea Scrolls (*Jub.* 1:17, 27, 29).[72] It is thus unlikely that the earliest recoverable form of the saying spoke only about the destruction of the temple.[73]

When this traditional saying was placed in the context of a scholastic dialogue set on the temple mount, however, its form was modified to fit this context.[74] The emphasis here, perhaps in anticipation of vv. 5b-37, is on the destruction of the current temple, and there is no mention of a new temple. It is likely that the evangelist gave the saying in v. 2 its present form.[75] It is sometimes

claimed that the prediction in this verse corresponds to what actually happened and thus is prophecy *ex eventu*.[76] Pesch and others have referred to Josephus's report that "Caesar ordered the whole city and the temple to be razed to the ground" (κελεύει Καῖσαρ ἤδη τήν τε πόλιν ἅπασαν καὶ τὸν νεὼν κατασκάπτειν) (*Bell.* 7.1.1 §1).[77] Josephus, however, goes on to say that Titus deliberately left the three great towers standing, as well as the part of the wall that enclosed the city on the west. Even with regard to the temple, the prophecy of 13:2 does not correspond to what actually happened, since the western wall is, in effect, part of the foundation of the temple and still stands today. Theissen recognized this problem and argued that the prediction is qualified by the word ὧδε ("here").[78] But since the text describes Jesus as leaving the temple precinct, rather than standing next to the ναός (the "temple" building proper) itself, this argument is not persuasive. The wording of the prophecy is best taken as hyperbolic, and it is impossible to determine by comparison with Josephus whether it was coined before or after the destruction.

The implication is that v. 2 was not necessarily written after the temple was destroyed in 70 CE. It could have been written during the Roman siege of Jerusalem or even earlier. The current form of the saying could well have been inspired by the military isolation of Jerusalem by Vespasian in the first half of 68 or by the march of

---

68 Gerd Theissen, *Social Reality and the Early Christians: Theology, Ethics and the World of the New Testament* (Minneapolis, MN: Fortress, 1992) 104–5 n. 21.

69 Cf. Bultmann, *History*, 36, 120–21, 128.

70 Ibid., 401, and the literature cited there.

71 4QFlorilegium (4Q174) 1:6-7 may also refer to the definitive, eschatological temple that would be established on Mount Zion by God and that would be like the garden of Eden (Adela Yarbro Collins, "The Dream of a New Jerusalem at Qumran," in James H. Charlesworth, ed., *The Bible and the Dead Sea Scrolls*, vol. 3: *The Scrolls and Christian Origins* [Waco, TX: Baylor University Press, 2006] 244–46). The temple in the *Description of the New Jerusalem* (2Q24, etc.) is probably also the definitive, everlasting temple (Yarbro Collins, "Dream of a New Jerusalem," 246–48).

72 See James C. VanderKam, "The Temple Scroll and the Book of Jubilees," in George J. Brooke, ed., *Temple Scroll Studies: Papers presented at the International Symposium on the Temple Scroll, Manchester, December*

1987 (JSPSup 7; Sheffield: JSOT Press, 1989) 211–36, esp. 232, 236 n. 51.

73 John R. Donahue argued that the double form of the saying, containing prophecies of both the destruction of the temple and the building of a new temple, resulted from the combination of two originally separate sayings (*Are You the Christ?* 103–13).

74 Bultmann, *History*, 36, 120; Theissen, *Social Reality*, 95 n. 3.

75 So also, to some degree, Pesch, 2:272.

76 E.g., Pesch, 2:272.

77 Text and trans. from Thackeray, *Josephus*, 3:504–5; Pesch, 2:271.

78 Theissen, *Gospels in Context*, 259 (= *Lokalkolorit*, 271). In a later work, Theissen argued that v. 2 is not "a pure prophecy after the event" (*Social Reality*, 96 n. 4).

Titus and his legions against the city in the first half of 70. Mark could have anticipated the destruction of Jerusalem and the temple at any time after 68 and have seen the hand of God in that pending destruction.

In any case, the saying, especially the phrase "a stone upon a stone" ($\lambda i\theta o\varsigma$ $\dot{\epsilon}\pi\dot{\iota}$ $\lambda i\theta o\nu$), does not correspond to any surviving description of the destruction of the First or Second Temple. Rather, it depicts a reversal of the allusion to the building of the Second Temple in Haggai:

And now call to mind, from this day backward, before the placing of a stone upon a stone in the temple of the Lord, what sort of people were you? ($\kappa\alpha\dot{\iota}$ $\nu\hat{\upsilon}\nu$ $\theta\dot{\epsilon}\sigma\theta\epsilon$ $\delta\dot{\eta}$ $\epsilon\dot{\iota}\varsigma$ $\tau\dot{\alpha}\varsigma$ $\kappa\alpha\rho\delta i\alpha\varsigma$ $\dot{\upsilon}\mu\hat{\omega}\nu$ $\dot{\alpha}\pi\dot{o}$ $\tau\hat{\eta}\varsigma$ $\dot{\eta}\mu\dot{\epsilon}\rho\alpha\varsigma$ $\tau\alpha\dot{\upsilon}\tau\eta\varsigma$ $\kappa\alpha\dot{\iota}$ $\dot{\upsilon}\pi\epsilon\rho\dot{\alpha}\nu\omega$ $\pi\rho\dot{o}$ $\tau o\hat{\upsilon}$ $\theta\epsilon\hat{\iota}\nu\alpha\iota$ $\lambda i\theta o\nu$ $\dot{\epsilon}\pi\dot{\iota}$ $\lambda i\theta o\nu$ $\dot{\epsilon}\nu$ $\tau\hat{\omega}$ $\nu\alpha\hat{\omega}$ $\kappa\upsilon\rho i o\upsilon$ $\tau i\nu\epsilon\varsigma$ $\hat{\eta}\tau\epsilon$). (Hag 2:15-16a LXX)[79]

■ **3-4** As noted above, vv. 3-37 constitute a scholastic dialogue that focuses on an apocalyptic discourse, rather than on a single prophetic saying, as the one in vv. 1-2 does.[80] In v. 3, Jesus is depicted as seated, the conventional ancient posture of the teacher.[81] He is also portrayed as sitting opposite the temple mount. As noted above, this detail foreshadows the subject matter of this second, longer scholastic dialogue and thus links it with the one in vv. 1-2.[82]

Peter, James, John, and Andrew are portrayed as asking Jesus a question.[83] They ask it "privately" ($\kappa\alpha\tau$' $\dot{\iota}\delta i\alpha\nu$). Simon (Peter) and his brother Andrew were the first two disciples called by Jesus; James and his brother John were called immediately afterward (Mark 1:16-20).[84] In the list of the Twelve, Simon, who is at that point given the name "Peter," is listed first, followed by James

and John. Andrew is mentioned as the fourth (3:16-18). Only Peter, James, and John were allowed to accompany Jesus when he went to heal Jairus's daughter (5:37). Only these three were present at the transfiguration of Jesus (9:2).

The phrase $\kappa\alpha\tau$' $\dot{\iota}\delta i\alpha\nu$ ("privately") occurs six other times in Mark (4:34; 6:31, 32; 7:33; 9:2, 28). Of these, only two passages (4:34; 9:28), like this one, are occasions on which Jesus is teaching the disciples. The only other passage in which a limited group of disciples and the phrase $\kappa\alpha\tau$' $\dot{\iota}\delta i\alpha\nu$ ("privately") are combined is 9:2. The data suggest that the apocalyptic discourse of vv. 5b-37 is important teaching but also something revelatory, like the experience of the transfiguration.

Mark seems to have composed the question of the disciples in v. 4 in such a way as to link the discourse of vv. 5b-37 with the anecdote of vv. 1-2. The question has two parts. The first asks *when* "this" or "these things" ($\tau\alpha\hat{\upsilon}\tau\alpha$) will be; the second, what the *sign* is that will indicate when "all these things" ($\tau\alpha\hat{\upsilon}\tau\alpha$ . . . $\pi\dot{\alpha}\nu\tau\alpha$) are about to be accomplished. The $\tau\alpha\hat{\upsilon}\tau\alpha$ ("this" or "these things") in the first part of the question refers back to the prophecy of v. 2 and thus to the destruction of the temple. The second part of the question anticipates the discourse itself. It presupposes that the destruction of the temple is part of a sequence of eschatological events: $\tau\alpha\hat{\upsilon}\tau\alpha$ . . . $\pi\dot{\alpha}\nu\tau\alpha$ ("all these things"). The verb $\sigma\upsilon\nu$-$\tau\epsilon\lambda\epsilon\hat{\iota}\sigma\theta\alpha\iota$ ("to be accomplished") seems to have eschatological connotations here.[85]

■ **5-6** The speech of Jesus does not begin with a rhetorical introduction (*proemium* or *exordium*). Rather, it opens abruptly but powerfully with an admonition that would be equally at home in a prophetic oracle or wisdom book: "Watch out, so that no one deceives you" ($\beta\lambda\dot{\epsilon}\pi\epsilon\tau\epsilon$ $\mu\dot{\eta}$ $\tau\iota\varsigma$ $\dot{\upsilon}\mu\hat{\alpha}\varsigma$ $\pi\lambda\alpha\nu\dot{\eta}\sigma\eta$). This admonition (v. 5b) forms a

79 Pesch, 2:271.
80 See "Literary Context and Genre" above.
81 He is seated "on the Mount" ($\epsilon\dot{\iota}\varsigma$ $\tau\dot{o}$ $\ddot{o}\rho o\varsigma$); $\epsilon\dot{\iota}\varsigma$ ("into" or "to") is often used in early Christian literature where $\dot{\epsilon}\nu$ ("on") would be expected (BAGD, s.v. $\epsilon\dot{\iota}\varsigma$, sect. 1.a.$\delta$).
82 See "Literary Context and Genre" above.
83 The use of the singular verb $\dot{\epsilon}\pi\eta\rho\dot{\omega}\tau\alpha$ ("he asked") suggests that Peter was the one who actually spoke (Swete, 296).
84 Taylor, 502. The four appear also in 1:29.

85 Cf. *1 Enoch* 10:12 in the Greek text of Georgius Syncellus (Black, *Apocalypsis Henochi Graece*, 25). See also Denis and Janssens, *Concordance grecque*, 820 (as *Liber Henochi* 10B:12); *T. Dan* 6:4 (de Jonge, *Testaments of the Twelve Patriarchs*; Denis and Janssens, 843).

small unit with v. 6, which gives the explanation for the warning. The explanation follows without a connecting particle. In this brief opening unit, a specific warning is expressed that seems to relate to concrete historical circumstances in the future, followed by a brief explanation of those historical circumstances (v. 6).

On one level, vv. 5b-37 is a speech of Jesus, as a character in the narrative, to four named disciples. On another level, as is now widely acknowledged among New Testament scholars, the evangelist indirectly provides his audience with an interpretation of the first Jewish war with Rome. What moved Mark to write, the rhetorical exigence with which he was faced, was the appearance of popular prophets and claimants to messianic status during this war.[86] In the situation of the evangelist, the persons whom he viewed as false prophets and messiahs had acquired a significant following. If Jesus was the messiah, this situation ought not to have occurred. The evangelist found himself obliged to reassert, legitimate, and interpret the attribution of messianic and prophetic status to Jesus and to challenge the claims of pretenders to such status.

The explanation given in v. 6 is difficult to interpret. There are two main possibilities. The first is to paraphrase the main clause with the words "Many will come and speak in my name" by analogy with passages in the LXX in which a prophet is said to speak in the name of the Lord, presumably a reference to the typical introduction of an oracle, "Thus says the Lord."[87] The "many" in Mark would then be early Christian prophets who spoke in the name of the risen Jesus. The dependent clause, λέγοντες ὅτι ἐγώ εἰμι, could then be translated either absolutely, "saying, 'I am,'" and taken as a claim to divinity, or "saying, 'I am he'" and taken as a claim to be Jesus returning as the glorious Son of Man.[88] The latter claim could be understood in the historical context of the expectation of the return of Elijah, the tradition that John the Baptist was Elijah returned, and the statement in Mark's Gospel that Herod Antipas thought that Jesus was John returned from the dead (6:16).[89] The main problem with this interpretation is that it does not explain how this warning is linked to the prediction of wars, rumors of wars, and the related eschatological traditions that follow in vv. 7-8.

The second approach is to paraphrase the main clause with the words "Many will come with the power and authority of Jesus" by analogy with two passages in the LXX that also use verbs of motion in connection with the phrase ἐπὶ τῷ ὀνόματι ("in the name"). The first is 1 Sam 17:45 in which David says to Goliath:

> You come to me with a sword and a spear and a shield; but I come to you in the name of the Lord God of hosts of the army of Israel, which you have mocked today (Σὺ ἔρχη πρός με ἐν ῥομφαίᾳ καὶ ἐν δόρατι καὶ ἐν ἀσπίδι, κἀγὼ πορεύομαι πρὸς σὲ ἐν ὀνόματι κυρίου σαβαωθ θεοῦ παρατάξεως Ισραηλ, ἣν ὠνείδισας σήμερον). (1 Kgdms 17:45 LXX)

The second is a passage in which Asa, the king of Judah, cries out to the Lord:

---

86 On the interpretation of Mark 13 in terms of the notion of a "rhetorical exigence," see Yarbro Collins, "Apocalyptic Rhetoric," 5–8. On the role of prophets in the Jewish war, see the commentary on vv. 21-23 below.

87 For the phrase "in my name" (ἐπὶ τῷ ὀνόματί μου) or the equivalent in this usage, see Exod 5:23; Deut 18:19; Jer 11:21; 14:14-15; 20:9; 23:13, 25; 33:16; 36:9; Dan 9:6 (OG); Zech 13:3; for an example of "Thus said the Lord" (οὕτως εἶπε κύριος), see Jer 34:4. For a study of the use of the phrase "in the name of Jesus Christ" (ἐπὶ τῷ ὀνόματί Ἰησοῦ Χριστοῦ) and similar phrases in early Christian baptism, see Lars Hartman, *"Auf den Namen des Herrn Jesus": Die Taufe in den neutestamentlichen Schriften* (SBS 148; Stuttgart: Katholisches Bibelwerk, 1992).

88 Pesch argued that the reference is to Christian false prophets who claimed to be the returning Jesus (2:279); see also idem, *Naherwartungen: Tradition und Redaktion in Mk 13* (KBANT; Düsseldorf: Patmos-Verlag, 1968) 111. Theodore Weeden also took this position following Pesch, Walter Grundmann, Eduard Schweizer, and Johannes Schreiber (*Mark–Traditions in Conflict*, 79–81). Kelber similarly argued that the reference is to Christians who arrogated to themselves the authority and identity of the messiah Jesus by enacting his parousia (*Kingdom*, 115).

89 See the commentary on 1:6; 6:14-16; and 9:12-13 above.

O Lord, it is not impossible for you to save with many or with few; strengthen us, O Lord our God, for we trust in you and in your name we have come against this great multitude (*Κύριε, οὐκ ἀδυνατεῖ παρὰ σοὶ σῴζειν ἐν πολλοῖς καὶ ἐν ὀλίγοις· κατίσχυσον ἡμᾶς, κύριε ὁ θεὸς ἡμῶν, ὅτι ἐπὶ σοὶ πεποίθαμεν καὶ ἐπὶ τῷ ὀνόματί σου ἤλθαμεν ἐπὶ τὸ πλῆθος τὸ πολὺ τοῦτο*). (2 Chr 14:10 LXX)

According to this interpretation, the many who come are warriors, those who claim to be the messiah of Israel and to exercise the power and authority which, from the point of view of Mark, only the risen Jesus has. The dependent clause would then be translated "saying, 'I am he,'" that is, the messiah, an interpretation attested by Matt 24:5. The historical context for this interpretation would then be the messianic pretenders who came forward during the Jewish war and the memory of similar figures around the time of the death of Herod the Great. Support for taking the many who come in Jesus' name as Jews and not followers of Jesus may be found in the fact that Mark speaks of a non-follower of Jesus performing exorcisms in the name of Jesus, presumably by coopting his power and authority (9:38-39).[90] Finally, the phrase "in my name" or "in your name" is used with reference to Jesus in five passages in Mark besides this one (9:37, 38, 39, 41; 13:13). In only one of these (9:41) does a particular name become explicit. Here the name is *χριστός* ("anointed" or "messiah"), rather than the proper name "Jesus." This usage supports the inference that, if any particular name is in view in 13:6, it is the messianic designation, rather than "Jesus," "Lord," or "Son of Man."

Thus, those coming in the name of Jesus should be understood as those who claimed to be the *χριστός*, the eschatological king of Israel.[91] Josephus gives evidence for such claimants, although he avoids associating this term and its eschatological connotations with such people.[92] At least two such pretenders put themselves forward and acquired a following shortly after the death of Herod in 4 BCE. One of these was Simon, a royal slave, and another was Athrongaeus, a former shepherd, like David.[93] A similar phenomenon emerged near the beginning of the first Jewish war with Rome. During the summer of 66 CE, while the rebels were besieging the pro-Roman faction in the palace where they had taken refuge, Menahem, a son or grandson of Judas the Galilean, who had led an uprising against the Romans after the death of Herod, seized arms from Masada and entered Jerusalem like a king to direct the siege of the palace (*Bell.* 2.17.7-8 §§430–34). His leadership lasted only a short time and he was executed by followers of Eleazar (*Bell.* 2.17.9 §§441–48).[94] The rise to power of John of Gischala should also be mentioned in this context. He began as a brigand leader and, after escaping from Titus's siege of Gischala in the autumn of 67, became a prominent figure among the Zealots in Jerusalem.[95] After the Zealots had converted the temple into their fortress and had defeated, with the help of the Idumeans, the attempt to overthrow them led by Ananus and Jesus son of Gamalas, John sought absolute sovereignty (*μοναρχία*).[96]

The major messianic figure during the Jewish war was of course Simon, son of Gioras. Like John of Gischala, Simon either began as or became a brigand leader.

---

90   In the report of John to Jesus, the phrase is *ἐν τῷ ὀνόματί σου* ("in your name"). In Jesus' reply, the phrase is *ἐπὶ τῷ ὀνόματί μου* ("in my name").

91   That there was expectation of such a figure in the first centuries BCE and CE is shown by the *Psalms of Solomon* 17–18 and various passages from the DSS. Among the latter are 4QpIsa[a], 1QSb 5, 4Q174, 4Q252, and CD 7:19. For discussion see Collins, *Scepter and the Star*, 74–101.

92   Josephus readily uses language of "kingship" and speaks of men putting on the *διάδημα* ("royal headband" or "crown"). On Simon donning the diadem, see *Bell.* 2.4.2 §57 and Athrongaeus doing the same, see *Bell.* 2.4.3 §62. He compares Athrongaeus' behavior to that of a king in *Bell.* 2.4.3 §61. On the

avoidance of the term *χριστός* by Josephus, see Louis H. Feldman, "Josephus' Portrait of David," *HUCA* 60 (1989) 129–74, esp. 131 and 173.

93   Simon is discussed in *Bell.* 2.4.2 §§57–59; Athrongaeus in *Bell.* 2.4.3 §§60–65.

94   According to Helmut Schwier, his rule lasted barely a month (*Tempel und Tempelzerstörung* [NTOA 11; Freiburg: Universitätsverlag Freiburg Schweiz; Göttingen: Vandenhoeck & Ruprecht, 1989] 7).

95   On his career as a brigand, see Josephus *Bell.* 2.21.1 §§585–89; on his leadership of the Zealots in Jerusalem, see 4.2.1–3.1 §§84–127.

96   On the temple as the Zealots' fortress, see *Bell.* 4.3.7 §151; on the defeat of Ananus and Jesus, see 4.3.11–6.1 §§193–365; on John's bid for absolute

According to Josephus, Simon was involved in the repulsion of the attack by the Syrian legate Cestius Gallus on Jerusalem in 66 (*Bell.* 2.19.2 §521). He was then active as a brigand in Acrabatene and Idumaea in the winter of 66–67 (*Bell.* 2.22.2 §§652–54). After the death of Ananus, the former high priest and leader of the pro-Roman faction during the war, Simon emerged as a messianic leader. His messianic pretensions can be discerned in the words of Josephus, "He, on the contrary, was aspiring to despotic power and cherishing high ambitions" (ὁ δὲ τυραννιῶν καὶ μεγάλων ἐφιέμενος) (*Bell.* 4.9.3 §508).[97] His acceptance as a messianic leader by many from various social statuses can be inferred from Josephus's statement:

> And now when he was becoming a terror to the towns, many men of standing were seduced by his strength and career of unbroken success into joining him; and his was no longer an army of mere serfs or brigands, but one including numerous citizen recruits, subservient to his command as to a king (κἀπειδὴ πόλεσιν ἤδη φοβερὸς ἦν, πολλοὶ πρὸς τὴν ἰσχὺν καὶ τὴν εὔροιαν τῶν κατορθωμάτων ἐφθείροντο δυνατοί, καὶ οὐκέτι ἦν δούλων μόνων οὐδὲ λῃστῶν στρατός, ἀλλὰ καὶ δημοτικῶν οὐκ ὀλίγων ὡς πρὸς βασιλέα πειθαρχία). (*Bell.* 4.9.4 §510)[98]

In the spring of 69, Simon was invited by an alliance of Idumeans and chief priests to enter Jerusalem and overcome the Zealots. He was acclaimed by the people as savior and protector (σωτὴρ . . . κηδεμών) (*Bell.* 4.9.11 §575).[99] During the desperate fighting in the spring of 70, Simon was regarded with such reverence and awe (αἰδὼς ἦν καὶ δέος) that those under his command were quite prepared to take their own lives if he commanded it (*Bell.* 5.7.1 §309).[100]

These messianic figures are the most likely referents of the "many" (πολλοί) in v. 6. Whether Mark actually feared that some of the followers of Jesus would reject

him and follow Simon, son of Gioras instead, is impossible to determine. In any case he defined Jesus' messiahship in contrast to the claims of these messianic pretenders.

■ **7-8** In v. 7 a new unit begins, marked by the use of δέ ("now" or "and" or "but") and a change in subject matter from those who deceive to wars and reports of wars. This unit extends through v. 8, since the use of δέ in v. 9, along with another change in subject matter, marks the beginning of yet another unit. The relation between the admonition with explanation (vv. 5b-6) and this unit (vv. 7-8) is not explicit, but the latter is probably meant to provide a context for the former.

The new unit consists of reassurance and instruction in relation to the prediction of eschatological events (vv. 7-8). The opening temporal clause, "Now when you hear of wars and reports of wars" (ὅταν δὲ ἀκούσητε πολέμους καὶ ἀκοὰς πολέμων) in v. 7a is an indirect prediction. The main clause is an expression of reassurance: "do not be disturbed" (μὴ θροεῖσθε). The statement "It must happen" (δεῖ γενέσθαι) in v. 7c is an allusion to Dan 2:28-29 (OG and Theodotion) and 45 (Theodotion). This appropriation of Daniel implies that, from the evangelist's point of view, the events revealed in the dream of Nebuchadnezzar, which "must happen" at the end of days, were only now occurring or about to occur. It also implies that the wars and reports of wars belong to the events of the last days. This statement is significant as the first emphatic declaration of an eschatological or apocalyptic character in this speech. It portrays Jesus as a teacher who clarifies eschatological tradition (based on scripture) for his disciples, as well as a prophet who has insight into the divine plan.[101] The declaration "but the end is not yet" (ἀλλ᾽ οὔπω τὸ τέλος) in v. 7d instructs the audience that the wars do not themselves constitute "the end," but only the first in a series of eschatological events. This statement should not be taken as antieschatological. It is rather part of an attempt to clarify, interpret, and actualize eschatological tradition. It

---

sovereignty, see 4.7.1 §§389–95; he confronted his adversaries as a rival sovereign (ἀντεβασίλευσεν [§395]).

97 Text and trans. from Thackeray, *Josephus*, 3:150–51.
98 Text and trans. from Thackeray, *Josephus*, 3:152–53.
99 Thackeray, *Josephus*, 3:170–71.
100 Thackeray, *Josephus*, 3:296–97.

101 Knowledge of signs and wonders (σημεῖα καὶ τέρατα) is also an attribute of wisdom (Wis 8:8 LXX).

does not necessarily imply that the author is refuting a claim that identified such wars with "the end" ($\tau \grave{o}$ $\tau \acute{\epsilon} \lambda o \varsigma$).[102] Rather, it is a device in the unfolding of the author's own presentation of the eschatological scenario.

The justification for the affirmation that the end is not yet is given in v. 8, as the use of the conjunction $\gamma \acute{\alpha} \rho$ ("for") indicates. The predictions in v. 8abc must be fulfilled before the end. Such predictions are typical of apocalypses, and the events predicted are understood as signs that the end, that is, the divine intervention, is near.[103] The events predicted in vv. 7-8 are interpreted collectively, $\tau \alpha \hat{v} \tau \alpha$ ("this" or "these things"), as the "the beginning of the birth-pains" ($\grave{\alpha} \rho \chi \grave{\eta} \grave{\omega} \delta \acute{\iota} \nu \omega \nu$) (v. 8d). This label reflects the attempt, typical of apocalypses, to organize the eschatological events into stages.[104] The events predicted in these verses thus constitute the first act of the eschatological drama.

As suggested above, the prediction of the many who will come "in the name" of Jesus refers to specific historical events, since the audience is warned not to be deceived by them. The predictions of vv. 7-8 seem to have a different function. They are very general apocalyptic commonplaces. It is usually easy for audiences to associate these motifs with historical events in their own immediate situation. Nevertheless, their purpose here seems to be primarily to define the appearance of the deceivers as one of the events of the last days. Placing them and their activity in such a context heightens the importance of recognizing their true character and behaving accordingly.

■ **9-13** A new unit begins in v. 9; the shift is indicated by the use of $\delta \acute{\epsilon}$ ("now" or "and" or "but") in this verse, along with the change in subject matter from catastrophes that affect humanity in general to the specific difficulties faced by the followers of Jesus. The $\delta \acute{\epsilon}$ ("and") in v. 13b expresses a contrast between the tribulations mentioned in vv. 12 and 13a, on the one hand, and the salvation promised to the one who endures, on the other. Since there is no change in subject matter, v. 13b is part of this unit. The $\delta \acute{\epsilon}$ of v. 14 marks the beginning of the next unit. The temporal relation between vv. 9-13 and 7-8 is not explicit, but they are probably meant to be contemporary. This hypothesis is supported by the similarity between the predictions of vv. 7a and 8abc, on the one hand, and v. 12, on the other.

The new unit (vv. 9-13) consists of admonition, prediction, instruction, and promise. The first part of this unit is similar in form to the first unit of the speech, vv. 5b-6. The admonition of v. 9a, "Now watch out for yourselves" ($\beta \lambda \acute{\epsilon} \pi \epsilon \tau \epsilon \delta \grave{\epsilon} \acute{v} \mu \epsilon \hat{\iota} \varsigma \grave{\epsilon} \alpha \upsilon \tau o \acute{v} \varsigma$), is similar to that of v. 5b, "Watch out, so that no one deceives you" ($\beta \lambda \acute{\epsilon} \pi \epsilon \tau \epsilon \mu \acute{\eta} \tau \iota \varsigma \acute{v} \mu \hat{\alpha} \varsigma \pi \lambda \alpha \nu \acute{\eta} \sigma \eta$). As the warning of v. 5b is followed by a prediction explaining the context of the admonition, so also that of v. 9a is followed by an analogous prediction in v. 9b, "They will hand you over, etc." ($\pi \alpha \rho \alpha \delta \acute{\omega} \sigma o \upsilon \sigma \iota \nu \acute{v} \mu \hat{\alpha} \varsigma, \kappa \tau \lambda .$). Verse 10, "And first it is necessary that the good news be proclaimed to all the nations" ($\kappa \alpha \grave{\iota} \epsilon \grave{\iota} \varsigma \pi \acute{\alpha} \nu \tau \alpha \tau \grave{\alpha} \acute{\epsilon} \vartheta \nu \eta \pi \rho \hat{\omega} \tau o \nu \delta \epsilon \hat{\iota} \kappa \eta \rho \upsilon \chi \vartheta \hat{\eta} - \nu \alpha \iota \tau \grave{o} \epsilon \grave{v} \alpha \gamma \gamma \acute{\epsilon} \lambda \iota o \nu$), is a declaration of eschatological teaching, like that of v. 7c, concerning the sequence of events in the time before the divine intervention. The point seems to be that, during the period of political,

102   Contra Marxsen, *Der Evangelist Markus,* 116–17; ET *Mark the Evangelist,* 172–73. His argument is persuasive, however, that the destruction of the temple was one of the last things for Mark, that this destruction was in the immediate future from Mark's point of view, and that thus v. 2 is not a prophecy after the fact (ibid., 113–15; ET 167–70). Cilliers Breytenbach also argues that vv. 14-27 are still future from the point of view of Mark (*Nachfolge und Zukunftserwartung nach Markus: Eine methodenkritische Studie* [AThAnt 71; Zurich: Theologischer Verlag Zürich, 1984] 282).

103   2 Esdr 13:21-58 (note esp. the prediction in vv. 30–31 that the dwellers on the earth will make war on one another, city against city, place against place, people against people, and kingdom against kingdom); 2 Esdr 8:63–9:13 (note esp. the earthquakes,

tumult of peoples, and intrigues of nations in 9:3); *2 Baruch* 25–30 (note esp. the famine and withholding of rain in 27:6 and the earthquakes and terrors in 27:7); *2 Baruch* 70 (note esp. the prediction in 70:8 that everyone who saves himself from the war will die in an earthquake, and he who saves himself from the earthquake will be burned by fire, and he who saves himself from the fire will perish by famine). See also the Jewish oracle in *Sib. Or.* 2:154-76; note the combination of famines and wars (line 155) with deceivers (line 165). For discussion, see Hartman, *Prophecy Interpreted,* 30–31, 71–101.

104   See, e.g., *2 Baruch* 26–30 in which the tribulation has twelve parts. For further examples and discussion, see Adela Yarbro Collins, "Numerical Symbolism in Jewish and Early Christian Apocalyptic Literature," *ANRW* 2.21.2 (1984) 1221–87, esp.

social, and economic upheaval, the task of the followers of Jesus is to be the proclamation of the good news to all the nations and that the occasion for this will be official interrogation by Jewish and various Gentile authorities. Only after this task is accomplished will the divine intervention occur, and only those who do not succumb to the opposition involved will experience that intervention as blessing. It would appear, then, that the events predicted in vv. 9-13 also belong to the period characterized as the "beginning of the birth-pains" (ἀρχὴ ὠδίνων) in v. 8d.

Like those of v. 8, the events predicted in v. 12 are apocalyptic commonplaces.[105] It may have been possible for Mark's audience to consider this prophecy fulfilled in experiences related to persecution, just as Josephus could use similar phrases in describing the internal conflict of the Jewish people during the war with Rome.[106] But again, the primary purpose in evoking such motifs seems to be to place the persecution of the followers of Jesus and the proclaiming of the good news to all nations in the context of the last days, the prelude to the divine intervention. Verse 13 then returns to the specific situation of the followers of Jesus. The statement that you will be hated "on account of my name" (διὰ τὸ ὄνομά μου) is illuminated by 9:41. The latter is a promise of reward to those who give a cup of water "on the ground that you belong to Christ" (ἐν ὀνόματι ὅτι χριστοῦ ἐστε). The analogy between 13:13a and 9:41 supports the hypothesis that the "name" of Jesus referred to in 13:6, if any, is χριστός ("Christ" or "messiah").

This section also portrays the followers of Jesus as sharing in the fate that he suffered. Like him, they "will be handed over" (vv. 9, 11, 12).[107]

■ **14-20** A new unit begins in v. 14, indicated by δέ ("now" or "and" or "but") and the shift in subject matter from the activity of the followers of Jesus and the hard-

ships that they will suffer among the nations to events in Jerusalem and Judea. Verse 14 not only begins a new literary unit in the speech, but it also marks the shift from the discussion of the first stage of the eschatological scenario, the "beginning of the birth-pains" (ἀρχὴ ὠδίνων), to that of the second stage. This shift is evident in the contrasting parallel between v. 14 and v. 7. Verse 7 begins with "Now when you hear" (ὅταν δὲ ἀκούσητε), and v. 14 with "Now when you see" (ὅταν δὲ ἴδητε). In v. 7, the audience is told not to be alarmed, because the end is not yet. On the contrary, in v. 14 and what follows, it is implied that they *should* be alarmed! They are commanded to flee without delay, a woe is pronounced on pregnant and nursing women, and the audience is to pray that the event in question not happen in winter. All these expressions stir the emotions in a way analogous to the rhetorical figure of speech called *exsuscitatio* ("arousal") in *Rhet. Her.* (4.43.55-56).[108] According to the instruction in v. 19, this second stage may be called the "tribulation" (θλῖψις). As with vv. 5b-6, the interpretation of this section requires a judgment about its relation to the social and historical situation of the author of Mark and his perspective on that situation.

As noted above, some have argued that the prediction placed in the mouth of Jesus in v. 2 implies that the temple had already been destroyed when Mark wrote his Gospel.[109] Such a conclusion is not necessary and not the most illuminating hypothesis for the interpretation of vv. 14-20. That the conclusion is not necessary is shown by the comments above and also by a remark of Josephus, who observed that the speeches of John of Gischala seduced most of the youth and incited them to war:

but of the sober and elder men there was not one who did not foresee the future and mourn for the city as if

---

1234–47; reprinted in eadem, *Cosmology and Eschatology*, 55–138, esp. 69–89.

105   *1 Enoch* 100:2; 2 Esdr 5:9; 6:24. Cf. also the Jewish oracle in *Sib. Or.* 2:154-76, especially the remark in lines 158-59 that children will feed on their parents. This apocalyptic motif may have been inspired in part by Mic 7:6; cf. Matt 10:21, 35-36. The particular form it takes in *Sib. Or.* 2.158-59 is similar to Ezek 5:10.

106   Josephus *Bell.* 4.3.2 §§131–34; cf. 5.10.3 §§429–30; 6.3.3–4 §§193–213.

107   See the commentary on 3:19 and 9:31 above and on 15:27 below.

108   Text and trans. from Harry Caplan, [*Cicero*], vol. 1, *Ad Herrennium* (LCL; Cambridge, MA: Harvard University Press; London: Heinemann, 1954) 366–69; this is suggested for v. 18, using the Greek equivalent ἀνάστασις ("arousal"), by Black, "Oration at Olivet," 88.

109   See the commentary on vv. 1-2 above.

it had already met its doom (τῶν δὲ σωφρονούντων καὶ γηραιῶν οὐκ ἦν ὅστις οὐ τὰ μέλλοντα προορώμενος ὡς ἤδη τῆς πόλεως οἰχομένης ἐπένθει). (*Bell.* 4.3.2 §128)[110]

Surely Josephus's remark owes something to hindsight, but once the war had begun, anyone, especially one who knew the Jewish scriptures, could have come to the conclusion that it would end in the destruction of the temple and the city of Jerusalem.

It is necessary, then, to consider what the reference to "the desolating sacrilege" (τὸ βδέλυγμα τῆς ἐρημώσεως) in v. 14a suggests about the historical context of Mark. It has been argued that the parenthesis in v. 14b, "let the reader understand" (ὁ ἀναγινώσκων νοείτω), is strong evidence for the use of a written source, for example, a kind of apocalyptic broadsheet or flier. This argument is not compelling.[111] The clause is better taken as an aside from the evangelist to the individual who read the Gospel aloud to a group of assembled followers of Jesus (directly) and to his audience (indirectly), a hypothesis supported by the concluding statement in v. 37, which makes clear that the speech is directed to a broader audience than the four disciples named in v. 3.

The phrase "the desolating sacrilege" (τὸ βδέλυγμα τῆς ἐρημώσεως) alludes either to the book of Daniel or to an apocalyptic tradition inspired by it.[112] The book of Daniel does not make clear what this abomination was. More information is given in 1 Macc 1:54, "they erected a desolating sacrilege on the altar of burnt offering" (ᾠκοδόμησαν βδέλυγμα ἐρημώσεως ἐπὶ τὸ θυσιαστήριον).[113] This remark may be complemented by the report of Josephus, although he does not use the term "desolating sacrilege" (βδέλυγμα ἐρημώσεως). He

states, "The king also built a pagan altar upon the temple altar, and slaughtered swine thereon" (ἐποικοδομήσας δὲ καὶ τῷ θυσιαστηρίῳ βωμὸν ὁ βασιλεὺς σύας ἐπ᾽ αὐτοῦ κατέσφαξε) (*Ant.* 12.5.4 §253).[114] It seems likely, then, that the term in Daniel originally referred to a pagan altar built upon the altar in the temple in Jerusalem. It is doubtful, however, that the author of Mark was aware of this interpretation. Even if he was aware of it, he may still have preferred another interpretation.

Given the eschatological perspective of Mark and the analogies in the Dead Sea Scrolls, it is likely that the evangelist read the *ex eventu* prophecy of Dan 9:27 as a genuine prophecy of an event to take place in the last days. In the context of vv. 14-20, it is implied that this event will initiate the second stage of the eschatological scenario, the "tribulation" (θλῖψις). Those who understand v. 2 as an *ex eventu* prophecy conclude that v. 14 is another of the same type. But the tribulation inaugurated by this event does not seem to be equivalent to the first Jewish war with Rome as a whole, since at least part of this war belongs to the first stage, the "beginning of the birth-pains" (ἀρχὴ ὠδίνων), as argued above.[115] Some argue that the desolating sacrilege is the destruction of the temple as such, but this theory cannot explain the shift from the neuter noun to the masculine participle or why the sacrilege or abomination is said to be "standing."[116] Another possibility is that the term βδέλυγμα ("sacrilege" or "abomination") refers to Titus's inspection of "the holy place of the sanctuary" (τοῦ ναοῦ τὸ ἅγιον) when the chambers surrounding the temple were already burning (*Bell.* 6.4.7 §§260–61).[117] But what sense would it make to encourage those in Judea to flee

---

110 Text and trans. from Thackeray, *Josephus*, 3:38–39.

111 See "Sources, Composition, and Performance" above; see also Yarbro Collins, *Beginning of the Gospel*, 77–81.

112 The wording of the phrase in Mark 13:14 is closest to Dan 12:11; cf. Dan 9:27; 11:31; 1 Macc 1:54.

113 Text cited from Rahlfs (modified); he reads ᾠκοδόμησεν, following S*; the reading adopted here is from A S^c pl., ᾠκοδόμησαν; trans. from NRSV. See also 1 Macc 6:7.

114 Text and trans. from Ralph Marcus, in Thackeray, *Josephus*, 7:128–31. 2 Macc 6:5 also mentions unlawful sacrifices, but does not mention a new altar

superimposed on that of the temple. For discussion, see Collins, *Daniel*, 357–58.

115 See the commentary on vv. 5-6 and 7-8 above.

116 Lührmann argued that the abomination refers to the destruction of the city and the temple, which had already occurred when Mark was written; the masculine participle represents the Roman general or his army (222).

117 Text and trans. from Thackeray, *Josephus*, 3:450–51. Joel Marcus mentions this possibility, but rejects it ("The Jewish War and the *Sitz im Leben* of Mark," *JBL* 111 [1992] 441–62, esp. 454). Glenn S. Holland argued that the "desolating sacrilege" occurred when

at that late stage of the war? And what would they be fleeing from?[118]

Martin Hengel argued that the perspective of vv. 14-19 does not fit the situation during or after the conquest of the temple and the city, which took place in the period extending from July to September of 70 CE. Since Vespasian had subdued Judea and isolated Jerusalem already in 68 CE, an exhortation to its inhabitants to flee to the mountains in the desert of Judea would already at that time have made little sense. Once the siege was in place, refugees would have had to flee into the arms of the Romans or, if they managed to escape them, they might have encountered the equally murderous *sicarii* in and around Masada. In fact, in the period before the siege, rather than fleeing to the mountains, the rural population fled *into* the city. Those who remained in the countryside, who were not active rebels, no longer had to fear for their lives, and thus flight was more dangerous than staying put. Hengel concluded that the Gospel was written after the inauguration of the siege, between the winter of 68/69 and the winter of 69/70, but in a distant place (that is, in Rome), since the author evidently knew so little about the actual circumstances and events of the war.[119] He also left open the possibility that the vivid imperatives in vv. 15-18 are to be actualized by the audience allegorically.[120]

Hengel himself, however, recognized that the command to flee immediately is combined with a picture of the sudden occurrence of disaster, which is itself incompatible with the approach or siege of a Roman army. He noted that the combination of the elements of sudden-

ness and indeterminate time of occurrence makes the event analogous to the parousia. He concluded, however, that v. 14 therefore has nothing to do with the siege or conquest of the temple by Titus, but rather alludes to the appearance of the Antichrist.[121] If, however, the event in question is a divine intervention in the war that would involve the destruction of the city and its surrounding land, the new situation of massive destruction and confusion might well make flight not only feasible but essential for those destined to survive. The evangelist would then have been calling for a reversal of the movement of the people as well as of their expectation that the city would be protected. This point will be discussed further below.

Joel Marcus has argued that there was a point during the war at which flight from Judea would make sense, namely, during the winter of 67–68, after Eleazar, son of Simon, had moved into the temple but before Vespasian had completely conquered the area around Jerusalem and thus isolated the city.[122] He argued further that the reference to the "abomination of desolation standing where he should not" in v. 14 reflects a series of events, especially the occupation of the temple by Eleazar and his allies in the winter of 67–68. He cited several passages in which Josephus uses the language of defilement to speak of the presence of the revolutionaries in the temple and argued that one of these passages implies that they went where they should not.[123]

This interpretation is not entirely satisfactory. First of all, v. 14 implies that the abomination is standing where it ought not to be in an absolute sense. The passage cited by

---

Titus's soldiers erected their standards in the courtyard of the temple in 70 CE (*The Tradition That You Received from Us: 2 Thessalonians in the Pauline Tradition* [HUTh 24; Tübingen: Mohr Siebeck, 1988] 138).

118 Cf. Marcus, "Jewish War," 454.

119 Martin Hengel, "Entstehungszeit und Situation des Markusevangeliums," in Cancik, *Markus-Philologie*, 1–45, esp. 25–26, 43, 45; ET idem, *Studies in Mark*, 16–17, 28–29.

120 Hengel, "Entstehungszeit," 31; idem, *Studies in Mark*, 20; so also Pesch, *Naherwartungen*, 147–49.

121 Hengel, "Entstehungszeit," 27, 29; idem, *Studies in Mark*, 17–19. For criticism of this hypothesis, see the commentary on vv. 21-23 below.

122 Marcus, "Jewish War," 453–54, with reference to *Bell.* 4.9.1 §§486–90.

123 Marcus, "Jewish War," 454–55. A similar argument

had already been made by Otto Pfleiderer, in an article in which he argued that the verse referring to the abomination of desolation was part of a Jewish-Christian apocalypse, written at the end of 67 CE, which had been combined with eschatological sayings of Jesus ("Ueber die Composition der eschatologicschen Rede Matth. 24, 4ff.," *Jahrbücher für Deutsche Theologie* 13 [1868] 134–49, esp. 139–41). In a later work, Pfleiderer rejected his earlier interpretation of the abomination as the pollution of the temple by the Zealots and argued instead that it alluded to the setting up of a statue in the temple, an event that did not occur during the first Jewish war, but which was feared because of Gaius's attempt to do so earlier (*Das Urchristenthum, seine Schriften und Lehren* [Berlin: Reimer, 1887] 402-7).

Marcus (*Bell.* 4.3.10 §§182–83)[124] does not imply that the revolutionaries should not "walk about in the midst of the holy places" (ἐμπεριπατεῖν μέσοις τοῖς ἁγίοις) in an absolute sense, but only that they should not have been there with hands still hot from the blood of their countrymen whom they had slaughtered. In any case, the burden of the passage is to point out the irony of the fact that the friends of the people (the Romans) were outside the walls of the city, whereas the nation's enemies (the Zealots) were inside.

The hypothesis that the "desolating sacrilege" (βδέ-λυγμα τῆς ἐρημώσεως) is a statue of a deity fits the remark that it was "where it/he should not be" (ὅπου οὐ δεῖ) better than the theory that it reflects the Zealot occupation of the temple. Such a statue was tolerable in a sanctuary dedicated to the relevant deity but not in the temple of Jerusalem. Further, the modifier "standing" (ἑστηκότα) fits a statue better than a political or military leader. Finally, Marcus dates Mark to a time shortly after the destruction of the temple in 70 CE.[125] What relevance would a command to flee from Judea have at that time? This problem is especially acute if the aside to the reader in v. 14 was composed by Mark, as has been argued here and elsewhere.[126] This aside implies that the abomination and the command to flee were of immediate relevance to the audience at the time of writing.

The hypothesis that the "sacrilege" refers to a statue is supported by one well-attested usage of the term βδέ-λυγμα in the LXX, namely, to designate the image of a foreign god.[127] Especially significant for v. 14 is the fact that the term may refer both to the image and to the deity that it represents.[128] Thus, the shift from the neuter noun βδέλυγμα ("sacrilege") to the masculine participle ἑστηκώς ("standing") may be explained in terms of this equivalence. The masculine participle would thus refer to the divinized emperor or to the deity he claimed to be or to represent.[129]

Another possibility was suggested by Günther Zuntz. He argued that v. 14 alludes to Gaius Caligula's attempt to have his statue set up in the temple in Jerusalem. He concluded from this allusion that the whole Gospel was written in 40 CE.[130] Others who argue that v. 14 refers to Caligula's attempt have concluded that the source used by Mark in chapter 13 was written in 40 CE.[131] Neither of the latter two hypotheses is compelling. The position taken here is that Mark was written in the late 60s CE and that Caligula's attempt on the temple was a widespread living memory at that time. In any case, Zuntz's theory was that the masculine participle represents "the statue of the king/emperor" (ὁ ἀνδριὰς τοῦ βασιλέως).[132] Although he does not say so, the use of the noun ἀνδριάς ("statue") by Philo and Josephus in their accounts of this crisis supports the idea that this is another credible way to explain the shift from the neuter to the masculine.[133]

Doubts must also be raised about the theory held by Hengel and others that Mark was written during the Jewish war, but in Rome. If the interpretation proposed above of vv. 5b-6 is correct, that the warning expressed there concerns messianic pretenders during the Jewish war, then another hypothesis fits better with those verses, namely, that the evangelist was aware of the

---

124 Text and trans. (modified) from Thackeray, *Josephus,* 3:56–57.

125 Marcus, "Jewish War," 460.

126 See "Sources, Composition, and Performance" above and Yarbro Collins, *Beginning of the Gospel,* 78, 85–86.

127 Deut 7:25-26; 27:14-15; 29:15-16 (vv. 16-17 in English); Isa 2:8, 20; 44:19; cf. Jer 7:30; Ezek 8:10; 20:30.

128 Deut 32:16-17; 3 Kgdms 11:6 (v. 5 in English), 33; 4 Kgdms 23:13; Wis 14:8-11.

129 The reference may be to an image of the emperor as Zeus. Compare the description of Philopator, the Ptolemaic king who ruled from 221 to 205 BCE, as a "living image of Zeus" (εἰκὼν ζῶσα τοῦ Δι[ός]) (S. R. Llewelyn, ed., *New Documents Illustrating Early Christianity,* vol. 9: *A Review of the Greek Inscriptions and Papyri Published in 1986–87* [North Ryde, N.S.W., Australia: Ancient History Documentary Research Centre, Macquarie University; Grand Rapids: Eerdmans, 2002] 36–38).

130 Günther Zuntz, "Wann wurde das Evangelium Marci geschrieben?" in Cancik, *Markus-Philologie,* 47–71, esp. 47–48.

131 See "Sources, Composition, and Performance" above.

132 Zuntz, "Wann wurde das Evangelium Marci geschrieben," 47–48.

133 Philo *Legat.* 29 §188; Josephus *Ant.* 18.8.2 §261.

course of events in the war and was writing in some proximity to them. He wrote not primarily to portray present or past events as prophecy after the fact but to place in the mouth of Jesus a prophecy of the turning point in the war which was still future from his perspective.

When the desolating sacrilege appears, the faithful must take to headlong flight. Hartman has suggested that this flight is patterned on Lot's flight from Sodom. The idea that links Genesis 19, Dan 9:27, and Mark 13 is that an ungodly place or thing will be destroyed by God's wrathful judgment. The flight commanded in vv. 14-16, therefore, is a matter of escaping from the punishment of God that will befall the ungodly thing.[134] But Hartman did not address the question how this expected punishment relates to the historical situation of Mark. As argued above, Mark expected the Romans to set up a statue in the temple. The apocalyptic rhetoric of chapter 13 implies that this act would evoke the wrathful punishment of God, that is, the destruction of the temple and its environs by fire, a destruction analogous to that of Sodom. Jan Lambrecht concluded that, although the evangelist adapted tradition that used the story of Lot typologically, he did not preserve a clear allusion to the story. Nevertheless, Lambrecht points out that the words "on account of the elect" (διὰ τοὺς ἐκλεκτούς) in v. 20 recall the "righteous" (δίκαιοι) in Genesis 18.[135]

Such an expectation fits the typological thinking of apocalyptic writers and early Christians. The Book of the Watchers (1 Enoch 1-36) seems to imply that there will be a catastrophe in the last days like the flood in the time of Noah (1 Enoch 1:2-9).[136] The Synoptic Sayings Source (Q), followed by Matthew and Luke, compared the arrival of the days of the Son of Man to the flood in the days of Noah, and Luke adds (or also preserves) a

comparison to the destruction of Sodom, when fire and brimstone rained from heaven.[137] Furthermore, Josephus gives ample evidence that those who rebelled against Rome expected a divine intervention during the war that would preserve the temple from destruction. This expectation is clearly described in *Bell.* 5.11.2 §459. Two other passages allude to it (*Bell.* 5.7.3 §306; 6.2.1 §98).[138] It is likely that this intervention was also expected to be the inauguration of the new age.

In an expression of pathos or emotion (πάθος) analogous to vv. 14-18, Josephus stated his belief that, had the Romans delayed in destroying the city, either the earth would have opened up and swallowed it, or it would have been swept away by a flood, or it would have had a share in the thunderbolts of Sodom (*Bell.* 5.13.6 §566). In addition to the well-known stories of Noah and Lot, Josephus alludes here typologically to the story of Korah and his companions in Numbers 16. He presented these hypothetical disasters as punishment upon the leaders of the revolt, especially John of Gischala, for what Josephus perceived to be temple robbery or sacrilege.[139] Thus, both Josephus and Mark imagined a destructive, miraculous, divine intervention against the city, but for different reasons and perhaps with a different degree of seriousness.

The designation of the faithful as "the elect" (οἱ ἐκλεκτοί) occurs only in this chapter of Mark (vv. 20, 22, 27). The oracle that introduces the book known as *1 Enoch* (chapters 1–5) uses the term "the elect" or "the chosen" (οἱ ἐκλεκτοί) as the designation of the eschatological community, who are identified as the righteous remnant of Israel (1:1, 3, 8; 5:7-8).[140] The Apocalypse of Weeks (1 Enoch 93:1-10; 91:11-17) also uses the term for the eschatological community that will receive revelation in the end-time (93:1, 10).[141] The Parables or Similitudes

---

134 Hartman, *Prophecy Interpreted*, 151-54.

135 Lambrecht, *Redaktion*, 159, 165 n. 2. On the use of the term "the elect" (ἐκλεκτοί), see below.

136 See also the description of the renovation of the earth after the flood in 10:16—11:2, which seems to apply also the definitive new age.

137 Matt 24:37-39||Luke 17:26-27 on Noah; Luke 17:28 on Lot. See Robinson et al., *Critical Edition of Q*, 512-17.

138 Schwier argues that Josephus tried to minimize it (*Tempel und Tempelzerstörung*, 30 n. 14). Further, the way in which Simon, son of Gioras, is described as presenting himself to the Romans seems to indicate

that he thought of himself as the messianic king and expected a divine intervention (7.2.2 §29). Josephus says that he wore a purple mantle and emerged from the ground on the very spot where the temple had stood.

139 Ἱεροσυλία (*Bell.* 5.13.6 §562).

140 Nickelsburg, *1 Enoch 1*, 135, 162–63. See also 25:5; Nickelsburg, *1 Enoch 1*, 315. All of these verses survive in Greek; for the Greek text, see Black, *Apocalypsis Henochi Graece*, 19–20; Denis and Janssens, *Concordance grecque*, 818–22.

141 Nickelsburg, *1 Enoch 1*, 135, 441, 447–48. The Greek text of these verses has not survived.

of Enoch also use the term "the elect" or "the chosen," along with "the righteous," for the eschatological community.[142] The community (יחד) of the Dead Sea Scrolls considered itself to be a remnant of the people of Israel with whom God had made a new covenant.[143] In some texts, the community refers to itself as "the chosen" (בחירים).[144]

The author of Mark was familiar with the designation of the eschatological community as "the elect" in written or oral contexts and used the term to describe the faithful who would endure to the end and be gathered by the angels that the Son of Man would send out when he came with the clouds.[145]

Popular Prophets in the First Century CE

Josephus provides an account of the prophet Theudas, who was active while Fadus was governor of Judea (44–46 CE). Josephus labels him an "imposter" (γόης) but reports that he claimed to be a "prophet" (προφήτης) (*Ant.* 20.5.1 §§97–98).[146] Although Josephus does not use the term, Theudas may have presented his predicted parting of the Jordan River as a "sign" (σημεῖον). Josephus does comment that he deceived many (πολλοὺς ἠπάτησεν). In a discussion of events in the 50s, Josephus speaks of "deceivers and imposters" (πλάνοι γὰρ ἄνθρωποι καὶ ἀπατεῶνες), who under the pretense of divine inspiration advocated revolutionary changes. These led many people out into the desert where, as they had predicted, God would show them "signs of deliverance" (σημεῖα ἐλευθερίας) (*Bell.* 2.13.4 §§258–60).[147] Immediately after this summary, Josephus gives a brief account of an Egyptian who, like Theudas, claimed to be a prophet. Josephus's evaluation is similar to those already cited; he calls the Egyptian a "false prophet" (ψευδοπροφήτης) and an "imposter" (γόης) and speaks of those deceived by him (ἠπατημένοι) (*Bell.* 2.13.5 §§261–63).[148] The account in the *Jewish War* implies that this leader had kingly aspirations and that he planned to take Jerusalem by force (2.13.5 §§262–63). The account in the *Antiquities*, however, implies that he promised to perform a miraculous deed, namely, to cause the walls of Jerusalem to fall at his command (20.8.6 §170). Once again, although Josephus does not use the word, such an event may have been promised as a "sign" (σημεῖον).

In Josephus's account of the events of 70 CE, when the temple was already on fire, he tells how a large number of people had taken refuge on the one remaining portico of the outer court. When the Roman soldiers set fire to it, they all perished. Josephus blames their destruction on a certain false prophet (ψευδοπροφήτης τις) who had proclaimed that very day to the people in the city that God commanded them to go up to the sanctuary where they would receive "signs of their deliverance" (τὰ σημεῖα τῆς σωτηρίας) (*Bell.* 6.5.2 §§283–85).[149]

Very interesting in light of the pairing of false messiahs and false prophets in Mark 13:22 is Josephus's

---

142 *1 Enoch* 38:2-4; 39:6-7; 40:5; 41:2; 48:1, 9; 50:1; 51:5; 56:6, 8; 58:1-3; 60:6, 8; 61:4, 12-13; 62:7-8, 11-15; 70:3; Nickelsburg, *1 Enoch 1*, 135–36. The Greek text of these verses has not survived.

143 James C. VanderKam, *The Dead Sea Scrolls Today* (Grand Rapids: Eerdmans; London: SPCK, 1994) 111.

144 1QpHab 5:4; 9:11-12; 10:12-13; 1QpMic (1Q14) frg. 10, lines 5-6; 4QpNah (4Q169) frgs. 1-2, 2:8; on these texts, respectively, see Maurya P. Horgan, *Pesharim: Qumran Interpretations of Biblical Books* (CBQMS 8; Washington, DC: Catholic Biblical Association of America, 1979) 15, 32; 18, 44; 19, 48; 57, 61; 162, 170; eadem, "Habakkuk Pesher (1QpHab)," in Charlesworth, *Dead Sea Scrolls*, 6B:168–69, 176–77, 178–79; eadem, "Micah Pesher 1 (1Q14 = 1QpMic)," in Charlesworth, ibid., 134–35; eadem, "Nahum Pesher (4Q169 = 4QpNah)," in Charlesworth, ibid., 146–47.

145 Brandenburger assigned vv. 20 and 27 to a written source used by Mark, but v. 22 to Markan redaction (*Markus 13 und die Apokalyptik*, 23–24, 167). On the use of a written source in this chapter, see "Sources, Composition, and Performance" above.

146 Text and trans. from Louis Feldman, in Thackeray, *Josephus*, 9:440–43. Theudas is mentioned also in the Acts of the Apostles (5:36), but his activity is misdated there. See also the section of the introduction above on "Jesus as Prophet"; Horsley and Hanson, *Bandits*, 164–67.

147 Text and trans. (modified) from Thackeray, *Josephus*, 2:422–25.

148 Text and trans. (modified) from Thackeray, *Josephus*, 2:424–25; cf. *Ant.* 20. 8.6 §§169–71. See also the section of the introduction above on "Jesus as Prophet"; Horsley and Hanson, *Bandits*, 167–70.

149 Text and trans. (modified) from Thackeray, *Josephus*, 3:458–59.

remark that numerous prophets were instigated by "the tyrants" (οἱ τύραννοι) to create the expectation in the people of imminent divine aid (*Bell.* 6.5.2 §286).[150] It is likely that such prophets and the messianic leader they supported, Simon son of Gioras, actually believed that God would intervene on their behalf. But from Josephus's point of view they acted in bad faith; he calls them deceivers and pretended messengers of the deity (*Bell.* 6.5.3 §288). He then narrates a series of τέρατα ("wonders" or "portents") which these prophets apparently interpreted positively, but which Josephus argues were actually signs of the coming destruction (*Bell.* 6.5.3 §§288–300).

■ **21-23** Verse 21 is a variant of a Q saying. Its alleged "secondary" form, however, is not sufficient to support the hypothesis that Mark knew a written copy of Q.[151] The notion that false prophets will come and lead people astray by performing signs and wonders is based, at least in part, on Deut 13:2-6 (1-5 in English versions).[152] The motif became widespread in early Christian literature, especially in relation to the final eschatological adversary, later called the Antichrist (2 Thess 2:9-10; cf. Rev. 13:13-15).

Many scholars have treated vv. 5-6 and vv. 21-22 as doublets.[153] There is indeed a similarity between the warning about those who will come "in my name" (ἐπὶ τῷ ὀνόματί μου) in vv. 5b-6 and the warning about false messiahs and false prophets in vv. 21-22. As argued above, however, the prediction in the form of a warning in vv. 5b-6 is a prophecy after the fact that reflects the rise of messianic leaders during the first Jewish war with Rome. Some of those who take vv. 5-6 as prophecy after the fact assume that vv. 21-22 is a similar *ex eventu* prophecy and that the individuals alluded to are the same in both passages.

Lambrecht, for example, concluded that one should not emphasize the temporal aspect of καὶ τότε ("and at that time" or "and then") in v. 21a. Rather, v. 21 should

be taken as a downward movement from the climax in the preceding section and, as a repetition of a theme, it is also a rounding off, an *inclusio*. He argued that vv. 5b-23a constitute a unity with the schema a b c b' a'.[154] He thus inferred that vv. 21-22 do not describe events happening later than those of vv. 5-6; but he concluded that the events of vv. 14-20 happen later than those of vv. 7-8![155] The words καὶ τότε ("and at that time" or "and then") in v. 21a create a problem for this interpretation.

As argued above, vv. 5b-13 describe the first stage of the end-time, the "beginning of the birth-pains" (ἀρχὴ ὠδίνων) (v. 8). The second stage, the "tribulation" (θλῖψις) (v. 19), is described in vv. 14-20. The question then arises whether the appearance of the false messiahs and prophets in vv. 21-22 is a flashback to the first stage, belongs to the second stage, or constitutes the beginning of a third stage. A crucial issue in arriving at a conclusion on this matter is whether τότε in v. 21 means "at that time" or "then, thereupon."[156] Since v. 24 introduces the appearance of the Son of Man as taking place "after that tribulation," the meaning of τότε in v. 21 is most likely "at that time." In other words, it is predicted that the false messiahs and prophets will arrive during the tribulation, but those who are to come "in my name," according to v. 6, make their appearance during the first stage, the "beginning of the birth-pains." It would seem, then, that the two predictions do not concern the same persons, the same events, or the same historical situation, but that the experiences upon which the first is based, along with tradition, provide a model for the second.[157]

One might object that the signs and wonders described by Josephus in his account of the fall of Jerusalem in 70 CE so illuminate Mark 13:21-22 that the latter passage must reflect those events and thus have been written after 70. It is true that the first and most dramatic incident took place in 70 when parts of the temple grounds were already burning (*Bell.* 6.5.2

150 Text and trans. from Thackeray, *Josephus*, 3:458–59.

151 Contra Fleddermann, *Mark and Q*, 199–201; Neirynck is also skeptical about Mark's use of Q, at least in this case (ibid., 294). On the form of the saying in Q, see Robinson et al., *Critical Edition of Q*, 502.

152 The terms σημεῖον ("sign") and τέρας ("wonder") appear in Deut 13:2 LXX.

153 E.g., Kelber; see "Sources, Composition, and Performance" above.

154 Lambrecht, *Redaktion*, 168–69, 173.

155 Ibid., 295.

156 See BAGD, s.v.

157 Marxsen argued similarly (*Der Evangelist Markus*, 126 n. 1; *Mark the Evangelist*, 185 n. 132), as did Breytenbach (*Nachfolge und Zukunftserwartung*, 309).

§285),[158] but the subsequent comment concerning the collaboration between messianic pretenders and popular prophets probably refers to a longer period and not just to the final months, weeks, or days of the war (*Bell.* 6.5.2 §286).[159] This conclusion is supported by the following digression on portents, signs, and oracles (*Bell.* 6.5.3-4 §§288–315).[160] Josephus describes at least one portent that occurred at the Feast of Unleavened Bread before the war began and the appearance of a comet that lasted a year.[161]

Apparently, the evangelist imagined that, during the tribulation, a yet greater number of still more impressive and powerful messianic pretenders and popular prophets would arise. It should also be noted that the appearance of multiple false messiahs and false prophets at this point in the speech undercuts the hypothesis that the abomination in v. 14 is *the* Antichrist.[162]

The instruction concerning the second stage, the "tribulation," ends in v. 23 with a dramatic warning, "As for you, watch out then" (ὑμεῖς δὲ βλέπετε), and a summary, "I have told you everything beforehand" (προείρηκα ὑμῖν πάντα).[163] The latter summary statement does not imply that everything described up to this point is prophecy *ex eventu*.[164] The reason for a concluding formula at this point is that it is only during the first two stages that human beings still have the opportunity to choose a course of action in relation to the eschatological events. As Lambrecht pointed out, the section describing the arrival of the Son of Man excludes all human activity.[165]

■ **24-27** The interpretation of the tribulation offered above implies that the evangelist understood that second stage of the end-time as the execution of divine judgment. The subsequent manifestation of the Son of Man constitutes the third stage of the eschatological period, in which divine intervention for the salvation of the elect occurs. The temporal indicator, "But in those days after that tribulation" (ἀλλὰ ἐν ἐκείναις ταῖς ἡμέραις μετὰ τὴν θλῖψιν ἐκείνην), and the shift in subject matter in v. 24a mark the beginning of a new unit.

The cosmic phenomena predicted in vv. 24b-25 are typical of descriptions of theophany in older writings, but they had come to function as signs of the eschatological divine intervention in Jewish apocalyptic literature.[166] The appearance of the Son of Man in v. 26 is thus characterized as an eschatological divine intervention. The description of the gathering of the elect in v. 27 makes clear that this intervention is conceived by the evangelist as oriented to the salvation of the faithful rather than the judgment of sinners.[167] Such an orientation makes sense if the judgment has already been predicted as belonging to the second stage; the judgment of sinners is associated with the fiery destruction of the temple and its environs in vv. 14-20.[168] For these reasons, vv. 24-27 should be taken not only as a separate literary unit but also as the portrayal of the final stage in the eschatological drama.

As we have seen, chapter 13 involves a three-part eschatological scenario.[169] Hartman showed that a five-stage scenario could be inferred from a range of Jewish apocalyptic texts, but that all five stages or themes do not occur in every text. His five constituents are (1) the

---

158 See "Popular Prophets in the First Century CE" above.

159 The comment in §287 seems to return to the particular incident recounted in §285.

160 The term τέρατα ("wonders" or "portents") is used in 6.5.3 §288 and often; the term σημεῖα ("signs") in 6.5.4 §315.

161 The former is recounted in *Bell.* 6.5.3 §290; the latter in §289.

162 So also Lambrecht, *Redaktion*, 152 n. 1.

163 The drama of the warning is due in part to the emphatic superfluity of the ὑμεῖς; see Black, "Oration at Olivet," 88.

164 According to Lambrecht, προείρηκα ("I have told") is partly retrospective (*Redaktion*, 172 n. 1).

165 Ibid., 294.

166 Hartman, *Prophecy Interpreted*, 71–77; Brandenburger, *Markus 13 und die Apokalyptik*, 12, 56–65.

167 On the term οἱ ἐκλεκτοί ("the elect"), see the commentary on vv. 14-20 above.

168 The third person plural "they will see" (ὄψονται) in v. 26 may include a reference to the enemies of Jesus and his followers (cf. 14:62), but the emphasis is on the gathering of the elect, not the disconcerting or punishing of the wicked. Mark often uses an impersonal third person plural verb as equivalent to the passive; thus the trans. "will be seen" above.

169 Breytenbach, following Hahn, argues for a two-part scenario, the "beginning of the birth pangs" (v. 8) and "those days" (vv. 17-27) (*Nachfolge und Zukunftserwartung*, 283).

preliminary time of evil, (2) divine intervention, (3) the judgment, (4) the fate of sinners, and (5) the joy of the elect.[170] The eschatological scenario presupposed by the book of Revelation involves three stages: (1) persecution, (2) judgment of the persecutors, and (3) salvation of the faithful.[171] In the scenario of Mark 13, the first stage, the "beginning of the birth-pains," includes the themes of a preliminary time of evil (the beginning of the war, the deception of false messiahs in vv. 5b-6) as well as persecution (vv. 9-13). The second stage, the "tribulation," combines the themes of divine intervention, judgment, and the fate of sinners. The judgment on the city would also affect representative leaders of the persecution against the followers of Jesus, among both the Jews and the Romans. The third stage involves the appearance of the Son of Man, described in theophanic terms, and the gathering of the elect (vv. 24-27). Chapter 13 thus contains two divine interventions, an act of divine judgment without a mediator and an act of salvation through the mediation of the Son of Man and his angels. Jewish apocalypses involve both direct and mediated divine interventions, as Hartman has shown. That there should be more than one divine intervention in an early Christian apocalyptic text is not surprising, as the example of the book of Revelation amply shows.

The apocalyptic Son of Man saying in v. 26 is a clear allusion to and interpretation of Dan 7:13. It also narrates proleptically the coming of the Son of Man that was alluded to in 8:38. The prophetic saying of 8:38 lacks the detail of the clouds, which is present in 13:26. Both sayings include the motif of glory, but 8:38 specifies what is only implicit in 13:26, namely, that the glory belongs ultimately to the Father of the Son of Man. The saying of 8:38 states that the Son of Man will come "with the holy angels" (μετὰ τῶν ἀγγέλων τῶν ἁγίων). This feature is implied by 13:27, which states that the Son of Man will send the angels to gather the elect when he comes. The description of the coming of the Son of Man here is also related to the account of the parousia in 1 Thess 4:13-18.[172]

The focus of v. 27 is on the salvation of the remnant of Israel, "the elect."[173] The description of this salvation here, however, alludes to the motif of the gathering of all the exiles of Israel from the nations with the words "from the four winds, from (one) end of the earth to the other" (ἐκ τῶν τεσσάρων ἀνέμων ἀπ᾽ ἄκρου γῆς ἕως ἄκρου οὐρανοῦ).[174]

■ **28-31** These verses constitute an argument supporting imminent expectation. The use of δέ ("now" or "and" or "but") and the change in subject matter from the arrival of the Son of Man to the comparison involving the fig tree indicate that a new unit begins with v. 28. The comparison itself is contained in vv. 28-29. This comparison is followed closely, without a connecting conjunction or particle, by a solemn confirmatory saying (v. 30). A second solemn confirmation follows (v. 31), whose contrasting clauses are linked by δέ ("but"). This saying takes up one of the verbs of the previous saying, "pass away" (παρέρχεσθαι), and uses it in a related but different way. Another unit begins in v. 32 with δέ ("but"), which signals a contrast with the previous two sayings but also the introduction of a new topic, the time of the return of the Son of Man.

In the transition from v. 27 to v. 28, the language shifts from mythic-realistic prediction of events to a comparison between the sequence of events in nature and the sequence of events in human "history." The force and placement of the comparison may be illuminated by Aristotle's discussion of proofs (πίστεις) common to all kinds of rhetoric.[175] The Markan Jesus is, of course, neither exhorting nor dissuading, praising nor blaming, accusing nor defending, in the way that the speakers Aristotle had in mind would do.[176] He is rather revealing a divinely determined course of events and advocating a

---

170 Hartman, *Prophecy Interpreted*, 23–49.

171 Adela Yarbro Collins, *The Combat Myth in the Book of Revelation* (HDR 9; Missoula, MT: Scholars Press/Harvard Theological Review, 1976, reprinted Eugene, OR: Wipf & Stock, 2001).

172 See "History of the Tradition" above.

173 On "the elect" as the designation of the eschatological community understood as the faithful remnant of Israel, see the commentary on vv. 14-20 above.

174 Cf. Isa 11:11-12; Ezek 39:27-28; Hos 11:10-11; *1 Enoch* 57; 90:33; 2 Esdr 13:12-13, 39-40; Brandenburger, *Markus 13 und die Apokalyptik*, 60; Stone, *Fourth Ezra*, 387, 404.

175 Aristotle *Rhet.* 2.20 (1393a-1394a).

176 *Rhet.* 2.1 (1377b).

particular understanding of these events and a particular course of action in relation to them. Although Mark's Jesus speaks with authority rather than attempting to give evidence and proofs for his teaching, the speech does manifest attempts to awaken conviction in the audience and acceptance of the instruction and commands to action. One way in which this is done is the authoritative actualization of scripture. This approach is especially characteristic of vv. 7-8, 12-13, 14-20, 21-23, and 24-27. A different approach is taken in vv. 28-37. This approach has some affinities with Aristotle's advice about proofs.

Aristotle states that the proofs common to all sorts of speeches are of two kinds: the example (παράδειγμα) and the enthymeme (ἐνθύμημα), which includes the maxim (γνώμη). He suggests that there are two forms of examples: one involving things that have actually happened, the other fictional. Fictional examples are then divided into comparisons (παραβολαί) and fables (λόγοι). As an example of a comparison, Aristotle refers to the point made by Socrates, that choosing magistrates by lot would be as foolish as choosing athletes for competitions by lot.[177] This instance shows that the typical comparison, although invented by the speaker, is grounded in the normal events of daily life.

The παραβολή ("comparison" or "parable") in vv. 28-29 is similar. The starting point is a common phenomenon in nature, the invariable sequence of the fig tree sprouting, putting forth leaves, and the arrival of summer. The argument is that the events described in vv. 5b-27 will follow one another just as inevitably. The evangelist, whether consciously or unconsciously, has adapted to the context of apocalyptic rhetoric the commonplace cited by Aristotle: "for as a rule the future resembles the past" (ὅμοια γὰρ ὡς ἐπὶ τὸ πολὺ τὰ μέλλοντα τοῖς γεγονόσιν).[178]

The ταῦτα γινόμενα ("these things happening") of v. 29 corresponds to the sprouting of the fig tree and its putting forth leaves. The appearance of the Son of Man corresponds to the arrival of summer. It could be debated whether ταῦτα γινόμενα refers to all the events described in vv. 5b-25 or only to those in vv. 24b-25, which immediately precede the appearance of the Son of Man. It is likely that the phrase refers to all the events of vv. 5b-25, since it takes up the disciples' questions in v. 4, which also use the word ταῦτα ("these things" or "this"). Thus, the comparison is a kind of recapitulation of the speech up to that point. It is clear, however, that the response of Jesus does not correspond exactly to the questions of the disciples. As pointed out above, the first question asks when the destruction of the temple, predicted in v. 2, will take place. The second asks what the sign will be when the complex of eschatological events associated with the destruction of the temple is about to take place. In the part of the speech that extends from v. 5b to v. 27, Jesus does not name one event as *the* sign but rather a whole series of events that function as signs, although the occurrence alluded to in v. 14a is highlighted as particularly significant by the aside to the audience. Furthermore, the part of the comparison that makes the analogy (v. 29) puts the emphasis on the arrival of the Son of Man ("he is near, at the door"), rather than on the destruction of the temple. These discrepancies are not surprising and should not be used to distinguish sources from redaction or to infer the assertions of alleged opponents of Mark. Rather, they are normal in a rhetorical situation in which the authoritative teacher knows more than the disciples and answers their questions in a way intended to lead them closer to a full understanding of the issues involved.

The placement of the comparison in vv. 28-29 is also illuminated by the discussion of Aristotle. He argues that enthymemes should be placed first in a speech, since they are the more important proofs. The prophetic actualization of scripture functions in Mark 13 in a way analogous to the enthymemes. According to Aristotle, the examples should be used as a kind of epilogue to the enthymemes. Even a single example is effective at the end of a speech, like a single trustworthy witness.[179]

The speech moves from the quasi-argumentative mode employed in vv. 28-29 back to the mode of authoritative revelation in the two sayings of vv. 30 and 31. The saying of v. 30 confirms imminent expectation of the return of the Son of Man in a way analogous to the saying of 9:1. In both cases, imminent expectation is

177   *Rhet.* 2.20.1–4 (1393a-1393b).
178   *Rhet.* 2.20.8 (1394a); text and trans. (modified) from John Henry Freese, *Aristotle*, vol. 22, *The "Art" of* *Rhetoric* (LCL; Cambridge: Harvard University Press; London: Heinemann, 1926) 276–77.
179   *Rhet.* 2.20.9 (1394a).

legitimated by a solemn statement of Jesus. In the saying of 13:31, the speaker legitimates his own words and affirms their eternal validity. This saying is similar to the words of the angel in Rev 19:9b, to the words of God in Rev 21:5b, and to the words of the angel in Rev 22:6a.

These sayings do not necessarily imply that the destruction of Jerusalem had already taken place and that the assumption of the close connection of the end with that destruction had been called into question by events. One should not infer the position of opponents of Mark from these sayings. Rather, they may be understood more simply and more in keeping with the rest of the speech by taking them as consolation to those who are undergoing the hardships described in vv. 9-13. Their identity as belonging to Christ (cf. 13:13a with 9:41) and their teaching will be confirmed, their suffering will end, and all this soon, in their lifetimes. The two sayings make this point in an effective, hyperbolic, and emotional way.

■ **32-36** These verses make an argument for watchfulness in light of indefinite imminence. The question when the Son of Man would appear was already addressed indirectly in vv. 28-31. His appearance will follow the events predicted in vv. 5b-25 according to the analogy drawn in v. 29, and it will surely occur before the generation addressed by Jesus dies out (v. 30). The question exactly when the Son of Man would come is addressed in the last section of the speech (vv. 32-36). The opening saying declares that no one knows the exact time, not even the angels in heaven or the Son; only the Father knows it. This saying suggests that the date of the arrival of the Son of Man is a deeper and better-kept secret than the identity of Jesus, since not only Jesus but also the unclean spirits know who he is.[180]

The saying of v. 32 should not be understood as expressive of an alleged antiapocalyptic attitude on the part of the evangelist or as his attempt to dampen imminent expectation. That the evangelist shared the perspective of imminent expectation is amply shown by the saying in v. 30. Rather, the saying of v. 32 expresses oppo-

sition to the activity of calculating the date of the end and even to the impulse to do so. Such opposition is not antiapocalyptic but is characteristic of some forms of apocalyptic thinking and writing.[181] The calculation of the time of the end is reflected in the closing remarks of the angel in Dan 12:11-13. One calculation is given in v. 11 (1,290 days) and another in v. 12 (1,335 days). The most likely explanation is that, when the first deadline passed, the end was recalculated.[182] This passage in Daniel, along with 9:24-27, has given rise to many attempts to calculate the end and to divide history into periods.[183] Since expectation of the actualization of the desolating sacrilege of Dan 12:11 was alive in the evangelist and probably also in his audience, it may be that the impulse to calculate the end was present in his audience as well. The saying in v. 32 either responds to such an impulse or attempts to prevent it from arising. The saying may be an attempt to explain why Jesus did not make a specific prediction about the exact time at which the Son of Man would return. Or it may simply reflect a conviction about the limits of apocalyptic revelation.

This saying regarding the lack of knowledge concerning the time of the arrival of the Son of Man (v. 32) is followed immediately by its application to the behavior of Jesus' audience (v. 33a): "Watch out, stay awake" ($\beta\lambda\acute{\epsilon}\pi\epsilon\tau\epsilon$, $\mathring{\alpha}\gamma\rho\upsilon\pi\nu\epsilon\hat{\iota}\tau\epsilon$). The close connection between the two verses is indicated by the explanatory statement: "for you do not know when the time is" ($o\mathring{\upsilon}\kappa$ $o\mathring{\iota}\delta\alpha\tau\epsilon$ $\gamma\mathring{\alpha}\rho$ $\pi\acute{o}\tau\epsilon$ $\mathring{o}$ $\kappa\alpha\iota\rho\acute{o}\varsigma$ $\mathring{\epsilon}\sigma\tau\iota\nu$) (v. 33b). The asyndeton in v. 33a makes the utterance more vigorous and emphatic by producing the impression of a vehemence due to repeated outbursts of emotion.[184]

The imperatives of v. 33a recapitulate a theme developed earlier in the speech; in fact, the command "Watch out" ($\beta\lambda\acute{\epsilon}\pi\epsilon\tau\epsilon$) opens the speech (v. 5b). In vv. 5b and 23a, the command is to beware of deceivers. In v. 9a, it concerns proper behavior in the context of persecution. In v. 33a, the command is generalized to express the attitude that the followers of Jesus should adopt between the

---

180 See 1:23-24; 1:34; 3:11-12; 5:7; and the commentary on these verses above.

181 See, e.g., 2 Esdr 4:52; cf. 4:21.

182 See Collins, *Daniel*, 400–401.

183 See Yarbro Collins, "Numerical Symbolism," 1224–33, reprinted in eadem, *Cosmology and Eschatology*, 58–69.

184 Quintilian describes the effect of both asyndeton and polysyndeton in this way (9.3.50–54); this figure is pointed out by Black, "Oration at Olivet," 86. On asyndeton, see Smyth §3016; on polysyndeton, ibid., §3043.

resurrection of Jesus and his arrival as Son of Man. In this verse, "Watch out" (βλέπετε) is supplemented with the command "stay awake" (ἀγρυπνεῖτε), which points ahead to the comparison in vv. 34-36.

The reason given for the two commands, "for you do not know when the time is" (οὐκ οἴδατε γὰρ πότε ὁ καιρός ἐστιν) (v. 33b), indicates another shift from the language of authoritative pronouncement to a quasi-argumentative mode. The two imperatives may be seen as a recapitulatory statement of a theme or thesis: it is necessary for you to be on your guard and to keep awake. This statement is first defended with a reason (v. 33b) and then with a comparison. The theme is restated in v. 35a, "So keep awake" (γρηγορεῖτε οὖν), and the original reason is restated and elaborated in vv. 35b-36. The extension of the theme from the fictional audience (the four disciples mentioned in v. 3) to the actual audience (those who read the Gospel of Mark or hear it read aloud) functions as the ending of the section and of the speech as a whole (v. 37).[185]

The comparison in vv. 34-36 is somewhat less straightforward than the one in vv. 28-29, since the main clause associated with the ὡς-clause ("as-clause" or "like-clause") in v. 34 is omitted.[186] This omission is not, strictly speaking, an example of the rhetorical figure *praecisio* or ἀποσιώπησις ("breaking off abruptly").[187] The main point of comparison is clear enough: it is necessary for the followers of Jesus to remain alert, just as the doorkeeper must stay awake in the absence of his master. This comparison does, however, seem to be more complex than the first one and to have more than one point of analogy. The man away on a journey (v. 34) corresponds to the risen Jesus, and the man's household (v. 34) corresponds to the postresurrection community of the followers of Jesus, which is referred to with the same word in the application of the comparison in v. 35b. The man's slaves, each given authority by the master to do his or her task (v. 34), evoke on the second level of meaning the followers of Jesus. These presumably have a variety of tasks, but preaching the good news and endurance under persecution are emphasized in vv. 9-13. Perhaps even the doorkeeper (θυρωρός) has an analogue. The function of the doorkeeper was to protect the property of the master of the household.[188] This task may correspond to the warnings against false messiahs and prophets in vv. 5b-6 and 21-23, where the warning "watch out" (βλέπετε), analogous to the command "keep awake" (ἵνα γρηγορῇ) in v. 34, occurs. The leaders of the community, represented by the addressees of the speech in the narrative, Peter, James, John, and Andrew, are to be alert to discern false messiahs and prophets and to unmask the pretensions of such people in order to prevent the deception of the rest of the community. When the master returns, he expects to find them engaged in this task (v. 36). This discernment may be the special task of the leaders, but all are exhorted to be similarly watchful (v. 37).

It is clear that it is not necessary to read this comparison as a reflection of a situation involving a delay of the parousia. It fits perfectly well a situation during the first Jewish war with Rome, before the destruction of Jerusalem and the temple, when a popular messiah, Simon son of Gioras, and popular prophets were active and inciting even "the elect" to share their vision of the inauguration of the new age.

■ **37** This verse is a concluding address that includes a command. The speech of Jesus in chapter 13 does not have a typical rhetorical conclusion. The *Rhet. Her.* gives a convenient description of *conclusiones* or ἐπίλογοι ("conclusions" or "perorations") as means of bringing

---

185 Compare the illustration of the treatment of a theme in the *Rhet. Her.* 4.44.56–58.

186 See BDF §453 (4) and §482.

187 *Rhet. Her.* classifies *praecisio*, which is equivalent to ἀποσιώπησις ("breaking off abruptly") as a figure of diction (*exornatio verborum*; 4.13.18 and 4.30.41); Caplan, [*Cicero*], 1:274–75, 330–31. Black classified Mark 13:34 as an example of ἀποσιώπησις, which he described as a figure of thought (87), apparently following Quintilian (9.2.1; 9.2.54). The form and function of v. 34 seem, however, to be different from the examples given in these two ancient works; see also BDF §482.

188 At least such is the case in rabbinic literature; see Str-B, 2:47–48. Note also how the "doorkeeper" (θυρωρός) in the παροιμία ("proverb" or "figure" or "comparison") of John 10:1-6 is contrasted with the "thief" (κλέπτης) and the "robber" (λῃστής).

arguments to a close. They are tripartite and consist of the summing up (*enumeratio*), amplification (*amplificatio*), and appeal to pity (*commiseratio*).[189] This work also discusses the conclusion (*conclusio*) as a figure of diction. The latter is a brief argument that deduces the necessary consequences of what has been said or done beforehand. This argument takes the form of a condition: if X, then Y (4.30.41).[190]

As noted earlier, the concluding statement of the speech of Jesus (v. 37) rounds off both the last section (vv. 32-36) and the speech as a whole. Its connection with the last section is shown by the use of the imperative "keep awake" ($\gamma\rho\eta\gamma\rho\epsilon\hat{\iota}\tau\epsilon$), which takes up the task assigned to the doorkeeper, "keep awake" ($\gamma\rho\eta\gamma\rho\hat{\eta}$) in

v. 34, and repeats the command in the application of the comparison in v. 35a. Its relation to the speech as a whole is shown by the way in which the word $\hat{\upsilon}\mu\hat{\iota}\nu$ ("to you") alludes back to the four disciples of v. 3 whose questions in v. 4 evoke the discourse. The statement "Now what I say to you, I say to all" ($\hat{o}$ $\delta\grave{\epsilon}$ $\hat{\upsilon}\mu\hat{\iota}\nu$ $\lambda\acute{\epsilon}\gamma\omega$ $\pi\hat{\alpha}\sigma\iota\nu$ $\lambda\acute{\epsilon}\gamma\omega$) could mean that all the disciples in the narrative, not just these four, should be watchful. Since, however, v. 14 breaks through the fictional setting to address the reader of the text and the subject matter concerns the future from the point of view of the characters in the narrative, it is more likely that "to all" ($\pi\hat{\alpha}\sigma\iota\nu$) refers to all the followers of Jesus in the postresurrection period.

189 *Rhet. Her.* 2.30–31.47–50; Caplan, [*Cicero*], 1:144–53.
190 See also the conclusion of the illustration of a treatment of an idea in 4.44.57.

14

14:1-11 Conspiracy and Anointing

1/ Now the (feast of) Passover and Unleavened Bread was (to begin) after two days. And the chief priests and the scribes were looking for a way to arrest him by deceit and kill him. 2/ For they said, "Not during the festival, so there will not be a disturbance of the people."[a]

3/ And while he was in Bethany at the house of Simon the leper and was dining, a woman came with a small glass bottle of aromatic oil (extracted) from the spikenard plant, genuine and very expensive. She broke the bottle and poured the oil on his head. 4/ Now some became angry (and said) to one another,[b] "Why this waste of aromatic oil? 5/ For this oil could have been sold for more than three hundred denarii and (the money) given to the poor." And they reproved her. 6/ Jesus then said, "Leave her alone. Why do you cause trouble for her? She has done a good deed to me. 7/ For you always have the poor with you, and whenever you want, you can do good to them,[c] but you do not always have me. 8/ She did what she could. She anointed my body for burial beforehand. 9/ Truly I say to you, wherever the good news is proclaimed in the whole world, what this woman has done will also be spoken of in memory of her."

10/ And Judas Iscariot,[d] who was one of the twelve, went to the chief priests, in order to hand him over to them. 11/ So when they heard, they were glad, and they offered to give him money. And he was looking for a way to hand him over at an opportune time.

a The trans. is based on what is probably the earliest recoverable reading, μὴ ἐν τῇ ἑορτῇ, μήποτε ἔσται θόρυβος τοῦ λαοῦ ("Not during the festival, so there will not be a disturbance of the people"), attested by most MSS. This reading is problematic because, according to Mark, they did arrest Jesus during the festival. This problem may have given rise to the variant attested by D it, μήποτε ἐν τῇ ἑορτῇ ἔσται θόρυβος τοῦ λαοῦ ("Perhaps during the festival there will be a disturbance of the people"); cf. Taylor, ad loc.

b The reading ἀγανακτοῦντες πρὸς ἑαυτούς, "became angry (and said) to one another," attested by ℵ* B C* L et al., is elliptical and thus has given rise to variants. A C² W f^{1.13} 𝔐 et al. attest a reading in which καὶ λέγοντες ("and saying") has been added to introduce the following direct speech. Most of these MSS, however, have these words following πρὸς ἑαυτούς ("to one another"), so that the problem remains that ἀγανακτοῦντες πρὸς ἑαυτούς would normally mean "became angry at one another"; see BAGD, s.v. This problem was solved in another variant, attested by D 565 (it), οἱ δὲ μαθηταὶ αὐτοῦ διεπονοῦντο καὶ ἔλεγον ("His disciples then became annoyed and said"); cf. Taylor, ad loc.

c The earlier reading is the dative form, αὐτοῖς ("them"), attested by ℵ² B C D et al. The reading with the accusative form, αὐτούς ("them"), attested by A Θ 𝔐, is the result of a correction in light of classical Greek usage; see LSJ, s.v. ποιέω, B. 2; cf. Taylor, ad loc.

d Some MSS (K W 579. 1241 pm) include the definite article before Ἰούδας ("Judas") and others (A C² W f¹ 𝔐 et al.) before Ἰσκαριώτης ("Iscariot") or, in ℵ² L Θ et al., before Ἰσκαριώθ ("Iscariot"). Since it is more likely that the definite article would be added rather than omitted, the readings with the article are probably secondary.

There are also variants in the MSS of the surname or epithet; cf. note g on the trans. of 3:19 above. A C² W f^{1.13} 𝔐 et al. attest the reading Ἰσκαριώτης ("Iscariot"). This reading probably results from a secondary attempt to conform the spelling of the name to Greek usage. Thus, the spelling Ἰσκαριώθ ("Iscariot"), attested by ℵ*.² B C*^vid L Θ et al., is probably the earlier reading. The origin of the spelling Σκαριώτης ("Scariot"), attested by D lat, is obscure. These MSS read Σκαριώθ ("Scariot") in 3:19.

Excursus: The Passion Narrative

Many issues arise in the consideration of the passion narrative.[1] One of these is the question of composition, which asks whether the evangelist composed the passion narrative from small units of tradition, as he composed most of the rest of the Gospel, or whether he used an extended written source. If he used a source, further questions arise about the extent, nature, and origin of that source. Some have argued that the authors of Mark and John used a common, or similar, source. Another issue is what kind of narrative the passion narrative is and what models the author followed in composing it. Finally, the question of historical reliability is often raised, especially with regard to the allusions to passages of the OT. Some have argued that passages from the OT were called upon in the interpretation of events that actually happened, whereas others have argued that, with regard to details, the tradents or authors have fabricated events to accord with scripture.

Composition and History of the Tradition

Although the leading form critics all argued that Mark used some kind of written source in composing his passion narrative, they were divided about the extent and nature of this source. Karl Ludwig Schmidt argued that Mark and the other evangelists used an early, extended narrative account of Jesus' suffering and death, which was created by the oldest Christian community.[2] Dibelius agreed with Schmidt and argued that the pre-Markan passion narrative began with the plot to arrest Jesus (14:1-2) and the betrayal by Judas (14:10-11). He concluded that the narrative ended with an appearance of the risen Jesus to the disciples, and not with the story of the empty tomb.[3] Bultmann, however, argued that the passion story as we have it in the Synoptic Gospels is not an organic unity. He did argue, nevertheless, that Mark used a source consisting of an account of the passion, but it was a short narrative of historical reminiscence about the arrest, condemnation, and execution of Jesus. This narrative was then expanded in several stages, but it is not possible to determine which expansions are pre-Markan and which were carried out by Mark.[4]

Vincent Taylor adopted form criticism but considered the criticism of Bultmann and others "excessively radical."[5] He concluded that the Markan passion narrative is "relatively a unity," but that it "contains material of different kinds and origin."[6] The passion narrative is thus a "composite section" made up of "primary" and "secondary" elements, literarily speaking "without prejudice to historical considerations."[7] The primary element was a straightforward narrative that was probably composed for the community in Rome and found by Mark there. The secondary element consists of reminiscences of Peter that Mark inserted into the earlier narrative.[8]

Eta Linnemann pushed some of Bultmann's observations to their logical conclusion and argued that there was no pre-Markan passion narrative. In her view, Mark composed the passion account in the same way as he wrote the rest of the Gospel, by creating an extended narrative out of individual, originally independent units. She explained the greater coherence of the passion narrative in comparison with the rest of the Gospel by arguing that Mark used a different method in writing the former and that the course of events itself provided greater coherence.[9]

Ludger Schenke published a detailed study of Mark 14:1-42 and a shorter study of 14:53—15:47.[10] In the longer study, he concluded that Mark composed 14:1-31 by combining brief traditional units. The traditional part of the Gethsemane story was the first unit in the

---

1   The passion narrative of Mark is defined here as chaps. 14–16. The pre-Markan passion narrative, however, extended only from the anecdote set in Gethsemane to the tearing of the veil in 15:38. On the latter, see below.

2   Karl Ludwig Schmidt, "Die literarische Eigenart der Leidensgeschichte Jesu," *Die Christliche Welt* 32 (1918) 114–16, reprinted in Meinrad Limbeck, ed., *Redaktion und Theologie des Passionsberichtes nach den Synoptikern* (Wege der Forschung 481; Darmstadt: Wissenschaftliche Buchgesellschaft, 1981) 17–20; the reprint is cited here. For discussion, see Yarbro Collins, *Beginning of the Gospel*, 93, 100.

3   Dibelius, *From Tradition to Gospel*, 22–23, 178–80. For discussion, see Yarbro Collins, *Beginning of the Gospel*, 94, 103–4.

4   Bultmann, *History*, 275–79; for discussion, see Yarbro Collins, *Beginning of the Gospel*, 94–95, 104, 109–14, 116–17.

5   Taylor, vii.

6   Ibid., 526.

7   Ibid., 654.

8   Ibid., 654–64.

9   Eta Linnemann, *Studien zur Passionsgeschichte* (FRLANT 102; Göttingen: Vandenhoeck & Ruprecht, 1970) 24–28, 44–52, 146–58, 162–63, 169–70, 173–74; for discussion, see Yarbro Collins, *Beginning of the Gospel*, 96–98, 107, 111 n. 54, 112–13, 115–17.

10 Ludger Schenke, *Studien zur Passionsgeschichte des Markus: Tradition und Redaktion in Markus 14, 1–42* (FB 4; Würzburg: Echter Verlag; Stuttgart: Katho-

pre-Markan passion narrative.[11] In the briefer study, he discerned three layers of tradition in 14:53–15:47: the oldest account, a pre-Markan edition of the former, and a Markan edition.[12]

A group of scholars working in the United States published a collection of essays in which they emphasized the creativity of Mark as an author.[13] They concluded that, from the perspective of the history of the tradition, Mark 14–16 does not differ appreciably from what is known about the literary genesis and composition of chapters 1–13. The passion narrative also constitutes a theologically inseparable and homogeneous part of the Gospel.[14]

Rudolf Pesch took a position diametrically opposed to that of the volume edited by Kelber. He argued that Mark used a preexisting, historically reliable passion narrative, substantially preserved in 8:27–16:8. From 8:27 to 13:37, the evangelist made substantial additions to the source. Beginning with 14:1, he followed the source very closely.[15] In another work, he argued that the pre-Markan passion narrative was written before 37 CE in and for the oldest, Aramaic-speaking Christian community in Jerusalem.[16] Till Arend Mohr and Etienne Trocmé agreed with Pesch that the pre-Markan passion story may go back to the oldest Christian community.[17]

Joel Green concluded that Matthew used only Mark as a source for his passion narrative, whereas Luke used both Mark and a non-Markan source that had tradition-historical connections with John.[18] John used a source similar to Mark's, but it was an independent tradition.[19] Like Pesch, Green concluded that Mark was a cautious editor.[20] He also argued that the coherence of the passion narrative is due to the social setting for which it was formed and in which it was transmitted, the Lord's supper.[21] Finally, he suggested that the theme of atonement does not appear prominently in the written passion story because "the testimony of the eucharistic words" made "additional, explicit testimony" to the soteriological significance of Jesus' death unnecessary.[22]

A number of studies have argued that Mark and John used a common, or at least a similar, extensive written source in composing their passion narratives. Mohr concluded that Mark had at his disposal an extensive written account of the passion that had already been edited (B) and, in its original form (P), essentially agreed with the pre-Johannine passion narrative, which was independent of the Synoptic Gospels.[23] Mohr's methods have been criticized, for example, because he presupposed *both* that John knew the Synoptic Gospels *and* that he used an old passion source. Under such a presupposition, it is impossible to be certain when a particular passage is dependent on another Gospel and when it comes from the old passion source.[24]

Matti Myllykoski attempted to reconstruct the pre-

lisches Bibelwerk, 1971); idem, *Der gekreuzigte Christus: Versuch einer literarkritischen und traditionsgeschichtlichen Bestimmung der vormarkinischen Passionsgeschichte* (SBS 69; Stuttgart: Katholisches Bibelwerk, 1974).

11 For discussion, see Yarbro Collins, *Beginning of the Gospel*, 104, 106–7.

12 Schenke, *Der gekreuzigte Christus*, 135–45. For discussion, see Yarbro Collins, *Beginning of the Gospel*, 98, 108–17.

13 Werner H. Kelber, ed., *The Passion in Mark: Studies on Mark 14–16* (Philadelphia: Fortress, 1976).

14 For discussion, see Yarbro Collins, *Beginning of the Gospel*, 99–100. Johannes Schreiber also approched the passion narrative of Mark as the composition of the evangelist (*Die Markuspassion: Eine redaktionsgeschichtliche Untersuchung* [2nd ed.; BZNW 68; Berlin/New York: de Gruyter, 1993]).

15 Pesch, 2:1–27, 319.

16 Rudolf Pesch, *Das Evangelium der Urgemeinde: Wiederhergestellt und erläutert* (Freiburg/Basel/Vienna: Herder, 1979) 79–88.

17 Till Arend Mohr, *Markus- und Johannespassion: Redaktions- und traditionsgeschichtliche Untersuchung der Markinischen und Johanneischen Passionstradition* (AThANT 70; Zurich: Theologischer Verlag, 1982) 405; Etienne Trocmé, *The Passion as Liturgy: A Study in the Origin of the Passion Narratives in the Four Gospels* (London: SCM, 1983). Trocmé argues for a liturgical origin of "the archetype of the Passion narratives as we have them in the canonical Gospels" (ibid., 51). The social setting was the observance of Passover in Jerusalem by Jerusalem Christians and Christian pilgrims (ibid., 84).

18 Joel B. Green, *The Death of Jesus: Tradition and Interpretation in the Passion Narrative* (WUNT 2.33; Tübingen: Mohr Siebeck, 1988) 23, 102–3.

19 Ibid., 133–35.

20 Ibid., 216.

21 Ibid., 214–17.

22 Ibid., 322.

23 Mohr, *Markus- und Johannespassion*, 404.

24 Reinbold, *Der älteste Bericht*, 17 n. 19. The same criticism could be made of the work of Anton Dauer, *Die*

Markan passion narrative by means of literary-critical methods. The disruption of the narrative thread served as the main criterion for discerning secondary insertions. Once he had discerned pre-Markan narrative elements, he attempted to separate source and redaction in the passion narrative of John in a search for verification of the analyses of Mark.[25] He concluded that there was a short, old passion account (PB = *Passionsbericht*) that Mark used in a form that had already been edited and expanded (PG = *Passionsgeschichte*).[26] According to Myllykoski, the PB began with Jesus' entry into Jerusalem and ended with the crucifixion and the description of the charge against Jesus that was posted.[27] He argued that the PG began with the entry into Jerusalem and ended with an appearance of Jesus to the eleven disciples.[28] A further conclusion is that Mark and John used similar forms of the PG in constructing their passion narratives.[29] Myllykoski's source theory is that the fourth evangelist knew Mark, but used the PG rather than Mark in writing his passion narrative. Thus, like Mohr, Myllykoski has been criticized because of the difficulty in determining when John used Mark and when the PG.[30]

In order to avoid the methodological difficulty that calls the results of Mohr and Myllykoski into question, Wolfgang Reinbold made a case for the overall independence of John from the Synoptic Gospels.[31] He also concluded, with Green, that Matthew had no source besides Mark for his passion narrative, but also, against Green, that Luke had no special passion source.[32] In light of these conclusions, he was able to argue that the traditions attested by both Mark and John constitute a reliable core of the oldest passion tradition. This conclusion is unavoidable, he argued, because the extensive agreement between the Markan and Johannine passion narratives in content and wording cannot be coincidental. He applied to the comparison of those two passion narratives the methods that have been developed in studies of the Synoptic Sayings Source (Q). He designated the earliest recoverable account of the passion "PB" (*Passionsbericht*) and concluded that Mark and John used different recensions of the same document (PB[Mk] and PB[Joh]), since it is unlikely that all the differences are due to the redaction of the evangelists.[33]

According to Reinbold, the PB began with the decision to bring about the death of Jesus. It contained the entry into Jerusalem but not the "cleansing of the temple." It included the Last Supper, but it was not portrayed as a Passover meal. The account continued with the arrest, an interrogation of Jesus by the high priest, the denial of Peter, an interrogation by Pilate, including the Barabbas scene, the scourging and mocking, the crucifixion and death, and ended with the burial of Jesus.[34]

Gerd Theissen argued for a pre-Markan passion narrative on the basis of a conflict in chronology between the evangelist and his source. "According to Mark, Jesus died on the day of Passover [that is, during the day following the sacrifice of the paschal lambs]."[35] The tradition used by Mark, however, assumes that Jesus died on the day of preparation for Passover. Theissen supports this conclusion by arguing that "in 14:1-2, the Sanhedrin decides to kill Jesus before the feast in order to prevent unrest on the day of the feast."[36] He argues that this fits with the

---

Passionsgeschichte im Johannesevangelium: Eine traditionsgeschichtliche und theologische Untersuchung zu Joh 18,1–19,30 (SANT 30; Munich: Kösel, 1972). He raises the interesting possibility, however, that written texts were reabsorbed into oral tradition (ibid., 335–36).

25 Matti Myllykoski, *Die letzten Tagen Jesu: Markus und Johannes, ihre Traditionen und die historische Frage* (2 vols.; Suomalaisen Tiedeakatemian Toimituksia [Annales Academiae Scientiarum Fennicae] B. 256, 272; Helsinki: Suomalainen Tiedeakatemia, 1991, 1994) 1:36–37.

26 See, e.g., ibid., 1:66.

27 Ibid., 2:138–39.

28 Ibid., 2:162.

29 Ibid., 1:36; 2:138–74.

30 Reinbold, *Der älteste Bericht*, 19 n. 22.

31 Ibid., 27–48.

32 On Matthew, ibid., 25; on Luke, ibid., 49–72. He also rightly rejects the theory of John Dominic Crossan (*The Cross That Spoke: The Origins of the Passion Narrative* [San Francisco: Harper & Row, 1988]) that the earliest account of the passion can be reconstructed from the *Gos. Pet.*; Reinbold, *Der älteste Bericht*, 25–26 and n. 20.

33 Reinbold, *Der älteste Bericht*, 73–78.

34 Ibid., 92–215. See esp. the chart on p. 119.

35 Theissen, *Gospels in Context*, 166.

36 Ibid., 167.

portrayal of Simon of Cyrene coming in from the fields in 15:21, since he thinks that the implication is that Simon was coming in from work, whereas no work was done on Passover. He also argued that the "day of preparation," on which Jesus was buried according to 15:42, was originally the day of preparation for Passover, not for the Sabbath, as Mark explains it.

> The motive for removing Jesus from the cross and burying him before sundown would probably have been to have this work done before the beginning of the feast day, which would not make sense if it were already the day of Passover. Finally, the "trial" before the Sanhedrin presupposes that this was not a feast day, since no judicial proceedings could be held on that day.[37]

Thus, in his view, the chronology of Mark's source agrees with that of the passion narrative in John. He accepted the view that John is independent of the Synoptic Gospels and thus concluded "that Mark and John both presuppose an older account of the Passion, in which Jesus died on the day before Passover."[38] Theissen does not attempt to reconstruct this source and leaves open whether it began with the entry into Jerusalem, a decision to put Jesus to death or with the arrest of Jesus.[39]

There are problems with Theissen's argument. A more appropriate way of reading 14:1-2 is to conclude that the chief priests and scribes do not wish to arrest Jesus *openly* during the feast of Passover, lest there be a disturbance. Yet they hope to be able to arrest Jesus ἐν δόλῳ ("by deceit" or "in an underhanded way"), and that hope is fulfilled when Judas approaches them (14:10-11). At the time mentioned in 14:1, two days before Passover, the crowds would, in any case, already have assembled in Jerusalem and its environs.

The statement in 15:21 that Simon was coming ἀπ' ἀγροῦ could be translated "from the country" as well as "from the field(s)." In the former case, work is not necessarily implied. Theissen is right that no work was to be done on Abib = Nisan 15, which, according to Exodus

12–13, was both Passover and the first day of Unleavened Bread. Exod 12:16 says that no work shall be done on the first and last days of Unleavened Bread. But this prohibition is not as strict as the prohibition of work on the Sabbath. On these days, food may be prepared. Leviticus states that "you shall do no laborious work" on the first and last days of Unleavened Bread (Lev 23:7-8).[40] This is a more lenient statement than the formulation connected with the Sabbath and Yom Kippur. The latter proscribes every conceivable kind of exertion, whereas the former means that light work is permitted.[41]

The argument about the "day of preparation" is dubious because John 19:31 speaks of the day as one of preparation *both* for the Sabbath and for Passover. This issue is connected with the larger problem of the independence of John from the Synoptic Gospels and whether the chronology of John is to be preferred to that of the Synoptics.

Reinbold has made the best case for a passion source used by both Mark and John. This case, however, rests on the thesis that John is independent of Mark and the other Synoptic Gospels. He rightly concludes that the existence of special Johannine tradition is beyond doubt, even in the material that is similar to the Synoptic Gospels.[42] He admits, however, that the fact that John wrote a "Gospel" allows one to conclude that the evangelist knew about the existence of at least one writing of that literary type. Having granted that, he reasonably concludes that John did not use any Synoptic Gospel as a *literary* source.[43]

He notes, however, that there are very few pericopes in common between John and the Synoptic Gospels outside of the passion narrative and resurrection stories. In his consideration of the theory that John reproduced material from one or more Synoptic Gospels from memory, he admits that this model has the advantage of flexibility over against the "simple" model of literary dependence.[44] He also makes the interesting observation that the relatively stronger agreement between Mark and John after the arrest of Jesus is explicable by the hypothesis that neither of them (or neither PB[Mk] nor PB[Joh]) had

---

37   Ibid.
38   Ibid.
39   Ibid., 168.
40   Trans. from Milgrom, *Leviticus,* 3:1947.
41   Ibid., 1977–78.
42   Reinbold, *Der älteste Bericht,* 38.
43   Ibid., 39.
44   Ibid., 47.

special material that belonged in or could be adapted to (this part of) the passion narrative.[45]

Although a reasonable case can be made for the independence of John from the Synoptic Gospels, another explanation is also attractive, namely, that John is indirectly dependent on Mark (or another Synoptic Gospel), especially in the case of the passion narrative, in a context of the reoralization of the passion narrative after the composition and circulation of Mark.[46] The probable use of the passion narrative in liturgy and other oral, communal contexts would lead to a situation in which the story was well known.

It is likely that Mark used a written source in composing his passion narrative but that the source was a transitional text (between oral and literary production and performance) and was probably discarded eventually, just as the Synoptic Sayings Source (Q) was allowed to go out of existence.[47] Thus, Matthew and Luke relied primarily on Mark for their passion narratives and elaborated his version with details and new scenes that they either took from the ongoing, expansive oral tradition or composed themselves. It is likely that John, as well, relied primarily on the passion as narrated by Mark, but indirectly as mediated in contexts of reoralization. The author of John then modified the narrative according to other traditions known to him, his own historical convictions, theological perspective, and literary taste.

As Reinbold has shown so well, the lack of an external control has led to a wide divergence of opinion on the question of the extent and nature of the hypothetical pre-Markan passion narrative.[48] A verbal reconstruction of such a source is surely impossible, since Mark most likely made changes, or even rewrote it, to conform it to his own style and concerns. Certainty is probably unattainable even on the question of what incidents or "scenes" the pre-Markan source included. Given the lack of an external control (if one assumes that John was at least indirectly dependent on Mark), it seems best to use literary criteria exclusively to recover the outlines of the source, rather than to base arguments on what incidents the source "must have" or even "probably" contained.[49]

Schmidt was surely right in noting a significant literary difference between Mark 1–13 and 14–15. The first thirteen chapters provide minimal orientation in time and space, whereas temporal and spatial information is much more common and precise in chapters 14–16. In addition, chapters 14–15 have greater literary coherence and continuity than chapters 1–13.[50] It is noteworthy, however, that the location of the tomb of Jesus is not mentioned, which is strange after the great spatial specificity of 14:1–15:39.

It is unlikely that 14:1-2, 10-11 constituted the beginning of the pre-Markan passion narrative.[51] There are indications that the evangelist composed 14:1-31 using

---

45 Ibid., 96–97.

46 On the notion of "reoralization" in folklore studies, see Margaret A. Mills, "Domains of Folkloristic Concern: The Interpretation of Scriptures," in Susan Niditch, ed., *Text and Tradition: The Hebrew Bible and Folklore* (SBLSS; Atlanta: SBL/Scholars Press, 1990) 230–41, esp. 232, 237–38. Dan Ben-Amos stated that "oral texts cross into the domain of written literature . . . ; conversely, the oral circulation of songs and tales has been affected by print" ("Toward a Definition of Folklore in Context," in Américo Paredes and Richard Bauman, eds., *Toward New Perspectives in Folklore* [Austin: American Folklore Society/University of Texas Press, 1972] 3–15; quotation from 14; in antiquity, the reading (aloud) of manuscripts would affect oral forms, as print media do today. Susan Niditch, in discussing the creation of Israelite literature, speaks about "not only a process whereby oral becomes written but also a process whereby the written becomes oral and then that oral production is eventually recreated in fuller written form" (*Oral World and Written Word: Ancient Israelite Literature* [Library of Ancient Israel; Louisville: Westminster John Knox, 1996] 120). See also William A. Graham, *Beyond the Written Word: Oral Aspects of Scripture in the History of Religion* (Cambridge/New York: Cambridge University Press, 1987) esp. 156–57.

47 On "transitional texts," see Mills, "Domains of Folkloristic Concern," 232.

48 Reinbold, *Der älteste Bericht*, 8–14.

49 See the appendix to this commentary for a tentative reconstruction of the content of the pre-Markan narrative, without any claim to have discerned the original wording.

50 For details, see Yarbro Collins, *Beginning of the Gospel*, 100–102.

51 Ibid., 103–4; see also the criticism of Theissen's position above and the commentary below.

individual units of tradition.[52] It is likely, however, that an earlier form of the scene in Gethsemane constituted the beginning of the source. Verse 42, "Wake up; let us go. See, the one who is to hand me over has drawn near," is probably the earlier ending of the story, and this statement links it closely to the account of the arrest. It is thus likely that the Gethsemane story and the account of the arrest were already linked in Mark's source.[53]

An earlier form of the arrest story[54] was followed in Mark's source by the statement that they took Jesus to the high priest (14:53a). An earlier form of 15:1 then continued the story.[55] Next came an earlier form of the interrogation by Pilate (without the Barabbas story), which ended with Pilate's handing Jesus over to be whipped and crucified (15:15b).[56] The next scene was the mocking of Jesus by Roman soldiers. The only likely Markan addition is the explanation of "palace" ($\alpha \dot{v} \lambda \acute{\eta}$) in 15:16, "that is, the praetorium" ($\ddot{o} \, \dot{\epsilon} \sigma \tau \iota \nu \; \pi \rho \alpha \iota \tau \acute{\omega} \rho \iota o \nu$).[57]

The pre-Markan account of the crucifixion contained most, if not all, of what is preserved in 15:20b-27.[58] An earlier form of the account of the mocking by passersby and the two men crucified with Jesus followed next.[59] The pre-Markan passion narrative continued with a brief account of the death of Jesus, including the statements now preserved in 15:33, 34a, 37b.[60]

If one determines the end of Mark's source on literary grounds alone, two observations are important. First is the likelihood that 15:39 is a Markan composition.[61]

Second is the belated and artificial introduction of the women "observing from a distance" in 15:40 and the background that has then to be supplied in v. 41.[62] The literary nature of 15:40-41 suggests strongly that the story of the burial (15:42-47) and that of the empty tomb (16:1-8) were independent units of tradition that the evangelist added to his source.[63] The fact that the location of the tomb is not mentioned, in contrast to the topographical specificity of 14:32–15:39, supports this conclusion.

The earliest recoverable, and perhaps the actual, ending of the pre-Markan passion narrative thus appears to be 15:38. Schenke concluded that this verse is secondary because it signifies that the judgment of God upon the "old" temple has already begun. He supposes that the tearing of the curtain indicates that God has left the temple.[64] Pesch interpreted the "sign" as signifying judgment or punishment. In the pre-Markan passion narrative, it confirmed Jesus' messiahship and warned the Jewish leaders who were responsible for his death that they would be punished. Pesch concluded that, for Mark, it was a prophecy of the destruction of the temple after the fact.[65]

The pre-Markan passion narrative, as tentatively reconstructed above, did not contain a temple theme, as Mark in its present form does. Thus, v. 38, as part of that earlier narrative, is open to a quite different line of interpretation.[66] In Jewish literature written in Greek roughly

---

52   Schenke, *Passionsgeschichte*, 561; Yarbro Collins, *Beginning of the Gospel*, 104–5.

53   Yarbro Collins, *Beginning of the Gospel*, 106–7. In his first work on the passion narrative of Mark, Schenke concluded that, if there was a pre-Markan passion narrative, it must have begun with the scene in Gethsemane and not with some earlier event (*Passionsgeschichte*, 561). In his second book on this topic, he affirmed his earlier conclusion and modified it slightly by leaving open the possibility that something like 14:1a provided an introduction to the Gethsemane scene (*Der gekreuzigte Christus*, 126–27, 135).

54   Yarbro Collins, *Beginning of the Gospel*, 107–8.

55   Ibid., 108–9.

56   Ibid., 109–10.

57   Ibid., 110–11.

58   Ibid., 111–13. Mark 15:28 is not part of the earliest recoverable text of Mark; see ibid., 113, and the note on the trans. of 15:27 below.

59   Yarbro Collins, *Beginning of the Gospel*, 113–14.

60   Ibid., 114–17.

61   Ibid., 117.

62   The tensions in the lists of women's names in 15:40, 47; and 16:1 have often led exegetes to conclude that various traditions were here combined by Mark (Reinbold, *Der älteste Bericht*, 98, 100–102), but the lists can satisfactorily be explained as Markan composition; see Yarbro Collins, *Beginning of the Gospel*, 129–30, and the commentary below.

63   Mark 16:1-8 may be entirely Markan composition. See Yarbro Collins, *Beginning of the Gospel*, 127–34, and the commentary below.

64   Schenke, *Der gekreuzigte Christus*, 100–101.

65   Pesch, 2:498–99.

66   On the ambiguity of the sign, see Fowler, *Let the Reader Understand*, 202–3, 211. On the variety of interpretations, see Timothy J. Geddert, *Watchwords: Mark 13 in Markan Eschatology* (JSNTSup 26; Sheffield: JSOT Press, 1989) 140–43.

contemporary with Mark, the veil or curtain separating the inner sanctum, the Holy of Holies, from the rest of the temple proper (ναός) symbolized that which encloses the presence of God.[67] In this literature, which is often apologetic, the structure of the earthly tabernacle or temple has a deeper, symbolic meaning, usually cosmic or mystic. In Hebrews, this earthly reality also has a symbolic meaning, but a negative one. The prohibition of ordinary priests and the laity from entering the inner sanctum is interpreted to mean that the earthly temple could not provide true access to the presence of God. According to Heb 10:19-20, the death of Jesus opened "the way into the true, heavenly sanctuary, the path to glory."[68] Hebrews speaks about Jesus' ascent to heaven and interprets it metaphorically to mean an abstract realm in which God is truly worshiped.[69]

The tearing of the curtain of the sanctuary in v. 38 as part of the pre-Markan passion narrative may symbolize Jesus' ascent to heaven and entry into the presence of God. At the same time, it may symbolize the rending of the barrier between humanity and God. As in Hebrews, it may signify that the death of Jesus has made possible access to God for all humanity.[70]

Genre

The generic label "passion narrative" derives from the Christian notion of the redemptive suffering of Christ and from the Latin word *passio* in its Christian sense.

This label evokes a long history of liturgical reading and related musical performance of the accounts of Jesus' death in the four canonical Gospels. Since the term *passio* was used also for detailed accounts of early Christian martyrdoms,[71] the generic label "passion narrative" implies that the account of the suffering of Jesus was the first example of the genre "Christian martyrdom."[72] The strength and significance of this generic perception is evident in the fact that the Christian term "martyrdom" has been applied in the history of scholarship to Jewish, Greek, and Roman texts also, primarily to certain passages in 2 and 4 Maccabees and to the *Acta Alexandrinorum*, widely known as the *Acts of the Pagan Martyrs*.[73]

"In order to reconstruct the original genre, we have to eliminate from consciousness its subsequent states."[74] Doing so is of course impossible, but attempting to do so may be instructive. The following remarks will involve a search for the literary models of the passion narrative and distinctions between later and original terminology.[75]

A number of candidates for the literary model of the passion narrative have been proposed. Lothar Ruppert argued that the most important model for the pre-Markan passion narrative was the motif of the suffering just person (*passio iusti*) in the psalms and in chapters 2 and 5 of the Wisdom of Solomon. He referred to the source used in the composition of Wisdom 2 and 5 as a "diptych."[76] Ruppert does not seem to have had the

---

67   Attridge, *Hebrews,* 185.

68   Ibid., 240.

69   Ibid., 247–48.

70   See the discussion of the genre of the pre-Markan passion narrative below for a related reading of v. 38 as an evocation of Psalm 17 LXX. See also Yarbro Collins, "From Noble Death," 498–99; cf. R. H. Lightfoot, *The Gospel Message of St. Mark* (Oxford: Clarendon, 1950) 56.

71   See "Passional (Lat. *Liber Passionarius*)," in F. L. Cross and E. A. Livingstone, eds., *The Oxford Dictionary of the Christian Church* (2nd ed.; Oxford: Oxford University Press, 1974) 1039; and "Passions," ibid., 1040; see also Herbert Musurillo, *The Acts of the Christian Martyrs* (OECT; Oxford: Clarendon, 1972) xii, 86, 106, 176, 194, 214, 254, 260, 266, 294, 302, 344.

72   Schmidt identified the pre-Markan passion narrative as the first of a series of Christian acts of the martyrs ("Die literarische Eigenart," 18–20).

73   The Jewish texts include the deaths of Eleazar and of a nameless Jewish woman and her seven sons (2 Macc 6:18-31; 7:1-42; 4 Macc 5:1–7:23; 8:1–18:24); van Henten, *Maccabean Martyrs.* On the *Acta Alexandrinorum,* see Herbert A. Musurillo, *The Acts of the Pagan Martyrs* (Oxford: Clarendon, 1954).

74   Alastair Fowler, *Kinds of Literature: An Introduction to the Theory of Genres and Modes* (Cambridge, MA: Harvard University Press, 1982) 261.

75   See my earlier study of this topic, Adela Yarbro Collins, "The Genre of the Passion Narrative," *Studia Theologica* 47 (1993) 3–28. Much of what follows reproduces those results, with some modifications.

76   Lothar Ruppert, *Jesus als der leidende Gerechte? Der Weg Jesu im Lichte eines alt- und zwischentestamentlichen Motivs* (SBS 59; Stuttgart: Katholisches Bibelwerk, 1972) 48–59; see also idem, *Der leidende Gerechte: Eine motivgeschichtliche Untersuchung zum Alten Testament und zwischentestamentlichen Judentum*

question of genre as such in mind, since he spoke of the *Gestalt* of the passion narrative as an issue distinct from his concern for the motif that generated the text.[77] In aesthetic literary critical terms, his observations apply to the "inner form" of the text as opposed to its "outer form" or "external structure."[78] A problem with the alleged motif of the "suffering just person" is that it applies well enough to the Wisdom of Solomon, whereas the lamenter of the psalms is not consistently portrayed as "just" or "righteous." More importantly, the "righteous sufferer" may be more of a modern scholarly construct than a widespread ancient notion.[79]

George Nickelsburg has argued that the pre-Markan passion narrative belongs to a genre that he identified and labeled as "the story of the persecution and vindication of the righteous person."[80] Other instances of the genre in his view are the narratives about Joseph in Genesis, the story of Ahikar, the book of Esther, the story of the three young men in the fiery furnace in Daniel 3, the story about Daniel in the lion's den in Daniel 6, the story of Susanna, and, with some qualifications, the treatment of the righteous person in chapters 2, 4, and 5 of the Wisdom of Solomon. Nickelsburg identified the genre by noting that all these stories have a common theme and argued that this theme is emplotted by means of a limited number of narrative elements or components. This approach to genre focuses mainly on the plot of texts. Some of the narrative elements are expressed at such a high level of abstraction that major differences between the stories are obscured. For example, the narrative element "Rescue" applies both to stories in which the righteous person is rescued *from* death and to those in which he or she is vindicated *after* death.[81] It is noteworthy, however, that the *Martyrdom of Polycarp*, dating to the second century CE, makes an analogy between the situation of the martyr and the three young men in the fiery furnace.[82]

Detlev Dormeyer reconstructed three stages in the composition of the Markan passion narrative. He argued that the oldest stage is a mixture of two previously existing genres, the Jewish martyrdom and the acts of the pagan martyrs. The content, involving a detailed description of the conduct of a persecuted person during his execution, was influenced by the Jewish martyrdom. The form, consisting of an account of judicial proceedings placed in the context of a frame story, was modeled on the structure of the acts of the pagan martyrs. He argued further that the pre-Markan redaction of the earliest passion narrative was carried out under the influence of the biographies of the prophets in the OT. The product consisted of a kind of proto-Gospel. The Markan redaction resulted in a complex of individual scenes that constituted a cycle of Christian legends. In the process, Mark preserved the characterization of the death of Jesus as a martyrdom. Thus, a subtype of the legend, the martyr legend, came into being. According to Dormeyer, the Markan passion narrative in its final form became the model of all the later Christian martyr legends.[83]

The "Jewish martyrdom" and the "acts of the pagan martyrs" are promising candidates for the literary mod-

---

(FB 5; Würzburg: Echter Verlag/Katholisches Bibelwerk, 1972); idem, *Der leidende Gerechte und seine Feinde: Eine Wortfelduntersuchung* (Würzburg: Echter Verlag, 1973).

77   Ruppert, *Jesus als der leidende Gerechte?* 59.

78   Fowler cited Austin Warren for the distinction between "outer form" and "inner form" (*Kinds of Literature*, 55). He himself identified "external structure" as one of the features important for the understanding of genres or "kinds" of literature (ibid., 60).

79   Donald Juel argued with respect to the work of C. H. Dodd that the construct "Righteous Sufferer" in pre-Christian biblical exegesis may be a product of modern imaginations (*Messianic Exegesis: Christological Interpretation of the Old Testament in Early Christianity* [Philadelphia: Fortress, 1988] 22); see also Ahearne-Kroll, "Suffering of David," 1:5–12.

80   George W. E. Nickelsburg, "The Genre and Function of the Markan Passion Narrative," *HTR* 73 (1980) 153–84; idem, "Passion Narratives," *ABD* 5:172–77; idem, *Resurrection, Immortality and Eternal Life in Intertestamental Judaism* (HTS 26; Cambridge, MA: Harvard University Press; London: Oxford University Press, 1972) 48–111 (expanded ed. 2006, 67–140).

81   Nickelsburg, "Genre and Function," 155–56, 161.

82   *Mart. Pol.* 14–15; Jan Willem van Henten, "Daniel 3 and 6 in Early Christian Literature," in John J. Collins and Peter Flint, eds., *The Book of Daniel: Composition and Reception* (2 vols.; Supplements to Vetus Testamentum 83.1–2; Leiden: Brill, 2001) 1:149–69, esp. 156–58. See also van Henten, *Maccabean Martyrs*, 7–13.

83   Detlev Dormeyer, *Die Passion Jesu as Verhaltensmodell: Literarische und theologische Analyse der Traditions- und*

els of the passion narrative, but here we must confront the terminological problem. The later Christian notions of the μάρτυς ("witness" or "martyr") and the μαρτύριον ("testimony" or "martyrdom") have been retrojected onto texts that are in many cases earlier and in all cases of a different cultural origin. As Norbert Brox has shown, the Christian *Martyrdom of Polycarp* is the first text to use the term μάρτυς with the primary meaning "one who dies" and μαρτύριον with the primary meaning "death."[84]

The oldest Jewish text that Dormeyer identified as a "martyrdom" is the story about the prophet Zechariah, son of the priest Jehoiada, in 2 Chr 24:20-22. This text was probably written in the late Persian or early Greek period.[85] The passage may be described as an account of the death of a prophet. The references to conspiracy, the command of the king, and stoning may imply a judicial procedure. The context makes clear that the story is an integral part of the whole historical work. The scene does not appear in 2 Kings 12, the model for this portion of 2 Chronicles. It may be that it was composed under the influence of Persian or Greek historiography, both of which had developed an interest in biographical elements, including the deaths of famous men, by the fifth century BCE.[86]

One may then infer the existence of a literary genre, literary form, or micro-genre that may be labeled the "story of the death of a famous man." Herodotus provides evidence that such accounts were called τελευταί ("ends," a euphemism for "deaths") by Greeks from at least the fifth century BCE.[87] This label may refer either to portions of larger works or to stories that circulated independently and orally. Later such stories were collected, as we learn from Pliny the Younger. In Latin the genre was called *exitus illustrium virorum* ("departures of famous men").[88]

Herodotus's *History* contains several accounts in which a man's life as a whole is narrated,[89] each of which ends with a report of his death. The life of Cyrus is narrated in book 1 (1.107–30, 177–88, 201–14). The report concludes with his final campaign and fall in battle. His last words are not recorded, but those of Queen Tomyris, whose people he was attempting to conquer, are given along with a striking description of her insult to his corpse. The story of the life of Cambyses in book 3 ends with an account of his decline, followed by death from a wound accidentally self-inflicted, and last words (3.61-66). Sketches of the lives of a number of Greeks are given also, most of which include reports of their deaths.[90] The causes and manners of the deaths differ in these stories, and they have no fixed structure. This flexibility does not preclude the suggestion that these texts belong to the same "kind" of literature. It simply shows that the genre or micro-genre was closely linked to history and

---

Redaktionsgeschichte der Markuspassion (NTAbh n.F. 11; Münster: Aschendorff, 1974) 44–46, 243, 261–62, 273, 276.

84 Norbert Brox, *Zeuge und Märtyrer: Untersuchungen zur frühchristlichen Zeugnis-Terminologie* (SANT 5; Munich: Kösel, 1961) 41–42, 68–69, 106–9, 129–30, 172–73, 193–95, 230–37. *Mart. Pol.* belongs to the genre "letter." The later titles in the MSS refer to it as a μαρτύριον ("martyrdom"). The work was the first of a new genre, and a label was devised only later on. The date of *Mart. Pol.*, however, is contested (Musurillo, *Christian Martyrs*, xiii–xiv, lxiv n. 6). If the work dates to the second half of the third or to the fourth century, the question of the origin of the genre "martyrdom" will need to be rethought.

85 Ralph Klein dates the work to the fourth cent. BCE ("Chronicles, Book of 1–2," *ABD* 1:995). Jacob M. Myers dates it to the Persian period (c. 538–333 BCE) (*I Chronicles: Introduction, Translation, and Notes* [AB 12; Garden City, NY: Doubleday, 1965] LXXXVII–LXXXVIII).

86 Momigliano, *Greek Biography*, 28–36; Helene Homeyer, "Zu den Anfängen der griechischen Biographie," *Philologus* 106 (1962) 75–85.

87 Text and trans. from Godley, *Herodotus* 1:34–35. See the story of Solon and Croesus preserved by Herodotus in which Solon recounts the death of Tellus and says, "the end of his life was most splendid" (τελευτὴ τοῦ βίου λαμπροτάτη ἐπεγένετο) (1.30).

88 This is Pliny's description of a lost work by Fannius, entitled *exitus occisorum aut relegatorum a Nerone* ("departures of those killed or exiled by Nero") (*Letters* 5.5). Pliny comments that the style was intermediate between the colloquial and the historical (*inter sermonem historiamque medios*). According to Klaus Berger, Cicero already attests to the collection of such stories; "Hellenistische Gattungen," 1257.

89 Homeyer, "Anfängen," 76.

90 Miltiades the elder (Herodotus 6.34–38), Miltiades the younger (6.39–41, 103–4, 132–40), and Cleomenes (5.39–41; 6.73–84, 6.75 describes his self-inflicted death).

biography, and the variety associated with it reflects the variety of histories and lives.[91]

The death of Socrates and literary accounts of it in the fourth century had great impact on the development of the genre. The event itself and the accounts of it by Plato and Xenophon created an interest in a particular sort of death, beyond the older concern with the death of a famous man as an intrinsically important event, whatever sort it was. Even older than the historical and biographical interest in the τελευταί ("ends" or "deaths") of famous men was the notion of a noble death in accordance with the heroic ideal.[92] An important element in this idea of a noble death is the public honor given to the hero by his fellow citizens afterward.[93] The death of Socrates redefined the noble death in philosophical terms.

Plato's *Apology*, as Socrates' speech of self-defense before the citizens of Athens, gives an impressive picture of his attitude toward death and his behavior under the threat of condemnation to death. The *Phaedo* is a literary dialogue in which Phaedo reports to Echecrates Socrates' last dialogue and death, both of which took place in his prison. The subject of conversation is the nature of death and the immortality of the soul. The report ends with an account of Socrates' death. He drinks the poison readily and calmly. When his friends break down in tears, he maintains his composure and urges them to keep silence and to bear up. His last words are, "Crito, we owe a cock to Asclepius; pay it and do not neglect it."[94] The cock was a thank-offering that those who were cured of illness gave to the god of healing.

Socrates' last words are thus an ironic affirmation of his teaching that death is a good thing for the good person.[95]

The Greek and Roman genre "deaths of famous men" and the tradition regarding Socrates' death are important for understanding the texts usually described as Jewish martyrdoms. After the short text in 2 Chronicles, the oldest such accounts appear in 2 Maccabees. This book is an abridgment of a lost work in five volumes by an otherwise unknown author, Jason of Cyrene. Both the original work and its epitome were composed in Greek, and the summary manifests a refined rhetorical style. Jason's work was probably written not long after 161 BCE; the abridgment was certainly made before 63 BCE and probably before 124 BCE.[96] Both the original and the epitome belong to the genre "history." The summary reports events from the reign of Seleucus IV through the career of Judah the Maccabee, that is, from about 187 to 161 BCE. The deaths of Eleazar, the seven sons, and their mother are described as part of this sequence of events.

Chapter 6 begins with a summary of Antiochus's attempt to force the Jews to abandon the laws of God and their ancestors and to adopt Greek religious practices. It is in this context that the story of Eleazar is introduced (2 Macc 6:18-31). The general situation is similar to those of two of the wisdom tales of Daniel, the stories of the fiery furnace and the lion's den (Daniel 3 and 6). Religious Jews are being forced by a foreign king to perform an act forbidden by their tradition or to refrain from performing one that is commanded. None of the three cases involves a trial of the accused, but a decree of the monarch and obedience to it are at issue. The

---

91 Fowler has argued that the changing and interpenetrating nature of the genres makes their definition impossible, although we can apprehend them intuitively (*Kinds of Literature*, 25); he also suggests that a genre is usually characterized by very few "necessary" elements (ibid., 39).

92 Van Henten, *Maccabean Martyrs*, 208–9, esp. n. 108; Yarbro Collins, "From Noble Death," 482–84.

93 See the story of Tellus's death referred to above (Hdt. 1.30); cf. the honor given to Miltiades the elder by the people of the Chersonese as their founder (ibid., 6.38).

94 Plato *Phaed.* 117c-118; trans. (modified) from Harold North Fowler, *Plato*, vol. 1: *Euthyphro, Apology, Crito, Phaedo, Phaedrus* (12 vols.; LCL; Cambridge, MA: Harvard University Press; London: Heinemann, 1914) 398–403.

95 According to Arthur J. Droge and James D. Tabor, the implication is that death is the "cure" for life (*A Noble Death: Suicide and Martyrdom among Christians and Jews in Antiquity* [San Francisco: Harper Collins, 1992] 21). A spurious letter from Socrates' disciple Aeschines to Xenophon, which dates to the late second or early third cent. CE, explains that Socrates was in debt to Asclepius because of a vow given when he was ill after returning from the battle at Delium; see Malherbe, *Cynic Epistles*, 258–59; on the date, ibid., 28–29. This ancient explanation seems to miss the irony of Plato's text.

96 Schürer, *History*, 3:532.

emphasis in the Eleazar story on his noble death, however, gives it a striking similarity to the genre of the "deaths of famous men," especially to the tradition regarding Socrates' death.[97]

Like Socrates, Eleazar was at an advanced age when the threat of execution arose. Both made reference to the little time left to them to live. The narrator's comment that Eleazar welcomed death with honor rather than life with pollution recalls Socrates' argument that it is worse to behave unjustly than to die. Like Socrates, Eleazar was counseled by his friends to take action that would allow him to avoid death. One of his reasons for rejecting their suggestion is that to accept it would not be in keeping with the excellent life that he had led since childhood. Socrates did offer to pay a fine, but the whole tenor of his defense implies that he acted in his trial in a way consistent with his life up to that point. Eleazar made reference to his responsibility to God, as did Socrates. Eleazar emphasized that his death would be a noble example to the young, and the narrator commented that his death was an example of nobility and a memorial of courage, not only to the young but to the majority of his nation.[98] The same point is implied in the *Apology* and the *Phaedo*. Further, the death of Socrates did become a conscious and often cited example in accounts of the noble deaths of others. Eleazar's last words, uttered like those of Socrates just before the moment of death, in part focus on the distinction between body and soul, a point also made by Socrates but at an earlier stage of the narrative.[99]

It would seem, then, that the original genre of the story in 2 Maccabees is "death of a famous man" or an "account of a noble death." It is noteworthy that the account combines narration and direct speech and that only Eleazar's words are given in direct discourse. One of the most striking similarities between Plato's accounts of the trial and death of Socrates and the story of Eleazar is the way in which the situation is portrayed and exploited as a didactic opportunity.

Torture is a minor feature in the account of Eleazar; he dies from blows on the rack (2 Macc 6:30; cf. vv. 19, 28b). It is prominent in the account of the mother and her seven sons. They were being compelled by the king to perform an act forbidden by the Law under torture with whips and cords. The tongue of the eldest son was cut out; he was scalped; his hands and feet were cut off; and he was finally fried in a pan (2 Macc 7:1-5). The other brothers were tortured in a similar fashion. Their bravery and disregard of pain and death probably owe something to the noble-death tradition, but the detailed description of torture is a distinctive feature. Jason or the epitomizer employed here a motif that he took either from the melodramatic type of historiography that characterized the Hellenistic period (sometimes called "tragic history" or "pathetic history")[100] or from the emerging genre of the ancient novel or romance.[101] Although the latter genre reached its zenith in the second century CE, the first "proto-novels" may have appeared already in late Hellenistic times.[102] One of the main features of the Greek novel was a melodramatic emphasis on death, torture, attempted suicide, ordeal by fire, and similar trials.[103]

---

97 For a discussion of the similarities between Eleazar and Socrates, see Jonathan A. Goldstein, *II Maccabees: A New Translation with Introduction and Commentary* (AB 41A; Garden City, N.Y.: Doubleday, 1983) 285.

98 Socrates was seventy (*Ap.* 17d); Eleazar, eighty-nine (2 Macc 6:24). On the little time left, cf. *Ap.* 38c with 2 Macc 6:25; on death with honor, cf. *Ap.* 32a-33b, 39ab with 2 Macc 6:19; on avoiding death, cf. *Ap.* 37e-38c with 2 Macc 6:21-23; on responsibility to God, cf. *Ap.* 37e with 2 Macc 6:23, 26; on Eleazar as a "noble example" (ὑπόδειγμα γενναῖον), see 2 Macc 6:28; cf. vv. 24-25; as a "memorial of courage" (μνημόσυνον ἀρετῆς), see 2 Macc 6:31.

99 Plato *Phaed.* 115c-116a; 2 Macc 6:30.

100 For a discussion of 2 Maccabees as "tragic history," see Thomas Fischer, "First and Second Maccabees," *ABD* 4:445.

101 On the relation between historiography and the novels, see Bryan P. Reardon, "Chariton: Chaereas and Callirhoe; Introduction," in idem, ed., *Collected Ancient Greek Novels* (Berkeley: University of California Press, 1989) 18.

102 See the discussion by Reardon, "General Introduction," in *Ancient Greek Novels*, 5; cf. 17.

103 Chariton *Chaereas and Callirhoe* 3.4, 9; 4.2; ET by Reardon, *Ancient Greek Novels*, 56–57, 63, 67; Xenophon of Ephesus *An Ephesian Tale* 2.6; ET by Graham Anderson in Reardon, *Ancient Greek Novels*, 141–42; Achilles Tatius *Leucippe and Clitophon* 7.12; ET by John J. Winkler in Reardon, *Ancient Greek Novels*, 267. See the discussion in Musurillo, *Pagan Martyrs*, 253–54.

In the story of Eleazar, King Antiochus is entirely in the background, but in the story of the seven sons and their mother, the king is directly involved. He himself gives the orders for the tortures (2 Macc 7:3, 4, 5), and his reactions are described (2 Macc 7:3, 12, 24, 39). Much more than the story of Eleazar, this account is cast as a kind of contest or struggle between the heroes and heroine, on the one hand, and the king, who is cast in the role of a vicious tyrant, on the other.

The second story does not call the model of Socrates to mind as much as the first. The speeches of all seven sons and their mother are much more informed by contemporary Jewish values.[104] Nevertheless, important points of similarity with the death of Socrates remain. In general, they share the feature of fearless death because of commitment to high principles. In terms of more specific features, Socrates also predicted the punishment of those who condemned him[105] and faced death confident that his true self would go to share in the joys of the blessed.[106]

In spite of the characteristically Jewish historical setting and the predominantly Jewish values that inform the story, it does not seem necessary to conclude that the story of the mother and her seven sons was the first instance of a new genre, at least not in its own time. It seems best to take it as a creative adaptation of the noble-death type of literature to a Jewish cultural context.[107]

Although the influence of Socrates as a model in dying was great, the older interest in the death of a famous man, of whatever sort it was, did not die out. It has been argued that collections of the τελευταί ("ends" or "deaths") of philosophers and heroes were made in Alexandria in the Hellenistic period. One such collection was that of Hermippus of Smyrna, who flourished around 200 BCE; this work was one of the sources used by Diogenes Laertius in composing his *Lives and Opinions of Eminent Philosophers*.[108]

Like the Maccabean story of the seven brothers and their mother, some of the τελευταί ("ends" or "deaths") recounted by Diogenes have as their main feature the tension between the protagonist and a tyrant. According to several sources, Zeno of Elea plotted to overthrow a tyrant but was arrested. While being interrogated by the tyrant himself about his accomplices, Zeno said that he had something to tell him privately in his ear. When the tyrant offered his ear, the philosopher laid hold of it with his teeth and refused to let go until he was stabbed to death. According to another source, Zeno bit off his tongue and spat it at the tyrant (Diogenes Laertius 9.26-27).

Anaxarchus, the companion of Alexander, made himself an enemy of Nicocreon, the tyrant of Cyprus, by wishing out loud, though indirectly, that his head would be served at table. Later, when forced to land in Cyprus after Alexander's death, the philosopher was arrested and, at the order of Nicocreon, pounded to death in a mortar. When he was placed in the mortar, Anaxarchus said, "Pound, pound the pouch containing Anaxarchus; you pound not Anaxarchus." When the tyrant commanded that his tongue be cut out, the philosopher bit it off and spat it at him (ibid. 9.58-59).[109]

Such stories may have influenced the accounts in chapters 6–7 of 2 Maccabees. The general situation of conflict with a ruler is analogous; the story about Anaxarchus and the account of the death of the first of the seven sons share the motif of the command to cut out the protagonist's tongue. The purpose of this cruel deed is to put an end to speech that is offensive to the ruler.[110]

---

104 2 Macc 7:6, 9, 11, 14, 18, 23, 29, 32-33, 36a.

105 Cf. 2 Macc 7:14, 17, 19, 31 with *Ap.* 39c.

106 Cf. 2 Macc 7:9, 11, 14, 23, 29 with *Phaed.* 115d.

107 Ulrich Kellermann characterized 2 Maccabees 7 provisionally as a martyrological didactive narrative, but concluded that its closest parallel is the *exitus illustrium virorum* ("departures of famous men") (*Auferstandenen in den Himmel: 2 Makkabäer 7 und die Auferstehung der Märtyrer* [SBS 95; Stuttgart: Katholisches Bibelwerk, 1979] 35-40, 51-53).

108 Musurillo, *Pagan Martyrs*, 238; see also Herbert S. Long, "Introduction," in Hicks, *Diogenes Laertius*, 1:xxi; Robert William Sharples, "Hermippus (2)," *OCD* 692.

109 See also the story of Callisthenes, the historian, who was said to have spoken with too much frankness to Alexander. As a result, he was carried about in an iron cage until he became infested with vermin; eventually he was thrown to a lion and so died (*Diogenes Laertius,* 5.4-5).

110 On the relation of 2 Maccabees 7 to "philosophical martyrdoms," see Kellermann, *Auferstandenen in den Himmel,* 46-50.

4 Maccabees is also often associated with the notion of "Jewish martyrdom" or "Jewish martyrs." It was written around 100 CE, probably in Asia Minor.[111] In terms of literary form, it seems best to take it as the rhetorical development of the thesis stated in 1:1, "whether devout reason is sovereign over the emotions."[112] The argument combines later Stoic and Jewish values. The first part of the work is a discursive argument of the thesis (1:1—3:18). The second part argues the thesis with reference to a specific group of examples and treats them as worthy of praise. This second part then has elements of the encomium or panegyric speech.[113] The examples cited are the same faithful Jews whose stories are told in 2 Maccabees. In fact, it is generally agreed that the narrative portions of 4 Maccabees 5–18 are based on 2 Macc 6:12—7:42.[114]

In the story of Eleazar in 4 Maccabees, Antiochus is portrayed as a tyrant (4 Macc 5:1). As noted above, in 2 Maccabees 6 only the speech of Eleazar is given in direct discourse. In 4 Maccabees, the speech of Antiochus is also quoted so that the account contains an actual dialogue. As in 2 Maccabees, but even more so, Eleazar's speech is didactic. It provides instruction for the character Antiochus and, more importantly, for the audience of the work on the rationality of the Law and the Jewish way of life.[115]

In 2 Maccabees, the element of torture is a minor theme in the story of Eleazar. In 4 Maccabees, this element is elaborated (6:1-11). The emphasis on the old man's ability to endure pain and torture is related to the author's Stoic values.[116] As in 2 Maccabees, Eleazar in 4 Maccabees emphasizes that his noble death will be an example for the young. But his final words contain an important new element: his prayer that his death be accepted by God as vicarious suffering for the rest of the Jewish people (6:27-29). Like the accounts in 2 Maccabees, the stories of 4 Maccabees are $\tau\epsilon\lambda\epsilon\upsilon\tau\alpha\iota$ ("ends" or "deaths"), accounts of the deaths of famous or noble people that serve as examples to those who read or hear them.[117]

Besides the Jewish martyrdom, the "Hellenistic acts of the martyrs" is the other genre that Dormeyer proposed as a literary model for the early forms of the passion narrative. This genre is represented primarily by a group of texts often referred to as the *Acts of the Alexandrians* or the *Acts of the Pagan Martyrs*. In this context, the term "acts" refers to proceedings in a judicial setting. These texts were discovered in the nineteenth and twentieth centuries written in Greek on fragments of papyrus. Ulrich Wilcken published the first comprehensive study, in which he argued that four such fragmentary works had a family resemblance and could be classified together as the *Acts of the Alexandrians*.[118] Since then more than twenty additional fragments have been identified as belonging to this group, but scholars do not agree on the extent of the corpus. Wilcken believed that they were historical documents and identified them as extracts from $\dot{\upsilon}\pi\omega\mu\nu\eta\mu\alpha\tau\iota\sigma\mu\omega\iota$ ("memoranda" or "written records") or *commentarii Caesaris* ("imperial memoranda"), that is, from official records of legal proceedings. These are often referred to as "protocols" by modern scholars.[119]

Adolf Bauer was the first to apply the label "acts of the pagan martyrs" to these texts.[120] He argued that

---

111 Van Henten, *Maccabean Martyrs*, 78–81.

112 $\epsilon\dot{\iota}$ $\alpha\dot{\upsilon}\tau\omicron\delta\dot{\epsilon}\sigma\pi\omicron\tau\dot{\omicron}\varsigma$ $\dot{\epsilon}\sigma\tau\iota\nu$ $\tau\tilde{\omega}\nu$ $\pi\alpha\vartheta\tilde{\omega}\nu$ $\dot{\omicron}$ $\epsilon\dot{\upsilon}\sigma\epsilon\beta\dot{\eta}\varsigma$ $\lambda\omicron\gamma\iota\sigma\mu\dot{\omicron}\varsigma$; text from Rahlfs; trans. NRSV.

113 Van Henten, *Maccabean Martyrs*, 63.

114 Ibid., 70.

115 See esp. 4 Macc 5:22-24. The construction of a dialogue between Eleazar and Antiochus makes this part of 4 Maccabees more similar to the *Acts of the Alexandrians* than to the corresponding portion of 2 Maccabees; see below on the *Acts of the Alexandrians*.

116 Cf. Cicero *Tusc.* 2.42–65; Seneca *Ad Lucilium Epistulae Morales* 24. Cf. 4 Macc 6:1-11 with *Epistulae Morales* 24.14.

117 Cf. these accounts with the narrative about Cato in Seneca *Epistulae Morales* 24.

118 Ulrich Wilcken, *Zum alexandrinischen Antisemitismus* (ASGW 57.23; ASGW.PH 27.23; Leipzig: Teubner, 1909).

119 See the discussion by Musurillo, *Pagan Martyrs*, 259; cf. 249 on the protocol. An early but classic study is Hans Niedermeyer, *Über antike Protokoll-Literatur* (Göttingen: Kaestner, 1918); see also Berger, "Hellenistische Gattungen," 1248–49; Gary A. Bisbee, *Pre-Decian Acts of Martyrs and Commentarii* (HDR 22; Philadelphia: Fortress, 1988) 19–64, and the literature cited there.

120 Adolf Bauer, "Heidnische Märtyrerakten," *Archiv* 1 (1901) 29–47; see the discussion by Musurillo, *Pagan Martyrs*, 260–61, and by Theofrid Baumeister, *Martyr Invictus: Der Martyrer als Sinnbild der Erlösung in der*

these works belong to the same literary genre as the Christian acts of the martyrs. He argued further that some texts are actually based on protocols, but that others only imitate their literary form. In response to Bauer and others who took a literary approach, Wilcken conceded that the *Acts* were basically historical but showed evidence of the addition of a fictional framework and reworking at various stages. He admitted that some might not be based on protocols at all. The author of the most recent comprehensive study, Herbert Musurillo, takes a similar position with due allowance for the aspect of political propaganda.[121]

The *Acts of the Alexandrians* were composed between 41 CE and the end of the second century CE.[122] Their subject matter involves tension and conflict between citizens of Alexandria and the Roman government from the reign of Tiberius to that of Septimius Severus and between Alexandrian Greeks and Jews. Five of the texts usually included in the *Acts of the Alexandrians* are not really comparable in genre to the passion narrative.[123] But six of them do have some points of similarity.[124] All of these are fragmentary, so it is difficult to determine their structure and genre, but some features are clear. Five of the six contain part of an account of judicial proceedings, and each of these involves a dialogue between the accused and the emperor.[125] Only two contain part of a frame story.[126] One includes an account of a sign or wonder in its frame story.[127]

With regard to content, one work implies that the two accused men were sentenced to death, but their execution is not described in the surviving fragments (*Acts of Isidore*). In another, the emperor threatens the Alexandrian protagonist with death for his insolence, but the fragment does not describe his condemnation or execution (*Acts of Hermaiskos*). In a third, one of the accused is released and the other bound, apparently to be tortured (*Acts of Paul and Antoninus*). It is not clear whether the latter was eventually released or executed. The frame story of a fourth (*Acts of Appian*) describes how the accused is led off to be executed, but then called back by the emperor, not once, but twice.[128]

Although none of the *Acts of the Alexandrians* in its present form describes the death of the protagonist, the hero of one of the works does refer to three of the main characters of another one as having died before him.[129] So a few of them may have been τελευταί ("ends" or "deaths") in their original form, but we cannot be sure.

The genre or micro-genre involving accounts of the deaths of famous men continued to flourish as the *Acts of the Alexandrians* were being written. Pliny the Younger mentions a work by Fannius, otherwise unknown, consisting of a collection of stories about the deaths of those who had been killed or exiled under the emperor Nero.[130] He mentions another such work by Titinius Capito, which probably dealt with events during the reign of Domitian.[131] He himself composed an account of

---

Legende und im Kult der frühen koptischen Kirche (Forschungen zur Volkskunde 46; Münster: Regensberg, 1972) 20–21. According to Berger, Ulrich von Wilamowitz-Moellendorff used the term "Märtyrerakten" for these works ("Hellenistische Gattungen," 1250).

121 Musurillo, *Pagan Martyrs*, 260; he holds that the majority of the *Acta* fragments may be described as "reworked protocols" and that the "protocol form" is not merely a literary device (ibid., 275).

122 Dormeyer, *Die Passion Jesu*, 44.

123 The "Boule Papyrus," the "Interview with Flaccus," the "Gerousia *Acta*," the *Acts of Maximus*, and the *Acts of Athenodorus*.

124 The *Acts of Isidore*, the *Acts of Diogenes*, the *Acts of Hermias*, the *Acts of Hermaiskos*, the *Acts of Paul and Antoninus*, and the *Acts of Appian*.

125 All of the six except the *Acts of Diogenes*, which is a fragment of a speech of prosecution.

126 The *Acts of Hermaiskos* and the *Acts of Appian*.

127 The *Acts of Hermaiskos*.

128 The *Acts of Appian* is similar in this respect to the *Life of Secundus the Philosopher*; Secundus is led out to be executed, but saved at the last moment. The latter text is not one of the *Acts of the Alexandrians*; see Ben Edwin Perry, ed., *Secundus the Silent Philosopher: The Greek Life of Secundus Critically Edited and Restored so far as possible together with Translations of the Greek and Oriental Versions, the Latin and Oriental Texts, and a Study of the Tradition* (APA.PM 22; Ithaca, NY: American Philological Association/Cornell University Press, 1964).

129 Appian in the *Acts of Appian* speaks about Theon, Isidore, and Lampo in this way, all of whom appear in the *Acts of Isidore*.

130 *Exitus occisorum aut relegatorum a Nerone* ("departures of those killed or exiled by Nero") (Pliny *Letters* 5.5).

131 *Exitus illustrium virorum* ("departures of famous men") (Pliny *Letters*, 8.12).

the death of his uncle, Pliny the Elder.[132] There is reason to think that Tacitus and Pliny made use of collections of *exitus* ("departures" or "deaths") in their own writings.[133]

Tacitus's *Annals* contain accounts of the deaths of men during the reigns of Tiberius and Claudius that involved conspiracy and false accusations. The early books contain accounts of voluntary death; of judicial proceedings, sometimes leading to execution, sometimes to acquittal; and accounts of banishment. In the work as a whole, these narratives show how the absolute power of the principate led to abuses, either by the emperor himself or by those who were able to manipulate him for their own purposes. The *exitus* ("departures" or "deaths") go beyond this comprehensive, historical function by idealizing their protagonists and holding up their behavior as a model to be admired, if not imitated. Books 14–16 of the *Annals* contain accounts of notable people who died voluntarily, were murdered, or were exiled during the reign of Nero. The most famous of these is the forced suicide of Seneca (Tacitus *Ann.* 15.44-64, esp. 60-64). The account makes clear that the death of Seneca was intended to be a model for others. Socrates was equally clearly Seneca's model. His last words were that he was making a drink-offering to Jove the Liberator. He thus welcomed death as granting freedom from the tyrant (15.62).[134]

Having surveyed these Greek, Roman, and Jewish texts, we are in a position to consider the genre of the earliest recoverable passion narrative. Reinbold concluded that the oldest recoverable passion account is best characterized form-critically as a popular "historical account" (*Geschichtsbericht*). From an ancient point of view, appropriate designations include διήγησις ("account"), διήγημα ("story"), and ἱστορία ("historical narrative"). An ancient writer could have designated the work διήγησις περὶ τοῦ θανάτου Ἰησοῦ Χριστοῦ ("an account of the death of Jesus Christ").[135] He found it difficult to go beyond that form-critical definition and concluded that a clear categorization of the work in terms of one of the genres of contemporary literature is not possible. He admitted, however, that it includes motifs found in other literature of the time, especialy Old Testament/Jewish "death literature."[136]

Reinbold did not take the position that this popular historical account is objective and only interested in the facts related to Jesus' last days. He defined the central theme of the account as the narrative assertion that it was the chief priests who brought Jesus to the cross by co-opting the power of the Roman prefect. Further, the account makes the claim that Jesus was innocent and was executed only because he admitted to being the messiah, which is equivalent to being the king of the Jews. The early Christian community wanted to protect itself by making the point that its founder was not a common criminal.[137]

The pre-Markan passion narrative is reconstructed quite differently here from the results of Reinbold's study. Nevertheless, to some degree, the source as defined here fits his label "popular historical account." It begins with the scene in the Garden of Gethsemane, in which Jesus is portrayed as distressed and anxious. This portrait contrasts with the self-control and composure of the Maccabean heroes and heroine and most of the famous men of Greek and Roman tradition. In his distress, Jesus prays, at first asking his omnipotent Father to save him from death. This motif recalls the wisdom tales in which the protagonist is rescued from danger by divine power. Yet the prayer concludes with the serene acceptance of God's will; the finishing touches on the portrait thus call to mind Socrates and those who followed his example in meeting death with composure and courage.[138]

---

132 Ibid., 6.16; see the discussion by Richard Reitzenstein, "Ein Stück hellenistischer Kleinliteratur," *NGWG.PH* (Göttingen: Commissionsverlag der Dieterich'schen Universitätsbuchhandlung, 1904) 1:327.

133 Tacitus *Ann.* 4.68–70; 6.47–48; 11.1–3. F. A. Marx makes a case for Tacitus's use of such works ("Tacitus und die Literatur der exitus illustrium virorum," *Philologus* 92 [1937] 83–103); on Pliny's use of such material, see Musurillo, *Pagan Martyrs*, 241–42; and Berger, "Hellenistische Gattungen," 1257.

134 Cf. Cicero *Tusc.* 1.118; Epictetus *Diss.* 4.1.159–177.

135 Reinbold, *Der älteste Bericht*, 189.

136 Ibid., 193–94.

137 Ibid., 197–98.

138 The prayer is a relatively infrequent motif in τελευταί ("ends" or "deaths"). The only real prayer in the relevant portions of 2 and 4 Maccabees is the one uttered by Eleazar as his last words (4 Macc 6:27–29).

The arrival of Judas, one of the Twelve, who handed Jesus over, provides the transition to the second scene. In the Maccabean stories there is no betrayer or even accuser. In the Greek and Roman τελευταί, there is often an accuser and sometimes a conspiracy. The narrative element of betrayal by a disciple with a kiss gives poignancy to the simple narrative of the arrest, which most closely resembles a historical report or a biographical anecdote. This literary character does not necessarily imply historical accuracy or reliability. It is likely that Jesus was in fact arrested by a troop of temple police.[139] But the story about Judas may be legendary.

The narrative then relates that Jesus was taken to the high priest and implies that this event took place at night. In the morning the chief priests held a consultation. This language does not imply a judicial proceeding and no verdict is mentioned. The result of the consultation is that Jesus was sent bound to Pilate, the Roman prefect of Judea. These remarks, which follow the story of the arrest, resemble a historical report. The literary form does not guarantee reliability, but such a course of events is not implausible. Since the high priest and his council did not have the legal authority to impose the sentence of capital punishment, it is more likely that they took Jesus to Pilate and made a complaint against him than that they held a trial themselves.[140]

These remarks also serve as a frame story for the dialogue between Pilate and Jesus that follows. The scene involving this dialogue is unlike the ancient protocols in that it lacks a heading at the beginning and a verdict at the end. It does, however, represent in a plausible way the form of a typical *cognitio extra ordinem*, an informal judicial proceeding in which the Roman governor could interrogate a prisoner and make a decision without a formal legal trial.[141] In such a procedure, the governor would question the accused, as here. The first question concerns the accusation. The second gives the accused the opportunity to respond to the charge. Pilate's decision is implied in the last sentence of the scene, in the remark that he handed Jesus over to be whipped and crucified. The presiding official in a *cognitio extra ordinem* against someone who was not a Roman citizen did not need to formulate a precise legal charge.[142] Without a formal charge there would be no formal verdict. The whipping was apparently a standard prelude to crucifixion.[143] The content of the dialogue, however, is shaped by the later and, as Reinbold has shown, tendentious view that Jesus was condemned for claiming to be the messiah, that is, the king of the Jews. It is more likely that the informal charge was causing unrest, that is, stirring up a revolt (*seditio*).[144] The perspective of the pre-Markan narrative also comes through in the emphasis on the silence of Jesus, which is depicted as amazing Pilate. This silence contrasts strongly with the didactic speeches of the protagonists in many accounts of noble death. It is probably inspired by scripture.[145] The evocation of scripture of course is a narrative technique that belongs to the Jewish and eventually Christian cultural contexts. Formally analogous is the evocation of Socrates' death in the accounts of the death of Eleazar, especially in 2 Maccabees, and of Seneca.

After the scourging and before the crucifixion, there is an account describing how a cohort of Roman auxiliary soldiers mocked Jesus. This scene is analogous to incidents that took place in Alexandria. The first occurred in 38 CE and is reported by Philo (*Flacc.* 6 §§36–39).[146] Agrippa I, grandson of Herod the Great, had just been made king by the emperor Gaius Caligula. The Alexandrian Greeks instigated a public mockery of Agrippa, taking a harmless simpleton to the gymnasium,

---

139 Cf. Reinbold, *Der älteste Bericht*, 314.

140 Ibid.

141 Fergus Millar argued that there is no formal trial even in the Markan passion narrative ("Reflections on the Trials of Jesus," in Philip R. Davies and Richard T. White, eds., *A Tribute to Geza Vermes: Essays on Jewish and Christian Literature and History* [JSOTSup 100; Sheffield: JSOT Press, 1990] 366).

142 Musurillo, *Pagan Martyrs*, 113–14; Peter Garnsey, *Social Status and Legal Privilege in the Roman Empire* (Oxford: Clarendon, 1970) 5–6.

143 Livy 33.36; Josephus *Bell.* 2.14.9 §306; 5.11.1 §449; Taylor, 584; Hengel, *Crucifixion*, 29 and n. 21.

144 Reinbold, *Der älteste Bericht*, 314.

145 Ps 37:14-15 LXX (38:14-15 MT; 38:13-14 NRSV) is perhaps evoked here or Isa 53:7. See the commentary on 15:5 below.

146 Herbert Box, *Philonis Alexandrini: In Flaccum* (London/New York: Oxford University Press, 1939) xl–xliii, 91–92. On Agrippa I, see also David C. Braund, "Agrippa," *ABD* 1:98–99.

setting him up on high, putting on his head a sheet of papyrus, spread out wide like a royal crown, clothing him in a rug as a mantle, and giving him a papyrus rush that had been thrown on the road as a scepter. Some approached him, pretending to salute him, others to sue for justice, and others to consult him on state affairs. Then the crowd hailed him as "Marin," the name by which it is said that kings are called in Syria. Philo described the whole affair as similar to the theatrical mimes.

The other incident is mentioned in the *Acts of Paul and Antoninus,* one of the *Alexandrian Acts.* This work reports a speech by an Alexandrian about how the people of Alexandria had mocked a king by performing a mime. The king in question was probably the royal or messianic claimant who led the revolt in Cyrene.[147] This mime took place in about 117 CE. The similarities between the mocking of Agrippa and that of Jesus are probably due to the widespread popularity of the mime.[148] The mocking of Jesus also has similarities to ancient rituals and literary motifs related to the *pharmakos*.[149]

The next scene, the account of the crucifixion itself, resembles a historical report. It is not, of course, a matter of brute facts. The account of Jesus' death is historical in form even though it presents him as a crucified messiah and involves omens that interpret the event. If the wine flavored or drugged with myrrh offered to Jesus is meant to dull the pain, his refusal of it calls to mind the motif of despising pain prominent especially in the late Stoic τελευταί ("ends" or "deaths"). The soldiers divide his clothing, casting lots to see who would take what. The wording of this incident creates a strong allusion to Ps 21:19 LXX.[150] Once again, an old story helps to narrate and interpret Jesus' death in a complex way. The placard announcing the crime of Jesus is said to read "the king of the Jews." This statement links the crucifixion scene to

the proceedings before Pilate and likewise states the informal charge against Jesus in a historically tendentious way. The remark that Jesus was crucified between two bandits or rebels may evoke Isa 53:12, "he was numbered with the transgressors." There is not much evidence for other perceived instigators of unrest at the time of Jesus. If he alone was arrested, and his followers allowed to flee,[151] it is unlikely that he was crucified with others. The depiction of Jesus between two rebels or common criminals heightens the pathos of the scene for those who believe him to be innocent and the irony for those who believe him to be a king (messiah). The mocking of the passersby and the two bandits also evokes Psalm 21 LXX.[152]

The description of the death of Jesus involves a sign or wonder, darkness over the whole land for three hours. Such prodigies are relatively rare in accounts of the deaths of famous people (τελευταί), but not unknown. This incident recalls portrayals of the death of Julius Caesar. Virgil, for example, says that the sun "expressed mercy for Rome when Caesar was killed; he hid his shining head in gloom and the impious age feared eternal night" (*Georgics* 1.468).[153]

According to the tentative reconstruction offered here, the pre-Markan passion narrative did not contain a report of Jesus' last words. This lack is consonant with the virtual silence of Jesus during the proceedings before Pilate. He is simply portrayed as crying out with a loud voice and expiring. In place of the last words is another sign, the tearing of the curtain of the temple. It was suggested above that this sign, as the ending of the pre-Markan passion narrative, may symbolize Jesus' ascent to heaven and entry into the presence of God, as well as the rending of the barrier between humanity and God. Another possibility is that it suggests a metaphorical theophany.[154] The removing of the veil before the Holy of Holies reveals God. The sequence of the cry of Jesus

147 According to Eusebius, his name was Lukuas (*Hist. eccl.* 4.2); Cassius Dio says his name was Andreias (68.32.1–3).

148 Elaine Fantham, "Mime," *OCD* 982–83; Hermann Reich, *Der Mimus: Ein litterar-entwickelungs-geschichtlicher Versuch*, vol. 1, part 1: *Theorie des Mimus* (Berlin: Weidmann, 1903).

149 Yarbro Collins, "Finding Meaning," 186–87.

150 Ps 22:19 MT; 22:18 NRSV. See the commentary on 15:24 below.

151 Reinbold, *Der älteste Bericht*, 314–16.

152 Ps 21:7-9 LXX; Ps 22:7-9 MT; 22:6-8 NRSV. See the commentary on 15:29-30 below.

153 Trans. from David R. Cartlidge and David L. Dungan, *Documents for the Study of the Gospels* (Philadelphia: Fortress, 1980) 163. See also Plutarch *Vit. Caesar* 69.4–5.

154 Cf. Rev 11:19; 16:17-21; Yarbro Collins, *Beginning of the Gospel*, 116–17; eadem, "Genre," 16.

and the opening of the temple may evoke Psalm 17 LXX.[155] In that psalm, the speaker cries out to God, and God hears the cry in the temple. A theophany follows that leads to the deliverance of the speaker. The allusion to this psalm implies that God heard the cry of Jesus and vindicated him.

A number of proposals have been made with regard to the social setting of the pre-Markan passion narrative. Dibelius proposed that it was rooted in the preaching of the Christian message.[156] Green argued that it was composed for the celebration of the Lord's supper.[157] Trocmé opted for the annual celebration of Passover.[158] Reinbold concluded that a catechetical setting is most likely.[159] The view taken here is that a liturgical setting is most likely, although the document would have had missionary and catechetical significance as well.[160]

In terms of genre, the pre-Markan passion narrative may be categorized as a τελευτή ("end" or "death"), the story of the death of a prominent person. Jesus was not a noble person in the eyes of those who believed that his message and the crowds that he attracted constituted a threat to public order. For a long time after his death he remained an obscure person from the point of view of the general public in the Mediterranean world, so he hardly qualified as a famous man for them. But from the perspective of this document and his followers he was of noble rank; he was the messiah, the rejected king of Israel. The combination of his noble rank and the humiliation that he suffered creates a narrative of great pathos and irony.

Subtypes of the genre "account of the death of a famous person" may be defined according to the social role of the protagonists: rulers, rebellious subjects, philosophers. From the point of view of outsiders, the account of Jesus' death may be defined as belonging to the subtype, "death of a messianic pretender." Josephus includes several accounts of this subtype: the stories of Simon, the slave of Herod the Great;[161] Athronges the shepherd;[162] Menahem;[163] and Simon son of Giora.[164] None of these accounts includes a judicial proceeding, but Simon son of Giora was executed in the Roman forum at the climax of the triumph celebrated by Vespasian and Titus.

The presence of the scene with Pilate gives the pre-Markan passion narrative a certain similarity to the *Acts of the Alexandrians*, but the silence of Jesus is a striking difference. The detailed description of Jesus' death is analogous to the Maccabean stories, but the little emphasis on torture and the physical suffering of Jesus is a significant difference. Most of the differences between the pre-Markan passion narrative and other τελευταί ("ends" or "deaths") are connected with the frequent evocation of scripture in the former, especially the psalms. One could say that the external *form* of the narrative is the τελευτή, but its *tone* or internal form derives from the psalms of lament. Given the hermeneutics of the time, it is likely that these psalms were read by followers of Jesus as prophecies or prefigurations of the death of Jesus as messiah. They probably read them as songs of David, the prototypical king.[165]

From the point of view of genre, Mark altered his source in several significant ways. Perhaps the most notable is the addition of the empty-tomb story at the end. This scene is a Christian adaptation of a familiar genre in Greek and Roman traditions, disappearance stories that imply the protagonist's translation to heaven.[166]

In order to prepare for the empty-tomb story, Mark also added the account of Jesus' burial. Burial of the protagonist is rarely mentioned in the accounts of the deaths

155 Ps 17:7-20 LXX; 18:7-20 MT; 18:6-19 NRSV. See also Yarbro Collins, "From Noble Death," 498–99.

156 Dibelius, *From Tradition to Gospel*, 22–23, 178–79.

157 Green, *Death of Jesus*, 214–17.

158 Trocmé, *Passion as Liturgy*, 84.

159 Reinbold, *Der älteste Bericht*, 194–97.

160 Yarbro Collins, *Beginning of the Gospel*, 118.

161 Josephus *Bell.* 2.4.2 §§57–59 = *Ant.* 17.10.6 §§273–77. Simon the slave was decapitated while trying to flee from a battle with Roman soldiers.

162 *Bell.* 2.4.3 §§60–65 = *Ant.* 17.10.7 §§278–84. Josephus does not actually describe the death of Athronges, but it seems to be implied. He and his four brothers led a revolt; three of them were captured and one surrendered.

163 *Bell.* 2.17.8 §§433–48. Menachem was killed by partisans of Eleazar, one of the leaders of the revolt, joined by the people of Jerusalem.

164 *Bell.* 7.2.2 §§26–36; 7.5.6 §§153–57.

165 Juel, *Messianic Exegesis*, 116; Yarbro Collins, "Genre," 18.

166 Yarbro Collins, *Beginning of the Gospel*, 119–48.

of famous people.[167] The burial of Socrates is discussed before his death but not narrated (Plato *Phaedo* 115c–116a). In 4 Macc 17:8, the tomb(s) of Eleazar and the others is mentioned, and the author proposed a fitting inscription for it. The burial of Jesus in Mark may be an originally independent tradition. It may have a historically reliable core. Or it could be a legend making the point that Jesus really died.[168]

By adding the burial and disappearance/empty-tomb stories, Mark brought out much more clearly than the earlier passion narrative the divine vindication of Jesus. In a sense, this was a logical development of the genre. The account of the death of Julius Caesar in Suetonius (*Jul.* 80–82, 84, 88) is followed by a description of his funeral, cremation, and apotheosis.[169] For a Greek or Roman audience, the "disappearance" of Jesus' body assimilates him to their heroes and divinized founders and rulers.

Another important new scene is the trial before the high priest and the council (Sanhedrin). Mark states that the chief priests and the whole council were seeking testimony against Jesus in order that they might condemn him to death (14:55). Since the definite article is used, Mark refers not to an ad hoc group of the high priest's personal advisory council but to the provincial assembly of Judea, which ruled under the authority of and in cooperation with the Roman prefect.[170] The scene is similar to the Roman protocols and to some of the *Acts of the Alexandrians* in that the judicial proceeding is in part summarized and in part represented in direct discourse. The high point is the dialogue between Jesus and the high priest. The high priest first questions Jesus about the testimony of the witnesses. To this question Jesus gives no response, but when the high priest asks Jesus whether he is the messiah, he gives a decidedly positive response and adds a prophetic saying that plays a key role in the development of the Markan theme regarding Jesus' identity. With this brief speech of Jesus, Mark stretches the picture of the virtually silent Jesus of his source to the breaking point and also deviates from the Gospel's own theme of secrecy. This element makes the Markan form of the passion narrative more similar to the Maccabean accounts, in which the speeches of the dying heroes have a didactic function. It also makes this account of the death of Jesus more like the Hellenistic and Roman death stories in which the speech of the protagonist is often the major focus. The charge is informally stated as blasphemy.[171] The verdict is clearly stated: the members of the council unanimously condemned Jesus to death (14:64). This trial is most likely unhistorical.[172] In addition to its similarities to other death stories that include judicial proceedings, this scene also resonates with psalms that express the themes of false witnesses and the unjust condemnation of an innocent person (Pss 109:2-3, 6-7; 35:11; 69:4; 94:21).

As noted above, Mark expanded the story of the death of Jesus in a way that logically develops the genre: the divinely appointed and vindicated messiah of his source becomes the messiah translated to heaven whence he will return in glory as the Son of Man. Jesus' death is portrayed in 8:34—9:1 and 13:9-13 as one to be imitated by his followers. The same point is made in Luke-Acts, for example, by the way in which the account of Stephen's death is modeled on that of Jesus. These passages do not yet imply that Jesus was the first of a series of martyrs. On the contrary, they fit quite well in the tradition of the τελευτή ("end" or "death") and the *exitus* ("departure" or "death"). Those aspiring to die nobly model their attitudes and behavior on the great examples of the past.[173]

Comment

■ **1-2** As noted above, a number of scholars have concluded that the pre-Markan passion narrative began with 14:1-2.[174] One argument put forward in favor of that view is that the chronology of the passion implied by these

---

167 In some cases, cremation is mentioned or implied, e.g., Tacitus *Ann.* 11.3; 15.64. Burial is occasionally mentioned in passing, e.g., ibid., 16.11.

168 See the commentary on 15:42-47 below.

169 Cf. Plutarch *Vit. Caesar* 69.4.

170 Anthony J. Saldarini, "Sanhedrin," *ABD* 5:975–80.

171 For discussion see Yarbro Collins, "Charge of Blasphemy," 379–401, and the commentary below.

172 Reinbold, *Der älteste Bericht*, 258.

173 On the distinctiveness of the Markan passion narrative in relation to other types of death stories in the ancient world, see Yarbro Collins, "From Noble Death," 481–503.

174 See the section "Composition and History of the Tradition" in the excursus on the passion narrative above.

verses conflicts with that of Mark. As argued above, there is no real conflict.[175] It is much more likely that 14:1-2 is a Markan composition.[176]

Passover and Unleavened Bread were originally two distinct festivals. In scripture the two feasts are combined into a single holiday.[177] The opening statement of v. 1 reflects this unity.

Some interpreters of Mark have concluded that chapters 11–16 imply that Jesus entered Jerusalem on a Sunday ("Palm Sunday") and that the empty tomb was discovered on the following Sunday ("Easter Sunday").[178] It is true that Mark portrays Jesus' entry into Jerusalem as occuring on one day (11:1-11), the cursing of the fig tree and the actions in the temple on the next day (11:12-19), and the observation that the fig tree had withered on a third day (11:20), but there is no mention of a fourth day in the whole section from 11:20 to 13:37. The comment in 14:1 does not continue the clear sequence of one day following another. It is evident that Mark portrays the discovery of the empty tomb as occurring on a Sunday, but it is not clear that he portrays Jesus as spending only a week in Jerusalem. Such is a reasonable inference, but it is not certain. The exact chronology of Jesus' stay in Jerusalem does not appear to be a major concern of the evangelist.

The chief priests here probably represent the priestly aristocracy, members of the noble families from which the high priest was selected. Under Roman rule, the chief priests were leading members of the Sanhedrin and of the internal government generally.[179] The scribes here are probably "temple scribes," who may have been "concerned either with the financial and organizational functions of the Temple or with the recording and teaching of sacred traditions and laws. . . . That the scribes [were] dependent on Temple revenues and subordinate to the priests who controlled the Temple is certain and signifi-cant for understanding the scribes as they appear in the gospels for there too the scribes are located mainly in Jerusalem and allied with the chief priests."[180] It is unlikely that "scribes" associated with the Pharisees are meant here. The portrayal of the chief priests and scribes as wanting to arrest Jesus and to kill him links this verse with 11:18, where the same motivation is attributed to the same two groups. There the desire to eliminate Jesus is a response to his actions in the temple.

According to v. 1b, the chief priests and scribes were trying to arrest Jesus "by deceit" ($\dot{\epsilon}\nu$ $\delta\acute{o}\lambda\omega$). Their motivation is implied in v. 2: they did not want to arrest him publicly because doing so might cause a disturbance among the people. Verse 2 says that they did not want to arrest Jesus during the festival. The development of the narrative after this point suggests that they were not able to arrest Jesus in the short time remaining before the festival. When Judas offered to hand him over, they found a way to arrest Jesus "by deceit" and thus to avoid arresting him publicly, even though they had to arrest him during the festival.[181]

The motif of "deceit" ($\delta\acute{o}\lambda o\varsigma$) in the story of Jesus' death is a point of similarity to the story of the death of Aesop, whom the citizens of Delphi plotted to kill by deceit ($\delta\acute{o}\lambda o\varsigma$).[182] In this, as in other ways, the life of Jesus as presented in Mark is analogous to the typical life of a poet as presented in various ancient popular biographies and biographical traditions.[183]

■ **3-9** The placement of the story of the anointing between the two parts of the story about the plot against Jesus (vv. 1-2, 10-11) is a sign of Markan editing.[184] Luke has a variant of the story outside the passion narrative (7:36-50). These two pieces of evidence make it highly probable that the story was not in Mark's passion source and that it was an originally independent story that circulated in at least two variant forms.[185]

175 See the criticism of Theissen's formulation of this argument above (ibid.).
176 Schenke, *Passionsgeschichte*, 12–66.
177 For the scriptural evidence see Exodus 12–13; 23:10-19; 34:18-26; Lev 23:4-8; Ezra 6:19-22; Num 28:16-25. For discussion, see Baruch M. Bokser, "Unleavened Bread and Passover, Feasts of," *ABD* 6:755–65.
178 See the commentary on 11:12-14 above.
179 Schürer, *History*, 2:233–36.
180 Saldarini, *Pharisees*, 250. See also the commentary on 11:18 above.
181 See note a on the trans. of v. 2 above.
182 Yarbro Collins, "Finding Meaning," 192.
183 Ibid., 187–93.
184 Yarbro Collins, *Beginning of the Gospel*, 104.
185 Reinbold also concludes that the anointing was not part of the oldest recoverable passion account, but he thinks that it was added at an early stage and thus was part of Mark's and John's passion sources (*Der älteste Bericht*, 106–11).

Ernst von Dobschütz argued that Mark artfully heightened the suspense for the audience by not introducing the offer of Judas immediately after the description of the dilemma of the chief priests and scribes. He held them in suspense by narrating the quite different story of the anointing before introducing Judas' offer.[186] James R. Edwards emphasized the sharp contrast between the woman's devotion to Jesus and Judas' treachery.[187] Tom Shepherd spoke of "dramatized irony" in the contrast of the woman and Judas. A named member of the Twelve brings on the passion of Jesus, whereas an unnamed woman illustrates true discipleship, whose act of love prepares for Jesus' burial.[188]

For the development of the theme of Judas and his handing Jesus over, it is important to note that he is not mentioned by name in vv. 3-9. It is not suggested that the woman's deed plays a role in motivating Judas to go to the chief priests.[189]

With regard to genre, Dibelius defined vv. 3-9 as a pure paradigm.[190] Bultmann categorized it as a biographical apophthegm.[191] Tannehill, more helpfully, defined it as a hybrid pronouncement story that combines correction and commendation.[192]

■ **3** Since the construction with two genitive absolutes, one following immediately upon the other, is very awkward Greek, it is likely that one of them is a redactional addition by Mark. Since Mark has already indicated that Jesus was staying in Bethany (11:11-12; cf. 11:19), it is likely that the phrase "while he was in Bethany" (ὄντος αὐτοῦ ἐν Βηθανίᾳ) is the evangelist's addition to a traditional story.[193] The traditional form of the story, as it was known to Mark, began more or less as follows, "And as he was reclining at table in the house of Simon the leper" (καὶ κατακειμένου αὐτοῦ ἐν τῇ οἰκίᾳ Σίμονος τοῦ λέπρου).[194] Nothing more is known about this Simon.[195] Mark probably preserved this mention of Simon, who was known to the audience when this traditional story was composed.[196]

The statement that "a woman came" (ἦλθεν γυνή) is ambiguous, but probably indicates that she came to Jesus from outside the house of Simon and was an uninvited guest.[197] The fact that she brought a glass bottle of expensive aromatic oil suggests that she was rich.[198] The bottle probably did not need to be broken to be opened.[199]

It has been suggested that, in an earlier form of the

---

186 Von Dobschütz, "Erzählerkunst," 194–95.

187 Edwards, "Markan Sandwiches," 208–9. Elizabeth Struthers Malbon defines the same irony. In addition to the contrast with Judas, she suggests that there is an analogy between this woman and the widow in 12:41-44; both are exemplary women (*In the Company of Jesus*, 55–57).

188 Shepherd, *Markan Sandwich Stories*, 263. See also Kim Paffenroth, *Judas: Images of the Lost Disciple* (Louisville/London: Westminster John Knox, 2001) 7.

189 Paffenroth, *Judas*, 7; William Klassen, *Judas: Betrayer or Friend of Jesus?* (Minneapolis: Fortress, 1996) 89–90.

190 Dibelius *From Tradition to Gospel*, 43.

191 Bultmann, *History*, 36–37.

192 Tannehill, "Varieties," 1.1 (p. 103), 2.1 (p. 105).

193 With Schenke, *Passionsgeschichte*, 68–72, and against Bultmann, *History*, 65.

194 Schenke, *Passionsgeschichte*, 72.

195 Dibelius, *From Tradition to Gospel*, 49; Meier, *Marginal Jew*, 2:746 n. 96 (3), 869 n. 162.

196 Schenke, *Passionsgeschichte*, 70.

197 Bultmann, *History*, 66. Matthew maintains Mark's ambiguity (Matt 26:7); Luke's version of the story, which does not appear to be dependent on Mark's

version, implies, somewhat more clearly than Mark, that the woman was an uninvited guest (7:37-38). In John's version, the woman, Mary, the sister of Lazarus, is part of the household and serves at the table (12:2).

198 In contrast to the poor widow of Mark 12:41-44 (Malbon, *In the Company of Jesus*, 55–57). On the use of aromatic oil (perfume) in social contexts involving wealthy people, and on the nature and use of the ἀλάβαστρον ("small glass bottle [containing aromatic oil]"), see Marianne Sawicki, "Making Jesus," in Levine, *Feminist Companion*, 136–70, esp. 144–47.

199 David Daube argued that the breaking of the "box" and the pouring out of its entire contents fits the practice of anointing for burial better than the practice of anointing oneself [or a guest in preparation for a festive banquet] (*New Testament*, 315, 317). On the basis of published finds of ἀλάβαστρα ("small glass bottles" [containing aromatic oil = perfume]), Sawicki argued that the bottle did not need to be broken to be opened ("Making Jesus," 157).

story, the gesture of the woman signified an anointing of Jesus as the royal messiah.[200] But in the classic scriptural passages of royal anointing, what is poured on the king's head is "olive oil" ($\check{\epsilon}\lambda\alpha\iota\omicron\nu$), not "aromatic oil" ($\mu\acute{\upsilon}\rho\omicron\nu$) as here.[201] This may be one of the connotations of the woman's deed, but it is not the only one.[202]

Psalm 132 LXX, however, speaks of "aromatic oil" ($\mu\acute{\upsilon}\rho\omicron\nu$) flowing down from the head of Aaron over his beard and down to the edge of his garment. This abundance of aromatic oil, however, does not refer primarily to the ritual of anointing Aaron as high priest. It is a metaphor for plenitude and prosperity.[203] The psalm also uses language from the Song of Songs "to describe the family of the Lord at the feast in Jerusalem."[204] The term $\mu\acute{\upsilon}\rho\omicron\nu$ ("aromatic oil") is used five or six times in the Song of Songs LXX.[205] In 1:3-4 the female voice extols the aromatic oils on the body of her lover, which make him attractive. In 2:5 she asks him to support her or to feed her ($\sigma\tau\eta\rho\acute{\iota}\zeta\epsilon\iota\nu$) with aromatic oils. In 4:10, the male voice extols the fragrance of the aromatic oils of the one he calls "my sister, my bride" ($\grave{\alpha}\delta\epsilon\lambda\varphi\acute{\eta}$ $\mu\omicron\upsilon$ $\nu\acute{\upsilon}\mu\varphi\eta$). The potential allusion to the Song of Songs may indicate that Jesus is portrayed as a metaphorical bridegroom in this passage.[206] It is more likely, however, that the woman's gesture represents the custom of anointing the head in preparation for a joyous feast.[207]

■ **4-5** Some of those who witness the woman's extrava-gant gesture do not appreciate it. The tendency of the tradition seems to be in the direction of specifying the critic(s) of her action. In Codex Bezae and a few other manuscripts, "some" ($\tau\iota\nu\epsilon\varsigma$) has become "the disciples" ($\omicron\grave{\iota}$ $\mu\alpha\vartheta\eta\tau\alpha\acute{\iota}$).[208] The same change was made by Matthew (26:8). In John, the antagonist is Judas Iscariot (12:4).[209] "Some" are depicted in Mark as arguing that the aromatic oil should have been sold and the proceeds given to the poor. The larger context of the Gospel as a whole suggests that those who make this argument are admonishing the woman to put into effect the teaching that Jesus directed to the rich man in 10:21, "sell what you possess and give to the poor, and you will have treasure in heaven." They seem to be justified in reproving her.

■ **6** Jesus, however, corrects the attitude of those who reproved the woman by telling them to leave her alone and asking why they are causing trouble for her. Immediately following that correction, he commends the woman's action as "a good deed" ($\kappa\alpha\lambda\grave{\omicron}\nu$ $\check{\epsilon}\rho\gamma\omicron\nu$) done to him.[210]

■ **7** Jesus' speech continues as he explains, indirectly, why the principle of 10:21 does not apply in this case. "For you always have the poor with you," he says, "and whenever you want, you can do good to them, but you do not always have me." This saying is similar to the passage in which Jesus is compared to a bridegroom (2:18-22).[211] There fasting is presented as a pious activity in normal

---

200 Schüssler Fiorenza, *In Memory of Her*, xiii–xiv.

201 1 Kgdms 10:1a (the anointing of Saul by Samuel); 16:13 (the anointing of David by Samuel). The first high priest, Aaron, was also anointed with olive oil (Lev 8:12). The Hebrew noun שמן, used in all these passages in the MT, refers to oil in general and specifically to olive oil (BDB, s.v., 2.a).

202 Support for the argument that one of the connotations of the woman's gesture is an anointing of Jesus as king or messiah is the fact that, after the conclusion of the conspiracy story, the anointing is followed by the sending of two disciples to find a room for the celebration of the Passover (vv. 12-16). The latter story evokes 1 Kgdms 10:1b-8, as the former evokes 10:1a.

203 Ps 132:2 LXX (133:2 MT); Richard J. Clifford, *Psalms 73–150* (AOTC; Nashville: Abingdon, 2003) 260.

204 Ibid., 259–60.

205 Cant 1:3 (twice), 4; 2:5 (all MSS, but emended by Rahlfs following Grabe); 4:10 (Sinaiticus); 4:14.

206 Cf. 2:19-20, where Jesus is compared to a bridegroom.

207 Amos 6:6 LXX; Ps 22:5 LXX (23:5 MT); Isa 25:6-7 LXX; Josephus *Ant.* 19.4.1 §239. Cf. Luke 7:36, 46. On the use of aromatic oil as a personal adornment, see Jdt 10:3 LXX; cf. Wis 2:7, which may imply a banquet scene. Dennis R. MacDonald has argued that the woman recognized the necessity of Jesus' death, but the text gives no indication of that ("Renowned Far and Wide: The Women Who Anointed Odysseus and Jesus," in Levine, ed., *Feminist Companion*, 128–35).

208 See note b on the trans. of v. 4 above; Bultmann, *History*, 37.

209 The object and point of the criticism in Luke's version are different, but there the critic is Jesus' host, Simon the Pharisee (7:36, 39-40).

210 The passage is a hybrid pronouncement story; see the commentary on vv. 3-9 above. Daube argued that the notion of a "good deed" or "good work" was a technical one (*New Testament*, 315).

times. But when Jesus is present, it is a time not for fasting but rather a time for feasting, just as people feast at a wedding. So here, giving alms to the poor is normally a good deed. But now, it is a good deed to anoint Jesus' head in this extravagant way.

■ **8** Just as the bridegroom is "taken away" from those who rejoice with him (2:20), there will come a time when Jesus is no longer with those whom Jesus is correcting. Nothing can be done to prevent this absence of Jesus, but the woman "did what she could" (ὃ ἔσχεν ἐποίησεν). Finally, in v. 8b, Jesus explains why the woman's action is "a good deed" to him: "She anointed my body for burial beforehand" (προέλαβεν μυρίσαι τὸ σῶμά μου εἰς τὸν ἐνταφιασμόν). As noted above, aromatic oil (μύρον) was used to adorn oneself, especially for a festive meal.[212] It was also used to anoint the dead before burial.[213]

David Daube has interpreted this passage to mean that the action of the woman constitutes the actual burial rite of anointing in a kind of legal fiction. Thus, according to Mark, Joseph of Arimathea does not anoint the body (15:46), and the women who intended to do so arrived at the tomb too late (16:1-6).[214] He interprets the passages in which Josephus speaks of the "dishonorable burial" of the criminal as implying that the body of such a man was not anointed.[215] Further, he concludes that "the earliest tradition was that Jesus had been buried

unanointed, like a common criminal, 'dishonorably, by night.'"[216] Since this tradition was unbearable to the followers of Jesus, they denied it in different ways—Mark by the anointing of Jesus' body in advance, John by depicting an anointing by Joseph and Nicodemus.[217] Daube seems to be right at least with regard to the inference that Mark does not imply that Joseph anointed Jesus. Mark thus implies that he did not receive the usual anointing for burial. The action of the woman portrayed here takes the place of a practice that bestows honor on the deceased.

■ **9** After explaining why the action of the woman was a good deed done to Jesus, he goes on to commend her further. He affirms solemnly that "wherever the good news is proclaimed in the whole world, what this woman has done will also be spoken of in memory of her." The use of the verbs κηρύσσειν ("to proclaim") and λαλεῖν ("to speak of") seems to refer to an oral context, that is, to the oral proclamation of the gospel to which Paul refers frequently in his letters.[218] But the idea that the strictly oral gospel would include this pronouncement story seems unlikely. As noted above, this story was probably not included in the pre-Markan passion narrative, which makes its regular inclusion in the oral "gospel" unlikely.

Matthew reproduces this verse almost verbatim (26:13). He changed the order of the words in the last clause, a change that does not affect the meaning of the

---

211 See the commentary on v. 3 above.

212 See the commentary on v. 3 above.

213 2 Chr 16:13-14 LXX; Luke 23:56; Victor H. Matthews, "Perfumes and Spices," *ABD* 5:226–28, esp. 227. See also Rachel Hachlili, *Jewish Funerary Customs, Practices and Rites in the Second Temple Period* (JSJSup 94; Leiden/Boston: Brill, 2005) 376, 382, and esp. 383–85, 480.

214 Daube, *New Testament*, 313.

215 Josephus *Ant.* 4.8.6 §202 (this passage states ἀτίμως καὶ ἀφανῶς θαπτέσθω, "Let him . . . be . . . buried dishonorably and in obscurity"; text and trans. [modified] from Thackeray, *Josephus*, 4:572–73); *Ant.* 4.8.24 §264 (this passage simply says θαπτέσθω νυκτός, "let him be buried at night"; text and trans. from Thackeray, *Josephus*, 4:602–3); *Ant.* 5.1.14 §44 (this passage states that Achar [Josh 7:25-26] "at nightfall was given the dishonorable burial proper to the condemned" [ἐν νυκτὶ ταφῆς ἀτίμου καὶ καταδίκῳ πρεπούσης τυγχάνει] text and trans. [modified] from Thackeray, *Josephus*, 5:20–21).

216 Daube, *New Testament*, 314.

217 Ibid. Daube argued that John's account especially appears to be written in response to "disparaging talk on the part of Jewish opponents" (ibid., 316).

218 The following passages all contain the term "gospel" (εὐαγγέλιον); when a verb explicitly linking that noun with oral activity is used, that verb is specified. 1 Thess 1:5; 2:2 (λαλεῖν), 4 (λαλεῖν), 8, 9 (κηρύσσειν); 3:2; 1 Cor 4:15; 9:12, 14 (καταγγέλειν), 18 (εὐαγγελίζειν), 23; 15:1 (εὐαγγελίζειν); Gal 1:6, 7, 11 (εὐαγγελίζειν); 2:2 (κηρύσσειν), 5, 7, 14; 2 Cor 2:12; 4:3, 4; 8:18; 9:13; 10:14; 11:4, 7 (εὐαγγελίζειν); Phil 1:5, 7, 12, 16, 27; 2:22; 4:3, 15; Phlm 13; Rom 1:1, 9, 16; 2:16; 10:16; 11:28; 15:16, 19.

statement. His other change is more noteworthy. After the word εὐαγγέλιον ("good news" or "gospel"), he adds τοῦτο ("this"). It is conceivable that "this" here refers to the good news expressed in the story in Matt 26:6-13, which is parallel to Mark 14:3-9. It is more likely, however, that the addition of the demonstrative adjective narrows the meaning of the word "gospel" to the good news as expressed in the text of Matthew as a whole.

Many manuscripts of Mark have the word τοῦτο after εὐαγγέλιον also, but this is surely a later addition designed to conform the text of Mark to that of Matthew.[219] It seems likely, however, that the author of Mark, like Matthew, was referring here to the work he was composing in terms of the oral proclamation of the gospel. Such a reference would make sense in a social context in which the Gospel was read aloud and expounded, that is, in a social context of reoralization.[220] It would also make the claim more intelligible that "wherever the good news is proclaimed in the whole world, what this woman has done will also be spoken of in memory of her."

It seems likely, then, that here the author of Mark refers to his own work as a "gospel." This does not imply, however, that he was using the term as the designation of a (new) literary type or kind of literature. The usage simply shows that no great distinction was made by this author, and probably his audiences, between an oral summary of the gospel and a written Gospel.[221]

■ **10-11** Some scholars have argued that vv. 10-11 constituted the continuation of vv. 1-2 in the pre-Markan passion narrative.[222] It is more likely, however, that vv. 10-11, like vv. 1-2, were composed by Mark.[223]

The evangelist reproduces here the name "Judas Iscariot" (Ἰούδας Ἰσκαριώθ) from the traditional list of the Twelve that he used in composing 3:13-19.[224] He probably found the designation of Judas as "one of the Twelve" (εἷς τῶν δώδεκα) in his passion source (preserved in 14:43) and used it as a model in composing the titular form of it in v. 10, "the [notorious] one of the Twelve" (ὁ εἷς τῶν δώδεκα).[225]

No motivation is given for Judas' decision to hand Jesus over to the chief priests and scribes. Matthew apparently filled in that narrative gap by implying that Judas was a lover of money. He makes this point by having Judas ask the chief priests what they would give him if he handed Jesus over and by having the chief priests offer a specific amount of money.[226] Luke fills in the gap by stating that Satan entered into Judas (22:3). John makes the motivation of greed explicit, adding that Judas was a thief (12:4-6), and also presents Judas as under the power of the devil (6:70-71; 13:2, 27).

For Mark, however, the phrase "in order to hand him over to them" (ἵνα αὐτὸν παραδοῖ) was a sufficient interpretation. Although Judas was not relieved of responsibility, the allusion to Isa 53:6, 12 LXX implies that the death of Jesus was divinely ordained.[227] Verse 11

219 E.g., Alexandrinus (A), Ephraemi Syri Rescriptus (C), Coridethianus (Θ). Sinaiticus (ℵ), Vaticanus (B), Bezae (D), and Freerianus (W) have the shorter reading.

220 On the notion of reoralization, see Mills, "Domains of Folkloristic Concern," 232, 237–38; see the section "Composition and History of the Tradition" in the excursus on the passion narrative above.

221 See also the commentary on 1:1 above.

222 See the section "Composition and History of the Tradition" in the excursus on the passion narrative above.

223 Schenke, *Passionsgeschichte*, 119–40.

224 See note d on the trans. of 14:10, note g on the trans. of 3:19, and the commentary on 3:14-15, 19 above.

225 Schenke, *Passionsgeschichte*, 122–26. Cf. Klauck, *Judas*, 48.

226 Cf. Matt 26:14-16 with Mark 14:10-11. Note also that Matthew rewrote the probably unrealistic "more

than three hundred denarii" (ἐπάνω δηνάρια τριακόσια) of Mark 14:5 as simply "much" (πολλόν). Matthew's τριάκοντα ἀργύρια ("thirty silver [shekels]") may allude to the τριάκοντα ἀργυροῖ ("thirty silver [shekels]") of Zech 11:12 LXX (Davies and Allison, *Matthew*, 3:451). Howard Clark Kee concluded that Mark 14:11 alludes to the same passage, but that is unlikely ("The Function of Scriptural Quotations and Allusions in Mark 11–16," in E. Earle Ellis and Erich Gräßer, eds., *Jesus und Paulus: Festschrift für Werner Georg Kümmel zum 70. Geburtstag* [Göttingen: Vandenhoeck & Ruprecht, 1975] 169).

227 See the commentary on 3:19 above. See also Gnilka, 2:229; Klauck, *Judas*, 49; Klassen, *Judas*, 85.

vividly portrays the conspiracy in the details of the joy of the chief priests and Judas' active waiting for an opportunity to carry out his treacherous promise.

Mark has artfully combined tradition and his own composition in 14:1-11 in creating an effective prelude to the passion narrative. The intentions of the leaders of Jerusalem, especially the chief priests and the temple scribes, to arrest and put Jesus to death, expressed in 11:18; 12:12; and 14:1-2, are beginning to take a more concrete form and to be put into effect. The body of Jesus has already been anointed, and his close associate has begun his treacherous activity.[228]

---

228 Cf. Schenke, *Passionsgeschichte,* 149.

14

14:12-16 A Place to Eat the Passover Meal

12/ **And on the first day of (the feast of) Unleavened Bread, when the Passover lamb is sacrificed, his disciples said to him, "Where do you want us to go and prepare, so that you may eat the Passover meal?" 13/ And he sent two of his disciples and said to them, "Go into the city, and a man carrying a water-jug will come toward you; follow him, 14/ and wherever he goes in, say to the master of the house, 'The Teacher says, "Where is there a guest room for me, where I may eat the Passover meal with my disciples?"' 15/ And he will show you a large room upstairs, furnished and ready; and prepare for us there." 16/ And the (two) disciples went out and went into the city and found (matters) as he had said to them, and they prepared the Passover meal.**

Comment

■ **12-16** On the most general level, one can say that this story is a legend or that it has legendary features.[1] It is similar in form to the account of the finding of a young donkey in 11:1-7.[2] Some have argued that it was modeled on 1 Sam 10:1-10.[3] Ernst Lohmeyer emphasized the particularity of the story, in which the master, through his knowledge and will, guides what is not foreseeable, and to whom the improbable and the impossible submit.[4]

This passage was probably not in Mark's passion source.[5] The story may once have circulated independently.[6] If it was ever part of a larger account of a Passover meal celebrated by Jesus with his disciples, its continuation has been lost.

■ **12** The temporal reference here, "on the first day of (the feast of) Unleavened Bread, when the Passover lamb is sacrificed" ($\tau\hat{\eta}$ $\pi\rho\acute{\omega}\tau\eta$ $\dot{\eta}\mu\acute{\epsilon}\rho\alpha$ $\tau\hat{\omega}\nu$ $\dot{\alpha}\zeta\acute{\nu}\mu\omega\nu$, $\dot{\sigma}\tau\epsilon$ $\tau\dot{o}$ $\pi\acute{\alpha}\sigma\chi\alpha$ $\ddot{\epsilon}\theta\nu o\nu$), seems to confuse the day of preparation with the first day of the feast. The confusion may arise from the tension between the biblical day, or the day of ancient Israel, and the day as calculated in the late

---

1   Dibelius, *From Tradition to Gospel*, 121, 189; Bultmann speaks of "a fairy-tale motif, where some creature (mostly an animal) precedes the traveler and so shows him the way" (*History*, 264; cf. Nineham, 376).

2   Bultmann, *History*, 263; Lohmeyer, 299; Nineham, 376; Schenke, *Passionsgeschichte*, 181; Evans, 369–70.

3   Bultmann says that it is reminiscent of 1 Samuel 10, but prefers the explanation in terms of a fairy-tale motif (*History*, 263–64). D. E. Nineham speaks of 1 Sam 10:2, 3, 5 as a parallel to the foresight of Jesus here. See also Schenke, *Passionsgeschichte*, 181, and the literature cited there in n. 3; Evans, 374.

4   Lohmeyer, 299–300.

5   Contra Pesch (2:340), who argued that both this passage and 11:1-6 belonged to the pre-Markan passion narrative, and Mohr, *Markus- und Johannespassion*,

119, 162–63. Dibelius argued credibly that it was Mark who prefixed this "introductory Legend" to the Last Supper (*From Tradition to Gospel*, 189). Bultmann (*History*, 264, 434, first addition to p. 264) and Nineham (376) agreed that the account of the finding of the Passover room was not in the earliest form of the passion narrative. Matti Myllykoski does not include this account in either the oldest passion account or the expanded pre-Markan passion narrative (*Die letzten Tagen*, 1:191–92).

6   Yarbro Collins, *Beginning of the Gospel*, 104; Schenke, *Passionsgeschichte*, 181–94.

Second Temple period.[7] The biblical day was reckoned from morning to morning.[8] At some point after the end of the monarchy, Jews began to reckon the day from evening to evening.[9] If the days are reckoned from evening to evening, the day of preparation is Abib/Nisan 14 and the first day of the feast is Abib/Nisan 15.[10] But if the days are reckoned from morning to morning, the day of preparation and the eating of the Passover meal with unleavened bread could appear to occur on the same day.[11]

According to Pliny (*Hist. nat.* 2.79.188), the common people everywhere consider a "day" to be the period between dawn and dark.[12] So it may be that Mark bases the temporal reference under discussion on this reckoning in order to communicate with as wide an audience as possible.

In the present context of Mark as a whole, this temporal reference picks up the statement in 14:1 that "the (feast of) Passover and Unleavened Bread was (to begin) after two days" and indicates that now the feast has begun.

The disciples take the initiative here and ask where Jesus would like them to prepare a place for him to eat the Passover.[13] This formulation is compatible with the story being relatively old tradition.[14]

■ **13-14** Jesus, in response, sends two of his disciples and gives them instructions, as he did in 11:1-2. But here they are sent into the city (Jerusalem), rather than into a village (Bethphage). They will encounter a man carrying a water-jug, and they are instructed to follow him. The indefinite construction, "wherever he goes in" (ὅπου ἐὰν εἰσέλθῃ), that is, into whatever dwelling he may enter, tells against the theory of some that Jesus had pre-arranged with someone to eat the Passover in his home.[15] The literary context of Mark supports the hypothesis that this story is modeled on 1 Kgdms 10. In v. 1a of that chapter, Samuel pours oil on Saul's head, anointing him privately as king of Israel. He then describes what Saul will encounter after he leaves Samuel's presence, a story that resembles this one (1 Kgdms 10:1b-8).[16]

The disciples are to enter the place into which the man carrying the water-jug goes and to ask the master of the house for a guest room where "the teacher" may eat the Passover with his disciples. The statement that they are to make is analogous to the one in 11:3. There Jesus assumes that the people of Bethphage will allow him to take (or borrow) a donkey because of his status as "Lord" or perhaps "messiah."[17] Here, following Jesus' public teaching in Jerusalem, he expects hospitality to be provided because of his status as "teacher" (διδάσκαλος).[18]

■ **15-16** The detailed description of what they will find suggests Jesus' foreknowledge and sovereign control over events.[19] The master of the house will show them a large upstairs room. The room will be "furnished"

---

7   Or the tension may be between the day as reckoned by Jews at the time in Palestine, especially Judea (from evening to evening) and the day as reckoned by non-Jews in the rest of the Mediterranean world. If, as seems likely, Mark's audience included many Gentiles, the text may take their perspective with regard to the reckoning of days. These considerations make more likely that Mark composed this temporal reference than that it was in his source.

8   Roland de Vaux, *Ancient Israel*, vol. 1: *Social Institutions* (New York/Toronto: McGraw-Hill, 1961) 180–82; Milgrom, *Leviticus*, 3:1967.

9   De Vaux, *Ancient Israel*, 1:180–82; Milgrom, *Leviticus*, 3:1968.

10   Baruch M. Bokser, "Unleavened Bread and Passover, Feasts of," *ABD* 6:755–65.

11   Yarbro Collins, *Beginning of the Gospel*, 101–2; Jack Finegan, *Handbook of Biblical Chronology: Principles of Time Reckoning in the Ancient World and Problems of Chronology in the Bible* (Princeton, NJ: Princeton University Press, 1964) §452 (p. 290).

12   Finegan, *Biblical Chronology*, §11 (p. 8).

13   On the construction of the Greek, see note a on the trans. of 10:36 above.

14   Bultmann argued that the cases in which Jesus takes the initiative are relatively late; see the section "Genre, History of the Tradition, and Composition" in the commentary on 12:35-37 above.

15   Cranfield, 422; Pesch, 2:343; Evans, 374.

16   See the commentary on v. 3 above.

17   See the commentary on 11:2-3 above.

18   John Paul Heil puts great emphasis on the use of the article in the phrase ὁ διδάσκαλος ("*the* Teacher") ("Mark 14,1-52: Narrative Structure and Reader-Response," *Bib* 71 [1990] 305–32, esp. 315–16).

19   Cf. the interpretation of Lohmeyer cited in the commentary on vv. 12-16 above.

($\dot{\epsilon}\sigma\tau\rho\omega\mu\acute{\epsilon}\nu o\nu$), probably with dining couches upon which the guests could recline.[20] Jesus' final remark, "prepare for us there," returns to the disciples' question in v. 12b in a way that rounds off his speech.

The narrator's statement that the disciples went out, went into the city, and found things to be as he said con-firms the sovereignty of Jesus in a straightforward and unassuming way. The brevity of the confirmation is a sign that it can be taken for granted.[21] The story con-cludes with the statement that the two disciples then prepared the Passover meal.

14

14:17-21 The One Who Hands Jesus Over

17/ And when evening had come, he came with the Twelve. 18/ And while they were at table and eat-ing, Jesus said, "Truly I say to you, one of you will hand me over, who is eating with me." 19/ They began[a] to be distressed and to say to him, one by one, "Is it I?" 20/ He then said to them, "(It is) one of the Twelve, who is dipping with me in the bowl;[b] 21/ for the Son of Man goes as it is written about him, but woe to that man through whom the Son of Man is handed over; it would be better for him, if that man had not been born."

a   The earliest recoverable reading is that with no con-necting particle or conjunction (asyndeton), attested by ℵ B L Ψ 2427; see Turner, "Markan Usage," 28 (1926) 18 (Elliott, *Language and Style of Mark*, 77). C 892 *pc* sa^{mss} attest a reading that relieves the asyndeton by adding $\kappa\alpha\acute{\iota}$ ("and") before $\mathring{\eta}\rho\xi\alpha\nu\tau o$ ("they began"); cf. Matt 26:22. A D W Θ $f^{1.13}$ $\mathfrak{M}$ latt sy attest a reading with the addition of $o\acute{\iota}$ $\delta\acute{\epsilon}$ ("They then") instead.

b   The earliest recoverable reading is probably that attested by ℵ A C² D et al., $\epsilon\acute{\iota}\varsigma$ $\tau\grave{o}$ $\tau\rho\acute{\upsilon}\beta\lambda\iota o\nu$ ("in the bowl," lit., "into the bowl"). 047. 131. 179. 1424 et al. attest the reading $\dot{\epsilon}\nu$ $\tau\hat{\wp}$ $\tau\rho\upsilon\beta\lambda\acute{\iota}\wp$ ("in the bowl"); cf. Huck-Greeven, ad loc. This reading may have been inspired by the parallel in Matt 26:23. B C* Θ 565 attest the reading $\epsilon\acute{\iota}\varsigma$ $\tau\grave{o}$ $\hat{\epsilon}\nu$ $\tau\rho\acute{\upsilon}\beta\lambda\iota o\nu$ ("in the same bowl," lit., "into the one bowl"). Although this reading was accepted (in brackets) by Westcott and Hort, fol-lowed by Taylor, ad loc., and by Nestle-Aland (25th ed.) and Aland, *Synopsis*, it is likely that it arose from a marginal gloss suggesting the substitution of $\dot{\epsilon}\nu$ ("in") for $\epsilon\acute{\iota}\varsigma$ ("in" or "into"); see Turner, "Marcan Usage," 26 (1924) 20 (Elliott, *Language and Style*, 21).

Comment

■ **17-21** This account does not follow smoothly upon vv. 12-16. The major discontinuity is the lack of the typi-cal features of a Passover meal in vv. 17-21. The two sto-ries use different terms for Jesus' followers, "disciples" ($\mu\alpha\vartheta\eta\tau\alpha\acute{\iota}$) in vv. 12-16 and "the Twelve" ($o\acute{\iota}$ $\delta\acute{\omega}\delta\epsilon\kappa\alpha$) in vv. 17-21. The story in vv. 12-16 could be read as imply-ing that Jesus shared the meal with a larger group, but the account in vv. 17-21 assumes that he ate only with the Twelve. These tensions support the conclusion that the evangelist composed 14:1-31 by joining previously inde-pendent individual traditions.[22]

Bultmann defined this passage as a "faith legend" with an apologetic motive.[23] The scandal of the cross is dealt with by portraying it as the result of divine necessity.[24]

In the context of Mark as a whole, this passage contin-ues two themes. One is the portrayal of the rejection of Jesus. The development of this theme begins with the remark about Jesus' family thinking that he was out of his

20   BAGD, s.v. $\sigma\tau\rho\omega\nu\nu\acute{\upsilon}\omega/\sigma\tau\rho\acute{\omega}\nu\nu\upsilon\mu\iota$ (2).
21   Lohmeyer, 298.
22   Yarbro Collins, *Beginning of the Gospel*, 104–5; Bult-mann, *History*, 264–65.
23   Bultmann, *History*, 306. An ancient opponent of Christianity, Celsus, challenged the teaching that Jesus was divine or the son of the Most High God

on the basis of, among other things, the tradition that he was betrayed by one of his own disciples (Origen *Contra Celsum* 6.10; Yarbro Collins, "From Noble Death," 481–82).
24   See the literature cited by Schenke, *Passionsgeschichte*, 210–11. He himself concludes that only v. 21b in this passage is pre-Markan.

mind.[25] It continues with the offense taken and unbelief expressed by people in Jesus' hometown.[26] It becomes explicit in Jesus' statement to Peter, James, and John that the Son of Man "is to suffer much and be treated with contempt" in 9:12b. This saying is connected with the three passion predictions and explicitly refers to the rejection of the Son of Man as "written" (γέγραπται) concerning him.[27] The theme also appears in the *nimshal* (the application) of the parable about the vineyard and the tenants, "Have you not read this scripture, 'The stone that the builders rejected has become the cornerstone. . . .'"[28]

The other theme is that of Judas as the one who hands Jesus over to those who wish to put him to death. This theme begins with the introduction of Judas at the end of the list of the Twelve in 3:19. There, as here, the defining action of Judas is linked with scripture.[29] The theme is developed in 14:1-2, 10-11. In vv. 17-21, the theme of Judas is again connected to scripture, as the commentary on v. 18 below indicates.

■ **17** In spite of the tensions between this passage and the preceding one, it is clear that the evangelist intended this unit to follow upon and continue the account of the finding of the room. The depiction of the arrival of evening in this verse follows logically upon vv. 12-16, a series of events that took place earlier in the day. The main clause, "he came with the Twelve" (ἔρχεται μετὰ τῶν δώδεκα), presupposes the preceding account, in

spite of the difficulty of relating "the Twelve" to "the disciples."

■ **18** The description of Jesus and the Twelve "reclining and eating" (ἀνακειμένων αὐτῶν καὶ ἐσθιόντων) fits well with the prediction that the large room upstairs would be "furnished and ready" (ἐστρωμένον ἕτοιμον).[30] Once the scene is set, Jesus says to the Twelve, "Truly I say to you, one of you will hand me over, who is eating with me" (ἀμὴν λέγω ὑμῖν ὅτι εἷς ἐξ ὑμῶν παραδώσει με ὁ ἐσθίων μετ᾽ ἐμοῦ). Many have seen an allusion to Psalm 40 LXX (Psalm 41 MT) here, which reads:

> For even the man of my peace, upon whom I set my hope,
> the one who eats my bread, has magnified his cunning against me
> (καὶ γὰρ ὁ ἄνθρωπος τῆς εἰρήνης μου, ἐφ᾽ ὃν ἤλπισα,
> ὁ ἐσθίων ἄρτους μου, ἐμεγάλυνεν ἐπ᾽ ἐμὲ πτερνισμόν). (Ps 40:10 LXX)[31]

The significance of this allusion could be explained in various ways.[32] One common way has been to argue that the allusion expresses the idea that the death of Jesus and the events related to it were prophesied by scripture.[33] This interpretation presupposes that the author and audience of Mark understood the text of the

---

25 See the commentary on 3:20-21 above.

26 See the commentary on 6:1-6a above, esp. on 6:3.

27 See the commentary on 8:31 and 9:12-13 above.

28 See the commentary on 12:10-11 above.

29 See the commentary on 3:19 above.

30 See the commentary on vv. 15-16 above.

31 Those who see an allusion to this psalm include Lohmeyer, 301; Lindars, *New Testament Apologetic*, 98–99; Cranfield, 423; Douglas J. Moo, *The Old Testament in the Gospel Passion Narratives* (Sheffield: Almond, 1983) 237–38; Gnilka, 2:236; Best, *Temptation*, 92; Hooker, 336; Pesch, 2:349; Marcus, *Way of the Lord*, 172–73; Gundry, 827; Evans, 375; Donahue and Harrington, 394. Schenke doubts the allusion (*Passionsgeschichte*, 216–17). Against the likelihood of the allusion is its nonrecognition by Matthew (26:21); Gnilka argued that Matthew deliberately omitted it (2:236–37 n. 10). In favor of it is the explicit citation of the relevant verse in John 13:18. On the latter, see C. H. Dodd, *According to the Scrip-*

tures: The Sub-structure of New Testament Theology (London: Collins/Fontana Books, 1965; 1st ed. 1952) 100.

32 For a history of scholarship on Mark's use of scripture, see Thomas R. Hatina, *In Search of a Context: The Function of Scripture in Mark's Narrative* (JSNTSup 232; SSEJC 8; Sheffield: Sheffield Academic Press, 2002) 8–48.

33 Feigel, *Der Einfluss des Weissagungsbeweises*, 4–5, 47. Dodd spoke of certain passages from the OT that were treated by early Christians "as 'testimonies' to the Gospel facts, or in other words as disclosing that 'determinate counsel of God' which was fulfilled in those facts" (*According to the Scriptures*, 57). Margaret Daly-Denton spoke of "the synoptic concentration of psalm usage in the Passion Narrative" as evidence for "the earliest form of Christian *relecture* of details in the Psalter as prophetic of Jesus' sufferings" (*David*, 253). Richard B. Hays suggested that the "royal lament psalms" already underlie the

psalm as prophecy. It also presupposes or argues that the scandal of the cross was overcome by early Christians in part by showing that it occurred in fulfillment of scriptural prophecy.[34] Thus, an allusion such as this one constitutes an instance of "proof from prophecy."[35] There are two sayings of Jesus in Mark 14 that come close to expressing this idea: v. 21 and especially v. 49. But in other cases, the force of the allusions to the Old Testament is the notion that the death of Jesus and the events associated with it occurred "in accordance with the scriptures" ($\kappa\alpha\tau\grave{\alpha}$ $\tau\grave{\alpha}\varsigma$ $\gamma\rho\alpha\varphi\acute{\alpha}\varsigma$).[36]

Other scholars have constructed abstract schemata or complexes of themes from scripture. Eduard Schweizer argued that Jesus and his followers made use of a preexisting schema of abasement and exaltation of the suffer-

ing righteous one to make sense of his suffering and death. This schema was expressed in what Schweizer called "the psalms of the suffering righteous" person to which the passion narrative alludes.[37] Lothar Ruppert criticized Schweizer's thesis for combining disparate motifs, but he adopted the idea that the passion narrative in Mark portrays Jesus' destiny in terms of the suffering and rescued righteous person.[38] Ruppert's approach has also been criticized.[39]

Another approach is to interpret the allusion as a literary device that leads the audience to understand and experience the narrative in a particular way.[40] Pesch argued that the allusion to Ps 40:10 LXX brings into the narrative a motif from the theme of the suffering just one (*passio iusti*) that fits the situation in Mark well,

---

affirmation of the kerygma cited in 1 Cor 15:3-5 "that the death and resurrection of Jesus occurred $\kappa\alpha\tau\grave{\alpha}$ $\tau\grave{\alpha}\varsigma$ $\gamma\rho\alpha\varphi\acute{\alpha}\varsigma$ ['according to the scriptures']" ("Christ Prays the Psalms: Paul's Use of an Early Christian Exegetical Convention," in Abraham J. Malherbe and Wayne A. Meeks, eds., *The Future of Christology: Essays in Honor of Leander E. Keck* [Minneapolis: Fortress, 1993] 122–36, quotation from 127 n. 20).

34 Harold W. Attridge took the position that some psalms were used in the writings of the NT "as prophetic texts, fulfilled in Jesus or his early followers" ("Giving Voice to Jesus: Use of the Psalms in the New Testament," in idem and Margot E. Fassler, eds., *Psalms in Community: Jewish and Christian Textual, Liturgical, and Artistic Traditions* [SBLSymS 25; Atlanta: SBL, 2003] 101–12; quotation from 101; cf. 107). He also accepts the view that, in many cases, this usage belongs to the category of "literary apologetics" (ibid., 102; cf. 107).

35 Those whose interpretations of v. 18 follow the approach of proof from scripture include Vernon K. Robbins, "Last Meal: Preparation, Betrayal, and Absence (Mark 14:12-25)," in Kelber, *Passion*, 21–40, esp. 30; Gnilka 2:236–37; Best, *Temptation*, 92; Hooker, 336; Marcus, *Way of the Lord*, 173, 178; Gundry, 827; Evans, 376. More generally speaking, Dibelius, Bultmann, and Eta Linnemann also made use of this approach; see Adela Yarbro Collins, "The Appropriation of the Psalms of Individual Lament by Mark," in Tuckett, *Scriptures*, 223–41, esp. 228–29. Hays concluded that Ps 69:9 (MT) is depicted in John 2:17 "as a prophetic *prefiguration* of Jesus Christ" ("Christ Prays the Psalms," 125 [emphasis his]). Similarly, Jesus' thirst in John 19:28 "is appar-

ently likewise seen by the Fourth Evangelist as a fulfillment of Psalm 69 (ibid.).

36 Suhl, *Funktion*, 42–45, 65–66. Ellen Flesseman-van Leer argued similarly, but she also pointed out the congruence of the context of Ps 41:10 (MT) and the context of the allusion to it in Mark ("Die Interpretation der Passionsgeschichte vom Alten Testament aus," in Hans Conzelmann et al., *Zur Bedeutung des Todes Jesu: Exegetische Beiträge* [Gütersloh: Mohn, 1967] 81–96, esp. 83–84).

37 Eduard Schweizer, *Erniedrigung und Erhöhung bei Jesus und seinen Nachfolgern* (2nd ed.; AThANT 28; Zurich: Zwingli-Verlag, 1962); ET *Lordship and Discipleship* (SBT; Naperville, IL: Allenson, 1960); for discussion, see Yarbro Collins, "Psalms of Individual Lament," 229.

38 Lothar Ruppert, *Jesus als der leidende Gerechte? Der Weg Jesu im Lichte eines alt- und zwischentestamentlichen Motius* (SBS 59; Stuttgart: Katholisches Bibelwerk, 1972) 44, 50–52. Hays made use of this category ("the Righteous Sufferer") in discussing the use of Psalm 22 (MT) in the Markan passion narrative ("Christ Prays the Psalms," 126). For discussion of the category, see the section "Genre" of the excursus on the passion narrative above and Yarbro Collins, "Psalms of Individual Lament," 229–30.

39 Reinhard Feldmeier, *Die Krisis des Gottessohnes: Die Gethsemaneerzählung als Schlüssel der Markuspassion* (WUNT 2.21; Tübingen: Mohr Siebeck, 1987) 161–62; Juel (*Messianic Exegesis*, 21–22) raised some questions about Dodd's approach that apply also to Ruppert's; Yarbro Collins, "Psalms of Individual Lament," 230–31.

40 Those who focus on the literary effect of the allusion include Lohmeyer, 301; Pesch, 2:349–50;

namely, an outrageous offense against fellowship, especially meal fellowship.[41] His reference to the complex of themes associated with the suffering just one is open to criticism, as is the work of Ruppert. Pesch also claimed that in Jewish tradition the relevant psalm verse was applied to the betrayer of David, Ahithophel (2 Samuel 15–17).[42]

The tension between the two interpretations offered by Pesch raises the question of how the tradents of the passion tradition, Mark, and his audiences understood the voice of the speaker in the psalms. In a psalm of individual lament like Psalm 40 LXX, is the speaker a suffering righteous person whose voice Jesus takes on as one falsely accused and abandoned by his friends?[43] Or is the voice that of David, the prototypical king who had his moments of suffering as well as of glory?[44]

Here in v. 18, as many commentators have pointed out, the emphasis is on the outrageous deed of handing over a close associate, rather than on the person of Judas or even that of Jesus.[45] At this point in the narrative, it is enough to say that Jesus takes on the voice of the psalmist, however the psalmist's identity may be defined. That identity may become clearer in v. 21.

It should also be noted that the remark "one of you will hand me over" (εἷς ἐξ ὑμῶν παραδώσει με) continues the theme of the divine activity of "handing over" John the Baptist, Jesus, and his followers.[46]

■ **19-20** The distress of the Twelve and their sorrowful questions, one after another, pick up and heighten the pathos introduced by Jesus' allusion to Ps 40:10 LXX. Jesus' reply intensifies the pathos even more. The substance of what he says in v. 20 has already been expressed in v. 18, but here it is expressed in a more vivid and shocking way. "One of you" (εἷς ἐξ ὑμῶν) is restated more pointedly as "one of the Twelve" (εἷς τῶν δώδεκα). The latter phrase recalls the description of Judas in v. 10. Verse 20, in the context of this unit, impresses upon the audience the terrible significance of what was stated in v. 10. "Who is eating with me" (ὁ ἐσθίων μετ᾽ ἐμοῦ) in v. 18 has become "who is dipping with me in the bowl" (ὁ ἐμβαπτόμενος μετ᾽ ἐμοῦ εἰς τὸ τρύβλιον) in v. 20. The latter phrase expresses the intimacy of meal fellowship in a heightened way.[47]

■ **21** This saying is loosely connected to the statement of Jesus in v. 20.[48] The first part of the saying states that "the Son of Man goes as it is written about him" (ὁ μὲν υἱὸς τοῦ ἀνθρώπου ὑπάγει καθὼς γέγραπται περὶ αὐτοῦ). The verb ὑπάγειν ("to go") is not used in this absolute sense elsewhere in Mark. The phrase "as it is written" (καθὼς γέγραπται) is used in 1:2, but there, in contrast to the context here, an explicit citation of scripture follows. More similar to v. 21 is the statement in 9:13, "as it is written with reference to him" (καθὼς γέγραπται ἐπ᾽ αὐτόν).[49] This statement concerns Elijah explicitly and John the Baptist implicitly. With regard to the latter verse, no allusion to scripture is made in the context to which this statement could refer. In the preceding verse it is said, "how is it written with reference to the Son of Man that he is to suffer much and be treated with contempt?" (πῶς γέγραπται ἐπὶ τὸν υἱὸν τοῦ ἀνθρώπου ἵνα πολλὰ πάθῃ καὶ ἐξουδενηθῇ;). That saying refers most directly to 8:31, which itself alludes to scripture.[50]

Donahue and Harrington, 394; Ahearne-Kroll, "Suffering of David."

41 Pesch, 2:349.

42 Ibid., 2:350. So also Moo, *Old Testament*, 239.

43 The situation of the psalmist is a mortal illness; his enemies and even his friend assume that he will die. Note that the psalmist confesses his sin in 40:5 LXX (41:5 MT; 41:4 NRSV).

44 In 1QH 13 (5):23-24, the Teacher of Righteousness rewrote the same passage that is alluded to here (Ps 41:10 MT; 40:10 LXX; 41:9 NRSV) with himself as speaker, as a special individual with an important role to play in the last days (Yarbro Collins, "Psalms of Individual Lament," 226–27).

45 E.g., Moo, *Old Testament*, 239.

46 See the commentary on 3:19; 9:31; and 14:10-11 above and 15:27 below.

47 On meal fellowship in relation to communal bonding in societies related to the OT, see Alan W. Jenks, "Eating and Drinking in the Old Testament," *ABD* 2:250–54, esp. 252–53. On the pathos of this scene, see Heil, "Mark 14,1-52," 316–17.

48 On the awkwardness of the beginning of the saying of v. 21 with ὅτι ("for"), see Taylor, 542; Schenke, *Passionsgeschichte*, 237–38; Fleddermann, *Mark and Q*, 165.

49 Barnabas Lindars concluded that both 9:12 and 14:21 allude to Isaiah 53 and that the purpose is apologetic (*New Testament Apologetic*, 81, 88).

50 See the commentary on 9:12-13 above.

Here, however, there is an allusion to scripture in the immediate context. As noted above, v. 18 probably alludes to Ps 40:10 LXX.[51] The proximity of vv. 18 and 21 suggests that the speaker of the psalm is interpreted in v. 21 as "the Son of Man." This link favors the supposition that Mark and his audiences considered the speaker of the psalm to be David, the prototypical king,[52] because of the equivalence of "Son of Man" and "messiah" in Jewish and Christian tradition of the first century CE.[53] The alluding process initiated by v. 18 is complex and literary, but the statement of v. 21 implies that there is a divine plan to which the destiny of the Son of Man must conform. This divine necessity, however, does not release "that man" who hands Jesus over from responsibility.[54]

This opening clause (v. 21a) is linked to a woe saying (v. 21b) by the use of the connectives μέν ("on the one hand"; not translated above) and δέ ("on the other hand"; translated with "but" above). The woe saying states "but woe to that man through whom the Son of Man is handed over" (οὐαὶ δὲ τῷ ἀνθρώπῳ ἐκείνῳ δι' οὗ ὁ υἱὸς τοῦ ἀνθρώπου παραδίδοται). There is only one other woe saying in Mark, 13:17, and Schenke concluded that both are traditional.[55] The woe saying of v. 21b is joined to a "'better' saying" (v. 21c): "it would be better for him if that man had not been born" (καλὸν αὐτῷ εἰ οὐκ ἐγεννήθη ὁ ἄνθρωπος ἐκεῖνος).[56]

It is likely that v. 21 is a Markan rewriting, adaptation, and expansion of a traditional saying preserved in Luke 17:1b-2 and Matt 18:6-7. This saying was probably in the Synoptic Sayings Source (Q).[57] The Lukan version reads:

It is impossible to avoid the occurrence of temptations to sin, but woe to the one through whom [such a temptation] occurs; it would be better for him if a millstone were hung around his neck and he were thrown into the sea than that one of these little ones be caused to sin (ἀνένδεκτόν ἐστιν τοῦ τὰ σκάνδαλα μὴ ἐλθεῖν, πλὴν οὐαι δι' οὗ ἔρχεται· λυσιτελεῖ αὐτῷ εἰ λίθος μυλικὸς περίκειται περὶ τὸν τράχηλον αὐτοῦ καὶ ἔρριπται εἰς τὴν θάλασσαν ἢ ἵνα σκανδαλίσῃ τῶν μικρῶν τούτων ἕνα). (Luke 17:1b-2)[58]

Mark took a saying that dealt with the relations of members of the community among themselves and transformed it into a saying about the one who "handed over" Jesus.[59] The placement of significant responsibility upon an insider here is striking in relation to the attempt to shift the lion's share of the blame onto the Jewish leaders later in the passion narrative. This whole unit may recall for the audiences of Mark the apocalyptic event predicted in 13:12, "And brother will hand brother over to death, and a father (his) child, and children will rise in rebellion against (their) parents and put them to death." If so, this passage, on one level at least, is a warning, and the one who hands Jesus over becomes here a negative example for the audiences in relation to situations of interrogation and persecution.

---

51 Lindars concluded that 14:18 and 20 allude to this psalm and that thus v. 21 alludes to it as well as to Isaiah 53; he also argued that the "Judas-apologetic" manifested here is a secondary development from early Christian "Passion apologetic" (*New Testament Apologetic*, 98–99).

52 Ahearne-Kroll, "Suffering of David," 2:243–44.

53 See Adela Yarbro Collins, "The Influence of Daniel on the New Testament," in Collins, *Daniel*, 90–105.

54 Cf. Paul's discussion of "vessels of wrath made for destruction" (σκεύη ὀργῆς κατηρτισμένα εἰς ἀπώλειαν) in Rom 9:22.

55 Schenke, *Passionsgeschichte*, 263.

56 Sayings of this type occur in 9:42, 43b, 45b, 47b; see the commentary on 9:43 above.

57 Schenke, *Passionsgeschichte*, 263–64; Fleddermann,

Mark and Q, 164–66; Robinson et al., *Critical Edition of Q*, 472–77.

58 Mark apparently also made use of this traditional saying preserved by Luke in composing 9:42.

59 On the theme of the divine activity of "handing over," see the commentary on 3:19; 9:31; and 14:10-11 above and 15:27 below.

14

14:22-25 Sayings about the Bread and the Cup

22/ And while they were eating, he took bread,[a] gave praise (to God),[b] broke it, and gave[c] it to them and said, "Take,[d] this is my body." 23/ And he took a cup, gave thanks, and gave it to them, and they all drank from it. 24/ And he said to them, "This is my blood of the covenant[e] which is poured out for[f] many. 25/ Truly I say to you, I will surely not drink again[g] of the fruit of the vine until that day when I drink it new in the kingdom of God."

a   The trans. given here is based on the reading attested by $\aleph^1$ B D W et al. Most of the Greek MSS and many of the Latin and those of other versions have also the words ὁ Ἰησοῦς ("Jesus") after the word λαβών ("took"). These words are probably an addition that assimilated the text of Mark to that of Matthew.

b   A few MSS (U 579. 1012; see Huck-Greeven, ad loc.) read εὐχαριστήσας ("gave thanks") instead of εὐλογήσας ("gave praise [to God]"). The latter was probably changed to the former under the influence of the parallels in Luke 22:19 and 1 Cor 11:24. Or the former reading may have resulted from the assimilation of this verse to v. 23.

c   Some MSS (W $f^{1.13}$ 2542 pc) read ἐδίδου ("was giving, began to give") instead of ἔδωκεν ("gave"). The former reading may have arisen under the influence of Mark 6:41; 8:6; Matt 15:36 or Luke 9:16.

d   Γ 0116 f^{13} et al. have the word φάγετε ("eat") after the word λάβετε ("take"). The former is probably an addition inspired by Matt 26:26. The shorter text is attested by $\aleph$ A B C D et al.

e   The trans. given here is based on the reading attested by $\aleph$ B C D^C et al. D* W 2427 read τὸ τῆς διαθήκης ("which is of the covenant"). This reading probably arose as an improvement of the style. A $f^{1.13}$ $\mathfrak{M}$ et al. include the word καινῆς ("new") before the word διαθήκης ("covenant"). The latter reading probably results from an addition inspired by Luke 22:20 or 1 Cor 11:25. Cf. Metzger, *Textual Commentary*, 95.

f $\aleph$ B C D et al. attest the reading ὑπὲρ πολλῶν ("for many"). A f^1 $\mathfrak{M}$ sy^h attest the reading περὶ πολλῶν ("for many"). The latter reading probably arose as a stylistic variant; see BAGD, s.v., 1. f.

g   The trans. is based on the reading οὐκέτι οὐ μὴ πίω ("I will surely not drink again"), which is attested by A B $f^{1.13}$ et al. A number of MSS ($\aleph$ C L W et al.) lack οὐκέτι ("again"). A few, D (Θ, 565) a f, attest the reading οὐ μὴ προσθῶ πεῖν ("I will surely not drink again"). The latter reading is too weakly attested to be the earliest. The reading without οὐκέτι ("again") probably arose under the influence of Matt 26:29. Cf. Metzger, *Textual Commentary*, 95–96.

Comment

■ **22-25** This passage was probably not included in the pre-Markan passion narrative that the evangelist used as a source.[60] It does not follow smoothly upon either the story about the preparation for the meal (vv. 12-16) or upon the narrative concerning the one who would hand Jesus over (vv. 17-21). It does not follow coherently on vv. 12-16 because there is no indication that the loaf and the cup were part of a Passover meal.[61] It does not con-

---

60   With Schenke, *Der gekreuzigte Christus*, 135; Reinbold, *Der älteste Bericht*, 133, and Myllykoski, *Die letzten Tagen*, 2:162; contra Mohr, *Markus- und Johannespassion*, 185–212.

61   Bultmann, *History*, 265.

tinue vv. 17-21 in a simple and straightforward way because it reintroduces the meal scene in v. 22a, "And while they were eating" (καὶ ἐσθιόντων αὐτῶν).[62] This reintroduction would probably not be included if vv. 17-21 and 22-25 had originally been composed as a single account. These two units appear to be independent stories or units of tradition placed one after the other, rather than two parts of the same narrative describing the same meal.[63]

In terms of genre, Bultmann defined vv. 22-25 as "the cult legend of the Hellenistic circles" around Paul.[64] Nineham remarked, "For St Mark and his readers it went without saying that Jesus was here instituting a sacramental rite (cf. I Cor. 11:24, 25 which made this explicit)."[65] This view, however, is dubious and requires a closer look at 1 Cor 11:17-26. According to v. 20, the meal is called the "Lord's supper." This is not an innovation on Paul's part, since he argues that it is not *really* the Lord's supper as they are celebrating it. The term could imply that the meal was held on Sundays (cf. 16:2). More likely, it implies that the meal involves fellowship with the risen Lord; he is guest or host or both.[66] It is likely that the Corinthians had already learned from Paul to associate the meal with the death of Jesus, since he presupposes the association in his argument in 10:16-18. He says in 11:23 that he had (already) handed on to them the tradition about the meal "on the night on which he was betrayed." The fact that they had heard this tradition before, however, does not mean that they were recalling it in the context of the meal or repeating the words of Jesus. It is not certain to what the words "Do this in remembrance of me" in v. 24 refer.[67] It is not necessarily the case that they refer, or were understood as referring, to the repetition of Jesus' words about the bread and the cup. They may have been taken as referring simply to

sharing a communal meal with some understanding of the relation of that meal to Jesus. It is clear that Paul intended to instill a genuine sense of community involving respect for one another, especially consideration for those who lacked material goods. Verse 26 emphasizes that the meal is a commemoration of the *death* of Jesus; it involves a literal or figurative announcement of that death until he comes. This emphasis is meant to support rhetorically the reforms in the practice of the meal that Paul is advocating. So Paul had to remind his audience of the sayings about the bread and the cup and to clarify their relation to the Christian ritual meal. Note that not even he advocates the repetition of these words in the actual practice of the meal.[68]

This reading of 1 Cor 11:17-26 suggests that the corresponding passage in Mark is not a "cult legend" but rather an anecdote that serves to interpret Jesus' death beforehand in the context of the Gospel as a whole.[69] This reading is supported by the lack of the words "Do this in remembrance of me" in Mark. Matthew's account is similar. The presence of the command "Do this in remembrance of me" in Luke 22:19 suggests that the anecdote, for Luke, had some connection to a ritual meal, as it did for Paul. This link, however, does not necessarily imply that the participants or the presider at the meal were repeating Jesus' words.

The pre-Markan and pre-Pauline traditions of the sayings about the bread and the cup may have been "interpretive reflections or catacheses applied to the liturgical meal," but were probably not "prayer texts."[70]

■ **22** As noted above, the introduction to this anecdote, "And while they were eating" (Καὶ ἐσθιόντων αὐτῶν), indicates that it contains what was once independent tradition.[71]

---

62 Cf. v. 18a, καὶ ἀνακειμένων αὐτῶν καὶ ἐσθιόντων ("And while they were at table and eating," lit., "And while they were reclining [at table] and eating"). Bultmann, *History*, 265, 276.

63 Yarbro Collins, *Beginning of the Gospel*, 105.

64 Bultmann, *History*, 265.

65 Nineham, 381.

66 Cf. the quotation from Aelius Aristides cited by Hans Conzelmann, *1 Corinthians: A Commentary on the First Epistle to the Corinthians* (Hermeneia; Philadelphia: Fortress, 1975) 172 n. 20.

67 The same is true of the statement "Do this, as often

as you drink, in remembrance of me" in 1 Cor 11:25.

68 Cf. Andrew Brian McGowan, "'Is There a Liturgical Text in this Gospel?': The Institution Narratives and Their Early Interpretive Communities," *JBL* 118 (1999) 73-87, esp. 77-80.

69 Similarly, Donald Senior, *The Passion of Jesus in the Gospel of Mark* (Wilmington, DE: Michael Glazier, 1984) 53-54.

70 McGowan, "'Is There a Liturgical Text in this Gospel?'" 85.

71 See the commentary on 14:22-25 above.

The statement that Jesus "took bread, gave praise (to God), broke it, and gave it to [the Twelve]" (λαβὼν ἄρτον εὐλογήσας ἔκλασεν καὶ ἔδωκεν αὐτοῖς) is similar to the statement at the beginning of the first multiplication of loaves (6:41). There it is said that Jesus "took the five loaves and the two fish, looked up to heaven, gave praise (to God) and broke the loaves (into pieces) and gave (them) to his disciples" (λαβὼν τοὺς πέντε ἄρτους καὶ τοὺς δύο ἰχθύας ἀναβλέψας εἰς τὸν οὐρανὸν εὐλόγησεν καὶ κατέκλασεν τοὺς ἄρτους καὶ ἐδίδου τοῖς μαθηταῖς [αὐτοῦ]). In 6:41 there are five loaves instead of one; the gesture of looking up to heaven is found here, but not in 14:22; and the last two verbal forms differ slightly.

Verse 22 is also similar to 8:6, which says that Jesus "took the seven loaves, gave thanks, broke (them) and gave (them) to his disciples" (λαβὼν τοὺς ἑπτὰ ἄρτους εὐχαριστήσας ἔκλασεν καὶ ἐδίδου τοῖς μαθηταῖς αὐτοῦ). In 8:6 there are seven loaves instead of one; the word εὐχαριστεῖν ("to give thanks") is used instead of εὐλογεῖν ("to give praise [to God]"); and only the last verbal form differs slightly from the last one in v. 22.

Since the gestures are intelligible as common practices related to ordinary Jewish meals,[72] the significance of the similarities should not be pressed. They do suggest, however, that the gestures in v. 22 need not point to a liturgical rite.

After this series of gestures, Jesus said, "Take, this is my body" (λάβετε, τοῦτό ἐστιν τὸ σῶμά μου). This saying is terse, lacking the word φάγετε ("eat") found in Matt 26:26[73] and the phrase τὸ ὑπὲρ ὑμῶν ("which is for you") found in 1 Cor 11:24.[74]

The brief saying related to the bread in v. 22 is certainly metaphorical and symbolic, rather than propositional or metaphysical. No notions of transubstantiation or real presence have arisen at this early date. But what is the metaphorical meaning? Some of Paul's remarks in 1 Cor 11:27-32 may offer some guidance. These verses contain admonition backed up with threats. In v. 27, Paul

implies that eating the bread or drinking the cup in an unworthy manner (ἀναξίως) means practicing the abuses described in vv. 17-22. He goes on to say that anyone who does so will be "answerable" or "guilty of the body and blood of the Lord" (ἔνοχος ἔσται τοῦ σώματος καὶ τοῦ αἵματος τοῦ κυρίου). According to v. 29, those who eat and drink unworthily are liable to judgment, illustrated in v. 30 by illness and even death. How can such severe penalties be explained? Paul seems to be implying that those who eat in an unworthy manner will be guilty of committing a sacrilege against the body and blood of the Lord. He may be drawing here on the tradition that a sacrificial offering had to be eaten in a state of ritual purity according to scripture and Jewish tradition. He then adapts this tradition by reinterpreting ritual purity in terms of a communal ethic.

What kind of sacrificial offering is implied? The saying in 1 Cor 5:7 suggests the paschal lamb.[75] Another possibility is the sacrifice of well-being. Note that, according to Exod 24:5, burnt offerings and sacrifices of well-being were made on the occasion of the ceremony of covenant ratification at Sinai. According to Exod 24:11, the chief men of the people of Israel beheld God and ate and drank. Note also that, according to Exodus 32, burnt offerings and sacrifices of well-being were brought also to the golden calf. In the LXX, the phrase θυσία σωτηρίου ("sacrifice of deliverance" or "sacrifice of salvation") is used in both passages, marking them as contrasting rituals. Paul quotes Exod 32:6 in 1 Cor 10:7 and may allude to the passage again here. He may be using the biblical contrast between the two rituals to contrast the Lord's supper in the way the Corinthians celebrate it with the way it should be celebrated.

It is also important for the Markan passage that sacrifices of well-being were made in connection with the ratification of the covenant, according to Exod 24:5. Although the saying over the bread does not mention the covenant, the saying over the cup in v. 23 does.

The comparison with 1 Cor 11:27-32 suggests that the

---

72   See the commentary on 8:5-6 above.
73   See the note d on the trans. of v. 22 above.
74   The earliest recoverable reading of Luke 22:19 includes the phrase τὸ ὑπὲρ ὑμῶν διδομένον ("which is given for you").
75   Cf. John 1:29; Rev 5:6 and often. Flesseman-van Leer concluded that the bread and the wine compare

Jesus to the Passover lamb, since the present form of Mark defines the meal as a Passover meal ("Die Interpretation der Passionsgeschichte," 86).

metaphorical significance of the saying related to the bread is that the death of Jesus is like a sacrifice. This metaphorical or symbolic meaning should not be interpreted as a "spiritualization" or "rejection" of the allegedly flawed sacrificial worship of ancient Jews. Rather, it should be understood as a positive appropriation of or borrowing from Jewish sacrificial practices.[76]

■ **23-25** Just as Jesus "took" (λαβών) bread in v. 22, v. 23 says that he "took a cup" (λαβών ποτήριον). Here, however, instead of giving praise (to God) (εὐλογήσας) as in v. 22, he "gave thanks" (εὐχαριστήσας). Such variation is typical of Jewish prayers in the first century CE.[77] Language of "thanksgiving" later became typical of early Christian ritual meals.[78] It is noteworthy that the sayings related to the cup are narrated *after* all of the Twelve had drunk from it (v. 23). This order of events supports the reading of this passage proposed above, namely, as an interpretation of the death of Jesus before the event, not as a liturgical text.[79]

There are two sayings associated with the cup in Mark, one in v. 24 and one in v. 25. The first is more complex than the cup-saying in 1 Cor 11:25b. The form of the saying used by Paul interprets Jesus' death only as a covenant sacrifice.[80] The first part of the saying in Mark 14:24, "This is my blood of the covenant" (τοῦτό ἐστιν τὸ αἷμά μου τῆς διαθήκης), is similar to Paul's cup-saying. The earliest recoverable reading of this verse,

unlike the parallel in 1 Corinthians, does not include the word "new" (καινή).[81] At the least, however, the saying in Mark implies a renewal of the covenant.[82]

The second part of the first saying related to the cup, "which is poured out for many" (τὸ ἐκχυννόμενον ὑπὲρ πολλῶν), has sacrificial connotations.[83] It could be interpreted as an elaboration of the idea of the covenant: the blood is poured out for the benefit of many, with the result that they become members of a renewed covenant with God.[84] Although the phrase "for many" (ὑπὲρ πολλῶν) is not a technical term in the sacrificial tradition, the idea that a sacrifice can be performed on behalf of a specific group was widespread, and the preposition used by Mark, ὑπέρ ("for" or "on behalf of"), is used elsewhere to express this idea.[85]

There are two basic ways in which the expression "for many" (ὑπὲρ πολλῶν) may be understood. One is in terms of a metaphorical sacrifice effecting atonement for sin. The other is in terms of the vicarious suffering of a righteous person. Both are atoning, but the latter is not necessarily sacrificial.[86] In favor of a metaphorical sacrificial reading here is the presence of terminology pertaining to the pouring out of blood, which is technical sacrificial language, as pointed out above. Matthew understood the Markan phrase to imply atonement for sin and made this idea explicit by adding the phrase "for the forgiveness of sins" (εἰς ἄφεσιν ἁμαρτιῶν) (Matt 26:28).

---

76   Jonathan Klawans, "Interpreting the Last Supper: Sacrifice, Spiritualization, and Anti-Sacrifice," *NTS* 48 (2002) 1–17.

77   See the commentary on 6:41 and 8:5-6 above.

78   The term εὐχαριστία ("thanksgiving") is used in *Didache* 9–10 both for a type of ritual meal and for the prayer of thanksgiving associated with it; Ignatius used the term for a ritual meal in *Phld.* 4:1; *Smyrn.* 7:1; 8:1.

79   See the commentary on 14:22-25 above.

80   1 Cor 11:25b reads τοῦτο τὸ ποτήριον ἡ καινὴ διαθήκη ἐστιν ἐν τῷ ἐμῷ αἵματι ("This cup is the new covenant in my blood").

81   See note e on the trans. of v. 24 above.

82   The יחד ("community") associated with the DSS considered themselves to be members of a new covenant with the God of Israel (Joseph A. Fitzmyer, *The Dead Sea Scrolls and Christian Origins* [Grand Rapids/Cambridge: Eerdmans, 2000] 104–5). The idea of a new covenant among Jews in the Second Temple period and among the early followers of Jesus proba-

bly derives from Jer 31:31. On the covenant in the prophetic literature of the OT, in the Jewish literature of the Second Temple period, and at Qumran, see Kim Huat Tan, *The Zion Traditions and the Aims of Jesus* (SNTSMS 91; Cambridge: Cambridge University Press, 1997) 205–15.

83   Yarbro Collins, "Finding Meaning," 176.

84   Cf. Exod 24:6-8; the LXX uses the word προσχεῖν ("to pour [blood] to" or "to pour [blood] on" [the altar]). Flesseman-van Leer discusses the possibility that the allusion here is to Zech 9:11 ("Die Interpretation der Passionsgeschichte," 86–87). Dodd argued that Zech 9:11 "is probably one of the scriptures underlying the 'words of institution' . . . though the primary source is probably Exod. xxiv.8" (*According to the Scriptures*, 64). The "many" in Isa 53:11-12 also contributed to v. 24 (ibid., 93).

85   Yarbro Collins, "Finding Meaning," 176.

86   Cilliers Breytenbach, *Versöhnung: Eine Studie zur paulinischen Soteriologie* (WMANT 60; Neukirchen-Vluyn: Neukirchener Verlag, 1989) 36, 202, 205. He

The naming of Jesus' death as "a pouring out of his blood for many" may result from a combination of the terminology of sacrifice with the poem about the suffering servant of the Lord in Isaiah 53.[87] This part of the saying also echoes Mark 10:45, "the Son of Man did not come to be served, but to serve, and to give his life as a ransom in behalf of many" ($\kappa\alpha\grave{\iota}\ \delta o\hat{v}\nu\alpha\iota\ \tau\grave{\eta}\nu\ \psi\nu\chi\grave{\eta}\nu\ \alpha\grave{v}\tau o\hat{v}\ \lambda\acute{v}\tau\rho o\nu\ \grave{\alpha}\nu\tau\grave{\iota}\ \pi o\lambda\lambda\hat{\omega}\nu$).[88] The latter saying uses a different preposition in the statement about the beneficiaries of Jesus' death. Whereas 14:24 has the phrase $\grave{v}\pi\grave{\epsilon}\rho\ \pi o\lambda\lambda\hat{\omega}\nu$ ("for many" or "in behalf of many"), 10:45 has the phrase $\grave{\alpha}\nu\tau\grave{\iota}\ \pi o\lambda\lambda\hat{\omega}\nu$, which could be translated "in behalf of many" but also has the connotation of "instead of many" or "in place of many."[89]

The second saying associated with the cup (v. 25) is a solemn prophetic saying that is more similar in form to 9:1 than to the binding oath to abstain from something.[90] As a prediction, this saying is an indirect prophecy by Jesus of his own death; at the same time it looks forward to the full manifestation of the kingdom of God in the future.[91] Drinking wine as a symbol of eschatological ful-

fillment appears in Isa 25:6-8 and *2 Baruch* 29. The motif of drinking wine in the kingdom of God is analogous to the image of reclining at a festive banquet with Abraham, Isaac, and Jacob in the kingdom of God. This image is expressed in a Q-saying preserved in Matt 8:11-12 and Luke 13:28-29.[92] The images of eating and drinking in the kingdom of God do not necessarily imply a messianic kingdom on earth. Much ancient language about the afterlife, including that of Jews in the Second Temple period and followers of Jesus, tends to assume the continuation of a bodily existence of some sort.[93]

It does not appear to be possible to determine whether v. 25 is a pre-Markan tradition or whether the evangelist composed it himself. In any case, it is clear that he joined the saying to vv. 22-24 and thereby interpreted the tradition of the sayings about the bread and the cup.[94] The result is an emphasis on the absence of Jesus during the time between his death and resurrection, on the one hand, and his return as Son of Man, on the other.[95]

14

14:26-31 Predictions of Abandonment and Denial

26/ **And after they had sung a hymn, they went out to the Mount of Olives. 27/ And Jesus said to them, "You will all take offense,[a] for it is written, 'I will strike the shepherd, and the sheep will be scattered.'[b] 28/ But after I am**

a   The trans. is based on the shortest reading, which is attested by ℵ B C* D et al., $\sigma\kappa\alpha\nu\delta\alpha\lambda\iota\sigma\vartheta\acute{\eta}\sigma\epsilon\sigma\vartheta\epsilon$ ("you will take offense"). The longest reading, attested by A C² K (N) W Θ et al., $\sigma\kappa\alpha\nu\delta\alpha\lambda\iota\sigma\vartheta\acute{\eta}\sigma\epsilon\sigma\vartheta\epsilon\ \grave{\epsilon}\nu\ \grave{\epsilon}\mu o\grave{\iota}\ \grave{\epsilon}\nu\ \tau\hat{\eta}\ \nu\nu\kappa\tau\grave{\iota}\ \tau\alpha\acute{v}\tau\eta$ ("you will take offense at me during this night"), is probably due to the assimilation of Mark's text to the parallel in Matt 26:31. Ψ^C 28 et al. attest the reading $\sigma\kappa\alpha\nu\delta\alpha\lambda\iota\sigma\vartheta\acute{\eta}\sigma\epsilon\sigma\vartheta\epsilon\ \grave{\epsilon}\nu\ \grave{\epsilon}\mu o\grave{\iota}$ ("you will take offense at me"). This reading may have arisen

---

argues that Paul and Greek-speaking Jews before him interpreted both Isaiah 53 and Jesus' death in terms of a vicarious atoning death of a righteous person.

87   Yarbro Collins, "Finding Meaning," 177; Moo, *Old Testament*, 130–32.

88   See the commentary on 10:45 above.

89   Cf. 4 Macc 6:28-29; for discussion, see Yarbro Collins, "Finding Meaning," 179–80.

90   Pesch, 2:355–56; see also the commentary on 9:1 above. On the binding oaths in the future tense, see Benovitz, *KOL NIDRE*, 10. On the semitizing, "biblical" language of this saying, see Marinus de Jonge, "Mark 14:25 among Jesus' Words about the Kingdom of God," in William Petersen et al., eds., *Say-*

ings of Jesus: Canonical and Non-Canonical; Essays in Honour of Tjitze Baarda (NovTSup 89; Leiden: Brill, 1997) 123–35, esp. 125–26. De Jonge also concluded that the saying is not a vow of abstinence (ibid., 128).

91   Cf. Pesch, 2:360–61; Schenke, *Passionsgeschichte*, 332–33.

92   Robinson et al., *Critical Edition of Q*, 414–17. For discussion, see de Jonge, "Mark 14:25," 129.

93   Lehtipuu, *Afterlife Imagery*. On images of the afterlife as a banquet involving wine, see 216–17. On the variety of interpretations of v. 25 in the early church, see the literature cited by de Jonge, "Mark 14:25," 130.

94   Schenke, *Passionsgeschichte*, 302–6.

95   Cf. 2:20 and the commentary on that verse above.

raised, I will go ahead of you to Galilee." 29/ Peter then said to him, "Even if they all take offense, I at least will not." 30/ And Jesus said to him, "Truly I say to you, today,[c] in this night before the cock crows twice,[d] you will deny me three times." 31/ But he said vehemently, "Even if it be necessary for me to die with you, I will surely not deny you." Then they all also began to speak likewise.

through the accidental omission of the words $\dot{\epsilon} \nu \ \tau \hat{\eta} \ \nu \nu \kappa \tau \dot{\iota} \ \tau \alpha \dot{\nu} \tau \eta$ ("during this night"). Other MSS (pc vgst bo^{mss}) attest the reading $\sigma \kappa \alpha \nu \delta \alpha \lambda \iota \sigma \vartheta \dot{\eta} \sigma \epsilon \sigma \vartheta \epsilon \ \dot{\epsilon} \nu \ \tau \hat{\eta} \ \nu \nu \kappa \tau \dot{\iota} \ \tau \alpha \dot{\nu} \tau \eta$ ("you will take offense during this night"). This reading may have arisen in an analogous way through accidental omission of the words $\dot{\epsilon} \nu \ \dot{\epsilon} \mu o \acute{\iota}$ ("at me").

b The earliest recoverable reading is probably $\tau \grave{\alpha} \ \pi \rho \acute{o} \beta \alpha \tau \alpha \ \delta \iota \alpha \sigma \kappa o \rho \pi \iota \sigma \vartheta \acute{\eta} \sigma o \nu \tau \alpha \iota$ ("the sheep will be scattered"), attested by ℵ B C D et al. The word order has been changed in the reading attested by A K f^1 𝔐 lat, possibly under the influence of the text alluded to in this verse, Zech 13:7 LXX.

c The word $\sigma \acute{\eta} \mu \epsilon \rho o \nu$ ("today") is lacking in D Θ f^{13} et al., but the longer reading is well attested and is, in any case, typical of Markan style. See Neirynck, *Duality in Mark*, 95.

d ℵ C* D W et al. lack the word $\delta \acute{\iota} \varsigma$ ("twice"). This reading is probably due to an assimilation of the text of Mark to the parallel in Matt 26:34, Luke 22:34, or John 13:38. See also below on 14:68 and 72. Cf. Metzger, *Textual Commentary*, 96.

Excursus: Galilee[96] and Jerusalem in Mark

The occasion for this excursus is the mention of Galilee in v. 28 and the debate about its significance in this context and also in 16:7. Since the topic involves exegesis of Mark as well as premises and conclusions about the history of Galilee and its ethnic and religious character in the first century CE, both aspects will be treated briefly here.

In the latter part of the nineteenth and early part of the twentieth century, scholars were troubled by the fact that some canonical and extracanonical Gospels reported appearances of the risen Jesus only in Jerusalem and others only in Galilee.[97] Friedrich Spitta argued that the saying preserved in Mark 14:28 continues the image of the shepherd and his flock from v. 27, which is taken from Zech 13:7. He concluded, therefore, that v. 28 signified that Jesus would lead his flock from Jerusalem to Galilee. Thus, the

saying originally made the point that Jesus would meet his disciples after the resurrection first of all in Jerusalem, not Galilee. When Peter and the others returned to Galilee without the risen Jesus (an event he inferred from Luke 22:32), however, the saying was transformed to express the same view as 16:7.[98] Johannes Weiss challenged the consensus of his time that Mark 14:27-28 is good evidence for the flight of the disciples to Galilee after the arrest of Jesus.[99] He pointed out that 16:7 presumes that Peter and the other disciples were still in Jerusalem and implies that they went to Galilee in response to a command of Jesus, not in headlong flight. The interpretation of 14:28 in 16:7, however, was based on a misunderstanding. The original meaning of 14:28, in his view, was a promise that Jesus, after his resurrection, would meet his disciples in Jerusalem and then lead them back to Galilee for the coming of the kingdom of God.[100] The

---

96 The name "Galilee" (Greek $\Gamma \alpha \lambda \iota \lambda \alpha \acute{\iota} \alpha$) comes from the Hebrew גָּלִיל, which means "circuit" or "district." On the Hebrew term, see, e.g., Hans Walter Wolff, *Joel and Amos: A Commentary on the Books of the Prophets Joel and Amos* (Hermeneia; Philadelphia: Fortress, 1977) 78.

97 Ernst Lohmeyer, *Galiläa und Jerusalem* (Göttingen: Vandenhoeck & Ruprecht, 1936) 5–8.

98 Friedrich Spitta, *Die synoptische Grundschrift in ihrer Überlieferung durch das Lukasevangelium* (Leipzig: Hinrichs, 1912) 387; cf. 450; cited by Günter Stem-

berger, "Galilee—Land of Salvation?" Appendix IV in W. D. Davies, *The Gospel and the Land* (Berkeley: University of California Press, 1974) 410.

99 Johannes Weiss, *Das Urchristentum* (Göttingen: Vandenhoeck & Ruprecht, 1917) 11–12; ET *Earliest Christianity: A History of the Period A.D. 30–150* (New York: Harper & Brothers, 1959; 1st ed. 1937) 1:16–17.

100 Weiss, *Urchristentum*, 12; *Earliest Christianity*, 1:17–18.

tradition in Matthew 28 and John 21 about resurrection appearances in Galilee arose from the same misunderstanding of the saying preserved in 14:28.[101] Francis C. Burkitt argued that the appearances could not have taken place in Galilee because, if they had, Galilee would have been the center of the earliest community of the followers of Jesus, rather than Jerusalem. That Jerusalem was in fact its center is attested by Acts and the letters of Paul. An appearance of Jesus in or near Jerusalem would make it, not Galilee, holy ground. He also emphasized that there is no evidence for an established Christian community in Galilee until the time when Christians were to be found in all parts of the empire.[102] Kirsopp Lake was critical of Weiss's position.[103] He found Burkitt's position to be "more subtle and more acceptable."[104] He conceded that one might expect the church to have its center in Galilee, not Jerusalem, if the risen Lord had been seen in Galilee, but he rightly raised the question whether at least a partial reply to Burkitt's argument may be that it was eschatological expectation that led the disciples back to Jerusalem.[105] Although Burkitt's arguments made him waver in his opinion,[106] ultimately Lake continued to maintain that Mark 14:28 and 16:7 "imply the expectation of appearances in Galilee, not an appearance near Jerusalem before Galilee was reached."[107]

Lohmeyer approached the question of the significance of Galilee and Jerusalem in Mark under the influence of Burkitt's historical discussion of the resurrection appearances. In the exegetical part of his study, Lohmeyer stated that 14:28 seems to be an insertion into an alien context.[108] He noted that, in the context of 16:7, the first part of the prophecy of 14:28 is fulfilled: Jesus has risen (16:6). The second part, that Jesus will go before the Twelve[109] to Galilee, is in the process of being fulfilled.[110] In the reprise of 14:28 in 16:7, a further prophecy is added, namely, "there you will see him" ($\dot{\epsilon}\kappa\epsilon\hat{\iota}$ $\alpha\dot{\upsilon}\tau\dot{\text{o}}\nu$ $\ddot{\text{o}}\psi\epsilon\sigma\vartheta\epsilon$).[111] It is clear that the author of Matthew interpreted this prophecy to mean that the risen Jesus would appear to the eleven in Galilee (Matt 28:10, 16-20), but that may not have been the understanding of Mark.[112] Lohmeyer admitted that resurrection appearances are sometimes described with the active voice of $\dot{\text{o}}\rho\dot{\alpha}\omega$ ("to see"), the recipient of the appearance being the subject of that verbal form (1 Cor 9:1; John 20:18, 25, 29).[113] He pointed out, however, that the phrase $\ddot{\text{o}}\psi\epsilon\sigma\vartheta\epsilon$ $\alpha\dot{\upsilon}\tau\dot{\text{o}}\nu$ ("you will see him") is sometimes used of the parousia (Mark 14:62).[114] He concluded from this allegedly fixed formula that the angel in 16:7 refers not to a resurrection appearance but to the parousia.[115]

Lohmeyer rightly concluded that the resurrection of Jesus, for Mark and other early Christian writers, is one in a series of eschatological events. It was

---

101 Weiss, *Urchristentum*, 12–13; *Earliest Christianity*, 1:18. See also the brief discussion of Weiss's views in Lohmeyer, *Galiläa und Jerusalem*, 8, and the more extensive one in Stemberger, "Galilee—Land of Salvation?" 410.

102 Francis C. Burkitt, *Christian Beginnings: Three Lectures by F. C. Burkitt* (London: University of London Press, 1924) 78–97; cited by Lohmeyer, *Galiläa und Jerusalem*, 8.

103 Kirsopp Lake, "Note II. The Command Not to Leave Jerusalem and the 'Galilean Tradition,'" in Frederick J. Foakes Jackson and Kirsopp Lake, eds., *The Beginnings of Christianity*, Part I: *The Acts of the Apostles*, vol. 5, Kirsopp Lake and Henry J. Cadbury, eds., *Additional Notes to the Commentary* (reprint, Grand Rapids: Baker Book House, 1979; the edition used by Lohmeyer was published in 1933) 7–16, esp. 9–12.

104 Ibid., 12.

105 Ibid., 12–13.

106 Ibid., 8, 13, 14.

107 Ibid., 13; cf. 15.

108 Lohmeyer took the position that the sayings in both 14:28 and 16:7 are pre-Markan (*Galiläa und Jerusalem*, 29).

109 So 14:28, in context. In 16:7, Jesus is said to be going before "his disciples and Peter" ($\text{o}\dot{\iota}$ $\mu\alpha\vartheta\eta\tau\alpha\dot{\iota}$ $\alpha\dot{\upsilon}\tau\text{o}\hat{\upsilon}$ $\kappa\alpha\dot{\iota}$ $\dot{\text{o}}$ $\Pi\dot{\epsilon}\tau\rho\text{o}\varsigma$).

110 Note the use of the present tense of $\pi\rho\text{o}\dot{\alpha}\gamma\omega$ ("to go before") in 16:7; Lohmeyer, *Galiläa und Jerusalem*, 10; cf. 12–13.

111 Ibid., 10–11.

112 Ibid., 11.

113 Ibid.

114 Cf. Mark 13:26 par.; Matt 16:28; 1 John 3:2; Rev 1:7; Lohmeyer, *Galiläa und Jerusalem*, 11–12. He claimed that the same usage occurs in John 16:16 (ibid., 11). The use of the image of labor-pains in the context supports this claim; but the evangelist or editor may have reinterpreted the usage so that it refers to the resurrection appearances of Jesus, rather than to the parousia.

115 Ibid., 12. Lohmeyer also cited *T. Zeb.* 9:8 in support of this hypothesis, but that passage is probably Christian, not Jewish, as he supposed. See Hollander and de Jonge, 125 (on *T. Sim.* 6:5), 273 (on *T. Zeb.* 9:8).

preceded, for example, by the suffering and death of Jesus and would be succeeded by others.[116] But it does not necessarily follow, as he argued, that Jesus' movement toward Galilee is to be interpreted as part of the next eschatological event, the parousia,[117] rather than as part of the resurrection event itself, that is, a resurrection appearance that confirms the resurrection for the disciples and grants them a commission and the insight and strength to fulfill it. Lohmeyer went on to claim that Mark implies that the parousia will take place in Galilee, the latter being the holy land where Jesus would live forever with his followers.[118]

In order to support this dubious exegetical conclusion, Lohmeyer attempted to discern the perspective of each of the canonical evangelists on Galilee and Jerusalem.[119] In a brief historical and cultural preface to those studies, he remarked that Galilee was religiously ostracized or condemned by influential and devout Jews of Jerusalem.[120] He based this conclusion on Isa 8:23 (NRSV 9:1) and Matt 4:15.

Before discussing the interpretation of Lohmeyer further, I would like to turn to George H. Boobyer's study of Galilee and Galileans in Mark, which treats the evidence of the LXX and expresses opinions on the nature of the population of Galilee in the first

century CE. His work on this topic was influenced by Lohmeyer and R. H. Lightfoot (see below on the latter), and it has been quite influential in its own right.[121] Boobyer pointed out that, like the MT, the LXX in Judg 1:30 and 33 "mentions that the tribes of Zebulon and Naphtali did not drive the Canaanites from amongst them."[122] Against the repeated assertion in Judg 1:27-33 that they "did not dispossess" the inhabitants of the Canannite cities, however, "the text of Joshua asserts twice that they 'could not'" (Josh 15:63; 17:12).[123]

Boobyer interprets Joel 4:4 LXX (3:4 NRSV) as an indictment of "Galilee as a Gentile land which conspired with other Gentile lands against Judah."[124] Joel 4:4a MT reads:

Furthermore: What are you to me, Tyre and Sidon and all the districts of Philistia?

[125](וגם מה־אתם לי צר וצידון וכל גלילות פלשׁת)

The LXX reads:

καὶ τί καὶ ὑμεῖς ἐμοί, Τύρος καὶ Σιδὼν καὶ πᾶσα Γαλιλαία ἀλλοφύλων;[126]

---

116 Lohmeyer, *Galiläa und Jerusalem*, 12–13.

117 Ibid., 13. Lohmeyer recognized that 1 Cor 15:3-7 supports the idea that the resurrection of Jesus was closely linked in the pre-Pauline tradition to resurrection appearances. He attempted to minimize this evidence by claiming that the appearances belong to a missionary context and not to the fundamentals of Christian faith (ibid.).

118 Ibid. He concluded further, as a consequence of his interpretation of 16:7, that Mark, the oldest Gospel, does not yet attest the tradition of resurrection appearances in Galilee (ibid., 14).

119 Ibid., 25–46.

120 Ibid., 26. He also comments on religiously positive aspects of Galilee in this context, especially after 70 CE. Stemberger also speaks about the "bad name which Galilee had among the Jews of Judaea" ("Galilee—Land of Salvation?" 436). This view of Galilee has persisted until quite recently (Robert W. Funk, *Honest to Jesus: Jesus for a New Millennium* [San Francisco: HarperSanFrancisco, 1996] 33; cf. 79); see the discussion in Chancey, *Gentile Galilee*, 1–7, esp. 2.

121 See the discussion by Stemberger, "Galilee—Land of Salvation?" 436 and n. 81.

122 George H. Boobyer, "Galilee and Galileans in St. Mark's Gospel," *BJRL* 35 (1952–53) 334–48; reprinted in *Galilee and Galileans in St. Mark's Gospel* (Manchester: John Rylands Library/Manchester Uni-

versity Press, 1953); quotation from 335 (the reprint has the same page numbering).

123 Robert G. Boling, *Judges: Introduction, Translation, and Commentary* (AB 6A; Garden City, NY: Doubleday, 1975) 66. Although the cities mentioned in Judg 1:30 have not been identified (ibid., 60), Zebulun's territory "was a part of the poorer southern flank of the Galilee mountains together with a contiguous wedge out of the Jezreel plain" (Robert G. Boling and G. Ernest Wright, *Joshua: A New Translation with Notes and Commentary* [AB 6; Garden City, NY: Doubleday, 1982] 443). The two cities mentioned in Judg 1:33 also "resist location" (Boling, *Judges*, 60). According to Boling and Wright, "Naphtali must have been the nerve center of the Yahwist movement in Galilee." They place Naphtali's territory "in the southern part of Upper Galilee" (*Joshua*, 460). In that area "new, small, unfortified settlements of the Iron I period were first discovered" (ibid.).

124 Boobyer, "Galilee and Galileans," 335.

125 Text from *BHS*; trans. from Wolff, *Joel and Amos*, 72. Wolff argued that 4:4-8 is a later addition to Joel and dated it between 400 and 343 BCE (ibid., 74–75, 78). John Barton also takes it as a later addition to the book and dates it between 400 and 350 BCE (*Joel and Obadiah: A Commentary* [OTL; Louisville: Westminster John Knox, 2001] 100–101).

126 BAGD notes that the term ἀλλόφυλος ("alien" or

Boobyer's remark presupposes a translation as follows:

> And what indeed [are] you to me, Tyre and Sidon and all Galilee of [the] Gentiles?

In the LXX, however, the vast majority of the occurrences of ἀλλόφυλοι translates פלשתים ("Philistines"). So, from the point of view of the LXX as a translation, a more accurate rendering of Joel 4:4a is the following:

> And what indeed [are] you to me, Tyre and Sidon and all the district of [the] Philistines? (or "and all the district of the aliens?").

There are a few instances in Codex Vaticanus in which פלשתים ("Philistines") is translated Φυλιστιιμ ("Philistines") (Judg 10:6, 7, 11; 13:1, 5). In all of these cases, Codex Alexandrinus reads ἀλλόφυλοι ("Philistines," lit., "aliens"). In all the other instances of פלשתים in Judges, Vaticanus, like Alexandrinus, reads ἀλλόφυλοι.

It is likely that the translator of Joel, who probably lived in Egypt, intended πᾶσα γαλιλαία ἀλλοφύλων to mean "all the district of the Philistines" and did not intend to refer to Galilee. The choice of a general word like ἀλλόφυλοι shows a lack of concern about differentiating the various non-Israelite ethnic groups. At a later time and a different place, however, the phrase was open to being understood as a reference to Galilee.[127]

More to the point, Boobyer noted that 1 Macc 5:21 "reports that Simon Maccabaeus did battle in Galilee with Gentiles who lived there."[128] He also interprets Γαλιλαία τῶν ἀλλοφύλων in 1 Macc 5:15 as a reference to "Galilee of the Gentiles."

1 Macc 5:1-2, 13 describes how, when neighboring Gentiles heard that the altar in Jerusalem had been rebuilt and the sanctuary rededicated, they began to kill "the descendants of Jacob" (τὸ γένος Ιακωβ) who lived among them and to plunder their property (5:2 NRSV). In this context, messengers came to Judas and his brothers from Galilee:

> . . . and see, other messengers arrived from Galilee with torn clothing and reported in accordance with these words, saying [that] [people] from Ptolemais and Tyre and Sidon and [the] whole district of the Phoenicians (or "all Galilee of [the] aliens") had gathered together against them "in order to destroy us utterly" (. . . καὶ ἰδοὺ ἄγγελοι ἕτεροι παρεγένοντο ἐκ τῆς Γαλιλαίας διερρηχότες τὰ ἱμάτια ἀπαγγέλλοντες κατὰ τὰ ῥήματα ταῦτα λέγοντες ἐπισυνῆχθαι ἐπ᾽ αὐτοὺς ἐκ Πτολεμαίδος καὶ Τύρου καὶ Σιδῶνος καὶ πᾶσαν Γαλιλαίαν ἀλλοφύλων τοῦ ἐξαναλῶσαι ἡμᾶς). (1 Macc 5:14-15)

Boobyer translated the phrase Γαλιλαία τῶν ἀλλοφύλων in this passage with "Galilee of the Gentiles." It should be noted, however, that the Greek phrase used here is different from the one used in Isa 8:23 (9:1).[129]

The text then goes on to say that Judas sent Simon with three thousand men to rescue the Galilean Jews. The report of Simon's actions in 5:21-22 could be interpreted in either of two ways. One is to take it as implying that residents of the cities or territories of Ptolemais, Tyre, Sidon, and other coastal cities had attacked Jews living in Galilee. The other is to take it as implying that residents of those areas gathered to assist non-Jews of Galilee in their attacks on the Jews living there. In any case, the statement that Simon, after defeating the Gentile forces, brought the Jews of Galilee to Judea (5:23) may indicate that the Jews were a minority in Galilee in the second century BCE.[130]

"Gentile" [from a Jewish perspective]) is used in the LXX of the Philistines.

127 Chancey concluded that Joel 4:4 LXX "suggests that at the time of translation, the part of Galilee near the coast was known as Γαλιλαία ἀλλοφύλων" (*Gentile Galilee*, 38).

128 Boobyer, "Galilee and Galileans," 335.

129 See below for a discussion of Isa 8:23 (9:1). Aryeh Kasher concluded, following Albrecht Alt and Klein, that the Greek phrase καὶ Τύρου καὶ Σιδῶνος καὶ πᾶσαν Γαλιλαίαν ἀλλοφύλων ("and Tyre and Sidon and all Galilee of [the] aliens") was probably written in imitation of a biblical expression, similar to the LXX of Joel 4:4, "Tyre and Sidon and all the districts of Philistia" (*Jews and Hellenistic Cities in Eretz-Israel: Relations of the Jews in Eretz-Israel with the*

Hellenistic Cities during the Second Temple Period (332 BCE–70 CE) [TSAJ 21; Tübingen: Mohr Siebeck, 1990] 68 n. 40). The implication is that the coastal region traditionally called "Phoenicia" is referred to here with a biblical formula that originally designated Philistia.

130 So Schürer, *History*, 1:142; 2:8. Kasher concluded from the same passage that the Jewish population of Galilee was quite large at the time; or they may have had considerable support among the non-Jewish rural population in the vicinity (the Ituraeans) (*Jews and Hellenistic Cities*, 68). Chancey concluded that the phrase Γαλιλαία ἀλλοφύλων in 1 Maccabees may reflect archaizing language and that it is "related to the author's emphasis on 'the nations roundabout' Israel." He also argued that the phrase

Boobyer also called attention to Josh 12:23, arguing that the MT intended a reference to "Galilee of the Gentiles," whereas the translator of the LXX took גוים to be a proper name.[131] The text of the relevant part of the verse in the MT is apparently corrupt and reads מלך־גוים לגלגל. Wright and Boling declare the phrase to be unintelligible and omit it from their translation.[132] The Greek translation reads: βασιλέα Γωιμ τῆς Γαλιλαίας ("king of the *Gôyîm* of Galilee"; or, the translation presupposed by Boobyer, "king Goyim of Galilee") (Josh 12:23b LXX).[133] Boling and Wright also mention that the reading of the LXX recalls Isa 8:23 (9:1).[134] This text is one of the two on which Lohmeyer based his understanding of the attitude toward Galilee on the part of religious leaders in Judea in the first century CE. It is also mentioned by Boobyer. It is a well-known text on this topic, since it is cited by Matthew (4:15). In the MT, a poem (Isa 9:1-6 [9:2-7]) celebrates the birth of an heir to the throne. This poem is introduced by an editorial comment in prose (8:23 [9:1]).[135] The introductory comment speaks about how former rulers (probably foreigners) treated the land of Zebulun and Naphtali with contempt and oppressed the following territories: "the way of the sea, the land across the Jordan, Galilee of the nations" (דרך הים עבר הירדן גליל הגוים) (Isa 8:23 MT [9:1 RSV]).[136] This prose introduction "refers to two phases of military disaster for parts of the Kingdom of Samaria." The second "almost certainly alludes to the annexation of Israelite territory during Tiglath-pileser's campaign of 732 B.C.E. resulting in the formation of the Assyrian provinces of Duru (Dor, 'the way of the sea'), Galʿazu (Gilead, 'the land across the Jordan') and Magidu (Megiddo, 'Galilee of the nations')."[137] The poem probably celebrates the birth of Hezekiah and expresses political and military aspirations.[138]

The translation of the prose comment in the LXX seems to be corrupt and there are many variant readings. Rahlfs's text reads:

> Do this first, do [it] quickly, district of Zebulon, the land of Naphtali, [those who inhabit] the way of the sea and the rest who dwell along the sea-coast and beyond the Jordan, Galilee of the nations [or "Gentiles"], the region of Judea (Τοῦτο πρῶτον ποίει, ταχὺ ποίει, χώρα Ζαβουλων, ἡ γῆ Νεφθαλιμ ὁδὸν θαλάσσης καὶ οἱ λοιποὶ οἱ τὴν παραλίαν κατοικοῦντες καὶ πέραν τοῦ Ιορδάνου, Γαλιλαία τῶν ἐθνῶν, τὰ μέρη τῆς Ιουδαίας). (Isa 8:23 LXX)

The phrase "Galilee of the nations" or "Galilee of the Gentiles" here may reflect the circumstance that, in the preexilic period, Galilee was a part of the Israelite kingdom that was inhabited primarily by Gentiles.[139] Another interpretation of the phrase is that the ordinary peasantry were Israelite, but they had no aristocracy or city-states of their own. Thus, the non-Jewish rulers and city-states within and surrounding the area competed for political and economic domination over it.[140] 1 Macc 5:9-23 shows that circumstances were similar in the second century BCE.[141] Schürer argued that the Hasmonean king Aristobulos I (104–103 BCE) seized Galilee from the Itureans and forced the inhabitants to be circumcised and to live in accordance with the Jewish way of life.[142] Seán Freyne, however, has argued that Galilee was already substantially Jewish in the time of John Hyrcanus (134–105 BCE). The task was not, therefore, to seize and convert Galilee but only to incorporate Galilee into the emerging Jewish state.[143]

Both Freyne and Richard A. Horsley have argued, primarily on the basis of literary sources, including inscriptions and letters, that people who practiced the

---

does not clearly denote "the larger region of Galilee" and that it was not "the common name for the entire region" (*Gentile Galilee*, 39).

131 Boobyer, "Galilee and Galileans," 335–36.

132 Boling and Wright, *Joshua*, 320, 322.

133 First trans. from Boling and Wright, *Joshua*, 329. They state that this reading suggests the name of the town of Sisera, mentioned in Judg 4:2, "Harosheth-haggoyim."

134 Boling and Wright, *Joshua*, 329.

135 Blenkinsopp, *Isaiah 1–39*, 247–48.

136 Trans. from Blenkinsopp, *Isaiah 1–39*, 245.

137 Ibid.

138 Ibid., 247–49.

139 Unlike Boling and Wright (see above), Schürer goes so far as to say that the region was never inhabited by Israelites in the preexilic period (*History*, 2:7). For

criticism of this view, see Freyne, *Galilee*, 55 n. 47; idem, "Galilee in the Hellenistic through Byzantine Periods," *OEANE* 2:370–76, esp. 372. Richard A. Horsley (*Galilee: History, Politics, People* [Valley Forge, PA: Trinity Press International, 1995] 295–96 n. 25) supports Schürer in part.

140 Horsley, *Galilee*, 20.

141 See the discussion above; see also Schürer, *History*, 1:142; 2:8.

142 Ibid., 2:9–10. Seth Schwartz concluded that by 100 BCE the Hasmoneans ruled both Lower and Upper Galilee; before that time, the population of Galilee had been, apart from "the Judeans" there, "a mixture or patchwork of Arabs, Greeks, and Syrian pagans (some of remotely Israelite descent)" and "now became in some sense Jewish" (*Imperialism and Jewish Society, 200 B.C.E. to 640 C.E.* [Princeton/

worship of Yahweh lived continuously in both Upper and Lower Galilee from the beginnings in the twelfth century BCE until the first century BCE (and later).[144] Both recognized that the surface survey by Zvi Gal has called the hypothesis of continuity into question.[145] Freyne's initial response was that "[o]nly additional stratified digs will decide whether this population gap was the result of the Assyrian aggression or was due to the migration of the country people to larger settlements."[146] Horsley's was that "[m]ore decisive evidence for the hypothesis of near-total depopulation of Galilee under the Assyrian empire would have to come from concrete excavations of Iron II sites not mentioned in the Assyrian annals that could prove a sudden and prolonged break in the occupation of those sites."[147] Jonathan L. Reed concluded that "the settlement patterns of Galilean sites from the Iron Age through the Roman Period, which reveal an almost complete abandonment of the region at the close of the Iron Age, essentially rul[e] out any direct continuity between the northern Israelites and the first-century Galileans."[148]

Horsley argued, on the one hand, that Galilee was not primarily a Gentile region in the Second Temple period, but, on the other, that the Galileans belonged to a different *ethnos* from the Judeans (Jews).[149] The latter thesis, especially, has proved controversial.[150] Meyers and Sanders agree that the Galilee of Antipas (the time of Jesus) was thoroughly Jewish.[151] Chancey concluded that the evidence does not support the conclusion "that Early Roman Galilee had a mixed population; in fact, it suggests the opposite case. In the first century CE, its inhabitants seem to have been primarily Jewish, with only a few pagans."[152] Josephus's statement that Galilee was "encircled by foreign nations" is supported "by specific details in his writings as well as by numerous archaeological finds. These areas were predominantly Gentile, though all had Jewish minorities."[153] Some "contact with Gentiles did occur in ancient Galilee," especially in border towns and villages. But for most residents of Galilee such contact was not frequent.[154] Reed concluded that "Galilee's material culture was clearly distinct, yet its closest parallel was that of Judea . . . Galilee's essentially Jewish character was shared with Judea."[155]

Related issues are the questions whether the Galilean Jews had a distinctive halakah that differed significantly from Judean halakah and whether the Galilean Jews, on the whole, were lax in their observance of the Law.[156] Lawrence Schiffman reexamined all the passages in tannaitic literature that refer explicitly to Galilean halakic practices in order to answer

Oxford: Princeton University Press, 2001] 36; see also n. 46).

143 Freyne, *Galilee*, 41–44. In this, his first study of Galilee, Freyne argued that the Assyrians had not deported the ordinary Israelites of rural Galilee, so there was no disruption of the religious character of the region throughout the centuries (24–26). In his more recent work, he has acknowledged that archaeological evidence challenges his earlier view, following Alt and based on literary sources, that "the Israelite population in the Galilee was relatively undisturbed throughout" the period from the Assyrian conquest to the rise of the Hasmoneans ("Galilee in the Hellenistic through Byzantine Periods," 371). He also concluded that Jewish settlements in both Upper and Lower Galilee increased beginning at least in the late Hellenistic period (ibid., 372). See also the discussion of Freyne's work in Chancey, *Gentile Galilee*, 23–24.

144 Freyne, *Galilee*, 24–26; Horsley, *Galilee*, 21–22, 25–29.

145 Freyne, "Galilee in the Hellenistic through Byzantine Periods," 371; Horsley, *Galilee*, 26, 290 n. 13.

146 Freyne, "Galilee in the Hellenistic through Byzantine Periods," 371.

147 Horsley, *Galilee*, 290 n. 13. See also his renewed argument based on literary sources (ibid., 26–27).

148 Jonathan L. Reed, *Archaeology and the Galilean Jesus:*

A Re-examination of the Evidence (Harrisburg, PA: Trinity Press International, 2000) 27.

149 Horsley, *Galilee*, 34–61, esp. 49–51. For the early Roman period, see 61–88.

150 Chancey, *Gentile Galilee*, 25. Schwartz argued that, under Hasmonean rule, the Idumeans "became Jewish but remained simultaneously Idumaeans" (*Imperialism and Jewish Society*, 39). Presumably, one could say the same of the Galileans: they were Jewish (Judean) but at the same time Galileans. On the loyalty of the Galileans and the Idumeans to the temple and their willingness to risk death or enslavement to protect it during the first revolt, see Schwartz, *Imperialism and Jewish Society*, 61. But he concluded that the Galileans had been less willing than the Judeans "to hand over their surplus production to the temple and its staff" (ibid., 52).

151 See the summary of their views and the citation of their works by Chancey, *Gentile Galilee*, 25–26.

152 Ibid., 61. On the archaeological evidence that supports this conclusion, see 63–119.

153 Ibid., 165.

154 Ibid., 166.

155 Reed, *Archaeology*, 216–17.

156 On the role of Torah and temple in Galilee prior to 70 CE, see Schwartz, *Imperialism and Jewish Society*, 72–73. With regard to an analogous issue, Birger A. Pearson concluded that "there was no significant

these questions.[157] He acknowledged that his conclusions do not apply to the entire population of Galilee. There was diversity among Jews in the region, at least until tannaitic practices became dominant. Hellenized Jews and the peasants of Galilee may have had distinctive practices. Schiffman concluded that Galilean Jews who followed tannaitic traditions adhered to the same rulings as the tannaitic Jews of the south in the vast majority of cases.[158] In cases in which the Galileans differed from the Judeans, a higher degree of stringency in halakic observance is attributed to the Galileans.[159] The tannaitic evidence, however, may not be relevant to the times of Jesus and Mark, since it is at least post-70 CE and possibly dating to the second century CE.

We return now to Boobyer's use of the evidence of the LXX. He interpreted Isa 8:23—9:6 as depicting Galilee of the Gentiles "as specially appointed to receive salvation in the messianic age, and, further, as a land which will be one of the first to experience God's deliverance."[160] This reading certainly does not correspond to the significance that the passage had for its author and first audiences. It does not represent Matthew's reading of it very precisely either. Matthew associates the fulfillment of this scripture with Jesus' move to Capernaum (4:13), which he explicitly states is "the [city or small town] located by the sea in the region of Zebulon and Naphtali" (τὴν παραθαλασσίαν ἐν ὁρίοις Ζαβουλὼν καὶ Νεφθαλίμ). He also associates it with Jesus' proclamation of repentance and the kingdom of heaven (4:17) from that time onward. There is no particular emphasis on Galilee in general or on Gentiles. At most, the passage indicates that the proclamation of Jesus will eventually bring salvation to the Gentiles.[161]

Finally, Boobyer concluded that "Galilee had a mixed population in Mark's day" and assumed extensive contact between Gentiles and Jews in that region.[162] Freyne, however, has argued that it was the few *cities* in Galilee that were heavily hellenized, as opposed to the rural areas, villages, and small towns, and that most of the non-Jewish population lived in them. These cities, however, did not have significant impact on the practices and lifestyles of the Jews who lived in the rural areas of Upper and Lower Galilee.[163] In any case, Boobyer's conclusion that Mark 14:28 and 16:7 signify that the disciples should go to Galilee after the resurrection "chiefly for the purpose of commencing the Gentile mission" is dubious.[164]

Let us now return to Lohmeyer's study. His claim that Galilee was religiously ostracized or condemned by influential and devout Jews of Jerusalem does not seem to be supported by Isa 8:23 (9:1) or Matt 4:15. Freyne concluded that, although Galilean Jews "may not have followed Pharisaic regulations concerning the half shekel offering and do not appear to have been too scrupulous in regard to tithing," they were loyal to the practices related to the temple in Jerusalem.[165] The presence of stoneware and stepped pools in early Roman contexts of Galilean sites supports the conclusion that Galilean Jews observed dietary and purity regulations.[166]

In his discussion of Mark as a whole, Lohmeyer argued that in 1:14—9:50 Galilee is presented not only

---

difference in terms of beliefs and practices between Jesus-believing Jews in Galilee and in Jerusalem" ("A Q Community in Galilee?" *NTS* 50 [2004] 476–94; quotation is from the abstract on 476).

157 Lawrence H. Schiffman, "Was There a Galilean Halakhah?" in Lee I. Levine, ed., *The Galilee in Late Antiquity* (New York/Jerusalem: Jewish Theological Seminary of America; Cambridge, MA/London: Harvard University Press, 1992) 143–56. I am grateful to my colleague, Steven Fraade, for bringing this article to my attention.

158 Schiffman noted that A. Oppenheimer, E. E. Urbach, and Klein came to the same conclusions ("Was There a Galilean Halakhah?" 144–45 n. 5).

159 Ibid., 144–45, 156.

160 Boobyer, "Galilee and Galileans," 336.

161 Luz, *Matthew 1–7*, 195. The apologetic tone found in the text by Davies and Allison is by no means obvious (*Matthew*, 1:370–80).

162 Boobyer, "Galilee and Galileans," 337.

163 Freyne, *Galilee*, 138–45. Horsley concluded that

"there may have been little more than a thin veneer of cosmopolitan culture even in the cities of Lower Galilee in the early first century C.E. . . . Critical consideration of Josephus' accounts of events in 4 B.C.E. and 66–67 C.E. . . . indicates a widespread and long-standing reaction against the urban-based rulers and their culture (*Archaeology, History, and Society in Galilee* [Valley Forge, PA: Trinity Press International, 1996] 179). Kasher concluded that the relations between the Jews and the Hellenistic cities in the Second Temple period were characterized by "a powerful religious hostility," "age-old religious conflict," and rivalry and hatred of an ethnic-cultural character (*Jews and Hellenistic Cities*, 313). See also the discussion of Chancey's conclusions above.

164 Boobyer, "Galilee and Galileans," 338.

165 Freyne, *Galilee*, 293.

166 Chancey, *Gentile Galilee*, 118.

as the beginning and center of Jesus' activity but also as the "holy land of the gospel, the place of its fulfillment."[167] In contrast, Jerusalem is portrayed as "the place of sin and of death"[168] and "of deadly enmity to Jesus."[169] Lohmeyer recognized that Galilee is also described as a place where there was resistance to and rejection of Jesus. But he argued that these features only darkened, but did not destroy, the faith that Galilee was the place chosen to have a key eschatological role.[170] He did not note, however, that the Gospel of Mark begins with the activity of John the Baptist, which is clearly presented as the first eschatological event. This activity does not take place in Galilee.[171]

But the main problem with Lohmeyer's interpretation of Mark is that he oversimplifies the narrative techniques used by the evangelist to tell the story of Jesus and then makes too much of the result. Opposition to Jesus is a prominent theme introduced early in the narrative.[172] The lack of understanding of the majority of the people is a theme in 4:1-34; and the misunderstanding of the disciples becomes acute already in 6:52.[173] In order to claim that most of Jesus' activity of proclamation (κηρύσσειν) and miracle-working takes place in Galilee, Lohmeyer has to speak of "greater Galilee" and to assume that the events narrated in regions around Galilee in Mark contribute to its status as a chosen, holy land of eschatological fulfillment.

Lohmeyer's study has been very influential. Light-foot agreed with him almost entirely.[174] Willi Marxsen, like Lohmeyer, had historical interests in the topic and attempted to refine the analysis of it with redaction-critical methods. He solved the problem of the lack of early attestation of an important community in Galilee by arguing that Mark 16:7 must be understood in terms of the situation of the evangelist and his audience, not in terms of an earlier time. He put forward the hypothesis that this saying is closely related to the oracle mentioned by Eusebius, instructing the community in Jerusalem to emigrate. Marxsen argued that the oracle originally contained two elements: a command to leave Jerusalem and an announcement of the imminent parousia. Mark narrated only the first part of the oracle (the instruction to go to Galilee). Since the parousia had not yet occurred, he could not narrate that event. Thus 16:8 is an appropriate ending for the Gospel.[175] Paul did not know about an important community in Galilee because one arose only in the late 60s CE.[176] Marxsen could link Mark 16:7 with the oracle described by Eusebius only by assuming that Mark did not define Galilee narrowly; thus he could associate Pella (in the region of the Decapolis),[177] where Eusebius says the community of Jerusalem resettled, with Galilee.[178] Like Lohmeyer, Marxsen concluded that 16:7 (and thus 14:28 as well) referred, not to a resurrection appearance, but to the expected parousia.[179]

---

167 Lohmeyer, *Galiläa und Jerusalem*, 28–29; quotation from 29. See also the detailed discussion in support of this conclusion (ibid., 29–36).

168 Ibid., 33.

169 Ibid., 34.

170 Ibid., 32–33.

171 See the commentary on 1:2-15 and on 9:9-13 above. Elizabeth Struthers Malbon noted that "the narrative [of Mark], in fact, opens in Judea and closes with past and future looks to Galilee" ("Galilee and Jerusalem: History and Literature in Marcan Interpretation," *CBQ* 44 [1982] 242–55; quotation from 250–51).

172 See the section "Narrative Unity and Literary History of 2:1–3:6" in the commentary on 2:1-12 above; Stemberger, "Galilee—Land of Salvation?" 431–35; Seán Freyne, "The Geography of Restoration: Galilee—Jerusalem Relations in Early Jewish and Christian Experience," *NTS* 47 (2001) 289–311, esp. 306. See also the commentary on 3:20-30 above.

173 See the commentary on those passages, as well as that on 8:16-21 above.

174 Robert Henry Lightfoot, *Locality and Doctrine in the Gospels* (New York/London: Harper & Brothers, 1938) esp. 111–25. He later changed his mind, interpreting 14:28 and 16:7 as referring to resurrection appearances that enable the disciples at last to understand the Lord and to do his work (*Gospel Message*, 115–16). See also the brief discussion of Lightfoot's views in Stemberger, "Galilee—Land of Salvation?" 413, 438.

175 Marxsen, *Der Evangelist Markus,* 75–77; ET *Mark the Evangelist*, 114–16.

176 Ibid., 70 n. 3; ET 107 n. 158.

177 Finegan, *Archaeology*, 117.

178 Marxsen, *Der Evangelist Markus*, 70; *Mark the Evangelist*, 107.

179 Ibid., 54, 73; ET 85, 111. See also the summary of Marxsen's views in Stemberger, "Galilee—Land of Salvation?" 413–14. Another scholar who agreed with most of Lohmeyer's major theses is Philip Carrington, *The Primitive Christian Calendar: A Study in the Making of the Marcan Gospel*, vol. 1: *Introduction & Text* (Cambridge: Cambridge University Press, 1952) 81–82. In contrast, Leonard E. Elliott-Binns concluded that 14:28 and 16:7 imply resurrection appearances in Galilee (*Galilean Christianity* [SBT; Chicago: Allenson, 1956] 39). See the discussion in Stemberger, "Galilee—Land of Salvation?" 414 and n. 19. For further scholars influenced by Lohmeyer, see Yarbro Collins, *Beginning of the Gospel*, 136 n. 57.

Werner Kelber followed Lohmeyer and Marxsen in interpreting 14:28 and 16:7 in terms of the coming of the kingdom of God in Galilee and the establishment of the eschatological reunion in that place.[180]

Elizabeth Struthers Malbon studied the geography and theology of Mark, but she did not focus on "Marcan geography [as] an indicator of the historical world of the text," but rather on "Marcan geography in the context of the text as a literary world."[181] Following Claude Lévi-Strauss, she includes in her analysis diachronic investigation (the chronological order in which events occur from 1:1 to 16:8) and synchronic analysis (of the "latent content" involving the fundamental opposition the story seeks to mediate).[182] Her analysis and conclusions are in some ways more precise than Lohmeyer's, but they seem to replicate some of his major theses in another key. Her diachronic investigation led to the conclusion that "the Marcan diachronic pattern reverses [the cultural] expectation [that the action should culminate in Jerusalem]: Judean actions culminate in Galilee (14:28; 16:7)."[183] The synchronic analysis led to the conclusion that "[t]he Marcan narrative . . . reverses the expected associations of Galilee and Judea."[184] In Mark, Galilee "is the center of order," and "Judea is linked with the chaos-pole of the fundamental opposition."[185] She interprets 16:7 neither in terms of resurrection appearances nor parousia, but symbolically: "At the close of the Gospel of Mark, Jesus' spatial location is neither Jerusalem nor Galilee, but somewhere in between; Jesus is in movement; he is 'going before' (16:7); he is on the way."[186]

In the same year that Kelber's first book on Mark appeared, Stemberger published a critical assessment of the interpretation of Galilee by Lohmeyer and his followers.[187] With regard to Lohmeyer's theory of a "greater Galilee," Stemberger concluded that one cannot prove such a notion from Mark, since the evangelist "clearly distinguishes Galilee from the surrounding regions, the country across the Jordan, the lake, the Decapolis, the region of Caesarea Philippi and that of Tyre and Sidon. This leaves no room for a larger Galilee."[188] Further, "neither Matthew nor Mark thought of a larger Galilee, and consequently the first half of the ministry of Christ in these two gospels reveals no geographical unity: most important events like the transfiguration take place outside Galilee."[189]

One of the weakest aspects of Lohmeyer's theory is that, acording to Mark, "Galileans" were equivalent to "Christians" (*populus christianus*) and that Galilee was Christian territory (*terra christiana*).[190] This part of his overall interpretation of Galilee in Mark was based on the statement of those who were standing by when Peter was in the courtyard of the high priest, "You really are one of them, for you are a Galilean" (ἀληθῶς ἐξ αὐτῶν εἶ, καὶ γὰρ Γαλιλαῖος εἶ) in 14:70. In the narrative context of Mark, this statement does not imply that all Galileans were followers of Jesus. It is the combination of Peter's presence in the high priest's residence while Jesus was there (cf. 14:54) with his Galilean identity that led to the conclusion that he was one of the group around Jesus.[191] Stemberger doubted that there was an organized Christian community in Galilee when Mark wrote his Gospel.[192]

With regard to the thesis that Mark expected the parousia in Galilee, Stemberger concluded that, in Jewish tradition, it "was the land of Palestine where one expected the end. . . . If one wanted to be more precise, then only Jerusalem, and more exactly Mount Sion, the Temple, could be the place of the final manifestation. . . . Thus the interpretation of Mark 14:28; 16:7 of the parousia seems *a priori* unlikely."[193] He concludes that the resurrection appearances in Galilee narrated in Matthew and John "do not express the association of Galilee with the coming end."[194]

On the historical question, Stemberger argued that it is easier to explain why appearances originally connected with Galilee would be transferred to

---

180 Kelber, *Kingdom*, xi, 105, 107, 129, 144–47; see the summary and assessment of Kelber's treatment of the polarity between Galilee and Jerusalem by Malbon, "Galilee and Jerusalem," 245–47. See also Kelber, *Mark's Story*, 74–75; in this work the kingdom of God is demythologized, and thus the eschatology is immanent, rather than imminent; see esp. 84. A similar perspective is expressed in Kelber, *Gospel*, 215.

181 Malbon, "Galilee and Jerusalem," 247.

182 Ibid., 248.

183 Ibid., 251.

184 Ibid., 252–53.

185 Ibid., 253.

186 Ibid. On the theme of Galilee and Jerusalem, see also Malbon, *Narrative Space*, 15–49.

187 Stemberger, "Galilee—Land of Salvation?" 409–38. Stemberger also referred to earlier critics of this interpretation (ibid., 409 n. 3).

188 Ibid., 419.

189 Ibid., 421.

190 Lohmeyer, *Galiläa und Jerusalem*, 28.

191 14:67 may imply that the female servant had seen Peter with Jesus previously and recognized him. Cf. Stemberger, "Galilee—Land of Salvation?" 421.

192 Ibid., 421–25.

193 Ibid., 426–27.

194 Ibid., 431.

Jerusalem than the other way around.[195] He suggested that "there was a tradition that Christ had been seen in Galilee after his resurrection (cf. Mark 14:28; 16:7), but that details were no longer known."[196]

In a later work, Lightfoot changed his mind about the significance of 14:28 and 16:7.[197] Stemberger agreed with his articulation of the double function of 16:7; it recalls the beginnings of Christ's ministry and suggests that the task of the audience in the future is to carry on that work.[198]

The position taken in this commentary is that, from a historical point of view, resurrection appearances did take place in Galilee, in the sense that Peter, and probably others, had experiences there that convinced them that Jesus had been raised from the dead. The author of Mark and his early audiences were familiar with the oral proclamation of appearance accounts. The lack of narration of such accounts in the earliest recoverable form of Mark may be explained in a variety of ways: the evangelist had no details about these appearances; or he wanted to portray the present as a time in which Jesus is absent; or his focus was on the story of Jesus, which, in his view, ended with the resurrection.[199] In ancient literature, it was not unusual to end a narrative without including subsequent events that were well known to both the author and the audience. Homer's *Iliad* is a good example of such a technique.[200] The remarks about Jesus going before the disciples to Galilee allude to the resurrection appearances (14:28; 16:7) that Mark does not narrate.[201]

The lack of attestation for an important community in Galilee in the early period and the association of Peter and other prominent disciples with Jerusalem can be explained by the hypothesis that, soon after the resurrection-appearances, the disciples moved to Jerusalem. The move may have been motivated by the expectation that Jerusalem would be the beginning point or center of the parousia.[202] Another possibility is that they chose Jerusalem as an appropriate starting point and center of their missionary activities. The two explanations are, of course, not mutually exclusive.

Comment

■ **26-31** This unit has important links with subsequent incidents in the passion narrative.[203] Jesus' prediction that all the disciples would take offense and be scattered (v. 27) is fulfilled in the account of the arrest (v. 50). The promise that, after he was raised, Jesus would go before them to Galilee (v. 28) is repeated by the "young man" in the tomb in 16:7. Peter's denial, predicted in v. 30, is narrated in vv. 54, 66-72. These connections would seem to support the idea that this unit was part of the pre-Markan passion narrative that the evangelist used as a source. The main problem with drawing such a conclusion is that the passage does not fit smoothly in its context. It is not historically certain that "Gethsemane" originally designated a place on the Mount of Olives. The name of the traditional pilgrimage site, the Garden of Gethsemane, next to the Church of All Nations on the Mount of Olives, derives from a conflation of Mark's "Gethsemane" in 14:32 and John's κῆπος ("garden" or "orchard") in 18:1.[204] In any case, it has often been suspected that the association of "Gethsemane" with the "Mount of Olives" is a result, rather than a cause, of the association of the two place-names in Mark 14.[205] The

195 Ibid., 429.

196 Ibid., 430.

197 Lightfoot, *Gospel Message*, 115–16.

198 Stemberger, "Galilee—Land of Salvation?" 438.

199 See the commentary on 16:8 below.

200 J. Lee Magness, *Sense and Absence: Structure and Suspension in the Ending of Mark's Gospel* (SBLSS; Atlanta: SBL/Scholars Press, 1986) 25–47.

201 Yarbro Collins, *Beginning of the Gospel*, 136–37.

202 Such an expectation could have been based on an exegesis of Zech 14:4. See also Hans Conzelmann's conclusion, against Lohmeyer, that "Jerusalem" in Luke is to be interpreted from the point of view of eschatology, not Christology (*Die Mitte der Zeit: Studien zur Theologie des Lukas* [Beiträge zur historischen Theologie 17; Tübingen: Mohr Siebeck,

1954] 61 n. 1; ET *The Theology of St Luke* [London: Faber & Faber, 1960] 74 n. 1).

203 Yarbro Collins, *Beginning of the Gospel*, 105–6.

204 Mark's χωρίον in v. 32 simply means an unpopulated place. Joan E. Taylor has argued recently that the location of Jesus' arrest was not the Garden of Gethsemane mentioned above, but the Cave of Gethsemane, which had one or two olive oil presses (the name "Gethsemane" probably means "oil press" [BAGD, s.v. Γεθσημανί]) ("The Garden of Gethsemane Not the Place of Jesus' Arrest," *BAR* 21.4 [July/August 1995] 26–35, 62). According to Donald A. D. Thorsen, there were four rival locations claiming to be the authentic site, but none of them can be traced back prior to the fourth cent. ("Gethsemane," *ABD* 2:997–98).

205 Schenke, *Passionsgeschichte*, 353.

presence of the two place-names in two different units, without any comment on the relation between them, suggests that the two passages have been joined secondarily.

Furthermore, the Gethsemane story does not follow smoothly on vv. 26-31. The transition is rough, and the failure of the disciples to stay awake is not an illustration or a fulfillment of the prophecy that they would take offense. The tension between these two passages could be resolved either by taking vv. 26-31 as a Markan composition to prepare for later elements in the passion narrative (whether those elements are pre-Markan or redactional) or by taking the Gethsemane story (vv. 32-42) as an insertion into an earlier sequence in which the arrest followed immediately on the predictions of vv. 26-31.[206]

Vincent Taylor concluded that vv. 27-31 lacked the vividness of instances of the classic form-critical oral types.[207] Bultmann described the same passage as "an historical account with legendary traits"[208] and also defined it as a "faith-legend" because of its apologetic motives.[209] Since the Gethsemane story is clearly linked to the following arrest story, and probably was already so connected in Mark's source, it is likely that Mark placed vv. 26-31 in their present position.[210] In order to reconstruct the "faith-legend" or pre-Markan "historical account," Bultmann had to argue that v. 28 is secondary to the context.[211] The simpler hypothesis seems to be the conclusion that Mark composed vv. 26-31, as Schenke has argued.

With regard to its present position as part of Mark as a whole, this passage continues the theme of the rejec-tion of Jesus.[212] He is the shepherd who will be struck and the one who will be denied. He is to be vindicated through resurrection. From another point of view, one notes that the emphasis in this passage seems to be on the disciples. As in Zech 13:7-9, the text evoked in v. 17, the emphasis is on the "flock" or the "sheep" that will be scattered, rather than on the shepherd. The focus is on Peter especially, the "Rock" of 3:16, who once refused to accept the idea of a suffering messiah, but now professes his commitment to that necessity and his willingness to die with Jesus. The tension between his statements and those of Jesus here continues the theme of the misunderstanding of the disciples.[213]

■ **26** The participle ὑμνήσαντες ("after they had sung a hymn") in this transitional verse was probably composed by Mark to round off the account of the last meal of Jesus with his disciples.[214] It alludes generally to the practice of singing hymns, probably psalms, during the Passover meal and thus picks up the story about the preparation for the celebration of that meal in vv. 12-16.

According to the Mishnah, the Levites sang the *Hallel* (Psalms 113–118) in the temple court while the people were slaughtering the Passover offering.[215] The Mishnah also states that four cups of wine must be drunk during the Passover meal.[216] The first part of the *Hallel* should be sung in connection with the second cup.[217] The school of Shammai says that this first part included only to the end of Psalm 113; the school of Hillel says to the end of Psalm 114.[218] The remainder of the *Hallel* was to be sung over the fourth cup.[219] It is not certain, however, that the *Hallel* was sung during the meal already in the time of

---

206 In his Additional Note "J. The Construction of the Passion and Resurrection Narrative," Taylor argues that this passage (vv. 26-31) was part of the pre-Markan passion narrative and that the Gethsemane story (vv. 32-42) was one of the Petrine reminiscences added later by Mark (660, 662–63). In the introduction and the commentary proper, he concluded that vv. 26-31 do not comprise an old oral narrative, but a construction by Mark or a predecessor based on tradition (82–83, 548). Schenke argued that vv. 26-31 were composed by Mark on the basis of the tradition of the arrest (vv. 43-52) and the denial of Peter (vv. 66-72) (*Passionsgeschichte*, 353, 423). E. J. Pryke attributed all of vv. 26-31 to Markan redaction, noting that part of Jesus' statement in v. 30 and Peter's statement in v. 31 are possibly from a source (*Redactional Style*, 172).

207 Taylor, 82–83.
208 Bultmann, *History*, 267.
209 Ibid., 306.
210 Yarbro Collins, *Beginning of the Gospel*, 106–7.
211 Bultmann, *History*, 267.
212 See the commentary on vv. 17-21 above.
213 See the commentary on vv. 29–31 below.
214 Schenke, *Passionsgeschichte*, 349.
215 *M. Pesaḥ.* 5.7; Danby, *Mishnah*, 142 and n. 9.
216 *M. Pesaḥ.* 10.1.
217 Ibid., 10.4–6.
218 Ibid., 10.6; Danby, *Mishnah*, 151 and nn. 3 and 4.
219 *M. Pesaḥ.* 10.7.

Mark.[220] Philo states that the Passover meal included prayers and hymns ($\epsilon\dot{v}\chi\alpha\acute{i}\ \tau\epsilon\ \kappa\alpha\grave{i}\ \ddot{v}\mu\nu o\iota$) (*Spec. leg.* 2.27 §148).[221]

The rest of v. 26, "they went out to the Mount of Olives" ($\dot{\epsilon}\xi\tilde{\eta}\lambda\vartheta o\nu\ \epsilon\dot{i}\varsigma\ \tau\dot{o}\ \ddot{o}\rho o\varsigma\ \tau\tilde{\omega}\nu\ \dot{\epsilon}\lambda\alpha\iota\tilde{\omega}\nu$), is probably also Markan redaction.[222] Beginning with 11:11, Jesus is portrayed as spending his days in Jerusalem, primarily on the temple mount, and his nights in Bethany. In 11:1, Bethany, Bethphage, and the Mount of Olives are closely associated.[223] Here Jesus and his disciples are portrayed as leaving the city of Jerusalem, as in 11:19, and heading for the Mount of Olives/Bethany.[224] Mark does not specify "Bethany" in v. 26 because he wants to link vv. 26-31 with the traditional scene in Gethsemane, preserved in vv. 32-42, a place that, he infers, was located on the Mount of Olives.

■ **27** At some unspecified place on the Mount of Olives,[225] Jesus says to the disciples, "You will all take offense" ($\sigma\kappa\alpha\nu\delta\alpha\lambda\iota\sigma\vartheta\acute{\eta}\sigma\epsilon\sigma\vartheta\epsilon$).[226] He then elaborates this prediction with an explicit citation of scripture, "for it is written, 'I will strike the shepherd, and the sheep will be scattered'" ($\ddot{o}\tau\iota\ \gamma\acute{\epsilon}\gamma\rho\alpha\pi\tau\alpha\iota\cdot\ \pi\alpha\tau\acute{\alpha}\xi\omega\ \tau\grave{o}\nu\ \pi o\iota\mu\acute{\epsilon}\nu\alpha\ \kappa\alpha\grave{i}\ \tau\grave{\alpha}\ \pi\rho\acute{o}\beta\alpha\tau\alpha\ \delta\iota\alpha\sigma\kappa o\rho\pi\iota\sigma\vartheta\acute{\eta}\sigma o\nu\tau\alpha\iota$). The text cited is from the first half of Zech 13:7b,[227] which reads:

"strike the shepherds and draw out the sheep" (or "and remove the sheep by force") ($\pi\alpha\tau\acute{\alpha}\xi\alpha\tau\epsilon\ \tau o\grave{v}\varsigma\ \pi o\iota\mu\acute{\epsilon}\nu\alpha\varsigma\ \kappa\alpha\grave{i}\ \dot{\epsilon}\kappa\sigma\pi\acute{\alpha}\sigma\alpha\tau\epsilon\ \tau\grave{\alpha}\ \pi\rho\acute{o}\beta\alpha\tau\alpha$). (Zech 13:7b LXX)

The Hebrew reads:

Strike the shepherd so that the flock may be scattered

(הַךְ אֶת־הָרֹעֶה וּתְפוּצֶיןָ הַצֹּאן).
(Zech 13:7b MT)[228]

Instead of $\pi\alpha\tau\acute{\alpha}\xi\alpha\tau\epsilon$ ("strike" [second person plural]), Codex Alexandrinus and the corrected text of Sinaiticus read $\pi\alpha\tau\acute{\alpha}\xi o\nu$ ("strike" [second person sing.]), and instead of $\tau o\grave{v}\varsigma\ \pi o\iota\mu\acute{\epsilon}\nu\alpha\varsigma$ ("the shepherds"), $\tau\grave{o}\nu\ \pi o\iota\mu\acute{\epsilon}\nu\alpha$ ("the shepherd"). The singular readings, however, especially the latter one, may result from an attempt to conform the LXX to Matt 26:31 and Mark 14:27.[229] So Mark may have modified the LXX text known to him to fit the situation of Jesus better, or he may have known an early Greek version that was more similar to the Hebrew text than the earliest recoverable reading of the LXX that has come down to us.[230]

The meaning of Zech 13:7b in its original context is highly ambiguous. It is not clear whether the image of the shepherd represents a prophet or a ruler, though the latter is more likely.[231] If Mark approached this text with a hermeneutic of prophecy and fulfillment, this ambiguity would make it attractive as a text whose true meaning becomes apparent only as it is fulfilled in the story of Jesus.[232] The context in Zechariah of the two clauses that are cited in v. 27 begins with a disaster brought about by the decree of Yahweh (13:7-9a) and concludes with the

---

220 Bradshaw, *Search*, 23, 51.
221 Text and trans. from Colson and Whitaker, *Philo,* 7:396–97.
222 Schenke, *Passionsgeschichte*, 349–54.
223 See the commentary on 11:1 above.
224 Schenke, *Passionsgeschichte*, 351–53.
225 Or on the way to the Mount of Olives; so Schenke, *Passionsgeschichte*, 561–62.
226 On the priority of the shortest reading, see note a on the trans. of v. 27 above.
227 Dodd referred to this passage as "an important *testimonium*" in the writings of the NT (*According to the Scriptures*, 65–66).
228 Text from *BHS*; trans. from Meyers and Meyers, *Zechariah 9–14*, 361.
229 See the apparatus to Zech 13:7 in Rahlfs.
230 It is of course also possible that he was familiar with a Hebrew form of Zechariah. Moo argued that Mark may be dependent here on "a pre-Christian Palestin-

ian Jewish Greek recension" (*Old Testament*, 183–84). On the possibility that Mark was dependent here on a Greek version of the OT "which had been, in places, revised toward the Hebrew text," see David S. New, *Old Testament Quotations in the Synoptic Gospels, and the Two-Document Hypothesis* (SBLSCS 37; Atlanta: Scholars Press, 1993) 122–23.
231 Meyers and Meyers, *Zechariah 9–14*, 384–89; Petersen, *Zechariah 9–14*, 128–33.
232 Suhl is right that the notion of prophecy and fulfillment is not explicit here (*Funktion*, 65). But 14:49 makes clear that Mark is familiar with the idea.

reaffirmation of the relation of the remnant with their God (13:9b). Two-thirds of the people will perish, but one-third, after severe testing, will survive (13:8b-9a). The image of testing fits the role of the disciples, whose loyalty to Jesus will be severely tested by his arrest and crucifixion. The image of scattering (not present in the earliest recoverable form of the LXX as it has come down to us) fits the flight of the disciples narrated in v. 50.

It is noteworthy that both the MT and the LXX portray God as instructing his agent or agents to strike the shepherd, whereas Mark has God say, "I will strike the shepherd."[233] The Markan formulation is a clear indication that, for the evangelist, the death of Jesus is willed by God.[234]

The idea that the events of the passion narrative took place in accordance with the scriptures may be at work here as a way for the author and the audience to make sense of the death of Jesus and to understand him as a sovereign and willing subject in the events rather than a humiliated and disgraced object of forces beyond his control.

The scriptural citation of v. 27, however, also has a noteworthy literary effect. Like the passion predictions, especially the first and the third, this prediction by Jesus, linked to scripture, foreshadows the events to be narrated in the rest of chapter 14 (the flight of the disciples, the denial of Peter) and in chapter 15 (the death of Jesus).[235] As a divine oracle in some ancient novels catches the attention of the audience and arouses their interest in the detailed narration of the events that will unfold later in the narrative,[236] so this prediction by Jesus arouses interest in the details of the fate of Jesus and the behavior of the disciples. For those who know the story well, the prediction adds pathos to Jesus' saying in v. 27 and irony to the protestations of Peter and the disciples in vv. 29 and 31.

The introductory statement of Jesus interprets the flight of the disciples in v. 50 and the denial of Peter in vv. 54, 66-72 as "taking offense" ($\sigma\kappa\alpha\nu\delta\alpha\lambda\iota\sigma\vartheta\hat{\eta}\nu\alpha\iota$). The Twelve are thus like "the ones sown on stony ground" described by Jesus in 4:17—"when tribulation or persecution on account of the word occurs, they immediately take offense." They are also like the people of Nazareth who "take offense" at Jesus according to 6:3. Thus, their taking offense belongs to the theme of the misunderstanding or lack of understanding on the part of the disciples of Jesus.[237]

■ 28 The first brief speech of Jesus in this passage is completed in this verse: "But after I am raised, I will go ahead of you to Galilee" ($\dot{\alpha}\lambda\lambda\dot{\alpha}$ $\mu\epsilon\tau\dot{\alpha}$ $\tau\dot{o}$ $\dot{\epsilon}\gamma\epsilon\rho\vartheta\hat{\eta}\nu\alpha\acute{\iota}$ $\mu\epsilon$ $\pi\rho\sigma\acute{\alpha}\xi\omega$ $\dot{\upsilon}\mu\hat{\alpha}\varsigma$ $\epsilon\dot{\iota}\varsigma$ $\tau\dot{\eta}\nu$ $\Gamma\alpha\lambda\iota\lambda\alpha\acute{\iota}\alpha\nu$). This statement is analogous to the predictions of Jesus' resurrection in the three passion predictions (8:31; 9:31; 10:33-34). Here a new detail is the implied instruction that the disciples should go to Galilee after Jesus' death to meet him, risen, in that place. This saying prepares for 16:7, where the phrase "there you will see him" ($\dot{\epsilon}\kappa\epsilon\hat{\iota}$ $\alpha\dot{\upsilon}\tau\dot{o}\nu$ $\check{o}\psi\epsilon\sigma\vartheta\epsilon$) implies a resurrection appearance.

Many scholars have argued that v. 28 is not original in this context.[238] The context of the clauses cited from Zech 13:7b, however, suggests that a reassurance about a

---

233 In the MT, it is the sword addressed in v. 7 that is the subject of the imperative "strike" (Meyers and Meyers, *Zechariah 9–14*, 384, 387).

234 Such is the case even if the primary motivation for the change was simply adaptation to the new context; cf. Moo, *Old Testament*, 184. On the rejection of Jesus, the passion of Jesus, and the flight of the disciples as willed by God according to Mark, see Gudrun Guttenberger, *Die Gottesvorstellung im Markusevangelium* (BZNW 123; Berlin/New York: de Gruyter, 2004) 54, 116. This reading of v. 27 fits with v. 21 and the first passion prediction (8:31); see the commentary on those verses above. Flesseman-van Leer also makes this point; in addition, she points out a degree of similarity between the situation of Zech 13:7-9 and the one in Mark ("Die Interpretation der Passionsgeschichte," 87–88).

235 See the commentary on 8:31 and 10:33-34 above.

236 As Mary Ann Tolbert has pointed out, the "oracles or narrative reassurances of a successful conclusion" in the ancient novels and in Mark give away the ending of the story. "The concern of the audience in both cases is not *what* is going to happen but *how* it will happen" (*Sowing the Gospel*, 67; emphasis original). See also Heil, "Mark 14,1-52," 310.

237 Cf. Schenke, *Passionsgeschichte*, 428.

238 For discussion of this issue, see Schenke, *Passionsgeschichte*, 370–73; he himself concluded that v. 28, like the whole of vv. 27-31, is Markan redaction (ibid., 374–423).

positive outcome in the future is to be expected at this point.[239]

Lohmeyer argued that 14:28 and 16:7 are prophecies of the parousia which is to take place in Galilee.[240] This interpretation, however, is highly unlikely. The parousia, as it is described in 13:24-27, is portrayed by Mark as a cosmic event. Its effects reach as far as "the four winds, from (one) end of the earth to the other."[241] The language of "power" (δύναμις) and "glory" (δόξα) associated with the parousia elsewhere in Mark (9:1; 13:26; cf. 14:62) does not occur here or in 16:7. The parousia and Galilee are not associated anywhere else in the Gospel.[242] Further, the interpretation of 14:28 and 16:7 as referring to a resurrection appearance is more appropriate to the context in each case.[243]

■ **29** Peter contradicts Jesus here, at least with regard to his own case. In an analogous way, Peter rejected Jesus' revelation of the mystery that the Son of Man must suffer.[244] Here he accepts the idea that God will "strike the shepherd," but he refuses to accept the notion that he will take offense when that event begins to take place. The implication is that Peter still lacks understanding concerning who Jesus is and how great the test will be to which the Twelve will be subjected. One could say that the statement, in the context of Mark as a whole, implies a lack of self-knowledge as well. Similarly, James and John affirmed that they were able to drink the cup that Jesus was about to drink and to be baptized with the baptism with which he was about to be baptized (10:38-39a). The account of the passion of Jesus, however, reveals that none of the three prove to be able to live up to their promises. Their failure is not definitive, however. Jesus predicts that James and John will (eventually) suffer as he

will.[245] The instruction given to the women by the "young man" in 16:7 implies that "the disciples and Peter" will have a second chance.[246] Similarly, the predictions and instructions of 13:9-13 imply that the failures of Peter, James, John, and Andrew (13:3) and the other disciples at the time of Jesus' arrest and crucifixion are not absolute.

In any case, in the passion narrative the Twelve serve as negative examples for the audience because they fail to deny themselves, take up their crosses, and follow Jesus. They seek to save their lives, rather than losing them for the sake of Jesus and the good news. Instead, they prove themselves to be ashamed of Jesus (Mark 8:34-38).[247]

Verse 28 indicates that the turning point for the disciples will be the encounter with the risen Jesus, who is also the crucified one (16:6). By means of that encounter, the disciples are finally enabled to receive the divine revelation and to act on it, which previously their human weakness and hardness of heart prevented them from grasping.[248]

■ **30** Jesus' second speech in this passage is both a reply to Peter's affirmation in v. 29 and a further prediction, this time without reference to scripture. The "introductory Amen" gives the saying solemnity and emphasis. It does not necessarily indicate that the saying goes back to the historical Jesus.[249] This statement also heightens the theme of "taking offense" in v. 27 to outright denial on the part of Peter.

The pronoun "you" (σύ), the subject of the verb "will deny" (ἀπαρνήσῃ), does not need to be expressed and so is emphatic here, especially after σοι ("[Truly I say] to you"). The temporal expressions move from specific, "today" (σήμερον), to more specific, "in this night"

---

239 See the commentary on v. 27 above. See also Moo, *Old Testament*, 216–17.

240 Lohmeyer, *Galiläa und Jerusalem*, 11–13; Lohmeyer, 355–56. See the "Excursus: Galilee and Jerusalem in Mark" above.

241 Lit., "from (one) end of the earth to (one) end of the sky." Cf. Stemberger, "Galilee—Land of Salvation?" 428–29.

242 Yarbro Collins, *Beginning of the Gospel*, 136–37.

243 Schenke, *Passionsgeschichte*, 436–41.

244 See the commentary on 8:32a, 32b-33 above.

245 See the commentary on 10:38-40 above.

246 This is the case even when one takes 16:8 with full seriousness. The granting of resurrection appear-

ances to the disciples and Peter is not dependent on the women conveying the message of the "young man." See the commentary on 16:8 below.

247 Cf. Schenke, *Passionsgeschichte*, 429; Heil, "Mark 14,1-52," 320.

248 See the commentary on 6:51-52 above; cf. Schenke, *Passionsgeschichte*, 433–36; Heil, "Mark 14,1-52," 321–22; Agustí Borrell, *The Good News of Peter's Denial: A Narrative and Rhetorical Reading of Mark 14:54.66–72* (SFISFCJ 7; Atlanta: Scholars Press/University of South Florida, 1998) 43–44.

249 See n. 147 in the commentary on 3:28-30 above.

(ταύτῃ τῇ νυκτί), to most specific, "before the cock crows twice" (πρὶν ἢ δὶς ἀλέκτορα φωνῆσαι).[250] These redundant and emphatic references to Peter and to the exact time when he will deny Jesus are ironic in relation to Peter's bold and self-confident assertion that even if everyone else takes offense at what happens to Jesus, he will not.

According to Mark, Peter would deny Jesus three times before the cock crowed twice. Matthew and Luke both retain the triple denial, but refer to a single cock-crow (Matt 26:34; Luke 22:34).[251] Mark's formulation of the prediction probably seemed too complicated and was thus simplified. The complexity and concreteness of the prediction in Mark, however, give it vividness and verisimilitude. Further, the fact that Peter ignores the first cock-crow heightens the impression of his weakness and self-absorption in the narration of the fulfillment of Jesus' prediction in vv. 66-72.

This detailed and concrete prediction by Jesus has a literary effect analogous to those of the prophecies of vv. 27-28. As noted above, v. 27 captures the attention of the audience and awakens their interest in finding out exactly how God "will strike the shepherd" and how the disciples will "take offense" and "be scattered." Verse 28 similarly awakens anticipation on the part of the audience as to how Jesus will be raised and what "going before you to Galilee" means. The prediction of Peter's denial here is quite detailed with regard to "when," but piques the interest of the audience in finding out "where" and "how" the denial will take place. For those familiar with the story, the prophecy increases the pathos of its narrative fulfillment.

■ 31 In v. 29, Peter had simply asserted that he would not take offense when "the shepherd" is "struck." Here he goes much further and affirms "vehemently" (ἐκπερισσῶς) that, even if it be necessary for Peter to die with him, Peter will surely not deny him. All of the Twelve say the same.[252] The mention of "all" the other disciples, although only the denial of Peter is narrated, supports the interpretation given above, that this passage is an important instance of the theme of the misunderstanding of the disciples.[253]

---

250 Matthew omitted σήμερον ("today"), probably because it seemed redundant (26:34); see the first note on the trans. of v. 30 above.

251 See note c on the trans. of v. 30 above.

252 Or eleven of the Twelve, if the audience is supposed to infer that Judas left Jesus and the others at some point so that he could lead the crowd with swords and clubs from the chief priests and the scribes and the elders to Gethsemane and arrest Jesus "by deceit" (ἐν δόλῳ) (vv. 1, 43). John made explicit what Mark, Matthew, and Luke probably assume (John 13:27-30).

253 See the commentary on vv. 26-31, v. 27 and v. 29 above.

14

14:32-42 The Agony in Gethsemane

32/ And they went to a place named Gethsemane, and he said to his disciples, "Sit here, while I pray." 33/ And he took Peter and James and John with him and began to be distressed and anxious, 34/ and he said to them, "My soul is exceedingly sorrowful to the point of death; stay here and keep awake." 35/ And he went a little farther on, fell upon the ground, and prayed that, if it was possible, the hour would pass away from him. 36/ And he said, "Abba! Father! All things are possible for you; remove this cup from me. But (let) not what I want (be), but what you want." 37/ And he went and found them sleeping and said to Peter, "Simon, are you sleeping? Were you not strong enough to keep awake for one hour? 38/ Keep awake and pray that you not be put to the test. The spirit is willing, but the flesh is weak." 39/ And again he went away and prayed, saying the same saying. 40/ And he went again and found them sleeping, for their eyes were heavy, and they did not know how they should respond to him. 41/ And he went a third time and said to them, "Sleep now[a] and rest; it is enough.[b] The hour has come; see, the Son of Man is to be handed over into the hands of the sinners. 42/ Get up; let us go. See, the one who is to hand me over has drawn near."

a   The trans. is based on the reading τὸ λοιπόν ("now," lit., "henceforward" or "hereafter"), attested by ℵ B K et al. This command is in tension with the command and exhortation in v. 42, and this tension has given rise to the variant λοιπόν ("then" or "well, then"), attested by A C D L W et al. Both readings also occur in the MSS of Matt 26:45. The latter reading allows the preceding verb more easily to be taken as an indicative statement or question; this construal then relieves the tension with v. 42. See the discussion in Taylor, ad loc.

b   The earliest recoverable reading is ἀπέχει ("it is enough"), attested by ℵ A B and the majority of the MSS. This absolute impersonal construction is difficult to construe, and this difficulty gave rise to variants. Some MSS (Ψ 892 et al.) simply omit ἀπέχει, perhaps under the influence of the parallel in Matt 26:45. (W) Θ f¹³ et al. attest a reading in which the words τὸ τέλος ("the end") have been added after ἀπέχει, to give the sense "it is the end (of the matter)"; see BDF §129. Cf. Metzger, *Textual Commentary*, 96.

Comment

■ **32-42** It is likely that the Gethsemane story was the first unit of the pre-Markan passion narrative, although it was heavily edited by Mark.[1]

When this passage is read as part of Mark as a whole, it is striking that this is the first time that Jesus is portrayed as having any distress or anxiety about his impending suffering and death.[2] Here he is portrayed in

1   Schenke, *Passionsgeschichte*, 353, 360–62, 561; Yarbro Collins, *Beginning of the Gospel*, 106–7. Reinhard Feldmeier took the position that the story was the first part of a probably pre-Markan passion narrative; he concluded, however, that one cannot determine with any certainty whether Mark edited the story (*Die Krisis des Gottessohnes: Die Gethsemaneerzählung als Schlüssel der Markuspassion* [WUNT 2.21; Tübingen: Mohr Siebeck, 1987] 111–12, 126–27).

2   There is no indication of this in the passion predictions or their contexts: 8:31-33; 9:30-32; 10:32-45. Nor is there evidence of such in the praise of the anointing woman or the predictions of betrayal, abandonment, and denial on the part of the disciples (14:8-9, 17-21, 26–31). On this whole issue and scholarly attempts to deal with it, see Jung-Sik Cha, "Confronting Death: The Story of Gethsemane in Mark 14:32-42 and Its Historical Legacy" (2 vols.; Ph.D. diss., University of Chicago, 1996) 1:1–27.

terms of his ordinary humanity and weakness,[3] in contrast to his miracle-working power and confidence in the power of faith or trust in other parts of the narrative.[4]

Bultmann argued that the story was originally independent and that it had a thoroughly legendary character.[5] At a later stage, the story was shaped by Christian faith and worship and played a role as "a faith- or cult-legend" expressing in narrative form the "Christ-myth" of Phil 2:8, "having become obedient unto death" ($\gamma\epsilon\nu\acute{o}$-$\mu\epsilon\nu o\varsigma$ $\dot{v}\pi\acute{\eta}\kappa oo\varsigma$ $\mu\acute{\epsilon}\chi\rho\iota$ $\vartheta\alpha\nu\acute{\alpha}\tau o\upsilon$).[6]

Dibelius argued that the scene does not "bear witness to a disillusionment—for then it would not have been accepted into the Gospel at all—but to a certain understanding of revelation. Like the entire Markan Passion it is orientated not psychologically but soteriologically."[7] He concluded that the story is unhistorical because there are no witnesses to "the essential part of the scene, since the witnesses are asleep."[8] Unlike Bultmann, he argued that the story never circulated independently and thought it likely that it was in the passion source used by Mark.[9] He suggested that the story, like Heb 5:7 but independently, was constructed on the model of certain "Psalms of suffering," such as Psalms 22, 31, and 69, all of which "speak of cries and in addition to that of extreme stress and of a prayer for deliverance."[10] The main problem with this theory is that the Gethsemane story alludes to Psalms 42–43 but not to Psalm 22, 31, or 69.

Like Bultmann, Eta Linnemann argued that the Gethsemane story was originally independent. Following Bultmann, she concluded that the original ending of the story was "The account is closed; the hour has come" ($\dot{\alpha}\pi\acute{\epsilon}\chi\epsilon\iota$ $\mathring{\eta}\lambda\vartheta\epsilon\nu$ $\mathring{\eta}$ $\mathring{\omega}\rho\alpha$). She interpreted this ending as

signifying that Jesus accepted God's will. This reading enabled her to conclude that the story was composed to make sense of Jesus' passion as a whole.[11] But such an ending leaves the audience hanging, so it is unlikely that the story ever circulated independently. It is best understood as an interpretation of the whole passion of Jesus as an introduction to an extensive account of it, probably already in its pre-Markan form, as argued above.[12]

In a challenge to the form-critical assumption that there was a continuous passion narrative prior to Mark, Werner Kelber set out to demonstrate that Mark was "the sole creator and composer of the Gethsemane story, relying at best upon a minimal core of tradition."[13] Following the position taken by Dibelius and Eduard Lohse, he concluded that "Mark is not merely the redactor, but to a high degree the creator and composer of the Gethsemane story."[14] He argued that the "kerygmatic force" of the passage is a matter of "discipleship theology," in particular, "the incorrigible blindness of the disciples."[15] Finally, he suggested, following Joseph B. Tyson and Theodore Weeden, that the author of Mark made a big issue of the disciples' failure in order to dramatize a dispute between "Peter-Christians," who rejected a passion Christology and probably constituted "the mother church of Jerusalem," and the perspective represented by Mark, which was associated with a northern, "Christian Galilean" tradition.[16]

In a later article, Kelber interpreted the Gethsemane story with a focus on its present form in Mark.[17] He concluded that the narrative has two foci; one is Jesus' "plea for release from the passion" which "raises the question whether [he] will live out the truth of the Gospel of the Kingdom which is contingent upon his suffering and

3   Jesus' human weakness, in every way except sin, is explored in Heb 4:14–5:10, esp. 4:15 and 5:7; Attridge, *Hebrews*, 140–41, 148–49.

4   Contrast this passage with 1:21-28, 29-34, 40-45; 2:1-12; 3:7-12; 4:35-41; 5:1-20, 21-43; 6:31-56; 8:1-9; 8:31–9:1; 9:2-8. Note especially the sayings about all things being possible for those who have faith or trust (9:23; 11:22-23).

5   Bultmann, *History*, 267.

6   Ibid., 305–6; quotations from 306.

7   Dibelius, *From Tradition to Gospel*, 211.

8   Ibid.

9   Ibid., 212.

10   Ibid.

11   Linnemann, *Studien zur Passionsgeschichte*, 24–28.

12   Yarbro Collins, *Beginning of the Gospel*, 107. Cf. Schenke, *Passionsgeschichte*, 551–52.

13   Werner H. Kelber, "Mark 14:32-42: Gethsemane: Passion Christology and Discipleship Failure," *ZNW* 63 (1972) 166–87; quotation from 166.

14   Ibid., 176; see the discussion of Dibelius and Lohse, 168–69.

15   Ibid., 176–81; quotations from 176 and 180.

16   Ibid., 181–87; quotations from 186 and n. 61.

17   Werner H. Kelber, "The Hour of the Son of Man and the Temptation of the Disciples (Mark 14:32-42)," in idem, *Passion*, 41–60.

death."[18] The other is "the disciples' continuing lack of understanding," which marks "a pivotal point on their collision course with Jesus."[19] He interpreted this double focus in terms of the Markan setting.[20] He concluded that one dimension of the story is the testing Jesus undergoes in preparation for the passion. Mark forced "Jesus to the brink of recanting his passion identity because the Evangelist deals with Christians who are indifferent or hostile toward a suffering Messiah."[21] It is more likely that the passage presents Jesus as a positive model and the disciples as a negative model for the audiences of Mark who are in constant danger of being accused before local authorities.[22]

The passage has an unusually large number of doublets and apparent contradictions or tensions between various pairs of elements.[23] These have led many scholars to conclude that the story was composed by combining two sources or to attempt to distinguish a single source and a Markan redaction.[24] Frans Neirynck's study of "duality" as an aspect of Markan style has seriously called into question theories concerning the combination of two sources to create the Markan version of the story.[25] It does not, however, rule out hypotheses that distinguish between source and redaction, since Mark may have created his customary "duality" in the rewriting or editing of a source.

■ **32-33a** As noted above, Gethsemane may have been linked to the Mount of Olives for the first time by Mark.[26] One may infer from v. 32a, which is probably pre-Markan, only that it was an unpopulated place (χωρίον)

and that there was an olive press there, since the name "Gethsemane" probably means "oil press."[27]

The second half of v. 32, "and he said to his disciples, 'Sit here, while I pray'" (καὶ λέγει τοῖς μαθηταῖς αὐτοῦ· καθίσατε ὧδε ἕως προσεύξωμαι) is probably redactional, since it prepares for the remark that he took Peter and James and John with him in v. 33a.[28] The latter is very likely to be a Markan addition, since the special role of these three disciples is a Markan theme. The other passages that mention the three are probably Markan compositions (5:37; 9:2; 13:3).[29]

■ **33b** The narrative indicates the emotional state of Jesus with the words ἐκθαμβεῖσθαι (usually, "to be amazed"; here, "to be distressed") and ἀδημονεῖν ("to be anxious"). This portrait contrasts with the accounts of the deaths of the Maccabean heroes and famous Greeks and Romans who display composure and bravery.[30] Oscar Cullmann contrasted Socrates and Jesus in relation to the scene in Gethsemane. Socrates considered death the great liberator because it allowed the soul to return to its eternal home. Nothing is seen of death's terror in Plato's *Phaedo* because death is the soul's great friend. The Jesus of the passion narrative trembled and was distressed because he is so thoroughly human that he shares the natural fear of death.[31]

It has been argued that v. 33b is redactional because the construction ἄρχομαι with an infinitive ("to begin" to do something) is typical of Mark, as is the unusual word ἐκθαμβεῖσθαι ("to be amazed").[32] But when the latter verb and its simple form θαμβεῖσθαι ("to be

---

18 Ibid., 46.
19 Ibid., 53.
20 Ibid., 58.
21 Ibid., 59.
22 See the commentary below, esp. on vv. 37-38.
23 Kelber, "Hour of the Son of Man," 41.
24 Ibid. and the literature cited in n. 1; Neirynck, *Duality in Mark*, 30–31, 63–64, 70–71.
25 Karl Georg Kuhn argued that Mark combined two source reports in fashioning the story in its present form as a prelude to the passion source, which began with the arrest ("Jesus in Gethsemane," *EvTh* 12 [1952–53] 260–85).
26 See the commentary on vv. 26-31 above.
27 BAGD, s.v. Γεθσημανί; Donald A. D. Thorsen, "Gethsemane," *ABD* 2:997–98.
28 See the tentative reconstruction of the content (not necessarily the wording) of the pre-Markan version

of this story in the appendix to the commentary below. The motif of Jesus at prayer occurs also in 1:35; 6:46. Even if these passages are traditional, they could be the basis for the redactional addition of the explicit motif in v. 32b.
29 Schenke, *Passionsgeschichte*, 483–85; Yarbro Collins, *Beginning of the Gospel*, 106.
30 See "Excursus: The Passion Narrative" above.
31 Oscar Cullmann, "Immortality of the Soul or Resurrection of the Dead: The Witness of the New Testament," in Krister Stendahl, ed., *Immortality and Resurrection* (New York: Macmillan, 1965) 9–53, esp. 12–20; Yarbro Collins, "From Noble Death," 485–86. For a discussion of the Gethsemane story in relation to analogous texts in Greco-Roman literature, see Cha, "Confronting Death," 1:147–77.
32 Dwyer, *Wonder*, 179.

amazed") are used elsewhere in Mark, the ordinary sense of being amazed or astounded fits the context quite well,[33] but here the usual sense does not fit the context.[34] In Sir 30:9, ἐκθαμβεῖν is used in synonymous parallelism with λυπεῖν ("to grieve" or "to vex"). The context suggests a meaning of "to distress" for the former verb. This sense fits the context of v. 33b quite well and is supported by its being paired with ἀδημονεῖν ("to be anxious").[35] The use of the construction ἄρχομαι with an infinitive ("to begin" to do something) could be a result of Mark's rewriting of his source.

This is the first time in Mark that Jesus is portrayed as distressed and anxious. The narrative portrayal of v. 33b prepares the audience for the anguish that follows in this passage and for the account of Jesus' suffering and death in chapter 15.

■ 34a After the narrator's description of Jesus' anguished state, his lament is given in direct speech: "My soul is exceedingly sorrowful to the point of death" (περίλυπός ἐστιν ἡ ψυχή μου ἕως θανάτου). This statement of Jesus evokes the refrain of one of the psalms of individual lament:

> Why are you exceedingly sorrowful, O soul, and why do you disturb me? (ἵνα τί περίλυπος εἶ, ψυχή, καὶ ἵνα τί συνταράσσεις με;).[36]

Jesus' speech echoes another psalm of individual lament:

> And my soul is extremely disturbed;
> and you, Lord, how long?

Turn, Lord, rescue my life,
save me on account of your mercy
(καὶ ἡ ψυχή μου ἐταράχθη σφόδρα·
καὶ σύ, κύριε, ἕως πότε;
ἐπίστρεψον, κύριε, ῥῦσαι τὴν ψυχήν μου,
σῶσόν με ἕνεκεν τοῦ ἐλέους σου). (Ps 6:4-5 [6:3-4 NRSV])

The first two lines quoted from this psalm express a lament similar to that of Jesus in v. 34. The second two lines are analogous to the summary of Jesus' prayer in v. 35 and to its expression in direct speech in v. 36.

The expression ἕως θανάτου ("to the point of death") occurs also in two books of the LXX:

> Is it not a sorrow to the point of death when a friend turns to enmity? (οὐχὶ λύπη ἔνι ἕως θανάτου ἑταῖρος καὶ φίλος τρεπόμενος εἰς ἔχθραν;). (Sir 37:2 LXX)[37]

The phrase occurs also in Jonah:

> And God said to Jonah, "Have you become extremely sorrowful because of the [gourd-]vine?" And he said, "I have become extremely sorrowful to the point of death" (καὶ εἶπεν ὁ θεὸς πρὸς Ιωναν Εἰ σφόδρα λελύπησαι σὺ ἐπὶ τῇ κολοκύνθῃ; καὶ εἶπεν Σφόδρα λελύπημαι ἐγὼ ἕως θανάτου). (Jonah 4:9 LXX)[38]

The evocation of the refrain of Psalm(s) 41–42 LXX has the effect of making Jesus the speaker of the traditional

---

33   Mark 1:27; 10:24, 32 (θαμβεῖσθαι); 9:15; 16:5, 6 (ἐκθαμβεῖσθαι).

34   Contra Dwyer, who interprets the verb here as signifying "shuddering awe at an encounter with the holy" (*Wonder*, 178–79).

35   So also BAGD, s.v. ἐκθαμβέω.

36   Pss 41:6a, 12a; 42:5a LXX (42:6a, 12a; 43:5a MT; 42:5a, 11a; 43:5a NRSV). Although they have been transmitted as two psalms, Pss 41–42 (42–43) constitute a single poem (Richard J. Clifford, *Psalms 73–150* [AOTC; Nashville: Abingdon, 2003] 214). On the psalms of individual lament or complaint, see Erhard S. Gerstenberger, *Psalms: Part I with an Introduction to Cultic Poetry* (FOTL 14; Grand Rapids: Eerdmans, 1988) 9–10, 11–14, 174; Ahearne-Kroll, "Suffering of David," 1:159–68. On the echoes of

"these twin psalms" in v. 34 and in John 12:27, see Dodd, *According to the Scriptures*, 100–101.

37   Patrick W. Skehan and Alexander A. Di Lella translate (from the Hebrew) "Is it not a sorrow to bring death close when your other self becomes your enemy?" (*The Wisdom of Ben Sira: A New Translation with Notes* [AB 39; New York: Doubleday, 1987] 424).

38   Jack M. Sasson translates Jonah's reply (from the Hebrew) "Dejected enough to want death" (*Jonah: A New Translation with Introduction, Commentary, and Interpretation* [AB 24B; New York: Doubleday, 1990] 300). Since the Hebrew expression is rare and translated faithfully by the versions, Sasson concludes that Mark 14:34 actually alludes to this part of Jonah (ibid., 307); he referred to v. 33, but presumably meant v. 34.

lament.[39] Since David was considered to be the author of the psalms by Jews of the late Second Temple period,[40] it could well be that Mark and his audiences would understand v. 34 in terms of Jesus, as suffering messiah, speaking in the voice of David, the lamenting prototypical king.[41] The Markan Jesus already associated himself indirectly with David in 2:25-26, hinting at Jesus' messianic status.[42] The relation of Jesus to David is taken up again in the healing of blind Bartimaeus, who addresses him as "son of David." This address serves as an acclamation, in effect, that prepares for the scene of Jesus' entry into Jerusalem, in which the crowd blesses "the coming kingdom of our father David."[43] The narrative of Mark, from 2:25 until 11:10, has hinted quite strongly that Jesus is the son of David, the messiah of Israel.[44] In 12:35-37, however, Jesus raises the question how the messiah can be the son of David, since David calls him "Lord" (Ps 110:1). This passage does not signify that Jesus is not the son of David for Mark and his audiences. It does, however, play a role in the redefinition of the notion of the messiah of Israel, which takes place throughout the Gospel.[45]

The allusion to Jonah contrasts with the context here in one particularly striking way. In the context of the evoked text in Jonah, God initiates the dialogue with Jonah and both parties speak. In the context in Mark, Jesus initiates the dialogue, but God does not respond.[46] In the context of Jonah, God's activity is contingent.

Mark implies that, in some important respects at least, the divine activity is predetermined.[47]

■ **34b-35** After his lament, Jesus asks Peter, James, and John to stay in a particular spot and to keep awake (v. 34b). Kelber pointed out that the verb γρηγορεῖν ("to stay awake") occurs in Mark only in the parable about the doorkeeper (13:33-37) and here in the scene at Gethsemane. He concluded, on the basis of this observation, that "the disciples' 'sleeping' and failure to 'wake' have eschatological repercussions."[48] The contexts and rhetorical force of the two passages, however, are quite different. The parable refers to a time when Jesus is absent and the disciples must "stay awake" or be watchful in order to be prepared when he returns as the heavenly and glorious Son of Man. Here Jesus is present in all his humanity, distressed and anxious. The force of the instruction to "remain here and stay awake" is that he needs these leading disciples, these close friends, to stay nearby and awake in order to provide him company and support.

Although the disciples' nearness is important to the suffering Markan Jesus, he goes a little distance from the threesome in order to pray, presumably in private. It is only the omniscient narrator who is able to report what Jesus said in his prayer. He is also described as falling on the ground. This gesture signifies a highly emotional state and occurs also in an ancient novel, *Chaereas and Callirhoe* 3.6.6; 5.2.4.[49]

39 Richard B. Hays, "Christ Prays the Psalms: Paul's Use of an Early Christian Exegetical Convention," in Abraham J. Malherbe and Wayne A. Meeks, eds., *The Future of Christology: Essays in Honor of Leander E. Keck* (Minneapolis: Fortress, 1993) 122–36, esp. 125–26; see also Harold W. Attridge, "Giving Voice to Jesus: Use of the Psalms in the New Testament," in idem and Margot E. Fassler, eds., *Psalms in Community: Jewish and Christian Textual, Liturgical, and Artistic Traditions* (SBLSymS 25; Atlanta: SBL, 2003) 101–12, esp. 102. He points out that this phenomenon occurs only in passages "that focus on the passion of Jesus" (ibid., 102).

40 Daly-Denton, *David*, 59–113; Ahearne-Kroll, "Suffering of David," 1:69–71.

41 Cf. Ahearne-Kroll, "Suffering of David," 2:256–58. Dibelius did not argue that Jesus speaks here in the voice of David, but he did argue that Jesus' struggle in Gethsemane was understood by early Christians as proof of his messiahship ("Gethsemane," in idem,

Botschaft und Geschichte: Gesammelte Aufsätze, vol. 1: *Zur Evangelienforschung* [Tübingen: Mohr Siebeck, 1953] 258–71, esp. 261–63).

42 See the commentary on 2:25-26 and 28 above.

43 See the commentary on 10:47-49 and 11:9-10 above.

44 See the section of the introduction "Jesus as Messiah" above.

45 See the commentary on 12:37 above.

46 Feldmeier emphasizes the silence of God and God's handing Jesus over into human hands (*Die Krisis*, 126, 187–91, 216–29, 252).

47 Cf. Yarbro Collins, "From Noble Death," 491.

48 Kelber, "Hour of the Son of Man," 48–49. See also Lightfoot, *Gospel Message*, 54–55.

49 See the ET by Bryan P. Reardon in idem, *Ancient Greek Novels*, 59, 77. See also the discussion of scenes of violent emotion, including throwing oneself on the ground, by Musurillo, *Pagan Martyrs*, 254, iii.2b; cf. 255, ii.6. André Feuillet interpreted the gesture primarily as a sign of overwhelming distress

The narrator first summarizes Jesus' prayer: "[he] prayed that, if it was possible, the hour would pass away from him" (προσηύχετο ἵνα εἰ δυνατόν ἐστιν παρέλθῃ ἡ ὥρα). In praying to be spared "the hour," Jesus seeks to avoid the suffering and death that he announced to the disciples and explained to them so carefully in chapters 8–10. The "hour" is interpreted in v. 41 as the time when the Son of Man is to be handed over into the hands of sinners.[50] On one level, this "handing over" refers to the arrest of Jesus and his being taken into custody.[51] On another level, "the hour" is a symbol of the whole passion of Jesus, from the arrest to the cross.[52] The term has an eschatological connotation as the fulfillment of Jesus' prophecies in 8:31; 9:31; 10:33-34. The saying in 8:31, especially, implies that a divine plan "must" be carried out and alludes to scripture.[53]

The qualification in the prayer summary, "if it is possible" (εἰ δυνατόν ἐστιν), contrasts with part of the prayer in direct speech in v. 36, "All things are possible for you" (πάντα δυνατά σοι).

■ **36** After the summary in v. 35b, the narrator gives Jesus' prayer in direct speech: "Abba! Father! All things are possible for you; remove this cup from me. But [let] not what I want [be], but what you want" (αββα ὁ πατήρ, πάντα δυνατά σοι· παρένεγκε τὸ ποτήριον τοῦτο ἀπ᾽ ἐμοῦ· ἀλλ᾽ οὐ τί ἐγὼ θέλω ἀλλὰ τί σύ).

The term αββα is a Greek transliteration of an Aramaic word that is a vocative form of אב ("father"). Joachim Jeremias argued that the use of αββα (אבא in Aramaic, "Father!") was a distinctive usage of Jesus, since the term was not used in contemporary Jewish texts or prayers; that it was central to his teaching; and that it expresses a particular intimacy with God because of its origin in the speech of a young child.[54] The last point was criticized by James Barr.[55] The first two points have been criticized by Mary Rose D'Angelo.[56]

This is the only occurrence of αββα ("Father!") in the Gospels.[57] It could be that Jesus did use the term, but its usage here does not imply that the saying introduced by it goes back to Jesus. As noted above, Jesus' prayer in direct speech is presented as solitary and private.[58] At most, it represents what the author of the pre-Markan passion narrative (or Mark) imagined Jesus' prayer to have been. It may reflect the usage of the term in early

---

(*L'Agonie de Gethsémani* [Paris: Gabalda, 1977] 83); Feldmeier concluded that it expresses both affliction (*Gebeugtsein*) and homage (*Selbstbeugung*) (*Die Krisis*, 166).

50   Kelber, "Hour of the Son of Man," 44. It is likely that both the narrator's summary of Jesus' prayer (v. 35b) and the saying about the Son of Man being handed over (v. 41c) are Markan additions to his passion source (see Yarbro Collins, *Beginning of the Gospel*, 106–7). On the the motif of "the hour" here and in 13:32-33 and on the schema of hours in 13:35 and in the passion narrative, see Lightfoot, *Gospel Message*, 52–53. Lightfoot suggests that these parallels indicate that chaps. 14–15 constitute a first "fulfillment" of chap. 13 as a "sign, a seal of assurance, and a sacrament of the ultimate fulfillment" (ibid., 54). The position taken here is rather that the parallels suggest that Jesus' behavior in Gethsemane and in the passion narrative is presented as a model for the disciples and the audiences to imitate in their own trials.

51   BAGD, s.v. παραδίδωμι, 1.b.

52   Kelber, "Hour of the Son of Man," 44.

53   See the commentary on 8:31 above. Kelber also concluded that "the hour" has an eschatological sense, but he based his conclusion on the use of the word "hour" in 15:25, 33, 34 and 13:11, 32 ("Hour of the Son of Man," 44). Although the context is eschato-

logical in chap. 13, the word ὥρα ("hour") is used in the two relevant passages in the ordinary sense. The same is true of the occurrences in chap. 15. If the term has a symbolic sense, it is a different one from that in 14:35, 41. In John the same term is used to "refer to a special period in Jesus' life, a period best defined in xiii 1—the hour of return to the Father" (Raymond E. Brown, *The Gospel according to John (i-xii): Introduction, Translation, and Notes* [AB 29; Garden City, NY: Doubleday, 1966] 517).

54   Joachim Jeremias, *Abba: Studien zur neutestamentlichen Theologie und Zeitgeschichte* (Göttingen: Vandenhoeck & Ruprecht, 1966) 15–67; ET *The Prayers of Jesus* (SBT 2nd series 6; Naperville, IL: Allenson, 1967) 11–65.

55   James Barr, "'Abbā Isn't Daddy," *JTS* n.s. 39 (1988) 28–47.

56   Mary Rose D'Angelo, "*Abba* and 'Father': Imperial Theology and the Traditions about Jesus," *JBL* 111 (1992) 611-30; eadem, "Theology in Mark and Q: *Abba* and 'Father' in Context," *HTR* 85 (1992) 149–74.

57   The only other occurrences in the NT are Gal 4:6 and Rom 8:15.

58   Mary Ann Tolbert defined it as "a narrative soliloquy" dramatizing "internal struggle" (*Sowing the Gospel*, 214).

Christian prayers at the time and place the pre-Markan passion narrative was composed or in Mark's context.[59]

Paul's two uses of the term αββα ("Father!") explicitly state that this form of address is used in a context of ecstatic prayer, that is, prayer in the divine spirit that the baptized have received (Gal 4:6; Rom 8:15-16). It is noteworthy that both Paul and Mark, although writing in Greek, preserve the Aramaic word and translate it. As argued above, Mark used or preserved Aramaic words in the miracle stories because they were believed to be powerful words.[60] It could well be that a prayer involving the Aramaic expression αββα was believed to be an especially powerful prayer.[61]

Following the address of God as αββα ὁ πατήρ ("Father!"), the Markan Jesus says, "All things are possible for you" (πάντα δυνατά σοι). This prayerful statement recalls Jesus' remark to the father of the demon-possessed young man in 9:23, "All things are possible for the one who trusts" (πάντα δυνατὰ τῷ πιστεύοντι). In 14:36 the motif is used in a more typical way: it is only for God or the gods that all things are possible.[62] But as spoken by Jesus and in a context of prayer, it also echoes Jesus' instruction to the disciples on prayer: "Have trust in God. Truly I say to you, that whoever says to this mountain, 'Be lifted up and thrown into the sea,' and does not doubt in his mind, but trusts that what he says will come to pass, it will be (so) for him. For this reason I say to you, whatever you pray and ask for, trust that you will obtain it, and it will be (so) for you" (11:22b-24).[63]

The prayer summary in v. 35b, however, has already prepared the audience for a modification of Jesus' earlier teaching on trust and prayer. The last clause of Jesus' prayer, "But (let) not what I want (be), but what you want" (ἀλλ' οὐ τί ἐγὼ θέλω ἀλλὰ τί σύ), introduces an element of resignation that is missing from the healing of the epileptic boy in chapter 9 and the instruction on prayer in chapter 11. In an ancient Jewish context, this last statement may be seen as an expression of perfect obedience. Compare the following passage in the *Damascus Document*:

> For having walked in the stubbornness of their hearts the Watchers of the heavens fell; . . . Abraham did not walk in it, and was counted as a friend for keeping God's precepts and not following the desire of his spirit

> (בלכתם בשרירות לבם נפלו עירי השמים . . .
> אברהם לא הלך בה ויעל אוהב בשמרו מצות אל ולא
> בחר ברצון רוחו).
> (*CD* 2:17-18; 3:2-3)[64]

In a Hellenistic philosophical context, such an attitude is necessary to achieve freedom from fear:

> Who is there, then, that I *can* any longer be afraid of? . . . Because, if anyone will not receive me, I do not care to go in, but always I want rather the thing which takes place. For I regard that which God wants as better than what I (want) (Τίνα οὖν ἔτι φοβηθῆναι δύναμαι; . . . Ὅτι ἂν μή τίς με δέχηται, οὐ θέλω εἰσελθεῖν, ἀλλ' ἀεὶ μᾶλλον ἐκεῖνο θέλω τὸ γινόμενον. κρεῖττον γὰρ ἡγοῦμαι ὃ ὁ θεὸς θέλει ἢ ὅ ἐγώ). (Epictetus *Diss.* 4.7.19-20)[65]

According to a retelling of the story of Joseph in Genesis, he was handed over to foreigners, who consumed his strength and broke all his bones. In this situation:

> And he became wear[y. . .] and he summoned the powerful God to save him from their hands. And he

---

59   This hypothesis is supported by Gal 4:6 and Rom 8:15, which seem to represent prayers in use in the communities addressed; cf. D'Angelo, "Theology in Mark and Q," 160.

60   See the section "Genres" in the commentary on 5:21-43 above; see also the commentary on 5:40b-43 and 7:34 above.

61   Cf. D'Angelo, "Theology in Mark and Q," 157, 160.

62   See the commentary on 9:21-24 above.

63   See the commentary on these verses above.

64   Text and trans. from García Martínez and Tigchelaar, *Dead Sea Scrolls*, 1:552–53. Carolyn Sharp

concluded that the statement about Abraham is an allusion to the binding of Isaac ("Phinehan Zeal and Rhetorical Strategy in *4QMMT*," *RevQ* 70 [1997] 207–22, esp. 210). Cullmann argued that Jesus' statement "Yet not as I will, but as thou wilt" does not mean that, at the last, he came to regard death as a friend or liberator; rather it means that, if it is God's will, he will submit to the greatest of all terrors ("Immortality of the Soul," 15–16; Yarbro Collins, "From Noble Death," 485).

65   Text and trans (modified) from William A. Oldfather, *Epictetus: The Discourses as Reported by Arrian*,

said, <<My father and my God, do not abandon me in the hands of gentiles [. . .]. . . >>

ויוע[ף . . .] וקרא אל אל גבור להושיעו מידם ויאמר
אבי ואלהי אל תעזבני ביד גוים [. . .].

(4QApocryphon of Joseph[b] [4Q372] frg.1, lines 15-16)[66]

Eileen Schuller has pointed out the similarity between the prayer of Joseph in this text and that of Jesus in Mark 14:36.[67] D'Angelo has called attention to the analogy between Joseph's prayer that God not abandon him and Jesus' cry from the cross in 15:34.[68]

The request addressed to God, "remove this cup from me" ($\pi\alpha\rho\acute{\epsilon}\nu\epsilon\gamma\kappa\epsilon\ \tau\grave{o}\ \pi o\tau\acute{\eta}\rho\iota ov\ \tauo\hat{v}\tauo\ \dot{\alpha}\pi'\acute{\epsilon}\mu o\hat{v}$) recalls the question the Markan Jesus put to the sons of Zebedee in 10:38, when they requested that they be allowed to sit on his right and left in his glory: "Are you able to drink the cup which I am about to drink?" ($\delta\acute{v}\nu\alpha\sigma\vartheta\epsilon\ \pi\iota\epsilon\hat{\iota}v\ \tau\grave{o}\ \pi o\tau\acute{\eta}\rho\iota ov\ \grave{o}\ \dot{\epsilon}\gamma\grave{\omega}\ \pi\acute{\iota}\nu\omega$). It is not clear whether Mark, or the author of the pre-Markan passion narrative (with regard to 14:36), adopted a symbol from the Old Testament, the cup of wrath, or whether 10:38 and 14:36 reflect the emergence of a new symbol, the cup of suffering.[69] Leonhard Goppelt assumed the latter.[70] It seems likely that the foundation of Mark's usage is the imagery of the cup of wrath in the Old Testament.[71] This image is associated with the theme of the judgment of the nations. The experience of the judicial wrath of God is compared to extreme intoxication.[72] Thus, the image of drinking a cup in v. 36 suggests that

Jesus, though innocent, will take upon himself the wrath that others deserve. This idea, which may already have been present in the pre-Markan passion narrative, is analogous to the interpretation of Jesus' death in the second part of the cup-saying in v. 24.[73] It is also analogous to the ransom saying in 10:45.[74]

■ **37-38** In these verses, the focus gradually shifts from Jesus to the sleeping disciples. In the pre-Markan passion narrative, Jesus addressed Peter as representative of all the disciples who came to Gethsemane with Jesus (cf. v. 32). In the Markan form of the story, Peter represents the three leading disciples that Jesus took aside as particular companions in his distress.[75]

The first part of Jesus' address to Peter, "Simon, are you sleeping?" ($\Sigma\acute{\iota}\mu\omega\nu,\ \kappa\alpha\vartheta\epsilon\acute{v}\delta\epsilon\iota\varsigma;$), still belongs to the theme of Jesus' anguish, since the audience may infer his disappointment in the failure of Peter and the others to support him in his time of need. The address of Peter as "Simon" may already signal a shift of emphasis. The narrator refers to the man as "Peter" in conformity with the new name that Jesus gave him when he appointed the Twelve.[76] The fact that Jesus calls him by his old name may be an ironic expression of the observation that he is not living up to his new name, "Rock." The second question Jesus puts to him reinforces this impression, "Were you not strong enough to keep awake for one hour?" ($o\dot{v}\kappa\ \ddot{\iota}\sigma\chi v\sigma\alpha\varsigma\ \mu\acute{\iota}\alpha v\ \ddot{\omega}\rho\alpha v\ \gamma\rho\eta\gamma o\rho\hat{\eta}\sigma\alpha\iota;$). The use of the verb $\dot{\iota}\sigma\chi\acute{v}\omega$ ("to be strong") prepares for the proverbial saying in v. 38b.

Both of Jesus' questions to Peter in v. 37b use verbs in the second person singular. In the exhortation of v. 38,

the Manual, and Fragments (2 vols.; LCL; Cambridge, MA: Harvard University Press; London: Heinemann, 1928) 2:366–67; emphasis original.

66 Text and trans. from García Martínez and Tigchelaar, Dead Sea Scrolls, 2:736–37.

67 Eileen Schuller, "4Q372 1: A Text about Joseph," RevQ 14 (1990) 349–76.

68 Evoking Ps 22:2 (MT); 22:1 (NRSV); 21:2 LXX; D'Angelo, "Theology in Mark and Q," 159.

69 Or the cup of death; Death identifies himself to Abraham as "the bitter cup of death" in T. Abr. 16:11. E. P. Sanders dated this work to c. 100 CE ("Testament of Abraham," in OTP 1:875; trans. from 892). On the use of the phrase "cup of death" in Targum Neofiti, see Roger David Aus, The Wicked Tenants and Gethsemane (ISFCJ 4; Atlanta: Scholars

Press, 1996) 96–97. Aus also associates the cup of v. 36 with Ps 116:13 MT and the targum of Ps 116:13a (ibid., 99–10).

70 Leonhard Goppelt, "$\pi\acute{\iota}\nu\omega\ \kappa\tau\lambda$.," TDNT 6 (1968) 135–60, esp. 144, 152–53.

71 So also Best, Temptation, lxv–lxviii, 156.

72 See the commentary on 10:38-40 above. See also Goppelt's discussion of the use of this metaphor in the book of Revelation ("$\pi\acute{\iota}\nu\omega\ \kappa\tau\lambda$.," 149–52).

73 See the commentary on vv. 23-25 above.

74 See the commentary on 10:45 above.

75 See Yarbro Collins, Beginning of the Gospel, 106–7.

76 See the commentary on 3:16 above.

"Keep awake and pray that you not be put to the test" (γρηγορεῖτε καὶ προσεύχεσθε, ἵνα μὴ ἔλθητε εἰς πειρασμόν), second person plural verbal forms are used. The audiences could infer that Jesus begins to address James and John here, as well as Peter, but the use of the second person plural makes it even easier for the audiences to identify with the disciples and to apply Jesus' words to their own situation. Although it is not the original reading, most MSS of 13:33 read "stay awake and pray" (ἀγρυπνεῖτε καὶ προσεύχεσθε).[77] This reading indicates that many scribes saw a connection between 13:33-37 and 14:38. The perceived connection suggests that v. 38 was indeed read as applying to the situation of the audiences of Mark, who, unlike the disciples in the narrative, did not experience the presence of the human Jesus, but awaited his return as Son of Man, as the door-keeper needed to stay awake in anticipation of his master's return.[78]

The disciples and the audiences are instructed to pray ἵνα μὴ ἔλθητε εἰς πειρασμόν ("that you not be put to the test" or "that you not come into temptation").[79] This prayer is reminiscent of part of the Lord's Prayer in Matt 6:13 and Luke 11:4.[80] This association would encourage the audiences of Mark to apply this instruction to themselves. A result of this application is that Jesus in this scene becomes a model of faithful prayer.[81] In the narrative context of Mark, it may mean that the disciples are to pray that they not be arrested and interrogated as Jesus will be.

The warrant for staying awake and praying is given in the saying "The spirit is willing, but the flesh is weak"

(τὸ μὲν πνεῦμα πρόθυμον ἡ δὲ σὰρξ ἀσθενής). This saying recalls the tension in vv. 26-31 between Jesus' prediction that all the disciples would take offense (v. 27) and the affirmation of all of them that they would die with Jesus and not deny him (v. 31b). The tension is especially strong between Jesus' prediction that Peter would deny him (v. 30) and Peter's vehement statement that, if necessary, he would die with Jesus and would surely not deny him (v. 31a). The predictions of Jesus and their narrative fulfillment constitute a good illustration of the spirit being willing but the flesh being weak. This example of the application of the saying suggests that πειρασμός ("testing" or "temptation") has to do with suffering discipleship.[82] The instruction to pray that one not be put to the test (or come into temptation) thus implies that the audiences should not seek out the opportunity to suffer like Jesus. Nevertheless, for some that opportunity will come, as the Markan Jesus predicts in 13:9, 12-13a. The teaching on discipleship in 8:34-38 and 13:13b calls for endurance and loyalty to the gospel and to Jesus when followers of Jesus are put to the test.[83]

■ **39-41a** The present form of the narrative makes use of the folkloric pattern of three in telling the story of Gethsemane. The effect of the use of this pattern is twofold. It increases the pathos of the portrait of Jesus struggling alone without the support of his friends. It also emphasizes the weakness and failure of the disciples.

In v. 40, when Jesus finds the disciples sleeping for the second time, the narrator comments "for their eyes were heavy" (ἦσαν γὰρ αὐτῶν οἱ ὀφθαλμοὶ καταβαρυνόμενοι). Kelber suggested that, on the level of

77   See note s on the trans. of 13:33 above.

78   On later Christian interpretations of the Gethsemane tradition, see Cha, "Confronting Death," 2:239-332.

79   Feldmeier argued that the clause is final: pray *in order that* you not come into temptation (*Die Krisis*, 197-98). But the use of the same construction in 13:18 makes it likely that ἵνα here takes the place of the infinitve (similarly Matt 24:20; 26:41). Note that Luke changed the Markan construction with ἵνα in 13:18 to one with the infinitive (Luke 22:40). Thus, when Luke uses the construction with ἵνα in the parallel to Mark 14:38, it may well have a final sense; but that does not necessarily mean that it does in Mark.

80   Betz, *Sermon*, 405. Matthew gives the prayer of Jesus

in direct speech a second time (26:42); in this formulation, he modifies the last clause to make it more similar to the Lord's Prayer: "your will be done" (γενηθήτω τὸ θέλημά σου). This redactional change has been pointed out by many, e.g., Günter Bader, *Symbolik des Todes Jesu* (HUTh 25; Tübingen: Mohr Siebeck, 1988) 217.

81   Cf. the discussion of Heb 5:7 by Attridge, "Giving Voice to Jesus," 110, and of Rom 15:3 and 9 (ibid., 111-12).

82   See the commentary on vv. 26-31 and 8:34-38 above.

83   Dibelius argued that the test in question is the great eschatological time of testing ("Gethsemane," 263).

discourse, this comment suggests that the disciples are blind to what is taking place in Gethsemane.[84] Although the point should not be pressed, there is a certain analogy between the portrayal of the disciples here and, for example, Jesus' question in 8:18a, "Having eyes, do you not see?"

The inability to resist the power of sleep is also quintessentially human. Compare the story of Gilgamesh, who visits Utnapishtim in search of immortality. Utnapishtim says that he must not sleep for six days and seven nights. Gilgamesh proves unable to stay awake for that long, even though he is half-divine and only half-human.[85] Dibelius contrasts the disciples with Jesus in this scene and argues that only the disciples are presented as weak in the typically human way.[86]

The narrator adds a further comment in v. 40, "and they did not know how they should respond to him" (καὶ οὐκ ᾔδεισαν τί ἀποκριθῶσιν αὐτῷ). This remark is reminiscent of the narrator's comment in 9:6 that Peter did not know how he should respond to the transfiguration and the voice from heaven.[87] More significant is the contrast between the disciples' bewilderment here and their ready response in 14:19 to Jesus' prophecy that one of the Twelve would betray him: they began to be distressed and each to ask "Is it I?" Similarly, there is a contrast between their speechlessness here and their response to the prediction that they would all take offense in vv. 29-31: Peter takes the lead, but they all affirm their loyalty. In v. 40, the weakness of the flesh seems to be overpowering the willingness of the spirit.[88]

■ **41b-42** When Jesus comes the third time, he says, "Sleep now and rest; it is enough" (v. 41b). This remark appears to be in tension with the command and exhortation in v. 42a, "Get up; let us go."[89] This tension signifies, at least for the text in its Markan form, that the remark "Sleep now and rest" is ironic, perhaps even sarcastic. Jesus is portrayed as exasperated and realizes that "it is enough," that is, that he has been unsuccessful in exhorting the disciples to keep awake.

The next saying (v. 41c) announces to the disciples that the hour has come, namely, the hour when the Son of Man is "handed over into the hands of the sinners."[90] In 9:31, the Markan Jesus had simply said that he would be handed over into the hands of humans (ἄνθρωποι). In 10:33, he says that after the chief priests and scribes have condemned him to death, they will hand him over to the nations or to Gentiles (ἔθνη). It is likely that the "sinners" (ἁμαρτωλοί) in v. 41 refers primarily to "Gentiles." Paul expressed the typically Jewish view in speaking of "Gentile sinners" (ἐξ ἐθνῶν ἁμαρτωλοί) (Gal 2:15).[91] Thus, Jesus' execution by the Romans may be in view here.[92] Another possibility is that the word "sinners" is used here in allusion to the language of the Psalms.[93]

Jesus continues to speak, saying "Get up; let us go." The verb ἄγειν ("to go") is used in the sense of motion away from a position,[94] but the goal is not expressed. It is highly unlikely that flight is meant.[95] Jesus' final statement in this scene, which links the Gethsemane story to the account of the arrest that follows, is "See, the one who is to hand me over has drawn near." The implication

84   Kelber, "Hour of the Son of Man," 49.

85   Stephanie Dalley, *Myths from Mesopotamia: Creation, the Flood, Gilgamesh and Others* (Oxford/New York: Oxford University Press, 1989) 116–17.

86   Dibelius, "Gethsemane," 259.

87   Ibid. See also the commentary on 9:5-6 above.

88   The struggle between "spirit" and "flesh" portrayed here is analogous to Paul's use in Romans 7 of the Platonic tradition concerning the battle between the mind and the emotions; on the latter, see Emma Wasserman, "The Death of the Soul in Romans 7: Sin, Death, and the Law in Light of Hellenistic Moral Psychology" (Ph.D. diss., Yale University, 2005).

89   See note a on the trans. of v. 41 above.

90   On this "handing over" as ultimately a divine activity, see the commentary above on 3:19, 9:31, and 14:10-11 and below on 15:27.

91   See also the prayer of Joseph in 4Q372, cited above, in which Joseph prays that God will save him from the hands of the Gentiles.

92   Swete (348) concluded that the disciples would have understood Jesus to mean "Gentiles," but that Jesus no doubt meant to include the scribes and priests (presumably those who rejected him).

93   Cf. Pss 35:12; 70:4; 81:4 LXX; cf. Gnilka, 2:263.

94   BAGD, s.v. ἄγω, 5.

95   Swete, 349.

is that Jesus plans to meet Judas and those with him and assumes that the disciples, for the moment, will remain in Jesus' company. The use of the expression "the one who is to hand me over" (ὁ παραδιδούς με) instead of Judas' name heightens the drama of the unfolding events and links them to the passion predictions.[96]

14

14:43-52 The Arrest

43/ And immediately, while he was still speaking, Judas, one of the Twelve, arrived. And with him was a crowd with swords and clubs from the chief priests and the scribes and the elders. 44/ Now the one who was about to hand him over had given them a signal, saying, "The one whom I kiss is he; arrest him and lead him away under guard." 45/ And he came immediately, went up to him and said, "Rabbi," and kissed him. 46/ They then laid hands on him and arrested him. 47/ Now a certain one[a] of those who were standing by drew his sword and struck the slave of the high priest and cut off his ear. 48/ And Jesus said to them, "You have come out to seize me with swords and clubs as you would (come out) against a robber. 49/ Every day I was with you in the temple precinct teaching and you did not arrest me. But (it is occurring) in order that the scriptures may be fulfilled." 50/ And they all left him and fled. 51/ And a certain young man was accompanying him, wearing a linen cloth over his naked body,[b] and they arrested him. 52/ But he left the linen cloth behind and fled naked.[c]

a The trans. is based on the reading εἷς δέ τις ("Now a certain one"), attested by B C Θ et al. This reading was apparently perceived as redundant or inelegant, and this perception gave rise to variants. The expression, however, is characteristic of Markan style; see Neirynck, *Duality in Mark*, 106. The redundancy is eliminated through the omission of τις ("a certain one") in the reading attested by ℵ A L et al. The same effect is achieved by changing the εἷς δέ τις ("Now a certain one") to καί τις ("and a certain one") in the reading attested by D (it). In the reading attested by W (*f*¹), the apparent redundancy is preserved, but the awkwardness of the separation of εἷς ("one") and τις ("a certain one") by δέ ("now") is removed by changing δέ ("now") to καί ("and").

b The earliest recoverable reading is probably ἐπὶ γυμνοῦ ("over his naked body"); see BAGD, s.v. γυμνός, 1. The shorter reading, γυμνός ("naked"), attested by Θ *f*¹³ et al., probably arose through an accidental assimilation of this passage to v. 52. The words ἐπὶ γυμνοῦ ("over his naked body") are lacking in W *f*¹ et al.; this shortest reading is due either to accidental omission or deliberate revision because the phrase seemed obscure, unnecessary, or misleading; contra Taylor, ad loc.

c The reading ἀπ᾽ αὐτῶν ("from them"), although very well attested by A D W Θ et al., is probably an early, clarifying expansion.

Comment

■ **43-52** The story of the arrest of Jesus was probably the second unit of the pre-Markan passion narrative. It seems to contain a number of Markan expansions.[97] Bult-mann argued that a briefer account of the arrest began the primitive narrative that constituted the oldest account of the passion.[98] Jeremias concluded, on the basis of a comparison of Mark and John, "that at a very

---

96 Kelber argued that the statement "the one who is to hand me over draws near" (ὁ παραδιδούς με ἤγγικεν) in v. 42b signifies that "[t]he 'coming' of the passion is thus correlated with the 'coming' of the Kingdom [in 1:14-15], and Jesus' being 'delivered up' is given an eschatological perspective" ("Hour of the Son of Man," 45). The link between 14:42 and 1:14-15, however, is not strong.

97 Yarbro Collins, *Beginning of the Gospel*, 107–8. For a tentative reconstruction of the form of the story in Mark's passion source, see the appendix to this commentary. See also Detlev Dormeyer, "Joh 18.1-14 par Mk 14.43-53: Methodologische Überlegungen zur Rekonstruktion einer vorsynoptischen Passionsgeschichte," *NTS* 41 (1995) 218–39, esp. 234–36.

98 Bultmann, *History*, 275, 279.

early stage the Passion story began with the arrest of Jesus."[99] Gerhard Schneider affirmed the conclusions of Bultmann and Jeremias, but also presupposed that the Gethsemane story and the arrest story were already linked in Mark's source.[100]

■ **43** The opening two words, "And immediately" ($Καὶ$ $εὐθύς$), are quite likely to be Markan.[101] Ludger Schenke concluded that the genitive absolute, $ἔτι$ $αὐτοῦ$ $λαλοῦντος$ ("while he was still speaking"), could be a Markan addition, since the same phrase occurs in 5:35.[102] But the phrase in 5:35 may well have been in Mark's source.[103] The identification of Judas as "one of the Twelve" was probably already in Mark's source.[104] In the source, those who sent the crowd with Judas were probably described simply as "the chief priests" ($οἱ$ $ἀρχιερεῖς$). "The crowd" is most likely equivalent to temple police, and it was the chief priests who had authority over them. So the reference to "the scribes and the elders" ($οἱ$ $γραμματεῖς$ $καὶ$ $οἱ$ $πρεσβύτεροι$) is probably a Markan addition.[105]

In the present form of the text, this verse links the arrest of Jesus closely to the scene in Gethsemane, especially to vv. 41 ("the hour has come") and 42 ("the one who is to hand me over has drawn near"). The description of Judas as "one of the Twelve" recalls v. 10, which tells how Judas went to the chief priests and offered to hand Jesus over to them. So v. 43 begins the narration of the event planned at that time. Without mentioning Judas by name, Jesus had predicted that "one of the Twelve" would hand him over (vv. 18-20). The pathos of that scene is recalled and revived by the use of the phrase here.

■ **44-46** There are no obvious redactional elements in v. 44.[106] It is a flashback, explaining how the cooperation between Judas and the armed crowd was planned and how it would be put into action. This aside, however, is not intrusive, but constitutes an integral element of the story.[107] The signal devised by Judas affects the meaning of his act of kissing Jesus in v. 45.

The oldest and most common social context of kissing in antiquity was the affectionate kiss between members of the same family.[108] Kisses given to a political or social superior expressed the honor and respect accorded by the inferior to the superior; the privilege of being allowed to kiss a superior also brought honor upon the inferior person.[109] When the kiss is a mark of honor, it is usually on the hands, the breast, the knee, or the feet.[110] The most common occasions of kissing are greeting and parting.[111] "On reception into a closed circle the kiss is a sign of brotherhood."[112]

It is not entirely clear what social custom can explain the kiss of Judas on its first level of meaning. It could

---

99 Joachim Jeremias, *The Eucharistic Words of Jesus* (New York: Macmillan, 1955) 66. But see the argument by Dormeyer that the author of John knew Mark, especially with regard to the account of the arrest ("Joh 18.1-14 par Mk 14.43-53," 222–27).

100 Gerhard Schneider, "Die Verhaftung Jesu: Traditionsgeschichte von Mk 14.43-52," *ZNW* 63 (1972) 188–209, esp. 200, 207–8.

101 Ibid., 199.

102 Schenke, *Passionsgeschichte*, 359. Schneider concluded that it was a Markan addition ("Die Verhaftung Jesu," 193, 199–200).

103 See the commentary on 5:35-36 above.

104 With Schneider ("Die Verhaftung Jesu," 196) and Wolfgang Trilling, "Zur Entstehung des Zwölferkreises: Eine geschichtskritische Überlegung," in Rudolf Schnackenburg, Josef Ernst, and Joachim Wanke, eds., *Die Kirche des Anfangs: Festschrift für Heinz Schürmann zum 65. Geburtstag* (Leipzig: St. Benno, 1977) 201–22, esp. 206. Schenke leaves open the possibility that the phrase is Markan (*Passionsgeschichte*, 233–34, 359). See the commentary on vv. 10-11 above.

105 Schneider, "Die Verhaftung Jesu," 200.

106 The designation of Judas as "the one who was about to hand him over" ($ὁ$ $παραδιδοὺς$ $αὐτοῦ$) fits well with Mark's theme of the ultimately divine activity of "handing over," but the characterization of Judas in this way was most likely already in Mark's sources; see the commentary on 3:16-19 and on 14:10-11 above.

107 Schneider, "Die Verhaftung Jesu," 197.

108 Gustav Stählin, "$φιλέω$ $κτλ$.," *TDNT* 9 (1974) 113–71, esp. 119–20, 126. On the kiss in ancient Judaism and in Greco-Roman society, see also William Klassen, "Kiss (NT)," *ABD* 4:89–92, esp. 90–91. On the kiss among kin and friends, see L. Edward Phillips, "The Ritual Kiss in Early Christian Worship" (Ph.D. diss., University of Notre Dame, 1992) 15–17, 23–24, 34.

109 Stählin, "$φιλέω$ $κτλ$.," 120; Str-B, 1:995; Phillips, "Ritual Kiss," 17–18, 35–36.

110 Stählin, "$φιλέω$ $κτλ$.," 121; Str-B, 1:995–96.

111 Stählin, "$φιλέω$ $κτλ$.," 121, 126–27; Phillips, "Ritual Kiss," 24–25.

112 Stählin, "$φιλέω$ $κτλ$.," 122.

have been an expression of respect for Jesus as "Rabbi," since that is how Judas greets him in v. 45.[113] It could be a kiss of greeting.[114] Since the disciples are not portrayed as kissing Jesus in the canonical Gospels elsewhere, it may be that the kiss here is portrayed as "an unusual act undertaken ad hoc." Its significance would then be a pretended expression of affection and reverence, the misuse of a sign of love as a treacherous signal.[115] If any of the audiences of Mark were practicing the ritual kiss mentioned in some of the letters of Paul, this would increase the impression of treachery in Judas' kiss.[116]

When Judas gave the signal by kissing Jesus, the armed crowd was supposed to arrest Jesus and lead him away under guard (v. 44b). The use of the word $\kappa\rho\alpha\tau\epsilon\hat{\iota}\nu$ ("to arrest") links this passage with the reaction of the chief priests, scribes, and elders to the parable about the vineyard and the tenants, when they begin to try to arrest Jesus (12:12). It also recalls 14:1, when the chief priests and the scribes were looking for a way to arrest Jesus and kill him. In the immediate context, it prepares for the narration of the arrest of Jesus in v. 46. Judas' command "to lead him away under guard" ($\dot{\alpha}\pi\dot{\alpha}\gamma\epsilon\tau\epsilon$ $\dot{\alpha}\sigma\phi\alpha\lambda\hat{\omega}\varsigma$) anticipates v. 53, which tells how those who arrested Jesus then led him away to the high priest.[117]

Verse 46 then narrates, simply and straightforwardly, the actions of the armed crowd, actions that correspond to the aside in v. 44 about the agreement between Judas

and those who came with him. The expression "they laid hands on him" is not a Semitism.[118]

■ **47** The expression $\epsilon\hat{\iota}\varsigma$ $\delta\acute{\epsilon}$ $\tau\iota\varsigma$ ("Now a certain one") is awkward, but characteristic of Markan style.[119] The vague reference to one of the bystanders is odd. It is usually assumed that the person who drew his sword and struck a slave of the high priest was one of the disciples of Jesus and that the gesture signifies an effort to defend him and to prevent his arrest.[120] Linnemann, however, inferred from the fact that this person is not described as one of the Twelve or as a disciple that the verse presupposes a context different from the setting described in v. 32.[121] She remarked that one would expect a disciple who drew a sword at this point to attack Judas rather than some slave of the high priest.[122] It is also odd that the action described in this verse is not anticipated or prepared for earlier in the narrative and that no consequences of it are described in what follows. In v. 48, Jesus addresses the arresting party, not the person who drew the sword, and seems to ignore the incident.[123] Gerd Theissen concluded that the incident is historical and that the person who drew the sword is kept anonymous for his protection, since he had "run afoul of the 'police.'"[124]

In any case, in the present form of Mark, the gesture implies that the disciples do not understand the plan of God, which includes the necessity of the suffering and

---

113 Such could be the case even if "Rabbi" does not mean "teacher" here; cf. Stählin, "$\varphi\iota\lambda\acute{\epsilon}\omega$ $\kappa\tau\lambda$.," 141 and the literature cited in n. 245. See the commentary on 9:5-6 above.

114 Stählin, "$\varphi\iota\lambda\acute{\epsilon}\omega$ $\kappa\tau\lambda$.," 141; Stählin thinks it unlikely that the kiss was a greeting, since such kisses normally took place after a longer separation than the context implies. But Matthew's addition of $\chi\alpha\hat{\iota}\rho\epsilon$ ("hello") suggests that he interpreted the kiss as one of greeting (26:49).

115 Ibid. See the examples of "the false kiss of the deceiver" from the OT, Philo, and other texts that Stählin gives in n. 243. On false kisses, see also Str-B, 1:996; Klauck, *Judas*, 65–66; Phillips, "Ritual Kiss," 36, 87.

116 1 Thess 5:26; 1 Cor 16:20; 2 Cor 13:12; Rom 16:16; on this ritual practice, see Phillips, "Ritual Kiss," 43–76.

117 Schneider, "Die Verhaftung Jesu," 198, 207; Klauck, *Judas*, 64.

118 Lohmeyer, 322 n. 4; Schneider, "Die Verhaftung Jesu," 199.

119 See note a on the trans. of v. 47 above; Theissen, *Gospels in Context*, 184 (*Lokalkolorit*, 196).

120 Matthew (26:51-54) and Luke (22:49-51) interpret Mark in this way. John identifies the individual with Peter (18:10-11); Theissen, *Gospels in Context*, 184–85 (*Lokalkolorit*, 196).

121 Linnemann, *Studien zur Passionsgeschichte*, 41. She concluded that vv. 47, 50-52 are fragments from another story about Jesus' arrest (ibid., 46).

122 Ibid., 46; similarly, Schneider, "Die Verhaftung Jesu," 191. He concluded that v. 47 is a pre-Markan addition to the oldest form of the story, which consisted of vv. 43-46 (53a); the addition was intended to excuse the disciples and to stigmatize Judas (ibid., 207–8).

123 Linnemann, *Studien zur Passionsgeschichte*, 41. She concluded that vv. 43, 48-49 constituted a biographical apophthegm that Mark used as a source in composing his account of the arrest. See also Schneider, "Die Verhaftung Jesu," 191–92.

124 Theissen, *Gospels in Context*, 186–87 (*Lokalkolorit*, 198).

death of Jesus. The misunderstanding of the disciple who drew his sword is analogous to that of Peter when he rebuked Jesus in 8:32.[125] The use of the diminutive ὠτάριον ("ear"), instead of the ordinary noun οὖς ("ear"), is typical of Markan style[126] and may be an indication that this verse is redactional.

■ **48-49** These verses are probably Markan additions to his source.[127] The first statement of Jesus addressed to the arresting party (v. 48) is a reproach for coming out against him as they would against a λῃστής ("robber," "bandit," or "revolutionary"). This reproach reflects the situation of the evangelist and his aim of contrasting Jesus with the revolutionaries who engaged in the revolt that led to the first Jewish war with Rome.[128]

The second statement of Jesus (v. 49a) refers to the fact that he was teaching "every day" in the temple precinct in their[129] presence, yet they did not arrest him.[130] This statement is open to at least two readings in the context of Mark as a whole. It could refer to his teaching about the temple, that it should be a house of prayer and not a den of robbers (11:17). The term λῃστής ("robber," "bandit," or "revolutionary") links this passage with that one. In that case, the statement would be a reproach for their lack of courage in arresting him on that occasion, because of his popularity with the crowd (11:18; cf. 12:12), and especially for their conspiracy to arrest him "by deceit," instead of openly (14:1). The

other way of reading the statement is as a reproach for arresting him at all, since there was nothing unlawful in his public teaching. The remark may remind the audience about how his interlocutors failed "to catch him in a statement" in questioning him about paying taxes to Caesar (12:13-17).[131] The two readings are not mutually exclusive. These reproaches are, at the same time, statements of self-defense on the part of the Markan Jesus. They thus represent a kind of passion apologetic emphasizing the innocence of Jesus.

The final statement of Jesus (v. 49b) in this short speech implies that his arrest is taking place "in order that the scriptures may be fulfilled" (ἵνα πληρωθῶσιν αἱ γραφαί). Although the point is disputed, this seems to be the clearest statement in Mark of the idea that the events of the passion of Jesus take place in fulfillment of the scriptures read as prophecies.[132] Hugh Anderson argued that the phrase ἀλλ᾽ ἵνα πληρωθῶσιν αἱ γραφαί ought to be translated "But let the scriptures be fulfilled." He argued that it was "not apparently Mark's way, as it is Matthew's, to reflect on past events as the exact fulfillment of Old Testament predictions."[133] Schneider argued similarly, concluding that the construction with ἵνα here has an imperatival sense.[134] The Greek phrase, however, may also be taken as elliptical and as implying a verb analogous to Matthew's γέγονεν ("it has taken place").[135] It is certainly the case that Mark

125 Yarbro Collins, *Beginning of the Gospel*, 107–8; see also the commentary on 8:32b-33 above; Schneider, "Die Verhaftung Jesu," 208.

126 BDF §111 (3).

127 Yarbro Collins, *Beginning of the Gospel*, 108; Schneider, "Die Verhaftung Jesu," 202–4. Reinhold Liebers, however, argued that vv. 48-49 are pre-Markan (*"Wie geschrieben steht"*, 134–47, 384, 391).

128 See the commentary on 11:17 and on 13:5-6 above. See also Schneider, "Die Verhaftung Jesu," 195.

129 The armed crowd, historically best interpreted as temple police, are here addressed as equivalent to the chief priests, by whom they were sent.

130 For the phrase ἐν τῷ ἱερῷ διδάσκων ("teaching in the temple precinct"), cf. 12:35; Schneider, "Die Verhaftung Jesu," 203.

131 Ibid.

132 Liebers argued, for the pre-Markan stage, that "fulfillment" here does not signify the idea of a proof from prophecy, since no particular text is evoked. What is "fulfilled" is the destiny of the righteous one

(*"Wie geschrieben steht"*, 388). But the category of "the righteous one" has been criticized; see the commentary on v. 18 above.

133 Hugh Anderson, "The Old Testament in Mark's Gospel," in James M. Efird, ed., *The Use of the Old Testament in the New and Other Essays: Studies in Honor of William Franklin Stinespring* (Durham, NC: Duke University Press, 1972) 280–306; quotation from 293. Alfred Suhl also minimizes the significance of this verse and of v. 21 (*Funktion*, 45, 65). Schneider concluded that the phrase signifies not the schema of prophecy and fulfillment but the idea of the fulfillment of God's will as revealed in scripture ("Die Verhaftung Jesu," 195).

134 Schneider, "Zur Verhaftung Jesu," 204 n. 86. Cf. BDF §387 (3).

135 BDF §448 (7).

does not develop the idea of the fulfillment of scripture to the extent that Matthew does, but he does seem to express the notion here.

Erich Klostermann suggested that v. 49b evokes Isa 53:12, which is cited in Luke 22:37.[136] Alfred Suhl objected to that hypothesis on the basis of the use of the plural, αἱ γραφαί ("the scriptures"), here as in 1 Cor 15:3-4. He concluded that in neither case was there an allusion to a specific passage. Rather, the claim that certain events of Jesus' life occurred in accordance with the scriptures simply expressed the conviction of the early Christians that in these events, God was active in bringing about their salvation. In v. 49b, the idea of prophecy and fulfillment is present, but it has not yet been developed into a proof from prophecy.[137] Liebers, like Suhl, has argued that no specific scripture or early Jewish text is alluded to in v. 49b.[138]

Since vv. 48-49 were probably composed by Mark, it makes sense to consider what the context suggests about what scriptural text is alluded to here. The hypothesis that the allusion is to Zech 13:7b is attractive because the scene in vv. 27-31 was probably composed by Mark in order to foreshadow the following events of the passion narrative in general and the arrest and flight of the disciples in particular.[139] The passage, as cited in v. 27, has two parts: "I will strike the shepherd" and "the sheep will be scattered." The first part is fulfilled in the arrest of Jesus in v. 46; the second in the flight of the disciples in v. 50.[140] Jesus' saying about the scriptures being fulfilled is placed after the account of the arrest[141] and before the narration of the flight of the disciples, thus linking the two.

■ **50** Grammatically and syntactically speaking, the word πάντες ("all") should refer to the arresting party, who are addressed in the short speech of Jesus in vv. 48-49.

Another oddity is that the disciples flee immediately after Jesus' statement.[142] Contextually speaking, however, it is obvious that the disciples are meant. Further, as suggested above, the placement of the disciples' flight is meant to demonstrate the fulfillment of the scripture referred to in v. 49b and of Jesus' prophecy in v. 27.[143]

Schneider argued that v. 50 is in some tension with vv. 51-52 and is certainly not in full accord with the account of the denial of Peter in vv. 54, 66-72. He rejected the suggestion of Hans-Martin Schenke that v. 50, at the pre-Markan stage, followed directly on v. 46 because the disciples are not mentioned in vv. 43-46. He concluded that v. 50 was added by Mark in connection with his interest in the themes of the misunderstanding and failure of the disciples.[144] If, however, as seems likely, the arrest story was the second, not the first, scene in the pre-Markan passion narrative, the disciples would not need to be mentioned explicitly in v. 50, since they have already been placed at the scene with Jesus in Gethsemane. Further, it is unlikely that an account of the arrest of Jesus would lack any mention of the reaction and whereabouts of Jesus' followers.[145] Whatever tension there may be between v. 50 and vv. 51-52, 54, 66-72 can be explained by the hypothesis that v. 50 is pre-Markan and that Mark added vv. 51-52 to elaborate the brief statement of v. 50 and by the hypothesis that the denial of Peter is also a Markan addition to the passion account. Finally, the flight of the disciples is certainly plausible historically.[146] Thus, although Mark probably did not compose v. 50, he was able to make use of it in developing the themes of the misunderstanding and failure of the disciples.

Schneider also argued, in favor of the Markan composition of v. 50, that the verse is thoroughly Markan in style.[147] One of the allegedly Markan features is the use

---

136 Klostermann, 153; he refers to Isa 53:7, but presumably he meant 53:12.

137 Suhl, *Funktion*, 41–42, 43–44.

138 Liebers, *"Wie geschrieben steht"*, 13, 384–89.

139 See the commentary on vv. 26-31 and on v. 27 above; cf. Gnilka, 2:271; Vorster, "Function," 62–72, esp. 63.

140 Schneider, "Die Verhaftung Jesu," 204.

141 Except for the intervening saying about the person who drew a sword in v. 47.

142 Schneider, "Die Verhaftung Jesu," 192.

143 Note the use of the word πάντες ("all") in v. 27, as

well as in v. 50. One could argue that Mark inserted vv. 48-49 before v. 50, which was already in his source, or, as Schneider argues, that Mark added all three verses to make that demonstration ("Die Verhaftung Jesu," 204–5).

144 Schneider, "Die Verhaftung Jesu," 195, 204–5.

145 Schenke, *Passionsgeschichte*, 358–59.

146 Reinbold, *Der älteste Bericht*, 225 n. 17.

147 Schneider, "Die Verhaftung Jesu," 205.

of the singular or plural aorist active participle of ἀφίημι followed by a finite verb, which he says occurs only eight times in the New Testament, six of which are in Mark. Although he acknowledged that the construction occurs once in redactional material in Matthew (26:44), he failed to mention another case of the latter type (Matt 13:36). Although Luke rewrote Mark 1:16-20 thoroughly, he nevertheless used this construction in the concluding sentence of the pericope (5:11). In special Lukan material, the construction is used, but with the participle following the main verb (10:30). Further, Luke uses the construction in 18:28, even though the parallel in Mark has two finite verbs instead. Paul also uses the construction (Rom 1:27). The fact that the precise form ἔφυγον ("they fled") occurs only once in the NT (Heb 11:34) apart from Mark and passages dependent on Mark does not seem to be significant. Other forms of this verb, which is used relatively infrequently in the New Testament, occur, notably the singular ἔφυγεν ("he/she/it fled"). Although v. 50 fits very well into the Markan context, that fit can be explained just as well on the hypothesis that Mark used an element from a source in constructing the relevant themes as on the hypothesis of Markan composition.

■ **51-52** The only other place in Mark where the word νεανίσκος ("young man") is used is 16:5. In v. 51 the young man is introduced in a way that signifies that he has not yet been mentioned in the story.[148] The phrase συνηκολούθει αὐτῷ could be translated "was accompanying him," "was following him," or "was attempting to accompany/follow him."[149] The significance could be either that the young man was in the entourage of Jesus up to the time of his arrest or that, when Jesus was arrested, he tried to follow him by joining the group taking him away.[150] The word σινδών may be translated

either "piece of linen cloth" or "garment made of linen."[151] This word occurs twice in this passage and twice in 15:46. These are the only places where it occurs in Mark. The phrase περιβεβλημένος σινδόνα ἐπὶ γυμνοῦ[152] is ambiguous. The word περιβεβλημένος could be translated literally, signifying that the young man had a piece of linen or other fine cloth wrapped around himself, or, in accordance with its frequent usage, with "dressed in" or "wearing." One way in which the audience could understand the phrase ἐπὶ γυμνοῦ is as equivalent to ἐπὶ γυμνοῦ ἐνδύματος ("upon the covering of his nakedness" or "upon the garment of his nakedness"). In this understanding, the young man would be wearing a light, upper garment over his underwear.[153] Or they could understand it as equivalent to ἐπὶ γυμνοῦ τοῦ σώματος ("over his naked body").[154] The "crowd" with swords and clubs "arrest" or "seize" (κρατεῖν) the young man, just as they arrested or seized Jesus (v. 46). When they take hold of him, the young man flees naked, leaving the cloth or garment behind (v. 52). "Naked" (γυμνός) here could mean either "in his underwear" or literally "naked."

Excursus: Scholarship on 14:51-52

Epiphanius identified the young man as James the brother of the Lord. Ambrose, John Chrysostom, and Bede identified him as John, the son of Zebedee.[155] The anonymous author of a seventh-century commentary on Mark that was attributed to Jerome in the Middle Ages says regarding our passage:

> This is proper to Mark. This is like the case of Joseph, who leaving behind his tunic, fled in the nude from the hands of the shameless mistress of the house. Whoever wants to escape from the hands of wicked people, let them mentally abandon the things of the world, and flee after Jesus

---

148 This point holds also for the textual variants (Sellew, "*Secret Mark*," 251–52).

149 LSJ, s.v. ἀκολουθέω; Smyth §§1889, 1895.

150 W. C. Allen, *The Gospel according to Saint Mark* (Oxford Church Biblical Commentary; London: Rivingtons, 1915) 178.

151 LSJ, s.v. σινδών.

152 On the variants, see note b on the trans. of v. 51 above.

153 Klostermann, 153; Allen, 178; Str-B, 2:50–51. *M. Kelim* 29.1 provides evidence that Jews wore under-

wear at least by the end of the second cent. CE. According to Joshua Schwartz (personal communication), since practices related to material culture are conservative, it is likely that Jews normally wore underwear in the first century CE.

154 Thucydides 2.49.5; Klostermann, 153; Allen, 178; Str-B, 2:50–51.

155 Swete, 354; Frans Neirynck, "La Fuite du jeune homme en Mc 14,51-52," *EThL* 55 (1979) 43–66, esp. 55–56.

(Hoc proprie Marcus. Sic et Ioseph relicto pallio nudus de manibus inpudicae dominae effugit. Qui uult effugere manus iniquorum, relinquens mente quae mundi sunt, fugiat post Iesum).[156]

Like Epiphanius and other ancient writers, many modern authors have taken this passage as a historical reminiscence.[157] Theissen raised the question whether the relationship of the young man to Jesus was "meant to remain shadowy."[158] He considered the anonymity of this disciple to be striking and explained it in terms of "protective anonymity." He had "run afoul of the 'police.'" He offered resistance and therefore was in danger. It would be inopportune to mention his name or even to admit that he was a member of the Christian community.[159] This hypothesis does not explain why the young man was dressed (or nearly undressed) in the way he was.[160]

Other scholars have seen the evocation of scripture as a key to the significance of the passage. Loisy interpreted it as a messianic application of prophecy to the events of the passion. He argued that this brief narrative is based on the Hebrew version of Amos 2:16 and noted Rev 16:15 as a parallel.[161] Klostermann suggested that the author wished to enrich the account of the flight of all those around Jesus in v. 50 with a prophetic motif based on the Greek version of Amos 2:16.[162] He also referred to Mark 13:16 as an analogy. Linnemann concluded that it was impossible to be sure that Amos 2:16 was a factor in the origin of this passage, but she considered it at least possible.[163] Schneider argued that vv. 51-52 constitute a traditional story formulated by Mark. He concluded that it belongs, as a special case, to the theme of the flight of the disciples. In his view, the notion of the eschatological tribulation, perhaps following Amos 2:16 and Mark 13:14-16, also plays a role in this story.[164] Gnilka rejected the hypothesis that this story is connected with Amos 2:16 because Amos plays no role otherwise in the theological interpretation of the passion.[165] He argued, however, that the flight of the young man makes an impression of chaos and is an instance of an apocalyptic motif.[166]

A number of scholars have concluded that the incident is symbolic. John Knox suggested that the "whimsical story of the young man and the linen cloth" is a cryptic reference to the empty tomb.[167] In a later study, he argued that "Mark likes to describe events in proleptic fasion, or at any rate to make cryptic references to coming future events."[168] Both Jesus and the young man were "seized" by the arresting party. Just as the young man broke free, leaving the linen cloth behind, so Jesus "was likewise destined to escape the hands of his enemies, leaving only the linen cloth in which he was wrapped."[169] He noted that the σινδών ("linen cloth") in which Jesus was buried is mentioned in 15:46, but not in 16:1-8. But both 14:51-52 and 16:5 refer to a νεανίσκος . . . περιβεβλημένος ("young man . . . clothed"). He also referred to John 20:5-7, Acts of Pilate 15:6, and a quotation by Jerome from the

---

156 The allusion is to Gen 39:6-20. Text from Cahill, *Expositio Evangelii*, 66; trans. from idem, *First Commentary*, 109–10; on authorship and date of the commentary, see *First Commentary*, 4–7.

157 E.g., Gould, 276; cf. xvi (John Mark); Swete, 354 (John Mark or another eyewitness); Allen, 178; cf. 3 (John Mark); Lohmeyer, 324 (an eyewitness); Cranfield, 438–39; cf. 5–6 (an eyewitness, perhaps John Mark); Taylor, 562 (an eyewitness known to Mark); Schweizer, 316–17 (a young man arrested with Jesus who later joined the church); Pesch, 2:402 (a curious youth who lived nearby); Michael J. Haren, "The Naked Young Man: A Historian's Hypothesis on Mark 14,51-5," *Bib* 79 (1998) 525–31 (Lazarus).

158 Theissen, *Gospels in Context*, 185 (*Lokalkolorit*, 197).

159 Ibid., 186–87 (198–99).

160 The implausible speculations on the part of most of the authors who consider vv. 51-52 to be an historical reminiscence discredit this hypothesis.

161 Loisy, 425.

162 Klostermann, 153. He notes that Greek MSS of Amos belonging to the Lucian group read φεύξεται ("will flee") rather than διώξεται ("will be pursued"). See the citation of Amos 2:16 LXX below.

163 Linnemann, *Studien zur Passionsgeschichte*, 52.

164 Schneider, "Die Verhaftung Jesu," 205–6.

165 Gnilka, 2:271; but the motif of the darkness at noon in Mark 15:33 seems to evoke Amos 8:9.

166 Ibid., 2:267, citing Rev 6:15-16; *1 Enoch* 62:10; Mark 13:14-20. He takes the position that the earliest passion narrative was revised in an apocalyptic direction before Mark received it (ibid.); he cites with approval, however, Schneider's conclusion that vv. 51-52 constitute a Markan formulation of traditional material (ibid., n. 5).

167 John Knox, *Christ the Lord: The Meaning of Jesus in the Early Church* (Chicago/New York: Willett, Clark, 1945) 100 n. 18.

168 John Knox, "A Note on Mark 14:51-52," in Sherman E. Johnson, ed., *The Joy of Study: Papers on New Testament and Related Subjects Presented to Honor Frederick Clifton Grant* (New York: Macmillan, 1951) 27–30; quotation from 28.

169 Ibid., 29.

Gospel according to the Hebrews in support of his interpretation.[170]

Apparently independently of Knox, but inspired by Austin Farrer's focus on the editing of tradition by the evangelist, Albert Vanhoye came to a similar conclusion, that this episode is an enigmatic prefiguration of the destiny of Jesus.[171] He commented on the same similarities that were noted by Knox; in addition, he concluded that Mark's use of the unusual verb συνακολουθεῖν ("to accompany" or "to follow along with") links the young man closely to Jesus.[172] The last two words of the story, γυμνὸς ἔφυγεν ("he fled naked"), express a situation of extreme distress and humiliation. It is shameful to flee, all the more so naked. At the same time, there is a positive element: the escape from danger and the exultation such a deliverance brings. The ridicule falls upon the enemies, who are left with a piece of cloth in their hands. In such a situation, nudity loses its shame and takes on the connotation of liberation. In reading the passage, one thinks first of a negative interpretation, but it also contains a promise.[173]

Robin Scroggs and Kent Groff argued that "when seen against the backdrop of Christian baptismal practices, the appearance of the young man in both instances can best be explained as a symbolic pointer to the Christian initiate. The nakedness and flight in 14:51-52 symbolize dying with Christ; the reappearance of the young man in a new garment in 16:5 symbolizes rising with Christ."[174] The rite of Christian baptism, however, is not explicitly mentioned in Mark. One could argue that the baptism of Jesus in 1:9-11 serves as a model for the Christian rite and that John's saying in 1:8 alludes to Christian baptism "in Holy Spirit," but the notion of dying and rising in baptism does not occur in chapter 1. In 10:38-39, the terms βαπτίζειν ("to immerse" or "to baptize") and βάπτισμα ("immersion" or "baptism") are associated with the death of Jesus, but these terms are used metaphorically in that context and do not refer to the ritual of baptism.[175] The passion predictions speak about the death and resurrection of Jesus, and the disciple is expected to follow Jesus in suffering (8:34—9:1), but the idea of the disciple dying and rising with Jesus is not explicitly present.[176] Further, as the authors recognize, there is no early evidence for the practice of "the actual stripping off of the clothes of the candidate before immersion and the robing in a white garment after he had emerged from the water."[177] *Didache* 7 says nothing about such a ritual act in its discussion of of baptism. The *Apostolic Tradition* attributed to Hippolytus seems to imply that those

---

170 Ibid., 29–30. In *Acts of Pilate* 15:6, the risen Jesus appears to Joseph of Arimathea and shows him the place where he had laid Jesus, the clean linen cloth in which he had wrapped Jesus, and the cloth he had placed on Jesus' face (*NTApoc*, 1:518). The relevant quotation of Jerome from the *Gospel according to the Hebrews* says regarding the risen Jesus: "And when the Lord had given the linen cloth to the servant of the priest, he went to James [the Just] and appeared to him" (Jerome *De viris illustribus* 2 [*NTApoc*, 1:178]).

171 Albert Vanhoye, "La fuite du jeune homme nu (Mc 14,51-52)," *Bib* 52 (1971) 401–6, esp. 405. Similarly, Adela Yarbro Collins, "Mysteries in the Gospel of Mark," in David Hellholm, Halvor Moxnes, and Turid Karlsen Seim, eds., *Mighty Minorities: Minorities in Early Christianity–Positions and Strategies: Essays in Honour of Jacob Jervell on His 70th Birthday* (Oslo/Copenhagen/Stockholm/Boston: Scandinavian University Press, 1995) 11–23, esp. 19–20. Michelangelo Merisi da Caravaggio (1571–1610) portrayed Jesus and the young man who fled in such a way as to suggest their identity in his painting *The Taking of the Christ* (1602) (on indefinite loan to the National Gallery of Ireland from the Jesuit Community, Leeson Street, Dublin). I am grateful to Turid Karlsen Seim for bringing this painting to my attention. Ernst L. Schnellbächer argued that the young man of 14:51-52 is identical with the one who appears in

16:5; the two episodes illustrate the two main aspects of the evangelist's message: crucifixion and resurrection ("Das Rätsel des νεανίσκος bei Markus," *ZNW* 73 [1982] 127–35). Wolfgang Schenk, however, had already pointed out that, if the young man in 16:5 were the same as the one in 14:51-52, there would be a definite article in 16:5 referring back to the introduction of the figure (*Der Passionsbericht nach Markus: Untersuchungen zur Überlieferungsgeschichte der Passionstraditionen* [Gütersloh: Mohn, 1974] 210).

172 Vanhoye, "La fuite du jeune homme nu," 404. He also observed that περιβάλλειν ("to put on") is found in Mark only in 14:51 and 16:5. Less helpfully, he notes that φεύγειν ("to flee") creates another verbal contact between the two passages: the young man fled and so did the women who found the empty tomb (ibid., 404–5).

173 Ibid., 405–6.

174 Robin Scroggs and Kent I. Groff, "Baptism in Mark: Dying and Rising with Christ," *JBL* 92 (1973) 531–48; quotation from 540.

175 See the commentary on 10:38-40 above.

176 Harry Fleddermann rightly concluded that the dying and rising motif is not one of the "known Markan concerns" ("The Flight of a Naked Young Man [Mark 14:51-52]," *CBQ* 41 [1979] 412–18; quotation from 415).

177 Scroggs and Groff, "Baptism in Mark," 537.

who are baptized put the same clothes on again after the rite.[178]

Frank Kermode also took the incident to be fictional, but in a quite different way. He suggested that the young man's appearance represents the kind of random event that characterizes ordinary experience and is analogous to the man in the macintosh in James Joyce's *Ulysses*, who just keeps popping up, although he has no significant narrative role.[179] Although Mark's narrative style is realistic,[180] the technique Kermode identifies is characteristic of modern literature. Mark does not seem otherwise to include random characters.

Other scholars have seen the incident of vv. 51-52 as a literary expression of the theme of the misunderstanding and failure of the disciples. As noted above, Schneider took this position with regard to the role of the passage in its present context in Mark.[181] Robert C. Tannehill argued that the "flight of the naked young man probably dramatizes the shamefulness of the disciple's flight and satirizes the pretensions of Christians who claim to be ready for martyrdom."[182] He noted the occurrence of σινδών ("linen cloth") in the scene describing Jesus' burial (15:46) and inferred from it "that this man is so sure of his loyalty that he comes all dressed for death, but suddenly changes his mind when death is a real prospect." At the same time, he argued that the man's nakedness emphasizes the shamefulness of his flight.[183]

Harry T. Fleddermann argued that the flight of the young man is a "commentary on 14:50" and "a dramatization of the universal flight of the disciples."[184] Thus, the passage belongs to the "theme of the failure of the disciples to understand and accept the passion and their consequent falling into unbelief."[185] Against Knox and Vanhoye, who see in the young man a prefiguration of the risen Jesus,

Fleddermann argued that "[t]he fleeing young man is in contrast to Jesus who accepts the passion as God's will (14:36)."[186] Against Scroggs and Groff, he claimed that the youth "is not a symbol of the Christian initiate approaching baptism, he is a symbol of those who oppose God's will in the passion."[187] With regard to the use of the word σινδών ("linen cloth") twice in 14:51-52 and twice in 15:46, he concluded that the remarks about Jesus' clothing in the passion narrative imply that he was crucified naked. Again there is a contrast between the young man who was arrested and stripped but flees, and Jesus, who "is arrested and stripped and crucified."[188]

Stephen Hatton argued that the verb συνακολουθεῖν ("to accompany" or "to follow along with") suggests that "following," that is, "discipleship" is a subtext of the passage.[189] He proposed that "[t]o write that all fled and then to write of one who did not flee is a comic use of 'all.'" This "obvious incongruity" is one of the features of this pericope that links it to comedy.[190] Its "humorous metalanguage" interrupts "the reader's progress and abandons denotative signification."[191] Hatton conjectured that it may have been Mark's objective to downplay "the importance of discipleship and 'following.'" This objective "is achieved by emphasis on the physical when the story-level context calls for an emphasis on the spiritual, by exaggerated detail, by a focus on the embarrassing . . . , textual materiality, and textual self-reference."[192]

Donahue and Harrington concluded that the young man "represents concretely the group of disciples whose flight was described in 14:50. Rather than symbolizing Jesus or the Christian, he stands for those who desert Jesus in time of trouble." The fact that he fled naked indicates "the shame that the young man will experience." He chose "shame over fidelity to Jesus."[193]

---

178 *Apostolic Tradition* 21.3–20; see the translation in Paul F. Bradshaw, Maxwell E. Johnson, and L. Edward Phillips, *The Apostolic Tradition: A Commentary* (Hermeneia; Minneapolis: Fortress, 2002) 112–19. The core of this document goes back to the second century CE (ibid., 14–15).

179 Kermode, *Genesis of Secrecy*, 49–73.

180 See the discussion in Vanhoye, "La fuite du jeune homme nu," 401.

181 Schneider, "Die Verhaftung Jesu," 205–6.

182 Tannehill, "Disciples in Mark," 403.

183 Ibid., 403 n. 38.

184 Fleddermann, "Flight of a Naked Young Man," 415.

185 Ibid., 416, citing Schenke, *Passionsgeschichte*, 401–4, in n. 26.

186 Fleddermann, "Flight of a Naked Young Man," 416.

187 Ibid., 417.

188 Ibid.

189 Stephen B. Hatton, "Mark's Naked Disciple: The Semiotics and Comedy of Following," *Neotestamentica* 35 (2001) 35–48, esp. 36–44. Contrast the conclusion of Pesch, that the verb is to be taken literally and not as connoting discipleship (2:402); so also Neirynck, "La Fuite du jeune homme," 53–55.

190 Hatton, "Mark's Naked Disciple," 45.

191 Ibid., 35 (abstract).

192 Ibid., 47. Cf. the comment of Knox, "Anyone who has read this Markan narrative (chaps. 14–15) to a congregation on Good Friday is bound to have felt tempted to omit this apparently whimsical passage" ("A Note on Mark 14:51-52," 27), and Vanhoye's description of the scene as ridiculous and indecent ("La fuite du jeune homme nu," 401).

193 Donahue and Harrington, 417.

Since the publication in 1973 of a fragment of a letter ostensibly written by Clement of Alexandria that contains quotations from a work described by Clement as a secret Gospel of Mark, scholars have made use of that fragment to make sense of vv. 51-52.[194] The author of the letter says that this Gospel (τὸ μυστικὸν εὐαγγέλιον) contains a passage following Mark 10:34 that tells how Jesus raised a young man (νεανίσκος) from the dead. The text goes on to say that "after six days, Jesus told him what to do and in the evening the youth comes to him, wearing a linen cloth over his naked body (περιβεβλημένος σινδόνα ἐπὶ γυμνοῦ). And he remained with him that night, for Jesus taught him the mystery of the kingdom of God."[195]

In an addendum to their article, Scroggs and Groff refer to this passage and argue that "*at least* the framers of the added story understood 14:51-52 as also alluding to a ritual event" and that this event "is, or is related to, baptism."[196] Helmut Koester argued that the incident involving the young man fleeing naked in vv. 51-52 was added by the editor or reviser who transformed "Proto-Mark" into "the *Secret Gospel of Mark*" early in the second century. These verses were not eliminated by the redactor of canonical Mark, although he omitted the first passage about the young man, which followed 10:34.[197]

Before Schenke became acquainted "with Smith's letter of Clement," he was already inclined to think that the incident in vv. 51-52 constitutes "the now incomprehensible remains of something that was originally more extensive, which had been eliminated, and may have been of a highly mythological nature."[198] He concluded that v. 51 supports Koester's theory about the relation between canonical Mark and Secret Mark, arguing that it is "unnatural" to argue, as others do, that "the clothing of the youth in the resurrection nar-rative was taken over from Mark 14:51f."[199] The redactor, "in purifying the Secret Gospel of Mark," did not omit 14:51-52 because he no longer saw the connection between the two passages about the young man with the linen cloth, but understood 14:51-52 to be reporting a historical event. Schenke himself concluded that the latter passage is "the true conclusion" to the story about the young man raised from the dead and taught the mystery of the kingdom of God by Jesus.[200] He suggested that both passages belong to "a separately circulating 'apocryphal' resurrection story" in which the young man, at one stage in the literary history of the story, "appears as a prototype and a symbol of all those who are to be initiated into the higher discipleship of Jesus."[201]

Marvin Meyer concluded that "[t]he key to understanding the significance of the word σινδών ('linen') in the *Secret Gospel of Mark* and Mark 14:51 may be found in . . . Mark 15:46 . . . the σινδών ['linen cloth' or 'linen garment'] of the νεανίσκος ['young man'] is quite the same as Jesus' shroud: the νεανίσκος participates in baptism as an experience of sharing in the suffering and death of Christ, and wears ritual clothing appropriate for such an experience."[202] Yet he disagrees, following Smith, with Scroggs and Groff that vv. 51-52 allude to baptism. Rather, the passage signifies "the forsaking of baptismal loyalties: the paradigmatic disciple is scandalized by the suffering of Jesus no less than the other disciples, and even abandons his sacramental clothes symbolizing his participation in Jesus' passion and death. The viability of discipleship itself seems in doubt as the tension builds in Mark 14."[203]

Scott Brown argued, against Koester, Schenke, and others, that "longer Mark," that is, the secret or spiritual Gospel alluded to by Clement in the letter fragment, is later than canonical Mark.[204] He argued

---

194 See "Excursus: The Secret Gospel of Mark" above after the commentary on 10:32b-34.

195 Text and trans. from Smith, *Clement of Alexandria,* 447, 452.

196 Scroggs and Groff, "Baptism in Mark," 547–48.

197 Koester, "History and Development," 41, 54–57; see also idem, *Gospels,* 277, 301.

198 Hans-Martin Schenke, "The Mystery of the Gospel of Mark," *Second Century* 4 (1984) 65–82; quotation from 69.

199 Ibid., 74.

200 Ibid., 77.

201 Ibid., 77–78.

202 Marvin W. Meyer, "The Youth in the *Secret Gospel of Mark,*" in Ron Cameron, ed., *The Apocryphal Jesus and Christian Origins, Semeia* 49 (1990) 129–53; quotation from 142.

203 Ibid., 145–46. In another study, Meyer concluded that "the prototype or 'historical model' of the Beloved Disciple may best be understood as the νεανίσκος ("young man") in Secret Mark and as Lazarus in John" ("The Youth in Secret Mark and the Beloved Disciple in John," in James E. Goehring et al., eds., *Gospel Origins and Christian Beginnings: In Honor of James M. Robinson* [Sonoma, CA: Polebridge, 1990] 94–105, esp. 104).

204 Scott G. Brown, *Mark's Other Gospel: Rethinking Morton Smith's Controversial Discovery* (Studies in Christianity and Judaism 15; Waterloo, ON: Wilfrid Laurier University Press/Canadian Corporation for Studies in Religion, 2005) 3–22, 105–20, 215–38; idem, "On the Composition History of the Longer ("Secret") Gospel of Mark," *JBL* 122 (2003) 89–110. See also idem, "The More Spiritual Gospel: Markan Literary

against Schenke that the incident in vv. 51-52 is unlikely to be a remnant of the story about the raising of a young man that follows 10:34 in the spiritual Gospel.[205] Rather, the incident in canonical Mark seems to be deliberately enigmatic and to evoke a series of questions on the part of the audience. Longer Mark is designed to offer answers to these questions. Brown argued that 14:51-52 was added to the canonical version of Mark by the evangelist as "a deliberate enigma designed to entice catechumens to inquire more deeply into the truths conveyed in this story through study of the more spiritual Gospel," after he had decided to produce a more esoteric version (longer Mark).[206]

Comment

■ **51-52** It is likely that this passage is a Markan insertion, but the question must be left open whether it was invented by the evangelist or results from his reformulation of an older tradition.[207] In either case, the question of the ingredients, prototypes, or sources of inspiration of the story must be distinguished from the issue of the meaning of the scene as part of Mark as a whole.

The lack of any attempt on the evangelist's part to explain how the young man happened to be at the scene of Jesus' arrest and especially why he was dressed in the way he was makes it unlikely that the brief narrative is a historical reminiscence.[208] Frederick Field proposed that περιβεβλημένος σινδόνα ἐπὶ γυμνοῦ be translated "having a sheet *wrapped about* his naked body" by analogy with a brief narrative concerning Crates' manner of dressing.[209] In the latter text, περιβάλλομαι and ἀμφίεσμαι ("to have put round oneself" or "to have on") are used interchangeably.[210] Galen recommended sleeping not naked (γυμνός) but wrapped in a sheet (περιβεβλημένος σινδόνα).[211]

Hatton's remarks on the comic effect of the incident are well taken, but they do not address the question of the sources or inspiration of the details of the scene.[212] Linnemann rightly concluded, following Georg Bertram, that flight after leaving behind one's garment is a motif typical of folklore.[213] To that extent, vv. 51-52 are similar to the story of Joseph escaping the advances of Potiphar's wife (Gen 39:6-20).[214]

There seems also to be a relationship between this passage and Amos 2:12-16:

Techniques in the Longer Gospel of Mark" (Ph.D. diss., University of Toronto, 1999) 58–62, 256–61, 297–98.

205 Brown, "On the Composition History," 107–8.

206 Ibid., 109 and n. 56. In his later work, Brown argued that Mark added the story about Jesus' raising the young man (after 10:34) and the incident about the young man fleeing naked (14:51-52) to canonical Mark at the same time (*Mark's Other Gospel*, 230, 233).

207 Yarbro Collins, *Beginning of the Gospel*, 107–8.

208 But see the interpretation of Neirynck, who argues that ἐπὶ γυμνοῦ ("over his naked body") was not part of the earliest recoverable reading of v. 51 and that σινδών ("linen cloth/garment") in vv. 51-52 refers to the young man's mantle ("La Fuite du jeune homme," 60–65). Cf. a text cited by Klostermann (153), Demosthenes *Or.* 21.216 (p. 583): "that I was startled by your clamour, Athenians, and let my cloak drop so that I was half-naked in my tunic, trying to get away from his grasp" (ὦ ἄνδρες Ἀθηναῖοι, φοβηθέντα τὸν ὑμέτερον θόρυβον θοἰμάτιον προέσθαι καὶ μικροῦ γυμνὸν ἐν τῷ χιτωνίσκῳ γενέσθαι, φεύγοντ᾽ ἐκεῖνον ἕλκοντά με); text and trans. from J. H. Vince, *Demosthenes* (LCL; Cambridge, MA: Harvard University Press;

London: Heinemann, 1935) 144–45. If the σινδών ("linen cloth" or "linen garment") in vv. 51-52 were the young man's mantle or cloak, one would expect v. 52 to read something like μικρὸς γυμνός ("half-naked"), rather than γυμνός ("naked").

209 Diogenes Laertius *Vit. Phil.* 6.90; Frederick Field, *Notes on the Translation of the New Testament: Being the Otium Norvicense (Pars Tertia)* (Cambridge: Cambridge University Press, 1899) 40; cited by Swete, 354. Field also refers to Acts 12:8 (ibid.).

210 For text and trans., see Hicks, *Diogenes Laertius*, 2:93–95.

211 Or, as Johann Jacob Wettstein translates, *Veste dormitoria* ("in sleeping attire") (*Novum Testamentum Graecum* [2 vols.; Amstelaedami: Ex Officina Dommeriana, 1751–52] 1:265; cited by Swete, 631). Wettstein also lists Amos 2:16 as a parallel (ibid.).

212 See "Excursus: Scholarship on 14:51-52" above.

213 Linnemann, *Studien zur Passionsgeschichte*, 51; Georg Bertram, *Die Leidensgeschichte Jesu und der Christuskult: Eine formgeschichtliche Untersuchung* (FRLANT 32; Göttingen: Vandenhoeck & Ruprecht, 1922) 51 n. 4.

214 See the interpretation of vv. 51-52 in the anonymous commentary on Mark discussed in the "Excursus: Scholarship on 14:51-52" above. Herman Waetjen,

And you gave wine to the consecrated ones to drink and you commanded the prophets saying "Do not prophesy." Therefore, see, I am rolling under you, in the way a wagon rolls along which is full of the stalk of wheat; and flight will fail the runner, and the mighty will surely not be master of his strength, and the warrior will surely not save his life, and the archer will surely not endure, and the swift of foot will surely not be preserved, even the cavalryman will surely not save his life, and he will find his heart in mighty deeds, the naked will be pursued[215] on that day,' says the Lord (καὶ ἐποτίζετε τοὺς ἡγιασμένους οἶνον καὶ τοῖς προφήταις ἐνετέλλεσθε λέγοντες Οὐ μὴ προφητεύσητε. διὰ τοῦτο ἰδοὺ ἐγὼ κυλίω ὑποκάτω ὑμῶν, ὃν τρόπον κυλίεται ἡ ἅμαξα ἡ γέμουσα καλάμης· καὶ ἀπολεῖται φυγὴ ἐκ δρομέως, καὶ ὁ κραταιὸς οὐ μὴ κρατήσῃ τῆς ἰσχύος αὐτοῦ, καὶ ὁ μαχητὴς οὐ μὴ σώσῃ τὴν ψυχὴν αὐτοῦ, καὶ ὁ τοξότης οὐ μὴ ὑποστῇ, καὶ ὁ ὀξὺς τοῖς ποσὶν αὐτοῦ οὐ μὴ διασωθῇ, οὐδὲ ὁ ἱππεὺς οὐ μὴ σώσῃ τὴν ψυχὴν αὐτοῦ, καὶ εὑρήσει τὴν καρδίαν αὐτοῦ ἐν δυναστείαις, ὁ γυμνὸς διώξεται[216] ἐν ἐκείνῃ τῇ ἡμέρᾳ, λέγει κύριος). (Amos 2:12-16 LXX)

Since the motif of the darkness at noon in 15:33 seems to evoke Amos 8:9, it is likely that there is an evocation of Amos 2:16 and its context here.[217]

In the context of Amos, read historically, the Hebrew version of this passage refers to "the immobility and helplessness of the entire Israelite army."[218] The text, however, has eschatological and cosmic overtones as well.[219] The connotations of the phrase "on that day" (ἐν ἐκείνῃ τῇ ἡμέρᾳ) make it likely that Mark evokes the passage in a reference to the woes of the end-time.[220] Such woes are not eschatological in the same way that the coming of the Son of Man in 13:24-27 is an eschatological event. They could, however, be connected with the idea that "the hour" in which the Son of Man is handed over (v. 41) is part of the eschatological scenario. The Hebrew expression translated "shall flee naked" means to "flee unarmed."[221] The evangelist may have assumed that γυμνός meant literally "naked" or may have interpreted the word that way deliberately for maximum effect.

With regard to the role of this passage in Mark as a whole, it does not seem prudent to base an interpretation on the fragmentary letter of Clement, as long as its authenticity is in doubt.[222] The best starting points for a contextual understanding are the hypotheses that the incident involving the young man running away naked is an instance of the general flight of the disciples and that it is part of the theme of their misunderstanding and refusal to accept the passion of Jesus and their duty to follow him in suffering that cannot honorably be avoided.

---

however, goes too far in arguing that there was a *Gattung* or genre of νεανίσκος stories, that Joseph is predominant among these ideal young men, and that there is a typological relationship between Joseph's humiliation and exaltation and Jesus' destiny in Mark ("The Ending of Mark and the Gospel's Shift in Eschatology," *Annual of the Swedish Theological Institute* 4 [1965] 114–31, esp. 118–21).

215 Some MSS support the reading φεύξεται ("will flee"); see the following note.

216 The Lucianic group of MSS (22-36-48-51-231-719-763), the Sahidic (Coptic) version, three early Christian writers and three later Greek translations support the reading φεύξεται ("will flee") (Joseph Ziegler, ed., *Duodecim prophetae* [Septuaginta: Vetus Testamentum Graecum Auctoritate Societas Litterarum Gottingensis 13; Göttingen: Vandenhoeck & Ruprecht, 1943] 185–86).

217 Contra Gnilka, 2:271. Neirynck argued that a direct influence of Amos 2:16 is improbable because the text of the LXX differs considerably from that of the MT; he preferred to take Mark 13:16 as the

model for vv. 51-52 ("La Fuite du jeune homme," 65 and n. 292).

218 Shalom M. Paul, *Amos: A Commentary on the Book of Amos* (Hermeneia; Minneapolis: Fortress, 1991) 95.

219 Francis I. Andersen and David Noel Freedman, *Amos: A New Translation with Introduction and Commentary* (AB 24A; New York/London: Doubleday, 1989) 343, 357.

220 J. M. Ross took the position that the incident is historical, but it was remembered and included by Mark "because it showed that the crucifixion was a 'day of the Lord' such as Amos had foretold" ("The Young Man Who Fled Naked: Mark 15:51-2," *Irish Biblical Studies* 13 [1991] 170–74; quotation from 173). Schenk also combined the hypothesis of historical reminiscence with that of allusion to scripture (*Der Passionsbericht nach Markus*, 210–12).

221 Paul, *Amos*, 98. Cf. 2 Macc 11:12, where γυμνοί ("naked") has the same meaning (Swete, 354).

222 See "Excursus: The Secret Gospel of Mark" above after the commentary on 10:32b-34.

Even though the words νεανίσκος ("young man") and περιβάλλειν ("to put on") occur only in 14:51 and 16:5 in Mark, the two passages are not similar enough otherwise to warrant the conclusion either that the two young men are identical or that they are part of the same symbolic complex of ideas.[223] More fruitful are the observations that both Jesus and the young man are "arrested" or "seized" (κρατεῖν) and that both are associated with a σινδών ("linen cloth" or "linen garment"), a term that occurs twice in vv. 51-52 and twice in 15:46 and only in those places in Mark.[224] Rather than representing Jesus, the paradigmatic disciple or the Christian initiate, the young man is best interpreted as one whose flight and abandonment of his linen cloth contrast dramatically with Jesus' obedience in submitting to being arrested, stripped, and crucified.[225]

---

223 They are linked only to the extent that the one in 14:51-52 contrasts with Jesus, whereas the one in 16:5 is comparable to Jesus. See the commentary on 16:5 below.

224 See the discussion of the work of Knox, Vanhoye, and especially Fleddermann in "Excursus: Scholarship on 14:51-52" above.

225 Cf. the discussion of Fleddermann's interpretation above. See also Borrell, *Peter's Denial*, 136.

53/ And they led Jesus away to the high priest, and all the chief priests and the elders and the scribes gathered.[a] 54/ And Peter followed him from a distance right into the courtyard of the high priest. And he was sitting with the servants and warming himself at the fire.

55/ Now the chief priests and the whole (Judean) council were looking for testimony against Jesus, in order that they might put him to death, and yet they could not find (any). 56/ For many were bearing false witness against him, and yet their testimony was not consistent. 57/ And some stood up and bore false witness against him, saying, 58/ "We heard him saying, 'I will destroy this sanctuary, which is made with hands, and in the course of three days I will build[b] another, which is not made with hands.'" 59/ And not even so was their testimony consistent. 60/ And the high priest stood up (and went) to the center and asked Jesus, saying, "Have you no response to what[c] these are testifying against you?" 61/ But he remained silent and did not answer anything. Again the high priest asked him and said to him, "Are you the messiah, the son of the Blessed?" 62/ Jesus then said, "I am,[d] and you will see the Son of Man sitting on the right of the Power and coming with the clouds of heaven." 63/ The high priest tore his clothes and said, "Why do we need witnesses any longer? 64/ You heard the blasphemy. How does it seem to you?" They all then condemned him as being deserving of death.

65/ And some began to spit on his face[e] and to punch him and to say to him, "Prophesy!"[f] and the servants got him with slaps.[g]

66/ And while Peter was below in the courtyard, one of the female servants of the high priest came 67/ and, when she saw Peter warming himself, she looked at him intently and said, "You also were with the man from Nazareth, Jesus." 68/ He then denied (the fact), saying, "I nei-ther know nor understand what

a   The longer reading with αὐτῷ ("to him"), attested by A B Ψ 2427 𝔐, is probably the result of a secondary expansion, like the longer reading of v. 52 (see above). The reading of C, πρὸς αὐτόν ("to him"), is either a stylistic variant of the former reading or an independent, analogous expansion. The reading of 1, αὐτοῦ ("of him"), is probably a mistake for αὐτῷ ("to him").

b   The earliest recoverable reading is probably οἰκοδομήσω ("I will build"), attested by the majority of the MSS. D it attest the reading ἀναστήσω ("I will raise"); this reading may have resulted from the influence of an interpretation of the saying in which the new sanctuary is a metaphor for the risen body of Jesus; cf. John 2:21.

c   The earliest recoverable reading is probably the indirect interrogative τί ("what"), attested by the majority of the MSS. The sentence is probably a single question (contra Taylor, ad loc.), with an ellipsis in which τί ("what") stands for πρὸς τί ("to what"). The readings ὅτι and ὅ τι ("that which"), attested by B P^(c vid) W Ψ 2427 are stylistic variants. Turner accepted ὅτι ("that which") as the earliest reading and interpreted it as an indirect interrogative ("Marcan Usage," 27 [1926] 59 [Elliott, *Language and Style*, 64]).

d   The trans. is based on the shorter reading, ἐγώ εἰμι ("I am"), attested by the majority of the MSS. Θ f^13 et al. attest the reading σὺ εἶπας ὅτι ἐγώ εἰμι ("You say that I am"). This reading seems to be a conflation of the earlier reading of Mark (see above) and that of the parallel in Matt 26:64.

e   The trans. is based on the reading attested by D (Θ) et al., ἐμπτύειν τῷ προσώπῳ αὐτοῦ ("to spit on his face") and on the shorter reading attested by D a f sy^s bo^(pt), which lacks the words καὶ περικαλύπτειν αὐτοῦ τὸ πρόσωπον ("and to blindfold him"). The earliest recoverable reading of the words spoken to Jesus later in this verse (see next note) lacks the indirect question τίς ἐστιν ὁ παίσας σε ("who it is who hit you"). This question is found in the parallel in Matt 26:68 with no variants. If Matthew had read the words about Jesus being blindfolded in Mark, it is unlikely that he would have omitted them, since, if Jesus could not see his tormentors at all, the question makes even more sense. Note also that Matthew reads ἐνέπτυσαν εἰς τὸ πρόσωπον αὐτοῦ ("they spit in his face"), which supports the reading of D (Θ) et al. It seems likely that Luke introduced the comment about Jesus being blindfolded and that it entered the text of Mark later under the influence of the parallel in Luke 22:64. See the discussions by Turner, "Western Readings," 10–11; and Taylor, ad loc.

f   The shortest reading, προφήτευσον ("Prophesy!"), is probably the earliest. It is attested by ℵ A B C D et al. This statement was then expanded in various ways. The longest reading, προφήτευσον ἡμῖν νῦν, you are saying." And he went out-side into the entrance hall and a cock crowed.[h] 69/ And the female servant saw him and began again to say to those who were stand-ing by, "This man is one of them." 70/ He then again denied (the fact). And again after a little while, those who were standing by said to Peter, "You really are one of them, for you are a Galilean."[i] 71/ He then began to curse and swear, "I do not know this man you are talking about." 72/ And immediately, for the sec-ond time,[j] a cock crowed. And Peter remembered the statement, how Jesus had said to him, "Before a cock crows twice, you will deny me three times."[k] And he set to[l] and wept.

$X\rho\iota\sigma\tau\acute{\epsilon}, \tau\acute{\iota}\varsigma \,\dot{\epsilon}\sigma\tau\iota\nu \,\dot{o} \,\pi\alpha\acute{\iota}\sigma\alpha\varsigma \,\sigma\epsilon$ ("Prophesy to us now, messiah, who it is who hit you"), is attested by W f^{13} pc. The same reading, except that $\nu\hat{\nu}\nu$ ("now") is lacking, is attested by N X (Δ) Θ f^{13} et al. The $\nu\hat{\nu}\nu$ ("now") is apparently an independent, early expansion. It is also attested by G f^1 pc (sy^s). The $\dot{\eta}\mu\hat{\iota}\nu$ ("to us") probably came into the text of Mark from the parallel in Matt 26:68. It is also attested for Mark by Ψ et al. The mocking address $X\rho\iota\sigma\tau\acute{\epsilon}$ ("messiah") and the indirect question $\tau\acute{\iota}\varsigma \,\dot{\epsilon}\sigma\tau\iota\nu \,\dot{o} \,\pi\alpha\acute{\iota}\sigma\alpha\varsigma \,\sigma\epsilon$ ("who it is who hit you") were also added to the text of Mark under the influence of the parallel in Matt 26:68. Cf. Metzger, *Textual Commentary*, 97. For an argument that $X\rho\iota\sigma\tau\acute{\epsilon}$ ("messiah") was added to the text of Mark to empha-size that it was the Christ who suffered, see Ehrman, *Orthodox Corruption*, 154.

g The trans. is based on the reading $\dot{\rho}\alpha\pi\acute{\iota}\sigma\mu\alpha\sigma\iota\nu$ $\alpha\dot{\upsilon}\tau\dot{o}\nu \,\ddot{\epsilon}\lambda\alpha\beta o\nu$ ("got him with slaps"), attested by $\aleph$ A B et al. The expression is colloquial. The variant $\ddot{\epsilon}\beta\alpha\lambda o\nu$, "(the servants) beat (him with slaps)," lit., "drove (him)," attested by E 33. et al., is either a stylis-tic variant or the result of an attempt to clarify or improve the style.

h $\aleph$ B L W et al. attest a reading in which the words $\kappa\alpha\grave{\iota}$ $\dot{\alpha}\lambda\acute{\epsilon}\kappa\tau\omega\rho \,\dot{\epsilon}\phi\acute{\omega}\nu\eta\sigma\epsilon\nu$ ("and a cock crowed") are lack-ing. Of these $\aleph$ W 579 also lack the word $\delta\acute{\iota}\varsigma$ ("twice") in 14:30 (see note d on the trans. of that verse above). $\aleph$ also lacks the words $\dot{\epsilon}\kappa \,\delta\epsilon\upsilon\tau\acute{\epsilon}\rho o\upsilon$ ("for the second time") and $\delta\acute{\iota}\varsigma$ ("twice") in 14:72. W reads the former, but not the latter. The reading including $\kappa\alpha\grave{\iota} \,\dot{\alpha}\lambda\acute{\epsilon}\kappa$-$\tau\omega\rho \,\dot{\epsilon}\phi\acute{\omega}\nu\eta\sigma\epsilon\nu$ ("and a cock crowed") in 14:68 is attested by A C D et al. In spite of the fact that it includes the narration of two cock-crows, C* lacks the word $\delta\acute{\iota}\varsigma$ ("twice") in 14:30 and the words $\dot{\epsilon}\kappa$ $\delta\epsilon\upsilon\tau\acute{\epsilon}\rho o\upsilon$ ("for the second time") and $\delta\acute{\iota}\varsigma$ ("twice") in 14:72. D also narrates the two cock-crows, although it lacks $\delta\acute{\iota}\varsigma$ ("twice") in 14:30 and 14:72; it does, how-ever, read $\dot{\epsilon}\kappa \,\delta\epsilon\upsilon\tau\acute{\epsilon}\rho o\upsilon$ ("for the second time") in v. 72. This state of affairs implies that $\aleph$ is the only major MS of Mark to be consistently revised to con-form to the other three Gospels, which narrate three denials of Peter, but speak of and narrate only one cock-crow.

Some other MSS of Mark were influenced only par-tially by the other accounts. See the discussion by Turner, "Marcan Usage," 26 (1925) 344–45 (Elliott, *Language and Style*, 60–61). Cf. also Taylor, ad loc.; Metzger, *Textual Commentary*, 97.

i The earliest recoverable reading is probably $\kappa\alpha\grave{\iota} \,\gamma\grave{\alpha}\rho$ $\Gamma\alpha\lambda\iota\lambda\alpha\hat{\iota}o\varsigma \,\epsilon\hat{\iota}$ ("for you are a Galilean"), attested by $\aleph$ B C D et al. The significance of this remark is unex-plained, and this lack gave rise to variants. W 2427 et al. simply omit these words. Matthew rewrote the remark so that it became self-explanatory: $\kappa\alpha\grave{\iota} \,\gamma\grave{\alpha}\rho \,\dot{\eta}$ $\lambda\alpha\lambda\iota\acute{\alpha} \,\sigma o\upsilon \,\delta\hat{\eta}\lambda\acute{o}\nu \,\sigma\epsilon \,\pi o\iota\epsilon\hat{\iota}$ ("for your speech gives you away"); Matt 26:73. The reading attested by A Θ f^{13} et al., καὶ γὰρ Γαλιλαῖος εἶ καὶ ἡ λαλιά σου ὁμοιάζει, "for you are a Galilean and your speech is like (the speech of the Galileans)," reflects the addition of an explanation, which was either an independent expansion or inspired by the parallel in Matthew. For a different opinion, see Taylor, ad loc.

j   ℵ C*vid L et al. lack the words ἐκ δευτέρου ("for the second time"). See note d on 14:30 and note n on v. 68 above; see also Metzger, *Textual Commentary*, 97–98.

k   The earliest recoverable reading is φωνῆσαι δὶς τρίς με ἀπαρνήσῃ ("crows twice, you will deny me three times"), attested by C2vid L et al. Many MSS change the

order of words in order to improve the style and euphony; see Metzger, *Textual Commentary*, 98. ℵ C*vid W et al., however, attest a reading which lacks δίς ("twice"), and D a attest a reading that lacks the words ὅτι πρὶν ἀλέκτορα φωνῆσαι δὶς τρίς με ἀπαρνήσῃ ("Before a cock crows twice, you will deny me three times"). On these omissions, see notes d on 14:30 and note n on 14:68 above.

l   The trans. is based on the reading ἐπιβαλών ("he set to," lit., "setting to" or "rushing"), attested by ℵ*2 A B C L W et al. The variant attested by D Θ 565 et al., ἤρξατο κλαίειν ("he began to weep") clarifies the sense. Cf. Metzger, *Textual Commentary*, 98.

Literary Context and Unity

The first clause of v. 53, "And they led Jesus away to the high priest" (καὶ ἀπήγαγον τὸν Ἰησοῦν πρὸς τὸν ἀρχιερέα), tightly links this unit with the arrest scene. It depicts the last of the three events foreshadowed in the narrator's aside about the plan that Judas and the agents of the chief priests had made: "The one whom I kiss is he; arrest him and lead him away under guard" (ὃν ἂν φιλήσω αὐτός ἐστιν, κρατήσατε αὐτὸν καὶ ἀπάγετε ἀσφαλῶς). Both clauses of v. 53 together introduce the account of Jesus' trial before the Judean council, which then continues in vv. 55-65.[1] Verse 54 introduces the story of Peter's denial, which is taken up again in v. 66 and completed in v. 72.[2]

This unit is one of the clearest examples of the Markan technique of inserting one story within another (intercalation).[3] According to Ernst von Dobschütz, the events of Peter's denial and Jesus' trial before the Judean

council occurred, or were believed to occur, simultaneously. It is difficult to depict that simultaneity in a narrative, which normally portrays one event after another. He thus explained this passage as an effective way of dealing with that problem.[4] James R. Edwards commented that Mark "opens the account of Jesus before the council with a tantalizing reference to Peter's standing 'in the courtyard of the high priest . . . warming himself by the fire' (14:54)."[5] The combination of the two stories, in his view, highlights the contrast between Peter's repudiation of Jesus, which is the first open denial of him, and Jesus' confession before the high priest, which is the first time that Jesus openly declares his identity.[6] Tom Shepherd noted the irony in the juxtaposition of Jesus' being mocked as a (false) prophet in v. 65 with the denial of Peter in vv. 66-72, which fulfills an earlier prophecy of Jesus (v. 30).[7] He also argued that there is dramatic irony in the contrasting characterizations of Jesus as innocent, though falsely accused, and of Peter as failing morally

---

1   Tom Shepherd pointed out and discussed the fact that this intercalation (see the next paragraph) is unusual in that the inner story is introduced before the outer story (*Markan Sandwich Stories*, 267, 278–80).

2   The pattern of the intercalation here (see next paragraph) is A1-B1-A2-B2 (Borrell, *Peter's Denial*, 47–48).

3   See "Narrative Unity" in the commentary on 3:20-35, "Literary Relationship between the Two Stories" in the commentary on 5:21-43, "The Literary Unity of 6:6b-30," "The Literary Relationship between the Two Stories" in the commentary on 11:12-25, and the commentary on 14:3-9 above. See also Kim E. Dewey, "Peter's Curse and Cursed Peter (Mark 14:53-54, 66-72)," in Kelber, *Passion*, 96–114, esp. 97 and n. 2.

4   Von Dobschütz, "Erzählerkunst," 197–98; he notes that Matthew follows Mark and also describes and evaluates Luke's and John's treatments of the same events. On the simultaneity of the two events, see Borrell, *Peter's Denial*, 48–49, and the literature cited there (48 n. 11).

5   Edwards, "Markan Sandwiches," 212; Shepherd described this effect as the opening of a gap "as to what will happen" to Peter (*Markan Sandwich Stories*, 277).

6   Edwards, "Markan Sandwiches," 212.

7   Shepherd, *Markan Sandwich Stories*, 283.

when questioned.[8] The insertion of the trial of Jesus into the account of the denial of Peter is a literary technique for portraying simultaneous events that has the effect, in this case, of making audiences aware of contrasts between the two stories and their main characters. The contrast between Jesus and Peter here reinforces the conclusion reached above that the arrest story creates a contrast between the young man who fled naked and Jesus, who did not evade his captors.

History of the Tradition and Historical Reliability

A consideration of Jesus' case by the chief priests is mentioned twice (14:53, 55-64; and 15:1). Mistreatment of Jesus by his captors is also mentioned twice (14:65 and 15:16-20a). As noted above, the insertion of the story of Jesus' trial before the council into the account of Peter's denial is a typically Markan literary technique. These observations suggest that Mark added the denial of Peter and the trial before the Judean council to the earlier passion narrative that he used as a source.[9] The remark that "all the chief priests and the elders and the scribes gathered" in v. 53b is probably a Markan addition, serving to introduce the trial scene.[10]

From the point of view of historical reconstruction, Mark's account of a trial before the Judean council is not based on any historically reliable tradition.[11] It develops

further an apologetic tendency in the pre-Markan passion narrative to depict the death of Jesus as a miscarriage of justice. Mark and his predecessors wanted to protect the communities of followers of Jesus by making the point that their founder was not a criminal.[12] Mark 14-15 makes a narrative argument that it was the chief priests who brought Jesus to the cross, making use of the power of the Roman prefect, because of their envy of his success with the people.[13] It is unlikely that the Judean council would have held a formal trial of Jesus, if his death were the goal, because only the Roman governor had the right to hear capital cases and the power to impose the death penalty.[14] The evangelist, perhaps following his source on this point, implicates the Jewish leaders in the death of Jesus because he wants to argue that the grounds for Jesus' death were primarily religious and not political in the narrow sense. For the same reason, he portrays Jesus as innocent in the eyes of the Romans.[15]

Historically speaking, Pilate alone had the responsibility for the execution of Jesus. It is likely, however, that the high priest co-operated with the Roman governor in dealing with Jesus. A likely scenario[16] is that Jesus was arrested by a troop of Jewish temple police and taken to the house of the high priest, Caiaphas.[17] There he was interrogated. Afterward, he was taken to Pilate with a report that he was stirring up the people. Pilate decided

---

8 Ibid., 284–86. Geert van Oyen rightly criticized Shepherd's thesis that the events in this unit take place one after the other and that the events of the two stories are not simultaneous ("Intercalation and Irony in the Gospel of Mark," in van Segbroeck et al., *Four Gospels 1992*, 2:949–74, esp. 967–71). He also has a good discussion of the relationship between story and discourse in this unit (ibid., 972–74).

9 Cf. Yarbro Collins, *Beginning of the Gospel*, 108. On the unit as Markan composition in its present form, see Donahue, *Are You the Christ?* 54–63; idem, "Temple, Trial, and Royal Christology (Mark 14:53-65)," in Kelber, *Passion*, 61–79, esp. 64, 78.

10 Schenke, *Der gekreuzigte Christus*, 32; Donahue, *Are You the Christ?* 63–67; idem, "Temple, Trial," 65.

11 Reinbold, *Der älteste Bericht*, 249–58, 308–9. Paul Winter argued that Mark's depiction of a meeting of the council in the residence of the high priest "conflicts with all the information available concerning the procedural activities of the senatorial assembly"

(*On the Trial of Jesus* [2nd ed.; Studia Judaica 1; Berlin/New York: de Gruyter, 1974] 28).

12 Reinbold, *Der älteste Bericht*, 197–98.

13 See esp. 15:10. Anselm C. Hagedorn and Jerome H. Neyrey have provided an illuminating cultural and literary contextualization of the comment about envy ("'It Was Out of Envy'"). Their conclusion that this Markan explanation of the reason for Jesus' death is historically reliable (55–56, esp. the abstract), however, is mistaken. See the discussion immediately below and the commentary on 15:9-10.

14 Awareness of this political and legal fact is reflected in the famous passage in Josephus that mentions Jesus (*Ant.* 18.3.3 §§63–64); see the discussion in Reinbold, *Der älteste Bericht*, 297–300, also 197–98, 306.

15 Cf. Reinbold, *Der älteste Bericht*, 198–99, 281.

16 Cf. ibid., 314.

17 On Caiaphas, see William Horbury, "The 'Caiaphas' Ossuaries and Joseph Caiaphas," *Palestine Exploration Quarterly* 126 (1994) 32–48; James C. VanderKam,

the matter in a *cognitio extra ordinem*, an informal legal proceeding often used by Roman governors in cases involving ordinary provincials.[18] He came to the conclusion that Jesus was deserving of death on account of *seditio* (sedition or revolt). So he had Jesus whipped and then handed him over to his soldiers for crucifixion.[19]

Although the story of the denial of Peter was probably not part of Mark's source, this account may be based on tradition.[20]

Comment

■ **53** The substance of v. 53a, "And they led Jesus away to the high priest," comes from Mark's passion source, although he may have reformulated the statement in his own style.[21] In the present context, this statement connects the account of Jesus' trial before the Judean council to the arrest scene. In addition to the link with Judas' statement in v. 44,[22] it is to be expected that "a crowd . . . from the chief priests" (v. 44), the arresting party, would take Jesus to *the* chief (or high) priest.

In Mark's source, an earlier form of 15:1 probably followed directly on v. 53a.[23] Verse 53b is a Markan addi-

tion, composed to introduce the account of the trial before the Judean council that he has composed, using older traditions.[24] This introduction accomplishes several things. First, it indicates that Jesus' first passion prediction is beginning to be fulfilled.[25] It also continues the narrative theme of the desire of these groups to destroy Jesus and their eventual conspiracy to accomplish that aim.[26] Finally, it anticipates the explicit introduction of "the whole (Judean) council" (ὅλος τὸ συνέδριον) in v. 55 and implies that it was made up of these three groups. This council was "the highest assembly and court" of the people of Judea. When the temple still stood, it was made up of "the traditional priestly and aristocratic leaders" who met in council "to rule, guide, supervise, and judge the Jewish community in its internal and external social relations."[27]

■ **54** In composing the account about Peter's denial, the evangelist made no attempt to reconcile the statement that Peter followed Jesus from a distance with the remark in v. 50 that all (the disciples) left him and fled. Peter "followed" (ἠκολούθησεν) Jesus here, just as Simon and Andrew (1:18) and Levi (2:14) did when Jesus called

From Joshua to Caiaphas: High Priests after the Exile (Minneapolis: Fortress; Assen, Netherlands: Van Gorcum, 2004) 426–36.

18 On the *cognitio extra ordinem*, see Adolf Berger, Barry Nicholas, and Andrew W. Lintott, "Law and Procedure, Roman," *OCD* 827–34, esp. 833; Adrian N. Sherwin-White, *Roman Society and Roman Law in the New Testament* (Oxford: Clarendon, 1963) 12–23; Richard A. Bauman, *Crime and Punishment in Ancient Rome* (London: Routledge, 1996) 5–6; see the index under *cognitio extraordinaria/extra ordinem* for further discussions.

19 Cf. the co-operation of Jewish leaders and the governor Albinus in the case of Jesus, son of Ananias, in the account of Josephus *Bell.* 6.5.3 §§300–305 (Reinbold, *Der älteste Bericht*, 314). Reinbold argued that one should not speak about the sentencing and execution of Jesus as judicial murder; if Pilate perceived that Jesus was a threat to public order, he was right, according to the laws of the time, to pass sentence on him (ibid., 310 n. 12).

20 Donahue, *Are You the Christ?* 67–68; Dewey, "Peter's Curse," 96–114. Reinbold concluded that the core of the tradition concerning the denial of Peter is probably historical; the exact course of events, however, is unknown (*Der älteste Bericht*, 317). Dewey, in con-

trast, argued that "no judgments can be made regarding the historicity" of the traditional denial story "or any of its parts" ("Peter's Curse," 105).

21 See "Literary Context and Unity" above. On v. 53a as a Markan redaction of a traditional statement, see Donahue, *Are You the Christ?* 63–64.

22 See "Literary Context and Unity" above.

23 Yarbro Collins, *Beginning of the Gospel*, 108; Schenke, *Der gekreuzigte Christus*, 31.

24 Donahue, *Are You the Christ?* 5–102 (66–67 on v. 53b); idem, "Temple, Trial," 61–79 (65 on v. 53b).

25 Mark 8:31 speaks about the same three groups, although the elders are mentioned first and the chief priests second. Cf. 10:33, which says that the Son of Man will be handed over to the chief priests and the scribes.

26 See 11:18 (the chief priests and the scribes); 12:12 (the chief priests and the scribes and the elders, as specified in 11:27); 14:1 (the chief priests and the scribes); 14:10 (the chief priests).

27 Anthony J. Saldarini, "Sanhedrin," *ABD* 5:975–80; quotations from 978, 979. This council usually met on the temple mount (ibid., 978). Mark, however, implies that it met at the high priest's house on this occasion (cf. vv. 54 and 66). This depiction is one of a number of reasons for doubting the historicity of

them.[28] Yet his following "from a distance" (ἀπὸ μακρόθεν) already portrays his fear and desire to preserve his life (cf. 8:35). Nevertheless, his following Jesus "right into the courtyard of the high priest" and sitting with the servants at their fire were risky things to do, as will become apparent when Peter's story is taken up again in v. 66.

■ **55-56** These verses do two things, in literary terms. First, they reintroduce the account of Jesus' trial after the digression in v. 54 that begins the story of Peter's denial.[29] Second, they summarize and prepare the audience for the more detailed account of the false witnesses in vv. 57-59.[30] The bald statement of v. 55 is an apologetic accusation that the members of the council departed from their proper judicial role in actively seeking testimony against Jesus and in perverting justice by deciding in advance what the outcome of the trial should be.[31] This attempt, however, proved to be futile. As v. 56 explains, although they found many willing to come forward to bear false witness against Jesus, the various testimonies were inconsistent. This statement implies that the council wished to preserve at least the semblance of justice.

■ **57-58** Although v. 56 has summarized the first part of the trial in advance, the actual narration of the judicial proceedings begins with vv. 57-58. The first stage of the trial involves testimony that Mark explicitly labels as

false: "We heard him saying 'I will destroy this sanctuary,[32] which is made with hands, and in the course of three days I will build another, which is not made with hands.'" This statement is in some tension with 13:2, where Jesus is portrayed as predicting the destruction of the temple.[33] A striking difference between the reported testimony and the saying of Jesus in 13:2 is that, in the latter case, Jesus is not portrayed as saying "I will destroy" the temple.[34] Rather, he uses two verbs in the passive voice, οὐ μὴ ἀφεθῇ ("there surely will not be left") and οὐ μὴ καταλυθῇ ("that will not be thrown down"). These formulations may be taken as instances of the "divine passive," signifying that God is the ultimate agent of the destruction of the temple. Such an interpretation fits with the description of the tribulation in 13:14-20.[35] The saying of 13:2 does not mention a new temple that will replace the one that is to be destroyed, but such an idea is culturally appropriate for the teaching of Jesus and may well be implied by the report here of the false testimony. Again, the falsity lies in the accusation that Jesus said, "I will build another." Traditions current at the time spoke about a final, definitive, or eschatological temple to be established by God.[36]

The cultural situation thus implies that the false witnesses are making a (possibly indirect, but still clear) accusation of blasphemy. The accusation that Jesus spoke about and aimed at a destruction of the temple that he

---

Mark's account; see "History of the Tradition and Historical Reliability" above.

28 All three passages use the same verb, ἀκολουθεῖν ("to follow"), in the aorist tense; cf. 3:7.

29 Borrell calls this technique "resumptive repetition" (German: *Wiederaufnahme*; French: *reprise*) (*Peter's Denial*, 51–52).

30 Donahue isolates v. 55 as performing these transitional functions and includes v. 56 with the following detailed account (*Are You the Christ?* 68).

31 This accusation is not historically reliable; see "History of the Tradition and Historical Reliability" above.

32 The term "sanctuary" translates ναός here, the "temple" in the narrower sense of the main building in the complex.

33 Donahue, *Are You the Christ?* 71–72. The saying of 13:2 apparently applies to the whole temple precinct (τὸ ἱερόν).

34 Note the emphatic ἐγώ ("I") at the beginning of Jesus' quoted speech in v. 58.

35 See the commentary on 13:14-20 above. It is also consistent with the OT and the Animal Apocalypse; see *1 Enoch* 90:28-29, where it is implied that God ("the owner of the sheep") removes or destroys Jerusalem and replaces it with a new Jerusalem (Tiller, *Animal Apocalypse*, 373–76); but note that here, as in Revelation 21–22, the new Jerusalem does not contain a temple. See also Gundry, 899.

36 *Jub.* 1:17, 27, 29; 11QT^a (11Q19) 29:6-10. 4QFlorilegium (4Q174) 1:1-7; see the commentary on 13:1-2 above. Note that 4QFlor 1:2-3 quotes Exod 15:17, which addresses the Lord and speaks about the sanctuary "which your hands have established" (כוננו ידיך). The LXX version reads ὃ ἡτοίμασαν αἱ χεῖρές σου ("which your hands have prepared"). Cf. Pesch, 2:435; Gundry, 899–900; Evans, 445–46. See also Adela Yarbro Collins, "The Dream of a New Jerusalem at Qumran," in James H. Charlesworth, ed., *The Bible and the Dead Sea Scrolls*, vol. 3: *The Scrolls and Christian Origins* (Waco, TX: Baylor University Press, 2006) 244–48.

himself would carry out would be an implicit charge of blasphemy, since the temple was God's house and was thus associated with the presence of God. The other accusation is analogous. The alleged claim of Jesus to be able to build a new temple in a short time ("in the course of three days")[37] implies that he will employ miraculous power in doing so. This claim, which contrasts with the idea of the divine origin of the final temple, could also be seen as blasphemous, since Jesus would be arrogating to himself an activity attributed to God.[38] The fact that the messiah was expected to be God's agent in carrying out the divine plan for the last days in contemporary apocalyptic literature prepares for the high priest's question in v. 61b. It does not, however, mitigate the implication of blasphemy in the saying of v. 58, since the members of the council do not accept Jesus' messiahship. Thus, his alleged claim to have the power and the authority to do these things would be unauthorized and thus an offense against God.[39]

If the saying of v. 58 is based on a saying of the historical Jesus, it is likely that it was a prophetic or apocalyptic saying that concerned the replacement of Herod's temple with a new, definitive temple to be established by divine power.[40] If the contrast between the two temples was expressed at that stage already with the terms χειροποίητος ("made with hands") and ἀχειροποίητος ("not made with hands"), or with expressions roughly equivalent to these in Hebrew or Aramaic, the contrast at that stage of the history of the tradition would be between human agency and divine agency. In the context of Mark as a whole, the saying may be interpreted as still having this significance.[41]

It could be argued that, at the Markan stage, the use of the term χειροποίητος ("made with hands") is a polemical indictment of the cult of the temple in Jerusalem as equivalent to idolatry.[42] The term occurs in Lev 26:1 LXX as a substantive with the sense of "(gods) made with hands" or "idols".[43] But such a connotation is plausible only if one overinterprets Jesus' actions in the temple in relation to the cursing of the fig tree.[44] Although such a reading of Mark is not well supported by the text, it does seem to be an aspect of the significance of the speech of Stephen in Acts. Stephen is accused by false witnesses of saying that Jesus will destroy the temple (6:13-14). In his defense, he tells how the wilderness generation asked Aaron to "make gods" for them (ποίησον ἡμῖν θεούς) (7:40). They made a golden calf, offered sacrifice to the idol and "rejoiced in the works of their hands" (εὐφραίνοντο ἐν τοῖς ἔργοις τῶν χειρῶν αὐτῶν) (7:41). In criticism of the temple built by Solomon, Stephen cites Isa 66:1-2 (7:49-50). In introducing this quotation, he says, "But the Most High does not dwell in (temples)[45] made by hands" (ἀλλ᾽ οὐχ ὁ ὕψιστος ἐν χειροποιήτοις κατοικεῖ) (7:48). If v. 48 alludes back

---

37   Cranfield, 442. The temporal designation in v. 58 is διὰ τριῶν ἡμερῶν ("in the course of three days"). In the passion predictions the temporal phrase is consistently μετὰ τρεῖς ἡμέρας ("after three days"); see the notes on the trans. and the commentary on 8:30-31, 9:31, and 10:32b-34 above. The similarity between the two phrases suggests that a short time is indicated in each case; cf. the phrase ἐν τρισὶν ἡμέραις ("in three days") in the paraphrase of v. 58 in 15:29. The differences make it unlikely that the implied reader is supposed to interpret v. 58 in light of the passion predictions and to conclude that the temple not made with hands is the resurrected body of Jesus (as in John 2:21) or the community of his followers (as in 1 Cor 3:16); with Pesch, 2:434; Gundry, 900–901; contra Gnilka, 2:280; Donahue and Harrington, 421–22.

38   For a discussion of the various interpretations of blasphemy in the cultural context of Mark in relation to the trial before the Judean council, see Yarbro Collins, "Charge of Blasphemy," 379–401.

39   Cf. Pesch, 2:435 n. 24.

40   See the commentary on 13:1-2 above.

41   Donahue and Harrington, 421.

42   Evans, 446.

43   The same usage occurs in Isa 46:6 LXX in the plural and in Wis 14:8 in the singular. The phrase εἴδωλα χειροποίητα ("idols made with hands") occurs in Bel and the Dragon 5 (Θ not OG); Sib. Or. 3.605–6. In Sib. Or. 3.618, the phrase ἔργα χειροποίητα ("works made with hands") occurs. In the latter context, such works are contrasted with "God the great immortal king" (trans. John J. Collins, in OTP 1:375). In Sib. Or. 4.28, people who reject all temples and "handmade images" (ἀγάλματα χειροποίητα) are praised (trans. ibid., 384); text from Aloisius Rzach, ed., ΧΡΗΣΜΟΙ ΣΙΒΥΛΛΙΑΚΟΙ: Oracula Sibyllina (Pragae/Vindobonae: F. Tempsky; Lipsiae: G. Freytag, 1891) 80, 93.

44   See "The Literary Relationship between the Two Stories" and the commentary on 11:12-25 above.

45   Cf. Acts 17:24-25, where the noun ναοί ("temples")

to v. 41, as seems likely, the implication is that having a material temple is a kind of idolatry.

Whereas the author and audience of *Jubilees* and the community at Qumran apparently expected a glorious temple built by God to be established in the earthly Jerusalem, Paul and the author of Hebrews used the term ἀχειροποίητος ("not made with hands") to speak of eternal entities in the heavenly world (2 Cor 5:1; Heb 9:11, 24). Heb 9:11 says that Christ has entered "through the greater and more perfect tabernacle, which is not made with hands, that is, not of this creation" (διὰ τῆς μείζονος καὶ τελειοτέρας σκηνῆς οὐ χειροποιήτου, τοῦτ᾽ ἔστιν οὐ ταύτης τῆς κτίσεως) (Heb 9:11).[46] This greater and more perfect tabernacle is "the heavenly or spiritual archetype of the earthly tabernacle" or "a more abstract 'heaven,' represented in its entirety by the σκηνή" ("tabernacle").[47] In 2 Cor 5:1, the οἰκοδομὴ ἐκ θεοῦ ("building from God") is either a spiritual body that God will grant each of the faithful when they die (or at least the special dead, like Paul) or the heavenly temple into which the faithful dead will be incorporated (cf. Rev 3:12).

Somewhat different from the biblical, Second Temple Jewish, and early Christian distinctions between that which is "made with hands" and that which is "not made with hands" is the form that distinction took in Hellenistic critiques of traditional cults. In the latter, what is "not made with hands" is the universe or cosmos as a whole.[48]

The most likely meaning for "the temple not made with hands" in v. 58 at the Markan stage is the apocalyptic notion of an eschatological, eternal temple of divine origin. The narrator of Mark calls the saying attributed to Jesus "false" primarily because of the emphatic first person singular form the saying takes in both its parts. Another factor may be that the author no longer expects

the appearance of such a temple on earth; calling the testimony "false" creates or recognizes some distance between the traditional saying behind the testimony and the views of the author and audiences of Mark.

■ **59** Although only one form of the testimony was cited in v. 58, the narrator informs the audience in v. 59 that even when only "some" (τινες) were actually allowed to come forward to testify, even these few did not agree in their testimony. Thus, v. 58 is presented as only one among two or more versions of the statements made by those few.

■ **60-61a** The second stage of the proceedings begins when the high priest, as the foremost among the members of the council acting as judges, rises up, goes to the center of the room and questions Jesus. Apparently, the high priest's question[49] is intended to evoke a comment from Jesus about the temple. Since he cannot be convicted on the basis of conflicting testimony, the high priest attempts to induce him to make a statement similar to what he is accused of saying, so that he could be convicted of blasphemy.[50] Jesus, however, "remained silent and did not answer anything" (ἐσιώπα καὶ οὐκ ἀπεκρίνατο οὐδέν).

The silence of Jesus here could be interpreted as another way in which the narrator (possibly representing the views of the author and audiences) creates distance from the two prophecies Jesus is alleged to have made.[51] Another possibility is that the silence is a tactic of self-defense.[52]

It is noteworthy, however, that this silence is unusual in comparison with texts of the same or related genres.[53] In the accounts of the noble deaths of Eleazar and the anonymous heroes in 2 and 4 Maccabees and of the trials of various leaders in the *Acts of the Alexandrians*, the individuals being threatened with execution or put on trial

---

is explicitly used with the adjective χειροποίητοι ("made with hands").

46 Trans. by Attridge (modified), *Hebrews*, 244.

47 Ibid., 247; cf. Heb 9:24.

48 Attridge, *Hebrews*, 222–23, 247.

49 See note c on the trans. of v. 60 above.

50 The scene is not historically reliable; see "History of the Tradition and Historical Reliability" above. The comments on v. 60 deal with the logic or rhetoric of the narrative.

51 See the closing comments on vv. 57-58 above.

52 William Sanger Campbell, "Engagement, Disengagement and Obstruction: Jesus' Defense Strategies in Mark's Trial and Execution Scenes (14.53–64; 15.1-39)," *JSNT* 26 (2004) 283–300, esp. 286–87.

53 See the section "Genre" of "Excursus: The Passion Narrative" in the commentary on 14:1-11 above.

give speeches explaining their values and reasons for resisting the tyrant. This contrast suggests that the silence of Jesus may be motivated by another factor, namely, the voice of David in the psalms of individual lament:

> But I, like a deaf man, did not hear,
> and (I am) like a mute who does not open his mouth,
> and I became like a man who does not hear
> and who has no refutations in his mouth
> (ἐγὼ δὲ ὡσεὶ κωφὸς οὐκ ἤκουον
> καὶ ὡσεὶ ἄλαλος οὐκ ἀνοίγων τὸ στόμα αὐτοῦ
> καὶ ἐγενόμην ὡσεὶ ἄνθρωπος οὐκ ἀκούων
> καὶ οὐκ ἔχων ἐν τῷ στόματι αὐτοῦ ἐλεγμούς).
> (Ps 37:14-15)[54]

That Psalm 37 LXX is evoked here is likely because the situation and language in the context of Mark are similar to elements in two other Psalms of individual lament:

> Do not hand me over to the intentions of those who oppress me,
> for unjust witnesses have risen up against me,
> and [their] injustice falsifies itself
> (μὴ παραδῷς με εἰς ψυχὰς θλιβόντων με,
> ὅτι ἐπανέστησάν μοι μάρτυρες ἄδικοι,
> καὶ ἐψεύσατο ἡ ἀδικία ἑαυτῇ). (Ps 26:12 LXX)[55]

> Unjust witnesses rose up and questioned me about things I know nothing about
> (ἀναστάντες μάρτυρες ἄδικοι ἃ οὐκ ἐγίνωσκον ἠρώτων με). (Ps 34:11 LXX)[56]

The implication is that what is happening to Jesus is in accordance with the scriptures. Just as the prototypical king, David, suffered, so must the messiah.

■ **61b-62** When Jesus does not respond to the high priest's question about the testimony against him, he asks Jesus directly, "Are you the messiah, the son of the Blessed?" (σὺ εἶ ὁ χριστὸς ὁ υἱὸς τοῦ εὐλογητοῦ;). The question whether Jesus is the messiah is related to the false testimony in the first stage of the proceedings of the Judean council against Jesus in the sense that the messiah could be expected to do the things mentioned in the accusation of v. 58 as the eschatological agent of God.[57] The high priest's use of the phrase ὁ εὐλογητός ("the Blessed one") may be intended to represent the Jewish custom of avoiding pronouncing the name of the deity. Although it is not a phrase commonly attested in Second Temple Jewish texts, it has an analogy in Philo's reference to God as ὁ πάντα μακάριος ("the All-blessed") (Som. 2.18 §130).[58] The expression may be related to formulas of benediction.[59]

Jesus responds to the high priest with a strongly affirmative statement, "I am,[60] and you will see the Son of Man sitting on the right of the Power and coming with the clouds of heaven" (ἐγώ εἰμι, καὶ ὄψεσθε τὸν υἱὸν τοῦ ἀνθρώπου ἐκ δεξιῶν καθήμενον τῆς δυνάμεως καὶ ἐρχόμενον μετὰ τῶν νεφελῶν τοῦ οὐρανοῦ). The Markan Jesus had already indirectly affirmed Peter's identification of Jesus as the messiah, there, as here, employing the term "Son of Man" as equivalent to "messiah."[61] In that context, however, he rebuked the disciples, signifying that this identity must be kept secret for the time being. Here Jesus explicitly affirms his identity as the messiah to outsiders, the high priest in particular, and the Judean council in general. In 8:27-31, it is implied that Jesus' identity must be kept secret temporarily, because the meaning of the term "messiah" must be reinterpreted in terms of the hiddenness of the heavenly messiah, the Son of Man, and of the necessity of his suffering. Here, when Jesus is on the verge of being

---

54 Ps 38:14-15 MT; 38:13-14 NRSV. Cf. Yarbro Collins, "Genre," 15, 26 n. 93.

55 Ps 27:12 MT and NRSV. Cf. Donahue, *Are You the Christ?* 75.

56 Ps 35:11 MT and NRSV. Cf. Donahue, *Are You the Christ?* 75.

57 See the commentary on vv. 57-58 above.

58 Text and trans. from Colson and Whitaker, *Philo*, 5:500–501.

59 *1 Enoch* 77:1; 2 Cor 11:31; Rom 1:25; 9:5; Allen, 180; Str-B, 2:51; Klostermann, 156.

60 See note d on the trans. of v. 62 above. The statement ἐγώ εἰμι ("I am") here is not a claim to divinity, but an affirmation that "I am the messiah, the son of the Blessed." The same phrase in 13:6 is also unlikely to represent a divine claim; see the commentary on 13:5-6 above.

61 See the commentary on 8:30-31 above.

"rejected by the elders and the chief priests and the scribes," as he predicted in 8:31, his affirmation is a preview of his exaltation and return as Son of Man.[62]

The prediction that the members of the council will see the Son of Man "sitting on the right of the Power" (ἐκ δεξιῶν καθήμενον τῆς δυνάμεως) evokes Ps 110:1 (109:1 LXX), one of the two psalms evoked in 12:36.[63] There Jesus raised the question how the scribes could say that the messiah is David's son, if David addressed him as "Lord" (κύριος). The question received no explicit answer at that time. As argued above, the question is part of the reinterpretation of the contemporary notion of the "Davidic messiah" or "the messiah of Israel" in Mark as a whole.[64] Two important aspects of that reinterpretation are the idea that the messiah must suffer and that, after his suffering and death, he will be exalted to a heavenly state. Jesus' reply to the high priest is part of the narrative reinterpretation of the "messiah" in Mark. The high priest asks whether Jesus is the messiah. In a context in which Jesus is about to suffer, he refers to the messiah as "Son of Man" and describes his future exalted state in terms of Ps 110:1.

Jesus' reply also includes the affirmation that he, as the messiah-Son of Man, will return, "coming with the clouds of heaven" (ἐρχόμενον μετὰ τῶν νεφελῶν τοῦ οὐρανοῦ). Not only will he be exalted, but he will return in the glorious state of the "one like a son of man" in Dan 7:13.[65] The statement "you will see" (ὄψεσθε) does not necessarily imply that Jesus will return as judge to punish his enemies. Note that chapter 13 does not portray Jesus executing such a judgment when he returns as Son of Man (13:24-27). Rather, the activity he comes to carry out is the gathering of the elect. The force of "you will see" is that Jesus will be vindicated in their eyes.

■ **63-64** In biblical and Second Temple literature, the tearing of one's clothes is first and foremost a sign of grief.[66] The same gesture with the same significance also occurs in Greek and Latin literature, inscriptions, and papyri.[67] According to Lev 10:6 and 21:10, the chief priests or the high priest were commanded not to tear their garments as a sign of grief or mourning at the death of even very close relatives. They apparently did tear their garments, or were thought to do so, in cases in which the honor of God was threatened.[68] The high priest's tearing of his clothes in v. 63a thus prepares for his speech in vv. 63b-64a.

The opening question and the first statement of the high priest, "Why do we need witnesses any longer? You heard the blasphemy," supports the inference drawn above, that the false witnesses were accusing Jesus of blasphemy.[69] Witnesses are no longer needed to convict Jesus of blasphemy because he himself has blasphemed in the hearing of the judges. These remarks make clear that the high priest is interpreting the statement of Jesus in 14:62 as blasphemous.[70]

According to the Mishnah (m. Sanh 7.5), Jesus' statement would not be blasphemous, since blasphemy is defined as pronouncing the name of God (יהוה).[71] In his statement, Jesus, like the high priest, used a circumlocution instead of the divine name or even the Greek

62 Harry L. Chronis defines Jesus' statement to the high priest as a "formal disclosure of his identity" and the statement of the centurion in 15:39 as the "material disclosure" ("To Reveal and To Conceal: A Literary-Critical Perspective on 'the Son of Man' in Mark," NTS 51 [2005] 459–81; quotations from 473 and n. 44).

63 See the commentary on 12:35-37 above. On the distinctiveness of Mark's use the word δύναμις ("Power") here, see Raymond E. Brown, The Death of the Messiah: From Gethsemane to the Grave; A Commentary on the Passion Narratives in the Four Gospels (2 vols.; ABRL; New York/London: Doubleday, 1994) 1:496–97.

64 For a discussion of contemporary messianic expectations, see the section of the introduction entitled "Jesus as Messiah" above.

65 Martin Albl concluded, agreeing with Norman Perrin, that v. 62 conflates Zech 12:10; Dan 7:13; and Ps 110 (109):1 ("And Scripture Cannot Be Broken," 258). He thought it likely that this conflation was borrowed by the evangelist from a written testimony collection (ibid.).

66 Gen 37:29; Jdt 14:19; Esth 4:1; Philo Jos. 37 §217; Josephus Bell. 2.15.4 §322; BAGD, s.v. δια(ρ)ρήγνυμι/διαρήσσω.

67 Klostermann, 156; BAGD, s.v., δια(ρ)ρήγνυμι/διαρήσσω.

68 Josephus Bell. 2.15.4 §322; Klostermann, 156. Cf. Str-B, 1:1007–8.

69 See the commentary on vv. 57-58 above.

70 Yarbro Collins, "Charge of Blasphemy," 381, 398.

71 The passage concerns the punishment of "the blasphemer" (המגדף); text from Blackman, Mishnayoth, vol. 4: Order Nezikin, 269; see also Yarbro Collins, "Charge of Blasphemy," 381, 400.

word "God" (ὁ θεός).[72] He has clearly not blasphemed according to the regulations of the Mishnah. Such a definition of blasphemy was indeed current in the first century CE.,[73] but this definition was by no means the only or official one. The chief priests in this passage are portrayed as holding to a broader definition.

Josephus provides evidence that the Pharisees were more lenient in judgments than the Sadducees. It is likely that the Pharisees limited the definition of blasphemy, in a way similar to the later Mishnah cited above, in order to limit or even eliminate the use of the death penalty. Josephus says that the Sadducees, on the contrary, were "more cruel than any of the other Jews . . . when they sit in judgment" (*Ant.* 20.9.1 §199).[74] In the same context, Josephus says that the high priest, the younger Ananus, who executed James the brother of Jesus, was a Sadducee (ibid.).[75] Although one cannot say that all Sadducees were priests or that all priests were Sadducees, many scholars associate the two groups.[76] So, although the account of the trial of Jesus before the Judean council is not historically reliable,[77] it has verisimilitude in assigning to the chief priests a broad understanding of blasphemy and in holding to the death penalty for that offense.

Evidence for the currency of a broader understanding of blasphemy in the late Second Temple period is provided by Philo.[78] Although he uses the word-group βλασφημεῖν ("to insult" or "to blaspheme") in other ways as well, on two occasions he uses it to mean a spe-cific kind of insult to God, namely, speech that compromises the Jewish affirmation that only the God of Israel is divine. Specifically, this insult involves a human being claiming a greater degree of authority and power than he has a right to do and, directly or indirectly, claiming divine status for himself.[79]

Jesus' saying in v. 62, from the point of view of the high priest and the other members of the council as characters in the narrative, fits the broader definition of blasphemy attested by Philo. In this saying, Jesus claims to be a messiah of the heavenly type, who will be exalted to the right hand of God (Ps 110:1). Being seated at the right hand of God implies being equal to God, at least in terms of authority and power. The allusion to Dan 7:13 reinforces the heavenly messianic claim. The "coming on the clouds" has a dual role. On the one hand, this motif, typical of divine beings, signifies the universal power that Jesus as messiah will have. On the other, the statement that the members of the council "will see" him applies especially to his "coming on the clouds" in a public manifestation of his messianic power and glory.[80]

The high priest closes his speech in vv. 63b–64a with another question, "How does it seem to you?" He had already abandoned the position of neutrality appropriate for a chief justice by declaring Jesus guilty of blasphemy in advance. Not surprisingly, the other members of the council (πάντες) affirmed his judgment by condemning Jesus "as deserving of death" (v. 64b).[81] The narrative presupposes that the penalty for blasphemy was death.[82]

---

72 The high priest uses the circumlocution "the Blessed" (ὁ εὐλογητός) (v. 61); Jesus, "the Power" (ἡ δύναμις) (v. 62). In the parallel passage, Matthew portrays the high priest as putting Jesus under oath "by the living God" (κατὰ τοῦ θεοῦ τοῦ ζῶντος); he also uses the expression "son of God" (ὁ υἱὸς θεοῦ) in the question of the high priest, but follows Mark in using "the Power" in the reply of Jesus (Matt 26:63-64).

73 Josephus *Ant.* 4.8.6 §202; Yarbro Collins, "Charge of Blasphemy," 392.

74 Trans. (modified) from Louis Feldman, in Thackeray, *Josephus*, 9:495. See also *Ant.* 13.10.6 §294. For more detailed discussion, see Yarbro Collins, "Charge of Blasphemy," 393–94.

75 This event took place in 62 CE.

76 Gary G. Porton, "Sadducees," *ABD* 5:892–95, esp. 894.

77 See "History of the Tradition and Historical Reliability" above.

78 Philo *Leg. Gaj.* 46 §368; *Som.* 2.18 §§130–32.

79 Yarbro Collins, "Charge of Blasphemy," 386–90, 395.

80 Ibid., 398–401.

81 That they are portrayed as condemning Jesus as "deserving of death" (κατέκριναν αὐτὸν ἔνοχον εἶναι θανάτου) rather than simply as condemning him to death (κατέκριναν αὐτὸν θανάτῳ) (cf. 10:33) may signify a belated recognition that the council had no authority over capital cases. Only the Roman governor could impose and carry out the death sentence. See "History of the Tradition and Historical Reliability" above; cf. Klostermann, 156.

82 It is likely that both Pharisees and Sadducees agreed on this point; where they differed may have been in the definition of blasphemy. See the discussion above. See also Richard Bauckham, "For What Offense Was James Put to Death?" in Bruce Chilton and Craig A. Evans, eds., *James the Just and Christian*

The narrative of Jesus' trial before the Judean council is ironic in the sense that what is blasphemy from the point of view of the council is true from the perspective of the audiences of Mark. For them, the first part of 14:62 had already been fulfilled in the resurrection and exaltation of Jesus to the right hand of God. The evangelist advocates the acceptance of the second part as soon to be fulfilled (Mark 9:1; 13:30).[83]

■ **65** This verse portrays some (τινες) of the members of the council as lapsing into behavior that characterizes them as a kind of lynch mob, abusing the prisoner. They spit on his face, punch him, and demand that he prophesy.[84] Then even the servants (οἱ ὑπηρέται), presumably of the high priest (cf. v. 54), join in and "get him with slaps."[85] The command to prophesy may be equivalent to "Prophesy again about the temple!"[86]

This scene has in common with the mocking of Jesus by soldiers in 15:16-20 the acts of spitting at Jesus[87] and of striking him.[88] In the later scene, the soldiers' activity in 15:17-19 is explicitly described in 15:20 as mocking (ἐμπαίζειν). The command of "some" in v. 65 that Jesus prophesy may be understood as mocking, even if it is not explicitly so characterized.

As was noted above, the third passion prediction summarizes the passion narrative and prepares the audience for it.[89] In that prediction, it is said that, after the chief priests and the scribes condemn Jesus to death, they will hand him over to the nations; only then will the mocking and spitting upon him take place (10:33-34). Thus the fulfillment of the relevant part of the third passion prediction of Jesus is narrated in 15:16-20, not in 14:65.[90]

The brief scene of 14:65 thus seems to be a doublet that Mark has constructed in order to make the two trial scenes analogous.[91] Both scenes evoke a passage in Isaiah spoken by the servant of the Lord:

My back I gave to strokes with a whip, and my cheeks to slaps, and my face I did not turn away from the disgrace of being spit upon (τὸν νῶτόν μου δέδωκα εἰς μάστιγας, τὰς δὲ σιαγόνας μου εἰς ῥαπίσματα, τὸ δὲ πρόσωπόν μου οὐκ ἀπέστρεψα ἀπὸ αἰσχύνης ἐμπτυσμάτων). (Isa 50:6 LXX)[92]

The motif of giving his back to strokes with a whip is evoked by the statement in 15:15 that Pilate had Jesus whipped before having him crucified. The scene with the soldiers apparently takes place between the whipping and the crucifixion. The ῥαπίσματα ("slaps" or "blows") of the text from Isaiah are evoked by the slaps (ῥαπίσματα) with which the servants "get" (ἔλαβον) Jesus in 14:65. The disgrace of being spit upon is evoked in 14:65 and 15:19. The association of the word πρόσωπον ("face") with spitting occurs in both Isa 50:6 LXX and 14:65.[93]

■ **66-67** The scene shifts in v. 66 to Peter, who is also at the high priest's house, below in the courtyard (κάτω ἐν τῇ αὐλῇ).[94] A female servant (μία[95] τῶν παιδισκῶν) of the high priest comes along and sees Peter warming himself (at the fire) (v. 67). This description of Peter's activity resumes the depiction of him in v. 54 and thus deliberately takes up his story again. When she noticed him, "she looked at him intently and said, 'You also were

---

Origins (NovTSup 98; Leiden: Brill, 1999) 199–232, esp. 223; Yarbro Collins, "Charge of Blasphemy," 393–94.

83   Yarbro Collins, "Charge of Blasphemy," 381, 401.

84   See notes e, f, and g on the trans. of v. 65 above.

85   The expression is unusual, although not entirely unparalleled. Swete (362) refers to a Greek papyrus of the first cent. CE that contains the phrase (αὐτὸν) κονδύλοις ἔλαβεν ("he gave him a thrashing," lit., "he got him with knuckles"); for this wording of the phrase and a reference to the papyrus, see Moulton-Milligan, s.v. ῥάπισμα. Some scholars have considered it to be a Latinism; BDF §5 (3b), 198 (3). Swete translates the Markan expression with "they caught Him with blows" (362).

86   Klostermann, 157.

87   Cf. 14:65a with 15:19b.

88   In 14:65, two different groups strike Jesus with their hands; in 15:19a, the soldiers strike him on the head with a reed.

89   See the commentary on 10:32b-34 above.

90   Klostermann, 156.

91   Loisy, 436; Klostermann, 157.

92   Loisy, 437.

93   Donahue, *Are You the Christ?* 98. Donahue concluded that the mocking scene of 14:65 is based on an element of tradition (ibid.).

94   The repetition of elements from v. 54 in v. 66 is resumptive (Borrell, *Peter's Denial*, 52).

95   Here μία ("a," lit., "one") is equivalent to τις (the indefinite article); this usage is acceptable Greek; BAGD, s.v. εἷς, 3.

with the man from Nazareth, Jesus.'"[96] This portrayal suggests that she had seen him before and recognized him.

■ **68** Peter's response is his first denial of Jesus: "I neither know nor understand what you are saying."[97] It was noted above that Peter's following Jesus "at a distance" (ἀπὸ μακρόθεν) seems to be a narrative way of depicting his fear.[98] Here his fear is portrayed by the narration of his movement away from the servant in order to avoid her and her remarks: "And he went outside (the boundaries of the courtyard) into the entrance hall" (καὶ ἐξῆλθεν ἔξω εἰς τὸ προαύλιον). Peter has taken one step, both physically and metaphorically, away from Jesus. He has not yet left the house of the high priest, but he is on the verge of doing so. At that moment, a cock crowed.[99] Both the denial and the crowing of the cock signify to the audiences that the prediction made by Jesus in v. 30 is beginning to be fulfilled.[100]

■ **69-70a** Although he has moved away from the presence of the female servant, she can still see him, and he can still hear her. Perhaps his fearful movement has confirmed her identification of him as an associate of Jesus. In any case, she repeats that identification (πάλιν) by telling those standing by, "This man is one of them." The narrator informs the audience that Peter denied what she had said a second time (πάλιν).

■ **70b-71** After a short while, Peter is identified a third time (πάλιν), in this instance by the bystanders. They are convinced that he is "one of them" because they recognize him as a Galilean (v. 70b). The text does not inform the audiences how those standing by could determine that he was from Galilee. Lohmeyer inferred from this passage that, from the point of view of Mark, "Galilean" was equivalent to "Christian," but this hypothesis is unlikely.[101] Matthew fills this gap by having those

standing there say "for your speech reveals (who) you (are)" (καὶ γὰρ ἡ λαλιά σου δῆλόν σε ποίει). John's version of the story has one of the slaves of the high priest say to Peter, "Did I not see you in the garden with him?" (Matt 26:73; John 18:26).

There is a dramatic escalation in Peter's three denials. The first time, he simply says, in effect, I don't know what you are talking about. The second time, the narrator just informs the audiences that Peter denied what the female servant had said. This third time, the denial is strong and unmistakable (v. 71). Part of it is quoted in direct speech: "I do not know this man you are talking about."[102] The narrator introduces this quotation by saying, "He then began to curse and swear" (ὁ δὲ ἤρξατο ἀναθεματίζειν καὶ ὀμνύναι). The implication is that Peter put himself under a curse, if what he said was not true.[103] In addition, he took an oath that what he said was true; in other words, he called upon God as a witness to his truthfulness.[104] The only other occasion on which a character in Mark takes an oath is the time Herod Antipas[105] swore to his daughter that he would give her anything she asked for.[106] That foolish oath led to an evil deed, the unjust execution of John the Baptist. Here the oath itself is an evil deed, in that Peter calls on God to witness to the truth of a false statement. Such an oath also involved calling divine punishment down upon oneself if one is swearing falsely.

This is surely the lowest point in the development of the theme of the failure of the disciples in Mark. This failure has been interpreted in a wide variety of ways. Theodore Weeden argued that "it is the denial of Peter that underscores the complete and utter rejection of Jesus and [the type of messiahship to which he committed himself] by the disciples."[107] He interprets the denial in terms of Peter's "initial rebuke of Jesus' christology

---

96 The epithet Ναζαρηνός ("coming from Nazareth," "Nazarene," or "inhabitant of Nazareth") always occurs in Mark with the name Ἰησοῦς ("Jesus"). In the other three occurrences, 1:24; 10:47; 16:6, the name consistently precedes the epithet, whereas here it follows it.

97 According to BDF §445 (2), the construction in א B D L W, namely, οὔτε . . . οὔτε ("neither . . . nor") is incorrect; the construction of A K M is proper: οὐκ . . . οὐδέ ("not . . . or").

98 See the commentary on v. 54 above.

99 See note h on the trans. of v. 68 above.

100 See the commentary on v. 30 above.

101 See the discussion of Lohmeyer's views in "Excursus: Galilee and Jerusalem in Mark" in the commentary on vv. 26-31 above.

102 This statement is ironic in the sense that the most important, leading disciple of Jesus claims that he does not know him (Fowler, *Let the Reader Understand*, 159).

103 BAGD, s.v. ἀναθεματίζω.

104 Ibid., s.v. ὀμνύω.

105 See the commentary on 6:14-16 above.

106 See the commentary on 6:22-23 above.

(8:31)." The denial restates the rebuke "in even more hardened and final terms. He is true to his character. . . . He joins the Sanhedrin (14:53 ff.) in rejecting Jesus." The tears of v. 72 are appropriate because, since he has been ashamed of Jesus, the Son of Man will also be ashamed of him in the future.[108] This interpretation fits with Weeden's thesis that "Mark is assiduously involved in a vendetta against the disciples. He is intent on totally discrediting them. . . . As the coup de grace, Mark closes his Gospel without rehabilitating the disciples."[109] This thesis is part of Weeden's overall interpretation of Mark as a response to and an attack on a divine-man Christology. He discredits the disciples because his "opponents" claim the disciples as the authority for their position.[110]

Under the influence of Weeden, Werner Kelber interpreted Mark in an analogous way. He concluded, "Far from experiencing a change of heart, the disciples, under the leadership of Peter, play out their roles of outsiders to the bitter end. . . . Peter, the last hope, denies Jesus while the latter makes his fateful confession before the high priest (14:53-72).[111] Because the women fail to deliver the message given them by the young man at the tomb, the disciples "never learn that the signal has been given for the reunion with the resurrected one. They are thereby effectively eliminated as apostolic representatives of the risen Lord."[112] The interweaving of the trial of Jesus and the denial of Peter results in "an incomparable dramatization of the depth of Peter's tragedy. This last time the leader of the Twelve features in the gospel's story, he is placed in irreconcilable opposition to Jesus." Jesus gives his life by his confession, but Peter tries to save his by his denials.[113] "Broken hearted and weeping, Peter is phased out of the gospel story."[114]

Quite different interpretations have been offered by Robert C. Tannehill and Norman R. Petersen. Tannehill also recognizes that Peter, who follows Jesus from afar, is the last hope—in the narrative of chapter 14 at least—for

faithful discipleship. Likewise, he contrasts Peter's denial with Jesus' "fearless disclosure (14:62),"[115] but he notes that chapter 13 presupposes "a continuing role for the disciples beyond the disaster of chapter 14."[116] Further, he argues, "The construction of the denial narrative itself encourages both sympathetic awareness of Peter's plight, as he struggles to escape the persistent accusations, and full recognition of the horrible thing that he is doing. . . . The composition of the story promotes both the reader's sympathetic involvement and an emphatically negative evaluation of Peter's act."[117] He concludes that in one sense, the story of the disciples is over, since they do not appear again in the narrative. In another sense, "their story is *not* over" because there "are features of the story which hold the future open."[118]

Petersen notes that the disciples are absent "from the narrative after 14:72, leaving suspended the question of when they would overcome their ignorance. Yet intruding into this suspense-full question is now the suspense attending the one unfulfilled prediction of Jesus going before the disciples to Galilee after his resurrection."[119] Since so many of Jesus' predictions have been fulfilled "in plotted time," that is, in the narrative message of Mark, the audiences "cannot doubt that all of those yet to be fulfilled by the end of plotted time will be fulfilled in story time," that is, in the "narrative world" that the text signifies or to which it refers.[120] Thus, it is at the implied meeting in Galilee that the disciples' ignorance will be overcome.

Various features of Mark's narrative support the interpretations of Tannehill and Petersen, not least the conclusion of the account of Peter's denial.

■ **72** Immediately after Peter's vehement and shocking third denial, with a curse and an oath, a cock crowed for the second time.[121] Although Peter did not react to the first crowing of the cock (v. 68), the second cock-crow seems to shock him into recognition of the evil thing

107 Weeden, *Traditions in Conflict*, 38–39.
108 Ibid., 69.
109 Ibid., 50–51.
110 Ibid., 162.
111 Kelber, *Gospel*, 128.
112 Ibid., 129.
113 Kelber, *Mark's Story*, 79.
114 Ibid., 80.
115 Tannehill, "Disciples in Mark," 403.

116 Ibid., 402.
117 Ibid., 403.
118 Emphasis his; he cites in this connection 14:28 and 16:7 (ibid.).
119 Petersen, *Literary Criticism*, 76.
120 Ibid., 77; cf. 39, 43, 47. See also Borrell, *Peter's Denial*, 42–43.
121 See notes j and k on the trans. of v. 72 above.

that he has done: he "remembered" ($\dot{\alpha}\nu\epsilon\mu\nu\dot{\eta}\sigma\vartheta\eta$) the prediction that Jesus had made on the Mount of Olives after the last supper (v. 30).

The "explicit citation" of Jesus' earlier words (v. 30) here (v. 72b) immediately following the narration of the events (vv. 66-72a) is the third element in a pattern of "forecast, enactment, report."[122]

The participle $\dot{\epsilon}\pi\iota\beta\alpha\lambda\dot{\omega}\nu$ is a case of the intransitive (reflexive) use of a transitive verb of motion.[123] The textual variant $\ddot{\eta}\rho\xi\alpha\tau o \ \kappa\lambda\alpha\dot{\iota}\epsilon\iota\nu$ ("he began to weep") captures the sense,[124] but the earlier reading "set to" is more vivid.[125] The implication is that as soon as Peter remembered Jesus' prediction he wept as vehemently as he had denied Jesus a short time before.

As Tannehill suggested, Peter's weeping creates empathy in the audiences of Mark.[126] The evocation of this empathetic response is related to the features of the scene in Gethsemane that encourage identification with the disciples, especially Simon Peter.[127] The inability to resist the power of sleep in that scene may be interpreted as a quintessentially human weakness. Similarly here,

Peter's fear and desire to preserve his life are reactions to a dangerous situation with which most members of the audiences could identify. In both passages, Peter is a negative example, but one that encourages others to try to do better than he was able to do on that occasion. The portrayal of Peter as weeping suggests that he also will try to do better in the future. Mark implies, however, that human effort is insufficient. The ability to endure and to let go of the desire to save one's life is granted on the occasion of the appearance of the risen Jesus to the disciples in Galilee.[128] As Petersen argued, although this event is not narrated, the plot of Mark implies strongly that it did take place.[129]

The major rhetorical effect of 14:53-72 is the contrast between Jesus and Peter as characters in the narrative. This narrative contrast is related to the more discursive rhetorical technique of the $\sigma\dot{\upsilon}\gamma\kappa\rho\iota\sigma\iota\varsigma$ ("comparison") of two famous persons.[130] Jesus accepts his death, whereas Peter seeks to save his life. Jesus manifests courage, or at least endurance, and loyalty to the will of God, whereas Peter is weak and fearful.[131]

---

122 Borrell, *Peter's Denial*, 82.

123 BDF §308.

124 Ibid.; Klostermann, 157.

125 Allen, 181. Allen's hypothesis of the mistranslation of an Aramaic word is unnecessary.

126 See the commentary on vv. 70b-71 above. Such empathy played a major role in the history of the interpretation of this passage; see Robert W. Herron, Jr., *Mark's Account of Peter's Denial of Jesus: A History of Its Interpretation* (Lanham/New York/London: University Press of America, 1991) e.g., 124. Con-

trast John 18:25-27, which does not portray Peter as weeping after the cock crowed.

127 See the commentary on vv. 37-38 and 39-41a above.

128 Cf. Borrell, *Peter's Denial*, 170.

129 See the commentary on vv. 70b-71 above and on 16:1-8 below.

130 See Plutarch's *Lives*. See also Borrell, *Peter's Denial*, 144–45.

131 Borrell, *Peter's Denial*, 145. On the rhetorical effect of the narrative on the reader, see ibid., 202–6.

15 15:1-15 The Trial before Pilate and the
Amnesty of Barabbas

1/ So then, early in the morning, the
chief priests held a consultationᵃ
with the elders and scribes and
the whole (Judean) council,
bound Jesus, brought him, and
handed him over to Pilate. 2/ And
Pilate asked him, "Are you the
king of the Jews?" He then said
to him, "You say (so)." 3/ And the
chief priests accused him of many
things. 4/ Pilate then asked him
again, saying, "Have you no
response? Look how many accusations they make against you."
5/ But Jesus no longer made any
response, so that Pilate marveled.

6/ Now at each (Passover) festival he
would release for them a prisoner
for whom they would ask.
7/ Now a man called Barabbas
was imprisoned along with the
rebels who had committed murder in the rebellion. 8/ And the
crowd went upᵇ and began to ask
(that he do) as he would do for
them (at the festival). 9/ Pilate
then answered them, saying "Do
you want me to release for you
the king of the Jews?" 10/ For he
knew that the chief priestsᶜ had
handed him over on account of
envy. 11/ The chief priests then
incited the crowd, so that he
would release Barabbas for them
instead. 12/ So Pilate again said
to them, "What then do you
wantᵈ me to do with the king of
the Jews?"ᵉ 13/ They then cried
out again, "Crucify him!"
14/ Pilate then said to them,
"What evil has he done?" But
they cried out even louder, "Crucify him!" 15/ So Pilate, intending
to satisfy the crowd, released
Barabbas for them, and he had
Jesus whipped and handed him
over to be crucified.

a   The earliest recoverable reading is probably συμβούλιον ποιήσαντες ("held a consultation," lit., "having
held a consultation"), attested by A B W et al. A reading with the finite verb ἐποίησαν, "held (a consultation)," which has virtually the same meaning, is
attested by D 565. 2542ˢ *pc* it; Or. These readings are
difficult, because they seem to ignore the fact that a
meeting of the whole council had already taken place.
This difficulty apparently gave rise to the reading
συμβούλιον ἑτοιμάσαντες ("having reached a decision"), attested by ℵ C L 892 *pc*, which relieves the tension. Cf. Taylor, ad loc.

b   The trans. is based on the reading ἀναβάς ("went
up"), attested by ℵ* B D 892. 2427 lat co. The variant
ἀναβοήσας ("called out"), attested by ℵ² A C W Θ et
al., arose either by mistake or because the topographical information seemed unintelligible or irrelevant.
Cf. Taylor, ad loc.; Metzger, *Textual Commentary*, 98.
Another possibility is that it results from a deliberate
change in order to prepare for the statement in v. 13
that πάλιν ἔκραξαν, "(the crowd) cried out again."

c   The words οἱ ἀρχιερεῖς ("the chief priests") are lacking in B 1. 579 *pc* syˢ bo. This shorter reading is probably due to stylistic improvement of the earlier text,
since the next sentence begins with οἱ δὲ ἀρχιερεῖς
("The chief priests then"). Cf. Taylor, ad loc. For a different opinion, see Turner, "Marcan Usage," 25 (1924)
385–86 (Elliott, *Language and Style*, 11–12).

d   The trans. is based on the reading θέλετε ("you
want"), attested by A D Θ 0250 𝔐 latt sy. This word is
lacking in the reading attested by ℵ B C W et al. Westcott and Hort, followed by Taylor, ad loc., adopt the
shorter reading. Tischendorf adopted the longer reading, which is likely to be original, since the construction is in keeping with Markan style; cf. 10:36, 51;
14:12; 15:9. The shorter reading may have been
inspired by the parallel in Matt 27:22. See Turner,
"Marcan Usage," 28 (1926) 21 n. 1 (Elliott, *Language
and Style*, 80 n. 12). Nestle-Aland (27th ed.) includes
θέλετε ("you want") in brackets; cf. Metzger, *Textual
Commentary*, 98.

e   The earliest recoverable reading is probably the
shorter one attested by A D W et al., which lacks the
words ὃν λέγετε ("whom you call"). This reading is
supported by representatives of three of the four textual groups, namely, groups "A," "C," and "D"; on the
groups, see Epp, "Dynamic View." Furthermore, since
most readers, ancient and modern, would infer that
Pilate did not accept Jesus as the "king of the Jews"
and since this epithet was not a favored designation of
Jesus among his followers, it is easier to see why an
editor or scribe would add such a phrase rather than
delete it. Cf. Taylor, ad loc.; Metzger, *Textual Commentary*, 99.

Comment

■ **1-15** As noted above, in the pre-Markan passion narrative, an earlier form of 15:1 probably followed directly upon the substance of the statement preserved in 14:53a.[1] It is likely that Mark's source mentioned only the chief priests in v. 1.[2] Since Jesus had been taken by the "crowd sent by the chief priests"[3] to "the high priest" (14:53a), it is likely that the pre-Markan passion narrative continued with the remark that, early in the morning, the chief priests (the high priest and the other chief priests) held a consultation. The words "with the elders and scribes and the whole council" ($\mu\epsilon\tau\grave{\alpha}$ $\tau\hat{\omega}\nu$ $\pi\rho\epsilon\sigma$-$\beta\upsilon\tau\acute{\epsilon}\rho\omega\nu$ $\kappa\alpha\grave{\iota}$ $\gamma\rho\alpha\mu\mu\alpha\tau\acute{\epsilon}\omega\nu$ $\kappa\alpha\grave{\iota}$ $\acute{\text{o}}\lambda\text{o}\nu$ $\tau\grave{\text{o}}$ $\sigma\upsilon\nu\acute{\epsilon}\delta\rho\iota\text{o}\nu$) were probably added by Mark. The repetition of "the elders and scribes" resumes 14:53b, and the reference to "the whole council" takes up 14:55. In other words, the evangelist reconnected the thread of the narrative after inserting the interwoven stories of the trial of Jesus before the Judean council and the denial of Peter. He was not concerned about the awkwardness of the council holding another session after they had already passed a verdict upon Jesus.[4]

The episode concerning Barabbas is inserted into the account of the judicial proceedings conducted by Pilate. This literary technique again suggests Markan redaction.[5] Ludger Schenke and Matti Myllykoski concluded that the Barabbas episode was not part of the oldest form of the passion narrative.[6]

■ **1** The opening words "So then" ($K\alpha\grave{\iota}$ $\epsilon\grave{\upsilon}\theta\acute{\upsilon}\varsigma$) are probably Markan, just as the same opening words in 14:43 are likely to be.[7] As noted above, mention of the elders, scribes, and the whole council in v. 1 is likely to be a Markan addition as well.[8] In Mark's source, the consultation among the chief priests in the early morning was their only activity after Jesus was arrested and brought to the high priest during the previous night and before he was handed over to Pilate[9] thereafter. There was no trial before the Judean council in the source.[10]

The precaution of binding Jesus ($\delta\acute{\eta}\sigma\alpha\nu\tau\epsilon\varsigma$ $\tau\grave{\text{o}}\nu$ $\mathit{I}\eta\sigma\text{o}\hat{\upsilon}\nu$) recalls the narrator's comment in 14:44 that Judas had instructed the arresting party "to lead him away under guard" ($\grave{\alpha}\pi\acute{\alpha}\gamma\epsilon\tau\epsilon$ $\grave{\alpha}\sigma\varphi\alpha\lambda\hat{\omega}\varsigma$). The notice that "they brought him and handed him over to Pilate" ($\grave{\alpha}\pi\acute{\eta}\nu\epsilon\gamma\kappa\alpha\nu$ $\kappa\alpha\grave{\iota}$ $\pi\alpha\rho\acute{\epsilon}\delta\omega\kappa\alpha\nu$) is significant on two levels. On the one hand, it accurately reflects the historical situation in which the council had no jurisdiction over capital cases; only the Roman governor had authority to impose the death sentence.[11] On the other, it takes up a term that appears to be used with a double meaning in Mark. For example, in the second passion prediction, Jesus foretold that "the Son of Man will be handed over into human hands" ($\acute{\text{o}}$ $\upsilon\acute{\iota}\grave{\text{o}}\varsigma$ $\tau\text{o}\hat{\upsilon}$ $\grave{\alpha}\nu\theta\rho\acute{\omega}\pi\text{o}\upsilon$ $\pi\alpha\rho\alpha\delta\acute{\iota}\delta\text{o}\tau\alpha\iota$ $\epsilon\grave{\iota}\varsigma$ $\chi\epsilon\hat{\iota}\rho\alpha\varsigma$ $\grave{\alpha}\nu\theta\rho\acute{\omega}\pi\omega\nu$). The term $\pi\alpha\rho\alpha\delta\iota\delta\acute{\text{o}}\nu\alpha\iota$ is sometimes used, as in 15:1, to mean "to hand over a person into the custody of officials." At the same time, in a number of passages in Mark it evokes Isa 53:12 LXX, according to which the servant of the Lord is handed over to death.[12] Further, the handing of Jesus over to Pilate by the chief priests here fulfills the next part of the most detailed prediction of the passion, 10:33: "and they will hand him over to the nations" ($\kappa\alpha\grave{\iota}$ $\pi\alpha\rho\alpha\delta\acute{\omega}\sigma\text{o}\upsilon\sigma\iota\nu$ $\alpha\grave{\upsilon}\tau\grave{\text{o}}\nu$ $\tau\text{o}\hat{\iota}\varsigma$ $\acute{\epsilon}\theta\nu\epsilon\sigma\iota\nu$).[13]

---

1   See the commentary on 14:53 above.

2   Contra Schenke, who argued that the source read "the high priest and the whole Sanhedrin" (*Der gekreuzigte Christus*, 31).

3   See the commentary on 14:43 above.

4   See note a on the trans. of v. 1 above.

5   Yarbro Collins, *Beginning of the Gospel*, 109.

6   Schenke, *Der gekreuzigte Christus*, 47–49; Myllykoski, *Die letzten Tagen*, 2:25. Gerd Theissen includes it in his reconstruction of the earliest passion narrative and discusses the historicity of the passage; he does not take a strong stand on the question but seems to presuppose that it is historical (*Gospels in Context*, 182 n. 37; *Lokalkolorit*, 194 n. 37).

7   See the commentary on 14:43 above.

8   See the commentary on 15:1-15 above.

9   On the historical Pilate, see Daniel R. Schwartz, "Pontius Pilate," *ABD* 5:395–401. See also Helen K. Bond, *Pilate in History and Interpretation* (SNTSMS 100; Cambridge: Cambridge University Press, 1998).

10 See the section "Composition and History of the Tradition" in the excursus on the passion narrative in the commentary on 14:1-11 and the section "History of the Tradition and Historical Reliability" in the commentary on 14:53-72 above.

11 See "History of the Tradition and Historical Reliability" in the commentary on 14:53-72 above.

12 See the commentary on 9:31 above.

13 The immediately preceding part of the prediction, "and [the chief priests and the scribes] will condemn him to death" ($\kappa\alpha\grave{\iota}$ $\kappa\alpha\tau\alpha\kappa\rho\iota\nu\text{o}\hat{\upsilon}\sigma\iota\nu$ $\alpha\grave{\upsilon}\tau\grave{\text{o}}\nu$ $\theta\alpha\nu\acute{\alpha}\tau\omega$), was fulfilled in 14:53-72.

■ **2** Without preliminaries, the account moves directly from Jesus' being handed over to Pilate to the governor's question, "Are you the king of the Jews?" (σὺ εἶ ὁ βασιλεὺς τῶν Ἰουδαίων;). Bultmann argued that this question, as well as Jesus' answer, is an addition to the earliest story of the interrogation of Jesus by Pilate.[14] This conclusion fits with his understanding of the development of the passion narrative. First was the proclamation of the passion in the kerygma. Next came "a short narrative of historical reminiscence about the Arrest, Condemnation and Execution of Jesus."[15] Verse 2 is an addition because it is related to the perspective of 14:55-64, according to which Jesus was executed for his messianic claims.[16]

It is likely, however, that the earliest passion narrative was shaped not only by historical reminiscence but by an apologetic perspective as well. This apologetic perspective included the idea that Jesus was executed because he admitted that he was the messiah, which is equivalent to "the king of the Jews."[17] Even if 14:62 was not part of the pre-Markan passion narrative, Pilate's question presupposes that the chief priests have informed him of Jesus' crime.[18]

Jesus' answer, "You say (so)" (σὺ λέγεις), is ambiguous. It is neither a denial nor an affirmation. W. C. Allen argued that Jesus answered ambiguously because "He claimed to be the Messiah, but in a sense different from any current meaning attached to the title."[19] Although the notion of the Davidic messiah or the messiah of Israel is reinterpreted in Mark,[20] the reason for Jesus'

ambiguous answer may lie in its similarity to his response to the question about paying the taxes to Caesar. His answer there is equally evasive. He avoided saying anything that would provide grounds for a charge against him before the Roman governor.[21] Mark portrays Jesus as replying boldly, clearly, and fully to the high priest in 14:62. The ambiguous answer here may be due to the evangelist's, or more likely his source's, recognition of the social reality that provincials needed to be wary when dealing with the representatives of imperial power.[22]

■ **3** The statement that "the chief priests accused him of many things" (κατηγόρουν αὐτοῦ οἱ ἀρχιερεῖς πολλά) is the beginning of a theme that will be developed extensively in this account, namely, that Pilate believed Jesus to be innocent but condemned him to death because of pressure from the chief priests and the crowd manipulated by them.[23]

■ **4-5** Pilate's next statement follows well upon the narrator's comment about the chief priests' allegations, "Have you no response? Look how many accusations they make against you" (οὐκ ἀποκρίνῃ οὐδέν; ἴδε πόσα σου κατηγοροῦσιν). It was the responsibility of a Roman official in a legal proceeding to attempt to determine the facts and to give the accused an opportunity to respond to the charges.[24] It was usually in the interest of the accused to refute the charges, if possible. So it is to be expected that Jesus' silence would be surprising to Pilate.

The narrative does not give any explicit interpretation of Jesus' lack of response to the accusations.[25] This sec-

14   Bultmann, *History*, 272.
15   Ibid., 275.
16   Ibid., 272.
17   Reinbold, *Der älteste Bericht*, 197.
18   Historically speaking, the crime would most likely have been expressed as *seditio* ("stirring up a revolt"). See "History of the Tradition and Historical Reliability" in the commentary on 14:53-72 above.
19   Allen, 182.
20   See the section of the introduction entitled "Jesus as Messiah" and the commentary on 12:35-37 above.
21   See the commentary on 12:16-17 above.
22   In the present context, the continuation of the narrative in vv. 3-5 makes clear that Jesus' response in v. 2 is understood as being ambiguous. Gustaf Dalman's discussion of σὺ εἶπας ("You have said [so]") in the trial before the Judean council (Matt 26:64) is not relevant to Mark's σὺ λέγεις ("You say [so]") in

this quite different context (*The Words of Jesus Considered in the Light of Post-Biblical Jewish Writings and the Aramaic Language* [Edinburgh: T & T Clark, 1902] 309–11).
23   This portrayal is not historical; see "History of the Tradition and Historical Reliability" in the commentary on 14:53-72 above. On the rhetorical impact of the motif of the reluctant executioner, see Whitney T. Shiner, "The Ambiguous Pronouncement of the Centurion and the Shrouding of Meaning in Mark," *JSNT* 78 (2000) 3–22, esp. 13–14.
24   A. N. Sherwin-White, *Roman Society and Roman Law in the New Testament* (Oxford: Clarendon, 1963) 25–26. See also Haim Cohn, *The Trial and Death of Jesus* (New York/London: Harper & Row, 1971) 157.
25   William Sanger Campbell argued that Jesus' refusal to answer is a disengagement from the judicial proceedings, a strategy of self-defense, as in 14:61a

ond exchange between Pilate and Jesus is similar to the first exchange between Jesus and the high priest in the trial before the Judean council. It was argued above that the latter exchange, in context, evoked the voice of David in several psalms of individual lament and implied that what was happening to Jesus occurred in accordance with the scriptures.[26] One could argue that the same psalms are evoked here, since the context is analogous. A further passage that may be evoked comes from the depiction of the Suffering Servant in Isaiah:

And he does not open his mouth because of the wrong done (to him); as a sheep is led to slaughter, and as a lamb makes no sound in front of the one who shears it, so he does not open his mouth (καὶ αὐτὸς διὰ τὸ κεκακῶσθαι οὐκ ἀνοίγει τὸ στόμα· ὡς πρόβατον ἐπὶ σφαγὴν ἤχθη καὶ ὡς ἀμνὸς ἐναντίον τοῦ κείροντος αὐτὸν ἄφωνος οὕτως οὐκ ἀνοίγει τὸ στόμα αὐτοῦ). (Isa 53:7 LXX)

If that passage is alluded to here, it may be that the author of the pre-Markan passion narrative, and tradents of the tradition before him, interpreted the Suffering Servant in messianic terms.[27]

■ **6** This verse is an aside by the narrator that sets the scene for the incident concerning Barabbas that is about to be narrated. The hearing described in vv. 2-5 had not yet issued in a decision by Pilate. With v. 6, the narrative focus shifts from the hearing of Jesus' case to the question of the release of a particular prisoner at the time of the festival.[28]

It is generally agreed that there is no evidence outside of the canonical Gospels for the specific custom mentioned here, that is, Pilate's (or any other governor of Judea) releasing a particular prisoner at the request of the people each year at the time of Passover.[29] Craig A. Evans argued, in support of the historicity of the custom, that it is attested in two separate streams of tradition: Mark, followed by Matthew and Luke, and John.[30] Matthew indeed follows Mark, but the earliest recoverable text of Luke omits the allusion to this custom (Matt 27:15).[31] John does mention the practice (18:39), but it is not certain that John is independent of Mark, at least with respect to the passion narrative.[32]

The hypothesis that Mark composed the incident involving Barabbas is supported by the connection between Jesus' remarks at the time of his arrest and this story. In the arrest story, the Markan Jesus distances himself from the social category "bandit" (λῃστής).[33] It is clear from the writings of Josephus that this term was used in the first century CE as a designation of a kind of insurrectionist.[34] In 15:7, Barabbas is associated with rebels (στασιασταί), and Jesus is contrasted with Barabbas in the episode as a whole. Since it was apparently Mark who added 14:48-49, it is likely that he inserted this incident as well. The lack of evidence for the specific practice mentioned in this verse supports the conclusion that Mark not only inserted the story but composed it as well. Further support comes from the fact that bandits and rebels were much more of a problem in the time of Mark than in the time of Jesus.[35]

A good story, however, must be true to life. Robert

("Engagement, Disengagement and Obstruction," 290–91).

26   See the commentary on 14:60-62 above.

27   Yarbro Collins, "From Noble Death," 494.

28   Cf. Schenke, *Der gekreuzigte Christus*, 47.

29   E.g., Allen, 182; Bond, *Pilate*, 200; Roger David Aus, *"Caught in the Act": Walking on the Sea and the Release of Barabbas Revisited* (SFSHJ 157; Atlanta: Scholars Press, 1998) 138. For further literature, see Robert L. Merritt, "Jesus Barabbas and the Paschal Pardon," *JBL* 104 (1985) 57–68, esp. 58–59 n. 5. See esp. the critical history of scholarship by the legal scholar Johannes Merkel, "Die Begnadigung am Passahfeste," *ZNW* 6 (1905) 293–316, esp. 293–308. Winter declared, "The *privilegium paschale* is nothing but a figment of the imagination. No such custom existed" (*Trial*, 134).

30   Evans, 479.

31   Luke 23:17 is probably a secondary expansion of the text; see Nestle-Aland A (27th ed.) ad loc.; Fitzmyer, *Luke*, 2:1485–86.

32   See "Composition and History of the Tradition" in "Excursus: The Passion Narrative" in the commentary on 14:1-11 above.

33   See the commentary on 14:48-49 above.

34   Horsley and Hanson, *Bandits*, 48–87.

35   Lührmann, 256.

Merritt has collected evidence for practices involving the release of a single prisoner during religious festivals in Babylonian and Assyrian texts and of multiple prisoners in relation to specific Greek festivals.[36] One of these Greek festivals was the City or the Great Dionysia, which was celebrated, like Passover, in March.[37] The observance of this festival continued at least until the first century CE.[38] The criteria for choosing prisoners to be released and the details of their release are sparsely attested. It seems, however, that only those worthy of participating in the festival would be released. Furthermore, "the release was merely a parole for the duration of the festival and not an amnesty, with bond required to be furnished on behalf of the released prisoner."[39] In the Barabbas episode of Mark, however, the release appears to be an amnesty, not just a temporary parole. Merritt also discussed the evidence for Roman practices involving the release of multiple prisoners at festivals.[40] According to Livy, at the first celebration of the *lectisternium* in 399 BCE, prisoners were released at least for the duration of the festival.[41]

Mark may also have been aware of the ad hoc release of prisoners in certain political circumstances and the occasional role of demands by crowds in such cases.[42] An obscure papyrus is often cited in this regard.[43] A Roman prefect in Egypt at some point between 86 and 88 CE, C. Septimius Vegetus, heard a case brought by a certain Phibion. Phibion's father had lent the father of another man one hundred artabas of wheat. When the other man refused to repay the loan, Phibion took the law into his own hands by confining the man and seizing his property. The papyrus is a record of the subsequent hearing. The account ends with a direct quotation of Septimius Vegetus's final statement to Phibion, followed by a statement (in the third person) about the decision of the prefect:

> You may be worthy of whipping, since you confined a man of high standing and women on your own authority, but I graciously give you to the crowds and will be more kind than you; you present this document after forty years; I graciously give you half of that time; you shall return to me in twenty years. And he commanded that the bond be cancelled (Ἄξιος μ[ὲ]ν ἧς μαστιγωθῆναι, διὰ σεαυτοῦ [κ]ατασχὼν ἄνϑρωπον εὐσχήμονα καὶ γυν[αῖ]κας· χαρίζομαι

36 Merritt, "Jesus Barabbas," 59–63.

37 Ibid., 62; Richard A. S. Seaford, "Dionysia," *OCD* 476.

38 Merritt, "Jesus Barabbas," 62.

39 Ibid., 63. It is likely that reference to "one whom they have promised to bring out of prison" in *m. Pesaḥ* 8.6 also concerns a temporary release (trans. from Danby, *Mishnah*, 147). See the critical comments of Merkel, "Die Begnadigung am Passahfeste," 306–7. Cf. Evans, 479–80. Winter presupposed that the release was absolute, but he argued that the text is irrelevant to the Barabbas story (*Trial*, 131–32); similarly, Horace Abram Rigg, "Barabbas," *JBL* 64 (1945) 417–56, esp. 421–22 and n. 17. The interpretation of Charles B. Chavel is overly speculative ("The Releasing of a Prisoner on the Eve of Passover in Ancient Jerusalem," *JBL* 60 [1941] 273–78); the same holds for that of August Strobel, *Die Stunde der Wahrheit: Untersuchungen zum Strafverfahren gegen Jesus* (WUNT 21; Tübingen: Mohr Siebeck, 1980) 120–24.

40 Merritt, "Jesus Barabbas," 65–66.

41 Livy 5.13.8: "even prisoners were loosed from their chains for those days, and they scrupled thenceforth to imprison men whom the gods had thus befriended" (vinctis quoque demta in eos dies vincula; religioni deinde fuisse quibus eam opem di tulissent vinciri) (text and trans. from B. O. Foster, *Livy*, vol. 3 (LCL; Cambridge, MA: Harvard University Press; London: Heinemann, 1924) 48–49; Merritt, "Jesus Barabbas," 65–66. Cf. Lohmeyer, 336; Klostermann, 159; and esp. Merkel, "Die Begnadigung am Passahfeste," 304–5. On the *lectisternium*, see Jerzy Linderski, "Lectisternium," *OCD* 837.

42 Cf. Schenke, *Der gekreuzigte Christus*, 47 n. 2.

43 It is cited by Adolf Deissmann, *Licht vom Osten: Das Neue Testament und die neuentdeckten Texte der hellenistisch-römischen Welt* (4th ed.; Tübingen: Mohr Siebeck, 1923) 229 n. 7; ET *Light from the Ancient East: The New Testament Illustrated by Recently Discovered Texts of the Graeco-Roman World* (London: Hodder & Stoughton, 1927) 269 n. 7; Wolfgang Waldstein, *Untersuchungen zum römischen Begnadigungsrecht: abolitio, indulgentia, venia* (Commentationes Aenipontanae 18; Innsbruck: Universitätsverlag Wagner, 1964) 42 n. 12; Evans (480) from Deissmann; and by Lohmeyer (336–37) and Klostermann (159) from *Papiri greco-egizii*, Vol. 1: *Papiri fiorentini* no. 61 (see next note).

δέ σε τοῖς ὄχλοις καὶ φιλανθρωπ[ότ]ερ[ό]ς σοι
ἔσομαι· διὰ τεσ[σ]εράκοντα ἐτῶν ἐπιφέ[ρε]ις
ἐπίσταλ[μ]α· τὸ ἥμισ[ύ] σοι τοῦ χρόνου χαρί-
ζομαι· [μ]ετὰ εἴκοσι ἔτη ἐπανελεύσῃ πρὸς ἐμέ.
Καὶ ἐκ[έ]λευσε τό χειρ[ό]γραφον χιασθῆναι).[44]

The comment about granting twenty years and returning
in twenty years is probably facetious.[45] The role of the
crowd in this case is not clear.[46]

Furthermore, Roman law allowed for the cancellation
of a charge before the verdict (*abolitio*) and for a pardon
after the verdict had been reached (*indulgentia*).[47] Ernst
Lohmeyer stated that *abolitio* was exercised especially at
festivals, but according to Theodor Mommsen, it was
only at the end of the first century that a general cancellation of charges (*abolitio publica*) was practiced, on the
occasion of specially fortunate events. This cancellation
had to be voted by the senate and approved by the
emperor. It was still later that the *abolitio publica* began to
be regularly granted at festivals.[48] Pliny the Younger
accepted oral testimony that some governors (*proconsules*)
of Nicomedia and Nicea, or their legates, had released
people condemned to the mines, the public games, or
similar punishments and had allowed them to become
slaves of certain cities and to draw an annual stipend for
their work as such. Trajan, however, assumed that if
there were no written records of the sentences being
reversed, that the people in question had been released
without authority.[49] These cases, however, do not count
as evidence that Pilate undertook to release one prisoner
annually at Passover.[50]

Josephus makes the following statement about a later
governor, Albinus (62–64 CE):

When Albinus heard that Gessius Florus was coming
to succeed him, he sought to gain a name as one who
had done some service to the inhabitants of
Jerusalem. He therefore brought out those prisoners
who clearly deserved to be put to death and sentenced
them to execution, but released for a personal consideration those who had been cast into prison for a tri-
fling and commonplace offence. Thus the prison was
cleared of inmates and the land was infested with brigands (Ὡς δ᾽ ἤκουσεν Ἀλβῖνος διάδοχον αὐτῷ Γέσ-
σιον Φλῶρον ἀφικνεῖσθαι, βουλόμενος δοκεῖν τι
τοῖς Ἱεροσολυμίταις παρεσχῆσθαι προαγαγὼν

---

44 Text from D. Comparetti and G. Vitelli, eds., *Papiri
greco-egizii* (Supplementi filologico-storici ai monu-
menti antichi), Vol. 1: Girolamo Vitelli, ed., *Papiri
fiorentini* (Milan: Ulrico Hoepli/Editore-librario
della real casa e della r. Accademia dei Lincei, 1906;
reprinted Torino: Bottega d'Erasmo, 1960) No. 61,
lines 59–66 (p. 116); my trans. Underlining indicates
undertain letters.

45 Cf. Vitelli, *Papiri fiorentini*, 114.

46 Ibid., 116, note on line 61.

47 Lohmeyer, 337. According to Theodor Mommsen,
however, the governors' authority to exercise *abolitio*
was limited (*Römisches Strafrecht* [Systematisches
Handbuch der deutschen Rechtswissenschft 1.4;
Leipzig: Duncker & Humblot, 1899] 454 n. 1; on
indulgentia, see 455 n. 6). Waldstein concluded that
the legal notion of *indulgentia* is irrelevant to the
practice attributed to Pilate because it is first
attested in the late second century CE (*Untersuchungen*, 44). He argued that a practice like that reported
in the Gospels could have established itself in particular circumstances under the rubric of *venia* ("pardon") (ibid., 44). See the discussion of Seneca's
distinction between *clementia* ("clemency") and *venia*
("pardon") and his argument that the "wise man
does not remit a punishment that he ought to

impose" in Richard A. Bauman, *Crime and Punishment in Ancient Rome* (London: Routledge, 1996) 78–
79. For the similar view of another Stoic, Thrasea
Paetus, see ibid., 84–85. In the second century,
Marcus, Verus, and Commodus were more willing to
grant pardons (ibid., 104–5).

48 Mommsen, *Römisches Strafrecht*, 455; the general cancellation of accusations did not include capital cases.
The accuser in all cases was free to reinstate the
charge after thirty days (ibid., 455–56). Waldstein
concluded that the *abolitio publica* has no direct connection with the issue of the practice attributed to
Pilate in the Gospels (*Untersuchungen*, 44 and n. 18).

49 Pliny *Letters* 10.31–32; Lohmeyer, 337; Waldstein,
Untersuchungen, 42 n. 7. Unscrupulous governors,
like Marius Priscus, proconsul of Africa, apparently
accepted bribes to condemn and even execute innocent people (Pliny *Letters* 2.11; Waldstein, *Untersuchungen*, 42 and n. 9). Cf. the discussion of the
case of Albinus below.

50 Contra Waldstein, *Untersuchungen*, 42–43.

τοὺς δεσμώτας, ὅσοι ἦσαν αὐτῶν προδήλως θανεῖν ἄξιοι, τούτους προσέταξεν ἀναιρεθῆναι, τοὺς δ' ἐκ μικρᾶς καὶ τῆς τυχούσης αἰτίας εἰς τὴν εἱρκτὴν κατατεθέντας χρήματα λαμβάνων αὐτὸς ἀπέλυεν. Καὶ οὕτως ἡ μὲν φυλακὴ τῶν δεσμωτῶν ἐκαθάρθη, ἡ δὲ χώρα δὲ λῃστῶν ἐπληρώθη). (*Ant.* 20.9.5 §215)[51]

There is clearly tension between the positive assessment of Albinus in the first part of this passage and the negative comment in the last sentence. This tension is resolved in a negative direction in the parallel passage, which states that he accepted money from the relatives of those who had been arrested by local councils or former governors for revolutionary banditry (λῃστεία). The only people who continued to be held were those who could not or would not pay for their release.[52] The latter report may be exaggerated; in any case, nothing similar is reported about Pilate.[53]

Johannes Merkel suggested that the focus on one person being released at the request of a crowd was inspired by an element of Roman law, namely, the granting of amnesty to a criminal or the emancipation of a slave *per acclamationem populi* ("by the shout [of approval] of the people").[54] This practice was later outlawed, apparently by Diocletian.[55] Merritt proposed that the narrative,

"built on familiarity with the existence of" customs regarding the release of prisoners, "also was reinforced by widespread knowledge of the choice given to the crowd at Roman gladiatorial games, the choice to determine whether a wounded gladiator would be killed or allowed to live."[56]

The invention of a custom in order to develop a narrative's plot is known from Greek, Roman, and Second Temple Jewish literature. The alleged practice of Pilate here is another example of the same literary technique.[57]

■ **7** The narrator's aside, begun in v. 6, continues here, giving further information needed for the comprehension of the episode in which Barabbas plays a role.

It is unusual for Mark to use the definite article, as here, with the name of a person who has not yet been mentioned in the narrative.[58] The participial form λεγό-μενος ("called") is not used anywhere else in Mark. P. W. Schmiedel argued that these two problems can be solved by concluding that the meaning of ὁ λεγόμενος here is "He who, for distinction's sake (though it was not his proper name) was called Barabbas."[59] Since many manuscripts of Matt 27:16 and 17 refer to the man in question as "Jesus Barabbas," some scholars have concluded that the Markan text of v. 7 either once contained the name "Jesus" before "Barabbas" or that the phrase presupposes the knowledge that "Jesus" was the man's proper

51 Text and trans. from Louis Feldman, in Thackeray, *Josephus*, 9:502–3; cf. Evans, 480. Evans also cites *Ant.* 17.8.4 §204, which concerns a request for the release of people arrested by Herod that was granted by Archelaus in an attempt to gain the good will of the people when he had just succeeded his father.

52 Josephus *Bell.* 2.14.1 §§272–73.

53 Schwartz, "Pontius Pilate," 398–400.

54 Suetonius *Tib.* 37; 47; Merkel, "Die Begnadigung am Passahfeste," 308–9; Klostermann, 159. Cf. Claudius's practice of obtaining "verdicts from the praetorian cohorts by acclamation" (Bauman, *Crime and Punishment*, 71; cf. 106–7, 114). On the use of acclamation in judicial contexts, see also David Potter, "Performance, Power, and Justice in the High Empire," in William J. Slater, ed., *Roman Theater and Society: E. Togo Salmon Papers I* (Ann Arbor: University of Michigan Press, 1996) 129–59, esp. 138, 140–41; see 150–51 on the trial of Jesus in John.

55 Merkel, "Die Begnadigung am Passahfeste," 309. Cohn is certainly right in rejecting Blinzler's view

that Roman judges, including governors, "invariably inquired for the *vox populi* and adjudicated according to the will of the people assembled" (Cohn, *Trial*, 150, 157–58; cf. 162–63). But the practice, as described by Merkel, may have played a role in the construction of Mark's narrative and those dependent, directly or indirectly, on it.

56 Merritt, "Jesus Barabbas," 68.

57 Johannes B. Bauer, "'Literarische' Namen und 'literarische' Bräuche (zu Joh 2,10 und 18,39)," *BZ* n.F. 26 (1982) 258–64; Roger David Aus, *Barabbas and Esther and Other Studies in the Judaic Illumination of Earliest Christianity* (SFSHJ 54; Atlanta: Scholars Press, 1992) 3 and n. 11.

58 Cf., e.g., 1:4 with 1:6; 1:9 with 1:14; Sellew, "*Secret Mark*," 251–52 and n. 35.

59 P. W. Schmiedel, cited by Merritt, "Jesus Barabbas," 57 n. 1; similarly, Nineham, 416. Theissen argued that the phrase indicates that Barabbas was well known to the author and audience of Mark's source (*Gospels in Context*, 182–84; *Lokalkolorit*, 193–95).

name.[60] Some scholars have even argued that Jesus of Nazareth and Jesus Barabbas were the same person.[61]

Βαραββᾶς ("Barabbas") is the Greek form of an Aramaic name, בר אבא ("son of Abba").[62] A likely interpretation of the name is that the father of the man so designated was named "Abba." Israel Abrahams has argued, following Bacher, that the proper name "Abba" does not necessarily mean "father" and that it is attested "early enough."[63] The name "bar Abba" as a patronymic is also well attested.[64] As to the origin of the name "Abba," Abrahams mentions two possibilities. The first is that it was originally an honorary title ("father" = "master" = Rabbi). The other is that it is an abbreviation for Abraham.[65]

Regardless of what the actual derivation was, the name "Barabbas" was open to the interpretation "the son of the father," and it may have been chosen by Mark because of that potential connotation. Since Jesus addresses God as "Abba" in Gethsemane, the name

"Barabbas (bar Abba)" suggests that Jesus and this other prisoner are rival claimants to be the son of God, that is the Messiah,[66] and that they are to be compared and contrasted as such.

Just as it is surprising that the definite article is used to introduce Barabbas, it is also odd that definite articles are used to introduce "the rebels" (οἱ στασιασταί) and "the rebellion" (ἡ στάσις).[67] In the latter two related cases, many scholars have been inclined to infer that an actual uprising in the time of Pilate is presumed here, even though there is no corroborating evidence outside of the Gospels.[68] It could well be, however, that the use of these articles is part of a vivid storytelling technique.[69] Dieter Lührmann argued that "the rebels" and "the rebellion" signify for Mark the Jewish war with Rome that began in 66 CE.[70]

The narrator's aside in v. 7 also informs the audiences that Barabbas was imprisoned "along with the rebels who had committed murder" (μετὰ τῶν στασιαστῶν . . .

---

60 So Schmiedel (cited by Merritt, 57 n. 1); Nineham, 416; for further literature, see Merritt (ibid.).

61 Rigg, "Barabbas," 435–53; Hyam Z. Maccoby, "Jesus and Barabbas," *NTS* 16 (1969–70) 55–60; idem, *Revolution in Judaea: Jesus and the Jewish Resistance* (London: Ocean Books, 1973) 214; Stevan L. Davies, "Who Is Called Bar Abbas?" *NTS* 27 (1980–81) 260–62; see the discussion in Merritt, "Jesus Barabbas," 57–58 and n. 2.

62 For other theories about the derivation from Aramaic, see Michael J. Wilkins, "Barabbas," *ABD* 1:607.

63 *M. Pe'a* 2.6; Abrahams, *Studies in Pharisaism*, 2:201.

64 Judah bar Abba (some MSS of *m. 'Ed.* 6.1; Abrahams, *Studies in Pharisaism*, 2:201); Abba bar Abba (*b. Ber.* 18b; Abrahams, *Studies in Pharisaism*, 2:201–2). See also Str-B, 1:1031; Swete, 370. The name "Joseph son of Abba" (דאבא . . . יוסף) occurs in an Aramaic donor inscription from the synagogue in Dura-Europos dated to c. 244/245 CE; David Noy and Hanswulf Bloedhorn, eds., *Inscriptiones Judaicae Orientis*, vol. 3: *Syria und Cyprus* (TSAJ 102; Tübingen: Mohr Siebeck, 2004) Syr89 (pp. 152–54). The same or an ostensibly similar name (cited by BAGD, s.v. Βαραββᾶς) is attested in the spelling βαρραβας ("Barrabas") in a graffito on one of the north walls of the older tower of the temple of the Palmyrene gods at Dura-Europos: μνησθ(είης) Βαρράβας (on one line), πρὸς Διί (on a second line) ("Remember [O Zeus] Barrabas, in the presence of Zeus"); text from Clark Hopkins, "IV. Inscriptions," in Paul V. C. Baur and Michael I. Rostovtzeff, eds., *The Excava-*

tions at Dura-Europos Conducted by Yale University and the French Academy of Inscriptions and Letters: Preliminary Report of Second Season of Work October 1928–April 1929 (New Haven: Yale University Press; London: Humphrey Milford/Oxford University Press, 1931) H. 28 (Block 28), p. 106 = *Supplementum Epigraphicum Graecum*, vol. 7, no. 489 (p. 79); my trans. based on Hopkins's interpretation. On the date of the graffito, see Clark Hopkins, "The Building Periods," in *Preliminary Report of Second Season*, 20–31, esp. 24.

65 Abrahams, *Studies in Pharisaism*, 2:202. The latter hypothesis is supported by passages that refer to Abraham as "father" or imply such an appellation; Matt 3:9; Luke 16:24, 27, 30; Gal 3:7, 16, 29; Tertullian *Adversus Marcion* 4.34.11–14.

66 Yarbro Collins, "Son of God among Jews," 393–408.

67 Klostermann, 159.

68 E.g., Lohmeyer, 337; Schürer, *History*, 1:385; Theissen, *Gospels in Context*, 183 (*Lokalkolorit*, 195); Schwartz, "Pontius Pilate," 399; Aus, *"Caught in the Act"*, 136.

69 Cf. Klostermann, 159–60.

70 Lührmann, 256. Theissen argued that, for the community related to the earliest passion narrative, the story about Barabbas could be updated in the generation after Jesus (the 40s) with reference to the rebellious elements in the country (*Gospels in Context*, 196–96; *Lokalkolorit*, 208–9).

οἵτινες . . . φόνον πεποιήκεισαν). The indefinite relative pronoun, οἵτινες ("who") characterizes the men: they were such that they had gone so far as to commit murder to achieve their aims.[71] The text does not clearly state that Barabbas had personally committed murder,[72] but he was the sort who would, or at least he associated with men who had. Mark perhaps avoids saying explicitly that Barabbas was himself an insurrectionist and guilty of murder because, in that case, Pilate's offer to release him would lack verisimilitude.

■ **8** Here the narrator returns to the sequence of events being narrated. In vv. 2-5, the setting and circumstances are rather vague. Pilate, Jesus, and the chief priests are mentioned as being present. In v. 8, suddenly "the crowd" (ὁ ὄχλος) appears on the scene. The proceedings in vv. 2-5 could have been understood as a closed hearing with only those present who are named.[73] Verse 8, however, implies that the proceedings were open to the public.[74]

The earliest recoverable reading of this verse indicates that the crowd "went up" (ἀναβάς) in order to make a petition to Pilate concerning the release of a prisoner.[75] Their "going up" would make sense if Pilate's official residence was commonly known to have been on high ground.[76] It could have been the Hasmonean fortress connected to the temple, rebuilt and renamed "Antonia" by Herod.[77] Or, when he was in Jerusalem, Pilate may

have resided in Herod's Lower Palace or his Upper Palace.[78] Both were at the disposal of the Roman governors after Judea became a Roman province in 6 CE.[79] Jack Finegan concluded that the Lower Palace was the residence of official administration, both for Herod and the Roman governors, whereas the Upper Palace in the far western part of the city was a luxurious private residence.[80] Emil Schürer concluded, in contrast, that the praetorium of Jerusalem was "the palace of Herod in the west of the city."[81] Both palaces, however, were in the upper city, whereas the ordinary people lived in the lower city.[82] So the crowd could be described as "going up" to Pilate with reference to any one of these three locations.

Some scholars have found it problematic that the crowd here petitions for Barabbas instead of Jesus, since the high priests earlier feared that there would be a disturbance among the people if Jesus were arrested openly during the festival (14:2) and "the mass of the people" (ὁ πολὺς ὄχλος) heard him gladly (12:37). In light of this tension and the statement in Acts 13:27 that the residents of Jerusalem and their leaders rejected Jesus, Lohmeyer concluded that those who supported Jesus were mainly pilgrims from Galilee.[83] This seems to be an overinterpretation. In the ancient world crowds were proverbially unstable.[84] Thus Mark could portray a fickle crowd with verisimilitude. Verse 8 leaves open the

---

71 BDF §293 (2); Swete, 370–71.

72 Theissen recognized this (*Gospels in Context*, 182–83; *Lokalkolorit*, 194).

73 On the private, or even secret, character of judicial proceedings that took place in a governor's *praetorium*, see Cohn, *Trial*, 145–46. His insistence that no Jew could have been present (ibid., 144–45), however, goes beyond the evidence; see "History of the Tradition and Historical Reliability" in the commentary on 14:53-72 above.

74 This tension between vv. 2-5 and vv. 6-15 is one of the grounds for concluding that the Barabbas story is an expansion of an older account of the hearing before Pilate (Schenke, *Der gekreuzigte Christus*, 47–48). See also the commentary on 15:1-15 and on v. 6 above.

75 See note b on the trans. of v. 8 and the commentary on v. 6 above.

76 Klostermann, 160.

77 Lohmeyer, 337; Taylor, 581; on this structure, see Finegan, *Archaeology*, 248; Lichtenberger, *Baupolitik*, 35–39.

78 Finegan, *Archaeology*, 248–49. Herod's Lower Palace had been built by the Hasmoneans above the bridge that linked the upper city with the temple mount. He himself built a new palace (the Upper Palace) on the western hill; on the latter see Lichtenberger, *Baupolitik*, 93–98.

79 On the establishment of Judea as a Roman province, see Schürer, *History*, 1:356–57.

80 Finegan, *Archaeology*, 248; see the map on 184.

81 Schürer, *History*, 1:361.

82 The wealthy families resided in the upper city (Finegan, *Archaeology*, 248).

83 Lohmeyer, 337.

84 Artemidorus *Oneirocritica* 3.16; see the citation of this text in "Cultural Contexts" in the commentary on 6:45-52 above.

identity of the prisoner whose release they came to request, but v. 11 indicates that the crowd was "incited" or "stirred up" (ἀνασείειν) by the chief priests. It may even be implied that the chief priests organized the crowd so that they would ask for Barabbas. Such a portrayal would be in keeping with Mark's account of the trial before the Judean council, which implies that the members of the council sought false witnesses to testify against Jesus.[85]

■ **9-10** The construction θέλετε ἀπολύσω ὑμῖν ("Do you want me to release for you") is typical of Mark's style.[86]

Historically speaking, it is very odd that Pilate takes the initiative here. If there were a custom like the one presupposed in vv. 6 and 8, one would expect the people to take the initiative and to ask for a particular prisoner, rather than the governor proposing that they ask for the release of some individual.[87]

It is also surprising that Pilate refers to Jesus here as "the king of the Jews" (ὁ βασιλεὺς τῶν Ἰουδαίων). Jerry Camery-Hoggatt interpreted the reference as ironic because Jesus is mocked as a "king" by soldiers in the next scene (vv. 16-20),[88] but vv. 9 and 10 are closely linked by the conjunction γάρ ("for") in v. 10. The narrator explains the question of Pilate with the remark that "he knew that the chief priests had handed him over on account of envy."[89] This explanation implies that Pilate expected the people to ask for Jesus. The envy of the chief priests, the implied reader is expected to infer, is due to Jesus' popularity with the crowd. The narrative overlooks the historical fact that Pilate's authority would also be threatened if the people were to recognize Jesus as their king.

Mark narrates the story in this way in order to construct a scene in which the people of Jerusalem have a choice between Jesus and Barabbas and all that each signifies.

■ **11** The portrayal of the chief priests "stirring up" (ἀνασείειν) the crowd may imply that they had gathered a specific group of people and influenced or bribed them to ask for Barabbas. Or the text may simply imply that there were a few supporters of Barabbas in the crowd and the chief priests were able to get them shouting for Barabbas and the others to go along with them. In any case, the account is historically implausible.[90]

■ **12** The construction τί οὖν θέλετε ποιήσω ("What then do you want me to do") is similar to the one in v. 9 and is typical of Markan style.[91]

This response of Pilate to the request of the crowd for Barabbas is even stranger than his proposal that he release "the king of the Jews" for them in v. 9. Here, in effect, he abdicates his authority as governor acting as judge and leaves it to the crowd to determine what the verdict should be regarding Jesus. It is historically unlikely that Pilate or any other Roman governor would have done such a thing. Mark could put such a question in Pilate's mouth only because of the analogies of amnesty and emancipation by *acclamatio* and the role of the crowd in the determination of the fate of gladiators.[92]

Mark's purpose in composing this question is to continue the construction of a scene in which the crowd, standing for the people of Jerusalem or for all the rebels in the Jewish war that began in 66 CE, is faced with a choice between Jesus and Barabbas.[93]

■ **13-14** It is striking that the sentence of Jesus (crucifix-

---

85 Neither of these motifs is historical; see "History of the Tradition and Historical Reliability" in the commentary on 14:53-72 above. Cf. Cohn's arguments for the conclusion that the Gospels' portrayal of the role of the crowd here is apologetic and not historical (*Trial*, 161–63).

86 See note a on the trans. of 10:36 above.

87 Winter, *Trial*, 133–34; Cohn, *Trial*, 165.

88 Camery-Hoggatt, *Irony*, 174; cf. Fowler, *Let the Reader Understand*, 159. Swete described the remark as "cynical" (371).

89 On the double meaning of "hand over" (παραδιδόναι), see the commentary on v. 1 above; see also the commentary on 3:19 and 9:31 above and on 15:27

below. On the notion of envy in antiquity, see Matthew W. Dickie, "Envy," *ABD* 2:528–32, and esp. Hagedorn and Neyrey, "'It Was Out of Envy.'" But the conclusion of the latter that Mark's remark is a historically reliable explanation for the death of Jesus is untenable. See "History of the Tradition and Historical Reliability" in the commentary on 14:53-72 above.

90 See the commentary on v. 8 above.

91 See note d on the trans. of v. 12 and the commentary on v. 9 above.

92 See the commentary on v. 6 above.

93 See the commentary on vv. 9-10 above.

ion) is determined here by the crowd and not by Pilate, who, as governor, was the only person with the authority to pass such a sentence at the time. Pilate's question in v. 14, "What evil has he done?" ($\tau i \ \gamma \grave{\alpha} \rho \ \dot{\epsilon} \pi o i \eta \sigma \epsilon \nu \ \kappa \alpha \kappa \acute{o} \nu;$), is a clear indication that, from the perspective of the narrative, Pilate believed Jesus to be innocent and that he ought to have been released.

The shifting of the responsibility for the death of Jesus from Pilate to the Jewish crowd[94] was motivated by the need to make the point that Jesus was indeed innocent; he was not a criminal justly convicted by a Roman official. This was important lest his followers and the movement in his name be defined in criminal terms.[95]

■ **15** The construction used here, $\tau \grave{o} \ \dot{\iota} \kappa \alpha \nu \grave{o} \nu \ \pi o \iota \epsilon \hat{\iota} \nu$ ("to satisfy") is a Latinism (*satisfacere*).[96] The use of the participle $\beta o \upsilon \lambda \acute{o} \mu \epsilon \nu o \varsigma$ ("intending") implies a consciously chosen course of action.[97]

The formulation of the first clause (v. 15a) reinforces the impression created by vv. 12-14 that the release of Barabbas and the condemnation of Jesus to death by crucifixion were actions that Pilate took only because of pressure from the crowd. His own preference was to do the opposite.

The ambiguity about whether Barabbas was actually guilty of insurrection and murder noted above in the discussion of v. 7 may be explained by the supposition that Mark hesitated to depict Pilate as releasing someone clearly guilty of such crimes. Such a depiction would per-

haps have been incredible to at least some in his audiences.

In any case, the contrast drawn in this verse between the fate of Barabbas and the fate of Jesus increases the likelihood that this scene is another example of rhetorical $\sigma \acute{u} \nu \kappa \rho \iota \sigma \iota \varsigma$ (comparison) in narrative form.[98] In this case, the focus is on the choice made by the crowd. It is likely that the evangelist, who probably wrote during the first Jewish war with Rome, created this scene to address the subject of that war in the light of the rejection of Jesus as messiah by the majority of the Jewish people. Instead of accepting Jesus, who taught the way of self-denial and endurance of unavoidable suffering, the people chose leaders like Barabbas, who led them into a brutal and destructive war.

The substance of v. 15b represents the conclusion to the account of the interrogation of Jesus before Pilate that Mark found in his source.[99] The verb $\pi \alpha \rho \alpha \delta \iota \delta \acute{o} \nu \alpha \iota$ ("to hand over") may have been used in the source.[100] It could, however, have been introduced by Mark in his reformulation of the statement, in keeping with the thematic use of the verb with a double meaning.[101]

The verb $\varphi \rho \alpha \gamma \epsilon \lambda \lambda o \hat{u} \nu$ ("to whip") is a loanword from Latin (*flagellare*).[102] The indication that Pilate had Jesus whipped is a fulfillment of another part of his third prophecy of his destiny.[103] In some cases, beating was the main penalty, and a person sentenced to this punishment was to be beaten to death.[104] Often, as here, whipping

---

94 This shift is even more pronounced in Matthew, which has the additional saying "His blood be upon us and upon our children" (27:25). Originally, the saying probably expressed the conviction of some followers of Jesus that the destruction of Jerusalem and the temple was divine punishment for the rejection of Jesus as messiah. This significance is already difficult in its lack of empathy with those who suffered in that war and in its overreaching claim to know the divine will. The saying had even more terrible consequences in the later history of relations between Christians and Jews. See the discussion of the increasing tendency in the speeches of Acts to blame the Jews for Jesus' death in Reinbold, *Der älteste Bericht*, 297.

95 Cf. Reinbold, *Der älteste Bericht*, 197-99.

96 BAGD, s.v. $\dot{\iota} \kappa \alpha \nu \acute{o} \varsigma$; BDF §5 (3b); Moulton, 20-21.

97 BAGD, s.v. $\beta o \acute{u} \lambda o \mu \alpha \iota$ 2a.

98 See the commentary on 14:72 above.

99 Bultmann, *History*, 279.

100 Yarbro Collins, *Beginning of the Gospel*, 110.

101 See the commentary on v. 1 above.

102 BAGD, s.v. $\varphi \rho \alpha \gamma \epsilon \lambda \lambda \acute{o} \omega$. Josephus uses the Greek word with the same meaning, $\mu \alpha \sigma \tau \iota \gamma \acute{o} \omega$; see below. According to Mommsen, the punishment of beating (*verbera*) differed in form for slaves and free persons, respectively. In all periods, "whipping" (*flagella*) was typically done to slaves (*Römisches Strafrecht*, 983). In the fourth century, even in cases of free people, leaden balls were attached to the whips, which increased the danger of death (ibid., 983-84). *Verbera/verberare* and the synonym *caedere* were the most general terms for punishment involving a beating of some kind (Manfred Fuhrmann, "Verbera," in PW, *Supplementband IX: Acilius bis Utis* [Stuttgart: Alfred Druckenmüller, 1962] 1589-97, esp. 1589).

103 $\kappa \alpha \grave{\iota} \ \mu \alpha \sigma \tau \iota \gamma \acute{\omega} \sigma o \upsilon \sigma \iota \nu \ \alpha \dot{\upsilon} \tau \acute{o} \nu$ ("and they will whip him") in 10:34.

104 Nero was sentenced to this type of execution, but he committed suicide before the sentence could be

was a prelude to the punishment of crucifixion.[105] Josephus says that the governor Gessius Florus (64–66 CE), after a conflict between Jews and Greeks in Caesarea, whipped and crucified many peaceful citizens of Jerusalem, including some of equestrian rank:

whom he crucified after he mistreated them beforehand with whips . . . . For Florus ventured that day to do what none had ever done before, namely, to whip before his tribunal and nail to the cross men of equestrian rank, men who, if Jews by birth, were at least invested with that Roman dignity (οὓς μάστιξιν προαικισάμενος ἀνεσταύρωσεν . . . ὃ γὰρ μηδεὶς πρότερον τότε Φλῶρος ἐτόλμησεν, ἄνδρας ἱππικοῦ τάγματος μαστιγῶσαί τε πρὸ τοῦ βήματος

καὶ σταυρῷ προσηλῶσαι, ὧν εἰ καὶ τὸ γένος Ἰουδαῖον ἀλλὰ γοῦν τὸ ἀξίωμα Ῥωμαϊκὸν ἦν). (Bell. 2.14.9 §§306–8)[106]

According to ancient sources, crucifixion was a cruel form of execution, practiced by "barbarians."[107] The procedures and terminology vary.[108] The penalty was imposed for crimes such as "desertion to the enemy, the betraying of secrets, incitement to rebellion, murder, prophecy about the welfare of rulers (*de salute dominorum*), nocturnal impiety (*sacra impia nocturna*), magic (*ars magica*), serious cases of the falsification of wills etc."[109] It was most often inflicted on slaves, people of low social status (*humiliores*) and foreigners (*peregrini*).[110]

15

| | 15:16-20 Soldiers Mock Jesus | a |

16/ **Then the soldiers led Jesus into the courtyard, that is, the praetorium, and called together the whole cohort. 17/ And they dressed him in a purple cloak, wove an acanthus crown and put it on him. 18/ And they began to greet him, "Welcome, king[a] of the Jews!" 19/ And they hit him on the head with a reed and spat on him and, kneeling, showed him reverence. 20/ And when they had mocked him, they took the purple cloak off of him and put his clothes on him. And they led him out to crucify him.**

The earliest recoverable reading is probably that attested by ℵ B D et al., according to which the soldiers address Jesus as king using the vocative case, βασιλεῦ ("king" or "O king"), and thus ironically acknowledge his royal dignity. In the parallel account in the Gospel of John, the irony is weaker, since the nominative case, ὁ βασιλεύς ("the king"), is used, instead of the vocative. A C K N et al. have the same reading for Mark, perhaps under the influence of John 19:3. Cf. Taylor, ad loc., who does not appreciate the irony.

carried out. See Suetonius *Nero* 2: *corpus virgis ad necem caedi*, "beaten to death with rods" (text and trans. from Rolfe, *Suetonius*, 2:170–71); Mommsen, *Römisches Strafrecht*, 920 n. 5, also 939; Livy 1.26; Suetonius *Dom.* 8.3–4; Fuhrmann, "Verbera," 1591; Hengel, *Crucifixion*, 43 n. 10.

105 Cicero *Against Verres* 2.5.61–63 §§158–64; *Pro Rabirio* 16; Hengel, *Crucifixion*, 25, 41–45. According to Mommsen, a whipping preceded all forms of capital punishment in the republican period (*Römisches Strafrecht*, 938). Further types of torture often took place, especially in cases of the execution of slaves, at the whim of higher and lower officials (ibid., 939). Whipping regularly preceded execution also in the imperial period (Fuhrmann, "Verbera," 1592).

106 Text and trans. (modified) from Thackeray, *Josephus*, 2:442–43. During the siege of Jerusalem by Titus,

some Jews who left the city to search for food in the surrounding ravines were captured, whipped, subjected to torture and crucified opposite the walls of the city (*Bell.* 5.11.1 §§446–51). For further references to crucifixion in Josephus, see Hengel, *Crucifixion*, 26 n. 17. See also Lucian *Pisc.* 2; BAGD, s.v. φραγελλόω.

107 Greek and Roman writers downplay the use of this penalty by their own people (Hengel, *Crucifixion*, 22–23).

108 Ibid., 24–32.

109 Ibid., 34.

110 Ibid., 34–35, 46–50, 51–63. But see Hengel, "Crucifixion and Roman Citizens," ibid., 39–45.

Comment

■ **16-20** This scene is the fulfillment of two more parts of Jesus' third prediction of the passion: "and they will mock him and spit upon him" (καὶ ἐμπαίξουσιν αὐτῷ καὶ ἐμπτύσουσιν αὐτῷ) (10:34).

The question of the historical reliability of this passage is often linked to the issue of its presence in the earliest passion narrative or in Mark's source and to the topic of its similarity to other texts. Bultmann argued that this scene is a secondary expansion of the earliest account of the passion, which was added to explain and elaborate the mention of whipping in v. 15b.[111] The narrative can equally well be understood as implying that, after the whipping ordered by Pilate (v. 15b), the governor handed Jesus over to the soldiers to be crucified. Before leading him out to crucify him (v. 20b), they mocked him, on the assumption that he had claimed to be the king of the Jews (vv. 16-20a).

In contrast to Bultmann, others have concluded that this scene was part of the earliest recoverable passion narrative.[112] Vincent Taylor argued that the passage may have been added by Mark, but that it is historically reliable.[113] It is certainly credible that soldiers mocked Jesus, but the details of the scene cannot be assumed to be historically reliable, especially since they develop the literary theme of the ironic kingship of Jesus.

Hugo Grotius already remarked on the similarity between the account of the mocking of Jesus in the Gospels and Philo's description of the mocking of

Agrippa I (Herod's grandson) in Alexandria in 38 CE, just after he had been given the northern domains of Philip the tetrarch and the title of king (*Flacc.* 6 §§36–39).[114] Philo says that this impromptu mocking was similar to "theatrical mimes" (θεατρικοὶ μῖμοι) (*Flacc.* 6 §38).[115] Another text describes how the people of Alexandria had mocked a king by performing a mime (*Acts of Paul and Antoninus* col. 1).[116] The king in question was probably the royal or messianic pretender who led the revolt in Cyrene, whose name was Lukuas according to Eusebius or Andreias as Cassius Dio says. This mime probably took place in about 117 CE.[117] These two texts suggest that there may have been a type of mime that could be called "the mocked king" and that it served as a model for this scene.[118] This passage also has similarities to ancient rituals and literary texts related to the notion of a scapegoat or φαρμακός.[119]

Cassius Dio reports an incident that allegedly occurred in 69 CE, around the time that Mark was written. When Vitellius was in hiding, knowing that he would be deposed and perhaps murdered, soldiers (στρατιῶται) found him, tore off the ragged and filthy clothing in which he had disguised himself, tied "his hands behind his back and put a rope around his neck." Some slapped (ῥαπίζειν) him, "some plucked at his beard; all mocked (σκώπτειν) him, all insulted (ὑβρίζειν) him. . . ."[120] The soldiers mocked him further, murdered him, cut off his head, and carried it around Rome. Dio notes the irony of the striking reversal in Vitellius's fortune, but this is a different kind of irony from that in the mocking of Jesus.

111 Bultmann, *History*, 272; Klostermann, 161.
112 Schenke, *Der gekreuzigte Christus*, 54–55; Pesch, 2:468; Mohr, *Markus- und Johannespassion*, 302–8; Yarbro Collins, *Beginning of the Gospel*, 110–11; Reinbold, *Der älteste Bericht*, 119, 164–66.
113 Taylor, 584–85.
114 Hugo Grotius, *Annotationes in Novum Testamentum* (denuo emendatius editae; 9 vols.; Groningae: W. Zuidema, 1826–34) 2:356 (ad Matt 27:28-29); Yarbro Collins, "Genre," 15. Cf. Klostermann, 161; Taylor, 646–48. See also the section "Genre" in the excursus on the passion narrative in the commentary on 14:1-11 above.
115 Text and trans. (modified) from Colson and Whitaker, *Philo*, 9:322–23.
116 Text in Musurillo, *Pagan Martyrs*, 49–50; trans. ibid., 57.
117 Ibid., 182–85. See "Genre" in the excursus on the

passion narrative in the commentary on 14:1-11 above.
118 Yarbro Collins, "From Noble Death," 494–95. On the ancient mimes in general, see Walter Headlam and Alfred D. Knox, *The Mimes and Fragments: Herodas* (London: Bristol Classic Press, 2001); Frank-Joachim Simon, *τὰ κύλλ᾽ ἀείδειν: Interpretationen zu den Mimiamben des Herodas* (Frankfurt am Main: Lang, 1991); Alfred D. Knox, *Herodas, Cercidas, and the Greek Cholimabic Poets* (London: Heinemann; New York: Putnam's Sons, 1929); Hermann Reich, *Der Mimus: Ein litterar-entwickelungsgeschichtlicher Versuch*, vol. 1, part 1: *Theorie des Mimus* (Berlin: Weidmann, 1903).
119 See Yarbro Collins, "Finding Meaning," 181–87.
120 Cassius Dio 64.20; text and trans. from Earnest Cary and Herbert B. Foster, *Dio's Roman History* (9 vols.; LCL; Cambridge, MA: Harvard University Press;

■ 16 The "soldiers" (στρατιῶται) were Greek-speaking eastern provincials, not Latin-speaking Romans or Italians. The core of the Roman army was made up of legions, and normally only Roman citizens served in them.[121] The rest of the soldiers were auxiliaries. Auxiliary troops were made up of provincials who were recruited locally.[122] Jews were exempt from this service.[123] The infantrymen of both legions and auxiliaries were organized into cohorts, and the cavalry into *alae* ("wings").[124] The auxiliaries of Augustus were organized in three types of units: the *cohors peditata* (troop of foot soldiers), the *cohors equitata* (a troop containing foot soldiers and some mounted soldiers), and the *ala* (cavalry).[125] The cohorts and *alae* of the auxiliaries recruited in the western provinces were named after the tribe or region from which they came; those in the eastern provinces after a city.[126] Before the war that reached its climax in the destruction of Jerusalem in 70 CE, the governors were prefects (until the reign of Claudius) and procurators (from then until the end of the war) from the equestrian order.[127] Before the war, only auxiliary troops were stationed in Judea, and they served under the command of the governor. Troops from Samaria-Sebaste (Σεβαστηνοί) and Caesarea (Καισαρεῖς) played the largest role.[128] One cohort of auxiliaries was stationed permanently in Jerusalem, and they resided in the

London: Heinemann, 1925) 8:252–55. The reference to 65.20 in Pesch (2:472) is incorrect.

121 Henry M. D. Parker, *The Roman Legions* (Cambridge: W. Heffer and Sons, 1958) 9–46. In the second century, legionary soldiers were recruited from Galatia and Cappadocia and given Roman citizenship as individuals (ibid., 149, 160, 169–71, 181–82, 184–85). Under Hadrian "the difference of status between legions and *auxilia* was greatly modified and finally disappeared" (ibid., 171, 243–44); George R. Watson, *The Roman Soldier* (Aspects of Greek and Roman Life; London: Thames & Hudson, 1969) 16, 24; George L. Cheesman, *The Auxilia of the Roman Imperial Army* (Oxford: Clarendon, 1914; reprinted Chicago: Ares, 1975) 133; Lawrence Keppie, *The Making of the Roman Army: From Republic to Empire* (London: B. T. Batsford, 1984) 185–86. See also Denis B. Saddington, "Roman Military and Administrative Personnel in the New Testament," *ANRW* 2.26.3 (1996) 2409–35.

122 Paul A. Holder, *The Auxilia from Augustus to Trajan* (BAR International Series 70; Oxford: B.A.R., 1980) 121, 123. "Many regiments [of the auxiliaries] served at first in or close to their own tribal zone" (Keppie, *Making of the Roman Army*, 185). After the first Jewish war with Rome, Vespasian transferred the locally recruited troops to other provinces and brought in troops recruited elsewhere, some from the far western part of the empire (Schürer, *History*, 1:367; Cheesman, *Auxilia of the Roman Imperial Army*, 58–59, 61, 162–63, 170, 182). On the deployment of legions in the Roman campaign to put down the rebellion, see Parker, *Roman Legions*, 138–40. When the revolt had been put down, only one legion (X Fretensis) was stationed in Judea (Josephus *Bell.* 7.1.2 §5; Parker, 149, 158). Another legion (VI Ferrata) was sent to Galilee at the end of Trajan's reign; after the revolt under Hadrian, Judea had two

legions (VI Ferrata and X Fretensis; Parker, 149, 162–63). On the titles, emblems, and formation of these legions, see Keppie, *Making of the Roman Army*, 207–8. According to Graham Webster, VI Ferrata was established at Bostra (Busra) in 106 CE, when the Nabatean state was annexed to the empire (*The Roman Imperial Army of the First and Second Centuries A.D.* [3rd ed.; London: A & C Black, 1985] 65; see also fig. 9 [86]).

123 Schürer, *History*, 1:362. Appian, however, says that there were Jews in Pompey's auxiliary army (Denis B. Saddington, *The Development of the Roman Auxiliary Forces from Caesar to Vespasian (49 B.C.–A.D. 79)* [Harare, Zimbabwe: University of Zimbabwe, 1982] 9). These may have been slaves (cf. ibid., 8).

124 Cheesman, *Auxilia of the Roman Imperial Army*, 22–23; Watson, *Roman Soldier*, 15, 24–25; Keppie, *Making of the Roman Army*, 182; Webster, *Roman Imperial Army*, 145–49.

125 Holder, *Auxilia from Augustus to Trajan*, 5–9. On the *cohors equitata*, see also Cheesman, *Auxilia of the Roman Imperial Army*, 30.

126 Keppie, *Making of the Roman Army*, 182; cf. Schürer, *History*, 1:362; Cheesman, *Auxilia of the Roman Imperial Army*, 46.

127 Schwartz, "Pontius Pilate," 397; after the war, the governor of the province of Judea was a legate of senatorial rank (Schürer, *History*, 1:367).

128 Schürer, *History*, 1:363–65; Saddington, *Development of the Roman Auxiliary Forces*, 50. Note that Herod's army included Thracian, German, and Gallic troops (Josephus *Ant.* 17.8.3 §198). Some at least of these troops may have served later as auxiliaries under the Romans (Holder, *Auxilia from Augustus to Trajan*, 14). According to Holder, the auxiliary units raised in Judea were in existence from an early date, including three different series of cohorts from Iturea (ibid., 113; see the list of regiments and the date of

Antonia, the fortress located just north of the temple.[129] When Pilate visited Jerusalem, the troops that accompanied him would have stayed with him in the praetorium.[130]

The term αὐλή normally refers to the "court" or "forecourt" attached to an ordinary house. Although some take it to mean "palace" here,[131] it is more likely that it means "courtyard."[132] The view that it means "palace" seems to be based on the identification of the αὐλή with the "praetorium" in v. 16. In the present context, the audiences infer that the interrogation of Jesus by Pilate and the scene in which the crowd asks for Barabbas take place outside the praetorium in public space of some sort. The pre-Markan passion narrative, however, lacked the scene concerning Barabbas, and the setting of the interrogation is unclear. In that context, the audiences may have inferred that the interrogation took place in a room inside the building. When Jesus is delivered to the soldiers, they take him outside, that is, into the courtyard, for the whipping and then the mocking. The impression that the whipping took place somewhere other than the courtyard may be due to Mark's rewriting of v. 15b.

The term πραιτώριον (Latin *praetorium*) means, in this context, the headquarters of the provincial governor, Pilate.[133] The primary residence and headquarters of Pilate were in Caesarea, as was the case with all the Roman governors. He had a secondary residence and headquarters in Jerusalem, where he went occasionally, especially during the main festivals to ensure that order was maintained.[134]

The main verb of v. 16a, which sets the scene, is in the aorist tense: ἀπήγαγον ("they led him" or "they led him away"). The main verb of the next clause, συγκαλοῦσιν ("they called together," lit., "they call together"), is in the present tense. The shift to the present tense indicates that the mocking itself is beginning; the historical present is used to create a vivid effect and to involve the audience.

The word σπεῖρα was a technical military term. In the NT and early Christian literature, it is probably equivalent to a "cohort."[135] A cohort was, in principle, the tenth part of a legion. Since a legion consisted of five thousand to six thousand men,[136] a legionary cohort would normally be five hundred to six hundred men. The cohorts of the auxiliary troops varied in number from five hundred to one thousand men.[137] In the first century CE, the smaller size was more common.[138] The depiction of the gathering of roughly five hundred troops supports the interpretation of the αὐλή here as a courtyard.[139] T. E. Schmidt has argued that the gathering of the *whole* cohort in the praetorium is meant to evoke the presence of the entire praetorian guard at an imperial triumph.[140] The parallel, however, seems far-fetched.

■ **17** The use of the historical present continues in this verse. Although it is not stated in v. 17,[141] v. 20a implies

---

their first attestation in Palestine in Appendix III, on p. 232).

129 Schürer, *History*, 1:366.

130 Ibid., 1:361–62.

131 BAGD, s.v. αὐλή; Allen, 183; Pesch, 2:471.

132 Moulton-Milligan, s.v. αὐλή; Taylor, 585; Lührmann, 257; Gundry, 942.

133 On the history of the Latin term and its various usages, see John B. Campbell, "Praetorium," *OCD* 1241.

134 Schürer, *History*, 1:361. See also the commentary on v. 8 above.

135 BAGD, s.v. σπεῖρα. According to Saddington, Josephus used σπεῖρα or σπεῖρα πεζῶν for *cohors* and ἴλη or ἴλη ἱππέων for *ala* (*Development of the Roman Auxiliary Forces*, 49).

136 Watson, *Roman Soldier*, 13; Keppie, *Making of the Roman Army*, 173.

137 Schürer, *History*, 1:362; Cheesman, *Auxilia of the*

138 Cheesman, *Auxilia of the Roman Imperial Army*, 25. According to Keppie, most auxiliary cohorts under Augustus numbered 480–500 men; perhaps "from the time of Nero, or more certainly from the Flavian period," they ranged in size from eight hundred to one thousand men (*Making of the Roman Army*, 182).

139 Finegan notes that broad courtyards in the fortress Antonia "provided accommodation for troops" and that a cohort of soliders was permanently stationed there (*Archaeology*, 196), citing Josephus *Bell.* 5.5.8 §241.

140 T. E. Schmidt, "Mark 15.16-32: The Crucifixion Narrative and the Roman Triumphal Procession," *NTS* 41 (1995) 1–18, esp. 6.

141 Pesch comments that Jesus' clothes would already have been removed for the whipping (2:472); so also Gundry, 942.

Roman Imperial Army, 25–26; Watson, *Roman Soldier*, 15, 25.

that Jesus' own clothing was removed before the soldiers put some kind of purple garment ($\pi o\rho\varphi\acute{v}\rho\alpha$) on him.[142]

In the East, kings allowed their deputies and local leaders under their patronage and control to wear purple clothing.[143] The higher magistrates in Rome wore togas bordered with purple.[144] Victorious commanders in triumphal processions wore the *toga picta* or *trabea triumphalis*, which was made of purple wool and gold thread.[145]

The crown ($\sigma\tau\acute{\epsilon}\varphi\alpha\nu o\varsigma$) complements the purple garment as another emblem of rulers subordinate to the great kings of the East.[146] In Christian tradition, the "crown of thorns" has been viewed as an instrument of torture, as well as of the mocking of Jesus as a king.[147] The context, however, suggests that it was primarily, if not entirely, an instrument of mocking.[148] The soldiers wove the crown out of material that they found near at hand ($\pi\lambda\acute{\epsilon}\xi\alpha\nu\tau\epsilon\varsigma$ $\acute{\alpha}\kappa\acute{\alpha}\nu\vartheta\iota\nu o\nu$ $\sigma\tau\acute{\epsilon}\varphi\alpha\nu o\nu$).[149] The plant that they used was probably the Syrian acanthus.[150] Although the acanthus was sometimes depicted in decorative art (Aristeas 70), it was a weed and of no utilitarian value.[151] This element of the narrative is analogous to the use of the twigs of the wild fig tree to drive out the human scapegoat, the *pharmakos*.[152]

■ **18** Here the narrator shifts from the historical present to the typically Markan use of the aorist of $\acute{\alpha}\rho\chi\epsilon\sigma\vartheta\alpha\iota$ ("to begin") with the infinitive.[153] The vividness of the narrative is maintained by quoting the words of the soldiers in direct speech, "Welcome, king of the Jews!" ($\chi\alpha\hat{\iota}\rho\epsilon$, $\beta\alpha\sigma\iota\lambda\epsilon\hat{v}$ $\tau\hat{\omega}\nu$ $\emph{I}ov\delta\alpha\acute{\iota}\omega\nu$). The Alexandrians similarly mocked the surrogate Agrippa I by pretending to greet him, as well as to bring legal cases to him and to converse with him on state affairs.[154]

The address of Jesus here as "king of the Jews" takes up the question Pilate put to Jesus in v. 2 and the questions he addresses to the crowd in vv. 9 and 12. The soldiers, as characters in the narrative, parody the claim that Jesus is the messiah or king of the Jews. They force him to mimic the dress of a king, and they themselves mimic the interaction of subjects with their king. In these activities, they attempt to expose the supposed pretension or falsity in the claim that Jesus is a king. The passage, as a text, is ironic in its deployment of the rhetorical device in which the perspective of the author is in sharp contrast to the literal meaning, in this case, to the parody of Jesus' kingship. This device depends on the collaboration of the audiences, who, along with the author, know that Jesus is indeed a king.[155]

■ **19** In this verse, the mocking turns to mistreatment. The main verbs are in the imperfect tense. The imperfect

---

142 Cf. the dressing of the simpleton with a rug ($\chi\alpha\mu\alpha\acute{\iota}\sigma\tau\rho\omega\tau o\varsigma$) in lieu of a royal mantle ($\chi\lambda\alpha\mu\acute{v}\varsigma$) in the mocking of Agrippa I (Philo *Flacc.* 6 §37; Colson and Whitaker, *Philo,* 9:322–23).

143 Dan 5:7, 29; 1 Macc 10:20, 62, 64; 11:58; 14:43-44; contrast 1 Macc 8:14; Swete, 375; Klostermann, 162; Pesch, 1:472. See also Josephus *Ant.* 11.6.10 §§256–57; 13.2.2 §45; Josef Blinzler, *Der Prozess Jesu* (4th ed.; Regensburg: Pustet, 1969) 325–26 and nn. 27–28.

144 LS, s.v. *praetexo*; Hero Granger-Taylor, "Toga," *OCD* 1533; Ludwig A. Moritz, "Purple," ibid., 1280.

145 Granger-Taylor, "Toga," 1533. Schmidt argued that the combination of purple robe and crown here also evokes the Roman triumph ("Mark 15.16-32," 7; see the commentary on v. 16 above). The mockery of Jesus as king of the Jews, however, evokes the practice of local rulers subject to the Romans more strongly than the Roman triumph.

146 $\sigma\tau\acute{\epsilon}\varphi\alpha\nu o\varsigma$ $\chi\rho\nu\sigma o\hat{v}\varsigma$ ("golden crown"): Esth 8:15; 1 Macc 10:20. See also Josephus *Ant.* 13.2.2 §45; Blinzler, *Der Prozess Jesu,* 326 and n. 27.

147 Walter Grundmann, "$\sigma\tau\acute{\epsilon}\varphi\alpha\nu o\varsigma$, $\sigma\tau\epsilon\varphi\alpha\nu\acute{o}\omega$," *TDNT* 7 (1971) 632.

148 Loisy, 453; Blinzler, *Der Prozess Jesu,* 326.

149 Cf. the use of a sheet of papyrus as a mock diadem and the way in which the rioters picked up a papyrus rush that someone had thrown away and gave it to the surrogate Agrippa I as a scepter (Philo *Flacc.* 6 §37).

150 Irene Jacob and Walter Jacob, "Flora," *ABD* 2:803–17. The Syrian acanthus is discussed on 815; the material of the "crown of thorns" is traditionally defined as the *Ziziphus spina-christi* (Heb. ʾāṭād) (ibid., 805). See also Pesch, 2:472.

151 Jacob and Jacob, "Flora," 815.

152 Yarbro Collins, "Finding Meaning," 186–87.

153 Pryke, *Redactional Style,* 79–87. This usage here may simply be an indication of Mark's reformulation of the source material in his own words and style.

154 The same verb is used as in Mark: $\acute{\alpha}\sigma\pi\acute{\alpha}\zeta\epsilon\sigma\vartheta\alpha\iota$ ("to greet"); Philo *Flacc.* 6 §38 (Colson and Whitaker, *Philo,* 9:322–23).

155 Yarbro Collins, "From Noble Death," 495–96.

could be used here as equivalent to the aorist, or it could perhaps be iterative.[156]

The reed (κάλαμος) suggests a mock scepter,[157] but instead of giving it to Jesus to hold, they hit his head with it. The point does not seem to be to cause him pain, but to insult and humiliate him.[158] This gesture may be related to an opaque prophetic text:

> Now (the) daughter of Ephraim will be barricaded with a blockade; affliction he has appointed for us; with a rod they will strike the tribes of Israel on the cheek (νῦν ἐμφραχθήσεται θυγάτηρ Εφραιμ ἐν φραγμῷ, συνοχὴν ἔταξεν ἐφ᾽ ἡμᾶς, ἐν ῥάβδῳ πατάξουσιν ἐπὶ σιαγόνα τὰς φυλὰς τοῦ Ισραηλ). (Mic 4:14 LXX; 5:1 NRSV)

The Hebrew version refers to בַת־גְּדוּד ("daughter of gĕdûd"). The translation is disputed, but it is likely that the phrase refers to Zion.[159] The last clause in the Hebrew version reads:

בַּשֵּׁבֶט יַכּוּ עַל־הַלְּחִי אֵת שֹׁפֵט יִשְׂרָאֵל

("With a staff they are striking the cheek of the judge of Israel"). (Mic 4:14 MT)[160]

The "judge of Israel" here may be the king of Judah.[161] It may be that Mark was familiar with the Hebrew version or with a Greek version closer to the Hebrew than the LXX. The obscurity of the text may have invited interpretive activity identifying the one struck on the cheek with Jesus.[162]

The sermon collection known as *Pesiqta de Rab Kahana* alludes to Mic 4:14 (5:1) and interprets the one being struck with a rod on the cheek as the prophet Micah himself.[163] Rab Kahana belonged to the second generation of Babylonian Amoraim. The sermon collection, however, is of a later date.[164] The basis for this collection may be a midrashic compilation made by R. Tanḥum(a) bar Abba, one of the fifth-century Amoraim.[165] The work probably derives from Palestine in the fifth century CE.[166]

After hitting Jesus with a reed, the soldiers spit on him. Like 14:65, this gesture evokes part of a speech attributed to the Servant of the Lord:

> My back I gave to strokes with a whip, and my cheeks to slaps, and my face I did not turn away from the disgrace of being spit upon (τὸν νῶτόν μου δέδωκα εἰς μάστιγας, τὰς δὲ σιαγόνας μου εἰς ῥαπίσματα, τὸ δὲ πρόσωπόν μου οὐκ ἀπέστρεψα ἀπὸ αἰσχύνης ἐμπτυσμάτων). (Isa 50:6 LXX)[167]

The reference to being whipped on the back may have been seen as fulfilled in the whipping ordered by Pilate (v. 15b), and the slaps on the cheeks in the slaps with which the servants of the high priest "get" Jesus (14:65).[168] The disgrace of being spit upon is then evoked

---

156 On the use of the imperfect as equivalent to the aorist in Mark, see Swete, l. Gundry assumes the iterative usage (940). On the iterative imperfect (repeated action), see Smyth §1790.

157 Cf. the papyrus rush given to the surrogate Agrippa I to hold as a scepter (Philo *Flacc.* 6 §37).

158 Cf. the punching and slapping of Jesus by members of the council and the servants of the high priest; see the commentary on 14:65 above.

159 Delbert R. Hillers, *Micah: A Commentary on the Book of the Prophet Micah* (Hermeneia; Philadelphia: Fortress, 1984) 62, n. a; Francis I. Andersen and David Noel Freedman, *Micah: A New Translation with Introduction and Commentary* (AB 24E; New York/London: Doubleday, 2000) 459.

160 Mic 4:14 MT; text from *BHS*; trans. from Hillers, *Micah*, 62.

161 Hillers, *Micah*, 63; Andersen and Freedman, *Micah*, 461.

162 Cf. Loisy, 453–54.

163 *Pesiq. R. Kah.* 16.4; William G. (Gershon Zev) Braude and Israel J. Kapstein, *Pĕsiḳta dĕ Rab-Kahăna: R. Kahana's Compilation of Discourses for Sabbaths and Festal Days* (Philadelphia: Jewish Publication Society of America, 2002/5762) 391.

164 Herman L. Strack and Günter Stemberger, *Introduction to the Talmud and Midrash* (Edinburgh: T & T Clark, 1991) 95; cf. 321.

165 Ibid., 106.

166 Ibid., 321.

167 See also Yarbro Collins, "From Noble Death," 494 and n. 51.

168 On the trans. of this unusual phrase, see note 85 on the commentary on 14:65 above.

or fulfilled here in the mistreatment of Jesus by the soldiers (v. 19b). The spitting upon Jesus here also fulfills his own prophecy in the third passion prediction.[169]

In the last clause of v. 19, the activity of the soldiers returns to mocking parody: "and, kneeling, showed him reverence" (καὶ τιθέντες τὰ γόνατα προσεκύνουν αὐτῷ). The usage τιθέναι τὰ γόνατα ("to kneel") is probably a Latinism (genua ponere).[170] The main verb, προσκυνεῖν ("to show reverence"), is typically Greek.[171] It can imply prostrating oneself on the ground.[172] Here, however, combined with the gesture of kneeling, it probably means a deep bow on bended knee.

The Greeks used the term προσκυνεῖν ("to do reverence") in relation to their adoration of the gods. They rejected the Persian practice of showing reverence or submission to the great king by prostrating oneself or bowing deeply (προσκυνεῖν),[173] but the Persians did not consider their kings to be divine.[174] The Achaemenids presented themselves only as having a divine mandate to rule. It was the Sasanid rulers (beginning around 224 CE) who first claimed to have a divine lineage.[175] Thus, the gesture of the soldiers should be interpreted as a parody of an extravagant gesture of reverence to a king in the cultural region of the eastern Mediterranean world. It is unlikely that the idea of divinity plays any role here.[176]

Like the address of Jesus as "the king of the Jews" in v. 18, this last gesture of the soldiers is ironic in the passage as text. The author and the ideal audiences recognize that Jesus' power and authority are appropriately acknowledged by such a gesture. When the Gerasene demoniac bowed down before Jesus, it was the demon paying tribute to Jesus' status as "son of the most high God" and his power to cast out the unclean spirit.[177]

■ **20** The narrator's comment, "And when they had mocked him" (καὶ ὅτε ἐνέπαιξαν αὐτῷ), explicitly marks all or some of the actions of the soldiers as parody. The audience no longer needs help in recognizing the nature of these actions.[178] The explicit reference to "mocking" (ἐμπαίζειν) may be a stimulus to the audiences to recall Jesus' prophecy that, after he is handed over to the nations, they will mock him (ἐμπαίξουσιν αὐτῷ) (10:33-34).

The soldiers remove the purple garment from Jesus and put his own clothes back on him. It is not stated that they remove the acanthus crown from his head. The text thus leaves open the possibility that Jesus continued to wear the crown as he was led out to be crucified and during his crucifixion.[179] If so, the crucifixion itself becomes highly ironic. The prisoner goes to his death and dies on the cross, having been whipped and wearing an improvised mock-crown. This image is "a secret epiphany" of Jesus as the royal messiah.[180] It reveals and conceals the mystery of the kingdom of God, announced to the disciples at Caesarea Philippi, that the kingship of the earthly Jesus is characterized by rejection, suffering, and death.

The statement that "they led him out to crucify him" (ἐξάγουσιν αὐτὸν ἵνα σταυρώσωσιν αὐτόν) signifies primarily that the soldiers led Jesus out of the praetorium. Secondarily, it also means that they led him out of the city of Jerusalem. It is highly likely that the place of Jesus' crucifixion was outside of the current walls of the city.[181]

---

169 See the commentary on 10:34 above; see also Gundry, 940–41.

170 BDF §5.3b; BAGD, s.v. τίθημι 1.b.γ; Gundry, 943.

171 The only other place in which Mark uses the word is 5:6; see the commentary above.

172 BAGD, s.v. προσκυνέω; Heinrich Greeven, "προσκυνέω, προσκυνητής," TDNT 6 (1968) 758–66, esp. 759, 760–61.

173 Greeven, "προσκυνέω, προσκυνητής," 759.

174 Contra BAGD, s.v. προσκυνέω.

175 William W. Malandra, "Religion and Politics: Iran," in Sarah Iles Johnston, ed., Religions of the Ancient World (Cambridge, MA/London: Belknap Press of Harvard University Press, 2004) 555–56.

176 Similarly, Gundry, 943.

177 See the commentary on 5:6-7 above.

178 Cf. Fowler, Let the Reader Understand, 157.

179 Gundry, 943.

180 Dibelius used this term with regard to the Gospel of Mark as a whole (From Tradition to Gospel, 230, 260, 297), especially with regard to the first section (1:1-13) (ibid., 231).

181 Such a location fits the context, in which the soldiers leading Jesus out encounter Simon coming in from the country (v. 21). Cf. Acts 7:58. For further evidence and arguments, see Brown, Death, 2:912–13. See also the commentary on v. 22 below.

In his effort to make a case that the crucifixion of Jesus in Mark is an "anti-triumph," Schmidt argued that the verb ἐξάγειν ("to lead out") is used "commonly in the NT and elsewhere to denote a procession involving the accompaniment of a key figure by others."[182] This remark, however, is a misrepresentation of the use of this verb in the passages from the NT that he cites.

---

182 Schmidt, "Mark 15.16-32," 8 and n. 23.

15

15:21-39 The Crucifixion and Death
of Jesus

21/ And they forced a certain passerby,
Simon of Cyrene, who was com-
ing from the country, the father of
Alexander and Rufus, to carry his
cross. 22/ And they brought him
to the place Golgotha, that is,
translated, the place that is called
Skull. 23/ And they tried to give
him wine to which myrrh had
been added, but he did not take
it. 24/ And they crucified him and
divided his clothes, casting lots
for them (to determine) who
would take what. 25/ Now it was
the third[a] hour when they crucified[b] him. 26/ And the inscription
of the offense of which he had
been found guilty was posted:
"the king of the Jews." 27/ And
they crucified two robbers with
him, one on his right and one on
his left.[c]

29/ And those who passed by reviled
him, shaking their heads and saying, "Hah! You who are about to
destroy the sanctuary and build
(another) in three days, 30/ save
yourself by coming down from
the cross!" 31/ Similarly, the
chief priests also mocked him
among themselves along with
the scribes, saying, "He saved
others; himself he cannot save;
32/ let the messiah, the king of
Israel, come down now from the
cross, in order that we may see
and believe." And those who
were crucified with him also
insulted him.

33/ And at the sixth hour, darkness
came upon the whole land until
the ninth hour. 34/ And at the
ninth hour, Jesus cried out with a
loud voice, "Eloi, Eloi,[d] lema[e]
sabachthani?,"[f] that is, translated,
"My God, my God, why have you
abandoned me?"[g] 35/ And some
of those who were standing by
heard (him) and said, "Look, he is
calling Elijah." 36/ Then one (of
them) ran, filled a sponge with
sour wine, placed it on a reed,
and tried to give it to him to
drink, saying, "Let us see whether
Elijah is coming to take him
down." 37/ But Jesus uttered a
loud cry and expired. 38/ And the
curtain of the sanctuary was
split in two from top to bottom.
39/ When the centurion who was
standing by opposite him[h] saw

a   The reading ἕκτη ("sixth"), attested by Θ *pc* sy[hmg], is
probably due to a correction of Mark's text in light of
John 19:14; see the discussion in Taylor, ad loc.; cf.
Metzger, *Textual Commentary*, 99. ·

b   The earliest recoverable reading is probably καὶ
ἐσταύρωσαν ("when they crucified him," lit., "and
they crucified him"), attested by the majority of the
MSS. This statement is repetitive, especially if the καὶ
("when," lit., "and") is taken as coordinating rather
than subordinating; for the use of coordination
instead of subordination with temporal designations,
see BDF §442 (4). The difficulty of this reading has
given rise to two variants: *f*[13] *pc* aur sy[p] sa[mss] attest a
reading in which ὅτε ("when") has been substituted
for καὶ ("when," lit., "and"). D it sa[mss] attest the reading καὶ ἐφύλασσον, "and they kept watch over
(him)." It is more likely that this reading was inspired
by the parallel in Matt 27:36 than that it represents
the text of Mark that Matthew read (contra Turner,
"Western Readings," 11; cf. Taylor, ad loc.).

c   In the traditional text of Mark, v. 28 follows, attested
by L Θ 083. 0250 *f*[1.13] 33 𝔐 et al., which reads καὶ
ἐπληρώθη ἡ γραφὴ ἡ λέγουσα· καὶ μετὰ ἀνόμων
ἐλογίσθη ("and the scripture was fulfilled which says,
'and he was considered to be among the lawless'").
The lack of the passage in ℵ A B C D et al. and the
agreement in the wording of the citation from Isa
53:12 is an indication that this verse was added under
the influence of Luke 22:37; see Taylor, ad loc.; Metzger, *Textual Commentary*, 99.

d   The transliteration here is based on the reading
attested by the majority of the MSS, ελωι ελωι ("Eloi,
Eloi"), which reflects a Hebraized Aramaic expression
meaning "my God." D Θ 059. 565 et al. attest the
reading ηλι ηλι ("Eli, Eli"), which is a transliteration
of the equivalent Hebrew expression. The latter reading probably arose under the direct influence of the
parallel in Matt 27:46 and the indirect influence of
the Hebrew of Ps 22:2. Cf. Metzger, *Textual Commentary*, 99–100. For a different opinion, see Turner,
"Western Readings," 12; idem, "Marcan Usage," 26
(1925) 154 n. 2 (Elliott, *Language and Style*, 33 n. 7).
Taylor concluded that the former reading is the earliest reading in Mark, even though he thought that the
latter better represents what the historical Jesus said
(ad loc.).

e   The transliteration is based on the reading λεμα
("lema"), attested by ℵ C L et al., which is a transitera-
tion of the Aramaic לְמָא ("why"). B D Θ et al. attest
the reading λαμα ("lama"), which is a transliteration
of the Hebrew לְמָה ("why"). A *f*[13] 33 𝔐 sy[h] attest the
reading λιμα ("lima"), which may be a variant transliteration of the Aramaic לְמָא ("why"). It is difficult to
decide which of these is the earliest reading. On the
one hand, the transliteration of an Aramaic word

that he had expired in this way,[i]
he said, "This man really was
God's son."

would fit well with the previous earlier reading in this verse, ελωι ελωι ("Eloi, Eloi"). On the other hand, the earliest recoverable reading of the parallel in Matthew combines the transliteration of the Hebrew ηλι ηλι ("Eli, Eli") with that of the Aramaic λεμα ("lema"). It seems most likely that Matthew read ελωι ελωι λεμα ("Eloi, Eloi, lema") in Mark and changed only the first two words to conform more closely to the Hebrew. Then later, Mark's λεμα ("lema") was changed in some MSS to conform to the Hebrew.

f   The transliteration is based on the reading σαβαχθανι ("sabachthani"), attested by C L Δ Θ et al., which is a transliteration of the Aramaic שבקתני, meaning "you have abandoned me." The readings σαβακτανι ("sabaktani") attested by ℵ* and σιβακθανι ("sibaktani") attested by A are variant transliterations of the Aramaic; for a listing of variants, see Tischendorf, ad loc. The reading ζαφθανι ("zaphthani"), attested by D (i) vg^mss, probably reflects the assimilation of the text of Mark to the Hebrew עזבתני ("you have abandoned me") of Ps 22:2. The reading ζαβαφθανι ("zabaphthani"), attested by B, may also show the influence of the Hebrew. Cf. Metzger, *Textual Commentary*, 100.

g   The trans. is based on the reading ἐγκατέλιπές με ("have you abandoned me"), attested by ℵ B (L) et al. The variant word order, με ἐγκατέλιπες ("have you abandoned me"), attested by (A) C (K) Θ f^1.13 et al., probably arose under the influence of the parallel in Matt 27:46; cf. Metzger, *Textual Commentary*, 100. The reading ὠνείδισάς με ("have you insulted me"), attested by D c (i) k, is probably due to a deliberate revision, although the rationale is difficult to determine; contra Turner, "Western Readings," 12; cf. Taylor, ad loc.; Metzger, *Textual Commentary*, 100. For an argument that the change was made to oppose the Gnostic use of the text in support of their separationist Christology, see Ehrman, *Orthodox Corruption*, 143–45.

h   The trans. is based on the reading ἐξ ἐναντίας αὐτοῦ ("opposite him"), attested by the majority of MSS. This is a classical Greek ellipsis, in which χώρας ("place") is to be supplied; see BDF §241 (1). Perhaps because this expression was unfamiliar, or because it seemed cumbersome, two variants occur. W f^1 et al. attest the reading αὐτῷ, "(standing by) him." D Θ 565 et al. attest the reading ἐκεῖ, "(standing by) there."

i   W Θ 565. et al. attest a reading that lacks the word οὕτως ("in this way"). Since the longer reading is strongly attested by ℵ A B C D et al., however, it is likely to be the earlier reading; cf. Turner, "Western Readings," 12. It is more difficult to determine whether some form of the verb κράζω ("cry out") belongs to the earliest recoverable form of the text. A C W Θ et al. attest a reading with the nominative participle, κράξας ("having cried out"); D attests a reading with the accusative participle, κράξαντα ("having cried out"); and k the finite verb, ἔκραξεν ("he cried out"). It is true that the witnesses for a reading without any form of this verb, ℵ B L Ψ 892 *pc* sa (bo), belong primarily to a single textual group, group "B"; on textual groups, see Epp, "Dynamic View." But the variation in the form of κράζω ("cry out") suggests that the three other readings may be independent expansions; contra Turner, "Western Readings," 12–13; and Taylor, ad loc. Since the verb is so common, it is not necessary to conclude that it was directly inspired by Matt 27:50; contra Metzger, *Textual Commentary*, 100–101. A major difficulty with the reading of ℵ B L et al. is the lack of clarity about what led the centurion to conclude that Jesus was God's son; i.e., the referent of οὕτως ("in this way") is ambiguous. The addition of some form of the verb κράζω reflects an attempt to fill this gap: it must have been what Jesus said, which Mark does not report, that led the centurion to his insight. Luke then more effectively filled the gap by reporting words suitable to the context (Luke 23:46). Turner harmonized the two Gospels by concluding that Luke reports what Jesus actually said, whereas Mark's informant could hear the cry, but could not make out the words ("Western Readings," 13).

History of the Tradition and Historical Reliability

The main issues regarding the history of the tradition and historical reliability are (1) the character of the earliest recoverable account of Jesus' death; (a) whether it was a reliable historical report or already an interpretation with apologetic and dogmatic concerns; (b) whether it was culturally unified or complex, that is, whether it was produced by and for the earliest Aramaic-speaking community alone or for a variety of audiences, including both Aramaic- and Greek-speaking followers of Jesus; (2) whether the passages that evoke scripture represent historical events that are described in scriptural terms or whether they are fictions designed to interpret Jesus' death and to deal with the scandal that it caused; (3) in what detail it is possible to reconstruct the history of the tradition, that is, whether one can distinguish three stages of composition or only two; (4) whether repetition is usually a sign of secondary editing and expansion or whether, at least some of the time, it is a technique of primary (original, unitary) composition.

Bultmann took the position that the earliest account of Jesus' death was a neutral, that is, reliable, historical account. He considered all strongly interpretive elements to be later legendary elaborations. For example, he classi-fied any passage that alludes to scripture as a secondary expansion based on dogmatic or apologetic motives. He assigned some parts of the text to the oldest account and some to Mark, but did not attempt to describe the history of the composition of the text in any detail beyond that.

He assigned vv. 20b-24a to the oldest account.[1] The depiction of the soldiers casting lots for Jesus' clothing evokes Ps 21:19 LXX (22:18 NRSV); therefore, in his view, v. 24b is a later addition and not likely to be historical.[2] He made similar judgments about the mocking of the passersby in v. 29 (Ps 21:8 LXX [22:7]; Lam 2:15),[3] Jesus' last cry in v. 34 (Ps 21:2 LXX [22:1]),[4] and the drinking of "vinegar" in v. 36a (Ps 68:22 [69:21]).[5] It could well be that all the allusions to scripture are historically unreliable, but whoever wishes to make a case for reliability or unreliability must do so in each specific case. It is problematic to argue that the earliest recoverable narrative of the passion contained no allusions to scripture and that it was primarily a historical account and thus a reliable one. It is not clear why any of the followers of Jesus would have been interested in creating a "neutral" account of the passion. Historical reliability is not a criterion for literary priority.[6]

One of the scriptural allusions, however, seems likely

---

1   Bultmann, *History*, 273; cf. 279.
2   Ibid., 273, 281.
3   Ibid., 273, 281.
4   Ibid., 281.
5   Ibid., 273, 281.
6   Linnemann, *Studien zur Passionsgeschichte*, 136–37; Yarbro Collins, "From Noble Death," 488–89.

to be a Markan addition. Bultmann remained undecided whether the statement in v. 27 that Jesus was crucified between two criminals (or rebels) was historical or inspired by Isa 53:12.[7] On the one hand, there are historical problems with the portrayal, since there is no evidence for a revolt in the time of Jesus.[8] On the other, Mark would have had a reason to invent such a picture, since λῃσταί ("robbers" or "bandits" or "rebels") play an important role in the Markan passion narrative elsewhere.[9]

Bultmann also argued that the references to the time of day in vv. 25, 33, and 34 are Markan additions.[10] With respect to v. 25, he based this conclusion on the fact that the last clause of this verse, καὶ ἐσταύρωσαν αὐτόν ("when they crucified him," lit., "and they crucified him"),[11] repeats what is said in v. 24.[12] He does not make his reasoning explicit with regard to the same motif in vv. 33 and 34, but it seems to be that, if the temporal reference in v. 25 is Markan, then those of vv. 33-34 must be due to the evangelist's editing as well. The repetition in v. 25 may indeed seem awkward to some, but it can be explained as characteristic of a writing style influenced by oral communication.[13] Such repetition is especially understandable in a context such as this one, in which the narrative has slowed down to describe terrible and awesome events in some detail. Linnemann is more likely to be correct in her argument that the schema of the hours is a narrative device for telling the story of the crucifixion when little information was available.[14] Another possibility is that the schema is used for dramatic effect.[15]

In accordance with his view that the earliest account of the passion was historically oriented, Bultmann defined v. 26, with its mention of the charge against Jesus, "the king of the Jews," as a legendary expansion similar to v. 2.[16] He labeled this motif "dogmatic" and interpreted it as an expression of the faith of the church.[17] If the earliest account, however, was not a neutral description of historical events, then the specific motif of Jesus' execution for claiming to be the messiah is likely to be early, as well as apologetic and dogmatic.[18]

Bultmann used a literary argument in his treatment of vv. 34-35, 36b. He defined Jesus' cry of abandonment in v. 34 as a secondary elaboration of the wordless or unreported cry in v. 37. If v. 34 is secondary, then vv. 35, 36b must have been added at the same time.[19]

Returning to his thesis about the character of the oldest account, Bultmann argued that vv. 33, 38, and 39 are legendary expansions concerning the wonders (τέρατα) that took place at the death of Jesus and impressed "the Gentile onlookers."[20] In the section consisting of vv. 33-39, only v. 37 is "neutral," and it is impossible to tell whether it "ever had a place in an older (relatively) legend-free tradition."[21] If, as argued above, the schema of the hours is a narrative device attributable to the earliest recoverable form of the passion narrative and if the position that the oldest account was historically oriented is untenable, there is no good reason for defining v. 33 as secondary.[22] The same argument holds for the tearing of the curtain of the temple in v. 38.[23] The statement of the centurion in v. 39, however, is probably a Markan addition.[24]

---

7 Bultmann, *History*, 281. Linnemann concluded that v. 27 is secondary, but that it was already in Mark's source (*Studien zur Passionsgeschichte*, 157–58, 168–69).

8 See the commentary on v. 7 above.

9 See 14:48; 15:6-15; and the commentary on those verses above. See also the commentary on 11:17.

10 Bultmann, *History*, 273–74.

11 See note b on the trans. of v. 25 above.

12 Bultmann, *History*, 273.

13 See "Sources, Composition, and Performance" in the commentary on 13:1-37 above.

14 Linnemann, *Studien zur Passionsgeschichte*, 155–57; Yarbro Collins, *Beginning of the Gospel*, 97, 111–12.

15 See the commentary on vv. 34-39 below.

16 Bultmann, *History*, 272.

17 Ibid., 284.

18 See the commentary on v. 2 above; see also Yarbro Collins, *Beginning of the Gospel*, 109–10, 112–13.

19 Bultmann, *History*, 273, 313.

20 Ibid., 273–74. He also described the wonders as "novelistic motifs" (ibid., 282). Further, he interpreted v. 39 as the expression of a dogmatic motif (ibid., 283–84). For critical discussion of Bultmann's argument that v. 38 is secondary, see Yarbro Collins, *Beginning of the Gospel*, 116.

21 Ibid., 274.

22 Yarbro Collins, *Beginning of the Gospel*, 114–15.

23 Ibid., 116.

24 Ibid., 117.

Ludger Schenke was more confident than Bultmann about the feasibility of reconstructing the history of the tradition of the passion narrative. He discerned three layers or stages of composition: the oldest account, a pre-Markan expanded edition of the oldest account, and the Markan form of the passion narrative.[25] He rejected Bultmann's thesis that the oldest account was a neutral historical report. Instead, Schenke concluded that the earliest passion narrative had a polemical and apologetic character. Its main dogmatic emphasis was an apologetic insistence that the crucified one is the messiah. Against Lothar Ruppert, he concluded that it does not portray Jesus primarily as "the suffering just one," but he followed Ruppert in concluding that the destiny of the messiah is described in terms of that motif.[26]

With regard to the cultural character of the oldest account, Schenke concluded that it was written in and for the "Hebrews" mentioned in Acts, namely, Aramaic-speaking Jews among the post-Easter followers of Jesus in Jerusalem.[27] He attributed the pre-Markan expansion of the passion narrative to the followers of Jesus among the "Hellenists," or Greek-speaking Jews, in the earliest community in Jerusalem, who were led by Stephen and also mentioned in Acts.[28]

Schenke agreed with many of Bultmann's judgments about the account of Jesus' crucifixion and death.[29] The points on which he disagreed with Bultmann will be discussed briefly here. For literary and other reasons, Schenke argued that v. 21 is an addition to the oldest account. In his view, after the mention of Simon of Cyrene in v. 21, it is not clear whether the word αὐτόν ("him") in the phrase Καὶ φέρουσιν αὐτὸν ἐπὶ τὸν Γολγοθᾶν τόπον ("And they brought him to the place Golgotha") refers to Jesus or to Simon.[30] This is a weak argument, since the story is mainly about Jesus, and it is clear that Jesus is the one being taken to Golgotha to be crucified. He argued further that v. 21 is present because Hellenistic circles in the oldest community were interested in the Hellenistic Jew "Simon of Cyrene" and his sons, who probably played a particular role in those circles.[31] Verse 21 was added, with a critical undertone against the disciples, to make the point that the Hellenistic Jewish community could boast that one of their own had performed a service of true discipleship for Jesus.[32] He also argued that the presence of Greek translations of Aramaic words and phrases is evidence for the conclusion that the oldest account was written in Aramaic. Therefore, he concluded, the translation of the place-name "Golgotha" as "the place of (the) Skull" in v. 22b and the translation of Jesus' words of abandonment in v. 34b are secondary; that is, they belong to the pre-Markan second edition of the narrative.[33]

The presence of translations of Aramaic words and phrases in the passion narrative, however, does not necessarily imply that the earliest form of the narrative was composed in Aramaic. It could just as well have been composed in Greek by bilingual followers of Jesus who translated the Aramaic elements for the benefit of members of the audience who spoke Greek but not Aramaic. The mention of Simon of Cyrene is likely to be historical reminiscence. The memory of his forced service was maintained because his sons, Alexander and Rufus, were known to the earliest audiences of the narrative. The fact that Mark retains the reference to the sons suggests that they were known to the evangelist and to at least some members of his audiences.[34]

Unlike Bultmann, Schenke concluded that the passages that allude to scripture belong to the oldest account. He included in his reconstruction the depiction of the casting of lots for Jesus' clothing in v. 24b; the two

25 Schenke, *Der gekreuzigte Christus*, 22–23, 49–51, 141–45.
26 Ibid., 74–75, 137–40. For Ruppert's position and criticism of it, see the commentary on 14:18 above.
27 Schenke, *Der gekreuzigte Christus*, 84, 92, 140.
28 Ibid., 91–92, 143.
29 Schenke included the description of Jesus' death in v. 37 in the earliest account, whereas Bultmann remained agnostic on the issue. Cf. Schenke, *Der gekreuzigte Christus*, 98, 102, 137 with Bultmann, *History*, 274.
30 Schenke, *Der gekreuzigte Christus*, 83.
31 Ibid., 84.
32 Ibid., 91–92.
33 Ibid., 84, 90–91.
34 The fact that Matthew and Luke lack the names of the two sons may be explained by the hypothesis that they were no longer known to those two evangelists and their audiences (Matt 27:32; Luke 23:26). They retained the account of Simon of Cyrene's carrying of the cross-beam as a noteworthy historical reminiscence.

robbers crucified on either side of Jesus in v. 27; the mocking of the passersby in vv. 29a, 31b-32; the Aramaic part of Jesus' cry of abandonment in v. 34a, and the giving of vinegar to drink in v. 36a.[35]

As noted above, Bultmann concluded that all three temporal references are secondary. Schenke agreed that the references to the third hour in v. 25 and to the sixth hour in v. 33 are secondary, but he agreed with Vincent Taylor that the reference to the ninth hour in v. 34a is original.[36] As argued above, it is likely that all three temporal references are original.[37]

Because Schenke viewed the oldest account as apologetic, he included, on good grounds and against Bultmann, the description of the charge against Jesus, "king of the Jews," in v. 26.[38] He also accepted v. 39, the statement of the centurion, as part of the oldest account. As noted above, however, there are good reasons for concluding that v. 39 is a Markan addition.

Schenke attributed the tearing of the temple veil to the pre-Markan, Hellenistic-Jewish Christian edition of the passion narrative.[39] He assigned to the same source other passages dealing with the temple (14:57-59; 15:29b).[40] The position taken in this commentary is that the attempt to discern three layers or stages in the composition of the Markan passion narrative goes beyond the limits of the available evidence. As argued above, the scene containing Jesus' trial before the Judean council was composed and added by Mark.[41] Thus, it was the evangelist who added the theme of the destruction and replacement of the temple to the pre-Markan form of the passion narrative (14:58; 15:29b). Schenke concluded

that v. 38 is secondary because he interpreted that verse as signifying that divine judgment on the old temple had already begun.[42] If, however, 14:57-59 and 15:29b were not part of the pre-Markan passion narrative, the event of the tearing of the veil can be read quite differently. As argued above, the tearing of the veil in the pre-Markan account may be interpreted as symbolizing Jesus' ascent to heaven and entry into the presence of God. At the same time, it may symbolize the rending of the barrier between humanity and God.[43]

It is likely that the pre-Markan passion narrative ended with the death of Jesus and the event symbolized by the rending of the veil in v. 38.[44]

Comment

■ **21** The verb ἀγγαρεύειν is a Persian loanword meaning to requisition or press into service and thus to compel someone to perform some service for representatives of the imperial power.[45] The name Σίμων ("Simon") is the Greek equivalent of the Hebrew name שמעון ("Simeon" or "Symeon"). Both the Greek and the Hebrew forms of the name were very common among Jews in the first century CE.[46] The individual mentioned here was evidently a Jew from the Diaspora, specifically from the city of Cyrene or the territory in North Africa associated with it. Cyrene was the major Greek colony in Africa. It submitted to Alexander the Great and became a dependency of the Ptolemaic kingdom upon his death. In 96 BCE, it came under Roman rule. Under Augustus, Cyrenaica was combined with Crete to form a senatorial

---

35   Schenke, *Der gekreuzigte Christus*, 137.

36   Ibid., 84–85, 92, 95, 137.

37   See also Yarbro Collins, *Beginning of the Gospel*, 111–12, 114–15.

38   Schenke, *Der gekreuzigte Christus*, 102, 137. Detlev Dormeyer also included v. 26 in his reconstruction of the earliest form of the passion narrative (*Die Passion Jesu*, 195). Eta Linnemann's arguments for the secondary character of v. 26 are not compelling (*Studien zur Passionsgeschichte*, 147).

39   Schenke, *Der gekreuzigte Christus*, 141.

40   Ibid., 142.

41   See "History of the Tradition and Historical Reliability" in the commentary on 14:53-72 above.

42   Schenke, *Der gekreuzigte Christus*, 100, 142.

43   See the end of the section "Composition and His-

tory of the Tradition" in the excursus on the passion narrative in the commentary on 14:1-11 above.

44   See the section of this commentary cited in the previous note; see also Yarbro Collins, *Beginning of the Gospel*, 100–101, 116–17; Yarbro Collins, "From Noble Death," 497–99.

45   BAGD, s.v. ἀγγαρεύω; Moulton-Milligan, s.v. ἀγγαρεύω; BDF §6. The term occurs in the parallel in Matt 27:32 and also in the Sermon on the Mount (Betz, *Sermon*, 291).

46   See the commentary on 3:16 above.

province with a proconsul as governor.[47] Literary and inscriptional evidence attests to a substantial Jewish community in the city of Cyrene and more broadly in Cyrenaica.[48] It is possible that Simon was in Jerusalem as a pilgrim for the feast of Passover, but it is more likely that he had settled in Jerusalem. The latter situation could better explain the fact that the sons of Simon were apparently known to the author and audience of the pre-Markan passion narrative and also to the evangelist and at least some in his audiences.[49] Acts 6:9 (cf. 24:12) supports the conclusion that there was a synagogue in Jerusalem for the exclusive or joint use of Jews from Cyrenaica who had settled in Jerusalem.[50]

Simon is portrayed as a passer-by, coming from the country ($\pi\alpha\rho\acute{\alpha}\gamma o\nu\tau\acute{\alpha} \tau\iota\nu\alpha \ldots \acute{\epsilon}\rho\chi\acute{o}\mu\epsilon\nu o\nu \ \acute{\alpha}\pi$ $\mathaccent'\alpha\gamma\rho o\tilde{\upsilon}$). Gerd Theissen translated the latter phrase "coming in from the fields" and argued that Simon is depicted as coming from his work. He uses this datum to support the hypothesis that, according to the oldest account of the passion, Jesus died on the day of preparation for Passover, not on the first day of the feast itself, as in Mark.[51] The statement is not precise enough to make clear what the exact circumstances of Simon's activity were. Furthermore, evidence is lacking for the hypothesis that the earliest account placed Jesus' death on the day of preparation.[52]

As Theissen has pointed out, the best explanation for the identification of Simon as "the father of Alexander and Rufus" ($\acute{o} \ \pi\alpha\tau\grave{\eta}\rho \ \mathaccent'\!A\lambda\epsilon\xi\acute{\alpha}\nu\delta\rho o\upsilon \ \kappa\alpha\grave{\iota} \ \mathaccent'P o\acute{\upsilon}\varphi o\upsilon$) is that the two sons were better known to the author and audiences of the passion narrative than the father.[53] $\mathaccent'\!A\lambda\epsilon\xi\acute{\alpha}\nu\delta\rho o\varsigma$ ("Alexander") was of course a famous Greek name. It was common among Jews as well as Gentiles.[54] The name Alexander occurs on three of the eleven ossuaries found in a family tomb in the Kidron Valley used for burials in the first century CE, before the destruction of the temple. It is likely that the family came from one of the large diaspora communities in Egypt or Cyrenaica, more likely the latter.[55] "Rufus" was originally a Latin name, but it was common among Greeks as well.[56] A Roman example is the Annius Rufus who was prefect of Judea from about 12 to 15 CE.[57] A freeborn Gentile Christian named $\mathaccent'P o\tilde{\upsilon}\varphi o\varsigma$ ("Rufus"), who probably emigrated from the East to Rome, is greeted by Paul in Rom 16:13.[58] He is probably not the same person as the Rufus mentioned here, since the latter was Jewish.[59]

47 Joyce M. Reynolds, "Cyrene," *OCD* 421–22; W. Ward Gasque, "Cyrene," *ABD* 1:1230–31; BAGD, s.v. $K\upsilon\rho\acute{\eta}\nu\eta$.

48 Schürer, *History*, 3:60–62.

49 See "History of the Tradition and Historical Reliability" above. Gerd Theissen points out that the mention of his place of origin would be sufficient to identify Simon. The only reason the sons are named is that "they are known to the traditionists of the Passion story" (*Gospels in Context*, 176–77; *Lokalkolorit*, 188).

50 Schürer, *History*, 2:428; 3:61; Ernst Haenchen, *The Acts of the Apostles: A Commentary* (Philadelphia: Westminster, 1971; 14th Germ. ed. 1965) 271 and n. 1.

51 Theissen, *Gospels in Context*, 167; *Lokalkolorit*, 177–78.

52 See the discussion of both points in "Composition and History of the Tradition" in the excursus on the passion narrative in the commentary on 14:1–11 above.

53 Theissen, *Gospels in Context*, 176–77; *Lokalkolorit*, 188. Theissen, however, connects this familiarity with the sons to the oldest account, which, in his view, was composed in Jerusalem between 41 and 44 CE (ibid., 197–98; *Lokalkolorit*, 209–10). The position taken here is that the sons were known both to the author and audiences of the pre-Markan passion narrative and to the evangelist and at least some in his audiences; see "History of the Tradition and Historical Reliability" above.

54 BAGD, s.v. $\mathaccent'\!A\lambda\acute{\epsilon}\xi\alpha\nu\delta\rho o\varsigma$; Acts 4:6; 19:33; Haenchen, *Acts of the Apostles*, 216, 574–75; 1 Tim 1:20; 2 Tim 4:14; Dibelius-Conzelmann, *Pastoral Epistles*, 33–34, 123. See also Schürer, *History*, 3:896–97.

55 Nahman Avigad, "A Depository of Inscribed Ossuaries in the Kidron Valley," *IEJ* 12 (1962) 1–12.

56 BAGD, s.v. $\mathaccent'P o\tilde{\upsilon}\varphi o\varsigma$; Moulton-Milligan, s.v. $\mathaccent'P o\tilde{\upsilon}\varphi o\varsigma$. Rufus of Ephesus was a Greek physician active in the second half of the first cent. CE (Vivian Nutton and Ludwig Edelstein, "Rufus," *OCD* 1337).

57 Josephus *Ant.* 18.2.2 §33; Schürer, *History*, 1:382. The historian Cluvius Rufus, who was consul in 39 or 40 CE, is mentioned in *Ant.* 19.1.13 §§91–92; Josephus may have used a work of his in the long account about the conspiracy against Gaius and the accession of Claudius (Schürer, *History*, 1:51 and n. 17). Q. Tineius Rufus was governor of Judea at the time of the revolt of Bar Kokhba (ibid., 1:518, 547–49, 551).

58 Peter Lampe, "Rufus," *ABD* 5:839.

59 Ibid. Polycarp mentions a Rufus, whom the Philippians saw with their own eyes "practicing all

According to v. 21, Simon was forced to carry Jesus' "cross" (σταυρός). The Greek word usually refers to the pole or stake driven into the ground at the site where the penalty of crucifixion is to be carried out.[60] Older Latin writers speak about the condemned person carrying the cross-beam (*patibulum*) to the place of execution, where the stake had already been erected.[61] The reason why the soldiers conscripted Simon is not stated in the text. It is usually thought to be that Jesus was too weak to carry the cross-beam, perhaps because of a severe whipping.[62] William Sanger Campbell argued that Jesus deliberately refused to carry the cross-beam as a protest against the injustice of his condemnation.[63]

T. E. Schmidt argued that Mark's text implies that Simon's role was divinely planned. This "practically official function" recalls, in his view, the official who would walk alongside the bull to be sacrificed in the imperial triumph, carrying "over his shoulder the double-bladed axe, the instrument of the victim's death."[64] There is no hint, however, in Mark's narrative that Simon's role was divinely planned. The chance conscription of Simon by the soldiers is not at all like an "official function." It is highly unlikely that Mark's audiences would have perceived an evocation of the Roman imperial triumph in Simon's role.

■ **22** The verb in the first clause of this verse that describes the action taken by the soldiers in relation to

Jesus is φέρειν. This verb has a wide range of meanings.[65] Campbell argued that the verb has the sense of "carry" here. Jesus obstructed the effort to crucify him by refusing to walk to Golgatha, "forcing the soldiers responsible for his execution to carry him there."[66] In support of this conclusion, he argued further that, elsewhere in Mark, when the verb is used with living persons, the person who is the object of the action "is sick, physically or mentally infirm or challenged, or a child, and the term conveys the sense of literal or figurative 'carrying', that is, the individual could not or would not 'move from one position to another' independently."[67] There is a significant difference, however, between literal and figurative "carrying." Furthermore, the conclusion that "the individual could not or would not 'move from one position to another' independently" is a considerable overstatement. In 7:32, for example, it is unlikely that the people who entreated Jesus to lay his hand upon the man who was deaf and impeded in his speech had literally to carry the man to Jesus. At the same time, it is not implied that he could not or would not go to Jesus independently. The implication of the description seems rather to be that other people took the initiative and the man in need of healing was subordinated to them.[68] In the case of the blind man in 8:22, the narrative may imply that he needed assistance in finding Jesus, but not that he needed to be carried. The significance of the

---

endurance" (ἀσκεῖν πᾶσαν ὑπομονήν), as also Ignatius and Zosimus did (*Phil.* 9.1); text and trans. from Ehrman, *Apostolic Fathers*, 1:344–45. Joseph B. Lightfoot inferred from *Phil.* 1.1 that Zosimus and Rufus were among those whom the Philippians received as they passed through in chains on their way to Rome; he also noted that they are mentioned in the *Martyrol. Roman.* (*The Apostolic Fathers: Clement, Ignatius, and Polycarp: Revised Texts with Introductions, Notes, Dissertations, and Translations* [2nd ed.; 2 parts in 3 vols.; London/New York: Macmillan, 1889–90; reprinted Grand Rapids: Baker, 1981] part 2, vol. 3, p. 337). William R. Schoedel gives references to inscriptions in which the names Zosimus and Rufus occur (*The Apostolic Fathers: A New Translation and Commentary*, vol. 5: *Polycarp, Martyrdom of Polycarp, Fragments of Papias* [London/Camden, NJ: Nelson & Sons, 1967] 28).

60 BAGD, s.v. σταυρός.
61 John J. Collins, S.J., "The Archaeology of the Crucifixion," *CBQ* 1 (1939) 154–59, esp. 156–57;

Johannes Schneider, "σταυρός, κτλ.," *TDNT* 7 (1971) 572–84, esp. 573; Brown, *Death*, 2:913; George R. Watson and Andrew W. Lintott, "Crucifixion," *OCD* 411; Donald G. Kyle, *Spectacles of Death in Ancient Rome* (London/New York: Routledge, 1998) 53. Cf. Gerald G. O'Collins, "Crucifixion," *ABD* 1:1207–10, esp. 1208–9.

62 Brown, *Death*, 2:914–15.
63 Campbell, "Engagement," 291–94.
64 T. E. Schmidt, "Mark 15.16-32: The Crucifixion Narrative and the Roman Triumphal Procession," *NTS* 41 (1995) 1–18, esp. 9.
65 BAGD, s.v. φέρω.
66 Campbell, "Engagement," 294.
67 Ibid., 295.
68 The case is similar with regard to 9:17; since a seizure is described in v. 18, the occurrences of the verb in vv. 19 and 20 could be interpreted as literal carrying.

verb φέρειν in v. 22 is that Jesus was under the authority of the soldiers and that it was due to their initiative that he moved from the praetorium to Golgotha.

T. E. Schmidt argued that the verb should be translated "they bore (φέρουσιν) him to . . . Golgotha." This detail, in his view, signifies not only "the growing physical weakness of Jesus but also the custom of the triumphator being borne in a portable *curule* chair which was placed in his chariot. Thus the 'litter' of the Afflicted One is in reality the *curule chair* of the Conquering One."[69] Since, however, no litter is mentioned, the likelihood that the verb φέρουσιν (in this case to be translated "they brought") evokes the chair and chariot of the triumphator is quite small.

The name "Golgotha" (Γολγοθᾶ) probably comes from an Aramaic name. The Greek transliteration presupposes the form גֻּלְגָּלְתָּא, which seems to derive from גֻּלְגֻּלְתָּא or גֻּלְגָּלְתָּא, which would be the Aramaic definite form of the Hebrew גֻּלְגֹּלֶת ("skull").[70] The Greek equivalent, κρανίον, is in the genitive case used here in apposition with τόπος ("place").[71] Neither the Hebrew nor the Greek word necessarily signifies a skull in the sense of the dried-out head of a skeleton. The Latin equivalent, *calvaria*, can also be used of the skull of a living person.[72] The original significance of the name "Golgotha" cannot be determined.[73]

The phrase ὅ ἐστιν μεθερμηνευόμενον ("that is, translated") occurs also in 5:41 and 15:34. It is difficult to determine whether these instances were composed by Mark or found by him in his sources. The position tentatively taken here is that the instances of the phrase in

5:41 and 15:22 come from Mark's sources and that the instance in 15:34 was composed by Mark on the model of 15:22.[74]

As noted above, it is likely that, in the time of Jesus, Golgotha was located outside of the walls of Jerusalem.[75] The Gospel of John states that there was a garden "in the place where Jesus was crucified" (ἐν τῷ τόπῳ ὅπου ἐσταυρώθη κῆπος) (John 19:41a). It goes on to say that there was a new tomb in that garden, in which no one had yet been laid. "On account of the day of preparation of the Jews" (διὰ τὴν παρασκευὴν τῶν Ἰουδαίων), they buried Jesus in that tomb because it was nearby (John 19:41b-42). The tomb alleged to be that of Jesus at the pilgrimage site called the Garden Tomb has been shown to date from the Iron Age, so it cannot support the historical reliability of the burial account in John.[76]

The emperor Constantine built, from 325 to 335 CE, a sacred complex in Jerusalem including a basilica called the Martyrion, a "garden with a colonnaded rotunda centered on the" alleged tomb of Jesus called the Anastasis, and a rock or hill "thought to be the hill of Golgotha." The Crusaders rebuilt the complex from 1099 to 1149, and the remodeled construction is called the Church of the Holy Sepulchre.[77] There has been considerable debate about whether the site of the church includes the actual sites of Jesus' crucifixion and burial.

A crucial point in the debate has been whether the site of the Church of the Holy Sepulchre lay inside or outside of the walls of the city at the time Jesus was crucified. According to Philip King, "The topography of Jerusalem's walls is controversial."[78] Josephus wrote, at

69   Schmidt, "Mark 15.16-32," 9.

70   BAGD, s.v. Γολγοθᾶ; BDF §39 (6); Brown, *Death*, 2:936 n. 5. The Hebrew גֻּלְגֹּלֶת was also used in the Hebrew Bible to mean "head" or "poll (in counting, taxing etc.)" (BDB, s.v.). See also Gundry, 955; Schmidt, "Mark 15.16-32," 10–11; and Joan Taylor, "Golgotha: A Reconsideration of the Evidence for the Sites of Jesus' Crucifixion and Burial," *NTS* 44 (1998) 180–203, esp. 182–83.

71   BAGD, s.v. κρανίον; Smyth §1322.

72   E.g., Celsus *De Medicina* 8.1.1; Schmidt, "Mark 15.16-32," 10 n. 31.

73   For a discussion of various theories, see Brown, *Death*, 2:937.

74   On the use of a source in 5:21-43, see "Literary Relationship between the Two Stories" in the commen-

tary on that passage above. On the credibility of the phrase in 15:22 as part of the earliest recoverable form of the passion narrative, see the section "History of the Tradition and Historical Reliability" above. For reasons supporting the conclusion that Mark added the evocation of Ps 22:1 and its translation in v. 34, see Yarbro Collins, *Beginning of the Gospel*, 115–16, and the commentary below.

75   See the commentary on 15:20 above.

76   Taylor, "Golgotha," 180 and n. 1. The consensus is that the site of the Garden Tomb is inauthentic (Brown, *Death*, 2:938–39).

77   Brown, *Death*, 2:937–38; see also Taylor, "Golgotha," 180–82 and fig. 1.

78   Philip J. King, "Jerusalem," *ABD* 3:747–66, esp. 760–61.

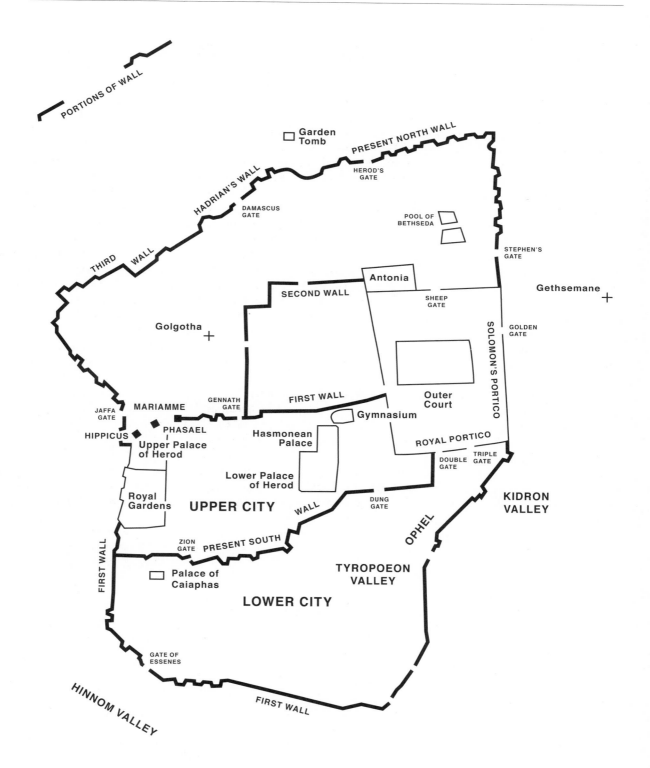

PORTIONS OF WALL

Garden
Tomb

PRESENT NORTH WALL

HEROD'S
GATE

HADRIAN'S WALL

DAMASCUS
GATE

POOL OF
BETHSEDA

STEPHEN'S
GATE

THIRD WALL

Gethsemane +

Antonia

SECOND WALL

SHEEP
GATE

GOLDEN
GATE

Golgotha +

SOLOMON'S PORTICO

Outer
Court

GENNATH
GATE

FIRST WALL

JAFFA
GATE

MARIAMME

Gymnasium

ROYAL PORTICO

PHASAEL

Hasmonean
Palace

HIPPICUS

DOUBLE
GATE

TRIPLE
GATE

Upper Palace
of Herod

Lower Palace
of Herod

KIDRON
VALLEY

Royal
Gardens

UPPER CITY

WALL

DUNG
GATE

OPHEL

ZION
GATE

PRESENT SOUTH

FIRST WALL

TYROPOEON
VALLEY

Palace of
Caiaphas

LOWER CITY

GATE OF
ESSENES

HINNOM VALLEY

FIRST WALL

739

some point between 70 and 80 CE,[79] that there were three (successive) walls fortifying the city, except in the places where it was enclosed by steep ravines (*Bell.* 5.4.1 §136).[80] The oldest and innermost wall, surrounding the whole city, is the least controversial and was in place in the time of Jesus.[81] This wall ran "roughly S from the present-day Citadel (Jaffa Gate), around Mount Zion, along the Hinnom valley, to the Kidron valley; from the crest of the E hill, to the SE corner of the Temple Mount; then from Wilson's arch on the W wall of the Temple Mount [it ran westward] back to the Phasael Tower (present-day Citadel)."[82]

The second wall is crucial for the authenticity of the site of the Church of the Holy Sepulchre as, more or less, the actual site of Jesus' crucifixion.[83] The exact course of this wall "is uncertain and controversial."[84] It probably ran first northward and then eastward from "the present-day Citadel by way of the present-day Damascus Gate, to the Antonia at the NW corner of the Temple."[85] The wall was probably built in Herodian times. It was fortified by a quarry which lay at its foot to the west, which functioned like a moat. Traces of this quarry have been found south of the church, so it is likely that its site was outside the walls of the city in Jesus' time.[86]

Ernest Martin proposed that the site of the crucifixion of Jesus was a little hill on the summit of the Mount of Olives. A major reason for his selection of this site is his assumption that the centurion mentioned in v. 39 must have been able to see the curtain of the temple and its rending in two.[87] Mark, however, does not necessarily imply that the centurion could see the curtain. Furthermore, it is unlikely that a site in view of the temple would have been chosen for crucifixions, because of the sacred character of the temple mount.[88]

More plausible is Joan Taylor's suggestion that the name "Golgotha" referred not to a rock or a hill shaped like a head or a skull but to the whole quarry that lay to the west of the city outside and north of the first wall and outside and west of the second wall.[89] Along the first wall was the west road and along the second wall was the old north road, from which passersby could have seen Jesus on the cross. Taylor suggests that the quarry was near the Gennath Gate (Garden Gate) mentioned by Josephus (*Bell.* 5.4.2 §146).[90] She concludes that Jesus was likely to have been crucified about two hundred meters south of the traditional site, at a point near the west road and the Gennath Gate, where the sign stating Jesus' crime could be read by passersby.[91] This site would fit the usual Roman practice of crucifying criminals "at well-traveled public roadways, offering a stark contrast to the hallowed burials of good citizens nearby."[92]

■ **23** This verse is open to a variety of interpretations. It is likely that the first finite verb, ἐδίδουν, is a conative imperfect and should be translated "they tried to give."[93] The subject of this verb, however, is ambiguous. The context suggests that it is the soldiers who give Jesus the drink.[94] This could, however, be a case of the indefinite or impersonal plural, a usage that occurs occasionally in Mark and seems to be equivalent to the passive voice.[95] On the basis of a passage in the Babylonian Talmud, a

79   According to Louis H. Feldman, Josephus wrote *Bell.* in the decade following the destruction of the temple in 70 CE ("Josephus," *ABD* 3:981–98, esp. 982).

80   King, "Jerusalem," 760.

81   This wall is usually dated to 100 BCE (King, "Jerusalem," 760).

82   Ibid.; cf. Josephus *Bell.* 5.4.2 §§142–45. See the depiction of the first wall in the plan of Jerusalem in the time of Jesus in Finegan, *Archaeology,* 184.

83   King, "Jerusalem," 760–61; Brown, *Death,* 2:938.

84   King, "Jerusalem," 760.

85   Ibid., 761; Finegan, *Archaeology,* 184. Cf. Josephus *Bell.* 5.4.2 §146.

86   King, "Jerusalem," 761; see also Brown, *Death,* 2:938.

87   Ernest L. Martin, *Secrets of Golgotha: The Forgotten History of Christ's Crucifixion* (Alhambra, CA: ASK Publications, 1988) 12–19, 58–64.

88   For further criticism of Martin's thesis, see Brown, *Death,* 2:938–39. On the concern to avoid showing disrespect to the eastern gate of the temple mount, see *m. Ber.* 9.5; *t. Ber.* 61b; cf. *m. Mid.* 2.4.

89   Taylor, "Golgotha," 184–86 and fig. 3.

90   Ibid., 186.

91   Ibid., 186–88.

92   Kyle, *Spectacles of Death,* 53.

93   So Swete, 379; Klostermann, 163; Dormeyer, *Die Passion Jesu,* 193; Pesch, 2:478; Gundry, 944; Brown, *Death,* 2:940. On the conative imperfect, see Smyth §1895; BDF §326.

94   So Wilhelm Michaelis, "σμύρνα, σμυρνίζω," *TDNT* 7 (1971) 457–59, esp. 459; Gnilka, 2:316; Gundry, 944; Brown, *Death,* 2:940–41; Evans, 501; Donahue and Harrington, 442.

95   On the apparently impersonal use of third person plural verbs, see Taylor, 47–48; Lane concludes that

number of commentators have concluded that the drink was offered to Jesus by Jewish women.[96]

There is also ambiguity with regard to the properties, effects, and cultural significance of ἐσμυρνισμένος[97] οἶνος ("wine to which myrrh had been added").[98] One line of interpretation is based on the remarks of Pliny the Elder on myrrh. For the most part, he implies that myrrh is valued for its scent as a perfume (*Hist. nat.* 12.33-35 §§66–71). In spite of his opinion that good myrrh has a slightly bitter taste, he states, "The finest wines in early days were those spiced with scent of myrrh."[99] He also says, "I also find that aromatic wine is constantly made from almost exactly the same ingredients as perfumes—first from myrrh, as we have already said. . . ." He also mentions "savoury wines" or "peppered wines."[100]

Robert H. Gundry based his interpretation on the observations of Pliny and concluded that the account of the soldiers giving Jesus wine spiced with myrrh "adds to his dignity, for such wine is a delicacy."[101] Craig A. Evans also took his cue from Pliny but argued that "the offer of fine wine to Jesus was in fact part of the ongoing mockery (cf. vv. 29-32). In effect, the soldiers were offering the finest wine to the 'king of the Jews.'"[102]

Schmidt links the offer of this "expensive delicacy" to Jesus with the libation of wine associated with the sacrifice of a bull at the climax of the celebration of a triumph.[103] In order to make this rather far-fetched parallel seem stronger, he states that, just prior to the sacrifice that concluded the triumphal procession, the triumphator "was offered a cup of wine, which he would refuse and then pour on the altar."[104] He does not cite evidence, however, to support the idea that the wine is offered first to the one celebrating the triumph, or to one offering some other kind of sacrifice, who refuses it. Rather, the libation is intended for one or more deities from the outset and by definition.[105]

Another line of interpretation is based on the idea

the verb ἐδίδουν in v. 23 is an "indefinite plural" (564 n. 50).

96 Lane, 564; Hooker, 372–73. Pesch leaves open the question concerning who tried to give Jesus the drink (2:478).

97 The verb σμυρνίζειν is rare outside the Bible and does not occur in the LXX. It is used in Dioscorides *De materia medica* 1.66.1, where it means "to be like myrrh" (Michaelis, "σμύρνα, σμυρνίζω," 458 n. 1). On Dioscorides, see below.

98 According to Michael Zohary, myrrh is native to Arabia, Ethiopia, and Somaliland; in antiquity it was imported from South Arabia; it was the most precious and popular resin and was employed as perfume and medicine (*Plants of the Bible* [London/New York: Cambridge University Press, 1982] 41–42, 200); see also James Innes Miller, *The Spice Trade of the Roman Empire, 29 B.C. to A.D. 641* (Oxford: Clarendon, 1969) 104–5; A. Steier, "Myrrha (2)," PW 16 (1935) 1134–46; Erkki Koskenniemi, Kirsi Nisula, and Jorma Toppari, "Wine Mixed with Myrrh (Mark 15.23) and *Crurifragium* (John 19.31–32): Two Details of the Passion Narratives," *JSNT* 27 (2005) 379–91, esp. 382–84.

99 Lautissima apud priscos vina erant myrrhae odore condita (Pliny *Hist. nat.* 14.15 §92; text and trans. from Harris Rackham, *Pliny: Natural History*, vol. 4 [LCL; Cambridge, MA: Harvard University Press; London: Heinemann, 1938] 248–49). On the bitter taste of good myrrh, see *Hist. nat.* 12.35 §70. In his work *On Odors*, Theophrastus attested the practice

of adding spices, including myrrh, to wine to flavor it (Miller, *Spice Trade*, 3–4, 108). Spiced wine is also mentioned in Cant 8:2 (Johannes Döller, "Der Wein in Bibel und Talmud," *Bib* 4 [1923] 143–67, 267–99, esp. 164–65; Marvin H. Pope, *Song of Songs: A New Translation with Introduction and Commentary* [AB 7C; Garden City, NY: Doubleday, 1977] 653, 659).

100 Aromatiten quoque invenio factitatum tantum non unguentorum compositione, primo ex murra, ut diximus. . . . (*Hist. nat.* 14.19 §107; text and trans. from Rackham, *Pliny*, 4:256–57). He mentions what some people call "savoury wines" (*condita*) and others "peppered wines" (*piperata*) in *Hist. nat.* 14.19 §108 (Rackham, *Pliny*, 4:256–57). Pliny seems to imply, however, that this type of spiced wine was no longer made in his time (first cent. CE) (Steier, "Myrrha (2)," 1144).

101 Gundry, 944.

102 Evans, 501.

103 Schmidt, "Mark 15.16-32," 11–12.

104 Ibid., 11.

105 Inez Scott Ryberg does not mention such a gesture in her discussions of the monuments depicted in the figures cited by Schmidt ("Mark 15.16-32," 11 n. 33) (Ryberg, *Rites of the State Religion in Roman Art* [Memoirs of the American Academy in Rome 22; Rome: American Academy in Rome, 1955], e.g., 143 and fig. 77d [Plate L]).

that the wine or the myrrh or both were intended to deaden the pain. The book of Proverbs is often cited in this regard:

> Give strong drink to those in pain
> and wine to drink to those in distress,
> so that they may forget their poverty
> and not remember their sufferings any more
> (δίδοτε μέθην τοῖς ἐν λύπαις
> καὶ οἶνον πίνειν τοῖς ἐν ὀδύναις,
> ἵνα ἐπιλάθωνται τῆς πενίας
> καὶ τῶν πόνων μὴ μνησθῶσιν ἔτι). (Prov 31:6-7
>   LXX)

These verses could be interpreted as applying either to physical pain or to mental anguish or both. The main reason that this passage is regularly cited in comments on Mark 15:23 is its appearance in a passage of the Talmud related to *m. Sanh.* 6.1:

> Again, what of R. Ḥiyya b. Ashi's dictum in R. Ḥisda's name: When one is led out to execution, he is given a goblet of wine containing a grain of frankincense, in order to benumb his senses, for it is written, *Give strong drink unto him that is ready to perish, and wine unto the bitter in soul* [Prov 31:6]. And it has also been taught: The noble women in Jerusalem used to donate and bring it. If these did not bring it, who provided it?—As for that, it is certainly logical that it should be provided out of the public [funds]: since it is written, *"Give,"* [the implication is] of what is theirs. (b. Sanh. 43a [section b])[106]

Many commentators take this passage as evidence for a custom practiced at the time of Jesus, but the text only shows that rabbis at a considerably later time than that of Jesus used the passage from Proverbs to construct part of their ideology regarding how those condemned to death should be treated.[107]

Some who take this line of interpretation cite Dioscorides, who wrote a scientific treatise on medicines in the first century CE.[108] According to him, myrrh has a narcotic effect (δύναμις καρωτική) (*De materia medica* 1.64.3).[109] Others have concluded that it was the wine itself that "was intended to have a narcotic effect."[110] Yet others seem to imply that the wine, given by the soldiers, was intended to stimulate an exhausted prisoner on the way to the place of execution.[111] This last theory is unlikely, since the context implies that Jesus and the soldiers have already arrived at Golgotha.

Erkki Koskenniemi, Kirsi Nisula, and Jorma Toppari have argued that the wine mixed with myrrh was offered to Jesus by the soldiers as a means of torture. This interpretation is dependent on the presupposition that a large quantity of myrrh was used to make the wine extremely bitter and undrinkable, rather than a small amount to flavor or preserve it.[112] The intention was to frustrate the great thirst of the person being executed.[113]

---

106 Trans. by Jacob Schachter in Isidore Epstein, ed., *The Babylonian Talmud: Seder Neziḳin. Sanhedrin* (London: Soncino, 1935–52). Cited by Str-B, 1:1037; Michaelis, "σμύρνα, σμυρνίζω," 459 (but he disputes its relevance to Mark 15:23); Swete, 379; Klostermann, 163; Taylor, 589; Lane, 564; Dormeyer, *Die Passion Jesu*, 193; Gnilka, 1:316; Hooker, 372–73; Pesch, 2:478; Evans, 500–501.

107 On the subject of the rabbis' reflections on the death penalty, see Beth A. Berkowitz, *Execution and Invention: Death Penalty Discourse in Early Rabbinic and Christian Cultures* (Oxford/New York: Oxford University Press, 2006) esp. chaps. 3–6.

108 On Dioscorides, see John M. Riddle, "Dioscorides (2) (Pedanius Dioscorides)," *OCD* 483–84.

109 For a critical Greek text, see Max Wellmann, ed., *Pedanii Dioscuridis Anazarbei de materia medica libri quinque* (5 parts in 3 vols.; Berolini: Apud Weidmannos, 1906–14 [vol. 1, 1907]; reprinted Hildesheim: Weidmann, 1999) 1:58; this passage is the middle part of 1.77 in Robert T. Gunther, ed., *The Greek Herbal of Dioscorides: Illustrated by a Byzantine A.D. 512, Englished by John Goodyer A.D. 1655, Edited and First Printed A.D. 1933* (Oxford: John Johnson/Oxford University Press, 1934; reprinted New York: Hafner, 1959) 42–43. See also Lane, 564; Gnilka, 2:316 and n. 37; Pesch, 2:478. Cf. Brown, *Death*, 2:941; Schmidt, "Mark 15.16-32," 11 n. 32.

110 Donahue and Harrington, 442; so, apparently, Brown, *Death*, 2:940–44.

111 Michaelis, "σμύρνα, σμυρνίζω," 458–59; Gould seems to imply something similar (291).

112 See Koskenniemi et al., "Wine Mixed with Myrrh," 384, and the literature cited there on the use of myrrh as a preservative.

113 Ibid., 385–86.

There are also a variety of interpretations of the statement that Jesus refused the drink. Some commentators seem to assume that the account is historically reliable and to conclude that Jesus rejected the offer because the pain "belonged to the cup which the Father's Will had appointed (xiv. 36 ff.) of which he would abate nothing."[114] C. E. B. Cranfield also argued that "his refusal to drink may be explained as due to his vow recorded in xiv. 25."[115] Others speak about Mark's or the narrator's intention to portray Jesus as wanting to endure everything consciously or accepting the path of suffering willingly.[116]

It is likely that this verse was part of the pre-Markan passion narrative.[117] It is also likely that this account was influenced to some degree by ancient ideas about noble death.[118] Under those assumptions and from the perspective of the pre-Markan narrative, it is credible to argue that the wine to which myrrh was added is offered to dull the pain of the crucifixion that was about to take place.[119] From the same perspective, the verb ἐδίδουν ("they tried to give") may be taken as an indefinite or impersonal verb, implying that individuals other than the soldiers who had mocked Jesus made the offer. Jesus' refusal would then call to mind the motif of despising pain prominent especially in the late Stoic death accounts.[120]

Once this verse became part of Mark's narrative as a whole, Jesus' refusal could call to mind for the audiences his prophecy that he would surely not drink of the fruit of the vine until that day when he drinks it new in the kingdom of God (14:25), but for those in the audiences familiar with the noble death tradition, the gesture would still carry the connotation of disdaining pain and any effort to minimize it.

Tertullian provides indirect evidence that some Christians in North Africa around 213 CE[121] not only interpreted this verse in Mark to mean that the wine to which myrrh had been added was offered to Jesus to dull the pain of his suffering, but also imitated that event themselves in their treatment of prospective martyrs. This evidence lies in Tertullian's report of a practice of which he disapproved:

> Your practice is obviously to provide cook-shops (*popinas*) in the prisons for unreliable martyrs, in case they miss their usual comforts, tire of life, and stumble over the novel discipline of abstinence, with which not even Pristinus—your martyr, not a Christian one—had ever had contact. He had long been stuffed, thanks to "free custody" (*libera custodia*), and I suspect owed money to all the bathhouses (as if they were better than baptism), and to all the haunts of excess (as if they were more secret than the church), and to all the enticements of this life (as if they were worthier than those of eternal life). Since he was unwilling to die, at noon on the last day of trial you premedicated him with doctored wine [aromatic or spiced wine] as an antidote. He was so completely enervated that on being tickled—for his intoxication made it feel like that—with a few claws, he was no longer able to tell the magistrate interrogating him just whom he confessed to be Lord. Put on the rack as a result, when he could only manage hiccups and belches, he expired in the

---

114 Swete, 380; similarly Cranfield, 455; Taylor, 589; Lane, 564, who also refers to 10:38; Gnilka, 2:316, who cites 10:32-33; Gundry, 944. Pesch accepts as historical that Jesus refused an analgesic drink, but he emphasizes that the text does not give a motivation (2:478–79). Evans says that Jesus "refuses to drink because he refuses to participate in the mockery" and compares this refusal to Jesus' silence before the priests and Pilate (501).

115 Cranfield, 455. See the commentary on 14:25 above, where it is argued that the saying of Jesus is more of a prophecy than a vow.

116 Klostermann, 163; Dormeyer speaks about the tradition in v. 23b (*Die Passion Jesu*, 193); Lührmann speaks about the narrator (260); Hooker, like Klostermann, speaks about Mark (372–73).

117 Bultmann, *History*, 273; Schenke, *Der gekreuzigte Christus*, 137; Dormeyer, *Die Passion Jesu*, 193; Mohr, *Markus- und Johannespassion*, 349; Myllykoski, *Die letzten Tagen*, 2:162.

118 See the section "Genre" in the excursus on the passion narrative in the commentary on 14:1-11 above.

119 The claim here is only that the drink was believed to be able to dull the pain, not that it actually would do so.

120 Yarbro Collins, "Genre," 16; see also eadem, "From Noble Death," 482–84.

121 On the date of *De ieiunio*, see Andrew McGowan, "Discipline and Diet: Feeding the Martyrs in Roman Carthage," *HTR* 96 (2003) 455–76, esp. 462 and n. 32.

very act of denial (Plane uestrum est in carceribus popinas exhibere martyribus incertis, ne consuetudinem quaerant, ne taedeat uitae, ne noua abstinentiae disciplina scandalizentur, quam nec ille Pristinus uester non Christianus martyr adtigerat, quem ex facultate custodiae liberae aliquamdiu fartum, omnibus balneis quasi baptismate melioribus et omnibus luxuriae secessibus quasi ecclesia secretioribus et omnibus uitae istius inlecebris quasi aeterna dignioribus hoc puto obligatum, ne mori uellet, postremo ipso tribunalis die luce summa condito mero[122] tamquam antidoto praemedicatum ita eneruastis, ut paucis ungulis titillatus (hoc enim ebrietas sentiebat) quem dominum confiteretur interroganti praesidi respondere non potuerit amplius, atque ita de hoc iam extortus, cum singultus et ructus solos haberet, in ipsa negatione discessit). (De ieiunio 12.3)[123]

Tertullian's depiction of Pristinus as *uester non Christianus martyr* ("your martyr, not a Christian one") may be read as a contrast between Pristinus, who accepted the offer of drugged wine, and Jesus, who refused it.

The Martyrdom of Fructuosus and Companions provides evidence for how our text was understood by Christians in Spain and perhaps elsewhere in the fourth century.[124] The relevant passage reads:

As Bishop Fructuosus was being taken to the amphitheatre with his deacons, the people began to sympathize with him, for he was much beloved of pagans and Christians alike. For he was all that the Holy Spirit, through Paul, *the vessel of election* [Acts 9:15] and *the teacher of the Gentiles* [2 Tim 1:11], declared that a bishop should be. For this reason his brothers, who knew that he was going on to such great glory, were happy rather than sad. Many out of

brotherly affection offered him a cup of drugged wine [aromatic or spiced wine] to drink, but he said: "It is not yet the time for breaking the fast." For it was still in the fourth hour, and in gaol they duly observed the stational fast on Wednesdays. And so on Friday he was hastening joyfully and confidently to break his fast with the martyrs and prophets in heaven, which *the Lord has prepared for those who love Him* [1 Cor 2:9] (Et cum duceretur Fructuosus cum diaconibus suis ad amphitheatrum, populus Fructuosum episcopum dolere coepit quia talem amorem habebat non tantum a fratribus sed etiam ab ethnicis. talis enim erat qualem Spiritus sanctus per beatum Paulum apostolum, *uas electionis, doctorem gentium*, <episcopum> debere esse declarauit. propter quod etiam fratres qui sciebant illum ad tantam gloriam pergere gaudebant potius quam dolebant. Cumque multi ex fraterna caritate ei offerrent ut conditi permixti poculum sumeret, respondit: Non est, inquit, hora soluendi stationis. (agebatur enim hora diei quarta, siquidem in carcerem quarta feria stationem sollemniter celebrauerat). igitur sexta feria laetus atque securus festinabat, uti cum martyribus et prophetis in paradiso *quem praeparauit Deus amantibus se* solueret stationem). (3.1-3)[125]

In this text, in contrast to Pristinus in the text cited above, Fructuosus is Christlike in his refusal of the wine. His observance of the fast and the narrator's comment about breaking the fast in Paradise evoke Jesus' prophecy in Mark 14:25.

■ **24** Even though Jesus is depicted as despising pain in v. 23, the account, unlike 2 and 4 Maccabees, does not describe the methods of torture and execution in any detail. Verse 24a simply states, "And they crucified him" (Καὶ σταυροῦσιν αὐτόν).[126]

---

122 *Conditum merum* is seasoned wine not mixed with water; the Romans considered drinking unmixed wine to be a sign of gluttony; only wine mixed with a high proportion of water was suitable for decent, temperate men (Döller, "Der Wein in Bibel und Talmud," 273).

123 Text from CChrSL 2, *Tertulliani Opera*, pars 2, *Opera Montanistica* (Turnholt: Brepols, 1954) 1271; trans. from McGowan, "Discipline and Diet," 463.

124 Fructuosus was bishop of Tarragona (Tarraco) in

Spain; on the date of the *Martyrdom*, see Musurillo, *Christian Martyrs*, xxxii.

125 Text and trans. from Musurillo, *Christian Martyrs*, 178–81. McGowan refers to this text in relation to Tertullian *De ieiunio* 12.3 ("Discipline and Diet," 463 n. 34).

126 For evidence concerning the practice of crucifixion, see the commentary on v. 21 above and the literature cited there; see also James F. Strange, "Crucifixion, Method of," *IDB*, Supplementary vol.

Verse 24b reports that the soldiers crucified Jesus and divided his clothes among themselves, casting lots for them. As noted above, Bultmann argued that v. 24b was not part of the earliest passion narrative because he viewed the oldest account as a historical report and considered all the "proofs from prophecy" to be secondary.[127] Schenke and Wolfgang Reinbold, however, included it in their reconstructions of the oldest version of the passion.[128]

It is widely recognized that v. 24b evokes Psalm 21 LXX:

They divided my clothes among themselves
and for my clothing they cast lots
(διεμερίσαντο τὰ ἱμάτιά μου ἑαυτοῖς
καὶ ἐπὶ τὸν ἱματισμόν μου ἔβαλον κλῆρον).
(Ps 21:19 LXX)[129]

Although the portrayal of the incident has been shaped by this scripture, it is credible that it is based on a historical event. Apparently, it was customary for the executioners to take whatever the condemned person had with him. If the person was executed for treason (*maiestas*), his property was taken by the state.[130] Hadrian issued new regulations concerning the *spolia* or *pannicularia*, that is, the goods that the condemned wore or carried on his own person.[131] Since Hadrian set limits on what the torturers and executioners could take, it is credible that, prior to that time, there were few, if any, limits. The new regulations stipulated that the executioners could only take stuff that did not exceed the value of five gold coins. Valuable articles exceeding that amount were to be taken by the governor and to be employed for the benefit of his office, not for his personal use.

In the context of Psalm 21, the verse cited above expresses the idea that his acquaintances are sure that the speaker of the psalm will die by portraying them as already dividing his goods among themselves.[132] The allusion to Ps 21:19 LXX is the first clear allusion to that psalm in Mark.[133]

The significance of the allusion can be explained in various ways.[134] One way is to say that it presupposes the idea that God prophesied through the psalmist (as prophet) what would happen to Jesus and that the prophecy is fulfilled in the event narrated.[135] Alfred Suhl rejected this interpretation in the case of this verse, arguing that it simply involves "description in the colors of the OT," that is, the use of Old Testament language in the narration of the event.[136] Others have argued that the evocation of Psalm 21 has the effect of portraying Jesus as the righteous sufferer or the suffering pious one.[137] In general, Barnabas Lindars argued that scripture played a major role in early Christian apologetic, that is, in defending elements of the kerygma in debates

(Nashville: Abingdon, 1976) 199–200; Hengel, *Crucifixion*, 22–63; Brown, *Death*, 2:945–52; Evans, 501–2.

127 See "History of the Tradition and Historical Reliability" above.

128 Schenke, *Der gekreuzigte Christus*, 137; Reinbold, *Der älteste Bericht*, 166. Alfred Suhl concluded that v. 24b is pre-Markan (*Funktion*, 65).

129 Note that the Synoptic Gospels take the two synonymously parallel lines cited from the psalm as portraying one event, whereas John 19:23-24 depicts the two lines as describing two distinct but related events (Brown, *Death*, 2:954).

130 Tacitus *Ann.* 6.29; Justinian *Digest* 48.4.11; for a critical Latin text and ET, see Theodor Mommsen, Paul Krueger, and Alan Watson, eds., *The Digest of Justinian* (4 vols.; Philadelphia: University of Pennsylvania Press, 1985) 4:804; Josef Blinzler, *Der Prozess Jesu* (4th ed.; Regensburg: Pustet, 1969) 369 n. 47. The property of any man condemned to death is confiscated and put into the imperial treasury (*Digest*

48.20.1; Mommsen et al., *Digest of Justinian*, 4:854; Brown, *Death*, 2:955; cf. Evans, 502).

131 Justinian *Digest* 48.20.6 (Mommsen et al., *Digest of Justinian*, 4:855); Blinzler, *Der Prozess Jesu*, 369 n. 47. Cf. Brown, *Death*, 2:955; Evans, 502.

132 On the motif of the division of clothing as an image, see Feigel, *Der Einfluss des Weissagungsbeweises*, 70.

133 There may be an allusion to Ps 21:7 LXX in 9:12; see the commentary on 9:12-13 above.

134 Cf. the discussion of the allusion to Ps 40:10 LXX in the commentary on 14:18 above.

135 Feigel, *Der Einfluss des Weissagungsbeweises*, 6, 70–72; Grundmann, 314; Dodd, *According to the Scriptures*, 97–98.

136 Suhl, *Funktion*, 47–48. Willem S. Vorster argued that Mark uses material from the OT to characterize Jesus and his opponents and "to get his story told" ("Function," 70–71; quotation from 71).

137 Lohmeyer, 343; Lührmann, 260; Gnilka, 2:316–17; Marcus, *Way of the Lord*, 172–75; Pesch interprets the allusion both as a fulfillment of scripture and as a

with (other) Jews.[138] He also interpreted Psalm 22 (21 LXX), originally and in its New Testament usage, as "the psalm of the righteous sufferer."[139] He described its role here, however, as "a quarry for pictorial detail in writing the story of the Passion."[140]

Donald Juel's starting point is similar to the conclusions of Suhl and Lindars. Like the form critics, he distinguished between the confessional tradition and the narrative tradition. He concluded that the psalms provided "language and imagery" not for the confessional tradition but for narratives. He argued, however, that the use of Psalms 22; 31; and 69 (21; 30; and 68 LXX) in the passion narrative is exegetical at root and that these psalms were read "from the outset," that is, soon after the death of Jesus, as "messianic." In other words, they were applied to Jesus not as the righteous sufferer, but as the messiah.[141] Jesus was executed as a messianic pretender, and the psalms "were in all likelihood employed from the earliest stages of the tradition to recount the death of Jesus as the King."[142] The hypothesis that Psalm 21 is used here to portray Jesus as a king is supported by the likelihood that the author of the pre-Markan passion narrative, Mark, and their audiences assumed that David, the prototypical king, was the author of the psalms.[143]

■ **25** As argued above, it is likely that this verse was part of the pre-Markan passion narrative.[144] Verse 24 opens with the statement Καὶ σταυροῦσιν αὐτόν (lit., "And they crucify him"). Verse 25 ends with the remark καὶ ἐσταύρωσαν αὐτόν (lit., "And they crucified him"). This repetition conveys the horror and magnitude of the event without recounting it in any detail.[145] The two similar clauses also surround the description of the dividing of Jesus' clothes and the announcement about the time of Jesus' crucifixion, forming a kind of *inclusio*. Such writing is close to oral communication.

The καί (lit., "and") of v. 25b plays the role here of a subordinate, temporal conjunction.[146] It may occur here under the influence of one or more Semitic languages, but it does not count as evidence for the original composition of the passion narrative in Aramaic or Hebrew.[147]

Verse 25 as a whole states that Jesus was crucified at the third hour. In both Latin and Greek texts, a "day," in ordinary language, signified the period of daylight, and this period was divided into twelve equal parts called "hours."[148] At the latitude of Jerusalem around the spring equinox, the first "hour" would begin around what we would call 6:00 A.M. So, according to Mark, Jesus was crucified around 9:00 A.M.[149] As argued above, the use of the schema of three-hour periods in vv. 25, 33, and 34 was a device for narrating the crucifixion when little information was available.[150] The placement of the crucifixion at around 9:00 A.M., however, is compatible with the remark, also in Mark's passion source, that the chief priests held a consultation "early in the morning" (πρωΐ) and took Jesus to Pilate thereafter.[151]

According to John 19:14, Pilate handed Jesus over to be crucified at about noon. Mark and John differ not only as to the time of the crucifixion but also about the day. According to the Synoptics, Jesus was crucified on the day of the feast of Passover, whereas John places the

portrayal of Jesus as the suffering righteous one (2:481).

138 Lindars, *New Testament Apologetic*, 19.

139 Ibid., 89.

140 Ibid., 90–91. In this last view, he is close to Suhl (see above).

141 Juel, *Messianic Exegesis*, 90.

142 Ibid.; similarly, Yarbro Collins, "From Noble Death," 487–89, 490–96.

143 Daly-Denton, *David*, 59–113; Ahearne-Kroll, "Suffering of David," 1:69–71.

144 See "History of the Tradition and Historical Reliability" above.

145 For a discussion of the remains of a crucified man discovered by archaeologists, see Jodi Magness, "What Did Jesus' Tomb Look Like?" *BAR* 32.1 (2006) 38–49, 70, esp. 46–48.

146 BDF §442 (4).

147 Cf. Beyer, *Semitische Syntax*, 33 n. 4, 259–71; Dormeyer, *Die Passion Jesu*, 194.

148 Brown, *Death*, 2:959 n. 61.

149 Schmidt, "Mark 15.16-32," 12. John Pobee argued that the third hour was the time of the morning sacrifice ("The Cry of the Centurion—A Cry of Defeat," in Ernst Bammel, ed., *The Trial of Jesus: Cambridge Studies in Honour of C. F. D. Moule* (SBT 2nd series 13; London: SCM; Naperville, IL: Alec R. Allenson, 1970) 91–102, esp. 95. The morning sacrifice may, however, have still been offered at the break of day, in accordance with the biblical stipulation (Schürer, *History*, 2:300–301), but see the commentary on v. 33 below.

150 See "History of the Tradition and Historical Reliability" above.

151 See the commentary on 15:1 above.

crucifixion on the day of preparation for the feast. Both the day and the time of the crucifixion have symbolic significance in John. Jesus is crucified at the time that the Passover lambs were slaughtered.[152] The symbolic character of John's chronology, however, does not necessarily mean that Mark's is historically reliable. It was known and remembered that Jesus was crucified in Jerusalem around the time of Passover, but reliable information about the exact timing may not have survived.

■ **26** The redundancy of ἐπιγραφή . . . ἐπιγεγραμμένη (lit., "an inscription was inscribed") is typical of Markan style.[153] If this verse was part of Mark's source, as seems likely, it was rewritten by the evangelist in his own words.[154] The term ἐπιγραφή ("inscription") is equivalent to the Latin *titulus*, which is sometimes used to mean "placard" or "notice."[155] The Greek word αἰτία can mean "charge" or "accusation," but here the sense is "the offense of which he had been found guilty."[156]

According to Suetonius, Gaius Caligula immediately handed over to the executioners a slave who had stolen a strip of silver from the dining couches at a public banquet, ordering that his hands be cut off and hung around his neck. He was also to be "led around among the guests, preceded by a placard giving the reason for his punishment" (praecedente titulo qui causam poenae indicaret, per coetus epulantium circumduceretur) (*C. Caligula* 32.2).[157] The placard and the public display are intended to deter others from committing the same offense.[158]

The use of a placard (*titulus*) is attested also in an anecdote about Domitian:

A householder who said that a Thracian gladiator was a match for the *murmillo* [a kind of gladiator who fought with a Thracian], but not for the giver of the games, [Domitian] caused to be dragged from his seat and thrown into the arena to dogs, with this placard: "A favourer of the Thracians who spoke impiously (Patrem familias, quod Thraecem murmilloni parem, munerario imparem dixerat, detractum spectaculis in harenam canibus obiecit cum hoc titulo: "Impie locutus parmularius"). (Suetonius *Dom.* 10.1)[159]

The letter from the churches of Vienne and Lyon to Christians in Asia and Phrygia describes several martyrdoms, including that of Attalus of Pergamum. Before the governor became aware that he was a Roman citizen:

He was conducted around the arena behind a sign on which there was written in Latin, "This is Attalus, the Christian" (καὶ περιαχθεὶς κύκλῳ τοῦ ἀμφιθεάτρου, πίνακος αὐτὸν προάγοντος ἐν ᾧ ἐγέγραπτο Ῥωμαϊστί· οὗτός ἐστιν Ἄτταλος ὁ Χριστιανός). (Eusebius *Hist. eccl.* 5.1.44)[160]

It is credible that a placard was made indicating the crime of which Jesus was convicted. It could conceivably have read "the king of the Jews," using an ironic tone to insult Jesus, as Domitian insulted the Roman householder in the passage cited above.[161] It is more likely, however, that the portrayal of the inscription or placard as reading "the king of the Jews" originated in the apologetic and polemical perspective of the pre-Markan

152 Cf. John 1:29; Raymond E. Brown, *The Gospel according to John (xiii–xxi): Introduction, Translation, and Notes* (AB 29A; Garden City, NY: Doubleday, 1970) 882–83.

153 Neirynck, *Duality in Mark*, 77; Brown, *Death*, 2:962.

154 See "History of the Tradition and Historical Reliability" above; see also Yarbro Collins, *Beginning of the Gospel*, 112–13.

155 LS, s.v. *titulus*. The loanword from Latin, τίτλος ("inscription"), is used in John 19:19.

156 Winter, *Trial*, 153.

157 Text and trans. from Rolfe, *Suetonius*, 1:466–67.

158 Brown, *Death*, 2:963.

159 Text and trans. from Rolfe, *Suetonius*, 2:340–41. Rolfe notes that the householder's remark implied that Domitian was unfair because he favored the Thracians and that the use of the term *parmularius*

(lit., "one armed with the buckler," "a Thracian") in the *titulus* was an added insult to the Roman citizen (ibid., nn. b and c). See also Cassius Dio 54.3.6–7, which tells how Caepio's father "led a slave through the midst of the Forum with an inscription making known the reason why he was to be put to death and afterwards crucified him (διά τε τῆς ἀγορᾶς μέσης μετὰ γραμμάτων τὴν αἰτίαν τῆς θανατώσεως αὐτοῦ δηλούντων διαγαγόντος καὶ μετὰ ταῦτα ἀνασταυρώσαντος); text and trans. from Earnest Carey and Herbert B. Foster, *Dio's Roman History* (9 vols.; LCL; Cambridge, MA: Harvard University Press, 1954–61) 6:290–91.

160 Text and trans. from Musurillo, *Christian Martyrs*, 74–75.

161 For arguments in favor of the historicity of the

passion narrative.[162] It fits with the pre-Markan portrayal of the interrogation of Jesus by Pilate and the governor's question, "Are you the king of the Jews?" (15:2). It also follows well upon the mockery of the soldiers, and the audiences could infer that they were the ones who made the placard.[163] In the present form of Mark, the placard may be seen, from the point of view of the soldiers as characters, as a parody of Jesus' claim to be the messiah (cf. 14:61-62).[164] For the evangelist and his audiences, however, the inscription is ironic, because it unwittingly expresses the truth that Jesus is a king.[165]

■ **27** This depiction of Jesus crucified between two robbers (λῃσταί) seems to evoke a passage from Isaiah:

> For this reason he will be the heir of many and will distribute the spoils of the mighty, because he was handed over to death and he was considered to be among the lawless; and he bore the sins of many and was handed over on account of their sins (διὰ τοῦτο αὐτὸς κληρονομήσει πολλοὺς καὶ τῶν ἰσχυρῶν μεριεῖ σκῦλα, ἀνθ' ὧν παρεδόθη εἰς θάνατον ἡ ψυχὴ αὐτοῦ, καὶ ἐν τοῖς ἀνόμοις ἐλογίσθη· καὶ αὐτὸς ἁμαρτίας πολλῶν ἀνήνεγκεν καὶ διὰ τὰς ἁμαρτίας αὐτῶν παρεδόθη). (Isa 53:12 LXX)

It is likely that this depiction is an addition by the evangelist for several reasons. The passage from Isaiah just cited is apparently one of the sources and prototypes of the Markan theme of the divine activity of "handing over," which involves John the Baptist, Jesus, and the followers of Jesus being "handed over" to human adversaries who kill them.[166] Another reason why Mark may have added the passage is the role that "robbers" or "bandits" or "rebels" (λῃσταί) play in his account of Jesus' time in Jerusalem and the contrast that he draws

between them and Jesus. In his account of Jesus' actions in the temple, he implicitly contrasts Jesus' efforts to restore and preserve the purity and holiness of the temple with the sacrilegious occupation of the temple by the rebels during the Jewish war.[167] Similarly, when Jesus is arrested, Mark puts a saying in his mouth that contrasts his behavior with that of the rebels and indicts the authorities for treating him as if he were like them.[168] Further, Mark constructed a narrative σύνκρισις ("rhetorical comparison") of Barabbas and Jesus in order to contrast the nonviolent messiahship of Jesus with the misguided and destructive leadership of the instigators of the revolt, symbolized by Barabbas.[169] Finally, this portrayal of Jesus' crucifixion between two robbers reprises the request of James and John in 10:37 that they be granted the privilege of sitting, one on Jesus' right and one on his left in his glory (εἷς σου ἐκ δεξιῶν καὶ εἷς ἐξ ἀριστερῶν καθίσωμεν ἐν τῇ δόξῃ σου).[170] Here there are "two robbers, one on his right and one on his left" (δύο λῃστάς, ἕνα ἐκ δεξιῶν καὶ ἕνα ἐξ εὐωνύμων αὐτοῦ). The evocation of the earlier text in the account of the crucifixion elaborates the ironic portrayal of Jesus as king that already characterized Mark's source. Jesus hangs on a cross with a placard announcing his kingship, but James and John are not with him. Because of their fear of suffering and death, they abandoned him and the places of honor are filled by men who are unworthy.

■ **28** The traditional text of Mark includes v. 28, and the majority of the manuscripts contain it: "and the scripture was fulfilled which says, 'and he was considered to be among the lawless'" (καὶ ἐπληρώθη ἡ γραφὴ ἡ λέγουσα· καὶ μετὰ ἀνόμων ἐλογίσθη). Although this verse was not part of the earliest recoverable text of

---

inscription, see Blinzler, *Der Prozess Jesu*, 367–68; Winter, *Trial*, 154–56; Brown, *Death*, 2:962–68.

162 Reinbold, *Der älteste Bericht*, 273–76, 280–81.

163 Schmidt, "Mark 15.16-32," 13. Schmidt does not discuss the question of a pre-Markan passion narrative. The position taken here is that the mocking of the soldiers in 15:16-20 was part of Mark's source; see the comment on that unit above. See also the section "Composition and History of the Tradition" in the excursus on the passion narrative in the commentary on 14:1-11 above.

164 See also the discussion of the mocking of Jesus as

parody from the perspective of the soldiers in the commentary on v. 18 above.

165 Cf. Yarbro Collins, "From Noble Death," 495.

166 Mark 1:14; 3:19; 9:31; 10:33 (twice); 13:9, 11, 12; 14:10, 11, 18, 21, 41, 42, 44; 15:1, 10, 15. See also the commentary on 3:19; 9:31; and 14:10-11 above.

167 See the commentary on 11:17 above.

168 See the commentary on 14:48-49 above.

169 See the commentary on 15:6-15 above.

170 Similarly, Frank J. Matera, *The Kingship of Jesus: Composition and Theology in Mark 15* (SBLDS 66; Chico, CA: Scholars Press, 1982) 62, 171–72 n. 8.

Mark,[171] its addition demonstrates that later editors and scribes of Mark recognized in v. 27 an allusion to Isa 53:12 LXX.

■ **29-32** The present form of this passage is the result of Mark's expansion of his source. The source read something like the following:

And those who passed by reviled[172] him, shaking their heads and saying, "He saved others, himself he cannot save; let the messiah, the king of Israel, come down now from the cross, in order that we may see and believe" (Καὶ οἱ παραπορευόμενοι ἐβλασφήμουν αὐτὸν κινοῦντες τὰς κεφαλὰς αὐτῶν καὶ λέγοντες· ἄλλους ἔσωσεν, ἑαυτὸν οὐ δύναται σῶσαι· ὁ χριστὸς ὁ βασιλεὺς Ἰσραὴλ καταβάτω νῦν ἀπὸ τοῦ σταυροῦ, ἵνα ἴδωμεν καὶ πιστεύσωμεν).[173]

The appearance of random passersby fits with the probable location of Golgotha outside the walls of the city and near a gate and one or more roads.[174] The portrayal of the passersby as reviling Jesus and shaking their heads evokes a psalm that plays an important role elsewhere in Mark:

All who saw me sneered at me,
they spoke with their lips, they shook their heads,
"He based his hope on the Lord, let Him rescue him;
let Him save him, if He cares for him"
(πάντες οἱ θεωροῦντές με ἐξεμυκτήρισάν με,
ἐλάλησαν ἐν χείλεσιν, ἐκίνησαν κεφαλήν
Ἤλπισεν ἐπὶ κύριον, ῥυσάσθω αὐτόν·
σωσάτω αὐτόν, ὅτι θέλει αὐτόν). (Ps 21:8-9 LXX)[175]

The two passages share the motifs of shaking the head (κινεῖν κεφαλήν) and the saving or rescuing of Jesus (σῴζειν). This part of the (pre-)Markan text is also similar to another psalm:

And I became an object of insult for them;
they saw me, they shook their heads.
Help me, Lord, my God,
save me in accordance with your mercy
(καὶ ἐγὼ ἐγενήθην ὄνειδος αὐτοῖς·
εἴδοσάν με, ἐσάλευσαν κεφαλὰς αὐτῶν.
βοήθησόν μοι, κύριε ὁ θεός μου,
σῶσόν με κατὰ τὸ ἔλεός σου). (Ps 108:25 LXX)

Both of these psalms and the (pre-)Markan text refer to a sequence of seeing and shaking the head; each has a different word for "seeing," and Psalm 108 has a different term for "shaking." All three have some form of the word σῴζειν ("save" or "rescue") in relation to the one who is being reviled, sneered at, or insulted. Psalm 108 and the expanded Markan text both have a term from the word-group ὀνειδίζειν/ὄνειδος ("to insult"/"object of insulting"). The pre-Markan text may evoke both psalms. It is highly likely that the evangelist recognized the evocation of Psalm 21, given its role in the Gospel as a whole.

It may be that, from the perspective of the pre-Markan passion narrative, both the allusion to Ps 21:19 LXX in v. 24 and that to Ps 21:8-9 in vv. 29a, 31b-32a are instances of "messianic exegesis."[176] In other words, these evocations of older texts make a narrative argument that Jesus is indeed the messiah, as testified by scripture, a reality to which the soldiers and passersby inadvertently attest by their actions and words. If so, the evangelist may have been aware of and affirmed that narrative exegesis. It is at least clear that in both cases, there is a figurative relationship between scripture and the events that happened to Jesus. A new story is told by adapting an old story. The link between the two unifies the old expressions of hardship, rejection, and lament with the new story of the rejection and mistreatment of the messiah.

The statement "He saved others, himself he cannot save" in the pre-Markan text alludes to the traditions

---

171 See note c on the trans. of v. 27 above.
172 The primary meaning of βλασφημεῖν here is "revile," not "blaspheme"; see Yarbro Collins, "Charge of Blasphemy," 396.
173 Schenke, *Der gekreuzigte Christus*, 92–94; Yarbro Collins, *Beginning of the Gospel*, 113–14. The reconstruction offered here differs from those just cited in omitting the reference to those crucified with Jesus insulting him. If v. 27 was added by the evan-

gelist, he probably added this reference as well. See the commentary on v. 27 above.
174 See the commentary on v. 22 above.
175 This psalm is also evoked in 9:12; 15:24, 34; see the commentary on these passages.
176 See the commentary on v. 24 above.

concerning Jesus' mighty deeds of exorcising, healing, and perhaps also raising from the dead. In its present context in Mark, it recalls the miracle stories that occur so frequently in chapters 1–8.[177] The mocking intensifies with the challenge to "come down now from the cross, in order that we may see and believe." One of the major aims of the Markan narrative as a whole seems to be the reinterpretation of messiahship to include the degrading suffering and death experienced by Jesus.[178] The passion predictions, the teaching that follows each of them, and the scene in Gethsemane make clear to sympathetic audiences that Jesus was not unable to save himself as he hung on the cross. Rather, he chose to submit himself to the mysterious plan of God.[179]

In the pre-Markan passion narrative, the address of Jesus as "the messiah, the king of Israel" is ironic and continues the apologetic and polemical theme that Jesus was crucified because he claimed to be the messiah.[180] This theme begins with Pilate's question, "Are you the king of the Jews?" and continues with the mocking of Jesus as the king of the Jews by the soldiers. Its climax is the announcement concerning the inscription that publicized Jesus' "crime": being "king of the Jews." The mocking of Jesus as a king shifts from "king of the Jews," an expression appropriate on the lips of non-Judeans and non-Jews,[181] to "the messiah, the king of Israel," an appellation that expresses an inner-Jewish perspective. The passersby are apparently portrayed as Jews, but not as followers of Jesus who would affirm that Jesus truly is the messiah.

The premise of the mockery in v. 32, that seeing is believing, is not a theme that is directly addressed anywhere else in Mark.[182] It could well be pre-Markan, as is assumed here. In its present context in Mark, it appears to be ironic in the sense that, even if these outsiders did see Jesus come down from the cross, they probably would still not believe. Such a premise seems to be implied by the evocation of Isa 6:9-10 in 4:11-12, "To you has been given the mystery of the kingdom of God, but to those who are outside, everything happens in parables, in order that, seeing, they may see and not perceive, and hearing, they may hear and not comprehend, lest they turn and it be forgiven them." It is also implied by the account of the reaction of the people of Gerasa to Jesus' healing of the demoniac. Even though they saw the former demoniac clothed and in his right mind, instead of believing in Jesus, they ask him to leave their region (5:14-17). Even insiders are portrayed as seeing and not believing, which in the context seems to be equivalent to not understanding. The disciples see Jesus walking on the sea, but they think he is a ghost. Even when they recognize him, they still do not understand; instead their hearts are hardened (6:49-52).

Mark apparently expanded an earlier scene involving one mocking voice to an account of a triple mockery. He begins, like his source, with the passersby, but gives them a new script. What they say is in part new and in part modeled on the old speech, which is now transferred to the chief priests and scribes. The new part is the opening statement, "Hah! You who are about to throw down the sanctuary and build (another) in three days (οὐὰ ὁ καταλύων τὸν ναὸν καὶ οἰκοδομῶν ἐν τρισὶν ἡμέραις), save yourself by coming down from the cross!" (v. 29b). This part reprises the statement of the false witnesses in 14:58, "We heard him saying 'I will destroy this sanctuary, which is made with hands, and in the course of three days I will build another, which is not made with hands'" (ἐγὼ καταλύσω τὸν ναὸν τοῦτον τὸν χειροποίητον καὶ διὰ τριῶν ἡμερῶν ἄλλον ἀχειροποίητον οἰκοδομήσω). The second part of their statement is

---

177 On the association of the messiah with miracle-working, see "Jesus as Messiah" in the introduction to the commentary above.

178 See the commentary on 8:30-31 above.

179 See the excursus on the messianic secret following the commentary on 1:24 above.

180 See "Genre" in the excursus on the passion narrative in the commentary on 14:1-11 and "History of the Tradition and Historical Reliability" in the commentary on 14:53-72 above.

181 When Ἰουδαῖοι is used primarily as a geographical, social, and political term, "Judeans" is an appropriate translation; when it is used primarily as a religious term, "Jews" is a better translation. English cannot capture this double significance of Ἰουδαῖοι.

182 The closest parallel is the exclamation of the bystanders in 2:12, "We have never seen anything like this!" Since they glorify God, it is implied that they accept Jesus as God's agent, but it is not said that they "believe."

based on elements of the original speech, which is now attributed to the chief priests and the elders: "Save yourself by coming down from the cross!" in v. 30 seems to be a rewriting and combination of "He saved others; himself he cannot save" in v. 31b and "Let the messiah, the king of Israel, come down now from the cross" in v. 32a.[183]

Mark's source already connected the scene of the crucifixion with the trial before Pilate through the theme of Jesus as the "king of the Jews." As argued above, Mark composed and added to his source the account of the trial before the Judean council and the denial of Peter.[184] The reprise of the false testimony against Jesus regarding the temple serves to link that trial with the account of the crucifixion as well. The speech of the passersby as a whole effectively reviles Jesus by contrasting his alleged claim to miraculous power, to be exercised by removing the current temple and building the definitive, eschatological temple, with his current weakness and humiliation.

In v. 31a, Mark introduces the second voice, in this case explicitly mocking Jesus (ἐμπαίζειν), belonging to the chief priests and the scribes. This part of the scene is a bit awkward for two reasons. The chief priests and scribes would be more likely to know about the false testimony against Jesus than random passersby. Furthermore, the idea that chief priests and scribes, presumably temple scribes,[185] would go out of the city to observe Jesus' crucifixion and to mock him lacks verisimilitude. Such exalted personages would be unlikely to take part in such a sordid scene.[186] It is credible that Mark would have introduced the chief priests and scribes as characters here, since they play the role of typical opponents of Jesus in the Gospel as a whole, especially in the part set in Jerusalem and in Markan additions to the passion narrative.[187]

The third voice in the scene of mockery is that of the two men who were crucified with Jesus (v. 32b). This reference takes up and continues the introduction of them as characters in v. 27, a Markan addition inspired by Isa 53:12, as argued above. James and John were unable to take up their crosses and follow Jesus because they wished to save their lives. The two robbers or rebels are even more unworthy to be on Jesus' left and right because they behave like the passersby, the chief priests, and the scribes when they insult Jesus.

■ 33 As argued above, this verse was probably in the pre-Markan passion narrative.[188] The sixth hour would be the midpoint of the period of daylight when the sun was at its height.[189] The depiction of darkness coming upon the land at midday evokes a passage in Amos:

> And on that day, says the Lord God, the sun will set at midday, and the light will grow dark upon the land at daytime (καὶ ἔσται ἐν ἐκείνῃ τῇ ἡμέρᾳ, λέγει κύριος ὁ θεός, καὶ δύσεται ὁ ἥλιος μεσημβρίας, καὶ συσκοτάσει ἐπὶ τῆς γῆς ἐν ἡμέρᾳ τὸ φῶς). (Amos 8:9 LXX)

If the evangelist recognized an evocation of Amos here in his source, this perception may have led him to evoke another passage from Amos in his depiction of the young man who ran away naked on the occasion of Jesus' arrest.[190]

The significance of this evocation may be articulated in various ways. The context in Amos concerns a day of judgment and punishment.[191] If that context is evoked, and if the passage alluded to is not adapted atomistically, the motif of darkness at noon could be related to the image of the cup (of wrath) in 14:36, which was probably

---

183 Schenke, *Der gekreuzigte Christus*, 84–85.
184 See the commentary on 14:53-72 above.
185 See the commentary on 14:1-2 above.
186 Schenke comments that the portrayal of people reviling Jesus who just happen to pass by is more realistic than the artificial depiction of the chief priests and scribes coming out of the city specifically to mock him (*Der gekreuzigte Christus*, 84).
187 See 8:31; 10:33; 11:18, 27; 14:1, 43, 53; 15:1.
188 See "History of the Tradition and Historical Reliability" above; see also Yarbro Collins, *Beginning of the Gospel*, 114.
189 See the commentary on v. 25 above for the reckon-

ing of the hours of the day in Greek and Roman cultural contexts.
190 Or the evocation of Amos may be part of a pre-Markan tradition; see the commentary on 14:51-52 above.
191 Shalom M. Paul, *Amos: A Commentary on the Book of Amos* (Hermeneia; Minneapolis, MN: Fortress, 1991) 262. Hans Walter Wolff interprets the oracle in relation to the destruction of the (northern) kingdom of Israel (*Joel and Amos: A Commentary on the Books of the Prophets Joel and Amos* [Hermeneia; Philadelphia: Fortress, 1977] 329).

also part of the pre-Markan passion narrative.[192] In that case, the darkness could symbolize Jesus taking the wrath of God upon himself.[193] Or it could symbolize mourning for a "beloved" or "only son," a motif that occurs in Amos 8:10.[194] This interpretation is supported for the Markan stage by the heavenly voice in 1:11, which addresses Jesus as "my beloved son" (ὁ υἱός μου ὁ ἀγαπητός) and also by the voice from the cloud at the transfiguration, which announces, "This is my beloved son" (οὗτός ἐστιν ὁ υἱός μου ὁ ἀγαπητός).[195]

If the passage from Amos is evoked in an atomistic way, the darkness may be interpreted as a sign, wonder, or prodigy expressing the great significance of Jesus and his death.[196] This interpretation is supported by the hypothesis that the pre-Markan passion narrative shared features with accounts of the deaths of famous people circulating in the cultural context of the early Roman empire in the eastern Mediterranean world. The death of Caesar was associated with darkness or the weakening of the sun.[197] Darkness and other signs were also associated with the death of Alexander the Great.[198] Some said that, when Romulus died or disappeared, an eclipse of the sun occurred.[199] Diogenes Laertius made the following remark about the death of the philosopher Carneades:

At the time he died the moon is said to have been eclipsed, and one might well say that the brightest luminary in heaven next to the sun thereby gave token of her sympathy (τελευτῶντος δ᾽ αὐτοῦ φασιν ἔκλειψιν γενέσθαι σελήνης, συμπάθειαν, ὡς ἂν εἴποι τις, αἰνιττομένου τοῦ μεθ᾽ ἥλιον καλλίστου τῶν ἄστρων). (Vit. Phil. 4.64)[200]

The depiction of the darkness as lasting from the sixth hour to the ninth hour (from noon until roughly 3:00 P.M.) should probably be understood as a way of moving the narrative along.[201] The association of the death of Jesus with the ninth hour, however, may have symbolic significance. The narrative links the death of Jesus with the ninth hour or implies that he died between the ninth and the tenth hour. This was the time of the afternoon Tamid, the second daily sacrifice of a lamb in the temple.[202] It is impossible to tell whether this

---

192 On the image of the cup of wrath, see the commentary on 14:36 above. On darkness symbolizing divine wrath, see Brown, *Death*, 2:1035.

193 Yarbro Collins, "From Noble Death," 497.

194 In the commentary on Lam 1:1 in *Lam. Rab.*, a *mashal* is cited in which God clothes the skies in blackness and darkens the sun, moon, and stars to express divine mourning; see the ET in Stern, *Parables in Midrash*, 126.

195 Mark 9:7; see also the parable of the vineyard and the tenants, according to which the owner of the vineyard sends, as a last resort, his "beloved son" (υἱὸς ἀγαπητός) (12:6).

196 Such as the one that occurred when Cleomenes, king of Sparta, was killed and then crucified: a large serpent coiled itself around his head so that no bird of prey could land on it (Plutarch *Vit. Cleomenes* 39); Bultmann, *History*, 274 n. 1. See the citation of this passage in the commentary on v. 39 below. For further examples of signs, wonders, or prodigies accompanying the deaths of famous people, see Bultmann, *History*, 282 nn. 3–4; Klostermann, 166; Shiner, "Ambiguous Pronouncement," 8–10.

197 Virgil *Georgics* 1.463–68; Plutarch *Vit. Caesar* 69.4–5; Yarbro Collins, "Genre," 16, 27 n. 102; Taylor, 593; Shiner, "Ambiguous Pronouncement," 10.

198 *Alexander Romance* 3.33.5; Talbert, "Biographies,"

1633–34. For the Greek text and a German trans., see Helmut van Thiel, *Leben und Taten Alexanders von Makedonien: Der griechische Alexanderroman nach der Handschrift L* (TzF 13; Darmstadt: Wissenschaftliche Buchgesellschaft, 1983) 164–65; for an ET, see Pseudo-Callisthenes, *The Greek Alexander Romance* (trans. with an introduction and notes by Richard Stoneman; London/New York: Penguin Books, 1991) 157.

199 Plutarch *Vit. Romulus* 27.6. The case of Pelopidas is different. An eclipse of the sun occurred when he was about to set out with an army from Thebes (Plutarch *Vit. Pelopidas* 31.1–3 = p. 295A); this was interpreted by the seers and the citizens as an omen that he should not go to war against Alexander of Pherae. He did go to battle and was victorious, but lost his life. See also Christopher J. Tuplin, "Pelopidas," *OCD* 1132–33.

200 Text and trans. from Hicks, *Diogenes Laertius*, 1:440–41; Taylor, 593; Shiner, "Ambiguous Pronouncement," 10.

201 See the discussion of the schema of hours in vv. 25, 33, and 34 in "History of the Tradition and Historical Reliability" above.

202 Josephus *Ant.* 14.4.3 §65; cf. *Ant.* 3.10.1 §237; Acts 3:1; Schürer, *History*, 2:300–301.

association was deliberate on the part of the author of the pre-Markan passion narrative or whether the evangelist was conscious of it, although it seems likely. In that case, the implication would be that Jesus' death is a metaphorical sacrifice.[203]

■ **34-39** Like vv. 29-32, the present form of this passage is probably due to Mark's expansion of his source. The pre-Markan passion narrative probably read something like the following:

> And at the ninth hour, Jesus cried out with a loud voice and expired. And the curtain of the sanctuary was split in two from top to bottom (καὶ τῇ ἐνάτῃ ὥρᾳ ἐβόησεν ὁ Ἰησοῦς φωνῇ μεγάλῃ καὶ ἐξέπνευσεν. Καὶ τὸ καταπέτασμα τοῦ ναοῦ ἐσχίσθη εἰς δύο ἀπ᾽ ἄνωθεν ἕως κάτω).

The announcement of Jesus' death at the ninth hour, roughly equivalent to 3:00 P.M., is the climax of the schema of hours that began in v. 25 with the remark that Jesus was crucified at the third hour. The drama is heightened with the depiction in v. 33 of darkness over the whole land from the sixth hour until the ninth hour. Jesus' death at the ninth hour is then followed by another portent: the tearing of the temple veil. The schema of hours provides a framework for the events and makes their depiction more impressive.

Jesus' cry of abandonment in v. 34 is probably a secondary elaboration of the wordless or unreported cry in v. 37.[204] The lack of a report of Jesus' last words in the earlier account fits with the depiction of Jesus as virtually silent during his interrogation by Pilate. The second portent, the rending of the veil, takes the place of the last words.[205] The depiction of this event was probably the end of the pre-Markan passion narrative. It implied the vindication of Jesus, not the destruction of the temple.[206]

The remark of some of the bystanders that Jesus was calling Elijah is linked to the cry of abandonment by a play on words. Since the whole unit regarding the misunderstanding of Jesus' cry and its significance develops the Gospel's Elijah theme, it is likely to be Markan composition. If the latter unit is Markan, the cry of abandonment probably is too. It appears that the cry of Jesus in v. 34 was added, among other reasons, to prepare for the deliberate misunderstanding and mockery reported in vv. 35-36.[207]

The saying of the centurion in v. 39 also expresses the vindication of Jesus. Since it fits so well with the theme of Jesus as Son of God in the Gospel as a whole, it was probably added by Mark.[208]

■ **34** The evangelist was not content to describe Jesus' death with a wordless cry, as his source did. As argued above, a version of the Gethsemane story was already part of Mark's passion source.[209] The story depicted Jesus as distressed and anxious, asking God to remove the cup from him. In that scene, Jesus speaks the language of scripture in expressing his anguish: "My soul is exceedingly sorrowful to the point of death" (περίλυπός ἐστιν ἡ ψυχή μου ἕως θανάτου).[210] In Gethsemane, Jesus is portrayed as sharing the weakness and fear of most ordinary human beings in the face of death. He experienced the terror of death in the core of his being. With difficulty, he was able to say in his prayer that he was willing to accept what God had ordained for him.

Taking his cue from the depiction of Jesus in Gethsemane, Mark has Jesus speak the language of scripture in his last words:[211]

> "Eloi, Eloi, lema sabachthani?," that is, translated, "My God, my God, why have you abandoned me?" (ἐλωι

---

203 See the commentary on 14:22 above.

204 See "History of the Tradition and Historical Reliability" above.

205 Yarbro Collins, "Genre," 16.

206 See "Composition and History of the Tradition" in the excursus on the passion narrative in the commentary on 14:1-11 above. See also Yarbro Collins, *Beginning of the Gospel*, 116–17; eadem, "From Noble Death," 497–99.

207 Yarbro Collins, *Beginning of the Gospel*, 115–16.

208 Ibid., 117; eadem, "From Noble Death," 497. On the theme of Jesus as the Son of God in Mark, see Yarbro Collins, "Son of God among Greeks and Romans," 85–100; and eadem, "Son of God among Jews," 393–408.

209 See the commentary on 14:32-42 above.

210 This statement apparently evokes Psalms 6; 41–42; Sir 37:2 and Jonah 4:9, all from the LXX. See the discussion in the commentary on 14:34a above.

211 Bultmann erred in denying that there were *any* allusions to scripture in the earliest account of Jesus' death; Schenke erred by assuming that *all* the allusions are pre-Markan; see "History of the Tradition and Historical Reliability" above; for a discussion of

ελωι λεμα σαβαχθανι; ὅ ἐστιν μεθερμηνευό-
μενον· ὁ θεός μου, ὁ θεός μου, εἰς τί ἐγκατέλιπές
με).

Like the words of Jesus in Gethsemane quoted above, Jesus' dying words evoke a psalm of individual lament:

O God, my God, give heed to me; why have you abandoned me? (ὁ θεὸς ὁ θεός μου, πρόσχες μοι· ἵνα τί
ἐγκατέλιπές με;). (Ps 21:2a LXX)[212]

Matthew follows Mark in having Jesus express a sense of abandonment by God in his last words (Matt 27:46). Luke substitutes a more edifying and exemplary saying, "Father, into your hands I entrust my spirit" (πάτερ, εἰς χεῖράς σου παρατίθεμαι τὸ πνεῦμά μου), which is taken from a psalm with some elements of lament (Luke 23:46; Ps 30:6 LXX). John puts last words in the mouth of Jesus that fit with his characterization in that Gospel as a whole: "It is accomplished" (τετέλεσται) (John 19:30).[213] In the history of interpretation of Mark and Matthew, many have resisted the implication that Jesus was or felt abandoned by God.[214]

We have no way of knowing what the historical Jesus actually felt as he died or what his last words on the cross, if any, were.[215] What is clear is that Mark did not portray Jesus' last words on the model of the noble death. Jesus' last words in Mark are passionate, express-ing both the loneliness of intense suffering and a bold and demanding challenge addressed to God. Contrast the beautiful death of Socrates and his ironic saying

about sacrificing a cock to Asclepius, which expresses the idea that death is a good thing for a good person.[216] Con-trast also the last words of Eleazar in 2 Maccabees, full of trust and submission, in spite of divine knowledge of his innocent suffering (2 Macc 6:30).[217] The seven brothers express threats and challenges to Antiochus, who kills them unjustly, but only trust and confidence toward God.[218]

It is also clear that Jesus' death in Mark is quite differ-ent from the idealized accounts of the deaths of the later martyrs. Only a few examples can be cited here. Although the martyrdom of Polycarp is explicitly com-pared with the death of Jesus (*Mart. Pol.* 1.1-2; 6.2; 7.1), in his prayer he is calm and undisturbed (5.1-2; 7.2–8.1), unlike Jesus in Gethsemane. Polycarp did "not collapse in terror" at the governor's threats to throw him to wild animals and to burn him alive.[219] When he is burned to death, he shows no sign of pain or mental anguish; the account is highly idealized (*Mart. Pol.* 15–16). Contrast-ing with Polycarp's courage is the apostasy of a Phrygian named Quintus, which is attributed to his becoming cow-ardly (δειλιᾶν) and to the fact that he gave himself up, rather than waiting to be "handed over" or "arrested" (παρα-διδόναι) (*Mart. Pol.* 4; cf. 1.2). Another work tells how, when Carpus was hung up and being scraped, he kept shouting only "I am a Christian" (ὁ δὲ ἔκραξεν· Χριστιανός εἰμι) until he was too exhausted to say any-thing more. When Papylus had to undergo the same kind of torture, the narrator says that he "did not utter a sound; like a noble athlete he received the angry onslaught of his adversary."[220] They both die cheerfully

---

Schenke's conclusions regarding 15:34, see also Yarbro Collins, *Beginning of the Gospel*, 115.

212 On the wording of Jesus' cry in Aramaic, see notes d, e, and f on the trans. of v. 34 above; see also Brown, *Death*, 2:1051-54; Swete, 385.

213 Brown, *Death*, 2:1072.

214 See Brown, *Death*, 2:1047–51.

215 Yarbro Collins, "From Noble Death," 500.

216 Plato *Phaedo* 117c-118; Yarbro Collins, "Genre," 7. See also eadem, "From Noble Death," 485–86. Compare also the death of Seneca, which was modeled on that of Socrates; Tacitus *Annals* 15.44–64, esp. 60–64; Yarbro Collins, "Genre," 13.

217 Cf. also Eleazar's calm and altruistic statement in 4 Macc 6:27-29.

218 2 Macc 7:6, 9, 11, 14, 16-17, 18-19, 30-38; similarly 4 Macc 9:1-9, 15, 17, 23-24, 29-32; 10:10-11, 14–16,

18-21; 11:2-6, 20-27; 12:11-18. Their mother, even though forced to witness the torture and deaths of her seven sons, also expresses unshaken confidence in the compassion and mercy of God (7:22-23, 27-29). See also the encomium on the mother in 4 Macc 14:11–17:6, esp. the speech attributed to her in 16:16-23.

219 οὐ . . . μὴ συμπεσεῖν ταραχθέντα ὑπὸ τῶν λεγομένων πρὸς αὐτόν (*Mart. Pol.* 12.1; text and trans. from Musurillo, *Christian Martyrs*, 10–11).

220 φωνὴν οὐκ ἔδωκεν, ἀλλ᾽ ὡς γενναῖος ἀθλητὴς ἀπεδέχετο τὸν θυμὸν τοῦ ἀντικειμένου (*Martyr-dom of Saints Carpus, Papylus, and Agathonice*, Greek recension, 23; 35; Musurillo, *Christian Martyrs*, 24–27).

and in peace. The letter of the churches of Lyons and Vienne says that Blandina, a slave, suffered extreme tortures "like a noble athlete" (ὡς γενναῖος ἀθλητής) and a barbaric execution, strengthened by "her intimacy with Christ" (ὁμιλία πρὸς Χριστόν).[221]

Mark does, nevertheless, contain hints that the death of Jesus should serve as a model for his followers. They are to take up their crosses and follow him and to lose their lives because of Jesus and the gospel, rather than try to save them (Mark 8:34—9:1). When they are arrested and interrogated, they should speak the truth and endure torture and death, rather than deny Jesus as Peter did (13:9-13; 14:53-72). In the interwoven stories of Jesus' trial before the Judean council and Peter's denial, the two characters are contrasted in a narrative form of the rhetorical practice of comparing two individuals. The implication is that Jesus' behavior is a model to be followed, whereas Peter's is to be avoided.[222] The author of Luke-Acts also implies that Jesus' death is to be imitated by modeling the account of Stephen's death on that of Jesus (Acts 7:54-60).[223]

While it is clear that Jesus' cry in v. 34 expresses a sense of abandonment by God, that expression should not be confused with despair. The despairing person retreats into silence, whereas Jesus speaks. Although his speech is anguished and confrontational, it is still a kind of prayer and still a cry for help and support.[224]

The fact that the prayer is given in both Aramaic and Greek suggests that at least some in Mark's audiences could understand Aramaic, whereas others could not. The use of Aramaic is necessary to introduce the misunderstanding of Jesus' cry as calling upon Elijah: there is a play on the words ελωι ("Eloi") and Ἡλίας ("Elijah").[225]

■ **35** The first part of this verse refers to "some of those who were standing by" (τινες τῶν παρεστηκότων). This reference is quite vague. Verse 29 refers to "those who passed by" (οἱ παραπορευόμενοι), who seem to be different from those "standing by." Verse 31 refers to the chief priests and scribes who were with them, but no indication is given that they stayed on the scene.[226] The soldiers who crucified Jesus are the ones most likely to be "standing by," but those referred to in v. 35 appear to be Jews, since they know traditions and perhaps texts about Elijah.

The speech of the passersby is explicitly described as reviling in v. 29 and implicitly defined as mocking in v. 31: "Similarly, the chief priests also mocked him" (ὁμοίως καὶ οἱ ἀρχιερεῖς ἐμπαίζοντες). In vv. 35-36, there is no explicit characterization of what is said as mocking. The statement in v. 35b, however, is surely ironic.[227] One way in which it is ironic is that the characters are portrayed as *hearing* what Jesus said and saying, *see*, he is calling Elijah. Like the outsiders of 4:11-12, however, they neither hear nor see rightly.[228] Another ironic dimension of the text is that the speakers, whether seriously or mockingly, imply that Jesus is calling Elijah to rescue him in a miraculous show of power.[229] They evoke the traditions of Elijah as a miracle-worker, as one taken up to heaven by a chariot in a whirlwind and as one who will return in the last days as God's agent. The powerful, miraculous interpretation of Elijah, however, has already been rejected by the Markan Jesus. Elijah has already

---

221 Eusebius *Hist. eccl.* 5.1.19; 5.1.56; Musurillo, *Christian Martyrs*, 66–67, 78–81.

222 See the commentary on 14:53-72 above, esp. on v. 72.

223 Yarbro Collins, "Genre," 20.

224 According to Hindy Najman, lamentation itself is the beginning of the recovery of intimacy with the divine; in Lam 3:22, for example, a prayer begins in the midst of lament (personal communication).

225 This is the case even if the misunderstanding is implausible. Matthew's change of ελωι ("Eloi") to ηλι ("Eli") in 27:46 is an attempt to make the misunderstanding more intelligible. See note d on the trans. of v. 34 above; see also Brown, *Death*, 2:1051–54; Swete, 385; Hooker, 376.

226 Schenke argued that the bystanders are the chief priests and the scribes, but this conclusion is dubious (*Der gekreuzigte Christus*, 98–99). Since Mark is

not averse to repetition, if he meant them to be so understood, he would probably have made the point explicitly.

227 It is not necessarily ironic in the sense that the characters are portrayed as consciously using irony; it is ironic in the sense that "elements of the story-line provoke the reader to see beneath the surface of the text to deeper significances" (Camery-Hoggatt, *Irony*, 1). Jerry Camery-Hoggatt refers to this type of irony as "dramatic irony" (ibid., 2). See also Yarbro Collins, "From Noble Death," 495, for a discussion of this type of irony in 15:16-20.

228 Fowler, *Let the Reader Understand*, 122. See also ibid., 109.

229 This implication links the remarks about Elijah to the challenges addressed to Jesus in vv. 29b-32a to do something miraculous.

returned, as John the Baptist, and has suffered and died in accordance with scripture, just as the Son of Man must also suffer and be treated with contempt.[230]

■ **36** The speech of the person who offered the drink to Jesus clarifies the portrayal of the character. The opening word, ἄφετε, can be taken either independently or as closely related to the following word, ἴδωμεν. If it is taken separately, it is elliptical and thus ambiguous. It could mean either "Let (me give him this)" or "Let (him alone)."[231] If it is taken with ἴδωμεν, the sense would be "Let us see."[232] The latter is more likely.[233]

If ἄφετε ἴδωμεν is translated "Let us see (whether Elijah is coming to take him down)," then the person who offered the drink to Jesus must be one of the bystanders mentioned in v. 35. He associates himself with them by using the first person plural and knows traditions about Elijah as they do. It is thus probable that this character is one of those Jewish bystanders and not one of the soldiers.[234]

The bystander gives Jesus ὄξος to drink. The term ὄξος in Greek and its counterparts in Hebrew (חמץ) and Latin (*acetum*) were used for sour wine of varying qualities and acidity. This sour wine, when diluted with water,

"formed the ordinary drink of the common people."[235] When mixed with water, and especially if made from good wine, it was a pleasant, thirst-quenching drink, quite different from modern vinegar.[236] Precisely speaking, sour wine mixed with water was called ὀξύκρατον or ὀξύκραμα in Greek.[237] But ὄξος is sometimes used to mean the same thing.[238]

According to the book of Numbers, the Nazirite is to abstain from wine (οἶνος) and from sour wine or wine-vinegar (ὄξος ἐξ οἴνου) (Num 6:3 LXX).[239] In the book of Ruth, Boaz invites Ruth to "come here and eat some bread and dip your morsel in the sour wine" (πρόσελθε ὧδε καὶ φάγεσαι τῶν ἄρτων καὶ βάψεις τὸν ψωμόν σου ἐν τῷ ὄξει) (Ruth 2:14 LXX).[240]

Pliny the Elder spoke of the great cooling qualities of sour wine and indicated that it was used as a remedy for various ailments (*Hist. nat.* 23.27 §§54–58). Schmidt's contention, that Pliny supports the conclusion that sour wine was understood to deaden pain, is misleading.[241] Pliny says rather that it can heal various painful ailments.

In a play by Plautus, the slave of a young Athenian is envious of the slaves of a soldier because they are drunk on wine (*vinum*):

230 See the commentary on 9:11-13 above. See also Christine E. Joynes, "A Question of Identity: 'Who Do People Say That I Am?' Elijah, John the Baptist and Jesus in Mark's Gospel," in Christopher Rowland and Crispin H. T. Fletcher-Louis, eds., *Understanding, Studying and Reading: New Testament Essays in Honour of John Ashton* (JSNTSup 153; Sheffield: Sheffield Academic Press, 1998) 15–29, esp. 27. Mark F. Whitters argued that vv. 35-36 constitute a rejection of one of several inadequate titles for Jesus: "a revived Elijah or *Elias redivivus*" and that the "confusion of the bystanders is an intentional rhetorical device that prepares the reader for the resolution of Jesus' identity provided by the centurion" in v. 39; "Why Did the Bystanders Think Jesus Called upon Elijah before He Died (Mark 15:34-36)? The Markan Position," *HTR* 95 (2002) 119–24; quotations from 123–24.

231 Gould took the former position (295). Cranfield entertained the second as a possibility, but rejected it (459).

232 Cranfield, 459.

233 Cf. ἄφες with the subjunctive in Matt 7:4/Luke 6:42; Taylor, 595; see also Moulton-Milligan, s.v. ἀφίημι; Pesch, 2:497; Brown, *Death*, 2:1064, and the literature that Pesch and Brown cite.

234 With Pesch, 2:496, and contra Klostermann, 166; Cranfield, 459; Taylor, 594; Lane, 573; Gnilka, 2:323; Hooker, 376.

235 W. G. Spencer, "List of Alimenta: *Vinum acetum, posca*," in idem, *Celsus: De medicina* (3 vols.; LCL; Cambridge, MA: Harvard University Press; London: Heinemann, 1935) 1:498; similarly, Jean Colin, "Il soldato della Matrona d'Efeso e l'aceto dei crocifissi (Petronio III)," *Rivista di Filologia e Istruzione Classica* 81 (1953) 97–128, esp. 105. See also BAGD and Moulton-Milligan, s.v. ὄξος.

236 Hans Wolfgang Heidland, "ὄξος," *TDNT* 5 (1967) 288–89, esp. 288.

237 LSJ, s.v. ὀξύκραμα and ὀξύκρατον; J. Colin, "Essig," *RAC* 6 (1966) 635–46, esp. 636.

238 Colin, "Essig," 636–37.

239 See the trans. and discussion of the MT in Levine, *Numbers 1–20*, 216, 219–20.

240 See the trans. and discussion of the MT in Edward F. Campbell, *Ruth: A New Translation with Introduction and Commentary* (AB 7; Garden City, NY: Doubleday, 1975) 87, 102.

241 Schmidt, "Mark 15.16-32," 11 n. 32.

Some folks get gloriously drunk, while others are always bibbing diluted sour wine (Alii ebrii sunt, alii poscam potitant). (*Miles gloriosus* 837–38, Act 3, Scene 2)[242]

In another play, three young men are all in love with a courtesan. The city man sends her gifts, which make the soldier, also her suitor, jealous. He says to her:

Can you, you, for a scrubby gift of greens, fodder and sour wine, deign to love a soft seducer with crinkled locks, an indoorsportsman, a thrummer of the tambourine, a makeshift of a male? (tun tantilli doni causa, holerum atque escarum et poscarum, moechum malacum, cincinnatum, umbraticulum, tympanotribam amas, hominem non nauci?). (Plautus *Truculentus* 609–10, Act 2, Scene 7)[243]

In his characterization of Marcus Cato, Plutarch says:

Water was what he drank on his campaigns, except that once in a while, in a raging thirst, he would call for sour wine, or, when his strength was failing, would add a little wine (ὕδωρ δ' ἔπινεν ἐπὶ στρατείας, πλὴν εἴποτε διψήσας περιφλεγῶς ὄξος αἰτήσειεν ἢ τῆς ἰσχύος ἐνδιδούσης ἐπιλάβοι μικρὸν οἰνάριον). (*Vit. Cato Major* 1.7 [pp. 336–37])[244]

It is likely that the ὄξος of v. 36 is the sour wine used regularly by ordinary people in antiquity.[245] Considering the narrative context in light of the uses of sour wine in antiquity leads to the conclusion that the implied reason for giving Jesus the sour wine was to cool any fever he may have had, to quench his thirst, and thus to extend his life a bit longer so that the bystanders could see whether Elijah would come.[246] There is no evidence that sour wine was considered in antiquity to be a stimulant.[247]

It is not clear whether the saying of the one who offered Jesus a drink is mocking, like the saying of the bystanders in v. 35, or expressing a genuine curiosity.[248] In any case, both sayings are ironic in the sense that the audiences of the narrative know that Elijah has already come, in the person of John the Baptist, and that he has already been "handed over."[249] They know that Elijah will not come, since suffering and death are ordained both for Elijah (John the Baptist) and for Jesus.[250]

The placement of the sponge on a reed presupposes that Jesus was crucified on a cross that was high enough that one could not extend him a drink with the upraised arm alone.[251] The imperfect ἐπότιζεν is conative, like ἐδίδουν in v. 23, and thus is translated "tried to give (it to him) to drink."[252]

It is often assumed or argued that v. 36 recalls Ps

---

242 Text and trans. (modified) from Paul Nixon, *Plautus* (5 vols.; LCL; London: Heinemann; Cambridge, MA: Harvard University Press, 1924) 3:210–11; Lohmeyer, 346 n. 3.

243 Text and trans. (modified) from Nixon, *Plautus*, 5:286–87; Lohmeyer, 346 n. 3.

244 Text and trans. (modified) from Perrin, *Plutarch's Lives*, 2:306–7.

245 Gould, 295 n. 2; Gustav Wohlenberg, *Das Evangelium des Markus* (KNT 2; Leipzig: Deichert, 1910) 377; Swete, 386; Döller, "Der Wein in Bibel und Talmud," 165, 278–79; Lohmeyer, 346 n. 3; Grundmann, 316; Cranfield, 459; Taylor, 594–95; Heidland, "ὄξος," 288; Lane, 573–74; Pesch, 2:496; Hooker, 376–77. Douglas J. Moo mistakenly defines *posca* ("sour wine") as "wine diluted with vinegar" (*Old Testament*, 279). Perhaps he refers to the practice of using vinegar to season wine; Pliny *Hist. nat.* 14.24 §120; Colin, "Essig," 636; cf. *Hermas Man.* 10.3.3. Brown recognizes that ὄξος here means a common drink ("*posca* or red peasant wine"), but

concludes that the context and the allusion to Ps 69:22 [MT] make it likely that the offer was "not a friendly gesture" and that is was "mockery" (*Death*, 2:1063–64).

246 Gould, 295; Grundmann, 316; Pesch, 2:496.

247 With Heidland, "ὄξος," 288–89; Pesch, 2:496; Gnilka, 2:323; contra Lohmeyer, 346; Evans, 508.

248 Lohmeyer, 346; Grundmann, 316; Donahue and Harrington, 448. See also the commentary on v. 35 above.

249 Lührmann, 263.

250 Öhler argued that vv. 35-36 were composed to counteract the magical idea, current in Mark's audiences or in their cultural contexts, that Jesus was rescued from death, i.e., raised from the dead, by a good demon or secret name of God (*Elia*, 139–53); this hypothesis is unnecessary and implausible.

251 Pesch, 2:496; for a description of the high type of cross (*crux sublimis*), see Collins, S.J., "Archaeology of the Crucifixion," 154.

252 Klostermann, 167; Taylor, 595; Pesch, 2:496; Gundry, 948.

68:22 LXX[253] or that the evangelist deliberately alluded to it.[254] Some of those who take this position infer, on the basis of the evocation of that psalm, that the drink offered to Jesus either is meant to torment or torture him[255] or is a mocking gesture.[256] The verse from the psalm reads as follows:

> And they gave me gall [or bile] for food
> and for my thirst they gave me sour wine to drink
> (καὶ ἔδωκαν εἰς τὸ βρῶμά μου χολὴν
> καὶ εἰς τὴν δίψαν μου ἐπότισάν με ὄξος). (Ps 68:22 LXX)

The only verbal similarities between Mark 15:36 and the verse from the psalm are the common use of the noun ὄξος ("sour wine") and the verb ποτίζειν ("to give to drink"). Since the use of sour wine, and thus the word for it, was common in the evangelist's cultural milieu, and since he uses the verb ποτίζειν elsewhere in the same sense (9:41), the argument for the evocation of the psalm is tenuous. The likely evocation of Ps 68:9 LXX in 3:21, however, supports the conclusion that another verse from the same psalm is evoked here as well.[257]

Assuming that the verse from the psalm is evoked here, one must ask what the significance of that evocation is. How can the portrayal of the sour wine in Mark as a refreshing drink that would ameliorate Jesus' fever and wounds be reconciled with an allusion to Ps 68:22? Johannes Döller tried to reconcile the two by arguing that Ps 68:22 was meant to be understood figuratively. "Gall" or "bile" in v. 22a stands for ridicule and mockery. The "sour wine" of v. 22b signifies hurtful or wounding speech. *Acetum* ("sour wine") is also used in a metaphorical sense to mean biting wit.[258] The same verse is evoked in the thanksgiving psalms from Qumran, where the term under discussion is interpreted figuratively. In the relevant passage,[259] the speaker, who is probably the Teacher of Righteousness,[260] thanks God for revealing God's covenant and God's self to the Teacher.[261] He then talks about others, the leaders of an opposing party in Jerusalem,[262] who teach the people of Israel falsehoods. He calls them "mediators of fraud and seers of deceit" (והמה מליצי כוב וחוזי רמיה) (1QH 12:9-10).[263] In the same context, Ps 69:22 MT is evoked:

> they have denied the drink of knowledge to the thirsty, but for their thirst they have given them sour wine to drink
>
> (ויעצורו משקה דעת מצמאים ולצמאם ישקום חומיץ).
> (1QH 12:11)[264]

The "sour wine" or vinegar here signifies false or inadequate teaching.

Hans Heidland argued that Mark was not consciously referring to Ps 69:21 (68:22 LXX). He interpreted Luke 23:36-37, however, as implying that the "drink itself is contemptuous—sour wine offered to the King of the

---

253 Swete, "perhaps" (387); Lohmeyer, 346; Klostermann, 167; Pesch, "subtle allusion" (2:496); Moo, *Old Testament*, 278–79; Lührmann, 263; Juel, *Messianic Exegesis*, 96; Gnilka, 2:323; Gundry, 948; Brown, "less specific" [than Matthew and the *Gospel of Peter*] (*Death*, 2:1059); Evans, 508; Donahue and Harrington, "very likely" (448).

254 According to Hooker, all four evangelists saw the incident as a fulfillment of Ps 69:21 (68:22 LXX) (377).

255 Gnilka, 2:323.

256 Klostermann, 167; Lührmann, 263; Brown, *Death*, 2:1059; Evans, 508.

257 See the commentary on 3:20-21 above. See also the discussion regarding the evocation of Ps 68:22 LXX in Mark 15:36 by Stephen Ahearne-Kroll, "Suffering of David," 1:101–4.

258 Döller, "Der Wein in Bibel und Talmud," 278–79.

259 According to García Martínez and Tigchelaar, there

is a blank at the beginning of line 5 of 1QH (1QH^a), col. 12 (*Dead Sea Scrolls*, 1:166–67). Vermes defines 12:5 (formerly 4:5) as the beginning of *Hymn* 12 (formerly 7) (*Dead Sea Scrolls*, 263). Michael C. Douglas and the scholars he cites, however, define 12:7 as the beginning of a unit ("The Teacher Hymn Hypothesis Revisited: New Data for an Old Crux," *DSD* 6 [1999] 239–66); they do not, however, include 12:5-6. Lines 5-6 will be taken into account here.

260 Douglas, "Teacher Hymn Hypothesis," 246–66.

261 1QH 12:5-6; these lines may be the ending of the previous hymn; see n. 259 above.

262 Douglas, "Teacher Hymn Hypothesis," 259–65.

263 Text and trans. from García Martínez and Tigchelaar, *Dead Sea Scrolls*, 1:168–69.

264 Text and trans. (modified) from García Martínez and Tigchelaar, *Dead Sea Scrolls*, 1:168–69.

Jews."[265] Since the gesture of offering sour wine to Jesus in the Lukan passage is framed by the statement, "The soldiers also mocked him" (ἐνέπαιξαν δὲ αὐτῷ καὶ οἱ στρατιῶται), and by their taunting him as "the king of the Jews" (ὁ βασιλεὺς τῶν Ἰουδαίων), it is a reasonable inference that the offer of sour wine itself is a mockery of Jesus' kingship from the point of view of the soldiers as characters in the narrative of Luke.

In Mark, there is no indication that the individual who offered Jesus sour wine did so in mockery, but we may have here another case of dramatic irony.[266] The individual offers Jesus the sour wine in order to extend his life long enough for Elijah to appear, if Jesus' cry, as understood by the bystanders, is to be answered. The audiences of Mark know, however, that sour wine is not a fit drink for Jesus, the king of the Jews, that is, the messiah.[267] Ps 68:22 could be understood along the same lines from the perspective of the Markan scene. According to its superscription, it is a psalm of David. As a king, David, the speaker of the psalm, deserved better than sour wine to drink. Jesus, who, according to the early Christian interpretation, is the subject of the psalm and the messiah, exercises his kingship ironically, at this stage of the eschatological scenario. The offer of sour wine, even if well intentioned, is one small detail in the ironic contrast between Jesus' identity and the way he is treated.[268]

■ **37** The Markan Jesus does "not go gentle into that good night."[269] He dies with a loud, probably wordless cry. His death puts an end to the bystanders' expectation of the coming of Elijah, whether feigned or genuine. It also frustrates the attempt of the individual with the sponge on a reed to give Jesus a drink. Perhaps not incidentally, the frustration of that attempt fulfills Jesus'

prophecy in 14:25 that he would surely not drink again of the fruit of the vine until that day when he drinks it new in the kingdom of God.[270]

The description of Jesus' death fulfills one main element of the passion predictions in 8:31; 9:31; and 10:33-34. It may also be seen as the culmination of the theme of the rejection and suffering of Jesus in the Gospel as a whole.[271]

■ **38** The depiction of "the curtain of the sanctuary" (τὸ καταπέτασμα τοῦ ναοῦ) being split is ambiguous and probably symbolic. The ambiguity of such prodigies is shown by the fact that portents occurring during the Jewish war were interpreted negatively by Josephus (presumably with the benefit of hindsight) and positively by the people during the course of the war (Josephus *Bell.* 6.5.3 §§288–300).

It is not clear which curtain is meant.[272] Josephus, in his description of the tabernacle constructed in the wilderness at the command of God, says that the Holy of Holies (τὸ ἄδυτον), the innermost part of the tabernacle, was an imitation of heaven, which is devoted to God (*Ant.* 3.6.4 §§122–23). He refers to the curtain that conceals this space as the "first one" (πρῶτον) (*Ant.* 3.6.4 §125).[273] The second curtain hung before the entrance to the tabernacle or dwelling (σκηνή) as a whole, the covered part of the tent, which corresponded to the sanctuary or temple proper (ναός). This curtain hung only to the middle of the pillars so that the priests could pass under it. He also says that a linen curtain hung over the second or outer curtain to protect it from the weather. On great days (ἐπίσημοι ἡμέραι), presumably feast days, he says that it was drawn to one side so as not to obstruct the view of the main part of the inner tabernacle (*Ant.* 3.6.4 §§127–29).

265 Heidland, "ὄξος," 289.

266 See the commentary on v. 35 above.

267 Juel argues that this and other psalms evoked in the passion narrative were read messianically (*Messianic Exegesis*, 96–117); he does not propose a specific interpretation of the evocation of Ps 69:22 (68:22) in v. 36. Pesch (2:496), Lührmann (263), and Brown (*Death*, 2:1059–60) interpret the evocation as characterizing Jesus as the suffering just one.

268 Ahearne-Kroll interprets the allusion to Ps 68:22 LXX in relation to the whole psalm, especially the psalmist's cry to God "for deliverance in the midst of suffering" ("Suffering of David," 2:292–95).

269 Dylan Thomas, "Do not go gentle into that good night," in idem, *The Collected Poems of Dylan Thomas* (New York: New Directions, 1957) 128.

270 Cf. v. 23 above; see also the commentary on 14:25 and 15:23 above.

271 Harry L. Chronis, "The Torn Veil: Cultus and Christology in Mark 15:37-39," *JBL* 101 (1982) 97–114, esp. 99–100.

272 Pesch takes the position that it cannot be determined to which veil v. 38 refers (2:498).

273 He uses the word τὸ ὕφος for curtain in §§124–25 and the word τὸ φάρσος in §126.

In his description of Herod's temple, Josephus says that the sanctuary (ναός) had golden doors before which hung a curtain (καταπέτασμα) made of materials that typified the universe (ἀλλ᾽ ὥσπερ εἰκόνα τῶν ὅλων) (*Bell.* 5.5.4 §212).[274] On this woven cloth (πέπλος) "was portrayed a panorama of the heavens, the signs of the Zodiac excepted."[275] He states that the innermost part of the temple, the Holy of Holies, was also screened by a curtain (καταπέτασμα) (*Bell.* 5.5.5 §219).[276] Since both of these curtains were part of the temple proper, it is not appropriate to argue that only the outer curtain could be described as the curtain of the temple (τὸ καταπέτασμα τοῦ ναοῦ).[277]

Scholars have been divided on whether v. 38 refers to the outer veil or the inner one. Some have concluded that the inner veil is meant;[278] others the outer veil.[279] Some of the latter group have argued that, in its context in the present form of Mark, it must refer to the outer veil because the centurion's statement in v. 39 is inspired by his actually seeing the tearing of the veil. The inner veil would not be visible to those outside the temple, so the reference must be to the outer veil.[280] Given the location of Golgotha, however, and the likelihood of the

evangelist's being aware of it, it is improbable that he intended the audiences to infer that the centurion could actually see the curtain tearing. The temple was on the eastern edge of the city, facing east. Golgotha was outside the city to the west.[281] Furthermore, the presentation of the event in Mark seems to have little interest in the effect of the tearing of the veil on the characters in the narrative. It is the audiences of Mark who are expected to reflect on its significance.[282]

Carl Schneider pointed out that the outer curtain had no special cultic significance. The inner curtain, in contrast, had great cultic meaning because it was the only entity separating the holy place and the Holy of Holies. It alone conceals the inner sanctum, and only the high priest, on one day in the year, could pass beyond it. This contrast between the two curtains makes it highly likely that the inner curtain is meant in v. 38.[283]

A number of interpretations were offered above for the significance of this event as part of the pre-Markan passion narrative. It may symbolize the rending of the barrier between humanity and God. Like the letter to the Hebrews, it may signify that the death of Jesus has made possible access to God for all humanity.[284] A related inter-

274 The colors or origins of the materials represented the four elements: fire, earth, air, and sea.

275 κατεγέγραπτο δ᾽ ὁ πέπλος ἅπασαν τὴν οὐράνιον θεωρίαν πλὴν τῶν ζῳδίων (Josephus *Bell.* 5.5.4 §214); text and trans. from Thackeray, *Josephus*, 3:264–65.

276 Thackeray, *Josephus*, 3:266–67. On the symbolism, see Otfried Hofius, *Katapausis: Die Vorstellung vom endzeitlichen Ruheort im Hebräerbrief* (WUNT 11; Tübingen: Mohr Siebeck, 1970).

277 Contra Donahue, *Are You the Christ?* 202–3. In his later work, Donahue argued that the veil of v. 38 could be either the inner or the outer veil (Donahue and Harrington, 448).

278 BAGD, s.v. καταπέτασμα; Lightfoot, *Gospel Message*, 56; Taylor and the first group of authors he cites (596); Chronis, "Torn Veil," 110 n. 67; Linnemann, *Studien zur Passionsgeschichte*, 159; Malbon, *Narrative Space*, 108.

279 Theodor Zahn, *Das Evangelium des Matthäus* (KNT 1; 3rd ed.; Leipzig: Deichert, 1910) 713–14; Lohmeyer, 347; Gösta Lindeskog, "The Veil of the Temple," in *Seminarium Neotestamenticum Upsaliense*, ed., *In honorem Antonii Fridrichsen, sexagenarii* (Coniectanea Neotestamentica 11; Lund: Gleerup; Copenhagen: Munksgaard, 1947) 132–37, esp. 132; Klostermann,

167; Otto Michel, "ναός," *TDNT* 4 (1967) 880–90, esp. 885 n. 21 (following Zahn); Donahue, *Are You the Christ?* 202–3; Donald Juel, *Messiah and Temple: The Trial of Jesus in the Gospel of Mark* (SBLDS 31; Missoula, MT: Scholars Press/SBL, 1977) 140–42; Howard M. Jackson, "The Death of Jesus in Mark and the Miracle from the Cross," *NTS* 33 (1987) 16–37, esp. 24; Stephen Motyer, "The Rending of the Veil: A Markan Pentecost?" *NTS* 33 (1987) 155–57; Gundry, 950.

280 Lohmeyer, 347; Jackson, "Death of Jesus in Mark," 24; David Ulansey, "The Heavenly Veil Torn: Mark's Cosmic *Inclusio*," *JBL* 110 (1991) 123–25, esp. 124; Gundry, 950.

281 See the commentary on v. 22 above.

282 Linnemann, *Studien zur Passionsgeschichte*, 159. See also the commentary on v. 39 below.

283 Carl Schneider, "καταπέτασμα," *TDNT* 3 (1965) 628–30, esp. 629. Similarly, Linnemann, *Studien zur Passionsgeschichte*, 159; Christian Maurer, "σχίζω, σχίσμα," *TDNT* 7 (1971) 959–64, esp. 961.

284 See "Composition and History of the Tradition" in the excursus on the passion narrative in the commentary on 14:1-11 above. Lindeskog argued that v. 38 and Hebrews have a common source, namely, "an early Christian *theologoumenon* implying that the

pretation is that the portrayal of this event signifies the revelation of God or hints at a divine theophany.[285] Similarly, the link of the cry of Jesus with the opening of the temple may evoke Psalm 17 LXX. Such an evocation would imply that God heard Jesus' plea and that God would vindicate him.[286]

The interpretation of v. 38 as part of the Gospel of Mark as a whole depends on what other passage or passages the interpreter considers to be key to its significance. Ernst Lohmeyer linked this verse to 15:29-30 and (implicitly) 14:58 and concluded that the splitting of the curtain signifies the destruction of the temple and thus the beginning of the fulfillment of Jesus' prophecy, "I will destroy the temple." The event also implies that soon the second half of the prophecy will be fulfilled: Jesus is the eschatological bringer of fulfillment in that he ended the old sacrificial cult and inaugurated the new one.[287]

Otto Michel argued that "the feature is to be interpreted against the background of the *kerygma* of Jesus

(Mk. 13:1ff.). God's judgment has fallen on the temple."[288] John R. Donahue placed v. 38 in what he saw as a Markan "anti-temple theme" beginning with 11:1, "in which Jesus is pictured in opposition to the Jerusalem temple, predicting its destruction and being condemned to death because of this prediction." Verse 38 is the culmination of this theme, signifying that "[w]hat has been destroyed in anticipation is now destroyed in fact."[289] It is not so clear, however, that there is an "anti-temple" theme in chapters 11–15. The prediction in 13:1-2 of the destruction of the temple and the saying in 14:58 regarding destroying this temple and building another do not imply a rejection of the temple as such. In chapter 11, the problem is the disobedience of the leaders of the people, especially the priests. In chapter 13, the revolt and the pending destruction of the temple are interpreted in terms that recall the disobedience alluded to in chapter 11. In 14:58, the talk about a new temple, probably the eschatological, definitive temple, implies that the

---

death of Christ on the Cross opens the Gate to Heaven" ("Veil of the Temple," 134). See the criticism of Lindeskog by Linnemann, *Studien zur Passionsgeschichte*, 162 n. 94. A seventh-century commentary on Mark interprets the tearing of the veil of the temple as heaven being opened; see Cahill, *Expositio Evangelii*, 77; and idem, *First Commentary*, 123.

285   See "Genre" in the excursus on the passion narrative in the commentary on 14:1-11 above.

286   See Yarbro Collins, "From Noble Death," 497–98; see also the section "Genre" in the excursus on the passion narrative in the commentary on 14:1-11 above.

287   Lohmeyer, 347, citing on the last point, Epiphanius 30.16 and Hebrews. On the passage from Epiphanius, see Albert F. J. Klijn and Gerrit J. Reinink, *Patristic Evidence for Jewish-Christian Sects* (NovTSup 36; Leiden: Brill, 1973) 182–83. Maurer's interpretation ("σχίζω, σχίσμα," 961) is similar to Lohmeyer's; so also Lentzen-Deis, *Die Taufe Jesu*, 280–81. Pesch took the position that, in the pre-Markan passion narrative, the tearing of the veil was a "sign" that verified Jesus' messiahship and foretold the punishment of the Jewish leaders who were responsible for his death; as part of Mark, it is a "sign," after the fact, of the destruction of the temple (2:498–99). James R. Edwards interpreted v. 38 in association with the story about the withering of the fig tree and concluded that both events foreshadow the destruction of the temple. His conclu-

sion is that "Jesus himself has replaced the temple as the center of Israel's faith (15:38-39); salvation is found in him, not in the temple" ("Markan Sandwiches," 208). See "The Literary Relationship between the Two Stories" in the commentary on 11:12-25 above. Motyer connected v. 38 with 13:2 and interpreted it as a foreshadowing of the destruction of the temple ("Rending of the Veil," 155).

288   Michel, "ναός," 885. Similarly, Evans, 509.

289   Donahue, *Are You the Christ?* 203. The last quotation reflects Donahue's premise that Mark was composed after the temple was actually destroyed in 70 CE. See also the discussion of the interpretations of Schenke and Pesch in the section "Composition and History of the Tradtion" in the excursus on the passion narrative in the commentary on 14:1-11 above. Juel concluded that the tearing of the curtain is "a culmination of the temple theme" and "a portent of the impending destruction of the temple." He argued further that the temple not made with hands mentioned in 14:58 refers to the Christian community (*Messiah and Temple*, 137–39; cf. 169). Chronis argued that the rending of the veil is presented by Mark as "the ultimate theophany." Its link with vv. 37 and 39 implies that the self-revelation of Jesus in his death is a christophany. He combined this interpretation with the theme of "temple destruction and rebuilding" and concluded that Jesus' death is "the end of the temple because the revelation of God's 'face' *on the cross* shatters the Jewish cultus at its very foundation" ("Torn Veil," 110–11). The move from

temple and its cult are to be renewed, not abolished.[290] The interpretation of the rending of the veil in terms of the destruction of the temple and in other terms that imply the supersession of Jewish ideas and practices by Christian ones arose in the context of the early church, when Christians were attempting to forge a new identity vis-à-vis Jewish communities.[291]

A number of scholars have argued that there is a link between the baptism and the death of Jesus, in particular between the splitting ($\sigma\chi\ell\zeta\epsilon\iota\nu$) of the heavens in 1:10 and the splitting ($\sigma\chi\ell\zeta\epsilon\iota\nu$) of the curtain in 15:38.[292] All three Synoptic Gospels use this verb in the account of the death of Jesus (Mark 15:38||Matt 27:51||Luke 23:45). Mark is the only one, however, who uses it in the account of his baptism (1:10).[293] It is likely that Mark is dependent on tradition in both passages.[294] Since the use of the verb $\mathring{\alpha}\nu o\acute{\iota}\gamma\nu\nu\mu\iota/\mathring{\alpha}\nu o\acute{\iota}\gamma\omega$ ("to open") is more common in connection with the heavens,[295] it is likely that Mark formulated the tradition about Jesus' baptism in his own words and chose to use the verb $\sigma\chi\ell\zeta\epsilon\iota\nu$ ("to split"). The common diction suggests that v. 38 is meant to recall 1:10.[296] It is noteworthy that the link between the two passages also connects the beginning and the end of Jesus' public activity.[297] David Ulansey argued that the two passages are also linked by the fact, attested by Josephus, that the outer veil depicted the appearance of the entire heaven or sky. Thus, for those members of the audiences who had seen or heard about this curtain, the announcement of the rending of the curtain would evoke an image of "*the heavens being torn* and [they] would immediately have been reminded" of the account of Jesus' baptism.[298] This theory is ingenious, but it should be recalled that the Holy of Holies, according to Josephus' description of the tabernacle, was an imitation of heaven, which is devoted to God (*Ant.* 3.6.4 §§122–23).[299] Thus, the tearing of the inner veil could also symbolize the rending of the heavens.

Without mentioning the link between v. 38 and 1:10, Gould argued that the rending of the veil, which he took to be the inner one, signified "the removal of the separation between God and the people, and the access into his presence.[300] Similarly, Taylor favors the interpretation that the torn veil "symbolizes the opening of the way to God effected by the death of Christ."[301] Linnemann

---

divine theophany to christophany in this interpretation is forced, as is the combination of the theophany with the theme of the destruction of the temple.

290 See the commentary on 11:11; 11:12-25; 13:1-2, 14-20, and 14:57-58 above.

291 See the passages cited by Lohmeyer and Klostermann, ad loc. See also the interpretation of Pobee and the early Christian texts he cites in support of it ("Cry of the Centurion," 97–98 and nn. 26–27).

292 Malbon, *Narrative Space*, 187 n. 93; Jackson, "Death of Jesus in Mark," 27; Motyer, "Rending of the Veil," 155; Ulansey, "Heavenly Veil Torn," 123; Johannes Heidler, "Die Verwendung von Psalm 22 im Kreuzigungsbericht des Markus: Ein Beitrag zur Frage nach der Christologie des Markus," in Hartmut Genest, ed., *Christi Leidenspsalm: Arbeiten zum 22. Psalm; Festschrift zum 50. Jahr des Bestehens des Theologischen Seminars "Paulinum" Berlin* (Neukirchen-Vluyn: Neukirchener Verlag, 1996) 26–34; Shiner, "Ambiguous Pronouncement," 20 and the literature cited in n. 32. Lightfoot interpreted the two passages in theological, doctrinal terms; 1:10 "is Mark's description of the incarnation," and 15:38 "describes the at-one-ment between God and man, which He by His death has thus effected" (*Gospel Message*, 56). Lightfoot also noted that the baptism, the transfiguration, and the

centurion's "confession" are the three main passages in which "the divine sonship is directly ascribed to the Lord; and it is probably no accident that they occur at the beginning, in the middle, and at the close of the book" (ibid., 57).

293 Matthew and Luke use different forms of $\mathring{\alpha}\nu$-$o\acute{\iota}\gamma\nu\nu\mu\iota/\mathring{\alpha}\nu o\acute{\iota}\gamma\omega$ (Matt 3:16||Luke 3:21).

294 See the commentary on 1:9-11 and "Composition and History of the Tradition" in the excursus on the passion narrative in the commentary on 14:1-11 above.

295 Isa 63:19 LXX (64:1); Ezek 1:1 LXX; *T. Levi* 2:6; 5:1; 18:6; *T. Jud.* 24:2; John 1:51; Acts 7:56; Rev 4:1; 11:19; 19:11.

296 Motyer suggests more similarities between the two passages ("Rending of the Veil," 155–57); see also the summary in Ulansey, "Heavenly Veil Torn," 123. Although some are tenuous, these suggestions are plausible enough, especially that concerning the evocation of Elijah in both contexts.

297 Motyer, "Rending of the Veil," 155; Ulansey, "Heavenly Veil Torn," 123.

298 Ulansey, "Heavenly Veil Torn," 125.

299 See the discussion of this passage above.

300 Gould, 295. Similarly, Nineham, 430; Schneider, "$\kappa\alpha\tau\alpha\pi\acute{\epsilon}\tau\alpha\sigma\mu\alpha$," 630; Schweizer, 355.

301 Taylor, 596. He also entertains the possibility that, at

argued that the function of the inner veil was not to act as a barrier between God and humanity, but rather to veil the majesty of God. It was dangerous for sinful and finite human beings to come in contact with that majesty. The significance of the opening of the veil, at the pre-Markan stage, is that, at the moment of Jesus' greatest lack of power, the full majesty of God becomes manifest.[302] Gnilka took the position that the tearing of the veil means that Jesus' death effected an opening of access to God and God's revelation of God's self in the cross of God's Son.[303] Donahue and Daniel J. Harrington concluded that the rending of the veil signified two things. First, because of the similarity between v. 38 and 1:11 and 9:7, it means that "God has opened definitively the way between heaven and earth through Jesus' death on the cross." Second, it "is probably also an expression of divine judgment on the continuing efficacy of worship at the Jerusalem temple. This has been a major theme since Jesus' entrance into Jerusalem in Mark 11, and it comes to a certain anticipatory fulfillment in the rending of the sanctuary veil."[304]

Howard M. Jackson argued that, according to Mark, "Jesus' earthly ministry as Son of God is initiated by the descent into him of God's Spirit, which tears the heavens in its descent, and it is brought to a close by the ascent of that Spirit out of him in his dying breath, which tears the Temple curtain at its departure. . . ."[305] Similarly, Gundry argued that "just as the force of the Spirit's coming down ($\kappa\alpha\tau\alpha$-) caused the heavens to be rent ($\sigma\chi\iota\zeta o\mu\acute{e}\nu o\nu\varsigma$– 1:10), so the force of the Spirit's exhalation by Jesus causes the veil of the temple to be rent ($\grave{e}\sigma\chi\acute{\iota}\sigma\vartheta\eta$) from the top downward ($\kappa\acute{\alpha}\tau\omega$; cf. the force of Jesus' expulsion by the Spirit into the wilderness–1:12)."[306] Evans adopted a similar interpretation: "The power of Jesus is displayed in his death audibly in the loud shout of v. 37, but it is

displayed even more impressively and more tangibly in the tearing of the $\kappa\alpha\tau\alpha\pi\acute{e}\tau\alpha\sigma\mu\alpha$ $\tau o\hat{\upsilon}$ $\nu\alpha o\hat{\upsilon}$, 'veil of the temple.' That the tearing of the veil is the result of Jesus' sudden expiration, and not merely a coincidental omen, is probable."[307]

There are serious problems with this strange hypothesis. The use of the word $\grave{e}\xi\acute{e}\pi\nu\epsilon\upsilon\sigma\epsilon\nu$ (from $\grave{e}\kappa\pi\nu\acute{e}\omega$) may indeed evoke the context of Jesus' baptism, when the Spirit ($\tau\grave{o}$ $\pi\nu\epsilon\hat{\upsilon}\mu\alpha$) came down into Jesus, but the word itself is simply an elevated and somewhat euphemistic way of saying that someone died,[308] being analogous to the English word "expired." The idea that a strong wind came forth from Jesus directed specifically and only at the veil of the temple is bizarre.

The depiction of the baptismal scene (1:10) does not imply that the dove split the heavens by force as it descended. The reason for the choice of the word $\sigma\chi\acute{\iota}\zeta\epsilon\iota\nu$ ("to split" or "to rend") may be to evoke Isa 63:19b MT or a Greek translation of it closer to the Hebrew than the LXX:

O that you would tear open the heavens and come down, so that the mountains would quake at your presence

(לוא־קרעת שמים ירדת מפניך הרים נזלו).
(Isa 63:19b MT)[309]

By evoking this text, which is similar to the traditional and typical theophanies of the Hebrew Bible, the Markan text suggests that the desire for the self-revelation of God expressed by Isaiah is fulfilled, in a quiet and less traditional way, in the descent of the Spirit into Jesus.

The similarities between 1:10 and 15:38 in vocabulary

the same time, the torn veil symbolizes "the end of the Temple system"; he thinks it less likely that it signifies the destruction of the temple (ibid.).

302 Linnemann, *Studien zur Passionsgeschichte*, 162–63. Her argument that $\sigma\chi\acute{\iota}\zeta\epsilon\sigma\vartheta\alpha\iota$ here can mean "separate" or "open," rather than "split" or "tear" (ibid., 161–62) is linguistically possible but unlikely, since Josephus's description of the curtains in the temple makes clear that they each constituted one large curtain, not two that could be drawn either open or closed.

303 Gnilka, 2:324.

304 Donahue and Harrington, 452. See the discussion of the alleged anti-temple theme above.

305 Jackson, "Death of Jesus in Mark," 27.

306 Gundry, 949–50 (Jackson is cited in the paragraph following this quotation).

307 Evans, 508–9; he cites Gundry on this point.

308 As Gundry notes (949).

309 Text from *BHS*; trans. from NRSV (64:1).

and in the themes in each of their contexts strongly suggest that v. 38, in the context of Mark as a whole, should be read not as a sign of the destruction of the temple but as another nontraditional theophany. Indeed, one could say that it is an ironic theophany. The death of Jesus on the cross is accompanied by a real, but ambiguous and mysterious, theophany, which suggests that the will of God is fulfilled in the apparently shameful death of Jesus on the cross. The presence of God is signified in the baptism and transfiguration of Jesus by the voice from heaven, but God's absence at the cross is implied by Jesus' cry in v. 34. The absence of God at the cross suggests that how and why Jesus' death is the will of God are difficult to understand and to express. In classic theological terms, God as the One who requires Jesus' death is the *deus absconditus*.[310]

■ **39** This verse is probably a Markan addition to the pre-Markan passion narrative.[311] It is the climax of the Markan theme of Jesus as the Son of God.[312]

An important question for interpretation is how the evangelist and his first audiences would have understood the social and cultural location of the centurion. The first thing to notice is that the word κεντυρίων ("centurion") is a Latin loanword.[313] It is a military term taken over directly from the Latin *centurio*, which means "the commander of a century," that is, of a hundred soldiers, "occupying a station below the tribunus."[314]

As noted above, before the war that broke out in 66 CE, only auxiliary troops were stationed in Judea.[315] The auxiliary cohorts, like those of the legions, were subdivided into centuries.[316] Throughout the first two centuries CE, the auxiliary centurions were usually men who had been promoted from the lower ranks, although occasionally legionaries were appointed to this rank in the auxiliary regiments.[317] The auxiliary centurions would have been provincials, if they had been promoted from the ranks.[318] According to Paul A. Holder, in the majority of cases, it is not possible to determine whether the centurion of an auxiliary century was a Roman citizen or not, especially when he has a common Latin cognomen.[319] In the pre-Flavian period, that is, prior to Vespasian's accession as emperor in 69 CE, there is evidence

310 Gudrun Guttenberger, *Die Gottesvorstellung im Markusevangelium* (BZNW 123; Berlin/New York: de Gruyter, 2004) 343–44. See also Yarbro Collins, "Finding Meaning," 195–96.

311 Yarbro Collins, *Beginning of the Gospel*, 117.

312 Yarbro Collins, "Son of God among Jews," 406.

313 BAGD, s.v. κεντυρίων. As they note, the Latinism was used by Polybius, and the equivalent Greek term is ἑκατοντάρχης. The latter term was used by Josephus (Denis B. Saddington, *The Development of the Roman Auxiliary Forces from Caesar to Vespasian [49 B.C.–A.D. 79]* [Harare, Zimbabwe: University of Zimbabwe, 1982] 51; 210 n. 109. Matthew and Luke read ἑκατόνταρχος and ἑκατοντάρχης respectively (Matt 27:54||Luke 23:47). Both of the latter terms occur in the LXX; Hatch-Redpath, s.v. ἑκατοντάρχης, ἑκατόνταρχος; Swete, 388.

314 BDF §5 (1); quotation from LS, s.v. *centurio*. On the centurions as officers of the Roman legions, see Henry M. D. Parker, *The Roman Legions* (Cambridge: W. Heffer and Sons, 1958) 199–205; George R. Watson, *The Roman Soldier* (Aspects of Greek and Roman Life; London: Thames and Hudson, 1969) 86–88. On their uniform, see ibid., 130–31.

315 See the commentary on v. 16 above.

316 Graham Webster, *The Roman Imperial Army of the First and Second Centuries A.D.* (3rd ed.; London: A & C Black, 1985) 148–49.

317 George L. Cheesman, *The Auxilia of the Roman Impe-* *rial Army* (Oxford: Clarendon, 1914; reprinted Chicago: Ares, 1975) 37–38.

318 See the commentary on v. 16 above.

319 Paul A. Holder, *The Auxilia from Augustus to Trajan* (BAR International Series 70; Oxford: B.A.R., 1980) 86. Holder listed the known citizen and peregrine centurions in table 7.2 (p. 102); those whose status cannot be determined are listed as "nondescript." Among the latter are an "Antonius" and a "Cornelius" (cf. nos. 1606 and 1607 in the Prosopography on p. 311). Josephus mentions a centurion by the name of Antonius, who was killed by treachery at Jotapata (*Bell.* 3.7.35 §§333–35). This man, however, may well have been a legionary, since Vespasian's army included three complete legions during the war (Schürer, *History*, 1:492). A centurion by the name of Cornelius is mentioned in Acts 10:1. Haenchen notes that the Italian Cohort, to which he belonged, was supplemented by Syrians from 69 down into the second century. It is thus not as clear as Haenchen claims that Cornelius possessed Roman citizenship (*Acts of the Apostles*, 346 n. 2). See also Conzelmann, *Acts of the Apostles*, 80–81. Dennis B. Saddington follows Sherwin-White in concluding that Cornelius was a provincial (*Development of the Roman Auxiliary Forces from Caesar to Vespasian [49 B.C.–A.D. 79]* [Harare: Zimbabwe: University of Zimbabwe, 1982] 210 n. 111).

for thirteen citizen centurions and seven peregrines.[320] All but one of the peregrine centurions are of the same ethnic origin as the unit in which they serve and thus were probably promoted within the unit.[321]

The auxiliary soldiers and centurions who were not Roman citizens no doubt retained non-Roman characteristics but were also to some degree Romanized. "Roman military ideas and something of the ethos of the Roman army would be absorbed by the foreign troops' association with the Romans and by the training given to some of them."[322]

The centurion is depicted as a bystander (ὁ παρεστηκώς), like those who think Jesus is calling Elijah in v. 35 (τινες τῶν παρεστηκότων).[323] A centurion is not mentioned in vv. 15-20 or in the following material, which belonged to the pre-Markan passion narrative. Mark introduces him here, and it becomes clear in vv. 44-45 that the centurion is portrayed as being in charge of the group of soldiers who take Jesus out of the city and crucify him.[324]

Harry L. Chronis argued that "Mark's description of the position of the centurion vis-à-vis the dying Jesus, ἐξ ἐναντίας αὐτοῦ (15:39), may possess a subtly cultic force. It utilizes, at any rate, one of the idiomatic expressions for entering the temple, for standing 'in the presence' or 'before the face' of God."[325] Yet, as Chronis notes, the LXX "seems to favor ἐναντίον for cultic force."[326] The only case in which the phrase ἐξ ἐναντίας has cultic force is 1 Kgdms 26:20, in which David implores Saul not to let his blood fall to the ground "away from the presence of the Lord" (ἐξ ἐναντίας προσώπου κυρίου). In virtually all the other occurrences

of the phrase in the LXX, it is used to express the spatial position of human individuals or groups. An example comes from a psalm attributed to David:

Before me you have prepared a table opposite those who afflict me (ἡτοίμασας ἐνώπιόν μου τράπεζαν ἐξ ἐναντίας τῶν θλιβόντων με). (Ps 22:5 LXX)

Many of the usages of the phrase in the LXX occur in narrative contexts describing battles.[327] So the spatial description of the centurion as standing opposite Jesus (ἐξ ἐναντίας αὐτοῦ), if it has any symbolic or metaphorical force at all, may well signify the initial role of the centurion as an enemy of Jesus or as one who afflicts him.

The object of the participle ἰδών ("When he saw") is the clause ὅτι οὕτως ἐξέπνευσεν ("that he had expired in this way"). The referent of the word οὕτως ("in this way") is unclear, and this unclarity has given rise to variants in the text.[328] Gould argued that "The only thing narrated by Mark" to which it can refer is "the darkness over all the land."[329] Bultmann concluded that it referred to the darkness and possibly to the splitting of the curtain as well.[330]

The cultural milieu of Mark supports the inference that the centurion's statement about Jesus is a response to one or more omens. According to Plutarch, Cleomenes, king of Sparta,[331] committed suicide when he failed to win the favor and support of Ptolemy IV Philopator.[332] After his death, Ptolemy ordered that his body be flayed and hung up (κρεμάσαι), that is, crucified.

---

320 Holder, *Auxilia from Augustus to Trajan*, 87. The term *peregrinus* was used by the Romans for the free citizens of any other community than the Roman people (Adrian N. Sherwin-White and Andrew W. Lintott, "*peregrini*," *OCD* 1138). See also Saddington, *Development of the Roman Auxiliary Forces*, 254, addendum to 58 n. 22, 212 (concerning the peregrine Caeno, who reached the rank of centurion).

321 Holder, *Auxilia from Augustus to Trajan*, 87.

322 Saddington, *Development of the Roman Auxiliary Forces*, 187–88; quotation from 188.

323 As argued above, vv. 34-35 are also Markan additions; see the commentary on vv. 34-39 above.

324 Cf. Pesch, 2:499. It was customary for soldiers to keep watch over one who had been crucified;

325 Plutarch *Vit. Cleomenes* 39.1–2 (cited below on v. 39); Colin, "Essig," 641.

325 Chronis, "Torn Veil," 110.

326 Ibid., n. 66.

327 Hatch-Redpath, s.v. ἐναντίος (incl. ἐξ ἐναντίας).

328 See note i on the trans. of v. 39 above.

329 Gould, 295.

330 Bultmann, *History*, 274.

331 Cleomenes III; see Paul A. Cartledge, "Cleomenes (2) III," *OCD* 346.

332 Ibid. See also Perrin, *Plutarch's Lives*, 10:125 n. 1.

And a few days afterwards those who were keeping watch upon the crucified body of Cleomenes saw a serpent of great size coiling itself about the head and hiding away the face so that no ravening bird of prey could light upon it. In consequence of this, the king was seized with superstitious fear, and thus gave the women occasion for various rites of purification, since they felt that a man had been taken off who was of a superior nature and beloved of the gods. And the Alexandrians actually worshipped him, coming frequently to the spot and addressing Cleomenes as a hero and a child of the gods (ὀλίγαις δὲ ὕστερον ἡμέραις οἱ τὸ σῶμα τοῦ Κλεομένους ἀνεσταυρωμένον παραφυλάττοντες εἶδον εὐμεγέθη δράκοντα τῇ κεφαλῇ περιπεπλεγμένον καὶ ἀποκρύπτοντα τὸ πρόσωπον, ὥστε μηδὲν ὄρνεον ἐφίπτασθαι σαρκοφάγον. ἐκ δὲ τούτου δεισιδαιμονία προσέπεσε τῷ βασιλεῖ καὶ φόβος, ἄλλων καθαρμῶν ταῖς γυναιξὶν ἀρχὴν παρασχών, ὡς ἀνδρὸς ἀνῃρημένου θεοφιλοῦς καὶ κρείττονος τὴν φύσιν. οἱ δὲ Ἀλεξανδρεῖς καὶ προσετρέποντο φοιτῶντες ἐπὶ τὸν τόπον, ἥρωα τὸν Κλεομένη καὶ θεῶν παῖδα προσαγορεύοντες). (Plutarch Vit. Cleomenes 39.1–2)[333]

In the second century CE, the motif was widespread enough for Lucian to satirize it.[334]

It may well be, however, that the οὕτως ("in this way") is "a simple 'thus' (so RSV) with resumptive or restorative rather than recapitulative force."[335] In other words, the purpose of the adverb is simply to take up the thread of the narrative again after the brief digression of v. 38.[336] In this case, the emphasis in the interpretation of the participle ἰδών ("When he saw") should be not so much on exactly *what* the centurion saw as on the implication of the text that he saw *rightly* in contrast to the other bystanders mentioned in vv. 35–36.[337] The identification of the speakers in v. 35 as "bystanders" (παρεστηκότες) and the use of the same participle in characterizing the centurion may be an indication that we have here another case of narrative rhetorical comparison of two characters.[338] The group of bystanders who think that Jesus is calling Elijah *see* (and hear), but not with insight. The centurion, in contrast, *sees* (and hears) with insight into the significance of Jesus' suffering and his identity.

That insight is expressed in the statement, "This man really was God's son" (ἀληθῶς οὗτος ὁ ἄνθρωπος υἱὸς θεοῦ ἦν). The first issue that arises in relation to this statement is whether the phrase υἱὸς θεοῦ ("God's son") is indefinite ("a son of God" or "a son of a god") or definite ("the Son of God"). Both nouns lack the article.[339] But the definite article in ancient Greek was not used in the same way as in modern English. Greek was flexible in this regard and a phrase may be definite even without the article.[340] The manuscripts that contain the words υἱοῦ θεοῦ in the opening verse of Mark do not use the article with υἱοῦ ("Son"), although many use it with θεοῦ ("of God").[341] In spite of the lack of an article with the first noun, the phrase probably means "the Son of God."[342] Further, Ernest C. Colwell argued that the noun phrase in v. 39 lacks the article because a predicate nominative lacks the article, even if it is definite, in order to

---

333 Text and trans. (modified) from Perrin, *Plutarch's Lives*, 10:140–41; Bultmann, *History*, 274 n. 1; Hengel, *Crucifixion*, 74; cf. Shiner, "Ambiguous Pronouncement," 8.

334 Lucian *Pergr. mort.* 39–40; Shiner, "Ambiguous Pronouncement," 8, 11.

335 Chronis, "Torn Veil," 99 n. 8.

336 Verse 38 appears to be a digression in the present form of Mark. In his source, it served to interpret the death of Jesus. The evangelist retained this climactic verse, but added a second interpretation in v. 39. The links with v. 37 show that the statement of the centurion in v. 39 is a reaction to the death of Jesus and not to the splitting of the curtain of the temple.

337 See the commentary on v. 35 above. That he saw rightly does not necessarily imply that his insight

was complete; it only implies that he is on the right track, in contrast to the other bystanders; similarly, Shiner, "Ambiguous Pronouncement," 15.

338 See the commentary on 14:72 and 15:15 above.

339 If a noun follows another and the second is in the genitive case, the second noun usually follows the first in having or lacking the article.

340 See Smyth §§1126–52; BDF §§253–62.

341 See note a on the trans. of 1:1 above.

342 Tae Hun Kim has argued that the phrase υἱὸς θεοῦ, both in 1:1 and in 15:39, was intended to echo the language of the Roman imperial cult ("The Anarthrous υἱὸς θεοῦ in Mark 15,39 and the Roman Imperial Cult," *Bib* 79 [1998] 221–41). On the usage of the imperial cult, see immediately below.

distinguish it from the subject of the clause.[343] Consequently, he argued that the statement of the centurion
should be translated "the Son of God," not "a son of
god." Earl S. Johnson, however, has rightly pointed out
that grammar alone cannot eliminate the possibility that
the author of Mark intended the centurion's reference to
Jesus' divine sonship to be indefinite.[344]

Another issue is whether the centurion's statement is
presented as a Christian confession of faith in Jesus. In
3:11, the unclean spirits address Jesus, saying, "You are
the Son of God!" ($\sigma\grave{v}$ $\epsilon\hat{\iota}$ $\acute{o}$ $\upsilon\grave{\iota}\grave{o}\varsigma$ $\tau o\hat{v}$ $\vartheta\epsilon o\hat{v}$). This saying is
closer to what one could call a Christian confession, even
though it is spoken by demons. Both nouns have the article, so the noun phrase is clearly definite. Another difference between the two passages is that the statement of
the unclean spirits is in the present tense, which is what
we would expect in a statement of faith. The remark of
the centurion, however, fits the narrative context in
using the imperfect tense, since Jesus has just died.[345]
The centurion's statement shows no expectation of the
resurrection.[346]

If the statement is read as part of the Gospel of Mark
as a whole, especially from the point of view of audiences knowledgeable about Jewish traditions from the
period of the Second Temple, the centurion can be
understood as recognizing Jesus' messiahship.[347] "Son of
God," "king," and "messiah" are synonyms in those traditions.[348] The theme of Jesus as a king is prominent in
chapter 15. If, however, the cultural and social likelihood
of the centurion's being a Gentile is taken seriously, the
noun phrase would not have the meaning "king of the
Jews" or "messiah" for such a character.

Gould concluded that the centurion's statement signifies that "the portent(s) accompanying the death of Jesus
convinced the centurion that he was $\upsilon\grave{\iota}\grave{o}\varsigma$ $\vartheta\epsilon o\hat{v}$, not *the
Son of God*, but *a son of God*, a hero after the heathen con-
ception."[349] One of the Roman stories about an extraordinary death accompanied by portents concerns
Romulus.[350] Actually, the story implies that he did not
die, but disappeared and became a god. This tradition
served as a prototype for the later stories about the
apotheosis, or deification, of Roman emperors.[351]

There is another link between the centurion's state-
ment and the imperial cult.[352] The phrase $\upsilon\grave{\iota}\grave{o}\varsigma$ $\vartheta\epsilon o\hat{v}$, or
more commonly, $\vartheta\epsilon o\hat{v}$ $\upsilon\grave{\iota}\acute{o}\varsigma$ ("God's son"), was used of
emperors. When Julius Caesar died, he was deified and
given the new name *Divus Iulius*. In origin *divus* was simply another form of *deus* and thus meant "god." But following the deification of Julius Caesar, it came to mean a
god who had previously been a man.[353] In the Greek
East, *divus* was usually translated as $\vartheta\epsilon\acute{o}\varsigma$ ("god").[354]
After the official deification of Caesar in 42 BCE, Octa-
vian began to call himself officially *Divi filius*. This
phrase identified Octavian as the (adopted) son of the

343 Ernest C. Colwell, "A Definite Rule for the Use of
the Article in the Greek New Testament," *JBL* 52
(1933) 12–21; Moulton-Turner, 3.183. See also
Shiner, "Ambiguous Pronouncement," 5–6, and the
literature cited in n. 7.

344 Earl S. Johnson, "Is Mark 15.39 the Key to Mark's
Christology?" *JSNT* 31 (1987) 3–22, esp. 6–7.

345 Robert C. Tannehill argued that "the past tense indicates that [the remark of the centurion] is a retrospective statement. It is a comment on the story
narrated to this point, declaring that Jesus has fulfilled the commission given to him by God" ("The
Gospel of Mark as Narrative Christology," *Semeia* 16
[1979] 57–95; quotation from 88).

346 Yarbro Collins, "Son of God among Greeks and
Romans," 41; cf. Johnson, "Is Mark 15.39 the Key to
Mark's Christology?" 7–8; Shiner, "Ambiguous Pro-
nouncement," 5.

347 Yarbro Collins, "Son of God among Jews," 393–408,
esp. 405–6.

348 This equivalence is maintained in John 1:49.

349 Gould, 295; Yarbro Collins, "Son of God among
Greeks and Romans," 94; Shiner, "Ambiguous Pronouncement," 7.

350 Plutarch *Vit. Romulus* 27.6–7; Shiner, "Ambiguous
Pronouncement," 8.

351 See the discussion of the death and apotheosis of
Augustus in Talbert, "Biographies," 1634. See also
"Excursus: Resurrection in Ancient Cultural Con-
texts" in the commentary on 16:1-8 below.

352 Yarbro Collins, "Son of God among Greeks and
Romans," 94–96; Kim, "Anarthrous $\upsilon\grave{\iota}\grave{o}\varsigma$ $\vartheta\epsilon o\hat{v}$,"
225–38.

353 Stefan Weinstock, *Divus Julius* (Oxford: Clarendon,
1971) 391–92.

354 See, for example, the letter of the emperor Claudius
to the Alexandrians, which dates to 41 CE, in which
the deified Augustus is referred to as ($\acute{o}$) $\vartheta\epsilon\grave{o}\varsigma$
$\Sigma\epsilon\beta\alpha\sigma\tau\acute{o}\varsigma$, "(the) god Augustus"; the papyrus was
published by Harold Idris Bell in 1912; the Greek
text and an English translation are given in John L.
White, *Light from Ancient Letters* (Philadelphia:

deified Julius Caesar, but literally translated it could signify "God's son" or "son of a god."[355]

It is clear from a bilingual inscription from Alexandria dated to 10 or 11 CE that θεοῦ υἱός ("God's son" or "a son of a god") is a translation of the Latin *divi filius*.[356] But this does not mean that the Greek phrase was limited to the denotation of the Latin expression and to its usage in Rome and the West. Rather, as Simon Price has shown, the phrase θεοῦ υἱός as an epithet of the emperor must be understood in a Greek cultural framework. The fact that the living emperor could be called θεός ("god") already indicates a profound difference between the Latin and the Greek cultural contexts. *Divus* could be applied only to a dead emperor, and thus θεός, when applied to the living emperor, cannot be a translation (narrowly defined) of *divus*.[357] The epithet θεός was added to the name of the emperor and on its own it could refer to a specific emperor. Both practices also occur in contemporary usage with regard to the traditional gods. Calling the emperor θεός ("god") was accompanied by other linguistic practices: he was assimilated to particular named deities; he, like the traditional deities, was sometimes described as ἐπιφανής ("distinguished" or "manifest") and ἐπιφανέστατος τῶν θεῶν ("the most distinguished of the gods"); and a whole system of cults was devised to show εὐσέβεια ("reverence" or "piety") toward the emperors.[358]

The noun phrase in the statement of the centurion in v. 39 is ambiguous. It may be understood as a definite reference to the Son of God, as Colwell argued, but for those familiar with the terminology of the imperial cult, the lack of the articles recalls the imperial epithet θεοῦ υἱός ("God's son" or "a son of a god"). The earliest recoverable reading of Mark's text has the nouns in the opposite order, υἱὸς θεοῦ, but some manuscripts, including Codex Bezae and most of the Old Latin manuscripts, attest a reading in which the phrase has the same form as the imperial title: θεοῦ υἱός.[359] Those members of the audiences of Mark familiar with the imperial cult would understand that the centurion recognized Jesus, rather than the emperor, as the true ruler of the known world. The cultural expectation that the centurion would be Roman or a Romanized provincial supports the hypothesis that there is an allusion to the imperial cult here. Living memory and the material continuation by his heirs of the imperial cults dedicated to Augustus by Herod the Great in Palestine could have evoked the imperial cult even for audiences of Mark living in that area.[360]

Another issue is whether the centurion's statement is presented as a serious one or as another instance of mocking. Johnson argued that the statement of the centurion is ironic in the same sense as the statements of the chief priests, scribes, and those who think that Jesus is calling Elijah.[361] That the statements of the priests and

Fortress, 1986) no. 88, pp. 131–37; the citation is from line 59.

355 Weinstock, *Divus Julius*, 399; see also the bronze coin of Philippi, dated tentatively to 2 BCE, which contains on the obverse the legend "Aug. Divi f. Divo Iul(io)" (ibid., plate 29, coin no. 12). See also Harold Mattingly, *Coins of the Roman Empire in the British Museum*, vol. 1, *Augustus to Vitellius* (London: British Museum, 1923) mint of Rome: no. 275 (p. 50); coins from the East: nos. 589–616 (pp. 97–101); mint of Ephesus: nos. 691–93 (p. 112). An inscription from Acanthus in Macedonia is dedicated to Augustus: (αὐτοκράτορι Καίσ)α(ρι θ)ε̂ωι θεοῦ (υἱῶι) Σεβαστῷ ("to the emperor Caesar, god, son of god, Augustus") (Victor Ehrenberg and Arnold H. M. Jones, *Documents Illustrating the Reigns of Augustus and Tiberius* [2nd ed.; Oxford: Clarendon, 1955] no. 108 [p. 91]; cf. 115 [p. 93]).

356 See Franz Josef Dölger, *ΙΧΘΥΣ: Das Fischsymbol in frühchristlicher Zeit*, vol. 1: *Religionsgeschichtliche und epigraphische Untersuchungen* (Supplement to Römi-

sche Quartalschrift; Freiburg im Breisgau: Herder; Rome: Spithöver, 1910) 391.

357 Simon R. F. Price, "Gods and Emperors: The Greek Language of the Roman Imperial Cult," *JHS* 104 (1984) 79–95, esp. 79.

358 Ibid., 93.

359 The introduction of the reading θεοῦ υἱός may be explained in either of two ways: it could be influenced by the usage of the imperial cult or it could be due to the use of the acronym ἰχθύς ("fish") for Ἰησοῦς Χριστὸς Θεοῦ Υἱὸς Σωτήρ ("Jesus Christ God's Son Savior"); see Dölger, *ΙΧΘΥΣ*, 1:403–5.

360 See the commentary on 8:27a above.

361 Johnson, "Is Mark 15.39 the Key to Mark's Christology?" 16. Similarly, Donald H. Juel, *A Master of Surprise: Mark Interpreted* (Minneapolis: Fortress, 1994) 74 n. 7.

scribes are ironic in the sense of mocking is clearly signaled by the participle ἐμπαίζοντες ("mocking") in v. 31. The remarks of those who think that Jesus is calling Elijah are clearly marked as based on a misunderstanding, since the audiences are informed in v. 34 about what Jesus actually said. The statement of the centurion, however, has no marker indicating mocking or misunderstanding.

Rather than taking the statement of the centurion as mocking, it is more appropriate to take it as ironic in the dramatic sense.[362] The real Son of God, the real ruler of the world, has died a shameful and horrifying death on a cross. The irony is mitigated only by the darkness and the splitting of the temple curtain, portents that manifest a divine response to this death.[363]

Bultmann argued that the positive response of the centurion to the death of Jesus "has its parallels in the literature of martyrdom."[364] It is important to distinguish here between texts that are older than or roughly contemporary with Mark and later texts. It is also appropriate to distinguish martyrdoms from other genres. Daniel 3 is the story of the three young men who are thrown into a fiery furnace because they refuse to worship the golden statue set up by Nebuchadnezzer. Its genre is best defined as a legendary court tale,[365] although the text is used in the interpretation of the martyrdom of Polycarp.[366] When the king sees that the three young men are preserved in the fiery furnace by the angel (or messenger) of their God, he blesses their God and decrees that anyone who blasphemes (or reviles) their God shall be punished (Dan 3:28-30 MT; 3:95-96

LXX).[367] In this story, the king is impressed by the trust and obedience of the young men and especially by the power of their God to deliver them. In the crucifixion scene in Mark, Jesus is not presented as calm and trusting like the three young men. Rather, he cries out loudly to God and charges God with abandoning him. God does not deliver him from the cross and the death that follows shortly.

Analogously to the story of the three young men, Daniel 6 tells how Daniel was cast into the lions' den because he worshiped someone other than King Darius. The crisis is brought about by other officials who are envious because the king plans to set Daniel over his whole kingdom, and therefore they conspire against him. When Daniel is miraculously preserved from the lions, the king throws the conspirators into the den along with their children and wives. They are destroyed by the lions. Then the king issues a decree praising the God of Daniel. In this legendary court tale, the king is already favorably disposed toward Daniel and his God before the conspiracy. The conspirators do not change from hostility to admiration.[368] Again, it is Daniel's preservation from death by miraculous power that leads to the king's reverence for his God.

3 Maccabees (which is not actually about the Maccabees) is a tale about the life of the Jewish minority in the Egyptian Diaspora. On his way home from a battle with Antiochus III, Ptolemy IV Philopator visited Jerusalem and was greatly offended because he was not allowed to enter the temple. When he arrived home, incited by bad advisers, he decided to assemble and put

---

362 See the commentary on v. 35 above. See also Shiner, "Ambiguous Pronouncement," 15–17, 19. Joel Marcus has suggested that parody and mockery of a crucified prisoner could actually lead to a positive impression on the onlookers when the prisoner "responded to his torture with unaccountable dignity" ("Crucifixion as Parodic Exaltation," *JBL* 125 [2006] 73–87; quotation from 87).

363 Cf. Shiner, "Ambiguous Pronouncement," 14–15.

364 Bultmann, *History*, 282. See also Pobee, "Cry of the Centurion," 101–2; Shiner, "Ambiguous Pronouncement," 11–15.

365 Collins, *Daniel*, 192.

366 See "Genre" in the excursus on the passion narrative in the commentary on 14:1-11 above.

367 Shiner takes this story as an example of "conversions

that occur through martyrdom or near martyrdom" ("Ambiguous Pronouncement," 12). The king shows reverence for the God of Daniel, but the text does not imply that he "converted" to the worship of that God in any strong sense. The acclamations of those who observe the martyrdoms of the apostles in the apocryphal acts are similar to the reactions of the kings in Daniel 3 and 6; see Erik Peterson, *ΕΙΣ ΘΕΟΣ: Epigraphische, formgeschichtliche und religionsgeschichtliche Untersuchungen* (FRLANT n.F. 24; Göttingen: Vandenhoeck & Ruprecht, 1926) 184–85; Bultmann, *History*, 282 n. 5. In these cases, however, the worshiper of the true God actually dies. These texts are considerably later than Mark and may be indirectly influenced by the Gospels.

368 Shiner interprets this text in the same way as Daniel

to death all the Jews living in Alexandria and in the countryside (3:1). When he is about to carry out this plan, God sends two glorious angels who oppose the forces of the king and terrify the king himself. The king then has a change of heart, not because of the behavior of the Jews, but because of the miraculous, divine defense afforded them by their God (3 Macc 6:16—7:9).[369]

The accounts of the deaths of Eleazar, the seven brothers, and their mother in 2 and 4 Maccabees are Jewish adaptations of the theme of the noble death.[370] In 2 Maccabees, no response to the death of Eleazar on the part of the authorities is narrated. In 4 Maccabees, the king falls into a violent rage when he is unable to compel Eleazar to eat defiling foods (8:2). The resolve of the seven brothers and their mother provokes rage in the king, according to 2 Maccabees (7:3, 39). He and those with him are astonished at the endurance of the third brother (2 Macc 7:12). Although the king is favorably disposed to the seven brothers in 4 Maccabees at first, he becomes infuriated when they reject his advice and express their willingness to die (4 Macc 9:10).[371] Yet all marvel at the courage of the first brother (9:26).

Depictions of noble deaths were no doubt received at times as accounts to be admired, but containing exploits that ordinary people could not emulate. Nevertheless, the stories were at least sometimes presented as models to be imitated.[372] The astonishment of the king and his friends at the endurance of the third brother in 2 Macc 7:12 and the marveling of the bystanders at the courage of the first brother in 4 Macc 9:26 come closest to the reaction of the centurion in v. 39.

It seems, then, that the characterization of the centurion in v. 39 is something new. It takes motifs such as those of astonishment and marveling in 2 and 4 Maccabees further by putting a statement in the mouth of the centurion that acknowledges Jesus' extraordinary status as a hero or a ruler. This new development was later elaborated in the accounts of Christian martyrdoms. For example, in the *Martyrdom of Saints Perpetua and Felicitas*, even before Perpetua and the others were martyred, Pudens, the adjutant in charge of the prison, had already become a believer (*iam et ipso optione carceris credente*).[373] In some texts, the influence of the Gospels is clear. Those texts indicate that their authors and audiences interpreted the statement of the centurion as a serious acknowledgment of the significance of Jesus.[374]

Similar motifs occur in post–New Testament Jewish texts. The following story occurs in the Babylonian Talmud:

[The Roman officials in Caesarea] found R. Ḥanina b. Teradion sitting and occupying himself with the Torah, publicly gathering assemblies, and keeping a scroll of the Law in his bosom. Straightaway they took hold of him, wrapt him in the Scroll of the Law, placed bundles of branches round him and set them on fire. They then brought tufts of wool, which they had soaked in water, and placed them over his heart, so that he should not expire quickly. . . . The executioner then said to him, "Rabbi, if I raise the flame and take away the tufts of wool from over your heart, will you cause me to enter into the life to come?" "Yes," he replied. "Then swear to me" [he urged]. He swore to him. He thereupon raised the flame and removed the tufts of wool from over his heart, and his soul departed speedily. The executioner then jumped and threw himself into the fire. And a *bath-kol* [voice from heaven] exclaimed: R. Ḥanina b. Teradion and the executioner have been assigned to the world to come. (*b. ʿAbod. Zar.* 18a)[375]

3; see the previous note. But he has a good discussion of the rhetorical effect of the depiction of Darius and the jealous courtiers ("Ambiguous Pronouncement," 13–14).

369 Shiner's interpretation is the same as in the case of Daniel 3 and 6; see the previous two notes.

370 See "Genre" in the excursus on the passion narrative in the commentary on 14:1-11 above.

371 The torturers similarly become enraged at the boldness of the third brother (4 Macc 10:5).

372 E.g., the account of the death of Eleazar in 2 Macc 6:18-31; see esp. vv. 24-25, 28, 31.

373 *Passio Sanctarum Perpetuae et Felicitatis* 16.4; text from Musurillo, *Christian Martyrs*, 124; the adjutant is introduced in 9.1; Adolf von Harnack, *Militia Christi: Die christliche Religion und der Soldatenstand in den ersten drei Jahrhunderten* (Tübingen: Mohr Siebeck, 1905) 75, with more examples on pp. 74–75. See also Luke 23:39-43 and the discussion by Shiner, "Ambiguous Pronouncement," 14.

374 Candida R. Moss, personal communication.

375 Trans. (modified) from A. Mischon in Isidore Epstein, ed., *The Babylonian Talmud: Seder Neziḳin. ʿAboda Zara* (London: Soncino, 1935–52); Shiner,

Although this text does not manifest dependence on the Gospels, it may be that there was interaction and mutual influence between Christians and Jews who wrote, read, or listened to stories about martyrs.[376]

Much is often made of the fact that the centurion is implicitly portrayed as a Gentile. An interpretation that fits the context is one that links this portrayal to Psalm 21 LXX, the psalm to which Jesus' cry in v. 34 alludes. Psalm 21 concludes with a vow of praise, on the condition that God respond to the laments and pleas of the psalmist.[377] The following statement belongs to the vow of praise:

All the ends of the earth will remember and will turn to the Lord, and all the peoples of the nations will worship before You, for kingly rule is the Lord's, and he is master of the nations (μνησθήσονται καὶ ἐπι-στραφήσονται πρὸς κύριον πάντα τὰ πέρατα τῆς γῆς καὶ προσκυνήσουσιν ἐνώπιόν σου πᾶσαι αἱ πατριαὶ τῶν ἐθνῶν, ὅτι τοῦ κυρίου ἡ βασιλεία, καὶ αὐτὸς δεσπόζει τῶν ἐθνῶν). (Ps 21:28-29 LXX)[378]

The revelation of the divine majesty in v. 38 and the centurion's positive statement in v. 39 together recall the words of Jesus in 11:17, "Is it not written, 'My house shall be called a house of prayer for all the nations'?"

Mark does not portray the centurion as a convert in the sense that he joins the disciples of Jesus or an early Christian community. Later Christian legend, however, assumed that he did. In *The Letter of Pilate to Herod*, he is called "the believing centurion" and is given the name Longinus.[379] By the time of Chrysostom, he was reckoned as a saint and martyr.[380]

"Ambiguous Pronouncement," 12. See also *Gen. Rab.* 65.22 and the discussion by Shiner (ibid.). Both of these texts were written centuries later than Mark, but the point made by Shiner is worth making, namely, that the divine voice vindicating R. Ḥanina b. Teradion contrasts with the ambiguous, human pronouncement of the centurion in v. 39 (ibid., 20).

376 Daniel Boyarin, *Dying for God: Martyrdom and the Making of Christianity and Judaism* (Stanford: Stanford University Press, 1999) esp. 1–21. Boyarin discusses the first part of *b. ʿAbod. Zar.* 18a, but not the part involving the executioner (ibid., 58–59, 121).

377 Ps 21:23-32 LXX; Ahearne-Kroll, "Suffering of David," 1:117–47, esp. 136–45.

378 Lührmann, 264; Daniel Guichard, "La reprise du Psalm 22 dans le récit de la mort de Jésus (Marc 15,21-41)," *Foi et Vie* 87 (1988) 59–65, esp. 64.

379 See the ET in James K. Elliott, *The Apocryphal New Testament* (Oxford: Clarendon Press, 1993) 223. He is also mentioned in an apocryphal letter of Paul to the Corinthians (ibid., 382). See also Swete, 388.

380 Swete, 388.

15

40/ Now there were also women observing from a distance, among whom were both Mary of Magdala and Mary, the mother of James the younger and Joses,[a] and Salome, 41/ who (plural) followed him when he was in Galilee and served him, and many other women who had come up with him to Jerusalem.

42/ And when it was already evening, because it was a day of preparation, that is, the day before the Sabbath, 43/ Joseph of Arimathea,[b] a prominent councilor, who also was himself awaiting the kingdom of God, went and dared to go in to Pilate and ask for the body[c] of Jesus. 44/ Pilate then marveled that he was already dead; he summoned the centurion and asked him whether he had died very long ago.[d] 45/ And when he had found out from the centurion (that he was dead), he granted the corpse[e] to Joseph.[f] 46/ And he bought a linen cloth, took him down (from the cross) and wrapped him in the linen cloth and put him in a tomb that had been cut out of the rock and rolled a stone up to the entrance of the tomb. 47/ Now Mary of Magdala and Mary the (mother) of Joses[g] observed where he put (him).

a   The trans. is based on the reading Ἰωσῆτος, "(the mother of James the younger and) Joses," attested by ℵ² D L et al. B Ψ attest a reading in which the article precedes the second name, with the result that the text refers to four women instead of three. The slight support for this reading makes it unlikely to be the earlier. Variant spellings of the second name are also attested; ℵ* A C W Ψ 𝔐 sa attest the spelling Ἰωσῆ ("Joses") and lat sy^s the spelling Ἰωσήφ ("Joseph"); see the second note on the trans. of 6:3 above.

b   The earliest recoverable reading is Ἰωσήφ ἀπὸ Ἀριμαθαίας ("Joseph of Arimathea," lit., "Joseph from Arimathea"), attested by B D W^c et al. The reading Ἰωσήφ ὁ ἀπὸ Ἀριμαθαίας ("Joseph of Arimathea," lit., "Joseph, the one from Arimathea"), attested by ℵ A C L W* et al., is an improvement of the style, perhaps designed to avoid the impression that the meaning is that Joseph had just come from Arimathea. Cf. Taylor, ad loc.

c   The trans. is based on the reading of the majority of the MSS, σῶμα ("body"). D k sy^s attest the reading πτῶμα ("corpse"). C. H. Turner argued that the latter reading is earlier, and that Matthew, Luke, and most of the MSS of Mark substituted σῶμα ("body") for πτῶμα ("corpse"), presumably because the former is more respectful ("Western Readings," 13). But πτῶμα ("corpse") may have been substituted for σῶμα ("body") in order to bring v. 43 into conformity with v. 45, in which the reading more likely to be earlier is πτῶμα ("corpse"); cf. Taylor, ad loc.

d   The trans. is based on the reading εἰ πάλαι, "whether (he had died) very long ago," attested by the majority of the MSS. B D W et al. attest the reading εἰ ἤδη, "whether (he had) already (died)." 544 pc sy^s attest a reading with εἰ ("whether") only. Δ reads καὶ εἶπεν, "and he said, ('Did he die?')." The reading that best explains the origin of the others is εἰ πάλαι, "whether (he had died) very long ago," since the use of the word πάλαι ("very long ago") seemed inappropriate here and this problem was dealt with in various ways; cf. Metzger, *Textual Commentary*, 101. Taylor (ad loc.) argued that ἤδη ("already") is the earliest recoverable reading, and that it was omitted or replaced to avoid repetition, since the word also appears earlier in the verse.

e   The trans. is based on the reading πτῶμα ("corpse"), attested by ℵ B D et al. A C W et al. attest the reading σῶμα ("body"). The latter was probably substituted for the former, because σῶμα ("body") seemed more respectful; see the second note on v. 43 above. In v. 45, the somewhat harsh τὸ πτῶμα ("the corpse") is softened in the reading attested by D sy^s by the addition of αὐτοῦ ("his").

f   B W attest the spelling Ἰωσῆ ("Joses") instead of Ἰωσήφ ("Joseph"). See the note on v. 40 above.

g   The trans. is based on the reading Ἰωσῆτος ("of Joses"), attested by ℵ² B L et al. Since this woman was described as ἡ Ἰακώβου τοῦ μικροῦ καὶ Ἰωσῆτος μήτηρ ("the mother of James the younger and Joses") in v. 40, this reading gave rise to variants. D *pc* et al. attest a reading in which Ἰακώβου ("of James") has been substituted for Ἰωσῆτος ("of Joses"), possibly because the former name at least, if not the person, was better known. Θ *f*¹³ et al. attest the reading Ἰακώβου καὶ Ἰωσῆτος ("of James and Joses"); this reading is due to a partial assimilation of this verse to v. 40. C W et al. attest the alternate spelling Ἰωση ("of Joses"); see note a on v. 40 above. W *f*¹³ et al. attest a reading in which μήτηρ ("mother") has been added; this reading is another partial assimilation of this verse to v. 40.

History of the Tradition

In Bultmann's judgment, the introduction and description of the women in vv. 40-41 constitute "an isolated piece of tradition" that has no historical basis.[1] In contrast, he concluded that the description of the burial is a historical account that does not give the impression that it is a legend. It does, however, have legendary features in its present form: first of all, the mention of the women who appear again as witnesses in v. 47. He also argued that vv. 44-45 are legendary and that those verses were not in the copies of Mark known to Matthew and Luke. He did not think that the account of the burial "was devised with the Easter story in mind."[2] The comment that Joseph rolled a stone up to the entrance of the tomb could be understood in that way, "though that can also be simply a descriptive touch."[3] The fact that "the women who are eyewitnesses" are mentioned by name "in three successive stories . . . (and with differences in detail at that!). . . clearly shows that individual stories have been brought together here."[4]

Vincent Taylor concluded that vv. 40-41 belong to the "supplementary details derived from the reminiscences of Peter," which Mark added to the primitive passion narrative that he found in Rome.[5] Most of the account of the burial, vv. 42-46, he assigned to the primitive passion narrative, but agreed with Bultmann that Mark had added v. 47.[6] He disagreed with Bultmann's conclusion that vv. 44-45 are also later additions.[7]

According to Eta Linnemann, Mark added vv. 40-41 to a source narrating the crucifixion. He may have composed them himself, or they may have come from an independent tradition.[8] Ludger Schenke concluded that the oldest form of the passion narrative ended with an account of the burial, roughly equivalent to vv. 42-47.[9] Detlev Dormeyer also argued that the earliest form of the passion narrative ended with the burial (v. 46).[10] He attributed the substance of v. 40 to the oldest account and v. 41 to Markan redaction.[11] Rudolf Pesch included vv. 40-47 in his reconstruction of the pre-Markan passion narrative.[12] Like Dormeyer, Till Arend Mohr attributed v. 40 to the earliest form of the passion narrative and v. 41 to Mark.[13] Joel B. Green argued that the primitive passion account included the statement about the women at the crucifixion site, but not the burial or resurrection stories.[14] Wolfgang Reinbold concluded that the oldest account of the passion mentioned two women in connection with the crucifixion, Mary Magdalene and another Mary.[15] Like Bultmann, he ascribed vv. 44-45a to Markan redaction.[16] He believed that v. 47 was already part of the later edition of the old passion account used by Mark.[17]

The position taken here is that the earliest recoverable ending of the pre-Markan passion narrative is v. 38. After the high degree of specificity with regard to place in

1   Bultmann, *History*, 274.
2   Ibid.
3   Ibid.
4   Mark 15:40-41; 15:47; 16:1; Bultmann, *History*, 276.
5   Taylor, 658; on his view, see also Yarbro Collins, *Beginning of the Gospel*, 96.
6   Taylor, 599, 658.
7   Ibid., 599.
8   Linnemann, *Studien zur Passionsgeschichte*, 169.
9   Schenke, *Der gekreuzigte Christus*, 74, 77–83, 137.
10   Dormeyer, *Die Passion Jesu*, 229.
11   Ibid., 209.
12   Rudolf Pesch, *Das Evangelium der Urgemeinde: Wiederhergestellt und erläutert* (Freiburg/Basel/Vienna: Herder, 1979) 41, 212–15.
13   Mohr, *Markus- und Johannespassion*, 348–49.
14   Joel B. Green, *The Death of Jesus: Tradition and Interpretation in the Passion Narrative* (WUNT 2.33; Tübingen: Mohr Siebeck, 1988) 310–13.
15   Reinbold, *Der älteste Bericht*, 167, 172–73.
16   Ibid., 175.
17   Ibid., 176.

14:1–15:39, the vagueness about the location of the tomb of Jesus is striking.[18] This lack of specificity suggests that the story about the burial was not part of the pre-Markan passion narrative. The account of the burial is more like the individual units that make up chapters 1–12 in their lack of topographical specificity and the loose manner in which they are linked to one another. Verse 38 would make a fitting conclusion to a narrative that focused on the significance of the death of Jesus.[19] Such a focus would fit the most likely social setting of the text, either an annual commemoration of Jesus' death held in conjunction with Passover or the more frequent ritual of the Lord's Supper. The resurrection or exaltation of Jesus was probably assumed, but not narrated in this early document.[20]

Comment

■ **40-41** The comment in v. 40 that there were women watching from afar looks very much like an afterthought. Such afterthoughts are typical of oral style, but that only reinforces the impression that this verse and what follows were not in the pre-Markan passion narrative that the evangelist probably used as a written source.[21] Mark apparently added vv. 40-41 to prepare for the narrative about the discovery of the empty tomb.[22]

The author of Luke apparently noticed the roughness of the transition in Mark and improved it in several ways. First, he introduces a group of women, including Mary Magdalene, as companions of Jesus during his activity in Galilee (8:1-3). Second, he eliminates the multiple mentions of the names of the women, with confusing variations, who are connected to the crucifixion, the burial, and the discovery of the empty tomb. He mentions in 23:49 a nameless group of women observing the crucifixion, in a way that reminds the audiences of their introduction in 8:1-3. He refers to them next as observers of

the burial, as "the women who had come with him from Galilee," again with no names, in 23:55-56. The names of some of the women in the group are given for the first time in 24:10, as eyewitnesses of the empty tomb and the appearance of the two angels. Three women are named, two of whom are also mentioned in 8:1-3, Mary Magdalene and Joanna. The third woman mentioned in chapter 24 has a name that overlaps with Mark 15:40, Mary, the (mother) of James ($Μαρία ἡ Ἰακώβου$).

Mark names three of the women in the group he portrays as observers of the crucifixion, "Mary of Magdala and Mary, the mother of James the younger and Joses,[23] and Salome" ($Μαρία ἡ Μαγδαληνὴ καὶ Μαρία ἡ Ἰακώβου τοῦ μικροῦ καὶ Ἰωσῆτος μήτηρ καὶ Σαλώμη$).[24] Magdala, the native town of the first Mary, also called Tarichea, was a fishing center on the Sea of Galilee, about two miles north of Tiberias and three miles south of Capernaum.[25] This verse is the first time in Mark that Mary Magdalene is mentioned.

The second Mary is sometimes thought to be the mother of Jesus, since his mother's name is given as Mary ($Μαρία$) in 6:3. Further, Jesus is said in the same verse to have brothers named James ($Ἰάκωβος$) and Joses ($Ἰωσῆς$). The brother of Jesus mentioned in 6:3, however, is not called "James the younger" ($Ἰάκωβος ὁ μικρός$). In fact, it could be that James the younger was so designated to distinguish him from James the brother of the Lord, who played an important role in the postresurrection community. Further, if Mark was aware that the second Mary was the mother of Jesus, he would most likely have referred to her explicitly as such. Finally, all three names were relatively common in the first century CE. So the second Mary should not be identified with the mother of Jesus.

In v. 41, Mark describes the group of women introduced in v. 40 as those who followed and served Jesus in Galilee and who came up with him to Jerusalem. The

---

18 Yarbro Collins, *Beginning of the Gospel*, 100–102.
19 See the commentary on v. 39 above.
20 Yarbro Collins, *Beginning of the Gospel*, 117.
21 See "History of the Tradition" above. On afterthoughts in oral stories, see the commentary on 5:8 above.
22 Yarbro Collins, *Beginning of the Gospel*, 129.
23 See note a on the trans. of v. 40 above.
24 On the ambiguity of the Greek with regard to the second Mary, see Theissen, *Gospels in Context*, 177–78.
25 Mordechai Aviam, "Magdala," *OEANE* 3:399–400; James F. Strange, "Magdala," *ABD* 4:463–64; Jürgen Zangenberg, *Magdala am See Gennesaret: Überlegungen zur sogenannten "mini-synagoga" und einige andere Beobachtungen zum kulturellen Profil des Ortes in neutestamentlicher Zeit* (Kleine Arbeiten zum Alten und Neuen Testament 2; Waltrop: Spenner, 2001).

only woman that Mark portrays earlier in the narrative as serving Jesus is the mother-in-law of Simon (1:31). He does not mention any women traveling with Jesus from Galilee to Jerusalem in 10:1–11:11. It seems unlikely that Mark simply made up the names of the three women. It is clear, however, that these names did not come to him in the more or less fixed traditions that he had received.[26]

Matthew appears to identify the Salome of Mark with the mother of the sons of Zebedee, although he never mentions the name Salome (cf. Matt 27:56 with 20:20-21). This identification could simply be a conjecture on Matthew's part. Luke's "Mary the (mother) of James" in 24:10 is dependent on Mark's virtually identical phrase in 16:1. Matthew and Luke are probably dependent on Mark with regard to Salome and the other Mary.[27] John shares with Mark the portrayal of Mary Magdalene as discovering the empty tomb. But John may be dependent on Mark indirectly, through reoralization of the passion narrative of Mark.[28]

Mark was apparently the first to attempt to incorporate the resurrection of Jesus into an extended narrative. Because of his understanding of the nature of Jesus' resurrection, he assumed that the tomb was empty, an assumption that Paul may not have made. Mark chose not to narrate appearances of the resurrected Jesus. He also portrayed the (male) disciples as having abandoned Jesus at the time of his arrest and thus as not being present for the crucifixion and burial.[29] Assuming that the tomb was empty, Mark chose to depict its discovery by female followers of Jesus.[30]

■ **42-46** There is evidence that the Roman practice of crucifixion at least some of the time involved leaving the crucified corpse on the cross to be "torn to pieces by wild animals and birds of prey."[31] Some have argued that crucifixion was associated "with denial of burial; the victim loses contact with the earth, is denied acceptance in the realm of the dead below, and wanders the earth near the site of death."[32]

Paul's statement that Jesus was buried (1 Cor 15:4) does not necessarily indicate that he knew traditions about the empty tomb. Followers of Jesus may have emphasized that he was buried because of the belief, current at the time, that the shades of those who were unburied could not enter Hades but wandered the earth and could thus be invoked in magic rituals.[33] They also probably wanted to minimize the dishonor and shame associated with death by crucifixion.

The harsh practices of exposure of the body to animals and the refusal of burial were sometimes mitigated. Philo stated that he knew cases in which, on the eve of a holiday such as the birthday of an emperor, the bodies of those who had been crucified were taken down and given to their relatives for burial and the usual rites. He complained that Flaccus did not make this humane concession with respect to the Jews whom he had crucified near the birthday of Gaius (*Flacc.* 10 §§81–83).[34]

The practice of leaving the corpse on the cross for days or even longer was in tension with the commandment of Deut 21:22-23, as it was interpreted in the time of Jesus.[35] Josephus criticized the Idumeans for denying

---

26 Assuming that 15:47 and 16:1 are also Markan compositions; see Yarbro Collins, *Beginning of the Gospel*, 119–48.

27 It is clear that Luke has an independent tradition about Mary of Magdala and Joanna (8:2–3). It is not clear, however, that Joanna was associated with the empty tomb in the tradition known to Luke.

28 See "Composition and History of the Tradition" in the excursus on the passion narrative in the commentary on 14:1-11 above.

29 This characterization of the disciples of Jesus contrasts with the portrayal of the disciples of John, who take their teacher's corpse and place it in a tomb (6:29).

30 Yarbro Collins, *Beginning of the Gospel*, 119–48.

31 Donald G. Kyle, *Spectacles of Death in Ancient Rome* (London/New York: Routledge, 1998) 182 nn. 95

and 96; quotation from n. 95. See also Brown, *Death*, 2:1207–9.

32 Kyle, *Spectacles of Death*, n. 95. See also Douglas W. Geyer, *Fear, Anomaly, and Uncertainty in the Gospel of Mark* (ATLAMS 47; Lanham, MD: Scarecrow, 2002) 27–28.

33 Tertullian *De anima* 56–57; Geyer, *Fear, Anomaly, and Uncertainty*, 8–9; Sarah Ihles Johnston, *Restless Dead: Encounters between the Living and the Dead in Ancient Greece* (Berkeley: University of California Press, 1999) 9–10, 27, 30–31, 83. Those who died violently were also believed to torment the living, especially their murderers (ibid., 127–28).

34 John J. Collins, S.J., "The Archaeology of the Crucifixion," *CBQ* 1 (1939) 154–59, esp. 157.

35 Brown, *Death of the Messiah*, 1:532–34; 2:1209.

burial to the bodies of the high priest Ananus and Jesus, another chief priest, after they had killed them:

They actually went so far in their impiety as to cast out the corpses without burial, although the Jews are so careful about funeral rites that even malefactors who have been sentenced to crucifixion are taken down and buried before sunset (προῆλθον δὲ εἰς τοσοῦτον ἀσεβείας, ὥστε καὶ ἀτάφους ῥῖψαι, καίτοι τοσαύτην Ἰουδαίων περὶ τὰς ταφὰς πρόνοιαν ποιουμένων, ὥστε καὶ τοὺς ἐκ καταδίκης ἀνεσταυρωμένους πρὸ δύντος ἡλίου καθελεῖν τε καὶ θάπτειν). (Bell. 4.5.2 §317)[36]

Josephus's remark makes clear that the request of Joseph of Arimathea for the body of Jesus in order to bury it may be interpreted as an act of piety in obedience to the law.[37] It does not necessarily imply acceptance of Jesus as God's agent or of Jesus' message.[38] Mark's comment in v. 43 that Joseph was waiting for the kingdom of God may be an inference from his charitable act, if indeed the account is based on a historical event. The descriptions of Joseph as a disciple of Jesus in Matthew and John provide early evidence for the growth of a legend about him (Matt 27:57; John 19:38).[39]

In his interpretation of the Law of Moses, Josephus says the following about the blasphemer:

Let him that blasphemeth God be stoned, then hung for a day, and buried ignominiously and in obscurity (Ὁ δὲ βλασφημήσας θεὸν καταλευσθεὶς κρεμάσθω δι᾽ ἡμέρας καὶ ἀτίμως καὶ ἀφανῶς θαπτέσθω). (Ant. 4.8.6 §202)[40]

Mark's account of the trial before the Judean council and Jesus' conviction on the charge of blasphemy, however, is unlikely to be historical.[41]

Some of the details of Mark's account have verisimilitude, at least. Joseph, as a pious Jew, would have wanted to bury Jesus before sunset. He purchased a linen cloth in which to wrap the body, but he did not take the time to anoint it with fragrant spices and perfumed oil, or did not grant the body the honor of being so anointed.[42] He may have used a tomb cut out of rock because it was nearby and available to him, for example, because it belonged to his family.[43] Such tombs were used by Jewish families of sufficient means.[44] The use of a rolling rock to close the entrance was not common, but it is attested.[45] This architectural feature is limited to the tombs of the wealthy. Mark's characterization of Joseph of Arimathea as "a prominent councilor" (εὐσχήμων βουλευτής) indicates high social status and thus probably wealth as well.[46]

■ **42-43** "Evening" (ὀψία) signifies the time between late afternoon and darkness.[47] The second clause of v. 42

---

36 Cf. Bell. 3.8.5 §§375–77; Ant. 4.8.24 §§264–65; Brown, Death, 2:1209.

37 Cf. Mark's account of Joseph's good deed with the self-characterization of Tobit in Tob 1:3-20, esp. vv. 16-20.

38 The type of burial that Joseph gives Jesus, however, may imply that he had some sympathy with him; see the commentary on vv. 42-43 below.

39 The legendary character of these passages is not recognized by Stanley E. Porter, "Joseph of Arimathea," ABD 3:971–72.

40 Brown, Death, 2:1211.

41 See "History of the Tradition and Historical Reliability" in the commentary on 14:53-72 above.

42 On the use of oil and perfume in the preparation of the corpse for burial, see Rachel Hachlili, Jewish Funerary Customs, Practices and Rites in the Second Temple Period (JSJSup 94; Leiden/Boston: Brill, 2005) 480.

43 Matthew apparently inferred from Mark's account that the tomb belonged to Joseph (Matt 27:60).

According to Jodi Magness, all such rock-cut tombs were family tombs ("What Did Jesus' Tomb Look Like?" BAR 32.1 [2006] 38–49, 70, esp. 48).

44 Hachlili, Jewish Funerary Customs, 1–73, 235–310, 447–79, 522–26; Byron R. McCane, Roll Back the Stone: Death and Burial in the World of Jesus (Harrisburg, PA/London/New York: Trinity Press International/Continuum, 2003) 32–37.

45 McCane, Roll Back the Stone, 33. See the photograph of a tomb with a rolling stone that closes the entrance on the opening two pages of Magness, "What Did Jesus' Tomb Look Like?" 38–39. The tomb is dated to the Herodian era and is located in a necropolis under the Convent of the Sisters of Nazareth in Nazareth (ibid., 40).

46 Matthew evidently inferred from Mark's text that Joseph was rich (πλούσιος [Matt 27:57]).

47 BAGD, s.v. ὄψιος.

indicates that Jesus died on a Friday, a day of preparation for the Sabbath.[48] Verses 42-43 imply that Joseph was eager to bury Jesus before sunset because the next day was the Sabbath.[49] This statement is in tension with the evidence that it was customary to bury the body of a deceased person before sunset on the day of death, whether it was a day of preparation or not.[50] A remark by Josephus allows a resolution of this tension. In his summary of the Mosaic code of laws, he stipulates the punishment of a youth who rebels against his parents and who ignores their oral admonition to cease rebelling:

> let him be led forth by their own hands outside the city, followed by the multitude, and stoned to death; and, after remaining for the whole day exposed to the general view, let him be buried at night. Thus shall it be too with all who howsoever are condemned by the laws to be put to death (προαχθεὶς ὑπ᾽ αὐτῶν τούτων ἔξω τῆς πόλεως τοῦ πλήθους ἑπομένου καταλευέσθω καὶ μείνας δι᾽ ὅλης τῆς ἡμέρας εἰς θέαν τὴν ἁπάντων θαπτέσθω νυκτός. οὕτως δὲ καὶ οἱ ὁπωσοῦν ὑπὸ τῶν νόμων ἀναιρεθῆναι κατακριθέντες). (Ant. 4.8.24 §§264–65)[51]

This passage suggests that it was customary for at least some executed criminals to be buried at night, rather than before sunset on the day of death.[52] One may infer, however, that when the Sabbath was to begin at sunset on such a day, burial at night was not an option.

The opening participial clause of v. 43 could be read as signifying that Joseph came from Arimathea to Jerusalem to ask for the body of Jesus.[53] Alternatively, the phrase ἀπὸ Ἁριμαθαίας ("from Arimathea") could indicate that he was a native of Arimathea.[54] The Markan narrator describes this man as "a prominent councilor" (εὐσχήμων βουλευτής). This portrayal is also ambiguous. It could imply that Joseph was a member of the governing council of the town of Arimathea or that he was a member of the Judean council that met in Jerusalem.[55]

The town of Arimathea is the place mentioned as the birthplace of Samuel in 1 Sam 1:1. The Hebrew name of the town, הרמתים, was rendered Ἀρμαθαιμ in the LXX (1 Kgdms 1:1).[56] 1 Samuel locates it in the hill country of Ephraim, that is, in the Shephelah, about twenty miles east of modern Jaffa.[57] In the Second Temple period, it was part of Samaria. In 145 BCE, the Syrian king Demetrius II Nicator granted three Samaritan toparchies, one of which included Arimathea, to the Maccabean leader Jonathan (1 Macc 11:28-34).[58] It is likely that the town had a local governing council in the first century CE, if only a traditional council of elders.[59] The portrayal of Joseph as having access to a tomb, probably a family tomb, just outside Jerusalem, however, suggests that he and his family had moved to that city at some point.[60]

In addition, the narrator says that Joseph "also was himself awaiting the kingdom of God" (ὃ καὶ αὐτὸς ἦν προσδεχόμενος τὴν βασιλείαν τοῦ θεοῦ). This remark could be a legendary inference from the good deed that he performed by burying Jesus. Or it could be a reliable indication that Joseph had views related to the hope for an eschatological restoration of Israel or even less

---

48 BAGD, s.v. παρασκευή.

49 Assuming that ἐπεί should be taken causally (BAGD, s.v.).

50 See the commentary on vv. 42-46 above; see also Hachlili, *Jewish Funerary Customs*, 480.

51 Text and trans. (modified) from Thackeray, *Josephus*, 4:602–3; cited by Pesch, 2:512.

52 Cf. Josephus's remarks about the execution and burial of the blasphemer quoted in the commentary on vv. 42-46 above.

53 See note b on the trans. of v. 43 above.

54 Matthew seems to interpret Mark 15:43 as indicating that Joseph came from Arimathea to ask for the body of Jesus (Matt 27:57), whereas Luke takes the phrase as signifying that Joseph was a native of Arimathea (Luke 23:51). John is similar to Luke on this point (19:38).

55 Matthew describes Joseph simply as a rich man (ἄνθρωπος πλούσιος) and not as a councilor (27:57). Luke portrays Joseph as a member of the Judean council (23:50-51); this may not be independent, historically reliable information, however, but could simply be an inference from the text of Mark. In John, Joseph is presented as a hidden disciple of Jesus (μαθητὴς τοῦ Ἰησοῦ κεκρυμμένος) and not as a councilor (19:38).

56 Jerry A. Pattengale, "Arimathea," *ABD* 1:378.

57 Ibid.

58 Josephus *Ant.* 13.4.9 §§125–28; Pattengale, "Arimathea," 378.

59 Cf. Schürer, *History*, 2:86, 184.

60 Without discussing the tomb, Schürer assumed that Joseph was a member of the council of Jerusalem (*History*, 2:206).

worldly apocalyptic views. Although, judging from the text of Mark, he did not become a follower of Jesus, he may have had sympathy with Jesus' teaching and respect for his person. Such a historical inference fits with the datum that Joseph placed Jesus in a tomb cut from the rock and equipped with a rolling stone to cover the entrance.[61]

The last two clauses of v. 43 remark on how Joseph "dared" ($τολμήσας$) to go in to Pilate and ask for the body of Jesus. This account is similar to the perhaps less daring[62] portrayal of the disciples of John the Baptist, who, it is implied, asked Herod Antipas for the body of John in order to bury it (6:29). It contrasts with the cowardice of Jesus' male disciples, who have fled and do not dare to ask Pilate for the body. Historically speaking, it would make sense that Joseph would "dare" to approach Pilate if he were a wealthy man of high social standing, especially if he were a member of the Judean council, motivated by the desire to observe the traditional Jewish practice of prompt burial of a corpse. It is noteworthy that family members are not portrayed as having a role in the burials of John and Jesus.[63]

■ **44-45** When Joseph asks Pilate for the body of Jesus, Pilate marvels at the implication that Jesus is already dead. He does not grant Joseph the body until he has verified, by consultation with the centurion, that Jesus is actually dead. Bultmann concluded that these two verses are not only legendary but were not even in the texts of Mark used by Matthew and Luke, since neither of those Gospels contains a parallel to them.[64]

It may be, however, that the other two Synoptic evangelists omitted the substance of these two verses because they did not find them intelligible or significant. As argued above, the centurion did not appear in the pre-Markan passion narrative. Mark introduces him in v. 39 and again here.[65] A plausible explanation for Mark's introduction of the motif that Pilate marveled at how soon Jesus had died is that the relatively quick death is portrayed as a divine response to Jesus' complaint in v. 34 that God had abandoned him. The death of Jesus follows so soon after that cry that the bystander who "runs" ($δραμών$) to get some sour wine for Jesus is too late to offer it to him (vv. 35-37).

Although Bultmann's hypothesis that vv. 44-45 constitute a later addition to the text of Mark is to be rejected, his conclusion that the material is legendary is most likely correct.

■ **46** When Joseph has received permission from Pilate to take charge of the body of Jesus, he first goes to buy a linen cloth ($καὶ ἀγοράσας σινδόνα$). Both Matthew and Luke omit this detail, probably because it seemed superfluous.

Next he takes the body down from the cross ($καθελὼν αὐτόν$). Luke keeps the participle but omits the pronoun. Matthew instead says "And Joseph took the body" ($καὶ λαβὼν τὸ σῶμα ὁ Ἰωσήφ$).

After the two participles, the first finite verb of this verse portrays Joseph as wrapping the body of Jesus in a linen cloth ($σινδών$). The word $σινδών$ is emphasized here, since it is used twice. The only other time this word occurs in Mark is in 14:51-52, where it also occurs twice. The lexical connection is probably not intended to express a similarity between Jesus and the young man of chapter 14. Rather, it expresses a contrast.[66] Whereas the young man escaped death by fleeing at the time of his arrest and shamefully leaving the $σινδών$ behind, Jesus did not flee when he was arrested, but endured humiliation, suffering, and death so that, at the end of his ordeal, his body was wrapped in a $σινδών$.

For the activity of wrapping the body, Mark uses the verb $ἐνειλέω$. Matthew and Luke both use a different verb, $ἐντυλίσσω$. This minor agreement against Mark, however, does not necessarily signify that the copies of Mark used by the two later evangelists were different on this point from the text that has come down to us. Since $ἐνειλέω$ was sometimes used in a forcible and thus bad sense, the later evangelists may independently have preferred the more seemly $ἐντυλίσσω$.[67]

---

61   Unless that tomb was used simply because of haste and convenience; see the commentary on vv. 42-46 above.

62   The narrative of Mark portrays Herod Antipas as sympathetic to John.

63   Assuming that the second Mary was not the mother of Jesus; see the commentary on vv. 40-41 above.

64   See "History of the Tradition" above.

65   See the commentary on vv. 38 and 39 above.

66   See the commentary on 14:51-52 above.

67   Moulton-Milligan, s.v. $ἐνειλέω$ and esp. $ἐντυλίσσω$.

No mention is made of washing the body or of anointing it with perfumed oil or spices, as was customary.[68] Brown has argued that these rituals were omitted because the burial was a dishonorable one, the type afforded a criminal.[69] It could be, however, that the usual rituals were omitted simply because of lack of time.[70]

As noted above, the type of tomb depicted here, with a rolling rock to close the entrance, was relatively rare and expensive.[71]

■ **47** This verse, like vv. 40-41, was composed by Mark in order to prepare for the empty-tomb story.[72] In v. 47, only two of the three women introduced in vv. 40-41 are mentioned: Mary of Magdala and Mary the (mother) of Joses (ἡ δὲ Μαρία ἡ Μαγδαληνὴ καὶ Μαρία ἡ

Ἰωσῆτος). Salome (Σαλώμη) is missing here. The name of Salome is omitted and the description of the second Mary is simplified here for the same reason.[73] Since the designation of the second Mary in v. 40 is so long, it is understandable that it would be shortened here. The variations in the descriptions of the women in vv. 40 and 47 are fully explicable on the assumption that both verses were composed by the evangelist.

The statement that these two women saw where Joseph buried Jesus is necessary to explain how the women were able to find the tomb when the Sabbath had ended and to discover that Jesus' body was no longer there.

16

16:1-8 The Empty Tomb

1/ And when the Sabbath was over, Mary of Magdala and Mary, the (mother) of James, and Salome[a] bought aromatic (oils), so that they could go and anoint him. 2/ And very early in the morning on the first day of the week, they went to the tomb, when the sun had risen. 3/ And they said to one another, "Who will roll the stone away from the entrance of the tomb for us?" 4/ And they looked up and observed that the stone had been rolled away; for it was extremely large.[b] 5/ And they went into the tomb and saw a young man sitting on the right, wearing a white robe, and they were amazed. 6/ He then said to them, "Do not be amazed; you are looking for Jesus of Nazareth[c] who has been crucified. He is risen; he is not here. Look, the

a D (k) n attest a reading that lacks the words διαγενομένου τοῦ σαββάτου Μαρία ἡ Μαγδαληνὴ καὶ Μαρία ἡ τοῦ Ἰακώβου καὶ Σαλώμη, "when the Sabbath was over, Mary of Magdala and Mary, the (mother) of James, and Salome." Turner argued that this is the earliest recoverable reading and that, if Salome's name had stood here in the text of Mark, it is odd that neither Matthew nor Luke mentions her in their resurrection narratives ("Western Readings," 13). But her name stands in Mark 15:40, and neither Matthew nor Luke mentions her in the parallels to that passage, unless it be supposed that Matthew understood Salome to be the mother of the sons of Zebedee. Turner argued further that the reading attested by the majority of the MSS arose under the influence of the text of Matthew. He made the ingenious suggestion that the third mention of the women in Matt 28:1 is a repetition of the second mention in Matt 27:61; the third mention is an addition by Matthew, made to pick up the thread of the narrative after the insertion of the story of the sealing of the tomb. One or more later editors or scribes added the third mention to Mark, because, if Matthew

---

68 See the commentary on vv. 42-46 above. Matthew and Luke also do not mention washing or anointing (Matt 27:59-60; Luke 23:53). It is clear that Mark and Luke do not presuppose anointing, since they mention that the women planned to anoint the body after the Sabbath (Mark 16:1; Luke 23:56; 24:1). The account of lavish anointing with a mixture of myrrh and aloes by Joseph and Nicodemus before burial in John 19:39-40 reflects a legendary elaboration either of the reoralized text of Mark or of tradition similar to that used by Mark.

69 Raymond E. Brown, "The Burial of Jesus (Mark 15:42-47)," *CBQ* 50 (1988) 233–45; Yarbro Collins, *Beginning of the Gospel*, 130–31.

70 See the commentary on v. 42 above.

71 See the commentary on vv. 42-46 above.

72 Yarbro Collins, *Beginning of the Gospel*, 129–30; see also "History of the Tradition" above.

73 In v. 40, the second Mary is identified as Μαρία ἡ Ἰακώβου τοῦ μικροῦ καὶ Ἰωσῆτος μήτηρ ("Mary, the mother of James the younger and Joses"). See the commentary on vv. 40-41 above.

place where they put him.[d] 7/ So go and say to his disciples and to Peter, 'He is going ahead of you to Galilee; there you will see him, as he said to you.'" 8/ And they went out and fled from the tomb, for trembling[e] and amazement had seized them; and they said nothing to anyone;[f] for they were afraid.[g]

mentioned the women three times, Mark must do so as well. Since interpolators are fond of fullness, the three names from Matt 27:56 = Mark 15:40 are added rather than the two from Matt 27:61 (ibid., 14). Although this theory is attractive, it is undercut by Turner's remark that the text of Mark is more intelligible without the third mention of the names and that these names are not necessary, since there is no interval between Mark 15:47 and 16:1. This is exactly the type of reasoning that probably led an editor or scribe to omit the words from $\delta\iota\alpha\gamma\epsilon\nu\upsilon\mu\acute{\epsilon}\nu\upsilon$, "when (the Sabbath) was over," to $\Sigma\alpha\lambda\acute{\omega}\mu\eta$ ("Salome"), unless they were simply omitted by accident. Cf. Taylor, ad loc.; Metzger, *Textual Commentary*, 101.

b   The trans. is based on the reading $\kappa\alpha\grave{\iota}$ $\mathring{\alpha}\nu\alpha\beta\lambda\acute{\epsilon}\psi\alpha\sigma\alpha\iota$ $\theta\epsilon\omega\rho\upsilon\hat{\upsilon}\sigma\iota\nu$ $\mathring{\upsilon}\tau\iota$ $\mathring{\alpha}\pi\upsilon\kappa\epsilon\kappa\acute{\upsilon}\lambda\iota\sigma\tau\alpha\iota$ $\mathring{\upsilon}$ $\lambda\acute{\iota}\theta\upsilon\varsigma\cdot$ $\mathring{\eta}\nu$ $\gamma\grave{\alpha}\rho$ $\mu\acute{\epsilon}\gamma\alpha\varsigma$ $\sigma\phi\acute{\upsilon}\delta\rho\alpha$ ("And they looked up and observed that the stone had been rolled away; for it was extremely large"), attested by the majority of the MSS. D Θ 565 et al. attest the reading $\mathring{\eta}\nu$ $\gamma\grave{\alpha}\rho$ $\mu\acute{\epsilon}\gamma\alpha\varsigma$ $\sigma\phi\acute{\upsilon}\delta\rho\alpha$ $\kappa\alpha\grave{\iota}$ $\mathring{\epsilon}\rho\chi\upsilon\nu\tau\alpha\iota$ $\kappa\alpha\grave{\iota}$ $\epsilon\mathring{\upsilon}\rho\acute{\iota}\sigma\kappa\upsilon\upsilon\sigma\iota\nu$ $\mathring{\alpha}\pi\upsilon$-$\kappa\epsilon\kappa\upsilon\lambda\iota\sigma\mu\acute{\epsilon}\nu\upsilon\nu$ $\tau\grave{\upsilon}\nu$ $\lambda\acute{\iota}\theta\upsilon\nu$ ("For it was extremely large; and they went and found the stone rolled away"). This reading results from an attempt to improve the logical sequence of thought in the earlier Markan text; the remark about the size of the stone follows more appropriately immediately after the question posed by the women in v. 3.

c   The earliest recoverable reading is $\tau\grave{\upsilon}\nu$ $N\alpha\zeta\alpha\rho\eta\nu\acute{\upsilon}\nu$ ("of Nazareth"), attested by the majority of the MSS. ℵ* D lack these words; this lack is due to accidental omission, simplification of the text, or the influence of the parallel in Matt 28:5.

d   The trans. is based on the reading $\mathring{\iota}\delta\epsilon$ $\mathring{\upsilon}$ $\tau\acute{\upsilon}\pi\upsilon\varsigma$ ("Look, the place"), attested by the majority of the MSS. Since this expression is elliptical, it gave rise to clarifying variants. D(*) (c ff²) attest the reading $\epsilon\mathring{\iota}\delta\epsilon\iota\tau\epsilon$ $\mathring{\epsilon}\kappa\epsilon\hat{\iota}$ $\tau\grave{\upsilon}\nu$ $\tau\acute{\upsilon}\pi\upsilon\nu$ $\alpha\mathring{\upsilon}\tau\upsilon\hat{\upsilon}$ ("You have seen there his place"). W (Θ 565) attest the reading $\epsilon\mathring{\iota}\delta\epsilon\iota\tau\epsilon\cdot$ $\mathring{\epsilon}\kappa\epsilon\hat{\iota}$ $\mathring{\upsilon}$ $\tau\acute{\upsilon}\pi\upsilon\varsigma$ $\alpha\mathring{\upsilon}\tau\upsilon\hat{\upsilon}$ $\mathring{\epsilon}\sigma\tau\iota\nu$ ("You have seen; there is his place").

e   The trans. is based on the reading $\tau\rho\acute{\upsilon}\mu\upsilon\varsigma$ ("trembling"), attested by the majority of the MSS. D W et al. attest the reading $\phi\acute{\upsilon}\beta\upsilon\varsigma$ ("fear"). The latter is due to an effort to clarify or improve the text.

f   The words $\kappa\alpha\grave{\iota}$ $\upsilon\mathring{\upsilon}\delta\epsilon\nu\grave{\iota}$ $\upsilon\mathring{\upsilon}\delta\grave{\epsilon}\nu$ $\epsilon\mathring{\iota}\pi\alpha\nu$ ("and they said nothing to anyone") are omitted by k. This omission was deliberate; see the commentary below on the shorter (additional) ending.

g   The earliest recoverable ending of the Gospel of Mark is $\mathring{\epsilon}\phi\upsilon\beta\upsilon\hat{\upsilon}\nu\tau\upsilon$ $\gamma\acute{\alpha}\rho$ ("for they were afraid"). ℵ B et al. attest this ending, which is the shortest; cf. James K. Elliott, "The Text and Language of the Endings to Mark's Gospel," in idem, *Language and Style*, 204; Metzger, *Textual Commentary*, 102–6. Although some scholars think that the author did not intend to end the Gospel at this point, most agree that this is the earliest ending that can be reconstructed on the basis of the available evidence. It is accepted as the earliest surviving ending because its priority explains the origin of the other extant endings. Since the shortest ending was perceived as abrupt, inadequate, or incomplete, various editors or scribes supplied what they perceived to be more appropriate endings. These additional endings are also translated and commented upon below because of their historical and theological importance.

History of the Tradition

According to Bultmann, the oldest tradition about the resurrection of Jesus consisted of proclamation that Jesus had appeared to individuals, first of all to Peter. This proclamation made no distinction between the resurrection and exaltation of Jesus, so the question of the status of the tomb of Jesus did not arise. Furthermore, the appearances were understood and proclaimed as demonstrations of the reality of the resurrection of Jesus (1 Cor 15:5-7).[74]

In Bultmann's view, the second stage of the tradition involved the story of the empty tomb. He concluded that the unit of vv. 1-8 represents a complete, pre-Markan tradition that had "its original and organic conclusion in v. 8."[75] His reasons for coming to this conclusion were the following: (1) the fact that the women are named again in 16:1 shows that the story was not originally connected to the preceding sections of Mark; (2) the intention of the women to anoint the body "does not agree with 15:46 where there is never so much as a thought that the burial was incomplete or provisional"; and (3) v. 7 is a Markan addition to the preexisting story, comparable to 14:28.

The first argument is not persuasive because it overlooks the fact that Mark's style is repetitive and that series of three are common in the Gospel.[76] The three mentions of the women in 15:40, 47, and 16:1 link the crucifixion scene from the pre-Markan passion narrative with the originally independent tradition about Jesus' burial and with the narration of the discovery of the empty tomb. The second argument is not compelling because there are indeed reasons to think that the burial is portrayed as incomplete.[77] Third, the saying about the risen Jesus going before the disciples to Galilee in 14:28 is integral to its context, not a secondary addition.[78] The statement of 16:7 also fits well in its context.[79]

John Dominic Crossan concluded more plausibly that Mark created the tradition of the empty tomb.[80] Verses 1-8 constitute a unified and effective composition.[81] The author of Mark was heir to the astounding but terse proclamation that God had raised Jesus from the dead, an announcement supported by traditions that the risen Jesus had appeared at least to Peter and the Twelve. His aim in composing what we know as the Gospel according to Mark was to provide an extended narrative expressing the good news ($\varepsilon\dot{\nu}\alpha\gamma\gamma\dot{\varepsilon}\lambda\iota o\nu$ [1:1, 14-15]) of God's activity through Jesus, God's eschatological agent.[82] As the first to write such an extended account, Mark was faced with the challenge of expressing the proclamation of Jesus' resurrection in narrative form. He chose to do so by narrating the discovery of the absence of Jesus' body in the tomb because his understanding of resurrection, unlike Paul's, involved the revival and transformation of Jesus' earthly body, as well as the exaltation of his inner self. Thus, Paul's idea of the provision of a new spiritual body is rendered superfluous.[83] Since the absence of Jesus' body could be explained in a variety of ways,[84]

74 Bultmann, *History*, 288, 290. See also Yarbro Collins, *Beginning of the Gospel*, 123–27.
75 Bultmann, *History*, 285 n. 2.
76 See, e.g., Neirynck, *Duality in Mark*, 110–12. See also note a on the trans. of v. 1 above and Yarbro Collins, *Beginning of the Gospel*, 129 n. 31.
77 See the commentary on vv. 42-47 above.
78 See the commentary on 14:28 above. See also Yarbro Collins, *Beginning of the Gospel*, 127–34.
79 Ibid., 136–38.
80 John Dominic Crossan, "Empty Tomb and Absent Lord (Mark 16:1-8)," in Kelber, *Passion*, 135–52. Although other conclusions in Crossan's article are dubious, he is persuasive on this point.
81 Yarbro Collins, *Beginning of the Gospel*, 134–38.
82 See the section on "Genre" in the introduction above.
83 Yarbro Collins, *Beginning of the Gospel*, 145–46.
84 Matthew (27:62-66; 28:11-15) provides evidence that,

Mark chose to express the significance of that absence by portraying a "young man" taking the role of an interpreting angel. This standard apocalyptic character makes clear that the women have come to the right tomb and that Jesus' body has not been removed or stolen. Rather, the crucified one is risen (ἠγέρϑη).[85]

Excursus: Resurrection in Ancient Cultural Contexts

It is important to recognize the difference between English and ancient Greek with regard to language about rising from the dead. In English, "resurrection" is virtually a technical term for "the rising again of Christ after His death and burial" or for the general resurrection on the last day.[86] Many readers of the New Testament today assume that "resurrection," by definition, means "bodily" in a strong sense. The two main Greek words used to express the idea of resurrection from the dead are ἐγείρω and ἀνίστημι. Both of these verbs are used metaphorically when applied to rising from the dead. Ἐγείρω has the basic meanings of "to cause someone to wake from sleep" and "to cease sleeping."[87] The basic meanings of ἀνίστημι are "to cause to stand" and "to stand up" or "rise" from a reclining or sitting position.[88] This linguistic difference should alert twenty-first-century readers of the New Testament that ancient expressions about resurrection are unlikely to be clear and distinct ideas belonging to a philosophically systematic body of thought.

It is also worthy of note that thought about the afterlife in ancient Israel and ancient Greece had two main stages, broadly speaking. In the earlier stage, in both cultures, the fate of all the dead was believed to be similar, regardless of their way of life. Social status in the afterworld reflected social status in this world, but there was no ethical differentiation and thus there were no rewards or punishments. In both the Hebrew Sheol[89] and the Greek Hades,[90] the dead have a shadowy existence in a dark, gloomy place.

The shift to the later stage began early and was a gradual process over several centuries. Eventually the view became widespread that the righteous or virtuous would have a happy afterlife and sinners or the wicked would suffer torments in the next world.[91] At the same time, the old view survived.[92] In both cultures there was great variety in the imagery of the afterlife and little attempt to create clear and coherent systems of thought.[93] From the Persian period onward, Jews and the various Jewish subcultures became hellenized, both in the Diaspora and in Palestine. Nevertheless, Jews and Jewish writings in the Second Temple period maintained some distinctive perspectives and traditions.

Even the specific notion of resurrection in Jewish tradition was not a unified concept. Texts, including those of roughly the same date, differ on key issues, that is, on whether the entity that rises is the earthly person as a whole, including the earthly body; or the inner person, referred to as the "soul" (ψυχή), the "spirit" (πνεῦμα), or simply with a personal pronoun or the equivalent. Texts appearing to presuppose that only the inner person is raised differ on whether that

---

at least by the time of the composition of that Gospel, opponents (or skeptics) of the proclamation of Jesus' resurrection argued that the disciples had stolen the body in order to claim that he was risen. John 20:2 expresses the possibility of misunderstanding the empty tomb as due to the removal of the body by outsiders.

85 Yarbro Collins, *Beginning of the Gospel*, 135–36.

86 *The Compact Edition of the Oxford English Dictionary* (2 vols.; New York: Oxford University Press, 1971) 2:2518.

87 BAGD, s.v. ἐγείρω.

88 Ibid., s.v. ἀνίστημι.

89 Ps 6:6(5); Ps 89:49(48); Isa 38:18; Job 17:13-16; Eccl 9:4-10; cf. Ps 30:10(9); Ps 88:11-13(10-12); Ps 115:17; Job 7:9; 10:20-22; 14:12-14; Eccl 3:20; Sir 17:27; 41:4; Richard Bauckham, "Hades, Hell," *ABD* 3:14–16, esp. 14; Theodore J. Lewis, "Dead, Abode of the," *ABD* 2:101–5, esp. 102–4; Lehtipuu, *Afterlife Imagery*, 120; Collins, *Daniel*, 394 and n. 225.

90 Homer *Il.* 23.65–107; *Od.* 11.14–19, 204–8, 488–91;

Lehtipuu, *Afterlife Imagery*, 57–58; Ihles Johnston, *Restless Dead*, 7–14.

91 For the Israelite-Jewish traditions, see Roland E. Murphy, "Death and Afterlife in the Wisdom Literature," in Alan J. Avery-Peck and Jacob Neusner, eds., *Judaism in Late Antiquity*, part 4: *Death, Life-after-Death, Resurrection and the World-to-Come in the Judaisms of Antiquity* (HO 1, Der Nahe und Mittlere Osten/The Near and Middle East 49; Leiden: Brill, 2000) 101–16; John J. Collins, "The Afterlife in Apocalyptic Literature" (ibid., 119–39); George W. E. Nickelsburg, "Judgment, Life-after-Death, and Resurrection in the Apocrypha and the Non-Apocalyptic Pseudepigrapha" (ibid., 141–62). On the Greek tradition, see Ihles Johnston, *Restless Dead*, 98; Lehtipuu, *Afterlife Imagery*, 62–75.

92 Lehtipuu, *Afterlife Imagery*, 155–56; Martin, *Corinthian Body*, 109.

93 Lehtipuu, *Afterlife Imagery*, 58–62, 81–97.

entity receives a new body or remains disembodied.[94] Another important issue on which the texts differ is where the dead live after they are raised—on earth; on a transformed or newly created earth; in Eden, or some other normally inaccessible earthly place; or in heaven.

The oldest Jewish text that clearly expresses the idea of the resurrection of individual, physically dead persons is the Book of the Watchers, which was later incorporated into a composite work known today as *1 Enoch*.[95] It also differentiates clearly between the fate of the righteous dead and that of the sinful dead. In this work, the angel Raphael shows Enoch the ends of the earth, places normally inaccessible to human beings. In the course of the tour, Enoch sees the places of the dead:

> And from there I went to another place, and he showed me, toward the west, another great and high mountain of hard rock. And there were four hollow places in it, which were deep and smooth. Three of them were dark, and one was bright, and there was a spring of water in the middle of it. And I said, "How is it that these hollow places are smooth and very deep and dark in appearance?" Raphael, the one of the holy angels who was with me, then answered and said to me, "These hollow places (exist) so that the spirits of the souls of the dead may be gathered into them. For the same reason, they were selected, that all the souls of human beings[96] be gathered here. And these places, they made (them) for their reception until the day of their judgment and until the limit and until (the) determined time, at which the great judgment will take place with respect to them" (κἀκεῖθεν ἐφώδευσα εἰς ἄλλον τόπον, καὶ ἔδειξέν μοι πρὸς δυσμὰς ἄλλο ὄρος μέγα καὶ ὑψηλόν, πέτρας στερεάς. καὶ τέσσαρες τόποι ἐν αὐτῷ

κοῖλοι, βάθος ἔχοντες καὶ λίαν λεῖοι, τρεῖς αὐτῶν σκοτινοὶ καὶ εἰς φωτινός, καὶ πηγὴ ὕδατος ἀνὰ μέσον αὐτοῦ. καὶ εἶπον Πῶς λεῖα τὰ κοιλώματα ταῦτα καὶ ὁλοβαθῆ καὶ σκοτινὰ τῇ ὁράσει; τότε ἀπεκρίθη Ῥαφαὴλ, ὁ εἰς τῶν ἁγίων ἀγγέλων ὃς μετ᾽ ἐμοῦ ἦν, καὶ εἶπέν μοι Οὗτοι οἱ τόποι οἱ κοῖλοι, ἵνα ἐπισυνάγωνται εἰς αὐτοὺς τὰ πνεύματα τῶν ψυχῶν τῶν νεκρῶν. εἰς αὐτὸ τοῦτο ἐκρίθησαν, ὧδε ἐπισυνάγεσθαι πάσας τὰς ψυχὰς τῶν ἀνθρώπων. καὶ οὗτοι οἱ τόποι εἰς ἐπισύνσχεσιν αὐτῶν ἐποίησαν μέχρι τῆς ἡμέρας τῆς κρίσεως αὐτῶν καὶ μέχρι τοῦ διορισμοῦ καὶ διορισμένου χρόνου ἐν ᾧ ἡ κρίσις ἡ μεγάλη ἔσται ἐν αὐτοῖς). (*1 Enoch* 22:1-4)[97]

The one hollow place with light and a spring of water is the place where the spirits of the righteous dead await judgment. The three dark places are for the spirits of the wicked (*1 Enoch* 22:5-13).[98] The souls of the wicked will not rise again from their hollow places (οὐδὲ μὴ μετεγερθῶσιν ἐντεῦθεν) (22:13).

Later, Enoch went to another place, where he saw seven glorious mountains (*1 Enoch* 24:2). According to the Greek version, the seventh mountain, in the midst of the other six, was like the seat of a throne, and it was surrounded by beautiful trees (24:3). According to both the Greek and the Ethiopic versions, there was one especially beautiful and fragrant tree among them (24:4). The angel Michael informed Enoch that the seventh mountain is the place where God will sit at the final judgment and that the beautiful, fragrant tree will be given to the righteous (25:3-4).

> Its fruit (will be) for the elect, for life toward the north, and it will be transplanted in a holy place beside the house of God, the eternal king. Then they will rejoice and be glad, and they will enter

---

94 "Disembodied" here does not necessarily mean "immaterial." See the discussion of "soul" (ψυχή) and "spirit" (πνεῦμα) as finer and lighter forms of "stuff" than "flesh" (σάρξ), but still "stuff," in Martin, *Corinthian Body*, 3–37, 128. Furthermore, in many ancient texts of the Hellenistic and early Roman periods from a variety of cultures, the disembodied dead are described in bodily terms (Lehtipuu, *Afterlife Imagery*, 81–154). In other words, their "shades" or "souls" are depicted as eating, drinking, being physically punished, etc.

95 The Book of the Watchers, preserved in *1 Enoch* 1–36, dates to the third or early second cent. BCE (Collins, "Afterlife in Apocalyptic Literature," 121).

96 An Aramaic frg. from Qumran, 4Q206 (4QEn^c ar = *4QEnoch^e*), reads "[the soul]s of the sons of men"

(אנשא בני ח[שפ]); text and trans. from García Martínez and Tigchelaar, *Dead Sea Scrolls*, 1:424–25; cited by Michael A. Knibb, *The Ethiopic Book of Enoch: A New Edition in Light of the Aramaic Dead Sea Fragments* (2 vols.; Oxford: Clarendon, 1978) 2:108, note on 22:3.

97 Text from Black, *Apocalypsis Henochi Graece*, 33; cf. Denis and Janssens, *Concordance grecque*, 821–22; my trans.; cf. the trans. of the Ethiopic version in Nickelsburg and VanderKam, 42; see also Knibb, *Enoch*, 2:108–9; Nickelsburg, *1 Enoch 1*, 300.

98 Black, *Apocalypsis Henochi Graece*, 34.

the holy place. (The tree's) fragrance (will be) in their bones, and they will live a longer life upon the earth than your fathers lived, and in their days no torments nor plagues nor suffering will touch them (ὁ καρπὸς αὐτοῦ τοῖς ἐκλεκτοῖς εἰς ζωὴν εἰς βορρᾶν, καὶ μεταφυτευθήσεται ἐν τόπῳ ἁγίῳ παρὰ τὸν οἶκον τοῦ θεοῦ βασιλέως τοῦ αἰῶνος. τότε εὐφρανθήσονται εὐφραινόμενοι καὶ χαρήσονται καὶ εἰς τὸ ἅγιον εἰσελεύσονται· αἱ ὀσμαὶ αὐτοῦ ἐν τοῖς ὀστέοις αὐτῶν καὶ ζωὴν πλείονα ζήσονται ἐπὶ γῆς ἣν ἔζησαν οἱ πατέρες σου, καὶ ἐν ταῖς ἡμέραις αὐτῶν καὶ βάσανοι καὶ πληγαὶ καὶ μάστιγες οὐχ ἅψονται αὐτῶν). (1 Enoch 25:5-6)[99]

1 Enoch 25:3-6 implies that, before the final judgment, the tree of life is inaccessible to all human beings. After that event, it will be given to the righteous. The location of the tree when Enoch sees it seems to be in Eden or an inaccessible place similar to it.[100] After the judgment, the tree of life will be transplanted to Jerusalem, near the temple.[101] Apparently the new life of the righteous will be lived in that place.

The statement that the fragrance of the tree of life will be in the bones of the righteous seems to imply bodily resurrection, but the term "bones" could also signify "the self" or "the soul."[102] It is unclear whether eternal life is also implied.[103] It is said that the risen righteous will live longer lives than those of the patriarchs before the flood. To a modern reader, this statement seems to imply that they will eventually die. Another passage in the Book of the Watchers, however, suggests that no distinction was made between "eternal life" and a very long life. In instructing Gabriel to destroy the giants, the offspring of the watchers by human women, God says:

For they hope to live an eternal life and that each of them will live for five hundred years (ὅτι ἐλπίζουσιν ζῆσαι ζωὴν αἰώνιον, καὶ ὅτι ζήσεται ἕκαστος αὐτῶν ἔτη πεντακόσια). (1 Enoch 10:10)[104]

Here a life of five hundred years in length appears to be equivalent to "eternal life" (ζωὴ αἰώνιος).

The book of Daniel, which received its present form between 167 and 164 BCE,[105] also speaks about the resurrection of individual, physically dead people:

Many of those who sleep in the dusty earth will awake, some to everlasting life and some to reproach and everlasting disgrace. The wise shall shine like the splendour of the firmament, and those who lead the common people to righteousness like the stars forever and ever

(ורבים מישני אדמת־עפר יקיצו
אלה לחיי עולם ואלה לחרפות לדראון עולם
והמשכלים יזהרו כזהר הרקיע
ומצדיקי הרבים ככוכבים לעולם ועד).

(Dan 12:2-3)[106]

Here we see the metaphor of "sleep" for "death." The reading "the dusty earth" is probably a conflation of two readings found in different exemplars. Some apparently read "in the dust" and others "in the earth."[107] The reading "in the dust" may be understood as "in Sheol," since "dust" is used in synonymous parallelism with "Sheol" in Job 17:16.[108] In any case, early audiences of Daniel could well have taken both "in the earth" and "in the dust" to mean "in Sheol," rather than thinking of the bodies of the dead in their graves.[109]

This interpretation is supported by the fact that

---

99 Text from Black, *Apocalypsis Henochi Graece*, 35; cf. Denis and Janssens, *Concordance grecque*, 822; my trans.; cf. the trans. of the Ethiopic version in Nickelsburg and VanderKam, 45; see also Knibb, *Enoch*, 2:114; Nickelsburg, *1 Enoch 1*, 312.

100 Nickelsburg refers to it as "the mountain paradise of God" (*1 Enoch 1*, 328).

101 Nickelsburg speaks of "the new Jerusalem, the locus of eternal life in the future" (*1 Enoch 1*, 328), since the passage is based on Isaiah 65 and presupposes a new Jerusalem, a new heaven, and a new earth (ibid., 315).

102 Ibid., 315.

103 Nickelsburg infers that eternal life is implied (ibid., 315, 328).

104 Text from Black, *Apocalypsis Henochi Graece*, 25; cf. Denis and Janssens, *Concordance grecque*, 819; my trans.

105 Collins, *Daniel*, 38.

106 Trans. from Collins, *Daniel*, 369.

107 The OG reads "in the breadth of the earth" (ἐν τῷ πλάτει τῆς γῆς); Θ reads "in the dust of the earth" (ἐν γῆς χώματι). The Syriac version reads "in the dust" (Collins, *Daniel*, 369 n. 7).

108 Collins, *Daniel*, 392.

109 Richard Bauckham argued that "earth" and "dust" were both synonyms of "Sheol" ("Hades, Hell," 14), citing, e.g., 2 Bar. 42:8, "And the dust will be summoned and told, Give up what is not yours, and surrender everything you have guarded until its appointed time" (trans. from Robert H. Charles and Leonard H. Brockington, "The Syriac Apocalypse of Baruch," in *AOT*, 862). See also Yarbro Collins, *Beginning of the Gospel*, 125–26.

the context does not say anything about the earthly bodies of "the wise." Rather, they "shall shine like the splendour of the firmament" and "like the stars." According to Dan 8:10, the stars are identical with the host of heaven; thus the resurrected "wise" will have an existence like that of the angels.[110] There is nothing in this text to indicate that the "soul" (שֶׁפֶשׁ) of the individual was made of ether, fire, or pneuma and returned to its place of origin after death.[111] The heavenly existence of "the wise" is probably envisaged as bodily in some way, but it is not simply a matter of the revival or even the transformation of the earthly bodies. The idea of resurrection expressed here may be the transformation of the "soul" into an astral or heavenly "stuff" like that of the angels. The "soul" (שֶׁפֶשׁ) could be considered to be of divine origin on the basis of Gen 2:7. But Dan 12:1-3 places great weight on divine intervention in delivering those found "written in the book" from the time of trouble (v. 1), in raising "many" from the dead, and in shaming the wicked and exalting the righteous (vv. 2-3).

About the same time as Daniel, the Animal Apocalypse was written, a work that was later joined with the Book of the Watchers and other short works to form *1 Enoch*.[112] The Animal Apocalypse is an extended allegory of the history of Israel that ends with a series of eschatological events. In the allegory, Adam and the patriarchs before the flood are represented by white bulls. The children of Israel are depicted as sheep and "men" are angels. After the judgment of the wicked angels and the apostate Israelites, "the Lord of the sheep" replaces the "old house" (historical Jerusalem) with "a new house" (the eschatological, new Jerusalem) (*1 Enoch* 90:28-29).[113] Then "all that had been destroyed and dispersed . . . gathered in that house . . ." (90:33).[114] The reference to the gathering of the sheep that had been destroyed probably presup-

poses their resurrection.[115] Since these are then transformed into "white bulls" or "white cattle," the transformation of their earthly bodies into more glorious bodies seems to be implied (90:38).[116] They will enjoy resurrected life in the new Jerusalem (90:34-38).

Another work in the same tradition as the Book of the Watchers and the Animal Apocalypse, the Epistle of Enoch, was composed at some point in the second century BCE.[117] Like those works, it implies that only the souls or spirits of the righteous will experience resurrection:

> I [Enoch] swear to you . . . . I understand this mystery; for I read the tablets of heaven and I saw the necessary writing; I came to know what is written in them and what is engraved concerning you, that good things and joy and honor are prepared and recorded for the souls of the pious who have died. They will rejoice and their spirits will surely not perish, and the memory (of them) (will surely not perish) from the presence of the Great One for all the generations of the ages. Therefore, do not fear their insults (ἐγὼ ὀμνύω ὑμῖν . . . . ἐπίσταμαι τὸ μυστήριον τοῦτο· ἀν[έγνων] γὰρ τὰς πλάκας τοῦ οὐρανοῦ καὶ εἶδον τὴν γραφὴν ἀναγκαίαν· ἔγνων τὰ γ[εγραμμέ]να ἐν αὐταῖς καὶ ἐγκεκολαμμέν[α περὶ] ὑμῶν, ὅτι ἀγαθὰ καὶ χαρὰ καὶ ἡ τ[ιμὴ] ἡτοίμασται καὶ ἐγγέγραπται ταῖς ψ[υχαῖς] τῶν ἀποθανόντων εὐσεβῶν· καὶ χαιρήσονται καὶ οὐ μὴ ἀπόλωνται τὰ πνεύματα αὐτῶν οὐδὲ τὸ μνημόσυνον ἀπὸ προσώπου τοῦ μεγάλου εἰς πάσας τὰς γενεὰς τῶν αἰώνων. μὴ οὖν φοβεῖσθε τοὺς ὀνειδισμοὺς αὐτῶν). (*1 Enoch* 103:1-4)[118]

The understanding of resurrection expressed here involves the exaltation of the spirits of the dead from Sheol to heaven.[119] Another passage in the same work

---

110 This motif may be a Jewish adaptation of the Greek notion of astral immortality (Collins, *Daniel*, 393–94; Martin, *Corinthian Body*, 117–20).

111 As Cicero, Philo, and others believed (Martin, *Corinthian Body*, 119–20).

112 The Animal Apocalypse is now found in *1 Enoch* 85–90; it was composed around 165 BCE (Nickelsburg, *1 Enoch 1*, 8; Tiller, *Animal Apocalypse*, 78–79).

113 Trans. from Nickelsburg and VanderKam, 135; see also Knibb, *Enoch*, 2:215. On the "house" as Jerusalem, see Tiller, *Animal Apocalypse*, 376; Nickelsburg, *1 Enoch 1*, 404.

114 Trans. from Nickelsburg and VanderKam, 135–36; see also Knibb, *Enoch*, 2:216.

115 Collins, "Afterlife in Apocalyptic Literature," 123; Nickelsburg, *1 Enoch 1*, 405–6.

116 Knibb translates "white bulls" (*Enoch*, 2:216); Tiller translates "white cattle" (*Animal Apocalypse*, 383); so also Nickelsburg and VanderKam, 136.

117 The Epistle of Enoch is preserved in *1 Enoch* 92–105; Nickelsburg, *1 Enoch 1*, 8, 427–28.

118 Text from Black, *Apocalypsis Henochi Graece*, 42; see also Denis and Janssens, *Concordance grecque*, 824; my trans. See also the trans. of the corresponding Ethiopic text in Nickelsburg and VanderKam, 159; Knibb, *Enoch*, 2:240; and in Nickelsburg, *1 Enoch 1*, 511. See also the Greek frgs. from Qumran, 7Q4, 8, 11–14; text and trans. in García Martínez and Tigchelaar, *Dead Sea Scrolls*, 2:1162–63.

119 Collins, "Afterlife in Apocalyptic Literature," 124; Nickelsburg, *1 Enoch 1*, 519, 523.

states that the righteous "will shine like the luminaries of heaven," "will have great joy like the angels of heaven" and "will be companions of the host of heaven" (*1 Enoch* 104:2-6).[120] This passage, like Dan 12:3, portrays the resurrected righteous as being in an angelic state.[121]

Similar to the type of resurrection envisaged in the Epistle of Enoch is that portrayed in the book of *Jubilees*. This work was written between 170 and 150 BCE.[122] In a digression after the account of the death of Abraham, "an angel of the presence" reveals to Moses (cf. *Jub.* 1:27) a future evil generation followed by a generation that repents and is blessed (*Jub.* 23:8-32).[123] Among the blessings of the latter generation is their postmortem experience:

> Their bones will rest in the earth and their spirits will be very happy. They will know that the Lord is one who executes judgment but shows kindness to hundreds and thousands and to all who love him. (23:31)[124]

If this text presupposes any kind of resurrection or conscious afterlife, as seems likely, the earthly bodies are not included in the resurrected or exalted state.

Texts of the first centuries BCE and CE also express varied points of view. 2 Maccabees was composed between 100 and 63 BCE and treats the events of the persecution under Antiochus.[125] This work presupposes that the persecution was divine punishment for the sins of the people, yet it focuses on the sufferings and death of Eleazar, seven brothers, and their mother. These were not sinners but righteous and pious people. Their innocent suffering and their prayers moved God to bring about an end to the persecution through the military might of the Maccabees.[126]

The topic of resurrection is mentioned in connection with the suffering and death of the second brother (2 Macc 7:7-9). With his last breath he said:

> You, an offender against heaven, do indeed send us away from the life of the present, but the king

of the world will raise us to an eternal renewal of life because we have died for the sake of his laws (Σὺ μέν, ἀλάστωρ, ἐκ τοῦ παρόντος ἡμᾶς ζῆν ἀπολύεις, ὁ δὲ τοῦ κόσμου βασιλεὺς ἀποθανόντας ἡμᾶς ὑπὲρ τῶν αὐτοῦ νόμων εἰς αἰώνιον ἀναβίωσιν ζωῆς ἡμᾶς ἀναστήσει). (2 Macc 7:9 LXX)

The third brother was commanded to put out his tongue and to put forth his hands. As he did so, he said:

> I acquired these from heaven and, on account of his laws, I disdain them as not worthy of notice; and from him I hope to get them back again (Ἐξ οὐρανοῦ ταῦτα κέκτημαι καὶ διὰ τοὺς αὐτοῦ νόμους ὑπερορῶ ταῦτα καὶ παρ᾽ αὐτοῦ ταῦτα πάλιν ἐλπίζω κομίσασθαι). (2 Macc 7:11 LXX)

This remark is a clear expression of the expectation of a bodily resurrection in the sense of a restoration of the earthly body (see also 2 Macc 7:14, 23, 29).

The youngest brother makes the following statement before he dies in a speech addressed to Antiochus:

> For now our brothers, after enduring a little pain, have inherited eternal life under the terms of God's covenant; but you, because of the judgment of God, will win for yourself the just penalties of arrogance (οἱ μὲν γὰρ νῦν ἡμέτεροι ἀδελφοὶ βραχὺν ὑπενέγκαντες πόνον ἀενάου ζωῆς ὑπὸ διαθήκην θεοῦ πεπτώκασιν· σὺ δὲ τῇ τοῦ θεοῦ κρίσει δίκαια τὰ πρόστιμα τῆς ὑπερηφανίας ἀποίσῃ). (2 Macc 7:36 LXX)[127]

If the text is emended, with the result that the brothers are said "to have drunk" (reading πεπώκασιν rather than πεπτώκασιν) of "everflowing" (another usage of ἀέναος, the adjective translated here with "eternal") life, one could argue that the text envisages the resurrection as taking place immediately after death. There is no textual support for this emenda-

---

120 Trans. from Nickelsburg, *1 Enoch 1*, 512.

121 Cf. Collins, "Afterlife in Apocalyptic Literature,"124; Nickelsburg, *1 Enoch 1*, 529-30.

122 VanderKam, *Book of Jubilees*, V–VI.

123 See Orval S. Wintermute, "Jubilees," *OTP* 2:35, 100–102.

124 Trans. from VanderKam, *Book of Jubilees*, 149; similarly Collins, "Afterlife in Apocalyptic Literature," 124. Wintermute concludes that the verse is ambiguous; it could be "a description of spirits that remain conscious and aware of postmortem events while their bones rest in peace. It could also be under-

stood as an example of poetic hyperbole, describing those who die with assurance that justice has been done" ("Jubilees," 102 n. p).

125 Nickelsburg, "Judgment, Life-after-Death, and Resurrection in the Apocrypha and the Non-Apocalyptic Pseudepigrapha," in Avery-Peck and Neusner, *Judaism in Late Antiquity*, part 4, 148; Goldstein, *I Maccabees*, 62–89; idem, *II Maccabees*, 71–83.

126 Van Henten, *Maccabean Martyrs*. Cf. Nickelsburg, "Judgment, Life-after-Death, and Resurrection," 148–49.

127 On the trans. of πεπτώκασιν ("they have inherited,"

tion, however, and the notion of "inheriting eternal life" is ambiguous. It could mean that they enjoy their inheritance immediately or that they will receive it at the time of the resurrection of all the righteous at the end of days.

The Similitudes or Parables of Enoch is a work that was incorporated into *1 Enoch* at some point.[128] Since no fragments of it have been found in the caves near Qumran, the Dead Sea Scrolls provide no evidence regarding its date or relation to the other Enochic works in their history of reception. The book is often dated to the end of the first century BCE, but could have been composed as late as the mid-first century CE[129] or even somewhat later. The introductory chapter contains a self-description as "a vision of wisdom" (chap. 37).[130] As a whole, however, it has the form of a heavenly journey. It is organized into three "similitudes" or "parables" plus two epilogues in chaps. 70–71.[131] The term "similitude" or "parable" in this work has the sense of an instruction that is in some sense figurative.

On his journey, Enoch saw "the dwellings of the holy ones and the resting places of the righteous." He saw "their dwellings with his righteous angels and their resting places with the holy ones" (*1 Enoch* 39:4-5).[132] According to some manuscripts, the place of the chosen, the place of their dwelling, is also described as "beneath the wings of the Lord of Spirits" (39:7).[133] All manuscripts state that "all the righteous and chosen shone [or were mighty] before [the Lord of Spirits] like fiery lights" (39:7).[134]

This passage, like Dan 12:3 and the Epistle of Enoch (*1 Enoch* 104:2-6), envisages the resurrected state of the righteous in terms of likeness to and association with the angels.[135] Another passage states that the righteous will enjoy eternal life in the company of "that Son of Man" (*1 Enoch* 71:16-17).[136]

Another important resource for understanding Jewish ideas about afterlife in the Second Temple period is the group of manuscripts and fragments discovered in caves near Khirbet Qumran. Most of the documents came to light between 1947 and 1956.[137] The individual scrolls have been dated paleographically from the mid-third century BCE to the third quarter of the first century CE.[138]

The *Community Rule* seems to presuppose both a judgment immediately after the death of each individual and a public, final judgment.[139] After the individual judgment, the one judged will already experience eternal reward or punishment. The final judgment will presumably complete and confirm that process. The reward of those who walk in the spirit of truth is described in 1QS 4:6-8; the punishment of those who walk in the spirit of deceit is depicted in 4:11-14. The public, final judgment is announced in 4:18-19.[140] It will be followed by the triumph of truth and the renewal of creation (4:19-23, 25-26). Some of the rewards of the sons of truth may apply to life on the earth before death: "healing, plentiful peace in a long life, fruitful offspring with all everlasting blessings" (1QS 4:6-7).[141] The last two, however, seem to belong to the afterlife: "eternal enjoyment with endless life, and a crown of glory with majestic raiment in eternal light" (4:7-8). The first punishment of the wicked could refer to life in this world: "abundance of afflictions at the hands of the angels of destruction" (4:12).

---

lit., "they have fallen"), see Goldstein, *II Maccabees*, 291, 316–17; van Henten, *Maccabean Martyrs*, 175 n. 219; Nickelsburg, "Judgment, Life-after-Death, and Resurrection," 149 n. 24.

128 It is preserved in *1 Enoch* 37–71.

129 Cf. Collins, *Apocalyptic Imagination*, 177–78. The argument for dating the work prior to 66 CE rests on the lack of any mention of the first Jewish war with Rome.

130 Collins, *Apocalyptic Imagination*, 178–79.

131 The first "parable" is given in 38:1–44:1; the second in 45:1–57:3; the third in 58:1–69:29.

132 Trans. from Nickelsburg and VanderKam, 52; see also Knibb, *Enoch*, 2:126.

133 According to other MSS, it is the Chosen One, the messiah, whose place is beneath the wings of the Lord of Spirits (Nickelsburg and VanderKam, 52–53).

134 Nickelsburg and VanderKam choose the reading "were mighty" (53); Knibb chooses "shone" (*Enoch*, 2:126).

135 Cf. Collins, "Afterlife in Apocalyptic Literature," 124–25.

136 Trans. from Knibb, *Enoch*, 2:167; cf. Nickelsburg and VanderKam, 95. See the discussion in Collins, "Afterlife in Apocalyptic Literature," 125.

137 John J. Collins, "Dead Sea Scrolls," *ABD* 2:85–101, esp. 86.

138 Ibid., 86.

139 Another important rule book, the *Damascus Document*, also appears to envisage both individual judgments and a final, definitive judgment (CD 2:3-13) (John J. Collins, *Apocalypticism in the Dead Sea Scrolls* [The Literature of the Dead Sea Scrolls; London/New York: Routledge, 1997] 118).

140 For discussion, see Collins, *Apocalypticism*, 116–17.

141 Trans. in this paragraph are from García Martínez and Tigchelaar, *Dead Sea Scrolls*, 1:77.

The rest seem to belong to the afterlife because of the language of eternity and the mention of "the fire of the dark regions" (4:12-14). In both lists, the dead are spoken of in bodily terms. This language, however, does not necessarily imply resurrection of the earthly body, since the "shades," "souls," or "spirits" of the dead are often spoken of in bodily terms.[142]

Column 4 of the *Community Rule* thus expresses a continuity between what the righteous and the wicked experience in this life and what they will experience in the next. The emphasis, however, seems to be on the future, definitive distribution of rewards and punishments. In the hymn of columns 10–11, however, a kind of realized eschatology is expressed:

> My eyes have observed what always is, wisdom that has been hidden from mankind, knowledge and prudent understanding (hidden) from the sons of man, fount of justice and well of strength and spring of glory (hidden) from the assembly of flesh. To those whom God has selected he has given them as everlasting possession; and he has given them an inheritance in the lot of the holy ones. He unites their assembly to the sons of the heavens in order (to form) the council of the Community and a foundation of the building of holiness to be an everlasting plantation throughout all future ages. (1QS 11:5-9)[143]

This passage clearly states that God has united the assembly of the community on earth with the angels. This signifies that, from the point of view of the community of the Dead Sea Scrolls, they are already enjoying the fellowship with the angels described in the Epistle of Enoch (*1 Enoch* 104:2-6)[144] and in the Similitudes or Parables of Enoch (39:4-7)[145] as characteristic of the resurrected state.[146] For the community of the Dead Sea Scrolls, their glory had yet to be manifested, but they already enjoyed fellowship with the angels.[147] The same sentiment is expressed in the Thanksgiving Hymns (*Hôdāyôt*) from Qumran:

> For the sake of your glory, you have purified man from offence, so that he can make himself holy for you from every impure abomination and guilt of unfaithfulness, to become united wi[th] the sons of your truth and in the lot with your holy ones, to raise the worm of the dead from the dust, to an ever[lasting] community, and from a depraved spirit, to [your] knowledge, so that he can take his place in your presence with the perpetual host and the [everlasting] spirits, to renew him with everything that will exist, and with those who know in a community of jubilation. (1QH 19:10-14)[148]

Émile Puech has argued that, among other passages from the Dead Sea Scrolls, 1QH 19:12 (11:12) expresses the idea of resurrection, rather than the joining of the life of the community with "life on the height" in the present. He focuses especially on the phrase תולעת מתים ("worm of dead ones").[149] This phrase is an allusion to Isaiah: "Your dead shall live, their corpses shall rise. O dwellers in the dust, awake and sing for joy!" (Isa 26:19 NRSV). It is likely that the statement in Isaiah was meant metaphorically.[150] The adaptation of the verse in 1QH 19:12 could thus also be metaphorical.[151]

Thus, the texts most characteristic of the community do not speak clearly about resurrection as such. Two other texts found at Qumran, however, do. The so-called *Messianic Apocalypse* (4Q521) is one of these. The surviving portion of this text begins with the statement that "[the heav]ens and the earth will listen to his anointed one."[152] A few lines later, a list of the things that the Lord will do in the future is given, based on Ps 146:7c-8b (4Q521 frg. 2 2:8).[153] A bit later, the following comment is made:

> And the Lord will perform marvellous acts such as have not existed, just as he sa[id,] [for] he will heal the badly wounded and will make the dead live, he will proclaim good news to the poor

142 See n. 94 above.

143 Trans. from García Martínez and Tigchelaar, *Dead Sea Scrolls*, 1:97.

144 See the discussion above.

145 See the discussion above.

146 Although Dan 12:1-3 does not speak explicitly about fellowship with the angels, the angelic state of "the wise" after being raised probably implies it.

147 Collins, *Apocalypticism*, 117–18.

148 Trans. (modified) from García Martínez and Tigchelaar, *Dead Sea Scrolls*, 1:189. See also 1QH 11:19-23 (formerly 3:19-23); Collins, *Apocalypticism*, 119–20.

149 Émile Puech, *La Croyance des esséniens en la vie future, immortalité, résurrection, vie éternelle? Histoire d'une croyance dans le judaïsme ancien* (2 vols.; EtB n.s. 21–22; Paris: Librairie Lecoffre/Gabalda, 1993) 2:375–81.

150 Blenkinsopp, *Isaiah 1–39*, 371.

151 Collins, *Apocalypticism*, 121; George W. E. Nickelsburg, "Resurrection," *EDSS* 2:764–67, esp. 766.

152 Or "will obey" (4Q521 frg. 2 2:1); trans. from García Martínez and Tigchelaar, *Dead Sea Scrolls*, 2:1045.

153 Collins, *Apocalypticism*, 88.

(וֹנכבדות שלוֹא היו יעשׂה אדני כאשׂר ה[בר]
[כיْ] ירפֹא חללים ומתים יחיה ענוים יבשׂר).
(4Q521 frg. 2 2:11-12)[154]

Puech argued that the anointed one in this text is the royal messiah, but the allusion to Isa 61:1 in the lines just quoted makes it more likely that the anointed one is "an anointed eschatological prophet, either Elijah or a prophet like Elijah."[155] In any case, no further indication of what is meant by "he will make the dead live" (ומתים יחיה) is given.

The other text is Pseudo-Ezekiel (4Q385). A fragment of this work reads:

[that I am YHWH,] who rescued my people, giving them the covenant. *Blank* [And I said: "YHWH,] I have seen many in Israel who love your name and walk on the paths of [justice.] When will [the]se things happen? And how will they be rewarded for their loyalty?" And YHWH said to me: "I will make the children of Israel see and they will know that I am YHWH." *Blank* [And he said:] "Son of man, prophesy over the bones and say: May a bone [connect] with its bone and a joint [with its joint."] And s[o it happe]ned. And he said a second time: "Prophesy, and sinews will grow on them and they will be covered with skin [all over." And so it happened.] And again he s[a]id: "Prophesy over the four winds of the sky and the wind[s] [of the sky] will blow [upon them and they will live] and a large crowd of men will r[i]se and bless YHWH Sebaoth wh[o] [caused them to live." *Blank*? And] I said: "O YHWH, when will these things happen?" And YHWH said to me [. . .] [. . .] . . . a tree will bend over and straighten up [. . .]. (4Q385 frg. 2 lines 1–10)[156]

This text is an interpretation of the vision of the dry bones in Ezekiel 37. Since the new context in which interpretation takes place involves the question of the reward of those loyal to God, it is likely that the resurrection of dead individuals is implied.[157] This work was probably not composed by a member of the community but was read by its members.[158]

The evidence supports the conclusion that the leaders of the community associated with the Dead Sea Scrolls had no problem with reading texts containing language about resurrection in the future. Some of the texts found in the caves spoke about the resurrection of the soul, spirit, or inner self.[159] Others spoke of the resurrection of the earthly body,[160] but texts that were composed by leaders of the community did not use terminology involving the revival of the earthly body or even the "rising" of the soul or spirit. They assume continuity from this life to the next without commenting on the transition (*Community Rule* and *Damascus Document*), or they speak about exaltation to a life in association with the angels already in the present (*Thanksgiving Hymns*).

The Jewish texts discussed so far focus on the resurrection of the righteous, pious, elect, or "sons of truth." In his first letter to the Corinthians, Paul, a Jew of the first century CE who believed that Jesus was the primary agent of God as messiah and Lord, wrote about the resurrection of "those who belong to Christ" (οἱ τοῦ Χριστοῦ) and also seems to have presupposed that a general resurrection to rewards and punishments would take place afterward: "(The) last enemy to be destroyed is Death" (ἔσχατος ἐχϑρὸς καταργεῖται ὁ ϑάνατος) (1 Cor 15:23, 26; cf. Rom 2:5-8). Paul's understanding of resurrection was refined and perhaps modified in conversation with members of the Corinthian community, some of whom were educated in Greek philosophy and science.[161]

Presumably, all the members of the Corinthian community founded by Paul accepted the idea that Jesus had been raised from the dead or exalted to heaven and glorified.[162] Some of them, however, denied "the resurrection of the dead" (ἀνάστασις νεκρῶν), that is, the resurrection of "those in Christ" and the general resurrection at the end (1 Cor 15:12). They probably understood this phrase to mean "the bringing to life of human corpses."[163] The reason they disbelieved is what Martin called their hierarchical view of the universe and what Asher called the doctrine of cosmological polarity. No human body can

---

154 Trans. from García Martínez and Tigchelaar, *Dead Sea Scrolls*, 2:1045.

155 Collins, *Apocalypticism*, 88–89.

156 Trans. from García Martínez and Tigchelaar, *Dead Sea Scrolls*, 2:769. See also 4Q386.

157 Nickelsburg, "Resurrection," 766; Collins, *Apocalypticism*, 126–27.

158 Collins, *Apocalypticism*, 127–28; Nickelsburg, "Resurrection," 766.

159 Daniel, the Epistle of Enoch (*1 Enoch* 92–105), *Jubilees*; see the discussion of these texts above.

160 The Book of the Watchers (*1 Enoch* 1–36), the Animal Apocalypse (*1 Enoch* 85–90); see the discussion of these texts above.

161 Asher, *Polarity and Change*, 91–205; cf. Martin, *Corinthian Body*, 104–36.

162 Cf. Martin, *Corinthian Body*, 107–8, 122.

163 Ibid., 122.

participate in immortality because, in Plutarch's words, "to mix heaven with earth is foolish" (οὐρανῷ δὲ μιγνύειν γῆν ἀβέλτερον) (*Vit. Rom.* 28.6).[164] They believed it impossible to raise "a terrestrial body to the celestial realm."[165]

Paul responds to the objection by correcting the views in question, while also accommodating his position to these views.[166] After laying out three types of evidence in favor of the resurrection of the dead in 1 Cor 15:1-34,[167] Paul turns to the specific issue of the impossibility of resurrection in the context of cosmological polarity. In v. 35a, Paul "uses a dialogical technique to frame an objection in the form of a question."[168] In v. 35b, he restates the question "in more neutral terms" in order to "direct the subsequent discussion" in the direction Paul wants to take it.[169] The element of correction is clear in the use of a strong invective, "Fool!" (ἄφρων), in v. 36a, immediately following the restatement of the question, a usage typical of educational contexts. The particular term of invective chosen prepares for the argument that the prudent person recognizes "the creative power of God."[170]

The correct answer, from Paul's point of view, to the reformulated question is given in vv. 36b-38, the comparison of resurrection to the planting of a seed and the growth of a plant from that seed. The new idea that Paul introduces here in order to resolve the problem at issue is the notion of the transition or transformation of bodies.[171] Paul accepts the idea that earthly bodies cannot share in immortality and cannot exist in the heavenly world (cf. 1 Cor 15:33b-36 with v. 50). His thinking about the seed and the plant and about the transformation that makes resurrection possible, however, is different from that of modern people and from educated ancient people. He does not seem to assume that each kind of seed automatically grows into a specific kind of plant because of its intrinsic nature. Nor does he seem to think that each kind of human soul or spirit goes to the place after death that corresponds to its physical nature, which is determined by its way of life. Rather, he emphasizes

the creative power of God, in giving to each kind of seed and to each kind of soul or spirit the body that God has chosen (ὁ δὲ θεὸς δίδωσιν αὐτῷ σῶμα καθὼς ἠθέλησεν, καὶ ἑκάστῳ τῶν σπερμάτων ἴδιον σῶμα) (v. 38).[172]

After correcting the relevant members of the community in vv. 36b-38, Paul lays out an argument in vv. 39-49 that accommodates the notion of resurrection to the cosmological view of his interlocutors.[173] In vv. 39-41, he summarizes a standard cosmology held by educated people in antiquity. This cosmology involves the view that all things are divided into the earthly and the heavenly (v. 40). Earthly beings are characterized by "flesh" (σάρξ), and there are various categories of "flesh"—one kind for humans (ἄνθρωποι), another for domesticated animals (κτήνη), another for birds (πτηνά) and another for fish (ἰχθύες) (v. 39). Heavenly beings, like the sun (ἥλιος), the moon (σελήνη), and the stars (ἀστέρες), have "bodies" (σώματα), but not "flesh" (σάρξ) (vv. 40-41). Both earthly beings and heavenly beings have "glory" or "honor" (δόξα), but of different kinds. The heavenly beings can also be divided into categories, using the criterion of "glory" or "brightness" (δόξα) (v. 41). In these verses, Paul accepts the cosmology apparently presupposed by those who deny the resurrection of the dead and prepares to discuss resurrection in that context.[174]

In 1 Cor 15:42-44a, Paul applies the illustration of the seed and the plant (vv. 36b-38) and the discussion of cosmology (vv. 39-41) to the resurrection of the dead.[175] The antithetical structure of the clauses in vv. 42bc-44a recalls the antithesis between the seed and the plant in the illustration. These antitheses also reflect the polarity of the earthly and the heavenly in the summary of the standard Hellenistic cosmology. The resurrection of the dead is possible in the context of that cosmology because "the creative activities of God comply with the metaphysical strictures" of the locative polarity that characterizes it.[176]

1 Cor 15:44a expresses an antithesis between a body characterized by an earthly soul (σῶμα ψυχικόν)

---

164 Trans. from Perrin, *Plutarch's Lives,* 1:180–81; cited by Martin, *Corinthian Body,* 113.

165 Asher, *Polarity and Change,* 91.

166 Ibid., 30–90.

167 Mitchell, *Rhetoric of Reconciliation,* 286. Asher argues that this section is devoted to showing the Corinthians that it is inconsistent to deny the resurrection of the dead while affirming the resurrection of Christ (*Polarity and Change,* 59–63).

168 Asher, *Polarity and Change,* 66.

169 Ibid. Asher shows that the word "body" (σῶμα) is introduced by Paul in his restatement of the ques-

tion and that this word was a neutral formulation, acceptable both to Paul and to those who denied the resurrection of the dead (*Polarity and Change,* 69–71).

170 Ibid., 77–78; quotation from 78.

171 Ibid., 80–81.

172 Cf. *1 Clement* 24.5, cited in the commentary on 4:8 above.

173 Asher, *Polarity and Change,* 81–88, 103–6.

174 Ibid., 105–6.

175 Ibid., 106–10.

176 Ibid., 108.

and a body characterized by spirit ($\sigma\hat{\omega}\mu\alpha$ $\pi\nu\epsilon\upsilon$-$\mu\alpha\tau\iota\kappa\acute{o}\nu$). This contrast prepares for a shift from a spatial, cosmological argument (vv. 42-44a) to a temporal, eschatological argument (vv. 44b-49).[177] In the temporal part of his argument, Paul evokes the account of the creation of Adam.

> And God made the man by molding soil from the earth and blew breath of life into his face, and the man became a living being ($\kappa\alpha\grave{\iota}$ $\check{\epsilon}\pi\lambda\alpha\sigma\epsilon\nu$ $\acute{o}$ $\vartheta\epsilon\grave{o}\varsigma$ $\tau\grave{o}\nu$ $\check{\alpha}\nu\vartheta\rho\omega\pi\sigma\nu$ $\chi\sigma\hat{\upsilon}\nu$ $\grave{\alpha}\pi\grave{o}$ $\tau\hat{\eta}\varsigma$ $\gamma\hat{\eta}\varsigma$ $\kappa\alpha\grave{\iota}$ $\grave{\epsilon}\nu\epsilon\varphi\acute{\upsilon}\sigma\eta$-$\sigma\epsilon\nu$ $\epsilon\grave{\iota}\varsigma$ $\tau\grave{o}$ $\pi\rho\acute{o}\sigma\omega\pi\sigma\nu$ $\alpha\grave{\upsilon}\tau\sigma\hat{\upsilon}$ $\pi\nu\sigma\grave{\eta}\nu$ $\zeta\omega\hat{\eta}\varsigma$, $\kappa\alpha\grave{\iota}$ $\grave{\epsilon}\gamma\acute{\epsilon}\nu\epsilon\tau\sigma$ $\acute{o}$ $\check{\alpha}\nu\vartheta\rho\omega\pi\sigma\varsigma$ $\epsilon\grave{\iota}\varsigma$ $\psi\upsilon\chi\grave{\eta}\nu$ $\zeta\hat{\omega}\sigma\alpha\nu$). (Gen 2:7 LXX)

By connecting this passage with a typology of the first Adam and the last Adam (Christ), Paul is able to show that the resurrection fits with a temporal succession of opposites as well as with the spatial, simultaneous existence of the two elements of the cosmological polarity of earth and heaven.[178]

In v. 44b, Paul makes the point "that the existence of one opposite demands the existence of its counterpart:"[179] "If there is a body characterized by an earthly soul, there is also a body characterized by spirit" ($E\grave{\iota}$ $\check{\epsilon}\sigma\tau\iota\nu$ $\sigma\hat{\omega}\mu\alpha$ $\psi\upsilon\chi\iota\kappa\acute{o}\nu$, $\check{\epsilon}\sigma\tau\iota\nu$ $\kappa\alpha\grave{\iota}$ $\pi\nu\epsilon\upsilon\mu\alpha\tau\iota\kappa\acute{o}\nu$). Paul assumes that his interlocutors will accept that premise. In v. 45, he presupposes another premise that he and they have in common: that Christ has been raised from the dead and therefore has or is "a spiritual body" ($\sigma\hat{\omega}\mu\alpha$ $\pi\nu\epsilon\upsilon\mu\alpha\tau\iota\kappa\acute{o}\nu$). From these premises, the argument of v. 45 infers that, as the first man, Adam, became a(n earthly) living being (Gen 2:7), the last Adam (Christ) became a (heavenly) life-giving spirit ($\pi\nu\epsilon\hat{\upsilon}\mu\alpha$ $\zeta\omega\sigma\pi\sigma\iota\sigma\hat{\upsilon}\nu$). Verses 46-47 clarify and elaborate the inference of v. 45.

Why Christ may be called a *life-giving* spirit is clarified in vv. 48-49. All human beings after Adam have been of the soil of the earth, as he was. That is, as he possessed an earthly body, so have they.[180] They share his characteristics, including death. Christ, however, because of his resurrection, is heavenly.[181] Just as the first Adam influenced all people after him so that they die, so also will the second Adam influence people after him so that they will rise from the dead

(v. 49). The inference is based on the premise that one opposite presupposes its counterpart.[182]

Verse 50 both concludes the discussion to that point and introduces what follows. The statement "flesh and blood cannot inherit the kingdom of God" ($\sigma\grave{\alpha}\rho\xi$ $\kappa\alpha\grave{\iota}$ $\alpha\hat{\iota}\mu\alpha$ $\beta\alpha\sigma\iota\lambda\epsilon\acute{\iota}\alpha\nu$ $\vartheta\epsilon\sigma\hat{\upsilon}$ $\kappa\lambda\eta\rho\sigma\nu\sigma\mu\hat{\eta}\sigma\alpha\iota$ $\sigma\grave{\upsilon}$ $\delta\acute{\upsilon}\nu\alpha\tau\alpha\iota$) concludes the argument in vv. 35-49 and summarizes Paul's opinion on the relation between the resurrection and the earthly body in the form of a principle. On this point he agrees with those who objected to the idea of the resurrection of the dead on the grounds of the standard cosmology of the time. The second antithesis of v. 50, "and corruption shall not inherit incorruptibility" ($\sigma\grave{\upsilon}\delta\grave{\epsilon}$ $\acute{\eta}$ $\varphi\vartheta\sigma\rho\grave{\alpha}$ $\tau\grave{\eta}\nu$ $\grave{\alpha}\varphi\vartheta\alpha\rho\sigma\acute{\iota}\alpha\nu$ $\kappa\lambda\eta\rho\sigma\nu\sigma\mu\epsilon\hat{\iota}$), introduces the remarks in vv. 51-57.[183] The two antitheses of v. 50 are most likely synonymously parallel and thus clearly state that no earthly body can ascend to the heavenly realm.[184]

The remarks in 1 Cor 15:51-57 do not constitute a new argument but continue the one begun in v. 35.[185] It is important to note that Paul does not simply argue that the lower elements of the earthly human being—flesh ($\sigma\acute{\alpha}\rho\xi$), blood ($\alpha\hat{\iota}\mu\alpha$), soul ($\psi\upsilon\chi\acute{\eta}$)—will be stripped off or left behind. Rather, he uses language of change ($\grave{\alpha}\lambda\lambda\acute{\alpha}\sigma\sigma\omega$) in vv. 50, 51, and 52 and language of investiture ($\grave{\epsilon}\nu\delta\acute{\upsilon}\omega$) in vv. 53 and 54. This language must mean either (1) that one (e.g., flesh) or more of the earthly elements will be transformed into a heavenly element ($\pi\nu\epsilon\hat{\upsilon}\mu\alpha$) or (2) that the earthly stuff will be removed and the heavenly stuff will be added.[186] Both possibilities are also compatible with what Paul says in 2 Cor 4:16—5:5.[187]

The story of the empty tomb in Mark is compatible with Paul's view as expressed in 1 Corinthians 15 only if Paul's language of change and investiture signifies the transformation of the earthly body into a heavenly body.

In addition to the texts discussed so far in this excursus, one should be aware of the possibility of the influence on Mark 16:1-8 of ancient notions of the translation or transference of the body of a favored person to the ends of the earth or to heaven, where he or she is made immortal.[188] Ancient notions

---

177 Ibid., 109–10.
178 Asher, *Polarity and Change*, 111–12.
179 Ibid., 112; see also 113–14.
180 Ibid., 115.
181 He is "of heaven" ($\grave{\epsilon}\xi$ $\sigma\grave{\upsilon}\rho\alpha\nu\sigma\hat{\upsilon}$) (v. 47) and "heavenly" ($\grave{\epsilon}\pi\sigma\upsilon\rho\acute{\alpha}\nu\iota\sigma\varsigma$) (v. 48).
182 Asher, *Polarity and Change*, 115.
183 Ibid., 151–52.
184 Ibid., 152–53.

185 Ibid., 147–55.
186 Ibid., 156 n. 20.
187 Furnish, *II Corinthians*, 261–71, 288–301.
188 Yarbro Collins, *Beginning of the Gospel*, 138–43. In addition to the texts cited there, see the story about Heracles in Diodorus Siculus 4.38.3–39.4.

of deification or apotheosis may also have influenced the story of the empty tomb.

One example of the expression of the latter idea occurs in a Jewish work attributed to the Gentile writer Phocylides, probably written in the first century CE.[189]

> For in fact we hope that the remains of the departed will soon come to the light again out of the earth. And afterwards they become gods (καὶ τάχα δ᾽ ἐκ γαίης ἐλπίζομεν ἐς φάος ἐλθεῖν λείψαν᾽ ἀποιχομένων· ὀπίσω δὲ θεοὶ τελέθονται).[190]

The first sentence clearly refers to the resurrection of the earthly body. Since angels are referred to as "gods" (אלים) in the Dead Sea Scrolls, the second sentence could be interpreted as expressing the idea that the resurrected righteous become angels.[191] Or the point could be that those who are resurrected become immortal, like the gods. In any case, the combination of the idea of bodily resurrection with elevation to a divine status in this text is similar to the empty-tomb story in Mark, with its presupposition of the transformation of Jesus' body and the idea that he has been exalted to the right of God (12:35-37 and 14:62).

The notion of deification or apotheosis played a role in the legend of Alexander the Great. In the life of Alexander attributed to Callisthenes, it is said that just before he died, a star and an eagle were seen coming down from heaven. Then, "the statue in Babylon, which was called the statue of Zeus, trembled." When the star went back up to the sky, along with the eagle, Alexander died.[192] These events were portrayed as Alexander's ascent to heaven, which was interpreted as an answer to his prayer to Zeus: "And if it be thy will, receive me too in heaven, as the third mortal."[193]

In Roman tradition, a similar account of the end of Romulus, the founder of the city of Rome, was related. Romulus "disappeared" (ἠφανίσθη) on the Nones of July, the month then called Quintilis. Because of tension between Romulus and the patricians, they were suspected of murdering him (Plutarch *Vit. Rom.* 27.3). A noble and reputable patrician, Julius Proculus, however, testified that Romulus had appeared to him as he was traveling on the road, dressed "in bright and shining armour" (ὅπλοις δὲ λαμπροῖς καὶ φλέγουσι κεκοσμημένος) (ibid. 28.1).[194] Romulus told Proculus that it was the will of the gods that he should dwell again in heaven, whence he had come. Proculus's testimony was accepted, and thereafter the Roman people honored Romulus as a god (ibid. 28.2-3).[195]

The same notion played a role in the institution and cult of the emperors in the early imperial period. According to Pliny the Elder, during games in honor of Mother Venus after the death of Julius Caesar, a comet was visible in the northern part of the sky for seven days. It rose each day about an hour before sunset, and it was so bright that it could be seen from all lands. The common people believed that this star signified that the soul (*anima*) of Caesar was received among the spirits (*numina*) of the immortal gods. For this reason, a star was added to the bust of Caesar that was dedicated shortly thereafter in the forum (Pliny *Hist. nat.* 2.23 §94).[196] Suetonius reported that, the night before he was murdered, Caesar dreamed "now

189 John J. Collins, *Between Athens and Jerusalem: Jewish Identity in the Hellenistic Diaspora* (2nd ed.; Grand Rapids/Cambridge: Eerdmans, 2000) 108. P. W. van der Horst dates the work to the period from 30 BCE to 14 CE (*The Sentences of Pseudo-Phocylides with Introduction and Commentary* [SVTP 4; Leiden: Brill, 1978] 81–82).

190 *Sentences of Phocylides* 103–4; text and trans. from van der Horst, *Sentences of Pseudo-Phocylides*, 94–95; cf. 185. See also John J. Collins, "Life after Death in Pseudo-Phocylides," in idem, *Jewish Cult and Hellenistic Culture: Essays on the Jewish Encounter with Hellenism and Roman Rule* (JSJSup 100; Leiden/Boston: Brill, 2005) 128–42. Collins translates τάχα in line 103 with "perhaps," rather than "soon" (ibid., 128).

191 Cf. the discussion above of Dan 12:2-3, the Epistle of Enoch (*1 Enoch* 104:2-6) and the Similitudes or Parables of Enoch (*1 Enoch* 39:4-7). See also Yarbro Collins, *Beginning of the Gospel*, 143.

192 Pseudo-Callisthenes *Alexander Romance* 3.33; trans. from Richard Stoneman, *The Greek Alexander Romance* (London/New York: Penguin Books, 1991) 157.

193 In other words, Alexander prayed that he might join the company of the Olympian gods as Heracles and Dionysos did (Talbert, "Biographies," 1633–34 and n. 74). Cf. Rev 22:16, where the risen Jesus says that he is "the bright morning star" (ὁ ἀστὴρ ὁ λαμπρὸς ὁ προϊνός).

194 Text and trans. from Perrin, *Plutarch's Lives*, 1:178–79.

195 Plutarch himself did not believe that a body could ascend to heaven (*Vit. Rom.* 28.6-8); see the discussion of 1 Corinthians 15 above. See also the discussion of *Vit. Rom.* 27.6-7 in the commentary on 15:39 above.

196 See Harris Rackham, *Pliny, the Elder: Natural History* (LCL; Cambridge, MA: Harvard University Press, 1938–63) 1:236–37. Dio Cassius has the same story (47.7.1). See Earnest Cary, *Dio's Roman History* (LCL; Cambridge, MA: Harvard University Press, 1914–27) 4:418–19.

that he was flying above the clouds, and now that he was clasping the hand of Jupiter" (Ea vero nocte, cui inluxit dies caedis, et ipse sibi visus est per quietem interdum supra nubes volitare, alias cum Iove dextram iungere) (*Jul.* 81.3).[197] Regarding Caesar's deification, he says:

> He died in the fifty-sixth year of his age, and was numbered among the gods, not only by a formal decree, but also in the conviction of the common people. For at the first of the games which his heir Augustus gave in honor of his apotheosis, a comet shone for seven successive days, rising about the eleventh hour [about an hour before sunset] and was believed to be the soul of Caesar, who had been taken to heaven; and this is why a star is set upon the crown of his head in his statue (Periit sexto et quinquagensimo aetatis anno atque in deorum numerum relatus est, non ore modo decernentium sed et persuasione volgi. Siquidem ludis, quos primos consecrato ei heres Augustus edebat, stella crinita per septem continuos dies fulsit exoriens circa undecimam horam, creditumque est animam esse Caesaris in caelum recepti; et hac de causa simulacro eius in vertice additur stella). (*Jul.* 88)[198]

Regarding Augustus's death, Suetonius says:

> There was even an ex-praetor who took oath that he had seen the form of the Emperor, after he had been reduced to ashes, on its way to heaven (Nec defuit vir praetorius, qui se effigiem cremati euntem in caelum vidisse iuraret). (*Aug.* 100.4)[199]

Dio says that soon after Augustus's death, they declared him to be immortal (ἀθανατίσαντες αὐτόν) and assigned to him priests and sacred rites. He also says that Numenius Atticus, a senator and ex-praetor, swore that he had seen Augustus ascending to heaven in the way that tradition says Proculus swore about Romulus (Dio Cassius 56.46).[200] Tacitus simply says that after Augustus's funeral, a decree followed, endowing him with a temple and divine rites (*templum et caelestes religiones decernuntur*) (Tacitus *Ann.* 1.10 [end]).[201]

Claudius, Vespasian, and Titus were also deified after their deaths.[202] The arch of Titus in Rome has an inscription that indicates that it was dedicated to the deified Titus.[203] At the vertex of the inner roof of the arch is a relief that depicts the apotheosis of Titus with the image of an eagle carrying him to heaven.[204] The arch also commemorates the triumph celebrated by Vespasian and Titus in relation to their victory over Judea.[205] The monument was probably dedicated early in the reign of Domitian.[206]

The author of Mark was probably aware of the idea that some Roman emperors had ascended to heaven and become gods. He may also have known that their deifications were modeled on that of Romulus.

---

197 Text and trans. from Rolfe, *Suetonius,* 1:136–38.

198 Rolfe, *Suetonius,* 1:146–47. See the coins minted under Augustus portraying Caesar with a star above his head in Charles T. Seltman in Stanley A. Cook et al., eds., *The Cambridge Ancient History: Plates IV* (Cambridge: Cambridge University Press, 1934) 200–201 (j). The altar of the Augustan Lares depicts the apotheosis of Caesar with the image of his chariot ascending to heaven (ibid., 130–31 [a]).

199 Rolfe, *Suetonius,* 1:304–5.

200 Cary, *Dio's Roman History,* 7:104–5.

201 Clifford H. Moore and John Jackson, *Tacitus* (LCL; Cambridge, MA: Harvard University Press, 1931–37) 264–65.

202 Suetonius *Claud.* 45; Seneca mocked the deification of Claudius, calling it a "pumpkinification" (*apocolocyntosis*); for a text and trans. see William H. D. Rouse, *Petronius and Seneca. Apocolocyntosis* (LCL; London: Heinemann; New York: Macmillan, 1913). Leighton D. Reynolds, Miriam Griffin, and Elaine Fantham define the work as "a Menippean satire" ("Annaeus Seneca [2], Lucius," *OCD* 96–98, esp. 97). For coins issued by Nero celebrating the apotheosis of Claudius, see Larry Kreitzer, "Apotheosis of the Roman Emperor," *Biblical Archaeologist* 53 (1990) 210–17, esp. 215–16 and the sketch of one of these coins on 216 top.

Suetonius *Vesp.* 23.4. Suetonius does not explicitly mention the deification of Vespasian after his death, but the remark "Woe is me; I think I am becoming a god" ("Vae," inquit, "puto deus fio"), in the passage cited, as well as the title of this part of Suetonius's *The Twelve Caesars*, namely, *The Deified Vespasian* (*Divus Vespasianus*), imply that it was voted. Text and trans. (modified) from Rolfe, *Suetonius,* 2:300–301.

Suetonius *Titus* 11; again, deification is implied in that passage, though not explicitly stated. Note also the title *The Deified Titus* (*Divus Titus*).

203 Michael Pfanner, *Der Titusbogen* (Beiträge zur Erschließung hellenistischer und kaiserzeitlicher Skulptur und Architektur 2; Mainz am Rhein: Philipp von Zabern, 1983) 1, 16.

204 Ibid., 1, and plates 68–69.

205 Ibid., 1, and plates 45–67.

206 Ibid., 91–92.

The Jewish texts referring to resurrection discussed above portray a collective resurrection in the future, of the righteous alone,[207] of both the especially righteous and the especially wicked (Dan 12:2-3), or of all the dead (1 Cor 15:21-22, 26). The only possible exception is 2 Maccabees.[208] The affirmation of followers of Jesus concerning him was that he had been raised from the dead as a single individual. Apart from the context of the collective resurrection, this affirmation seemed quite similar to the claims that Enoch, Elijah, Moses, Romulus, and others had been taken, including their earthly bodies, to heaven. Since the earliest recoverable form of Mark does not depict Jesus as walking the earth in bodily form, it is likely that the author assumed that his earthly body had been transformed.[209]

Comment

■ **1** The genitive absolute διαγενομένου τοῦ σαββάτου ("when the Sabbath was over") connects this scene with the burial, where mention is made of the approaching Sabbath (v. 42). The women see the place where Jesus is buried (v. 47) and return after the Sabbath to anoint him. Their intention to anoint the body of Jesus is problematic, since they arrive after the body has been in the tomb for two nights and a day,[210] but this aim fits well in the overall narrative. It is motivated by the fact that the body of Jesus was not anointed when he was buried.[211] At the same time, the narrated intention of the women is an instance of dramatic irony. The body is not there to be anointed. Furthermore, Jesus declared earlier in the narrative that his body had already been anointed for burial (14:8).

The three women who go to the tomb are the same three who are introduced in 15:40 as observing the crucifixion of Jesus from afar. The designation here of the first woman, Mary of Magdala, is identical with the one

in 15:40. The second woman is the same one mentioned in that verse, but here her identification is abbreviated. The full designation, as given in 15:40, is "Mary, the mother of James the younger and Joses" (Μαρία ἡ Ἰακώβου τοῦ μικροῦ καὶ Ἰωσῆτος μήτηρ). In 15:47, this woman's identification is abbreviated by omitting the name of the first son, James the younger: "Mary the (mother) of Joses" (Μαρία ἡ Ἰωσῆτος). Here it is abbreviated by leaving out the name of the second son, Joses, and by omitting the characterization of the first son as "the younger": "Mary, the (mother) of James" (Μαρία ἡ [τοῦ] Ἰακώβου). "Salome" (Σαλώμη), who appears in 15:40 but whose name is left out in 15:47—probably for the sake of brevity—reappears here.

As Joseph is portrayed as purchasing a linen cloth (σινδών) before taking Jesus' body down from the cross and burying it in 15:46, the women are portrayed here as buying "aromatic (oils)" (ἀρώματα) before they go to the tomb. The time of the women's purchase is not made explicit.

■ **2** Since the women go to the tomb "very early in the morning" (λίαν πρωΐ), "when the sun had risen" (ἀνατείλαντος τοῦ ἡλίου), it may be implied that they purchased the aromatic oils the evening before, once the Sabbath had ended. The tradition concerning the burial of Jesus by Joseph of Arimathea clearly assumes that the day is calculated from evening to evening.[212] It may be that Mark, in contrast, calculates the day from morning to morning. In that case, vv. 1-2 would imply that the Sabbath ended only with the rising of the sun on "the first day of the week" (τῇ μιᾷ τῶν σαββάτων). Audiences who understood a "day" to mean the time from morning to morning, or simply the period of daylight, would infer that the women bought the aromatic oils early in the morning, rather than the evening before.[213]

---

207 The Book of the Watchers (see *1 Enoch* 22:5—25:6; the sinful dead will not arise from the hollows where their spirits or souls are kept after death according to 22:13); also the Animal Apocalypse, unless the judgment of the wicked before they are cast into the abyss of fire implies their resurrection (*1 Enoch* 90:26-27). The Epistle of Enoch speaks about the resurrection of the righteous (*1 Enoch* 103:1-4) and says that the souls of the sinners will be made to go down to Sheol, where they will suffer torments and burning flames (103:5-8). Pseudo-Ezekiel (4Q385 frg. 2 lines 1–10) speaks only about the resurrection of the

righteous. 2 Macc 7:14 explicitly excludes the resurrection of Antiochus.

208 As noted above, some argue that 2 Maccabees 7 implies that the resurrections of the seven brothers and their mother take place immediately after their deaths.

209 Yarbro Collins, *Beginning of the Gospel*, 146–47.

210 Bultmann, *History*, 285 n. 1.

211 See the commentary on v. 46 above.

212 Verses 42-43 imply that Joseph wanted to bury Jesus before sunset, when the Sabbath would begin. See the commentary on these verses above.

Some have argued that this verse is "overloaded" with temporal indicators and that this characteristic indicates the use of a source.[214] But the construction is a typically Markan two-step progression, in which the second phrase qualifies the first: (1) early in the morning (on the first day of the week); (2) after the sun had risen.[215]

■ **3-4** The women's question to one another, "Who will roll the stone away from the entrance of the tomb for us?," like the mention of the end of the Sabbath in v. 1, connects this narrative to the previous one. In 15:46, Joseph is described as rolling a stone in front of the entrance to the tomb. From a mundane perspective, the women's question is problematic, since it shows a lack of planning and forethought on their part. The evangelist, however, is less interested in reporting how things would ideally happen than in constructing a dramatic narrative. The question creates dramatic tension and leads the audiences to expect something extraordinary to occur.[216]

The arrival of the women at the tomb is narrated in a striking manner. They look up and observe that the stone has already been rolled away from the entrance to the tomb. The extraordinary character of this situation is emphasized by the remark that the stone was "extremely large" ($\mu\epsilon\gamma\alpha\varsigma$ $\sigma\phi\delta\rho\alpha$). In the cultural context of this narrative and the preceding one, it may well be assumed that Joseph, as a prominent and wealthy man, did not accomplish the burial and closing of the tomb by himself alone. He would have taken the initiative and overseen the procedures but would have had the help of servants or slaves.[217]

■ **5-6** When the women entered the tomb they saw "a young man sitting on the right, wearing a white robe" ($\nu\epsilon\alpha\nu\iota\sigma\kappa o\nu$ $\kappa\alpha\vartheta\eta\mu\epsilon\nu o\nu$ $\epsilon\nu$ $\tau o\iota\varsigma$ $\delta\epsilon\xi\iota o\iota\varsigma$ $\pi\epsilon\rho\iota\beta\epsilon\beta\lambda\eta$-$\mu\epsilon\nu o\nu$ $\sigma\tau o\lambda\eta\nu$ $\lambda\epsilon\nu\kappa\eta\nu$). The only other time the word $\nu\epsilon\alpha\nu\iota\sigma\kappa o\varsigma$ ("young man") is used in Mark is in 14:51, the description of the young man who ran away naked. The same is true of the verb $\pi\epsilon\rho\iota\beta\alpha\lambda\lambda o\mu\alpha\iota$ ("to wrap around onself" or "to wear"). But if the young man here were identical with the young man of chapter 14, he would be introduced as $\dot{o}$ $\nu\epsilon\alpha\nu\iota\sigma\kappa o\varsigma$ ("*the* young man," that is, the one mentioned earlier) and not simply as $\nu\epsilon\alpha\nu\iota\sigma\kappa o\varsigma$ ("a young man").[218]

The young man of 14:51-52 is a character constructed in *contrast* to Jesus.[219] The young man here is portrayed as symbolically *similar* to the risen Jesus. Just as the risen Jesus is enthroned at the right hand of God, as 12:35-37 implies ($\kappa\alpha\vartheta o\nu$ $\epsilon\kappa$ $\delta\epsilon\xi\iota\omega\nu$ $\mu o\nu$), so this young man is described as "sitting on the right" ($\kappa\alpha\vartheta\eta\mu\epsilon\nu o\nu$ $\epsilon\nu$ $\tau o\iota\varsigma$ $\delta\epsilon\xi\iota o\iota\varsigma$). Since this description has little or no realistic significance in the narrative, the audiences are led to reflect on its symbolic import and to recall the citation of Ps 110:1 (109:1 LXX) earlier in the narrative. The white robe worn by the young man here ($\sigma\tau o\lambda\eta$ $\lambda\epsilon\nu\kappa\eta$) recalls the clothing of Jesus during his transfiguration: "and his clothes became very white and they shone" ($\kappa\alpha\iota$ $\tau\alpha$ $\iota\mu\alpha\tau\iota\alpha$ $\alpha\nu\tau o\nu$ $\epsilon\gamma\epsilon\nu\epsilon\tau o$ $\sigma\tau\iota\lambda\beta o\nu\tau\alpha$ $\lambda\epsilon\nu\kappa\alpha$ $\lambda\iota\alpha\nu$). One way of interpreting the transfiguration is to say that it anticipates Jesus' glorified state after his death.[220] The women do not see the risen Jesus, but the young man communicates to them his resurrected status, both in words and in his person.

Besides representing Jesus symbolically, the young man is a character in the narrative best defined as an angel. The motif of white or shining clothing typically characterizes angels and other heavenly beings.[221] In Second Temple Jewish texts it was a widespread convention to speak of angels as "men" or "young men."[222] Certain characteristics of the narrative reinforce the impression that the "young man" is an angel. When the women see him, they are amazed ($\epsilon\xi\epsilon\vartheta\alpha\mu\beta\eta\vartheta\eta\sigma\alpha\nu$).

---

213 Cf. the commentary on 14:12 above.

214 See the discussion in Yarbro Collins, *Beginning of the Gospel*, 131–32.

215 Neirynck, *Duality in Mark*, 94–96; Yarbro Collins, *Beginning of the Gospel*, 131–32.

216 Bultmann, *History*, 286; Yarbro Collins, *Beginning of the Gospel*, 135.

217 This conjecture is confirmed by the use of the plural in v. 6, "they put him" ($\epsilon\vartheta\eta\kappa\alpha\nu$).

218 Yarbro Collins, *Beginning of the Gospel*, 135 n. 50.

219 See the part of the commentary on 14:51-52 above that follows the "Excursus: Scholarship on 14:51-52."

220 See the commentary on 9:2 above.

221 See "History of the Tradition" in the commentary on 9:2-8 above.

222 The OG of Dan 8:15-16 refers to Gabriel and to another heavenly being, respectively, as $\alpha\nu\vartheta\rho\omega\pi o\varsigma$ ("a man" or "a human being"); Θ uses the term $\alpha\nu\eta\rho$ ("a man") instead. Both versions refer to Gabriel as $\alpha\nu\eta\rho$ in 9:21. A mighty angel, probably Gabriel, is referred to in 10:5 in the OG as $\alpha\nu\vartheta\rho\omega$-$\pi o\varsigma$ ("a man" or "a human being") and in Θ as $\alpha\nu\eta\rho$ ("a man"). Two heavenly messengers of God are referred to as $\nu\epsilon\alpha\nu\iota\alpha\iota$ ("young men") in 2 Macc

Awe, fear or being overwhelmed is a typical reaction ascribed to human beings in accounts of epiphanies of heavenly beings.[223] In such cases, the heavenly being often strengthens or reassures the recipient of the epiphany, as the young man does here: "Do not be amazed" (μὴ ἐκθαμβεῖσθε).[224]

As noted above,[225] the young man is portrayed here as taking the role of the interpreting angel, a stock character in apocalypses and works influenced by them.[226] This role sometimes involves the interpretation of a vision.[227] In other texts, as here, it involves the explanation of a situation.[228] In Acts 1:10-11, the same device is used to comment on the significance of Jesus' ascension.

After comforting the women, the young man says "you are looking for Jesus of Nazareth who has been crucified" (Ἰησοῦν ζητεῖτε τὸν Ναζαρηνὸν τὸν ἐσταυρωμένον). The angel thus reveals that he knows the motivation of the women for coming to the tomb. Indirectly, he also affirms that the tomb in which they find themselves is indeed the one in which Jesus was buried.

Then comes the proclamation, in narrative context, of the resurrection of Jesus, "He is risen" (ἠγέρθη). The following two statements elaborate the proclamation: "he is not here. Look, the place where they put him" (οὐκ ἔστιν ὧδε· ἴδε ὁ τόπος ὅπου ἔθηκαν αὐτόν).[229] They also may be understood as proofs of the reality of Jesus' resurrection.[230]

■ 7 Bultmann argued that this verse is an addition to older tradition by the evangelist, as he believed 14:28 to be.[231] He also regarded v. 7 as secondary because it is based on the assumption that the disciples remained in

Jerusalem after the death of Jesus, whereas older tradition "told of their flight to Galilee, and placed the appearances of the risen Lord there."[232] As argued above, however, 14:28 is not a secondary addition to its context.[233] With regard to the second point, Mark portrays all the male disciples as fleeing when Jesus is arrested, but the text does not indicate whether they fled immediately to Galilee or rather hid themselves somewhere in or near Jerusalem. One can make a case that the earliest tradition placed the resurrection appearances in Galilee,[234] but there is no evidence on which one could base a historical judgment as to whether the disciples fled to Galilee immediately after the arrest of Jesus, immediately after his death, or after the conclusion of the seven days of Passover and Unleavened Bread. The same holds for determining what the earliest tradition said on this matter, if it addressed it at all.

This verse expresses the second announcement of the young man, "So go and say to his disciples and to Peter, 'He is going ahead of you to Galilee; there you will see him, as he said to you'" (ἀλλὰ ὑπάγετε εἴπατε τοῖς μαθηταῖς αὐτοῦ καὶ τῷ Πέτρῳ ὅτι προάγει ὑμᾶς εἰς τὴν Γαλιλαίαν· ἐκεῖ αὐτὸν ὄψεσθε, καθὼς εἶπεν ὑμῖν). There has been a debate about whether προάγει should be translated "he is going ahead of you to Galilee," as translated here, or "he will lead you to Galilee." This debate was occasioned in part by the historical interest in determining where the first resurrection appearances occurred, in Jerusalem or in Galilee.[235] Linguistically, either translation is possible, since προάγω can be employed either transitively or intransi-

---

3:26, 33. In rewriting Judges 13, Josephus said that "an apparition" (φάντασμα) appeared to the wife of Manoah, an angel or messenger of God (ἄγγελος τοῦ θεοῦ), in the likeness of a young man (νεανίας) (*Ant.* 5.8.2 §277). In describing the heavenly being's second visit, he refers to the angel as a νεανίσκος ("young man") (5.8.3 §279).

223 Exod 20:18-21; Ps 47:5-8 LXX (48:4-7 NRSV); Dan 8:15-17 (the OG uses the verb θορυβέομαι; Θ has θαμβέομαι); Dan 10:7-9; *Jos. Asen.* 14:10; 2 Esdr 10:25-28; *Apoc. Abr.* 10:1-2. Cf. 2 Esdr 5:14; *Apoc. Abr.* 16:1; *1 Enoch* 14:9, 14, 24; 21:8.

224 Dan 8:17-18; 10:10-11; *Jos. Asen.* 14:11; 2 Esdr 10:29-31; *Apoc. Abr.* 9:2-4; 10:3-8; *1 Enoch* 14:24—15:2. Cf. 2 Esdr 5:15; 6:33; *Apoc. Abr.* 16:2-4; *1 Enoch* 21:9-10.

225 See "History of the Tradition" above.

226 Bultmann, *History*, 287, 290; Yarbro Collins, *Beginning of the Gospel*, 135-36.

227 Dan 7:15-27; 8:15-26; 2 Esdr 10:27-59.

228 Dan 9:20-27; 10:2—12:4; 12:5-13; 2 Esdr 3:1—5:13; 5:21—6:28; 6:35—9:22.

229 Yarbro Collins, *Beginning of the Gospel*, 136.

230 Bultmann, *History*, 287.

231 See "History of the Tradition" above. See also "Excursus: Galilee and Jerusalem in Mark" and the commentary on 14:26-31 and 14:28 above.

232 Bultmann, *History*, 285.

233 See the commentary on 14:28 above.

234 See "Excursus: Galilee and Jerusalem in Mark" following the trans. of 14:26-31 above.

235 Ibid.

796

tively.[236] Further, Lohmeyer and others have argued that the phrase ἐκεῖ αὐτὸν ὄψεσθε ("there you will see him") refers to the parousia.[237] This interpretation is unlikely because language of "power" (δύναμις) and "glory" (δόξα) associated with the parousia (the coming of the Son of Man) elsewhere in Mark does not occur here (9:1; 13:26; cf. 14:62). In addition, the parousia and Galilee are not associated anywhere else in the Gospel. It is more likely that the promise "there you will see him" refers to the same tradition of appearances (14:28; 16:7) cited by Paul in 1 Cor 15:5.[238]

It was standard literary practice in ancient writings to allude to well-known events that occurred after those being narrated in the text, without actually narrating those later events. The best-known example of this technique is the *Iliad*.[239] Thus, the fact that the appearances of the risen Jesus are not narrated in Mark does not necessarily mean that the author believed that they did not occur or wanted to suppress the tradition that they did. The decision not to narrate them, however, does have the effect of emphasizing the absence of Jesus in the time of the author and audiences (cf. 2:19-20).[240]

The second announcement of the young man, quoted above, indicates the significance of the empty tomb for the disciples. It is the first stage in the fulfillment of the prophecy that Jesus gave them on the Mount of Olives (14:28). At the moment in which the angel is speaking to the women in the tomb, the first part of Jesus' prophecy, "after I am raised" (μετὰ τὸ ἐγερθῆναί με), has been fulfilled. The women are instructed to give the message "to his disciples and to Peter" (τοῖς μαθηταῖς αὐτοῦ καὶ τῷ Πέτρῳ). This instruction, along with the remark at the end, "as he said to you" (καθὼς εἶπεν ὑμῖν), makes clear that the young man's words recall Jesus' saying in 14:28, both for the disciples as characters in the narrative and for the audiences of Mark. The explicit mention of Peter is an indication that Jesus is reaching out to him, through the angel, in spite of his triple denial (14:66-72). The implication is that his failure is not permanent. He will have opportunities in the future to deny himself, to take up his cross, to follow Jesus, and to show that he is not ashamed of Jesus and his words (8:34-38). The same applies to the other disciples who abandoned Jesus at the time of his arrest (14:50).

In comparison with 14:28, a new element in v. 7 is the prediction "there you will see him" (ἐκεῖ αὐτὸν ὄψεσθε). This phrase makes explicit what the earlier saying only implied, that the disciples, perhaps Peter first of all, would see the risen Jesus in Galilee.[241]

■ 8 The two main issues related to the interpretation of v. 8 are whether it is the original ending of Mark[242] and how to interpret it, in general[243] and in relation to v. 7. Most scholars agree that v. 8 is the earliest recoverable ending for a variety of reasons, including the fact that its priority can explain how all the other variants arose.[244] A number of scholars, however, have concluded that v. 8 was not the original conclusion to Mark.[245]

236 BAGD, s.v., προάγω.

237 See "Excursus: Galilee and Jerusalem in Mark" above.

238 Pheme Perkins, *Resurrection: New Testament Witness and Contemporary Reflection* (Garden City, NY: Doubleday, 1984) 120; Yarbro Collins, *Beginning of the Gospel*, 137.

239 J. Lee Magness, *Sense and Absence: Structure and Suspension in the Ending of Mark's Gospel* (SBLSS; Atlanta: SBL/Scholars Press, 1986) 30–31.

240 Crossan, "Empty Tomb and Absent Lord," 145–52.

241 See 1 Cor 15:5 and the discussion above.

242 For a review of scholarship on this issue, see Steven Lynn Cox, *A History and Critique of Scholarship concerning the Markan Endings* (Lewiston, NY: Edwin Mellen, 1993).

243 For a study on "the experience of the ending," see Donald Harrisville Juel, "A Disquieting Silence: The Matter of the Ending," in Beverly Roberts Gaventa and Patrick D. Miller, eds., *The Ending of Mark and the Ends of God: Essays in Memory of Donald Harrisville Juel* (Louisville, KY: Westminster John Knox, 2005) 1–13. Joan L. Mitchell concludes that the fear of the women "is not failed disbelief but a numinous threshold of commitment" (*Beyond Fear and Silence: A Feminist-Literary Approach to the Gospel of Mark* [New York/London: Continuum, 2001] 115).

244 See note g on the trans. of v. 8 above. See also Taylor, 610; Kurt Aland, "Bemerkungen zum Schluss des Markusevangeliums," in Ellis and Wilcox, *Neotestamentica et Semitica*, 157–80; Kurt Aland, "Der Schluss des Markusevangeliums," in Sabbe, *L'Évangile selon Marc*, 435–70; Pesch, 1:40–47; D. C. Parker, *The Living Text of the Gospels* (Cambridge: Cambridge University Press, 1997) 124–47.

245 E.g., Swete, 398–99; Bultmann, *History*, 285; Cranfield, 470–71; Gundry, 1009–12; Evans, 539; Croy, *Mutilation*, 165.

Robert H. Gundry argued that v. 8, in the autograph of Mark, was not the conclusion to the pericope that began with v. 1, but the beginning of a new unit, "the rest of which is now lost."[246] He gives twelve arguments in support of this hypothesis.[247] In the tenth argument, he acknowledges that a "sentence, paragraph, or section may end in γάρ, 'for.'"[248] He argues, nevertheless, that no other book has γάρ as its last word, mentioning Plot. *Enn.* 5.5 as a "possible exception" with reference to an article by P. W. van der Horst.[249] In that article, van der Horst took the position that, "if a sentence can end with γάρ, a book can end with such a sentence."[250] As an example, he pointed to the above-mentioned text, the thirty-second treatise of Plotinus, as edited by Porphyry (*Enneads* 5.5), which ends with γάρ.[251] Following R. Harder, he acknowledges that treatises 30, 31, 32, and 33 constitute one large treatise.[252] But there is evidence that these treatises were originally four separate lectures on the same topic.[253] The lecture in question, presented as a distinct treatise (#32) by Porphyry, ends as follows: "For that which acts is better than that which is acted upon. For it is more perfect" (κρεῖττον γὰρ τὸ ποιοῦν τοῦ ποιουμένου· τελειότερον γάρ).[254]

N. Clayton Croy concluded that the most significant analogies to 16:8 are the Plotinus passage and the twelfth essay of Musonius Rufus.[255] The latter concerns sexual indulgence (περὶ ἀφροδισίων). This short essay (or fragment of an essay) ends with a question followed by a short statement:

What need is there to say that it is an act of licentiousness and nothing less for a master to have relations with a slave? Everyone knows that (ὅτι δ' ἀκρασίας ἔργον καὶ οὐδενὸς ἄλλου ἐστὶ τὸ δεσπότην δούλῃ πλησιάζειν, τί δεῖ καὶ λέγειν; γνώριμον γάρ).[256]

Croy also noted, as others had before him, that a work attributed to Demetrius on epistolary types ends with γάρ, but he found this fact "deceptive," since the final sentence, "For I am in your debt" (ὀφείλω γάρ), is actually the last sentence of a sample letter of the thankful type.[257]

Croy argued that a book *could* end with γάρ, but concluded that the rarity of sentences ending with that conjunction "in narrative prose and their extreme rarity at the end of narrative works" makes it unlikely that Mark originally ended with 16:8. He suggested that the "narrative went on to relate the action of the women, who reported the news to the other disciples. The lost ending contained at least one resurrection appearance story," located in Galilee and focusing on Peter.[258] Kelly Iverson has argued persuasively, however, that the argument from the infrequency of final γάρ in narrative literature does not make it probable that 16:8 is not the original ending of Mark.[259]

246 Gundry, 1009. Evans (539) follows Gundry in this judgment.

247 Gundry, 1009–12.

248 Ibid., 1011, following Thomas E. Boomershine and Gilbert L. Bartholomew, "The Narrative Technique of Mark 16:8," *JBL* 100 (1981) 213–23, esp. the literature cited in 213–14 n. 4. Note that two of the references on 214 are incorrect. The correct references are Carl H. Kraeling, "A Philological Note on Mark 16:8," *JBL* 44 (1925) 357–58; Henry J. Cadbury, "Mark 16:8," *JBL* 46 (1927) 344–45. See also Aland, "Der Schluss des Markusevangeliums," 461–64. Using computer technology, Cox has shown that over a thousand sentences in Greek literature from Homer through the fourteenth century CE end with γάρ (*A History and Critique of Scholarship*, 152–57, 203–4, 223–27). Especially noteworthy are the examples from the LXX: Gen 18:15; 45:3; Isa 29:11; cited by Morton S. Enslin, "ἐφοβοῦντο γάρ, Mark 16:8," *JBL* 46 (1927) 62–68, esp. 63. Cf. R. R. Ottley, "εφοβουντο γαρ [sic] Mark xvi 8," *JTS* 27 (1925–26) 407–9.

249 Gundry, 1011.

250 P. W. van der Horst, "Can a Book End with γάρ? A Note on Mark xvi. 8," *JTS* n.s. 23 (1972) 121–24; quotation from 122. Cox also took this position (*History and Critique of Scholarship*, 211).

251 Van der Horst, "Can a Book End with γάρ?" 123.

252 Ibid.

253 Ibid., 124.

254 Ibid., 123.

255 Croy, *Mutilation*, 48–49.

256 Text and trans. from Cora E. Lutz, *Musonius Rufus: "The Roman Socrates"* (Yale Classical Studies 10; New Haven: Yale University Press, 1947) 84–89; quotation from 88–89.

257 Pseudo-Demetrius, *Epistolary Types* 21; text and trans. from Abraham J. Malherbe, *Ancient Epistolary Theorists* (SBLSBS 19; Atlanta: Scholars Press, 1988) 40–41. See the discussion by Croy, *Mutilation*, 66 n. 14; van der Horst, "Can a Book End with γάρ?" 123.

258 Croy, *Mutilation*, 165.

259 Kelly R. Iverson, "A Further Word on Final *Γάρ* (Mark 16:8)," *CBQ* (2006) 79–94.

In light of the evidence, it seems best to regard v. 8 as the original ending of Mark and to interpret the additional endings as products of later times.[260] The alternative is to argue that (1) the author was prevented from completing his Gospel, or (2) that he did continue after 16:8, but that the continuation was lost or detached at an early date. These hypotheses have already been refuted decisively.[261]

The issue of the relation between v. 8 and v. 7 in the Easter narrative of Mark has also been important in the interpretation of v. 8. Bultmann argued that, in the present form of Mark, the statement "they said nothing to anyone" in v. 8 implies that the women did not carry out the angel's instructions. But he rejected the conclusion that this implication was the original meaning of the empty-tomb story and thus of v. 8. Further, he concluded that the original ending of Mark "must have recounted the appearance of Jesus in Galilee."[262] The evidence led J. M. Creed to argue in the opposite direction. According to him, vv. 7 and 8 contradict each other, and no consistent continuation of the narrative is possible. Thus Mark must have ended with v. 8.[263] What is needed, however, is an interpretation that makes sense of both v. 7 and v. 8 in their present context.

Before the issue of interpretation can be addressed, a few more philological or stylistic details should be discussed. With regard to the issue of the concluding sentence ending with "for" (γάρ), it should be noted that the Gospel of Mark includes many explanatory comments linked to their contexts with this conjunction.[264]

Since these comments follow the statement that they are explaining or elaborating, the force of this observation is that the use of this conjunction in 16:8 does not require any continuation of the narrative to fulfill its role in the context.[265]

Some opponents of the thesis that v. 8 is the original conclusion of the Gospel have argued that the verb "they were afraid" (ἐφοβοῦντο) is incomplete as it stands and must have been followed originally by an object, an infinitive, or a clause introduced with the conjunction μή ("that . . . [not]" or "lest"). Apart from 16:8, the verb "to be afraid" (φοβεῖσθαι) occurs eleven times in Mark. It is used with a personal object four times (6:20; 11:18, 32; 12:12).[266] Once it is used in the phrase ἐφοβήθησαν φόβον μέγαν ("they were very fearful"; lit. "they feared a great fear") (4:41).[267] On one occasion it is used with the infinitive: "they were afraid to ask him" (ἐφοβοῦντο αὐτὸν ἐπερωτῆσαι) (9:32).[268] This verb is never used with the conjunction μή ("that . . . [not]" or "lest") in Mark. It is used five times absolutely, as in 16:8.[269] In each of these cases, the cause of the fear is at least somewhat ambiguous. This is especially true in 10:32.[270]

In 16:8, however, the cause of the fear is clear from the context. It points backward, not forward. In the first part of the verse, it is clear that the trembling and amazement that seized the women were caused by what they had seen and heard in the tomb. The disappearance of Jesus' body, the presence of an angel, and the announcement that Jesus had risen from the dead are events that go beyond, or even contradict, ordinary expectations and

---

260 On vv. 9-20 as a composition of the second century, see Kelhoffer, *Miracle and Mission*, 243–480.

261 Lightfoot, *Gospel Message*, 80–85; Aland, "Der Schluss des Markusevangeliums," 455–61.

262 Bultmann, *History*, 285.

263 J. M. Creed, "The Conclusion of the Gospel according to Saint Mark," *JTS* 31 (1930) 175–80. He assumed that the empty-tomb story is pre-Markan and that Mark interpolated v. 7 into it, not noticing the contradiction that he had introduced (180).

264 Mark 1:16, 38; 2:15; 3:21; 5:8, 28, 42; 6:18, 20, 31, 48, 50; 7:3; 9:6 (ἔκφοβοι γὰρ ἐγένοντο), 34; 11:13, 18 (ἐφοβοῦντο γὰρ αὐτόν), 32; 12:12; 14:2, 40; 15:10; 16:4; cited by Olof Linton, "Der vermißte Markusschluß," *Theologische Blätter* 8 (1929) 229–34, esp. 230. Boomershine and Bartholomew have a similar list, which lacks 1:38; 6:50; 11:18, 32; 12:12 and has, in addition, 1:22; 6:17; 10:22; 14:56 ("Narrative

Technique," 215). They designate these explanatory comments as "narrative commentary" and describe them as communication between the narrator and his audience (214). The statement that "[n]arrative comments introduced by γάρ are almost always used to explain *confusing or surprising events* which have been reported in previous sentences" does not apply to all of their examples (215; emphasis added).

265 Linton, "Der vermißte Markusschluß," 230.

266 See ibid.

267 Ibid.

268 Ibid.

269 Mark 5:15, 33, 36; 6:50; 10:32. See Linton, "Der vermißte Markusschluß," 230.

270 Cf. the use of the verb "to be amazed" (ἐκθαμβεῖσθαι) in 9:15; Linton, "Der vermißte Markusschluß," 230.

experience. The second part of v. 8, "and they said nothing to anyone; for they were afraid," continues the description of the impact that the experience at the tomb had on the women. Their silence is a result of their being struck with awe at the extraordinary events.[271] The tension between the commission given the women by the angel in v. 7 and the silence of the women in v. 8 is due to the depiction of the overwhelming effect of the overall experience on the women. The text does not address the question whether the women eventually gave the disciples and Peter the message. It focuses rather on the numinous and shocking character of the event of Jesus' resurrection from the dead.

This interpretation is supported by primary texts within and outside of Mark. In the account of the stilling of the storm, the disciples are presented indirectly as having an ordinary fear of the storm when they wake Jesus and say "don't you care that we are perishing?" (4:38). When Jesus has put a stop to the storm, however, they experience a different kind of fear (4:41). They are terrified when they see Jesus, whom they presume to be an ordinary human being, act with divine power.[272] Furthermore, a reaction of amazement or awe is typical of the responses of those present to the mighty deeds of Jesus.[273] This kind of reaction is related to the typical human response to a theophany or epiphany.

A good example of overwhelmed, awestruck flight in response to a divine epiphany occurs in a hymn to Demeter by Callimachus. Demeter, disguised as her priestess, warns a youth to stop cutting down her sacred trees. Rather than desist, he defies her:

But Demeter was unspeakably enraged, and took on her godlike shape again: her steps touched the ground, but her head touched Olympus. When they [the young man and his servants] saw the goddess they started away, half-dead with fear, leaving their bronze implements in the trees (Δαμάτηρ δ᾽ ἄφατόν τι κοτέσσατο, γείνατο δ᾽ αὖ θεύς· ἴθματα μὲν χέρσω, κεφαλὰ δέ οἱ ἅψατ᾽ Ὀλύμπω. οἱ μὲν ἄρ᾽ ἡμιθνῆτες, ἐπεὶ τὰν πότνιαν εἶδον, ἐξαπίνας ἀπόρουσαν ἐνὶ δρυσὶ χαλκὸν ἀφέντες). (Callimachus Hymn VI [to Demeter] 57–60)[274]

In Greek literature, "Fear is a common reaction to divine epiphany."[275] In biblical literature, the appearance of an angel is analogous to the Greek divine epiphany.[276]

Gundry, following and citing C. E. B. Cranfield, argued that "it is highly improbable that Mark intended to conclude his gospel without at least one account of a Resurrection appearance" since resurrection appearances were part of the early Christian kerygma.[277] This type of argument was already well refuted by Olof Linton.[278] One can observe a progression from Mark, to Matthew and John, to Luke-Acts, to apocryphal Gospels. The earliest tradition about the resurrection linked it indissolubly with the exaltation of Jesus (Phil 2:9-11; Rom 1:3-4; Mark 14:62). Later, accounts of the resurrection appearances began to imply that, when Jesus rose from the dead, he returned to a bodily existence much like the one he had had before his death (Luke 24:37-43; John 20:20, 25-27).[279] The apocryphal Gospels and related texts elaborate the beginning and the ending of

---

271 Similarly, Linton, "Der vermißte Markusschluß," 230–31.

272 The fear of the Gerasenes in 5:15 and the fear of the disciples in 10:32 may be analogous to that of the women here (ibid., 231). See also the commentary on 4:41; 5:14-17; and 10:32a above.

273 Mark 1:27; 2:12; 5:42; 6:51; 7:37.

274 Text and trans. from Neil Hopkinson, *Callimachus, Hymn to Demeter: Edited with an Introduction and Commentary* (Cambridge Classical Texts and Commentaries 27; Cambridge: Cambridge University Press, 1984) 66–67; see also Alexander W. Mair, *Callimachus, Hymns and Epigrams* (LCL; Cambridge, MA: Harvard University Press; London: Heinemann, 1921) 128–29.

275 Hopkinson, *Callimachus*, 132 on lines 59–60.

276 E.g., Judg 6:21-23; Dan 8:17; 10:4-19. Note that the trans. of the latter text attributed to Theodotion speaks about Daniel's companions fleeing in fear (καὶ ἔφυγον ἐν φόβῳ) when his vision commences (10:7), in a way analogous to the flight of the women in Mark, even though Daniel alone saw the vision. The OG of 10:7 is also analogous: "and a mighty fear fell upon them, and they ran away in haste" (καὶ φόβος ἰσχυρὸς ἐπέπεσεν ἐπ᾽ αὐτούς, καὶ ἀπέδρασαν ἐν σπουδῇ).

277 Gundry (1012) citing Cranfield, 471.

278 Linton, "Der vermißte Markusschluß," 232.

279 Matt 28:9 implies a solid body, so that the women can take hold of Jesus' feet; but the appearance to the eleven in 28:16-20 is more spiritual and is a kind of vision, like the appearances as described by Paul (1 Cor 15:4-8).

the story of Jesus as found in the canonical Gospels more than the account of his ministry. Furthermore, Luke-Acts distinguishes between the resurrection of Jesus and his exaltation explicitly, by narrating his definitive ascension to heaven in Acts 1:9-11.

For the author of Mark, writing near the beginning of this process, the tradition about the appearances of Jesus did not seem to be an integral part of the story of Jesus. This is already clear from the predictions of the passion, which mention his death and resurrection, but not appearances (8:31; 9:31; 10:33-34). A shift in focus can also be noted in the kerygma as summarized by Paul in 1 Cor 15:3-8. The first part focuses on Jesus, and it is the predicates that change: "he died" ($\dot{\alpha}\pi\acute{\epsilon}\vartheta\alpha\nu\epsilon\nu$), "he was buried" ($\dot{\epsilon}\tau\acute{\alpha}\varphi\eta$), and "he rose" ($\dot{\epsilon}\gamma\acute{\eta}\gamma\epsilon\rho\tau\alpha\iota$). In the second part, the focus is on those to whom the risen Jesus appeared. The predicate stays the same, "he appeared" ($\ddot{\omega}\varphi\vartheta\eta$), and it is the indirect objects that change: "to Cephas (Peter)" ($K\eta\varphi\tilde{\alpha}$), "to the Twelve" ($\tau o\hat{\iota}\varsigma \delta\acute{\omega}\delta\epsilon\kappa\alpha$), "to more than five hundred brothers (and sisters)" ($\dot{\epsilon}\pi\acute{\alpha}\nu\omega \pi\epsilon\nu\tau\alpha\kappa o\sigma\acute{\iota}o\iota\varsigma \dot{\alpha}\delta\epsilon\lambda\varphi o\hat{\iota}\varsigma$), "to James" ($I\alpha\kappa\acute{\omega}\beta\omega$), "to all the apostles" ($\tau o\hat{\iota}\varsigma \dot{\alpha}\pi o\sigma\tau\acute{o}\lambda o\iota\varsigma \pi\hat{\alpha}\sigma\iota\nu$) "and to me (Paul)" ($\kappa\dot{\alpha}\mu o\acute{\iota}$). The explicit marking of sequence in the list of appearances, "then" ($\epsilon\hat{\iota}\tau\alpha$) . . . , "thereupon" ($\ddot{\epsilon}\pi\epsilon\iota\tau\alpha$), suggests that the appearance to Peter is the first in a series. Paul's concern to include himself in the list implies that such appearances, at least in the case of certain individuals, endowed their recipients with authority in the early communities of those who accepted Jesus as the messiah.

Mark drew the line, that is, ended his Gospel, after the first part of the kerygma: "he rose."[280] The author of Luke-Acts drew another kind of line after the appearance(s) to the Twelve. Up to that point, the appearances are bodily. Thereafter, they are more spiritual: the descent of the Holy Spirit on a group (the five hundred?) in Acts 2:1-4 and the visions that Paul has of the risen Lord, which are described quite differently from the association of the risen Jesus with the Twelve in Luke 24 and Acts 1.

The evangelist alludes to the appearance(s) in 14:28 and 16:7. He did not need actually to narrate one or more appearance accounts because he wrote for an audience that knew the tradition about appearances of the risen Lord from the oral proclamation.[281] As argued above, the "young man" is best understood as an angel and probably was so understood by early audiences. Thus, his prediction, or promise, that the disciples and Peter would see Jesus (experience a resurrection appearance) in Galilee can be taken as reliable.[282] How exactly the appearance would take place, even in light of the women's silence, would probably not have been an issue for the early audiences. It was only after Matthew, Luke, and John became widely known that the ending of Mark seemed deficient. It was this new perception that led to the addition of further material after 16:8.

The conclusion that Mark ended with 16:8 is supported by the emphasis throughout the Gospel on the "numinous" or on the human response of "wonder" to the manifestation of heavenly power in an earthly context.[283]

---

280 "He rose"; $\dot{\epsilon}\gamma\acute{\eta}\gamma\epsilon\rho\tau\alpha\iota$ in 1 Cor 15:3 and $\mathring{\eta}\gamma\acute{\epsilon}\rho\vartheta\eta$ in Mark 16:6. Although his reasons are different, Larry W. Hurtado also concludes that a resurrection appearance was not necessary to fulfill the narrative purposes of Mark ("The Women, the Tomb, and the Climax of Mark," in Anne Fitzpatrick McKinley, Margaret Daly Denton, Brian McGing, and Zuleika Rodgers, eds., [Festschrift for Sean Freyne; Leiden: Brill, forthcoming, p. 45 of MS]).

281 Compare the evident assumption that the audience knows what "gospel" or "good news" ($\epsilon\dot{\upsilon}\alpha\gamma\gamma\acute{\epsilon}\lambda\iota o\nu$) means in 1:1; see the commentary on that verse above.

282 Linton argued that the angel's command in v. 7 does not *prepare* for appearance accounts but rather *represents* them ("Der vermißte Markusschluß," 232-33).

283 Ibid., 233-34; Dwyer, *Wonder*, 195.

16

The Shorter (Additional) Ending

They then promptly reported to those around Peter all the things that had been commanded. And afterward, through their agency, Jesus himself also sent forth the holy and imperishable proclamation of eternal salvation from the east as far as the west. Amen.[a]

a   The Greek text appears in Nestle-Aland (27th ed.) in double brackets following 16:8. The raised numeral 1 after the opening double brackets indicates that this is the first of two additional endings of Mark.

Comment

There is only one known manuscript that contains Mark 16:1-8 plus this shorter (additional) ending alone, namely, Codex Bobiensis. This codex is one of the Old Latin manuscripts and is referred to in the critical apparatus of the Greek New Testament with the letter k. It dates to the fourth or fifth century. It continues from v. 8 to this additional ending without a break or any text-critical indication of separation or difference in origin. In order to prepare for the additional ending, this manuscript omits the Latin equivalent of the words "and they said nothing to anyone" (καὶ οὐδενὶ οὐδὲν εἶπαν) in v. 8.[1] This ending, however, is attested also by a number of manuscripts that contain 16:8 + the shorter (additional) ending + 9-20, the longer (additional) ending. These manuscripts represent a conflation of the text of one or more exemplars that contained only the shorter ending and one or more others that contained only the longer ending. They include a number of Ethiopic, Coptic, Syriac, and Greek manuscripts.[2] In all these witnesses, the shorter ending is placed before the longer.[3] The shorter (additional) ending probably originated in the second century CE.[4] The location of its origin is uncertain. Codex Bobiensis (k) was apparently written in North Africa.[5] Its Latin version of the shorter (addi-

tional) ending is probably based on a Greek exemplar.[6] Another Old Latin manuscript, Codex Vercellensis (a), is now defective but probably once contained the shorter ending. This manuscript was probably written in Europe in the fourth century CE.[7]

The phrase "those around Peter" (οἱ περὶ τὸν Πέτρον) also occurs in a letter of Ignatius:

For I know and believe that he was in the flesh even after the resurrection. And when he came to those around Peter, he said to them, "Reach out, touch me and see that I am not a bodiless daimon" (Ἐγὼ γὰρ μετὰ τὴν ἀνάστασιν ἐν σαρκὶ αὐτὸν οἶδα καὶ πιστεύω ὄντα. καὶ ὅτε πρὸς τοὺς περὶ Πέτρον ἦλθεν, ἔφη αὐτοῖς· λάβετε, ψηλαφήσατέ με καὶ ἴδετε, ὅτι οὐκ εἰμὶ δαιμόνιον ἀσώματον). (Smyrn. 3.1–2)[8]

Since the context in Ignatius is reminiscent of Luke 24:37-39, it is likely that "those around Peter" are the eleven, the Twelve without Judas.[9] The same group is likely to be meant in the shorter ending.[10]

The expression "from the east as far as the west" (ἀπὸ ἀνατολῆς ἄχρι δύσεως) is similar to a phrase in Ps 112:3 LXX, "from the east as far as the west," literally "from the rising of the sun as far as (its) setting" (ἀπὸ ἀνατολῶν ἡλίου μέχρι δυσμῶν).[11] This is probably not a case of

---

1   Kurt Aland, "Der Schluss des Markusevangeliums," in Sabbe, *L'Évangile selon Marc*, 435–70, esp. 441. See also Kurt Aland, "Bemerkungen zum Schluss des Markusevangeliums," in Ellis and Wilcox, *Neotestamentica et Semitica*, 157–80, esp. 162–63.

2   See the apparatus to the shorter ending in Nestle-Aland (27th ed.); see also Aland, "Der Schluss des Markusevangeliums," 447–48.

3   Aland, "Der Schluss des Markusevangeliums," 448.

4   Aland, "Bemerkungen," 177–78.

5   Ibid., 169.

6   Ibid., 176.

7   Ibid., 176–77.

8   Text and trans. (modified) from Ehrman, *Apostolic Fathers*, 1:298–99. In an earlier Loeb edition, Lake translated δαιμόνιον with "phantom," rather than "daimon." This passage is cited by Aland, "Bemerkungen," 179.

9   The eleven are specifically mentioned in Mark 16:14; cf. Luke 24:9 (Aland, "Bemerkungen," 179).

10 See the analogous expressions in Acts 2:14; 5:29 (Aland, "Bemerkungen," 179).

11 Aland, "Bemerkungen," 173. He refers also to *1 Clem.* 5:6 and rejects a literary connection to the shorter ending in both cases.

literary dependence or even allusion, since it is an old and widespread formula expressing the totality of space.[12]

The word "proclamation" (κήρυγμα) is not uncommon in early Christian literature.[13] It occurs in Rom 16:25, part of a passage (vv. 25-27) that is not Pauline, but arose in the process of the collection of Paul's letters. It may be that "it is connected with the elimination of the destination in 1:7, 15 and thus presents the 'catholic' significance of the epistle as a whole."[14] This passage, like the shorter (additional) ending of Mark, may date to the second century.

The entire phrase, "the holy and imperishable proclamation" (τὸ ἱερὸν καὶ ἄφθαρτον κήρυγμα), is quite unusual and distinctive,[15] but the notion of "eternal salvation" (ἡ αἰώνιος σωτηρία) is similar to Heb 5:9 and may derive from Isa 45:17.[16] Heb 5:9 speaks about the "perfected" Christ as "the cause of eternal salvation" for those who are obedient to him (καὶ τελειωθεὶς ἐγένετο πᾶσιν τοῖς ὑπακούουσιν αὐτῷ αἴτιος σωτηρίας αἰωνίου). Isa 45:17 LXX states that "Israel is saved by the Lord (who thus effects) an eternal salvation" (Ἰσραηλ σῴζεται ὑπὸ κυρίου σωτηρίαν αἰώνιον).

The scribe or editor who added this ending evidently did not understand that the silence of the women is a way of emphasizing the overwhelming mystery of the resurrection of Jesus and the terror inspired by the presence of an angel in the tomb announcing that event.[17]

The silence of the women was perceived as so problematic that the relevant words were omitted in at least one manuscript. This ending resolves the problem of the silence by affirming that the women did carry out the angel's instructions and gave the message to Peter and the rest of the eleven.

The author of the shorter (additional) ending was probably familiar with at least one of the Gospels that later became canonical and perceived the ending of Mark with 16:8 to be deficient in comparison with them. In the other Gospels, the risen Jesus gives the disciples a commission. In Matthew, it has to do with making disciples (μαθητεύειν) and teaching (διδάσκειν) (Matt 28:19-20). In Luke, it concerns proclaiming repentance for the forgiveness of sins (κηρύσσειν μετάνοιαν εἰς ἄφεσιν ἁμαρτιῶν) (Luke 24:47). In John, the disciples are to forgive or retain sins (ἀφεῖναι/κρατεῖν τὰς ἁμαρτίας) by the Holy Spirit (John 20:21-23). Very tersely, in the implied setting of an appearance of the risen Jesus, an analogous commission is added in this ending. Although it is expressed in a different style and for a later cultural context, the sending out of "the holy and imperishable proclamation of eternal salvation" by the risen Jesus through the disciples is a fitting concluding commission for Mark, in which "good news" (εὐαγγέλιον) and "proclaiming" (κηρύσσειν) play an important role.[18]

---

16   The Longer (Additional) Ending and the Freer Logion

9/ When he rose, early on the first day of the week, he appeared first to Mary of Magdala, from whom he had driven out seven demons. 10/ She went and reported to those who had been with him, who were mourning and weeping. 11/ But they, when they heard that he had become alive

---

12   See the comment on Ps 113:3 MT by Kraus, *Psalms 60–150*, 368. See also Isa 45:6 LXX.

13   Matt 12:41||Luke 11:32 (proclamation of Jonah); Rom 16:25; 1 Cor 1:21; 2:4; 15:14; 2 Tim 4:17; Tit 1:3; *Barn.* 12:6; *Hermas Sim.* 8.3.2; 9.15.4; 9.16.5. For further references, see Aland, "Bemerkungen," 173–74.

14   Ernst Käsemann, *Commentary on Romans* (Grand Rapids: Eerdmans, 1980; ET of German 4th ed. 1980) 423.

15   Aland, "Bermerkungen," 173–75.

16   Ibid., 173; Attridge, *Hebrews*, 154.

17   See the commentary on 16:8 above.

18   Cf. Mark 1:1, 14, 15; 8:35; 10:29; 13:10; 14:9 for "good news" (εὐαγγέλιον) and 1:4, 7, 14, 38, 39, 45; 3:14; 5:20; 6:12; 7:36; 13:10; 14:9 for "proclaiming" (κηρύσσειν).

12/ Afterward, he appeared in a different form to two of them as they were walking, going into the country. 13/ They also went and reported to the rest. They did not believe them either.

14/ Later, he appeared to the eleven themselves while they were at table and censured their unbelief and hardness of heart because they did not believe those who had seen him after he had risen. 15/ And he said to them, "Go to all the world and proclaim the gospel to all creation. 16/ The one who believes and is baptized will be saved, but the one who refuses to believe will be condemned. 17/ These signs then will attend those who believe: in my name they will drive out demons, they will speak in unknown languages, 18/ they will pick up snakes; even if they drink something deadly, it will surely not harm them; they will lay their hands upon ill people, and they will be well."

19/ The Lord Jesus then, after he had spoken to them, was taken up into heaven and sat on the right of God. 20/ They then went out and proclaimed in all directions, while the Lord worked together (with them) and confirmed the word through the accompanying signs.

Attestation of the Longer (Additional) Ending

The longer ending of Mark is attested in four different ways:

1. following 16:1-8, but set off by text-critical signs or annotations;
2. following 16:1-8 in a continuous text;
3. 16:1-8 + 9-14 + the Freer Logion + 15b-20;
4. 16:1-8 + the shorter ending + 9-20.[19]

In the first text form, asterisks, obeli, annotations, or other means are used to indicate doubt about the authenticity of vv. 9-20, that is, about whether those verses originally belonged to the text of Mark.[20] The manuscripts that take this form have been divided into six types:

a. In three minuscules,[21] two from the twelfth cent. and one from the eleventh, vv. 9-20 are set off from vv. 1-8 with obeli or asterisks by a later hand;[22]

---

19 Aland, "Der Schluss des Markusevangeliums," 436.
20 Ibid., 442.
21 "Minuscules" are MSS dating from the ninth to the sixteenth cent. that were written in a script of smaller letters (than had been customary beforehand) in a running hand (Metzger and Ehrman, *Text*, 17–21; Aland and Aland, 81).
22 Aland, "Der Schluss des Markusevangeliums," 443.

b. In minuscule 199 (twelfth cent.), the following note appears in the margin by v. 9: "in some of the copies this is not found; rather, it stops here" (ἔν τισι τῶν ἀντιγράφων οὐ κεῖται τούτω [sic]. ἀλλ᾽ ἐνταῦθα καταπαύει).[23]

c. In two minuscules of the eleventh cent., which contain the Gospels with commentary, a note was placed secondarily between the block of text and the commentary on it: "(the material) from here until the end is not found in some of the copies; but in the old ones, all (of it) is found without exception" (ἐντεῦθεν ἕως τοῦ τέλους ἔν τισι τῶν ἀντιγράφων οὐ κεῖται· ἐν δὲ τοῖς ἀρχαίοις πάντα ἀπαράλειπτα κεῖται).[24]

d. The minuscules of Family 1 contain the following note: "In some of the copies, the evangelist is set out fully up to this place; Eusebius also, the (pupil of) Pamphilus, only went this far in his canons; but in many (copies) this also is in circulation" (ἔν τισι μὲν τῶν ἀντιγράφων ἕως ὧδε πληροῦται ὁ εὐαγγελιστής· ἕως οὗ καὶ εὐσέβιος ὁ παμφίλου ἐκανόνισεν· ἐν πολλοῖς δὲ καὶ ταῦτα φέρεται).[25] In most of the manuscripts, this note occurs between 16:8 and 16:9. Occasionally, it is highlighted with ornamental frames or asterisks.[26]

e. Many manuscripts give an indirect witness to the (original) ending of Mark with 16:8 by the evidence that they provide that the canons of Eusebius ended at that point.[27]

f. In the fifth cent., Victor of Antioch fashioned a commentary on Mark that consisted of a series of excerpts from exegetical and homiletic writings of earlier authors. Most manuscripts that contain this commentary have a note to the following effect: "In most copies this additional material in the Gospel according to Mark is not found, so that some have considered it to be spurious. But we, inasmuch as we have found it in most of the accurate copies in accordance with the Palestinian Gospel of Mark, have included it, as the truth requires, and (have included) the additional (account of the) resurrection of the Lord in it after the (words) 'for they were afraid'" (παρὰ πλείστοις ἀντιγράφοις οὐ κεῖνται ταῦτα ἐπιφερόμενα ἐν τῷ κατὰ μάρκον εὐαγγελίῳ, ὡς νόθα νομίσαντες αὐτὰ τινες εἶναι· ἡμεῖς δὲ ἐξ ἀκριβῶν ἀντιγράφων ὡς ἐν πλείστοις εὑρόντες αὐτὰ κατὰ τὸ παλαιστιναῖον εὐαγγέλιον μάρκου, ὡς ἔχει ἡ ἀλήθεια συντεθείκαμεν, καὶ τὴν ἐν αὐτῷ ἐπιφερομένην δεσποτικὴν ἀνάστασιν μετὰ τὸ ἐφοβοῦντο γάρ).[28] This comment is found in manuscripts dating from the tenth to the sixteenth century.[29]

The second text form, which has vv. 9-20 following directly on v. 8 in a continuous text, became the normal form of the text in the church. This form is attested by the overwhelming majority of the manuscripts.[30]

The third text form has 16:1-8 + 9-14 + the Freer Logion + 15b-20. At present, this form is attested in only one manuscript, Codex Freerianus, represented by "W" in the apparatus. It was copied in the fourth or fifth cent.[31] Jerome, however, wrote that he found this text form in "certain copies and especially in Greek codices" (quibusdam exemplaribus et maxime in graecis codicibus).[32]

In this manuscript, the phrase "and he said to them" (καὶ εἶπεν αὐτοῖς) at the beginning of v. 15 is omitted. Between v. 14 and the rest of v. 15, the following speech of the disciples is inserted:

---

23 Text from Aland (ibid; my trans.).

24 Text from Aland (ibid.; my trans.). Aland notes that, even though these MSS describe the situation in terms opposite to the actual historical circumstances, they nevertheless attest to the existence of MSS at the time that ended with 16:8 (ibid).

25 Text from Aland, "Der Schluss des Markusevangeliums," 443; see also Nestle-Aland (27th ed.), apparatus to second additional ending; my trans.

26 Aland, "Der Schluss des Markusevangeliums," 443; on Family 1, see also Aland and Aland, 129. On the Eusebian canons, see Metzger and Ehrman, Text, 38–39.

27 These include, e.g., Codex Sinaiticus (Aland, "Der Schluss des Markusevangeliums," 443–44).

28 Text from Aland, "Der Schluss des Markusevangeliums," 444; my trans. See the discussion, ibid., 444–46.

29 Aland, "Der Schluss des Markusevangeliums," 445.

30 Ibid., 446.

31 Ibid., 446; on Codex Freerianus (W), see Metzger and Ehrman, Text, 80–81.

32 Text from Aland, "Der Schluss des Markusevangeliums," 447; my trans.

But they defended themselves, saying, "This age of lawlessness and unbelief is under (the power of) Satan, who does not permit, by the agency of the unclean spirits, the truth (and) power of God[33] to be grasped. For this reason, reveal your righteousness now," they said to Christ. And Christ replied to them, "The limit of the years of the authority of Satan has been reached, but other afflictions are drawing near. And I was handed over to death for those who had sinned in order that they might return to the truth and no longer sin so that they might inherit the spiritual and imperishable glory of righteousness which is in heaven" (κακεινοι απελογουντο λεγοντες οτι ο αιων ουτος της ανομιας και της απιστιας υπο σαταναν εστιν, τον μη εωντα υπο των πνευματων ακαθαρτων την αληθειαν[34] του θεου καταλαβεσθαι δυναμιν· δια τουτο αποκαλυψον σου την δικαιοσυνην ηδη, εκεινοι ελεγον τω χριστω. και ο χριστος εκεινοις προσελεγεν οτι πεπληρωται ο ὅρος των ετων της εξουσιας του σατανα, ἀλλὰ ἐγγιζει ἄλλα δεινα· καὶ υπερ ων εγω αμαρτησαντων παρεδοθην εις θανατον ινα υποστρεψωσιν εις την αληθειαν και μηκετι αμαρτησωσιν ινα την εν τω ουρανω πνευματικην και αφθαρτον της δικαιοσυνης δοξαν κληρονομησωσιν).[35]

The word "But" (ἀλλά) is then added in order to take up the command in v. 15, "Go to all the world etc.," and to indicate that the preceding discussion is a settled matter.[36]

The Freer Logion is clearly an expansion of the longer ending and not an independent additional ending to Mark.[37] It was added apparently to soften the transition from v. 14 to v. 15 in the longer ending.[38]

The Authenticity of the Longer Ending

The authenticity of the longer ending was rarely questioned from the second half of the second century until the nineteenth century.[39] The emergence of the disciplines of paleography and textual criticism, however, led to a consensus that the earliest recoverable ending of Mark is 16:8. A major factor in the establishment of this new consensus was the publication of a critical edition of the Greek New Testament by Westcott and Hort.[40] In reaction, John William Burgon defended the longer ending of Mark (and the Textus Receptus) in 1871.[41] The vast majority, however, accepted the "short ending," that is, at 16:8, as the earliest recoverable.

When Kenneth Clark stated in his presidential address to the SBL in 1965 that the authenticity of the longer ending was still an open question, William Farmer was inspired to write a monograph defending its genuineness, published in 1974.[42] Although his work has been heavily criticized,[43] his stylistic analyses provided a basis for further work.[44]

---

33 Or "the true power of God."

34 Or, if the text is emended, αληθινην.

35 Text from apparatus to the second additional ending (on v. 14) in Nestle-Aland (27th ed.), with some emendations suggested there in parentheses; my trans.

36 See the apparatus to v. 15 in Nestle-Aland (27th ed.); on this use of ἀλλά, see BAGD, s.v., 3.

37 Aland, "Der Schluss des Markusevangeliums," 447.

38 See the commentary on v. 15 and the Freer Logion below.

39 Kelhoffer, *Miracle and Mission*, 6; Steven Lynn Cox, *A History and Critique of Scholarship concerning the Markan Endings* (Lewiston, NY: Edwin Mellen, 1993) 13–51; Croy, *Mutilation*, 19–20.

40 Westcott and Hort; Croy, *Mutilation*, 19–21. On "The Fall of the 'Textus Receptus' (1831–1934)," see Léon Vaganay and Christian-Bernard Amphoux, *An Introduction to New Testament Textual Criticism* (2nd ed.; Cambridge/New York: Cambridge University Press, 1991) 145–61.

41 Kelhoffer, *Miracle and Mission*, 17–18; Cox, *History and Critique*, 56–72; John William Burgon, *The Last Twelve Verses of the Gospel according to S. Mark: Vindicated against Recent Critical Objectors and Established* (Oxford/London: James Parker, 1871; reprinted Ann Arbor, MI: Associated Publishers and Authors, 1959).

42 Kelhoffer, *Miracle and Mission*, 32–33; Cox, *History and Critique*, 81–84; Kenneth W. Clark, "The Theological Relevance of Textual Variation in Current Criticism of the Greek New Testament," *JBL* 85 (1966) 1–16; William Farmer, *The Last Twelve Verses of Mark* (SNTSMS 25; Cambridge: Cambridge University Press, 1974).

43 Cox, *History and Critique*, 84–90.

44 Kelhoffer, *Miracle and Mission*, 34 n. 133.

A few scholars have argued that the original ending of Mark is contained in the longer ending. Eta Linnemann argued that the Gospel originally ended with 16:1-8, plus the substance of Matt 28:16-17, followed by Mark 16:15-20.[45] Her argument was refuted by Kurt Aland.[46] In 1986, Paul Mirecki argued that 16:9a, 10-15 and 20a constituted the original ending of Mark, which followed directly upon 15:47. In his view, 16:1-8 was inserted later.[47]

James A. Kelhoffer has argued persuasively that the author of the longer ending used copies of all four of the Gospels that eventually became canonical in composing this addition to Mark.[48] He has made a good case for the unity of this ending and for its composition by a single author at some point between 120 and 150 CE.[49] Finally, his contextual study of the passage in relation to apocryphal acts and the writings of the apologists shows that it is best understood as a work composed in the second century.[50]

Literary Structure

Apart from the conclusion in vv. 19-20, the longer ending is divided into three scenes: vv. 9-11; vv. 12-13; and vv. 14-18. Each of the three scenes involves an appearance of the risen Jesus. The first two scenes are structured in a parallel manner: (1) Jesus appears to one or two disciples; (2) the individual(s) to whom Jesus appears report the experience to the disciples, the eleven, or the "rest" (οἱ λοιποί); (3) those who receive the report do not believe.

Each section is introduced with an indication of temporal sequence: "first" (πρῶτον) in v. 9; "afterward" (μετὰ δὲ ταῦτα) in v. 12; and "later" (ὕστερον) in v. 14.[51] The conclusion also opens with temporal sequencing, "after he had spoken to them" (μετὰ τὸ λαλῆσαι αὐτοῖς). The simple reports of the appearances of Jesus in the first two sections are parallel to but greatly heightened in the response of the disciples to the appearance and commission of Jesus in the conclusion: they go forth and proclaim (the gospel) in all directions (ἐκεῖνοι δὲ ἐξελθόντες ἐκήρυξαν πανταχοῦ) (v. 20a).[52]

The lack of smooth continuity from v. 14 to v. 15 is insufficient grounds for denying the unity of the longer ending as a whole.[53] The break at this point in the narrative is the likely occasion for the addition of the Freer Logion.[54]

Comment

■ **9** The shorter (additional) ending makes a direct link with v. 8 by stating that "they," presumably the three women mentioned in v. 1, promptly did what the angel had commanded them to do. As noted above, this link is made more plausible by the omission of the words "and they said nothing to anyone" (καὶ οὐδενὶ οὐδὲν εἶπαν) in v. 8.[55] The longer ending, in contrast, does not make a direct or clearly continuous link. It simply states, "When he rose, . . . he appeared first to Mary of Magdala" (Ἀναστὰς δὲ . . . ἐφάνη πρῶτον Μαρίᾳ τῇ Μαγδαληνῇ). Members of the audience could infer that this

---

45   Eta Linnemann, "Der (wiedergefundene) Markusschluß," *ZThK* 66 (1969) 255–87.

46   See the discussions in Kelhoffer, *Miracle and Mission*, 35; Cox, *History and Critique*, 116–19; Kurt Aland, "Der wiedergefundene Markusschluß? Eine methodologische Bermerkung zur textkritischen Arbeit," *ZTK* 67 (1970) 3–13.

47   See the summary, appreciation of the literary analysis of vv. 9-20, and criticism of Mirecki in Kelhoffer, *Miracle and Mission*, 42–45; Paul Allan Mirecki, "Mark 16:9-20: Composition, Tradition and Redaction" (Th.D. diss., Harvard University, 1986).

48   Kelhoffer, *Miracle and Mission*, 48–156.

49   Ibid., 157–244, 473–80.

50   Ibid., 245–472.

51   See the partial agreement on this point of Kelhoffer

(*Miracle and Mission*, 36 and n. 141, 164–65) with Joseph Hug, *La finale de l'évangile de Marc: Mc 16,9-20* (EtB; Paris: Gabalda, 1978) 33–38.

52   That they proclaim the "gospel" (τὸ εὐαγγέλιον) is implied by v. 15. See the partial agreement of Kelhoffer (*Miracle and Mission*, 167–68) with Mirecki (*Miracle and Mission*, 167–68).

53   Ibid., 168–69.

54   See the section "Attestation of the Longer (Additional) Ending" above.

55   See the commentary on "The Shorter (Additional) Ending" above.

appearance took place after the women had seen and heard the angel (vv. 5-7) and left the tomb (v. 8), but this is not made explicit. The temporal setting, "early on the first day of the week" (πρωΐ πρώτη σαββάτου), however, resumes the temporal setting of v. 2 and could indicate a slightly later time.[56]

The statement that the risen Jesus appeared "first" (πρῶτον) to Mary Magdalene is an indication that the author of the longer ending is summarizing and dependent on John 20:1-18.[57] The characterization of Mary as one "from whom Jesus had driven out seven demons" (παρ' ἧς ἐκβεβλήκει ἑπτὰ δαιμόνια) is probably dependent on the last phrase of Luke 8:2, "from whom seven demons had come out" (ἀφ' ἧς δαιμόνια ἑπτὰ ἐξεληλύθει), which also characterizes "Mary, the one called Magdalene" (Μαρία ἡ καλουμένη Μαγδαληνή).[58]

■ **10-11** As the shorter (additional) ending portrays the women "reporting" (ἐξήγγειλαν) to those around Peter what the angel had commanded, the longer ending depicts Mary Magdalene "going" (πορευθεῖσαι) and "reporting" (ἀπήγγειλεν) to the disciples (that the risen Jesus had appeared to her). Both passages are directly or indirectly dependent on John 20:18 (ἔρχεται . . . ἀγγέλλουσα) and Matt 28:8 (ἀπελθοῦσαι . . . ἔδραμον ἀπαγγεῖλαι).[59]

The designation of the disciples as "those who had been with him" (οἱ μετ' αὐτοῦ γενόμενοι) probably derives from Mark 3:14, which states that Jesus appointed Twelve "in order that they might be with him" (ἵνα ὦσιν μετ' αὐτοῦ).[60]

The disciples are portrayed as "mourning and weeping" (πενθοῦσι καὶ κλαίουσιν), presumably on account of the death of Jesus. Such a response to death is presented as the usual one in the account of the raising of

Jairus's daughter.[61] As the mourners in Jairus's house laugh at Jesus when he says that the girl is sleeping and not dead (5:39-40), the disciples in the longer ending refuse to believe Mary's report. At the same time, v. 11 is probably dependent on Luke 24:11. In that context, when the three women who had discovered the empty tomb reported to the disciples, "these words seemed to them like nonsense, and they refused to believe the (women)" (ἐφάνησαν ἐνώπιον αὐτῶν ὡσεὶ λῆρος τὰ ῥήματα ταῦτα, καὶ ἠπίστουν αὐταῖς).[62]

■ **12-13** As noted above, this second scene is structurally parallel to the first one (vv. 9-11).[63] Here, Jesus appears "to two of them" (δυσὶν ἐξ αὐτῶν). The group in question evidently is "those who had been with him" (οἱ μετ' αὐτοῦ γενόμενοι), that is, the eleven, the remainder of the Twelve after the defection of Judas. Verse 12 is a summary of the Emmaus story in Luke 24:13-31.[64]

As the eleven refuse to believe Mary, the nine who did not experience the second appearance do not believe the two who did.

■ **14** The connection of the appearance to Mary Magdalene with the discovery of the empty tomb[65] and the way that the appearance to the two disciples in vv. 12-13 evokes Luke 24 would suggest to audiences that the first two appearances described in the longer ending occurred in Jerusalem. This third appearance, however, has no particular link to Jerusalem. The vague temporal indication, "later" (ὕστερον), leaves open the possibility that this appearance occurred in Galilee. This location is suggested by the similarities between vv. 14-18 and Matt 28:16-20. Both mention "the eleven" (οἱ ἕνδεκα); both recount an appearance of the risen Jesus to them; and in both Jesus commissions them, during the appearance, to go forth and proclaim or teach and to baptize.[66]

The censuring of the disciples' unbelief and hardness

56   In v. 2, the word "very" (λίαν) precedes "early" (πρωΐ). Another difference is the use of ἡ μία instead of πρώτη for "the first day (of the week)" in v. 2.

57   Kelhoffer, *Miracle and Mission*, 69–71.

58   Ibid., 70–71.

59   Ibid., 71–73.

60   Ibid., 73.

61   When Jesus entered the house, "he saw a disturbance and people who were weeping and wailing loudly" (θεωρεῖ θόρυβον καὶ κλαίοντας καὶ ἀλαλάζοντας πολλά) (5:38). The phrase in the

longer ending is a less vivid depiction of an analogous scene.

62   See also John 20:25; Kelhoffer, *Miracle and Mission*, 79–84.

63   See the section "Literary Structure" above; see also Kelhoffer, *Miracle and Mission*, 84–85.

64   Cf., for instance, the "two of them" in v. 12 with "two of them" (δύο ἐξ αὐτῶν) in Luke 24:13. On the dependence of vv. 12-13 on the Emmaus story, see Kelhoffer, *Miracle and Mission*, 85–90.

65   See the commentary on v. 9 above.

66   Kelhoffer, *Miracle and Mission*, 94–95; he suggests

of heart is harsh but does not go far beyond the characterization of the disciples in Mark. The context suggests that ἀπιστία here should be translated "unbelief." In the account of the stilling of the storm, after Jesus has rebuked the wind and sea and created a great calm, he asks the disciples, οὔπω ἔχετε πίστιν; (4:40). In that context, the question is best translated "Do you not yet have trust?" It could also be translated "Do you not yet have faith?" or "Do you not yet have belief?" The exact word translated "hardness of heart" (σκληροκαρδία) in 16:14 is used in 10:5 in a way that implicates the whole people of Israel, not just the Pharisees, who are Jesus' partners in dialogue in the discussion of divorce. The same idea is evoked in relation to the disciples on two occasions in Mark. The first occurs in the narrator's comment about the disciples at the end of the story about Jesus' walking on the water: "For they did not comprehend with regard to the loaves, but their hearts had become hardened" (οὐ γὰρ συνῆκαν ἐπὶ τοῖς ἄρτοις, ἀλλ᾽ ἦν αὐτῶν ἡ καρδία πεπωρωμένη) (6:52). The other occasion occurs in the passage designated "The Question of a Sign and Bread" in this commentary (8:10-21). As Jesus and the disciples are crossing from Dalmanoutha to the other shore, they misunderstand his warning against the leaven of the Pharisees and the leaven of Herod. So he asks them, "Do you have hardened hearts?" (πεπωρωμένην ἔχετε τὴν καρδίαν ὑμῶν;) (8:17).

The criticism of the disciples' failure to believe those who had seen the risen Jesus in this verse refers back to vv. 11 and 13, bringing the theme of refusal or inability to believe to a climax and close.

Verse 15 and the Freer Logion

In the earliest recoverable form of the longer ending, the risen Jesus moves directly from the censure of the disciples' unbelief concerning the resurrection in v. 14 to his commissioning them to proclaim the gospel to the whole world. The text apparently assumes that, when the eleven have all seen the risen Lord themselves, their unbelief is overcome, and they are able to fulfill their commission. The promise of signs attending those who believe in vv. 17-18 and the comment that "the Lord worked together (with them) and confirmed the word through the accompanying signs" (τοῦ κυρίου συνεργοῦντος καὶ τὸν λόγον βεβαιοῦντος διὰ τῶν ἐπακολουθούντων σημείων) in v. 20 provide an indirect explanation concerning the transformation of the disciples from unbelievers to confident and effective missionaries.

The scribe or editor who added the Freer Logion, however, evidently found the transition from v. 14 to v. 15 too harsh.[67] The added material suggests a reason why the disciples disbelieved the reports that Jesus had risen: "This age of lawlessness and unbelief is under (the power of) Satan, who does not permit, by the agency of the unclean spirits, the truth (and) power of God[68] to be grasped." The implication is that it was Satan who prevented their belief. This explanation recalls the interpretation of "the ones who (are) along the road" (οἱ παρὰ τὴν ὁδόν) in the parable of the sower: "when they hear, immediately Satan comes and takes away the word which has been sown in them" (ὅταν ἀκούσωσιν, εὐθὺς ἔρχεται ὁ σατανᾶς καὶ αἴρει τὸν λόγον τὸν ἐσπαρμένον εἰς αὐτούς) (4:15).

The solution to this problem that the disciples propose is that Christ should "reveal your righteousness now" (ἀποκάλυψον σου τὴν δικαιοσυνην ηδη). Christ's "righteousness" entails his activity as a just judge. The particular aspect of judgment in view here is the definitive punishment of the evil spirits, including their leader, Satan.[69] Thus, the request that Christ reveal his righteousness is a plea that the judgment, at least of Satan, take place immediately.

Christ replies, in effect, that the time for the definitive judgment has not yet arrived: "The limit of the years of the authority of Satan has been reached, but other afflictions are drawing near" (πεπληρωται ο ορος των

---

that the author of the longer ending does not mention the locations of the appearances because he knows traditions relating both to Jerusalem and to Galilee and does not wish "to follow one explicitly while contradicting the other" (ibid., 95 n. 149).

67 Kelhoffer, *Miracle and Mission*, 166 n. 33.

68 Or "the true power of God." See "Attestation of the

Longer (Additional) Ending" above for a full ET and the Greek text of the Freer Logion.

69 Cf. the Book of the Watchers, according to which Azazel, the leader of the fallen angels, will "be led away to the burning conflagration" on the great day of judgment (*1 Enoch* 10:6); trans. from Nickelsburg and VanderKam, 28; cf. Knibb, *Enoch*, 2:88. See also

ετων της εξουσιας του σατανα, ἀλλὰ εγγιζει ἄλλα δεινα). In the meantime, the vicarious death of Jesus is what should enable sinners, including the disciples, to live rightly so that they may inherit imperishable glory: "And I was handed over to death for those who had sinned in order that they might return to the truth and no longer sin so that they might inherit the spiritual and imperishable glory of righteousness which is in heaven" (καὶ υπερ ων εγω αμαρτησαντων παρεδοθην εις θανατον ινα υποστρεψωσιν εις την αληθειαν και μηκετι αμαρτησωσιν ινα την εν τω ουρανω πνευματικην και αφθαρτον της δικαιοσυνης δοξαν κληρονομησωσιν). With the problem of the disciples' unbelief dealt with, if not resolved, the version of the longer ending with the Freer Logion turns then to their commission in v. 15.[70]

The command of the risen Jesus that the eleven "Go to all the world and proclaim the gospel to all creation" (πορευθέντες εἰς τὸν κόσμον ἅπαντα κηρύξατε τὸ εὐαγγέλιον πάσῃ τῇ κτίσει) makes explicit what is implied in the discourse about the fall of the temple in chapter 13. In a passage predicting the persecution of the disciples and other followers of Jesus, it is said in a brief digression, "And first it is necessary that the good news be proclaimed to all the nations" (καὶ εἰς πάντα τὰ ἔθνη πρῶτον δεῖ κηρυχθῆναι τὸ εὐαγγέλιον) (13:10).[71]

■ **16** In this verse the risen Jesus pronounces a prophetic saying regarding the responses the disciples will encounter in their missionary work. The saying is expressed in two parallel clauses: "The one who believes and is baptized will be saved, but the one who refuses to believe will be condemned" (ὁ πιστεύσας καὶ βαπτισθεὶς σωθήσεται, ὁ δὲ ἀπιστήσας κατακριθήσεται). The first clause expresses a promise, the second

a threat. In the literary context, the saying functions to reassure the disciples that their proclamation will be effective, bringing salvation to those who respond favorably and judgment to those who reject their message.[72] The focus on belief and disbelief here is typical of the longer ending; at the same time it is similar to John 3:18ab.[73]

It is noteworthy that the saying in John 3:18 focuses on the present, whereas the one in Mark 16:16 focuses on the future. The latter emphasis may be due to the literary context, in which the missionary activity of the disciples is future from the point of view of the risen Jesus as the speaker. It seems likely, however, that the future tenses also allude to the future, definitive judgment of all. The latter interpretation would be especially clearly evoked by the Freer Logion in manuscripts where it was present.[74]

The Gospel of Mark in its earliest recoverable form does not say much, if anything, about the ritual of baptism in the postresurrection communities.[75] A statement attributed to John the baptizer, however, would probably have brought that ritual to mind for the audiences: "I have baptized you with water, but (the one stronger than I who is coming after me) will baptize you in the Holy Spirit" (ἐγὼ ἐβάπτισα ὑμᾶς ὕδατι, αὐτὸς δὲ βαπτίσει ὑμᾶς ἐν πνεύματι ἁγίῳ) (1:8).

The linking of believing and being baptized reflects widespread practice in the communities of those who accepted Jesus as the messiah or as Lord.[76] According to Luke-Acts, baptism is the means by which acceptance of the proclamation and repentance are expressed, sins are forgiven, and the gift of the Holy Spirit is granted (Acts 2:37-38). Paul warned against placing too much emphasis on the person who performs the baptismal ritual but

---

1 Enoch 10:12-14, where the leader is named Semyaza; cf. also 2 Pet 2:4; Jude 6.

70 On the modifications of the longer ending to provide transitions into and out of the Freer Logion, see "Attestation of the Longer (Additional) Ending" above.

71 Kelhoffer argues for dependence also on Matthew 28, Luke 24, John 20, and Mark 6:6b-13 (*Miracle and Mission*, 97–100). He also points out that the language and style of v. 15 are not like Mark's, except for the phrase "proclaim the gospel" (κηρύξατε τὸ εὐαγγέλιον) (ibid., 100).

72 Cf. the two-part saying with promise and threat in Matt 10:32-33 || Luke 12:8-9. A related form of the saying occurs in Mark with only one part, the threat; see the commentary on 8:38 above.

73 Kelhoffer, *Miracle and Mission*, 101.

74 Only one MS (W) with the Freer Logion survives, but Jerome's comment indicates that there were more. See "Attestation of the Longer (Additional) Ending" above.

75 Kelhoffer, *Miracle and Mission*, 101–2.

76 Kelhoffer speaks of baptism as "a requirement" in v. 16 (*Miracle and Mission*, 101–2).

assumed that the ritual was a common experience of all the members of the communities he addressed.[77]

■ **17-18** These verses contain a further promise, in addition to the one in v. 16 that the one who believes will be saved. The further promise is that "signs" (σημεῖα) will attend those who believe (v. 17a). This idea is similar to the teaching of Jesus on miracle-working trust in 11:22-23.[78]

Paul attests to the Romans that he performed "signs and wonders" (σημεῖα καὶ τέρατα) through the power of the Spirit of God "to win obedience from the Gentiles" (εἰς ὑπακοὴν ἐθνῶν) (Rom 15:18-19). So, as in the longer ending, Paul associates "signs" with effectiveness in mission. The portrait of Paul in Acts is similar. In depicting the activity of Paul and Barnabas in Iconium, the narrator states, "So they spent a considerable period of time speaking fearlessly about the Lord, who was bearing witness to the word about his graciousness by causing signs and wonders to occur through their hands" (ἱκανὸν μὲν οὖν χρόνον διέτριψαν παρρησιαζόμενοι ἐπὶ τῷ κυρίῳ τῷ μαρτυροῦντι (ἐπὶ) τῷ λόγῳ τῆς χάριτος αὐτοῦ, διδόντι σημεῖα καὶ τέρατα γίνεσθαι διὰ τῶν χειρῶν αὐτῶν) (Acts 14:3).

Paul states to the Corinthians that "the apostolic signs were performed among you with utmost endurance, by signs and wonders and powerful works" (τὰ μὲν σημεῖα τοῦ ἀποστόλου κατειργάσθη ἐν ὑμῖν ἐν πάσῃ ὑπομονῇ, σημείοις τε καὶ τέρασιν καὶ δυνάμεσιν) (2 Cor 12:12).[79] One could get the impression from the latter statement that such signs were performed only by apostles, but, since speaking in tongues was apparently one of the signs in question (1 Cor 14:22-23), it seems that believers could perform them as well.

2 Cor 12:12, cited above, is an indication that the more usual "signs and wonders"[80] or, as in that verse, "signs, wonders and deeds of power"[81] could be referred to—in shorthand, so to speak—simply as "signs."[82] The use of "signs" alone in vv. 17 and 20 of the longer ending, however, may also reflect the distinctive use of this term for the mighty deeds or miracles of Jesus in the Gospel of John.[83] Jesus' miracles are also called "works" (ἔργα) in John. The first instance occurs in 5:20, where "these (works)" (οὗτοι) include at least the healing recounted in 5:2-9.[84] Raymond E. Brown has argued that "works" is the Johannine Jesus' own designation for his miracles, not "signs."[85]

In the Farewell Discourse, Jesus speaks about his miracles as evidence that the Father dwells in him (14:10-11). He goes on to say that "the one who believes in me will do the works that I am doing and will do greater works than these because I am going to the Father" (ὁ πιστεύων εἰς ἐμὲ τὰ ἔργα ἃ ἐγὼ ποιῶ κἀκεῖνος ποιήσει καὶ μείζονα τούτων ποιήσει, ὅτι ἐγὼ πρὸς τὸν πατέρα πορεύομαι) (John 14:12).[86] Like v. 17 of the longer ending, this passage in John links belief and extraordinary events—"signs" (σημεῖα) in the longer ending and "works" (ἔργα) in John.[87]

Form-critically speaking, vv. 17b-18 constitute a

---

77 Caution about the baptizer is expressed in 1 Cor 1:13-17. Paul's assumption that all his addressees had been baptized is evident in Rom 6:3-4; 1 Cor 12:13; Gal 3:27. The use of ὅσοι ("as many as") in Rom 6:3 and Gal 3:27 does not indicate that only some members of the community were baptized; in these contexts, the term is equivalent to "all" (Betz, *Galatians*, 186).

78 See the commentary on 11:22-23 above. Cf. the discussion in Kelhoffer, *Miracle and Mission*, 103 n. 167.

79 Trans. (modified) by Furnish, *II Corinthians*, 552; see the discussion of the syntax of this verse (ibid., 553).

80 Acts 2:43 (in the opposite order); 4:30; 5:12; 6:8 (opposite order); 8:6; 8:13 ("signs and great, powerful deeds"; σημεῖα καὶ δυνάμεις μεγάλας); 15:12.

81 The same three terms, in a different order, occur in Acts 2:22, where Peter characterizes Jesus as "a man attested by God to you by means of powerful works and wonders and signs" (ἄνδρα ἀποδεδειγμένον ἀπὸ τοῦ θεοῦ εἰς ὑμᾶς δυνάμεσι καὶ τέρασι καὶ σημείοις). See also Heb 2:3-4, which has the three terms in the same order as 2 Cor 12:12.

82 See also Acts 4:16, 22, where "sign" (σημεῖον) refers to the healing of a crippled beggar in the temple (3:1-10).

83 John 2:11, 23; 3:2; 4:54; 6:2, 14; 7:31; 9:16; 11:47; 12:18, 37; 20:30; see the discussion in Kelhoffer, *Miracle and Mission*, 103, 261–66.

84 Raymond E. Brown, *The Gospel according to John (i–xii): Introduction, Translation, and Notes* (AB 29; Garden City, NY: Doubleday, 1966) 214.

85 Ibid., 224. In addition to 5:20, see 5:36; 7:21; 9:3; 10:25, 32, 37-38; 14:10-11; 15:24. But note that the brothers of Jesus also speak about his miracles as "works," yet do not believe in him (7:3).

86 See the commentary on 11:24 above.

87 Kelhoffer, *Miracle and Mission*, 104, 121–22, 262, 338.

"miracle-list."[88] Isa 35:5-7 is part of a visionary and poetic description of an ideal future.[89] At least from a later perspective, these verses may be understood as a miracle-list.[90] Such lists occur elsewhere in early Christian literature.[91] The closest analogies to vv. 17b-18 are found in the work of Irenaeus (*Haer.* 2.31.2–32.4) and a passage in the *Pistis Sophia* (3.110) probably composed in the second half of the third century CE.[92]

Irenaeus refers to the ability of Jesus to raise the dead and the ability of the apostles to do the same by prayer (*Haer.* 2.31.2). Not only that, but he seems to imply that members of "the brotherhood," presumably in his own day, have done likewise "frequently":

> the entire Church in that particular locality entreating [the boon] with much fasting and prayer, the spirit of the dead man has returned, and he has been bestowed in answer to the prayers of the saints (ea quae est in quoquo loco Ecclesia uniuersa postulante per ieiunium et supplicationem multam, reuersus est spiritus mortui et donatus est homo orationibus sanctorum). (*Haer.* 2.31.2)[93]

In the same context, Irenaeus again seems to refer to miracles worked by Christians in his own day:

> Wherefore, also, those who are in truth His disciples, receiving grace from Him, do in his name perform [miracles], so as to promote the welfare of other men, according to the gift which each one has received from Him. For some do certainly and truly drive out devils, so that those who have been cleansed from evil spirits frequently both believe [in Christ] and join themselves to the Church. Others have foreknowledge of things to come: they see visions, and utter prophetic expressions. Others still, heal the sick by laying their hands upon them, and they are made whole. Yea, moreover, as I have said, the dead even have been raised up, and remained among us for many years (Quapropter et in illius nomine qui uere illius sunt discipuli, ab ipso accipientes gratiam, perficiunt ad beneficia reliquorum hominum, quemadmodum unusquisque accepit donum ab eo. Alii enim daemonas excludunt firmissime et uere, ut etiam saepissime credant ipse qui emundati sunt a nequissimis spiritibus et sint in Ecclesia; alii autem et praescientiam habent futurorum et uisiones et dictiones propheticas; alii autem laborantes aliqua infirmitate per manus impositionem curant et sanos restituunt; iam etiam, quemadmodum diximus, et mortui resurrexerunt et perseuerauerunt nobiscum annis multis). (*Haer.* 2.32.4)[94]

The work known as *Pistis Sophia* survives in a Coptic version in a parchment manuscript of the second half of

---

88 Ibid., 199–227.

89 Blenkinsopp, *Isaiah 1–39*, 456–57.

90 Kelhoffer, *Miracle and Mission*, 204–5.

91 Matt 10:8; Matt 11:5 || Luke 7:22; Matt 15:31; *Sib. Or.* 1:351-59 (for an introduction and ET, see John J. Collins, "Sibylline Oracles," in *OTP* 1:330-34, 343); *Sib. Or.* 6:13-16 (Collins, "Sibylline Oracles," 406–7; for a Greek text and discussion, see Kelhoffer, *Miracle and Mission*, 205–6); *Sib. Or.* 8:269-81 (Collins, "Sibylline Oracles," 415–17, 424); *Epistula Apostolorum* 4–5 (for an introduction and ET, see C. Detlef G. Muller, "Epistula Apostolorum," in *NTApoc*, 1:249–51, 253); *Acts of Andrew and Matthias* 10 (for introduction and bibliography, see J. K. Elliott, *The Apocryphal New Testament* [Oxford: Clarendon, 1993] 24–42; Aurelio de Santos Otero, "Later Acts of Apostles," in *NTApoc*, 2:443–47; Kelhoffer, *Miracle and Mission*, 206–7); *Acts of Peter and Paul* 41 (for a brief introduction and bibliography, see Elliott, *Apocryphal New Testament*, 428–29; de Santos Otero, "Later Acts of Apostles," 440–42; Kelhoffer, *Miracle*

and Mission, 207). For further primary references, see Kelhoffer, *Miracle and Mission*, 210 nn. 161 and 162, 216–17; see also his discussion of the secondary literature (ibid., 199–227).

92 On the date of the latter work, see Henri-Charles Puech and Beate Blatz, "Other Gnostic Gospels and Related Literature," in *NTApoc*, 1:362. On the similarity of these texts to vv. 17b-18, see Kelhoffer, *Miracle and Mission*, 210–11.

93 Text from Adelin Rousseau and Louis Doutreleau, eds., *Irénée de Lyon: Contre les Hérésies Livre II* (SC 294; Paris: Cerf, 1982) 328, 330; trans. from Coxe, *Apostolic Fathers*, 407. For a discussion of these statements in the context of Irenaeus's argument, see Kelhoffer, *Miracle and Mission*, 212–14.

94 Text from Rousseau and Doutreleau, *Contre les Hérésies*, 340; trans. from Coxe, *Apostolic Fathers*, 409.

the fourth century, the Codex Askewianus. It was purchased in a London bookstore in 1773 by an English collector, Dr. A. Askew. Since 1785, it has been in the British Museum in London.[95] In the third book of this work, Mary asks the risen Jesus about the "mysteries" that he has brought to the world. In her question, the term "mysteries" includes miracles, although it may have a broader range. She continues:

> So that when we go to *places* of the *country*, and they do not *believe* us and they do not listen to our words, and we perform a *mystery* of this kind in those *places*, then they know *truly* and verily that we are *preaching* the words <of the God> of All. (3.110)[96]

Like the longer ending of Mark, this text links the occurrence of extraordinary events ("signs" in the longer ending and "mysteries" in *Pistis Sophia*) with effective missionary work. Jesus then replies to Mary as follows:

> Concerning this *mystery* upon which you question me, I gave it to you once, *but* I will repeat again and say the word to you. *Now* at this time, Maria, *not only* you *but* all men who will complete the *mystery* of the raising of the dead: this *cures demons* and all pains and all sicknesses and the blind and the lame and the maimed and the dumb and the deaf, this I have given to you once. He who will take a *mystery* and complete it, if now afterwards he *asks* for anything: poverty and riches, weakness and strength, *plague* or sound *body*, and all *cures* of the *body*, and the raising of the dead, and *curing* of the lame and the blind and the *deaf* and the dumb and all sickness and pains, *in a word*, he

who completes that *mystery* and *asks* for any thing which I have said, it will happen to him *with speed*. (3.110)[97]

Like Mark 11:22-24 and John 14:12-14, this passage implies that any faithful follower of Jesus can perform extraordinary deeds by means of prayer. In addition to praying or asking for a miracle, the passage in the *Pistis Sophia* adds the expectation that the person "complete a *mystery*," in particular, "the *mystery* of the raising of the dead," but it is not clear what such a process would entail.

The first "sign" mentioned in v. 17b is "in my name they will drive out demons" (ἐν τῷ ὀνόματί μου δαιμόνια ἐκβαλοῦσιν). The idea that the disciples are able to drive out demons is expressed in the earliest recoverable form of Mark (6:7, 13a; see also Luke 9:1). The disciples were not able to drive a "mute spirit" (πνεῦμα ἄλαλον) from a man's son, but Jesus gave them instruction on how to deal with such difficult cases (9:14-29). According to 9:38, a man who was not following Jesus was able to drive out demons in his name. Justin Martyr refers a number of times to exorcisms performed in his own time by calling upon the name of Jesus Christ (e.g., Justin *Dial.* 30.3).[98]

The second sign (v. 17c) is "they will speak in unknown[99] languages" (γλώσσαις λαλήσουσιν καιναῖς). This sign seems to be a summary of Acts 2:1-11 and an extension of that event to the early Christian mission in general.[100] Acts 2:4 states that "they were all filled with the Holy Spirit and began to speak other[101] languages to the degree that the Spirit enabled them to do so" (ἐπλήσθησαν πάντες πνεύματος ἁγίου καὶ

For discussion, see Kelhoffer, *Miracle and Mission*, 322–26.

95 Puech and Blatz, "Other Gnostic Gospels," 361–62. For a history of the Askew Codex and a description of the MS, see Carl Schmidt (editor of the text) and Violet MacDermot (translation and notes), *Pistis Sophia* (NHS 9; Leiden: Brill, 1978) XI–XIV.

96 Trans. from Schmidt and MacDermot, *Pistis Sophia*, 279. The italicized words are of Greek origin; pointed brackets indicate conjectural emendations. For discussion of the passage, see Kelhoffer, *Miracle and Mission*, 214–16.

97 Trans. from Schmidt and MacDermot, *Pistis Sophia*, 279.

98 Kelhoffer, *Miracle and Mission*, 317. For discussion of similar passages in Theophilus of Antioch, Irenaeus, Tertullian, and Origen, see ibid., 321–37.

99 The Greek word καινός is often translated "new." Here it has the sense of languages new to the speaker, i.e., languages previously unknown.

100 Kelhoffer argues that the author of the longer ending adapted Mark 6 and Luke 9 in the same way (*Miracle and Mission*, 224). See also ibid., 266–67.

101 The Greek word ἕτερος, often translated "other," has the sense here of languages other than the speaker's native language. The ability to speak other languages is clearly presented as miraculous.

ἤρξαντο λαλεῖν ἑτέραις γλώσσαις καθὼς τὸ πνεῦμα ἐδίδου ἀποφθέγγεσθαι αυτοῖς). In both the longer ending and Acts 2, the ability to speak in various languages is linked to effectiveness in mission.[102] A difference between them is that the phenomenon is attributed to the agency of the Holy Spirit in Acts, whereas it is the risen Jesus who empowers believers in this way according to the longer ending.[103]

It is unlikely that the third sign (v. 18a), "they will pick up snakes" (ὄφεις ἀροῦσιν), derives from any passage in the New Testament. The only candidates are Luke 10:19 and Acts 28:1-10. In the former, Jesus declares that he has given the seventy missionaries the power to step on snakes (ὄφεις) and scorpions. The latter is illustrated in the story concerning how Paul survived the bite of a snake (ἔχιδνα). Although neither of these is similar enough to v. 18a to suggest literary dependence, the reaction of the people of Malta to the incident involving Paul is illuminating for understanding the assumption of the author of the longer ending that outsiders would be impressed by an ability to pick up snakes without being harmed.[104] There is evidence that the handling of snakes in public situations was known in antiquity as a way of impressing onlookers.[105]

The fourth sign (v. 18b) is a promise that "even if they drink something deadly, it will surely not harm them" (κἂν θανάσιμόν τι πίωσιν οὐ μὴ αὐτοὺς βλάψῃ). It is not clear whether "something deadly" refers to a substance that is harmful in a physical manner or to something deadly in a metaphorical way.[106] It is also uncertain whether the promise envisages believers drinking "something deadly" willingly, their being forced to do so, or whether both types of situation are presupposed.[107]

Ignatius urged the Trallians as follows:

make use only of Christian food and abstain from a foreign plant, which is heresy. Even though such persons seem to be trustworthy, they mingle Jesus Christ with themselves, as if giving a deadly drug mixed with honeyed wine, which the unsuspecting gladly takes with evil pleasure, but then dies (μόνῃ τῇ χριστιανῇ τροφῇ χρῆσθε, ἀλλοτρίας δὲ βοτάνης ἀπέχεσθε, ἥτις ἐστὶν αἵρεσις· οἳ ἑαυτοῖς παρεμπλέκουσιν Ἰησοῦν Χριστὸν καταξιοπιστευόμενοι, ὥσπερ θανάσιμον φάρμακον διδόντες μετὰ οἰνομέλιτος, ὅπερ ὁ ἀγνοῶν ἡδέως λαμβάνει ἐν ἡδονῇ κακῇ τὸ ἀποθανεῖν). (*Trall.* 6:1-2)[108]

It is unlikely, however, that the promise in v. 18b of the longer ending refers to immunity from heresy. Since the other "signs" refer to extraordinary abilities, this one probably does also. Immunity from heresy, even if perceived as rampant and beguiling, does not fit the context of the longer ending.

In a version of the story about Joseph and Potiphar's wife, she sends him "food prepared in sorcery" (βρῶμα ἐν γοητείᾳ πεφυραμένον).[109] An angel appears to Joseph to warn him not to eat the food. When the woman comes and sees that he has not eaten it, she asks him why he has not done so. He replies, "Because you filled it with death. How can you say, 'I do not draw near to the idols, but only to the Lord?'" (Ὅτι ἐπλήρωσας αὐτὸ θανάτου· καὶ πῶς εἶπας, ὅτι οὐκ ἐγγίζω εἰδώλοις, ἀλλὰ κυρίῳ μόνῳ;) (*T. Jos.* 6:5).[110] The statement that the food was prepared in sorcery indicates that the woman made use of magical utterances, herbs and plants with magical power, magical performances, or all of these in order to arouse love for herself in Joseph.[111] In his remark that she had filled the food with death,

---

102 Cf. Paul's remark in 1 Cor 14:22 that speaking in tongues takes place as a "sign" (σημεῖον) for unbelievers (i.e., those who have not yet believed), not for believers.

103 Kelhoffer, *Miracle and Mission*, 267.

104 Ibid., 402–3.

105 Ibid., 408, 415.

106 On the metaphorical use of terms signifying poison in the OT, OT apocrypha, and DSS, see Kelhoffer, *Miracle and Mission*, 421–22. The metaphorical usage occurs in the NT in Rom 3:13b, citing Ps 139:4b LXX; Jas 3:8 (ibid., 432).

107 Ibid., 419–20.

108 Text and trans. from Ehrman, *Apostolic Fathers*, 1:260–63.

109 Or "food mixed with sorcery" (*T. 12 Patr.*, *T. Jos.* 6:1; my trans.; text from de Jonge, *Testaments of the Twelve Patriarchs*, 149).

110 Trans. (modified) from Kee, "Testaments," *OTP* 1:820; text from de Jonge, *Testaments of the Twelve Patriarchs*, 150.

111 On magic and magical techniques, see H. S. Versnel, "Magic," *OCD* 908–10.

"death" is meant metaphorically either in recognition that the magical power of the food could have led him into adultery or on the assumption that the magical substances and techniques were connected with supernatural beings and that eating the food would thus be equivalent to idolatry. After praying aloud, Joseph ate the food, apparently with no ill effects. The woman fell at his feet weeping and agreed not to commit such an impiety again. Although this text is older than the beginning of the third century CE, its exact date and cultural context remain uncertain.[112] It is analogous to the longer ending in its association of drinking something deadly with an attempt to bring about a change in an observer.[113]

A closer analogy may be found in a quotation from Papias by Philip of Side:

> Papias, who has been mentioned [above], related, as having received [it] from the daughters of Philip, that Barsabbas, who [is] also called Justus, when he was tested by the unbelievers and *drank viper's venom*, was by the name of Christ protected from harm. And he relates also other wonders . . . (Παπίας ὁ εἰρημένος ἱστόρησεν ὡς παραλαβὼν ἀπὸ τῶν θυγατέρων Φιλίππου, ὅτι Βαρσαβᾶς ὁ καὶ Ἰοῦστος, δοκιμαζόμενος ὑπὸ τῶν ἀπίστων ἰὸν ἐχίδνης πιὼν, ἐν ὀνόματι τοῦ Χριστοῦ ἀπαθὴς διεφυλάχθη. ἱστορεῖ δὲ καὶ ἄλλα θαύματα . . .).[114]

It is not clear whether Justus Basabbas initiated contact with the unbelievers in a missionary setting or was forced to drink poison in a context of persecution. In any case, it was known in antiquity that drinking a serpent's venom is not deadly. Such knowledge may explain why Eusebius, in quoting the same text, changed "viper's venom" (ἰὸν ἐχίδνης) to "a harmful drug" (δηλητήριον φάρμακον).[115]

Although the exact origin of this tradition cannot be determined, it may be that the protection of Odysseus by Hermes against the "evil drugs" (κακὰ φάρμακα) of Circe has, at least in part, inspired both v. 18b and *T. Jos.* 6.[116]

Like the first and second "signs," the fifth (v. 18c) is familiar from other early Christian texts: "they will lay their hands upon ill people, and they will be well" (ἐπὶ ἀρρώστους χεῖρας ἐπιθήσουσιν καὶ καλῶς ἕξουσιν). In fact, this promise is similar to two passages in the earliest recoverable form of Mark. In 6:12-13, a summary of the mission of the Twelve is given, "And they went out and proclaimed that (people) should repent, and they drove out many demons, and they anointed many ill people with oil and healed them" (Καὶ ἐξελθόντες ἐκήρυξαν ἵνα μετανοῶσιν, καὶ δαιμόνια πολλὰ ἐξέβαλλον, καὶ ἤλειφον ἐλαίῳ πολλοὺς ἀρρώστους καὶ ἐθεράπευον). The structure of 16:15-18 may owe something to 6:12-13; proclaiming is mentioned in v. 15, as it is in 6:12, and the first and last of the five "signs" in vv. 17-18 are similar to the two types of mighty deeds mentioned in 6:13.[117]

The second text is the statement about the limitation put on Jesus' ability to perform mighty deeds in Nazareth by the people's unbelief: "And he was not able to do any powerful work there, except that he laid his hands on a few who were ill and healed them" (καὶ οὐκ ἐδύνατο ἐκεῖ ποιῆσαι οὐδεμίαν δύναμιν, εἰ μὴ ὀλίγοις ἀρρώστοις ἐπιθεὶς τὰς χεῖρας ἐθεράπευσεν). Both this text and v. 18c speak about "laying on hands" (χεῖρας ἐπιτιθέναι) on those who are "ill" (ἄρρωστοι).[118] The verbal similarity is greater between 6:5 and v. 18c, but the contexts are more similar in 6:12-13 and v. 18c, since the mighty deeds are performed by disciples who are commissioned to go forth and proclaim in both cases.

■ **19-20** The promise concerning the occurrence of the five types of "signs" (σημεῖα) in vv. 17-18 concludes the commissioning speech of Jesus, as well as the third main section, that is, the third appearance account in the longer ending. Verses 19-20 form the conclusion to the

---

112 Hollander and de Jonge, 82–85.

113 Kelhoffer speaks about "the taking of poison to persuade another" as common to both (*Miracle and Mission*, 429).

114 Philip of Side (Philippus Sidetes), frg. 6; text and trans. from Kelhoffer, *Miracle and Mission*, 437–38 (emphasis his).

115 Ibid., 433–42.

116 Homer *Od.* 10.212–13, 274–306; cf. Kelhoffer, *Miracle and Mission*, 423–25, 470.

117 Kelhoffer, *Miracle and Mission*, 224.

118 Ibid.

longer ending as a whole. Verse 19 provides a smooth transition from vv. 14-18 with the words "after he had spoken to them" (μετὰ τὸ λαλῆσαι αὐτοῖς). It is linked to v. 20 by the coordinated and slightly contrasting particles μέν and δέ.[119]

In the earliest recoverable form of the longer ending, that is, without the Freer Logion,[120] the risen Jesus is named for the first time in v. 19: "The Lord Jesus" (Ὁ μὲν οὖν κύριος Ἰησοῦς).[121] The references to him in the earlier part of the longer ending by means of the unexpressed subject of finite verbs and participles make an impression of continuity with the preceding Gospel of Mark as a whole. The use of the epithet "Lord" and the personal name "Jesus" gives this verse emphasis and lends it a climactic impact.

Two events are narrated in v. 19. The first is the translation or transference of Jesus from earth to heaven: "(The Lord Jesus) was taken up into heaven" (ἀνελήμφθη εἰς τὸν οὐρανόν). Acts 1:1-2 refers to Luke 24:1 using the same verb: "I wrote the first book, O Theophilus, about all the things that Jesus began to do and to teach until the day on which he was taken up, after giving instructions through the Holy Spirit to the apostles whom he had chosen" (Τὸν μὲν πρῶτον λόγον ἐποιησάμην περὶ πάντων, ὦ Θεόφιλε, ὧν ἤρξατο ὁ Ἰησοῦς ποιεῖν τε καὶ διδάσκειν, ἄχρι ἧς ἡμέρας ἐντειλάμενος τοῖς ἀποστόλοις διὰ πνεύματος ἁγίου οὓς ἐξελέξατο ἀνελήμφθη).[122]

In terms of substance, v. 19a is similar to the account of Jesus' ascension in Acts 1:9, "And having said these things, while they were watching, he was lifted up, and a cloud took him up, out of their sight" (Καὶ ταῦτα εἰπὼν βλεπόντων αὐτῶν ἐπήρθη καὶ νεφέλη ὑπέλαβεν αὐτὸν ἀπὸ τῶν ὀφθαλμῶν αὐτῶν). Although the substance is similar, the vocabulary differs.[123] The verb used in v. 19, "to be taken up" (ἀναλαμβάνεσθαι) is also used in the account of the translation of Elijah to heaven: "and Elijah was taken up in a whirlwind as it were into heaven" (καὶ ἀνελήμφθη Ἡλιου ἐν συσσεισμῷ ὡς εἰς τὸν οὐρανόν) (4 Kgdms 2:11 LXX).[124] The similarity to the account of the translation of Elijah here is interesting in light of the appearance of Elijah along with Moses at the transfiguration of Jesus (9:2-8). As argued above, an important purpose of the transfiguration account is to foreshadow the transformation of Jesus' body and his translation to heaven. Elijah and Moses appear, at least in part, because they were both believed at the time of Mark to have been translated to heaven.[125] The use of vocabulary in v. 19 also found in the account of the transference of Elijah to heaven may indicate that the author of the longer ending understood Jesus' ascent to heaven as analogous to that of Elijah. This hypothesis of course does not exclude the likelihood of the author's use of Luke 24 and Acts 1.[126]

The second event narrated in v. 19 is Jesus' taking his seat on the right of God (καὶ ἐκάθισεν ἐκ δεξιῶν τοῦ θεοῦ). This statement recalls the teaching of Jesus in 12:35-37. The command or invitation attributed to God in the citation of Ps 109:1 LXX, "Sit on my right" (Κάθου ἐκ δεξιῶν μου), in 12:36 is accepted and carried out in v. 19b. The latter also serves as a partial fulfillment of the prediction of Jesus in 14:62, "and you will

119 Kelhoffer argues that this construction implies "a direct relationship between the journey of Jesus to the right hand of God (v. 19) and the risen Lord's continued self-manifestation among the disciples (v. 20) (Miracle and Mission, 110).

120 See the commentary on v. 15 and the Freer Logion above; see also "Attestation of the Longer (Additional) Ending" above.

121 Kelhoffer considers the word "Jesus" (Ἰησοῦς) to be a secondary expansion of the text (Miracle and Mission, 4 n. 14). He also concludes that the use of the expression "the Lord" (ὁ . . . κύριος) in v. 19 is dependent on John 20–21 (ibid., 110).

122 The same verb is used again in Acts 1:22. It is also used in 1 Tim 3:16; on the relevance of the latter, see Kelhoffer, Miracle and Mission, 111 n. 86.

123 Both v. 19 and Luke 24:51 have the phrase "into heaven" (εἰς τὸν οὐρανόν), but the verbs differ. The Lukan passage reads, "And while he was blessing them, he departed from them and he was brought up into heaven" (καὶ ἐγένετο ἐν τῷ εὐλογεῖν αὐτὸν αὐτοὺς διέστη ἀπ᾽ αὐτῶν καὶ ἀνεφέρετο εἰς τὸν οὐρανόν). On the relation of v. 19a to Luke 24:51, see Kelhoffer, Miracle and Mission, 111–14, 229, and the literature cited in n. 206.

124 See also 1 Macc 2:58; Sir 48:9, where the same verb is used. It is also used of the translation of Enoch to heaven in Sir 49:14. See Kelhoffer, Miracle and Mission, 111–12, and the literature cited there.

125 See the commentary on 9:4 above.

126 See the arguments of Kelhoffer for the latter conclusion (Miracle and Mission, 113–14).

see the Son of Man sitting on the right of the Power and coming with the clouds of heaven" (καὶ ὄψεσθε τὸν υἱὸν τοῦ ἀνθρώπου ἐκ δεξιῶν καθήμενον τῆς δυνάμεως καὶ ἐρχόμενον μετὰ τῶν νεφελῶν τοῦ οὐρανοῦ).[127] The vision of Stephen in Acts 7:55-56 is similar to v. 19b in that "Jesus" (v. 55)/"the Son of Man" (v. 56) is depicted as being "on the right of God" (ἐκ δεξιῶν τοῦ θεοῦ). A difference between the two passages lies in the portrayal of Jesus/the Son of Man as "standing" (ἑστῶς) in Acts, rather than sitting as in v. 19b.

Verse 20 describes the activity of the eleven after Jesus was taken up into heaven: "They then went out and proclaimed in all directions, while the Lord worked together (with them) and confirmed the word through the accompanying signs" (ἐκεῖνοι δὲ ἐξελθόντες ἐκήρυξαν πανταχοῦ, τοῦ κυρίου συνεργοῦντος καὶ τὸν λόγον βεβαιοῦντος διὰ τῶν ἐπακολουθούντων σημείων). The going out of the eleven and their proclaiming in all directions contrasts markedly with their unbelief in vv. 11 and 13.[128] The reason for the change presupposed by the author of the longer ending may be that their unbelief turns into belief once they all have seen the risen Jesus. Another explanation may be inferred from v. 20 itself: that they were able to believe and proclaim because the Lord was working together with them.[129]

The statement that "they went out and proclaimed" (ἐξελθόντες ἐκήρυξαν) agrees in its wording with 6:12, the first part of the summary of the mission of the Twelve. That they proclaimed "in all directions" (πανταχοῦ) is reminiscent of Jesus' fame going out "in all directions" (πανταχοῦ) in 1:28. A passage in Luke, however, has the same word in the context of the mission of the Twelve (9:6), which is a closer analogue to v. 20.[130]

The idea of the Lord "confirming the word through the accompanying signs" (τὸν λόγον βεβαιοῦντος διὰ τῶν ἐπακολουθούντων σημείων) is similar in substance to a passage in Hebrews:

For if the word spoken by angels was valid and every transgression and act of disobedience received its just recompense, how shall we escape, if we neglect such a great salvation, which, after originally being proclaimed [lit. "spoken"] by the Lord, was validated for us by those who heard it, while God corroborated the testimony with signs and wonders and various powerful deeds and distributions of holy spirit according to his will (εἰ γὰρ ὁ δι᾽ ἀγγέλων λαληθεὶς λόγος ἐγένετο βέβαιος καὶ πᾶσα παράβασις καὶ παρακοὴ ἔλαβεν ἔνδικον μισθαποδοσίαν, πῶς ἡμεῖς ἐκφευξόμεθα τηλικαύτης ἀμελήσαντες σωτηρίας, ἥτις ἀρχὴν λαβοῦσα λαλεῖσθαι διὰ τοῦ κυρίου ὑπὸ τῶν ἀκουσάντων εἰς ἡμᾶς ἐβεβαιώθη, συνεπιμαρτυροῦντος τοῦ θεοῦ σημείοις τε καὶ τέρασιν καὶ ποικίλαις δυνάμεσιν καὶ πνεύματος ἁγίου μερισμοῖς κατὰ τὴν αὐτοῦ θέλησιν;). (Heb 2:2-4)[131]

The use of the term "salvation" (σωτηρία) in Heb 2:3 may be a case of metonymy, in which it takes the place of "the word" (λόγος), since the two notions are closely related.[132] In any case, this salvation is "spoken" (λαλεῖσθαι).[133] The fact that God is portrayed in Hebrews as the one who confirms the word with signs, whereas it is the risen Jesus who does so in the longer ending, is a minor difference, given the widespread idea of Jesus as God's agent or deputy.[134]

The association of miracles and missionary activity, however, is not peculiar to traditions of the first century but is common in the second century also, especially in apocryphal acts and apologetic writings, broadly defined.[135]

Like the shorter (additional) ending, the longer ending was appended to Mark because 16:8 seemed to be a deficient conclusion in comparison with those of Matthew, Luke, and John.[136] It was composed by the

---

127 Kelhoffer argues that the narration of the session of Jesus in v. 19b (v. 19c in his reckoning) is modeled on 14:62 (ibid., 116–17).

128 Ibid., 118.

129 See the commentary on v. 15 and the Freer Logion above.

130 Kelhoffer, *Miracle and Mission*, 118.

131 Trans. from Attridge, *Hebrews*, 63.

132 On metonymy, see Smyth §3033.

133 Attridge, *Hebrews*, 66.

134 See, e.g., Acts 2:22. On the similarities and differences between 16:20 and Heb 2:2-4, see Kelhoffer, *Miracle and Mission*, 279–80.

135 On the apocryphal acts, see ibid., 281–310; on apologetic writings, ibid., 310–37.

136 See the commentary on the shorter (additional) ending above.

adaptation of ideas and motifs from Mark, Matthew, Luke, John, and Acts.[137] It affirms that one of the three women who discovered the empty tomb, Mary of Magdala, also received an appearance of the risen Jesus. It is perhaps implied that it was this appearance that enabled her to overcome her fear and report to the disciples. The first appearance account (vv. 9-11) is a partial harmonization of (extended) Mark with John 20. In both texts, Mary is the first one to see the risen Lord. Unlike the longer ending, John 20:8 speaks about the belief of "the other disciple" (ὁ ἄλλος μαθητής), although the statement in v. 9 qualifies his belief.

The second appearance account (vv. 12-13) is, in effect, a partial harmonization of Mark with Luke, since it summarizes the story of the appearance at Emmaus in Luke 24:13-35.[138] The third appearance account is the most distinctive, although it also had its literary models.[139] It harmonizes Mark with Matthew, Luke, and John insofar as it, like them, presents an appearance of the risen Jesus to the eleven remaining disciples of the inner circle.

The perceived need for a better conclusion to Mark, especially when the four Gospels began to be collected, made it difficult, if not impossible, to read 16:1-8 as a distinctively Markan and sufficient ending. Two additional endings were produced, the shorter and longer. These competed for centuries, but the longer eventually won out as the one better suited to assimilate Mark to the other three most authoritative Gospels in the church.

---

137 Kelhoffer, *Miracle and Mission*, 48–156.
138 See the commentary on vv. 12-13 above.

139 See the commentary on vv. 14-18 above.

A Tentative Reconstruction and Translation of the Content (not necessarily the wording) of the Pre-Markan Passion Narrative

They went to a place named Gethsemane, and Jesus began to be distressed and anxious, and he said to them, "My soul is exceedingly sorrowful to the point of death; stay here and keep awake." He went a little farther on, fell upon the ground, began to pray and said, "Abba, father, all things are possible for you; remove this cup from me; but (let) not what I want (be), but what you want." And he went and found them sleeping and said to Peter, "Simon, are you sleeping? Were you not strong enough to keep awake for one hour? Wake up, let us go. See, the one who hands me over has drawn near."

While he was still speaking, Judas, one of the Twelve, arrived. With him was a crowd with swords and clubs, sent by the chief priests. Now the one who was about to hand him over had given them a signal, saying, "The one whom I kiss is he; arrest him and take him securely into custody." And when he arrived, he immediately went to Jesus and said, "Rabbi," and kissed him. The others laid hands on him and arrested him. And all (the disciples) left him and fled.

And they led Jesus away to the high priest. Early in the morning, the chief priests took counsel, bound Jesus, brought him, and handed him over to Pilate. And Pilate asked him, "Are you the king of the Jews?" He then said to him, "You say (so)." And the chief priests accused him of many things. Pilate asked him again, saying, "Have you no response? Look how many accusations they make against you." But Jesus no longer made any response, so that Pilate marveled. He had Jesus whipped and handed him over to be crucified.

The soldiers led him into the courtyard and called together the whole cohort. And they dressed him in a purple cloak, wove an acanthus crown and put it on him. And they began to greet him, "Welcome, king of the Jews!" And they hit him on the head with a reed and spat on him and, kneeling, showed him reverence. And when they had mocked him, they took the purple cloak off of him and put his (own) clothes on him.

And they led him out to crucify him. And they forced a certain passerby, Simon of Cyrene, who was coming from the country, the father of Alexander and Rufus, to carry his cross. And they brought him to the place Golgotha, that is, translated, the place that is called Skull. And they tried to give him wine flavored with myrrh, but he did not take it. And they crucified him and divided his clothes, casting lots for them (to determine) who would take what. Now it was the third hour when they crucified him. And the inscription of the charge against him was posted: the king of the Jews. And those who passed by reviled him, shaking their heads and saying, "He saved others, himself he cannot save; let the messiah, the king of Israel, come down now from the cross, in order that we may see and believe."

And at the sixth hour, darkness came upon the whole land until the ninth hour. And at the ninth hour, Jesus cried out with a loud voice and expired. And the curtain of the sanctuary was split in two from top to bottom.

Bibliography
Indices

Under "Commentaries," only major critical treatments are listed. Under "Studies," the emphasis is on recent critical contributions.

1. Commentaries

a. Patristic

Victor of Antioch (6th century)
Petrus Possinus and Michael Hercules, *Catena Graecorum Patrum in Evangelium Secundum Marcum* (Romae: Typis Barberinis excudebat Michael Hercules, 1673).[1]

Christian Friedrich Matthaei (Matthäi), Βίκτωρος πρεσβυτέρου Ἀντιοχείας καὶ ἄλλων τινῶν ἁγίων πατέρων ἐξήγησις εἰς τὸ κατὰ Μάρκον ἅγιον εὐαγγέλιον (2 vols.; Moskow, 1775).

John Anthony Cramer, "Catena in Evangelium S. Marci e codd. Bodl. et Paris.," in idem, *Catenae Graecorum Patrum in Novum Testamentum* (8 vols.; Oxonii: E Typographeo Academico, 1840; reprinted Hildesheim: Georg Olms, 1967), vol. 1: *Catenae in Evangelia S. Matthaei et S. Marci ad fidem Codd. MSS*, 259–447.[2]

b. Medieval

Albertus Magnus (13th century)
Steph. Caes. Aug. Borgnet, ed., *Enarrationes in Matthaeum (XXI–XXVIII)–in Marcum* in *Opera Omnia*, vol. 21 (Paris: Apud Ludovicum Vives, Bibliopolam Editorem, 1894) 339–761.

Bede (8th century)
Patrologia latina, 92:131–302.

D. Hurst, ed., *Bedae Venerabilis Opera*, pars 2.3: *Opera Exegetica: In Lucae Evangelium Expositio; In Marci Evangelium Expositio* (CChrSL 120; Turnhout: Brepols, 1960).

Comianus? (Pseudo-Jerome) (7th century)
Patrologia latina, 30:589–644.

Michael Cahill, ed., *Expositio Evangelii secundum Marcum* (CChrSL 82; Scriptores Celtigenae, pars 2; Turnholt: Brepols, 1997).

Michael Cahill, *The First Commentary on Mark: An Annotated Translation* (New York/Oxford: Oxford University Press, 1998).

Pseudo-Jerome and Pseudo-Walafrid Strabo (7th century)
Patrologia latina, 30:560–67 and *Patrologia latina*, 114:887–94.

Sedulius Scottus (9th century)
Patrologia latina, 103:279–86.

Angelo Mai, ed., *Scriptorum veterum nova collectio*, vol. 9 (Rome: Typis Vaticanis, 1837) 170–75.

Theophylact (11th century)
Patrologia graeca 123:487–682.

The Explanation by Blessed Theophylact, Archbishop of Ochrid and Bulgaria, of the Holy Gospel according to St. Mark; translated from the original Greek (Bl. Theophylact's Explanation of the New Testament 2; House Springs, MO; Chrysostom Press, 1993).

c. Renaissance and Reformation

Erasmus (16th century)
Joannis Leclerc, ed., *Desiderii Erasmi Roterodami opera omnia* (10 vols.; Leiden: Petri Vander Aa, 1703–6) vol. 7.

Erika Rummel, trans. and annotator, *Paraphrase on Mark* (NT Scholarship of Erasmus: Collected Works of Erasmus 49; Toronto/Buffalo/London: University of Toronto Press, 1988).

Marlorat, Augustin
A Catholike and Ecclesiasticall Exposition of the Holy

---

1   This book is available at the libraries of Boston College, University of Oxford, and Cambridge University.

2   According to Joseph Reuss, Cramer's edition is the most extensive and also the worst (*Matthäus-, Markus- und Johannes-Katenen nach den handschriftlichen Quellen untersucht* [NTAbh 18.4-5; Münster: Aschendorff, 1941] 137–38). John W. Burgon praised Matthaei's edition as having been produced "with his usual skill and accuracy," but noted that it had "become of extraordinary rarity." He praised Cramer's edition as "by far the fullest and most satisfactory exhibition of the Commentary of Victor of Antioch which has hitherto appeared" but regretted that the work is "disfigured in every page with errors so gross as to be even scandalous, and with traces of slovenly editorship which are simply unintelligible" (*The Last Twelve Verses of the Gospel according to S. Mark Vindicated against Recent Critical Objectors and Established* [Oxford and London: James Parker, 1871] 271).

Gospell after S. Marke and Luke: Gathered out of all the singular and approued deuines, vvhich the Lorde hath geuen to hys Church by Augustine Marlorat (trans. Thomas Timme; London: Thomas Marsh, 1583).[3]

Piscator, Johannes
Analysis Logica Evangelii secundum Marcum Una cum Scholiis et Observationibus Locorum Doctrinae (Londoni: Ex officina typographica Richardi Field, 1595).[4]

d. Seventeenth Century

Jansenius, Cornelius
"In Evangelium Iesu Christi secundum Marcum," in idem, *Tretrateuchus, sive Commentarius in sancta Iesu Christi evangelia* (Lovanii: Typis ac sumptibus Iacobi Zegeri, 1639) 407–46.

Lapide, Cornelius Corneliià
Commentarivs in Qvatvor Evangelia (Antverpiae: Apud Haered. Martini NvtI, 1639).[5]

Commentarii in S. Marci Evangelium in *Commentarii in Sacram Scripturam*, vol. 8: *Complectens Commentaria in Quattuor Evangelia: Matthaei, Marci, Lucae et Joannis* (Melitae: Typis Societatis Bibliographicae, 1849–50), pars II, pp. 571–620.

The Great Commentary of Cornelius à Lapide (trans. Thomas W. Mossman; London: John Hodges, 1881), vol. 3: *S. Matthew's Gospel Chaps 22–28; S. Mark's Gospel Complete*, pp. 355–448.

Commentaria in Quattuor Evangelia (ed. Antonius Padovani; 3rd rev. ed.; 2 vols.; Augustae Taurinorum: Sumptibus et typis Petri Marietti, 1922) 2:1–84.

Lightfoot, John
Horae Hebraicae et Talmudicae Impensae in Evangelium Sancti Marci (Cantabrigiae: Excudebat Johannes Field . . . prostant apud Thomam Danks, 1663).

Horae Hebraicae et Talmudicae: Hebrew and Talmudical Exercitations upon the Gospels, the Acts, Some Chapters of St. Paul's Epistle to the Romans and the First Epistle to the Corinthians (new ed. by Robert Gandell; 4 vols.; Oxford: Oxford University Press, 1859).

A Commentary on the New Testament from the Talmud and Hebraica, Matthew–1 Corinthians (reprint of the 1859 ed.; introd. by R. Laird Harris; 4 vols.; Grand Rapids: Baker, 1979), vol. 2: *Matthew and Mark*, pp. 385–480.

Pas, Angelus del
In sacrosanctum Evangelium secundum Marcum: Libri XV (ed. Luca Waddingo [Lucas Wadding] and Antonio Hiquaeo; Rome, 1623).[6]

Veil, Carolus Maria de
Explicatio literalis Evangelii secundum Matthaeum & Marcum, ex ipsis scripturarum fontibus, Hebraeorum ritibus & idiomatis, veterum & recentiorum monumentis eruta (Londini, 1678).[7]

e. Eighteenth Century

Elsner, Jacob
Ferdinandus Stosch, ed. *Jacob Elsner Magni Nominis Theologi Commentarius Critico-Philologicus in Euangelium Marci: Tomus Tertius* (Trajecti ad Rhenum: apud J. C. ten Bosch, 1773).

f. Nineteenth Century

Gould, Ezra P.
A Critical and Exegetical Commentary on the Gospel according to St. Mark (ICC; Edinburgh: T & T Clark; New York: Charles Scribner's Sons, 1896).

Hilgenfeld, Adolf B. C. C.
Das Markusevangelium nach seiner Composition, seiner Stellung in der Evangelien-Literatur, seinem Ursprung und Charakter (Leipzig: Breitkopf und Härtel, 1850).

Holtzmann, Heinrich Julius
Hand-commentar zum Neuen Testament, bearbeitet von H. J. Holtzmann, R. J. Lipsius, P. W. Schmiedel [und] H. von Soden (Freiburg i. B.: J. C. B. Mohr, 1889–91; 2nd rev. ed. 1892–93).

Klostermann, August
Das Markusevangelium nach seinem Quellenwerthe für die evangelische Geschichte (Göttingen: Vandenhoeck & Ruprecht, 1867).

Knabenbauer, Joseph
Commentarius in quattuor S. Evangelia Domini N. Iesu

---

3   As of October 5, 2006, this book was available as an online book at http://gateway.proquest.com/openurl?ctx_ver=Z39.88-2003&res_id=xri:eebo&rft_id=xri:eebo:image:1180 and at http://eebo.chadwyck.com/search/full_rec?SOURCE=pgimages.cfg&ACTION=ByID&ID=V1180.

4   As of October 16, 2006, this book was available online at http://gateway.proquest.com/openurl?

ctx%5Fver=Z39.88-2003&res%5Fid=xri:eebo&rft%5Fval%5Ffmt=&rft%5Fid=xri:eebo:image:12243.

5   This book is available in the library of Brown University.

6   This book is available in the library of Cambridge University.

7   This book is available in the library of Cambridge University.

Christi, vol. 2: *Evangelium secundum S. Marcum* (Paris: Lethielleux, 1894; 2nd ed. 1907).

Patrizi, Francesco Saverio
Francisci Xaverii Patritii e Societate Iesu in Marcum commentarium: cum duabus apendicibus (Rome: apud Iosephum Spithoever, 1862).

Paulus, Heinrich Eberhard Gottlob
Philologisch-kritischer und historischer Commentar über das Neue Testament (4 vols.; Lübeck: J. F. Bohn, 1804–5).[8]

Swete, Henry Barclay
The Gospel according to St. Mark: The Greek Text with Introduction, Notes and Indices (London: Macmillan, 1898; reprinted from the 1913 ed. as *Commentary on Mark: The Greek Text with Introduction, Notes and Indexes* (Grand Rapids: Kregel, 1977).

Weiss, Bernhard
Das Marcusevangelium und seine synoptischen Parallelen erklärt (Berlin: Hertz [Besser], 1872).

Weiss, Bernhard, and Johannes Weiss
Die Evangelien des Markus und Lukas (8th rev. ed.; MeyerK 1.2; Göttingen: Vandenhoeck & Ruprecht, 1892).

g. Twentieth Century

Achtemeier, Paul J.
Mark (Proclamation Commentaries; Philadelphia: Fortress, 1975; 2nd rev. ed. 1986).

Allen, Willoughby Charles
The Gospel according to Saint Mark: With Introduction, Notes and Map (Oxford Church Biblical Commentary; London: Rivingtons, 1915).

Cranfield, Charles E. B.
The Gospel according to Saint Mark (rev. ed.; CGTC; Cambridge/New York: Cambridge University Press, 1977; 1st ed. 1959).

Gnilka, Joachim
Das Evangelium nach Markus (2 vols.; EKK 2; Zurich: Benziger; Neukirchen-Vluyn: Neukirchener Verlag, 1978–79; 3rd rev. ed. 1989).

Grundmann, Walter
Das Evangelium nach Markus (ThHKNT 2; Berlin: Evangelische Verlagsanstalt, 1959).

Guelich, Robert A.
Mark 1–8:26 (WBC 34A; Dallas, TX: Word Books, 1989).

Gundry, Robert Horton
Mark: A Commentary on His Apology for the Cross (Grand Rapids: Eerdmans, 1993).

Hooker, Morna D.
The Gospel according to Saint Mark (BNTC 2; London: A & C Black; Peabody, MA: Hendrickson, 1991).

Hurtado, Larry W.
Mark (NIBC 2; Peabody, MA: Hendrickson, 1983).

Iersel, Bas M. F. van
Mark: A Reader-Response Commentary (Sheffield: Sheffield Academic Press, 1998).

Johnson, Sherman Elbridge
A Commentary on the Gospel according to St. Mark (HNTC; New York: Harper; London: A & C Black, 1960).

Juel, Donald
Mark (Augsburg Commentary on the New Testament; Minneapolis: Augsburg, 1990).

Klostermann, Erich
Das Markusevangelium erklärt (2nd rev. ed.; HNT 3; Tübingen: Mohr Siebeck, 1926; 3rd rev. ed. 1936; 4th ed. 1950).

Lagrange, Marie-Joseph
Évangile selon saint Marc (EtB; Paris: Victor Lecoffre, 1910; 4th rev. ed., Paris: Gabalda, 1928; 5th ed. 1929; reprinted 1966).

Lamarche, Paul
Évangile de Marc: Commentaire (EtB n.s. 33; Paris: Gabalda, 1996).

Lane, William L.
The Gospel according to Mark: The English Text with Introduction, Exposition and Notes (NICNT; Grand Rapids: Eerdmans, 1974).

Lohmeyer, Ernst
Das Evangelium des Markus übersetzt und erklärt (10th ed.; MeyerK 1.2; Göttingen: Vandenhoeck & Ruprecht, 1937; 17th ed. 1967).

Loisy, Alfred Firmin
L'Évangile selon Marc (Paris: Émile Nourry, 1912).

Lührmann, Dieter
Das Markusevangelium (HNT 3; Tübingen: Mohr Siebeck, 1987).

Mann, Christopher Stephen
Mark: A New Translation with Introduction and Commentary (AB 27; Garden City, NY: Doubleday, 1986).

Moule, Charles Francis Digby
The Gospel according to Mark (Cambridge Bible Commentary; Cambridge: Cambridge University Press, 1965).

Nineham, Dennis Eric
The Gospel of St. Mark (PGC; Harmondsworth, Middlesex; Baltimore: Penguin Books, 1963).

Pesch, Rudolf
Das Markusevangelium I. Teil: Einleitung und Kommentar zu Kap. 1,1–8,26 (HTK 2.1; Freiburg: Herder, 1976; 5th ed. 1989) and *Das Markusevangelium II. Teil: Kommentar zu Kap. 8,27–16,20* (HTK 2.2; Freiburg: Herder, 1977; 4th ed. 1991).

---

8   Vols. 1–3 contain a synoptic commentary on the Synoptic Gospels; vol. 4 is a commentary on the first half of John.

Rawlinson, Alfred Edward John
St. Mark: With Introduction, Commentary and Additional Notes (London: Methuen, 1925).

Schlatter, Adolf von
Die Evangelien nach Markus und Lukas ausgelegt für Bibelleser (Stuttgart: Calwer, 1947).

Schmid, Josef
Das Evangelium nach Markus übersetzt und erklärt (5th rev. ed.; RNT 2; Regensburg: F. Pustet, 1958); ET: *The Gospel according to Mark* (RNT; Staten Island, NY: Alba House, 1968).

Schmithals, Walter
Das Evangelium nach Markus (2 vols.; ÖTBK 2; Gütersloh: Mohn; Würzburg: Echter, 1979).

Schweizer, Eduard
Das Evangelium nach Markus übersetzt und erklärt (Das Neue Testament Deutsch 1; Göttingen: Vandenhoeck & Ruprecht, 1967); ET *The Good News according to Mark* (Atlanta: John Knox, 1970).

Taylor, Vincent
The Gospel according to St. Mark: The Greek Text with Introduction, Notes and Indexes (London: Macmillan, 1952; 2nd ed.; Grand Rapids: Baker, 1966).

Turner, Cuthbert Hamilton
The Gospel according to St. Mark: Introduction and Commentary (London: SPCK; New York: Macmillan, 1931).

Weiss, Bernhard
Commentary on the New Testament, vol. 1: *Matthew–Mark* (New York: Funk & Wagnalls, 1906).

Weiss, Johannes
Das Markusevangelium in vol. 1 of idem, *Die Schriften des Neuen Testaments* (2 vols.; Göttingen: Vandenhoeck & Ruprecht, 1906–7; 2nd rev. ed. 1907–8).

Wellhausen, Julius
Das Evangelium Marci übersetzt und erklärt (Berlin: G. Reimer, 1903; 2nd ed. 1909).

Wohlenberg, Gustav
Das Evangelium nach Markus (KNT 2; Leipzig: A. Deichert, 1910).

h. Twenty-First Century

Boring, M. Eugene
Mark: A Commentary (NTL; Louisville: Westminster John Knox , 2006).

Donahue, John R., and Daniel J. Harrington
The Gospel of Mark (SacP 2; A Michael Glazier Book; Collegeville, MN: Liturgical Press, 2002).

Dowd, Sharyn Echols
Reading Mark: A Literary and Theological Commentary on the Second Gospel (Reading the New Testament; Macon, GA: Smyth & Helwys, 2000).

Evans, Craig A.
Mark 8:27–16:20 (WBC 34B; Nashville: Thomas Nelson, 2001).

France, R. T.
The Gospel of Mark: A Commentary on the Greek Text
(New International Greek Commentary; Grand Rapids: Eerdmans; Carlisle, Cumbria, UK, 2002).

Marcus, Joel
Mark 1–8: A New Translation with Introduction and Commentary (AB 27; New York: Doubleday, 2000).

Moloney, Francis J.
The Gospel of Mark: A Commentary (Peabody, MA: Hendrickson, 2002).

Schenke, Ludger
Das Markusevangelium: Literarische Eigenart–Text und Kommentierung (Stuttgart: Kohlhammer, 2005).

2. Studies

Achtemeier, Paul J.
"'And He Followed Him': Miracles and Discipleship in Mark 10:46-52," *Semeia* 11 (1978) 115–45.

Idem
"'He Taught Them Many Things': Reflections on Marcan Christology," *CBQ* 42 (1980) 465–81.

Idem
"The Origin and Function of the Pre-Markan Miracle Catenae," *JBL* 91 (1972) 198–221.

Idem
"Toward the Isolation of Pre-Markan Miracle Catenae," *JBL* 89 (1970) 265–91.

Ahearne-Kroll, Stephen P.
"'Who Are My Mother and My Brothers?' Family Relations and Family Language in the Gospel of Mark," *JR* 81 (2001) 1–25.

Aland, Kurt
"Bemerkungen zum Schluss des Markusevangeliums," in E. Earle Ellis and Max Wilcox, eds., *Neotestamentica et Semitica: Studies in Honour of Matthew Black* (Edinburgh: T & T Clark, 1969) 157–80.

Idem
"Der Schluss des Markusevangeliums," in Maurits Sabbe, ed., *L'Évangile selon Marc: tradition et redaction* (BEThL 34; 2nd rev. ed.; Leuven: Leuven University Press/Peeters, 1988; 1st ed. 1974) 435–70.

Albertz, Martin
Die synoptischen Streitgespräche: Ein Beitrag zur Formengeschichte des Urchristentums (Berlin: Trowitzsch & Sohn, 1921).

Allison, Dale C., Jr.
"Mark 12.28-31 and the Decalogue," in Craig A. Evans and W. Richard Stegner, eds., *The Gospels and the Scriptures of Israel* (JSNTSup 104; SSEJC 3; Sheffield: Sheffield Academic Press, 1994) 270–78.

Anderson, Hugh
"The Old Testament in Mark's Gospel," in James M. Efird, ed., *The Use of the Old Testament in the New and Other Essays: Studies in Honor of William Franklin Stinespring* (Durham, NC: Duke University Press, 1972) 280–306.

Anderson, Janice Capel, and Stephen D. Moore, eds.
Mark & Method: New Approaches in Biblical Studies (Minneapolis: Fortress, 1992).

Aus, Roger David
"Caught in the Act": Walking on the Sea and the Release of Barabbas Revisited (SFSHJ 157; Atlanta: Scholars Press, 1998).

Idem
The Stilling of the Storm: Studies in Early Palestinian Judaic Traditions (ISFCJ; Binghamton, NY: Global Publications, 2000).

Idem
The Wicked Tenants and Gethsemane (ISFCJ 4; Atlanta: Scholars Press, 1996).

Backhaus, Knut
"'Lösepreis für viele' (Mk 10,45): Zur Heilsbedeutung des Todes Jesu bei Markus," in Thomas Söding, ed., *Der Evangelist als Theologe: Studien zum Markusevangelium* (SBS 163; Stuttgart: Katholisches Bibelwerk, 1995) 91–118.

Bacon, Benjamin Wisner
The Gospel of Mark: Its Composition and Date (New Haven: Yale University Press, 1925).

Idem
"After Six Days: A New Clue for Gospel Critics," *HTR* 8 (1915) 94–121.

Baltzer, Klaus
Die Biographie der Propheten (Neukirchen-Vluyn: Neukirchener Verlag, 1975).

Idem
The Covenant Formulary in Old Testament, Jewish, and Early Christian Writings (Oxford: Basil Blackwell, 1971).

Barr, James
"ʾAbbā Isn't Daddy," *JTS* n.s. 39 (1988) 28–47.

Barrett, Charles Kingsley
"The Background of Mark 10:45," in Angus J. B. Higgins, ed., *New Testament Essays: Studies in Memory of Thomas Walter Manson 1893–1958* (Manchester: Manchester University Press, 1959) 1–18.

Barton, Stephen C.
Discipleship and Family Ties in Mark and Matthew (SNTSMS 80; Cambridge: Cambridge University Press, 1994).

Bauckham, Richard J.
The Gospels for All Christians: Rethinking the Gospel Audiences (Grand Rapids: Eerdmans, 1998).

Bauernfeind, Otto
Die Worte der Dämonen im Markusevangelium (BWANT 44; Stuttgart: Kohlhammer, 1927).

Beasley-Murray, George R.
Jesus and the Last Days: The Interpretation of the Olivet Discourse (Peabody, MA: Hendrickson, 1993).

Becker, Eve-Marie
Das Markus-Evangelium im Rahmen antiker Historiographie (WUNT 194; Tübingen: Mohr Siebeck, 2006).

Belo, Fernando
A Materialist Reading of the Gospel of Mark (Maryknoll, NY: Orbis, 1981; 2nd rev. French ed. 1975).

Berger, Klaus
"Die königlichen Messiastraditionen des Neuen Testaments," *NTS* 20 (1973) 1–44.

Best, Ernest
Disciples and Discipleship: Studies in the Gospel according to Mark (Edinburgh: T & T Clark, 1986).

Idem
Following Jesus: Discipleship in the Gospel of Mark (JSNTSup 4; Sheffield: JSOT Press, 1981).

Idem
Mark: The Gospel as Story (Edinburgh: T & T Clark, 1983).

Idem
The Temptation and the Passion: The Markan Soteriology (2nd ed.; SNTSMS 2; Cambridge: Cambridge University Press, 1990; 1st ed. 1965).

Black, C. Clifton
The Disciples according to Mark: Markan Redaction in Current Debate (JSNTSup 27; Sheffield: JSOT Press/Sheffield Academic Press, 1989).

Idem
Mark: Images of an Apostolic Interpreter (Studies on Personalities of the New Testament; Columbia: University of South Carolina Press, 1994).

Idem
"An Oration at Olivet: Some Rhetorical Dimensions of Mark 13," in Duane F. Watson, ed., *Persuasive Artistry: Studies in New Testament Rhetoric in Honor of George A. Kennedy* (JSNTSup 50; Sheffield: Sheffield Academic Press, 1991) 66–92.

Blackburn, Barry
Theios Anēr and the Markan Miracle Traditions (WUNT 2.40; Tübingen: Mohr Siebeck, 1991).

Blenkinsopp, Joseph
"The Oracle of Judah and the Messianic Entry," *JBL* 80 (1961) 55–64.

Bond, Helen K.
Pilate in History and Interpretation (SNTSMS 100; Cambridge: Cambridge University Press, 1998).

Boobyer, George Henry
"Galilee and Galileans in St. Mark's Gospel," *BJRL* 35 (1952–53) 334–48; reprinted as *Galilee and Galileans in St. Mark's Gospel* (Manchester: John Rylands Library/Manchester University Press, 1953). The reprint has the same page numbering as the original publication.

Boomershine, Thomas E., and Gilbert L. Bartholomew
"The Narrative Technique of Mark 16:8," *JBL* 100 (1981) 213–23.

Booth, Roger P.
Jesus and the Laws of Purity: Tradition History and Legal History in Mark 7 (JSNTSup 13; Sheffield: JSOT Press, 1986).

Boring, M. Eugene
Truly Human/Truly Divine: Christological Language and the Gospel Form (St. Louis, MO: CBP Press, 1984).

Idem

"The Unforgivable Sin Logion Mark III 28-29/ Matt XII 31-32/Luke XII 10: Formal Analysis and History of the Tradition," *NovT* 18 (1976) 258-79.

Bornkamm, Günther

"Das Doppelgebot der Liebe," in *Neutestamentliche Studien für Rudolf Bultmann* (2nd rev. ed.; BZNW 21; Berlin: Töpelmann, 1957) 85-93.

Borrell, Agustí

The Good News of Peter's Denial: A Narrative and Rhetorical Reading of Mark 14:54.66-72 (SFISFCJ 7; Atlanta: Scholars Press/University of South Florida, 1998).

Brandenburger, Egon

Markus 13 und die Apokalyptik (Göttingen: Vandenhoeck & Ruprecht, 1984).

Breytenbach, Cilliers

"Das Markusevangelium als episodische Erzählung: Mit Überlegungen zum 'Aufbau' des zweiten Evangeliums," in Ferdinand Hahn, ed., *Der Erzähler des Evangeliums: Methodische Neuansätze in der Markusforschung* (SBS 118/119; Stuttgart: Katholisches Bibelwerk, 1985) 137-69.

Idem

"Das Markusevangelium als Traditionsgebundene Erzählung? Anfragen an die Markusforschung der achtziger Jahre," in Camille Focant, ed., *The Synoptic Gospels: Source Criticism and the New Literary Criticism* (BEThL 110; Leuven: Leuven University Press/Peeters, 1993) 77-110.

Idem

Nachfolge und Zukunftserwartung nach Markus: eine methodenkritische Studie (AThANT 71; Zurich: Theologischer Verlag, 1984).

Broadhead, Edwin K.

Teaching with Authority: Miracles and Christology in the Gospel of Mark (JSNTSup 74; Sheffield: JSOT Press, 1992).

Brooke, George J.

"4Q500 1 and the Use of Scripture in the Parable of the Vineyard," *DSD* 2 (1995) 268-94.

Brown, Raymond E.

"The Burial of Jesus (Mark 15:42-47)," *CBQ* 50 (1988) 233-45.

Idem

The Semitic Background of the Term "Mystery" in the New Testament (FBBS 21; Philadelphia: Fortress, 1968).

Brown, Schuyler

"'The Secret of the Kingdom of God' (Mark 4:11)," *JBL* 92 (1973) 60-74.

Brown, Scott G.

Mark's Other Gospel: Rethinking Morton Smith's Controversial Discovery (Studies in Christianity and Judaism 15; Waterloo: Wilfrid Laurier University Press/Canadian Corporation for Studies in Religion, 2005).

Idem

"The More Spiritual Gospel: Markan Literary Techniques in the Longer Gospel of Mark" (Ph.D. diss., University of Toronto, 1999).

Idem

"On the Composition History of the Longer ('Secret') Gospel of Mark," *JBL* 122 (2003) 89-110.

Bruce, Frederick Fyvie

"Render to Caesar," in Ernst Bammel and Charles F. D. Moule, eds., *Jesus and the Politics of His Day* (Cambridge/New York: Cambridge University Press, 1984) 249-63.

Burchard, Christoph

"Das doppelte Liebesgebot in der frühen christlichen Überlieferung," in Eduard Lohse, ed., *Der Ruf Jesu und die Antwort der Gemeinde: Exegetische Untersuchungen Joachim Jeremias zum 70. Geburtstag* (Göttingen: Vandenhoeck & Ruprecht, 1970) 39-62.

Burger, Christoph

Jesus als Davidssohn: Eine traditionsgeschichtliche Untersuchung (FRLANT 98; Göttingen: Vandenhoeck & Ruprecht, 1970).

Burkill, T. Alec

Mysterious Revelation: An Examination of the Philosophy of St. Mark's Gospel (Ithaca, NY: Cornell University Press, 1963).

Cahill, Michael, ed.

Expositio Evangelii secundum Marcum (CChrSL 82; Scriptores Celtigenae pars 2; Turnhout: Brepols, 1997).

Idem, trans. and ed.

The First Commentary on Mark: An Annotated Translation (New York/Oxford: Oxford University Press, 1998).

Callahan, Allen Dwight

"The *Acts of Saint Mark*: An Introduction and Commentary" (Ph.D. diss., Harvard University, 1992).

Idem

"The Acts of Saint Mark: An Introduction and Translation," *Coptic Church Review* 14 (1993) 3-10.

Camery-Hoggatt, Jerry

Irony in Mark's Gospel: Text and Subtext (SNTSMS 72; Cambridge/New York: Cambridge University Press, 1992).

Campbell, William Sanger

"Engagement, Disengagement and Obstruction: Jesus' Defense Strategies in Mark's Trial and Execution Scenes (14.53-64; 15.1-39)," *JSNT* 26 (2004) 283-300.

Cancik, Hubert, ed.

Markus-Philologie: historische, literargeschichtliche und stilistische Untersuchungen zum zweiten Evangelium (WUNT 33; Tübingen: Mohr Siebeck, 1984).

Carlston, Charles Edwin

"Transfiguration and Resurrection," *JBL* 80 (1961) 233-40.

Casey, Maurice

Aramaic Sources of Mark's Gospel (SNTSMS 102; Cambridge: Cambridge University Press, 1998).

Idem

"Idiom and Translation: Some Aspects of the Son of Man Problem," *NTS* 41 (1995) 164–82.

Idem

Son of Man: The Interpretation and Influence of Daniel 7 (London: SPCK, 1979) 224–40.

Idem

"The Son of Man Problem," *ZNW* 67 (1976) 147–54.

Cha, Jung-Sik

"Confronting Death: The Story of Gethsemane in Mark 14:32-42 and Its Historical Legacy" (2 vols.; Ph.D. diss., University of Chicago, 1996).

Charlesworth, James H.

"The Son of David: Solomon and Jesus (Mark 10.47)," in Peder Borgen and Søren Giversen, eds., *The New Testament and Hellenistic Judaism* (Peabody, MA: Hendrickson, 1995) 72–87.

Chilton, Bruce

"Jesus *ben David*: Reflections on the *Davidssohnfrage*," *JSNT* 14 (1982) 88–112.

Chronis, Harry L.

"To Reveal and To Conceal: A Literary-Critical Perspective on 'the Son of Man' in Mark," *NTS* 51 (2005) 459–81.

Idem

"The Torn Veil: Cultus and Christology in Mark 15:37-39," *JBL* 101 (1982) 97–114.

Collins, Adela Yarbro

"The Apocalyptic Rhetoric of Mark 13 in Historical Context," *BR* 41 (1996) 5–36.

Eadem

The Beginning of the Gospel: Probings of Mark in Context (Minneapolis: Fortress, 1992).

Eadem

"The Charge of Blasphemy in Mark 14.64," in *JSNT* 26 (2004) 379–401.

Eadem

"Establishing the Text: Mark 1:1," in Tord Fornberg and David Hellholm, eds., *Texts and Contexts: The Function of Biblical Texts in Their Textual and Situative Contexts* (Oslo: Scandinavian University Press, 1995) 111–27.

Eadem

"From Noble Death to Crucified Messiah," *NTS* 40 (1994) 481–503.

Eadem

"Jesus' Action in Herod's Temple," in eadem and Margaret M. Mitchell, eds., *Antiquity and Humanity: Essays on Ancient Religion and Philosophy Presented to Hans Dieter Betz on His 70th Birthday* (Tübingen: Mohr Siebeck, 2001) 45–61.

Eadem

"Mark and His Readers: The Son of God among Greeks and Romans," *HTR* 93 (2000) 85–100.

Eadem

"Mark and His Readers: The Son of God among Jews," *HTR* 92 (1999) 393–408.

Eadem

"Messianic Secret and the Gospel of Mark: Secrecy in Jewish Apocalypticism, the Hellenistic Mystery Religions, and Magic," in Elliott R. Wolfson, ed., *Rending the Veil: Concealment and Secrecy in the History of Religions* (New York/London: Seven Bridges, 1999) 11–30.

Eadem

"The Signification of Mark 10:45 among Gentile Christians," in François Bovon, ed., *Jesus' Sayings in the Life of the Early Church: Papers Presented in Honor of Helmut Koester's Seventieth Birthday, HTR* 90 (1997) 371–82.

Cook, John G.

The Structure and Persuasive Power of Mark: A Linguistic Approach (SBLSS; Atlanta: Scholars Press, 1995).

Cook, Michael J.

Mark's Treatment of the Jewish Leaders (NovTSup 51; Leiden: Brill, 1978).

Cotter, Wendy J.

"The Markan Sea Miracles: Their History, Formation, and Function in the Literary Context of Greco-Roman Antiquity" (Ph.D. diss., University of St. Michael's College, Toronto, 1991).

Cox, Steven Lynn

A History and Critique of Scholarship concerning the Markan Endings (Lewiston, NY: Edwin Mellen, 1993).

Crossley, James G.

"Halakah and Mark 7.4: '. . . and Beds,'" *JSNT* 25 (2003) 433–47.

Croy, N. Clayton

The Mutilation of Mark's Gospel (Nashville: Abingdon, 2003).

D'Angelo, Mary Rose

"*Abba* and 'Father': Imperial Theology and the Traditions about Jesus," *JBL* 111 (1992) 611–30.

Eadem

"Gender and Power in the Gospel of Mark: The Daughter of Jairus and the Woman with the Flow of Blood," in John C. Cavadini, ed., *Miracles in Jewish and Christian Antiquity: Imagining Truth* (Notre Dame Studies in Theology 3; Notre Dame, IN: University of Notre Dame Press, 1999) 83–109.

Eadem

"Theology in Mark and Q: *Abba* and 'Father' in Context," *HTR* 85 (1992) 149–74.

Danove, Paul L.

The End of Mark's Story: A Methodological Study (BIS 3; Leiden: Brill, 1993).

Davidsen, Ole

The Narrative Jesus: A Semiotic Reading of Mark's Gospel (Aarhus: Aarhus University Press, 1993).

Delorme, Jean

"Évangile et récit: la narration evangélique en Marc," *NTS* 43 (1997) 367–84.

Idem

"Prises de parole et parler vrai dans un récit de Marc (1, 21-28)," in Pietro Bovati and Roland Meynet, eds., *Ouvrir les écritures: mélanges offerts à Paul Beauchamp* (LD 162; Paris: Cerf, 1995) 179–99.

Idem

"La tête de Jean-Baptiste ou la parole pervertie: lecture d'un récit (Marc 6. 14-29)," in Pierre-Marie Baude, ed., *La Bible en littérature: Actes du colloque international de Metz* (Paris: Cerf; Metz: Université de Metz, 1997).

Deming, Will

"Mark 9.42–10.12; Matthew 5.27-32, and *B. Nid.* 13b: A First Century Discussion of Male Sexuality," *NTS* 36 (1990) 130–41.

Dewey, Joanna

"'Let Them Renounce Themselves and Take Up Their Cross': A Feminist Reading of Mark 8.34 in Mark's Social and Narrative World," in Amy-Jill Levine, ed., *A Feminist Companion to Mark* (Sheffield: Sheffield Academic Press, 2001) 23–36.

Eadem

Markan Public Debate: Literary Technique, Concentric Structure, and Theology in Mark 2:1–3:6 (SBLDS 48; Chico, CA: Scholars Press, 1980).

Dobschütz, Ernst von

"Zur Erzählerkunst des Markus," *ZNW* 27 (1928) 193–98.

Donahue, John R.

Are You the Christ? The Trial Narrative in the Gospel of Mark (SBLDS 10; Missoula, MT: Scholars Press, 1973).

Idem

"A Neglected Factor in the Theology of Mark," *JBL* 101 (1982) 563–94.

Dormeyer, Detlef

"Die Familie Jesu und der Sohn der Maria im Markusevangelium (3,20f.31-35; 6,3), in Hubert Frankemölle und Karl Kertelge, eds., *Vom Urchristentum zu Jesus: Für Joachim Gnilka* (Freiburg/Basel/Vienna: Herder, 1989) 109–35.

Idem

"Joh 18.1-14 par Mk 14.43-53: Methodologische Überlegungen zur Rekonstruktion einer vorsynoptischen Passionsgeschichte," *NTS* 41 (1995) 218–39.

Idem

"Die Kompositionsmetapher 'Evangelium Jesu Christi, des Sohnes Gottes' Mark 1.1: Ihre theologische und literarische Aufgabe in der Jesus-Biographie des Markus," *NTS* 33 (1987) 452–68.

Idem

Das Markusevangelium als Idealbiographie vom Jesus Christus, dem Nazarener (SBB 43; Stuttgart: Katholisches Bibelwerk, 1999).

Idem

"Mk 1,1-15 als Prolog des ersten idealbiographischen Evangeliums von Jesus Christus," *Biblical Interpretation* 5 (1997) 181–211.

Idem

Die Passion Jesu as Verhaltensmodell: Literarische und theologische Analyse der Traditions- und Redaktionsgeschichte der Markuspassion (NTAbh n.F. 11; Münster: Aschendorff, 1974).

Doudna, John Charles

The Greek of the Gospel of Mark (SBLMS 12; Philadelphia: SBL, 1961).

Dowd, Sharyn Echols

Prayer, Power, and the Problem of Suffering: Mark 11:22-25 in the Context of Markan Theology (SBLDS 105; Atlanta: Scholars Press, 1988).

Eadem and Elizabeth Struthers Malbon

"The Significance of Jesus' Death in Mark: Narrative Context and Authorial Audience," *JBL* (2006) 271–97.

Duff, Paul Brooks

"The March of the Divine Warrior and the Advent of the Greco-Roman King: Mark's Account of Jesus' Entry into Jerusalem," *JBL* 111 (1992) 55–71.

Duling, Dennis C.

"Solomon, Exorcism, and the Son of David," *HTR* 68 (1975) 235–52.

Dungan, David Laird

"Mark—The Abridgement of Matthew and Luke," in David G. Buttrick, ed., *Jesus and Man's Hope* (2 vols.; Pittsburgh: Pittsburgh Theological Seminary, 1970-71) 1:51–97.

Dwyer, Timothy

The Motif of Wonder in the Gospel of Mark (JSNTSup 128; Sheffield: Sheffield Academic Press, 1996).

Ebeling, Hans Jürgen

Das Messiasgeheimnis und die Botschaft des Marcus-Evangelisten (Berlin: A. Töpelmann, 1939).

Edwards, James R.

"Markan Sandwiches: The Significance of Interpolations in Markan Narratives," *NovT* 31 (1989) 193–216.

Ehrman Bart

"The Text of Mark in the Hands of the Orthodox," in Mark Burrows and Paul Rorem, eds., *Biblical Hermeneutics in Historical Perspective: Essays in Honor of Karlfried Froehlich* (Grand Rapids: Eerdmans, 1991) 19–31; reprinted, *LQ* 5 (1991) 143–56.

Elliott, James Keith

"An Eclectic Textual Commentary on the Greek Text of Mark's Gospel," in idem, ed., *The Language and Style of the Gospel of Mark: An Edition of C. H. Turner's "Notes on Marcan Usage" Together with Other Comparable Studies* (NovTSup 71; Leiden: Brill, 1993) 189–201.

Idem

"Mark 1.1-3—A Later Addition to the Gospel?" *NTS* 46 (2000) 584–88.

Idem

"The Text and Language of the Endings to Mark's Gospel," in idem, ed., *The Language and Style of the Gospel of Mark: An Edition of C. H. Turner's "Notes on*

Marcan Usage" Together with Other Comparable Studies (NovTSup 71; Leiden: Brill, 1993) 203–11.

Esler, Philip F.
"The Incident of the Withered Fig Tree in Mark 11: A New Source and Redactional Explanation," *JSNT* 28 (2005) 41–67.

Fander, Monika
Die Stellung der Frau im Markusevangelium unter besonderer Berücksichtigung kultur- und religions- geschichtlicher Hintergründe (2nd ed.; Altenberge: Telos, 1990).

Farmer, William Rueben
The Last Twelve Verses of Mark (London/New York: Cambridge University Press, 1974).

Farrer, Austin Marsden
A Study in St. Mark (Westminster, UK: Dacre, 1951).

Feigel, Friedrich Karl
Der Einfluss des Weissagungsbeweises und anderer Motive auf die Leidensgeschichte: Ein Beitrag zur Evan- gelienkritik (Tübingen: Mohr Siebeck, 1910).

Feldmeier, Reinhard
Die Krisis des Gottessohnes: Die Gethsemaneerzählung als Schlüssel der Markuspassion (WUNT 2.21; Tübin- gen: Mohr Siebeck, 1987).

Fleddermann, Harry T.
"The Discipleship Discourse (Mark 9:33-50), *CBQ* 43 (1981) 57–75.

Idem
"The Flight of a Naked Young Man (Mark 14:51- 52)," *CBQ* 41 (1979) 412–18.

Idem
Mark and Q: A Study of the Overlap Texts (BEThL 122; Leuven: Leuven University Press/Peeters, 1995).

Fowler, Robert M.
Let the Reader Understand: Reader-Response Criticism and the Gospel of Mark (Minneapolis: Fortress, 1991).

Idem
Loaves and Fishes: The Function of the Feeding Stories in the Gospel of Mark (SBLDS 54; Chico, CA: Schol- ars Press, 1981).

Frickenschmidt, Dirk
Evangelium als Biographie: Die vier Evangelien im Rahmen antiker Erzählkunst (TANZ 22; Tübingen/Basel: A. Francke, 1997).

Garrett, Susan R.
The Temptations of Jesus in Mark's Gospel (Grand Rapids: Eerdmans, 1998).

Geddert, Timothy J.
Watchwords: Mark 13 in Markan Eschatology (JSNTSup 26; JSOT Press, 1989).

Geyer, Douglas W.
Fear, Anomaly, and Uncertainty in the Gospel of Mark (ATLAMS 47; Lanham, MD/London: Scarecrow, 2002).

Giblin, Charles Homer
"The Beginning of the Ongoing Gospel (Mk 1,2–

16,8), in Frans van Segbroeck, Christopher M. Tuckett, G. van Belle, and J. Verheyden, eds., *The Four Gospels 1992: Festschrift Frans Neirynck* (3 vols.; BEThL 100; Leuven: Leuven University Press/Peeters, 1992) 2:975–85.

Gibson, Jeffrey B.
"Jesus' Refusal to Produce a 'Sign' (Mk 8.11-13)," *JSNT* 38 (1990) 37–66.

Idem
"Jesus' Wilderness Temptation according to Mark," *JSNT* 53 (1994) 3–34.

Idem
"The Rebuke of the Disciples in Mark 8.14-21," *JSNT* 27 (1986) 31–47.

Gillman, Florence Morgan
Herodias: At Home in That Fox's Den (Interfaces; Col- legeville, MN: Liturgical Press, 2003).

Glancy, Jennifer A.
"Unveiling Masculinity: The Construction of Gen- der in Mark 6:14-29," *BI* 2 (1994) 34–50.

Goodacre, Mark S.
The Case against Q: Studies in Markan Priority and the Synoptic Problem (Harrisburg, PA: Trinity Press International, 2002).

Gundry-Volf, Judith M.
"The Least and the Greatest: Children in the New Testament," in Marcia J. Bunge, ed., *The Child in Christian Thought* (Grand Rapids: Eerdmans, 2001) 29–60.

Guttenberger, Gudrun
Die Gottesvorstellung im Markusevangelium (BZNW 123; Berlin/New York: de Gruyter, 2004).

Haber, Susan
"A Woman's Touch: Feminist Encounters with the Hemorrhaging Woman in Mark 5:24-34," *JSNT* 26 (2003) 171–92.

Hagedorn, Anselm C., and Jerome H. Neyrey
"'It Was Out of Envy That They Handed Jesus Over' (Mark 15:10): The Anatomy of Envy and the Gospel of Mark," *JSNT* 69 (1998) 15–56.

Haren, Michael J.
"The Naked Young Man: A Historian's Hypothesis on Mark 14,51-5," *Bib* 79 (1998) 525–31.

Harrington, Daniel J.
What Are They Saying about Mark? (New York: Paulist, 2004).

Hartman, Lars
"Das Markusevangelium, 'für die lectio sollemnis im Gottesdienst abgefaßt'?" in idem, *Text-Centered New Testament Studies: Text-theoretical Essays on Early Jewish and Early Christian Literature* (ed. David Hell- holm; WUNT 102; Tübingen: Mohr Siebeck, 1997) 25–51.

Idem
Prophecy Interpreted: The Formation of Some Jewish Apocalyptic Texts and of the Eschatological Discourse Mark 13 Par. (CBNTS 1; Lund: Gleerup, 1966).

Idem

"Some Reflections on the Problem of the Literary Genre of the Gospels," in idem, *Text-Centered New Testament Studies* (ed. David Hellholm; Tübingen: Mohr Siebeck, 1997) 3–23.

Hatina, Thomas R.

In Search of a Context: The Function of Scripture in Mark's Narrative (JSNTSup 232; SSEJC 8; Sheffield: Sheffield Academic Press, 2002).

Hatton, Stephen B.

"Mark's Naked Disciple: The Semiotics and Comedy of Following," *Neotestamentica* 35 (2001) 35–48.

Hawkins, John C.

Horae Synopticae: Contributions to the Study of the Synoptic Problem (2nd ed.; Oxford: Clarendon, 1909).

Head, Peter M.

"A Text-Critical Study of Mark 1.1: 'The Beginning of the Gospel of Jesus Christ,'" *NTS* 37 (1991) 621–29.

Hedrick, Charles W.

"Parable and Kingdom: A Survey of the Evidence in Mark," *Perspectives in Religious Studies* 27 (2000) 179–99.

Idem

"The Role of 'Summary Statements' in the Composition of the Gospel of Mark: A Dialog with Karl Schmidt and Norman Perrin," *NovT* 26 (1984) 289–311.

Idem

"What Is a Gospel? Geography, Time and Narrative Structure," *Perspectives in Religious Studies* 10 (1983) 255–68.

Heidler, Johannes

"Die Verwendung von Psalm 22 im Kreuzigungsbericht des Markus: Ein Beitrag zur Frage nach der Christologie des Markus," in Hartmut Genest, ed., *Christi Leidenspsalm: Arbeiten zum 22. Psalm: Festschrift zum 50. Jahr des Bestehens des Theologischen Seminars "Paulinum" Berlin* (Neukirchen-Vluyn: Neukirchener Verlag, 1996) 26–34.

Heil, John Paul

Jesus Walking on the Sea: Meaning and Gospel Functions of Matt 14:22-33, Mark 6:45-52 and John 6:15b-21 (AnBib 87; Rome: Biblical Institute Press, 1981).

Idem

"Mark 14,1-52: Narrative Structure and Reader-Response," *Bib* 71 (1990) 305–32.

Idem

The Transfiguration of Jesus: Narrative Meaning and Function of Mark 9:2-8, Matt 17:1-8 and Luke 9:28-36 (AnBib 144; Rome: Pontificio Istituto Biblico, 2000).

Henaut, Barry W.

Oral Tradition and the Gospels: The Problem of Mark 4 (JSNTSup 82; Sheffield: JSOT Press, 1993).

Henderson, Suzanne Watts

"'Concerning the Loaves': Comprehending Incomprehension in Mark 6:45-52," *JSNT* 83 (2001) 3–26.

Hengel, Martin

Die Evangelienüberschriften (Vorgetragen am 18. Oktober, 1981; SHAW.PH 1984, 3; Heidelberg: Carl Winter/Universitätsverlag, 1984); ET: *Studies in the Gospel of Mark* (Philadelphia: Fortress, 1985) 64–84.

Idem

"Das Gleichnis von den Weingärtnern Mc 12 1-12 im Lichte der Zenonpapyri und der rabbinischen Gleichnisse," *ZNW* 59 (1968) 1–39.

Idem

"Jesus, the Messiah of Israel," in idem, *Studies in Early Christology* (Edinburgh: T & T Clark, 1995) 1–72.

Idem

Studies in the Gospel of Mark (Philadelphia: Fortress, 1985).

Herron, Robert W., Jr.

Mark's Account of Peter's Denial of Jesus: A History of Its Interpretation (Lanham, MD/New York/London: University Press of America, 1991).

Hilgert, Earle

"The Son of Timaeus: Blindness, Sight, Ascent, Vision in Mark," in Elizabeth A. Castelli and Hal Taussig, eds., *Reimagining Christian Origins: A Colloquium Honoring Burton L. Mack* (Valley Forge, PA: Trinity Press International, 1996) 185–98.

Horst, Pieter Willem van der

"Can a Book End with γάρ? A Note on Mark xvi. 8," *JTS* n.s. 23 (1972) 121–24.

Hughes, Kirk T.

"Framing Judas," *Semeia* 54 (1991) 222–33.

Hull, John M.

Hellenistic Magic and the Synoptic Tradition (SBT, 2nd series, 28; Naperville, IL: Allenson, 1974).

Hurtado, Larry W.

"Following Jesus in the Gospel of Mark—and Beyond," in Richard N. Longenecker, ed., *Patterns of Discipleship in the New Testament* (Grand Rapids: Eerdmans, 1996) 9–29.

Idem

"Greco-Roman Textuality and the Gospel of Mark: A Critical Assessment of Werner Kelber's *The Oral and the Written Gospel*," *Bulletin for Biblical Research* 7 (1997) 91–106.

Idem

"The Women, the Tomb, and the Climax of Mark," in Anne Fitzpatrick McKinley, Margaret Daly Denton, Brian McGing, and Zuleika Rodgers, eds., [Festschrift for Sean Freyne] (Leiden: Brill, forthcoming).

Iersel, Bas van

"The Gospel according to St. Mark—Written for a Persecuted Community?" *Nederlands Theologisch Tijdschrift* 34 (1980) 15–36.

Idem

Reading Mark (Edinburgh: T & T Clark; Collegeville, MN: Liturgical Press, 1988).

Incigneri, Brian J.
   The Gospel to the Romans: The Setting and Rhetoric of Mark's Gospel (BIS 65; Leiden/Boston: Brill, 2003).

Iverson, Kelly R.
   "A Further Word on Final Γάρ (Mark 16:8)," *CBQ* 68 (2006) 79–94.

Jackson, Howard M.
   "The Death of Jesus in Mark and the Miracle from the Cross," *NTS* 33 (1987) 16–37.

Janzen, J. Gerald
   "Resurrection and Hermeneutics: On Exodus 3.6 in Mark 12.26," *JSNT* 23 (1985) 43–58.

Jeffery, Peter
   The Secret Gospel of Mark Unveiled: Imagined Rituals of Sex, Death, and Madness in a Biblical Forgery (New Haven: Yale University Press, 2007).

Johnson, Earl S.
   "Is Mark 15.39 the Key to Mark's Christology?" *JSNT* 31 (1987) 3–22.

Idem
   "Mark VIII. 22-26: The Blind Man from Bethsaida," *NTS* 25 (1978–79) 370–83.

Idem
   "Mark 10:46-52: Blind Bartimaeus," *CBQ* 40 (1978) 191–204.

Jonge, Henk J. de
   "The Cleansing of the Temple in Mark 11:15 and Zechariah 14:21," in Christopher Tuckett, ed., *The Book of Zechariah and Its Influence* (Aldershot, Hampshire/Burlington, VT: Ashgate, 2003) 87–99.

Jonge, Marinus de
   "Mark 14:25 among Jesus' Words about the Kingdom of God," in William Petersen et al., eds., *Sayings of Jesus: Canonical and Non-Canonical: Essays in Honour of Tjitze Baarda* (NovTSup 89; Leiden: Brill, 1997) 123–35.

Joynes, Christine E.
   "A Question of Identity: 'Who Do People Say That I Am?' Elijah, John the Baptist and Jesus in Mark's Gospel," in Christopher Rowland and Crispin H. T. Fletcher-Louis, eds., *Understanding, Studying and Reading: New Testament Essays in Honour of John Ashton* (JSNTSup 153; Sheffield: Sheffield Academic Press, 1998) 15–29.

Eadem
   "The Reception History of Mark's Gospel," *Scripture Bulletin* 36 (2006) 24–32.

Eadem
   "The Returned Elijah? John the Baptist's Angelic Identity in the Gospel of Mark," *SJT* 58 (2005) 1–13.

Juel, Donald
   A Master of Surprise: Mark Interpreted (Minneapolis: Fortress, 1994).

Idem
   Messiah and Temple: The Trial of Jesus in the Gospel of Mark (SBLDS 31; Missoula, MT: Scholars Press, 1977).

Idem
   Messianic Exegesis: Christological Interpretation of the Old Testament in Early Christianity (Philadelphia: Fortress, 1988).

Kealy, Seán P.
   Mark's Gospel: A History of Its Interpretation from the Beginning until 1979 (New York: Paulist, 1982).

Keck, Leander E.
   "The Introduction to Mark's Gospel," *NTS* 12 (1965–66) 352–70.

Idem
   "Mark 3:7-12 and Mark's Christology," *JBL* 84 (1965) 341–58.

Kee, Howard Clark
   Community of the New Age: Studies in Mark's Gospel (Philadelphia: Westminster, 1977).

Idem
   "The Function of Scriptural Quotations and Allusions in Mark 11–16," in E. Earle Ellis and Erich Gräßer, eds., *Jesus und Paulus: Festschrift für Werner Georg Kümmel zum 70. Geburtstag* (Göttingen: Vandenhoeck & Ruprecht, 1975).

Idem
   "The Terminology of Mark's Exorcism Stories," *NTS* 14 (1967–68) 232–46.

Idem
   "The Transfiguration in Mark: Epiphany or Apocalyptic Vision?" in John Reumann, ed., *Understanding the Sacred Text: Essays in Honor of Morton S. Enslin on the Hebrew Bible and Christian Beginnings* (Valley Forge, PA: Judson, 1972) 135–52.

Kelber, Werner H.
   The Kingdom in Mark (Philadelphia: Fortress, 1974).

Idem
   "Mark 14:32-42: Gethsemane: Passion Christology and Discipleship Failure," *ZNW* 63 (1972) 166–87.

Idem
   Mark's Story of Jesus (Philadelphia: Fortress, 1979).

Idem
   The Oral and the Written Gospel (Philadelphia: Fortress, 1983).

Idem, ed.
   The Passion in Mark: Studies on Mark 14–16 (Philadelphia: Fortress, 1976).

Kelhoffer, James A.
   "'How Soon a Book' Revisited: ΕΥΑΓΓΕΛΙΟΝ as a Reference to 'Gospel' Materials in the First Half of the Second Century," *ZNW* 95 (2004) 1–34.

Idem
   The Diet of John the Baptist: "Locusts and Wild Honey" in Synoptic and Patristic Interpretation (WUNT 176; Tübingen: Mohr Siebeck, 2005)

Idem
   Miracle and Mission: The Authentication of Missionaries and Their Message in the Longer Ending of Mark (WUNT 2.112; Tübingen: Mohr Siebeck, 2000).

Kermode, Frank
   The Genesis of Secrecy: On the Interpretation of

Narrative (Cambridge, MA/London: Harvard University Press, 1979).

Kertelge, Karl
Die Wunder Jesu im Markusevangelium: Eine redaktionsgeschichtliche Untersuchung (SANT 23; Munich: Kösel, 1970).

Kilpatrick, George Dunbar
"Recitative λέγων," in James K. Elliott, ed., *The Language and Style of the Gospel of Mark: An Edition of C. H. Turner's "Notes on Marcan Usage" Together with Other Comparable Studies* (NovTSup 71; Leiden: Brill, 1993) 175–77.

Idem
"Some Notes on Marcan Usage," in James K. Elliott, ed., *The Language and Style of the Gospel of Mark: An Edition of C. H. Turner's "Notes on Marcan Usage" Together with Other Comparable Studies* (NovTSup 71; Leiden: Brill, 1993) 159–74.

Kim, Tae Hun
"The Anarthrous υἱὸς θεοῦ in Mark 15,39 and the Roman Imperial Cult," *Bib* 79 (1998) 221–41.

Kingsbury, Jack Dean
The Christology of Mark's Gospel (Philadelphia: Fortress, 1983).

Kinukawa, Hisako
Women and Jesus in Mark: A Japanese Feminist Perspective (Maryknoll, NY: Orbis, 1994).

Klauck, Hans-Josef
Vorspiel im Himmel? Erzähltechnik und Theologie im Markusprolog (Biblisch-Theologische Studien 32; Neukirchen-Vluyn: Neukirchener Verlag, 1997).

Kloppenborg, John S.
"*Evocatio deorum* and the Date of Mark," *JBL* 124 (2005) 419–50.

Idem
"Self-Help or *Deus ex Machina* in Mark 12.9?" *NTS* 50 (2004) 495–518.

Knox, John
"A Note on Mark 14:51-52," in Sherman E. Johnson, ed., *The Joy of Study: Papers on New Testament and Related Subjects Presented to Honor Frederick Clifton Grant* (New York: Macmillan, 1951) 27–30.

Koch, Dietrich-Alex
Die Bedeutung der Wundererzählungen für die Christologie des Markusevangeliums (BZNW 42; Berlin/New York: de Gruyter, 1975).

Koch, Klaus
"Spätisraelitisch-jüdische und urchristliche Danielrezeption vor und nach der Zerstörung des zweiten Tempels," in Reinhard Gregor Kratz und Thomas Krüger, eds., *Rezeption und Auslegung im Alten Testament und in seinem Umfeld: Ein Symposium aus Anlass des 60. Geburtstags von Odil Hannes Steck* (Orbis Biblicus et Orientalis 153; Freiburg, Schweiz: Universitätsverlag; Göttingen: Vandenhoeck & Ruprecht, 1997) section 5, "Daniel im Markusevangelium" (107–13).

Koester, Helmut
"History and Development of Mark's Gospel," in

Bruce Corley, ed., *Colloquy on New Testament Studies: A Time for Reappraisal and Fresh Approaches* (Macon, GA: Mercer University Press, 1983) 35–57.

Idem
"Mark 9:43-47 and Quintilian 8.3.75," *HTR* 71 (1978) 151–53.

Idem
"The Text of the Synoptic Gospels in the Second Century," in William L. Petersen, ed., *Gospel Traditions in the Second Century: Origins, Recensions, Text, and Transmission* (CJA 3; Notre Dame, IN: University of Notre Dame Press, 1989) 19–37.

Kollmann, Bernd
"Jesu Schweigegebote an die Dämonen," *ZNW* 82 (1991) 267–73.

Koskenniemi, Erkki, Kirsi Nisula, and Jorma Toppari
"Wine Mixed with Myrrh (Mark 15.23) and *Crurifragium* (John 19.31-32): Two Details of the Passion Narratives," *JSNT* 27 (2005) 379–91.

Kotansky, Roy
"Jesus and Heracles in Cádiz (τὰ Γάδειρα): Death, Myth, and Monsters at the 'Straits of Gibraltar' (Mark 4:35–5:43)," in Adela Yarbro Collins, ed., *Ancient and Modern Perspectives on the Bible and Culture: Essays in Honor of Hans Dieter Betz* (Scholars Press Homage Series; Atlanta: Scholars Press, 1998) 160–229.

Krause, Deborah
"Narrated Prophecy in Mark 11.12-21: The Divine Authorization of Judgment," in Craig A. Evans and W. Richard Stegner, eds., *The Gospels and the Scriptures of Israel* (JSNTSup 104; SSEJC 3; Sheffield: Sheffield Academic Press, 1994) 235–48.

Eadem
"Simon Peter's Mother-in-law—Disciple or Domestic Servant? Feminist Biblical Hermeneutics and the Interpretation of Mark 1.29-31," in Amy-Jill Levine, ed., *A Feminist Companion to Mark* (Sheffield: Sheffield Academic Press, 2001) 37–53.

Kuhn, Heinz-Wolfgang
Ältere Sammlungen im Markusevangelium (StUNT 8; Göttingen: Vandenhoeck & Ruprecht, 1971).

Idem
"Neuere Wege in der Synoptiker-Exegese am Beispiel des Markusevangeliums," in Friedrich Wilhelm Horn, ed., *Bilanz und Perspektiven gegenwärtiger Auslegung des Neuen Testaments: Symposion zum 65. Geburtstag von Georg Strecker* (BZNW 75; Berlin/New York: de Gruyter, 1995) 60–90.

Künze, Martin
Das Naherwartungslogion Markus 9,1 par: Geschichte seiner Auslegung (BGBE 21; Tübingen: Mohr Siebeck, 1977).

Lambrecht, Jan
Die Redaktion der Markus-Apokalypse: Literarische Analyse und Strukturuntersuchung (AnBib 28; Rome: Pontifical Biblical Institute, 1967).

Levine, Amy-Jill
"Discharging Responsibility: Matthean Jesus, Bibli-

cal Law, and Hemorrhaging Woman," in David R. Bauer and Mark Allan Powell, eds., *Treasures New and Old: Recent Contributions to Matthean Studies* (SBLSymS 1; Atlanta: Scholars Press, 1996) 379–97.

Eadem, ed.

A Feminist Companion to Mark (Sheffield: Sheffield Academic Press, 2001).

Liew, Tat-Siong Benny

Politics of Parousia: Reading Mark Inter(con)textually (Leiden/Boston: Brill, 1999).

Idem

"Tyranny, Boundary and Might: Colonial Mimicry in Mark's Gospel," *JSNT* 73 (1999) 7–31.

Lightfoot, Robert Henry

The Gospel Message of St. Mark (Oxford: Clarendon, 1950).

Idem

Locality and Doctrine in the Gospels (New York: Harper & Brothers, 1938).

Linton, Olof

"The Demand for a Sign from Heaven (Mk 8, 11-12 and Parallels)," *StTh* 19 (1965) 112–29.

Idem

"Der vermißte Markusschluß," *Theologische Blätter* 8 (1929) 229–34.

Lohmeyer, Ernst

Galiläa und Jerusalem (Göttingen: Vandenhoeck & Ruprecht, 1936).

Idem

"Und Jesus ging vorüber," *Nieuw Theologisch Tijdschrift* 23 (1934) 206–24; reprinted in idem, *Urchristliche Mystik: Neutestamentliche Studien* (Darmstadt: Hermann Gentner, 1956) 57–79.

Löhr, Hermut

"Bermerkungen zur Elia-Erwartung in den Evangelien: Ausgehend von Mk 9,11-13," in Klaus Grünwaldt and Harald Schroeter, eds., *Was suchst du hier, Elia? Ein hermeneutisches Arbeitsbuch* (Hermeneutica 4; Rheinbach-Merzbach: CMZ-Verlag, 1995) 85–95.

Longstaff, Thomas R. W.

Evidence of Conflation in Mark? A Study in the Synoptic Problem (SBLDS 28; Missoula, MT: Scholars Press, 1977).

Lövestam, Evald

Spiritus Blasphemia: Eine Studie zu Mk 3,28f par Mt 12,31f, Lk 12,10 (Lund: Gleerup, 1968).

Idem

"The ἡ γενεὰ αὕτη: Eschatology in Mk 13,30 parr.," in Jan Lambrecht, ed., *L'Apocalypse johannique et l'Apocalyptique dans le Nouveau Testament* (BEThL 53; Gembloux/Paris: Duculot; Leuven/Louvain: Leuven University Press, 1980) 403–13.

Luz, Ulrich

"Das Geheimnismotiv und die markinische Christologie," *ZNW* 56 (1965) 9–30; ET "The Secrecy Motif and the Markan Christology," in Christopher M. Tuckett, ed., *The Messianic Secret* (Issues in Reli-

gion and Theology; Philadelphia: Fortress; London: SPCK, 1983).

Idem

"Das Jesusbild der vormarkinischen Tradition," in Georg Strecker, ed., *Jesus Christus in Historie und Theologie: Neutestamentliche Festschrift für Hans Conzelmann zum 60. Geburtstag* (Tübingen: Mohr Siebeck, 1975) 347–74.

MacDonald, Dennis R.

The Homeric Epics and the Gospel of Mark (New Haven/London: Yale University Press, 2000).

Mack, Burton L.

A Myth of Innocence: Mark and Christian Origins (Philadelphia: Fortress, 1988).

Magness, J. Lee

Sense and Absence: Structure and Suspension in the Ending of Mark's Gospel (SBLSS; Atlanta: Scholars Press, 1986).

Malbon, Elizabeth Struthers

In the Company of Jesus: Characters in Mark's Gospel (Louisville, KY: Westminster John Knox, 2000).

Eadem

"Galilee and Jerusalem: History and Literature in Marcan Interpretation," *CBQ* 44 (1982) 242–55.

Eadem

Hearing Mark: A Listener's Guide (Harrisburg, PA: Trinity Press International, 2002).

Eadem

Narrative Space and Mythic Meaning in Mark (San Francisco, CA: Harper & Row, 1986).

Maloney, Elliott C.

Semitic Interference in Marcan Syntax (SBLDS 51; Chico, CA: Scholars Press, 1981).

Marcus, Joel

"The Beelzebul Controversy and the Eschatologies of Jesus," in Bruce D. Chilton and Craig A. Evans, eds., *Authenticating the Activities of Jesus* (Leiden/Boston: Brill, 1999) 247–77.

Idem

"Crucifixion as Parodic Exaltation," *JBL* 125 (2006) 73–87.

Idem

"The Jewish War and the *Sitz im Leben* of Mark," *JBL* 111 (1992) 441–62.

Idem

"Mark 4:10-12 and Markan Epistemology," *JBL* 103 (1984) 557–74.

Idem

The Mystery of the Kingdom of God (SBLDS 90; Atlanta: Scholars Press, 1986).

Idem

The Way of the Lord: Christological Exegesis of the Old Testament in the Gospel of Mark (Louisville: Westminster John Knox, 1992).

Marshall, Christopher D.

Faith as a Theme in Mark's Narrative (SNTSMS 64; Cambridge/New York: Cambridge University Press, 1989).

Marxsen, Willi
Mark the Evangelist: Studies on the Redaction History of the Gospel (Nashville: Abingdon, 1969). ET of idem, *Der Evangelist Markus: Studien zur Redaktionsgeschichte des Evangeliums* (2nd ed.; Göttingen: Vandenhoeck & Ruprecht, 1959; 1st ed. 1956).

Matera, Frank
"The Incomprehension of the Disciples and Peter's Confession (Mark 6,14–8,30)," *Bib* 70 (1989) 153–72.

Idem
The Kingship of Jesus: Composition and Theology in Mark 15 (SBLDS 66; Chico, CA: Scholars Press, 1982).

Idem
"The Prologue as the Interpretive Key to Mark's Gospel," *JSNT* 34 (1988) 3–20.

McCurley, Foster R., Jr.
"'And after Six Days' (Mk. 9:2): A Semitic Literary Device," *JBL* 93 (1974) 67–81.

McGowan, Andrew
"'Is There a Liturgical Text in this Gospel?' The Institution Narratives and Their Early Interpretive Communities," *JBL* 118 (1998) 73–87.

Meier, John P.
"The Circle of the Twelve: Did It Exist during Jesus' Public Ministry?" *JBL* 116 (1997) 635–72.

Idem
"The Debate on the Resurrection of the Dead: An Incident from the Ministry of the Historical Jesus?" *JSNT* 77 (2000) 3–24.

Idem
"The Historical Jesus and the Historical Law: Some Problems within the Problem," *CBQ* 65 (2003) 52–79.

Merritt, Robert L.
"Jesus Barabbas and the Paschal Pardon," *JBL* 104 (1985) 57–68.

Mitchell, Joan L.
Beyond Fear and Silence: A Feminist-Literary Approach to the Gospel of Mark (New York/London: Continuum, 2001).

Mitchell, Margaret M., and Patricia A. Duncan
"Chicago's 'Archaic Mark' (MS 2427): A Reintroduction to Its Enigmas and a Fresh Collation of Its Readings," *NovT* 48 (2006) 1–35.

Moeser, Marion C.
The Anecdote in Mark, the Classical World and the Rabbis (JSNTSup 227; Sheffield: Sheffield Academic Press, 2002).

Mohr, Till Arend
Markus- und Johannespassion: Redaktions- und traditionsgeschichtliche Untersuchung der Markinischen und Johanneischen Passionstradition (AThANT 70; Zürich: Theologischer Verlag, 1982).

Moloney, Francis J.
"Mark 6:6b-30: Mission, the Baptist, and Failure," *CBQ* 63 (2001) 647–63.

Moo, Douglas J.
The Old Testament in the Gospel Passion Narratives (Sheffield: Almond, 1983).

Moss, Candida R.
"The Transfiguration: An Exercise in Markan Accommodation," *Biblical Interpretation* 12 (2004) 69–89.

Motyer, Stephen
"The Rending of the Veil: A Markan Pentecost?" *NTS* 33 (1987) 155–57.

Myers, Ched
Binding the Strong Man: A Political Reading of Mark's Story of Jesus (Maryknoll, NY: Orbis, 1988).

Myllykoski, Matti
Die letzten Tage Jesu: Markus, Johannes, ihre Traditionen und die historische Frage (2 vols.; Suomalaisen Tiedeakatemian Toimituksia [Annales Academiae Scientiarum Fennicae] B. 256, 272; Helsinki: Suomalainen Tiedeakatemia, 1991, 1994).

Neirynck, Frans
"The Apocryphal Gospels and the Gospel of Mark," in Jean-Marie Sevrin, ed., *The New Testament in Early Christianity: La réception des écrits néotestamentaires dans le christianisme primitif* (BEThL 86; Leuven: Leuven University Press/Peeters, 1989) 123–75.

Idem
Duality in Mark: Contributions to the Study of the Markan Redaction (BEThL 31; Leuven: Leuven University Press/Peeters, 1972; rev. ed. with supplementary notes, 1988).

Idem
"La Fuite du jeune homme en Mc 14,51-52," *EThL* 55 (1979) 43–66.

Idem
"Marc 13: Examen critique de l'interpretation de R. Pesch," in Jan Lambrecht, ed., *L'Apocalypse johannique et l'Apocalyptique dans le Nouveau Testament* (BEThL 53; Gembloux: Duculot; Leuven: Leuven University Press, 1980) 369–401.

Idem
"Papyrus Egerton and the Healing of the Leper," *EThL* 61 (1985) 153–60; reprinted in idem, *Evangelica II* (BEThL 99; Leuven: Leuven University Press; Leuven: Peeters, 1991) 773–83.

Idem
"The Tradition of the Sayings of Jesus: Mark 9, 33-50," in *The Dynamism of Biblical Tradition* (New York: Paulist Press, 1967) = *Concilium* 20 (1967) 62–74.

Idem, ed., with Theo Hansen and Frans van Segbroeck
The Minor Agreements of Matthew and Luke against Mark with a Cumulative List (BEThL 37; Leuven: Leuven University Press, 1974).

Idem and Jozef Verheyden, Frans van Segbroeck, Geert van Oyen, and R. Corstjens
The Gospel of Mark: A Cumulative Bibliography 1950-

1990 (BEThL 102; Leuven: Leuven University Press/Peeters, 1992).

New, David S.
Old Testament Quotations in the Synoptic Gospels, and the Two-Document Hypothesis (SBLSCS 37; Atlanta: Scholars Press, 1993).

Nickelsburg, George W. E.
"The Genre and Function of the Markan Passion Narrative," *HTR* 73 (1980) 153-84.

Niederwimmer, Kurt
"Johannes Markus und die Frage nach dem Verfasser des zweiten Evangeliums," *ZNW* 58 (1967) 172-88.

Oden, Thomas C., and Christopher A. Hall, eds.
Mark (Ancient Christian Commentary on Scripture, NT 2; Downers Grove, IL: InterVarsity, 1998).

Oyen, Geert van
The Interpretation of the Feeding Miracles in the Gospel of Mark (Collectanea Biblica et Religiosa Antiqua 4; Brussel: Wetenschappelijk Comité voor Godsdienstwetenschappen Koninklijke Vlaamse Academie van België voor Wetenschappen en Kunsten, 1999).

Idem and Tom Shepherd, eds.
The Trial and Death of Jesus: Essays on the Passion Narrative in Mark (Leuven: Peeters, 2006).

Perrin, Norman
"Mark XIV.62: The End Product of a Christian Pesher Tradition?" *NTS* 12 (1965-66) 150-55; reprinted in idem, *A Modern Pilgrimage in New Testament Christology* (Philadelphia: Fortress, 1974) 10-22.

Idem
A Modern Pilgrimage in New Testament Christology (Philadelphia: Fortress, 1974).

Idem
"Towards an Interpretation of the Gospel of Mark," in Hans Dieter Betz, ed., *Christology and a Modern Pilgrimage: A Discussion with Norman Perrin* (Claremont, CA: New Testament Colloquium, 1971) 1-78.

Idem
What Is Redaction Criticism? (GBS; Philadelphia: Fortress, 1969).

Pesch, Rudolf
Der Besessene von Gerasa (SBS 56; Stuttgart: Katholisches Bibelwerk, 1972).

Idem
Das Evangelium der Urgemeinde: Wiederhergestellt und erläutert (Freiburg/Basel/Vienna: Herder, 1979).

Idem
Naherwartungen: Tradition und Redaktion in Mark 13 (KBANT; Düsseldorf: Patmos, 1968).

Peterson, Dwight N.
The Origins of Mark: The Markan Community in Current Debate (BIS 48; Leiden/Boston: Brill, 2000).

Pryke, E. J.
Redactional Style in the Markan Gospel (SNTSMS 33; Cambridge: Cambridge University Press, 1978).

Quesnell, Quentin
The Mind of Mark: Interpretation and Method through the Exegesis of Mark 6:52 (AnBib 38; Rome: Pontifical Biblical Institute, 1969).

Räisänen, Heikki
"Jesus and the Food Laws: Reflections on Mark 7.15," *JSNT* 16 (1982) 79-100.

Idem
The 'Messianic Secret' in Mark (Studies of the New Testament and Its World; Edinburgh: T & T Clark, 1990).

Rhoads, David
Reading Mark, Engaging the Gospel (Minneapolis: Fortress, 2004).

Idem, Joanna Dewey, and Donald Michie
Mark as Story: An Introduction to the Narrative of a Gospel (2nd ed.; Minneapolis: Fortress, 1999).

Robbins, Vernon K.
"The Healing of Blind Bartimaeus (10:46-52) in the Marcan Theology," *JBL* 92 (1973) 224-43.

Idem
Jesus the Teacher: A Socio-Rhetorical Interpretation of Mark (Philadelphia: Fortress, 1984).

Idem
"Pronouncement Stories and Jesus' Blessing of the Children: A Rhetorical Approach," *Semeia* 29 (1983) 43-74.

Robinson, James M.
The Problem of History in Mark (SBT; Naperville, IL: Allenson, 1957); reprinted in idem, *The Problem of History in Mark and Other Markan Studies* (Philadelphia: Fortress, 1982).

Rogers, T. J.
"Shaking the Dust off the Markan Mission Discourse," *JSNT* 27 (2004) 169-92.

Roloff, Jürgen
"Das Markusevangelium als Geschichtsdarstellung," *EvTh* 27 (1969) 73-93.

Roskam, Hendrika Nicoline
The Purpose of the Gospel of Mark in Its Historical and Social Context (NovTSup 114; Leiden/Boston: Brill, 2004).

Ross, J. M.
"The Young Man Who Fled Naked: Mark 15:51-2," *Irish Biblical Studies* 13 (1991) 170-74.

Sabbe, Maurits
L'Évangile selon Marc: tradition et redaction (BEThL 34; 2nd rev. ed.; Leuven: Leuven University Press/Peeters, 1988; 1st ed. 1974).

Schenk, Wolfgang
Der Passionsbericht nach Markus: Untersuchungen zur Überlieferungsgeschichte der Passionstraditionen (Gütersloh: Mohn, 1974).

Schenke, Hans-Martin
"The Mystery of the Gospel of Mark," *Second Century* 4 (1984) 65-82.

Schenke, Ludger
Der gekreuzigte Christus: Versuch einer literarkritischen

und traditionsgeschichtlichen Bestimmung der vormarkinischen Passionsgeschichte (SBS 69; Stuttgart:
Katholisches Bibelwerk, 1974).

Idem

*Studien zur Passionsgeschichte des Markus: Tradition
und Redaktion in Markus 14, 1-42* (FB 4; Würzburg:
Echter Verlag; Stuttgart: Katholisches Bibelwerk,
1971).

Idem

Die Wundererzählungen des Markusevangeliums (SBB;
Stuttgart: Katholisches Bibelwerk, 1974).

Schildgen, Brenda Deen

*Power and Prejudice: The Reception of the Gospel of
Mark* (Detroit: Wayne State University Press, 1999).

Schmidt, Karl Ludwig

"Die literarische Eigenart der Leidensgeschichte
Jesu," *Die Christliche Welt* 32 (1918) 114–16;
reprinted in Meinrad Limbeck, ed., *Redaktion und
Theologie des Passionsberichtes nach den Synoptikern*
(Wege der Forschung 481; Darmstadt: Wis-
senschaftliche Buchgesellschaft, 1981) 17–20.

Idem

*Der Rahmen der Geschichte Jesu: Literarkritische Unter-
suchungen zur ältesten Jesusüberlieferung* (Berlin:
Trowitzsch & Sohn, 1919; reprinted Darmstadt:
Wissenschaftliche Buchgesellschaft, 1964).

Schmidt, T. E.

"Mark 15.16-32: The Crucifixion Narrative and the
Roman Triumphal Procession," *NTS* 41 (1995) 1–
18.

Schmithals, Walter

*Wunder und Glaube: Eine Auslegung von Markus
4,35—6,6a* (BSt 59; Neukirchen-Vluyn: Neukirchener Verlag, 1970).

Schneck, Richard

Isaiah in the Gospel of Mark I–VIII (BIBAL Dissertation Series 1; Vallejo, CA: BIBAL, 1994).

Schneider, Gerhard

"Die Verhaftung Jesu: Traditionsgeschichte von Mk
14.43-52," *ZNW* 63 (1972) 188–209.

Schnellbächer, Ernst L.

"Das Rätsel des *νεανίσκος* bei Markus," *ZNW* 73
(1982) 127–35.

Scholtissek, Klaus

"'Er ist nicht ein Gott der Toten, sondern der
Lebenden' (Mk 12,27): Grundzüge der markini-
schen Theologie," in Thomas Söding, ed., *Der
lebendige Gott: Studien zur Theologie des Neuen
Testaments; Festschrift für Wilhelm Thüsing zum 75.
Geburtstag* (Münster: Aschendorff, 1996) 71–100.

Idem

*Die Vollmacht Jesu: Traditions- und redaktions-
geschichtliche Analysen zu einem Leitmotiv markinischer
Christologie* (NTAbh 25; Münster: Aschendorff,
1992).

Schreiber, Johannes

*Die Markuspassion: Eine redaktionsgeschichtliche Unter-
suchung* (2nd ed.; BZNW 68; Berlin/New York: de
Gruyter, 1993).

Schwankl, Otto

*Die Sadduzäerfrage (Mk 12, 18-27 parr): Eine
exegetisch-theologische Studie zur Auferstehungserwartung* (BBB 66; Frankfurt: Athenäum, 1987).

Schwier, Helmut

Tempel und Tempelzerstörung (NTOA 11; Freiburg:
Universitätsverlag; Göttingen: Vandenhoeck &
Ruprecht, 1989).

Scroggs, Robin, and Kent I. Groff

"Baptism in Mark: Dying and Rising with Christ,"
JBL 92 (1973) 531–48.

Seeley, David

"Rulership and Service in Mark 10:41-45," *NovT* 35
(1993) 234–50.

Sellew, Philip

"Oral and Written Sources in Mark 4.1-34," *NTS* 36
(1990) 234–67.

Idem

"*Secret Mark* and the History of Canonical Mark,"
in Birger A. Pearson, ed., *The Future of Early Christianity: Essays in Honor of Helmut Koester* (Minneapolis: Fortress, 1991) 242–57.

Senior, Donald

The Passion of Jesus in the Gospel of Mark (Wilmington, DE: Michael Glazier, 1984).

Shepherd, Tom

*Markan Sandwich Stories: Narration, Definition, and
Function* (AUSDDS 18; Berrien Springs, MI:
Andrews University Press, 1993).

Shiner, Whitney Taylor

"The Ambiguous Pronouncement of the Centurion
and the Shrouding of Meaning in Mark," *JSNT* 78
(2000) 3–22.

Idem

Follow Me! Disciples in Markan Rhetoric (SBLDS 145;
Atlanta: Scholars Press, 1995).

Idem

*Proclaiming the Gospel: First Century Performance of
Mark* (Harrisburg, PA: Trinity Press International,
2003).

Skeat, Theodore C.

"*ΑΡΤΟΝ ΦΑΓΕΙΝ*: A Note on Mark iii. 20-21," in
Traianos Gagos and Roger S. Bagnall, eds., *Essays
and Texts in Honor of J. David Thomas* (American
Studies in Papyrology 42; Oakville, CT: American
Society of Papyrologists, 2001) 29–30.

Smith, Morton

Clement of Alexandria and a Secret Gospel of Mark
(Cambridge, MA: Harvard University Press, 1973).

Smith, Stephen H.

"The Function of the Son of David Tradition in
Mark's Gospel," *NTS* 42 (1996) 523–39.

Idem

*A Lion with Wings: A Narrative-Critical Approach to
Mark's Gospel* (Biblical Seminar 38; Sheffield:
Sheffield Academic Press, 1996).

Snodgrass, Klyne R.

The Parable of the Wicked Tenants (WUNT 27; Tübingen: Mohr Siebeck, 1983).

Sorensen, Eric
Possession and Exorcism in the New Testament and Early Christianity (WUNT 2.157; Tübingen: Mohr Siebeck, 2002).

Standaert, Benoit H. M. G. M.
L'Évangile selon Marc: Composition et genre litteraire (Nijmegen: Stichting Studentenpers Nijmegen, 1978).

Stegner, William Richard
"The Use of Scripture in Two Narratives of Early Jewish Christianity (Matthew 4.1-11; Mark 9.2-8)," in Craig A. Evans and James A. Sanders, eds., *Early Christian Interpretation of the Scriptures of Israel: Investigations and Proposals* (JSNTSup 148; SSEJC 5; Sheffield: Sheffield Academic Press, 1997) 98–120.

Stein, Robert H.
"Is the Transfiguration (Mark 9:2-8) a Misplaced Resurrection-Account?" *JBL* 95 (1976) 79–96.

Stock, Klemens
Boten aus dem Mit-Ihm Sein: Das Verhältnis zwischen Jesus und den Zwölf nach Markus (AnBib 70; Rome: Biblical Institute Press, 1975).

Strelan, Rick
"A Greater than Caesar: Storm Stories in Lucan and Mark," *ZNW* 91 (2000) 166–79.

Suhl, Alfred
Die Funktion der alttestamentlichen Zitate und Anspielungen im Markusevangelium (Gütersloh: Mohn, 1965).

Sundwall, Johannes
Die Zusammensetzung des Markusevangeliums (AAABO.H 9.2; Åbo: Åbo Akademi, 1934).

Svartvik, Jesper
Mark and Mission: Mk 7:1-23 in its Narrative and Historical Contexts (CBNTS 32; Stockholm: Almqvist & Wiksell, 2000).

Swanson, Reuben J., ed.
New Testament Greek Manuscripts: Variant Readings Arranged in Horizontal Lines against Codex Vaticanus, Mark (Sheffield: Sheffield Academic Press; Pasadena, CA: William Carey International University Press, 1995).

Tannehill, Robert C.
"The Disciples in Mark: The Function of a Narrative Role," *JR* 57 (1977) 386–405.

Idem
"The Gospel of Mark as Narrative Christology," *Semeia* 16 (1979) 57–95.

Taylor, Joan E.
"The Garden of Gethsemane Not the Place of Jesus' Arrest," *BAR* 21.4 (July/August 1995) 26–35, 62.

Eadem
"Golgotha: A Reconsideration of the Evidence for the Sites of Jesus' Crucifixion and Burial," *NTS* 44 (1998) 180–203.

Eadem
The Immerser: John the Baptist within Second Temple Judaism (Grand Rapids/Cambridge: Eerdmans, 1997).

Taylor, Justin
"The Coming of Elijah, Mt 17,10-13 and Mk 9,11-13: The Development of the Texts," *RB* 98 (1991) 107–19.

Telford, William Rodgers
The Barren Temple and the Withered Tree: A Redaction-critical Analysis of the Cursing of the Fig-Tree Pericope in Mark's Gospel and Its Relation to the Cleansing of the Temple Tradition (JSNTSup 1; Sheffield: JSOT Press, 1980).

Idem
Interpretation of Mark (2nd ed.; Edinburgh: T & T Clark, 1995).

Idem
The Theology of the Gospel of Mark (Cambridge: Cambridge University Press, 1999).

Theissen, Gerd
"Die pragmatische Bedeutung der Geheimnismotive im Markusevangelium: Ein wissenssoziologischer Versuch," in Hans G. Kippenberg and Guy G. Stroumsa, eds., *Secrecy and Concealment: Studies in the History of Mediterranean and Near Eastern Religions* (SHR 65; Leiden: Brill, 1995) 225–45.

Thrall, Margaret E.
"Elijah and Moses in Mark's Account of the Transfiguration," *NTS* 16 (1970) 305–17.

Tillesse, G. Minette de
Le secret messianique dans L'Évangile de Marc (LD 47; Paris: Cerf, 1968).

Tilly, Michael
Johannes der Täufer und die Biographie der Propheten: Die synoptische Täuferüberlieferung und das jüdische Prophetenbild zur Zeit des Täufers (BWANT 137; Stuttgart: Kohlhammer, 1994).

Tolbert, Mary Ann
Sowing the Gospel: Mark's World in Literary-Historical Perspective (Minneapolis: Fortress, 1989).

Trakatellis, Demetrios
Authority and Passion: Christological Aspects of the Gospel according to Mark (Brookline, MA: Holy Cross Orthodox Press, 1987).

Trocmé, Etienne
The Formation of the Gospel according to Mark (Philadelphia: Westminster, 1975). ET of idem, *La formation de l'Évangile selon Marc* (Paris: Presses Universitaires de France, 1963).

Idem
The Passion as Liturgy: A Study in the Origin of the Passion Narratives in the Four Gospels (London: SCM, 1983).

Tuckett, Christopher
"Thomas and the Synoptics," *NovT* 30 (1988) 132–57.

Idem, ed.
The Messianic Secret (London: SPCK; Philadelphia: Fortress, 1983).

Turner, Cuthbert Hamilton
"Did Codex Vercellensis (a) Contain the Last Twelve Verses of St. Mark?" *JTS* 29 (1927) 16–18.

Idem
"Marcan Usage: Notes, Critical and Exegetical, on the Second Gospel," *JTS* 25 (1924) 377–86; 26 (1924) 12–20; 26 (1925) 145–56, 225–40, 337–46; 27 (1926) 58–62; 28 (1926) 9–30; 28 (1927) 349–62; 29 (1928) 275–89; 346–61; reprinted in James K. Elliott, ed., *The Language and Style of the Gospel of Mark: An Edition of C. H. Turner's "Notes on Marcan Usage" Together with Other Comparable Studies* (NovTSup 71; Leiden: Brill, 1993) 3–136.

Idem
"A Textual Commentary on Mark 1," *JTS* 28 (1927) 145–58.

Idem
"Western Readings in the Second Half of St. Mark's Gospel," *JTS* 29 (1927) 1–16.

Ulansey, David.
"The Heavenly Veil Torn: Mark's Cosmic *Inclusio*," *JBL* 110 (1991) 123–25.

Vanhoye, Albert
"La fuite du jeune homme nu (Mc 14,51-52)," *Bib* 52 (1971) 401–6.

Verheyden, Joseph
"Describing the Parousia: The Cosmic Phenomena in Mk 13,24-25," in Christopher M. Tuckett, ed., *The Scriptures in the Gospels* (BEThL 131; Leuven: Leuven University Press/Peeters, 1997) 527–550.

Idem
"Persecution and Eschatology: Mk 13,9-13," in Frans van Segbroeck, Christopher M. Tuckett, G. van Belle, and Joseph Verheyden, eds., *The Four Gospels 1992: Festschrift Frans Neirynck* (3 vols.; Leuven: Leuven University Press/Peeters, 1992) 2:1141–59.

Via, Dan O., Jr.
The Ethics of Mark's Gospel—in the Middle of Time (Philadelphia: Fortress, 1985).

Vines, Michael E.
The Problem of Markan Genre: The Gospel of Mark and the Jewish Novel (SBLAB 3; Leiden/Boston: Brill, 2002).

Vorster, Willem S.
"The Function of the Use of the Old Testament in Mark," *Neotestamentica* 14 (1980).

Idem
"Literary Reflections on Mark 13:5-37: A Narrated Speech of Jesus," *Neotestamentica* 21 (1987) 91–112.

Waetjen, Herman
"The Ending of Mark and the Gospel's Shift in Eschatology," *Annual of the Swedish Theological Institute* 4 (1965) 114–31.

Wahlde, Urban C. von
"Mark 9:33-50: Discipleship: The Authority That Serves," *BZ* n.F. 29 (1985) 49–67.

Watts, Rikki E.
"Jesus' Death, Isaiah 53, and Mark 10:45: A Crux Revisited," in William H. Bellinger, Jr., and William R. Farmer, eds., *Jesus and the Suffering Servant: Isaiah 53 and Christian Origins* (Harrisburg, PA: Trinity Press International, 1998) 125–51.

Weeden, Theodore J., Sr.
Mark—Traditions in Conflict (Philadelphia: Fortress, 1971).

Wegener, Mark I.
Cruciformed: The Literary Impact of Mark's Story of Jesus and His Disciples (Lanham, MD: University Press of America, 1995).

Weiss, Johannes
Das älteste Evangelium: Ein Beitrag zum Verständnis des Markusevangeliums und der ältesten evangelischen Überlieferung (Göttingen: Vandenhoeck & Ruprecht, 1903).

Weiss, Wolfgang
"Eine neue Lehre in Vollmacht": Die Streit- und Schulgespräche des Markus-Evangeliums (BZNW 52; Berlin/New York: de Gruyter, 1989).

Whitters, Mark F.
"Why Did the Bystanders Think Jesus Called upon Elijah before He Died (Mark 15:34-36)? The Markan Position," *HTR* 95 (2002) 119–24.

Wiarda, Timothy
"Peter as Peter in the Gospel of Mark," *NTS* 45 (1999) 19–37.

Wilke, Christian Gottlob
Der Urevangelist oder exegetisch kritische Untersuchung über das Verwandtschaftsverhältniss der drei ersten Evangelien (Dresden/Leipzig: Gerhard Fleischer, 1838).

Wills, Lawrence M.
The Quest for the Historical Gospel: Mark, John, and the Origins of the Gospel Genre (London/New York: Routledge, 1997).

Wischmeyer, Oda
"Herrschen als Dienen—Mk 10,41-45," *ZNW* 90 (1999) 28–44.

Wrede, William
The Messianic Secret (Cambridge/London: James Clarke, 1971). ET of idem, *Das Messiasgeheimnis in den Evangelien: Zugleich ein Beitrag zum Verständnis des Markusevangeliums* (Göttingen: Vandenhoeck & Ruprecht, 1901; reprinted 1969).

Wright, Addison G.
"The Widow's Mites: Praise or Lament?—A Matter of Context," *CBQ* 44 (1982) 256–65.

Wuellner, Wilhelm H.
The Meaning of "Fishers of Men" (NTL; Philadelphia: Westminster, 1967).

Yeung, Maureen W.
Faith in Jesus and Paul: A Comparison with Special Reference to 'Faith that Can Remove Mountains' and 'Your Faith Has Healed/Saved You' (WUNT 2.147; Tübingen: Mohr Siebeck, 2002).

Zager, Werner
Gottesherrschaft und Endgericht in der Verkündigung Jesu: Eine Untersuchung zur markinischen Jesusüber-

lieferung einschliesslich der Q-Parallelen (BZNW 82; Berlin: de Gruyter, 1996).

Zeller, Dieter

"Bedeutung und religionsgeschichtlicher Hintergrund der Verwandlung Jesu (Markus 9:2-8)," in Bruce D. Chilton and Craig A. Evans, eds., *Authenticating the Activities of Jesus* (NTTS 28.2; Leiden/Boston: Brill, 1999) 303–21.

Idem

"Die Beseitigung des Handels im Tempel (Mk 11,15-19): Ein Beispiel für die umstrittene Stellung Jesu zum jüdischen Kult," in Reinhard Wunderlich

and Bernd Feininger, eds., *Variationen des Christseins—Wege durch die Kirchengeschichte* (Frankfurt am Main: Peter Lang, 2006) 65–81.

Idem

"Die Handlungsstruktur der Markuspassion," *Tübinger theologische Quartalschrift* 159 (1979) 213–27.

Zerwick, Max

Untersuchungen zum Markus-Stil: Ein Beitrag zur stilistischen Durcharbeitung des Neuen Testaments (Scripta Pontificii Instituti Biblici; Romae: E Pontificio Instituto Biblico, 1937).

Index[1]

---

1   Superscripted numbers refer to footnotes in this volume.

34:14	22[75]	18:22	451	15:25, 26	185[27]
34:21	201[122]	18:24-30	358	15:32-36	207, 208[161]
34:28	151	19:14	361[184]	15:37-41	338[133], 573
34:29	417[20]	19:15. 35	359	15:39-40	573
40:34-35	425	19:16a	359	15:41	573[73]
		19:17, 18	574	16	611
Leviticus		19:18	566, 570,	18:8-20	345[37]
2:3 LXX	443[i]		572, 574[86]	18:15	502[130]
4:20	185	19:20	501	18:28	563
4:26, 31, 35	185[27]	19:22	185[27]	19:2	518
4:27-35	208[163]	19:31	228, 229[115]	19:7	138[25]
4:27	207[155]	20:9 LXX	351	19:8	138[25]
5:6, 10, 13,		20:10	469	24:15-19	54
16, 18, 26	185[27]	20:21	560	24:17	48
5:14-16	352	20:27	208, 228,	25:1-18	223
6:1-7 (5:20-26			229	25:15	218[35]
LXX)	478	21:7, 13-14	463	27:17	319
8:12	642[201]	21:10	705	28:16-25	640[177]
10:6	705	22:6	138[25]	31:8	218[35]
11:32	349	23:4-8	640[117]	34:11	156[1]
11:22	145[65]	23:7-8	624	35:2-5	201[122]
14:1-32	179	23:43	424[81]	35:29-34	258[157]
14:2, 4	179	25:5-9	203[132]	35:31-34	501, 502
14:9	138[25]	25:24	501		
14:12-13 LXX	139	25:26	501[124]	Deuteronomy	
14:12	139	25:51-52	501	1:15	324[33], 325
14:16	138	26:1	702	4	142[44]
15	349[78]	26:40-45	144[56]	4:35	575
15:4, 21, 23, 26	349	27:31 LXX	500	5	478[44], 568
15:8, 11	348			5:8	528
15:13	138[25]	Numbers		5:16	351
15:16	138[25]	1:2, 20	326	5:12-16	201[122]
15:18	138[25]	1:6	218[36]	5:16-20	474[c]
15:25-30	283	2:12	218[36]	5:16	479
16	232[132]	3:11-13 LXX	502	5:17	478
16:4	138[25]	3:12	502	5:18	478
16:24	138[25]	3:35	218[36]	5:19	358, 478
16:26	138[25]	3:40-51	502[131]	5:20	478
16:27-28	138[25]	3:46, 48, 49, 51	502[131]	6:3	146[66]
16:29, 31	198	6:3	756	6:4-9	573
18:5	477	11:16-25	348	6:4-5	570, 572,
18:6-20, 22-23	358	11:25	148		573[73]
18:12-13	306[89]	11:26-30	448	6:4	135[7], 137,
18:16	306, 307,	11:38-50	448		571-73, 575
	560	13:27	146[66]	6:5	566, 567,
18:18	461, 463	14:19	185[23]		572-574,
		14:22	384[53]		576, 590

844

851

17–18	51
17	51[56]
17:21-25	51[56], 55
17:21-24	63, 65
17:27	51
17:32	55, 66
17:43	66
18:8-9	66

Sibylline Oracles

1.103	453[118]
1.351-59	812[91]
2.154-76	606[103], 607[105]
2.158-59	607[105]
2.187-89	423[69]
3.591-94	346
3.605-6	702[43]
3.618	702[43]
4.28	702[43]
4:152-70	141, 144[54]
4:171-78	146
4.186	453[118]
6.13-16	812[91]
8.269-81	812[91]
frg. 3, lines 46-49	476

Testament of the Twelve Patriarchs

Testament of Benjamin

3:1-3	566[9]
10:3	566
10:5-6	564

Testament of Dan

5	233[143]
5:3	566
5:10-11	233[141]
6:4	602[85]

Testament of Issachar

5:1-2	566
5:2	566
7:6	566[9]

Testament of Joseph

6	815

6:1	814[109]
6:5	814
11:1	566[9]

Testament of Judah

24:2	762[295]
25:1	564[150]

Testament of Levi

2:6	148[80], 762[295]
5:1	762[295]
18:6	148[80], 762[295]
18:12	233[143]

Testament of Simeon

6:5	659[115]

Testament of Zebulon

5:1	566[12], 575[89]
7:6	575[89]
9:8	659[115]

Testament of Abraham

16:11	680[69]

Testament of Isaac

2:1-6	564
12:1—13:1	564

Testament of Solomon

2:1	168
2:8	230[122]
3:5-6	168
4:3-7	168[67]
5:2-3	168
5:5	170[75]
6:2	230
6:4	230
7:1-7	169[68]
8:1-12	168[67]
9:1-2	168[67]
10:1-2	169
11	269
11:1-7	169[70]
12:1-5	168[67]
12:2	439

13:1-7	169[68]
14:1-8	168[67]
15:1-6	168[67]
16	262
16:3	231
17:1-5	168[67]
18:1-42	168[67]
20:1-21	170[75]
20:12	170
22:16-19	168[67]
25:1-4	168[67]

Vitae prophetarum

3	321
21:6	320[10]
22:8	320[10]

c) Dead Sea Scrolls and Related Texts

1QapGen

20:16-17, 26	49[43]
20:28-29	370
20:28	49, 172[95]
21:2	268[60]

1QH

9:21	246
11:9-18	259
11:14	259[18]
11:15	259[15]
11:19-23	788[148]
12:5-6	758[261]
12:9-10	758
12:11	758
13:8-9	159[15]
13:23-24 (=5:23-24)	651[44]
14:14-16	244
14:22-24	259
14:30 (=6:30)	64[97]
19:10-14	788
19:12	788

1QpHab

2:1-2	223[81]
2:3-10	411[140]

27:64	440[a]	6:14-16	218[26]	9:44	440
28:1	779[a]	6:15	215[f], 221[66]	9:49-50	447
28:2-3	416[12]	6:16	222	10:1	222, 293[a]
28:3	416[11]	6:17	211[b]	10:7	300, 600[64]
28:5	780[c]	6:20-26	480	10:8	354[123]
28:8	808	6:20-21	472	10:11	301
28:9	800[279]	6:27-36	575	10:12	301
28:10	659	6:38	253[a]	10:17	439
28:11-15	781[84]	6:46	555[59]	10:19	113, 814
28:16-20	659, 800[279],	7:12-15	106	10:25-28	565[3]
	808	7:17	174[103]	10:25	572
28:16-17	807	7:20	133[c]	10:27	572
28:16	414	7:22	812[91]	11:4	188[50], 681
28:19-20	365[6], 803	7:27	136[16]	11:10	536[124]
		7:33	133[c], 198[111]	11:15	230[121]
Luke		7:34	197	11:21-22	228[105]
1:1	16	7:36, 46	642[207]	11:23	447
1:2	42[186]	8:2	808	11:24-26	439[110]
1:3	85	8:9	247[a]	11:29-30	260[23]
1:11	422[60]	8:12	250[b]	11:29	348
1:35	425	8:17	105	11:32	803[13]
3:11	299[26]	8:24	259	11:38	348
3:16-17	146[68]	8:25	257[e]	11:47-51	21[36]
3:16	133[f], 146	8:26	263[a]	11:47-48	546[70]
3:21	762[293]	8:39	265[m]	12:1	386
3:22	134[h]	8:41	274	12:8-9	410, 810[72]
3:25-26	221[59]	8:46	283[153]	12:11-12	595
4:23-24	291	9:1	214[c], 813	12:49-50	497
4:38-39	174[106]	9:3	300	13:6-9	525
4:38	174[a]	9:5	293[d], 300[38],	13:20	475[21]
4:41	161[d], 175[a]		301, 302[48]	13:28-29	657
5:1-11	507	9:9	294[j]	13:34-35	21[36]
5:1	156[l], 318[q]	9:7	294[k]	14:7-11	583
5:11	156	9:13	315	14:27	396[d], 408
5:12-16	178	9:16	317[i], 325,	14:31	264[c]
5:14	178[c]		653[c]	14:34-35	455
5:20	181[d]	9:19	133[c], 396[a]	15:1-2	194[82]
5:27, 29	190	9:22	396[c], 440	15:22	583[173]
5:30	194[82]	9:23-24	408	16:16	412[154]
5:34	196[a]	9:23	396[d], 408	16:18	458[e], 469-70
5:37	196[b]	9:24	396[e], 409[113]	16:19-31	564
5:38	196[c]	9:25-26	409[119]	16:24, 27, 30	718[65]
6:1	200[a]	9:26	410	17:1b-2	652
6:4	200[b], 756[233]	9:29	414[a]	17:3-4	188[50]
6:5	200[d]	9:39	161[d]	17:6	522[c], 532
6:6	205[a]	9:41	437	17:11-19	178[123]
6:13	214[a]	9:43	440[4]	17:12	264[c]

Acts (*cont.*)

26:16	422
27:35	379[18]
28:1-10	814
28:3-6	113
28:4	260[21]
28:6	375[111]

Romans

1:1-7	20
1:1	15[5], 134[k], 643[218]
1:3-4	800
1:9	15[7], 643[218]
1:16	365[7], 411[134], 643[218]
1:25	704[59]
1:27	688
1:29	359
2:5-8	789
2:16	643[218]
3:24-25	503, 504
3:25-26	503
5:20	374[100]
6:3-4	811[77]
6:3	811[77]
7:1-3	469
7:4	252[67]
8:3-4, 14-15, 17	147[78]
8:15-16	679
8:15	678[57], 679[59]
9:5	704[59]
9:22	652[54]
10:16	643[218]
10:20-21	267[53]
11:7-8	209
11:25-26	106
11:28	643[218]
12:9-10	575
13:8-10	575
13:10	109[82]
13:13	360[179]
14:1-4	356[140]
15:3	681[81]
15:9	681[81]
15:16	15[5], 134[k], 643[218]

15:18-19	811
15:19	15[7], 643[218]
15:24	299
16:13	736
16:16	685[116]
16:25	803

1 Corinthians

1:1	298[18]
1:12	101, 218[30]
1:13-17	811[77]
1:21	803[13]
2:4	803[13]
2:9	744
3:7-10	548
3:13, 15	454
3:16	702[37]
3:22	101, 218[30]
4:15	482, 643[218]
5:5	455[134]
5:6-8	386
5:7	83, 655
6:11	147
6:20	503[139]
7:7-10	459
7:10-11	470[110]
7:10	468
7:27	469
8:8	356
9:1	315[157], 659
9:5	101, 218[30], 292
9:12	15[7], 643[218]
9:14	600, 643[218]
9:18	643[218]
9:19-23	499
9:23	643[218]
10:7	655
10:16-18	654
10:20	197[101]
10:21	380
11:17-26	654
11:23-24	379[17]
11:23	654
11:24	653-55
11:25	654[67], 656
11:27-32	655

12:13	811[77]
13:2	532, 535[118]
14:22-23	811
14:22	814[102]
14:27	598[40]
15:1-34	790
15:1-4	80[1]
15:1	643[218]
15:3-7	660[117]
15:3-5	650[33]
15:3-4	687
15:3	80, 801[280]
15:4-8	800[279]
15:4	399, 405, 440[a], 775
15:5-7	781
15:5	217, 218[30], 224, 422[59], 797
15:7-8	315[157]
15:7	292[225]
15:12	789
15:14	
15:21-22, 26	794
15:23	789
15:24-28	582[168]
15:25-27	579
15:26	789
15:33	192[70]
15:33b-36	790
15:42-44a	790
15:43	421
15:44a	790
15:44b-49	791
15:49	421
15:50	790
15:51-57	791
15:51-53	421
16:2	654
16:6	299
16:11	299
16:20	685[116]

2 Corinthians

1:1	298[18]
2:12	15[5]
3:18	415[9], 421[51]

Dioscorides
De material medica
1.64.3   742
1.66.1   741[97]

Empedocles
Καθαρμοί ("Purifications")
Frg. 102   212[3]
Frg. 112   212[3]

Epictetus
Dissertationes
3.6.6   479
3.22.10   78
3.22.22   78
3.22.23-24   79
3.22.26-49   74[12]
3.22.39   79
3.22.43-44   79
3.22.45-47   78
3.22.69   79
3.23.23-38   195[89]
4.1.159-177   635[134]
4.4.33   479
4.6.34   479[55]
4.7.19-20   679

Enchiridion
1   479[55]

Euripides
Bacchae
704–13   321

Hecuba
294–95   499

Galen
De locis affectis
4.9   373

On the Natural Faculties
3.7 §163   370

On Tromos, Palmos, Spasmos, and Rigos
On the Differences between Symptoms   280[136]

Herodotus
History
1.4   40
1.23-24   36[149], 39[169]
1.30   630[93]
1.41.1   419
1.107-30   629
1.177-88   629
1.201-14   629
2.123, 125   36[149]
3.9   36[149]
3.61-66   629
4.36   283[152]
6.38   630[93]
7.34-35   261
7.56   331
7.152   36[149]
9.109   309

Hesiod
Opera et Dies
336   587[217]

Scutum Herculis
168   270[82]

Hippocrates
ἀφορισμοί ("Aphorisms")
3.16   435[55]
3.20   435[55]
3.22   435[55]
3.29   435[55]
5.7   435[55]

Precepts
3   245
4, 6   281

Morbus Sacer
1.10   435[58]
2.1-5   435[59]
3.6-7   435[60]
4.29-32   435[62]
5.7-8   435[63]
8.1-2   435[63]
10.3-6   435[61]

15.1-14   438[93]
15.1-8   435[60]
21.26   436[69]

Homer
Iliad
2.353   221[54]
6.266   344[33]
13.23-31   328
15.128-29   387[83]
18.375   322[15]
20.81-81   418
20.131   418
23.65-107   782[90]

Odyssey
7.20   418
10.1-69   258
10.47-49   259[16]
10.212-13   815[116]
10.274-306   815[116]
11.14-19   782[90]
11.204-8   782[90]
11.488-91   782[90]
13.73-80   259[16]
13.222-23   418
13.288-89   418
17.485-87   418
20.102-5   221[54]

Hom. Hymn
2.268-74   418
2.275-80   418
22   262[34]
31.10-13   422
33.8-10   259[19]
33.11-12   259[15]

Iamblichus
Vita Pythagorae
6.30   213[4]
92   282
28.135   335[114]

Inscriptiones Graecae
IV², 1.4   392[109]
IV², 1.9   392[109]

Xenophon
Memorabilia Socratis
(*cont.*)
4.5.1   215[12]
4.6.1   215[12]
4.7.1   215[12]
4.8.7   215[12]

k) Medieval, Reformation, Renaissance and Early Modern (through 1799)

Albertus Magnus
Secundum Marcum
ad 8:1-3   113

Bede
ad 14:51-52   688
Homily
I.1   111[107]
II.6   111[108]

John Calvin
Commentarius in harmonium evangelicam
ad 4:26   114
ad 7:31-37   115

Philip of Side
frg. 6   815[114]

Martin Luther
ad 7:31-37   114
ad 8:1   114
ad 10:35-45   114
ad 16:14   114

Pseudo-Jerome
Expositio Evangelii secundum Marcum
ad 7:32-36   107
ad 14:51-52   688-89

Theophylact
Explanation by Blessed Theophylact
ad 4:26-29   107[54], 112
ad 6:6b-7   298[19]
ad 16:18-20   113

Victor of Antioch
ad 4:26-29   107
ad 7:31-37   107
ad 16:8-20   805

2. Greek Words

ἀββᾶ
678–80

ἀγαπητός
150, 426, 543,
546–47, 752

ἀγρός
624, 736

αἰών
483

αἷμα
280

ἅλας
455

ἁμαρτωλός
411, 682

ἀναστενάζω
384

ἀνδριάς
13, 610

ἀνίστημι
405, 782

ἀποκάλυψις
19

ἀπολύω
470

ἀποστέλλω
296, 297, 314–15

ἀρχή
42, 130–31,
606–608

ἀσέλγεια
360

ἀφροσύνη
362

αὐλή
725

βαπτίζω, βάπτισμα
496–97, 690

βδέλυγμα
13, 597, 608–10

Βεελζεβούλ
229–30

βίος
22–23, 28–29, 237,
590

βλασφημέω,
βλασφημία
361, 706, 749

Βοανηργές
219–20

γέεννα
453

γραμματεύς
73, 75, 164, 571

γράφω, γραφή
430–31, 649–50,
687

γρηγορέω
618–19, 677

γυμνός
688, 693–94

δεσμός
372–73

δέω
233

διδάσκω,
διδάσκαλος
74–77, 215, 296,
440, 647

διήγησις
16, 635

δόλος
359–60, 640

δύναμις
282–83, 574

ἐκλεκτός
49, 70, 611

ἐπιγραφή
747

εὐαγγέλιον
3, 15–17, 20,
129–30, 246

εὐλογέω
379

εὐχαριστέω
325, 379

ἐξουδενέω
431

θηρίον
153

θλῖψις
43, 607–8, 613

ἴδιος
593, 602

ἱλαστήριον
503–4

ἱμάτιον
511, 583

ἱστορία
16, 17, 36

ἰσχύς, ἰσχυρός
64, 65, 146, 233,
590

καλέω
196

καρδία
355–57

κηρύσσω
79

κλοπή
358

κοινόω, κοινός
343–44

κοδράντης
589

κύριος
469, 518, 547, 705

κύων
366–67, 371

λῃστής
532[82], 686, 714,
748

λόγος
251, 599–600, 817

λύτρον
81, 500–503

μάστιξ
213, 282

μεταμορφόω
418

μετανοέω
155

μοιχεία
358

μύρον
642

μυστήριον
209, 247–48,
403

ναός
759–60

ὁδός
398

οἶκος, οἰκία
226, 481, 584

ὁμολογέω
143, 410

ὄξος
756–58

παιδίον
449, 473, 560

παραβολή
231, 240–42, 616

παραδίδωμι
81, 154, 440, 485,
712

παράδοσις
347–50

παρρησία
300, 312, 406

παρουσία
515–17

πάσχω
404

πειράζω
151, 459

πίστις
258, 288, 507

πλεονεξία
358–59

πονηρία
359

πορνεία
358

πορφύρα
726

πούς
453

προσκυνέω,
προσευχή
163, 728

πῶλος
517–18

ῥαββί
76, 511

3. Subjects[2]

---

2   The following list does not repeat page numbers for subjects given in the table of contents but may include additional references to them.

880

611, 613, 623, 625, 652

Temple
344–35, 351–53, 399–400, 521–32, 538–39, 587–88, 601–2, 607–11, 626–27, 700–703, 759–64

Touch, communication of power by
107–8, 178–79, 276–79, 280–85, 338, 370, 393–94, 471, 473

Trust. *See* "faith"

4. Authors[3]

Abrahams, I.
149[83], 164[47], 191[66], 194, 203[136], 204, 324[30], 424[73], 476[30], 477, 574[86], 584[190], 585[197], 718,

Achtemeier, P.
4, 91, 174[102], 258, 265, 276, 284[164], 286[187], 288, 289[195], 326–27, 338[131], 364, 369[51], 374, 378–81, 383, 394, 505[147], 506[159], 507–8, 510[211], 524, 551[20], 578[178], 582[169]

Ahearne-Kroll, S.
481[73], 652[52], 759[268], 771[377]

Aland, K.
122, 124[45], 802–5, 807

Aland, B.
122

Albertz, M.
182–83, 550–51

Albl, M.
579–81, 705[6]

Albright, W.
229[119]

Alkier, S.
553, 556[76], 589

Alexander, L.
130[4]

Alexander, P.
167, 233[139], 272, 569[38], 572[69], 575[94]

Allen, W.
688, 710[125], 713,

Allison, D.
131[7], 403[62], 430[21], 452[108], 453[110]

Amandry, M.
553, 554[43], 556[69], 589

Andersen, F.
694[219]

Andersen, Ø.
202[127], 205[143]

Anderson, H.
430, 686

Appold, M.
390[94]

Arav, R.
390, 393[120]

Ariel, D.
528[47], 553[38], 554

Asher, J.
244[25], 421[51], 789–91

Atkinson, K.
51[56], 163[33]

Attridge, H.
15[3], 205[141], 579[141], 600[66], 627[67], 650[34], 674, 677[39], 681[81], 703[48], 803[16], 817[133]

Aune, D.
21[33], 22, 25–26, 30[104], 85, 86[6], 392[118], 393

Aus, R.
157[6], 680[59], 714[29], 717[59]

Avigad, N.
736[55]

Aviam, M.
774[25]

Bacon, B.
100, 420

Baird, W.
94[3], 115–16

Balch, D.
445[38], 446, 459[16], 465

Baltzer, K.
29–30, 144[53]

Barclay, J.
12[17]

Barr, J.
678

Barrett, C.
500[120]

Barton, J.
660[125]

Bauckham, R.
97–98, 100, 150, 360[179], 415[3], 505, 784[109]

Bauer, A.
633–34

Bauer, J.
717[57]

Bauernfeind, O.
169, 173, 360

Bauman, R.
700[18], 717[54]

Baumgärtel, F.
149[85], 355[135], 387[81]

Baumgarten, J.
544

Beasley-Murray, G.
595

Becker, E.-M.
33–35, 36[149], 80[3], 82[11], 130[1]

Bedenbender, A.
171[86], 266[51], 383[34], 517

Behm, J.
356, 387[81]

Benovitz, M.
352, 353[110]

Berger, K.
26[76], 160[18], 304, 510[205], 567, 568[26], 634[120]

Berlin, A.
400[27]

Bernardin, J.
426

Best, E.
117, 182[3], 443[18], 458[41], 490, 597, 680[71]

Betz, H.
269[72], 361[181], 421[43], 450[91], 452, 454[128], 507, 537, 585, 681[80]

Betz, O.
139

Beyer, H.
361

Beyer, K.
429[9], 450[89], 452[109]

Bilezikian, G.
91

Billerbeck, P.
301, 509, 561

Binder, D.
163, 164[39]

Bird, P.
186[33], 204[141]

Bischoff, B.
108–10

3   The following contains modern studies that receive some significant discussion.

Turner, C. H.
174, 176, 211[a],
263[a], 389, 473, 522,
538, 540, 550, 696,
730–32, 767[343],
772[c], 780[a]
Tzaferis, V.
399–400

Udoh, F.
553
Ulansey, D.
762
Ulmer, R.
361[182]
Ulrich, E.
460[23]

Vamosh, M.
544[54]
Van der Horst, P.
798
Van Henten, J. W.
232[133], 504, 564[151],
630[92], 633, 786[126]
Vanhoye, A.
690–91
van Iersel, B.
88[22], 90, 91, 102[75],
135[4], 400[39]
Van Oyen, G.
699[8]
Van Seters, J.
30[101], 37–39, 41[181],
42
VanderKam, J.
59, 61[63], 70[131],
153[109], 167[57],
232[133], 234[145],
612[143], 786[122]
Vermes, G.
461[29], 462
Versnel, H.
327[62]
Vielhauer, P.
20–22, 187, 217,
410

Vines, M.
42[185]
Volkmar, G.
508, 509[194]
Von Dobbeler, S.
145
Von Dobschütz, E.
226, 276[114], 295,
296, 303[55], 521[82],
523, 524, 641, 698
Von Soden, F.
123, 389[d]
Von Wahlde, U.
455
Votaw, C.
24–26, 27[77]

Waetjen, H.
96
Walbank, W.
40[178]
Walker, D.
518[47], 553
Warren, A.
27
Wasserman, E.
195[88], 454[125]
Watson, G.
724, 725
Watts, R.
501[120]
Webster, G.
724, 764[316]
Weeden, T.
97[15], 366, 415, 674,
708–9
Wegener, M.
16[10], 33[125]
Wehrli, F.
23[46]
Weinfeld, M.
499, 567
Weinfeld, M.
567[15], 568[27]
Weinreich, D.
271, 283[154], 393[129]

Weinsäcker, C.
597
Weinstock, S.
767[353], 768[355]
Weiser, W.
554[42], 589[231]
Weiss, J.
22, 24, 25, 658–59
Weisse, C.
116
Wellek, R.
27
Wellhausen, J.
187[36], 188[49], 204[139],
234, 266, 271, 285,
372[79], 414, 420,
422, 425, 426[90],
454[133], 509, 527,
560[112], 562, 597–98
Wenham, D.
599
Westerholm, S.
164[46]
Wiarda, T.
406[89]
Wibbing, S.
357–62
Wilcox, M.
503[137]
Wilder, A.
117
Wilson, R.
533[100]
Windisch, H.
386
Winston, D.
376[117]
Winter, P.
720[87], 747[156]
Wise, M.
144[56], 167[58], 230[120]
Wong, E.
470[110]
Wrede, W.
34, 69[125], 96, 116,
170–72, 186, 403,
429, 513

Yadin, Y.
461
Yarbro Collins, A.
12[16], 83, 94[1], 268[63],
290[204], 327–28,
332[89], 388[90], 418,
421–22, 426[95], 431,
441[11], 455[134], 513[5],
527, 528, 531[48],
541[21], 560[115], 594,
598[49], 600[66], 601[71],
615[171], 626–27,
630[92], 637–40,
646[6], 647[10], 648,
651[44], 654[63],
656–57, 667,
668[210], 671[242],
674[12], 683[97], 686,
693[207], 704–7, 723,
726, 733, 752–55,
764, 767, 774, 775,
779, 781, 794–97
Yardeni, A.
464
Yeung, M.
535
Ysebaert, J.
224[91]

Zager, W.
450, 452
Zahn, T.
760[279]
Ziesler, J.
447
Zimmerli, W.
54, 256[74], 533[100]
Zuntz, G.
610

In the design of the visual aspects of *Hermeneia*, consideration has been given to relating the form to the content by symbolic means.

The letters of the logotype *Hermeneia* are a fusion of forms alluding simultaneously to the letter forms of Hebrew (dotted vowel markings) and Greek (geometric round shapes). In their modern treatment they remind us of the electronic age, the vantage point from which this investigation of the past begins.

The Lion of Judah used as visual identification for the series is based on the Seal of Shema. The version for *Hermeneia* is again a fusion of Hebrew calligraphic forms, especially the legs of the lion, and Greek elements characterized by the geometric. In the sequence of arcs, which can be understood as scroll-like images, the first is the lion's mouth. It is reasserted and accelerated in the whorl and returns in the aggressively arched tail: tradition is passed from one age to the next, rediscovered and re-formed.

"Who is worthy to open the scroll and break
    its seals. . . ."
Then one of the elders said to me
    "weep not; lo, the Lion of the tribe of David,
    the Root of David, has conquered,
    so that he can open the scroll
    and its seven seals."

Rev. 5:2, 5

To celebrate the signal achievement in biblical scholarship which Hermeneia represents, the entire series by its color will constitute a signal on the theologian's bookshelf: the Old Testament will be bound in yellow and the New Testament in red, traceable to a commonly used color coding for synagogue and church in medieval painting; in pure color terms, varying degrees of intensity of the warm segment of the color spectrum. The colors interpenetrate when the binding color for the Old Testament is used to imprint volumes from the New and vice versa.

Wherever possible, a photograph of the oldest extant manuscript, or a historically significant document pertaining to the biblical sources, will be displayed on the end papers of each volume to give a feel for the tangible reality and beauty of the source material.

The title-page motifs are expressive derivations from the Hermeneia logotype, repeated seven times to form a matrix and debossed on the cover of each volume. These sifted-out elements are in their exact positions within the parent matrix.

The type has been set with unjustified right margins to preserve the internal consistency of word spacing. This is a major factor in both legibility and aesthetic quality; the resultant uneven line endings are only slight impairments to legibility by comparison. In this respect the type resembles the handwritten manuscripts where the quality of the calligraphic writing is dependent on establishing and holding to integral spacing patterns.

All of the type faces in common use today have been designed between 1500 C.E. and the present. For the biblical text a face was chosen which does not date the text arbitrarily, but rather is uncompromisingly modern and unembellished, giving it a universal feel. The type style is Univers by Adrian Frutiger.

The expository texts and footnotes are set in Baskerville, chosen for its compatibility with the many brief Greek and Hebrew insertions. The double-column format and the shorter line length facilitate speed reading and the wide margins to the left of footnotes provide for the scholar's own notations.

Kenneth Hiebert

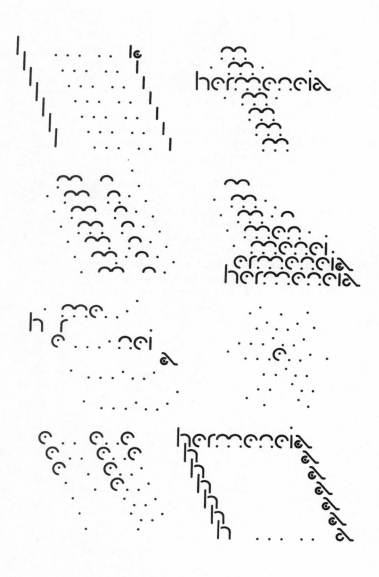

Category of biblical writing,
key symbolic characteristic,
and volumes so identified.

1
Law
(boundaries described)
  Genesis
  Exodus
  Leviticus
  Numbers
  Deuteronomy

2
History
(trek through time and space)
  Joshua
  Judges
  Ruth
  1 Samuel
  2 Samuel
  1 Kings
  2 Kings
  1 Chronicles
  2 Chronicles
  Ezra
  Nehemiah
  Esther

3
Poetry
(lyric emotional expression)
  Job
  Psalms
  Proverbs
  Ecclesiastes
  Song of Songs

4
Prophets
(inspired seers)
  Isaiah
  Jeremiah
  Lamentations
  Ezekiel
  Daniel
  Hosea
  Joel
  Amos
  Obadiah
  Jonah
  Micah
  Nahum
  Habakkuk
  Zephaniah
  Haggai
  Zechariah
  Malachi

5
New Testament Narrative
(focus on One)
  Matthew
  Mark
  Luke
  John
  Acts

6
Epistles
(directed instruction)
  Romans
  1 Corinthians
  2 Corinthians
  Galatians
  Ephesians
  Philippians
  Colossians
  1 Thessalonians
  2 Thessalonians
  1 Timothy
  2 Timothy
  Titus
  Philemon
  Hebrews
  James
  1 Peter
  2 Peter
  1 John
  2 John
  3 John
  Jude

7
Apocalypse
(vision of the future)
  Revelation

8
Extracanonical Writings
(peripheral records)